COMMITTEE ON FOREIGN AFFAIRS

COMMITTEE ON FOREIGN RELATIONS

Legislation on Foreign Relations Through 2005

JULY 2009

VOLUME V

TREATIES AND RELATED MATERIAL

U.S. House of Representatives

U.S. Senate

Printed for the use of the Committees on Foreign Affairs and Foreign Relations of the House of Representatives and the Senate respectively

U.S. GOVERNMENT PRINTING OFFICE

WASHINGTON : 2009

39–710 PS

For sale by the Superintendent of Documents, U.S. Government Printing Office
Internet: bookstore.gpo.gov Phone: toll free (866) 512–1800; DC area (202) 512–1800
Fax: (202) 512–2104 Mail: Stop IDCC, Washington, DC 20402–0001

COMMITTEE ON FOREIGN AFFAIRS

HOWARD L. BERMAN, California, *Chairman*

GARY L. ACKERMAN, New York
ENI F.H. FALEOMAVAEGA, American Samoa
DONALD M. PAYNE, New Jersey
BRAD SHERMAN, California
ROBERT WEXLER, Florida
ELIOT L. ENGEL, New York
BILL DELAHUNT, Massachusetts
GREGORY W. MEEKS, New York
DIANE E. WATSON, California
RUSS CARNAHAN, Missouri
ALBIO SIRES, New Jersey
GERALD E. CONNOLLY, Virginia
MICHAEL E. McMAHON, New York
JOHN S. TANNER, Tennessee
GENE GREEN, Texas
LYNN WOOLSEY, California
SHEILA JACKSON LEE, Texas
BARBARA LEE, California
SHELLEY BERKLEY, Nevada
JOSEPH CROWLEY, New York
MIKE ROSS, Arkansas
BRAD MILLER, North Carolina
DAVID SCOTT, Georgia
JIM COSTA, California
KEITH ELLISON, Minnesota
GABRIELLE GIFFORDS, Arizona
RON KLEIN, Florida

ILEANA ROS-LEHTINEN, Florida
CHRISTOPHER H. SMITH, New Jersey
DAN BURTON, Indiana
ELTON GALLEGLY, California
DANA ROHRABACHER, California
DONALD A. MANZULLO, Illinois
EDWARD R. ROYCE, California
RON PAUL, Texas
JEFF FLAKE, Arizona
MIKE PENCE, Indiana
JOE WILSON, South Carolina
JOHN BOOZMAN, Arkansas
J. GRESHAM BARRETT, South Carolina
CONNIE MACK, Florida
JEFF FORTENBERRY, Nebraska
MICHAEL T. McCAUL, Texas
TED POE, Texas
BOB INGLIS, South Carolina
GUS BILIRAKIS, Florida

RICHARD J. KESSLER, *Staff Director*
YLEEM POBLETE, *Republican Staff Director*

COMMITTEE ON FOREIGN RELATIONS

JOHN F. KERRY, Massachusetts, *Chairman*

CHRISTOPHER J. DODD, Connecticut
RUSSELL D. FEINGOLD, Wisconsin
BARBARA BOXER, California
ROBERT MENENDEZ, New Jersey
BENJAMIN L. CARDIN, Maryland
ROBERT P. CASEY, JR., Pennsylvania
JIM WEBB, Virginia
JEANNE SHAHEEN, New Hampshire
EDWARD E. KAUFMAN, Delaware
KIRSTEN E. GILLIBRAND, New York

RICHARD G. LUGAR, Indiana
Republican Leader designee
BOB CORKER, Tennessee
JOHNNY ISAKSON, Georgia
JAMES E. RISCH, Idaho
JIM DEMINT, South Carolina
JOHN BARRASSO, Wyoming
ROGER F. WICKER, Mississippi

DAVID MCKEAN, *Staff Director*
KENNETH A. MYERS, JR., *Republican Staff Director*

FOREWORD

This volume of treaties and related material is part of a five volume set of laws and related material frequently referred to by the Committees on Foreign Affairs of the House of Representatives and Foreign Relations of the Senate, amended to date and annotated to show pertinent history or cross references.

Volumes I (A and B), II (A and B), III and IV contain legislation and related material and are republished with amendments and additions on a regular basis. Volume V, which contains treaties and related material, will be revised as necessary.

We wish to express our appreciation to Larry Q. Nowels and Dianne E Rennack of the Foreign Affairs, Defense, and Trade Division of the Congressional Research Service of the Library of Congress and Suzanne Kayne of the U.S. Government Printing Office who prepared volume V of this year's compilation.

HOWARD L. BERMAN,
Chairman, Committee on Foreign Affairs.

JOHN F. KERRY,
Chairman, Committee on Foreign Relations.

July 1, 2009.

EXPLANATORY NOTE

All treaties included in this volume, except as noted below, are currently in force. The texts of the treaties have been codified, with footnoting, to show them in amended form. Treaties included in the volume but not presently in force for the United States are the Convention Relating to the Status of Refugees, the Treaty for the Prohibition of Nuclear Weapons in Latin America with Additional Protocols I and II, and the Interim Agreement on Certain Measures With Respect to the Limitation of Strategic Offensive Arms. All other material in this volume is in force as of December 31, 2005.

Corrections may be sent to Dianne E Rennack at the Library of Congress, Congressional Research Service, Washington, D.C., 20540–7460, or by e-mail at drennack@crs.loc.gov.

ABBREVIATIONS

Bevans	Treaties and Other International Agreements of the United States of America, 1776–1949, compiled under the direction of Charles I. Bevans.
CFR	Code of Federal Regulations.
EAS	Executive Agreement Series.
F.R	Federal Register.
LNTS	League of Nations Treaty Series.
I Malloy, II Malloy	Treaties, Conventions, International Acts, Protocols, and Agreements Between the United States of America and Other Powers, 1776–1909, compiled under the direction of the United States Senate by William M. Malloy.
R.S	Revised Statutes.
Stat	United States Statutes at Large.
TIAS	Treaties and Other International Acts Series.
TS	Treaty Series.
UNTS	United Nations Treaty Series.
U.S.C	United States Code.
UST	United States Treaties and Other International Agreements.

CONTENTS

A. FOREIGN ASSISTANCE

(See Volume I for all Material on This Subject)

B. AGRICULTURAL COMMODITIES

CONTENTS

1. Agreement Establishing the International Fund for Agricultural Development

Done at Rome June 13, 1976; Signed by the President August 15, 1977; Instrument of acceptance deposited October 4, 1977; Entered into force November 30, 1977;[1] Amended March 11, 1987,[2] February 20, 1997, and February 21, 1997

PREAMBLE

RECOGNIZING that the continuing food problem of the world is afflicting a large segment of the people of the developing countries and is jeopardizing the most fundamental principles and values associated with the right to life and human dignity;

CONSIDERING the need to improve the conditions of life in the developing countries and to promote socio-economic development within the context of the priorities and objectives of the developing countries, giving due regard to both economic and social benefits;

BEARING IN MIND the responsibility of the Food and Agriculture Organization of the United Nations within the United Nations system, to assist the efforts of developing countries to increase food and agricultural production, as well as that organization's technical competence and experience in this field;

CONSCIOUS of the goals and objectives of the International Development Strategy for the Second United Nations Development Decade and especially the need to spread the benefits of assistance to all;

BEARING IN MIND paragraph (f) of part 2 ("Food") of Section I of General Assembly resolution 3202 (S–VI) on the Programme of Action on the Establishment of a new International Economic Order;

BEARING IN MIND also the need for effecting transfer of technology for food and agricultural development and Section V ("Food and Agriculture") of General Assembly resolution 3362 (S–VII) on development and international economic co-operation, with particular reference to paragraph 6 thereof regarding the establishment of an International Fund for Agricultural Development;

RECALLING paragraph 13 of General Assembly resolution 3348 (XXIX) and resolutions I and II of the World Food Conference on the objectives and strategies of food production and on the priorities for agricultural and rural development;

RECALLING resolution XIII of the World Food Conference which recognized:

(i) the need for a substantial increase in investment in agriculture for increasing food and agricultural production in the developing countries;

---

[1] 28 UST 8435; TIAS 8765.
[2] TIAS 12068.

(ii) that provision of an adequate supply and proper utilization of food are the common responsibility of all members of the international community, and

(iii) that the prospects of the world food situation call for urgent and co-ordinated measures by all countries;

and which resolved:

that an International Fund for Agricultural Development should be established immediately to finance agricultural development projects primarily for food production in the developing countries;

THE CONTRACTING PARTIES have agreed to establish the International Fund for Agricultural Development, which shall be governed by the following provisions:

ARTICLE 1

DEFINITIONS

For the purposes of this Agreement the terms set out below shall have the following meaning, unless the context otherwise requires:

(a) "Fund" shall mean the International Fund for Agricultural Development;

(b) "food production" shall mean the production of food including the development of fisheries and livestock;

(c) "State" shall mean any State, or any grouping of States eligible for membership of the Fund in accordance with Section 1(*b*) of Article 3;

(d) "freely convertible currency" shall mean:

(i) currency of a Member which the Fund determines, after consultation with the International Monetary Fund, is adequately convertible into the currencies of other Members for the purposes of the Fund's operations; or

(ii) currency of a Member which such Member agrees, on terms satisfactory to the Fund, to exchange for the currencies of other Members for the purposes of the Fund's operations.

"Currency of a Member" shall, in respect of a Member that is a grouping of States, mean the currency of any member of such grouping;

(e) "Governor" shall mean a person whom a Member has designated as its principal representative at a session of the Governing Council;

(f) "votes cast" shall mean affirmative and negative votes.

ARTICLE 2

OBJECTIVE AND FUNCTIONS

The objective of the Fund shall be to mobilize additional resources to be made available on concessional terms for agricultural development in developing Member States. In fulfilling this objective the Fund shall provide financing primarily for projects and programmes specifically designed to introduce, expand or improve food production systems and to strengthen related policies and institutions within the framework of national priorities and strategies, taking into consideration: the need to increase food production in the poorest food deficit countries; the potential for increasing food production in other developing countries; and the importance of improving the nutritional level of the poorest populations in developing countries and the conditions of their lives.

ARTICLE 3

MEMBERSHIP

Section 1—Eligibility for membership

(a) Membership of the Fund shall be open to any State member of the United Nations or of any of its specialized agencies, or of the International Atomic Energy Agency.

(b) Membership shall also be open to any grouping of States whose members have delegated to it powers in fields falling within the competence of the Fund, and which is able to fulfill all the obligations of a Member of the Fund.

Section 2—Original Members and non-original Members

(a) Original Members of the Fund shall be those States listed in Schedule I, which forms an integral part of this Agreement, that become parties to this Agreement in accordance with Section 1(*b*) of Article 13.

(b) Non-original Members of the Fund shall be those other States that, after approval of their membership by the Governing Council, become parties to this Agreement in accordance with Section 1(*c*) of Article 13.

Section 3—Limitation of liability [3]

No Member shall be liable, by reason of its membership, for acts or obligations of the Fund.

ARTICLE 4

RESOURCES

Section 1—Resources of the Fund

The resources of the Fund shall consist of:

(i) initial contributions;

(ii) additional contributions;

(iii) special contributions from non-member States and from other sources;

(iv) funds derived or to be derived [4] from operations or otherwise accruing to the Fund.

Section 2—Initial contributions

(a) [5] The amount of an initial contribution of an original and a non-original Member shall be the amount and in the currency of such contribution specified by the Member in its instrument of ratification, acceptance, approval or accession deposited by that Member pursuant to Section 1(b) and (c) of Article 13 of this Agreement.

---

[3] Amendment of February 20, 1997 struck out sec. 3 and redesignated sec. 4 as sec. 3. Sec. 3 had previously related to the classification of members.

[4] Amendment of February 21, 1997 inserted "or to be derived".

[5] Amendment of February 20, 1997 amended and restated subsec. (a), struck out subsec. (b), and redesignated subsec. (c) as subsec. (b).

(b)[5] The initial contribution of each Member shall be due and payable in the forms set forth in Section 5 (b) and (c) of this Article, either in a single sum or, at the option of the Member, in three equal annual instalments. The single sum or the first annual instalment shall be due on the thirtieth day after this Agreement enters into force with respect to that Member; any second and third instalments shall be due on the first and on the second anniversary of the date on which the first instalment was due.

Section 3—Additional contributions

In order to assure continuity in the operations of the Fund, the Governing Council shall periodically, at such intervals as it deems appropriate, review the adequacy of the resources available to the Fund; the first such review shall take place not later than three years after the Fund commences operations. If the Governing Council, as a result of such a review, deems it necessary or desirable, it may invite Members to make additional contributions to the resources of the Fund on terms and conditions consistent with Section 5 of this Article. Decisions under this Section shall be taken by a two-thirds majority of the total number of votes.

Section 4—Increases in contributions

The Governing Council may authorize, at any time, a Member to increase the amount of any of its contributions.

Section 5—Conditions governing contributions

(a) Contributions shall be made without restrictions as to use and shall be refunded to contributing Members only in accordance with Section 4 of Article 9.

(b) Contributions shall be made in freely convertible currencies.[6]

(c) Contributions to the Fund shall be made in cash or, to the extent that any part of such contributions is not needed immediately by the Fund in its operations, such part may be paid in the form of non-negotiable, irrevocable, non-interest bearing promissory notes or obligations payable on demand. In order to finance its operations, the Fund shall draw down all contributions (regardless of the form in which they are made) as follows:

(i) contributions shall be drawn down on a *pro rata* basis over reasonable periods of time as determined by the Executive Board;

(ii) where a contribution is paid partly in cash, the part so paid shall be drawn down, in accordance with paragraph (i), before the rest of the contribution. Except to the extent that the part paid in cash is thus drawn down, it may be deposited or invested by the Fund to produce income to help defray its administrative and other expenditures;

(iii) all initial contributions, as well as any increases in them, shall be drawn down before any additional contributions are drawn down. The same rule shall apply to further additional contributions.

[6] Amendment of February 20, 1997 struck out "except that Members in category III may pay contributions in their own currency whether or not it is freely convertible".

Section 6—Special contributions

The resources of the Fund may be increased by special contributions from non-member States or other sources on such terms and conditions, consistent with Section 5 of this Article, as shall be approved by the Governing Council on the recommendation of the Executive Board.

ARTICLE 5

CURRENCIES

Section 1—Use of currencies

(a) Members shall not maintain or impose any restriction on the holding or use by the Fund of freely convertible currencies.

(b)[7] The non-convertible currency contributions of a Member made to the Fund on account of that Member's initial or additional contributions prior to 26 January 1995 may be used by the Fund, in consultation with the Member concerned, for the payment of administrative expenditures and other costs of the Fund in the territories of that Member, or, with the consent of that Member, for the payment of goods or services produced in its territories and required for activities financed by the Fund in other States.

Section 2—Valuation of currencies

(a) The unit of account of the Fund shall be the Special Drawing Right of the International Monetary Fund.

(b) For the purposes of this Agreement, the value of a currency in terms of the Special Drawing Right shall be calculated in accordance with the method of valuation applied by the International Monetary Fund, provided that:

(i) in the case of the currency of a member of the International Monetary Fund for which such value is not available on a current basis, the value shall be calculated after consultation with the International Monetary Fund;

(ii) in the case of the currency of a non-member of the International Monetary Fund, the value of the currency in terms of the Special Drawing Right shall be calculated by the Fund on the basis of an appropriate exchange rate relationship between that currency and the currency of a member of the International Monetary Fund for which a value is calculated as specified above.

ARTICLE 6

ORGANIZATION AND MANAGEMENT

Section 1—Structure of the Fund

The Fund shall have: (a) A Governing Council; (b) an Executive Board; and (c) a President and such staff as shall be necessary for the Fund to carry out its functions.

[7] Amendment of February 20, 1997 amended and restated subsec. (b).

Section 2—The Governing Council

(a) Each Member shall be represented on the Governing Council and shall appoint one Governor and an alternate. An alternate may vote only in the absence of his principal.

(b) All the powers of the Fund shall be vested in the Governing Council.

(c) The Governing Council may delegate any of its powers to the Executive Board with the exception of the power to:

(i) adopt amendments to this Agreement;

(ii) approve membership;[8]

(iii) suspend a member;

(iv) terminate the operations of the Fund and distribute its assets;

(v) decide appeals from decisions made by the Executive Board concerning the interpretation or application of this Agreement;

(vi) determine the remuneration of the President.

(d) The Governing Council shall hold an annual session, and such special sessions as it may decide, or as are called by Members having at least one fourth of the total number of votes in the Governing Council, or as requested by the Executive Board by a two-thirds majority of the votes cast.

(e) The Governing Council may by regulation establish a procedure whereby the Executive Board may obtain a vote of the Council on a specific question without calling a meeting of the Council.

(f) The Governing Council may, by a two-thirds majority of the total number of votes, adopt such regulations and by-laws not inconsistent with this agreement as may be appropriate to conduct the business of the Fund.

(g) A quorum for any meeting of the Governing Council shall be constituted by Governors exercising two-thirds of the total votes of all its members.[9]

Section 3—Voting in the Governing Council

(a)[10] The total number of votes in the Governing Council shall be comprised of Original Votes and Replenishment Votes. All Members shall have equal access to those votes on the following basis:

(i) Original Votes shall consist of a total of one thousand eight hundred (1 800) votes made up of membership votes and contribution votes:

(A) membership votes shall be distributed equally among all Members; and

(B) contribution votes shall be distributed among all Members in the proportion that each Member's cumulative paid contributions to the resources of the Fund, authorized by the Governing Council prior to 26 January 1995 and made by Members in accordance with Sections 2, 3 and 4 of Article 4 of this Agreement, bear to the aggregate of the total of the said contributions paid by all Members;

[8] Amendment of February 20, 1997 struck out "and determine the classification or reclassification of Members".

[9] Amendment of February 20, 1997 struck out ", provided that Governors exercising one half of the total votes of the members in each categories I, II and III are present".

[10] Amendment of February 20, 1997 amended and restated subsec. (a).

(ii) Replenishment Votes shall be made up of membership votes and contribution votes in a total amount of votes to be decided by the Governing Council upon each occasion that it calls for additional contributions under Section 3 of Article 4 of this Agreement (a "replenishment" commencing with the fourth such replenishment. Except as the Governing Council shall by a two-thirds majority of the total number of votes otherwise decide, the votes for each replenishment shall be established in the ratio of one hundred (100) votes for the equivalent of each one hundred and fifty eight million United States dollars (USD 158 000 000) contributed to the total amount of that replenishment, or a fraction thereof:

(A) membership votes shall be distributed equally among all Members on the same basis as that set forth in provision (i)(A) above; and

(B) contribution votes shall be distributed among all Members in the proportion that each Member's paid contribution to the resources contributed to the Fund by Members for each replenishment bears to the aggregate of the total contributions paid by all Members to the said replenishment; and

(iii) The Governing Council shall decide the total number of votes to be allocated as membership votes and contribution votes under paragraphs (i) and (ii) of this Section. Upon any change in the number of Members of the Fund, the membership votes and contribution votes distributed under paragraphs (i) and (ii) of this Section shall be redistributed in accordance with the principles laid down in the said paragraphs. In the allocation of votes, the Governing Council shall ensure that those Members classified as members of Category III before 26 January 1995 receive one-third of the total votes as membership votes.

(b) Except as otherwise specified in this Agreement, decisions of the Governing Council shall be taken by a simple majority of the total number of votes.

Section 4—Chairman of the Governing Council

The Governing Council shall elect a Chairman from among the Governors, who shall serve for two years.

Section 5—Executive Board

(a)[11] The Executive Board shall be composed of 18 members and up to 18 alternate members, elected from the Members of the Fund at the annual session of the Governing Council. The seats in the Executive Board shall be distributed by the Governing Council from time to time as specified in Schedule II to this Agreement. The members of the Executive Board and their alternates, who may vote only in the absence of a member, shall be elected and appointed in accordance with the procedures set forth in Schedule II hereto, which forms an integral part of this Agreement.

---

[11] Amendment of February 20, 1997 amended and restated subsec. (a).

(b) Members of the Executive Board shall serve for a term of three years.[12]

(c) The Executive Board shall be responsible for the conduct of the general operations of the fund, and for this purpose shall exercise the powers given to it by this Agreement or delegated to it by the Governing Council.

(d) The Executive Board shall meet as often as the business of the Fund may require.

(e) The representatives of a member or of an alternate member of the Executive Board shall serve without remuneration from the Fund. However, the Governing Council may decide the basis on which reasonable travel and subsistence expenses may be granted to one such representative of each member and of each alternate member.

(f) A quorum for any meeting of the Executive Board shall be constituted by members exercising two thirds of the total votes of all its members.[13]

Section 6—Voting in the Executive Board

(a)[14] The Governing Council shall, from time to time, decide the distribution of votes among the members of the Executive Board in accordance with the principles established in Section 3(a) of Article 6 of this Agreement.

(b) Except as otherwise specified in this Agreement, decisions of the Executive Board shall be taken by a majority of three fifths of the votes cast, provided that such majority is more than one half of the total number of votes of all members of the Executive Board.

Section 7—Chairman of the Executive Board

The President of the Fund shall be the Chairman of the Executive Board and shall participate in its meetings without the right to vote.

Section 8—President and staff

(a) The Governing Council shall appoint the President by a two-thirds majority of the total number of votes. He shall be appointed for a term of four[15] years and shall be eligible for reappointment for only one further term. The appointment of the President may be terminated by the Governing Council by a two-thirds majority of the total number of votes.

(b)[16] Notwithstanding the restriction on the term of office of the President of four years, contained in paragraph (a) of this Section, the Governing Council may, under special circumstances, on the recommendation of the Executive Board, extend the term of office of the President beyond the duration prescribed in paragraph (a) above. Any such extension shall be for no more than six months.

---

[12] Amendment of February 20, 1997 struck out "However, unless otherwise provided in or in accordance with Schedule II, at the first election two members in each category shall be designated to serve for one year, and two to serve for two years.".

[13] Amendment of February 20, 1997 struck out ", provided that members exercising one half of the total votes of the members in each of categories I, II and III are present".

[14] Amendment of February 20, 1997 amended and restated subsec. (a).

[15] Amendment of March 11, 1987 struck "three" and inserted in lieu thereof "four".

[16] Amendment of March 11, 1987 added subsec. (b) and redesignated subsecs. (b) through (h) as subsecs. (c) through (i).

(c)[16] The President may appoint a Vice-President, who shall perform such duties as shall be assigned to him by the President.

(d)[16] The President shall head the staff and, under the control and direction of the Governing Council and the Executive Board, shall be responsible for conducting the business of the Fund. The President shall organize the staff and shall appoint and dismiss members of the staff in accordance with regulations adopted by the Executive Board.

(e)[16] In the employment of the staff and in the determination of the conditions of service consideration shall be given to the necessity of securing the highest standards of efficiency, competence and integrity as well as to the importance of observing the criterion of equitable geographical distribution.

(f)[16] The President and the staff, in the discharge of their functions, owe their duty exclusively to the Fund and shall neither seek nor receive instructions in regard to the discharge thereof from any authority external to the Fund. Each Member of the Fund shall respect the international character of this duty and shall refrain from any attempt to influence them in the discharge of their duties.

(g)[16] The President and the staff shall not interfere in the political affairs of any Member. Only development policy considerations shall be relevant to their decisions and these considerations shall be weighed impartially in order to achieve the objective for which the Fund was established.

(h)[16] The President shall be the legal representative of the Fund.

(i)[16] The President, or a representative designated by him, may participate, without the right to vote, in all meetings of the Governing Council.

Section 9—Seat of the Fund

The Governing Council shall determine the permanent seat of the Fund by a two-thirds majority of the total number of votes. The provisional seat of the Fund shall be in Rome.

Section 10—Administrative budget

The President shall prepare an annual administrative budget which he shall submit to the Executive Board for transmission to the Governing Council for approval by a two-thirds majority of the total number of votes.

Section 11—Publication of reports and provision of information

The Fund shall publish an annual report containing an audited statement of its accounts and, at appropriate intervals, a summary statement of its financial position and of the results of its operations. Copies of such reports, statements and other publications connected therewith shall be distributed to all Members.

ARTICLE 7

OPERATIONS

Section 1—Use of resources and conditions of financing

(a) The resources of the Fund shall be to achieve the objective specified in Article 2.

(b) Financing by the Fund shall be provided only to developing States that are Members of the Fund or to intergovernmental organizations in which such Members participate. In the case of a loan to an intergovernmental organization, the Fund may require suitable governmental or other guarantees.

(c) The Fund shall make arrangements to ensure that the proceeds of any financing are used only for the purposes for which the financing was provided, with due attention to considerations of economy, efficiency and social equity.

(d) In allocating its resources the Fund shall be guided by the following priorities:

(i) the need to increase food production and to improve the nutritional level of the poorest populations in the poorest food deficit countries;

(ii) the potential for increasing food production in other developing countries. Likewise, emphasis shall be placed on improving the nutritional level of the poorest populations in these countries and the conditions of their lives.

Within the framework of the above-mentioned priorities, eligibility for assistance shall be on the basis of objective economic and social criteria with special emphasis on the needs of the low income countries and their potential for increasing food production, as well as due regard to a fair geographic distribution in the use of such resources.

(e) Subject to the provisions of this Agreement, financing by the Fund shall be governed by broad policies, criteria and regulations laid down, from time to time, by the Governing Council by a two-thirds majority of the total number of votes.

Section 2—Forms and terms of financing

(a) Financing by the Fund shall take the form of loans and grants, which shall be provided on such terms as the Fund deems appropriate, having regard to the economic situation and prospects of the Member and to the nature and requirements of the activity concerned.

(b) The proportion of the Fund's resources to be committed in any financial year for financing operations in either of the forms referred to in subsection (a) shall be decided from time to time by the Executive Board with due regard to the long-term viability of the Fund and the need for continuity in its operations. The proportion of grants shall not formally exceed one-eighth of the resources committed in any financial year. A large proportion of the loans shall be provided on highly concessional terms.

(c) The President shall submit projects and programmes to the Executive Board for consideration and approval.

(d) Decisions with regard to the selection and approval of projects and programmes shall be made by the Executive Board. Such decisions shall be made on the basis of the broad policies, criteria and regulations established by the Governing Council.

(e) For the appraisal of projects and programmes presented to it for financing, the Fund shall, as a general rule, use the services of international institutions and may, where appropriate, use the services of other competent agencies specialized in this field. Such institutions and agencies shall be selected by the Executive Board after consultations with the recipient concerned and shall be directly responsible to the Fund in performing the appraisal.

(f) The loan agreement shall be concluded in each case by the Fund and the recipient, which shall be responsible for the execution of the project or programme concerned.

(g) The Fund shall entrust the administration of loans, for the purposes of the disbursement of the proceeds of the loan and the supervision of the implementation of the project or programme concerned, to competent international institutions. Such institutions shall be of a world-wide or regional character and shall be selected in each case with the approval of the recipient. Before submitting the loan to the Executive Board for approval, the Fund shall assure itself that the institution to be entrusted with the supervision agrees with the results of the appraisal of the project or programme concerned. This shall be arranged between the Fund and the institution or agency in charge of the appraisal as well as with the institution to be entrusted with the supervision.

(h) For the purposes of subsections (f) and (g) above, references to "loans" shall be deemed to include "grants".

(i) The Fund may extend a line of credit to a national development agency to provide and administer subloans for the financing of projects and programmes within the terms of the loan agreement and the framework agreed to by the Fund. Before the Executive Board approves the extension of such a line of credit, the national development agency concerned and its programme shall be appraised in accordance with the provisions of subsection (e). Implementation of the said programme shall be subject to supervision by the institutions selected in accordance with the provisions of subsection (g).

(j) The Executive Board shall adopt suitable regulations for procuring goods and services to be financed from the resources of the Fund. Such regulations shall, as a general rule, conform to the principles of international competitive bidding and shall give appropriate preference to experts, technicians and supplies from developing countries.

Section 3—Miscellaneous operations

In addition to the operations specified elsewhere in this Agreement, the Fund may undertake such ancillary activities and exercise such powers incidental to its operations as shall be necessary in furtherance of its objective.

Article 8

RELATIONS WITH THE UNITED NATIONS AND WITH OTHER ORGANIZATIONS, INSTITUTIONS AND AGENCIES

Section 1—Relations with the United Nations

The Fund shall enter into negotiations with the United Nations with a view to concluding an agreement to bring it into relationship with the United Nations as one of the specialized agencies referred to in Article 57 of the Charter of the United Nations. Any agreements concluded in accordance with Article 63 of the Charter require the approval of the Governing Council, by a two-thirds majority of the total number of votes, upon the recommendation of the Executive Board.

Section 2—Relations with other organizations, institutions, and agencies

The Fund shall cooperate closely with the Food and Agriculture Organization of the United Nations and other organizations of the United Nations system. It shall also cooperate closely with other intergovernmental organizations, international financial institutions, nongovernmental organizations and governmental agencies concerned with agricultural development. To this end, the Fund will seek the collaboration in its activities of the Food and Agriculture Organization of the United Nations and the other bodies referred to above, and may enter into agreements or establish working arrangements with such bodies, as may be decided by the Executive Board.

ARTICLE 9

WITHDRAWAL, SUSPENSION OF MEMBERSHIP, TERMINATION OF OPERATIONS

Section 1—Withdrawal

(a) Except as provided in section 4(a) of this Article, a Member may withdraw from the Fund by depositing an instrument of denunciation of this Agreement with the Depositary.

(b) Withdrawal of a Member shall take effect on the date specified in its instrument of denunciation, but in no event less than six months after deposit of such instrument.

Section 2—Suspension of Membership

(a) If a Member fails to fulfill any of its obligations to the Fund, the Governing Council may, by a three-fourths majority of the total number of votes, suspend its membership. The Member so suspended shall automatically cease to be a Member one year from the date of its suspension, unless the Council decides by the same majority of the total number of votes to restore the Member to good standing.

(b) While under suspension, a Member shall not be entitled to exercise any rights under this Agreement except the right of withdrawal, but shall remain subject to all of its obligations.

Section 3—Rights and duties of States ceasing to be Members

Whenever a State ceases to be a Member, whether by withdrawal or through the operation of Section 2 of this Article, it shall have no rights under this Agreement except as provided in this Section or in Section 2 of Article 11, but it shall remain liable for all financial obligations undertaken by it to the Fund, whether as Member, borrower or otherwise.

Section 4—Termination of operations and distribution of assets

(a) The Governing Council may terminate the Fund's operations by a three-fourths majority of the total number of votes. After such termination of operations the Fund shall forthwith cease all activities, except those incidental to the orderly realization and conservation of its assets and the settlement of its obligations. Until final settlement of such obligations and the distribution of such assets, the Fund shall remain in existence and all rights and obligations of the Fund and its Members under this Agreement shall continue unimpaired, except that no Member may be suspended or may withdraw.

(b) No distribution of assets shall be made to Members until all liabilities to creditors have been discharged or provided for. The Fund shall distribute its assets to contributing Members *pro rata* to the contributions that each Member has made to the resources of the Fund. Such distribution shall be decided by the Governing Council by a three-fourths majority of the total number of votes and shall be effected at such times, and in such currencies or other assets as the Governing Council shall deem fair and equitable.

ARTICLE 10

LEGAL STATUS, PRIVILEGES AND IMMUNITIES

Section 1—Legal status

The Fund shall possess international legal personality.

Section 2—Privileges and immunities

(a) The Fund shall enjoy in the territory of each of its Members such privileges and immunities as are necessary for the exercise of its functions and for the fulfillment of its objective. Representatives of Members, the President and the staff of the Fund shall enjoy such privileges and immunities as are necessary for the independent exercise of their functions in connection with the Fund.

(b) The privileges and immunities referred to in paragraph (a) shall:

(i) in the territory of any Member that has acceded to the Convention on the Privileges and Immunities of the specialized Agencies in respect of the Fund, be as defined in the standard clauses of that Convention as modified by an annex thereto approved by the Governing Council;

(ii) in the territory of any Member that has acceded to the Convention on the Privileges and Immunities of the Specialized Agencies only in respect of agencies other than the Fund, be as defined in the standard clauses of that Convention, except if such Member notifies the Depositary that such clauses shall not apply to the Fund or shall apply subject to such modifications as may be specified in the notification;

(iii) be as defined in other agreements entered into by the Fund.

(c) In respect of a Member that is a grouping of States, it shall ensure that the privileges and immunities referred to in this Article are applied in the territories of all members of the grouping.

ARTICLE 11

INTERPRETATION AND ARBITRATION

Section 1—Interpretation

(a) Any question of interpretation or application of the provisions of this Agreement arising between any Member and the Fund or between Members of the Fund, shall be submitted to the Executive Board for decision. If the question particularly affects any Member of the Fund not represented on the Executive Board, that Member shall be entitled to be represented in accordance with regulations to be adopted by the Governing Council.

(b) Where the Executive Board has given a decision pursuant to subsection (a), any Member may require that the question be referred to the Governing Council, whose decision shall be final. Pending the decision of the Governing Council, the Fund may, so far as it deems necessary, act on the basis of the decision of the Executive Board.

Section 2—Arbitration

In the case of a dispute between the Fund and a State that has ceased to be a Member, or between the Fund and any Member upon the termination of the operations of the Fund, such dispute shall be submitted to arbitration by a tribunal of three arbitrators. One of the arbitrators shall be appointed by the Fund, another by the Member or former Member concerned and two parties shall appoint the third arbitrator, who shall be the Chairman. If within 45 days of receipt of the request for arbitration either party has not appointed an arbitrator, or if within 30 days of the appointment of two arbitrators the third arbitrator has not been appointed, either party may request the President of the International Court of Justice, or such other authority as may have been prescribed by regulations adopted by the Governing Council, to appoint an arbitrator. The procedure of the arbitration shall be fixed by the arbitrators, but the Chairman shall have full power to settle all questions of procedure in any case of disagreement with respect thereto. A majority vote of the arbitrators shall be sufficient to reach a decision, which shall be final and binding upon the parties.

ARTICLE 12

AMENDMENTS

(a) Except in respect of Schedule II:

(i) Any proposal to amend this Agreement made by a Member or by the Executive Board shall be communicated to the President who shall notify all Members. The President shall refer proposals to amend this Agreement made by a Member to the Executive Board, which shall submit its recommendation thereon to the Governing Council.

(ii) Amendments shall be adopted by the Governing Council by a four-fifths majority of the total number of votes. Amendments shall enter into force three months after their adoption unless otherwise specified by the Governing Council except that any amendment modifying:

(A) the right to withdraw from the Fund;

(B) the voting majority requirements provided for in this Agreement;

(C) the limitation on liability provided for in Section 3 [17] of Article 3;

(D) the procedure for amending this Agreement;

shall not come into force until written acceptance of such amendment by all Members is received by the President.

(b) In respect of the several parts of Schedule II, amendments shall be proposed and adopted as provided in such parts.

(c) The President shall immediately notify all Members and the Depositary of any amendments that are adopted and of the date of entry into force of any such amendments.

ARTICLE 13

FINAL CLAUSES

Section 1—Signature, ratification, acceptance, approval, and accession

(a) This Agreement may be initialed on behalf of the States listed in Schedule I to this Agreement at the United Nations Conference on the establishment of the Fund and shall be open for signature at the Headquarters of the United Nations in New York by the States listed in that Schedule as soon as the initial contributions indicated therein to be made in freely convertible currencies amount to at least the equivalent of 1,000 million United States dollars (valued as of 10 June 1976). If the foregoing requirement has not been fulfilled by 30 September 1976 the Preparatory Commission established by that Conference shall convene by 31 January 1977 a meeting of the States listed in Schedule I, which may by a two-thirds majority of each category reduce the above specified amount and may also establish other conditions for the opening of this Agreement for signature.

(b) Signatory States may become parties by depositing an instrument of ratification, acceptance or approval; non-signatory States listed in Schedule I may become parties by depositing an instrument of accession. Instruments of ratification, acceptance, approval and accession by States in category I or II shall specify the amount of the initial contribution the State undertakes to make. Signatures may be affixed and instruments of ratification, acceptance, approval or accession deposited by such States until one year after the entry into force of this Agreement.

(c) States listed in Schedule I that have not become parties to this Agreement within one year after its entry into force and States that are not so listed, may, after approval of their membership by the Governing Council, become parties by depositing an instrument of accession.

Section 2

(a) The Secretary-General of the United Nations shall be the Depositary of this Agreement.

[17] Amendment of February 20, 1997 struck out "4" and inserted in lieu thereof "3".

(b) The Depositary shall send notifications concerning this Agreement:

(i) until one year after its entry into force, to the States listed in Schedule I to this Agreement, and after such entry into force to all States parties to this Agreement as well as to those approved for membership by the Governing Council;

(ii) To the Preparatory Commission established by the United Nations Conference on the Establishment of the Fund, as long as it remains in existence, and thereafter to the President.

Section 3—Entry into force

(a) This Agreement shall enter into force upon receipt by the Depositary of instruments of ratification, acceptance, approval or accession from at least 6 States in category I, 6 States in category II and 24 States in category III, provided that such instruments have been deposited by States in categories I and II the aggregate of whose initial contributions specified in such instruments amounts to at least the equivalent of 750 million United States dollars (valued as of 10 June 1976), and further provided that the foregoing requirements have been fulfilled within 18 months of the date on which this Agreement is opened for signature or by such later date as the States that have deposited such instruments by the end of that period may decide, by a two-thirds majority of each category, and as they notify to the Depositary.

(b) For States that deposit an instrument of ratification, acceptance, approval or accession subsequent to the entry into force of this Agreement, it shall enter into force on the date of such deposit.

(c)[18] The obligations accepted by original and non-original Members under this Agreement prior to 26 January 1995 shall remain unimpaired and shall be the continuing obligations of each Member to the Fund.

(d)[18] References throughout this Agreement to categories or to Categories I, II and III shall be deemed to refer to the categories of Members prevailing prior to 26 January 1995, as set out in Schedule III hereto, which forms an integral part of this Agreement.

Section 4—Reservations

Reservations may only be made to Section 2 of Article 11 of this Agreement.

Section 5—Authoritative texts

The versions of this Agreement in the Arabic, English, French and Spanish languages shall each be equally authoritative.

In witness whereof, the undersigned being duly authorized thereto, have signed this Agreement in a single original in the Arabic, English, French, and Spanish languages.

[18] Amendment of February 20, 1997 added subsecs. (c) and (d).

Schedule I

Part I—States eligible for original membership

Category I

Australia
Austria
Belgium
Canada
Denmark
Finland
France
Germany [19]
Ireland
Italy
Luxembourg
Japan
Netherlands
New Zealand
Norway
Spain
Sweden
Switzerland
United Kingdom of Great Britain and Northern Ireland
United States of America

Category II

Algeria
Gabon
Indonesia
Iran
Iraq
Kuwait
Libyan Arab Jamahiriya [20]
Nigeria
Qatar
Saudi Arabia
United Arab Emirates
Venezuela

Category III

Argentina
Bangladesh
Bolivia
Botswana
Brazil
Cameroon [21]
Cape Verde
Chad
Chile
Colombia
Congo
Costa Rica
Cuba
Dominican Republic
Ecuador
Egypt
El Salvador
Ethiopia
Ghana
Greece
Guatemala
Guinea
Haiti
Honduras
India
Israel [1]
Jamaica
Kenya
Liberia
Mali
Malta
Mexico
Morocco
Nicaragua
Pakistan
Panama
Papua New Guinea
Peru
Philippines
Portugal
Republic of Korea
Romania
Rwanda
Senegal
Sierra Leone
Somalia
Sri Lanka
Sudan
Swaziland
Syrian Arab Republic
Thailand
Tunisia
Turkey
Uganda
United Republic of Tanzania
Uruguay
Yugoslavia
Zaire
Zambia

[1] With reference to Article 7, Section 1(b) on the use of resources of the Fund for "developing countries", this country will not be included under this Section and will not seek or receive financing from the Fund.

---

[19] Amendment of February 20, 1997 struck out ", Federal Republic of".

[20] Amendment of February 20, 1997 struck out "Republic" and inserted in lieu thereof "Jamahiriya".

[21] Amendment of February 20, 1997 inserted Cameroon at this point. Previously, the country had been listed as the United Republic of Cameroon.

PART II—PLEDGES OF INITIAL CONTRIBUTIONS [2]

State and currency unit	Amount in currency	Equivalent in SDRs [3]	
		Freely convertible	Not freely convertible
Category I			
Australia: Australian dollar	[a] 8,000,000	8,609,840	
Austria: U.S. dollar	[a] 4,800,000	4,197,864	
Belgium:			
Belgian franc	500,000,000	11,930,855	
U.S. dollar	[a] 1,000,000		
Canada: Canadian dollar	[a] 33,000,000	29,497,446	
Denmark: U.S. dollar	[a] 7,500,000	6,559,163	
Finland: Finnish markka	[a] 12,000,000	2,692,320	
France: U.S. dollar	25,000,000	21,863,875	
Germany [19]: U.S. dollar	[a,b] 55,000,000	48,100,525	
Ireland: Pound sterling	[a] 570,000	883,335	
Italy: U.S. dollar	[a] 25,000,000	21,863,875	
Japan: U.S. dollar	[a] 55,000,000	48,100,525	
Luxembourg: Special Drawing Right	[a] 320,000	320,000	
Netherlands:			
Dutch guilder	100,000,000	34,594,265	
U.S. dollar	3,000,000		
New Zealand: New Zealand dollar	[a] 2,000,000	1,721,998	
Norway:			
Norwegian Kroner	[a] 75,000,000	20,612,228	
U.S. dollar	9,981,851		
Spain: U.S. dollar	[c] 2,000,000	1,749,110	
Sweden:			
Swedish kroner	100,000,000	22,325,265	
U.S. dollar	3,000,000		
Switzerland: Swiss franc	[a] 22,000,000	7,720,790	
United Kingdom: Pound sterling	18,000,000	27,894,780	
United States: U.S. dollar	200,000,000	174,911,000	
Subtotal		496,149,059	
Category II			
Algeria: U.S. dollar	10,000,000	8,745,550	
Gabon: U.S. dollar	500,000	437,278	
Indonesia: U.S. dollar	1,250,000	1,093,194	
Iran: U.S. dollar	124,750,000	109,100,736	
Iraq: U.S. dollar	20,000,000	17,491,100	
Kuwait: U.S. dollar	36,000,000	31,483,980	
Libyan Arab Jamahiriya [20]: U.S. dollar	20,000,000	17,491,100	
Nigeria: U.S. dollar	26,000,000	22,738,430	
Qatar: U.S. dollar	9,000,000	7,870,995	
Saudi Arabia: U.S. dollar	105,500,000	92,265,553	
United Arab Emirates: U.S. dollar	16,500,000	14,430,158	

State and currency unit	Amount in currency	Equivalent in SDRs[3]	
		Freely convertible	Not freely convertible
Venezuela: U.S. dollar	66,000,000	57,720,630	
Subtotal		380,868,704	
Category III			
Argentina: Argentine peso	[d] 240,000,000		1,499,237
Bangladesh: Taka (equivalent of U.S. dollar)	500,000		437,278
Cameroon:[21] U.S. dollar	10,000	8,746	
Chile: U.S. dollar	50,000	43,728	
Ecuador: U.S. dollar	25,000	21,864	
Egypt: Egyptian pound (equivalent of U.S. dollar)	300,000		262,367
Ghana: U.S. dollar	100,000	87,456	
Guinea: Syli	[a] 25,000,000		1,012,145
Honduras: U.S. dollar	25,000	21,864	
India:			
U.S. dollar	2,500,000	2,186,388	
Indian rupee (equivalent of U.S. dollar)	2,500,000		2,186,388
Israel: Israel pound (equivalent of U.S. dollar)	[a,e] 150,000		131,183
Kenya: Kenya shilling (equivalent of U.S. dollar)	1,000,000		874,555
Mexico: U.S. dollar	5,000,000	4,372,775	
Nicaragua: Cordoba	200,000		24,894
Pakistan:			
U.S. dollar	500,000	437,278	
Pakistan rupee (equivalent of U.S. dollar)	500,000		437,278
Philippines: U.S. dollar[f]	[f] 250,000	43,728	174,911
Republic of Korea:			
U.S. dollar	100,000	87,456	
Chon (equivalent of U.S. dollar)	100,000		87,456
Romania: Leu (equivalent of U.S. dollar)	1,000,000		874,555
Sierra Leone: Leone	20,000		15,497
Sri Lanka:			
U.S. dollar	500,000	437,278	
Sri Lanka rupee (equivalent of U.S. dollar)	500,000		437,278
Syrian Arab Republic: Syrian pound	500,000		111,409
Thailand: U.S. dollar	100,000	87,456	
Tunisia: Tunisian dinar	50,000		100,621
Turkey: Turkish lira (equivalent of U.S. dollar)	100,000		87,456
Uganda: Uganda shilling	200,000		20,832
United Republic of Tanzania: Tanzania shilling	300,000		31,056

State and currency unit	Amount in currency	Equivalent in SDRs[3]	
		Freely convertible	Not freely convertible
Yugoslavia: Yugoslav dinar (equivalent of U.S. dollar)	300,000		262,367
Subtotal		7,836,017	9,068,763
Total freely convertible		*884,853,780	
Grand total (freely and not freely convertible)		893,922,543	

[2] Subject to obtaining, where required, the necessary legislative approval.

[3] Special Drawing Rights (SDRs) of the International Monetary Fund valued as of 10 June 1976. These equivalent values are stated merely for information in the light of Section 2(a) of Article 5 of the Agreement, with the understanding that the initial contributions pledged will be payable in accordance with Section 2(a) of Article 4 of the Agreement in the amount and currency specified by the State concerned.

[a] Payable in three instalments.

[b] This amount includes an additional pledge of $US 3 million, which was made subject to the necessary budgetary arrangements in the fiscal year 1977.

[c] Payable in two instalments.

[d] To be spent within the territory of Argentina for goods or services required by the Fund.

[e] Usable for technical assistance.

[f] $US 200,000 of this pledge was stated to be subject to confirmation, including the terms of payment and the type of currency. This amount has consequently been entered in the "not freely convertible" column.

* Equivalent of $US 1,011,776,023 valued as of 10 June 1976.

SCHEDULE II[22]

DISTRIBUTION OF VOTES AND ELECTION OF EXECUTIVE BOARD MEMBERS

1. The Governing Council, in accordance with the procedures specified in paragraph 29 of this Schedule, shall decide, from time to time, the distribution of seats and alternate seats among the Members of the Fund, taking into account: (i) the need to strengthen and safeguard the mobilization of resources for the Fund; (ii) the equitable geographic distribution of the said seats; and (iii) the role of developing Member Countries in the governance of the Fund.

2. *Distribution of Votes in the Executive Board.* Each member of the Executive Board shall be entitled to cast the votes of all of the Members that it represents. Where the member represents more than one Member, it may cast separately the votes of the Members that it represents.

3. (a) *Lists of Member Countries.* The Member Countries shall be divided, form time to time, into Lists A, B and C for the purposes of this Schedule. Upon joining the Fund, a new Member shall decide on which List it wishes to be placed and, after consultation

[22] Amendment of February 20, 1997 amended and restated Schedule II.

with the Members of that List, shall provide appropriate notification thereof to the President of the Fund in writing. A Member may, at the time of each election for the members and alternate members representing the List of Member Countries to which it belongs, decide to withdraw from one List of Member Countries and place itself upon another List of Member Countries, with the approval of the Members therein. In such event, the concerned Member shall inform the President of the Fund in writing of such change, who shall, from time to time, inform all Members of the composition of all the Lists of Member Countries.

(b) *Distribution of Seats in the Executive Board.* The eighteen (18) members and up to eighteen (18) alternate members of the Executive Board shall be elected or appointed from the Members of the Fund and of whom:

(i) eight (8) members and up to eight (8) alternate members shall be elected or appointed from among those Members set forth in the List A of Member Countries, to be established from time to time;

(ii) four (4) members and four (4) alternate members shall be elected or appointed from among those Members set forth in the List B of Member Countries, to be established from time to time; and

(iii) six (6) members and six (6) alternate members shall be elected or appointed from among those Members set forth in the List C of Member Countries, to be established from time to time.

4. *Procedures for the Election of Executive Board Members.* The procedures that shall apply for the election or appointment of members and alternate members to vacant seats on the Executive Board shall be those set forth below for the respective Members of each List of Member Countries.

A. ELECTION OF MEMBERS OF THE EXECUTIVE BOARD AND THEIR ALTERNATIVES

Part I—List A Member Countries

5. All of the members and alternate members of the Executive Board from List A of Member Countries shall serve for a term of three years.

6. List A Member Countries shall form constituencies and, on the basis of procedures agreed by the List A Member Countries and its constituencies, shall appoint eight members to the Executive Board and shall also appoint up to eight alternates.

7. *Amendments.* The Governors representing List A Member Countries may by a unanimous decision amend the provisions of Part I of this Schedule (paragraphs 5 to 6). Unless otherwise decided, the amendment shall have immediate effect. The President of the Fund shall be informed of any amendment to Part I of this Schedule.

Part II—List B Member Countries

8. All of the members and alternate members of the Executive Board from List B of Member Countries shall serve for a term of three years.

9. The Members of List B shall form themselves into a number of constituencies equal to the number of seats allocated to the List, with each constituency represented by one member and one alternate member in the Executive Board. The President of the Fund shall be informed of the composition of each constituency and any changes thereto that may be made by the Members of List B from time to time.

10. The Members of List B shall decide on the procedures that shall apply for the election or appointment of members and alternate members to vacant seats on the Executive Board and shall provide a copy thereof to the President of the Fund.

11. *Amendments.* The provisions of Part II of this Schedule (paragraphs 8 to 10) may be amended by a vote of the Governors representing two-thirds of the List B Member Countries whose contributions (made in accordance with Section 5(c) of Article 4) amount to seventy per cent (70%) of the contributions of all List B Member Countries. The President of the Fund shall be informed of any amendments to Part II of this Schedule.

Part III—List C Member Countries

Elections

12. All the members and alternate members of the Executive Board from List C of Member Countries shall serve for a term of three years.

13. Except as decided otherwise by the Member Countries of List C, of the six (6) members and six (6) alternate members of the Executive Board elected or appointed from among the List C Member Countries, two (2) members and two (2) alternate members shall be from each of the following regions, as these are set forth in each of the sub-Lists of List C Member Countries:

Africa (sub-List C1);
Europe, Asia and the Pacific (sub-List C2); and
Latin America and the Caribbean (sub-List C3).

14. (a) In accordance with the provisions contained in paragraphs 1 and 27 of this Schedule, the Member Countries of List C shall elect from the countries of its sub-List two members and two alternate members to represent the interests of the whole of the said sub-List, including at least one member or one alternate member from among the Member Countries in that sub-List making the highest substantial contributions to the resources of the Fund.

(b) The Members of List C may review at any time but not later than the Sixth Replenishment of the Fund's Resources, the provisions of sub-paragraph (a) above, taking into account the experience of each sub-List in the implementation of the said sub-paragraph and, if necessary, amended keeping in view the relevant principles contained in Resolution 86/XVIII of the Governing Council.

15. Balloting shall first take place for all members to be elected from each sub-List for which there is a vacancy and for which countries from each sub-List shall nominate candidates. Balloting for each seat shall take place among the Members of the List C.

16. After all members have been elected, balloting shall take place for electing alternate members in the same orders indicated in paragraph 15 above.

17. Election shall require a simple majority of the valid votes cast, not counting abstentions.

18. If no candidate obtains in the first ballot the majority specified in paragraph 17 above, successive ballots shall be held, from each of which that candidate shall be eliminated who receives the lowest number of votes in the previous ballot.

19. In case of a tide vote, the ballot shall, if necessary, be repeated and, if the tide persists in that ballot and on one subsequent one, a decision shall be taken by drawing lots.

20. If at any stage there is only one candidate for a vacancy, he may be declared elected without a ballot, if no Governor objects.

21. Meetings of the List C Member Countries for electing or appointing members and alternate members of the Executive Board shall be held in private. The Members of the List C shall appoint by consensus a Chairman for these meetings.

22. The Members of each sub-List shall appoint by consensus, the Chairman of the respective sub-List meeting.

23. The names of the members and alternate members elected shall be furnished to the President of the Fund along with the term of office of each member and alternate member and the list of principals and alternates.

Casting of Votes in the Executive Board

24. For the purpose of casting votes in the Executive Board, the total number of votes of the countries of each sub-List shall be divided equally between the members of the sub-List concerned.

Amendments

25. Part III of this Schedule (paragraphs 12 to 24) may be amended from time to time by a two-thirds majority of the List C Member Countries. The President of the Fund shall be informed of any amendments to Part III of this Schedule.

B. GENERAL PROVISIONS APPLICABLE TO LIST A, B, AND C

26. The names of the members and alternate members elected or appointed by Lists A, B and C of Member Countries, respectively, shall be furnished to the President of the Fund.

27. Notwithstanding anything to the contrary in paragraphs 5 to 25 above, at the time of each election, the Members of a List of Member Countries or the members of a constituency within a List may decide to appoint a specified number of Members making the highest substantial contribution to the Fund from that List as a member or alternate member of the Executive Board for that List of Member Countries in order to encourage Members to contribute to the resources of the Fund. In such event, the result of that decision shall be notified in writing to the President of the Fund.

28. Once a new Member Country had joined a List of Member Countries, its Governor may designate an existing member of the Executive Board for that List of Member Countries to represent it

and cast its votes until the next election of members of the Executive Board for that List. During such period, a member so designated shall be deemed to have been elected or appointed by the Governor which so designated it and the Member Country shall be deemed to have joined that member's constituency.

29. *Amendments to Paragraphs 1 to 4, 7, 11 and 25 to 29.* The procedures set forth in paragraphs 1 to 4, 7, 11 and 25 to 29 inclusive herein may be amended from time to time by a two-thirds majority of the total votes of the governing Council. Unless otherwise decided, any amendment of paragraphs 1 to 4, 7, 11 and 25 to 29 inclusive shall take effect immediately upon adoption thereof.

SCHEDULE III [23]

DISTRIBUTION OF MEMBER STATES AMONG CATEGORIES AS AT 26 JANUARY 1995

Category I

Australia
Austria
Belgium
Canada
Denmark
Finland
France
Germany
Greece
Ireland
Italy
Japan
Luxembourg
Netherlands
New Zealand
Norway
Portugal
Spain
Sweden
Switzerland
United Kingdom
United States

Category II

Algeria
Gabon
Indonesia
Iran
Iraq
Kuwait
Libyan Arab Jamahiriya [20]
Nigeria
Qatar
Saudi Arabia
United Arab Emirates
Venezuela

Category III

Afghanistan
Albania
Angola
Antigua and Barbuda
Argentina
Armenia
Azerbaijan
Bangladesh
Barbados
Belize
Benin
Bhutan
Bolivia
Bosnia and Herzegovina
Botswana
Brazil
Burkina Faso
Burundi
Cambodia
Cameroon
Cape Verde
Central African Republic
Chad
Chile
China
Colombia
Comoros
Congo
Cook Islands
Costa Rica
Cote d'Ivoire
Croatia
Cuba
Cyprus
D.P.R. Korea
Djibouti
Dominica
Dominican Republic
Ecuador
Egypt
El Salvador
Equatorial Guinea
Eritrea
Ethiopia
Fiji
Gambia, The
Georgia
Ghana
Grenada
Guatemala
Guinea
Guinea Bissau
Guyana
Haiti
Honduras
India
Israel
Jamaica
Joran
Kenya
Kyrgyzstan
Laos
Lebanon
Lesotho
Liberia
Madagascar
Malawi
Malaysia
Maldives

[23] Amendment of February 20, 1997 added Schedule III.

Mali
Malta
Mauritania
Mauritius
Mexico
Mongolia
Morocco
Mozambique
Myanmar
Namibia
Nepal
Nicaragua
Niger
Oman
Pakistan
Panama
Papua New Guinea
Paraguay
Peru
Philippines
Republic of Korea
Romania
Rwanda
Saint Christopher and Nevis
Saint Lucia
Saint Vincent and the Grenadines
Sao Tome and Principe
Senegal
Seychelles
Sierra Leone
Solomon Islands
Somalia
Sri Lanka
Sudan
Suriname
Swaziland
Syria
Tajikistan
Tanzania, United Republic of
Thailand
The Former Yugoslavia Republic of Macedonia
Togo
Tonga
Trinidad and Tobago
Tunisia
Turkey
Uganda
Uruguay
Viet Nam
Western Samoa
Yemen
Yugoslavia
Zaire
Zambia
Zimbabwe

2. Grains Trade Convention, 1995

Done at London December 7, 1994; Entered into force July 1, 1995; Entered into force for the United States May 27, 1999[1]

PREAMBLE[2]

The signatories to this agreement

CONSIDERING that the International Wheat Agreement, 1949 was revised, renewed, updated or extended on successive occasions leading to the conclusion of the International Wheat Agreement, 1986

CONSIDERING that the provisions of the International Wheat Agreement, 1986, consisting of the Wheat Trade Convention, 1986, on the one hand, and the Food Aid Convention, 1986, on the other, as extended, will expire on 30th June 1995, and that it is desirable to conclude an agreement for a new period,

HAVE AGREED that the International Wheat Agreement, 1986 shall be updated and renamed the International Grains Agreement, 1995, which shall consist of two separate legal instruments

(a) the Grains Trade Convention, 1995 and

(b) the Food Aid Convention, 1995,

and that each of these two Conventions, or either of them as appropriate, shall be submitted for signature and ratification, acceptance or approval, in conformity with their respective constitutional or institutional procedures, by the Governments concerned.

GRAINS TRADE CONVENTION, 1995

PART I—GENERAL

ARTICLE 1

Objectives

The objectives of this Convention are:

(a) to further international co-operation in all aspects of trade in grains, especially insofar as these affect the food grain situation;

(b) to promote the expansion of international trade in grains, and to secure the freest possible flow of this trade, including the elimination of trade barriers and unfair and discriminatory practices, in the interest of all members, in particular developing members;

(c) to contribute to the fullest extent possible to the stability of international grain markets in the interests of all members, to enhance world food security, and to contribute to the development of

[1] The Grains Trade Convention, 1995, is a constituent instrument of the International Grains Agreement, 1995, which also included the Food Aid Convention, 1995. The Food Aid Convention, 1995, was re-opened for negotiation in December 1996 and resulted in the Food Aid Convention, 1999 (see below for text). The Food Aid Convention, 1999, also remains a constituent instrument of the International Grains Agreement, 1995.

[2] This preamble is the preamble to the International Grains Agreement, 1995, and precedes the text of the Grains Trade Convention, 1995.

countries whose economies are heavily dependent on commercial sales of grain; and

(d) to provide a forum for exchange of information and discussion of members' concerns regarding trade in grains.

ARTICLE 2

Definitions

For the purposes of this Convention:

(1)(a) "Council" means the International Grains Council established by the International Wheat Agreement, 1949 and continued in being by Article 9;

(b)(i) "member" means a party to this Convention;

(ii) "exporting member" means a member so designated under Article 12;

(iii) "importing member" means a member so designated under Article 12;

(c) "executive Committee" means the Committee established under Article 15;

(d) "Market Conditions Committee" means the Committee established under Article 16;

(e) "grain" or "grains" means barley, maize, millet, oats, rye, sorghum, triticale and wheat, and their products, and such other grains and products as the Council may decide;

(f)(i) "purchase" means a purchase of grain for import, or the quantity of grain so purchased, as the context requires;

(ii) "sale" means a sale of grain for export, or the quantity of such grain so sold, as the context requires;

(iii) where reference is made in this Convention to a purchase or sale, it shall be understood to refer not only to purchases or sales concluded between the Governments concerned, but also to purchases or sales concluded between private traders, and to purchases or sales concluded between a private trader and the Government concerned;

(g) "special vote" means a vote requiring at least two thirds of the votes (as calculated under Article 12) cast by the exporting members present and voting, and at least two thirds of the votes (as calculated under Article 12) cast by the importing members present and voting, counted separately;

(h) "crop year" or "fiscal year" means the period from 1 July to the following 30 June;

(i) "working day" means a working day at the headquarters of the Council.

(2) Any reference in this Convention to a "Government" or "Governments" or "member" shall be construed as including a reference to the European Community (hereinafter referred to as the EC). Accordingly, any reference in this Convention to "signature" or to the "deposit of instruments of ratification, acceptance, or approval" or "an instrument of accession" or "a declaration of provisional application" by a Government shall, in the case of the EC, be construed as including signature or declaration of provisional application on behalf of the EC by its competent authority and the deposit of the instrument required by the institutional procedures of the

EC to be deposited for the conclusion of an international agreement.

(3) Any reference in this Convention to a "Government", or "Governments", or "member", shall be understood, where appropriate, to include a reference to any separate customs territory within the meaning of the General Agreement on Tariffs and Trade or of the Agreement Establishing The World Trade Organization.

ARTICLE 3

Information, reports and studies

(1) To facilitate the achievement of the objectives in Article 1, make possible a fuller exchange of views at Council sessions, and provide information on a continuing basis to serve the general interest of members, arrangements shall be made for regular reports and exchange of information, and also special studies, as appropriate, covering grains, focusing primarily upon the following:

(a) supply, demand and market conditions;

(b) developments in national policies and their effects on the international market;

(c) developments concerning the improvement and expansion of trade, utilization, storage and transportation, especially in developing countries.

(2) To improve the collection and presentation of information for those reports and studies referred to in paragraph (1) of this Article, to make it possible for more members to participate directly in the work of the Council, and to supplement the guidance already given by the Council in the course of its sessions, there shall be established a Market Conditions Committee, whose meetings shall be open to all members of the Council. The Committee shall have the functions specified in Article 16.

ARTICLE 4

Consultations on market developments

(1) If the Market Conditions Committee, in the course of its continuous review of the market under Article 16, is of the opinion that developments in the international grain market seriously threaten to affect the interests of members, or if such developments are called to the Committee's attention by the Executive Director on his own initiative or at the request of any member of the Council, it shall immediately report the facts concerned to the Executive Committee. The Market Conditions Committee, in so informing the Executive Committee, shall give particular regard to those circumstances which threaten to affect the interests of members.

(2) The Executive Committee shall meet within ten working days to review such developments and, if it deems it appropriate, request the Chairman of the Council to convene a session of the Council to consider the situation.

ARTICLE 5

Commercial purchases and special transactions

(1) A commercial purchase for the purposes of this Convention is a purchase as defined in Article 2 which conforms to the usual commercial practices in international trade and which does not include those transactions referred to in paragraph (2) of this Article.

(2) A special transaction for the purposes of this Convention is one which includes features introduced by the Government of a member concerned which do not conform to usual commercial practices. Special transactions include the following:

(a) sales on credit in which, as a result of government intervention, the interest rate, period of payment, or other related terms do not conform to the commercial rates, periods or terms prevailing in the world market;

(b) sales in which the funds for the purchase of grain are obtained under a loan from the Government of the exporting member tied to the purchase of grain;

(c) sales for currency of the importing member which is not transferable or convertible into currency or goods for use in the exporting member;

(d) sales under trade agreements with special payments arrangements which include clearing accounts for settling credit balances bilaterally through the exchange of goods, except where the exporting member and the importing member concerned agree that the sale shall be regarded as commercial;

(e) barter transactions:

(i) which result from the intervention of Governments where grain is exchanged at other than prevailing world prices, or

(ii) which involve sponsorship under a government purchase programme, except where the purchase of grain results from a barter transaction in which the country of final destination was not named in the original barter contract;

(f) a gift of grain or a purchase of grain out of a monetary grant by the exporting member made for that specific purpose;

(g) any other categories of transactions, as the Council may prescribe, that include features introduced by the Government of a member concerned which do not conform to usual commercial practices.

(3) Any question raised by the Executive Director or by any member as to whether a transaction is a commercial purchase as defined in paragraph (1) of this Article or a special transaction as defined in paragraph (2) of this Article shall be decided by the Council.

ARTICLE 6

Guidelines relating to concessional transactions

(1) Members undertake to conduct any concessional transactions in grains in such a way as to avoid harmful interference with normal patterns of production and international commercial trade.

(2) To this end both supplying and recipient members shall undertake appropriate measures to ensure that concessional transactions are additional to commercial sales which could reasonably be anticipated in the absence of such transactions, and would increase consumption or stocks in the recipient country. Such measures shall, for countries which are members of the Food and Agriculture Organization (FAO), be consistent with the FAO Principles of Surplus Disposal and Guiding Lines and the consultative obligations of FAO members, and may include the requirement that a specified level of commercial imports of grains agreed with the recipient country be maintained on a global basis by that country. In establishing or adjusting this level, full regard shall be had to the commercial import levels in a representative period, to recent trends in utilisation and imports, and to the economic circumstances of the recipient country, including, in particular, its balance-of-payments situation.

(3) Members, when engaging in concessional export transactions, shall consult with exporting members whose commercial sales might be affected by such transactions to the maximum possible extent before such arrangements are concluded with recipient countries.

(4) The Secretariat shall periodically report to the Council on developments in concessional transactions in grains.

ARTICLE 7

Reporting and recording

(1) Members shall provide regular reports, and the Council shall maintain records for each crop year, showing separately commercial and special transactions, of all shipments of grain by members and all imports of grain from non-members. The Council shall also maintain, to the extent possible, records of all shipments between non-members.

(2) Members shall provide, as far as possible, such information as the Council may require concerning their grain supply and demand, and report promptly all changes in their national grain policies.

(3) For the purposes of this Article:

(a) members shall send to the Executive Director such information concerning the quantities of grain involved in commercial sales and purchases and special transactions as the Council within its competence may require, including:

(i) in relation to special transactions, such detail of the transactions as will enable them to be classified in accordance with Article 5;

(ii) such information as may be available as to the type, class, grade and quality of the grains concerned;

(b) any member when exporting grain shall send to the Executive Director such information relating to their export prices as the Council may require;

(c) the council shall obtain regular information on currently prevailing grain transportation costs, and members shall report such supplementary information as the council may require.

(4) In the case of any grain which reaches the country of final destination after resale in, passage through, or transhipment from the ports of, a country other than that in which it originated, members shall to the maximum extent possible make available such information as will enable the shipment to be entered in the records as a shipment between the country of origin and the country of final destination. In the case of a resale, the provisions of this paragraph shall apply if the grain originated in the country of origin during the same crop year.

(5) The Council shall make rules of procedure for the reports and records referred to in this Article. Those rules shall prescribe the frequency and the manner in which those reports shall be made and shall prescribe the duties of members with regard thereto. The Council shall also make provision for the amendment of any records or statements kept by it, including provision for the settlement of any dispute arising in connection therewith. If any member repeatedly and unreasonably fails to make reports as required by this Article, the Executive Committee shall arrange consultations with that member to remedy the situation.

ARTICLE 8

Disputes and complaints

(1) Any dispute concerning the interpretation or application of this Convention which is not settled by negotiation shall, at the request of any member which is a party to the dispute, be referred to the Council for decision.

(2) Any member which considers that its interests as a party to this Convention have been seriously prejudiced by actions of any one or more members affecting the operation of this Convention may bring the matter before the Council. In such a case, the Council shall immediately consult with the members concerned in order to resolve the matter. If the matter is not resolved through such consultations, the Council shall consider the matter further and may make recommendations to the members concerned.

PART II—ADMINISTRATION

ARTICLE 9

Constitution of the Council

(1) The Council (formerly the International Wheat Council, as established by the International Wheat Agreement, 1949, and now renamed the International Grains Council) shall continue in being for the purposes of administering this Convention with the membership, powers and functions provided in this Convention.

(2) Members may be represented at Council meetings by delegates, alternates and advisers.

(3) The Council shall elect a Chairman and a Vice-Chairman who shall hold office for one crop year. The Chairman shall have no vote and the Vice-Chairman shall have no vote while acting as Chairman.

ARTICLE 10

Powers and functions of the Council

(1) The Council shall establish its Rules of Procedure.

(2) The Council shall keep such records as are required by the terms of this Convention and may keep such other records as it considers desirable.

(3) In order to enable the Council to discharge its functions under this Convention, the Council may request, and members undertake to supply, subject to the provisions of paragraph (2) of Article 7, such statistics and information as are necessary for this purpose.

(4) The Council may, by special vote, delegate to any of its committees, or to the Executive Director, the exercise of powers or functions other than the following:

(a) decisions on matters under Article 8;

(b) review, under Article 11, of the votes of members listed in the Annex;

(c) determination of exporting and importing members and distribution of their votes under Article 12;

(d) location of the seat of the Council under paragraph (1) of Article 13;

(e) appointment of the Executive Director under paragraph (2) of Article 17;

(f) adoption of the budget and assessment of members' contributions under Article 21;

(g) suspension of the voting rights of a member under paragraph (6) of Article 21;

(h) any request to the Secretary-General of UNCTAD to convene a negotiating conference under Article 22;

(i) exclusion of a member from the Council under Article 30;

(j) recommendation of an amendment under Article 32;

(k) extension or termination of this Convention under Article 33. The Council may at any time revoke such delegation by a majority of the votes cast.

(5) Any decision made under any powers or functions delegated by the Council in accordance with paragraph (4) of this Article shall be subject to review by the Council at the request of any member made within a period which the Council shall prescribe. Any decision in respect of which no request for review has been made within the prescribed period shall be binding on all members.

(6) In addition to the powers and functions specified in this Convention the Council shall have such other powers and perform such other functions as are necessary to carry out the terms of this Convention.

ARTICLE 11

Votes for entry into force and budgetary procedures

(1) For the purposes of the entry into force of this Convention, the calculations under paragraph (1) of Article 28 shall be based on the votes as set out in part A of the Annex.

(2) For the purposes of the assessment of financial contributions under Article 21, the votes of members shall be based on those set

out in the Annex, subject to the provisions of this Article and the associated Rules of Procedure.

(3) Whenever this Convention is extended under paragraph (2) of Article 33, the Council shall review and adjust the votes of members under this Article. Such adjustments shall bring the distribution of votes more closely into line with current grain trade patterns, and shall be in accordance with the methods specified in the Rules of Procedure.

(4) If the Council decides that a significant shift in world grain trading patterns has occurred it shall review, and may adjust, the votes of members. Such adjustments shall be regarded as amendments to this Convention, and shall be subject to the provisions of Article 32, except that an adjustment of votes may take effect only at the beginning of a fiscal year. After any adjustment to member's votes under this paragraph has taken effect, no further such adjustment may be put into effect before three years have elapsed.

(5) All redistributions of votes under this Article shall be conducted in accordance with the Rules of Procedure.

(6) For all purposes regarding the administration of this Convention, other than its entry into force under paragraph (1) of Article 28 and the assessment of financial contributions under Article 21, the votes to be exercised by members shall be as determined under Article 12.

ARTICLE 12

Determination of exporting and importing members and distribution of their votes

(1) At the first session held under this Convention, the Council shall establish which members shall be exporting members and which members shall be importing members for the purposes of this Convention. In so deciding, the Council shall take account of the grain trading patterns of those members and of their own views.

(2) As soon as the Council has determined which members shall be exporting and which shall be importing members under this Convention, the exporting members, on the basis of their votes under Article 11, shall divide their votes among them as they shall decide, subject to the conditions laid down in paragraph (3) of this Article, and the importing members shall similarly divide their votes.

(3) For the purposes of the allocation of votes under paragraph (2) of this Article, the exporting members shall together hold 1,000 votes, and the importing members shall together hold 1,000 votes. No member shall hold more than 333 votes as an exporting member or more than 333 votes as an importing member. There shall be no fractional votes.

(4) The lists of exporting and importing members shall be reviewed by the Council, in the light of changing patterns in their grain trade, after a period of three years following the entry into force of this Convention. They shall also be reviewed whenever this Convention is extended under paragraph (2) of Article 33.

(5) At the request of any member, the Council may, at the beginning of any fiscal year, agree by special vote to the transfer of that

member from the list of exporting members to the list of importing members, or from the list of importing members to the list of exporting members, as appropriate.

(6) The distribution of the votes of exporting and importing members shall be reviewed by the Council whenever the lists of the exporting and importing members are changed under paragraphs (4) or (5) of this Article. Any redistribution of votes under this paragraph shall be subject to the conditions set out in paragraph (3) of this Article.

(7) Whenever any Government becomes, or ceases to be, a party to this Convention, the Council shall redistribute the votes of the other exporting or importing members, as appropriate, in proportion to the number of votes held by each member, subject to the conditions set out in paragraph (3) of this Article.

(8) Any exporting member may authorize any other exporting member, and any importing member may authorise any other importing member, to represent its interests and to exercise its votes at any meeting or meetings of the Council. Satisfactory evidence of such authorisation shall be submitted to the Council.

(9) If at any meeting of the Council a member is not represented by an accredited delegate and has not authorized another member to exercise its votes in accordance with paragraph (8) of this Article, or if at the date of any meeting any member has forfeited, has been deprived of, or has recovered its votes under any provisions of this Convention, the total votes to be exercised by the exporting members at that meeting shall be adjusted to a figure equal to the total of votes to be exercised at that meeting by the importing members and redistributed among exporting members in proportion to their votes.

ARTICLE 13

Seat, sessions and quorum

(1) The seat of the Council shall be in London unless the Council decides otherwise.

(2) The Council shall meet at least once during each half of each fiscal year and at such other times as the Chairman may decide, or as otherwise required by this Convention.

(3) The Chairman shall convene a session of the Council if so requested by (a) five members or (b) one or more members holding a total of not less than 10 per cent of the total votes or (c) the Executive Committee.

(4) The presence of delegates with a majority of the votes held by the exporting members and a majority of the votes held by the importing members, prior to any adjustment of votes under paragraph (9) of Article 12, shall be necessary to constitute a quorum at any meeting of the Council.

ARTICLE 14

Decisions

(1) Except where otherwise specified in this Convention, decisions of the Council shall be by a majority of the votes cast by the

exporting members and a majority of the votes cast by the importing members, counted separately.

(2) Without prejudice to the complete liberty of action of any member in the determination and administration of its agricultural and price policies, each member undertakes to accept as binding all decisions of the Council under the provisions of this Convention.

ARTICLE 15

Executive Committee

(1) The Council shall establish an Executive Committee consisting of not more than six exporting members elected annually by the exporting members and not more than eight importing members elected annually by the importing members. The Council shall appoint the Chairman of the Executive Committee and may appoint a Vice-Chairman.

(2) The Executive Committee shall be responsible to and work under the general direction of the Council. It shall have such powers and functions as are expressly assigned to it under this Convention and such other powers and functions as the Council may delegate to it under paragraph (4) of Article 10.

(3) The exporting members on the Executive Committee shall have the same total number of votes as the importing members. The votes of the exporting members on the Executive Committee shall be divided among them as they shall decide, provided that no such exporting member shall have more than 40 per cent of the total votes of those exporting members. The votes of the importing members on the Executive Committee shall be divided among them as they shall decide, provided that no such importing member shall have more than 40 per cent of the total votes of those importing members.

(4) The Council shall prescribe rules of procedure regarding voting in the Executive Committee and may make such other provision regarding rules of procedure in the Executive Committee as it thinks fit. A decision of the Executive Committee shall require the same majority of votes as this Convention prescribes for the Council when making a decision on a similar matter.

(5) Any member of the Council which is not a member of the Executive Committee may participate, without voting, in the discussion of any question before the Executive Committee whenever the latter considers that the interests of that member are affected.

ARTICLE 16

Market Conditions Committee

(1) The Council shall establish a Market Conditions Committee, which shall be a Committee of the whole. The Chairman of the Market Conditions Committee shall be the Executive Director, unless the Council decides otherwise.

(2) Invitations to attend the meetings of the Market Conditions Committee as observers may be extended to representatives of non-member Governments and international organizations, as the Chairman of the Committee considers appropriate.

(3) The Committee shall keep under continuous review, and report to members on, all matters affecting the world grain economy. The Committee shall take account in its review of relevant information supplied by any member of the Council.

(4) The Committee shall supplement the guidance given by the Council to assist the Secretariat in carrying out the work envisaged in Article 3.

(5) The Committee shall advise in accordance with the relevant Articles of this Convention and on any matters which the Council or the Executive Committee may refer to it.

ARTICLE 17

Secretariat

(1) The Council shall have a Secretariat consisting of an Executive Director, who shall be its chief administrative officer, and such staff as may be required for the work of the Council and its Committees.

(2) The Council shall appoint the Executive Director who shall be responsible for the performance of the duties devolving upon the Secretariat in the administration of this Convention, and for the performance of such other duties as are assigned to him by the Council and its Committees.

(3) The staff shall be appointed by the Executive Director in accordance with regulations established by the Council.

(4) It shall be a condition of employment of the Executive Director and of the staff that they do not hold or shall cease to hold financial interest in the grain trade and that they shall not seek or receive instructions regarding their duties under this Convention from any Government or from any other authority external to the Council.

ARTICLE 18

Admission of observers

The Council may invite any non-member State, and any intergovernmental organization, to attend any of its meetings as an observer.

ARTICLE 19

Co-operation with other intergovernmental organisations

(1) The Council may make whatever arrangements are appropriate for consultation or co-operation with the United Nations, its organs, and such other specialized agencies and intergovernmental organisations as may be appropriate, in particular the United Nations Conference on Trade and Development, the Food and Agriculture Organization, the Common Fund for Commodities and the World Food Programme.

(2) The Council, bearing in mind the particular role of the United Nations Conference on Trade and Development in international commodity trade, will, as it considers appropriate, keep the United

Nations Conference on Trade and Development informed of its activities and programmes of work.

(3) If the Council finds that any terms of this Convention are materially inconsistent with such requirements as may be laid down by the United Nations through its appropriate organs or by its specialised agencies regarding intergovernmental commodity agreements, the inconsistency shall be deemed to be a circumstance affecting adversely the operation of this Convention and the procedure prescribed in Article 32 shall be applied.

ARTICLE 20

Privileges and immunities

(1) The Council shall have legal personality. It shall in particular have the capacity to contract, acquire and dispose of movable and immovable property and to institute legal proceedings.

(2) The status, privileges and immunities of the Council in the territory of the United Kingdom shall continue to be governed by the Headquarters Agreement between the Government of the United Kingdom of Great Britain and Northern Ireland and the International Wheat Council signed at London on 28 November 1968.

(3) The Agreement referred to in paragraph (2) of this Article shall be independent of the present Convention. It shall however terminate:

(a) by agreement between the Government of the United Kingdom of Great Britain and Northern Ireland and the Council, or

(b) in the event of the seat of the Council being moved from the United Kingdom, or

(c) in the event of the Council ceasing to exist.

(4) In the event of the seat of the Council being moved from the United Kingdom, the Government of the member in which the seat of the Council is situated shall conclude with the Council an international agreement relating to the status, privileges and immunities of the Council, its Executive Director, its staff and representatives of members at meetings convened by the Council.

ARTICLE 21

Finance

(1) The expenses of delegations to the Council and of representatives on its Committees and working groups shall be met by their respective Governments. The other expenses necessary for the administration of this Convention shall be met by annual contributions from all members. The contribution of each member for each fiscal year shall be in the proportion which the number of its votes in the Annex bears to the total of the votes of members in the Annex, as adjusted under Article 11 to reflect the membership of the Convention at the time when the budget for that fiscal year is adopted.

(2) At its first session after this Convention comes into force, the Council shall approve its budget for the fiscal year ending 30 June 1996, and assess the contribution to be paid by each member.

(3) The Council shall, at a session during the second half of each fiscal year, approve its budget for the following fiscal year and assess the contribution to be paid by each member for that fiscal year.

(4) The initial contribution of any member acceding to this Convention under paragraph (2) of Article 27 shall be assessed on the basis of the votes agreed with the Council as a condition for its accession, and the period of the current fiscal year remaining at the time of accession, but the assessments of contributions to be paid by the other members in that fiscal year shall not be altered.

(5) Contributions shall be payable immediately upon assessment.

(6) If, at the end of six months following the date on which its contribution is due in accordance with paragraph (5) of this Article, a member has not paid its full contribution, the Executive Director shall request the member to make payment as quickly as possible. If, at the expiration of six months after the request of the Executive Director, the member has still not paid its contribution, its voting rights in the Council and in the Executive Committee shall be suspended until such time as it has made full payment of the contribution.

(7) A member whose voting rights have been suspended under paragraph (6) of this Article shall not be deprived of any of its other rights or relieved of any of its obligations under this Convention, unless the Council so decides by special vote. It shall remain liable to pay its contribution and to meet any other of its financial obligations under this Convention.

(8) The Council shall, each fiscal year, publish an audited statement of its receipts and expenditures in the previous fiscal year.

(9) The Council shall, prior to its dissolution, provide for the settlement of its liabilities and the disposal of its records and assets.

ARTICLE 22

Economic provisions

The Council may, at an appropriate time, examine the possibility of the negotiation of a new international agreement or convention with economic provisions, and report to members, making such recommendations as it deems appropriate. The Council may, when it is judged that such a negotiation could be successfully concluded, request the Secretary-General of the United Nations Conference on Trade and Development to convene a negotiating conference.

PART III—FINAL PROVISIONS

ARTICLE 23

Depositary

(1) The Secretary-General of the United Nations is hereby designated as the depositary of this Convention.

(2) The depositary shall notify all signatory and acceding Governments of each signature, ratification, acceptance, approval, provisional application of, and accession to, this Convention, as well as each notification and notice received under Articles 29 and 32.

ARTICLE 24

Signature

This Convention shall be open for signature at United Nations Headquarters from 1 May 1995 until and including 30 June 1995 by the Governments listed in the Annex.

ARTICLE 25

Ratification, acceptance, approval

(1) This Convention shall be subject to ratification, acceptance or approval by each signatory Government in accordance with its respective constitutional procedures.

(2) Instruments of ratification, acceptance or approval shall be deposited with the depositary not later than 30 June 1995. The Council may, however, grant one or more extensions of time to any signatory Government which is unable to deposit its instrument by that date. The Council shall inform the depositary of all such extensions of time.

ARTICLE 26

Provisional application

Any signatory Government and any other Government eligible to sign this Convention, or whose application for accession is approved by the Council, may deposit with the depositary a declaration of provisional application. Any Government depositing such a declaration shall provisionally apply this Convention in accordance with its laws and regulations and be provisionally regarded as a party thereto.

ARTICLE 27

Accession

(1) Any Government listed in the Annex may accede to the present Convention until and including 30 June 1995, except that the Council may grant one or more extensions of time to any Government which has not deposited its instrument by that date.

(2) This Convention shall be open for accession after 30 June 1995 by the Governments of all States upon such conditions as the Council considers appropriate. Accession shall be effected by the deposit of an instrument of accession with the depositary. Such instruments of accession shall state that the Government accepts all the conditions established by the Council.

(3) Where, for the purposes of the operation of this Convention, reference is made to members listed in the Annex, any member the Government of which has acceded to this Convention on conditions

prescribed by the Council in accordance with this Article shall be deemed to be listed in the Annex.

ARTICLE 28

Entry into force

(1) This Convention shall enter into force on 1 July 1995 if instruments of ratification, acceptance, approval or accession, or declarations of provisional application have been deposited not later than 30 June 1995 on behalf of Governments listed in part A of the Annex holding, at least, 88 per cent of the total votes set out in part A of the Annex.

(2) If this Convention does not enter into force in accordance with paragraph (1) of this Article, the Governments which have deposited instruments of ratification, acceptance, approval or accession, or declarations of provisional application, may decide by mutual consent that it shall enter into force between themselves.

ARTICLE 29

Withdrawal

Any member may withdraw from this Convention at the end of any fiscal year by giving written notice of withdrawal to the depositary at least ninety days prior to the end of that fiscal year, but shall not thereby be released from any obligations under this Convention which have not been discharged by the end of that fiscal year. The member shall simultaneously inform the Council of the action it has taken.

ARTICLE 30

Exclusion

If the Council finds that any member is in breach of its obligations under this Convention and decides further that such breach significantly impairs the operation of this Convention, it may, by special vote, exclude such member from the Council. The Council shall immediately notify the depositary of any such decision. Ninety days after the date of the Council's decision, that member shall cease to be a member of the Council.

ARTICLE 31

Settlement of accounts

(1) The Council shall determine any settlement of accounts which it finds equitable with a member which has withdrawn from this Convention or which has been excluded from the Council, or has otherwise ceased to be a party to this Convention. The Council shall retain any amounts already paid by such member. Such member shall be bound to pay any amounts due from it to the Council.

(2) Upon termination of this Convention, any member referred to in paragraph (1) of this Article shall not be entitled to any share of the proceeds of the liquidation or the other assets of the Council;

nor shall it be burdened with any part of the deficit, if any, of the Council.

ARTICLE 32

Amendment

(1) The Council may by special vote recommend to members an amendment of this Convention. The amendment shall become effective 100 days after the depositary has received notifications of acceptance from exporting members which hold two thirds of the votes of the exporting members and by importing members which hold two thirds of the votes of the importing members, or on such later date as the Council may have determined by special vote. The Council may fix a time within which each member shall notify the depositary of its acceptance of the amendment and, if the amendment has not become effective by such time, it shall be considered withdrawn. The Council shall provide the depositary with the information necessary to determine whether the notifications of acceptance received are sufficient to make the amendment effective.

(2) Any member on behalf of which notification of acceptance of an amendment has not been made by the date on which such amendment becomes effective shall as of that date cease to be a party to this Convention, unless such member has satisfied the Council that acceptance could not be secured in time owing to difficulties in completing its constitutional procedures and the Council decides to extend for such member the period fixed for acceptance. Such member shall not be bound by the amendment before it has notified its acceptance thereof.

ARTICLE 33

Duration, extension and termination

(1) This Convention shall remain in force until 30 June 1998, unless extended under paragraph (2) of this Article, or terminated earlier under paragraph (3) of this Article, or replaced before that date by a new agreement or convention negotiated under Article 22.

(2) The Council may, by special vote, extend this Convention beyond 30 June 1998 for successive periods not exceeding two years on each occasion. Any member which does not accept such extension of this Convention shall so inform the Council at least thirty days prior to the extension coming into force. Such a member shall cease to be a party to this Convention from the beginning of the period of extension, but it shall not thereby be released from any obligations under this Convention which have not been discharged prior to that date.

(3) The Council may at any time decide, by special vote, to terminate this Convention with effect from such date and subject to such conditions as it may determine.

(4) Upon termination of this Convention, the Council shall continue in being for such time as may be required to carry out its liquidation and shall have such powers and exercise such functions as may be necessary for that purpose.

(5) The Council shall notify the depositary of any action taken under paragraph (2) or paragraph (3) of this Article.

ARTICLE 34

Relationship of Preamble to Convention

This Convention includes the Preamble to the International Grains Agreement, 1995.

3. Food Aid Convention, 1999

Done at London April 13, 1999; Entered into force July 1, 1999; Entered into force for the United States January 5, 2001[1]

PREAMBLE

The Parties to this Convention,

HAVING reviewed the Food Aid Convention, 1995 and its objective of securing at least 10 million tonnes of food aid annually in the form of grain suitable for human consumption, and wishing to confirm their desire to maintain international co-operation on food aid matters among member governments;

RECALLING the Declaration on World Food Security and the World Food Summit Plan of Action adopted in Rome in 1996, in particular the commitment to achieve food security for all and to an ongoing effort to eradicate hunger;

DESIRING to enhance the capacity of the international community to respond to food emergency situations and to improve world food security, through the assurance of supplies of food aid irrespective of world food price and supply fluctuations;

RECALLING that, in their 1994 Marrakesh decision on measures concerning least-developed countries and net food-importing developing countries, Ministers of WTO member countries agreed to review the level of food aid established under the Food Aid Convention as further elaborated at the 1996 Singapore Ministerial Conference;

RECOGNISING that the recipients and members have their own policies on food aid and related matters, and that the ultimate objective of food aid is the elimination of the need for food aid itself;

DESIRING to improve the effectiveness and quality of food aid as a tool in support of food security in developing countries, particularly to alleviate poverty and hunger of the most vulnerable groups, and to improve member co-ordination and co-operation in the field of food aid;

HAVE AGREED ON THE FOLLOWING:

[1] The Food Aid Convention, 1999, is a contstituent instrument of the International Grains Agreement, 1995, which also includes the Grain Trade Convention, 1995. The Food Aid Convention, 1995, was re-opened for negotiation in December 1996 and resulted in the Food Aid Convention, 1999.

PART I—OBJECTIVES AND DEFINITIONS

ARTICLE I

Objectives

The objectives of this Convention are to contribute to world food security and to improve the ability of the international community to respond to emergency food situations and other food needs of developing countries by:

(a) making appropriate levels of food aid available on a predictable basis, as determined by the provisions of this Convention;

(b) encouraging members to ensure that the food aid provided is aimed particularly at the alleviation of poverty and hunger of the most vulnerable groups, and is consistent with agricultural development in those countries;

(c) including principles for maximising the impact, the effectiveness and quality of the food aid provided as a tool in support of food security; and,

(d) providing a framework for co-operation, co-ordination and information-sharing among members on food aid related matters to achieve greater efficiency in all aspects of food aid operations and better coherence between food aid and other policy instruments.

ARTICLE II

Definitions

(a) Under this Convention, unless the context otherwise requires, any reference to:

(i) "c.i.f." means cost, insurance and freight;

(ii) "Commitment" means the minimum amount of food aid to be provided annually by a member under Article III (e);

(iii) "Committee" means the Food Aid Committee referred to in Article XV;

(iv) "Contribution" means the amount of food aid provided and reported to the Committee by a member annually in accordance with the provisions of this Convention;

(v) "Convention" means the Food Aid Convention, 1999;

(vi) "DAC" means the Development Assistance Committee of OECD;

(vii) "Developing country" means any country or territory eligible to receive food aid under Article VII;

(viii) "Eligible product" means a product, referred to in Article IV, which may be provided as food aid by a member as its contribution under this Convention;

(ix) "Executive Director" means the Executive Director of the International Grains Council;

(x) "f.o.b." means free on board;

(xi) "Food" or "food aid" includes, as appropriate, a reference to seed for food crops;

(xii) "Member" means a party to this Convention;

(xiii) "Micronutrients" means vitamins and minerals used to fortify or complement food aid products which are eligible, under Article IV (c), to be counted as a member's contribution;

(xiv) "OECD" means the Organisation for Economic Co-operation and Development;

(xv) "Products of primary processing" include:

cereal flours;

cereal groats and cereal meal;

other worked cereal grains (e.g. rolled, flaked, polished, pearled and kibbled, but not further prepared) except husked, glazed, polished or broken rice;

germ of cereals, whole, rolled, flaked or ground;

bulgur; and

any other similar grain product which the Committee may decide;

(xvi) "Products of secondary processing" include:

macaroni, spaghetti and similar products; and

any other product, whose manufacture involves the use of a product of primary processing, which the Committee may decide;

(xvii) "Rice" includes husked, glazed, polished or broken rice;

(xviii) "Secretariat" means the Secretariat of the International Grains Council;

(xix) "Tonne" means a metric ton of 1,000 kilograms;

(xx) "Transport and other operational costs", as listed in Annex A, mean costs beyond the f.o.b. stage or, in the case of local purchases, beyond the point of purchase, associated with a food aid operation, which may be counted in whole or in part towards a member's contribution;

(xxi) "Value" means the commitment of a member in a convertible currency;

(xxii) "Wheat equivalent" means the amount of a member's commitment or contribution as evaluated in accordance with Article V;

(xxiii) "WTO" means the World Trade Organization;

(xxiv) "Year" means the period from 1 July to the following 30 June, unless otherwise stated.

(b) Any reference in this Convention to a "Government" or "Governments" or "member" shall be construed as including a reference to the European Community (hereinafter referred to as the EC). Accordingly, any reference in this Convention to "signature" or to the "deposit of instruments of ratification, acceptance, or approval" or "an instrument of accession" or "a declaration of provisional application" by a Government shall, in the case of the EC, be construed as including signature or declaration of provisional application on behalf of the EC by its competent authority and the deposit of the instrument required by the institutional procedures of the EC to be deposited for the conclusion of an international agreement.

(c) Any reference in this Convention to a "Government", or "Governments", or "member", shall be understood, where appropriate, to include a reference to any separate customs territory within the meaning of the General Agreement on Tariffs and Trade or of the Agreement Establishing The World Trade Organization.

PART II—CONTRIBUTIONS AND NEEDS

ARTICLE III

Quantities and Quality

(a) Members agree to provide food aid to developing countries or the cash equivalent thereof in the minimum annual amounts specified in paragraph (e) below (hereinafter referred to as "he commitment".

(b) The commitment of each member shall be expressed in either tonnes of wheat equivalent or in value or in a combination of tonnage and value. Members expressing their commitment in value terms shall also specify a guaranteed annual tonnage.

(c) In the case of members expressing their commitment in value terms or in a combination of tonnage and value, the value may include the transport and other operational costs associated with the food aid operations.

(d) Whether its commitment is expressed in tonnage, in value, or in a combination of tonnage and value, a member may also include an indicative value representing its total estimated cost, including the transport and other operational costs associated with the food aid operations.

(e) Subject to the provisions of Article VI, the commitment of each member shall be:

Member	Tonnage [1] (wheat equivalent)	Value [1] (millions)	Total indicative value (millions)
Argentina	35,000	—	
Australia	250,000	—	[2] A$ 90
Canada	420,000	—	[2] C$ 150
European Community and its member States	1,320,000	[2] €130	[2] €422
Japan	300,000	—	
Norway	30,000	—	[2] NOK 59
Switzerland	40,000	—	
United States of America	2,500,000	—	[2] US$ 900–1,000

[1] Members shall report their food aid operations in line with the relevant Rules of Procedure

[2] Includes transport and other operational costs

(f) Transport and other operational costs, when counted towards a member's commitment, must be incurred as part of a food aid operation which is also eligible to be counted towards a member's commitment.

(g) In respect of transport and other operational costs, a member cannot count more than the acquisition cost of eligible products towards its commitment, except in the case of internationally recognised emergency situations.

(h) Any member which has acceded to this Convention under paragraph (b) of Article XXIII shall be deemed to be listed in paragraph (e) of this Article, together with its commitment.

(i) The commitment of an acceding member referred to in paragraph (h) of this Article shall not be less than 20,000 tonnes or an appropriate value as the Committee may approve. This will normally apply in full starting in the first year during which the country is deemed by the Committee to have acceded to the Convention. However, to facilitate the accession of Governments other than those referred to in paragraph (e) of this Article, the Committee may agree that an acceding member's commitment should be phased in over a period of not more than three years, provided that the commitment is at least 10,000 tonnes or an appropriate value in the first year, and increases by at least 5,000 tonnes a year or an appropriate value in each succeeding year.

(j) All products provided as food aid shall meet international quality standards, be consistent with the dietary habits and nutritional needs of recipients and, with the exception of seeds, shall be suitable for human consumption.

ARTICLE IV

Products

(a) The following products are eligible to be supplied under this Convention, subject to the specifications set out in the relevant Rules of Procedure:

(i) grains (wheat, barley, maize, millet, oats, rye, sorghum or triticale) or rice;

(ii) grain and rice products of primary or secondary processing;

(iii) pulses;

(iv) edible oil;

(v) root crops (cassava, round potatoes, sweet potatoes, yams, or taro), where these are supplied in triangular transactions or in local purchases;

(vi) skimmed milk powder;

(vii) sugar;

(viii) seed for eligible products; and,

(ix) within the limits of paragraph (b) below, products which are a component of the traditional diet of vulnerable groups, or a component of supplementary feeding programmes, and which meet the requirements set out in Article III (j) of this Convention.

(b) The amount of food aid provided by a member in any year in fulfilling its commitment in the form of:

(i) all products included in paragraph (a) (vi) to (viii) of this Article shall not together exceed 15%, and no product category may individually exceed 7%, of its commitment excluding transport and other operational costs;

(ii) all products included in paragraph (a) (ix) of this Article shall not together exceed 5%, and no product may individually exceed 3%, of its commitment excluding transport and other operational costs;

(iii) in the case of commitments expressed as a combination of tonnage and value, the percentages in sub-paragraphs (i) and (ii) above shall be calculated separately for tonnage and value, excluding transport and other operational costs.

(c) For the purposes of fulfilment of their commitments, members may provide micro-nutrients in conjunction with eligible products. They are encouraged to provide, when appropriate, fortified food aid products, particularly in emergency situations and targeted development projects.

ARTICLE V

Equivalence

(a) Contributions shall be counted in terms of their wheat equivalent, as follows:

(i) grain for human consumption shall be equal to wheat;

(ii) rice shall be determined by the international export price relationship between rice and wheat, in accordance with the methods set out in the Rules of Procedure;

(iii) products of primary or secondary processing of grains or of rice shall be determined by their respective grain or rice content, in accordance with the specifications set out in the Rules of Procedure;

(iv) pulses, seed of grain, rice or other food crops, and all other eligible products, shall be based on the costs of acquisition in accordance with the methods set out in the Rules of Procedure.

(b) In the case of contributions in the form of blends or mixtures of products, only the proportion of the blend or mixture which is made from eligible products shall be counted towards a member's contribution.

(c) The Committee shall establish a Rule of Procedure to determine the wheat equivalent of fortified products and micro-nutrients.

(d) Contributions of cash for the purchase of eligible products supplied as food aid shall be evaluated either in accordance with the wheat equivalent of these products, or at prevailing international market prices of wheat, in accordance with the methods laid down in the Rules of Procedure.

ARTICLE VI

Carryover and Carryforward

(a) Each member shall ensure that operations in respect of its commitment for one year are made to the maximum extent possible within that year.

(b) If a member is unable to provide the amount specified in paragraph (e) of Article III in a particular year, it shall report the circumstances to the Committee as soon as possible and, in any case, no later than the first session held after the end of that year. Unless the Committee decides otherwise, the unfulfilled amount shall be added to the member's commitment for the following year.

(c) If a member's contribution exceeds its commitment for any year, up to 5% of its overall commitment, or the amount of the excess, whichever is the smaller, may be counted as part of the member's commitment for the following year.

ARTICLE VII

Eligible Recipients

(a) Food aid under this Convention may be provided to the developing countries and territories which are listed in Annex B, namely:

(i) least-developed countries;

(ii) low-income countries;

(iii) lower middle-income countries, and other countries included in the WTO list of Net Food-Importing Developing Countries at the time of negotiation of this Convention, when experiencing food emergencies or internationally recognised financial crises leading to food shortage emergencies, or when food aid operations are targeted on vulnerable groups.

(b) For purposes of paragraph (a) above, any changes made to the DAC list of Developing Countries and Territories in Annex B (a) to (c) shall also apply to the list of eligible recipients under this Convention.

(c) When allocating their food aid, members shall give priority to least-developed countries and low-income countries.

ARTICLE VIII

Needs

(a) Food aid should only be provided when it is the most effective and appropriate means of assistance.

(b) Food aid should be based on an evaluation of needs by the recipient and the members, within their own respective policies, and should be aimed at enhancing food security in recipient countries. In responding to those needs, members shall pay attention to meeting the particular nutritional needs of women and children.

(c) Food aid for free distribution should be targeted on vulnerable groups.

(d) The provision of food aid in emergency situations should take particular account of longer-term rehabilitation and development objectives in the recipient countries and should respect basic humanitarian principles. Members shall aim to ensure that the food aid provided reaches the intended recipients in a timely manner.

(e) To the maximum extent possible, non-emergency food aid shall be provided by members on a forward planning basis, so that recipient countries may be able to take account, in their development programmes, of the likely flow of food aid they will receive during each year of this Convention.

(f) If it appears that, because of a substantial production shortfall or other circumstances, a particular country, region or regions is faced with exceptional food needs, the matter shall be considered by the Committee. The Committee may recommend that members should respond to the situation by increasing the amount of food aid provided.

(g) At the time of the identification of food aid needs, members or their partners shall endeavour to consult with each other at the regional and recipient country level, with a view to developing a common approach to needs analysis.

(h) Members agree, where appropriate, to identify priority countries and regions under their food aid programmes. Members will ensure transparency as to their priorities, policies and programmes, by providing information for other donors.

(i) Members will consult with each other, directly or through their relevant partners, on the possibilities for the establishment of common action plans for priority countries, if possible on a multi-annual basis.

ARTICLE IX

Forms and Terms of Aid

(a) Food aid under this Convention may be supplied as:

(i) grants of food or of cash to be used to purchase food for or by the recipient country;

(ii) sales of food for the currency of the recipient country, which is not transferable and is not convertible into currency or goods and services for use by the donor members;

(iii) sales of food on credit, with payment to be made in reasonable annual amounts over periods of 20 years or more and with interest at rates which are below commercial rates prevailing in world markets.

(b) With respect only to food aid counted against a member's commitment, all food aid provided to least-developed countries shall be made in the form of grants.

(c) Food aid under this Convention provided in the form of grants shall represent not less than 80 per cent of a member's contribution and, to the extent possible, members will seek progressively to exceed this percentage.

(d) Members shall undertake to conduct all food aid transactions under this Convention in such a way as to avoid harmful interference with normal patterns of production and international commercial trade.

(e) Members shall ensure that:

(i) the provision of food aid is not tied directly or indirectly, formally or informally, explicitly or implicitly, to commercial exports of agricultural products or other goods and services to recipient countries;

(ii) food aid transactions, including bilateral food aid which is monetised, are carried out in a manner consistent with the FAO "principles of Surplus Disposal and Consultative Obligations"

ARTICLE X

Transport and Delivery

(a) The costs of transporting and delivering food aid beyond the f.o.b. stage shall, to the extent possible, be borne by the donors, particularly in the case of emergency food aid or food aid provided to priority recipient countries.

(b) In planning food aid operations, due account shall be taken of potential difficulties which may affect transport, processing or storage of food aid, and the effects that the delivery of the aid may have on marketing of local harvests in the recipient country.

(c) In order to make optimum use of available logistical capacity, members shall establish, as far as possible, with other food aid donors, recipient countries, and any other parties involved in the delivery of the food aid, a co-ordinated timetable for the delivery of their aid.

(d) Due reference to the payment of transport and other operational costs shall be made in any review of the performance of members under this Convention.

(e) Transport and other operational costs must be incurred as part of a food aid operation which is also eligible to be reported as part of a member's contribution.

ARTICLE XI

Channelling

(a) Members may provide their food aid bilaterally, through intergovernmental or other international organisations, or non-governmental organisations.

(b) Members shall give full consideration to the advantages of directing food aid through multilateral channels, in particular the World Food Programme.

(c) In developing and implementing their food aid operations, members shall make use, whenever possible, of information and competencies available within the relevant international organisations, whether inter-governmental or non-governmental, active in the field of food aid.

(d) Members are encouraged to co-ordinate their food aid policies and activities in relation to international organisations active in the field of food aid, with a view to strengthening the coherence of food aid operations.

ARTICLE XII

Local Purchases and Triangular Transactions

(a) In order to promote local agricultural development, strengthen regional and local markets and enhance the longer-term food security of recipient countries, members shall give consideration to using or directing their cash contributions for the purchase of food:

(i) for supply to the recipient country from other developing countries ("triangular transactions"); or,

(ii) in one part of a developing country for supply to a deficit area in that country ("local purchases").

(b) Cash contributions shall not normally be made to purchase food which is of the same type that the country which is the source of supply has received as bilateral or multilateral food aid in the same year as the purchase, or in a previous year if the food aid then received is still being used.

(c) To facilitate the purchase of food from developing countries, members shall, to the extent possible, provide to the Secretariat such information as is available to them on food surpluses that may exist, or are anticipated, in developing countries.

(d) Members shall pay particular attention to avoiding harmful effects on low-income consumers due to price changes resulting from local purchases.

ARTICLE XIII

Effectiveness and Impact

(a) In all food aid transactions, members shall pay particular attention to:

(i) avoiding harmful effects on local harvests, production and marketing structures, by appropriately timing the distribution of food aid;

(ii) respecting local food habits and nutritional needs of the beneficiaries and minimising any possible negative effects on their eating habits; and

(iii) facilitating the participation of women in the decision-making process and in the implementation of food aid operations, thus strengthening food security at the household level.

(b) Members shall endeavour to support the efforts of governments in recipient countries to develop and implement food aid programmes in a manner consistent with this Convention.

(c) Members should support and, where appropriate, contribute to strengthening the capacity and competence of recipient governments and the respective civil societies to develop and implement food security strategies to enhance the impact of food aid programmes.

(d) When food aid is sold within a recipient country, the sale shall be carried out, as far as possible, through the private sector and be based on market analysis. In targeting proceeds from such sales, priority shall be given to projects aiming to improve the food security of beneficiaries.

(e) Consideration should be given to reinforcing food aid by other means (financial aid, technical assistance etc.) in order to strengthen its capacity to enhance food security and to increase the capacity of governments and civil society to develop food security strategies at all levels.

(f) Members shall endeavour to ensure coherence between food aid policies and policies in other sectors such as development, agriculture and trade.

(g) Members agree to consult to the extent possible with all partners concerned at the level of each recipient country to ensure monitoring of the co-ordination of food aid programmes and operations.

(h) Members shall endeavour to carry out joint evaluations of their food aid programmes and operations. Such evaluation should be based on agreed international principles.

(i) When carrying out evaluations of their food aid programmes and operations, members shall take into consideration the provisions of this Convention relating to the effectiveness and impact of those food aid programmes and operations.

(j) Members are encouraged to assess the impact of their food aid programmes, channelled bilaterally or multilaterally or through non-governmental organisations, using appropriate indicators such as the nutritional status of the beneficiaries and other indicators related to world food security.

ARTICLE XIV

Information and Co-ordination

(a) Members shall provide regular and timely reports to the Committee on the amount, content, channelling, costs including transport and other operational costs, forms and terms of their contributions in accordance with the Rules of Procedure.

(b) Members undertake to supply such statistical and other information that may be required for the operation of this Convention, in particular regarding their:

(i) aid deliveries, including the purchase of products made as the result of cash contributions, local purchases or triangular operations, and those channelled through international organisations;

(ii) arrangements entered into for the future supply of food aid;

(iii) policies affecting the provision and distribution of food aid. To the extent possible, these reports shall be submitted in writing to the Executive Director before each regular session of the Committee.

(c) Members who make contributions in the form of multilateral cash contributions to international organisations shall report the fulfilment of their obligations in accordance with the Rules of Procedure.

(d) Members shall exchange information on their food aid policies and programmes and the results of their evaluations of these policies and programmes, and shall endeavour to ensure the coherence of their food aid programmes with food security strategies at national, regional, local and household levels.

(e) Members shall indicate to the Committee, in advance, the amount of their commitment which is not made in the form of grants and the terms of any such aid.

PART III—ADMINISTRATION

ARTICLE XV

Food Aid Committee

(a) The Food Aid Committee, established by the Food Aid Convention of the International Grains Arrangement, 1967, shall continue in being for the purpose of administering this Convention, with the powers and functions provided in this Convention.

(b) The membership of the Committee shall consist of all parties to this Convention.

(c) Each member shall designate a representative resident at the seat of the Committee to whom the Secretariat's notices and other communications related to the work of the Committee shall normally be addressed. Other arrangements may be adopted by any member in agreement with the Executive Director.

ARTICLE XVI

Powers and Functions

(a) The Committee shall take such decisions and perform such functions as are required to carry out the provisions of this Convention. It shall establish such Rules of Procedure as are necessary for this purpose.

(b) The decisions of the Committee shall be reached by consensus.

(c) The Committee shall keep the requirements for food aid in developing countries and the ability of members to respond to those requirements under review.

(d) The Committee shall keep under review the progress made in attaining the objectives set out in Article I of this Convention, and the fulfilment of the provisions of this Convention.

(e) The Committee may receive information from recipient countries and consult with them.

ARTICLE XVII

Chairman and Vice-Chairman

(a) At the last statutory session held in each year, the Committee shall appoint a Chairman and a Vice-Chairman for the following year.

(b) The duties of the Chairman shall be:

(i) to approve the draft agenda for each session;

(ii) to preside at sessions;

(iii) to declare the opening and closing of each meeting and of each session;

(iv) to submit the draft agenda to the Committee for adoption at the beginning of each session;

(v) to direct the discussions and to ensure observance of the Rules of Procedure;

(vi) to accord the right to speak and to decide all questions of order in accordance with the relevant Rules of Procedure;

(vii) to put questions and announce decisions; and,

(viii) to rule on points of order that delegates may raise.

(c) If the Chairman is absent from a session or any part thereof, or is temporarily unable to fill the office of Chairman, the Vice-Chairman shall act as Chairman. In the absence of the Chairman and the Vice-Chairman, the Committee shall appoint a temporary Chairman.

(d) If, for any reason, the Chairman is unable to continue to fill the office of Chairman, the Vice-Chairman shall act as Chairman pending the appointment of a new Chairman by the Committee.

(e) The Vice-Chairman, when acting as Chairman, or the temporary Chairman, shall have the same powers and duties as the Chairman.

ARTICLE XVIII

Sessions

(a) The Committee shall meet at least twice a year in conjunction with the statutory sessions of the International Grains Council. The Committee shall meet also at such other times either as the Chairman shall decide, at the request of three members, or as otherwise required by this Convention.

(b) The presence of delegates representing two thirds of the membership of the Committee shall be necessary to constitute a quorum at any session of the Committee.

(c) The Committee may, when appropriate, invite any non-member government and representatives from other international intergovernmental organisations to attend its open meetings as observers.

(d) The seat of the Committee shall be in London.

ARTICLE XIX

Secretariat

(a) The Committee shall use the services of the Secretariat of the International Grains Council for the performance of such administrative duties as the Committee may request, including the processing and distribution of documentation and reports.

(b) The Executive Director shall carry out the directions of the Committee and shall perform such duties as are laid down in the Convention and the Rules of Procedure.

ARTICLE XX

Defaults and Disputes

(a) In the case of a dispute concerning the interpretation or application of this Convention, or of a default in obligations under this Convention, the Committee shall meet and take appropriate action.

(b) Members shall take account of the recommendations and conclusions reached by consensus by the Committee in cases of disagreement as to the application of the provisions of this Convention.

PART IV—FINAL PROVISIONS

ARTICLE XXI

Depositary

The Secretary-General of the United Nations is hereby designated as the depositary of this Convention.

ARTICLE XXII

Signature and Ratification

(a) This Convention shall be open for signature from 1 May 1999 until and including 30 June 1999 by the Governments referred to in paragraph (e) of Article III.

(b) This Convention shall be subject to ratification, acceptance or approval by each signatory Government in accordance with its constitutional procedures. Instruments of ratification, acceptance or approval shall be deposited with the depositary not later than 30 June 1999, except that the Committee may grant one or more extensions of time to any signatory Government that has not deposited its instrument of ratification, acceptance or approval by that date.

(c) Any signatory Government may deposit with the depositary a declaration of provisional application of this Convention. Any such Government shall provisionally apply this Convention in accordance with its laws and regulations and be provisionally regarded as a party thereto.

(d) The depositary shall notify all signatory and acceding Governments of each signature, ratification, acceptance, approval, provisional application of, and accession to, this Convention.

ARTICLE XXIII

Accession

(a) This Convention shall be open for accession by any Government referred to in paragraph (e) of Article III that has not signed this Convention. Instruments of accession shall be deposited with the depositary not later than 30 June 1999, except that the Committee may grant one or more extensions of time to any Government that has not deposited its instrument of accession by that date.

(b) Once this Convention has entered into force in accordance with Article XXIV, it shall be open for accession by any Government other than those referred to in paragraph (e) of Article III, upon such conditions as the Committee considers appropriate. Instruments of accession shall be deposited with the depositary.

(c) Any Government acceding to this Convention under paragraph (a) of this Article, or whose accession has been agreed by the Committee under paragraph (b) of this Article, may deposit with the depositary a declaration of provisional application of this Convention pending the deposit of its instrument of accession. Any such Government shall provisionally apply this Convention in accordance with its laws and regulations and be provisionally regarded as a party thereto.

ARTICLE XXIV

Entry into force

(a) This Convention shall enter into force on 1 July 1999 if by 30 June 1999 the Governments, whose combined commitments, as listed in paragraph (e) of Article III, equal at least 75% of the total commitments of all governments listed in that paragraph, have deposited instruments of ratification, acceptance, approval or accession, or declarations of provisional application, and provided that the Grains Trade Convention, 1995 is in force.

(b) If this Convention does not enter into force in accordance with paragraph (a) of this Article, the Governments which have deposited instruments of ratification, acceptance, approval or accession, or declarations of provisional application, may decide by unanimous consent that it shall enter into force among themselves provided that the Grains Trade Convention, 1995 is in force.

ARTICLE XXV

Duration and Withdrawal

(a) This Convention shall remain in force until and including 30 June 2002, unless extended under paragraph (b) of this Article or terminated earlier under paragraph (f) of this Article, provided that the Grains Trade Convention, 1995, or a new Grains Trade Convention replacing it, remains in force until and including that date.

(b) The Committee may extend this Convention beyond 30 June 2002 for successive periods not exceeding two years on each occasion, provided that the Grains Trade Convention, 1995, or a new Grains Trade Convention replacing it, remains in force during the period of the extension.

(c) If this Convention is extended under paragraph (b) of this Article, the commitments of members under paragraph (e) of Article III may be subject to review by members before the entry into force of each extension. Their respective commitments, as reviewed, shall remain unchanged for the duration of each extension.

(d) The operation of this Convention shall be kept under review, in particular with reference to the results of any multilateral negotiations bearing on the provision of food aid, including especially on concessional credit terms, and the need to apply the results thereof.

(e) The situation with respect to all food aid operations and, in particular, those under concessional credit terms, shall be reviewed before deciding on any extension of this Convention or any new convention.

(f) In the event of this Convention being terminated, the Committee shall continue in being for such time as may be required to carry out its liquidation, and shall have such powers, and exercise such functions, as may be necessary for that purpose.

(g) Any member may withdraw from this Convention at the end of any year by giving written notice of withdrawal to the depositary at least ninety days prior to the end of that year. That member shall not thereby be released from any obligations incurred under this Convention which have not been discharged by the end of that year. The member shall simultaneously inform the Committee of the action it has taken.

(h) Any member which withdraws from this Convention may thereafter rejoin by giving written notice to the Committee and to the depositary. It shall be a condition of rejoining the Convention that the member shall be responsible for fulfilling its commitment with effect from the year in which it rejoins.

ARTICLE XXVI

International Grains Agreement

This Convention shall replace the Food Aid Convention, 1995, as extended, and shall be one of the constituent instruments of the International Grains Agreement, 1995.

ARTICLE XXVII

Authentic texts

The texts of this Convention in the English, French, Russian and Spanish languages shall all be equally authentic.

ANNEX A

TRANSPORT AND OTHER OPERATIONAL COSTS

The following transport and other operational costs associated with food aid contributions are included under Articles II (a)(vii), III, X and XIV of this Convention:

(a) Transport Costs

freight, including loading and discharge
demurrage and dispatch
trans-shipment
bagging
insurance and superintendance
port charges and storage fees in port
temporary warehouse facilities and fees in port and on-route
in-country transport, vehicle hire, tolls and escort, convoy and border fees
equipment hire
aircraft, airlifts

(b) Other Operational Costs

non-food items (NFIs) utilised by beneficiaries (tools, utensils, agricultural inputs)
NFIs provided to implementing partners (vehicles, storage facilities)
costs of counterpart training
implementing partners' operational costs, not otherwise covered as transport costs
milling and other special costs
in-country NGO costs
technical support services and logistics management
project preparation, appraisal, monitoring and evaluation
beneficiary registration
in-country technical services

ANNEX B

ELIGIBLE RECIPIENTS

Eligible food aid recipients under Article VII of this Convention refer to Developing Countries and Territories listed as aid recipients by the Development Assistance Committee (DAC) of the OECD, effective as of 1 January 1997, and to countries included in the WTO list of Net Food-Importing Developing Countries, effective as of 1 March 1999.

(a) Least-Developed Countries.—Afghanistan, Angola, Bangladesh, Benin, Bhutan, Burkina Faso, Burundi, Cambodia, Cape Verde, Central African Republic, Chad, Comoros, Congo Dem. Rep., Djibouti, Equatorial Guinea, Eritrea, Ethiopia, Gambia, Guinea, Guinea-Bissau, Haiti, Kiribati, Laos, Lesotho, Liberia, Madagascar, Malawi, Maldives, Mali, Mauritania, Mozambique, Myanmar, Nepal, Niger, Rwanda, Sao Tome and Principe, Sierra Leone, Solomon Islands, Somalia, Sudan, Tanzania, Togo, Tuvalu, Uganda, Vanuatu, Western Samoa, Yemen, Zambia.

(b) Low-Income Countries.—Albania, Armenia, Azerbaijan, Bosnia and Herzegovina, Cameroon, China, Congo Rep, Côte d'Ivoire, Georgia, Ghana, Guyana, Honduras, India, Kenya, Kyrgyz Rep, Mongolia, Nicaragua, Nigeria, Pakistan, Senegal, Sri Lanka, Tajikistan, Viet Nam and Zimbabwe.

(c) Lower Middle-Income Countries.—Algeria, Belize, Bolivia, Botswana, Colombia, Costa Rica, Cuba, Dominica, Dominican Republic, Ecuador, Egypt, El Salvador, Fiji, Grenada, Guatemala, Indonesia, Iran, Iraq, Jamaica, Jordan, Kazakhstan, Korea (Democratic Republic of), Lebanon, Macedonia (former Yugoslav Republic), Marshall Islands, Micronesia Federated States, Moldova, Morocco, Namibia, Niue, Palau Islands, Palestinian Administered Areas, Panama, Papua New Guinea, Paraguay, Peru, Philippines, St Vincent & Grenadines, Suriname, Swaziland, Syria, Thailand, Timor, Tokelau, Tonga, Tunisia, Turkey, Turkmenistan, Uzbekistan, Venezuela, Wallis and Futuna, and Yugoslavia Federal Republic.

(d) WTO Net Food-Importing Developing Countries (not included above).—Barbados, Mauritius, St Lucia, Trinidad & Tobago.

Secretariat's note

In accordance with Article VII (c) of the FAC, 1999, changes made by the Development Assistance Committee (DAC) of OECD in its lists of aid recipients are to be reflected in the lists of eligible FAC recipients. The table in Annex B above applied in respect of aid provided in 1999/2000 only. Current lists of eligible recipients may be obtained from the IGC Secretariat.

C. THE PEACE CORPS

(SEE VOLUME I–B FOR ALL MATERIAL ON THIS SUBJECT)

D. DEPARTMENT OF STATE

CONTENTS

1. State Department Procedures on Treaties and Other International Agreements; Partial Text, Circular 175, 11 Foreign Affairs Manual, Chapter 700, "Treaties and Other International Agreements," as revised

700—TREATIES AND OTHER INTERNATIONAL AGREEMENTS

711 PURPOSE

a. The purpose of this chapter is to facilitate the application of orderly and uniform measures and procedures for the negotiation, conclusion, publication, and registration of treaties and other international agreements of the United States. It is also designed to facilitate the maintenance of complete and accurate records on treaties and agreements and the publication of authoritative information regarding them.

b. The chapter is not a catalog of all the essential guidelines or information pertaining to the making and application of international agreements. It is limited to guidelines or information necessary for general guidance.

712 AUTHORITIES

Legal authorities underlying the provisions of the 11 FAM 700 include but are not limited to:

(1) U.S. Constitution, Article II;
(2) 1 U.S.C. 112a; 1 U.S.C. 112b;
(3) Vienna Convention on the Law of Treaties;
(4) 22 CFR Part 181; and
(5) Delegation of Authority No. 205 (September 1, 1993).

713 ROLE OF THE OFFICE OF THE LEGAL ADVISER

713.1 Legal Review of Draft Agreements

As soon as tentative provisions for an agreement are considered or drafted, the Office of the Legal Adviser will make available the services of an attorney-adviser to insure that the agreement is properly drafted and agreed policy is expressed clearly and fully. The Office of the Legal Adviser often prepares a draft in the first instance upon the request of another office.

713.2 Legal Clearance Required

Any draft of a proposed treaty or agreement, or any action regarding the negotiation, conclusion, ratification or approval, or termination, as well as the existence, status, and application, of any international agreement to which the United States is or may become a party, should be cleared with the Office of the Legal Adviser (including the Assistant Legal Adviser for Treaty Affairs as appropriate) and with other appropriate bureaus or offices and, as appropriate, with any other agency concerned with the treaty or international agreement.

714 DISCLAIMER

This chapter is intended solely as a general outline of measures and procedures ordinarily followed. This outline cannot anticipate all circumstances or situations that may arise. Deviation or derogation from the provisions of this chapter will not invalidate actions taken by officers or affect the validity of negotiations engaged in or of treaties or other agreements concluded.

720 NEGOTIATION AND CONCLUSION

721 CIRCULAR 175 PROCEDURE

This subchapter is a codification of the substance of Department Circular No. 175, December 13, 1955, as amended, on the negotiation and conclusion of treaties and other international agreements. It may be referred to for convenience and continuity as the "Circular 175 Procedure." The C–175 procedure facilitates the application of orderly and uniform measures to the negotiation, conclusion, reporting, publication, and registration of U.S. treaties and international agreements, and facilitates the maintenance of complete and accurate records on such agreements.

722 GENERAL OBJECTIVES

The objectives are:

(1) That the making of treaties and other international agreements for the United States is carried out within constitutional and other appropriate limits;

(2) That particular treaties or international agreements are not in conflict with other international agreements or U.S. law;

(3) That the objectives to be sought in the negotiation of particular treaties and other international agreements are approved by the Secretary or an officer specifically authorized by him for that purpose;

(4) That timely and appropriate consultation is had with congressional leaders and committees on treaties and other international agreements;

(5) That where, in the opinion of the Secretary of State or a designee, the circumstances permit, other agencies and the public be given an opportunity to comment on treaties and other international agreements;

(6) That firm positions departing from authorized positions are not undertaken without the approval of the Legal Adviser (L) and interested assistant secretaries or their deputies;

(7) That the final texts developed are approved by the Office of the Legal Adviser (L) and the interested assistant secretaries or their deputies and, when required, brought a reasonable time before signature to the attention of the Secretary or an officer specifically designated by the Secretary for that purpose;

(8) That authorization to sign the final text is obtained and appropriate arrangements for signature are made; and

(9) That there is compliance with the requirements of 1 U.S.C. 112b, as amended, on the transmission of the texts of international agreements other than treaties to the Congress (see 11 FAM 726); the law on the publication of treaties and other international agreements (see 1 U.S.C. 112a and 11 FAM 727); and treaty provisions on registration (see 11 FAM 753.3).

723 EXERCISE OF THE INTERNATIONAL AGREEMENT POWER

723.1 Determination of Type of Agreement

The following considerations will be taken into account along with other relevant factors in determining whether an international agreement shall be dealt with by the United States as a treaty to be brought into force with the advice and consent of the Senate or as an agreement to be brought into force on some other constitutional basis.

723.2 Constitutional Requirements

There are two procedures under the Constitution through which the United States becomes a party to international agreements. Those procedures and the constitutional parameters of each are found below.

723.2–1 Treaties

International agreements (regardless of their title, designation, or form) whose entry into force with respect to the United States takes place only after the Senate has given its advice and consent are "treaties." The President, with the advice and consent of two-thirds of the Senators present, may enter into an international agreement on any subject genuinely of concern in foreign relations, so long as the agreement does not contravene the United States Constitution;

723.2–2 International Agreements Other Than Treaties

International agreements brought into force with respect to the United States on a constitutional basis other than with the advice and consent of the Senate are "international agreements other than treaties." (The term "sole executive agreement" is appropriately reserved for agreements made solely on the basis of the constitutional authority of the President.) There are three constitutional bases for international agreements other than treaties as set forth below. An international agreement may be concluded pursuant to one or more of these constitutional bases:

(1) Treaty;
(2) Legislation;
(3) Constitutional authority of the President.

723.2–2(A) Agreements Pursuant to Treaty

The President may conclude an international agreement pursuant to a treaty brought into force with the advice and consent of the Senate, the provisions of which constitute authorization for the agreement by the Executive without subsequent action by the Congress.

723.2–2(B) Agreements Pursuant to Legislation

The President may conclude an international agreement on the basis of existing legislation or subject to legislation to be adopted by the Congress, or upon the failure of Congress to adopt a disapproving joint or concurrent resolution within designated time periods.

723.2–2(C) Agreements Pursuant to the Constitutional Authority of the President

The President may conclude an international agreement on any subject within his constitutional authority so long as the agreement is not inconsistent with legislation enacted by the Congress in the exercise of its constitutional authority. The constitutional sources of authority for the President to conclude international agreements include:

(1) The President's authority as Chief Executive to represent the nation in foreign affairs;

(2) The President's authority to receive ambassadors and other public ministers, and to recognize foreign governments;

(3) The President's authority as "Commander-in-Chief"; and

(4) The President's authority to "take care that the laws be faithfully executed."

723.3 Considerations for Selecting Among Constitutionally Authorized Procedures

In determining a question as to the procedure which should be followed for any particular international agreement, due consideration is given to the following factors along with those in 11 FAM 723.2:

(1) The extent to which the agreement involves commitments or risks affecting the nation as a whole;

(2) Whether the agreement is intended to affect state laws;

(3) Whether the agreement can be given effect without the enactment of subsequent legislation by the Congress;

(4) Past U.S. practice as to similar agreements;

(5) The preference of the Congress as to a particular type of agreement;

(6) The degree of formality desired for an agreement;

(7) The proposed duration of the agreement, the need for prompt conclusion of an agreement, and the desirability of concluding a routine or short-term agreement; and

(8) The general international practice as to similar agreements.

In determining whether any international agreement should be brought into force as a treaty or as an international agreement other than a treaty, the utmost care is to be exercised to avoid any invasion or compromise of the constitutional powers of the President, the Senate, and the Congress as a whole.

723.4 Questions as to Type of Agreement To Be Used; Consultation With Congress

a. All legal memoranda accompanying Circular 175 requests (see 11 FAM 724.3, paragraph h) will discuss thoroughly the legal authorities underlying the type of agreement recommended.

b. When there is any question whether an international agreement should be concluded as a treaty or as an international agreement other than a treaty, the matter is brought to the attention, in the first instance, of the Legal Adviser for Treaty Affairs. If the Assistant Legal Adviser for Treaty Affairs considers the question to be a serious one that may warrant formal congressional consultation, s/he or an appropriate representative of the Office of the Legal Adviser (L) will consult with the Assistant Secretary for Legislative Affairs (H) (or designee) and other affected bureaus. Upon receiving their views on the subject, the Legal Adviser will, if the matter has not been resolved, transmit a memorandum thereon to the Secretary (or designee) for a decision. Every practicable effort will be made to identify such questions at the earliest possible date so that consultations may be completed in sufficient time to avoid last-minute consideration.

c. Consultations on such questions will be held with congressional leaders and committees as may be appropriate. Arrangements for such consultations shall be made by the Assistant Secretary for Legislative Affairs and shall be held with the assistance of the Office of the Legal Adviser (L) and such other offices as may be determined. Nothing in this section shall be taken as derogating from the requirement of appropriate consultations with the Congress in accordance with 11 FAM 725.1, subparagraph (5), in connection with the initiation of, and developments during negotiations for international agreements, particularly where the agreements are of special interest to the Congress.

724 ACTION REQUIRED IN NEGOTIATION, CONCLUSION, AND TERMINATION OF TREATIES AND INTERNATIONAL AGREEMENTS

724.1 Authorization Required to Undertake Negotiations

Negotiations of treaties, or other "significant" international agreements, or for their extension or revision, are not to be undertaken, nor any exploratory discussions undertaken with representatives of another government or international organization, until authorized in writing by the Secretary or an officer specifically authorized by the Secretary for that purpose.

724.2 Scope of Authorization

Approval of a request for authorization to negotiate a treaty or other international agreement does not constitute advance approval of the text nor authorization to agree upon a date for signature or to sign the treaty or agreement. Authorization to agree upon a given date for, and to proceed with, signature must be specifically requested in writing, as provided in 11 FAM 724.3. This applies to treaties and other agreements to be signed abroad as well as those to be signed at Washington. Special instructions may be required, because of the special circumstances involved, for multilateral conventions or agreements to be signed at international conferences.

724.3 *Request for Authorization to Negotiate and/or Sign Action Memorandum*

a. A request for authorization to negotiate and/or conclude a treaty or other international agreement takes the form of an action memorandum addressed to the Secretary or other principal to whom such authority has been delegated, as appropriate, and cleared with the Office of the Legal Adviser (L) (including the Assistant Legal Adviser for Treaty Affairs), the Office of the Assistant Secretary for Legislative Affairs, other appropriate bureaus, and any other agency (such as Defense, Commerce, etc.) which has primary responsibility or a substantial interest in the subject matter.

b. The action memorandum may request one of the following:

(1) Authority to negotiate;
(2) Authority to conclude; or
(3) Authority to negotiate and conclude.

The request in each instance states that any substantive changes in the draft text will be cleared with the Office of the Legal Adviser and other specified regional and/or functional bureaus before definitive agreement is reached. Drafting offices should consult closely with the Office of the Legal Adviser (L) to ensure that all legal requirements are met.

c. The action memorandum indicates what arrangements have been made and/or are planned as to: (1) congressional consultation and (2) opportunity for public comment on the treaty or agreement being negotiated, signed, or acceded to.

d. The action memorandum shall indicate whether a proposed treaty or agreement embodies a commitment to furnish funds, goods, or services beyond or in addition to those authorized in an approved budget; and if so, what arrangements are being planned or carried out concerning consultation with the Office of Management and Budget (OMB) for such commitment. The Department will not authorize such commitments without confirmation that the relevant budget approved by the President requests or provides funds adequate to fulfill the proposed commitment or that the President has made a determination to seek the required funds.

e. The action memorandum shall indicate whether a proposed treaty or agreement embodies a commitment that could reasonably be expected to require (for its implementation) the issuance of a "significant regulatory action" (as defined in section 3 of Executive Order 12866); and if so, what arrangements are being planned or carried out concerning timely consultation with OMB. The Department will not authorize such commitments without confirmation that OMB has been consulted in a timely manner concerning the proposed commitment.

f. Where it appears that there may be issues regarding the public disclosure of the text of an agreement upon its signature or entry into force, the action memorandum shall include an explanation thereof (see 11 FAM 725.2 and 11 FAM 725.3).

g. An action memorandum dealing with an agreement that has a potential for adverse environmental impact should contain a statement indicating whether the agreement will significantly affect the quality of the human environment.

h. The action memorandum is accompanied by:

(1) The U.S. draft, if available, of any agreement or other instrument intended to be negotiated; or

(2) The text of any agreement and related exchange of notes, agreed minutes, or other document to be signed (with appropriate clearances, including that of the Assistant Legal Adviser for Treaty Affairs); and

(3) A memorandum of law prepared in the Office of the Legal Adviser.

i. These provisions shall apply whether a proposed international agreement is to be concluded in the name of the U.S. Government or in the name of a particular agency of the U.S. Government. However, in the latter case, the action memorandum may be addressed to the interested Assistant Secretary or Secretaries of State, or their designees in writing, unless such official(s) judge that consultation with the Secretary, Deputy Secretary or an Under Secretary is necessary. (See 22 CFR 181.4.)

724.4 Separate Authorizations

When authorization is sought for a particular treaty or other agreement, either multilateral or bilateral, the action memorandum for this purpose outlines briefly and clearly the principal features of the proposed treaty or other agreements, indicates any special problems which may be encountered, and, if possible, the contemplated solutions of those problems.

724.5 Blanket Authorizations

a. In general, blanket authorizations are appropriate only in those instances where, in carrying out or giving effect to provisions of law or policy decisions, a series of agreements of the same general type is contemplated; that is, a number of agreements to be negotiated according to a more or less standard formula (for example, Public Law 480 Agricultural Commodities Agreements; Educational Exchange Agreements; Investment Guaranty Agreements; Weather Station Agreements) or a number of treaties to be negotiated according to a more or less standard formula (for example, consular conventions, extradition treaties, etc.). Each request for blanket authorization shall specify the office or officers to whom the authority is to be delegated.

b. The basic precepts under 11 FAM 724.3 and 11 FAM 724.4 apply equally to requests for blanket authorizations. The specific terms of any blanket authorization, i.e., that the text of any particular agreement shall be cleared by the Office of the Legal Adviser (L) and other interested bureaus before signature, shall be observed in all cases.

724.6 Certificate on Foreign Language Text

a. Before any treaty or other agreement containing a foreign language text is laid before the Secretary (or any person authorized by the Secretary) for signature, either in the Department or at a post, a signed memorandum must be obtained from a responsible language officer of the Department certifying that the foreign language text and the English language text are in conformity with each other and that both texts have the same meaning in all substantive respects. A similar certification must be obtained for exchanges of notes that set forth the terms of an agreement in two languages.

b. In the case of treaties or international agreements that expressly provide that the English language text prevails in the case of a divergence between the language texts, the certification described in paragraph a of this section may not be required.

c. In exceptional circumstances the Department can authorize the certification to be made at a post.

724.7 Transmission of Texts to the Secretary

The texts of treaties and other international agreements must be completed and approved in writing by all responsible officers concerned sufficiently in advance to give the Secretary, or the person to whom authority to approve the text has been delegated, adequate time before the date of signing to examine the text and dispose of any questions that arise. Posts must transmit the texts to the Department as expeditiously as feasible to assure adequate time for such consideration. Except as otherwise specifically authorized by the Secretary, a complete text of a treaty or other international agreement must be delivered to the Secretary or other person authorized to approve the text, before any such text is agreed upon as final or any date is agreed upon for its signature.

724.8 Authorization to Terminate Treaties or International Agreements

Terminations of treaties or other international agreements are not to be undertaken, nor any exploratory discussions undertaken with representatives of another government or international organization, until authorized by the Secretary or an officer specifically authorized by the Secretary for that purpose. A Circular 175 memorandum (as well as accompanying documents) should be prepared that takes into account the views of the relevant government agencies and interested bureaus within the Department (including the Office of the Legal Adviser (L) and the Bureau of Legislative Affairs).

725 RESPONSIBILITY OF OFFICE OR OFFICER CONDUCTING NEGOTIATIONS

725.1 Conduct of Negotiations

The office or officer responsible for any negotiations keeps in mind that:

(1) During the negotiations no position is communicated to a foreign government or to an international organization as a U.S. position that goes beyond any existing authorization or instructions;

(2) No proposal is made or position is agreed to beyond the original authorization without appropriate clearance (see 11 FAM 722.3, paragraph a);

(3) All significant policy-determining memoranda and instructions to the field on the subject of the negotiations have appropriate clearance (see 11 FAM 724.3, paragraph a);

(4) The Secretary or other principal, as appropriate, is kept informed in writing of important policy decisions and developments, including any particularly significant departures from substantially standard drafts that have evolved;

(5) With the advice and assistance of the Assistant Secretary for Legislative Affairs, the appropriate congressional leaders and committees are advised of the intention to negotiate significant new international agreements, consulted concerning such agreements, and kept informed of developments affecting them, including especially whether any legislation is considered necessary or desirable for the implementation of the new treaty or agreement. Where the proposal for any especially important treaty or other international agreement is contemplated, the Office of the Assistant Secretary for Legislative Affairs will be informed as early as possible by the office responsible for the subjects;

(6) The interest of the public be taken into account and, where in the opinion of the Secretary of State or his or her designee the circumstances permit, the public be given an opportunity to comment;

(7) In no case, after accord has been reached on the substance and wording of the texts to be signed, do the negotiators sign an agreement or exchange notes constituting an agreement until a request under 11 FAM 724.3 for authorization to conclude has been approved and, if at a post abroad, until instructed by the Department to do so as stated in 11 FAM 731.3. If an agreement is to be signed in two languages, each language text must be cleared in full with the Language Services Division or, if at a post abroad, with the Department before signature, as stated in 11 FAM 724.6;

(8) Due consideration is given also to the provisions of 11 FAM 725.2 through 11 FAM 725.9, 11 FAM 731.3, and 11 FAM 732 of this chapter; and

(9) In any case where any other department or agency is to play a primary or significant role or has a major interest in negotiation of an international agreement, the appropriate official or officials in such department or agency are informed of the provisions of this subchapter.

725.2 Publication and Registration

The objective of avoiding any commitment incompatible with the law requiring publication (1 U.S.C. 112a) and with the treaty provisions requiring registration (see 11 FAM 753.3) should be borne in mind by U.S. negotiators. Although negotiations may be conducted and draft texts may be exchanged on a confidential basis, efforts must be made to assure that any definitive agreement or commitment entered into will be devoid of any aspect which would prevent the publication and registration of the agreement. Classified agreements are not published.

725.3 Public Release of International Agreements

a. The Office of the Assistant Legal Adviser for Treaty Affairs (L/T) receives numerous inquiries for copies of unclassified U.S. treaties and international agreements. Unclassified international agreements that have entered into force generally will be released upon request. These agreements are reported to Congress under the Case Act and, unless classified, generally are published by the Office of the Assistant Legal Adviser for Treaty Affairs.

b. Unclassified international agreements that enter into force upon signature generally will be released once there is a signed agreement.

c. A more detailed analysis will be required for those unclassified international agreements that do not enter into force upon signature:

(1) Many international agreements do not enter into force upon signature, but still require some sort of Presidential (or Executive) action prior to being brought into force ("PA Agreements"). Some agreements require further action by the Executive on the international plane, such as an exchange of notes between the parties confirming completion of their respective domestic procedures or the deposit of an instrument of ratification or acceptance, before the agreements enter into force. Other agreements require that the President also take certain domestic actions after signature and before the agreement enters into force. For example, the President may need to seek the advice and consent of the Senate to ratify a treaty. For other types of agreements, the President may need to transmit an agreement to Congress for a mandatory review period;

(2) With respect to signed PA Agreements that (a) have not been submitted to Congress, (b) are not publicly available from other sources, and (c) require Presidential or Executive action before they enter into force, the Office of the Assistant Legal Adviser for Treaty Affairs will consult with relevant offices within the Department, other agencies, the White House, and possibly the foreign government to identify potential sensitivities about public release of these agreements. When sensitivities are identified, the office will work with other relevant offices to determine whether such agreements properly should be classified or otherwise withheld under any applicable exemption under the Freedom of Information Act, perhaps on a temporary basis until they enter into force. Where no sensitivities or issues are identified, the office will release a copy of the agreement.

d. Classified international agreements are not subject to public release.

725.4 Public Statements

No public statement is to be made indicating that agreement on a text has been reached, or that negotiations have been successfully completed, before authorization is granted to sign the treaty or other agreement. If such authorization has been granted subject to a condition that no substantive change in the proposed text is made without appropriate clearance (see 11 FAM 724.3, paragraph a), no such public statement is to be made until definitive agreement on the text has been reached and such clearance has been received. Normally, such a public statement is made only at the time a treaty or other agreement is actually signed, inasmuch as it remains possible that last-minute changes will be made in the text.

Any such statement prior to that time must have the appropriate clearance, and the approval of the Secretary or the Department principal who originally approved the action memorandum request under "Circular 175 Procedure."

725.5 English-Language Text

Negotiators will assure that every bilateral treaty or other international agreement to be signed for the United States contains an English-language text. If the language of the other country concerned is one other than English, the text is done in English and, if desired by the other country, in the language of that country. A U.S. note that constitutes part of an international agreement effected by exchange of notes is always in the English language. If it quotes a foreign government note, the quotation is to be rendered in English translation. A U.S. note is not in any language in addition to English, unless specifically authorized (with the clearance of the Assistant Legal Adviser for Treaty Affairs). The note of the other government concerned may be in whatever language that government desires.

725.6 Electronic Reporting of Signature of Treaty or Exchange of Notes

The officer responsible for the signature of a treaty or other international agreement or for the exchange of notes constituting an international agreement shall as soon as possible, in any event within twenty-four hours of the signature or exchange, report electronically to the address that follows: the title of the signed treaty or other international agreement or the subject matter and names of the parties to the exchange of notes, as well as the date and place where the signature or exchange took place. The reporting address is treatyoffice@state.gov.

725.7 Transmission of Signed Texts to Assistant Legal Adviser for Treaty Affairs

a. The officer responsible for the negotiation of a treaty or other agreement at any post must transmit, as expeditiously as possible, the signed original text, together with all accompanying papers such as agreed minutes, exchanges of notes, plans, etc. (indicating full names of persons who signed), to the Assistant Legal Adviser for Treaty Affairs. Where originals are not available, the officer must obtain accurate certified copies and transmit them as in the case of the original. (See 11 FAM 725.8, 11 FAM 725.9, and 11 FAM 725.10.)

b. Any officer in the Department having possession of or receiving from any source a signed original or certified copy of a treaty or agreement or of a note or other document constituting a part of a treaty or agreement must forward such documents immediately to the Assistant Legal Adviser for Treaty Affairs.

725.8 Transmission of Certified Copies to the Department

a. When an exchange of diplomatic notes between the mission and a foreign government constitutes an agreement or has the effect of extending, modifying, or terminating an agreement to which the United States is a party, a properly certified copy of the note from the mission to the foreign government, and the signed original of the note from the foreign government are sent, as soon as practicable (indicating full names of persons who signed) [remove italics] to the Department for attention of the Assistant Legal Adviser for Treaty Affairs. Likewise, if, in addition to the treaty or other international agreement signed, notes related thereto are exchanged (either at the same time, beforehand, or thereafter), particularly bringing an agreement into force, a properly certified copy (copies) of the note(s) from the mission to the foreign government is transmitted with the signed original(s) of the note(s) from the foreign government.

b. In each instance, the mission retains for its files certified copies of the note exchanged. The U.S. note is prepared in accordance with the rules prescribed in 5 FAH–1, Correspondence Handbook. The note of the foreign government is prepared in accordance with the style of the foreign ministry and usually in the language of that country. Whenever practicable, arrangements are made for the notes to bear the same date.

725.9 Certification of Copies

If a copy of a note is a part of an international agreement, such copy is certified by a duly commissioned and qualified Foreign Service officer either (a) by a certification on the document itself, or (b) by a separate certification attached to the document. A certification on the document itself is placed at the end of the document. It indicates, either typed or rubber stamped, that the document is a true copy of the original signed (or initialed) by (INSERT FULL NAME OF OFFICER WHO SIGNED DOCUMENT), and it is signed by the certifying officer. If a certification is typed on a separate sheet of paper, it briefly describes the document certified and states that it is a true copy of the original signed (or initialed) by (FULL NAME), and it is signed and dated by the certifying officer. The certification may be stapled to the copy of the note.

725.10 Preparation of Copies for Certification

For purposes of accuracy of the Department's records and publication and registration, a certified copy must be an exact copy of the signed original. It must be communicated in a form that renders information accessible so as to be usable for subsequent reference, either as a PDF file e-mailed to treatyoffice@state.gov or as a facsimile reproduction on white durable paper and must be clearly legible. In the case of notes, the copy shows the letterhead, the date and, if signed, an indication of the signature or, if merely initialed, the initials which appear on the original. It is suggested that, in the case of a note from the mission to the foreign government, the copy for certification and transmission to the Department be made at the same time the original is prepared. If the copy is made at the same time, the certificate prescribed in 11 FAM 725.9 may state that the document is a true and correct copy of the signed original. If it is not possible to make a copy at the same time the original is prepared, the certificate indicates that the document is a true and correct copy of the copy on file in the mission. The word "(Copy)" is not placed on the document which is being certified; the word "(Signed)" is not placed before the indication of signatures.

726 TRANSMISSION OF INTERNATIONAL AGREEMENTS OTHER THAN TREATIES TO CONGRESS: COMPLIANCE WITH THE CASE-ZABLOCKI ACT

All officers will be especially diligent in cooperating to assure compliance with Public Law 92–403 "An Act to require that international agreements other than treaties, hereafter entered into by the United States, be transmitted to the Congress within sixty days after the execution thereof." That act, popularly known as the Case-Zablocki Act, approved August 22, 1972 (86 Stat. 619; 1 U.S.C. 112b, as amended), provides in relevant part:

The Secretary of State shall transmit to the Congress the text of any international agreement The Secretary of State shall transmit to the Congress the text of any international agreement (including the text of any oral international agreement, which agreement shall be reduced to writing) other than a treaty to which the United States is a party as soon as practicable after such agreement has entered into force with respect to the United States but in no event later than sixty days thereafter. However, any such agreement the immediate public disclosure of which would in the opinion of the President, be prejudicial to the national security of the United States shall not be so transmitted to the Congress but shall be transmitted to the Committee on Foreign Relations of the Senate and the Committee on International Relations of the House of Representatives under an appropriate injunction of secrecy to be removed only upon due notice from the President. Any department or agency of the United States government which enters into any international agreement on behalf of the United States shall transmit to the Department of State the text of such agreement not later than twenty days after such agreement has been signed.

727 PUBLICATION AND INTERNET AVAILABILITY OF TREATIES AND OTHER INTERNATIONAL AGREEMENTS OF THE UNITED STATES

The attention of all officers is directed to the requirements of the Act of September 23, 1950 (64 Stat. 979; 1 U.S.C. 112a), which provides in relevant part:

(a) The Secretary of State shall cause to be compiled, edited, indexed, and published, beginning as of January 1, 1950, a compilation entitled "United States Treaties and Other International Agreements," which shall contain all treaties to which the United States is a party that have been proclaimed during each calendar year, and all international agreements other than treaties to which the United States is a party that have been signed, proclaimed, or with reference to which any other final formality has been executed, during each calendar year. The said United States Treaties and Other International Agreements shall be legal evidence of the treaties, international agreements other than treaties, and proclamations by the President of such treaties and agreements, therein contained, in all the courts of the United States, the several

States, and the Territories and insular possessions of the United States.

* * * * * * *

(d) The Secretary of State shall make publicly available through the Internet website of the Department of State each treaty or international agreement proposed to be published in the compilation entitled "United States Treaties and Other International Agreements" not later than 180 days after the date on which the treaty or agreement enters into force.

730 GUIDELINES FOR CONCLUDING INTERNATIONAL AGREEMENTS

731 BILATERAL AND MULTILATERAL AGREEMENTS

731.1 Method of Concluding Bilateral and Multilateral Agreements

An agreement may be concluded through bilateral negotiations, which result either in the signing of a single instrument in duplicate or in an exchange of diplomatic notes, or through multilateral negotiations, usually at an international conference to which the governments concerned send official delegations to formulate and adopt or sign an instrument of agreement.

731.2 Bilateral Treaties and Agreements

731.2–1 Negotiation and Background Assistance

Whenever the negotiation of a new international agreement is under consideration, the Department office or the post having primary responsibility informs the Legal Adviser and may, if considered necessary, request background material and advice regarding relevant provisions in existing treaties and agreements, the general treaty relations of this Government with the government or governments concerned, and other pertinent information.

731.3 Instructions to Negotiators

a. When an agreement is to be concluded at a foreign capital, the Department designates the U. S. negotiator or negotiators, and the negotiator or negotiators are given appropriate instructions. If the agreement to be negotiated is a treaty that will be referred to the Senate, the Secretary of State may at some time prior to or during the negotiations issue or request the President to issue a "full power" (see 11 FAM 733) constituting formal authorization for the United States negotiators to sign the agreement. Such a "full power" is not customary with respect to an international agreement other than a treaty. Receiving or possessing a "full power" is never to be considered as a final authorization to sign.

b. The Department gives that authorization by a written or telegraphic instruction, and no signature is affixed in the absence of such instruction. If the proposal for an agreement originates with the United States, the U.S. negotiators as a rule furnish a tentative draft of the proposed agreement for submission to the other government for its consideration. The negotiators submit to the Department any modification of the draft or any counterproposal made by the other government and await instructions from the Department. If the original proposal emanates from a foreign government, the mission forwards The proposal to the Department and awaits its instructions.

731.4 Preparation of Texts for Signature

a. If an agreement is to be signed at a post abroad as a single instrument (in duplicate), preparing the documents to be signed is customarily done in the foreign ministry on paper supplied by it, along with a binding and ribbons to tie the pages in place. However, the mission may lend assistance if the foreign ministry so desires. There is no universal standard as to the kind or size of paper which must be used (each foreign ministry has its own "treaty paper"). For every bilateral agreement there must be two originals, one for each government. Each original must embody the full text of the agreement in all the languages in which the agreement is to be signed, and must be exactly the same as the other original subject only to the principle of the "alternat."

b. In the case of an agreement effected by an exchange of notes, the U.S. notes are prepared in English and in accordance with 5 FAM 220 through 224 and the rules prescribed in 5 FAH–1, Correspondence Handbook. The note of the foreign government is prepared in accordance with the style of the foreign ministry and usually in the language of that country. Whenever practicable, arrangements are made for the notes to bear the same date.

731.5 Arrangement of Texts and Principle of the Alternat

731.5–1 Arrangement of Texts

When English and a language other than English are both used, the texts in the two languages are placed:

(1) in "tandem" fashion, that is, with one text following the other (the tandem procedure is the most widely used as it is the most expeditious); or

(2) in parallel, vertical columns on the same page, the columns being approximately of equal width; or

(3) on opposite facing pages of the document the entire width of the type or printed space on the page.

If the two languages are placed "tandem" fashion, the English text is placed first in the U.S. original, and conversely in the foreign government's original.

If parallel columns are used, the English text is placed in the left column of each page in the original to be retained by the United States, and the foreign text appears in the right column. In the other original, to be retained by the foreign government, the foreign text appears in the left column, and the English text in the right column.

If the two languages are placed on opposite facing pages of the document, the English text occupies the left-hand page and the foreign text the right-hand page in the U.S. original, and conversely in the foreign government's original. If either the "tandem" or the "opposite facing page" style is used, the concluding part (usually beginning "IN WITNESS WHEREOF," "DONE," etc.) should appear in parallel columns on the page on which the signatures will appear, so that only one set of signatures is required for each separately bound document (see 11 FAM Exhibit 731.5, page 8). If parallel signature columns are not feasible, the concluding paragraphs can be placed in "tandem" fashion on the page on which the signatures appear (see 11 FAM Exhibit 731.5, page 9).

If a foreign text is one which, from the occidental viewpoint, reads from back to front, it may be possible to join the two texts in a single binding so that the signatures appear, roughly speaking, in the center of the document. If this is not feasible, the negotiators should seek instructions from the Office of the Assistant Legal Adviser for Treaty Affairs (L/T).

731.5–2 Arrangement of Names and Signatures and Use of Titles

a. In the original that the United States retains, the United States is named first in both the English and foreign texts, wherever the names of the countries occur together conjunctively or disjunctively, and the signature of the plenipotentiary of the United States appears on the left and that of the foreign plenipotentiary on the right of the original that the United States retains. Conversely, throughout both of the language texts of the original that the foreign government retains, that government is named first and its plenipotentiary's signature appears to the left of the signature of the U.S. plenipotentiary. The position of full sentences, paragraphs, or subparagraphs in the text is never transposed in the alternat procedure.

b. The general practice and preference of the Department of State is not to use titles along with signatures, especially where the President or the Secretary of State signs. However, if preferred by the other party or parties concerned, titles may be typed BELOW where each will sign (with ample space allowed for the signature). Generally, only one person signs for each party.

732 CONFORMITY OF TEXTS

After the documents have been prepared for signature on the basis of agreed texts, and before the agreement is signed, the negotiators or other responsible officers on each side make sure that the texts in both originals of the prepared agreement are in exact conformity with each other and with the texts in the drafts agreed to, and especially that where a foreign language is included, that text and the English text are in conformity in all substantive respects. Prior to document preparation, it should have been determined that the foreign-language text is essentially (that is, as a matter of substance) in accord with the English text, and that it has received the clearance of the Department as required in 11 FAM 722.6.

733 EXCHANGE OR EXHIBITION OF FULL POWERS

a. Each representative who is to sign a treaty is furnished a full power signed by the head of state, head of government, or minister for foreign affairs. More than one representative should be named in a single instrument of full power. On occasion, formal full powers may be (but customarily are NOT in U.S. practice) issued for signing certain agreements other than treaties. When issued, the full power is formal evidence of the authority of the representative to sign on behalf of the representative's government. It names the representative, with title, and gives a clear indication of the particular instrument of agreement that the representative is entitled to sign. Full powers for representatives of the United States are prepared by the Office of the Assistant Legal Adviser for Treaty Affairs (L/T) and generally are signed by the Secretary or Acting Secretary of State. On occasion, full powers are signed by the President.

b. If the agreement itself requires the exchange of full powers, they are exchanged. If not, they may be either exchanged or exhibited by the representatives on the occasion of signing the agreement, as may be preferred by the foreign representative. If a full power is required, the U.S. representative shall NOT proceed to sign the treaty until the full power is in hand, or the Department specially instructs otherwise. If exchanged, the original full power of the foreign representative is forwarded to the Department with the U.S. original of the signed agreement. If the representatives retain the original of the respective full powers, each representative should supply the other representative with a copy or a certified copy of the full power.

734 SIGNATURE AND SEALING

After a treaty or other international agreement that is to be signed as a single instrument has been completed, the host government makes mutually convenient arrangements for its signature. In the case of treaties, the signatures of the representatives may be accompanied by their respective seals, ribbons being fastened in the seals and binding the documents. The same procedure may be followed for other agreements signed as single instruments. It is not essential that seals be affixed, unless the agreement specifically so requires (the preference of the Department of State is NOT to use seals). The representative's personal seal, if available, is used when seals accompany the signatures, except that if the other government concerned prefers official seals, the seal of the mission may be used.

(NOTE.—A personal seal may consist of a signet ring with initial(s) or family crest, written initials, etc.)

735 EXCHANGE OF RATIFICATIONS

735.1 Time and Place for Exchange

It is customary for a treaty to contain a simple provision to the effect that the instruments of ratification will be exchanged as soon as possible at a designated capital, and that the treaty will enter into force on the date of such exchange or at the expiration of a specified number of days or months following the date of exchange. (As all treaties signed on the part of the United States are subject to ratification by and with the advice and consent of the Senate, and as the time required for action on any particular treaty cannot be foreseen, it is preferable that provision is made in the treaty that the instruments of ratification are to be exchanged "as soon as possible" rather than within a specified period.)

735.2 Effecting the Exchange

a. In exchanging instruments of ratification, the representative of the United States hands to the representative of the foreign government a duplicate original of the President's instrument of ratification. In return, the representative of the foreign government hands to the representative of the United States the instrument of ratification executed by the head or the chief executive of the foreign government. A protocol, sometimes called "Protocol of Exchange of Ratifications" or procès-verbal, attests that the exchange has been signed by the two representatives. No full power is required for this purpose.

b. The protocol of exchange is signed in duplicate originals, one for each government, and the principle of the alternat is observed as in the treaty. Before making the exchange and signing the procès-verbal or protocol of exchange, the diplomatic representative of the United States must be satisfied that the ratification of the foreign government is an unqualified ratification, or subject only to such reservations or understandings as have been agreed to by the two governments.

735.3 Notification of Date of Exchange

In all cases, but particularly in those in which the treaty enters into force on the day of the exchange, it is essential that the mission formally notify the Department by whatever means practicable when arrangements have been completed for the exchange, and also when the exchange actually takes place. By the first pouch after the exchange takes place, the mission should forward to the Department the instrument of ratification of the foreign government and the U.S. Government's original of the signed procès-verbal or protocol of exchange.

740 MULTILATERAL TREATIES AND AGREEMENTS

741 GENERAL PROCEDURES

The procedures for making multilateral agreements are in many respects the same as those for making bilateral agreements; for example, the general requirements in regard to full powers, ratification, proclamation, and publication. This subchapter covers certain procedures that vary with bilateral procedures.

742 NEGOTIATION

742.1 Function of International Conference

The international conference is the device usually employed for negotiating multilateral agreements. The greater the number of countries involved, the greater the necessity for such a conference. If only three or four countries are involved, it may be convenient to conduct the preliminary negotiations through correspondence and have a joint meeting of plenipotentiaries to complete the negotiations and to sign the document.

742.2 Invitation

Traditionally, the international conference is convened by one government extending to other interested governments an invitation (acceptance usually assured beforehand) to participate, the host government bearing most, if not all, of the expense incident to the physical aspects of the conference. This is still often the practice, but increasing numbers of conferences have been convened under the auspices and at the call of international organizations.

742.3 Statement of Purpose

When a call is made or invitations are extended for a conference to formulate a multilateral agreement, it is customary for a precise statement of purpose to accompany the call or the invitations. Sometimes, the invitation is also accompanied by a draft agreement to be used as a basis for negotiations. If the conference is called under the auspices of an international organization, the precise statement of purpose or the draft agreement may be prepared in preliminary sessions of the organization or by the secretariat of the organization.

742.4 Instructions to Negotiators

The U.S. delegation to a conference may be comprised of one or more representatives. As a rule, the U.S. delegation is furnished written instructions by the Department prior to the conference in the form of a position paper for the U.S. delegation cleared with the Secretary or an officer specifically authorized by him or her and other appropriate Department officers for that purpose, under the procedures described in 11 FAM 722.3. The Office of the Legal Adviser (L) in all instances reviews drafts of international conventions to be considered in meetings of an international organization of which the United States is a member; when necessary, it also provides legal assistance at international conferences and meetings.

742.5 Final Acts of Conference

The “Final Act” of a conference should not contain international commitments. A Final Act generally is limited to such matters as a statement or summary of the proceedings of the conference, the names of the states that participated, the organization of the conference and the committees established, resolutions adopted, the drafts of international agreements formulated for consideration by governments concerned, and the like. If an international agreement is to be opened for signature at the close of the conference, a text thereof may be annexed to the Final Act but must not be incorporated in the body thereof; the text to be signed must be prepared and bound separately for that purpose. Where a final Act appears to embody international commitments, the U.S. representative reports the same to the Department and awaits specific instructions before taking any further action.

743 OFFICIAL AND WORKING LANGUAGES

743.1 General Procedures

The working languages of the conference and the official languages of the conference documents are determined by the conference. A conference does not necessarily adopt all of the languages for both purposes. It is customary and preferable for all the official languages in which the final document is prepared for signature to be designated as having equal authenticity. It is possible, however, for the conference to determine, because of special circumstances, that in the event of dispute one of the languages is to prevail and to include in the text of the agreement a provision to that effect. Before a U.S. delegation concurs in any such proposal, it must request instructions from the Department.

743.2 English-Language Text

Negotiators will use every practicable effort to assure that an English-language text is part of the authentic text of any multilateral treaty negotiated for the United States. Where any question exists on this subject, the negotiators should seek further instructions.

744 PREPARATION OF DOCUMENTS FOR SIGNATURE

744.1 Language or Languages Used in Texts

The multilateral agreement drawn up at an international conference is prepared for signature in the official language or languages adopted by the conference. (See 11 FAM 743.) The document preparation ordinarily will be done by the conference secretariat.

744.2 Principle of the Alternat

The principle of the alternat (see 11 FAM 731.5) does not apply in regards to a multilateral agreement, except in the remote case when an agreement between three or four governments is prepared for signature in the language of all the signatories and each of those governments receives a signed original of the agreement. Customarily, a multilateral agreement is prepared for signature in a single original, comprising all the official languages. That original is placed in the custody of a depositary (either a government or an international organization) that furnishes certified copies to all governments concerned.

744.2–1 Arrangements of Texts

The arrangement of multilateral agreement texts varies, depending largely on the number of languages used. As in the case of bilateral agreements, however, the basic alternatives in the case of multilateral agreements are "tandem," parallel columns, or facing pages, as follows:

744.2–1(A) Tandem

If an agreement is to be signed in two languages, and especially if signed in three or more languages, the texts may be arranged in tandem style, that is, one complete text following the other. This allows readily for any number of official texts; the tandem style precedent of the Charter of the United Nations is followed for preparing agreements formulated under the UN auspices. It is desirable, whenever practicable, that the concluding part of each text be placed with the concluding part of each of the other texts in parallel columns on the page on which the first of the signatures appears, although the tandem arrangement described at the end of 11 FAM 744.2–1C can be used.

744.2–1(B) Parallel Columns

If an agreement is to be signed in only two languages, the traditionally preferred method of arrangement of the texts has been parallel, vertical columns. This method may be used also if only three languages are used, but the three columns are necessarily so narrow that the method has been rarely used in such cases. When there are four official languages, However, it is possible to use the parallel column method by placing two of the language texts on a left-hand page and the other two language texts on the facing right-hand page; this method has been used often and to good advantage in various inter-American agreements with English, Spanish, French, and Portuguese.

744.2–1(C) Facing Pages

If an agreement is to be signed in only two languages, and circumstances make it necessary or desirable, the facing page method may be used for preparing the texts for signature, so that one of the language texts will be on a left-hand page and the other will be on the facing right-hand page. When this method is used, it is desirable that at least the concluding part (usually beginning "IN WITNESS WHEREOF," "DONE," etc.) be prepared in parallel columns on the page at the end of the texts in both languages so that only one set of signatures is required. If parallel columns are not feasible, the concluding paragraphs can be placed tandem fashion (one language text after another) on the page at the end of the texts in both languages.

744.2–2 Arrangements of Names and Signatures

a. The arrangement of names and signatures, although seemingly a minor matter, sometimes presents difficulties in the case of multilateral agreements. There may be variations of arrangements, depending on particular factors, but the arrangement most generally used is alphabetical according to the names of the countries concerned. An alphabetical listing, however, presents the further question, even when there are only two languages, of what language is to be used in determining the arrangement.

b. It is a common practice to use the language of the host government or for an agreement formulated under the auspices of an international organization, to follow the precedents established by that organization. It is possible, in the event that agreement could not be reached regarding the arrangement of names of countries and signatures of plenipotentiaries, to have a drawing of lots, a device seldom used. In any event, the question is one to be determined by the conference.

744.3 Conformity of Texts

It is the primary responsibility of the delegations, acting in conference, to determine the conformity of the agreement texts that are to be signed. However, the conference secretariat has a responsibility for checking the texts carefully to insure that, when put in final form for signature, the texts are in essential conformity.

745 FULL POWERS

a. In the case of a multilateral agreement drawn up at an international conference, this Government customarily (almost invariably, in the case of a treaty) issues to one or more of its representatives at the conference an instrument of full power authorizing signature of the agreement on behalf of the United States. In some instances, issuance of the full power is deferred until it is relatively certain that the agreement formulated is to be signed for the United States. (See 11 FAM 733.) Ordinarily, that full power is presented by the representatives to the secretary general of the conference upon arrival of the delegation at the conference site. It may be submitted in advance of arrival, but usually that is not necessary.

b. When the conference has formally convened, it usually appoints a credentials committee, to which all full powers and other evidence of authorization are submitted for examination. The full powers and related documents are retained by the credentials committee or the secretary general until the close of the conference. At the close of the conference, the full powers, related documents, and the signed original of the agreement are turned over to the government or the international organization designated in the agreement as the depositary authority, to be placed in its archives.

746 SIGNATURE AND SEALING

746.1 Signature

Most multilateral agreements are signed. Some, however, are adopted by a conference or organization after which governments become parties by adherence, accession, acceptance, or some other method not requiring signature (for example, conventions drawn up and adopted at sessions of the International Labor Organization). Procedures for the deposit of an instrument of adherence, accession, or acceptance are similar to procedures for the deposit of instruments of ratification. In some cases, accession or approval can be accomplished by formal notice through diplomatic channels.

746.2 Seals

Multilateral treaties do not usually provide for the use of seals along with the signatures of representatives. The large number of signatures would make the use of seals difficult and cumbersome.

747 DISPOSITION OF FINAL DOCUMENTS OF CONFERENCE

a. At the close of a conference, the remaining supply of working documents (for example, records of committee meetings, verbatim minutes, etc.) usually is placed in the custody of the host government or the organization that called the conference for appropriate disposition. It is not proper for definitive commitments constituting part of the agreement to be embodied in such working documents. Definitive commitments must be incorporated only in a final document to be signed or adopted as an international agreement.

b. The final documents of the conference may include a Final Act (see 11 FAM 742.5) and separately, the text(s) of any agreement(s). The practice of signing a Final Act is still followed in many cases. In any event, any agreement formulated at the conference must be prepared as a separate document and signed or adopted. The signed or adopted originals of the final documents of the conference are submitted to the government or international organization designated in such documents as depositary. If the conference is not held under the auspices of an organization, it is customary for the host government to be designated depositary, but it might be appropriate, even in such case, to name an organization, such as the United Nations, as depositary. The decision is made by the conference, with the concurrence of the government or international organization concerned.

748 PROCEDURE FOLLOWING SIGNATURE

748.1 Understandings or Reservations

If it is necessary to inform other governments concerned, and perhaps obtain their consent, with respect to an understanding, interpretation, or reservation included by the Senate in its resolution of advice and consent, this Government communicates with the depositary, which then carries on the necessary correspondence with the other governments concerned.

748.2 Deposit of Ratification

a. When the depositary for a multilateral agreement is a foreign government or an international organization, the U.S. instrument of ratification (or adherence, accession, acceptance, etc.) is sent by the Office of the Assistant Legal Adviser for Treaty Affairs (L/T) to the appropriate Foreign Service mission or to the U.S. representative to the organization if there is a permanent representative. The mission or the representative deposits it with the depositary authority in accordance with the terms of the accompanying instruction from the Department concerning the time of deposit.

b. When this Government is depositary for a multilateral agreement, posts are not authorized to accept instruments of ratification of foreign governments; that is, the foreign government cannot deposit its instrument with the post. If a post is requested to transmit an instrument of ratification to the Department, it must make clear to the foreign government that the post is acting only as a transmitting agent and that the ratification cannot be considered as accepted for deposit until received and examined by the Department.

748.3 Registration

It is generally recognized that the depositary for a multilateral agreement has a primary responsibility for its registration. Normally, the depositary has custody not only of the original document of agreement but also of instruments of ratification and other formal documents. Consequently, the depositary is the most authoritative source of information and documentation. (See also 11 FAM 753.3.)

750 RESPONSIBILITIES OF THE ASSISTANT LEGAL ADVISER FOR TREATY AFFAIRS (L/T)

751 PREPARATION OF DOCUMENTS, CEREMONIES, AND INSTRUCTIONS

Carrying out and providing advice and assistance respecting the provisions of this chapter is the responsibility of the Assistant Legal Adviser for Treaty Affairs (L/T), who:

(1) Reviews all drafts of international agreements, proposals by other governments or international organizations, instructions and position papers, all Circular 175 requests (see 11 FAM 721), and accompanying memoranda of law;

(2) Makes arrangements for and/or supervises ceremonies at Washington, DC for the signature of treaties or other international agreements; and supervises the preparation of texts of treaties and other agreements to be signed at Washington, DC;

(3) Supervises preparation of the Secretary of State's reports to the President and the President's messages to the Senate to transmit treaties for advice and consent to ratification;

(4) Prepares full powers, protocols of exchange, instruments of ratification or adherence, instruments or notifications of acceptance or approval, termination notices, and proclamations with respect to treaties or other international agreements;

(5) Makes arrangements for the exchange or deposit of instruments of ratification, deposit of instruments of adherence, the receipt or deposit of instruments or notifications of acceptance or approval, termination notices, and proclamations with respect to treaties or other international agreements;

(6) Prepares instructions to posts abroad and notes to foreign diplomatic missions at Washington, DC respecting matters stated in paragraph e;

(7) Prepares and signs transmittals to the Congress of all international agreements other than treaties, as required by the Case-Zablocki Act, 1 U.S.C. 112b (see 11 FAM 726);

(8) Takes appropriate steps required for the publication and registration of treaties and other international agreements to which the United States is a party, including making them available on the Department's Internet Web site (see 11 FAM 727 and 11 FAM 753.3); and

(9) Consults periodically with Congress on the full range of treaty issues, including matters of treaty priorities for the Administration; significant negotiations; the appropriate form of an international agreement; and the attachment of reservations, understandings, or declarations to treaties before the Senate for its advice and consent.

752 PREPARING DOCUMENTS FOR SIGNATURE

a. After the text of a treaty or other agreement is approved in writing in accordance with 11 FAM 724.7, the document is normally prepared at the capital at which it is to be signed.

b. Adequate time (normally 7 business days) is allowed for the preparation (printing on treaty paper), comparing, etc., of the treaty or other agreement to be signed, in order to assure sufficient time for the preparation of accurate texts in duplicate for signature, including, in the case of documents to be signed in a foreign language, sufficient time for the Language Services Division to prepare any translations required; check any existing foreign-language draft; and check the prepared foreign-language text. If any question arises as to the time necessary to complete the preparation of texts at Washington, DC, the matter will be referred to the Assistant Legal Adviser for Treaty Affairs (L/T).

753 PUBLICATION AND REGISTRATION

753.1 Publication of Texts

After the necessary action has been taken to bring into force the treaty or other international agreement concluded by the United States, it is published in the Treaties and Other International Acts Series issued by the Department. After publication in that series, the text of the treaty or other agreement is printed in the annual volume(s) (which may consist of two or more bindings) of United States Treaties and Other International Agreements, as required by law (see 11 FAM 727). Treaties and other agreements concluded prior to January 1, 1950, were published in the United States Statutes at Large and for easy reference were reprinted in Bevans, Treaties and Other International Agreements of the United States of America, 1776-1949.

753.2 Responsibility for Other Treaty Publications

The Office of the Assistant Legal Adviser for Treaty Affairs (L/T) prepares and maintains the annual publication, Treaties in Force, an authoritative guide to the text and status of treaties and other international agreements currently in force for the United States. It also compiles and has published, in addition to the text referred to in 11 FAM 753.1, other volumes containing texts of treaties and other agreements as required or authorized by law. The "Treaty Actions" information on the Department of State Web site is compiled by that office.

753.3 Registration

The Office of the Assistant Legal Adviser for Treaty Affairs (L/T) is responsible for registering U.S. treaties and international agreements:

(1) Article 102 of the United Nations Charter requires that every treaty and every international agreement entered into by a member of the United Nations be registered, as soon as possible, with the Secretariat and published by it; and

(2) Article 83 of the Chicago Convention on International Civil Aviation of 1944 requires registering aviation agreements

with the Council of the International Civil Aviation Organization.

753.4 United States as Depositary

a. Inquiries from foreign diplomatic missions at Washington, DC and from U.S. diplomatic missions abroad with respect to the preparation or deposit of instruments relating to any multilateral agreement for which the United States is depositary are referred to the Office of the Assistant Legal Adviser for Treaty Affairs (L/T). Notify L/T immediately when any such document is received anywhere in the Department. As the depositary office, the Office of the Assistant Legal Adviser for Treaty Affairs (L/T) is required to ascertain whether those documents are properly executed before accepting them for deposit; to keep accurate records regarding them; and to inform other concerned governments of the order and date it received such documents.

b. Before any arrangements are proposed or agreed to for the United States to serve as depositary for any international agreement, obtain the views of the Assistant Legal Adviser for Treaty Affairs (L/T).

753.5 Records and Correspondence Custody

a. The Assistant Legal Adviser for Treaty Affairs compiles and maintains authoritative records regarding the negotiation, signature, transmission to the Senate, and ratification or approval, as well as the existence, status, and application, of all international agreements to which the United States is or may become a party. Inquiries on these subjects are addressed to, and outgoing communications cleared with, the Office of the Legal Adviser (L).

b. To insure that the records regarding the matters described in this section are complete and up to date, it is important that all relevant papers be referred to the Office of the Legal Adviser (L).

c. The Assistant Legal Adviser for Treaty Affairs is responsible for the custody of originals of bilateral agreements and certified copies of multilateral agreements pending entry into force and completion of manuscripts for publication. Following publication, such originals and certified copies are transferred to the National Archives. The Assistant Legal Adviser for Treaty (L/T) Affairs retains custody of signed originals of multilateral agreements for which the United States is depositary, together with relevant instruments of ratification, adherence, acceptance, or approval, as long as those agreements remain active.

2. Vienna Convention on Diplomatic Relations [1]

Done at Vienna April 18, 1961; Entered into force April 24, 1964; Entered into force for the United States December 13, 1972

The States Parties to the present Convention,

RECALLING that peoples of all nations from ancient times have recognized the status of diplomatic agents,

HAVING IN MIND the purposes and principles of the Charter of the United Nations concerning the sovereign equality of States, the maintenance of international peace and security, and the promotion of friendly relations among nations,

BELIEVING that an international convention on diplomatic intercourse, privileges and immunities would contribute to the development of friendly relations among nations, irrespective of their differing constitutional and social systems,

REALIZING that the purpose of such privileges and immunities is not to benefit individuals but to ensure the efficient performance of the functions of diplomatic missions as representing States,

AFFIRMING that the rules of customary international law should continue to govern questions not expressly regulated by the provisions of the present Convention,

HAVE AGREED AS FOLLOWS:

Article 1

For the purpose of the present Convention, the following expressions shall have the meanings hereunder assigned to them:

(a) the "head of the mission" is the person charged by the sending State with the duty of acting in that capacity;

(b) the "members of the mission" are the head of the mission and the members of the staff of the mission;

(c) the "members of the staff of the mission" are the members of the diplomatic staff, of the administrative and technical staff and of the service staff of the mission;

(d) the "members of the diplomatic staff" are the members of the staff of the mission having diplomatic rank;

(e) a "diplomatic agent" is the head of the mission or a member of the diplomatic staff of the mission;

(f) the "members of the administrative and technical staff" are the members of the staff of the mission employed in the administrative and technical service of the mission;

(g) the "members of the service staff" are the members of the staff of the mission in the domestic service of the mission;

[1] 23 UST 3227; TIAS 7502.

(h) a "private servant" is a person who is in the domestic service of a member of the mission and who is not an employee of the sending State;

(i) the "premises of the mission" are the buildings or parts of buildings and the land ancillary thereto, irrespective of ownership, used for the purposes of the mission including the residence of the head of the mission.

Article 2

The establishment of diplomatic relations between States, and of permanent diplomatic missions, takes place by mutual consent.

Article 3

1. The functions of a diplomatic mission consist inter alia in:

(a) representing the sending State in the receiving State;

(b) protecting in the receiving State the interests of the sending State and of its nationals, within the limits permitted by international law;

(c) negotiating with the Government of the receiving State;

(d) ascertaining by all lawful means conditions and developments in the receiving State, and reporting thereon to the Government of the sending State;

(e) promoting friendly relations between the sending State and the receiving State, and developing their economic, cultural and scientific relations.

2. Nothing in the present Convention shall be construed as preventing the performance of consular functions by a diplomatic mission.

Article 4

1. The sending State must make certain that the *agrement* of the receiving State has been given for the person it proposes to accredit as head of the mission to that State.

2. The receiving State is not obliged to give reasons to the sending State for a refusal of *agrment*.

Article 5

1. The sending State may, after it has given due notification to the receiving States concerned, accredit a head of mission or assign any member of the diplomatic staff, as the case may be, to more than one State, unless there is express objection by any of the receiving States.

2. If the sending State accredits a head of mission to one or more other States it may establish a diplomatic mission headed by a charge d'affaires ad interim in each State where the head of mission has not his permanent seat.

3. A head of mission or any member of the diplomatic staff of the mission may act as representative of the sending State to any international organization.

Article 6

Two or more States may accredit the same person as head of mission to another State, unless objection is offered by the receiving State.

Article 7

Subject to the provisions of Articles 5, 8, 9 and 11, the sending State may freely appoint the members of the staff of the mission. In the case of military, naval or air attaches, the receiving State may require their names to be submitted beforehand, for its approval.

Article 8

1. Members of the diplomatic staff of the mission should in principle be of the nationality of the sending State.
2. Members of the diplomatic staff of the mission may not be appointed from among persons having the nationality of the receiving State, except with the consent of that State which may be withdrawn at any time.
3. The receiving State may reserve the same right with regard to nationals of a third State who are not also nationals of the sending State.

Article 9

1. The receiving State may at any time and without having to explain its decision, notify the sending State that the head of the mission or any member of the diplomatic staff of the mission is persona non grata or that any other member of the staff of the mission is not acceptable. In any such case, the sending State shall, as appropriate, either recall the person concerned or terminate his functions with the mission. A person may be declared non grata or not acceptable before arriving in the territory of the receiving State.
2. If the sending State refuses or fails within a reasonable period to carry out its obligations under paragraph 1 of this Article, the receiving State may refuse to recognize the person concerned as a member of the mission.

Article 10

1. The Ministry for Foreign Affairs of the receiving State, or such other ministry as may be agreed, shall be notified of:

(a) the appointment of members of the mission, their arrival and their final departure or the termination of heir functions with the mission;

(b) the arrival and final departure of a person belonging to the family of a member of the mission and, where appropriate, the fact that a person becomes or ceases to be a member of the family of a member of the mission;

(c) the arrival and final departure of private servants in the employ of persons referred to in sub-paragraph (a) of this paragraph and, where appropriate, the fact that they are leaving the employ of such persons;

(d) the engagement and discharge of persons resident in the receiving State as members of the mission or private servants entitled to privileges and immunities.

2. Where possible, prior notification of arrival and final departure shall also be given.

Article 11

1. In the absence of specific agreement as to the size of the mission, the receiving State may require that the size of a mission be kept within limits considered by it to be reasonable and normal, having regard to circumstances and conditions in the receiving State and to the needs of the particular mission.

2. The receiving State may equally, within similar bounds and on a nondiscriminatory basis, refuse to accept officials of a particular category.

Article 12

The sending State may not, without the prior express consent of the receiving State, establish offices forming part of the mission in localities other than those in which the mission itself is established.

Article 13

1. The head of the mission is considered as having taken up his functions in the receiving State either when he has presented his credentials or when he has notified his arrival and a true copy of his credentials has been presented to the Ministry for Foreign Affairs of the receiving State, or such other ministry as may be agreed, in accordance with the practice prevailing in the receiving State which shall be applied in a uniform manner.

2. The order of presentation of credentials or of a true copy thereof will be determined by the date and time of the arrival of the head of the mission.

Article 14

1. Heads of mission are divided into three classes, namely:

(a) that of ambassadors or nuncios accredited to Heads of State, and other heads of mission of equivalent rank;

(b) that of envoys, ministers and internuncios accredited to Heads of State;

(c) that of charges d'affaires accredited to Ministers for Foreign Affairs.

2. Except as concerns precedence and etiquette, there shall be no differentiation between heads of mission by reason of their class.

Article 15

The class to which the heads of their missions are to be assigned shall be agreed between States.

Article 16

1. Heads of mission shall take precedence in their respective classes in the order of the date and time of taking up their functions in accordance with Article 13.

2. Alterations in the credentials of a head of mission not involving any change of class shall not affect his precedence.

3. This article is without prejudice to any practice accepted by the receiving State regarding the precedence of the representative of the Holy See.

Article 17

The precedence of the members of the diplomatic staff of the mission shall be notified by the head of the mission to the Ministry for Foreign Affairs or such other ministry as may be agreed.

Article 18

The procedure to be observed in each State for the reception of heads of mission shall be uniform in respect of each class.

Article 19

1. If the post of head of the mission is vacant, or if the head of the mission is unable to perform his functions, a charge d'affaires ad interim shall act provisionally as head of the mission. The name of the charge d'affaires ad interim shall be notified, either by the head of the mission or, in case he is unable to do so, by the Ministry for Foreign Affairs of the sending State to the Ministry for Foreign Affairs of the receiving State or such other ministry as may be agreed.

2. In cases where no member of the diplomatic staff of the mission is present in the receiving State, a member of the administrative and technical staff may, with the consent of the receiving State, be designated by the sending State to be in charge of the current administrative affairs of the mission.

Article 20

The mission and its head shall have the right to use the flag and emblem of the sending State on the premises of the mission, including the residence of the head of the mission, and on his means of transport.

Article 21

1. The receiving State shall either facilitate the acquisition on its territory, in accordance with its laws, by the sending State of premises necessary for its mission or assist the latter in obtaining accommodation in some other way.

2. It shall also, where necessary, assist missions in obtaining suitable accommodation for their members.

Article 22

1. The premises of the mission shall be inviolable. The agents of the receiving State may not enter them, except with the consent of the head of the mission.

2. The receiving State is under a special duty to take all appropriate steps to protect the premises of the mission against any intrusion or damage and to prevent any disturbance of the peace of the mission or impairment of its dignity.

3. The premises of the mission, their furnishings and other property thereon and the means of transport of the mission shall be immune from search, requisition, attachment or execution.

Article 23

1. The sending State and the head of the mission shall be exempt from all national, regional or municipal dues and taxes in respect of the premises of the mission, whether owned or leased, other than such as represent payment for specific services rendered.

2. The exemption from taxation referred to in this Article shall not apply to such dues and taxes payable under the law of the receiving State by persons contracting with the sending State or the head of the mission.

Article 24

The archives and documents of the mission shall be inviolable at any time and wherever they may be.

Article 25

The receiving State shall accord full facilities for the performance of the functions of the mission.

Article 26

Subject to its laws and regulations concerning zones entry into which is prohibited or regulated for reasons of national security, the receiving State shall ensure to all members of the mission freedom of movement and travel in its territory.

Article 27

1. The receiving State shall permit and protect free communication on the part of the mission for all official purposes. In communicating with the Government and the other missions and consulates of the sending State, wherever situated, the mission may employ all appropriate means, including diplomatic couriers and messages in code or cipher. However, the mission may install and use a wireless transmitter only with the consent of the receiving State.

2. The official correspondence of the mission shall be inviolable. Official correspondence means all correspondence relating to the mission and its functions.

3. The diplomatic bag shall not be opened or detained.

4. The packages constituting the diplomatic bag must bear visible external marks of their character and may contain only diplomatic documents or articles intended for official use.

5. The diplomatic courier, who shall be provided with an official document indicating his status and the number of packages constituting the diplomatic bag, shall be protected by the receiving State in the performance of his functions. He shall enjoy personal inviolability and shall not be liable to any form of arrest or detention.

6. The sending State or the mission may designate diplomatic couriers ad hoc. In such cases the provisions of paragraph 5 of this Article shall also apply, except that the immunities therein mentioned shall cease to apply when such a courier has delivered to the consignee the diplomatic bag in his charge.

7. A diplomatic bag may be entrusted to the captain of a commercial aircraft scheduled to land at an authorized port of entry. He shall be provided with an official document indicating the number of packages constituting the bag but he shall not be considered to be a diplomatic courier. The mission may send one of its members to take possession of the diplomatic bag directly and freely from the captain of the aircraft.

Article 28

The fees and charges levied by the mission in the course of its official duties shall be exempt from all dues and taxes.

Article 29

The person of a diplomatic agent shall be inviolable. He shall not be liable to any form of arrest or detention. The receiving State shall treat him with due respect and shall take all appropriate steps to prevent any attack on his person, freedom or dignity.

Article 30

1. The private residence of a diplomatic agent shall enjoy the same inviolability and protection as the premises of the mission.

2. His papers, correspondence and, except as provided in paragraph 3 of Article 31, his property, shall likewise enjoy inviolability

Article 31

1. A diplomatic agent shall enjoy immunity from the criminal jurisdiction of the receiving State. He shall also enjoy immunity from its civil and administrative jurisdiction, except in the case of:

(a) a real action relating to private immovable property situated in the territory of the receiving State, unless he holds it on behalf of the sending State for the purposes of the mission;

(b) an action relating to succession in which the diplomatic agent is involved as executor, administrator, heir or legatee as a private person and not on behalf of the sending State;

(c) an action relating to any professional or commercial activity exercised by the diplomatic agent in the receiving State outside his official functions.

2. A diplomatic agent is not obliged to give evidence as a witness.

3. No measures of execution may be taken in respect of a diplomatic agent except in the cases coming under sub-paragraphs (a), (b) and (c) of paragraph 1 of this Article, and provided that the measures concerned can be taken without infringing the inviolability of his person or of his residence.

4. The immunity of a diplomatic agent from the jurisdiction of the receiving State does not exempt him from the jurisdiction of the sending State.

Article 32

1. The immunity from jurisdiction of diplomatic agents and of persons enjoying immunity under Article 37 may be waived by the sending State.

2. Waiver must always be express.

3. The initiation of proceedings by a diplomatic agent or by a person enjoying immunity from jurisdiction under Article 37 shall preclude him from invoking immunity from jurisdiction in respect of any counter-claim directly connected with the principal claim.

4. Waiver of immunity from jurisdiction in respect of civil or administrative proceedings shall not be held to imply waiver of immunity in respect of the execution of the judgment, for which a separate waiver shall be necessary.

Article 33

1. Subject to the provisions of paragraph 3 of this Article, a diplomatic agent shall with respect to services rendered for the sending State be exempt from social security provisions which may be in force in the receiving State.

2. The exemption provided for in paragraph 1 of this Article shall also apply to private servants who are in the sole employ of a diplomatic agent, on condition:

(a) that they are not nationals of or permanently resident in the receiving State; and

(b) that they are covered by the social security provisions which may be in force in the sending State or a third State.

3. A diplomatic agent who employs persons to whom the exemption provided for in paragraph 2 of this Article does not apply shall observe the obligations which the social security provisions of the receiving State impose upon employers.

4. The exemption provided for in paragraphs 1 and 2 of this Article shall not preclude voluntary participation in the social security system of the receiving State provided that such participation is permitted by that State.

5. The provisions of this Article shall not affect bilateral or multilateral agreements concerning social security concluded previously and shall not prevent the conclusion of such agreements in the future.

Article 34

A diplomatic agent shall be exempt from all dues and taxes, personal or real, national, regional or municipal, except:

(a) indirect taxes of a kind which are normally incorporated in the price of goods or services;

(b) dues and taxes on private immovable property situated in the territory of the receiving State, unless he holds it on behalf of the sending State for the purposes of the mission;

(c) estate, succession or inheritance duties levied by the receiving State, subject to the provisions of paragraph 4 of Article 39;

(d) dues and taxes on private income having its source in the receiving State and capital taxes on investments made in commercial undertakings in the receiving State;

(e) charges levied for specific services rendered;

(f) registration, court or record fees, mortgage dues and stamp duty, with respect to immovable property, subject to the provisions of Article 23.

Article 35

The receiving State shall exempt diplomatic agents from all personal services, from all public service of any kind whatsoever, and from military obligations such as those connected with requisitioning, military contributions and billeting.

Article 36

1. The receiving State shall, in accordance with such laws and regulations as it may adopt, permit entry of and grant exemption from all customs duties, taxes, and related charges other than charges for storage, cartage and similar services, on:

(a) articles for the official use of the mission;

(b) articles for the personal use of a diplomatic agent or members of his family forming part of his household, including articles intended for his establishment.

2. The personal baggage of a diplomatic agent shall be exempt from inspection, unless there are serious grounds for presuming that it contains articles not covered by the exemptions mentioned in paragraph 1 of this Article, or articles the import or export of which is prohibited by the law or controlled by the quarantine regulations of the receiving State. Such inspection shall be conducted only in the presence of the diplomatic agent or of his authorized representative.

Article 37

1. The members of the family of a diplomatic agent forming part of his household shall, if they are not nationals of the receiving State, enjoy the privileges and immunities specified in Articles 29 to 36.

2. Members of the administrative and technical staff of the mission, together with members of their families forming part of their respective households, shall, if they are not nationals of or permanently resident in the receiving State, enjoy the privileges and immunities specified in Articles 29 to 35, except that the immunity from civil and administrative jurisdiction of the receiving State specified in paragraph 1 of Article 31 shall not extend to acts performed outside the course of their duties. They shall also enjoy the privileges specified in Article 36, paragraph 1, in respect of articles imported at the time of first installation.

3. Members of the service staff of the mission who are nationals of or permanently resident in the receiving State shall enjoy immunity in respect of acts performed in the course of their duties, exemption from dues and taxes on the emoluments they receive by reason of their employment and the exemption contained in Article 33.

4. Private servants of members of the mission shall, if they are not nationals of or permanently resident in the receiving State, be exempt from dues and taxes on the emoluments they receive by reason of their employment. In other respects, they may enjoy privileges and immunities only to the extent admitted by the receiving State. However, the receiving State must exercise its jurisdiction over those persons in such a manner as not to interfere unduly with the performance of the functions of the mission.

Article 38

1. Except insofar as additional privileges and immunities may be granted by the receiving State, a diplomatic agent who is a national of or permanently resident in that State shall enjoy only immunity from jurisdiction, and inviolability, in respect of official acts performed in the exercise of his functions.

2. Other members of the staff of the mission and private servants who are nationals of or permanently resident in the receiving State shall enjoy privileges and immunities only to the extent admitted by the receiving State. However, the receiving State must exercise its jurisdiction over those persons in such a manner as not to interfere unduly with the performance of the functions of the mission.

Article 39

1. Every person entitled to privileges and immunities shall enjoy them from the moment he enters the territory of the receiving State on proceeding to take up his post or, if already in its territory, from the moment when his appointment is notified to the Ministry for Foreign Affairs or such other ministry as may be agreed.

2. When the functions of a person enjoying privileges and immunities have come to an end, such privileges and immunities shall normally cease at the moment when he leaves the country, or on expiry of a reasonable period in which to do so, but shall subsist until that time, even in case of armed conflict. However, with respect to acts performed by such a person in the exercise of his functions as a member of the mission, immunity shall continue to subsist.

3. In case of the death of a member of the mission, the members of his family shall continue to enjoy the privileges and immunities to which they are entitled until the expiry of a reasonable period in which to leave the country.

4. In the event of the death of a member of the mission not a national of or permanently resident in the receiving State or a member of his family forming part of his household, the receiving State shall permit the withdrawal of the movable property of the

deceased, with the exception of any property acquired in the country the export of which was prohibited at the time of his death. Estate, succession and inheritance duties shall not be levied on movable property the presence of which in the receiving State was due solely to the presence there of the deceased as a member of the mission or as a member of the family of a member of the mission.

Article 40

1. If a diplomatic agent passes through or is in the territory of a third State, which has granted him a passport visa if such visa was necessary, while proceeding to take up or to return to his post, or when returning to his own country, the third State shall accord him inviolability and such other immunities as may be required to ensure his transit or return. The same shall apply in the case of any members of his family enjoying privileges or immunities who are accompanying the diplomatic agent, or travelling separately to join him or to return to their country.

2. In circumstances similar to those specified in paragraph 1 of this Article, third States shall not hinder the passage of members of the administrative and technical or service staff of a mission, and of members of their families, through their territories.

3. Third States shall accord to official correspondence and other official communications in transit, including messages in code or cipher, the same freedom and protection as is accorded by the receiving State. They shall accord to diplomatic couriers, who have been granted a passport visa if such visa was necessary, and diplomatic bags in transit the same inviolability and protection as the receiving State is bound to accord.

4. The obligations of third States under paragraphs 1, 2 and 3 of this Article shall also apply to the persons mentioned respectively in those paragraphs, and to official communications and diplomatic bags, whose presence in the territory of the third State is due to force majeure.

Article 41

1. Without prejudice to their privileges and immunities, it is the duty of all persons enjoying such privileges and immunities to respect the laws and regulations of the receiving State. They also have a duty not to interfere in the internal affairs of that State.

2. All official business with the receiving State entrusted to the mission by the sending State shall be conducted with or through the Ministry for Foreign Affairs of the receiving State or such other ministry as may be agreed.

3. The premises of the mission must not be used in any manner incompatible with the functions of the mission as laid down in the present Convention or by other rules of general international law or by any special agreements in force between the sending and the receiving State.

Article 42

A diplomatic agent shall not in the receiving State practice for personal profit any professional or commercial activity.

Article 43

The function of a diplomatic agent comes to an end, inter alia:

(a) on notification by the sending State to the receiving State that the function of the diplomatic agent has come to an end;

(b) on notification by the receiving State to the sending State that, in accordance with paragraph 2 of Article 9, it refuses to recognize the diplomatic agent as a member of the mission.

Article 44

The receiving State must, even in case of armed conflict, grant facilities in order to enable persons enjoying privileges and immunities, other than nationals of the receiving State, and members of the families of such persons irrespective of their nationality, to leave at the earliest possible moment. It must, in particular, in case of need, place at their disposal the necessary means of transport for themselves and their property.

Article 45

If diplomatic relations are broken off between two States, or if a mission is permanently or temporarily recalled:

(a) the receiving State must, even in case of armed conflict, respect and protect the premises of the mission, together with its property and archives;

(b) the sending State may entrust the custody of the premises of the mission, together with its property and archives, to a third State acceptable to the receiving State;

(c) the sending State may entrust the protection of its interests and those of its nationals to a third State acceptable to the receiving State.

Article 46

A sending State may with the prior consent of a receiving State, and at the request of a third State not represented in the receiving State, undertake the temporary protection of the interests of the third State and of its nationals.

Article 47

1. In the application of the provisions of the present Convention, the receiving State shall not discriminate as between States.

2. However, discrimination shall not be regarded as taking place:

(a) where the receiving State applies any of the provisions of the present Convention restrictively because of a restrictive application of that provision to its mission in the sending State;

(b) where by custom or agreement States extend to each other more favourable treatment than is required by the provisions of the present Convention.

Article 48

The present Convention shall be open for signature by all States Members of the United Nations or of any of the specialized agencies or Parties to the Statute of the International Court of Justice, and by any other State invited by the General Assembly of the United Nations to become a Party to the Convention, as follows: until 31 October 1961 at the Federal Ministry for Foreign Affairs of Austria and subsequently, until 31 March 1962, at the United Nations Headquarters in New York.

Article 49

The present Convention is subject to ratification. The instruments of ratification shall be deposited with the Secretary-General of the United Nations.

Article 50

The present Convention shall remain open for accession by any State belonging to any of the four categories mentioned in Article 48. The instruments of accession shall be deposited with the Secretary-General of the United Nations.

Article 51

1. The present Convention shall enter into force on the thirtieth day following the date of deposit of the twenty-second instrument of ratification or accession with the Secretary-General of the United Nations.

2. For each State ratifying or acceding to the Convention after the deposit of the twenty-second instrument of ratification or accession, the Convention shall enter into force on the thirtieth day after deposit by such State of its instrument of ratification or accession.

Article 52

The Secretary-General of the United Nations shall inform all States belonging to any of the four categories mentioned in Article 48:

(a) of signatures to the present Convention and of the deposit of instruments of ratification or accession, in accordance with Articles 48, 49 and 50;

(b) of the date on which the present Convention will enter into force, in accordance with Article 51.

Article 53

The original of the present Convention, of which the Chinese, English, French, Russian and Spanish texts are equally authentic, shall be deposited with the Secretary-General of the United Nations, who shall send certified copies thereof to all States belonging to any of the four categories mentioned in Article 48.

IN WITNESS WHEREOF the undersigned Plenipotentiaries, being duly authorized thereto by their respective Governments, have signed the present Convention.

DONE at Vienna, this eighteenth day of April one thousand nine hundred and sixty-one.

Optional Protocol to the Vienna Convention on Diplomatic Relations, Concerning Acquisition of Nationality

Done at Vienna, April 18, 1961.

The States Parties to the present Protocol and to the Vienna Convention on Diplomatic Relations, hereinafter referred to as "the Convention", adopted by the United Nations Conference held at Vienna from 2 March to 14 April 1961,

EXPRESSING their wish to establish rules between them concerning acquisition of nationality by the members of their diplomatic missions and of the families forming part of the household of those members,

HAVE AGREED AS FOLLOWS:

Article I

For the purpose of the present Protocol, the expression "members of the mission" shall have the meaning assigned to it in Article 1, sub-paragraph (b), of the Convention, namely "the head of the mission and the members of the staff of the mission".

Article II

Members of the mission not being nationals of the receiving State, and members of their families forming part of their household, shall not, solely by the operation of the law of the receiving State, acquire the nationality of that State.

Article III

The present Protocol shall be open for signature by all States which may become Parties to the Convention, as follows: until 31 October 1961 at the Federal Ministry for Foreign Affairs of Austria and subsequently, until 31 March 1962, at the United Nations Headquarters in New York.

Article IV

The present Protocol is subject to ratification. The instruments of ratification shall be deposited with the Secretary-General of the United Nations.

Article V

The present Protocol shall remain open for accession by all States which may become Parties to the Convention. The instruments of accession shall be deposited with the Secretary-General of the United Nations.

Article VI

1. The present Protocol shall enter into force on the same day as the Convention or on the thirtieth day following the date of deposit of the second instrument of ratification or accession to the Protocol with the Secretary-General of the United Nations, whichever date is the later.

2. For each State ratifying or acceding to the present Protocol after its entry into force in accordance with paragraph 1 of this Article, the Protocol shall enter into force on the thirtieth day after deposit by such State of its instrument of ratification or accession.

Article VII

The Secretary-General of the United Nations shall inform all States which may become Parties to the Convention:

(a) of signatures to the present Protocol and of the deposit of instruments of ratification or accession, in accordance with Articles III, IV and V;

(b) of the date on which the present Protocol will enter into force, in accordance with Article VI.

Article VIII

The original of the present Protocol, of which the Chinese, English, French, Russian and Spanish texts are equally authentic, shall be deposited with the Secretary-General of the United Nations, who shall send certified copies thereof to all States referred to in Article III.

IN WITNESS WHEREOF the undersigned Plenipotentiaries, being duly authorized thereto by their respective Governments, have signed the present Protocol.

DONE at Vienna, this eighteenth day of April one thousand nine hundred and sixty-one.

Optional Protocol to the Vienna Convention on Diplomatic Relations, Concerning the Compulsory Settlement of Disputes[2]

Done at Vienna, April 18, 1961; Entered into force April 24, 1964; Entered into force for the United States December 13, 1972

The States Parties to the present Protocol and to the Vienna Convention on Diplomatic Relations, hereinafter referred to as "the Convention", adopted by the United Nations Conference held at Vienna from 2 March to 14 April 1961,

EXPRESSING their wish to resort in all matters concerning them in respect of any dispute arising out of the interpretation or application of the Convention to the compulsory jurisdiction of the International Court of Justice, unless some other form of settlement has been agreed upon by the parties within a reasonable period,

HAVE AGREED AS FOLLOWS:

Article I

Disputes arising out of the interpretation or application of the Convention shall lie within the compulsory jurisdiction of the International Court of Justice and may accordingly be brought before the Court by an application made by any party to the dispute being a Party to the present Protocol.

[2] 23 UST 3374; TIAS 7502.

Article II

The parties may agree, within a period of two months after one party has notified its opinion to the other that a dispute exists, to resort not to the International Court of Justice but to an arbitral tribunal. After the expiry of the said period, either party may bring the dispute before the Court by an application.

Article III

1. Within the same period of two months, the parties may agree to adopt a conciliation procedure before resorting to the International Court of Justice.
2. The conciliation commission shall make its recommendations within five months after its appointment. If its recommendations are not accepted by the parties to the dispute within two months after they have been delivered, either party may bring the dispute before the Court by an application.

Article IV

States Parties to the Convention, to the Optional Protocol concerning Acquisition of Nationality, and to the present Protocol may at any time declare that they will extend the provisions of the present Protocol to disputes arising out of the interpretation or application of the Optional Protocol concerning Acquisition of Nationality. Such declarations shall be notified to the Secretary-General of the United Nations.

Article V

The present Protocol shall be open for signature by all States which may become Parties to the Convention, as follows: until 31 October 1961 at the Federal Ministry for Foreign Affairs of Austria and subsequently, until 31 March 1962, at the United Nations Headquarters in New York.

Article VI

The present Protocol is subject to ratification. The instruments of ratification shall be deposited with the Secretary-General of the United Nations.

Article VII

The present Protocol shall remain open for accession by all States which may become Parties to the Convention. The instruments of accession shall be deposited with the Secretary-General of the United Nations.

Article VIII

1. The present Protocol shall enter into force on the same day as the Convention or on the thirtieth day following the date of deposit of the second instrument of ratification or accession to the Protocol with the Secretary-General of the United Nations, whichever day is the later.

2. For each State ratifying or acceding to the present Protocol after its entry into force in accordance with paragraph 1 of this Article, the Protocol shall enter into force on the thirtieth day after deposit by such State of its instrument of ratification or accession.

Article IX

The Secretary-General of the United Nations shall inform all States which may become Parties to the Convention:

(a) of signatures to the present Protocol and of the deposit of instruments of ratification or accession, in accordance with Articles V, VI and VII;

(b) of declarations made in accordance with Article IV of the present Protocol;

(c) of the date on which the present Protocol will enter into force, in accordance with Article VIII.

Article X

The original of the present Protocol, of which the Chinese, English, French, Russian and Spanish texts are equally authentic, shall be deposited with the Secretary-General of the United Nations, who shall send certified copies thereof to all States referred to in Article V.

IN WITNESS WHEREOF the undersigned Plenipotentiaries, being duly authorized thereto by their respective Governments, have signed the present Protocol.

3. Vienna Convention on Consular Relations and Optional Protocols[1]

Done at Vienna April 24, 1963; Entered into force March 19, 1967; Entered into force for the United States December 24, 1969

THE STATES PARTIES TO THE PRESENT CONVENTION,

RECALLING that consular relations have been established between peoples since ancient times,

HAVING IN MIND the Purposes and Principles of the Charter of the United Nation concerning the sovereign equality of States, the maintenance of international peace and security, and the promotion of friendly relations among nations,

CONSIDERING that the United Nations Conference on Diplomatic Intercourse and Immunities adopted the Vienna Convention on Diplomatic Relations which was opened for signature on 18 April 1961,

BELIEVING that an international convention on consular relations, privileges and immunities would also contribute to the development of friendly relations among nations, irrespective of their differing constitutional and social systems,

REALIZING that the purpose of such privileges and immunities is not to benefit individuals but to ensure the efficient performance of functions by consular posts on behalf of their respective States,

AFFIRMING that the rules of customary international law continue to govern matters not expressly regulated by the provisions of the present Convention,

HAVE AGREED as follows:

Article 1

Definitions

1. For the purposes of the present Convention, the following expressions shall have the meanings hereunder assigned to them:

(a) "consular post" means any consulate-general, consulate, vice-consulate or consular agency;

(b) "consular district" means the area assigned to a consular post for the exercise of consular functions;

(c) "head of consular post" means the person charged with the duty of acting in that capacity;

(d) "consular officer" means any person, including the head of a consular post, entrusted in that capacity with the exercise of consular functions;

(e) "consular employee" means any person employed in the administrative or technical service of a consular post;

(f) "member of the service staff" means any person employed in the domestic service of a consular post;

[1] 21 UST 77; TIAS 6820.

(g) "members of the consular post" means consular officers, consular employees and members of the service staff;

(h) "members of the consular staff" means consular officers, other than the head of a consular post, consular employees and members of the service staff;

(i) "member of the private staff" means a person who is employed exclusively in the private service of a member of the consular post;

(j) "consular premises" means the buildings or parts of buildings and the land ancillary thereto, irrespective of ownership, used exclusively for the purposes of the consular post;

(k) "consular archives" includes all the papers, documents, correspondence, books, films, tapes and registers of the consular post, together with the ciphers and codes, the card-indexes and any article of furniture intended for their protection or safekeeping.

2. Consular officers are of two categories, namely career consular officers and honorary consular officers. The provisions of Chapter II of the present Convention apply to consular posts headed by career consular officers; the provisions of Chapter III govern consular posts headed by honorary consular officers.

3. The particular status of members of the consular posts who are nationals or permanent residents of the receiving State is governed by Article 71 of the present Convention.

CHAPTER I

CONSULAR RELATIONS IN GENERAL

SECTION I

ESTABLISHMENT AND CONDUCT OF CONSULAR RELATIONS

Article 2

Establishment of consular relations

1. The establishment of consular relations between States takes place by mutual consent.

2. The consent given to the establishment of diplomatic relations between two States implies, unless otherwise stated, consent to the establishment of consular relations.

3. The severance of diplomatic relations shall not ipso facto involve the severance of consular relations.

Article 3

Exercise of consular functions

Consular functions are exercised by consular posts. They are also exercised by diplomatic missions in accordance with the provisions of the present Convention.

Article 4

Establishment of a consular post

1. A consular post may be established in the territory of the receiving State only with that State's consent.

2. The seat of the consular post, its classification and the consular district shall be established by the sending State and shall be subject to the approval of the receiving State.

3. Subsequent changes in the seat of the consular post, its classification or the consular district may be made by the sending State only with the consent of the receiving State.

4. The consent of the receiving State shall also be required if a consulate-general or a consulate desires to open a vice-consulate or a consular agency in a locality other than that in which it is itself established.

5. The prior express consent of the receiving State shall also be required for the opening of an office forming part of an existing consular post elsewhere than at the seat thereof.

Article 5

Consular functions

Consular functions consist in:

(a) protecting in the receiving State the interests of the sending State and of its nationals, both individuals and bodies corporate, within the limits permitted by international law;

(b) furthering the development of commercial, economic, cultural and scientific relations between the sending State and the receiving State and otherwise promoting friendly relations between them in accordance with the provisions of the present Convention;

(c) ascertaining by all lawful means conditions and developments in the commercial, economic, cultural and scientific life of the receiving State, reporting thereon to the Government of the sending State and giving information to persons interested;

(d) issuing passports and travel documents to nationals of the sending State, and visas or appropriate documents to persons wishing to travel to the sending State;

(e) helping and assisting nationals, both individuals and bodies corporate, of the sending State;

(f) acting as notary and civil registrar and in capacities of a similar kind, and performing certain functions of an administrative nature, provided that there is nothing contrary thereto in the laws and regulations of the receiving State;

(g) safeguarding the interests of nationals, both individuals and bodies corporate, of the sending State in cases of succession mortis causa in the territory of the receiving State, in accordance with the laws and regulations of the receiving State;

(h) safeguarding, within the limits imposed by the laws and regulations of the receiving State, the interests of minors and other persons lacking full capacity who are nationals of the sending State, particularly where any guardianship or trusteeship is required with respect to such persons;

(i) subject to the practices and procedures obtaining in the receiving State, representing or arranging appropriate representation for nationals of the sending State before the tribunals and other authorities of the receiving State, for the purpose of obtaining, in accordance with the laws and regulations of the receiving State, provisional measures for the preservation of the rights and interests of these nationals, where, because of absence or any other reason, such nationals are unable at the proper time to assume the defence of their rights and interests;

(j) transmitting judicial and extrajudicial documents or executing letters rogatory or commissions to take evidence for the courts of the sending State in accordance with international agreements in force or, in the absence of such international agreements, in any other manner compatible with the laws and regulations of the receiving State;

(k) exercising rights of supervision and inspection provided for in the laws and regulations of the sending State in respect of vessels having the nationality of the sending State, and of aircraft registered in that State, and in respect of their crews;

(l) extending assistance to vessels and aircraft mentioned in sub-paragraph (k) of this Article and to their crews, taking statements regarding the voyage of a vessel, examining and stamping the ship's papers, and, without prejudice to the powers of the authorities of the receiving State, conducting investigations into any incidents which occurred during the voyage, and settling disputes of any kind between the master, the officers and the seamen in so far as this may be authorized by the laws and regulations of the sending State;

(m) performing any other functions entrusted to a consular post by the sending State which are not prohibited by the laws and regulations of the receiving State or to which no objection is taken by the receiving State or which are referred to in the international agreements in force between the sending State and the receiving State.

Article 6

Exercise of consular functions outside the consular district

A consular officer may, in special circumstances, with the consent of the receiving State, exercise his functions outside his consular district.

Article 7

Exercise of consular functions in a third state

The sending State may, after notifying the States concerned, entrust a consular post established in a particular State with the exercise of consular functions in another State, unless there is express objection by one of the States concerned.

Article 8

Exercise of consular functions on behalf of a third state

Upon appropriate notification to the receiving State, a consular post of the sending State may, unless the receiving State objects, exercise consular functions in the receiving State on behalf of a third State.

Article 9

Classes of heads of consular posts

1. Heads of consular posts are divided into four classes, namely:
   (a) consuls-general;
   (b) consuls;
   (c) vice-consuls;
   (d) consular agents.

2. Paragraph 1 of this Article in no way restricts the right of any of the Contracting Parties to fix the designation of consular officers other than the heads of consular posts.

Article 10

Appointment and admission of heads of consular posts

1. Heads of consular posts are appointed by the sending State and are admitted to the exercise of their functions by the receiving State.

2. Subject to the provisions of the present Convention, the formalities for the appointment and for the admission of the head of a consular post are determined by the laws, regulations and usages of the sending State and of the receiving State respectively.

Article 11

The consular commission or notification of appointment

1. The head of a consular post shall be provided by the sending State with a document, in the form of a commission or similar instrument, made out for each appointment, certifying his capacity and showing, as a general rule, his full name, his category and class, the consular district and the seat of the consular post.

2. The sending State shall transmit the commission or similar instrument through the diplomatic or other appropriate channel to the Government of the State in whose territory the head of a consular post is to exercise his functions.

3. If the receiving State agrees, the sending State may, instead of a commission or similar instrument, send to the receiving State a notification containing the particulars required by paragraph 1 of this Article.

Article 12

The exequatur

1. The head of a consular post is admitted to the exercise of his functions by an authorization from the receiving State termed an exequatur, whatever the form of this authorization.

2. A State which refuses to grant an exequatur is not obliged to give to the sending State reasons for such refusal.

3. Subject to the provisions of Articles 13 and 15, the head of a consular post shall not enter upon his duties until he has received an exequatur.

Article 13

Provisional admission of heads of consular posts

Pending delivery of the exequatur, the head of a consular post may be admitted on a provisional basis to the exercise of his functions. In that case, the provisions of the present Convention shall apply.

Article 14

Notification to the authorities of the consular district

As soon as the head of a consular post is admitted even provisionally to the exercise of his functions, the receiving State shall immediately notify the competent authorities of the consular district. It shall also ensure that the necessary measures are taken to enable the head of a consular post to carry out the duties of his office and to have the benefit of the provisions of the present Convention.

Article 15

Temporary exercise of the functions of the head of a consular post

1. If the head of a consular post is unable to carry out his functions or the position of head of consular post is vacant, an acting head of post may act provisionally as head of the consular post.

2. The full name of the acting head of post shall be notified either by the diplomatic mission of the sending State or, if that State has no such mission in the receiving State, by the head of the consular post, or, if he is unable to do so, by any competent authority of the sending State, to the Ministry for Foreign Affairs of the receiving State or to the authority designated by that Ministry. As a general rule, this notification shall be given in advance. The receiving State may make the admission as acting head of post of a person who is neither a diplomatic agent nor a consular officer of the sending State in the receiving State conditional on its consent.

3. The competent authorities of the receiving State shall afford assistance and protection to the acting head of post. While he is in charge of the post, the provisions of the present Convention shall apply to him on the same basis as to the head of the consular post concerned. The receiving State shall not, however, be obliged to grant to an acting head of post any facility, privilege or immunity

which the head of the consular post enjoys only subject to conditions not fulfilled by the acting head of post.

4. When, in the circumstances referred to in paragraph 1 of this Article, a member of the diplomatic staff of the diplomatic mission of the sending State in the receiving State is designated by the sending State as an acting head of post, he shall, if the receiving State does not object thereto, continue to enjoy diplomatic privileges and immunities.

Article 16

Precedence as between heads of consular posts

1. Heads of consular posts shall rank in each class according to the date of the grant of the exequatur.

2. If, however, the head of a consular post before obtaining the exequatur is admitted to the exercise of his functions provisionally, his precedence shall be determined according to the date of the provisional admission; this precedence shall be maintained after the granting of the exequatur.

3. The order of precedence as between two or more heads of consular posts who obtained the exequatur or provisional admission on the same date shall be determined according to the dates on which their commissions or similar instruments or the notifications referred to in paragraph 3 of Article 11 were presented to the receiving State.

4. Acting heads of posts shall rank after all heads of consular posts and, as between themselves, they shall rank according to the dates on which they assumed their functions as acting heads of posts as indicated in the notifications given under paragraph 2 of Article 15.

5. Honorary consular officers who are heads of consular posts shall rank in each class after career heads of consular posts, in the order and according to the rules laid down in the foregoing paragraphs.

6. Heads of consular posts shall have precedence over consular officers not having that status.

Article 17

Performance of diplomatic acts by consular officers

1. In a State where the sending State has no diplomatic mission and is not represented by a diplomatic mission of a third State, a consular officer may, with the consent of the receiving State, and without affecting his consular status, be authorized to perform diplomatic acts. The performance of such acts by a consular officer shall not confer upon him any right to claim diplomatic privileges and immunities.

2. A consular officer may, after notification addressed to the receiving State, act as representative of the sending State to any inter-governmental organization. When so acting, he shall be entitled to enjoy any privileges and immunities accorded to such a representative by customary international law or by international agreements; however, in respect of the performance by him of any

consular function, he shall not be entitled to any greater immunity from jurisdiction than that to which a consular officer is entitled under the present Convention.

Article 18

Appointment of the same person by two or more states as a consular officer

Two or more States may, with the consent of the receiving State, appoint the same person as a consular officer in that State.

Article 19

Appointment of members of consular staff

1. Subject to the provisions of Articles 20, 22 and 23, the sending State may freely appoint the members of the consular staff.
2. The full name, category and class of all consular officers, other than the head of a consular post, shall be notified by the sending State to the receiving State in sufficient time for the receiving State, if it so wishes, to exercise its rights under paragraph 3 of Article 23.
3. The sending State may, if required by its laws and regulations, request the receiving State to grant an exequatur to a consular officer other than the head of a consular post.
4. The receiving State may, if required by its laws and regulations, grant an exequatur to a consular officer other than the head of a consular post.

Article 20

Size of the consular staff

In the absence of an express agreement as to the size of the consular staff, the receiving State may require that the size of the staff be kept within limits considered by it to be reasonable and normal, having regard to circumstances and conditions in the consular district and to the needs of the particular post.

Article 21

Precedence as between consular officers of a consular post

The order of precedence as between the consular officers of a consular post and any change thereof shall be notified by the diplomatic mission of the sending State or, if that State has no such mission in the receiving State, by the head of the consular post, to the Ministry for Foreign Affairs of the receiving State or to the authority designated by that Ministry.

Article 22

Nationality of consular officers

1. Consular officers should, in principle, have the nationality of the sending State.

2. Consular officers may not be appointed from among persons having the nationality of the receiving State except with the express consent of that State which may be withdrawn at any time.

3. The receiving State may reserve the same right with regard to nationals of a third State who are not also nationals of the sending State.

Article 23

Persons declared "non grata"

1. The receiving State may at any time notify the sending State that a consular officer is persona non grata or that any other member of the consular staff is not acceptable. In that event, the sending State shall, as the case may be, either recall the person concerned or terminate his functions with the consular post.

2. If the sending State refuses or fails within a reasonable time to carry out its obligations under paragraph 1 of this Article, the receiving State may, as the case may be, either withdraw the exequatur from the person concerned or cease to consider him as a member of the consular staff.

3. A person appointed as a member of a consular post may be declared unacceptable before arriving in the territory of the receiving State or, if already in the receiving State, before entering on his duties with the consular post. In any such case, the sending State shall withdraw his appointment.

4. In the cases mentioned in paragraphs 1 and 3 of this Article, the receiving State is not obliged to give to the sending State reasons for its decision.

Article 24

Notification of the receiving state of appointments, arrivals and departures

1. The Ministry for Foreign Affairs of the receiving State or the authority designated by that Ministry shall be notified of:

(a) the appointment of members of a consular post, their arrival after appointment to the consular post, their final departure or the termination of their functions and any other changes affecting their status that may occur in the course of their service with the consular post;

(b) the arrival and final departure of a person belonging to the family of a member of a consular post forming part of his household and, where appropriate, the fact that a person becomes or ceases to be such a member of the family;

(c) the arrival and final departure of members of the private staff and, where appropriate, the termination of their service as such;

(d) the engagement and discharge of persons resident in the receiving State as members of a consular post or as members of the private staff entitled to privileges and immunities.

2. When possible, prior notification of arrival and final departure shall also be given.

SECTION II

END OF CONSULAR FUNCTIONS

Article 25

Termination of the functions of a member of a consular post

The functions of a member of a consular post shall come to an end inter alia:

(a) on notification by the sending State to the receiving State that his functions have come to an end;

(b) on withdrawal of the exequatur;

(c) on notification by the receiving State to the sending State that the receiving State has ceased to consider him as a member of the consular staff.

Article 26

Departure from the territory of the receiving state

The receiving State shall, even in case of armed conflict, grant to members of the consular post and members of the private staff, other than nationals of the receiving State, and to members of their families forming part of their households irrespective of nationality, the necessary time and facilities to enable them to prepare their departure and to leave at the earliest possible moment after the termination of the functions of the members concerned. In particular, it shall, in case of need, place at their disposal the necessary means of transport for themselves and their property other than property acquired in the receiving State the export of which is prohibited at the time of departure.

Article 27

Protection of consular premises and archives and of the interests of the sending state in exceptional circumstances

1. In the event of the severance of consular relations between two States:

(a) the receiving State shall, even in case of armed conflict, respect and protect the consular premises, together with the property of the consular post and the consular archives;

(b) the sending State may entrust the custody of the consular premises, together with the property contained therein and the consular archives, to a third State acceptable to the receiving State;

(c) the sending State may entrust the protection of its interests and those of its nationals to a third State acceptable to the receiving State.

2. In the event of the temporary or permanent closure of a consular post, the provisions of sub-paragraph (a) of paragraph 1 of this Article shall apply. In addition,

(a) if the sending State, although not represented in the receiving State by a diplomatic mission, has another consular post in the territory of that State, that consular post may be entrusted with the custody of the premises of the consular post which has been closed, together with the property contained therein and the consular archives, and, with the consent of the receiving State, with the exercise of consular functions in the district of that consular post; or

(b) if the sending State has no diplomatic mission and no other consular post in the receiving State, the provisions of sub-paragraphs (b) and (c) of paragraph 1 of this Article shall apply.

CHAPTER II

FACILITIES, PRIVILEGES AND IMMUNITIES RELATING TO CONSULAR POSTS, CAREER CONSULAR OFFICERS AND OTHER MEMBERS OF A CONSULAR POST

SECTION I

FACILITIES, PRIVILEGES AND IMMUNITIES RELATING TO A CONSULAR POST

Article 28

Facilities for the work of the consular post

The receiving State shall accord full facilities for the performance of the functions of the consular post.

Article 29

Use of national flag and coat-of-arms

1. The sending State shall have the right to the use of its national flag and coat-of-arms in the receiving State in accordance with the provisions of this Article.

2. The national flag of the sending State may be flown and its coat-of-arms displayed on the building occupied by the consular post and at the entrance door thereof, on the residence of the head of the consular post and on his means of transport when used on official business.

3. In the exercise of the right accorded by this Article regard shall be had to the laws, regulations and usages of the receiving State.

Article 30

Accommodation

1. The receiving State shall either facilitate the acquisition on its territory, in accordance with its laws and regulations, by the sending State of premises necessary for its consular post or assist the latter in obtaining accommodation in some other way.

2. It shall also, where necessary, assist the consular post in obtaining suitable accommodation for its members.

Article 31

Inviolability of the consular premises

1. Consular premises shall be inviolable to the extent provided in this Article.

2. The authorities of the receiving State shall not enter that part of the consular premises which is used exclusively for the purpose of the work of the consular post except with the consent of the head of the consular post or of his designee or of the head of the diplomatic mission of the sending State. The consent of the head of the consular post may, however, be assumed in case of fire or other disaster requiring prompt protective action.

3. Subject to the provisions of paragraph 2 of this Article, the receiving State is under a special duty to take all appropriate steps to protect the consular premises against any intrusion or damage and to prevent any disturbance of the peace of the consular post or impairment of its dignity.

4. The consular premises, their furnishings, the property of the consular post and its means of transport shall be immune from any form of requisition for purposes of national defence or public utility. If expropriation is necessary for such purposes, all possible steps shall be taken to avoid impeding the performance of consular functions, and prompt, adequate and effective compensation shall be paid to the sending State.

Article 32

Exemption from taxation of consular premises

1. Consular premises and the residence of the career head of consular post of which the sending State or any person acting on its behalf is the owner or lessee shall be exempt from all national, regional or municipal dues and taxes whatsoever, other than such as represent payment for specific services rendered.

2. The exemption from taxation referred to in paragraph 1 of this Article shall not apply to such dues and taxes if, under the law of the receiving State, they are payable by the person who contracted with the sending State or with the person acting on its behalf.

Article 33

Inviolability of the consular archives and documents

The consular archives and documents shall be inviolable at all times and wherever they may be.

Article 34

Freedom of movement

Subject to its laws and regulations concerning zones entry into which is prohibited or regulated for reasons of national security, the receiving State shall ensure freedom of movement and travel in its territory to all members of the consular post.

Article 35

Freedom of communications

1. The receiving State shall permit and protect freedom of communication on the part of the consular post for all official purposes. In communicating with the Government, the diplomatic missions and other consular posts, wherever situated, of the sending State, the consular post may employ all appropriate means, including diplomatic or consular couriers, diplomatic or consular bags and messages in code or cipher. However, the consular post may install and use a wireless transmitter only with the consent of the receiving State.

2. The official correspondence of the consular post shall be inviolable. Official correspondence means all correspondence relating to the consular post and its functions.

3. The consular bag shall be neither opened nor detained. Nevertheless, if the competent authorities of the receiving State have serious reason to believe that the bag contains something other than the correspondence, documents or articles referred to in paragraph 4 of this Article, they may request that the bag be opened in their presence by an authorized representative of the sending State. If this request is refused by the authorities of the sending State, the bag shall be returned to its place of origin.

4. The packages constituting the consular bag shall bear visible external marks of their character and may contain only official correspondence and documents or articles intended exclusively for official use.

5. The consular courier shall be provided with an official document indicating his status and the number of packages constituting the consular bag. Except with the consent of the receiving State he shall be neither a national of the receiving State, nor, unless he is a national of the sending State, a permanent resident of the receiving State. In the performance of his functions he shall be protected by the receiving State. He shall enjoy personal inviolability and shall not be liable to any form of arrest or detention.

6. The sending State, its diplomatic missions and its consular posts may designate consular couriers ad hoc. In such cases the provisions of paragraph 5 of this Article shall also apply except that the immunities therein mentioned shall cease to apply when such a courier has delivered to the consignee the consular bag in his charge.

7. A consular bag may be entrusted to the captain of a ship or of a commercial aircraft scheduled to land at an authorized port of entry. He shall be provided with an official document indicating the number of packages constituting the bag, but he shall not be considered to be a consular courier. By arrangement with the appropriate local authorities, the consular post may send one of its members to take possession of the bag directly and freely from the captain of the ship or of the aircraft.

Article 36

Communication and contact with national of the sending state

1. With a view to facilitating the exercise of consular functions relating to nationals of the sending State:

(a) consular officers shall be free to communicate with nationals of the sending State and to have access to them. Nationals of the sending State shall have the same freedom with respect to communication with and access to consular officers of the sending State;

(b) if he so requests, the competent authorities of the receiving State shall, without delay, inform the consular post of the sending State if, within its consular district, a national of that State is arrested or committed to prison or to custody pending trial or is detained in any other manner. Any communication addressed to the consular post by the person arrested, in prison, custody or detention shall also be forwarded by the said authorities without delay. The said authorities shall inform the person concerned without delay of his rights under this subparagraph;

(c) consular officers shall have the right to visit a national of the sending State who is in prison, custody or detention, to converse and correspond with him and to arrange for his legal representation. They shall also have the right to visit any national of the sending State who is in prison, custody or detention in their district in pursuance of a judgment. Nevertheless, consular officers shall refrain from taking action on behalf of a national who is in prison, custody or detention if he expressly opposes such action.

2. The rights referred to in paragraph 1 of this Article shall be exercised in conformity with the laws and regulations of the receiving State, subject to the proviso, however, that the said laws and regulations must enable full effect to be given to the purposes for which the rights accorded under this Article are intended.

Article 37

Information in cases of deaths, guardianship or trusteeship, wrecks and air accidents

If the relevant information is available to the competent authorities of the receiving State, such authorities shall have the duty:

(a) in the case of the death of a national of the sending State, to inform without delay the consular post in whose district the death occurred;

(b) to inform the competent consular post without delay of any case where the appointment of a guardian or trustee appears to be in the interests of a minor or other person lacking full capacity who is a national of the sending State. The giving of this information shall, however, be without prejudice to the operation of the laws and regulations of the receiving State concerning such appointments;

(c) if a vessel, having the nationality of the sending State, is wrecked or runs aground in the territorial sea or internal waters of the receiving State, or if an aircraft registered in the sending State suffers an accident on the territory of the receiving State, to inform without delay the consular post nearest to the scene of the occurrence.

Article 38

Communication with the authorities of the receiving state

In the exercise of their functions, consular officers may address:

(a) the competent local authorities of their consular district;

(b) the competent central authorities of the receiving State if and to the extent that this is allowed by the laws, regulations and usages of the receiving State or by the relevant international agreements.

Article 39

Consular fees and charges

1. The consular post may levy in the territory of the receiving State the fees and charges provided by the laws and regulations of the sending State for consular acts.

2. The sums collected in the form of the fees and charges referred to in paragraph 1 of this Article, and the receipts for such fees and charges, shall be exempt from all dues and taxes in the receiving State.

SECTION II

FACILITIES, PRIVILEGES AND IMMUNITIES RELATING TO CAREER CONSULAR OFFICERS AND OTHER MEMBERS OF A CONSULAR POST

Article 40

Protection of consular officers

The receiving State shall treat consular officers with due respect and shall take all appropriate steps to prevent any attack on their person, freedom or dignity.

Article 41

Personal inviolability of consular officers

1. Consular officers shall not be liable to arrest or detention pending trial, except in the case of a grave crime and pursuant to a decision by the competent judicial authority.

2. Except in the case specified in paragraph 1 of this Article, consular officers shall not be committed to prison or liable to any other form of restriction on their personal freedom save in execution of a judicial decision of final effect.

3. If criminal proceedings are instituted against a consular officer, he must appear before the competent authorities. Nevertheless, the proceedings shall be conducted with the respect due to him by

reason of his official position and, except in the case specified in paragraph 1 of this Article, in a manner which will hamper the exercise of consular functions as little as possible. When, in the circumstances mentioned in paragraph 1 of this Article, it has become necessary to detain a consular officer, the proceedings against him shall be instituted with the minimum of delay.

Article 42

Notification of arrest, detention or prosecution

In the event of the arrest or detention, pending trial, of a member of the consular staff, or of criminal proceedings being instituted against him, the receiving State shall promptly notify the head of the consular post. Should the latter be himself the object of any such measure, the receiving State shall notify the sending State through the diplomatic channel.

Article 43

Immunity from jurisdiction

1. Consular officers and consular employees shall not be amenable to the jurisdiction of the judicial or administrative authorities of the receiving State in respect of acts performed in the exercise of consular functions.

2. The provisions of paragraph 1 of this Article shall not, however, apply in respect of a civil action either:

(a) arising out of a contract concluded by a consular officer or a consular employee in which he did not contract expressly or impliedly as an agent of the sending State; or

(b) by a third party for damage arising from an accident in the receiving State caused by a vehicle, vessel or aircraft.

Article 44

Liability to give evidence

1. Members of a consular post may be called upon to attend as witnesses in the course of judicial or administrative proceedings. A consular employee or a member of the service staff shall not, except in the cases mentioned in paragraph 3 of this Article, decline to give evidence. If a consular officer should decline to do so, no coercive measure or penalty may be applied to him.

2. The authority requiring the evidence of a consular officer shall avoid interference with the performance of his functions. It may, when possible, take such evidence at his residence or at the consular post or accept a statement from him in writing.

3. Members of a consular post are under no obligation to give evidence concerning matters connected with the exercise of their functions or to produce official correspondence and documents relating thereto. They are also entitled to decline to give evidence as expert witnesses with regard to the law of the sending State.

Article 45

Waiver of privileges and immunities

1. The sending State may waive, with regard to a member of the consular post, any of the privileges and immunities provided for in Articles 41, 43 and 44.

2. The waiver shall in all cases be express, except as provided in paragraph 3 of this Article, and shall be communicated to the receiving State in writing.

3. The initiation of proceedings by a consular officer or a consular employee in a matter where he might enjoy immunity from jurisdiction under Article 43 shall preclude him from invoking immunity from jurisdiction in respect of any counter-claim directly connected with the principal claim.

4. The waiver of immunity from jurisdiction for the purposes of civil or administrative proceedings shall not be deemed to imply the waiver of immunity from the measures of execution resulting from the judicial decision; in respect of such measures, a separate waiver shall be necessary.

Article 46

Exemption from registration of aliens and residence permits

1. Consular officers and consular employees and members of their families forming part of their households shall be exempt from all obligations under the laws and regulations of the receiving State in regard to the registration of aliens and residence permits.

2. The provisions of paragraph 1 of this Article shall not, however, apply to any consular employee who is not a permanent employee of the sending State or who carries on any private gainful occupation in the receiving State or to any member of the family of any such employee.

Article 47

Exemption from work permits

1. Members of the consular post shall, with respect to services rendered for the sending State, be exempt from any obligations in regard to work permits imposed by the laws and regulations of the receiving State concerning the employment of foreign labour.

2. Members of the private staff of consular officers and of consular employees shall, if they do not carry on any other gainful occupation in the receiving State, be exempt from the obligations referred to in paragraph 1 of this Article.

Article 48

Social security exemption

1. Subject to the provisions of paragraph 3 of this Article, members of the consular post with respect to services rendered by them for the sending State, and members of their families forming part of their households, shall be exempt from social security provisions which may be in force in the receiving State.

2. The exemption provided for in paragraph 1 of this Article shall apply also to members of the private staff who are in the sole employ of members of the consular post, on condition:

(a) that they are not nationals of or permanently resident in the receiving State; and

(b) that they are covered by the social security provisions which are in force in the sending State or a third State.

3. Members of the consular post who employ persons to whom the exemption provided for in paragraph 2 of this Article does not apply shall observe the obligations which the social security provisions of the receiving State impose upon employers.

4. The exemption provided for in paragraphs 1 and 2 of this Article shall not preclude voluntary participation in the social security system of the receiving State, provided that such participation is permitted by that State.

Article 49

Exemption from taxation

1. Consular officers and consular employees and members of their families forming part of their households shall be exempt from all dues and taxes, personal or real, national, regional or municipal, except:

(a) indirect taxes of a kind which are normally incorporated in the price of goods or services;

(b) dues or taxes on private immovable property situated in the territory of the receiving State, subject to the provisions of Article 32;

(c) estate, succession or inheritance duties, and duties on transfers, levied by the receiving State, subject to the provisions of paragraph (b) of Article 51;

(d) dues and taxes on private income, including capital gains, having its source in the receiving State and capital taxes relating to investments made in commercial or financial undertakings in the receiving State;

(e) charges levied for specific services rendered;

(f) registration, court or record fees, mortgage dues and stamp duties, subject to the provisions of Article 32.

2. Members of the service staff shall be exempt from dues and taxes on the wages which they receive for their services.

3. Members of the consular post who employ persons whose wages or salaries are not exempt from income tax in the receiving State shall observe the obligations which the laws and regulations of that State impose upon employers concerning the levying of income tax.

Article 50

Exemption from customs duties and inspection

1. The receiving State shall, in accordance with such laws and regulations as it may adopt, permit entry of and grant exemption from all customs duties, taxes, and related charges other than charges for storage, cartage and similar services, on:

(a) articles for the official use of the consular post;

(b) articles for the personal use of a consular officer or members of his family forming part of his household, including articles intended for his establishment. The articles intended for consumption shall not exceed the quantities necessary for direct utilization by the persons concerned.

2. Consular employees shall enjoy the privileges and exemptions specified in paragraph 1 of this Article in respect of articles imported at the time of first installation.

3. Personal baggage accompanying consular officers and members of their families forming part of their households shall be exempt from inspection. It may be inspected only if there is serious reason to believe that it contains articles other than those referred to in sub-paragraph (b) of paragraph 1 of this Article, or articles the import or export of which is prohibited by the laws and regulations of the receiving State or which are subject to its quarantine laws and regulations. Such inspection shall be carried out in the presence of the consular officer or member of his family concerned.

Article 51

Estate of a member of the consular post or of a member of his family

In the event of the death of a member of the consular post or of a member of his family forming part of his household, the receiving State:

(a) shall permit the export of the movable property of the deceased, with the exception of any such property acquired in the receiving State the export of which was prohibited at the time of his death;

(b) shall not levy national, regional or municipal estate, succession or inheritance duties, and duties on transfers, on movable property the presence of which in the receiving State was due solely to the presence in that State of the deceased as a member of the consular post or as a member of the family of a member of the consular post.

Article 52

Exemption from personal services and contributions

The receiving State shall exempt members of the consular post and members of their families forming part of their households from all personal services, from all public service of any kind whatsoever, and from military obligations such as those connected with requisitioning, military contributions and billeting.

Article 53

Beginning and end of consular privileges and immunities

1. Every member of the consular post shall enjoy the privileges and immunities provided in the present Convention from the moment he enters the territory of the receiving State on proceeding

to take up his post or, if already in its territory, from the moment when he enters on his duties with the consular post.

2. Members of the family of a member of the consular post forming part of his household and members of his private staff shall receive the privileges and immunities provided in the present Convention from the date from which he enjoys privileges and immunities in accordance with paragraph 1 of this Article or from the date of their entry into the territory of the receiving State or from the date of their becoming a member of such family or private staff, whichever is the latest.

3. When the functions of a member of the consular post have come to an end, his privileges and immunities and those of a member of his family forming part of his household or a member of his private staff shall normally cease at the moment when the person concerned leaves the receiving State or on the expiry of a reasonable period in which to do so, whichever is the sooner, but shall subsist until that time, even in case of armed conflict. In the case of the persons referred to in paragraph 2 of this Article, their privileges and immunities shall come to an end when they cease to belong to the household or to be in the service of a member of the consular post provided, however, that if such persons intend leaving the receiving State within a reasonable period thereafter, their privileges and immunities shall subsist until the time of their departure.

4. However, with respect to acts performed by a consular officer or a consular employee in the exercise of his functions, immunity from jurisdiction shall continue to subsist without limitation of time.

5. In the event of the death of a member of the consular post, the members of his family forming part of his household shall continue to enjoy the privileges and immunities accorded to them until they leave the receiving State or until the expiry of a reasonable period enabling them to do so, whichever is the sooner.

Article 54

Obligations of third states

1. If a consular officer passes through or is in the territory of a third State, which has granted him a visa if a visa was necessary, while proceeding to take up or return to his post or when returning to the sending State, the third State shall accord to him all immunities provided for by the other Articles of the present Convention as may be required to ensure his transit or return. The same shall apply in the case of any member of his family forming part of his household enjoying such privileges and immunities who are accompanying the consular officer or travelling separately to join him or to return to the sending State.

2. In circumstances similar to those specified in paragraph 1 of this Article, third States shall not hinder the transit through their territory of other members of the consular post or of members of their families forming part of their households.

3. Third States shall accord to official correspondence and to other official communications in transit, including messages in code or cipher, the same freedom and protection as the receiving State

is bound to accord under the present Convention. They shall accord to consular couriers who have been granted a visa, if a visa was necessary, and to consular bags in transit, the same inviolability and protection as the receiving State is bound to accord under the present Convention.

4. The obligations of third States under paragraphs 1, 2 and 3 of this Article shall also apply to the persons mentioned respectively in those paragraphs, and to official communications and to consular bags, whose presence in the territory of the third State is due to force majeure.

Article 55

Respect for the laws and regulations of the receiving state

1. Without prejudice to their privileges and immunities, it is the duty of all persons enjoying such privileges and immunities to respect the laws and regulations of the receiving State. They also have a duty not to interfere in the internal affairs of that State.

2. The consular premises shall not be used in any manner incompatible with the exercise of consular functions.

3. The provisions of paragraph 2 of this Article shall not exclude the possibility of offices of other institutions or agencies being installed in part of the building in which the consular premises are situated, provided that the premises assigned to them are separate from those used by the consular post. In that event, the said offices shall not, for the purposes of the present Convention, be considered to form part of the consular premises.

Article 56

Insurance against third party risks

Members of the consular post shall comply with any requirement imposed by the laws and regulations of the receiving State in respect of insurance against third party risks arising from the use of any vehicle, vessel or aircraft.

Article 57

Special provisions concerning private gainful occupation

1. Career consular officers shall not carry on for personal profit any professional or commercial activity in the receiving State.

2. Privileges and immunities provided in this Chapter shall not be accorded:

(a) to consular employees or to members of the service staff who carry on any private gainful occupation in the receiving State;

(b) to members of the family of a person referred to in subparagraph (a) of this paragraph or to members of his private staff;

(c) to members of the family of a member of a consular post who themselves carry on any private gainful occupation in the receiving State.

CHAPTER III

REGIME RELATING TO HONORARY CONSULAR OFFICERS AND CONSULAR POSTS HEADED BY SUCH OFFICERS

Article 58

General provision relating to facilities, privileges and immunities

1. Articles 28, 29, 30, 34, 35, 36, 37, 38 and 39, paragraph 3 of Article 54 and paragraphs 2 and 3 of Article 55 shall apply to consular posts headed by an honorary consular officer. In addition, the facilities, privileges and immunities of such consular posts shall be governed by Articles 59, 60, 61 and 62.

2. Articles 42 and 43, paragraph 3 of Article 44, Articles 45 and 53 and paragraph 1 of Article 55 shall apply to honorary consular officers. In addition, the facilities, privileges and immunities of such consular officers shall be governed by Articles 63, 64, 65, 66 and 67.

3. Privileges and immunities provided in the present Convention shall not be accorded to members of the family of an honorary consular officer or of a consular employee employed at a consular post headed by an honorary consular officer.

4. The exchange of consular bags between two consular posts headed by honorary consular officers in different States shall not be allowed without the consent of the two receiving States concerned.

Article 59

Protection of the consular premises

The receiving State shall take such steps as may be necessary to protect the consular premises of a consular post headed by an honorary consular officer against any intrusion or damage and to prevent any disturbance of the peace of the consular post or impairment of its dignity.

Article 60

Exemption from taxation of consular premises

1. Consular premises of a consular post headed by an honorary consular officer of which the sending State is the owner or lessee shall be exempt from all national, regional or municipal dues and taxes whatsoever, other than such as represent payment for specific services rendered.

2. The exemption from taxation referred to in paragraph 1 of this Article shall not apply to such dues and taxes if, under the laws and regulations of the receiving State, they are payable by the person who contracted with the sending State.

Article 61

Inviolability of consular archives and documents

The consular archives and documents of a consular post headed by an honorary consular officer shall be inviolable at all times and wherever they may be, provided that they are kept separate from other papers and documents and, in particular, from the private correspondence of the head of a consular post and of any person working with him, and from the materials, books or documents relating to their profession or trade.

Article 62

Exemption from customs duties

The receiving State shall, in accordance with such laws and regulations as it may adopt, permit entry of, and grant exemption from all customs duties, taxes, and related charges other than charges for storage, cartage and similar services on the following articles, provided that they are for the official use of a consular post headed by an honorary consular officer: coats-of-arms, flags, signboards, seals and stamps, books, official printed matter, office furniture, office equipment and similar articles supplied by or at the instance of the sending State to the consular post.

Article 63

Criminal procedures

If criminal proceedings are instituted against an honorary consular officer, he must appear before the competent authorities. Nevertheless, the proceedings shall be conducted with the respect due to him by reason of his official position and, except when he is under arrest or detention, in a manner which will hamper the exercise of consular functions as little as possible. When it has become necessary to detain an honorary consular officer, the proceedings against him shall be instituted with the minimum of delay.

Article 64

Proection of honorary consular officers

The receiving State is under a duty to accord to an honorary consular officer such protection as may be required by reason of his official position.

Article 65

Exemption from registration of aliens and residence permits

Honorary consular officers, with the exception of those who carry on for personal profit any professional or commercial activity in the receiving State, shall be exempt from all obligations under the laws and regulations of the receiving State in regard to the registration of aliens and residence permits.

Article 66

Exemption from taxation

An honorary consular officer shall be exempt from all dues and taxes on the remuneration and emoluments which he receives from the sending State in respect of the exercise of consular functions.

Article 67

Exemption from personal services and contributions

The receiving State shall exempt honorary consular officers from all personal services and from all public services of any kind whatsoever and from military obligations such as those connected with requisitioning, military contributions and billeting.

Article 68

Optional character of the institution of honorary consular officers

Each State is free to decide whether it will appoint or receive honorary consular officers.

CHAPTER IV

GENERAL PROVISIONS

Article 69

Consular agents who are not heads of consular posts

1. Each State is free to decide whether it will establish or admit consular agencies conducted by consular agents not designated as heads of consular post by the sending State.

2. The conditions under which the consular agencies referred to in paragraph 1 of this Article may carry on their activities and the privileges and immunities which may be enjoyed by the consular agents in charge of them shall be determined by agreement between the sending State and the receiving State.

Article 70

Exercise of consular functions by diplomatic missions

1. The provisions of the present Convention apply also, so far as the context permits, to the exercise of consular functions by a diplomatic mission.

2. The names of members of a diplomatic mission assigned to the consular section or otherwise charged with the exercise of the consular functions of the mission shall be notified to the Ministry for Foreign Affairs of the receiving State or to the authority designated by that Ministry.

3. In the exercise of consular functions a diplomatic mission may address:

(a) the local authorities of the consular district;

(b) the central authorities of the receiving State if this is allowed by the laws, regulations and usages of the receiving State or by relevant international agreements.

4. The privileges and immunities of the members of a diplomatic mission referred to in paragraph 2 of this Article shall continue to be governed by the rules of international law concerning diplomatic relations.

Article 71

Nationals or permanent residents of the receiving state

1. Except in so far as additional facilities, privileges and immunities may be granted by the receiving State, consular officers who are nationals of or permanently resident in the receiving State shall enjoy only immunity from jurisdiction and personal inviolability in respect of official acts performed in the exercise of their functions, and the privilege provided in paragraph 3 of Article 44. So far as these consular officers are concerned, the receiving State shall likewise be bound by the obligation laid down in Article 42. If criminal proceedings are instituted against such a consular officer, the proceedings shall, except when he is under arrest or detention, be conducted in a manner which will hamper the exercise of consular functions as little as possible.

2. Other members of the consular post who are nationals of or permanently resident in the receiving State and members of their families, as well as members of the families of consular officers referred to in paragraph 1 of this Article, shall enjoy facilities, privileges and immunities only in so far as these are granted to them by the receiving State. Those members of the families of members of the consular post and those members of the private staff who are themselves nationals of or permanently resident in the receiving State shall likewise enjoy facilities, privileges and immunities only in so far as these are granted to them by the receiving State. The receiving State shall, however, exercise its jurisdiction over those persons in such a way as not to hinder unduly the performance of the functions of the consular post.

Article 72

Non-discrimination

1. In the application of the provisions of the present Convention the receiving State shall not discriminate as between States.

2. However, discrimination shall not be regarded as taking place:

(a) where the receiving State applies any of the provisions of the present Convention restrictively because of a restrictive application of that provision to its consular posts in the sending State;

(b) where by custom or agreement States extend to each other more favourable treatment than is required by the provisions of the present Convention.

Article 73

Relationship between the present convention and other international agreements

1. The provisions of the present Convention shall not affect other international agreements in force as between States parties to them.

2. Nothing in the present Convention shall preclude States from concluding international agreements confirming or supplementing or extending or amplifying the provisions thereof.

CHAPTER V

FINAL PROVISIONS

Article 74

Signature

The present Convention shall be open for signature by all States Members of the United Nations or of any of the specialized agencies or Parties to the Statute of the International Court of Justice, and by any other State invited by the General Assembly of the United Nations to become a Party to the Convention, as follows until 31 October 1963 at the Federal Ministry for Foreign Affairs of the Republic of Austria and subsequently, until 31 March 1964, at the United Nations Headquarters in New York.

Article 75

Ratification

The present Convention is subject to ratification. The instruments of ratification shall be deposited with the Secretary-General of the United Nations.

Article 76

Accession

The present Convention shall remain open for accession by any State belonging to any of the four categories mentioned in Article 74. The instruments of accession shall be deposited with the Secretary-General of the United Nations.

Article 77

Entry into force

1. The present Convention shall enter into force on the thirtieth day following the date of deposit of the twenty-second instrument of ratification or accession with the Secretary-General of the United Nations.

2. For each State ratifying or acceding to the Convention after the deposit of the twenty-second instrument of ratification or accession, the Convention shall enter into force on the thirtieth day after deposit by such State of its instrument of ratification or accession.

Article 78

Notifications by the Secretary-General

The Secretary-General of the United Nations shall inform all States belonging to any of the four categories mentioned in Article 74:

(a) of signatures to the present Convention and of the deposit of instruments of ratification or accession, in accordance with Articles 74, 75 and 76;

(b) of the date on which the present Convention will enter into force, in accordance with Article 77.

Article 79

Authentic texts

The original of the present Convention, of which the Chinese, English, French, Russian and Spanish texts are equally authentic, shall be deposited with the Secretary-General of the United Nations, who shall send certified copies thereof to all States belonging to any of the four categories mentioned in Article 74.

IN WITNESS WHEREOF the undersigned Plenipotentiaries, being duly authorized thereto by their respective Governments, have signed the present Convention.

Optional Protocol to the Vienna Convention on Diplomatic Relations, Concerning Acquisition of Nationality

Done at Vienna, April 18, 1961

The States Parties to the present Protocol and to the Vienna Convention on Diplomatic Relations, hereinafter referred to as "the Convention", adopted by the United Nations Conference held at Vienna from 2 March to 14 April 1961,

EXPRESSING their wish to establish rules between them concerning acquisition of nationality by the members of their diplomatic missions and of the families forming part of the household of those members,

HAVE AGREED AS FOLLOWS:

Article I

For the purpose of the present Protocol, the expression "members of the mission" shall have the meaning assigned to it in Article 1, sub-paragraph (b), of the Convention, namely "the head of the mission and the members of the staff of the mission".

Optional Protocol to the Vienna Convention on Consular Relations Concerning Acquisition of Nationality

Done at Vienna, 24 April 1963

The States Parties to the present Protocol and to the Vienna Convention on Consular Relations, hereinafter referred to as "the Convention" adopted by the United Nations Conference held at Vienna from 4 March to 22 April 1963,

EXPRESSING their wish to establish rules between them concerning acquisition of nationality by members of the consular post and by members of their families forming part of their households,

HAVE AGREED AS FOLLOWS:

Article I

For the purposes of the present Protocol, the expression "members of the consular post" shall have the meaning assigned to it in sub-paragraph (g) of paragraph 1 of Article 1 of the Convention, namely, "consular officers, consular employees and members of the service staff".

Article II

Members of the consular post not being nationals of the receiving State, and members of their families forming part of their households, shall not, solely by the operation of the law of the receiving State, acquire the nationality of that State.

Article III

The present Protocol shall be open for signature by all States which may become Parties to the Convention, as follows: until 31 October 1963 at the Federal Ministry for Foreign Affairs of the Republic of Austria and, subsequently, until 31 March 1964, at the United Nations Headquarters in New York.

Article IV

The present Protocol is subject to ratification. The instruments of ratification shall be deposited with the Secretary-General of the United Nations.

Article V

The present Protocol shall remain open for accession by all States which may become Parties to the Convention. The instruments of accession shall be deposited with the Secretary-General of the United Nations.

Article VI

1. The present Protocol shall enter into force on the same day as the Convention or on the thirtieth day following the date of deposit of the second instrument of ratification of or accession to the Protocol with the Secretary-General of the United Nations, whichever date is the later.

2. For each State ratifying or acceding to the present Protocol after its entry into force in accordance with paragraph 1 of this Article, the Protocol shall enter into force on the thirtieth day after deposit by such State of its instrument of ratification or accession.

Article VII

The Secretary-General of the United Nations shall inform all States which may become Parties to the Convention:

(a) of signatures to the present Protocol and of the deposit of instruments of ratification or accession, in accordance with Articles III, IV and V;

(b) of the date on which the present Protocol will enter into force, in accordance with Article VI.

Article VIII

The original of the present Protocol, of which the Chinese, English, French, Russian and Spanish texts are equally authentic, shall be deposited with the Secretary-General of the United Nations, who shall send certified copies thereof to all States referred to in Article III.

IN WITNESS WHEREOF the undersigned plenipotentiaries, being duly authorized thereto by their respective Governments, have signed the present Protocol.

Optional Protocol to the Vienna Convention on Consular Relations Concerning the Compulsory Settlement of Disputes

Done at Vienna, 24 April 1963

The States Parties to the present Protocol and to the Vienna Convention on Consular Relations, hereinafter referred to as "the Convention", adopted by the United Nations Conference held at Vienna from 4 March to 22 April 1963,

EXPRESSING their wish to resort in all matters concerning them in respect of any dispute arising out of the interpretation or application of the Convention to the compulsory jurisdiction of the International Court of Justice, unless some other form of settlement has been agreed upon by the parties within a reasonable period,

HAVE AGREED AS FOLLOWS:

Article I

Disputes arising out of the interpretation or application of the Convention shall lie within the compulsory jurisdiction of the International Court of Justice and may accordingly be brought before the Court by an application made by any party to the dispute being a Party to the present Protocol.

Article II

The parties may agree, within a period of two months after one party has notified its opinion to the other that a dispute exists, to resort not to the International Court of Justice but to an arbitral tribunal. After the expiry of the said period, either party may bring the dispute before the Court by an application.

Article III

1. Within the same period of two months, the parties may agree to adopt a conciliation procedure before resorting to the International Court of Justice.

2. The conciliation commission shall make its recommendations within five months after its appointment. If its recommendations

are not accepted by the parties to the dispute within two months after they have been delivered, either party may bring the dispute before the Court by an application.

Article IV

States Parties to the Convention, to the Optional Protocol concerning Acquisition of Nationality, and to the present Protocol may at any time declare that they will extend the provisions of the present Protocol to disputes arising out of the interpretation or application of the Optional Protocol concerning Acquisition of Nationality. Such declarations shall be notified to the Secretary-General of the United Nations.

Article V

The present Protocol shall be open for signature by all States which may become Parties to the Convention as follows: until 31 October 1963 at the Federal Ministry for Foreign Affairs of the Republic of Austria and, subsequently, until 31 March 1964, at the United Nations Headquarters in New York.

Article VI

The present Protocol is subject to ratification. The instruments of ratification shall be deposited with the Secretary-General of the United Nations.

Article VII

The present Protocol shall remain open for accession by all States which may become Parties to the Convention. The instruments of accession shall be deposited with the Secretary-General of the United Nations.

Article VIII

1. The present Protocol shall enter into force on the same day as the Convention or on the thirtieth day following the date of deposit of the second instrument of ratification or accession to the Protocol with the Secretary-General of the United Nations, whichever date is the later.

2. For each State ratifying or acceding to the present Protocol after its entry into force in accordance with paragraph 1 of this Article, the Protocol shall enter into force on the thirtieth day after deposit by such State of its instrument of ratification or accession.

Article IX

The Secretary-General of the United Nations shall inform all States which may become Parties to the Convention:

(a) of signatures to the present Protocol and of the deposit of instruments of ratification or accession, in accordance with Articles V, VI and VII;

(b) of declarations made in accordance with Article IV of the present Protocol;

(c) of the date on which the present Protocol will enter into force, in accordance with Article VIII.

Article X

The original of the present Protocol, of which the Chinese, English, French, Russian and Spanish texts are equally authentic, shall be deposited with the Secretary-General of the United Nations, who shall send certified copies thereof to all States referred to in Article V.

IN WITNESS WHEREOF the undersigned plenipotentiaries, being duly authorised thereto by their respective Governments, have signed the present Protocol.

4. Organization and Administration

a. Interdepartmental Operations of the U.S. Government Overseas

(1) The National Security Council System (Presidential Directive/NSPD–1, February 13, 2001)

MEMORANDUM FOR THE VICE PRESIDENT
THE SECRETARY OF STATE
THE SECRETARY OF THE TREASURY
THE SECRETARY OF DEFENSE
THE ATTORNEY GENERAL
THE SECRETARY OF AGRICULTURE
THE SECRETARY OF COMMERCE
THE SECRETARY OF HEALTH AND HUMAN SERVICES
THE SECRETARY OF TRANSPORTATION
THE SECRETARY OF ENERGY
ADMINISTRATOR, ENVIRONMENTAL PROTECTION AGENCY
DIRECTOR OF THE OFFICE OF MANAGEMENT AND BUDGET
UNITED STATES TRADE REPRESENTATIVE
CHAIRMAN, COUNCIL OF ECONOMIC ADVISERS
DIRECTOR, NATIONAL DRUG CONTROL POLICY
CHIEF OF STAFF TO THE PRESIDENT
DIRECTOR OF CENTRAL INTELLIGENCE
DIRECTOR, FEDERAL EMERGENCY MANAGEMENT AGENCY
ASSISTANT TO THE PRESIDENT FOR NATIONAL SECURITY AFFAIRS
ASSISTANT TO THE PRESIDENT FOR ECONOMIC POLICY
COUNSEL TO THE PRESIDENT
CHIEF OF STAFF AND ASSISTANT TO THE VICE PRESIDENT FOR NATIONAL SECURITY AFFAIRS
DIRECTOR, OFFICE OF SCIENCE AND TECHNOLOGY POLICY
CHAIRMAN, BOARD OF GOVERNORS OF THE FEDERAL RESERVE
CHAIRMAN, COUNCIL ON ENVIRONMENTAL QUALITY
CHAIRMAN, EXPORT-IMPORT BANK
CHAIRMAN OF THE JOINT CHIEFS OF STAFF
COMMANDANT, U.S. COAST GUARD
ADMINISTRATOR, NATIONAL AERONAUTICS AND SPACE ADMINISTRATION
CHAIRMAN, NUCLEAR REGULATORY COMMISSION
DIRECTOR, PEACE CORPS
DIRECTOR, FEDERAL BUREAU OF INVESTIGATION

DIRECTOR, NATIONAL SECURITY AGENCY
DIRECTOR, DEFENSE INTELLIGENCE AGENCY
PRESIDENT, OVERSEAS PRIVATE INVESTMENT CORPORATION
CHAIRMAN, FEDERAL COMMUNICATIONS COMMISSION
COMMISSIONER, U.S. CUSTOMS SERVICE
ADMINISTRATOR, DRUG ENFORCEMENT ADMINISTRATION
PRESIDENT'S FOREIGN INTELLIGENCE ADVISORY BOARD
ARCHIVIST OF THE UNITED STATES
DIRECTOR, INFORMATION SECURITY OVERSIGHT OFFICE

SUBJECT: Organization of the National Security Council System

This document is the first in a series of National Security Presidential Directives. National Security Presidential Directives shall replace both Presidential Decision Directives and Presidential Review Directives as an instrument for communicating presidential decisions about the national security policies of the United States.

National security includes the defense of the United States of America, protection of our constitutional system of government, and the advancement of United States interests around the globe. National security also depends on America's opportunity to prosper in the world economy. The National Security Act of 1947, as amended, established the National Security Council to advise the President with respect to the integration of domestic, foreign, and military policies relating to national security. That remains its purpose. The NSC shall advise and assist me in integrating all aspects of national security policy as it affects the United States—domestic, foreign, military, intelligence, and economics (in conjunction with the National Economic Council (NEC)). The National Security Council system is a process to coordinate executive departments and agencies in the effective development and implementation of those national security policies.

The National Security Council (NSC) shall have as its regular attendees (both statutory and non-statutory) the President, the Vice President, the Secretary of State, the Secretary of the Treasury, the Secretary of Defense, and the Assistant to the President for National Security Affairs. The Director of Central Intelligence and the Chairman of the Joint Chiefs of Staff, as statutory advisors to the NSC, shall also attend NSC meetings. The Chief of Staff to the President and the Assistant to the President for Economic Policy are invited to attend any NSC meeting. The Counsel to the President shall be consulted regarding the agenda of NSC meetings, and shall attend any meeting when, in consultation with the Assistant to the President for National Security Affairs, he deems it appropriate. The Attorney General and the Director of the Office of Management and Budget shall be invited to attend meetings pertaining to their responsibilities. For the Attorney General, this includes both those matters within the Justice Department's jurisdiction and those matters implicating the Attorney General's responsibility under 28 U.S.C. 511 to give his advice and opinion on questions of law when required by the President. The heads of other executive departments and agencies, as well as other senior officials, shall be invited to attend meetings of the NSC when appropriate.

The NSC shall meet at my direction. When I am absent from a meeting of the NSC, at my direction the Vice President may preside. The Assistant to the President for National Security Affairs shall be responsible, at my direction and in consultation with the other regular attendees of the NSC, for determining the agenda, ensuring that necessary papers are prepared, and recording NSC actions and Presidential decisions. When international economic issues are on the agenda of the NSC, the Assistant to the President for National Security Affairs and the Assistant to the President for Economic Policy shall perform these tasks in concert.

The NSC Principals Committee (NSC/PC) will continue to be the senior interagency forum for consideration of policy issues affecting national security, as it has since 1989. The NSC/PC shall have as its regular attendees the Secretary of State, the Secretary of the Treasury, the Secretary of Defense, the Chief of Staff to the President, and the Assistant to the President for National Security Affairs (who shall serve as chair). The Director of Central Intelligence and the Chairman of the Joint Chiefs of Staff shall attend where issues pertaining to their responsibilities and expertise are to be discussed. The Attorney General and the Director of the Office of Management and Budget shall be invited to attend meetings pertaining to their responsibilities. For the Attorney General, this includes both those matters within the Justice Department's jurisdiction and those matters implicating the Attorney General's responsibility under 28 U.S.C. 511 to give his advice and opinion on questions of law when required by the President. The Counsel to the President shall be consulted regarding the agenda of NSC/PC meetings, and shall attend any meeting when, in consultation with the Assistant to the President for National Security Affairs, he deems it appropriate. When international economic issues are on the agenda of the NSC/PC, the Committee's regular attendees will include the Secretary of Commerce, the United States Trade Representative, the Assistant to the President for Economic Policy (who shall serve as chair for agenda items that principally pertain to international economics), and, when the issues pertain to her responsibilities, the Secretary of Agriculture. The Chief of Staff and National Security Adviser to the Vice President shall attend all meetings of the NSC/PC, as shall the Assistant to the President and Deputy National Security Advisor (who shall serve as Executive Secretary of the NSC/PC). Other heads of departments and agencies, along with additional senior officials, shall be invited where appropriate.

The NSC/PC shall meet at the call of the Assistant to the President for National Security Affairs, in consultation with the regular attendees of the NSC/PC. The Assistant to the President for National Security Affairs shall determine the agenda in consultation with the foregoing, and ensure that necessary papers are prepared. When international economic issues are on the agenda of the NSC/PC, the Assistant to the President for National Security Affairs and the Assistant to the President for Economic Policy shall perform these tasks in concert.

The NSC Deputies Committee (NSC/DC) will also continue to serve as the senior sub-Cabinet interagency forum for consideration of policy issues affecting national security. The NSC/DC can prescribe and review the work of the NSC interagency groups discussed later in this directive. The NSC/DC shall also help ensure that issues being brought before the NSC/PC or the NSC have been properly analyzed and prepared for decision. The NSC/DC shall have as its regular members the Deputy Secretary of State or Under Secretary of the Treasury or Under Secretary of the Treasury for International Affairs, the Deputy Secretary of Defense or Under Secretary of Defense for Policy, the Deputy Attorney General, the Deputy Director of the Office of Management and Budget, the Deputy Director of Central Intelligence, the Vice Chairman of the Joint Chiefs of Staff, the Deputy Chief of Staff to the President for Policy, the Chief of Staff and National Security Adviser to the Vice President, the Deputy Assistant to the President for International Economic Affairs, and the Assistant to the President and Deputy National Security Advisor (who shall serve as chair). When international economic issues are on the agenda, the NSC/DC's regular membership will include the Deputy Secretary of Commerce, a Deputy United States Trade Representative, and, when the issues pertain to his responsibilities, the Deputy Secretary of Agriculture, and the NSC/DC shall be chaired by the Deputy Assistant to the President for International Economic Affairs for agenda items that principally pertain to international economics. Other senior officials shall be invited where appropriate.

The NSC/DC shall meet at the call of its chair, in consultation with the other regular members of the NSC/DC. Any regular member of the NSC/DC may also request a meeting of the Committee for prompt crisis management. For all meetings the chair shall determine the agenda in consultation with the foregoing, and ensure that necessary papers are prepared.

The Vice President and I may attend any and all meetings of any entity established by or under this directive.

Management of the development and implementation of national security policies by multiple agencies of the United States Government shall usually be accomplished by the NSC Policy Coordination Committees (NSC/PCCs). The NSC/PCCs shall be the main day-to-day fora for interagency coordination of national security policy. They shall provide policy analysis for consideration by the more senior committees of the NSC system and ensure timely responses to decisions made by the President. Each NSC/PCC shall include representatives from the executive departments, offices, and agencies represented in the NSC/DC.

Six NSC/PCCs are hereby established for the following regions: Europe and Eurasia, Western Hemisphere, East Asia, South Asia, Near East and North Africa, and Africa. Each of the NSC/PCCs shall be chaired by an official of Under Secretary or Assistant Secretary rank to be designated by the Secretary of State.

Eleven NSC/PCCs are hereby also established for the following functional topics, each to be chaired by a person of Under Secretary or Assistant Secretary rank designated by the indicated authority:

Democracy, Human Rights, and International Operations (by the Assistant to the President for National Security Affairs);

International Development and Humanitarian Assistance (by the Secretary of State);

Global Environment (by the Assistant to the President for National Security Affairs and the Assistant to the President for Economic Policy in concert);

International Finance (by the Secretary of the Treasury);

Transnational Economic Issues (by the Assistant to the President for Economic Policy);

Counter-Terrorism and National Preparedness (by the Assistant to the President for National Security Affairs);

Defense Strategy, Force Structure, and Planning (by the Secretary of Defense);

Arms Control (by the Assistant to the President for National Security Affairs);

Proliferation, Counterproliferation, and Homeland Defense (by the Assistant to the President for National Security Affairs);

Intelligence and Counterintelligence (by the Assistant to the President for National Security Affairs); and

Records Access and Information Security (by the Assistant to the President for National Security Affairs).

The Trade Policy Review Group (TPRG) will continue to function as an interagency coordinator of trade policy. Issues considered within the TPRG, as with the PCCs, will flow through the NSC and/or NEC process, as appropriate.

Each NSC/PCC shall also have an Executive Secretary from the staff of the NSC, to be designated by the Assistant to the President for National Security Affairs. The Executive Secretary shall assist the Chairman in scheduling the meetings of the NSC/PCC, determining the agenda, recording the actions taken and tasks assigned, and ensuring timely responses to the central policymaking committees of the NSC system. The Chairman of each NSC/PCC, in consultation with the Executive Secretary, may invite representatives of other executive departments and agencies to attend meetings of the NSC/PCC where appropriate.

The Assistant to the President for National Security Affairs, at my direction and in consultation with the Vice President and the Secretaries of State, Treasury, and Defense, may establish additional NSC/PCCs as appropriate.

The Chairman of each NSC/PCC, with the agreement of the Executive Secretary, may establish subordinate working groups to assist the PCC in the performance of its duties.

The existing system of Interagency Working Groups is abolished.

The oversight of ongoing operations assigned in PDD/NSC–56 to Executive Committees of the Deputies Committee will be performed by the appropriate regional NSC/PCCs, which may create subordinate working groups to provide coordination for ongoing operations.

The Counter-Terrorism Security Group, Critical Infrastructure Coordination Group, Weapons of Mass Destruction Preparedness, Consequences Management and Protection Group, and the interagency working group on Enduring Constitutional Government are reconstituted as various forms of the NSC/PCC on Counter-Terrorism and National Preparedness.

The duties assigned in PDD/NSC–75 to the National Counterintelligence Policy Group will be performed in the NSC/PCC on Intelligence and Counterintelligence, meeting with appropriate attendees.

The duties assigned to the Security Policy Board and other entities established in PDD/NSC–29 will be transferred to various NSC/PCCs, depending on the particular security problem being addressed.

The duties assigned in PDD/NSC–41 to the Standing Committee on Nonproliferation will be transferred to the PCC on Proliferation, Counterproliferation, and Homeland Defense.

The duties assigned in PDD/NSC–35 to the Interagency Working Group for Intelligence Priorities will be transferred to the PCC on Intelligence and Counterintelligence.

The duties of the Human Rights Treaties Interagency Working Group established in E.O. 13107 are transferred to the PCC on Democracy, Human Rights, and International Operations.

The Nazi War Criminal Records Interagency Working Group established in E.O. 13110 shall be reconstituted, under the terms of that order and until its work ends in January 2002, as a Working Group of the NSC/PCC for Records Access and Information Security.

Except for those established by statute, other existing NSC interagency groups, ad hoc bodies, and executive committees are also abolished as of March 1, 2001, unless they are specifically reestablished as subordinate working groups within the new NSC system as of that date. Cabinet officers, the heads of other executive agencies, and the directors of offices within the Executive Office of the President shall advise the Assistant to the President for National Security Affairs of those specific NSC interagency groups chaired by their respective departments or agencies that are either mandated by statute or are otherwise of sufficient importance and vitality as to warrant being reestablished. In each case the Cabinet officer, agency head, or office director should describe the scope of the activities proposed for or now carried out by the interagency group, the relevant statutory mandate if any, and the particular NSC/PCC that should coordinate this work. The Trade Promotion Coordinating Committee established in E.O. 12870 shall continue its work, however, in the manner specified in that order. As to those committees expressly established in the National Security Act, the NSC/PC and/or NSC/DC shall serve as those committees and perform the functions assigned to those committees by the Act.

To further clarify responsibilities and effective accountability within the NSC system, those positions relating to foreign policy that are designated as special presidential emissaries, special envoys for the President, senior advisors to the President and the Secretary of State, and special advisors to the President and the Secretary of State are also abolished as of March 1, 2001, unless they are specifically redesignated or reestablished by the Secretary of State as positions in that Department.

This Directive shall supersede all other existing presidential guidance on the organization of the National Security Council system. With regard to application of this document to economic matters, this document shall be interpreted in concert with any Executive Order governing the National Economic Council and with presidential decision documents signed hereafter that implement either this directive or that Executive Order.

[SIGNED: GEORGE W. BUSH]

5. Control on Persons Leaving or Entering the United States

Presidential Proclamation 3004, January 17, 1953, 18 F.R. 489

By the President of the United States of America

Whereas section 215 of the Immigration and Nationality Act, enacted on June 27, 1952 (Public Law 414, 82nd Congress; 66 Stat. 163, 190)[1] authorizes the President to impose restrictions and prohibitions in addition to those otherwise provided by that Act upon the departure of persons from, and their entry into, the United States when the United States is at war or during the existence of any national emergency proclaimed by the President or, as to aliens, whenever there exists a state of war between or among two or more States, and when the President shall find that the interests of the United States so require; and

Whereas the national emergency the existence of which was proclaimed on December 16, 1950, by Proclamation 2914 still exists; and

Whereas because of the exigencies of the international situation and of the national defense then existing Proclamation No. 2523 of November 14, 1941, imposed certain restrictions and prohibitions, in addition to those otherwise provided by law, upon the departure of persons from and their entry into the United States; and

Whereas the exigencies of the international situation and of the national defense still require that certain restrictions and prohibitions, in addition to those otherwise provided by law, be imposed upon the departure of persons from and their entry into the United States:

Now, therefore, I, Harry S. Truman, President of the United States of America, acting under and by virtue of the authority vested in me by section 215 of the Immigration and Nationality Act and by section 301 of title 3 of the United States Code, do hereby find and publicly proclaim that the interests of the United States require that restrictions and prohibitions, in addition to those otherwise provided by law, be imposed upon the departure of persons from and their entry into, the United States; and I hereby prescribe and make the following rules, regulations, and orders with respect thereto:

(1) The departure and entry of citizens and nationals of the United States from and into the United States, including the Canal Zone, and all territory and waters, continental or insular, subject to the jurisdiction of the United States, shall be subject to the regulations prescribed by the Secretary of State and published as sections 53.1 to 53.9, inclusive, of title 22 of the Code of Federal Regulations. Such regulations are hereby incorporated into and made a

[1] For text, see *Legislation on Foreign Relations*, volume II–A.

part of this proclamation; and the Secretary of State is hereby authorized to revoke, modify, or amend such regulations as he may find the interests of the United States to require.

(2) The departure of aliens from the United States, including the Canal Zone, and all territory and waters, continental or insular, subject to the jurisdiction of the United States, shall be subject to the regulations prescribed by the Secretary of State, with the concurrence of the Attorney General, and published as sections 53.61 to 53.71, inclusive, of title 22 of the Code of Federal Regulations. Such regulations are hereby incorporated into and made a part of this proclamation; and the Secretary of State, with the concurrence of the Attorney General, is hereby authorized to revoke, modify, or amend such regulations as he may find the interests of the United States to require.

(3) The entry of aliens into the Canal Zone and American Samoa shall be subject to the regulations prescribed by the Secretary of State, with the concurrence of the Attorney General, and published as sections 53.21 to 53.41, inclusive, of title 22 of the Code of Federal Regulations. Such regulations are hereby incorporated into and made a part of this proclamation; and the Secretary of State, with the concurrence of the Attorney General, is hereby authorized to revoke, modify, or amend such regulations as he may find the interests of the United States to require.

(4) Proclamation No. 2523 of November 14, 1941, as amended by Proclamation No. 2850 of August 17, 1949, is hereby revoked, but such revocation shall not affect any order, determination, or decision relating to an individual, or to a class of individuals, issued in pursuance of such proclamations prior to the revocation thereof, and shall not prevent prosecution for any offense committed, or the imposition of any penalties or forfeitures, liability for which was incurred under such proclamations prior to the revocation thereof; and the provisions of this proclamation, including the regulations of the Secretary of State incorporated herein and made a part thereof, shall be in addition, to, and shall not be held to revoke, supersede, modify, amend, or suspend, any other proclamation, rule, regulation, or order heretofore issued relating to the departure of persons from, or their entry into, the United States; and compliance with the provisions of this proclamation, including the regulations of the Secretary of State incorporated herein and made a part hereof, shall not be considered as exempting any individual from the duty of complying with the provisions of any other statute, law, proclamation, rule, regulation, or order heretofore enacted or issued and still in effect.

(5) I hereby direct all departments and agencies of the Government to cooperate with the Secretary of State in the execution of his authority under this proclamation and any subsequent proclamation, rule, regulation, or order issued in pursuance hereof; and such departments and agencies shall upon request make available to the Secretary of State for that purpose the services of their respective officials and agents. I enjoin upon all officers of the United States charged with the execution of the laws thereof the utmost diligence in preventing violations of section 215 of the Immigration and Nationality Act and this proclamation, including the regulations of the Secretary of State incorporated herein and made a part

hereof, and in bringing to trial and punishment any person violating any provision of that section or of this proclamation.

To the extent permitted by law, this proclamation shall take effect as of December 24, 1952.

IN WITNESS WHEREOF, I have hereunto set my hand and caused the Seal of the United States of America to be affixed.

DONE at the City of Washington this 17th day of January in the year of our Lord nineteen hundred and fifty-three and of the Independence of the United States of America the one hundred and seventy-seventh.

[SEAL]

HARRY S. TRUMAN.

By the President:

DEAN ACHESON,
Secretary of State.

6. Migration and Refugee Assistance

a. Protocol Relating to the Status of Refugees [1] (with reservation)

Done at New York January 31, 1967; Accession advised by the Senate of the United States of America subject to certain reservations, October 4, 1968; Accession approved by the President of the United States of America, subject to said reservations, October 15, 1968; Accession of the United States of America deposited with the Secretary-General of the United Nations, with the said reservations, November 1, 1968; Proclaimed by the President of the United States of America, November 6, 1968; Entered into force with respect to the United States of America, November 1, 1968

PROTOCOL RELATING TO THE STATUS OF REFUGEES

The States Parties to the present Protocol,

CONSIDERING that the Convention relating to the Status of Refugees done at Geneva on 28 July 1951 [2] (hereinafter referred to as the Convention) covers only those persons who have become refugees as a result of events occurring before 1 January 1951,

CONSIDERING that the new refugee situations have arisen since the Convention was adopted and that the refugees concerned may therefore not fall within the scope of the Convention,

CONSIDERING that it is desirable that equal status should be enjoyed by all refugees covered by the definition in the Convention irrespective of the dateline 1 January 1951,

HAVE AGREED AS FOLLOWS:

ARTICLE I

GENERAL PROVISION

1. The States Parties to the present Protocol undertake to apply articles 2 to 34 inclusive to the Convention to refugees as hereinafter defined.

2. For the purpose of the present Protocol, the term "refugee" shall, except as regards the application of paragraph 3 of this article, mean any person within the definition of article 1 of the Convention as if the words "As a result of events occurring before 1 January 1951 and . . ." and the words ". . . as a result of such events", in article 1A(2) were omitted.

---

[1] 19 UST 6223; TIAS 6577. For states which are party to the Protocol, see Department of State publication, *Treaties in Force*. See also material concerning migration and refugee assistance in *Legislation on Foreign Relations*, volume II–A.

[2] 189 UNTS 150.

3. The present Protocol shall be applied by the States Parties hereto without any geographic limitation, save that existing declarations made by States already Parties to the Convention in accordance with article 1B(1)(a) of the Convention, shall, unless extended under article 1B(2) thereof, apply also under the present Protocol.

ARTICLE II

CO-OPERATION OF THE NATIONAL AUTHORITIES WITH THE UNITED NATIONS

1. The States Parties to the present Protocol undertake to co-operate with the Office of the United Nations High Commission for Refugees, or any other agency of the United Nations which may succeed it, in the exercise of its functions, and shall in particular facilitate its duty of supervising the application of the provisions of the present Protocol.

2. In order to enable the Office of the High Commissioner, or any other agency of the United Nations which may succeed it, to make reports to the competent organs of the United Nations, the States Parties to the present Protocol undertake to provide them with the information and statistical data requested, in the appropriate form, concerning:

(a) The condition of refugees;

(b) The implementation of the present protocol;

(c) Laws, regulations and decrees which are, or may hereafter be, in force relating to refugees.

ARTICLE III

INFORMATION ON NATIONAL LEGISLATION

The States Parties to the present Protocol shall communicate to the Secretary-General of the United Nations the laws and regulations which they may adopt to ensure the application of the present Protocol.

ARTICLE IV

SETTLEMENT OF DISPUTES

Any dispute between States Parties to the present Protocol which relates to its interpretation or application and which cannot be settled by other means shall be referred to the International Court of Justice at the request of any one of the parties to the dispute.

ARTICLE V

ACCESSION

The present Protocol shall be open for accession on behalf of all States Parties to the Convention and of any other State Member of the United Nations or member of any of the specialized agencies or to which an invitation to accede may have been addressed by the General Assembly of the United Nations. Accession shall be effected by the deposit of an instrument of accession with the Secretary-General of the United Nations.

Article VI

FEDERAL CLAUSE

In the case of Federal or non-unitary State, the following provisions shall apply:

(a) With respect to those articles of the Convention to be applied in accordance with article I, paragraph 1, of the present Protocol that come within the legislative jurisdiction of the federal legislative authority, the obligations of the Federal Government shall to this extent be the same as those of States Parties which are not Federal States;

(b) With respect to those articles of the Convention to be applied in accordance with article I, paragraph 1, of the present Protocol that come within the legislative jurisdiction of constituent States, provinces or cantons which are not, under the constitutional system of the federation, bound to take legislative action, the Federal Government shall bring such articles with a favourable recommendation to the notice of the appropriate authorities of States, provinces or cantons at the earliest possible moment;

(c) A Federal State Party to the present Protocol shall, at the request of any other State Party hereto transmitted through the Secretary-General of the United Nations, supply a statement of the law and practice of the Federation and its constituent units in regard to any particular provision of the Convention to be applied in accordance with article I, paragraph 1, of the present Protocol, showing the extent to which effect has been given to that provision by legislative or other action.

Article VII

RESERVATIONS AND DECLARATIONS

1. At the time of accession, any State may make reservations in respect of article IV of the present Protocol and in respect of the application in accordance with article I of the present Protocol of any provision of the Convention other than those contained in articles 1, 3, 4, 16(1) and 33 thereof, provided that in the case of a State Party to the Convention reservations made under this article shall not extend to refugees in respect of whom the Convention applies.

2. Reservations made by the States Parties to the Convention in accordance with article 42 thereof shall, unless withdrawn, be applicable in relation to their obligations under the present Protocol.

3. Any State making a reservation in accordance with paragraph 1 of this article may at any time withdraw such reservation by a communication to that effect addressed to the Secretary-General of the United Nations.

4. Declaration made under article 40, paragraphs 1 and 2, of the Convention by a State Party thereto which accedes to the present Protocol shall be deemed to apply in respect of the present Protocol, unless upon accession a notification to the contrary is addressed by the State Party concerned to the Secretary-General of the United Nations. The provisions of article 40, paragraphs 2 and 3, and of

article 44, paragraph 3, of the Convention shall be deemed to apply *mutatis mutandis* to the present Protocol.

ARTICLE VIII

ENTRY INTO FORCE

1. The present Protocol shall come into force on the day of deposit of the sixth instrument of accession.

2. For each State acceding to the Protocol after the deposit of the sixth instrument of accession, the Protocol shall come into force on the date of deposit by such State of its instrument of accession.

ARTICLE IX

DENUNCIATION

1. Any State Party hereto may denounce this Protocol at any time by a notification addressed to the Secretary-General of the United Nations.

2. Such denunciation shall take effect for the State Party concerned one year from the date on which it is received by the Secretary-General of the United Nations.

ARTICLE X

NOTIFICATIONS BY THE SECRETARY-GENERAL OF THE UNITED NATIONS

The Secretary-General of the United Nations shall inform the States referred to in article V above of the date of entry into force, accessions, reservations and withdrawals of reservations to and denunciations of the present Protocol, and of declarations and notifications relating hereto.

ARTICLE XI

DEPOSIT IN THE ARCHIVES OF THE SECRETARIAT OF THE UNITED NATIONS

A copy of the present Protocol, of which the Chinese, English, French, Russian and Spanish texts are equally authentic, signed by the President of the General Assembly and by the Secretary-General of the United Nations, shall be deposited in the archives of the Secretariat of the United Nations. The Secretary-General will transmit certified copies thereof to all States Members of the United Nations and to the other States referred to in article V above.

RESERVATION AS STATED IN PROCLAMATION

WHEREAS the Senate of the United States of America by its resolution of October 4, 1968, two-thirds of the Senators present concurring therein, did advise and consent to accession to the Protocol with the following reservations:

"The United States of America construes Article 29 of the Convention as applying only to refugees who are resident in the United States and reserves the right to tax refugees who are not residents of the United States in accordance with its general rules relating to nonresident aliens."

"The United States of America accepts the obligation of paragraph 1(b) of Article 24 of the Convention except insofar as that paragraph may conflict in certain instances with any provision of title II (old age, survivors' and disability insurance) or title XVIII (hospital and medical insurance for the aged) of the Social Security Act. As to any such provision, the United States will accord to refugees lawfully staying in its territory treatment no less favorable than is accorded aliens generally in the same circumstances."

b. Convention Relating to the Status of Refugees [1]

Done at Geneva, July 28, 1951

Preamble

The High Contracting Parties,

CONSIDERING that the Charter of the United Nations and the Universal Declaration of Human Rights approved on 10 December 1948 by the General Assembly have affirmed the principle that human beings shall enjoy fundamental rights and freedoms without discrimination,

CONSIDERING that the United Nations has, on various occasions, manifested its profound concern for refugees and endeavored to assure refugees the widest possible exercise of these fundamental rights and freedoms,

CONSIDERING that it is desirable to revise and consolidate previous international agreements relating to the status of refugees and to extend the scope of and the protection accorded by such instruments by means of a new agreement,

CONSIDERING that the grant of asylum may place unduly heavy burdens on certain countries, and that a satisfactory solution of a problem of which the United Nations has recognized the international scope and nature cannot therefore be achieved without international co-operation,

EXPRESSING the wish that all States, recognizing the social and humanitarian nature of the problem of refugees, will do everything within their power to prevent this problem from becoming a cause of tension between States,

NOTING that the United Nations High Commissioner for Refugees is charged with the task of supervising international conventions providing for the protection of refugees, and recognizing that the effective co-ordination of measures taken to deal with this problem will depend upon the co-operation of States with the High Commissioner.

HAVE AGREED AS FOLLOWS:

[1] 19 UST 6260; TIAS 6577; 606 UNTS 267. The United States is not a party to this Convention. However, the United States is a party to the Protocol Relating to the Status of Refugees, which incorporates Articles 2 through 34 of this Convention. See also material concerning migration and refugee assistance in *Legislation on Foreign Relations*, volume II–A.

Chapter I

GENERAL PROVISIONS

Article 1

Definition of the Term "Refugee"

A. For the purposes of the present Convention, the term "refugee" shall apply to any person who:

(1) Has been considered a refugee under the Arrangements of 12 May 1926[2] and 30 June 1928[3] or under the Conventions of 28 October 1933[4] and 10 February 1938,[5] the Protocol of 14 September 1939[6] or the Constitution of the International Refugee Organization;[7]

Decisions of non-eligibility taken by the International Refugee Organization during the period of its activities shall not prevent the status of refugee being accorded to persons who fulfill the conditions of paragraph 2 of this section;

(2) As a result of events occurring before 1 January 1951 and owing to well-founded fear of being persecuted for reasons of race, religion, nationality, membership of a particular social group or political opinion, is outside the country of his nationality and is unable or, owing to such fear, is unwilling to avail himself of the protection of that country; or who, not having a nationality and being outside the country of his former habitual residence as a result of such events, is unable or, owing to such fear, is unwilling to return to it.

In the case of a person who has more than one nationality, the term "the country of his nationality" shall mean each of the countries of which he is a national, and a person shall not be deemed to be lacking the protection of the country of his nationality if, without any valid reason based on well-founded fear, he has not availed himself of the protection of one of the countries of which he is a national.

B. (1) For the purposes of this Convention, the words "events occurring before 1 January 1951" in article 1, section A, shall be understood to mean either

(a) "events occuring in Europe before 1 January 1951"; or

(b) "events occurring in Europe or elsewhere before 1 January 1951";

and each Contracting State shall make a declaration at the time of signature, ratification or accession, specifying which of these meanings it applies for the purpose of its obligations under this Convention.

(2) Any Contracting State which has adopted alternative (a) may at any time extend its obligations by adopting alternative (b) by means of a notification addressed to the Secretary-General of the United Nations.

---

[2] 89 LNTS 47.
[3] 89 LNTS 63.
[4] 159 LNTS 199.
[5] 192 LNTS 59.
[6] 198 LNTS 141.
[7] TIAS 1846; 62 Stat. (3) 3037.

C. This Convention shall cease to apply to any person falling under the terms of section A if:

(1) He has voluntarily re-availed himself of the protection of the country of his nationality; or

(2) Having lost his nationality, he has voluntarily reacquired it; or

(3) He has acquired a new nationality, and enjoys the protection of the country of his new nationality; or

(4) He has voluntarily re-established himself in the country which he left or outside which he remained owing to fear of persecution; or

(5) He can no longer, because the circumstances in connection with which he has been recognized as a refugee have ceased to exist, continue to refuse to avail himself of the protection of the country of his nationality;

Provided that this paragraph shall not apply to a refugee falling under section A(1) of this article who is able to invoke compelling reasons arising out of previous persecution for refusing to avail himself of the protection of the country of nationality;

(6) Being a person who has no nationality he is, because the circumstances in connexion with which he has been recognized as a refugee have ceased to exist, able to return to the country of his former habitual residence;

Provided that this paragraph shall not apply to a refugee falling under section A(1) of this article who is able to invoke compelling reasons arising out of previous persecutions for refusing to return to the country of his former habitual residence.

D. This Convention shall not apply to persons who are at present receiving from organs or agencies of the United Nations other than the United Nations High Commissioner for Refugees protection or assistance.

When such protection or assistance has ceased for any reason, without the position of such persons being definitively settled in accordance with the relevant resolutions adopted by the General Assembly of the United Nations, these persons shall *ipso facto* be entitled to the benefits of this Convention.

E. This Convention shall not apply to a person who is recognized by the competent authorities of the country in which he has taken residence as having the rights and obligations which are attached to the possession of the nationality of that country.

F. The provisions of this Convention shall not apply to any person with respect to whom there are serious reasons for considering that:

(a) he has committed a crime against peace, a war crime, or a crime against humanity, as defined in the international instruments drawn up to make provision in respect of such crimes;

(b) he has committed a serious non-political crime outside the country of refuge prior to his admission to that country as a refugee;

(c) he has been guilty of acts contrary to the purposes and principles of the United Nations.

ARTICLE 2

General Obligations

Every refugee has duties to the country in which he finds himself, which require in particular that he conform to its laws and regulations as well as to measures taken for the maintenance of public order.

ARTICLE 3

Non-discrimination

The Contracting States shall apply the provisions of this Convention to refugees without discrimination as to race, religion or country of origin.

ARTICLE 4

Religion

The Contracting States shall accord to refugees within their territories treatment at least as favourable as that accorded to their nationals with respect to freedom to practice their religion and freedom as regard the religious education of their children.

ARTICLE 5

Rights Granted Apart from this Convention

Nothing in this Convention shall be deemed to impair any rights and benefits granted by a Contracting State to refugees apart from this Convention.

ARTICLE 6

The Term "in the same circumstances"

For the purpose of this Convention, the term "in the same circumstances" implies that any requirements (including requirements as to length and conditions of sojourn or residence) which the particular individual would have to fulfill for the enjoyment of the right in question, if he were not a refugee, must be fulfilled by him, with the exception of requirements which by their nature a refugee is incapable of fulfilling.

ARTICLE 7

Exemption from Reciprocity

1. Except where this Convention contains more favourable provisions, a Contracting State shall accord to refugees the same treatment as is accorded to aliens generally.
2. After a period of three years' residence, all refugees shall enjoy exemption from legislative reciprocity in the territory of the Contracting States.
3. Each Contracting State shall continue to accord to refugees the rights and benefits to which they were already entitled, in the

absence of reciprocity, at the date of entry into force of this Convention for that State.

4. The Contracting States shall consider favourably the possibility of according to refugees, in the absence of reciprocity, rights and benefits beyond those to which they are entitled according to paragraphs 2 and 3, and to extending exemption from reciprocity to refugees who do not fulfill the conditions provided for in paragraphs 2 and 3.

5. The provisions of paragraphs 2 and 3 apply both to the rights and benefits referred to in articles 13, 18, 19, 21 and 22 of this Convention and to rights and benefits for which this Convention does not provide.

ARTICLE 8

Exemption from Exceptional Measures

With regard to exceptional measures which may be taken against the persons, property or interests of nationals of a foreign State, the Contracting States shall not apply such measures to a refugee who is formally a national of the said State solely on account of such nationality. Contracting States which, under their legislation, are prevented from applying the general principle expressed in this article, shall, in appropriate cases, grant exemptions in favour of such refugees.

ARTICLE 9

Provisional Measures

Nothing in this Convention shall prevent a Contracting State, in time of war or other grave and exceptional circumstances, from taking provisionally measures which it considers to be essential to the national security in the case of a particular person, pending a determination by the Contracting State that that person is in fact a refugee and that the continuance of such measures is necessary in his case in the interests of national security.

ARTICLE 10

Continuity of Residence

1. Where a refugee has been forcibly displaced during the Second World War and removed to the territory of a Contracting State, and is resident there, the period of such enforced sojourn shall be considered to have been lawful residence within that territory.

2. Where a refugee has been forcibly displaced during the Second World War from the territory of a Contracting State and has, prior to the date of entry into force of this Convention, returned there for the purpose of taking up residence, the period of residence before and after such enforced displacement shall be regarded as one uninterrupted period for any purposes for which uninterrupted residence is required.

Article 11

Refugee Seamen

In the case of refugees regularly serving as crew members on board a ship flying the flag of a Contracting State, that State shall give sympathetic consideration to their establishment on its territory and the issue of travel documents to them or their temporary admission to its territory particularly with a view to facilitating their establishment in another country.

Chapter II

JURIDICAL STATUS

Article 12

Personal Status

1. The personal status of a refugee shall be governed by the law of the country of his domicile or, if he has no domicile, by the law of the country of his residence.

2. Rights previously acquired by a refugee and dependent on personal status, more particularly rights attaching to marriage, shall be respected by a Contracting State, subject to compliance, if this be necessary, with the formalities required by the law of that State, provided that the right in question is one which would have been recognized by the law of that State had he not become a refugee.

Article 13

Movable and Immovable Property

The Contracting States shall accord to a refugee treatment as favourable as possible and, in any event, not less favourable than that accorded to aliens generally in the same circumstances, as regards the acquisition of movable and immovable property and other rights pertaining thereto, and to leases and other contracts relating to movable and immovable property.

Article 14

Artistic Rights and Industrial Property

In respect to the protection of industrial property, such as inventions, designs or models, trade marks, trade names, and of rights in literary, artistic and scientific works, a refugee shall be accorded in the country in which he has his habitual residence the same protection as is accorded to nationals of that country. In the territory of any other Contracting State, he shall be accorded the same protection as is accorded in that territory to nationals of the country in which he has his habitual residence.

Article 15

Rights of Association

As regards non-political and non-profitmaking associations and trade unions the Contracting States shall accord to refugees lawfully staying in their territory the most favourable treatment accorded to nationals of a foreign country, in the same circumstances.

Article 16

Access to Courts

1. A refugee shall have free access to the courts of law on the territory of all Contracting States.
2. A refugee shall enjoy in the Contracting State in which he has his habitual residence the same treatment as a national in matters pertaining to access to the Courts, including legal assistance and exemption from *cautio judicatun solvi.*
3. A refugee shall be accorded in the matters referred to in paragraph 2 in countries other than that in which he has his habitual residence the treatment granted to a national of the country of his habitual residence.

Chapter III

GAINFUL EMPLOYMENT

Article 17

Wage-earning Employment

1. The Contracting States shall accord to refugees lawfully staying in their territory the most favourable treatment accorded to nationals of a foreign country in the same circumstances, as regards the right to engage in wage-earning employment.
2. In any case, restrictive measures imposed on aliens or the employment of aliens for the protection of the national labour market shall not be applied to a refugee who was already exempt from them at the date of entry into force of this Convention for the Contracting State concerned, or who fulfils one of the following conditions:
   (a) He has completed three years' residence in the country.
   (b) He has a spouse possessing the nationality of the country of residence. A refugee may not invoke the benefit of this provision if he has abandoned his spouse;
   (c) He has one or more children possessing the nationality of the country of residence.
3. The Contracting States shall give sympathetic consideration to assimilating the rights of all refugees with regard to wage-earning employment to those of nationals, and in particular of those refugees who have entered their territory pursuant to programmes of labour recruitment or under immigration schemes.

ARTICLE 18

Self-employment

The Contracting States shall accord to a refugee lawfully in their territory treatment as favourable as possible and, in any event, not less favourable than that accorded to aliens generally in the same circumstances, as regards the right to engage on his own account in agriculture, industry, handicrafts and commerce and to establish commercial and industrial companies.

ARTICLE 19

Liberal Professions

1. Each Contracting State shall accord to refugees lawfully staying in their territory who hold diplomas recognized by the competent authorities of that State, and who are desirous of practising a liberal profession, treatment as favourable as possible and, in any event, not less favourable than that accorded to aliens generally in the same circumstances.

2. The Contracting States shall use their best endeavours consistently with their laws and constitutions to secure the settlement of such refugees in the territories, other than the metropolitan territory, for whose international relations they are responsible.

Chapter IV

WELFARE

ARTICLE 20

Rationing

Where a rationing system exists, which applies to the population at large and regulates the general distribution of products in short supply, refugees shall be accorded the same treatment as nationals.

ARTICLE 21

Housing

As regards housing, the Contracting States, in so far as the matter is regulated by laws or regulations or is subject to the control of public authorities, shall accord to refugees lawfully staying in their territory treatment as favourable as possible and, in any event, not less favourable than that accorded to aliens generally in the same circumstances.

ARTICLE 22

Public Education

1. The Contracting States shall accord to refugees the same treatment as is accorded to nationals with respect to elementary education.

2. The Contracting States shall accord to refugees treatment as favourable as possible, and, in any event, not less favourable than

that accorded to aliens generally in the same circumstances, with respect to education other than elementary education and, in particular, as regards access to studies, the recognition of foreign school certificates, diplomas and degrees, the remission of fees and charges and the award of scholarships.

ARTICLE 23

Public Relief

The Contracting States shall accord to refugees lawfully staying in their territory the same treatment with respect to public relief and assistance as is accorded to their nationals.

ARTICLE 24

Labour Legislation and Social Security

1. The Contracting States shall accord to refugees lawfully staying in their territory the same treatment as is accorded to nationals in respect of the following matters:

(a) In so far as such matters are governed by laws or regulations or are subject to the control of administrative authorities: remuneration, including family allowances where these form part of remuneration, hours of work, overtime arrangements, holidays with pay, restrictions on home work, minimum age of employment, apprenticeship and training, women's work and the work of young persons, and the enjoyment of the benefits of collective bargaining;

(b) Social security (legal provisions in respect of employment injury, occupational diseases, maternity, sickness, disability, old age, death, unemployment, family responsibilities and any other contingency which, according to national laws or regulations, is covered by a social security scheme), subject to the following limitations;

(i) There may be appropriate arrangements for the maintenance of acquired rights and rights in course of acquisition;

(ii) National laws or regulations of the country of residence may prescribe special arrangements concerning benefits or portions of benefits which are payable wholly out of public funds, and concerning allowances paid to persons who do not fulfill the contribution conditions prescribed for the award of a normal pension.

2. The right to compensation for the death of a refugee resulting from employment injury or from occupational disease shall not be affected by the fact that the residence of the beneficiary is outside the territory of the Contracting State.

3. The Contracting States shall extend to refugees the benefits of agreements concluded between them, or which may be concluded between them in the future, concerning the maintenance of acquired rights and rights in the process of acquisition in regard to social security, subject only to the conditions which apply to nationals of the States signatory to the agreements in question.

4. The Contracting States will give sympathetic consideration to extending to the refugees so far as possible the benefits of similar agreements which may at any time be in force between such Contracting States and noncontracting States.

Chapter V

ADMINISTRATIVE MEASURES

ARTICLE 25

Administrative Assistance

1. When the exercise of a right by a refugee would normally require the assistance of authorities of a foreign country to whom he cannot have recourse, the Contracting States in whose territory he is residing shall arrange that such assistance be afforded to him by their own authorities or by an international authority.
2. The authority or authorities mentioned in paragraph 1 shall deliver or cause to be delivered under their supervision to refugees such documents or certifications as would normally be delivered to aliens by or through their national authorities.
3. Documents or certifications so delivered shall stand in the stead of the official instruments delivered to aliens by or through their national authorities, and shall be given credence in the absence of proof to the contrary.
4. Subject to such exceptional treatment as may be granted to indigent persons fees may be charged for the services mentioned herein, but such fees shall be moderate and commensurate with those charged to nationals for similar services.
5. The provisions of this article shall be without prejudice to articles 27 and 28.

ARTICLE 26

Freedom of Movement

Each Contracting State shall accord to refugees lawfully in its territory the right to choose their place of residence and to move freely within its territory, subject to any regulations applicable to aliens generally in the same circumstances.

ARTICLE 27

Identity Papers

The Contracting States shall issue identity papers to any refugee in their territory who does not possess a valid travel document.

ARTICLE 28

Travel Documents

1. The Contracting States shall issue to refugees lawfully staying in their territory travel documents for the purpose of travel outside their territory, unless compelling reasons of national security or public order otherwise require, and the provisions of the Schedule

to this Convention shall apply with respect to such documents. The Contracting States may issue such a travel document to any other refugee in their territory; they shall in particular give sympathetic consideration to the issue of such a travel document to refugees in their territory who are unable to obtain a travel document from the country of their lawful residence.

2. Travel documents issued to refugees under previous international agreements by parties thereto shall be recognized and treated by the Contracting States in the same way as if they had been issued pursuant to this article.

Article 29

Fiscal Charges

1. The Contracting States shall not impose upon refugees duties, charges or taxes, of any description whatsoever, other or higher than those which are or may be levied on their nationals in similar situations.

2. Nothing in the above paragraph shall prevent the application to refugees of the laws and regulations concerning charges in respect of the issue to aliens of administrative documents including identity papers.

Article 30

Transfer of Assets

1. A Contracting State shall, in conformity with its laws and regulations, permit refugees to transfer assets which they have brought into its territory, to another country where they have been admitted for the purposes of resettlement.

2. A Contracting State shall give sympathetic consideration to the application of refugees for permission to transfer assets wherever they may be and which are necessary for their resettlement in another country to which they have been admitted.

Article 31

Refugees Unlawfully in the Country of Refuge

1. The Contracting States shall not impose penalties, on account of their illegal entry or presence, on refugees who, coming directly from a territory where their life or freedom was threatened in the sense of article 1, enter or are present in their territory without authorization, provided they present themselves without delay to the authorities and show good cause for their illegal entry or presence.

2. The Contracting States shall not apply to the movements of such refugees restrictions other than those which are necessary and such restrictions shall only be applied until their status in the country is regularized or they obtain admission into another country. The Contracting States shall allow such refugees a reasonable period and all the necessary facilities to obtain admission into another country.

Article 32

Expulsion

1. The Contracting States shall not expel a refugee lawfully in their territory save on grounds of national security or public order.

2. The expulsion of such a refugee shall be only in pursuance of a decision reached in accordance with due process of law. Except where compelling reasons of national security otherwise require, the refugee shall be allowed to submit evidence to clear himself, and to appeal to and be represented for the purpose before competent authority or a person or persons specially designated by the competent authority.

3. The Contracting States shall allow such a refugee a reasonable period within which to seek legal admission into another country. The Contracting States reserve the right to apply during that period such internal measures as they may deem necessary.

Article 33

Prohibition of Expulsion or Return ("Refoulement")

1. No Contracting State shall expel or return ("refouler") a refugee in any manner whatsoever to the frontiers of territories where his life or freedom would be threatened on account of his race, religion, nationality, membership of a particular social group or political opinion.

2. The benefit of the present provision may not, however, be claimed by a refugee whom there are reasonable grounds for regarding as a danger to the security of the country in which he is, or who, having been convicted by a final judgment of a particularly serious crime, constitutes a danger to the community of that country.

Article 34

Naturalization

The Contracting States shall as far as possible facilitate the assimilation and naturalization of refugees. They shall in particular make every effort to expedite naturalization proceedings and to reduce as far as possible the charges and costs of such proceedings.

Chapter VI

EXECUTORY AND TRANSITORY PROVISIONS

Article 35

Co-operation of the National Authorities with the United Nations

1. The Contracting States undertake to co-operate with the Office of the United Nations High Commissioner for Refugees, or any other agency of the United Nations which may succeed it, in the exercise of its functions, and shall in particular facilitate its duty of supervising the application of the provisions of this Convention.

2. In order to enable the Office of the High Commissioner or any other agency of the United Nations which may succeed it, to make reports to the competent organs of the United Nations, the Contracting States undertake to provide them in the appropriate form with information and statistical data requested concerning:

(a) the condition of refugees,

(b) the implementation of this Convention, and

(c) laws, regulations and decrees which are, or may hereafter be, in force relating to refugees.

Article 36

Information on National Legislation

The Contracting States shall communicate to the Secretary-General of the United Nations the laws and regulations which they may adopt to ensure the application of this Convention.

Article 37

Relation to Previous Convention

Without prejudice to article 28, paragraph 2, of this Convention, this Convention replaces, as between parties to it, the Arrangements of 5 July 1922,[8] 31 May 1924, 12 May 1926, 30 June 1928 and 30 July 1935, the Conventions of 28 October 1933 and 10 February 1938, the Protocol of 14 September 1939 and the Agreement of 15 October 1946.[9]

Chapter VII

FINAL CLAUSES

Article 38

Settlement of Disputes

Any dispute between parties to this Convention relating to its interpretation of application, which cannot be settled by other means, shall be referred to the International Court of Justice at the request of any one of the parties to the dispute.

Article 39

Signature, Ratification and Accession

1. This Convention shall be opened for signature at Geneva on 28 July 1951 and shall thereafter be deposited with the Secretary-General of the United Nations. It shall be open for signature at the European Office of the United Nations from 28 July to 31 August 1951 and shall be re-opened for signature at the Headquarters of the United Nations from 17 September 1951 to 31 December 1952.

2. This Convention shall be open for signature on behalf of all States Members of the United Nations, and also on behalf of any

[8] 13 LNTS 237.
[9] 11 LNTS 73.

other State invited to attend the Conference of Plenipotentiaries on the Status of Refugees and Stateless Persons or to which an invitation to sign will have been addressed by the General Assembly. It shall be ratified and the instruments of ratification shall be deposited with the Secretary-General of the United Nations.

3. This Convention shall be open from 28 July 1951 for accession by the States referred to in paragraph 2 of this article. Accession shall be effected by the deposit of an instrument of accession with the Secretary-General of the United Nations.

Article 40

Territorial Application Clause

1. Any State may, at the time of signature, ratification or accession, declare that this Convention shall extend to all or any of the territories for the international relations of which it is responsible. Such a declaration shall take effect when the Convention enters into force for the State concerned.

2. At any time thereafter any such extension shall be made by notification addressed to the Secretary-General of the United Nations and shall take effect as from the ninetieth day after the day of receipt by the Secretary-General of the United Nations of this notification, or as from the date of entry into force of the Convention for the State concerned, whichever is the later.

3. With respect to those territories to which this Convention is not extended at the time of signature, ratification or accession, each State concerned shall consider the possibility of taking the necessary steps in order to extend the application of this Convention to such territories, subject, where necessary for constitutional reasons, to the consent of the Government of such territories.

Article 41

Federal Clause

In the case of a Federal or non-unitary State, the following provisions shall apply:

(a) With respect to those articles of this Convention that come within the legislative jurisdiction of the federal legislative authority, the obligations of the Federal Government shall to this extent be the same as those of Parties which are not Federal States;

(b) With respect to those articles of this Convention that come within the legislative jurisdiction of constituent States, provinces or cantons which are not, under the constitutional system of the federation, bound to take legislative action, the Federal Government shall bring such articles with a favourable recommendation to the notice of the appropriate authorities of States, provinces or cantons at the earliest possible moment.

(c) A Federal State Party to this Convention shall, at the request of any other Contracting State transmitted through the Secretary-General of the United Nations, supply a statement of the law and practice of the Federation and its constituent units in regard to any particular provision of the Convention showing the extent to which effect has been given to that provision by legislative or other action.

Article 42

Reservations

1. At the time of signature, ratification or accession, any State may make reservations to articles of the Convention other than to articles 1, 3, 4, 16(I), 33, 36–46 inclusive.
2. Any State making a reservation in accordance with paragraph 1 of this article may at any time withdraw the reservation by a communication to that effect addressed to the Secretary-General of the United Nations.

Article 43

Entry into Force

1. This Convention shall come into force on the ninetieth day following the day of deposit of the sixth instrument of ratification or accession.
2. For each State ratifying or acceding to the Convention after the deposit of the sixth instrument of ratification or accession, the Convention shall enter into force on the ninetieth day following the date of deposit by such State of its instrument of ratification or accession.

Article 44

Denunciation

1. Any Contracting State may denounce this Convention at any time by a notification addressed to the Secretary-General of the United Nations.
2. Such denunciation shall take effect for the Contracting State concerned one year from the date upon which it is received by the Secretary-General of the United Nations.
3. Any State which has made a declaration or notification under article 40 may, at any time thereafter, by a notification to the Secretary-General of the United Nations, declare that the Convention shall cease to extend to such territory one year after the date of receipt of the notification by the Secretary-General.

Article 45

Revision

1. Any Contracting State may request revision of this Convention at any time by a notification addressed to the Secretary-General of the United Nations.
2. The General Assembly of the United Nations shall recommend the steps, if any, to be taken in respect of such request.

ARTICLE 46

Notifications by the Secretary-General of the United Nations

The Secretary-General of the United Nations shall inform all Members of the United Nations and non-member States referred to in article 39:

(a) Of declaration and notifications in accordance with section B of article 1;

(b) Of signature, ratifications and accessions in accordance with article 39;

(c) Of declarations and notifications in accordance with article 40;

(d) Of reservations and withdrawals in accordance with article 42;

(e) Of the date on which this Convention will come into force in accordance with article 43;

(f) Of denunciations and notifications in accordance with article 44;

(g) Of requests for revision in accordance with article 45.

IN FAITH WHEREOF the undersigned, duly authorized, have signed this Convention on behalf of their respective Governments,

DONE at Geneva, this twenty-eighth day of July, one thousand nine hundred and fifty-one, in a single copy, of which the English and French texts are equally authentic and which shall remain deposited in the archives of the United Nations, and certified true copies of which shall be delivered to all Members of the United Nations and to the non-member States referred to in article 39.

SCHEDULE

Paragraph 1

1. The travel document referred to in article 28 of this Convention shall be similar to the specimen annexed hereto.

2. The document shall be made out in at least two languages, one of which shall be English or French.

Paragraph 2

Subject to the regulations obtaining in the country of issue, children may be included in the travel document of a parent or, in exceptional circumstances, of another adult refugee.

Paragraph 3

The fees charged for issue of the document shall not exceed the lowest scale of charges for national passports.

Paragraph 4

Save in special or exceptional cases, the document shall be made valid for the largest possible number of countries.

Paragraph 5

The document shall have a validity of either one or two years, at the discretion of the issuing authority.

Paragraph 6

1. The renewal or extension of the validity of the document is a matter for the authority which issued it, so long as the holder has not established lawful residence in another territory and resides lawfully in the territory of the said authority. The issue of a new document is, under the same conditions, a matter for the authority which issued the former document.
2. Diplomatic or consular authorities, specially authorized for the purpose, shall be empowered to extend, for a period not exceeding six months, the validity of travel documents issued by their Governments.
3. The Contracting States shall give sympathetic consideration to renewing or extending the validity of travel documents or issuing new documents to refugees no longer lawfully resident in their territory who are unable to obtain a travel document from the country of their lawful residence.

Paragraph 7

The Contracting States shall recognize the validity of the documents issued in accordance with the provisions of article 28 of this Convention.

Paragraph 8

The competent authorities of the country to which the refugee desires to proceed shall, if they are prepared to admit him and if a visa is required, affix a visa on the document of which he is the holder.

Paragraph 9

1. The Contracting States undertake to issue transit visas to refugees who have obtained visas for a territory of final destination.
2. The issue of such visas may be refused on grounds which would justify refusal of a visa to any alien.

Paragraph 10

The fees for the issue of exit, entry or transit visas shall not exceed the lowest scale of charges for visas on foreign passports.

Paragraph 11

When a refugee has lawfully taken up residence in the territory of another Contracting State, the responsibility for the issue of a new document, under the terms and conditions of article 28, shall be that of the competent authority of that territory, to which the refugee shall be entitled to apply.

Paragraph 12

The authority issuing a new document shall withdraw the old document and shall return it to the country of issue if it is stated in the document that it should be so returned; otherwise it shall withdraw and cancel the document.

Paragraph 13

1. Each Contracting State undertakes that the holder of a travel document issued by it in accordance with article 28 of this Convention shall be readmitted to its territory at any time during the period of its validity.

2. Subject to the provisions of the preceding sub-paragraph, a Contracting State may require the holder of the document to comply with such formalities as may be prescribed in regard to exit from or return to its territory.

3. The Contracting States reserve the right, in exceptional cases, or in cases where the refugee's stay is authorized for a specific period, when issuing the document, to limit the period during which the refugee may return to a period of not less than three months.

Paragraph 14

Subject only to the terms of paragraph 13, the provisions of this Schedule in no way affect the laws and regulations governing the conditions of admission to, transit through, residence and establishment in, and departure from, the territories of the Contracting States.

Paragraph 15

Neither the issue of the document nor the entries made thereon determine or affect the status of the holder, particularly as regards nationality.

Paragraph 16

The issue of the document does not in any way entitle the holder to the protection of the diplomatic or consular authorities of the country of issue, and does not confer on these authorities a right of protection.

Paragraph 12

The authority issuing a new document shall withdraw the old document and shall return it to the country of issue if it is stated in the document that it should be so returned; otherwise it shall withdraw and cancel the document.

Paragraph 13

1. Each Contracting State undertakes that the holder of a travel document issued by it in accordance with article 28 of this Convention shall be readmitted to its territory at any time during the period of its validity.

2. Subject to the provisions of the preceding sub-paragraph, a Contracting State may require the holder of the document to comply with such formalities as may be prescribed in regard to exit from or return to its territory.

3. The Contracting States reserve the right, in exceptional cases, or in cases where the refugee's stay is authorized for a specific period, when issuing the document, to limit the period during which the refugee may return to a period of not less than three months.

Paragraph 14

Subject only to the terms of paragraph 13, the provisions of this Schedule in no way affect the laws and regulations governing the conditions of admission to, transit through, residence and establishment in, and departure from, the territories of the Contracting States.

Paragraph 15

Neither the issue of the document nor the entries made thereon determine or affect the status of the holder, particularly as regards nationality.

Paragraph 16

The issue of the document does not in any way entitle the holder to the protection of the diplomatic or consular authorities of the country of issue, and does not confer on these authorities a right of protection.

E. INFORMATION AND EDUCATIONAL AND CULTURAL EXCHANGE PROGRAMS

CONTENTS

1. Agreement for Facilitating the International Circulation of Visual and Auditory Materials of an Educational, Scientific and Cultural Character (Beirut Agreement of 1949) [1]

Agreement and Protocol opened for signature at Lake Success July 15, 1949; Signed on behalf of the United States, September 13, 1949; Ratification advised by the Senate, May 26, 1960; Ratified by the President, September 30, 1966; Acceptance by the United States deposited with the Secretary-General of the United Nations October 14, 1966; Proclaimed by the President, October 14, 1966; Date of entry into force with respect to the United States, January 12, 1967

The Governments of the States signatory to the present Agreement,

BEING CONVINCED that in facilitating the international circulation of visual and auditory materials of an educational, scientific and cultural character, the free flow of ideas by word and image will be promoted and the mutual understanding of peoples thereby encouraged, in conformity with the aims of the United Nations Educational, Scientific and Cultural Organization,

HAVE AGREED AS FOLLOWS:

ARTICLE I

The present Agreement shall apply to visual and auditory materials of the types specified in article II which are of an educational, scientific or cultural character.

Visual and auditory materials shall be deemed to be of an educational, scientific or cultural character:

(a) When their primary purpose or effect is to instruct or inform through the development of a subject or aspect of a subject, or when their content is such as to maintain, increase or diffuse knowledge, and augment international understanding and good will; and

(b) When the materials are representative, authentic, and accurate; and

(c) When the technical quality is such that it does not interfere with the use made of the material.

ARTICLE II

The provisions of the preceding Article shall apply to visual and auditory materials of the following types and forms:

(a) Films, filmstrips and microfilm in either negative form, exposed and developed, or positive form, printed and developed;

(b) Sound recordings of all types and forms;

[1] 17 UST 1578; TIAS 6116; 197 UNTS 3. For a list of states which are parties to the Agreement, see Department of State publication, *Treaties in Force*.

(c) Glass slides; models, static and moving; wall charts, maps and posters.

These materials are hereinafter referred to as material.

ARTICLE III

1. Each of the contracting States shall accord, within six months from the coming into force of the present Agreement with respect to that State exemption from all Customs duties and quantitative restrictions and from the necessity of applying for an import license in respect of the importation, either permanent or temporary, of material originating in the territory of any of the other contracting States.

2. Nothing in this Agreement shall exempt material from those taxes, fees, charges or exactions which are imposed on the import of all articles without exception and without regard to their nature and origin, even though such articles are exempt from customs duties; such taxes, fees and exactions shall include, but are not limited to, nominal statistical fees and stamp duties.

3. Material entitled to the privileges provided by paragraph 1 of this article shall be exempt, in the territory of the country of entry, from all internal taxes, fees, charges or exactions other or higher than those imposed on like products of that country, and shall be accorded treatment no less favourable than that accorded like products of that country in respect of all internal laws, regulations or requirements affecting its sale, transportation or distribution or affecting its processing, exhibition or other use.

4. Nothing in this Agreement shall require any contracting State to deny the treatment provided for in this article to like material of an educational, scientific or cultural character originating in any State not a party to this Agreement in any case in which the denial of such treatment would be contrary to an international obligation or to the commercial policy of such contracting State.

ARTICLE IV

1. To obtain the exemption, provided under the present Agreement for material for which admission into the territory of a contracting State is sought, a certificate that such material is of an educational, scientific or cultural character within the meaning of article I, shall be filed in connection with the entry.

2. The certificate shall be issued by the appropriate governmental agency of the State wherein the material to which the certificate relates originated, or by the United Nations Educational, Scientific and Cultural Organization as provided for in paragraph 3 of this article, and in the forms annexed hereto. The prescribed forms of certificate may be amended or revised upon mutual agreement of the contracting States, provided such amendment or revision is in conformity with the provisions of this Agreement.

3. Certificates shall be issued by the United Nations Educational, Scientific and Cultural Organization for material of educational, scientific or cultural character produced by international organizations recognized by the United Nations or by any of the specialized agencies.

4. On the filing of any such certificate, there will be a decision by the appropriate governmental agency of the contracting State into which entry is sought as to whether the material is entitled to the privilege provided by article III, paragraph 1, of the present Agreement. This decision shall be made after consideration of the material and through the application of the standards provided in article I. If, as a result of that consideration, such agency of the contracting State into which entry is sought intends not to grant the privileges provided by article III, paragraph 1, to that material because it does not concede its educational, scientific and cultural character, the Government of the State which certified the material, or UNESCO, as the case may be, shall be notified prior to any final decision in order that it may make friendly representations in support of the exemption of that material to the Government of the other State into which entry is sought.

5. The governmental agency of the contracting State into which entry is sought shall be entitled to impose regulations upon the importer of the material to ensure that it shall only be exhibited or used for non-profit-making purposes.

6. The decision of the appropriate governmental agency of the contracting State into which entry is sought, provided for in paragraph 4 of this article shall be final, but in making its decision the said agency shall give due consideration to any representations made to it by the Government certifying the material or by UNESCO as the case may be.

Article V

Nothing in the present Agreement shall affect the right of the contracting States to censor material in accordance with their own laws or to adopt measures to prohibit or limit the importation of material for reasons of public security or order.

Article VI

Each of the contracting States shall send to the United Nations Educational, Scientific and Cultural Organization a copy of each certificate which it issues to material originating within its own territory and shall inform the United Nations Educational, Scientific and Cultural Organization of the decisions taken and the reasons for any refusals in respect of certified materials from other contracting States for which entry is sought into its own territory. The United Nations Educational, Scientific and Cultural Organization shall communicate this information to all contracting States and shall maintain and publish in English and French catalogues of material showing all the certifications and decisions made in respect of them.

Article VII

The contracting States undertake jointly to consider means of reducing to a minimum the restrictions that are not removed by the present Agreement which might interfere with the international circulation of the material referred to in article I.

ARTICLE VIII

Each contracting State shall communicate to the United Nations Educational, Scientific and Cultural Organization, within the period of six months following the coming into force of the present Agreement the measures taken in their respective territories to ensure the execution of the provisions of the present Agreement. The United Nations Educational, Scientific and Cultural Organization shall communicate this information as it receives it to all contracting States.

ARTICLE IX

1. All disputes arising out of the interpretation or application of the present Agreement between States which are both parties to the Statute of the International Court of Justice,[2] except as to Articles IV and V, shall be referred to the International Court of Justice unless in any specific case it is agreed by the parties to have recourse to another mode of settlement.

2. If the contracting States between which a dispute has arisen are not parties or any one of them is not party to the Statute of the International Court of Justice, the dispute shall, if the States concerned so desire, be submitted, in accordance with the constitutional rules of each of them, to an arbitral tribunal established in conformity with the Convention for the Pacific Settlement of International Disputes signed at The Hague on 18 October 1907,[3] or to any other arbitral tribunal.

ARTICLE X

The present Agreement is open to acceptance by the signatory States. The instrument of acceptance shall be deposited with the Secretary-General of the United Nations who shall notify all the Members of the United States of each deposit and the date thereof.

ARTICLE XI

1. On or after 1 January 1950 any Member of the United Nations not a signatory to the present Agreement, and any non-member State to which a certified copy of the present Agreement has been communicated by the Secretary-General of the United Nations, may accede to it.

2. The instrument of accession shall be deposited with the Secretary-General of the United Nations, who shall notify all the Members of the United Nations and the non-Member States, referred to in the preceding paragraph, of each deposit and the date thereof.

ARTICLE XII

1. The present Agreement shall come into force ninety days after the Secretary-General of the United Nations has received at least ten instruments of acceptance or accession in accordance with article X or article XI. As soon as possible thereafter the Secretary-

[2] TS 993; 59 Stat. 1055.
[3] TS 536; 36 Stat. 2199.

General shall draw up a *procès-verbal* specifying the date on which, in accordance with this paragraph, the present Agreement shall have come into force.

2. In respect of each State on behalf of which an instrument of acceptance or accession is subsequently deposited, the present Agreement shall come into force ninety days after the date of the deposit of such instrument.

3. The present Agreement shall be registered with the Secretary-General of the United Nations on the day of its entry into force in accordance with article 102 of the Charter[4] and the regulations made thereunder by the General Assembly.

ARTICLE XIII

1. The present Agreement may be denounced by any contracting State after the expiration of a period of three years from the date on which it comes into force in respect of that particular State.

2. The denunciation of the Agreement by any contracting States shall be effected by a written notification addressed by that State to the Secretary-General of the United Nations who shall notify all the Members of the United Nations and all non-member States referred to in article XI of each notification and the date of the receipt thereof.

3. The denunciation shall take effect one year after the receipt of the notification by the Secretary-General of the United Nations.

ARTICLE XIV

1. Any contracting State may declare, at the time of signature, acceptance, or accession, that in accepting the present Agreement it is not assuming any obligation in respect of all or any territories, for which such contracting State has international obligations. The present Agreement shall, in that case, not be applicable to the territories named in the declaration.

2. The contracting States in accepting the present Agreement do not assume responsibility in respect of any or all Non-Self-Governing territories for which they are responsible but may notify the acceptance of the Agreement by any or all of such territories at the time of acceptance by such contracting States or at any time thereafter. The present Agreement shall, in such cases, apply to all the territories named in the notification ninety days after the receipt thereof by the Secretary-General of the United Nations.

3. Any contracting State may at any time after the expiration of the period of three years provided for in article XIII declare that it desires the present Agreement to cease to apply to all or any territories for which such contracting State has international obligations or to any or all Non-Self-Governing territories for which it is responsible. The present Agreement shall, in that case, cease to apply to the territories named in the declaration six months after the receipt thereof by the Secretary-General of the United Nations.

4. The Secretary-General of the United Nations shall communicate to all the Members of the United Nations and to all non-

[4] TS 993; 59 Stat. 1052.

member States referred to in article XI the declarations and notifications received in virtue of the present article, together with the dates of the receipt thereof.

ARTICLE XV

Nothing in this Agreement shall be deemed to prohibit the contracting States from entering into agreements or arrangements with the United Nations or any of its specialized agencies which would provide for facilities, exemptions, privileges or immunities with respect to material emanating from or sponsored by the United Nations or by any of its specialized agencies.

ARTICLE XVI

The original of the present Agreement shall be deposited in the archives of the United Nations and shall be opened for signature at Lake Success on 15 July 1949 where it shall remain open for signature until 31 December 1949. Certified copies of the present Agreement shall be furnished by the Secretary-General of the United Nations to each of the Members of the United Nations and to such other Governments as may be designated by agreement between the Economic and Social Council of the United Nations and the Executive Board of the United Nations Educational, Scientific and Cultural Organization.

IN WITNESS WHEREOF, the undersigned plenipotentiaries, having deposited their full powers found to be in due and proper form, sign the present Agreement in the English and French languages, each being equally authentic, on behalf of their respective Governments, on the dates appearing opposite their respective signatures.

2. Agreement on the Importation of Educational, Scientific and Cultural Materials (Florence Agreement), with Reservation and Annexed Protocol [1]

Agreement and Protocol opened for signature at Lake Success November 22, 1950; Signed on behalf of the United States, June 24, 1959; Ratification advised by the Senate, February 23, 1960; Ratified by the President, October 14, 1966; Ratification of the United States deposited with the Secretary General of the United Nations, November 2, 1966; Proclaimed by the President, November 3, 1966; Entered into force with respect to the United States, November 2, 1966

PREAMBLE

The contracting States,

CONSIDERING that the free exchange of ideas and knowledge and, in general, the widest possible dissemination of the diverse forms of self-expression used by civilizations are vitally important both for intellectual progress and international understanding, and consequently for the maintenance of world peace;

CONSIDERING that this interchange is accomplished primarily by means of books, publications and educational, scientific and cultural materials;

CONSIDERING that the Constitution of the United Nations Educational, Scientific and Cultural Organization urges co-operation between nations in all branches of intellectual activity, including "the exchange of publications, objects of artistic and scientific interest and other materials of information" and provides further that the Organization shall "collaborate in the work of advancing the mutual knowledge and understanding of peoples, though all means of mass communication and to that end recommend such international agreements as may be necessary to promote the flow of ideas by word and image";

RECOGNIZE that these aims will be effectively furthered by an international agreement facilitating the free flow of books, publications and educational, scientific and cultural materials; and

HAVE, THEREFORE, AGREED TO THE FOLLOWING PROVISIONS:

ARTICLE I

1. The contracting States undertake not to apply customs duties or other charges on, or in connection with, the importation of:

(a) Books, publications and documents, listed in annex A to this Agreement;

(b) Educational, scientific and cultural materials, listed in annexes B, C, D and E to this Agreement;

[1] 17 UST 1835; TIAS 6129; 131 UNTS 25. For a list of states which are parties to the Agreement, see Department of State publication, *Treaties in Force*.

which are the products of another contracting State, subject to the conditions laid down in those annexes.

2. The provisions of paragraph 1 of this article shall not prevent any contracting State from levying on imported materials:

(a) Internal taxes or any other internal charges of any kind, imposed at the time of importation or subsequently, not exceeding those applied directly or indirectly to like domestic products;

(b) Fees and charges, other than customs duties, imposed by governmental authorities on, or in connection with, importation, limited in amount to the approximate cost of the services rendered, and representing neither an indirect protection to domestic products nor a taxation of imports for revenue purposes.

Article II

1. The contracting States undertake to grant the necessary licences and/or foreign exchange for the importation of the following articles:

(a) Books and publications consigned to public libraries and collections and to the libraries and collections of public educational, research or cultural institutions;

(b) Official government publications, that is, official parliamentary and administrative documents published in their country of origin;

(c) Books and publications of the United Nations or any of its specialized agencies;

(d) Books and publications received by the United Nations Educational, Scientific and Cultural Organization and distributed free of charge by it or under its supervision;

(e) Publications intended to promote tourist travel outside the country of importation, sent and distributed free of charge;

(f) Articles for the blind:

(i) Books, publications and documents of all kinds in raised characters for the blind;

(ii) Other articles specially designed for the educational, scientific or cultural advancement of the blind, which are imported directly by institutions or organizations concerned with the welfare of the blind, approved by the competent authorities of the importing country for the purpose of duty-free entry of these types of articles.

2. The contracting States which at any time apply quantitative restrictions and exchange control measures undertake to grant, as far as possible, foreign exchange and licenses necessary for the importation of other educational, scientific or cultural materials, and particularly the materials referred to in the annexes to this Agreement.

Article III

1. The contracting States undertake to give every possible facility to the importation of educational, scientific or cultural materials, which are imported exclusively for showing at a public exhibition approved by the competent authorities of the importing country and for subsequent re-exportation. These facilities shall include the

granting of the necessary licenses and exemption from customs duties and internal taxes and charges of all kinds payable on importation, other than fees and charges corresponding to the approximate cost of services rendered.

2. Nothing in this article shall prevent the authorities of an importing country from taking such steps as may be necessary to ensure that the materials in question shall be re-exported at the close of their exhibition.

Article IV

The contracting States undertake that they will as far as possible:

(a) Continue their common efforts to promote by every means the free circulation of educational, scientific or cultural materials, and abolish or reduce any restrictions to that free circulation which are not referred to in this Agreement;

(b) Simplify the administrative procedure governing the importation of educational, scientific or cultural materials;

(c) Facilitate the expeditious and safe customs clearance of educational, scientific or cultural materials.

Article V

Nothing in this Agreement shall affect the right of contracting States to take measures, in conformity with their legislation, to prohibit or limit the importation, or the circulation after importation, of articles on grounds relating directly to national security, public order or public morals.

Article VI

This Agreement shall not modify or affect the laws and regulations of any contracting State or any of its international treaties, conventions, agreements or proclamations, with respect to copyright, trademarks or patents.

Article VII

Subject to the provisions of any previous conventions to which the contracting States may have subscribed for the settlement of disputes, the contracting States undertake to have recourse to negotiations or conciliation, with a view to settlement of any disputes regarding the interpretation or the application of this Agreement.

Article VIII

In case of a dispute between contracting States relating to the educational, scientific or cultural character of imported materials, the interested Parties may, by common agreement, refer it to the Director-General of the United Nations Educational, Scientific and Cultural Organization for an advisory opinion.

Article IX

1. This Agreement, of which the English and French texts are equally authentic, shall bear today's date and remain open for signature by all Member States of the United Nations Educational, Scientific and Cultural Organization, all Member States of the United Nations and any non-member State to which an invitation may have been addressed by the Executive Board of the United Nations Educational, Scientific and Cultural Organization.

2. The Agreement shall be ratified on behalf of the signatory States in accordance with their respective constitutional procedures.

3. The instruments of ratification shall be deposited with the Secretary-General of the United Nations.

Article X

The States referred to in paragraph 1 of article IX may accept this Agreement from 22 November 1950. Acceptance shall become effective on the deposit of a formal instrument with the Secretary-General of the United Nations.

Article XI

This Agreement shall come into force on the date on which the Secretary-General of the United Nations receives instruments of ratification or acceptance from ten States.

Article XII

1. The States Parties to this Agreement on the date of its coming into force shall each take all the necessary measures for its fully effective operation within a period of six months after that date.

2. For States which may deposit their instruments of ratification or acceptance after the date of the Agreement coming into force, these measures shall be taken within a period of three months from the date of deposit.

3. Within one month of the expiration of the periods mentioned in paragraphs 1 and 2 of this article, the contracting States to this Agreement shall submit a report to the United Nations Educational, Scientific and Cultural Organization of the measures which they have taken for such fully effective operation.

4. The United Nations Educational, Scientific and Cultural Organization shall transmit this report to all signatory States to this Agreement and to the International Trade Organization (provisionally, to its Interim Commission).

Article XIII

Any contracting State may, at the time of signature or the deposit of its instrument of ratification or acceptance, or at any time thereafter, declare by notification addressed to the Secretary-General of the United Nations that this Agreement shall extend to all or any of the territories for the conduct of whose foreign relations that contracting State is responsible.

Article XIV

1. Two years after the date of the coming into force of this Agreement, any contracting State may, on its own behalf or on behalf of any of the territories for the conduct of whose foreign relations that contracting State is responsible, denounce this Agreement by an instrument in writing deposited with the Secretary-General of the United Nations.

2. The denunciation shall take effect one year after the receipt of the instrument of denunciation.

Article XV

The Secretary-General of the United Nations shall inform the States referred to in paragraph 1 of Article IX, as well as the United Nations Educational, Scientific and Cultural Organization, and the International Trade Organization (provisionally, its Interim Commission), of the deposit of all the instruments of ratification and acceptance provided for in articles IX and X, as well as of the notifications and denunciations provided for respectively in articles XIII and XIV.

Article XVI

At the request of one-third of the contracting States to this Agreement, the Director-General of the United Nations Educational, Scientific and Cultural Organization shall place on the agenda of the next session of the General Conference of that Organization, the question of convoking a meeting for the revision of this Agreement.

Article XVII

Annexes A, B, C, D, and E, as well as the Protocol annexed to this Agreement are hereby made an integral part of this Agreement.

Article XVIII

1. In accordance with Article 102 of the Charter of the United Nations,[2] this Agreement shall be registered by the Secretary-General of the United Nations on the date of its coming into force.

2. In faith whereof the undersigned, duly authorized, have signed this Agreement on behalf of their respective Governments.

Done at Lake Success, New York, this twenty-second day of November one thousand nine hundred and fifty in a single copy, which shall remain deposited in the archives of the United Nations, and certified true copies of which shall be delivered to all the States referred to in paragraph 1 of article IX, as well as to the United Nations Educational, Scientific and Cultural Organization and to the International Trade Organization (provisionally, to its Interim Commission).

---

[2] TS 993; 59 Stat. 1052.

ANNEX A

BOOKS, PUBLICATIONS AND DOCUMENTS

(i) Printed books.

(ii) Newspapers and periodicals.

(iii) Books and documents produced by duplicating processes other than printing.

(iv) Official government publications, that is, official, parliamentary and administrative documents published in their country of origin.

(v) Travel posters and travel literature (pamphlets, guides, timetables, leaflets and similar publications), whether illustrated or not, including those published by private commercial enterprises, whose purpose is to stimulate travel outside the country of importation.

(vi) Publications whose purpose is to stimulate study outside the country of importation.

(vii) Manuscripts, including typescripts.

(viii) Catalogues of books and publications, being books and publications offered for sale by publishers or booksellers established outside the country of importation.

(ix) Catalogues of films, recordings or other visual and auditory material of an educational, scientific or cultural character, being catalogues issued by or on behalf of the United Nations or any of its specialized agencies.

(x) Music in manuscript or printed form, or reproduced by duplicating processes other than printing.

(xi) Geographical, hydrographical or astronomical maps and charts.

(xii) Architectural, industrial or engineering plans and designs, and reproductions thereof, intended for study in scientific establishments or educational institutions approved by the competent authorities of the importing country for the purpose of duty-free admission of these types of articles.

(The exemptions provided by annex A shall not apply to:

(a) Stationery;

(b) Books, publications and documents (except catalogues, travel posters and travel literature referred to above) published by or for a private commercial enterprise, essentially for advertising purposes;

(c) Newspapers and periodicals in which the advertising matter is in excess of 70 per cent by space;

(d) All other items (except catalogues referred to above) in which the advertising matter is in excess of 25 per cent by space. In the case of travel posters and literature, this percentage shall apply only to private commercial advertising matter.)

ANNEX B

WORKS OF ART AND COLLECTORS' PIECES OF AN EDUCATIONAL, SCIENTIFIC OR CULTURAL CHARACTER

(i) Paintings and drawings, including copies, executed entirely by hand, but excluding manufactured decorated wares.

(ii) Hand-printed impressions, produced from hand-engraved or hand-etched blocks, plates or other material, and signed and numbered by the artist.

(iii) Original works of art of statuary or sculpture, whether in the round, in relief, or in intaglio, excluding mass-produced reproductions and works of conventional craftsmanship of a commercial character.

(iv) Collectors' pieces and objects or art consigned to public galleries, museums and other public institutions, approved by the competent authorities of the importing country for the purpose of duty-free entry of these types of articles, not intended for resale.

(v) Collections and collectors' pieces in such scientific fields as anatomy, zoology, botany, mineralogy, palaeontology, archaeology and ethnography, not intended for resale.

(vi) Antiques, being articles in excess of 100 years of age.

ANNEX C

VISUAL AND AUDITORY MATERIALS OF AN EDUCATIONAL, SCIENTIFIC OR CULTURAL CHARACTER

(i) Films, filmstrips, microfilms, and slides of an educational, scientific or cultural character, when imported by organizations (including, at the discretion of the importing country, broadcasting organizations), approved by the competent authorities of the importing country for the purpose of duty-free admission of these types of articles, exclusively for exhibition by these organizations or by other public or private educational, scientific or cultural institutions or societies approved by the aforesaid authorities.

(ii) Newsreels (with or without sound track), depicting events of current news value at the time of importation, and imported in either negative form, exposed and developed, or positive form, printed and developed, when imported by organizations (including, at the discretion of the importing country, broadcasting organizations) approved by the competent authorities of the importing country for the purpose of duty-free admission of such films, provided that free entry may be limited to two copies of each subject for copying purposes.

(iii) Sound recordings of an educational, scientific or cultural character for use exclusively in public or private educational, scientific or cultural institutions or societies (including, at the discretion of the importing country, broadcasting organizations) approved by the competent authorities of the importing country for the purpose of duty-free admission of these types of articles.

(iv) Films, filmstrips, microfilms and sound recordings of an educational, scientific or cultural character produced by the United Nations or any of its specialized agencies.

(v) Patterns, models and wall charts for use exclusively for demonstrating and teaching purposes in public or private educational, scientific or cultural institutions approved by the competent authorities of the importing country for the purpose of duty-free admission of these types of articles.

Annex D

Scientific Instruments or Apparatus

Scientific instruments or apparatus, intended exclusively for educational purposes or pure scientific research, provided:

(a) That such scientific instruments or apparatus are consigned to public or private scientific or educational institutions approved by the competent authorities of the importing country for the purpose of duty-free entry of these types of articles, and used under the control and responsibility of these institutions;

(b) That instruments or apparatus of equivalent scientific value are not being manufactured in the country of importation.

Annex E

Articles for the Blind

(i) Books, publications and documents of all kinds in raised characters for the blind.

(ii) Other articles specially designed for the educational, scientific or cultural advancement of the blind, which are imported directly by institutions or organizations concerned with the welfare of the blind, approved by the competent authorities of the importing country for the purpose of duty-free entry of these types of articles.

Protocol Annexed to the Agreement on the Importation of Educational, Scientific and Cultural Materials

The contracting States,

In the interest of facilitating the participation of the United States of America in the Agreement on the Importation of Educational, Scientific and Cultural Materials, have agreed to the following:

1. The United States of America shall have the option of ratifying this Agreement, under article IX, or of accepting it, under article X, with the inclusion of the reservation hereunder.

2. In the event of the United States of America becoming Party to this Agreement with the reservation provided for in the preceding paragraph 1, the provisions of that reservation may be invoked by the Government of the United States of America with regard to any of the contracting States to this Agreement, or by any contracting State with regard to the United States of America, provided that any measure imposed pursuant to such reservation shall be applied on a non-discriminatory basis.

(TEXT OF THE RESERVATION)

(a) *If, as a result of the obligations incurred by a contracting State under this Agreement, any product covered by this Agreement is being imported into the territory of a contracting State in such relatively increased quantities and under such conditions as to cause or threaten serious injury to the domestic industry in that territory producing like or directly competitive products, the contracting State, under the conditions provided for by paragraph 2 above, shall be free, in respect of such product and to the extent and for such time as may be necessary to prevent or remedy such injury, to suspend, in whole or in part, any obligation under this Agreement with respect to such product.*

(b) *Before any contracting State shall take action pursuant to the provisions of paragraph* (a) *above, it shall give notice in writing to the United Nations Educational, Scientific and Cultural Organization as far in advance as may be practicable and shall afford the Organization and the contracting States which are Parties to this Agreement an opportunity to consult with it in respect of the proposed action.*

(c) *In critical circumstances where delay would cause damage which it would be difficult to repair, action under paragraph* (a) *above may be taken provisionally without prior consultation, on the condition that consultation be effected immediately after taking such action.*

3. Protocol to the Agreement on the Importation of Educational, Scientific and Cultural Materials [1]

Adopted at Nairobi November 26, 1976; Opened for signature at the United Nations March 1, 1977; Signed on behalf of the United States, October 25, 1982; Ratification of the United States deposited with the Secretary General of the United Nations, May 5, 1989; Entered into force with respect to the United States, November 15, 1989

The contracting States parties to the Agreement on the Importation of Educational Scientific and Cultural Materials, adopted by the General Conference of the United Nations Educational, Scientific and Cultural Organization at its fifth session held in Florence in 1950,

REAFFIRMING the principles on which the Agreement, hereinafter called "the Agreement," is based,

CONSIDERING that this Agreement has proved to be an effective instrument in lowering customs barriers and reducing other economic restrictions that impede the exchange of ideas and knowledge,

CONSIDERING, nevertheless, that in the quarter of a century following the adoption of the Agreement, technical progress has changed the ways and means of transmitting information and knowledge, which is the fundamental objective of that Agreement,

CONSIDERING, further, that the developments that have taken place in the field of international trade during this period have, in general, been reflected in greater freedom of exchanges,

CONSIDERING that since the adoption of the Agreement, the international situation has changed radically owing to the development of the international community, in particular through accession of many States to independence,

CONSIDERING that the needs and concerns of the developing countries should be taken into consideration, with a view to giving them easier and less costly access to education, science, technology and culture,

RECALLING the provisions of the Convention on the means of prohibiting and preventing the illicit import, export and transfer of ownership of cultural property, adopted by the General Conference of UNESCO in 1970, and those of the Convention concerning the protection of the world cultural and natural heritage, adopted by the General Conference in 1972,

RECALLING, moreover, the customs conventions concluded under the auspices of the Custom Co-operation Council, in consultation

[1] Senate Treaty Doc. 97–2. This Protocol amends and substantially expands the Agreement on the Importation of Educational Scientific and Cultural Materials (Florence Agreement) by (1) extending the exemption from customs duties to additional materials listed in nine Annexes; (2) by providing optional provisions regarding internal charges or taxes on certain products; and (3) by providing an optional provision (in Part IV) for the furnishing of import licenses and foreign exchange for additional items not previously covered.

with the United Nations Educational, Scientific and Cultural Organization, concerning the temporary importation of educational, scientific and cultural materials,

CONVINCED that the new arrangements should be made and that such arrangements will contribute even more effectively to the development of education, science and culture which constitute the essential bases of economic and social progress,

RECALLING resolution 4.112 adopted by the General Conference of UNESCO at its eighteenth session,

HAVE AGREED AS FOLLOWS:

I

1. The contracting States undertake to extend to the materials listed in annexes A, B, D, and E and also, where the annexes in question have not been the subject of a declaration under the paragraph 16(a) below, annexes C.1, F, G and H, to the present Protocol exemption from customs duties and other charges on, or in connection with their importation, as set out in article I, Paragraph 1, of the Agreement, provided such materials fulfill the conditions laid down in these annexes and are the products of another contracting State.

2. The provisions of paragraph 1 of this Protocol shall not prevent any contracting State from levying on imported materials:

(a) internal taxes or any other internal charges of any kind, imposed at the time of importation or subsequently, not exceeding those applied directly or indirectly to like domestic products;

(b) fees and charges, other than customs duties, imposed by governmental or administrative authorities on, or in connection with, importation, limited in amount to the approximate cost of the services rendered, and representing neither an indirect protection to domestic products nor a taxation of imports for revenue purposes.

II

3. Notwithstanding paragraph 2(a) of this Protocol, the contracting States undertake not to levy on the materials listed below any internal taxes or other internal charges of any kind, imposed at the time of importation or subsequently:

(a) books and publications consigned to the libraries referred to in paragraph 5 of this Protocol;

(b) official, parliamentary and administrative documents published in their country of origin:

(c) books and publications of the United Nations or any of its specialized agencies;

(d) books and publications received by the United Nations Educational, Scientific and Cultural Organization and distributed free of charge by it or under its supervision;

(e) publications intended to promote tourist travel outside the country of importation, sent and distributed free of charge;

(f) articles for the blind and other physically and mentally handicapped persons:

(i) books, publications and documents of all kinds in raised characters for the blind;

(ii) other articles specially designed for the educational, scientific or cultural advancement of the blind and other physically or mentally handicapped persons which are imported directly by institutions or organizations concerned with the education of, or assistance to the blind and other physically or mentally handicapped persons approved by the competent authorities of the importing country for the purpose of duty-free entry of these types of articles.

III

4. The contracting States undertake not to levy on the articles and materials referred to in the annexes to this Protocol any customs duties, export duties or duties levied on goods leaving the country, or other internal taxes of any kind, levied on such articles and materials when they are intended for export to other contracting States.

IV

5. The contracting States undertake to extend the granting of the necessary licenses and/or foreign exchange provided for in article II, paragraph 1, of the Agreement, to the importation of the following materials:

(a) books and publications consigned to libraries serving the public interest, including the following:

(i) national libraries and other major research libraries;

(ii) general and specialized academic libraries, including university libraries, college libraries, institute libraries and university extra-mural libraries;

(iii) public libraries;

(iv) school libraries;

(v) special libraries serving a group of readers who form an entity, having particular and identifiable subjects of interest, such as government libraries, public authority libraries, industrial libraries, and libraries of professional bodies;

(vi) libraries for the handicapped and for readers who are unable to move around, such as libraries for the blind, hospital libraries and prison libraries;

(vii) music libraries, including record libraries;

(b) books adopted or recommended as textbooks in higher educational establishments and imported by such establishments;

(c) books in foreign languages, with the exception of books in the principle native language or languages of the importing country;

(d) films, slides, video-tapes and sound recordings of an educational, scientific or cultural nature, imported by organizations approved by the competent authorities of the importing country for the purpose of duty-free entry of these types of articles.

V

6. The contracting States undertake to extend the granting of the facilities provided for in article III of the Agreement to materials and furniture imported exclusively for showing at a public exhibition of objects of an educational, scientific or cultural nature approved by the competent authorities of the importing country and for subsequent re-exportation.

7. Nothing in the foregoing paragraph shall prevent the authorities of an importing country from taking such steps as may be necessary to ensure that the materials and furniture in question will in fact be re-exported at the close of the exhibition.

VI

8. The contracting States undertake:

(a) to extend to the importation of the articles covered by the present Protocol the provisions of article IV of the Agreement;

(b) to encourage through appropriate measures the free flow and distribution of educational, scientific and cultural objects and materials produced in the developing countries.

VII

9. Nothing in this Protocol shall affect the right of contracting States to take measures, in conformity with their legislation, to prohibit or limit the importation of articles, or their circulation after importation, on grounds relating directly to national security, public order or public morals.

10. Notwithstanding other provisions of this Protocol, a developing country, which is defined as such by the practice established by the General Assembly of the United Nations and which is a party to the Protocol, may suspend or limit the obligations under this Protocol relating to importation of any object or material if such importation causes or threatens to cause serious injury to the nascent indigenous industry in that developing country. The country concerned shall implement such action in an non-discriminatory manner. It shall notify the Director-General of the United Nations Educational, Scientific and Cultural Organization of any such action, as far as practicable in advance of implementation, and the Director-General of the United Nations Educational, Scientific and Cultural Organization shall notify all Parties to the Protocol.

11. This Protocol shall not modify or affect the laws and regulations of any contracting State or any of its international treaties, conventions, agreements or proclamations, with respect to copyright, trade marks or patents.

12. Subject to the provisions of any previous conventions to which they may have subscribed for the settlements of disputes, the contracting States undertake to have recourse to negotiation or conciliation with a view to settlement of any disputes regarding the interpretation of application of this Protocol.

13. In case of a dispute between contracting States relating to the educational, scientific or cultural character of imported materials, the interested parties may, by common agreement refer it to the Director-General of the United Nations Educational, Scientific and Cultural Organization for an advisory opinion.

VIII

14. (a) This Protocol, of which the English and French texts are equally authentic, shall bear today's date and shall be open to signature by all States Parties to the Agreement, as well as by customs or economic unions, provided that all the member States constituting them are also Parties to the Protocol.

The term "State" or "Country" as used in this Protocol, or in the Protocol referred to in paragraph 18, shall be taken to refer also, as the context may require, to the customs or economics unions and, in all matters which fall within their competence with regard to the scope of this Protocol, to the whole of the territories of the member States which constitute them, and not to the territory of each of those States.

It is understood that, in becoming a contracting Party to this Protocol, such customs or economics unions will also apply the provisions of the Agreement on the same basis as is provided in the preceding paragraph with respect to the Protocol.

(b) This Protocol shall be subject to ratification or acceptance by the signatory States in accordance with their respective constitutional procedures.

(c) The instruments of ratification or acceptance shall be deposited with the Secretary-General of the United Nations.

15. (a) The States referred to in paragraph 14(a) which are not signatories of this Protocol may accede to this Protocol.

(b) Accession shall be effected by the deposit of a formal instrument with the Secretary-General of the United Nations.

16. (a) The States referred to in paragraph 14 (a) of this Protocol may, at the time of signature, ratification, acceptance, or accession, declare that they will not be bound by part II, part IV, annex C.1, annex F, annex G, and annex H, or by any of those parts or annexes. They may also declare that they will not be bound by annex C.1 only in respect of contracting States which have themselves accepted that annex.

(b) Any contracting State which has made such a declaration may withdraw it, in whole or in part, at any timely notification to the Secretary-General of the United Nations, specifying the date on which such withdrawal takes effect.

(c) States which have declared, in accordance with subparagraph (a) of this paragraph, that they will not be bound by annex C.1 shall necessarily be bound by annex C.2. Those which have declared that they will be bound by annex C.1 only in respect of contracting States which have themselves accepted that annex shall necessarily be bound by annex C.2 in respect of contracting States which have not accepted annex C.1.

17. (a) This Protocol shall come into force six months after the date of deposit of the fifth instrument of ratification, acceptance, or accession with the Secretary-General of the United Nations.

(b) It shall come into force for every other State six months after the date of the deposit of its instrument of ratification, acceptance or accession.

(c) Within one month following the expiration of the periods mentioned in subparagraphs (a) and (b) of this paragraph, the contracting States to this Protocol shall submit a report to the United

Nations Educational, Scientific and Cultural Organization on the measures which they have taken to give full effect to the Protocol.

(d) The United Nations Educational, Scientific, and Cultural Organization shall transmit these reports to all States Parties to this Protocol.

18. The Protocol annexed to the Agreement, and made an integral part thereof, as provided for in article XVII of the Agreement, is hereby made an integral part of this Protocol and shall apply to obligations incurred under this Protocol and to products covered by this Protocol.

19. (a) Two years after the date of the coming into force of this Protocol, any contracting State may denounce this Protocol by an instrument in writing deposited with the Secretary-General of the United Nations.

(b) The denunciation shall take effect one year after the receipt of the instrument of denunciation.

(c) Denunciation of the Agreement pursuant to article XIV thereof shall automatically imply denunciation of this Protocol.

20. The Secretary-General of the United Nations shall inform the States referred to in paragraph 14(a), as well as the United Nations Educational, Scientific and Cultural Organization, of the deposit of all the instruments of ratification, acceptance or accession referred to in paragraphs 14 and 15; of declarations made and withdrawn under paragraph 16 of the dates of entry into force of this Protocol in accordance with paragraph 17 (a) and (b); and of the denunciations provided for in paragraph 19.

21. (a) This Protocol may be revised by the General Conference of the United Nations Educational, Scientific and Cultural Organization. Any such revision, however, shall be binding only upon States that become parties to the revising Protocol.

(b) Should the General Conference adopt a new protocol revising this Protocol either totally or in part, and unless the new protocol provides otherwise, the present Protocol shall cease to be open to signature, ratification, acceptance or accession as from the date of the coming into force of the new revising protocol.

22. This Protocol shall not change or modify the Agreement.

23. Annexes A, B, C.1, C.2, D, E, F, G and H are hereby made an integral part of this Protocol.

24. In accordance with Article 102 of the Charter of the United Nations, this Protocol shall be registered by the Secretary-General of the United Nations on the date of its coming into force.

IN FAITH WHEREOF the undersigned, duly authorized, have signed this Protocol on behalf of their respective Governments.

DONE at United Nations Headquarters, New York, this first day of March one thousand nine hundred and seventy-seven, in a single copy.

ANNEX A

Books, publications and documents

(i) Printed books, irrespective of the language in which they are printed and whatever amount of space given over to illustrations, including the following:

(a) luxury editions;

(b) books printed abroad from the manuscript of an author resident in the importing country;

(c) children's drawing and painting books;

(d) school exercise books (workbooks) with printed texts and blank spaces to be filled in by the pupils;

(e) crossword puzzle books containing printed texts;

(f) loose illustrations and printed pages in the form of loose or bound sheets and reproduction proofs or reproductions films to be used for the production of books.

(ii) Printed documents or reports of an non-commercial character.

(iii) Microforms of the articles listed under items (i) and (ii) of this annex, as well as of those listed under items (i) to (vi) of annex A to the Agreement.

(iv) Catalogues of films, recordings or other visual and auditory material of a educational, scientific or cultural character.

(v) Maps and charts of interest in scientific fields such as geology, zoology, botany, mineralogy, palaeontology, archaeology, ethnology, meteorology, climatology and geophysics, and also meteorological and geophysical diagrams.

(vi) Architectural, industrial or engineering plans and designs and reproductions thereof.

(vii) Bibliographical information material for distribution free of charge.

ANNEX B

Works of art and collectors' pieces of an educational, scientific or cultural character

(i) Paintings and drawings, whatever the nature of the materials on which they have been executed entirely by hand, including copies executed by hand, but excluding manufactured decorated wares.

(ii) Ceramics and mosaics on wood, being original works of art.

(iii) Collectors' pieces and objects of art consigned to galleries, museums and other institutions approved by the competent authorities of the importing country for the purpose of duty-free entry of those types of materials, on condition they are not resold.

ANNEX C.1

Visual and auditory materials

(i) Films,[2] filmstrips, microforms and slides.

(ii) Sound recordings.

(iii) Patterns, models and wall charts of an educational, scientific or cultural character, except toy models.

(iv) Other visual and auditory materials, such as:

(a) video-tapes, kinescopes, video-discs, videograms and other forms of visual and sound recordings;

(b) microcards, microfiches and magnetic or other information storage media required in computerized information and documentation services;

[2] The duty-free entry of exposed and developed cinematographic films for public commercial exhibition or sale may be limited to negatives, it being understood that this limitation shall not apply to films (including newsreels) when admitted duty-free under the provisions of annex C.2 to this Protocol.

(c) materials for programmed instruction, which may be presented in kit form, with the corresponding printed materials, including video-cassettes and audio-cassettes;

(d) transparencies, including those intended for direct projection or for viewing through optical devices;

(e) holograms for laser projection;

(f) mock-ups or visualizations of abstract concepts such as molecular structures or mathematical formulae;

(g) multi-media kits;

(h) materials for the promotion of tourism, including those produced by private concerns, designed to encourage the public to travel outside the country of importation.

The exemptions provided for in the present annex C.1 shall not apply to:

(a) unused microform stock and unused visual and auditory recording media and their specific packaging such as cassettes, cartridges, reels;

(b) visual and auditory recordings with the exception of materials for the promotion of tourism covered by paragraph (iv) (h), produced by or for a private commercial enterprise, essentially for advertising purposes;

(c) visual and auditory recordings in which the advertising matter is in excess of 25 percent by time. In the case of materials for the promotion of tourism covered by paragraph (iv) (h), this percentage applies only to private commercial publicity.

ANNEX C.2

Visual and auditory materials of an educational, scientific or cultural character

Visual and auditory materials of an educational, scientific, or cultural character, when imported by organizations (including, at the discretion of the importing country, broadcasting and television organizations) or by any other public or private institution or association, approved by the competent authorities of the importing country for the purpose of duty-free admission of these types of materials or when produced by the United Nations or any of its specialized agencies and including the following:

(i) films, filmstrips, microfilms and slides;

(ii) newsreels (with or without sound track) depicting events of current news value at the time of importation, and imported in either negative form, exposed and developed, or positive form, printed and developed, it being understood that duty free entry may be limited to two copies of each subject for copying purposes;

(iii) archival film materials (with or without sound track) intended for use in connection with newsreel films;

(iv) recreational films particularly suited for children and youth;

(v) sound recordings;

(vi) video-tapes, kinescopes, video-discs, videograms and other forms of visual and sound recordings;

(vii) microcards, microfiches and magnetic or other information storage media required in computerized information and documentation services;

(viii) materials for programmed instruction, which may be presented in kit form, with the corresponding printed materials, including video-cassettes and audio-cassettes;

(ix) transparencies, including those intended for direct projection or for viewing through optical devices;

(x) holograms for laser projection;

(xi) mock-ups or visualizations of abstract concepts such as molecular structures or mathematical formulae;

(xii) multi-media kits.

ANNEX D

Scientific instruments or apparatus

(i) Scientific instruments or apparatus, provided:

(a) that they are consigned to public or private scientific or educational institutions approved by the competent authorities of the importing country for the purposes of duty-free entry of these types of articles, and used for non-commercial purposes under the control and responsibility of these institutions;

(b) that instruments or apparatus of equivalent scientific value are not being manufactured in the country of importation.

(ii) Spare parts, components or accessories specifically matching scientific instruments or apparatus, provided these spare parts, components or accessories are imported at the same time as such instruments and apparatus, or if imported subsequently, that they are identifiable as intended for instruments or apparatus previously admitted duty-free or entitled to duty-free entry.

(iii) Tools to be used for the maintenance, checking, gauging, or repair of scientific instruments, provided these tools are imported at the same time as such instruments and apparatus or, if imported subsequently, that they are identifiable as intended for the specific instruments or apparatus previously admitted duty-free or entitled to duty-free entry, and further provided that tools of equivalent scientific value are not being manufactured in the country of importation.

ANNEX E

Articles for the blind and other handicapped persons

(i) All articles specially designed for the educational, scientific or cultural advancement of the blind which are imported directly by institutions or organizations concerned with the education of, or assistance to, the blind, approved by the competent authorities of the importing country for the purpose of duty-free entry of these types of articles, including:

(a) talking books (discs, cassettes or other sound reproductions) and large-print books;

(b) phonographs and cassette players, specially designed or adapted for the blind and other handicapped persons and required to play the talking books;

(c) equipment for the reading of normal print by the blind and partially sighted, such as electronic reading machines, television-enlargers and optical aids;

(d) equipment for the mechanical or computerized production of braille and recorded material, such as stereo-typing machines, electronic braille, transfer and pressing machines; braille computer terminals and displays;

(e) braille paper, magnetic tapes and cassettes for the production of braille and talking books;

(f) aids for improving the mobility of the blind, such as electronic orientation and obstacle detection appliances and white canes;

(g) technical aids for the education, rehabilitation, vocational training and employment of the blind, such as braille watches, braille typewriters, teaching and learning aids, games and other instruments specifically adapted for the use of the blind.

(ii) All materials specially designed for the education, employment and social advancement of other physically or mentally handicapped persons, directly imported by institutions or organizations concerned with the education of, or assistance to, such persons, approved by the competent authorities of the importing country for the purpose of duty-free entry of these types of articles, provided that equivalent objects are not being manufactured in the importing country.

ANNEX F

Sports equipment

Sports equipment intended exclusively for amateur sports associations or groups approved by the competent authorities of the importing country for the purpose of duty-free entry of these types of articles, provided that equivalent materials are not being manufactured in the importing country.

ANNEX G

Musical instruments and other musical equipment

Musical instruments and other musical equipment intended solely for cultural institutions or music schools approved by the competent authorities of the importing country for the purpose of duty-free entry of these types of articles, provided that equivalent instruments and other equipment are not being manufactured in the importing country.

ANNEX H

Material and machines used for the production of books, publications and documents

(i) Material used for the production of books, publications and documents (paper pulp, recycled paper, newsprint, and other types of paper used for printing, printing inks, glue, etc.).

(ii) Machines for the processing of paper pulp and paper and also printing and binding machines, provided that machines of equivalent technical quality are not being manufactured in the importing country.

I hereby certify that the foregoing text is a true copy of the Protocol to the Agreement on the Importation of Educational, Scientific and Cultural Materials, adopted by the General Conference of the United Nations Educational, Scientific and Cultural Organization at its nineteenth session held at Nairobi from 26 October 1976 to 30 November 1976, the original of which is deposited with the Secretary-General of the United Nations.

For the Secretary-General: The Legal Counsel.

UNITED NATIONS, *New York, March 1, 1977.*

F. ARMS CONTROL AND DISARMAMENT

CONTENTS

1. Limits on Nuclear Testing

a. Limited Nuclear Test Ban Treaty [1]

Treaty Banning Nuclear Weapon Tests in the Atmosphere, in Outer Space and Under Water; Done at Moscow, U.S.S.R., on August 5, 1963; Ratification advised by the Senate September 24, 1963; Ratified by the President of the United States October 7, 1963; Ratifications of the Governments of the United States, the United Kingdom of Great Britain and Northern Ireland, and the Union of Soviet Socialist Republics deposited with the said Governments at Washington, London, and Moscow October 10, 1963; Proclaimed by the President October 10, 1963; Entered into force October 10, 1963

The Governments of the United States of America, the United Kingdom of Great Britain and Northern Ireland, and the Union of Soviet Socialist Republics, hereinafter referred to as the "Original Parties",

PROCLAIMING as their principal aim the speediest possible achievement of an agreement on general and complete disarmament under strict international control in accordance with the objectives of the United Nations which would put an end to the armaments race and eliminate the incentive to the production and testing of all kinds of weapons, including nuclear weapons,

SEEKING to achieve the discontinuance of all test explosions of nuclear weapons for all time, determined to continue negotiations to this end, and desiring to put an end to the contamination of man's environment by radioactive substances,

HAVE AGREED AS FOLLOWS:

ARTICLE I

1. Each of the Parties to this Treaty undertakes to prohibit, to prevent, and not to carry out any nuclear weapon test explosion, or any other nuclear explosions at any place under its jurisdiction or control:

(a) in the atmosphere; beyond its limits, including outer space; or underwater, including territorial waters or high seas; or

(b) in any other environment if such explosion causes radioactive debris to be present outside the territorial limits of the State under whose jurisdiction or control such explosion is conducted.

It is understood in this connection that the provisions of this subparagraph are without prejudice to the conclusion of a treaty resulting in the permanent banning of all nuclear test explosions, including all such explosions underground, the conclusion of which,

[1] 14 UST 1313; TIAS 5433; 480 UNTS 43. For a list of states which are parties to the Treaty, see Department of State publication, *Treaties in Force*.

as the Parties have stated in the Preamble to this Treaty, they seek to achieve.

2. Each of the Parties to this Treaty undertakes furthermore to refrain from causing, encouraging, or in any way participating in, the carrying out of any nuclear weapon test explosion, or any other nuclear explosion, anywhere which would take place in any of the environments described, or have the effect referred to, in paragraph 1 of this Article.

ARTICLE II

1. Any Party may propose amendments to this Treaty. The text of any proposed amendment shall be submitted to the Depositary Governments which shall circulate it to all Parties to this Treaty. Thereafter, if requests to do so by one-third or more of the Parties, the Depositary Governments shall convene a conference to which they shall invite all the Parties, to consider such amendment.

2. Any amendment to this Treaty must be approved by a majority of the votes of all the Parties to this Treaty, including the votes of all of the Original Parties. The amendment shall enter into force for all Parties upon the deposit of instruments of ratification by a majority of all the Parties, including the instruments of ratification of all of the Original Parties.

ARTICLE III

1. This Treaty shall be open to all States for signature. Any State which does not sign this Treaty before its entry into force in accordance with paragraph 3 of this Article may accede to it at any time.

2. This Treaty shall be subject to ratification by signatory States. Instruments of ratification and instruments of accession shall be deposited with the Governments of the Original Parties—the United States of America, the United Kingdom of Great Britain and Northern Ireland, and the Union of Soviet Socialist Republics—which are hereby designated the Depositary Governments.

3. This Treaty shall enter into force after its ratification by all the Original Parties and the deposit of their instruments of ratification.

4. For States whose instruments of ratification or accession are deposited subsequent to the entry into force of this Treaty, it shall enter into force on the date of the deposit of their instruments of ratification or accession.

5. The Depositary Governments shall promptly inform all signatory and acceding States of the date of each signature, the date of deposit of each instrument of ratification of and accession to this Treaty, the date of its entry into force, and the date of receipt of any requests for conferences or other notices.

6. This Treaty shall be registered by the Depositary Governments pursuant to Article 102 of the Charter of the United Nations.

ARTICLE IV

This Treaty shall be of unlimited duration.

Each Party shall in exercising its national sovereignty have the right to withdraw from the Treaty if it decides that extraordinary events, related to the subject matter of this Treaty, have jeopardized the supreme interests of its country. It shall give notice of such withdrawal to all other Parties to the Treaty three months in advance.

ARTICLE V

This Treaty, of which the English and Russian texts are equally authentic, shall be deposited in the archives of the Depositary Governments. Duly certified copies of this Treaty shall be transmitted by the Depositary Governments to the Governments of the signatory and acceding States.

IN WITNESS WHEREOF the undersigned, duly authorized, have signed this Treaty.

DONE in triplicate at the city of Moscow the fifth day of August, one thousand nine hundred and sixty-three.

b. Threshold Test Ban Treaty and the Protocol Thereto

Treaty Between the United States and the Union of Soviet Socialist Republics on the Limitation of Underground Nuclear Weapon Tests; Done at Moscow, U.S.S.R., July 3, 1974; Ratification advised by the Senate, September 25, 1990; President ratified, December 8, 1990; Ratifications exchanged and entered into force, December 11, 1990

The United States of America and the Union of Soviet Socialist Republics, hereinafter referred to as the Parties,

DECLARING their intention to achieve at the earliest possible date the cessation of the nuclear arms race and to take effective measures toward reductions in strategic arms, nuclear disarmament, and general and complete disarmament under strict and effective international control,

RECALLING the determination expressed by the Parties to the 1963 Treaty Banning Nuclear Weapon Tests in the Atmosphere, in Outer Space and Under Water in its Preamble to seek to achieve the discontinuance of all test explosions of nuclear weapons for all time, and to continue negotiations to this end,

NOTING that the adoption of measures for the further limitation of underground nuclear weapon tests would contribute to the achievement of these objectives and would meet the interests of strengthening peace and the further relaxation of international tension,

REAFFIRMING their adherence to the objectives and principles of the Treaty Banning Nuclear Weapon Tests in the Atmosphere, in Outer Space and Under Water and of the Treaty of the Non-Proliferation of Nuclear Weapons,

HAVE AGREED AS FOLLOWS:

ARTICLE I

1. Each Party undertakes to prohibit, to prevent, and not to carry out any underground nuclear weapon test having a yield exceeding 150 kilotons at any place under its jurisdiction or control, beginning March 31, 1976.

2. Each Party shall limit the number of its underground nuclear weapon tests to a minimum.

3. The Parties shall continue their negotiations with a view toward achieving a solution to the problem of the cessation of all underground nuclear weapon tests.

ARTICLE II

1. For the purpose of providing assurance of compliance with the provisions of this Treaty, each Party shall use national technical means of verification at its disposal in a manner consistent with the generally recognized principles of international law.

2. Each Party undertakes not to interfere with the national technical means of verification of the other Party operating in accordance with paragraph 1 of this Article.

3. To promote the objectives and implementation of the provisions of this Treaty the Parties shall, as necessary, consult with each other, make inquiries and furnish information in response to such inquiries.

ARTICLE III

The provisions of this Treaty do not extend to underground nuclear explosions carried out by the Parties for peaceful purposes. Underground nuclear explosions for peaceful purposes shall be governed by an agreement which is to be negotiated and concluded by the Parties at the earliest possible time.

ARTICLE IV

This Treaty shall be subject to ratification in accordance with the constitutional procedures of each Party. This Treaty shall enter into force on the day of the exchange of instruments of ratification.

ARTICLE V

1. This Treaty shall remain in force for a period of five years. Unless replaced earlier by an agreement in implementation of the objectives specified in paragraph 3 of Article I of this Treaty, it shall be extended for successive five-year periods unless either Party notifies the other of its termination no later than six months prior to the expiration of the Treaty. Before the expiration of this period the Parties may, as necessary, hold consultations to consider the situation relevant to the substance of this treaty and to introduce possible amendments to the text of the Treaty.

2. Each Party shall, in exercising its national sovereignty, have the right to withdraw from this Treaty if it decides that extraordinary events related to the subject matter of this Treaty have jeopardized its supreme interests. It shall give notice of its decision to the other Party six months prior to withdrawal from this Treaty. Such notice shall include a statement of the extraordinary events the notifying Party regards as having jeopardized its supreme interests.

3. This Treaty shall be registered pursuant to Article 102 of the Charter of the United Nations.

DONE at Moscow on July 3, 1974, in duplicate, in the English and Russian languages, both texts being equally authentic.

PROTOCOL TO THE TREATY BETWEEN THE UNITED STATES OF AMERICA AND THE UNION OF SOVIET SOCIALIST REPUBLICS ON THE LIMITATION OF UNDERGROUND NUCLEAR WEAPON TESTS

The United States of America and the Union of Soviet Socialist Republics, hereinafter referred to as the Parties,

CONFIRMING the provisions of the Treaty Between the United States of America and the Union of Soviet Socialist Republics on the Limitation of Underground Nuclear Weapon Tests of July 3, 1974, hereinafter referred to as the Treaty,

CONVINCED of the necessity to ensure effective verification of compliance with the Treaty,

HAVE AGREED AS FOLLOWS:

SECTION I. DEFINITIONS

For the purposes of this Protocol:

1. The term "test site" means a geographical area for the conduct of underground nuclear weapon tests, specified in paragraph 2 of Section II of this Protocol.

2. The term "underground nuclear weapon test," hereinafter "test," means either a single underground nuclear explosion conducted at a test site, or two or more underground explosions conducted at a test site within an area delineated by a circle having a diameter of two kilometers and conducted within a total period of time of 0.1 second. The yield of a test shall be the aggregate yield of all explosions in the test.

3. The term "explosion" means the release of nuclear energy from an explosive canister.

4. The term "explosive canister" means, with respect to every explosion, the container or covering for one or more nuclear explosives.

5. The term "Testing Party" means the Party conducting a test.

6. The term "Verifying Party" means the Party entitled to carry out, in accordance with this Protocol, activities related to verification of compliance with the Treaty by the Testing Party.

7. The term "Designated Personnel" means personnel appointed by the Verifying Party form among its nationals and included on its list of Designated Personnel, in accordance with Section IX of the Protocol, to carry out activities related to verification in accordance with this Protocol in the territory of the Testing Party.

8. The term "Transport Personnel" means personnel appointed by the Verifying Party from among its nationals and included on its list of Transport Personnel, in accordance with Section IX of this Protocol, to provide transportation for Designated Personnel, their baggage and equipment of the Verifying Party between the territory of the Verifying Party and the point of entry in the territory of the Testing Party.

9. The term "point of entry" means Washington, D.C. (Dulles International Airport), for Designated Personnel and Transport Personnel, and Travis Air Force Base, California, for Designated Personnel and Transport Personnel and for equipment specified in Section VIII of this Protocol, with respect to the United States of America; and Moscow (Sheremetyevo–2 International Airport) for Designated Personnel and Transport Personnel and for equipment specified in Section VIII of this Protocol, and Leningrad (Pulkovo–2 International Airport) for Designated Personnel and Transport Personnel, with respect to the Union of Soviet Socialist Republics. Other locations may serve as points of entry for specific tests, as agreed by the Parties.

10. The term "hydrodynamic yield measurement method" means the method whereby the yield of a test is derived from on-site, direct measurement of the properties of the shock wave as a function of time during the hydrodynamic phase of the ground motion produced by the test.

11. The term "seismic measurement yield method" means the method whereby the yield of a test is derived from measurement of parameters of elastic ground motion produced by the test.

12. The term "on-site inspection" means activities carried out by the Verifying Party at the test site of the Testing Party, in accordance with Section VII of this Protocol, for the purposes of independently obtaining data on conditions under which the test will be conducted and for confirming the validity of data provided by the Testing Party.

13. The term "emplacement hole" means any drill-hole, shaft, adit or tunnel in which one or more explosive canisters, associated cables, and other equipment are installed for the purposes of conducting a test.

14. The term "end of the emplacement hole" means the reference point established by the Testing Party beyond the planned location of each explosive canister along the axis of the emplacement hole.

15. The term "satellite hole" means any drill-hole, shaft, adit or tunnel in which sensing elements and cables and transducers are installed by the Verifying Party for the purposes of hydrodynamic measurement of the yield of a specific test.

16. The term "standard configuration" means either the standard vertical configuration or the standard horizontal configuration of a test described in paragraph 2 or 3 of Section V of this Protocol.

17. The term "non-standard configuration" means a configuration of a test different from that described in paragraph 2 or 3 of Section V of this Protocol.

18. The term "hydrodynamic measurement zone" means a region, the dimensions of which are specified in paragraph 1 of Section V of this Protocol, within which hydrodynamic yield measurements are carried out.

19. The term "reference test" means a test, identified by the Testing Party as a reference test, that meets the requirements of paragraph 8 of Section V of this Protocol.

20. The term "emplacement point" means the point in the emplacement hole that coincides with the center point of an emplaced explosive canister.

21. The term "choke section" means a barrier designed to restrict the flow of energy form an explosive canister.

22. The term "area of a pipe" or "area of a cableway" means the area of the external cross section of that pipe or cableway measured in a plane perpendicular to the axis of that pipe or cableway at the point within the zone specified in paragraph 2(c), 3(e), or 3(f) of Section V of this Protocol where its cross section is largest.

23. The term "sensing elements and cables" means switches, cables, and cable segments that provide direct measurement of the position of a shock front as a function of time, and are installed in a satellite hole by the Verifying Party for the purposes of use of the hydrodynamic yield measurement method.

24. The term "transducer" means a device that converts physical properties of a shock wave, such as stress and particle velocity, into a recordable signal, and is installed in a satellite hole by the Verifying Party, with associated power supplies, for the purposes of the use of the hydrodynamic yield measurement method, with respect to explosions having a planned yield exceeding 50 kilotons and characteristics differing from those set forth in paragraph 2 or 3 of Section V of this Protocol.

25. The term "core sample" means an intact cylindrical sample of geological material having dimensions no less than two centimeters in diameter and two centimeters in length.

26. The term "rock fragment" means a sample of geological material having an irregular shape and a volume no less than 10 cubic centimeters.

27. The term "geodetic measurements" means the determination of the geometric position of points within tunnels or cavities.

28. The term "Designated Seismic Station" means any one of the seismic stations designated by each Party, in accordance with Section VI of this Protocol, at which activities related to verification are carried out.

29. The term "Bilateral Consultative Commission" means the Commission established in accordance with Section XI of this Protocol.

30. The term "Coordinating Group" means a working group of the Bilateral Consultative Commission that is established for each test with respect to which activities related to verification are carried out.

31. The term "coordinated schedule" means the schedule, including the specific times and durations for carrying out activities related to verification for a specific test, established in the Coordinating Group as specified in paragraph 12 of Section XI of this Protocol.

32. The term "Nuclear Risk Reduction Centers" means the Centers located in Washington, D.C., and Moscow, established in accordance with the Agreement Between the United States of America and the Union of Soviet Socialist Republics on the Establishment of Nuclear Risk Reduction Centers of September 15, 1987.

SECTION II. TEST SITES

1. The test sites for the Parties are: the Nevada Test Site, for the United States of America; and the Northern Test Site (Novaya Zemlya) and the Semipalatinsk Test Site, for the Union of Soviet Socialist Republics. Upon entry into force of the Treaty, each Party, for each of its test sites, shall provide the other Party with:

(a) a precise written description of the boundaries; and

(b) a diagram with geographic coordinates of the boundaries to the nearest second, to a scale of no smaller than 1:250,000.

2. Following entry into force of the Treaty, if a Party decides to establish a new test site or to change the boundaries of a test site specified in paragraph 1 of this Section, the description and diagram specified in paragraph 1 of this Section shall be transmitted to the other Party no less than 12 months prior to the planned date

for conducting the first test at the new site or area of expansion of a previously specified test site.

3. A test site of a Party shall be located only within its territory. All tests shall be conducted solely within test sites specified in paragraph 1 or in accordance with paragraph two of this Section.

4. For the purposes of the Treaty and this Protocol, all underground nuclear explosions at test sites specified in paragraph 1 or in accordance with paragraph 2 of this Section shall be considered underground nuclear weapon tests and shall be subject to all provisions of the Treaty and this Protocol.

SECTION III. VERIFICATION MEASURES

1. For purposes of verification of compliance with the Treaty, in addition to using available national technical means, the Verifying Party shall have the right, with respect to tests that are conducted 200 days or more following entry into force of the Treaty:

(a) with respect to a test having a planned yield exceeding 50 kilotons, to carry out any or all of the verification activities associated with the use of the hydrodynamic yield measurement method, in accordance with Section V of this Protocol, with respect too each explosion in the test;

(b) with respect to a test having a planned yield exceeding 50 kilotons, to carry out any or all of the verification activities associated with the use of the seismic yield measurement method, in accordance with Section V of this Protocol; and

(c) with respect to a test having a planned yield exceeding 35 kilotons, to carry out any or all of the verification activities associated with on-site inspection, in accordance with Section VII of this Protocol, with respect to each explosion in the test, except that such activities may be carried out with respect to a test having a planned yield exceeding 50 kilotons only if the Verifying Party does not use the hydrodynamic yield measurement method.

2. In addition to the rights specified in paragraph 1 of this Section, for the purposes of building confidence in the implementation of this Protocol and improving its national technical means of verification, the Verifying Party shall have the right:

(a) if, in each of the five calendar years immediately following entry into force of the Treaty, the Testing Party does not conduct at least two tests having a planned yield exceeding 50 kilotons, to use the hydrodynamic yield measurement method, in accordance with Section V of this Protocol, with respect to two tests from among those having the highest planned yields that the Testing Party conducts in that calendar year;

(b) if, in the sixth calendar year following entry into force of the Treaty and in each calendar year thereafter, unless the Parties otherwise agree, the Testing Party does not conduct at least one test having a planned yield exceeding 50 kilotons, to use the hydrodynamic yield measurement method, in accordance with Section V of this Protocol, with respect to one test from among those having the highest planned yield that the Testing Party conducts in that calendar year;

(c) if, in any calendar year, the testing Party postpones a test having a planned yield of 50 kilotons or less to the following calendar year, after having been notified by the Verifying Party of its intent to use the hydrodynamic yield measurement method with respect to that test, to use such method with respect to that test in the following calendar year. This right shall be additional to the rights specified in paragraph 1(a) of this Section and in subparagraphs (a) and (b) of this paragraph; and

(d) in addition to the rights specified in subparagraphs (a), (b), and (c) of this paragraph, if, in each of the five calendar years beginning with the conduct of the first test by the Testing Party at a new test site, the Testing Party does not conduct at least two tests having a planned yield exceeding 50 kilotons at the new test site, the Verifying Party shall have the right to use the hydrodynamic yield measurement method, in accordance with Section V of this Protocol, with respect to two tests from among those having the highest planned yields that the Testing Party conducts at the new site in that calendar year.

3. If the Verifying Party has notified the Testing Party that it intends to use the hydrodynamic yield measurement method with respect to a specific test including more than one explosion, unless the Parties agree on verification measures with respect to such a test:

(a) the distance between the closest points of any two adjacent explosive canisters shall be no less than 50 meters; and

(b) the time of each explosion shall be established by the Testing Party so as to permit the carrying out of hydrodynamic yield measurements for each explosion for a distance of no less than 30 meters in the satellite hole closest to the emplacement hole with which it is associated.

4. If the Verifying Party has notified the Testing Party that it intends to use the hydrodynamic yield measurement method with respect to a specific test, and if that test is conducted in more than one emplacement hole, the Testing Party shall have the right to conduct that test only if no more than one emplacement hole has characteristics or contains explosive canisters having characteristics differing from those set forth in paragraph 2 or 3 of Section V of this Protocol with respect to a test of standard configuration, unless the Parties agree on verification measures with respect to such a test.

5. The Testing Party shall have the right to conduct a test having a planned yield exceeding 35 kilotons within a time period of less than two seconds of any other test having a planned yield exceeding 35 kilotons only if the Parties agree on verification measures with respect to such tests. No test shall be conducted within 15 minutes prior to or following a reference test, unless the Parties otherwise agree.

6. The Testing Party shall have the right to conduct a test having a planned yield exceeding 35 kilotons in a cavity having a volume exceeding 20,000 cubic meters only if the Parties agree on verification measures with respect to such a test.

7. The Verifying Party, by notifying the Testing Party that it intends to use the hydrodynamic yield measurement method with respect to a test of non-standard configuration having a planned yield exceeding 50 kilotons, shall have the right to require a reference test for this non-standard test, in order to compare the yields measured through its national technical means for these two associated tests with the yield obtained by carrying out hydrodynamic yield measurement of the reference test. The right of the Verifying Party to a reference test shall be independent of whether or not it actually carries out hydrodynamic yield measurements of the test of non-standard configuration.

8. With respect to the requirement for a reference test:

(a) if the Testing Party, at the time it provides notification of a test, identifies that test as a reference test for a future test of non-standard configuration, and if the Verifying Party does not use the hydrodynamic yield measurement method with respect to the identified reference test, the Verifying Party shall forfeit its right to require a reference test for that test of non-standard configuration and foe any subsequent test of non-standard configuration that would be associated with that reference test, if the Testing Party conducts the identified reference test;

(b) the Testing Party shall have the right to identify only one test of standard configuration as a reference test not associated with any specific test of non-standard configuration until it has conducted an associated test of non-standard configuration for which this tests serves as a reference test, or unless it simultaneously provides notification of the associated test of non-standard configuration; and

(c) If the Testing Party, at the time it provides notification of a test of standard configuration, indicates that the test will satisfy a requirement for a reference test for a previously conducted test of non-standard configuration, and if the Verifying Party notifies the Testing Party of its intent not to use the hydrodynamic yield measurement method with respect to the reference test, the Verifying Party shall forfeit its right to require a reference test for the previously conducted test of non-standard configuration. In that case, the Testing Party shall have the right to cancel that reference test.

9. Following notification by the Verifying Party, in accordance with paragraph 5 of Section IV of this Protocol, of whether or not it intends to carry out any of the activities related to verification for a specific test, and, if so, which activities, the Verifying Party shall forfeit its right to revise that notification unless the Testing Party changes the previously declared location of that test by more than one minute of latitude or longitude or changes the planned yield of a test form 50 kilotons or less to a planned yield exceeding 50 kilotons. If the Testing Party makes any such change, the Verifying Party shall have the right to revise its previous notification and to carry out any of the activities specified in paragraph 1 or 2 of this Section and, if the Verifying Party notifies the Testing Party that it intends to carry out activities related to verification with respect to that test, in accordance with paragraph

20 of Section IV of this Protocol, the Testing Party shall not conduct the test less than 180 days following the date of the revised notification by the Verifying Party, unless the Parties otherwise agree.

10. Designated Personnel shall have the right to carry out activities related to verification in accordance with the Protocol, 24 hours a day, provided such activities are consistent with the safety requirements of the Testing Party at the test site or Designated Seismic Station. All operations and procedures that require the participation of Designated Personnel and personnel of the Testing Party shall be carried out in accordance with the technical operations and practices at the testing site or the Designated Seismic Station of the Testing Party, and in this connection:

(a) Designated Personnel:

(i) shall not interfere with activities of personnel of the Testing Party at the test site or Designated Seismic Station; and

(ii) shall be responsible for the working of their equipment, its timely installation and operation, participation in such operations, including dry runs, as the Testing Party may request, and recording of data; and

(b) the Testing Party:

(i) shall be under no obligation to delay the test because of any malfunction of the equipment of the Verifying Party or inability of Designated Personnel to carry out their functions, unless the Testing Party caused such a situation to arise; and

(ii) shall bear full responsibility for the preparation and conduct of the test and shall have exclusive control over it.

11. If the Verifying Party has notified the Testing Party that it intends to carry out activities related to verification of a specific test, the Testing Party shall have the right to make changes in the timing of its operations related to the conduct of the test, except that the Testing Party shall not make changes in the timing of its operations related to the conduct of that test that would preclude Designated Personnel from carrying out their rights related to verification provided in this Protocol. If the Testing Party notifies the Verifying Party of a change in the timing of its operations that the Verifying Party deems would either preclude or significantly limit the exercise of such rights, the Coordinating Group shall meet at the request to the Representative of the Verifying Party to the Coordinating Group, to consider the change in order to ensure that the rights of the Verifying Party are preserved. If the Coordinating Group cannot agree on a revision to the coordinated schedule that will ensure the rights of both Parties as provided in this Protocol, there shall be no advancement of events within the coordinated schedule due to such a change. Either Party may request that the Bilateral Consultative Commission consider any such change in timing of operations or in the coordinated schedule, in accordance with paragraph 15 of Section XI of this Protocol.

SECTION IV. NOTIFICATIONS AND INFORMATION RELATING TO TESTS

1. Unless otherwise provided in this Protocol, all notifications required by this Protocol shall be transmitted through the Nuclear Risk Reduction Centers. The Nuclear Risk Reduction Centers may also be used, as appropriate, to transmit other information provided in accordance with this Protocol.

2. Not later than June 1 immediately following entry into force of the Treaty, and not later than June 1 of each year thereafter, each Party shall provide the other Party with the following information on tests that it intends to conduct in the following calendar year:

(a) the projected number of tests having a planned yield exceeding 35 kilotons;

(b) the projected number of tests having a planned yield exceeding 50 kilotons; and

(c) if the number of tests declared in accordance with subparagraphs (a) and (b) of this paragraph is less than the number of tests for which rights are specified in paragraph 2 of Section III of this Protocol, whether it intends to conduct a sufficient number of other tests to permit the Verifying Party to exercise fully the rights specified in paragraph 2 of Section III of this Protocol.

3. On the date of entry into force of the Treaty each Party shall provide the other Party with the information specified in paragraphs 2(a) and 2(b) of this Section for the remainder of the calendar year in which the Treaty enters into force, and, if the Treaty enters into force after June 1, information specified in paragraph 2 of this Section for the following calendar year.

4. No less than 200 days prior to the planned date of any test with respect to which the Verifying Party has the right to carry out any activity related to verification in accordance with this Protocol, the Testing Party shall provide the Verifying Party with the following information to the extent and degree of accuracy available at that time:

(a) the planned date of the test and its designation;

(b) the planned date of the beginning of emplacement of explosive canisters;

(c) the location of the test, expressed in geographic coordinates to the nearest minute;

(d) whether the planned yield of the test exceeds 35 kilotons;

(e) whether the planned yield of the test exceeds 50 kilotons;

(f) whether the planned yield is 50 kilotons or less, whether the test is one of the tests with respect to which the Verifying Party has the right to use the hydrodynamic yield measurement method, in accordance with paragraph 2 of Section III of this Protocol;

(g) the planned depth of each emplacement hole to the nearest 10 meters;

(h) the type or types of rock in which the test will be conducted, including the depth of the water table;

(i) whether the test will be of standard or non-standard configuration; and

(j) whether the test will serve as a reference test for:

(i) a previously conducted test of non-standard configuration with which such a reference test is associated;

(ii) a future test of non-standard configuration for which notification has been provided or is being simultaneously provided in accordance with paragraph 8(b) of Section III of this Protocol; or

(iii) a future test of non-standard configuration for which the Testing Party has not yet provided notification.

5. Within 20 days following receipt of information specified in paragraph 4 of this Section, the Verifying Party shall inform the Testing Party, in a single notification, whether or not it intends to carry out, with respect to this test, any activities related to verification that it has a right to carry out, in accordance with Section III of this Protocol, and if so, whether it intends:

(a) to use the hydrodynamic yield measurement method, in accordance with Section V of this Protocol;

(b) to use the seismic yield measurement method, in accordance with Section VI of this Protocol; and

(c) to carry out on-site inspection, in accordance with Section VII of this Protocol.

6. Within 30 days following notification by the Verifying Party, in accordance with paragraph 11 of Section XI of this Protocol, that it requires a reference test for a test of non-standard configuration, the Testing Party shall notify the Verifying Party whether it will meet the requirement test through:

(a) the identification of a previously conducted reference test;

(b) the identification of a previously conducted test of standard configuration, meeting the requirements for a reference test, with respect to which the Verifying Party carried out hydrodynamic yield measurements;

(c) the identification of a previously notified test of standard configuration, meeting the requirements for a reference test, with respect to which the Verifying Party has notified the Testing Party of its intent to carry out hydrodynamic yield measurements; or

(d) the conduct of a reference test within 12 months of the non-standard test, whose identification as a reference test will be made in the notification, in accordance with paragraph 4(j) of this section.

7. If the Verifying Party notifies the Testing Party that it intends to use the hydrodynamic yield measurement method, the Testing Party shall provide the Verifying Party, no less than 120 days prior to the planned date of the test, with the following information:

(a) a description of the geological and geophysical characteristics of the test location, which shall include: the depth of the water table; the stratigraphic column, including the lithologic description of each formation; the estimated physical parameters of the rock, including bulk density, grain density, compressional velocity, porosity, and total water content; and information on any known geophysical discontinuities in the media within each hydrodynamic measurement zone;

(b) the planned cross-sectional dimensions of each emplacement hole in each hydrodynamic measurement zone;

(c) the location and configuration of any known voids larger than one cubic meter within each hydrodynamic measurement zone;

(d) a description of materials, including their densities, to be used to stem each emplacement hole within each hydrodynamic measurement zone;

(e) whether it is planned that each emplacement hole will be fully or partially cased, and if so, a description of materials of this casing;

(f) whether it is planned that each satellite hole will be fully or partially cased, and if so, a description of materials of this casing;

(g) a topographic map to a scale of no smaller than 1:25,000 and a contour interval of 10 meters or less showing:

(i) an area with a radius of no less than two kilometers centered on the entrance to each emplacement hole, that shall include the area delineated by a circle having a radius of 300 meters centered directly above the planned emplacement point of each explosive canister; and

(ii) a one-kilometer wide corridor centered on the planned location of the above-ground cables of the Verifying Party;

(h) overall drawings showing the external dimensions of each explosive canister and each choke section, and any pipes or cableways passing through a choke section, as well as any other pipes and cableways connected to that explosive canister and located within five meters of that explosive canister;

(i) the specific locations, referenced to the entrance to each vertical satellite hole or to the surface location of the entrance to each horizontal emplacement hole, at which individual gas-blocking devices shall be installed if such devices are used on the electrical cables specified in paragraphs 3(a) and 3(b) of Section VIII of this Protocol; and

(j) whether the Testing Party will provide satellite communications as specified in paragraph 13 of Section X of this Protocol for use by Designated Personnel.

8. If the Verifying Party notifies the Testing Party that it intends to use the seismic yield measurement method, the Testing Party shall provide the Verifying Party, no less than 120 days prior to the planned date of the test, with the information specified in paragraphs 9(a), 9(b), and 9(c) of this Section.

9. If the Verifying Party notifies the Testing Party that it intends to carry out on-site inspection, the Testing Party shall provide the Verifying Party, no less than 120 days prior to the planned date of the test, with the following information:

(a) a description of the geological and geophysical characteristics of the test location, which shall include: the depth of the water table; the stratigraphic column, including the lithologic description of each formation; the estimated physical parameters of the rock, including bulk density, grain density, compressional velocity, porosity, and total water content; and information on any known geophysical discontinuities in the media within a radius of 300 meters of the planned emplacement point of each explosive canister.

(b) the planned cross-sectional dimensions of each emplacement hole in the portion within 300 meters of the planned emplacement point of each explosive canister;

(c) the location and configuration of any known voids larger than 1000 cubic meters within a radius of 300 meters of the planned emplacement point of each explosive canister;

(d) whether it is planned that each emplacement hole will be fully or partially cased, and, if so, a description of materials of this casing;

(e) a topographic map to a scale of no smaller than 1:25,000 and a contour interval of 10 meters or less showing an area with a radius of no less than two kilometers centered on the entrance to each emplacement hole, that shall include the are delineated by a circle having a radius of 300 meters centered directly above the planned emplacement point of each explosive canister; and

(f) whether the Testing Party will provide satellite communications as specified in paragraph 13 of Section X of this Protocol for use by Designated Personnel.

10. The Testing Party shall immediately notify the Verifying Party of any change in any information provided in accordance with paragraph 2, 3, 4(a), 4(c), 4(e), 4(f), or 4(j) of this Section, and:

(a) if the Verifying Party has notified the Testing Party that it intend to carry out activities related to verification in accordance with Section V of this Protocol, of any change in information provided in accordance with paragraph 4(b), 4(g), 4(h), 4(i), 6 or 7 of this Section, or paragraph 10 of Section XI of this Protocol;

(b) if the Verifying Party has notified the Testing Party that it intend to carry out activities related to verification in accordance with Section VI of this Protocol, of any change in information provided in accordance with paragraph 4(g), 4(h) or 8 of this Section; and

(c) if the Verifying Party has notified the Testing Party that it intend to carry out activities related to verification in accordance with Section VII of this Protocol, of any change in information provided in accordance with paragraph 4(b), 4(g), 4(h) or 9 of this Section, or paragraph 10(a) of Section XI of this Protocol.

11. If the Testing Party makes changes in the information specified in paragraph 4(a), 10(a), 10(b) or 10(c) of this Section related to a specific test for which Designated Personnel are present in the territory of the Testing Party, it shall also immediately notify, in writing, the Designated Personnel Team Leader carrying out activities related to verification of that test at the test site and at each Designated Seismic Station of such changes.

12. The Testing Party shall immediately inform the Verifying party of any change in the timing of its operations related to the conduct of a specific test that affects the coordinated schedule, and if Designated Personnel are present in the territory of the Testing Party, it shall also immediately notify, in writing, the Designated Personnel Team Leader carrying out activities related to verification of that test at the test site and at each Designated Seismic Station.

13. If, in carrying out activities related to verification of a specific test, Designated Personnel are present at the test site or any Designated Seismic Station:

(a) no less than 48 hours prior to the initial planned time of the test, the Testing Party notify shall each Designated Personnel Team Leader, in writing, of the time for beginning the period of readiness for the test and the planned time of the test, to the nearest second. This and all subsequent notifications shall be referenced to Universal Time Coordinated and to local time at the test site or the Designated Seismic Station;

(b) except as otherwise provided on this Section, if the Testing Party changes the planned time of the test, it shall immediately notify each Designated Personnel Team Leader, in writing, of the new planned time of the test;

(c) the Testing Party shall conduct the test only within a period of readiness;

(d) unless the Parties otherwise agree, the period of readiness shall begin:

(i) no less than six days following completion of stemming of the hydrodynamic measurement zone of all satellite holes, if verification activities in accordance with Section V of this Protocol are carried out; and

(ii) no more than five days prior to the planned date of the test, if verification activities in accordance with Section VI of this Protocol are carried out;

(e) the Testing Party may terminate the period of readiness at any time. The Testing Party shall then immediately notify each Designated Personnel Team Leader, in writing, that the period of readiness has been terminated; and

(f) if the Testing Party terminates the period of readiness or changes the time for the beginning of the period of readiness, it shall provide notice of the time for beginning a new period of readiness to each Designated Personnel Team Leader, in writing, no less than 12 hours prior to beginning this new period of readiness.

14. Following notification in accordance with paragraph 13(a) or 13(b) of this Section, the Testing Party, without further notification may advance the time of the test by no more than five minutes.

15. After the event readiness signal specified in paragraph 10(b) of Section V of this Protocol has been started:

(a) if the Testing Party delays the test and terminates the event readiness signal at least one second prior to the planned time of the test, it may carry out the test, without further notification, at any time within no more than 60 minutes after the planned time of the test, provided it generates a new event readiness signal; and

(b) if the Testing Party subsequently delays the test without ending the event readiness signal at least one second prior to the planned time of the test, the Testing Party shall end the event readiness signal and shall not begin a new event readiness signal within 20 minutes following that planned time of the test. The Testing Party shall notify each Designated Personnel Team Leader, in writing, of the new planned time of the test, at least 10 minutes prior to the beginning of the new event readiness signal for that test.

16. Following notification in accordance with paragraph 13(a) or 13(b) of this Section, if the test is delayed by more than 60 minutes the Testing Party shall notify each Designated Personnel Team Leader, in writing, of the new planned time of the test no less than 30 minutes prior to the new planned time of the test.

17. During the period of readiness, if a test is delayed by more than three hours from the last notification of the planned time of the test, the Testing Party shall notify each Designated Personnel Team Leader, in writing, of the period during which the test will not be conducted.

18. No less than one hour following the test, the Testing Party shall notify each Designated Personnel Team Leader, in writing, of the actual time of the test to the nearest 0.1 second.

19. For each test for which notification has been provided in accordance with paragraph 4 of this Section, no less than 48 hours prior to the initial planned time of the test, the Testing Party shall notify the Verifying Party of the time of the planned test to the nearest one second. If the Testing Party subsequently delays the planned time of the test by more than 24 hours, it shall immediately notify the Verifying Party of the new planned time of the test to the nearest one second. No less than three days following the test, the Testing Party shall notify the Verifying Party of the actual time of the test, referenced to Universal Time Coordinated, to the nearest 0.1 second.

20. The Testing Party shall immediately notify the Verifying Party of a change in the location of a test by more than one minute of latitude or longitude or of a change in the planned yield of a test from 50 kilotons or less to a planned yield exceeding 50 kilotons. The Verifying Party shall notify the Testing Party, within 20 days following receipt of notification of such a change in the location or planned yield of the test, whether it intends to carry out for this test any activities related to verification in accordance with paragraph 9 of Section III of this Protocol. If the Verifying Party, in this revised notification, notifies the Testing Party that it intends to carry out any activities related to verification that it has a right to carry out in accordance with Section III of this Protocol, the Testing Party shall provide the Verifying Party with the information that it is required to provide in accordance with paragraphs 7, 8, and 9 of this Section and paragraph 10 of Section XI of this Protocol.

21. If the Verifying Party has notified the Testing Party that it intends to use the hydrodynamic yield measurement method, the beginning of emplacement of sensing elements and cables shall not occur less than 90 days after notification of any change in the location of the test by more than one minute of latitude or longitude, unless the Parties otherwise agree.

22. If the Verifying Party has notified the Testing Party that it does not intend to carry out hydrodynamic yield measurements for a specific test, the Testing Party shall have the right to change the configuration of that test from standard to non-standard or vice-versa, without notifying the Verifying Party of such change.

23. If the Verifying Party has notified the Testing Party that it intends to carry out hydrodynamic yield measurements for a specific test, the Testing Party shall immediately notify the Verifying Party of a change in the configuration of that test from standard to non-standard or vice-versa, or of any increase in the number of emplacement holes or explosive canisters of the test. The Verifying Party shall, within five days of notification of any such change, notify the Testing Party whether it will revise its initial notification and whether it deems that this change would either preclude or significantly limit the exercise of its rights provided in this Protocol. If so, the Coordinating Group shall immediately meet to consider a revision in the coordinated schedule that will ensure the rights of both Parties provided in this Protocol. If the Parties cannot agree on a revised coordinated schedule within 15 days following notification by the Testing Party of such a change, the date of notification of the change shall be deemed the initial notification of a test in accordance with paragraph 4 of this Section, and the test shall be conducted no less than 180 days following the date of notification.

24. If the Verifying Party has notified the Testing Party that it intends to carry out on-site inspection with respect to a specific test, and if the Testing Party notifies the Verifying Party of an increase in the number of explosive canisters or an increase in the number of emplacement holes, the Verifying Party shall, within five days of any such change, notify the Testing Party whether it deems that this change would significantly limit the exercise of its rights provided in this Protocol. If so, the Coordinating Group shall immediately meet to consider a revision in the coordinated schedule that will ensure the rights of both Parties provided in this Protocol. If the Parties cannot agree on a revised coordinated schedule within 15 days following notification by the Verifying Party that it deems that, as a result of such an increase, its rights would be significantly limited, the date of that notification shall be deemed notification by the Verifying Party that it intends to carry out on-site inspection in accordance with paragraph 5 of this Section, and the test shall be conducted no less than 165 days following the date of such notification.

25. The Verifying Party may at any time, but no later than one year following a test, request from the Testing Party clarification of any point of information provided in accordance with this Section. Such clarification shall be provided in the shortest possible time, but no later than 30 days following the receipt of the request.

SECTION V. HYDRODYNAMIC YIELD MEASUREMENT METHOD

1. The hydrodynamic measurement zone is:

(a) with respect to a test of standard configuration, described in paragraph 2 or 3 of this Section, as well as with respect to any explosion having a planned yield of 50 kilotons less;

(i) if an emplacement hole is vertical, the cylindrical region 25 meters in diameter whose axis is midway between the axes of the emplacement hole and the satellite hole, extending from a point 30 meters below the end of the emplacement hole to a point 100 meters from the end of the emplacement hole in the direction of the entrance to the emplacement hole; or

(ii) if an emplacement hole is horizontal, the cylindrical region 25 meters in diameter whose axis is midway between the axes of the emplacement hole and the satellite hole, extending from a point 15 meters beyond the end of the emplacement hole to a point 65 meters from the end of the emplacement hole in the direction of the entrance to the emplacement hole; and

(b) with respect to a test of non-standard configuration having a planned yield exceeding 50 kilotons:

(i) if an emplacement hole is vertical, the cylindrical region 200 meters in diameter coaxial with the emplacement hole, extending from a point 30 meters below the end of the emplacement hole to a point 100 meters from the center point of the explosive canister in the direction of the entrance to the emplacement hole; or

(ii) if an emplacement hole is horizontal, the cylindrical region 130 meters in diameter whose axis is coaxial with the emplacement hole, extending from a point 15 meters beyond the end of the emplacement hole to a point 65 meters from the center point of the explosive canister in the direction of the entrance to the emplacement hole.

2. For the purposes of the use of the hydrodynamic yield measurement method, a test shall be deemed of standard vertical configuration if:

(a) each emplacement hole is vertical and cylindrical, and is drilled or excavated with a diameter no greater than four meters;

(b) the bottom of each emplacement hole is filled with stemming material having a bulk density no less than 60 percent of the average density of the surrounding rock, to form a plug no less than three meters thick, and the top of this plug of stemming material is the end of the emplacement hole for the explosive canister emplaced farthest from the entrance to the emplacement hole;

(c) any pipe or cableway connected to an explosive canister passes through a choke section. This choke section is installed on the top of the explosive canister and has the following characteristics:

(i) the diameter of the choke section is no less than that of the explosive canister;

(ii) the choke section is no less than one meter thick;

(iii) the sum of the areas of all pipes and cableways within the choke section does not exceed 0.5 square meters;

(iv) the area of each pipe or cableway within the choke section does not exceed 0.3 square meters;

(v) the part of the choke section in contact with the explosive canister consists of a steel plate having a thickness no less than 0.005 meters; and

(vi) the choke section, except for pipes and cableways, is filled, prior to emplacement, with stemming material having a bulk density no less than 60 percent of the average density of the surrounding rock, and has a product of density and thickness no less than 250 grams per square centimeter;

(d) the length of each explosive canister does not exceed 12 meters and, after an explosive canister is emplaced, the lowest part of the choke section is no more than 12 meters above the end of the emplacement hole;

(e) the diameter of each explosive canister does not exceed three meters;

(f) each emplacement hole has been drilled or excavated with a diameter, within each hydrodynamic measurement zone, no more than one meter greater than the diameter of each explosive canister; or, if an emplacement hole has been cased, the inside diameter of the casing, within each hydrodynamic measurement zone, is no more than one meter greater than the diameter of each explosive canister. Within the 15-meter segment above the end of each emplacement hole for each explosive canister, no washouts penetrate more than one meter into the wall of the emplacement hole;

(g) all voids in or connected to an emplacement hole, within each hydrodynamic measurement zone, external to:

(i) any explosive canister;

(ii) any choke sections;

(iii) any diagnostic canisters; and

(iv) associated cables and pipes are filled with stemming material having a bulk density no less than 60 percent of the average density of the surrounding rock;

(h) within each hydrodynamic measurement zone, all voids greater than 10 cubic meters, external and unconnected to an emplacement hole or a satellite hole, and all voids greater than one cubic meter, within two meters of the wall of a satellite hole or any part of an explosive canister, are filled with stemming material having a bulk density no less than 70 percent of the average density of the surrounding rock; and

(i) within each hydrodynamic measurement zone, the distance between a satellite hole and any other drilled hole or excavation is no less than the distance between that satellite hole and the emplacement hole with which it is associated.

3. For the purposes of the use of the hydrodynamic yield measurement method, a test shall be deemed of standard horizontal configuration if:

(a) each emplacement hole is horizontal, with an excavated cross section, measured in the plane perpendicular to its axis, no greater than five meters by five meters for the first 65 meters from the end of the emplacement hole for each explosive canister, except that any diagnostic canister associated with it shall occupy, in an emplacement hole, space having a cross section no greater than 3.5 meters by 3.5 meters for the first 50 meters of the emplacement hole from the choke section of each explosive canister in the direction of the entrance to the emplacement hole;

(b) the end of each emplacement hole is either:

(i) unsupported native rock, the surface of which is essentially perpendicular to the axis of the emplacement hole; or

(ii) the surface of a plug no less than three meters thick, formed of stemming material having a bulk density no less than 60 percent of the average density of the surrounding rock;

(c) the length of each explosive canister does not exceed 12 meters and, after it is emplaced, the end of the explosive canister farthest from the entrance to the emplacement hole is no less than one meter and no more than two meters from the end of the emplacement hole;

(d) the cross section of each explosive canister measured in the plane perpendicular to the axis of the emplacement hole does not exceed three meters by three meters;

(e) any pipe or cableway connected to an explosive canister and lying entirely within the emplacement hole passes through a choke section. This choke section is installed at the end of the explosive canister nearest to the entrance of the emplacement hole and has the following characteristics:

(i) the dimensions of the choke section perpendicular to the axis of the emplacement hole are no less than those of the explosive canister;

(ii) the choke section is no less than one meter thick;

(iii) the sum of the areas of all pipes and cableways within the choke section, plus the sum of the areas of pipes and cableways specified in subparagraph (f) of this paragraph, does not exceed 0.5 square meters;

(iv) the area of each pipe or cableway within the choke section does not exceed 0.3 square meters; and

(v) the choke section, except for pipes and cableways meeting the requirements of subparagraphs (e) (iii) and (e) (iv) of this paragraph, is filled with stemming material having a bulk density no less than 60 percent of the average density of the surrounding rock, and has a product of density and thickness no less than 250 grams per square centimeter;

(f) any pipe or cableway connected to any surface of an explosive canister and not lying entirely within the emplacement hole has the following characteristics:

(i) the area of each pipe or cableway within five meters of the explosive canister does not exceed 0.05 square meters; and

(ii) the sum of the areas of all such pipes and cableways within five meters of the explosive canister does not exceed 0.1 square meters;

(g) any diagnostic canister connected to the pipes or cableways specified in subparagraph (f) of this paragraph lies entirely outside the hydrodynamic measurement zone;

(h) all voids in or connected to an emplacement to hole, including any bypass or access tunnels within the hydrodynamic measurement zone, external to:

(i) any explosive canister;

(ii) any choke sections;
(iii) any diagnostic canisters; and
(iv) associated cables and pipes
are filled with stemming material having a bulk density no less than 60 percent of the average density of the surrounding rock;

(i) within each hydrodynamic measurement zone, all voids greater than 10 cubic meters, external and unconnected to an emplacement hole or a satellite hole, and all voids greater than one cubic meter, within two meters of the wall of a satellite hole or any part of an explosive canister, are filled with stemming material having a bulk density no less than 70 percent of the average density of the surrounding rock; and

(j) with the portion of each hydrodynamic measurement zone extending from the end of the emplacement hole in the direction of the entrance to the emplacement hole, the distance between a satellite hole and any other tunnel or excavation is no less than the distance between that satellite hole and the emplacement hole with which it is associated.

4. With respect to a test of standard configuration, as well as with respect to any explosion having a planned yield of 50 kilotons or less:

(a) personnel of the Testing Party, using their own equipment, shall drill or excavate a satellite hole associated with each emplacement hole, at a time of their own choosing. The Testing Party shall have the right to complete drilling or excavation of a satellite hole for a specific test prior to the arrival of Designated Personnel at the test site to carry out activities related to use of the hydrodynamic yield measurement method for that test. Each satellite hole shall meet the following requirements:

(i) if an emplacement hole is vertical, the axis of the associated satellite hole shall be located 11 meters, plus or minus three meters, from the axis of the emplacement hole within each hydrodynamic measurement zone. If an emplacement hole is horizontal, the axis of the associated satellite hole shall be located 11 meters, plus or minus two meters, from the axis of the emplacement hole within each hydrodynamic measurement zone, and it may be drilled or excavated either as a single continuous hole or in separate consecutive segments associated with each hydrodynamic measurement zone. The axis of any satellite hole shall be no less than six meters from the wall of any drilled or excavated cavity or hole;

(ii) its end shall be no less than 30 meters below the level of the end of the associated vertical emplacement hole farthest from the entrance to the emplacement hole, or no less than 15 meters beyond the point at which the satellite hole is closest to the end of the associated horizontal emplacement hole farthest from the entrance to the emplacement hole;

(iii) if it is prepared by drilling, it shall be drilled no less than 0.3 meters and no more than 0.5 meters in diameter.

Within each hydrodynamic measurement zone, no washouts shall penetrate more than one meter into the wall of the hole; and

(iv) if it is prepared by excavation, it shall have an excavated cross section, measured in the plane perpendicular to its axis, no greater than 2.5 meters by 2.5 meters within each hydrodynamic measurement zone;

(b) Designated Personnel shall have the right to observe the activities of the personnel of the Testing Party carried out to meet the specifications set forth in paragraph 2(b) of this Section and, if applicable, set forth in paragraph 3(b) (ii) of this Section. A representative sample of no less than 1000 cubic centimeters in volume of the stemming material used to form the plugs specified in paragraphs 2(b) and 3(b) (ii) of this Section shall be provided to Designated Personnel for retention;

(c) Designated Personnel shall have the right to carry out, under observation of personnel of the Testing Party and with their assistance, if such assistance is requested by Designated Personnel, directional surveys and geodetic measurements of each satellite hole and emplacement hole prior to the planned date of the beginning of emplacement of sensing elements and cables;

(d) equipment specified in paragraph 3 of Section VIII of this Protocol shall be operated by Designated Personnel and shall be installed, in accordance with installation instructions provided in accordance with paragraph 6(c) of Section VIII of this Protocol, by Designated Personnel under observation of personnel of the Testing Party and with their assistance, if such assistance is requested by Designated Personnel. The location of each hydrodynamic recording facility and the command and monitoring facility of the Verifying Party and the instrumentation facility of the Testing Party specified in paragraph 10 (l) of this Section shall be determined by the Testing Party in consultation with the Verifying Party in the Coordinating Group no less than 90 days prior to the beginning of emplacement of sensing elements and cables. Areas for the installation of these facilities, cable supports, and cableways for protection of cables of the Verifying Party, specified in paragraphs 3(b), 3(f), and 3(g) of Section VIII of this protocol, shall be prepared by the Testing Party in accordance with requirements agreed upon in the Coordinating Group. Only cables of the Verifying Party shall be installed in these cableways. Designated Personnel shall have access, under observation of personnel of the Testing Party, to the cables specified in paragraphs 3(f) and 3(g) of Section VIII of this Protocol and to the cableways in which they are installed, at all times. Personnel of the Testing Party shall have access to these cableways only under observation of Designated Personnel;

(e) Designated Personnel shall have the right to use their own primary electrical power sources to supply electrical power to hydrodynamic equipment specified in paragraph 3 of Section VIII of this Protocol. At the request of the Verifying Party, the Testing Party shall supply electrical power from the standard electrical network of its test site through converters provided by the Verifying Party or, by agreement of the Parties, by the Testing Party;

(f) for each test, the only equipment installed in a satellite hole shall be that of the Verifying Party specified in paragraphs 3(a) and 3(h) of Section VIII of this Protocol. If an emplacement hole is vertical, the end point of the equipment farthest from the entrance to the satellite hole shall be installed no less than 30 meters below the level of the end of the emplacement hole farthest from the entrance to the emplacement hole. If an emplacement hole is horizontal, the end point of this equipment shall be installed no less than 15 meters beyond the point at which a satellite hole is closest to the end of the emplacement hole farthest from the entrance to the emplacement hole. For each satellite hole, Designated Personnel shall have the right to install no more than six sensing elements and cables, without regard to the number of switches. Personnel of each Party shall have the right to measure the location of the installed sensing elements and cables;

(g) Designated Personnel shall have the right to conduct a final directional survey and geodetic measurements of each satellite hole upon completion of installation of sensing elements and cables;

(h) personnel of the Testing Party, under observation of Designated Personnel, shall fill all voids in or connected to each satellite hole within each hydrodynamic measurement zone with a stemming material agreed upon by the Parties, having a bulk density no less than 70 percent of the average density of the surrounding rock. A representative sample of no less than 1000 cubic centimeters in volume of each stemming material used in each hydrodynamic measurement zone shall be provided to Designated Personnel for retention. The methods and materials used for stemming satellite holes and any hydrodynamic measurement equipment emplacement pipe shall:

(i) be consistent with the containment practices of the Testing Party;

(ii) be chosen to minimize voids around sensing elements and cables; and

(iii) be chosen to avoid damage to the sensing elements and cables;

(i) Designated Personnel shall have the right to observe the stemming of the hydrodynamic measurement zones of each emplacement hole in accordance with paragraphs 2(g) and 3(h) of this Section. A representative sample of no less than 1000 cubic centimeters in volume of each stemming material used in each hydrodynamic measurement zone shall be provided to Designated Personnel for retention;

(j) the Testing Party shall have the right to case or line each emplacement hole; and

(k) the Testing Party shall have the right to case or line each satellite hole, provided that:

(i) sensing elements and cable can be installed as specified in subparagraph (f) of this paragraph;

(ii) casing or lining material in each hydrodynamic measurement zone is agreed upon by the Parties; and

(iii) casing or lining in each hydrodynamic measurement zone is affixed to the surrounding formation with material agreed upon by the Parties.

5. In preparation for the use of the hydrodynamic yield measurement method with respect to a test of standard configuration, as well as with respect to any explosion having a planned yield of 50 kilotons of less:

(a) upon their arrival at the test site, no less than 10 days prior to the planned date of the beginning of emplacement of sensing elements and cables, Designated Personnel shall provide the Testing Party with a description of the recording format and the computer program, to enable the Testing Party to read digital data if digital recordings of hydrodynamic data will be made by Designated Personnel;

(b) the Testing Party shall provide Designated Personnel upon their arrival at the test site with the results of any studies of core samples and rock fragments extracted from each emplacement hole and satellite hole and any exploratory holes and tunnels, and the results of logging and geodetic measurements carried out in each emplacement hole, each satellite hole, and any exploratory holes and tunnels, relevant to the geology and geophysics of each hydrodynamic measurement zone, if the Testing Party carried out such studies and measurements;

(c) using their own equipment and under observation of personnel of the Testing Party, Designated Personnel shall have the right to carry out:

(i) if an emplacement hole is vertical, in the emplacement hole and associated satellite hole, caliper logs, directional surveys, geodetic measurements, and depth or distance measurements to determine the dimensions and the relative locations of the emplacement hole and satellite hole, as well as measurements to determine the location and volume of all voids within each hydrodynamic measurement zone, using, in a non-destructive way, such methods as electromagnetic measurements, radar, and acoustic sounding;

(ii) if an emplacement hole is vertical, within the hydrodynamic measurement zones of either the emplacement hole or, at the option of the Testing Party, of the satellite hole, gamma-gamma, gamma, neutron, electrical resistivity, magnetic susceptibility, gravity, acoustic, and television logging;

(iii) if an emplacement hole is horizontal, in the emplacement hole and associated satellite hole, as well as in the drilled holes specified in subparagraph (e)(ii) of this paragraph, caliper logs, directional surveys, geodetic measurements, and distance measurements to determine the dimensions and relative location of these holes, as well as measurements to determine the location and volume of all voids within each hydrodynamic measurement zone using, in a non-destructive way, such methods as electromagnetic measurements, radar, and acoustic sounding; and

(iv) if an emplacement hole is horizontal, in the drilled holes specified in subparagraph (e)(ii) of this paragraph, and within the hydrodynamic measurement zones of the emplacement hole, or, at the option of the Testing Party, of the satellite hole, gamma-gamma, gamma, neutron, electrical resistivity, magnetic susceptibility, gravity, and acoustic logging;

(d) all logging data and geometrical measurements obtained by Designated Personnel, in accordance with subparagraph (c) of this paragraph, including calibration data, shall be duplicated, and a copy of the data shall be provided to personnel of the Testing Party prior to departure from the test site of Designated Personnel who have carried out these measurements. Calibration data shall include information necessary to confirm the sensitivity of logging equipment under the conditions in which it is used;

(e) Designated Personnel shall have the right to receive:

(i) if an emplacement hole is vertical, core samples or, at the option of Designated Personnel, rock fragments from the emplacement hole or, at the option of the Testing Party, from the satellite hole, extracted at no more than 10 depths within each hydrodynamic measurement zone, specified by Designated Personnel. The total volume of core samples or rock fragments extracted at each depth shall be no less than 400 cubic centimeters and no more than 3000 cubic centimeters, unless the Parties otherwise agree; and

(ii) if an emplacement hole is horizontal, core samples or, at the option of Designated Personnel, rock fragments from the emplacement hole or, at the option of the Testing Party, the satellite hole within each hydrodynamic measurement zone. If core samples are extracted from the emplacement hole or, at the option of the Testing Party, from the excavated satellite hole, they shall be extracted during drilling from each of no more than 10 holes drilled at stations specified by Designated Personnel. The diameter of each drilled hole shall be no less than 0.09 meters and no more than 0.15 meters, and the depth of each hole shall be no more than the diameter of the emplacement hole or satellite hole at this station. Core samples shall be extracted at locations specified by Designated Personnel along each drilled hole. If core samples are extracted from a drilled satellite hole, they shall be extracted by personnel of the Testing Party during the drilling of the satellite hole, within each hydrodynamic measurement zone, at no more than 10 stations specified by Designated Personnel and under their observation. Rock fragments shall be extracted from the emplacement hole or an excavated satellite hole at each of no more than 10 stations specified by Designated Personnel. Core samples and rock fragments may be taken from no more than a total of 10 stations. If an emplacement hole or an excavated satellite hole is lined at any station specified by Designated Personnel for extracting core samples or rock fragments, personnel of the Testing Party shall enable Designated Personnel to extract core samples or rock fragments at such a station from native rock. The total volume of core samples or rock fragments extracted at each station shall be no less than 400 cubic centimeters and no more than 3000 cubic centimeters, unless the Parties otherwise agree;

(f) core samples of rock fragments may be extracted in accordance with subparagraph (e) of this paragraph by personnel of the Testing Party, under observation of Designated Personnel, or by Designated Personnel, at the option of the Testing Party;

(g) if personnel of the Testing Party do not extract core samples or rock fragments in accordance with subparagraph (e) of this paragraph, Designated Personnel shall have the right, using their own equipment, to extract such core samples or rock fragments in accordance with subparagraph (e) of this paragraph, under observation of personnel of the Testing Party;

(h) if an emplacement hole is vertical, and if the Testing Party, prior to arrival of Designated Personnel at the test site:

(i) has cased a total of 20 meters or more of the emplacement hole or the satellite hole within any hydrodynamic measurement zone, Designated Personnel shall have the right to carry out, in the uncased hole, the activities specified in subparagraph (c)(ii) of this paragraph and to receive core samples or rock fragments from the uncased hole, extracted in accordance with subparagraphs (e), (f), and (g) of this paragraph; or

(ii) has cased a total of 20 meters or more of both the emplacement hole and the satellite hole within any hydrodynamic measurement zone, the Testing Party shall provide an uncased hole with respect to which Designated Personnel shall have the same rights as those specified for the emplacement hole and the satellite hole in subparagraphs (c), (e), (f), and (g) of this paragraph. The axis of this uncased hole shall be within 22 meters of the axes of the emplacement hole and the satellite hole within each hydrodynamic measurement zone. If personnel of the Testing Party, under observation of Designated Personnel, extract core samples through coring during the drilling of this uncased hole, the diameter of the hole shall be no less than 0.09 meters. If Designated Personnel, under observation of personnel of the Testing Party, extract core sample from this uncased hole following drilling, the diameter of the uncased hole shall be no less than 0.3 meters;

(i) Designated Personnel shall have the right to retain core sample and rock fragments specified in subparagraphs (e), (f), (g), and (h) of this paragraph. Any such core samples of rock fragments shall be prepared in accordance with procedures agreed upon by the Parties for shipment to the territory of the Verifying Party; and

(j) logging, directional surveys, geodetic measurements, and extracting of core samples or rock fragments carried out in accordance with subparagraphs (c), (e), (f), (g), (h), and (i) of this paragraph shall begin at times chosen by the Testing Party and specified in the coordinated schedule. Designated Personnel shall have the right, within a period not to exceed 21 days, to carry out logging, directional surveys, geodetic measurements, and coring activities, unless the Parties otherwise agree and so specify in the coordinated schedule. The Testing Party shall not emplace any explosive until the activities specified in this paragraph have been completed.

6. With respect to any explosion having a planned yield exceeding 50 kilotons and characteristics differing from those set forth in paragraph 2 or 3 of this Section with respect to a test of standard configuration:

(a) personnel of the Testing Party, using their own equipment and at a time of their own equipment and at a time of their own choosing, shall drill or excavate up to three satellite holes associated with the emplacement hole. The location of the satellite holes shall be determined in accordance with paragraph 11(b)(i) of Section XI of this Protocol. The Testing Party shall have the right to complete drilling or excavation of satellite holes for the specific test prior to the arrival of Designated Personnel at the test site for that test. The satellite holes shall meet the following requirements:

(i) with respect to the first satellite hole, its length shall be as specified in paragraph 4(a)(ii) of this Section;

(ii) with respect to the second and third satellite holes, if such are required by the Verifying Party, the axis of each satellite hole shall be within three meters of the axis specified by the Verifying Party. Its length shall be specified by the Verifying Party and in no case shall it extend beyond the hydrodynamic measurement zone associated with that explosion;

(iii) within each hydrodynamic measurement zone, the axis of each satellite hole shall be essentially parallel to the axis of the emplacement hole, if the emplacement hole is vertical, or shall be essentially straight, if the emplacement hole is horizontal. Within each hydrodynamic measurement zone, its axis shall be no less than eight meters from the axis of the emplacement hole, if the emplacement hole is vertical, or no less than 10 meters from the axis of the emplacement hole, if the emplacement hole is horizontal, and no less than six meters from the wall of any drilled or excavated cavity or hole;

(iv) with respect to a drilled satellite hole, it shall be drilled no less than 0.3 meters and no more than 0.5 meters in diameter, unless the Parties otherwise agree. Within each hydrodynamic measurement zone, no washouts shall penetrate more than one meter into the wall of the hole;

(v) with respect to an excavated satellite hole, it shall have a cross section, measured in the plane perpendicular to its axis, no greater than 2.5 meters by 2.5 meters within each hydrodynamic measurement zone; and

(vi) within each hydrodynamic measurement zone, except for any drilled or excavated cavity or hole, all voids, external and unconnected to any satellite hole, greater than 10 cubic meters in volume, within six meters of the axis of any satellite hole, and all voids greater than one cubic meter in volume, within two meters of the axis of any satellite hole, shall be filled with stemming material having a bulk density no less than 70 percent of the average density of the surrounding rock;

(b) Designated Personnel shall have the right to carry out, under observation of personnel of the Testing Party and with their assistance, if such assistance is requested by Designated Personnel, directional surveys and geodetic measurements of each satellite hole and emplacement hole prior to the beginning of emplacement of sensing elements and cables and transducers;

(c) equipment specified in paragraph 3 of Section VIII of this Protocol shall be operated by Designated Personnel and shall be installed, in accordance with installation instructions provided in accordance with paragraph 6(c) of Section VIII of this Protocol, by Designated Personnel under observation of personnel of the Testing Party and with their assistance, if such assistance is requested by Designated Personnel. The location of each hydrodynamic recording facility and the command and monitoring facility of the Verifying Party and the instrumentation facility of the Testing Party specified in paragraph 10(l) of this Section shall be determined by the Testing Party in consultation with the Verifying Party in the Coordinating Group no less than 90 days prior to the beginning of emplacement of sensing elements and cables. Areas for the installation of these facilities, cable supports, and cableways for protection of cables of the Verifying Party specified in paragraphs 3(b), 3(f), and 3(g) of Section VIII of this Protocol shall be prepared by the Testing Party in accordance with requirements agreed upon in the Coordinating Group. Only cables of the Verifying Party shall be installed in these cableways. Designated Personnel shall have access, under observation of personnel of the Testing Party, to the cables specified in paragraphs 3(f) and 3(g) of Section VIII of this Protocol and to the cableways in which they are installed, at all times. Personnel of the Testing Party shall have access to these cableways only under observation of Designated Personnel;

(d) Designated Personnel shall have the right to use their own primary electrical power sources to supply electrical power to hydrodynamic equipment specified in paragraph 3 of Section VIII of this Protocol. At the request of the Verifying Party, the Testing Party shall supply electrical power from the standard electrical network of its test site through converters provided by the Verifying Party or, upon agreement of the Parties, by the Testing Party;

(e) for each test, the only equipment installed in each satellite hole shall be that of the Verifying Party specified in paragraphs 3(a) and 3(h) of Section VIII of this Protocol. This equipment shall be installed in each satellite hole at the locations specified by Designated Personnel. Designated Personnel shall have the right to install in each satellite hole no more than six sensing elements and cables, without regard to the number of switches, and no more than six transducers together with no more than 14 cables for information transmission and power supply. The total number of cable in each satellite hole shall not exceed 20. Personnel of each Party shall have the right to measure the location of the installed sensing elements and cables and transducers;

(f) Designated Personnel shall have the right to conduct a final directional survey and geodetic measurements of each satellite hole upon completion of installation of sensing elements and cables and transducers;

(g) personnel of the Testing Party, under observation of Designated Personnel, shall fill all voids in or connected to each satellite hole within each hydrodynamic measurement zone with a stemming material agreed upon by the Parties, having a bulk density no less than 70 percent of the average density of the surrounding rock. A representative sample of no less than 1000 cubic centimeters in volume of each stemming material used in each hydrodynamic measurement zone shall be provided to Designated Personnel for retention. The methods and materials used for stemming satellite holes and any hydrodynamic measurement equipment emplacement pipe shall:

(i) be consistent with the containment practices of the Testing Party;

(ii) be chosen to minimize voids around sensing elements and cables and transducers; and

(iii) be chosen to avoid damage to the sensing elements and cables and transducers;

(h) Designated Personnel shall have the right to observe the stemming of the hydrodynamic measurement zones of each emplacement hole in accordance with paragraph 9(d) of this Section. A representative sample of no less than 1000 cubic centimeters in volume of each stemming material used in each hydrodynamic measurement zone shall be provided to Designated Personnel for retention;

(i) the Testing Party shall have the right to case or line each emplacement hole; and

(j) the Testing Party shall have the right to case or line each satellite hole, provided that:

(i) sensing elements and cables and transducers can be installed as specified in subparagraph (e) of this paragraph;

(ii) casing or lining material in each hydrodynamic measurement zone is agreed upon by the Parties; and

(iii) casing or lining in each hydrodynamic measurement zone is affixed to the surrounding formation with material agreed upon by the Parties.

7. In preparation for the use of the hydrodynamic yield measurement method with respect to any explosion having a planned yield exceeding 50 kilotons and characteristics differing from those set forth in paragraph 2 or 3 of this Section with respect to a test of standard configuration:

(a) upon their arrival at the test site, no less than 10 days prior to the planned date of the beginning of emplacement of sensing elements and cables and transducers, Designated Personnel shall provide the Testing Party with a description of the recording format and the computer program, to enable the Testing Party to read digital data if digital recordings of hydrodynamic data will be made by Designated Personnel;

(b) the Testing Party shall provide Designated Personnel upon their arrival at the test site with the results of any studies of core samples and rock fragments extracted from each emplacement hole and satellite hole and any exploratory holes and tunnels, and the results of logging and geodetic measurements carried out in each emplacement hole, each satellite hole, and any exploratory holes and tunnels, relevant to the geology and geophysics of each hydrodynamic measurement zone, if the Testing Party carried out such studies and measurements;

(c) using their own equipment and under observation of personnel of the Testing Party, Designated Personnel shall have the right to carry out:

(i) if an emplacement hole is vertical, in the emplacement hole and each associated satellite hole, caliper logs, directional surveys, geodetic measurements, and depth or distance measurements to determine the dimensions and the relative locations of the emplacement hole and each satellite hole, as well as measurements to determine the location and volume of all voids within each hydrodynamic measurement zone, using, in a non-destructive way, such methods as electromagnetic measurements, radar, and acoustic sounding;

(ii) if an emplacement hole is vertical, within the hydrodynamic measurement zones of the emplacement hole and each associated satellite hole, gamma-gamma, gamma, neutron, electrical resistivity, magnetic susceptibility, gravity, acoustic, and television logging;

(iii) if an emplacement hole is horizontal, in the emplacement hole and each associated satellite hole, as well as in the drilled holes specified in subparagraph (e)(ii) of this paragraph, caliper logs, directional surveys, geodetic measurements, and distance measurements to determine the dimensions and relative location of these holes, as well as measurements to determine the location and volume of all voids in each hydrodynamic measurement zone using, in a non-destructive way, such methods as electromagnetic measurements, radar, and acoustic sounding;

(iv) if an emplacement hole is horizontal, in the drilled holes specified in subparagraph (e)(ii) of this paragraph, and within the hydrodynamic measurement zones of the emplacement hole and each associated satellite hole, gamma-gamma, gamma, neutron, electrical resistivity, magnetic susceptibility, gravity, and acoustic logging; and

(v) magnetic surveys, in vertical satellite holes and drilled horizontal satellite holes, to obtain information necessary for the installation and positioning of transducers;

(d) all logging data and geometrical measurements obtained by Designated Personnel, in accordance with subparagraph (c) of this paragraph, including calibration data, shall be duplicated, and a copy of the data shall be provided to personnel of the Testing Party prior to departure from the test site of Designated Personnel who have carried out these measurements. Calibration data shall include information necessary to confirm the sensitivity of logging equipment under the conditions in which it is used;

(e) Designated Personnel shall have the right to receive:

(i) if an emplacement hole is vertical, core sample or, at the option of Designated Personnel, rock fragments from the emplacement hole and from each satellite hole, extracted at no more than 10 depths within each hydrodynamic measurement zone, specified by Designated Personnel. The total volume of core samples or rock fragments extracted at each depth shall be no less than 400 cubic centimeters and no more than 3000 cubic centimeters, unless the Parties otherwise agree; and

(ii) if an emplacement hole is horizontal, core samples or, at the option of Designated Personnel, rock fragments from the emplacement hole and each satellite hole within each hydrodynamic measurement zone. If core samples are extracted from the emplacement hole or an excavated satellite hole, they shall be extracted during drilling from each of no more than 10 holes drilled at stations specified by Designated Personnel. The diameter of each drilled hole shall be no less than 0.09 meters and no more than 0.15 meters, and the depth of each hole shall be no more than the diameter of the emplacement hole or satellite hole at this station. Core samples shall be extracted at locations specified by Designated Personnel along each drilled hole. If core samples are extracted form a drilled satellite hole, they shall be extracted by personnel of the Testing Party during the drilling of the satellite hole, within each hydrodynamic measurement zone, at no more than 10 stations specified by Designated Personnel and under their observation. Rock fragments shall be extracted from the emplacement hole or an excavated satellite hole at each of no more than 10 stations specified by Designated Personnel. Core samples and rock fragments may be taken from no more than a total of 10 stations for each hole. If an emplacement hole or an excavated satellite hole is lined at any station specified by Designated Personnel for extracting core samples or rock fragments, personnel of the Testing Party shall enable Designated Personnel to extract core samples or rock fragments at such a station from native rock. The total volume of core samples or rock fragments extracted at each station shall be no less than 400 cubic centimeters, unless the Parties otherwise agree;

(f) core samples or rock fragments may be extracted in accordance with subparagraph (e) of this paragraph by personnel of the Testing Party, under observation of Designated Personnel, or by Designated Personnel, at the option of the Testing Party;

(g) if personnel of the Testing Party do not extract core samples or rock fragments in accordance with subparagraph (e) of this paragraph, Designated Personnel shall have the right, using their own equipment, to extract such core samples or rock fragments in accordance with subparagraph (e) of this paragraph, under observation of personnel of the Testing Party;

(h) if an emplacement hole is vertical, and if the Testing Party, prior to arrival of Designated Personnel at the test site, has cased a total of 20 meters or more of the emplacement hole or any satellite hole within any hydrodynamic measurement zone, and if within 22 meters from this cased hole there is no uncased hole with a diameter no less than 0.3 meters, the Testing Party shall provide an uncased hole for each hole so cased, with respect to which the Verifying Party shall have the same rights as those specified in subparagraphs (c), (e), (f), and (g) of this paragraph. Within each hydrodynamic measurement zone the axis of each uncased hole shall be no less than 11 and no more than 22 meters from such a cased hole. If personnel of the Testing Party, under observation of Designated Personnel, extract core samples through coring during the drilling of this uncased hole, the diameter of the hole shall be no less than 0.09 meters. If Designated Personnel, under observation of personnel of the Testing Party, extract core samples from this uncased hole following drilling, the diameter of the uncased hole shall be no less than 0.3 meters;

(i) Designated Personnel shall have the right to retain core samples and rock fragments specified in subparagraphs (c), (e), (f), (g), and (h) of this paragraph. Any such core samples or rock fragments shall be prepared in accordance with procedures agreed upon by the Parties for shipment to the territory of the Verifying Party; and

(j) logging, directional surveys, magnetic surveys, geodetic measurements, and extracting of core samples or rock fragments carried out in accordance with subparagraphs (e), (f), (g), (h), and (i) of this paragraph shall begin at times chosen by the Testing Party and specified in the coordinated schedule. Designated Personnel shall have the right, within a period not to exceed 25 days, to carry out logging, directional surveys, magnetic surveys, geodetic measurements, and coring activities, unless the Parties otherwise agree and so specify in the coordinated schedule. The Testing Party shall not emplace any explosive until the activities specified in this paragraph have been completed.

8. If the Verifying Party has notified the Testing Party that it intends to use the hydrodynamic yield measurement method with respect to a test of non-standard configuration having a planned yield exceeding 50 kilotons, and that it requires a reference test in accordance with paragraph 7 of Section III of this Protocol, the Testing Party shall provide for such a reference test for the non-standard test. To serve as a reference test, a test shall:

(a) have a planned yield exceeding 50 kilotons;

(b) be of standard configuration;

(c) have a single explosive canister;

(d) meet the following spacing criteria:

(i) the horizontal separation between the emplacement point of the reference test and each emplacement point of the non-standard test at which any explosive canister or its emplacement conditions differ from those specified for a test of standard configuration shall be no less than 300 meters and no more than 2000 meters.

(ii) each explosive canister of the test of non-standard configuration and the explosive canister of the associated reference test shall all be emplaced above the water table or shall all be emplaced below the water table; and

(iii) the depth of all emplacement points of the test of non-standard configuration shall be within 150 meters of the depth of the emplacement point of its associated reference tests; and

(e) be conducted either prior to, or within 12 months following, the conduct of the test of non-standard configuration for which it serves as a reference test.

9. Designated Personnel shall have the right:

(a) to have access along agreed routes to the location of the test to carry out activities related to use of the hydrodynamic yield measurement method;

(b) to have access to their equipment associated with the hydrodynamic yield measurement method from the time of its delivery to Designated Personnel at the test site, until it is transferred to personnel of the Testing Party in accordance with paragraph 7(i) of Section VIII of this Protocol, unless otherwise provided in this Protocol;

(c) with respect to a test of standard configuration, as well as with respect to any explosion having a planned yield of 50 kilotons or less:

(i) if an emplacement hole is vertical, prior to the lowering of the explosive canister into the emplacement hole, to confirm by direct measurement the external dimensions of each explosive canister; to inspect visually the entire structure of that canister and the choke section; to confirm by direct measurement that the choke section conforms to the specifications set forth in paragraph 2(c) of this Section; to observe continuously the explosive canister and any choke section from the time inspections and measurements, carried out in accordance with this subparagraph, begin; to observe the emplacement of the explosive canister into the emplacement hole and stemming of the emplacement hole from the time the entire explosive canister is last visible above the entrance of the emplacement hole until completion of stemming of each hydrodynamic measurement zone of the emplacement hole; to determine by direct measurement the depth of emplacement of the bottom part of any choke section; and to observe the stemming of the entire satellite hole; and

(ii) if an emplacement hole is horizontal, following placement of explosive canisters in the emplacement hole, and prior to the beginning of stemming around explosive canisters, to confirm by direct measurement the external dimensions of each explosive canister; to inspect visually the entire external structure of each explosive canister; to confirm by direct measurement that each choke section confirms to the specifications set forth in paragraph 3(e) of this Section; to observe continuously each explosive canister and each choke section from the time inspections and measurements, carried out in accordance with this subparagraph, begin, until the completion of stemming around each explosive canister and choke section, or, at the option of the Testing Party, until the explosive canister and choke section are fixed in place with solidified stemming material, in which case, after a period of no more than 24 hours for placement of explosives, to observe the explosive canister, the choke section, and the completion of stemming around each explosive canister and choke section; and to observe the stemming of each hydrodynamic measurement zone of the emplacement hole, the stemming of any access or bypass drifts, the stemming of any voids in each hydrodynamic measurement zone connected to the emplacement hole; and to observe the entire stemming of each associated satellite hole;

(d) with respect to any explosion having a planned yield exceeding 50 kilotons and characteristics differing from those set forth in paragraph 2 or 3 of this Section with respect to a test of standard configuration:

(i) if an emplacement hole is vertical, prior to the lowering of an explosive canister into the emplacement hole, to confirm by direct measurement the external dimensions of each explosive canister; to inspect visually the external structure of each canister and each choke section; to confirm by direct measurement that each choke section conforms to any specifications provided by the Testing Party in accordance with paragraph 10(c)(iii) of Section XI of this Protocol; to observe continuously each explosive canister and each choke section from the time inspections and measurements, carried out in accordance with this subparagraphs, begin; to observe the emplacement of each explosive canister into the emplacement hole and the stemming of the emplacement hole from the time an entire explosive canister is last visible above the entrance of the emplacement hole until completion of stemming of each hydrodynamic measurement zone of the emplacement hole; to determine by direct measurement the depth of emplacement of the upper surface of each explosive canister; and to observe the entire stemming of each associated satellite hole;

(ii) if an emplacement hole is horizontal, following placement of all explosive canisters in the emplacement hole and prior to the beginning of stemming around the explosive canisters to confirm by direct measurement the external dimensions of each explosive canister; to inspect visually the entire external structure of each explosive canister; to confirm by direct measurement that each choke section conforms to any specifications provided by the Testing Party in accordance with paragraph 10(c)(iii) of Section XI of this Protocol; to observe continuously each explosive canister and each choke section from the time inspections and measurements, carried out in accordance with this subparagraph, begin, until the completion of stemming around each explosive canister and choke section, or, at the option of the Testing Party, until the explosive canister and choke section are fixed in place with solidified stemming material, in which case, after a period of no more than 24 hours for placement of explosives, to observe the explosive canister, the choke section, and the completion of stemming around each explosive canister and choke section; and to observe the stemming of each hydrodynamic measurement zone of the emplacement hole, except those voids and any access or bypass drifts designated by the Testing Party to remain unstemmed in accordance with paragraph 10(c) of Section XI of this Protocol; and to observe the entire stemming of each associated satellite hole; and

(iii) if a test is conducted in a cavity, to measure the shape and volume of the cavity after excavation and once again immediately prior to placement of explosive canisters with explosives or placement of explosives into canisters. After placement of explosive canisters with explosives or placement of explosives into explosive canisters, Designated Personnel shall have the right to observe explosive canisters and to observe the stemming of each hydrodynamic measurement zone of the emplacement hole and any access or bypass drifts, and of any voids connected to the emplacement hole, within hydrodynamic measurement zone, except those voids and any access or bypass drifts designated by the Testing Party to remain unstemmed, in accordance with paragraph 10(c) of Section XI of this Protocol; and to observe the entire stemming of each associated satellite hole;

(e) with respect to a test of standard configuration, as well as with respect to any explosion having a planned yield of 50 kilotons or less:

(i) if an emplacement hole is vertical, to unobstructed visual observation of the entrance to the emplacement hole and associated satellite hole from completion of stemming of the satellite hole and of the hydrodynamic measurement zones of the emplacement hole until departure of all personnel from the test location prior to the test; and

(ii) if an emplacement hole is horizontal, to unobstructed visual observation of sensing elements and cables and transducers until completion of stemming of all associated satellite holes, and of cables specified in paragraph 3(b) of Section VIII of this Protocol until completion of their installation in protective cableways specified in paragraph 4(d) of this Section of the Protocol, as well as the entrance to the emplacement hole and associated satellite hole from completion of stemming of all satellite holes and of the hydrodynamic measurement zones of the emplacement hole until departure of all personnel from the test location prior to the test;

(f) with respect to any explosion having a planned yield exceeding 50 kilotons and characteristics differing from those set forth in paragraph 2 or 3 of this Section with respect to a test of standard configuration:

(i) if an emplacement hole is vertical, to unobstructed visual observation of the entrance to the emplacement hole and associated satellite hole from completion of stemming of all satellite holes and of the hydrodynamic measurement zones of the emplacement hole until departure of all personnel from the test location prior to the test; and

(ii) if an emplacement hole is horizontal, to unobstructed visual observation of sensing elements and cables and transducers until completion of stemming of all associated satellite holes, and of cables specified in paragraph 3(b) of Section VIII of this Protocol until completion of their installation in protective cableways specified in paragraph 6(c) of this Section of the Protocol, as well as the entrance to the emplacement hole and associated satellite hole from completion of stemming of all satellite holes and of the hydrodynamic measurement zones of the emplacement hole until departure of all personnel from the test location prior to the test;

(g) to monitor electrically the integrity and performance of their equipment specified in paragraphs 3(a), 3(b), 3(c), 3(d), 3(e), 3(f), and 3(g) of Section VIII of this Protocol and to observe continuously the cables specified in paragraphs 3(f) and 3(g) of Section VIII of this Protocol and the cableways in which they are installed as specified in paragraphs 4(d) and 6(c) of this Section, from the time emplacement of sensing elements and cables and transducers begins until departure of all personnel from the test location. Following departure of personnel and until reentry of personnel to the test location following the test, Designated Personnel shall have the right to observe remotely, by means of closed-circuit television, the surface area containing their hydrodynamic yield measurement equipment;

(h) to monitor electrically the integrity and performance of their equipment specified in paragraphs 3(a), 3(b), 3(c), 3(d), 3(f), and 3(g) of Section VIII of this Protocol from the command and monitoring facility specified in paragraph 3(e) of Section VIII of this Protocol, from commencement of its use by Designated Personnel until completion of the activities specified in paragraphs 9(m) and 14(b) of this Section;

(i) to transmit from the command and monitoring facility to each hydroponic recording facility the commands required for operation of that hydroponic recording facility;

(j) to use channels provided by the Testing Party within its telemetry system for transmission of information specified in subparagraphs (h), (i), (k), and (l) of this paragraph, if such a system is used at the test site of the Testing Party, or to use for these purposes its own cables, specified in paragraph 3(g) of Section VIII of this Protocol;

(k) to carry out hydrodynamic yield measurements and to record the hydrodynamic data;

(l) to transmit the hydrodynamic yield measurement data from each hydrodynamic recording facility to the command and monitoring facility; and

(m) to reenter the area containing each hydrodynamic recording facility at the same time as personnel of the Testing Party, and to have access, in accordance with procedures agreed upon by the Parties and accompanied by personnel of the Testing Party, to each hydrodynamic recording facility, for the purposes of retrieving and verifying the authenticity of recorded data and assessing the performance of the equipment of the Verifying Party during data recording and transmission.

10. During the carrying out of hydrodynamic yield measurements:

(a) the Representative of the Testing Party shall notify, in writing, the Designated Personnel Team Leader at the test site of the beginning of the period of readiness and the planned time of the test, in accordance with paragraph 13 of Section IV of this Protocol;

(b) the Testing Party shall produce an event readiness signal in the interval from seven to 15 minutes prior to the planned time of the test, as specified by the Verifying Party, with an accuracy of plus or minus 100 milliseconds. The parameters for this signal, produced by the Testing Party, and procedures for its transmission shall be agreed upon by the Parties;

(c) Designated Personnel shall have the right to generate, using the trigger conditioner devices approved by the Parties, a timing reference signal using an electromagnetic pulse from their sensing elements and cables. This timing reference signal shall be generated, transmitted, and used by Designated Personnel without intervention by personnel of the Testing Party. For each explosion in a test, the trigger conditioner shall receive signals from one or two hydrodynamic yield measurement cables;

(d) Designated Personnel, under observation of personnel of the Testing Party, shall have the right to install the trigger conditioner devices. From the time of installation of these devices until the time of the test:

(i) Designated Personnel shall have the right to test and monitor the operation of the devices;

(ii) personnel of the Testing Party shall have the right to monitor the operation of the devices and to monitor and record the timing reference signal; and

(iii) neither Designated Personnel nor personnel of the Testing Party shall have physical access to the devices, except under observation of personnel of the other Party;

(e) the Testing Party shall provide, at the request of the Verifying Party, an electrical plus corresponding to the nuclear explosion zero-time, with an accuracy of plus or minus one microsecond, for each explosion. The parameters for this signal and procedures for its transmission and reception shall be agreed upon by the Parties;

(f) the Testing Party shall have exclusive control over the generation of signals specified in subparagraphs (b) and (e) of this paragraph;

(g) Designated Personnel, under observation of personnel of the Testing Party, shall install in each cable from each satellite hole to a hydrodynamic recording facility an anti-intrusiveness device for interrupting the transmission, from the sensing elements and cables and transducers to the hydrodynamic recording facility of the Verifying Party, of any signal unrelated to hydrodynamic yield measurements. These devices shall be provided by the Testing Party from among those approved by both Parties and shall not interfere with the ability of Designated Personnel to record data required for hydrodynamic yield measurements of each explosion in a test. From the time of installation of these devices until the final dry run, personnel of each Party shall have the right to test and monitor the operation of the devices and to have physical access to them only under observation of personnel of the other Party. Sole control over the triggering of these devices shall be transferred to the Testing Party at the time of departure of all personnel from the test location prior to the test;

(h) each hydrodynamic recording facility shall have an independent grounding loop with an impedance no greater than 10 ohms;

(i) the shields of all cables associated with sensing elements and cables and transducers of the Verifying Party shall be grounded:

(i) at the input to each hydrodynamic recording facility of the Verifying Party;

(ii) at the output of each anti-intrusiveness device;

(iii) at the input of each trigger conditioner device; and

(iv) in those cables associated with sensing elements and cables in which no trigger conditioner device is installed, at the input of the anti-intrusiveness device;

(j) grounding of each hydrodynamic recording facility, as well as grounding of cables associated with the sensing elements and cables and transducers of the Verifying Party, shall be carried out by Designated Personnel under observation of personnel of the Testing Party. The grounding system of each hydrodynamic recording facility, as well as of cables associated with the sensing elements and cables and transducers shall be under the joint control of the Parties;

(k) Designated Personnel shall have the right to install, under observation of personnel of the Testing Party, an isolation transformer at the input of each anti-intrusiveness device or trigger conditioner device. From the time of installation of these devices until the time of the test, neither Designated Personnel nor personnel of the Testing Party shall have physical access to these devices, except under observation of personnel of the other Party;

(l) The Testing Party shall have the right to install, at a distance of no less than 50 meters from each hydrodynamic recording facility, a facility containing instrumentation for monitoring and recording the timing reference signal, for controlling and monitoring the operation of the anti-intrusiveness devices, and for the transmission of control and trigger signals. Signals between the instrumentation facility of the Testing Party and each hydrodynamic recording facility shall be transmitted over fiber optic cables. The Testing Party shall provide for the installation, in each hydrodynamic recording facility, of terminal devices for converting optical signals into electrical signals produced in accordance with subparagraphs (b) and (e) of this paragraph, and for monitoring the interval of interruption and for monitoring the power supply of the anti-intrusiveness device, in accordance with subparagraph (g) of this paragraph. The Verifying Party shall provide for the installation in the facility of the Testing Party of a terminal device for converting an optical signal into an electrical time referencing signal provided in accordance with subparagraph (d)(ii) of this paragraph. These provided devices shall be installed under observation of personnel of both Parties and sealed by the Party providing the device. The instrumentation facilities specified in this subparagraph shall be under the exclusive control of the Testing Party; and

(m) upon arrival at the test site, Designated Personnel shall provide the Testing Party with a copy of the block diagram of the equipment configuration for hydrodynamic yield measurements for the test together with notification of any changes from the block diagram approved during the familiarization process provided in paragraph 6(d)(i) of Section VIII of this Protocol. No less that two days prior to the final dry run, Designated Personnel shall notify the Testing Party, in writing, of any additional changes in this block diagram. In the event of any changes in the block diagram, the Testing Party shall have the right, within one day following such notification, to disapprove any changes it finds inconsistent with its non-intrusiveness, containment, safety, or security requirements. Such disapproval shall be provided, in writing, to the Designated Personnel Team Leader, stating the specific reasons for disapproval. Any changes not disapproved shall be deemed accepted. If a change is disapproved, Designated Personnel shall configure the equipment in accordance with the block diagram previously approved in accordance with paragraph 6(d)(i) of Section VIII of this Protocol, unless the Testing Party otherwise agrees.

11. Personnel of the Testing Party shall have the right to observe used of equipment by Designated Personnel at the test site, with access to each hydrodynamic recording facility and the command

and monitoring facility of the Verifying Party subject to the following:

(a) at any time prior to the test that Designated Personnel are not present in these facilities, these facilities shall be sealed by the seals of both Parties. Seals shall be removed only under observation of personnel of both Parties;

(b) prior to the test, except for periods specified in subparagraphs (c) and (d) of this paragraph, personnel of the Testing Party may enter these facilities only with the agreement of the Designated Personnel Team Leader and when accompanied by the Team Leader or his designated representative;

(c) for the period of two hours prior to the final dry run, and for the period of two hours prior to the time fixed for withdrawal of all personnel to the area designated for occupation during the test, personnel of the Testing Party, not to exceed two, shall have the right to join Designated Personnel in each hydrodynamic recording facility, to observe final preparations of the equipment and to confirm the agreed configuration of that equipment. All personnel shall leave the facility together; and

(d) for a period beginning two hours prior to a test and ending upon completion of the activities specified in paragraphs 9(m) and 14(b) of this Section, personnel of the Testing Party, not to exceed two, shall have the right to join Designated Personnel in the command and monitoring of the recording equipment and acquisition and duplication of data, and to receive a copy of these data.

12. Designated Personnel shall have the right to obtain photographs taken by personnel of the Testing Party using photographic cameras of the Testing Party or, at the option of the Testing Party, photographic cameras provided by the Verifying Party. These photographs shall be taken under the following conditions:

(a) the Testing Party shall identify those of its personnel who will take photographs;

(b) photographs shall be taken at the request and under observation of Designated Personnel. If requested by Designated Personnel, such photographs shall show the size of an object by placing a measuring scale, provided by Designated Personnel, alongside that object during the photographing;

(c) Designated Personnel shall determine whether photographs conform to those requested, and if not, repeat photographs shall be taken; and

(d) before completion of any photographed operation related to emplacement, and prior to the time at which an object that is being photographed becomes permanently hidden from view, Designated Personnel shall determine whether requested photographs are adequate. If they are not adequate, before the operation shall proceed additional photographs shall be taken until the Designated Personnel determine that the photographs of that operation are adequate. This photographic process shall be undertaken as expeditiously as possible, and in no case shall the cumulative delay resulting from this process exceed two hours for each of the operations specified in paragraphs 13(a), 13(b), 13(d), 13(e), and 13(f) of this Section, unless the Parties otherwise agree, except that stemming shall not be interrupted as a result of the photographic process.

13. Designated Personnel shall have the right to obtain photographs, taken in accordance with paragraph 12 of this Section, of the following:

(a) the emplacement and installation of equipment associated with the hydrodynamic yield measurement method, including all sensing elements and cables and transducers and their connections, each hydrodynamic recording facility, the command and monitoring facility, anti-intrusiveness devices, and trigger conditioner devices;

(b) the stemming of all satellite holes;

(c) all choke sections and the exterior of each explosive canister;

(d) if an emplacement hole is vertical, the emplacement of each explosive canister and the stemming of the hydrodynamic measurement zones of the emplacement hole;

(e) if an emplacement hole is horizontal, the interior of the emplacement hole within 20 meters of the emplacement point of each installed explosive canister and the stemming of each hydrodynamic measurement zones of the emplacement hole;

(f) core samples and rock fragments obtained in accordance with paragraphs 5(e), 5(f), 5(g), 5(h), 7(e), 7(f), 7(g), and 7(h) of this Section, the equipment and activities associated with extracting such samples, as well as the interior of the emplacement hole, if an emplacement hole is horizontal, at the stations where core samples or rock fragments were extracted; and

(g) with the agreement of the Testing Party, other activities of Designated Personnel directly related to the use of the hydrodynamic yield measurement method.

14. The following procedures shall apply to the recovery and transfer of data:

(a) no later than the final dry run, Designated Personnel shall inform personnel of the Testing Party of the procedures for recovering and verifying the authenticity of data and shall advise personnel of the Testing Party, at the time of data recovery, of any changes Designated Personnel make in those procedures and the reasons for such changes;

(b) following the test, Designated Personnel, in the presence of personnel of the Testing Party, shall enter the hydrodynamic recording facility and recover all recordings of data taken at the time of the test. Designated Personnel shall prepare two identical copies of such data. Personnel of the Testing Party shall select one of the two identical copies. Designated Personnel shall retain the other copy, but no other such data; and

(c) following the completion of the activities specified in paragraph 9(m) of this Section and subparagraph (b) of this paragraph, Designated Personnel shall leave the hydrodynamic recording facility and the command and monitoring facility at the same time as personnel of the Testing Party. Designated Personnel shall have no further access to their hydrodynamic recording facility, command and monitoring facility, or equipment until these are returned to the Verifying Party in accordance with paragraph 7(i)(ii) of Section VIII of this Protocol, unless the Parties otherwise agree, in which case access by Designated Personnel to their facilities and equipment shall be under observation of personnel of the Testing Party.

15. Designated Personnel shall not be present in areas from which all personnel of the Testing Party have been withdrawn in connection with the test, but shall have the right to reenter those areas, as provided in this Protocol, at the same time as personnel of the Testing Party.

16. All hydrodynamic yield measurement activities shall be carried out in accordance with the coordinated schedule. Designated Personnel who will carry out the activities specified in this Section and in paragraph 7(e) of Section VIII of this Protocol shall arrive at the test site in accordance with the coordinated schedule, but no less than three days prior to the date specified by the Testing Party for the beginning of these activities.

17. The number of Designated Personnel carrying out hydrodynamic yield measurements with respect to a test of standard configuration conducted in a single emplacement hole, without regard to the number of ends of that emplacement hole, as these are specified in paragraph 3(b) of this Section, shall not exceed, at any time, 35 individuals, and the number of Designated Personnel, at any time, carrying out hydrodynamic yield measurements with respect to a test of non-standard configuration or a test conducted in more than one emplacement hole shall not exceed, at any time, 45 individuals, unless the Parties otherwise agree. Within these totals, the coordinated schedule shall be developed so as to ensure that the number of Designated Personnel for carrying out hydrodynamic yield measurements with respect to a specified test shall not exceed:

(a) if a test is of standard configuration, for carrying out activities related to hydrodynamic yield measurements, other than activities specified in paragraphs 5(j) of this Section, 26 individuals and, for carrying out activities specified in paragraph 5(j) of this Section:

(i) if an emplacement hole is vertical, 18 individuals; or

(ii) if an emplacement hole is horizontal, 22 individuals; or

(b) if a test is of non-standard configuration or is conducted in more than one emplacement hole, for carrying out activities related to hydrodynamic yield measurements other than activities specified in paragraph 5(j) or 7(j) of this Section, 35 individuals and, for carrying out activities specified in paragraph 5(j) or 7(j) of this Section, 26 individuals; and

(c) Designated Personnel shall include at least two individuals fluent in the language of the Party.

SECTION VI. SEISMIC YIELD MEASUREMENT METHOD

1. For the purposes of the use of the seismic yield measurement method, the Verifying Party shall have the right to carry out independent measurements at three Designated Seismic Stations in the territory of the Testing Party, in accordance with this Section. Designated Seismic Stations of each Party shall meet the following criteria:

(a) be located within its continental territory;

(b) each shall have an Lg-wave signal-to-noise ration not less than nine for any test in its territory having a yield of 150 kilotons. The signal-to-noise ratio shall be defined as one-half of the maximum peak amplitude of the Lg-wave signal divided by the root-mean-square value of the seismic noise in the recording segment immediately preceding the arrival of the P-wave signal and having a duration of no less than one minute. The signals and the noise shall be measured on a vertical component of the recording in the frequency range typical of Lg-waves recorded at the Designated Seismic Station;

(c) ensure wide azimuthal coverage of each of its test sites, insofar as permitted by their geographic location; and

(d) be chosen from those existing seismic stations that provide earthquake and other seismic event data, including tests, to archives in the territory of the Testing Party, accessible to the Verifying Party.

2. The United States of America designates the following three seismic stations as meeting the criteria specified in paragraph 1 of this Section: Tulsa, Oklahoma (TUL) (35°55′N; 095°48′W); Black Hills, South Dakota (RSSD) (44°07′N; 104°02′W); and Newport Washington, (NEW) 48°16′N); 117°07′W).

3. The Union of Soviet Socialist Republics designates the following three seismic stations as meeting the criteria specified in paragraph 1 of this Section: Arti (ARU) (56°26′N; 058°34′E); Novosibirsk (NVS) (54°51′N; 083°16′E); and Obninsk (OBN) (55°07′N; 036°34′E).

4. Upon entry into force of the Treaty each Party shall provide the other Party with the following information on each of its Designated Seismic Stations:

(a) a site diagram of the station showing the areas assigned for use by Designated Personnel;

(b) elevation above mean sea level to the nearest 10 meters; and

(c) types of rock on which it is located.

5. The Testing Party shall have the right to replace one or more of its Designated Seismic Stations, provided:

(a) the new Designated Seismic Station meets all the criteria specified in paragraph 1 of this Section;

(b) notification of the decision of the Testing Party to select a new Designated Seismic Station, together with the station name and its reference code, the station coordinates to the nearest one minute of geographic latitude and longitude, and the information and site diagram for the new station specified in paragraph 4 of this Section, is provided to the Verifying Party no less than 90 days prior to the planned date of any test with respect to which the Verifying Party has notified the Testing Party that it intends to use the seismic yield measurement method and for which this Designated Seismic Station would be used; and

(c) seismic data, for the period from entry into force of the Treaty until the new designated Seismic Station, are placed in archives in the territory of the Testing Party, accessible to the Verifying Party. If a Designated Seismic Station is replaced within the first four years of operation of the new Designated Seismic Station shall be placed in archives in the territory of the Testing Party, accessible to the Verifying Party.

6. If any Designated Seismic Station does not meet the criteria specified in paragraph 1 of this Section, the Verifying Party shall have the right to request its replacement with another Designated Seismic Station that meets such criteria. Any request by the Verifying Party for replacement shall state the reasons this Designated Seismic Station does not meet the criteria specified in paragraph 1 of this Section, and shall be transmitted to the Testing Party through the Nuclear Risk Reduction Centers. If the Parties are unable to resolve the issue of replacement of a Designated Seismic Station, it shall immediately be referred to the Bilateral Consultative Commission in accordance with paragraph 1( ) of Section XI of this Protocol for resolution.

7. The Testing Party shall bear the costs of replacing any Designated Seismic Station in its territory, including any costs of eliminating the previous Designated Seismic Station and the costs of preparing a new Designated Seismic Station in accordance with paragraph 6 of this Section.

8. If requested by the Verifying Party, the Testing Party shall provide, according to agreed technical specifications, at each Designated Station for the exclusive use of Designated Personnel:

(a) a surface vault and pier for installation of seismic sensors, to be located not less than 100 meters and not more than 200 meters from the seismometers of the Testing Party, unless the Parties otherwise agree;

(b) a borehole for installation of seismic senders, to be located not less than 100 meters and not more than 200 hundred meters from the seismometers of the Verifying Party, unless the Parties otherwise agree;

(c) a working facility with an area not less than 20 square meters, for the installation and operation of equipment by Designated Personnel and situated not less than 75 meters and not more than 125 meters from the seismometers of the Verifying Party, unless the Parties otherwise agree;

(d) a covered cableway that will allow Designated Personnel to connect devices in the facilities specified in subparagraphs (a), (b), and (c) of this paragraph;

(e) a facility for the storage of shipping containers and spare parts for the use of Designated Personnel while carrying out their activities at the Designated Seismic Stations; and

(f) electrical power from its standard electrical network through converters provided by the Verifying Party or, by agreement of the Parties, by the Testing Party.

9. At each Designated Seismic Station, personnel of the Testing Party shall:

(a) have the right to observe the installation and calibration of equipment by Designated Personnel, but at all other times they may be present only at the invitation of the Designated Personnel Team Leader and when accompanied by the Designated Personnel Team Leader or his designated representative;

(b) not to interfere with the activities of Designated Personnel with regard to the installation, calibration, adjustment, and operation of equipment; and

(c) provide assistance and logistical support to Designated Personnel in accordance with paragraph 13 of Section XI of this Protocol, and, by agreement of the Parties, other assistance and logistical support requested by Designated Personnel.

10. In carrying out seismic measurements at the Designated Seismic Stations, Designated Personnel shall have the right to:

(a) confirm that the agreed technical specifications for the installation and operation of the equipment have been met during the time periods specified in the coordinated schedule;

(b) have access to their equipment from the time of the arrival of Designated Personnel at, and until their departure from, each Designated Seismic Station, unless otherwise provided in this Protocol;

(c) install, calibrate, adjust, and continuously operate their equipment;

(d) record seismic signals and universal time signals continuously from the time their equipment is installed until two hours after the test, as well as process data to monitor the quality of recorded data and retrieve and copy all recorded data;

(e) use their own electrical sources to supply electrical power to their equipment specified in paragraph 4 of Section VIII of this Protocol;

(f) install and operated tamper-detection equipment and observe the cableway and exterior of the facility in which the seismic sensors are installed;

(g) assess the integrity and performance of their equipment and confirm that there has been no interference with seismic measurements and the recording of such measurements; and

(h) lock and seal the facilities specified in paragraphs 8(a), 8(b), 8(c), and 8(e) of this Section with their own seals.

11. The Representative of the Testing Party shall notify, in writing and referenced to Universal Time Coordinated, the Designated Personnel Team Leader at each Designated Seismic Station of the beginning of the period of event readiness and the planned time of the test, to the nearest one second, in accordance with paragraph 13 of Section IV of this Protocol.

12. At each Designated Seismic Station, Designated Personnel shall:

(a) upon arrival, provide the Representative of the Testing Party with a description of the recording format and the computer program to enable the Testing Party to read digital data, if digital recordings of data are made;

(b) prior to departure, provide the Representative of the Testing Party with the following:

(i) a copy of all data recorded by all equipment used by Designated Personnel, on the same medium as that on which these data were recorded;

(ii) a graphic representation on a paper medium of the seismic data of the test for a period of time beginning one minute prior to the test and ending 30 minutes following the test; and

(iii) the results of the calibration of all seismic equipment, including the amplitude-frequency characteristics of the equipment used to measure and record the seismic data; and

(c) prior to their departure, prepare for inspection, storage in accordance with conditions chosen by the Testing Party, or shipment of their equipment.

13. Designated Personnel shall have the right to acquire photographs of operations and activities related to seismic yield measurement at the Designated Seismic Stations. Photographs shall be taken by personnel of the Testing Party, using their own photographic cameras or, at the option of the Testing Party, by Designated Personnel using their own photographic cameras.

(a) If the testing party takes photographs, the following conditions shall be met:

(i) the Testing Party shall identify those of its personnel who will take photographs;

(ii) photographs shall be taken at the request and under observation of Designated Personnel. If requested by Designated Personnel, such photographs shall show the size of an object being photographed by placing a measuring scale, provided by Designed Personnel, alongside that object during the photographing; and

(iii) Designated Personnel shall determine whether photographs that were taken conform to those requested, and, if not, repeat photographs shall be taken.

(b) If Designated Personnel take photographs, the following conditions shall be met:

(i) the Verifying Party shall identify those of its Designated Personnel who will take photographs; and

(ii) photographs shall be taken under observation of personnel of the Testing Party, unless otherwise agreed by the Parties.

14. All activities of Designated Personnel at the Designated Seismic Stations shall be carried out in accordance with the coordinated schedule. Designated Personnel shall arrive at the Designated Seismic Stations in accordance with this schedule, but no less than 10 days prior to the planned date of the test. Designated Personnel shall depart the Designated Seismic Station within two days following the test.

15. If the planned date of a test is postponed by more than 10 days following receipt of the most recent notification, Designated Personnel shall have the right to leave the Designated Seismic Stations or, if requested by the Representative of the Testing Party, shall depart the Designated Seismic Stations for a mutually agreed

location within the territory of the Testing Party or depart the territory of the Testing Party through the point of entry. If Designated Personnel leave the Designated Seismic Stations, they shall have the right to seal their equipment located at the stations. The seals shall not be broken except by Designated Personnel under observation of personnel of the Testing Party. Designated Personnel shall have the right to reoccupy the Designated Seismic Stations no less than 72 hours prior to the next planned time of the test.

16. The number of Designated Personnel carrying out seismic measurements at each Designated Seismic Station shall not exceed five. At least one individual fluent in the language of the Testing Party shall be among Designated Personnel at each Designated Seismic Station.

SECTION VII. ON-SITE INSPECTION

1. In carrying out on-site inspections, the Verifying Party shall have the right to confirm the validity of the geological, geophysical, and geometrical information provided in accordance with paragraphs 4 and 9 of Section IV of this Protocol, in accordance with the following procedures:

(a) the Testing Party shall provide Designated Personnel, upon their arrival at the test site, with the result of any studies of core samples and rock fragments extracted from each emplacement hole and any exploratory holes and tunnels, and the results of logging and geodetic measurements carried out in each emplacement hole and any exploratory holes and tunnels, relevant to the geology and geophysics of the emplacement medium, if the Testing Party carried out such studies and measurements;

(b) using their own equipment and under observation of personnel of the Testing Party, Designated Personnel shall have the right to carry out:

(i) if an emplacement hole is vertical, in the emplacement hole, from the end of the hole to the entrance to the hole, gamma-gamma, gamma, neutron, electrical resistivity, magnetic susceptibility, gravity, acoustic, television, and caliper logging, and measurements of the depth and cross section of the emplacement hole, as well as measurements to determine the location and volume of voids, using, in a non-destructive way, such methods as electromagnetic measurements, radar, and acoustic sounding; and

(ii) if an emplacement hole is horizontal, in the holes specified in subparagraph (d)(ii) of this paragraph, and in the emplacement hole in the regions extending from each end of the emplacement hole to a point located 300 meters from the corresponding emplacement point in the direction of the entrance to the emplacement hole, gamma-gamma, gamma, neutron, electrical resistivity, magnetic susceptibility, gravity, acoustic, and caliper logging, and measurements of the length and cross section of the emplacement hole, as well as measurements to determine the location and volume of voids, using, in a non-destructive way, such methods as electromagnetic measurements, radar, and acoustic sounding;

(c) all logging and geometrical measurement data obtained by Designated Personnel in accordance with subparagraph (b) of this paragraph, including calibration data, shall be duplicated, and a copy of these data shall be provided to personnel of the Testing Party prior to the departure from the test site of Designated Personnel who have carried out those measurements. Calibration data shall include information needed to confirm the sensitivity of logging equipment under the conditions in which it is used;

(d) Designated Personnel shall have the right to receive:

(i) if an emplacement hole is vertical, core samples or rock fragments, at the option of Designated Personnel, extracted from the emplacement hole at 10 depths specified by Designated Personnel, plus one additional depth for every complete 50-meter distance between the uppermost and lowest emplacement points. The total volume of core samples or rock fragments extracted at each of the specified depths shall be no less than 400 cubic centimeters and no more than 3,000 cubic centimeters, unless the Parties otherwise agree; and

(ii) if an emplacement hole is horizontal, core samples or rock fragments, at the option of Designated Personnel, from the emplacement hole in the regions extending from each end of the emplacement hole to a point located 300 meters from the corresponding emplacement point in the direction of the entrance to the emplacement hole. Core samples shall be extracted during drilling form each of five holes drilled at stations in the emplacement hole, specified by Designated Personnel. These five stations shall be separated from each other by no less than 5 meters. At each station the hole shall be drilled in a direction specified by Designated Personnel, except that at each station within 65 meters of each emplacement point the Testing Party shall have the right to exclude two 90-degree sectors separated by a sector of 90 degrees. The diameter of each drilled hole shall be no less than 0.09 meters and no more than 0.15 meters, and the depth of each hole shall be no more than the diameter of the emplacement hole at that station. Core samples shall be extracted at locations specified by Designated Personnel along the drilled hole. Rock fragments shall be extracted from the walls of the emplacement hole at five stations specified by Designated Personnel. The total volume of core samples or rock fragments extracted at each station shall be no less than 400 cubic centimeters and no more than 3,000 cubic centimeters, unless the Parties otherwise agree.

(e) core samples or rock fragments, at the option of Designated Personnel, shall be extracted, in accordance with subparagraph (d) of this paragraph, by personnel of the Testing Party, under observation of Designated Personnel, or by Designated Personnel, at the option of the Testing Party;

(f) if the Testing Party does not extract core samples or rock fragments in accordance with subparagraph (d) of this paragraph, Designated Personnel shall have the right to do so, using their own equipment and under observation of personnel of Testing Party;

(g) if, prior to arrival of Designated Personnel at the test site, the Testing Party has cased more than a total of 20 meters within any 100-meter segment of a vertical emplacement hole in the region extending from the end of the emplacement hole to a point 300 meters from the planned emplacement point in the direction of the entrance to the emplacement hole, the Testing Party shall provide an uncased hole with respect to which the Verifying Party shall have the same rights as those specified for an emplacement hole in subparagraphs (b), (d), (e), and (f) of this paragraph. This uncased hole shall be located no more than 50 meters from the emplacement hole and shall have a depth no less than that of the emplacement hole. If personnel of the Testing Party, under observation of Designated Personnel, extract core samples through coring during the drilling of this uncased hole, the diameter of this hole shall be no less than 0.09 meters. If Designated Personnel, under observation of personnel of the Testing Party, extract core samples from this uncased hole following drilling, the diameter of this uncased hole shall be no less than 0.3 meters; and

(h) Designated Personnel shall have the right to retain core samples and rock fragments specified in subparagraphs (d), (e), (f), and (g) of this paragraph. Any such core samples or rock fragments shall be prepared in accordance with the procedures agreed upon by the Parties for shipment to the territory of the Verifying Party.

2. Designated Personnel shall have the right:

(a) if an emplacement hole is vertical, to observe the emplacement of each explosive canister into the emplacement hole from the time the bottom of the canister is last visible above the entrance of the emplacement hole, and to determine by direct measurement the depth of emplacement of the bottom of the canister;

(b) if an emplacement hole is horizontal, to determine by direct measurement the location of each explosive canister in the emplacement hole, and to confirm the presence of at least 1 meters of stemming, as specified in subparagraph (c)(ii) of this paragraph, in any previously stemmed tunnel that had provided access to an explosive canister, using, in a non-destructive way, such methods as electromagnetic measurements, radar, and acoustic sounding;

(c) to observe stemming of each emplacement hole:

(i) if an emplacement hole is vertical, until a solid concrete plug no less than three meters thick is installed above the explosive canister closest to the entrance to the emplacement hole; and

(ii) if an emplacement hole is horizontal, until access to any explosive canister has been prevented by installation of stemming material for a distance no less than 10 meters, including the installation of a solid concrete plug no less than three meters thick;

(d) to have access along agreed routes to the location of the test to carry out activities related to on-site inspection;

(e) to have access to their equipment associated with the carrying out of on-site inspection from the time of its transfer to Designated Personnel at the test site, until it is transferred to personnel of the Testing Party in accordance with paragraph 9(g) of Section VIII of this Protocol, unless otherwise provided in this Protocol;

(f) if an emplacement hole is vertical, to have access, for the purpose of visual inspection of the ground surface, to the area delineated by a circle having a radius of 300 meters, centered on the entrance to the emplacement hole; and

(g) if an emplacement hole is horizontal, to have access, for the purpose of visual inspection of the ground surface, to the area delineated by a circle having a radius of 300 meters, centered directly above the emplacement point of each explosive canister.

3. Designated Personnel shall have the right to obtain photographs associated with on-site inspection, which shall be taken in accordance with paragraph 12 of Section V of this Protocol, of the following:

(a) if an emplacement hole is vertical, the emplacement of each explosive canister and the stemming of the emplacement hole specified in paragraph 2(c)(i) of this Section;

(b) if an emplacement hole is horizontal, the interior of the emplacement hole within 20 meters of the emplacement point of each explosive canister, and the stemming of the emplacement hole specified in paragraph 2(c)(ii) of this Section;

(c) core samples and rock fragments, extracted in accordance with paragraphs 1(d), 1(e), 1(f), and 1(g) of this Section, the equipment and activities associated with extracting such samples, as well as the interior of the emplacement hole, if the emplacement hole is horizontal, at the stations where core samples and rock fragments were extracted; and

(d) with the agreement of the Testing Party, other activities of Designated Personnel directly related to on-site inspection.

4. In no case shall the cumulative delay resulting from the photographic process specified in paragraph 3 of this Section exceed two hours for each of the operations specified in paragraph 3 of this Section, unless the Parties otherwise agree, except that stemming shall not be interrupted as a result of the photographic process.

5. All on-site inspection activities shall be carried out in accordance with the coordinated schedule. Designated Personnel shall have the right within a period not to exceed 15 days, to carry out logging and coring activities specified in paragraph 1 of this Section, unless the Parties otherwise agree and so specify in the coordinated schedule. These activities shall be completed no less than one day prior to the beginning of emplacement of explosives. Upon completion of the activities specified in paragraph 1 of this Section, Designated Personnel shall depart the territory of the Testing Party, except that Designated Personnel who will also participate

in the activities specified in paragraph 2 of this Section shall remain at the test site, if the Parties decide that this is required by the coordinated schedule. Otherwise, Designated Personnel shall depart the territory of the Testing Party or, if agreed by the Parties, they may depart to another point within the territory of the Testing Party. All Designated Personnel who will carry out the activities specified in paragraph 2 of this Section shall arrive at the test site in accordance with the coordinated schedule, but no less than three days prior to the date specified by the Testing Party for the beginning of these activities.

6. The number of Designated Personnel carrying out the activities specified in paragraph 1 of this Section shall not exceed 23 at any time. The number of Designated Personnel carrying out activities specified in paragraphs 2(a), 2(b), and 2(c) of this Section shall not exceed five at any time. At least one individual fluent in the language of the Testing Party shall be among Designated Personnel.

SECTION VIII. EQUIPMENT

1. Designated Personnel, in carrying out activities related to verification in accordance with this Protocol, shall have the right to bring into the territory of the Testing Party, install, and use:

(a) if the Verifying Party has provided notification of its intent to use the hydrodynamic yield measurement method, part or all of the equipment specified in paragraph 3 of this Section;

(b) if the Verifying Party has provided notification of its intent to use the seismic yield measurement method, part or all of the equipment specified in paragraph 4 of this Section;

(c) if the Verifying Party has provided notification of its intent to carry out on-site inspection, part or all of the equipment specified in paragraph 5 of this Section;

(d) maintenance and support equipment and spare parts necessary for the installation and functioning of equipment of the Verifying Party;

(e) electrical power supplies, converters, and associated cables;

(f) photographic equipment, if the Testing Party does not provide such equipment;

(g) locks, seals, and equipment necessary for installing seals of the Verifying Party and checking their integrity;

(h) medical and health physics equipment and supplies, personal protective gear, recreational items, and such other items as may be agreed upon by the Parties;

(i) office equipment and supplies, including, but not limited to, copying and facsimile machines, and personal computers;

(j) closed-circuit television equipment for the purpose of carrying out remote observation by Designated Personnel, in accordance with paragraph 9(g) of Section V of this Protocol, if the Testing Party does not provide such equipment; and

(k) satellite communications equipment, if the Testing Party does not provide satellite communications for Designated Personnel.

2. During the first meeting of the Coordinating Group for a specific test, the Parties shall agree, within 15 days, upon such additional materials, temporary structures, and equipment as may be requested in writing by the Verifying Party and which shall be supplied by the Testing Party for use by Designated Personnel. Such additional materials, temporary structures, and equipment, with their descriptions and operating instructions, shall be provided to Designated Personnel in accordance with the coordinated schedule.

3. The list of equipment for the purposes of the use of the hydrodynamic yield measurement methods in accordance with Section V of this Protocol shall include:

(a) sensing elements and cables and transducers;

(b) electrical cables for transmission of hydrodynamic data from the entrance of each horizontal satellite hole to the entrance of the horizontal emplacement hole with which it is associated;

(c) the hydrodynamic recording facilities, with equipment, including computers, for acquiring, recording, and processing data and timing signals, as well as for transmitting and receiving hydrodynamic data and command and monitoring signals between each hydrodynamic recording facility and the command and monitoring facility, and the shock mitigation platforms for installing each hydrodynamic recording facility, and with equipment for distributing electrical analogs of the signals arriving from the instrumentation facility of the Testing Party;

(d) trigger conditioner devices for generating a timing reference signal from the electrical cables of the Verifying Party, and terminal devices for converting an optical signal into an electrical signal;

(e) the command and monitoring facility, with equipment, including computers, for generating and recording command and monitoring signals, for transmitting and receiving command and monitoring signals between each hydrodynamic recording facility and the command and monitoring facility, as well as for retrieving, storing, and processing hydrodynamic data;

(f) electrical cables for transmission of hydrodynamic data from the entrance of each vertical satellite hole or from the entrance of each horizontal emplacement hole to the hydrodynamic recording facility of the Verifying Party;

(g) electrical cables for the grounding of equipment and for above-ground transmission of electrical power, and electrical and fiber optic cables for above-ground transmission of command and monitoring signals and hydrodynamic data;

(h) measuring and calibration instrumentation, support equipment, and equipment for installing and positioning sensing elements and cables and transducers;

(i) equipment specified in paragraph 5 of this Section for confirming the characteristics of emplacement holes and satellite holes; and

(j) directional survey and magnetic survey equipment and equipment for determining the distance between emplacement holes and satellite holes, and equipment for detecting voids and determining their relative locations and volumes

4. The list of equipment for the purposes of the use of the seismic yield measurement method at each Designated Seismic Station in accordance with Section VI of this Protocol shall include:

(a) seismic sensors capable of recording ground movements in three orthogonal directions within the frequency range from 0.1 to 10 hertz;

(b) equipment for amplifying, filtering, and digitizing the output signals of the seismic sensors;

(c) equipment for recording seismic data, and cables for interconnecting the equipment described in this paragraph;

(d) equipment for controlling sensors and recorders and for calibrating equipment;

(e) means of recording Universal Time Coordinated and referencing the recorded seismic data to it;

(f) equipment, including computers, to process data, to monitor the quality of the recorded data, as well as to display, store, and copy data; and

(g) equipment, including that using digital algorithms, for assessing the validity of recorded seismic data.

5. The list of equipment for the purposes of carrying out on-site inspection in accordance with Section VII of this Protocol shall include:

(a) equipment for obtaining the following logging data: gamma-gamma, gamma, neutron, electrical resistivity, magnetic susceptibility, gravity, television, acoustic, and caliper, as well as equipment for measuring the depth and cross section of emplacement holes and for measuring the volume of voids;

(b) equipment, including computers, for calibrating logging equipment, for monitoring the quality of the recorded data, as well as for recording, displaying, and copying data from logging equipment;

(c) equipment for extracting core samples and rock fragments; and

(d) geologist's field tools and kits, and equipment for the recording of field data.

6. The Testing Party shall have the right, for the purposes of an initial familiarization, to inspect the equipment and every component thereof that the Verifying Party intends to use in carrying out activities related to verification, and thereafter shall have the right to familiarize itself with the equipment and every component thereof that had not previously been provided for this purpose in accordance with this paragraph. For these purposes:

(a) the equipment subject to familiarization by the Testing Party shall include:

(i) a set of equipment for hydrodynamic yield measurements, specified in paragraph 3 of this Section;

(ii) a set of equipment for seismic yield measurements, specified in paragraph 4 of this Section;

(iii) a set of equipment for on-site inspection, specified in paragraph 5 of this Section; and

(iv) the equipment specified in paragraphs 1(d), 1(e), 1(f), 1(g), 1(h), 1(i), 1(j), and 1(k) of this Section;

(b) the Verifying Party shall initiate the familiarization process by notifying the Testing Party no less than 30 days prior to the date on which it intends to deliver equipment to the point of entry. This notification shall include a preliminary inventory of the equipment and the planned date of its delivery;

(c) no less tan seven days prior to the date of delivery of equipment, the Verifying Party shall provide a complete inventory of such equipment, which shall also specify which equipment, in accordance with paragraph 7(h) of this Section, will be removed from the facilities of the Verifying Party immediately prior to the beginning of the final dry run and immediately prior to the test. At the same time the Verifying Party shall provide instructions on the installation and operation of equipment with functional and technical descriptions and specifications, including electrical diagrams, as well as block diagrams of the system and its components;

(d) no more than 45 days following receipt of the equipment, the Testing Party, taking into account the equipment specified for removal in subparagraph (c) of this paragraph, shall specify, in writing, to the Verifying Party:

(i) the equipment approved by it for use by Designated Personnel in accordance with the information provided in accordance with subparagraph (c) of this paragraph; and

(ii) the characteristics of any equipment component it finds unacceptable because it is inconsistent with its non-intrusiveness, containment, safety, or security requirements;

(e) no more than 50 days following its initial delivery to the point of entry, equipment shall be returned, in the same condition as that in which it was received, to the Verifying Party at the point of entry; and

(f) following receipt of the written evaluation provided by the Testing Party in accordance with subparagraph (d)(ii) of this paragraph, the Verifying Party may deliver to the Testing Party, for familiarization in accordance with procedures specified in subparagraphs (b) and (c) of this paragraph, modified or replacement equipment to eliminate the unacceptable characteristics specified in subparagraphs (d) and (e) of this paragraph shall be followed with respect to the modified or replacement equipment.

7. The following procedures shall apply to equipment for use of the hydrodynamic yield measurement method:

(a) with the exception of that equipment that the Verifying Party intends to use from the equipment stored in accordance with subparagraph (j) of this paragraph, no less than 60 days prior to the planned date of the beginning of emplacement of sensing elements and cables or the planned date of the beginning of emplacement of explosives, whichever occurs earlier, unless the Parties otherwise agree, the Verifying Party shall deliver in sealed containers to the point of entry, at its option, either one or two sets of all or part of the equipment specified in paragraphs 1(d), 1(e), 1(f), 1(g), 1(h), 1(i), 1(k), 3(i), and 3(j) of this section;

(b) with the exception of that equipment that the Verifying Party intends to use from the equipment stored in accordance with subparagraph (j) of this paragraph, no less than 45 days prior to the planned date of the beginning of emplacement of sensing elements and cables, unless the Parties otherwise agree, the Verifying Party shall deliver in sealed containers to the point of entry two identical sets of the equipment specified in paragraphs 3(a), 3(b), 3(c), 3(d), and 3(e) of this Section, and, at its option, either one or two sets of the equipment specified in paragraphs 1(j), 3(f), 3(g), and 3(h) of this Section, and, if it has not been delivered in accordance with subparagraph (a) of this paragraph, the equipment specified in paragraphs 1(d), 1(e), 1(f), 1(g), 1(h), 1(i), and 1(k) of this Section;

(c) these sets of equipment shall have the same components with the same functional and technical descriptions and specifications as the equipment approved by the Testing Party in accordance with paragraph 6(d)(i) of this Section;

(d) no less than seven days prior to the date of delivery of equipment to the point of entry, the Verifying Party shall provide a complete inventory of this equipment, specifying which equipment, in accordance with subparagraph (h) of this paragraph, will be removed from the facilities of the Verifying Party immediately prior to the beginning of the final dry run and immediately prior to the test;

(e) if the Verifying Party provides two identical sets of equipment:

(i) the Testing party shall choose, at the point of entry, one of the two identical sets of each type of equipment for use by Designated Personnel, with the exception of the equipment specified in paragraphs 3(a) and 3(b) of this Section, and shall affix its own seals to the sealed containers in which that set of equipment arrived. The set of equipment not chosen by the Testing Party for use by Designated Personnel shall be subject to inspection by the Testing Party. Seals of the Verifying Party shall be removed from equipment chosen by the Testing Party for inspection, in the presence of personnel of both Parties, and thereafter this equipment shall be retained for inspection by the Testing Party without the presence of Designated Personnel for a period of no more than 30 days, after which time it shall be returned, in the same condition as that in which it was received, to the Verifying Party at the point of entry;

(ii) with respect to the equipment specified in paragraphs 3(a) and 3(b) of this Section, the Testing Party, under observation of Designated Personnel, shall remove the seals of the Verifying Party, combine the two sets of equipment, and randomly redistribute the items of each type of such equipment in order to produce two new identical sets. The Testing Party shall choose one of these new identical sets for use by Designated Personnel, and both Parties shall affix their own seals to the containers of that set. The set of equipment not chosen by the Testing Party for use by Designated Personnel shall be subject to inspection by the Testing Party in accordance with procedures specified in subparagraph (e)(iii) of this paragraph;

(iii) if the Verifying Party has delivered the equipment specified in paragraphs 3(a) and 3(b) of this Section with individual gas-blocking devices installed in the cables, Designated Personnel, under observation of personnel of the Testing Party, shall cut each cable at points three meters on either side of each gas-blocking device and shall place these gas-blocking devices and their attached cable segments in separate containers. If the Verifying Party delivered this equipment without individual gas-blocking devices installed, Designated Personnel, under observation of the personnel of the Testing Party, shall cut a three-meter segment from each end of each cable and shall place these segments in separate containers. Personnel of each Party, under observation of personnel of the other Party, shall seal these separate containers of cable segments or gas-blocking devices with cable segments. The remainder of this equipment shall be retained for inspection by the Testing Party in accordance with subparagraph (e)(i) of this paragraph, except that during inspection of this equipment the Testing Party may remove up to 150 meters of cable from the set chosen for inspection, in no more segments than twice the number of cables in that set; the set of equipment not chosen by the Testing Party for use by Designated Personnel shall be subject to inspection by the Testing Party;

(iv) the Testing Party shall ensure protection of the equipment chosen by it for use by Designated Personnel and the sealed containers specified in subparagraph (e)(iii) of this paragraph while they are in its territory, and shall transport this equipment to the test site in such a manner as the ensure that it is delivered to Designated Personnel in the same condition as that in which it was received by the Testing Party. Prior to shipment to the test site, and from the time of its arrival at the test site until the time of its transfer to Designated Personnel, this equipment shall be kept sealed, in storage under conditions agreed upon by the Parties;

(v) personnel of the Testing Party shall consult with the Designated Personnel regarding plans and schedule of shipment of the equipment no less than 48 hours prior to its shipment. Designated Personnel shall have the right to verify the integrity of their seals, to observe their equipment, and to accompany it from the point of entry to the test site. The equipment specified in subparagraph (a) of this paragraph shall be delivered to Designated Personnel for use at the test site no less than 25 days prior to the planned date of the beginning of emplacement of explosives or the planned date of the beginning of emplacement of sensing elements and cables, whichever occurs earlier, unless the Parties otherwise agree. The equipment specified in subparagraph (b) of this paragraph shall be delivered to Designated Personnel at the test site for use no later than 10 days prior to the planned date of the beginning of emplacement of sensing elements and cables, unless the Parties otherwise agree. Personnel of each Party shall remove their seals from the equipment under observation of personnel of the other Party. Prior to removing their seals, personnel of each Party shall have the right to verify the integrity of those seals, under observation of personnel of the other Party;

(vi) seals affixed to the equipment specified in paragraphs 3(a), 3(b), and 3(d) of this Section shall not be removed prior to either the conduct of pressure tests and non-destructive inspections, in accordance with subparagraphs (e)(vii) and (e)(viii) of this paragraph, or preparation for installation of such equipment, at which time personnel or each Party shall remove their seals, under observation of personnel of the other Party. Prior to removing their seals, personnel of each Party shall have the right to verify the integrity of those seals, under observation of personnel of the other Party. Thereafter, personnel of the Testing Party shall have the right to observe all activities of Designated Personnel related to this equipment;

(vii) the Testing Party shall have the right to conduct pressure tests on the portions of cables with individual gas-blocking devices specified in subparagraph (e)(iii) of this paragraph, in accordance with its technical operations and practices and under observation of Designated Personnel, to ensure that the individual gas-blocking devices meet the containment requirements of the Testing Party. These pressure test shall be conducted at a time specified by the Testing Party, at which time personnel of each Party shall verify the integrity of their seals on the containers specified in subparagraph (e)(iii) of this paragraph and shall remove their seals, under observation of personnel of the other Party. The Testing Party shall also have the right to conduct non-destructive inspections, under observation of Designated Personnel, on the set of cables chosen for use, to ensure that the cables chosen for use are identical in construction to those chosen for inspection. Such non-destructive inspections shall be carried out at a time specified by the Testing Party. All tests and non-destructive inspections related to the containment requirements of the Testing Party shall be completed, and the results communicated to the Designated Personnel Team Leader at the test site, no less than 10 days prior to the planned date for the beginning of emplacement of sensing elements and cables. If all of the individual gas-blocking devices removed from cables in the set chosen for inspection in accordance with subparagraph (e)(iii) of this paragraph, successfully meet the containment requirements, and if cables chosen for use are found to be identical in construction to those chosen for inspection, then the set chosen for use shall be sealed by the seals of both Parties, which shall not be removed prior to preparation for installation of such equipment. Following the pressure tests, the

Testing Party shall have the right to retain the individual gas-blocking devices with their attached cable segments from the set chosen for inspection;

(viii) if the Verifying Party delivered the equipment specified in paragraphs 3(a) and 3(b) of this Section without individual gas-blocking devices installed in the cables, the Testing Party shall have the right to conduct pressure tests, in accordance with its technical operations and practices, to ensure that the gas-blocking properties of these cables meet the containment requirements of the Testing Party. These tests shall be performed under observation of Designated Personnel on the segments of cables specified in subparagraph (e)(iii) of this paragraph as well as one three-meter segment of each cable of the set chosen for use, removed by Designated Personnel, under observation of personnel of the Testing Party, from the end of the cable that will extend to the ground surface. These pressure tests shall be conducted at a time specified by the Testing Party, at which time personnel of each Party shall verify the integrity of their seals on the containers specified in subparagraph (e)(iii) of this paragraph, as well as on the containers with the set of equipment chosen for use, specified in paragraphs 3(a) and 3(b), and shall remove their seals under observation of personnel of the other Party. All tests related to the containment requirements of the Testing Party shall be completed, and the results communicated to the Designated Personnel Team Leader at the test site, no less than 10 days prior to the planned date for the beginning of emplacement of sensing elements and cables. If all of the cable segments removed from the set chosen for use and the set chosen for inspection meet the containment requirements of the Testing Party, then the set chosen for use shall be sealed by the seals of both Parties, which shall not be removed prior to preparation for installation of such equipment and its use in hydrodynamic yield measurements; and

(ix) if, within one day following the completion of testing and non-destructive inspections specified in subparagraphs (e)(vii) and (e)(viii) of this paragraph, the Verifying Party so requests, the Testing Party shall provide cables that meet its containment requirements. The Testing Party shall deliver these cables to Designated Personnel at the test site no more than two days following the request of the Verifying Party but no less than seven days prior to the planned date for the beginning of emplacement of sensing elements and cables, unless the Parties otherwise agree;

(f) if the Verifying Party provides only one set of equipment:

(i) upon arrival of the equipment at the point of entry, the seals of the Verifying Party shall be removed from this equipment in the presence of personnel of both Parties, after which the Testing Party shall have the right to inspect this equipment for no more than 30 days, without the presence of Designated Personnel;

(ii) upon completion of the inspection, the Testing Party shall transport all approved equipment to the test site and deliver it, in the same condition as that in which it was received, to Designated Personnel. The equipment specified in subparagraph (a) of this paragraph shall be delivered to Designated Personnel no less than 25 days prior to the planned date of the beginning of emplacement of explosives or the planned date of the beginning of emplacement of sensing elements and cables, whichever occurs earlier, unless the Parties otherwise agree. The equipment specified in subparagraph (b) of this paragraph shall be delivered to Designated Personnel at the test site no less than 10 days prior to the planned date of the beginning of emplacement of sensing elements and cables, unless the Parties otherwise agree; and

(iii) within five days following delivery of equipment to Designated Personnel, the Team Leader shall certify, in writing, to the Representative of the Testing Party that the equipment delivered to the test site is in working condition or, in the event of damage to the equipment, shall report such damage in writing;

(g) upon completion of inspection of the equipment, in accordance with subparagraphs (e)(i) and (f)(i) of this paragraph, the Testing Party shall inform the Verifying Party, in writing, of any equipment that does not conform to that approved previously in accordance with paragraph 6(d)(i) of this Section and shall specify the non-conforming characteristics of any such equipment or component thereof. Prior to shipment to the test site, in the case of equipment provided in one set, or at the time of delivery to Designated Personnel at the test site of the set of equipment chosen for use, in the case of equipment provided in two sets, the equipment that does not conform to that approved previously shall be removed by Designated Personnel under seals of both Parties in storage at a location chosen by the Testing Party. Any such equipment shall be returned by the Testing Party to Designated Personnel at the point of entry following completion of the activity related to verification for which it was originally provided. Except as otherwise provided in this Protocol, equipment approved by the Testing Party shall remain under the exclusive control of Designated Personnel from the time of its delivery to Designated Personnel at the test site until it is transferred to the Testing Party in accordance with subparagraph (i) of this paragraph;

(h) immediately prior to the beginning of the final dry run, Designated Personnel, under observation of personnel of the Testing Party, shall remove from each hydrodynamic recording facility and the command and monitoring facility all items specified in accordance with paragraph 6(c) of this Section for removal at that time. These items shall be placed under the seals of both Parties and stored at a location chosen by the Testing Party. Upon departure of personnel of both Parties from each hydrodynamic recording facility immediately prior to the test, all remaining maintenance and support equipment and spare parts shall be removed by Designated Personnel, unless the Parties otherwise agree;

(i) personnel of the Testing Party shall have the right to inspect equipment after it has been used for carrying out activities related to hydrodynamic yield measurements, for a period of 30 days, without the presence of Designated Personnel. For these purposes:

(i) the equipment used for carrying out activities specified in paragraphs 4(g), 5(c), and 5(f) or 5(g) or 5(h), and 6(b), 6(f), 7(c), and 7(f) or 7(g) or 7(h) of Section V of this Protocol shall be transferred to the Testing Party upon completion of all these activities, unless the Parties agree that equipment for any specific activity may be transferred upon completion of that activity;

(ii) all other equipment, except that specified in paragraphs 1(e), 1(g), 1(h), 1(i), and 1(k) of this Section, shall be transferred to the Testing Party upon completion of all activities specified in paragraphs 9(m) and 14(b) of Section V of this Protocol;

(iii) equipment specified in paragraphs 1(e), 1(g), 1(h), 1(i), and 1(k) of this Section shall be transferred to the Testing Party upon completion of all activities of specified in Section V of this Protocol; and

(iv) during inspection of equipment specified in paragraphs 3(f) and 3(g) of this Section, after it has been used for carrying out activities related to hydrodynamic yield measurements, the Testing Party shall have the right to remove and retain no more than 150 meters of those cables, in no more segments than twice the number of cables in each set, with the exception of the fiber optic cables and the electrical cables for above-ground transmission of electrical power;

(j) the Verifying Party shall have the right to store for subsequent use part or all of its equipment in the territory of the Testing Party. Storage shall be under conditions agreed upon by the Parties, at a location chosen by the Testing Party and under this protection;

(k) with respect to inventory and shipment or storage of this equipment, the following procedures, at the option of the Verifying Party, shall be applied:

(i) upon transfer of equipment to the Testing Party for inspection, in accordance with subparagraph (i) of this paragraph, Designated Personnel shall provide complete inventories of equipment to be stored and equipment to be shipped to their territory. These inventories shall be signed by the Designated Personnel Team Leader and the Representative of the Testing Party, each of whom shall retain a copy of the inventories. Within five days following completion of inspection of equipment to be shipped, the Testing Party shall return this equipment to Designated Personnel at the point of entry, in the same condition as that in which it was received. Elimination of information stored in memories shall not be deemed damage to the equipment; or

(ii) within five days following completion of inspection of equipment in accordance with subparagraph (i) of this paragraph, the Testing Party shall return this equipment to Designated Personnel at a location chosen by the Testing Party, in the same condition as that in which it was received. Elimination of information stored in memories shall not be deemed damage to the equipment. Designated Personnel shall examine, inventory, and pack their equipment in containers. Personnel of the Testing Party shall have the right to observe these activities. Within five days following receipt of their equipment, Designated Personnel shall transfer to the Testing Party the packed containers, along with the equipment to be stored and the equipment to be shipped. These inventories shall be signed by the Designated Personnel Team Leader and the Representative of the Testing Party, each of whom shall retain a copy of the inventories. Within 10 days following receipt of the equipment to be shipped, the Testing Party shall deliver it to the point of entry; and

(l) if stored equipment is to be used for activities related to verification of a subsequent test, it shall be subject to further inspection only after such use. The equipment specified in subparagraph (a) of this paragraph shall be delivered, in the same condition as that in which it was received, to Designated Personnel for use at the test site no less than 25 days prior to the planned date of the beginning of emplacement of explosives or the planned date of the beginning of emplacement of sensing elements and cables, whichever occurs earlier, unless the Parties otherwise agree. The equipment specified in subparagraph (b) of this paragraph shall be delivered, in the same condition as that in which it was received, to Designated Personnel at the test site no later than 10 days prior to the planned date of the beginning of emplacement of sensing elements and cables, unless the Parties otherwise agree.

8. The following procedures shall apply to equipment for use of the seismic yield measurement method:

(a) with the exception of that equipment that the Verifying Party intends to use from the equipment stored in accordance with subparagraph (h) of this paragraph, no less than 45 days prior to the planned date of the test, unless the Parties otherwise agree, the Verifying Party shall deliver in sealed containers to the point of entry, at its option, either one or two sets of all or part of the equipment specified in paragraphs 1(d), 1(e), 1(f), 1(g), 1(h), 1(i), and 4 of this Section;

(b) these sets of equipment shall have the same components with the same functional and technical descriptions and specifications as the equipment approved by the Testing Party in accordance with paragraph 6(d)(i) of this Section;

(c) no less than seven days prior to the date of delivery of equipment to the point of entry, the Verifying Party shall provide a complete inventory of this equipment;

(d) if the Verifying Party provides two identical sets of equipment:

(i) the Testing Party shall choose, at the point of entry, one of the two identical sets of each type of equipment for use by Designated Personnel, and shall affix its own seals to the sealed containers in which that set of equipment arrived;

(ii) the Testing Party shall ensure protection of this equipment while it is in its territory, and shall transport this equipment to the Designated Seismic Stations in such a manner as to ensure that it is delivered to Designated Personnel in the same condition as that in which it was received by the Testing Party. Prior to shipment to the Designated Seismic Stations, and from the time of its arrival tat the Designated Seismic Stations until the time of its transfer to Designated Personnel, the set of equipment chosen by the Testing Party for use by Designated Personnel shall be kept sealed in storage under conditions agreed upon by the Parties;

(iii) personnel of the Testing Party shall consult with Designated Personnel regarding plans and schedule of shipment of the equipment no less than 48 hours prior to its shipment. Designated Personnel shall have the right to verify the integrity of their seals, to observe their equipment, and to accompany it from the point of entry to the Designated Seismic Stations. This equipment shall be delivered to Designated Personnel at Designated Seismic Stations for installation and use no less than 10 days prior to the planned date of the test. Personnel of each Party shall remove their seals from the equipment under observation of personnel of the other Party. Prior to removing their seals, personnel of each Party shall have the right to verify the integrity of those seals, under observation of personnel of the other Party; and

(iv) seals of the Verifying Party shall be removed from equipment chosen by the Testing Party for inspection, in the presence of personnel of both Parties, and thereafter this equipment shall be retained for inspection by the Testing Party without the presence of Designated Personnel for a period of no more than 30 days, after which time it shall be returned, in the same condition as that in which it was received, to the Verifying Party at the point of entry;

(e) if the Verifying Party provides only one set of equipment:

(i) upon arrival of the equipment at the point of entry, the seals of the Verifying Party shall be removed from this equipment in the presence of personnel of both Parties, after which the Testing Party shall have the right to inspect this equipment for no more than 30 days, without the presence of Designated Personnel;

(ii) upon completion of the inspection, the Testing Party shall transport all approved equipment to the Designated Seismic Stations and deliver it, in the same condition as that in which it was receive, to Designated Personnel no less than 10 days prior to the planned date of the test, unless the Parties otherwise agree; and

(iii) within three days following delivery of the equipment to Designated Personnel, the Designated Personnel Team Leader shall certify in writing to the Representative of the Testing Party that the equipment delivered to the Designated Seismic Station is in working condition or, in the event of damage to the equipment, shall report such damage in writing;

(f) upon completion of inspection of the equipment, in accordance with subparagraphs (d)(iv) and (e)(i) of this paragraph, the Testing Party shall inform the Verifying Party, in writing, of any equipment that does not conform to that approved previously in accordance with paragraph 6(d)(i) of this Section and shall specify the non-conforming characteristics of any such equipment or component thereof. Prior to shipment to the Designated Seismic Stations, in the case of equipment provided in one set, or at the time of delivery to Designated Personnel at the Designated Seismic Station of the set of equipment chosen for use, in the case of equipment provided in two sets, the equipment that does not conform to that approved previously shall be removed by Designated Personnel under observation of personnel of the Testing Party and placed under seals of both Parties in storage at a location chosen by the Testing Party. Any such equipment shall returned by the Testing Party to Designated Personnel at the point of entry following completion of the activity related to verification for which it was originally provided. Except as otherwise provided in this Protocol, equipment approved by the Testing Party shall remain under the exclusive control of Designated Personnel from the time of its delivery to Designated Personnel at a Designated Seismic Station until it is transferred to the Testing Party in accordance with subparagraphs (g) and (j) of this paragraph;

(g) personnel of the Testing Party shall have the right to inspect equipment after it has been used for activities related to seismic yield measurements for a period of 30 days, without the presence of Designated Personnel. If the Testing Party decides to inspect that equipment, it shall be transferred to the Testing Party upon completion of activities specified in Section VI of this Protocol;

(h) the Verifying Party shall have the right to store for subsequent use part or all of its equipment in the territory of the Testing Party. Storage shall be under conditions agreed upon by the Parties, at a location chosen by the Testing Party and under its protection;

(i) if the Testing Party inspects the equipment, with respect to inventory and shipment or storage of this equipment, the following procedures, at the option of the Verifying Party, shall be applied:

(i) upon transfer of equipment to the Testing Party for inspection in accordance with subparagraph (g) of this paragraph, Designated Personnel shall provide complete inventories of equipment to be stored and equipment to be shipped to their territory. These inventories shall be signed by the Designated Personnel Team Leader and the Representative of the Testing Party, each of whom shall retain a copy of the inventories. Within five days following completion of inspection of equipment to be shipped, the Testing Party shall return this equipment to Designated Personnel at the point of entry, in the same condition as that in which it was received. Elimination of information stored in memories shall not be deemed damage to the equipment; or

(ii) within five days following completion of inspection of equipment in accordance with subparagraph (g) of this paragraph, the Testing Party shall return this equipment to Designated Personnel at a location chosen by the Testing Party in the same condition as that in which it was received. Elimination of information stored in memories shall not be deemed damage to the equipment. Designated Personnel shall examine, inventory, and pack their equipment in containers. Personnel of the Testing Party shall have the right to observe these activities. Within five days following receipt of their equipment, Designated Personnel shall transfer to the Testing Party the packed containers, along with inventories of the equipment to be stored and the equipment to be shipped. These inventories shall be signed by the Designated Personnel Team Leader and the Representative of the Testing Party, each of whom shall retain a copy of the inventories. Within 10 days following receipt of equipment to be shipped, the Testing Party shall deliver it to the point of entry;

(j) if the Testing Party chooses not to inspect the equipment upon completion of activities related to seismic yield measurements, Designated Personnel shall prepare the equipment for storage or shipment to their territory prior to departure from the Designated Seismic Station and, upon transfer of equipment to the Testing Party, shall provide complete inventories of equipment to be stored and equipment to shipped. These inventories shall be signed by the Designated Personnel Team Leader and the Representative of the Testing Party, each of whom shall retain a copy of the inventories. Equipment to be shipped shall be returned to the Verifying Party at the point of entry within 10 days following departure of Designated Personnel from the Designated Seismic Station. Equipment to be stored shall be prepared for storage, in accordance with agreed procedures for the conditions of storage chosen by the Testing Party; and

(k) if stored equipment is to be used for activities related to verification of a subsequent test, it shall be subject to further inspection only after such use. This equipment shall be delivered, in the same condition as that in which it was received, to Designated Personnel for use at the Designated Seismic Stations no later than 10 days prior to the planned date of the test, unless the Parties otherwise agree.

9. The following procedures shall apply to equipment for carrying out on-site inspection:

(a) with the exception of that equipment that the Verifying Party intends to use from the equipment stored in accordance with subparagraph (h) of this paragraph, no less than 5 days prior to the planned date of the beginning of emplacement of explosives, unless the Parties otherwise agree, the Verifying Party shall deliver in sealed containers to the point of entry, at its option, either one or two sets of all or part of the equipment specified in paragraphs 1(d), 1(e), (f), 1(g), 1(h), 1(i), 1(k), and 5 of this Section;

(b) these sets of equipment shall have the same components with the same functional and technical descriptions and specifications as the equipment approved by the Testing Party in accordance with paragraph 6(d)(i) of this Section;

(c) no less than seven days prior to the date of delivery of equipment to the point of entry, the Verifying Party shall provide a complete inventory of this equipment;

(d) if the Verifying Party provides two identical sets of equipment;

(i) the Testing Party shall choose, at the point of entry, one of the two identical sets of each type of equipment for use by Designated Personnel, and shall affix its own seals to the sealed containers in which that set of equipment arrived;

(ii) the Testing Party shall ensure protection of this equipment while it is in its territory, and shall transport this equipment to the test site in such a manner as to ensure that it is delivered to Designated Personnel in the same condition as that in which it was received by the Testing Party. Prior to shipment to the test site, and from the time of its arrival at the test site until the time of its transfer to Designated Personnel, the set of equipment chosen by the Testing Party for use by Designated Personnel shall be kept sealed, in storage under conditions agreed upon by the Parties;

(iii) personnel of the Testing Party shall consult with Designated Personnel regarding plans and schedule of shipment of the equipment no less than 48 hours prior to its shipment. Designated Personnel shall have the right to verify the integrity of their seals, to observe their equipment, and to accompany it from the point of entry to the test site. This equipment shall be delivered to Designated Personnel at the test site no less than 20 days before the planned date of the beginning of emplacement of explosives, unless the Parties otherwise agree. Personnel of each Party shall remove their seals from the equipment under observation of personnel of the other Party. Prior to removing their seals, personnel of each Party shall have the right to verify the integrity of those seals, under observation of personnel of the other Party; and

(iv) seals of the Verifying Party shall be removed from equipment chosen by the Testing Party for inspection, in the presence of personnel of both Parties, and thereafter this equipment shall be retained for inspection by the testing Party without the presence of Designated Personnel for a period of no more than 30 days, after which time is shall be returned, in the same condition as that in which it was received, to the Verifying Party at the point of entry;

(e) if the Verifying Party provides only one set of equipment:

(i) upon arrival of the equipment at the point of entry, the seals of the Verifying Party shall be removed from this equipment in the presence of personnel of both Parties, after which the Testing Party shall have the right to inspect this equipment for no more than 30 days, without the presence of Designated Personnel;

(ii) upon completion of the inspection, the Testing Party shall transport all approved equipment to the test site and deliver it, in the same condition as that in which it was received, to Designated Personnel no less than 20 days prior to the planned date of the beginning of emplacement of explosives, unless the Parties otherwise agree; and

(iii) within five days following delivery of equipment to Designated Personnel, the Designated Personnel Team Leader shall certify, in writing, to the Representative of the Testing Party that the equipment delivered to the test site is in working condition or, in the event of damage to the equipment, shall report such damage in writing;

(f) upon completion of inspection of the equipment in accordance with subparagraphs (d)(iv) and (e)(i) of this paragraph, the Testing Party shall inform the Verifying Party, in writing, of any equipment that does not conform to that approved previously in accordance with paragraph 6(d)(i) of this Section and shall specify the non-conforming characteristics of any such equipment or component thereof. Prior to shipment to the test site, in the case of equipment provided in one set, or at the time of delivery to Designated Personnel at the test site of the set of equipment chosen for use, in the case of equipment provided in two sets, the equipment that does not conform to that approved previously shall be removed by Designated Personnel under observation of personnel of the Testing Party and placed under seals of both Parties in storage at a location chosen by the Testing Party. Any such equipment shall be returned by the Testing Party to Designated Personnel at the point of entry, following completion of the activity related to verification for which it was originally provided. Except as otherwise provided in this Protocol, equipment approved by the Testing Party shall remain under the exclusive control of Designated Personnel from the time of its delivery to Designated Personnel at the test site until it is transferred to the Testing Party in accordance with subparagraph (g) of this paragraph;

(g) personnel of the Testing Party shall have the right to inspect equipment after it has been used for carrying out activities related to on-site inspection, for a period of 30 days, without the presence of Designated Personnel. For these purposes:

(i) the equipment used for carrying out activities specified in paragraphs 1(b), 1(c), 1(e), 1(f), 1(g), and 1(h) of Section VII of this Protocol shall be transferred to the Testing Party upon completion of all these activities, unless the Parties agree that equipment for any specific activity may be transferred upon completion of that activity; and

(ii) all other equipment shall be transferred to the Testing Party upon completion of all activities of Designated Personnel specified in Section VII of this Protocol;

(h) the Verifying Party shall have the right to store for subsequent use part or all of its equipment in the territory of the Testing Party. Storage shall be under conditions agreed by the Parties, at a location chosen by the Testing Party and under its protection;

(i) with respect to inventory and shipment or storage of this equipment, the following procedures, at the option of the Verifying Party, shall be applied:

(i) upon transfer of equipment to the Testing Party for inspection in accordance with subparagraph (g) of this paragraph, Designated Personnel shall provide complete inventories of equipment to be stored and equipment to be shipped to their territory. These inventories shall be signed by the Designated Personnel Team Leader and the Representative of the Testing Party, each of whom shall retain a copy of the inventories. Within five days following completion of inspection of the equipment to be shipped, the Testing Party shall return this equipment to Designated Personnel at the point of entry, in the same condition as that in which it was received. Elimination of information stored in memories shall not be deemed damage to the equipment; or

(ii) within five days following completion of inspection of equipment in accordance with subparagraph (g) of this paragraph, the Testing Party shall return this equipment to Designated Personnel at a location chosen by the Testing Party, in the same condition as that in which it was received. Elimination of information stored in memories shall not be deemed damage to the equipment. Designated Personnel shall examine, inventory, and pack their equipment in containers. Personnel of the Testing Party shall have the right to observe these activities. Within five days following receipt of their equipment, Designated Personnel shall transfer to the Testing Party the packed containers, along with inventories of the equipment to be stored and the equipment to be shipped. These inventories shall be signed by the Designated Personnel Team Leader and the Representative of the Testing Party, each of whom shall retain a copy of the inventories. Within 10 days following receipt of the equipment to be shipped, the Testing Party shall deliver it to the point of entry; and

(j) if stored equipment is to be used for activities related to verification of a subsequent test, it shall be subject to further inspection only after such use. This equipment shall be delivered, in the same condition as that in which it was received, to Designated Personnel at the test site no less than 20 days prior to the planned date of the beginning of emplacement of explosives for that test, unless the Parties otherwise agree.

SECTION IX. DESIGNATED PERSONNEL AND TRANSPORT PERSONNEL

1. No later than 10 days following entry into force of the Treaty each Party shall provide the other Party with a list of its proposed Designated Personnel who will carry out activities in accordance with this Protocol and a list of its proposed Transport Personnel who will provide transportation for these Designated Personnel, their baggage, and equipment of the Verifying Party. These lists shall contain name, date of birth, and sex of each individual of its proposed Designated Personnel and Transport Personnel. The list of Designated Personnel shall at no time include more than 300 individuals, and the list of Transport Personnel shall at no time include more than 200 individuals.

2. Each Party shall review the list of Designated Personnel and the list of Transport Personnel proposed by the other Party. If the Party reviewing a list determines that an individual included thereon is acceptable to it, it shall so inform the Party providing the list within 20 days following receipt of the list, and such an individual shall be deemed accepted. If the Party reviewing a list determines that an individual included thereon is not acceptable to it, it shall so inform the Party providing the list of its objection within 20 days following receipt of the list, and such an individual shall be deemed unaccepted and shall be deleted from the list.

3. Each Party may propose the addition or substitution of individuals on its list of Designated Personnel or its list of Transport Personnel at any time, who shall be designated in the same manner as provided in paragraph 2 of this Section with regard to the initial lists. Annually, no more than 100 individuals from the list of Designated Personnel shall be subject to substitution. This limitation shall not apply to the replacement of individuals due to permanent physical incapacity or death, or to deletion of an individual from the list of Designated Personnel in accordance with paragraph 5 of this Section. Replacement of an individual due to permanent physical incapacity, death or deletion from the list shall be accomplished in the same manner as provided in paragraph 2 of this Section.

4. Following receipt of the initial list of Designated Personnel or the initial list of Transport Personnel or of subsequent changes thereto, the Party receiving such information shall prepare for the issuance of such visas and other documents as may be required to ensure that each individual on the list of Designated Personnel or the list of Transport Personnel who has been accepted may enter and remain in its territory for the purpose of carrying out activities in accordance with this Protocol. Such visas and documents shall be provided by the Testing Party only to the individuals who names are included in the notification provided by the Verifying Party, in accordance with paragraphs 2 and 3 of Section X of this Protocol, upon receipt of such notification. Such visas and documents shall be valid for multiple entry throughout the period required for Designated Personnel to carry out their activities related to verification of a specific test.

5. If a Party determines that an individual included on the list of Designated Personnel or the list of Transport Personnel of the

other Party has violated the provisions of this Protocol or has ever committed a criminal offense in its territory, or has ever been sentenced for committing a criminal offense, or has ever been expelled from its territory, the Party making such a determination shall notify the other Party of its objection to the continued inclusion of this individual is present in the territory of the Party raising the objection, then the other Party shall immediately recall this individual from the territory of the Party raising this objection and immediately thereafter delete that individual from the list of Designated Personnel or from the list of Transport Personnel.

6. Designated Personnel with their personal baggage and equipment of the Verifying Party shall be permitted to enter the territory of the Testing Party at the designated point of entry, to remain in that territory, and to exit that territory through the designated point of entry.

7. Designated Personnel and Transport Personnel shall be accorded the following privileges and immunities for the entire period they are in the territory of the Testing Party and thereafter with respect to acts previously performed in the exercise of their official functions as Designated Personnel or Transport Personnel:

(a) Designated Personnel and Transport Personnel shall be accorded the inviolability enjoyed by diplomatic agents pursuant to Article 29 of the Vienna Convention on Diplomatic Relations of April 18, 1961;

(b) living and working quarters occupied by Designated Personnel and Transport Personnel carrying out activities in accordance with this Protocol shall be accorded the inviolability and protection accorded the quarters of missions and diplomatic agents pursuant to Articles 22 and 30 of the Vienna Convention on Diplomatic Relations;

(c) archives, documents, papers, and correspondence of Designated Personnel and Transport Personnel shall enjoy the inviolability accorded the archives, documents, papers, and correspondence of missions and diplomatic agents pursuant to Articles 24 and 30 of the Vienna Convention of Diplomatic Relations. In addition, the aircraft or other transport vehicles of the Verifying Party shall be inviolable;

(d) Designated Personnel and Transport Personnel shall be accorded the immunities accorded diplomatic agents pursuant to paragraphs 1, 2, and 3 of Article 31 the Vienna Convention on Diplomatic Relations. Immunity from jurisdiction of Designated Personnel or Transport Personnel may be waived by the Verifying in those cases in which it is of the Opinion that immunity would impede the course of justice, and it can be waived without prejudice to the implementation of the provisions of this Protocol. Waiver must always be express;

(e) Designated Personnel and Transport Personnel carrying out their activities in accordance with this Protocol shall be accorded the exemption from dues and taxes accorded diplomatic agents pursuant to Article 34 of the Vienna Convention on Diplomatic Relations;

(f) living and working quarters occupied by Designated Personnel and Transport Personnel carrying out their activities in accordance with this Protocol shall be accorded the exemption from dues and taxes accorded mission premises pursuant to Article 23 of the Vienna Convention on Diplomatic Relations; and

(g) Designated Personnel and Transport Personnel shall be permitted to bring into the territory of the Testing Party, without payment of any customs duties or related charges, articles for their personal use, with the exception of articles the import or export of which is prohibited by law or controlled by quarantine regulations.

8. Designated Personnel and Transport Personnel shall not engage in any professional or commercial activity for personal profit in the territory of the Testing Party.

9. Without prejudice to their privileges and immunities, Designated Personnel and Transport Personnel shall be obliged to respect the laws and regulations of the Testing Party and shall be obliged not to interfere in the internal affairs of that Party.

10. If the Testing Party considers that there has been an abuse of privileges and immunities specified in paragraph 7 of this Section, consultations shall be held between the Parties to determine whether such an abuse has occurred and, if so determined, to prevent a repetition of such an abuse.

SECTION X. ENTRY, TRANSPORT, FOOD, LODGING, AND PROVISION OF SERVICES FOR DESIGNATED PERSONNEL AND TRANSPORT PERSONNEL

1. The Testing Party shall ensure Designated Personnel and Transport Personnel access to its territory for the purposes of carrying out activities related to verification in accordance with this Protocol, and shall provided these personnel with such other assistance as may be necessary to enable them to carry out these activities. Designated Personnel shall have the right to be present at the test site and at Designated Seismic stations in the territory of the Testing Party to carry out activities related to verification in accordance with this Protocol at such times and for such periods as required to carry out these activities. The specific times and periods for carrying out such activities shall be specified in the coordinated schedule.

2. No less than 20 days prior to the planned date of arrival of its Designated Personnel at the point of entry for participation in activities related to verification of a specific test, the Verifying Party shall provide the Testing Party with:

(a) a list of the names of the Designated Personnel with their passports and documentation, who will carry out activities related to verification of a specific test;

(b) the names of the Designated Personnel Team Leader or Leaders and the names of Designated Personnel who will escort equipment of the Verifying Party to the test site or each Designated Seismic Station;

(c) confirmation of the point of entry to be used;

(d) the planned date and the estimated time of arrival of these Designated Personnel at the point of entry; and

(e) the mode of transport to be used.

No more than 15 days following receipt of the list and passports and documentation specified in subparagraph (a) of this paragraph, the Testing Party shall return those passports to the Verifying Party with the visas and all necessary documents specified in paragraph 4 of Section IX of this Protocol.

3. No less than 20 days prior to the planned date of arrival of Transport Personnel at the point of entry, the Verifying Party shall provide the Testing Party with the number of Transport Personnel. No less than three days prior to the planned ate of arrival of Transport Personnel, the Verifying Party shall provide the testing Party with a list of the names of those Transport Personnel with their passports and documentation. No less than one day prior to the planned date of arrival of Transport Personnel, the Testing Party shall return those passports to the Verifying Party with the visas and all necessary documents specified in paragraph of Section IX of this Protocol.

4. The number of Designated Personnel present at a test site or Designated Seismic Station to carry out activities related to verification of a specific test shall be governed by the relevant restrictions specified in Sections V, VI, and VII of this Protocol. Designated Personnel shall leave the test site or Designated Seismic Station upon completion of activities related to verification of a specific test as specified in the coordinated schedule. Designated Personnel who have been present at the test site for a period of six consecutive weeks or more may be replaced by individuals included on the list submitted in accordance with paragraph 1 of Section IX of this Protocol. Designated Personnel who have not been present at the test site for a period of six consecutive weeks may be replaced only for reasons of injury, illness, or family emergency, and shall be replaced by individuals included on the list submitted in accordance with paragraph 1 of Section IX of this Protocol.

5. If a transport aircraft other than a regularly scheduled commercial aircraft is used by the Verifying Party for transportation between the territory of the Verifying Party and the point of entry, its flight path shall be along airways agreed upon by the Parties, and its flight plan shall be filed in accordance with the procedures of the International Civil Aviation Organization applicable to civil aircraft, including in the remarks section of the flight plan a confirmation that the appropriate clearance has been obtained. The Testing Party shall provide parking, security protection, servicing, and fuel for aircraft of the Verifying Party at the point of entry. The Verifying Party shall bear the cost of such fuel and servicing.

6. The Testing Party shall ensure that all necessary clearances or approvals are granted so as to enable Designated Personnel, their baggage, and equipment of the Verifying Party to arrive at the point of entry by the estimated arrival date and time.

7. The Testing Party shall assist Designated Personnel and Transport Personnel and their baggage in passage through customs without undue delay. The Testing Party shall provide transportation between the point of entry and the test site or the Designated Seismic Stations for Designated Personnel, their baggage, and equipment of the Verifying Party, so as to enable such personnel to exercise their rights and functions in the time periods provided in this Protocol and specified in the coordinated schedule.

8. The Testing Party shall have the right to assign its personnel to escort Designated Personnel and Transport Personnel while they are in its territory.

9. Except as otherwise provided in this Protocol, movement and travel of Designated Personnel and Transport Personnel in the territory of the Testing Party, from the time of their arrival at the point of entry until their departure from the territory of the Testing Party at the point of entry, shall be subject to the authorization of the Testing Party.

10. During the period Designated Personnel and Transport Personnel are in the territory of the Testing Party, the Testing Party shall provide food, hotel-like living accommodations, working facilities, transportation, and medical facilities for out-patient treatment and in-patient treatment, and also secure places for storing equipment. If the Verifying Party desires to provide its own food for its Designated Personnel and its Transport Personnel during their stay in the territory of the Testing Party, the Testing Party shall provide such assistance as may be necessary for such food to arrive at the appropriate locations. Designated Personnel shall have the use of a complete kitchen at all times during their stay at the test site and at each Designated Seismic Station.

11. The Verifying Party shall have the right to include among its Designated Personnel a medical specialist, who shall be allowed to bring medications, medical instruments, and portable medical equipment agreed upon by the Parties. If Designated Personnel are treated in a medical facility of the Testing Party, the medical specialist shall have the right to consult on the recommended treatment and monitor the course of medical treatment at all times. The medical specialist of the Verifying Party shall have the right to require the Testing Party to provide emergency evacuation of any individual of the Designated Personnel who is ill or has suffered an accident to a mutually agreed medical facility in the territory of the Testing Party or to the point of entry for emergency medical evacuation by the Verifying Party. Designated Personnel shall have the right to refuse any treatment prescribed by medical personnel of the Testing treatment prescribed by medical personnel of the Testing Party, and in this case the Testing Party shall not be responsible for any consequences of such refusal. Such refusal must always be express.

12. The Testing Party shall provide the Designated Personnel Team Leader or his designated representative at all times access to:

(a) telephone communications between the embassy of the Verifying Party in the territory of the Testing Party and the working facilities and living accommodations of Designated Personnel at each test site and each Designated Seismic Station; and

(b) an international telephone network from their working facilities and living accommodations at each test site and each Designated Seismic Station.

13. The Designated Personnel Team Leader or his designated representative shall have the right to use at all times satellite communications to ensure communications via the International Maritime Satellite Organization (INMARSAT) commercial satellite system, or a system of equivalent performance, between each test site in the territory of the Testing Party and the telephone communications system of the Verifying Party. If the Testing Party does not provide such communications, Designated Personnel shall have the right to use their own equipment specified in paragraph 1(k) of Section VIII of this Protocol. In this case, installation and alignment of all such equipment shall be done jointly. All equipment of this system, except the remote control unit, shall be locked and placed under seals of both Parties, and personnel of neither Party shall have access to this equipment except under observation of personnel of the other Party. Only Designated Personnel shall use the remote control unit. If the Verifying Party provides satellite communications equipment, personnel of the Testing Party shall have the right, under observation of Designated Personnel, to make the following modifications provided they do not degrade the quality of the communications:

(a) install bandpass filters, to limit the frequency range, in the antenna signal transmission and reception lines;

(b) modify the remote control unit to prevent manual tuning; and

(c) modify the satellite communications equipment to allow the Testing Party to monitor all transmissions.

14. The Testing Party shall provide the following for use by Designated Personnel:

(a) portable radios for communications at the test location;

(b) telephones for communications between work areas and between work areas and living quarters of Designated Personnel at the test site or Designated Seismic Stations; and

(c) access to Testing Party-controlled vehicle-mounted radios for communications with the test location, work areas, or living quarters while Designated Personnel are in transit at the test site.

15. At the test site and each Designated Seismic Station, Designated Personnel shall observe all safety rules and regulations applicable to the personnel of the Testing Party, as well as all those additional restrictions with regard to access and movement as may be established by the Testing Party. Designated Personnel shall have access only to the areas in which they will directly exercise their rights and functions in accordance with Sections V, VI, VII, and VIII of this Protocol. The areas at the test site or the Designated Seismic Station in which Designated Personnel shall have freedom of movement during the conduct of a specific test without the mandatory escort of personnel of the Testing Party shall be marked on the diagrams of the test site or the Designated Seismic Stations provided to the Verifying Party at the first meeting of the Coordinating Group specified in paragraph 10 of Section XI of this Protocol. In all other cases, the permission of the Representative of the Testing Party, and escort by, personnel of the Testing Party shall be required.

16. Designated Personnel shall not be given or seek access by physical, visual, or technical means to the interior of any explosive canister, to documentary or other information descriptive of the design of an explosive, or to equipment for control and firing of an explosive. The Testing Party shall not locate documentary or other information descriptive of the design of an explosive in such ways as to impede Designated Personnel in carrying out their activities in accordance with this Protocol.

17. Possession or use by Designated Personnel of firearms, ammunition, or substances containing narcotics, with the exception of those prescribed by a physician, in the territory of the Testing Party is prohibited. Except as otherwise provided in this Protocol, possession or use by Designated Personnel of the following items is also prohibited at the test site or a Designated Seismic Station:

(a) photographic and video recording equipment;

(b) radio transmitters or receivers other than those supplied by the Testing Party;

(c) sound recorders;

(d) teleoptical devices; and

(e) personal computers.

18. Except as otherwise provided in this Protocol or as may be approved in writing by the Representative of the Testing Party, Designated Personnel are prohibited from removing any of the following items from the test site or a Designated Seismic Station:

(a) soil samples;

(b) plant samples;

(c) water and air samples;

(d) animals;

(e) metal objects; and

(f) rock samples or debris.

19. Designated Personnel shall have the right to remove from the territory of the Testing Party all items, including data, obtained in accordance with this Protocol.

20. The Testing Party shall have the right to inspect, in the presence of Designated Personnel, baggage and personal possessions of Designated Personnel upon their entry to or departure from the test site or Designated Seismic Stations. The Testing Party shall also have the right to inspect, in the presence of Designated Personnel, any packages received by Designated Personnel during their stay at the test site or Designated Seismic Stations or prepared for shipment by Designated Personnel from the test site or Designated Seismic Stations.

21. Except as provided in paragraphs 22, 23, and 24 of this Section or unless the Parties otherwise agree, the Verifying Party shall bear all costs of verification activities of Designated Personnel and Transport Personnel set forth in the coordinated schedule, including costs for use of consumption of materials, equipment, transportation, food, living and working facilities, medical assistance, communications, and services requested by and provided to the costs associated with transport aircraft in accordance with paragraph 5 of this Section.

22. The Testing Party shall bear all costs related to the preparation of its test sites, Designated Seismic Stations, and equipment

storage facilities within its territory for the use of Designated Personnel as provided for in this Protocol.

23. With respect to a test of non-standard configuration:

(a) the Testing Party shall bear the costs of the activities specified in paragraph 6(a) of Section V of this Protocol that are carried out with respect to the second and third satellite holes, if requested by the Verifying Party in accordance with paragraph 11 of Section XI of this Protocol; and

(b) the Testing Party shall bear the costs related to the conduct of a test identified by it as a reference test to satisfy the request of the Verifying Party in accordance with paragraph 11 of Section XI of this Protocol.

24. The Testing Party shall bear all costs related to transportation of equipment of the Verifying Party between:

(a) the point of entry and the location at which such equipment is subject to familiarization or inspection by the Testing Party in accordance with Section VIII of this Protocol;

(b) the location for familiarization or inspection by the Testing Party and the location at which such equipment is returned to the Verifying Party;

(c) the location at which such equipment is turned over to the Testing Party for storage and the storage location; and

(d) the storage location and the location at which such equipment is returned to the Verifying Party.

25. If the Verifying Party decides not to carry out activities related to verification that it specified in its initial notification, after technical and logistical support for these activities has been agreed upon in the Coordinating Group in accordance with paragraph 12 of Section XI of this Protocol, the Verifying Party shall reimburse the Testing Party for the costs of such agreed technical and logistical support incurred by the Testing Party prior to receipt of notification that the Verifying Party will not carry out the initially declared activities related to verification.

SECTION XI. PROCEDURES FOR CONSULTATION AND COORDINATION

1. For the purposes of implementation of the Treaty and this Protocol, the Parties shall, immediately following entry into force of the Treaty, establish a Bilateral Consultative Commission, within the framework of which they shall meet, at the request of either Party, to:

(a) consider any questions relating to implementation of the Treaty and this Protocol;

(b) consider any suggestions for amendments to the Treaty or this Protocol;

(c) consider any technical or administrative changes to this Protocol of the nature provided in paragraph 2, 3, or 4 of this Section;

(d) consider any questions relating to compliance with the Treaty or this Protocol;

(e) consider any new verification technologies having a bearing on the Treaty or this Protocol;

(f) seek agreement on those matters specified in this Protocol as requiring agreement of the Parties; and

(g) seek agreement on questions related to costs for verification activities and procedures for reciprocal payments of such costs between the Parties.

2. If the Parties determine that the periods of time specified with respect to notifications in Section IV of this Protocol create practical difficulties and do not serve the interest of effective implementation of this Protocol, they may change such periods of time by agreement in the Bilateral Consultative Commission. Such agreed changes shall not be considered amendments to the Treaty or this Protocol.

3. If the Parties determine that, in the interest of effective implementation of this Protocol, the arrangements set forth in Section X of this Protocol regarding transportation, lodging, food, and services require modification, the provisions of Section X of this Protocol may be changed by agreement of the Parties in the Bilateral Consultative Commission. Such agreed changes shall not be considered amendments to the Treaty or this Protocol.

4. If the Parties determine that modifications to verification procedures, including modifications resulting from improvements in existing technologies, would enhance effective implementation of the basic aims of the Treaty or this Protocol, they may, in the Bilateral Consultative Commission, agree upon such modifications. Such agreed modifications shall not be considered amendments to the Treaty or this Protocol.

5. The Parties, through consultation, shall establish, and may amend as appropriate, regulations to govern the operations of the Bilateral Consultative Commission.

6. For each test with respect to which activities related to verification are carried out in accordance with this Protocol, the Parties shall establish a Coordinating Group of the Bilateral Consultative Commission that shall be responsible for coordinating the activities of the Verifying Party with the activities of the Testing Party. The Bilateral Consultative Commission may, as necessary, establish and amend procedures governing the activities of the Coordinating Group.

7. The Coordinating Group shall operate throughout the entire period of preparing and carrying out activities related to verification of a specific test, until departure of Designated Personnel from the territory of the Testing Party.

8. All members of the Coordinating Group from the Verifying Party shall be drawn from the list of Designated Personnel. The Representative of the Verifying Party to the Coordinating Group shall be the Principal Designated Personnel Team Leader, whose name shall be provided simultaneously with the notification of intent to carry out activities related to verification of a specific test. Within 15 days following receipt of this notification, the Testing Party shall provide the Verifying Party with the name of its Representative to the Coordinating Group.

9. The first meeting of the Coordinating Group shall be convened in the capital of the Testing Party within 25 days following notification by the Verifying Party that it intends to carry out activities

related to verification of a specific test. Thereafter, the Coordinating Group shall meet at the request of either Party.

10. On the first day of the first meeting of the Coordinating Group, the Testing Party shall present a list, including times and durations, of all activities it intends to carry out that could affect the rights of the Verifying Party provided in this Protocol with respect to activities declared by it and related to verification of a specific test. If the Verifying Party has provided notification of its intent:

(a) to use the hydrodynamic yield measurement method or carry out an on-site inspection, the Testing Party shall provide the Verifying Party with the following information:

(i) the number of emplacement holes for the specific test;

(ii) with respect to each emplacement hole, whether, for the purposes of this Protocol, the emplacement hole shall be deemed vertical or horizontal; and

(iii) the number of explosions included in the test and the location of each planned end of each emplacement hole and of the corresponding planned emplacement point, to the nearest 10 meters;

(b) to use the hydrodynamic yield measurement method with respect to a test of standard configuration that includes more than one explosion, the Testing Party shall provide, in addition to the information specified in subparagraph (a) of this paragraph, the following information:

(i) whether any explosion has a planned yield exceeding 50 kilotons, and, if so, which explosion or explosions; and

(ii) whether any explosion has a planned yield exceeding 35 kilotons, and, if so, which explosion or explosions; and

(c) to use the hydrodynamic yield measurement method with respect to a test of non-standard configuration, the Testing Party shall provide the information specified in subparagraphs (a) and (b) of this paragraph, as well as the following information:

(i) a detailed description, including dimensions, of each emplacement hole and any access or bypass tunnels connected to each emplacement hole if any portion of an access or bypass tunnel is within the hydrodynamic measurement zone;

(ii) the dimensions of each explosive canister and its orientation in the emplacement hole;

(iii) the density and dimensions of each choke section; and

(iv) the location and configuration of any access or bypass tunnels and any known voids with a volume larger than one cubic meter, within 50 meters of the wall of each emplacement hole within the hydrodynamic measurement zone, and the bulk density of the stemming material if these voids are to be stemmed.

11. Within 15 days following the convening of the first meeting of the Coordinating Group, the Verifying Party shall provide the Testing Party, in the Coordinating Group, with a list of the activities it intends to carry out, as well as those activities provided for in this Protocol that it intends not to carry out. The Verifying

Party shall also provide the Testing Party, in the Coordinating Group, with a preliminary statement of its requirements for technical and logistical support for the activities related to verification that it intends to carry out and whether it will require the Testing Party to provide the cables specified in paragraphs 3(a) and 3(b) of Section VIII of this Protocol for its use. If the Verifying Party has notified the Testing Party that it intends to use the hydrodynamic yield measurement method with respect to a test of non-standard configuration, the Verifying Party also shall inform the Testing Party:

(a) whether it requires a reference test; and

(b) whether it will actually carry out hydrodynamic yield measurements of the test of non-standard configuration, and, if so, which measurements, and:

(i) the number of satellite holes required and the specific distance and azimuth relative to the emplacement hole of the second and third satellite holes, if such are requested by the Verifying Party and, if the Testing Party is unable to prepare the first satellite hole in accordance with the conditions for such hole in the standard configuration, the distance and azimuth of that satellite hole relative to the emplacement hole; and

(ii) in which satellite holes the Verifying Party intends to use transducers and associated power supplies.

12. Within 10 days following receipt by the Testing Party of the information specified in paragraph 11 of this Section, the Parties, in the Coordinating Group, shall develop and agree upon a coordinated schedule, which shall include specific times and durations for carrying out activities related to verification, ensuring the rights of each Party provided in this Protocol, and taking into account the number of Designated Personnel that will carry out activities related to verification of a specific test in accordance with Sections V, VI, and VII of this Protocol. The coordinated schedule shall reflect those numbers.

13. Agreement of the Representative of each Party to the Coordinating Group shall constitute agreement of the Parties for the purposes of this Protocol with the exception of paragraphs 3, 4, 5, 6, and 9 of Section III of this Protocol and paragraph 2 of Section XII of this Protocol.

14. Upon completion of activities related to verification of a specific test, the Designated Personnel Team Leader at the test site or at each Designated Seismic Station shall prepare a written report, in the language of each Party. The report shall be factual. It shall list activities carried out by Designated Personnel, with dates of their completion, and shall include lists of information, data, photographs, and samples obtained by Designated Personnel or provided by the Testing Party in accordance with this Protocol. The report shall list technical and logistical activities carried out by the Testing Party in support of activities related to verification. The Designated Personnel Team Leader shall include in the report comments on any ambiguities not resolved during the carrying out of activities related to verification. The Representative of the Testing Party may include in the report comments responding to these ambiguities. The Designated Personnel Team Leader shall complete

the report prior to the scheduled departure of Designated Personnel from the test site or Designated Seismic Station. The Designated Personnel Team Leader and the Representative of the Testing Party shall each sign the report and retain a copy.

15. If, in the course of implementing activities related to verification of a specific test, in accordance with this Protocol, questions arise requiring prompt resolution, such questions shall be considered by the Coordinating Group. If the Coordinating Group is unable to resolve such questions, they shall immediately be referred to the Bilateral Consultative Commission for resolution.

SECTION XII. RELEASE OF INFORMATION

1. Nothing in the Treaty and this Protocol shall affect the proprietary rights of either Party in information provided by it in accordance with the Treaty and this Protocol, or in information that may be disclosed to the other Party or that may become known to the other Party in preparing for or conducting a test. Claims to such proprietary rights, however, shall not impede implementation of the provisions of the Treaty and this Protocol.

2. Public release of the information provided in accordance with this Protocol or publication of material using such information may take place only with the agreement of the Testing Party. Public release of the results of observation or measurements made by Designated Personnel may take place only with the agreement of both Parties.

SECTION XIII. ENTRY INTO FORCE

This Protocol is an integral part of the Treaty. It shall enter into force on the date of entry into force of the Treaty and shall remain in force as long as the Treaty remains in force.

DONE at Washington, a duplicate, this first day of June, 1990, in the English and Russian languages, both texts being equally authentic.

c. Treaty with the Union of Soviet Socialist Republics on Underground Nuclear Explosions for Peaceful Purposes, and the Protocol Thereto [1]

Done at Washington, D.C. and Moscow, U.S.S.R., May 28, 1976; Ratification advised by the Senate, September 25, 1990; President ratified, December 8, 1990; Exchange of ratifications and entered into force, December 11, 1990

The United States of America and the Union of Soviet Socialist Republics, hereinafter referred to as the Parties,

PROCEEDING from a desire to implement Article Ill of the Treaty between the United States of America and the Union of Soviet Socialist Republics on the Limitation of Underground Nuclear Weapon Tests, which calls for the earliest possible conclusion of an agreement on underground nuclear explosions for peaceful purposes,

REAFFIRMING their adherence to the objectives and principles of the Treaty Banning Nuclear Weapon Tests in the Atmosphere, in Outer Space and Under Water, the Treaty on Non-Proliferation of Nuclear Weapons, and the Treaty on the Limitation of Underground Nuclear Weapon Tests, and their determination to observe strictly the provisions of these international agreements,

DESIRING to assure that underground nuclear explosions for peaceful purposes shall not be used for purposes related to nuclear weapons,

DESIRING that utilization of nuclear energy be directed only toward peaceful purposes,

DESIRING to develop appropriately cooperation in the field of underground nuclear explosions for peaceful purposes,

HAVE AGREED AS FOLLOWS:

ARTICLE I

1. The Parties enter into this Treaty to satisfy the obligations in Article Ill of the Treaty on the Limitation of Underground Nuclear Weapon Tests, and assume additional obligations in accordance with the provisions of this Treaty.

2. This Treaty shall govern all underground nuclear explosions for peaceful purposes conducted by the Parties after March 31, 1976.

ARTICLE II

For the purposes of this Treaty:

(a) "explosion" means any individual or group underground nuclear explosion for peaceful purposes;

[1] 1714 UNTS 387.

(b) "explosive" means any device, mechanism or system for producing an individual explosion;

(c) "group explosion" means two or more individual explosions for which the time interval between successive individual explosions does not exceed five seconds and for which the emplacement points of all explosives can be interconnected by straight line segments, each of which joins two emplacement points and each of which does not exceed 40 kilometers.

ARTICLE III

1. Each Party, subject to the obligations assumed under this Treaty and other international agreements, reserves the right to:

(a) carry out explosions at any place under its jurisdiction or control outside the geographical boundaries of test sites specified under the provisions of the Treaty on the Limitation of Underground Nuclear Weapon Tests; and

(b) carry out, participate or assist in carrying out explosions in the territory of another State at the request of such other State.

2. Each Party undertakes to prohibit, to prevent and not to carry out at any place under its jurisdiction or control, and further undertakes not to carry out, participate or assist in carrying out anywhere:

(a) any individual explosion having a yield exceeding 150 kilotons;

(b) any group explosion:

(1) having an aggregate yield exceeding 150 kilotons except in ways that will permit identification of each individual explosion and determination of the yield of each individual explosion in the group in accordance with the provisions of Article IV of and the Protocol to this Treaty;

(2) having an aggregate yield exceeding one and one-half megatons;

(c) any explosion which does not carry out a peaceful application;

(d) any explosion except in compliance with the provisions of the Treaty Banning Nuclear Weapon Tests in the Atmosphere, in Outer Space and Under Water, the Treaty on the Non-Proliferation of Nuclear Weapons, and other international agreements entered into by that Party.

3. The question of carrying out any individual explosion having a yield exceeding the yield specified in paragraph 2(a) of this article will be considered by the Parties at an appropriate time to be agreed.

ARTICLE IV

1. For the purpose of providing assurance of compliance with the provisions of this Treaty, each Party shall:

(a) use national technical means of verification at its disposal in a manner consistent with generally recognized principles of international law; and

(b) provide to the other Party information and access to sites of explosions and furnish assistance in accordance with the provisions set forth in the Protocol to this Treaty.

2. Each Party undertakes not to interfere with the national technical means of verification of the other Party operating in accordance with paragraph 1(a) of this article, or with the implementation of the provisions of paragraph 1(b) of this article.

ARTICLE V

1. To promote the objectives and implementation of the provisions of this Treaty, the Parties shall establish promptly a Joint Consultative Commission within the framework of which they will:

(a) consult with each other, make inquiries and furnish information in response to such inquiries, to assure confidence in compliance with the obligations assumed;

(b) consider questions concerning compliance with the obligations assumed and related situations which may be considered ambiguous;

(c) consider questions involving unintended interference with the means for assuring compliance with the provisions of this Treaty;

(d) consider changes in technology or other new circumstances which have a bearing on the provisions of this Treaty; and

(e) consider possible amendments to provisions governing underground nuclear explosions for peaceful purposes.

2. The Parties through consultation shall establish, and may amend as appropriate, Regulations for the Joint Consultative Commission governing procedures, composition and other relevant matters.

ARTICLE VI

1. The Parties will develop cooperation on the basis of mutual benefit, equality, and reciprocity in various areas related to carrying out underground nuclear explosions for peaceful purposes.

2. The Joint Consultative Commission will facilitate this cooperation by considering specific areas and forms of cooperation which shall be determined by agreement between the Parties in accordance with their constitutional procedures.

3. The Parties will appropriately inform the International Atomic Energy Agency of results of their cooperation in the field of underground nuclear explosions for peaceful purposes.

ARTICLE VII

1. Each Party shall continue to promote the development of the international agreement or agreements and procedures provided for in Article V of the Treaty on the Non-Proliferation of Nuclear Weapons, and shall provide appropriate assistance to the International Atomic Energy Agency in this regard.

2. Each Party undertakes not to carry out, participate or assist in the carrying out of any explosion in the territory of another State unless that State agrees to the implementation in its territory of the international observation and procedures contemplated

by Article V of the Treaty on the Non-Proliferation of Nuclear Weapons and the provisions of Article IV of the Protocol to this Treaty, including the provision by that State of the assistance necessary for such implementation and of the privileges and immunities specified in the Protocol.

ARTICLE VIII

1. This Treaty shall remain in force for a period of five years, and it shall be extended for successive five-year periods unless either Party notifies the other of its termination no later than six months prior to its expiration. Before the expiration of this period the Parties may, as necessary, hold consultations to consider the situation relevant to the substance of this Treaty. However, under no circumstances shall either Party be entitled to terminate this Treaty while the Treaty on the Limitation of Underground Nuclear Weapon Tests remains in force.

2. Termination of the Treaty on the Limitation of Underground Nuclear Weapon Tests shall entitle either Party to withdraw from this Treaty at any time.

3. Each Party may propose amendments to this Treaty. Amendments shall enter into force on the day of the exchange of instruments of ratification of such amendments.

ARTICLE IX

1. This Treaty including the Protocol which forms an integral part hereof, shall be subject to ratification in accordance with the constitutional procedures of each Party. This Treaty shall enter into force on the day of the exchange of instruments of ratification which exchange shall take place simultaneously with the exchange of instruments of ratification of the Treaty on the Limitation of Underground Nuclear Weapon Tests.

2. This Treaty shall be registered pursuant to Article 102 of the Charter of the United Nations.

DONE at Washington and Moscow, on May 28, 1976, in duplicate, in the English and Russian languages, both texts being equally authentic.

THE PROTOCOL TO THE TREATY BETWEEN THE UNITED STATES OF AMERICA AND THE UNION OF SOVIET SOCIALIST REPUBLICS ON UNDERGROUND NUCLEAR EXPLOSIONS FOR PEACEFUL PURPOSES[2]

The United States of America and the Union of Soviet Socialist Republics, hereinafter referred to as the Parties,

CONFIRMING the provisions of the Treaty between the United States of America and the Union of Soviet Socialist Republics on Underground Nuclear Explosions for Peaceful Purposes of May 28, 1976, hereinafter referred to as the Treaty,

---

[2] 1714 UNTS 440.

TAKING into account the fact that nuclear explosions for peaceful purposes are conducted outside national nuclear tests sites under various geological conditions,

CONVINCED of the necessity to ensure effective verification of compliance with the Treaty,

HAVE AGREED AS FOLLOWS:

SECTION I. DEFINITIONS

In addition to the definitions of terms set forth in Article II of the Treaty, for the purposes of this Protocol:

1. The term "emplacement hole" means the entire interior of any drill hole, shaft, adit or tunnel in which an explosive, associated cables, and other equipment are installed for the purposes of carrying out an explosion.
2. The term "Verifying Party" means the Party entitled to carry out, in accordance with this Protocol, activities related to verification of compliance with the Treaty by the Party carrying out an explosion.
3. The term "Designated Personnel" means personnel appointed by the Verifying Party from among its nationals and included on its list of Designated Personnel, in accordance with Section IX of this Protocol, to carry out activities related to verification, in accordance with this Protocol, in the territory of the Party carrying out the explosion.
4. The term "Transport Personnel" means personnel appointed by the Verifying Party from among its nationals and included on its list of Transport Personnel, in accordance with this Protocol, to provide transportation for Designated Personnel, their baggage, and equipment of the Verifying Party between the territory of the Verifying Party and the point of entry in the territory of the Party carrying out the explosion.
5. The term "point of entry" means Washington, D.C. (Dulles International Airport) with respect to the United States of America; and Moscow (Sheremetyevo-2 Airport) with respect to the Union of Soviet Socialist Republics. Other locations may serve as points of entry for specific explosions, as agreed by the Parties.
6. The term "on-site inspection" means activities carried out by the Verifying Party in the territory of the Party carrying out the explosion, in accordance with Section VII of this Protocol, for the purposes of independently obtaining data on conditions under which the explosion will be conducted and confirming the validity of data provided by the Party carrying out the explosion.
7. The term "hydrodynamic yield measurement method" means the method whereby the yield of an explosion is derived from on-site, direct measurement of the position of the shock front as a function of time during the hydrodynamic phase of the ground motion produced by the explosion.
8. The term "local seismic network" means the array of seismic stations and the control point temporarily deployed, in accordance with this Protocol, for the purpose of identifying the number of individual explosions in a specific group explosion.
9. The term "Joint Consultative Commission" means the Commission established in accordance with Article V of the Treaty.

10. The term "Coordinating Group" means a working group of the Joint Consultative Commission, established in accordance with Section XI of this Protocol.

11. The term "Nuclear Risk Reduction Centers" means the Centers located in Washington, D.C., and Moscow, established in accordance with the Agreement Between the United States of America and the Union of Soviet Socialist Republics on the Establishment of Nuclear Risk Reduction Centers of September 15, 1987.

SECTION II. EXPLOSION DEPTH AND COMPOSITION

1. No explosion shall be conducted at a distance in meters from the ground surface less than 30 times the 3.4 root of the planned yield of that explosion in kilotons.

2. No group explosion shall have an aggregate yield exceeding 150 kilotons unless the Parties agree on specific procedures to implement appropriate provisions of this Protocol so as to permit identification of each individual explosion and determination of the yield of each individual explosion in the group.

3. No explosion having a planned yield exceeding 35 kilotons shall be conducted in a cavity having a volume exceeding 20,000 cubic meters, unless the Parties agree on verification measures for such an explosion.

SECTION III. VERIFICATION MEASURES

1. For the purposes of the Treaty, all underground nuclear explosions conducted outside national nuclear test sites shall be considered underground nuclear explosions for peaceful purposes subject to all the provisions of the Treaty. For purposes of verification of compliance with the Treaty, in addition to using available national technical means, the Verifying Party shall have the right:

(a) to use the hydrodynamic yield measurement method, in accordance with Section V of this Protocol, to measure the yield of each explosion that the Party carrying out the explosion notifies, in accordance with paragraph 3 of Section IV of this Protocol, to have a planned yield exceeding 50 kilotons;

(b) to use the hydrodynamic yield measurement method, in accordance with Section V of this Protocol, to monitor the yield of each individual explosion in a group explosion that the Party carrying out the explosion notifies, in accordance with paragraph 3 of Section IV of this Protocol, to have a planned aggregate yield exceeding 50 kilotons;

(c) to use, in conjunction with the use of the hydrodynamic yield measurement method, a local seismic network, in accordance with Section VI of this Protocol, for each group explosion that the Party carrying out the explosion notifies, in accordance with paragraph 3 of Section IV of this Protocol, to have a planned aggregate yield exceeding 150 kilotons, and

(d) to carry out on-site inspection, in accordance with Section VII of this Protocol, with respect to any explosion that the Party carrying out the explosion notifies, in accordance with paragraph 3 of Section IV of this Protocol, to have a planned yield exceeding 35 kilotons, and, with respect to any explosion having a planned yield exceeding 50 kilotons, only if the

Verifying Party has decided not to use the hydrodynamic yield measurement method.

2. The Party carrying out the explosion shall bear full responsibility for, and have exclusive control over, the conduct of the explosion.

3. Designated Personnel shall be responsible for the working of their equipment, its timely installation and operation, for participating in such operations, including dry runs, as the Party carrying out the explosion may request, and for recording data at the time of the explosion. The Party carrying out the explosion shall be under no obligation to change the time of the explosion because of any malfunction of the equipment of the Verifying Party or inability of Designated Personnel to carry out their functions, unless actions of the Party carrying out the explosion have caused such a situation to arise.

SECTION IV. NOTIFICATIONS AND INFORMATION RELATING TO EXPLOSIONS

1. Unless the Parties otherwise agree, all notifications provided for in this Protocol shall be transmitted through the Nuclear Risk Reduction Centers. The Nuclear Risk Reduction Centers may also be used, as appropriate, to transmit other information provided in accordance with this Protocol.

2. Not later than July 1 following entry into force of the Treaty, and each July 1 thereafter, each Party shall inform the other Party whether or not it intends to conduct, during the following calendar year, any individual or group explosion for peaceful purposes having a planned aggregate yield exceeding 35 kilotons, and if so, how many. On the date of entry into force of the Treaty, information specified by this paragraph shall be provided by each Party for the remainder of the calendar year in which the Treaty enters into force and for the period from January 1 through December 31 of the succeeding year. In the event of changes in the information provided in accordance with this paragraph, such changes shall be immediately provided to the other Party.

3. No less than 180 days prior to the planned date of the beginning of emplacement of the explosive or explosives for every explosion having a planned yield exceeding 35 kilotons, the Party carrying out the explosion shall notify the Verifying Party of its intention to carry out the explosion and shall provide the Verifying Party with the following information, to the extent and degree of accuracy available at the time when it is provided:

(a) the planned date of the explosion;

(b) the planned date of the beginning of emplacement of the explosive or explosives;

(c) the purpose of the explosion;

(d) the location of the explosion, expressed in geographic coordinates to the nearest minute;

(e) the planned yield of the explosion;

(f) the number of explosives, and the planned yield of each individual explosive;

(g) the planned depth of emplacement of each explosive to the nearest 10 meters;

(h) the type or types of rock in which the explosion will take place, including the depth of the water table; and

(i) a description of specific technological features of the project of which the explosion is a part that may affect determination of its yield and confirmation of its purpose.

4. Following receipt of information specified in paragraph 3 of this Section, the Verifying Party shall inform the Party carrying out the explosion, no less than 150 days prior to the planned date of the beginning of emplacement of explosives, in a single notification, whether or not it intends to carry out one of the following activities related to verification:

(a) with respect to an explosion having a planned yield exceeding 35 kilotons, to carry out on-site inspection in accordance with Section VII of this Protocol; or

(b) with respect to an explosion having a planned yield exceeding 50 kilotons, to use the hydrodynamic yield measurement method, in accordance with Section V of this Protocol, and, with respect to a group explosion having a planned aggregate yield exceeding 150 kilotons, to use, in conjunction with the hydrodynamic yield measurement method, a local seismic network, in accordance with Section VI of this Protocol.

5. If the Verifying Party:

(a) declares its intention not to conduct activities described in paragraphs 4(a) and 4(b) of this Section, it shall thereby forfeit its right to conduct such activities unless the Party carrying out the explosion provides notification, in accordance with paragraph 9 of this Section, of a change in the location by more than one minute of latitude or longitude or of a change in the planned date of the explosion that changes the date indicated in the initial notification by 60 days or more. Within 30 days of notification by the Party carrying out the explosion of any such change in location or planned date of the explosion, the Verifying Party shall have the right to revise the notification it provided in accordance with paragraph 4 of this Section. In the event the Verifying Party elects to revise its notification and to use the hydrodynamic yield measurement method or to carry out on-site inspection, the beginning of emplacement of explosives shall not occur less than 90 days from the date of the Verifying Party's revised notification, unless the Parties otherwise agree. The Party carrying out the explosion shall thereafter provide the Verifying Party with the information specified in paragraph 6 or 7 of this Section; or

(b) decides not to conduct the activities related to verification specified by it in its initial notification, after technical and logistical support requirements for these activities have been agreed upon in the Coordinating Group, in accordance with paragraph 6 of Section XI of this Protocol, the Verifying Party shall reimburse the Party carrying out the explosion for costs for such technical and logistical support incurred by the party carrying out the explosion prior to receipt of notification that the Verifying Party will not carry out the initially-declared activities related to verification.

6. In the event of receipt by the Party carrying out the explosion of notification from the Verifying Party of its intent to use the hydrodynamic yield measurement method, the Party carrying out the explosion shall provide the Verifying Party not less than 60 days prior to the planned date of the beginning of emplacement of explosives with the following information:

(a) the number of explosives; the planned yield of each explosive; the planned depth of emplacement of each explosive with an accuracy of 10 meters; the planned point of emplacement of each explosive to be used in a group explosion relative to all other explosives in the group with an accuracy of 10 percent of the distance between that explosive and the nearest other explosive, but in no case shall the error be greater than 100 meters; and the planned time intervals between individual explosions in each group explosion with an accuracy of 0.1 second;

(b) a description of the geological and geophysical characteristics of the site of each explosion that could influence determination of the yield, which shall include: the depth of the water table; a stratigraphic column above each emplacement point; the position of each emplacement point relative to nearby geological and other features than influenced the design of the project of which the explosion is a part; and the estimated physical parameters of the rock within each hydrodynamic measurement zone, including bulk density, grain density, compressional and shear-wave velocities, porosity, and total water content;

(c) the locations and purposes of facilities and installations that are associated with the conduct of the explosion;

(d) the planned date of the beginning of emplacement of each explosive;

(e) a topographic chart, marked with geographic coordinates accurate to one minute of latitude and longitude, of the areas circumscribed by circles of 15 kilometer radius centered on points on the surface of the earth above the points of emplacement of each explosive, at a scale of 1:24,000 or 1:25,000 with a contour interval of 10 meters or less. The planned location of each explosive shall be marked on this chart with an accuracy of 50 meters;

(f) the length of each canister in which an explosive will be contained, hereinafter referred to as an explosive canister;

(g) the dimensions of any pipe or other device that will be used to emplace each explosive canister;

(h) the planned cross-sectional dimensions of each emplacement hole within the hydrodynamic measurement zones;

(i) a description of materials, including their densities, to be used to stem the emplacement hole within each hydrodynamic measurement zone; and

(j) the location and configuration of any known voids larger in volume than one cubic meter within each hydrodynamic measurement zone.

7. In the event of receipt by the Party carrying out the explosion of notification from the Verifying Party of its intent to carry out on-site inspection, the Party carrying out the explosion shall provide

the Verifying Party, not less than 60 days prior to the planned date of the beginning of emplacement of explosives, with the following information:

(a) the number of explosives; the planned yield of each explosive; the planned depth of emplacement of each explosive with an accuracy of 10 meters; the planned point of emplacement of each explosive to be used in a group explosion relative to all other explosives in the group with an accuracy of 10 percent of the distance between that explosive and the nearest other explosive, but in no case shall the error be greater than 100 meters; and the planned time intervals between individual explosions in each group explosion with an accuracy of 0.1 second;

(b) a description of the geological and geophysical characteristics of the site of each explosion that could influence determination of the yield, which shall include: the depth of the water table; a lithologic column above each emplacement point; the position of each emplacement point relative to nearby geological and other features that influenced the design of the project of which the explosion is a part; and the estimated physical parameters of the rock within each hydrodynamic measurement zone, including bulk density, grain density, porosity, and total water content;

(c) the locations and purposes of facilities and installations that are associated with the conduct of the explosive;

(d) the planned date of the beginning of emplacement of each explosive;

(e) a topographic chart, marked with geographic coordinates accurate to one minute of latitude and longitude, of the areas circumscribed by circles of 15 kilometer radius centered on points on the surface of the earth above the points of emplacement of each explosive, at a scale of 1:24,000 or 1:25,000 with a contour interval of 10 meters or less. The planned location of each explosive shall be marked on this chart with an accuracy of 50 meters;

(f) the planned cross-sectional dimensions of each emplacement hole within the hydrodynamic measurement zones; and

(g) the location and configuration of any known voids larger in volume than one cubic meter within each hydrodynamic measurement zone.

8. For each explosion, the Party carrying out the explosion shall inform the Verifying Party, no less than two days prior to the explosion, of the planned time of detonation of each explosive, with an accuracy of 0.1 second. In the event the Party carrying the explosion decides to change the detonation time, the Verifying Party shall be notified of this change immediately after this decision has been taken. No more than 10 days following the explosion the Verifying Party shall be informed of the actual detonation time.

9. The Party carrying out the explosion shall immediately notify the Verifying Party of any change in any information provided in accordance with paragraph 3, 6, or 7 of this Section. If the Verifying Party has provided notification under paragraph 4 of this Section of its decision to use the hydrodynamic yield measurement

method or to carry out on-site inspection, the emplacement of explosives shall not begin less than 90 days following notification of any change in any information provided in accordance with paragraph 3, 6, or 7 of this Section that requires more extensive verification procedures than are required on the basis of initial information, unless an earlier date for the beginning of emplacement of explosives has been agreed upon by the Parties. Such changes include:

(a) change in the location of the explosion by more than one minute of latitude or longitude;

(b) change in the number of explosives in a group explosion;

(c) change in the yield of the explosion;

(d) change in the purpose of the explosion; and

(e) delay in the planned date of the explosion by more than 90 days.

10. In using an explosion to decrease the consequences of an emergency situation related to an unforeseen set of circumstances and requiring immediate action, by virtue of which it would be practically impossible to adhere to the requirements of paragraph 3 of this Section concerning the time period, the following conditions shall be fulfilled:

(a) the Party making the decision to carry out an explosion for such a purpose shall notify the Verifying Party of this decision immediately after it has been made and shall describe the circumstances and provide the planned yield for such an explosion;

(b) the planned aggregate yield for such an explosion shall not exceed 100 kilotons and the explosion shall not include more than three individual explosions, unless the Parties otherwise agree;

(c) the Party carrying out such an explosion shall provide the Verifying Party with the information specified in paragraphs 3 and 6 of this Section, to the extent such information is available, after making the decision on carrying out the explosion, but no less than 60 days prior to the beginning of emplacement of explosives; and

(d) if, within 15 days following receipt of notification of such an explosion, the Verifying Party has made the decision to carry out verification of that explosion using the hydrodynamic yield measurement method, it shall deliver hydrodynamic yield measurement equipment to the point of entry in the territory of the Party carrying out the explosion no less than 35 days prior to the planned date of the beginning of emplacement of explosives, in accordance with paragraphs 8(b), 8(c), 8(d), 8(e), and 8(f) of Section VIII of this Protocol. This equipment shall be handed over, in the same condition as that in which it was received, to Designated Personnel at the site of the explosion for emplacement, installation, and use no less than 20 days prior to the planned date of the beginning of emplacement of explosives.

11. The Party carrying out an explosion shall have the right to make changes in the schedule of operations related to the conduct of the explosion. In the event the Verifying Party exercises its rights to use the hydrodynamic yield measurement method or to

carry out on-site inspection, in accordance with Section III of this Protocol, the Party carrying out the explosion shall immediately inform the Verifying Party of any such change in the schedule of operations. In the event the Verifying Party has provided notification, under paragraph 5 of this Section, of its decision to use the hydrodynamic yield measurement method or to carry out on-site inspection, the explosion shall not be carried out more than five days prior to the planned date of the explosion indicated in the initial notification, unless the Parties otherwise agree.

12. The Verifying Party may at any time, but no more than one year after the explosion, request from the Party carrying out the explosion clarification of any point of information provided in accordance with this Section. Such clarification shall be provided in the shortest possible time, but no more than 30 days following receipt of a request.

SECTION V. HYDRODYNAMIC YIELD MEASUREMENT METHOD

1. The hydrodynamic measurement zone for each explosive means a cylindrical region coaxial with the emplacement hole of that explosive. This region extends in the direction of the entrance to the emplacement hole intersects a spherical surface whose radius, measured from the midpoint of the canister containing the explosive, is equal in meters to 10 times the cube root of the planned yield in kilotons of that explosive, or 25 meters, whichever is greater. The length of this region in the opposite direction from the same midpoint of the canister is equal in meters to three times the cube root of the planned yield in kilotons of that explosive, or 7.5 meters, whichever is greater. The radius of this region is equal in meters to three times the cube root of the planned yield in kilotons of that explosive, or 7.5 meters, whichever is greater.

2. For hydrodynamic yield measurement the following procedures shall apply:

(a) Designated Personnel shall emplace, for each explosive, the equipment specified in paragraph 5(a) of Section VIII of this Protocol in the same emplacement hole as the explosive. The equipment specified in paragraphs 5(a) and 5(b) of Section VIII of this Protocol shall be installed, in accordance with installation instructions provided in accordance with paragraph 8(a)(i) of Section VIII of this Protocol, by Designated Personnel under observation of personnel of the Party carrying out the explosion and with their assistance, if Designated Personnel have requested such assistance. The location of each recording facility and the command and monitoring facility of the Verifying Party shall be determined by agreement of the Parties with respect to each particular explosion. This equipment shall be operated by Designated Personnel;

(b) for each explosive, the equipment specified in paragraph 5(a) of Section VIII of this Protocol shall be installed so that the end point of the equipment farthest from the emplacement hole entrance is three meters from the surface of the explosive canister closest to the emplacement hole entrance as measured along the axis of the emplacement hold. The location of this equipment relative to the axis of the emplacement hole shall be agreed upon by the Parties. No more than six sensor channels shall be installed for each explosive. Each Party shall make documented records of measured distances to the sensors. These records shall be exchanged by the Parties;

(c) explosive canisters with a length greater than 10 meters or a diameter greater than three meters shall be used only if prior agreement has been reached between the Parties establishing, in each specific case, provisions for their use; and

(d) the Party carrying out the explosion shall fill all voids other than the explosive canister within the hydrodynamic measurement zone of each explosive in each emplacement hole with stemming material. This stemming material, beginning no more than three meters from each explosive canister cover towards the entrance of the hole, and proceeding in that direction, shall have a bulk density no less than 70 percent of the average density of the surrounding rock. An alternate stemming material may be used for filling the remainder of the hydrodynamic measurement zone of that explosive. For any explosive emplaced in an emplacement hole whose diameter is less than 30 centimeters and emplaced at a distance of more than 1.5 kilometers from the entrance of the hole, an alternate stemming material may be used for filling the entire hydrodynamic measurement zone of that explosive. If more than one explosive is emplaced in a single emplacement hole, the Parties shall agree upon an alternate stemming material for filling the entire hydrodynamic measurement zone of each explosive other than the explosive nearest the entrance of the emplacement hole is the emplacement hole diameter is greater than 30 centimeters but less than 60 centimeters. Any alternate stemming material shall have a bulk density no less than 1.2 grams per cubic centimeter. Pipes located within the hydrodynamic measurement zone need not be filled with stemming material if they have a cross-sectional area less than 10 square centimeters, or if they have a cross-sectional area less than 100 square centimeters and a length less than one meter. Costs incurred by the Party carrying out the explosion to ensure, within the hydrodynamic measurement zone, a density of stemming material no less than 70 percent of the average density of the surrounding rock shall be borne by the Verifying Party.

3. For a group explosion the Party carrying out the explosion shall ensure that the emplacement point of each explosive canister, the detonation sequence, and the time intervals between individual explosions are such that no explosion in the group shall interfere with the hydrodynamic yield measurement of any other individual explosion. With the exception of group explosions provided for in paragraph 2 of Section II of this Protocol, if the technological characteristics of the project of which the group explosion is a part make it impossible to satisfy this requirement, the Parties, prior to the beginning of emplacement of explosives, shall agree upon alternative hydrodynamic or other verification procedures.

4. In preparation for the use of the hydrodynamic yield measurement method, the Verifying Party shall have the right to confirm the validity of the geological and geophysical information provided

in accordance with Section IV of this Protocol, in accordance with the following procedures:

(a) Designated Personnel may analyze relevant studies and measurement data, including logging data, of the Party carrying out the explosion, the core samples or rock fragments extracted from each emplacement hole within the hydrodynamic measurement zone, as well as any logging data and core samples from existing exploratory holes, which shall be provided to Designated Personnel upon their arrival at the explosion site, if the Party carrying out the explosion carried out relevant studies, measurements, and coring; and

(b) Designated Personnel shall have the right to observe logging and the extraction of core samples or rock fragments from locations agreed upon by the Parties within the hydrodynamic measurement zone in the emplacement hole or from an exploratory hole at depth intervals agreed upon by the Parties. Any such exploratory hole shall be no farther from the emplacement hole than a distance in meters of 10 times the cube root of the planned yield in kilotons of the emplaced explosive; or

(c) if the Party carrying out the explosion does not take core samples or rock fragments in accordance with subparagraph (b) of this paragraph or does not drill an exploratory hole meeting the requirements specified in subparagraph (b) or this paragraph, the Verifying Party shall have the right to extract sidewall rock samples from the emplacement hole with its own equipment, to drill such an exploratory hole, and to core this hole. Such operations shall be conducted in the presence of personnel of the Party carrying out the explosion. Such an exploratory hole shall be stemmed by the Party carrying out the explosion, at the expense of the Verifying Party; and

(d) Designated Personnel shall have the right to examine and remove from the territory of the Party carrying out the explosion logging data, core samples, sidewall rock samples, and rock fragments referred to in subparagraphs (a), (b), and (c) of this paragraph, as selected by Designated Personnel.

5. While using the hydrodynamic yield measurement method, Designated Personnel shall have the right:

(a) to confirm by direct measurement the validity of the information provided in accordance with paragraphs 6(f), 6(g), and 6(h) of Section IV of this Protocol;

(b) to confirm the validity of the information provided in accordance with paragraph 6(i) of Section IV of this Protocol, and to receive, upon request, a sample of each batch of stemming material as this material is placed in the emplacement hole within the hydrodynamic measurement zone; and

(c) to confirm the validity of the information provided in accordance with paragraphs 6(b) and 6(j) of Section IV of this Protocol, by observing, upon request, relevant field measurements being made by the Party carrying out the explosion if such measurements are made by the Party carrying out the explosion, and by making field measurements with its own logging equipment, to include determination of the location and configuration of any voids within each hydrodynamic measurement zone or, at the option of the Verifying Party under leasing conditions, with the logging equipment of the Party carrying out the explosion, if the Party carrying out the explosion has such equipment. Such field measurements shall be made in the presence of personnel of both Parties. All of the data produced by either Party, including calibration data, shall be duplicated, and one copy of the data shall be provided to each Party. Calibration data for the equipment shall include information to confirm the sensitivity of the equipment under the conditions in which it is utilized for this explosion.

6. Designated Personnel shall have the right:

(a) to have access to the site of the explosion and to facilities and structures related to the conduct of the explosion, along agreed routes;

(b) to observe the emplacement of each explosive canister, to confirm, by direct measurement, the depth of emplacement of each explosive canister and, for explosives in a group, the relative location of their points of emplacement, and to observe the stemming of each emplacement hole;

(c) to have access to their equipment associated with the use of the hydrodynamic yield measurement method from commencement of its use by Designated Personnel at the explosion site until the departure of all personnel from the explosion area prior to the explosion;

(d) to unimpeded visual observation of the entrance area to each emplacement hole at any time from the moment of emplacement of each explosive until the departure of all personnel from the explosion area prior to the explosion;

(e) to observe remotely by means of closed-circuit television equipment their hydrodynamic yield measurement equipment specified in paragraphs 5(b) and 5(c) of Section VIII of this Protocol;

(f) to observe the explosion; and

(g) to monitor electrically the integrity and performance of their equipment in each recording facility from the command and monitoring facility, to transmit the hydrodynamic yield measurement data from each recording facility to the command and monitoring facility, and to transmit the commands required for operation of each recording facility from the command and monitoring facility to each recording facility.

7. The Party carrying out the explosion shall produce, at the request of the Verifying Party, a timing reference command signal to each recording facility at two minutes, plus or minus 100 milliseconds, before the moment of the explosion, or before the first explosion in a group, and a zero-time reference signal to each corresponding recording facility for each explosion, with an accuracy of plus or minus one microsecond. The parameters for these signals, produced by the Party carrying out the explosion, and procedures for their transmission and reception shall be agreed upon by the Parties. At the Verifying Party's option, it shall have the right to generate a timing reference signal for each explosion, using the electromagnetic pulse from its hydrodynamic measurement cables.

These timing reference signals shall be transmitted, used, and recorded by the Verifying Party with out intervention by the Party carrying out the explosion.

8. Designated Personnel shall have the right to acquire photographs taken by the Party carrying out the explosion, with photographic cameras provided by the Verifying Party, under the following conditions:

(a) the Party carrying out the explosion shall identify those of its personnel who will take photographs;

(b) photographs shall be taken as requested by, and in the presence of, Designated Personnel. If requested by Designated Personnel, such photographs shall show the size of an object by placing a measuring scale, provided by the Verifying Party, alongside that object during the photographing;

(c) Designated Personnel shall determine whether photographs conform to those requested and, if not, repeat photographs shall be taken; and

(d) before completion if any photographed operation related to emplacement, and prior to the time at which an object being photographed becomes permanently hidden from view, Designated Personnel shall determine whether requested photographs are adequate. If they are not adequate, before the operation shall proceed, additional photographs shall be taken until the Designated Personnel determine that the photographs of that operation are adequate. This photographic process shall be carried out as expeditiously as possible, and in no case shall the hours for each emplacement operation, unless the Parties otherwise agree.

9. Designated Personnel shall have the right to obtain photographs of the following:

(a) the exterior of installations and structures associated with the conduct of the explosion;

(b) the emplacement of each explosive canister and stemming of each emplacement hole as specified in paragraph 6(b) of this Section;

(c) geological samples used for confirming the validity of geological and geophysical information as provided for in paragraph 4 of this Section, and equipment used in obtaining such samples;

(d) emplacement and installation of hydrodynamic yield measurement method equipment and cables associated with it;

(e) containers, facilities and structures for storing and operating the equipment used by Designated Personnel; and

(f) with the agreement of the Party carrying out the explosion, other activities of Designated Personnel directly related to the use of the hydrodynamic yield measurement method.

10. Equipment identified by the Party carrying out the explosion, in accordance with paragraph 8(h) of Section VIII of this Protocol, as unacceptable for use at the time of the explosion shall be sealed by both Parties and placed in the custody of the Party carrying out the explosion at a time agreed upon by the Party carrying out the explosion and by Designated Personnel.

11. Two individuals from the Party carrying out the explosion shall have the right to join Designated Personnel in the command

and monitoring facility at the time of the explosion, to observe command and monitoring of the recording equipment and acquisition and duplication of data transmitted from each recording facility, and to receive a copy of the data. Designated Personnel, in the presence of personnel of the Party carrying out the explosion, shall recover all recordings of data taken at the time of the explosion and prepare two identical copies of such data. Personnel of the Party carrying out the explosion shall select one of the two identical copies by lot, and Designated Personnel shall retain the other copy. Designated Personnel shall retain no other such data, and shall have no further access to their recording facilities, their command and monitoring facility, and their equipment until these are returned to the Verifying Party, in accordance with paragraph 11 of Section VIII of this Protocol, unless the Parties otherwise agree, in which case access of the Designated Personnel to their recording facilities, their command and monitoring facility, and their equipment shall be under the observation of personnel of the Party carrying out the explosion. Designated Personnel shall provide the Party carrying out the explosion with information on sensor location in relation to the explosive canister. With respect to digital recording of signals, the Verifying Party shall provide a description of the recording format and a sample of the computer program for reading digital data. The program shall be provided by Designated Personnel upon their arrival at the point of entry.

12. Designated Personnel shall not be present in areas from which all personnel of the Party carrying out the explosion have been withdrawn in connection with carrying out an explosion, but shall have the right to reenter those areas at the same time as personnel of the Party carrying out the explosion.

SECTION VI. LOCAL SEISMIC NETWORK

1. For any group explosion that the Party carrying out the explosion has notified to have a planned aggregate yield exceeding 150 kilotons, and with respect to which the Verifying Party has notified its intention to measure the yield of the explosion using the hydrodynamic yield measurement method, Designated Personnel, in addition to using the hydrodynamic yield measurement method, shall have the right to install and use, under the observation and with the assistance of personnel of the Party carrying out the explosion if Designated Personnel request such assistance, a local seismic network.

2. Such a network shall be installed and used at locations agreed upon by the Parties within an area circumscribed by circles of 15 kilometer radius centered on points on the surface of the earth above the points of emplacement of the explosives. The number of stations of the network shall be determined by the Verifying Party, but shall not exceed the number of explosives in the group plus eight.

3. The control point of the local seismic network shall be installed at a location that the Parties agree is outside the areas specified in paragraph 12 of Section V of this Protocol and within the area specified in paragraph 2 of this Section, unless the Parties otherwise agree. Designated Personnel shall have the right to have

access to their equipment in the control point at any time from commencement of installation of the local seismic network until five days following the explosion, subject to the provisions of paragraph 12 of Section V, if applicable, and paragraph 10(e) of Section VIII of this Protocol.

4. Installation of a local seismic network may commence 20 days prior to the planned date of the explosion, and its operation shall continue no more than three days following the explosion, unless the Parties otherwise agree.

5. Designated Personnel shall have the right to use radio communication for the transmission and reception of data and control signals between seismic stations and the control point of the local seismic network. Frequencies and maximum power output of radio transmitters, frequency range and sensitivity of radio receivers, orientation of transmitting and receiving antennas, and period of operation of the local seismic network radio transmitters and radio receivers prior to the explosion shall be agreed upon by the Parties. Operation of the radio equipment following the explosion shall continue for no more than three days, unless the Parties otherwise agree.

6. Designated Personnel shall have access along agreed routes to the stations and the control point of the local seismic network for the purpose of carrying out activities related to the installation and use of the local seismic network.

7. In installing and using a local seismic network, Designated Personnel shall have the right to use and retain the topographic chart provided in accordance with paragraph 6(e) of Section IV of this Protocol.

8. Designated Personnel shall have the right to obtain photographs associated with the local seismic network, which shall be taken by the Party carrying out the explosion at the request of Designated Personnel in accordance with applicable provisions of paragraph 8 of Section V of this Protocol.

9. Within five days following the explosion, Designated Personnel shall provide the Party carrying out the explosion with the original and one copy of the data from the local seismic network stations recorded on the primary medium, graphic representation of recording materials on a paper medium, and the results of calibration of seismic channels. Upon receipt of these materials the Party carrying out the explosion, in the presence of Designated Personnel, shall select and retain either the copy or the original of each recording, graphic representation, and results of calibration of the seismic channels. The set of data not selected by the Party carrying out the explosion shall be retained by Designated Personnel. For digital recording of seismic signals, the Verifying Party shall provide the description of the recording format and a sample of the computer program for reading digital data. Designated Personnel shall provide the program sample upon arrival at the point of entry. Seismic recordings provided to the Party carrying out the explosion shall cover a time period beginning no less than 30 seconds prior to the time of arrival of the first explosion-generated P-wave at any station of the local seismic network and ending no more than three days after the explosion, unless the Parties otherwise

agree. All seismic recordings shall include a common time reference agreed upon by the Parties.

SECTION VII. ON-SITE INSPECTION

1. In carrying out on-site inspection, the Verifying Party shall have the right to confirm the validity of the geological and geophysical information provided in accordance with paragraphs 3 and 7 of Section IV of this Protocol in accordance with the following procedures:

(a) Designated Personnel may analyze relevant studies and measurement data, including logging data, of the Party carrying out the explosion, the core samples of rock fragments extracted from each emplacement hole from the bottom of the hole to a distance above the point of emplacement in meters equal to 40 times the cube root of the planned yield in kilotons of the emplaced explosive, as well as any logging data and core samples from existing exploratory holes, which shall be provided to Designated Personnel upon their arrival at the explosion site, if the Party carrying out the explosion carried out relevant studies, measurements, and coring;

(b) Designated Personnel shall have the right to observe logging and the extraction of core samples or rock fragments from locations agreed upon by the Parties within the portion of the emplacement hole specified in subparagraph (a) of this paragraph or from an exploratory hole, provided that it is located no farther from the emplacement hole than a distance in meters equal to 10 times the cube root of the planned yield in kilotons of the emplaced explosive at depth intervals agreed upon by the Parties if such operations are carried out by the Party carrying out the explosion;

(c) Designated Personnel shall have the right to use their own equipment for logging the emplacement hole and extracting sidewall rock samples within the portion of the emplacement hole identified in subparagraph (a) of this paragraph. Such operations shall be conducted in the presence of personnel of the Party carrying out the explosion; and

(d) all logging data produced by either Party, including calibration data, shall be duplicated, and one copy of the data shall be provided to each Party. Calibration data shall include information needed to confirm the sensitivity of the equipment under the conditions in which it is used. Designated Personnel shall have the right to examine and remove from the territory of the Party carrying out the explosion core samples, sidewall rock samples, and rock fragments specified in subparagraphs (a), (b), and (c) of this paragraph, as selected by Designated Personnel.

2. In carrying out on-site inspection, Designated Personnel shall have the right:

(a) to confirm by direct measurement the validity of the information provided in accordance with paragraph 7(f) of Section IV of this Protocol;

(b) to confirm the validity of the information provided in accordance with paragraph 7(g) of Section IV of this Protocol, by observing relevant measurements being made, and by having access to the data obtained if such measurements are conducted by the Party carrying out the explosion, and by making measurements with their own equipment to determine the location and configuration of any voids within each hydrodynamic measurement zone;

(c) to have access to the site of the explosion and to facilities and structures related to the conduct of the explosion, along agreed routes;

(d) to observe the emplacement of each explosive canister, to confirm the depth of its emplacement and the relative location of explosives in a group, and to observe the stemming of each emplacement hole;

(e) to have access to their equipment associated with carrying out on-site inspection from commencement of its use by Designated Personnel at the explosion site until the departure of all personnel from the explosion area prior to the explosion;

(f) to unimpeded visual observation of the entrance area to each emplacement hole at any time from the moment of emplacement of each explosive until the departure of all personnel from the explosion area prior to the explosion; and

(g) to observe the explosion.

3. Designated Personnel shall have the right to obtain photographs associated with carrying on-site inspection, which shall be taken by the Party carrying out the explosion at the request of Designated Personnel, in accordance with paragraphs 8 and 9 of Section V of this Protocol.

SECTION VIII. EQUIPMENT

1. Designated Personnel, in carrying out activities related to verification in accordance with this Protocol, shall have the right to bring into the territory of the Party carrying out the explosion, install, and use the following equipment:

(a) if the Verifying Party has provided notification of its intent to use the hydrodynamic yield measurement method, part or all of the equipment specified in paragraph 5 of this Section;

(b) if the Verifying Party has provided notification of its intent to use a local seismic network, part or all of the equipment specified in paragraph 6 of this Section;

(c) if the Verifying Party has provided notification of its intent to carry out on-site inspection, part or all of the equipment specified in paragraph 7 of this Section;

(d) geologist's field tools and kits, geodetic equipment topographic survey equipment, equipment for recording of field data, and equipment for rapid photo processing;

(e) portable short-range communication equipment, whose power and frequency shall conform to restrictions established by the Party carrying out the explosion;

(f) mobile work stations and temporary facilities;

(g) medical and health physics equipment and supplies, personal protective gear, personal computers, recreational and other items as may be agreed by the Parties; and

(h) satellite communications equipment, if the Party carrying out the explosion does not provide satellite communications for Designated Personnel.

2. At the choice of the Party carrying out the explosion, closed-circuit television equipment shall be provided by the Verifying Party or the Party carrying out the explosion, for the purpose of remote observation by the Verifying Party, in accordance with paragraph 6(e) of Section V of this Protocol.

3. Designated Personnel, in carrying out activities related to verification in accordance with this Protocol, shall have the right to bring into the territory of the Party carrying out the explosion, for use by the personnel of the Party carrying out the explosion in accordance with paragraph 8 of section V of this Protocol, photographic cameras, film, and related photographic equipment.

4. No less than 120 days prior to the planned date of the beginning of emplacement of explosives, the Parties shall agree upon the list of such additional equipment as may be requested by the Verifying Party, and which shall be supplied by the Party carrying out the explosion for use by Designated Personnel. Such additional equipment with its description and operating instructions shall be provided to Designated Personnel upon arrival at the site of the explosion.

5. The complete list of equipment for hydrodynamic yield measurement shall include:

(a) sensing elements and associated cables for use in the emplacement hole;

(b) the recording facility or facilities, including equipment for sending and recording commands, equipment for generation of a timing reference signal from hydrodynamic measurement cables, and equipment for data acquisition, recording and processing, and, with respect to a group explosion in which any individual explosion in the group is separated from any other explosion by more than two kilometers, radio equipment for monitoring the operational status of the equipment and for transmitting and receiving control signals. Frequencies and maximum power output of radio transmitters, frequency range and sensitivity of radio receivers, and orientation of transmitting and receiving antennas shall be agreed upon by the Parties. Operation of the radio equipment shall begin at the time of the beginning of emplacement of sensing elements and associated cables and shall end at the time of the explosion. Designated Personnel shall notify the Party carrying out the explosion in advance of any activation or deactivation of the radio equipment;

(c) cables for above-ground transmission of electrical power, control signals and data;

(d) electrical power supplies;

(e) measuring and calibration instruments, support equipment, maintenance equipment, and spare parts necessary for ensuring the functioning of sensing elements, cables and equipment of the recording facilities and the command and monitoring facility;

(f) logging and sidewall rock sampling equipment necessary for confirming geological and geophysical characteristics of the emplacement hole as well as for obtaining data on the spatial location of points of emplacement of each explosive canister;

(g) coring equipment and drilling equipment for the drilling of an exploratory hole for coring purposes. Upon agreement between the Parties, the Verifying Party, under leasing conditions, may use for these purposes the coring and drilling equipment of the Party carrying out the explosion; and

(h) the command and monitoring facility, with equipment, including computers, for generating and recording command and monitoring signals, for transmitting and receiving command and monitoring signals between each recording facility and the command and monitoring facility, as well as for retrieving, storing, and processing hydrodynamic data.

6. The complete list of equipment for a local seismic network shall include:

(a) seismic stations, each of which contains seismic instruments, and electrical power supply and associated cables, and radio equipment for receiving and transmitting control signals and data;

(b) equipment for the control point, including electrical power supplies, equipment for sending and recording control signals and data, and data processing equipment; and

(c) measuring and calibration instruments, support equipment, maintenance equipment, and spare parts necessary for ensuring the functioning of the complete network.

7. The complete list of equipment for on-site inspection shall include logging and sidewall rock sampling equipment necessary for confirming geological and geophysical characteristics of the emplacement hole as well as for obtaining data on the spatial location of points of emplacement of each explosive canister.

8. The following procedures shall be followed with respect to the equipment for hydrodynamic yield measurement, the equipment for on-site inspection, and the equipment for a local seismic network:

(a) no less than 140 days prior to the planned date of the beginning of emplacement of explosives, the Verifying Party, if it has declared its intention to use the hydrodynamic yield measurement method, shall provide the Party carrying out the explosion with the equipment and information specified in subparagraph (a)(i) of this paragraph and, if the Verifying Party has declared its intention to use local seismic network, the equipment and information specified in subparagraph (a)(ii) of this paragraph; or, if it has declared is intention to conduct on-site inspection, equipment and information specified in subparagraph (a)(iii) of this paragraph, in order to enable the Party carrying out the explosion to familiarize itself with such equipment, if such equipment and information have not previously been provided. If, upon completion of familiarization with the equipment provided in accordance with this subparagraph, the Party carrying out the explosion concludes that use of any element of the equipment provided would be inconsistent with its containment or security requirements, the Party carrying out the explosion shall promptly, but no less than 120 days prior to the planned date of the beginning of emplacement of explosives, so inform the Verifying Party, and shall specify the modifications that must be made in this equipment to satisfy the requirements of the Party carrying out the explosion. The equipment provided in accordance with this subparagraph shall be returned in the same condition as that in which it was received to the Verifying Party at the Point of entry no less than 90 days prior to the planned date of the beginning of emplacement of explosives. The following equipment and information shall be provided:

(i) one set of equipment specified in paragraphs 5(a), 5(b), 5(c), 5(d), 5(e), 5(f) and 5(h) of this Section, as well as electrical and mechanical design information, specifications, and installation and operating instructions for this equipment;

(ii) one set of equipment specified in paragraph 6 of this Section, including one seismic station, as well as electrical and mechanical design information, specifications, and installation and operating instructions for this equipment; and

(iii) one set of equipment specified in paragraph 7 of the Section, as well as electrical and mechanical design information, specifications, and operating instructions for this equipment;

(b) no less than 50 days prior to the planned date of the beginning of emplacement of explosives, the Verifying Party shall deliver in sealed containers, to the point of entry in the territory of the Party carrying out the explosion, two identical sets of each type of equipment that it intends to use for activities related to verification for that explosion, with a complete inventory of equipment, specifying any components that do not perform functions directly related to measurements during the explosion. These sets of equipment shall have the same components and technical characteristics as the equipment specified in subparagraph (a) of this paragraph, or, if specified by the Party carrying out the explosion in accordance with subparagraph (a) of this paragraph, shall contain modifications made in accordance with the requirements of the Party carrying out the explosion with regard to containment and security. Each of the two identical sets shall include the following:

(i) if the Verifying Party has provided notification of its intent to use the hydrodynamic yield measurement method, equipment specified in paragraphs 5(a), 5(b), and 5(h) of this Section; and

(ii) if the Verifying Party has provided notification of its intent to use a local seismic network, equipment specified in paragraphs 6(a) and 6(b) of this Section;

(c) the Party carrying out the explosion shall choose one of the two identical sets of each type of equipment for use by Designated Personnel;

(d) at the point of entry the Party carrying out the explosion shall affix its own seals to the sealed containers in which the equipment chosen for use arrived, shall ensure protection of this equipment throughout the entire period it is in the territory of the Party carrying out the explosion, and shall transport that equipment to the site of the explosion. Prior to shipment to the site of the explosion, the set of equipment chosen for use shall be kept sealed at the point of entry, and the time of its shipment to the site of the explosion shall be determined by the Party carrying out the explosion. The Party carrying out the explosion shall consult with Designated Personnel regarding plans and schedule of shipment of the equipment no less than 48 hours in advance of the shipment. Designated Personnel shall have the right to unimpeded verification of the integrity of their seals, to observe their equipment. This equipment shall be handed over to Designated Personnel at the site of the explosion for emplacement, installation, and use no less than 20 days prior to the planned date of the beginning of emplacement of explosives, and it shall thereafter remain under the control of Designated Personnel; seals affixed to the equipment specified in paragraph 5(a) of this Section shall not be removed prior to preparation for installation of such equipment, at which time the seals shall be removed by Designated Personnel in the presence of personnel of the Party carrying out the explosion, and personnel of the Party carrying out the explosion thereafter shall have the right to observe all activities relating to the installation of such equipment;

(e) seals of the Verifying Party shall be removed from equipment not chosen for use, in the presence of personnel of both Parties, and thereafter this equipment shall be retained for inspection by the Party carrying out the explosion without the presence of Designated Personnel for a period ending no more than 30 days following the explosion, at which time such equipment shall be returned in the same condition as that in which it was received to the Verifying Party at the point of entry;

(f) no less than 50 days prior to the planned date of the beginning of emplacement of explosives, the Verifying Party shall provide, at its option, either one or two sets of the equipment that the Verifying Party intends to use for activities related to verification for this explosion, other than equipment specified in paragraph 8(b) of this Section. A complete inventory of such equipment, specifying any components that do not perform functions directly related to measurements during the explosion, shall be provided to the Party carrying out the explosion at least one week prior to the planned arrival of the equipment at the point of entry. If only one set of equipment is provided by the Verifying Party, the Party carrying out the explosion shall have the right to inspect this equipment upon its arrival at the point of entry for up to 30 days, without the presence of Designated Personnel. Upon conclusion of the inspection, the Party carrying out the explosion shall identify any equipment that it deems unacceptable for delivery to the site of the explosion, in which case equipment shall be removed by the Verifying Party and returned to its territory. All equipment deemed acceptable for delivery to the site of the explosion shall be shipped to the site of the explosion so as to enable Designated Personnel to carry out their activities related to verification as set forth in the coordinated schedule specified in paragraph 6 of Section XI of this Protocol, but in no case less than 20 days prior to the beginning of emplacement of explosives. The Party carrying out the explosion shall transport this equipment in such a manner as to ensure that it is delivered to Designated Personnel in the same condition as that in which it was received. If two sets of equipment are provided by the Verifying Party, the procedures specified in paragraphs 8(b), 8(c), 8(d), and 8(e) of this Section for selection and inspection of equipment shall be followed. If the Verifying Party under leasing conditions uses coring and drilling equipment of the Party carrying out the explosion, such equipment shall be provided to Designated Personnel at the site of the explosion so as to enable Designated Personnel to carry out their activities related to verification as set forth in the coordinated schedule referred to in paragraph 6 of Section XI of this Protocol, but in no case less than 20 days prior to the beginning of emplacement of explosives, unless the Parties otherwise agree;

(g) with respect to the equipment specified in paragraphs 5(a) and 5(c) of this Section, the Party carrying out the explosion shall have the right to retain for its own purposes up to 150 meters of each type of cable in the set being inspected. The cable segments to be retained may be taken from any place along the length of the cable, but the number of individual segments shall not exceed the number of reels of cable in a set of equipment; and

(h) after inspecting the equipment in accordance with paragraphs 8(e) and 8(f) of this Section, the Party carrying out the explosion shall inform Designated Personnel what equipment of that delivered to the site of the explosion it deems unacceptable for use during the explosion.

9. Prior to the beginning of emplacement of explosives, Designated Personnel shall certify in writing to the personnel of the Party carrying out the explosion that the equipment delivered to the site of the explosion is in working condition.

10. Personnel of the Party carrying out the explosion shall have the right to observe use of equipment by Designated Personnel at the site of the explosion, with access to the recording facilities, the command and monitoring facility, the control point, and seismic stations of the local seismic network of the Verifying Party being subject to the following:

(a) at any time prior to the explosion that Designated Personnel are not present in the recording facilities, in the command and monitoring facility, in the control point, or at the seismic stations, these facilities, control point, and stations shall be sealed by the seals of both Parties. Seals may be removed by Designated Personnel only in the presence of personnel of the Party carrying out the explosion;

(b) prior to the explosion, personnel of the Party carrying out the explosion may enter the recording facilities, the command and monitoring facility, or the control point of the Verifying Party for the purpose of conducting operations that require the participation of both Parties only with the agreement of the Designated Personnel Team Leader and when accompanied by Designated Personnel Team Leader or his designated representative;

(c) at all other times prior to the explosion, personnel of the Party carrying out the explosion may enter the recording facilities, the command and monitoring facility, or the control point of the Verifying Party only at the express invitation of the Designated Personnel Team Leader or his designated representative;

(d) following the explosion, Designated Personnel shall have the right to enter the recording facilities for data recovery only when accompanied by personnel of the Party carrying out the explosion. No later than the final dry run, Designated Personnel shall inform the Party carrying out the explosion of procedures for recovering such data shall advise the Party carrying out the explosion at the time of data recovery of any changes the Designated Personnel make in both those procedures and the reasons for such changes. Personnel of the Party carrying out the explosion shall observe the process of data recovery from instrumentation in the recording facilities and the command and monitoring facility, and shall leave the recording and the command and monitoring facility at the same time as Designated Personnel; and

(e) at any time following the explosion, personnel of the Party carrying out the explosion shall have the right to observe the activities of Designated Personnel in the control point. Personnel of the Party carrying out the explosion shall be present in the control point to observe recovery of the initial data, which shall take place within one hour following the explosion. At any time following the explosion that Designated Personnel are not present in the control point, the control point shall be sealed with the seals of both Parties. The seals may be removed by Designated Personnel only in the presence of personnel of the Party carrying out the explosion. Within five days following the explosion, Designated Personnel shall leave the control point at the same time as personnel of the Party carrying out the explosion.

11. Following data recovery, the equipment used for activities related to verification in accordance with this Protocol may be retained by the Party carrying out the explosion and be subject to its exclusive control for a period ending no more than 30 days following data recovery, at which time this equipment shall be returned, in the same condition as that in which it was received, to the Verifying Party at the point of entry. Elimination of information stored in memories shall not be deemed damage to the equipment.

SECTION IX. DESIGNATED PERSONNEL AND TRANSPORT PERSONNEL

1. No later than 10 days following entry into force of the Treaty, each Party shall provide the other Party with a list of its proposed Designated Personnel who will carry out the activities related to

verification in accordance with this Protocol and a list of its proposed Transport Personnel who will provide transportation for these Designated Personnel, their baggage, and equipment of the Verifying Party. These lists shall contain name, date of birth, and sex of each individual of its proposed Designated Personnel and Transport Personnel. The list of Designated Personnel shall at no time include more than 200 individuals, and the list of Transport Personnel shall at no time include more than 200 individuals.

2. Each Party shall review the list of Designated Personnel and the list of Transport Personnel proposed by the other Party. If the Party reviewing a list determines that an individual included thereon is acceptable to it, it shall so inform the Party providing the list within 20 days following receipt of the list, and such an individual shall be deemed accepted. If the Party reviewing a list determines that an individual included thereon is not acceptable to it, it shall so inform the Party providing the list of its objection within 20 days following receipt of the list, and such an individual shall be deemed not accepted and shall be deleted from the list.

3. Each Party may propose the addition or substitution of individuals on its list of Designated Personnel or its list of Transport Personnel at any time, who shall be designated in the same manner as is provided for in paragraph 2 of this Section with regard to the initial lists. Annually, no more than 40 individuals from the list of Designated Personnel shall be subject to substitution. This limitation shall not apply to the replacement of individuals due to permanent physical incapacity or death, or to deletion of an individual from the list of Designated Personnel in accordance with paragraph 5 of this Section. Replacement of an individual due to permanent physical incapacity, death or deletion from the list shall be accomplished in the same manner as is provided for in paragraph 2 of this Section.

4. Following receipt of the initial list of Designated Personnel or the initial list of Transport Personnel or of subsequent changes thereto, the Party receiving such information shall prepare for the issuance of such visas and other documents as may be required to ensure that each individual on the list of Designated Personnel or the list of Transport Personnel to whom it has agreed may enter and remain in its territory for the purpose of carrying out activities related to verification in accordance with this Protocol. Such visas and documents shall be provided by the Party carrying out the explosion only to the individuals whose names are included on the lists provided by the Verifying Party, in accordance with paragraph 3 of Section X of this Protocol, upon receipt of such lists. Such visas and documents shall be valid for multiple entry throughout the period of preparation and conduct of the particular explosion.

5. If a Party determines that an individual included on the list of Designated Personnel or the list of Transport Personnel of the other Party has violated the provisions of this Protocol or has ever committed a criminal offense in its territory, or has ever been sentenced for committing a criminal offense, or has ever been expelled from its territory, the Party making such a determination shall so notify the other Party of its objection to the continued inclusion of this individual on the list. If at that time this individual is present in the territory of the Party raising the objection, the other Party

shall immediately recall this individual from the territory of the Party raising this objection and immediately thereafter delete that individual from the list of Designated Personnel or from the list of Transport Personnel.

6. Designated Personnel with their personal baggage and equipment of the Verifying Party shall be permitted to enter the territory of the Party carrying out the explosion at the designated point of entry, to remain in that territory and to exit through the designated point of entry.

7. Designated Personnel and Transport Personnel shall be accorded the following privileges and immunities for the entire period they are in the territory of the Party carrying out the explosion and thereafter with respect to acts previously performed in the exercise of their official functions as Designated Personnel or Transport Personnel:

(a) Designated Personnel and Transport Personnel shall be accorded the inviolability enjoyed by diplomatic agents pursuant to Article 29 of the Vienna Convention on Diplomatic Relations of April 18, 1961;

(b) living and working quarters occupied by Designated Personnel and Transport Personnel carrying out activities in accordance with this Protocol shall be accorded the inviolability and protection accorded the quarters of missions and diplomatic agents pursuant to Articles 22 and 30 of the Vienna Convention on Diplomatic Relations;

(c) archives, documents, papers and correspondence of Designated Personnel and Transport Personnel shall enjoy the inviolability accorded the archives, documents, papers and correspondence of missions and diplomatic agents pursuant to Articles 24 and 30 of the Vienna Convention on Diplomatic Relations. In addition, the aircraft or other transport vehicles of the Verifying Party shall be inviolable;

(d) Designated Personnel and Transport Personnel shall be accorded the immunities accorded diplomatic agents pursuant to paragraphs 1, 2, and 3 of Article 31 of the Vienna Convention on Diplomatic Relations. Immunity from jurisdiction of Designated Personnel or Transport Personnel may be waived by the Verifying Party in those cases in which it is of the opinion that immunity would impede the course of justice and it can be waived without prejudice to the implementation of the provisions of this Protocol. Waiver must always be express;

(e) Designated Personnel and Transport Personnel carrying out their activities in accordance with this Protocol shall be accorded the exemption from dues and taxes accorded diplomatic agents pursuant to Article 34 of the Vienna Convention on Diplomatic Relations;

(f) living and working quarters occupied by Designated Personnel and Transport Personnel carrying out their activities in accordance with this Protocol shall be accorded the exemption from dues and taxes accorded mission premises pursuant to Article 23 of the Vienna Convention on Diplomatic Relations; and

(g) Designated Personnel and Transport Personnel shall be permitted to bring into the territory of the Party carrying out the explosion, without payment of any customs duties or related charges, articles for their personal use, with the exception of articles the import or export of which is prohibited by law or controlled by quarantine regulations.

8. Designated Personnel and Transport Personnel shall not engage in any professional or commercial activity for personal profit in the territory of the Party carrying out the explosion.

9. Without prejudice to their privileges and immunities, Designated Personnel and Transport Personnel shall be obliged to carry out the explosion and shall be obliged not to interfere in the internal affairs of that Party.

10. If the Party carrying out the explosion considers that there has been an abuse of privileges and immunities specified in paragraph 7 of this Section, consultations shall be held between the Parties to determine whether such an abuse has occurred and, if so determined, to prevent a repetition of such an abuse.

SECTION X. ENTRY, TRANSPORT, FOOD, LODGING AND PROVISION OF SERVICES FOR DESIGNATED PERSONNEL AND TRANSPORT PERSONNEL

1. The Party carrying out the explosion shall ensure Designated Personnel and Transport Personnel access to its territory for the purposes of carrying out activities related to verification, in accordance with this Protocol, and shall provide these personnel with such other assistance as may be necessary to enable them to carry out these activities. Following notification by the Verifying Party of its intention to conduct hydrodynamic yield measurement or to carry out on-site inspection, Designated Personnel shall have the right to be present at the site of the explosion to carry out activities in accordance with this Protocol at such times and for such periods as required to carry out these activities. The specific times and periods for carrying out such activities shall be specified in the coordinated schedule specified in paragraph 6 of Section XI of this Protocol.

2. The number of Designated Personnel shall not exceed:

(a) when exercising their rights and functions associated with drilling, logging, hole surveying, and coring, if this work is carried out by Designated Personnel operating their own equipment or equipment leased from the Party carrying out the explosion, 25;

(b) when exercising their rights and functions associated with observing drilling, logging, hole surveying, and coring performed by the Party carrying out the explosion, or when Designated Personnel perform logging, hole surveying, or sidewall rock sampling, 10;

(c) when exercising their rights and functions associated with the confirmation of the validity of geological and geophysical information, the number of emplacement holes plus three;

(d) when exercising their rights and functions associated with the use of hydrodynamic yield measurement equipment, the number of explosives plus three, plus the number of recording facilities specified in paragraph 5 of Section VIII of this

Protocol multiplied by seven; and, with respect to group explosions in which radio controlled recording facilities are employed, three per recording facility, plus seven for the command and monitoring facility;

(e) when exercising their rights and functions associated with the use of a local seismic network, 15;

(f) for administrative, coordination, clerical, and health and safety matters, when Designated Personnel described in subparagraphs (a), (b), (c), (d), and (e) of this paragraph are present, eight; and

(g) if the Verifying Party provides food and housing for Designated Personnel identified in subparagraphs (a), (b), (c), (d), (e), and (f) of this paragraph, six.

3. No less than 20 days prior to the planned arrival of its Designated Personnel or equipment at the point of entry to carry out activities related verification of a particular explosion, the Verifying Party shall provide the Party carrying out the explosion with:

(a) a list of the names of the Designated Personnel, their passports and documentation, and a list of the names of the Transport Personnel, their passports and documentation, who will carry out activities related to verification of a particular explosion;

(b) the names of the Designated Personnel Team Leader and deputy team leader, and the names of those individuals from the Designated Personnel who will escort equipment of the Verifying Party to the site of the explosion;

(c) confirmation of the point of entry to be used;

(d) the scheduled date and the estimated time of arrival of Designated Personnel at the point of entry; and

(e) designation of the mode of transport to be used.

No more than 15 days following receipt of the lists, passports, and documentation specified in subparagraph (a) of this paragraph, the Party carrying out the explosion shall return those passports to the Verifying Party with visas and documents specified in paragraph 4 of Section IX of this Protocol.

4. If a transport aircraft other than a regularly scheduled commercial aircraft is used for transportation, its flight path shall be along airways that are agreed upon by the Parties, and its flight plan shall be filed in accordance with the procedures of the International Civil Aviation Organization applicable to civil aircraft, including in the remarks section of the flight plan a confirmation that the appropriate clearance has been obtained. The Party carrying out the explosion shall provide parking, security protection, servicing, and fuel for the aircraft of the Verifying Party at the point of entry. The Verifying Party shall bear the cost of such fuel and servicing.

5. The Party carrying out the explosion shall ensure that any necessary clearances or approvals are granted so as to enable Designated Personnel, their baggage, and equipment of the Verifying Party to arrive at the point of entry by the estimated arrival date and time.

6. The Party carrying out the explosion shall assist Designated Personnel and Transport Personnel and their baggage in passage

through customs without undue delay. The Party carrying out the explosion shall provide transportation between the point of entry and the site of the explosion for Designated Personnel, for their baggage and equipment of the Verifying Party, so as to enable such personnel to exercise their rights and functions in the time periods provided for in this Protocol.

7. The Party carrying out the explosion shall have the right to assign its personnel to escort Designated Personnel and Transport Personnel while they are in the territory of the Party carrying out the explosion.

8. Except as otherwise provided for in this Protocol, movement and travel of Designated Personnel and Transport Personnel shall be subject to the authorization of the Party carrying out the explosion.

9. During the period Designated Personnel and Transport Personnel are in the territory of the Party carrying out the explosion, the Party carrying out the explosion shall provide food, living and working facilities, secure places for storing equipment, transportation, and medical services for such personnel. If the Verifying Party desires to provide its own food or housing units for its Designated Personnel, or food for its Transport Personnel during their stay in the territory of the Party carrying out the explosion, the Party carrying out the explosion shall provide such assistance as may be necessary for such food and housing units to arrive at the appropriate locations. If the Verifying Party provides its own housing units, they shall be delivered to the point of entry no less than 30 days prior to the arrival of Designated Personnel. The Party carrying out the explosion shall have the right to inspect these housing units upon their arrival at the point of entry for a 30–day period, without the presence of personnel of the Verifying Party.

10. The Party carrying out the explosion shall ensure the Designated Personnel Team Leader or his designated representative access at all times to means of direct communications between the site of the explosion and the embassy of the Verifying Party, and shall provide Designated Personnel with telephone communications between their working facilities and living accommodations at the site of the explosion. The Designated Personnel Team Leader or his designated representative shall also have the right to use at all times satellite communications to ensure communications via the International Maritime Satellite Organization (INMARSAT) commercial satellite system, or a system of equivalent performance, between the site of the explosion and the telephone communications system of the Verifying Party. If the Party carrying out the explosion does not provide such communications, Designated Personnel shall have the right to use their own equipment specified in paragraph 1(h) of Section VIII of this Protocol. In this case, installation and alignment of all such equipment shall be done jointly. All equipment of this system, except the remote control unit, shall be locked and placed under seals of both Parties, and neither Party shall have access to this equipment except under the observation of personnel of the other Party. Designated Personnel shall have exclusive use of the remote control unit. If the Verifying Party provides satellite communications equipment, personnel of the Party

carrying out the explosion shall have the right, under the observation of Designate Personnel, to make the following modifications provided they do not degrade the quality of communications:

(a) install bandpass filters, to limit the frequency range, in the antenna signal transmission and reception lines;

(b) modify the remote control unit to prevent manual tuning; and

(c) modify the satellite communications equipment to allow the Party carrying out the explosion to monitor all transmissions.

11. At the site of the explosion, Designated Personnel shall observe all safety rules and regulations applicable to the personnel of the Party carrying out the explosion, as well as those additional restrictions with regard to access and movement as may be established by the Party carrying out the explosion. Designated Personnel shall have access only to the areas where they will directly exercise their rights and functions in accordance with Sections V, VI, and VII of this Protocol.

12. Designated Personnel shall not be given or seek access by physical, visual or technical means to the interior of the explosive canister, to documentary or other information descriptive of the design of an explosive, or to equipment for control and firing of explosives. The Party carrying out the explosion shall not locate documentary or other information descriptive of the design of an explosive in such ways as to impede Designated Personnel in carrying out their activities in accordance with this Protocol.

13. With the exception of those cases in which the Parties otherwise agree, all costs related to the activities of Designated Personnel and Transport Personnel carried out in accordance with the Protocol shall be borne by the Verifying Party, including costs for materials, equipment, leased equipment, and services that have been requested by and provided to the Verifying Party, as well as costs for transportation, food, living and working facilities, provision of medical assistance, and communications. These costs shall be billed at the standard or official rate existing in the territory of the Party carrying out the explosion.

14. The Verifying Party shall have the right to include among its Designated Personnel a medical specialist, who shall be allowed to bring medications, medical instruments, and portable medical equipment agreed upon by the Parties. If Designated Personnel are treated in a medical facility of the Party carrying out the explosion the medical specialist shall have the right to consult on the recommended treatment and monitor the course of medical treatment at all times. The medical specialist of the Verifying Party shall have the right to require the Party carrying out the explosion to provide emergency evacuation of any individual of Designated Personnel who is ill or suffered and accident to a mutually agreed medical facility in the territory of the Party carrying out the explosion or to the point of entry for emergency medical evacuation by the Verifying Party. Designated Personnel shall have the right to refuse any treatment prescribed by medical personnel of the Party carrying out the explosion, and in this case the Party carrying out the explosion shall not be responsible for any consequences of such refusal. Such refusal must always be express.

SECTION XI. PROCEDURES FOR CONSULTATION AND COORDINATION

1. To facilitate the implementation of this Protocol, the Parties shall use the Joint Consultative Commission, as provided for in the Treaty, that shall meet at the request of either Party. For each explosion for which activities are carried out in accordance with this Protocol, the Parties shall establish a Coordinating Group of this Commission.

2. The Coordinating Group shall be responsible for coordinating the activities of the Verifying Party with the activities of the Party carrying out the explosion.

3. The Coordinating Group shall operate throughout the entire period of preparing and carrying out of the activities related to verification for a particular explosion, until the departure of Designated Personnel from the territory of the Party carrying out the explosion.

4. The Representative of the Verifying Party to the Coordinating Group shall be the Designated Personnel Team Leader whose name shall be provided simultaneously with the notification of intent to carry out activities related to verification for a particular explosion. All members of the Coordinating Group from the Verifying Party shall be drawn from the list of Designated Personnel. Within 15 days following receipt of this notification, the Party carrying out the explosion shall provide the Verifying Party with the name of its Representative to the Coordinating Group.

5. The first meeting of the Coordinating Group shall be convened in the capital of the Party carrying out the explosion within 25 days following notification by the Verifying Party of its intent to conduct activities related to verification for a particular explosion. Thereafter, the Coordinating Group shall meet at the request of either Party.

6. At the first meeting of the Coordinating Group, the Party carrying out the explosion shall present a list, including times and durations, of all its planned activities that are to be carried out as from the first day of this meeting and affect the rights of the Verifying Party provided in this Protocol. The Verifying Party shall provide a preliminary statement of its requirements for technical and logistical support for the activities related to verification that it intends to carry out. Within 10 days the Parties shall develop and agree upon coordinated schedule, including specific times and durations for carrying out activities related to verification, that shall ensure the rights of each Party provided in this Protocol.

7. Agreement of the Representative of each Party in the Coordinating Group shall constitute agreement of the Parties with respect to the following specific provisions of this Protocol:

(a) Section I: paragraph 5;

(b) Section IV: paragraphs 9, 10(b), and 11;

(c) Section V: paragraphs 2, 3, 4(b), 6(a), 7, 8(d), 9(f), 10 and 11;

(d) Section VI: paragraphs 2, 3, 4, 5, 6, and 9;

(e) Section VII: paragraphs 1(b) and 2(c);

(f) Section VIII: paragraphs 1(g), 4, 5(b), 5(g), and 8(f);

(g) Section X: paragraphs 4 and 13; and

(h) Section XI: paragraph 6.

8. Upon completion of activities related to verification at the site of an explosion, the Designated Personnel Team Leader shall prepare, at his option, either at the site of the explosion or in the capital of the Party carrying out the explosion, a report of the activities provided for in this Protocol that were carried out by Designated Personnel. The report shall be factual, and shall list the types of activities in chronological order. Lists of information, of photographs, and of data required in accordance with this Protocol and provided by Designated Personnel to the Party carrying out the explosion and received by Designated Personnel from the Party carrying out the explosion in the course of conducting activities related to verification on the territory of the Party carrying out the explosion shall be appended to the report. The report shall be provided to the Party carrying out the explosion in its capital by the Designated Personnel Team Leader within 15 days following completion of activities related to verification at the site of the explosion.

9. If, in the course of implementing activities related to verification in accordance with this Protocol, questions arise requiring prompt resolution, such questions shall be considered by the Coordinating Group. If the Coordinating Group is unable to resolve such questions, they shall immediately be referred to the Joint Consultative Commission for resolution.

10. Within 30 days after the Party carrying out the explosion provides notification of its intent to carry out a group explosion having a planned aggregate yield exceeding 150 kilotons, a meeting of the Joint Consultative Commission shall be convened at the request of either Party with the goal of reaching agreement on specific procedures as specified in paragraph 2 of Section II of this Protocol. The explosion shall be conducted no less than 150 days following agreement of the Parties upon such procedures.

11. The Joint Consultative Commission may, as necessary, establish and amend procedure governing the activities of the Coordinating Group.

SECTION XII. RELEASE OF INFORMATION

1. Nothing in the Treaty and this Protocol shall affect the proprietary rights of either Party in information provided by it in accordance with the Treaty and this Protocol, or in information that may be disclosed to the other Party or that may be disclosed to the other Party or that may become known to the other Party in preparing for, or carrying out, explosions. Claims to such proprietary rights, however, shall not impede implementation of the provisions of the Treaty and this Protocol.

2. Public release of the information provided in accordance with this Protocol or publication of material using such information may take place only with the agreement of the Party carrying out an explosion. Public release of the results of observation or measurements made by Designated Personnel may take place only with the agreement of both Parties.

SECTION XIII. ENTRY INTO FORCE

This Protocol is an integral part of the Treaty. It shall enter into force on the date of entry into force of the Treaty and shall remain in force as long as the Treaty remains in force.

DONE at Washington, in duplicate, this first day of June, 1990, in the English and Russian languages, both texts being equally authentic.

2. SALT and Related Materials

a. Interim Agreement Between the United States of America and the Union of Soviet Socialist Republics on Certain Measures With Respect to the Limitation of Strategic Offensive Arms, With Associated Protocol[1]

Signed at Moscow, May 26, 1972; Related joint resolution approved, September 30, 1972 [Public Law 92–448]; Approved by the President, October 3, 1972; Entered into force, October 3, 1972

The United States of America and the Union of Soviet Socialist Republics, hereinafter referred to as the Parties,

CONVINCED that the Treaty on the Limitation of Anti-Ballistic Missile Systems and this Interim Agreement on Certain Measures with Respect to the Limitation of Strategic Offensive Arms will contribute to the creation of more favorable conditions for active negotiations on limiting strategic arms as well as to the relaxation of international tension and the strengthening of trust between States,

TAKING into account the relationship between strategic offensive and defensive arms,

MINDFUL of their obligations under Article VI of the Treaty on the Non-Proliferation of Nuclear Weapons,

HAVE AGREED AS FOLLOWS:

ARTICLE I

The Parties undertake not to start construction of additional fixed land-based intercontinental ballistic missile (ICBM) launchers after July 1, 1972.

ARTICLE II

The Parties undertake not to convert land-based launchers for light ICBMs, or ICBMs of older types deployed prior to 1964, into land-based launchers for heavy ICBMs of types deployed after that time.

ARTICLE III

The Parties undertake to limit submarine-launched ballistic missile (SLBM) launchers and modern ballistic missile submarines to the numbers operational and under construction on the date of signature of this Interim Agreement, and in addition to launchers and

[1] 23 UST 3462; TIAS 7504. The Interim Agreement expired on October 3, 1977. Both the United States and the Soviet Union, however, issued parallel statements announcing that they would continue to observe the limitations on strategic buildups which were contained in the Agreement.

submarines constructed under procedures established by the Parties as replacements for an equal number of ICBM launchers of older types deployed prior to 1964 or for launchers on older submarines.

ARTICLE IV

Subject to the provisions of this Interim Agreement, modernization and replacement of strategic offensive ballistic missiles and launchers covered by this Interim Agreement may be undertaken.

ARTICLE V

1. For the purpose of providing assurance of compliance with the provisions of this Interim Agreement, each Party shall use national technical means of verification at its disposal in a manner consistent with generally recognized principles of international law.

2. Each Party undertakes not to interfere with the national technical means of verification of the other Party operating in accordance with paragraph 1 of this Article.

3. Each Party undertakes not to use deliberate concealment measures which impede verification by national technical means of compliance with the provisions of this Interim Agreement. This obligation shall not require changes in current construction, assembly, conversion, or overhaul practices.

ARTICLE VI

To promote the objectives and implementation of the provisions of this Interim Agreement, the Parties shall use the Standing Consultative Commission established under Article XIII of the Treaty on the Limitation of Anti-Ballistic Missile Systems in accordance with the provisions of that Article.

ARTICLE VII

The Parties undertake to continue active negotiations for limitations on strategic offensive arms. The obligations provided for in this Interim Agreement shall not prejudice the scope or terms of the limitations on strategic offensive arms which may be worked out in the course of further negotiations.

ARTICLE VIII

1. This Interim Agreement shall enter into force upon exchange of written notices of acceptance by each Party, which exchange shall take place simultaneously with the exchange of instruments of ratification of the Treaty on the Limitation of Anti-Ballistic Missile Systems.

2. This Interim Agreement shall remain in force for a period of five years unless replaced earlier by an agreement on more complete measures limiting strategic offensive arms. It is the objective of the Parties to conduct active follow-on negotiations with the aim of concluding such an agreement as soon as possible.

3. Each Party shall, in exercising its national sovereignty, have the right to withdraw from this Interim Agreement if it decides

that extraordinary events related to the subject matter of this Interim Agreement have jeopardized its supreme interests. It shall give notice of its decision to the other Party six months prior to withdrawal from this Interim Agreement. Such notice shall include a statement of the extraordinary events the notifying Party regards as having jeopardized its supreme interests.

DONE at Moscow on May 26, 1972, in two copies, each in the English and Russian languages, both texts being equally authentic.

For the United States of America:

RICHARD NIXON,
President of the United States of America.

For the Union of Soviet Socialist Republics:

L. I. BREZHNEV,
General Secretary of the Central Committee of the CPSU.

Protocol to the Interim Agreement Between the United States of America and the Union of Soviet Socialist Republics on Certain Measures With Respect to the Limitation of Strategic Offensive Arms [2]

Signed at Moscow, May 26, 1972

The United States of America and the Union of Soviet Socialist Republics, hereinafter referred to as the Parties.

Having agreed on certain limitations relating to submarine-launched ballistic missile launchers and modern ballistic missile submarines, and to replacement procedures, in the Interim Agreement,

Have agreed as follows:

The Parties understand that, under Article III of the Interim Agreement, for the period during which that Agreement remains in force:

The U.S. may have no more than 710 ballistic missile launchers on submarines (SLBMs) and no more than 44 modern ballistic missile submarines. The Soviet Union may have no more than 950 ballistic missile launchers on submarines and no more than 62 modern ballistic missile submarines.

Additional ballistic missile launchers on submarines up to the above-mentioned levels, in the U.S.—over 656 ballistic missile launchers on nuclear-powered submarines, and in the U.S.S.R.—over 740 ballistic missile launchers on nuclear-powered submarines, operational and under construction, may become operational as replacements for equal numbers of ballistic missile launchers of older types deployed prior to 1964 or of ballistic missile launchers on older submarines.

The deployment of modern SLBMs on any submarine, regardless of type, will be counted against the total level of SLBMs permitted for the U.S. and the U.S.S.R.

This protocol shall be considered an integral part of the Interim Agreement.

---

[2] 23 UST 3469.

DONE at Moscow this 26th day of May, 1972.

For the United States of America:

RICHARD NIXON,

President of the United States of America.

For the Union of Soviet Socialist Republics:

L. I. BREZHNEV,

General Secretary of the Central Committee of the CPSU.

b. Joint Resolution on Interim Agreement [1]

Public Law 92–448 [H.J. Res. 1227], 86 Stat. 746, approved September 30, 1972

Resolved by the Senate and House of Representatives of the United States of America in Congress assembled, That the Congress hereby endorses those portions of the Declaration of Basic Principles of Mutual Relations Between the United States of America and the Union of Soviet Socialist Republics signed by President Nixon and General Secretary Brezhnev at Moscow on May 29, 1972, which relate to the dangers of military confrontation and which read as follows:

"The United States of America and the Union of Soviet Socialist Republics attach major importance to preventing the development of situations capable of causing a dangerous exacerbation of their relations . . ." and "will do their utmost to avoid military confrontations and to prevent the outbreak of nuclear war" and "will always exercise restraint in their mutual relations," and "on outstanding issues will conduct" their discussions and negotiations "in a spirit of reciprocity, mutual accommodation and mutual benefit," and

"Both sides recognize that efforts to obtain unilateral advantage at the expense of the other, directly or indirectly, are inconsistent with these objectives," and

"The prerequisites for maintaining and strengthening peaceful relations between the United States of America and the Union of Soviet Socialist Republics are the recognition of the security interests of the parties based on the principle of equality and the renunciation of the use or threat of force."

SEC. 2. The President is hereby authorized to approve on behalf of the United States the interim agreement between the United States of America and the Union of Soviet Socialist Republics on certain measures with respect to the limitation of strategic offensive arms, and the protocol related thereto, signed at Moscow on May 26, 1972, by Richard Nixon, President of the United States of America and Leonid I. Brezhnev, General Secretary of the Central Committee of the Communist Party of the Soviet Union.

SEC. 3. The Government and the people of the United States ardently desire a stable international strategic balance that maintains peace and deters aggression. The Congress supports the stated policy of the United States that, were a more complete strategic offensive arms agreement not achieved within the five years of the interim agreement, and were the survivability of the strategic deterrent forces of the United States to be threatened as a result of

[1] The Interim Agreement expired on October 3, 1977. Both the United States and the Soviet Union, however, issued parallel statements announcing that they would continue to observe the limitations on strategic buildups which were contained in the Interim Agreement.

such failure, this could jeopardize the supreme national interests of the United States; the Congress recognizes the difficulty of maintaining a stable strategic balance in a period of rapidly developing technology; the Congress recognizes the principle of United States-Soviet Union equality reflected in the antiballistic missile treaty, and urges and requests the President to seek a future treaty that, inter alia, would not limit the United States to levels of intercontinental strategic forces inferior to the limits provided for the Soviet Union: and the Congress considers that the success of these agreements and the attainment of more permanent and comprehensive agreements are dependent upon the maintenance under present world conditions of a vigorous research and development and modernization program as required by a prudent strategic posture.

SEC. 4. The Congress hereby commends the President for having successfully concluded agreements with the Soviet Union limiting the production and deployment of antiballistic missiles and certain strategic offensive armaments, and it supports the announced intention of the President to seek further limits on the production and deployment of strategic armaments at future Strategic Arms Limitation Talks. At the same time, the Senate takes cognizance of the fact that agreements to limit the further escalation of the arms race are only preliminary steps, however important, toward the attainment of world stability and national security. The Congress therefore urges the President to seek at the earliest practicable moment Strategic Arms Reduction Talks (START) with the Soviet Union, the People's Republic of China, and other countries, and simultaneously to work toward reductions in conventional armaments, in order to bring about agreements for mutual decreases in the production and development of weapons of mass destruction so as to eliminate the threat of large-scale devastation and the ever-mounting costs of arms production and weapons modernization, thereby freeing world resources for constructive, peaceful use.

SEC. 5. Pursuant to paragraph six of the Declaration of Principles of Nixon and Brezhnev on May 29, 1972, which states that the United States and the Union of Soviet Socialist Republics: "will continue to make special efforts to limit strategic armaments. Whenever possible, they will conclude concrete agreements aimed at achieving these purposes"; Congress considers that the success of the interim agreement and the attainment of more permanent and comprehensive agreements are dependent upon the preservation of longstanding United States policy that neither the Soviet Union nor the United States should seek unilateral advantage by developing a first strike potential.

c. Agreed Interpretations, Common Understandings, and Unilateral Statements

1. Agreed Interpretations

(a) Initialed Statements.—The document set forth below was agreed upon and initialed by the Heads of the Delegations on May 26, 1972:

Agreed Statements Regarding the Treaty Between the United States of America and the Union of Soviet Socialist Republics on the Limitation of Anti-Ballistic Missile Systems[1]

[A]

The Parties understand that, in addition to the ABM radars which may be deployed in accordance with subparagraph (a) of Article III of the Treaty, those non-phased-array ABM radars operational on the date of signature of the Treaty within the ABM system deployment area for defense of the national capital may be retained.

[B]

The Parties understand that the potential (the product of mean emitted power in watts and antenna area in square meters) of the smaller of the two large phased-array ABM radars referred to in subparagraph (b) of Article III of the Treaty is considered for purposes of the Treaty to be three million.

[C]

The Parties understand that the center of the ABM system deployment area centered on the national capital and the center of the ABM system deployment area containing ICBM silo launchers for each Party shall be separated by no less than thirteen hundred kilometers.

[D]

In order to insure fulfillment of the obligation not to deploy ABM systems and their components except as provided in Article III of the Treaty, the Parties agree that in the event ABM systems based on other physical principles and including components capable of substituting for ABM interceptor missiles, ABM launchers, or ABM

[1] 23 UST 3456; TIAS 7503.

radars are created in the future, specific limitations on such systems and their components would be subject to discussion in accordance with Article XIII and agreement in accordance with Article XIV of the Treaty.

[E]

The Parties understand that Article V of the Treaty includes obligations not to develop, test or deploy ABM interceptor missiles for the delivery by each ABM interceptor missile of more than one independently guided warhead.

[F]

The Parties agree not to deploy phased-array radars having a potential (the product of mean emitted power in watts and antenna area in square meters) exceeding three million, except as provided for in Articles III, IV and VI of the Treaty, or except for the purposes of tracking objects in outer space or for use as national technical means of verification.

[G]

The Parties understand that Article IX of the Treaty includes the obligation of the U.S. and the U.S.S.R. not to provide to other States technical descriptions or blueprints specially worked out for the construction of ABM systems and their components limited by the Treaty.

(b) Common Understandings.—Common understanding of the Parties on the following matters was reached during the negotiations:

A. LOCATION OF ICBM DEFENSES

The U.S. Delegation made the following statement on May 26, 1972:

"Article III of the ABM Treaty provides for each side one ABM system deployment area centered on its national capital and one ABM system deployment area containing ICBM silo launchers. The two sides have registered agreement on the following statement: 'The Parties understand that the center of the ABM system deployment area centered on the national capital and the center of the ABM system deployment area contained ICBM silo launchers for each Party shall be separated by no less than thirteen hundred kilometers.' In this connection, the U.S. side notes that its ABM system deployment area for defense of ICBM silo launchers, located west of the Mississippi River, will be centered in the Grand Forks ICBM silo launcher deployment area." (See Initialed Statement [C].)

B. ABM TEST RANGES

The U.S. Delegation made the following statement on April 26, 1972:

"Article IV of the ABM Treaty provides that 'the limitations provided for in Article III shall not apply to ABM systems or their components used for development or testing, and located within current or additionally agreed test ranges.' We believe it would be useful to assure that there is no misunderstanding as to current ABM test ranges. It is our understanding that ABM test ranges encompass the area within which ABM components are located for test purposes. The current U.S. ABM test ranges are at White Sands, New Mexico, and at Kwajalein Atoll, and the current Soviet ABM test range is near Sary Shagan in Kazakhstan. We consider that non-phased array radars of types used for range safety or instrumentation purposes may be located outside of ABM test ranges. We interpret the reference in Article IV to 'additionally agreed test ranges' to mean that ABM components will not be located at any other test ranges without prior agreement between our Governments that there will be such additional ABM test ranges."

On May 5, 1972, the Soviet Delegation stated that there was a common understanding on what ABM test ranges were, that the use of the types of non-ABM radars for range safety or instrumentation was not limited under the Treaty, that the reference in Article IV to "additionally agreed" test ranges was sufficiently clear, and that national means permitted identifying current test ranges.

C. MOBILE ABM SYSTEMS

On January 28, 1972, the U.S. Delegation made the following statement:

"Article V(I) of the Joint Draft Text of the ABM Treaty includes an undertaking not to develop, test, or deploy mobile land-based ABM systems and their components. On May 5, 1972, the U.S. side indicated that, in its view, a prohibition on deployment of mobile ABM systems and components would rule out the deployment of ABM launchers and radars which were not permanent fixed types. At that time, we asked for the Soviet view of this interpretation. Does the Soviet side agree with the U.S. side's interpretation put forward on May 5, 1971?"

On April 13, 1972, the Soviet Delegation said there is a general common understanding on this matter.

D. STANDING CONSULTATIVE COMMISSION

Ambassador Smith made the following statement on May 22, 1972:

"The United States proposes that the sides agree that, with regard to initial implementation of the ABM Treaty's Article XIII on the Standing Consultative Commission (SCC) and of the consultation Articles to the Interim Agreement on offensive arms and the Accidents Agreement,[2] agreement establishing the SCC will be worked out early in the follow-on SALT negotiations; until that is completed, the following arrangements will prevail: when SALT is in session, any consultation desired by either side under these Articles can be carried out by the two SALT Delegations: when SALT

[2] See Article 7 of Agreement on Measures to Reduce the Risk of Outbreak of Nuclear War Between the United States of America and the Union of Soviet Socialist Republics, signed September 30, 1971.

is not in session, *ad hoc* arrangements for any desired consultations under these Articles may be made through diplomatic channels."

Minister Semenov replied that, on an *ad referendum basis,* he could agree that the U.S. statement corresponded to the Soviet understanding.

E. STANDSTILL

On May 6, 1972, Minister Semenov made the following statement:

"In an effort to accommodate the wishes of the U.S. side, the Soviet Delegation is prepared to proceed on the basis that the two sides will in fact observe the obligations of both the Interim Agreement and the ABM Treaty beginning from the date of signature of these two documents."

In reply, the U.S. Delegation made the following statement on May 20, 1972:

"The U.S. agrees in principle with the Soviet statement made on May 6 concerning observance of obligations beginning from date of signature but we would like to make clear our understanding that this means that, pending ratification and acceptance, neither side would take any action prohibited by the agreements after they had entered into force. This understanding would continue to apply in the absence of notification by either signatory of its intention not to proceed with ratification or approval."

The Soviet Delegation indicated agreement with the U.S. statement.

2. UNILATERAL STATEMENTS

(a) The following noteworthy unilateral statements were made during the negotiations by the United States Delegation:

A. WITHDRAWAL FROM THE ABM TREATY

On May 9, 1972, Ambassador Smith made the following statement:

"The U.S. Delegation has stressed the importance the U.S. Government attaches to achieving agreement on more complete limitations on strategic offensive arms, following agreement on an ABM Treaty and on an Interim Agreement on certain measures with respect to the limitation of strategic offensive arms. The U.S. Delegation believes that an objective of the follow-on negotiations should be to constrain and reduce on a long-term basis threats to the survivability of our respective strategic retaliatory forces. The U.S.S.R. Delegation has also indicated that the objectives of SALT would remain unfulfilled without the achievement of an agreement providing for more complete limitations on strategic offensive arms. Both sides recognize that the initial agreements would be steps toward the achievement of more complete limitations on strategic arms. If an agreement providing for more complete strategic offensive arms limitations were not achieved within five years, U.S. supreme interests could be jeopardized. Should that occur, it would constitute a basis for withdrawal from the ABM Treaty. The U.S. does not wish to see such a situation occur, nor do we believe that the U.S.S.R. does. It is because we wish to prevent such a situation that we emphasize the importance the U.S. Government attaches to achievement of more complete limitations on strategic offensive arms. The U.S. Executive will inform the Congress, in connection with Congressional consideration of the ABM Treaty and the Interim Agreement, of this statement of the U.S. position."

B. TESTED IN ABM MODE

On April 7, 1972, the U.S. Delegation made the following statement:

"Article II of the Joint Text Draft uses the term 'tested in an ABM mode,' in defining ABM components, and Article VI includes certain obligations concerning such testing. We believe that the sides should have a common understanding of this phrase. First, we would note that the testing provisions of the ABM Treaty are intended to apply to testing which occurs after the date of signature of the Treaty, and not to any testing which may have occurred in the past. Next, we would amplify the remarks we have made on this subject during the previous Helsinki phase by setting forth the objectives which govern the U.S. view on the subject, namely, while prohibiting testing of non-ABM components for ABM purposes: Not to present testing of ABM components, and not to prevent testing non-ABM components for non-ABM purposes. To clarify our interpretation of 'tested in an ABM mode,' we note that we would consider a launcher, missile or radar to be 'tested in an ABM model' if, for example, any of the following events occur: (1) a launcher is used to launch an ABM interceptor missile, (2) an interceptor missile is flight tested against a target vehicle which has a flight trajectory with characteristics of a strategic ballistic missile flight trajectory, or is flight tested in conjunction with the test of an ABM interceptor missile or an ABM radar at the same test range, or is flight tested to an altitude inconsistent with interception of targets against which air defenses are deployed, (3) a radar makes measurements on a cooperative target vehicle of the kind referred to in item (2) above during the reentry portion of its trajectory or makes measurements in conjunction with the test of an ABM interceptor missile or an ABM radar at the same test range. Radars used for purposes such as range safety or instrumentation would be exempt from application of these criteria."

C. NO-TRANSFER ARTICLE OF ABM TREATY

On April 18, 1972, the U.S. Delegation made the following statement:

"In regard to this Article [IX], I have a brief and I believe self-explanatory statement to make. The U.S. side wishes to make clear that the provisions of this Article do not set a precedent for whatever provision may be considered for a Treaty on Limiting Strategic Offensive Arms. The question of transfer of strategic offensive arms is a far more complex issue, which may require a different solution."

D. NO INCREASE IN DEFENSE OF EARLY WARNING RADARS

On July 28, 1970, the U.S. Delegation made the following statement:

"Since Hen House radars [Soviet ballistic missile early warning radars] can detect and track ballistic missile warheads at great distances, they have a significant ABM potential. Accordingly, the U.S. would regard any increase in the defenses of such radars by surface-to-air missiles as inconsistent with an agreement."

---

1. AGREED INTERPRETATIONS

(a) Initialed Statements.—The document set forth below was agreed upon and initialed by the Heads of the Delegations on May 26, 1972.

AGREED STATEMENTS REGARDING THE INTERIM AGREEMENT BETWEEN THE UNITED STATES OF AMERICA AND THE UNION OF SOVIET SOCIALIST REPUBLICS ON CERTAIN MEASURES WITH RESPECT TO THE LIMITATION OF STRATEGIC OFFENSIVE ARMS [3]

[A]

The Parties understand that land-based ICBM launchers referred to in the Interim Agreement are understood to be launchers for strategic ballistic missiles capable of ranges in excess of the shortest distance between the northeastern border of the continental U.S. and the northwestern border of the continental U.S.S.R.

[B]

The Parties understand that fixed land based ICBM launchers under active construction as of the date of signature of the Interim Agreement may be completed.

[C]

The Parties understand that in the process of modernization and replacement the dimensions of land-based ICBM silo launchers will not be significantly increased.

[D]

The Parties understand that during the period of the Interim Agreement there shall be no significant increase in the number of ICBM or SLBM test and training launchers, or in the number of such launchers for modern land-based heavy ICBMs. The Parties further understand that construction or conversion of ICBM launchers at test ranges shall be undertaken only for purposes of testing and training.

---

[3] 23 UST 3478; TIAS 7504.

[E]

The Parties understand that dismantling or destruction of ICBM launchers of older types deployed prior to 1964 and ballistic missile launchers on older submarines being replaced by new SLBM launchers on modern submarines will be initiated at the time of the beginning of sea trials of a replacement submarine, and will be completed in the shortest possible agreed period of time. Such dismantling or destruction, and timely notification thereof, will be accomplished under procedures to be agreed in the Standing Consultative Commission.

(b) Common Understandings.—Common understanding of the Parties on the following matters was reached during the negotiations:

A. INCREASE IN ICBM SILO DIMENSIONS

Ambassador Smith made the following statement on May 26, 1972:

"The Parties agree that the term 'significantly increased' means that an increase will not be greater than 1015 percent of the present dimensions of land-based ICBM silo launchers."

Minister Semenov replied that this statement corresponded to the Soviet understanding.

B. STANDING CONSULTATIVE COMMISSION

[Here follows text identical to d. in the preceding ABM Treaty understandings]

C. STANDSTILL

[Here follows text identical to e. in the preceding ABM Treaty understandings]

2. UNILATERAL STATEMENTS

(a) The following noteworthy unilateral statements were made during the negotiations by the United States Delegation:

A. WITHDRAWAL FROM THE ABM TREATY

[Here follows text identical to the Unilateral Statements contained in the preceding ABM Treaty understandings]

B. LAND-MOBILE ICBM LAUNCHERS

The U.S. Delegation made the following statement on May 20, 1972:

"In connection with the important subject of land-mobile ICBM launchers, in the interest of concluding the Interim Agreement the U.S. Delegation now withdraws its proposal that Article I or an agreed statement explicitly prohibits the deployment of mobile land-based ICBM launchers. I have been instructed to inform you that, while agreeing to defer the question of limitation of operational land-mobile ICBM launchers to the subsequent negotiations on more complete limitations on strategic offensive arms, the U.S.

would consider the deployment of operational land-mobile ICBM launchers during the period of the Interim Agreement as inconsistent with the objectives of that Agreement."

C. COVERED FACILITIES

The U.S. Delegation made the following statement on May 20, 1972:

"I wish to emphasize the importance that the United States attaches to the provisions of Article V, including in particular their application to fitting out or berthing submarines."

D. "HEAVY" ICBM'S

The U.S. Delegation made the following statement on May 26, 1972:

"The U.S. Delegation regrets that the Soviet Delegation has not been willing to agree on a common definition of a heavy missile. Under these circumstances, the U.S. Delegation believes it necessary to state the following: The United States would consider any ICBM having a volume significantly greater than that of the largest light ICBM now operational on either side to be a heavy ICBM. The U.S. proceeds on the premise that the Soviet side will give due account to this consideration."

(b) The following noteworthy unilateral statement was made by the Delegation of the U.S.S.R. and is shown here with the U.S. reply:

On May 17, 1972, Minister Semenov made the following unilateral "Statement of the Soviet Side":

"Taking into account that modern ballistic missile submarines are presently in the possession of not only the U.S., but also of its NATO allies, the Soviet Union agrees that for the period of effectiveness of the Interim 'Freeze' Agreement the U.S. and its NATO allies have up to 50 such submarines with a total of up to 800 ballistic missile launchers thereon (including 41 U.S. submarines with 656 ballistic missile launchers). However, if during the period of effectiveness of the Agreement U.S. allies in NATO should increase the number of their modern submarines to exceed the numbers of submarines they would have operational or under construction on the date of signature of the Agreement, the Soviet Union will have the right to a corresponding increase in the number of its submarines. In the opinion of the Soviet side, the solution of the question of modern ballistic missile submarines provided for in the Interim Agreement only partially compensates for the strategic imbalance in the deployment of the nuclear-powered missile submarines of the U.S.S.R. and the U.S. Therefore, the Soviet side believes that this whole question, and above all the question of liquidating the American missile submarine bases outside the U.S., will be appropriately resolved in the course of follow-on negotiations."

On May 24, Ambassador Smith made the following reply to Minister Semenov:

"The United States side has studied the 'statement made by the Soviet side' of May 17 concerning compensation for submarine basing and SLBM submarines belonging to third countries. The United

States does not accept the validity of the considerations in that statement."

On May 26 Minister Semenov repeated the unilateral statement made on May 24. Ambassador Smith also repeated the U.S. rejection on May 26.

d. Standing Consultative Commission on Arms Limitation [1]

Memorandum of Understanding signed at Geneva December 21, 1972; Entered into force December 21, 1972

MEMORANDUM OF UNDERSTANDING BETWEEN THE GOVERNMENT OF THE UNITED STATES OF AMERICA AND THE GOVERNMENT OF THE UNION OF SOVIET SOCIALIST REPUBLICS REGARDING THE ESTABLISHMENT OF A STANDING CONSULTATIVE COMMISSION

I

The Government of the United States of America and the Government of the Union of Soviet Socialist Republics hereby establish a Standing Consultative Commission.

II

The Standing Consultative Commission shall promote the objectives and implementation of the provisions of the Treaty between the USA and the USSR on the Limitation of Anti-Ballistic Missile Systems of May 26, 1972, the Interim Agreement between the USA and the USSR on Certain Measures with Respect to the Limitation of Strategic Offensive Arms of May 26, 1972, and the Agreement on Measures to Reduce the Risk of Outbreak of Nuclear War between the USA and the USSR of September 30, 1971, and shall exercise its competence in accordance with the provisions of Article XIII of said Treaty, Article VI of said Interim Agreement, and Article 7 of said Agreement on Measures.

III

Each Government shall be represented on the Standing Consultative Commission by a Commissioner and a Deputy Commissioner, assisted by such staff as it deems necessary.

IV

The Standing Consultative Commission shall hold periodic sessions on dates mutually agreed by the Commissioners but no less than two times per year. Sessions shall also be convened as soon as possible, following reasonable notice, at the request of either Commissioner.

V

The Standing Consultative Commission shall establish and approve Regulations governing procedures and other relevant matters and may amend them as it deems appropriate.

[1] 24 UST 238; TIAS 7545.

VI

The Standing Consultative Commission will meet in Geneva. It may also meet at such other places as may be agreed.

DONE in Geneva, on December 21, 1972, in two copies, each in the English and Russian language, both texts being equally authentic.

e. Standing Consultative Commission on Arms Limitation: Regulations [1]

Protocol, with regulations, signed at Geneva May 30, 1973; Entered into force May 30, 1973

STANDING CONSULTATIVE COMMISSION

PROTOCOL

Pursuant to the provisions of the Memorandum of Understanding between the Government of the United States of America and the Government of the Union of Soviet Socialist Republics Regarding the Establishment of a Standing Consultative Commission, dated December 21, 1972, the undersigned, having been duly appointed by their respective Governments as Commissioners of said Standing Consultative Commission, hereby establish and approve, in the form attached, Regulations governing procedures and other relevant matters of the Commission, which Regulations shall enter into force upon signature of this Protocol and remain in force until and unless amended by the undersigned or their successors.

DONE in Geneva, on May 30, 1973, in two copies each in the English and Russian language, both texts being equally authentic.

[ATTACHMENT]

STANDING CONSULTATIVE COMMISSION

REGULATIONS

1. The Standing Consultative Commission, established by the Memorandum of Understanding between the Government of the United States of America and the Government of the Union of Soviet Socialist Republics Regarding the Establishment of a Standing Consultative Commission of December 21, 1972, shall consist of a U.S. component and Soviet component, each of which shall be headed by a Commissioner.

2. The Commissioners shall alternately preside over the meetings.

3. The Commissioners shall, when possible, inform each other in advance of the matters to be submitted for discussion, but may at a meeting submit for discussion any matter within the competence of the Commission.

4. During intervals between sessions of the Commission, each Commissioner may transmit written or oral communications to the other Commissioner concerning matters within the competence of the Commission.

---

[1] 24 UST 1124; TIAS 7637.

5. Each component of the Commission may invite such advisers and experts as it deems necessary to participate in a meeting.

6. The Commission may establish working groups to consider and prepare specific matters.

7. The results on the discussion of questions at the meetings of the Commission may, if necessary, be entered into records which shall be in two copies, each in the English and the Russian languages, both texts being equally authentic.

8. The proceedings of the Standing Consultative Commission shall be conducted in private. The Standing Consultative Commission may not make its proceedings public except with the express consent of both Commissioners.

9. Each component of the Commission shall bear the expenses connected with its participation in the Commission.

3. Treaty Between the United States of America and the Union of Soviet Socialist Republics on the Limitation of Anti-Ballistic Missile Systems,[1] With Associated Protocol

Signed at Moscow, May 26, 1972; Ratification advised by the Senate, August 3, 1972; Ratified by the President, September 30, 1972; Entered into force, October 3, 1972

The United States of America and the Union of Soviet Socialist Republics, hereinafter referred to as the Parties,

PROCEEDING from the premise that nuclear war would have devastating consequences for all mankind,

CONSIDERING that effective measures to limit anti-ballistic missile systems would be a substantial factor in curbing the race in strategic offensive arms and would lead to a decrease in the risk of outbreak of war involving nuclear weapons,

PROCEEDING from the premise that the limitation of anti-ballistic missile systems, as well as certain agreed measures with respect to the limitation of strategic offensive arms, would contribute to the creation of more favorable conditions for further negotiations on limiting strategic arms,

MINDFUL of their obligations under Article VI of the Treaty on the Non-Proliferation of Nuclear Weapons,

DECLARING their intention to achieve at the earliest possible date the cessation of the nuclear arms race and to take effective measures toward reductions in strategic arms, nuclear disarmament, and general and complete disarmament,

DESIRING to contribute to the relaxation of international tension and the strengthening of trust between States,

HAVE AGREED AS FOLLOWS:

ARTICLE I

1. Each Party undertakes to limit anti-ballistic missile (ABM) systems and to adopt other measures in accordance with the provisions of this Treaty.

2. Each Party undertakes not to deploy ABM systems for a defense of the territory of its country and not to provide a base for such a defense, and not to deploy ABM systems for defense of an individual region except as provided for in Article III of this Treaty.

ARTICLE II

1. For the purposes of this Treaty an ABM system is a system to counter strategic ballistic missiles or their elements in flight trajectory, currently consisting of:

[1] 23 UST 3435; TIAS 7503.

(a) ABM interceptor missiles, which are interceptor missiles constructed and deployed for an ABM role, or of a type tested in an ABM mode;

(b) ABM launchers, which are launchers constructed and deployed for launching ABM interceptor missiles; and

(c) ABM radars, which are radars constructed and deployed for an ABM role, or of a type tested in an ABM mode.

2. The ABM system components listed in paragraph 1 of this Article include those which are:

(a) operational;

(b) under construction;

(c) undergoing testing;

(d) undergoing overhaul, repair or conversion; or

(e) mothballed.

ARTICLE III

Each party undertakes not to deploy ABM systems or their components except that:

(a) within one ABM system deployment area having a radius of one hundred and fifty kilometers and centered on the Party's national capital, a Party may deploy; (1) no more than one hundred ABM launchers and no more than one hundred ABM interceptor missiles at launch sites, and (2) ABM radars within no more than six ABM radar complexes, the area of each complex being circular and have a diameter of no more than three kilometers; and

(b) within one ABM system deployment area having a radius of one hundred and fifty kilometers and containing ICBM silo launchers, a Party may deploy: (1) no more than one hundred ABM launchers and no more than one hundred ABM interceptor missiles at launch sites, (2) two large phased-array ABM radars comparable in potential to corresponding ABM radars operational or under construction on the date of signature of the Treaty in an ABM system deployment area containing ICBM silo launchers, and (3) no more than eighteen ABM radars each having a potential less than the potential of the smaller of the above-mentioned two large phased-array ABM radars.

ARTICLE IV

The limitations provided for in Article III shall not apply to ABM systems or their components used for development or testing, and located within current or additionally agreed test ranges. Each Party may have no more than a total of fifteen ABM launchers at test ranges.

ARTICLE V

1. Each Party undertakes not to develop, test, or deploy ABM systems or components which are sea-based, air-based, space-based, or mobile land-based.

2. Each Party undertakes not to develop, test, or deploy ABM launchers for launching more than one ABM interceptor missile at a time from each launcher, nor to modify deployed launchers to provide them with such a capability, nor to develop, test, or deploy

automatic or semi-automatic or other similar systems for rapid reload or ABM launchers.

Article VI

To enhance assurance of the effectiveness of the limitations on ABM systems and their components provided by this Treaty, each Party undertakes:

(a) not to give missiles, launchers, or radars, other than ABM interceptor missiles, ABM launchers, or ABM radars, capabilities to counter strategic ballistic missiles or their elements in flight trajectory, and not to test them in an ABM mode; and

(b) not to deploy in the future radars for early warning of strategic ballistic missile attack except at locations along the periphery of its national territory and oriented outward.

Article VII

Subject to the provisions of this Treaty, modernization and replacement of ABM systems or their components may be carried out.

Article VIII

ABM systems or their components in excess of the numbers or outside the areas specified in this Treaty, as well as ABM systems or their components prohibited by this Treaty, shall be destroyed or dismantled under agreed procedures within the shortest possible agreed period of time.

Article IX

To assure the viability and effectiveness of this Treaty, each Party undertakes not to transfer to other States, and not to deploy outside its national territory, ABM systems or their components limited by this Treaty.

Article X

Each Party undertakes not to assume any international obligations which would conflict with this Treaty.

Article XI

The Parties undertake to continue active negotiations for limitations on strategic offensive arms.

Article XII

1. For the purpose of providing assurance of compliance with the provisions of this Treaty, each Party shall use national technical means of verification at its disposal in a manner consistent with generally recognized principles of international law.

2. Each Party undertakes not to interfere with the national technical means of verification of the other Party operating in accordance with paragraph 1 of this Article.

3. Each Party undertakes not to use deliberate concealment measures which impede verification by national technical means of compliance with the provisions of this Treaty. This obligation shall

not require changes in current construction, assembly, conversion, or overhaul practices.

Article XIII

1. To promote the objectives and implementation of the provisions of this Treaty, the Parties shall establish promptly a Standing Consultative Commission, within the framework of which they will:

(a) consider questions concerning compliance with the obligations assumed and related situations which may be considered ambiguous;

(b) provide on a voluntary basis such information as either Party considers necessary to assure confidence in compliance with the obligations assumed;

(c) consider questions involving unintended interference with national technical means of verification;

(d) consider possible changes in the strategic situation which have a bearing on the provisions of this Treaty;

(e) agree upon procedures and dates for destruction or dismantling of ABM systems or their components in cases provided for by the provisions of this Treaty;

(f) consider, as appropriate, possible proposals for further increasing the viability of this Treaty, including proposals for amendments in accordance with the provisions of this Treaty;

(g) consider, as appropriate, proposals for further measures aimed at limiting strategic arms.

2. The Parties through consultation shall establish, and may amend as appropriate, Regulations for the Standing Consultative Commission governing procedures, composition and other relevant matters.

Article XIV

1. Each Party may propose amendments to this Treaty. Agreed amendments shall enter into force in accordance with the procedures governing the entry into force to this Treaty.

2. Five years after entry into force of this Treaty, and at five year intervals thereafter, the Parties shall together conduct a review of this Treaty.

Article XV

1. This Treaty shall be of unlimited duration.

2. Each Party shall, in exercising its national sovereignty, have the right to withdraw from this Treaty if it decides that extraordinary events related to the subject matter of this Treaty have jeopardized its supreme interests. It shall give notice of its decision to the other Party six months prior to withdrawal from the Treaty. Such notice shall include a statement of the extraordinary events the notifying Party regards as having jeopardized its supreme interests.

ARTICLE XVI

1. This Treaty shall be subject to ratification in accordance with the constitutional procedures of each Party. The Treaty shall enter into force on the day of the exchange of instruments of ratification.

2. This Treaty shall be registered pursuant to Article 102 of the Charter of the United Nations.

DONE at Moscow on May 26, 1972, in two copies, each in the English and Russian languages, both texts being equally authentic.

For the United States of America:

RICHARD NIXON,
President of the United States of America.

For the Union of Soviet Socialist Republics:

L. I. BREZHNEV,
General Secretary of the Central Committee of the CPSU.

Protocol to the Treaty Between the United States of America and the Union of Soviet Socialist Republics on the Limitation of Anti-Ballistic Missile Systems [2]

Signed at Moscow, July 3, 1974; Ratification advised by the Senate, November 10, 1975; Ratified by the President, March 19, 1976; Ratified by the Union of Soviet Socialist Republics, March 30, 1976; Ratifications exchanged at Washington, May 24, 1976; Proclaimed by the President, July 6, 1976; Entered into force, May 24, 1976

The United States of America and the Union of Soviet Socialist Republics, hereinafter referred to as the Parties,

PROCEEDING from the Basic Principles of Relations between the United States of America and the Union of Soviet Socialist Republics signed on May 29, 1972,

DESIRING to further the objectives of the Treaty between the United States of America and the Union of Soviet Socialist Republics on the Limitation of Anti-Ballistic Missile Systems signed on May 26, 1972, hereinafter referred to as the Treaty.

REAFFIRMING their conviction that the adoption of further measures for the limitation of strategic arms would contribute to strengthening international peace and security,

PROCEEDING from the premise that further limitation of anti-ballistic missile systems will create more favorable conditions for the completion of work on a permanent agreement on more complete measures for the limitation of strategic offensive arms,

HAVE AGREED AS FOLLOWS:

ARTICLE I

1. Each Party shall be limited at any one time to a single area out of the two provided in Article III of the Treaty for deployment of anti-ballistic missile (ABM) systems or their components and accordingly shall not exercise its rights to deploy an ABM system or its components in the second of the two ABM system deployment areas permitted by Article III of the Treaty, except as an exchange

---

[2] 27 UST 1645; TIAS 8276.

of one permitted area for the other in accordance with Article II of this Protocol.

2. Accordingly, except as permitted by Article II of this Protocol: the United States of America shall not deploy an ABM system or its components in the area centered on its capital, as permitted by Article III(a) of the Treaty, and the Soviet Union shall not deploy an ABM system or its components in the deployment area of intercontinental ballistic missile (ICBM) silo launchers permitted by Article III(b) of the Treaty.

Article II

1. Each Party shall have the right to dismantle or destroy its ABM system and the components thereof in the area where they are presently deployed and to deploy an ABM system or its components in the alternative area permitted by Article III of the Treaty, provided that prior to initiation of construction, notification is given in accord with the procedure agreed to by the Standing Consultative Commission, during the year beginning October 3, 1977, and ending October 2, 1978, or during any year which commences at five year intervals thereafter, those being the years for periodic review of the Treaty, as provided in Article XIV of the Treaty. This right may be exercised only once.

2. Accordingly, in the event of such notice, the United States would have the right to dismantle or destroy the ABM system and its components in the deployment area of ICBM silo launchers and to deploy an ABM system or its components in an area centered on its capital, as permitted by Article III(a) of the Treaty, and the Soviet Union would have the right to dismantle or destroy the ABM system and its components in the area centered on its capital and to deploy an ABM system or its components in an area containing ICBM silo launchers, as permitted by Article III(b) of the Treaty.

3. Dismantling or destruction and deployment of ABM systems or their components and the notification thereof shall be carried out in accordance with Article VIII of the ABM Treaty and procedures agreed to in the Standing Consultative Commission.

Article III

The rights and obligations established by the Treaty remain in force and shall be complied with by the Parties except to the extent modified by this Protocol. In particular, the deployment of an ABM system or its components within the area selected shall remain limited by the levels and other requirements established by the Treaty.

Article IV

This Protocol shall be subject to ratification in accordance with the constitutional procedures of each Party. It shall enter into force on the day of the exchange of instruments of ratification and shall thereafter be considered an integral part of the Treaty.

Done at Moscow on July 3, 1974, in duplicate, in the English and Russian languages, both texts being equally authentic.

For the United States of America:

RICHARD NIXON,
President of the United States of America.

For the Union of Soviet Socialist Republics:

L. I. BREZHNEV,
General Secretary of the Central Committee of the CPSU.

4. INF

a. Treaty Between the United States of America and the Union of Soviet Socialist Republics on the Elimination of Their Intermediate-Range and Shorter-Range Missiles[1]

Signed at Washington, December 8, 1987; Ratification advised by the Senate, May 27, 1988; Entered into force, June 1, 1988

The United States of America and the Union of Soviet Socialist Republics, hereinafter referred to as the Parties,

CONSCIOUS that nuclear war would have devastating consequences for all mankind,

GUIDED by the objective of strengthening strategic stability,

CONVINCED that the measures set forth in this Treaty will help to reduce the risk of outbreak of war and strengthen international peace and security, and

MINDFUL of their obligations under Article VI of the Treaty on the Non-Proliferation of Nuclear Weapons,

HAVE AGREED AS FOLLOWS:

ARTICLE I

In accordance with the provisions of this Treaty which includes the Memorandum of Understanding and Protocols which form an integral part thereof, each Party shall eliminate its intermediate-range and shorter-range missiles, not have such systems thereafter, and carry out the other obligations set forth in this Treaty.

ARTICLE II

For the purposes of this Treaty:

1. The term "ballistic missile" means a missile that has a ballistic trajectory over most of its flight path. The term "ground-launched ballistic missile (GLBM)" means a ground-launched ballistic missile that is a weapon-delivery vehicle.

2. The term "cruise missile" means an unmanned, self-propelled vehicle that sustains flight through the use of aerodynamic lift over most of its flight path. The term "ground-launched cruise missile (GLCM)" means a ground-launched cruise missile that is a weapon-delivery vehicle.

3. The term "GLBM launcher" means a fixed launcher or a mobile land-based transporter-erector-launcher mechanism for launching a GLBM.

4. The term "GLCM launcher" means a fixed launcher or a mobile land-based transporter-erector-launcher mechanism for launching a GLCM.

[1] Treaty Doc. 100–11; 1657 UNTS 2.

5. The term "intermediate-range missile" means a GLBM or a GLCM having a range capability in excess of 1000 kilometers but not in excess of 5500 kilometers.

6. The term "shorter-range missile" means a GLBM or a GLCM having a range capability equal to or in excess of 500 kilometers but not in excess of 1000 kilometers.

7. The term "deployment area" means a designated area within which intermediate-range missiles and launchers of such missiles may operate and within which one or more missile operating bases are located.

8. The term "missile operating base" means:

(a) in the case of intermediate-range missiles, a complex of facilities, located within a deployment area, at which intermediate-range missiles and launchers of such missiles normally operate, in which support structures associates with such missiles and launchers are also located and in which support equipment associated with such missiles and launchers is normally located; and

(b) in the case of shorter-range missiles, a complex of facilities, located any place, at which shorter-range missiles and launchers of such missiles normally operate and in which support equipment associated with such missiles and launchers is normally located.

9. The term "missile support facility," as regards intermediate-range or shorter-range missiles and launchers of such missiles, means a missile production facility or a launcher production facility, a missile repair facility or a launcher repair facility, a training facility, a missile storage facility or a launcher storage facility, a test range, or an elimination facility as those terms are defined in the Memorandum of Understanding.

10. The term "transit" means movement, notified in accordance with paragraph 5(f) of Article IX of this Treaty, of an intermediate-range missile or a launcher of such a missile between missile support facilities, between such a facility and a deployment area or between deployment areas, or of a shorter-range missile or a launcher of such a missile from a missile support facility or a missile operating base to an elimination facility.

11. The term "deployed missile" means an intermediate-range missile located within a deployment area or a shorter-range missile located at a missile operating base.

12. The term "non-deployed missile" means an intermediate-range missile located outside a deployment area or a shorter-range missile located outside a missile operating base.

13. The term "deployed launcher" means a launcher of an intermediate-range missile located within a deployment area or a launcher of a shorter-range missile located at a missile operating base.

14. The term "non-deployed launcher" means a launcher of an intermediate-range missile located outside a deployment area or a launcher of a shorter-range missile located outside a missile operating base.

15. The term "basing country" means a country other than the United States of America or the Union of Soviet Socialist Republics on whose territory intermediate-range or shorter-range missiles of

the Parties, launchers of such missiles or support structures associated with such missiles and launchers were located at any time after November 1, 1987. Missiles or launchers in transit are not considered to be "located."

ARTICLE III

1. For the purposes of this Treaty, existing types of intermediate-range missiles are:

(a) for the United States of America, missiles of the types designated by the United States of America as the Pershing II and the BGM–109G, which are known to the Union of Soviet Socialist Republics by the same designations; and

(b) for the Union of Soviet Socialist Republics, missiles of the types designated by the Union of Soviet Socialist Republics as the RSD–10, the R–12 and the R–14, which are known to the United States of America as the SS–20, the SS–4 and the SS–5, respectively.

2. For the purposes of this Treaty, existing types of shorter-range missiles are:

(a) for the United States of America, missiles of the type designated by the United States of America as the Pershing IA, which is known to the Union of Soviet Socialist Republics by the same designation; and

(b) for the Union of Soviet Socialist Republics, missiles of the types designated by the Union of Soviet Socialist Republics as the OTR–22 and the OTR–23, which are known to the United States of America as the SS–12 and the SS–23, respectively.

ARTICLE IV

1. Each Party shall eliminate all its intermediate-range missiles and launchers of such missiles, and all support structures and support equipment of the categories listed in the Memorandum of Understanding associated with such missiles and launchers, so that no later than three years after entry into force of this Treaty and thereafter no such missiles, launchers, support structures or support equipment shall be possessed by either Party.

2. To implement paragraph 1 of this Article, upon entry into force of this Treaty, both Parties shall begin and continue throughout the duration of each phase, the reduction of all types of their deployed and non-deployed intermediate-range missiles and deployed and non-deployed launchers of such missiles and support structures and support equipment associated with such missiles and launchers in accordance with the provisions of this Treaty. These reductions shall be implemented into two phases so that:

(a) by the end of the first phase, that is, no later than 29 months after entry into force of this Treaty:

(i) the number of deployed launchers of intermediate-range missiles for each Party shall not exceed the number of launchers that are capable of carrying or containing at one time missiles considered by the Parties to carry 171 warheads;

(ii) the number of deployed intermediate-range missiles for each Party shall not exceed the number of such missiles considered by the Parties to carry 180 warheads;

(iii) the aggregate number of deployed and non-deployed launchers of intermediate-range missiles for each Party shall not exceed the number of launchers that are capable of carrying or containing at one time missiles considered by the Parties to carry 200 warheads;

(iv) the aggregate number of deployed and non-deployed intermediate-range missiles for each Party shall not exceed the number of such missiles considered by the Parties to carry 200 warheads; and

(v) the ratio of the aggregate number of deployed and non-deployed intermediate-range GLBMs of existing types for each Party to the aggregate number of deployed and non-deployed intermediate-range missiles of existing types possessed by that Party shall not exceed the ratio of such intermediate-range GLBMs to such intermediate-range missiles for that Party as of November 1, 1987, as set forth in the Memorandum of Understanding; and

(b) by the end of the second phase, that is, no later than three years after entry into force of this Treaty, all intermediate-range missiles of each Party, launchers of such missiles and all support structures and support equipment of the categories listed in the Memorandum of Understanding associated with such missiles and launchers, shall be eliminated.

ARTICLE V

1. Each Party shall eliminate all its shorter-range missiles and launchers of such missiles, and all support equipment of the categories listed in the Memorandum of Understanding associated with such missiles and launchers, so that no later than 18 months after entry into force of this Treaty and thereafter no such missiles, launchers or support equipment shall be possessed by either Party.

2. No later than 90 days after entry into force of this Treaty, each Party shall complete the removal of all its deployed shorter-range missiles and deployed and non-deployed launchers of such missiles to elimination facilities and shall retain them at those locations until they are eliminated in accordance with the procedures set forth in the Protocol on Elimination. No later than 12 months after entry into force of this Treaty, each Party shall complete the removal of all its non-deployed shorter-range missiles to elimination facilities and shall retain them at those locations until they are eliminated in accordance with the procedures set forth in the Protocol on Elimination.

3. Shorter-range missiles and launchers of such missiles shall not be located at the same elimination facility. Such facilities shall be separated by no less than 1000 kilometers.

ARTICLE VI

1. Upon entry into force of this Treaty and thereafter, neither Party shall:

(a) produce or flight-test any intermediate-range missiles or produce any stages of such missiles or any launchers of such missiles; or

(b) produce, flight-test or launch any shorter-range missiles or produce any stages of such missiles or any launchers of such missiles.

2. Notwithstanding paragraph 1 of this Article, each Party shall have the right to produce a type of GLBM not limited by this Treaty which uses a stage which is outwardly similar to, but not interchangeable with, a stage of an existing type of intermediate-range GLBM having more than one stage, providing that that Party does not produce any other stage which is outwardly similar to, but not interchangeable with, any other stage of an existing type of intermediate-range GLBM.

ARTICLE VII

For the purposes of this Treaty:

1. If a ballistic missile or a cruise missile has been flight-tested or deployed for weapon delivery, all missiles of that type shall be considered to be weapon-delivery vehicles.

2. If a GLBM or GLCM is an intermediate-range missile, all GLBMs or GLCMs of that type shall be considered to be intermediate-range missiles. If a GLBM or GLCM is a shorter-range missile, all GLBMs or GLCMs of that type shall be considered to be shorter-range missiles.

3. If a GLBM is of a type developed and tested solely to intercept and counter objects not located on the surface of the earth, it shall not be considered to be a missile to which the limitations of this Treaty apply.

4. The range capability of a GLBM not listed in Article III of this Treaty shall be considered to be the maximum range to which it has been tested. The range capability of a GLCM not listed in Article III of this Treaty shall be considered to be the maximum distance which can be covered by the missile in its standard design mode flying until fuel exhaustion, determined by projecting its flight path onto the earth's sphere from the point of launch to the point of impact. GLBMs or GLCMs that have a range capability equal to or in excess of 500 kilometers but not in excess of 1000 kilometers shall be considered to be shorter-range missiles. GLBMs or GLCMs that have a range capability in excess of 1000 kilometers but not in excess of 5500 kilometers shall be considered to be intermediate-range missiles.

5. The maximum number of warheads an existing type of intermediate-range missile or shorter-range missile carries shall be considered to be the number listed for missiles of that type in the Memorandum of Understanding.

6. Each GLBM or GLCM shall be considered to carry the maximum number of warheads listed for a GLBM or GLCM of that type in the Memorandum of Understanding.

7. If a launcher has been tested for launching a GLBM or a GLCM, all launchers of that type shall be considered to have been tested for launching GLBMs or GLCMs.

8. If a launcher has contained or launched a particular type of GLBM or GLCM, all launchers of that type shall be considered to be launchers of that type of GLBM or GLCM.

9. The number of missiles each launcher of an existing type of intermediate-range missile or shorter-range missile shall be considered to be capable of carrying or containing at one time is the number listed for launchers of missiles of that type in the Memorandum of Understanding.

10. Except in the case of elimination in accordance with the procedures set forth in the Protocol on Elimination, the following shall apply:

(a) for GLBMs which are stored or moved in separate stages, the longest stage of an intermediate-range or shorter-range GLBM shall be counted as a complete missile;

(b) for GLBMs which are not stored or moved in separate stages, a canister of the type used in the launch of an intermediate-range GLBM, unless a Party proves to the satisfaction of the other Party that it does not contain such a missile, or an assembled intermediate-range or shorter-range GLBM, shall be counted as a complete missile; and

(c) for GLCMs, the airframe of an intermediate-range or shorter-range GLCM shall be counted as a complete missile.

11. A ballistic missile which is not a missile to be used in a ground-based mode shall not be considered to be a GLBM if it is test-launched at a test site from a fixed land-based launcher which is used solely for test purposes and which is distinguished from GLBM launchers. A cruise missile which is not a missile to be used in a ground-based mode shall not be considered to be a GLCM if it is test-launched at a test site from a fixed land-based launcher which is used solely for test purposes and which is distinguishable from GLCM launchers.

12. Each Party shall have the right to produce and use for booster systems, which might otherwise be considered to be intermediate-range or shorter-range missiles, only existing types of booster stages for such booster systems. Launchers of such booster systems shall not be considered to be flight-testing of intermediate-range or shorter-range missiles provided that:

(a) stages used in such booster systems are different from stages used in those missiles listed as existing types of intermediate-range or shorter-range missiles in Article III of this Treaty;

(b) such booster systems are used only for research and development purposes to test objects other than the booster systems themselves;

(c) the aggregate number of launchers for such booster systems shall not exceed 35 for each Party at any one time; and

(d) the launchers for such booster systems are fixed, emplaced above ground and located only at research and development launch sites which are specified in the Memorandum of Understanding.

Research and development launch sites shall not be subject to inspection pursuant to Article XI of this Treaty.

ARTICLE VIII

1. All intermediate-range missiles and launchers of such missiles shall be located in deployment areas, at missile support facilities or shall be in transit. Intermediate-range missiles or launchers of such missiles shall not be located elsewhere.

2. Stages of intermediate-range missiles shall be located in deployment areas, at missile support facilities or moving between deployment areas, between missile support facilities or between missile support facilities and deployment areas.

3. Until their removal to elimination facilities as required by paragraph 2 of Article V of this Treaty, all shorter-range missiles and launchers of such missiles shall be located at missile operating bases, at missile support facilities or shall be in transit. Shorter-range missiles or launchers of such missiles shall not be located elsewhere.

4. Transit of a missile or launcher subject to the provisions of this Treaty shall be completed within 25 days.

5. All deployment areas, missile operating bases and missile support facilities are specified in the Memorandum of Understanding or in subsequent updates of data pursuant to paragraphs 3, 5(a) or 5(b) of Article IX of this Treaty. Neither Party shall increase the number of, or change the location or boundaries of, deployment areas, missile operating bases or missile support facilities, except for elimination facilities, from those set forth in the Memorandum of Understanding. A missile support facility shall not be considered to be part of a deployment area even though it may be located within the geographic boundaries of a deployment area.

6. Beginning 30 days after entry into force of this Treaty, neither Party shall locate intermediate-range or shorter-range missiles, including stages of such missiles, or launchers of such missiles at missile production facilities, launcher production facilities or test ranges listed in the Memorandum of Understanding.

7. Neither Party shall locate any intermediate-range or shorter-range missiles at training facilities.

8. A non-deployed intermediate-range or shorter-range missile shall not be carried on or contained within a launcher of such a type of missile, except as required for maintenance conducted at repair facilities or for elimination by means of launching conducted at elimination facilities.

9. Training missiles and training launchers for intermediate-range or shorter-range missiles shall be subject to the same locational restrictions as are set forth for intermediate-range and shorter-range missiles and launchers of such missiles in paragraphs 1 and 3 of this Article.

ARTICLE IX

1. The Memorandum of Understanding contains categories of data relevant to obligations undertaken with regard to this Treaty and lists all intermediate-range and shorter-range missiles, launchers of such missiles, and support structures and support equipment associated with such missiles and launchers, possessed by the Parties as of November 1, 1987. Updates of that data and notification

required by this Article shall be provided according to the categories of data contained in the Memorandum of Understanding.

2. The Parties shall update that data and provide the notifications required by this Treaty through the Nuclear Risk Reduction Centers, established pursuant to the Agreement Between the United States of America and the Union of Soviet Socialist Republics on the Establishment of Nuclear Risk Reduction Centers of September 15, 1987.

3. No later than 30 days after entry into force of this Treaty, each Party shall provide the other Party with updated data, as of the date of entry into force of this Treaty, for all categories of data contained in the Memorandum of Understanding.

4. No later than 30 days after the end of each six-month interval following the entry into force of this Treaty, each Party shall provide updated data for all categories of data contained in the Memorandum of Understanding by informing the other Party of all changes, completed and in process, in that data, which have occurred during the six-month interval since the preceding data exchange, and the net effect of those changes.

5. Upon entry into force of this Treaty and thereafter, each Party shall provide the following notifications to the other Party:

(a) notification, no less than 30 days in advance, of the scheduled date of the elimination of a specific deployment area, missile operating base or missile support facility;

(b) notification, no less than 30 days in advance, of changes in the number or location of elimination facilities, including the location and scheduled date of each change;

(c) notification, except with respect to launchers of intermediate-range missiles for the purpose of their elimination, no less than 30 days in advance, of the scheduled date of the initiation of the elimination of intermediate-range and shorter-range missiles, and stages of such missiles, and launchers of such missiles and support structures and support equipment associated with such missiles and launchers, including:

(i) the number and type of items of missile systems to be eliminated;

(ii) the elimination site;

(iii) for intermediate-range missiles, the location from which such missiles, launchers of such missiles and support equipment associated with such missiles and launchers are moved to the elimination facility; and

(iv) except in the case of support structures, the point of entry to be used by an inspection team conducting an inspection pursuant to paragraph 7 of Article XI of this Treaty and the estimated time of departure of an inspection team from the point of entry to the elimination facility;

(d) notification, no less than ten days in advance, of the scheduled date of the launch, or the scheduled date of the initiation of a series of launches, of intermediate-range missiles for the purpose of their elimination, including:

(i) the type of missiles to be eliminated;

(ii) the location of the launch, or, if elimination is by a series of launches, the location of such launches and the number of launches in the series;

(iii) the point of entry to be used by an inspection team conducting an inspection pursuant to paragraph 7 of Article XI of this Treaty; and

(iv) the estimated time of departure of an inspection team from the point of entry to the elimination facility;

(e) notification, no later than 48 hours after they occur, of changes in the number of intermediate-range and shorter-range missiles, launchers of such missiles and support structures and support equipment associated with such missiles and launchers resulting from elimination as described in the Protocol on Elimination, including:

(i) the number and type of items of a missile system which were eliminated; and

(ii) the date and location of such elimination; and

(f) notification of transit of intermediate-range or shorter-range missiles or launchers of such missiles, or the movement of training missiles or training launchers for such intermediate-range and shorter-range missiles, no later than 48 hours after it has been completed, including:

(i) the number of missiles or launchers;

(ii) the points, dates and times of departure and arrival;

(iii) the mode of transport; and

(iv) the location and time at that location at least once every four days during the period of transit.

6. Upon entry into force of this Treaty and thereafter, each Party shall notify the other Party, no less than ten days in advance, of the scheduled date and location of the launch of a research and development booster system as described in paragraph 12 of Article VII of this Treaty.

ARTICLE X

1. Each Party shall eliminate its intermediate-range and shorter-range missiles and launchers of such missiles and support structures and support equipment associated with such missiles and launches in accordance with the procedures set forth in the Protocol on Elimination.

2. Verification by on-site inspection of the elimination of items of missiles systems specified in the Protocol on Elimination shall be carried out in accordance with Article XI of this Treaty, the Protocol on Elimination and the Protocol on Inspection.

3. When a Party removes its intermediate-range missiles, launchers of such missiles and support equipment associated with such missiles and launchers from deployment areas to elimination facilities for the purpose of their elimination, it shall do so in complete deployed organizational units. For the United States of America, these units shall be Pershing II batteries and BGM–109G flights. For the Union of Soviet Socialist Republics, these units shall be SS–20 regiments composed of two or three battalions.

4. Elimination of intermediate-range and shorter-range missiles and launchers of such missiles and support equipment associated

with such missiles and launchers shall be carried out at the facilities that are specified in the Memorandum of Understanding or notified in accordance with paragraph 5(b) of Article IX of this Treaty, unless eliminated in accordance with Section IV or V of the Protocol on Elimination. Support structures, associated with the missiles and launchers subject to this Treaty, that are subject to elimination shall be eliminated *in situ*.

5. Each Party shall have the right, during the first six months after entry into force of this Treaty, to eliminate by means of launching no more than 100 of its intermediate-range missiles.

6. Intermediate-range and shorter-range missiles which have been tested prior to entry into force of this Treaty, but never deployed, and which are not existing types of intermediate-range or shorter-range missiles listed in Article III of this Treaty, and launchers of such missiles, shall be eliminated within six months after entry into force of this Treaty in accordance with the procedures set forth in the Protocol on Elimination. Such missiles are:

(a) for the United States of America, missiles of the type designated by the United States of America as the Pershing IB, which is known to the Union of Soviet Socialist Republics by the same designation; and

(b) for the Union of Soviet Socialist Republics, missiles of the type designated by the Union of Soviet Socialist Republics as the RK–55, which is known to the United States of America as the SSC–X–4.

7. Intermediate-range and shorter-range missiles and launchers of such missiles and support structures and support equipment associated with such missiles and launchers shall be considered to be eliminated after completion of the procedures set forth in the Protocol on Elimination and upon the notification provided for in paragraph 5(e) of Article IX of this Treaty.

8. Each Party shall eliminate its deployment areas, missile operating bases and missile support facilities. A Party shall notify the other Party pursuant to paragraph 5(a) of Article IX of this Treaty once the conditions set forth below are fulfilled:

(a) all intermediate-range and shorter-range missiles, launchers of such missiles and support equipment associated with such missiles and launchers located there have been removed;

(b) all support structures associated with such missiles and launchers located there have been eliminated; and

(c) all activity related to production, flight-testing, training, repair, storage or deployment of such missiles and launchers has ceased there.

Such deployment areas, missile operating bases and missile support facilities shall be considered to be eliminated either when they have been inspected pursuant to paragraph 4 of Article XI of this Treaty or when 60 days have elapsed since the date of the scheduled elimination which was notified pursuant to paragraph 5(a) of Article IX of this Treaty. A deployment area, missile operating base or missile support facility listed in the Memorandum of Understanding that met the above conditions prior to entry into force of this Treaty, and is not included in the initial data exchange pursuant to paragraph 3 of Article IX of this Treaty, shall be considered to be eliminated.

9. If a Party intends to convert a missile operating base listed in the Memorandum of Understanding for use as a base associated with GLBM or GLCM systems not subject to this Treaty, then that Party shall notify the other Party, no less than 30 days in advance of the scheduled date of the initiation of conversion, of the scheduled date and the purpose for which the base will be converted.

ARTICLE XI

1. For the purpose of ensuring verification of compliance with the provisions of this Treaty, each Party shall have the right to conduct on-site inspections. The Parties shall implement on-site inspections in accordance with this Article, the Protocol on Inspection and the Protocol on Elimination.

2. Each Party shall have the right to conduct inspections provided for by this Article both within the territory of the other Party and within the territories of basing countries.

3. Beginning 30 days after entry into force of this Treaty, each Party shall have the right to conduct inspections at all missile operating bases and missile support facilities specified in the Memorandum of Understanding other than missile production facilities, and at all elimination facilities included in the initial data update required by paragraph 3 of Article IX of this Treaty. These inspections shall be completed no later than 90 days after entry into force of this Treaty. The purpose of these inspections shall be to verify the number of missiles, launchers, support structures and support equipment and other data, as of the date of entry into force of this Treaty, provided pursuant to paragraph 3 of Article IX of this Treaty.

4. Each Party shall have the right to conduct inspections to verify the elimination, notified pursuant to paragraph 5(a) of Article IX of this Treaty, of missile operating bases and missile support facilities other than missile production facilities, which are thus no longer subject to inspections pursuant to paragraph 5(a) of this Article. Such an inspection shall be carried out within 60 days after the scheduled date of the elimination of that facility. If a Party conducts an inspection at a particular facility pursuant to paragraph 3 of this Article after the scheduled date of the elimination of that facility, then no additional inspection of that facility pursuant to this paragraph shall be permitted.

5. Each Party shall have the right to conduct inspections pursuant to this paragraph for 13 years after entry into force of this Treaty. Each Party shall have the right to conduct 20 such inspections per calendar year during the first three years after entry into force of this Treaty, 15 such inspections per calendar year during the subsequent five years, and ten such inspections per calendar year during the last five years. Neither Party shall use more than half of its total number of these inspections per calendar year within the territory of any one basing country. Each Party shall have the right to conduct:

(a) inspections, beginning 90 days after entry into force of this Treaty, of missile operating bases and missile support facilities other than elimination facilities and missile production facilities, to ascertain, according to the categories of data specified in the Memorandum of Understanding, the numbers of missiles, launchers, support structures and support equipment located at each missile operating base or missile support facility at the time of the inspection; and

(b) inspections of former missile operating bases and former missile support facilities eliminated pursuant to paragraph 8 of Article X of this Treaty other than former missile production facilities.

6. Beginning 30 days after entry into force of this Treaty, each Party shall have the right, for 13 years after entry into force of this Treaty, to inspect by means of continuous monitoring:

(a) the portals of any facility of the other Party at which the final assembly of a GLBM using stages, any of which is outwardly similar to a stage of a solid-propellant GLBM listed in Article III of this Treaty, is accomplished; or

(b) if a Party has no such facility, the portals of an agreed former missile production facility at which existing types of intermediate-range or shorter-range GLBMs were produced.

The Party whose facility is to be inspected pursuant to this paragraph shall ensure that the other Party is able to establish a permanent continuous monitoring system at that facility within six months after entry into force of this Treaty or within six months of initiation of the process of final assembly described in subparagraph (a). If, after the end of the second year after entry into force of this Treaty, neither Party conducts the process of final assembly described in subparagraph (a) for a period of 12 consecutive months, then neither Party shall have the right to inspect by means of continuous monitoring any missile production facility for the other Party unless the process of final assembly as described in subparagraph (a) is initiated again. Upon entry into force of this Treaty, the facilities to be inspected by continuous monitoring shall be: in accordance with subparagraph (b), for the United States of America, Hercules Plant Number 1, at Magna, Utah; in accordance with subparagraph (a), for the Union of Soviet Socialist Republics, the Votkinsk Machine Building Plant, Udmurt Autonomous Soviet Socialist Republic, Russian Soviet Federative Socialist Republic.

7. Each Party shall conduct inspections of the process of elimination, including elimination of intermediate-range missiles by means of launching, of intermediate-range and shorter-range missiles and launchers of such missiles and support equipment associated with such missiles and launchers carried out at elimination facilities in accordance with Article X of this Treaty and the Protocol on Elimination. Inspectors conducting inspections provided for the elimination of the missiles, launchers and support equipment have been completed.

8. Each Party shall have the right to conduct inspections to confirm the completion of the process of elimination of intermediate-range and shorter-range missiles and launchers of such missiles

and support equipment associated with such missiles and launchers eliminated pursuant to Section V of the Protocol on Elimination, and of training missiles, training missile stages, training launch canisters and training launchers eliminated pursuant to Sections II, IV and V of the Protocol on Elimination.

ARTICLE XII

1. For the purpose of ensuring verification compliance with the provisions of this Treaty, each Party shall use national technical means of verification at its disposal in a manner consistent with generally recognized principles of international law.

2. Neither Party shall:

(a) interfere with national technical means of verification of the other Party operating in accordance with paragraph 1 of this Article; or

(b) use concealment measures which impede verification of compliance with the provisions of this Treaty by national technical means of verification carried out in accordance with paragraph 1 of this Article. This obligation does not apply to cover or concealment practices, within a deployment area, associated with normal training, maintenance and operations, including the use of environmental shelters to protect missiles and launchers.

3. To enhance observation by national technical means of verification, each Party shall have the right until a treaty between the Parties reducing and limiting strategic offensive arms enters into force, but in any event for no more than three years after entry into force of this Treaty, to request the implementation of cooperative measures at deployment bases for road-mobile GLBMs with a range capability in excess of 5500 kilometers, which are not former missile operating bases eliminated pursuant to paragraph 8 of Article X of this Treaty. The Party making such a request shall inform the other Party of the deployment base at which cooperative measures shall be implemented. The Party whose base is to be observed shall carry out the following cooperative measures:

(a) no later than six hours after such a request, the Party shall have opened the roofs of all fixed structures for launchers located at the base, removed completely all missiles on launchers from such fixed structures for launchers and displayed such missiles on launchers in the open without using concealment measures; and

(b) the Party shall leave the roofs open and the missiles on launchers in place until twelve hours have elapsed from the time of the receipt of a request for such an observation.

Each Party shall have the right to make six such requests per calendar year. Only one deployment base shall be subject to these cooperative measures at any one time.

ARTICLE XIII

1. To promote the objectives and implementation of the provisions of this Treaty, the Parties hereby establish the Special Verification Commission. The Parties agree that, if either Party so

requests, they shall meet within the framework of the Special Verification Commission to:

(a) resolve questions relating to compliance with the obligations assumed; and

(b) agree upon such measures as may be necessary to improve the viability and effectiveness of this Treaty.

2. The Parties shall use the Nuclear Risk Reduction Centers, which provide for continuous communication between the Parties, to:

(a) exchange data and provide notifications as required by paragraphs 3, 4, 5 and 6 of Article IX of this Treaty and the Protocol on Elimination;

(b) provide and receive the information required by paragraph 9 of Article X of this Treaty;

(c) provide and receive notifications of inspections as required by Article XI of this Treaty and the Protocol on Inspection; and

(d) provide and receive requests for cooperative measures as provided for in paragraph 3 of Article XII of this Treaty.

ARTICLE XIV

The Parties shall comply with the Treaty and shall not assume any international obligations or undertakings which would conflict with its provisions.

ARTICLE XV

1. This Treaty shall be of unlimited duration.

2. Each Party shall, in exercising its national sovereignty, have the right to withdraw from the Treaty if it decides that extraordinary events related to the subject matter of this Treaty have jeopardized its supreme interests. It shall give notice of its decision to withdraw to the other Party six months prior to withdrawal from this Treaty. Such notice shall include a statement of the extraordinary events the notifying Party regards as having jeopardizing its supreme interests.

ARTICLE XVI

Each Party may propose amendments to this Treaty. Agreed amendments shall enter into force in accordance with the procedures set forth in Article XVII governing the entry into force of this Treaty.

ARTICLE XVII

1. This Treaty, including the Memorandum of Understanding and Protocols, which form an integral part thereof, shall be subject to ratification in accordance with the constitutional procedures of each Party. This Treaty shall enter into force on the date of the exchange of instruments of ratification.

2. This Treaty shall be registered pursuant to Article 102 of the Charter of the United Nations.

DONE at Washington on December 8, 1987, in two copies, each in the English and Russian languages, both texts being equally authentic.

For the United States of America:

RONALD REAGAN,
President of the United States of America.

For the Union of Soviet Socialist Republics:

M GORBACHEV,
General Secretary of the Central Committee of the CPSU.

MEMORANDUM OF UNDERSTANDING REGARDING THE ESTABLISHMENT OF THE DATA BASE FOR THE TREATY BETWEEN THE UNION OF SOVIET SOCIALIST REPUBLICS AND THE UNITED STATES OF AMERICA ON THE ELIMINATION OF THEIR INTERMEDIATE-RANGE AND SHORTER-RANGE MISSILES

Pursuant to and in implementation of the Treaty Between the Union of Soviet Socialist Republics and the United States of America on the Elimination of their Intermediate-Range and Shorter-Range Missiles of December 8, 1987, hereinafter referred to as the Treaty, the Parties have exchanged data current as of November 1, 1987, on intermediate-range and shorter-range missiles and launchers of such missiles and support structures and support equipment associated with such missiles and launchers.

I. DEFINITIONS

For the purposes of this Memorandum of Understanding, the Treaty, the Protocol on Elimination and the Protocol on Inspection:

1. The term "missile production facility" means a facility for the assembly or production of solid-propellant intermediate-range or shorter-range GLBMs, or existing types of GLCMs.

2. The term "missile repair facility" means a facility at which repair or maintenance of intermediate-range or shorter-range missiles takes place other than inspection and maintenance conducted at a missile operating base.

3. The term "launcher production facility" means a facility for final assembly of launchers of intermediate-range or shorter-range missiles.

4. The term "launcher repair facility" means a facility at which repair or maintenance of launchers of intermediate-range or shorter-range missiles takes place other than inspection and maintenance conducted at a missile operating base.

5. The term "test range" means an area at which flight-testing of intermediate-range or shorter-range missiles takes place.

6. The term "training facility" means a facility, not at a missile operating base, at which personnel are trained in the use of intermediate-range or shorter-range missiles or launchers of such missiles and at which launchers of such missiles are located.

7. The term "missile storage facility" means a facility, not at a missile operating base, at which intermediate-range or shorter-range missiles or stages of such missiles are stored.

8. The term "launcher storage facility" means a facility, not at a missile operating base, at which launchers of intermediate-range or shorter-range missiles are stored.

9. The term "elimination facility" means a facility at which intermediate-range or shorter-range missiles, missile stages and launchers of such missiles or support equipment associated with such missiles or launchers are eliminated.

10. The term "support equipment" means unique vehicles and mobile or transportable equipment that support a deployed intermediate-range or shorter-range missile or a launcher of such a missile. Support equipment shall include full-scale inert training missiles, full-scale inert training missile stages, full-scale inert training launch canisters, and training launchers not capable of launching a missile. A listing of such support equipment associated with each existing type of missile, and launchers of such missiles, except for training equipment, is contained in Section VI of this Memorandum of Understanding.

11. The term "support structure" means a unique fixed structure used to support deployed intermediate-range missiles or launchers of such missiles. A listing of such support structures associated with each existing type of missile, and launchers of such missiles, except for training equipment, is contained in Section VI of this Memorandum of Understanding.

12. The term "research and development launch site" means a facility at which research and development booster systems are launched.

[DETAILED DATA * * *][2]

Each Party, in signing this Memorandum of Understanding, acknowledges it is responsible for the accuracy of only its own data. Signature of this Memorandum of Understanding constitutes acceptance of the categories of data and inclusion of the data contained herein.

This Memorandum of Understanding is an integral part of the Treaty. It shall enter into force on the date of entry into force of the Treaty and shall remain in force so long as the Treaty remains in force.

DONE at Washington on December 8, 1987, in two copies, each in the English and Russian languages, both texts being equally authentic.

For the United States of America:

RONALD REAGAN,
President of the United States of America.

For the Union of Soviet Socialist Republics:

M GORBACHEV,
General Secretary of the Central Committee of the CPSU.

---

[2] This section of the Memorandum of Understanding contains the detailed data that were required to be exchanged between the Parties pursuant to Article IX of the Treaty. See Treaty Doc. 100–11.

Protocol on Procedures Governing the Elimination of the Missile Systems Subject to the Treaty Between the United States of America and the Union of Soviet Socialist Republics on the Elimination of Their Intermediate-Range and Shorter-Range Missiles

Pursuant to and in implementation of the Treaty Between the United States of America and the Union of Soviet Socialist Republics on the Elimination of Their Intermediate-Range and Shorter-Range Missiles of December 8, 1987, hereinafter referred to as the Treaty, the Parties hereby agree upon procedures governing the elimination of the missile systems subject to the Treaty.

I. ITEMS OF MISSILE SYSTEMS SUBJECT TO ELIMINATION

The specific items for each type of missile system to be eliminated are:

1. For the United States of America:
   Pershing–II: Missile, launcher and launch pad shelter;
   BGM–109G: Missile, launch canister and launcher;
   Pershing IA: Missile and launcher; and
   Pershing IB: Missile.
2. For the Union of Soviet Socialist Republics:
   SS–20: Missile, launch canister, launcher, missile transporter vehicle and fixed structure for a launcher;
   SS–4: Missile, missile transporter vehicle, missile erector, launch stand and propellant tanks;
   SS–5: Missile;
   SSC–X–4: Missile, launch canister and launcher;
   SS–12: Missile, launcher and missile transporter vehicle; and
   SS–23: Missile, launcher and missile transporter vehicle.
3. For both Parties, all training missiles, training missile stages, training launch canisters and training launchers shall be subject to elimination.
4. For both Parties, all stages of intermediate-range and shorter-range GLBMs shall be subject to elimination.
5. For both Parties, all front sections of deployed intermediate-range and shorter-range missiles shall be subject to elimination.

II. PROCEDURES FOR ELIMINATION AT ELIMINATION FACILITIES

1. In order to ensure the reliable determination of the type and number of missiles, missile stages, front sections, launch canisters, launchers, missile transporter vehicles, missile erectors and launch stands, as well as training missiles, training missile stages, training launch canisters and training launchers, indicated in Section I of this protocol, being eliminated at elimination facilities, and to preclude the possibility of restoration of such items for purposes inconsistent with the provisions of the Treaty, the Parties shall fulfill the requirements below.

2. The conduct of the elimination procedures for the items of missile systems listed in paragraph 1 of this Section, except for training missiles, training missile stages, training launch canisters and training launchers, shall be subject to on-site inspection in accordance with Article XI of the Treaty and the Protocol on Inspection. The Parties shall have the right to conduct on-site inspections to

confirm the completion of the elimination procedures set forth in paragraph 11 of this Section for training missiles, training missile stages, training launch canisters and training launchers. The Party possessing such a training missile, training missile stage, training launch canister or training launcher shall inform the other Party of the name and coordinates of the elimination facility at which the on-site inspection may be conducted as well as the date on which it may be conducted. Such information shall be provided no less than 30 days in advance of that date.

3. Prior to a missile's arrival at the elimination facility, its nuclear warhead device and guidance elements may be removed.

4. Each Party shall select the particular technological means necessary to implement the procedures required in paragraphs 10 and 11 of this Section and to allow for on-site inspection of the conduct of the elimination procedures required in paragraph 10 of this Section in accordance with Article XI of the Treaty, this Protocol and the Protocol on Inspection.

5. The initiation of the elimination of the items of missile systems subject to this Section shall be considered to be the commencement of the procedures set forth in paragraph 10 or 11 of this Section.

6. Immediately prior to the initiation of the elimination procedures set forth in paragraph 10 of this Section, an inspector from the Party receiving the pertinent notification required by paragraph 5(c) of Article IX of the Treaty shall confirm and record the type and number of items of missile systems, listed in paragraph 1 of this Section, which are to be eliminated. If the inspecting Party deems it necessary, this shall include a visual inspection of the contents of launch canisters.

7. A missile stage being eliminated by burning in accordance with the procedures set forth in paragraph 10 of this Section shall not be instrumented for data collection. Prior to the initiation of the elimination procedures set forth in paragraph 10 of this Section, an inspector from the inspecting Party shall confirm that such missile stages are not instrumented for data collection. Those missile stages shall be subject to continuous observation by such an inspector from the time of that inspection until the burning is completed.

8. The completion of the elimination procedures set forth in this Section, except those for training missiles, training missile stages, training launch canisters and training launchers, along with the type and number of items of missile systems for which those procedures have been completed, shall be confirmed in writing by the representative of the Party carrying out the elimination and by the inspection team leader of the other Party. The elimination of a training missile, training missile stage, training launch canister or training launcher shall be considered to have been completed upon completion of the procedures set forth in paragraph 11 of this Section and notification as required by paragraph 5(e) of Article IX of the Treaty following the date specified pursuant to paragraph 2 of this Section.

9. The Parties agree that all United States and Soviet intermediate-range and shorter-range missiles and their associated reentry vehicles shall be eliminated within an agreed overall period

of elimination. It is further agreed that all such missiles shall, in fact, be eliminated fifteen days prior to the end of the overall period of elimination. During the last fifteen days, a Party shall withdraw to its national territory reentry vehicles which, by unilateral decision, have been released from existing programs of cooperation and eliminate them during the same timeframe in accordance with the procedures set forth in this Section.

10. The specific procedures for the elimination of the items of missile systems listed in paragraph 1 of this Section shall be as follows, unless the Parties agree upon different procedures to achieve the same result as the procedures identified in this paragraph:

For the Pershing II:

Missile:

(a) Missile stages shall be eliminated by explosive demolition or burning;

(b) Solid fuel, rocket nozzles and motor cases not destroyed in this process shall be burned, crushed, flattened or destroyed by explosion; and

(c) Front section, minus nuclear warhead device and guidance elements, shall be crushed or flattened.

Launcher:

(a) Erector-launcher mechanism shall be removed from launcher chassis;

(b) All components of erector-launcher mechanism shall be cut at locations that are not assembly joints into two pieces of approximately equal size;

(c) Missile launch support equipment, including external instrumentation compartments, shall be removed from launcher chassis; and

(d) Launcher chassis shall be cut at a location that is not an assembly joint into two pieces of approximately equal size.

For the BGM–109G:

Missile:

(a) Missile airframe shall be cut longitudinally into two pieces;

(b) Wings and tail section shall be severed from missile airframe at locations that are not assembly joints; and

(c) Front section, minus nuclear warhead device and guidance elements, shall be crushed or flattened.

Launch Canister:

Launch canister shall be crushed, flattened, cut into two pieces of approximately equal size or destroyed by explosion.

Launcher:

(a) Erector-launcher mechanism shall be removed from launcher chassis;

(b) All components of erector-launcher mechanism shall be cut at locations that are not assembly joints into two pieces of approximately equal size;

(c) Missile launch support equipment, including external instrumentation compartments, shall be removed from launcher chassis; and

(d) Launcher chassis shall be cut at a location that is not an assembly joint into two pieces of approximately equal size.

For the Pershing IA:

Missile:

(a) Missile stages shall be eliminated by explosive demolition or burning;

(b) Solid fuel, rocket nozzles and motor cases not destroyed in this process shall be burned, crushed, flattened or destroyed by explosion; and

(c) Front section, minus nuclear warhead device and guidance elements, shall be crushed or flattened.

Launcher:

(a) Erector-launcher mechanism shall be removed from launcher chassis;

(b) All components of erector-launcher mechanism shall be cut at locations that are not assembly joints into two pieces of approximately equal size;

(c) Missile launch support equipment, including external instrumentation compartments, shall be removed from launcher chassis; and

(d) Launcher chassis shall be cut at a location that is not an assembly joint into two pieces of approximately equal size.

For the Pershing IB:

Missile:

(a) Missile stage shall be eliminated by explosive demolition or burning;

(b) Solid fuel, rocket nozzle and motor case not destroyed in this process shall be burned, crushed, flattened or destroyed by explosion; and

(c) Front section, minus nuclear warhead device and guidance elements, shall be crushed or flattened.

For the SS–20:

Missile:

(a) Missile shall be eliminated by explosive demolition of the missile in its launch canister or by burning missile stages;

(b) Solid fuel, rocket nozzles and motor cases not destroyed in this process shall be burned, crushed, flattened or destroyed by explosion; and

(c) Front section, including reentry vehicles, minus nuclear warhead devices, and instrumentation compartment, minus guidance elements, shall be crushed or flattened.

Launch Canister:

Launch canister shall be destroyed by explosive demolition together with a missile, or shall be destroyed separately by explosion, cut into two pieces of approximately equal size, crushed or flattened.

Launcher:

(a) Erector-launcher mechanism shall be removed from launcher chassis;

(b) All components of erector-launcher mechanism shall be cut at locations that are not assembly joints into two pieces of approximately equal size;

(c) Missile launch support equipment, including external instrumentation compartments, shall be removed from launcher chassis;

(d) Mountings of erector-launcher mechanism and launcher leveling supports shall be cut off launcher chassis;

(e) Launcher leveling supports shall be cut at locations that are not assembly joints into two pieces of approximately equal size; and

(f) A portion of the launcher chassis, at least 0.78 meters in length, shall be cut off aft of the rear axle.

Missile Transporter Vehicle:

(a) All mechanisms associated with missile loading and mounting shall be removed from transporter vehicle chassis;

(b) All mountings of such mechanisms shall be cut off transporter vehicle chassis;

(c) All components of the mechanisms associated with missile loading and mounting shall be cut at locations that are not assembly joints into two pieces of approximately equal size;

(d) External instrumentation compartments shall be removed from transporter vehicle chassis;

(e) Transporter vehicle leveling supports shall be cut off transporter vehicle chassis and cut at locations that are not assembly joints into two pieces of approximately equal size; and

(f) A portion of the transporter vehicle chassis, at least 0.78 meters in length, shall be cut off aft of the rear axle.

For the SS–4:

Missile:

(a) Nozzles of propulsion system shall be cut off at locations that are not assembly joints;

(b) All propellant tanks shall be cut into two pieces of approximately equal size;

(c) Instrumentation compartment, minus guidance elements, shall be cut into two pieces of approximately equal size; and

(d) Front section, minus nuclear warhead device, shall be crushed or flattened.

Launch Stand:

Launch stand components shall be cut at locations that are not assembly joints into two pieces of approximately equal size.

Missile Erector:

(a) Jib, missile erector leveling supports and missile erector mechanism shall be cut off missile erector at locations that are not assembly joints; and

(b) Jib and missile erector leveling supports shall be cut into two pieces of approximately equal size.

Missile Transporter Vehicle:

Mounting components for a missile and for a missile erector mechanism as well as supports for erecting a missile onto a launcher shall be cut off transporter vehicle at locations that are not assembly joints.

For the SS–5:

Missile:

(a) Nozzles of propulsion system shall be cut off at locations that are not assembly joints;

(b) All propellant tanks shall be cut into two pieces of approximately equal size; and

(c) Instrumentation compartment, minus guidance elements, shall be cut into two pieces of approximately equal size.

For the SSC–X–4:

Missile:

(a) Missile airframe shall be cut longitudinally into two pieces;

(b) Wings and tail section shall be severed from missile airframe at locations that are not assembly joints; and

(c) Front section, minus nuclear warhead device and guidance elements, shall be crushed or flattened.

Launch Canister:

Launch canister shall be crushed, flattened, cut into two pieces of approximately equal size or destroyed by explosion.

Launcher:

(a) Erector-launcher mechanism shall be removed from launcher chassis;

(b) All components of erector-launcher mechanism shall be cut at locations that are not assembly joints from two pieces of approximately equal size;

(c) Missile launch support equipment, including external instrumentation compartments, shall be removed from launcher chassis;

(d) Mountings of erector-launcher mechanism and launcher leveling supports shall be cut off launcher chassis;

(e) Launcher leveling supports shall be cut at locations that are not assembly joints into two pieces of approximately equal size; and

(f) The launcher chassis shall be severed at a location determined by measuring no more than 0.70 meters rearward from the rear axle.

For the SS–12:

Missile:

(a) Missile shall be eliminated by explosive demolition or by burning missile stages;

(b) Solid fuel, rocket nozzles and motor cases not destroyed in this process shall be burned, crushed, flattened or destroyed by explosion; and

(c) Front section, minus nuclear warhead device, and instrumentation compartment, minus guidance elements, shall be crushed, flattened or destroyed by explosive demolition together with a missile.

Launcher:

(a) Erector-launcher mechanism shall be removed from launcher chassis;

(b) All components of erector-launcher mechanism shall be cut at locations that are not assembly joints into two pieces of approximately equal size;

(c) Missile launch support equipment, including external instrumentation compartments, shall be removed from launcher chassis;

(d) Mountings of erector-launcher mechanism and launcher leveling supports shall be cut off launcher chassis;

(e) Launcher leveling supports shall be cut at locations that are not assembly joints into two pieces of approximately equal size; and

(f) A portion of the launcher chassis, at least 1.10 meters in length, shall be cut off aft of the rear axle.

Missile Transporter Vehicle:

(a) All mechanisms associated with missile loading and mounting shall be removed from transporter vehicle chassis;

(b) All mountings of such mechanisms shall be cut off transporter vehicle chassis;

(c) All components of the mechanisms associated with missile loading and mounting shall be cut at locations that are not assembly joints into two pieces of approximately equal size;

(d) External instrumentation compartments shall be removed from transporter vehicle chassis;

(e) Transporter vehicle leveling supports shall be cut off transporter vehicle chassis and cut at locations that are not assembly joints into two pieces of approximately equal size; and

(f) A portion of the transporter vehicle chassis, at least 1.10 meters in length, shall be cut off aft of the rear axle.

For the SS–23:

Missile:

(a) Missile shall be eliminated by explosive demolition or by burning the missile stage;

(b) Solid fuel, rocket nozzle and motor case not destroyed in this process shall be burned, crushed, flattened or destroyed by explosion; and

(c) Front section, minus nuclear warhead device, and instrumentation compartment, minus guidance elements, shall be crushed, flattened, or destroyed by explosive demolition together with a missile.

Launcher:

(a) Erector-launcher mechanism shall be removed from launcher body;

(b) All components of erector-launcher mechanism shall be cut at locations that are not assembly joints into two pieces of approximately equal size;

(c) Missile launch support equipment shall be removed from launcher body;

(d) Mountings of erector-launcher mechanism and launcher leveling supports shall be cut off launcher body;

(e) Launcher leveling supports shall be cut at locations that are not assembly joints into two pieces of approximately equal size;

(f) Each environmental cover of the launcher body shall be removed and cut into two pieces of approximately equal size; and

(g) A portion of the launcher body, at least 0.85 meters in length, shall be cut off aft of the rear axle.

Missile Transporter Vehicle:

(a) All mechanisms associated with missile loading and mounting shall be removed from transporter vehicle body;

(b) All mountings of such mechanisms shall be cut off transporter vehicle body;

(c) All components of mechanisms associated with missile loading and mounting shall be cut at locations that are not assembly joints into two pieces of approximately equal size;

(d) Control equipment of the mechanism associated with missile loading shall be removed from transporter vehicle body;

(e) Transporter vehicle leveling supports shall be cut off transporter vehicle body and cut at locations that are not assembly joints into two pieces of approximately equal size; and

(f) A portion of the transporter vehicle body, at least 0.85 meters in length, shall be cut off aft of the rear axle.

11. The specific procedures for the elimination of the training missiles, training missile stages, training launch canisters and training launchers indicated in paragraph 1 of this Section shall be as follows:

Training Missile and Training Missile Stage:

Training missile and training missile stage shall be crushed, flattened, cut into two pieces of approximately equal size or destroyed by explosion.

Training Launch Canister:

Training launch canister shall be crushed, flattened, cut into two pieces of approximately equal size or destroyed by explosion.

Training Launcher:

Training launcher chassis shall be cut at the same location designated in paragraph 10 of this Section for launcher of the same type of missile.

III. ELIMINATION OF MISSILES BY MEANS OF LAUNCHING

1. Elimination of missiles by means of launching pursuant to paragraph 5 of Article X of the Treaty shall be subject to on-site inspection in accordance with paragraph 7 of Article XI of the Treaty and the Protocol on Inspection. Immediately prior to each launch conducted for the purpose of elimination, an inspector from the inspecting Party shall confirm by visual observation the type of missile to be launched.

2. All missiles being eliminated by means of launching shall be launched from designated elimination facilities to existing impact areas for such missiles. No such missile shall be used as a target vehicle for a ballistic missile interceptor.

3. Missiles being eliminated by means of launching shall be launched one at a time, and no less than six hours shall elapse between such launches.

4. Such launches shall involve ignition of all missile stages. Neither Party shall transmit or recover data from missiles being eliminated by means of launching except for unencrypted data used for range safety purposes.

5. The completion of the elimination procedures set forth in this Section, and the type and number of missiles for which those procedures have been completed, shall be confirmed in writing by the representative of the Party carrying out the elimination and by the inspection team leader of the other Party.

6. A missile shall be considered to be eliminated by means of launching after completion of the procedures set forth in this Section and upon notification required by paragraph 5(e) of Article IX of the Treaty.

IV. PROCEDURES FOR ELIMINATION IN SITU

1. *Support Structures:*

(a) Support structures listed in Section I of this Protocol shall be eliminated *in situ.*

(b) The initiation of the elimination of support structures shall be considered to be the commencement of the elimination procedures required in paragraph 1(d) of this Section.

(c) The elimination of support structures shall be subject to verification by on-site inspection in accordance with paragraph 4 of Article XI of the Treaty.

(d) The specific elimination procedures for support structures shall be as follows:

(i) the superstructure of the fixed structure or shelter shall be dismantled or demolished, and removed from its base or foundation;

(ii) the base or foundation of the fixed structure or shelter shall be destroyed by excavation or explosion;

(iii) the destroyed based or foundation of a fixed structure or shelter shall remain visible to national technical means of verification for six months or until completion of an on-site inspection conducted in accordance with Article XI of the Treaty; and

(iv) upon completion of the above requirements, the elimination procedures shall be considered to have been completed.

2. *Propellant Tanks for SS–4 Missiles:*

Fixed and transportable propellant tanks for SS–4 missiles shall be removed from launch sites.

3. *Training Missiles, Training Missile Stages, Training Launch Canisters and Training Launchers:*

(a) Training missiles, training missile stages, training launch canisters and training launchers not eliminated at elimination facilities shall be eliminated *in situ.*

(b) Training missiles, training missile stages, training launch canisters and training launchers being eliminated *in situ* shall be eliminated in accordance with the specific procedures set forth in paragraph 11 of Section II of this Protocol.

(c) Each Party shall have the right to conduct an on-site inspection to confirm the completion of the elimination procedures for training missiles, training missile stages, training launch canisters and training launchers.

(d) The Party possessing such a training missile, training missile stage, training launch canister or training launcher shall inform the other Party of the place-name and coordinates of the location at which the on-site inspection provided for in paragraph 3(c) of this Section may be conducted as well as the date on which it may be conducted. Such information shall be provided no less than 30 days in advance of that date.

(e) Elimination of a training missile, training missile stage, training launch canister or training launcher shall be considered to have been completed upon the completion of the procedures required by this paragraph and upon notification as required by paragraph 5(e) of Article IX of the Treaty following the date specified pursuant to paragraph 3(d) of this Section.

V. OTHER TYPES OF ELIMINATION

1. *Loss or Accidental Destruction:*

(a) If an item listed in Section I of this Protocol is lost or destroyed as a result of an accident, the possessing Party shall notify the other Party within 48 hours, as required in paragraph 5(e) of Article IX of the Treaty, that the item has been eliminated.

(b) Such notification shall include the type of the eliminated item, its approximate or assumed location and the circumstances related to the loss or accidental destruction.

(c) In such a case, the other Party shall have the right to conduct an inspection of the specific point at which the accident occurred to provide confidence that the item has been eliminated.

2. *Static Display:*

(a) The Parties shall have the right to eliminate missiles, launch canisters and launchers, as well as training missiles, training launch canisters and training launchers, listed in Section I of this Protocol by placing them on static display. Each Party shall be limited to a total of 15 missiles, 15 launch canisters and 15 launchers on such static display.

(b) Prior to being placed on static display, a missile, launch canister or launcher shall be rendered unusable for purposes inconsistent with the Treaty. Missile propellant shall be removed and erector-launcher mechanisms shall be rendered inoperative.

(c) The Party possessing a missile, launch canister or launcher, as well as a training missile, training launch canister or training launcher that is to be eliminated by placing it on static display shall provide the other Party with the place-name and coordinates of the location at which such a missile, launch canister or launcher is to be on static display, as well as the location at which the on-site inspection provided for in paragraph 2(d) of this Section, may take place.

(d) Each Party shall have the right to conduct an on-site inspection of such a missile, launch canister or launcher within 60 days of receipt of the notification required in paragraph 2(c) of this Section.

(e) Elimination of a missile, launch canister or launcher, as well as training missile, training launch canister or training launcher, by placing it on static display shall be considered to have been completed upon completion of the procedures required by this paragraph and notification as required by paragraph 5(e) of Article IX of the Treaty.

This Protocol is an integral part of the Treaty. It shall enter into force on the date of the entry into force of the Treaty and shall remain in force so long as the Treaty remains in force. As provided for in paragraph 1(b) of Article XIII of the Treaty, the Parties may agree upon such measures as may be necessary to improve the viability and effectiveness of this Protocol. Such measures shall not be deemed amendments to the Treaty.

DONE at Washington on December 8, 1987, in two copies, each in the English and Russian languages, both texts being equally authentic.

For the United States of America:

RONALD REAGAN,
President of the United States of America.

For the Union of Soviet Socialist Republics:

M GORBACHEV,
General Secretary of the Central Committee of the CPSU.

PROTOCOL REGARDING INSPECTIONS RELATING TO THE TREATY BETWEEN THE UNITED STATES OF AMERICA AND THE UNION OF SOVIET SOCIALIST REPUBLICS ON THE ELIMINATION OF THEIR INTERMEDIATE-RANGE AND SHORTER-RANGE MISSILES

Pursuant to and in implementation of the Treaty Between the United States of America and the Union of Soviet Socialist Republics on the Elimination of Their Intermediate-Range and Shorter-Range Missiles of December 8, 1987, hereinafter referred to as the Treaty, the Parties hereby agree upon procedures governing the conduct of inspections provided for in Article XI of the Treaty.

I. DEFINITIONS

For the purposes of this Protocol, the Treaty, the Memorandum of Understanding and the Protocol on Elimination:

1. The term "inspected Party" means the Party to the Treaty whose sites are subject to inspection as provided for by Article XI of the Treaty.

2. The term "inspecting Party" means the Party to the Treaty carrying out an inspection.

3. The term "inspector" means an individual designated by one of the Parties to carry out inspections and included on that Party's

list of inspectors in accordance with the provisions of Section III of this Protocol.

4. The term "inspection team" means the group of inspectors assigned by the inspecting Party to conduct a particular inspection.

5. The term "inspection site" means an area, location or facility at which an inspection is carried out.

6. The term "period of inspection" means the period of time from arrival of the inspection team at the inspection site until its departure from the inspection site, exclusive of time spent on any pre- and post-inspection procedures.

7. The term "point of entry" means: Washington, D.C., or San Francisco, California, the United States of America; Brussels (National Airport), The Kingdom of Belgium; Frankfurt (Rhein Main Airbase), The Federal Republic of Germany; Rome (Ciampino), The Republic of Italy; Schiphol, The Kingdom of the Netherlands; RAF Greenham Common, The United Kingdom of Great Britain and Northern Ireland; Moscow, or Irkutsk, the Union of Soviet Socialist Republics; Schkeuditz Airport, the German Democratic Republic; and International Airport Ruzyne, the Czechoslovak Socialist Republic.

8. The term "in-country period" means the period from the arrival of the inspection team at the point of entry until its departure from the country through the point of entry.

9. The term "in-country escort" means individuals specified by the inspected Party to accompany and assist inspectors and aircrew members as necessary throughout the in-country period.

10. The term "aircrew member" means an individual who performs duties related to the operation of an airplane and who is included on a Party's list of aircrew members in accordance with the provisions of Section III of this Protocol.

II. GENERAL OBLIGATIONS

1. For the purpose of ensuring verification of compliance with the provisions of the Treaty, each Party shall facilitate inspection by the other Party pursuant to this Protocol.

2. Each Party takes note of the assurances received from the other Party regarding understandings reached between the other Party and the basing countries to the effect that the basing countries have agreed to the conduct of inspections, in accordance with the provisions of this Protocol, on their territories.

III. PRE-INSPECTION REQUIREMENTS

1. Inspections to ensure verification of compliance by the Parties with the obligations assumed under the Treaty shall be carried out by inspectors designated in accordance with paragraphs 3 and 4 of this Section.

2. No later than one day after entry into force of the Treaty, each Party shall provide to the other Party: a list of its proposed inspectors who will carry out inspections pursuant to paragraphs 3, 4, 5, 7 and 8 of Article XI of the Treaty; and a list of its proposed inspectors who will carry out inspection activities pursuant to paragraph 6 of Article XI of the Treaty. None of these lists shall contain at any time more than 200 individuals.

3. Each Party shall review the lists of inspectors and aircrew members proposed by the other Party. With respect to an individual included on the list of proposed inspectors who will carry out inspection activities pursuant to paragraph 6 of Article XI of the Treaty, if such an individual is unacceptable to the Party reviewing the list, that Party shall, within 20 days, so inform the Party providing the list, and the individual shall be deemed not accepted and shall be deleted from the list. With respect to an individual on the list of proposed aircrew members or the list of proposed inspectors who will carry out inspections pursuant to paragraphs 3, 4, 5, 7 and 8 of Article XI of the Treaty, each Party, within 20 days after the receipt of such lists, shall inform the other Party of its agreement to the designation of each inspector and aircrew member proposed. Inspectors shall be citizens of the inspecting Party.

4. Each Party shall have the right to amend its lists of inspectors and aircrew members. New inspectors and aircrew members shall be designated in the same manner as set forth in paragraph 3 of this Section with respect to the initial lists.

5. Within 30 days of receipt of the initial lists of inspectors and aircrew members, or of subsequent changes thereto, the Party receiving such information shall provide, or shall ensure the provision of, such visas and other documents to each individual to whom it has agreed as may be required to ensure that each inspector or aircrew member may enter and remain in the territory of the Party or basing country in which an inspection site is located throughout the in-country period for the purpose of carrying out inspection activities in accordance with the provisions of this Protocol. Such visas and documents shall be valid for a period of at least 24 months.

6. To exercise their functions effectively, inspectors and aircrew members shall be accorded, throughout the in-country period, privileges and immunities in the country of the inspection site as set forth in the Annex to this Protocol.

7. Without prejudice to their privileges and immunities, inspectors and aircrew members shall be obliged to respect the laws and regulations of the State on whose territory an inspection is carried out and shall be obliged not to interfere in the internal affairs of that State. In the event the inspected Party determines that an inspector or aircrew member of the other Party has violated the conditions governing inspection activities set forth in this Protocol, or has ever committed a criminal offense on the territory of the inspected Party or a basing country, or has ever been sentenced for committing a criminal offense or expelled by the inspected Party or a basing country, the inspected Party making such a determination shall so notify the inspecting Party, which shall immediately strike the individual from the lists of inspectors or the list of aircrew members. If, at that time, the individual is on the territory of the inspected Party or a basing country, the inspecting Party shall immediately remove that individual from the country.

8. Within 30 days after entry into force of the Treaty, each Party shall inform the other Party of the standing diplomatic clearance number for airplanes of the party transporting inspectors and equipment necessary for inspection into and out of the territory of the Party or basing country in which an inspection site is located.

Aircraft routings to and from the designated point of entry shall be along established international airways that are agreed upon by the Parties as the basis for such diplomatic clearance.

IV. NOTIFICATIONS

1. Notification of an intention to conduct an inspection shall be made through the Nuclear Risk Reduction Centers. The receipt of this notification shall be acknowledged through the Nuclear Risk Reduction Centers by the inspected Party within one hour of its receipt.

(a) For inspections conducted pursuant to paragraphs 3, 4 or 5 of Article XI of the Treaty, such notifications shall be made no less than 16 hours in advance of the estimated time of arrival of the inspection team at the point of entry and shall include:

(i) the point of entry;

(ii) the date and estimated time of arrival at the point of entry;

(iii) the date and time when the specification of the inspection site will be provided; and

(iv) the names of inspectors and aircrew members.

(b) For inspections conducted pursuant to paragraphs 7 or 8 of Article XI of the Treaty, such notifications shall be made no less than 72 hours in advance of the estimated time of arrival of the inspection team at the point of entry and shall include:

(i) the point of entry;

(ii) the date and estimated time of arrival at the point of entry;

(iii) the site to be inspected and the type of inspection; and

(iv) the names of inspectors and aircrew members.

2. The date and time of the specification of the inspection site as notified pursuant to paragraph 1(a) of this Section shall fall within the following time intervals:

(a) for inspections conducted pursuant to paragraph 4 or 5 of Article XI of the Treaty, neither less than four hours nor more than 24 hours after the estimated date and time of arrival at the point of entry; and

(b) for inspections conducted pursuant to paragraph 3 of Article XI of the Treaty, neither less than four hours nor more than 48 hours after the estimated date and time of arrival at the point of entry.

3. The inspecting Party shall provide the inspected Party with a flight plan, through the Nuclear Risk Reduction Centers, for its flight from the last airfield prior to entering the airspace of the country in which the inspection site is located to the point of entry, no less than six hours before the scheduled departure time from that airfield. Such a plan shall be filed in accordance with the procedures of the International Civil Aviation Organization applicable to civil aircraft. The inspecting Party shall include in the remarks section of each flight plan the standing diplomatic clearance number and the notation: "Inspection aircraft. Priority clearance processing required."

4. No less than three hours prior to the scheduled departure of the inspection team from the last airfield prior to entering the airspace of the country in which the inspection is to take place, the inspected Party shall ensure that the flight plan filed in accordance with paragraph 3 of this Section is approved so that the inspection team may arrive at the point of entry by the estimated arrival time.

5. Either Party may change the point or points of entry to the territories of the countries within which its deployment areas, missile operating bases or missile support facilities are located, by giving notice of such change to the other Party. A change in a point of entry shall become effective five months after receipt of such notification by the other Party.

V. ACTIVITIES BEGINNING UPON ARRIVAL AT THE POINT OF ENTRY

1. The in-country escort and a diplomatic aircrew escort accredited to the Government of either the inspected Party or the basing country in which the inspection site is located shall meet the inspection team and aircrew members at the point of entry as soon as the airplane of the inspecting Party lands. The number of aircrew members for each airplane shall not exceed ten. The in-country escort shall expedite the entry of the inspection team and aircrew, their baggage, and equipment and supplies necessary for inspection, into the country in which the inspection site is located. A diplomatic aircrew escort shall have the right to accompany and assist aircrew members throughout the in-country period. In the case of an inspection taking place on the territory of a basing country, the in-country escort may include representatives of that basing country.

2. An inspector shall be considered to have assumed his duties upon arrival at the point of entry on the territory of the inspected Party or a basing country, and shall be considered to have ceased performing those duties when he has left the territory of the inspected Party or basing country.

3. Each Party shall ensure that equipment and supplies are exempt from all customs duties.

4. Equipment and supplies which the inspecting Party brings into the country in which an inspection site is located shall be subject to examination at the point of entry each time they are brought into that country. This examination shall be completed prior to the departure of the inspection team from the point of entry to conduct an inspection. Such equipment and supplies shall be examined by the in-country escort in the presence of the inspection team members to ascertain to the satisfaction of each Party that the equipment and supplies cannot perform functions unconnected with the inspection requirements of the Treaty. If it is established upon examination that the equipment or supplies are unconnected with these inspection requirements, then they shall not be cleared for use and shall be impounded at the point of entry until the departure of the inspection team from the country where the inspection is conducted. Storage of the inspecting Party's equipment and supplies at each point of entry shall be within tamper-proof containers

within a secure facility. Access to each secure facility shall be controlled by a "dual key" system requiring the presence of both Parties to gain access to the equipment and supplies.

5. Throughout the in-country period, the inspected Party shall provide, or arrange for the provision of, meals, lodging, work space, transportation and, as necessary, medical care for the inspection team and aircrew of the inspecting Party. All the costs in connection with the stay of inspectors carrying out inspection activities pursuant to paragraph 6 of Article XI of the Treaty, on the territory of the inspected Party, including meals, services, lodging, work space, transportation and medical care shall be borne by the inspecting Party.

6. The inspected Party shall provide parking, security protection, servicing and fuel for the airplane of the inspecting Party at the point of entry. The inspecting Party shall bear the cost of such fuel and servicing.

7. For inspections conducted on the territory of the Parties, the inspection team shall enter at the point of entry on the territory of the inspected Party that is closest to the inspection site. In the case of inspections carried out in accordance with paragraph 3, 4 or 5 of Article XI of the Treaty, the inspection team leader shall, at or before the time notified pursuant to paragraph 1(a)(iii) of Section IV of this Protocol, inform the inspected Party at the point of entry through the in-country escort of the type of inspection and the inspection site, by place-name and geographic coordinates.

VI. GENERAL RULES FOR CONDUCTING INSPECTIONS

1. Inspectors shall discharge their functions in accordance with this Protocol.

2. Inspectors shall not disclose information received during inspections except with the express permission of the inspecting Party. They shall remain bound by this obligation after their assignment as inspectors has ended.

3. In discharging their functions, inspectors shall not interfere directly with on-going activities at the inspection site and shall avoid unnecessarily hampering or delaying the operation of a facility or taking actions affecting its safe operation.

4. Inspections shall be conducted in accordance with the objectives set forth in Article XI of the Treaty as applicable for the type of inspection specified by the inspecting Party under paragraph 1(b) of Section IV or paragraph 7 of Section V of this Protocol.

5. The in-country escort shall have the right to accompany and assist inspectors and aircrew members as considered necessary by the inspected Party throughout the in-country period. Except as otherwise provided in this Protocol, the movement and travel of inspectors and aircrew members shall be at the discretion of the in-country escort.

6. Inspectors carrying out inspection activities pursuant to paragraph 6 of Article XI of the Treaty shall be allowed to travel within 50 kilometers from the inspection site with the permission of the in-country escort, and as considered necessary by the inspected Party, shall be accompanied by the in-country escort. Such travel shall be taken solely as a leisure activity.

7. Inspectors shall have the right throughout the period of inspection to be in communication with the embassy of the inspecting Party located within the territory of the country where the inspection is taking place using the telephone communications provided by the inspected Party.

8. At the inspection site, representatives of the inspected facility shall be included among the in-country escort.

9. The inspection team may bring onto the inspection site such documents as needed to conduct the inspection, as well as linear measurement devices; cameras; portable weighing devices; radiation detection devices; and other equipment, as agreed by the Parties. The characteristics and method of use of the equipment listed above, shall also be agreed upon within 30 days after entry into force of the Treaty. During inspections conducted pursuant to paragraph 3, 4, 5(a), 7 or 8 of Article XI of the Treaty, the inspection team may use any of the equipment listed above, except for cameras, which shall be for use only by the inspected Party at the request of the inspecting Party. During inspections conducted pursuant to paragraph 5(b) of Article XI of the Treaty, all measurements shall be made by the inspected Party at the request of the inspecting Party. At the request of inspectors, the in-country escort shall take photographs of the inspected facilities using the inspecting Party's camera systems which are capable of producing duplicate, instant development photographic prints. Each Party shall receive one copy of every photograph.

10. For inspections conducted pursuant to paragraphs 3, 4, 5, 7 or 8 of Article XI of the Treaty, inspectors shall permit the in-country escort to observe the equipment used during the inspection by the inspection team.

11. Measurements recorded during inspections shall be certified by the signature of a member of the inspection team and a member of the in-country escort when they are taken. Such certified data shall be included in the inspection report.

12. Inspectors shall have the right to request clarifications in connection with ambiguities that arise during an inspection. Such requests shall be made promptly through the in-country escort. The in-country escort shall provide the inspection team, during the inspection, with such clarifications as may be necessary to remove the ambiguity. In the event questions relating to an object or building located within the inspection site are not resolved, the inspected Party shall photograph the object or building as requested by the inspecting Party for the purpose of clarifying its nature and function. If the ambiguity cannot be removed during the inspection, then the question, relevant clarifications and a copy of any photographs taken shall be included in the inspection report.

13. In carrying out their activities, inspectors shall observe safety regulations established at the inspection site, including those for the protection of controlled environments within a facility and for personal safety. Individual protective clothing and equipment shall be provided by the inspected Party, as necessary.

14. For inspections pursuant to paragraphs 3, 4, 5, 7 or 8 of Article XI of the Treaty, pre-inspection procedures, including briefings and safety-related activities, shall begin upon arrival of the inspection team at the inspection site and shall be completed within one

hour. The inspection team shall begin the inspection immediately upon completion of the pre-inspection procedures. The period of inspection shall not exceed 24 hours, except for inspections pursuant to paragraph 6, 7, or 8 of Article XI of the Treaty. The period of inspection may be extended, by agreement with the in-country escort, by no more than eight hours. Post-inspection procedures, which include completing the inspection report in accordance with the provisions of Section XI of this Protocol, shall begin immediately upon completion of the inspection and shall be completed at the inspection site within four hours.

15. An inspection team conducting an inspection pursuant to Article XI of the Treaty shall include no more than ten inspectors, except for an inspection team conducting an inspection pursuant to paragraphs 7 or 8 of that Article, which shall include no more than 20 inspectors and an inspection team conducting inspection activities pursuant to paragraph 6 of that Article, which shall include no more than 30 inspectors. At least two inspectors on each team must speak the language of the inspected Party. An inspection team shall operate under the direction of the team leader and deputy team leader. Upon arrival at the inspection site, the inspection team may divide itself into subgroups consisting of no fewer than two inspectors each. There shall be no more than one inspection team at an inspection site at any time.

16. Except in the case of inspections conducted pursuant to paragraphs 3, 4, 7 or 8 of Article XI of the Treaty, upon completion of the post-inspection procedures, the inspection team shall return promptly to the point of entry from which it commenced inspection activities and shall then leave, within 24 hours, the territory of the country in which the inspection site is located, using its own airplane. In the case of inspections conducted pursuant to paragraphs 3, 4, 7 or 8 of Article XI of the Treaty, if the inspection team intends to conduct another inspection it shall either:

(a) notify the inspected Party of its intent upon return to the point of entry; or

(b) notify the inspected Party of the type of inspection and the inspection site upon completion of the post-inspection procedures. In this case it shall be the responsibility of the inspected Party to ensure that the inspection team reaches the next inspection site without unjustified delay. The inspected Party shall determine the means of transportation and route involved in such travel.

With respect to subparagraph (a), the procedures set forth in paragraph 7 of Section V of this Protocol and paragraphs 1 and 2 of Section VII of this Protocol shall apply.

VII. INSPECTIONS CONDUCTED PURSUANT TO PARAGRAPHS 3, 4 OR 5 OF ARTICLE XI OF THE TREATY

1. Within one hour after the time for the specification of the inspection site notified pursuant to paragraph 1(a) of Section IV of this Protocol, the inspected Party shall implement pre-inspection movement restrictions at the inspection site, which shall remain in

effect until the inspection team arrives at the inspection site. During the period that pre-inspection movement restrictions are in effect, missiles, stages of such missiles, launchers or support equipment subject to the Treaty shall not be removed from the inspection site.

2. The inspected Party shall transport the inspection team from the point of entry to the inspection site so that the inspection team arrives at the inspection site no later than nine hours after the time for the specification of the inspection site notified pursuant to paragraph 1(a) of Section IV of this Protocol.

3. In the event that an inspection is conducted in a basing country, the aircrew of the inspected Party may include representatives of the basing country.

4. Neither Party shall conduct more than one inspection pursuant to paragraph 5(b) of Article XI of the Treaty at any one time, more than one inspection pursuant to paragraph 5(b) of Article XI of the Treaty at any one time, or more than 10 inspections pursuant to paragraph 3 of Article XI of the Treaty at any one time.

5. The boundaries of the inspection site at the facility to be inspected shall be the boundaries of that facility set forth in the Memorandum of Understanding.

6. Except in the case of an inspection conducted pursuant to paragraphs 4 or 5(b) of Article XI of the Treaty, upon arrival of the inspection team at the inspection site, the in-country escort shall inform the inspection team leader of the number of missiles, stages of missiles, launchers, support structures and support equipment at the site that are subject to the Treaty and provide the inspection team leader with a diagram of the inspection site indicating the location of these missiles, stages of missiles, launchers, support structures and support equipment at the inspection site.

7. Subject to the procedures of paragraphs 8 through 14 of this Section, inspectors shall have the right to inspect the entire inspection site, including the interior of structures, containers or vehicles, or including covered objects, whose dimensions are equal to or greater than the dimensions specified in Section VI of the Memorandum of Understanding for the missiles, stages of such missiles, launchers or support equipment of the inspected Party.

8. A missile, a stage of such a missile or a launcher subject to the Treaty shall be subject to inspection only by external visual observation, including measuring, as necessary, the dimensions of such a missile, stage of such a missile or launcher. A container that the inspected Party declares to contain a missile or stage of a missile subject to the Treaty, and which is not sufficiently large to be capable of containing more than one missile or stage of such a missile of the inspected Party subject to the Treaty, shall be subject to inspection only by external visual observation, including measuring, as necessary, the dimensions of such a container to confirm that it cannot contain more than one missile or stage of such a missile of the inspected Party subject to the Treaty. Except as provided for in paragraph 14 of this Section, a container that is sufficiently large to contain a missile or stage of such a missile of the inspected Party subject to the Treaty that the inspected Party declares not to contain a missile or stage of such a missile subject to the Treaty shall be subject to inspection only by means of weighing or visual

observation of the interior of the container, as necessary, to confirm that it does not, in fact, contain a missile or stage of such a missile of the inspected Party subject to the Treaty. If such a container is a launch canister associated with a type of missile not subject to the Treaty, and declared by the inspected Party to contain such a missile, it shall be subject to external inspection only, including use of radiation detection devices, visual observation and linear measurement, as necessary, of the dimensions of such a canister.

9. A structure or container that is not sufficiently large to contain a missile, stage of such a missile or launcher of the inspected Party subject to the Treaty shall be subject to inspection only by external visual observation including measuring, as necessary, the dimensions of such a structure or container to confirm that it is not sufficiently large to be capable of containing a missile, stage of such a missile or launcher of the inspected Party subject to the Treaty.

10. Within a structure, a space which is sufficiently large to contain a missile, stage of such a missile or launcher of the inspected Party subject to the Treaty, but which is demonstrated to the satisfaction of the inspection team not to be accessible by the smallest missile, stage of a missile or launcher of the inspected Party subject to the Treaty shall not be subject to further inspection. If the inspected Party demonstrates to the satisfaction of the inspection team by means of a visual inspection of the interior of an enclosed space from its entrance that the enclosed space does not contain any missile, stage of such a missile or launcher of the inspected Party subject to the Treaty, such an enclosed space shall not be subject to further inspection.

11. The inspection team shall be permitted to patrol the perimeter of the inspection site and station inspectors at the exits of the site for the duration of the inspection.

12. The inspection team shall be permitted to inspect any vehicle capable of carrying missiles, stages of such missiles, launchers or support equipment of the inspected Party subject to the Treaty at any time during the course of an inspection and no such vehicle shall leave the inspection site during the course of the inspection until inspected at site exits by the inspection team.

13. Prior to inspection of a building within the inspection site, the inspection team may station subgroups at the exits of the building that are large enough to permit passage of any missile, stage of such a missile, launcher or support equipment of the inspected Party subject to the Treaty. During the time that the building is being inspected, no vehicle or object capable of containing any missile, stage of such a missile, launcher or support equipment of the inspected Party subject to the Treaty shall be permitted to leave the building until inspected.

14. During an inspection conducted pursuant to paragraph 5(b) of Article XI of the Treaty, it shall be the responsibility of the inspected Party to demonstrate that a shrouded or environmentally protected object which is equal to or larger than the smallest missile, stage of a missile or launcher of the inspected Party subject to the Treaty is not, in fact, a missile, stage of such a missile or launcher of the inspected Party subject to the Treaty. This may be accomplished by partial removal of the shroud or environmental

protection cover, measuring, or weighing the covered object or by other methods. If the inspected Party satisfies the inspection team by its demonstration that the object is not a missile, stage of such a missile or launcher of the inspected Party subject to the Treaty, then there shall be no further inspection of that object. If the container is a launch canister associated with a type of missile not subject to the Treaty, and declared by the inspected Party to contain such a missile, then it shall be subject to external inspection only, including use of radiation detection devices, visual observation and linear measurement, as necessary, of the dimensions of such a canister.

VIII. INSPECTIONS CONDUCTED PURSUANT TO PARAGRAPHS 7 OR 8 OF ARTICLE XI OF THE TREATY

1. Inspections of the process of elimination of items of missile systems specified in the Protocol on Elimination carried out pursuant to paragraph 7 of Article XI of the Treaty shall be conducted in accordance with the procedures set forth in this paragraph and the Protocol on Elimination.

(a) Upon arrival at the elimination facility, inspectors shall be provided with a schedule of elimination activities.

(b) Inspectors shall check the data which are specified in the notification provided by the inspected Party regarding the number and type of items of missile systems to be eliminated against the number and type of such items which are at the elimination facility prior to the initiation of the elimination procedures.

(c) Subject to paragraphs 3 and 11 of Section VI of this Protocol, inspectors shall observe the execution of the specific procedures for the elimination of the items of missile systems as provided for in the Protocol on Elimination. If any deviations from the agreed elimination procedures are found, the inspectors shall have the right to call the attention of the in-country escort to the need for strict compliance with the above-mentioned procedures. The completion of such procedures shall be confirmed in accordance with the procedures specified in the Protocol on Elimination.

(d) During the elimination of missiles by means of launching, the inspectors shall have the right to ascertain by visual observation that a missile prepared for launch is a missile of the type subject to elimination. The inspectors shall also be allowed to observe such a missile from a safe location specified by the inspected Party until the completion of its launch. During the inspection of a series of launches for the elimination of missiles by means of launching, the inspected Party shall determine the means of transport and route for the transportation of inspectors between inspection sites.

2. Inspections of the elimination of items of missile systems specified in the Protocol on Elimination carried out pursuant to paragraph 8 of Article XI of the Treaty shall be conducted in accordance with the procedures set forth in Sections II, IV or V of the Protocol on Elimination or as otherwise agreed by the Parties.

IX. INSPECTION ACTIVITIES CONDUCTED PURSUANT TO PARAGRAPH 6 OF ARTICLE XI OF THE TREATY

1. The inspected Party shall maintain an agreed perimeter around the periphery of the inspection site and shall designate a portal with not more than one rail line and one road which shall be within 50 meters of each other. All vehicles which can contain an intermediate-range GLBM or longest stage of such a GLBM of the inspected Party shall exit only through this portal.

2. For the purposes of this Section, the provisions of paragraph 10 of Article VII of the Treaty shall be applied to intermediate-range GLBMs of the inspected Party and the longest stage of such GLBMs.

3. There shall not be more than two other exits from the inspection site. Such exits shall be monitored by appropriate sensors. The perimeter of and exits from the inspection site may be monitored as provided for by paragraph 11 of Section VII of this Protocol.

4. The inspecting Party shall have the right to establish continuous monitoring systems at the portal specified in paragraph 1 of this Section and appropriate sensors at the exits specified in paragraph 3 of this Section and carry out necessary engineering surveys, construction, repair and replacement of monitoring systems.

5. The inspected Party shall, at the request of and at the expense of the inspecting Party, provide the following:

(a) all necessary utilities for the construction and operation of the monitoring systems, including electrical power, water, fuel, heating and sewage;

(b) basic construction materials including concrete and lumber;

(c) the site preparation necessary to accommodate the installation of continuously operating systems for monitoring the portal specified in paragraph 1 of this Section, appropriate sensors for other exits specified in paragraph 3 of this Section and the center for collecting data obtained during inspections. Such preparation may include ground excavation, laying of concrete foundations, trenching between equipment locations and utility connections;

(d) transportation for necessary installation tools, materials and equipment from the point of entry to the inspection site; and

(e) a minimum of two telephone lines and, as necessary, high frequency radio equipment capable of allowing direct communication with the embassy of the inspecting Party in the country in which the site is located.

6. Outside the perimeter of the inspection site, the inspecting Party shall have the right to:

(a) build no more than three buildings with a total floor space of not more than 150 square meters for a data center and inspection team headquarters, and one additional building with floor space not to exceed 500 square meters for the storage of supplies and equipment;

(b) install systems to monitor the exits to include weight sensors, vehicle, sensors, surveillance systems and vehicle dimensional measuring equipment;

(c) install at the portal specified in paragraph 1 of this Section equipment for measuring the length and diameter of missile stages contained inside of launch canisters or shipping containers;

(d) install at the portal specified in paragraph 1 of this Section non-damaging image producing equipment for imaging the contents of launch canisters or shipping containers declared to contain missiles or missile stages as provided for in paragraph 11 of this Section;

(e) install a primary and back-up power source and

(f) use, as necessary, data authentication devices.

7. During the installation or operation of the monitoring systems, the inspecting Party shall not deny the inspected Party access to any existing structures or security systems. The inspecting Party shall not take any actions with respect to such structures without consent of the inspected Party. If the Parties agree that such structures are to be rebuilt or demolished, either partially or completely, the inspecting Party shall provide the necessary compensation.

8. The inspected Party shall not interfere with the installed equipment or restrict the access of the inspection team to such equipment.

9. The inspecting Party shall have the right to use its own two-way systems of radio communication between inspectors patrolling the perimeter and the data collection center. Such systems shall conform to power and frequency restrictions established on the territory of the inspected Party.

10. Aircraft shall not be permitted to land within the perimeter of the monitored site except for emergencies at the site and with prior notification to the inspection team.

11. Any shipment existing through the portal specified in paragraph 1 of this Section which is large enough and heavy enough to contain an intermediate-range GLBM or longest stage of such a GLBM of the inspected Party shall be declared by the inspected Party to the inspection team before the shipment arrives at the portal. The declaration shall state whether such a shipment contains a missile or missile stage as large or larger than and as heavy or heavier than an intermediate-range GLBM or longest stage of such a GLBM of the inspected Party.

12. The inspection team shall have the right to weight and measure the dimensions of any vehicle, including railcars, exiting the site to ascertain whether it is large enough and heavy enough to contain an intermediate-range GLBM or longest stage of such a GLBM of the inspected Party. These measurements shall be performed so as to minimize the delay of vehicles exiting the site. Vehicles that are either not large enough or not heavy enough to contain an intermediate-range GLBM or longest stage of such a GLBM of the inspected Party shall not be subject to further inspection.

13. Vehicles exiting through the portal specified in paragraph 1 of this Section that are large enough and heavy enough to contain an intermediate-range GLBM or longest stage of such a GLBM of the inspected Party but that are declared not to contain a missile or missile stage as large or larger than and as heavy or heavier than an intermediate-range GLBM or longest stage of such a

GLBM of the inspected Party shall be subject to the following procedures.

(a) The inspecting Party shall have the right to inspect the interior of all such vehicles.

(b) If the inspecting Party can determine by visual observation or dimensional measurement that, inside a particular vehicle, there are no containers or shrouded objects large enough to be or to contain an intermediate-range GLBM or longest stage of such a GLBM of the inspected Party, then that vehicle shall not be subject to further inspection.

(c) If inside a vehicle there are one or more containers or shrouded objects large enough to be or to contain an intermediate-range GLBM or longest stage of such a GLBM of the inspected Party, it shall be the responsibility of the inspected Party to demonstrate that such containers or shrouded objects are not and do not contain intermediate-range GLBMs or the longest stages of such GLBMs of the inspected Party.

14. Vehicles exiting through the portal specified in paragraph 1 of this Section that are declared to contain a missile or missile stage as large or larger than and as heavy or heavier than an intermediate-range GLBM or longest stage of such a GLBM of the inspected Party shall be subject to the following procedures.

(a) The inspecting Party shall preserve the integrity of the inspected missile or stage of a missile.

(b) Measuring equipment shall be placed only outside of the launch canister or shipping container; all measurements shall be made by the inspecting Party using the equipment provided for in paragraph 6 of this Section. Such measurements shall be observed and certified by the in-country escort.

(c) The inspecting Party shall have the right to weigh and measure the dimensions of any launch canister or of any shipping container declared to contain such a missile or missile stage and to image the contents of any launch canister or of any shipping container declared to contain such a missile or missile stage; it shall have the right to view such missiles or missile stages contained in launch canisters or shipping containers eight times per calendar year. The in-country escort shall be present during all phases of such viewing. During such interior viewing:

(i) the front end of the launch canister or the cover of the shipping container shall be opened;

(ii) the missile or missile stage shall not be removed from its launch canister or shipping container; and

(iii) the length and diameter of the stages of the missile shall be measured in accordance with the methods agreed by the Parties so as to ascertain that the missile or missile stage is not an intermediate-range GLBM of the inspected Party, or the longest stage of such a GLBM, and that the missile has no more than one stage which is outwardly similar to a stage of an existing type of intermediate-range GLBM.

(d) The inspecting Party shall also have the right to inspect any other containers or shrouded objects inside the vehicle containing such a missile or missile stage in accordance with the procedures in paragraph 13 of this Section.

X. CANCELLATION OF INSPECTION

An inspection shall be canceled if, due to circumstances brought about by *force majeure,* it cannot be carried out. In the case of a delay that prevents an inspection team performing an inspection pursuant to paragraphs 3, 4 or 5 of Article XI of the Treaty, from arriving at the inspection site during the time specified in paragraph 2 of Section VII of this Protocol, the inspecting Party may either cancel or carry out the inspection. If an inspection is canceled due to circumstances brought about by *force majeure* or delay, then the number of inspections to which the inspecting Party is entitled shall not be reduced.

XI. INSPECTION REPORT

1. For inspections conducted pursuant to paragraphs 3, 4, 5, 7 or 8 of Article XI of the Treaty, during post-inspection procedures, and no later than two hours after the inspection has been completed, the inspection team leader shall provide the in-country escort with a written inspection report in both the English and Russian languages. The report shall be factual. It shall include the type of inspection carried out, the inspection site, the number of missiles, stages of missiles, launchers and items of support equipment subject to the Treaty observed during the period of inspection and any measurements recorded pursuant to paragraph 10 of Section VI of this Protocol. Photographs taken during the inspection in accordance with agreed procedures, as well as the inspection site diagram provided for by paragraph 6 of Section VII of this Protocol, shall be attached to this report.

2. For inspection activities conducted pursuant to paragraph 6 of Article XI of the Treaty, within 3 days after the end of each month, the inspection team leader shall provide the in-country escort with a written inspection report both in the English and Russian languages. The report shall be factual. It shall include the number of vehicles declared to contain a missile or stage of a missile as large or larger than and as heavy or heavier than an intermediate-range GLBM or longest stage of such a GLBM of the inspected Party that left the inspection site through the portal specified in paragraph 1 of Section IX of this Protocol during that month. The report shall also include any measurements of launch canisters or shipping containers contained in these vehicles recorded pursuant to paragraph 11 of Section VI of this Protocol. In the event the inspecting Party, under the provisions of paragraph 14(c) of Section IX of this Protocol, has viewed the interior of a launch canister or shipping container declared to contain a missile or stage of a missile as large or larger than and as heavy or heavier than an intermediate-range GLBM or longest stage of such a GLBM of the inspected Party, the report shall also include the measurements of the length and diameter of missile stages obtained during the inspection and recorded pursuant to paragraph 11 of Section VI of this Protocol.

Photographs taken during the inspection in accordance with agreed procedures shall be attached to this report.

3. The inspected Party shall have the right to include written comments in the report.

4. The Parties shall, when possible, resolve ambiguities regarding factual information contained in the inspection report. Relevant clarifications shall be recorded in the report. The report shall be signed by the inspection team leader and by one of the members of the in-country escort. Each Party shall retain one copy of the report.

This Protocol is an integral part of the Treaty. It shall enter into force on the date of entry into force of the Treaty and shall remain in force as long as the Treaty remains in force. As provided for in paragraph 1(b) of Article XIII of the Treaty, the Parties may agree upon such measures as may be necessary to improve the viability and effectiveness of this Protocol. Such measures shall not be deemed amendments to the Treaty.

DONE at Washington on December 8, 1987, in two copies, each in the English and Russian languages, both texts being equally authentic.

For the United States of America:

RONALD REAGAN,
President of the United States of America.

For the Union of Soviet Socialist Republics:

M GORBACHEV,
General Secretary of the Central Committee of the CPSU.

ANNEX—PROVISIONS ON PRIVILEGES AND IMMUNITIES OF INSPECTORS AND AIRCREW MEMBERS

In order to exercise their functions effectively, for the purpose of implementing the Treaty and not for their personal benefit, the inspectors and aircrew members referred to in Section III of this Protocol shall be accorded the privileges and immunities contained in this Annex. Privileges and immunities shall be accorded for the entire in-country period in the country in which an inspection site is located, and thereafter with respect to acts previously performed in the exercise of official functions as an inspector or aircrew member.

1. Inspectors and aircrew members shall be accorded the inviolability enjoyed by diplomatic agents pursuant to Article 29 of the Vienna Convention of Diplomatic Relations of April 18, 1961.

2. The living quarters and office premises occupied by an inspector carrying out inspection activities pursuant to paragraph 6 of Article XI of the Treaty shall be accorded the inviolability and protection accorded the premises of diplomatic agents pursuant to Article 30 of the Vienna Convention of Diplomatic Relations.

3. The papers and correspondence of inspectors and aircrew members shall enjoy the inviolability accorded to the papers and correspondence of diplomatic agents pursuant to Article 30 of the Vienna Convention of Diplomatic Relations. In addition, the aircraft of the inspection team shall be inviolable.

4. Inspectors and aircrew members shall be accorded the immunities accorded diplomatic agents pursuant to paragraphs 1, 2 and 3 of Article 31 of the Vienna Convention on Diplomatic Relations. The immunity from jurisdiction of an inspector or an aircrew member may be waived by the inspecting Party in those cases when it is of the opinion that immunity would impede the course of justice and that it can be waived without prejudice to the implementation of the provisions of the Treaty. Waiver must always be express.

5. Inspectors carrying out inspection activities pursuant to paragraph 6 of Article XI of the Treaty shall be accorded the exemption from dues and taxes accorded to diplomatic agents pursuant to Article 34 of the Vienna Convention on Diplomatic Relations.

6. Inspectors and aircrew members of a Party shall be permitted to bring into the territory of the other Party or a basing country in which an inspection site is located, without payment of any customs duties or related charges, articles for their personal use, with the exception of articles the import or export of which is prohibited by law or controlled by quarantine regulations.

7. An inspector or aircrew member shall not engage in any professional or commercial activity for personal profit on the territory of the inspected Party or that of the basing countries.

8. If the inspected Party considers that there has been an abuse of privileges and immunities specified in this Annex, consultations shall be held between the Parties to determine whether such an abuse has occurred and, if so determined, to prevent a repetition of such an abuse.

[PHOTOGRAPHS]

b. Agreement Among the United States of America and the Kingdom of Belgium, the Federal Republic of Germany, the Republic of Italy, the Kingdom of the Netherlands and the United Kingdom of Great Britain and Northern Ireland Regarding Inspections Relating to the Treaty Between the United States of America and the Union of Soviet Socialist Republics on the Elimination of Their Intermediate-Range and Shorter-Range Missiles and the Notes Exchanged Between the United States of America and both the German Democratic Republic and Czechoslovakia

Agreement signed at Brussels, December 11, 1987; Entered into force, June 1, 1988[1]

The United States of America, the Kingdom of Belgium, the Federal Republic of Germany, the Republic of Italy, the Kingdom of the Netherlands, and the United Kingdom of Great Britain and Northern Ireland, noting the terms agreed between the United States of America and the Union of Soviet Socialist Republics for the elimination of their intermediate-range and shorter-range missiles,

HAVE AGREED AS FOLLOWS:

ARTICLE I—GENERAL OBLIGATIONS

1. Inspection activities related to Article XI of the Treaty between the United States of America and the Union of Soviet Socialist Republics on the Elimination of Their Intermediate-Range and Shorter-Range Missiles, signed at Washington on December 8, 1987, may take place on the territory of the Kingdom of Belgium, the Federal Republic of Germany, the Republic of Italy, the Kingdom of the Netherlands and the United Kingdom of Great Britain and Northern Ireland and shall be carried out in accordance with the requirements, procedures and arrangements set forth in the Protocol Regarding Inspections Relating to the Treaty between the United States of America and the Union of Soviet Socialist Republics on the Elimination of Their Intermediate-Range and Shorter-Range Missiles and this Agreement.

2. The Kingdom of Belgium, the Federal Republic of Germany, the Republic of Italy, the Kingdom of the Netherlands and the United Kingdom of Great Britain and Northern Ireland, hereinafter the Basing Countries, hereby agree to facilitate the implementation by the United States of America of its obligations under the Treaty, including the Inspection Protocol thereto, on their territories in accordance with the requirements, procedures and arrangements set forth in this Agreement.

[1] This Agreement entered into force simultaneously with the entry into force of the Treaty and will remain in force for 13 years.

3. Except as herein agreed by the United States of America and the Basing Countries, nothing shall affect the sovereign authority of each state to enforce its laws and regulations with respect to persons entering, and activities taking place within, its jurisdiction.

4. The Basing Countries do not by this Agreement assume any obligations or grant any rights deriving from the Treaty or the Inspection Protocol other than those expressly undertaken or granted in this Agreement or otherwise with their specific consent.

5. The United States of America:

a) Remains fully responsible towards the Soviet Union for the implementation of its obligations under the Treaty and the Inspection Protocol in respect of United States facilities located on the territories of the Basing Countries;

b) Undertakes on request at any time to take such action, in exercise of its rights under the Treaty, including the Inspection Protocol, as may be required to protect and preserve the rights of the Basing Countries under this Agreement.

ARTICLE II—DEFINITIONS

For purposes of the present Agreement:

1. The term "Treaty" means the Treaty between the United States of America and the Union of Soviet Socialist Republics on the Elimination of Their Intermediate-Range and Shorter-Range Missiles;

2. The term "Inspection Protocol" means the Protocol Regarding Inspections Relating to the Treaty between the United States of America and the Union of Soviet Socialist Republics on the Elimination of Their Intermediate-Range and Shorter-Range Missiles;

3. The term "Inspected Party" means the United States of America;

4. The term "Inspecting Party" means the Union of Soviet Socialist Republics;

5. The term "inspection team" means those inspectors designated by the Inspecting Party to conduct a particular inspection activity;

6. The term "inspector" means an individual proposed by the Union of Soviet Socialist Republics to carry out inspections pursuant to Article XI of the Treaty, and included on its list of inspectors in accordance with Section III of the Inspection Protocol;

7. The term "diplomatic aircrew escort" means that individual accredited to the government of the Basing Country in which the inspection site is located who is designated by the Inspecting Party to assist the aircrew of the Inspecting Party;

8. The term "inspection site" means the area, facility, or location in a Basing Country at which an inspection provided for in Article XI of the Treaty is carried out;

9. The term "period of inspection" mean the period from initiation of the inspection at the inspection site until completion of the inspection at the inspection site, exclusive of time spent on any pre- and post-inspection procedures;

10. The term "point of entry" means: in respect of Belgium, Brussels (National); in respect of the Federal Republic of Germany, Frankfurt (Rhein Main Airbase); in respect of Italy, Rome (Ciampino); in respect of the Kingdom of the Netherlands,

Schiphol; and in respect of the United Kingdom of Great Britain and Northern Ireland, RAF Greenham Common;

11. The term "in-country period" means the period from the arrival of the inspection team at the point of entry until departure of the inspection team from the point of entry to depart the country;

12. The term "in-country escort" means the official or officials specified by the Inspected Party, one or more of whom may be nominated by the Basing Country within whose territory the inspection site is located, who shall accompany an inspection team throughout the in-country period and provide appropriate assistance to an inspection team, in accordance with the provisions of the Inspection Protocol, throughout the in-country period;

13. The term "aircrew member" means an individual, other than the members of an inspection team, diplomatic aircrew escort and in-country escort, on the aircraft of the Inspecting Party. The number of aircrew members per aircraft shall not exceed ten.

ARTICLE III—NOTIFICATIONS

1. Upon entry into force of this Agreement, the Inspected Party and each Basing Country shall establish channels which shall be available to receive and acknowledge receipt of notifications on a 24-hour continuous basis.

2. Immediately upon receipt of notice from the Inspecting Party of its intention to conduct an inspection in a Basing Country, the Inspected Party shall notify the Basing Country concerned thereof and of the date and estimated time of arrival of the inspection team at the point of entry, the date and estimated time of departure from the point of entry to the inspection site, the names of the aircrew and inspection team members, the flight plan (including the type of aircraft as specified therein) filed by the Inspecting Party in accordance with the International Civil Aviation Organization, hereinafter ICAO, procedures applicable to civil aircraft, and any other information relevant to the inspection provided by the Inspecting Party.

3. No less than one hour prior to the estimated time of departure of the inspection team from the point of entry for the inspection site, or in the case of successive inspections conducted pursuant to paragraphs 3, 4, 7 of 8 of Article XI of the Treaty no less than one hour prior to the inspection team's departure from an inspection site for another inspection site, the Inspected Party shall inform the Basing Country of the inspection site, described by place name and geographic coordinates, at which the inspection will be carried out.

ARTICLE IV—PRE-INSPECTION ARRANGEMENTS

1. The Inspected Party shall provide the Basing Countries with the initial lists of inspectors and aircrew members, or any modification thereto, proposed by the Inspecting Party immediately upon receipt thereof. Within 15 days of receipt of the initial lists or proposed additions thereto, each Basing Country shall notify the Inspected Party if it objects to the inclusion of any inspector or aircrew member on the basis that such individual had ever committed

a criminal offense on the territory of the Inspected Party or the Basing Country, or been sentenced for committing a criminal offense or expelled by the Inspected Party or the Basing Country. The Inspected Party shall thereupon exercise its right under the Inspection Protocol to prevent the named individual from serving as an inspector or aircrew member.

2. Within 25 days of receipt of the initial lists of inspectors or aircrew members, or of any subsequent change thereto, each Basing Country shall provide such visas and related documentation as may be necessary to ensure that each inspector or aircrew member may enter its territory for the purpose of carrying out inspection activities in accordance with the provisions of the Treaty and the Inspection Protocol. Such visas and documentation shall be valid for a period of at least 24 months. The Inspected Party shall immediately notify the Basing Countries of the removal of any individual from the Inspecting Party's lists of inspectors or aircrew members, and the Basing Countries may thereupon cancel forthwith any visas and related documentation issued to such person pursuant to this paragraph.

3. Within 25 days after entry into force of this Agreement, each Basing Country shall inform the Inspected Party of the standing diplomatic clearance number for the aircraft of the Inspecting Party which will transport inspectors and equipment into its territory. At the same time each Basing Country shall inform the Inspected Party of the established international airways along which aircraft of the Inspecting Party shall enter the airspace of the Basing Country for the purpose of carrying out inspection activities under the Treaty.

4. Each Basing Country shall accord inspectors and aircrew members of the Inspecting Party entering its territory for the purpose of conducting inspection activities pursuant to the Treaty, including the Inspection Protocol, the privileges and immunities set forth in the Privileges and Immunities Annex to this Agreement. In the event the Inspecting Party refuses or fails to carry out its obligation under Section III, paragraph 7 of the Inspection Protocol to remove an inspector or aircrew member who has violated the conditions governing inspections, the inspector or aircrew member may be refused continued recognition as being entitled to such privileges and immunities.

5. Each Basing Country shall issue, at the point of entry, appropriate authorizations waiving customs duties and expediting customs processing requirements in respect of all equipment relating to inspection activities.

6. Each Basing Country shall provide, if requested, facilities at the point of entry for lodging and the provision of food for inspectors and aircrew members.

7. The Basing Country in which the inspection is to take place shall have the right to examine jointly with the Inspected Party each item of equipment brought in by the Inspecting Party to ascertain that the equipment cannot be used to perform functions unconnected with the inspection requirements of the Treaty. If it is established upon examination that a piece of equipment is unconnected with these inspection requirements, it shall not be

cleared for use and shall be impounded at the point of entry until the departure of the inspection team from the country.

ARTICLE V—CONDUCT OF INSPECTIONS

1. Within 90 minutes of receipt from the Inspected Party of notification that a flight plan for an aircraft of the Inspecting Party has been filed in accordance with ICAO procedures applicable to civil aircraft, the Basing Country in whose territory the inspection site is located shall provide the Inspected Party with its approval for the aircraft of the Inspecting Party to proceed to the point of entry via the filed routing, or an amended routing if necessary.

2. The Basing Country in whose territory the inspection site is located shall facilitate the entry of inspectors and aircrew into the country, and shall take the steps necessary to ensure that the baggage and equipment of the inspection team is identified and transported expeditiously through customs.

3. Upon notification by the Inspected Party, in accordance with Article III above, of the inspection site, the Basing Country in whose territory the inspection is to take place shall take the steps necessary to ensure that the inspection team is granted all clearances and assistance necessary to enable it to proceed expeditiously to the inspection site and to arrive at the inspection site within nine hours of the Inspecting Party's notification of the site to be inspected. The Inspected Party and the Basing Country in which the inspection site is located shall consult with respect to the mode of transport to be utilized, and the Basing Country shall have the right to designate the routing between the point of entry and the inspection site.

4. Each Basing Country shall assist the inspected Party, as necessary, in providing two-way voice communication capability for an inspector team between an inspection site within its territory and the embassy of the Inspecting Party.

5. The Inspected Party and the Basing Country within whose territory an inspection site is located shall consult with respect to aircraft servicing and the provision of meals, lodging, and services for inspectors and aircrew members at the point of entry and inspection site. The cost of the foregoing requested by the Inspected Party and provided by the Basing Country shall be borne by the Inspected Party.

6. In the event the Inspecting Party requests an extension, which shall not exceed eight hours beyond the original 24-hour period of inspection as provided for in Section VI, paragraph 14 of the Inspection Protocol, the Inspected Party shall immediately notify the Basing Country in whose territory the inspection site is located of the extension.

ARTICLE VI—CONSULTATIONS

1. Within five days after entry into force of this Agreement, the Inspected Party and the Basing Countries shall meet to coordinate implementation of the inspection activities provided for by Article XI of the Treaty, the Inspection Protocol and this Agreement.

2. A meeting between the Inspected Party and any Basing Country do discuss implementation of this Agreement shall be held

within five days of a request for such a meeting by the Inspected Party of a Basing Country.

3. Should any question arise which in the opinion of a Basing Country requires immediate attention, the Basing Country may contact the inspection notification authority of the Inspected Party. The Inspected Party will immediately acknowledge receipt of the inquiry or question and give urgent attention to the question or problem.

4. In the event that a Basing Country determines that an inspector or aircrew member has violated the conditions governing inspection within its territory, the Basing Country may notify the Inspected Party which shall inform the Inspecting Party of the disqualification of the inspector or aircrew member. The name of the individual will be removed from the list of inspectors or aircrew members.

5. A Basing Country may change the point of entry for its territory by giving six months' notice of such change to the Inspected Party.

6. Upon completion of an inspection, the Inspected Party shall advise the Basing Country within whose territory the inspection took place that the inspection has been completed, and upon request of the Basing Country provide a briefing for the Basing Country on the inspection.

7. The United States of America shall not, without the express agreement of the Basing Countries, propose or accept any amendment to Article XI of the Treaty or to the Inspection Protocol that directly affects the rights, interests or obligations of the Basing Countries.

ARTICLE VII—ENTRY INTO FORCE AND DURATION

This Agreement shall be subject to approval in accordance with the constitutional procedures of each Party, which approval shall be notified by each Party to each of the other Parties. Following such notification by all Parties, the Agreement shall enter into force simultaneously with the entry into force of the Treaty and shall remain in force for a period of thirteen years.

DONE at Brussels, on the eleventh of December, 1987, in a single original which shall be deposited in the archives of the Government of the United States of America, which shall transmit a duly certified copy thereof to each of the other signatory Governments.

IN WITNESS WHEREOF, the undersigned, being duly authorized, have signed this Agreement.

For the Government of the Kingdom of Belgium:

For the Government of the Federal Republic of Germany:

For the Government of the Kingdom of the Netherlands:

For the Government of the United Kingdom of Great Britain and Northern Ireland:

For the Government of the United States of America:

Annex—Provisions on Privileges and Immunities of Inspectors and Aircrew Members

In order to exercise their functions effectively, for the purpose of implementing the Treaty and not for their personal benefit, inspectors and aircrew members shall be accorded the privileges and immunities contained herein. Privileges and immunities shall be accorded for the entire in-country period in the country in which an inspection site is located, and thereafter with respect to acts previously performed in the exercise of official functions as an inspector or aircrew member.

1. Inspectors and aircrew members shall be accorded the inviolability enjoyed by diplomatic agents pursuant to Article 29 of the Vienna Convention on Diplomatic Relations of April 18, 1961.

2. The papers and correspondence of inspectors and aircrew members shall enjoy the inviolability accorded to the papers and correspondence of diplomatic agents pursuant to Article 30 of the Vienna Convention on Diplomatic Relations. In addition, the aircraft of the inspection team shall be inviolable.

3. Inspectors and aircrew members shall be accorded the immunities accorded diplomatic agents pursuant to paragraphs (1), (2) and (3) of Article 31 of the Vienna Convention on Diplomatic Relations. The immunity from jurisdiction of an inspector or an aircrew member may be waived by the Inspecting Party in those cases when it is of the opinion that immunity would impede the course of justice and that it can be waived without prejudice to the implementation of the provisions of the Treaty. Waiver must always be express.

4. Inspectors and aircrew members of the Inspecting Party shall be permitted to bring into the territory of a Basing Country in which an inspection site is located, without payment of any customs duties or related changes, articles for their personal use, with the exception of articles the import or export of which is prohibited by law or controlled by quarantine regulations.

5. An inspector or aircrew member shall not engage in any professional or commercial activity for personal profit on the territory of the Basing Countries.

NOTE OF THE EMBASSY OF THE UNITED STATES OF AMERICA TO THE GERMAN DEMOCRATIC REPUBLIC TO THE MINISTRY OF FOREIGN AFFAIRS OF THE GERMAN DEMOCRATIC REPUBLIC

The Embassy of the United States of America presents its compliments to the Ministry of Foreign Affairs of the German Democratic Republic and has the honor to acknowledge receipt of the Ministry's note of December 23, 1987, as follows:

"The Ministry of Foreign Affairs of the German Democratic Republic presents its compliments to the Embassy of the United States of America and has the honor to state the following.

The Government of the German Democratic Republic has been informed by the Government of the Union of Soviet Socialist Republics of the arrangements agreed by the United States of America and the Union of Soviet Socialist Republics for the verification of their mutual obligations provided for in Article XI of the Treaty between the United States of America and the Union of Soviet Socialist Republics on the elimination of their intermediate-range and shorter-range missiles and in the Protocol on Inspection thereto.

As a strong supporter of balanced and verifiable measures of arms control and disarmament, the Government of the German Democratic Republic wholeheartedly endorses the said Treaty and Protocol on Inspection and has agreed to the application on its territory of inspections in accordance with that Treaty and the Protocol thereto.

The Ministry has the honor to inform you, therefore, that the Government of the German Democratic Republic is willing to accord to the Government of the United States of America and its inspectors and aircrew members the inspection rights provided for in the Protocol on Inspection upon receipt of an undertaking that the Government of the United States of America and its officials will, in relation to all activities to be carried out thereunder on the territory of the German Democratic Republic and in its airspace, strictly comply with the terms of that Protocol. It is understood in this connection that nothing therein affects, except as specifically provided, the enforcement of the laws and regulations of the German Democratic Republic.

The Ministry has the honor further to propose that the present note and the Embassy's note of reply to that effect shall be regarded as constituting an Agreement between the Governments of the German Democratic Republic and the United States of America. This Agreement shall enter into force simultaneously with the entry into force of the Treaty and shall remain in force until thirteen years following the date of entry into force of the Treaty.

The present Agreement shall not, however, in any way affect the exclusive obligations of the United States of America and the Union of Soviet Socialist Republics undertaken with regard to each other under the Treaty and the Protocol on Inspection.

The Ministry takes this opportunity to reassure the Embassy of its highest consideration."

In reply, the Embassy, on behalf of the Government of the United States of America, takes note of the willingness of the Government of the German Democratic Republic to facilitate the application to its territory of the inspections provided for in the Treaty and the Protocol on Inspection thereto.

The Embassy has the honor further, in consideration thereof, to inform the Ministry that the Government of the United States of America gives the Government of the German Democratic Republic the formal undertaking requested in the aforesaid note and has agreed that the note of the Ministry of December 23, 1987, and the present note of the Embassy be regarded as constituting an Agreement between the Government of the United States of America and the Government of the German Democratic Republic regarding inspection on the territory of the German Democratic Republic provided for by the Treaty between the United States of America and the Union of Soviet Socialist Republics on the elimination of their intermediate-range and shorter-range missiles and conducted in accordance with the Protocol on Inspection thereto. This Agreement shall enter into force simultaneously with the entry into force of the Treaty and shall remain in force until thirteen years following the date of entry into force of the Treaty.

The present Agreement shall not, however, in any way affect the exclusive obligations of the United States of America and the Union of Soviet Socialist Republics undertaken with regard to each other under the Treaty and the Protocol on Inspection.

The Embassy takes this opportunity to reassure the Ministry of its highest consideration.

EMBASSY OF THE UNITED STATES OF AMERICA, *Berlin, December 23, 1987.*

TEXT OF NOTE FROM THE EMBASSY OF THE UNITED STATES OF AMERICA TO THE FEDERAL MINISTRY OF FOREIGN AFFAIRS OF THE CZECHOSLOVAK SOCIALIST REPUBLIC

The Embassy of the United States of America presents its compliments to the Federal Ministry of Foreign Affairs of the Czechoslovak Socialist Republic and has the honor to acknowledge receipt of the ministry's note of December 18, 1987, as follows:

"The Federal Ministry of Foreign Affairs of the Czechoslovak Socialist Republic presents its compliments to the Embassy of the United States of America and has the honor to state the following.

"The Governments of the Czechoslovak Socialist Republic has been informed by the Government of the Union of Soviet Socialist Republics of the arrangements agreed by the United States of America and the Union of Soviet Socialist Republics for the verification of their mutual obligations provided for in Article XI of the Treaty between the United States of America and the Union of Soviet Socialist Republics on the Elimination of Their Intermediate-Range and Shorter-Range Missiles and in the Protocol on Inspection thereto.

"As a strong supporter of balanced and verifiable measures of arms control and disarmament, the Government of the Czechoslovak Socialist Republic wholeheartedly endorses the said Treaty and Protocol on Inspection and has agreed to the application on its territory of inspections in accordance with that Treaty and the Protocol thereto.

"The Ministry has the honor to inform you, therefore, that the Government of the Czechoslovak Socialist Republic is willing to accord to the Government of the United States of America and its inspectors and aircrew members the inspection rights provided for in the Protocol on Inspection upon receipt of an undertaking that the United States of America and its officials will, in relation to all activities to be carried out thereunder on the territory of the Czechoslovak Socialist Republic and in its airspace, strictly comply with the terms of that Protocol. It is understood in this connection that nothing therein affects, expect as specifically provided, the enforcement of the laws and regulations of the Czechoslovak Socialist Republic within its territory.

"The Ministry has the honor further to propose that the present note and the Embassy's note of reply to that effect shall be regarded as constituting an agreement between the Governments of the Czechoslovak Socialist Republic and of the United States of

America. This Agreement shall enter into force simultaneously with the entry into force of the Treaty and shall remain in force until thirteen years following the date of entry into force of the Treaty.

"The present agreement shall not, however, in any way affect the exclusive obligations of the United States of America and the Union of Soviet Socialist Republics undertaken with regard to each other under the Treaty and the Protocol on Inspection.

"The Ministry takes this opportunity to reassure the Embassy of its highest consideration."

In reply, the Embassy, on behalf of the Government of the United States of America takes note of the willingness of the Government of the Czechoslovak Socialist Republic to facilitate the application to its territory of the inspections provided for in the Treaty and the Protocol on Inspection thereto.

The Embassy has the honor further, in consideration thereof, to inform the Ministry that the Government of the United States of America gives the Government of the Czechoslovak Socialist Republic the formal undertaking requested in the aforesaid note and has agreed that the note of the Ministry of December 18, 1987, and the present note of the Embassy be regarded as constituting an agreement between the Government of the United States of America and the Government of the Czechoslovak Socialist Republic regarding inspections on the territory of the Czechoslovak Socialist Republic provided for by the Treaty between the United States of America and the Union of Soviet Socialist Republics on the Elimination of Their Intermediate-Range and Shorter-Range Missiles and conducted in accordance with the Protocol on Inspection thereto. This Agreement shall enter into force simultaneously with the entry into force of the Treaty and shall remain in force until thirteen years following the date of entry into force of the Treaty.

The present agreement shall not, however, in any way affect the exclusive obligations of the United States of America and the Union of Socialist Republics undertaken with regard to each other under the Treaty and the Protocol on Inspection.

The Embassy takes this opportunity to reassure the Ministry of its highest consideration.

EMBASSY OF THE UNITED STATES OF AMERICA, *Prague, January 4, 1988.*

5. Seabed Arms Control Treaty[1]

Treaty on the Prohibition of the Emplacement of Nuclear Weapons and Other Weapons of Mass Destruction on the Seabed and the Ocean Floor and in the Subsoil Thereof; Done at Washington, London and Moscow, February 11, 1971; Ratification advised by the Senate, February 15, 1972; Ratified by the President, April 26, 1972; Ratification of the United States deposited at Washington, London and Moscow, May 18, 1972; Entered into force, May 18, 1972

The States Parties to this Treaty,

RECOGNIZING the common interest of mankind in the progress of the exploration and use of the seabed and the ocean floor for peaceful purposes,

CONSIDERING that the prevention of a nuclear arms race on the seabed and the ocean floor serves the interests of maintaining world peace, reduces international tensions and strengthens friendly relations among States,

CONVINCED that this Treaty constitutes a step towards the exclusion of the seabed, the ocean floor and the subsoil thereof from the arms race,

CONVINCED that this Treaty constitutes a step towards a treaty on general and complete disarmament under strict and effective international control, and determined to continue negotiations to this end,

CONVINCED that this Treaty will further the purposes and principles of the Charter of the United Nations, in a manner consistent with the principles of international law and without infringing the freedoms of the high seas,

HAVE AGREED AS FOLLOWS:

ARTICLE I

1. The States Parties to this Treaty undertake not to emplant or emplace on the seabed and the ocean floor and in the subsoil thereof beyond the outer limit of a seabed zone, as defined in article II, any nuclear weapons or any other types of weapons of mass destruction as well as structures, launching installations or any other facilities specifically designed for storing, testing or using such weapons.

2. The undertakings of paragraph 1 of this article shall also apply to the seabed zone referred to in the same paragraph, except that within such seabed zone, they shall not apply either to the coastal State or to the seabed beneath its territorial waters.

3. The States Parties to this Treaty undertake not to assist, encourage or induce any State to carry out activities referred to in

[1] 23 UST 701; TIAS 7337; 955 UNTS 115. For a list of states which are parties to the Treaty, see Department of State publication, *Treaties in Force.*

paragraph 1 of this article and not to participate in any other way in such actions.

Article II

For the purpose of this Treaty, the outer limit of the seabed zone referred to in article I shall be coterminous with the twelve-mile outer limit of the zone referred to in part II of the Convention on the Territorial Sea and the Contiguous Zone, signed at Geneva on April 29, 1958, and shall be measured in accordance with the provisions of part I, section II, of that Convention and in accordance with international law.

Article III

1. In order to promote the objectives of and insure compliance with the provisions of this Treaty, each State Party to the Treaty shall have the right to verify through observation the activities of other States Parties to the Treaty on the seabed and the ocean floor and in the subsoil thereof beyond the zone referred to in article I, provided that observation does not interfere with such activities.

2. If after such observation reasonable doubts remain concerning the fulfillment of the obligations assumed under the Treaty, the State Party having such doubts and the State Party that is responsible for the activities giving rise to the doubts shall consult with a view to removing the doubts. If the doubts persist, the State Party having such doubts shall notify the other States Parties, and the Parties concerned shall cooperate on such further procedures for verification as may be agreed, including appropriate inspection of objects, structures, installations or other facilities that reasonably may be expected to be of a kind described in article I. The Parties in the region of the activities, including any coastal State, and any other Party so requesting, shall be entitled to participate in such consultation and cooperation. After completion of the further procedures for verification, an appropriate report shall be circulated to other Parties by the Party that initiated such procedures.

3. If the State responsible for the activities giving rise to the reasonable doubts is not identifiable by observation of the object, structure, installation or other facility, the State Party having such doubts shall notify and make appropriate inquires of States Parties in the region of the activities and of any other State Party. If it is ascertained through these inquiries that a particular State Party is responsible for the activities, that State Party shall consult and cooperate with other Parties as provided in paragraph 2 of this article. If the identity of the State responsible for the activities cannot be ascertained through these inquiries, then further verification procedures, including inspection, may be undertaken by the inquiring State Party, which shall invite the participation of the Parties in the region of the activities, including any coastal State, and of any other Party desiring to cooperate.

4. If consultation and cooperation pursuant to paragraphs 2 and 3 of this article have not removed the doubts concerning the activities and there remains a serious question concerning fulfillment of

the obligations assumed under this Treaty, a State Party may, in accordance with the provisions of the Charter of the United Nations, refer the matter to the Security Council, which may take action in accordance with the Charter.

5. Verification pursuant to this article may be undertaken by any State Party using its own means, or with the full or partial assistance of any other State Party, or through appropriate international procedures within the framework of the United Nations and in accordance with its Charter.

6. Verification activities pursuant to this Treaty shall not interfere with activities of other State Parties and shall be conducted with due regard for rights recognized under international law, including the freedoms of the high seas and the rights of coastal States with respect to the exploration and exploitation of their continental shelves.

Article IV

Nothing in this Treaty shall be interpreted as supporting or prejudicing the position of any State Party with respect to existing international conventions, including the 1958 Convention on the Territorial Sea and the Contiguous Zone, or with respect to rights or claims which such State Party may assert, or with respect to recognition or nonrecognition of rights or claims asserted by any other State, related to waters off its coasts, including, *inter alia*, territorial seas and contiguous zones, or to the seabed and the ocean floor, including continental shelves.

Article V

The Parties to this Treaty undertake to continue negotiations in good faith concerning further measures in the field of disarmament for the prevention of an arms race on the seabed, the ocean floor and the subsoil thereof.

Article VI

Any State Party may propose amendments to this Treaty. Amendments shall enter into force for each State Party accepting the amendments upon their acceptance by a majority of the States Parties to the Treaty and, thereafter, for each remaining State Party on the date of acceptance by it.

Article VII

Five years after the entry into force of this Treaty, a conference of Parties to the Treaty shall be held at Geneva, Switzerland, in order to review the operation of this Treaty with a view to assuring that the purposes of the preamble and the provisions of the Treaty are being realized. Such review shall take into account any relevant technological developments. The review conference shall determine, in accordance with the views of a majority of those Parties attending, whether and when an additional review conference shall be convened.

Article VIII

Each State Party to this Treaty shall in exercising its national sovereignty have the right to withdraw from this Treaty if it decides that extraordinary events related to the subject matter of this Treaty have jeopardized the supreme interests of its country. It shall give notice to such withdrawal to all other States Parties to the Treaty and to the United Nations Security Council three months in advance. Such notice shall include a statement of the extraordinary events it considers to have jeopardized its supreme interests.

Article IX

The provisions of this Treaty shall in no way affect the obligations assumed by States Parties to the Treaty under international instruments establishing zones free from nuclear weapons.

Article X

1. This Treaty shall be open for signature to all States. Any State which does not sign the Treaty before its entry into force in accordance with paragraph 3 of this article may accede to it at any time.

2. This Treaty shall be subject to ratification by signatory States. Instruments of ratification and of accession shall be deposited with the Governments of the United States of America, the United Kingdom of Great Britain and Northern Ireland, and the Union of Soviet Socialist Republics, which are hereby designated the Depository Governments.

3. This Treaty shall enter into force after the deposit of instruments of ratification by twenty-two Governments, including the Governments designated as Depositary Governments of this Treaty.

4. For States whose instruments of ratification or accession are deposited after the entry into force of this Treaty, it shall enter into force on the date of the deposit of their instruments of ratification or accession.

5. The Depositary Governments shall promptly inform the Governments of all signatory and acceding States of the date of each signature, of the date of deposit of each instrument of ratification or of accession, of the date of the entry into force of this Treaty, and of the receipt of other notices.

6. This Treaty shall be registered by the Depositary Governments pursuant to Article 102 of the Charter of the United Nations.

Article XI

This Treaty, the English, Russian, French, Spanish and Chinese texts of which are equally authentic, shall be deposited in the archives of the Depositary Governments. Duly certified copies of this Treaty shall be transmitted by the Depositary Governments to the Governments of the States signatory and acceding thereto.

In witness whereof the undersigned, being duly authorized thereto, have signed this Treaty.

DONE in triplicate, at the cities of Washington, London and Moscow, this eleventh day of February, one thousand nine hundred seventy-one.

6. Convention on the Prohibition of Military or Any Other Hostile Use of Environmental Modification Techniques [1]

Convention done at Geneva, May 18, 1977; Ratification advised by the Senate, November 28, 1979; Ratified by the President, December 13, 1979; Ratification of the United States deposited with the Secretary-General of the United Nations, January 17, 1980; Entered into force with respect to the United States, January 17, 1980; Proclaimed by the President, February 12, 1980

The States Parties to this Convention,

GUIDED by the interest of consolidating peace, and wishing to contribute to the cause of halting the arms race, and of bringing about general and complete disarmament under strict and effective international control, and of saying mankind from the danger of using new means of warfare,

DETERMINED to continue negotiations with a view to achieving effective progress towards further measures in the field of disarmament,

RECOGNIZING that scientific and technical advances may open new possibilities with respect to modification of the environment,

RECALLING the Declaration of the United Nations Conference on the Human Environment, adopted at Stockholm on 16 June 1972,

REALIZING that the use of environmental modification techniques for peaceful purposes could improve the interrelationship of man and nature and contribute to the preservation and improvement of the environment for the benefit of present and future generations,

RECOGNIZING, however, that military or any other hostile use of such techniques could have effects extremely harmful to human welfare,

DESIRING to prohibit effectively military or any other hostile use of environmental modification techniques in order to eliminate the dangers to mankind from such use, and affirming their willingness to work towards the achievement of this objective,

DESIRING also to contribute to the strengthening of trust among nations and to the further improvement of the international situation in accordance with the purposes and principles of the Charter of the United Nations,[2]

HAVE AGREED AS FOLLOWS:

Article I

1. Each State Party to this Convention undertakes not to engage in military or any other hostile use of environmental modification

[1] 31 UST 333; TIAS 9614. For a list of states that are parties to the Treaty, see Department of State publication, *Treaties in Force*.
[2] TS 993; 59 Stat. 1031.

techniques having widespread, long-lasting or severe effects as the means of destruction, damage or injury to any other State Party.

2. Each State Party to this Convention undertakes not to assist, encourage or induce any State, group of States or international organization to engage in activities contrary to the provisions of paragraph 1 of this article.

Article II

As used in article I, the term "environmental modification techniques" refers to any technique for changing—through the deliberate manipulation of natural processes—the dynamics, composition or structure of the Earth, including its biota, lithosphere, hydrosphere and atmosphere, or of outer space.

Article III

1. The provisions of this Convention shall not hinder the use of environmental modification techniques for peaceful purposes and shall be without prejudice to the generally recognized principles and applicable rules of international law concerning such use.

2. The States Parties to this Convention undertake to facilitate, and have the right to participate in, the fullest possible exchange of scientific and technological information on the use of environmental modification techniques for peaceful purposes. States Parties in a position to do so shall contribute, alone or together with other States or international organizations, to international economic and scientific co-operation in the preservation, improvement and peaceful utilization of the environment, with due consideration for the needs of the developing areas of the world.

Article IV

Each State Party to this Convention undertakes to take any measures it considers necessary in accordance with its constitutional processes to prohibit and prevent any activity in violation of the provisions of the Convention anywhere under its jurisdiction or control.

Article V

1. The States Parties to this Convention undertake to consult one another and to co-operate in solving any problems which may arise in relation to the objectives of, or in the application of the provisions of, the Convention. Consultation and co-operation pursuant to this article may also be undertaken through appropriate international procedures within the framework of the United Nations and in accordance with its Charter. These international procedures may include the services of appropriate international organizations, as well as of a Consultative Committee of Experts as provided for in paragraph 2 of this article.

2. For the purposes set forth in paragraph 1 of this article, the Depositary shall, within one month of the receipt of a request from any State Party to this Convention, convene a Consultative Committee of Experts. Any State Party may appoint an expert to the Committee whose functions and rules of procedure are set out in

the annex, which constitutes an integral part of this Convention. The Committee shall transmit to the Depositary a summary of its findings of fact, incorporating all views and information presented to the Committee during its proceedings. The Depositary shall distribute the summary to all States Parties.

3. Any State Party to this Convention which has reason to believe that any other State Party is acting in breach of obligations deriving from the provisions of the Convention may lodge a complaint with the Security Council of the United Nations. Such a complaint should include all relevant information as well as all possible evidence supporting its validity.

4. Each State Party to this Convention undertakes to co-operate in carrying out any investigation which the Security Council may initiate, in accordance with the provisions of the Charter of the United Nations, on the basis of the complaint received by the Council. The Security Council shall inform the States Parties of the results of the investigation.

5. Each State Party to this Convention undertakes to provide or support assistance, in accordance with the provisions of the Charter of the United Nations, to any State Party which so requests, if the Security Council decides that such Party has been harmed or is likely to be harmed as a result of violation of the Convention.

Article VI

1. Any State Party to this Convention may propose amendments to the Convention. The text of any proposed amendment shall be submitted to the Depositary, who shall promptly circulate it to all States Parties.

2. An amendment shall enter into force for all States Parties to this Convention which have accepted it, upon the deposit with the Depositary of instruments of acceptance by a majority of States Parties. Thereafter it shall enter into force for any remaining State Party on the date of deposit of its instrument of acceptance.

Article VII

This Convention shall be of unlimited duration.

Article VIII

1. Five years after the entry into force of this Convention, a conference of the States Parties to the Convention shall be convened by the Depositary at Geneva, Switzerland. The conference shall review the operation of the Convention with a view to ensuring that its purposes and provisions are being realized, and shall in particular examine the effectiveness of the provisions of paragraph 1 of article I in eliminating the dangers of military or any other hostile use of environmental modification techniques.

2. At intervals of not less than five years thereafter, a majority of the States Parties to this Convention may obtain, by submitting a proposal to this effect to the Depositary, the convening of a conference with the same objectives.

3. If no conference has been convened pursuant to paragraph 2 of this article within ten years following the conclusion of a previous conference, the Depositary shall solicit the views of all States

Parties to this Convention concerning the convening of such a conference. If one third or ten of the States Parties, whichever number is less, respond affirmatively, the Depositary shall take immediate steps to convene the conference.

Article IX

1. This Convention shall be open to all States for signature. Any State which does not sign the Convention before its entry into force in accordance with paragraph 3 of this article may accede to it at any time.
2. This Convention shall be subject to ratification by signatory States. Instruments of ratification or accession shall be deposited with the Secretary-General of the United Nations.
3. This Convention shall enter into force upon the deposit of instruments of ratification by twenty Governments in accordance with paragraph 2 of this article.
4. For those States whose instruments of ratification or accession are deposited after the entry into force of this Convention, it shall enter into force on the date of the deposit of their instruments of ratification or accession.
5. The Depositary shall promptly inform all signatory and acceding States of the date of each signature, the date of deposit of each instrument of ratification or accession and the date of the entry into force of this Convention and of any amendments thereto, as well as of the receipt of other notices.
6. This Convention shall be registered by the Depositary in accordance with Article 102 of the Charter of the United Nations.

Article X

This Convention, of which the English, Arabic, Chinese, French, Russian and Spanish texts are equally authentic, shall be deposited with the Secretary-General of the United Nations, who shall send duly certified copies thereof to the Governments of the signatory and acceding States.

IN WITNESS WHEREOF, the undersigned, being duly authorized thereto by their respective Governments, have signed this Convention, opened for signature at Geneva on the eighteenth day of May, one thousand nine hundred and seventy-seven.

Annex to the Convention

Consultative Committee of Experts

1. The Consultative Committee of Experts shall undertake to make appropriate findings of fact and provide expert views relevant to any problem raised pursuant to paragraph 1 of article V of this Convention by the State Party requesting the convening of the Committee.
2. The work of the Consultative Committee of Experts shall be organized in such a way as to permit it to perform the functions set forth in paragraph 1 of this annex. The Committee shall decide procedural questions relative to the organization of its work, where possible by consensus, but otherwise by a majority of those present and voting. There shall be no voting on matters of substance.

3. The Depositary or his representative shall serve as the Chairman of the Committee.

4. Each expert may be assisted at meetings by one or more advisers.

5. Each expert shall have the right, through the Chairman, to request from States, and from international organizations, such information and assistance as the expert considers desirable for the accomplishment of the Committee's work.

7. Treaty on the Non-Proliferation of Nuclear Weapons [1]

Done at Washington, London, and Moscow, July 1, 1968; Ratification advised by the Senate, March 13, 1969; Ratified by the President, November 24, 1969; Ratification of the United States deposited at Washington, London, and Moscow, March 5, 1970; Proclaimed by the President, March 5, 1970; Entered into force, March 5, 1970

The States concluding this Treaty, hereinafter referred to as the "Parties to the Treaty",

CONSIDERING the devastation that would be visited upon all mankind by a nuclear war and the consequent need to make every effort to avert the danger of such a war and to take measures to safeguard the security of peoples,

BELIEVING that the proliferation of nuclear weapons would seriously enhance the danger of nuclear war,

THE CONFORMITY with resolutions of the United Nations General Assembly calling for the conclusion of an agreement on the prevention of wider dissemination of nuclear weapons,

UNDERTAKING to cooperate in facilitating the application of International Atomic Energy Agency safeguards on peaceful nuclear activities,

EXPRESSING their support for research, development and other efforts to further the application, within the framework of the International Atomic Energy Agency safeguards system, of the principle of safeguarding effectively the flow of source and special fissionable materials by use of instruments and other techniques at certain strategic points.

AFFIRMING the principle that the benefits of peaceful applications of nuclear technology, including any technological by-products which may be derived by nuclear-weapon States from the development of nuclear explosive devices, should be available for peaceful purposes to all Parties to the Treaty, whether nuclear-weapon or non-nuclear-weapon States,

CONVINCED that, in furtherance of this principle, all Parties to the Treaty are entitled to participate in the fullest possible exchange of scientific information for, and to contribute alone or in cooperation with other States to, the further development of the applications of atomic energy for peaceful purposes,

DECLARING their intention to achieve at the earliest possible date the cessation of the nuclear arms race and to undertake effective measures in the direction of nuclear disarmament,

URGING the cooperation of all States in the attainment of their objective,

[1] 21 UST 483; TIAS 6839; 729 UNTS 161. For a list of states which are parties to the Treaty, see Department of State publication, *Treaties in Force*.

RECALLING the determination expressed by the Parties to the 1963 Treaty Banning Nuclear Weapon Tests in the Atmosphere in Outer Space and Under Water in its Preamble to seek to achieve the discontinuance of all test explosions of nuclear weapons for all time and to continue negotiations to this end,

DESIRING to further the easing of international tension and the strengthening of trust between States in order to facilitate the cessation of the manufacture of nuclear weapons, the liquidation of all their existing stockpiles, and the elimination from national arsenals of nuclear weapons and the means of their delivery pursuant to a treaty on general and complete disarmament under strict and effective international control,

RECALLING that, in accordance with the Charter of the United Nations, States must refrain in their international relations from the threat or use of force against the territorial integrity or political independence of any State, or in any other manner inconsistent with the Purposes of the United Nations, and that the establishment and maintenance of international peace and security are to be promoted with the least diversion for armaments of the world's human and economic resources,

HAVE AGREED AS FOLLOWS:

ARTICLE I

Each nuclear-weapon State Party to the Treaty undertakes not to transfer to any recipient whatsoever nuclear weapons or other nuclear explosive devices or control over such weapons or explosive devices directly, or indirectly; and not in any way to assist, encourage, or induce any non-nuclear-weapon State to manufacture or otherwise acquire nuclear weapons or other nuclear explosive devices, or control over such weapons or explosive devices.

ARTICLE II

Each non-nuclear-weapon State Party to the Treaty undertakes not to receive the transfer from any transferor whatsoever of nuclear weapons or other nuclear explosive devices or of control over such weapons or explosive devices directly, or indirectly; not to manufacture or otherwise acquire nuclear weapons or other nuclear explosive devices; and not to seek or receive any assistance in the manufacture of nuclear weapons or other nuclear explosive devices.

ARTICLE III

1. Each non-nuclear-weapon State Party to the Treaty undertakes to accept safeguards, as set forth in an agreement to be negotiated and concluded with the International Atomic Energy Agency in the cordance with the Statute of the International Atomic Energy Agency[2] and the Agency's safeguards system, for the exclusive purpose of verification of the fulfillment of its obligations assumed under this Treaty with a view to preventing diversion of nuclear energy from peaceful uses to nuclear weapons or other nuclear explosive devices. Procedures for the safeguards required by this article shall be followed with respect to source or special fissionable

[2] TIAS 3873; 8 UST 1093.

material whether it is being produced, processed or used in any principal nuclear facility or is outside any such facility. The safeguards required by this article shall be applied on all source or special fissionable material in all peaceful nuclear activities within the territory of such State, under its jurisdiction, or carried out under its control anywhere.

2. Each State Party to the Treaty undertakes not to provide: (a) source or special fissionable material, or (b) equipment or material especially designed or prepared for the processing, use or production of special fissionable material, to any non-nuclear-weapon State for peaceful purposes, unless the source or special fissionable material shall be subject to the safeguards required by this article.

3. The safeguards required by this article shall be implemented in a manner designed to comply with article IV of this Treaty, and to avoid hampering the economic or technological development of the Parties or international cooperation in the field of peaceful nuclear activities, including the international exchange of nuclear material and equipment for the processing, use or production of nuclear material for peaceful purposes in accordance with the provisions of this article and the principle of safeguarding set forth in the Preamble of the Treaty.

4. Non-nuclear-weapon States Party to the Treaty shall conclude agreements with the International Atomic Energy Agency to meet the requirements of this article either individually or together with other States in accordance with the Statute of the International Atomic Energy Agency. Negotiation of such agreements shall commence within 180 days from the original entry into force of this Treaty. For States depositing their instruments of ratification or accession after the 180-day period, negotiation of such agreements shall commence not later than the date of such deposit. Such agreements shall enter into force not later than eighteen months after the date of initiation of negotiations.

ARTICLE IV

1. Nothing in this Treaty shall be interpreted as affecting the inalienable right of all the Parties to the Treaty to develop research, production and use of nuclear energy for peaceful purposes without discrimination and in conformity with articles I and II of this Treaty.

2. All the Parties to the Treaty undertake to facilitate, and have the right to participate in, the fullest possible exchange of equipment, materials and scientific and technological information for the peaceful uses of nuclear energy. Parties to the Treaty in a position to do so shall also cooperate in contributing alone or together with other States or international organizations to the further development of the applications of nuclear energy for peaceful purposes, especially in the territories of non-nuclear-weapon States Party to the Treaty, with due consideration for the needs of the developing areas of the world.

ARTICLE V

Each Party to the Treaty undertakes to take appropriate measures to ensure that, in accordance with this Treaty, under appropriate international observation and through appropriate international procedures, potential benefits from any peaceful applications of nuclear explosions will be made available to non-nuclear-weapon States Party to the Treaty on a non-discriminatory basis and that the charge to such Parties for the explosive devices used will be as low as possible and exclude any charge for research and development. Non-nuclear-weapon States Party to the Treaty shall be able to obtain such benefits, pursuant to a special international agreement or agreements, through an appropriate international body with adequate representation of non-nuclear-weapon States. Negotiations of this subject shall commence as soon as possible after the Treaty enters into force. Non-nuclear-weapon States Party to the Treaty so desiring may also obtain such benefits pursuant to bilateral agreements.

ARTICLE VI

Each of the Parties to the Treaty undertakes to pursue negotiations in good faith on effective measures relating to cessation of the nuclear arms race at an early date and to nuclear disarmament, and on a treaty on general and complete disarmament under strict and effective international control.

ARTICLE VII

Nothing in this Treaty affects the right of any group of States to conclude regional treaties in order to assure the total absence of nuclear weapons in their respective territories.

ARTICLE VIII

1. Any Party to the Treaty may propose amendments to this Treaty. The text of any proposed amendment shall be submitted to the Depositary Governments which shall circulate it to all Parties to the Treaty. Thereupon, if requested to do so by one-third or more of the Parties to the Treaty, the Depositary Governments shall convene a conference, to which they shall invite all the Parties to the Treaty, to consider such an amendment.

2. Any amendment to this Treaty must be approved by a majority of the votes of all the Parties to the Treaty, including the votes of all nuclear-weapon States Party to the Treaty and all other Parties which, on the date the amendment is circulated, are members of the Board of Governors of the International Atomic Energy Agency. The amendment shall enter into force for each Party that deposits its instrument of ratification of the amendment upon the deposit of such instruments of ratification by a majority of all the Parties, including the instruments of ratification of all nuclear-weapon States Party to the Treaty and all other Parties which, on the date the amendment is circulated, are members of the Board of Governors of the International Atomic Energy Agency. Thereafter, it shall enter into force for any other Party upon the deposit of its instrument of ratification of the amendment.

3. Five years after the entry into force of this Treaty, a conference of Parties to the Treaty shall be held in Geneva, Switzerland, in order to review the operation of this Treaty with a view to assuring that the purposes of the Preamble and the provisions of the Treaty are being realized. At intervals of five years thereafter, a majority of the Parties to the Treaty may obtain, by submitting a proposal to this effect to the Depositary Governments, the convening of further conferences with the same objective of reviewing the operation of the Treaty.

ARTICLE IX

1. This Treaty shall be open to all States for signature. Any State which does not sign the Treaty before its entry into force in accordance with paragraph 3 of this article may accede to it at any time.

2. This Treaty shall be subject to ratification by signatory States. Instruments of ratification and instruments of accession shall be deposited with the Governments of the United States of America, the United Kingdom of Great Britain and Northern Ireland and the Union of Soviet Socialist Republics, which are hereby designated the Depositary Governments.

3. This Treaty shall enter into force after its ratification by the States, the Governments of which are designated Depositaries of the Treaty, and forty other States signatory to this Treaty and the deposit of their instruments of ratification. For the purposes of this Treaty, a nuclear-weapon State is one which has manufactured and exploded a nuclear weapon or other nuclear explosive device prior to January 1, 1967.

4. For States whose instruments of ratification or accession are deposited subsequent to the entry into force of this Treaty, it shall enter into force on the date of the deposit of their instruments of ratification or accession.

5. The Depositary Governments shall promptly inform all signatory and acceding States of the date of each signature, the date of deposit of each instrument of ratification or of accession, the date of the entry into force of this Treaty, and the date of receipt of any requests for convening a conference or other notices.

6. This Treaty shall be registered by the Depositary Governments pursuant to article 102 of the Charter of the United Nations.

ARTICLE X

1. Each Party shall in exercising its national sovereignty have the right to withdraw from the Treaty if it decides that extraordinary events, related to the subject matter of this Treaty, have jeopardized the supreme interests of its country. It shall give notice of such withdrawal to all other Parties to the Treaty and to the United Nations Security Council three months in advance. Such notice shall include a statement of the extraordinary events it regards as having jeopardized its supreme interests.

2. Twenty-five years after the entry into force of the Treaty, a conference shall be convened to decide whether the Treaty shall continue in force indefinitely, or shall be extended for an additional fixed period or periods. This decision shall be taken by a majority of the Parties of the Treaty.

ARTICLE XI

This Treaty, the English, Russian, French, Spanish and Chinese texts of which are equally authentic, shall be deposited in the archives of the Depositary Governments. Duly certified copies of this Treaty shall be transmitted by the Depositary Governments to the Government of the signatory and acceding States.

IN WITNESS WHEREOF the undersigned, duly authorized, have signed this Treaty.

DONE in triplicate, at the cities of Washington, London, and Moscow, the first day of July one thousand nine hundred sixty-eight.

8. Chemical and Biological Warfare

a. Geneva Protocol of 1925 (with reservation)

Protocol for the Prohibition of the Use in War of Asphyxiating, Poisonous or Other Gases, and of Bacteriological Methods of Warfare; Done at Geneva, June 17, 1925; Ratification advised by the Senate, December 16, 1974; Ratification deposited, April 10, 1975 [1]

The undersigned plenipotentiaries, in the name of their respective Governments:

Whereas the use in war of asphyxiating, poisonous or other gases, and of all analogous liquids, materials or devices, has been justly condemned by the general opinion of the civilised world; and

Whereas the prohibition of such use has been declared in Treaties to which the majority of Powers of the world are Parties; and

To the end that this prohibition shall be universally accepted as a part of International Law, binding alike the conscience and the practice of nations;

Declare:

> That the High Contracting Parties, so far as they are not already Parties to Treaties prohibiting such use, accept this prohibition, agree to extend this prohibition to the use of bacteriological methods of warfare and agree to be bound as between themselves according to the terms of this declaration.

The High Contracting Parties will exert every effort to induce other States to accede to the present Protocol. Such accession will be notified to the Government of the French Republic, and by the latter to all signatory and acceding Powers, and will take effect on the date of the notification by the Government of the French Republic.

The present Protocol, of which the French and English texts are both authentic, shall be ratified as soon as possible. It shall bear today's date.

The ratifications of the present Protocol shall be addressed to the Government of the French Republic, which will at once notify the deposit of such ratification to each of the signatory and acceding Powers.

The instruments of ratification of and accession to the present Protocol will remain deposited in the archives of the Government of the French Republic.

The present Protocol will come into force for each signatory Power as from the date of deposit of its ratification, and, from that moment, each Power will be bound as regards other Powers which have already deposited their ratifications.

---

[1] 26 UST 571; TIAS 8061; LNTS 65. For a list of states which are parties to the Protocol, see Department of State publication, *Treaties in Force*. See also Executive Order 11850 (Volume II–A of *Legislation on Foreign Relations*), which discusses U.S. policy on the uses of chemical herbicides and riot control agents.

IN WITNESS WHEREOF the Plenipotentiaries have signed the present Protocol.

DONE at Geneva in a single copy, this seventeenth day of June, One Thousand Nine Hundred and Twenty-Five.

Ratification of Geneva Protocol of 1925, with Reservation

Resolved, (two-thirds of the Senators present concurring therein), That the Senate advise and consent to the ratification of The Protocol for the Prohibition of the Use in War of Asphyxiating, Poisonous, or other Gases, and of Bacteriological Methods of Warfare, signed at Geneva on June 17, 1925 (Ex. J, 91–2) subject to the following reservation:

That the said Protocol shall cease to be binding on the Government of the United States with respect to the use in war of asphyxiating, poisonous or other gases, and of all analogous liquids, materials, or devices, in regard to an enemy State if such State or any of its allies fails to respect the prohibitions laid down in the Protocol.

b. Biological Weapons Convention

Convention on the Prohibition of the Development, Production and Stockpiling of Bacteriological (Biological) and Toxin Weapons and on Their Destruction; Done at Washington, London, and Moscow, April 10, 1972; Ratification advised by the Senate, December 16, 1974; Ratification deposited, March 26, 1975; Proclaimed by the President, March 26, 1975; Entered into force, March 26, 1975[1]

The States Parties to this Convention,

DETERMINED to act with a view to achieving effective progress towards general and complete disarmament, including the prohibition and elimination of all types of weapons of mass destruction, and convinced that the prohibition of the development, production and stockpiling of chemical and bacteriological (biological) weapons and their elimination, through effective measures, will facilitate the achievement of general and complete disarmament under strict and effective international control,

RECOGNIZING the important significance of the Protocol for the Prohibition of the Use of War of Asphyxiating, Poisonous or Other Gases, and of Bacteriological Methods of Warfare, signed at Geneva on June 17, 1925, and conscious also of the contribution which the said Protocol has already made, and continues to make, to mitigating the horrors of war,

REAFFIRMING their adherence to the principles and objectives of that Protocol and calling upon all States to comply strictly with them,

RECALLING that the General Assembly of the United Nations has repeatedly condemned all actions contrary to the principles and objectives of the Geneva Protocol of June 17, 1925,

DESIRING to contribute to the strengthening of confidence between peoples and the general improvement of the international atmosphere,

DESIRING also to contribute to the realization of the purposes and principles of the Charter of the United Nations,

CONVINCED of the importance and urgency of eliminating from the arsenals of States, through effective measures, such dangerous weapons of mass destruction as those using chemical or bacteriological (biological) agents,

RECOGNIZING that an agreement on the prohibition of bacteriological (biological) and toxin weapons represents a first possible step towards the achievement of agreement on effective measures

---

[1] 26 UST 583; TIAS 8062; 1015 UNTS 163. For a list of states which are parties to the Convention, see Department of State publication, *Treaties in Force*. See also Executive Order 11850 (Volume II–A of *Legislation on Foreign Relations*), which discusses U.S. policy on the uses of chemical herbicides and riot control agents.

also for the prohibition of the development, production and stockpiling of chemical weapons, and determined to continue negotiations to that end,

DETERMINED, for the sake of all mankind, to exclude completely the possibility of bacteriological (biological) agents and toxins being used as weapons,

CONVINCED that such use would be repugnant to the conscience of mankind and that no effort should be spared to minimize this risk,

HAVE AGREED AS FOLLOWS:

ARTICLE I

Each State Party to this Convention undertakes never in any circumstances to develop, produce, stockpile or otherwise acquire or retain:

(1) Microbial or other biological agents, or toxins whatever their origin or method of production, of types and in quantities that have no justification for prophylactic, protective or other peaceful purposes;

(2) Weapons, equipment or means of delivery designed to use such agents or toxins for hostile purposes or in armed conflict.

ARTICLE II

Each State Party to this Convention undertakes to destroy, or to divert to peaceful purposes, as soon as possible but not later than nine months after the entry into force of the Convention, all agents, toxins, weapons, equipment and means of delivery specified in article I of the Convention, which are in its possession or under its jurisdiction or control. In implementing the provisions of this article all necessary safety precautions shall be observed to protect populations and the environment.

ARTICLE III

Each State Party to this Convention undertakes not to transfer to any recipient whatsoever, directly or indirectly, and not in any way to assist, encourage, or induce any State, group of States or international organizations to manufacture or otherwise acquire any of the agents, toxins, weapons, equipment or means of delivery specified in article I of the Convention.

ARTICLE IV

Each State Party to this Convention shall, in accordance with its constitutional processes, take any necessary measures to prohibit and prevent the development, production, stockpiling, acquisition or retention of the agents, toxins, weapons, equipment and means of delivery specified in article I of the Convention, within the territory of such State, under its jurisdiction or under its control anywhere.

Article V

The States Parties to this Convention undertake to consult one another and to cooperate in solving any problems which may arise in relation to the objective of, or in the application of the provisions of, the Convention. Consultation and cooperation pursuant to this article may also be undertaken through appropriate international procedures within the framework of the United Nations and in accordance with its Charter.

Article VI

(1) Any State Party to this Convention which finds that any other State Party is acting in breach of obligations deriving from the provisions of the Convention may lodge a complaint with the Security Council of the United Nations. Such a complaint should include all possible evidence confirming its validity, as well as a request for its consideration by the Security Council.

(2) Each State Party to this Convention undertakes to cooperate in carrying out any investigation which the Security Council may initiate, in accordance with the provisions of the Charter of the United Nations, on the basis of the complaint received by the Council. The Security Council shall inform the States Parties to the Convention of the results of the investigation.

Article VII

Each State Party to this Convention undertakes to provide or support assistance, in accordance with the United Nations Charter, to any Party to the Convention which so requests, if the Security Council decides that such Party has been exposed to danger as a result of violation of the Convention.

Article VIII

Nothing in this Convention shall be interpreted as in any way limiting or detracting from the obligations assumed by any State under the Protocol for the Prohibition of the Use in War of Asphyxiating, Poisonous or Other Gases, and of Bacteriological Methods of Warfare, signed at Geneva on June 17, 1925.

Article IX

Each State Party to this Convention affirms the recognized objective of effective prohibition of chemical weapons and, to this end, undertakes to continue negotiations in good faith with a view to reaching early agreement on effective measures for the prohibition of their development, production and stockpiling and for their destruction, and on appropriate measures concerning equipment and means of delivery specifically designed for the production or use of chemical agents for weapons purposes.

Article X

(1) The States Parties to this Convention undertake to facilitate, and have the right to participate in, the fullest possible exchange

of equipment, materials and scientific and technological information for the use of bacteriological (biological) agents and toxins for peaceful purposes. Parties to the Convention in a position to do so shall also cooperate in contributing individually or together with other States or international organizations to the further development and application of scientific discoveries in the field of bacteriology (biology) for prevention of disease, or for other peaceful purposes.

(2) This Convention shall be implemented in a manner designed to avoid hampering the economic or technological development of States Parties to the Convention or international cooperation in the field of peaceful bacteriological (biological) activities, including the international exchange of bacteriological (biological) agents and toxins and equipment for the processing, use or production of bacteriological (biological) agents and toxins for peaceful purposes in accordance with the provisions of the Convention.

Article XI

Any State Party may propose amendments to this Convention. Amendments shall enter into force for each State Party accepting the amendments upon their acceptance by a majority of the States Parties to the Convention and thereafter for each remaining State Party on the date of acceptance by it.

Article XII

Five years after the entry into force of this Convention, or earlier if it is requested by a majority of Parties to the Convention by submitting a proposal to this effect to the Depositary Governments, a conference of States Parties to the Convention shall be held at Geneva, Switzerland, to review the operation of the Convention, with a view to assuring that the purposes of the preamble and the provisions of the Convention, including the provisions concerning negotiations on chemical weapons, are being realized. Such review shall take into account any new scientific and technological developments relevant to the Convention.

Article XIII

(1) This Convention shall be unlimited duration.

(2) Each State Party to this Convention shall in exercising its national sovereignty have the right to withdraw from the Convention if it decides that extraordinary events, related to the subject matter of the Convention, have jeopardized the supreme interests of its country. It shall give notice of such withdrawal to all other States Parties to the Convention and to the United Nations Security Council three months in advance. Such notice shall include a statement of the extraordinary events it regards as having jeopardized its supreme interests.

Article XIV

(1) This Convention shall be open to all States for signature. Any State which does not sign the Convention before its entry into force

in accordance with paragraph (3) of this Article may accede to it at any time.

(2) This Convention shall be subject to ratification by signatory States. Instruments of ratification and instruments of accession shall be deposited with the Governments of the United States of America, the United Kingdom of Great Britain and Northern Ireland and the Union of Soviet Socialist Republics, which are hereby designated the Depositary Governments.

(3) This Convention shall enter into force after the deposit of instruments of ratification by twenty-two Governments, including the Governments designated as Depositaries of the Convention.

(4) For States whose instruments of ratification or accession are deposited subsequent to the entry into force of this Convention, it shall enter into force on the date of the deposit of their instruments of ratification or accession.

(5) The Depositary Governments shall promptly inform all signatory and acceding States of the date of each signature, the date of deposit of each instrument of ratification or of accession and the date of the entry into force of this Convention, and of the receipt of other notices.

(6) This Convention shall be registered by the Depositary Governments pursuant to Article 102 of the Charter of the United Nations.

Article XV

This Convention, the English, Russian, French, Spanish and Chinese texts of which are equally authentic, shall be deposited in the archives of the Depositary Governments. Duly certified copies of the Convention shall be transmitted by the Depositary Governments to the Governments of the signatory and acceding States.

c. Convention on the Prohibition of the Development, Production, Stockpiling and Use of Chemical Weapons and on Their Destruction[1]

Convention on the Prohibition of the Development, Production, Stockpiling and Use of Chemical Weapons and on Their Destruction, with annexes; Signed at Paris, January 13, 1993; Ratification advised by the Senate, with conditions, April 24, 1997; Entered into force, April 29, 1997

PREAMBLE

The States Parties to this Convention,

DETERMINED to act with a view to achieving effective progress towards general and complete disarmament under strict and effective international control, including the prohibition and elimination of all types of weapons of mass destruction,

DESIRING to contribute to the realization of the purposes and principles of the Charter of the United Nations,

RECALLING that the General Assembly of the United Nations has repeatedly condemned all actions contrary to the principles and objectives of the Protocol for the Prohibition of the Use in War of Asphyxiation, Poisonous or Other Gases, and of Bacteriological Methods of Warfare, signed at Geneva on 17 June 1925 (the Geneva Protocol of 1925),

RECOGNIZING that this Convention reaffirms principles and objectives of and obligation assumed under the Geneva Protocol of 1925, and the Convention on the Prohibition of the Development, Production and Stockpiling of Bacteriological (Biological) and Toxin Weapons and on their Destruction signed at London, Moscow and Washington on 10 April 1972,

BEARING in mind the objective contained in Article IX of the Convention on the Prohibition of the Development, Production and Stockpiling of Bacteriological (Biological) and Toxin Weapons and their Destruction,

DETERMINED for the sake of all mankind, to exclude completely the possibility of the use of chemical weapons, through the implementation of the provisions of this Convention, thereby complementing the obligations assumed under the Geneva Protocol of 1925,

---

[1] Treaty Doc. 103–21. For a list of states that are parties to the Convention, see Department of State publication, *Treaties in Force*.

The Convention also includes three annexes: Annex on Chemicals; Annex on Implementation and Verification; and Annex on the Protection of Confidential Information. The complete text of these annexes is available at a web site maintained by the Departments of Commerce and State: http://www.cwc.gov/cwc_treaty.html.

Senate conditions to the ratification of the Convention can be found at the same web site: http://www.cwc.gov/cwc_authority_ratification.html.

RECOGNIZING the prohibition, embodied in the pertinent agreements and relevant principles of international law, of the use of herbicides as a method of warfare,

CONSIDERING that achievements in the field of chemistry should be used exclusively for the benefit of mankind,

DESIRING to promote free trade in chemicals as well as international cooperation and exchange of scientific and technical information in the field of chemical activities for purposes not prohibited under this Convention in order to enhance the economic and technological development of all States Parties,

CONVINCED that the complete and effective prohibition of the development, production, acquisition, stockpiling, retention, transfer and use of chemical weapons, and their destruction, represent a necessary step towards the achievement of these common objectives,

HAVE AGREED AS FOLLOWS:

ARTICLE I

GENERAL OBLIGATIONS

1. Each State Party to this Convention undertakes never under any circumstances:

(a) To develop, produce, otherwise acquire, stockpile or retain chemical weapons, or transfer, directly or indirectly, chemical weapons to anyone;

(b) To use chemical weapons;

(c) To engage in any military preparations to use chemical weapons;

(d) To assist, encourage or induce, in any way, anyone to engage in any activity prohibited to a State Party under this Convention.

2. Each State Party undertakes to destroy chemical weapons it owns or possesses, or that are located in any place under its jurisdiction or control, in accordance with the provisions of this Convention.

3. Each State Party undertakes to destroy all chemical weapons it abandoned on the territory of another State Party, in accordance with the provisions of this Convention.

4. Each State Party undertakes to destroy any chemical weapons production facilities it owns or possesses, or that are located in any place under its jurisdiction or control, in accordance with the provisions of this Convention.

5. Each State Party undertakes not to use riot control agents as a method of warfare.

ARTICLE II

DEFINITIONS AND CRITERIA

For the purposes of this Convention:

1. "Chemical Weapons" means the following, together or separately:

(a) Toxic chemicals and their precursors, except where intended for purposes not prohibited under this Convention, as long as the types and quantities are consistent with such purposes;

(b) Munitions and devices, specifically designed to cause death or other harm through the toxic properties of those toxic chemicals specified in subparagraph (a), which would be released as a result of the employment of such munitions and devices;

(c) Any equipment specifically designed for use directly in connection with the employment of munitions and devices specified in subparagraph (b).

2. "Toxic Chemical" means:

Any chemical which through its chemical action on life processes can cause death, temporary incapacitation or permanent harm to humans or animals. This includes all such chemicals, regardless of their origin or of their method of production, and regardless of whether they are produced in facilities, in munitions or elsewhere.

(For the purpose of implementing this Convention, toxic chemicals which have been identified for the application of verification measures are listed in Schedules contained in the Annex on Chemicals.)

3. "Precursor" means:

Any chemical reactant which takes part at any stage in the production by whatever method of a toxic chemical. This includes any key component of a binary or multicomponent chemical system.

(For the purpose of implementing this Convention, precursors which have been identified for the application of verification measures are listed in Schedules contained in the Annex on Chemicals.)

4. "Key Component of Binary or Multicomponent Chemical Systems" (hereinafter referred to as "key component") means:

The precursor which plays the most important role in determining the toxic properties of the final product and reacts rapidly with other chemicals in the binary or multicomponent system.

5. "Old Chemical Weapons" means:

(a) Chemical weapons which were produced before 1925; or

(b) Chemical weapons produced in the period between 1925 and 1946 that have deteriorated to such extent that they can no longer be used as chemical weapons.

6. "Abandoned Chemical Weapons" means:

Chemical weapons, including old chemical weapons, abandoned by a State after 1 January 1925 on the territory of another State without the consent of the latter.

7. "Riot Control Agent" means:

Any chemical not listed in a Schedule, which can produce rapidly in humans sensory irritation or disabling physical effects which disappear within a short time following termination of exposure.

8. "Chemical Weapons Production Facility":

(a) Means any equipment, as well as any building housing such equipment, that was designed, constructed or used at any time since 1 January 1946:

(i) As part of the stage in the production of chemicals ("final technological stage") where the material flows would contain, when the equipment is in operation:

(1) Any chemical listed in Schedule 1 in the Annex on Chemicals; or

(2) Any other chemical that has no use, above 1 tonne per year on the territory of a State Party or in any other place under the jurisdiction or control of a State Party, for purposes not prohibited under this Convention, but can be used for chemical weapons purposes; or

(ii) For filling chemical weapons, including, inter alia, the filling of chemicals listed in Schedule 1 into munitions, devices or bulk storage containers; the filling of chemicals into containers that form part of assembled binary munitions and devices or into chemical submunitions that form part of assembled unitary munitions and devices, and the loading of the containers and chemical submunitions into the respective munitions and devices;

(b) Does not mean:

(i) Any facility having a production capacity for synthesis of chemicals specified in subparagraph (a) (i) that is less than 1 tonne;

(ii) Any facility in which a chemical specified in subparagraph (a) (i) is or was produced as an unavoidable by-product of activities for purposes not prohibited under this Convention, provided that the chemical does not exceed 3 per cent of the total product and that the facility is subject to declaration and inspection under the Annex on Implementation and Verification (hereinafter referred to as "Verification Annex"); or

(iii) The single small-scale facility for production of chemicals listed in Schedule 1 for purposes not prohibited under this Convention as referred to in Part VI of the Verification Annex.

9. "Purposes Not Prohibited Under this Convention" means:

(a) Industrial, agricultural, research, medical, pharmaceutical or other peaceful purposes;

(b) Protective purposes, namely those purposes directly related to protection against toxic chemicals and to protection against chemical weapons;

(c) Military purposes not connected with the use of chemical weapons and not dependent on the use of the toxic properties of chemicals as a method of warfare;

(d) Law enforcement including domestic riot control purposes.

10. "Production Capacity" means:

The annual quantitative potential for manufacturing a specific chemical based on the technological process actually used or, if the process is not yet operational, planned to be used at the relevant facility. It shall be deemed to be equal to the nameplate capacity or, if the nameplate capacity is not available, to the design capacity. The nameplate capacity is the product output under conditions optimized for maximum quantity for the production facility, as demonstrated by one or more test-runs. The design capacity is the corresponding theoretically calculated product output.

11. "Organization" means the Organization for the Prohibition of Chemical Weapons established pursuant to Article VIII of this Convention.

12. For the purposes of Article VI:

(a) "Production" of a chemical means its formation through chemical reaction;

(b) "Processing" of a chemical means a physical process, such as formulation, extraction and purification, in which a chemical is not converted into another chemical;

(c) "Consumption" of a chemical means its conversion into another chemical via a chemical reaction.

ARTICLE III

DECLARATIONS

1. Each State Party shall submit to the Organization, not later than 30 days after this Convention enters into force for it, the following declarations, in which it shall:

(a) With respect to chemical weapons:

(i) Declare whether it owns or possesses any chemical weapons, or whether there are any chemical weapons located in any place under its jurisdiction or control;

(ii) Specify the precise location, aggregate quantity and detailed inventory of chemical weapons it owns or possesses, or that are located in any place under its jurisdiction or control, in accordance with Part IV (A), paragraphs 1 to 3, of the Verification Annex, except for those chemical weapons referred to in sub-subparagraph (iii);

(iii) Report any chemical weapons on its territory that are owned and possessed by another State and located in any place under the jurisdiction or control of another State, in accordance with Part IV (A), paragraph 4, of the Verification Annex;

(iv) Declare whether it has transferred or received, directly or indirectly, any chemical weapons since 1 January 1946 and specify the transfer or receipt of such weapons, in accordance with Part IV (A), paragraph 5, of the Verification Annex;

(v) Provide its general plan for destruction of chemical weapons that it owns or possesses, or that are located in any place under its jurisdiction or control, in accordance with Part IV (A), paragraph 6, of the Verification Annex;

(b) With respect to old chemical weapons and abandoned chemical weapons:

(i) Declare whether it has on its territory old chemical weapons and provide all available information in accordance with Part IV (B), paragraph 3, of the Verification Annex;

(ii) Declare whether there are abandoned chemical weapons on its territory and provide all available information in accordance with Part IV (B), paragraph 8, of the Verification Annex;

(iii) Declare whether it has abandoned chemical weapons on the territory of other States and provide all available information in accordance with Part IV (B), paragraph 10, of the Verification Annex;

(c) With respect to chemical weapons production facilities:

(i) Declare whether it has or has had any chemical weapons production facility under its ownership or possession, or that is or has been located in any place under its jurisdiction or control at any time since 1 January 1946;

(ii) Specify any chemical weapons production facility it has or has had under its ownership or possession or that is or has been located in any place under its jurisdiction or control at any time since 1 January 1946, in accordance with Part V, paragraph 1, of the Verification Annex, except for those facilities referred to in sub-subparagraph (iii);

(iii) Report any chemical weapons production facility on its territory that another State has or has had under its ownership and possession and that is or has been located in any place under the jurisdiction or control of another State at any time since 1 January 1946, in accordance with Part V, paragraph 2, of the Verification Annex;

(iv) Declare whether it has transferred or received, directly or indirectly, any equipment for the production of chemical weapons since 1 January 1946 and specify the transfer or receipt of such equipment, in accordance with Part V, paragraphs 3 to 5, of the Verification Annex;

(v) Provide its general plan for destruction of any chemical weapons production facility it owns or possesses, or that is located in any place under its jurisdiction or control, in accordance with Part V, paragraph 6, of the Verification Annex;

(vi) Specify actions to be taken for closure of any chemical weapons production facility it owns or possesses, or that is located in any place under its jurisdiction or control, in accordance with Part V, paragraph 1 (i), of the Verification Annex;

(vii) Provide its general plan for any temporary conversion of any chemical weapons production facility it owns or possesses, or that is located in any place under its jurisdiction or control, into a chemical weapons destruction facility, in accordance with Part V, paragraph 7, of the Verification Annex;

(d) With respect to other facilities:

Specify the precise location, nature and general scope of activities of any facility or establishment under its ownership or possession, or located in any place under its jurisdiction or control, and that has been designed, constructed or used since 1 January 1946 primarily for development of chemical weapons. Such declaration shall include, inter alia, laboratories and test and evaluation sites;

(e) With respect to riot control agents:

Specify the chemical name, structural formula and Chemical Abstracts Service (CAS) registry number, if assigned, of each chemical it holds for riot control purposes. This declaration shall be updated not later than 30 days after any change becomes effective.

2. The provisions of this Article and the relevant provisions of Part IV of the Verification Annex shall not, at the discretion of a State Party, apply to chemical weapons buried on its territory before 1 January 1977 and which remain buried, or which had been dumped at sea before 1 January 1985.

ARTICLE IV

CHEMICAL WEAPONS

1. The provisions of this Article and the detailed procedures for its implementation shall apply to all chemical weapons owned or possessed by a State Party, or that are located in any place under its jurisdiction or control, except old chemical weapons and abandoned chemical weapons to which Part IV (B) of the Verification Annex applies.

2. Detailed procedures for the implementation of this Article are set forth in the Verification Annex.

3. All locations at which chemical weapons specified in paragraph 1 are stored or destroyed shall be subject to systematic verification through on-site inspection and monitoring with on-site instruments, in accordance with Part IV (A) of the Verification Annex.

4. Each State Party shall, immediately after the declaration under Article III, paragraph 1 (a), has been submitted, provide access to chemical weapons specified in paragraph 1 for the purpose of systematic verification of the declaration through on-site inspection. Thereafter, each State Party shall not remove any of these chemical weapons, except to a chemical weapons destruction facility. It shall provide access to such chemical weapons, for the purpose of systematic on-site verification.

5. Each State Party shall provide access to any chemical weapons destruction facilities and their storage areas, that it owns or possesses, or that are located in any place under its jurisdiction or control, for the purpose of systematic verification through on-site inspection and monitoring with on-site instruments.

6. Each State Party shall destroy all chemical weapons specified in paragraph 1 pursuant to the Verification Annex and in accordance with the agreed rate and sequence of destruction (hereinafter referred to as "order of destruction"). Such destruction shall begin not later than two years after this Convention enters into force for it and shall finish not later than 10 years after entry into force of this Convention. A State Party is not precluded from destroying such chemical weapons at a faster rate.

7. Each State Party shall:

(a) Submit detailed plans for the destruction of chemical weapons specified in paragraph 1 not later than 60 days before each annual destruction period begins, in accordance with Part IV (A), paragraph 29, of the Verification Annex; the detailed plans shall encompass all stocks to be destroyed during the next annual destruction period;

(b) Submit declarations annually regarding the implementation of its plans for destruction of chemical weapons specified in paragraph 1, not later than 60 days after the end of each annual destruction period; and

(c) Certify, not later than 30 days after the destruction process has been completed, that all chemical weapons specified in paragraph 1 have been destroyed.

8. If a State ratifies or accedes to this Convention after the 10-year period for destruction set forth in paragraph 6, it shall destroy chemical weapons specified in paragraph 1 as soon as possible. The order of destruction and procedures for stringent verification for such a State Party shall be determined by the Executive Council.

9. Any chemical weapons discovered by a State Party after the initial declaration of chemical weapons shall be reported, secured and destroyed in accordance with Part IV (A) of the Verification Annex.

10. Each State Party, during transportation, sampling, storage and destruction of chemical weapons, shall assign the highest priority to ensuring the safety of people and to protecting the environment. Each State Party shall transport, sample, store and destroy chemical weapons in accordance with its national standards for safety and emissions.

11. Any State Party which has on its territory chemical weapons that are owned or possessed by another State, or that are located in any place under the jurisdiction or control of another State, shall make the fullest efforts to ensure that these chemical weapons are removed from its territory not later than one year after this Convention enters into force for it. If they are not removed within one year, the State Party may request the Organization and other States Parties to provide assistance in the destruction of these chemical weapons.

12. Each State Party undertakes to cooperate with other States Parties that request information or assistance on a bilateral basis or through the Technical Secretariat regarding methods and technologies for the safe and efficient destruction of chemical weapons.

13. In carrying out verification activities pursuant to this Article and Part IV (A) of the Verification Annex, the Organization shall consider measures to avoid unnecessary duplication of bilateral or multilateral agreements on verification of chemical weapons storage and their destruction among States Parties.

To this end, the Executive Council shall decide to limit verification to measures complementary to those undertaken pursuant to such a bilateral or multilateral agreement, if it considers that:

(a) Verification provisions of such an agreement are consistent with the verification provisions of this Article and Part IV (A) of the Verification Annex;

(b) Implementation of such an agreement provides for sufficient assurance of compliance with the relevant provisions of this Convention; and

(c) Parties to the bilateral or multilateral agreement keep the Organization fully informed about their verification activities.

14. If the Executive Council takes a decision pursuant to paragraph 13, the Organization shall have the right to monitor the implementation of the bilateral or multilateral agreement.

15. Nothing in paragraphs 13 and 14 shall affect the obligation of a State Party to provide declarations pursuant to Article III, this Article and Part IV (A) of the Verification Annex.

16. Each State Party shall meet the costs of destruction of chemical weapons it is obliged to destroy. It shall also meet the costs of verification of storage and destruction of these chemical weapons unless the Executive Council decides otherwise. If the Executive Council decides to limit verification measures of the Organization pursuant to paragraph 13, the costs of complementary verification and monitoring by the Organization shall be paid in accordance with the United Nations scale of assessment, as specified in Article VIII, paragraph 7.

17. The provisions of this Article and the relevant provisions of Part IV of the Verification Annex shall not, at the discretion of a State Party, apply to chemical weapons buried on its territory before 1 January 1977 and which remain buried, or which had been dumped at sea before 1 January 1985.

ARTICLE V

CHEMICAL WEAPONS PRODUCTION FACILITIES

1. The provisions of this Article and the detailed procedures for its implementation shall apply to any and all chemical weapons production facilities owned or possessed by a State Party, or that are located in any place under its jurisdiction or control.

2. Detailed procedures for the implementation of this Article are set forth in the Verification Annex.

3. All chemical weapons production facilities specified in paragraph 1 shall be subject to systematic verification through on-site inspection and monitoring with on-site instruments in accordance with Part V of the Verification Annex.

4. Each State Party shall cease immediately all activity at chemical weapons production facilities specified in paragraph 1, except activity required for closure.

5. No State Party shall construct any new chemical weapons production facilities or modify any existing facilities for the purpose of chemical weapons production or for any other activity prohibited under this Convention.

6. Each State Party shall, immediately after the declaration under Article III, paragraph 1 (c), has been submitted, provide access to chemical weapons production facilities specified in paragraph 1, for the purpose of systematic verification of the declaration through on-site inspection.

7. Each State Party shall:

(a) Close, not later than 90 days after this Convention enters into force for it, all chemical weapons production facilities specified in paragraph 1, in accordance with Part V of the Verification Annex, and give notice thereof; and

(b) Provide access to chemical weapons production facilities specified in paragraph 1, subsequent to closure, for the purpose of systematic verification through on-site inspection and monitoring with on-site instruments in order to ensure that the facility remains closed and is subsequently destroyed.

8. Each State Party shall destroy all chemical weapons production facilities specified in paragraph 1 and related facilities and equipment, pursuant to the Verification Annex and in accordance with an agreed rate and sequence of destruction (hereinafter referred to as "order of destruction"). Such destruction shall begin not later than one year after this Convention enters into force for it, and shall finish not later than 10 years after entry into force of this Convention. A State Party is not precluded from destroying such facilities at a faster rate.

9. Each State Party shall:

(a) Submit detailed plans for destruction of chemical weapons production facilities specified in paragraph 1, not later than 180 days before the destruction of each facility begins;

(b) Submit declarations annually regarding the implementation of its plans for the destruction of all chemical weapons production facilities specified in paragraph 1, not later than 90 days after the end of each annual destruction period; and

(c) Certify, not later than 30 days after the destruction process has been completed, that all chemical weapons production facilities specified in paragraph 1 have been destroyed.

10. If a State ratifies or accedes to this Convention after the 10-year period for destruction set forth in paragraph 8, it shall destroy chemical weapons production facilities specified in paragraph 1 as soon as possible. The order of destruction and procedures for stringent verification for such a State Party shall be determined by the Executive Council.

11. Each State Party, during the destruction of chemical weapons production facilities, shall assign the highest priority to ensuring the safety of people and to protecting the environment. Each State Party shall destroy chemical weapons production facilities in accordance with its national standards for safety and emissions.

12. Chemical weapons production facilities specified in paragraph 1 may be temporarily converted for destruction of chemical weapons in accordance with Part V, paragraphs 18 to 25, of the Verification Annex. Such a converted facility must be destroyed as soon as it is no longer in use for destruction of chemical weapons but, in any case, not later than 10 years after entry into force of this Convention.

13. A State Party may request, in exceptional cases of compelling need, permission to use a chemical weapons production facility specified in paragraph 1 for purposes not prohibited under this Convention. Upon the recommendation of the Executive Council, the Conference of the States Parties shall decide whether or not to approve the request and shall establish the conditions upon which approval is contingent in accordance with Part V, Section D, of the Verification Annex.

14. The chemical weapons production facility shall be converted in such a manner that the converted facility is not more capable of being reconverted into a chemical weapons production facility

than any other facility used for industrial, agricultural, research, medical, pharmaceutical or other peaceful purposes not involving chemicals listed in Schedule 1.

15. All converted facilities shall be subject to systematic verification through on-site inspection and monitoring with on-site instruments in accordance with Part V, Section D, of the Verification Annex.

16. In carrying out verification activities pursuant to this Article and Part V of the Verification Annex, the Organization shall consider measures to avoid unnecessary duplication of bilateral or multilateral agreements on verification of chemical weapons production facilities and their destruction among States Parties.

To this end, the Executive Council shall decide to limit the verification to measures complementary to those undertaken pursuant to such a bilateral or multilateral agreement, if it considers that:

(a) Verification provisions of such an agreement are consistent with the verification provisions of this Article and Part V of the Verification Annex;

(b) Implementation of the agreement provides for sufficient assurance of compliance with the relevant provisions of this Convention; and

(c) Parties to the bilateral or multilateral agreement keep the Organization fully informed about their verification activities.

17. If the Executive Council takes a decision pursuant to paragraph 16, the Organization shall have the right to monitor the implementation of the bilateral or multilateral agreement.

18. Nothing in paragraphs 16 and 17 shall affect the obligation of a State Party to make declarations pursuant to Article III, this Article and Part V of the Verification Annex.

19. Each State Party shall meet the costs of destruction of chemical weapons production facilities it is obliged to destroy. It shall also meet the costs of verification under this Article unless the Executive Council decides otherwise. If the Executive Council decides to limit verification measures of the Organization pursuant to paragraph 16, the costs of complementary verification and monitoring by the Organization shall be paid in accordance with the United Nations scale of assessment, as specified in Article VIII, paragraph 7.

ARTICLE VI

ACTIVITIES NOT PROHIBITED UNDER THIS CONVENTION

1. Each State Party has the right, subject to the provisions of this Convention, to develop, produce, otherwise acquire, retain, transfer and use toxic chemicals and their precursors for purposes not prohibited under this Convention.

2. Each State Party shall adopt the necessary measures to ensure that toxic chemicals and their precursors are only developed, produced, otherwise acquired, retained, transferred, or used within its territory or in any other place under its jurisdiction or control for purposes not prohibited under this Convention. To this end, and

in order to verify that activities are in accordance with obligations under this Convention, each State Party shall subject toxic chemicals and their precursors listed in Schedules 1, 2 and 3 of the Annex on Chemicals, facilities related to such chemicals, and other facilities as specified in the Verification Annex, that are located on its territory or in any other place under its jurisdiction or control, to verification measures as provided in the Verification Annex.

3. Each State Party shall subject chemicals listed in Schedule 1 (hereinafter referred to as "Schedule 1 chemicals") to the prohibitions on production, acquisition, retention, transfer and use as specified in Part VI of the Verification Annex. It shall subject Schedule 1 chemicals and facilities specified in Part VI of the Verification Annex to systematic verification through on-site inspection and monitoring with on-site instruments in accordance with that Part of the Verification Annex.

4. Each State Party shall subject chemicals listed in Schedule 2 (hereinafter referred to as "Schedule 2 chemicals") and facilities specified in Part VII of the Verification Annex to data monitoring and on-site verification in accordance with that Part of the Verification Annex.

5. Each State Party shall subject chemicals listed in Schedule 3 (hereinafter referred to as "Schedule 3 chemicals") and facilities specified in Part VIII of the Verification Annex to data monitoring and on-site verification in accordance with that Part of the Verification Annex.

6. Each State Party shall subject facilities specified in Part IX of the Verification Annex to data monitoring and eventual on-site verification in accordance with that Part of the Verification Annex unless decided otherwise by the Conference of the States Parties pursuant to Part IX, paragraph 22, of the Verification Annex.

7. Not later than 30 days after this Convention enters into force for it, each State Party shall make an initial declaration on relevant chemicals and facilities in accordance with the Verification Annex.

8. Each State Party shall make annual declarations regarding the relevant chemicals and facilities in accordance with the Verification Annex.

9. For the purpose of on-site verification, each State Party shall grant to the inspectors access to facilities as required in the Verification Annex.

10. In conducting verification activities, the Technical Secretariat shall avoid undue intrusion into the State Party's chemical activities for purposes not prohibited under this Convention and, in particular, abide by the provisions set forth in the Annex on the Protection of Confidential Information (hereinafter referred to as "Confidentiality Annex").

11. The provisions of this Article shall be implemented in a manner which avoids hampering the economic or technological development of States Parties, and international cooperation in the field of chemical activities for purposes not prohibited under this Convention including the international exchange of scientific and technical information and chemicals and equipment for the production, processing or use of chemicals for purposes not prohibited under this Convention.

ARTICLE VII

NATIONAL IMPLEMENTATION MEASURES

General undertakings

1. Each State Party shall, in accordance with its constitutional processes, adopt the necessary measures to implement its obligations under this Convention. In particular, it shall:

(a) Prohibit natural and legal persons anywhere on its territory or in any other place under its jurisdiction as recognized by international law from undertaking any activity prohibited to a State Party under this Convention, including enacting penal legislation with respect to such activity;

(b) Not permit in any place under its control any activity prohibited to a State Party under this Convention; and

(c) Extend its penal legislation enacted under subparagraph (a) to any activity prohibited to a State Party under this Convention undertaken anywhere by natural persons, possessing its nationality, in conformity with international law.

2. Each State Party shall cooperate with other States Parties and afford the appropriate form of legal assistance to facilitate the implementation of the obligations under paragraph 1.

3. Each State Party, during the implementation of its obligations under this Convention, shall assign the highest priority to ensuring the safety of people and to protecting the environment, and shall cooperate as appropriate with other States Parties in this regard.

Relations between the State Party and the Organization

4. In order to fulfill its obligations under this Convention, each State Party shall designate or establish a National Authority to serve as the national focal point for effective liaison with the Organization and other States Parties. Each State Party shall notify the Organization of its National Authority at the time that this Convention enters into force for it.

5. Each State Party shall inform the Organization of the legislative and administrative measures taken to implement this Convention.

6. Each State Party shall treat as confidential and afford special handling to information and data that it receives in confidence from the Organization in connection with the implementation of this Convention. It shall treat such information and data exclusively in connection with its rights and obligations under this Convention and in accordance with the provisions set forth in the Confidentiality Annex.

7. Each State Party undertakes to cooperate with the Organization in the exercise of all its functions and in particular to provide assistance to the Technical Secretariat.

ARTICLE VIII

THE ORGANIZATION

A. GENERAL PROVISIONS

1. The States Parties to this Convention hereby establish the Organization for the Prohibition of Chemical Weapons to achieve the object and purpose of this Convention, to ensure the implementation of its provisions, including those for international verification of compliance with it, and to provide a forum for consultation and cooperation among States Parties.

2. All States Parties to this Convention shall be members of the Organization. A State Party shall not be deprived of its membership in the Organization.

3. The seat of the Headquarters of the Organization shall be The Hague, Kingdom of the Netherlands.

4. There are hereby established as the organs of the Organization: the Conference of the States Parties, the Executive Council, and the Technical Secretariat.

5. The Organization shall conduct its verification activities provided for under this Convention in the least intrusive manner possible consistent with the timely and efficient accomplishment of their objectives. It shall request only the information and data necessary to fulfill its responsibilities under this Convention. It shall take every precaution to protect the confidentiality of information on civil and military activities and facilities coming to its knowledge in the implementation of this Convention and, in particular, shall abide by the provisions set forth in the Confidentiality Annex.

6. In undertaking its verification activities the Organization shall consider measures to make use of advances in science and technology.

7. The costs of the Organization's activities shall be paid by States Parties in accordance with the United Nations scale of assessment adjusted to take into account differences in membership between the United Nations and this Organization, and subject to the provisions of Articles IV and V. Financial contributions of States Parties to the Preparatory Commission shall be deducted in an appropriate way from their contributions to the regular budget. The budget of the Organization shall comprise two separate chapters, one relating to administrative and other costs, and one relating to verification costs.

8. A member of the Organization which is in arrears in the payment of its financial contribution to the Organization shall have no vote in the Organization if the amount of its arrears equals or exceeds the amount of the contribution due from it for the preceding two full years. The Conference of the States Parties may, nevertheless, permit such a member to vote if it is satisfied that the failure to pay is due to conditions beyond the control of the member.

B. THE CONFERENCE OF THE STATES PARTIES

Composition, procedures and decision-making

9. The Conference of the States Parties (hereinafter referred to as "the Conference") shall be composed of all members of this Organization. Each member shall have one representative in the Conference, who may be accompanied by alternates and advisers.

10. The first session of the Conference shall be convened by the depositary not later than 30 days after the entry into force of this Convention.

11. The Conference shall meet in regular sessions which shall be held annually unless it decides otherwise.

12. Special sessions of the Conference shall be convened:

(a) When decided by the Conference;

(b) When requested by the Executive Council;

(c) When requested by any member and supported by one third of the members; or

(d) In accordance with paragraph 22 to undertake reviews of the operation of this Convention.

Except in the case of subparagraph (d), the special session shall be convened not later than 30 days after receipt of the request by the Director-General of the Technical Secretariat, unless specified otherwise in the request.

13. The Conference shall also be convened in the form of an Amendment Conference in accordance with Article XV, paragraph 2.

14. Sessions of the Conference shall take place at the seat of the Organization unless the Conference decides otherwise.

15. The Conference shall adopt its rules of procedure. At the beginning of each regular session, it shall elect its Chairman and such other officers as may be required. They shall hold office until a new Chairman and other officers are elected at the next regular session.

16. A majority of the members of the Organization shall constitute a quorum for the Conference.

17. Each member of the Organization shall have one vote in the Conference.

18. The Conference shall take decisions on questions of procedure by a simple majority of the members present and voting. Decisions on matters of substance should be taken as far as possible by consensus. If consensus is not attainable when an issue comes up for decision, the Chairman shall defer any vote for 24 hours and during this period of deferment shall make every effort to facilitate achievement of consensus, and shall report to the Conference before the end of this period. If consensus is not possible at the end of 24 hours, the Conference shall take the decision by a two-thirds majority of members present and voting unless specified otherwise in this Convention. When the issue arises as to whether the question is one of substance or not, that question shall be treated as a matter of substance unless otherwise decided by the Conference by the majority required for decisions on matters of substance.

Powers and functions

19. The Conference shall be the principal organ of the Organization. It shall consider any questions, matters or issues within the scope of this Convention, including those relating to the powers and functions of the Executive Council and the Technical Secretariat. It may make recommendations and take decisions on any questions, matters or issues related to this Convention raised by a State Party or brought to its attention by the Executive Council.

20. The Conference shall oversee the implementation of this Convention, and act in order to promote its object and purpose. The Conference shall review compliance with this Convention. It shall also oversee the activities of the Executive Council and the Technical Secretariat and may issue guidelines in accordance with this Convention to either of them in the exercise of their functions.

21. The Conference shall:

(a) Consider and adopt at its regular sessions the report, programme and budget of the Organization, submitted by the Executive Council, as well as consider other reports;

(b) Decide on the scale of financial contributions to be paid by States Parties in accordance with paragraph 7;

(c) Elect the members of the Executive Council;

(d) Appoint the Director-General of the Technical Secretariat (hereinafter referred to as "the Director-General");

(e) Approve the rules of procedure of the Executive Council submitted by the latter;

(f) Establish such subsidiary organs as it finds necessary for the exercise of its functions in accordance with this Convention;

(g) Foster international cooperation for peaceful purposes in the field of chemical activities;

(h) Review scientific and technological developments that could affect the operation of this Convention and, in this context, direct the Director-General to establish a Scientific Advisory Board to enable him, in the performance of his functions, to render specialized advice in areas of science and technology relevant to this Convention, to the Conference, the Executive Council or States Parties. The Scientific Advisory Board shall be composed of independent experts appointed in accordance with terms of reference adopted by the Conference;

(i) Consider and approve at its first session any draft agreements, provisions and guidelines developed by the Preparatory Commission;

(j) Establish at its first session the voluntary fund for assistance in accordance with Article X;

(k) Take the necessary measures to ensure compliance with this Convention and to redress and remedy any situation which contravenes the provisions of this Convention, in accordance with Article XII.

22. The Conference shall not later than one year after the expiry of the fifth and the tenth year after the entry into force of this Convention, and at such other times within that time period as may be decided upon, convene in special sessions to undertake reviews of the operation of this Convention. Such reviews shall take into

account any relevant scientific and technological developments. At intervals of five years thereafter, unless otherwise decided upon, further sessions of the Conference shall be convened with the same objective.

C. THE EXECUTIVE COUNCIL

Composition, procedures and decision-making

23. The Executive Council shall consist of 41 members. Each State Party shall have the right, in accordance with the principle of rotation, to serve on the Executive Council. The members of the Executive Council shall be elected by the Conference for a term of two years. In order to ensure the effective functioning of this Convention, due regard being specially paid to equitable geographical distribution, to the importance of chemical industry, as well as to political and security interests, the Executive Council shall be composed as follows:

(a) Nine States Parties from Africa to be designated by States Parties located in this region. As a basis for this designation it is understood that, out of these nine States Parties, three members shall, as a rule, be the States Parties with the most significant national chemical industry in the region as determined by internationally reported and published data; in addition, the regional group shall agree also to take into account other regional factors in designating these three members;

(b) Nine States Parties from Asia to be designated by States Parties located in this region. As a basis for this designation it is understood that, out of these nine States Parties, four members shall, as a rule, be the States Parties with the most significant national chemical industry in the region as determined by internationally reported and published data; in addition, the regional group shall agree also to take into account other regional factors in designating these four members;

(c) Five States Parties from Eastern Europe to be designated by States Parties located in this region. As a basis for this designation it is understood that, out of these five States Parties, one member shall, as a rule, be the State Party with the most significant national chemical industry in the region as determined by internationally reported and published data; in addition, the regional group shall agree also to take into account other regional factors in designating this one member;

(d) Seven States Parties from Latin America and the Caribbean to be designated by States Parties located in this region. As a basis for this designation it is understood that, out of these seven States Parties, three members shall, as a rule, be the States Parties with the most significant national chemical industry in the region as determined by internationally reported and published data; in addition, the regional group shall agree also to take into account other regional factors in designating these three members;

(e) Ten States Parties from among Western European and other States to be designated by States Parties located in this region. As a basis for this designation it is understood that, out of these 10 States Parties, 5 members shall, as a rule, be the States Parties with the most significant national chemical industry in the region as determined by internationally reported and published data; in addition, the regional group shall agree also to take into account other regional factors in designating these five members;

(f) One further State Party to be designated consecutively by States Parties located in the regions of Asia and Latin America and the Caribbean. As a basis for this designation it is understood that this State Party shall be a rotating member from these regions.

24. For the first election of the Executive Council 20 members shall be elected for a term of one year, due regard being paid to the established numerical proportions as described in paragraph 23.

25. After the full implementation of Articles IV and V the Conference may, upon the request of a majority of the members of the Executive Council, review the composition of the Executive Council taking into account developments related to the principles specified in paragraph 23 that are governing its composition.

26. The Executive Council shall elaborate its rules of procedure and submit them to the Conference for approval.

27. The Executive Council shall elect its Chairman from among its members.

28. The Executive Council shall meet for regular sessions. Between regular sessions it shall meet as often as may be required for the fulfillment of its powers and functions.

29. Each member of the Executive Council shall have one vote. Unless otherwise specified in this Convention, the Executive Council shall take decisions on matters of substance by a two-thirds majority of all its members. The Executive Council shall take decisions on questions of procedure by a simple majority of all its members. When the issue arises as to whether the question is one of substance or not, that question shall be treated as a matter of substance unless otherwise decided by the Executive Council by the majority required for decisions on matters of substance.

Powers and functions

30. The Executive Council shall be the executive organ of the Organization. It shall be responsible to the Conference. The Executive Council shall carry out the powers and functions entrusted to it under this Convention, as well as those functions delegated to it by the Conference. In so doing, it shall act in conformity with the recommendations, decisions and guidelines of the Conference and assure their proper and continuous implementation.

31. The Executive Council shall promote the effective implementation of, and compliance with, this Convention. It shall supervise the activities of the Technical Secretariat, cooperate with the National Authority of each State Party and facilitate consultations and cooperation among States Parties at their request.

32. The Executive Council shall:

(a) Consider and submit to the Conference the draft programme and budget of the Organization;

(b) Consider and submit to the Conference the draft report of the Organization on the implementation of this Convention, the report on the performance of its own activities and such special reports as it deems necessary or which the Conference may request;

(c) Make arrangements for the sessions of the Conference including the preparation of the draft agenda.

33. The Executive Council may request the convening of a special session of the Conference.

34. The Executive Council shall:

(a) Conclude agreements or arrangements with States and international organizations on behalf of the Organization, subject to prior approval by the Conference;

(b) Conclude agreements with States Parties on behalf of the Organization in connection with Article X and supervise the voluntary fund referred to in Article X;

(c) Approve agreements or arrangements relating to the implementation of verification activities, negotiated by the Technical Secretariat with States Parties.

35. The Executive Council shall consider any issue or matter within its competence affecting this Convention and its implementation, including concerns regarding compliance, and cases of non-compliance, and, as appropriate, inform States Parties and bring the issue or matter to the attention of the Conference.

36. In its consideration of doubts or concerns regarding compliance and cases of non-compliance, including, inter alia, abuse of the rights provided for under this Convention, the Executive Council shall consult with the States Parties involved and, as appropriate, request the State Party to take measures to redress the situation within a specified time. To the extent that the Executive Council considers further action to be necessary, it shall take, inter alia, one or more of the following measures:

(a) Inform all States Parties of the issue or matter;

(b) Bring the issue or matter to the attention of the Conference;

(c) Make recommendations to the Conference regarding measures to redress the situation and to ensure compliance.

The Executive Council shall, in cases of particular gravity and urgency, bring the issue or matter, including relevant information and conclusions, directly to the attention of the United Nations General Assembly and the United Nations Security Council. It shall at the same time inform all States Parties of this step.

D. THE TECHNICAL SECRETARIAT

37. The Technical Secretariat shall assist the Conference and the Executive Council in the performance of their functions. The Technical Secretariat shall carry out the verification measures provided for in this Convention. It shall carry out the other functions entrusted to it under this Convention as well as those functions delegated to it by the Conference and the Executive Council.

38. The Technical Secretariat shall:

(a) Prepare and submit to the Executive Council the draft programme and budget of the Organization;

(b) Prepare and submit to the Executive Council the draft report of the Organization on the implementation of this Convention and such other reports as the Conference or the Executive Council may request;

(c) Provide administrative and technical support to the Conference, the Executive Council and subsidiary organs;

(d) Address and receive communications on behalf of the Organization to and from States Parties on matters pertaining to the implementation of this Convention;

(e) Provide technical assistance and technical evaluation to States Parties in the implementation of the provisions of this Convention, including evaluation of scheduled and unscheduled chemicals.

39. The Technical Secretariat shall:

(a) Negotiate agreements or arrangements relating to the implementation of verification activities with States Parties, subject to approval by the Executive Council;

(b) Not later than 180 days after entry into force of this Convention, coordinate the establishment and maintenance of permanent stockpiles of emergency and humanitarian assistance by States Parties in accordance with Article X, paragraphs 7 (b) and (c). The Technical Secretariat may inspect the items maintained for serviceability. Lists of items to be stockpiled shall be considered and approved by the Conference pursuant to paragraph 21 (i) above;

(c) Administer the voluntary fund referred to in Article X, compile declarations made by the States Parties and register, when requested, bilateral agreements concluded between States Parties or between a State Party and the Organization for the purposes of Article X.

40. The Technical Secretariat shall inform the Executive Council of any problem that has arisen with regard to the discharge of its functions, including doubts, ambiguities or uncertainties about compliance with this Convention that have come to its notice in the performance of its verification activities and that it has been unable to resolve or clarify through its consultations with the State Party concerned.

41. The Technical Secretariat shall comprise a Director-General, who shall be its head and chief administrative officer, inspectors and such scientific, technical and other personnel as may be required.

42. The Inspectorate shall be a unit of the Technical Secretariat and shall act under the supervision of the Director-General.

43. The Director-General shall be appointed by the Conference upon the recommendation of the Executive Council for a term of four years, renewable for one further term, but not thereafter.

44. The Director-General shall be responsible to the Conference and the Executive Council for the appointment of the staff and the organization and functioning of the Technical Secretariat. The paramount consideration in the employment of the staff and in the determination of the conditions of service shall be the necessity of

securing the highest standards of efficiency, competence and integrity. Only citizens of States Parties shall serve as the Director-General, as inspectors or as other members of the professional and clerical staff. Due regard shall be paid to the importance of recruiting the staff on as wide a geographical basis as possible. Recruitment shall be guided by the principle that the staff shall be kept to a minimum necessary for the proper discharge of the responsibilities of the Technical Secretariat.

45. The Director-General shall be responsible for the organization and functioning of the Scientific Advisory Board referred to in paragraph 21 (h). The Director-General shall, in consultation with States Parties, appoint members of the Scientific Advisory Board, who shall serve in their individual capacity. The members of the Board shall be appointed on the basis of their expertise in the particular scientific fields relevant to the implementation of this Convention. The Director-General may also, as appropriate, in consultation with members of the Board, establish temporary working groups of scientific experts to provide recommendations on specific issues. In regard to the above, States Parties may submit lists of experts to the Director-General.

46. In the performance of their duties, the Director-General, the inspectors and the other members of the staff shall not seek or receive instructions from any Government or from any other source external to the Organization. They shall refrain from any action that might reflect on their positions as international officers responsible only to the Conference and the Executive Council.

47. Each State Party shall respect the exclusively international character of the responsibilities of the Director-General, the inspectors and the other members of the staff and not seek to influence them in the discharge of their responsibilities.

E. PRIVILEGES AND IMMUNITIES

48. The Organization shall enjoy on the territory and in any other place under the jurisdiction or control of a State Party such legal capacity and such privileges and immunities as are necessary for the exercise of its functions.

49. Delegates of States Parties, together with their alternates and advisers, representatives appointed to the Executive Council together with their alternates and advisers, the Director-General and the staff of the Organization shall enjoy such privileges and immunities as are necessary in the independent exercise of their functions in connection with the Organization.

50. The legal capacity, privileges, and immunities referred to in this Article shall be defined in agreements between the Organization and the States Parties as well as in an agreement between the Organization and the State in which the headquarters of the Organization is seated. These agreements shall be considered and approved by the Conference pursuant to paragraph 21 (i).

51. Notwithstanding paragraphs 48 and 49, the privileges and immunities enjoyed by the Director-General and the staff of the Technical Secretariat during the conduct of verification activities shall be those set forth in Part II, Section B, of the Verification Annex.

ARTICLE IX

CONSULTATIONS, COOPERATION AND FACT-FINDING

1. States Parties shall consult and cooperate, directly among themselves, or through the Organization or other appropriate international procedures, including procedures within the framework of the United Nations and in accordance with its Charter, on any matter which may be raised relating to the object and purpose, or the implementation of the provisions, of this Convention.

2. Without prejudice to the right of any State Party to request a challenge inspection, States Parties should, whenever possible, first make every effort to clarify and resolve, through exchange of information and consultations among themselves, any matter which may cause doubt about compliance with this Convention, or which gives rise to concerns about a related matter which may be considered ambiguous. A State Party which receives a request from another State Party for clarification of any matter which the requesting State Party believes causes such a doubt or concern shall provide the requesting State Party as soon as possible, but in any case not later than 10 days after the request, with information sufficient to answer the doubt or concern raised along with an explanation of how the information provided resolves the matter. Nothing in this Convention shall affect the right of any two or more States Parties to arrange by mutual consent for inspections or any other procedures among themselves to clarify and resolve any matter which may cause doubt about compliance or gives rise to a concern about a related matter which may be considered ambiguous. Such arrangements shall not affect the rights and obligations of any State Party under other provisions of this Convention.

Procedure for requesting clarification

3. A State Party shall have the right to request the Executive Council to assist in clarifying any situation which may be considered ambiguous or which gives rise to a concern about the possible non-compliance of another State Party with this Convention. The Executive Council shall provide appropriate information in its possession relevant to such a concern.

4. A State Party shall have the right to request the Executive Council to obtain clarification from another State Party on any situation which may be considered ambiguous or which gives rise to a concern about its possible non-compliance with this Convention. In such a case, the following shall apply:

(a) The Executive Council shall forward the request for clarification to the State Party concerned through the Director-General not later than 24 hours after its receipt;

(b) The requested State Party shall provide the clarification to the Executive Council as soon as possible, but in any case not later than 10 days after the receipt of the request;

(c) The Executive Council shall take note of the clarification and forward it to the requesting State Party not later than 24 hours after its receipt;

(d) If the requesting State Party deems the clarification to be inadequate, it shall have the right to request the Executive

Council to obtain from the requested State Party further clarification;

(e) For the purpose of obtaining further clarification requested under subparagraph (d), the Executive Council may call on the Director-General to establish a group of experts from the Technical Secretariat, or if appropriate staff are not available in the Technical Secretariat, from elsewhere, to examine all available information and data relevant to the situation causing the concern. The group of experts shall submit a factual report to the Executive Council on its findings;

(f) If the requesting State Party considers the clarification obtained under subparagraphs (d) and (e) to be unsatisfactory, it shall have the right to request a special session of the Executive Council in which States Parties involved that are not members of the Executive Council shall be entitled to take part. In such a special session, the Executive Council shall consider the matter and may recommend any measure it deems appropriate to resolve the situation.

5. A State Party shall also have the right to request the Executive Council to clarify any situation which has been considered ambiguous or has given rise to a concern about its possible non-compliance with this Convention. The Executive Council shall respond by providing such assistance as appropriate.

6. The Executive Council shall inform the States Parties about any request for clarification provided in this Article.

7. If the doubt or concern of a State Party about a possible non-compliance has not been resolved within 60 days after the submission of the request for clarification to the Executive Council, or it believes its doubts warrant urgent consideration, notwithstanding its right to request a challenge inspection, it may request a special session of the Conference in accordance with Article VIII, paragraph 12 (c). At such a special session, the Conference shall consider the matter and may recommend any measure it deems appropriate to resolve the situation.

Procedures for challenge inspections

8. Each State Party has the right to request an on-site challenge inspection of any facility or location in the territory or in any other place under the jurisdiction or control of any other State Party for the sole purpose of clarifying and resolving any questions concerning possible non-compliance with the provisions of this Convention, and to have this inspection conducted anywhere without delay by an inspection team designated by the Director-General and in accordance with the Verification Annex.

9. Each State Party is under the obligation to keep the inspection request within the scope of this Convention and to provide in the inspection request all appropriate information on the basis of which a concern has arisen regarding possible non-compliance with this Convention as specified in the Verification Annex. Each State Party shall refrain from unfounded inspection requests, care being taken to avoid abuse. The challenge inspection shall be carried out for the sole purpose of determining facts relating to the possible non-compliance.

10. For the purpose of verifying compliance with the provisions of this Convention, each State Party shall permit the Technical Secretariat to conduct the on-site challenge inspection pursuant to paragraph 8.

11. Pursuant to a request for a challenge inspection of a facility or location, and in accordance with the procedures provided for in the Verification Annex, the inspected State Party shall have:

(a) The right and the obligation to make every reasonable effort to demonstrate its compliance with this Convention and, to this end, to enable the inspection team to fulfill its mandate;

(b) The obligation to provide access within the requested site for the sole purpose of establishing facts relevant to the concern regarding possible non-compliance; and

(c) The right to take measures to protect sensitive installations, and to prevent disclosure of confidential information and data, not related to this Convention.

12. With regard to an observer, the following shall apply:

(a) The requesting State Party may, subject to the agreement of the inspected State Party, send a representative who may be a national either of the requesting State Party or of a third State Party, to observe the conduct of the challenge inspection.

(b) The inspected State Party shall then grant access to the observer in accordance with the Verification Annex.

(c) The inspected State Party shall, as a rule, accept the proposed observer, but if the inspected State Party exercises a refusal, that fact shall be recorded in the final report.

13. The requesting State Party shall present an inspection request for an on-site challenge inspection to the Executive Council and at the same time to the Director-General for immediate processing.

14. The Director-General shall immediately ascertain that the inspection request meets the requirements specified in Part X, paragraph 4, of the Verification Annex, and, if necessary, assist the requesting State Party in filing the inspection request accordingly. When the inspection request fulfills the requirements, preparations for the challenge inspection shall begin.

15. The Director-General shall transmit the inspection request to the inspected State Party not less than 12 hours before the planned arrival of the inspection team at the point of entry.

16. After having received the inspection request, the Executive Council shall take cognizance of the Director-General's actions on the request and shall keep the case under its consideration throughout the inspection procedure. However, its deliberations shall not delay the inspection process.

17. The Executive Council may, not later than 12 hours after having received the inspection request, decide by a three-quarter majority of all its members against carrying out the challenge inspection, if it considers the inspection request to be frivolous, abusive or clearly beyond the scope of this Convention as described in paragraph 8. Neither the requesting nor the inspected State Party shall participate in such a decision. If the Executive Council decides against the challenge inspection, preparations shall be stopped, no further action on the inspection request shall be taken, and the States Parties concerned shall be informed accordingly.

18. The Director-General shall issue an inspection mandate for the conduct of the challenge inspection. The inspection mandate shall be the inspection request referred to in paragraphs 8 and 9 put into operational terms, and shall conform with the inspection request.

19. The challenge inspection shall be conducted in accordance with Part X or, in the case of alleged use, in accordance with Part XI of the Verification Annex. The inspection team shall be guided by the principle of conducting the challenge inspection in the least intrusive manner possible, consistent with the effective and timely accomplishment of its mission.

20. The inspected State Party shall assist the inspection team throughout the challenge inspection and facilitate its task. If the inspected State Party proposes, pursuant to Part X, Section C, of the Verification Annex, arrangements to demonstrate compliance with this Convention, alternative to full and comprehensive access, it shall make every reasonable effort, through consultations with the inspection team, to reach agreement on the modalities for establishing the facts with the aim of demonstrating its compliance.

21. The final report shall contain the factual findings as well as an assessment by the inspection team of the degree and nature of access and cooperation granted for the satisfactory implementation of the challenge inspection. The Director-General shall promptly transmit the final report of the inspection team to the requesting State Party, to the inspected State Party, to the Executive Council and to all other States Parties. The Director-General shall further transmit promptly to the Executive Council the assessments of the requesting and of the inspected States Parties, as well as the views of other States Parties which may be conveyed to the Director-General for that purpose, and then provide them to all States Parties.

22. The Executive Council shall, in accordance with its powers and functions, review the final report of the inspection team as soon as it is presented, and address any concerns as to:

(a) Whether any non-compliance has occurred;

(b) Whether the request had been within the scope of this Convention; and

(c) Whether the right to request a challenge inspection had been abused.

23. If the Executive Council reaches the conclusion, in keeping with its powers and functions, that further action may be necessary with regard to paragraph 22, it shall take the appropriate measures to redress the situation and to ensure compliance with this Convention, including specific recommendations to the Conference. In the case of abuse, the Executive Council shall examine whether the requesting State Party should bear any of the financial implications of the challenge inspection.

24. The requesting State Party and the inspected State Party shall have the right to participate in the review process. The Executive Council shall inform the States Parties and the next session of the Conference of the outcome of the process.

25. If the Executive Council has made specific recommendations to the Conference, the Conference shall consider action in accordance with Article XII.

ARTICLE X

ASSISTANCE AND PROTECTION AGAINST CHEMICAL WEAPONS

1. For the purposes of this Article, "Assistance" means the coordination and delivery to States Parties of protection against chemical weapons, including, inter alia, the following: detection equipment and alarm systems; protective equipment; decontamination equipment and decontaminants; medical antidotes and treatments; and advice on any of these protective measures.

2. Nothing in this Convention shall be interpreted as impeding the right of any State Party to conduct research into, develop, produce, acquire, transfer or use means of protection against chemical weapons, for purposes not prohibited under this Convention.

3. Each State Party undertakes to facilitate, and shall have the right to participate in, the fullest possible exchange of equipment, material and scientific and technological information concerning means of protection against chemical weapons.

4. For the purposes of increasing the transparency of national programmes related to protective purposes, each State Party shall provide annually to the Technical Secretariat information on its programme, in accordance with procedures to be considered and approved by the Conference pursuant to Article VIII, paragraph 21 (i).

5. The Technical Secretariat shall establish, not later than 180 days after entry into force of this Convention and maintain, for the use of any requesting State Party, a data bank containing freely available information concerning various means of protection against chemical weapons as well as such information as may be provided by States Parties.

The Technical Secretariat shall also, within the resources available to it, and at the request of a State Party, provide expert advice and assist the State Party in identifying how its programmes for the development and improvement of a protective capacity against chemical weapons could be implemented.

6. Nothing in this Convention shall be interpreted as impeding the right of States Parties to request and provide assistance bilaterally and to conclude individual agreements with other States Parties concerning the emergency procurement of assistance.

7. Each State Party undertakes to provide assistance through the Organization and to this end to elect to take one or more of the following measures:

(a) To contribute to the voluntary fund for assistance to be established by the Conference at its first session;

(b) To conclude, if possible not later than 180 days after this Convention enters into force for it, agreements with the Organization concerning the procurement, upon demand, of assistance;

(c) To declare, not later than 180 days after this Convention enters into force for it, the kind of assistance it might provide in response to an appeal by the Organization. If, however, a State Party subsequently is unable to provide the assistance envisaged in its declaration, it is still under the obligation to provide assistance in accordance with this paragraph.

8. Each State Party has the right to request and, subject to the procedures set forth in paragraphs 9, 10 and 11, to receive assistance and protection against the use or threat of use of chemical weapons if it considers that:

(a) Chemical weapons have been used against it;

(b) Riot control agents have been used against it as a method of warfare; or

(c) It is threatened by actions or activities of any State that are prohibited for States Parties by Article I.

9. The request, substantiated by relevant information, shall be submitted to the Director-General, who shall transmit it immediately to the Executive Council and to all States Parties. The Director-General shall immediately forward the request to States Parties which have volunteered, in accordance with paragraphs 7 (b) and (c), to dispatch emergency assistance in case of use of chemical weapons or use of riot control agents as a method of warfare, or humanitarian assistance in case of serious threat of use of chemical weapons or serious threat of use of riot control agents as a method of warfare to the State Party concerned not later than 12 hours after receipt of the request. The Director-General shall initiate, not later than 24 hours after receipt of the request, an investigation in order to provide foundation for further action. He shall complete the investigation within 72 hours and forward a report to the Executive Council. If additional time is required for completion of the investigation, an interim report shall be submitted within the same time-frame. The additional time required for investigation shall not exceed 72 hours. It may, however, be further extended by similar periods. Reports at the end of each additional period shall be submitted to the Executive Council. The investigation shall, as appropriate and in conformity with the request and the information accompanying the request, establish relevant facts related to the request as well as the type and scope of supplementary assistance and protection needed.

10. The Executive Council shall meet not later than 24 hours after receiving an investigation report to consider the situation and shall take a decision by simple majority within the following 24 hours on whether to instruct the Technical Secretariat to provide supplementary assistance. The Technical Secretariat shall immediately transmit to all States Parties and relevant international organizations the investigation report and the decision taken by the Executive Council. When so decided by the Executive Council, the Director-General shall provide assistance immediately. For this purpose, the Director-General may cooperate with the requesting State Party, other States Parties and relevant international organizations. The States Parties shall make the fullest possible efforts to provide assistance.

11. If the information available from the ongoing investigation or other reliable sources would give sufficient proof that there are victims of use of chemical weapons and immediate action is indispensable, the Director-General shall notify all States Parties and shall take emergency measures of assistance, using the resources the Conference has placed at his disposal for such contingencies. The

Director-General shall keep the Executive Council informed of actions undertaken pursuant to this paragraph.

ARTICLE XI

ECONOMIC AND TECHNOLOGICAL DEVELOPMENT

1. The provisions of this Convention shall be implemented in a manner which avoids hampering the economic or technological development of States Parties, and international cooperation in the field of chemical activities for purposes not prohibited under this Convention including the international exchange of scientific and technical information and chemicals and equipment for the production, processing or use of chemicals for purposes not prohibited under this Convention.

2. Subject to the provisions of this Convention and without prejudice to the principles and applicable rules of international law, the States Parties shall:

(a) Have the right, individually or collectively, to conduct research with, to develop, produce, acquire, retain, transfer, and use chemicals;

(b) Undertake to facilitate, and have the right to participate in, the fullest possible exchange of chemicals, equipment and scientific and technical information relating to the development and application of chemistry for purposes not prohibited under this Convention;

(c) Not maintain among themselves any restrictions, including those in any international agreements, incompatible with the obligations undertaken under this Convention, which would restrict or impede trade and the development and promotion of scientific and technological knowledge in the field of chemistry for industrial, agricultural, research, medical, pharmaceutical or other peaceful purposes;

(d) Not use this Convention as grounds for applying any measures other than those provided for, or permitted, under this Convention nor use any other international agreement for pursuing an objective inconsistent with this Convention;

(e) Undertake to review their existing national regulations in the field of trade in chemicals in order to render them consistent with the object and purpose of this Convention.

ARTICLE XII

MEASURES TO REDRESS A SITUATION AND TO ENSURE COMPLIANCE, INCLUDING SANCTIONS

1. The Conference shall take the necessary measures, as set forth in paragraphs 2, 3 and 4, to ensure compliance with this Convention and to redress and remedy any situation which contravenes the provisions of this Convention. In considering action pursuant to this paragraph, the Conference shall take into account all information and recommendations on the issues submitted by the Executive Council.

2. In cases where a State Party has been requested by the Executive Council to take measures to redress a situation raising problems with regard to its compliance, and where the State Party fails to fulfill the request within the specified time, the Conference may, inter alia, upon the recommendation of the Executive Council, restrict or suspend the State Party's rights and privileges under this Convention until it undertakes the necessary action to conform with its obligations under this Convention.

3. In cases where serious damage to the object and purpose of this Convention may result from activities prohibited under this Convention, in particular by Article I, the Conference may recommend collective measures to States Parties in conformity with international law.

4. The Conference shall, in cases of particular gravity, bring the issue, including relevant information and conclusions, to the attention of the United Nations General Assembly and the United Nations Security Council.

ARTICLE XIII

RELATION TO OTHER INTERNATIONAL AGREEMENTS

Nothing in this Convention shall be interpreted as in any way limiting or detracting from the obligations assumed by any State under the Protocol for the Prohibition of the Use in War of Asphyxiating, Poisonous or Other Gases, and of Bacteriological Methods of Warfare, signed at Geneva on 17 June 1925, and under the Convention on the Prohibition of the Development, Production and Stockpiling of Bacteriological (Biological) and Toxin Weapons and on Their Destruction, signed at London, Moscow and Washington on 10 April 1972.

ARTICLE XIV

SETTLEMENT OF DISPUTES

1. Disputes that may arise concerning the application or the interpretation of this Convention shall be settled in accordance with the relevant provisions of this Convention and in conformity with the provisions of the Charter of the United Nations.

2. When a dispute arises between two or more States Parties, or between one or more States Parties and the Organization, relating to the interpretation or application of this Convention, the parties concerned shall consult together with a view to the expeditious settlement of the dispute by negotiation or by other peaceful means of the parties' choice, including recourse to appropriate organs of this Convention and, by mutual consent, referral to the International Court of Justice in conformity with the Statute of the Court. The States Parties involved shall keep the Executive Council informed of actions being taken.

3. The Executive Council may contribute to the settlement of a dispute by whatever means it deems appropriate, including offering its good offices, calling upon the States Parties to a dispute to start the settlement process of their choice and recommending a time-limit for any agreed procedure.

4. The Conference shall consider questions related to disputes raised by States Parties or brought to its attention by the Executive Council. The Conference shall, as it finds necessary, establish or entrust organs with tasks related to the settlement of these disputes in conformity with Article VIII, paragraph 21 (f).

5. The Conference and the Executive Council are separately empowered, subject to authorization from the General Assembly of the United Nations, to request the International Court of Justice to give an advisory opinion on any legal question arising within the scope of the activities of the Organization. An agreement between the Organization and the United Nations shall be concluded for this purpose in accordance with Article VIII, paragraph 34 (a).

6. This Article is without prejudice to Article IX or to the provisions on measures to redress a situation and to ensure compliance, including sanctions.

ARTICLE XV

AMENDMENTS

1. Any State Party may propose amendments to this Convention. Any State Party may also propose changes, as specified in paragraph 4, to the Annexes of this Convention. Proposals for amendments shall be subject to the procedures in paragraphs 2 and 3. Proposals for changes, as specified in paragraph 4, shall be subject to the procedures in paragraph 5.

2. The text of a proposed amendment shall be submitted to the Director-General for circulation to all States Parties and to the Depositary. The proposed amendment shall be considered only by an Amendment Conference. Such an Amendment Conference shall be convened if one third or more of the States Parties notify the Director-General not later than 30 days after its circulation that they support further consideration of the proposal. The Amendment Conference shall be held immediately following a regular session of the Conference unless the requesting States Parties ask for an earlier meeting. In no case shall an Amendment Conference be held less than 60 days after the circulation of the proposed amendment.

3. Amendments shall enter into force for all States Parties 30 days after deposit of the instruments of ratification or acceptance by all the States Parties referred to under subparagraph (b) below:

(a) When adopted by the Amendment Conference by a positive vote of a majority of all States Parties with no State Party casting a negative vote; and

(b) Ratified or accepted by all those States Parties casting a positive vote at the Amendment Conference.

4. In order to ensure the viability and the effectiveness of this Convention, provisions in the Annexes shall be subject to changes in accordance with paragraph 5, if proposed changes are related only to matters of an administrative or technical nature. All changes to the Annex on Chemicals shall be made in accordance with paragraph 5. Sections A and C of the Confidentiality Annex, Part X of the Verification Annex, and those definitions in Part I of the Verification Annex which relate exclusively to challenge inspections, shall not be subject to changes in accordance with paragraph 5.

5. Proposed changes referred to in paragraph 4 shall be made in accordance with the following procedures:

(a) The text of the proposed changes shall be transmitted together with the necessary information to the Director-General. Additional information for the evaluation of the proposal may be provided by any State Party and the Director-General. The Director-General shall promptly communicate any such proposals and information to all States Parties, the Executive Council and the Depositary;

(b) Not later than 60 days after its receipt, the Director-General shall evaluate the proposal to determine all its possible consequences for the provisions of this Convention and its implementation and shall communicate any such information to all States Parties and the Executive Council;

(c) The Executive Council shall examine the proposal in the light of all information available to it, including whether the proposal fulfills the requirements of paragraph 4. Not later than 90 days after its receipt, the Executive Council shall notify its recommendation, with appropriate explanations, to all States Parties for consideration. States Parties shall acknowledge receipt within 10 days;

(d) If the Executive Council recommends to all States Parties that the proposal be adopted, it shall be considered approved if no State Party objects to it within 90 days after receipt of the recommendation. If the Executive Council recommends that the proposal be rejected, it shall be considered rejected if no State Party objects to the rejection within 90 days after receipt of the recommendation;

(e) If a recommendation of the Executive Council does not meet with the acceptance required under subparagraph (d), a decision on the proposal, including whether it fulfills the requirements of paragraph 4, shall be taken as a matter of substance by the Conference at its next session;

(f) The Director-General shall notify all States Parties and the Depositary of any decision under this paragraph;

(g) Changes approved under this procedure shall enter into force for all States Parties 180 days after the date of notification by the Director-General of their approval unless another time period is recommended by the Executive Council or decided by the Conference.

ARTICLE XVI

DURATION AND WITHDRAWAL

1. This Convention shall be of unlimited duration.

2. Each State Party shall, in exercising its national sovereignty, have the right to withdraw from this Convention if it decides that extraordinary events, related to the subject-matter of this Convention, have jeopardized the supreme interests of its country. It shall give notice of such withdrawal 90 days in advance to all other States Parties, the Executive Council, the Depositary and the United Nations Security Council. Such notice shall include a statement of the extraordinary events it regards as having jeopardized its supreme interests.

3. The withdrawal of a State Party from this Convention shall not in any way affect the duty of States to continue fulfilling the obligations assumed under any relevant rules of international law, particularly the Geneva Protocol of 1925.

ARTICLE XVII

STATUS OF THE ANNEXES

The Annexes form an integral part of this Convention. Any reference to this Convention includes the Annexes.

ARTICLE XVIII

SIGNATURE

This Convention shall be open for signature for all States before its entry into force.

ARTICLE XIX

RATIFICATION

This Convention shall be subject to ratification by States Signatories according to their respective constitutional processes.

ARTICLE XX

ACCESSION

Any State which does not sign this Convention before its entry into force may accede to it at any time thereafter.

ARTICLE XXI

ENTRY INTO FORCE

1. This Convention shall enter into force 180 days after the date of the deposit of the 65th instrument of ratification, but in no case earlier than two years after its opening for signature.

2. For States whose instruments of ratification or accession are deposited subsequent to the entry into force of this Convention, it shall enter into force on the 30th day following the date of deposit of their instrument of ratification or accession.

ARTICLE XXII

RESERVATIONS

The Articles of this Convention shall not be subject to reservations. The Annexes of this Convention shall not be subject to reservations incompatible with its object and purpose.

ARTICLE XXIII

DEPOSITARY

The Secretary-General of the United Nations is hereby designated as the Depositary of this Convention and shall, *inter alia*:

(a) Promptly inform all signatory and acceding States of the date of each signature, the date of deposit of each instrument of ratification or accession and the date of the entry into force of this Convention, and of the receipt of other notices;

(b) Transmit duly certified copies of this Convention to the Governments of all signatory and acceding States; and

(c) Register this Convention pursuant to Article 102 of the Charter of the United Nations.

ARTICLE XXIV

AUTHENTIC TEXTS

This Convention, of which the Arabic, Chinese, English, French, Russian and Spanish texts are equally authentic, shall be deposited with the Secretary-General of the United Nations.

IN WITNESS WHEREOF the undersigned, being duly authorized to that effect, have signed this Convention.

DONE at Paris on the thirteenth day of January, one thousand nine hundred and ninety-three.

9. Treaty on Conventional Armed Forces in Europe (CFE) [1]

Treaty on Conventional Armed Forces in Europe (CFE), With Protocols on Existing Types (With Annex), Aircraft Reclassification, Reduction, Helicopter Recategorization, Information Exchange (With Annex), Inspection, the Joint Consultative Group, and Provisional Application; Signed at Paris, November 19, 1990; Ratification advised by the Senate, November 25, 1991; Entered into force, November 9, 1992

The Kingdom of Belgium, the Republic of Bulgaria, Canada, the Czech and Slovak Federal Republic, the Kingdom of Denmark, the French Republic, the Federal Republic of Germany, the Hellenic Republic, the Republic of Hungary, the Republic of Iceland, the Italian Republic, the Grand Duchy of Luxembourg, the Kingdom of the Netherlands, the Kingdom of Norway, the Republic of Poland, the Portuguese Republic, Romania, the Kingdom of Spain, the Republic of Turkey, the Union of Soviet Socialist Republics, the United Kingdom of Great Britain and Northern Ireland and the United States of America, hereinafter referred to as the State Parties,

GUIDED by the Mandate for Negotiation on Conventional Armed Forces in Europe of January 10, 1989, and having conducted this negotiation in Vienna beginning on March 9, 1989,

GUIDED by the objectives and the purposes of the Conference on Security and Cooperation in Europe, within the framework of which the negotiation of this Treaty was conducted,

RECALLING their obligation to refrain in their mutual relations, as well as in their international relations in general, from the threat or use of force against the territorial integrity or political independence of any State, or in any other manner inconsistent with the purposes and principles of the Charter of the United Nations,

CONSCIOUS of the need to prevent any military conflict in Europe,

CONSCIOUS of the common responsibility which they all have for seeking to achieve greater stability and security in Europe,

STRIVING to replace military confrontation with a new pattern of security relations among all the States Parties based on peaceful cooperation and thereby to contribute to overcoming the division of Europe,

COMMITTED to the objectives of establishing a secure and stable balance of conventional armed forces in Europe at lower levels than

---

[1] Treaty Doc. 102–8. For a list of states that are parties to the Treaty, see Department of State publication, *Treaties in Force*.

The Treaty also includes protocols and annexes, the complete text of which is available at a web site maintained by the Federation of American Scientists: http://www.fas.org/nuke/control/cfe/text/index.html.

Senate conditions to the ratification of the Convention can be found at the same web site: http://www.fas.org/nuke/control/cfe/congress/22c4.htm#IX.

heretofore, of eliminating disparities prejudicial to stability and security and of eliminating, as a matter of high priority, the capability for launching surprise attack and for initiating large-scale offensive action in Europe,

RECALLING that they signed or acceded to the Treaty of Brussels of 1948, the Treaty of Washington of 1949 or the Treaty of Warsaw of 1955 and that they have the right to be or not to be a party to treaties of alliance,

COMMITTED to the objective of ensuring that the numbers of conventional armaments and equipment limited by the Treaty within the area of application of this Treaty do not exceed 40,000 battle tanks, 60,000 armoured combat vehicles, 40,000 pieces of artillery, 13,600 combat aircraft and 4,000 attack helicopters,

AFFIRMING that this Treaty is not intended to affect adversely the security interests of any State,

AFFIRMING their commitment to continue the conventional arms control process including negotiations, taking into account future requirements for European stability and security in the light of political developments in Europe,

HAVE AGREED AS FOLLOWS:

Article I

1. Each State Party shall carry out the obligations set forth in this Treaty in accordance with its provisions, including those obligations relating to the following five categories of conventional armed forces: battle tanks, armoured combat vehicles, artillery, combat aircraft and combat helicopters.

2. Each State Party also shall carry out the other measures set forth in this Treaty designed to ensure security and stability both during the period of reduction of conventional armed forces and after the completion of reductions.

3. This Treaty incorporates the Protocol on Existing Types of Conventional Armaments and Equipment, hereinafter referred to as the Protocol on Existing Types, with an Annex thereto, the Protocol on Procedures Governing the Reclassification of Specific Models or Versions of Combat-Capable Trainer Aircraft Into Unarmed Trainer Aircraft, hereinafter referred to as the Protocol on Aircraft Reclassification; the Protocol on Procedures Governing the Reduction of Conventional Armaments and Equipment Limited by the Treaty on Conventional Armed Forces in Europe, hereinafter referred to as the Protocol on Reduction; the Protocol on Procedures Governing the Categorization of Combat Helicopters and the Recategorization of Multi-Purpose Attack Helicopter, hereinafter referred to as the Protocol on Helicopter Recategorization; the Protocol on Notification and Exchange of Information, hereinafter referred to as the Protocol on Information Exchange, with an Annex on the Format for the Exchange of Information, hereinafter referred to as the Annex on Format; the Protocol on Inspection, the Protocol on the Joint Consultative Group; and the Protocol on the Provisional Application of Certain Provisions of the Treaty on Conventional Armed Forces in Europe, hereinafter referred to as the Protocol on

Provisional Application. Each of these documents constitutes an integral part of this treaty.

Article II

1. For the purposes of this Treaty:

(A) The term "group of States Parties" means the group of States Parties that signed the Treaty of Warsaw[2] of 1955 consisting of the Republic of Bulgaria, the Czech and Slovak Federal Republic, the Republic of Hungary, the Republic of Poland, Romania and the Union of Soviet Socialist Republics, or the group of States Parties that signed or acceded to the Treaty of Brussels[3] of 1948 or the Treaty of Washington[4] of 1949 consisting of the Kingdom of Belgium, Canada, the Kingdom of Denmark, the French Republic, the Federal Republic of Germany, the Hellenic Republic, the Republic of Iceland, the Italian Republic, the Grand Duchy of Luxembourg, the Kingdom of the Netherlands, the Kingdom of Norway, the Portuguese Republic, the Kingdom of Spain, the Republic of Turkey, the United Kingdom of Great Britain and Northern Ireland and the United States of America.

(B) The term "area of application" means the entire land territory of the States Parties in Europe from the Atlantic Ocean to the Ural Mountains, which includes all the European island territories of the States Parties, including the Faroe Islands of the Kingdom of Denmark, Svalbard including BearIsland of the Kingdom of Norway, the islands of Azores and Madeira of the Portuguese Republic, the Canary Islands of the Kingdom of Spain and Franz Josef Land and Novaya Zemlya of the Union of Soviet Socialist Republics. In the case of the Union of Soviet Socialist Republics, the area of application includes all territory lying west of the Ural River and the Caspian Sea. In the case of the Republic of Turkey north and west of a line extending from the point of intersection of the Turkish border with the 39th parallel to Muradiye, Patnos, Karayazi, Tekman, Kemaliye, Feke, Ceyhan, Dogankent, Gozne and thence to the sea.

(C) The term "battle tank" means a self-propelled armoured fighting vehicle, capable of heavy firepower, primarily of a high muzzle velocity direct fire main gun necessary to engage armoured and other targets, with high cross-country mobility, with a high level of self-protection, and which is not designed and equipped primarily to transport combat troops. Such armoured vehicles serve as the principal weapon system of ground-force tank and other armoured formations.

Battle tanks are tracked armoured fighting vehicles which weigh at least 16.5 metric tonnes unladen weight and which are armed with a 360-degree traverse gun of at least 75 millimetres calibre. In addition, any wheeled armoured fighting vehicles entering into service which

[2] The Treaty of Friendship, Cooperation and Mutual Assistance signed in Warsaw, May 14, 1955.

[3] The Treaty of Economic, Social and Cultural Collaboration and Collective Self-Defence signed in Brussels, March 17, 1948.

[4] The North Atlantic treaty signed in Washington, April 4, 1949.

meet all the other criteria stated above shall also be deemed battle tanks.

(D) The term "armoured combat vehicle" means a self-propelled vehicle with armoured protection and cross-country capability. Armoured combat vehicles include armoured personnel carriers, armoured infantry fighting vehicles and heavy armament combat vehicles.

The term "armoured personnel carrier" means an armoured combat vehicle which is designed and equipped to transport a combat infantry squad and which, as a rule, is armed with an integral or organic weapon of less than 20 millimetres calibre.

The term "armoured infantry fighting vehicle" means an armoured combat vehicle which is designed and equipped primarily to transport a combat infantry squad, which normally provides the capability for the troops to deliver fire from inside the vehicle under armoured protection, and which is armed with an integral or organic cannon of at least 20 millimetres calibre and sometimes an antitank missile launcher. Armoured infantry fighting vehicles serve as the principal weapon system of armoured infantry or mechanised infantry or motorised infantry formations and units of ground forces.

The term "heavy armament combat vehicle" means an armoured combat vehicle with an integral or organic direct fire gun of at least 75 millimetres calibre, weighing at least 6.0 metric tonnes unladen weight, which does not fall within the definitions of an armoured personnel carrier, or an armoured infantry fighting vehicle or a battle tank.

(E) The term "unladen weight" means the weight of a vehicle excluding the weight of ammunition; fuel, oil and lubricants; removable reactive armour; spare parts, tools, accessories; removable snorkeling equipment; and crew and their personal kit.

(F) The term "artillery" means large calibre systems capable of engaging ground targets by delivering primarily indirect fire. Such artillery systems provide the essential indirect fire support to combined arms formations.

Large calibre artillery systems are guns, howitzers, artillery pieces combining the characteristics of guns and howitzers, mortars and multiple launch rocket systems with a calibre of 100 millimetres and above. In addition, any future large calibre direct fire system which has a secondary effective indirect fire capability shall be counted against the artillery ceilings.

(G) The term "stationed conventional armed forces" means conventional armed forces of a State Party that are stationed within the area of application on the territory of another State Party.

(H) The term "designated permanent storage site" means a place with a clearly defined physical boundary containing conventional armaments and equipment limited by the Treaty, which are counted within overall ceilings but which are not subject to limitations on conventional armaments and equipment limited by the Treaty in active units.

(I) The term "armoured launched bridge" means a self-propelled armoured transporter-launcher vehicle capable of carrying and, through built-in mechanisms, of emplacing and retrieving a bridge structure. Such a vehicle with a bridge structure operates as an integrated system.

(J) The term "conventional armaments and equipment limited by the Treaty" means battle tanks, armoured combat vehicles, artillery, combat aircraft and attack helicopters subject to the numerical limitations set forth in Articles IV, V and VI.

(K) The term "combat aircraft" means a fixed-wing or variable-geometry wing aircraft armed and equipped to engage targets by employing guided missiles, unguided rockets, bombs, guns, cannons, or other weapons of destruction, as well as any model or version of such an aircraft which performs other military functions such as reconnaissance or electronic warfare. The term "combat aircraft" does not include primary trainer aircraft.

(L) The term "combat helicopter" means a rotary wing aircraft armed and equipped to engage targets or equipped to perform other military functions. The term "combat helicopter" comprises attack helicopters and combat support helicopters. The term "combat helicopter" does not include unarmed transport helicopters.

(M) The term "attack helicopter" means a combat helicopter equipped to employ anti-armour, air-to-ground, or air-to-air guided weapons and equipped with an integrated fire control and aiming system for these weapons. The term "attack helicopter" comprises specialised attack helicopters and multi-purpose attack helicopters.

(N) The term "specialised attack helicopter" means an attack helicopter that is designed primarily to employ guided weapons.

(O) The term "multi-purpose attack helicopter" means an attack helicopter designed to perform multiple military functions and equipped to employ guided weapons.

(P) The term "combat support helicopter" means a combat helicopter which does not fulfill the requirements to qualify as an attack helicopter and which may be equipped with a variety of self-defence and area suppression weapons, such as guns, cannons and unguided rockets, bombs or cluster bombs, or which may be equipped to perform other military functions.

(Q) The term "conventional armaments and equipment subject to the Treaty" means battle tanks, armoured combat vehicles, artillery, combat aircraft, primary trainer aircraft, unarmed trainer aircraft, combat helicopters, unarmed transport helicopters, armoured vehicle launched bridges, armoured personnel carrier look-alikes and armoured infantry fighting vehicle look-alikes subject to information exchange in accordance with the Protocol on Information Exchange.

(R) The term "in service" as it applies to conventional armed forces and conventional armaments and equipment, means battle tanks, armoured combat vehicles, artillery, combat aircraft, primary trainer aircraft, unarmed trainer aircraft, combat helicopters, unarmed transport helicopters, armoured vehicle launched bridges, armoured personnel carrier look-alikes and armoured infantry fighting vehicle look-alikes that are within the area of application, except for those that are held by organisations designed and structured to perform in peacetime internal security functions or that meet any of the exceptions set forth in Article III.

(S) The terms "armoured personnel carrier look-alike" and "armoured infantry fighting vehicle look-alike" mean an armoured vehicle based on the same chassis as, and externally similar to, an armoured personnel carrier or armoured infantry fighting vehicle, respectively, which does not have a cannon or gun of 20 millimetres calibre or greater and which has been constructed or modified in such a way as not to permit the transportation of a combat infantry squad. Taking into account the provisions of the Geneva Convention "For the Amelioration of the Conditions of the Wounded and Sick in Armed Forces in the Field" of 12 August 1949 that confer a special status on ambulances, armoured personnel carrier ambulances shall not be deemed armoured combat vehicles or armoured personnel carrier look-alikes.

(T) The term "reduction site" means a clearly designated location where the reduction of conventional armaments and equipment limited by the Treaty in accordance with Article VIII takes place.

(U) The term "reduction liability" means the number in each category of conventional armaments and equipment limited by the Treaty that a State Party commits itself to reduce during the period of 40 months following the entry into force of this Treaty in order to ensure compliance with Article VII.

2. Existing types of conventional armaments and equipment subject to the Treaty are listed in the Protocol on Existing Types. The lists of existing types shall be periodically updated in accordance with Article XVI, paragraph 2, subparagraph (D) and Section IV of the Protocol on Existing Types. Such updates to the existing types lists shall not be deemed amendments to this Treaty.

3. The existing types of combat helicopters listed in the Protocol on Existing Types shall be categorised in accordance with Section I of the Protocol on Helicopter Recategorisation.

Article III

1. For the purposes of this Treaty, the States Parties shall apply the following counting rules:

All battle tanks, armoured combat vehicles, artillery, combat aircraft and attack helicopters, as defined in Article II, within the area of application shall be subject to the numerical limitations and other provisions set forth in Articles IV, V and VI, with the exception of those which in a manner consistent with a State Party's normal practices:

(A) are in the process of manufacture, including manufacturing-related testing;

(B) are used exclusively for the purposes of research and development;

(C) belong to historical collections;

(D) are awaiting disposal, having been decommissioned from service in accordance with the provisions of Article IX;

(E) are awaiting, or are being refurbished for, export or re-export and are temporarily retained within the area of application. Such battle tanks, armoured combat vehicles, artillery, combat aircraft and attack helicopters shall be located elsewhere than at sites declared under the terms of Section V of the Protocol on Information Exchange or at no than 10 such declared sites which shall have been notified in the previous year's annual information exchange. In the latter case, they shall be separately distinguishable from conventional armaments and equipment limited by the Treaty;

(F) are, in the case of armoured personnel carriers, armoured infantry fighting vehicles, heavy armament combat vehicles or multi-purpose attack helicopters, held by organisations designed and structured to perform in peacetime internal security functions; or

(G) are in transit through the area of application from a location outside the area of application to a final destination outside the area of application, and are in the area of application for no longer than a total of seven days.

2. If, in respect of any such battle tanks, armoured combat vehicles, artillery, combat aircraft or attack helicopters, the notification of which is required under Section IV of the Protocol on Information Exchange, a State Party notifies an unusually high number in more than two successive annual information exchanges, it shall explain the reasons in the Joint Consultative Group, if so requested.

Article IV

1. Within the area of application, as defined in Article II, each State Party shall limit and, as necessary, reduce its battle tanks, armoured combat vehicles, artillery, combat aircraft and attack helicopters so that, 40 months after entry into force of this Treaty and thereafter, for the group of States Parties to which it belongs, as defined in Article II, the aggregate numbers do not exceed:

(A) 20,000 battle tanks, of which no more than 16.500 shall be in active units;

(B) 30,000 armoured combat vehicles, of which no more than 27,300 shall be in active units. Of the 30,000 armoured combat vehicles, no more than 18,000 shall be armoured infantry fighting vehicles and heavy armament combat vehicles; of armoured infantry fighting vehicles and heavy armament combat vehicles, no more than 1,500 shall be heavy armament combat vehicles;

(C) 20,000 pieces of artillery, of which no more 17,000 shall be in active units;

(D) 6,800 combat aircraft; and

(E) 2,000 attack helicopters.

Battle tanks, armoured combat vehicles and artillery not in active units shall be placed in designated permanent storage sites, as defined in Article II, and shall be located only in the area described in paragraph 2 of this Article. Such designated permanent storage sites may also be located in that part of the territory of the Union of Soviet Socialist Republics comprising the Odessa Military District and the southern part of the Leningrad Military District. In the Odessa Military District, no more than 400 battle tanks and no more than 500 pieces of artillery may be thus stored. In the southern part of the Leningrad Military District, no more than 600 battle tanks, no more than 800 armoured combat vehicles, including no more than 300 armoured combat vehicles of any type with the remaining number consisting of armoured personnel carriers, and no more than 400 pieces of artillery may be thus stored. The southern part of the Leningrad Military District is understood to mean the territory within that military district south of the line East-West 60 degrees 15 minutes northern latitude.

2. Within the area consisting of the entire land territory in Europe, which includes all the European island territories, of the Kingdom of Belgium, the Czech and Slovak Federal Republic, the Kingdom of Denmark including the Faroe Islands, the French Republic, the Federal Republic of Germany, the Republic of Hungary, the Italian Republic, the Grand Duchy of Luxembourg, the Kingdom of the Netherlands, the Republic of Poland, the Portuguese Republic including the islands of Azores and Madeira, the Kingdom of Spain including the Canary Islands, the United Kingdom of Great Britain and Northern Ireland and that part of the territory of the Union of Soviet Socialist Republics west of the Ural Mountains comprising the Baltic, Byelorussian, Carpathian, Kiev, Moscow and Volga-Ural Military Districts, each State Party shall limit and, as necessary, reduce its battle tanks, armoured combat vehicles and artillery so that, 40 months after entry into force of this Treaty and thereafter, for the group of States Parties to which it belongs the aggregate numbers do not exceed:

(A) 15,300 battle tanks, of which no more than 11,800 shall be in active units;

(B) 24,100 armoured combat vehicles, of which no more than 21,400 shall be in active units; and

(C) 14,000 pieces of artillery, of which no more than 11,000 shall be in active units.

3. Within the area consisting of the entire land territory in Europe, which includes all the European island territories, of the Kingdom of Belgium, the Czech and Slovak Federal Republic, the Kingdom of Denmark including the Faroe Islands, the French Republic, the Federal Republic of Germany, the Republic of Hungary, the Italian Republic, the Grand Duchy of Luxembourg, the Kingdom of the Netherlands, the Republic of Poland, the United Kingdom of Great Britain and Northern Ireland and that part of the territory of the Union of Soviet Socialist Republics comprising the Baltic, Byelorussian, Carpathian and Kiev Military Districts, each State Party shall limit and, as necessary, reduce its battle tanks, armoured combat vehicles and artillery so that, 40 months after entry into force of this Treaty and thereafter, for the group of

States Parties to which it belongs the aggregate numbers do not exceed:

(A) 10,300 battle tanks;

(B) 19,260 armoured combat vehicles; and

(C) 9,100 pieces of artillery; and

(D) in the Kiev Military District, the aggregate numbers in active units and designated permanent storage sties together shall not exceed:

(1) 2,250 battle tanks;

(2) 2,500 armoured combat vehicles; and

(3) 1,500 pieces of artillery.

4. Within the area consisting of the entire land territory of Europe, which includes all the European island territories of the Kingdom of Belgium, the Czech and Slovak Federal Republic, the Federal Republic of Germany, the Republic of Hungary, the Grand Duchy of Luxembourg, the Kingdom of the Netherlands and the republic of Poland, each State Party shall limit and, as necessary, reduce its battle tanks, armoured combat vehicles and artillery so that, 40 months after entry into force of this Treaty and thereafter, for the group of States Parties to which it belongs the aggregate numbers in active units do not exceed:

(A) 7,500 battle tanks;

(B) 11,250 armoured combat vehicles; and

(C) 5,000 pieces of artillery.

5. States Parties belonging to the same group of States Parties may locate battle tanks, armoured combat vehicles and artillery in active units in each of the areas described in this Article and Article V, paragraph 1, subparagraph (A) up to the numerical limitations applying in that area, consistent with the maximum levels for holdings notified pursuant to Article VII and provided that no State Party stations conventional armed forces on the territory of another State Party without the agreement of that State Party.

6. If a group of States Parties' aggregate number of battle tanks, armoured combat vehicles and artillery in active units within the area described in paragraph 4 of this Article are less than the numerical limitations set forth in paragraph 4 of this Article, and provided that no State Party is thereby prevented from reaching its maximum levels for holdings notified in accordance with Article VII, paragraphs 2, 3 and 5, then amounts equal to the difference between the aggregate numbers in each of the categories of battle tanks, armoured combat vehicles and artillery and the specified numerical limitations for that area may be located by States Parties belonging to that group of States Parties in the area described in paragraph 3 of this Article, consistent with the numerical limitations specified in paragraph 3 of this Article.

Article V

1. To ensure that the security of each State Party is not affected adversely at any stage:

(A) within the area consisting of the entire land territory in Europe, which includes all the European island territories, of the Republic of Bulgaria, the Hellenic Republic, the Republic of Iceland, the Kingdom of Norway, Romania, the part of the

Republic of Turkey within the area of application and that part of the Union of Soviet Socialist Republics, comprising the Leningrad, Odessa, Transcaucasus and North Caucasus Military Districts, each State Party shall limit and, as necessary, reduce its battle tanks, armoured combat vehicles and artillery so that, 40 months after entry into force of this Treaty and thereafter, for the group of States Parties to which it belongs the aggregate numbers in active units do not exceed the difference between the overall numerical limitations set forth in Article IV, paragraph 1, and those in Article IV, paragraph 2, that is:

(1) 4,700 battle tanks;
(2) 5,900 combat vehicles; and
(3) 6,000 pieces of artillery;

(B) notwithstanding the numerical limitations set forth in subparagraph (A) of this paragraph, a State Party or States Parties may on a temporary basis deploy into the territory belonging to the members of the same group of States Parties within the area described in subparagraph (A) of this paragraph additional aggregate numbers in active units for each group of States Parties not to exceed:

(1) 459 battle tanks;
(2) 723 armoured combat vehicles; and
(3) 420 pieces of artillery; and

(C) provided that for each group of States Parties no more than one-third of each of these additional aggregate numbers shall be deployed to any State Party with territory within the area described in subparagraph (A) of this paragraph, that is:

(1) 153 battle tanks;
(2) 241 armoured combat vehicles; and
(3) 140 pieces of artillery.

2. Notification shall be provided to all other States Parties no later than at the start of the deployment by the State Party or States Parties conducting the deployment and by the recipient State Party or States Parties, specifying the total number in each category of battle tanks, armoured combat vehicles and artillery deployed. Notification also shall be provided to all other States Parties by the State Party or States Parties conducting the deployment and by the recipient State Party or States Parties within 30 days of the withdrawal of those battle tanks, armoured combat vehicles and artillery that were temporarily deployed.

Article VI

With the objective of ensuring that no single State Party possesses more than approximately one-third of the conventional armaments and equipment limited by the Treaty within the area of application, each State Party shall limit and, as necessary, reduce its battle tanks, armoured combat vehicles, artillery, combat aircraft and attack helicopters so that, 40 months after entry into force of this Treaty and thereafter, the numbers within the area of application for that State Party do not exceed:

(A) 13,300 battle tanks;
(B) 20,000 armoured combat vehicles;
(C) 13,700 pieces of artillery;

(D) 5,150 combat aircraft; and
(E) 1,500 attack helicopters.

Article VII

1. In order that the limitations set forth in Articles IV, V and VI are not exceeded, no State Party shall exceed, from 40 months after entry into force of this Treaty, the maximum levels which it has previously agreed upon within its group of States Parties, in accordance with paragraph 7 of this Article, for its holdings of conventional armaments and equipment limited by the Treaty and of which it has provided notification pursuant to the provisions of this Article.

2. Each State Party shall provide at the signature of this Treaty notification to all other States Parties of the maximum levels for its holdings of conventional armaments and equipment limited by the Treaty. The notification of the maximum levels for holdings of conventional armaments and equipment limited by the Treaty provided by each State Party at the signature of this Treaty shall remain valid until the date specified in a subsequent notification pursuant to paragraph 3 of this Article.

3. In accordance with the limitations set forth in Articles IV, V and VI, each State Party shall have the right to change the maximum levels for its holdings of conventional armaments and equipment limited by the Treaty. Any change in the maximum levels for holdings of a State Party shall be notified by that State Party to all other States Parties at least 90 days in advance of the date, specified in the notification, on which such a change takes effect. In order not to exceed any of the limitations set forth in Articles IV and V, any increase in the maximum levels for holdings of a State Party that would otherwise cause those limitations to be exceeded shall be preceded or accompanied by a corresponding reduction in the previously notified maximum levels for holdings of conventional armaments and equipment limited by the Treaty of one or more States Parties belonging to the same group of States Parties. The notification of a change in the maximum levels for holdings shall remain valid from the date specified in the notification until the date specified in a subsequent notification of change pursuant to this paragraph.

4. Each notification required pursuant to paragraph 2 or 3 of this Article for armoured combat vehicles shall also include maximum levels for the holdings of armoured infantry fighting vehicles and heavy armament combat vehicles of the State Party providing the notification.

5. Ninety days before expiration of the 40-month period of reductions set forth in Article VIII and subsequently at the time of any notification of a change pursuant to paragraph 3 of this Article, each State Party shall provide notification of the maximum levels for its holdings of battle tanks, armoured combat vehicles and artillery with respect to each of the areas described in Article IV, paragraphs 2 to 4, and Article V, paragraph 1, subparagraph (A).

6. A decrease in the number of conventional armaments and equipment limited by the treaty held by a State Party and subject to notification pursuant to the Protocol on Information Exchange

shall by itself confer no right on any other State Party to increase the maximum levels for its holdings subject to notification pursuant to this Article.

7. It shall be the responsibility solely of each individual State Party to ensure that the maximum levels for its holdings notified pursuant to the provisions of this Article are not exceeded. States Parties belonging to the same group of States Parties shall consult in order to ensure that the maximum levels for holdings notified pursuant to the provisions of this Article, taken together as appropriate, do not exceed the limitations set forth in Articles IV, V and VI.

Article VIII

1. The numerical limitations set forth in Articles IV, V and VI shall be achieved only by means of reduction in accordance with the Protocol on Reduction, the Protocol on Helicopter Recategorisation, the Protocol on Aircraft Reclassification, the Footnote to Section I, paragraph 2, subparagraph (A) of the Protocol on Existing Types and the Protocol on Inspection.

2. The categories of conventional armaments and equipment subject to reductions are battle tanks, armoured combat vehicles, artillery, combat aircraft and attack helicopters. The specific types are listed in the Protocol on Existing Types.

(A) Battle tanks and armoured combat vehicles shall be reduced by destruction, conversion for non-military purposes, placement on static display, use as ground targets, or, in the case of armoured personnel carriers, modification in accordance with the Footnote to Section I, paragraph 2, subparagraph (A) of the Protocol of Existing Types.

(B) Artillery shall be reduced by destruction or placement on static display, or, in the case of self-propelled artillery, by use as ground targets.

(C) Combat aircraft shall be reduced by destruction, placement on static display, use for ground instructional purposes, or, in the case of specific models or versions of combat-capable trainer aircraft, reclassification into unarmed trainer aircraft.

(D) Specialised attack helicopters shall be reduced by destruction, placement on static display, or use for ground instructional purposes.

(E) Multi-purpose attack helicopters shall be reduced by destruction, placement on static display, use for ground instructional purposes, or recategorisation.

3. Conventional armaments and equipment limited by the Treaty shall be deemed to be reduced upon execution of the procedures set forth in the Protocols listed in paragraph 1 of this Article and upon notification as required by these Protocols. Armaments and equipment reduced shall no longer be counted against the numerical limitations set forth in Articles IV, V and VI.

4. Reductions shall be effected in three phases and completed no later than 40 months after entry into force of this Treaty, so that:

(A) by the end of the first reduction phase, that is, no later than 16 months after entry into force of this Treaty, each State Party shall have ensured that at least 25 percent of its total reduction liability in each of the categories of conventional armaments and equipment limited by the Treaty has been reduced;

(B) by the end of the second reduction phase, that is, no later than 28 months after entry into force of this Treaty, each State Party shall have ensured that at least 60 percent of its total reduction liability in each of the categories of conventional armaments and equipment limited by the Treaty has been reduced;

(C) by the end of the third reduction phase, that is, no later than 40 months after entry into force of this Treaty, each State Party shall have reduced its total reduction liability in each of the categories of conventional armaments and equipment limited by the Treaty. States Parties carrying out conversion for non-military purposes shall have ensured that the conversion of all battle tanks in accordance with Section VIII of the Protocol on Reduction shall have been completed by the end of the third reduction phase; and

(D) armoured combat vehicles deemed reduced by reason of having been partially destroyed in accordance with Section VIII, paragraph 6 of the Protocol on Reduction shall have been fully converted for non-military purposes, or destroyed in accordance with Section IV of the Protocol on Reduction, no later than 64 months after entry into force of this Treaty.

5. Conventional armaments and equipment limited by the Treaty to be reduced shall have been declared present within the area of application in the exchange of information at signature of this Treaty.

6. No later than 30 days after entry into force of this Treaty, each State Party shall provide notification to all other States Parties of its reduction liability.

7. Except as provided for in paragraph 8 of this Article, a State Party's reduction liability in each category shall be no less than the difference between its holdings notified, in accordance with the Protocol on Information Exchange, at signature or effective upon entry into force of this Treaty, whichever is the greater, and the maximum levels for holdings it notified pursuant to Article VII.

8. Any subsequent revision of a State Party's holdings notified pursuant to the Protocol on Information Exchange or of its maximum levels for holdings notified pursuant to Article VII shall be reflected by a notified adjustment to its reduction liability. Any notification of a decrease in a State Party's reduction liability shall be preceded or accompanied by either a notification of a corresponding increase in holdings not exceeding the maximum levels for holdings notified pursuant to Article VII by one or more States Parties belonging to the same group of States Parties, or a notification of a corresponding increase in the reduction liability of one or more such States Parties.

9. Upon entry into force of this Treaty, each State Party shall notify all other States Parties, in accordance with the Protocol on Information Exchange, of the locations of its reduction sites, including those where the final conversion of battle tanks and armoured combat vehicles for non-military purposes will be carried out.

10. Each State Party shall have the right to designate as many reduction sites as it wishes, to revise without restriction its designation of such sites and to carry out reduction and final conversion simultaneously at a maximum of 20 sites. States Parties shall have the right to share or co-locate reduction sites by mutual agreement.

11. Notwithstanding paragraph 10 of this Article, during the baseline validation period, that is, the interval between entry into force of this Treaty and 120 days after entry into force of this Treaty, reduction shall be carried out simultaneously at no more than two reduction sites for each State Party.

12. Reduction of conventional armaments and equipment limited by the Treaty shall be carried out at reduction sites, unless otherwise specified in the Protocols listed in paragraph I of this Article, within the area of application.

13. The reduction process, including the results of the conversion of conventional armaments and equipment limited by the Treaty for non-military purposes both during the reduction period and in the 24 months following the reduction period, shall be subject to inspection, without right of refusal, in accordance with the Protocol on Inspection.

Article IX

1. Other than removal from service in accordance with the provisions of Article VIII, battle tanks, armoured combat vehicles, artillery, combat aircraft and attack helicopters within the area of application shall be removed from service only by decommissioning, provided that:

(A) such conventional armaments and equipment limited by the Treaty are decommissioned and awaiting disposal at no more than eight sites which shall notified as declared sites in accordance with the Protocol on Information Exchange and shall be identified in such notifications as holding areas for decommissioned conventional armaments and equipment limited by the Treaty. If sites containing conventional armaments and equipment limited by the Treaty decommissioned from service also contain any other conventional armaments and equipment subject to the Treaty, the decommissioned conventional armaments and equipment limited by the Treaty shall be separately distinguishable; and

(B) the number of such decommissioned conventional armaments and equipment limited by the Treaty do not exceed, in the case of any individual State Party, one percent of its notified holdings of conventional armaments and equipment limited by the Treaty, or a total of 250, whichever is greater, of which no more than 200 shall be battle tanks, armoured combat vehicles and pieces of artillery, and no more than 50 shall be attack helicopters and combat aircraft.

2. Notification of decommissioning shall include the number and type of conventional armaments and equipment limited by the Treaty decommissioned and the location of decommissioning and

shall be provided to all other States Parties in accordance with Section IX, paragraph 1, subparagraph (B) of the Protocol on Information Exchange.

Article X

1. Designated permanent storage sites shall be notified in accordance with the Protocol on Information Exchange to all other States Parties by the State Party to which the conventional armaments and equipment limited by the Treaty contained at designated permanent storage sites belong. The notification shall include the designation and location, including geographic coordinates of designated permanent storage sites and the numbers by type of each category of its conventional armaments and equipment limited by the Treaty at each such storage site.

2. Designated permanent storage sites shall contain only facilities appropriate for the storage and maintenance of armaments and equipment (e.g., warehouses, garages, workshops and associated stores as well as other support accommodation). Designated permanent storage sites shall not contain firing ranges or training areas associated with conventional armaments and equipment limited by the Treaty. Designated permanent storage sites shall contain only armaments and equipment belonging to the conventional armed forces of a State Party.

3. Each designated permanent storage site shall have a clearly defined physical boundary that shall consist of a continuous perimeter fence at least 1.5 metres in height. The perimeter fence shall have no more than three gates providing the sole means of entrance and exit for armaments and equipment.

4. Conventional armaments and equipment limited by the Treaty located within designated permanent storage sites shall be counted as conventional armaments and equipment limited by the Treaty not in active units, including when they are temporarily removed in accordance with paragraphs 7, 8, 9 and 10 of this Article. Conventional armaments and equipment limited by the treaty in storage other than in designated permanent storage sites shall be counted as conventional armaments and equipment limited by the Treaty in active units.

5. Active units or formations shall not be located within designated permanent storage sites, except as provided for in paragraph 6 of this Article.

6. Only personnel associated with the security or operation of designated storage sites, or the maintenance of the armaments and equipment stored therein, shall be located within the designated permanent storage sites.

7. For the purpose of maintenance, repair or modification of conventional armaments and equipment limited by the Treaty located within designated permanent storage sites, each State Party shall have the right, without prior notification, to remove from and retain outside designated permanent storage sites simultaneously up to 10 percent, rounded up to the nearest even whole number, of the notified holdings of each category of conventional armaments and equipment limited by the Treaty in each designated permanent

storage site, or 10 items of the conventional armaments and equipment limited by the Treaty in each category in each designated permanent storage site, whichever is less.

8. Except as provided for in paragraph 7 of this Article, no State Party shall remove conventional armaments and equipment limited by the Treaty from designated permanent storage sites unless notification has been provided to all other States Parties at least 42 days in advance of such removal. Notification shall be given by the State Party to which the conventional armaments and equipment limited by the Treaty belong. Such notification shall specify:

(A) the location of the designated permanent storage site from which conventional armaments and equipment limited by the Treaty are to be removed and the numbers by type of conventional armaments and equipment limited by the Treaty of each category to be removed;

(B) the dates of removal and return of conventional armaments and equipment limited by the Treaty; and

(C) the intended location and use of conventional armaments and equipment limited by the Treaty while outside the designated permanent storage site.

9. Except as provided for in paragraph 7 of this Article, the aggregate numbers of conventional armaments and equipment limited by the Treaty removed from and retained outside designated permanent storage sites by States Parties belonging to the same group of States Parties shall at no time exceed the following levels:

(A) 550 battle tanks;

(B) 1,000 armoured combat vehicles; and

(C) 300 pieces of artillery.

10. Conventional armaments and equipment limited by the Treaty removed from designated permanent storage sites pursuant to paragraphs 8 and 9 of this Article shall be returned to designated permanent storage sites no later than 42 days after their removal, except for those items of conventional armaments and equipment limited by the Treaty removed for industrial rebuild. Such items shall be returned to designated permanent storage sites immediately on completion of the rebuild.

11. Each State Party shall have the right to replace conventional armaments and equipment limited by the Treaty located in designated permanent storage sites. Each State Party shall notify all other States Parties, at the beginning of replacement, of the number, location, type and disposition of conventional armaments and equipment limited by the Treaty being replaced.

Article XI

1. Each State Party shall limit its armoured vehicle launched bridges so that, 40 months after entry into force of this Treaty and thereafter, for the group of States Parties to which it belongs the aggregate number of armoured vehicle launched bridges in active units within the area of application does not exceed 740.

2. All armoured vehicle launched bridges within the area of application in excess of the aggregate number specified in paragraph 1 of this Article for each group of States Parties shall be placed in designated permanent storage sites, as defined in Article II. When

armoured vehicle launched bridges are placed in a designated permanent storage site, either on their on or together with conventional armaments and equipment limited by the Treaty, Article X, paragraphs 1 to 6 shall apply to armoured vehicle launched bridges as well as to conventional armaments and equipment limited by the Treaty. Armoured vehicle launched bridges placed in designated permanent storage sites shall not be considered as being in active units.

3. Except as provide for in paragraph 6 of this Article, armoured vehicle launched bridges may be removed, subject to the provisions of paragraphs 4 and 5 of this Article, from designated permanent storage sites only after notification has been provided to all other States Parties at least 42 days prior to such removal. This notification shall specify:

(A) the locations of the designated permanent storage sites from which armoured vehicle launched bridges are to be removed and the numbers of armoured vehicle launched bridges to be removed from each such site:

(B) the dates of removal of armoured vehicle launched bridges from and return to designated permanent storage sites; and

(C) the intended use of armoured vehicle launched bridges during the period of their removal from designated permanent storage sites.

4. Except as provided for in paragraph 6 of this Article, armoured vehicle launched bridges removed from designated permanent storage sites shall be returned to them no later than 42 days after the actual date of removal.

5. The aggregate number of armoured vehicle launched bridges removed from and retained outside of designated permanent storage sites by each group of States Parties shall not exceed 50 at any one time.

6. States Parties shall have the right, for the purpose of maintenance or modification, to remove and have outside of designated permanent storage sites simultaneously up to 10 percent, rounded up to the nearest even whole number, of their notified holdings of armoured vehicle launched bridges in each designated permanent storage site, or 10 armoured vehicle launched bridges from each designated permanent storage site, whichever is less.

7. In the event of natural disasters involving flooding or damage to permanent bridges, States parties shall have the right to withdraw armoured vehicle launched bridges from designated permanent storage sites. Notification to all other States Parties of such withdrawals shall be given at the time of withdrawal.

Article XII

1. Armoured infantry fighting vehicles held by organisations of a State Party designed and structured to perform in peacetime internal security functions, which are not structured and organised for ground combat against an external enemy, are not limited by this Treaty. The foregoing notwithstanding, in order to enhance the implementation of this Treaty and to provide assurance that the number of such armaments held by such organisations shall not be

used to circumvent the provisions of this Treaty, any such armaments in excess of 1,000 armoured infantry fighting vehicles assigned by a State Party to organisations designed and structured to perform in peacetime internal security functions shall constitute a portion of the permitted levels specified in Articles IV, V and VI. No more than 600 such armoured infantry fighting vehicles of a State Party, assigned to such organisations, may be located in that part of the area of application described in Article V, paragraph 1, subparagraph (A). Each State Party shall further ensure that such organisations refrain from the acquisition of combat capabilities in excess of those necessary for meeting internal security requirements.

2. A State Party that intends to reassign battle tanks, armoured infantry fighting vehicles, artillery, combat aircraft, attack helicopters and armoured vehicle launched bridges in service with its conventional armed forces to any organisation of that State Party not a part of its conventional armed forces shall notify all other States Parties no later than the date such reassignment takes effect. Such notification shall specify the effective date of the reassignment, conventional armaments and equipment limited by the Treaty being reassigned.

Article XIII

1. For the purpose of ensuring verification of compliance with the provisions of this Treaty, each State Party shall provide notifications and exchange information pertaining to its conventional armaments and equipment in accordance with the Protocol on Information Exchange.

2. Such notifications and exchange of information shall be provided in accordance with Article XVII.

3. Each State Party shall be responsible for its own information; receipt of such information and of notifications shall not imply validation or acceptance of the information provided.

Article XIV

1. For the purpose of ensuring verification of compliance with the provisions of this Treaty, each State Party shall have the right to conduct, and the obligation to accept, within the area of application, inspections in accordance with the provisions of the Protocol on Inspection.

2. The purpose of such inspections shall be:

(A) to verify, on the basis of the information provided pursuant to the Protocol on Information Exchange, the compliance of States Parties with the numerical limitations set forth in Articles IV, V and VI;

(B) to monitor the process of reduction of battle tanks, armoured combat vehicles, artillery, combat aircraft and attack helicopters carried out at reduction sites in accordance with Article VIII and the Protocol on Reduction; and

(C) to monitor the certification of recategorised multi-purpose attack helicopters and reclassified combat-capable trainer aircraft carried out in accordance with the Protocol on Helicopter Recategorisation and the Protocol on Aircraft Reclassification, respectively.

3. No State Party shall exercise the rights set forth in paragraphs 1 and 2 of this Article in respect of States Parties which belong to the group of States Parties to which it belongs in order to elude the objectives of the verification regime.

4. In the case of an inspection conducted jointly by more than one State Party, one of them shall be responsible for the execution of the provisions of this Treaty.

5. The number of inspections pursuant to Sections VII and VIII of the Protocol on Inspection which each State Part shall have the right to conduct and the obligation to accept during each specified time period shall be determined in accordance with the provisions of Section II of that Protocol.

6. Upon completion of the 120-day residual level validation period, each State Party shall have the right to conduct, and each State Party with territory within the area of application shall have the obligation to accept, an agreed number of aerial inspections within the area of application. Such agreed numbers and other applicable provisions shall be developed during negotiations referred to in Article XVIII.

Article XV

1. For the purpose of ensuring verification of compliance with the provisions of this Treaty, a State Party shall have the right to use, in addition to the procedures referred to in Article XIV, national or multinational technical means of verification at its disposal in a manner consistent with generally recognised principles of international law.

2. A State Party shall not interfere with national or multinational technical means of verification of another State Party operating in accordance with paragraph 1 of this Article.

3. A State Party shall not use concealment measures that impede verification of compliance with the provisions of this Treaty by national or multinational technical means of verification of another State Party operating in accordance with paragraph 1 of this Article. This obligation does not apply to cover or concealment practices associated with normal personnel training, maintenance or operations involving conventional armaments and equipment limited by the Treaty.

Article XVI

1. To promote the objectives and implementation of the provisions of this Treaty, the States Parties hereby establish a Joint Consultative Group.

2. Within the framework of the Joint Consultative Group, the States Parties shall:

(A) address questions relating to compliance with or possible circumvention of the provisions of this Treaty;

(B) seek to resolve ambiguities and differences of interpretation that may become apparent in the way this Treaty is implemented;

(C) consider and, if possible, agree on measures to enhance the viability and effectiveness of this Treaty;

(D) update the lists contained in the Protocol on Existing Types, as required by Article II, paragraph 2;

(E) resolve technical questions in order to seek common practices among the States Parties in the way this Treaty is implemented;

(F) work out or revise, as necessary, rules of procedure, working methods, the scale of distribution of expenses of the Joint Consultative Group and of conferences convened under this Treaty and the distribution of costs of inspections between or among States Parties;

(G) consider and work out appropriate measures to ensure that information obtained through exchanges of information among the States Parties or as a result of inspections pursuant to this Treaty is used solely for the purposes of this Treaty, taking into account the particular requirements of each State Party in respect of safeguarding information which that State Party specifies as being sensitive;

(H) consider, upon the request of any State Party, any matter that a State Party wishes to propose for examination by any conference to be convened in accordance with Article XXI; such consideration shall not prejudice the right of any State Party to resort to the procedures set forth in Article XXI; and

(I) consider matters of dispute arising out of the implementation of this Treaty.

3. Each State Party shall have the right to raise before the Joint Consultative Group, and have placed on its agenda, any issue relating to this Treaty.

4. The Joint Consultative Group shall take decisions or make recommendations by consensus. Consensus shall be understood to mean the absence of any objection by any representative of a State Party to the taking of a decision or the making of a recommendation.

5. The Joint Consultative Group may propose amendments to this Treaty for consideration and confirmation in accordance with Article XX. The Joint consultative Group may also agree on improvements to the viability and effectiveness of this Treaty, consistent with its provisions. Unless such improvements relate only to minor matters of an administrative or technical nature, they shall be subject to consideration and confirmation in accordance with Article XX before they can take effect.

6. Nothing in this Article shall be deemed to prohibit or restrict any State Party from requesting information from or undertaking consultations with other States Parties on matters relating to this Treaty and its implementation in channels or fora other than the Joint Consultative Group.

7. The Joint Consultative Group shall follow the procedures set forth in the Protocol on the Joint Consultative Group.

Article XVII

The States Parties shall transmit information and notifications required by this Treaty in written form. They shall use diplomatic channels or other official channels designated by them, including in particular a communications network to be established by a separate arrangement.

Article XVIII

1. The States Parties, after signature of this Treaty, shall continue the negotiations on conventional armed forces with the same Mandate and with the goal of building on this Treaty.

2. The objective for these negotiations shall be to conclude an agreement on additional measures aimed at further strengthening security and stability in Europe, and pursuant to the Mandate, including measures to limit the personnel strength of their conventional armed forces within the area of application.

3. The States Parties shall seek to conclude these negotiations no later than the follow-up meeting of the Conference on Security and Cooperation in Europe to be held in Helsinki in 1992.

Article XIX

1. This Treaty shall be of unlimited duration. It may be supplemented by a further treaty.

2. Each State Party shall, in exercising its national sovereignty, have the right to withdraw from this Treaty if it decides that extraordinary events related to the subject matter of this Treaty have jeopardised its supreme interests. A State Party intending to withdraw shall give notice of its decision to do so to the Depositary and to all other States Parties. Such notice shall be given at least 150 days prior to the intended withdrawal from this Treaty. It shall include a statement of the extraordinary events the State Party regards as having jeopardised its supreme interests.

3. Each State Party shall, in particular, in exercising its national sovereignty, have the right to withdraw from this Treaty if another State Party increases its holdings in battle tanks, armoured combat vehicles, artillery, combat aircraft or attack helicopters, as defined in Article II, which are outside the scope of the limitations of this Treaty, in such proportions as to pose an obvious threat to the balance of forces within the area of application.

Article XX

1. Any State Party may propose amendments to this Treaty. The text of a proposed amendment shall be submitted to the Depositary, which shall circulate it to all the States Parties.

2. If an amendment is approved by all the States Parties, it shall enter into force in accordance with the procedures set forth in Article XXII governing the entry into force of this Treaty.

Article XXI

1. Forty-six months after entry into force of this Treaty, and at five-year intervals thereafter, the Depositary shall convene a conference of the States Parties to conduct a review of the operations of this Treaty.

2. The Depositary shall convene an extraordinary conference of the States Parties, if requested to do so by any State Party which

considers that exceptional circumstances relating to this Treaty have arisen, in particular, in the event that a State Party has announced its intention to leave its group of States Parties or to join the other group of States Parties, as defined in Article II, paragraph 1, subparagraph (A). In order to enable the other States Parties to prepare for this conference, the request shall include the reasons why that State Party deems an extraordinary conference to be necessary. The conference shall consider the circumstances set forth in the request and their effect on the operation of this Treaty. The conference shall open no later than 15 days after receipt of the request and, unless it decides otherwise, shall last no longer than three weeks.

3. The Depositary shall convene a conference of the States Parties to consider an amendment proposed pursuant to Article XX, if requested to do so by three or more States Parties. Such a conference shall open no later than 21 days after receipt of the necessary requests.

4. In the event that a State Party gives notice of its decision to withdraw from this Treaty pursuant to Article XIX, the Depositary shall convene a conference of the States Parties which shall open no later than 21 days after receipt of the notice of withdrawal in order to consider questions relating to the withdrawal from this Treaty.

Article XXII

1. This Treaty shall be subject to ratification by each State Party in accordance with its constitutional procedures. Instruments of ratification shall be deposited with the Government of the Kingdom of the Netherlands, hereby designated the Depositary.

2. This Treaty shall enter into force 10 days after instruments of ratification have been deposited by all States Parties listed in the Preamble.

3. The Depositary shall promptly inform all States Parties of:

(A) the deposit of each instrument of ratification;

(B) the entry into force of this Treaty;

(C) any withdrawal in accordance with Article XIX and its effective date;

(D) the text of any amendment proposed in accordance with Article XX;

(E) the entry into force of any amendment to this Treaty;

(F) any request to convene a conference in accordance with Article XXI;

(G) the convening of a conference pursuant to Article XXI; and

(H) any other matter of which the Depositary is required by this Treaty to inform the States Parties.

4. This Treaty shall be registered by the Depositary pursuant to Article 102 of the Charter of the United Nations.

Article XXIII

The original of this Treaty, of which the English, French, German, Italian, Russian and Spanish texts are equally authentic, shall be deposited in the archives of the Depositary. Duly certified copies of this Treaty shall be transmitted by the Depositary to all the States Parties.

10. Antarctic Treaty [1]

Signed at Washington December 1, 1959; Ratification of the United States deposited, August 18, 1960; Proclaimed by the President, June 23, 1961; Entered into force, June 23, 1961

The Governments of Argentina, Australia, Belgium, Chile, the French Republic, Japan, New Zealand, Norway, the Union of South Africa, the Union of Soviet Socialist Republics, the United Kingdom of Great Britain and Northern Ireland, and the United States of America,

RECOGNIZING that it is in the interest of all mankind that Antarctica shall continue forever to be used exclusively for peaceful purposes and shall not become the scene or object of international discord;

ACKNOWLEDGING the substantial contributions to scientific knowledge resulting from international cooperation in scientific investigation in Antarctica;

CONVINCED that the establishment of a firm foundation for the continuation and development of such cooperation on the basis of freedom of scientific investigation in Antarctica as applied during the International Geophysical Year accords with the interests of science and the progress of all mankind;

CONVINCED also that a treaty ensuring the use of Antarctica for peaceful purposes only and the continuance of international harmony in Antarctica will further the purposes and principles embodied in the Charter of the United Nations;

HAVE AGREED AS FOLLOWS:

ARTICLE I

1. Antarctica shall be used for peaceful purposes only. There shall be prohibited, *inter alia*, any measures of a military nature, such as the establishment of military bases and fortifications, the carrying out of military maneuvers, as well as the testing of any type of weapons.

2. The present Treaty shall not prevent the use of military personnel or equipment for scientific research or for any other peaceful purpose.

ARTICLE II

Freedom of scientific investigation in Antarctica and cooperation toward that end, as applied during the International Geophysical Year, shall continue, subject to the provisions of the present Treaty.

---

[1] 12 UST 794; TIAS 4780; 402 UNTS 71. For a list of states that are parties to this Treaty, see Department of State publication, *Treaties in Force*.

ARTICLE III

1. In order to promote international cooperation in scientific investigation in Antarctica, as provided for in Article II of the present Treaty, the Contracting Parties agree that, to the greatest extent feasible and practicable:

(a) information regarding plans for scientific programs in Antarctica shall be exchanged to permit maximum economy and efficiency of operations;

(b) scientific personnel shall be exchanged in Antarctica between expeditions and stations;

(c) scientific observations and results from Antarctica shall be exchanged and made freely available.

2. In implementing this Article, every encouragement shall be given to the establishment of cooperative working relations with those Specialized Agencies of the United Nations and other international organizations having a scientific or technical interest in Antarctica.

ARTICLE IV

1. Nothing contained in the present Treaty shall be interpreted as:

(a) a renunciation by any Contracting Party of previously asserted rights of or claims to territorial sovereignty in Antarctica;

(b) a renunciation or diminution by any Contracting Party of any basis of claim to territorial sovereignty in Antarctica which it may have whether as a result of its activities or those of its nationals in Antarctica, or otherwise;

(c) prejudicing the position of any Contracting Party as regards its recognition or non-recognition of any other State's right of or claim or basis of claim to territorial sovereignty in Antarctica.

2. No acts or activities taking place while the present Treaty is in force shall constitute a basis for asserting, supporting or denying a claim to territorial sovereignty in Antarctica or create any rights of sovereignty in Antarctica. No new claim, or enlargement of an existing claim, to territorial sovereignty in Antarctica shall be asserted while the present Treaty is in force.

ARTICLE V

1. Any nuclear explosions in Antarctica and the disposal there of radioactive waste material shall be prohibited.

2. In the event of the conclusion of international agreements concerning the use of nuclear energy, including nuclear explosions and the disposal of radioactive waste material, to which all of the Contracting Parties whose representatives are entitled to participate in the meetings provided for under Article IX are parties, the rules established under such agreements shall apply in Antarctica.

ARTICLE VI

The provisions of the present Treaty shall apply to the area south of 60° South Latitude, including all ice shelves, but nothing in the present Treaty shall prejudice or in any way affect the rights, or the exercise of the rights, of any State under international law with regard to the high seas within that area.

Article VII

1. In order to promote the objectives and ensure the observance of the provisions of the present Treaty, each Contracting Party whose representatives are entitled to participate in the meetings referred to in Article IX of the Treaty shall have the right to designate observers to carry out any inspection provided for by the present Article. Observers shall be nationals of the Contracting Parties which designate them. The names of observers shall be communicated to every other Contracting Party having the right to designate observers, and like notice shall be given of the termination of their appointment.

2. Each observer designated in accordance with the provisions of paragraph 1 of this Article shall have complete freedom of access at any time to any or all areas of Antarctica.

3. All areas of Antarctica, including all stations, installations and equipment within those areas, and all ships and aircraft at points of discharging or embarking cargoes or personnel in Antarctica, shall be open at all times to inspection by any observers designated in accordance with paragraph 1 of this Article.

4. Aerial observation may be carried out at any time over any or all areas of Antarctica by any of the Contracting Parties having the right to designate observers.

5. Each Contracting Party shall, at the time when the present Treaty enters into force for it, inform the other Contracting Parties, and thereafter shall give them notice in advance, of

(a) all expeditions to and within Antarctica, on the part of its ships or nationals, and all expeditions to Antarctica organized in or proceeding from its territory;

(b) all stations in Antarctica occupied by its nationals; and

(c) any military personnel or equipment intended to be introduced by it into Antarctica subject to the conditions prescribed in paragraph 2 of Article I of the present Treaty.

Article VIII

1. In order to facilitate the exercise of their functions under the present Treaty, and without prejudice to the respective positions of Contracting Parties relating to jurisdiction over all other persons in Antarctica, observers designated under paragraph 1 of Article VII and scientific personnel exchanged under subparagraph 1(b) of Article III of the Treaty, and members of the staffs accompanying any such persons, shall be subject only to the jurisdiction of the Contracting Party of which they are nationals in respect to all acts or omissions occurring while they are in Antarctica for the purpose of exercising their functions.

2. Without prejudice to the provisions of paragraph 1 of this Article, and pending the adoption of measures in pursuance of subparagraph 1(e) of Article IX, the Contracting Parties concerned in any

case of dispute with regard to the exercise of jurisdiction in Antarctica shall immediately consult together with a view to reaching a mutually acceptable solution.

ARTICLE IX

1. Representatives of the Contracting Parties named in the preamble to the present Treaty shall meet at the City of Canberra within two months after the date of entry into force of the Treaty, and thereafter at suitable intervals and places, for the purpose of exchanging information, consulting together on matters of common interest pertaining to Antarctica, and formulating and considering, and recommending to their Governments, measures in furtherance of the principles and objectives of the Treaty, including measures regarding:

(a) use of Antarctica for peaceful purposes only;

(b) facilitation of scientific research in Antarctica;

(c) facilitation of international scientific cooperation an Antarctica;

(d) facilitation of the exercise of the rights of inspection provided for in Article VII of the Treaty;

(e) questions relating to the exercise of jurisdiction in Antarctica;

(f) preservation and conservation of living resources in Antarctica;

2. Each Contracting Party which has become a party to the present Treaty by accession under Article XIII shall be entitled to appoint representatives to participate in the meetings referred to in paragraph 1 of the present Article, during such time as that Contracting Party demonstrates its interest in Antarctica by conducting substantial scientific research activity there, such as the establishment of a scientific station or the dispatch of a scientific expedition.

3. Reports from the observers referred to in Article VII of the present Treaty shall be transmitted to the representatives of the Contracting Parties participating in the meetings referred to in paragraph 1 of the present Article.

4. The measures referred to in paragraph 1 of this Article shall become effective when approved by all the Contracting Parties whose representatives were entitled to participate in the meetings held to consider those measures.

5. Any or all of the rights established in the present Treaty may be exercised as from the date of entry into force of the Treaty whether or not any measures facilitating the exercise of such rights have been proposed, considered or approved as provided in this Article.

ARTICLE X

Each of the Contracting Parties undertakes to exert appropriate efforts, consistent with the Charter of the United Nations, to the end that no one engages in any activity in Antarctica contrary to the principles or purposes of the present Treaty.

Article XI

1. If any dispute arises between two or more of the Contracting Parties concerning the interpretation or application of the present Treaty, those Contracting Parties shall consult among themselves with a view to having the dispute resolved by negotiation, inquiry, mediation, conciliation, arbitration, judicial settlement or other peaceful means of their own choice.

2. Any dispute of this character not so resolved shall, with the consent, in each case, of all parties to the dispute, be referred to the International Court of Justice for settlement; but failure to reach agreement on reference to the International Court shall not absolve parties to the dispute from the responsibility of continuing to seek to resolve it by any of the various peaceful means referred to in paragraph 1 of this Article.

Article XII

1. (a) The present Treaty may be modified or amended at any time by unanimous agreement of the Contracting Parties whose representatives are entitled to participate in the meetings provided for under Article IX. Any such modification or amendment shall enter into force when the depositary Government has received notice from all such Contracting Parties that they have ratified it.

(b) Such modification or amendment shall hereafter enter into force as to any other Contracting Party when notice of ratification by it has been received by the depositary Government. Any such Contracting Party from which no notice of ratification is received within a period of two years from the date of entry into force of the modification or amendment in accordance with the provisions of subparagraph 1(a) of this Article shall be deemed to have withdrawn from the present Treaty on the date of expiration of such period.

2. (a) If after the expiration of thirty years from the date of entry into force of the present Treaty, any of the Contracting Parties whose representatives are entitled to participate in the meetings provided for under Article IX so requests by a communication addressed to the depositary Government, a Conference of all the Contracting Parties shall be held as soon as practicable to review the operation of the Treaty.

(b) Any modification or amendment to the present Treaty which is approved at such a Conference by a majority of the Contracting Parties there represented, including a majority of those whose representatives are entitled to participate in the meetings provided for under Article IX, shall be communicated by the depositary Government to all the Contracting Parties immediately after the termination of the Conference and shall enter into force in accordance with the provisions of paragraph 1 of the present Article.

(c) If any such modification or amendment has not entered into force in accordance with the provisions of subparagraph 1(a) of this Article within a period of two years after the date of its communication to all the Contracting Parties, any Contracting Party may at any time after the expiration of that period give notice to the depositary Government of its withdrawal from the present Treaty;

and such withdrawal shall take effect two years after the receipt of the notice by the depositary Government.

Article XIII

1. The present Treaty shall be subject to ratification by the signatory States. It shall be open for accession by any State which is a Member of the United Nations, or by any other State which may be invited to accede to the Treaty with the consent of all the Contracting Parties whose representatives are entitled to participate in the meetings provided for under Article IX of the Treaty.

2. Ratification of or accession to the present Treaty shall be effected by each State in accordance with its constitutional processes.

3. Instruments of ratification and instruments of accession shall be deposited with the Government of the United States of America, hereby designated as the depositary Government.

4. The depositary Government shall inform all signatory and acceding States of the date of each deposit of an instrument of ratification or accession, and the date of entry into force of the Treaty and of any modification or amendment thereto.

5. Upon the deposit of instruments of ratification by all the signatory States, the present Treaty shall enter into force for those States and for States which have deposited instruments of accession. Thereafter the Treaty shall enter into force for any acceding State upon the deposit of its instrument of accession.

6. The present Treaty shall be registered by the depositary Government pursuant to Article 102 of the Charter of the United Nations.

Article XIV

The present Treaty, done in the English, French, Russian and Spanish languages, each version being equally authentic, shall be deposited in the archives of the Government of the United States of America, which shall transmit duly certified copies thereof to the Governments of the signatory and acceding States.

In witness whereof, the undersigned Plenipotentiaries, duly authorized, have signed the present Treaty.

Done at Washington this first day of December, one thousand nine hundred and fifty-nine.

11. Prohibition of Nuclear Weapons in Latin America

a. Treaty for the Prohibition of Nuclear Weapons in Latin America [1]

Done at Mexico, February 14, 1967

Preamble

In the name of their peoples and faithfully interpreting their desires and aspirations, the Governments of the States which sign the Treaty for the Prohibition of Nuclear Weapons in Latin America,

DESIRING to contribute, so far as lies in their power, towards ending the armaments race, especially in the field of nuclear weapons, and toward strengthening a world at peace, based on the sovereign equality of States, mutual respect and good neighbourliness,

RECALLING that the United Nations General Assembly, in its Resolution 808 (IX), adopted unanimously as one of the three points of a coordinated programme of disarmament "the total prohibition of the use and manufacture of nuclear weapons and weapons of mass destruction of every type",

RECALLING that militarily denuclearized zones are not an end in themselves but rather a means for achieving general and complete disarmament at a later stage,

RECALLING United Nations General Assembly Resolution 1911 (XVIII), which established that the measures that should be agreed upon for the denuclearization of Latin America should be taken "in the light of the principles of the Charter of the United Nations and of regional agreements",

RECALLING United Nations General Assembly Resolution 2028 (XX), which established the principle of an acceptable balance of mutual responsibilities and duties for the nuclear and non-nuclear powers, and

RECALLING that the Charter of the Organization of American States proclaims that it is an essential purpose of the Organization to strengthen the peace and security of the hemisphere.

Convinced:

That the incalculable destructive power of nuclear weapons has made it imperative that the legal prohibition of war should be strictly observed in practice if the survival of civilization and of mankind itself is to be assured,

[1] 22 UST 762; TIAS 7137. The United States is not a party to this Treaty. The United States is, however, a party to Additional Protocols I and II of this Treaty that refer to specific articles of the Treaty.

That nuclear weapons, whose terrible effects are suffered, indiscriminately and inexorably, by military forces and civilian population alike, constitute, through the persistence of the radioactivity they release, an attack on the integrity of the human species and ultimately may even render the whole earth uninhabitable,

That general and complete disarmament under effective international control is a vital matter which all the peoples of the world equally demand,

That the proliferation of nuclear weapons, which seems inevitable unless States, in the exercise of the sovereign rights, impose restrictions on themselves in order to prevent it, would make any agreement on disarmament enormously difficult and would increase the danger of the outbreak of a nuclear conflagration,

That the establishment of militarily denuclearized zones is closely linked with the maintenance of peace and security in the respective regions,

That the military denuclearization of vast geographical zones, adopted by the sovereign decision of the States comprised therein, will exercise a beneficial influence on other regions where similar conditions exist,

That the privileged situation of the signatory States, whose territories are wholly free from nuclear weapons, imposes upon them the inescapable duty of preserving that situation both in their own interests and for the good of mankind,

That the existence of nuclear weapons in any country of Latin America would make it a target for possible nuclear attacks and would inevitably set off, throughout the region, a ruinous race in nuclear weapons which would involve the unjustifiable diversion, for warlike purposes, of the limited resources required for economic and social development,

That the foregoing reasons, together with the traditional peace-loving outlook of Latin America, give rise to an inescapable necessity that nuclear energy should be used in that region exclusively for peaceful purposes, and that the Latin American countries should use their right to the greatest and most equitable possible access to this new source of energy in order to expedite the economic and social development of their peoples,

Convinced finally:

That the military denuclearization of Latin American—being understood to mean the undertaking entered into internationally in this Treaty to keep their territories forever free from nuclear weapons—will constitute a measure which will spare their peoples from the squandering of their limited resources on nuclear armaments and will protect them against possible nuclear attacks on their territories, and will also constitute a significant contribution towards preventing the proliferation of nuclear weapons and a powerful factor for general and complete disarmament, and

That Latin America, faithful to its tradition of universality, must not only endeavour to banish from its homelands the scourge of a nuclear war, but must also strive to promote the well-being and advancement of its peoples, at the same time co-operating in the fulfillment of the ideals of mankind, that is to say, in the consolidation of a permanent peace based on equal rights, economic fairness and social justice for all, in accordance with the principles and purposes set forth in the Charter of the United Nations and in the Charter of the Organization of American States,

Have agreed as follows:

Obligations

ARTICLE 1

1. The Contracting Parties hereby undertake to use exclusively for peaceful purposes the nuclear material and facilities which are under their jurisdiction, and to prohibit and prevent in their respective territories:

(a) The testing, use, manufacture, production or acquisition by any means whatsoever of any nuclear weapons, by the Parties themselves, directly or indirectly, on behalf of anyone else or in any way, and

(b) The receipt, storage, installation, deployment and any form of possession of any nuclear weapons, directly, or indirectly, by the Parties themselves, by anyone on their behalf or in any other way.

2. The Contracting Parties also undertake to refrain from engaging in, encouraging or authorizing, directly or indirectly, or in any way participating in the testing, use, manufacture, production, possession or control of any nuclear weapons.

Definition of the Contracting Parties

ARTICLE 2

For the purposes of this Treaty the Contracting Parties are those for whom the Treaty is in force.

Definition of territory

ARTICLE 3

For the purposes of this Treaty, the term "territory" shall include the territorial sea, air space and any other space over which the State exercises sovereignty in accordance with its own legislation.

Zone of application

ARTICLE 4

1. The zone of application of this Treaty is the whole of the territories for which the Treaty is in force.

2. Upon fulfillment of the requirements of article 28, paragraph 1, the zone of application of this Treaty shall also be that which is situated in the western hemisphere within the following limits (except the continental part of the territory of the United States of America and its territorial waters): starting at a point located at 35° north latitude, 75° west longitude; from this point directly southward to a point at 30° north latitude, 75° west longitude; from there, directly eastward to a point at 30° north latitude, 50° west longitude; from there, along a loxodromic line to a point at 5° north latitude, 20° west longitude; from there, directly southward to a

point at 60° south latitude, 20° west longitude; from there, directly westward to a point at 60° south latitude, 115° west longitude; from there, directly northward to a point at 0 latitude, 115° west longitude; from there, along a loxodromic line to a point at 35° north latitude, 150° west longitude; from there directly eastward to a point at 35° north latitude, 75° west longitude.

Definition of nuclear weapons

ARTICLE 5

For the purposes of this Treaty, a nuclear weapon is any device which is capable of releasing nuclear energy in an uncontrolled manner and which has a group of characteristics that are appropriate for use for warlike purposes. An instrument that may be used for the transport or propulsion of the device is not included in this definition if it is separable from the device and not an indivisible part thereof.

Meeting of signatories

ARTICLE 6

At the request of any of the signatory States of it the Agency established by article 7 should so decide, a meeting of all the signatories may be convoked to consider in common questions which may affect the very essence of this instrument, including possible amendments to it. In either case, the meeting will be convoked by the General Secretary.

Organization

ARTICLE 7

1. In order to ensure compliance with the obligations of this Treaty, the Contracting Parties hereby establish an international organization to be known as the "Agency for the Prohibition of Nuclear Weapons in Latin America," hereinafter referred to as "the Agency." Only the Contracting Parties shall be affected by its decisions.

2. The Agency shall be responsible for the holding of periodic or extraordinary consultations among Member States on matters relating to the purposes, measures and procedures set forth in this Treaty and to the supervision of compliance with the obligations arising therefrom.

3. The Contracting Parties agree to extend to the Agency full and prompt co-operation in accordance with the provisions of this Treaty, of any agreements they may conclude with the Agency and of any agreements the Agency may conclude with any other international organization or body.

4. The headquarters of the Agency shall be in Mexico City.

Organs

ARTICLE 8

1. There are hereby established as principal organs of the Agency a General Conference, a Council and a Secretariat.

2. Such subsidiary organs as are considered necessary by the General Conference may be established within the purview of this Treaty.

The General Conference

ARTICLE 9

1. The General Conference, the supreme organ of the Agency, shall be composed of all the Contracting Parties; it shall hold regular sessions every two years, and may also hold special sessions whenever this Treaty so provides or, in the opinion of the Council the circumstances so require.

2. The General Conference:

(a) May consider and decide on any matters or questions covered by this Treaty, within the limits thereof, including those referring to powers and functions of any organ provided for in this Treaty.

(b) Shall establish procedures for the control system to ensure observance of this Treaty in accordance with its provisions.

(c) Shall elect the Members of the Council and the General Secretary.

(d) May remove the General Secretary from office if the proper functioning of the Agency so requires.

(e) Shall receive and consider the biennial and special reports submitted by the Council and General Secretary.

(f) Shall initiate and consider studies designed to facilitate the optimum fulfillment of the aims of this treaty, without prejudice to the power of the General Secretary independently to carry out similar studies for submission and to consideration by the Conference.

(g) Shall be the organ competent to authorize the conclusion of agreements with Governments and other international organization and bodies.

3. The General Conference shall adopt the Agency's budget and fix the scale of financial contributions to be paid by Member States, taking into account the systems and criteria used for the same purpose by the United Nations.

4. The General Conference shall elect its officers for each session and may establish such subsidiary organs as it deems necessary for the performance of its functions.

5. Each Member of the Agency shall have one vote. The decisions of the General Conference shall be taken by a two-thirds majority of the Members present and voting in the case of matters relating to the control system and measures referred to in article 20, the admission of new Members, the election or removal of the General Secretary, adoption of the budget and matters related thereto. Decisions on other matters, as well as procedural questions and also determination of which questions must be decided by a two-thirds majority, shall be taken by a simple majority of the Members present and voting.

6. The General Conference shall adopt its own rules procedure.

The Council

ARTICLE 10

1. The Council shall be composed of five Members of the Agency elected by the General Conference from among the Contracting Parties, due account being taken of equitable geographic distribution.

2. The Members of the Council shall be elected for a term of four years. However, in the first election three will be elected for two years. Outgoing Members may not be re-elected for the following period unless the limited number of States for which the Treaty is in force so requires.

3. Each Member of the Council shall have one representative.

4. The Council shall be so organized as to be able to function continuously.

5. In addition to the functions conferred upon it by this Treaty and to those which may be assigned to it by the General Conference, the Council shall, through the General Secretary, ensure the proper operation of the control system in accordance with the provisions of this Treaty and with the decisions adopted by the General Conference.

6. The Council shall submit an annual report on its work to the General Conference as well as such special reports as it deems necessary or which the General Conference requests of it.

7. The Council shall elect its officers for each session.

8. The decisions of the Council shall be taken by a simple majority of its Members present and voting.

9. The Council shall adopt its own rules of procedure.

The Secretariat

ARTICLE 11

1. The Secretariat shall consist of a General Secretary, who shall be the chief administrative officer to the Agency, and of such staff as the agency may require. The term of office of the General Secretary shall be four years and he may be re-elected for a single additional term. The General Secretary may not be a national of the country in which the Agency has its headquarters. In case the office of General Secretary becomes vacant, a new election shall be held to fill the office for the remainder of the term.

2. The staff of the Secretariat shall be appointed by the General Secretary, in accordance with rules laid down by the General Conference.

3. In addition to the functions conferred upon him by this Treaty and to those which may be assigned to him by the General Conference—the General Secretary shall ensure, as provided by article 10, paragraph 5, the proper operation of the control system established by this Treaty, in accordance with the provisions of the Treaty and the decisions taken by the General Conference.

4. The General Secretary shall act in that capacity in all meetings of the General Conference and of the Council and shall make an annual report to both bodies on the work of the Agency and any

special reports requested by the General Conference or the Council or which the General Secretary may deem desirable.

5. The General Secretary shall establish the procedures for distributing to all Contracting Parties information received by the Agency from governmental sources and such information from non-governmental sources as may be of interest to the Agency.

6. In the performance of their duties the General Secretary and the staff shall not seek or receive instructions from any Government or from any other authority external to the Agency and shall refrain from any action which might reflect on their position as international officials responsible only to the Agency; subject to their responsibility to the Agency, they shall not disclose any industrial secrets or other confidential information coming to their knowledge by reason of their official duties in the Agency.

7. Each of the Contracting Parties undertakes to respect the exclusively international character of the responsibilities of the General Secretary and the staff and not to seek to influence them in the discharge of their responsibilities.

Control system

ARTICLE 12

1. For the purpose of verifying compliance with the obligations entered into by the Contracting Parties in accordance with article 1, a control system shall be established which shall be put into effect in accordance with the provisions of articles 1318 of this Treaty.

2. The control system shall be used in particular for the purpose of verifying:

(a) That devices, services and facilities intended for peaceful uses of nuclear energy are not used in the testing or manufacture of nuclear weapons,

(b) That none of the activities prohibited in article 1 of this Treaty are carried out in the territory of the Contracting Parties with nuclear materials or weapons introduced from abroad, and

(c) That explosions for peaceful purposes are compatible with article 18 of this Treaty.

IAEA safeguards

ARTICLE 13

Each Contracting Party shall negotiate multilateral or bilateral agreements with the International Atomic Energy Agency for the application of its safeguards to its nuclear activities. Each Contracting Party shall initiate negotiations within a period of 180 days after the date of the deposit of its instrument of ratification of this Treaty. These agreements shall enter into force, for each Party, not later than eighteen months after the date of the initiation of such negotiations except in case of unforeseen circumstances or *force majeure*.

Reports of the Parties

ARTICLE 14

1. The Contracting Parties shall submit to the Agency and to the International Atomic Energy Agency, for their information, semi-annual reports stating that no activity prohibited under this Treaty has occurred in their respective territories.

2. The Contracting Parties shall simultaneously transmit to the Agency a copy of any report they may submit to the International Atomic Energy Agency which relates to matters that are the subject of this Treaty and to the application of safeguards.

3. The Contracting Parties shall also transmit to the Organization of American States, for its information, any reports that may be of interest to it, in accordance with the obligations established by the Inter-American System.

Special reports requested by the General Secretary

ARTICLE 15

1. With the authorization of the Council, the General Secretary may request any of the Contracting Parties to provide the Agency with complementary or supplementary information regarding any event or circumstance connected with compliance with this Treaty, explaining his reasons. The Contracting Parties undertake to co-operate promptly and fully with the General Secretary.

2. The General Secretary shall inform the Council and the Contracting Parties forthwith of such requests and of the respective replies.

Special inspections

ARTICLE 16

1. The International Atomic Energy Agency and the Council established by this Treaty have the power of carrying out special inspections in the following cases:

(a) In the case of the International Atomic Energy Agency, in accordance with the agreements referred to in article 13 of this Treaty:

(b) In the case of the Council:

(i) When so requested, the reasons for the request being stated, by any Party which suspects that some activity prohibited by this Treaty has been carried out or is about to be carried out, either in the territory of any other Party or in any other place on such latter Party's behalf, the Council shall immediately arrange for such an inspection in accordance with article 10, paragraph 5.

(ii) When requested by any Party which has been suspected of or charged with having violated this Treaty, the Council shall immediately arrange for the special inspection requested in accordance with article 10, paragraph 5.

The above requests will be made to the Council through the General Secretary.

2. The costs and expenses of any special inspection carried out under paragraph 1, sub-paragraph (b), sections (i) and (ii) of this article shall be borne by the requesting Party or Parties, except where the Council concludes on the basis of the report on the special inspection that, in view of the circumstances existing in the case, such costs and expenses should be borne by the Agency.

3. The General Conference shall formulate the procedures for the organization and execution of the special inspections carried out in accordance with paragraph 1, sub-paragraph (b), sections (i) and (ii) of this article.

4. The Contracting Parties undertake to grant the inspectors carrying out such special inspections full and free access to all places and all information which may be necessary for the performance of their duties and which are directly and intimately connected with the suspicion of violating this Treaty. If so requested by the authorities of the Contracting Party in whose territory the inspection is carried out, the inspectors designated by the General Conference shall be accompanied by representatives of said authorities, provided that this does not in any way delay or hinder the work of the inspectors.

5. The Council shall immediately transmit to all the Parties through the General Secretary, a copy of any report resulting from special inspections.

6. Similarly, the Council shall send through the General Secretary to the Secretary-General of the United Nations, for transmission to the United Nations Security Council and General Assembly, and to the Council of the Organization of American States, for its information, a copy of any report resulting from any special inspection carried out in accordance with paragraph 1, sub-paragraph (b), sections (i) and (ii) of this article.

7. The Council may decide, or any Contracting Party may request, the convening of a special session of the General Conference for the purpose of considering the reports resulting from any special inspection. In such a case, the General Secretary shall take immediate steps to convene the special session requested.

8. The General Conference, convened in special session under this article, may make recommendations to the Contracting Parties and submit reports to the Secretary-General of the United Nations to be transmitted to the United Nations Security Council and the General Assembly.

Use of nuclear energy for peaceful purposes

ARTICLE 17

Nothing in the provisions of this Treaty shall prejudice the rights of the Contracting Parties, in conformity with this Treaty, to use nuclear energy for peaceful purposes, in particular for their economic development and social progress.

Explosions for peaceful purposes

ARTICLE 18

1. The Contracting Parties may carry out explosions of nuclear devices for peaceful purposes—including explosions which involve

devices similar to those used in nuclear weapons—or collaborate with third parties for the same purpose, provided that they do so in accordance with the provisions of this article and the other articles of the Treaty, particularly articles 1 and 5.

2. Contracting Parties intending to carry out, or to co-operate in carrying out, such an explosion shall notify the Agency and the International Atomic Energy Agency, as far in advance as the circumstances require, of the date of the explosion and shall at the same time provide the following information:

(a) The nature of the nuclear device and the source from which it was obtained,

(b) The place and purpose of the planned explosion,

(c) The procedures which will be followed in order to comply with paragraph 3 of this article,

(d) The expected force of the device, and

(e) The fullest possible information on any possible radioactive fall-out that may result from the explosion or explosions, and measures which will be taken to avoid danger to the population, flora, fauna and territories of any other Party or Parties.

3. The General Secretary and the technical personnel designated by the Council and the International Atomic Energy Agency may observe all the preparations, including the explosion of the device, and shall have unrestricted access to any area in the vicinity of the site of the explosion in order to ascertain whether the device and the procedures followed during the explosion are in conformity and the information supplied under paragraph 2 of this article and the other provisions of this Treaty.

4. The Contracting Parties may accept the collaboration of third parties for the purpose set forth in paragraph 1 of the present article, in accordance with paragraphs 2 and 3 thereof.

Relations with other international organizations

ARTICLE 19

1. The Agency may conclude such agreements with the International Atomic Energy Agency as are authorized by the General conference and as it considers likely to facilitate the efficient operation of the control system established by this Treaty.

2. The Agency may also enter into relations with any international organization or body, especially any which may be established in the future to supervise disarmament or measures for the control of armaments in any part of the world.

3. The Contracting Parties may, if they see fit, request the advice of the Inter-American Nuclear Energy Commission on all technical matters connected with the application of this Treaty with which the Commission is competent to deal under its Statute.

Measures in the event of violation of the Treaty

ARTICLE 20

1. The General Conference shall take note of all cases in which, in its option, any Contracting Party is not complying fully with its

obligations under this Treaty and shall draw the matter to the attention of the Party concerned, making such recommendations as it deems appropriate.

2. If, in its opinion, such non-compliance constitutes a violation of this Treaty which might endanger peace and security, the General Conference shall report thereon simultaneously to the United Nations Security Council and the General Assembly through the Secretary-General of the United Nations, The General Conference shall likewise report to the International Atomic Energy Agency for such purposes as are relevant in accordance with its Statute.

United Nations and Organization of American States

ARTICLE 21

None of the provisions of this Treaty shall be construed as impairing the rights and obligations of the Parties under the Charter of the United Nations or, in the case of the States Members of the Organization of American States, under existing regional treaties.

Privileges and immunities

ARTICLE 22

1. The Agency shall enjoy in the territory of each of the Contracting Parties such legal capacity and such privileges and immunities as may be necessary for the exercise of its functions and the fulfillment of its purposes.

2. Representatives of the Contracting Parties accredited to the Agency and officials of the Agency shall similarly enjoy such privileges and immunities as are necessary for the performance of their functions.

3. The Agency may conclude agreements with the Contracting Parties with a view to determining the details of the application of paragraphs 1 and 2 of this article.

Notification of other agreements

ARTICLE 23

Once this Treaty has entered into force, the Secretariat shall be notified immediately of any international agreement concluded by any of the Contracting Parties on matters with which this Treaty is concerned; the Secretariat shall register it and notify the other Contracting Parties.

Settlement of disputes

ARTICLE 24

Unless the Parties concerned agree on another mode of peaceful settlement, any question or dispute concerning the interpretation or application of this Treaty which is not settled shall be referred to the International Court of Justice with the prior consent of the Parties to the controversy.

Signature

ARTICLE 25

1. This Treaty shall be open indefinitely for signature by:

(a) All the Latin American Republics, and

(b) All other sovereign States situated in their entirety south of latitude 35° north in the western hemisphere; and, except as provided in paragraph 2 of this article, all such States which become sovereign, when they have been admitted by the General Conference.

2. The General Conference shall not take any decision regarding the admission of a political entity part or all of whose territory is the subject, prior to the date when this Treaty is opened for signatures of a dispute or claim between an extra-continental country and one or more Latin American States, so long as the dispute has not been settled by peaceful means.

Ratification and deposit

ARTICLE 26

1. This Treaty shall be subject to ratification by signatory States in accordance with their respective constitutional procedures.

2. This Treaty and the instruments of ratification shall be deposited with the Government of the Mexican United States, which is hereby designated the Depositary Government.

3. The Depositary Government shall send certified copies of this Treaty of the Governments of Signatory States and shall notify them of the deposit of each instrument of ratification.

Reservations

ARTICLE 27

This Treaty shall not be subject to reservations.

Entry into force

ARTICLE 28

1. Subject to the provisions of paragraph 2 of this article this Treaty shall enter into force among the States that have ratified it as soon as the following requirements have been met:

(a) Deposit of the instruments of ratification of this Treaty with the Depositary Government by the Governments of the States mentioned in article 25 which are in existence on the date when this Treaty is opened for signature and which are not affected by the provisions of article 25, paragraph 2;

(b) Signature and ratification of Additional Protocol I annexed to this Treaty by all extra-continental or continental States having *de jure* or *de facto* international responsibility for territories situated in the zone of application of the Treaty;

(c) Signature and ratification of the Additional Protocol II annexed to this Treaty by all powers possessing nuclear weapons;

(d) Conclusion of bilateral or multilateral agreements on the application of the Safeguards System of the International Atomic Energy Agency in accordance with article 13 of this Treaty.

2. All signatory States shall have the imprescriptible right to waive, wholly or in part, the requirements laid down in the preceding paragraph. They may do so by means of a declaration which shall be annexed to their respective instrument of ratification and which may be formulated at the time of deposit of the instrument or subsequently. For these States which exercise this right, this Treaty shall enter into force upon deposit of the declaration, or as soon as those requirements have been met which have not been expressly waived.

3. As soon as this Treaty has entered into force in accordance with the provisions of paragraph 2 for eleven States, the Depositary Government shall convene a preliminary meeting of those States in order that the Agency may be set up and commence its work.

4. After the entry into force of this Treaty for all the countries of the zone, the rise of a new power possessing nuclear weapons shall have the effect of suspending the execution of this Treaty for those countries which have ratified it without waiving requirements of paragraph 1, sub-paragraph (c) of this article, and which request such suspension; the Treaty shall remain suspended until the new power on its own initiative or upon request by the General Conference, ratifies the annexed Additional Protocol II.

Amendments

Article 29

1. Any Contracting Party may propose amendments to this Treaty and shall submit its proposals to the Council through the General Secretary, who shall transmit them to all the other Contracting Parties and, in addition, to all other signatories in accordance with article 6. The Council, through the General Secretary, shall immediately following the meeting of signatories convene a special session of the General Conference to examine the proposals made, for the adoption of which a two-thirds majority of the Contracting parties present and voting shall be required.

2. Amendments adopted shall enter into force as soon as the requirements set forth in article 28 of this Treaty have been complied with.

Duration and denunciation

Article 30

1. This Treaty shall be of a permanent nature and shall remain in force indefinitely, but any Party may denounce it by notifying the General Secretary of the Agency if, in the opinion of the denouncing State, there have arisen or may arise circumstances connected with the content of this Treaty or of the annexed Additional Protocols I and II which affect its supreme interest or the peace and security of one or more Contracting Parties.

2. The denunciation shall take effect three months after the delivery to the General Secretary of the Agency of the notification to the other Contracting Parties and to the Secretary-General of the United Nations for the information of the United Nations Security Council and the General Assembly. He shall also communicate it to the Secretary-General of the Organization of American States.

Authentic texts and registration

ARTICLE 31

This Treaty, of which the Spanish, Chinese, English, French, Portuguese and Russian texts are equally authentic, shall be registered by the Depositary Government in accordance with article 102 of the United Nations Charter. The Depositary Government shall notify the Secretary-General of the United Nations of the signatures, ratifications and amendments relating to this Treaty and shall communicate them to the Secretary-General of the Organization of American States for its information.

TRANSITIONAL ARTICLE

Denunciation of the declaration referred to in article 28, paragraph 2, shall be subject to the same procedures as the denunciation of this Treaty, except that it will take effect on the date of delivery of the respective notification.

IN WITNESS WHEREOF the undersigned Plenipotentiaries, having deposited their full powers, found in good and due form, sign this Treaty on behalf of their respective Governments.

DONE at Mexico, Distrito Federal, on the Fourteenth day of February, one thousand nine hundred and sixty-seven.

b. Additional Protocol II[1]

Done at Mexico, February 14, 1967; Ratification advised by the Senate, with understandings and declarations, April 19, 1971; Ratified by the President, with understandings and declarations, May 8, 1971; Ratification of the United States deposited at Mexico, with understandings and declarations, May 12, 1971; Entered into force for the United States, May 12, 1971; Proclaimed by the President, June 11, 1971

The undersigned Plenipotentiaries, furnished with full powers by their respective Governments,

CONVINCED, That the Treaty for the Prohibition of Nuclear Weapons in Latin America,[2] negotiated and signed in accordance with the recommendations of the General Assembly of the United Nations in Resolution 1911 (XVIII) of 27 November 1963, represents an important step towards ensuring the non-proliferation of nuclear weapons,

AWARE, That the non-proliferation of nuclear weapons is not an end in itself but, rather, a means of achieving general and complete disarmament at a later stage, and

DESIRING, To contribute, so far as lies in their power, towards ending the armaments race, especially in the field of nuclear weapons, and towards promoting and strengthening a world at peace, based on mutual respect and sovereign equality of States,

HAVE AGREED AS FOLLOWS:

Article 1. The statute of denuclearization of Latin America in respect of warlike purposes, as defined, delimited and set forth in the Treaty for the Prohibition of Nuclear Weapons in Latin America of which this instrument is an annex, shall be fully respected by the Parties to this Protocol in all its express aims and provisions.

Article 2. The Governments represented by the undersigned Plenipotentiaries undertake, therefore not to contribute in any way to the performance of acts involving a violation of the obligations of article 1 of the Treaty in the territories to which the Treaty applies in accordance with article 4 thereof.

Article 3. The Governments represented by the undersigned Plenipotentiaries also undertake not to use or threaten to use nuclear weapons against the Contracting Parties of the Treaty for the Prohibition of Nuclear Weapons in Latin America.

Article 4. The duration of this Protocol shall be the same as that of the Treaty for the Prohibition of Nuclear Weapons in Latin America of which this Protocol is an annex, and the definitions of territory and nuclear weapons set forth in articles 3 and 5 of the

[1] 22 UST 754; TIAS 7137; 634 UNTS 364. For a list of states that are parties to this Protocol, see Department of State publication, *Treaties in Force*.

[2] The United States is not a party to the Treaty for the Prohibition of Nuclear Weapons in Latin America (the Treaty of Tlatelolco). The United States has ratified Additional Protocols I and II. China, France, the Soviet Union and the United Kingdom are the other parties to Protocol II.

Treaty shall be applicable to this Protocol, as well as the provisions regarding ratification, reservations, denunciation, authentic texts and registration contained in articles 26, 27, 30 and 31 of the Treaty.

Article 5. This Protocol shall enter into force, for the States which have ratified it, on the date of the deposit of their respective instruments of ratification.

IN WITNESS WHEREOF, the undersigned Plenipotentiaries, having deposited their full powers, found to be in good and due form, sign this Additional Protocol on behalf of their respective Governments.

Understandings and Declarations Included in the U.S. Instrument of Ratification[2]

The Senate of the United States of America by its resolution of April 19, 1971, two-thirds of the Senators present concurring, gave its advice and consent to the ratification of Additional Protocol II, with the following understandings and declarations:

I

That the United States Government understands the reference in Article 3 of the treaty to "its own legislation" to relate only to such legislation as is compatible with the rules of international law and as involves an exercise of sovereignty consistent with those rules, and accordingly that ratification of Additional Protocol II by the United States Government could not be regarded as implying recognition, for the purposes of this treaty and its protocols or for any other purpose, of any legislation which did not, in the view of the United States, comply with the relevant rules of international law.

That the United States Government takes note of the Preparatory Commission's interpretation of the treaty, as set forth in the Final Act, that, governed by the principles and rules of international law, each of the Contracting Parties retains exclusive power and legal competence, unaffected by the terms of the treaty, to grant or deny non-Contracting Parties transit and transport privileges.

That as regards the undertaking in Article 3 of Protocol II not to use or threaten to use nuclear weapons against the Contracting Parties, the United States Government would have to consider that an armed attack by a Contracting Party, in which it was assisted by a nuclear-weapon state, would be incompatible with the Contracting Party's corresponding obligations under Article 1 of the treaty.

II

That the United States Government considers that the technology of making nuclear explosive devices for peaceful purposes is indistinguishable from the technology of making nuclear weapons, and that nuclear weapons and nuclear explosive devices for peaceful purposes are both capable of releasing nuclear energy in an uncontrolled manner and have the common group of characteristics of

---

[2] 22 UST 760; TIAS 7137.

large amounts of energy generated instantaneously from a compact source. Therefore the United States Government understands the definition contained in Article 5 of the treaty as necessarily encompassing all nuclear explosive devices. It is also understood that Articles 1 and 5 restrict accordingly the activities of the Contracting Parties under paragraph 1 of Article 18.

That the United States Government understands that paragraph 4 of Article 18 of the treaty permits, and that United States adherence to Protocol II will not prevent, collaboration by the United States with Contracting Parties for the purpose of carrying out explosions of nuclear devices for peaceful purposes in a manner consistent with a policy of not contributing to the proliferation of nuclear weapons capabilities. In this connection, the United States Government notes Article V of the Treaty on the Non-Proliferation of Nuclear Weapons, under which it joined in an undertaking to take appropriate measures to ensure that potential benefits of peaceful applications of nuclear explosions would be made available to non-nuclear-weapon states party to that treaty, and reaffirms its willingness to extend such undertaking, on the same basis, to states precluded by the present treaty from manufacturing or acquiring any nuclear explosive device.

III

That the United States Government also declares that, although not required by Protocol II, it will act with respect to such territories of Protocol I adherents as are within the geographical area defined in paragraph 2 of Article 4 of the treaty in the same manner as Protocol II requires it to act with respect to the territories of Contracting Parties.

The President ratified Additional Protocol II on May 8, 1971, with the above-recited understandings and declarations, in pursuance of the advice and consent of the Senate.

It is provided in Article 5 of Additional Protocol II that the Protocol shall enter into force, for the States which ratified it, on the date of the deposit of their respective instruments of ratification.

The instrument of ratification of the United Kingdom of Great Britain and Northern Ireland was deposited on December 11, 1969 with understandings and a declaration, and the instrument of ratification of the United States of America was deposited on May 12, 1971 with the above-recited understandings and declarations.

In accordance with Article 5 of Additional Protocol II, the Protocol entered into force for the United States of America on May 12, 1971, subject to the above-recited understandings and declarations.

* * * * * * *

c. Additional Protocol I[1]

Done at Mexico, February 14, 1967; Ratification advised by the Senate, with understandings, November 13, 1981; Ratification of the United States deposited with Mexico, with understandings, November 23, 1981; Entered into force with respect to the United States, November 23, 1981; Proclaimed by the President, December 14, 1981

The undersigned Plenipotentiaries, furnished with full powers by their respective Governments,

CONVINCED that the Treaty for the Prohibition of Nuclear Weapons in Latin America,[2] negotiated and signed in accordance with the recommendations of the General Assembly of the United Nations in Resolution 1911 (XVIII) of 27 November 1963, represents an important step towards ensuring the non-proliferation of nuclear weapons.

AWARE that the non-proliferation of nuclear weapons is not an end in itself but, rather, a means of achieving general and complete disarmament at a later stage, and

DESIRING to contribute, so far as lies in their power, towards ending the armaments race, especially in the field of nuclear weapons, and towards strengthening a world at peace, based on mutual respect and sovereign equality of States,

HAVE AGREED AS FOLLOWS:

ARTICLE 1. To undertake to apply the statute of denuclearization in respect of warlike purposes as defined in articles 1, 3, 5 and 13 of the Treaty for the Prohibition of Nuclear Weapons in Latin America in territories for which, *de jure* or *de facto,* they are internationally responsible and which lie within the limits of the geographical zone established in that Treaty.

ARTICLE 2. The duration of this Protocol shall be the same as that of the Treaty for the Prohibition of Nuclear Weapons in Latin America of which this Protocol is an annex, and the provisions regarding ratification and denunciation contained in the Treaty shall be applicable to it.

---

[1] 33 UST 1796; TIAS 10147; 634 UNTS 362. For a list of states that are parties to this Protocol, see Department of State publication, *Treaties in Force.*

The Senate of the United States of America gave its advice and consent to the ratification of Additional Protocol I, with the following understandings:

"(1) That the provisions of the Treaty made applicable by this Additional Protocol do not affect the exclusive power and legal competence under international law of a State adhering to this Protocol to grant or deny transit and transport privileges to its own or any other vessels or aircraft irrespective of cargo or armaments.

"(2) That the provisions of the Treaty made applicable by this Additional Protocol do not affect rights under international law of a State adhering to this Protocol regarding the exercise of the freedom of the seas, of regarding passage through or over waters subject to the sovereignty of a State.

"(3) That the understandings and declarations attached by the United States to its ratification of Additional Protocol II apply also to its ratification of Additional Protocol I.".

[2] The United States is not a party to the Treaty for the Prohibition of Nuclear Weapons in Latin America (the Treaty of Tlatelolco) but has ratified Additional Protocols I and II to such Treaty.

ARTICLE 3. This Protocol shall enter into force, for the States which have ratified it, on the date of the deposit of their respective instruments of ratification.

IN WITNESS WHEREOF the undersigned Plenipotentiaries, having deposited their full powers, found in good and due form, sign this Protocol on behalf of their respective Governments.

12. U.S.-U.S.S.R. Bilateral Arms Control Agreements

a. Agreement on Measures To Reduce the Risk of Outbreak of Nuclear War Between the United States of America and the Union of Soviet Socialist Republics [1]

Signed at Washington, September 30, 1971; Entered into force, September 30, 1971

The United States of America and the Union of Soviet Socialist Republics, hereinafter referred to as the Parties:

TAKING into account the devastating consequences that nuclear war would have for all mankind, and recognizing the need to exert every effort to avert the risk of outbreak of such a war, including measures to guard against accidental or unauthorized use of nuclear weapons,

BELIEVING that agreement on measures for reducing the risk of outbreak of nuclear war serves the interests of strengthening international peace and security, and is in no way contrary to the interests of any other country,

BEARING in mind that continued efforts are also needed in the future to seek ways of reducing the risk of outbreak of nuclear war,

HAVE AGREED AS FOLLOWS:

ARTICLE 1

Each Party undertakes to maintain and to improve, as it deems necessary, its existing organizational and technical arrangements to guard against the accidental or unauthorized use of nuclear weapons under its control.

ARTICLE 2

The Parties undertake to notify each other immediately in the event of an accidental, unauthorized or any other unexplained incident involving a possible detonation of a nuclear weapon which could create a risk of outbreak of nuclear war. In the event of such an incident, the Party whose nuclear weapon in involved will immediately make every effort to take necessary measures to render harmless or destroy such weapon without its causing damage.

ARTICLE 3

The Parties undertake to notify each other immediately in the event of detection by missile warning systems of unidentified objects, or in the event of signs of interference with these systems or with related communications facilities, if such occurrences could create a risk of outbreak of nuclear war between the two countries.

[1] 22 UST 1590; TIAS 7186; 807 UNTS 57.

ARTICLE 4

Each Party undertakes to notify the other Party in advance of any planned missile launches if such launches will extend beyond it national territory in the direction of the other Party.

ARTICLE 5

Each Party, in other situations involving unexplained nuclear incidents, undertakes to act in such a manner as to reduce the possibility of its actions being misinterpreted by the other Party. In any such situation, each Party may inform the other Party or request information when, in its view, this is warranted by the interests of averting the risk of outbreak of nuclear war.

ARTICLE 6

For transmission of urgent information, notifications and requests for information in situations requiring prompt clarification, the Parties shall make primary use of the Direct Communications Link between the Governments of the United States of America and the Union of Soviet Socialist Republics.

For transmission of other information, notifications and requests for information, the Parties, at their own discretion, may use any communications facilities, including diplomatic channels, depending on the degree of urgency.

ARTICLE 7

The Parties undertake to hold consultations, as mutually agreed, to consider questions relating to implementation of the provisions of this Agreement, as well as to discuss possible amendments thereto aimed at further implementation of the purposes of this Agreement.

ARTICLE 8

This Agreement shall be of unlimited duration.

ARTICLE 9

This Agreement shall enter into force upon signature.

DONE at Washington on September 30, 1971, in two copies, each in the English and Russian languages, both texts being equally authentic.

b. Agreement Between the United States of America and the Union of Soviet Socialist Republics on the Prevention of Nuclear War [1]

Agreement signed at Washington, June 22, 1973; Entered into force, June 22, 1973

The United States of America and the Union of Soviet Socialist Republics, hereinafter referred to as the Parties,

GUIDED by the objectives of strengthening world peace and international security,

CONSCIOUS that nuclear war would have devastating consequences for mankind,

PROCEEDING from the desire to bring about conditions in which the danger of an outbreak of nuclear war anywhere in the world would be reduced and ultimately eliminated,

PROCEEDING from their obligations under the charter of the United Nations regarding the maintenance of peace, refraining from the threat or use of force, and the avoidance of war, and in conformity with the agreements to which either Party has subscribed,

PROCEEDING from the Basic Principles of Relations between the United States of America and the Union of Soviet Socialist Republics signed in Moscow on May 29, 1972,[2]

REAFFIRMING that the development of relations between the United States of America and the Union of Soviet Socialist Republics is not directed against other countries and their interests,

HAVE AGREED AS FOLLOWS:

ARTICLE I

The United States and the Soviet Union agree that an objective of their policies is to remove the danger of nuclear war and of the use of nuclear weapons.

Accordingly, the Parties agree that they will act in such a manner as to prevent the development of situations capable of causing a dangerous exacerbation of their relations, as to avoid military confrontations, and as to exclude the outbreak of nuclear war between them and between either of the Parties and other countries.

ARTICLE II

The Parties agree, in accordance with Article I and to realize the objective stated in that Article, to proceed from the premise that each Party will refrain from the threat or use of force against the other Party, against the allies of the other Party and against other

[1] 24 UST 1478; TIAS 7654.
[2] *Department of State Bulletin*, June 26, 1972, p. 898.

countries, in circumstances which may endanger international peace and security. The Parties agree that they will be guided by these considerations in the formulation of their foreign policies and in their actions in the field of international relations.

ARTICLE III

The Parties undertake to develop their relations with each other and with other countries in a way consistent with the purposes of this Agreement.

ARTICLE IV

If at any time relations between the Parties or between either Party and other countries appear to involve the risk of a nuclear conflict, or if relations between countries not parties to this Agreement appear to involve the risk of nuclear war between the United States of America and the Union of Soviet Socialist Republics or between either Party and other countries, the United States and the Soviet Union, acting in accordance with the provisions of this Agreement, shall immediately enter into urgent consultations with each other and make every effort to avert this risk.

ARTICLE V

Each Party shall be free to inform the Security Council of the United Nations, the Secretary General of the United Nations and the Governments of allied or other countries of the progress and outcome of consultations initiated in accordance with Article IV of this Agreement.

ARTICLE VI

Nothing in this Agreement shall affect or impair:

(a) the inherent right of individual or collective self-defense as envisaged by Article 51 of the Charter of the United Nations.[3]

(b) the provisions of the Charter of the United Nations, including those relating to the maintenance or restoration of international peace and security, and

(c) the obligations undertaken by either Party towards its allies or other countries in treaties, agreements, and other appropriate documents.

ARTICLE VII

This Agreement shall be of unlimited duration.

ARTICLE VIII

This Agreement shall enter into force upon signature.

DONE at Washington on June 22, 1973, in two copies, each in the English and Russian languages, both texts being equally authentic.

[3] TS 993; 59 Stat. 1044.

c. Agreement Between the United States of America and the Union of Soviet Socialist Republics on the Establishment of Nuclear Risk Reduction Centers with Protocols I and II

Agreement signed at Washington, September 15, 1987; Entered into force, September 15, 1987

The United States of America and the Union of Soviet Socialist Republics, hereinafter referred to as the Parties,

AFFIRMING their desire to reduce and ultimately eliminate the risk of outbreak of nuclear war, in particular, as a result of misinterpretation, miscalculation, or accident,

BELIEVING that a nuclear war cannot be won and must never be fought,

BELIEVING that agreement on measures for reducing the risk of outbreak of nuclear war serves the interests of strengthening international peace and security,

REAFFIRMING their obligations under the Agreement on Measures to Reduce the Risk of Outbreak of Nuclear War between the United States of America and the Union of Soviet Socialist Republics on September 30, 1971,[1] and the Agreement between the Government of the United States of America and the Government of the Union of Soviet Socialist Republics on the Prevention of Incidents on and over the High Seas of May 25, 1972,[2]

HAVE AGREED AS FOLLOWS:

ARTICLE 1

Each party shall establish, in its capital, a national Nuclear Risk Reduction Center that shall operate on behalf of and under the control of its respective Government.

ARTICLE 2

The Parties shall use the Nuclear Risk Reduction Centers to transmit notifications identified in Protocol I which constitutes an integral part of this Agreement.

In the future, the list of notifications transmitted through the Centers may be altered by agreement between the Parties, as relevant new agreements are reached.

ARTICLE 3

The Parties shall establish a special facsimile communications link between their national Nuclear Risk Reduction Centers in accordance with Protocol II which constitutes an integral part of this Agreement.

---

[1] 22 UST 1590; TIAS 7186.
[2] 23 UST 1168; TIAS 7379.

ARTICLE 4

The Parties shall staff their national Nuclear Risk Reduction Centers as they deem appropriate, so as to ensure their normal functioning.

ARTICLE 5

The Parties shall hold regular meetings between representatives of the Nuclear Risk Reduction Centers at least once each year to consider matters related to the functioning of such Centers.

ARTICLE 6

This Agreement shall not affect the obligations of either Party under other agreements.

ARTICLE 7

This Agreement shall enter into force on the date of its signature.

The duration of this Agreement shall not be limited.

This Agreement may be terminated by either Party upon 12 months written notice to the other Party.

DONE at Washington on September 15, 1987,[3] in two copies, each in the English and Russian languages, both texts being equally authentic.

For the United States of America

GEORGE P. SHULTZ

For the Union of Soviet Socialist Republics

EDUARD A. SHEVARDNADZE

PROTOCOL I TO THE AGREEMENT BETWEEN THE UNITED STATES OF AMERICA AND THE UNION OF SOVIET SOCIALIST REPUBLICS ON THE ESTABLISHMENT OF NUCLEAR RISK REDUCTION CENTERS

Pursuant to the provisions and in implementation of the Agreement between the United States of America and the Union of Soviet Socialist Republics on the Establishment of Nuclear Risk Reduction Centers, the Parties have agreed as follows:

ARTICLE 1

The Parties shall transmit the following types of notifications through the Nuclear Risk Reduction Centers:

(a) notification of ballistic missile launches under Article 4 of the Agreement on Measures to Reduce the Risk of Outbreak of Nuclear War between the United States of America and the Union of Soviet Socialist Republics of September 30, 1971;

(b) notifications of ballistic missile launches under paragraph 1 of Article VI of the Agreement between the Government of the United States of America and the Government of the Union of Soviet Socialist Republics on the Prevention of Incidents on and over the High Seas of May 25, 1972.

---

[3] *Department of State Bulletin*, November, 1987, p. 34.

ARTICLE 2

The scope and format of the information to be transmitted through the Nuclear Risk Reduction Centers shall be agreed upon.

ARTICLE 3

Each Party also may, at its own discretion as a display of good will and with a view to building confidence, transmit through the Nuclear Risk Reduction Centers communications other than those provided for under Article 1 of this Protocol.

ARTICLE 4

Unless the Parties agree otherwise, all communications transmitted through and communications procedures of the Nuclear Risk Reduction Centers' communication link will be confidential.

ARTICLE 5

This Protocol shall enter into force on the date of its signature and shall remain in force as long as the Agreement between the United States of America and the Union of Soviet Socialist Republics on the Establishment of Nuclear Risk Reduction Centers of September 15, 1987, remains in force.

DONE at Washington on September 15, 1987, in two copies, each in the English and Russian languages, both texts being equally authentic.

For the United States of America

GEORGE P. SHULTZ

For the Union of Soviet Socialist Republics

EDUARD A. SHEVARDNADZE

PROTOCOL II TO THE AGREEMENT BETWEEN THE UNITED STATES OF AMERICA AND THE UNION OF SOVIET SOCIALIST REPUBLICS ON THE ESTABLISHMENT OF NUCLEAR RISK REDUCTION CENTERS

Pursuant to the provisions and in implementation of the Agreement between the United States of America and the Union of Soviet Socialist Republics on the Establishment of Nuclear Risk Reduction Centers, the Parties have agreed as follows:

ARTICLE 1

To establish and maintain for the purpose of providing direct facsimile communications between their national Nuclear Risk Reduction Centers, established in accordance with Article 1 of this Agreement, hereinafter referred to as the national Centers, an INTELSAT satellite circuit and a STATSIONAR satellite circuit, each with a secure orderwire communications capability for operational monitoring. In this regard:

(a) There shall be terminals equipped for communication between the national Centers:

(b) Each Party shall provide communications circuits capable of simultaneously transmitting and receiving 4800 bits per second;

(c) Communication shall begin with test operation of the INTELSAT satellite circuit, as soon as purchase, delivery, and installation of the necessary equipment by the Parties are completed. Thereafter, taking into account the results of test operations, the Parties shall agree on the transition to a fully operational status;

(d) To the extent practicable, test operation of the STATSIONAR satellite circuit shall begin simultaneously with test operation of the INTELSAT satellite circuit. Taking into account the results of test operations, the Parties shall agree on the transition to a fully operational status.

ARTICLE 2

To employ agreed-upon information security devices to assure secure transmission of facsimile messages. In this regard:

(a) The information security devices shall consist of microprocessors that will combine the digital message output with buffered random data read from standard 5¼ inch floppy disks;

(b) Each Party shall provide, through its Embassy, necessary keying material to the other.

ARTICLE 3

To establish and maintain at each operating end of the two circuits, facsimile terminals of the same make and model. In this regard:

(a) Each Party shall be responsible for the purchase, installation, operation, and maintenance of its own terminals, the related information security devices, and local transmission circuits appropriate to the implementation of the Protocol;

(b) A Group III facsimile unit which meets CCITT Recommendations T.4 and T.30 and operates at 4800 bits per second shall be used;

(c) Direct facsimile messages from the USSR national Center the U.S. national Center shall be transmitted and received in the Russian language, and from the U.S. national Center to the USSR national Center in the English language;

(d) Transmission and operating procedures shall be in conformity with procedures employed on the Direct Communications Link and adapted as necessary for the purpose of communications between the national Centers.

ARTICLE 4

To establish and maintain a secure orderwire communications capability necessary to coordinate facsimile operation. In this regard:

(a) The orderwire terminals used with the information security devices described in paragraph (a) of Article 2 shall incorporate standard USSR Cyrillic and United States Latin keyboards and cathode ray tube displays to permit the exchange of messages between operators. The specific layout of the Cyrillic keyboard shall be as specified by the Soviet side;

(b) To coordinate the work of operators, the orderwire shall be configured so as to permit, prior to the transmission and reception of messages, the exchange of all information pertinent to the coordination of such messages;

(c) Orderwire messages concerning transmissions shall be encoded using the same information security devices specified in paragraph (a) of Article 2;

(d) The orderwire shall use the same modem and communications link as used for facsimile message transmission;

(e) A printer shall be included to provide a record copy of all information exchanged on the orderwire.

ARTICLE 5

To use the same type of equipment and the same maintenance procedures as currently in use for the Direct Communications Link for the establishment of direct facsimile communications between the national Centers. The equipment, security devices, and spare parts necessary for telecommunications links and the orderwire shall be provided by the United States side to the Soviet side in return for payment of costs thereof by the Soviet side.

ARTICLE 6

To ensure the exchange of information necessary for the operation and maintenance of the telecommunication system and equipment configuration.

ARTICLE 7

To take all possible measures to assure the continuous, secure, and reliable operation of the equipment and communications link, including the orderwire, for which each Party is responsible in accordance with this Protocol.

ARTICLE 8

To determine, by mutual agreement between technical experts of the Parties, the distribution and calculation of expenses for putting into operation the communication link, its maintenance and further development.

ARTICLE 9

To convene meetings of technical experts of the Parties in order to consider initially questions pertaining to the practical implementation of the activities provided for in this Protocol and, thereafter, by mutual agreement and as necessary for the purpose of improving telecommunications and information technology in order to achieve the mutually agreed functions of the national Centers.

ARTICLE 10

This Protocol shall enter into force on the date of its signature and shall remain in force as long as the Agreement between the

United States of America and the Union of Soviet Socialist Republics on the Establishment of Nuclear Risk Reduction Centers of September 15, 1987, remains in force.

DONE at Washington on September 15, 1987, in two copies, each in the English and Russian languages, both texts being equally authentic.

For the United States of America

GEORGE P. SHULTZ

For the Union of Soviet Socialist Republics

EDUARD A. SHEVARDNADZE

d. Agreement Between the United States of America and the Union of Soviet Socialist Republics on Notifications of Launches of Intercontinental Ballistic Missiles and Submarine-Launched Ballistic Missiles

Agreement signed at Moscow, May 31, 1988; Entered into force, May 31, 1988

The United States of America and the Union of Soviet Socialist Republics, hereinafter referred to as the Parties,

AFFIRMING their desire to reduce and ultimately eliminate the risk of outbreak of nuclear war, in particular, as a result of misinterpretation, miscalculation, or accident,

BELIEVING that a nuclear war cannot be won and must never be fought,

BELIEVING that agreement on measures for reducing the risk of outbreak of nuclear war serves the interests of strengthening international peace and security,

REAFFIRMING their obligations under the Agreement on Measures to Reduce the Risk of Outbreak of Nuclear War between the United States of America and the Union of Soviet Socialist Republics of September 30, 1971, the Agreement between the Government of the United States of America and the Government of the Union of Soviet Socialist Republics on the Prevention of Incidents on and over the High Seas of May 25, 1972, and the Agreement between the United States of America and the Union of Soviet Socialist Republics on the Establishment of Nuclear Risk Reduction Centers of September 15, 1987,

HAVE AGREED AS FOLLOWS:

ARTICLE I

Each Party shall provide the other Party notification, through the Nuclear Risk Reduction Centers of the United States of America and the Union of Soviet Socialist Republics, no less than twenty-four hours in advance, of the planned date, launch area, and area of impact for any launch of a strategic ballistic missile: an intercontinental ballistic missile (hereinafter "ICBM") or a submarine-launched ballistic missile (hereinafter "SLBM").

ARTICLE II

A notification of a planned launch of an ICBM or an SLBM shall be valid for four days counting from the launch date indicated in such a notification. In case of postponement of the launch date within the indicated four days, or cancellation of the launch, no notification thereof shall be required.

ARTICLE III

1. For launches of ICBMs or SLBMs from land, the notification shall indicate the area from which the launch is planned to take place.

2. For launches of SLBMs from submarines, the notification shall indicate the general area from which the missile will be launched. Such notification shall indicate either the quadrant within the ocean (that is, the ninety-degree sector encompassing approximately one-fourth of the area of the ocean) or the body of water (for example, sea or bay) from which the launch is planned to take place.

3. For all launches of ICBMs or SLBMs, the notification shall indicate the geographic coordinates of the planned impact area or areas of the reentry vehicles. Such an area shall be specified either by indicating the geographic coordinates of the boundary points of the area, or by indicating the geographic coordinates of the center of a circle with a radius specified in kilometers or nautical miles. The size of the impact area shall be determined by the notifying Party at its discretion.

ARTICLE IV

The Parties undertake to hold consultations, as mutually agreed, to consider questions relating to implementation of the provisions of this Agreement, as well as to discuss possible amendments thereto aimed at furthering the implementation of the objectives of this Agreement. Amendments shall enter into force in accordance with procedures to be agreed upon.

ARTICLE V

This Agreement shall not affect the obligations of either Party under other agreements.

ARTICLE VI

This Agreement shall enter into force on the date of its signature.

The duration of this Agreement shall not be limited.

This Agreement may be terminated by either Party upon 12 months written notice to the other Party.

DONE at Moscow on May 31, 1988, in two copies, each in the English and Russian languages, both texts being equally authentic.

For the United States of America:

GEORGE P. SHULTZ

For the Union of Soviet Socialist Republics:

EDUARD A. SHEVARDNADZE

13. U.S.-Russia Bilateral Arms Control Agreements

a. Agreement Between the United States of America and the Russian Federation Concerning the Safe and Secure Transportation, Storage and Destruction of Weapons and the Prevention of Weapons Proliferation

Agreement signed at Washington, June 17, 1992; Extended by the Protocol of June 15/16, 1999; Further extended by the Protocol of June 16, 2006

The United States of America and the Russian Federation, hereinafter referred to as the Parties,

DESIRING to facilitate the safe and secure transportation and storage of nuclear, chemical, and other weapons in the Russian Federation in connection with their destruction,

INTENDING to build upon the framework for cooperation set forth in the Agreement Between the Government of the United States of America and the Government of the Russian Federation Regarding Cooperation to Facilitate the Provision of Assistance of April 4, 1992,

HAVE AGREED AS FOLLOWS:

ARTICLE I

The Parties shall cooperate in order to assist the Russian Federation in achieving the following objectives:

a. the destruction of nuclear, chemical, and other weapons;

b. the safe and secure transportation and storage of such weapons in connection with their destruction; and

c. the establishment of additional verifiable measures against the proliferation of such weapons that pose a risk of proliferation.

ARTICLE II

1. The Parties, through their Executive Agents, shall enter into implementing agreements as appropriate to accomplish the objectives set forth in Article I of this Agreement. The implementing agreements shall include, inter alia:

a. a description of the activities to be undertaken;

b. provisions concerning the sequence of activities;

c. provisions concerning access to material, training or services provided at sites of their use, if possible, for monitoring and inspection; and

d. other provisions as appropriate.

2. In case of any inconsistency between this Agreement and any implementing agreements, the provisions of this Agreement shall prevail.

ARTICLE III

Each Party shall designate an Executive Agent to implement this Agreement. For the United States of America, the Executive Agent shall be the Department of Defense. For the Russian Federation, with respect to nuclear weapons, the Executive Agent shall be the Ministry of Atomic Energy.

ARTICLE IV

Except as otherwise provided in this Agreement or in an implementing agreement, the terms of this Agreement shall apply to all material, training, or services provided in accordance with this Agreement or implementing agreements, and to all related activities and personnel.

ARTICLE V

1. The Russian Federation shall facilitate the entry and exit of employees of the Government of the United States of America and contractor personnel of the United States of America into and out of the territory of the Russian Federation for the purpose of carrying out activities in accordance with this Agreement.

2. Aircraft and vessels, other than regularly scheduled commercial aircraft and vessels, used by the United States of America in connection with activities pursuant to this Agreement in the Russian Federation shall, in accordance with international law, be free of customs inspections, customs charges, landing fees, navigation charges, port charges, tolls, and any other charges by the Russian Federation or any of its instrumentalities.

3. If an aircraft other than a regularly scheduled commercial aircraft is used by the United States of America for transportation to the Russian Federation, its flight plan shall be filed in accordance with the procedures of the International Civil Aviation Organization applicable to civil aircraft, including in the remarks section of the flight plan confirmation that the appropriate clearance has been obtained. The Russian Federation shall provide parking, security protection, servicing, and fuel for aircraft of the United States of America.

ARTICLE VI

Unless the written consent of the United States of America has first been obtained, the Russian Federation shall not transfer title to, or possession of, any material, training or services provided pursuant to this Agreement to any entity, other than an officer, employee or agent of a Party to this Agreement and shall not permit the use of such material, training or services for purposes other than those for which it has been furnished.

ARTICLE VII

1. The Russian Federation shall, in respect of legal proceedings and claims, other than contractual claims, hold harmless and bring no legal proceedings against the United States of America and personnel, contractors, and contractors' personnel of the United States

of America, for damage to property owned by the Russian Federation, or death or injury to any personnel of the Russian Federation, arising out of activities pursuant to this Agreement.

2. Claims by third parties, arising out of the acts or omissions of any employees of the United States of America or contractors or contractors' personnel of the United States of America done in the performance of official duty, shall be the responsibility of the Russian Federation.

3. The provisions of the Article shall not prevent the Parties from providing compensation in accordance with their national laws.

4. The Parties may consult, as appropriate, on claims and proceedings under this Article.

5. Nothing in this Article shall be construed to prevent legal proceedings or claims against nationals of the Russian Federation or permanent residents of the Russian Federation.

ARTICLE VIII

The activities of the United States of America under this Agreement are subject to availability of appropriated funds.

ARTICLE IX

Employees of the Government of the United States of America present in the territory of the Russian Federation for activities related to this Agreement shall be accorded privileges and immunities equivalent to that accorded administrative and technical staff personnel in accordance with the Vienna Convention on Diplomatic Relations of April 18, 1961.

ARTICLE X

1. The United States of America, its personnel, contractors, and contractors' personnel shall note be liable to pay any tax or similar charge by the Russian Federation or any of its instrumentalities on activities undertaken in accordance with this Agreement.

2. The United States of America, its personnel, contractors, and contractors' personnel may import into, and export out of, the Russian Federation any equipment, supplies, material or services required to implement this Agreement. Such importation and exportation of articles or services shall not be subject to any licenses, other restrictions, customs, duties, taxes or any other charges or inspections by the Russian Federation or any of its instrumentalities.

ARTICLE XI

In the event that a Party awards contracts for the acquisition of articles and services, including construction, to implement this Agreement, such contracts shall be awarded in accordance with the laws and regulations of that Party. Acquisition of articles and services in the Russian Federation by or on behalf of the United States of America in implementing this Agreement shall not be subject to any taxes, customs, duties or similar charges by the Russian Federation or its instrumentalities.

ARTICLE XII

The Russian Federation shall take all reasonable measures within its power to ensure the security of material, training or services provided pursuant to this Agreement and shall protect them against seizure or conversion.

ARTICLE XIII

Upon request, representatives of the Government of the United States of America shall have the right to examine the use of any material, training or other services provided in accordance with this Agreement, if possible at sites of their location or use, and shall have the right to inspect any and all related records or documentation during the period of this Agreement and for three years thereafter. These inspections shall be carried out in accordance with procedures to be agreed upon by the Parties.

ARTICLE XIV

This Agreement shall enter into force upon signature and shall remain in force for seven years. This Agreement may be amended or extended by the written agreement of the Parties and may be terminated by either Party upon ninety days written notification to the other Party of its intention to do so. Notwithstanding the termination of this Agreement or the implementing agreements, the obligations of the Russian Federation in accordance with Articles VI, VII, IX, X, XII of this Agreement shall continue to apply without respect to time, unless otherwise agreed in writing by the Parties.

DONE at Washington this 17th day of June 1992, in two copies, each in the English and Russian languages, both texts being equally authentic.

b. Treaty Between the United States and the Russian Federation on Strategic Offensive Reductions

Done at Moscow, May 24, 2002; Ratification advised by the Senate, March 6, 2003; Entered into force, June 1, 2003

The United States of America and the Russian Federation, hereinafter referred to as the Parties,

EMBARKING upon the path of new relations for a new century and committed to the goal of strengthening their relationship through cooperation and friendship,

BELIEVING that new global challenges and threats require the building of a qualitatively new foundation for strategic relations between the Parties,

DESIRING to establish a genuine partnership based on the principles of mutual security, cooperation, trust, openness, and predictability,

COMMITTED to implementing significant reductions in strategic offensive arms,

PROCEEDING from the Joint Statements by the President of the United States of America and the President of the Russian Federation on Strategic Issues of July 22, 2001 in Genoa and on a New Relationship between the United States and Russia of November 13, 2001 in Washington,

MINDFUL of their obligations under the Treaty Between the United States of America and the Union of Soviet Socialists Republics on the Reduction and Limitation of Strategic Offensive Arms of July 31, 1991, hereinafter referred to as the START Treaty,

MINDFUL of their obligations under Article VI of the Treaty on the Non-Proliferation of Nuclear Weapons of July 1, 1968, and

CONVINCED that this Treaty will help to establish more favorable conditions for actively promoting security and cooperation, and enhancing international stability,

HAVE AGREED AS FOLLOWS:

ARTICLE I

Each Party shall reduce and limit strategic nuclear warheads, as stated by the President of the United States of America on November 13, 2001 and as stated by the President of the Russian Federation on November 13, 2001 and December 13, 2001 respectively, so that by December 31, 2012 the aggregate number of such warheads does not exceed 1700–2200 for each Party. Each Party shall determine for itself the composition and structure of its strategic offensive arms, based on the established aggregate limit for the number of such warheads.

ARTICLE II

The Parties agree that the START Treaty remains in force in accordance with its terms.

ARTICLE III

For purposes of implementing this Treaty, the Parties shall hold meetings at least twice a year of a Bilateral Implementation Commission.

ARTICLE IV

1. This Treaty shall be subject to ratification in accordance with the constitutional procedures of each Party. This Treaty shall enter into force on the date of the exchange of instruments of ratification.
2. This Treaty shall remain in force until December 31, 2012 and may be extended by agreement of the Parties or superseded earlier by a subsequent agreement.
3. Each Party, in exercising its national sovereignty, may withdraw from this Treaty upon three months written notice to the other Party.

ARTICLE V

This Treaty shall be registered pursuant to Article 102 of the Charter of the United Nations.

DONE at Moscow on May 24, 2002, in two copies, each in the English and Russian languages, both texts being equally authentic.

FOR THE UNITED STATES OF AMERICA

GEORGE W. BUSH

FOR THE RUSSIAN FEDERATION

VLADIMIR V. PUTIN

14. Convention on Prohibitions or Restrictions on the Use of Certain Conventional Weapons Which May be Deemed to be Excessively Injurious or to Have Indiscriminate Effects with Protocol I

Convention adopted at Geneva, October 10, 1980; Entered into force, December 2, 1983; Ratification advised by the Senate, March 24, 1995; Entered into force for the United States, September 24, 1995

The High Contracting Parties,

RECALLING that every State has the duty, in conformity with the Charter of the United Nations, to refrain in its international relations from the threat or use of force against the sovereignty, territorial integrity or political independence of any State, or in any other manner inconsistent with the purposes of the United Nations,

FURTHER RECALLING the general principle of the protection of the civilian population against the effects of hostilities,

BASING themselves on the principle of international law that the right of the parties to an armed conflict to choose methods or means of warfare is not unlimited, and on the principle that prohibits the employment in armed conflicts of weapons, projectiles and material and methods of warfare of a nature to cause superfluous injury or unnecessary suffering,

ALSO RECALLING that it is prohibited to employ methods or means of warfare which are intended, or may be expected, to cause widespread, long-term and severe damage to the natural environment,

CONFIRMING their determination that in cases not covered by this Convention and its annexed Protocols or by other international agreements, the civilian population and the combatants shall at all times remain under the protection and authority of the principles of international law derived from established custom, from the principles of humanity and from the dictates of public conscience,

DESIRING to contribute to international détente, the ending of the arms race and the building of confidence among States, and hence to the realization of the aspiration of all peoples to live in peace,

RECOGNIZING the importance of pursuing every effort which may contribute to progress towards general and complete disarmament under strict and effective international control,

REAFFIRMING the need to continue the codification and progressive development of the rules of international law applicable in armed conflict,

WISHING to prohibit or restrict further the use of certain conventional weapons and believing that the positive results achieved in this area may facilitate the main talks on disarmament with a view to putting an end to the production, stockpiling and proliferation of such weapons,

EMPHASIZING the desirability that all States become parties to this Convention and its annexed Protocols, especially the militarily significant States,

BEARING in mind that the General Assembly of the United Nations and the United Nations Disarmament Commission may decide to examine the question of a possible broadening of the scope of the prohibitions and restrictions contained in this Convention and its annexed Protocols,

FURTHER BEARING in mind that the Committee on Disarmament may decide to consider the question of adopting further measures to prohibit or restrict the use of certain conventional weapons,

HAVE AGREED AS FOLLOWS:

Article 1

Scope of application

This Convention and its annexed Protocols shall apply in the situations referred to in Article 2 common to the Geneva Conventions of 12 August 1949 for the Protection of War Victims, including any situation described in paragraph 4 of Article 1 of Additional Protocol 1 to these Conventions.

Article 2

Relations with other international agreements

Nothing in this Convention or its annexed Protocols shall be interpreted as detracting from other obligations imposed upon the High Contracting Parties by international humanitarian law applicable in armed conflict.

Article 3

Signature

This Convention shall be open for signature by all States at United Nations Headquarters in New York for a period of twelve months from 10 April 1981.

Article 4

Ratification, acceptance, approval or accession

1. This Convention is subject to ratification, acceptance or approval by the Signatories. Any State which has not signed this Convention may accede to it.
2. The instruments of ratification, acceptance, approval or accession shall be deposited with the Depositary.
3. Expressions of consent to be bound by any of the Protocols annexed to this Convention shall be optional for each State, provided that at the time of the deposit of its instrument of ratification, acceptance or approval of this Convention or of accession thereto,

that State shall notify the Depositary of its consent to be bound by any two or more of these Protocols.

4. At any time after the deposit of its instrument of ratification, acceptance or approval of this Convention or of accession thereto, a State may notify the Depositary of its consent to be bound by any annexed Protocol by which it is not already bound.

5. Any Protocol by which a High Contracting Party is bound shall for that Party form an integral part of this Convention.

Article 5

Entry into force

1. This Convention shall enter into force six months after the date of deposit of the twentieth instrument of ratification, acceptance, approval or accession.

2. For any State which deposits its instrument of ratification, acceptance, approval or accession after the date of the deposit of the twentieth instrument of ratification, acceptance, approval or accession, this Convention shall enter into force six months after the date on which that State has deposited its instrument of ratification, acceptance, approval or accession.

3. Each of the Protocols annexed to this Convention shall enter into force six months after the date by which twenty States have notified their consent to be bound by it in accordance with paragraph 3 or 4 of Article 4 of this Convention.

4. For any State which notifies its consent to be bound by a Protocol annexed to this Convention after the date by which twenty States have notified their consent to be bound by it, the Protocol shall enter into force six months after the date on which that State has notified its consent so to be bound.

Article 6

Dissemination

The High Contracting Parties undertake, in time of peace as in time of armed conflict, to disseminate this Convention and those of its annexed Protocols by which they are bound as widely as possible in their respective countries and, in particular, to include the study thereof in their programmes of military instruction, so that those instruments may become known to their armed forces.

Article 7

Treaty relations upon entry into force of this Convention

1. When one of the parties to a conflict is not bound by an annexed Protocol, the parties bound by this Convention and that annexed Protocol shall remain bound by them in their mutual relations.

2. Any High Contracting Party shall be bound by this Convention and any Protocol annexed thereto which is in force for it, in any situation contemplated by Article 1, in relation to any State which is not a party to this Convention or bound by the relevant annexed

Protocol, if the latter accepts and applies this Convention or the relevant Protocol, and so notifies the Depositary.

3. The Depositary shall immediately inform the High Contracting Parties concerned of any notification received under paragraph 2 of this Article.

4. This Convention, and the annexed Protocols by which a High Contracting Party is bound, shall apply with respect to an armed conflict against that High Contracting Party of the type referred to in Article 1, paragraph 4, of Additional Protocol 1 to the Geneva Convention of 12 August 1949 for the Protection of War Victims:

(a) Where the High Contracting Party is also a party to Additional Protocol 1 and an authority referred to in Article 96, paragraph 3, of that Protocol has under-taken to apply the Geneva Conventions and Additional Protocol 1 in accordance with Article 96, paragraph 3, of the said Protocol, and undertakes to apply this Convention and the relevant annexed Protocols in relation to that conflict; or

(b) Where the High Contracting Party is not a party to Additional Protocol 1 and an authority of the type referred to in subparagraph (a) above accepts and applies the obligations of the Geneva Conventions and of this Convention and the relevant annexed Protocols in relation to that conflict. Such an acceptance and application shall have in relation to that conflict the following effects:

(i) The Geneva Conventions and this Convention and its relevant annexed Protocols are brought into force for the parties to the conflict with immediate effect;

(ii) The said authority assumes the same rights and obligations as those which have been assumed by a High Contracting Party to the Geneva Conventions, this Convention and its relevant annexed Protocols; and

(iii) The Geneva Conventions, this Convention and its relevant annexed Protocols are equally binding upon all parties to the conflict.

The High Contracting Party and the authority may also agree to accept and apply the obligations of Additional Protocol 1 to the Geneva Conventions on a reciprocal basis.

Article 8

Review and amendments

1. (a) At any time after the entry into force of this Convention any High Contracting Party may propose amendments to this Convention or any annexed Protocol by which it is bound.. Any proposal for an amendment shall be communicated to the Depositary, who shall notify it to all the High Contracting Parties and shall seek their views on whether a conference should be convened to consider the proposal. If a majority, that shall not be less than eighteen of the High Contracting Parties so agree, he shall promptly convene a conference to which all High Contracting Parties shall be invited. States not parties to this Convention shall be invited to the conference as observers.

(b) Such a conference may agree upon amendments which shall be adopted and shall enter into force in the same manner as this

Convention and the annexed Protocols, provided that amendments to this Convention may be adopted only by the High Contracting Parties and that amendments to a specific annexed Protocol may be adopted only by the High Contracting Parties which are bound by that Protocol.

2. (a) At any time after the entry into force of this Convention any High Contracting Party may propose additional protocols relating to other categories of conventional weapons not covered by the existing annexed protocols. Any such proposal for an additional protocol shall be communicated to the Depositary, who shall notify it to all the High Contracting Parties in accordance with subparagraph 1 (a) of this Article. If a majority, that shall not be less than eighteen of the High Contracting Parties so agree, the Depositary shall promptly convene a conference to which all States shall be invited.

(b) Such a conference may agree, with the full participation of all States represented at the conference, upon additional protocols which shall be adopted in the same manner as this Convention, shall be annexed thereto and shall enter into force as provided in paragraphs 3 and 4 of Article 5 of this Convention.

3. (a) If, after a period of ten years following the entry into force of this Convention, no conference has been convened in accordance with subparagraph 1 (a) or 2 (a) of this Article, any High Contracting Party may request the Depositary to convene a conference to which all High Contracting Parties shall be invited to review the scope and operation of this Convention and the Protocols annexed thereto and to consider any proposal for amendments of this Convention or of the existing Protocols. States not parties to this Convention shall be invited as observers to the conference. The conference may agree upon amendments which shall be adopted and enter into force in accordance with subparagraph 1 (b) above.

(b) At such conference consideration may also be given to any proposal for additional protocols relating to other categories of conventional weapons not covered by the existing annexed Protocols. Ali States represented at the conference may participate fully in such consideration. Any additional protocols shall be adopted in the same manner as this Convention, shall be annexed thereto and shall enter into force as provided in paragraphs 3 and 4 of Article 5 of this Convention.

(c) Such a conference may consider whether provision should be made for the convening of a further conference at the request of any High Contracting Party if, after a similar period to that referred to in subparagraph 3 (a) of this Article, no conference has been convened in accordance with subparagraph 1 (a) or 2 (a) of this Article.

Article 9

Denunciation

1. Any High Contracting Party may denounce this Convention or any of its annexed Protocols by so notifying the Depositary.

2. Any such denunciation shall only take effect one year after receipt by the Depositary of the notification of denunciation. If, however, on the expiry of that year the denouncing High Contracting

Party is engaged in one of the situations referred to in Article 1, the Party shall continue to be bound by the obligations of this Convention and of the relevant annexed Protocols until the end of the armed conflict or occupation and, in any case, until the termination of operations connected with the final release, repatriation or re-establishment of the persons protected by the rules of international law applicable in armed conflict, and in the case of any annexed Protocol containing provisions concerning situations in which peace-keeping, observation or similar functions are performed by United Nations forces or missions in the area concerned, until the termination of those functions.

3. Any denunciation of this Convention shall be considered as also applying to all annexed Protocols by which the denouncing High Contracting Party is bound.

4. Any denunciation shall have effect only in respect of the denouncing High Contracting Party.

5. Any denunciation shall not affect the obligations already incurred, by reason of an armed conflict, under this Convention and its annexed Protocols by such denouncing High Contracting Party in respect of any act committed before this denunciation becomes effective.

Article 10

Depositary

1. The Secretary-General of the United Nations shall be the Depositary of this Convention and of its annexed Protocols.

2. In addition to his usual functions, the Depositary shall inform all States of:

(a) Signatures affixed to this Convention under Article 3;

(b) Deposits of instruments of ratification, acceptance or approval of or accession to this Convention deposited under Article 4;

(c) Notifications of consent to be bound by annexed Protocols under Article 4;

(d) The dates of entry into force of this Convention and of each of its annexed Protocols under Article 5; and

(e) Notifications of denunciation received under Article 9 and their effective date.

Article 11

Authentic texts

The original of this Convention with the annexed Protocols, of which the Arabic, Chinese, English, French, Russian and Spanish texts are equally authentic, shall be deposited with the Depositary, who shall transmit certified true copies thereof to all States.

Protocol on Non-Detectable Fragments (Protocol I) [1]

Protocol adopted at Geneva October 10, 1980; Entered into force December 2, 1983; Ratification advised by the Senate March 24, 1995; Entered into force for the United States September 24, 1995

It is prohibited to use any weapon the primary effect of which is to injure by fragments which in the human body escape detection by X-rays.

[1] 1342 UNTS 168.

G. WAR POWERS, COLLECTIVE SECURITY TREATIES, AND RELATED MATERIAL

CONTENTS

1. Latin America

a. Inter-American Treaty of Reciprocal Assistance (Rio Treaty) [1]

Opened for signature at Rio de Janeiro, September 2, 1947; Ratification advised by the Senate, December 8, 1947; Ratified by the President, December 12, 1947; Ratification of the United States deposited with the Pan American Union, December 30, 1947; Entered into force, December 3, 1948; Proclaimed by the President, December 9, 1948

INTER-AMERICAN TREATY OF RECIPROCAL ASSISTANCE

In the name of their Peoples, the Governments represented at the Inter-American Conference for the Maintenance of Continental Peace and Security, desirous of consolidating and strengthening their relations of friendship and good neighborliness, and

CONSIDERING:

That Resolution VIII of the Inter-American Conference on Problems of War and Peace, which met in Mexico City, recommended the conclusion of a treaty to prevent and repel threats and acts of aggression against any of the countries of America;

That the High Contracting Parties reiterate their will to remain united in an inter-American system consistent with the purposes and principles of the United Nations, and reaffirm the existence of the agreement which they have concluded concerning those matters relating to the maintenance of international peace and security which are appropriate for regional action;

That the High Contracting Parties reaffirm their adherence to the principles of inter-American solidarity and cooperation, and especially to those set forth in the preamble and declarations of the Act of Chapultepec, all of which should be understood to be accepted as standards of their mutual relations and as the juridical basis of the Inter-American System;

That the American States propose, in order to improve the procedures for the pacific settlement of their controversies, to conclude the treaty concerning the "Inter-American Peace System" envisaged in Resolutions IX and XXXIX of the Inter-American Conference on Problems of War and Peace.

That the obligation of mutual assistance and common defense of the American Republics is essentially related to their democratic ideals and to their will to cooperate permanently in the fulfillment of the principles and purposes of a policy of peace;

---

[1] 62 Stat. 1681; TIAS 1838; 4 Bevans 559; 21 UNTS 77. For a list of states which are parties to the Treaty, see Department of State publication, *Treaties in Force*.

A Protocol of Amendment to this Treaty was signed at San José, Costa Rica, July 26, 1975, and ratified by the United States on April 17, 1978. It was never ratified, however, by the necessary two-thirds of the member states.

That the American regional community affirms as a manifest trust that juridical organization is a necessary prerequisite of security and peace, and that peace is founded on justice and moral order and, consequently, on the international recognition and protection of human rights and freedoms, on the indispensable well-being of the people, and on the effectiveness of democracy for the international realization of justice and security;

HAVE RESOLVED, in conformity with the objectives stated above, to conclude the following Treaty, in order to assure peace, through adequate means, to provide for effective reciprocal assistance to meet armed attacks against any American State, and in order to deal with threats of aggression against any of them:

ARTICLE 1

The High Contracting Parties formally condemn war and undertake in their international relations not to resort to the threat or the use of force in any manner inconsistent with the provisions of the Charter of the United Nations or of this Treaty.

ARTICLE 2

As a consequence of the principle set forth in the preceding Article, the High Contracting Parties undertake to submit every controversy which may arise between them to methods of peaceful settlement and to endeavor to settle any such controversy among themselves by means of the procedures in force in the Inter-American System before referring it to the General Assembly or the Security Council of the United Nations.

ARTICLE 3

1. The High Contracting Parties agree that an armed attack by any State against an American State shall be considered as an attack against all the American States and, consequently, each one of the said Contracting Parties undertakes to assist in meeting the attack in the exercise of the inherent right of individual or collective self-defense recognized by Article 51 of the Charter of the United Nations.

2. On the request of the State or States directly attacked and until the decision of the Organ of Consultation of the Inter-American System, each one of the Contracting Parties may determine the immediate measures which it may individually take in fulfillment of the obligation contained in the preceding paragraph and in accordance with the principle of continental solidarity. The Organ of Consultation shall meet without delay for the purpose of examining those measures and agreeing upon the measures of a collective character that should be taken.

3. The provisions of this Article shall be applied in case of any armed attack which takes place within the region described in Article 4 or within the territory of an American State. When the attack takes place outside of the said areas, the provisions of Article 6 shall be applied.

4. Measures of self-defense provided for under this Article may be taken until the Security Council of the United Nations has

taken the measures necessary to maintain international peace and security.

ARTICLE 4

The region to which this Treaty refers is bounded as follows: beginning at the North Pole; thence due south to a point 74 degrees north latitude, 10 degrees west longitude; thence by a rhumb line to a point 47 degrees 30 minutes north latitude, 50 degrees west longitude; thence by a rhumb line to a point 35 degrees north latitude, 60 degrees west longitude; thence due south to a point 20 degrees north latitude; thence by a rhumb line to a point 5 degrees north latitude, 24 degrees west longitude; thence due south to the South Pole; thence due north to a point 30 degrees south latitude, 90 degrees west longitude; thence by a rhumb line to a point on the Equator at 97 degrees west longitude; thence by a rhumb line to a point 15 degrees north latitude, 120 degrees west longitude; thence by a rhumb line to a point 50 degrees north latitude, 170 degrees east longitude; thence due north to a point in 54 degrees north latitude; thence by a rhumb line to a point 65 degrees 30 minutes north latitude, 168 degrees 58 minutes 5 seconds west longitude; thence due north to the North Pole.

ARTICLE 5

The High Contracting Parties shall immediately send to the Security Council of the United Nations, in conformity with Articles 51 and 54 of the Charter of the United Nations, complete information concerning the activities undertaken or in contemplation in the exercise of the right of self-defense or for the purpose of maintaining inter-American peace and security.

ARTICLE 6

If the inviolability or the integrity of the territory or the sovereignty or political independence of any American State should be affected by an aggression which is not an armed attack or by an extra-continental or intra-continental conflict, or by any other fact or situation that might endanger the peace of America, the Organ of Consultation shall meet immediately in order to agree on the measures which must be taken in case of aggression to assist the victim of the aggression or, in any case, the measures which should be taken for the common defense and for the maintenance of the peace and security of the Continent.

ARTICLE 7

In the case of a conflict between two or more American States, without prejudice to the right of self-defense in conformity with Article 51 of the Charter of the United Nations, the High Contracting Parties, meeting in consultation shall call upon the contending States to suspend hostilities and restore matters to the *status quo ante bellum*, and shall take in addition all other necessary measures to reestablish or maintain inter-American peace and security and for the solution of the conflict by peaceful means. The rejection of the pacifying action will be considered in the determination of the aggressor and in the application of the measures which the consultative meetings may agree upon.

ARTICLE 8

For the purposes of this Treaty, the measures on which the Organ of Consultation may agree will comprise one or more of the following: recall of chiefs of diplomatic missions; breaking of diplomatic relation; breaking of consular relations; partial or complete interruption of economic relations or of rail, sea, air, postal, telegraphic, telephonic, and radiotelephonic or radiotelegraphic communications; and use of armed force.

ARTICLE 9

In addition to other acts which the Organ of Consultation may characterize an aggression, the following shall be considered as such:

a. Unprovoked armed attack by a State against the territory, the people, or the land, sea or air forces of another State;

b. Invasion, by the armed forces of a State, of the territory of an American State, through the trespassing of boundaries demarcated in accordance with a treaty, judicial decision, or arbitral award, or, in the absence of frontiers thus demarcated, invasion affecting a region which is under the effective jurisdiction of another State.

ARTICLE 10

None of the provisions of this Treaty shall be construed as impairing the rights and obligations of the High Contracting Parties under the Charter of the United Nations.

ARTICLE 11

The consultations to which this Treaty refers shall be carried out by means of the Meetings of Ministers of Foreign Affairs of the American Republics which have ratified the Treaty, or in the manner or by the organ which in the future may be agreed upon.

ARTICLE 12

The Governing Board of the Pan American Union may act provisionally as an organ of consultation until the meeting of the Organ of Consultation referred to in the preceding Article takes place.

ARTICLE 13

The consultations shall be initiated at the request addressed to the Governing Board of the Pan American Union by any of the Signatory States which has ratified the Treaty.

ARTICLE 14

In the voting referred to in this Treaty only the representatives of the Signatory States which have ratified the Treaty may take part.

ARTICLE 15

The Governing Board of the Pan American Union shall act in all matters concerning this Treaty as an organ of liaison among the Signatory States which have ratified this Treaty and between these States and the United Nations.

ARTICLE 16

The decisions of the Governing Board of the Pan American Union referred to in Articles 13 and 15 above shall be taken by an absolute majority of the Members entitled to vote.

ARTICLE 17

The Organ of Consultation shall take its decisions by a vote of two-thirds of the Signatory States which have ratified the Treaty.

ARTICLE 18

In the case of a situation or dispute between American States, the parties directly interested shall be excluded from the voting referred to in two preceding Articles.

ARTICLE 19

To constitute a quorum in all the meetings referred to in the previous Articles, it shall be necessary that the number of States represented shall be at least equal to the number of votes necessary for the taking of the decision.

ARTICLE 20

Decisions which require the application of the measures specified in Article 8 shall be binding upon all the Signatory States which have ratified this Treaty, with the sole exception that no State shall be required to use armed force without its consent.

ARTICLE 21

The measures agreed upon by the Organ of Consultation shall be executed through the procedures and agencies now existing or those which may in the future be established.

ARTICLE 22

This Treaty shall come into effect between the States which ratify it as soon as the ratification of two-thirds of the Signatory States have been deposited.

ARTICLE 23

This Treaty is open for signature by the American States at the city of Rio de Janeiro, and shall be ratified by the Signatory States as soon as possible in accordance with their respective constitutional processes. The ratifications shall be deposited with the Pan American Union, which shall notify the Signatory States of each deposit. Such notification shall be considered as an exchange of ratifications.

ARTICLE 24

The present Treaty shall be registered with the Secretariat of the United Nations through the Pan American Union, when two-thirds of the Signatory States have deposited their ratifications.

ARTICLE 25

This Treaty shall remain in force indefinitely, but may be denounced by any High Contracting Party by a notification in writing to the Pan American Union, which shall reform all the other High Contracting Parties of each notification of denunciation received. After the expiration of two years from the date of the receipt by the Pan American Union of a notification of denunciation by any High Contracting Party, the present Treaty shall cease to be in force and with respect to such State, but shall remain in full force and effect with respect to all the other High Contracting Parties.

ARTICLE 26

The principles and fundamental provisions of this Treaty shall be incorporated in the Organic Pact of the Inter-American System.

IN WITNESS THEREOF, the undersigned Plenipotentiaries, having deposited their full powers found to be in due and proper form, sign this Treaty on behalf of their respective Governments, on the dates appearing opposite their signatures.

DONE in the city of Rio de Janeiro, in four texts respectively in the English, French, Portuguese and Spanish languages, on the second of September nineteen hundred forty-seven.

RESERVATION OF HONDURAS:

The Delegation of Honduras, in signing the present Treaty and in connection with Article 9, section (b), does so with the reservation that the boundary between Honduras and Nicaragua is definitely demarcated by the Joint Boundary Commission of nineteen hundred and nineteen hundred and one, starting from a point in the Gulf of Fonseca, in the Pacific Ocean, to Portillo de Teotecacinte and, from this point to the Atlantic, by the line that His Majesty the King of Spain's arbitral award established on the twenty third of December of nineteen hundred and six.

b. Charter of the Organization of American States [1] as amended by Protocols of Amendment [2] (with reservations)

Charter signed at Bogotá, April 30, 1948; Ratification advised by the Senate, with a reservation, August 28, 1950; Ratified by the President, subject to said reservation, June 15, 1951; Ratification of the United States deposited with the Pan American Union, June 19, 1951; Entered into force, December 13, 1951; Proclaimed by the President, December 27, 1951

In the name of their Peoples, the States represented at the Ninth International Conference of American States,

CONVINCED that the historic mission of America is to offer to man a land of liberty and a favorable environment for the development of his personality and the realization of his just aspirations;

CONSCIOUS that that mission has already inspired numerous agreements, whose essential value lies in the desire of the American peoples to live together in peace and, through their mutual understanding and respect for the sovereignty of each one, to provide for the betterment of all, in independence, in equality and under law;

CONVINCED that representative democracy is an indispensable condition for the stability, peace and development of the region;

CONFIDENT that the true significance of American solidarity and good neighborliness can only mean the consolidation on this continent, within the framework of democratic institutions, of a system of individual liberty and social justice based on respect for the essential rights of man;

PERSUADED that their welfare and their contribution to the progress and the civilization of the world will increasingly require intensive continental cooperation;

RESOLVED to persevere in the noble undertaking that humanity has conferred upon the United Nations, whose principles and purposes they solemnly reaffirm;

CONVINCED that juridical organization is a necessary condition for security and peace founded on moral order and on justice; and

IN ACCORDANCE with Resolution IX of the Inter-American Conference on Problems of War and Peace, held in Mexico City,

HAVE AGREED UPON THE FOLLOWING:

---

[1] 2 UST 2394; TIAS 2361; 119 UNTS 3.

[2] The OAS Charter has been amended through four Protocols: "Protocol of Buenos Aires", signed on February 27, 1967, at the Third Special Inter-American Conference (21 UST 607; TIAS 6847); "Protocol of Cartagena de Indias", approved on December 5, 1985, at the Fourteenth Special Session of the General Assembly; "Protocol of Washington", approved on December 14, 1992, at the Sixteenth Special Session of the General Assembly, and the "Protocol of Managua", adopted on June 10, 1993, at the Nineteenth Special Session of the General Assembly. The "Protocol of Cartagena de Indias" did not enter into force for the United States.

PART ONE

Chapter I. Nature and Purposes

ARTICLE 1

The American States establish by this Charter the international organization that they have developed to achieve an order of peace and justice, to promote their solidarity, to strengthen their collaboration, and to defend their sovereignty, their territorial integrity, and their independence. Within the United Nations, the Organization of American States is a regional agency.

The Organization of American States has no powers other than those expressly conferred upon it by this Charter, none of whose provisions authorizes it to intervene in matters that are within the internal jurisdiction of the Member States.

ARTICLE 2

The Organization of American States, in order to put into practice the principles on which it is founded and to fulfill its regional obligations under the Charter of the United Nations, proclaims the following essential purposes:

(a) To strengthen the peace and security of the continent;

(b) To promote and consolidate representative democracy, with due respect for the principle of nonintervention;

(c) To prevent possible causes of difficulties and to ensure the pacific settlement of disputes that may arise among the Member States;

(d) To provide for common action on the part of those States in the event of aggression;

(e) To seek the solution of political, juridical, and economic problems that may arise among them;

(f) To promote, by cooperative action, their economic, social, and cultural development;

(g) To eradicate extreme poverty, which constitutes an obstacle to the full democratic development of the peoples of the hemisphere; and

(h) To achieve an effective limitation of conventional weapons that will make it possible to devote the largest amount of resources to the economic and social development of the Member States.

Chapter II. Principles

ARTICLE 3

The American States reaffirm the following principles:

(a) International law is the standard of conduct of States in their reciprocal relations;

(b) International order consists essentially of respect for the personality, sovereignty, and independence of States, and the faithful fulfillment of obligations derived from treaties and other sources of international law;

(c) Good faith shall govern the relations between States;

(d) The solidarity of the American States and the high aims which are sought through it require the political organization of those States on the basis of the effective exercise of representative democracy;

(e) Every State has the right to choose, without external interference, its political, economic, and social system and to organize itself in the way best suited to it, and has the duty to abstain from intervening in the affairs of another State. Subject to the foregoing, the American States shall cooperate fully among themselves, independently of the nature of their political, economic, and social systems;

(f) The elimination of extreme poverty is an essential part of the promotion and consolidation of representative democracy and is the common and shared responsibility of the American States;

(g) The American States condemn war of aggression: victory does not give rights;

(h) An act of aggression against one American State is an act of aggression against all the other American States;

(i) Controversies of an international character arising between two or more American States shall be settled by peaceful procedures;

(j) Social justice and social security are bases of lasting peace;

(k) Economic cooperation is essential to the common welfare and prosperity of the peoples of the continent;

(l) The American States proclaim the fundamental rights of the individual without distinction as to race, nationality, creed, or sex;

(m) The spiritual unity of the continent is based on respect for the cultural values of the American countries and requires their close cooperation for the high purposes of civilization;

(n) The education of peoples should be directed toward justice, freedom, and peace.

CHAPTER III. MEMBERS

ARTICLE 4

All American States that ratify the present Charter are Members of the Organization.

ARTICLE 5

Any new political entity that arises from the union of several Member States and that, as such, ratifies the present Charter, shall become a Member of the Organization. The entry of the new political entity into the Organization shall result in the loss of membership of each one of the States which constitute it.

ARTICLE 6

Any other independent American State that desires to become a Member of the Organization should so indicate by means of a note addressed to the Secretary General, in which it declares that it is willing to sign and ratify the Charter of the Organization and to accept all the obligations inherent in membership, especially those relating to collective security expressly set forth in Articles 28 and 29 of the Charter.

ARTICLE 7

The General Assembly, upon the recommendation of the Permanent Council of the Organization, shall determine whether it is appropriate that the Secretary General be authorized to permit the applicant State to sign the Charter and to accept the deposit of the corresponding instrument of ratification. Both the recommendation of the Permanent Council and the decision of the General Assembly shall require the affirmative vote of two thirds of the Member States.

ARTICLE 8

Membership in the Organization shall be confined to independent States of the Hemisphere that were Members of the United Nations as of December 10, 1985, and the nonautonomous territories mentioned in document OEA/Ser. P, AG/doc.1939/85, of November 5, 1985, when they become independent.

ARTICLE 9

A Member of the Organization whose democratically constituted government has been overthrown by force may be suspended from the exercise of the right to participate in the sessions of the General Assembly, the Meeting of Consultation, the Councils of the Organization and the Specialized Conferences as well as in the commissions, working groups and any other bodies established.

(a) The power to suspend shall be exercised only when such diplomatic initiatives undertaken by the Organization for the purpose of promoting the restoration of representative democracy in the affected Member State have been unsuccessful;

(b) The decision to suspend shall be adopted at a special session of the General Assembly by an affirmative vote of two-thirds of the Member States;

(c) The suspension shall take effect immediately following its approval by the General Assembly;

(d) The suspension notwithstanding, the Organization shall endeavor to undertake additional diplomatic initiatives to contribute to the re-establishment of representative democracy in the affected Member State;

(e) The Member which has been subject to suspension shall continue to fulfill its obligations to the Organization;

(f) The General Assembly may lift the suspension by a decision adopted with the approval of two-thirds of the Member States;

(g) The powers referred to in this article shall be exercised in accordance with this Charter.

Chapter IV. Fundamental Rights and Duties of States

ARTICLE 10

States are juridically equal, enjoy equal rights and equal capacity to exercise these rights, and have equal duties. The rights of each

State depend not upon its power to ensure the exercise thereof, but upon the mere fact of its existence as a person under international law.

ARTICLE 11

Every American State has the duty to respect the rights enjoyed by every other State in accordance with international law.

ARTICLE 12

The fundamental rights of States may not be impaired in any manner whatsoever.

ARTICLE 13

The political existence of the State is independent of recognition by other States. Even before being recognized, the State has the right to defend its integrity and independence, to provide for its preservation and prosperity, and consequently to organize itself as it sees fit, to legislate concerning its interests, to administer its services, and to determine the jurisdiction and competence of its courts. The exercise of these rights is limited only by the exercise of the rights of other States in accordance with international law.

ARTICLE 14

Recognition implies that the State granting it accepts the personality of the new State, with all the rights and duties that international law prescribes for the two States.

ARTICLE 15

The right of each State to protect itself and to live its own life does not authorize it to commit unjust acts against another State.

ARTICLE 16

The jurisdiction of States within the limits of their national territory is exercised equally over all the inhabitants, whether nationals or aliens.

ARTICLE 17

Each State has the right to develop its cultural, political, and economic life freely and naturally. In this free development, the State shall respect the rights of the individual and the principles of universal morality.

ARTICLE 18

Respect for and the faithful observance of treaties constitute standards for the development of peaceful relations among States. International treaties and agreements should be public.

ARTICLE 19

No State or group of States has the right to intervene, directly or indirectly, for any reason whatever, in the internal or external affairs of any other State. The foregoing principle prohibits not only armed force but also any other form of interference or attempted threat against the personality of the State or against its political, economic, and cultural elements.

ARTICLE 20

No State may use or encourage the use of coercive measures of an economic or political character in order to force the sovereign will of another State and obtain from it advantages of any kind.

ARTICLE 21

The territory of a State is inviolable; it may not be the object, even temporarily, of military occupation or of other measures of force taken by another State, directly or indirectly, on any grounds whatever. No territorial acquisitions or special advantages obtained either by force or by other means of coercion shall be recognized.

ARTICLE 22

The American States bind themselves in their international relations not to have recourse to the use of force, except in the case of self-defense in accordance with existing treaties or in fulfillment thereof.

ARTICLE 23

Measures adopted for the maintenance of peace and security in accordance with existing treaties do not constitute a violation of the principles set forth in Articles 19 and 21.

CHAPTER V. PACIFIC SETTLEMENT OF DISPUTES

ARTICLE 24

International disputes between Member States shall be submitted to the peaceful procedures set forth in this Charter.

This provision shall not be interpreted as an impairment of the rights and obligations of the Member States under Articles 34 and 35 of the Charter of the United Nations.

ARTICLE 25

The following are peaceful procedures: direct negotiation, good offices, mediation, investigation and conciliation, judicial settlement, arbitration, and those which the parties to the dispute may especially agree upon at any time.

ARTICLE 26

In the event that a dispute arises between two or more American States which, in the opinion of one of them, cannot be settled through the usual diplomatic channels, the parties shall agree on some other peaceful procedure that will enable them to reach a solution.

ARTICLE 27

A special treaty will establish adequate means for the settlement of disputes and will determine pertinent procedures for each peaceful means such that no dispute between American States may remain without definitive settlement within a reasonable period of time.

CHAPTER VI. COLLECTIVE SECURITY

ARTICLE 28

Every act of aggression by a State against the territorial integrity or the inviolability of the territory or against the sovereignty or political independence of an American State shall be considered an act of aggression against the other American States.

ARTICLE 29

If the inviolability or the integrity of the territory or the sovereignty or political independence of any American State should be affected by an armed attack or by an act of aggression that is not an armed attack, or by an extracontinental conflict, or by a conflict between two or more American States, or by any other fact or situation that might endanger the peace of America, the American States, in furtherance of the principles of continental solidarity or collective self-defense, shall apply the measures and procedures established in the special treaties on the subject.

CHAPTER VII. INTEGRAL DEVELOPMENT

ARTICLE 30

The Member States, inspired by the principles of inter-American solidarity and cooperation, pledge themselves to a united effort to ensure international social justice in their relations and integral development for their peoples, as conditions essential to peace and security. Integral development encompasses the economic, social, educational, cultural, scientific, and technological fields through which the goals that each country sets for accomplishing it should be achieved.

ARTICLE 31

Inter-American cooperation for integral development is the common and joint responsibility of the Member States, within the framework of the democratic principles and the institutions of the inter-American system. It should include the economic, social, educational, cultural, scientific, and technological fields, support the achievement of national objectives of the Member States, and respect the priorities established by each country in its development plans, without political ties or conditions.

ARTICLE 32

Inter-American cooperation for integral development should be continuous and preferably channeled through multilateral organizations, without prejudice to bilateral cooperation between Member States.

The Member States shall contribute to inter-American cooperation for integral development in accordance with their resources and capabilities and in conformity with their laws.

ARTICLE 33

Development is a primary responsibility of each country and should constitute an integral and continuous process for the establishment of a more just economic and social order that will make possible and contribute to the fulfillment of the individual.

ARTICLE 34

The Member States agree that equality of opportunity, the elimination of extreme poverty, equitable distribution of wealth and income and the full participation of their peoples in decisions relating to their own development are, among others, basic objectives of integral development. To achieve them, they likewise agree to devote their utmost efforts to accomplishing the following basic goals:

(a) Substantial and self-sustained increase of per capita national product;

(b) Equitable distribution of national income;

(c) Adequate and equitable systems of taxation;

(d) Modernization of rural life and reforms leading to equitable and efficient land-tenure systems, increased agricultural productivity, expanded use of land, diversification of production and improved processing and marketing systems for agricultural products; and the strengthening and expansion of the means to attain these ends;

(e) Accelerated and diversified industrialization, especially of capital and intermediate goods;

(f) Stability of domestic price levels, compatible with sustained economic development and the attainment of social justice;

(g) Fair wages, employment opportunities, and acceptable working conditions for all;

(h) Rapid eradication of illiteracy and expansion of educational opportunities for all;

(i) Protection of man's potential through the extension and application of modern medical science;

(j) Proper nutrition, especially through the acceleration of national efforts to increase the production and availability of food;

(k) Adequate housing for all sectors of the population;

(l) Urban conditions that offer the opportunity for a healthful, productive, and full life;

(m) Promotion of private initiative and investment in harmony with action in the public sector; and

(n) Expansion and diversification of exports.

ARTICLE 35

The Member States should refrain from practicing policies and adopting actions or measures that have serious adverse effects on the development of other Member States.

ARTICLE 36

Transnational enterprises and foreign private investment shall be subject to the legislation of the host countries and to the jurisdiction of their competent courts and to the international treaties and agreements to which said countries are parties, and should conform to the development policies of the recipient countries.

ARTICLE 37

The Member States agree to join together in seeking a solution to urgent or critical problems that may arise whenever the economic development or stability of any Member State is seriously affected by conditions that cannot be remedied through the efforts of that State.

ARTICLE 38

The Member States shall extend among themselves the benefits of science and technology by encouraging the exchange and utilization of scientific and technical knowledge in accordance with existing treaties and national laws.

ARTICLE 39

The Member States, recognizing the close interdependence between foreign trade and economic and social development, should make individual and united efforts to bring about the following:

(a) Favorable conditions of access to world markets for the products of the developing countries of the region, particularly through the reduction or elimination, by importing countries, of tariff and nontariff barriers that affect the exports of the Member States of the Organization, except when such barriers are applied in order to diversify the economic structure, to speed up the development of the less-developed Member States, and intensify their process of economic integration, or when they are related to national security or to the needs of economic balance;

(b) Continuity in their economic and social development by means of:

i. Improved conditions for trade in basic commodities through international agreements, where appropriate; orderly marketing procedures that avoid the disruption of markets, and other measures designed to promote the expansion of markets and to obtain dependable incomes for producers, adequate and dependable supplies for consumers, and stable prices that are both remunerative to producers and fair to consumers;

ii. Improved international financial cooperation and the adoption of other means for lessening the adverse impact of sharp fluctuations in export earnings experienced by the countries exporting basic commodities;

iii. Diversification of exports and expansion of export opportunities for manufactured and semimanufactured products from the developing countries; and

iv. Conditions conducive to increasing the real export earnings of the Member States, particularly the developing countries of the region, and to increasing their participation in international trade.

ARTICLE 40

The Member States reaffirm the principle that when the more developed countries grant concessions in international trade agreements that lower or eliminate tariffs or other barriers to foreign trade so that they benefit the less-developed countries, they should not expect reciprocal concessions from those countries that are incompatible with their economic development, financial, and trade needs.

ARTICLE 41

The Member States, in order to accelerate their economic development, regional integration, and the expansion and improvement of the conditions of their commerce, shall promote improvement and coordination of transportation and communication in the developing countries and among the Member States.

ARTICLE 42

The Member States recognize that integration of the developing countries of the Hemisphere is one of the objectives of the inter-American system and, therefore, shall orient their efforts and take the necessary measures to accelerate the integration process, with a view to establishing a Latin American common market in the shortest possible time.

ARTICLE 43

In order to strengthen and accelerate integration in all its aspects, the Member States agree to give adequate priority to the preparation and carrying out of multinational projects and to their financing, as well as to encourage economic and financial institutions of the inter-American system to continue giving their broadest support to regional integration institutions and programs.

ARTICLE 44

The Member States agree that technical and financial cooperation that seeks to promote regional economic integration should be based on the principle of harmonious, balanced, and efficient development, with particular attention to the relatively less-developed countries, so that it may be a decisive factor that will enable them to promote, with their own efforts, the improved development of their infrastructure programs, new lines of production, and export diversification.

ARTICLE 45

The Member States, convinced that man can only achieve the full realization of his aspirations within a just social order, along with economic development and true peace, agree to dedicate every effort to the application of the following principles and mechanisms:

(a) All human beings, without distinction as to race, sex, nationality, creed, or social condition, have a right to material well-being and to their spiritual development, under circumstances of liberty, dignity, equality of opportunity, and economic security;

(b) Work is a right and a social duty, it gives dignity to the one who performs it, and it should be performed under conditions, including a system of fair wages, that ensure life, health, and a decent standard of living for the worker and his family, both during his working years and in his old age, or when any circumstance deprives him of the possibility of working;

(c) Employers and workers, both rural and urban, have the right to associate themselves freely for the defense and promotion of their interests, including the right to collective bargaining and the workers' right to strike, and recognition of the juridical personality of associations and the protection of their freedom and independence, all in accordance with applicable laws;

(d) Fair and efficient systems and procedures for consultation and collaboration among the sectors of production, with due regard for safeguarding the interests of the entire society;

(e) The operation of systems of public administration, banking and credit, enterprise, and distribution and sales, in such a way, in harmony with the private sector, as to meet the requirements and interests of the community;

(f) The incorporation and increasing participation of the marginal sectors of the population, in both rural and urban areas, in the economic, social, civic, cultural, and political life of the nation, in order to achieve the full integration of the national community, acceleration of the process of social mobility, and the consolidation of the democratic system. The encouragement of all efforts of popular promotion and cooperation that have as their purpose the development and progress of the community;

(g) Recognition of the importance of the contribution of organizations such as labor unions, cooperatives, and cultural, professional, business, neighborhood, and community associations to the life of the society and to the development process;

(h) Development of an efficient social security policy; and

(i) Adequate provision for all persons to have due legal aid in order to secure their rights.

ARTICLE 46

The Member States recognize that, in order to facilitate the process of Latin American regional integration, it is necessary to harmonize the social legislation of the developing countries, especially in the labor and social security fields, so that the rights of the workers shall be equally protected, and they agree to make the greatest efforts possible to achieve this goal.

ARTICLE 47

The Member States will give primary importance within their development plans to the encouragement of education, science, technology, and culture, oriented toward the overall improvement of the individual, and as a foundation for democracy, social justice, and progress.

ARTICLE 48

The Member States will cooperate with one another to meet their educational needs, to promote scientific research, and to encourage technological progress for their integral development. They will consider themselves individually and jointly bound to preserve and enrich the cultural heritage of the American peoples.

ARTICLE 49

The Member States will exert the greatest efforts, in accordance with their constitutional processes, to ensure the effective exercise of the right to education, on the following bases:

(a) Elementary education, compulsory for children of school age, shall also be offered to all others who can benefit from it. When provided by the State it shall be without charge;

(b) Middle-level education shall be extended progressively to as much of the population as possible, with a view to social improvement. It shall be diversified in such a way that it meets the development needs of each country without prejudice to providing a general education; and

(c) Higher education shall be available to all, provided that, in order to maintain its high level, the corresponding regulatory or academic standards are met.

ARTICLE 50

The Member States will give special attention to the eradication of illiteracy, will strengthen adult and vocational education systems, and will ensure that the benefits of culture will be available to the entire population. They will promote the use of all information media to fulfill these aims.

ARTICLE 51

The Member States will develop science and technology through educational, research, and technological development activities and information and dissemination programs. They will stimulate activities in the field of technology for the purpose of adapting it to the needs of their integral development. They will organize their cooperation in these fields efficiently and will substantially increase exchange of knowledge, in accordance with national objectives and laws and with treaties in force.

ARTICLE 52

The Member States, with due respect for the individuality of each of them, agree to promote cultural exchange as an effective means of consolidating inter-American understanding; and they recognize that regional integration programs should be strengthened by close ties in the fields of education, science, and culture.

PART TWO

CHAPTER VIII. THE ORGANS

ARTICLE 53

The Organization of American States accomplishes its purposes by means of:

(a) The General Assembly;

(b) The Meeting of Consultation of Ministers of Foreign Affairs;

(c) The Councils;

(d) The Inter-American Juridical Committee;

(e) The Inter-American Commission on Human Rights;

(f) The General Secretariat;

(g) The Specialized Conferences; and

(h) The Specialized Organizations.

There may be established, in addition to those provided for in the Charter and in accordance with the provisions thereof, such subsidiary organs, agencies, and other entities as are considered necessary.

CHAPTER IX. THE GENERAL ASSEMBLY

ARTICLE 54

The General Assembly is the supreme organ of the Organization of American States. It has as its principal powers, in addition to such others as are assigned to it by the Charter, the following:

(a) To decide the general action and policy of the Organization, determine the structure and functions of its organs, and consider any matter relating to friendly relations among the American States;

(b) To establish measures for coordinating the activities of the organs, agencies, and entities of the Organization among themselves, and such activities with those of the other institutions of the inter-American system;

(c) To strengthen and coordinate cooperation with the United Nations and its specialized agencies;

(d) To promote collaboration, especially in the economic, social, and cultural fields, with other international organizations whose purposes are similar to those of the Organization of American States;

(e) To approve the program-budget of the Organization and determine the quotas of the Member States;

(f) To consider the reports of the Meeting of Consultation of Ministers of Foreign Affairs and the observations and recommendations presented by the Permanent Council with regard to the reports that should be presented by the other organs and entities, in accordance with the provisions of Article 91.f, as well as the reports of any organ which may be required by the General Assembly itself;

(g) To adopt general standards to govern the operations of the General Secretariat; and

(h) To adopt its own rules of procedure and, by a two-thirds vote, its agenda.

The General Assembly shall exercise its powers in accordance with the provisions of the Charter and of other inter-American treaties.

ARTICLE 55

The General Assembly shall establish the bases for fixing the quota that each Government is to contribute to the maintenance of the Organization, taking into account the ability to pay of the respective countries and their determination to contribute in an equitable manner. Decisions on budgetary matters require the approval of two thirds of the Member States.

ARTICLE 56

All Member States have the right to be represented in the General Assembly. Each State has the right to one vote.

ARTICLE 57

The General Assembly shall convene annually during the period determined by the rules of procedure and at a place selected in accordance with the principle of rotation. At each regular session the date and place of the next regular session shall be determined, in accordance with the rules of procedure.

If for any reason the General Assembly cannot be held at the place chosen, it shall meet at the General Secretariat, unless one of the Member States should make a timely offer of a site in its territory, in which case the Permanent Council of the Organization may agree that the General Assembly will meet in that place.

ARTICLE 58

In special circumstances and with the approval of two thirds of the Member States, the Permanent Council shall convoke a special session of the General Assembly.

ARTICLE 59

Decisions of the General Assembly shall be adopted by the affirmative vote of an absolute majority of the Member States, except in those cases that require a two-thirds vote as provided in the Charter or as may be provided by the General Assembly in its rules of procedure.

ARTICLE 60

There shall be a Preparatory Committee of the General Assembly, composed of representatives of all the Member States, which shall:

(a) Prepare the draft agenda of each session of the General Assembly;

(b) Review the proposed program-budget and the draft resolution on quotas, and present to the General Assembly a report thereon containing the recommendations it considers appropriate; and

(c) Carry out such other functions as the General Assembly may assign to it.

The draft agenda and the report shall, in due course, be transmitted to the Governments of the Member States.

CHAPTER X. THE MEETING OF CONSULTATION OF MINISTERS OF FOREIGN AFFAIRS

ARTICLE 61

The Meeting of Consultation of Ministers of Foreign Affairs shall be held in order to consider problems of an urgent nature and of common interest to the American States, and to serve as the Organ of Consultation.

ARTICLE 62

Any Member State may request that a Meeting of Consultation be called. The request shall be addressed to the Permanent Council of the Organization, which shall decide by an absolute majority whether a meeting should be held.

ARTICLE 63

The agenda and regulations of the Meeting of Consultation shall be prepared by the Permanent Council of the Organization and submitted to the Member States for consideration.

ARTICLE 64

If, for exceptional reasons, a Minister of Foreign Affairs is unable to attend the meeting, he shall be represented by a special delegate.

ARTICLE 65

In case of an armed attack on the territory of an American State or within the region of security delimited by the treaty in force, the Chairman of the Permanent Council shall without delay call a meeting of the Council to decide on the convocation of the Meeting of Consultation, without prejudice to the provisions of the Inter-American Treaty of Reciprocal Assistance with regard to the States Parties to that instrument.

ARTICLE 66

An Advisory Defense Committee shall be established to advise the Organ of Consultation on problems of military cooperation that may arise in connection with the application of existing special treaties on collective security.

ARTICLE 67

The Advisory Defense Committee shall be composed of the highest military authorities of the American States participating in the Meeting of Consultation. Under exceptional circumstances the Governments may appoint substitutes. Each State shall be entitled to one vote.

ARTICLE 68

The Advisory Defense Committee shall be convoked under the same conditions as the Organ of Consultation, when the latter deals with matters relating to defense against aggression.

ARTICLE 69

The Committee shall also meet when the General Assembly or the Meeting of Consultation or the Governments, by a two-thirds majority of the Member States, assign to it technical studies or reports on specific subjects.

CHAPTER XI. THE COUNCILS OF THE ORGANIZATION

COMMON PROVISIONS

ARTICLE 70

The Permanent Council of the Organization and the Inter-American Council for Integral Development are directly responsible to the General Assembly, and each has the authority granted to it in the Charter and other inter-American instruments, as well as the functions assigned to it by the General Assembly and the Meeting of Consultation of Ministers of Foreign Affairs.

ARTICLE 71

All Member States have the right to be represented on each of the Councils. Each State has the right to one vote.

ARTICLE 72

The Councils may, within the limits of the Charter and other inter-American instruments, make recommendations on matters within their authority.

ARTICLE 73

The Councils, on matters within their respective competence, may present to the General Assembly studies and proposals, drafts of international instruments, and proposals on the holding of specialized conferences, on the creation, modification, or elimination of specialized organizations and other inter-American agencies, as well as on the coordination of their activities. The Councils may also present studies, proposals, and drafts of international instruments to the Specialized Conferences.

ARTICLE 74

Each Council may, in urgent cases, convoke Specialized Conferences on matters within its competence, after consulting with the Member States and without having to resort to the procedure provided for in Article 122.

ARTICLE 75

The Councils, to the extent of their ability, and with the cooperation of the General Secretariat, shall render to the Governments such specialized services as the latter may request.

ARTICLE 76

Each Council has the authority to require the other Council, as well as the subsidiary organs and agencies responsible to them, to provide it with information and advisory services on matters within their respective spheres of competence. The Councils may also request the same services from the other agencies of the inter-American system.

ARTICLE 77

With the prior approval of the General Assembly, the Councils may establish the subsidiary organs and the agencies that they consider advisable for the better performance of their duties. When the General Assembly is not in session, the aforesaid organs or agencies may be established provisionally by the corresponding Council. In constituting the membership of these bodies, the Councils, insofar as possible, shall follow the criteria of rotation and equitable geographic representation.

ARTICLE 78

The Councils may hold meetings in any Member State, when they find it advisable and with the prior consent of the Government concerned.

ARTICLE 79

Each Council shall prepare its own statutes and submit them to the General Assembly for approval. It shall approve its own rules of procedure and those of its subsidiary organs, agencies, and committees.

CHAPTER XII. THE PERMANENT COUNCIL OF THE ORGANIZATION

ARTICLE 80

The Permanent Council of the Organization is composed of one representative of each Member State, especially appointed by the respective Government, with the rank of ambassador. Each Government may accredit an acting representative, as well as such alternates and advisers as it considers necessary.

ARTICLE 81

The office of Chairman of the Permanent Council shall be held by each of the representatives, in turn, following the alphabetic order in Spanish of the names of their respective countries. The office of Vice Chairman shall be filled in the same way, following reverse alphabetic order.

The Chairman and the Vice Chairman shall hold office for a term of not more than six months, which shall be determined by the statutes.

ARTICLE 82

Within the limits of the Charter and of inter-American treaties and agreements, the Permanent Council takes cognizance of any matter referred to it by the General Assembly or the Meeting of Consultation of Ministers of Foreign Affairs.

ARTICLE 83

The Permanent Council shall serve provisionally as the Organ of Consultation in conformity with the provisions of the special treaty on the subject.

ARTICLE 84

The Permanent Council shall keep vigilance over the maintenance of friendly relations among the Member States, and for that purpose shall effectively assist them in the peaceful settlement of their disputes, in accordance with the following provisions.

ARTICLE 85

In accordance with the provisions of this Charter, any party to a dispute in which none of the peaceful procedures provided for in the Charter is under way may resort to the Permanent Council to obtain its good offices. The Council, following the provisions of the preceding article, shall assist the parties and recommend the procedures it considers suitable for peaceful settlement of the dispute.

ARTICLE 86

In the exercise of its functions and with the consent of the parties to the dispute, the Permanent Council may establish ad hoc committees.

The ad hoc committees shall have the membership and the mandate that the Permanent Council agrees upon in each individual case, with the consent of the parties to the dispute.

ARTICLE 87

The Permanent Council may also, by such means as it deems advisable, investigate the facts in the dispute, and may do so in the territory of any of the parties, with the consent of the Government concerned.

ARTICLE 88

If the procedure for peaceful settlement of disputes recommended by the Permanent Council or suggested by the pertinent ad hoc committee under the terms of its mandate is not accepted by one of the parties, or one of the parties declares that the procedure has not settled the dispute, the Permanent Council shall so inform the General Assembly, without prejudice to its taking steps to secure agreement between the parties or to restore relations between them.

ARTICLE 89

The Permanent Council, in the exercise of these functions, shall take its decisions by an affirmative vote of two thirds of its Members, excluding the parties to the dispute, except for such decisions as the rules of procedure provide shall be adopted by a simple majority.

ARTICLE 90

In performing their functions with respect to the peaceful settlement of disputes, the Permanent Council and the respective ad hoc committee shall observe the provisions of the Charter and the principles and standards of international law, as well as take into account the existence of treaties in force between the parties.

ARTICLE 91

The Permanent Council shall also:

(a) Carry out those decisions of the General Assembly or of the Meeting of Consultation of Ministers of Foreign Affairs the implementation of which has not been assigned to any other body;

(b) Watch over the observance of the standards governing the operation of the General Secretariat and, when the General Assembly is not in session, adopt provisions of a regulatory nature that enable the General Secretariat to carry out its administrative functions;

(c) Act as the Preparatory Committee of the General Assembly, in accordance with the terms of Article 60 of the Charter, unless the General Assembly should decide otherwise;

(d) Prepare, at the request of the Member States and with the cooperation of the appropriate organs of the Organization, draft agreements to promote and facilitate cooperation between the Organization of American States and the United Nations or between the Organization and other American agencies of recognized international standing. These draft agreements shall be submitted to the General Assembly for approval;

(e) Submit recommendations to the General Assembly with regard to the functioning of the Organization and the coordination of its subsidiary organs, agencies, and committees;

(f) Consider the reports of the Inter-American Council for Integral Development, of the Inter-American Juridical Committee, of the Inter-American Commission on Human Rights, of the General Secretariat, of specialized agencies and conferences, and of other bodies and agencies, and present to the General Assembly any observations and recommendations it deems necessary; and

(g) Perform the other functions assigned to it in the Charter.

ARTICLE 92

The Permanent Council and the General Secretariat shall have the same seat.

CHAPTER XIII. THE INTER-AMERICAN COUNCIL FOR INTEGRAL DEVELOPMENT

ARTICLE 93

The Inter-American Council for Integral Development is composed of one principal representative, of ministerial or equivalent rank, for each Member State, especially appointed by the respective Government.

In keeping with the provisions of the Charter, the Inter-American Council for Integral Development may establish the subsidiary bodies and the agencies that it considers advisable for the better performance of its duties.

ARTICLE 94

The purpose of the Inter-American Council for Integral Development is to promote cooperation among the American States for the purpose of achieving integral development and, in particular, helping to eliminate extreme poverty, in accordance with the standards of the Charter, especially those set forth in Chapter VII with respect to the economic, social, educational, cultural, scientific, and technological fields.

ARTICLE 95

In order to achieve its various goals, especially in the specific area of technical cooperation, the Inter-American Council for Integral Development shall:

(a) Formulate and recommend to the General Assembly a strategic plan which sets forth policies, programs, and courses of action in matters of cooperation for integral development, within the framework of the general policy and priorities defined by the General Assembly;

(b) Formulate guidelines for the preparation of the program-budget for technical cooperation and for the other activities of the Council;

(c) Promote, coordinate, and assign responsibility for the execution of development programs and projects to the subsidiary bodies and relevant organizations, on the basis of the priorities identified by the Member States, in areas such as:

(1) Economic and social development, including trade, tourism, integration and the environment;

(2) Improvement and extension of education to cover all levels, promotion of scientific and technological research, through technical cooperation, and support for cultural activities; and

(3) Strengthening of the civic conscience of the American peoples, as one of the bases for the effective exercise of democracy and for the observance of the rights and duties of man.

These ends shall be furthered by sectoral participation mechanisms and other subsidiary bodies and organizations established by the Charter and by other General Assembly provisions.

(d) Establish cooperative relations with the corresponding bodies of the United Nations and with other national and international agencies, especially with regard to coordination of inter-American technical cooperation programs.

(e) Periodically evaluate cooperation activities for integral development, in terms of their performance in the implementation of policies, programs, and projects, in terms of their impact, effectiveness, efficiency, and use of resources, and in terms of the quality, inter alia, of the technical cooperation services provided; and report to the General Assembly.

ARTICLE 96

The Inter-American Council for Integral Development shall hold at least one meeting each year at the ministerial or equivalent level. It shall also have the right to convene meetings at the same level for the specialized or sectorial topics it considers relevant, within its province or sphere of competence. It shall also meet when convoked by the General Assembly or the Meeting of Consultation of Foreign Ministers, or on its own initiative, or for the cases envisaged in Article 37 of the Charter.

ARTICLE 97

The Inter-American Council for Integral Development shall have the nonpermanent specialized committees which it decides to establish and which are required for the proper performance of its functions. Those committees shall operate and shall be composed as stipulated in the Statutes of the Council.

ARTICLE 98

The execution and, if appropriate, the coordination, of approved projects shall be entrusted to the Executive Secretariat for Integral Development, which shall report on the results of that execution to the Council.

CHAPTER XIV. THE INTER-AMERICAN JURIDICAL COMMITTEE

ARTICLE 99

The purpose of the Inter-American Juridical Committee is to serve the Organization as an advisory body on juridical matters; to promote the progressive development and the codification of international law; and to study juridical problems related to the integration of the developing countries of the Hemisphere and, insofar as may appear desirable, the possibility of attaining uniformity in their legislation.

ARTICLE 100

The Inter-American Juridical Committee shall undertake the studies and preparatory work assigned to it by the General Assembly, the Meeting of Consultation of Ministers of Foreign Affairs, or the Councils of the Organization. It may also, on its own initiative, undertake such studies and preparatory work as it considers advisable, and suggest the holding of specialized juridical conferences.

ARTICLE 101

The Inter-American Juridical Committee shall be composed of eleven jurists, nationals of Member States, elected by the General Assembly for a period of four years from panels of three candidates presented by Member States. In the election, a system shall be used that takes into account partial replacement of membership and, insofar as possible, equitable geographic representation. No two Members of the Committee may be nationals of the same State.

Vacancies that occur for reasons other than normal expiration of the terms of office of the Members of the Committee shall be filled by the Permanent Council of the Organization in accordance with the criteria set forth in the preceding paragraph.

ARTICLE 102

The Inter-American Juridical Committee represents all of the Member States of the Organization, and has the broadest possible technical autonomy.

ARTICLE 103

The Inter-American Juridical Committee shall establish cooperative relations with universities, institutes, and other teaching centers, as well as with national and international committees and entities devoted to study, research, teaching, or dissemination of information on juridical matters of international interest.

ARTICLE 104

The Inter-American Juridical Committee shall draft its statutes, which shall be submitted to the General Assembly for approval.

The Committee shall adopt its own rules of procedure.

ARTICLE 105

The seat of the Inter-American Juridical Committee shall be the city of Rio de Janeiro, but in special cases the Committee may meet at any other place that may be designated, after consultation with the Member State concerned.

CHAPTER XV. THE INTER-AMERICAN COMMISSION ON HUMAN RIGHTS

ARTICLE 106

There shall be an Inter-American Commission on Human Rights, whose principal function shall be to promote the observance and protection of human rights and to serve as a consultative organ of the Organization in these matters.

An inter-American convention on human rights shall determine the structure, competence, and procedure of this Commission, as well as those of other organs responsible for these matters.

CHAPTER XVI. THE GENERAL SECRETARIAT

ARTICLE 107

The General Secretariat is the central and permanent organ of the Organization of American States. It shall perform the functions assigned to it in the Charter, in other inter-American treaties and agreements, and by the General Assembly, and shall carry out the duties entrusted to it by the General Assembly, the Meeting of Consultation of Ministers of Foreign Affairs, or the Councils.

ARTICLE 108

The Secretary General of the Organization shall be elected by the General Assembly for a five-year term and may not be reelected more than once or succeeded by a person of the same nationality. In the event that the office of Secretary General becomes vacant, the Assistant Secretary General shall assume his duties until the General Assembly shall elect a new Secretary General for a full term.

ARTICLE 109

The Secretary General shall direct the General Secretariat, be the legal representative thereof, and, notwithstanding the provisions of Article 91.b, be responsible to the General Assembly for the proper fulfillment of the obligations and functions of the General Secretariat.

ARTICLE 110

The Secretary General, or his representative, may participate with voice but without vote in all meetings of the Organization.

The Secretary General may bring to the attention of the General Assembly or the Permanent Council any matter which in his opinion might threaten the peace and security of the Hemisphere or the development of the Member States.

The authority to which the preceding paragraph refers shall be exercised in accordance with the present Charter.

ARTICLE 111

The General Secretariat shall promote economic, social, juridical, educational, scientific, and cultural relations among all the Member States of the Organization, with special emphasis on cooperation for the elimination of extreme poverty, in keeping with the actions and policies decided upon by the General Assembly and with the pertinent decisions of the Councils.

ARTICLE 112

The General Secretariat shall also perform the following functions:

(a) Transmit ex officio to the Member States notice of the convocation of the General Assembly, the Meeting of Consultation of Ministers of Foreign Affairs, the Inter-American Council for Integral Development, and the Specialized Conferences;

(b) Advise the other organs, when appropriate, in the preparation of agenda and rules of procedure;

(c) Prepare the proposed program-budget of the Organization on the basis of programs adopted by the Councils, agencies, and entities whose expenses should be included in the program-budget and, after consultation with the Councils or their permanent committees, submit it to the Preparatory Committee of the General Assembly and then to the Assembly itself;

(d) Provide, on a permanent basis, adequate secretariat services for the General Assembly and the other organs, and carry out their directives and assignments. To the extent of its ability, provide services for the other meetings of the Organization;

(e) Serve as custodian of the documents and archives of the inter-American Conferences, the General Assembly, the Meetings of Consultation of Ministers of Foreign Affairs, the Councils, and the Specialized Conferences;

(f) Serve as depository of inter-American treaties and agreements, as well as of the instruments of ratification thereof;

(g) Submit to the General Assembly at each regular session an annual report on the activities of the Organization and its financial condition; and

(h) Establish relations of cooperation, in accordance with decisions reached by the General Assembly or the Councils, with the Specialized Organizations as well as other national and international organizations.

ARTICLE 113

The Secretary General shall:

(a) Establish such offices of the General Secretariat as are necessary to accomplish its purposes; and

(b) Determine the number of officers and employees of the General Secretariat, appoint them, regulate their powers and duties, and fix their remuneration.

The Secretary General shall exercise this authority in accordance with such general standards and budgetary provisions as may be established by the General Assembly.

ARTICLE 114

The Assistant Secretary General shall be elected by the General Assembly for a five-year term and may not be reelected more than once or succeeded by a person of the same nationality. In the event that the office of Assistant Secretary General becomes vacant, the Permanent Council shall elect a substitute to hold that office until the General Assembly shall elect a new Assistant Secretary General for a full term.

ARTICLE 115

The Assistant Secretary General shall be the Secretary of the Permanent Council. He shall serve as advisory officer to the Secretary General and shall act as his delegate in all matters that the Secretary General may entrust to him. During the temporary absence or disability of the Secretary General, the Assistant Secretary General shall perform his functions.

The Secretary General and the Assistant Secretary General shall be of different nationalities.

ARTICLE 116

The General Assembly, by a two-thirds vote of the Member States, may remove the Secretary General or the Assistant Secretary General, or both, whenever the proper functioning of the Organization so demands.

ARTICLE 117

The Secretary General shall appoint, with the approval of the Inter-American Council for Integral Development, an Executive Secretary for Integral Development.

ARTICLE 118

In the performance of their duties, the Secretary General and the personnel of the Secretariat shall not seek or receive instructions from any Government or from any authority outside the Organization, and shall refrain from any action that may be incompatible with their position as international officers responsible only to the Organization

ARTICLE 119

The Member States pledge themselves to respect the exclusively international character of the responsibilities of the Secretary General and the personnel of the General Secretariat, and not to seek to influence them in the discharge of their duties.

ARTICLE 120

In selecting the personnel of the General Secretariat, first consideration shall be given to efficiency, competence, and integrity; but at the same time, in the recruitment of personnel of all ranks, importance shall be given to the necessity of obtaining as wide a geographic representation as possible.

ARTICLE 121

The seat of the General Secretariat is the city of Washington, D.C.

CHAPTER XVII. THE SPECIALIZED CONFERENCES

ARTICLE 122

The Specialized Conferences are intergovernmental meetings to deal with special technical matters or to develop specific aspects of inter-American cooperation. They shall be held when either the General Assembly or the Meeting of Consultation of Ministers of Foreign Affairs so decides, on its own initiative or at the request of one of the Councils or Specialized Organizations.

ARTICLE 123

The agenda and rules of procedure of the Specialized Conferences shall be prepared by the Councils or Specialized Organizations concerned and shall be submitted to the Governments of the Member States for consideration.

CHAPTER XVIII. THE SPECIALIZED ORGANIZATIONS

ARTICLE 124

For the purposes of the present Charter, Inter-American Specialized Organizations are the intergovernmental organizations established by multilateral agreements and having specific functions with respect to technical matters of common interest to the American States.

ARTICLE 125

The General Secretariat shall maintain a register of the organizations that fulfill the conditions set forth in the foregoing Article, as determined by the General Assembly after a report from the Council concerned.

ARTICLE 126

The Specialized Organizations shall enjoy the fullest technical autonomy, but they shall take into account the recommendations of the General Assembly and of the Councils, in accordance with the provisions of the Charter.

ARTICLE 127

The Specialized Organizations shall transmit to the General Assembly annual reports on the progress of their work and on their annual budgets and expenses.

ARTICLE 128

Relations that should exist between the Specialized Organizations and the Organization shall be defined by means of agreements concluded between each organization and the Secretary General, with the authorization of the General Assembly.

ARTICLE 129

The Specialized Organizations shall establish cooperative relations with world agencies of the same character in order to coordinate their activities. In concluding agreements with international agencies of a worldwide character, the Inter-American Specialized Organizations shall preserve their identity and their status as integral parts of the Organization of American States, even when they perform regional functions of international agencies.

ARTICLE 130

In determining the location of the Specialized Organizations consideration shall be given to the interest of all of the Member States and to the desirability of selecting the seats of these organizations on the basis of a geographic representation as equitable as possible.

PART THREE

CHAPTER XIX. THE UNITED NATIONS

ARTICLE 131

None of the provisions of this Charter shall be construed as impairing the rights and obligations of the Member States under the Charter of the United Nations.

CHAPTER XX. MISCELLANEOUS PROVISIONS

ARTICLE 132

Attendance at meetings of the permanent organs of the Organization of American States or at the conferences and meetings provided for in the Charter, or held under the auspices of the Organization, shall be in accordance with the multilateral character of the aforesaid organs, conferences, and meetings and shall not depend on the bilateral relations between the Government of any Member State and the Government of the host country.

ARTICLE 133

The Organization of American States shall enjoy in the territory of each Member such legal capacity, privileges, and immunities as are necessary for the exercise of its functions and the accomplishment of its purposes.

ARTICLE 134

The representatives of the Member States on the organs of the Organization, the personnel of their delegations, as well as the Secretary General and the Assistant Secretary General shall enjoy the privileges and immunities corresponding to their positions and necessary for the independent performance of their duties.

ARTICLE 135

The juridical status of the Specialized Organizations and the privileges and immunities that should be granted to them and to their personnel, as well as to the officials of the General Secretariat, shall be determined in a multilateral agreement. The foregoing shall not preclude, when it is considered necessary, the concluding of bilateral agreements.

ARTICLE 136

Correspondence of the Organization of American States, including printed matter and parcels, bearing the frank thereof, shall be carried free of charge in the mails of the Member States.

ARTICLE 137

The Organization of American States does not allow any restriction based on race, creed, or sex, with respect to eligibility to participate in the activities of the Organization and to hold positions therein.

ARTICLE 138

Within the provisions of this Charter, the competent organs shall endeavor to obtain greater collaboration from countries not Members of the Organization in the area of cooperation for development.

Chapter XXI. Ratification and Entry Into Force

ARTICLE 139

The present Charter shall remain open for signature by the American States and shall be ratified in accordance with their respective constitutional procedures. The original instrument, the Spanish, English, Portuguese, and French texts of which are equally authentic, shall be deposited with the General Secretariat, which shall transmit certified copies thereof to the Governments for purposes of ratification. The instruments of ratification shall be deposited with the General Secretariat, which shall notify the signatory States of such deposit.

ARTICLE 140

The present Charter shall enter into force among the ratifying States when two thirds of the signatory States have deposited their ratifications. It shall enter into force with respect to the remaining States in the order in which they deposit their ratifications.

ARTICLE 141

The present Charter shall be registered with the Secretariat of the United Nations through the General Secretariat.

ARTICLE 142

Amendments to the present Charter may be adopted only at a General Assembly convened for that purpose. Amendments shall enter into force in accordance with the terms and the procedure set forth in article 140.

ARTICLE 143

The present Charter shall remain in force indefinitely, but may be denounced by any Member State upon written notification to the General Secretariat, which shall communicate to all the others each notice of denunciation received. After two years from the date on which the General Secretariat receives a notice of denunciation, the present Charter shall cease to be in force with respect to the denouncing State, which shall cease to belong to the Organization after it has fulfilled the obligations arising from the present Charter.

Chapter XXII. Transitory Provisions

ARTICLE 144

The Inter-American Committee on the Alliance for Progress shall act as the permanent executive committee of the Inter-American Economic and Social Council as long as the Alliance is in operation.

ARTICLE 145

Until the inter-American convention on human rights, referred to in Chapter XV, enters into force, the present Inter-American Commission on Human Rights shall keep vigilance over the observance of human rights.

ARTICLE 146

The Permanent Council shall not make any recommendation nor shall the General Assembly take any decision with respect to a request for admission on the part of a political entity whose territory became subject, in whole or in part, prior to December 18, 1964, the date set by the First Special Inter-American Conference, to litigation or claim between an extracontinental country and one or more Member States of the Organization, until the dispute has been ended by some peaceful procedure. This article shall remain in effect until December 10, 1990.

RESERVATIONS MADE AT THE TIME OF RATIFICATION

NOTE.—The original Charter was signed April 30, 1948, for the Argentine Republic, Bolivia, Brazil, Chile, Colombia, Costa Rica, Cuba,[3] the Dominican Republic, Ecuador, El Salvador, Guatemala, Haiti, Honduras, Mexico, Nicaragua, Panama, Paraguay, Peru, the United States of America, Uruguay, and Venezuela and the following reservations were made at the time of ratifying:

Guatemala

None of the stipulations of the present Charter of the Organization of American States may be considered as an impediment to Guatemala's assertion of its rights over the territory of Belize by such means as at any time it may deem advisable.[4]

Peru

With the reservation that the principles of inter-American solidarity and cooperation and essentially those set forth in the preamble and declarations of the Act of Chapultepec constitute standards for the mutual relations between the American States and juridical bases on the inter-American system.

[3] The present Government in Cuba is excluded from participation in the inter-American system by Resolution VI of the 8th Meeting of the Consultation of Ministers of Foreign Affairs, Punta del Este, Uruguay, January 22–31, 1962.

[4] With respect to this reservation, the Pan American Union consulted the signatory governments, in accordance with the procedure established by para. 2 of Resolution XXIX of the Eighth International Conference of American States, to ascertain whether they found it acceptable or not. At the request of the Government of Guatemala, this consultation was accompanied by a formal declaration of that Government to the effect that its reservation did not imply any alteration in the Charter of the Organization of American States, and that Guatemala is ready to act at all times within the bounds of international agreements to which it is a party. In view of this declaration, the States that previously did not find the reservation acceptable expressed their acceptance.

United States

That the Senate give its advice and consent to ratification of the Charter with the reservation that none of its provisions shall be considered as enlarging the powers of the Federal Government of the United States or limiting the powers of the several states of the Federal Union with respect to any matters recognized under the Constitution as being within the reserved powers of the several states.

c. Act of Bogotá

Act of Bogotá, Recommending Measures for Social Improvement and Economic Development within the Framework of Operation Pan America; Adopted by the Council of the Organization of American States, September 13, 1960; Approved by the Council, October 11, 1960 [1]

The Special Committee to Study the Foundation of New Measures for Economic Cooperation,

RECOGNIZING that the preservation and strengthening of free and democratic institutions in the American republics requires the acceleration of social and economic progress in Latin America adequate to meet the legitimate aspirations of the peoples of the Americas for a better life and to provide them the fullest opportunity to improve their status;

RECOGNIZING that the interests of the American republics are so interrelated that sound social and economic progress in each is of importance to all and that lack of it in any American republic may have serious repercussions in others;

COGNIZANT of the steps already taken by many American republics to cope with the serious economic and social problems confronting them, but convinced that the magnitude of these problems calls for redoubled efforts by governments and for a new and vigorous program of inter-American cooperation;

RECOGNIZING that economic development programs, which should be urgently strengthened and expanded, may have a delayed effect on social welfare, and that accordingly early measures are needed to cope with social needs;

RECOGNIZING that the success of a cooperative program of economic and social progress will require maximum self-help efforts on the part of the American republics and, in many cases, the improvement of existing institutions and practices, particularly in the fields of taxation, the ownership and use of land, education and training, health and housing;

BELIEVING it opportune to give further practical expression to the spirit of Operation Pan America by immediately enlarging the opportunities of the people of Latin America for social progress, thus strengthening of their hopes for the future;

CONSIDERING it advisable to launch a program for social development, in which emphasis should be given to those measures that meet social needs and also promote increases in productivity and strengthen economic development,

RECOMMENDS to the Council of the Organization of American States:

[1] *Department of State Bulletin*, October 3, 1960, p. 537; *American Foreign Policy, Current Documents 1960*, pp. 293–299.

I. Measures for Social Improvement

An inter-American program for social development should be established which should be directed to the carrying out of the following measures of social improvement in Latin America, as considered appropriate in each country:

A. *Measures for the improvement of conditions of rural living and land use*

1. The examination of existing legal and institutional systems with respect to:

a. land tenure legislation and facilities with a view to ensuring a wider and more equitable distribution of the ownership of land, in a manner consistent with the objectives of employment, productivity and economic growth;

b. agricultural credit institutions with a view to providing adequate financing to individual farmers or groups of farmers;

c. tax systems and procedures and fiscal policies with a view to assuring equity of taxation and encouraging improved use of land, especially of privately-owned land which is idle.

2. The initiation or acceleration of appropriate programs to modernize and improve the existing legal and institutional framework to ensure better conditions of land tenure, extend more adequate credit facilities and provide increased incentives in the land tax structure.

3. The acceleration of the preparation of projects and programs for:

a. land reclamation and land settlement, with a view to promoting more widespread ownership and efficient use of land, particularly of unutilized or under-utilized land;

b. the increase of the productivity of land already in use; and

c. the construction of farm-to-market and access roads.

4. The adoption or acceleration of other government service programs designed particularly to assist the smaller farmer, such as new or improved marketing organizations; extension services; research and basic surveys; and demonstration, education, and training facilities.

B. *Measures for the improvement of housing and community facilities*

1. The examination of existing policies in the field of housing and community facilities, including urban and regional planning, with a view to improving such policies, strengthening public institutions and promoting private initiative and participation in programs in these fields. Special consideration should be given to encouraging financial institutions to invest in low-cost housing on a long-term basis and in building and construction industries.

2. The strengthening of the existing legal and institutional framework for mobilizing financial resources to provide better housing and related facilities for the people and to create new institutions for this purpose when necessary. Special consideration should be given to legislation and measures which would encourage the establishment and growth of:

a. private financing institutions, such as building and loan associations;

b. institutions to insure sound housing loans against loss;

c. institutions to serve as a secondary market for home mortgages;

d. institutions to provide financial assistance to local communities for the development of facilities such as water supply, sanitation and other public works.

Existing national institutions should be utilized, wherever practical and appropriate, in the application of external resources to further the development of housing and community facilities.

3. The expansion of home building industries through such measures as the training of craftsmen and other personnel, research, the introduction of new techniques, and the development of construction standards for low- and medium-cost housing.

4. The lending of encouragement and assistance to programs, on a pilot basis for aided self-help housing, for the acquisition and subdivision of land for low-cost housing developments, and for industrial housing projects.

C. *Measures for the improvement of educational systems and training facilities*

1. The reexamination of educational systems, giving particular attention to:

a. the development of modern methods of mass education for the eradication of illiteracy;

b. the adequacy of training in the industrial arts and sciences with due emphasis on laboratory and work experience and on the practical application of knowledge for the solution of social and economic problems;

c. the need to provide instruction in rural schools not only in basic subjects but also in agriculture, health, sanitation, nutrition, and in methods of home and community improvement;

d. the broadening of courses of study in secondary schools to provide the training necessary for clerical and executive personnel in industry, commerce, public administration, and community service;

e. specialized trade and industrial education related to the commercial and industrial needs of the community;

f. vocational agricultural instruction;

g. advanced education of administrators, engineers, economists, and other professional personnel of key importance to economic development.

D. *Measures for the improvement of public health*

1. The reexamination of programs and policies of public health, giving particular attention to:

a. strengthening the expansion of national and local health services, especially those directed to the reduction of infant mortality;

b. the progressive development of health insurance systems, including those providing for maternity, accident and disability insurance, in urban and rural areas;

c. the provision of hospital and health service in areas located away from main centers of population;

d. the extension of public medical services to areas of exceptional need;

e. the strengthening of campaigns for the control or elimination of communicable diseases with special attention to the eradication of malaria;

f. the provision of water supply facilities for purposes of health and economic development;

g. the training of public health officials and technicians;

h. the strengthening of programs of nutrition for low-income groups.

E. *Measures for the mobilization of domestic resources*

1. This program shall be carried out within the framework of the maximum creation of domestic savings and of the improvement of fiscal and financial practices;

2. The equity and effectiveness of existing tax schedules, assessment practices and collection procedures shall be examined with a view to providing additional revenue for the purpose of this program;

3. The allocation of tax revenues shall be reviewed, having in mind an adequate provision of such revenues to the areas of social development mentioned in the foregoing paragraphs.

II. Creation of a Special Fund for Social Development

1. The delegations of the Governments of the Latin American republics welcome the decision of the Government of the United States to establish a special inter-American fund for social development, with the Inter-American Development Bank to become the primary mechanism for the administration of the fund.

2. It is understood that the purpose of the special fund would be to contribute capital resources and technical assistance on flexible terms and conditions, including repayment in local currency and the relending of repaid funds, in accordance with appropriate and selective criteria in the light of the resources available, to support the efforts of the Latin American countries that are prepared to initiate or expand effective institutional improvements and to adopt measures to employ efficiently their own resources with a view to achieving greater social progress and more balanced economic growth.

III. Measures for Economic Development

The Special Committee,

Having in view Resolution VII adopted at the Seventh Meeting of Consultation of Ministers of Foreign Affairs expressing the need for the maximum contribution of member countries in hemisphere cooperation in the struggle against underdevelopment, in pursuance of the objectives of Operation Pan America,

EXPRESSES ITS CONVICTION

1. That within the framework of Operation Pan America, the economic development of Latin America requires prompt action of exceptional breadth in the field of international cooperation and domestic effort comprising:

a. additional public and private financial assistance on the part of capital exporting countries of America, Western Europe, and international lending agencies within the framework of their charters, with special attention to:

i. the need for loans on flexible terms and conditions, including, whenever advisable in the light of the balance of payments situation of individual countries, the possibility of repayment in local currency,

ii. the desirability of the adequate preparation and implementation of development projects and plans, within the framework of the monetary, fiscal and exchange policies necessary for their effectiveness, utilizing as appropriate the technical assistance of inter-American and international agencies.

iii. the advisability, in special cases, of extending foreign financing for the coverage of local expenditures;

b. mobilization of additional domestic capital, both public and private;

c. technical assistance by the appropriate international agencies in the preparation and implementation of national and regional Latin American development projects and plans;

d. the necessity for developing and strengthening credit facilities for small and medium private business, agriculture and industry.

RECOMMENDS:

1. That special attention be given to an expansion of long-term lending, particularly in view of the instability of exchange earnings of countries exporting primary products and of the unfavourable effect of the excessive accumulation of short- and medium-term debt on continuing and orderly economic development.

2. That urgent attention be given to the search for effective and practical ways, appropriate to each commodity, to deal with the problem of the instability of exchange earnings of countries heavily dependent upon the exportation of primary products.

IV. MULTILATERAL COOPERATION FOR SOCIAL AND ECONOMIC PROGRESS

The Special Committee,

CONSIDERING the need for providing instruments and mechanisms for the implementation of the program of inter-American economic and social cooperation which would periodically review the progress made and propose measures for further mobilization of resources,

RECOMMENDS:

1. That the Inter-American Economic and Social Council undertake to organize annual consultative meetings to review the social

and economic progress of member countries, to analyze and discuss the progress achieved and the problems encountered in each country, to exchange opinions on possible measures that might be adopted to intensify further social and economic progress, within the framework of Operation Pan America, and to prepare reports on the outlook for the future. Such annual meetings should begin with an examination by experts and terminate with a session at the ministerial level.

2. That the Council of the Organization of American States convene within 60 days of the date of this Act a special meeting of senior government representatives to find ways of strengthening and improving the ability of the Inter-American Economic and Social Council to render effective assistance to governments with a view to achieving the objectives enumerated below, taking into account the proposal submitted by the delegation of Argentina in Document CECE/III–13:

a. To further the economic and social development of Latin American countries;

b. To promote trade between the countries of the Western Hemisphere as well as between them and extra-continental countries;

c. To facilitate the flow of capital and the extension of credits to the countries of Latin America both from the Western Hemisphere and from extra-continental sources.

3. The special meeting shall:

a. Examine the existing structure of the Inter-American Economic and Social Council, and of the units of the Secretariat of the Organization of American States working in the economic and social fields, with a view to strengthening and improving the Inter-American Economic and Social Council;

b. Determine the means of strengthening inter-American economic and social cooperation by an administrative reform of the Secretariat, which should be given sufficient technical, administrative and financial flexibility for the adequate fulfillment of its tasks;

c. Formulate recommendations designed to assure effective coordination between the Inter-American Economic and Social Council, the Economic Commission for Latin America, the Inter-American Development Bank, the United Nations and its Specialized Agencies and other agencies offering technical advice and services in the Western Hemisphere.

d. Propose procedures designed to establish effective liaison of the Inter-American Economic and Social Council and other regional American organizations with other international organizations for the purpose of study, discussion and consultation in the fields of international trade and financial and technical assistance;

e. And formulate appropriate recommendations to the Council of the Organization of American States.

In approving the Act of Bogotá the Delegations to the Special Committee, convinced that the people of the Americas can achieve a better life only within the democratic system, renew their faith in the essential values which lie at the base of Western civilization, and re-affirm their determination to assure the fullest measure of well-being to the people of the Americas under conditions of freedom and respect for the supreme dignity of the individual.

d. Charter of Punta del Este [1]

Signed in Punta del Este, Uruguay August 17, 1961

ESTABLISHING THE ALLIANCE FOR PROGRESS WITHIN THE FRAMEWORK OF OPERATION PAN AMERICA

PREAMBLE

We, the American Republics, hereby proclaim our decision to unite in a common effort to bring our people accelerated economic progress and broader social justice within the framework of personal dignity and political liberty.

Almost two hundred years ago we began in this Hemisphere the long struggle for freedom which now inspires people in all parts of the world. Today, in ancient lands, men moved to hope by the revolutions of our young nations search for liberty. Now we must give a new meaning to that revolutionary heritage. For America stands at a turning point in history. The men and women of our Hemisphere are reaching for the better life which today's skills have placed within their grasp. They are determined for themselves and their children to have decent and ever more abundant lives, to gain access to knowledge and equal opportunity for all, to end those conditions which benefit the few at the expense of the needs and dignity of the many. It is our inescapable task to fulfill these just desires—to demonstrate to the poor and forsaken of our countries, and of all lands, that the creative powers of free men hold the key to their progress and to the progress of future generations. And our certainty of ultimate success rests not alone on our faith in ourselves and in our nations but on the indomitable spirit of free man which has been the heritage of American civilization.

Inspired by these principles, and by the principles of Operation Pan America and the Act of Bogotá, the American Republics hereby resolve to adopt the following program of action to establish and carry forward an Alliance for Progress.

TITLE I. OBJECTIVES OF THE ALLIANCE FOR PROGRESS

It is the purpose of the Alliance for Progress to enlist the full energies of the peoples and governments of the American republics in a great cooperative effort to accelerate the economic and social development of the participating countries of Latin America, so that

[1] *Department of State Bulletin*, September 11, 1961, p. 463; *American Foreign Policy, Current Documents 1961*, pp. 395–409. The special meeting of the Inter-American Economic and Social Council which began at Punta del Este, Uruguay, on August 5, 1961, was concluded on August 17, 1961 with the signing of a declaration and a charter by all members of the Organization of American States except Cuba. The signatories are: Argentina, Bolivia, Brazil, Colombia, Costa Rica, Chile, Dominican Republic, Ecuador, El Salvador, Guatemala, Haiti, Honduras, Mexico, Nicaragua, Panama, Paraguay, Peru, United States, Uruguay, and Venezuela.

they may achieve maximum levels of well-being, with equal opportunities for all, in democratic societies adapted to their own needs and desires.

The American Republics agree to work toward the achievement of the following fundamental goals in the present decade:

1. To achieve in the participating Latin American countries a substantial and sustained growth of per capita income at a rate designed to attain, at the earliest possible date, levels of income capable of assuring self-sustaining development, and sufficient to make Latin American income levels constantly larger in relation to the levels of the more industrialized nations. In this way the gap between the living standards of Latin America and those of the more developed countries can be narrowed. Similarly, presently existing differences in income levels among the Latin American countries will be reduced by accelerating the development of the relatively less developed countries and granting them maximum priority in the distribution of resources and in international cooperation in general. In evaluating the degree of relative development, account will be taken not only of average levels of real income and gross product per capita, but also of indices of infant mortality, illiteracy, and per capita daily caloric intake.

It is recognized that, in order to reach these objectives within a reasonable time, the rate of economic growth in any country of Latin America should be not less than 2.5 percent per capita per year, and that each participating country should determine its own growth target in the light of its stage of social and economic evolution, resource endowment, and ability to mobilize national efforts for development.

2. To make the benefits of economic progress available to all citizens of all economic and social groups through a more equitable distribution of national income, raising more rapidly the income and standard of living of the needier sectors of the population, at the same time that a higher proportion of the national product is devoted to investment.

3. To achieve balanced diversification in national economic structures, both regional and functional, making them increasingly free from dependence on the export of a limited number of primary products and the importation of capital goods while attaining stability in the prices of exports or in income derived from exports.

4. To accelerate the process of rational industrialization so as to increase the productivity of the economy as a whole, taking full advantage of the talents and energies of both the private and public sectors, utilizing the natural resources of the country and providing productive and remunerative employment for unemployed or part-time workers. Within this process of industrialization, special attention should be given to the establishment and development of capital-goods industries.

5. To raise greatly the level of agricultural productivity and output and to improve related storage, transportation, and marketing services.

6. To encourage, in accordance with the characteristics of each country, programs of comprehensive agrarian reform leading to the effective transformation, where required, of unjust structures and systems of land tenure and use, with a view to replacing latifundia

and dwarf holdings by an equitable system of land tenure so that, with the help of timely and adequate credit, technical assistance and facilities for the marketing and distribution of products, the land will become for the man who works it the basis of his economic stability, the foundation of his increasing welfare, and the guarantee of his freedom and dignity.

7. To eliminate adult illiteracy and by 1970 to assure, as a minimum, access to 6 years of primary education for each school-age child in Latin America; to modernize and expand vocational, technical, secondary and higher educational and training facilities, to strengthen the capacity for basic and applied research; and to provide the competent personnel required in rapidly-growing societies.

8. To increase life expectancy at birth by a minimum of 5 years, and to increase the ability to learn and produce, by improving individual and public health. To attain this goal it will be necessary, among other measures, to provide adequate potable water supply and sewage disposal to not less than 70 percent of the urban and 50 percent of the rural population; to reduce the present mortality rate of children less than 5 years of age by at least one-half; to control the more serious communicable diseases, according to their importance as a cause of sickness, disability, and death; to eradicate those illnesses, especially malaria, for which effective techniques are known; to improve nutrition; to train medical and health personnel to meet at least minimum requirements; to improve basic health services at national and local levels; and to intensify scientific research and apply its results more fully and effectively to the prevention and cure of illness.

9. To increase the construction of low-cost houses for low-income families in order to replace inadequate and deficient housing and to reduce housing shortages; and to provide necessary public services to both urban and rural centers of population.

10. To maintain stable price levels, avoiding inflation or deflation and the consequent social hardships and maldistribution of resources, always bearing in mind the necessity of maintaining an adequate rate of economic growth.

11. To strengthen existing agreements on economic integration, with a view to the ultimate fulfillment of aspirations for a Latin American common market that will expand and diversify trade among the Latin American countries and thus contribute to the economic growth of the region.

12. To develop cooperative programs designed to prevent the harmful effects of excessive fluctuations in the foreign exchange earnings derived from exports of primary products, which are of vital importance to economic and social development; and to adopt the measures necessary to facilitate the access of Latin American exports to international markets.

Title II. Economic and Social Development

CHAPTER I. BASIC REQUIREMENTS FOR ECONOMIC AND SOCIAL DEVELOPMENT

The American Republics recognize that to achieve the foregoing goals it will be necessary:

1. That comprehensive and well-conceived national programs of economic and social development, aimed at the achievement of self-sustaining growth, be carried out in accordance with democratic principles.

2. That national programs of economic and social development be based on the principle of self-help—as established in the Act of Bogotá—and on the maximum use of domestic resources, taking into account the special conditions of each country.

3. That in the preparation an execution of plans for economic and social development, women should be placed on an equal footing with men.

4. That the Latin American countries obtain sufficient external financial assistance, a substantial portion of which should be extended on flexible conditions with respect to periods and terms of repayment and forms of utilization, in order to supplement domestic capital formation and reinforce their import capacity; and that, in support of well-conceived programs, which include the necessary structural reforms and measures for the mobilization of internal resources, a supply of capital from all external sources during the coming 10 years of at least 20 billion dollars be made available to the Latin American countries, with priority to the relatively less developed countries. The greater part of this sum should be in public funds.

5. That institutions in both the public and private sectors, including labor organizations, cooperatives, and commercial, industrial, and financial institutions, be strengthened and improved for the increasing and effective use of domestic resources, and that the social reforms necessary to permit a fair distribution of the fruits of economic and social progress be carried out.

CHAPTER II. NATIONAL DEVELOPMENT PROGRAMS

1. Participating Latin American countries agree to introduce or strengthen systems for the preparation, execution, and periodic revision of national programs for economic and social development consistent with the principles, objectives, and requirements contained in this document. Participating Latin American countries should formulate, if possible within the next eighteen months, long-term development programs. Such programs should embrace, according to the characteristics of each country, the elements outlined in the Appendix.

2. National development programs should incorporate self-help efforts directed to:

a. Improvement of human resources and widening of opportunities by raising general standards of education and health; improving and extending technical education and professional training with emphasis on science and technology; providing adequate remuneration for work performed, encouraging the talents of managers, entrepreneurs, and wage earners; providing more productive employment for underemployed manpower; establishing effective systems of labor relations, and procedures for consultation and collaboration among public authorities, employer associations, and labor organizations; promoting the establishment and expansion of local institutions for basic and applied research; and improving the standards of public administration.

b. Wider development and more efficient use of natural resources, especially those which are now idle or under-utilized, including measures for the processing of raw materials.

c. The strengthening of the agricultural base, progressively, extending the benefits of the land to those who work it, and ensuring in countries with Indian populations the integration of these populations into the economic, social, and cultural processes of modern life. To carry out these aims, measures should be adopted, among others, to establish or improve, as the case may be, the following services: extension, credit, technical assistance, agricultural research and mechanization; health and education; storage and distribution; cooperatives and farmers' associations; and community development.

d. More effective, rational and equitable mobilization and use of financial resources through the reform of tax structures, including fair and adequate taxation of large incomes and real estate, and the strict application of measures to improve fiscal administration. Development programs should include the adaptation of budget expenditures to development needs, measures for the maintenance of price stability, the creation of essential credit facilities at reasonable rates of interest, and the encouragement of private savings.

e. Promotion through appropriate measures, including the signing of agreements for the purpose of reducing or eliminating double taxation, of conditions that will encourage the flow of foreign investments and help to increase the capital resources of participating countries in need of capital.

f. Improvement of systems distribution and sales in order to make markets more competitive and prevent monopolistic practices.

CHAPTER III. IMMEDIATE AND SHORT-TERM ACTION MEASURES

1. Recognizing that a number of Latin American countries, despite their best efforts, may require emergency financial assistance, the United States will provide assistance from the funds which are or may be established for such purposes. The United States stands ready to take prompt action on applications for such assistance. Applications relating to existing situations should be submitted within the next 60 days.

2. Participating Latin American countries should, in addition to creating or strengthening machinery for long-term development programing, immediately increase their efforts to accelerate their development by giving special emphasis to the following objectives:

a. The completion of projects already underway and the initiation of projects for which the basic studies have been made, in order to accelerate their financing and execution.

b. The implementation of new projects which are designed:

(1) To meet the most pressing economic and social needs and benefit directly the greatest number of people;

(2) To concentrate efforts within each country in the less developed or more depressed areas in which particularly serious social problems exist;

(3) To utilize idle capacity or resources, particularly under-employment manpower; and

(4) To survey and assess natural resources.

c. The facilitation of the preparation and execution of long-term programs through measures designed:

(1) To train teachers, technicians, and specialists;

(2) To provide accelerated training to workers and farmers;

(3) To improve basic statistics;

(4) To establish needed credit and marketing facilities; and

(5) To improve services and administration.

3. The United States will assist in carrying out these short-term measures with a view to achieving concrete results from the Alliance for Progress at the earliest possible moment. In connection with the measures set forth above, and in accordance with the statement of President Kennedy, the United States will provide assistance under the Alliance, including assistance for the financing of short-term measures, totaling more than one billion dollars in the year ending march 1962.

CHAPTER IV. EXTERNAL ASSISTANCE IN SUPPORT OF NATIONAL DEVELOPMENT PROGRAMS

1. The economic and social development of Latin America will require a large amount of additional public and private financial assistance on the part of capital-exporting countries, including the members of the Development Assistance Group and international lending agencies. The measures provided for in the Act of Bogotá and the new measures provided for in this Charter, are designed to create a framework within which such additional assistance can be provided and effectively utilized.

2. The United States will assist those participating countries whose development programs establish self-help measures and economic and social policies and programs consistent with the goals and principles of this Charter. To supplement the domestic efforts of such countries, the United States is prepared to allocate resources which, along with those anticipated from other external sources, will be of a scope and magnitude adequate to realize the goals envisaged in this Charter. Such assistance will be allocated to both social and economic development and, where appropriate, will take the form of grants or loans on flexible terms and conditions. The participating countries will request the support of other capital-exporting countries and appropriate institutions so that they may provide assistance for the attainment of these objectives.

3. The United States will assist in the financing of technical assistance projects proposed by a participating country or by the General Secretariat of the Organization of American States for the purpose of:

a. Providing experts contracted in agreement with governments to work under their direction and to assist them in the preparation of specific investment projects and the strengthening of national mechanisms for preparing projects, using specialized engineering firms where appropriate;

b. Carrying out, pursuant to existing agreements for cooperation among the General Secretariat of the Organization of American States, the Economic Commission for Latin America, and the Inter-American Development Bank, field investigations and studies, including those relating to development problems, the organization of national agencies for the preparation of development programs, agrarian reform and rural development, health, cooperatives, housing, education and professional training, and taxation and tax administration; and

c. Convening meetings of experts and officials on development and related problems.

The governments or above mentioned organizations should, when appropriate, seek the cooperation of the United Nations and its specialized agencies in the execution of these activities.

4. The participating Latin American countries recognize that each has in varying degree a capacity to assist fellow republics by providing technical and financial assistance. They recognize that this capacity will increase as their economies grow. They therefore affirm their intention to assist fellow republics increasingly as their individual circumstances permit.

CHAPTER V. ORGANIZATION AND PROCEDURES

1. In order to provide technical assistance for the formulation of development programs, as may be requested by participating nations, the Organization of American States, the Economic Commission for Latin America, and the Inter-American Development Bank will continue and strengthen their agreements for coordination in this field in order to have available a group of programming experts whose service can be used to facilitate the implementation of this Charter. The participating countries will also seek an intensification of technical assistance from the specialized agencies of the United Nations for the same purpose.

2. The Inter-American Economic and Social Council, on the joint nomination of the Secretary General of the Organization of American States, the President of the Inter-American Development Bank, and the Executive Secretary of the United Nations Economic Commission for Latin America, will appoint a panel of nine high-level experts, exclusively on the basis of their experience, technical ability, and competence in the various aspects of economic and social development. The experts may be of any nationality, though if of Latin American origin an appropriate geographical distribution will be sought. They will be attached to the Inter-American Economic and Social Council, but will nevertheless enjoy complete autonomy in the performance of their duties. They may not hold any other remunerative position. The appointment of these experts will be for a period of three years, and may be renewed.

3. Each government, if it so wishes, may present its program for economic and social development for consideration by an ad hoc committee, composed of no more than three members drawn from the panel of experts referred to in the preceding paragraph together with an equal number of experts not on the panel. The experts who compose the ad hoc committee will be appointed by the Secretary General of the Organization of American States at the request of the interested government and with its consent.

4. The committee will study the development program, exchange opinions with the interested government as to possible modifications and, with the consent of the government, report its conclusions to the Inter-American Development Bank and to other governments and institutions that may be prepared to extend external financial and technical assistance in connection with the execution of the program.

5. In considering a development program presented to it, the ad hoc committee will examine the consistency of the program with the principles of the Act of Bogotá and of this Charter, taking into account the elements in the Appendix.

6. The General Secretariat of the Organization of American States will provide the personnel needed by the experts referred to in paragraphs 2 and 3 of this Chapter in order to fulfill their tasks. Such personnel may be employed specifically for this purpose or may be made available from the permanent staffs of the Organization of American States, the Economic Commission for Latin America, and the Inter-American Development Bank, in accordance with the present liaison arrangements between the three organizations. The General Secretariat of the Organization of American States may seek arrangements with the United Nations Secretariat, its specialized agencies and the Inter-American Specialized organizations for the temporary assignment of necessary personnel.

7. A government whose development program has been the object of recommendations made by the ad hoc committee with respect to external financing requirements may submit the program to the Inter-American Development Bank so that the Bank may undertake the negotiations required to obtain such financing, including the organization of a consortium of credit institutions and government disposed to contribute to the continuing and systematic financing, on appropriate terms, of the development program. However, the government will have full freedom to resort through any other channels to all sources of financing, for the purpose of obtaining, in full or in part, the required resources.

The ad hoc committee shall not interfere with the right of each government to formulate its own goals, priorities, and reforms in its national development programs.

The recommendations of the ad hoc committee will be of great importance in determining the distribution of public funds under the Alliance for Progress which contribute to the external financing of such programs. These recommendations shall give special consideration to Title I.1.

The participating governments will also use their good offices to the end that these recommendations may be accepted as a factor of great importance in the decisions taken, for the same purpose, by inter-American credit institutions, other international credit agencies, and other friendly governments which may be potential sources of capital.

8. The Inter-American Economic and Social Council will review annually the progress achieved in the formulation, national implementation, and international financing of development programs; and will submit to the Council of the Organization of American States such recommendations as it deems pertinent.

APPENDIX

ELEMENTS OF NATIONAL DEVELOPMENT PROGRAMS

1. The establishment of mutually consistent targets to be aimed at over the program period in expanding productive capacity in industry, agriculture, mining, transport, power and communications, and in improving conditions of urban and rural life, including better housing, education and health.

2. The assignment of priorities and the description of methods to achieve the targets, including specific measures and major projects. Specific development projects should be justified in terms of their relative costs and benefits, including their contribution to social productivity.

3. The measures which will be adopted to direct the operations of the public sector and to encourage private action in support of the development program.

4. The estimated cost, in national and foreign currency, of major projects and of the development program as a whole, year by year over the program period.

5. The internal resources, public and private, estimated to become available for the execution of the programs.

6. The direct and indirect effects of the program on the balance of payments, and the external financing, public and private, estimated to be required for the execution of the program.

7. The basic fiscal and monetary policies to be followed in order to permit implementation of the program within a framework of price stability.

8. The machinery of public administration—including relationships with local governments, decentralized agencies and nongovernmental organizations, such as labor organizations, cooperatives, business and industrial organizations—to be used in carrying out the program, adapting it to changing circumstances and evaluating the progress made.

TITLE III. ECONOMIC INTEGRATION OF LATIN AMERICA

The American Republics consider that the broadening of present national markets in Latin America is essential to accelerate the process of economic development in the Hemisphere. It is also an appropriate means for obtaining greater productivity through specialized and complementary industrial production which will, in turn, facilitate the attainment of greater social benefits for the inhabitants of the various regions of Latin America. The broadening of markets will also make possible the better use of resources under the Alliance for Progress. Consequently, the American Republics recognize that:

1. The Montevideo Treaty (because of its flexibility and because it is open to adherence of all of the Latin American nations) and the Central American Treaty of Economic Integration are appropriate instruments for the attainment of these objectives, as was recognized in Resolution No. 11 (III) of the Ninth Session of the Economic Commission for Latin America.

2. The integration process can be intensified and accelerated not only by the specialization resulting from the broadening of markets

through the liberalization of trade but also through the use of such instruments as the agreements for complementary production within economic sectors provided for in the Montevideo Treaty.

3. In order to insure the balanced and complementary economic expansion of all of the countries involved, the integration process should take into account, on a flexible basis, the condition of countries at a relatively less advanced stage of economic development, permitting them to be granted special, fair, and equitable treatment.

4. In order to facilitate economic integration in Latin America, it is advisable to establish effective relationships between the Latin American Free Trade Association and the group of countries adhering to the Central American Economic Integration Treaty, as well as between either of these groups and other Latin American countries. These arrangements should be established within the limits determined by these instruments.

5. The Latin American countries should coordinate their actions to meet the unfavorable treatment accorded to their foreign trade in world markets, particularly that resulting from certain restrictive and discriminatory policies of extra-continental countries and economic groups.

6. In the application of resources under the Alliance for Progress, special attention should be given not only to investments for multinational projects that will contribute to strengthening the integration process in all its aspects, but also to the necessary financing of industrial production, and to the growing expansion of trade in industrial products within Latin America.

7. In order to facilitate the participation of countries at a relatively lower stage of economic development in multinational Latin American economic cooperation programs, and in order to promote the balanced and harmonious development of the Latin American integration process, special attention should be given to the needs of these countries in the administration of financial resources provided under the Alliance for Progress, particularly in connection with infrastructure programs and the promotion of new lines of production.

8. The economic integration process implies a need for additional investment in various fields of economic activity and funds provided under the Alliance for Progress should cover these needs as well as those required for the financing of national development programs.

9. When groups of Latin American countries have their own institutions for financing economic integration, the financing referred to in the preceding paragraph should preferably be channeled through these institutions. With respect to regional financing designed to further the purposes of existing regional integration instruments, the cooperation of the Inter-American Development Bank should be sought in channeling extra-regional contributions which may be granted for these purposes.

10. One of the possible means for making effective a policy for the financing of Latin American integration would be to approach the International Monetary Fund and other financial sources with

a view to providing a means for solving temporary balance-of-payments problems that may occur in countries participating in economic integration arrangements.

11. The promotion and coordination of transportation and communications systems is an effective way to accelerate the integration process. In order to counteract abusive practices in relation to freight rates and tariffs, it is advisable to encourage the establishment of multinational transport and communication enterprises in the Latin American countries, or to find other appropriate solutions.

12. In working toward economic integration and complementary economies, efforts should be made to achieve an appropriate coordination of national plans, or to engage in joint planning for various economies through the existing regional integration organizations. Efforts should also be made to promote an investment policy directed to the progressive elimination of unequal growth rates in the different geographic areas, particularly in the case of countries which are relatively less developed.

13. It is necessary to promote the development of national Latin American enterprises, in order that they may compete on an equal footing with foreign enterprises.

14. The active participation of the private sector is essential to economic integration and development, and except in those countries in which free enterprise does not exist, development planning by the pertinent national public agencies, far from hindering such participation, can facilitate and guide it, thus opening new perspectives for the benefit of the community.

15. As the countries of the Hemisphere still under colonial domination achieve their independence, they should be invited to participate in Latin American economic integration programs.

Title IV. Basic Export Commodities

The American Republics recognize that the economic development of Latin America requires expansion of its trade, a simultaneous and corresponding increase in foreign exchange incomes received from exports, a lessening of cyclical of seasonal fluctuations in the incomes of those countries that still depend heavily on the export of raw materials, and the correction of the secular deterioration in their terms of trade.

They, therefore, agree that the following measures should be taken:

I. NATIONAL MEASURES

National measures affecting commerce in primary products should be directed and applied in order to:

1. Avoid undue obstacles to the expansion of trade in these products;
2. Avoid market instability;
3. Improve the efficiency of international plans and mechanisms for stabilization; and
4. Increase their present markets and expand their area of trade at a rate compatible with rapid development.

Therefore:

A. Importing member countries should reduce and if possible eliminate, as soon as feasible, all restrictions and discriminatory practices affecting the consumption and importation of primary products, including those with the highest possible degree of processing in the country of origin, except when these restrictions are imposed temporarily for purposes of economic diversification, to hasten the economic development of less developed nations, or to establish basic national reserves. Importing countries should also be ready to support, by adequate regulations, stabilization programs for primary products that may be agreed upon with producing countries.

B. Industrialized countries should give special attention to the need for hastening economic development of less developed countries. Therefore, they should make maximum efforts to create conditions, compatible with their international obligations, through which they may extend advantages to less developed countries so as to permit the rapid expansion of their markets. In view of the great need for this rapid development, industrialized countries should also study ways in which to modify, wherever possible, international commitments which prevent the achievement of this objective.

C. Producing member countries should formulate their plans for production and exports, taking account of their effect on world markets and of the necessity of supporting and improving the effectiveness of international stabilization programs and mechanisms. Similarly they should try to avoid increasing the uneconomic production of goods which can be obtained under better conditions in the less developed countries of the Continent, in which the production of these goods is an important source of employment.

D. Member countries should adopt all necessary measures to direct technological studies toward finding new uses and by-products of those primary commodities that are most important to their economies.

E. Member countries should try to reduce, and, if possible, eliminate within a reasonable time export subsidies and other measures which cause instability in the markets for basic commodities and excessive fluctuations in prices and income.

II. INTERNATIONAL COOPERATION MEASURES

1. Member countries should make coordinated, and if possible, joint efforts designed:

a. To eliminate as soon as possible undue protection of the production of basic products;

b. To eliminate taxes and reduce excessive domestic prices which discourage the consumption of imported basic products;

c. To seek to end preferential agreements and other measures which limit world consumption of Latin American basic products and their access to international markets, especially the markets of Western European countries in process of economic integration, and of countries with centrally planned economies; and

d. To adopt the necessary consultation mechanisms so that their marketing policies will not have damaging effects on the stability of the markets for basic commodities.

2. Industrialized countries should give maximum cooperation to less developed countries so that their raw material exports will have the greatest degree of processing that is economic.

3. Through their representation in international financial organizations, member countries should suggest that these organizations, when considering loans for the promotion of production for export, take into account the effect of such loans on products which are in surplus in world markets.

4. Member countries should support the efforts being made by international commodity study groups and by the Commission on International Commodity Trade of the United Nations. In this connection, it should be considered that producing and consuming nations bear a joint responsibility for taking national and international steps to reduce market instability.

5. The Secretary General of the Organization of American States shall convene a group of experts appointed by their respective Governments to meet before November 30, 1961 and to report, not later than March 31, 1962 on measures to provide an adequate and effective means of offsetting the effects of fluctuations in the volume and prices of exports of basic products. The experts shall:

a. Consider the questions regarding compensatory financing raised during the present meeting;

b. Analyze the proposal for establishing an international fund for the stabilization of export receipts contained in the Report of the Group of Experts to the Special Meeting of the Inter-American Economic and Social Council, as well as any other alternative proposals;

c. Prepare a draft plan for the creation of mechanisms for compensatory financing. This draft plan should be circulated among the member Governments and their opinions obtained well in advance of the next meeting of the Commission on International Commodity Trade.

6. Member countries should support the efforts under way to improve and strengthen international commodity agreements and should be prepared to cooperate in the solution of specific commodity problems. Further more, they should endeavor to adopt adequate solutions for the short- and long-term problems affecting markets for such commodities so that the economic interests of producers and consumers are equally safeguarded.

7. Members countries should request other producer and consumer countries to cooperate in stabilization programs, bearing in mind that the raw materials of the Western Hemisphere are also produced and consumed in other parts of the world.

8. Member countries recognize that the disposal of accumulated reserves and surpluses can be a means of achieving the goals outlined in the first chapter of this Title, provided that, along with the generation of local resources, the consumption of essential products in the receiving countries is immediately increased. The disposal of surpluses and reserves should be carried out in an orderly manner, in order to:

a. Avoid disturbing existing commercial markets in member countries; and

b. Encourage expansion of the sale of their products to other markets.

However, it is recognized that:

a. The disposal of surpluses should not displace commercial sales of identical products traditionally carried out by other countries; and

b. Such disposal cannot substitute for large scale financial and technical assistance programs.

IN WITNESS WHEREOF this Charter is signed, in Punta del Este, Uruguay, on the seventeenth day of August, nineteen hundred sixty-one.

The original texts shall be deposited in the archives of the Pan American Union, through the Secretary General of the Special Meeting, in order that certified copies may be sent to the Governments of the Member States of the Organization of American States.

e. Panama Canal Treaties and Related Material

(1) Panama Canal: Permanent Neutrality and Operation [1]

Signed at Washington, with Attached Protocol, September 7, 1977; Ratification advised by the Senate, with amendments, conditions, reservations, and understandings, March 16, 1978; Ratified by the President, subject to such amendments, conditions, reservations, and understandings, June 15, 1978; Ratifications exchanged with Protocol signed at Panama, June 16, 1978, effective April 1, 1979; Proclaimed by the President, September 24, 1979; Entered into force, October 1, 1979

BY THE PRESIDENT OF THE UNITED STATES OF AMERICA

A PROCLAMATION

CONSIDERING THAT:

The Treaty Concerning the Permanent Neutrality and Operation of the Panama Canal was signed at Washington on September 7, 1977, the text of which is hereto annexed;

The Senate of the United States of America by its resolution of March 16, 1978, two-thirds of the Senators present concurring therein, gave its advice and consent to the ratification of the Neutrality Treaty, subject to the following—

(a) AMENDMENTS:

(1) At the end of Article IV, insert the following:

"A correct and authoritative statement of certain rights and duties of the Parties under the foregoing is contained in the Statement of Understanding issued by the Government of the United States of America on October 14, 1977, and by the Government of the Republic of Panama on October 18, 1977, which is hereby incorporated as an integral part of this Treaty, as follows:

"'Under the Treaty Concerning the Permanent Neutrality and Operation of the Panama Canal (the Neutrality Treaty), Panama and the United States have the responsibility to assure that the Panama Canal will remain open and secure to ships of all nations. The correct interpretation of this principle is that each of the two countries shall, in accordance with their respective constitutional processes, defend the Canal against any threat to the regime of neutrality, and consequently shall have the right to act against any aggression or threat directed against the Canal or against the peaceful transit of vessels through the Canal.

"'This does not mean, nor shall it be interpreted as, a right of intervention of the United States in the internal affairs of Panama. Any United States action will be directed at insuring that the Canal will remain open, secure, and accessible, and it

[1] 33 UST 1; TIAS 10029; 1161 UNTS 177.

shall never be directed against the territorial integrity or political independence of Panama.'."

(2) At the end of the first paragraph of Article VI, insert the following:

"In accordance with the Statement of Understanding mentioned in Article IV above: 'The Neutrality Treaty provides that the vessels of war and auxiliary vessels of the United States and Panama will be entitled to transit the Canal expeditiously. This is intended, and it shall so be interpreted, to assure the transit of vessels through the Canal as quickly as possible, without any impediment, with expedited treatment, and in case of need or emergency, to go to the head of the line of vessels in order to transmit the Canal rapidly.'."

(b) CONDITIONS:

(1) Notwithstanding the provisions of Article V or any other provision of the Treaty, if the Canal is closed, or its operations are interfered with, the United States of America and the Republic of Panama, shall each independently have the right to take such steps as each deems necessary, in accordance with its constitutional processes, including the use of military force in the Republic of Panama, to reopen the Canal or restore the operations of the Canal, as the case may be.

(2) The instruments of ratification of the Treaty shall be exchanged only upon the conclusion of a Protocol of Exchange, to be signed by authorized representatives of both Governments, which shall constitute an integral part of the Treaty documents and which shall include the following:

> "Nothing in the Treaty shall preclude the Republic of Panama and the United States of America from making, in accordance with their respective constitutional processes, any agreement or arrangement between the two countries to facilitate performance at any time after December 31, 1999, of their responsibilities to maintain the regime of neutrality established in the Treaty, including agreements or arrangements for the stationing of any United States military forces or the maintenance of defense sites after that date in the Republic of Panama that the Republic of Panama and the United States of America may deem necessary or appropriate.".

(c) RESERVATIONS:

(1) Before the date of entry into force of the Treaty, the two Parties shall begin to negotiate for an agreement under which the American Battle Monuments Commission would, upon the date of entry into force of such agreement and thereafter, administer, free of all taxes and other charges and without compensation to the Republic of Panama and in accordance with the practices, privileges, and immunities associated with the administration of cemeteries outside the United States of America by the American Battle Monuments Commission, including the display of the flag of the United States of America, such part of Corozal Cemetery in the former Canal Zone as encompasses the remains of citizens of the United States of America.

(2) The flag of the United States of America may be displayed, pursuant to the provisions of paragraph 3 of Article VII of the Panama Canal Treaty, at such part of Corozal Cemetery in the former Canal Zone as encompasses the remains of citizens of the United States of America.

(3) The President—

(A) shall have announced, before the date of entry into force of the Treaty, his intention to transfer, consistent with an agreement with the Republic of Panama, and before the date of termination of the Panama Canal Treaty, to the American Battle Monuments Commission the administration of such part of Corozal Cemetery as encompasses the remains of citizens of the United States of America; and

(B) shall have announced, immediately after the date of exchange of the instrument of ratification, plans, to be carried out at the expense of the Government of the United States of America, for—

(i) removing, before the date of entry into force of the Treaty, the remains of citizens of the United States of America from Mount Hope Cemetery to such part of Corozal Cemetery as encompasses such remains, except that the remains of any citizen whose next of kin objects in writing to the Secretary of the Army not later than three months after the date of exchange of the instruments of ratification of the Treaty shall not be removed; and

(ii) transporting to the United States of America for reinterment, if the next of kin so requests, not later than thirty months after the date of entry into force of the Treaty, any such remains encompassed by Corozal Cemetery and, before the date of entry into force of the Treaty, any remains removed from Mount Hope Cemetery pursuant to subclause (i); and

(C) shall have fully advised, before the date of entry into force of the Treaty, the next of kin objecting under clause (B)(i) of all available options and their implications.

(4) To carry out the purposes of Article III of the Treaty of assuring the security, efficiency, and proper maintenance of the Panama Canal, the United States of America and the Republic of Panama, during their respective periods of responsibility for Canal operation and maintenance, shall, unless the amount of the operating revenues of the Canal exceeds the amount needed to carry out the purposes of such Article, use such revenues of the Canal only for purposes consistent with the purposes of Article III.

(d) UNDERSTANDINGS:

(1) Paragraph 1(c) of Article III of the Treaty shall be construed as requiring, before any adjustment in tolls for use of the Canal, that the effects of any such toll adjustment on the trade patterns of the two Parties shall be given full consideration, including consideration of the following factors in a manner consistent with the regime of neutrality:

(A) the costs of operating and maintaining the Panama Canal;

(B) the competitive position of the use of the Canal in relation to other means of transportation;

(C) the interests of both Parties in maintaining their domestic fleets;

(D) the impact of such an adjustment on the various geographical areas of each of the two Parties; and

(E) the interests of both Parties in maximizing their international commerce.

The United States of America and the Republic of Panama shall cooperate in exchanging information necessary for the consideration of such factors.

(2) The agreement "to maintain the regime of neutrality established in this Treaty" in Article IV of the Treaty means that either of the two Parties to the Treaty may, in accordance with its constitutional processes, take unilateral action to defend the Panama Canal against any threat, as determined by the Party taking such action.

(3) The determination of "need or emergency" for the purpose of any vessel of war or auxiliary vessel of the United States of America or the Republic of Panama going to the head of the line of vessels in order to transit the Panama Canal rapidly shall be made by the nation operating such vessel.

(4) Nothing in the Treaty, in Annex A or B thereto, in the Protocol relating to the Treaty, or in any agreement relating to the Treaty, obligates the United States of America to provide any economic assistance, military grant assistance, security supporting assistance, foreign military sales credits, or international military education and training education and training to the Republic of Panama.

(5) The President shall include all amendments, conditions, reservations, and understandings incorporated by the Senate in this resolution of ratification in the instrument of ratification to be exchanged with the Government of the Republic of Panama.

Treaty Concerning the Permanent Neutrality and Operation of the Panama Canal[2]

The United States of America and the Republic of Panama have agreed upon the following:

Article I

The Republic of Panama declares that the Canal, as an international transit waterway, shall be permanently neutral in accordance with the regime established in this Treaty. The same regime of neutrality shall apply to any other international waterway that may be built either partially or wholly in the territory of the Republic of Panama.

Article II

The Republic of Panama declares the neutrality of the Canal in order that both in time of peace and in time of war it shall remain secure and open to peaceful transit by the vessels of all nations on terms of entire equality, so that there will be no discrimination against any nation, or its citizens or subjects, concerning the conditions or charges of transit, or for any other reason, and so that the Canal, and therefore the Isthmus of Panama, shall not be the target of reprisals in any armed conflict between other nations of the world. The foregoing shall be subject to the following requirements:

(a) Payment of tolls and other charges for transit and ancillary services, provided they have been fixed in conformity with the provisions of Article III(c);

(b) Compliance with applicable rules and regulations, provided such rules and regulations are applied in conformity with the provisions of Article III;

(c) The requirement that transiting vessels commit no acts of hostility while in the Canal; and

(d) Such other conditions and restrictions as are established by this Treaty.

Article III

1. For purposes of the security, efficiency and proper maintenance of the Canal the following rules shall apply:

(a) The Canal shall be operated efficiently in accordance with conditions of transit through the Canal, and rules and regulations that shall be just, equitable and reasonable, and limited to those necessary for safe navigation and efficient, sanitary operation of the Canal;

(b) Ancillary services necessary for transit through the Canal shall be provided;

(c) Tolls and other charges for transit and ancillary services shall be just, reasonable, equitable and consistent with the principles of international law;

(d) As a pre-condition of transit, vessels may be required to establish clearly the financial responsibility and guarantees for

[2] TIAS 10029.

payment of reasonable and adequate indemnification, consistent with international practice and standards, for damages resulting from acts or omissions of such vessels when passing through the Canal. In the case of vessels owned or operated by a State or for which it has acknowledged responsibility, a certification by that State that it shall observe its obligations under international law to pay for damages resulting from the act or omission of such vessels when passing through the Canal shall be deemed sufficient to establish such financial responsibility;

(e) Vessels of war and auxiliary vessels of all nations shall at all times be entitled to transit the Canal, irrespective of their internal operation, means of propulsion, origin, destination or armament, without being subjected as a condition of transit, to inspection, search or surveillance. However, such vessels may be required to certify that they have complied with all applicable health, sanitation and quarantine regulations. In addition, such vessels shall be entitled to refuse to disclose their internal operation, origin, armament, cargo or destination. However, auxiliary vessels may be required to present written assurances, certified by an official at a high level of the government of the State requesting the exemption, that they are owned or operated by that government and in this case are being used only on government non-commercial service.

2. For the purposes of this Treaty, the terms "Canal," "vessel of war," "auxiliary vessel," "internal operation," "armament" and "inspection" shall have the meanings assigned them in Annex A to this Treaty.

ARTICLE IV[3]

The United States of America and the Republic of Panama agree to maintain the regime of neutrality established in this Treaty, which shall be maintained in order that the Canal shall remain permanently neutral, notwithstanding the termination of any other treaties entered into by the two Contracting Parties.

ARTICLE V

After the termination of the Panama Canal Treaty, only the Republic of Panama shall operate the Canal and maintain military forces, defense sites and military installations within its national territory.

ARTICLE VI[3]

1. In recognition of the important contributions of the United States of America and of the Republic of Panama to the construction, operation, maintenance, and protection and defense of the Canal, vessels of war and auxiliary vessels of those nations shall, notwithstanding any other provisions of this Treaty, be entitled to transit the Canal irrespective of their internal operation, means of propulsion, origin, destination, armament or cargo carried. Such

---

[3] In its resolution of ratification to the Treaties the Senate included amendments to Article IV and Article VI.

vessels of war and auxiliary vessels will be entitled to transit the Canal expeditiously.

2. The United States of America, so long as it has responsibility for the operation of the Canal, may continue to provide the Republic of Columbia toll-free transit through the Canal for its troops, vessels, and materials of war. Thereafter, the Republic of Panama may provide the Republic of Columbia and the Republic of Costa Rica with the right of toll-free transit.

Article VII

1. The United States of America and the Republic of Panama shall jointly sponsor a resolution in the Organization of American States opening to accession by all nations of the world the Protocol to this Treaty whereby all the signatories will adhere to the objectives of this Treaty, agreeing to respect the regime of neutrality set forth herein.

2. The Organization of American States shall act as the depositary for this Treaty and related instruments.

Article VIII

This Treaty shall be subject to ratification in accordance with the constitutional procedures of the two Parties. The instruments of ratification of this Treaty shall be exchanged at Panama at the same time as the instruments of ratification of the Panama Canal Treaty, signed this date, are exchanged. This Treaty shall enter into force, simultaneously with the Panama Canal Treaty, six calendar months from the date of the exchange of the instruments of ratification.

[Translation]

Done at Washington, this 7th day of September, 1977, in the English and Spanish languages, both texts being equally authentic.

Annex A

1. "Canal" includes the existing Panama Canal, the entrances thereto and the territorial seas of the Republic of Panama adjacent thereto, as defined on the map annexed hereto (Annex B), and any other inter-oceanic waterway in which the United States of America is a participant or in which the United States of America has participated in connection with the construction or financing, that may be operated wholly or partially within the territory of the Republic of Panama, the entrances thereto and the territorial seas adjacent thereto.

2. "Vessel of war" means a ship belonging to the naval forces of a State, and bearing the external marks distinguishing warships of its nationality, under the command of an officer duly commissioned by the government and whose name appears in the Navy List, and manned by a crew which is under regular naval discipline.

3. "Auxiliary vessel" means any ship, not a vessel of war, that is owned or operated by a State and used, for the time being, exclusively on government non-commercial service.

4. "Internal operation" encompasses all machinery and propulsion systems, as well as the management and control of the vessel, including its crew. It does not include the measures necessary to transit vessels under the control of pilots while such vessels are in the Canal.

5. "Armament" means arms, ammunitions, implements of war and other equipment of a vessel which possess characteristics appropriate for use for warlike purposes.

6. "Inspection" includes on-board examination of vessel structure, cargo, armament and internal operation. It does not include those measures strictly necessary for admeasurement, nor those measures strictly necessary to assure safe, sanitary transit and navigation, including examination of deck and visual navigation equipment, nor in the case of live cargoes, such as cattle or other livestock that may carry communicable diseases, those measures necessary to assure that health and sanitation requirements are satisfied.

[MAPPING GRAPHICS]

* * * * * * *

[TRANSLATION]

Protocol to the Treaty Concerning the Permanent Neutrality and Operation of the Panama Canal

WHEREAS the maintenance of the neutrality of the Panama Canal is important not only to the commerce and security of the United States of America and the Republic of Panama, but to the peace and security of the Western Hemisphere and to the interests of world commerce as well;

WHEREAS the regime of neutrality which the United States of America and the Republic of Panama have agreed to maintain will ensure permanent access to the Canal by vessels of all nations on the basis of entire equality; and

WHEREAS the said regime of effective neutrality shall constitute the best protection for the Canal and shall ensure the absence of any hostile act against it;

The Contracting Parties to this Protocol have agreed upon the following:

ARTICLE I

The Contracting Parties hereby acknowledge the regime of permanent neutrality for the Canal established in the Treaty Concerning the Permanent Neutrality and Operation of the Panama Canal and associate themselves with its objectives.

ARTICLE II

The Contracting Parties agree to observe and respect the regime of permanent neutrality of the Canal in time of war as in time of peace, and to ensure that vessels of their registry strictly observe the applicable rules.

ARTICLE III

This Protocol shall be open to accession by all States of the world, and shall enter into force for each State at the time of deposit of its instrument of accession with the Secretary General of the Organization of American States.

[TRANSLATION]

Protocol of Exchange of Instruments of Ratification Regarding the Treaty Concerning the Permanent Neutrality and Operation of the Panama Canal and the Panama Canal Treaty

The undersigned, Jimmy Carter, President of the United States of America, and Omar Torrijos Herrera, Head of Government of the Republic of Panama, in the exercise of their respective constitutional authorities, have met for the purpose of delivering to each other the instrument of ratification of their respective government of the Treaty Concerning the Permanent Neutrality and Operation of the Panama Canal and of the Panama Canal Treaty (the "Treaties").

The respective instruments of ratification of the Treaties have been carefully compared and found to be in due form. Delivery of the respective instruments took place this day, it being understood and agreed by the United Sates of America and the Republic of Panama that, unless the Parties otherwise agree through an exchange of Notes in conformity with the resolution of the Senate of the United Sates of America of April 18, 1978, the exchange of the instruments of ratification shall be effective on April 1, 1979, and the date of the exchange of the instruments of ratification for the purposes of Article VIII of the Treaty Concerning the Permanent Neutrality and Operation of the Panama Canal and Article II of the Panama Canal Treaty shall therefore be April 1, 1979.

The ratifications by the Government of the United Sates of America of the Treaties recite in their entirety the amendments, conditions, reservations and understandings contained in the resolution of March 16, 1978, of the Senate of the United States of America advising and consenting to ratification of the Panama Canal Treaty

Said amendments, conditions, reservations and understandings have been communicated by the Government of the United Sates of America to the Government of the Republic of Panama. Both governments agree that the Treaties, upon entry into force in accordance with their provisions, will be applied in accordance with the above-mentioned amendments, conditions, reservations and understandings.

Pursuant to the resolution of the Senate of the United States of America of March 16, 1978, the following text contained in the instrument of ratification of the United States of America of the Treaty Concerning the Permanent Neutrality and Operation of the

Panama Canal and agreed upon by both governments is repeated herewith:

"Nothing in the Treaty shall preclude the Republic of Panama and the United States of America from making, in accordance with their respective constitutional processes, any agreement or arrangement between the two countries to facilitate performance at any time after December 31, 1999, of their responsibilities to maintain the regime of neutrality established in the Treaty, including agreements or arrangements for the stationing of any United States military forces or the maintenance of defense sites after that date in the Republic of Panama that the Republic of Panama and the United States of America may deem necessary or appropriate.".

The Republic of Panama agrees to the exchange of the instruments of ratification of the Panama Canal Treaty and of the Treaty Concerning the Permanent Neutrality and Operation of the Panama Canal on the understanding that there are positive rules of public international law contained in multilateral treaties to which both the Republic of Panama and the United States of America are Parties and which consequently both States are bound to implement in good faith, such as Article 1, paragraph 2 and Article 2, paragraph 4 of the Charter of the United Nations, and Articles 18 and 20 of the Charter of the Organization of American States.

It is also the understanding of the Republic of Panama that the actions which either Party may take in the exercise of its rights and the fulfillment of its duties in accordance with the aforesaid Panama Canal Treaty and the Treaty Concerning the Permanent Neutrality and Operation of the Panama Canal, including measures to reopen the Canal or to restore its normal operation, if it should be interrupted or obstructed, will be effected in a manner consistent with the principles of mutual respect and cooperation on which the new relationship established by those Treaties is based.

IN WITNESS THEREOF, the respective Plenipotentiaries have signed this Protocol of Exchange at Panama, in duplicate, in the English and Spanish languages on this sixteenth day of June, 1978, both texts being equally authentic.

(2) Panama Canal Treaty [1]

Signed at Washington, September 7, 1977; Ratification advised by the Senate, subject to Reservations and Understandings, April 18, 1978; Ratifications exchanged, June 16, 1978, effective April 1, 1979; Entered into force, October 1, 1979

BY THE PRESIDENT OF THE UNITED STATES OF AMERICA

A PROCLAMATION

CONSIDERING THAT:

The Treaty Concerning the Permanent Neutrality and Operation of the Panama Canal was signed at Washington on September 7, 1977, the text of which is hereto annexed;

The Senate of the United States of America by its resolution of April 18, 1978, two-thirds of the Senators present concurring therein, gave its advice and consent to the ratification of the Treaty, subject to the following—

(a) RESERVATIONS:

(1) Pursuant to its adherence to the principle of nonintervention, any action taken by the United States of America in the exercise of its rights to assure that the Panama Canal shall remain open, neutral, secure, and accessible, pursuant to the provisions of the Panama Canal Treaty, the Treaty Concerning the Permanent Neutrality and Operation of the Panama Canal, and the resolutions of ratification thereto, shall be only for the purpose of assuring that the Canal shall remain open, neutral, secure, and accessible, and shall not have as its purpose or be interpreted as a right of intervention in the internal affairs of the Republic of Panama or interference with its political independence or sovereign integrity.

(2) The instruments of ratification of the Panama Canal Treaty to be exchanged by the United States of America and the Republic of Panama shall each include provisions whereby each party agrees to waive its right and release the other Party from its obligations under paragraph 2 of Article XII of the Treaty.

(3) Notwithstanding any provision of the Treaty, no funds may be drawn from the Treasury of the United States of America for payment under paragraph 4 of Article XIII without statutory authorization.

(4) Any accumulated unpaid balance under paragraph 4(c) of Article XIII of the Treaty at the date of termination of the Treaty shall be payable only to the extent of any operating surplus in the last year of the duration of the Treaty, and nothing

[1] TIAS 10030. The Panama Canal Treaty terminated on December 31, 1999. The Panama Canal Act of 1979 (Public Law 96–70), which provided implementing legislation for this Treaty, can be found in *Legislation on Foreign Relations*, vol. II–B, sec. G.

in such paragraph may be construed as obligating the United States of America to pay, after the date of the termination of the Treaty, any such unpaid balance which shall have accrued before such date.

(5) Exchange of the instruments of ratification of the Panama Canal Treaty and the Treaty Concerning the Permanent Neutrality and Operation of the Panama Canal shall not be effective earlier than March 31, 1979, and such Treaties shall not enter into force prior to October 1, 1979, unless legislation necessary to implement the provisions of the Panama Canal Treaty shall have been enacted by the Congress of the United States of America before March 31, 1979.

(6) After the date of entry into force of the Treaty, the Panama Canal Commission shall, unless otherwise provided by legislation enacted by the Congress of the United States of America, be obligated to reimburse the Treasury of the United States of America, as nearly as possible, for the interest costs of the funds or other assets directly invested in the Commission by the Government of the United States of America and for the interest cost of the funds or other assets directly invested in the predecessor Panama Canal Company by the Government of the United States of America and not reimbursed before the date of entry into force of the Treaty. Such reimbursement for such interest costs shall be made at a rate determined by the Secretary of the Treasury of the United States of America and at annual intervals to the extent earned, and if not earned, shall be made from subsequent earnings. For purposes of this reservation, the phrase "funds or other assets directly invested" shall have the same meaning as the phrase "net direct investment" has under section 62 of title 2 of the Canal Zone Code.

(b) UNDERSTANDINGS:

(1) Before the first day of the three-year period beginning on the date of entry into force of the Treaty and before each three-year period following thereafter, the two Parties shall agree upon specific levels and quality of services, as are referred to in paragraph 5 of Article III of the Treaty, to be provided during the following three-year period and, except for the first three-year period, on the reimbursement to be made for the costs of such services, such services to be limited to such as are essential to the effective functioning of the Canal operating areas and the housing areas referred to in paragraph 5 of Article III. If payments made under paragraph 5 of Article III for the preceding three-year period, including the initial three-year period, exceed or are less than the actual costs to the Republic of Panama for supplying, during such period, the specific levels and quality of services agreed upon, then the Panama Canal Commission shall deduct from or add to the payment required to be made to the Republic of Panama for each of the following three years one-third of such excess or deficit, as the case may be. There shall be an independent and binding audit, conducted by an auditor mutually selected by both Parties, of any costs of services disputed by the two Parties pursuant to the reexamination of such costs provided for in this understanding.

(2) Nothing in paragraph 3, 4, or 5 of Article IV of the Treaty may be construed to limit either the provisions of the first paragraph of Article IV providing that each Party shall act, in accordance with its constitutional processes, to meet danger threatening the security of the Panama Canal, or the provisions of paragraph 2 of Article IV providing that the United States of America shall have primary responsibility to protect and defend the Canal for the duration of the Treaty.

(3) Nothing in paragraph 4(c) of Article XIII of the Treaty shall be construed to limit the authority of the United States of America, through the United States Government agency called the Panama Canal Commission, to make such financial decisions and incur such expenses as are reasonable and necessary for the management, operation, and maintenance of the Panama Canal. In addition, toll rates established pursuant to paragraph 2(d) of Article III need not be set at levels designed to produce revenues to cover the payment to the Republic of Panama described in paragraph 4(c) of Article III.

(4) Any agreement concluded pursuant to paragraph 11 of Article IX of the Treaty with respect to the transfer of prisoners shall be concluded in accordance with the constitutional processes of both Parties.

(5) Nothing in the Treaty, in the Annex or Agreed Minute relating to the Treaty, or in any other agreement relating to the Treaty obligates the United States of America to provide any economic assistance, military grant assistance, security supporting assistance, foreign military sales credits, or international military education and training to the Republic of Panama.

(6) The President shall include all reservations and understandings incorporated by the Senate in this resolution of ratification in the instrument of ratification to be exchanged with the Government of the Republic of Panama.

Panama Canal Treaty

The United States of America and the Republic of Panama,

Acting in the spirit of the Joint Declaration of April 3, 1964, by the Representatives of the Governments of the United States of America and the Republic of Panama, and of the Joint Statement of Principles of February 7, 1974, initialed by the Secretary of State of the United States of America and the Foreign Minister of the Republic of Panama, and

Acknowledging the Republic of Panama's sovereignty over its territory,

Have decided to terminate the prior Treaties pertaining to the Panama Canal and to conclude a new Treaty to serve as the basis for a new relationship between them and, accordingly, have agreed upon the following:

Article I—Abrogation of Prior Treaties and Establishment of a New Relationship

1. Upon its entry into force, this Treaty terminates and supersedes:

(a) The Isthmian Canal Convention between the United States of America and the Republic of Panama, signed at Washington, November 18, 1903;

(b) The Treaty of Friendship and Cooperation, signed at Washington, March 2, 1936, and the Treaty of Mutual Understanding and Cooperation and the related Memorandum of Understandings Reached, signed at Panama, January 25, 1955, between the United States of America and the Republic of Panama;

(c) All other treaties, conventions, agreements and exchanges of notes between the United States of America and the Republic of Panama concerning the Panama Canal which were in force prior to the entry into force of this Treaty; and

(d) Provisions concerning the Panama Canal which appear in other treaties, conventions, agreements and exchanges of notes between the United States of America and the Republic of Panama which were in force prior to the entry into force of this Treaty.

2. In accordance with the terms of this Treaty and related agreements, the Republic of Panama, as territorial sovereign, grants to the United States of America, for the duration of this Treaty, the rights necessary to regulate the transit of ships through the Panama Canal, and to manage, operate, maintain, improve, protect and defend the Canal. The Republic of Panama guarantees to the United States of America the peaceful use of the land and water areas which it has been granted the rights to use for such purposes pursuant to this Treaty and related agreements.

3. The Republic of Panama shall participate increasingly in the management and protection and defense of the Canal, as provided in this Treaty.

4. In view of the special relationship established by this Treaty, the United States of America and the Republic of Panama shall cooperate to assure the uninterrupted and efficient operation of the Panama Canal.

ARTICLE II—RATIFICATION, ENTRY INTO FORCE, AND TERMINATION

1. This Treaty shall be subject to ratification in accordance with the constitutional procedures of the two Parties. The instruments of ratification of this Treaty shall be exchanged at Panama at the same time as the instruments of ratification of the Treaty Concerning the Permanent Neutrality and Operation of the Panama Canal, signed this date, are exchanged. This Treaty shall enter into force, simultaneously with the Treaty Concerning the Permanent Neutrality and Operation of the Panama Canal, six calendar months from the date of the exchange of the instruments of ratification.

2. This Treaty shall terminate at noon, Panama time, December 31, 1999.

ARTICLE III—CANAL OPERATION AND MANAGEMENT

1. The Republic of Panama, as territorial sovereign, grants to the United States of America the rights to manage, operate, and maintain the Panama Canal, its complementary works, installations and equipment and to provide for the orderly transit of vessels through the Panama Canal. The United States of America accepts the grant of such rights and undertakes to exercise them in accordance with this Treaty and related agreements.

2. In carrying out the foregoing responsibilities, the United States of America may:

(a) Use for the aforementioned purposes, without cost except as provided in this Treaty, the various installations and areas (including the Panama Canal) and waters, described in the Agreement in Implementation of this Article, signed this date, as well as such other areas and installations as are made available to the United States of America under this Treaty and related agreements, and take the measures necessary to ensure sanitation of such areas;

(b) Make such improvements and alterations to the aforesaid installations and areas as it deems appropriate, consistent with the terms of this Treaty;

(c) Make and enforce all rules pertaining to the passage of vessels through the Canal and other rules with respect to navigation and maritime matters, in accordance with the Treaty and related agreements. The Republic of Panama will lend its cooperation, when necessary, in the enforcement of such rules;

(d) Establish, modify, collect and retain tolls for the use of the Panama Canal, and other charges, and establish and modify methods of their assessment;

(e) Regulate relations with employees of the United States Government;

(f) Provide supporting services to facilitate the performance of its responsibilities under this Article;

(g) Issue and enforce regulations for the effective exercise of the rights and responsibilities of the United States of America under this Treaty and related agreements. The Republic of Panama will lend its cooperation, when necessary, in the enforcement of such rules; and

(h) Exercise any other right granted under this Treaty, or otherwise agreed upon between the two Parties.

3. Pursuant to the foregoing grant of rights, the United States of America shall, in accordance with the terms of this Treaty and the provisions of United States law, carry out its responsibilities by means of a United States Government agency called the Panama Canal Commission, which shall be constituted by and in conformity with the laws of the United States of America.

(a) The Panama Canal Commission shall be supervised by a Board composed of nine members, five of whom shall be nationals of the United States of America, and four of whom shall be Panamanian nationals proposed by the Republic of Panama for appointment to such positions by the United States of America in a timely manner.

(b) Should the Republic of Panama request the United States of America to remove a Panamanian national from membership on the Board, the United States of America shall agree to such request. In that event, the Republic of Panama shall propose another Panamanian national for appointment by the United States of America to such position in a timely manner. In case of removal of a Panamanian member of the Board at the initiative of the United States of America, both Parties will consult in advance in order to reach agreement concerning such removal, and the Republic of Panama shall propose another Panamanian national for appointment by the United States of America in his stead.

(c) The United States of America shall employ a national of the United States of America as Administrator of the Panama Canal Commission, and a Panamanian national as Deputy Administrator, through December 31, 1989. Beginning January 1, 1990, a Panamanian national shall be employed as the Administrator and a national of the United States of America shall occupy the position of Deputy Administrator. Such Panamanian nationals shall be proposed to the United States of America by the Republic of Panama for appointment to such positions by the United States of America.

(d) Should the United States of America remove the Panamanian national from his position as Deputy Administrator, or Administrator, the Republic of Panama shall propose another Panamanian national for appointment to such position by the United States of America.

4. An illustrative description of the activities the Panama Canal Commission will perform in carrying out the responsibilities and rights of the United States of America under this Article is set forth at the Annex. Also set forth in the Annex are procedures for the discontinuance or transfer of those activities performed prior to the entry into force of this Treaty by the Panama Canal Company or the Canal Zone Government which are not to be carried out by the Panama Canal Commission.

5. The Panama Canal Commission shall reimburse the Republic of Panama for the costs incurred by the Republic of Panama in providing the following public services in the Canal operating areas and in housing areas set forth in the Agreement in Implementation of Article III of this Treaty and occupied by both United States and Panamanian citizen employees of the Panama Canal Commission: police, fire protection, street maintenance, street lighting, street cleaning, traffic management and garbage collection. The Panama Canal Commission shall pay the Republic of Panama the sum of ten million United States dollars ($10,000,000) per annum for the foregoing services. It is agreed that every three years from the date that this Treaty enters into force, the costs involved in furnishing said services shall be reexamined to determine whether adjustment of the annual payment should be made because of inflation and other relevant factors affecting the cost of such services.

6. The Republic of Panama shall be responsible for providing, in all areas comprising the former Canal Zone, services of a general jurisdictional nature such as customs and immigration, postal services, courts and licensing, in accordance with this Treaty and related agreements.

7. The United States of America and the Republic of Panama shall establish a Panama Canal Consultative Committee, composed of an equal number of high-level representatives of the United States of America and the Republic of Panama, and which may appoint such subcommittees as it may deem appropriate. This Committee shall advise the United States of America and the Republic of Panama on matters of policy affecting the Canal's operation. In view of both Parties' special interest in the continuity and efficiency of the Canal operation in the future, the Committee shall advise on matters such as general tolls policy, employment and training policies to increase the participation of Panamanian nationals in the operation of the Canal, and international policies on matters concerning the Canal. The Committee's recommendation shall be transmitted to the two Governments, which shall give such recommendations full consideration in the formulation of such policy decisions.

8. In addition to the participation of Panamanian nationals at high management levels of the Panama Canal Commission, as provided for in paragraph 3 of this Article, there shall be growing participation of Panamanian nationals at all other levels and areas of employment in the aforesaid commission, with the objective of preparing, in an orderly and efficient fashion, for the assumption by the Republic of Panama of full responsibility for the management, operation and maintenance of the Canal upon the termination of this Treaty.

9. The use of the areas, waters and installations with respect to which the United States of America is granted rights pursuant to this Article, and the rights and legal status of United States Government agencies and employees operating in the Republic of Panama pursuant to this Article, shall be governed by the Agreement in Implementation of this Article, signed this date.

10. Upon entry into force of this Treaty, the United States Government agencies known as the Panama Canal Company and the Canal Zone Government shall cease to operate within the territory

of the Republic of Panama that formerly constituted the Canal Zone.

ARTICLE IV—PROTECTION AND DEFENSE

1. The United States of America and the Republic of Panama commit themselves to protect and defend the Panama Canal. Each Party shall act, in accordance with its constitutional processes, to meet the danger resulting from an armed attack or other actions which threaten the security of the Panama Canal or of ships transiting it.

2. For the duration of this Treaty, the United States of America shall have primary responsibility to protect and defend the Canal. The rights of the United States of America to station, train, and move military forces within the Republic of Panama are described in the Agreement in Implementation of this Article, signed this date. The use of areas and installations and the legal status of the armed forces of the United States of America in the Republic of Panama shall be governed by the aforesaid Agreement.

3. In order to facilitate the participation and cooperation of the armed forces of both Parties in the protection and defense of the Canal, the United States of America and the Republic of Panama shall establish a Combined Board comprised of an equal number of senior military representatives of each party. These representatives shall be charged by their respective governments with consulting and cooperating on all matters pertaining to the protection and defense of the Canal, and with planning for actions to be taken in concert for that purpose. Such combined protection and defense arrangements shall not inhibit the identity or lines of authority of the armed forces of the United States of America or the Republic of Panama. The Combined Board shall provide for coordination and cooperation concerning such matters as:

(a) The preparation of contingency plans for the protection and defense of the Canal based upon the cooperative efforts of the armed forces of both Parties;

(b) The planning and conduct of combined military exercises; and

(c) The conduct of United States and Panamanian military operations with respect to the protection and defense of the Canal.

4. The Combined Board shall, at five-year intervals throughout the duration of this Treaty, review the resources being made available by the two Parties for the protection and defense of the Canal. Also, the Combined Board shall make appropriate recommendations to the two Governments respecting projected requirements, the efficient utilization of available resources of the two Parties, and other matters of mutual interest with respect to the protection and defense of the Canal.

5. To the extent possible consistent with its primary responsibility for the protection and defense of the Panama Canal, the United States of America will endeavor to maintain its armed forces in the Republic of Panama in normal times at a level not in excess of that of the armed forces of the United States of America

in the territory of the former Canal Zone immediately prior to the entry into force of this Treaty.

ARTICLE V—PRINCIPLE OF NON-INTERVENTION

Employees of the Panama Canal Commission, their dependents and designated contractors of the Panama Canal Commission, who are nationals of the United States of America, shall respect the laws of the Republic of Panama and shall abstain from any activity incompatible with the spirit of this Treaty. Accordingly, they shall abstain from any political activity in the Republic of Panama as well as from any intervention in the internal affairs of the Republic of Panama. The United States of America shall take all measures within its authority to ensure that the provisions of this Article are fulfilled.

ARTICLE VI—PROTECTION OF THE ENVIRONMENT

1. The United States of America and the Republic of Panama commit themselves to implement this Treaty in a manner consistent with the protection of the natural environment of the Republic of Panama. To this end, they shall consult and cooperate with each other in all appropriate ways to ensure that they shall give due regard to the protection and conservation of the environment.

2. A Joint Commission on the Environment shall be established with equal representation from the United States of America and the Republic of Panama, which shall periodically review the implementation of this Treaty and shall recommend as appropriate to the two Governments ways to avoid or, should this not be possible, to mitigate the adverse environmental impacts which result from their respective actions pursuant to the Treaty.

3. The United States of America and the Republic of Panama shall furnish the Joint Commission on the Environment complete information on any action taken in accordance with this Treaty which, in the judgment of both, might have a significant effect on the environment. Such information shall be made available to the Commission as far in advance of the contemplated action as possible to facilitate the study by the Commission of any potential environmental problems and to allow for consideration of the recommendation of the Commission before the contemplated action is carried out.

ARTICLE VII—FLAGS

1. The entire territory of the Republic of Panama, including the areas the use of which the Republic of Panama makes available to the United States of America pursuant to this Treaty and related agreements, shall be under the flag of the Republic of Panama, and consequently such flag always shall occupy the position of honor.

2. The flag of the United States of America may be displayed, together with the flag of the Republic of Panama, at the headquarters of the Panama Canal Commission, at the site of the Combined Board and as provided in the Agreement in Implementation of Article IV of this Treaty.

3. The flag of the United States of America also may be displayed at other places and on some occasions, as agreed by both Parties.

Article VIII—Privileges and Immunities

1. The installations owned or used by the agencies or instrumentalities of the United States of America operating in the Republic of Panama pursuant to this Treaty and related agreements, and their official archives and documents, shall be inviolable. The two Parties shall agree on procedures to be followed in the conduct of any criminal investigation at such locations by the Republic of Panama.

2. Agencies and instrumentalities of the Government of the United States of America operating in the Republic of Panama pursuant to this Treaty and related agreements shall be immune from the jurisdiction of the Republic of Panama.

3. In addition to such other privileges and immunities as are afforded to employees of the United States Government and their dependents pursuant to this Treaty, the United States of America may designate up to twenty officials of the Panama Canal Commission who, along with their dependents, shall enjoy the privileges and immunities accorded to diplomatic agents and their dependents under international law and practice. The United States of America shall furnish to the Republic of Panama a list of the names of said officials and their dependents, identifying the positions they occupy in the Government of the United States of America, and shall keep such list current at all times.

Article IX—Applicable Laws and Law Enforcement

1. In accordance with the provisions of this Treaty and related agreements, the law of the Republic of Panama shall apply in the areas made available for the use of the United States of America pursuant to this Treaty. The law of the Republic of Panama shall be applied to matters or events which occurred in the former Canal Zone prior to the entry into force of this Treaty only to the extent specifically provided in prior treaties and agreements.

2. Natural or juridical persons who, on the date of entry into force of this Treaty, are engaged in business or non-profit activities at locations in the former Canal Zone may continue such business or activities at those locations under the same terms and conditions prevailing prior to the entry into force of this Treaty for a thirty-month transition period from its entry into force. The Republic of Panama shall maintain the same operating conditions as those applicable to the aforementioned enterprises prior to the entry into force of this Treaty in order that they may receive licenses to do business in the Republic of Panama subject to their compliance with the requirements of its law. Thereafter, such persons shall receive the same treatment under the law of the Republic of Panama as similar enterprises already established in the rest of the territory of the Republic of Panama without discrimination.

3. The rights of ownership, as recognized by the United States of America, enjoyed by natural or juridical private persons in buildings and other improvements to real property located in the former

Canal Zone shall be recognized by the Republic of Panama in conformity with its laws.

4. With respect to buildings and other improvements to real property located in the Canal operating areas, housing areas or other areas subject to the licensing procedure established in Article IV of the Agreement in Implementation of Article III of this Treaty, the owners shall be authorized to continue using the land upon which their property is located in accordance with the procedures established in that Article.

5. With respect to buildings and other improvements to real property located in areas of the former Canal Zone to which the aforesaid licensing procedure is not applicable, or may cease to be applicable during the lifetime or upon termination of this Treaty, the owners may continue to use the land upon which their property is located, subject to the payment of a reasonable charge to the Republic of Panama. Should the Republic of Panama decide to sell such land, the owners of the buildings or other improvements located thereon shall be offered a first option to purchase such land at a reasonable cost. In the case of non-profit enterprises, such as churches and fraternal organizations, the cost of purchase will be nominal in accordance with the prevailing practice in the rest of the territory of the Republic of Panama.

6. If any of the aforementioned persons are required by the Republic of Panama to discontinue their activities or vacate their property for public purposes, they shall be compensated at fair market value by the Republic of Panama.

7. The provisions of paragraphs 26 above shall apply to natural or juridical persons who have been engaged in business or non-profit activities at locations in the former Canal Zone for at least six months prior to the date of signature of this Treaty.

8. The Republic of Panama shall not issue, adopt or enforce any law, decree, regulation, or international agreement or take any other action which purports to regulate or would otherwise interfere with the exercise on the part of the United States of America of any right granted under this Treaty or related agreements.

9. Vessels transiting the Canal, and cargo, passengers and crews carried on such vessels shall be exempt from any taxes, fees, or other charges by the Republic of Panama. However, in the event such vessels call at a Panamanian port, they may be assessed charges incident thereto, such as charges for services provided to the vessel. The Republic of Panama may also require the passengers and crew disembarking from such vessels to pay such taxes, fees and charges as are established under Panamanian law for persons entering its territory. Such taxes, fees and charges shall be assessed on a nondiscriminatory basis.

10. The United States of America and the Republic of Panama will cooperate in taking such steps as may from time to time be necessary to guarantee the security of the Panama Canal Commission, its property, its employees and their dependents, and their property, the Forces of the United States of America and the members thereof, the civilian component of the United States Forces, the dependents of members of the Forces and the civilian components, and their property, and the contractors of the Panama Canal Commission and of the United States Forces, their dependents, and

their property. The Republic of Panama will seek from its Legislative Branch such legislation as may be needed to carry out the foregoing purposes and to punish any offenders.

11. The Parties shall conclude an agreement whereby nationals of either State, who are sentenced by the courts of the other State, and who are not domiciled therein, may elect to serve their sentences in their State of nationality.

ARTICLE X—EMPLOYMENT WITH THE PANAMA CANAL COMMISSION

1. In exercising its rights and fulfilling its responsibilities as the employer, the United States of America shall establish employment and labor regulations which shall contain the terms, conditions and prerequisites for all categories of employees of the Panama Canal Commission. These regulations shall be provided to the Republic of Panama prior to their entry into force.

2. (a) The regulations shall establish a system of preference when hiring employees, for Panamanian applicants possessing the skills and qualifications required for employment by the Panama Canal Commission. The United States of America shall endeavor to ensure that the number of its employees will conform to the proportion established for foreign enterprises under the law of the Republic of Panama.

(b) The terms and conditions of employment to be established will in general be no less favorable to persons already employed by the Panama Canal Company or Canal Zone Government prior to the entry into force of this Treaty, than those in effect immediately prior to that date.

3. (a) The United States of America shall establish an employment policy for the Panama Canal Commission that shall generally limit the recruitment of personnel outside of the Republic of Panama to persons possessing requisite skills and qualifications which are not available in the Republic of Panama.

(b) The United States of America will establish training programs for Panamanian employees and apprentices in order to increase the number of Panamanian nationals qualified to assume positions with the Panama Canal Commission, as positions become available.

(c) Within five years from the entry into force of this Treaty, the number of United States nationals employed by the Panama Canal Commission who were previously employed by the Panama Canal Company shall be at least twenty percent less than the total number of United States nationals working for the Panama Canal Company immediately prior to the entry into force of this Treaty.

(d) The United States of America shall periodically inform the Republic of Panama, through the Coordinating Committee, established pursuant to the Agreement in Implementation of Article III of this Treaty, of available positions within the Panama Canal Commission. The Republic of Panama shall similarly provide the United States of America any information it may have as to the availability of Panamanian nationals claiming to have skills and qualifications that might be required by the Panama Canal Commission, in order that the United States of America may take this information into account.

4. The United States of America will establish qualification standards for skills, training and experience required by the Panama Canal Commission. In establishing such standards, to the extent they include a requirement for a professional license, the United States of America, without prejudice to its right to require additional professional skills and qualifications, shall recognize the professional licenses issued by the Republic of Panama.

5. The United States of America shall establish a policy for the periodic rotation, at a maximum of every five years, of United States citizen employees and other non-Panamanian employees, hired after the entry into force of this Treaty. It is recognized that certain exceptions to the said policy of rotation may be made for sound administrative reasons, such as in the case of employees holding positions requiring certain non-transferable or nonrecruitable skills.

6. With regard to wages and fringe benefits, there shall be no discrimination on the basis of nationality, sex, or race. Payments by the Panama Canal Commission of additional remuneration, or the provision of other benefits, such as home leave benefits, to United States nationals employed prior to entry into force of this Treaty, or to persons of any nationality, including Panamanian nationals who are thereafter recruited outside of the Republic of Panama and who change their place of residence, shall not be considered to be discrimination for the purpose of this paragraph.

7. Persons employed by the Panama Canal Company or Canal Zone Government prior to the entry into force of this Treaty, who are displaced from their employment as a result of the discontinuance by the United States of America of certain activities pursuant to this Treaty, will be placed by the United States of America, to the maximum extent feasible, in other appropriate jobs with the Government of the United States in accordance with United States Civil Service regulations. For such persons who are not United States nationals, placement efforts will be confined to United States Government activities located within the Republic of Panama. Likewise, persons previously employed in activities for which the Republic of Panama assumes responsibility as a result of this Treaty will be continued in their employment to the maximum extent feasible by the Republic of Panama. The Republic of Panama shall, to the maximum extent feasible, ensure that the terms and conditions of employment applicable to personnel employed in the activities for which it assumes responsibility are no less favorable than those in effect immediately prior to the entry into force of this Treaty. Non-United States nationals employed by the Panama Canal Company or Canal Zone Government prior to the entry into force of this Treaty who are involuntarily separated from their positions because of the discontinuance of an activity by reason of this Treaty, who are not entitled to an immediate annuity under the United States Civil Service Retirement System, and for whom continued employment in the Republic of Panama by the Government of the United States of America is not practicable, will be provided special job placement assistance by the Republic of Panama for employment in positions for which they may be qualified by experience and training.

8. The Parties agree to establish a system whereby the Panama Canal Commission may, if deemed mutually convenient or desirable by the two Parties, assign certain employees of the Panama Canal Commission, for a limited period of time, to assist in the operation of activities transferred to the responsibility of the Republic of Panama as a result of this Treaty or related agreements. The salaries and other costs of employment of any such persons assigned to provide such assistance shall be reimbursed to the United States of America by the Republic of Panama.

9. (a) The right of employees to negotiate collective contracts with the Panama Canal Commission is recognized. Labor relations with employees of the Panama Canal Commission shall be conducted in accordance with forms of collective bargaining established by the United States of America after consultation with employee unions.

(b) Employee unions shall have the right to affiliate with international labor organizations.

10. The United States of America will provide an appropriate early optional retirement program for all persons employed by the Panama Canal Company or Canal Zone Government immediately prior to the entry into force of this Treaty. In this regard, taking into account the unique circumstances created by the provisions of this Treaty, including its duration, and their effect upon such employees, the United States of America shall, with respect to them:

(a) determine that conditions exist which invoke applicable United States law permitting early retirement annuities and apply such law for a substantial period of the duration of the Treaty;

(b) seek special legislation to provide more liberal entitlement to, and calculation of, retirement annuities than is currently provided for by law.

ARTICLE XI—PROVISIONS FOR THE TRANSITION PERIOD

1. The Republic of Panama shall reassume plenary jurisdiction over the former Canal Zone upon entry into force of this Treaty and in accordance with its terms. In order to provide for an orderly transition to the full application of the jurisdictional arrangements established by this Treaty and related agreements, the provisions of this Article shall become applicable upon the date this Treaty enters into force, and shall remain in effect for thirty calendar months. The authority granted in this Article to the United States of America for this transition period shall supplement, and is not intended to limit, the full application and effect of the rights and authority granted to the United States of America elsewhere in this Treaty and in related agreements.

2. During this transition period, the criminal and civil laws of the United States of America shall apply concurrently with those of the Republic of Panama in certain of the areas and installations made available for the use of the United States of America pursuant to this Treaty, in accordance with the following provisions:

(a) The Republic of Panama permits the authorities of the United States of America to have the primary right to exercise criminal jurisdiction over United States citizen employees of the Panama Canal Commission and their dependents, and members of the United States Forces and civilian component and their dependents, in the following cases:

(i) for any offense committed during the transition period within such areas and installations, and

(ii) for any offense committed prior to that period in the former Canal Zone.

The Republic of Panama shall have the primary right to exercise jurisdiction over all other offenses committed by such persons, except as otherwise provided in this Treaty and related agreements or as may be otherwise agreed.

(b) Either Party may waive its primary right to exercise jurisdiction in a specific case or category of cases.

3. The United States of America shall retain the right to exercise jurisdiction in criminal cases relating to offenses committed prior to the entry into force of this Treaty in violation of the laws applicable in the former Canal Zone.

4. For the transition period, the United States of America shall retain police authority and maintain a police force in the aforementioned areas and installations. In such areas, the police authorities of the United States of America may take into custody any person not subject to their primary jurisdiction if such person is believed to have committed or to be committing an offense against applicable laws or regulations, and shall promptly transfer custody to the police authorities of the Republic of Panama. The United States of America and the Republic of Panama shall establish joint police patrols in agreed areas. Any arrests conducted by a joint patrol shall be the responsibility of the patrol member or members representing the Party having primary jurisdiction over the person or persons arrested.

5. The courts of the United States of America and related personnel, functioning in the former Canal Zone immediately prior to the entry into force of this Treaty may continue to function during the transition period for the judicial enforcement of the jurisdiction to be exercised by the United States of America in accordance with this Article.

6. In civil cases, the civilian courts of the United States of America in the Republic of Panama shall have no jurisdiction over new cases of a private civil nature, but shall retain full jurisdiction during the transition period to dispose of any civil cases, including admiralty cases, already instituted and pending before the courts prior to the entry into force of this Treaty.

7. The laws, regulations, and administrative authority of the United States of America applicable in the former Canal Zone immediately prior to the entry into force of this Treaty shall, to the extent not inconsistent with this Treaty and related agreements, continue in force for the purpose of the exercise by the United States of America of law enforcement and judicial jurisdiction only during the transition period. The United States of America may amend, repeal or otherwise change such laws, regulations and administrative authority. The two Parties shall consult concerning procedural and substantive matters relative to the implementation of this Article, including the disposition of cases pending at the end of the transition period and, in this respect, may enter into appropriate agreements by an exchange of notes or other instrument.

8. During this transition period, the United States of America may continue to incarcerate individuals in the areas and installations made available for the use of United States of America by the Republic of Panama pursuant to this Treaty and related agreements, or to transfer them to penal facilities in the United States of America to serve their sentences.

ARTICLE XII—A SEA-LEVEL CANAL OR A THIRD LANE OF LOCKS

1. The United States of America and the Republic of Panama recognize that a sea-level canal may be important for international navigation in the future. Consequently, during the duration of this Treaty, both Parties commit themselves to study jointly the feasibility of a sea-level canal in the Republic of Panama, and in the event they determine that such a waterway is necessary, they shall negotiate terms, agreeable to both Parties, for its construction.

2. The United States of America and the Republic of Panama agree on the following:

(a) No new interoceanic canal shall be constructed in the territory of the Republic of Panama during the duration of this Treaty, except in accordance with the provisions of this Treaty, or as the two Parties may otherwise agree; and

(b) During the duration of this Treaty, the United States of America shall not negotiate with third States for the right to construct an interoceanic canal on any other route in the Western Hemisphere, except as the two Parties may otherwise agree.

3. The Republic of Panama grants to the United States of America the right to add a third lane of locks to the existing Panama Canal. This right may be exercised at any time during the duration of this Treaty, provided that the United States of America has delivered to the Republic of Panama copies of the plans for such construction.

4. In the event the United States of America exercises the right granted in paragraph 3 above, it may use for that purpose, in addition to the areas otherwise made available to the United States of America pursuant to this Treaty, such other areas as the two Parties may agree upon. The terms and conditions applicable to Canal operating areas made available by the Republic of Panama for the use of the United States of America pursuant to Article III of this Treaty shall apply in a similar manner to such additional areas.

5. In the construction of the aforesaid works, the United States of America shall not use nuclear excavation techniques without the previous consent of the Republic of Panama.

ARTICLE XIII—PROPERTY TRANSFER AND ECONOMIC PARTICIPATION BY THE REPUBLIC OF PANAMA

1. Upon termination of this Treaty, the Republic of Panama shall assume total responsibility for the management, operation, and maintenance of the Panama Canal, which shall be turned over in operating condition and free of liens and debts, except as the two Parties may otherwise agree.

2. The United States of America transfers, without charge, to the Republic of Panama all right, title and interest the United States

of America may have with respect to all real property, including nonremovable improvements thereon, as set forth below:

(a) Upon the entry into force of this Treaty, the Panama Railroad and such property that was located in the former Canal Zone but that is not within the land and water areas the use of which is made available to the United States of America pursuant to this Treaty. However, it is agreed that the transfer on such date shall not include buildings and other facilities, except housing, the use of which is retained by the United States of America pursuant to this Treaty and related agreements, outside such areas;

(b) Such property located in an area of a portion thereof at such time as the use by the United States of America of such area or portion thereof ceases pursuant to agreement between the two Parties.

(c) Housing units made available for occupancy by members of the Armed Forces of the Republic of Panama in accordance with paragraph 5(b) of Annex B to the Agreement in Implementation of Article IV of this Treaty at such time as such units are made available to the Republic of Panama.

(d) Upon termination of this Treaty, all real property and non-removable improvements that were used by the United States of America for the purposes of this Treaty and related agreements and equipment related to the management, operation and maintenance of the Canal remaining in the Republic of Panama.

3. The Republic of Panama agrees to hold the United States of America harmless with respect to any claims which may be made by third parties relating to rights, title and interest in such property.

4. The Republic of Panama shall receive, in addition, from the Panama Canal Commission a just and equitable return on the national resources which it has dedicated to the efficient management, operation, maintenance, protection and defense of the Panama Canal, in accordance with the following:

(a) An annual amount to be paid out of Canal operating revenues computed at a rate of thirty hundredths of a United States dollar ($0.30) per Panama Canal net ton, or its equivalency, for each vessel transiting the Canal after the entry into force of this Treaty, for which tolls are charged. The rate of thirty hundredths of a United States dollar ($0.30) per Panama Canal net ton, or its equivalency, will be adjusted to reflect changes in the United States wholesale price index for total manufactured goods during biennial periods. The first adjustment shall take place five years after entry into force of this Treaty, taking into account the changes that occurred in such price index during the preceding two years. Thereafter, successive adjustments shall take place at the end of each biennial period. If the United States of America should decide that another indexing method is preferable, such method shall be proposed to the Republic of Panama and applied if mutually agreed.

(b) A fixed annuity of ten million United States dollars ($10,000,000) to be paid out of Canal operating revenues. This amount shall constitute a fixed expense of the Panama Canal Commission.

(c) An annual amount of up to ten million United States dollars ($10,000,000) per year, to be paid out of Canal operating revenues to the extent that such revenues exceed expenditures of the Panama Canal Commission including amounts paid pursuant to this Treaty. In the event Canal operating revenues in any year do not produce a surplus sufficient to cover this payment, the unpaid balance shall be paid from operating surpluses in future years in a manner to mutually agreed.

Article XIV—Settlement of Disputes

In the event that any question should arise between the Parties concerning the interpretation of this Treaty or related agreements, they shall make every effort to resolve the matter through consultation in the appropriate committees established pursuant to this Treaty and related agreements, or, if appropriate, through diplomatic channels. In the event the Parties are unable to resolve a particular matter through such means, they may, in appropriate cases, agree to submit the matter to conciliation, mediation, arbitration, or such other procedure for the peaceful settlement of the dispute as they may mutually deem appropriate.

[Translation]

Done at Washington, this 7th day of September, 1977, in duplicate, in the English and Spanish languages, both texts being equally authentic.

Annex

Procedures for the Cessation or Transfer of Activities Carried out by the Panama Canal Company and the Canal Zone Government and Illustrative List of the Functions that may be Performed by the Panama Canal Commission

1. The laws of the Republic of Panama shall regulate the exercise of private economic activities within the areas made available by the Republic of Panama for the use of the United States of America pursuant to this Treaty. Natural or juridical persons who, at least six months prior to the date of signature of this Treaty, were legally established and engaged in the exercise of economic activities in the former Canal Zone, may continue such activities in accordance with the provisions of paragraphs 2–7 of Article IX of this Treaty.

2. The Panama Canal Commission shall not perform governmental or commercial functions as stipulated in paragraph 4 of this Annex, provided, however, that this shall not be deemed to limit in any way the right of the United States of America to perform those functions that may be necessary for the efficient management, operation and maintenance of the Canal.

3. It is understood that the Panama Canal Commission, in the exercise of the rights of the United States of America with respect to the management, operation and maintenance of the Canal, may

perform functions such as are set forth below by way of illustration:

a. Management of the Canal enterprise.

b. Aids to navigation in Canal waters and in proximity thereto.

c. Control of vessel movement.

d. Operation and maintenance of the locks.

e. Tug service for the transit of vessels and dredging for the piers and docks of the Panama Canal Commission.

f. Control of the water levels in Gatun, Alajuela (Madden) and Miraflores Lakes.

g. Non-commercial transportation services in Canal waters.

h. Meteorological and hydrographic services.

i. Admeasurement.

j. Non-commercial motor transportation and maintenance.

k. Industrial security through the use of watchmen.

l. Procurement and warehousing.

m. Telecommunications.

n. Protection of the environment by preventing and controlling the spillage of oil and substances harmful to human or animal life and of the ecological equilibrium in areas used in operation of the Canal and the anchorages.

o. Non-commercial vessel repair.

p. Air conditioning services in Canal installations.

q. Industrial sanitation and health services.

r. Engineering design, construction and maintenance of Panama Canal Commission installations.

s. Dredging of the Canal channel, terminal ports and adjacent waters.

t. Control of the banks and stabilizing of the slopes of the Canal.

u. Non-commercial handling of cargo on the piers and docks of the Panama Canal Commission.

v. Maintenance of public areas of the Panama Canal Commission, such as parks and gardens.

w. Generation of electric power.

x. Purification and supply of water.

y. Marine salvage in Canal waters.

z. Such other functions as may be necessary or appropriate to carry out, in conformity with this Treaty and related agreements, the rights and responsibilities of the United States of America with respect to the management, operation and maintenance of the Panama Canal.

4. The following activities and operations carried out by the Panama Canal Company and the Canal Zone Government shall not be carried out by the Panama Canal Commission, effective upon the dates indicated therein:

(a) Upon the date of entry into force of this Treaty:

(i) Wholesale and retail sales, including those through commissaries, food stores, department stores, optical shops and pastry shops;

(ii) The production of food and drink, including milk products and bakery products;

(iii) The operation of public restaurants and cafeterias and the sale of articles through vending machines;

(iv) The operation of movie theaters, bowling alleys, pool rooms and other recreational and amusement facilities for the use of which a charge is payable;

(v) The operation of laundry and dry cleaning plants other than those operated for official use;

(vi) The repair and service of privately owned automobiles or the sale of petroleum or lubricants thereto, including the operation of gasoline stations, repair garages and tire repair and recapping facilities, and the repair and service of other privately owned property, including applicants, electronic devices, boats, motors, and furniture;

(vii) The operation of cold storage and freezer plants other than those operated for official use;

(viii) The operation of freight houses other than those operated for official use;

(ix) The operation of commercial services to and supply of privately owned and operated vessels, including the construction of vessels, the sale of petroleum lubricants and the provision of water, tug services not related to the Canal or other United States Government operations, and repair of such vessels, except in situations where repairs may be necessary to remove disabled vessels from the Canal;

(x) Printing services other than for official use;

(xi) Maritime transportation for the use of the general public;

(xii) Health and medical services provided to individuals, including hospitals, leprosariums, veterinary, mortuary and cemetery services;

(xiii) Educational services not for professional training, including schools and libraries;

(xiv) Postal services;

(xv) Immigration, customs and quarantine controls, except those measures necessary to ensure the sanitation of the Canal;

(xvi) Commercial pier and dock services such as the handling of cargo and passengers; and

(xvii) Any other commercial activity of a similar nature, not related to the management, operation or maintenance of the Canal.

(b) Within thirty calendar months from the date of entry into force of this Treaty, governmental services such as:

(i) Police;

(ii) Courts; and

(iii) Prison system.

5. (a) With respect to those activities or functions described in paragraph 4 above, or otherwise agreed upon by the two Parties, which are to be assumed by the Government of the Republic of Panama or by private persons subject to its authority, the two Parties shall consult prior to the discontinuance of such activities or functions by the Panama Canal Commission to develop appropriate

arrangements for the orderly transfer and continued efficient operation or conduct thereof.

(b) In the event that appropriate arrangements cannot be arrived at to ensure the continued performance of a particular activity or function described in paragraph 4 above which is necessary to the efficient management, operation or maintenance of the Canal, the Panama Canal Commission may, to the extent consistent with the other provisions of this Treaty and related agreements, continue to perform such activity or function until such arrangements can be made.

[TRANSLATION]

LETTER DESCRIBING APPLICATION OF THE WHOLESALE PRICE INDEX REFERRED TO IN PARAGRAPH 4(A) OF ARTICLE XIII OF THE PANAMA CANAL TREATY

DEPARTMENT OF STATE,
AMBASSADOR AT LARGE,
Washington, September 7, 1977.

His Excellency RÓMULO ESCOBAR BETHANCOURT,
Chief Treaty Negotiator for Panama.

DEAR AMBASSADOR ESCOBAR:

As was discussed during our negotiations, I am pleased to furnish information on the application of the Wholesale Price Index referred to in paragraph 4(A) of Article XIII of the new Panama Canal Treaty.

The Wholesale Price Index for Total Manufactured Goods of the United States is understood by the United States to refer to the seasonally adjusted figure for Total Manufactured Goods found in Table 3, "Wholesale Price Indexes for Selected Groupings Unadjusted and Seasonally Adjusted," of the monthly report of the Department of Labor "Wholesale Prices and Price Indexes." Enclosed is a copy of the latest monthly report published by the Department of Labor entitled "Wholesale Prices and Price Indexes" which describes the method of calculation of the indexes.

The new rate shall be determined by multiplying the rate of 30 cents per Panama Canal ton by a fraction the numerator of which is the average index for the twelve months ending the biennial period and the denominator of which is the average index of the twelve months preceding the first biennial period.

Sincerely,

ELLSWORTH BUNKER.

Enclosure: Wholesale Prices and Price Indexes [2]

---

[2] Not printed here.

(A) Panama Canal Treaty—Implementation of Article III[1] (with Agreed Minute)

Agreement signed at Washington, September 7, 1977; Entered into force, October 1, 1979

AGREEMENT IN IMPLEMENTATION OF ARTICLE III OF THE PANAMA CANAL TREATY

WHEREAS, pursuant to Article III of the Panama Canal Treaty, signed this date, the Republic of Panama, as territorial sovereign, grants to the United States of America the rights necessary to manage, operate, and maintain the Panama Canal,

The United States of America and the Republic of Panama have agreed upon the following:

ARTICLE I—DEFINITIONS

For the purposes of this Agreement it shall be understood that:

1. "Panama Canal Commission" (hereinafter referred to as "the Commission") means the agency or agencies of the Government of the United States responsible for carrying out the responsibilities and rights of the United States under the Panama Canal Treaty with respect to the management, operation, and maintenance of the Panama Canal.

2. "United States citizen employees" means (a) nationals of the United States, to whom United States passports have been issued, who are employed by the Commission and assigned for duty in the Republic of Panama (including employees of other civilian agencies of the United States who are on temporary duty with the Commission or are otherwise visiting the area on official business of the United States), and (b) other categories of persons which may be agreed upon by the two Parties.

3. "Dependents" means the spouse and children of United States citizen employees, and other relatives who depend on them for their subsistence and who habitually live with them under the same roof.

ARTICLE II—COORDINATING COMMITTEE

1. A Coordinating Committee shall be established upon the entry into force of this Agreement to be composed of one representative of the United States and one representative of the Republic of Panama, of equal authority within the Committee, each of whom may have one or more deputies, on a parity basis.

2. The Coordinating Committee shall perform the functions specifically indicated by the provisions of this Agreement, and others

[1] TIAS 10031. The Panama Canal Treaty terminated on December 31, 1999.

entrusted to it by both Governments concerning implementation of this Agreement.

3. The Coordinating Committee shall establish its rules of procedure within the spirit of this Agreement and may designate such subcommittees as it may deem necessary for the fulfillment of its functions.

4. The Coordinating Committee shall be organized so that it may meet promptly and at any time upon request of the representative of the United States or of the Republic of Panama. The Coordinating Committee shall send periodic reports on its activities to the Governments of the United States and the Republic of Panama.

5. The Coordinating Committee shall refer any matters which it has not been able to resolve to the two Governments for their consideration through appropriate channels.

Article III—Use of Land and Water Areas

1. Canal Operating Areas: With respect to the areas and installations described in paragraph 1 of Annex A of this Agreement (hereinafter referred to as the "Canal operating areas"), the following provisions will be applicable:

(a) The United States shall have the right to use such areas and installations for the purposes of exercising its rights and fulfilling its responsibilities, under the Panama Canal Treaty and related agreements, concerning the management, operation and maintenance of the Panama Canal, and for such other purposes as the two Parties may agree upon.

(b) The United States shall have the right to use any portion of the Canal operating areas for military training, when such use is determined by the United States to be compatible with continued efficient operation of the Panama Canal.

2. Housing Areas: The areas and installations set forth in paragraph 2 of Annex A of this Agreement (hereinafter referred to as "housing areas") shall be dedicated to the primary purpose of housing United States citizen employees and dependents. The housing areas shall be administered in accordance with the regime of civil coordination established in Article VI of this Agreement.

3. Accessory Facilities and Installations: The United States may continue to use those accessory facilities or installations used in connection with the management, operation and maintenance of the Canal on the date this Agreement enters into force, but which are located outside the areas and installations otherwise made available for the use of the United States pursuant to the Panama Canal Treaty. A description of such facilities is set forth in paragraph 3 of Annex A to this Agreement. The United States, at its expense, may maintain, improve, replace, expand or remove these facilities and installations. The United States shall have unimpeded access to these and all other facilities and installations used in connection with the management, operation, or maintenance of the Canal.

4. Anchorages: The United States shall have free and unimpeded access to and use of the anchorages described in paragraph 4 of Annex A, for the purposes of exercising its rights and fulfilling its responsibilities concerning the movement and anchoring of vessels

under the Panama Canal Treaty and related agreements. The United States may own, use, operate, inspect, maintain or replace equipment, facilities and navigational aids in these areas. The United States shall have the right to increase the size of the anchorages as may be necessary or convenient, within the areas described in paragraph 5 of Annex A.

5. Special Areas: Those additional land and water areas set forth in paragraph 6 of Annex A are subject to the procedures set forth in Article IV of this Agreement in order that activities incompatible with the efficient management, operation, or maintenance of the Canal shall be precluded.

6. Annex A of this Agreement shall be examined every five years or by agreement between the two Parties, and shall be revised by exchange of notes or other instrument to reflect any agreed elimination or change in areas. The United States may notify the Republic of Panama at any time that the use of an area, or of a specified portion thereof, or other right granted by the Republic of Panama, is no longer required. Under such circumstances, such use or other right shall cease on the date determined by the two Parties.

7. (a) The United States may, at any time, remove from the Republic of Panama, or, in accordance with such conditions as may be agreed upon by the two Parties, dispose of in the Republic of Panama, any equipment, material, supplies or other removable property brought into, acquired or constructed in the Republic of Panama by or for the Commission. In case of disposal within the Republic of Panama, preference will be given to the Government of the Republic of Panama.

(b) All equipment, installations, material, supplies or removable property left by the United States in an area made available under this Agreement beyond 90 days from the date the use of such area by the United States ceases shall, unless agreed otherwise by the two Parties, become the property of the Republic of Panama.

8. The Commission may employ watchmen to protect the security of selected installations within the areas made available for the use of the United States under this Agreement, it being understood that such installations do not include housing or other installations not devoted to the management, operation or maintenance of the Panama Canal. Such watchmen shall not have powers of arrest or other general police powers. They may, however, temporarily detain persons believed to be committing or to have just committed an offense against applicable laws or regulations, and shall promptly transfer custody to the appropriate police authorities. The Commission shall provide to the authorities of the Republic of Panama through the Coordinating Committee a list identifying the individuals employed by it as watchmen, and shall promptly notify the Republic of Panama of any changes in such list. In the performance of their duties, such watchmen shall not bear firearms except handguns.

9. The Coordinating Committee shall constitute the means of communication and information between the two Parties with regard to matters pertaining to the implementation of this Article.

ARTICLE IV—LICENSING OF OTHER LAND USES

1. Without prejudice to the rights of the United States concerning use of areas and installations within the Republic of Panama under the Panama Canal Treaty and related agreements, the areas and installations set forth in Annex A may be used for other purposes compatible with the continuous efficient management, operation and maintenance of the Panama Canal, under land use licenses to be issued by the Republic of Panama in accordance with the following procedure:

(a) The Republic of Panama shall refer to the Coordinating Committee any requests it may receive from private concerns, or from agencies of the Republic of Panama, to undertake specific activities within the areas subject to this procedure.

(b) If the United States and the Republic of Panama, acting through the Coordinating Committee, determine that the proposed use, including its terms and conditions, is compatible with the continuous efficient management, operation and maintenance of the Panama Canal, the Republic of Panama shall issue a revocable land license for the specific use agreed upon. The United States must approve the license, in writing, before it becomes effective.

2. The Republic of Panama may terminate the land license for reasons arising under its laws.

3. At any time that the United States decides that a licensed land use is no longer compatible with the continuous efficient management, operation, or maintenance of the Panama Canal, or that the licensed area is necessary for a Panama Canal Treaty-related purpose, it may withdraw its concurrence in the land license, at which time the Republic of Panama shall cause the license to be terminated.

4. In the event that the United States withdraws its concurrence in a land license issued under the procedure established in this Article, the Republic of Panama shall take all measures necessary to ensure that the area is promptly vacated, in accordance with such rules as may be established by the two Parties through the Coordinating Committee.

5. The provisions of this Article shall not limit in any manner the authority of the United States to use the areas made available for its use under this Agreement, or to permit their use by its contractors, in the exercise of its rights and the fulfillment of its responsibilities under the Panama Canal Treaty and related Agreements.

ARTICLE V—BALBOA AND CRISTOBAL PORTS AND THE PANAMA RAILROAD

1. As provided in Article XIII of the Panama Canal Treaty, all right, title and interest of the United States in property, installations and equipment in the Ports of Balboa and Cristobal, the boundaries of which are set forth in paragraph 1 of Annex B of this Agreement, is transferred without charge to the Republic of Panama.

2. The Republic of Panama shall have the responsibility for the management, operation and maintenance of the Ports of Balboa

and Cristobal, subject, however, to the following terms and conditions:

(a) The Republic of Panama shall exercise its jurisdictional rights over vessels within the lands and waters areas of the Ports of Balboa and Cristobal. Movement of vessels to or from the piers and docks of the Ports of Balboa and Cristobal shall be subject to appropriate approval by the port authorities of the Republic of Panama.

(b) The Republic of Panama grants to the United States the following technical powers: the authority and responsibility for marine traffic control within the waters of the Canal operating areas and defense sites and within the ports of Balboa and Cristobal and to or from and within the anchorages and emergency beaching areas. Such authority and responsibility of the United States includes the right to require that vessels moving in such waters be under the direction of Commission pilots.

(c) The United States may use, for the management, operation, maintenance, protection and defense of the Canal, those port installations and equipment managed, operated, and maintained by the Republic of Panama which are described in paragraph 2 of Annex B of this Agreement. The Republic of Panama shall maintain such port installations and equipment in efficient operating condition.

(d) The United States is guaranteed use of the Port installations described in paragraph 3 of Annex B of this Agreement for normal maintenance of its equipment, in accordance with schedules established by the Commission or, when necessary for emergency repairs, at any time. The United States may use its employees to perform services in such installations. United States use of such installations and equipment shall be free of cost other than reimbursement for labor and services provided to the United States at rates which shall not exceed those charged the most favored customer on a commercial basis.

(e) In order to facilitate the optimum scheduling of vessel transits, the Republic of Panama shall ensure that vessels transiting the Canal receive port services at Balboa and Cristobal on a priority basis.

(f) The Republic of Panama shall control and supervise the activities to be carried out under its responsibility in the Ports of Balboa and Cristobal to ensure that such activities are compatible with the efficient management, operation, maintenance, protection and defense of the Canal. The Republic of Panama shall take the measures necessary to prevent, or to terminate, any activity that is incompatible with such purposes.

(g) In the event of emergencies relating to the protection and defense of the Canal, the Republic of Panama shall, at the request of the United States, make the installations and equipment of the Naval Industrial Reserve Shipyard available, without delay, to the United States for as long as may be necessary. In any such case, the United States shall reimburse the Republic of Panama for labor or services provided to it at rates which shall not exceed those charged the most favored customer on a commercial basis.

3. As provided in Article XIII of the Panama Canal Treaty, all right, title and interest of the United States in the property, installations and equipment of the Panama Railroad is transferred without charge to the Republic of Panama.

4. The Republic of Panama shall have the responsibility for the management, operation, and maintenance of the Panama Railroad (hereinafter referred to as the "Railroad"), subject, however, to the following terms and conditions:

(a) The Republic of Panama shall maintain the Railroad in efficient operating condition. The Railroad will continue to provide the levels and frequency of service necessary for efficient management, operation, and maintenance, and effective protection and defense of the Canal.

(b) The United States shall have the right to use and maintain the existing installations, including the 44KV electrical transmission lines and towers, and to construct, use and maintain additional installations along the Railroad right of way, and may have access thereto for such purposes.

(c) The Republic of Panama shall permit the United States to use the Railroad and its equipment, on a priority basis, for the purposes of maintaining such transmission lines and other installations, and of transporting equipment, supplies and personnel related to the management, operation, maintenance, or protection and defense of the Canal. The United States shall pay the costs resulting from such use in accordance with rates which shall not exceed those charged by the Railroad to its most favored customer on a commercial basis.

(d) Spur tracks, sidings and related equipment serving the installations in areas made available to the United States pursuant to the Panama Canal Treaty shall remain the responsibility of the United States. Railroad access to such trackage shall be subject to the approval of the responsible United States authorities.

(e) If the Republic of Panama decides, at any time, that its continued operation of the Railroad at the minimum levels of service agreed upon by the two Parties is no longer viable, the United States shall have the right to reassume management and operation of the Railroad.

5. A Ports and Railroad Committee, to be established as a subcommittee of the Coordinating Committee in accordance with paragraph 3 of Article II of this Agreement and composed of an equal number of representatives of each Party, shall be responsible *inter alia* for coordination of the activities of the Panama Canal Commission and the National Port Authority of the Republic of Panama concerning the operation of the Ports of Balboa and Cristobal and the Panama Railroad, and shall have the following functions:

(a) To consider and, upon agreement, to coordinate the termination of United States rights with respect to the use of areas or installations in, or in the vicinity of, the Ports of Balboa and Cristobal which the Republic of Panama might desire to use for port activities, or with respect to the use of areas and installations appertaining to the Railroad.

(b) To consider and, upon agreement, to coordinate any change in the use of lands or waters in the Ports of Balboa and

Cristobal or in areas or installations appertaining to the Railroad, or any initiation of, change in, or termination of Port or Railroad services. Consequently, change in the use of such lands and waters and the initiation of, changes in, or termination of such services shall occur only in accordance with the decisions reached by the Ports and Railroad Committee. Until such time as the Committee agrees upon new levels and frequency of Railroad services, the levels and frequency of service scheduled for 1977 shall be maintained.

(c) To maintain adequate standards of safety, fire prevention and oil pollution. Until such time as the Committee issues new regulations, the safety, fire prevention and oil pollution standards in force prior to the entry into force of this Agreement shall remain in force.

(d) To establish procedures and mechanisms to facilitate the movement of vessels in accordance with the rights and responsibilities of the Parties set forth in paragraph 2 above.

(e) To coordinate the use by the United States of those installations specified in paragraph 3 of Annex B that are located within the Ports of Balboa and Cristobal and the activities of the National Port Authority of the Republic of Panama in these Ports.

In considering these matters, the representatives of the two Parties on the Ports and Railroad Committee shall be guided by the principle that the operation of the Ports and Railroad shall be consistent with the continued efficient management, operation, maintenance, protection and defense of the Canal.

Article VI—Regime of Civil Coordination for Housing Areas

1. As provided in Article XIII of the Panama Canal Treaty, title to all housing within the housing areas, owned by the Panama Canal Company immediately prior to the entry into force of this Agreement, is transferred to the Republic of Panama. The housing areas shall, however, continue to be dedicated, for the duration of this Agreement, to the primary purpose of housing employees of the Commission in accordance with the provisions of this Article.

2. The Republic of Panama hereby places at the disposal of the United States, without cost, the use of such housing, within the housing areas, as the United States may deem necessary for United States citizen employees and dependents throughout the duration of this Agreement. The United States may continue to manage, maintain, improve, rent and assign such housing for United States citizen employees and dependents.

3. The use of housing units beyond those required by the United States for housing United States citizen employees and dependents at the date of entry into force of this Agreement, shall pass to the Republic of Panama on that date. Within five years from the entry into force of this Agreement, the use of at least twenty percent of the housing units located in the former Canal Zone, formerly owned by the Panama Canal Company, shall have passed to the Republic of Panama. Thereafter, the use of additional units shall pass to the Republic of Panama in accordance with the following schedule:

(a) Within ten years from the entry into force of this Agreement, the use of a total of at least thirty percent of such units shall have passed.

(b) Within fifteen years, the use of a total of at least forty-five percent shall have passed.

(c) Within twenty years, the use of a total of at least sixty percent shall have passed.

4. In order to protect the interests and welfare of employees of the United States who are not United States citizen employees and who, on the date of entry into force of this Agreement, are occupying housing units, the use of which is transferred to the Republic of Panama, the Republic of Panama shall give such persons the following special treatment:

(a) The opportunity to occupy, by lease or rental, or in the event the Republic of Panama decides to sell, to acquire by purchase at reasonable prices, the units which they are occupying on the date of entry into force of this Agreement.

(b) In cases of purchase, the opportunity to obtain long-term financing arrangements.

(c) In cases where continued occupancy of a particular housing unit is not feasible, the opportunity to obtain other adequate housing within such areas at reasonable cost, on a preferential or priority basis.

5. In addition to housing its United States citizen employees and dependents, the United States may use the housing areas for other purposes related to the management, operation and maintenance of the Canal. The housing areas may also be used for other activities complementary to or compatible with the primary purpose of housing employees of the Commission under revocable land licenses to be issued in accordance with the procedures set forth in Article IV of this Agreement.

6. In coordination with the appropriate authorities of the Republic of Panama, the Commission may continue to provide public services such as maintenance of streets, sidewalks and other public areas within the housing areas. Since the utilities systems in the housing areas are fully integrated with those of the Canal, the Commission shall, on behalf of the utilities agencies of the Republic of Panama, continue to provide utilities such as power, water, and sewers to industrial and commercial enterprises and other persons in the area, other than United States citizen employees and dependents. The utilities agencies of the Republic of Panama shall be responsible for setting rates for and billing such customers, and shall reimburse the Commission for its cost in providing such services.

7. The Coordinating Committee shall serve as the channel for consultation and coordination between the two Parties with respect to matters arising under the regime of civil coordination established in this Article.

Article VII—Water Rights

1. The United States shall have unimpaired use, free of cost, of the waters of the Canal and of Alajuela (Madden), Gatun and Miraflores Lakes, and of the waters of their tributary streams, for

the purposes of the management, operation and maintenance of the Panama Canal, including the generation of electric power, spilling to provide flood or pollution control, and the supplying of potable water, taking into account the needs of the Republic of Panama for potable water.

2. The United States may:

(a) Raise the surface of Alajuela (Madden) Lake to 260 feet above precise level datum (PLD) and of Gatun Lake to 100 feet above PLD, and lower the surfaces of these lakes down to elevations of 190 feet and 76 feet, respectively, for the purposes stated in paragraph 1 of this Article. The Parties shall consult and coordinate concerning the measures necessary to assure the supply of potable water to the Republic of Panama.

(b) Erect, operate, maintain, improve, expand, remove and replace rainfall and river gauging stations in the watersheds of the lakes and their tributaries, the data and information obtained from which shall be made available promptly to the Republic of Panama.

(c) Maintain and improve the saddle dams serving Gatun, Miraflores and Alajuela (Madden) Lakes and any new impoundment areas. The Republic of Panama agrees to take the necessary measures to prevent any activity that might endanger the stability of the saddle dams.

(d) Apply herbicides and conduct other water weed control and sanitation programs in the lakes, their watershed and tributaries. In the conduct of these programs the United States shall take into account the environmental protection and water standards of the Republic of Panama to the extent feasible and consistent with the efficient management, operation and maintenance of the Canal.

(e) Conduct flood control operations, to include periodic flushing of the rivers, and a routine maintenance program up to the 100 foot contour line along the Chagres River between Gamboa and Madden Dam, and up to the 30 foot contour line along the Chagres River between Gatun Dam and the Caribbean Sea.

(f) Use such land and water areas as may be necessary for the purpose of constructing new dams, including the proposed Trinidad, Manguito Point, and Panama Railroad Causeway dams, and impounding such water as may be required to develop and regulate the water supply of the Canal for the purposes stated in paragraph 1 of this Article. If new dams are constructed in accordance with this Agreement, any generation of electric power in connection with such dams shall be the prerogative of the Republic of Panama in the manner agreed upon between the two Parties.

3. The Republic of Panama shall take the necessary measures to ensure that any other land or water use of the Canal's watershed will not deplete the water supply necessary for the continuous efficient management, operation or maintenance of the Canal, and shall not interfere with the water use rights of the United States in the Canal's watershed.

ARTICLE VIII—SOCIAL SECURITY

1. Concerning Social Security and retirement benefits applicable to employees of the Commission who are not United States citizen employees, the following provisions shall apply:

(a) Such persons who are employed by the Commission subsequent to the entry into force of this Agreement shall, as of their date of employment, be covered by the Social Security System of the Republic of Panama.

(b) Such persons who were employed prior to the entry into force of this Agreement by the Panama Canal Company or Canal Zone Government and who were covered under the Civil Service Retirement System of the United States shall continue to be covered by that system until their retirement or until the termination of their employment with the Commission for any other reason.

(c) The Commission shall collect and transfer in a timely manner to the Social Security System of the Republic of Panama the employer's and employees' contributions for those of its employees who are covered by the Social Security System of the Republic of Panama.

2. Concerning health benefits applicable to employees of the Commission who are not United States citizen employees and who are covered by the Civil Service Retirement System of the United States the following provisions shall apply:

(a) For the duration of a transitional period of thirty calendar months following the entry into force of this Agreement, all such persons shall continue to be provided health insurance and medical benefits under the same general arrangements in effect prior to the entry into force of this Agreement.

(b) At the termination of the aforementioned transitional period, none of the above-mentioned persons shall be eligible to receive health or medical benefits from facilities operated by the United States in the Republic of Panama.

(c) Such persons shall have the right, during the aforementioned transitional period, to elect either to continue their coverage under the Federal Employees' Health Benefits Plan or to terminate their coverage under that program and enroll in the Health and Maternity Benefits Program under the Social Security System of the Republic of Panama, effective upon the termination of the transitional period.

(d) The Commission shall collect and transfer in a timely manner to the Social Security System of the Republic of Panama the employer's and employees' contributions to the Health and Maternity Benefits Program of that institution for such persons who enroll in that program. The employer's contribution shall be equal to that which the employer would have paid had the employee continued under the Federal Employees Health Benefits Plan.

3. (a) Following the entry into force of this Agreement, employees of the Panama Canal Company or Canal Zone Government, regardless of their nationality, who become employees of the Republic of Panama as the result either of a transfer of a function or activity to the Republic of Panama from the Panama Canal Company or

Canal Zone Government or through job placement efforts of the Commission or the Republic of Panama, shall be covered by the Social Security System of the Republic of Panama through a special regime identical in eligibility requirements, benefits, and employer/employee contributions to the United States Civil Service Retirement System in which the employee was previously enrolled.

(b) In those instances in which an employee has been separated from employment with the Commission and is due a refund of his contributions to the Civil Service Retirement System of the United States, said refund shall, upon the written request of the employee, be transferred by the Civil Service authorities of the United States to the Social Security System of the Republic of Panama for the purpose of the employee's purchase of an equity, which shall be financially equal to the total of the amounts transferred.

(c) When such employee of the Panama Canal Company or Canal Zone Government, regardless of his nationality, is separated from his employment with the Commission as the result of the implementation of the Panama Canal Treaty and becomes an employee of the Republic of Panama as the result either of a transfer of a function or activity to the Republic of Panama from the Panama Canal Company or the Canal Zone Government or through a job placement assistance program, and elects to purchase an equity in the Social Security System of the Republic of Panama, through a special regime identical in requirements for eligibility, benefits, and employer/employee contributions to the Civil Service Retirement System of the United States in which the employee was previously enrolled, the United States shall provide an equal sum to assist the employee in acquiring such an equity, provided, however, that:

(i) The employee is not eligible for an immediate retirement annuity under the United States Civil Service Retirement System.

(ii) The employee has not elected a deferred annuity under the United States Civil Service Retirement System.

(iii) The employee has been credited with at least five years of Federal service under the United States Civil Service Retirement System.

(iv) The employee elects to withdraw the entire amount of his capitalized contributions to the Civil Service Retirement System of the United States and transfer them to the Social Security System of the Republic of Panama.

(v) The contribution provided by the United States shall be the same as the amount withdrawn by the employee from the United States Civil Service Retirement Fund and contributed by the employee to the Panamanian Social Security System.

(d) Employees eligible for an immediate annuity under the Civil Service Retirement System of the United States shall begin to receive retirement pay at the time of their termination of their employment by the Government of the United States.

4. Except as otherwise provided in the Panama Canal Treaty or this Agreement, there shall be no loss or limitation of rights, options and benefits to which employees of the Commission who were employed by the Panama Canal Company or the Canal Zone Government may be entitled under applicable laws and regulations of

the United States. These rights, options and benefits include the rights, where appropriate under applicable laws and regulations of the United States, to optional or voluntary retirement, discontinued service retirement following involuntary separation, disability retirement, and deferred retirement.

5. Non-United States citizen employees of the Panama Canal Commission who were, prior to the entry into force of this Agreement, employed by the Panama Canal Company or the Canal Zone Government, and who continue to be covered by the United States Civil Service Retirement System, shall continue to be covered by United States Workmen's Compensation and may, if they so desire, continue their coverage under the Federal Employees' Group Life Insurance program in the same manner as prior to the entry into force of this Agreement.

ARTICLE IX—ACQUISITION OF PANAMANIAN SUPPLIES AND SERVICES

1. In procuring supplies and services, the Commission shall give preference to those obtainable in the Republic of Panama. Such preference shall apply to the maximum extent possible when such supplies and services are available as required, and are comparable in quality and price to those which may be obtained from other sources. For the comparison of prices there shall be taken into account the cost of transport to the Republic of Panama, including freight, insurance, and handling, of the supplies and services which compete with Panamanian supplies and services. In the acquisition of goods in the Republic of Panama, preference shall be given to goods having a larger percentage of components of Panamanian origin.

2. Any regulations which may be necessary to carry out this preference shall be agreed upon in the Coordinating Committee.

ARTICLE X—TELECOMMUNICATIONS

1. The Republic of Panama, in the exercise of its sovereign power over telecommunications, authorizes the United States, for the duration of this Agreement, to use communications networks and communications-electronics installations within the Canal operating areas, and the radio frequencies authorized or in use, and transportable equipment in use, immediately prior to the entry into force of this Agreement and as may be necessary for its requirements, in order to accomplish the purposes of the management, operation and maintenance of the Canal, and as the two Parties may otherwise agree. The Coordinating Committee may adopt regulations to govern the use of such transportable equipment outside of such areas.

2. The Republic of Panama also authorizes the United States to use installations such as those described in the preceding paragraph already existing outside the Canal operating areas, including those operated and maintained by the United States Forces or by contractors, which serve to accomplish the purposes of the management, operation or maintenance of the Canal, and as the two Parties may otherwise agree. The United States authorities shall have access to such installations for appropriate operation, maintenance and replacement.

3. Upon the termination of this Agreement, all telecommunication equipment and facilities necessary for purposes of operation of the Canal, which are the property of the United States, shall be transferred to the Republic of Panama. The United States, after consultation with the Republic of Panama, will institute a program to train Panamanian nationals to operate and maintain such telecommunications equipment, including ship-to-shore facilities.

4. Provided that they are available and suitable for the purpose, the Commission shall use, to the maximum extent practicable, the telecommunications services of public or private enterprise in the Republic of Panama in order to meet its growth needs, but the applicable rates shall be no less favorable than those charged to governmental agencies of the Republic of Panama.

5. The United States shall provide the Republic of Panama a list of all frequencies authorized or in use by it pursuant to this Article. This list shall be submitted through the Coordinating Committee in ascending frequency order and shall contain as a minimum information concerning the power, bandwidth, and type of emission being used in those frequencies.

6. The Republic of Panama undertakes not to authorize the use of any frequency which would interfere with those in use by or for the Commission or which it may use in the future in accordance with the Panama Canal Treaty and this Agreement.

7. All provisions regarding telecommunications in this Article shall be in accordance with the obligations of both Parties as members of the International Telecommunication Union and with the various relevant international agreements to which both are parties.

8. Any communication with the International Telecommunication Union regarding the subject matter of this Article shall be effected exclusively by the Republic of Panama.

9. The Coordinating Committee may adopt any further regulations as may be necessary to implement the provisions of this Article, including necessary technical coordination.

ARTICLE XI—CONTRACTORS AND CONTRACTORS' PERSONNEL

1. Whenever the Commission enters into contracts for the performance of services or the procurement of supplies, it shall adhere to the preferences for Panamanian sources set forth in Article IX of this Agreement.

2. Whenever contracts are awarded by the Commission to natural persons who are nationals or permanent residents of the United States or to corporations or other legal entities organized under the laws of the United States and under the effective control of such persons, such contractors shall be so designated by the United States and such designations shall be communicated to the authorities of the Republic of Panama through the Coordinating Committee. Designated contractors shall be subject to the laws and regulations of the Republic of Panama except with respect to the special regime established by this Agreement, which includes the following obligations and benefits:

(a) The contractor must engage exclusively in activities related to the execution of the work for which he has been contracted by the Commission or related to other works or activities authorized by the Republic of Panama.

(b) The contractor must refrain from carrying out practices which may constitute violations of the laws of the Republic of Panama.

(c) The contractor shall enter and depart from the territory of the Republic of Panama in accordance with procedures prescribed for United States citizen employees in Article XII of this Agreement.

(d) The contractor must obtain a document indicating his identity as a contractor which the proper authorities of the United States shall issue when they are satisfied he is duly qualified. This certificate shall be sufficient to permit him to operate under Panamanian law as a contractor of the United States. Nevertheless, the authorities of the Republic of Panama may require the registration of the appropriate documents to establish juridical presence in the Republic of Panama.

(e) The contractor shall not be obliged to pay any tax or other assessment to the Republic of Panama or income derived under a contract with the Commission, so long as he is taxed in the United States at a rate substantially equivalent to the corresponding taxes and assessments of the Republic of Panama.

(f) The contractor may move freely within the Republic of Panama, and shall have exemptions from customs duties and other charges, as provided for United States citizen employees in Article XIV and XVI of this Agreement.

(g) The contractor may use public services and installations in accordance with the terms and conditions of Article XIII of this Agreement and, on a non-discriminatory basis, shall pay the Republic of Panama highway tolls and taxes on plates for private vehicles.

(h) The contractor shall be exempt from any taxes imposed on depreciable assets belonging to him, other than real estate, which are used exclusively for the execution of contracts with the United States.

(i) The contractor may use the services and facilities provided for in Articles X and XVIII of the Agreement in Implementation of Article IV of the Panama Canal Treaty, signed this date, to the extent such use is authorized by the United States; provided, however, that after five years from the entry into force of this Agreement, the use of military postal services by such contractors shall be limited to that related to the execution of contracts with the United States.

3. The Commission shall withdraw the designation of a contractor when any of the following circumstances occur:

(a) Completion of termination of the contracts with the Commission.

(b) Proof that during the life of the contract such contractors have engaged in the Republic of Panama in business activities not related to their contracts with the United States nor authorized by the Republic of Panama.

(c) Proof that such contractors are engaged in practices which in the view of the Republic of Panama constitute serious violations of the laws of the Republic of Panama.

4. The authorities of the United States shall notify the authorities of the Republic of Panama whenever the designation of a contractor has been withdrawn. If, within sixty days after notification of withdrawal of the designation of a contractor who entered the territory of the Republic of Panama in the capacity of a contractor, the authorities of the Republic of Panama require such contractor to leave its territory, the United States shall ensure that the Republic of Panama shall not incur any expense due to the cost of transportation.

5. The provisions of this Article shall similarly apply to the subcontractors and to the employees of the contractors and subcontractors and their dependents who are nationals or residents of the United States. These employees and dependents shall not be subject to the Panamanian Social Security system.

ARTICLE XII—ENTRY AND DEPARTURE

1. The United States may bring into the territory of the Republic of Panama United States citizen employees and dependents for the specific purposes of the Panama Canal Treaty and as the two Parties may agree upon.

2. In order to enter or leave the territory of the Republic of Panama, such persons shall be required to bear only a valid passport and a special entry/exit permit issued by the Republic of Panama. Such documentation, upon entry into or departure from the territory of the Republic of Panama, shall be presented to the appropriate authorities of the Republic of Panama.

3. Such entry/exit permits shall authorize the bearer an unlimited number of entries into and exits from the territory of the Republic of Panama for the duration of the employment or other duties with the Commission of the bearer, or of his sponsor. Such permits shall remain valid until such time as United States authorities notify the appropriate authorities of the Republic of Panama of the termination of the employment or duties with the Commission of the bearer, or of his sponsor.

4. The Republic of Panama agrees to issue such special entry/exit permits to the persons described in paragraph 1 of this Article, upon written request by the authorities of the United States, and to implement special procedures to ensure such expeditious issuance.

5. Whenever the status of any person described in paragraph 1 of this Article is altered so that he is no longer entitled to remain in the territory of the Republic of Panama, the authorities of the United States shall promptly notify the authorities of the Republic of Panama, and shall ensure that the special entry/exit permit in question is returned to the Republic of Panama. If requested by the Republic of Panama within a period of sixty days following such notice, the authorities of the United States shall ensure that transportation of any such person from the Republic of Panama will be provided at no cost to the Republic of Panama.

6. The persons described in paragraph 1 of this Article shall be exempted from fiscal charges relating to their entry, stay in, or departure from the territory of the Republic of Panama, except from nondiscriminatory charges established or which may be established for use of airports. Similarly, they shall be exempted from obligatory services established in favor of the Republic of Panama. They shall not acquire any right to permanent residence or domicile in the Republic of Panama.

7. United States citizen employees who enter the Republic of Panama to execute professional services exclusively for the United States, or on its behalf, shall not be subject to the licensing regimes of the Republic of Panama, but their professional activity shall be limited to such services with the United States for the specific purposes of the Panama Canal Treaty, or as the two Parties may otherwise agree.

ARTICLE XIII—SERVICES AND INSTALLATIONS

1. The Commission, its United States citizen employees and dependents may use the public services and installations belonging to or regulated by the Republic of Panama, and the terms and conditions of use, prices, rates and tariffs and priorities shall not be unfavorable in relation to those charged other users.

2. The Commission may use the facilities and services of the United States Forces for official purposes and may establish and operate the supporting services and facilities it requires within the areas used under this Agreement, and exceptionally, with the authorization of the Republic of Panama, outside such areas.

3. The United States may furnish to United States citizen employees and dependents the services provided for in Article XVIII of the Agreement in Implementation of Article IV of the Panama Canal Treaty signed this date, and authorize their use of the facilities provided for in Article X and Article XI of that Agreement provided, however, that their use of military postal services, commissaries, and military exchanges may not be authorized after five years from the entry into force of this Agreement.

4. The facilities and services of the Commission may be made available, exclusively for official purposes, to other agencies of the Government of the United States operating in the Republic of Panama, including the United States Forces.

ARTICLE XIV—MOVEMENT, LICENSES, AND REGISTRATION OF VESSELS, AIRCRAFT AND VEHICLES

1. (a) When in the performance of official duties the vessels and aircraft operated by or for the Commission may move freely through Panamanian air space and waters, without the obligation of payment of taxes, tolls, landing or pier charges or other charges to the Republic of Panama except for reimbursement for specific services requested and received and without any other impediment.

(b) Such vessels and aircraft shall be exempt from customs inspections or other inspections. Whenever they carry cargo, crews or passengers who are not entitled to the exemptions provided for in this Agreement, timely notice shall be given to the appropriate authorities of the Republic of Panama. Both Parties shall adopt procedures to ensure that the customs laws and regulations of the Republic of Panama are not violated.

2. (a)(i) Similarly, the vehicles and equipment of the Commission may, when in the performance of official duties, move freely in the Republic of Panama, without the obligation of payment of taxes, tolls or other charges to the Republic of Panama and without any other impediment. Such vehicles and equipment shall be exempt from mechanical or other inspection.

(ii) Claims arising from damage caused by the Commission to the Panamanian road network outside the Canal operating areas, in excess of the usual wear and tear by reason of time and its appropriate use, shall be settled as provided for in Article XVIII of this Agreement.

(b) Such vehicles and equipment of the Commission shall not be assessed any license or registration fees. These vehicles shall bear means of identification as may be agreed upon by the Coordinating Committee, to be issued under the authority of said Coordinating Committee and distributed by the Commission.

3. (a) The plates, individual marks and registration documents issued by the United States for vehicles, trailers, vessels and aircraft which are the property of the Commission shall be accepted by the Republic of Panama.

(b) The Republic of Panama shall recognize as sufficient the valid licenses, permits, certificates or other official classifications from the United States, possessed by operators of vehicles, vessels and aircraft which are property of the United States.

4. (a) The vehicles, trailers, vessels and aircraft belonging to the United States citizen employees or dependents shall also move freely within the Republic of Panama, in compliance with the traffic regulations and those regarding the annual mechanical inspection. The license plate fee and other obligations shall not be discriminatory.

(b) The Republic of Panama shall issue the appropriate documents of title and registration of vehicles, trailers, vessels and aircraft which are the property of United States citizen employees or dependents when the latter present title and registration issued by the federal or state authorities of the United States or by the authorities of the former Canal Zone. Applicants may retain such documents provided they leave with the authorities of the Republic of Panama a copy authenticated by the Commission, duly translated into Spanish. While the corresponding request is being processed and within a term which may not exceed ninety days after entry into force this Agreement or after the arrival of the means of transportation mentioned above in the Republic of Panama, it may be operated with the plates or distinctive marks issued by the federal or state authorities of the United States or by the authorities of the former Canal Zone.

(c) United States citizen employees and dependents who bear valid documents such as drivers' licenses, vessel operators' permits, amateur radio licenses, or licenses and classifications of air pilots issued by the federal or state authorities of the United States or by the authorities of the former Canal Zone, shall receive equivalent Panamanian licenses, permits and classifications without being subjected to new tests or payments of the new fees. The applicants may retain the licenses, permits and classifications of the United States or the former Canal Zone provided that they leave with the authorities of the Republic of Panama a copy authenticated by the Commission and duly translated into Spanish. United States citizen employees and dependents shall be permitted to drive vehicles, vessels or aircraft in the Republic of Panama with such licenses, permits and classifications during the ninety days following the entry into force of this Agreement or their first arrival in the Republic of Panama. During this period the processing of the application in the Republic of Panama for a drivers license, vessel operator's permit, or license and classification as an air pilot shall be completed.

(d) The Panamanian licenses, permits or classifications shall be valid for the period of time indicated in the Panamanian law and, during the continuous presence of the bearer in the Republic of Panama, shall, to preserve their validity, be renewed in accordance with Panamanian laws. Whenever Panamanian laws require medical certifications for the renewal of licenses, permits or classifications, the Republic of Panama shall accept the certifications issued by the medical services of the United States, provided that said certifications are submitted in Spanish translation.

(e) The Republic of Panama shall issue drivers' licenses, vessel operators' permits, and licenses and other classifications of air pilots to United States citizen employees and dependents when they do not possess valid documents. If any test is required as a prerequisite for the issuance of the documents mentioned, the Republic of Panama shall permit the interested persons to take the examination in Spanish or in English. Any material which the Republic of Panama may generally issue in preparation for such examinations shall be furnished, in Spanish or in English, as the applicant may request. The fees for such documents shall not be discriminatory.

5. The Coordinating Committee may agree on rules and procedures that may be necessary to implement this Article.

Article XV—Taxation

1. By virtue of this Agreement, the Commission, its contractors and subcontractors, are exempt from payment in the Republic of Panama of all taxes, fees or other charges on their activities or property.

2. United States citizen employees and dependents shall be exempt from any taxes, fees, or other charges on income received as a result of their work for the Commission. Similarly, they shall be exempt from payment of taxes, fees or other charges on income derived from sources outside the Republic of Panama.

3. United States citizen employees and dependents shall be exempt from taxes, fees or other charges on gifts or inheritance or on personal property, the presence of which within the territory of the Republic of Panama is due solely to the stay therein of such person on account of their sponsor's work with the Commission.

4. The Coordinating Committee may establish such regulations as may be appropriate for the implementation of this Article.

ARTICLE XVI—IMPORT DUTIES

1. Except for the exemptions provided for in this Agreement, United States citizen employees and dependents shall be subject to the customs laws and regulations of the Republic of Panama.

2. All property imported for the official use or benefit of the Commission, including that imported by its contractors or subcontractors in connection with the various activities authorized under this Agreement, shall be exempt from the payment of all customs duties or other import taxes and charges and from all license requirements. The Commission shall issue a certificate, following the form adopted by the Coordinating Committee, stating that the property being imported is for these purposes.

3. Property consigned to or imported for the personal use of United States citizen employees or dependents shall be subject to the payment of import duties or other import taxes, except for the following:

(a) Furniture, household goods and personal effects imported by such persons for their private use within six months following their first arrival in the Republic of Panama.

(b) Vehicles imported by such persons for their private use. The Coordinating Committee shall establish the limitations on the quantity and frequency of additional imports of vehicles and shall authorize such importation of at least one vehicle every two years.

(c) A reasonable quantity of articles for the private use of such persons, imported as personal baggage or sent into the Republic of Panama through the mails.

(d) Such other imports as may be expressly authorized by the competent authorities of the Republic of Panama at the request of the Commission.

4. The exemptions granted in paragraph 3 of this Article apply only to cases involving the importation of articles exempted at the time of entry and shall not be construed as obligating the Republic of Panama to reimburse customs duties and domestic taxes collected by the Republic of Panama in connection with the purchase of goods from Panamanian sources subsequent to their importation.

5. Customs inspections shall not be made in the following cases:

(a) United States citizen employees traveling on official business who enter or depart from the Republic of Panama;

(b) Official documents under official seal, and mail sent through the military postal channels of the United States;

(c) Cargo consigned to the Commission.

6. Property imported under this Article and subsequently transferred to a person who is not entitled to duty-free importation shall be subject to the payment of import duties and other taxes according to the laws and regulations of the Republic of Panama.

7. All property imported in the Republic of Panama free of customs duties and other taxes pursuant to paragraphs 2 and 3 of this

Article may be exported free of customs duties, export permits, export taxes, and other assessments. All property acquired in the Republic of Panama by, or in the name of, the Commission, or acquired by United States citizen employees or dependents for their private use, may be exported free of customs duties, export licenses, and other export taxes or charges.

8. The authorities of the United States agree to cooperate with the authorities of the Republic of Panama and shall take, within their legal authority, all steps necessary to prevent the abuse of the privileges granted under this Article to United States citizen employees or dependents, which measure may include dismissal of such employees.

9. In order to prevent violations of the customs laws and regulations of the Republic of Panama, the two Parties agree as follows:

(a) The competent authorities of the United States and the authorities of the Republic of Panama shall mutually assist one another in the conduct of investigations and the collection of evidence.

(b) The authorities of the United States shall take, within their legal authority, all necessary measures to ensure that articles subject to seizure by or in the name of the customs authorities of the Republic of Panama are delivered to these authorities.

(c) The authorities of the United States shall take, within their legal authority, all necessary measures to ensure the payment by United States citizen employees, and dependents, of such import duties, taxes, and fines as may be duly determined by the authorities of the Republic of Panama.

10. Vehicles and articles belonging to the Commission that are seized from a person by the authorities of the Republic of Panama in connection with a violation of its customs or tax laws or regulations shall be delivered to the competent authorities of the Commission.

11. The Coordinating Committee will constitute the means of communication and information between the two Parties with regard to matters pertaining to the implementation of this Article.

Article XVII—Surveys

The United States may carry out topographic, hydrographic, agrologic and other surveys (including the taking of aerial photographs) within the area made available for the use of the United States pursuant to this Agreement and within the watershed basin of Gatun, Alajuela (Madden) and Miraflores Lakes. Surveys in other areas of the Republic of Panama shall require authorization from the Republic of Panama and shall be carried out in the manner agreed upon in the Coordinating Committee. The Republic of Panama shall, at its option, designate a representative to be present during such surveys. The United States shall furnish a copy of the data resulting from such surveys to the Republic of Panama at no cost.

ARTICLE XVIII—CLAIMS

1. (a) Each Party shall settle claims against it for damage to any property owned and used by the other Party in the following circumstances:

(i) If the damage was caused by an employee of the Government, against which the claim is made, in the performance of his official duties; or

(ii) If the damage arose from the use of any vehicle, vessel or aircraft owned and used by the said Government, provided either that the vehicle, vessel or aircraft causing the damage was being used for official purposes, or that the damage was caused to property being so used.

(b) If it is not settled in due course, the claim may be pursued through diplomatic channels. Both Parties hereby waive the collection of any claims for an amount less than $1,400 U.S., or B/. 1,400, whichever may be the currency of greater value.

2. In cases of maritime salvage, each Party waives its claims against the other if the vessel or cargo salved was the property of the other Party and was used for official purposes.

3. For the purposes of this Article, any vessel chartered, requisitioned or seized in prize by a Party shall be considered its property (except to the extent that the risk of loss or liability is assumed by some other person than such Party).

4. United States citizen employees shall be subject to the jurisdiction of the civil courts of the Republic of Panama except in matters which arise from the performance of their official duty. In cases in which payment has been accepted in full satisfaction of the claim, the civil courts of the Republic of Panama shall dismiss any proceeding concerning such matter.

5. Non-contractual claims arising from damages caused in the performance of their official duties by employees of the Commission to third parties shall be presented by the injured party through the Coordinating Committee to the appropriate authorities of the Commission for settlement. The authorities of the Republic of Panama may submit advice and recommendations on Panamanian law to the claims authorities of the Commission for the use in evaluating liability and amount of damages. The Commission shall assure payment of the appropriate damages if any are due.

6. Contractual claims against the Commission shall be settled in accordance with the dispute clause of the contracts, and in the absence of such clause through presentation of claims to the Commission.

7. The Commission shall require contractors and subcontractors referred to in Article XI of this Agreement to obtain appropriate insurance to cover the civil liabilities that may be incurred in the territory of the Republic of Panama as a result of acts or omissions done in the performance of official duty by their employees. The Coordinating Committee shall establish the general standards for such insurance.

8. The authorities of both Parties shall cooperate in the investigation and procurement of evidence for a fair disposition of claims under this Article.

ARTICLE XIX—CRIMINAL JURISDICTION

1. The Republic of Panama shall exercise, in the manner herein indicated, its jurisdiction over United States citizen employees and dependents with respect to all offenses arising from acts or omissions committed by them within the territory of the Republic of Panama and punishable under the laws of the Republic of Panama.

2. Concerning offenses committed by United States citizen employees or dependents that are punishable under the laws of both Parties, the authorities of the United States may request the Republic of Panama to waive its jurisdiction in favor of the authorities of the United States. Said authorities shall, in their request, state the reasons therefor, and the republic of Panama shall give favorable consideration to such requests in the following cases:

(a) If the offense arises out of an act or omission done in the performance of official duty. In such cases, when requested by the authorities of the Republic of Panama or when the authorities of the United States may deem it necessary, the latter shall issue a certificate establishing that the offense originated from an act or omission occurring in the performance of official duty. The Republic of Panama shall consider this certificate as sufficient proof for the purposes of this paragraph, or shall request a review by the Coordinating Committee, within ten days of the date of receipt of the certificate. The Coordinating Committee shall complete its review within ten days from the date of receipt of the request, except when more thorough consideration may be necessary, in which case the Coordinating Committee shall complete its review within thirty days. A substantial deviation from the duties which a person is required to perform in a specific mission shall generally indicate an act or omission not occurring in the performance of official duty and, consequently, the authorities of the United States will not consider it necessary to issue a certificate of official duty.

(b) If the offense is solely against the property or security of the United States and is committed in a Canal operating area or in a housing area. It is understood that offenses against the security of the United States include: treason or sabotage against the United States, espionage or violation of any law relating to official secrets of the United States or to secrets relating to the national defense of the United States.

3. In any case in which the authorities of the Republic of Panama waive jurisdiction to the United States, or in cases in which the offense constitutes a crime under the laws of the United States, but not under the laws of the Republic of Panama, the accused United States citizens employee or dependent shall be tried outside of the territory of the Republic of Panama.

4. (a) The authorities of the Republic of Panama shall notify the authorities of the United States as promptly as possible of the arrest of any United States citizen employee or dependent.

(b) The following procedures shall govern the custody of an accused United States citizen employee or dependent over whom the Republic of Panama is to exercise its jurisdiction:

(i) If the accused is detained by the authorities of the Republic of Panama he shall, except when charged with murder, rape, robbery with violence, trafficking in drugs, or crimes against the security of the Panamanian State, be handed over on request to the authorities of the United States in whose custody he shall remain until completion of all judicial proceedings and thereafter until custody is requested by authorities of the Republic of Panama for the execution of a sentence.

(ii) When charged with murder, rape, robbery with violence, trafficking in drugs, or crimes against the security of the Panamanian State, the accused will remain in the custody of the authorities of the Republic of Panama. In these cases, the authorities of the Republic of Panama shall give sympathetic consideration to requests for custody by the authorities of the United States.

5. (a) The authorities of the United States shall give full consideration to special requests made by the authorities of the Republic of Panama regarding conditions of custody of any detainee in the custody of the United States.

(b) When the accused is in the custody of the authorities of the United States, he must, upon request by the authorities of the Republic of Panama, be made available to them for the purposes of investigation and trial. This obligation of the United States to ensure the appearance of an accused United States citizen employee, or dependent shall be deemed to satisfy the bail requirement set by the laws of the Republic of Panama.

6. (a) The authorities of the United States and of the Republic of Panama shall assist each other in carrying out all necessary investigations of offenses and in the collection and production of evidence, including the seizure and, in proper cases, the delivery of objects connected with an offense and the appearance of witnesses as necessary.

(b) The authorities of the United States and of the Republic of Panama shall, upon request by the other Party, inform each other of the status of cases referred to under the provisions of this Article.

7. As is provided in the laws of the Republic of Panama, a United States citizen employee or a dependent who has been convicted by a Panamanian court shall not be subject to the death penalty or to any form of cruel and unusual punishment or treatment.

8. When an accused United States citizen employee or dependent has been tried in accordance with the provisions of this Article by the authorities of the United States or by the authorities of the Republic of Panama and has been acquitted, or has been convicted and is serving, or has served, his sentence, or has been pardoned, he shall not be tried again for the same offense within the territory of the Republic of Panama.

9. Whenever an accused United States citizen employee or a dependent is tried by the authorities of the Republic of Panama he shall be entitled to the procedural guarantees listed in Annex C of this Agreement.

10. During the detention by the authorities of the Republic of Panama of a United States citizen employee or a dependent the authorities of the Republic of Panama shall permit members of his

immediate family to visit him weekly. Material and medical assistance (such as food, clothing and comfort items) which the authorities of the United States and members of his immediate family may consider desirable, and any other assistance which is in accordance with or allowed by Panamanian prison regulations, may be provided to him on such visits.

11. The Coordinating Committee will constitute the channel of communication and information between the two Parties with regard to matters pertaining to the implementation of this Article.

ARTICLE XX—GENERAL PROVISIONS

1. The activities of the United States in the Republic of Panama shall be carried out with adequate attention to public health and safety, and consequently, within the areas made available for the use of the United States under this Agreement, the authorities of the United States shall have the right to take appropriate sanitation measures. The authorities of the United States shall cooperate with the authorities of the Republic of Panama for these purposes.

2. United States citizen employees and dependents may bear private arms in accordance with applicable Panamanian laws and regulations.

3. The Commission shall establish regulations to provide for the handling of matters under its competence in the English and Spanish languages, as appropriate.

ARTICLE XXI—DURATION

This Agreement shall enter into force simultaneously with the entry into force of the Panama Canal Treaty, signed this date, and shall remain in force throughout the period that the aforesaid Treaty remains in force.

DONE at Washington, this 7th day of September 1977, in duplicate, in the English and Spanish languages, both being equally authentic.

ANNEX A—CANAL OPERATING AREAS, HOUSING AREAS, ACCESSORY FACILITIES AND INSTALLATIONS, AND ANCHORAGES

The Canal operating areas, housing areas, accessory facilities and installations, and anchorages, the use of which is made available by the Republic of Panama to the United States by this Agreement, are described below and identified, but not definitively, on the maps attached hereto and referenced herein.[2] When areas or installations are depicted on more than one map of different scales, the identification on the map with the largest scale shall be controlling. More precise identifications and exact boundaries shall be agreed upon as soon as practicable by the Coordinating Committee established in Article II of this Agreement, after a joint survey to be conducted by representatives of the two Parties. When the aforementioned identifications have been completed and agreed upon,

---

[2] The maps referred to in this Annex are not reproduced in this volume. See TIAS 10031, attachment 1 [pocket].

The map atlas is deposited in the archives of the Department of State where it is available for reference.

they shall be controlling as to the boundaries of the installations and areas described in this Annex.

1. (a) The Canal operating areas are described generally as follows:

(i) A continuous area generally following the course of the Panama Canal and generally contiguous to it, running from the Atlantic Ocean to the Pacific Ocean, and including the Atlantic entrance, Gatun Locks, dam, spillway and power station, portions of Gatun Lake, Gaillard Cut, Pedro Miguel Locks, Miraflores Lake, Miraflores Locks, spillway filtration plant and power station, and the Pacific entrance, as well as the land and water areas encompassing them.

(ii) Certain areas not contiguous to the Canal, including the Brazos Brook area, the Gatun tank area, the Madden Dam and power station area, the Corozal/Cardenas area, and the Sosa hill area.

The Canal operating area described generally above, with the two exceptions hereinafter referred to, is identified on the map which is attached hereto as Attachment No. 1 in the manner indicated on the legend thereof. Although not so identified on the referenced map, the land and water areas which lie beneath the Thatcher Ferry Bridge and any new bridge that is constructed along the Panama/Arraijan right of way, to the extent that they are within the boundaries of the Canal operating area described in subparagraph 1(a)(i), above, are included in, and are parts of, that Canal operating area.

(iii) Barro Colorado Island, in the event and at such time as the Smithsonian Tropical Research Institute or an organization of similar purpose discontinues its activities there. This island is identified by name on the map attached hereto as Attachment No. 1.

(iv) Summit Naval Radio Station, at such time as use of the area is no longer required by the United States Forces. For purposes of this provision, this area is identified by name on the map attached hereto as Attachment No. 1.

(b) The Canal Zone Penitentiary shall cease to be a part of the Canal operating areas three years following the entry into force of this Agreement. For the purposes of this provision, the approximate center of this area is located at Coordinate 441069 on the map attached hereto as Attachment No. 1.

(c) The following areas shall cease to be a part of the Canal operating area five years following the entry into force of this Agreement:

(i) The Mount Hope warehouse area; and

(ii) The Mount Hope motor transportation area.

For the purposes of this provision, the Mount Hope warehouse area is identified on the map attached hereto as Attachment No. 2, SK 529–25–14A, in the manner indicated on the legend thereof, and the Mount Hope motor transportation area is identified on the map attached hereto as Attachment No. 3, SK 529–25–13A, in the manner indicated on the legend thereof.

(d) The following installations not contiguous to the Canal operating areas described in subparagraph 1(a) above shall be subject to the provisions of the Panama Canal Treaty and this Agreement applicable to the Canal operating areas:

(i) Retirement Office (449–X);
(ii) Sanitation Buildings (428, 428–X);
(iii) Health Bureau Official Quarters (286, 288, 286–G);
(iv) Pump House, Chilled Water (278);
(v) Treasurer's Office (287, 287–X);
(vi) Central Employment Office (363);
(vii) Payroll Branch Office (365);
(viii) Personnel Bureau Office (366);
(ix) Grounds Maintenance Building (361);
(x) Distribution Substation (367);
(xi) District Court Building (310);
(xii) Community Welfare (Red Cross) (0610–B);
(xiii) Motor Transportation Facilities (0625–A through K, 0630–C);
(xiv) Grounds Maintenance Office (0630–B);
(xv) Sewage Treatment Plant (0626, 0626–A, 0626–B);
(xvi) Grounds Maintenance Building (0586–X); and
(xvii) Maintenance Field Shop (234).

The installations which are described immediately above are identified on the map attached hereto as Attachment No. 4, SK 529–5–1, in the manner indicated on the legend thereof.

(xviii) Administration Building (101);
(xix) Balboa Filtered Water—Pump Station (634);
(xx) Community Service Office Building (635);
(xxi) Training Center (0600, 0602, 0604);
(xxii) Ancon Water Reservoir;
(xxiii) Grounds Maintenance Buildings (106, 108–X); and
(xxiv) Garage (628–X).

The installations which are described immediately above are identified on the map attached hereto as Attachment No. 5, SK 529–25–2, in the manner indicated on the legend thereof.

(xxv) Buildings (725, 726);
(xxvi) Community Health Center Building (721);
(xxvii) Maintenance Shop (1437);
(xxviii) Garage Buildings (0900, 711–X, 761–X, 786–X, 787–X, 788–X, 789–X, 797–X, 1435);
(xxix) Storage Sheds and Toilets (1559–X, 0773, 0849, 1435–X);
(xxx) Community Service Youth Facilities (0910);
(xxxi) Sewage Pump Station (0755);
(xxxii) Magistrates Court (803);
(xxxiii) Balboa Police Station (801, 801–R, 801–S, 801–T, 801–U); and
(xxxiv) Water Tanks—Ancon Hill.

The installations which are described immediately above are identified on the map attached hereto as Attachment No. 6, SK 529–25–3, in the manner indicated on the legend thereof.

(xxxv) Docks 12, 13 and 19;
(xxxvi) Harbor Master Building (43–A);
(xxxvii) Construction Division Offfice (29–X)
(xxxviii) Port Engineer Building (31);
(xxxix) Instrument Repair Shop (1–J);

(xl) Apprentice Training Facilities (2A and 3);

(xli) Warehouses (5, 19, 4, 44–B and 42 including yard area and miscellaneous small support buildings);

(xlii) Supply Management office (28);

(xliii) Refrigeration and Air Conditioning Repair Facility (14);

(xliv) Maintenance Facilities (8 and 10);

(xlv) Toilets (21);

(xlvi) Pilots Carport (39–B);

(xlvii) Rigging Shed, supporting Dock 19 (51);

(xlviii) Furniture Storage, Lubrication Warehouse (78);

(xlix) Community Service Balboa recreational Tennis Courts;

(l) Pier 20 Area (including 57 and 57–X);

(li) Electronic Repair Facility (40);

(lii) Core Storage (12);

(liii) Central Air Conditioning Plant and Cooling Tower (9);

(liv) Maintenance Equipment Storage (13);

(lv) Sand Blasting Shed (12–A);

(lvi) Community Service Recreational Facility (9–A);

(lvii) Electrical Division Buildings (66–A, 66–B, 66–C, 66–D, 66–E, 38 and 36);

(lviii) Chilled Water Pump house 972);

(lix) Telephone Exchange Building (69); and

(lx) Building (37).

The installations which are described immediately above are identified on the map attached hereto as Attachment No. 7, SK 529–25–4, in the manner indicated on the legend thereof.

(lxi) Toilets and Storage (1256);

(lxii) Community Service Youth Facilities (0791);

(lxiii) Foam Storage Facility (1254);

(lxiv) Sewage Pump Station No. 2 (1208);

(lxv) Dock 4;

(lxvi) Printing and Duplicating Center (911); and

(lxvii) Marine Traffic Control Center (909, 910).

The installations which are described immediately above are identified on the map attached hereto as Attachment No. 8, SK 529–25–5, in the manner indicated on the legend thereof.

(lxviii) Records Storage (42–D);

(lxix) Warehouse and Office (42–G, 42–F);

(lxx) Quarters Maintenance Shop (5052);

(lxxi) Toilets and Storage (5546);

(lxxii) Storage and Warehouse (5553);

(lxxiii) Surveying Office and Storage (5250);

(lxxiv) Community Service Center (5051, 5051–X);

(lxxv) Diablo Power Substation (5300);

(lxxvi) Office Building (5140); and

(lxxvii) Storage Warehouse (42–E).

The installations which are described immediately above are identified on the map attached hereto as Attachment No. 9, SK 529–25–6, in the manner indicated on the legend thereof.

(lxxviii) Water Tanks;

(lxxix) Water Pump Station (6219);

(lxxx) Toilets and Storage (6423);

(lxxxi) Community Welfare—AA (6550); and

(lxxxii) Los Rios Power Substation (6464).

The installations which are described immediately above are identified on the map attached hereto as Attachment No. 10, SK 529–25–7, in the manner indicated on the legend thereof.

(lxxxiii) Telephone Exchange (52);

(lxxxiv) Communication Field Office (53);

(lxxxv) Fire Station (62);

(lxxxvi) Community Service Center (65–A) and B.S.A. (729);

(lxxxvii) Gas Station, Noncommercial (57);

(lxxxviii) Housing Office, Maintenance Shops (58);

(lxxxix) Toilet and Storage (77–A, 0277–X, 332);

(xc) Sanitation Building (64); and

(xci) Community Health Center (63).

The installations which are described immediately above are identified on the map attached hereto as Attachment No. 11, SK 529–25–10, in the manner indicated on the legend thereof.

(xcii) Grounds Maintenance Offices, Toilets and Storage (40–A, 40–G, 141;

(xciii) Garages (29, 29–A, 108, 140);

(xciv) Telephone Exchange (102–X);

(xcv) A.R.S. (71, 74, 104, 135, 150, 208, 210, 220, 233–X, 236–X, 262, 355, 373, UX–1, UX–2, UX–3) and B.S.A. (122);

(xcvi) Public Toilet (385);

(xcvii) Fire Station (161);

(xcviii) Community Service Center (206); and

(xcix) Gatun Power Substation (100).

The installations which are described immediately above are identified on the map attached hereto as Attachment No. 12, SK 529–25–11, in the manner indicated on the legend thereof.

(c) Construction Division Office (7998);

(ci) Quarters Maintenance Shop and Office (7999);

(cii) Toilets and Storage (8038–X, 8471);

(ciii) Community Service Center (8040);

(civ) Sewage Pump Station (8140); and

(cv) Community Service Center Building Garage (8040–X).

The installations which are described immediately above are identified on the map attached hereto as Attachment No. 13, SK 529–251–2, in the manner indicated on the legend thereof.

(cvi) Engineering Survey Building (9212);

(cvii) Telephone Building (9214); and

(cviii) Fire Station Building (9100).

The installations which are described immediately above are identified on the map attached hereto as Attachment No. 14, SK 529–25–8, in the manner indicated on the legend thereof.

(cix) Filtered Water Pump House (308); and

(cx) Paraiso Power Substations.

The installations which are described immediately above are identified on the map attached hereto as Attachment No. 15, SK 529–25–9, in the manner indicated on the legend thereof.

(cxi) Motor Transportation Facilities (5046, 5063, 5064, 5064–A, 5065, 5067, 5077); and

(cxii) Canal/IRHE Power Interconnect Station.

The installations which are described immediately above are identified on the map attached hereto as Attachment No. 16, SK 529–25–13, in the manner indicated on the legend thereof.

(cxiii) Mount Hope Warehouse Complex (7018, 7020, 7021, 7022, 7025–A, 7025–B, 7025–C, 7030, 7031, 7032, 7033);

(cxiv) Fire Station (7029);

(cxv) Mount Hope Water Filtration Plant (7035, 7037 and Water Tanks 1 and 2);

(cxvi) Air Conditioning and Refrigeration Maintenance (7024); and

(cxvii) Electrical Field Facilities (7051, 7051–A, 7051–B, 7051–C, 7051–D, 7056).

The installations which are described immediately above are identified on the map attached hereto as Attachment No. 17, SK 529–25–14, in the manner indicated on the legend thereof.

(cxviii) Tugboat Personnel Parking Area and Shed;

(cxix) Harbor Master Office and Boat House (1013);

(cxx) Administration Building (1105); (3339);

(cxxi) Dredging Division Office and Dock (3339);

(cxxii) Maintenance Facilities (1707, 1707–C, 1707–D, 1707–E, 1709, 1726, 1728, 1730, 1708);

(cxxiii) Telephone Exchange (1907);

(cxxiv) Signal Station—Top of Pier 6;

(cxxv) Tug Landings at ends of Piers 6 and 7; and

(cxxvi) Police Training Center (1107).

The installations which are described immediately above are identified on the map attached hereto as Attachment No. 18, SK 529–25–15, in the manner indicated on the legend thereof.

(cxxvii) Buildings (22, 100, 82);

(cxxviii) Toilets and Storage (53);

(cxxix) Community Service Center and Telephone Exchange (1140);

(cxxx) Coco Solo Power Substation (3);

(cxxxi) Maintenance Shop (130); and

(cxxxii) Imhoff Tanks (86, 91).

The installations which are described immediately above are identified on the map attached hereto as Attachment No. 19, SK 529–25–16, in the manner indicated on the legend thereof.

(cxxxiii) Toilet and Storage (0349).

The installation which is described immediately above is identified on the map attached hereto as Attachment No. 20, SK 529–25–18, in the manner indicated on the legend thereof.

(cxxxiv) Amador Causeway and roadway south from southern tip of Fort Amador (Coordinates 601873 to 627847);

(cxxxv) Naos Island landing facilities, including dispatcher building, piers, float, breakwater and access roadway (Coordinate 611858);

(cxxxvi) Flamenco Island Signal Station (Coordinate 627847);

(cxxvii) Farfan Spillway (Coordinate 577868);

(cxxxviii) Madden Wye Facilities (101, 102, 104, 105, 106, 107, 108, 109, 111, 112, 113, 114, 127, 128, 129, 149, 172, 173) (Coordinate 499016);

(cxxxix) Summit Power Substation (Coordinate 495013);

(cxl) Summit Explosive Storage Facilities (1, 2, and 3) (Coordinate 477030);

(cxli) 44 KV Power Transmission Line (Coordinates 519183 to 495013);

(cxlii) Coco Solito Water Meterhouse (6201) (Coordinate 229323); and

(cxliii) South Coco Solo Power Substation (1116) (Coordinate 232345).

The approximate center or locations of the installations described immediately above are identified by the accompanying coordinates, as located on the map attached hereto as Attachment No. 1.

(e) The following installations that are described in subparagraph 1(d) above shall cease to be installations subject to the provisions of this Agreement applicable to the Canal operating areas as stated below:

(i) Thirty calendar months following the entry into force of this Agreement:

(A) The Balboa Police Station Complex (801, 801–R, 801–S, 801–T and 801–U).

(B) The Balboa Magistrates Court (803).

For the purposes of this provision, the Balboa Police Station complex and the Balboa Magistrates Court are identified on the map attached hereto as Attachment No. 21, SK 529–25–3A, in the manner indicated on the legend thereof.

(ii) Three years following the entry into force of this Agreement:

(A) The Ancon District Court (310).

(B) The Cristobal Police Training Center (1107).

For the purposes of this provision, the Ancon District Court is identified on the map attached hereto as Attachment No. 22, SK 529–25–1A, in the manner indicated on the legend thereof, and the Cristobal Police Training Center is identified on the map attached hereto as Attachment No. 23, SK 529–25–15A, in the manner indicated on the legend thereof.

(iii) At such time as the United States ceases to use such installations:

(A) The Balboa Commissary Installation (725 and 726).

(B) The Coco Solo Commissary installation (100 and 22).

For the purposes of this provision, the Balboa Commissary Installation is identified on the map attached hereto as Attachment No. 21, SK 529–25–3A, and the Coco Solo Commissary installation is identified on the map attached hereto as Attachment No. 24, SK 529–25–16A.

(iv) At such times the following areas and installations are required by the Republic of Panama for expansion of the Port of Balboa.

(A) The Pier 20 area (including 57 and 57–X).

(B) The Scrap Yard area (less 42).

For the purposes of this provision, these areas and installations are identified on the map attached hereto as Attachment No. 25, SK 529–25–4A in the manner indicated on the legend thereof.

2. The Housing Areas are as follows:

(a) Coco Solo, as identified on the map attached hereto as Attachment No. 19, SK 529–25–16, in the manner indicated on the legend thereof.

(b) France Field (Gold Hill), as identified on the map attached hereto as Attachment No. 20, SK 529–25–18, in the manner indicated on the legend thereof.

(c) Margarita, as identified on the map attached hereto as Attachment No. 13, SK 529–25–12, in the manner indicated on the legend thereof.

(d) Mindi, as located on the map attached hereto as Attachment No. 1 (approximate center at Coordinate 202286).

(e) Gatun, as identified on the map attached hereto as Attachment No. 12, SK 529–25–11, in the manner indicated on the legend thereof.

(f) Gamboa, as identified on the map attached hereto as Attachment No. 11, SK 529–25–10, in the manner indicated on the legend thereof.

(g) Cardenas (Commission housing), as identified on the map attached hereto as Attachment No. 26, SK 529–25–7A, in the manner indicated on the legend thereof.

(h) Los Rios, as identifed on the map attached hereto as Attachment No. 10, SK 529–25–7, in the manner indicated on the legend thereof.

(i) Corozal, as identified on the map attached hereto as Attachment No. 10, SK 529–25–7, in the manner indicated on the legend thereof.

(j) Diablo, as identified on the map attached hereto as Attachment No. 9, SK 529–25–6, in the manner indicated on the legend thereof.

(k) Balboa (La Boca), as identified on the maps attached hereto as Attachments Nos. 6 and 8, SK 529–25–3 and SK 529–25–5, in the manner indicated on the legends thereof.

(l) Balboa Heights, as identifed on the map attached hereto as Attachment No. 5, SK 529–25–2, in the manner indicated on the legend thereof.

(m) Ancon, as identified on the map attached hereto as Attachment No. 4, SK 529–25–1, in the manner indicated on the legend thereof.

(n) 18 housing units located within the area identified as the "Summit Naval Radio Station" on the map attached hereto as Attachment No. 1, in the event, and at such time as the area ceases to be a Military Area of Coordination.

(o) Cardenas (FAA housing), as identified on the map attached hereto as Attachment No. 27, SK 529–25–7AA, in the manner indicated on the legend thereof, in the event and at such time as the use of said housing area by the Federal Aviation Administration terminates and the area ceases to be an area subject to a separate bilateral agreement.

3. The accessory installations and facilities outside the areas made available for the use of the United States which the United States may continue to use are as follows:

(a) aids to navigation;

(b) triangulation stations;

(c) hydrographic stations and telemetering stations;

(d) spoil dump areas;
(e) ship beaching areas;
(f) saddle dams, dikes and water control structures;
(g) piers and docks;
(h) bank stability surveillance and protection systems;
(i) support facilities; and
(j) other existing facilities and installation required for the management, operation, or maintenance of the Canal (such as maintenance facilities, utility lines, and pipelines).

4. The Anchorages are as follows:

(a) The Pacific anchorage area, as identified on navigational chart No. 21603, attached hereto as Attachment No. 28, in the manner indicated on the legend thereof.

(b) The Atlantic anchorage area, as identified on navigational chart No. 26068, attached hereto as Attachment No. 29, in the manner indicated on the legend thereof.

5. The areas for expansion of the Anchorages are as follows:

(a) The Pacific anchorage expansion area, as indentified on the navigation chart attached hereto as Attachment No. 28, in the manner indicated on the legend thereof.

(b) The Atlantic anchorage expansion area, as identified on the navigational chart attached hereto as Attachment No. 29, in the manner indicated on the legend thereof.

(c) The Limon Bay anchorage expansion area, as identified on the navigational chart attached hereto as Attachment No. 29, in the manner indicated on the legend thereof.

6. The following land and water areas outside of the areas made available for the use of the United States pursuant to the Panama Canal Treaty are also subject to the land use licensing procedure set forth in Article V of this Agreement as stated:

(a) As of the entry into force of this Agreement:

(i) The Chagres River between Gamboa and Madden Dam to the 100 foot contour line. The Chagres River between Gatun Dam and the Caribbean Sea to the 30 foot contour line.

(ii) Near to the Atlantic entrance to the Canal:

—Within Limon Bay, those areas west of the Canal's channel that are not within the Canal operating area.

—Outside Limon Bay, for a distance of 3 kilometers on each side of the center line of the Canal's channel from the breakwater north for a distance of 3 nautical miles.

(iii) Near the Pacific entrance of the Canal:

—Along the east bank of the Canal from Balboa Port south to the Amador causeway, 30 miles inland from the high water mark.

—Along that portion of the Amador causeway extending from the southern limit of the Fort Amador mainland to Naos Island, the area northeast of the causeway for a distance of 1 kilometer.

—The water areas within a distance of 3 kilometers each side of the center line of the Canal channel from a point (Coordinate 603855) near Naos Island extending southeast paralleling the Canal center line for a distance of 3 nautical miles.

—The water areas between the easterly boundary of the Howard Air Force Base-Fort Kobbe Complex and the Canal channel.

(b) Three years after the entry into force of this Agreement: Canal Zone Penitentiary area (Gamboa), as described in subparagraph 1(b) above.

Annex B—Ports of Balboa and Cristobal

The areas and installations of the Ports of Balboa and Cristobal, as well as certain specific use rights and guarantees granted by the Republic of Panama to the United States in connection therewith, are described below and, in the case of the said areas and installation, are identified, but not definitively, on the maps attached hereto and referenced herein and on various maps attached to Annex A. When areas or installations are depicted on more than one map of different scales, the identification on the map with the largest scale shall be controlling. More precise identifications and exact boundaries shall be agreed upon as soon as practicable and in the same manner as described in Annex A. When the aforementioned identifications have been completed and agreed upon, they shall be controlling as to the boundaries of the installations and areas described in this Annex.

1. The boundaries of the Ports of Balboa and Cristobal are identified on the maps attached hereto as Attachments Nos. 1 and 2 respectively, in the manner indicated on the legend thereof.

2. The United States shall have the right to use, for the management, operation, maintenance, protection and defense of the Canal, the following port installations and equipment which the Republic of Panama shall maintain in efficient operating condition:

(a) Docks 6, 7, 14, 15, 16, 17, and Pier 18, including fendering systems, capstans, camels, bollards, bits, and wearing surfaces, railroad spurs, crane tracks, signal lights, water lines, sewers, compressed air lines, power cables, telephone cables, duct lines and material handling equipment, tunnels, and switch gear.

(b) Facilities.

(i) Drydock No. 1, including all of the following facilities, equipment and utilities required to support its operation:

(A) Drydock Miter Gates and two electric motors and mechanical systems for opening and closing the gates.

(B) Fifty keel blocks and one hundred and fifty hauling blocks, including all hauling block tracks, chain sheaves, brackets, hauling chains, and blocking dogs.

(C) Ten capstans.

(D) Flooding/dewatering tunnels.

(E) Four dewatering pumps, two drainage pumps, and one salt water pump.

(F) All valves, bulkheads, and screens in the flooding and dewatering system.

(G) Three stationary 1,600 CFM Joy Air Compressors.

(H) One elevator.

(I) Sixteen portable rain sheds.

(J) Dock 8.

(K) All electrical switch gear, lighting and power systems, water and compressed air piping, and hydraulic control systems located in Building 29, the Drydock and Dock 8.

(ii) Buildings:

Numbers	Description
1	Machine shop.
1–C	Facilities building (storage).
1–D	Launch repair.
1–G	Pipe shop.
1–H	Central toolcrib. Hose and blower room; power tool repair shop.
29	Pump and compressor plant.
32	Drydock block storage shed.
17, 18, 20, 25, and 30	Toilet and locker rooms.

All utility tunnels, electrical air and water systems which serve these buildings.

(c) Machine Tools and Equipment:

(i) Cranes D–4 (50-tons, steam) and D–19–N (30-ton, diesel-electric) and all trackage.

(ii) Portable 5-ton electric cranes (US–28 and 52).

(iii) Overhead Cranes: Two in bldg. 29; two in Bldg. 1.

(iv) Scaffolding and gangways.

(v) Bolt cutting and threading machine, M–569–N.

(vi) Grinding machine, M–723–N.

(vii) Band saws: T2–22–N, T2–27–N, XT–627, N–27, and BR–65.

(viii) Lathes: M–267, M–539–N, M–820–N, L–121–N, L–132, XM–729–N, XM–741–N, XM–808–N.

(ix) Milling machines: M–575–N, L–99–N, L–100–N, and L–118–N.

(x) Planers: M–178 and M–824–N.

(xi) Drill presses: M–578–N, M–701, and M–709–N.

(xii) Wood lathe, N–36.

(xiii) Wood planer, N–24.

(xiv) Wood jointer, M–197–N.

(xv) Jointer-Planer, BR–64.

(xvi) Wood saw, M–29–N.

(xvii) Bench saw, BR–66.

(xviii) Disc sander, N–32.

(xix) Surfacing machine, L–207.

(xx) Threading machines, L–194 and T2–23–N.

(xxi) Shear, XT2–90.

(xxii) Dynamometer, L–172.

(xxiii) Bolt-heading machine, F–174–N.

(xxiv) Grinding machines, XW–599–N and XM–758.

(xxv) Bending machine, T2–31–N.

(xxvi) Mortising machine, XW–707–N.
(xxvii) Router and boring machine, XW–820–N.
(xviii) Edge planer, XB–872.
(xxix) Table saw, S–572–N.

3. The United States shall have the right, on a guaranteed basis, to use the following installations and port services in accordance with the Commission's maintenance schedules or for emergency repairs:

(a) The facilities listed in paragraph 2(b) of this Annex.

(b) The machine tools and equipment listed in paragraph 2(c) of this annex.

(c) Access.

(i) Paved yard area adjacent to Drydock No. 1 and to the buildings listed in subparagraph 2(b)(ii) of this Annex.

(ii) Required water access for floating equipment and vessels from canal operating area to Drydock No. 1 includes water depth sufficient to clear gate sill (−39.5 feet PLD) and sufficient clearance between Docks 7 and 8 to permit safe entry.

ANNEX C—PROCEDURAL GUARANTEES

A United States citizen employee, or a dependent, prosecuted by the Panamanian authorities shall be entitled to the following procedural guarantees:

(a) To a prompt and speedy trial.

(b) To be informed, in advance of trial, of the specific charge or charges made against him.

(c) To be confronted with and to be allowed to cross-examine the witnesses against him.

(d) To have evidence and witnesses in his favor presented. The authorities shall submit such evidence and call the witnesses if they are within the Republic of Panama.

(e) To have legal representation of his own choice for his defense during all investigative and judicial phases from the time of submission to questioning and throughout the entire proceedings; or, if he indicates he lacks funds for his defense, to be defended by the appropriate public defender.

(f) To have the services of a competent interpreter if he considers it necessary.

(g) To communicate with a representative of the Government of the United States to have such a representative present, as an observer, at his trial.

(h) Not to be held guilty on account of any act or omission which did not constitute a criminal offense under the law of the Republic of Panama at the time it was committed.

(i) To be present at his trial which shall be public. However, without prejudice to the procedural guarantees in this Annex, persons whose presence is not necessary may be excluded, if the court so decides for reasons of public orders or morality.

(j) In his proceedings to have the total burden of proof laden upon the Public Prosecutor or the prosecution.

(k) To have the court consider only voluntary confessions and evidence properly obtained in accordance with the requirements of the law.

(l) Not to be compelled to testify against or otherwise incriminate himself.

(m) Not to be required to stand trial if he is not physically or mentally fit to stand trial and participate in his defense.

(n) Not to be tried or punished more than once for the same offense.

(o) To have the right to appeal a conviction or sentence.

(p) To have credited to any sentence for confinement his entire period of pretrial custody.

(q) Not to be subject to the application of martial law or trial by military courts or special tribunals.

(r) To enjoy all other guarantees and rights provided for in the Constitution, Judicial Code and other laws of the Republic of Panama.

[TRANSLATION]

AGREED MINUTE TO THE AGREEMENT IN IMPLEMENTATION OF ARTICLE III OF THE PANAMA CANAL TREATY

1. With reference to paragraph 2 of Article I, it is agreed that skilled, technical or professional employees of the Commission, who are nationals of States other than the United States or the Republic of Panama, and their dependents, shall have the same rights and privileges as United States citizen employees and dependents under the Panama Canal Treaty and the Agreement in Implementation of Article III of that Treaty (hereinafter referred to as "the Agreement"). Presence in connection with employment by the Commission shall not be considered as residence in the Republic of Panama. However, this provision shall not apply to nationals of third States recruited within the Republic of Panama after the entry into force of the Agreement.

2. With reference to Article II, it is contemplated that the United States may be represented on the Coordinating Committee by a senior United States citizen official or employee of the Commission and that the Republic of Panama will be represented by a citizen of the Republic of Panama of corresponding level or rank.

3. With reference to Article VI:

(a) It is understood that during the five years following the entry into force of the Panama Canal Treaty, certain United States nationals employed by the United States Forces, such as employees of medical and educational facilities, and the dependents, shall be considered to be United States citizen employees and dependents.

(b) It is understood that a housing unit is an individual family apartment, bachelor apartment or bachelor room in a single or multi-dwelling building. The minimum percentages of housing units, the use of which will pass to the Republic of Panama, have been calculated on the basis of an estimated inventory of approximately 4,300 housing units owned by the Panama Canal Company immediately prior to entry into force of the Agreement.

4. With reference to paragraph 3 of Article XIII, concerning educational services that may be furnished to United States citizen employees and their dependents, it is understood that the United States may continue to furnish such services to dependents of any person, regardless of nationality, in those cases in which such dependents were enrolled in the school system of the former Canal Zone Government prior to the entry into force of the Agreement.

5. With reference to paragraph 2 of Article XIX, it is understood that, as a matter of general policy, the Republic of Panama will waive jurisdiction to the United States, at its request, in cases arising under that paragraph.

6. With reference to paragraph 4(b) of Article XIX, the five offenses under Panamanian law referred to are understood to be:

(a) Murder—the intentional killing of one person by another.

(b) Rape—the commission of an act of sexual intercourse by violence or threat and without consent with a person not his spouse, or with a person who is not capable of resisting by reason of mental or physical illness, or with a minor less than twelve years old.

(c) Robbery with violence—the act of appropriating an object of value belonging to someone else with the purpose of depriving its owner of his possession and deriving benefit from it, using violence against such person or a third person present at the scene of the act.

(d) Trafficking in drugs—the unlawful sale, exchange, or transfer for gain of marihuana, hashish, heroin, cocaine, amphetamines, barbiturates, or L.S.D.

(e) Crimes against the security of the Panamanian State—espionage, sabotage, or terrorism directed against the constituted powers or authorities of the Republic of Panama, with the purpose of overthrowing them.

7. With reference to Annex A, it is understood that the United States may continue to provide utility services, in coordination with the appropriate authorities of the Republic of Panama, for certain of those areas and facilities transferred to the Republic of Panama as provided in Article XIII of the Panama Canal Treaty. It is further understood that since the utilities systems serving many of these areas and facilities are fully integrated with those of the Canal, the United States may, on behalf of the utilities agencies of the Republic of Panama, continue to provide utilities such as power, water, and sewers to private persons or to agencies of the Government of Panama in such areas. It is further understood that the utilities agencies of the Republic of Panama will be responsible for setting rates for and billing such of its customers, and will reimburse the United States for its cost in providing such services.

8. With reference to subparagraph 1(a) of Annex A:

(a) it is understood that the Republic of Panama may construct (i) an Atlantic Coast Highway through a right-of-way to be agreed upon by the Parties, at such time as the Republic of Panama is prepared to begin construction of that highway, and (ii) a new highway on the Pacific side of the Isthmus through a right-of-way to be agreed upon by the Parties at such time as the Republic of Panama is prepared to begin construction of that highway. It is further understood that the bridge over the Canal, in each case, will be constructed sufficiently high to as not to interfere with the operation of the Canal or with any improvements that may be made to the Canal.

(b) it is understood that the National Port Authority of the Republic of Panama will have the right to use, free of cost, the marine bunkering facilities located on Pier 16, Cristobal, for discharging petroleum products, subject always to the right of the United States to use those facilities on a priority basis. It is further understood that, in connection with its use of those facilities, the Republic of Panama will not alter or modify Pier 16, the marine bunkering facilities or the utilities thereon, except as mutually agreed, and will reimburse the United States for any damage caused as a result of the Republic of Panama's use of such facilities.

9. With reference to paragraphs 1(d) (xxxiii) and 1(e)(i)(A) of Annex A, it is understood that the United States shall make available to the Republic of Panama appropriate areas within the Balboa Police Station Complex for police liaison purposes for the thirty-month transition period following the entry into force of the Agreement. It is understood that at the end of that period, the provisions of paragraph 2(b) of Article XIII of the Panama Canal Treaty shall apply. With reference to paragraph 1(d)(cxx) of Annex A, it is understood that the United States shall, if requested by the Republic of Panama, make available to the Republic of Panama appropriate areas within the Cristobal Police Station (located in Building 1105) for police liaison purposes for the aforesaid thirty-month period and, thereafter, for general police functions.

10. With reference to subparagraph 1(e)(iv) (A) and (B) of Annex A, it is understood that at such time as Pier 20 and the Scrap Yard area referred to therein cease to be areas subject to the provisions of the Agreement applicable to the Canal operating areas, the Republic of Panama will provide comparable and acceptable pier space in Balboa Harbor and scrap yard areas for the use of the Commission at no charge.

11. With reference to paragraph 2 of Annex A, it is understood that the United States may continue to operate and maintain noncommercial recreational and community service areas and facilities for the benefit of all occupants of the housing areas and all employees of the Commission, and their dependents, on a nondiscriminatory basis. It is further understood that recreational and community service activities conducted in such areas and facilities will be noncommercial, and there will be no user charges associated therewith unless otherwise agreed by the Parties.

12. With reference to subparagraph 3(d) of Annex A, it is understood that such spoil dump areas include the spoil dump areas

identified on the navigational charts attached thereto as Attachments 28 and 29, in the manner indicated on the legend thereof.

13. With reference to subparagraph 3(j) of Annex A, it is understood that the Republic of Panama will not undertake or permit any construction, excavation or other activity which may endanger or encroach upon underground or aboveground installations, including pipes, ducts, culverts, cables, microwave paths and transmission lines, except as may be otherwise agreed in the Coordinating Committee.

14. With reference to Attachment Nos. 1 and 6 of Annex A, it is understood that the Republic of Panama shall continue to use the Balboa Fire Station (Building 703, Attachment No. 6) and the Coco Solito Fire Station (Building 96, Attachment No. 1, Coordinates 231328) as fire protection installations throughout the life of the Agreement, unless otherwise agreed by the Parties. The provisions of paragraph 2(a) of Article XIII of the Panama Canal Treaty apply to such fire stations. It is further understood that the United States, which may continue to provide fire protection of Commission areas and installations, and the Republic of Panama, which is responsible for fire protection generally throughout its territory, will review periodically the most effective allocation of both Parties' fire protection resources, and, if appropriate, the United States will transfer to the Republic of Panama such other fire stations as are excess to its needs. The Republic of Panama shall continue the use of any installations so transferred as fire protection installations for the life of the Agreement, unless otherwise agreed. It is understood also that both Parties will cooperate fully in ensuring effective and efficient delivery of fire protection services throughout the vicinity of the Canal.

15. With reference to Attachments 1, 14 and 15 to Annex A, it is understood that prior to authorizing any new use of or activities in the townsites of Pedro Miguel (Attachment No. 14) or Paraiso (Attachment No. 15) or (a) the land areas within a distance of 3 kilometers each side of the center line of the Canal channel from a point (Coordinate 603855) near Naos Island extending southeast paralleling the Canal center line for a distance of 3 nautical miles or (b) the land areas between the easterly boundary of the Howard Air Force Base-Fort Kobbe Complex and the Canal channel, the Republic of Panama shall ensure that the Commission concurs in writing that the proposed use or activity would be compatible with the efficient management, operation, maintenance, protection and defense of the Canal. It is further understood that the Republic of Panama (a) shall control and supervise the activities to be carried out under its responsibility in the aforementioned townsites and areas to ensure that such activities are compatible with such purposes, and (b) shall take the measures necessary to prevent, or to terminate, any activity that, in the opinion of the Commission, is incompatible with such purposes. It is further understood that, with reference to the aforementioned townsites of Pedro Miguel and Paraiso, the provisions of paragraphs 4 and 6 of Article VI of the Agreement will apply thereto.

16. With reference to Attachment No. 4 to Annex A, it is understood that for thirty calendar months following the entry into force of the Agreement the United States may, for activities related to

the management, operation or maintenance of the Panama Canal, continue to use certain office space located in the Civil Affairs Building (Building No. 0610), title to which is transferred to the Republic of Panama upon the entry into force of the Agreement as provided in Article XIII of the Panama Canal Treaty. It is further understood that, notwithstanding paragraph 4(xiii) of the Annex to the Panama Canal Treaty, the Commission may use such building to operate and maintain the museum and library collections which are located therein upon the entry into force of the Agreement.

17. With reference to Attachment No. 6 to Annex A:

(a) it is understood that the Republic of Panama shall ensure that recreational and entertainment activities comparable to those currently provided will continue to be provided in the Bowling Alley, Cafeteria, and Theater located in Balboa (Buildings 717–X, 727, and 727–C) throughout the life of the Agreement, unless otherwise agreed by the Parties. The provisions of paragraph 2(a) of Article XIII of the Panama Canal Treaty apply to such facilities.

(b) it is understood that the Republic of Panama shall continue use of the Balboa Post Office (Building 724) and the Gamboa Post Office (Building 61) as postal service installations throughout the life of the Agreement, unless otherwise agreed by the Parties. The provisions of paragraph 2(a) of Article XIII of the Panama Canal Treaty apply to such post offices.

18. With reference to Attachment 7 to Annex A, it is understood that the Republic of Panama will permit access to and scheduled use of the baseball and softball fields located in the Port of Balboa by organized leagues until such time as the area in which such fields are located is converted to other use. It is further understood that at such time as any of such fields is converted to other use, the Republic of Panama will make available, without charge, other areas suitable for the use of organized leagues.

19. With reference to Attachment No. 18 of Annex A, it is understood that appropriate areas in the Cristobal Administration Building (Building 1105) shall be made available to the postal service system of the Republic of Panama for postal service purposes.

20. With reference to Attachment 1 to Annex B:

(a) It is understood that the Ports and Railroads Committee will not approve any activity within the area which constituted the Corozal Antenna Field, prior to the entry into force of the Agreement, which would require construction of piers, docks, quays, or any similar structure along the banks of the Canal or within 250 feet of such banks.

(b) It is understood that the installation, shipyards, buildings, and equipment within said buildings, which make up the Naval Industrial Reserve Shipyard and which, in accordance with Article V of the Agreement, shall be made available to the United States in event of a defense emergency, include the following facilities: Drydocks 1, 2, and 3; Docks 7, 8, 12, and 13; Cranes D–4 and D–19–N; Buildings 1, 1A, 1C, 1D, 1G, 1H, 1J, 30, 17, 31, 20, 18, 2, 2A, 3, 4, 4B, 29, 25, 16, 11, 23, 12, 29B, 12A,

12X, and 13; the transfer table and capstans. It is understood, however, that only those of the above facilities which have been transferred to the Republic of Panama shall be deemed to be included within the Naval Industrial Reserve Shipyard for the purposes of paragraph 2(g) of Article V of the Agreement.

(c) It is understood that the Republic of Panama will permit the American Legion and the Balboa Yacht Club to continue their operations in Building 1370 and the adjacent facilities, unless otherwise agreed in the Ports and Railroads Committee.

21. With reference to Attachment 2 to Annex B, it is understood that the United States may use Pier 8 in the Port of Cristobal for berthing and handling cargo for the SS Cristobal, or for any successor to it, on a priority basis.

(B) Panama Canal Treaty—Implementation of Article IV[1]

Agreement signed at Washington, September 7, 1977; Entered into force, October 1, 1979

AGREEMENT IN IMPLEMENTATION OF ARTICLE IV OF THE PANAMA CANAL TREATY

Whereas, the Republic of Panama and the United States of America have signed on this date the "Panama Canal Treaty" to regulate the system pertaining to the operation, maintenance, administration, protection and defense of the Panama Canal in harmony with the Charter of the United Nations;

Whereas, the Republic of Panama shall permit the United States to use certain parts of its territory for the protection and defense of the Panama Canal, with the participation of the Panamanian Armed Forces as is established under Article IV of the "Panama Canal Treaty" subscribed under Article IV of the "Panama Canal Treaty" subscribed on this date;

Whereas, in order to determine the system applicable to the members of the Armed Forces of the United States, the civilian component, and dependents, accompanying them during their stay in the Republic of Panama for the specific purposes of the Panama Canal Treaty, and as the two Governments may otherwise agree, and for the purpose of regulating the use of the defense sites;

Pursuant to the "Panama Canal Treaty," the following has been agreed upon:

ARTICLE I—DEFINITIONS

(1) DEFENSE SITES: Those areas, and the installations within them, which the Republic of Panama by this Agreement permits the United States Forces to use for the specific purposes of the Panama Canal Treaty, and as the two Governments may otherwise agree, a list of which is set forth in paragraph (1) of Annex A of this Agreement.

(2) UNITED STATES FORCES: The land, sea and air armed services of the United States of America.

(3) MEMBERS OF THE FORCES: The military personnel of the United States Forces on active duty who are in the Republic of Panama for the specific purposes of the Panama Canal Treaty, and as the two Governments may otherwise agree.

This term includes those military personnel of the United States Forces on active duty and present in the Republic of Panama on temporary duty from other stations, or on board aircraft or vessels of the United States which are in transit or visiting on official business.

[1] TIAS 10032. The Panama Canal Treaty terminated on December 31, 1999.

Solely for purposes of the privileges authorized under Articles X, XI, and XVIII of this Agreement, this term also includes those military personnel of the United States Forces on active duty, assigned to other stations and present in the Republic of Panama on official leave.

(4) MEMBERS OF THE CIVILIAN COMPONENT:

(a) Nationals of the United States, to whom United States passports have been issued, who are employed by the United States Forces and assigned to the defense sites in the Republic of Panama.

(b) Nationals of third countries employed by the United States forces, who are assigned to the defense sites and who are not habitual residents of the Republic of Panama.

(c) Other categories of persons which could be agreed upon as exceptions by the two Governments.

This term includes personnel on temporary duty and civilian crew members of aircraft and vessels of the United States Forces which are in transit or visiting on official business.

For the purpose of this definition, presence in connection with employment by the United States Forces shall not be considered as residence in the Republic of Panama.

(5) DEPENDENTS: The spouse and children of members of the Forces or of the civilian component, and other relatives who depend on them for their subsistence and who habitually live with them under the same roof.

ARTICLE II—NON-INTERVENTION PRINCIPLE

The members of the Forces or the civilian component, dependents, and designated contractors of the United States Forces shall respect the laws of the Republic of Panama and shall refrain from any activity inconsistent with the spirit of this Agreement. Especially, they shall abstain from all political activity in the Republic of Panama as well as from any interference in the internal affairs of the Republic.

The United States shall take all measures within its authority to ensure that the provisions of this Article are fulfilled.

ARTICLE III—JOINT COMMITTEE

(1) A Joint Committee shall be established which shall start to function upon the entry into force of this Agreement and which shall be composed of a representative of the Republic of Panama and of the United States of America at the level and rank to be agreed upon by both Governments, and who may have one or more deputies, on a parity basis.

(2) The Joint Committee shall perform the functions specifically indicated by the provisions of this Agreement, and others entrusted to it by both Governments concerning the implementation of this Agreement.

(3) The Joint Committee shall determine its rules of procedure within the spirit of this Agreement and may designate the subcommittees it may deem necessary for the fulfillment of its functions.

(4) The Joint Committee shall be organized in such a manner that it may meet promptly and at any time upon request of the representative of the Republic of Panama or of the United States. The Joint Committee shall send a monthly report on its activities to the Governments of the Republic of Panama and the United States.

(5) The Joint Committee shall refer to the two Governments, for their consideration through appropriate channels, any matters which it has not been able to resolve.

Article IV—Use of Defense Sites

(1) The United States Forces may use the defense sites listed in paragraph (2) of Annex A of this Agreement. Moreover, Annex A includes a list of military areas of coordination which may be used by the Armed Forces of both Governments in accordance with Annex B of this Agreement.

(2) Annex A of this Agreement shall be examined every two years or upon the request of either Government, and shall be revised to reflect any agreed elimination or change in areas. The United States Forces may notify the Republic of Panama at any time that the use of a defense site or a military area of coordination or of a specified portion thereof, or other right granted by the Republic of Panama is no longer required. Under such circumstances, said use or other right shall cease on the date determined by the two Governments.

(3) The United States Government may, at any time, remove from the Republic of Panama, or dispose of in the Republic of Panama in accordance with conditions to be agreed upon by the two Governments, all equipment, installations, material, supplies or other removable property brought into, acquired or constructed in the Republic of Panama by or for the United States Forces. Property left by the United States in a defense site after the date the use of such site by United States Forces ceases shall, unless agreed otherwise by the two Governments, become the property of the Republic of Panama.

(4) At the termination of any activities or operations under this Agreement, the United States shall be obligated to take all measures to ensure insofar as may be practicable that every hazard to human life, health and safety is removed from any defense site or a military area of coordination or any portion thereof, on the date the United States Forces are no longer authorized to use such site. Prior to the transfer of any installation, the two Governments will consult concerning: (a) its conditions, including removal of hazards to human life, health and safety; and (b) compensation for its residual value, if any exists.

(5) The United States Forces shall have responsibility for control of entry to the defense sites. The Republic of Panama may share in the exercise of this control, in a manner to be agreed upon in the Joint Committee. Necessary signs, in Spanish and English, requested by the United States Forces through the Joint Committee will be erected outside the defense sites, expressing that the sign is erected under the authority of the Republic of Panama.

(6) Since the Republic of Panama is a signatory to the Latin American Denuclearization Treaty (Tlatelolco), the United States shall emplace no type of nuclear armament on Panamanian territory.

(7) The Joint Committee will constitute the means of communication and information between the two Governments with regard to matters pertaining to the implementation of this Article.

Article V—Flags

(1) All of the territory of the Republic of Panama, including the defense sites, shall be under the flag of the Republic of Panama and, consequently, within such sites the Panamanian flag shall always occupy the position of honor. Within the defense sites, the flag of the United States shall also be flown jointly with the Panamanian flag. The Joint Committee shall determine the manner of displaying the flags.

(2) At the entrances, outside the defense sites, only the flag of the Republic of Panama will be flown.

Article VI—Criminal Jurisdiction

(1) The authorities of the Republic of Panama shall have jurisdiction over members of the Forces or the civilian component, and dependents, with respect to offenses arising from acts or omissions committed in the Republic of Panama and punishable under the laws of the Republic of Panama. Nevertheless, the Republic of Panama permits the authorities of the United States to exercise criminal jurisdiction within defense sites, and, consequently, to have the primary right to exercise jurisdiction over acts which are criminal acts according to United States law, and which are committed within such sites by members of the Forces or the civilian component, or dependents.

(2) The Republic of Panama also permits the authorities of the United States to have the primary right to exercise criminal jurisdiction over members of the Forces or the civilian component, and dependents, for any offense committed outside the defense sites, in the following cases:

(a) If the offense is solely against the property or security of the United States. It is understood that offenses against the security of the United States include: treason or sabotage against the United States, espionage or violation of any law relating to official secrets of the United States or to secrets relating to the national defense of the United States.

(b) If the offense is solely against the person or property of a member of the Forces or the civilian component, or a dependent.

(c) If the offense arises out of an act or omission done in the performance of official duty, in which case, when requested by the Panamanian authorities or when the military authorities of the United States may deem it necessary, the military authorities of the United States shall issue a certificate establishing that the offense originated from an act or omission occurring in the performance of official duty. Panama shall consider this certificate as sufficient proof for the purposes of this paragraph, or shall request a review by the Joint Committee within ten days from the receipt of the certificate. The Joint Committee shall complete its review within ten days from the receipt of the request, except when more thorough consideration is required, in which case the Joint Committee shall complete its review within thirty days.

A substantial deviation from the duties which a person is required to perform in a specific mission shall generally indicate an act or omission not occurring in the performance of official duty, and, consequently, the military authorities of the United States will not consider it necessary to issue a certificate of official duty.

(3) The provisions of this Article notwithstanding, the Republic of Panama shall always reserve the right to exercise jurisdiction over members of the civilian component and dependents who are Panamanian nationals or habitual residents of Panama.

(4) The authorities of the Government having the primary right to exercise jurisdiction over an offense shall give sympathetic consideration to any request from the authorities of the other Government for permission to exercise jurisdiction. Such requests may be discussed in the Joint Committee.

(5)(a) The appropriate authorities of the Republic of Panama and of the United States shall assist each other in the arrest of members of the Forces or the civilian component, and dependents, and in their delivery to the authority which is to have custody in accordance with the provisions of this Article.

(b) The authorities of the Republic of Panama shall notify the authorities of the United States as promptly as possible of the arrest of any member of the Forces or the civilian component, or a dependent.

(c) The following procedure shall govern the custody of an accused member of the Forces or the civilian component, or a dependent, over whom the Republic of Panama is to exercise jurisdiction:

(i) If the accused is detained by the United States authorities, he shall, except when charged with murder, rape, robbery with violence, trafficking in drugs, or crimes against the security of the Panamanian State remain with such authorities pending the conclusion of all judicial proceedings and thereafter until custody is requested by the authorities of the Republic of Panama for the execution of a sentence.

(ii) If the accused is detained by the authorities of the Republic of Panama he shall, except when charged with murder, rape, robbery with violence, trafficking in drugs, or crimes against the security of the Panamanian State, be handed over on request to the United States authorities in whose custody he shall remain until completion of all judicial proceedings and thereafter until custody is requested by authorities of the Republic of Panama for the execution of a sentence.

(iii) When charged with murder, rape, robbery with violence, trafficking in drugs, or crimes against the security of the Panamanian State, the accused shall be handed over to Panamanian authorities upon their request, or if already in their custody, shall remain with them. In these cases the authorities of the Republic of Panama shall give sympathetic consideration to requests for custody by the United States authorities.

(6)(a) The United States authorities shall give full consideration to special requests regarding conditions of custody made by the authorities of the Republic of Panama.

(b) When the accused is in the custody or has been delivered into the custody of the United States authorities he must, upon request by the authorities of the Republic of Panama, be made available to them for the purposes of investigation and trial. This obligation of the United States to ensure the appearance of an accused member of the Forces or the civilian component, or a dependent, will be deemed to satisfy the bail requirement set by the laws of the Republic of Panama.

(7)(a) The authorities of the Republic of Panama and the United States shall assist each other in carrying out all necessary investigations of offenses and in the collection and production of evidence, including the seizure and, in proper cases, the delivery of objects connected with an offense and the appearance of witnesses as necessary.

(b) The authorities of the Republic of Panama and the United States shall, upon request by the other Government, inform each other of the status of cases referred to under the provisions of this Article.

(8) The authorities of the United States shall not carry out a death sentence in the Republic of Panama. As is provided in the laws of the Republic of Panama, a member of the Forces or the civilian component, or a dependent, who has been convicted by a Panamanian court shall not be subject to the death penalty or to any form of cruel and unusual punishment or treatment.

(9) When an accused member of the Forces or the civilian component, or a dependent, has been tried in accordance with the provisions of this Article by the authorities of the Republic of Panama or by authorities of the United States and has been acquitted, or has been convicted and is serving, or has served, his sentence, or has been pardoned, he shall not be tried again for the same offense within the territory of the Republic of Panama. However, nothing in this paragraph shall prevent the military authorities of the United States from trying a member of the Forces for any violation of rules of discipline arising from an act or omission which constituted an offense for which he was tried by the authorities of the Republic of Panama.

(10) Whenever a member of the Forces or the civilian component, or a dependent, is tried by the Panamanian authorities, he shall be entitled to the procedural guarantees listed in Annex D of this Agreement.

(11) At any time during the detention by the authorities of the Republic of Panama of a member of the Forces or the civilian component, or a dependent, the Panamanian authorities shall permit the military authorities of the United States to visit said member or dependent. Members of the immediate family may visit him weekly. Material and medical assistance (such as food, clothing and comfort items) which the United States authorities and members of

his immediate family may consider desirable, and any other assistance which is in accordance with or allowed by Panamanian prison regulations, may be provided to him on such visits.

(12) The Joint Committee will constitute the means of communication and information between the two governments with regard to matters pertaining to the implementation of this Article.

Article VII—Civilian Employment

The following principles shall govern civilian employment by the United States Forces:

(1) In order to set forth their rights and obligations as the employer, the United States forces shall draw up regulations which shall contain the terms, conditions and prerequisites for all categories of their civilian employees. These regulations shall be provided to the Republic of Panama through the Joint Committee.

(2) In conformity with the principles of the labor laws of the Republic of Panama, such regulations shall establish employment preferences in all levels for Panamanian applicants possessing the requisite skills and qualifications. Accordingly, the United States Forces shall endeavor to ensure that the number of Panamanian nationals employed by them in relation to the total number of civilian employees will conform to the proportion established under Panamanian law. Similarly, the terms, conditions and prerequisites for the employment of Panamanian personnel shall conform with the general principles contained in the labor laws of the Republic of Panama.

(3) All civilian employees of the United States Forces, except those who are nationals of the Republic of Panama or who have obtained permanent resident status therein, shall be subject to a system of periodic rotation which will limit their period of employment by the United States Forces in the Republic of Panama. The regulations providing for such rotation shall be provided to the Republic of Panama through the Joint Committee.

(4) With regard to wages, there shall be no discrimination on the basis of nationality, sex or race. Payments by the United States Forces of additional remunerations to persons of any nationality, including Panamanian citizens, who are recruited outside of Panama and must therefore change their place of residence, shall not be considered to be discrimination for the purposes of this Article.

(5) The United States Forces shall take the measures called for under the laws of the Republic of Panama with regard to the application of the tax and social security laws to their employees who are subject to Panama's taxation and social security system, including withholding of tax or social security payments from their salaries.

Article VIII—Acquisition of Panamanian Supplies and Services

(1) The United States Forces shall give preference to the procurement of supplies and services obtainable in the Republic of Panama. Such preference shall apply to the maximum extent possible when such supplies and services are available as required, and are comparable in quality and price to those which may be obtained

from other sources. For the comparison of prices there will be taken into account the cost of transport to the Republic of Panama, including freight, insurance and handling, of the supplies and services. In the acquisition of goods in the Republic of Panama, preference shall be given to goods having a larger percentage of components of Panamanian origin.

(2) Any regulations which may be necessary to carry our preference shall be agreed upon in the Joint Committee.

ARTICLE IX—TELECOMMUNICATIONS

(1) The Republic of Panama, in the exercise of its sovereign power over its telecommunications, authorizes the United States Forces to use the communications networks and communications-electronics installations within the defense sites, and to use the radio frequencies and transportable equipment as may be necessary for their requirements, in order to accomplish the specific purposes of the defense of the Canal, and as the two Governments may otherwise agree. The Joint Committee may adopt regulations to govern the use of such transportable equipment outside of the defense sites.

Any use presently being exercised of such networks, installations, frequencies and equipment, for purposes other than those herein authorized, shall be subject to the provisions contained in the Panama Canal Treaty, including those relating to any separation of nonmilitary telecommunications that may be deemed necessary.

(2) The Republic of Panama also authorizes the United States Forces to use installations such as those described in the preceding paragraph already existing outside the defense sites, which serve to accomplish the purposes of the defense of the Canal, and as the two Governments may otherwise agree.

Those already existing installations outside the defense sites may be guarded by authorities of the Republic of Panama. The United States Forces shall have access to such installations for appropriate operation, maintenance, and replacement.

(3) Provided that they are available and suitable for the purpose, the United States Forces shall use, to the maximum extent possible, the telecommunications services of the Republic of Panama in order to meet their needs, but the applicable rates shall be no less favorable than those charged to governmental agencies of the Republic of Panama.

(4) The United States Forces shall provide the Government of the Republic of Panama a list of all frequencies authorized or in use by the United States Forces. This list shall be submitted through the Joint Committee in ascending frequency order and shall contain as a minimum the power, bandwidth, and type of emission.

(5) The Republic of Panama undertakes not to authorize the use of any frequency which would interfere with those in use by or for the United States Forces or which they may use in the future in accordance with the Panama Canal Treaty and this Agreement.

(6) The Republic of Panama authorizes the United States Forces to use codes, ciphers and other secure cryptographic means necessary for the specific purposes of the defense of the Panama Canal, and as the two Governments may otherwise agree.

(7) All provisions regarding telecommunications in this Article shall be in accordance with the obligations of both Governments as members of the International Telecommunication Union and the various relevant international agreements to which both Governments are signatories.

(8) Any communication with the International Telecommunication Union regarding the subject matter of this Article shall be effected exclusively by the Republic of Panama.

(9) The radio and television services of the United States Forces operating within the Republic of Panama, will:

(a) Announce at the start and termination of each day's broadcast that the emissions are authorized by the Republic of Panama; and

(b) In television programs originating locally, not use announcers appearing in military uniform.

(10) The Joint Committee may adopt any further regulations as may be necessary to implement the provisions of this Article, including necessary technical coordination.

Article X—Military Post Offices

(1) The United States may establish, maintain and operate, within the defense sites, military post offices for the exclusive use of the United States Forces, the members of the Forces or the civilian component, and dependents, and for the use of such other persons and agencies as may be agreed upon as exceptions by the two Governments through the Joint Committee. Such post offices shall transmit mail only between themselves or between themselves and other United States post offices.

(2) The United States Forces shall take all necessary measures to prevent the unauthorized use of the military post offices. The Panamanian authorities shall periodically inform the authorities of the United States, through the Joint Committee, of all applicable provisions of Panamanian laws, and the United States Forces shall, within their legal capacity, ensure that such provisions are complied with.

(3) The military post offices in the Republic of Panama shall not have direct representation before any international postal organization.

(4) The Republic of Panama may establish post offices within the defense sites, the location of which shall be agreed upon in the Joint Committee, for the transmission of mail between the defense sites and any other areas not authorized to the military post offices by this Agreement.

Article XI—Commissaries, Military Exchanges and Other Service Installations

(1) The United States may establish, regulate and use within the defense sites, commissaries, military exchanges, military banking facilities, credit unions, recreational, social and athletic facilities,

schools, sanitation and medical facilities, and other categories of service facilities as may be periodically agreed upon by the two Governments through the Joint Committee, for the exclusive use of the members of the Forces or the civilian component, and dependents, and for such other persons as may be agreed upon by the two Governments as exceptions through the Joint Committee. These service facilities and their activities such as the import, purchase, sale and distribution of merchandise, medicine and services, shall be free of taxes, duties, liens, licenses, fees and other charges imposed by the Republic of Panama or any of its political subdivisions.

In order to take advantage of existing installations, the United States Forces may continue to use those installations already in existence outside of the defense sites, which are specified in paragraph (3) of Annex A.

(2) The military banking facilities shall be branches or agencies of banking entities duly authorized to engage in the banking business in Panama. The Government of the Republic of Panama may authorize the installation and operation within the defense sites, at locations agreed upon by the Joint Committee, of branches or agencies of Banco Nacional or other official banking entities of the Republic of Panama.

(3) It is the express objective and purpose of both Governments that the articles and services sold or provided at the commissaries and military exchanges be for the exclusive use of authorized persons. To that end the United States Forces shall, upon request, inform the Panamanian authorities, through the Joint Committee, as to the classification, nature and quantity of certain articles and services sold or provided at such establishments.

(4) With respect to the preceding paragraph, the Republic of Panama and the United States shall jointly take all the necessary measures to prevent the unauthorized use of such services and the abuse by those who are authorized. Such measures shall include the obtaining of pertinent information and the carrying out of any verifications that may be necessary by Panamanian authorities. The procedure to be followed for these purposes shall be agreed upon by the Joint Committee.

(5) The Government of the United States shall apply appropriate disciplinary sanctions to the members of the Forces or the civilian component, and dependents, or other persons authorized as exceptions who abuse the privileges granted in this Article and commit violations in that respect. In such cases, the United States authorities shall give sympathetic consideration to requests from the Panamanian Government to exercise jurisdiction.

(6) The service facilities referred to in the Article shall grant to Panamanian supplies and services the preference referred to in Article VIII.

Article XII—Contractors and Contractors' Personnel

(1) Whenever contracts are required by the United States Forces for the performance of services or the procurement of supplies, the United States Forces shall adhere to the preferences for Panamanian sources set forth in Article VIII of this Agreement.

(2) Whenever contracts are awarded by the United States Forces to natural persons who are nationals or permanent residents of the United States or to corporations or other legal entities organized under the laws of the United States and under the effective control of such persons, such contractors shall be so designated by the United States Forces and such designations shall be communicated to the Panamanian authorities through the Joint Committee. Such contractors shall be subject to the laws and regulations of the Republic of Panama except with respect to the special regime established by this Agreement, which includes the following obligations and benefits:

(a) The contractor must engage exclusively in activities related to the execution of the work for which he has been contracted by the United States Forces, or related to other works or activities authorized by the Republic of Panama.

(b) The contractor must refrain from carrying out practices which may constitute violations of the laws of the Republic of Panama.

(c) The contractor shall enter and depart from the territory of the Republic of Panama in accordance with procedures prescribed for members of the civilian component in Article XIII of this Agreement.

(d) The contractor must obtain a certificate of professional identity which the proper authorities of the United States Forces shall issue when they are satisfied he is duly qualified. This certificate shall be sufficient to permit him to operate under Panamanian law as a contractor of the Forces. Nevertheless, the Panamanian authorities may require the registration of the appropriate documents to establish juridical presence in the Republic of Panama.

(e) The contractor shall not be obliged to pay any tax or other assessment to the Republic of Panama on income derived under a contract with the United States Forces as long as he is taxed at a substantially equivalent rate in the United States.

(f) The contractor may move freely within the Republic of Panama, and shall have exemptions from customs duties and other charges, as provided for members of the civilian component in Articles XV and XVII of this Agreement.

(g) The contractor may use public services and installations in accordance with the terms and conditions of Article XIV of the Agreement, but shall pay no-discriminatory highway tolls and taxes on plates for private vehicles.

(h) The contractor shall be exempt from any taxes imposed on depreciable assets belonging to him, other than real estate, which are used exclusively for the execution of contracts with the United States Forces.

(i) The contractor may use the services and facilities provided for in Articles X and XVIII of this Agreement to the extent such use is authorized by the United States Forces.

(3) The United States Forces shall withdraw the designation of a contractor when any of the following circumstances occur:

(a) Upon completion or termination of the contracts with the United States Forces.

(b) Upon proof that such contractors are engaged in business activities in the Republic of Panama other than those pertaining to the United States Forces, without authorization of the Republic of Panama.

(c) Upon proof that such contractors are engaged in practices which in the view of the Republic of Panama constitute serious violations of the applicable laws of the Republic of Panama.

(4) The authorities of the United States shall notify the authorities of the Republic of Panama whenever the designation of a contractor has been withdrawn. If, within sixty days after notification of the withdrawal of the designation of a contractor who entered Panama in the capacity of a contractor, the authorities of the Republic of Panama require such contractor to leave its territory, the United States Government shall ensure that the Republic of Panama shall not incur any expense due to the cost of transportation.

(5) The provisions of the Article shall similarly apply to the subcontractors and to the employees of the contractors and subcontractors and their dependents who are nationals or residents of the United States. These employees and dependents shall not be subject to the Panamanian Social Security system.

Article XIII—Entry and Departure

(1) The United States may bring into the territory of the Republic of Panama members of the Forces or the civilian component, and dependents, for the specific purposes of the Panama Canal Treaty, and as the two Governments may otherwise agree.

(2)(a) In order to enter or leave the territory of the Republic of Panama, the members of the Forces shall be obligated to bear only a personal identity card and individual or collective travel documentation issued by the military authorities of the United States. Such documentation must be presented to the Panamanian authorities. The two Governments shall establish through the Joint Committee the procedure to be followed in exceptional cases.

(b) To enter or leave the territory of the Republic of Panama, the members of the civilian component and dependents must possess, in addition to the travel documentation issued by the United States military authorities, a valid passport. Such documentation shall be presented to the appropriate authorities of the Republic of Panama.

(c) The United States Forces shall furnish each member of the Forces or the civilian component, and dependent, who remains in the Republic of Panama for longer than thirty days, an identity card which shall be issued under the authority of the Joint Committee in Spanish and English. Children under the age of ten years may be included on the identity card of a parent at the option of the parent. These identity cards shall be shown to the appropriate authorities of the Republic of Panama upon request.

The authorities of the Republic of Panama may request information concerning the number of such cards outstanding and the validity of any particular card. The Joint Committee and the United States Forces shall provide such information.

(3) Whenever the status of any member of the Forces or the civilian component, or dependent, is altered so that, at the time of such alteration, he is no longer entitled to remain in the Republic of

Panama, the United States Forces shall promptly notify the Panamanian authorities, and shall, if requested within a period sixty days thereafter, ensure that transportation from the Republic of Panama will be provided at no cost to the Government of the Republic of Panama.

(4)(a) The members of the Forces or the civilian component, and dependents, shall be exempted from fiscal charges relating to their entry, stay in, or departure from the territory of the Republic of Panama. Similarly they will be exempted from obligatory services established in favor of the Republic of Panama. They shall not acquire any right to permanent residence or domicile in the Republic of Panama.

(b) Members of the Forces or the civilian component who enter the Republic of Panama to execute professional services exclusively for the United States Forces, or in its behalf, shall not be subject to the licensing regimes of the Republic of Panama, but they shall limit their professional activity to such services with the United States Forces for the specific purposes of the Panama Canal Treaty, or as the two Governments may otherwise agree.

ARTICLE XIV—SERVICES AND INSTALLATIONS

(1) The United States Forces, members of the Forces or civilian component, and dependents, may use the public services and installations belonging to or regulated by the Government of the Republic of Panama, but the terms and conditions of use, prices, rates and tariffs and priorities shall not be unfavorable in relation to those charged other users.

(2) For the use of public services and installations made available through a plant acquired or constructed, or equipment furnished, by the United States Government and subsequently transferred free to the Government of the Republic of Panama, preferential charges shall be granted to the United States Forces taking these circumstances into account.

(3) The United States Forces may establish and operate the supporting services and facilities it requires within the defense sites, and exceptionally, with the authorization of the Government of the Republic of Panama, outside such sites.

(4) The Republic of Panama will permit the United States Forces to continue to use in an adequate manner, accessory facilities, such as pipelines, communications, sanitation services and utilities, which serve the defense sites and are installed on land outside the defense sites. The United States Forces shall, at their cost, maintain and repair these facilities as necessary, in coordination with the proper entities of the Republic of Panama. Detailed identification of such facilities shall be made through the Joint Committee, within a period of six months from the entry into force of this Agreement unless extended by the Joint Committee for exceptional circumstances. The two Governments shall agree, through the Joint Committee, upon procedures to govern the appropriate use, access, maintenance and repair of these facilities. Similarly, procedures shall be agreed upon for coordination between the United States Forces and the competent Panamanian entities, concerning the use, access, maintenance and repair of such facilities as may

serve the Republic of Panama and are situated within the defense sites.

ARTICLE XV—MOVEMENT, LICENSES AND REGISTRATION OF VESSELS, AIRCRAFT AND VEHICLES

(1)(a) When in the performance of official duties, the vessels and aircraft operated by or for the United States Forces may move freely through Panamanian air space and waters, without the obligation of payment of taxes, tolls, landing or pier charges or other charges to the Republic of Panama and without any other impediment.

(b) Such vessels and aircraft shall be exempt from customs inspections or other inspections. Whenever the same carry freight, crews or passengers who are not entitled to the exemptions provided for in this Agreement, prior notice shall be given to the appropriate Panamanian authorities. Both Governments shall adopt procedures to ensure that the laws and regulations of the Republic of Panama are not violated.

(2)(a) Similarly, the vehicles and equipment of the United States Forces may, when in the performance of official duties, move freely in the Republic of Panama, without the obligation of payment of taxes, tolls or other charges to the Republic of Panama and without any other impediment. These vehicles and equipment shall be exempt from mechanical or other inspection.

Claims arising from damage caused by the United States Forces to the Panamanian road network outside the defense sites, in excess of the usual wear and tear by reason of time and its appropriate use, shall be settled as provided for in Article XX.

(b) Such official vehicles and equipment shall not be assessed any license or registration fees. These vehicles shall bear their customary United States military identification marks and an additional means of identification as may be agreed upon by the Joint Committee, to be issued under the authority of said Joint Committee and distributed by the United States Forces.

(c) In connection with the movement of any military convoys, or any large number of vehicles as a single unit, outside of the defense sites, the United States Forces shall consult with the Combined Military Board so that, if time and circumstances permit, proper traffic arrangements will be made, including accompaniment by Panamanian traffic patrols.

(3)(a) The plates, individual marks and registration documents issued by the United States for vehicles, trailers, vessels and aircraft which are the property of the United States Forces shall be accepted by the Republic of Panama.

(b) The Republic of Panama shall recognize as sufficient, the valid licenses, permits, certificates or other official classifications from the United States Government, possessed by operators of vehicles, vessels and aircraft which are property of the United States Government.

(4)(a) The vehicles, trailers, vessels and aircraft belonging to the members of the Forces or the civilian component, or dependents, shall also move freely within the Republic of Panama, in compliance with the traffic regulations and those regarding the annual mechanical inspection. The license plate fee and other obligations shall not be discriminatory.

(b) The Republic of Panama shall issue, in accordance with its laws, the appropriate documents of title and registration of vehicles, trailers, vessels and aircraft which are the property of the members of the Forces or the civilian component, or dependents, when the latter present title and registration, issued by the federal or state authorities of the United States or by the authorities of the former Canal Zone. Applicants may retain such documents provided they leave with the Panamanian authorities a copy authenticated by the United States Forces, duly translated into Spanish.

While the corresponding request is being processed and within a term which may not exceed thirty days after its arrival in the Republic of Panama, the means of transportation mentioned above may be operated with the plates or distinctive marks issued by the United States federal or state authorities.

(c) The members of the Forces or the civilian component, and dependents, who bear drivers' licenses, vessel operators' permits, or licenses and classifications of air pilots issued by the federal or state authorities of the United States or by the authorities of the former Canal Zone, shall receive equivalent Panamanian licenses, permits and classifications without being subjected to new tests or payments of new fees. The applicants may retain the licenses, permits and classifications of the United States or the former Canal Zone provided that they leave with the Panamanian authorities a copy authenticated by the United States Forces and duly translated into Spanish. Members of the Forces or the civilian component, and dependents, shall be permitted to drive vehicles, vessels or aircraft in the Republic of Panama with such licenses, permits and classifications during the thirty days following their first arrival in the Republic of Panama and during the subsequent period necessary for the processing of the application in Panama for a driver's license, vessel operator's permit, or license and classification as an air pilot.

(d) The Panamanian licenses, permits or classifications shall be valid for the period of time indicated in the Panamanian law and, during the continuous presence of the bearer in Panama, shall, to preserve their validity, be renewed in accordance with Panamanian laws.

Whenever Panamanian laws may require medical certifications for the renewal of licenses, permits or classifications the Republic of Panama shall accept the certifications issued by the medical services of the United States Forces, provided that said certifications are issued in Spanish.

(e) The Republic of Panama shall issue, in accordance with its laws, drivers' licenses, vessel operators' permits, and licenses and other classifications of air pilots to members of the Forces or the civilian component, and dependents, when they do not possess such documents. If any test is required as a prerequisite for the issuance of the documents mentioned, Panama shall permit the interested persons to take the examination in Spanish or English. Any material which the Republic of Panama may generally issue in preparation for such examinations shall be furnished, in Spanish or English, as the applicant may request.

(5) Aircraft other than those of Panama and the United States may use the runways of the defense sites only after obtaining appropriate authorization from the Republic of Panama. When deemed convenient, the two Governments shall adopt, through the Joint Committee, regulations governing the use by such aircraft.

(6) The installation, change of position or alteration of lights and other signal installations to assist in navigation of aircraft, placed or established in the defense sites or in their surroundings, shall be subject to previous consultation between the appropriate authorities of both Governments.

(7) The Republic of Panama shall adopt such measures as may be appropriate to coordinate air traffic in the Republic of Panama, so that, in a manner consistent with the mission of the United States Forces, maximum safety shall be offered to civil and military air navigation. All systems of control and coordination of military air traffic shall be developed jointly as needed for the fulfillment of the specific purposes of this Agreement. The procedures needed to bring about this coordination shall be agreed upon by the appointed authorities of both Governments, respecting always the sovereignty of the Republic of Panama over all its air space.

The Republic of Panama agrees that, for security reasons, at the request of the United States Forces it shall restrict overflights of certain of the defense sites.

(8) The Joint Committee may agree on rules and procedures that may be necessary to implement this Article.

ARTICLE XVI—TAXATION

(1) By virtue of this Agreement, the United States Forces are exempt from payment in the Republic of Panama of all taxes, fees or other charges on their activities or property, including those imposed through contractors or subcontractors.

(2) Members of the Forces or the civilian component, and dependents, shall be exempt from any taxes, fees, or other charges on income received as a result of their work for the United States Forces or for any of the service facilities referred to in Articles XI or XVIII of this Agreement. Similarly, as is provided by Panamanian law, they shall be exempt from payment of taxes, fees or other charges on income derived from sources outside the Republic of Panama.

(3) Members of the Forces or the civilian component, and dependents, shall be exempt from taxes, fees or other charges on gifts or inheritance or on personal property, the presence of which within the territory of the Republic of Panama is due solely to the stay therein of such persons on account of their or their sponsor's work with the United States Forces.

(4) The Joint Committee may establish such regulations as may be appropriate for the implementation of this Article.

ARTICLE XVII—IMPORT DUTIES

(1) Except for the exemptions provided for in this Agreement, the members of the Forces or the civilian component, and dependents shall be subject to the laws and regulations administered by the customs authorities of the Republic of Panama.

(2) All property imported for the official use or benefit of the United States Forces, including that imported by their contractors or subcontractors, in connection with the various activities authorized under this Agreement, shall be exempt from the payment of all customs duties or other import taxes and charges and from all license requirements

The United States Forces shall issue a certificate, following the form adopted by the Joint Committee, stating that the property being imported is for these purposes.

(3) Property consigned to or imported for the personal use of the members of the Forces or the civilian component, or dependents shall be subject to the payment of import duties or other import taxes, except for the following:

(a) Furniture, household goods and personal effects imported by such persons for their private use within six months following their first arrival in the Republic of Panama. In the case of persons who are unable to obtain adequate housing when they first arrive in the Republic of Panama, an additional period of six months from the time they obtain adequate housing shall be granted them for the importation of such articles, provided that the United States Forces issue a certificate stating that the person concerned has not accomplished such importation and indicating the date upon which he obtained adequate housing and its address.

(b) Vehicles imported by such persons for their private use, and the spare parts required for proper maintenance of such vehicles. The Joint Committee shall establish the limitations on the quantity and frequency of imports of such vehicles and parts;

(c) A reasonable quantity of articles for the private use of such persons, imported as personal baggage or sent into the Republic of Panama through the military post offices of the United States;

(d) Such other imports as may be expressly authorized by the competent authorities of the Republic of Panama at the request of the United States Forces.

(4) The exemptions granted in paragraph (3) of this Article shall apply only to cases involving the importation of articles exempted at the time of entry and shall not be construed as obligating the Republic of Panama to reimburse customs duties and domestic taxes collected by the Republic of Panama in connection with purchases of goods from Panamanian sources subsequent to their importation.

(5) Customs inspections shall not be made in the following cases:

(a) Members of the Forces traveling under orders, other than leave orders, who enter or depart from the Republic of Panama;

(b) Official documents under official seal and mail sent through the military postal channels of the United States;

(c) Cargo consigned to the United States Forces.

(6) Property imported under this Article and subsequently transferred to a person who is not entitled to duty-free importation shall be subject to the payment of import duties and other taxes according to the laws and regulations of the Republic of Panama. Such

sales shall not be permitted when they are motivated by commercial purposes.

(7) All property imported into the Republic of Panama free of customs duties and other taxes pursuant to paragraphs (2) and (3) of this Article may be exported free of customs duties, export permits, or other export taxes and assessments. All property acquired in the Republic of Panama by, or in the name of the United States Forces, or acquired by members of the Forces or the civilian component, or dependents, for their private use may be exported free of customs duties, export licenses or other export taxes and charges.

(8) The authorities of the United States agree to cooperate with the authorities of the Republic of Panama and shall take, within their legal authority, all such steps as may be necessary to prevent the abuse of the privileges granted under the Article to the members of the Forces or the civilian component, or dependents.

(9) In order to prevent violations of the laws and regulations administered by the customs authorities of the Republic of Panama, the two Governments agree as follows:

(a) The authorities of the Republic of Panama and the competent authorities of the United States shall mutually assist one another in the conduct of investigations and the collection of evidence.

(b) The authorities of the United States shall take, within their legal authority, all necessary measures to ensure that articles subject to seizure by or in the name of the customs authorities of the Republic of Panama are delivered to these authorities.

(c) The authorities of the United States shall take, within their legal authority, all necessary measures to ensure the payment by members of the Forces or the civilian component, and dependents, of such import duties, taxes, and fines as may be duly determined by the Panamanian authorities.

(10) Vehicles and articles belonging to the United States Forces that are seized from a person by the authorities of the Republic of Panama in connection with a violation of its customs or tax laws or regulations shall be delivered to the competent authorities of the United States Forces.

(11) The Joint Committee will constitute the means of communication and information between the two Governments with regard to matters pertaining to the implementation of this Article.

ARTICLE XVIII—HEALTH, SANITATION AND EDUCATION

(1) The United States Forces may furnish educational, sanitary and medical services, including veterinary services, to the members of the Forces or the civilian component, and dependents, and other persons as may be agreed upon as exceptions by the two Governments through the Joint Committee.

(2) Matters of mutual interest relative to the control and prevention of diseases and the coordination of other public health, quarantine, sanitation and education services shall be the subject of coordination in the Joint Committee.

(3) The Republic of Panama authorizes the United States Forces, in rendering such health, sanitation and education services, to apply its own regulations.

Article XIX—Surveys

The United States may carry our topographic, hydrographic, agrologic and other surveys (including taking of aerial photographs) within the defense sites. Surveys in other areas of the Republic of Panama shall require authorization from the Republic of Panama, in the manner agreed upon in the Joint Committee, and the Republic of Panama shall, at its option, designate a representative to be present. The United States shall furnish a copy of the data resulting from such surveys to the Republic of Panama at no cost.

Article XX—Claims

(1) Each Government waives its claims against the other Government for damage to any property owned by it and used by its land, sea or air armed services, in the following circumstances;

(a) If the damage was caused by a member or an employee of the armed services of the other Government, in the performance of his official duties; or,

(b) If the damage arose from the use of any vehicle, vessel or aircraft owned by the other Government and used by its armed services, provided either that the vehicle, vessel or aircraft causing the damage was being used for official purposes, or that the damage was caused to property being so used.

(2) In the case of damage caused or arising as stated in paragraph (1), to other property owned by either Government and located in the Republic of Panama, the claims shall be settled by the Government against which the claim is made. If it is not settled in due course, the claim may be pursued through diplomatic channels. Both Governments hereby waive the collection of any claims for an amount less than $1,400 U.S. or B/.1,400 which are of equal value.

(3) In cases of maritime salvage, each Government waives its claims against the other if the vessel or cargo salved was the property of the other Government and was used by its armed services for official purposes.

(4) For the purposes of this Article, any vessel chartered, requisitioned or seized in prize by a Government shall be considered its property (except to the extent that the risk of loss or liability is assumed by some other persons than such Government).

(5) Each Government waives its claims against the other Government for injury or death suffered by any member of its armed services while said member was engaged in the performance of his official duties.

(6) The members of the Forces and the civilian employees of the United States Forces shall be subject to the jurisdiction of the civil courts of the Republic of Panama except in matters which arise from the performance of their official duty. In cases where payment has been accepted in full satisfaction of the claim, the civil courts

of the Republic of Panama shall dismiss any proceedings concerning the matter.

(7) When personal private property subject to seizure or attachment by order of a competent authority under Panamanian law is within the defense sites, the United States authorities shall render, upon request of the Panamanian authorities, all assistance within their power in order that such property is turned over promptly to the Panamanian authorities. This paragraph shall not apply to personal property which, although privately owned, is in use by or on behalf of the United States Forces.

(8) Non-contractual claims arising from damages caused in the performance of their official duties by members or civilian employees of the United States Forces to third parties other than the two Governments shall be presented by the injured party through the Joint Committee to the appropriate authorities of the United States Forces for settlement. The authorities of the Republic of Panama may submit advice and recommendations on Panamanian law to the claim authorities of the United States for their use in evaluating liability and amount of damages.

(9) For other non-contractual claims against the members of the Forces or the civilian component, the authorities of the United States, following consultation with the appropriate authorities of the Government of Panama, shall consider the claim and, if appropriate, offer an *ex gratia* payment.

(10) The authorities of both Governments shall cooperate in the investigation and procurement of evidence for a fair disposition of claims under this Article.

(11) Contractual claims against the United States Forces shall be settled in accordance with the dispute clause of the contracts, and in the absence of such clause, through presentation of claims to the United States authorities through the appropriate channels.

(12) The United States Government shall require contractors and subcontractors referred to in Article XII of this Agreement to obtain appropriate insurance to cover the civil liabilities that may be incurred in Panamanian territory as a result of acts or omissions done in the performance of official duty by their employees. The Joint Committee shall establish the general standards for such insurance.

Article XXI—General Provisions

(1) The activities and operations of the United States Government shall be carried out with adequate attention to public health and safety in the Republic of Panama. Within the defense sites, whose use Panama makes available to the United States by virtue of this Agreement, the United States authorities shall adopt all the appropriate measures to cooperate for these purposes with the authorities of the Republic of Panama.

(2) When required by their official duties, members of the Forces or the civilian component may possess and carry official arms and they will conform to any standards which the Joint Committee establishes. The members of the Forces or the civilian component,

and dependents, may bear private arms in accordance with applicable Panamanian laws and regulations, and regulations of the United States Forces.

(3) The members of the Forces shall be obliged to observe proper conduct in accordance with the order and discipline required by Panamanian laws and the military laws and regulations of the United States. The authorities of the Republic of Panama shall maintain vigilance that Panamanian laws and regulations shall be observed at all times.

When the order and discipline referred to in this paragraph should be breached by members of the Forces outside the defense sites, and the authorities of the Republic of Panama, for reasons of language differences or other circumstances, consider it convenient they may request the presence of personnel of the police of the United States Forces to cooperate in the reestablishment of order and discipline, and, in such cases, the United States Forces shall be obliged to send them.

Within the defense sites, the police function shall be primarily exercised by the police of the United States Forces. The Panamanian authorities shall cooperate with the United States Forces in the fulfillment of this function, for which purpose they may locate members of the Panamanian police within the defense sites at the headquarters of the police of the United States Forces or as the Joint Committee agrees. Such cooperation shall be rendered particularly in those cases involving Panamanian nationals.

The Joint Committee may also agree on a procedure so that members of the Panamanian police and the police of the United States Forces may jointly conduct routine inspections for the maintenance of order and discipline in those places where vigilance is especially required.

(4) The United States Forces shall restrict, to the maximum extent possible, the wearing of military uniforms so that they will be worn only when necessary. The Joint Committee shall adopt standards regarding the wearing of military uniforms in other cases, as exceptions.

ARTICLE XXII—DURATION

This Agreement shall enter into force when the Panama Canal Treaty signed on this date enters into force and shall terminate at noon, Panama time, on December 31, 1999.

DONE at Washington, this 7th day of September, 1977, in duplicate in the English and Spanish languages, both texts being equally authentic.

ANNEX A—DEFENSE SITES, MILITARY AREAS OF COORDINATION AND OTHER INSTALLATIONS

(1) The defense sites, military areas of coordination, and other installations, the use of which is made available by the Republic of Panama to the United States, are described below and identified,

but not definitively, on the maps attached hereto[2] and referenced herein, in the manner indicated on the legends thereof. When areas or installations are depicted on more than one map of different scales, the identification on the map with the largest scale shall be controlling. More precise identifications and exact boundaries shall be agreed upon as soon as practicable by the Joint Committee established in Article II of this Agreement after a Joint Survey to be conducted by representatives of the two Parties. When the aforementioned identifications have been completed and agreed upon, they shall be controlling as to the boundaries of the installations and areas described in this Annex.

(2) The defense sites are described generally as follows:

(a) Howard Air Force Base—Fort Kobbe—Farfan (including the Farfan Radio Receiver Facility, Farfan Annex), and United States Naval Station, Rodman, and Marine Barracks (including 193rd Brigade Ammunition Storage Area, Cocoli Housing Area and Arraijan Tank Farm) (Attachment 1);

(b) Fort Clayton—Corozal Army Reservation and Albrook Air Force Station (west) (Attachments 1, 2 and 3);

(c) For William D. Davis Military Reservation, to include Dock 45 and the adjacent water area and Atlantic general depot areas, (Attachments 1 and 4);

(d) Fort Sherman Military Reservation, (Attachment 1); and

(e) Galeta Island; United States Navy Transisthmian Pipeline; and Semaphore Hill Long-Range Radar and Communications Link, (Attachment 1).

(3)(a) The Military Areas of Coordination are described generally as follows:

(i) General Military Areas of Coordination:

(aa) Quarry Heights, except for housing made available to Panama pursuant to paragraph (5)(b) of Annex B to this agreement (Attachments 1 and 5);

(bb) United States Naval Station, Panama Canal, Fort Amador (Attachments 1 and 6); and

(cc) Fort Gulick (Attachments 1 and 7).

(ii) Military Areas of Coordination for Training (Attachment 1):

(aa) Empire Range;

(bb) Piña Range;

(cc) Fort Sherman West; and

(dd) Fort Clayton Training Area.

(iii) Military Areas of Coordination for Housing:

(aa) Curundu Heights, except for housing made available to the Republic of Panama pursuant to paragraph (5)(b) of Annex B to this Agreement (Attachments 1 and 8);

(bb) Herrick Heights (Attachments 1 and 9);

(cc) Coco Solo South (Attachments 1 and 10);

(dd) Fort Amador, except for Buildings 1 through 9, 45 through 48, 51, 57, 64, and 93, and for housing made

[2] The maps referred to in this Annex are not reproduced in this volume. See TIAS 10031, attachment 1 [pocket].

available to the Republic of Panama pursuant to paragraph (5)(b) of Annex B to this Agreement (Attachments 1 and 11);

(ee) France Field (Attachments 1 and 12); and

(ff) Curundu Flats (Attachments 1 and 8).

(iv) Special Facilities:

(aa) Curundu Antenna Farm (Attachments 1 and 3);

(bb) United States Navy Communications Station, Balboa (Attachments 1 and 6);

(cc) Summit Naval Radio Station (Attachment 1);

(dd) Quarry Heights Communications Facility (tunnel) (Attachments 1 and 5);

(ee) Ancon Hill Communications Facilities (Attachments 1 and 5);

(ff) Battery Pratt Communications Facility (Coordinate 119326) (Attachment 1);

(gg) Ammunition Supply Point, Fort Gulick (Attachments 1 and 13);

(hh) Navy Communications-Electric Repair Facility (Building 43–F) (Attachments 1 and 14);

(ii) United States Army Transport-Shipping Facility (Building 39–C) (Attachments 1 and 14);

(jj) Gorgas Hospital Complex (Buildings 223, 233, 237, 238, 240, 240–A, 241, 241–A, 242, 253, 254, 255, 257, 257–G, 261, hospital grounds, and building 424) (Attachments 1 and 9);

(kk) Coco Solo Hospital (Buildings 8900, 8901, 8902, 8904, 8905, 8906, 8907, 8908, 8910, 8912, 8914, 8916, 8918, 8920, 8922, 8926, tennis court, grounds and miscellaneous buildings and structures) (Attachment 1);

(ll) Balboa High School (Buildings 74, 701, 702, 704, 705, 706, 707, 713–X, Stadium, 723, 723–A, 723–B, 723–C, 723–D, 723–E, 723–F, 723–G, parking area, and play slab) (Attachments 1, 14, 15 and 16);

(mm) Curundu Junior High School (Buildings 061–5A, 061–5B, 061–5C, 061–5D, 061–5F, cooling tower structure, playgrounds, tennis courts, and equipment, storage and music buildings, swimming pool and bathhouse, and parking areas (Attachments 1 and 8);

(nn) Cristobal Junior High School (Buildings 1141, 1143, 1149, 1150, 1151, 1153, 1154, 1156, 1239, 1158, 1186, 1288, 2000, playfield, and parking areas) (Attachments 1 and 10);

(oo) Balboa Elementary School (Buildings 709, 710, playground, and parking area) (Attachments 1, 15 and 16);

(pp) Diablo Elementary school (Buildings 5534, 5536, 5634, 5636, 5638, playground, air conditioning building, and parking area) (Attachments 1 and 17);

(qq) Los Rios Elementary School (Buildings 6225, 6226, playground, parking area and chilled water building) (Attachments 1 and 18);

(rr) Gamboa Elementary School (Buildings 56, 56–A, playground, and parking area) (Attachments 1 and 19);

(ss) Coco Solo Elementary School (Buildings 98, 98–A, parking area, playground and chilled water building) (Attachments 1 and 20);

(tt) Margarita Elementary School (Buildings 8350, 8352, playground, parking area, chilled water building and storage building) (Attachments 1 and 21);

(uu) Fort Gulick Elementary School (Buildings 350, 351, 352, playground and parking area) (Attachments 1 and 7);

(vv) Canal Zone College (Buildings 1030, 1031, 1032, 1033, 1034, 1035, 980, 982, 838, athletic field and parking lots) (Attachments 1, 15 and 22);

(ww) Ancon School Administration Office (Partial use of Panama Canal Commission Building 0610) (Attachments 1 and 9);

(xx) Margarita Community Health Center (Partial use of Panama Canal Commission Building 7998) (Attachments 1 and 21);

(yy) Gamboa Community Health Clinic (Use of Panama Canal Commission Building 63) (Attachments 1 and 19);

(zz) Ancon Dental Clinic (Building 287–X, partial use of Panama Canal Commission Building 287) (Attachments 1 and 9);

(aaa) Corozal Mental Health Center (Buildings 6521, 6523, 6524, 6525, 6526, 6537 and grounds) (Attachments 1, 18 and 23);

(bbb) Corozal Animal Care Station/Veterinary Hospital (Buildings 6553, 6554, 6555, and grounds) (Attachments 1 and 18);

(ccc) Corozal Cemetery (Buildings and facilities) (Attachments 1, 18 and 23);

(ddd) Balboa Community Health Center (Use of Panama Canal Commission Building 721) (Attachments 1 and 15); and

(eee) Coco Solo Community Health Center (Room in Building 1140) (Attachments 1 and 20).

(b) The following installations, not contiguous to the defense sites or military Areas of Coordination, which shall be subject to the provisions of the Panama Canal Treaty and this Agreement applicable to the Military Areas of Coordination are described generally as follows:

(i) Buildings 430, 433 and 435 in the Corozal Antenna Field (Attachments 1 and 2);

(ii) AAFES Warehouse, Building 1008 and 1009 (Attachments 1 and 3);

(iii) United States Army Meddac Warehouses, Buildings 490 and 1010 (Attachments 1 and 3);

(iv) Defense Mapping Agency—Inter-American Geodetic Survey Headquarters and warehouse, Buildings 1019, 1007 and 1022 (Attachments 1 and 3);

(v) Balboa West bombing range, as defined by coordinates PA 350056, PA 381074, PV 433990 and PV 404799 (Attachment 1);

(vi) United States Navy Salvage Storage Area, Building 29–B (Attachments 1 and 14);

(vii) United States Army NBC Chambers, Buildings 922, 923, 924, 925, 926 and 927 (Attachments 1 and 8);

(viii) United States Air Force Communications Group storage/training facility, Building 875 (Attachments 1 and 8);

(ix) Inter-American Air Force Academy Jet Engine Test Cell, Building 1901 (Attachments 1 and 8);

(x) Quarry Heights Motor Pool (Building 159) (Attachments 1 and 5);

(xi) Ammunition Transfer Point, Cerro Pelado (Coordinates 415083) (Attachment 1); and

(xii) Fort Amador (Buildings S–103, 104, 105, 105–A, 105–B, 107, 110, 190, 218, 228, 229, 268, 270) (Attachments 1 and 11).

(c) The following areas described in paragraph (a) above shall cease to be Military Areas of Coordination three years from the entry into force of this Agreement:

(i) Curundu Antenna Farm;

(ii) Curundu Heights Housing; and

(iii) Barracks facilities at Fort Gulick for a company of the Forces of the Republic of Panama in specific buildings as agreed in the Joint Committee.

(d) The following areas described in paragraph (a) above shall cease to be Military Areas of Coordination five years from the entry into force of this Agreement:

(i) Fort Gulick, except for family housing, community service areas, and the ammunition storage facility; and

(ii) France Field.

(e) The following areas described in paragraph (a) above shall cease to be Military Areas of Coordination during the life of this Agreement:

(i) Fort Clayton Training Area;

(ii) Fort Amador;

(iii) Fort Gulick Family Housing, community service areas and the ammunition storage facility;

(iv) Coco Solo Family Housing; and

(v) That portion of the Curundu Flats Housing Area comprising the contractor's trailer housing area.

(4) The installations outside of the defense sites, which may be used as provided in Article XI, are described generally as follows:

(a) Miscellaneous facilities as follows: Post Exchange Facility in Building 100, Coco Solo; packing and crating Building 406, Albrook; Post Exchange warehouse, Building 304; household goods crating warehouse, Building 1081; Contractor's air conditioning facility, Building 1002; and household goods warehouse, Building 1067 (Attachments 1, 3, 8 and 20);

(b) Recreational Facilities as follows: Camp Chagres Boy Scout Camp at Madden Dam; and Surfside Theater at Naos Island (Attachment 1); and

(c) Post Exchange Facility, Curundu, Buildings 1025, 1026 and 1027; Photo Shop Building 821 (Attachments 1, 3 and 8).

ANNEX B—TERMS FOR ADMINISTRATION OF MILITARY AREAS OF COORDINATION

(1) PURPOSE: To establish and delineate the respective responsibilities of the United States Forces and the Forces of the Republic of Panama concerning certain areas which the Republic of Panama makes available for coordinated use by the United States Forces and the Forces of the Republic of Panama.

(2) DEFINITIONS:

(a) Military Areas of Coordination (sometimes hereinafter referred to as "Areas") are those areas, and the facilities within them, outside of defense sites, which the Republic of Panama by this Agreement authorizes the United States to use for purposes of communications and military training, and for housing and support of members of the Forces, the civilian component, and dependents; and for other purposes, as the two Parties may agree. A list of these Areas is set forth in Annex A to this Agreement.

(b) Security includes those measures taken to provide physical protection and limit access to or egress from a Military Area of Coordination.

(c) Exterior security measures area applicable only outside the boundaries of Military Areas of Coordination.

(d) Interior security measures are applicable only inside the boundaries of Military Areas of Coordination.

(3) GENERAL CONDITIONS:

(a) The Republic of Panama authorizes the United States to use and maintain Military Areas of Coordination for the purposes of the Panama Canal Treaty. Signs exterior to Military Areas of Coordination will indicate that such Areas are operated under a grant of authority from the Republic of Panama. Only the flag of the Republic of Panama shall be flown in Military Areas of Coordination, including at their entrances, except that, as provided in Article VII of the Panama Canal Treaty, the flags of both the Republic of Panama and the United States may be flown at the site of the Combined Board, which shall be located at Quarry Heights.

(b) All rights, privileges and immunities, which the United States possesses with respect to defense sites under this Agreement shall apply equally with respect to the Military Areas of Coordination, except as limited or excluded in this Annex.

(c) The security of the Military Areas of Coordination shall be the combined responsibility of the United States Forces and the Forces of the Republic of Panama. The Forces of the Republic of Panama shall have the responsibility for maintaining exterior security for these Areas, except where the boundary of such an area coincides with the boundary of a defense site. The United States Forces may assist the Forces of the Republic of Panama in combined stations and patrols as mutually agreed. The senior United States Commander shall have the responsibility for interior security, including control of access to these Areas. Joint United States/Republic of Panama Military police patrols will be used within the Military Areas of Coordination, except within the Special Facilities referred to in paragraph 6 of this Annex. The United States Forces shall be responsible for the command, supervision and protection of their personnel, facilities and equipment within the Areas. The Forces of the Republic of Panama shall be responsible for the command, supervision, and the protection of their personnel and equipment and of the facilities they use within the Areas. The members of the Forces, civilian component and dependents, shall have free unrestricted access to the Areas.

(d) No change in the basic character and functions of Military Areas of Coordination shall be made except by mutual consent of the United States Forces and Forces of the Republic of Panama through the Joint Committee or in accordance with Article IV of this Agreement.

(e) The Combined Board, which is established in Article IV of the Panama Canal Treaty, will be the body in which the United States Forces and the Forces of the Republic of Panama will consult regarding joint training in the Military Areas of Coordination, including construction of new training facilities.

(f) The Joint Committee, established in Article III of this Agreement will be the body in which the United States Forces and the Armed Forces of the Republic of Panama will consult for the purpose of administration of the Military Areas of Coordination.

(g) All signs, posters, and notices of general interest within, and at the entrances to, Military Areas of Coordination will be written in the Spanish and English languages.

(h) A Liaison Office of the Forces of the Republic of Panama may be established within each Military Area of Coordination, as mutually agreed.

(i) The Republic of Panama authorizes the United States Forces to apply its own regulations concerning fire prevention, safety, and sanitation standards in Military Areas of Coordination.

(4) MILITARY AREAS OF COORDINATION FOR TRAINING:

(a) The Military Areas of Coordination for Training identified in Annex A to this Agreement will be available to both the United States Forces and the Forces of the Republic of Panama for the conduct of training.

(b) The United States Forces shall have the responsibility for scheduling the use of the Training Areas for the duration of this Agreement.

(c) The United States agrees to increased use of Training Areas by the Forces of the Republic of Panama over the life of this Agreement, in accordance with agreed arrangements of the Combined Board.

(d) Except as otherwise provided in this Annex, the United States Forces shall have the responsibility for internal control and management of the Training Areas.

(e) The Commanding Officer of the forces using the Training Areas at any given time will be responsible for the safety of all ranges and firing positions during such use, in accordance with established regulations, subject to the authority of the responsible United States Forces Commander only with respect to matters related to safety.

(5) MILITARY AREAS OF COORDINATION FOR HOUSING:

(a) Military Areas of Coordination for Housing are separately identified in Annex A to this Agreement.

(b) These areas shall be available for occupancy by members of the Forces or the civilian component, and dependents. Selected housing units will be made available to the Republic of Panama, as may be mutually agreed.

(c) No new housing units will be constructed in Military Areas of Coordination by the United States.

(6) SPECIAL FACILITIES:

(a) Special facilities located in Military Areas of Coordination are separately identified in Annex A to this Agreement.

(b) With respect to such special facilities, the United States authorities shall be responsible for all interior security to include entrance and exit guards. Only authorized personnel as determined by the United States authorities will be admitted to such facilities.

ANNEX C—APPLICATION OF PANAMANIAN SOCIAL SECURITY

(1) The provisions for Employee Social Security, retirement benefits, and health benefits coverage, set forth in paragraphs 1.4 of Article VIII of the Agreement in Implementation of Article III of the Panama Canal Treaty shall be applicable, *mutatis mutandis*, to employees of the United States Forces and to those employees who may be transferred from the Panama Canal Commission to the United States Forces.

(2)(a) Non-United States citizen employees who are not covered by the Civil Service Retirement System of the United States, or employees paid by United States non-appropriated fund instrumentalities, shall be covered by Panamanian Social Security from the date this Agreement enters into force, with contributions paid by the insured and the employer according to the rates established by the Social Security Laws of the Republic of Panama.

(b) The United States shall request the necessary legislation to pay each such employee at retirement similar to that of the Social Security System of the Republic of Panama.

ANNEX D—PROCEDURAL GUARANTEES

A member of the Forces or the civilian component, or a dependent, prosecuted by the Panamanian authorities shall be entitled to the following procedural guarantees:

(a) To a prompt and speedy trial.

(b) To be informed, in advance of trial, of the specific charge or charges made against him.

(c) To be confronted with and to be allowed to cross-examine the witnesses against him.

(d) To have evidence and witnesses in his favor presented. The authorities shall submit such evidence and call the witnesses if they are within the Republic of Panama.

(e) To have legal representation of his own choice for his defense during all investigative and judicial phases from the time of submission to questioning and throughout the entire proceedings; or, if he indicates he lacks funds for his defense, to be defended by the appropriate public defender.

(f) To have the services of a competent interpreter if he considers it necessary.

(g) To communicate with a representative of the Government of the United States and to have such a representative present, as an observer, at his trial.

(h) Not to be held guilty on account of any act or omission which did not constitute a criminal offense under the law of the Republic of Panama at the time it was committed.

(i) To be present at his trial which shall be public. However, without prejudice to the procedural guarantees in this Annex, persons whose presence is not necessary may be excluded, if the court so decides for reasons of public order or morality.

(j) In his proceedings to have the total burden of proof laden upon the Public Prosecutor or the prosecution.

(k) To have the court consider only voluntary confessions and evidence properly obtained in accordance with the requirements of the law.

(l) Not to be compelled to testify against or otherwise incriminate himself.

(m) Not to be required to stand trial if he is not physically or mentally fit to stand trial and participate in his defense.

(n) Not to be tried or punished more than once for the same offense.

(o) To have the right to appeal a conviction or sentence.

(p) To have credited to any sentence for confinement his entire period of pre-trial custody.

(q) Not to be subject to application of martial law or trial by military courts of special tribunals.

(r) To enjoy other guarantees and rights provided for in the Constitution, Judicial Code and other laws of the Republic of Panama.

Agreed Minute to the Agreement in Implementation of Article IV of the Panama Canal Treaty

1. With reference to paragraph 5(c) of Article VI of the Agreement in Implementation of Article IV of the Panama Canal Treaty (hereinafter referred to as "the Agreement"), the five offenses under Panamanian law referred to therein are understood to be:

(a) "Murder" means the intentional killing of one person by another.

(b) "Rape" means the commission of an act of sexual intercourse by violence or threat and without consent with a person not his spouse, or with a person who is not capable of resisting by reason of mental or physical illness, or with a minor less than twelve years old.

(c) "Robbery with violence" means the act of appropriating an object of value belonging to someone else with the purpose of depriving its owner of his possession and deriving benefit from it, using violence against such person or a third person present at the scene of the act.

(d) "Trafficking in drugs" means the unlawful sale, exchange or transfer for gain of marihuana, hashish, heroin, cocaine, amphetamines, barbiturates, or L.S.D.

(e) "Crime against the security of the Panamanian State" means espionage, sabotage, or terrorism directed against the constituted powers or authorities of Panama, with the purpose of overthrowing them.

2. With reference to paragraphs (2) and (3) of Annex A, it is understood that the United States agrees to the construction by the Republic of Panama of an Atlantic Coast Highway, and a new highway on the Pacific side of the Isthmus, at locations and with right of way widths to be mutually agreed. It is further understood that the bridge over the Canal, in each case, will be of a design sufficiently high so that it will not interfere with the operation of the Canal or with any improvement that may be made to the Canal.

3. With reference to paragraph (2)(a) of Annex A, it is understood that the United States agrees to the construction by the Republic of Panama of a road from Panama City to Vera Cruz at a location to be agreed upon by the Parties, the use of which will be subject to certain agreed conditions and restrictions, which will include the following:

The right of way through the defense site shall be used only for the construction, use and maintenance of the road.

The United States Forces shall have access to the right of way and the right to cross it at any point.

It is understood that upon completion of such road, the access road through Howard Air Force Base to Vera Cruz may be closed by the United States to through traffic. It is further understood that the Republic of Panama will preclude any activity in the coastal areas in the vicinity of Kobbe and Venado Beaches which, in the determination of the United States Forces, might interfere technically with the activities of the United States Navy Receiver Site at Farfan, the United States Air Force communications activity in the vicinity of the Howard/Kobbe Defense Sites, and aircraft operations at Howard Air Force Base.

An illustrative listing of activities which would interfere with aircraft operations at Howard Air Force Base is as follows:

Any construction within 1 kilometer on either side of the runway as extended to the sea.

Construction to structures or objects more than 8 meters high in an area from 1 to 3 kilometers east of the runway as extended to the sea.

Construction of structures or objects more than 8 meters high in an area from 1 to 2 kilometers west of the runway as extended to the sea.

It is further understood that the general public shall have free access to those portions of Venado and Kobbe Beaches lying within defense sites, in accordance with procedures to be developed by the Joint Committee.

4. With reference to paragraph (2)(b) of Annex A, it is understood that the airstrip at Albrook Air Force Station which is transferred

to the Republic of Panama as provided in Article XIII of the Panama Canal Treaty, will not be used for any aviation flight purposes other than helicopter operations. It is further understood that the United States Forces may conduct helicopter operations on the west taxiways, adjacent grassy areas and runway at Albrook Air Force Station until such time as the Republic of Panama determines that development of this area adversely affects flight safety.

5. With reference to paragraphs (2)(c), (2)(d), (3)(a)(ii)(bb) and (3)(a)(ii)(cc) of Annex A, it is understood that the general public shall have free access to and use of the R–6, 836, R–2, S–10, S–2, and S–8 Roads.

6. With reference to paragraph (2)(e) of Annex A:

(a) it is understood that the Republic of Panama will restrict any activity within a 6,000 foot radius of the Galeta operating antenna (coordinates 238393) which, in the determination of the United States Forces, might interfere technically with the communications at Galeta. It is further understood that there will be no construction within a 10,500 foot radius of the Galeta operating antenna for a purpose of heavy industry or of installations with high voltage electrical emission, unless the two parties otherwise agree;

(b) it is understood that the Republic of Panama shall keep the R–12 Road open from Coco Solo to Galeta Island; and

(c) it is understood that the United States will consider authorizing use by the Republic of Panama of the Navy pipelines, under terms and conditions to be mutually agreed.

7. With reference to paragraph (3)(a)(i)(aa) of Annex A, it is understood that the United States shall have use of and access rights to a helicopter landing site at grid coordinates 596898, in accordance with procedures to be developed by the Joint Committee.

8. With reference to paragraphs (3)(a)(i)(bb) and (3)(a)(iii)(dd) of Annex A, it is understood that the United States Forces and the Forces of the Republic of Panama will permit the general public to have free access to the Amador Road. It is further understood that the Joint Committee shall agree upon the location and operating procedure for a joint control point. Until such a new control point is established, the present entrance control point shall remain in operation and members of the Forces of the Republic of Panama shall participate with the United States Forces in its manning. It is also understood that joint patrols of the United States Forces and of the Forces of the Republic of Panama shall patrol the Amador Road. Such joint patrols shall be conducted in accordance with the procedures established for joint patrols in Article XI of the Panama Canal Treaty. It is further understood that the members of the Forces of the Republic of Panama and of the United States Forces, the civilian component, and dependents shall have free access to and use of the beach at Naos Island.

9. With reference to paragraphs (3)(a)(ii)(bb) and (cc) of Annex A, it is understood that the Republic of Panama shall maintain the S–10 Road open from Escobal north along the West Bank of the Canal from coordinates 140115 to 160228 in order to permit access to and from Piña Range and Fort Sherman West Training Area.

10. With reference to paragraph 3(a)(iii)(ff) of Annex A, it is understood that joint military patrols of the United States Forces and

the Forces of the Republic of Panama shall patrol the C–12 Road from coordinates 591939 to 601927. Such joint patrols shall be conducted in accordance with the procedures established for joint patrols in Article XI of the Panama Canal Treaty.

11. With reference to paragraph (3)(a)(iv)(ee) of Annex A, it is understood that the Republic of Panama will preclude any activity on Ancon Hill which, in the determination of the United States Forces, might interfere technically with the communications activity of the United States Forces or of the Federal Aviation Administration on Ancon Hill.

12. With reference to paragraphs (3)(b)(ii), (iii) and (iv) and (3)(b)(vi) of Annex A, it is understood that the following facilities shall cease to be areas of coordination as stated:

United States Navy Salvage storage Area, Building 29B—Five years from the entry into force of the Agreement.

Buildings 1008 and 1009—Three years from the entry into force of the Agreement.

Buildings 490 and 1010—Two years from the entry into force of the Agreement.

Buildings 1019, 1007 and 1022—One year from the entry into force of the Agreement.

13. With reference to paragraph (3)(b)(v) of Annex A, it is understood that the Balboa West Bombing Range will cease to be subject to the provisions of Annex B to this Agreement at such time as the Republic of Panama provides an alternative facility, acceptable to the United States, for the use of the United States Forces as a bombing range.

14. With reference to paragraph (5)(b) of Annex B, it is understood that the selected housing units to be made available by the United States to the Republic of Panama shall include:

(1) Upon entry into force of the Agreement:

(a) Two family housing units at Quarry Heights for officers of the Forces of the Republic of Panama serving on the combined Board;

(b) Eight family housing units in Fort Amador for members of the Forces of the Republic of Panama assigned to Fort Amador. It is further understood that the members of the Forces of the Republic of Panama residing at Fort Amador may use the community facilities at Fort Amador under the same conditions as are applicable to the United States Forces.

(c) Twenty family housing units at Curundu Heights.

(2) Within three years after the entry into force of the Agreement, all family housing units at Curundu Heights. It is understood that the laundry and the Bachelor Officers' housing units at Curundu Heights are not family housing units and will remain under the control of United States Forces for the duration of the Agreement.

(3) Documents Associated with the Panama Canal Treaties

CONTENTS

DOCUMENTS IMPLEMENTING THE PANAMA CANAL TREATY

OTHER DOCUMENTS

EXCHANGE OF NOTES RELATING TO POSTAL SERVICES

DEPARTMENT OF STATE,
Washington, September 7, 1977.

His Excellency RÓMULO ESCOBAR BETHANCOURT,
Chief Negotiator.

EXCELLENCY: I have the honor to confirm our understanding, reached during the negotiations of the Panama Canal Treaty, that the postal services of the United States Forces and of the Republic of Panama shall establish appropriate arrangements through the Joint Committee whereby mail being handled by both postal systems may be delivered by the Postal Service of the Republic of Panama through existing postal facilities in the Canal operating areas and housing areas.

Further, it is understood, with respect to Article X of the Agreement in Implementation of Article IV of the Panama Canal Treaty, that the Republic of Panama will furnish space in the Balboa Post Office (Building 724) and within the area in the Cristobal Administration Building (Building 1105) made available to the Postal Service System of the Republic of Panama, which the United States Forces may use for bulk mail sorting and as postal distribution points, under procedures to be developed by the Joint Committee.

If the foregoing is acceptable to you, I have the honor to suggest that this note and your reply thereto indicating acceptance shall constitute an agreement between our two Governments concerning this matter, which will enter into force on the date of the entry into force of the Panama Canal Treaty.

Accept, Excellency, the renewal assurance of my highest consideration.

For the Secretary of State:

ELLSWORTH BUNKER,
Ambassador at Large.

[TRANSLATION]

EMBASSY OF PANAMA,
Washington, D.C., September 7, 1977.

His Excellency ELLSWORTH BUNKER,
Ambassador at Large of the United States of America.

EXCELLENCY: I have the honor to acknowledge receipt of Your Excellency's note of today's date, which reads as follows:

[There follows Ambassador Bunker's note, quoted in English.]

I also have the honor to confirm on behalf of my Government the foregoing arrangements and to concur that Your Excellency's note and this note shall constitute an agreement between our two Governments concerning this matter, which shall take effect on the date of the entry into force of the Panama Canal Treaty.

Accept, Excellency, the renewed assurances of my most distinguished consideration.

RÓMULO ESCOBAR B.,
Chief Negotiator.

EXCHANGE OF NOTES RELATING TO USE OF COMMISSARY AND POST EXCHANGE FACILITIES

DEPARTMENT OF STATE,
Washington, D.C., September 7, 1977.

His Excellency RÓMULO ESCOBAR BETHANCOURT,
Chief Negotiator.

EXCELLENCY: I have the honor to confirm that with respect to Article XII of the Agreement in Implementation of Article III of the Panama Canal Treaty, it is understood that immediately following the exchange of instruments of ratification, the United States Forces will conduct a thorough study of the feasibility of accommodating the persons authorized to use commissary and post exchange facilities at installations within the defense sites and other areas which the Republic of Panama permits the United States to use in accordance with the Agreement in Implementation of Article IV of the Panama Canal Treaty.

Following the entry into force of that Treaty, the United States will take all practicable steps to accommodate such persons at facilities within defense sites and such other areas. If the United

States Forces find that such persons cannot practicably be so accommodated, the United States Forces may, for the purpose of providing commissary and post exchange services, use the installations listed in paragraphs 1(c)(iii)(A) and 1(e)(iii)(B) of Annex A to the Agreement in Implementation of Article III of the Panama Canal Treaty for a period of six months following the entry into force of the Treaty.

The Republic of Panama agrees that upon the written request of the United States, through the Joint Committee, that six month period of use will be extended until such time as the United States Forces determine it to be practicable to accommodate such persons within the defense sites and such other areas. In no event, however, will the total period of such use exceed 30 calendar months following the entry into force of the Treaty, unless the two Parties otherwise mutually agree.

If the foregoing proposal is acceptable to you, I have the honor to suggest that this note and your reply thereto indicating acceptance shall constitute an agreement between our two Governments concerning this matter, which will enter into force on the date of the exchange of ratification of the Panama Canal Treaty, and shall become effective on the date of the entry into force of the Panama Canal Treaty.

Accept, Excellency, the renewed assurances of my highest consideration.

For the Secretary of State:

ELLSWORTH BUNKER,
Ambassador at Large.

[TRANSLATION]

EMBASSY OF PANAMA,
Washington, D.C., September 7, 1977.

His Excellency ELLSWORTH BUNKER,
Ambassodor at Large of the United States of America.

EXCELLENCY: I have the honor to acknowledge receipt of Your Excellency's note of today's date, which reads as follows:

[There follows Ambassador Bunker's note, quoted in English.]

I also have the honor to confirm on behalf of my Government the foregoing arrangements and to concur that Your Excellency's note and this note shall constitute an agreement between our two Governments concerning this matter, which will enter into force on the date of the exchange of the instruments of ratification of the Panama Canal Treaty, and shall take effect on the date of the entry into force of the Panama Canal Treaty.

Accept, Excellency, the renewed assurances of my most distinguished consideration.

RÓMULO ESCOBAR B.,
Chief Negotiator.

Letter Regarding Termination of Article XVII of the United States-Panama Air Transport Services Agreement

Department of State,
Washington, September 7, 1977.

His Excellency Dr. Rómulo Escobar Bethancourt,
Chief Negotiator.

Dear Dr. Escobar: This is to confirm our understanding, reached in connection with the negotiation of the Panama Canal Treaty, that upon entry into force of that Treaty, Article XVII of the United States-Panama Air Transport Services Agreement, signed at Panama March 31, 1949, will have no further application.

Sincerely,

Ellsworth Bunker,
Ambassador at Large.

OTHER DOCUMENTS

Agreement on Certain Activities of the United States of America in the Republic of Panama [1]

Taking account of the Panama Canal Treaty and related agreements signed this date by representatives of the United States of America and the Republic of Panama, the two Governments confirm their understanding that, in addition to the activities directly related to the specific purpose of the Panama Canal Treaty, the United States may conduct certain other activities in the Republic of Panama. Such other activities shall be conducted in accordance with the provisions of this Agreement.

1. The United States may conduct the following activities in the Republic of Panama:

(a) Tropic testing;

(b) Telecommunications, meteorological, navigational, and oceanographic activities;

(c) Activities of the Inter-American Geodetic Survey;

(d) Humanitarian relief operations, including search and rescue;

(e) Schooling of Latin American military personnel.

2. In order to carry out these activities, the United States may use installations within defense sites and military areas of coordination, and in such other areas of the Republic of Panama as may be mutually agreed.

3. The Agreement in Implementation of Article IV of the Panama Canal Treaty shall apply to the conduct of these activities in the Republic of Panama, except as otherwise provided by arrangements between the two Parties.

(a) Active duty military personnel of the United States armed services assigned to these activities shall be considered to be "members of the Forces" within the meaning of the Agreement in Implementation of Article IV.

(b) Employees of the United States assigned to these activities who are nationals of the United States to whom United

---

[1] TIAS 10039.

States passports have been issued or who are nationals of third countries who are not habitual residents of the Republic of Panama shall be considered to be "members of the civilian component" within the meaning of the Agreement in Implementation of Article IV.

(c) The spouse and children of persons referred to in subparagraphs (a) and (b) above, and other relatives of such persons who depend on them for their subsistence and who habitually live with them under the same roof, shall be considered to be "dependents" within the meaning of the Agreement in Implementation of Article IV.

(d) Military personnel of other Latin American countries assigned to school duty in the Republic of Panama pursuant to paragraph (1)(e) of this Agreement shall be entitled to the privileges authorized under Articles XI and XVIII of the Agreement in Implementation of Article IV.

4. Changes in the activities listed above may be agreed upon by the two Parties through the Joint Committee created by Article III of the Agreement in Implementation of Article IV.

This Agreement shall enter into force simultaneously with the entry into force of the Panama Canal Treaty, and expire when that Treaty expires; provided, however, that the authority of the United States to conduct schooling of Latin American military personnel in the United States Army School of the Americas shall expire five years after the entry into force of the Panama Canal Treaty unless the two Governments otherwise agree.

ATTACHMENT

The following is an illustrative description of the manner in which the activities listed in paragraph 1 of the Agreement on Certain Activities of the United States in Panama presently conducted:

A. Tropic Testing

1. The United States Army Tropic Test Center (USATTC) plans, conducts and reports on tropic environmental phases of development tests and provides advice and guidance on tropic test and evaluation matters to material developers, material producers, other services, and private industry.

2. Many of the marked climatic, seismic, and biological variations which exist in tropical areas of the world are represented in Panama, providing a singular geographic area in which military hardware can be subjected to tropic environmental extremes.

3. The Center occupies office, barracks, laboratory, maintenance and supply building space, and uses outlying test facilities consisting of 18,868 acres of real estate. These outlying test facilities are: Chiva Chiva test area; Battery McKenzie; Firing Point #6, Empire Range; and Gamboa test area. The latter area consists of approximately 7500 hectares of land located along both sides of the pipeline road from the town site of Gamboa to Gatun Lake, bounded approximately by map coordinates 410085, 355080, 282198, 310217, 375164, 410110. It has been used for developmental tests and for methodology studies which provide background for studying the effects of a tropic environment on men and materiel. Range

areas of the 193d Infantry Brigade, Empire Range, Pinas Light Artillery Range and Pinas Beach are also used by USATTC.

B. Telecommunications, Meteorological, Navigational, and Oceanographic Activities

1. Military Affiliate Radio Station (MARS): serves as a backup communication capability for the military services. Provides morale, health, and welfare communication for military services. Has capability to link with MARS affiliates in the United States.

2. USSOUTHCOM Mission Radio Station: provides voice communications between USSOUTHCOM elements in Panama and United States Military Groups in Central and South America.

3. Inter-American Military Networks:

a. The Inter-American Military Network (RECIM) Station.

b. The Inter-American Telecommunications System for the Air Force (SITFA) Station.

c. The Inter-American Naval Telecommunications Network (IANTN).

These United States military stations in three international networks provide a rapid means of communications among the military services of Latin America on military matters. Most Latin American countries operate their own station in each of these networks.

4. United States Navy Timation Station: A Navy satellite tracking site sponsored by the Navy Research Laboratory (NRL). The tracking station is part of an overall Department of Defense program called the NAVSTAR Global Positioning System (GPS). The GPS program is directed toward the development and ultimate establishment, by the 1980's, of a system of 24 navigational satellites.

5. United States Army Atmospheric Sciences Laboratory Team: provides meteorological data from Central and South America.

6. Harbor Survey Assistance Program (HARSAP): a United States Naval oceanographic program which assists Western-Hemisphere countries to develop a hydrographic capability by conducting hydrographic surveys of harbors and waters. Data from these surveys are used to produce charts required to support Department of Defense and United States Merchant Marine operations. Additionally, under HARSAP, a new automated hydrographic survey collection and processing system is used to supplement in-country HARSAP survey efforts. This new system, the Hydrographic Survey and Charting System (HYSURCH), consists of a computer processing van, two boats, one officer, six enlisted personnel, six civilian engineers and technicians, and trainees from the host country.

7. Foreign Broadcast Information Service: monitors and translates into English reports appearing in the foreign public media.

C. Inter-American Geodetic Survey (IAGS)

IAGS is a regional activity, with headquarters for Latin American operations located in Panama. It is the nucleus for topographical activities conducted by the various Latin American nations. An IAGS cartography school is also conducted for Latin American students.

D. Humanitarian Relief Operations, Including Search and Rescue

United States military forces in Panama provide humanitarian relief to other Latin American countries in the event of natural disasters and to conduct searches for missing vessels in the waters of various Latin American nations.

E. Schooling for Latin American Military Personnel

1. Inter-American Naval Telecommunications Network Training Facility: conducts a formal course of instruction for operators and technicians of IANTN membership. This facility is supported by the IANTN communication assistance team, whose members are all bilingual.

2. The United States Army School of the Americas (USARSA): provides professional military training in Spanish for the armed forces of 17 Latin American states, accomplished through courses based on United States Army doctrine ranging from the Command and General Staff College Course, Advanced and Basic Officers Courses, and the Cadet Senior-Year Course, to the Non-Commissioned Officer Leadership Course. In addition to this emphasis on professional training, the School of the Americas provides specialized training in resources management at the national level, small unit tactics, and technical skills. This latter type of skill training is responsive to particular needs of Latin American states.

3. Inter-American Air Force Academy (IAFFA): provided professional education in Spanish for officers and technical training in aeronautical specialties for airmen of all the Latin American Republics.

Technical training in Spanish is provided from the unskilled level through the full spectrum of proficiency to the supervisory level, including transition training in new weapons systems. Approximately five percent of the Academy's 100-member instructor corps is composed of guest instructors who assist United States Air Force officers and airmen in conducting the courses. Specialized transition training is offered in the A/T–37, C–130, and UH–1H.

4. Small Craft Instruction and Technical Team (SCIATT): provides to the navies of Central America training in the operation and maintenance of small size boats.

DONE at Washington, this 7th day of September, 1977, in duplicate, in the English and Spanish languages, both texts being equally authentic.

For the United States of America:

ELLSWORTH BUNKER.
SOL. M. LINOWITZ.

For the Republic of Panama:

RÓMULO ESCOBAR BETHANCOURT.
ARISTIDES ROYO.

AGREEMENT PURSUANT TO ARTICLE VI OF THE CONVENTION ON NATURE PROTECTION AND WILDLIFE PRESERVATION IN THE WESTERN HEMISPHERE

The Governments of the United States of America and the Republic of Panama.

RECALLING that both are parties to the Convention on Nature Protection and Wildlife Preservation in the Western Hemisphere of October 12, 1940;

DESIRING to promote and advance the purposes of that Convention;

NOTING that Article VI of the Convention provides that the Parties may, when circumstances warrant, enter into agreements with one another in order to increase the effectiveness of their collaboration to this end;

AWARE of the unique importance to the international scientific community of the biological reserve located at Barro Colorado Island in Gatun Lake in the Republic of Panama; and

CONSIDERING that the Panama Canal Treaty and related agreements signed this date between them make desirable a further agreement between them to ensure preservation of this biological reserve;

HAVE AGREED UPON THE FOLLOWING:

ARTICLE I

1. The area known as Barro Colorado Island in Gatun Lake in the Republic of Panama is declared to be a Nature Monument as defined in Article I of the Convention, to be known as the Barro Colorado Nature Monument. Upon the termination of the Panama Canal Treaty signed this date, this Nature Monument shall also include the adjacent areas known as Orchid and Point Salud Islands; Bohio, Buena Vista, and Frijoles Points; and the smaller islets adjacent to them. The aforementioned adjacent areas shall be made available during the life of the Panama Canal Treaty for the purposes of this Agreement, through the issuance of land use licenses, as provided for in Article IV of the Agreement in Implementation of Article III of the Panama Canal Treaty. The Republic of Panama shall issue an appropriate land use license or make other arrangements to afford similar use of the peninsula immediately south of Maiz Island, which upon termination of the Panama Canal Treaty, shall also become a part of the aforementioned Nature Monument.

2. As used hereafter in this Agreement, the term "Nature Monument" shall refer to the Nature Monument defined in paragraph 1 of this Article.

ARTICLE II

The Governments pledge themselves to seek, in accordance with their respective national legislative processes, such legislation by each of them as may be necessary to ensure the preservation and protection of the Nature Monument as envisioned in the Convention and to take no action which would derogate in any way from its protected status, except as hereinafter provided.

ARTICLE III

The Governments agree to collaborate in use of the Nature Monument for the purposes of scientific research and investigation, and to assist each other's scientists and scientific institutions in carrying out such activities in the Nature Monument. The Governments shall agree from time to time on such arrangements as may be mutually convenient and desirable to facilitate such collaboration.

ARTICLE IV

The Governments agree that, consistent with the purposes of Article VI of the Convention, they shall make available to all the American Republics equally through publication or otherwise the scientific knowledge resulting from their cooperative efforts to establish and maintain the Nature Monument.

ARTICLE V

The Governments, mindful of their mutual interest in the efficient operation of the Panama Canal, agree that, in executing their responsibilities under the Panama Canal Treaty, they shall take account of this Agreement. It is understood that use of areas included in the Nature Monument for the purpose of maintaining existing facilities relating to the operation of the Panama Canal shall not be considered to derogate from the protected status of the Nature Monument. In the event either Government at any time considers that the efficient operation of the Panama Canal necessitates any other action materially affecting any part of the Nature Monument, the Governments agree to consult promptly and to agree to measures necessary for the protection of the overall integrity of the Nature Monument and furtherance of the purpose of this Agreement.

ARTICLE VI

The Governments agree that they shall jointly transmit copies of this Agreement to the Inter-American Economic and Social Council of the Organization of American States, and shall request that the Organization notify the Contracting Parties to the Convention of this Agreement.

ARTICLE VII

This Agreement shall enter into force simultaneously with the entry into force of the Panama Canal Treaty, and shall remain in force for ten years and, thereafter, for as long as both Governments are parties to the Convention on Nature Protection and Wildlife Preservation in the Western Hemisphere.

DONE at Washington, this 7th day of September, 1977, in duplicate, in the English and Spanish languages, both texts being equally authentic.

For the United States of America:

ELLSWORTH BUNKER.
SOL M. LINOWITZ.

For the Republic of Panama:

RÓMULO ESCOBAR BETHANCOURT.
ARISTIDES ROYO.

NOTE REGARDING ECONOMIC AND MILITARY COOPERATION

DEPARTMENT OF STATE,
Washington.

His Excellency GABRIEL LEWIS GALINDO,
Ambassador of Panama.

EXCELLENCY: I have the honor to refer to our recent discussions concerning programs designed to enhance cooperation between the United States of America and the Republic of Panama in the economic and military spheres. As a result of these discussions, I am authorized to inform you that my government is prepared to agree, within the limitations of applicable United States legislation and subject to compliance with applicable legal requirements and, where necessary, to the availability of appropriate funds, that:

The United States Government will consider applications from the Republic of Panama for housing investment guarantees with a view to approval of specific projects with an aggregate value of not to exceed $75 million over a five year period. Approval of specific projects shall be subject to conformance with any applicable administrative and legislative criteria.

The Overseas Private Investment Corporation would guarantee borrowing of not to exceed $20 million in United States private capital by the National Finance Corporation of Panama (COFINA) for use in financing productive projects in the private sector in Panama, subject to terms and conditions as shall be agreed upon by the Overseas Private Investment Corporation and COFINA, and approved by the Overseas Private Investment Corporation's Board of Directors.

The Export-Import Bank of the United States is prepared to offer a letter of intent to provide loans, loan guarantees, and insurance, aggregating not to exceed $200 million over a five year period beginning October 1, 1977 and ending September 30, 1982, for the purpose of financing the U.S. export value of sales to Panama. Such financing shall, at the discretion of the Board of Directors of the Export-Import Bank, be in the form of loans, loan guarantees, or insurance for individual products or projects approved by such Board.

The United States Government will issue repayment guarantees under its foreign military sales program in order to facilitate the extension of loans to the Government of Panama by eligible lenders for the purpose of financing the purchase by the Government of Panama of defense articles and defense services. The aggregate principal amount of loans guaranteed by the United States Government in accordance with this paragraph shall not exceed $50 million over a ten year period.

It is understood that the undertakings of the United States provided for herein will enter into force upon the exchange of Notes to that effect between our two governments.

Accept, Excellency, the renewed assurance of my highest consideration.

CYRUS VANCE.

EXCHANGE OF NOTES RELATING TO AIR TRAFFIC CONTROL SERVICES

DEPARTMENT OF STATE,
Washington, September 7, 1977.

His Excellency RÓMULO ESCOBAR BETHANCOURT,
Chief Negotiator.

EXCELLENCY: I have the honor to refer to the Panama Canal Treaty signed this date by representatives of the United States of America and the Republic of Panama. In that connection, my Government proposes that negotiations relating to continued air traffic control services commence as soon as possible and that a definitive arrangement on this subject be concluded prior to the exchange of instruments of ratification of the Panama Canal Treaty.

If the foregoing proposal is acceptable to the Government of Panama, I shall be grateful to have an affirmative response from Your Excellency.

Accept, Excellency, the renewed assurances of my highest consideration.

For the Secretary of State:

ELLSWORTH BUNKER,
Ambassador at Large.

[TRANSLATION]

EMBASSY OF PANAMA,
Washington, D.C., September 7, 1977.

His Excellency ELLSWORTH BUNKER,
Ambassador at Large of the United States of America.

EXCELLENCY: I have the honor to refer to your note of today's date concerning continued air traffic control services, and to confirm that my Government agrees to commence negotiations as soon as possible and to conclude a definitive arrangement on this subject prior to the exchange of instruments of ratification of the Panama Canal Treaty.

Accept, Excellency, the renewed assurances of my highest consideration.

RÓMULO ESCOBAR B.,
Chief Negotiator.

NOTE REGARDING THE ESTABLISHMENT OF THE PANAMA BUREAU OF THE UNITED STATES FOREIGN BROADCAST INFORMATION SERVICE

DEPARTMENT OF STATE,
Washington, September 7, 1977.

The Department of State of the United States of America has the honor to inform the foreign Ministry of the Republic of Panama that, upon the entry into force of the Panama Canal Treaty, it is the intention of the United States of America to establish the Panama Bureau of the United States Foreign Broadcast Information Service (FBIS) as an integral part of the Embassy of the United States of America in the Republic of Panama. The Bureau would form part of the diplomatic mission, in a manner similar to that of other agencies of the United States Government currently operating in the Republic of Panama, under the authority of the United States Ambassador.

The Foreign Broadcast Information Service is an agency of the United States Government with worldwide responsibility for monitoring and translating into English available foreign public media, including (a) transmissions by major press agencies, (b) public radio and television broadcasts, and (c) selected articles from newspapers and other publications. These translated materials are made available in the United States of America and abroad to interested persons in both governmental and private sectors. FBIS executes this responsibility from fourteen bureaus located in foreign countries, most of which are established as integral parts of the United States diplomatic missions to those countries.

The Panama Bureau of FBIS will have responsibility for providing this service for an area which includes most countries of Central America and northern South America, and a part of the African continent. The Bureau Staff currently consists of four United States citizen employees (a Bureau Chief, a Deputy Chief and two editors) assigned for rotational tours of two to four years. There are no locally-hired American employees. United States citizen personnel of the Bureau shall have the same privileges and immunities, and be subject to the same conditions, as other American personnel currently assigned to the various agencies forming parts of the Embassy of the United States of America in the Republic of Panama. the Bureau also currently employs three locally-hired third country nationals resident in Panama, and twenty-nine Panamanian citizens. FBIS anticipates no perceptible expansion of its American or local staff in the foreseeable future.

At the present time, the Panama Bureau of FBIS is located on a single parcel of land, comprising some 320 acres and including the Bureau office and the Chiva Chiva radio antenna field, located on the Fort Clayton Military Reservation.

E. B.

EXCHANGE OF NOTES RELATING TO THE GORGAS MEMORIAL INSTITUTE OF TROPICAL AND PREVENTIVE MEDICINE, INCORPORATED, AND TO THE GORGAS MEMORIAL LABORATORY

DEPARTMENT OF STATE,
Washington, September 7, 1977.

His Excellency RÓMULO ESCOBAR BETHANCOURT,
Chief Negotiator.

EXCELLENCY: I have the honor to refer to the Gorgas Memorial Institute of Tropical and Preventive Medicine, Incorporated, and its subsidiary, the Gorgas Memorial Laboratory. The Institute and Laboratory were established in memory of Dr. William C. Gorgas for research on diseases endemic to Central America and northern

South America. The Institute receives from the Government of the United States an annual contribution in Dr. Gorgas' memory for the operation and maintenance of the Laboratory.

The Gorgas Memorial Laboratory is established and operates in Panama under provisions of Law 15 of October 16, 1930, Law 5 of February 5, 1953 and Law 84 of September 20, 1973 of the Republic of Panama. The Institute has informed the United States of its desire to continue its operations in Panama pursuant to the provisions of these laws.

I refer further to the Panama Canal Treaty and related agreements signed this date by representatives of the Governments of the United States and Panama, and, in that connection, propose that our Governments agree that, subsequent to the entry into force of the Treaty, the Gorgas Memorial Institute and Laboratory shall continue to enjoy the sole and exclusive use, without charge, of the following areas of lands and waters, and installations, being used by the Institute and Laboratory prior to the entry into force of the Treaty:

Juan Mina Plantation, approximately 15 acres of land, and one multi-purpose building situated thereon, located on the east side of the Charges River in the Balboa East District; and Building 265, a laboratory building adjacent to the Gorgas Hospital, Ancon, and adjacent land.

It is understood that this arrangement shall continue for an initial period of five years, and will be renewed upon request at least one year in advance by the Gorgas Memorial Institute.

I propose further that in the event the Republic of Panama establishes any means whereby any legal or natural person other than the Government of the Republic of Panama may acquire title under the laws of the Republic of Panama to any areas of lands and waters, or other real property located thereon, which prior to the entry into force of the Panama Canal Treaty formed part of the Canal Zone, our Governments agree that the Gorgas Memorial Institute shall be permitted by the Republic of Panama to acquire title to the above-mentioned areas the use of which it enjoys. Such title shall be accorded by the Republic of Panama pursuant to an arrangement not less favorable than that accorded by the Republic of Panama to any other such legal or natural person.

I propose further that our Governments agree to the issuance of a license to the Gorgas Memorial Institute in accordance with the procedures set forth in Article IV of the Agreement in Implementation of Article III of the Panama Canal Treaty to permit the use, without charge, by the Gorgas Memorial Laboratory to Abogado and Aojeta Islands, located in Gatun Lake, for the purposes of the Laboratory.

I further propose that our Governments agree that the United States may permit the Gorgas Memorial Institute and Laboratory to enjoy the privilege of making official purchases for the Laboratory's operations in the United States military commissaries and exchanges established pursuant to the Agreement in Implementation of Article IV of the Panama Canal Treaty, and that the United States may provide to the Institute and Laboratory for official purposes such other supplies or services of the United States Forces or the Panama Canal Commission as may be convenient. It is understood that this agreement will not extend to personal purchases by individual members of the staff and employees of the Gorgas Memorial Laboratory, regardless of their nationality.

If the foregoing proposals relating to the status and operations of the Gorgas Memorial Institute and Laboratory are acceptable to the Government of the Republic of Panama, I have the honor to propose that this note, and Your Excellency's affirmative response, shall constitute an agreement between our Governments concerning this matter, which will enter into force on the date of entry into force of the Panama Canal Treaty.

Accept, Excellency, the renewed assurances of my highest consideration.

For the Secretary of State:

ELLSWORTH BUNKER,
Ambassador at Large.

[TRANSLATION]

EMBASSY OF PANAMA,
Washington, D.C., September 7, 1977.

His Excellency ELLSWORTH BUNKER,
Ambassador at Large of the United States of America.

EXCELLENCY: I have the honor to acknowledge receipt of Your Excellency's note of today's date, which reads as follows:

[There follows Ambassador Bunker's note, quoted in English.]

I have the honor to confirm that my Government accepts the foregoing proposals, and that Your Excellency's note and this note shall constitute an agreement between our two Governments which will enter into force on the date of the entry into force of the Panama Canal Treaty.

Accept, Excellency, the renewed assurances of my highest consideration.

RÓMULO ESCOBAR B.,
Chief Negotiator.

EXCHANGE OF NOTES RELATING TO SCIENTIFIC ACTIVITIES IN PANAMA OF THE SMITHSONIAN TROPICAL RESEARCH INSTITUTE

DEPARTMENT OF STATE,
Washington, September 7, 1977.

His Excellency RÓMULO ESCOBAR BETHANCOURT,
Chief Negotiator.

EXCELLENCY: As you are aware, the Smithsonian Tropical Research Institute, a trust instrumentality of the United States of America, hereinafter called "the Institute," has, for several years, carried out experimental and research activities of an exclusively scientific nature in various parts of the Republic of Panama. Those activities are described and authorized in Contract No. 1, January 5, 1977, signed by Dr. Abraham Saied, Minister of Health, and Dr. Ira Rubinoff, Director of the Institute. As set forth in the seventh clause of the contract, its duration is indefinite, but it may be terminated if one of the parties so desires, provided that it notify the other one year in advance of the date selected for termination.

Despite the foregoing, it is obvious that the Institute's legal situation and the development of its activities will be affected by the entry into force of the Panama Canal Treaty and related agreements, signed September 7, 1977 by representatives of the Republic of Panama and the United States of America. In anticipation of that eventuality, I thought it pertinent to propose to you, in compliance with precise instructions from my Government, that the Republic of Panama and the United States of America agree on the Institute's continuation of its scientific activities in the Republic of Panama, after entry into force of the Panama Canal Treaty and related agreements, in accordance with the provisions of the abovementioned contract and in order to achieve the objectives therein set forth.

The agreement which I present to you for consideration would remain in effect for five years from the date of the entry into force of the Panama Canal Treaty and would be extended automatically for 5 year periods until either Government gave notice of termination, at least one year before the date of automatic extension.

I consider it advisable to propose to Your Excellency that if one of the parties to the contract should wish to terminate it on the basis of the seventh clause thereof while the Panama Canal Treaty is in force, our Governments agree that, unless there is a mutual understanding to replace the contract, the contract and the agreement proposed in this note shall remain in force.

It could also be agreed, and I so propose to Your Excellency, that, if either party wishes to terminate the aforementioned contract after the expiration of the Panama Canal Treaty, our Governments shall immediately initiate consultations concerning the future legal situation of the Institute and its facilities, properties, and personnel in the Republic of Panama, before the contract expires.

With respect to facilities and land and water areas in various parts of the Isthmus of Panama listed and described in the annex to this note, the use of which has not been granted by the Republic of Panama to the United States of America by any other means, I propose that they be made available to the Institute for its exclusive use. It is understood that this agreement will not affect the right of the parties to the contract to enter into subsequent agreements on the terms of the Institute's utilization of other facilities and land and water areas in the Republic of Panama which the latter may consider it desirable to make available to the Institute for the uses and purposes defined in the contract.

I wish to propose that our Governments agree that, as long as the Panama Canal Treaty remains in force, the United States of America may permit the Institute to use any portion of the lands and waters, and of the facilities located therein, situated within the land and water areas the use of which is granted by the Treaty to the United States of America, for purposes of the aforementioned contract, subject to terms and conditions consistent with the Panama Canal Treaty, as the United States of America may define them.

I further wish to propose to Your Excellency that upon cessation, under the Panama Canal Treaty, of the right of the United States to use any land and water areas and facilities located therein which are being used by the Institute, our Governments immediately begin talks intended to reach agreements permitting the Institute to continue to use such areas of facilities.

The possibility should be considered, Your Excellency, that the Republic of Panama may establish procedures whereby any natural or legal person could acquire, in accordance with the laws of Panama, title to land and water areas or properties located therein which were formerly a part of the territory constituting the Panama Canal Zone. I therefore propose to you that, such being the case, our Governments agree that the Republic of Panama, subject to the applicable laws, shall grant the Institute rights, other than real property title, with respect to any land and water areas or properties in use by the Institute at the time when such procedures are established. These rights will be granted by the Republic of Panama by an agreement or other means, not less favorable than the most favorable granted by the Republic of Panama to any other natural or juristic person.

Finally, Your Excellency, I should like to propose that in the event that the Republic of Panama does not establish such procedures for transfer of title to land and water areas or properties located therein to natural or legal persons other than the Government of the Republic of Panama, the two Governments agree that the Government of the Republic of Panama shall place at the disposal of the Institute, free of cost, the use of all areas and facilities referred to in this letter, and any others that may be used by the Institute for the purposes defined in the aforementioned contract.

An exception will be made for cases in which the two Governments or the parties to the aforementioned contract might reach a mutual agreement on other terms.

If the aforementioned proposals relating to the operation in the Republic of Panama of the Smithsonian Tropical Research Institute are acceptable to your Government, I should like to propose that this note and Your Excellency's affirmative reply constitute an agreement between our Governments concerning this matter.

Accept, Excellency, the renewed assurances of my highest consideration.

For the Secretary of State:

ELLSWORTH BUNKER,
Ambassador at Large.

ANNEX

The following facilities and lands and waters shall be made available for the continued exclusive use of the Smithsonian Tropical Research Institute.

1. Smithsonian Tropical Research Institute Headquarters, shops, administrative offices, cages and laboratories on Gorgas Road.
2. Tivoli Site. Comprises approximately 4.8 acres at the site of the former Tivoli Hotel and adjacent Tivoli Kitchen structure.
3. Naos Island. All facilities and areas being used by the Smithsonian Tropical Research Institute on the date the Panama Canal Treaty enters into force.

4. Flamenco Island. All facilities and areas being used by the Smithsonian Tropical Research Institute on the date the Panama Canal Treaty enters in force.

5. Pipeline Road Reserve. Approximately 37 acres of land near Pipeline Road at coordinates PA 391116 (Sheet 4243 II, Gamboa).

[TRANSLATION]

EMBASSY OF PANAMA,
Washington, D.C., September 7, 1977.

His Excellency ELLSWORTH BUNKER,
Ambassador at Large of the United States of America.

EXCELLENCY: I have the honor to refer to Your Excellency's note of today's date concerning the activities of the Smithsonian Tropical Research Institute in the Republic of Panama, which reads as follows:

[There follows Ambassador Bunker's note, quoted in English.]

I have the honor to confirm the acceptance by my Government of the proposals contained in this note and its agreement that your note and this reply shall constitute an agreement between our two Governments.

Accept, Excellency, the renewed assurance of my highest consideration.

RÓMULO ESCOBAR B.,
Chief Negotiator.

EXCHANGE OF NOTES RELATING TO CUSTODIANSHIP OF THE BARRO COLORADO NATIVE MONUMENT BY THE SMITHSONIAN TROPICAL RESEARCH INSTITUTE [2]

DEPARTMENT OF STATE,
Washington, September 7, 1977.

His Excellency RÓMULO ESCOBAR BETHANCOURT,
Chief Negotiator.

EXCELLENCY: I have the honor to refer to the Agreement pursuant to Article VI of the Convention on Nature Protection and Wildlife Preservation in the Western Hemisphere, and to the Panama Canal Treaty and related agreements signed on September 7, 1977 by representatives of the United States of America and the Republic of Panama. Article III of the Agreement relating to the Convention on Nature Protection provides that our Governments may agree from time to time on such arrangements as may be mutually convenient and desirable to facilitate their collaboration in the use of the Barro Colorado Nature Monument for the purposes of scientific research and investigation.

I consider it desirable within the spirit of the aforementioned Convention and for the purposes of the Agreement based thereon that our Governments agree that the Smithsonian Tropical Research Institute (STRI), a trust instrumentality of the United States of America, which I shall hereinafter call the Institute, be

---

[2] TIAS 10036.

designated by both Governments as custodian of the Barro Colorado Nature Monument. I propose that our Governments further agree that the Institute shall, during the period of its custodianship, have sole responsibility to act on behalf of our Governments in authorizing use of the Nature Monument for the purposes of scientific research and investigation and for its protection as envisaged in the aforementioned Convention and our Agreement based thereon. In the event that one of the Parties should attempt to take any action related to the efficient operation of the Panama Canal as provided for in Article V of our Agreement, I propose that the Institute, as custodian, be advised in advance and invited to comment on the potential impact of such action on the overall integrity of the Nature Monument.

I consider it desirable and to that end I propose to Your Excellency that, during the period of its custodianship, the Institute be authorized to employ scientific and support staff, to include game wardens, as necessary to enforce such laws and regulations as may apply to the protection of the Nature Monument. Persons violating the integrity of the Nature Monument contrary to the provisions of such laws or regulations shall be promptly delivered to the authorities of the Republic of Panama by game wardens employed by the Institute for appropriate action under the laws of the Republic of Panama.

I further consider it desirable and I therefore propose to Your Excellency that our Governments agree to designate the Institute as custodian for the Barro Colorado Nature Monument for an initial period of five years, to be extended for additional 5-year periods upon request by the Institute at least one year in advance of the date of expiration of the period, or until such time as our Governments may mutually agree on other understandings for the administration of the Nature Monument. If, subsequent to the termination of the Panama Canal Treaty, the Republic of Panama should desire to terminate the custodianship of the Institute of the Nature Monument, I consider it desirable and I therefore propose that our Governments agree that the decision take effect one year after the day on which the Republic of Panama shall inform the United States of this intent.

If the foregoing understanding proposed for custodianship of the Barro Colorado Nature Monument by STRI are acceptable to the Government of the Republic of Panama, I propose that this note and Your Excellency's affirmative response constitute an agreement between our Governments concerning this matter.

Accept, Excellency, the renewed assurance of my highest consideration.

For the Secretary of State:

ELLSWORTH BUNKER,
Ambassador at Large.

[TRANSLATION]

EMBASSY OF PANAMA,
Washington, D.C., September 7, 1977.

His Excellency ELLSWORTH BUNKER,
Ambassador at Large of the United States of America.

EXCELLENCY: I have the honor to refer to Your Excellency's note of today's date concerning the designation of the Smithsonian Tropical Research Institute as custodian of the Barro Colorado Nature Monument, which reads as follows:

[There follows Ambassador Bunker's note, quoted in English.]

I have the honor to confirm that my Government accepts the understanding set forth in Your Excellency's note, and that your note and this note in reply shall constitute an agreement between our two Governments.

Accept, Excellency, the renewed assurances of my highest consideration.

RÓMULO ESCOBAR B.,
Chief Negotiator.

2. North Atlantic

a. North Atlantic Treaty[1]

Signed at Washington, April 4, 1949; Ratification advised by the Senate, July 21, 1949; Ratified by the President, July 25, 1949; Proclaimed by the President and entered into force, August 24, 1949; as amended February 15, 1952[2]

The Parties to this Treaty reaffirm their faith in the purposes and principles of the Charter of the United Nations and their desire to live in peace with all peoples and all governments.

They are determined to safeguard the freedom, common heritage and civilization of their peoples, founded on the principles of democracy, individual liberty and the rule of law.

They seek to promote stability and well-being in the North Atlantic area.

They are resolved to unite their efforts for collective defense and for the preservation of peace and security.

They therefore agree to this North Atlantic Treaty:

ARTICLE 1

The Parties undertake, as set forth in the Charter of the United Nations, to settle any international disputes in which they may be involved by peaceful means in such a manner that international peace and security, and justice, are not endangered, and to refrain in their international relations from the threat or use of force in any manner inconsistent with the purposes of the United Nations.

ARTICLE 2

The Parties will contribute toward the further development of peaceful and friendly international relations by strengthening their free institutions, by bringing about a letter understanding of the principles upon which these institutions are founded, and by promoting conditions of stability and well-being. They will seek to eliminate conflict in their international economic policies and will encourage economic collaboration between any or all of them.

[1] 63 Stat. 2241; TIAS 1964; 4 Bevans 828; 34 UNTS 243. For a list of states that are parties to the Treaty, see Department of State publication, *Treaties in Force*.

[2] 3 UST 43; TIAS 2390; 126 UNTS 350. Protocol to the North Atlantic Treaty on the accession of Greece and Turkey which was done at London October 17, 1951; ratification advised by the Senate of the United States of America February 7, 1952; ratified by the President of the United States of America February 11, 1952; proclaimed by the President of the United States of America March 4, 1952; entered into force February 15, 1952.

ARTICLE 3

In order more effectively to achieve the objectives of this Treaty, the Parties, separately and jointly, by means of continuous and effective self-help and mutual aid, will maintain and develop their individual and collective capacity to resist armed attack.

ARTICLE 4

The Parties will consult together whenever, in the opinion of any of them, the territorial integrity, political independence or security of any of the Parties is threatened.

ARTICLE 5

The Parties agree that an armed attack against one or more of them in Europe or North America shall be considered an attack against them all; and consequently they agree that, if such an armed attack occurs, each of them, in exercise of the right of individual or collective self-defense recognized by Article 51 of the Charter of the United Nations, will assist the Party or Parties so attacked by taking forthwith, individually and in concert with the other Parties, such action as it deems necessary, including the use of armed force, to restore and maintain the security of the North Atlantic area.

Any such armed attack and all measures taken as a result thereof shall immediately be reported to the Security Council. Such measures shall be terminated when the Security Council has taken the measures necessary to restore and maintain international peace and security.

ARTICLE 6[3]

For the purpose of Article 5, an armed attack on one or more of the Parties is deemed to include an armed attack—

(i) on the territory of any of the Parties in Europe or North America, on the Algerian Departments of France, on the territory of Turkey or the islands under the jurisdiction of any of the Parties in the North Atlantic area north of the Tropic of Cancer;

(ii) on the forces, vessels or aircraft of any of the Parties, when in or over these territories or any other area in Europe in which occupation forces of any of the Parties were stationed on the date when the Treaty entered into force or the Mediterranean Sea or the North Atlantic area north of the Tropic of Cancer.

---

[3] As modified by the Protocol on the Accession of Greece and Turkey, which entered into force February 15, 1952. The Article originally read as follows:

"ARTICLE 6

"For the purpose of Article 5 an armed attack on one or more of the Parties is deemed to include an armed attack on the territory of any of the Parties in Europe or North America, on the Algerian Departments of France, on the occupation forces of any Party in Europe, on the islands under the jurisdiction of any Party in the North Atlantic area north of the Tropic of Cancer or on the vessels or aircraft in this area of any of the Parties.".

ARTICLE 7

The Treaty does not affect, and shall not be interpreted as affecting in any way the rights and obligations under the Charter of the Parties which are members of the United Nations, or the primary responsibility of the Security Council for the maintenance of international peace and security.

ARTICLE 8

Each Party declares that none of the international engagements now in force between it and any other of the Parties or any third state is in conflict with the provisions of this Treaty, and undertakes not to enter into any international engagements in conflict with this Treaty.

ARTICLE 9

The Parties hereby establish a council, on which each of them shall be represented, to consider matters concerning the implementation of this Treaty. The council shall be so organized as to be able to meet promptly at any time. The council shall set up such subsidiary bodies as may be necessary; in particular it shall establish immediately a defense committee which shall recommend measures for the implementation of Articles 3 and 5.

ARTICLE 10

The Parties may, by unanimous agreement, invite any other European state in a position to further the principles of this Treaty and to contribute to the security of the North Atlantic area to accede to this Treaty. Any state so invited may become a party to the Treaty by depositing its instrument of accession with the Government of the United States of America. The Government of the United States of America will inform each of the Parties of the deposit of each such instrument of accession.

ARTICLE 11

This Treaty shall be ratified and its provisions carried out by the Parties in accordance with their respective constitutional processes. The instruments of ratification shall be deposited as soon as possible with the Government of the United States of America, which will notify all the other signatories of each deposit. The Treaty shall enter into force between the states which have ratified it as soon as the ratification of the majority of the signatories, including the ratifications of Belgium, Canada, France, Luxembourg, the Netherlands, the United Kingdom and the United States, have been deposited and shall come into effect with respect to other states on the date of deposit of their ratifications.

ARTICLE 12

After the Treaty has been in force for ten years, or at any time thereafter, the Parties shall, if any of them so requests, consult together for the purpose of reviewing the Treaty, having regard for the factors then affecting peace and security in the North Atlantic area, including the development of universal as well as regional arrangements under the Charter of the United Nations for the maintenance of international peace and security.

ARTICLE 13

After the Treaty has been in force for twenty years, any Party may cease to be a party one year after its notice of denunciation has been given to the Government of the United States of America, which will inform the Governments of the other Parties of the deposit of each notice of denunciation.

ARTICLE 14

This Treaty, of which the English and French texts are equally authentic, shall be deposited in the Archives of the Government of the United States of America. Duly certified copies thereof will be transmitted by that Government to the Governments of the other signatories.

IN WITNESS WHEREOF, the undersigned Plenipotentiaries have signed this Treaty.

DONE at Washington, the fourth day of April, 1949.

b. Protocol to the North Atlantic Treaty on the Accession of Greece and Turkey [1]

Done at London, October 17, 1951; Ratification advised by the Senate, February 7, 1952; Ratified by the President, February 11, 1952; Entered into force, February 15, 1952; Proclaimed by the President, March 4, 1952

The Parties to the North Atlantic Treaty, signed at Washington on April 4, 1949

Being satisfied that the security of the North Atlantic area will be enhanced by the accession of the Kingdom of Greece and the Republic of Turkey to that Treaty, agree as follows:

ARTICLE 1

Upon the entry into force of this Protocol, the Government of the United States of America shall, on behalf of all the Parties, communicate to the Government of the Kingdom of Greece and the Government of the Republic of Turkey an invitation to accede to the North Atlantic Treaty, as it may be modified by Article 2 of the present Protocol. Thereafter the Kingdom of Greece and the Republic of Turkey shall each become a Party on the date when it deposits its instruments of accession with the Government of the United States of America in accordance with Article 10 of the Treaty.

ARTICLE 2

If the Republic of Turkey becomes a Party to the North Atlantic Treaty, Article 6 of the Treaty shall, as from the date of the deposit by the Government of the Republic of Turkey of its instruments of accession with the Government of the United States of America, be modified to read as follows:

For the purpose of Article 5, an armed attack on one or more of the Parties is deemed to include an armed attack:

1. on the territory of any of the Parties in Europe or North America, on the Algerian Departments of France, on the territory of Turkey or on the islands under the jurisdiction of any of the Parties in the North Atlantic area north of the Tropic of Cancer;

2. on the forces, vessels, or aircraft of any of the Parties, when in or over these territories or any other area in Europe in which occupation forces of any of the Parties were stationed on the date when the Treaty entered into force or the Mediterranean Sea or the North Atlantic area north of the Tropic of Cancer.

[1] 3 UST 43; TIAS 2390; 126 UNTS 350.

ARTICLE 3

The present Protocol shall enter into force when each of the Parties to the North Atlantic Treaty has notified the Government of the United States of America of its acceptance thereof. The Government of the United States of America shall inform all the Parties to the North Atlantic Treaty of the date of the receipt of each such notification and of the date of the entry into force of the present Protocol.

ARTICLE 4

The present Protocol, of which the English and French texts are equally authentic, shall be deposited in the Archives of the Government of the United States of America. Duly certified copies thereof shall be transmitted by that Government to the Governments of all the Parties to the North Atlantic Treaty.

c. Protocol to the North Atlantic Treaty on the Accession of the Federal Republic of Germany [1]

Signed at Paris, October 23, 1954; Entered into force for the United States, May 5, 1955

The Parties to the North Atlantic Treaty signed at Washington on April 4, 1949,

Being satisfied that the security of the North Atlantic area will be enhanced by the accession of the Federal Republic of Germany to that Treaty, and Having noted that the Federal Republic of Germany has, by a declaration dated October 3, 1954, accepted the obligations set forth in Article 2 of the Charter of the United Nations and has undertaken upon its accession to the North Atlantic Treaty to refrain from any action inconsistent with the strictly defensive character of that Treaty, and

Having further noted that all member governments have associated themselves with the declaration also made on October 3, 1954, by the Governments of the United States of America, the United Kingdom of Great Britain and Northern Ireland and the French Republic in connection with the aforesaid declaration of the Federal Republic of Germany, Agree as follows:

Article 1

Upon the entry into force of the present Protocol, the Government of the United States of America shall on behalf of all the Parties communicate to the Government of the Federal Republic of Germany an invitation to accede to the North Atlantic Treaty. Thereafter the Federal Republic of Germany shall become a Party to that Treaty on the date when it deposits its instruments of accession with the Government of the United States of America in accordance with Article 10 of the Treaty.

Article 2

The present Protocol shall enter into force, when

1. each of the Parties to the North Atlantic Treaty has notified to the Government of the United States of America its acceptance thereof,
2. all instruments of ratification of the Protocol modifying and completing the Brussels Treaty have been deposited with the Belgian Government, and
3. all instruments of ratification or approval of the Convention on the Presence of Foreign Forces in the Federal Republic of Germany have been deposited with the Government of the Federal Republic of Germany.

[1] 6 UST 5707; TIAS 3428; 243 UNTS 308.

The Government of the United States of America shall inform the other Parties to the North Atlantic Treaty of the date of the receipt of each notification of acceptance of the present Protocol and of the date of the entry into force of the present Protocol.

Article 3

The present Protocol, of which the English and French texts are equally authentic, shall be deposited in the Archives of the Government of the United States of America. Duly certified copies thereof shall be transmitted by that Government to the Governments of the other Parties to the North Atlantic Treaty.

d. Protocol to the North Atlantic Treaty on the Accession of Spain[1]

Signed at Brussels, December 10, 1981; Ratification advised by the Senate, March 16, 1982; Ratified by the President, April 1, 1982; Entered into force, May 29, 1982

The Parties to the North Atlantic Treaty, signed at Washington on April 4, 1949,

Being satisfied that the security of the North Atlantic area will be enhanced by the accession of the Kingdom of Spain to that Treaty,

Agree as follows:

ARTICLE 1

Upon the entry into force of this Protocol, the Secretary General of the North Atlantic Treaty Organization shall, on behalf of all the Parties, communicate to the Government of the Kingdom of Spain an invitation to accede to the North Atlantic Treaty. In accordance with Article 10 of the Treaty, the Kingdom of Spain shall become a Party on the date when it deposits its instrument of accession with the Government of the United States of America.

ARTICLE 2

The present Protocol shall enter into force when each of the Parties to the North Atlantic Treaty has notified the Government of the United States of America of its acceptance thereof. The Government of the United States of America shall inform all the Parties to the North Atlantic Treaty of the date of receipt of each such notification and of the date of the entry into force of the present Protocol.

ARTICLE 3

The present Protocol, of which the English and French texts are equally authentic, shall be deposited in the Archives of the Government of the United States of America. Duly certified copies thereof shall be transmitted by that Government to the Governments of all the Parties to the North Atlantic Treaty.

[1] TIAS 10564.

e. Protocol to the North Atlantic Treaty on the Accession of the Czech Republic[1]

Signed at Brussels, December 16, 1997; Ratification advised by the Senate, April 30, 1998; Entered into force, December 4, 1998

The Parties to the North Atlantic Treaty, signed at Washington on April 4, 1949,

Being satisfied that the security of the North Atlantic area will be enhanced by the accession of the Czech Republic to that Treaty,

Agree as follows:

ARTICLE I

Upon the entry into force of this Protocol, the Secretary General of the North Atlantic Treaty Organization shall, on behalf of all the Parties, communicate to the Government of the Czech Republic an invitation to accede to the North Atlantic Treaty. In accordance with article 10 of the Treaty, the Czech Republic shall become a Party on the date when it deposits its instrument of accession with the Government of the United States of America.

ARTICLE II

The present Protocol shall enter into force when each of the Parties to the North Atlantic Treaty has notified the Government of the United States of America of its acceptance thereof. The Government of the United States of America shall inform all the Parties to the North Atlantic Treaty of the date of receipt of each such notification and of the date of the entry into force of the present Protocol.

ARTICLE III

The present Protocol, of which the English and French texts are equally authentic, shall be deposited in the Archives of the Government of the United States of America. Duly certified copies thereof shall be transmitted by that Government to the Governments of all the Parties to the North Atlantic Treaty.

[1] Treaty Doc. 105–36.

f. Protocol to the North Atlantic Treaty on the Accession of Hungary[1]

Signed at Brussels, December 16, 1997; Ratification advised by the Senate, April 30, 1998; Entered into force, December 4, 1998

The Parties to the North Atlantic Treaty, signed at Washington on April 4, 1949,

Being satisfied that the security of the North Atlantic area will be enhanced by the accession of the Republic of Hungary to that Treaty,

Agree as follows :

ARTICLE I

Upon the entry into force of this Protocol, the Secretary General of the North Atlantic Treaty Organization shall, on behalf of all the Parties, communicate to the Government of the Republic of Hungary an invitation to accede to the North Atlantic Treaty. In accordance with article 10 of the Treaty, the Republic of Hungary shall become a Party on the date when it deposits its instrument of accession with the Government of the United States of America.

ARTICLE II

The present Protocol shall enter into force when each of the Parties to the North Atlantic Treaty has notified the Government of the United States of America of its acceptance thereof. The Government of the United States of America shall inform all the Parties to the North Atlantic Treaty of the date of receipt of each such notification and of the date of the entry into force of the present Protocol.

ARTICLE III

The present Protocol, of which the English and French texts are equally authentic, shall be deposited in the Archives of the Government of the United States of America. Duly certified copies thereof shall be transmitted by that Government to the Governments of all the Parties to the North Atlantic Treaty.

---

[1] Treaty Doc. 105–36.

g. Protocol to the North Atlantic Treaty on the Accession of Poland[1]

Signed at Brussels, December 16, 1997; Ratification advised by the Senate, April 30, 1998; Entered into force, December 4, 1998

The Parties to the North Atlantic Treaty, signed at Washington on April 4, 1949,

Being satisfied that the security of the North Atlantic area will be enhanced by the accession of the Republic of Poland to that Treaty,

Agree as follows :

ARTICLE I

Upon the entry into force of this Protocol, the Secretary General of the North Atlantic Treaty Organization shall, on behalf of all the Parties, communicate to the Government of the Republic of Poland an invitation to accede to the North Atlantic Treaty. In accordance with article 10 of the Treaty, the Republic of Poland shall become a Party on the date when it deposits its instrument of accession with the Government of the United States of America.

ARTICLE II

The present Protocol shall enter into force when each of the Parties to the North Atlantic Treaty has notified the Government of the United States of America of its acceptance thereof. The Government of the United States of America shall inform all the Parties to the North Atlantic Treaty of the date of receipt of each such notification and of the date of the entry into force of the present Protocol.

ARTICLE III

The present Protocol, of which the English and French texts are equally authentic, shall be deposited in the Archives of the Government of the United States of America. Duly certified copies thereof shall be transmitted by that Government to the Governments of all the Parties to the North Atlantic Treaty.

[1] Treaty Doc. 105–36.

h. Protocol to the North Atlantic Treaty on the Accession of Bulgaria[1]

Signed at Brussels, March 26, 2003; Ratification advised by the Senate, May 8, 2003; Entered into force, February 27, 2004

The Parties to the North Atlantic Treaty, signed at Washington on April 4, 1949,

Being satisfied that the security of the North Atlantic area will be enhanced by the accession of the Republic of Bulgaria to that Treaty,

Agree as follows:

Article I

Upon the entry into force of this Protocol, the Secretary General of the North Atlantic Treaty Organisation shall, on behalf of all the Parties, communicate to the Government of the Republic of Bulgaria an invitation to accede to the North Atlantic Treaty. In accordance with Article 10 of the Treaty, the Republic of Bulgaria shall become a Party on the date when it deposits its instrument of accession with the Government of the United States of America.

Article II

The present Protocol shall enter into force when each of the Parties to the North Atlantic Treaty has notified the Government of the United States of America of its acceptance thereof. The Government of the United States of America shall inform all the Parties to the North Atlantic Treaty of the date of receipt of each such notification and of the date of the entry into force of the present Protocol.

Article III

The present Protocol, of which the English and French texts are equally authentic, shall be deposited in the Archives of the Government of the United States of America. Duly certified copies thereof shall be transmitted by that Government to the Governments of all the Parties to the North Atlantic Treaty.

[1] Treaty Doc. 108–4.

i. Protocol to the North Atlantic Treaty on the Accession of Estonia [1]

Signed at Brussels, March 26, 2003; Ratification advised by the Senate, May 8, 2003; Entered into force, February 27, 2004

The Parties to the North Atlantic Treaty, signed at Washington on April 4, 1949,

Being satisfied that the security of the North Atlantic area will be enhanced by the accession of the Republic of Estonia to that Treaty,

Agree as follows:

ARTICLE I

Upon the entry into force of this Protocol, the Secretary General of the North Atlantic Treaty Organisation shall, on behalf of all the Parties, communicate to the Government of the Republic of Estonia an invitation to accede to the North Atlantic Treaty. In accordance with Article 10 of the Treaty, the Republic of Estonia shall become a Party on the date when it deposits its instrument of accession with the Government of the United States of America.

ARTICLE II

The present Protocol shall enter into force when each of the Parties to the North Atlantic Treaty has notified the Government of the United States of America of its acceptance thereof. The Government of the United States of America shall inform all the Parties to the North Atlantic Treaty of the date of receipt of each such notification and of the date of the entry into force of the present Protocol.

ARTICLE III

The present Protocol, of which the English and French texts are equally authentic, shall be deposited in the Archives of the Government of the United States of America. Duly certified copies thereof shall be transmitted by that Government to the Governments of all the Parties to the North Atlantic Treaty.

[1] Treaty Doc. 108–4.

j. Protocol to the North Atlantic Treaty on the Accession of Latvia [1]

Signed at Brussels, March 26, 2003; Ratification advised by the Senate, May 8, 2003; Entered into force, February 27, 2004

The Parties to the North Atlantic Treaty, signed at Washington on April 4, 1949,

Being satisfied that the security of the North Atlantic area will be enhanced by the accession of the Republic of Latvia to that Treaty,

Agree as follows:

ARTICLE I

Upon the entry into force of this Protocol, the Secretary General of the North Atlantic Treaty Organisation shall, on behalf of all the Parties, communicate to the Government of the Republic of Latvia an invitation to accede to the North Atlantic Treaty. In accordance with Article 10 of the Treaty, the Republic of Latvia shall become a Party on the date when it deposits its instrument of accession with the Government of the United States of America.

ARTICLE II

The present Protocol shall enter into force when each of the Parties to the North Atlantic Treaty has notified the Government of the United States of America of its acceptance thereof. The Government of the United States of America shall inform all the Parties to the North Atlantic Treaty of the date of receipt of each such notification and of the date of the entry into force of the present Protocol.

ARTICLE III

The present Protocol, of which the English and French texts are equally authentic, shall be deposited in the Archives of the Government of the United States of America. Duly certified copies thereof shall be transmitted by that Government to the Governments of all the Parties to the North Atlantic Treaty.

[1] Treaty Doc. 108–4.

k. Protocol to the North Atlantic Treaty on the Accession of Lithuania [1]

Signed at Brussels, March 26, 2003; Ratification advised by the Senate, May 8, 2003; Entered into force, February 27, 2004

The Parties to the North Atlantic Treaty, signed at Washington on April 4, 1949,

Being satisfied that the security of the North Atlantic area will be enhanced by the accession of the Republic of Lithuania to that Treaty,

Agree as follows:

ARTICLE I

Upon the entry into force of this Protocol, the Secretary General of the North Atlantic Treaty Organisation shall, on behalf of all the Parties, communicate to the Government of the Republic of Lithuania an invitation to accede to the North Atlantic Treaty. In accordance with Article 10 of the Treaty, the Republic of Lithuania shall become a Party on the date when it deposits its instrument of accession with the Government of the United States of America.

ARTICLE II

The present Protocol shall enter into force when each of the Parties to the North Atlantic Treaty has notified the Government of the United States of America of its acceptance thereof. The Government of the United States of America shall inform all the Parties to the North Atlantic Treaty of the date of receipt of each such notification and of the date of the entry into force of the present Protocol.

ARTICLE III

The present Protocol, of which the English and French texts are equally authentic, shall be deposited in the Archives of the Government of the United States of America. Duly certified copies thereof shall be transmitted by that Government to the Governments of all the Parties to the North Atlantic Treaty.

[1] Treaty Doc. 108–4.

l. Protocol to the North Atlantic Treaty on the Accession of Romania[1]

Signed at Brussels, March 26, 2003; Ratification advised by the Senate, May 8, 2003; Entered into force, February 27, 2004

The Parties to the North Atlantic Treaty, signed at Washington on April 4, 1949,

Being satisfied that the security of the North Atlantic area will be enhanced by the accession of Romania to that Treaty,

Agree as follows:

ARTICLE I

Upon the entry into force of this Protocol, the Secretary General of the North Atlantic Treaty Organisation shall, on behalf of all the Parties, communicate to the Government of Romania an invitation to accede to the North Atlantic Treaty. In accordance with Article 10 of the Treaty, Romania shall become a Party on the date when it deposits its instrument of accession with the Government of the United States of America.

ARTICLE II

The present Protocol shall enter into force when each of the Parties to the North Atlantic Treaty has notified the Government of the United States of America of its acceptance thereof. The Government of the United States of America shall inform all the Parties to the North Atlantic Treaty of the date of receipt of each such notification and of the date of the entry into force of the present Protocol.

ARTICLE III

The present Protocol, of which the English and French texts are equally authentic, shall be deposited in the Archives of the Government of the United States of America. Duly certified copies thereof shall be transmitted by that Government to the Governments of all the Parties to the North Atlantic Treaty.

[1] Treaty Doc. 108–4.

m. Protocol to the North Atlantic Treaty on the Accession of the Slovak Republic [1]

Signed at Brussels, March 26, 2003; Ratification advised by the Senate, May 8, 2003; Entered into force, February 27, 2004

The Parties to the North Atlantic Treaty, signed at Washington on April 4, 1949,

Being satisfied that the security of the North Atlantic area will be enhanced by the accession of the Slovak Republic to that Treaty,

Agree as follows:

ARTICLE I

Upon the entry into force of this Protocol, the Secretary General of the North Atlantic Treaty Organisation shall, on behalf of all the Parties, communicate to the Government of the Slovak Republic an invitation to accede to the North Atlantic Treaty. In accordance with Article 10 of the Treaty, the Slovak Republic shall become a Party on the date when it deposits its instrument of accession with the Government of the United States of America.

ARTICLE II

The present Protocol shall enter into force when each of the Parties to the North Atlantic Treaty has notified the Government of the United States of America of its acceptance thereof. The Government of the United States of America shall inform all the Parties to the North Atlantic Treaty of the date of receipt of each such notification and of the date of the entry into force of the present Protocol.

ARTICLE III

The present Protocol, of which the English and French texts are equally authentic, shall be deposited in the Archives of the Government of the United States of America. Duly certified copies thereof shall be transmitted by that Government to the Governments of all the Parties to the North Atlantic Treaty.

[1] Treaty Doc. 108–4.

n. Protocol to the North Atlantic Treaty on the Accession of Slovenia[1]

Signed at Brussels, March 26, 2003; Ratification advised by the Senate, May 8, 2003; Entered into force, February 27, 2004

The Parties to the North Atlantic Treaty, signed at Washington on April 4, 1949,

Being satisfied that the security of the North Atlantic area will be enhanced by the accession of the Republic of Slovenia to that Treaty,

Agree as follows:

ARTICLE I

Upon the entry into force of this Protocol, the Secretary General of the North Atlantic Treaty Organisation shall, on behalf of all the Parties, communicate to the Government of the Republic of Slovenia an invitation to accede to the North Atlantic Treaty. In accordance with Article 10 of the Treaty, the Republic of Slovenia shall become a Party on the date when it deposits its instrument of accession with the Government of the United States of America.

ARTICLE II

The present Protocol shall enter into force when each of the Parties to the North Atlantic Treaty has notified the Government of the United States of America of its acceptance thereof. The Government of the United States of America shall inform all the Parties to the North Atlantic Treaty of the date of receipt of each such notification and of the date of the entry into force of the present Protocol.

ARTICLE III

The present Protocol, of which the English and French texts are equally authentic, shall be deposited in the Archives of the Government of the United States of America. Duly certified copies thereof shall be transmitted by that Government to the Governments of all the Parties to the North Atlantic Treaty.

[1] Treaty Doc. 108–4.

o. Treaty on the Final Settlement with Respect to Germany and Its Related Agreed Minute [1]

Signed by the United States, the Federal Republic of Germany, the German Democratic Republic, the French Republic, the Union of Soviet Socialist Republics, and the United Kingdom of Great Britain and Northern Ireland in Moscow, September 12, 1990; Ratification advised in the Federal Republic of Germany and the German Democratic Republic, September 20, 1990; Declaration suspending the occupation of quadripartite rights and responsibilities signed at New York, October 1, 1990; Entered into force, October 3, 1990; Ratification advised by the Senate, October 10, 1990; Ratified by the President, October 18, 1990; U.S.S.R. ratified on March 4, 1991; Instruments of ratification deposited and entered into force, March 15, 1991

The Federal Republic of Germany, the German Democratic Republic, the French Republic, the Union of Soviet Socialist Republics, the United Kingdom of Great Britain and Northern Ireland and the United States of America,

CONSCIOUS of the fact that their peoples have been living together in peace since 1945;

MINDFUL of the recent historic changes in Europe which make it possible to overcome the division of the continent;

HAVING REGARD to the rights and responsibilities of the Four Powers relating to Berlin and to Germany as a whole, and the corresponding wartime and post-war agreements and decisions of the Four Powers;

RESOLVED, in accordance with their obligations under the Charter of the United Nations to develop friendly relations among nations based on respect for the principle of equal rights and self-determination of peoples, and to take other appropriate measures to strengthen universal peace;

RECALLING the principles of the Final Act of the Conference on Security and Cooperation in Europe, signed in Helsinki;

RECOGNIZING that those principles have laid firm foundations for the establishment of a just and lasting peaceful order in Europe;

DETERMINED to take account of everyone's security interests;

CONVINCED of the need finally to overcome antagonism and to develop cooperation in Europe;

CONFIRMING their readiness to reinforce security, in particular by adopting effective arms control, disarmament and confidence-building measures; their willingness not to regard each other as adversaries but to work for a relationship of trust and cooperation; and accordingly their readiness to consider positively setting up appropriate institutional arrangements within the framework of the Conference on Security and Cooperation in Europe;

[1] 1686 UNTS 115.

WELCOMING the fact that the German people, freely exercising their right of self-determination, have expressed their will to bring about the unity of Germany as a state so that they will be able to serve the peace of the world as an equal and sovereign partner in a united Europe;

CONVINCED that the unification of Germany as a state with definitive borders is a significant contribution to peace and stability in Europe;

INTENDING to conclude the final settlement with respect to Germany;

RECOGNIZING that thereby, and with the unification of Germany as a democratic and peaceful state, the rights and responsibilities of the Four Powers relating to Berlin and to Germany as a whole lose their function;

REPRESENTED by their Ministers for Foreign Affairs who, in accordance with the Ottawa Declaration of 13 February 1990, met in Bonn on 5 May 1990, in Berlin on 22 June 1990, in Paris on 17 July 1990 with the participation of the Minister for Foreign Affairs of the Republic of Poland, and in Moscow on 12 September 1990;

HAVE AGREED AS FOLLOWS:

ARTICLE 1

(1) The united Germany shall comprise the territory of the Federal Republic of Germany, the German Democratic Republic and the whole of Berlin. Its external borders shall be the borders of the Federal Republic of Germany and the German Democratic Republic and shall be definitive from the date on which the present Treaty comes into force. The confirmation of the definitive nature of the borders of the united Germany is an essential element of the peaceful order in Europe.

(2) The united Germany and the Republic of Poland shall confirm the existing border between them in a treaty that is binding under international law.

(3) The united Germany has no territorial claims whatsoever against other states and shall not assert any in the future.

(4) The Governments of the Federal Republic of Germany and the German Democratic Republic shall ensure that the constitution of the united Germany does not contain any provision incompatible with these principles. This applies accordingly to the provisions laid down in the preamble, the second sentence of Article 23, and Article 146 of the Basic Law for the Federal Republic of Germany.

(5) The Governments of the French Republic, the Union of Soviet Socialist Republics, the United Kingdom of Great Britain and Northern Ireland and the United States of America take formal note of the corresponding commitments and declarations by the Governments of the Federal Republic of Germany and the German Democratic Republic and declare that their implementation will confirm the definitive nature of the united Germany's borders.

ARTICLE 2

The Governments of the Federal Republic of Germany and the German Democratic Republic reaffirm their declarations that only peace will emanate from German soil. According to the constitution of the united Germany, acts tending to and undertaken with the intent to disturb the peaceful relations between nations, especially to prepare for aggressive war, are unconstitutional and a punishable offence. The Governments of the Federal Republic of Germany and the German Democratic Republic declare that the united Germany will never employ any of its weapons except in accordance with its constitution and the Charter of the United States.

ARTICLE 3

(1) The Governments of the Federal Republic of Germany and the German Democratic Republic reaffirm their renunciation of the manufacture and possession of and control over nuclear, biological and chemical weapons. They declare that the united Germany, too, will abide by these commitments. In particular, rights and obligations arising from the Treaty on the Non-Proliferation of Nuclear Weapons of 1 July 1968 will continue to apply to the united Germany.

(2) The Government of the Federal Republic of Germany, acting in full agreement with the Government of the German Democratic Republic, made the following statement on 30 August 1990 in Vienna at the Negotiations on Conventional Armed Forces in Europe:

> The Government of the Federal Republic of Germany undertakes to reduce the personnel strength of the armed forces of the united Germany to 370,000 (ground, air and naval forces) within three to four years. This reduction will commence on the entry into force of the first CFE agreement. Within the scope of this overall ceiling no more than 345,000 will belong to the ground and air forces which, pursuant to the agreed mandate, alone are the subject to the Negotiations on Conventional Armed Forces in Europe. The Federal Government regards its commitment to reduce ground and air forces as a significant German contribution to the reduction of conventional armed forces in Europe. It assumes that in follow-on negotiations the other participants in the negotiations, too, will render their contribution to enhancing security and stability in Europe, including measures to limit personnel strengths. The Government of the German Democratic Republic has expressly associated itself with this statement.

(3) The Governments of the French Republic, the Union of Soviet Socialist Republics, the United Kingdom of Great Britain and Northern Ireland and the United States of America take note of these statements by the Governments of the Federal Republic of Germany and the German Democratic Republic.

ARTICLE 4

(1) The Governments of the Federal Republic of Germany, the German Democratic Republic and the Union of Soviet Socialist Republics state that the united Germany and the Union of Soviet Socialist Republics will settle by treaty the conditions for and the duration of the presence of Soviet armed forces on the territory of the present German Democratic Republic and of Berlin, as well as the

conduct of the withdrawal of these armed forces which will be completed by the end of 1994, in connection with the implementation of the undertaking of the Federal Republic of Germany and the German Democratic Republic referred to in paragraph 2 of Article 3 of the present Treaty.

(2) The Governments of the French Republic, the United Kingdom of Great Britain and Northern Ireland and the United States of America take note of this statement.

ARTICLE 5

(1) Until the completion of the withdrawal of the Soviet armed forces for the territory of the present German Democratic Republic and of Berlin in accordance with Article 4 of the present Treaty, only German territorial defence units which are not integrated into the alliance structures to which German armed forces in the rest of German territory are assigned will be stationed in that territory as armed forces of the united Germany. During that period and subject to the provisions of paragraph 2 of this Article, armed forces of other states will not be stationed in that territory or carry out any other military activity there.

(2) For the duration of the presence of Soviet armed forces in the territory of the present German Democratic Republic and of Berlin, armed forces of the French Republic, the United Kingdom of Great Britain and Northern Ireland and the United States of America will, upon German request, remain stationed in Berlin by agreement to this effect between the Government of the united Germany and the Governments of the states concerned. The number of troops and the amount of equipment of all non-German armed forces stationed in Berlin will not be greater than at the time of signature of the present Treaty. New categories of weapons will not be introduced there by non-German armed forces. The Government of the united Germany will conclude with the Governments of those states which have armed forces stationed in Berlin treaties with conditions which are fair taking account of the relations existing with the states concerned.

(3) Following the completion of the withdrawal of the Soviet armed forces from the territory of the present German Democratic Republic and of Berlin, units of German armed forces assigned to military alliance structures in the same way as those in the rest of German territory may also be stationed in that part of Germany, but without nuclear weapon carriers. This does not apply to conventional weapon systems which may have other capabilities in addition to conventional ones but which in that part of Germany are equipped for a conventional role and designated only for such. Foreign armed forces and nuclear weapons or their carriers will not be stationed in that part of Germany or deployed there.

ARTICLE 6

The right of the united Germany to belong to alliances, with all the rights and responsibilities arising therefrom, shall not be affected by the present Treaty.

ARTICLE 7

(1) The French Republic, the Union of Soviet Socialist Republics, the United Kingdom of Great Britain and Northern Ireland and the United States of America hereby terminate their rights and responsibilities relating to Berlin and to Germany as a whole. As a result, the corresponding, related quadripartite agreements, decisions and practices are terminated and all related Four Power institutions are dissolved.

(2) The United Germany shall have accordingly full sovereignty over its internal and external affairs.

ARTICLE 8

(1) The present Treaty is subject to ratification or acceptance as soon as possible. On the German side it will be ratified by the united Germany. The Treaty will therefore apply to the united Germany.

(2) The instruments of ratification or acceptance shall be deposited with the Government of the united Germany. That Government shall inform the Governments of the other Contracting Parties of the deposit of each instrument of ratification or acceptance.

ARTICLE 9

The present Treaty shall enter into force for the united Germany, the French Republic, the Union of Soviet Socialist Republics, the United Kingdom of Great Britain and Northern Ireland and the United States of America on the date of deposit of the last instrument of ratification or acceptance by these states.

ARTICLE 10

The original of the present Treaty, of which the English, French, German and Russian texts are equally authentic, shall be deposited with the Government of the Federal Republic of Germany, which shall transmit certified true copies to the Governments of the other Contracting Parties.

AGREED MINUTE TO THE TREATY ON THE FINAL SETTLEMENT WITH RESPECT TO GERMANY OF 12 SEPTEMBER 1990

Any questions with respect to the application of the word "deployed" as used in the last sentence of paragraph 3 of Article 5 will be decided by the Government of the united Germany in a reasonable and responsible way taking into account the security interests of each Contracting Party as set forth in the preamble.

3. Security Treaty Between Australia, New Zealand,[1] and the United States of America (ANZUS Pact)[2]

Signed at San Francisco, September 1, 1951; Ratification advised by the Senate, March 20, 1952; Ratified by the President, April 15, 1952; Ratification of the United States deposited with the Government of Australia at Canberra, April 29, 1952; Entered into force, April 29, 1952; Proclaimed by the President, May 9, 1952

RATIFIED BY AUSTRALIA, NEW ZEALAND, AND THE UNITED STATES OF AMERICA

The Parties to this Treaty,

REAFFIRMING their faith in the purposes and principles of the Charter of the United Nations and their desire to live in peace with all peoples and all Governments, and desiring to strengthen the fabric of peace in the Pacific Area,

NOTING that the United States already has arrangements pursuant to which its armed forces are stationed in the Philippines, and has armed forces and administrative responsibilities in the Ryukyus, and upon the coming into force of the Japanese Peace Treaty may also station armed forces in and about Japan to assist in the preservation of peace and security in the Japan Area,

RECOGNIZING that Australia and New Zealand as members of the British Commonwealth of Nations have military obligations outside as well as within the Pacific Area,

DESIRING to declare publicly and formally their sense of unity, so that no potential aggressor could be under the illusion that any of them stand alone in the Pacific Area, and

DESIRING further to coordinate their efforts for collective defense for the preservation of peace and security pending the development of a more comprehensive system of regional security in the Pacific Area,

THEREFORE DECLARE AND AGREE AS FOLLOWS:

ARTICLE I

The Parties undertake, as set forth in the Charter of the United Nations, to settle any international disputes in which they may be involved by peaceful means in such a manner that international peace and security and justice are not endangered and to refrain in their international relations from the threat or use of force in any manner inconsistent with the purposes of the United Nations.

[1] As of September 17, 1986, the United States has suspended obligations under this treaty between the United States and New Zealand.

[2] 3 UST 3420; TIAS 2493; 131 UNTS 83.

ARTICLE II

In order more effectively to achieve the objective of this Treaty the Parties separately and jointly by means of continuous and effective self-help and mutual aid will maintain and develop their individual and collective capacity to resist armed attack.

ARTICLE III

The Parties will consult together whenever in the opinion of any of them the territorial integrity, political independence or security of any of the Parties is threatened in the Pacific.

ARTICLE IV

Each Party recognizes that an armed attack in the Pacific Area on any of the Parties would be dangerous to its own peace and safety and declares that it would act to meet the common danger in accordance with its constitutional processes.

Any such armed attack and all measures taken as a result thereof shall be immediately reported to the Security Council of the United Nations. Such measures shall be terminated when the Security Council has taken the measures necessary to restore and maintain international peace and security.

ARTICLE V

For the purpose of Article IV, an armed attack on any of the Parties is deemed to include an armed attack on the metropolitan territory of any of the Parties, or on the island territories under its jurisdiction in the Pacific or on its armed forces, public vessels or aircraft in the Pacific.

ARTICLE VI

This Treaty does not affect and shall not be interpreted as affecting in any way the rights and obligations of the Parties under the Charter of the United Nations or the responsibility of the United Nations for the maintenance of international peace and security.

ARTICLE VII

The Parties hereby establish a Council, consisting of their Foreign Ministers or their Deputies, to consider matters concerning the implementation of this Treaty. The Council should be so organized as to be able to meet at any time.

ARTICLE VIII

Pending the development of a more comprehensive system of regional security in the Pacific Area and the development by the United Nations of more effective means to maintain international peace and security, the Council, established by Article VII, is authorized to maintain a consultative relationship with States, Regional Organizations, Associations of States or other authorities in the Pacific Area in a position to further the purposes of this Treaty and to contribute to the security of that Area.

Article IX

This Treaty shall be ratified by the Parties in accordance with their respective constitutional processes. The instruments of ratification shall be deposited as soon as possible with the Government of Australia, which will notify each of the other signatories of such deposit. The Treaty shall enter into force as soon as the ratifications of the signatories have been deposited.

Article X

This Treaty shall remain in force indefinitely. Any Party may cease to be a member of the Council established by Article VII one year after notice has been given to the Government of Australia, which will inform the Governments of the other Parties of the deposit of such notice.

Article XI

This Treaty in the English language shall be deposited in the archives of the Government of Australia. Duly certified copies thereof will be transmitted by that Government to the Governments of each of the other signatories.

In witness whereof, the undersigned Plenipotentiaries have signed this Treaty.

Done at the City of San Francisco this first day of September, 1951.

4. Asia

a. Mutual Defense Treaty Between the United States of America and the Republic of the Philippines [1]

Signed at Washington, August 30, 1951; Ratification advised by the Senate, March 20, 1952; Ratified by the President, April 15, 1952; Ratified by the Republic of the Philippines, August 27, 1952; Ratifications exchanged at Manila, August 27, 1952; Entered into force, August 27, 1952; Proclaimed by the President, September 15, 1952

The Parties to this Treaty,

REAFFIRMING their faith in the purposes and principles of the Charter of the United Nations and their desire to live in peace with all peoples and all Governments, and desiring to strengthen the fabric of peace in the Pacific Area,

RECALLING with mutual pride the historic relationship which brought their two peoples together in a common bond of sympathy and mutual ideals to fight side-by-side against imperialist aggression during the last war,

DESIRING to declare publicly and formally their sense of unity and their common determination to defend themselves against external armed attack, so that no potential aggressor could be under the illusion that either of them stands alone in the Pacific Area,

DESIRING further to strengthen their present efforts for collective defense for the preservation of peace and security pending the development of a more comprehensive system of regional security in the Pacific Area,

AGREEING that nothing in this present instrument shall be considered or interpreted as in any way or sense altering or diminishing any existing agreements or understandings between the United States of America and the Republic of the Philippines,

HAVE AGREED AS FOLLOWS:

ARTICLE I

The Parties undertake, as set forth in the Charter of the United Nations, to settle any international disputes in which they may be involved by peaceful means in such a manner that international peace and security and justice are not endangered and to refrain in their international relations from the threat or use of force in any manner inconsistent with the purposes of the United Nations.

ARTICLE II

In order more effectively to achieve the objective of this Treaty, the Parties separately and jointly by self-help and mutual aid will

[1] 3 UST 3947; TIAS 2529; 177 UNTS 133.

maintain and develop their individual and collective capacity to resist armed attack.

ARTICLE III

The Parties, through their Foreign Ministers or their deputies, will consult together from time to time regarding the implementation of this Treaty and whenever in the opinion of either of them the territorial integrity, political independence or security of either of the Parties is threatened by external armed attack in the Pacific.

ARTICLE IV

Each Party recognizes that an armed attack in the Pacific Area on either of the Parties would be dangerous to its own peace and safety and declares that it would act to meet the common dangers in accordance with its constitutional processes.

Any such armed attack and all measures taken as a result thereof shall be immediately reported to the Security Council of the United Nations. Such measures shall be terminated when the Security Council has taken the measures necessary to restore and maintain international peace and security.

ARTICLE V

For the purpose of Article IV, an armed attack on either of the Parties is deemed to include an armed attack on the metropolitan territory of either of the Parties, or on the island territories under its jurisdiction in the Pacific or on its armed forces, public vessels or aircraft in the Pacific.

ARTICLE VI

This Treaty does not affect and shall not be interpreted as affecting in any way the rights and obligations of the Parties under the Charter of the United Nations or the responsibility of the United Nations for the maintenance of international peace and security.

ARTICLE VII

This Treaty shall be ratified by the United States of America and the Republic of the Philippines in accordance with their respective constitutional processes and will come into force when instruments of ratification thereof have been exchanged by them at Manila.

ARTICLE VIII

This Treaty shall remain in force indefinitely. Either Party may terminate it one year after notice has been given to the other Party.

b. Mutual Defense Treaty Between the United States of America and the Republic of Korea[1]

Signed at Washington, October 1, 1953; Ratification advised, with an understanding, by the Senate, January 26, 1954; Ratified by the Republic of Korea, January 29, 1954; Ratified, subject to the said understanding, by the President, February 5, 1954; Ratifications exchanged in Washington, November 17, 1954; Entered into force November 17, 1954; Proclaimed by the President, December 1, 1954

The Parties to this Treaty,

REAFFIRMING their desire to live in peace with all peoples and all governments, and desiring to strengthen the fabric of peace in the Pacific area,

DESIRING to declare publicly and formally their common determination to defend themselves against external armed attack so that no potential aggressor could be under the illusion that either of them stands alone in the Pacific area,

DESIRING further to strengthen their efforts for collective defense for the preservation of peace and security pending the development of a more comprehensive and effective system of regional security in the Pacific area,

HAVE AGREED AS FOLLOWS:

ARTICLE I

The Parties undertake to settle any international disputes in which they may be involved by peaceful means in such a manner that international peace and security and justice are not endangered and to refrain in their international relations from the threat or use of force in any manner inconsistent with the Purposes of the United Nations, or obligations assumed by any Party toward the United Nations.

ARTICLE II

The Parties will consult together whenever, in the opinion of either of them, the political independence or security of either of the Parties is threatened by external armed attack. Separately and jointly, by self help and mutual aid, the Parties will maintain and develop appropriate means to deter armed attack and will take suitable measures in consultation and agreement to implement this Treaty and to further its purposes.

ARTICLE III

Each Party recognizes that an armed attack in the Pacific area on either of the Parties in territories now under their respective administrative control, or hereafter recognized by one of the Parties

[1] 5 UST 2368; TIAS 3097; 238 UNTS 199.

as lawfully brought under the administrative control of the other, would be dangerous to its own peace and safety and declares that it would act to meet the common danger in accordance with its constitutional processes.

ARTICLE IV

The Republic of Korea grants, and the United States of America accepts, the right to dispose United States land, air and sea forces in and about the territory of the Republic of Korea as determined by mutual agreement.

ARTICLE V

This Treaty shall be ratified by the United States of America and the Republic of Korea in accordance with their respective constitutional processes and will come into force when instruments of ratification thereof have been exchanged by them at Washington.

ARTICLE VI

This Treaty shall remain in force indefinitely. Either Party may terminate it one year after notice has been given to the other Party.

IN WITNESS WHEREOF, the undersigned Plenipotentiaries have signed this Treaty.

DONE in duplicate at Washington, in the English and Korean languages, this first day of October 1953.

UNDERSTANDING AS STATED IN THE PROCLAMATION

WHEREAS the Senate of the United States of America by their resolution of January 26, 1954, two-thirds of the Senators present concurring therein, did advise and consent to the ratification of the said Treaty with the following understanding:

"It is the understanding of the United States that neither party is obligated, under Article III of the above Treaty, to come to the aid of the other except in case of an external armed attack against such party; nor shall anything in the present Treaty be construed as requiring the United States to give assistance to Korea except in the event of an armed attack against territory which has been recognized by the United States as lawfully brought under the administrative control of the Republic of Korea."

c. Southeast Asia Collective Defense Treaty[1] with Understanding and Protocol (SEATO)[2]

Signed at Manila, September 8, 1954; Ratification advised by the Senate, February 1, 1955; Ratified by the President, February 4, 1955; Ratification deposited, February 19, 1955; Entered into force, February 19, 1955; Proclaimed by the President, March 2, 1955

The Parties to this Treaty,

RECOGNIZING the sovereign equality of all the Parties,

REITERATING their faith in the purposes and principles set forth in the Charter of the United Nations and their desire to live in peace with all peoples and all governments,

REAFFIRMING that, in accordance with the Charter of the United Nations, they uphold the principle of equal rights and self-determination of peoples, and declaring that they will earnestly strive by every peaceful means to promote self-government and to secure the independence of all countries whose peoples desire it and are able to undertake its responsibilities,

DESIRING to strengthen the fabric of peace and freedom and to uphold the principles of democracy, individual liberty and the rule of law, and to promote the economic well-being and development of all peoples in the Treaty area,

INTENDING to declare publicly and formally their sense of unity, so that any potential aggressor will appreciate that the Parties stand together in the area, and

DESIRING further to coordinate their efforts for collective defense for the preservation of peace and security,

THEREFORE AGREE AS FOLLOWS:

ARTICLE I

The Parties undertake, as set forth in the Charter of the United Nations, to settle any international disputes in which they may be involved by peaceful means in such a manner that international peace and security and justice are not endangered, and to refrain in their international relations from the threat or use of force in any manner inconsistent with the purposes of the United Nations.

[1] 6 UST 81; TIAS 3170; 209 UNTS 28. For a list of states which are parties to the Treaty, see Department of State publication, *Treaties in Force*.

[2] SEATO, by decision of the SEATO Council (September 24, 1975), ceased to exist as of June 30, 1977. The collective defense treaty remains in force.

Article II

In order more effectively to achieve the objectives of this Treaty the Parties, separately and jointly, by means of continuous and effective self-help and mutual aid will maintain and develop their individual and collective capacity to resist armed attack and to prevent and counter subversive activities directed from without against their territorial integrity and political stability.

Article III

The Parties undertake to strengthen their free institutions and to cooperate with one another in the further development of economic measures, including technical assistance, designed both to promote economic progress and social well-being and to further the individual and collective efforts of governments toward these ends.

Article IV

1. Each Party recognizes that aggression by means of armed attack in the treaty area against any of the Parties or against any State or territory which the Parties by unanimous agreement may hereafter designate, would endanger its own peace and safety, and agrees that it will in that event act to meet the common danger in accordance with its constitutional processes. Measures taken under this paragraph shall be immediately reported to the Security Council of the United Nations.

2. If, in the opinion of any of the Parties, the inviolability or the integrity of the territory or the sovereignty or political independence of any Party in the treaty area or of any other State or Territory to which the provisions of paragraph 1 of this Article from time to time apply is threatened in any way other than by armed attack or is affected or threatened by any fact or situation which might endanger the peace of the area, the Parties shall consult immediately in order to agree on the measures which should be taken for the common defense.

3. It is understood that no action on the territory of any State designated by unanimous agreement under paragraph 1 of this Article or on any territory so designated shall be taken except at the invitation or with the consent of the government concerned.

Article V

The Parties hereby establish a Council, on which each of them shall be represented, to consider matters concerning the implementation of this Treaty. The Council shall provide for consultation with regard to military and any other planning as the situation obtaining in the treaty area may from time to time require. The Council shall be so organized as to be able to meet at any time.

Article VI

This Treaty does not affect and shall not be interpreted as affecting in any way the rights and obligations of any of the Parties under the Charter of the United Nations or the responsibility of the

United Nations for the maintenance of international peace and security. Each Party declares that none of the international engagements now in force between it and any other of the Parties or any third party is in conflict with the provisions of this Treaty, and undertakes not to enter into any international engagements in conflict with this Treaty.

Article VII

Any other State in a position to further the objectives of this Treaty and to contribute to the security of the area may, by unanimous agreement of the Parties, be invited to accede to this Treaty. Any State so invited may become a Party to the Treaty by depositing its instrument of accession with the Government of the Republic of the Philippines. The Government of the Republic of the Philippines shall inform each of the Parties of the deposit of each such instrument of accession.

Article VIII

As used in this Treaty, the "treaty area" is the general area of Southeast Asia, including also the entire territories of the Asian Parties, and the general area of the Southwest Pacific not including the Pacific area north of 21 degrees 30 minutes north latitude. The Parties may, by unanimous agreement, amend this Article to include within the treaty area the territory of any State acceding to this Treaty in accordance with Article VII or otherwise to change the treaty area.

Article IX

1. This Treaty shall be deposited in the archives of the Government of the Republic of the Philippines. Duly certified copies thereof shall be transmitted by the government to the other signatories.

2. The Treaty shall be ratified and its provisions carried out by the Parties in accordance with their respective constitutional processes. The instruments of ratification shall be deposited as soon as possible with the Government of the Republic of the Philippines, which shall notify all of the other signatories of such deposit.

3. The Treaty shall enter into force between the States which have ratified it as soon as the instruments of ratification of a majority of the signatories shall have been deposited, and shall come into effect with respect to each other State on the date of the deposit of its instrument of ratification.

Article X

This Treaty shall remain in force indefinitely, but any Party may cease to be a Party one year after its notice of denunciation has been given to the Government of the Republic of the Philippines, which shall inform the Governments of the other Parties of the deposit of each notice of denunciation.

Article XI

The English text of this Treaty is binding on the Parties, but when the Parties have agreed to the French text thereof and have so notified the Government of the Republic of the Philippines, the French text shall be equally authentic and binding on the Parties.

Understanding of the United States of America

The United States of America in executing the present Treaty does so with the understanding that its recognition of the effect of aggression and armed attach and its agreement with reference thereto in Article IV, paragraph 1, apply only to communist aggression but affirms that in the event of other aggression or armed attack it will consult under the provisions of Article IV, paragraph 2.

IN WITNESS WHEREOF, the undersigned Plenipotentiaries have signed this Treaty.

DONE at Manila, this eighth day of September, 1954.

Protocol to the Southeast Asia Collective Defense Treaty

DESIGNATION OF STATES AND TERRITORY AS TO WHICH PROVISIONS OF ARTICLE IV AND ARTICLE III ARE TO BE APPLICABLE

The Parties to the Southeast Asia Collective Defense Treaty unanimously designate for the purposes of Article IV of the Treaty the States of Cambodia and Laos and the free territory under the jurisdiction of the State of Vietnam.

The Parties further agree that the above mentioned states and territory shall be eligible in respect of the economic measures contemplated by Article III.

This Protocol shall enter into force simultaneously with the coming into force of the Treaty.

IN WITNESS WHEREOF, the undersigned Plenipotentiaries have signed this Protocol to the Southeast Asia Collective Defense Treaty.

DONE at Manila, this eighth day of September, 1954.

d. Treaty of Mutual Cooperation and Security Between the United States of America and Japan,[1] With Agreed Minute and Exchanges of Notes

Signed at Washington, January 19, 1960; Ratified by Japan, June 21, 1960; Ratification advised by the Senate, June 22, 1960; Ratified by the President, June 22, 1960; Ratifications exchanged at Tokyo, June 23, 1960; Entered into force June 23, 1960; Proclaimed by the President, June 27, 1960

The United States of America and Japan,

DESIRING to strengthen the bonds of peace and friendship traditionally existing between them, and to uphold the principles of democracy, individual liberty, and the rule of law,

DESIRING further to encourage closer economic cooperation between them and to promote conditions of economic stability and well-being in their countries,

REAFFIRMING their faith in the purposes and principles of the Charter of the United Nations, and their desire to live in peace with all peoples and all governments,

RECOGNIZING that they have the inherent right of individual or collective self-defense as affirmed in the Charter of the United Nations,

CONSIDERING that they have a common concern in the maintenance of international peace and security in the Far East,

HAVING resolved to conclude a treaty of mutual cooperation and security,

THEREFORE AGREE AS FOLLOWS:

ARTICLE I

The Parties undertake, as set forth in the Charter of the United Nations, to settle any international disputes in which they may be involved by peaceful means in such a manner that international peace and security and justice are not endangered and to refrain in their international relations from the threat or use of force against the territorial integrity or political independence of any state, or in any other manner inconsistent with the purposes of the United Nations.

The Parties will endeavor in concert with other peace-loving countries to strengthen the United Nations so that its mission of maintaining international peace and security may be discharged more effectively.

ARTICLE II

The Parties will contribute toward the further development of peaceful and friendly international relations by strengthening their

[1] 11 UST 1632; TIAS 4509; 373 UNTS 186.

free institutions, by bringing about a better understanding of the principles upon which these institutions are founded, and by promoting conditions of stability and well-being. They will seek to eliminate conflict in their international economic policies and will encourage economic collaboration between them.

Article III

The Parties, individually and in cooperation with each other, by means of continuous and effective self-help and mutual aid will maintain and develop, subject to their constitutional provisions, their capacities to resist armed attack.

Article IV

The Parties will consult together from time to time regarding the implementation of this Treaty, and, at the request of either Party, whenever the security of Japan or international peace and security in the Far East is threatened.

Article V

Each Party recognizes that an armed attack against either Party in the territories under the administration of Japan would be dangerous to its own peace and safety and declares that it would act to meet the common danger in accordance with its constitutional provisions and processes.

Any such armed attack and all measures taken as a result thereof shall be immediately reported to the Security Council of the United Nations in accordance with the provisions of Article 51 of the Charter. Such measures shall be terminated when the Security Council has taken the measures necessary to restore and maintain international peace and security.

Article VI

For the purpose of contributing to the security of Japan and the maintenance of international peace and security in the Far East, the United States of America is granted the use by its land, air and naval forces of facilities and areas in Japan.

The use of these facilities and areas as well as the status of United States armed forces in Japan shall be governed by a separate agreement,[2] replacing the Administrative Agreement[3] under Article III of the Security Treaty[4] between the United States of America and Japan, signed at Tokyo on February 28, 1952, as amended, and by such other arrangements as may be agreed upon.

Article VII

This Treaty does not affect and shall not be interpreted as affecting in any way the rights and obligations of the Parties under the Charter of the United Nations or the responsibility of the United Nations for the maintenance of international peace and security.

---

[2] TIAS 4510; 11 UST 1652.
[3] TIAS 2492; 3 UST 3341.
[4] TIAS 2491; 3 UST 3332.

ARTICLE VIII

This Treaty shall be ratified by the United States of America and Japan in accordance with their respective constitutional processes and will enter into force on the date on which the instruments of ratification thereof have been exchanged by them in Tokyo.

ARTICLE IX

The Security Treaty between the United States of America and Japan signed at the city of San Francisco on September 8, 1951 shall expire upon the entering into force of this Treaty.

ARTICLE X

This Treaty shall remain in force until in the opinion of the Governments of the United States of America and Japan there shall have come into force such United Nations arrangements as will satisfactorily provide for the maintenance of international peace and security in the Japan area.

However, after the Treaty has been in force for ten years, either Party may give notice to the other Party of its intention to terminate the Treaty, in which case the Treaty shall terminate one year after such notice has been given.

Agreed Minute to the Treaty of Mutual Cooperation and Security

Japanese Plenipotentiary:

While the question of the status of the islands administered by the United States under Article 3 of the Treaty of Peace with Japan has not been made a subject of discussion in the course of treaty negotiations, I would like to emphasize the strong concern of the Government and people of Japan for the safety of the people of these islands since Japan possesses residual sovereignty over these islands. If an armed attack occurs or is threatened against these islands, the two countries will of course consult together closely under Article IV of the Treaty of Mutual Cooperation and Security. In the event of an armed attack, it is the intention of the Government of Japan to explore with the United States measures which it might be able to take for the welfare of the islanders.

United States Plenipotentiary:

In the event of an armed attack against these islands, the United States Government will consult at once with the Government of Japan and intends to take the necessary measures for the defense of these islands, and to do its utmost to secure the welfare of the islanders.

Exchanges of Notes Between the United States and Japan Dated January 19, 1960

EXCELLENCY:

I have the honour to refer to the Treaty of Mutual Cooperation and Security between Japan and the United States of America signed today, and to inform Your Excellency that the following is the understanding of the Government of Japan concerning the implementation of Article VI thereof:

> Major changes in the deployment into Japan of United States armed forces, major changes in their equipment, and the use of facilities and areas in Japan as bases for military combat operations to be undertaken from Japan other than those conducted under Article V of the said Treaty, shall be the subjects of prior consultation with the Government of Japan.

I should be appreciative if Your Excellency would confirm on behalf of your Government that this is also the understanding of the Government of the United States of America.

I avail myself of this opportunity to renew to Your Excellency the assurance of my highest consideration.

NOBUSUKE KISHI.

His Excellency
CHRISTIAN A. HERTER,
Secretary of State
of the United States of America.

EXCELLENCY:

I have the honor to acknowledge the receipt of Your Excellency's Note of today's date, which reads as follows:

[There follows the Prime Minister's note, quoted in English.]

I have the honor to confirm on behalf of my Government that the foregoing is also the understanding of the Government of the United States of America.

Accept, Excellency, the renewed assurances of my highest consideration.

CHRISTIAN A. HERTER,
Secretary of State of the
United States of America.

His Excellency
NOBUSUKE KISHI,
Prime Minister of Japan.

EXCELLENCY:

I have the honor to refer to the Security Treaty between the United States of America and Japan signed at the city of San Francisco on September 8, 1951, the exchange of notes effected on the same date between Mr. Shigeru Yoshida, Prime Minister of Japan, and Mr. Dean Acheson, Secretary of State of the United States of America, and the Agreement Regarding the Status of the United Nations Forces in Japan signed at Tokyo on February 19, 1954, as well as the Treaty of Mutual Cooperation and Security between the United States of America and Japan signed today. It is the understanding of my Government that:

1. The above-mentioned exchange of notes will continue to be in force so long as the Agreement Regarding the Status of the United Nations Forces in Japan remains in force.
2. The expression "those facilities and areas the use of which is provided to the United States of America under the Security

Treaty between Japan and the United States of America" in Article V, paragraph 2 of the above-mentioned Agreement is understood to mean the facilities and areas the use of which is granted to the United States of America under the Treaty of Mutual Cooperation and Security.

3. The use of the facilities and areas by the United States armed forces under the Unified Command of the United Nations established pursuant to the Security Council Resolution of July 7, 1950, and their status in Japan are governed by arrangements made pursuant to the Treaty of Mutual Cooperation and Security.

I should be grateful if Your Excellency would confirm on behalf of your Government that the understanding of my Government stated in the foregoing numbered paragraphs is also the understanding of your Government and that this understanding shall enter into operation on the date of the entry into force of the Treaty of Mutual Cooperation and Security signed at Washington on January 19, 1960.

Accept, Excellency, the renewed assurances of my highest consideration.

CHRISTIAN A. HERTER,
Secretary of State of the
United States of America.

His Excellency
NOBUSUKE KISHI,
Prime Minister of Japan.

EXCELLENCY:

I have the honour to acknowledge the receipt of Your Excellency's Note of today's date, which reads as follows:

[There follows the Secretary of State's note, quoted in English.]

I have the honour to confirm on behalf of my Government that the foregoing is also the understanding of the Government of Japan.

I avail myself of this opportunity to renew to Your Excellency the assurance of my highest consideration.

NOBUSUKE KISHI.

His Excellency
CHRISTIAN A. HERTER,
Secretary of State
of the United States of America.

DEAR SECRETARY HERTER:

I wish to refer to the Treaty of Mutual Cooperation and Security between Japan and the United States of America signed today. Under Article IV of the Treaty, the two Governments will consult together from time to time regarding the implementation of the Treaty, and, at the request of either Government, whenever the security of Japan or international peace and security in the Far East is threatened. The exchange of notes under Article VI of the Treaty specifies certain matters as the subjects of prior consultation with the Government of Japan.

Such consultations will be carried on between the two Governments through appropriate channels. At the same time, however, I feel that the establishment of a special committee which could as appropriate be used for these consultations between the Governments would prove very useful. This committee, which would meet whenever requested by either side, could also consider any matters underlying and related to security affairs which would serve to promote understanding between the two Governments and contribute to the strengthening of cooperative relations between the two countries in the field of security.

Under this proposal the present "Japanese-American Committee on Security" established by the Governments of the United States and Japan on August 6, 1957, would be replaced by this new committee which might be called "The Security Consultative Committee". I would also recommend that the membership of this new committee be the same as the membership of the "Japanese-American Committee on Security", namely on the Japanese side, the Minister for Foreign Affairs, who will preside on the Japanese side, and the Director General of the Defense Agency, and on the United States side, the United States Ambassador to Japan, who will serve as Chairman on the United States side, and the Commander-in-Chief, Pacific, who will be the Ambassador's principal advisor on military and defense matters. The Commander, United States Forces, Japan, will serve as alternate for the Commander-in-Chief, Pacific.

I would appreciate very much your views on this matter.

Most sincerely,

NOBUSUKE KISHI.

His Excellency
CHRISTIAN A. HERTER,
Secretary of State
of the United States of America.

DEAR MR. PRIME MINISTER:

The receipt is acknowledged of your Note of today's date suggesting the establishment of "The Security Consultative Committee". I fully agree to your proposal and share your view that such a committee can contribute to strengthening the cooperative relations between the two countries in the field of security. I also agree to your proposal regarding the membership of this committee.

Most sincerely,

CHRISTIAN A. HERTER.

His Excellency
NOBUSUKE KISHI,
Prime Minister of Japan.

5. Agreement Between the United States of America and the Multinational Force and Observers [1]

Effected by Exchange of Letters Signed at Washington, with Related Letters, March 26, 1982; Entered into force, March 26, 1982

THE DIRECTOR GENERAL OF THE MULTINATIONAL FORCE AND OBSERVERS TO THE SECRETARY OF STATE

MULTINATIONAL FORCE AND OBSERVERS
POST OFFICE BOX 11258
Alexandria, Virginia 22312
(703) 642-8300
March 26, 1982

The Honorable ALEXANDER M. HAIG, JR.
The Secretary of State
Washington, D.C. 20520

Dear Mr. Secretary:

I have the honor to refer to the Treaty of Peace between Egypt and Israel signed March 26, 1979, and to the enclosed Protocol between Egypt and Israel which provided for the establishment of a Multinational Force and Observers (MFO).

In accordance with the Protocol and with the agreement of the Parties, the Director General is to request those nations agreeable to the Parties to supply contingents to the MFO and to receive the agreement of contributing nations that the contingents will conduct themselves in accordance with the terms of the Protocol. Therefore, based on previous communications and discussions, I accept with appreciation the offer of the Government of the United States of America to provide to the MFO an infantry battalion task force of approximately eight hundred personnel, a logistics support element of approximately three hundred fifty personnel, staff personnel, and civilian observers, as provided in Annexes I and III to this letter.

As you are aware, the principles concerning the establishment, functions and responsibilities of the MFO are set out in the Protocol between Egypt and Israel. In accordance with paragraph 3 of the Annex to the Protocol, I would appreciate your confirmation that the United States units shall conduct themselves in accordance with the terms of the Protocol. Also, I would like to emphasize the importance of continuity of service of units in the MFO and to seek your agreement that the United States units will not be withdrawn without adequate prior notification to the Director General of the MFO.

I draw your attention as well to the Appendix to the Protocol, which stipulates the privileges and immunities of the MFO and the

[1] TIAS 10557.

duties of members of the MFO. Of particular importance is paragraph 11 concerning criminal jurisdiction, and its subparagraph c, which directs the Director General to obtain the assurance of each participating state that it will be prepared to take the necessary measures to assure proper discipline of its personnel and to exercise jurisdiction with respect to any crime or offense which might be committed by its personnel.

With regard to paragraph 42 of the Appendix to the Protocol, I assure you that I intend to act in accordance with the wishes of the participating state concerning the disposition of the bodies of its members who die in the service of the MFO, and their personal property.

The financial arrangements between the MFO and the Government of the United States concerning its military contribution and the civilian observers are set forth at Annexes II and III.

My separate letter of today's date confirms my understanding with respect to various aspects of participation in the MFO.

The enclosed Aide Memoire sets forth guidelines on procedures used by the MFO and is provided for the use of the Government of the United States in preparing and deploying its units for service in the MFO.

I have the honor to propose that this letter, including its attached Annexes I, II, and III, and your reply confirming the agreement of your Government to the terms thereof shall constitute an agreement between the Government of the United States and the MFO, which shall enter into force on the date of your reply.

With assurances of my highest consideration,

Sincerely,

LEAMON R. HUNT
Director General
Multinational Force and Observers

Attachments:
Annex I: United States Military Contribution
Annex II: Financial Arrangements for United States Military Contribution
Annex III: Civilian Observers

Enclosures:
Protocol
Aide Memoire

ANNEX I

UNITED STATES MILITARY CONTRIBUTION

A. INFANTRY BATTALION TASK FORCE

1. The Government of the United States of America shall provide to the MFO an infantry battalion task force, which shall be responsible for patrolling by foot, light vehicle, and helicopter; establishing and manning observation posts and check points; and conducting other activities as directed by the Force Commander in accordance with the Protocol between Egypt and Israel, signed August 3, 1981.

2. The infantry battalion task force shall consist of an infantry battalion headquarters and its associated headquarters company, three rifle companies, a combat support company, a helicopter support element, and signal support element. The total number of personnel of the infantry battalion task force shall not exceed 808.

3. The infantry battalion task force shall be equipped with its normal infantry battalion equipment and weapons, as mutually agreed, less its heavy (4.2″) mortars, heavy (TOW) anti-tank missiles, and air defense missiles (REDEYE/STINGER), subject to the following:

a. A maximum of 10 unarmed utility helicopters may be deployed to provide movement of personnel, equipment and supplies; medical evacuation; and command-control, observation, and liaison.

b. The infantry battalion task force shall deploy with sufficient light/utility vehicles to meet its operational ground transportation needs. The MFO shall supplement the infantry battalion task force's vehicles with additional vehicles as necessary to provide adequate logistical support.

c. The infantry battalion task force shall be sufficiently equipped and manned to perform at least organizational maintenance on all its deployed equipment, including helicopters. All other maintenance capability shall be provided by the MFO, as may be required.

B. LOGISTICS SUPPORT ELEMENT

1. The Government of the United States shall provide to the MFO a Logistics Support Element which shall be responsible for: explosive ordnance disposal; movements control; airlift control; operation of a central supply facility for all classes of supply, except post exchange supplies and alcoholic beverages; provision of agreed mail services; maintenance of all U.S.-standard small arms deployed with MFO contingents; operation of heavy vehicles; provision of medical services, including operation of central medical facilities at both primary base camps; and provision of food and sanitation inspection services.

2. The total number of personnel of the Logistics Support Element shall not exceed 356.

3. The Logistics Support Element shall be equipped with the equipment necessary to perform its mission, as described above, subject to the following:

a. The MFO shall provide sufficient equipment to meet the operational communications needs of the Logistics Support Element.

b. The MFO shall provide those vehicles required by the Logistics Support Element to perform its mission.

c. The Logistics Support Element shall be responsible for providing organizational maintenance for its deployed equipment, and operator maintenance for equipment provided to it by the MFO. The MFO shall be responsible for providing additional maintenance of equipment used by the Logistics Support Element.

d. All members of the Logistic Support Element shall be armed with their normally assigned individual weapons.

C. ADDITIONAL PROVISIONS

1. The mission, equipment and armament of the military units described herein may not be changed except with the consent of the Government of the United States and the MFO.

2. The commanders of the infantry battalion task force and of the Logistics Support Element shall have direct access to the Force Commander.

3. The Government of the United States shall also provide staff-trained military officers to the MFO Force Commander's staff for mutually acceptable positions.

4. The organizational criteria set forth in this Annex may from time to time be modified by mutual consent.

ANNEX II

FINANCIAL ARRANGEMENTS FOR UNITED STATES MILITARY CONTRIBUTION

1. The Government of the United States shall remain responsible for the payment to the United States military personnel, without cost to the MFO, of the salaries, benefits, subsistence and/or allowances which would normally be paid such personnel when stationed in the United States.

2. The MFO shall pay to the Government of the United States an amount equivalent to the cost to the Government of the United States of special pay and allowances paid to the United States military personnel pursuant to applicable United States law.

3. The Government of the United States shall provide, without cost to the MFO, those items of capital equipment required for the performance of missions assigned to United States units, in accordance with Annex I.

4. The MFO shall pay to the Government of the United States the actual cost of such special preparation and modification of equipment necessary for Sinai operation as has been mutually determined, and of the removal of such special preparation and modification upon cessation of deployment.

5. The MFO shall provide for the initial transportation to and final transportation from the Sinai of capital equipment and support equipment of the United States military units, without cost to the United States. Any non-maintenance-related rotation of such

equipment will be the responsibility of the Government of the United States.

6. Damage to or loss of capital equipment supplied by the Government of the United States shall be the responsibility of the MFO when any such damage or loss occurs in connection with official MFO business.

7. The MFO shall provide, without cost to the Government of the United States, equipment which is required by the United States units to perform their assigned missions, but which is not standard issue to United States military units.

8. The MFO shall provide for the transportation of the United States military personnel assigned to the MFO, their individual weapons and kit, without cost to the United States, from the designated point of departure to their stations in the Sinai and return, in accordance with the mutually established rotation schedule.

9. The MFO shall provide food and lodging to the United States military personnel in the Sinai, as well as base support, without cost to the United States.

10. In consideration of the food, lodging, base support, and other services, supplies and equipment to be provided the United States units by the MFO pursuant to this Annex, the Government of the United States shall credit to the account of the MFO an amount equivalent to the costs which would normally have been incurred by the Government of the United States for food and lodging, base support, and operations and maintenance for such units when stationed in the United States.

11. The net amount payable by the MFO in accordance with this Annex and the financial provisions of such other agreements as may be entered into between the Government of the United States and the MFO shall be determined on a fiscal year basis, and real costs shall be payable quarterly. The first such payment shall be made by July 1, 1982, and subsequent installments shall be paid quarterly thereafter.

12. Accounting, reimbursement and other administrative arrangements related to this Annex shall be agreed upon between designated representatives of the Government of the United States and the MFO.

Agreed Minute

With reference to paragraph 2 of Annex II of the letter of the Director General of the MFO to the Secretary of State of the Government of the United States, it is understood that the special pay and allowances to be paid to the personnel of the United States armed forces assigned to the MFO pursuant to applicable United States law will be:

(a) overseas pay for enlisted personnel, initially ranging from $8.00 to $22.50 per person per month, depending on grade;

(b) a separate maintenance allowance for married personnel of $30.00 per person per month.

With reference to paragraph 4 of Annex II, it is understood that the costs incurred in preparing equipment for use in the Sinai (i.e., painting vehicles and painting MFO insignia on equipment) will be calculated on the basis of actual cost incurred.

With reference to paragraph 8 of Annex II, it is understood that when air transportation for personnel, supplies and equipment is provided by the Government of the United States on a space available basis at no additional cost to the Government of the United States, no reimbursement will be required from the MFO.

With reference to paragraph 10 of Annex II, it is understood that the costs which would normally have been incurred by the Government of the United States for maintaining the United States personnel in the United States will be computed on the following basis:

(a) Costs for the budgeted support will be computed on the basis of factors set forth in the Army Force Planning Cost Handbook (AFPCH).

(b) Budgeted support costs for operations and maintenance of aviation units will be computed on the basis of United States Army Forces Command (FORSCOM) historical flying hour and standard United States Department of the Army cost factors.

(c) Budgeted support costs for operations and maintenance of the Logistics Support Element will be based on FORSCOM historical experience for each specific unit; provided, however, that the AFPCH will be the basis for computing costs for the Explosive Ordnance Disposal team.

(d) Budgeted costs for subsistence will be computed at the standard United States Department of the Army per person per day rate.

(e) Budgeted costs for base operations will be computed on the basis of a cost allocation factor of $50.00 per person per month.

ANNEX III

CIVILIAN OBSERVERS

The Government of the United States of America shall assist the MFO in recruiting, or otherwise ensure the provision of, approximately 25 United States Government personnel, on transfer or detail, to serve as civilian observers and support personnel in accordance with the Protocol between Egypt and Israel signed August 3, 1981. During their assignment with the MFO, the civilian observers shall be responsible to the Director General of the MFO in accordance with such organizational arrangements as he may establish, consistent with the Protocol, and shall have no responsibility to the Government of the United States with respect to the performance of their functions. It is understood that the civilian observers shall report directly to the Force Commander and that all civilian observers shall be citizens of the United States.

With respect to the financial arrangements for the civilian observers, the MFO shall be responsible for all costs related to their employment with the MFO, in accordance with the terms of employment as agreed between the individual employee and the MFO.

In the case of employees on detail to the MFO, the MFO will reimburse the United States Government for all costs related to the detail, including salaries, allowances, benefits, travel and transportation. The MFO will be responsible for all costs such as travel and support incident to the performance of duties while on detail to or employed by the MFO.

ENCLOSURE 1

PROTOCOL

[to the Treaty of Peace between Egypt and Israel]

In view of the fact that the Egyptian-Israeli Treaty of Peace dated March 26, 1979 (hereinafter, "the Treaty"), provides for the fulfillment of certain functions by the United Nations Forces and Observers and that the President of the Security Council indicated on May 18, 1981, that the Security Council was unable to reach the necessary agreement on the proposal to establish the UN Forces and Observers, Egypt and Israel, acting in full respect for the purposes and principles of the United Nations Charter, have reached the following agreement:

1. A Multinational Force and observers (hereinafter, "MFO") is hereby established as an alternative to the United Nations Forces and Observers. The two Parties may consider the possibility of replacing the arrangements hereby established with alternative arrangements by mutual agreement.

2. The provisions of the Treaty which relate to the establishment and functions and responsibilities of the UN Forces and observers shall apply mutatis mutandis to the establishment and functions and responsibilities of the MFO or as provided in this Protocol.

3. The provisions of Article IV of the Treaty and the Agreed Minute thereto shall apply to the MFO. In accordance with paragraph 2 of this Protocol, the words "through the procedures indicated in paragraph 4 of Article IV and the Agreed Minute thereto" shall be substituted for "by the Security Council of the United Nations with the affirmative vote of the five permanent members" in paragraph 2 of Article IV of the Treaty.

4. The Parties shall agree on the nations from which the MFO will be drawn.

5. The mission of the MFO shall be to undertake the functions and responsibilities stipulated in the Treaty for the United Nations Forces and observers. Details relating to the international nature, size, structure and operation of the MFO are set out in the attached Annex.

6. The Parties shall appoint a Director-General who shall be responsible for the direction of the MFO. The Director-General shall, subject to the approval of the Parties, appoint a Commander, who shall be responsible for the daily command of the MFO. Details relating to the Director-General and the Commander are set out in the attached Annex.

7. The expenses of the MFO which are not covered by other sources shall be borne equally by the Parties.

8. Disputes arising from the interpretation and application of this Protocol shall be resolved according to Article VII of the Treaty.

9. This Protocol shall enter into force when each Party has notified the other that all its Constitutional requirements have been fulfilled. The attached Annex shall be regarded as an integral part hereof. This Protocol shall be communicated to the Secretary General of the United Nations for registration in accordance with the provisions of Article 102 of the Charter of the United Nations.[2]

Signed for the Governments of the Arab Republic of Egypt and the State of Israel; witnessed by the Government of the United States of America

ANNEX

[to the Protocol to the Treaty of Peace between Egypt and Israel]

Director-General

1. The Parties shall appoint a Director-General of the MFO within one month of the signing of this Protocol. The Director-General shall serve a term of four years, which may be renewed. The Parties may replace the Director-General prior to the expiration of his term.

2. The Director-General shall be responsible for the direction of the MFO in the fulfillment of its functions and in this respect is authorized to act on behalf of the MFO. In accordance with local laws and regulations and the privileges and immunities of the MFO, the Director-General is authorized to engage an adequate staff, to institute legal proceedings, to contract, to acquire and dispose of property, and to take those other actions necessary and proper for the fulfillment of his responsibilities. The MFO shall not own immovable property in the territory of either Party without the agreement of the respective government. The Director-General shall determine the location of his office, subject to the consent of the country in which the office will be located.

3. Subject to the authorization of the Parties, the Director-General shall request those nations agreeable to the Parties to supply contingents to the MFO and to receive the agreement of contributing nations that the contingents will conduct themselves in accordance with the terms of this Protocol. The Director-General shall impress upon contributing nations the importance of continuity of service in units with the MFO so that the Commander may be in a position to plan his operations with knowledge of what units will be available. The Director-General shall obtain the agreement of contributing nations that the national contingents shall not be withdrawn without adequate prior notification to the Director-General.

4. The Director-General shall report to the Parties on developments relating to the functioning of the MFO. He may raise with either or both Parties, as appropriate, any matter concerning the functioning of the MFO. For this purpose, Egypt and Israel shall

[2] TS 993; 59 Stat. 1053; 3 Bevans 1176.

designate senior responsible officials as agreed points of contact for the Director-General. In the event that either Party or the Director-General requests a meeting, it will be convened in the location determined by the Director-General within 48 hours. Access across the international boundary shall only be permitted through entry checkpoints designated by each Party. Such access will be in accordance with the laws and regulations of each country. Adequate procedures will be established by each Party to facilitate such entries.

Military Command Structure

5. In accordance with paragraph 6 of the Protocol, the Director-General shall appoint a Commander of the MFO within one month of the appointment of the Director-General. The Commander will be an officer of general rank and shall serve a term of three years which may, with the approval of the Parties, be renewed or curtailed. He shall not be of the same nationality as the Director-General.

6. Subject to paragraph 2 of this Annex, the Commander shall have full command authority over the MFO, and shall promulgate its Standing Operating Procedures. In making the command arrangements stipulated in paragraph 9 of Article VI of Annex I of the Treaty (hereinafter "Annex I"), the Commander shall establish a chain of command for the MFO linked to the commanders of the national contingents made available by contributing nations. The members of the MFO, although remaining in their national service, are, during the period of their assignment to the MFO, under the Director-General and subject to the authority of the Commander through the chain of command.

7. The Commander shall also have general responsibility for the good order of the MFO. Responsibility for disciplinary action in national contingents provided for the MFO rests with the commanders of the national contingents.

Functions and Responsibilities of the MFO

8. The mission of the MFO shall be to undertake the functions and responsibilities stipulated in the Treaty for the United Nations Forces and Observers.

9. The MFO shall supervise the implementation of Annex I and employ its best efforts to prevent any violation of its terms.

10. With respect to the MFO, as appropriate, the Parties agree to the following arrangements:

(a) Operation of checkpoints, reconnaissance patrols, and observation posts along the international boundary and Line B, and within Zone C.

(b) Periodic verification of the implementation of the provisions of Annex I will be carried out not less than twice a month unless otherwise agreed by the Parties.

(c) Additional verifications within 48 hours after the receipt of a request from either Party.

(d) Ensuring the freedom of navigation through the Strait of Tiran in accordance with Article V of the Treaty of Peace.

11. When a violation has been confirmed by the MFO, it shall be rectified by the respective Party within 48 hours. The Party shall notify the MFO of the rectification.

12. The operations of the MFO shall not be construed as substituting for the undertakings by the Parties described in paragraph 2 of Article III of the Treaty. MFO personnel will report such acts by individuals as described in that paragraph in the first instance to the police of the respective Party.

13. Pursuant to paragraph 2 of Article II of Annex I, and in accordance with paragraph 7 of Article VI of Annex I, at the checkpoints at the international boundary, normal border crossing functions, such as passport inspection and customs control, will be carried out by officials of the respective Party.

14. The MFO operating in the Zones will enjoy freedom of movement necessary for the performance of its tasks.

15. MFO support flights to Egypt or Israel will follow normal rules and procedures for international flights. Egypt and Israel will undertake to facilitate clearances for such flights.

16. Verification flights by MFO aircraft in the Zones will be cleared with the authorities of the respective Party, in accordance with procedures to ensure that the flights can be undertaken in a timely manner.

17. MFO aircraft will not cross the international boundary without prior notification and clearance by each of the Parties.

18. MFO reconnaissance aircraft operating in Zone C will provide notification to the civil air control center and, thereby, to the Egyptian liaison officer therein.

Size and Organization

19. The MFO shall consist of a headquarters, three infantry battalions totalling not more than 2,000 troops, a coastal patrol unit and an observer unit, an aviation element and logistics and signal units.

20. The MFO units will have standard armament and equipment appropriate to their peacekeeping missions as stipulated in this Annex.

21. The MFO headquarters will be organized to fulfill its duties in accordance with the Treaty and this Annex. It shall be manned by staff-trained officers of appropriate rank provided by the troop contributing nations as part of their national contingents. Its organization will be determined by the Commander, who will assign staff positions to each contributor on an equitable basis.

Reports

22. The Commander will report findings simultaneously to the Parties as soon as possible, but not later than 24 hours, after a verification or after a violation has been confirmed. The Commander will also provide the Parties simultaneously a monthly report summarizing the findings of the checkpoints, observation posts, and reconnaissance patrols.

23. Reporting formats will be worked out by the Commander with the Parties in the Joint Commission. Reports to the Parties will be transmitted to the liaison offices to be established in accordance with paragraph 31 below.

Financing, Administration and Facilities

24. The budget for each financial year shall be prepared by the Director-General and shall be approved by the Parties. The financial year shall be from October 1 through September 30. Contributions shall be paid in U.S. dollars, unless the Director-General requests contributions in some other form. Contributions shall be committed the first day of the financial year and made available as the Director-General determines necessary to meet expenditures of the MFO.

25. For the period prior to October 1, 1981, the budget of the MFO shall consist of such sums as the Director-General shall receive. Any contributions during that period will be credited to the share of the budget of the contributing state in Financial Year 1982, and thereafter as necessary, so that the contribution is fully credited.

26. The Director-General shall prepare financial and administrative regulations consistent with this Protocol and submit them no later than December 1, 1981, for the approval of the Parties. These financial regulations shall include a budgetary process which takes into account the budgetary cycles of the contributing states.

27. The Commander shall request the approval of the respective Party for the use of facilities on its territory necessary for the proper functioning of the MFO. In this connection, the respective Party, after giving its approval for the use by the MFO of land or existing buildings and their fixtures, will not be reimbursed by the MFO for such use.

Responsibilities of the Joint Commission Prior to Its Dissolution

28. In accordance with Article IV of the Appendix to Annex I, the Joint Commission will supervise the implementation of the arrangements described in Annex I and its Appendix, as indicated in subparagraphs b, c, h, i and j of paragraph 3 of Article IV.

29. The Joint Commission will implement the preparations required to enable the Liaison System to undertake its responsibilities in accordance with Article VII of Annex I.

30. The Joint Commission will determine the modalities and procedures for the implementation of Phase Two, as described in paragraph 3(b) of Article I of Annex I, based on the modalities and procedures that were implemented in Phase One.

Liaison System

31. The Liaison System will undertake the responsibilities indicated in paragraph I of Article VII of Annex I, and may discuss any other matters which the Parties by agreement may place before it. Meetings will be held at least once a month. In the event that either Party or the Commander requests a special meeting, it will be convened within 24 hours. The first meeting will be held in El-Arish not later than two weeks after the MFO assumes its functions. Meetings will alternate between El-Arish and Beer Sheba, unless the Parties otherwise agree. The Commander shall be invited to any meeting in which subjects concerning the MFO are discussed, or when either Party requests MFO presence. Decisions will be reached by agreement of Egypt and Israel.

32. The Commander and each chief liaison officer will have access to one another in their respective offices. Adequate procedures will be worked out between the Parties with a view to facilitating the entry for this purpose of the representatives of either Party to the territory of the other.

Privileges and Immunities

33. Each Party will accord to the MFO the privileges and immunities indicated in the attached Appendix.

Schedule

34. The MFO shall assume its functions at 1300 hours on April 25, 1982.

35. The MFO shall be in place by 1300 hours, on March 20, 1982.

APPENDIX

[to the Protocol to the Treaty of Peace between Egypt and Israel]

Definitions

1. The "Multinational Force and Observers" (hereinafter referred to as "the MFO") is that organization established by the Protocol.

2. For the purposes of this Appendix, the term "Member of the MFO" refers to the Director-General, the Commander and any person, other than a resident of the Receiving State, belonging to the military contingent of a Participating State or otherwise under the authority of the Director-General, and his spouse and minor children, as appropriate.

3. The "Receiving State" means the authorities of Egypt or Israel as appropriate, and the territories under their control. "Government authorities" includes all national and local, civil and military authorities called upon to perform functions relating to the MFO under the provisions of this Appendix, without prejudice to the ultimate responsibility of the Government of the Receiving State.

4. "Resident of the Receiving State" includes (a) a person with citizenship of the Receiving State, (b) a person resident therein or (c) a person present in the territory of the Receiving State other than a member of the MFO.

5. "Participating State" means a State that contributes personnel to the MFO.

Duties of MFO in the Receiving State:

6. (a) Members of the MFO shall respect the laws and regulations of the Receiving State and shall refrain from any activity of a political character in the Receiving State and from any action incompatible with the international nature of their duties or inconsistent with the spirit of the present arrangements. The Director-General shall take all appropriate measures to ensure the observance of these obligations.

(b) In the performance of their duties for the MFO, members of the MFO shall receive their instructions only from the Director-General and the chain of command designated by him.

(c) Members of the MFO shall exercise the utmost discretion in regard to all matters relating to their duties and functions. They shall not communicate to any person any information known to them by reason of their position with the MFO which has not been made public, except in the course of their duties or by authorization of the Director-General. These obligations do not cease upon the termination of their assignment with the MFO.

(d) The Director-General will ensure that in the Standing Operating Procedures of the MFO, there will be arrangements to avoid accidental or inadvertent threats to the safety of MFO members.

Entry and Exit: Identification

7. Individual or collective passports shall be issued by the Participating States for members of the MFO. The Director-General shall notify the Receiving State of the names and scheduled time of arrival of MFO members, and other necessary information. The Receiving State shall issue an individual or collective multiple entry visa as appropriate prior to that travel. No other documents shall be required for a member of the MFO to enter or leave the Receiving State. Members of the MFO shall be exempt from immigration inspection and restrictions on entering or departing from the territory of the Receiving State. They shall also be exempt from any regulations governing the residence of aliens in the Receiving State, including registration, but shall not be considered as acquiring any right to permanent residence or domicile in the Receiving State. The Receiving State shall also provide each member of the Force with a personal identity card prior to or upon his arrival.

8. Members of the MFO will at all times carry their personal identity cards issued by the Receiving State. Members of the MFO may be required to present, but not to surrender, their passport or identity cards upon demand of an appropriate authority of the Receiving State. Except as provided in paragraph 7 of this Appendix, the passport or identity card will be the only document required for a member of the MFO.

9. If a member of the MFO leaves the services of the Participating State to which he belongs and is not repatriated, the Director-General shall immediately inform the authorities of the Receiving State, giving such particulars as may be required. The Director-General shall similarly inform the authorities of the Receiving State of any member of the MFO who has absented himself for more than 21 days. if an expulsion order against the ex-member of the MFO has been made, the Director-General shall be responsible for ensuring that the person concerned shall be received within the territory of the Participating State concerned.

Jurisdiction

10. The following arrangements respecting criminal and civil jurisdiction are made having regard to the special functions of the MFO and not for the personal benefit of the members of the MFO. The Director-General shall cooperate at all times with the appropriate authorities of the Receiving State to facilitate the proper administration of justice, secure the observance of laws and regulations and prevent the occurrence of any abuse in connection with

the privileges, immunities and facilities mentioned in this Appendix.

Criminal Jurisdiction

11. (a) Military members of the MFO and members of the civilian observer group of the MFO shall be subject to the exclusive jurisdiction of their respective national states in respect of any criminal offenses which may be committed by them in the Receiving State. Any such person who is charged with the commission of a crime will be brought to trial by the respective Participating State, in accordance with Its laws.

(b) Subject to Paragraph 25, other members of the MFO shall be immune from the criminal jurisdiction of the Receiving State in respect of words spoken or written and all acts performed by them in their official capacity.

(c) The Director-General shall obtain the assurances of each Participating State that it will be prepared to take the necessary measures to assure proper discipline of its personnel and to exercise jurisdiction with respect to any crime or offense which might be committed by its Personnel. The Director-General shall comply with requests of the Receiving State for the withdrawal from its territory of any member of the MFO who violates its laws, regulations, customs or traditions. The Director-General, with the consent of the Participating State, may waive the immunity of a member of the MFO.

(d) Without prejudice to the foregoing, a Participating State may enter into a supplementary arrangement with the Receiving State to limit or waive the immunities of its members of the MFO who are on periods of leave while in the Receiving State.

Civil Jurisdiction

12. (a) Members of the MFO shall not be subject to the civil jurisdiction of the courts of the Receiving State or to other legal process in any matter relating to their official duties. In a case arising from a matter relating to official duties and which involves a members of the MFO and a resident of the Receiving State, and in other disputes as agreed, the procedure provided in paragraph 38(b) of this Appendix shall apply to the settlement.

(b) If the Director-General certifies that a member of the MFO is unable because of official duties or authorized absence to protect his interests in a civil proceeding in which he is a participant, the court or authority shall at his request suspend the proceeding until the elimination of the disability, but for not more than ninety days. Property of a member of the MFO which is certified by the Director-General to be needed by him for the fulfillment of his official duties shall be free from seizure for the satisfaction of a Judgment decision or order, together with other property not subject thereto under the law of the Receiving State. The personal liberty of a member of the MFO shall not be restricted by a court or other authority of the Receiving State in a civil proceeding, whether to enforce a judgment, decision or order, to compel an oath of disclosure, or for any other reason.

(c) In the cases provided for in sub-paragraph (b) above, the claimant may elect to have his claim dealt with in accordance with the procedure set out in paragraph 38(b) of this Appendix. Where a claim adjudicated or an award made in favor of the claimant by a court of the Receiving State or the Claims Commission under paragraph 38(b) of this Appendix has not been satisfied, the authorities of the Receiving State may, without prejudice to the claimant's rights, seek the good offices of the Director-General to obtain satisfaction.

Notification: Certification

13. If any civil proceeding is instituted against a member of the MFO, before any court of the Receiving State having jurisdiction, notification shall be given to the Director-General. The Director-General shall certify to the court whether or not the proceeding is related to the official duties of such member.

Military Police: Arrest: Transfer of Custody and Mutual Assistance

14. The Director-General shall take all appropriate measures to ensure maintenance of discipline and good order among members of the MFO. To this end military police designated by the Director-General shall police the premises referred to in paragraph 19 of this Appendix, and such areas where the MFO is functioning.

15. The military police of the MFO shall immediately transfer to the civilian police of the Receiving State any individual, who is not a member of the MFO, of whom it takes temporary custody.

16. The police of the Receiving State shall immediately transfer to the MFO any member of the MFO, of whom it takes temporary custody, pending a determination concerning jurisdiction.

17. The Director-General and the authorities of the Receiving State shall assist each other concerning all offenses in respect of which either or both have an interest, including the production of witnesses, and in the collection and production of evidence, including the seizure and, in proper cases, the handing over, of things connected with an offense. The handing over of any such things may be made subject to their return within the time specified by the authority delivering them. Each shall notify the other of the disposition of any case in the outcome of which the other may have an interest or in which there has been a transfer of custody under the provisions of paragraphs 15 and 16 of this Appendix.

18. The government of the Receiving State will ensure the prosecution of persons subject to its criminal jurisdiction who are accused of acts in relation to the MFO or its members which, if committed in relation to the forces of the Receiving State or their members, would have rendered them liable to prosecution. The Director-General will take the measures within his power with respect to crimes or offenses committed against citizens of the Receiving State by members of the MFO.

Premises of the MFO

19. Without prejudice to the fact that all the premises of the MFO remain the territory of the Receiving State, they shall be inviolable and subject to the exclusive control and authority of the Director-General, who alone may consent to the entry of officials to perform duties on such premises.

MFO Flag

20. The Receiving States permit the MFO to display a special flag or insignia, of a design agreed upon by them, on its headquarters, camps, posts, or other premises, vehicles, boats and otherwise as decided by the Director-General. Other flags or pennants may be displayed only in exceptional cases and in accordance with conditions prescribed by the Director-General. Sympathetic consideration will be given to observations or requests of the authorities of the Receiving State concerning this last-mentioned matter. If the MFO flag or other flag is flown, the flag of the Receiving State shall be flown alongside it.

Uniform: Vehicle, Boats and Aircraft Markings and Registration: Operating Permits

21. Military members of the MFO shall normally wear their national uniform with such identifying MFO insignia as the Director-General may prescribe. The conditions on which the wearing of civilian dress is authorized shall be notified by the Director-General to the authorities of the Receiving State and sympathetic consideration will be given to observations or requests of the authorities of the Receiving State concerning this matter. Members of the MFO shall wear civilian dress while outside the areas where they are functioning. Service vehicles, boats and aircraft shall not carry the marks or license plates of any Participating State, but shall carry the distinctive MFO identification mark and license which shall be notified by the Director-General to the authorities of the Receiving State. Such vehicles, boats and aircraft shall not be subject to registration and licensing under the laws and regulations of the Receiving State. Authorities of the Receiving State shall accept as valid, without a test or fee, a permit or license for the operation of service vehicles, boats and aircraft issued by the Director-General. MFO drivers shall be given permits by the Receiving State to enable them to drive outside the areas where they are functioning, if these permits are required by the Receiving State.

Arms

22. Members of the MFO who are off-duty shall not carry arms while outside the areas where they are functioning.

Privileges and Immunities of the MFO

23. The MFO shall enjoy the status, privileges and immunities accorded in Article II of the Convention on the Privileges and Immunities of the United Nations (hereinafter, "the Convention"). The provisions of Article II of the Convention shall also apply to the property, funds and assets of Participating States used in the Receiving State in connection with the activities of the MFO. Such Participating States may not acquire immovable property in the Receiving State without agreement of the government of the Receiving State. The government of the Receiving State recognizes that the right of the MFO to import free of duty equipment for the MFO and provisions supplies and other goods for the exclusive use of members of the MFO, includes the right of the MFO to establish,

maintain and operate at headquarters, camps and posts, service institutes providing amenities for the members of the MFO. The amenities that may be provided by service institutes shall be goods of a consumable nature (tobacco and tobacco products, beer, etc.), and other customary articles of small value. To the end that duty-free importation for the MFO may be effected with the least possible delay, having regard to the interests of the government of the Receiving State, a mutually satisfactory procedure, including documentation, shall be arranged between the Director-General and the customs authorities of the Receiving State. The Director-General shall take all necessary measures to prevent any abuse of the exemption and to prevent the sale or resale of such goods to persons other than the members of the MFO. Sympathetic consideration shall be given by the Director-General to observations or requests of the authorities of the Receiving State concerning the operation of service institutes.

Privileges and Immunities and Delegation of Authority of Director-General

24. The Director-General of the MFO may delegate his powers to other members of the MFO.

25. The Director-General, his deputy, the Commander, and his deputy, shall be accorded in respect of themselves, their spouses and minor children, the Privileges and immunities, exemptions and facilities accorded to diplomatic envoys in accordance with international law.

Members of the MFO: Taxation, Customs and Fiscal Regulations

26. Members of the MFO shall be exempt from taxation by the Receiving State on the pay and emoluments received from their national governments or from the MFO. They shall also be exempt from all other direct taxes, fees, and charges, except for those levied for services rendered.

27. Members of the MFO shall have the right to import free of duty their personal effects in connection with their first taking up their post in the Receiving State. They shall be subject to the laws and regulations of the Receiving State governing customs and foreign exchange with respect to personal property not required by them by reason of their presence in the Receiving State with the MFO. Special facilities for entry or exit shall be granted by the immigration, customs and fiscal authorities of the Receiving State to regularly constituted units of the MFO provided that the authorities concerned have been duly notified sufficiently in advance. Members of the MFO on departure from the area may, notwithstanding the foreign exchange regulations, take with then such funds as the Director-General certifies were received in pay and emoluments from their respective national governments or from the MFO and are a reasonable residue thereof. Special arrangements between the Director-General and the authorities of the Receiving State shall be made for the implementation of the foregoing provisions in the interests of the government of the Receiving State and members of the MFO.

28. The Director-General will cooperate with the customs and fiscal authorities of the Receiving State and will render all assistance

within his power in ensuring the observance of the customs and fiscal laws and regulations of the Receiving State by the members of the MFO in accordance with this Appendix or any relevant supplemental arrangements.

Communications and Postal Services

29. The MFO shall enjoy the facilities in respect to communications provided for in Article III of the Convention. The Director-General shall have authority to install and operate communications systems as are necessary to perform its functions subject to the provisions of Article 35 of the International Telecommunication Convention of April 11, 1973, relating to harmful interference. The frequencies on which any such station may be operated will be duly communicated by the MFO to the appropriate authorities of the Receiving State. Appropriate consultations will be held between the MFO and the authorities of the Receiving State to avoid harmful interference. The right of the Director-General is likewise recognized to enjoy the priorities of government telegrams and telephone calls as provided for the United Nations in Article 39 and Annex 3 of the latter Convention and in Article 5, No. 10 of the telegraph regulations annexed thereto.

30. The MFO shall also enjoy, within the areas where it is functioning, the right of unrestricted communication by radio, telephone, telegraph or any other means, and of establishing the necessary facilities for maintaining such communications within and between premises of the MFO, including the laying of cables and land lines and the establishment of fixed and mobile radio sending and receiving stations. It is understood that the telegraph and telephone cables and lines herein referred to will be situated within or directly between the premises of the MFO and the areas where it is functioning, and that connection with the system of telegraphs and telephones of the Receiving State will be made in accordance with arrangements with the appropriate authorities of the Receiving State.

31. The government of the Receiving State recognizes the right of the MFO to make arrangements through its own facilities for the processing and transport of private mail addressed to or emanating from members of the MFO. The government of the Receiving State will be informed of the nature of such arrangements. No interference shall take place with, and no censorship shall be applied to, the mail of the MFO by the government of the Receiving State. In the event that postal arrangements applying to private mail of members of the MFO are extended to operations involving transfer of currency, or transport of packages or parcels from the Receiving State, the conditions under which such operations shall be conducted in the Receiving State will be agreed upon between the government of the Receiving State and the Director-General.

Motor Vehicle Insurance

32. The MFO will take necessary arrangements to ensure that all MFO motor vehicles shall be covered by third party liability insurance in accordance with the laws and regulations of the Receiving State.

Use of Roads, Waterways, Port Facilities, Airfields and Railways

33. When the MFO uses roads, bridges, port facilities and airfields it shall not be subject to payment of dues, tolls or charges either by way of registration or other-wise, in the areas where it is functioning and the normal points of access, except for charges that are related directly to services rendered. The authorities of the Receiving State, subject to special arrangements, will give the most favorable consideration to requests for the grant to members of the MFO of traveling facilities on its railways and of concessions with regard to fares.

Water, Electricity and Other Public Utilities

34. The MFO shall have the right to the use of water, electricity and other public utilities at rates not less favorable to the MFO than those to comparable consumers. The authorities of the Receiving State will, upon the request of the Director-General, assist the MFO in obtaining water, electricity and other utilities required, and in the case of interruption or threatened interruption of service, will give the same priority to the needs of the MFO as to essential government services. The MFO shall have the right where necessary to generate, within the premises of the MFO either on land or water, electricity for the use of the MFO and to transmit and distribute such electricity as required by the MFO.

Currency of the Receiving State

35. The Government of the Receiving State will, if requested by the Director-General, make available to the MFO, against reimbursement in U.S. dollars or other currency mutually acceptable, currency of the Receiving State required for the use of the MFO, including the pay of the members of the national contingents, at the rate of exchange most favorable to the MFO that is officially recognized by the government of the Receiving State.

Provisions, Supplies and Services

36. The authorities of the Receiving State will, upon the request of the Director-General, assist the MFO in obtaining equipment, provisions, supplies and other goods and services required from local sources for its subsistence and operation. Sympathetic consideration will be given by the Director-General in purchases on the local market to requests or observations of the authorities of the Receiving State in order to avoid any adverse effect on the local economy. Members of the MFO may purchase locally goods necessary for their own consumption, and such services as they, need, under conditions prevailing in the open market.

If members of the MFO should require medical or dental facilities beyond those available within the MFO, arrangements shall be made with the appropriate authorities of the Receiving State under which such facilities may be made available. The Director-General and the appropriate local authorities will cooperate with respect to sanitary services. The Director-General and the authorities of the Receiving State shall extend to each other the fullest cooperation in matters concerning health, particularly with respect to the control of communicable diseases in accordance with international conventions; such cooperation shall extend to the exchange of relevant information and statistics.

Locally Recruited Personnel

37. The MFO may recruit locally such personnel as required. The authorities of the Receiving State will, upon the request of the Director-General, assist the MFO in the recruitment of such personnel. Sympathetic consideration will be given by the Director-General in the recruitment of local personnel to requests or observations of authorities of the Receiving State in order to avoid any adverse effect on the local economy. The terms and conditions of employment for locally recruited personnel shall be prescribed by the Director-General and shall generally, to the extent practicable, be no less favorable than the practice prevailing in the Receiving State.

Settlement of Disputes or Claims

38. Disputes or claims of a private law character shall be settled in accordance with the following provisions:

(a) The MFO shall make provisions for the appropriate modes of settlement of disputes or claims arising out of contract or other disputes or claims of a private law character to which the MFO is a party other than those covered in subparagraph (b) and paragraph 39 following. When no such provisions have been made with the contracting party, such claims shall be settled according to subparagraph (b) below.

(b) Any claim made by:

(i) a resident of the Receiving State against the MFO or a member thereof, in respect of any damages alleged to result from an act or omission of such member of the MFO relating to his official duties;

(ii) the Government of the Receiving State against a member of the MFO;

(iii) the MFO or the Government of the Receiving State against one another, that is not covered by paragraph 40 of this Appendix;

shall be settled by a Claims Commission established for that purpose. One member of the Commission shall be appointed by the Director-General, one member by the Government of the Receiving State and a Chairman jointly by the two. If the Director-General and the Government of the Receiving State fail to agree on the appointment of a chairman, the two members selected by them shall select a chairman from the list of the Permanent Court of Arbitration. An award made by the Claims Commission against the MFO or a member or other employee thereof or against the Government of the Receiving State shall be notified to the Director-General or the authorities of the Receiving State as the case may be, to make satisfaction thereof.

39. Disputes concerning the terms of employment and conditions of service of locally recruited personnel shall be settled by administrative procedure to be established by the Director-General.

40. All disputes between the MFO and the Government of the Receiving State concerning the interpretation or application of this Appendix which are not settled by negotiation or other agreed mode of settlement shall be referred for final settlement to a tribunal of three arbitrators, one to be named by the Director-General, one by the Government of the Receiving State, and an umpire to be chosen jointly who shall preside over the proceedings of this tribunal.

41. If the two parties fail to agree on the appointment of the umpire within one month of the proposal of arbitration by one of the parties, the two members selected by them shall select a chairman from the list of the Permanent Court of Arbitration. Should a vacancy occur for any reason, the vacancy shall be filled within thirty days by the methods laid down in this paragraph for the original appointment. The tribunal shall come into existence upon the appointment of the chairman and at least one of the other members of the tribunal. Two members of the tribunal shall constitute a quorum for the performance of its functions, and for all deliberations and decisions of the tribunal a favorable vote of two members shall be sufficient.

Deceased Members: Disposition of Personal Property

42. The Director-General shall have the right to take charge of and dispose of the body of a member of the MFO who dies in the territory of the Receiving State and may dispose of his personal property after the debts of the deceased person incurred in the territory of the Receiving State and owing to residents of the Receiving State have been settled.

Supplemental Arrangements

43. Supplemental details for the carrying out of this Appendix shall be made as required between the Director-General and appropriate authorities designated by the Government of the Receiving State.

Effective Date and Duration

44. This Appendix shall take effect from the date of the entry into force of the Protocol and shall remain in force for the duration of the Protocol. The provisions of paragraphs 38, 39, 40 and 41 of this Appendix, relating to the settlement of disputes, however, shall remain in force until all claims arising prior to the date of termination of this Appendix and submitted prior to or within three months following the date of termination, have been settled.

AIDE MEMOIRE

GUIDELINES FOR THE GOVERNMENT OF THE UNITED STATES

PLANNING FOR THE MULTINATIONAL FORCE AND OBSERVERS (MFO)

INTRODUCTION

The following are guidelines to governments preparing to assign troops for service with the MFO. The actual composition of such contingents being prepared will depend on the military policy, equipment and other national characteristics of the country concerned. Adherence to these guidelines where possible would ease to a very great extent the administrative problems of the contingent in the initial stages of its service with the MFO and enhance its operational efficiency. It would also be useful if representatives from national military headquarters were to hold further discussions with the MFO before proceeding to their assignment in the Sinai.

AIM

To provide the necessary guidelines to the Government of the United States to enable it to organize its MFO contingent which will, to the maximum extent possible, be capable of supporting itself administratively and operationally.

ORGANIZATION

A. The basic *mission* of the military units, their suggested organizational structures, and required capital and support equipment are as set forth in Annex I to the Director General's letter of 26 March, 1982, to the Government of the United States. The basic mission of the civilian observer unit is as set forth in Annex III to this letter.

B. *Role of Unit Commanders*. Each unit commander will have direct access to the MFO Force Commander. Each commander's rank should be appropriate to the unit's size and function but should not exceed Lt. Colonel, since staff section chiefs and battalion commanders will be of that rank.

C. *Contribution to MFO Headquarters*. In order to ensure equitable representation of all contingents at all levels, a number of staff officers will be assigned by each troop-contributing state to the force headquarters. Accordingly, the Government of the United States is requested to provide a number of officers to be agreed for this purpose. The officers nominated to fill these posts must be staff trained.

D. *Common Language of MFO*. English will be the common working language of this multinational force. All officers should be able to speak, read and write English.

E. *Clothing*. Personnel should be fully equipped in accordance with their national scales of issue. Since the weather may vary from hot and dry to cold and wet, an appropriate range of items of clothing should be provided.

The MFO accepts responsibility for providing the following items of clothing for all ranks:

- beret, MFO color—one
- field cap, MFO color—one
- hat badge, flash—one
- cloth shoulder patch—six
- armlet, olive drab—two
- scarf, MFO color—two

The MFO will send to the troop-contributing state a minimum amount of berets, scarves, hat badges and shoulder patches to ensure that each individual may be given an initial partial issue. The remainder of the issue items will be obtained on arrival. It is imperative that the Director General be informed soonest of the address to enable the initial issue to be air-freighted and arrive before the departure of the advance party.

GENERAL INFORMATION

A. *Communications*. The MFO will provide communications among MFO elements working throughout the area of operations. The MFO will also provide access to the international telephone system for communications between national contingents and their home countries. Unless otherwise agreed, the contingent will provide equipment necessary to meet its internal communications requirements. Should it be decided by the government to have its own national radio link to its contingent, it may do so subject to MFO approval of equipment and frequency and on the understanding it will meet all the related costs without reimbursement by the MFO.

B. *Basic Equipment*. The following stores/equipment will be provided by the MFO as necessary (this list is not all-inclusive):

- Generators
- Freezers and refrigeration
- Defense stores
- Tentage (as required)
  - Personnel (sleeping accommodation)
  - Messing
  - Administration
  - Workshops
  - Stores
  - Medical inspection
- Quartermaster stores (as required)
  - Mosquito netting
  - Wardrobes
  - Tables
  - Desks
  - Chairs
  - Beds, blankets, sheets, etc.
  - Disinfectants, cleaning material, fumigants
  - Chemical toilets
- Office equipment (as required)
  - Desks
  - Tables
  - Filing cabinets
  - Typewriters
  - Calculators
  - Fans
  - Safes
- Special Equipment (as required)
  - Fire-fighting
  - Water purification
  - Observation (field, survey and night vision binoculars, and night observation devices)
  - Riot control equipment
  - Tradesmen's tools (saws, drills, etc.)
  - Compressor with auxiliary equipment

C. *Personal Identification.* While in transit to and from the mission area, contingent personnel should be in possession of identification in accordance with their national regulations. On arrival, personnel will be issued an MFO identification card which will be the identity document required within Egypt and Israel. To expedite issuance, it is recommended that each individual possess a minimum of six recent photographs approximately 3 cm by 3 cm.

D. *Passports.* Individual passports will be required for members of troop contingents if they wish to travel in the two countries outside the MFO's immediate area of operations. Members of the troop contingents may arrive or leave the Sinai under the "collective passport" referred to in the Protocol (Appendix, para 7), but if a soldier wishes to take leave either in Egypt or Israel, or would like to be prepared for emergencies requiring travel outside the area, he must have his own passport and visa from the appropriate country.

E. *Medical.* The contingent must be fully immunized against yellow fever. It is strongly recommended that immunization against tetanus, typhoid and polio be included. Gammaglobulin against hepatitis should be given every three months. Malaria prophylaxis and salt tablets are recommended while in the area. MFO will provide these pharmaceuticals while the unit is in the area.

Preliminary planning is for the MFO to provide a central medical facility and staff. Medical support at the field-hospital level and above will be provided through the Governments of Israel and Egypt.

F. *Ground Transport.* The contingent will provide such vehicles as necessary to perform its mission. The MFO will supplement those vehicles as necessary for unit support needs.

G. *Personal Services.* Haircuts, laundry, ablution and sanitation services will be provided by the MFO.

H. *Water.* It is anticipated that water in base camps will be provided through a pipeline system. Adequate water tank trucks, water trailers, water purification equipment, if required, and waterpumps with hoses will also be provided as necessary. Jerry cans or similar containers will be provided as necessary for water distribution.

I. *Rations.* Rations will be supplied by the MFO in accordance with the "MFO Ration Scale" which may be modified to be compatible with the home scales of contingents and to cater to national food tastes and religious dietary customs. In this regard it is requested that the troop-contributing government provide the Director General with a copy of the national ration scale as soon as possible.

J. *Transportation to and from the MFO Area.* Initial movement into the area will be by air or sea as required. The MFO will coordinate the transportation into the area and from the area to the home country on the completion of the tour of duty and will cover all costs attendant thereto, unless otherwise agreed.

1. *Airlift Arranged by the MFO.* In the event that the initial deployment is by air and the transportation as provided by the MFO, the following details are required by MFO as soon as they become available:

—Place of embarkation and name of airport;

—Dates troops and equipment will be ready for airlift;

—Dimensions and weights of large pieces of equipment;
—Total weight of equipment and stores to be airlifted; and,
—Type and amount of dangerous cargo such as ammunition, acid, batteries, kerosene, fuel and oil.

2. *Movement Control*. It is requested that the senior member on each flight have a completed manifest showing the number of passengers on board and the amount and type of cargo. This manifest will be given to the MFO movement control personnel on arrival. In addition, personnel familiar with movement control activities should be deployed on the first aircraft and be prepared to assist with subsequent arrivals of their contingent.

K. *Rotation*. Contingents are normally rotated after serving a period of at least six months with the Force. These rotations are arranged by the MFO either by chartered commercial aircraft or by military airlift. It is the responsibility of the contingent's home government to inform the MFO at least six weeks prior to the rotation of the exact dates they propose for the rotation and the number of troops to be rotated each way. The rotation will involve only the personnel and their personal gear (including personal weapons) up to 45 kgs (unit equipment is not rotated.)

A reasonable amount of additional freight may be allowed by air up to the available capacity of the aircraft after accommodating the passengers with their personal baggage. Contractual arrangements with commercial airlines are made by the MFO. Experience has shown the paramount need for close liaison with the MFO on all transportation arrangements. Failure to provide the required information in time to carry out the arrangements could delay the acquisition of airlift and the diplomatic overflight clearances.

L. *Accommodation*. Accommodations shall be provided in accordance with the policy decided for the MFO. Generally, accommodation is arranged in accordance with the local conditions and availability of facilities. It may be concentrated into platoon, company, or contingent camps according to the operational role of the contingent. If civilian accommodation must be rented, arrangements will be concluded by the chief administrative officer of the MFO.

M. *Local Resources*. If a contingent requires contractual services, the contingent commanding officer should forward his request to MFO headquarters. Contracts for services, supplies, equipment and other requirements will be made only through the chief administrative officer. Such matters include procurement of:

Land and accommodation;
Petrol, oil and lubricants;
Fresh rations;
Water supply;
Rentals;
Public service facilities;
Laundry and cleaning;
Civilian labor;
Garbage disposal;
Hair cutting;
Cobbler services;
Tailoring.

N. *Control of Resources*. It should be stressed that once a contingent enters the MFO area of operation and becomes a part of the

MFO, all equipment and supplies required thereafter (except for self-sufficiency) for the continued operational support of the contingent—and which would normally involve a charge to the MFO—should be requisitioned through the Director General's administrative channels. Since the Force Commander and the chief administrative officer work in close cooperation with the Director General, who in turn ensures liaison with governments, the operational needs of the various contingents in the field would be served most efficiently by centralizing, as is usual with peacekeeping forces, all requisitions of military supplies in this manner.

O. *Pay and Allowances.* Governments providing troops are responsible for making payment of pay and allowances to all their unit personnel in accordance with their own national legislation. Normal salaries, benefits and allowances that would be paid to troops serving at home will be at the expense of the troop-contributing state; special pay and allowances required under existing national legislation for service abroad will be reimbursed to the troop-contributing state by the MFO.

P. *Maintenance in the Sinai.* The MFO will provide for troops assigned to the Sinai all necessary food, lodging, and base support, and will absorb the costs of operations and maintenance. However, the troop-contributing state will pay the MFO an amount equivalent to the normal costs of maintaining the deployed personnel at home, with respect to base support, operations and maintenance, food and lodging.

Q. *Reimbursement for Equipment and Supplies.* The troop-contributing state will provide, at its own expense, all capital and support equipment required for the performance of its assigned mission. The MFO will pay for the transport of this equipment to the Sinai, and its eventual return to the troop-contributing state. All consumable supplies brought in by the national contingent at MFO request will be inspected by the MFO upon arrival in the area of operations and reimbursement will be paid on the basis of demonstrated cost.

R. *Payments for Death, Injury, Disability or Illness.* Reimbursement for payments mace by government bases upon national legislation and/or regulations for death, injury, disability or illness attributable to service with the MFO will be as follows. Where periodic payments are called for under national legislation or regulations, reimbursement will be made in a lump sum based on actuarial data. In respect of death and disability awards, a governmental claim is required to enable reimbursement of payments due or made by the government concerned to beneficiaries in accordance with national legislation and/or regulations. This claim should be appropriately certified by the government's auditor-general or an official of equivalent rank/position.

S. *Official Travel of MFO Personnel.* Members of the contingent who are required to make official duty trips to points where MFO food and lodging facilities cannot be provided will be paid at appropriate rates established by the MFO.

T. *Airline tickets* will be provided by the MFO in some circumstances for members and escorts if repatriation is authorized for medical, compassionate or other reason by the Force Commander.

U. *MFO Orders*. The Force Commander is empowered to issue orders consistent with the authority granted by the Director General of the MFO implementing the Protocol between the Arab Republic of Egypt and State of Israel. Such orders may be revised from time to time and are binding upon all members of the Force.

V. *Postal*. The MFO provides for members of the Force the free dispatch to the home country of a limited amount of personal mail. Contingents may avail themselves of this service, if desired, once an agreement has been concluded between the troop-contributing state and the MFO. Each troop-contributing state is required to designate a special postal address in the home country.

Handling of mail to and from troop-contributing countries is governed by local conditions, available means of transportation, and any agreements between the troop-contributing state and the postal authorities of the Receiving State.

W. *Currency Exchanges*. Currency regulations vary from country to country. Regulations for currency exchange are established to ensure that national currency regulations are respected in the area as well as in neighboring countries which the members may visit on leave or on duty. Regulations pertaining to the MFO will be obtained upon arrival in the MFO area.

X. *Recreational Equipment*. The MFO encourages units to bring sports equipment, personal musical instruments, and other recreational supplies for the use of their own units, for both intramural and extramural competitions.

The Secretary of State to the Director General

of the Multinational Force and Observers

THE SECRETARY OF STATE

WASHINGTON

March 26, 1982

Mr. LEAMON R. HUNT
Director General
Multinational Force and Observers
6121 Lincolnia Road
Alexandria, Virginia 22312

DEAR MR. HUNT:

Thank you for your letter of March 26, 1982. I wish to confirm to you that the Government of the United States of America will contribute to the MFO an infantry battalion task force, a logistics support element, staff personnel, and civilian observers as provided in Annexes I and III to your letter.

I confirm to you as well as that the Government of the United States hereby provides the agreements and assurances concerning its participation in the MFO which you requested in accordance with the terms of the Protocol.

I acknowledge receipt of the Aide Memoire enclosed with your letter. The guidelines contained in the Aide Memoire will be of use to my Government in preparing and deploying its units for service in the MFO.

Finally, my Government concurs with your proposal that your letter of March 26, 1982, including its attached Annexes I, II, and III, together with this reply, shall constitute an agreement between the Government of the United States and the MFO which shall enter into force on this date.

With assurances of my highest consideration.

Sincerely,

ALEXANDER M. HAIG, JR.

Multinational Force and Observers
Post Office Box 11258
Alexandria, Virginia 22312
(703) 642-8300

March 26, 1982

The Honorable ALEXANDER M. HAIG, JR.
The Secretary of State
Washington, D. C. 20520

DEAR MR. SECRETARY:

With reference to my letter of today's date accepting your government's offer to contribute to the MFO in accordance with the Protocol to the Treaty of Peace between Egypt and Israel signed on March 26, 1979, it may assist if I confirm our understanding with respect to various aspects of participation in the MFO.

(1) it is understood that, as provided in paragraph 12 of the Appendix to the Egypt-Israel Protocol of August 3, 1981, the courts or other legal process of Egypt or Israel in any matters relating to their official duties. It is also understood that, as provided in paragraph 38 of that Appendix, claims against a member of the MFO made by the Government of Egypt or Israel or by residents thereof in respect of damages alleged to result from an act or omission of such member relating to his official duties shall be settled according to the claims provisions of the Appendix. An award made by the claims commission against a member of the MFO shall be notified to the Director General for payment by the MFO. Accordingly, neither the individual member nor the participating state of which he is a national shall incur any liability in such official duty cases.

(2) With reference to paragraph 6 of the Annex to the Protocol, it is understood that national contingents provided to the MFO shall be placed under the operational control of the Force Commander. The Force Commander will issue orders to the national contingents through the appropriate national contingent commander in accordance with the chain of command established by him pursuant to the Protocol.

(3) It is understood that in exercising his functions under paragraphs 12(b), 13 and 42 of the Appendix, the Director General will seek relevant information from the appropriate national contingent commander through the Force Commander.

(4) It is understood that in the application of paragraph 20 of the Appendix, the Director General intends to follow the regulations and practices of the United Nations in its peacekeeping organizations so far as the display of flags and ensigns is concerned.

(5) With reference to paragraph 21 of the Appendix, it is understood that service vehicles, boats and aircraft serving with the

MFO shall be painted MFO colors, shall carry MFO identification marks and, in addition, shall carry only those marks or insignia as are necessary to satisfy international legal requirements applicable to state aircraft and boats.

(6) With reference to paragraph 24 of the Appendix, it is understood that the Director General does not intend to delegate any of his powers directly to members of national contingents who are under the command of the national contingent commander.

(7) It is understood that where supplementary arrangements are to be made, as provided in paragraph 43 of the Appendix, which substantially affect a national contingent, the Director General will first consult with the government of the affected participating state.

(8) It is understood that the Director General intends to establish a consultative mechanism whereby he will meet with representatives designated by participating states accredited to the country where his headquarters will be located for briefing and discussion of issues of general concern. In addition, the Director General and his staff will be available at any time to hold bilateral consultations with participating state representatives on substantive issues of mutual concern.

(9) It is understood that any disputes which may arise between a participating state and the MFO which cannot properly be resolved through normal administrative channels may be raised by either the MFO or the participating government for resolution at the diplomatic level between the Director General and the designated diplomatic representative of the participating government.

I would appreciate your reply confirming the above understandings.

Sincerely,

LEAMON R. HUNT
DIRECTOR GENERAL
Multinational Force and Observers

THE SECRETARY OF STATE

WASHINGTON

March 26, 1982

Mr. LEAMON R. HUNT
Director General
Multinational Force and Observers
6121 Lincolnia Road
Alexandria, Virginia 22312

DEAR MR. HUNT:

This is in reply to your letter of March 26, 1982 which sets forth a number of understandings concerning participation in the MFO. I am pleased to advise you that my government confirms the understandings set forth in our letter.

Sincerely,

ALEXANDER M. HAIG, JR.

H. UNITED NATIONS AND OTHER INTERNATIONAL ORGANIZATIONS

CONTENTS

1. Charter of the United Nations [1]

Signed at San Francisco, June 26, 1945; Ratification advised by the Senate, July 28, 1945; Ratified by the President, August 8, 1945; Ratification deposited, August 8, 1945; Entered into force, October 24, 1945; Proclaimed by the President, October 31, 1945; Amended, December 17, 1963,[2] December 20, 1965,[3] and December 20, 1971 [4]

WE THE PEOPLES OF THE UNITED NATIONS
DETERMINED

to save succeeding generations from the scourge of war, which twice in our lifetime has brought untold sorrow to mankind, and

to reaffirm faith in fundamental human rights, in the dignity and worth of the human person, in the equal rights of men and women and of nations large and small, and

to establish conditions under which justice and respect for the obligations arising from treaties and other sources of international law can be maintained, and

to promote social progress and better standards of life in larger freedom,

AND FOR THESE ENDS

to practice tolerance and live together in peace with one another as good neighbors, and

to unite our strength to maintain international peace and security, and

to ensure, by the acceptance of principles and the institution of methods, that armed force shall not be used, save in the common interest, and

to employ international machinery for the promotion of the economic and social advancement of all peoples,

HAVE RESOLVED TO COMBINE OUR EFFORTS TO ACCOMPLISH THESE AIMS.

Accordingly, our respective Governments, through representatives assembled in the city of San Francisco, who have exhibited their full powers found to be in good and due form, have agreed to the present Charter of the United Nations and to hereby establish an international organization to be known as the United Nations.

CHAPTER I—PURPOSES AND PRINCIPLES

ARTICLE 1

The Purposes of the United Nations are:

1. To maintain international peace and security, and to that end: to take effective collective measures for the prevention

[1] TS 993; 59 Stat. 1031; 3 Bevans 1153.
[2] Articles 23, 27 and 61 amended at 16 UST 1134; TIAS 5857; 557 UNTS 143.
[3] Article 109 amended at 19 UST 5450; TIAS 6529.
[4] Article 61 amended further at 24 UST 2225; TIAS 2255.

and removal of threats to the peace, and for the suppression of acts of aggression or other breaches of the peace, and to bring about by peaceful means, and in conformity with the principles of justice and international law, adjustment or settlement of international disputes or situations which might lead to a breach of the peace;

2. To develop friendly relations among nations based on respect for the principle of equal rights and self-determination of peoples, and to take other appropriate measures to strengthen universal peace;

3. To achieve international cooperation in solving international problems of an economic, social, cultural, or humanitarian character, and in promoting and encouraging respect for human rights and for fundamental freedoms for all without distinction as to race, sex, language, or religion; and

4. To be a center for harmonizing the actions of nations in the attainment of these common ends.

ARTICLE 2

The Organization and its Members, in pursuit of the Purposes stated in Article 1, shall act in accordance with the following Principles.

1. The Organization is based on the principle of the sovereign equality of all its Members.

2. All Members, in order to ensure to all of them the rights and benefits resulting from membership, shall fulfill in good faith the obligations assumed by them in accordance with the present Charter.

3. All Members shall settle their international disputes by peaceful means in such a manner that international peace and security, and justice, are not endangered.

4. All Members shall refrain in their international relations from the threat or use of force against the territorial integrity or political independence of any state, or in any other manner inconsistent with the Purposes of the United Nations.

5. All Members shall give the United Nations every assistance in any action it takes in accordance with the present Charter, and shall refrain from giving assistance to any state against which the United Nations is taking preventive or enforcement action.

6. The Organization shall ensure that states which are not Members of the United Nations act in accordance with these Principles so far as may be necessary for the maintenance of international peace and security.

7. Nothing contained in the present Charter shall authorize the United Nations to intervene in matters which are essentially within the domestic jurisdiction of any state or shall require the Members to submit such matters to settlement under the present Charter; but this principle shall not prejudice the application of enforcement measures under Chapter VII.

CHAPTER II—MEMBERSHIP

ARTICLE 3

The original Members of the United Nations shall be the states which, having participated in the United Nations Conference on International Organization at San Francisco, or having previously signed the Declaration by United Nations of January 1, 1942, sign the present Charter and ratify it in accordance with Article 110.

ARTICLE 4

1. Membership in the United Nations is open to all other peace-loving states which accept the obligations contained in the present Charter and, in the judgment of the Organization, are able and willing to carry out these obligations.

2. The admission of any such state to membership in the United Nations will be effected by a decision of the General Assembly upon the recommendation of the Security Council.

ARTICLE 5

A Member of the United Nations against which preventive or enforcement action has been taken by the Security Council may be suspended from the exercise of the rights and privileges of membership by the General Assembly upon the recommendation of the Security Council. The exercise of these rights and privileges may be restored by the Security Council.

ARTICLE 6

A Member of the United Nations which has persistently violated the Principles contained in the present Charter may be expelled from the Organization by the General Assembly upon the recommendation of the Security Council.

CHAPTER III—ORGANS

ARTICLE 7

1. There are established as the principal organs of the United Nations: a General Assembly, a Security Council, an Economic and Social Council, a Trusteeship Council, an International Court of Justice, and a Secretariat.

2. Such subsidiary organs as may be found necessary may be established in accordance with the present Charter.

ARTICLE 8

The United Nations shall place no restrictions on the eligibility of men and women to participate in any capacity and under conditions of equality in its principal and subsidiary organs.

CHAPTER IV—THE GENERAL ASSEMBLY

Composition

ARTICLE 9

1. The General Assembly shall consist of all the Members of the United Nations.

2. Each Member shall have not more than five representatives in the General Assembly.

Functions and Powers

ARTICLE 10

The General Assembly may discuss any questions or any matters within the scope of the present Charter or relating to the powers and functions of any organs provided for in the present Charter, and except as provided in Article 12, may make recommendations to the Members of the United Nations or to the Security Council or to both on any such questions or matters.

ARTICLE 11

1. The General Assembly may consider the general principles of cooperation in the maintenance of international peace and security, including the principles governing disarmament and the regulation of armaments, and may make recommendations with regard to such principles to the Members or to the Security Council or to both.

2. The General Assembly may discuss any questions relating to the maintenance of international peace and security brought before it by any Member of the United Nations, or by the Security Council, or by a state which is not a Member of the United Nations in accordance with Article 35, paragraph 2, and except as provided in Article 12, may make recommendations with regard to any such questions to the state or states concerned or to the Security Council or to both. Any such question on which action is necessary shall be referred to the Security Council by the General Assembly either before or after discussion.

3. The General Assembly may call the attention of the Security Council to situations which are likely to endanger international peace and security.

4. The powers of the General Assembly set forth in this Article shall not limit the general scope of Article 10.

ARTICLE 12

1. While the Security Council is exercising in respect of any dispute or situation the functions assigned to it in the present Charter, the General Assembly shall not make any recommendation with regard to that dispute or situation unless the Security Council so requests.

2. The Secretary-General, with the consent of the Security Council, shall notify the General Assembly at each session of any matters relative to the maintenance of international peace and security

which are being dealt with by the Security Council and shall similarly notify the General Assembly, or the Members of the United Nations if the General Assembly is not in session, immediately the Security Council ceases to deal with such matters.

ARTICLE 13

1. The General Assembly shall initiate studies and make recommendations for the purpose of:

a. promoting international cooperation in the political field and encouraging the progressive development of international law and its codification;

b. promoting international cooperation in the economic, social, cultural, educational, and health fields, and assisting in the realization of human rights and fundamental freedoms for all without distinction as to race, sex, language, or religion.

2. The further responsibilities, functions, and powers of the General Assembly with respect to matters mentioned in paragraph 1(b) above are set forth in Chapters IX and X.

ARTICLE 14

Subject to the provisions of Article 12, the General Assembly may recommend measures for the peaceful adjustment of any situation, regardless of origin, which it deems likely to impair the general welfare or friendly relations among nations, including situations resulting from a violation of the provisions of the present Charter setting forth the Purposes and Principles of the United Nations.

ARTICLE 15

1. The General Assembly shall receive and consider annual and special reports from the Security Council; these reports shall include an account of the measures that the Security Council has decided upon or taken to maintain international peace and security.

2. The General Assembly shall receive and consider reports from the other organs of the United Nations.

ARTICLE 16

The General Assembly shall perform such functions with respect to the international trusteeship system as are assigned to it under Chapters XII and XIII, including the approval of the trusteeship agreements for areas not designated as strategic.

ARTICLE 17

1. The General Assembly shall consider and approve the budget of the Organization.

2. The expenses of the Organization shall be borne by the Members as apportioned by the General Assembly.

3. The General Assembly shall consider and approve any financial and budgetary arrangements with specialized agencies referred to in Article 57 and shall examine the administrative budgets of such specialized agencies with a view to making recommendations to the agencies concerned.

Voting

ARTICLE 18

1. Each member of the General Assembly shall have one vote.

2. Decisions of the General Assembly on important questions shall be made by a two-thirds majority of the members present and voting. These questions shall include: recommendations with respect to the maintenance of international peace and security, the election of the non-permanent members of the Security Council, the election of the members of the Economic and Social Council, the election of members of the Trusteeship Council in accordance with paragraph 1(c) of Article 86, the admission of new Members to the United Nations, the suspension of the rights and privileges of membership, the expulsion of Members, questions relating to the operation of the trusteeship system, and budgetary questions.

3. Decisions on other questions, including the determination of additional categories of questions to be decided by a two-thirds majority, shall be made by a majority of the members present and voting.

ARTICLE 19

A Member of the United Nations which is in arrears in the payment of its financial contributions to the Organization shall have no vote in the General Assembly if the amount of the arrears equals or exceeds the amount of the contributions due from it for the preceding two full years. The General Assembly may, nevertheless, permit such a Member to vote if it is satisfied that the failure to pay is due to conditions beyond the control of the Member.

Procedure

ARTICLE 20

The General Assembly shall meet in regular annual sessions and in such special sessions as occasion may require. Special sessions shall be convoked by the Secretary-General at the request of the Security Council or of a majority of the Members of the United Nations.

ARTICLE 21

The General Assembly shall adopt its own rules of procedure. It shall elect its President for each session.

ARTICLE 22

The General Assembly may establish such subsidiary organs as it deems necessary for the performance of its functions.

CHAPTER V—THE SECURITY COUNCIL

Composition

ARTICLE 23 [5]

1. The Security Council shall consist of fifteen Members of the United Nations. The Republic of China, France, and the Union of Soviet Socialist Republics, the United Kingdom of Great Britain and Northern Ireland, and the United States of America shall be permanent members of the Security Council. The General Assembly shall elect ten other Members of the United Nations to be non-permanent members of the Security Council, due regard being specially paid, in the first instance to the contribution of Members of the United Nations to the maintenance of international peace and security and to the other purposes of the Organization, and also to equitable geographical distribution.

2. The non-permanent members of the Security Council shall be elected for a term of two years. In the first election of the non-permanent members after the increase of the membership of the Security Council from eleven to fifteen, two of the four additional members shall be chosen for a term of one year. A retiring member shall not be eligible for immediate re-election.

3. Each member of the Security Council shall have one representative.

Functions and Powers

ARTICLE 24

1. In order to ensure prompt and effective action by the United Nations, its Members confer on the Security Council primary responsibility for the maintenance of international peace and security, and agree that in carrying out its duties under this responsibility the Security Council acts on their behalf.

2. In discharging these duties the Security Council shall act in accordance with the Purposes and Principles of the United Nations. The specific powers granted to the Security Council for the discharge of these duties are laid down in Chapters VI, VII, VIII, and XII.

---

[5] 24 UST 2225; TIAS 7739. Amendments to Articles 23, 27 and 61 of the Charter of the United Nations, adopted by the General Assembly on December 17, 1963, came into force on August 31, 1965. The amendment to Article 23 enlarged the membership of the Security Council from 11 to 15. The amended Article 27 provides that decisions of the Security Council on procedural matters shall be made by an affirmative vote of nine members (formerly seven) and on all other matters by an affirmative vote of nine members (formerly seven), including the concurring votes of the five permanent members of the Security Council. The amendment to Article 61 enlarged the membership of the Economic and Social Council from 18 to 27. Another amendment, approved May 8, 1967 corrected an oversight. When the U.N. Charter amendments approved by the Senate in 1965 increased the membership of the Security Council from 11 to 15, at the same time there was an increase from seven to nine in the number of affirmative votes required for Council decisions. Inadvertently, the United Nations failed to include in its Amendments a conforming change in Security Council voting requirements in Article 109, para. 1, which was subsequently accomplished by Amendment to Article 109 adopted by the General Assembly to the United Nations December 20, 1965 (TIAS 6529).

A further amendment to Article 61 of the Charter of the United Nations, adopted by the General Assembly on December 20, 1971, came into force on September 24, 1973. The amendment enlarged the membership of the Economic and Social Council from 27 to 54.

3. The Security Council shall submit annual and, when necessary, special reports to the General Assembly for its consideration.

ARTICLE 25

The Members of the United Nations agree to accept and carry out the decisions of the Security Council in accordance with the present Charter.

ARTICLE 26

In order to promote the establishment and maintenance of international peace and security with the least diversion for armaments of the world's human and economic resources, the Security Council shall be responsible for formulating, with the assistance of the Military Staff Committee referred to in Article 47, plans to be submitted to the Members of the United Nations for the establishment of a system for the regulation of armaments.

Voting

ARTICLE 27 [5]

1. Each member of the Security Council shall have one vote.
2. Decisions of the Security Council on procedural matters shall be made by an affirmative vote of nine members.
3. Decisions of the Security Council on all other matters shall be made by an affirmative vote of nine members including the concurring votes of the permanent members; provided that, in decisions under Chapter VI, and under paragraph 3 of Article 52, a party to a dispute shall abstain from voting.

Procedure

ARTICLE 28

1. The Security Council shall be so organized as to be able to function continuously. Each member of the Security Council shall for this purpose be represented at all times at the seat of the Organization.
2. The Security Council shall hold periodic meetings at which each of its members may, if it so desires, be represented by a member of the government or by some other specially designated representative.
3. The Security Council may hold meetings at such places other than the seat of the Organization as in its judgment will best facilitate its work.

ARTICLE 29

The Security Council may establish such subsidiary organs as it deems necessary for the performance of its functions.

ARTICLE 30

The Security Council shall adopt its own rules of procedure, including the method of selecting its President.

ARTICLE 31

Any Member of the United Nations which is not a member of the Security Council may participate, without vote, in the discussion of any question brought before the Security Council whenever the latter considers that the interests of that Member are specially affected.

ARTICLE 32

Any Member of the United Nations which is not a member of the Security Council or any state which is not a Member of the United Nations, if it is a party to a dispute under consideration by the Security Council, shall be invited to participate, without vote, in the discussion relating to the dispute. The Security Council shall lay down such conditions as it deems just for the participation of a state which is not a Member of the United Nations.

CHAPTER VI—PACIFIC SETTLEMENT OF DISPUTES

ARTICLE 33

1. The parties to any dispute, the continuance of which is likely to endanger the maintenance of international peace and security, shall, first of all, seek a solution by negotiation, enquiry, mediation, conciliation, arbitration, judicial settlement, resort to regional agencies or arrangements, or other peaceful means of their own choice.
2. The Security Council shall, when it deems necessary, call upon the parties to settle their dispute by such means.

ARTICLE 34

The Security Council may investigate any dispute, or any situation which might lead to international friction or give rise to a dispute, in order to determine whether the continuance of the dispute or situation is likely to endanger the maintenance of international peace and security.

ARTICLE 35

1. Any Member of the United Nations may bring any dispute, or any situation of the nature referred to in Article 34, to the attention of the Security Council or of the General Assembly.
2. A state which is not a Member of the United Nations may bring to the attention of the Security Council or the General Assembly any dispute to which it is a party if it accepts in advance, for the purposes of the dispute, the obligations of pacific settlement provided in the present Charter.
3. The proceedings of the General Assembly in respect of matters brought to its attention under this Article will be subject to the provisions of Articles 11 and 12.

ARTICLE 36

1. The Security Council may, at any stage of a dispute of the nature referred to in Article 33 or of a situation of like nature, recommend appropriate procedures or methods of adjustment.

2. The Security Council should take into consideration any procedures for the settlement of the dispute which have already been adopted by the parties.

3. In making recommendations under this Article the Security Council should also take into consideration that legal disputes should as a general rule be referred by the parties to the International Court of Justice in accordance with the provisions of the Statute of the Court.

ARTICLE 37

1. Should the parties to a dispute of the nature referred to in Article 33 fail to settle it by the means indicated in that Article, they shall refer it to the Security Council.

2. If the Security Council deems that the continuance of the dispute is in fact likely to endanger the maintenance of international peace and security, it shall decide whether to take action under Article 36 or to recommend such terms of settlement as it may consider appropriate.

ARTICLE 38

Without prejudice to the provisions of Articles 33 to 37, the Security Council may, if all the parties to any dispute so request, make recommendations to the parties with a view to a pacific settlement of the dispute.

CHAPTER VII—ACTION WITH RESPECT TO THREATS TO THE PEACE, BREACHES OF THE PEACE, AND ACTS OF AGGRESSION

ARTICLE 39

The Security Council shall determine the existence of any threat to the peace, breach of the peace, or act of aggression and shall make recommendations, or decide what measures shall be taken in accordance with Articles 41 and 42, to maintain or restore international peace and security.

ARTICLE 40

In order to prevent an aggravation of the situation, the Security Council may, before making the recommendation or deciding upon the measures provided for in Article 39, call upon the parties concerned to comply with such provisional measures as it deems necessary or desirable. Such provisional measures shall be without prejudice to the rights, claims, or position of the parties concerned. The Security Council shall duly take account of failure to comply with such provisional measures.

ARTICLE 41

The Security Council may decide what measures not involving the use of armed force are to be employed to give effect to its decisions and it may call upon the Members of the United Nations to apply such measures. These may include complete or partial interruption of economic relations and of rail, sea, air, postal, telegraphic, radio, and other means of communication, and the severance of diplomatic relations.

ARTICLE 42

Should the Security Council consider that measures provided for in Article 41 would be inadequate or have proved to be inadequate, it may take such action by air, sea, or land forces as may be necessary to maintain or restore international peace and security. Such action may include demonstrations, blockade, and other operations by air, sea, or land forces of Members of the United Nations.

ARTICLE 43

1. All Members of the United Nations, in order to contribute to the maintenance of international peace and security, undertake to make available to the Security Council, on its call and in accordance with a special agreement or agreements, armed forces, assistance, and facilities, including rights of passage, necessary for the purpose of maintaining international peace and security.

2. Such agreement or agreements shall govern the numbers and types of forces, their degree of readiness and general location, and the nature of the facilities and assistance to be provided.

3. The agreement or agreements shall be negotiated as soon as possible on the initiative of the Security Council. They shall be concluded between the Security Council and Members or between the Security Council and groups of Members and shall be subject to ratification by the signatory states in accordance with their respective constitutional processes.

ARTICLE 44

When the Security Council has decided to use force it shall, before calling upon a Member not represented on it to provide armed forces in fulfillment of the obligations assumed under Article 43, invite that Member, if the Member so desires, to participate in the decisions of the Security Council concerning the employment of contingents of that Member's armed forces.

ARTICLE 45

In order to enable the United Nations to take urgent military measures, Members shall hold immediately available national air-force contingents for combined international enforcement action. The strength and degree of readiness of these contingents and plans for their combined action shall be determined, within the limits laid down in the special agreement or agreements referred to in Article 43, by the Security Council with the assistance of the Military Staff Committee.

ARTICLE 46

Plans for the application of armed force shall be made by the Security Council with the assistance of the Military Staff Committee.

ARTICLE 47

1. There shall be established a Military Staff Committee to advise and assist the Security Council on all questions relating to the Security Council's military requirements for the maintenance of international peace and security, the employment and command of

forces placed at its disposal, the regulation of armaments and possible disarmament.

2. The Military Staff Committee shall consist of the Chiefs of Staff of the permanent members of the Security Council or their representatives. Any Member of the United Nations not permanently represented on the Committee shall be invited by the Committee to be associated with it when the efficient discharge of the Committee's responsibilities requires the participation of that Member in its work.

3. The Military Staff Committee shall be responsible under the Security Council for the strategic direction of any armed forces placed at the disposal of the Security Council. Questions relating to the command of such forces shall be worked out subsequently.

4. The Military Staff Committee, with the authorization of the Security Council and after consultation with appropriate regional agencies, may establish regional subcommittees.

ARTICLE 48

1. The action required to carry out the decisions of the Security Council for the maintenance of international peace and security shall be taken by all the Members of the United Nations or by some of them, as the Security Council may determine.

2. Such decisions shall be carried out by the Members of the United Nations directly and through their action in the appropriate international agencies of which they are members.

ARTICLE 49

The Members of the United Nations shall join in affording mutual assistance in carrying out the measures decided upon by the Security Council.

ARTICLE 50

If preventive or enforcement measures against any state are taken by the Security Council, any other state, whether a Member of the United Nations or not, which finds itself confronted with special economic problems arising from the carrying out of those measures shall have the right to consult the Security Council with regard to a solution of those problems.

ARTICLE 51

Nothing in the present Charter shall impair the inherent right of individual or collective self-defense if an armed attack occurs against a Member of the United Nations, until the Security Council has taken the measures necessary to maintain international peace and security. Measures taken by Members in the exercise of this right of self-defense shall be immediately reported to the Security Council and shall not in any way affect the authority and responsibility of the Security Council under the present Charter to take at any time such action as it deems necessary in order to maintain or restore international peace and security.

Chapter VIII—Regional Arrangements

ARTICLE 52

1. Nothing in the present Charter precludes the existence of regional arrangements or agencies for dealing with such matters relating to the maintenance of international peace and security as are appropriate for regional action, provided that such arrangements or agencies and their activities are consistent with the Purposes and Principles of the United Nations.

2. The Members of the United Nations entering into such arrangements or constituting such agencies shall make every effort to achieve pacific settlement of local disputes through such regional arrangements or by such regional agencies before referring them to the Security Council.

3. The Security Council shall encourage the development of pacific settlement of local disputes through such regional arrangements or by such regional agencies either on the initiative of the states concerned or by reference from the Security Council.

4. This Article in no way impairs the application of Articles 34 and 35.

ARTICLE 53

1. The Security Council shall, where appropriate, utilize such regional arrangements or agencies for enforcement action under its authority. But no enforcement action shall be taken under regional arrangements or by regional agencies without the authorization of the Security Council, with the exception of measures against any enemy state, as defined in paragraph 2 of this Article, provided for pursuant to Article 107 or in regional arrangements directed against renewal of aggressive policy on the part of any such state, until such time as the Organization may, on request of the Governments concerned, be charged with the responsibility for preventing further aggression by such a state.

2. The term enemy state as used in paragraph 1 of this Article applies to any state which during the Second World War has been an enemy of any signatory of the present Charter.

ARTICLE 54

The Security Council shall at all times be kept fully informed of activities undertaken or in contemplation under regional arrangements or by regional agencies for the maintenance of international peace and security.

Chapter IX—International Economic and Social Cooperation

ARTICLE 55

With a view to the creation of conditions of stability and well-being which are necessary for peaceful and friendly relations among nations based on respect for the principle of equal rights and self-determination of peoples, the United Nations shall promote:

a. higher standards of living, full employment, and conditions of economic and social progress and development;

b. solutions of international economic, social, health, and related problems; and international cultural and educational co-operation; and

c. universal respect for, and observance of, human rights and fundamental freedoms for all without distinction as to race, sex, language, or religion.

ARTICLE 56

All Members pledge themselves to take joint and separate action in cooperation with the Organization for the achievement of the purposes set forth in Article 55.

ARTICLE 57

1. The various specialized agencies, established by intergovernmental agreement and having wide international responsibilities, as defined in their basic instruments, in economic, social, cultural, educational, health, and related fields, shall be brought into relationship with the United Nations in accordance with the provisions of Article 63.

2. Such agencies thus brought into relationship with the United Nations are hereinafter referred to as specialized agencies.

ARTICLE 58

The Organization shall make recommendations for the coordination of the policies and activities of the specialized agencies.

ARTICLE 59

The Organization shall, where appropriate, initiate negotiations among the states concerned for the creation of any new specialized agencies required for the accomplishment of the purposes set forth in Article 55.

ARTICLE 60

Responsibility for the discharge of the functions of the Organization set forth in this Chapter shall be vested in the General Assembly and, under the authority of the General Assembly, in the Economic and Social Council, which shall have for this purpose the powers set forth in Chapter X.

CHAPTER X—THE ECONOMIC AND SOCIAL COUNCIL

Composition

ARTICLE 61[5]

1. The Economic and Social Council shall consist of fifty-four Members of the United Nations elected by the General Assembly.

2. Subject to the provisions of paragraph 3, eighteen members of the Economic and Social Council shall be elected each year for a term of three years. A retiring member shall be eligible for immediate re-election.

3. At the first election after the increase in the membership of the Economic and Social Council from twenty-seven to fifty-four members, in addition to the members elected in place of the nine

members whose term of office expires at the end of that year, twenty-seven additional members shall be elected. Of these twenty-seven additional members, the term of office of nine members so elected shall expire at the end of one year, and of nine other members at the end of two years, in accordance with arrangements made by the General Assembly.

4. Each member of the Economic and Social Council shall have one representative.

Functions and Powers

ARTICLE 62

1. The Economic and Social Council may make or initiate studies and reports with respect to international economic, social, cultural, educational, health, and related matters and may make recommendations with respect to any such matters to the General Assembly, to the Members of the United Nations, and to the specialized agencies concerned.

2. It may make recommendations for the purpose of promoting respect for, and observance of, human rights and fundamental freedoms for all.

3. It may prepare draft conventions for submission to the General Assembly, with respect to matters falling within its competence.

4. It may call, in accordance with the rules prescribed by the United Nations, international conferences on matters falling within its competence.

ARTICLE 63

1. The Economic and Social Council may enter into agreements with any of the agencies referred to in Article 57, defining the terms on which the agency concerned shall be brought into relationship with the United Nations. Such agreements shall be subject to approval by the General Assembly.

2. It may coordinate the activities of the specialized agencies through consultation with and recommendations to such agencies and through recommendations to the General Assembly and to the Members of the United Nations.

ARTICLE 64

1. The Economic and Social Council may take appropriate steps to obtain regular reports from the specialized agencies. It may make arrangements with the Members of the United Nations and with the specialized agencies to obtain reports on the steps taken to give effect to its own recommendations and to recommendations on matters falling within its competence made by the General Assembly.

2. It may communicate its observations on these reports to the General Assembly.

ARTICLE 65

The Economic and Social Council may furnish information to the Security Council and shall assist the Security Council upon its request.

ARTICLE 66

1. The Economic and Social Council shall perform such functions as fall within its competence in connection with the carrying out of the recommendations of the General Assembly.

2. It may, with the approval of the General Assembly, perform services at the request of Members of the United Nations and at the request of specialized agencies.

3. It shall perform such other functions as are specified elsewhere in the present Charter or as may be assigned to it by the General Assembly.

Voting

ARTICLE 67

1. Each member of the Economic and Social Council shall have one vote.

2. Decisions of the Economic and Social Council shall be made by a majority of the members present and voting.

Procedure

ARTICLE 68

The Economic and Social Council shall set up commissions in economic and social fields and for the promotion of human rights, and such other commissions as may be required for the performance of its functions.

ARTICLE 69

The Economic and Social Council shall invite any Member of the United Nations to participate, without vote, in its deliberations on any matter of particular concern to that Member.

ARTICLE 70

The Economic and Social Council may make arrangements for representatives of the specialized agencies to participate, without vote, in its deliberations and in those of the commissions established by it, and for its representatives to participate in the deliberations of the specialized agencies.

ARTICLE 71

The Economic and Social Council may make suitable arrangements for consultation with non-governmental organizations which are concerned with matters within its competence. Such arrangements may be made with international organizations and, where appropriate, with national organizations after consultation with the Member of the United Nations concerned.

ARTICLE 72

1. The Economic and Social Council shall adopt its own rules of procedure, including the method of selecting its President.

2. The Economic and Social Council shall meet as required in accordance with its rules, which shall include provision for the convening of meetings on the request of a majority of its members.

CHAPTER XI—DECLARATION REGARDING NON-SELF-GOVERNING TERRITORIES

ARTICLE 73

Members of the United Nations which have or assume responsibilities for the administration of territories whose peoples have not yet attained a full measure of self-government recognize the principle that the interests of the inhabitants of these territories are paramount, and accept as a sacred trust the obligation to promote to the utmost, within the system of international peace and security established by the present Charter, the well-being of the inhabitants of these territories, and, to this end:

a. to ensure, with due respect for the culture of the peoples concerned, their political, economic, social, and educational advancement, their just treatment, and their protection against abuses;

b. to develop self-government, to take due account of the political aspirations of the peoples, and to assist them in the progressive development of their free political institutions, according to the particular circumstances of each territory and its peoples and their varying stages of advancement;

c. to further international peace and security;

d. to promote constructive measures of development, to encourage research, and to cooperate with one another and, when and where appropriate, with specialized international bodies with a view to the practical achievement of the social, economic, and scientific purposes set forth in this Article; and

e. to transmit regularly to the Secretary-General for information purposes subject to such limitation as security and constitutional considerations may require, statistical and other information of a technical nature relating to economic, social, and educational conditions in the territories for which they are respectively responsible other than those territories to which Chapters XII and XIII apply.

ARTICLE 74

Members of the United Nations also agree that their policy in respect of the territories to which this Chapter applies, no less than in respect of their metropolitan areas, must be based on the general principle of good-neighborliness, due account being taken of the interests and well-being of the rest of the world, in social, economic, and commercial matters.

CHAPTER XII—INTERNATIONAL TRUSTEESHIP SYSTEM

ARTICLE 75

The United Nations shall establish under its authority an international trusteeship system for the administration and supervision of such territories as may be placed thereunder by subsequent individual agreements. These territories are hereinafter referred to as trust territories.

ARTICLE 76

The basic objectives of the trusteeship system, in accordance with the Purposes of the United Nations laid down in Article 1 of the present Charter, shall be:

a. to further international peace and security;

b. to promote the political, economic, social, and educational advancement of the inhabitants of the trust territories, and their progressive development towards self-government or independence as may be appropriate to the particular circumstances of each territory and its peoples and the freely expressed wishes of the peoples concerned, and as may be provided by the terms of each trusteeship agreement;

c. to encourage respect for human rights and for fundamental freedoms for all without distinction as to race, sex, language, or religion, and to encourage recognition of the interdependence of the peoples of the world; and

d. to ensure equal treatment in social, economic, and commercial matters for all Members of the United Nations and their nationals, and also equal treatment for the latter in the administration of justice, without prejudice to the attainment of the foregoing objectives and subject to the provisions of Article 80.

ARTICLE 77

1. The trusteeship system shall apply to such territories in the following categories as may be placed thereunder by means of trusteeship agreements:

a. territories now held under mandate;

b. territories which may be detached from enemy states as a result of the Second World War; and

c. territories voluntarily placed under the system by states responsible for their administration.

2. It will be a matter for subsequent agreement as to which territories in the foregoing categories will be brought under the trusteeship system and upon what terms.

ARTICLE 78

The trusteeship system shall not apply to territories which have become Members of the United Nations, relationship among which shall be based on respect for the principle of sovereign equality.

ARTICLE 79

The terms of trusteeship for each territory to be placed under the trusteeship system, including any alteration or amendment, shall be agreed upon by the states directly concerned, including the mandatory power in the case of territories held under mandate by a Member of the United Nations, and shall be approved as provided for in Articles 83 and 85.

ARTICLE 80

1. Except as may be agreed upon in individual trusteeship agreements, made under Articles 77, 79, and 81, placing each territory under the trusteeship system, and until such agreements have been concluded, nothing in this Chapter shall be construed in or of itself to alter in any manner the rights whatsoever of any states or any peoples or the terms of existing international instruments to which Members of the United Nations may respectively be parties.

2. Paragraph 1 of this Article shall not be interpreted as giving grounds for delay or postponement of the negotiation and conclusion of agreements for placing mandated and other territories under the trusteeship system as provided for in Article 77.

ARTICLE 81

The trusteeship agreement shall in each case include the terms under which the trust territory will be administered and designate the authority which will exercise the administration of the trust territory. Such authority, hereinafter called the administering authority, may be one or more states or the Organization itself.

ARTICLE 82

There may be designated, in any trusteeship agreement, a strategic area or areas which may include part or all of the trust territory to which the agreement applies, without prejudice to any special agreement or agreements made under Article 43.

ARTICLE 83

1. All functions of the United Nations relating to strategic areas, including the approval of the terms of the trusteeship agreements and of their alteration or amendment, shall be exercised by the Security Council.

2. The basic objectives set forth in Article 76 shall be applicable to the people of each strategic area.

3. The Security Council shall, subject to the provisions of the trusteeship agreements and without prejudice to security considerations, avail itself of the assistance of the Trusteeship Council to perform those functions of the United Nations under the trusteeship system relating to political, economic, social, and educational matters in the strategic areas.

ARTICLE 84

It shall be the duty of the administering authority to ensure that the trust territory shall play its part in the maintenance of international peace and security. To this end the administering authority may make use of volunteer forces, facilities, and assistance from the trust territory in carrying out the obligations toward the Security Council undertaken in this regard by the administering authority, as well as for local defense and the maintenance of law and order within the trust territory.

ARTICLE 85

1. The functions of the United Nations with regard to trusteeship agreements for all areas not designated as strategic, including the approval of the terms of the trusteeship agreements and of their alteration or amendment, shall be exercised by the General Assembly.

2. The Trusteeship Council, operating under the authority of the General Assembly, shall assist the General Assembly in carrying out these functions.

CHAPTER XIII—THE TRUSTEESHIP COUNCIL

Composition

ARTICLE 86

1. The Trusteeship Council shall consist of the following Members of the United Nations:

a. those Members administering trust territories;

b. such of those Members mentioned by name in Article 23 as are not administering trust territories; and

c. as many other Members elected for three-year terms by the General Assembly as may be necessary to ensure that the total number of members of the Trusteeship Council is equally divided between those Members of the United Nations which administer trust territories and those which do not.

2. Each member of the Trusteeship Council shall designate one specially qualified person to represent it therein.

Functions and Powers

ARTICLE 87

The General Assembly and, under its authority, the Trusteeship Council, in carrying out their functions, may:

a. consider reports submitted by the administering authority;

b. accept petitions and examine them in consultation with the administering authority;

c. provide for periodic visits to the respective trust territories at times agreed upon with the administering authority; and

d. take these and other actions in conformity with the terms of the trusteeship agreements.

ARTICLE 88

The Trusteeship Council shall formulate a questionnaire on the political, economic, social, and educational advancement of the inhabitants of each trust territory, and the administering authority for each trust territory within the competence of the General Assembly shall make an annual report to the General Assembly upon the basis of such questionnaire.

Voting

ARTICLE 89

1. Each member of the Trusteeship Council shall have one vote.
2. Decisions of the Trusteeship Council shall be made by a majority of the members present and voting.

Procedure

ARTICLE 90

1. The Trusteeship Council shall adopt its own rules of procedure, including the method of selecting its President.
2. The Trusteeship Council shall meet as required in accordance with its rules, which shall include provision for the convening of meetings on the request of a majority of its members.

ARTICLE 91

The Trusteeship Council shall, when appropriate, avail itself of the assistance of the Economic and Social Council and of the specialized agencies in regard to matters with which they are respectively concerned.

CHAPTER XIV—THE INTERNATIONAL COURT OF JUSTICE

ARTICLE 92

The International Court of Justice shall be the principal judicial organ of the United Nations. It shall function in accordance with the annexed Statute, which is based upon the Statute of the Permanent Court of International Justice and forms as integral part of the present Charter.

ARTICLE 93

1. All Members of the United Nations are *ipso facto* parties to the Statute of the International Court of Justice.
2. A state which is not a Member of the United Nations may become a party to the Statute of the International Court of Justice on conditions to be determined in each case by the General Assembly upon the recommendation of the Security Council.

ARTICLE 94

1. Each Member of the United Nations undertakes to comply with the decision of the International Court of Justice in any case to which it is a party.
2. If any party to a case fails to perform the obligations incumbent upon it under a judgment rendered by the Court, the other party may have recourse to the Security Council, which may, if it deems necessary, make recommendations or decide upon measures to be taken to give effect to the judgment.

ARTICLE 95

Nothing in the present Charter shall prevent Members of the United Nations from entrusting the solution of their differences to other tribunals by virtue of agreements already in existence or which may be concluded in the future.

ARTICLE 96

1. The General Assembly or the Security Council may request the International Court of Justice to give an advisory opinion on any legal question.

2. Other organs of the United Nations and specialized agencies, which may at any time be so authorized by the General Assembly, may also request advisory opinions of the Court on legal questions arising within the scope of their activities.

CHAPTER XV—THE SECRETARIAT

ARTICLE 97

The Secretariat shall comprise a Secretary-General and such staff as the Organization may require. The Secretary-General shall be appointed by the General Assembly upon the recommendation of the Security Council. He shall be the chief administrative officer of the Organization.

ARTICLE 98

The Secretary-General shall act in that capacity in all meetings of the General Assembly, of the Security Council, of the Economic and Social Council, and of the Trusteeship Council, and shall perform such other functions as are entrusted to him by these organs. The Secretary-General shall make an annual report to the General Assembly on the work of the Organization.

ARTICLE 99

The Secretary-General may bring to the attention of the Security Council any matter which in his opinion may threaten the maintenance of international peace and security.

ARTICLE 100

1. In the performance of their duties the Secretary-General and the staff shall not seek or receive instructions from any government or from any other authority external to the Organization. They shall refrain from any action which might reflect on their position as international officials responsible only to the Organization.

2. Each Member of the United Nations undertakes to respect the exclusive international character of the responsibilities of the Secretary-General and the staff and not to seek to influence them in the discharge of their responsibilities.

ARTICLE 101

1. The staff shall be appointed by the Secretary-General under regulations established by the General Assembly.

2. Appropriate staffs shall be permanently assigned to the Economic and Social Council, the Trusteeship Council, and, as required, to other organs of the United Nations. These staffs shall form a part of the Secretariat.

3. The paramount consideration in the employment of the staff and in the determination of the conditions of service shall be the necessity of securing the highest standards of efficiency, competence, and integrity. Due regard shall be paid to the importance of recruiting the staff on as wide a geographical basis as possible.

CHAPTER XVI—MISCELLANEOUS PROVISIONS

ARTICLE 102

1. Every treaty and every international agreement entered into by any Member of the United Nations after the present Charter comes into force shall as soon as possible be registered with the Secretariat and published by it.

2. No party to any such treaty or international agreement which has not been registered in accordance with the provisions of paragraph 1 of this Article may invoke that treaty or agreement before any organ of the United Nations.

ARTICLE 103

In the event of a conflict between the obligations of the Members of the United Nations under the present Charter and their obligations under any other international agreement, their obligations under the present Charter shall prevail.

ARTICLE 104

The Organization shall enjoy in the territory of each of its Members such legal capacity as may be necessary for the exercise of its functions and the fulfillment of its purposes.

ARTICLE 105

1. The Organization shall enjoy in the territory of each of its Members such privileges and immunities as are necessary for the fulfillment of its purposes.

2. Representatives of the Members of the United Nations and officials of the Organization shall similarly enjoy such privileges and immunities as are necessary for the independent exercise of their functions in connection with the Organization.

3. The General Assembly may make recommendations with a view to determining the details of the application of paragraphs 1 and 2 of this Article or may propose conventions to the Members of the United Nations for this purpose.

CHAPTER XVII—TRANSITIONAL SECURITY ARRANGEMENTS

ARTICLE 106

Pending the coming into force of such special agreements referred to in Article 43 as in the opinion of the Security Council enable it to begin the exercise of its responsibilities under Article 42, the parties to the Four-Nation Declaration, signed in Moscow, October 30, 1943, and France, shall, in accordance with the provisions of paragraph 5 of that Declaration, consult with one another and as occasion requires with other Members of the United Nations with a view to such joint action on behalf of the Organization as may be necessary for the purpose of maintaining international peace and security.

ARTICLE 107

Nothing in the present Charter shall invalidate or preclude action, in relation to any state which during the Second World War has been an enemy of any signatory to the present Charter, taken or authorized as a result of that war by the Governments having responsibility for such action.

CHAPTER XVIII—AMENDMENTS

ARTICLE 108

Amendments to the present Charter shall come into force for all Members of the United Nations when they have been adopted by a vote of two thirds of the members of the General Assembly and ratified in accordance with their respective constitutional processes by two thirds of the Members of the United Nations, including all the permanent members of the Security Council.

ARTICLE 109 [5]

1. A General Conference of the Members of the United Nations for the purpose of reviewing the present Charter may be held at a date and place to be fixed by a two-thirds vote of the members of the General Assembly and by a vote of any nine members of the Security Council. Each Member of the United Nations shall have one vote in the conference.

2. Any alteration of the present Charter recommended by a two-thirds vote of the conference shall take effect when ratified in accordance with their respective constitutional processes by two-thirds of the Members of the United Nations including all the permanent members of the Security Council.

3. If such a conference has not been held before the tenth annual session of the General Assembly following the coming into force of the present Charter, the proposal to call such a conference shall be placed on the agenda of that session of the General Assembly, and the conference shall be held if so decided by a majority vote of the members of the General Assembly and by a vote of any seven members of the Security Council.

CHAPTER XIX—RATIFICATION AND SIGNATURE

ARTICLE 110

1. The present Charter shall be ratified by the signatory states in accordance with their respective constitutional processes.

2. The ratification shall be deposited with the Government of the United States of America, which shall notify all the signatory states of each deposit as well as the Secretary-General of the Organization when he has been appointed.

3. The present Charter shall come into force upon the deposit of ratifications by the Republic of China, France, the Union of Soviet Socialist Republics, the United Kingdom of Great Britain and

Northern Ireland, and the United States of America, and by a majority of other signatory states. A protocol of the ratifications deposited shall thereupon be drawn up by the Government of the United States of America which shall communicate copies thereof to all the signatory states.

4. The states signatory to the present Charter which ratify it after it has come into force will become original Members of the United Nations on the date of the deposit of their respective ratifications.

ARTICLE 111

The present Charter, of which the Chinese, French, Russian, English, and Spanish texts are equally authentic, shall remain deposited in the archives of the Government of the United States of America. Duly certified copies thereof shall be transmitted by that Government to the Governments of the other signatory states.

2. International Court of Justice

a. Statute of the International Court of Justice[1] (with reservation)[2]

Signed at San Francisco, June 26, 1945; Ratification advised by the Senate, July 28, 1945; Ratified by the President, August 8, 1945; Ratification deposited, August 8, 1945; Effective, October 24, 1945; Proclaimed by the President, October 31, 1945

ARTICLE 1

The International Court of Justice established by the Charter of the United Nations as the principle judicial organ of the United nations shall be constituted and shall function in accordance with the provisions of the present Statute.

CHAPTER I—ORGANIZATION OF THE COURT

ARTICLE 2

The Court shall be composed of a body of independent judges, elected regardless of their nationality from among persons of high moral character, who possess the qualifications required in their respective countries for appointment to the highest judicial offices, or are jurisconsults of recognized competence in international law.

ARTICLE 3

1. The Court shall consist of fifteen members, no two of whom may be nationals of the same state.
2. A person who for the purposes of membership in the Court could be regarded as a national of more than one state shall be deemed to be a national of the one in which he ordinarily exercises civil and political rights.

ARTICLE 4

1. The members of the Court shall be elected by the General Assembly and by the Security Council from a list of persons nominated by the national groups in the Permanent Court of Arbitration, in accordance with the following provisions.
2. In the case of Members of the United Nations not represented in the Permanent Court of Arbitration, candidates shall be nominated by national groups appointed for this purpose by their governments under the same conditions as those prescribed for members of the Permanent Court of Arbitration by Article 44 of the

[1] 59 Stat. 1055; TS 993: 3 Bevans 1153 at 1179. Also see chapter XIV of the Charter of the United Nations. The Statute of the International Court of Justice is annexed to the Charter of the United Nations.

[2] Declaration with Connally Reservation signed by the President August 14, 1956 (61 Stat. 1218; TIAS 1598; 4 Bevans 140; 1 UNTS 9).

Convention of The Hague of 1907 for the pacific settlement of international disputes.

3. The conditions under which a state which is a party to the present Statute but is not a Member of the United Nations may participate in electing the members of the Court shall, in the absence of a special agreement, be laid down by the General Assembly upon recommendation of the Security Council.

ARTICLE 5

1. At least three months before the date of the election, the Secretary-General of the United Nations shall address a written request to the members of the Permanent Court of Arbitration belonging to the states which are parties to the present Statute, and to the members of the national groups appointed under Article 4, paragraph 2, inviting them to undertake, within a given time, by national groups, the nomination of persons in a position to accept the duties of a member of the Court.

2. No group may nominate more than four persons, not more than two of whom shall be of their own nationality. In no case may the number of candidates nominated by a group be more than double the number of seats to be filled.

ARTICLE 6

Before making these nominations, each national group is recommended to consult its highest court of justice, its legal faculties and schools of law, and its national academies and national sections of international academies devoted to the study of law.

ARTICLE 7

1. The Secretary-General shall prepare a list in alphabetical order of all the persons thus nominated. Save as provided in article 12, paragraph 2, these shall be the only persons eligible.

2. The Secretary-General shall submit this list to the General Assembly and to the Security Council.

ARTICLE 8

The General Assembly and the Security Council shall proceed independently of one another to elect the members of the Court.

ARTICLE 9

At every election, the electors shall bear in mind not only that the persons to be elected should individually possess the qualifications required, but also that in the body as a whole the representation of the main forms of civilization and of the principal legal systems of the world should be assured.

ARTICLE 10

1. Those candidates who obtain an absolute majority of votes in the General Assembly and in the Security Council shall be considered as elected.

2. Any vote of the Security Council, whether for the election of judges or for the appointment of members of the conference envisaged in article 12, shall be taken without any distinction between permanent and non-permanent members of the Security Council.

3. In the event of more than one national of the same state obtaining an absolute majority of the votes both of the General Assembly and of the Security Council, the eldest of these only shall be considered as elected.

ARTICLE 11

If, after the first meeting held for the purpose of the election, one or more seats remain to be filled, a second and, if necessary, a third meeting shall take place.

ARTICLE 12

1. If, after the third meeting, one or more seats still remain unfilled, a joint conference consisting of six members, three appointed by the General Assembly and three by the Security Council, may be formed at any time at the request of either the General Assembly or the Security Council, for the purpose of choosing by the vote of an absolute majority one name for each seat still vacant, to submit to the General Assembly and the Security Council for their respective acceptance.

2. If the joint conference is unanimously agreed upon any person who fulfills the required conditions, he may be included in its list, even though he was not included in the list of nominations referred to in Article 7.

3. If the joint conference is satisfied that it will not be successful in procuring an election, those members of the Court who have already been elected shall, within a period to be fixed by the Security Council, proceed to fill the vacant seats by selection from among those candidates who have obtained votes either in the General Assembly or in the Security Council.

4. In the event of an equality of votes among the judges, the eldest judge shall have a casting vote.

ARTICLE 13

1. The members of the Court shall be elected for nine years and may be re-elected; provided, however, that of the judges elected at the first election, the terms of five judges shall expire at the end of three years and the terms of five more judges shall expire at the end of six years.

2. The judges whose terms are to expire at the end of the abovementioned initial periods of three and six years shall be chosen by lot to be drawn by the Secretary-General immediately after the first election has been completed.

3. The members of the Court shall continue to discharge their duties until their places have been filled. Though replaced, they shall finish any cases which they may have begun.

4. In the case of the resignation of a member of the Court, the resignation shall be addressed to the President of the Court for transmission to the Secretary-General. This last notification makes the place vacant.

ARTICLE 14

Vacancies shall be filled by the same method as that laid down for the first election, subject to the following provision: the Secretary-General shall, within one month of the occurrence of the vacancy, proceed to issue the invitations provided for in Article 5, and the date of the election shall be fixed by the Security Council.

ARTICLE 15

A member of the Court elected to replace a member whose term of office has not expired shall hold office for the remainder of his predecessor's term.

ARTICLE 16

1. No member of the Court may exercise any political or administrative function, or engage in any other occupation of a professional nature.
2. Any doubt on this point shall be settled by the decision of the Court.

ARTICLE 17

1. No member of the Court may act as agent, counsel, or advocate in any case.
2. No member may participate in the decision of any case in which he has previously taken part as agent, counsel, or advocate for one of the parties, or as a member of a national or international court, or of a commission of enquiry, or in any other capacity.
3. Any doubt on this point shall be settled by the decision of the Court.

ARTICLE 18

1. No member of the Court can be dismissed unless, in the unanimous opinion of the other members, he has ceased to fulfill the required conditions.
2. Formal notification thereof shall be made to the Secretary-General by the Registrar.
3. This notification makes the place vacant.

ARTICLE 19

The members of the Court, when engaged on the business of the Court, shall enjoy diplomatic privileges and immunities.

ARTICLE 20

Every member of the Court shall, before taking up his duties, make a solemn declaration in open court that he will exercise his powers impartially and conscientiously.

ARTICLE 21

1. The Court shall elect its President and Vice-President for three years; they may be re-elected.
2. The Court shall appoint its Registrar and may provide for the appointment of such other officers as may be necessary.

ARTICLE 22

1. The seat of the Court shall be established at The Hague. This, however, shall not prevent the Court from sitting and exercising its functions elsewhere whenever the Court considers it desirable.

2. The President and the Registrar shall reside at the seat of the Court.

ARTICLE 23

1. The Court shall remain permanently in session, except during the judicial vacations, the dates and duration of which shall be fixed by the Court.

2. Members of the Court are entitled to periodic leave, the dates and duration of which shall be fixed by the Court, having in mind the distance between The Hague and the home of each judge.

3. Members of the Court shall be bound, unless they are on leave or prevented from attending by illness or other serious reasons duly explained to the President, to hold themselves permanently at the disposal of the Court.

ARTICLE 24

1. If, for some special reason, a member of the Court considers that he should not take part in the decision of a particular case, he shall so inform the President.

2. If the President considers that for some special reason one of the members of the Court should not sit in a particular case, he shall give him notice accordingly.

3. If in any such case the member of the Court and the President disagree, the matter shall be settled by the decision of the Court.

ARTICLE 25

1. The full Court shall sit except when it is expressly provided otherwise in the present Statute.

2. Subject to the condition that the number of judges available to constitute the Court is not thereby reduced below eleven, the Rules of the Court may provide for allowing one or more judges, according to circumstances and in rotation, to be dispensed from sitting.

3. A quorum of nine judges shall suffice to constitute the Court.

ARTICLE 26

1. The Court may from time to time form one or more chambers, composed of three or more judges as the Court may determine, for dealing with particular categories of cases; for example, labor cases and cases relating to transit and communications.

2. The Court may at any time form a chamber for dealing with a particular case. The number of judges to constitute such a chamber shall be determined by the Court with the approval of the parties.

3. Cases shall be heard and determined by the chambers provided for in this Article if the parties so request.

ARTICLE 27

A judgment given by any of the chambers provided for in Articles 26 and 29 shall be considered as rendered by the Court.

ARTICLE 28

The chambers provided for in Articles 26 and 29 may, with the consent of the parties, sit and exercise their functions elsewhere than at The Hague.

ARTICLE 29

With a view to the speedy dispatch of business, the Court shall form annually a chamber composed of five judges which, at the request of the parties, may hear and determine cases by summary procedure. In addition, two judges shall be selected for the purpose of replacing judges who find it impossible to sit.

ARTICLE 30

1. The Court shall frame rules for carrying out its function. In particular, it shall lay down rules of procedure.
2. The Rules of the Court may provide for assessors to sit with the Court or with any of its chambers, without the right to vote.

ARTICLE 31

1. Judges of the nationality of each of the parties shall retain their right to sit in the case before the Court.
2. If the Court includes upon the Bench a judge of the nationality of one of the parties, any other party may choose a person to sit as judge. Such person shall be chosen preferably from among those persons who have been nominated as candidates as provided in Articles 4 and 5.
3. If the Court includes upon the Bench no judge of the nationality of the parties, each of these parties may proceed to choose a judge as provided in paragraph 2 of this Article.
4. The provisions of this Article shall apply to the case of Articles 26 and 29. In such cases, the President shall request one or, if necessary, two of the members of the Court of the nationality of the parties concerned, and, failing such, or if they are unable to be present, to the judges specially chosen by the parties.
5. Should there be several parties in the same interest, they shall, for the purpose of the preceding provisions, be reckoned as one party only. Any doubt upon this point shall be settled by the decision of the Court.
6. Judges chosen as laid down in paragraphs 2, 3, and 4 of this Article shall fulfill the conditions required by Articles 2, 17 (paragraph 2), 20, and 24 of the present Statute. They shall take part in the decision on terms of complete equality with their colleagues.

ARTICLE 32

1. Each member of the Court shall receive an annual salary.
2. The President shall receive a special annual allowance.
3. The Vice-President shall receive a special allowance for every day on which he acts as President.

4. The judges chosen under Article 31, other than members of the Court, shall receive compensation for each day on which they exercise their functions.

5. These salaries, allowances, and compensation shall be fixed by the General Assembly. They may not be decreased during the term of office.

6. The salary of the Registrar shall be fixed by the General Assembly on the proposal of the Court.

7. Regulations made by the General Assembly shall fix the conditions under which retirement pensions may be given to members of the Court and to the Registrar, and the conditions under which members of the Court and the Registrar shall have their traveling expenses refunded.

8. The above salaries, allowances, and compensation shall be free of all taxation.

ARTICLE 33

The expenses of the Court shall be borne by the United Nations in such a manner as shall be decided by the General Assembly.

CHAPTER II—COMPETENCE OF THE COURT

ARTICLE 34

1. Only states may be parties before the Court.

2. The Court, subject to and in conformity with its Rules, may request of public international organizations information relevant to cases before it, and shall receive such information presented by such organizations on their own initiative.

3. Whenever the construction of the constituent instrument of a public international organization or of an international convention adopted thereunder is in question in a case before the Court, the Registrar shall so notify the public international organization concerned and shall communicate to it copies of all the written proceedings.

ARTICLE 35

1. The Court shall be open to the states parties to the present Statute.

2. The conditions under which the Court shall be open to other states shall, subject to the special provisions contained in treaties in force, be laid down by the Security Council, but in no case shall such conditions place the parties in a position of inequality before the Court.

3. When a state which is not a Member of the United Nations is a party to a case, the Court shall fix the amount which that party is to contribute towards the expenses of the Court. This provision shall not apply if such state is bearing a share of the expenses of the Court.

ARTICLE 36

1. The jurisdiction of the Court comprises all cases which the parties refer to it and all matters specifically provided for in the

Charter of the United Nations or in treaties and conventions in force.

2. The states parties to the present Statute may at any time declare that they recognize as compulsory *ipso facto* and without special agreement, in relation to any other state accepting the same obligation, the jurisdiction of the Court in all legal disputes concerning:

a. the interpretation of a treaty;

b. any question of international law;

c. the existence of any fact which, if established, would constitute a breach of an international obligation;

d. the nature or extent of the reparation to be made for the breach of an international obligation.

3. The declarations referred to above may be made unconditionally or on condition of reciprocity on the part of several or certain states, or for a certain time.

4. Such declarations shall be deposited with the Secretary-General of the United Nations, who shall transmit copies thereof to the parties to the Statute and to the Registrar of the Court.

5. Declarations made under Article 36 of the Statute of the Permanent Court of International Justice and which are still in force shall be deemed, as between the parties to the present Statute, to be acceptances to the compulsory jurisdiction of the International Court of Justice for the period which they still have to run in accordance with their terms.

6. In the event of a dispute as to whether the Court has jurisdiction, the matter shall be settled by the decision of the Court.

ARTICLE 37

Whenever a treaty or convention in force provides for reference of a matter to a tribunal to have been instituted by the League of Nations, or to the Permanent Court of International Justice, the matter shall, as between the parties to the present Statute, be referred to the International Court of Justice.

ARTICLE 38

1. The Court, whose function is to decide in accordance with international law such disputes as are submitted to it, shall apply:

a. international conventions, whether general or particular, establishing rules expressly recognized by the contesting states;

b. international custom, as evidence of a general practice accepted as law;

c. the general principles of law recognized by civilized nations;

d. subject to the provisions of Article 59, judicial decisions and the teachings of the most highly qualified publicists of the various nations, as subsidiary means for the determination of rules of law.

2. This provision shall not prejudice the power of the Court to decide a case *ex aequo et bono,* if the parties agree thereto.

CHAPTER III—PROCEDURE

ARTICLE 39

1. The official languages of the Court shall be French and English. If the parties agree that the case shall be conducted in French, the judgment shall be delivered in French. If the parties agree that the case shall be conducted in English, the judgment shall be delivered in English.

2. In the absence of an agreement as to which language shall be employed, each party may, in the pleadings, use the language which it prefers; the decision of the Court shall be given in French and English. In this case the Court shall at the same time determine which of the two texts shall be considered as authoritative.

3. The Court shall, at the request of any party, authorize a language other than French or English to be used by that party.

ARTICLE 40

1. Cases are brought before the Court, as the case may be, either by the notification of the special agreement or by a written application addressed to the Registrar. In either case the subject of the dispute and the parties shall be indicated.

2. The Registrar shall forthwith communicate the application to all concerned.

3. He shall also notify the Members of the United Nations through the Secretary-General, and also any other states entitled to appear before the Court.

ARTICLE 41

1. The Court shall have the power to indicate, if it considers that circumstances so require, any provisional measures which ought to be taken to preserve the respective rights of either party.

2. Pending the final decision, notice of the measures suggested shall forthwith be given to the parties and to the Security Council.

ARTICLE 42

1. The parties shall be represented by agents.

2. They may have the assistance of counsel or advocates before the Court.

3. The agents, counsel, and advocates of parties before the Court shall enjoy the privileges and immunities necessary to the independent exercise of their duties.

ARTICLE 43

1. The procedure shall consist of two parts: written and oral.

2. The written proceedings shall consist of the communication to the Court and to the parties of memorials, counter-memorials and, if necessary, replies; also all papers and documents in support.

3. These communications shall be made through the Registrar, in the order and within the time fixed by the Court.

4. A certified copy of every document produced by one party shall be communicated to the other party.

5. The oral proceedings shall consist of the hearing by the Court of witnesses, experts, agents, counsel, and advocates.

ARTICLE 44

1. For the service of all notices upon persons other than the agents, counsel, and advocates, the Court shall apply direct to the government of the state upon whose territory the notice has to be served.

2. The same provision shall apply whenever steps are to be taken to procure evidence on the spot.

ARTICLE 45

The hearing shall be under the control of the President or, if he is unable to preside, of the Vice-President; if neither is able to preside, the senior judge present shall preside.

ARTICLE 46

The hearing in Court shall be public, unless the Court shall decide otherwise, or unless the parties demand that the public be not admitted.

ARTICLE 47

1. Minutes shall be made at each hearing and signed by the Registrar and the President.

2. These minutes alone shall be authentic.

ARTICLE 48

The Court shall make orders for the conduct of the case, shall decide the form and time in which each party must conclude its arguments, and make all arrangements connected with the taking of evidence.

ARTICLE 49

The Court may, even before the hearing begins, call upon the agents to produce any document or to supply any explanations. Formal note shall be taken of any refusal.

ARTICLE 50

The Court may, at any time, entrust any individual, body, bureau, commission, or other organization that it may select, with the task of carrying out an enquiry or giving an expert opinion.

ARTICLE 51

During the hearing any relevant questions are to be put to the witnesses and experts under the conditions laid down by the Court in the rules of procedure referred to in Article 30.

ARTICLE 52

After the Court has received the proofs and evidence within the time specified for the purpose, it may refuse to accept any further oral or written evidence that one party may desire to present unless the other side consents.

ARTICLE 53

1. Whenever one of the parties does not appear before the Court, or fails to defend its case, the other party may call upon the Court to decide in favor of its claim.

2. The Court must, before doing so, satisfy itself, not only that it has jurisdiction in accordance with Articles 36 and 37, but also that the claim is well founded in fact and law.

ARTICLE 54

1. When, subject to the control of the Court, the agents, counsel, and advocates have completed their presentation of the case, the President shall declare the hearing closed.

2. The Court shall withdraw to consider the judgment.

3. The deliberations of the Court shall take place in private and remain secret.

ARTICLE 55

1. All questions shall be decided by a majority of the judges present.

2. In the event of an equality of votes, the President or the judge who acts in his place shall have a casting vote.

ARTICLE 56

1. The judgment shall state the reasons on which it is based.

2. It shall contain the names of the judges who have taken part in the decision.

ARTICLE 57

If the judgment does not represent in whole or in part the unanimous opinion of the judges, any judge shall be entitled to deliver a separate opinion.

ARTICLE 58

The judgment shall be signed by the President and by the Registrar. It shall be read in open court, due notice having been given to the agents.

ARTICLE 59

The decision of the Court has no binding force except between the parties and in respect of that particular case.

ARTICLE 60

The judgment is final and without appeal. In the event of dispute as to the meaning or scope of the judgment, the Court shall construe it upon the request of any party.

ARTICLE 61

1. An application for revision of a judgment may be made only when it is based upon the discovery of some fact of such a nature as to be a decisive factor, which fact was, when the judgment was

given, unknown to the Court and also to the party claiming revision, always provided that such ignorance was not due to negligence.

2. The proceedings for revision shall be open by a judgment of the Court expressly recording the existence of the new fact, recognizing that it has such a character as to lay the case open to revision, and declaring the application admissible on this ground.

3. The Court may require previous compliance with the terms of the judgment before it admits proceedings in revision.

4. The application for revision must be made at least within six months of the discovery of the new fact.

5. No application for revision may be made after the lapse of ten years from the date of the judgment.

ARTICLE 62

1. Should a state consider that it has an interest of a legal nature which may be affected by the decision in the case, it may submit a request to the Court to be permitted to intervene.

2. It shall be for the Court to decide upon this request.

ARTICLE 63

1. Whenever the construction of a convention to which states other than those concerned in the case are parties is in question, the Registrar shall notify all such states forthwith.

2. Every state so notified has the right to intervene in the proceedings; but if it uses this right, the construction given by the judgment will be equally binding upon it.

ARTICLE 64

Unless otherwise decided by the Court, each party shall bear its own costs.

Chapter IV—Advisory Opinions

ARTICLE 65

1. The Court may give an advisory opinion on any legal question at the request of whatever body may be authorized by or in accordance with the Charter of the United Nations to make such a request.

2. Questions upon which the advisory opinion of the Court is asked shall be laid before the Court by means of a written request containing an exact statement of the question upon which an opinion is required, and accompanied by all documents likely to throw light upon the question.

ARTICLE 66

1. The Registrar shall forthwith give notice of the request for an advisory opinion to all states entitled to appear before the Court.

2. The Registrar shall also, by means of a special and direct communication, notify any state entitled to appear before the Court or international organization considered by the Court, or, should it not be sitting, by the President, as likely to be able to furnish information on the question, that the Court will be prepared to receive,

within a time limit to be fixed by the President, written statements, or to hear, at a public sitting to be held for the purpose, oral statements relating to the question.

3. Should any such state entitled to appear before the Court have failed to receive the special communication referred to in paragraph 2 of this Article, such state may express a desire to submit a written statement or to be heard; and the Court will decide.

4. States and organizations having presented written or oral statements or both shall be permitted to comment on the statements made by other states or organizations in the form, to the extent, and within the time limits which the Court, or, should it not be sitting, the President, shall decide in each particular case. Accordingly, the Registrar shall in due time communicate any such written statements to states and organizations having submitted similar statements.

ARTICLE 67

The Court shall deliver its advisory opinions in open court, notice having been given to the Secretary-General and to the representatives of Members of the United Nations, of other states and of international organizations immediately concerned.

ARTICLE 68

In the exercise of its advisory functions the Court shall further be guided by the provisions of the present Statute which apply in contentious cases to the extent to which it recognizes them to be applicable.

CHAPTER V—AMENDMENT

ARTICLE 69

Amendments to the present Statute shall be effected by the same procedure as is provided by the Charter of the United Nations for amendments to that Charter, subject however to any provisions which the General Assembly upon recommendation of the Security Council may adopt concerning the participation of states which are parties to the present Statute but are not Members of the United Nations.

ARTICLE 70

The Court shall have power to propose such amendments to the present Statute as it may deem necessary, through written communications to the Secretary-General, for consideration in conformity with the provisions of Article 69.

b. Declaration of United States Recognition of Compulsory Jurisdiction [1] (with "Connally Reservation")

Declaration by the President, signed August 14, 1946, respecting recognition by the United States of America of the compulsory jurisdiction of the International Court of Justice. Deposited with the Secretary General of the United Nations, August 26, 1946

DECLARATION ON THE PART OF THE UNITED STATES OF AMERICA

I, Harry S. Truman, President of the United States of America, declare on behalf of the United States of America, under Article 36, paragraph 2, of the Statute of the International Court of Justice, and in accordance with the Resolution of August 2, 1946,[2] of the Senate of the United States of America (two-thirds of the Senators present concurring therein), that the United States of America recognizes as compulsory *ipso facto* and without special agreement, in relation to any other state accepting the same obligation, the jurisdiction of the International Court of Justice in all legal disputes hereafter arising concerning.

a. the interpretation of a treaty;

b. any question of international law;

c. the existence of any fact which, if established, would constitute a breach of an international obligation;

d. the nature or extent of the reparation to be made for the breach of an international obligation;

Provided, that this declaration shall not apply to

a. disputes the solution of which the parties shall entrust to other tribunals by virtue of agreements already in existence or which may be concluded in the future; or

b. disputes with regard to matters which are essentially within the domestic jurisdiction of the United States of America as determined by the United States [3] of America; or

c. disputes arising under a multilateral treaty, unless (1) all parties to the treaty affected by the decision are also parties to the case before the Court, or (2) the United States of America specially agrees to jurisdiction; and

Provided further, that this declaration shall remain in force for a period of five years and thereafter until the expiration of six months after notice may be given to terminate this declaration.

DONE at Washington this fourteenth day of August 1946.

HARRY S. TRUMAN.

---

[1] TIAS 1598; 4 Bevans 140.

[2] Senate Resolution 196, 79th Congress, adopted August 3, 1946 (61 Stat. 1218).

[3] The words "as determined by the United States" are often cited as the "Connally Reservation."

c. United States Modification Respecting Compulsory Jurisdiction

6 April 1984.

I have the honor on behalf of the Government of the United States of America to refer to the Declaration of my Government of August 26, 1946, concerning the acceptance of the United States of America of the compulsory jurisdiction of the International Court of Justice, and to state that the aforesaid Declaration shall not apply to disputes with any Central American State or arising out of or related to events in Central America, any of which disputes shall be settled in such manner as the parties to them may agree.

Notwithstanding the terms of the aforesaid Declaration, this *proviso* shall take effect immediately and shall remain in force for two years, so as to foster the continuing regional dispute settlement process which seeks a negotiated solution to the interrelated political, economic and security problems of Central America.

(*Signed*) GEORGE SHULTZ,
Secretary of State of the United States of America.

d. United States Termination of Declaration Respecting Compulsory Jurisdiction [1]

DEAR MR. SECRETARY-GENERAL: I have the honor on behalf of the Government of the United States of America to refer to the declaration of my Government of 26 August 1946, as modified by my note of 6 April 1984, concerning the acceptance by the United States of America of the compulsory jurisdiction of the International Court of Justice, and to state that the aforesaid declaration is hereby terminated, with effect six months from the date hereof.

Sincerely yours,

(*Signed*) GEORGE P. SHULTZ,
Secretary of State of the United States of America.

[1] Delivered to the Secretary-General of the United Nations at 10:30 A.M., October 7, 1985.

3. Agreement Between the United Nations and the United States Regarding the Headquarters of the United Nations [1]

Agreement with Annexes signed at Lake Success, N.Y., June 26, 1947; Entered into force, by an exchange of notes between the U.S. Representative to the United Nations, under instruction of the President and the Secretary-General of the United Nations, November 21, 1947; Supplemented by Agreements of February 9, 1966, as amended, August 28, 1969, and December 10, 1980

THE UNITED NATIONS AND THE UNITED STATES OF AMERICA,

Desiring to conclude an agreement for the purpose of carrying out the Resolution adopted by the General Assembly on 14 December 1946 to establish the seat of the United Nations in The City of New York and to regulate questions arising as a result thereof;

Have appointed as their representatives for this purpose:

The United Nations:
TRYGVE LIE,
Secretary-General,

and

The United States of America:
GEORGE C. MARSHALL,
Secretary of State,

Who have agreed as follows:

ARTICLE I—DEFINITIONS

SECTION 1

In this agreement:

(a) the expression "headquarters district" means (1) the area defined as such in Annex 1, (2) any other lands or buildings which from time to time may be included therein by supplemental agreement with the appropriate American authorities; [2]

[1] 61 Stat. 3416; TIAS 1676; 12 Bevans 956; 11 UNTS 11. The United Nations Headquarters Agreement Act (Public Law 80–357; 61 Stat. 756) authorizing this agreement can be found in *Legislation on Foreign Relations vol. II–B,* sec. H.

[2] An agreement supplementing the original agreement was signed at New York, February 9, 1966, and entered into force the same day (17 UST 74; TIAS 5961). The agreement adds new land to that described in Annex I of the original agreement signed June 26, 1947 in order to accommodate the United Nation's expanding needs. The additions include another building (801 United Nations Plaza) and part of the Alcoa Plaza Associates Building.

This supplement was amended by an agreement signed at New York December 8, 1966 and entered into force the same day (17 UST 2319; TIAS 6176). The agreement adds the sixth floor of the Alcoa Plaza Associates Building to the headquarters district.

On August 28, 1969 a second supplemental agreement regarding the U.N. Headquarters was signed at New York and entered into force (20 UST 2810; TIAS 6750; 687 UNTS 408). This agreement added three floors from two other buildings to those above. There was also a clause allowing further additions, if space became available in those two buildings.

A third supplemental agreement was signed and entered into force on December 10, 1980 (32 UST 4414; TIAS 9955). This agreement added to the Headquarters District, floor space from premises located at One United Plaza (UNDC Building), and 605 Third Avenue (Burroughs Building); all buildings located at 30–12 41st Avenue, Long Island City; and floor space at 331 East 38th Street (UNICEF Greeting Card Operation), 821 UN Plaza (Turkish Mission Building),

(b) the expression "appropriate American authorities" means such federal, state, or local authorities in the United States as may be appropriate in the context and in accordance with the laws and customs of the United States, including the laws and customs of the state and local government involved;

(c) the expression "General Convention" means the Convention on the Privileges and Immunities of the United Nations approved by the General Assembly of the United Nations 13 February 1946, as acceded to by the United States;

(d) the expression "United Nations" means the international organization established by the Charter of the United Nations, hereinafter referred to as the "Charter";

(e) the expression "Secretary-General" means the Secretary- General of the United Nations.

ARTICLE II—THE HEADQUARTERS DISTRICT

SECTION 2

The seat of the United Nations shall be the headquarters district.

SECTION 3

The appropriate American authorities shall take whatever action may be necessary to assure that the United Nations shall not be dispossessed of its property in the headquarters district, except as provided in Section 22 in the event that the United Nations ceases to use the same; provided that the United Nations shall reimburse the appropriate American authorities for any costs incurred, after consultation with the United Nations, in liquidating by eminent domain proceedings or otherwise any adverse claims.

SECTION 4

(a) The United Nations may establish and operate in the headquarters district:

(1) its own short-wave sending and receiving radio broadcasting facilities (including emergency link equipment) which may be used on the same frequencies (within the tolerances prescribed for the broadcasting service by applicable United States regulations) for radiotelegraph, radioteletype, radiotelephone, radiotelephoto, and similar services;

(2) one point-to-point circuit between the headquarters district and the office of the United Nations in Geneva (using single sideband equipment) to be used exclusively for the exchange of broadcasting programs and interoffice communications;

(3) low power micro-wave, low or medium frequency facilities for communication within headquarters buildings only, or such other buildings as may temporarily be used by the United Nations;

(4) facilities for point-to-point communication to the same extent and subject to the same conditions as permitted under applicable rules and regulations for amateur operation in the

345 Park Avenue South, 866 UN Plaza (ALCOA Building), 666 Third Avenue (Chrysler Building), 485 Lexington Avenue, and 801 United Nations Plaza.

United States, except that such rules and regulations shall not be applied in a manner consistent with the inviolability of the headquarters district provided by Section 9(a);

(5) such other radio facilities as may be specified by supplemental agreement between the United Nations and the appropriate American authorities.

(b) The United Nations shall make arrangements for the operation of the services referred to in this section with the International Telecommunications Union, the appropriate agencies of the Government of the United States and the appropriate agencies of other affected governments with regard to all frequencies and similar matters.

(c) The facilities provided for in this section may, to the extent necessary for efficient operation, be established and operated outside the headquarters district. The appropriate American authorities will, on request of the United Nations, make arrangements, on such terms and in such manner as may be agreed upon by supplemental agreement, for the acquisition or use by the United Nations of appropriate premises for such purposes and the inclusion of such premises in the headquarters district.

SECTION 5

In the event that the United Nations should find it necessary and desirable to establish and operate an aerodrome, the conditions for the location, use and operation of such an aerodrome and the conditions under which there shall be entry into and exit therefrom shall be the subject of a supplemental agreement.

SECTION 6

In the event that the United Nations should propose to organize its own postal service, the conditions under which such service shall be set up shall be the subject of a supplemental agreement.

ARTICLE III—LAW AND AUTHORITY IN THE HEADQUARTERS DISTRICT

SECTION 7

(a) The headquarters district shall be under the control and authority of the United Nations as provided in this agreement.

(b) Except as otherwise provided in this agreement or in the General Convention, the federal, state and local law of the United States shall apply within the headquarters district.

(c) Except as otherwise provided in this agreement or in the General Convention, the federal, state and local courts of the United States shall have jurisdiction over acts done and transactions taking place in the headquarters district as provided in applicable federal, state and local laws.

(d) The federal, state and local courts of the United States, when dealing with cases arising out of or relating to acts done or transactions taking place in the headquarters district, shall take into account the regulations enacted by the United Nations under Section 8.

SECTION 8

The United Nations shall have the power to make regulations, operative within the headquarters district, for the purpose of establishing therein conditions in all respects necessary for the full execution of its functions. No federal, state or local law or regulation of the United States which is inconsistent with a regulation of the United Nations authorized by this section shall, to the extent of such inconsistency, be applicable within the headquarters district. Any dispute, between the United Nations and the United States, as to whether a regulation of the United Nations is authorized by this section or as to whether a federal, state or local law or regulation is inconsistent with any regulation of the United Nations authorized by this section, shall be promptly settled as provided in Section 21. Pending such settlement, the regulation of the United Nations shall apply, and the federal, state or local law or regulation shall be inapplicable in the headquarters district to the extent that the United Nations claims it to be inconsistent with the regulation of the United Nations. This section shall not prevent the reasonable application of fire protection regulations of the appropriate American authorities.

SECTION 9

(a) The headquarters district shall be inviolable. Federal, state or local officers or officials of the United States, whether administrative, judicial, military or police, shall not enter the headquarters district to perform any official duties therein except with the consent of and under conditions agreed to by the Secretary-General. The service of legal process, including the seizure of private property, may take place within the headquarters district only with the consent of and under conditions approved by the Secretary-General.

(b) Without prejudice to the provisions of the General Convention or Article IV of this agreement, the United Nations shall prevent the headquarters district from becoming a refuge either for persons who are avoiding arrest under the federal, state, or local law of the United States or are required by the Government of the United States for extradition to another country, or for persons who are endeavoring to avoid service of legal process.

SECTION 10

The United Nations may expel or exclude persons from the headquarters district for violation of its regulations adopted under Section 8 or for other cause. Persons who violate such regulations shall be subject to other penalties or to detention under arrest only in accordance with the provisions of such laws or regulations as may be adopted by the appropriate American authorities.

Article IV—Communications and Transit

SECTION 11

The federal, state or local authorities of the United States shall not impose any impediments to transit to or from the headquarters district of (1) representatives of Members or officials of the United

Nations, or of specialized agencies as defined in Article 57, paragraph 2, of the Charter, or the families of such representatives or officials, (2) experts performing missions for the United Nations or for such specialized agencies, (3) representatives of the press, or of radio, film or other information agencies, who have been accredited by the United Nations (or by such a specialized agency) in its discretion after consultation with the United States, (4) representatives of nongovernmental organizations recognized by the United Nations for the purpose of consultation under Article 71 of the Charter, or (5) other persons invited to the headquarters district by the United Nations or by such specialized agency on official business. The appropriate American authorities shall afford any necessary protection to such persons while in transit to or from the headquarters district. This section does not apply to general interruptions of transportation which are to be dealt with as provided in Section 17, and does not impair the effectiveness of generally applicable laws and regulations as to the operation of means of transportation.[3]

SECTION 12

The provisions of Section 11 shall be applicable irrespective of the relations existing between the Governments of the persons referred to in that section and the Government of the United States.

SECTION 13

(a) Laws and regulations in force in the United States regarding the entry of aliens shall not be applied in such manner as to interfere with the privileges referred to in Section 11. When visas are required for persons referred to in that Section, they shall be granted without charge and as promptly as possible.

(b) Laws and regulations in force in the United States regarding the residence of aliens shall not be applied in such manner as to interfere with the privileges referred to in Section 11 and, specifically, shall not be applied in such manner as to require any such person to leave the United States on account of any activities performed by him in his official capacity. In case of abuse of such privileges of residence by any such person in activities in the United States outside his official capacity, it is understood that the privileges referred to in Section 11 shall not be construed to grant him exemption from the laws and regulations of the United States regarding the continued residence of aliens, provided that:

(1) No proceedings shall be instituted under such laws or regulations to require any such person to leave the United States except with the prior approval of the Secretary of State of the United States. Such approval shall be given only after consultation with the appropriate Member in the case of a representative of a Member (or a member of his family) or with the Secretary-General or the principal executive officer of the

[3] See 8 U.S.C. 1101(a)(15)(C), establishing as a nonimmigrant (non quota) alien "an alien who qualifies as a person entitled to pass in transit to and from the United Nations Headquarters District and foreign countries, under the provisions of paragraphs (3), (4) and (5) of sec. 11 of the Headquarters Agreement with the United Nations (61 Stat. 758); * * *".

appropriate specialized agency in the case of any other person referred to in Section 11;

(2) A representative of the Member concerned, the Secretary-General, or the principal executive officer of the appropriate specialized agency, as the case may be, shall have the right to appear in any such proceedings on behalf of the person against whom they are instituted;

(3) Persons who are entitled to diplomatic privileges and immunities under section 15 or under the General Convention shall not be required to leave the United States otherwise than in accordance with the customary procedure applicable to diplomatic envoys accredited to the United States.

(c) This section does not prevent the requirement of reasonable evidence to establish that persons claiming the rights granted by Section 11 come within the classes described in that section, or the reasonable application of quarantine and health regulations.

(d) Except as provided above in this section and in the General Convention, the United States retains full control and authority over the entry of persons or property into the territory of the United States and the conditions under which persons may remain or reside there.

(e) The Secretary-General shall, at the request of the appropriate American authorities, enter into discussions with such authorities, with a view to making arrangements for registering the arrival and departure of persons who have been granted visas valid only for transit to and from the headquarters district and sojourn therein and in its immediate vicinity.

(f) The United Nations shall, subject to the foregoing provisions of this section, have the exclusive right to authorize or prohibit entry of persons and property into the headquarters district and to prescribe the conditions under which persons may remain or reside there.

SECTION 14

The Secretary-General and the appropriate American authorities shall, at the request of either of them, consult as to methods of facilitating entrance into the United States, and the use of available means of transportation, by persons coming from abroad, who wish to visit the headquarters district and do not enjoy the rights referred to in this Article.

Article V—Resident Representatives to the United Nations

SECTION 15

(1) Every person designated by a Member as the principal resident representative to the United Nations of such Member or as a resident representative with the rank of ambassador or minister plenipotentiary,

(2) such resident members of their staffs as may be agreed upon between the Secretary-General, the Government of the United States and the Government of the Member concerned,

(3) every person designated by a Member of a specialized agency, as defined in Article 57, paragraph 2, of the Charter, as its principal resident representative, with the rank of ambassador or minister plenipotentiary, at the headquarters of such agency in the United States, and

(4) such other principal resident representatives of members to a specialized agency and such resident members of the staffs of representatives to a specialized agency as may be agreed upon between the principal executive officer of the specialized agency, the Government of the United States and the Government of the Member concerned, shall, whether residing inside or outside the headquarters district, be entitled in the territory of the United States to the same privileges and immunities, subject to corresponding conditions and obligations, as it accords to diplomatic envoys accredited to it. In the case of Members whose governments are not recognized by the United States, such privileges and immunities need be extended to such representatives, or persons on the staffs of such representatives, only within the headquarters district, at their residences and offices outside the district, in transit between the district and such residences and offices, and in transit on official business to or from foreign countries.

ARTICLE VI—POLICE PROTECTION OF THE HEADQUARTERS DISTRICT

SECTION 16

(a) The appropriate American authorities shall exercise due diligence to ensure that the tranquility of the headquarters district is not disturbed by the unauthorized entry of groups of persons from outside or by disturbances in its immediate vicinity and shall cause to be provided on the boundaries of the headquarters district such police protection as is required for these purposes.

(b) If so requested by the Secretary-General, the appropriate American authorities shall provide a sufficient number of police for the preservation of law and order in the headquarters district, and for the removal therefrom of persons as requested under the authority of the United Nations. The United Nations shall, if requested, enter into arrangements with the appropriate American authorities to reimburse them for the reasonable cost of such services.

ARTICLE VII—PUBLIC SERVICES AND PROTECTION OF THE HEADQUARTERS DISTRICT

SECTION 17

(a) The appropriate American authorities will exercise to the extent requested by the Secretary-General the powers which they possess with respect to the supplying of public services to ensure that the headquarters district shall be supplied on equitable terms with the necessary public services, including electricity, water, gas, post, telephone, telegraph, transportation, drainage, collection of refuse, fire protection, snow removal, et cetera. In case of any interruption or threatened interruption of any such services, the appropriate American authorities will consider the needs of the United

Nations as being of equal importance with the similar needs of essential agencies of the Government of the United States, and will take steps accordingly, to ensure that the work of the United Nations is not prejudiced.

(b) Special provisions with reference to maintenance of utilities and underground construction are contained in Annex 2.

SECTION 18

The appropriate American authorities shall take all reasonable steps to ensure that the amenities of the headquarters district are not prejudiced and the purposes for which the district is required are not obstructed by any use made of the land in the vicinity of the district. The United Nations shall on its part take all reasonable steps to ensure that the amenities of the land in the vicinity of the headquarters district are not prejudiced by any use made of the land in the headquarters district by the United Nations.

SECTION 19

It is agreed that no form of racial or religious discrimination shall be permitted within the headquarters district.

Article VIII—Matters Relating to the Operation of This Agreement

SECTION 20

The Secretary-General and the appropriate American authorities shall settle by agreement the channels through which they will communicate regarding the application of the provisions of this agreement and other questions affecting the headquarters district, and may enter into such supplemental agreements as may be necessary to fulfill the purposes of this agreement. In making supplemental agreements with the Secretary-General, the United States shall consult with the appropriate state and local authorities. If the Secretary-General so requests the Secretary of State of the United States shall appoint a special representative for the purpose of liaison with the Secretary-General.

SECTION 21

(a) Any dispute between the United Nations and the United States concerning the interpretation or application of this agreement or of any supplemental agreement, which is not settled by negotiation or other agreed mode of settlement, shall be referred for final decision to a tribunal of three arbitrators, one to be named by the Secretary-General, one to be named by the Secretary of State of the United States, and the third to be chosen by the two, or, if they should fail to agree upon a third, then by the President of the International Court of Justice.

(b) The Secretary-General or the United States may ask the General Assembly to request of the International Court of Justice an advisory opinion on any legal question arising in the course of such proceedings. Pending the receipt of the opinion of the Court, an interim decision of the arbitral tribunal shall be observed on both parties. Thereafter, the arbitral tribunal shall render a final decision, having regard to the opinion of the Court.

Article IX—Miscellaneous Provisions

SECTION 22

(a) The United Nations shall not dispose of all or any part of the land owned by it in the headquarters district without the consent of the United States. If the United States is unwilling to consent to a disposition which the United Nations wishes to make of all or any part of such land, the United States shall buy the same from the United Nations at a price to be determined as provided in paragraph (d) of this section.

(b) If the seat of the United Nations is removed from the headquarters district, all right, title and interest of the United Nations in and to real property in the headquarters district or any part of it shall, on request of either the United Nations or the United States, be assigned and conveyed to the United States. In the absence of such request, the same shall be assigned or, if such subdivision shall not desire it, then to the state in which it is located. If none of the foregoing desires the same, it may be disposed of as provided in paragraph (a) of this section.

(c) If the United Nations disposes of all or any part of the headquarters district, the provisions of other sections of this agreement which apply to the headquarters district shall immediately cease to apply to the land and buildings so disposed of.

(d) The price to be paid for any conveyance under this section shall, in default of agreement, be the then fair value of the land, buildings and installations, to be determined under the procedure provided in Section 21.

SECTION 23

The seat of the United Nations shall not be removed from the headquarters district unless the United Nations should so decide.

SECTION 24

This agreement shall cease to be in force if the seat of the United Nations is removed from the territory of the United States, except for such provisions as may be applicable in connection with the orderly termination of the operations of the United Nations at its seat in the United States and the disposition of its property therein.

SECTION 25

Whenever this agreement imposes obligations on the appropriate American authorities, the Government of the United States shall have the ultimate responsibility for the fulfillment of such obligations by the appropriate American authorities.

SECTION 26

The provisions of this agreement shall be complementary to the provisions of the General Convention. In so far as any provision of this agreement and any provisions of the General Convention relate to the same subject matter, the two provisions shall, wherever possible, be treated as complementary, so that both provisions shall be applicable and neither shall narrow the effect of the other; but in any case of absolute conflict, the provisions of this agreement shall prevail.

SECTION 27

This agreement shall be construed in the light of its primary purpose to enable the United Nations at its headquarters in the United States, fully and efficiently to discharge its responsibilities and fulfill its purposes.

SECTION 28

This agreement shall be brought into effect by an exchange of notes between the Secretary-General, duly authorized pursuant to a resolution of the General Assembly of the United Nations, and the appropriate executive officer of the United States, duly authorized pursuant to appropriate action of the Congress.

IN WITNESS WHEREOF the respective representatives have signed this Agreement and have affixed their seals hereto.

DONE in duplicate, in the English and French languages, both authentic, at Lake Success the twenty-sixth day of June 1947.

For the Government of the United States of America:

G. C. MARSHALL
Secretary of State

For the United Nations:

TRYGVE LIE
Secretary-General

ANNEX 1

The area referred to in Section 1(a)(1) consists of (a) the premises bounded on the East by the westerly side of Franklin D. Roosevelt Drive, on the West by the easterly side of First Avenue, on the North by the southerly side of East Forty-eighth Street, and on the South by the northerly side of East Forty-second Street, all as proposed to be widened, in the Borough of Manhattan, City and State of New York, and (b) an easement over Franklin D. Roosevelt Drive, above a lower limiting plane to be fixed for the construction and maintenance of an esplanade, together with the structures thereon and foundation and columns to support the same in locations below such limiting plane, the entire area to be more definitely defined by supplemental agreement between the United Nations and the United States of America.

ANNEX 2—MAINTENANCE OF UTILITIES AND UNDERGROUND CONSTRUCTION

SECTION 1

The Secretary-General agrees to provide passes to duly authorized employees of The City of New York, the State of New York, or any of their agencies or subdivisions, for the purposes of enabling them to inspect, repair, maintain, reconstruct and relocate utilities, conduits, mains and sewers within the headquarters district.

SECTION 2

Underground constructions may be undertaken by The City of New York, or the State of New York, or any of their agencies or subdivisions, within the headquarters district only after consultation with the Secretary-General, and under conditions which shall not disturb the carrying out of the functions of the United Nations.

4. Convention on Privileges and Immunities of the United Nations [1]

Adopted by the General Assembly of the United Nations, February 13, 1946; Ratification, subject to reservations, advised by the Senate, March 19, 1970; Ratified, subject to said reservations, by the President, April 15, 1970; Accession of the United States deposited with the Secretary-General of the United Nations, April 29, 1970; Entered into force with respect to the United States, April 29, 1970; Proclaimed by the President, July 9, 1970

WHEREAS Article 104 of the Charter of the United Nations provides that the Organization shall enjoy in the territory of each of its Members such legal capacity as may be necessary for the exercise of its functions and the fulfillment of its purposes and

WHEREAS Article 105 of the Charter of the United Nations provides that the Organization shall enjoy in the territory of each of its Members such privileges and immunities as are necessary for the fulfillment of its purposes and that representatives of the Members of the United Nations and officials of the Organization shall similarly enjoy such privileges and immunities as are necessary for the independent exercise of their functions in connection with the Organization.

CONSEQUENTLY the General Assembly by a Resolution adopted on the 13 February 1946, approved the following Convention and proposed it for accession by each Member of the United Nations.

ARTICLE I—JURIDICAL PERSONALITY

SECTION 1

The United Nations shall possess juridical personality. It shall have the capacity:

(a) to contract;

(b) to acquire and dispose of immovable and movable property;

(c) to institute legal proceedings.

ARTICLE II—PROPERTY, FUNDS AND ASSETS

SECTION 2

The United Nations, its property and assets wherever located and by whomsoever held, shall enjoy immunity from every form of legal process except insofar as in any particular case it has expressly waived its immunity. It is, however, understood that no waiver of immunity shall extend to any measure of execution.

[1] 21 UST 1418; TIAS 6900; 1 UNTS 16. For a list of states that are parties, see Department of State publication, *Treaties in Force*.

SECTION 3

The premises of the United Nations shall be inviolable. The property and assets of the United Nations, wherever located and by whomsoever held, shall be immune from search, requisition, confiscation, expropriation and any other form of interference, whether by executive, administrative, judicial or legislative action.

SECTION 4

The archives of the United Nations, and in general all documents belonging to it or held by it, shall be inviolable wherever located.

SECTION 5

Without being restricted by financial controls, regulations or moratoria of any kind,

(a) the United Nations may hold funds, gold or currency of any kind and operate accounts in any currency;

(b) the United Nations shall be free to transfer its funds, gold or currency from one country to another or within any country and to convert any currency held by it into any other currency.

SECTION 6

In exercising its rights under Section 5 above, the United Nations shall pay due regard to any representations made by the Government of any Member insofar as it is considered that effect can be given to such representations without detriment to the interests of the United Nations.

SECTION 7

The United Nations, its assets, income and other property shall be:

(a) exempt from all direct taxes; it is understood, however, that the United Nations will not claim exemption from taxes which are, in fact, no more than charges for public utility services;

(b) exempt from customs duties and prohibitions and restrictions on imports and exports in respect of articles imported or exported by the United Nations for its official use. It is understood, however, that articles imported under such exemption will not be sold in the country into which they were imported except under conditions agreed with the Government of that country;

(c) exempt from customs duties and prohibitions and restrictions on imports and exports in respect of its publications.

SECTION 8

While the United Nations will not, as a general rule, claim exemption from excise duties and from taxes on the sale of movable and immovable property which form part of the price to be paid, nevertheless when the United Nations is making important purchases for official use of property on which such duties and taxes have been charged or are chargeable, Members will, whenever possible, make appropriate administrative arrangements for the remission or return of the amount of duty or tax.

Article III—Facilities in Respect of Communications

SECTION 9

The United Nations shall enjoy in the territory of each Member for its official communications treatment not less favourable than that accorded by the Government of that Member to any other Government including its diplomatic mission in the matter of priorities, rates and taxes on mails, cables, telegrams, radiograms, telephotos, telephone and other communications; and press rates for information to the press and radio. No censorship shall be applied to the official correspondence and other official communications of the United Nations.

SECTION 10

The United Nations shall have the right to use codes and to dispatch and receive its correspondence by courier or in bags, which have the same immunities and privileges as diplomatic couriers and bags.

Article IV—The Representatives of Members

SECTION 11

Representatives of Members to the principal and subsidiary organs of the United Nations and to conferences convened by the United Nations, shall, while exercising their functions and during their journey to and from the place of meeting, enjoy the following privileges and immunities:

(a) immunity from personal arrest or detention and from seizure of their personal baggage, and, in respect of words spoken or written and all acts done by them in their capacity as representatives, immunity from legal process of every kind;

(b) inviolability for all papers and documents;

(c) the right to use codes and to receive papers or correspondence by courier or in sealed bags;

(d) exemption in respect of themselves and their spouses from immigration restrictions, alien registration or national service obligations in the state they are visiting or through which they are passing in the exercise of their functions;

(e) the same facilities in respect of currency or exchange restrictions as are accorded to representatives of foreign governments on temporary official missions;

(f) the same immunities and facilities in respect of their personal baggage as are accorded to diplomatic envoys, and also

(g) such other privileges, immunities and facilities not inconsistent with the foregoing as diplomatic envoys enjoy, except that they shall have no right to claim exemption from customs duties on goods imported (otherwise than as part of their personal baggage) or from excise duties or sales taxes.

SECTION 12

In order to secure, for the representatives of Members to the principal and subsidiary organs of the United Nations and to conferences convened by the United Nations, complete freedom of speech and independence in the discharge of their duties, the immunity from legal process in respect of words spoken or written and all acts done by them in discharging their duties shall continue to be accorded, notwithstanding that the persons concerned are no longer the representatives of Members.

SECTION 13

Where the incidence of any form of taxation depends upon residence, periods during which the representatives of Members to the principal and subsidiary organs of the United Nations and to conferences convened by the United Nations are present in a state for the discharge of their duties shall not be considered as periods of residence.

SECTION 14

Privileges and immunities are accorded to the representatives of Members not for the personal benefit of the individuals themselves, but in order to safeguard the independent exercise of their functions in connection with the United Nations. Consequently a Member not only has the right but is under a duty to waive the immunity of its representative in any case where in the opinion of the Member the immunity would impede the course of justice, and it can be waived without prejudice to the purpose for which the immunity is accorded.

SECTION 15

The provisions of Sections 11, 12 and 13 are not applicable as between a representative and the authorities of the state of which he is a national or of which he is or has been the representative.

SECTION 16

In this article the expression "representatives" shall be deemed to include all delegates, deputy delegates, advisers, technical experts and secretaries of delegations.

ARTICLE V—OFFICIALS

SECTION 17

The Secretary-General will specify the categories of officials to which the provisions of this Article and Article VII shall apply. He shall submit these categories to the General Assembly. Thereafter these categories shall be communicated to the Governments of all Members. The names of the officials included in these categories shall from time to time be made known to the Governments of Members.

SECTION 18

Officials of the United Nations shall:

(a) be immune from legal process in respect of words spoken or written and all acts performed by them in their official capacity;

(b) be exempt from taxation on the salaries and emoluments paid to them by the United Nations;

(c) be immune from national service obligations;

(d) be immune, together with their spouses and relatives dependent on them, from immigration restrictions and alien registration;

(e) be accorded the same privileges in respect of exchange facilities as are accorded to the officials of comparable ranks forming part of diplomatic missions to the Government concerned;

(f) be given, together with their spouses and relatives dependent on them, the same repatriation facilities in time of international crisis as diplomatic envoys;

(g) have the right to import free of duty their furniture and effects at the time of first taking up their post in the country in question.

SECTION 19

In addition to the immunities and privileges specified in Section 18, the Secretary-General and all Assistant Secretaries-General shall be accorded in respect of themselves, their spouses and minor children, the privileges and immunities, exemptions and facilities accorded to diplomatic envoys, in accordance with international law.

SECTION 20

Privileges and immunities are granted to officials in the interests of the United Nations and not for the personal benefit of the individuals themselves. The Secretary-General shall have the right and the duty to waive the immunity of any official in any case where, in his opinion, the immunity would impede the course of justice and can be waived without prejudice to the interests of the United Nations. In the case of the Secretary-General, the Security Council shall have the right to waive immunity.

SECTION 21

The United Nations shall co-operate at all times with the appropriate authorities of Members to facilitate the proper administration of justice, secure the observance of police regulations and prevent the occurrence of any abuse in connection with the privileges, immunities and facilities mentioned in this Article.

ARTICLE VI—EXPERTS ON MISSIONS FOR THE UNITED NATIONS

SECTION 22

Experts (other than officials coming within the scope of Article V) performing missions for the United Nations shall be accorded such privileges and immunities as are necessary for the independent exercise of their functions during the period of their missions, including the time spent on journeys in connection with their missions. In particular they shall be accorded:

(a) immunity from personal arrest or detention and from seizure of their personal baggage;

(b) in respect of words spoken or written and acts done by them in the course of the performance of their mission, immunity from legal process of every kind. This immunity from legal process shall continue to be accorded notwithstanding that the persons concerned are no longer employed on missions for the United Nations;

(c) inviolability for all papers and documents;

(d) for the purpose of their communications with the United Nations, the right to use codes and to receive papers or correspondence by courier or in sealed bags;

(e) the same facilities in respect of currency or exchange restrictions as are accorded to representatives of foreign governments on temporary official missions;

(f) the same immunities and facilities in respect of their personal baggage as are accorded to diplomatic envoys.

SECTION 23

Privileges and immunities are granted to experts in the interest of the United Nations and not for the personal benefit of the individuals themselves. The Secretary-General shall have the right and the duty to waive the immunity of any expert in any case where, in his opinion, the immunity would impede the course of justice and it can be waived without prejudice to the interests of the United Nations.

ARTICLE VII—UNITED NATIONS LAISSEZ-PASSER

SECTION 24

The United Nations may issue United Nations laissez-passer to its officials. These laissez-passer shall be recognized and accepted as valid travel documents by the authorities of Members, taking into account the provisions of Section 25.

SECTION 25

Applications for visas (where required) from the holders of United Nations laissez-passer, when accompanied by a certificate that they are travelling on the business of the United Nations, shall be dealt with as speedily as possible. In addition, such persons shall be granted facilities for speedy travel.

SECTION 26

Similar facilities to those specified in Section 25 shall be accorded to experts and other persons who, though not the holders of United Nations laissez-passer, have a certificate that they are travelling on the business of the United Nations.

SECTION 27

The Secretary-General, Assistant Secretaries-General and Directors travelling on United Nations laissez-passer on the business of the United Nations shall be granted the same facilities as are accorded to diplomatic envoys.

SECTION 28

The provisions of this article may be applied to the comparable officials of specialized agencies if the agreements for relationship made under Article 63 of the Charter so provide.

ARTICLE VIII—SETTLEMENT OF DISPUTES

SECTION 29

The United Nations shall make provisions for appropriate modes of settlement of:

(a) disputes arising out of contracts of other disputes of a private law character to which the United Nations is a party;

(b) disputes involving any official of the United Nations who by reason of his official position enjoys immunity, if immunity has not been waived by the Secretary-General.

SECTION 30

All differences arising out of the interpretation or application of the present convention shall be referred to the International Court of Justice, unless in any case it is agreed by the parties to have recourse to another mode of settlement. If a difference arises between the United Nations on the one hand and a Member on the other hand, a request shall be made for an advisory opinion on any legal question involved in accordance with Article 96 of the Charter and Article 65 of the Statute of the Court.[2] The opinion given by the Court shall be accepted as decisive by the parties.

FINAL ARTICLE

SECTION 31

This convention is submitted to every Member of the United Nations for accession.

SECTION 32

Accession shall be effected by deposit of an instrument with the Secretary-General of the United Nations and the convention shall come into force as regards each Member on the date of deposit of each instrument of accession.

SECTION 33

The Secretary-General shall inform all Members of the United Nations of the deposit of each accession.

[2] TS 993; 59 Stat. 1063.

SECTION 34

It is understood that, when an instrument of accession is deposited on behalf of any Member, the Member will be in a position under its own law to give effect to the terms of this convention.

SECTION 35

This convention shall continue in force as between the United Nations and every Member which has deposited an instrument of accession for so long as that Member remains a Member of the United Nations, or until a revised general convention has been approved by the General Assembly and that Member has become a party to this revised convention.

SECTION 36

The Secretary-General may conclude with any Member or Members supplementary agreements adjusting the provisions of this convention so far as that Member or those Members are concerned. These supplementary agreements shall in each case be subject to the approval of the General Assembly.

Reservations as Stated in the Proclamation of the United States

By its resolution of March 19, 1970, the Senate of the United States of America, two-thirds of the Senators present concurring, gave its advice and consent to the ratification of the Convention subject to the following reservations:

(1) Paragraph (b) of section 18 regarding immunity from taxation and paragraph (c) of section 18 regarding immunity from national service obligations shall not apply with respect to United States nationals and aliens admitted for permanent residence.

(2) Nothing in Article IV, regarding the privileges and immunities of representatives of Members, in Article V, regarding the privileges and immunities of United Nations officials, or in Article VI regarding the privileges and immunities of experts on missions for the United Nations, shall be construed to grant any person who has abused his privileges of residence by activities in the United States outside his official capacity exemption from the laws and regulations of the United States regarding the continued residence of aliens, provided that:

(a) No proceedings shall be instituted under such laws or regulations to require any such person to leave the United States except with the prior approval of the Secretary of State of the United States. Such approval shall be given only after consultation with the appropriate Member in the case of a representative of a Member (or a member of his family) or with the Secretary-General in the case of any person referred to in Articles V and VI;

(b) A representative of the Member concerned or the Secretary-General, as the case may be, shall have the right to appear in any such proceedings on behalf of the person against whom they are instituted;

(c) Persons who are entitled to diplomatic privileges and immunities under the Convention shall not be required to leave the United States otherwise than in accordance with the customary procedure applicable to members of diplomatic missions accredited or notified to the United States.

I. INTERNATIONAL CRIME AND LAW ENFORCEMENT

CONTENTS

1. Terrorism

a. OAS Convention to Prevent and Punish the Acts of Terrorism Taking the Form of Crimes Against Persons and Related Extortion That Are of International Significance[1]

Adopted at the 3d Special Session of the OAS General Assembly, Washington, D.C., January 25–February 2, 1971; Ratification advised by the Senate, June 12, 1972; Instrument of ratification deposited in the General Secretariat of the Organization of American States, October 20, 1976; Entered into force with respect to the United States, October 20, 1976

WHEREAS, The defense of freedom and justice and respect for the fundamental rights of the individual that are recognized by the American Declaration of the Rights and Duties of Man and the Universal Declaration of Human Rights are primary duties of states;

The General Assembly of the Organization, in Resolution 4, of June 30, 1970, strongly condemned acts of terrorism, especially the kidnapping of persons and extortion in connection with that crime, which it declared to be serious common crimes;

Criminal acts against persons entitled to special protection under international law are occurring frequently, and those acts are of international significance because of the consequences that may flow from them for relations among states;

It is advisable to adopt general standards that will progressively develop international law as regards cooperation in the prevention and punishment of such acts; and

In the application of those standards the institution of asylum should be maintained and, likewise the principle of nonintervention should not be impaired,

THE MEMBER STATES OF THE ORGANIZATION OF AMERICAN STATES HAVE AGREED UPON THE FOLLOWING ARTICLES:

ARTICLE 1

The contracting states undertake to cooperate among themselves by taking all the measures that they may consider effective, under their own laws, and especially those established in this convention, to prevent and punish acts of terrorism, especially kidnapping, murder, and other assaults against the life or physical integrity of those persons to whom the state has the duty according to international law to give special protection, as well as extortion in connection with those crimes.

[1] 27 UST 3949; TIAS 8413. For states that are parties in the Convention, see Department of State publication, *Treaties in Force.*

ARTICLE 2

For the purposes of this convention, kidnapping, murder, and other assaults against the life or personal integrity of those persons to whom the state has the duty to give special protection according to international law, as well as extortion in connection with those crimes, shall be considered common crimes of international significance, regardless of motive.

ARTICLE 3

Persons who have been charged or convicted for any of the crimes referred to in Article 2 of this convention shall be subject to extradition under the provisions of the extradition treaties in force between the parties or, in the case of states that do not make extradition dependent on the existence of a treaty, in accordance with their own laws.

In any case, it is the exclusive responsibility of the state under whose jurisdiction or protection such persons are located to determine the nature of the acts and decide whether the standards of this convention are applicable.

ARTICLE 4

Any person deprived of his freedom through the application of this convention shall enjoy the legal guarantees of due process.

ARTICLE 5

When extradition requested for one of the crimes specified in Article 2 is not in order because the person sought is a national of the requested state, or because of some other legal or constitutional impediment, that state is obliged to submit the case to its competent authorities for prosecution, as if the act had been committed in its territory. The decision of these authorities shall be communicated to the state that requested extradition. In such proceedings, the obligation established in Article 4 shall be respected.

ARTICLE 6

None of the provisions of this convention shall be interpreted so as to impair the right of asylum.

ARTICLE 7

The contracting states undertake to include the crimes referred to in Article 2 of this convention among the punishable acts giving rise to extradition in any treaty on the subject to which they agree among themselves in the future. The contracting states that do not subject extradition to the existence of a treaty with the requesting state shall consider the crimes referred to in Article 2 of this convention as crimes giving rise to extradition, according to the conditions established by the laws of the requested state.

ARTICLE 8

To cooperate in preventing and punishing the crimes contemplated in Article 2 of this convention, the contracting states accept the following obligations:

a. To take all measures within their power, and in conformity with their own laws, to prevent and impede the preparation in their respective territories of the crimes mentioned in Article 2 that are to be carried out in the territory of another contracting state.

b. To exchange information and consider effective administrative measures for the purpose of protecting the persons to whom Article 2 of this convention refers.

c. To guarantee to every person deprived of his freedom through the application of this convention every right to defend himself.

d. To endeavor to have the criminal acts contemplated in this convention included in their penal laws, if not already so included.

e. To comply most expeditiously with the requests for extradition concerning the criminal acts contemplated in this convention.

ARTICLE 9

This convention shall remain open for signature by the member states of the Organization of American States, as well as by any other state that is a member of the United Nations or any of its specialized agencies, or any state that is a party to the Statute of the International Court of Justice, or any other state that may be invited by the General Assembly of the Organization of American States to sign it.

ARTICLE 10

This convention shall be ratified by the signatory states in accordance with their respective constitutional procedures.

ARTICLE 11

The original instrument of this convention, the English, French, Portuguese, and Spanish texts of which are equally authentic, shall be deposited in the General Secretariat of the Organization of American States, which shall send certified copies of the signatory governments for purposes of ratification. The instruments of ratification shall be deposited in the General Secretariat of the Organization of American States, which shall notify the signatory governments of such deposit.

ARTICLE 12

This convention shall enter into force among the states that ratify it when they deposit their respective instruments of ratification.

Article 13

This convention shall remain in force indefinitely, but any of the contracting states may denounce it. The denunciation shall be transmitted to the General Secretariat of the Organization of American States, which shall notify the other contracting states thereof. One year following the denunciation, the convention shall cease to be in force for the denouncing state, but shall continue to be in force for the other contracting states.

Statement of Panama

The Delegation of Panama states for the record that nothing in this convention shall be interpreted to the effect that the right of asylum implies the right to request asylum from the United States authorities in the Panama Canal Zone, or that there is recognition of the right of the United States to grant asylum or political refuge in that part of the territory of the Republic of Panama that constitutes the Canal Zone.

In witness whereof, the undersigned plenipotentiaries, having presented their full powers, which have been found to be in due and proper form, sign this convention on behalf of their respective governments, at the city of Washington this second day of February of the year one thousand nine hundred seventy-one.

b. International Convention for the Suppression of Terrorist Bombings[1]

Adopted at New York, December 15, 1997; Signed on behalf of the United States, January 12, 1998; Entered into force generally, May 23, 2001; Ratification advised by the Senate, December 5, 2001; Entered into force for the United States, July 26, 2002

The States Parties to this Convention,

HAVING IN MIND the purposes and principles of the Charter of the United Nations concerning the maintenance of international peace and security and the promotion of good-neighbourliness and friendly relations and cooperation among States,

DEEPLY CONCERNED about the worldwide escalation of acts of terrorism in all its forms and manifestations,

RECALLING the Declaration on the Occasion of the Fiftieth Anniversary of the United Nations of 24 October 1995,

RECALLING ALSO the Declaration on Measures to Eliminate International Terrorism, annexed to General Assembly resolution 49/60 of 9 December 1994, in which, inter alia, "the States Members of the United Nations solemnly reaffirm their unequivocal condemnation of all acts, methods and practices of terrorism as criminal and unjustifiable, wherever and by whomever committed, including those which jeopardize the friendly relations among States and peoples and threaten the territorial integrity and security of States",

NOTING that the Declaration also encouraged States "to review urgently the scope of the existing international legal provisions on the prevention, repression and elimination of terrorism in all its forms and manifestations, with the aim of ensuring that there is a comprehensive legal framework covering all aspects of the matter",

RECALLING FURTHER General Assembly resolution 51/210 of 17 December 1996 and the Declaration to Supplement the 1994 Declaration on Measures to Eliminate International Terrorism, annexed thereto,

NOTING ALSO that terrorist attacks by means of explosives or other lethal devices have become increasingly widespread,

NOTING FURTHER that existing multilateral legal provisions do not adequately address these attacks,

BEING CONVINCED of the urgent need to enhance international cooperation between States in devising and adopting effective and practical measures for the prevention of such acts of terrorism, and for the prosecution and punishment of their perpetrators,

---

[1] For states that are parties to the Convention, see Department of State publication, *Treaties in Force.*

CONSIDERING that the occurrence of such acts is a matter of grave concern to the international community as a whole,

NOTING that the activities of military forces of States are governed by rules of international law outside the framework of this Convention and that the exclusion of certain actions from the coverage of this Convention does not condone or make lawful otherwise unlawful acts, or preclude prosecution under other laws,

HAVE AGREED AS FOLLOWS:

ARTICLE 1

For the purposes of this Convention:

1. "State or government facility" includes any permanent or temporary facility or conveyance that is used or occupied by representatives of a State, members of Government, the legislature or the judiciary or by officials or employees of a State or any other public authority or entity or by employees or officials of an intergovernmental organization in connection with their official duties.

2. "Infrastructure facility" means any publicly or privately owned facility providing or distributing services for the benefit of the public, such as water, sewage, energy, fuel or communications.

3. "Explosive or other lethal device" means:

(a) An explosive or incendiary weapon or device that is designed, or has the capability, to cause death, serious bodily injury or substantial material damage; or

(b) A weapon or device that is designed, or has the capability, to cause death, serious bodily injury or substantial material damage through the release, dissemination or impact of toxic chemicals, biological agents or toxins or similar substances or radiation or radioactive material.

4. "Military forces of a State" means the armed forces of a State which are organized, trained and equipped under its internal law for the primary purpose of national defence or security, and persons acting in support of those armed forces who are under their formal command, control and responsibility.

5. "Place of public use" means those parts of any building, land, street, waterway or other location that are accessible or open to members of the public, whether continuously, periodically or occasionally, and encompasses any commercial, business, cultural, historical, educational, religious, governmental, entertainment, recreational or similar place that is so accessible or open to the public.

6. "Public transportation system" means all facilities, conveyances and instrumentalities, whether publicly or privately owned, that are used in or for publicly available services for the transportation of persons or cargo.

ARTICLE 2

1. Any person commits an offence within the meaning of this Convention if that person unlawfully and intentionally delivers, places, discharges or detonates an explosive or other lethal device in, into or against a place of public use, a State or government facility, a public transportation system or an infrastructure facility:

(a) With the intent to cause death or serious bodily injury; or

(b) With the intent to cause extensive destruction of such a place, facility or system, where such destruction results in or is likely to result in major economic loss.

2. Any person also commits an offence if that person attempts to commit an offence as set forth in paragraph 1.

3. Any person also commits an offence if that person:

(a) Participates as an accomplice in an offence as set forth in paragraph 1 or 2; or

(b) Organizes or directs others to commit an offence as set forth in paragraph 1 or 2; or

(c) In any other way contributes to the commission of one or more offences as set forth in paragraph 1 or 2 by a group of persons acting with a common purpose; such contribution shall be intentional and either be made with the aim of furthering the general criminal activity or purpose of the group or be made in the knowledge of the intention of the group to commit the offence or offences concerned.

Article 3

This Convention shall not apply where the offence is committed within a single State, the alleged offender and the victims are nationals of that State, the alleged offender is found in the territory of that State and no other State has a basis under Article 6, paragraph 1, or Article 6, paragraph 2, of this Convention to exercise jurisdiction, except that the provisions of Articles 10 to 15 shall, as appropriate, apply in those cases.

Article 4

Each State Party shall adopt such measures as may be necessary:

(a) To establish as criminal offences under its domestic law the offences set forth in Article 2 of this Convention;

(b) To make those offences punishable by appropriate penalties which take into account the grave nature of those offences.

Article 5

Each State Party shall adopt such measures as may be necessary, including, where appropriate, domestic legislation, to ensure that criminal acts within the scope of this Convention, in particular where they are intended or calculated to provoke a state of terror in the general public or in a group of persons or particular persons, are under no circumstances justifiable by considerations of a political, philosophical, ideological, racial, ethnic, religious or other similar nature and are punished by penalties consistent with their grave nature.

Article 6

1. Each State Party shall take such measures as may be necessary to establish its jurisdiction over the offences set forth in Article 2 when:

(a) The offence is committed in the territory of that State; or

(b) The offence is committed on board a vessel flying the flag of that State or an aircraft which is registered under the laws of that State at the time the offence is committed; or

(c) The offence is committed by a national of that State.

2. A State Party may also establish its jurisdiction over any such offence when:

(a) The offence is committed against a national of that State; or

(b) The offence is committed against a State or government facility of that State abroad, including an embassy or other diplomatic or consular premises of that State; or

(c) The offence is committed by a stateless person who has his or her habitual residence in the territory of that State; or

(d) The offence is committed in an attempt to compel that State to do or abstain from doing any act; or

(e) The offence is committed on board an aircraft which is operated by the Government of that State.

3. Upon ratifying, accepting, approving or acceding to this Convention, each State Party shall notify the Secretary-General of the United Nations of the jurisdiction it has established in accordance with paragraph 2 under its domestic law. Should any change take place, the State Party concerned shall immediately notify the Secretary-General.

4. Each State Party shall likewise take such measures as may be necessary to establish its jurisdiction over the offences set forth in Article 2 in cases where the alleged offender is present in its territory and it does not extradite that person to any of the States Parties which have established their jurisdiction in accordance with paragraph 1 or 2.

5. This Convention does not exclude the exercise of any criminal jurisdiction established by a State Party in accordance with its domestic law.

Article 7

1. Upon receiving information that a person who has committed or who is alleged to have committed an offence as set forth in Article 2 may be present in its territory, the State Party concerned shall take such measures as may be necessary under its domestic law to investigate the facts contained in the information.

2. Upon being satisfied that the circumstances so warrant, the State Party in whose territory the offender or alleged offender is present shall take the appropriate measures under its domestic law so as to ensure that person's presence for the purpose of prosecution or extradition.

3. Any person regarding whom the measures referred to in paragraph 2 are being taken shall be entitled to:

(a) Communicate without delay with the nearest appropriate representative of the State of which that person is a national or which is otherwise entitled to protect that person's rights or, if that person is a stateless person, the State in the territory of which that person habitually resides;

(b) Be visited by a representative of that State;

(c) Be informed of that person's rights under subparagraphs (a) and (b).

4. The rights referred to in paragraph 3 shall be exercised in conformity with the laws and regulations of the State in the territory of which the offender or alleged offender is present, subject to the provision that the said laws and regulations must enable full effect to be given to the purposes for which the rights accorded under paragraph 3 are intended.

5. The provisions of paragraphs 3 and 4 shall be without prejudice to the right of any State Party having a claim to jurisdiction in accordance with Article 6, subparagraph 1(c) or 2(c), to invite the International Committee of the Red Cross to communicate with and visit the alleged offender.

6. When a State Party, pursuant to this Article, has taken a person into custody, it shall immediately notify, directly or through the Secretary-General of the United Nations, the States Parties which have established jurisdiction in accordance with Article 6, paragraphs 1 and 2, and, if it considers it advisable, any other interested States Parties, of the fact that such person is in custody and of the circumstances which warrant that person's detention. The State which makes the investigation contemplated in paragraph 1 shall promptly inform the said States Parties of its findings and shall indicate whether it intends to exercise jurisdiction.

ARTICLE 8

1. The State Party in the territory of which the alleged offender is present shall, in cases to which Article 6 applies, if it does not extradite that person, be obliged, without exception whatsoever and whether or not the offence was committed in its territory, to submit the case without undue delay to its competent authorities for the purpose of prosecution, through proceedings in accordance with the laws of that State. Those authorities shall take their decision in the same manner as in the case of any other offence of a grave nature under the law of that State.

2. Whenever a State Party is permitted under its domestic law to extradite or otherwise surrender one of its nationals only upon the condition that the person will be returned to that State to serve the sentence imposed as a result of the trial or proceeding for which the extradition or surrender of the person was sought, and this State and the State seeking the extradition of the person agree with this option and other terms they may deem appropriate, such a conditional extradition or surrender shall be sufficient to discharge the obligation set forth in paragraph 1.

ARTICLE 9

1. The offences set forth in Article 2 shall be deemed to be included as extraditable offences in any extradition treaty existing between any of the States Parties before the entry into force of this Convention. States Parties undertake to include such offences as extraditable offences in every extradition treaty to be subsequently concluded between them.

2. When a State Party which makes extradition conditional on the existence of a treaty receives a request for extradition from another State Party with which it has no extradition treaty, the requested State Party may, at its option, consider this Convention as a legal basis for extradition in respect of the offences set forth in Article 2. Extradition shall be subject to the other conditions provided by the law of the requested State.

3. States Parties which do not make extradition conditional on the existence of a treaty shall recognize the offences set forth in Article 2 as extraditable offences between themselves, subject to the conditions provided by the law of the requested State.

4. If necessary, the offences set forth in Article 2 shall be treated, for the purposes of extradition between States Parties, as if they had been committed not only in the place in which they occurred but also in the territory of the States that have established jurisdiction in accordance with Article 6, paragraphs 1 and 2.

5. The provisions of all extradition treaties and arrangements between States Parties with regard to offences set forth in Article 2 shall be deemed to be modified as between State Parties to the extent that they are incompatible with this Convention.

ARTICLE 10

1. States Parties shall afford one another the greatest measure of assistance in connection with investigations or criminal or extradition proceedings brought in respect of the offences set forth in Article 2, including assistance in obtaining evidence at their disposal necessary for the proceedings.

2. States Parties shall carry out their obligations under paragraph 1 in conformity with any treaties or other arrangements on mutual legal assistance that may exist between them. In the absence of such treaties or arrangements, States Parties shall afford one another assistance in accordance with their domestic law.

ARTICLE 11

None of the offences set forth in Article 2 shall be regarded, for the purposes of extradition or mutual legal assistance, as a political offence or as an offence connected with a political offence or as an offence inspired by political motives. Accordingly, a request for extradition or for mutual legal assistance based on such an offence may not be refused on the sole ground that it concerns a political offence or an offence connected with a political offence or an offence inspired by political motives.

ARTICLE 12

Nothing in this Convention shall be interpreted as imposing an obligation to extradite or to afford mutual legal assistance, if the requested State Party has substantial grounds for believing that the request for extradition for offences set forth in Article 2 or for mutual legal assistance with respect to such offences has been made for the purpose of prosecuting or punishing a person on account of that person's race, religion, nationality, ethnic origin or political opinion or that compliance with the request would cause prejudice to that person's position for any of these reasons.

ARTICLE 13

1. A person who is being detained or is serving a sentence in the territory of one State party whose presence in another State Party is requested for purposes of testimony, identification or otherwise providing assistance in obtaining evidence for the investigation or prosecution of offences under this Convention may be transferred if the following conditions are met:

(a) The person freely gives his or her informed consent; and

(b) The competent authorities of both States agree, subject to such conditions as those States may deem appropriate.

2. For the purposes of this Article:

(a) The State to which the person is transferred shall have the authority and obligation to keep the person transferred in custody, unless otherwise requested or authorized by the State from which the person was transferred;

(b) The State to which the person is transferred shall without delay implement its obligation to return the person to the custody of the State from which the person was transferred as agreed beforehand, or as otherwise agreed, by the competent authorities of both States;

(c) The State to which the person is transferred shall not require the State from which the person was transferred to initiate extradition proceedings for the return of the person;

(d) The person transferred shall receive credit for service of the sentence being served in the State from which he was transferred for time spent in the custody of the State to which he was transferred.

3. Unless the State Party from which a person is to be transferred in accordance with this Article so agrees, that person, whatever his or her nationality, shall not be prosecuted or detained or subjected to any other restriction of his or her personal liberty in the territory of the State to which that person is transferred in respect of acts or convictions anterior to his or her departure from the territory of the State from which such person was transferred.

ARTICLE 14

Any person who is taken into custody or regarding whom any other measures are taken or proceedings are carried out pursuant to this Convention shall be guaranteed fair treatment, including enjoyment of all rights and guarantees in conformity with the law of the State in the territory of which that person is present and applicable provisions of international law, including international law of human rights.

ARTICLE 15

States Parties shall cooperate in the prevention of the offences set forth in Article 2, particularly:

(a) By taking all practicable measures, including, if necessary, adapting their domestic legislation, to prevent and counter preparations in their respective territories for the commission of those offences within or outside their territories, including measures to prohibit in their territories illegal activities of persons, groups and organizations that encourage, instigate, organize, knowingly finance or engage in the perpetration of offences as set forth in Article 2;

(b) By exchanging accurate and verified information in accordance with their national law, and coordinating administrative and other measures taken as appropriate to prevent the commission of offences as set forth in Article 2;

(c) Where appropriate, through research and development regarding methods of detection of explosives and other harmful substances that can cause death or bodily injury, consultations on the development of standards for marking explosives in order to identify their origin in post-blast investigations, exchange of information on preventive measures, cooperation and transfer of technology, equipment and related materials.

Article 16

The State Party where the alleged offender is prosecuted shall, in accordance with its domestic law or applicable procedures, communicate the final outcome of the proceedings to the Secretary-General of the United Nations, who shall transmit the information to the other States Parties.

Article 17

The States Parties shall carry out their obligations under this Convention in a manner consistent with the principles of sovereign equality and territorial integrity of States and that of non-intervention in the domestic affairs of other States.

Article 18

Nothing in this Convention entitles a State Party to undertake in the territory of another State Party the exercise of jurisdiction and performance of functions which are exclusively reserved for the authorities of that other State Party by its domestic law.

Article 19

1. Nothing in this Convention shall affect other rights, obligations and responsibilities of States and individuals under international law, in particular the purposes and principles of the Charter of the United Nations and international humanitarian law.

2. The activities of armed forces during an armed conflict, as those terms are understood under international humanitarian law, which are governed by that law, are not governed by this Convention, and the activities undertaken by military forces of a State in the exercise of their official duties, inasmuch as they are governed by other rules of international law, are not governed by this Convention.

ARTICLE 20

1. Any dispute between two or more States Parties concerning the interpretation or application of this Convention which cannot be settled through negotiation within a reasonable time shall, at the request of one of them, be submitted to arbitration. If, within six months from the date of the request for arbitration, the parties are unable to agree on the organization of the arbitration, any one of those parties may refer the dispute to the International Court of Justice, by application, in conformity with the Statute of the Court.

2. Each state may at the time of signature, ratification, acceptance or approval of this Convention or accession thereto declare that it does not consider itself bound by paragraph 1. The other States Parties shall not be bound by paragraph 1 with respect to any State Party which has made such a reservation.

3. Any State which has made a reservation in accordance with paragraph 2 may at any time withdraw that reservation by notification to the Secretary-General of the United Nations.

ARTICLE 21

1. This Convention shall be open for signature by all States from 12 January 1998 until 31 December 1999 at United Nations Headquarters in New York.

2. This Convention is subject to ratification, acceptance or approval. The instruments of ratification, acceptance or approval shall be deposited with the Secretary-General of the United Nations.

3. This Convention shall be open to accession by any State. The instruments of accession shall be deposited with the Secretary-General of the United Nations.

ARTICLE 22

1. This Convention shall enter into force on the thirtieth day following the date of the deposit of the twenty-second instrument of ratification, acceptance, approval or accession with the Secretary-General of the United Nations.

2. For each State ratifying, accepting, approving or acceding to the Convention after the deposit of the twenty-second instrument of ratification, acceptance, approval or accession, the Convention shall enter into force on the thirtieth day after deposit by such State of its instrument of ratification, acceptance, approval or accession.

ARTICLE 23

1. Any State Party may denounce this Convention by written notification to the Secretary-General of the United Nations.

2. Denunciation shall take effect one year following the date on which notification is received by the Secretary-General of the United Nations.

Article 24

The original of this Convention, of which the Arabic, Chinese, English, French, Russian and Spanish texts are equally authentic, shall be deposited with the Secretary-General of the United Nations, who shall send certified copies thereof to all States.

In witness whereof, the undersigned, being duly authorized thereto by their respective Governments, have signed this Convention, opened for signature at New York on 12 January 1998.

c. International Convention for the Suppression of the Financing of Terrorism [1]

Adopted at New York, December 9, 1999; Signed on behalf of the United States, January 10, 2000; Ratification advised by the Senate, December 5, 2001; Entered into force generally, April 10, 2002; Entered into force for the United States, July 26, 2002

The General Assembly,

RECALLING all its relevant resolutions, including resolution 46/51 of 9 December 1991, resolution 49/60 of 9 December 1994, by which it adopted the Declaration on Measures to Eliminate International Terrorism, and resolutions 51/210 of 17 December 1996 and 53/108 of 8 December 1998,

HAVING CONSIDERED the text of the draft international convention for the suppression of the financing of terrorism prepared by the Ad Hoc Committee established by General Assembly resolution 51/210 of 17 December 1996 and the Working Group of the Sixth Committee,

1. Adopts the International Convention for the Suppression of the Financing of Terrorism annexed to the present resolution, and requests the Secretary-General to open it for signature at United Nations Headquarters in New York from 10 January 2000 to 31 December 2001;

2. Urges all States to sign and ratify, accept, approve or accede to the Convention.

ANNEX

INTERNATIONAL CONVENTION FOR THE SUPPRESSION OF THE FINANCING OF TERRORISM

PREAMBLE

The States Parties to this Convention,

BEARING in mind the purposes and principles of the Charter of the United Nations concerning the maintenance of international peace and security and the promotion of good-neighbourliness and friendly relations and cooperation among States,

DEEPLY concerned about the worldwide escalation of acts of terrorism in all its forms and manifestations,

RECALLING the Declaration on the Occasion of the Fiftieth Anniversary of the United Nations, contained in General Assembly resolution 50/6 of 24 October 1995,

RECALLING also all the relevant General Assembly resolutions on the matter, including resolution 49/60 of 9 December 1994 and the

[1] For states that are parties to the Convention, see Department of State publication, *Treaties in Force.*

annex thereto on the Declaration on Measures to Eliminate International Terrorism, in which the States Members of the United Nations solemnly reaffirmed their unequivocal condemnation of all acts, methods and practices of terrorism as criminal and unjustifiable, wherever and by whomever committed, including those which jeopardize the friendly relations among States and peoples and threaten the territorial integrity and security of States,

NOTING that the Declaration on Measures to Eliminate International Terrorism also encouraged States to review urgently the scope of the existing international legal provisions on the prevention, repression and elimination of terrorism in all its forms and manifestations, with the aim of ensuring that there is a comprehensive legal framework covering all aspects of the matter,

RECALLING paragraph 3 (f) of General Assembly resolution 51/210 of 17 December 1996, in which the Assembly called upon all States to take steps to prevent and counteract, through appropriate domestic measures, the financing of terrorists and terrorist organizations, whether such financing is direct or indirect through organizations which also have or claim to have charitable, social or cultural goals or which are also engaged in unlawful activities such as illicit arms trafficking, drug dealing and racketeering, including the exploitation of persons for purposes of funding terrorist activities, and in particular to consider, where appropriate, adopting regulatory measures to prevent and counteract movements of funds suspected to be intended for terrorist purposes without impeding in any way the freedom of legitimate capital movements and to intensify the exchange of information concerning international movements of such funds,

RECALLING also General Assembly resolution 52/165 of 15 December 1997, in which the Assembly called upon States to consider, in particular, the implementation of the measures set out in paragraphs 3 (a) to (f) of its resolution 51/210,

RECALLING further General Assembly resolution 53/108 of 8 December 1998, in which the Assembly decided that the Ad Hoc Committee established by General Assembly resolution 51/210 of 17 December 1996 should elaborate a draft international convention for the suppression of terrorist financing to supplement related existing international instruments,

CONSIDERING that the financing of terrorism is a matter of grave concern to the international community as a whole,

NOTING that the number and seriousness of acts of international terrorism depend on the financing that terrorists may obtain,

NOTING also that existing multilateral legal instruments do not expressly address such financing,

BEING convinced of the urgent need to enhance international cooperation among States in devising and adopting effective measures for the prevention of the financing of terrorism, as well as for its suppression through the prosecution and punishment of its perpetrators,

HAVE AGREED AS FOLLOWS:

ARTICLE 1

For the purposes of this Convention:

1. "Funds" means assets of every kind, whether tangible or intangible, movable or immovable, however acquired, and legal documents or instruments in any form, including electronic or digital, evidencing title to, or interest in, such assets, including, but not limited to, bank credits, travellers cheques, bank cheques, money orders, shares, securities, bonds, drafts and letters of credit.

2. "State or government facility" means any permanent or temporary facility or conveyance that is used or occupied by representatives of a State, members of Government, the legislature or the judiciary or by officials or employees of a State or any other public authority or entity or by employees or officials of an intergovernmental organization in connection with their official duties.

3. "Proceeds" means any funds derived from or obtained, directly or indirectly, through the commission of an offence set forth in article 2.

ARTICLE 2

1. Any person commits an offence within the meaning of this Convention if that person by any means, directly or indirectly, unlawfully and wilfully, provides or collects funds with the intention that they should be used or in the knowledge that they are to be used, in full or in part, in order to carry out:

(a) An act which constitutes an offence within the scope of and as defined in one of the treaties listed in the annex; or

(b) Any other act intended to cause death or serious bodily injury to a civilian, or to any other person not taking an active part in the hostilities in a situation of armed conflict, when the purpose of such act, by its nature or context, is to intimidate a population, or to compel a Government or an international organization to do or to abstain from doing any act.

2. (a) On depositing its instrument of ratification, acceptance, approval or accession, a State Party which is not a party to a treaty listed in the annex may declare that, in the application of this Convention to the State Party, the treaty shall be deemed not to be included in the annex referred to in paragraph 1, subparagraph (a). The declaration shall cease to have effect as soon as the treaty enters into force for the State Party, which shall notify the depositary of this fact;

(b) When a State Party ceases to be a party to a treaty listed in the annex, it may make a declaration as provided for in this article, with respect to that treaty.

3. For an act to constitute an offence set forth in paragraph 1, it shall not be necessary that the funds were actually used to carry out an offence referred to in paragraph 1, subparagraph (a) or (b).

4. Any person also commits an offence if that person attempts to commit an offence as set forth in paragraph 1 of this article.

5. Any person also commits an offence if that person:

(a) Participates as an accomplice in an offence as set forth in paragraph 1 or 4 of this article;

(b) Organizes or directs others to commit an offence as set forth in paragraph 1 or 4 of this article;

(c) Contributes to the commission of one or more offences as set forth in paragraph 1 or 4 of this article by a group of persons acting with a common purpose. Such contribution shall be intentional and shall either:

(i) Be made with the aim of furthering the criminal activity or criminal purpose of the group, where such activity or purpose involves the commission of an offence as set forth in paragraph 1 of this article; or

(ii) Be made in the knowledge of the intention of the group to commit an offence as set forth in paragraph 1 of this article.

ARTICLE 3

This Convention shall not apply where the offence is committed within a single State, the alleged offender is a national of that State and is present in the territory of that State and no other State has a basis under article 7, paragraph 1 or 2, to exercise jurisdiction, except that the provisions of articles 12 to 18 shall, as appropriate, apply in those cases.

ARTICLE 4

Each State Party shall adopt such measures as may be necessary:

(a) To establish as criminal offences under its domestic law the offences as set forth in article 2;

(b) To make those offences punishable by appropriate penalties which take into account the grave nature of the offences.

ARTICLE 5

1. Each State Party, in accordance with its domestic legal principles, shall take the necessary measures to enable a legal entity located in its territory or organized under its laws to be held liable when a person responsible for the management or control of that legal entity has, in that capacity, committed an offence as set forth in article 2. Such liability may be criminal, civil or administrative.

2. Such liability is incurred without prejudice to the criminal liability of individuals who have committed the offences.

3. Each State Party shall ensure, in particular, that legal entities liable in accordance with paragraph 1 above are subject to effective, proportionate and dissuasive criminal, civil or administrative sanctions. Such sanctions may include monetary sanctions.

ARTICLE 6

Each State Party shall adopt such measures as may be necessary, including, where appropriate, domestic legislation, to ensure that criminal acts within the scope of this Convention are under no circumstances justifiable by considerations of a political, philosophical, ideological, racial, ethnic, religious or other similar nature.

ARTICLE 7

1. Each State Party shall take such measures as may be necessary to establish its jurisdiction over the offences set forth in article 2 when:

(a) The offence is committed in the territory of that State;

(b) The offence is committed on board a vessel flying the flag of that State or an aircraft registered under the laws of that State at the time the offence is committed;

(c) The offence is committed by a national of that State.

2. A State Party may also establish its jurisdiction over any such offence when:

(a) The offence was directed towards or resulted in the carrying out of an offence referred to in article 2, paragraph 1, subparagraph (a) or (b), in the territory of or against a national of that State;

(b) The offence was directed towards or resulted in the carrying out of an offence referred to in article 2, paragraph 1, subparagraph (a) or (b), against a State or government facility of that State abroad, including diplomatic or consular premises of that State;

(c) The offence was directed towards or resulted in an offence referred to in article 2, paragraph 1, subparagraph (a) or (b), committed in an attempt to compel that State to do or abstain from doing any act;

(d) The offence is committed by a stateless person who has his or her habitual residence in the territory of that State;

(e) The offence is committed on board an aircraft which is operated by the Government of that State.

3. Upon ratifying, accepting, approving or acceding to this Convention, each State Party shall notify the Secretary-General of the United Nations of the jurisdiction it has established in accordance with paragraph 2. Should any change take place, the State Party concerned shall immediately notify the Secretary-General.

4. Each State Party shall likewise take such measures as may be necessary to establish its jurisdiction over the offences set forth in article 2 in cases where the alleged offender is present in its territory and it does not extradite that person to any of the States Parties that have established their jurisdiction in accordance with paragraphs 1 or 2.

5. When more than one State Party claims jurisdiction over the offences set forth in article 2, the relevant States Parties shall strive to coordinate their actions appropriately, in particular concerning the conditions for prosecution and the modalities for mutual legal assistance.

6. Without prejudice to the norms of general international law, this Convention does not exclude the exercise of any criminal jurisdiction established by a State Party in accordance with its domestic law.

ARTICLE 8

1. Each State Party shall take appropriate measures, in accordance with its domestic legal principles, for the identification, detection and freezing or seizure of any funds used or allocated for the

purpose of committing the offences set forth in article 2 as well as the proceeds derived from such offences, for purposes of possible forfeiture.

2. Each State Party shall take appropriate measures, in accordance with its domestic legal principles, for the forfeiture of funds used or allocated for the purpose of committing the offences set forth in article 2 and the proceeds derived from such offences.

3. Each State Party concerned may give consideration to concluding agreements on the sharing with other States Parties, on a regular or case-by-case basis, of the funds derived from the forfeitures referred to in this article.

4. Each State Party shall consider establishing mechanisms whereby the funds derived from the forfeitures referred to in this article are utilized to compensate the victims of offences referred to in article 2, paragraph 1, subparagraph (a) or (b), or their families.

5. The provisions of this article shall be implemented without prejudice to the rights of third parties acting in good faith.

ARTICLE 9

1. Upon receiving information that a person who has committed or who is alleged to have committed an offence set forth in article 2 may be present in its territory, the State Party concerned shall take such measures as may be necessary under its domestic law to investigate the facts contained in the information.

2. Upon being satisfied that the circumstances so warrant, the State Party in whose territory the offender or alleged offender is present shall take the appropriate measures under its domestic law so as to ensure that person's presence for the purpose of prosecution or extradition.

3. Any person regarding whom the measures referred to in paragraph 2 are being taken shall be entitled:

(a) To communicate without delay with the nearest appropriate representative of the State of which that person is a national or which is otherwise entitled to protect that person's rights or, if that person is a stateless person, the State in the territory of which that person habitually resides;

(b) To be visited by a representative of that State;

(c) To be informed of that person's rights under subparagraphs (a) and (b).

4. The rights referred to in paragraph 3 shall be exercised in conformity with the laws and regulations of the State in the territory of which the offender or alleged offender is present, subject to the provision that the said laws and regulations must enable full effect to be given to the purposes for which the rights accorded under paragraph 3 are intended.

5. The provisions of paragraphs 3 and 4 shall be without prejudice to the right of any State Party having a claim to jurisdiction in accordance with article 7, paragraph 1, subparagraph (b), or paragraph 2, subparagraph (b), to invite the International Committee of the Red Cross to communicate with and visit the alleged offender.

6. When a State Party, pursuant to the present article, has taken a person into custody, it shall immediately notify, directly or through the Secretary-General of the United Nations, the States Parties which have established jurisdiction in accordance with article 7, paragraph 1 or 2, and, if it considers it advisable, any other interested States Parties, of the fact that such person is in custody and of the circumstances which warrant that person's detention. The State which makes the investigation contemplated in paragraph 1 shall promptly inform the said States Parties of its findings and shall indicate whether it intends to exercise jurisdiction.

Article 10

1. The State Party in the territory of which the alleged offender is present shall, in cases to which article 7 applies, if it does not extradite that person, be obliged, without exception whatsoever and whether or not the offence was committed in its territory, to submit the case without undue delay to its competent authorities for the purpose of prosecution, through proceedings in accordance with the laws of that State. Those authorities shall take their decision in the same manner as in the case of any other offence of a grave nature under the law of that State.

2. Whenever a State Party is permitted under its domestic law to extradite or otherwise surrender one of its nationals only upon the condition that the person will be returned to that State to serve the sentence imposed as a result of the trial or proceeding for which the extradition or surrender of the person was sought, and this State and the State seeking the extradition of the person agree with this option and other terms they may deem appropriate, such a conditional extradition or surrender shall be sufficient to discharge the obligation set forth in paragraph 1.

Article 11

1. The offences set forth in article 2 shall be deemed to be included as extraditable offences in any extradition treaty existing between any of the States Parties before the entry into force of this Convention. States Parties undertake to include such offences as extraditable offences in every extradition treaty to be subsequently concluded between them.

2. When a State Party which makes extradition conditional on the existence of a treaty receives a request for extradition from another State Party with which it has no extradition treaty, the requested State Party may, at its option, consider this Convention as a legal basis for extradition in respect of the offences set forth in article 2. Extradition shall be subject to the other conditions provided by the law of the requested State.

3. States Parties which do not make extradition conditional on the existence of a treaty shall recognize the offences set forth in article 2 as extraditable offences between themselves, subject to the conditions provided by the law of the requested State.

4. If necessary, the offences set forth in article 2 shall be treated, for the purposes of extradition between States Parties, as if they had been committed not only in the place in which they occurred

but also in the territory of the States that have established jurisdiction in accordance with article 7, paragraphs 1 and 2.

5. The provisions of all extradition treaties and arrangements between States Parties with regard to offences set forth in article 2 shall be deemed to be modified as between States Parties to the extent that they are incompatible with this Convention.

ARTICLE 12

1. States Parties shall afford one another the greatest measure of assistance in connection with criminal investigations or criminal or extradition proceedings in respect of the offences set forth in article 2, including assistance in obtaining evidence in their possession necessary for the proceedings.

2. States Parties may not refuse a request for mutual legal assistance on the ground of bank secrecy.

3. The requesting Party shall not transmit or use information or evidence furnished by the requested Party for investigations, prosecutions or proceedings other than those stated in the request without the prior consent of the requested Party.

4. Each State Party may give consideration to establishing mechanisms to share with other States Parties information or evidence needed to establish criminal, civil or administrative liability pursuant to article 5.

5. States Parties shall carry out their obligations under paragraphs 1 and 2 in conformity with any treaties or other arrangements on mutual legal assistance or information exchange that may exist between them. In the absence of such treaties or arrangements, States Parties shall afford one another assistance in accordance with their domestic law.

ARTICLE 13

None of the offences set forth in article 2 shall be regarded, for the purposes of extradition or mutual legal assistance, as a fiscal offence. Accordingly, States Parties may not refuse a request for extradition or for mutual legal assistance on the sole ground that it concerns a fiscal offence.

ARTICLE 14

None of the offences set forth in article 2 shall be regarded for the purposes of extradition or mutual legal assistance as a political offence or as an offence connected with a political offence or as an offence inspired by political motives. Accordingly, a request for extradition or for mutual legal assistance based on such an offence may not be refused on the sole ground that it concerns a political offence or an offence connected with a political offence or an offence inspired by political motives.

ARTICLE 15

Nothing in this Convention shall be interpreted as imposing an obligation to extradite or to afford mutual legal assistance, if the requested State Party has substantial grounds for believing that the request for extradition for offences set forth in article 2 or for mutual legal assistance with respect to such offences has been made for the purpose of prosecuting or punishing a person on account of that person's race, religion, nationality, ethnic origin or political opinion or that compliance with the request would cause prejudice to that person's position for any of these reasons.

ARTICLE 16

1. A person who is being detained or is serving a sentence in the territory of one State Party whose presence in another State Party is requested for purposes of identification, testimony or otherwise providing assistance in obtaining evidence for the investigation or prosecution of offences set forth in article 2 may be transferred if the following conditions are met:

(a) The person freely gives his or her informed consent;

(b) The competent authorities of both States agree, subject to such conditions as those States may deem appropriate.

2. For the purposes of the present article:

(a) The State to which the person is transferred shall have the authority and obligation to keep the person transferred in custody, unless otherwise requested or authorized by the State from which the person was transferred;

(b) The State to which the person is transferred shall without delay implement its obligation to return the person to the custody of the State from which the person was transferred as agreed beforehand, or as otherwise agreed, by the competent authorities of both States;

(c) The State to which the person is transferred shall not require the State from which the person was transferred to initiate extradition proceedings for the return of the person;

(d) The person transferred shall receive credit for service of the sentence being served in the State from which he or she was transferred for time spent in the custody of the State to which he or she was transferred.

3. Unless the State Party from which a person is to be transferred in accordance with the present article so agrees, that person, whatever his or her nationality, shall not be prosecuted or detained or subjected to any other restriction of his or her personal liberty in the territory of the State to which that person is transferred in respect of acts or convictions anterior to his or her departure from the territory of the State from which such person was transferred.

ARTICLE 17

Any person who is taken into custody or regarding whom any other measures are taken or proceedings are carried out pursuant to this Convention shall be guaranteed fair treatment, including enjoyment of all rights and guarantees in conformity with the law of the State in the territory of which that person is present and applicable provisions of international law, including international human rights law.

ARTICLE 18

1. States Parties shall cooperate in the prevention of the offences set forth in article 2 by taking all practicable measures, inter alia,

by adapting their domestic legislation, if necessary, to prevent and counter preparations in their respective territories for the commission of those offences within or outside their territories, including:

(a) Measures to prohibit in their territories illegal activities of persons and organizations that knowingly encourage, instigate, organize or engage in the commission of offences set forth in article 2;

(b) Measures requiring financial institutions and other professions involved in financial transactions to utilize the most efficient measures available for the identification of their usual or occasional customers, as well as customers in whose interest accounts are opened, and to pay special attention to unusual or suspicious transactions and report transactions suspected of stemming from a criminal activity. For this purpose, States Parties shall consider:

(i) Adopting regulations prohibiting the opening of accounts, the holders or beneficiaries of which are unidentified or unidentifiable, and measures to ensure that such institutions verify the identity of the real owners of such transactions;

(ii) With respect to the identification of legal entities, requiring financial institutions, when necessary, to take measures to verify the legal existence and the structure of the customer by obtaining, either from a public register or from the customer or both, proof of incorporation, including information concerning the customer's name, legal form, address, directors and provisions regulating the power to bind the entity;

(iii) Adopting regulations imposing on financial institutions the obligation to report promptly to the competent authorities all complex, unusual large transactions and unusual patterns of transactions, which have no apparent economic or obviously lawful purpose, without fear of assuming criminal or civil liability for breach of any restriction on disclosure of information if they report their suspicions in good faith;

(iv) Requiring financial institutions to maintain, for at least five years, all necessary records on transactions, both domestic and international.

2. States Parties shall further cooperate in the prevention of offences set forth in article 2 by considering:

(a) Measures for the supervision, including, for example, the licensing, of all money-transmission agencies;

(b) Feasible measures to detect or monitor the physical cross-border transportation of cash and bearer negotiable instruments, subject to strict safeguards to ensure proper use of information and without impeding in any way the freedom of capital movements.

3. States Parties shall further cooperate in the prevention of the offences set forth in article 2 by exchanging accurate and verified information in accordance with their domestic law and coordinating administrative and other measures taken, as appropriate, to prevent the commission of offences set forth in article 2, in particular by:

(a) Establishing and maintaining channels of communication between their competent agencies and services to facilitate the secure and rapid exchange of information concerning all aspects of offences set forth in article 2;

(b) Cooperating with one another in conducting inquiries, with respect to the offences set forth in article 2, concerning:

(i) The identity, whereabouts and activities of persons in respect of whom reasonable suspicion exists that they are involved in such offences;

(ii) The movement of funds relating to the commission of such offences.

4. States Parties may exchange information through the International Criminal Police Organization (Interpol).

ARTICLE 19

The State Party where the alleged offender is prosecuted shall, in accordance with its domestic law or applicable procedures, communicate the final outcome of the proceedings to the Secretary-General of the United Nations, who shall transmit the information to the other States Parties.

ARTICLE 20

The States Parties shall carry out their obligations under this Convention in a manner consistent with the principles of sovereign equality and territorial integrity of States and that of non-intervention in the domestic affairs of other States.

ARTICLE 21

Nothing in this Convention shall affect other rights, obligations and responsibilities of States and individuals under international law, in particular the purposes of the Charter of the United Nations, international humanitarian law and other relevant conventions.

ARTICLE 22

Nothing in this Convention entitles a State Party to undertake in the territory of another State Party the exercise of jurisdiction or performance of functions which are exclusively reserved for the authorities of that other State Party by its domestic law.

ARTICLE 23

1. The annex may be amended by the addition of relevant treaties:

(a) That are open to the participation of all States;

(b) That have entered into force;

(c) That have been ratified, accepted, approved or acceded to by at least twenty-two States Parties to the present Convention.

2. After the entry into force of this Convention, any State Party may propose such an amendment. Any proposal for an amendment

shall be communicated to the depositary in written form. The depositary shall notify proposals that meet the requirements of paragraph 1 to all States Parties and seek their views on whether the proposed amendment should be adopted.

3. The proposed amendment shall be deemed adopted unless one third of the States Parties object to it by a written notification not later than 180 days after its circulation.

4. The adopted amendment to the annex shall enter into force 30 days after the deposit of the twenty-second instrument of ratification, acceptance or approval of such amendment for all those States Parties that have deposited such an instrument. For each State Party ratifying, accepting or approving the amendment after the deposit of the twenty-second instrument, the amendment shall enter into force on the thirtieth day after deposit by such State Party of its instrument of ratification, acceptance or approval.

Article 24

1. Any dispute between two or more States Parties concerning the interpretation or application of this Convention which cannot be settled through negotiation within a reasonable time shall, at the request of one of them, be submitted to arbitration. If, within six months from the date of the request for arbitration, the parties are unable to agree on the organization of the arbitration, any one of those parties may refer the dispute to the International Court of Justice, by application, in conformity with the Statute of the Court.

2. Each State may at the time of signature, ratification, acceptance or approval of this Convention or accession thereto declare that it does not consider itself bound by paragraph 1. The other States Parties shall not be bound by paragraph 1 with respect to any State Party which has made such a reservation.

3. Any State which has made a reservation in accordance with paragraph 2 may at any time withdraw that reservation by notification to the Secretary-General of the United Nations.

Article 25

1. This Convention shall be open for signature by all States from 10 January 2000 to 31 December 2001 at United Nations Headquarters in New York.

2. This Convention is subject to ratification, acceptance or approval. The instruments of ratification, acceptance or approval shall be deposited with the Secretary-General of the United Nations.

3. This Convention shall be open to accession by any State. The instruments of accession shall be deposited with the Secretary-General of the United Nations.

Article 26

1. This Convention shall enter into force on the thirtieth day following the date of the deposit of the twenty-second instrument of ratification, acceptance, approval or accession with the Secretary-General of the United Nations.

2. For each State ratifying, accepting, approving or acceding to the Convention after the deposit of the twenty-second instrument of ratification, acceptance, approval or accession, the Convention shall enter into force on the thirtieth day after deposit by such State of its instrument of ratification, acceptance, approval or accession.

Article 27

1. Any State Party may denounce this Convention by written notification to the Secretary-General of the United Nations.

2. Denunciation shall take effect one year following the date on which notification is received by the Secretary-General of the United Nations.

Article 28

The original of this Convention, of which the Arabic, Chinese, English, French, Russian and Spanish texts are equally authentic, shall be deposited with the Secretary-General of the United Nations who shall send certified copies thereof to all States.

In witness whereof, the undersigned, being duly authorized thereto by their respective Governments, have signed this Convention, opened for signature at United Nations Headquarters in New York on 10 January 2000.

Annex

1. Convention for the Suppression of Unlawful Seizure of Aircraft, done at The Hague on 16 December 1970.

2. Convention for the Suppression of Unlawful Acts against the Safety of Civil Aviation, done at Montreal on 23 September 1971.

3. Convention on the Prevention and Punishment of Crimes against Internationally Protected Persons, including Diplomatic Agents, adopted by the General Assembly of the United Nations on 14 December 1973.

4. International Convention against the Taking of Hostages, adopted by the General Assembly of the United Nations on 17 December 1979.

5. Convention on the Physical Protection of Nuclear Material, adopted at Vienna on 3 March 1980.

6. Protocol for the Suppression of Unlawful Acts of Violence at Airports Serving International Civil Aviation, supplementary to the Convention for the Suppression of Unlawful Acts against the Safety of Civil Aviation, done at Montreal on 24 February 1988.

7. Convention for the Suppression of Unlawful Acts against the Safety of Maritime Navigation, done at Rome on 10 March 1988.

8. Protocol for the Suppression of Unlawful Acts against the Safety of Fixed Platforms located on the Continental Shelf, done at Rome on 10 March 1988.

9. International Convention for the Suppression of Terrorist Bombings, adopted by the General Assembly of the United Nations on 15 December 1997.

d. Inter-American Convention Against Terrorism[1]

Adopted at Bridgetown, Barbados, June 3, 2002; Signed on behalf of the United States, June 3, 2002; Entered into force, July 10, 2003; Ratification advised by the Senate, October 7, 2005; Entered into force for the United States, December 15, 2005

The General Assembly,

REAFFIRMING the principles and provisions contained in the Charter of the Organization of American States and the Charter of the United Nations;

RECOGNIZING the threat that terrorism poses to democratic values and international peace and security, and that it is a source of profound concern to all member states;

CONVINCED that the Charter of the Organization of American States and international law constitute the appropriate framework for strengthening hemispheric cooperation for the prevention, combating, and elimination of terrorism in all its forms and manifestations;

BEARING IN MIND resolution RC.23/RES. 1/01 rev. 1 corr. 1, "Strengthening Hemispheric Cooperation to Prevent, Combat, and Eliminate Terrorism," of the Twenty-Third Meeting of Consultation of the Ministers of Foreign Affairs of September 21, 2001, which entrusted the Permanent Council with preparing a Draft Inter-American Convention against Terrorism;

RECALLING the Declaration of Lima to Prevent, Combat, and Eliminate Terrorism and the Plan of Action on Hemispheric Cooperation to Prevent, Combat, and Eliminate Terrorism, adopted within the framework of the First Inter-American Specialized Conference on Terrorism, in Lima, Peru, in April 1996, as well as the Commitment of Mar del Plata, adopted at the Second Inter-American Specialized Conference on Terrorism, and the work of the Inter-American Committee against Terrorism (CICTE);

CONSIDERING that terrorism is a serious criminal phenomenon, which is of deep concern to all member states; attacks democracy; impedes the enjoyment of human rights and fundamental freedoms; threatens the security of states, destabilizing and undermining the foundations of all society; and seriously impacts the economic and social development of the states in the region;

BEARING IN MIND that the Inter-American Democratic Charter recognizes the commitment by member states to promote and defend representative democracy and that no democratic state can be indifferent to the clear threat that terrorism poses to democratic institutions and freedoms;

[1] For states that are parties to the Convention, see Department of State publication, *Treaties in Force.*

REAFFIRMING that the fight against terrorism must be undertaken with full respect for national and international law, human rights, and democratic institutions, in order to preserve the rule of law, liberties and democratic values in the Hemisphere, which are essential components of a successful fight against terrorism;

CONVINCED that the adoption, ratification, and effective implementation of the Inter-American Convention against Terrorism contribute to the progressive development and the codification of international law;

UNDERSCORING the importance of effective action in cutting off the supply of funds for terrorism, and of coordinated action with international entities competent in the area of money laundering, especially the Inter-American Drug Abuse Control Commission (CICAD);

RECOGNIZING the urgency of strengthening and establishing new forms of regional cooperation against terrorism with a view to its eradication; and

RECOGNIZING the importance and timeliness of the existing international legal instruments on combating terrorism, including the 10 international instruments considered for the text of the Inter-American Convention against Terrorism itself, as well as the Convention to Prevent and Punish the Acts of Terrorism Taking the Forms of Crimes against Persons and Related Extortion That Are of International Significance, adopted by the General Assembly itself on February 2, 1971; the Convention on Offences and Certain Other Acts Committed on Board Aircraft, adopted in Tokyo on September 14, 1963; and the Convention on the Marking of Plastic Explosives for the Purpose of Detection, adopted in Montreal on March 1, 1991,

RESOLVES:

1. To adopt the Inter-American Convention against Terrorism attached to this resolution and to open it for signature by the member states on this date.

2. To urge member states to ratify the Convention as soon as possible, in accordance with their constitutional procedures.

3. To request the Secretary General to present a report to the General Assembly at its thirty-third regular session on progress made toward the Convention's entry into force.

Inter-American Convention Against Terrorism

The States Parties to this Convention,

BEARING IN MIND the purposes and principles of the Charter of the Organization of American States and the Charter of the United Nations;

CONSIDERING that terrorism represents a serious threat to democratic values and to international peace and security and is a cause of profound concern to all member states;

REAFFIRMING the need to adopt effective steps in the inter-American system to prevent, punish, and eliminate terrorism through the broadest cooperation;

RECOGNIZING that the serious economic harm to states which may result from terrorist acts is one of the factors that underscore the need for cooperation and the urgency of efforts to eradicate terrorism;

REAFFIRMING the commitment of the states to prevent, combat, punish, and eliminate terrorism; and

BEARING IN MIND resolution RC.23/RES. 1/01 rev. 1 corr. 1, "Strengthening Hemispheric Cooperation to Prevent, Combat, and Eliminate Terrorism," adopted at the Twenty-third Meeting of Consultation of Ministers of Foreign Affairs,

HAVE AGREED TO THE FOLLOWING:

ARTICLE 1

OBJECT AND PURPOSES

The purposes of this Convention are to prevent, punish, and eliminate terrorism. To that end, the states parties agree to adopt the necessary measures and to strengthen cooperation among them, in accordance with the terms of this Convention.

ARTICLE 2

APPLICABLE INTERNATIONAL INSTRUMENTS

1. For the purposes of this Convention, "offenses" means the offenses established in the international instruments listed below:

a. Convention for the Suppression of Unlawful Seizure of Aircraft, signed at The Hague on December 16, 1970.

b. Convention for the Suppression of Unlawful Acts against the Safety of Civil Aviation, signed at Montreal on September 23, 1971.

c. Convention on the Prevention and Punishment of Crimes against Internationally Protected Persons, including Diplomatic Agents, adopted by the General Assembly of the United Nations on December 14, 1973.

d. International Convention against the Taking of Hostages, adopted by the General Assembly of the United Nations on December 17, 1979.

e. Convention on the Physical Protection of Nuclear Material, signed at Vienna on March 3, 1980.

f. Protocol on the Suppression of Unlawful Acts of Violence at Airports Serving International Civil Aviation, supplementary to the Convention for the Suppression of Unlawful Acts against the Safety of Civil Aviation, signed at Montreal on February 24, 1988.

g. Convention for the Suppression of Unlawful Acts against the Safety of Maritime Navigation, done at Rome on March 10, 1988.

h. Protocol for the Suppression of Unlawful Acts against the Safety of Fixed Platforms Located on the Continental Shelf, done at Rome on March 10, 1988.

i. International Convention for the Suppression of Terrorist Bombings, adopted by the General Assembly of the United Nations on December 15, 1997.

j. International Convention for the Suppression of the Financing of Terrorism, adopted by the General Assembly of the United Nations on December 9, 1999.

2. Upon depositing its instrument of ratification to this Convention, a state party that is not a party to one or more of the international instruments listed in paragraph 1 of this article may declare that, in application of this Convention to such state party, that particular instrument shall be deemed not to be included in that paragraph. The declaration shall cease to have effect as soon as that instrument enters into force for that state party, which shall notify the depositary of this fact.

3. When a state party ceases to be a party to one of the international instruments listed in paragraph 1 of this article, it may make a declaration, as provided in paragraph 2 of this article, with respect to that instrument.

Article 3

Domestic measures

Each state party, in accordance with the provisions of its constitution, shall endeavor to become a party to the international instruments listed in Article 2 to which it is not yet a party and to adopt the necessary measures to effectively implement such instruments, including establishing, in its domestic legislation, penalties for the offenses described therein.

Article 4

Measures to prevent, combat, and eradicate the financing of terrorism

1. Each state party, to the extent it has not already done so, shall institute a legal and regulatory regime to prevent, combat, and eradicate the financing of terrorism and for effective international cooperation with respect thereto, which shall include:

a. A comprehensive domestic regulatory and supervisory regime for banks, other financial institutions, and other entities deemed particularly susceptible to being used for the financing of terrorist activities. This regime shall emphasize requirements for customer identification, record-keeping, and the reporting of suspicious or unusual transactions.

b. Measures to detect and monitor movements across borders of cash, bearer negotiable instruments, and other appropriate movements of value. These measures shall be subject to safeguards to ensure proper use of information and should not impede legitimate capital movements.

c. Measures to ensure that the competent authorities dedicated to combating the offenses established in the international instruments listed in Article 2 have the ability to cooperate and exchange information at the national and international levels within the conditions prescribed under its domestic law. To that end, each state party shall establish and maintain a financial intelligence unit to serve as a national center for the collection, analysis, and dissemination of pertinent money laundering and terrorist financing information. Each state party shall inform the Secretary General of the Organization of American States of the authority designated to be its financial intelligence unit.

2. When implementing paragraph 1 of this article, states parties shall use as guidelines the recommendations developed by specialized international and regional entities, in particular the Financial Action Task Force and, as appropriate, the Inter-American Drug Abuse Control Commission, the Caribbean Financial Action Task Force, and the South American Financial Action Task Force.

Article 5

Seizure and confiscation of funds or other assets

1. Each state party shall, in accordance with the procedures established in its domestic law, take such measures as may be necessary to provide for the identification, freezing or seizure for the purposes of possible forfeiture, and confiscation or forfeiture, of any funds or other assets constituting the proceeds of, used to facilitate, or used or intended to finance, the commission of any of the offenses established in the international instruments listed in Article 2 of this Convention.

2. The measures referred to in paragraph 1 shall apply to offenses committed both within and outside the jurisdiction of the state party.

Article 6

Predicate offenses to money laundering

1. Each state party shall take the necessary measures to ensure that its domestic penal money laundering legislation also includes as predicate offenses those offenses established in the international instruments listed in Article 2 of this Convention.

2. The money laundering predicate offenses referred to in paragraph 1 shall include those committed both within and outside the jurisdiction of the state party.

Article 7

Cooperation on border controls

1. The states parties, consistent with their respective domestic legal and administrative regimes, shall promote cooperation and the exchange of information in order to improve border and customs control measures to detect and prevent the international movement of terrorists and trafficking in arms or other materials intended to support terrorist activities.

2. In this context, they shall promote cooperation and the exchange of information to improve their controls on the issuance of travel and identity documents and to prevent their counterfeiting, forgery, or fraudulent use.

3. Such measures shall be carried out without prejudice to applicable international commitments in relation to the free movement of people and the facilitation of commerce.

Article 8

Cooperation among law enforcement authorities

The states parties shall work closely with one another, consistent with their respective domestic legal and administrative systems, to enhance the effectiveness of law enforcement action to combat the offenses established in the international instruments listed in Article 2. In this context, they shall establish and enhance, where necessary, channels of communication between their competent authorities in order to facilitate the secure and rapid exchange of information concerning all aspects of the offenses established in the international instruments listed in Article 2 of this Convention.

Article 9

Mutual legal assistance

The states parties shall afford one another the greatest measure of expeditious mutual legal assistance with respect to the prevention, investigation, and prosecution of the offenses established in the international instruments listed in Article 2 and proceedings related thereto, in accordance with applicable international agreements in force. In the absence of such agreements, states parties shall afford one another expeditious assistance in accordance with their domestic law.

Article 10

Transfer of persons in custody

1. A person who is being detained or is serving a sentence in the territory of one state party and whose presence in another state party is requested for purposes of identification, testimony, or otherwise providing assistance in obtaining evidence for the investigation or prosecution of offenses established in the international instruments listed in Article 2 may be transferred if the following conditions are met:

a. The person freely gives his or her informed consent; and

b. Both states agree, subject to such conditions as those states may deem appropriate.

2. For the purposes of this article:

a. The state to which the person is transferred shall have the authority and obligation to keep the person transferred in custody, unless otherwise requested or authorized by the state from which the person was transferred.

b. The state to which the person is transferred shall without delay implement its obligation to return the person to the custody of the state from which the person was transferred as agreed beforehand, or as otherwise agreed, by the competent authorities of both states.

c. The state to which the person is transferred shall not require the state from which the person was transferred to initiate extradition proceedings for the return of the person.

d. The person transferred shall receive, for time spent in the custody of the state to which he or she was transferred, credit toward service of the sentence being served in the state from which he or she was transferred.

3. Unless the state party from which a person is to be transferred in accordance with the present article so agrees, that person, whatever his or her nationality, shall not be prosecuted or detained or subjected to any other restriction of his or her personal liberty in the territory of the state to which that person is transferred in respect of acts or convictions prior to his or her departure from the territory of the state from which said person was transferred.

Article 11

Inapplicability of political offense exception

For the purposes of extradition or mutual legal assistance, none of the offenses established in the international instruments listed in Article 2 shall be regarded as a political offense or an offense connected with a political offense or an offense inspired by political motives. Accordingly, a request for extradition or mutual legal assistance may not be refused on the sole ground that it concerns a political offense or an offense connected with a political offense or an offense inspired by political motives.

Article 12

Denial of refugee status

Each state party shall take appropriate measures, consistent with the relevant provisions of national and international law, for the purpose of ensuring that refugee status is not granted to any person in respect of whom there are serious reasons for considering that he or she has committed an offense established in the international instruments listed in Article 2 of this Convention.

Article 13

Denial of asylum

Each state party shall take appropriate measures, consistent with the relevant provisions of national and international law, for the purpose of ensuring that asylum is not granted to any person in respect of whom there are reasonable grounds to believe that he or she has committed an offense established in the international instruments listed in Article 2 of this Convention.

Article 14

Nondiscrimination

None of the provisions of this Convention shall be interpreted as imposing an obligation to provide mutual legal assistance if the requested state party has substantial grounds for believing that the request has been made for the purpose of prosecuting or punishing a person on account of that person's race, religion, nationality, ethnic origin, or political opinion, or that compliance with the request would cause prejudice to that person's position for any of these reasons.

Article 15

Human rights

1. The measures carried out by the states parties under this Convention shall take place with full respect for the rule of law, human rights, and fundamental freedoms.

2. Nothing in this Convention shall be interpreted as affecting other rights and obligations of states and individuals under international law, in particular the Charter of the United Nations, the Charter of the Organization of American States, international humanitarian law, international human rights law, and international refugee law.

3. Any person who is taken into custody or regarding whom any other measures are taken or proceedings are carried out pursuant to this Convention shall be guaranteed fair treatment, including the enjoyment of all rights and guarantees in conformity with the law of the state in the territory of which that person is present and applicable provisions of international law.

Article 16

Training

1. The states parties shall promote technical cooperation and training programs at the national, bilateral, subregional, and regional levels and in the framework of the Organization of American States to strengthen the national institutions responsible for compliance with the obligations assumed under this Convention.

2. The states parties shall also promote, where appropriate, technical cooperation and training programs with other regional and international organizations conducting activities related to the purposes of this Convention.

Article 17

Cooperation through the Organization of American States

The states parties shall encourage the broadest cooperation within the pertinent organs of the Organization of American States, including the Inter-American Committee against Terrorism (CICTE), on matters related to the object and purposes of this Convention.

Article 18

Consultations among the parties

1. The states parties shall hold periodic meetings of consultation, as appropriate, with a view to facilitating:

   a. The full implementation of this Convention, including the consideration of issues of interest relating thereto identified by the states parties; and

   b. The exchange of information and experiences on effective means and methods to prevent, detect, investigate, and punish terrorism.

2. The Secretary General shall convene a meeting of consultation of the states parties after receiving the 10th instrument of ratification. Without prejudice to this, the states parties may hold consultations as they consider appropriate.

3. The states parties may request the pertinent organs of the Organization of American States, including CICTE, to facilitate the consultations referred to in the previous paragraphs and to provide other forms of assistance with respect to the implementation of this Convention.

Article 19

Exercise of jurisdiction

Nothing in this Convention entitles a state party to undertake in the territory of another state party the exercise of jurisdiction or performance of functions that are exclusively reserved to the authorities of that other state party by its domestic law.

Article 20

Depositary

The original instrument of this Convention, the English, French, Portuguese, and Spanish texts of which are equally authentic, shall be deposited with the General Secretariat of the Organization of American States.

Article 21

Signature and ratification

1. This Convention is open for signature by all member states of the Organization of American States.

2. This Convention is subject to ratification by the signatory states in accordance with their respective constitutional procedures. The instruments of ratification shall be deposited with the General Secretariat of the Organization of American States.

Article 22

Entry into force

1. This Convention shall enter into force on the 30th day following the date of deposit of the sixth instrument of ratification of the Convention with the General Secretariat of the Organization of American States.

2. For each state ratifying the Convention after deposit of the sixth instrument of ratification, the Convention shall enter into force on the 30th day following the deposit by such state of its instrument of ratification.

Article 23

Denunciation

1. Any state party may denounce this Convention by written notification to the Secretary General of the Organization of American

States. Denunciation shall take effect one year following the date on which notification is received by the Secretary General of the Organization.

2. Such denunciation shall not affect any requests for information or assistance made during the time the Convention is in force for the denouncing state.

2. United Nations Convention on the Prevention and Punishment of Crimes Against Internationally Protected Persons, Including Diplomatic Agents [1]

Adopted by the United Nations General Assembly, December 14, 1973; Signed on behalf of the United States, December 28, 1973; Ratification advised by the Senate, October 28, 1975; Instrument of ratification deposited with the Secretary-General of the United Nations, October 27, 1976; Entered into force, February 20, 1977

The States Parties to this Convention,

HAVING IN MIND the purposes and principles of the Charter of the United Nations concerning the maintenance of international peace and the promotion of friendly relations and co-operation among States,

CONSIDERING that crimes against diplomatic agents and other internationally protected persons jeopardizing the safety of these persons create a serious threat to the maintenance of normal international relations which are necessary for co-operation among States,

BELIEVING that the commission of such crimes is a matter of grave concern to the international community,

CONVINCED that there is an urgent need to adopt appropriate and effective measures for the prevention and punishment of such crimes,

HAVE AGREED AS FOLLOWS:

ARTICLE 1

For the purposes of this Convention:

1. "internationally protected person" means:

(a) a Head of State, including any member of a collegial body performing the functions of a Head of State under the constitution of the State concerned, a Head of Government or a Minister for Foreign Affairs, whenever any such person is in a foreign State, as well as members of his family who accompany him;

(b) any representative or official of a State or any official or other agent of an international organization of an intergovernmental character who, at the time when and in the place where a crime against him, his official premises, his private accommodation or his means of transport is committed, is entitled pursuant to international law to special protection from any attack on his person, freedom or dignity, as well as members of his family forming part of his household.

---

[1] 28 UST 1975; TIAS 8532; 1035 UNTS 167. For states that are parties to the Convention, see Department of State publication, *Treaties in Force*.

2. "alleged offender" means a person as to whom there is sufficient evidence to determine *prima facie* that he has committed or participated in one or more of the crimes set forth in article 2.

ARTICLE 2

1. The international commission of:

(a) a murder, kidnapping or other attack upon the person or liberty of an internationally protected person;

(b) a violent attack upon the official premises, the private accommodation or the means of transport of an internationally protected person likely to endanger his person or liberty;

(c) a threat to commit any such attack;

(d) an attempt to commit any such attack; and

(e) an act constituting participation as an accomplice in any such attack shall be made by each State Party a crime under its internal law.

2. Each State Party shall make these crimes punishable by appropriate penalties which take into account their grave nature.

3. Paragraphs 1 and 2 of this article in no way derogate from the obligations of States Parties under international law to take all appropriate measures to prevent other attacks on the person, freedom or dignity of an internationally protected person.

ARTICLE 3

1. Each State Party shall take such measures as may be necessary to establish its jurisdiction over the crimes set forth in article 2 in the following cases:

(a) when the crime is committed in the territory of that State or on board a ship or aircraft registered in that State;

(b) when the alleged offender is a national of that State;

(c) when the crime is committed against an internationally protected person as defined in article 1 who enjoys his status as such by virtue of functions which he exercise on behalf of that State.

2. Each State Party shall likewise take such measures as may be necessary to establish its jurisdiction over these crimes in cases where the alleged offender is present in its territory and it does not extradite him pursuant to article 8 to any of the States mentioned in paragraph 1 of this article.

3. This Convention does not exclude any criminal jurisdiction exercised in accordance with internal law.

ARTICLE 4

States Parties shall co-operate in the prevention of the crimes set forth in article 2, particularly by:

(a) taking all practicable measures to prevent preparations in their respective territories for the commission of those crimes within or outside their territories;

(b) exchanging information and co-ordinating the taking of administrative and other measures as appropriate to prevent the commission of those crimes.

ARTICLE 5

1. The State Party in which any of the crimes set forth in article 2 has been committed shall, if it has reason to believe that an alleged offender has fled from its territory, communicate to all other States concerned, directly or through the Secretary-General of the United Nations, all the pertinent facts regarding the crime committed and all available information regarding the identity of the alleged offender.

2. Whenever any of the crimes set forth in article 2 has been committed against an internationally protected person, any State Party which has information concerning the victim and the circumstances of the crime shall endeavor to transmit it, under the conditions provided for in its internal law, fully and promptly to the State Party on whose behalf he was exercising his functions.

ARTICLE 6

1. Upon being satisfied that the circumstances so warrant, the State Party in whose territory the alleged offender is present shall take the appropriate measures under its internal law so as to ensure his presence for the purpose of prosecution or extradition. Such measures shall be notified without delay directly or through the Secretary-General of the United Nations to:

(a) the State where the crime was committed;

(b) the State or States of which the alleged offender is a national or, if he is a stateless person, in whose territory he permanently resides;

(c) the State or States of which the internationally protected person concerned is a national or on whose behalf he was exercising his functions;

(d) all other States concerned; and

(e) the international organization of which the internationally protected person concerned is an official or an agent.

2. Any person regarding whom the measures referred to in paragraph 1 of this article are being taken shall be entitled:

(a) to communicate without delay with the nearest appropriate representative of the State of which he is a national or which is otherwise entitled to protect his rights or, if he is a stateless person, which he requests and which is willing to protect his rights; and

(b) to be visited by a representative of that State.

ARTICLE 7

The State Party in whose territory the alleged offender is present shall, if it does not extradite him, submit, without exception whatsoever and without undue delay, the case to its competent authorities for the purpose of prosecution, through proceedings in accordance with the laws of that State.

ARTICLE 8

1. To the extent that the crimes set forth in article 2 are not listed as extraditable offences in any extradition treaty existing between States Parties, they shall be deemed to be included as such

therein. States Parties undertake to include those crimes as extraditable offenses in every future extradition treaty to be concluded between them.

2. If a State Party which makes extradition conditional on the existence of a treaty receives a request for extradition from another State Party with which it has no extradition treaty, it may, if it decides to extradite, consider this Convention as the legal basis for extradition in respect of those crimes. Extradition shall be subject to the procedural provisions and the other conditions of the law of the requested State.

3. States Parties which do not make extradition conditional on the existence of a treaty shall recognize those crimes as extraditable offenses between themselves subject to the procedural provisions and the other conditions of the law of the requested State.

4. Each of the crimes shall be treated, for the purpose of extradition between States Parties, as if it had been committed not only in the place in which it occurred but also in the territories of the States required to establish their jurisdiction in accordance with paragraph 1 of article 3.

ARTICLE 9

Any person regarding whom proceedings are being carried out in connexion with any of the crimes set forth in article 2 shall be guaranteed fair treatment at all stages of the proceedings.

ARTICLE 10

1. States Parties shall afford one another the greatest measure of assistance in connexion with criminal proceedings brought in respect of the crimes set forth in article 2, including the supply of all evidence at their disposal necessary for the proceedings.

2. The provisions of paragraph 1 of this article shall not affect obligations concerning mutual judicial assistance embodied in any other treaty.

ARTICLE 11

The State Party where an alleged offender is prosecuted shall communicate the final outcome of the proceedings of the Secretary-General of the United Nations, who shall transmit the information to the other States Parties.

ARTICLE 12

The provisions of this Convention shall not affect the application of the Treaties on Asylum, in force at the date of the adoption of this Convention, as between the States which are parties to those Treaties; but a State Party to this Convention may not invoke those Treaties with respect to another State Party to this Convention which is not a party to those Treaties.

ARTICLE 13

1. Any dispute between two or more States Parties concerning the interpretation or application of this Convention which is not

settled by negotiation shall, at the request of one of them, be submitted to arbitration. If within six months from the date of the request for arbitration the parties are unable to agree on the organization of the arbitration, any one of those parties may refer the dispute to the International Court of Justice by request in conformity with the Statute of the Court.

2. Each State Party may at the time of signature or ratification of this Convention or accession thereto declare that it does not consider itself bound by paragraph 1 of this article. The other States Parties shall not be bound by paragraph 1 of this article with respect to any State Party which has made such a reservation.

3. Any State Party which has made a reservation in accordance with paragraph 2 of this article may at any time withdraw that reservation by notification to the Secretary-General of the United Nations.

Article 14

This Convention shall be open for signature by all States, until 31 December 1974 at United Nations Headquarters in New York.

Article 15

This Convention is subject to ratification. The instruments of ratification shall be deposited with the Secretary-General of the United Nations.

Article 16

This Convention shall remain open for accession by any State. The instruments of accession shall be deposited with the Secretary-General of the United Nations.

Article 17

1. This Convention shall enter into force on the thirtieth day following the date of deposit of the twenty-second instrument of ratification or accession with the Secretary-General of the United Nations.

2. For each State ratifying or acceding to the Convention after the deposit of the twenty-second instrument of ratification or accession, the Convention shall enter into force on the thirtieth day after deposit by such State of its instrument of ratification or accession.

Article 18

1. Any State Party may denounce this Convention by written notification to the Secretary-General of the United Nations.

2. Denunciation shall take effect six months following the date on which notification is received by the Secretary-General of the United Nations.

Article 19

The Secretary-General of the United Nations shall inform all States, *inter alia:*

(a) of signatures to this Convention, of the deposit of instruments of ratification or accession in accordance with articles 14, 15 and 16 and of notifications made under article 18.

(b) of the date on which this Convention will enter into force in accordance with article 17.

ARTICLE 20

The original of this Convention, of which the Chinese, English, French, Russian and Spanish texts are equally authentic, shall be deposited with the Secretary-General of the United Nations, who shall send certified copies thereof to all States.

IN WITNESS WHEREOF the undersigned, being duly authorized thereto by their respective Governments, have signed this Convention, opened for signature at New York on 14 December 1973.

3. International Convention Against the Taking of Hostages [1]

Adopted at New York, December 17, 1979; Signed on behalf of the United States, December 21, 1979; Ratification advised by the Senate, July 30, 1981; Entered into force generally, June 3, 1983; Entered into force for the United States, January 6, 1985

The States Parties to this Convention,

HAVING IN MIND the purposes and principles of the Charter of the United Nations concerning the maintenance of international peace and security and the promotion of friendly relations and co-operation among States,

RECOGNIZING in particular that everyone has the right to life, liberty and security of person, as set out in the Universal Declaration of Human Rights and the International Covenant on Civil and Political Rights,

REAFFIRMING the principle of equal rights and self-determination of peoples as enshrined in the Charter of the United Nations and the Declaration on Principles of International Law concerning Friendly Relations and Co-operation among States in accordance with the Charter of the United Nations, as well as in other relevant resolutions of the General Assembly,

CONSIDERING that the taking of hostages is an offence of grave concern to the international community and that, in accordance with the provisions of this Convention, any person committing an act of hostage taking shall either be prosecuted or extradited,

BEING CONVINCED that it is urgently necessary to develop international co-operation between States in devising and adopting effective measures for the prevention, prosecution and punishment of all acts of taking of hostages as manifestations of international terrorism,

HAVE AGREED AS FOLLOWS:

ARTICLE 1

1. Any person who seizes or detains and threatens to kill, to injure or to continue to detain another person (hereinafter referred to as the "hostage") in order to compel a third party, namely, a State, an international intergovernmental organization, a natural or juridical person, or a group of persons, to do or abstain from doing any act as an explicit or implicit condition for the release of the hostage commits the offence of taking of hostages ("hostage-taking") within the meaning of this Convention.

2. Any person who:

(a) attempts to commit an act of hostage-taking, or

[1] TIAS 11081. For states that are parties to the Convention, see Department of State publication, *Treaties in Force*.

(b) participates as an accomplice of anyone who commits or attempts to commit an act of hostage-taking likewise commits an offence for the purposes of this Convention.

ARTICLE 2

Each State Party shall make the offences set forth in article 1 punishable by appropriate penalties which take into account the grave nature of those offences.

ARTICLE 3

1. The State Party in the territory of which the hostage is held by the offender shall take all measures it considers appropriate to ease the situation of the hostage, in particular, to secure his release and, after his release, to facilitate, when relevant, his departure.

2. If any object which the offender has obtained as a result of the taking of hostages comes into the custody of a State Party, that State Party shall return it as soon as possible to the hostage or the third party referred to in article 1, as the case may be, or to the appropriate authorities thereof.

ARTICLE 4

States Parties shall co-operate in the prevention of the offences set forth in article 1, particularly by:

(a) taking all practicable measures to prevent preparations in their respective territories for the commission of those offences within or outside their territories, including measures to prohibit in their territories illegal activities of persons, groups and organizations that encourage, instigate, organize or engage in the perpetration of acts of taking of hostages;

(b) exchanging information and co-ordinating the taking of administrative and other measures as appropriate to prevent the commission of those offences.

ARTICLE 5

1. Each State Party shall take such measures as may be necessary to establish its jurisdiction over any of the offences set forth in article 1 which are committed:

(a) in its territory or on board a ship or aircraft registered in that State;

(b) by any of its nationals or, if that State considers it appropriate, by those stateless persons who have their habitual residence in its territory;

(c) in order to compel that State to do or abstain from doing any act; or

(d) with respect to a hostage who is a national of that State, if that State considers it appropriate.

2. Each State Party shall likewise take such measures as may be necessary to establish its jurisdiction over the offences set forth in article 1 in cases where the alleged offender is present in its territory and it does not extradite him to any of the States mentioned in paragraph 1 of this article.

3. This Convention does not exclude any criminal jurisdiction exercised in accordance with internal law.

ARTICLE 6

1. Upon being satisfied that the circumstances so warrant, any State Party in the territory of which the alleged offender is present shall, in accordance with its laws, take him into custody or take other measures to ensure his presence for such time as is necessary to enable any criminal or extradition proceedings to be instituted. That State Party shall immediately make a preliminary inquiry into the facts.

2. The custody or other measures referred to in paragraph 1 of this article shall be notified without delay directly or through the Secretary-General of the United Nations to:

(a) the State where the offence was committed;

(b) the State against which compulsion has been directed or attempted;

(c) the State of which the natural or juridical person against whom compulsion has been directed or attempted is a national;

(d) the State of which the hostage is a national or in the territory of which he has his habitual residence;

(e) the State of which the alleged offender is a national or, if he is a stateless person, in the territory of which he has his habitual residence;

(f) the international intergovernmental organization against which compulsion has been directed or attempted;

(g) all other States concerned.

3. Any person regarding whom the measures referred to in paragraph 1 of this article are being taken shall be entitled:

(a) to communicate without delay with the nearest appropriate representative of the State of which he is a national or which is otherwise entitled to establish such communication or, if he is a stateless person, the State in the territory of which he has his habitual residence;

(b) to be visited by a representative of that State.

4. The rights referred to in paragraph 3 of this article shall be exercised in conformity with the laws and regulations of the State in the territory of which the alleged offender is present subject to the proviso, however, that the said laws and regulations must enable full effect to be given to the purposes for which the rights accorded under paragraph 3 of this article are intended.

5. The provisions of paragraphs 3 and 4 of this article shall be without prejudice to the right of any State Party having a claim to jurisdiction in accordance with paragraph 1(b) of article 5 to invite the International Committee of the Red Cross to communicate with and visit the alleged offender.

6. The State which makes the preliminary inquiry contemplated in paragraph 1 of this article shall promptly report its findings to the States or organization referred to in paragraph 2 of this article and indicate whether it intends to exercise jurisdiction.

Article 7

The State Party where the alleged offender is prosecuted shall in accordance with its laws communicate the final outcome of the proceedings to the Secretary-General of the United Nations, who shall transmit the information to the other States concerned and the international intergovernmental organizations concerned.

Article 8

1. The State Party in the territory of which the alleged offender is found shall, if it does not extradite him, be obliged, without exception whatsoever and whether or not the offence was committed in its territory, to submit the case to its competent authorities for the purpose of prosecution, through proceedings in accordance with the laws of that State. Those authorities shall take their decision in the same manner as in the case of any ordinary offence of a grave nature under the law of that State.

2. Any person regarding whom proceedings are being carried out in connexion with any of the offences set forth in article 1 shall be guaranteed fair treatment at all stages of the proceedings, including enjoyment of all the rights and guarantees provided by the law of the State in the territory of which he is present.

Article 9

1. A request for the extradition of an alleged offender, pursuant to this Convention, shall not be granted if the requested State Party has substantial grounds for believing:

(a) that the request for extradition for an offence set forth in article 1 has been made for the purpose of prosecuting or punishing a person on account of his race, religion, nationality, ethnic origin or political opinion; or

(b) that the person's position may be prejudiced:

(i) for any of the reasons mentioned in subparagraph (a) of this paragraph, or

(ii) for the reason that communication with him by the appropriate authorities of the State entitled to exercise rights of protection cannot be effected.

2. With respect to the offences as defined in this Convention, the provisions of all extradition treaties and arrangements applicable between States Parties are modified as between States Parties to the extent that they are incompatible with this Convention.

Article 10

1. The offences set forth in article 1 shall be deemed to be included as extraditable offences in any extradition treaty existing between States Parties. States Parties undertake to include such offences as extraditable offences in every extradition treaty to be concluded between them.

2. If a State Party which makes extradition conditional on the existence of a treaty receives a request for extradition from another State Party with which it has no extradition treaty, the requested State may at its option consider this Convention as the legal basis

for extradition in respect of the offences set forth in article 1. Extradition shall be subject to the other conditions provided by the law of the requested State.

3. States Parties which do not make extradition conditional on the existence of a treaty shall recognize the offences set forth in article 1 as extraditable offences between themselves subject to the conditions provided by the law of the requested State.

4. The offences set forth in article 1 shall be treated, for the purpose of extradition between States Parties, as if they had been committed not only in the place in which they occurred but also in the territories of the States required to establish their jurisdiction in accordance with paragraph 1 of article 5.

Article 11

1. States Parties shall afford one another the greatest measure of assistance in connexion with criminal proceedings brought in respect of the offences set forth in article 1, including the supply of all evidence at their disposal necessary for the proceedings.

2. The provisions of paragraph 1 of this article shall not affect obligations concerning mutual judicial assistance embodied in any other treaty.

Article 12

In so far as the Geneva Conventions of 1949 for the protection of war victims or the Protocols Additional to those Conventions are applicable to a particular act of hostage-taking, and in so far as States Parties to this Convention are bound under those conventions to prosecute or hand over the hostage-taker, the present Convention shall not apply to an act of hostage-taking committed in the course of armed conflicts as defined in the Geneva Conventions of 1949 and the Protocols thereto, including armed conflicts mentioned in article 1, paragraph 4, of Additional Protocol I of 1977, in which peoples are fighting against colonial domination and alien occupation and against racist regimes in the exercise of their right of self-determination, as enshrined in the Charter of the United Nations and the Declaration on Principles of International Law concerning Friendly Relations and Co-operation among States in accordance with the Charter of the United Nations.

Article 13

This Convention shall not apply where the offence is committed within a single State, the hostage and the alleged offender are nationals of that State and the alleged offender is found in the territory of that State.

Article 14

Nothing in this Convention shall be construed as justifying the violation of the territorial integrity or political independence of a State in contravention of the Charter of the United Nations.

ARTICLE 15

The provisions of this Convention shall not affect the application of the Treaties on Asylum, in force at the date of the adoption of this Convention, as between the States which are parties to those Treaties; but a State Party to this Convention may not invoke those Treaties with respect to another State Party to this Convention which is not a party to those treaties.

ARTICLE 16

1. Any dispute between two or more States Parties concerning the interpretation or application of this Convention which is not settled by negotiation shall, at the request of one of them, be submitted to arbitration. If within six months from the date of the request for arbitration the parties are unable to agree on the organization of the arbitration, any one of those parties may refer the dispute to the International Court of Justice by request in conformity with the Statute of the Court.

2. Each State may at the time of signature or ratification of this Convention or accession thereto declare that it does not consider itself bound by paragraph 1 of this article. The other States Parties shall not be bound by paragraph 1 of this article with respect to any State Party which has made such a reservation.

3. Any State Party which has made a reservation in accordance with paragraph 2 of this article may at any time withdraw that reservation by notification to the Secretary-General of the United Nations.

ARTICLE 17

1. This Convention is open for signature by all States until 31 December 1980 at United Nations Headquarters in New York.

2. This Convention is subject to ratification. The instruments of ratification shall be deposited with the Secretary-General of the United Nations.

3. This Convention is open for accession by any State. The instruments of accession shall be deposited with the Secretary-General of the United Nations.

ARTICLE 18

1. This Convention shall enter into force on the thirtieth day following the date of deposit of the twenty-second instrument of ratification or accession with the Secretary-General of the United Nations.

2. For each State ratifying or acceding to the Convention after the deposit of the twenty-second instrument of ratification or accession, the Convention shall enter into force on the thirtieth day after deposit by such State of its instrument of ratification or accession.

ARTICLE 19

1. Any State Party may denounce this Convention by written notification to the Secretary-General of the United Nations.

2. Denunciation shall take effect one year following the date on which notification is received by the Secretary-General of the United Nations.

ARTICLE 20

The original of this Convention, of which the Arabic, Chinese, English, French, Russian and Spanish texts are equally authentic, shall be deposited with the Secretary-General of the United Nations, who shall send certified copies thereof to all States.

IN WITNESS WHEREOF, the undersigned, being duly authorized thereto by their respective Governments, have signed this Convention, opened for signature at New York on 18 December 1979.

4. United Nations Convention Against Illicit Traffic in Narcotic Drugs and Psychotropic Substances [1]

Adopted at Vienna, December 20, 1988; Ratification advised by the Senate, November 21, 1989; Entered into force, November 11, 1990

The Parties to this Convention,

DEEPLY concerned by the magnitude of and rising trend in the illicit production of, demand for and traffic in narcotic drugs and psychotropic substances, which pose a serious threat to the health and welfare of human beings and adversely affect the economic, cultural and political foundations of society,

DEEPLY concerned also by the steadily increasing inroads into various social groups made by illicit traffic in narcotic drugs and psychotropic substances, and particularly by the fact that children are used in many parts of the world as an illicit drug consumers market and for purposes of illicit production, distribution and trade in narcotic drugs and psychotropic substances, which entails a danger of incalculable gravity,

RECOGNIZING the links between illicit traffic and other related organized criminal activities which undermine the legitimate economies and threaten the stability, security and sovereignty of States,

RECOGNIZING also the illicit traffic is an international criminal activity, the suppression of which demands urgent attention and the highest priority,

AWARE that illicit traffic generates large financial profits and wealth enabling transnational criminal organizations to penetrate, contaminate and corrupt the structures of government, legitimate commercial and financial business, and society at all its levels,

DETERMINED to deprive persons engaged in illicit traffic of the proceeds of their criminal activities and thereby eliminate their main incentive for so doing,

DESIRING to eliminate the root causes of the problem of abuse of narcotic drugs and psychotropic substances, including the illicit demand for such drugs and substances and the enormous profits derived from illicit traffic,

CONSIDERING that measures are necessary to monitor certain substances, including precursors, chemicals and solvents, which are used in the manufacture of narcotic drugs and psychotropic substances, the ready availability of which has led to an increase in the clandestine manufacture of such drugs and substances,

DETERMINED to improve international co-operation in the suppression of illicit traffic by sea,

[1] For states that are parties to the Convention, see Department of State publication, *Treaties in Force*.

RECOGNIZING that eradication of illicit traffic is a collective responsibility of all States and that, to that end, coordinated action within the framework of international co-operation is necessary,

ACKNOWLEDGING the competence of the United Nations in the field of control of narcotic drugs and psychotropic substances and desirous that the international organs concerned with such control should be within the framework of that Organization,

REAFFIRMING the guiding principles of existing treaties in the field of narcotic drugs and psychotropic substances and the system of control which they embody,

RECOGNIZING the need to reinforce and supplement the measures provided in the Single Convention on Narcotic Drugs, 1961, that Convention as amended by the 1972 Protocol Amending the Single Convention on Narcotic Drugs, 1961, and the 1971 Convention on Psychotropic Substances, in order to counter the magnitude and extent of illicit traffic and its grave consequences,

RECOGNIZING also the importance of strengthening and enhancing effective legal means for international co-operation in criminal matters for suppressing the international criminal activities of illicit traffic,

DESIRING to conclude a comprehensive, effective and operative international convention that is directed specifically against illicit traffic and that considers the various aspects of the problem as a whole, in particular those aspects not envisaged in the existing treaties in the field of narcotic drugs and psychotropic substances,

HEREBY AGREE AS FOLLOWS:

ARTICLE 1—DEFINITIONS

Except where otherwise expressly indicated or where the context otherwise requires, the following definitions shall apply throughout this Convention:

(a) "Board" means the International Narcotics Control Board established by the Single Convention on Narcotic Drugs, 1961, and that Convention as amended by the 1972 Protocol Amending the Single Convention on Narcotic Drugs, 1961;

(b) "Cannabis plant" means any plant of the genus Cannabis;

(c) "Coca bush" means the plant of any species of the genus Erythroxylon;

(d) "Commercial carrier" means any person or any public, private or other entity engaged in transporting persons, goods or mails for remuneration, hire or any other benefit;

(e) "Commission" means the Commission on Narcotic Drugs of the Economic and Social Council of the United Nations;

(f) "Confiscation", which includes forfeiture where applicable, means the permanent deprivation of property by order of a court or other competent authority;

(g) "Controlled delivery" means the technique of allowing illicit or suspect consignments of narcotic drugs, psychotropic substances, substances in Table I and Table II annexed to this Convention, or substances substituted for them, to pass out of, through or into the territory of one or more countries, with the knowledge and under the supervision of their competent authorities, with a view to identifying persons involved in the commission of offences established in accordance with article 3, paragraph 1 of the Convention;

(h) "1961 Convention" means the Single Convention on Narcotic Drugs, 1961;

(i) "1961 Convention as amended" means the Single Convention on Narcotic Drugs, 1961, as amended by the 1972 Protocol Amending the Single Convention on Narcotic Drugs, 1961;

(j) "1971 Convention" means the Convention on Psychotropic Substances, 1971;

(k) "Council" means the Economic and Social Council of the United Nations;

(l) "Freezing" or "seizure" means temporarily prohibiting the transfer, conversion, disposition or movement of property or temporarily assuming custody or control of property on the basis of an order issued by a court or a competent authority;

(m) "Illicit traffic" means the offences set forth in article 3, paragraphs 1 and 2, of this Convention;

(n) "Narcotic drug" means any of the substances, natural or synthetic, in Schedules I and II of the Single Convention on Narcotic Drugs, 1961, and that Convention as amended by the 1972 Protocol Amending the Single Convention on Narcotic Drugs, 1961;

(o) "Opium poppy" means the plant of the species *Papaver somniferum* L;

(p) "Proceeds" means any property derived from or obtained, directly or indirectly, through the commission of an offence established in accordance with article 3, paragraph 1;

(q) "Property" means assets of every kind, whether corporeal or incorporeal, movable or immovable, tangible or intangible, and legal documents or instruments evidencing title to, or interest in, such assets;

(r) "Psychotropic substance" means any substance, natural or synthetic, or any natural material in Schedules I, II, III and IV of the Convention on Psychotropic Substances, 1971;

(s) "Secretary-General" means the Secretary-General of the United Nations;

(t) "Table I" and "Table II" means the correspondingly numbered lists of substances annexed to this Convention, as amended from time to time in accordance with article 12;

(u) "Transit State" means a State through the territory of which illicit narcotic drugs, psychotropic substances and substances in Table I and Table II are being moved, which is neither the place of origin nor the place of ultimate destination thereof.

ARTICLE 2—SCOPE OF THE CONVENTION

1. The purpose of this Convention is to promote co-operation among the Parties so that they may address more effectively the various aspects of illicit traffic in narcotic drugs and psychotropic substances having an international dimension. In carrying out

their obligations under the Convention, the Parties shall take necessary measures, including legislative and administrative measures, in conformity with the fundamental provisions of their respective domestic legislative systems.

2. The Parties shall carry out their obligations under this Convention in a manner consistent with the principles of sovereign equality and territorial integrity of States and that of non-intervention in the domestic affairs of other States.

3. A Party shall not undertake in the territory of another Party the exercise of jurisdiction and performance of functions which are exclusively reserved for the authorities of that other Party by its domestic law.

ARTICLE 3—OFFENCES AND SANCTIONS

1. Each Party shall adopt such measures as may be necessary to establish as criminal offences under its domestic law, when committed intentionally:

(a)(i) The productions, manufacture, extraction, preparation, offering, offering for sale, distribution, sale, delivery on any terms whatsoever, brokerage, dispatch, dispatch in transit, transport, importation or exportation of any narcotic drug or any psychotropic substance contrary to the provisions of the 1961 Convention, the 1961 Convention as amended or the 1971 Convention;

(ii) The cultivation of opium poppy, coca bush or cannabis plant for the purpose of the production of narcotic drugs contrary to the provisions of the 1961 Convention and the 1961 Convention as amended;

(iii) The possession or purchase of any narcotic drug or psychotropic substance for the purpose of any of the activities enumerated in (i) above;

(iv) The manufacture, transport or distribution of equipment, materials or of substances listed in Table I and Table II, knowing that they are to be used in or for the illicit cultivation, production, or manufacture of narcotic drugs or psychotropic substances;

(v) The organization, management or financing of any of the offences enumerated in (i), (ii), (iii) or (iv) above;

(b)(i) The conversion or transfer of property, knowing that such property is derived from any offence or offences established in accordance with subparagraph (a) of this paragraph, or from an act of participation in such offence or offences, for the purpose of concealing or disguising the illicit origin of the property or of assisting any person who is involved in the commission of such an offence or offences to evade the legal consequences of his actions;

(ii) The concealment or disguise of the true nature, source, location, disposition, movement, rights with respect to, or ownership of property, knowing that such property is derived from an offence or offences established in accordance with subparagraph (a) of this paragraph or from an act of participation in such an offence or offences;

(c) Subject to its constitutional principles and the basic concepts of its legal system:

(i) The acquisition, possession or use of property, knowing, at the time of receipt, that such property was derived from an offence or offences established in accordance with subparagraph (a) of this paragraph or from an act of participation in such offence or offences;

(ii) The possession of equipment or materials or substances listed in Table I and Table II, knowing that they are being or are to be used in or for the illicit cultivation, production or manufacture of narcotic drugs or psychotropic substances;

(iii) Publicly inciting or inducing others, by any means, to commit any of the offences established in accordance with this article or to use narcotic drugs or psychotropic substances illicitly;

(iv) Participation in, association or conspiracy to commit, attempts to commit and aiding, abetting, facilitating and counselling the commission of any of the offences established in accordance with this article.

2. Subject to its constitutional principles and the basic concepts of its legal system, each Party shall adopt such measures as may be necessary to establish as a criminal offence under its domestic law, when committed intentionally, the possession, purchase or cultivation of narcotic drugs or psychotropic substances for personal consumption contrary to the provisions of the 1961 Convention, the 1961 Convention as amended or the 1971 Convention.

3. Knowledge, intent or purpose required as an element of an offence set forth in paragraph 1 of this article may be inferred from objective factual circumstances.

4. (a) Each Party shall make the commission of the offences established in accordance with paragraph 1 of this article liable to sanctions which take into account the grave nature of these offences, such as imprisonment or other form of deprivation of liberty, pecuniary sanctions and confiscation.

(b) The Parties may provide, in addition to conviction or punishment, for an offence established in accordance with paragraph 1 of this article, that the offender shall undergo measures such as treatment, education, aftercare, rehabilitation or social reintegration.

(c) Notwithstanding the preceding subparagraphs, in appropriate cases of a minor nature, the Parties may provide, as alternatives to conviction or punishment, measures such as education, rehabilitation or social reintegration, as well as, when the offender is a drug abuser, treatment and aftercare.

(d) The Parties may provide, either as an alternative to conviction or punishment, or in addition to conviction or punishment of an offence established in accordance with paragraph 2 of this article, measures for the treatment, education, aftercare, rehabilitation or social reintegration of the offender.

5. The Parties shall ensure that their courts and other competent authorities having jurisdiction can take into account factual circumstances which make the commission of the offences established in accordance with paragraph 1 of this article particularly serious, such as:

(a) The involvement in the offence of an organized criminal group to which the offender belongs;

(b) The involvement of the offender in other international organized criminal activities;

(c) The involvement of the offender in other illegal activities facilitated by commission of the offence;

(d) The use of violence or arms by the offender;

(e) The fact that the offender holds a public office and that the offence is connected with the office in question;

(f) The victimization or use of minors;

(g) The fact that the offence is committed in a penal institution or in an educational institution or social service facility or in their immediate vicinity or in other places to which school children and students resort for educational, sports and social activities;

(h) Prior conviction, particularly for similar offences, whether foreign or domestic, to the extent permitted under the domestic law of a Party.

6. The Parties shall endeavour to ensure that any discretionary legal powers under their domestic law relating to the prosecution of persons for offences established in accordance with this article are exercised to maximize the effectiveness of law enforcement measures in respect of those offences and with due regard to the need to deter the commission of such offences.

7. The Parties shall ensure that their courts or other competent authorities bear in mind the serious nature of the offences enumerated in paragraph 1 of this article and the circumstances enumerated in paragraph 5 of this article when considering the eventuality of early release or parole of persons convicted of such offences.

8. Each Party shall, where appropriate, establish under its domestic law a long statute of limitations period in which to commence proceedings for any offence established in accordance with paragraph 1 of this article, and a longer period where the alleged offender has evaded the administration of justice.

9. Each Party shall take appropriate measures, consistent with its legal system, to ensure that a person charged with or convicted of an offence established in accordance with paragraph 1 of this article, who is found within it territory, its present at the necessary criminal proceedings.

10. For the purpose of co-operation among the Parties under this Convention, including, in particular, co-operation under articles 5, 6, 7 and 9, offences established in accordance with this article shall not be considered as fiscal offences or as political offences or regarded as politically motivated, without prejudice to the constitutional limitations and the fundamental domestic law of the Parties.

11. Nothing contained in this article shall affect the principle that the description of the offences to which it refers and of legal defences thereto is reserved to the domestic law of a Party and that such offences shall be prosecuted and punished in conformity with that law.

ARTICLE 4—JURISDICTION

1. Each Party:

(a) Shall take such measures, as may be necessary to establish its jurisdiction over the offences it has established in accordance with article 3, paragraph 1, when:

(i) The offence is committed in its territory;

(ii) The offence is committed on board a vessel flying its flag or an aircraft which is registered under its laws at the time the offence is committed;

(b) May take such measures as may be necessary to establish its jurisdiction over the offences it has established in accordance with article 3, paragraph 1, when:

(i) The offence is committed by one of its nationals or by a person who has his habitual residence in its territory;

(ii) The offence is committed on board a vessel concerning which that Party has been authorized to take appropriate action pursuant to article 17, provided that such jurisdiction shall be exercised only on the basis of agreements or arrangements referred to in paragraphs 4 and 9 of that article;

(iii) The offence is one of those established in accordance with article 3, paragraph 1, subparagraph (c)(iv), and is committed outside its territory with a view to the commission, within its territory, of an offence established in accordance with article 3, paragraph 1.

2. Each Party:

(a) Shall also take such measures as may be necessary to establish its jurisdiction over the offences it has established in accordance with article 3, paragraph 1, when the alleged offender is present in its territory and it does not extradite him to another Party on the ground:

(i) That the offence has been committed in its territory or on board a vessel flying its flag or an aircraft which was registered under its law at the time the offence was committed; or

(ii) That the offence has been committed by one of its nationals;

(b) May also take such measures as may be necessary to establish its jurisdiction over the offences it has established in accordance with article 3, paragraph 1, when the alleged offender is present in its territory and it does not extradite him to another Party.

3. This Convention does not exclude the exercise of any criminal jurisdiction established by a Party in accordance with its domestic law.

ARTICLE 5—CONFISCATION

1. Each Party shall adopt such measures as may be necessary to enable confiscation of:

(a) Proceeds derived from offences established in accordance with article 3, paragraph 1, or property the value of which corresponds to that of such proceeds;

(b) Narcotic drugs and psychotropic substances, materials and equipment or other instrumentalities used in or intended for use in any manner in offences established in accordance with article 3, paragraph 1.

2. Each Party shall also adopt such measures as may be necessary to enable its competent authorities to identify, trace, and freeze or seize proceeds, property, instrumentalities or any other things referred to in paragraph 1 of this article, for the purpose of eventual confiscation.

3. In order to carry out the measures referred to in this article, each Party shall empower its courts or other competent authorities to order that bank, financial or commercial records be made available or be seized. A Party shall not decline to act under the provisions of this paragraph on the ground of bank secrecy.

4. (a) Following a request made pursuant to this article by another Party having jurisdiction over an offence established in accordance with article 3, paragraph 1, the Party in whose territory proceeds, property, instrumentalities or any other things referred to in paragraph 1 of this article are situated shall:

(i) Submit the request to its competent authorities for the purpose of obtaining an order of confiscation and, if such order is granted, give effect to it; or

(ii) Submit to its competent authorities, with a view to giving effect to it to the extent requested, an order of confiscation issued by the requesting Party in accordance with paragraph 1 of this article, in so far as it relates to proceeds, property, instrumentalities or any other things referred to in paragraph 1 situated in the territory of the requested Party.

(b) Following a request made pursuant to this article by another Party having jurisdiction over an offence established in accordance with article 3, paragraph 1, the requested Party shall take measures to identify, trace, and freeze or seize proceeds, property, instrumentalities or any other things referred to in paragraph 1 of this article for the purpose of eventual confiscation to be ordered either by the requesting Party or, pursuant to a request under subparagraph (a) of this paragraph, by the requested Party.

(c) The decisions or actions provided for in subparagraph (a) and (b) of this paragraph shall be taken by the requested Party, in accordance with and subject to the provisions of its domestic law and its procedural rules or any bilateral or multilateral treaty, agreement or arrangement to which it may be bound in relation to the requesting Party.

(d) The provisions of article 7, paragraphs 6 to 19 are applicable *mutatis mutandis*. In addition to the information specified in article 7, paragraph 10, requests made pursuant to this article shall contain the following:

(i) In the case of a request pertaining to subparagraph (a)(i) of this paragraph, a description of the property to be confiscated and a statement of the facts relied upon by the requesting Party sufficient to enable the requested Party to seek the order under its domestic law;

(ii) In the case of a request pertaining to subparagraph (a)(ii), a legally admissible copy of an order of confiscation issued by the requesting Party upon which the request is based, a statement of the facts and information as to the extent to which the execution of the order is requested;

(iii) In the case of a request pertaining to subparagraph (b), a statement of the facts relied upon by the requesting Party and a description of the actions requested.

(e) Each Party shall furnish to the Secretary-General the text of any of its laws and regulations which give effect to this paragraph and the text of any subsequent changes to such laws and regulations.

(f) If a Party elects to make the taking of the measures referred to in subparagraphs (a) and (b) of this paragraph conditional on the existence of a relevant treaty, that Party shall consider this Convention as the necessary and sufficient treaty basis.

(g) The Parties shall seek to conclude bilateral and multilateral treaties, agreements or arrangements to enhance the effectiveness of international co-operation pursuant to this article.

5. (a) Proceeds or property confiscated by a Party pursuant to paragraph 1 or paragraph 4 of this article shall be disposed of by that Party according to its domestic law and administrative procedures.

(b) Then acting on the request of another Party in accordance with this article, a Party may give special consideration to concluding agreements on:

(i) Contributing the value of such proceeds and property, or funds derived from the sale of such proceeds or property, or a substantial part thereof, to intergovernmental bodies specializing in the fight against illicit traffic in and abuse of narcotic drugs and psychotropic substances;

(ii) Sharing with other Parties, on a regular or case-by-case basis, such proceeds or property, or funds derived from the sale of such proceeds or property, in accordance with its domestic law, administrative procedures or bilateral or multilateral agreements entered into for this purpose.

6. (a) If proceeds have been transformed or converted into other property, such property shall be liable to the measures referred to in this article instead of the proceeds.

(b) If proceeds have been intermingled with property acquired from legitimate sources, such property shall, without prejudice to any powers relating to seizure or freezing, be liable to confiscation up to the assessed value of the intermingled proceeds.

(c) Income or other benefits derived from:

(i) Proceeds;

(ii) Property into which proceeds have been transformed or converted; or

(iii) Property with which proceeds have been intermingled shall also be liable to the measures referred to in this article, in the same manner and to the same extent as proceeds.

7. Each Party may consider ensuring that the onus of proof be reversed regarding the lawful origin of alleged proceeds or other property, liable to confiscation, to the extent that such action is consistent with the principles of its domestic law and with the nature of the judicial and other proceedings.

8. The provisions of this article shall not be construed as prejudicing the rights of *bona fide* third parties.

9. Nothing contained in this article shall affect the principle that the measures to which it refers shall be defined and implemented

in accordance with and subject to the provisions of the domestic law of a Party.

ARTICLE 6—EXTRADITION

1. This article shall apply to the offences established by the Parties in accordance with article 3, paragraph 1.

2. Each of the offences to which this article applies shall be deemed to be included as an extraditable offence in any extradition treaty existing between Parties. The Parties undertake to include such offences as extraditable offences in every extradition treaty to be concluded between them.

3. If a Party which makes extradition conditional on the existence of a treaty receives a request for extradition from another Party with which it has no extradition treaty, it may consider this Convention as the legal basis for extradition in respect of any offence to which this article applies. The Parties which require detailed legislation in order to use this Convention as a legal basis for extradition shall consider enacting such legislation as may be necessary.

4. The Parties which do not make extradition conditional on the existence of a treaty shall recognize offences to which this article applies as extraditable offences between themselves.

5. Extradition shall be subject to the conditions provided for by the law of the requested Party or by applicable extradition treaties, including the grounds upon which the requested Party may refuse extradition.

6. In considering requests received pursuant to this article, the requested State may refuse to comply with such requests where there are substantial grounds leading its judicial or other competent authorities to believe that compliance would facilitate the prosecution or punishment of any person on account of his race, religion, nationality or political opinions, or would cause prejudice for any of those reasons to any person affected by the request.

7. The Parties shall endeavour to expedite extradition procedures and to simplify evidentiary requirements relating thereto in respect of any offence to which this article applies.

8. Subject to the provisions of its domestic law and its extradition treaties, the requested Party may, upon being satisfied that the circumstances so warrant and are urgent, and at the request of the requesting Party, take a person whose extradition is sought and who is present in its territory into custody or take other appropriate measures to ensure his presence at extradition proceedings.

9. Without prejudice to the exercise of any criminal jurisdiction established in accordance with its domestic law, a Party in whose territory an alleged offender is found shall:

(a) If it does not extradite him in respect of an offence established in accordance with article 3, paragraph 1, on the grounds set forth in article 4, paragraph 2, subparagraph (a), submit the case to its competent authorities for the purpose of prosecution, unless otherwise agreed with the requesting Party;

(b) If it does not extradite him in respect of such an offence and has established its jurisdiction in relation to that offence in accordance with article 4, paragraph 2, subparagraph (b), submit the case to its competent authorities for the purpose of prosecution, unless otherwise requested by the requesting Party for the purposes of preserving its legitimate jurisdiction.

10. If extradition, sought for purposes of enforcing a sentence, is refused because the person sought is a national of the requested Party, the requested Party shall if its law so permits and in conformity with the requirements of such law, upon application of the requesting Party, consider the enforcement of the sentence which has been imposed under the law of the requesting Party, or the remainder thereof.

11. The Parties shall seek to conclude bilateral and multilateral agreements to carry out or to enhance the effectiveness of extradition.

12. The Parties may consider entering into bilateral or multilateral agreements, whether *ad hoc* or general, on the transfer to their country of persons sentenced to imprisonment and other forms of deprivation of liberty for offences to which this article applies, in order that they may complete their sentences there.

ARTICLE 7—MUTUAL LEGAL ASSISTANCE

1. The Parties shall afford one another, pursuant to this article, the widest measure of mutual legal assistance in investigations, prosecutions and judicial proceedings in relation to criminal offences established in accordance with article 3, paragraph 1.

2. Mutual legal assistance to be afforded in accordance with this article may be requested for any of the following purposes:

(a) Taking evidence or statements from persons;

(b) Effecting service of judicial documents;

(c) Executing searches and seizures;

(d) Examining objects and sites;

(e) Providing information and evidentiary items;

(f) Providing originals or certified copies of relevant documents and records, including bank, financial, corporate or business records;

(g) Identifying or tracing proceeds, property, instrumentalities or other things for evidentiary purposes.

3. The Parties may afford one another any other forms of mutual legal assistance allowed by the domestic law of the requested Party.

4. Upon request, the Parties shall facilitate or encourage, to the extent consistent with their domestic law and practice, the presence or availability of persons, including persons in custody, who consent to assist in investigations or participate in proceedings.

5. A Party shall not decline to render mutual legal assistance under this article on the ground of bank secrecy.

6. The provisions of this article shall not affect the obligations under any other treaty, bilateral or multilateral, which governs or will govern, in whole or in part, mutual legal assistance in criminal matters.

7. Paragraphs 8 to 19 of this article shall apply to requests made pursuant to this article if the Parties in question are not bound by a treaty of mutual legal assistance. If these Parties are bound by

such a treaty, the corresponding provisions of that treaty shall apply unless the Parties agree to apply paragraphs 8 to 19 of this article in lieu thereof

8. Parties shall designate an authority, or when necessary authorities, which shall have the responsibility and power to execute requests for mutual legal assistance or to transmit them to the competent authorities for execution. The authority or the authorities designated for this purpose shall be notified to the Secretary General. Transmission of requests for mutual legal assistance and any communication related thereto shall be effected between the authorities designated by the Parties; this requirement shall be without prejudice to the right of a Party to require that such requests and communications be addressed to it through the diplomatic channel and, in urgent circumstances, where the Parties agree, through channels of the International Criminal Police Organization, if possible.

9. Requests shall be made in writing in a language acceptable to the requested Party. The language or languages acceptable to each Party shall be notified to the Secretary-General. In urgent circumstances, and where agreed by the Parties, requests may be made orally, but shall be confirmed in writing forthwith.

10. A request for mutual legal assistance shall contain:

(a) The identity of the authority making the request;

(b) The subject matter and nature of the investigation, prosecution or proceeding to which the request relates, and the name and the functions of the authority conducting such investigation, prosecution or proceeding;

(c) A summary of the relevant facts, except in respect of requests for the purpose of service of judicial documents;

(d) A description of the assistance sought and details of any particular procedure the requesting Party wishes to be followed;

(e) Where possible, the identity, location and nationality of any person concerned;

(f) The purpose for which the evidence, information or action is sought.

11. The requested Party may request additional information when it appears necessary for the execution of the request in accordance with its domestic law or when it can facilitate such execution.

12. A request shall be executed in accordance with the domestic law of the requested Party and, to the extent not contrary to the domestic law of the requested Party and where possible, in accordance with the procedures specified in the request.

13. The requesting Party shall not transmit nor use information or evidence furnished by the requested Party for investigations, prosecutions or proceedings other than those stated in the request without the prior consent of the requested Party.

14. The requesting Party may require that the requested Party keep confidential the fact and substance of the request, except to the extent necessary to execute the request. If the requested Party cannot comply with the requirement of confidentiality, it shall promptly inform the requesting Party.

15. Mutual legal assistance may be refused:

(a) If the request is not made in conformity with the provisions of this article;

(b) If the requested Party considers that execution of the request is likely to prejudice its sovereignty, security, *ordre public* or other essential interests;

(c) If the authorities of the requested Party would be prohibited by its domestic law from carrying out the action requested with regard to any similar offence, had it been subject to investigation, prosecution or proceedings under their own jurisdiction;

(d) If it would be contrary to the legal system of the requested Party relating to mutual legal assistance for the request to be granted.

16. Reasons shall be given for any refusal of mutual legal assistance.

17. Mutual legal assistance may be postponed by the requested Party on the ground that it interferes with an ongoing investigation, prosecution or proceeding. In such a case, the requested Party shall consult with the requesting Party to determine if the assistance can still be given subject to such terms and conditions as the requested Part deems necessary.

18. A witness, expert or other person who consents to give evidence in a proceeding or to assist in an investigation, prosecution or judicial proceeding in the territory of the requesting Party, shall not be prosecuted, detained, punished or subjected to any other restriction of his personal liberty in that territory in respect of acts, omissions or convictions prior to his departure from the territory of the requested Party. Such safe conduct shall cease when the witness, expert or other person having had, for a period of fifteen consecutive days, or for any period agreed upon by the Parties, from the date on which he has been officially informed that his presence is no longer required by the judicial authorities, an opportunity of leaving, has nevertheless remained, voluntarily in the territory or, having left it, has returned of his own free will.

19. The ordinary costs of executing a request shall be borne by the requested Party, unless otherwise agreed by the Parties concerned. If expenses of a substantial or extraordinary nature are or will be required to fulfill the request, the Parties shall consult to determine the terms and conditions under which the request will be executed as well as the manner in which the costs shall be borne.

20. The Parties shall consider, as may be necessary, the possibility of concluding bilateral or multilateral agreements or arrangements that would serve the purposes of, give practical effect to, or enhance the provisions of this article.

ARTICLE 8—TRANSFER OF PROCEEDINGS

The Parties shall give consideration to the possibility of transferring to one another proceedings for criminal prosecution of offences established in accordance with article 3, paragraph 1, in cases where such transfer is considered to be in the interests of a proper administration of justice.

ARTICLE 9—OTHER FORMS OF CO-OPERATION AND TRAINING

1. The Parties shall co-operate closely with one another, consistent with their respective domestic legal and administrative systems, with a view to enhancing the effectiveness of law enforcement action to suppress the commission of offences established in accordance with article 3, paragraph 1. They shall, in particular, on the basis of bilateral or multilateral agreements or arrangements:

(a) Establish and maintain channels of communication between their competent agencies and services to facilitate the secure and rapid exchange of information concerning all aspects of offences established in accordance with article 3, paragraph 1, including, if the Parties concerned deem it appropriate, links with other criminal activities;

(b) Co-operate with one another in conducting enquiries, with respect to offences established in accordance with article 3, paragraph 1, having an international character, concerning:

(i) The identity, whereabouts and activities of persons suspected of being involved in offences established in accordance with article 3, paragraph 1;

(ii) The movement of proceeds or property derived from the commission of such offences;

(iii) The movement of narcotic drugs, psychotropic substances, substances in Table I and Table II of this Convention and instrumentalities used or intended for use in the commission of such offences;

(c) In appropriate cases and if not contrary to domestic law, establish joint teams, taking into account the need to protect the security of persons and of operations, to carry out the provisions of this paragraph. Officials of any Party taking part in such teams shall act as authorized by the appropriate authorities of the Party in whose territory the operation is to take place; in all such cases, the Parties involved shall ensure that the sovereignty of the Party on whose territory the operation is to take place is fully respected;

(d) Provide, when appropriate, necessary quantities of substances for analytical or investigative purposes;

(e) Facilitate effective coordination between their competent agencies and services and promote the exchange of personnel and other experts, including the posting of liaison officers.

2. Each Party shall, to the extent necessary, initiate, develop or improve a specific training programmes for its law enforcement and other personnel, including customs, charged with the suppression of offences established in accordance with article 3, paragraph 1. Such programmes shall deal, in particular, with the following:

(a) Methods used in the detection and suppression of offences established in accordance with article 3, paragraph 1;

(b) Routes and techniques used by persons suspected of being involved in offences established in accordance with article 3, paragraph 1, particularly in transit States, and appropriate countermeasures;

(c) Monitoring of the import and export of narcotic drugs, psychotropic substances and substances in Table I and Table II;

(d) Detection and monitoring of the movement of proceeds and property derived from, and narcotic drugs, psychotropic substances and substances in Table I and Table II, and instrumentalities used or intended for use in, the commission of offences established in accordance with article 3, paragraph 1;

(e) Methods used for the transfer, concealment or disguise of such proceeds, property and instrumentalities;

(f) Collection of evidence;

(g) Control techniques in free trade zones and free ports;

(h) Modern law enforcement techniques.

3. The Parties shall assist one another to plan and implement research and training programmes designed to share expertise in the areas referred to in paragraph 2 of this article and, to this end, shall also, when appropriate, use regional and international conferences and seminars to promote co-operation and stimulate discussion on problems of mutual concern, including the special problems and needs of transit States.

ARTICLE 10—INTERNATIONAL CO-OPERATION AND ASSISTANCE FOR TRANSIT STATES

1. The Parties shall co-operate, directly or through competent international or regional organizations, to assist and support transit States and, in particular, developing countries in need of such assistance and support, to the extent possible, through programmes of technical co-operation on interdiction and other related activities.

2. The Parties may undertake, directly or through competent international or regional organizations, to provide financial assistance to such transit States for the purpose of augmenting and strengthening the infrastructure needed for effective control and prevention of illicit traffic.

3. The Parties may conclude bilateral or multilateral agreements or arrangements to enhance the effectiveness of international co-operation pursuant to this article and may take into consideration financial arrangements in this regard.

ARTICLE 11—CONTROLLED DELIVERY

1. If permitted by the basic principles of their respective domestic legal systems, the Parties shall take the necessary measures, within their possibilities, to allow for the appropriate use of controlled delivery at the international level, on the basis of agreements or arrangements mutually consented to, with a view to identifying persons involved in offences established in accordance with article 3, paragraph 1, and to taking legal action against them.

2. Decisions to use controlled delivery shall be made on a case-by-case basis and may, when necessary, take into consideration financial arrangements and understandings with respect to the exercise of jurisdiction by the Parties concerned.

3. Illicit consignments whose controlled delivery is agreed to may, with the consent of the Parties concerned, be intercepted and allowed to continue with the narcotic drugs or psychotropic substances intact or removed or replaced in whole or in part.

ARTICLE 12—SUBSTANCES FREQUENTLY USED IN THE ILLICIT MANUFACTURE OF NARCOTIC DRUGS OR PSYCHOTROPIC SUBSTANCES

1. The Parties shall take the measures they deem appropriate to prevent diversion of substances in Table I and Table II used for the purpose of illicit manufacture of narcotic drugs or psychotropic substances, and shall co-operate with one another to this end.

2. If a Party or the Board has information which in its opinion may require the inclusion of a substance in Table I or Table II, it shall notify the Secretary-General and furnish him with the information in support of that notification. The procedure described in paragraphs 2 to 7 of this article shall also apply when a Party or the Board has information justifying the deletion of a substance from Table I or Table II, or the transfer of a substance from one Table to the other.

3. The Secretary-General shall transmit such notification, and any information which he considers relevant, to the Parties, to the Commission, and, where notification is made by a Party, to the Board. The Parties shall communicate their comments concerning the notification to the Secretary-General, together with all supplementary information which may assist the Board in establishing an assessment and the Commission in reaching a decision.

4. If the Board, taking into account the extent, importance and diversity of the licit use of the substance, and the possibility and ease of using alternate substances both for licit purposes and for the illicit manufacture of narcotic drugs or psychotropic substances, finds:

(a) That the substance is frequently used in the illicit manufacture of a narcotic drug or psychotropic substance;

(b) That the volume and extent of the illicit manufacture of a narcotic drug or psychotropic substance creates serious public health or social problems, so as to warrant international action,

it shall communicate to the Commission an assessment of the substance, including the likely effect of adding the substance to either Table I or Table II on both licit use and illicit manufacture, together with recommendations of monitoring measures, if any, that would be appropriate in the light of its assessment.

5. The Commission, taking into account the comments submitted by the Parties and the comments and recommendations of the Board, whose assessment shall be determinative as to scientific matters, and also taking into due consideration any other relevant factors, may decide by a two-thirds majority of its members to place a substance in Table I or Table II.

6. Any decision of the Commission taken pursuant to this article shall be communicated by the Secretary-General to all States and other entities which are, or which are entitled to become, Parties to this Convention, and to the Board. Such decision shall become fully effective with respect to each Party one hundred and eighty days after the date of such communication.

7. (a) The decision of the Commission taken under this article shall be subject to review by the Council upon the request of any Party filed within one hundred and eighty days after the date of notification of the decision. The request for review shall be sent to

the Secretary-General, together with all relevant information upon which the request for review is based.

(b) The Secretary-General shall transmit copies of the request for review and the relevant information to the Commission, to the Board and to all the Parties, inviting them to submit their comments within ninety days. All comments received shall be submitted to the Council for consideration.

(c) The Council may confirm or reverse the decision of the Commission. Notification of the Council's decision shall be transmitted to all States and other entities which are, or which are entitled to become, Parties to this Convention, to the Commission and to the Board.

8. (a) Without prejudice to the generality of the provisions contained in paragraph 1 of this article and the provisions of the 1961 Convention, the 1961 Convention as amended and the 1971 Convention, the Parties shall take the measures they deem appropriate to monitor the manufacture and distribution of substances in Table I and Table II which are carried out within their territory.

(b) To this end, the Parties may:

(i) Control all persons and enterprises engaged in the manufacture and distribution of such substances;

(ii) Control under license the establishment and premises in which such manufacture or distribution may take place;

(iii) Require that licensees obtain a permit for conducting the aforesaid operations;

(iv) Prevent the accumulation of such substances in the possession of manufacturers and distributors, in excess of the quantities required for the normal conduct of business and the prevailing market conditions.

9. Each Party shall, with respect to substances in Table I and Table II, take the following measures:

(a) Establish and maintain a system to monitor international trade in substances in Table I and Table II in order to facilitate the identification of suspicious transactions. Such monitoring systems shall be applied in close co-operation with manufacturers, importers, exporters, wholesalers and retailers, who shall inform the competent authorities of suspicious orders and transactions;

(b) Provide for the seizure of any substance in Table I or Table II if there is sufficient evidence that it is for use in the illicit manufacture of a narcotic drug or psychotropic substance;

(c) Notify, as soon as possible, the competent authorities and services of the Parties concerned if there is reason to believe that the import, export or transit of a substance in Table I or Table II is destined for the illicit manufacture of narcotic drugs or psychotropic substances, including in particular information about the means of payment and any other essential elements which led to that belief;

(d) Require that imports and exports be properly labelled and documented. Commercial documents such as invoices, cargo manifests, customs, transport and other shipping documents shall include the names, as stated in Table I or Table II, of the substances being imported or exported, the quantity being imported or exported, and the name and address of the exporter, the importer and, when available, the consignee;

(e) Ensure that documents referred to in subparagraph (d) of this paragraph are maintained for a period of not less than two years and may be made available for inspection by the competent authorities.

10. (a) In addition to the provisions of paragraph 9, and upon request to the Secretary-General by the interested Party, each Party from whose territory a substance in Table I is to be exported shall ensure that, prior to such export, the following information is supplied by its competent authorities to the competent authorities of the importing country:

(i) Name and address of the exporter and importer and, when available, the consignee;

(ii) Name of the substance in Table I;

(iii) Quantity of the substance to be exported;

(iv) Expected point of entry and expected date of dispatch;

(v) Any other information which is mutually agreed upon by the Parties.

(b) A Party may adopt more strict or severe measures of control than those provided by this paragraph if, in its opinion, such measures are desirable or necessary.

11. Where a Party furnishes information to another Party in accordance with paragraphs 9 and 10 of this article, the Party furnishing such information may require that the Party receiving it keep confidential any trade, business, commercial or professional secret or trade process.

12. Each Party shall furnish annually to the Board, in the form and manner provided for by it and on forms made available by it, information on:

(a) The amounts seized of substances in Table I and Table II and, when known, their origin;

(b) Any substance not included in Table I or Table II which is identified as having been used in illicit manufacture of narcotic drugs or psychotropic substances, and which is deemed by the Party to be sufficiently significant to be brought to the attention of the Board;

(c) Methods of diversion and illicit manufacture.

13. The Board shall report annually to the Commission on the implementation of this article and the Commission shall periodically review the adequacy and propriety of Table I and Table II.

14. The provisions of this article shall not apply to pharmaceutical preparations, nor to other preparations containing substances in Table I or Table II that are compounded in such a way that such substances cannot be easily used or recovered by readily applicable means.

ARTICLE 13—MATERIALS AND EQUIPMENT

The Parties shall take such measures as they deem appropriate to prevent trade in and the diversion of materials and equipment for illicit production or manufacture of narcotic drugs and psychotropic substances and shall co-operate to this end.

ARTICLE 14—MEASURES TO ERADICATE ILLICIT CULTIVATION OF NARCOTIC PLANTS AND TO ELIMINATE ILLICIT DEMAND FOR NARCOTIC DRUGS AND PSYCHOTROPIC SUBSTANCES

1. Any measures taken pursuant to this Convention by Parties shall not be less stringent than the provisions applicable to the eradication of illicit cultivation of plants containing narcotic and psychotropic substances and to the elimination of illicit demand for narcotic drugs and psychotropic substances under the provisions of the 1961 Convention, the 1961 Convention as amended and the 1971 Convention.

2. Each Party shall take appropriate measures to prevent illicit cultivation of and to eradicate plants containing narcotic or psychotropic substances, such as opium poppy, coca bush and cannabis plants, cultivated illicitly in its territory. The measures adopted shall respect fundamental human rights and shall take due account of traditional licit uses, where there is historic evidence of such use, as well as the protection of the environment.

3. (a) The Parties may co-operate to increase the effectiveness of eradication efforts. Such co-operation may, *inter alia,* include support, when appropriate, for integrated rural development leading to economically viable, alternatives to illicit cultivation. Factors such as access to markets, the availability of resources and prevailing socioeconomic conditions should be taken into account before such rural development programmes are implemented. The Parties may agree on any other appropriate measures of co-operation.

(b) The Parties shall also facilitate the exchange of scientific and technical information and the conduct of research concerning eradication.

(c) Whenever they have common frontiers, the Parties shall seek to co-operate in eradication programmes in their respective areas along those frontiers.

4. The Parties shall adopt appropriate measures aimed at eliminating or reducing illicit demand for narcotic drugs and psychotropic substances, with a view to reducing human suffering and eliminating financial incentives for illicit traffic. These measures may be based, *inter alia,* on the recommendations of the United Nations, specialized agencies of the United Nations such as the World Health Organization, and other competent international organizations, and on the Comprehensive Multidisciplinary Outline adopted by the International Conference on Drug Abuse and Illicit Trafficking, held in 1987, as it pertains to governmental and nongovernmental agencies and private efforts in the fields of prevention, treatment and rehabilitation. The Parties may enter into bilateral or multilateral agreements or arrangements aimed at eliminating or reducing illicit demand for narcotic drugs and psychotropic substances.

5. The Parties may also take necessary measures for early destruction or lawful disposal of the narcotic drugs, psychotropic substances and substances in Table I and Table II which have been seized or confiscated and for the admissibility as evidence of duly certified necessary quantities of such substances.

ARTICLE 15—COMMERCIAL CARRIERS

1. The Parties shall take appropriate measures to ensure that means of transport operated by commercial carriers are not used in the commission of offences established in accordance with article 3, paragraph 1; such measures may include special arrangements with commercial carriers.

2. Each Party shall require commercial carriers to take reasonable precautions to prevent the use of their means of transport for the commission of offences established in accordance with article 3, paragraph 1. Such precautions may include:

(a) If the principal place of business of a commercial carrier is within the territory of the Party:

(i) Training of personnel to identify suspicious consignments or persons;

(ii) Promotion of integrity of personnel;

(b) If a commercial carrier is operating within the territory of the Party:

(i) Submission of cargo manifests in advance, whenever possible;

(ii) Use of tamper-resistant, individually verifiable seals on containers;

(iii) Reporting to the appropriate authorities at the earliest opportunity all suspicious circumstances that may be related to the commission of offences established in accordance with article 3, paragraph 1.

3. Each Party shall seek to ensure that commercial carriers and the appropriate authorities at points of entry and exit and other customs control areas co-operate, with a view to preventing unauthorized access to means of transport and cargo and to implementing appropriate security measures.

ARTICLE 16—COMMERCIAL DOCUMENTS AND LABELLING OF EXPORTS

1. Each Party shall require that lawful exports of narcotic drugs and psychotropic substances be properly documented. In addition to the requirements for documentation under article 31 of the 1961 Convention, article 31 of the 1961 Convention as amended and article 12 of the 1971 Convention, commercial documents such as invoices, cargo manifests, customs, transport and other shipping documents shall include the names of the narcotic drugs and psychotropic substances being exported as set out in the respective Schedules of the 1961 Convention, the 1961 Convention as amended and the 1971 Convention, the quantity being exported, and the name and address of the exporter, the importer and, when available, the consignee.

2. Each Party shall require that consignments of narcotic drugs and psychotropic substances being exported be not mislabeled.

ARTICLE 17—ILLICIT TRAFFIC BY SEA

1. The Parties shall co-operate to the fullest extent possible to suppress illicit traffic by sea, in conformity with the international law of the sea.

2. A Party which has reasonable grounds to suspect that a vessel flying its flag or not displaying a flag or marks of registry is engaged in illicit traffic may request the assistance of other Parties in suppressing its use for that purpose. The Parties so requested shall render such assistance within the means available to them.

3. A Party which has reasonable grounds to suspect that a vessel exercising freedom of navigation in accordance with international law and flying the flag or displaying marks of registry of another Party is engaged in illicit traffic may so notify the flag State, request confirmation of registry and, if confirmed, request authorization from the flag State to take appropriate measures in regard to that vessel.

4. In accordance with paragraph 3 or in accordance with treaties in force between them or in accordance with any agreement or arrangement otherwise reached between those Parties, the flag State may authorize the requesting State to, *inter alia:*

(a) Board the vessel;

(b) Search the vessel;

(c) If evidence of involvement in illicit traffic is found, take appropriate action with respect to the vessel, persons and cargo on board.

5. Where action is taken pursuant to this article, the Parties concerned shall take due account of the need not to endanger the safety of life at sea, the security of the vessel and the cargo or to prejudice the commercial and legal interests of the flag State or any other interested State.

6. The flag State may, consistent with its obligations in paragraph 1 of this article, subject its authorization to conditions to be mutually agreed between it and the requesting Party, including conditions relating to responsibility.

7. For the purposes of paragraphs 3 and 4 of this article, a Party shall respond expeditiously to a request from another Party to determine whether a vessel that is flying its flag is entitled to do so, and to requests for authorization made pursuant to paragraph 3. At the time of becoming a Party to this Convention, each Party shall designate an authority or, when necessary, authorities to receive and respond to such requests. Such designation shall be notified through the Secretary-General to all other Parties within one month of the designation.

8. A Party which has taken any action in accordance with this article shall promptly inform the flag State concerned of the results of that action.

9. The Parties shall consider entering into bilateral or regional agreements or arrangements to carry out, or to enhance the effectiveness of, the provisions of this article.

10. Action pursuant to paragraph 4 of this article shall be carried out only by warships or military aircraft, or other ships or aircraft clearly marked and identifiable as being on government service and authorized to that effect.

11. Any action taken in accordance with this article shall take due account of the need not to interfere with or affect the rights and obligations and the exercise of jurisdiction of coastal States in accordance with the international law of the sea.

ARTICLE 18—FREE TRADE ZONES AND FREE PORTS

1. The Parties shall apply measures to suppress illicit traffic in narcotic drugs, psychotropic substances and substances in Table I and Table II in free trade zones and in free ports that are no less stringent than those applied in other parts of their territories.

2. The Parties shall endeavour:

(a) To monitor the movement of goods and persons in free trade zones and free ports, and, to that end, shall empower the competent authorities to search cargoes and incoming and outgoing vessels, including pleasure craft and fishing vessels, as well as aircraft and vehicles and, when appropriate, to search crew members, passengers and their baggage;

(b) To establish and maintain a system to detect consignments suspected of containing narcotic drugs, psychotropic substances and substances in Table I and Table II passing into or out of free trade zones and free ports;

(c) To establish and maintain surveillance systems in harbour and dock areas and at airports and border control points in free trade zones and free ports.

ARTICLE 19—THE USE OF THE MAILS

1. In conformity with their obligations under the Conventions of the Universal Postal Union, and in accordance with the basic principles of their domestic legal systems, the Parties shall adopt measures to suppress the use of the mails for illicit traffic and shall cooperate with one another to that end.

2. The measures referred to in paragraph 1 of this article shall include, in particular:

(a) Coordinated action for the prevention and repression of the use of the mails for illicit traffic;

(b) Introduction and maintenance by authorized law enforcement personnel of investigative and control techniques designed to detect illicit consignments of narcotic drugs, psychotropic substances and substances in Table I and Table II in the mails;

(c) Legislative measures to enable the use of appropriate means to secure evidence required for judicial proceedings.

ARTICLE 20—INFORMATION TO BE FURNISHED BY THE PARTIES

1. The Parties shall furnish, through the Secretary-General, information to the Commission on the working of this Convention in their territories and, in particular:

(a) The text of laws and regulations promulgated in order to give effect to the Convention;

(b) Particulars of cases of illicit traffic within their jurisdiction which they consider important because of new trends disclosed, the quantities involved, the sources from which the substances are obtained, or the methods employed by persons so engaged.

2. The Parties shall furnish such information in such a manner and by such dates as the Commission may request.

ARTICLE 21—FUNCTIONS OF THE COMMISSION

The Commission is authorized to consider all matters pertaining to the aims of this Convention and, in particular:

(a) The Commission shall, on the basis of the information submitted by the Parties in accordance with article 20, review the operation of this Convention;

(b) The Commission may make suggestions and general recommendations based on the examination of the information received from the Parties;

(c) The Commission may call the attention of the Board to any matters which may be relevant to the functions of the Board;

(d) The Commission shall, on any matter referred to it by the Board under article 22, paragraph 1(b), take such action as it deems appropriate;

(e) The Commission may, in conformity with the procedures laid down in article 12, amend Table I and Table II;

(f) The Commission may draw the attention of non-Parties to decisions and recommendations which it adopts under this Convention, with a view to their considering taking action in accordance therewith.

ARTICLE 22—FUNCTIONS OF THE BOARD

1. Without prejudice to the functions of the Commission under article 21, and without prejudice to the functions of the Board and the Commission under the 1961 Convention, the 1961 Convention as amended and the 1971 Convention:

(a) If, on the basis of its examination of information available to it, to the Secretary-General or to the Commission, or of information communicated by United Nations organs, the Board has reason to believe that the aims of this Convention in matters related to its competence are not being met, the Board may invite a Party or Parties to furnish any relevant information;

(b) With respect to articles 12, 13 and 15:

(i) After taking action under subparagraph (a) of this article, the Board, if satisfied that it is necessary to do so, may call upon the Party concerned to adopt such remedial measures as shall seem under the circumstances to be necessary for the execution of the provisions of articles 12, 13 and 16;

(ii) Prior to taking action under (iii) below, the Board shall treat as confidential its communications with the Party concerned under the preceding subparagraphs;

(iii) If the Board finds that the Party concerned has not taken remedial measures which it has been called upon to take under this subparagraph, it may call the attention of the Parties, the Council and the Commission to the matter. Any report published by the Board under this subparagraph shall also contain the views of the Party concerned if the latter so requests.

2. Any Party shall be invited to be represented at a meeting of the Board at which a question of direct interest to it is to be considered under this article.

3. If in any case a decision of the Board which is adopted under this article is not unanimous, the views of the minority shall be stated.

4. Decisions of the Board under this article shall be taken by a two-thirds majority of the whole number of the Board.

5. In carrying out its functions pursuant to subparagraph 1(a) of this article, the Board shall ensure the confidentiality of all information which may come into its possession.

6. The Board's responsibility under this article shall not apply to the implementation of treaties or agreements entered into between Parties in accordance with the provisions of this Convention.

7. The provisions of this article shall not be applicable to disputes between Parties falling under the provisions of article 32.

ARTICLE 23—REPORTS OF THE BOARD

1. The Board shall prepare an annual report on its work containing an analysis of the information at its disposal and, in appropriate cases, an account of the explanations, if any, given by or required of Parties, together with any observations and recommendations which the Board desires to make. The Board may make such additional reports as it considers necessary. The reports shall be submitted to the Council through the Commission which may make such comments as it sees fit.

2. The reports of the Board shall be communicated to the Parties and subsequently published by the Secretary-General. The Parties shall permit their unrestricted distribution.

ARTICLE 24—APPLICATION OF STRICTER MEASURES THAN THOSE REQUIRED BY THIS CONVENTION

A Party may adopt more strict or severe measures than those provided by this Convention if, in its opinion, such measures are desirable or necessary for the prevention or suppression of illicit traffic.

ARTICLE 25—NON-DEROGATION FROM EARLIER TREATY RIGHTS AND OBLIGATIONS

The provisions of this Convention shall not derogate from any rights enjoyed or obligations undertaken by Parties to this Convention under the 1961 Convention, the 1961 Convention as amended and the 1971 Convention.

ARTICLE 26—SIGNATURE

This Convention shall be open for signature at the United Nations Office at Vienna, from 20 December 1988 to 28 February 1989, and thereafter at the Headquarters of the United Nations at New York, until 20 December 1989, by:

(a) All States;

(b) Namibia, represented by the United Nations Council for Namibia;

(c) Regional economic integration organizations which have competence in respect of the negotiation, conclusion and application of international agreements in matters covered by this Convention, references under the Convention to Parties, States or national services being applicable to these organizations within the limits of their competence.

ARTICLE 27—RATIFICATION, ACCEPTANCE, APPROVAL OR ACT OF FORMAL CONFIRMATION

1. This Convention is subject to ratification, acceptance or approval by States and by Namibia, represented by the United Nations Council for Namibia, and to acts of formal confirmation by regional economic integration organizations referred to in article 26, subparagraph (c). The instruments of ratification, acceptance or approval and those relating to acts of formal confirmation shall be deposited with the Secretary-General.

2. In their instruments of formal confirmation, regional economic integration organizations shall declare the extent of their competence with respect to the matters governed by this Convention. These organizations shall also inform the Secretary-General of any modification in the extent of their competence with respect to the matters governed by the Convention.

ARTICLE 28—ACCESSION

1. This Convention shall remain open for accession by any State, by Namibia, represented by the United Nations Council for Namibia, and by regional economic integration organizations referred to in article 26, subparagraph (c). Accession shall be effected by the deposit of an instrument of accession with the Secretary-General.

2. In their instruments of accession, regional economic integration organizations shall declare the extent of their competence with respect to the matters governed by this Convention. These organizations shall also inform the Secretary-General of any modification in the extent of their competence with respect to the matters governed by the Convention.

ARTICLE 29—ENTRY INTO FORCE

1. This Convention shall enter into force on the ninetieth day after the date of the deposit with the Secretary-General of the twentieth instrument of ratification, acceptance, approval or accession by States or by Namibia, represented by the Council for Namibia.

2. For each State or for Namibia, represented by the Council for Namibia, ratifying, accepting, approving or acceding to this Convention after the deposit of the twentieth instrument of ratification, acceptance, approval or accession, the Convention shall enter into force on the ninetieth day after the date of the deposit of its instrument of ratification, acceptance, approval or accession.

3. For each regional economic integration organization referred to in article 26, subparagraph (c) depositing an instrument relating to an act of formal confirmation or an instrument of accession, this Convention shall enter into force on the ninetieth day after such

deposit, or at the date the Convention enters into force pursuant to paragraph 1 of this article, whichever is later.

ARTICLE 30—DENUNCIATION

1. A Party may denounce this Convention at any time by a written notification addressed to the Secretary-General.

2. Such denunciation shall take effect for the Party concerned one year after the date of receipt of the notification by the Secretary-General.

ARTICLE 31—AMENDMENTS

1. Any Party may propose an amendment to this Convention. The text of any such amendment and the reasons therefor shall be communicated by that Party to the Secretary-General, who shall communicate it to the other Parties and shall ask them whether they accept the proposed amendment. If a proposed amendment so circulated has not been rejected by any Party within twenty-four months after it has been circulated, it shall be deemed to have been accepted and shall enter into force in respect of a Party ninety days after that Party has deposited with the Secretary-General an instrument expressing its consent to be bound by that amendment.

2. If a proposed amendment has been rejected by any Party, the Secretary-General shall consult with the Parties and, if a majority so requests, he shall bring the matter, together with any comments made by the Parties, before the Council which may decide to call a conference in accordance with Article 62, paragraph 4, of the Charter of the United Nations. Any amendment resulting from such a conference shall be embodied in a Protocol of Amendment. Consent to be bound by such a Protocol shall be required to be expressed specifically to the Secretary-General.

ARTICLE 32—SETTLEMENT OF DISPUTES

1. If there should arise between two or more Parties a dispute relating to the interpretation or application of this Convention, the Parties shall consult together with a view to settlement of the dispute by negotiation, enquiry, mediation, conciliation, arbitration, recourse to regional bodies, judicial process or other peaceful means of their own choice.

2. Any such dispute which cannot be settled in the manner prescribed in paragraph 1 of this article shall be referred, at the request of any one of the States Parties to the dispute, to the International Court of Justice for decision.

3. If a regional economic integration organization referred to in article 26, subparagraph (c) is a Party to a dispute which cannot be settled in the manner prescribed in paragraph 1 of this article, it may, through a State Member of the United Nations, request the Council to request an advisory opinion of the International Court of Justice in accordance with Article 65 of the Statute of the Court, which opinion shall be regarded as decisive.

4. Each State, at the time of signature or ratification, acceptance or approval of this Convention or accession thereto, or each regional economic integration organization, at the time of a signature

or deposit of an act of formal confirmation or accession, may declare that it does not consider itself bound by paragraphs 2 and 3 of this article. The other Parties shall not be bound by paragraphs 2 and 3 with respect to any Party having made such a declaration.

5. Any Party having made a declaration in accordance with paragraph 4 of this article may at any time withdraw the declaration by notification to the Secretary-General.

ARTICLE 33—AUTHENTIC TEXTS

The Arabic, Chinese, English, French, Russian and Spanish texts of this Convention are equally authentic.

ARTICLE 34—DEPOSITARY

The Secretary-General shall be the depositary of this Convention.

IN WITNESS WHEREOF the undersigned, being duly authorized thereto, have signed this Convention.

DONE at Vienna, in one original, this twentieth day of December, one thousand nine hundred and eighty-eight.

ANNEX

Revised Tables including the amendments made by the Commission on Narcotic Drugs in force as of 23 November 1992

Table I [1]	Table II [2]
N-acetylanthranilic acid	Acetic anhydride
Ephedrine	Acetone
Ergometrine	Anthranilic acid
Ergotamine	Ethyl ether
Isosafrole	Hydrochloric acid
Lysergic acid	Methyl ethyl ketone
3,4-methylenedioxyphenyl-2-propanone	Phenylacetic acid
1-phenyl-2-propanone	Piperidine
Piperonal	Potassium permanganate
Pseudoephedrine	Sulphuric acid
Safrole	Toluene

[1] The salts of the substances listed in this Table whenever the existence of such salts is possible.

[2] The salts of the substances listed in this Table whenever the existence of such salts is possible (the salts of hydrochloric acid and sulphuric acid are specifically excluded).

5. Inter-American Convention on Serving Criminal Sentences Abroad[1]

Adopted at Managua, Nicaragua, June 9, 1993; Signed on behalf of the United States, January 10, 1995; Entered into force generally, April 12, 1996; Ratification advised by the Senate, October 18, 2000; Entered into force for the United States, June 24, 2001

The Member States of the Organization of American States,

CONSIDERING that, according to Article 2.e of the OAS Charter, one of the essential purposes of the Organization of American States is to "seek the solution of political, juridical and economic problems that may arise among them";

INSPIRED BY THE DESIRE to cooperate to ensure improved administration of justice through the social rehabilitation of the sentenced persons;

PERSUADED that to attain these ends, it is advisable that the sentenced person be given an opportunity to serve the sentence in the country of which the sentenced person is a national; and

CONVINCED that the way to bring about this result is to transfer the sentenced person,

RESOLVES to adopt the following Inter-American Convention on Serving Criminal Sentences Abroad:

ARTICLE I—DEFINITIONS

For the purposes of this convention:

1. Sentencing state: means the state party from which the sentenced person would be transferred.

2. Receiving state: means the state party to which the sentenced person would be transferred.

3. Sentence: means the final judicial decision imposing, as a penalty for the commission of a criminal offense, imprisonment or a term of parole, probation, or other form of supervision without imprisonment. A sentence is understood to be final when no ordinary legal appeal against the conviction or sentence is pending in the sentencing state and the period for its appeal has expired.

4. Sentenced person: means the person who is to serve or is serving a sentence in the territory of a state party.

ARTICLE II—GENERAL PROVISIONS

In accordance with the provisions of this convention:

a. a sentence imposed in one state party upon a national of another state party may be served by the sentenced person in the state of which he or she is a national; and

[1] For states that are parties to the Convention, see Department of State publication, *Treaties in Force*.

b. the states parties undertake to afford each other the fullest co-operation in connection with the transfer of sentenced persons.

Article III—Conditions for the Application of this Convention

This convention shall be applicable only under the following conditions:

1. The sentence must be final, as defined in Article 1.3 of this convention.

2. The sentenced person must consent to the transfer, having been previously informed of the legal consequences thereof.

3. The act for which the person has been sentenced must also constitutes a crime in the receiving state. For this purpose, no account shall be taken of differences of terminology or of those that have no bearing on the nature of the offense.

4. The sentenced person must be a national of the receiving state.

5. The sentence to be served must not be the death penalty.

6. At least six months of the sentence must remain to be served at the time the request is made.

7. The administration of the sentence must not be contrary to domestic law in the receiving state.

Article IV—Provision of Information

1. Each state party shall inform any sentenced person covered by the provisions of this convention as to its content.

2. The states parties shall keep the sentenced person informed as to the processing of the transfer.

Article V—Procedure for Transfer

The transfer of a sentenced person from one state to another shall be subject to the following procedure:

1. The request for application of this convention may be made by the sentencing state, the receiving state, or the sentenced person. The procedures for the transfer may be initiated by the sentencing state or by the receiving state. In these cases, it is required that the sentenced person has expressed consent to the transfer.

2. The request for transfer shall be processed through the central authorities indicated pursuant to Article XI of this convention, or, in the absence thereof, through consular or diplomatic channels. In conformity with its domestic law, each state party shall inform those authorities it considers necessary as to the content of this convention. It shall also endeavor to establish mechanisms for co-operation among the central authority and the other authorities that are to participate in the transfer of the sentenced person.

3. If the sentence was handed down by a state or province with criminal jurisdiction independent from that of the federal government, the approval of the authorities of that state or province shall be required for the application of this transfer procedure.

4. The request for transfer shall furnish pertinent information establishing that the conditions of Article III have been met.

5. Before the transfer is made, the sentencing state shall permit the receiving state to verify, if it wishes, through an official designated by the latter, that the sentenced person has given consent to the transfer in full knowledge of the legal consequences thereof.

6. In taking a decision on the transfer of a sentenced person, the states parties may consider, among other factors, the possibility of contributing to the person's social rehabilitation; the gravity of the offense; the criminal record of the sentenced person, if any; the state of health of the sentenced person; and the family, social, or other ties the sentenced person may have in the sentencing state and the receiving state.

7. The sentencing state shall provide the receiving state with a certified copy of the sentence, including information on the amount of time already served by the sentenced person and on the time off that could be credited for reasons such as work, good behavior, or pre-trial detention. The receiving state may request such other information as it deems necessary.

8. Surrender of the sentenced person by the sentencing state to the receiving state shall be effected at the place agreed upon by the central authorities. The receiving state shall be responsible for custody of the sentenced person from the moment of delivery.

9. All expenses that arise in connection with the transfer of the sentenced person until that person is placed in the custody of the receiving state shall be borne by the sentencing state.

10. The receiving state shall be responsible for all expenses arising from the transfer of the sentenced person as of the moment that person is placed in the receiving state's custody.

Article VI—Refusal of Transfer Request

When a state party does not approve the transfer of a sentenced person, it shall notify the requesting state of its refusal immediately, and whenever possible and appropriate, explain its reasons for the refusal.

Article VII—Rights of the Sentenced Person Who is Transferred and Manner of Serving Sentence

1. A sentenced person who is transferred under the provisions of this convention shall not be arrested, tried, or sentenced again in the receiving state for the same offense upon which the sentence to be executed is based.

2. Except as provided in Article VIII of this convention, the sentence of a sentenced person who is transferred shall be served in accordance with the laws and procedures of the receiving state, including application of any provisions relating to reduction of time of imprisonment or of alternative service of the sentence.

No sentence may be enforced by a receiving state in such fashion as to lengthen the sentence beyond the date on which it would expire under the terms of the sentence of the court in the sentencing state.

3. The authorities of a sentencing state may request, by way of the central authorities, reports on the status of service of the sentence of any sentenced person transferred to a receiving state in accordance with this convention.

Article VIII—Review of Sentence and Effects in the Receiving State

The sentencing state shall retain full jurisdiction for the review of sentences issued by its courts. It shall also retain the power to grant pardon, amnesty, or mercy to the sentenced person. The receiving state, upon receiving notice of any decision in this regard, must take the corresponding measures immediately.

Article IX—Application of the Convention in Special Cases

This Convention may also be applicable to persons subject to supervision or other measures under the laws of one of the states parties relating to youthful offenders. Consent for the transfer shall be obtained from the person legally authorized to grant it.

By agreement between the parties, this convention may be applied to persons whom the competent authority has pronounced unindictable, for purposes of treatment of such persons in the receiving state. The parties shall, in accordance with their laws, agree on the type of treatment to be accorded such individuals upon transfer. For the transfer, consent must be obtained from a person legally authorized to grant it.

Article X—Transit

If the sentenced person, upon being transferred, must cross the territory of a another state party to this convention, the latter shall be notified by way of transmittal of the decision granting the transfer by the state under whose custody the transfer is to be effected. In such cases, the state of transit may or may not consent to the transit of the sentenced person through its territory.

Such notification shall not be necessary when air transport is used and no regular landing is scheduled in the territory of the state party that is to be overflown.

Article XI—Central Authority

Upon signing, ratifying, or acceding to this convention, the states parties shall notify the General Secretariat of the Organization of American States of the central authority designated to perform the functions provided herein. The General Secretariat shall distribute to the states parties to this convention a list of the designations it has received.

Article XII—Relationship to Other Agreements

None of the stipulations of this convention shall be construed to restrict other bilateral or multilateral treaties or other agreements between the parties.

Final Clauses

Article XIII

This convention is open to signature by the Member states of the Organization of American States.

Article XIV

This convention is subject to ratification. The instruments of ratification shall be deposited with the General Secretariat of the Organization of American States.

Article XV

This convention shall remain open to accession by any other state. The instruments of accession shall be deposited with the General Secretariat of the Organization of American States.

Article XVI

The States may set forth reservations to this convention at such time as they approve, sign, ratify, or accede to it, provided that the reservations are not incompatible with the object and purpose of this convention and that they relate to one or more specific provisions.

Article XVII

This convention shall enter into force for the ratifying states on the thirtieth day following the date on which the second instrument of ratification has been deposited.

For each state that ratifies the convention or accedes to it after the second instrument of ratification has been deposited, the convention shall enter into force on the thirtieth day following the day on which such states has deposited its instrument of ratification or accession.

Article XVIII

This convention shall remain in force indefinitely, but any state party may denounce it. The denunciation shall be registered with the General Secretariat of the Organization of American States. At the end of one year from the date of the denunciation, the convention shall cease to be in force for the denouncing state.

However, its provisions shall remain in force for the denouncing state with respect to sentenced persons transferred in accordance with this convention, until the respective sentences have been served.

Requests for transfer being processed at the time the denunciation of this convention is made will continue to be processed and executed, unless the parties agree to the contrary.

Article XIX

The original of this convention, whose texts in English, French, Portuguese, and Spanish are equally authentic, shall be deposited with the General Secretariat of the Organization of American States, which shall send a certified copy, for registry and publication, to the Secretariat of the United Nations, pursuant to Article 102 of the United Nations Charter. The General Secretariat of the Organization of American States shall notify the Member states of that Organization and the states that have acceded to the convention of the signatures affixed, the instruments of ratification, accession, or denunciation deposited, and the reservations set forth, if any.

IN WITNESS WHEREOF the undersigned Plenipotentiaries, being duly authorized thereto by their respective governments, have signed this Convention, which shall be called the "Inter-American Convention on Serving Criminal Sentences Abroad".

6. United Nations Convention Against Transnational Organized Crime[1]

Adopted at New York, November 15, 2000; Signed on behalf of the United States, December 13, 2000; Entered into force generally, September 29, 2003; Ratification advised by the Senate, October 7, 2005; Entered into force for the United States, December 3, 2005

ARTICLE 1

STATEMENT OF PURPOSE

The purpose of this Convention is to promote cooperation to prevent and combat transnational organized crime more effectively.

ARTICLE 2

USE OF TERMS

For the purposes of this Convention:

(a) "Organized criminal group" shall mean a structured group of three or more persons, existing for a period of time and acting in concert with the aim of committing one or more serious crimes or offences established in accordance with this Convention, in order to obtain, directly or indirectly, a financial or other material benefit;

(b) "Serious crime" shall mean conduct constituting an offence punishable by a maximum deprivation of liberty of at least four years or a more serious penalty;

(c) "Structured group" shall mean a group that is not randomly formed for the immediate commission of an offence and that does not need to have formally defined roles for its members, continuity of its membership or a developed structure;

(d) "Property" shall mean assets of every kind, whether corporeal or incorporeal, movable or immovable, tangible or intangible, and legal documents or instruments evidencing title to, or interest in, such assets;

(e) "'Proceeds of crime" shall mean any property derived from or obtained, directly or indirectly, through the commission of an offence;

(f) "Freezing" or "seizure" shall mean temporarily prohibiting the transfer, conversion, disposition or movement of property or temporarily assuming custody or control of property on the basis of an order issued by a court or other competent authority;

(g) "Confiscation", which includes forfeiture where applicable, shall mean the permanent deprivation of property by order of a court or other competent authority;

[1] For states that are parties to the Convention, see Department of State publication, *Treaties in Force.*

(h) "Predicate offence" shall mean any offence as a result of which proceeds have been generated that may become the subject of an offence as defined in article 6 of this Convention;

(i) "Controlled delivery" shall mean the technique of allowing illicit or suspect consignments to pass out of, through or into the territory of one or more States, with the knowledge and under the supervision of their competent authorities, with a view to the investigation of an offence and the identification of persons involved in the commission of the offence;

(j) "Regional economic integration organization" shall mean an organization constituted by sovereign States of a given region, to which its member States have transferred competence in respect of matters governed by this Convention and which has been duly authorized, in accordance with its internal procedures, to sign, ratify, accept, approve or accede to it; references to "States Parties" under this Convention shall apply to such organizations within the limits of their competence.

Article 3

Scope of application

1. This Convention shall apply, except as otherwise stated herein, to the prevention, investigation and prosecution of:

(a) The offences established in accordance with articles 5, 6, 8 and 23 of this Convention; and

(b) Serious crime as defined in article 2 of this Convention;
where the offence is transnational in nature and involves an organized criminal group.

2. For the purpose of paragraph 1 of this article, an offence is transnational in nature if:

(a) It is committed in more than one State;

(b) It is committed in one State but a substantial part of its preparation, planning, direction or control takes place in another State;

(c) It is committed in one State but involves an organized criminal group that engages in criminal activities in more than one State; or

(d) It is committed in one State but has substantial effects in another State.

Article 4

Protection of sovereignty

1. States Parties shall carry out their obligations under this Convention in a manner consistent with the principles of sovereign equality and territorial integrity of States and that of non-intervention in the domestic affairs of other States.

2. Nothing in this Convention entitles a State Party to undertake in the territory of another State the exercise of jurisdiction and performance of functions that are reserved exclusively for the authorities of that other State by its domestic law.

Article 5

Criminalization of participation in an organized criminal group

1. Each State Party shall adopt such legislative and other measures as may be necessary to establish as criminal offences, when committed intentionally:

(a) Either or both of the following as criminal offences distinct from those involving the attempt or completion of the criminal activity:

(i) Agreeing with one or more other persons to commit a serious crime for a purpose relating directly or indirectly to the obtaining of a financial or other material benefit and, where required by domestic law, involving an act undertaken by one of the participants in furtherance of the agreement or involving an organized criminal group;

(ii) Conduct by a person who, with knowledge of either the aim and general criminal activity of an organized criminal group or its intention to commit the crimes in question, takes an active part in:

a. Criminal activities of the organized criminal group;

b. Other activities of the organized criminal group in the knowledge that his or her participation will contribute to the achievement of the above-described criminal aim;

(b) Organizing, directing, aiding, abetting, facilitating or counselling the commission of serious crime involving an organized criminal group.

2. The knowledge, intent, aim, purpose or agreement referred to in paragraph 1 of this article may be inferred from objective factual circumstances.

3. States Parties whose domestic law requires involvement of an organized criminal group for purposes of the offences established in accordance with paragraph 1 (a) (i) of this article shall ensure that their domestic law covers all serious crimes involving organized criminal groups. Such States Parties, as well as States Parties whose domestic law requires an act in furtherance of the agreement for purposes of the offences established in accordance with paragraph 1 (a) (i) of this article, shall so inform the Secretary-General of the United Nations at the time of their signature or of deposit of their instrument of ratification, acceptance or approval of or accession to this Convention.

Article 6

Criminalization of the laundering of proceeds of crime

1. Each State Party shall adopt, in accordance with fundamental principles of its domestic law, such legislative and other measures as may be necessary to establish as criminal offences, when committed intentionally:

(a)(i) The conversion or transfer of property, knowing that such property is the proceeds of crime, for the purpose of concealing or disguising the illicit origin of the property or of helping any person who is involved in the commission of the predicate offence to evade the legal consequences of his or her action;

(ii) The concealment or disguise of the true nature, source, location, disposition, movement or ownership of or rights with respect to property, knowing that such property is the proceeds of crime;

(b) Subject to the basic concepts of its legal system:

(i) The acquisition, possession or use of property, knowing, at the time of receipt, that such property is the proceeds of crime;

(ii) Participation in, association with or conspiracy to commit, attempts to commit and aiding, abetting, facilitating and counselling the commission of any of the offences established in accordance with this article.

2. For purposes of implementing or applying paragraph 1 of this article:

(a) Each State Party shall seek to apply paragraph 1 of this article to the widest range of predicate offences;

(b) Each State Party shall include as predicate offences all serious crime as defined in article 2 of this Convention and the offences established in accordance with articles 5, 8 and 23 of this Convention. In the case of States Parties whose legislation sets out a list of specific predicate offences, they shall, at a minimum, include in such list a comprehensive range of offences associated with organized criminal groups;

(c) For the purposes of subparagraph (b), predicate offences shall include offences committed both within and outside the jurisdiction of the State Party in question. However, offences committed outside the jurisdiction of a State Party shall constitute predicate offences only when the relevant conduct is a criminal offence under the domestic law of the State where it is committed and would be a criminal offence under the domestic law of the State Party implementing or applying this article had it been committed there;

(d) Each State Party shall furnish copies of its laws that give effect to this article and of any subsequent changes to such laws or a description thereof to the Secretary-General of the United Nations;

(e) If required by fundamental principles of the domestic law of a State Party, it may be provided that the offences set forth in paragraph 1 of this article do not apply to the persons who committed the predicate offence;

(f) Knowledge, intent or purpose required as an element of an offence set forth in paragraph 1 of this article may be inferred from objective factual circumstances.

ARTICLE 7

MEASURES TO COMBAT MONEY-LAUNDERING

1. Each State Party:

(a) Shall institute a comprehensive domestic regulatory and supervisory regime for banks and non-bank financial institutions and, where appropriate, other bodies particularly susceptible to money-laundering, within its competence, in order to deter and detect all forms of money-laundering, which regime shall emphasize requirements for customer identification, record-keeping and the reporting of suspicious transactions;

(b) Shall, without prejudice to articles 18 and 27 of this Convention, ensure that administrative, regulatory, law enforcement and other authorities dedicated to combating money-laundering (including, where appropriate under domestic law, judicial authorities) have the ability to cooperate and exchange information at the national and international levels within the conditions prescribed by its domestic law and, to that end, shall consider the establishment of a financial intelligence unit to serve as a national centre for the collection, analysis and dissemination of information regarding potential money-laundering.

2. States Parties shall consider implementing feasible measures to detect and monitor the movement of cash and appropriate negotiable instruments across their borders, subject to safeguards to ensure proper use of information and without impeding in any way the movement of legitimate capital. Such measures may include a requirement that individuals and businesses report the cross-border transfer of substantial quantities of cash and appropriate negotiable instruments.

3. In establishing a domestic regulatory and supervisory regime under the terms of this article, and without prejudice to any other article of this Convention, States Parties are called upon to use as a guideline the relevant initiatives of regional, interregional and multilateral organizations against money-laundering.

4. States Parties shall endeavour to develop and promote global, regional, subregional and bilateral cooperation among judicial, law enforcement and financial regulatory authorities in order to combat money-laundering.

ARTICLE 8

CRIMINALIZATION OF CORRUPTION

1. Each State Party shall adopt such legislative and other measures as may be necessary to establish as criminal offences, when committed intentionally:

(a) The promise, offering or giving to a public official, directly or indirectly, of an undue advantage, for the official himself or herself or another person or entity, in order that the official act or refrain from acting in the exercise of his or her official duties;

(b) The solicitation or acceptance by a public official, directly or indirectly, of an undue advantage, for the official himself or herself or another person or entity, in order that the official act or refrain from acting in the exercise of his or her official duties.

2. Each State Party shall consider adopting such legislative and other measures as may be necessary to establish as criminal

offences conduct referred to in paragraph 1 of this article involving a foreign public official or international civil servant. Likewise, each State Party shall consider establishing as criminal offences other forms of corruption.

3. Each State Party shall also adopt such measures as may be necessary to establish as a criminal offence participation as an accomplice in an offence established in accordance with this article.

4. For the purposes of paragraph 1 of this article and article 9 of this Convention, "public official" shall mean a public official or a person who provides a public service as defined in the domestic law and as applied in the criminal law of the State Party in which the person in question performs that function.

Article 9

Measures against corruption

1. In addition to the measures set forth in article 8 of this Convention, each State Party shall, to the extent appropriate and consistent with its legal system, adopt legislative, administrative or other effective measures to promote integrity and to prevent, detect and punish the corruption of public officials.

2. Each State Party shall take measures to ensure effective action by its authorities in the prevention, detection and punishment of the corruption of public officials, including providing such authorities with adequate independence to deter the exertion of inappropriate influence on their actions.

Article 10

Liability of legal persons

1. Each State Party shall adopt such measures as may be necessary, consistent with its legal principles, to establish the liability of legal persons for participation in serious crimes involving an organized criminal group and for the offences established in accordance with articles 5, 6, 8 and 23 of this Convention.

2. Subject to the legal principles of the State Party, the liability of legal persons may be criminal, civil or administrative.

3. Such liability shall be without prejudice to the criminal liability of the natural persons who have committed the offences.

4. Each State Party shall, in particular, ensure that legal persons held liable in accordance with this article are subject to effective, proportionate and dissuasive criminal or non-criminal sanctions, including monetary sanctions.

Article 11

Prosecution, adjudication and sanctions

1. Each State Party shall make the commission of an offence established in accordance with articles 5, 6, 8 and 23 of this Convention liable to sanctions that take into account the gravity of that offence.

2. Each State Party shall endeavour to ensure that any discretionary legal powers under its domestic law relating to the prosecution of persons for offences covered by this Convention are exercised to maximize the effectiveness of law enforcement measures in respect of those offences and with due regard to the need to deter the commission of such offences.

3. In the case of offences established in accordance with articles 5, 6, 8 and 23 of this Convention, each State Party shall take appropriate measures, in accordance with its domestic law and with due regard to the rights of the defence, to seek to ensure that conditions imposed in connection with decisions on release pending trial or appeal take into consideration the need to ensure the presence of the defendant at subsequent criminal proceedings.

4. Each State Party shall ensure that its courts or other competent authorities bear in mind the grave nature of the offences covered by this Convention when considering the eventuality of early release or parole of persons convicted of such offences.

5. Each State Party shall, where appropriate, establish under its domestic law a long statute of limitations period in which to commence proceedings for any offence covered by this Convention and a longer period where the alleged offender has evaded the administration of justice.

6. Nothing contained in this Convention shall affect the principle that the description of the offences established in accordance with this Convention and of the applicable legal defences or other legal principles controlling the lawfulness of conduct is reserved to the domestic law of a State Party and that such offences shall be prosecuted and punished in accordance with that law.

Article 12

Confiscation and seizure

1. States Parties shall adopt, to the greatest extent possible within their domestic legal systems, such measures as may be necessary to enable confiscation of:

(a) Proceeds of crime derived from offences covered by this Convention or property the value of which corresponds to that of such proceeds;

(b) Property, equipment or other instrumentalities used in or destined for use in offences covered by this Convention.

2. States Parties shall adopt such measures as may be necessary to enable the identification, tracing, freezing or seizure of any item referred to in paragraph 1 of this article for the purpose of eventual confiscation.

3. If proceeds of crime have been transformed or converted, in part or in full, into other property, such property shall be liable to the measures referred to in this article instead of the proceeds.

4. If proceeds of crime have been intermingled with property acquired from legitimate sources, such property shall, without prejudice to any powers relating to freezing or seizure, be liable to confiscation up to the assessed value of the intermingled proceeds.

5. Income or other benefits derived from proceeds of crime, from property into which proceeds of crime have been transformed or converted or from property with which proceeds of crime have been

intermingled shall also be liable to the measures referred to in this article, in the same manner and to the same extent as proceeds of crime.

6. For the purposes of this article and article 13 of this Convention, each State Party shall empower its courts or other competent authorities to order that bank, financial or commercial records be made available or be seized. States Parties shall not decline to act under the provisions of this paragraph on the ground of bank secrecy.

7. States Parties may consider the possibility of requiring that an offender demonstrate the lawful origin of alleged proceeds of crime or other property liable to confiscation, to the extent that such a requirement is consistent with the principles of their domestic law and with the nature of the judicial and other proceedings.

8. The provisions of this article shall not be construed to prejudice the rights of bona fide third parties.

9. Nothing contained in this article shall affect the principle that the measures to which it refers shall be defined and implemented in accordance with and subject to the provisions of the domestic law of a State Party.

ARTICLE 13

INTERNATIONAL COOPERATION FOR PURPOSES OF CONFISCATION

1. A State Party that has received a request from another State Party having jurisdiction over an offence covered by this Convention for confiscation of proceeds of crime, property, equipment or other instrumentalities referred to in article 12, paragraph 1, of this Convention situated in its territory shall, to the greatest extent possible within its domestic legal system:

(a) Submit the request to its competent authorities for the purpose of obtaining an order of confiscation and, if such an order is granted, give effect to it; or

(b) Submit to its competent authorities, with a view to giving effect to it to the extent requested, an order of confiscation issued by a court in the territory of the requesting State Party in accordance with article 12, paragraph 1, of this Convention insofar as it relates to proceeds of crime, property, equipment or other instrumentalities referred to in article 12, paragraph 1, situated in the territory of the requested State Party.

2. Following a request made by another State Party having jurisdiction over an offence covered by this Convention, the requested State Party shall take measures to identify, trace and freeze or seize proceeds of crime, property, equipment or other instrumentalities referred to in article 12, paragraph 1, of this Convention for the purpose of eventual confiscation to be ordered either by the requesting State Party or, pursuant to a request under paragraph 1 of this article, by the requested State Party.

3. The provisions of article 18 of this Convention are applicable, mutatis mutandis, to this article. In addition to the information specified in article 18, paragraph 15, requests made pursuant to this article shall contain:

(a) In the case of a request pertaining to paragraph 1 (a) of this article, a description of the property to be confiscated and a statement of the facts relied upon by the requesting State Party sufficient to enable the requested State Party to seek the order under its domestic law;

(b) In the case of a request pertaining to paragraph 1 (b) of this article, a legally admissible copy of an order of confiscation upon which the request is based issued by the requesting State Party, a statement of the facts and information as to the extent to which execution of the order is requested;

(c) In the case of a request pertaining to paragraph 2 of this article, a statement of the facts relied upon by the requesting State Party and a description of the actions requested.

4. The decisions or actions provided for in paragraphs 1 and 2 of this article shall be taken by the requested State Party in accordance with and subject to the provisions of its domestic law and its procedural rules or any bilateral or multilateral treaty, agreement or arrangement to which it may be bound in relation to the requesting State Party.

5. Each State Party shall furnish copies of its laws and regulations that give effect to this article and of any subsequent changes to such laws and regulations or a description thereof to the Secretary-General of the United Nations.

6. f a State Party elects to make the taking of the measures referred to in paragraphs 1 and 2 of this article conditional on the existence of a relevant treaty, that State Party shall consider this Convention the necessary and sufficient treaty basis.

7. Cooperation under this article may be refused by a State Party if the offence to which the request relates is not an offence covered by this Convention.

8. The provisions of this article shall not be construed to prejudice the rights of bona fide third parties.

9. States Parties shall consider concluding bilateral or multilateral treaties, agreements or arrangements to enhance the effectiveness of international cooperation undertaken pursuant to this article.

Article 14

Disposal of confiscated proceeds of crime or property

1. Proceeds of crime or property confiscated by a State Party pursuant to articles 12 or 13, paragraph 1, of this Convention shall be disposed of by that State Party in accordance with its domestic law and administrative procedures.

2. When acting on the request made by another State Party in accordance with article 13 of this Convention, States Parties shall, to the extent permitted by domestic law and if so requested, give priority consideration to returning the confiscated proceeds of crime or property to the requesting State Party so that it can give compensation to the victims of the crime or return such proceeds of crime or property to their legitimate owners.

3. When acting on the request made by another State Party in accordance with articles 12 and 13 of this Convention, a State Party may give special consideration to concluding agreements or arrangements on:

(a) Contributing the value of such proceeds of crime or property or funds derived from the sale of such proceeds of crime or property or a part thereof to the account designated in accordance with article 30, paragraph 2 (c), of this Convention and to intergovernmental bodies specializing in the fight against organized crime;

(b) Sharing with other States Parties, on a regular or case-by-case basis, such proceeds of crime or property, or funds derived from the sale of such proceeds of crime or property, in accordance with its domestic law or administrative procedures.

ARTICLE 15

JURISDICTION

1. Each State Party shall adopt such measures as may be necessary to establish its jurisdiction over the offences established in accordance with articles 5, 6, 8 and 23 of this Convention when:

(a) The offence is committed in the territory of that State Party; or

(b) The offence is committed on board a vessel that is flying the flag of that State Party or an aircraft that is registered under the laws of that State Party at the time that the offence is committed.

2. Subject to article 4 of this Convention, a State Party may also establish its jurisdiction over any such offence when:

(a) The offence is committed against a national of that State Party;

(b) The offence is committed by a national of that State Party or a stateless person who has his or her habitual residence in its territory; or

(c) The offence is:

(i) One of those established in accordance with article 5, paragraph 1, of this Convention and is committed outside its territory with a view to the commission of a serious crime within its territory;

(ii) One of those established in accordance with article 6, paragraph 1 (b) (ii), of this Convention and is committed outside its territory with a view to the commission of an offence established in accordance with article 6, paragraph 1 (a) (i) or (ii) or (b) (i), of this Convention within its territory.

3. For the purposes of article 16, paragraph 10, of this Convention, each State Party shall adopt such measures as may be necessary to establish its jurisdiction over the offences covered by this Convention when the alleged offender is present in its territory and it does not extradite such person solely on the ground that he or she is one of its nationals.

4. Each State Party may also adopt such measures as may be necessary to establish its jurisdiction over the offences covered by this Convention when the alleged offender is present in its territory and it does not extradite him or her.

5. If a State Party exercising its jurisdiction under paragraph 1 or 2 of this article has been notified, or has otherwise learned, that one or more other States Parties are conducting an investigation,

prosecution or judicial proceeding in respect of the same conduct, the competent authorities of those States Parties shall, as appropriate, consult one another with a view to coordinating their actions.

6. Without prejudice to norms of general international law, this Convention does not exclude the exercise of any criminal jurisdiction established by a State Party in accordance with its domestic law.

ARTICLE 16

EXTRADITION

1. This article shall apply to the offences covered by this Convention or in cases where an offence referred to in article 3, paragraph 1 (a) or (b), involves an organized criminal group and the person who is the subject of the request for extradition is located in the territory of the requested State Party, provided that the offence for which extradition is sought is punishable under the domestic law of both the requesting State Party and the requested State Party.

2. If the request for extradition includes several separate serious crimes, some of which are not covered by this article, the requested State Party may apply this article also in respect of the latter offences.

3. Each of the offences to which this article applies shall be deemed to be included as an extraditable offence in any extradition treaty existing between States Parties. States Parties undertake to include such offences as extraditable offences in every extradition treaty to be concluded between them.

4. If a State Party that makes extradition conditional on the existence of a treaty receives a request for extradition from another State Party with which it has no extradition treaty, it may consider this Convention the legal basis for extradition in respect of any offence to which this article applies.

5. States Parties that make extradition conditional on the existence of a treaty shall:

(a) At the time of deposit of their instrument of ratification, acceptance, approval of or accession to this Convention, inform the Secretary-General of the United Nations whether they will take this Convention as the legal basis for cooperation on extradition with other States Parties to this Convention; and

(b) If they do not take this Convention as the legal basis for cooperation on extradition, seek, where appropriate, to conclude treaties on extradition with other States Parties to this Convention in order to implement this article.

6. States Parties that do not make extradition conditional on the existence of a treaty shall recognize offences to which this article applies as extraditable offences between themselves.

7. Extradition shall be subject to the conditions provided for by the domestic law of the requested State Party or by applicable extradition treaties, including, inter alia, conditions in relation to the minimum penalty requirement for extradition and the grounds upon which the requested State Party may refuse extradition.

8. States Parties shall, subject to their domestic law, endeavour to expedite extradition procedures and to simplify evidentiary requirements relating thereto in respect of any offence to which this article applies.

9. Subject to the provisions of its domestic law and its extradition treaties, the requested State Party may, upon being satisfied that the circumstances so warrant and are urgent and at the request of the requesting State Party, take a person whose extradition is sought and who is present in its territory into custody or take other appropriate measures to ensure his or her presence at extradition proceedings.

10. A State Party in whose territory an alleged offender is found, if it does not extradite such person in respect of an offence to which this article applies solely on the ground that he or she is one of its nationals, shall, at the request of the State Party seeking extradition, be obliged to submit the case without undue delay to its competent authorities for the purpose of prosecution. Those authorities shall take their decision and conduct their proceedings in the same manner as in the case of any other offence of a grave nature under the domestic law of that State Party. The States Parties concerned shall cooperate with each other, in particular on procedural and evidentiary aspects, to ensure the efficiency of such prosecution.

11. Whenever a State Party is permitted under its domestic law to extradite or otherwise surrender one of its nationals only upon the condition that the person will be returned to that State Party to serve the sentence imposed as a result of the trial or proceedings for which the extradition or surrender of the person was sought and that State Party and the State Party seeking the extradition of the person agree with this option and other terms that they may deem appropriate, such conditional extradition or surrender shall be sufficient to discharge the obligation set forth in paragraph 10 of this article.

12. If extradition, sought for purposes of enforcing a sentence, is refused because the person sought is a national of the requested State Party, the requested Party shall, if its domestic law so permits and in conformity with the requirements of such law, upon application of the requesting Party, consider the enforcement of the sentence that has been imposed under the domestic law of the requesting Party or the remainder thereof.

13. Any person regarding whom proceedings are being carried out in connection with any of the offences to which this article applies shall be guaranteed fair treatment at all stages of the proceedings, including enjoyment of all the rights and guarantees provided by the domestic law of the State Party in the territory of which that person is present.

14. Nothing in this Convention shall be interpreted as imposing an obligation to extradite if the requested State Party has substantial grounds for believing that the request has been made for the purpose of prosecuting or punishing a person on account of that person's sex, race, religion, nationality, ethnic origin or political opinions or that compliance with the request would cause prejudice to that person's position for any one of these reasons.

15. States Parties may not refuse a request for extradition on the sole ground that the offence is also considered to involve fiscal matters.

16. Before refusing extradition, the requested State Party shall, where appropriate, consult with the requesting State Party to provide it with ample opportunity to present its opinions and to provide information relevant to its allegation.

17. States Parties shall seek to conclude bilateral and multilateral agreements or arrangements to carry out or to enhance the effectiveness of extradition.

Article 17

Transfer of sentenced persons

States Parties may consider entering into bilateral or multilateral agreements or arrangements on the transfer to their territory of persons sentenced to imprisonment or other forms of deprivation of liberty for offences covered by this Convention, in order that they may complete their sentences there.

Article 18

Mutual legal assistance

1. States Parties shall afford one another the widest measure of mutual legal assistance in investigations, prosecutions and judicial proceedings in relation to the offences covered by this Convention as provided for in article 3 and shall reciprocally extend to one another similar assistance where the requesting State Party has reasonable grounds to suspect that the offence referred to in article 3, paragraph 1 (a) or (b), is transnational in nature, including that victims, witnesses, proceeds, instrumentalities or evidence of such offences are located in the requested State Party and that the offence involves an organized criminal group.

2. Mutual legal assistance shall be afforded to the fullest extent possible under relevant laws, treaties, agreements and arrangements of the requested State Party with respect to investigations, prosecutions and judicial proceedings in relation to the offences for which a legal person may be held liable in accordance with article 10 of this Convention in the requesting State Party.

3. Mutual legal assistance to be afforded in accordance with this article may be requested for any of the following purposes:

(a) Taking evidence or statements from persons;

(b) Effecting service of judicial documents;

(c) Executing searches and seizures, and freezing;

(d) Examining objects and sites;

(e) Providing information, evidentiary items and expert evaluations;

(f) Providing originals or certified copies of relevant documents and records, including government, bank, financial, corporate or business records;

(g) Identifying or tracing proceeds of crime, property, instrumentalities or other things for evidentiary purposes;

(h) Facilitating the voluntary appearance of persons in the requesting State Party;

(i) Any other type of assistance that is not contrary to the domestic law of the requested State Party.

4. Without prejudice to domestic law, the competent authorities of a State Party may, without prior request, transmit information relating to criminal matters to a competent authority in another State Party where they believe that such information could assist the authority in undertaking or successfully concluding inquiries and criminal proceedings or could result in a request formulated by the latter State Party pursuant to this Convention.

5. The transmission of information pursuant to paragraph 4 of this article shall be without prejudice to inquiries and criminal proceedings in the State of the competent authorities providing the information. The competent authorities receiving the information shall comply with a request that said information remain confidential, even temporarily, or with restrictions on its use. However, this shall not prevent the receiving State Party from disclosing in its proceedings information that is exculpatory to an accused person. In such a case, the receiving State Party shall notify the transmitting State Party prior to the disclosure and, if so requested, consult with the transmitting State Party. If, in an exceptional case, advance notice is not possible, the receiving State Party shall inform the transmitting State Party of the disclosure without delay.

6. The provisions of this article shall not affect the obligations under any other treaty, bilateral or multilateral, that governs or will govern, in whole or in part, mutual legal assistance.

7. Paragraphs 9 to 29 of this article shall apply to requests made pursuant to this article if the States Parties in question are not bound by a treaty of mutual legal assistance. If those States Parties are bound by such a treaty, the corresponding provisions of that treaty shall apply unless the States Parties agree to apply paragraphs 9 to 29 of this article in lieu thereof. States Parties are strongly encouraged to apply these paragraphs if they facilitate cooperation.

8. States Parties shall not decline to render mutual legal assistance pursuant to this article on the ground of bank secrecy.

9. States Parties may decline to render mutual legal assistance pursuant to this article on the ground of absence of dual criminality. However, the requested State Party may, when it deems appropriate, provide assistance, to the extent it decides at its discretion, irrespective of whether the conduct would constitute an offence under the domestic law of the requested State Party.

10. A person who is being detained or is serving a sentence in the territory of one State Party whose presence in another State Party is requested for purposes of identification, testimony or otherwise providing assistance in obtaining evidence for investigations, prosecutions or judicial proceedings in relation to offences covered by this Convention may be transferred if the following conditions are met:

(a) The person freely gives his or her informed consent;

(b) The competent authorities of both States Parties agree, subject to such conditions as those States Parties may deem appropriate.

11. For the purposes of paragraph 10 of this article:

(a) The State Party to which the person is transferred shall have the authority and obligation to keep the person transferred in custody, unless otherwise requested or authorized by the State Party from which the person was transferred;

(b) The State Party to which the person is transferred shall without delay implement its obligation to return the person to the custody of the State Party from which the person was transferred as agreed beforehand, or as otherwise agreed, by the competent authorities of both States Parties;

(c) The State Party to which the person is transferred shall not require the State Party from which the person was transferred to initiate extradition proceedings for the return of the person;

(d) The person transferred shall receive credit for service of the sentence being served in the State from which he or she was transferred for time spent in the custody of the State Party to which he or she was transferred.

12. Unless the State Party from which a person is to be transferred in accordance with paragraphs 10 and 11 of this article so agrees, that person, whatever his or her nationality, shall not be prosecuted, detained, punished or subjected to any other restriction of his or her personal liberty in the territory of the State to which that person is transferred in respect of acts, omissions or convictions prior to his or her departure from the territory of the State from which he or she was transferred.

13. Each State Party shall designate a central authority that shall have the responsibility and power to receive requests for mutual legal assistance and either to execute them or to transmit them to the competent authorities for execution. Where a State Party has a special region or territory with a separate system of mutual legal assistance, it may designate a distinct central authority that shall have the same function for that region or territory. Central authorities shall ensure the speedy and proper execution or transmission of the requests received. Where the central authority transmits the request to a competent authority for execution, it shall encourage the speedy and proper execution of the request by the competent authority. The Secretary-General of the United Nations shall be notified of the central authority designated for this purpose at the time each State Party deposits its instrument of ratification, acceptance or approval of or accession to this Convention. Requests for mutual legal assistance and any communication related thereto shall be transmitted to the central authorities designated by the States Parties. This requirement shall be without prejudice to the right of a State Party to require that such requests and communications be addressed to it through diplomatic channels and, in urgent circumstances, where the States Parties agree, through the International Criminal Police Organization, if possible.

14. Requests shall be made in writing or, where possible, by any means capable of producing a written record, in a language acceptable to the requested State Party, under conditions allowing that State Party to establish authenticity. The Secretary-General of the United Nations shall be notified of the language or languages acceptable to each State Party at the time it deposits its instrument

of ratification, acceptance or approval of or accession to this Convention. In urgent circumstances and where agreed by the States Parties, requests may be made orally, but shall be confirmed in writing forthwith.

15. A request for mutual legal assistance shall contain:

(a) The identity of the authority making the request;

(b) The subject matter and nature of the investigation, prosecution or judicial proceeding to which the request relates and the name and functions of the authority conducting the investigation, prosecution or judicial proceeding;

(c) A summary of the relevant facts, except in relation to requests for the purpose of service of judicial documents;

(d) A description of the assistance sought and details of any particular procedure that the requesting State Party wishes to be followed;

(e) Where possible, the identity, location and nationality of any person concerned; and

(f) The purpose for which the evidence, information or action is sought.

16. The requested State Party may request additional information when it appears necessary for the execution of the request in accordance with its domestic law or when it can facilitate such execution.

17. A request shall be executed in accordance with the domestic law of the requested State Party and, to the extent not contrary to the domestic law of the requested State Party and where possible, in accordance with the procedures specified in the request.

18. Wherever possible and consistent with fundamental principles of domestic law, when an individual is in the territory of a State Party and has to be heard as a witness or expert by the judicial authorities of another State Party, the first State Party may, at the request of the other, permit the hearing to take place by video conference if it is not possible or desirable for the individual in question to appear in person in the territory of the requesting State Party. States Parties may agree that the hearing shall be conducted by a judicial authority of the requesting State Party and attended by a judicial authority of the requested State Party.

19. The requesting State Party shall not transmit or use information or evidence furnished by the requested State Party for investigations, prosecutions or judicial proceedings other than those stated in the request without the prior consent of the requested State Party. Nothing in this paragraph shall prevent the requesting State Party from disclosing in its proceedings information or evidence that is exculpatory to an accused person. In the latter case, the requesting State Party shall notify the requested State Party prior to the disclosure and, if so requested, consult with the requested State Party. If, in an exceptional case, advance notice is not possible, the requesting State Party shall inform the requested State Party of the disclosure without delay.

20. The requesting State Party may require that the requested State Party keep confidential the fact and substance of the request, except to the extent necessary to execute the request. If the requested State Party cannot comply with the requirement of confidentiality, it shall promptly inform the requesting State Party.

21. Mutual legal assistance may be refused:

(a) If the request is not made in conformity with the provisions of this article;

(b) If the requested State Party considers that execution of the request is likely to prejudice its sovereignty, security, public order or other essential interests;

(c) If the authorities of the requested State Party would be prohibited by its domestic law from carrying out the action requested with regard to any similar offence, had it been subject to investigation, prosecution or judicial proceedings under their own jurisdiction;

(d) If it would be contrary to the legal system of the requested State Party relating to mutual legal assistance for the request to be granted.

22. States Parties may not refuse a request for mutual legal assistance on the sole ground that the offence is also considered to involve fiscal matters.

23. Reasons shall be given for any refusal of mutual legal assistance.

24. The requested State Party shall execute the request for mutual legal assistance as soon as possible and shall take as full account as possible of any deadlines suggested by the requesting State Party and for which reasons are given, preferably in the request. The requested State Party shall respond to reasonable requests by the requesting State Party on progress of its handling of the request. The requesting State Party shall promptly inform the requested State Party when the assistance sought is no longer required.

25. Mutual legal assistance may be postponed by the requested State Party on the ground that it interferes with an ongoing investigation, prosecution or judicial proceeding.

26. Before refusing a request pursuant to paragraph 21 of this article or postponing its execution pursuant to paragraph 25 of this article, the requested State Party shall consult with the requesting State Party to consider whether assistance may be granted subject to such terms and conditions as it deems necessary. If the requesting State Party accepts assistance subject to those conditions, it shall comply with the conditions.

27. Without prejudice to the application of paragraph 12 of this article, a witness, expert or other person who, at the request of the requesting State Party, consents to give evidence in a proceeding or to assist in an investigation, prosecution or judicial proceeding in the territory of the requesting State Party shall not be prosecuted, detained, punished or subjected to any other restriction of his or her personal liberty in that territory in respect of acts, omissions or convictions prior to his or her departure from the territory of the requested State Party. Such safe conduct shall cease when the witness, expert or other person having had, for a period of fifteen consecutive days or for any period agreed upon by the States Parties from the date on which he or she has been officially informed that his or her presence is no longer required by the judicial authorities, an opportunity of leaving, has nevertheless remained voluntarily in the territory of the requesting State Party or, having left it, has returned of his or her own free will.

28. The ordinary costs of executing a request shall be borne by the requested State Party, unless otherwise agreed by the States Parties concerned. If expenses of a substantial or extraordinary nature are or will be required to fulfill the request, the States Parties shall consult to determine the terms and conditions under which the request will be executed, as well as the manner in which the costs shall be borne.

29. The requested State Party:

(a) Shall provide to the requesting State Party copies of government records, documents or information in its possession that under its domestic law are available to the general public;

(b) May, at its discretion, provide to the requesting State Party in whole, in part or subject to such conditions as it deems appropriate, copies of any government records, documents or information in its possession that under its domestic law are not available to the general public.

30. States Parties shall consider, as may be necessary, the possibility of concluding bilateral or multilateral agreements or arrangements that would serve the purposes of, give practical effect to or enhance the provisions of this article.

Article 19

Joint investigations

States Parties shall consider concluding bilateral or multilateral agreements or arrangements whereby, in relation to matters that are the subject of investigations, prosecutions or judicial proceedings in one or more States, the competent authorities concerned may establish joint investigative bodies. In the absence of such agreements or arrangements, joint investigations may be undertaken by agreement on a case-by-case basis. The States Parties involved shall ensure that the sovereignty of the State Party in whose territory such investigation is to take place is fully respected.

Article 20

Special investigative techniques

1. If permitted by the basic principles of its domestic legal system, each State Party shall, within its possibilities and under the conditions prescribed by its domestic law, take the necessary measures to allow for the appropriate use of controlled delivery and, where it deems appropriate, for the use of other special investigative techniques, such as electronic or other forms of surveillance and undercover operations, by its competent authorities in its territory for the purpose of effectively combating organized crime.

2. For the purpose of investigating the offences covered by this Convention, States Parties are encouraged to conclude, when necessary, appropriate bilateral or multilateral agreements or arrangements for using such special investigative techniques in the context of cooperation at the international level. Such agreements or arrangements shall be concluded and implemented in full compliance

with the principle of sovereign equality of States and shall be carried out strictly in accordance with the terms of those agreements or arrangements.

3. In the absence of an agreement or arrangement as set forth in paragraph 2 of this article, decisions to use such special investigative techniques at the international level shall be made on a case-by-case basis and may, when necessary, take into consideration financial arrangements and understandings with respect to the exercise of jurisdiction by the States Parties concerned.

4. Decisions to use controlled delivery at the international level may, with the consent of the States Parties concerned, include methods such as intercepting and allowing the goods to continue intact or be removed or replaced in whole or in part.

Article 21

Transfer of criminal proceedings

States Parties shall consider the possibility of transferring to one another proceedings for the prosecution of an offence covered by this Convention in cases where such transfer is considered to be in the interests of the proper administration of justice, in particular in cases where several jurisdictions are involved, with a view to concentrating the prosecution.

Article 22

Establishment of criminal record

Each State Party may adopt such legislative or other measures as may be necessary to take into consideration, under such terms as and for the purpose that it deems appropriate, any previous conviction in another State of an alleged offender for the purpose of using such information in criminal proceedings relating to an offence covered by this Convention.

Article 23

Criminalization of obstruction of justice

Each State Party shall adopt such legislative and other measures as may be necessary to establish as criminal offences, when committed intentionally:

(a) The use of physical force, threats or intimidation or the promise, offering or giving of an undue advantage to induce false testimony or to interfere in the giving of testimony or the production of evidence in a proceeding in relation to the commission of offences covered by this Convention;

(b) The use of physical force, threats or intimidation to interfere with the exercise of official duties by a justice or law enforcement official in relation to the commission of offences covered by this Convention. Nothing in this subparagraph shall prejudice the right of States Parties to have legislation that protects other categories of public officials.

Article 24

Protection of witnesses

1. Each State Party shall take appropriate measures within its means to provide effective protection from potential retaliation or intimidation for witnesses in criminal proceedings who give testimony concerning offences covered by this Convention and, as appropriate, for their relatives and other persons close to them.

2. The measures envisaged in paragraph 1 of this article may include, inter alia, without prejudice to the rights of the defendant, including the right to due process:

(a) Establishing procedures for the physical protection of such persons, such as, to the extent necessary and feasible, relocating them and permitting, where appropriate, non-disclosure or limitations on the disclosure of information concerning the identity and whereabouts of such persons;

(b) Providing evidentiary rules to permit witness testimony to be given in a manner that ensures the safety of the witness, such as permitting testimony to be given through the use of communications technology such as video links or other adequate means.

3. States Parties shall consider entering into agreements or arrangements with other States for the relocation of persons referred to in paragraph 1 of this article.

4. The provisions of this article shall also apply to victims insofar as they are witnesses.

Article 25

Assistance to and protection of victims

1. Each State Party shall take appropriate measures within its means to provide assistance and protection to victims of offences covered by this Convention, in particular in cases of threat of retaliation or intimidation.

2. Each State Party shall establish appropriate procedures to provide access to compensation and restitution for victims of offences covered by this Convention.

3. Each State Party shall, subject to its domestic law, enable views and concerns of victims to be presented and considered at appropriate stages of criminal proceedings against offenders in a manner not prejudicial to the rights of the defence.

Article 26

Measures to enhance cooperation with law enforcement authorities

1. Each State Party shall take appropriate measures to encourage persons who participate or who have participated in organized criminal groups:

(a) To supply information useful to competent authorities for investigative and evidentiary purposes on such matters as:

(i) The identity, nature, composition, structure, location or activities of organized criminal groups;

(ii) Links, including international links, with other organized criminal groups;

(iii) Offences that organized criminal groups have committed or may commit;

(b) To provide factual, concrete help to competent authorities that may contribute to depriving organized criminal groups of their resources or of the proceeds of crime.

2. Each State Party shall consider providing for the possibility, in appropriate cases, of mitigating punishment of an accused person who provides substantial cooperation in the investigation or prosecution of an offence covered by this Convention.

3. Each State Party shall consider providing for the possibility, in accordance with fundamental principles of its domestic law, of granting immunity from prosecution to a person who provides substantial cooperation in the investigation or prosecution of an offence covered by this Convention.

4. Protection of such persons shall be as provided for in article 24 of this Convention.

5. Where a person referred to in paragraph 1 of this article located in one State Party can provide substantial cooperation to the competent authorities of another State Party, the States Parties concerned may consider entering into agreements or arrangements, in accordance with their domestic law, concerning the potential provision by the other State Party of the treatment set forth in paragraphs 2 and 3 of this article.

Article 27

Law enforcement cooperation

1. States Parties shall cooperate closely with one another, consistent with their respective domestic legal and administrative systems, to enhance the effectiveness of law enforcement action to combat the offences covered by this Convention. Each State Party shall, in particular, adopt effective measures:

(a) To enhance and, where necessary, to establish channels of communication between their competent authorities, agencies and services in order to facilitate the secure and rapid exchange of information concerning all aspects of the offences covered by this Convention, including, if the States Parties concerned deem it appropriate, links with other criminal activities;

(b) To cooperate with other States Parties in conducting inquiries with respect to offences covered by this Convention concerning:

(i) The identity, whereabouts and activities of persons suspected of involvement in such offences or the location of other persons concerned;

(ii) The movement of proceeds of crime or property derived from the commission of such offences;

(iii) The movement of property, equipment or other instrumentalities used or intended for use in the commission of such offences;

(c) To provide, when appropriate, necessary items or quantities of substances for analytical or investigative purposes;

(d) To facilitate effective coordination between their competent authorities, agencies and services and to promote the exchange of personnel and other experts, including, subject to bilateral agreements or arrangements between the States Parties concerned, the posting of liaison officers;

(e) To exchange information with other States Parties on specific means and methods used by organized criminal groups, including, where applicable, routes and conveyances and the use of false identities, altered or false documents or other means of concealing their activities;

(f) To exchange information and coordinate administrative and other measures taken as appropriate for the purpose of early identification of the offences covered by this Convention.

2. With a view to giving effect to this Convention, States Parties shall consider entering into bilateral or multilateral agreements or arrangements on direct cooperation between their law enforcement agencies and, where such agreements or arrangements already exist, amending them. In the absence of such agreements or arrangements between the States Parties concerned, the Parties may consider this Convention as the basis for mutual law enforcement cooperation in respect of the offences covered by this Convention. Whenever appropriate, States Parties shall make full use of agreements or arrangements, including international or regional organizations, to enhance the cooperation between their law enforcement agencies.

3. States Parties shall endeavour to cooperate within their means to respond to transnational organized crime committed through the use of modern technology.

Article 28

Collection, exchange and analysis of information on the nature of organized crime

1. Each State Party shall consider analysing, in consultation with the scientific and academic communities, trends in organized crime in its territory, the circumstances in which organized crime operates, as well as the professional groups and technologies involved.

2. States Parties shall consider developing and sharing analytical expertise concerning organized criminal activities with each other and through international and regional organizations. For that purpose, common definitions, standards and methodologies should be developed and applied as appropriate.

3. Each State Party shall consider monitoring its policies and actual measures to combat organized crime and making assessments of their effectiveness and efficiency.

Article 29

Training and technical assistance

1. Each State Party shall, to the extent necessary, initiate, develop or improve specific training programmes for its law enforcement personnel, including prosecutors, investigating magistrates

and customs personnel, and other personnel charged with the prevention, detection and control of the offences covered by this Convention. Such programmes may include secondments and exchanges of staff. Such programmes shall deal, in particular and to the extent permitted by domestic law, with the following:

(a) Methods used in the prevention, detection and control of the offences covered by this Convention;

(b) Routes and techniques used by persons suspected of involvement in offences covered by this Convention, including in transit States, and appropriate countermeasures;

(c) Monitoring of the movement of contraband;

(d) Detection and monitoring of the movements of proceeds of crime, property, equipment or other instrumentalities and methods used for the transfer, concealment or disguise of such proceeds, property, equipment or other instrumentalities, as well as methods used in combating money-laundering and other financial crimes;

(e) Collection of evidence;

(f) Control techniques in free trade zones and free ports;

(g) Modern law enforcement equipment and techniques, including electronic surveillance, controlled deliveries and undercover operations;

(h) Methods used in combating transnational organized crime committed through the use of computers, telecommunications networks or other forms of modern technology; and

(i) Methods used in the protection of victims and witnesses.

2. States Parties shall assist one another in planning and implementing research and training programmes designed to share expertise in the areas referred to in paragraph 1 of this article and to that end shall also, when appropriate, use regional and international conferences and seminars to promote cooperation and to stimulate discussion on problems of mutual concern, including the special problems and needs of transit States.

3. States Parties shall promote training and technical assistance that will facilitate extradition and mutual legal assistance. Such training and technical assistance may include language training, secondments and exchanges between personnel in central authorities or agencies with relevant responsibilities.

4. In the case of existing bilateral and multilateral agreements or arrangements, States Parties shall strengthen, to the extent necessary, efforts to maximize operational and training activities within international and regional organizations and within other relevant bilateral and multilateral agreements or arrangements.

Article 30

Other measures: implementation of the Convention through economic development and technical assistance

1. States Parties shall take measures conducive to the optimal implementation of this Convention to the extent possible, through international cooperation, taking into account the negative effects of organized crime on society in general, in particular on sustainable development.

2. States Parties shall make concrete efforts to the extent possible and in coordination with each other, as well as with international and regional organizations:

(a) To enhance their cooperation at various levels with developing countries, with a view to strengthening the capacity of the latter to prevent and combat transnational organized crime;

(b) To enhance financial and material assistance to support the efforts of developing countries to fight transnational organized crime effectively and to help them implement this Convention successfully;

(c) To provide technical assistance to developing countries and countries with economies in transition to assist them in meeting their needs for the implementation of this Convention. To that end, States Parties shall endeavour to make adequate and regular voluntary contributions to an account specifically designated for that purpose in a United Nations funding mechanism. States Parties may also give special consideration, in accordance with their domestic law and the provisions of this Convention, to contributing to the aforementioned account a percentage of the money or of the corresponding value of proceeds of crime or property confiscated in accordance with the provisions of this Convention;

(d) To encourage and persuade other States and financial institutions as appropriate to join them in efforts in accordance with this article, in particular by providing more training programmes and modern equipment to developing countries in order to assist them in achieving the objectives of this Convention.

3. To the extent possible, these measures shall be without prejudice to existing foreign assistance commitments or to other financial cooperation arrangements at the bilateral, regional or international level.

4. States Parties may conclude bilateral or multilateral agreements or arrangements on material and logistical assistance, taking into consideration the financial arrangements necessary for the means of international cooperation provided for by this Convention to be effective and for the prevention, detection and control of transnational organized crime.

Article 31

Prevention

1. States Parties shall endeavour to develop and evaluate national projects and to establish and promote best practices and policies aimed at the prevention of transnational organized crime.

2. States Parties shall endeavour, in accordance with fundamental principles of their domestic law, to reduce existing or future opportunities for organized criminal groups to participate in lawful markets with proceeds of crime, through appropriate legislative, administrative or other measures. These measures should focus on:

(a) The strengthening of cooperation between law enforcement agencies or prosecutors and relevant private entities, including industry;

(b) The promotion of the development of standards and procedures designed to safeguard the integrity of public and relevant private entities, as well as codes of conduct for relevant professions, in particular lawyers, notaries public, tax consultants and accountants;

(c) The prevention of the misuse by organized criminal groups of tender procedures conducted by public authorities and of subsidies and licences granted by public authorities for commercial activity;

(d) The prevention of the misuse of legal persons by organized criminal groups; such measures could include:

(i) The establishment of public records on legal and natural persons involved in the establishment, management and funding of legal persons;

(ii) The introduction of the possibility of disqualifying by court order or any appropriate means for a reasonable period of time persons convicted of offences covered by this Convention from acting as directors of legal persons incorporated within their jurisdiction;

(iii) The establishment of national records of persons disqualified from acting as directors of legal persons; and

(iv) The exchange of information contained in the records referred to in subparagraphs (d) (i) and (iii) of this paragraph with the competent authorities of other States Parties.

3. States Parties shall endeavour to promote the reintegration into society of persons convicted of offences covered by this Convention.

4. States Parties shall endeavour to evaluate periodically existing relevant legal instruments and administrative practices with a view to detecting their vulnerability to misuse by organized criminal groups.

5. States Parties shall endeavour to promote public awareness regarding the existence, causes and gravity of and the threat posed by transnational organized crime. Information may be disseminated where appropriate through the mass media and shall include measures to promote public participation in preventing and combating such crime.

6. Each State Party shall inform the Secretary-General of the United Nations of the name and address of the authority or authorities that can assist other States Parties in developing measures to prevent transnational organized crime.

7. States Parties shall, as appropriate, collaborate with each other and relevant international and regional organizations in promoting and developing the measures referred to in this article. This includes participation in international projects aimed at the prevention of transnational organized crime, for example by alleviating the circumstances that render socially marginalized groups vulnerable to the action of transnational organized crime.

Article 32

Conference of the Parties to the Convention

1. A Conference of the Parties to the Convention is hereby established to improve the capacity of States Parties to combat transnational organized crime and to promote and review the implementation of this Convention.

2. The Secretary-General of the United Nations shall convene the Conference of the Parties not later than one year following the entry into force of this Convention. The Conference of the Parties shall adopt rules of procedure and rules governing the activities set forth in paragraphs 3 and 4 of this article (including rules concerning payment of expenses incurred in carrying out those activities).

3. The Conference of the Parties shall agree upon mechanisms for achieving the objectives mentioned in paragraph 1 of this article, including:

(a) Facilitating activities by States Parties under articles 29, 30 and 31 of this Convention, including by encouraging the mobilization of voluntary contributions;

(b) Facilitating the exchange of information among States Parties on patterns and trends in transnational organized crime and on successful practices for combating it;

(c) Cooperating with relevant international and regional organizations and non-governmental organizations;

(d) Reviewing periodically the implementation of this Convention;

(e) Making recommendations to improve this Convention and its implementation.

4. For the purpose of paragraphs 3 (d) and (e) of this article, the Conference of the Parties shall acquire the necessary knowledge of the measures taken by States Parties in implementing this Convention and the difficulties encountered by them in doing so through information provided by them and through such supplemental review mechanisms as may be established by the Conference of the Parties.

5. Each State Party shall provide the Conference of the Parties with information on its programmes, plans and practices, as well as legislative and administrative measures to implement this Convention, as required by the Conference of the Parties.

Article 33

Secretariat

1. The Secretary-General of the United Nations shall provide the necessary secretariat services to the Conference of the Parties to the Convention.

2. The secretariat shall:

(a) Assist the Conference of the Parties in carrying out the activities set forth in article 32 of this Convention and make arrangements and provide the necessary services for the sessions of the Conference of the Parties;

(b) Upon request, assist States Parties in providing information to the Conference of the Parties as envisaged in article 32, paragraph 5, of this Convention; and

(c) Ensure the necessary coordination with the secretariats of relevant international and regional organizations.

Article 34

Implementation of the Convention

1. Each State Party shall take the necessary measures, including legislative and administrative measures, in accordance with fundamental principles of its domestic law, to ensure the implementation of its obligations under this Convention.

2. The offences established in accordance with articles 5, 6, 8 and 23 of this Convention shall be established in the domestic law of each State Party independently of the transnational nature or the involvement of an organized criminal group as described in article 3, paragraph 1, of this Convention, except to the extent that article 5 of this Convention would require the involvement of an organized criminal group.

3. Each State Party may adopt more strict or severe measures than those provided for by this Convention for preventing and combating transnational organized crime.

Article 35

Settlement of disputes

1. States Parties shall endeavour to settle disputes concerning the interpretation or application of this Convention through negotiation.

2. Any dispute between two or more States Parties concerning the interpretation or application of this Convention that cannot be settled through negotiation within a reasonable time shall, at the request of one of those States Parties, be submitted to arbitration. If, six months after the date of the request for arbitration, those States Parties are unable to agree on the organization of the arbitration, any one of those States Parties may refer the dispute to the International Court of Justice by request in accordance with the Statute of the Court.

3. Each State Party may, at the time of signature, ratification, acceptance or approval of or accession to this Convention, declare that it does not consider itself bound by paragraph 2 of this article. The other States Parties shall not be bound by paragraph 2 of this article with respect to any State Party that has made such a reservation.

4. Any State Party that has made a reservation in accordance with paragraph 3 of this article may at any time withdraw that reservation by notification to the Secretary-General of the United Nations.

Article 36

Signature, ratification, acceptance, approval and accession

1. This Convention shall be open to all States for signature from 12 to 15 December 2000 in Palermo, Italy, and thereafter at United Nations Headquarters in New York until 12 December 2002.

2. This Convention shall also be open for signature by regional economic integration organizations provided that at least one member State of such organization has signed this Convention in accordance with paragraph 1 of this article.

3. This Convention is subject to ratification, acceptance or approval. Instruments of ratification, acceptance or approval shall be deposited with the Secretary-General of the United Nations. A regional economic integration organization may deposit its instrument of ratification, acceptance or approval if at least one of its member States has done likewise. In that instrument of ratification, acceptance or approval, such organization shall declare the extent of its competence with respect to the matters governed by this Convention. Such organization shall also inform the depositary of any relevant modification in the extent of its competence.

4. This Convention is open for accession by any State or any regional economic integration organization of which at least one member State is a Party to this Convention. Instruments of accession shall be deposited with the Secretary-General of the United Nations. At the time of its accession, a regional economic integration organization shall declare the extent of its competence with respect to matters governed by this Convention. Such organization shall also inform the depositary of any relevant modification in the extent of its competence.

Article 37

Relation with protocols

1. This Convention may be supplemented by one or more protocols.

2. In order to become a Party to a protocol, a State or a regional economic integration organization must also be a Party to this Convention.

3. A State Party to this Convention is not bound by a protocol unless it becomes a Party to the protocol in accordance with the provisions thereof.

4. Any protocol to this Convention shall be interpreted together with this Convention, taking into account the purpose of that protocol.

Article 38

Entry into force

1. This Convention shall enter into force on the ninetieth day after the date of deposit of the fortieth instrument of ratification, acceptance, approval or accession. For the purpose of this paragraph, any instrument deposited by a regional economic integration

organization shall not be counted as additional to those deposited by member States of such organization.

2. For each State or regional economic integration organization ratifying, accepting, approving or acceding to this Convention after the deposit of the fortieth instrument of such action, this Convention shall enter into force on the thirtieth day after the date of deposit by such State or organization of the relevant instrument.

ARTICLE 39

AMENDMENT

1. After the expiry of five years from the entry into force of this Convention, a State Party may propose an amendment and file it with the Secretary-General of the United Nations, who shall thereupon communicate the proposed amendment to the States Parties and to the Conference of the Parties to the Convention for the purpose of considering and deciding on the proposal. The Conference of the Parties shall make every effort to achieve consensus on each amendment. If all efforts at consensus have been exhausted and no agreement has been reached, the amendment shall, as a last resort, require for its adoption a two-thirds majority vote of the States Parties present and voting at the meeting of the Conference of the Parties.

2. Regional economic integration organizations, in matters within their competence, shall exercise their right to vote under this article with a number of votes equal to the number of their member States that are Parties to this Convention. Such organizations shall not exercise their right to vote if their member States exercise theirs and vice versa.

3. An amendment adopted in accordance with paragraph 1 of this article is subject to ratification, acceptance or approval by States Parties.

4. An amendment adopted in accordance with paragraph 1 of this article shall enter into force in respect of a State Party ninety days after the date of the deposit with the Secretary-General of the United Nations of an instrument of ratification, acceptance or approval of such amendment.

5. When an amendment enters into force, it shall be binding on those States Parties which have expressed their consent to be bound by it. Other States Parties shall still be bound by the provisions of this Convention and any earlier amendments that they have ratified, accepted or approved.

ARTICLE 40

DENUNCIATION

1. A State Party may denounce this Convention by written notification to the Secretary-General of the United Nations. Such denunciation shall become effective one year after the date of receipt of the notification by the Secretary-General.

2. A regional economic integration organization shall cease to be a Party to this Convention when all of its member States have denounced it.

3. Denunciation of this Convention in accordance with paragraph 1 of this article shall entail the denunciation of any protocols thereto.

Article 41

Depositary and languages

1. The Secretary-General of the United Nations is designated depositary of this Convention.

2. The original of this Convention, of which the Arabic, Chinese, English, French, Russian and Spanish texts are equally authentic, shall be deposited with the Secretary-General of the United Nations.

In witness whereof, the undersigned plenipotentiaries, being duly authorized thereto by their respective Governments, have signed this Convention.

7. Convention on Combating Bribery of Foreign Public Officials in International Business Transactions [1]

Adopted at Paris, November 21, 1997; Signed on behalf of the United States, December 17, 1997; Ratification advised by the Senate, July 31, 1998; Entered into force, February 15, 1999

PREAMBLE

The Parties,

CONSIDERING that bribery is a widespread phenomenon in international business transactions, including trade and investment, which raises serious moral and political concerns, undermines good governance and economic development, and distorts international competitive conditions;

CONSIDERING that all countries share a responsibility to combat bribery in international business transactions;

HAVING REGARD to the Revised Recommendation on Combating Bribery in International Business Transactions, adopted by the Council of the Organisation for Economic Co-operation and Development (OECD) on 23 May 1997, C(97)123/FINAL, which, inter alia, called for effective measures to deter, prevent and combat the bribery of foreign public officials in connection with international business transactions, in particular the prompt criminalisation of such bribery in an effective and co-ordinated manner and in conformity with the agreed common elements set out in that Recommendation and with the jurisdictional and other basic legal principles of each country;

WELCOMING other recent developments which further advance international understanding and co-operation in combating bribery of public officials, including actions of the United Nations, the World Bank, the International Monetary Fund, the World Trade Organisation, the Organisation of American States, the Council of Europe and the European Union;

WELCOMING the efforts of companies, business organisations and trade unions as well as other non-governmental organisations to combat bribery;

RECOGNISING the role of governments in the prevention of solicitation of bribes from individuals and enterprises in international business transactions;

RECOGNISING that achieving progress in this field requires not only efforts on a national level but also multilateral co-operation, monitoring and follow-up; Recognising that achieving equivalence

[1] For states that are parties to the Convention, see Department of State publication, *Treaties in Force.*

among the measures to be taken by the Parties is an essential object and purpose of the Convention, which requires that the Convention be ratified without derogations affecting this equivalence;

HAVE AGREED AS FOLLOWS:

ARTICLE 1

THE OFFENCE OF BRIBERY OF FOREIGN PUBLIC OFFICIALS

1. Each Party shall take such measures as may be necessary to establish that it is a criminal offence under its law for any person intentionally to offer, promise or give any undue pecuniary or other advantage, whether directly or through intermediaries, to a foreign public official, for that official or for a third party, in order that the official act or refrain from acting in relation to the performance of official duties, in order to obtain or retain business or other improper advantage in the conduct of international business.

2. Each Party shall take any measures necessary to establish that complicity in, including incitement, aiding and abetting, or authorisation of an act of bribery of a foreign public official shall be a criminal offence. Attempt and conspiracy to bribe a foreign public official shall be criminal offences to the same extent as attempt and conspiracy to bribe a public official of that Party.

3. The offences set out in paragraphs 1 and 2 above are hereinafter referred to as "bribery of a foreign public official".

4. For the purpose of this Convention:

   a. "foreign public official" means any person holding a legislative, administrative or judicial office of a foreign country, whether appointed or elected; any person exercising a public function for a foreign country, including for a public agency or public enterprise; and any official or agent of a public international organisation;

   b. "foreign country" includes all levels and subdivisions of government, from national to local;

   c. "act or refrain from acting in relation to the performance of official duties" includes any use of the public official's position, whether or not within the official's authorised competence.

ARTICLE 2

RESPONSIBILITY OF LEGAL PERSONS

Each Party shall take such measures as may be necessary, in accordance with its legal principles, to establish the liability of legal persons for the bribery of a foreign public official.

ARTICLE 3

SANCTIONS

1. The bribery of a foreign public official shall be punishable by effective, proportionate and dissuasive criminal penalties. The range of penalties shall be comparable to that applicable to the bribery of the Party's own public officials and shall, in the case of

natural persons, include deprivation of liberty sufficient to enable effective mutual legal assistance and extradition.

2. In the event that, under the legal system of a Party, criminal responsibility is not applicable to legal persons, that Party shall ensure that legal persons shall be subject to effective, proportionate and dissuasive non-criminal sanctions, including monetary sanctions, for bribery of foreign public officials.

3. Each Party shall take such measures as may be necessary to provide that the bribe and the proceeds of the bribery of a foreign public official, or property the value of which corresponds to that of such proceeds, are subject to seizure and confiscation or that monetary sanctions of comparable effect are applicable.

4. Each Party shall consider the imposition of additional civil or administrative sanctions upon a person subject to sanctions for the bribery of a foreign public official.

Article 4

Jurisdiction

1. Each Party shall take such measures as may be necessary to establish its jurisdiction over the bribery of a foreign public official when the offence is committed in whole or in part in its territory.

2. Each Party which has jurisdiction to prosecute its nationals for offences committed abroad shall take such measures as may be necessary to establish its jurisdiction to do so in respect of the bribery of a foreign public official, according to the same principles.

3. When more than one Party has jurisdiction over an alleged offence described in this Convention, the Parties involved shall, at the request of one of them, consult with a view to determining the most appropriate jurisdiction for prosecution.

4. Each Party shall review whether its current basis for jurisdiction is effective in the fight against the bribery of foreign public officials and, if it is not, shall take remedial steps.

Article 5

Enforcement

Investigation and prosecution of the bribery of a foreign public official shall be subject to the applicable rules and principles of each Party. They shall not be influenced by considerations of national economic interest, the potential effect upon relations with another State or the identity of the natural or legal persons involved.

Article 6

Statute of Limitations

Any statute of limitations applicable to the offence of bribery of a foreign public official shall allow an adequate period of time for the investigation and prosecution of this offence.

ARTICLE 7

MONEY LAUNDERING

Each Party which has made bribery of its own public official a predicate offence for the purpose of the application of its money laundering legislation shall do so on the same terms for the bribery of a foreign public official, without regard to the place where the bribery occurred.

ARTICLE 8

ACCOUNTING

1. In order to combat bribery of foreign public officials effectively, each Party shall take such measures as may be necessary, within the framework of its laws and regulations regarding the maintenance of books and records, financial statement disclosures, and accounting and auditing standards, to prohibit the establishment of off-the-books accounts, the making of off-the-books or inadequately identified transactions, the recording of non-existent expenditures, the entry of liabilities with incorrect identification of their object, as well as the use of false documents, by companies subject to those laws and regulations, for the purpose of bribing foreign public officials or of hiding such bribery.

2. Each Party shall provide effective, proportionate and dissuasive civil, administrative or criminal penalties for such omissions and falsifications in respect of the books, records, accounts and financial statements of such companies.

ARTICLE 9

MUTUAL LEGAL ASSISTANCE

1. Each Party shall, to the fullest extent possible under its laws and relevant treaties and arrangements, provide prompt and effective legal assistance to another Party for the purpose of criminal investigations and proceedings brought by a Party concerning offences within the scope of this Convention and for non-criminal proceedings within the scope of this Convention brought by a Party against a legal person. The requested Party shall inform the requesting Party, without delay, of any additional information or documents needed to support the request for assistance and, where requested, of the status and outcome of the request for assistance.

2. Where a Party makes mutual legal assistance conditional upon the existence of dual criminality, dual criminality shall be deemed to exist if the offence for which the assistance is sought is within the scope of this Convention.

3. A Party shall not decline to render mutual legal assistance for criminal matters within the scope of this Convention on the ground of bank secrecy.

Article 10

Extradition

1. Bribery of a foreign public official shall be deemed to be included as an extraditable offence under the laws of the Parties and the extradition treaties between them.

2. If a Party which makes extradition conditional on the existence of an extradition treaty receives a request for extradition from another Party with which it has no extradition treaty, it may consider this Convention to be the legal basis for extradition in respect of the offence of bribery of a foreign public official.

3. Each Party shall take any measures necessary to assure either that it can extradite its nationals or that it can prosecute its nationals for the offence of bribery of a foreign public official. A Party which declines a request to extradite a person for bribery of a foreign public official solely on the ground that the person is its national shall submit the case to its competent authorities for the purpose of prosecution.

4. Extradition for bribery of a foreign public official is subject to the conditions set out in the domestic law and applicable treaties and arrangements of each Party. Where a Party makes extradition conditional upon the existence of dual criminality, that condition shall be deemed to be fulfilled if the offence for which extradition is sought is within the scope of Article 1 of this Convention.

Article 11

Responsible Authorities

For the purposes of Article 4, paragraph 3, on consultation, Article 9, on mutual legal assistance and Article 10, on extradition, each Party shall notify to the Secretary-General of the OECD an authority or authorities responsible for making and receiving requests, which shall serve as channel of communication for these matters for that Party, without prejudice to other arrangements between Parties.

Article 12

Monitoring and Follow-up

The Parties shall co-operate in carrying out a programme of systematic follow-up to monitor and promote the full implementation of this Convention. Unless otherwise decided by consensus of the Parties, this shall be done in the framework of the OECD Working Group on Bribery in International Business Transactions and according to its terms of reference, or within the framework and terms of reference of any successor to its functions, and Parties shall bear the costs of the programme in accordance with the rules applicable to that body.

Article 13

Signature and Accession

1. Until its entry into force, this Convention shall be open for signature by OECD members and by non-members which have been invited to become full participants in its Working Group on Bribery in International Business Transactions.

2. Subsequent to its entry into force, this Convention shall be open to accession by any non-signatory which is a member of the OECD or has become a full participant in the Working Group on Bribery in International Business Transactions or any successor to its functions. For each such non-signatory, the Convention shall enter into force on the sixtieth day following the date of deposit of its instrument of accession.

Article 14

Ratification and Depositary

1. This Convention is subject to acceptance, approval or ratification by the Signatories, in accordance with their respective laws.

2. Instruments of acceptance, approval, ratification or accession shall be deposited with the Secretary-General of the OECD, who shall serve as Depositary of this Convention.

Article 15

Entry into Force

1. This Convention shall enter into force on the sixtieth day following the date upon which five of the ten countries which have the ten largest export shares (see annex), and which represent by themselves at least sixty per cent of the combined total exports of those ten countries, have deposited their instruments of acceptance, approval, or ratification. For each signatory depositing its instrument after such entry into force, the Convention shall enter into force on the sixtieth day after deposit of its instrument.

2. If, after 31 December 1998, the Convention has not entered into force under paragraph 1 above, any signatory which has deposited its instrument of acceptance, approval or ratification may declare in writing to the Depositary its readiness to accept entry into force of this Convention under this paragraph 2. The Convention shall enter into force for such a signatory on the sixtieth day following the date upon which such declarations have been deposited by at least two signatories. For each signatory depositing its declaration after such entry into force, the Convention shall enter into force on the sixtieth day following the date of deposit.

Article 16

Amendment

Any Party may propose the amendment of this Convention. A proposed amendment shall be submitted to the Depositary which shall communicate it to the other Parties at least sixty days before convening a meeting of the Parties to consider the proposed amendment. An amendment adopted by consensus of the Parties, or by such other means as the Parties may determine by consensus, shall enter into force sixty days after the deposit of an instrument of ratification, acceptance or approval by all of the Parties, or in such other circumstances as may be specified by the Parties at the time of adoption of the amendment.

Article 17

Withdrawal

A Party may withdraw from this Convention by submitting written notification to the Depositary. Such withdrawal shall be effective one year after the date of the receipt of the notification. After withdrawal, co-operation shall continue between the Parties and the Party which has withdrawn on all requests for assistance or extradition made before the effective date of withdrawal which remain pending.

8. Inter-American Convention Against Corruption [1]

Adopted at Caracas, Venezuela, March 29, 1996; Signed on behalf of the United States, June 27, 1996; Entered into force generally, March 6, 1997; Ratification advised by the Senate, July 27, 2000; Entered into force for the United States, October 29, 2000

PREAMBLE

The Member States of the Organization of American States,

CONVINCED that corruption undermines the legitimacy of public institutions and strikes at society, moral order and justice, as well as at the comprehensive development of peoples;

CONSIDERING that representative democracy, an essential condition for stability, peace and development of the region, requires, by its nature, the combating of every form of corruption in the performance of public functions, as well as acts of corruption specifically related to such performance;

PERSUADED that fighting corruption strengthens democratic institutions and prevents distortions in the economy, improprieties in public administration and damage to a society's moral fiber;

RECOGNIZING that corruption is often a tool used by organized crime for the accomplishment of its purposes;

CONVINCED of the importance of making people in the countries of the region aware of this problem and its gravity, and of the need to strengthen participation by civil society in preventing and fighting corruption;

RECOGNIZING that, in some cases, corruption has international dimensions, which requires coordinated action by States to fight it effectively;

CONVINCED of the need for prompt adoption of an international instrument to promote and facilitate international cooperation in fighting corruption and, especially, in taking appropriate action against persons who commit acts of corruption in the performance of public functions, or acts specifically related to such performance, as well as appropriate measures with respect to the proceeds of such acts;

DEEPLY CONCERNED by the steadily increasing links between corruption and the proceeds generated by illicit narcotics trafficking which undermine and threaten legitimate commercial and financial activities, and society, at all levels;

BEARING IN MIND the responsibility of States to hold corrupt persons accountable in order to combat corruption and to cooperate with one another for their efforts in this area to be effective; and

[1] For states that are parties to the Convention, see Department of State publication, *Treaties in Force*.

DETERMINED to make every effort to prevent, detect, punish and eradicate corruption in the performance of public functions and acts of corruption specifically related to such performance,

HAVE AGREED TO ADOPT THE FOLLOWING

INTER-AMERICAN CONVENTION AGAINST CORRUPTION

ARTICLE I

DEFINITIONS

For the purposes of this Convention:

"Public function" means any temporary or permanent, paid or honorary activity, performed by a natural person in the name of the State or in the service of the State or its institutions, at any level of its hierarchy.

"Public official", "government official", or "public servant" means any official or employee of the State or its agencies, including those who have been selected, appointed, or elected to perform activities or functions in the name of the State or in the service of the State, at any level of its hierarchy.

"Property" means assets of any kind, whether movable or immovable, tangible or intangible, and any document or legal instrument demonstrating, purporting to demonstrate, or relating to ownership or other rights pertaining to such assets.

ARTICLE II

PURPOSES

The purposes of this Convention are:

1. To promote and strengthen the development by each of the States Parties of the mechanisms needed to prevent, detect, punish and eradicate corruption; and

2. To promote, facilitate and regulate cooperation among the States Parties to ensure the effectiveness of measures and actions to prevent, detect, punish and eradicate corruption in the performance of public functions and acts of corruption specifically related to such performance.

ARTICLE III

PREVENTIVE MEASURES

For the purposes set forth in Article II of this Convention, the States Parties agree to consider the applicability of measures within their own institutional systems to create, maintain and strengthen:

1. Standards of conduct for the correct, honorable, and proper fulfillment of public functions. These standards shall be intended to prevent conflicts of interest and mandate the proper conservation and use of resources entrusted to government officials in the performance of their functions. These standards shall also establish measures and systems requiring government officials to report to appropriate authorities acts of corruption in the performance of public functions. Such measures should help preserve the public's

confidence in the integrity of public servants and government processes.

2. Mechanisms to enforce these standards of conduct.

3. Instruction to government personnel to ensure proper understanding of their responsibilities and the ethical rules governing their activities.

4. Systems for registering the income, assets and liabilities of persons who perform public functions in certain posts as specified by law and, where appropriate, for making such registrations public.

5. Systems of government hiring and procurement of goods and services that assure the openness, equity and efficiency of such systems.

6. Government revenue collection and control systems that deter corruption.

7. Laws that deny favorable tax treatment for any individual or corporation for expenditures made in violation of the anticorruption laws of the States Parties.

8. Systems for protecting public servants and private citizens who, in good faith, report acts of corruption, including protection of their identities, in accordance with their Constitutions and the basic principles of their domestic legal systems.

9. Oversight bodies with a view to implementing modern mechanisms for preventing, detecting, punishing and eradicating corrupt acts.

10. Deterrents to the bribery of domestic and foreign government officials, such as mechanisms to ensure that publicly held companies and other types of associations maintain books and records which, in reasonable detail, accurately reflect the acquisition and disposition of assets, and have sufficient internal accounting controls to enable their officers to detect corrupt acts.

11. Mechanisms to encourage participation by civil society and nongovernmental organizations in efforts to prevent corruption.

12. The study of further preventive measures that take into account the relationship between equitable compensation and probity in public service.

Article IV

Scope

This Convention is applicable provided that the alleged act of corruption has been committed or has effects in a State Party.

Article V

Jurisdiction

1. Each State Party shall adopt such measures as may be necessary to establish its jurisdiction over the offenses it has established in accordance with this Convention when the offense in question is committed in its territory.

2. Each State Party may adopt such measures as may be necessary to establish its jurisdiction over the offenses it has established in accordance with this Convention when the offense is committed by one of its nationals or by a person who habitually resides in its territory.

3. Each State Party shall adopt such measures as may be necessary to establish its jurisdiction over the offenses it has established in accordance with this Convention when the alleged criminal is present in its territory and it does not extradite such person to another country on the ground of the nationality of the alleged criminal.

4. This Convention does not preclude the application of any other rule of criminal jurisdiction established by a State Party under its domestic law.

ARTICLE VI

ACTS OF CORRUPTION

1. This Convention is applicable to the following acts of corruption:

a. The solicitation or acceptance, directly or indirectly, by a government official or a person who performs public functions, of any article of monetary value, or other benefit, such as a gift, favor, promise or advantage for himself or for another person or entity, in exchange for any act or omission in the performance of his public functions;

b. The offering or granting, directly or indirectly, to a government official or a person who performs public functions, of any article of monetary value, or other benefit, such as a gift, favor, promise or advantage for himself or for another person or entity, in exchange for any act or omission in the performance of his public functions;

c. Any act or omission in the discharge of his duties by a government official or a person who performs public functions for the purpose of illicitly obtaining benefits for himself or for a third party;

d. The fraudulent use or concealment of property derived from any of the acts referred to in this article; and

e. Participation as a principal, coprincipal, instigator, accomplice or accessory after the fact, or in any other manner, in the commission or attempted commission of, or in any collaboration or conspiracy to commit, any of the acts referred to in this article.

2. This Convention shall also be applicable by mutual agreement between or among two or more States Parties with respect to any other act of corruption not described herein.

ARTICLE VII

DOMESTIC LAW

The States Parties that have not yet done so shall adopt the necessary legislative or other measures to establish as criminal offenses under their domestic law the acts of corruption described in

Article VI(1) and to facilitate cooperation among themselves pursuant to this Convention.

Article VIII

Transnational Bribery

Subject to its Constitution and the fundamental principles of its legal system, each State Party shall prohibit and punish the offering or granting, directly or indirectly, by its nationals, persons having their habitual residence in its territory, and businesses domiciled there, to a government official of another State, of any article of monetary value, or other benefit, such as a gift, favor, promise or advantage, in connection with any economic or commercial transaction in exchange for any act or omission in the performance of that official's public functions.

Among those States Parties that have established transnational bribery as an offense, such offense shall be considered an act of corruption for the purposes of this Convention.

Any State Party that has not established transnational bribery as an offense shall, insofar as its laws permit, provide assistance and cooperation with respect to this offense as provided in this Convention.

Article IX

Illicit Enrichment

Subject to its Constitution and the fundamental principles of its legal system, each State Party that has not yet done so shall take the necessary measures to establish under its laws as an offense a significant increase in the assets of a government official that he cannot reasonably explain in relation to his lawful earnings during the performance of his functions.

Among those States Parties that have established illicit enrichment as an offense, such offense shall be considered an act of corruption for the purposes of this Convention.

Any State Party that has not established illicit enrichment as an offense shall, insofar as its laws permit, provide assistance and cooperation with respect to this offense as provided in this Convention.

Article X

Notification

When a State Party adopts the legislation referred to in paragraph 1 of articles VIII and IX, it shall notify the Secretary General of the Organization of American States, who shall in turn notify the other States Parties. For the purposes of this Convention, the crimes of transnational bribery and illicit enrichment shall be considered acts of corruption for that State Party thirty days following the date of such notification.

Article XI

Progressive Development

1. In order to foster the development and harmonization of their domestic legislation and the attainment of the purposes of this Convention, the States Parties view as desirable, and undertake to consider, establishing as offenses under their laws the following acts:

a. The improper use by a government official or a person who performs public functions, for his own benefit or that of a third party, of any kind of classified or confidential information which that official or person who performs public functions has obtained because of, or in the performance of, his functions;

b. The improper use by a government official or a person who performs public functions, for his own benefit or that of a third party, of any kind of property belonging to the State or to any firm or institution in which the State has a proprietary interest, to which that official or person who performs public functions has access because of, or in the performance of, his functions;

c. Any act or omission by any person who, personally or through a third party, or acting as an intermediary, seeks to obtain a decision from a public authority whereby he illicitly obtains for himself or for another person any benefit or gain, whether or not such act or omission harms State property; and

d. The diversion by a government official, for purposes unrelated to those for which they were intended, for his own benefit or that of a third party, of any movable or immovable property, monies or securities belonging to the State, to an independent agency, or to an individual, that such official has received by virtue of his position for purposes of administration, custody or for other reasons.

2. Among those States Parties that have established these offenses, such offenses shall be considered acts of corruption for the purposes of this Convention.

3. Any State Party that has not established these offenses shall, insofar as its laws permit, provide assistance and cooperation with respect to these offenses as provided in this Convention.

Article XII

Effect on State Property

For application of this Convention, it shall not be necessary that the acts of corruption harm State property.

Article XIII

Extradition

1. This article shall apply to the offenses established by the States Parties in accordance with this Convention.

2. Each of the offenses to which this article applies shall be deemed to be included as an extraditable offense in any extradition

treaty existing between or among the States Parties. The States Parties undertake to include such offenses as extraditable offenses in every extradition treaty to be concluded between or among them.

3. If a State Party that makes extradition conditional on the existence of a treaty receives a request for extradition from another State Party with which it does not have an extradition treaty, it may consider this Convention as the legal basis for extradition with respect to any offense to which this article applies.

4. States Parties that do not make extradition conditional on the existence of a treaty shall recognize offenses to which this article applies as extraditable offenses between themselves.

5. Extradition shall be subject to the conditions provided for by the law of the Requested State or by applicable extradition treaties, including the grounds on which the Requested State may refuse extradition.

6. If extradition for an offense to which this article applies is refused solely on the basis of the nationality of the person sought, or because the Requested State deems that it has jurisdiction over the offense, the Requested State shall submit the case to its competent authorities for the purpose of prosecution unless otherwise agreed with the Requesting State, and shall report the final outcome to the Requesting State in due course.

7. Subject to the provisions of its domestic law and its extradition treaties, the Requested State may, upon being satisfied that the circumstances so warrant and are urgent, and at the request of the Requesting State, take into custody a person whose extradition is sought and who is present in its territory, or take other appropriate measures to ensure his presence at extradition proceedings.

Article XIV

Assistance and Cooperation

1. In accordance with their domestic laws and applicable treaties, the States Parties shall afford one another the widest measure of mutual assistance by processing requests from authorities that, in conformity with their domestic laws, have the power to investigate or prosecute the acts of corruption described in this Convention, to obtain evidence and take other necessary action to facilitate legal proceedings and measures regarding the investigation or prosecution of acts of corruption.

2. The States Parties shall also provide each other with the widest measure of mutual technical cooperation on the most effective ways and means of preventing, detecting, investigating and punishing acts of corruption. To that end, they shall foster exchanges of experiences by way of agreements and meetings between competent bodies and institutions, and shall pay special attention to methods and procedures of citizen participation in the fight against corruption.

Article XV

Measures Regarding Property

1. In accordance with their applicable domestic laws and relevant treaties or other agreements that may be in force between or among them, the States Parties shall provide each other the broadest possible measure of assistance in the identification, tracing, freezing, seizure and forfeiture of property or proceeds obtained, derived from or used in the commission of offenses established in accordance with this Convention.

2. A State Party that enforces its own or another State Party's forfeiture judgment against property or proceeds described in paragraph 1 of this article shall dispose of the property or proceeds in accordance with its laws. To the extent permitted by a State Party's laws and upon such terms as it deems appropriate, it may transfer all or part of such property or proceeds to another State Party that assisted in the underlying investigation or proceedings.

Article XVI

Bank Secrecy

1. The Requested State shall not invoke bank secrecy as a basis for refusal to provide the assistance sought by the Requesting State. The Requested State shall apply this article in accordance with its domestic law, its procedural provisions, or bilateral or multilateral agreements with the Requesting State.

2. The Requesting State shall be obligated not to use any information received that is protected by bank secrecy for any purpose other than the proceeding for which that information was requested, unless authorized by the Requested State.

Article XVII

Nature of the Act

For the purposes of articles XIII, XIV, XV and XVI of this Convention, the fact that the property obtained or derived from an act of corruption was intended for political purposes, or that it is alleged that an act of corruption was committed for political motives or purposes, shall not suffice in and of itself to qualify the act as a political offense or as a common offense related to a political offense.

Article XVIII

Central Authorities

1. For the purposes of international assistance and cooperation provided under this Convention, each State Party may designate a central authority or may rely upon such central authorities as are provided for in any relevant treaties or other agreements.

2. The central authorities shall be responsible for making and receiving the requests for assistance and cooperation referred to in this Convention.

3. The central authorities shall communicate with each other directly for the purposes of this Convention.

Article XIX

Temporal Application

Subject to the constitutional principles and the domestic laws of each State and existing treaties between the States Parties, the fact that the alleged act of corruption was committed before this Convention entered into force shall not preclude procedural cooperation in criminal matters between the States Parties. This provision shall in no case affect the principle of non-retroactivity in criminal law, nor shall application of this provision interrupt existing statutes of limitations relating to crimes committed prior to the date of the entry into force of this Convention.

Article XX

Other Agreements or Practices

No provision of this Convention shall be construed as preventing the States Parties from engaging in mutual cooperation within the framework of other international agreements, bilateral or multilateral, currently in force or concluded in the future, or pursuant to any other applicable arrangement or practice.

Article XXI

Signature

This Convention is open for signature by the Member States of the Organization of American States.

Article XXII

Ratification

This Convention is subject to ratification. The instruments of ratification shall be deposited with the General Secretariat of the Organization of American States.

Article XXIII

Accession

This Convention shall remain open for accession by any other State. The instruments of accession shall be deposited with the General Secretariat of the Organization of American States.

Article XXIV

Reservations

The States Parties may, at the time of adoption, signature, ratification, or accession, make reservations to this Convention, provided that each reservation concerns one or more specific provisions and is not incompatible with the object and purpose of the Convention.

Article XXV

Entry Into Force

This Convention shall enter into force on the thirtieth day following the date of deposit of the second instrument of ratification. For each State ratifying or acceding to the Convention after the deposit of the second instrument of ratification, the Convention shall enter into force on the thirtieth day after deposit by such State of its instrument of ratification or accession.

Article XXVI

Denunciation

This Convention shall remain in force indefinitely, but any of the States Parties may denounce it. The instrument of denunciation shall be deposited with the General Secretariat of the Organization of American States. One year from the date of deposit of the instrument of denunciation, the Convention shall cease to be in force for the denouncing State, but shall remain in force for the other States Parties.

Article XXVII

Additional Protocols

Any State Party may submit for the consideration of other States Parties meeting at a General Assembly of the Organization of American States draft additional protocols to this Convention to contribute to the attainment of the purposes set forth in Article II thereof.

Each additional protocol shall establish the terms for its entry into force and shall apply only to those States that become Parties to it.

Article XXVIII

Deposit of Original Instrument

The original instrument of this Convention, the English, French, Portuguese, and Spanish texts of which are equally authentic, shall be deposited with the General Secretariat of the Organization of American States, which shall forward an authenticated copy of its text to the Secretariat of the United Nations for registration and publication in accordance with Article 102 of the United Nations Charter. The General Secretariat of the Organization of American States shall notify its Member States and the States that have acceded to the Convention of signatures, of the deposit of instruments of ratification, accession, or denunciation, and of reservations, if any.

9. Mutual Legal Assistance Treaties

a. Countries with which the United States has a Mutual Legal Assistance Treaty in Criminal Matters

Country	Entered Into Force
Antigua and Barbuda	July 1, 1999
Argentina	February 9, 1993
Australia	September 30, 1999
Austria	August 1, 1998
Bahamas	July 18, 1990
Barbados	July 3, 2000
Belgium	January 1, 2000
Belize	July 2, 2003
Brazil	February 21, 2001
Canada	January 24, 1990
China	March 8, 2001
China (Hong Kong)	January 21, 2000
Cyprus	September 18, 2002
Czech Republic	May 7, 2000
Dominica	May 25, 2000
Egypt	November 29, 2001
Estonia	October 20, 2000
France	December 1, 2001
Greece	November 20, 2001
Grenada	September 14, 1999
Hungary	March 18, 1997
India	October 3, 2005
Israel	May 25, 1999
Italy	November 13, 1985
Jamaica	July 25, 1995
Korea	May 23, 1997
Latvia	September 17, 1999
Liechtenstein	August 1, 2003
Lithuania	August 26, 1999
Luxembourg	February 1, 2001
Mexico	May 3, 1991
Morocco	June 23, 1993
Netherlands	September 15, 1983
Nigeria	January 14, 2003
Panama	September 6, 1995
Philippines	November 22, 1996
Poland	September 17, 1999
Romania	October 17, 2001
Russia	January 31, 2002
Saint Kitts and Nevis	February 23, 2000
Saint Lucia	February 2, 2000
Saint Vincent and The Grenadines	September 8, 1999
South Africa	June 25, 2001
Spain	June 30, 1993
Switzerland	January 23, 1977
Thailand	June 10, 1993

Country	Entered Into Force
Trinidad and Tobago	November 29, 1999
Turkey	January 1, 1981
Ukraine	February 27, 2001
United Kingdom (concerning the Cayman Islands).	March 19, 1990
United Kingdom (concerning Anguilla, the British Virgin Islands, and the Turks and Caicos Islands).	November 9, 1990
United Kingdom (concerning Montserrat)	April 26, 1991
United Kingdom	February 2, 1996
United Kingdom (concerning the Isle of Man).	June 5, 2003
Uruguay	April 15, 1994

b. Treaty on Mutual Legal Assistance in Criminal Matters Between France and the United States of America [1]

Signed at Paris, December 10, 1998; Ratification advised by the Senate, October 18, 2000; Entered into force, December 1, 2001

The President of the French Republic and the President of the United States of America,

DESIRING to establish more effective cooperation in the area of mutual legal assistance in criminal matters;

HAVE DECIDED to conclude a treaty on mutual legal assistance in criminal matters and have appointed as their plenipotentiaries for this purpose:

The President of the French Republic:

The Honorable Elisabeth Guigou, Minister of Justice;

The President of the United States of America:

The Honorable Madeleine Albright, Secretary of State of the United States of America;

Who, having communicated to each other their respective full powers, which were found in good and due form,

HAVE AGREED as follows:

ARTICLE 1

SCOPE OF ASSISTANCE

1. The Contracting States undertake to afford each other, in accordance with the provisions of this Treaty, the widest measure of mutual assistance in investigations or proceedings in respect of criminal offenses the punishment of which, at the time of the request for assistance, is a matter for the judicial authorities of the Requesting State.

2. This Treaty does not apply to:

(a) the execution of requests for provisional arrest and extradition;

(b) the enforcement of criminal judgments except for forfeiture decisions referred to in Article 11; or,

(c) offenses under military law that do not constitute offenses under ordinary criminal law.

3. This Treaty is intended solely for mutual legal assistance between the States. The provisions of the Treaty shall not affect the exercise of rights otherwise available to private persons under the laws of the State presented with a claim based on such rights.

[1] 2172 UNTS 69. The full text of the Treaty on Mutual Legal Assistance in Criminal Matters Between France and the United States of America is set out in this volume as a model of the other 53 MLAT treaties that were in force for the United States as of December 31, 2005.

Article 2

Central Authorities

1. Each State shall designate a Central Authority to make and receive requests pursuant to this Treaty. For France, the Central Authority is the Ministry of Justice. For the United States of America, the Central Authority is the Attorney General or a person designated by the Attorney General. The Central Authorities shall communicate directly with one another for the purposes of this Treaty.

2. The Central Authorities shall consult, at times to which they mutually agree, to promote the most effective use of this Treaty. The Central Authorities shall agree on such practical measures as may be necessary to facilitate the implementation of this Treaty, in particular those related to the implementation of Article 9.

3. The Central Authorities shall provide each other with information regarding the execution of requests and each shall respond to the other's requests regarding progress toward execution of specific requests.

Article 3

Competent Authorities

The Central Authorities shall make requests emanating from competent authorities. For France, the competent authorities are the judicial authorities including the public prosecutor. For the United States of America, the competent authorities are prosecutors and authorities with statutory or regulatory responsibility for investigations of criminal offenses, including the referral of matters to prosecutors for criminal prosecution. The presentation by the Central Authority of the United States of America of a request coming from such authorities establishes the competence of those authorities.

Article 4

Contents of Requests

1. Requests for assistance shall be in writing and shall include the following information:

(a) the identity of the competent authority from whom the request emanates;

(b) a description of the nature of the investigation or proceeding, including the facts on which the request is based, and a statement of the purpose for which the assistance is sought;

(c) the text of the applicable criminal statute;

(d) insofar as possible, the identity and nationality of the person who is the subject of the investigation or proceeding;

(e) insofar as possible, the identity, nationality, and address or location of any person to be served or from whom assistance is sought;

(f) a description of the evidence or other assistance sought including, where appropriate, a list of questions if testimony of a witness or questioning of a person who is the subject of the investigation or proceeding is requested; and

(g) the details of any particular procedure that the Requesting State wishes to be followed.

2. Where appropriate, the Requesting State may indicate any time limit within which the assistance should be provided.

ARTICLE 5

TRANSMISSION OF REQUESTS

Requests shall be sent by the Central Authority of the Requesting State to the Central Authority of the Requested State. The results of execution shall be returned through the same channel unless the Central Authorities agree otherwise. In the event of urgency, an advance copy of a request may be transmitted by any means, including Interpol. Thereafter, the Central Authority of the Requesting State shall transmit the original request to the Central Authority of the Requested State.

ARTICLE 6

DENIAL OF ASSISTANCE

1. Legal assistance may be denied if the Requested State considers that:

(a) the offense to which the request relates is a political offense or an offense related to a political offense; or

(b) execution of the request would prejudice its sovereignty, security, public order, or other essential interests.

2. Before denial of a request for assistance, the Central Authority of the Requested State shall consult with the Central Authority of the Requesting State to consider whether assistance can be given subject to such conditions as the Requested State deems to be necessary.

3. If a request for assistance is denied, the Central Authority of the Requested State shall inform the Central Authority of the Requesting State of the reasons for the denial.

ARTICLE 7

POSTPONING EXECUTION

If the Requested State determines that execution of a request would interfere with an ongoing criminal investigation or proceeding in that State, it may, after consultations between the Central Authorities, postpone execution, including transmission, or make execution subject to conditions determined to be necessary. If the Requesting State accepts the assistance subject to the conditions, it shall comply with the conditions.

ARTICLE 8

EXECUTION OF REQUESTS

1. Requests shall be executed in accordance with the provisions of this Treaty and the laws of the Requested State.

2. The Central Authority of the Requested State shall make all necessary arrangements for a request to be presented to its competent administrative and judicial authorities for execution. Administrative and judicial authorities charged with the execution of a request shall use all necessary measures available under the laws of the Requested State to provide any form of assistance, not prohibited by its laws, necessary or useful for the execution of the request.

3. A person giving testimony or evidence in the Requested State may assert such claims of immunity, incapacity, or privilege as are available under its laws. If such person asserts a claim under the laws of the Requesting State, the person's testimony or evidence shall be taken and the claim recorded and preserved for consideration by the judicial authorities of the Requesting State. If, within a reasonable time prior to giving testimony or evidence, such person notifies the executing authority of the Requested State of the intention to assert such a claim, the Central Authorities may consult with respect thereto.

4. A person who gives false testimony in the execution of a request shall be subject to prosecution and punishment in the Requested State in accordance with its laws.

Article 9

Specific Procedures

1. If the Requesting State requests, the Requested State shall inform it of the dates and places of the execution of the request. The authorities and persons designated by the Requesting State may be permitted to be present at, and may assist in, the execution of the request if the Requested State consents. The Requested State shall permit such designated authorities and persons to be present at and assist in the taking of depositions for use in a judicial proceeding in the Requesting State subject to, in particular, the application of Articles 6 and 7.

2. The procedures specified in this paragraph and outlined in the request shall be carried out insofar as they are not contrary to the fundamental principles of a judicial proceeding in the Requested State. The Requested State, if the Requesting State requests, shall:

(a) take the testimony of witnesses or experts under oath, or question persons who are the subject of investigations or proceedings;

(b) allow a confrontation between a defendant, together with counsel, and a witness or expert whose testimony or evidence is taken for use against that defendant in a criminal prosecution in the Requesting State;

(c) ask questions submitted by the Requesting State, including questions proposed by authorities of the Requesting State present at the execution of the request;

(d) record or allow to be recorded the testimony, questioning, or confrontation; and

(e) produce or allow to be produced a verbatim transcript of the proceeding in which the testimony, questioning, or confrontation occurs.

3. If the Requesting State requests, the Requested State shall transmit original documents or records to the extent possible. Otherwise, the Requested State shall transmit true copies thereof.

4. If the Requesting State requests, business records, whether originals or copies, shall be accompanied by:

(a) a certificate such as Form A appended to this Treaty; or

(b) a procès-verbal containing the essential information sought in Form A. Such records shall be admissible in evidence in the Requesting State as proof of the truth of the matters set forth therein.

Article 10

Search and Seizure

1. The Requested State shall execute a request for the search, seizure, and delivery of any item to the Requesting State if the request includes the information justifying such search under the laws of the Requested State.

2. If the Requesting State requests, a competent authority in the Requested State shall provide a certificate or procès-verbal that:

(a) identifies the item seized;

(b) identifies every official who has had custody of the item seized; and

(c) describes the circumstances of custody.

If, after seizure, any transfer of custody of or material change in the item seized occurs, the competent authority in the Requested State shall provide an additional certificate or procès-verbal that describes the circumstances of such transfer of custody or material change. No further proof of the identity of the item, the continuity of custody, or the integrity of its condition shall be required. The certificates or procès-verbaux shall be admissible in evidence in the Requesting State as proof thereof.

Article 11

Proceeds of Offenses

1. Upon the request of the Requesting State, the Requested State shall provide assistance for proceedings related to the forfeiture of proceeds or instrumentalities of criminal offenses.

2. Upon the request of the Requesting State, the Requested State shall take appropriate measures, in accordance with its laws, to locate and identify proceeds or instrumentalities of offenses within the Requested State, The request shall specify the reasons for believing that proceeds or instrumentalities are within the Requested State. The Requested State shall inform the Requesting State of the results of its inquiry.

3. At the request of the Requesting State, the Requested State, based on facts that would constitute an offense under the laws of both States and to the extent permitted by its laws, may take protective measures to immobilize temporarily such proceeds or instrumentalities to ensure their availability for forfeiture.

4. At the request of the Requesting State, the Requested State may execute a final decision of forfeiture pronounced by judicial authorities of the Requesting State. The execution of such a request shall be in accordance with the laws of the Requested State.

5. The Requested State that executes a final forfeiture decision shall dispose of the forfeited proceeds and instrumentalities in accordance with its laws. As it determines appropriate, the Requested State also may transfer all or part of such assets, or the proceeds of their sale, to the Requesting State. Insofar as cooperation between the two States contributed to a final forfeiture decision, the forfeiting State, to the extent permitted by its laws and upon such terms as it deems to be appropriate, may transfer all or part of such assets, or the proceeds of their sale, to the other State.

ARTICLE 12

RETURN OF EVIDENCE

1. Articles of evidence, including original documents and records, transmitted pursuant to a request shall be retained by the Requesting State unless the Requested State asks at the time of transmission for their return.

2. The Requested State may require that the Requesting State agree to terms and conditions for the care and return of articles of evidence deemed to be necessary to protect third party interests.

ARTICLE 13

RESTITUTION

The States shall assist each other to the extent permitted by their respective laws to facilitate restitution.

ARTICLE 14

CONFIDENTIALITY

1. The Requested State shall use its best efforts to keep confidential a request and its contents if such confidentiality is requested by the Central Authority of the Requesting State. If the request cannot be executed without breaching such confidentiality, the Central Authority of the Requested State shall so inform the Central Authority of the Requesting State, which shall then determine whether the request should nevertheless be executed.

2. The Central Authority of the Requested State may request that information or evidence furnished under this Treaty be kept confidential or be used only subject to terms and conditions it may specify. If the Requesting State accepts the information or evidence subject to such conditions, the Requesting State shall use its best efforts to comply with the conditions.

3. The Central Authority of the Requested State may request that the Requesting State not use any information or evidence obtained under this Treaty in any investigation or proceeding other than that described in the request without the prior consent of the Requested State. In that event, the Requesting State shall comply with the condition,

4. Nothing in this Article shall preclude the use or disclosure of information or evidence to the extent that an obligation exists, for the United States under its Constitution or for France under its Constitution and general principles of its law having Constitutional value, to do so in a criminal proceeding. To the extent possible, the Requesting State shall notify the Requested State in advance of any such use or disclosure.

5. Information and evidence obtained under the conditions referred to in paragraphs 2 or 3 of this Article may be used for any purpose insofar as they have been made public within the framework of the proceeding for which they were transmitted to the Requesting State.

Article 15

Service of Procedural Documents and Judicial Decisions

1. The Requested State shall serve procedural documents and judicial decisions sent to it for this purpose by the Requesting State.

2. Service may be effected by simple transmission of the document or decision to its addressee. If the Requesting State requests, the Requested State shall serve the document using a method, provided by or compatible with its laws.

3. Proof of service shall consist of a receipt dated and signed by the addressee or a statement by the Requested State noting the fact, the method, and the date of service. Either of these documents shall be sent immediately to the Requesting State. If service could not be effected, the Requested State shall inform the Requesting State immediately of the reason.

4. The Central Authority of the Requesting State shall transmit a document requiring the appearance of a person in the Requesting State to the Central Authority of the Requested State at least 50 days before the date of the scheduled appearance. Upon the request of the Requesting State, the Central Authority of the Requested State may waive this requirement for persons other than defendants.

Article 16

Appearance in the Requesting State

1. If the Requesting State requests the personal appearance of a witness or an expert, the Requested State shall invite this witness or expert to appear. The Requested State shall inform the Central Authority of the Requesting State of the person's response.

2. Such a request shall mention the approximate amount of the invited person's travel and subsistence costs to be reimbursed. If the person so requests, the Requesting State may advance part or all of the funds to pay those expenses through its diplomatic or consular missions in the Requested State.

3. A witness or expert who fails to comply with a document requiring an appearance in the Requesting State, service of which has been effected pursuant to a request, shall not be subjected to any sanction or measure of restraint, even if the document contains

a notice of penalty, unless the person subsequently travels voluntarily to the Requesting State, is duly served, and again fails to comply.

Article 17

Safe Conduct

1. A witness or expert appearing in the Requesting State in response to a request shall not be subject to service of process, prosecuted, detained, or subjected to any other restriction of personal liberty in that State by reason of any acts or convictions that preceded the person's departure from the Requested State unless the Central Authority of the Requesting State limits such safe conduct and so notifies the Central Authority of the Requested State. Any such limitation of safe conduct shall be communicated to the witness or expert at the time the witness or expert is invited to appear.

2. A person appearing in the Requesting State in response to a document served to answer for acts, for which that person is the subject of a criminal investigation or prosecution, shall not be prosecuted, detained, or subjected to any other restriction of personal liberty for acts or convictions that preceded that person's departure from the Requested State other than those specified in the document served.

3. The safe conduct provided for by this Article shall cease if the person, being free to leave, has not left the Requesting State within a period of fifteen consecutive days after being officially advised that the person's presence was no longer necessary or, having left, has returned.

Article 18

Temporary transfer

1. Upon the request of either State, a person in custody in either State may be temporarily transferred to the receiving State to give testimony or evidence or otherwise provide assistance in investigations or proceedings in relation to a criminal matter.

2. Such transfer may be denied:

(a) if the person in custody does not consent;

(b) if the person's period of detention might be thereby extended ;

(c) if the person's presence is required for ongoing criminal proceedings; or

(d) for reasons of safety, security, or other imperative concerns.

3. Pursuant to this Treaty, the receiving State shall have the obligation and the authority to keep the person transferred in custody unless the sending State authorizes the person's release.

4. The receiving State shall require no proceeding to effect the return to the sending State of the person transferred. The return shall occur by the date specified by the sending State. This period may be extended by agreement between both States.

5. The sending State shall deduct from that person's sentence any time that the person transferred serves in the custody of the receiving State.

6. A person appearing in either State pursuant to this Article may receive the safe conduct authorized under Article 17.

Article 19

Transit

1. Upon the request of the Requesting State, the Requested State may authorize the transit through its territory of a person held in custody by the Requesting State or a third State whose personal appearance has been requested by the Requesting State to give testimony or evidence or otherwise provide assistance in investigations or proceedings in relation to a criminal matter.

2. Pursuant to this Treaty, the Requested State shall have the obligation and the authority to keep the person in custody during transit.

Article 20

Official Records

1. At the request of the Requesting State, the Requested State shall provide copies of records of any nature and in any form that are in the possession of its judicial authorities or government departments or agencies and that are accessible to the public.

2. At the request of the Requesting State, the Requested State may provide copies of records of any nature and in any form that are in the possession of its judicial authorities or government departments or agencies, but that are not accessible to the public, to the same extent and under the same conditions that would apply to its own competent authorities in obtaining such copies. The Requested State may in its discretion deny a request, pursuant to this paragraph, entirely or in part.

3. Official records produced pursuant to this Article and certified by a competent authority of the Requested State as official records, or true and correct copies thereof, shall be admissible in evidence in the Requesting State as proof of the truth of the matters set forth therein. No further authentication shall be necessary.

Article 21

Translation

The Requesting State shall translate the request and any supporting documents into the language of the Requested State.

Article 22

Legalization

Except as otherwise provided by this Treaty, evidence, in whatever form, transmitted pursuant to this Treaty shall be exempt from all legalization formalities.

Article 23

Costs

1. The Requested State shall meet the costs of executing requests except for:

(a) the allowances and expenses related to travel of witnesses and experts pursuant to Article 16 and the travel of persons in custody pursuant to Articles 18 and 19;

(b) the costs of interpretation and translation;

(c) the costs of services provided by private parties at the request of the Requesting State; and

(d) the fees of experts needed to fulfill a request.

2. If during the execution of a request it becomes apparent that execution will entail expenses of an extraordinary nature, the Central Authorities shall consult to determine the terms and conditions according to which execution may continue.

Article 24

Sanitation of criminal proceedings in the requested state

1. Each State may provide to the other State information and evidence relating to criminal acts and request that the other State submit the information and evidence to its competent authorities for the purpose of criminal investigation and prosecution where both States have jurisdiction to investigate and prosecute those acts. Such requests shall be transmitted through the respective Central Authorities.

2. The Requested State shall consider initiating an investigation or prosecution as appropriate under its laws.

3. The Requested State shall notify the Requesting State of any action taken pursuant to the request and transmit a copy of any decision rendered.

Article 25

Entry into force

Each State shall notify the other of the completion of the procedures required for the entry into force of this Treaty. This Treaty shall enter into force on the first day of the second month following the date of receipt of the latter of these notifications.

Article 26

Termination

Either State may terminate this Treaty at any time by forwarding through the diplomatic channel written notice of termination. Termination shall take effect six months after receipt of this notification.

In witness whereof, the respective Plenipotentiaries have signed this Treaty and affixed their seals thereto.

DONE at Paris this tenth day of December, 1998, in duplicate, in the French and English languages, both texts being equally authentic.

TABLE OF CONTENTS

FORM A

CERTIFICATION OF BUSINESS RECORDS

I, the undersigned, (name) with the understanding that I am subject to criminal penalty under the laws of (name of country) for an intentionally false declaration, declare that I am employed by/associated with: (name of business from which documents are sought) in the position of: (business position or title) and by reason of my position am authorized and qualified to make this declaration.

Each of the records attached hereto is a record in the custody of the above-named business that:

1. was made at or near the time of the occurrence of the matters set forth therein by (or from information transmitted by) a person with knowledge of those matters;
2. was kept in the course of a regularly conducted business activity;

3. was made by the business as a regular practice; and
4. if not an original record, is a duplicate of the original.

(date of execution)
(place of execution)
(signature)

EXPLANATORY NOTE ON THE TREATY ON MUTUAL LEGAL ASSISTANCE IN CRIMINAL MATTERS BETWEEN THE UNITED STATES OF AMERICA AND FRANCE

The following understandings regarding the application of certain provisions of the treaty are agreed between the Parties.

Article 1(3)

Both Parties understand that, for the United States, the provisions of the Treaty do not create a new right on the part of a private person to obtain assistance, to suppress or exclude any testimony or evidence, or to impede the execution of a request. However, such rights of private persons as otherwise exist under United States law in this regard continue in effect.

Article 3

During the negotiation of Article 3 of the Treaty, both Parties discussed the competent authorities from whom requests under the Treaty must emanate. The Parties noted the substantial number of authorities for the United States, aside from prosecutors, that were capable of being competent to initiate requests for mutual legal assistance. These authorities are not judicial authorities but are comparable to them since their requests, in accordance with Paragraph I of Article 1, are presented in the framework of "investigations or proceedings in respect of criminal offenses the punishment of which, at the time of the request for assistance, is a matter for the judicial authorities of the Requesting State." Under United States law, these authorities are those that are responsible for the investigations of criminal offenses, including the referral of matters to prosecutors for criminal prosecution.

The Parties accordingly agreed not to attempt to list exhaustively in the Treaty the numerous state and federal authorities that fall under this definition, particularly because the inadvertent omission of one from the list could diminish the value of the Treaty to the United States. To illustrate this diversity, the United States, however, has agreed to provide, for the purposes of illustration only, the following short list:

Bureau of Alcohol, Tobacco, and Firearms
Commodity Futures Trading Commission
Drug Enforcement Administration
Federal Bureau of Investigation
Federal Trade Commission
Food and Drug Administration
Immigration and Naturalization Service
Internal Revenue Service
Securities and Exchange Commission
Trustees in Bankruptcy.

In any case, to facilitate in the identification of competent authorities of the United States by France, the two States agreed that the requests that are presented by the Central Authority of the United States of America will establish the competence of the requesting authorities for the purposes of this Treaty.

Article 9

The first part of paragraph 1 sets forth the principle that, with the consent of the Requested State, persons designated by the Requesting State (for example, the requesting authority, the defendant, and the counsel for such persons) shall be allowed to travel to the territory of the Requested State to be present and to assist during the execution of the request. The request for legal assistance should request the presence of these persons. For purposes of this Article, the term "Requested State" refers to the authorities in the Requested State who are authorized to approve or consent to the requested presence.

The second part of paragraph 1 commits the two Parties to accommodate such a request so that the deposition obtained in the Requested State may be used in the Requesting State in compliance with its internal procedure. The scope of this commitment, however, may be limited, notable by the application of Articles 6 and 7 relating respectively to the denial of requests for legal assistance and to postponement of execution of such requests. This commitment does not preclude that, in certain cases, which in practice shall be most exceptional, the authority entrusted with the execution of the request may determine that the presence and assistance of the designated persons are not possible in a specific case.

Article 23(1)

The discussion relating to Article 23 demonstrated the Parties' concerns to execute requests for mutual legal assistance in the least expensive manner, in particular those requests to obtain depositions in the United States. As a result, the Parties agreed that the United States will arrange and pay for the audio recording of a deposition requested by French authorities and its transmission to French authorities. Sealed in a container, the audio recording will be accompanied by a report or a declaration of the competent authority in the United states certifying the circumstances in which the deposition was taken. This document will mention the name of the authority conducting the proceeding, the identity of the person being deposed, and a statement whether or not the person was deposed under oath. The document should be signed by the deponent or, in case the deponent refuses or is unable to sign the document, the document should contain a statement to that effect. On the other hand, the costs of services furnished by private parties, such as those resulting from the transcription of depositions by a "court reporter", will be paid for by French authorities.

10. Extradition Treaties

a. Countries With Which the United States Has an Extradition Treaty

Country	Entered Into Force
Albania	November 14, 1935
Antigua and Barbuda	July 1, 1999
Argentina	June 15, 2000
Australia	May 8, 1976
	December 21, 1992
Austria	January 1, 2000
Bahamas	September 22, 1994
Barbados	March 3, 2000
Belgium	September 1, 1997
Belize	March 27, 2001
Bolivia	November 21, 1996
Brazil	December 17, 1964
Bulgaria	June 24, 1924
	August 15, 1935
Burma	November 1, 1941
Canada	March 22, 1976
	November 26, 1991
	April 30, 2003
Chile	June 26, 1902
Colombia	March 4, 1982
Congo	July 27, 1911
	May 19, 1929
	September 24, 1936
	August 5, 1961
Costa Rica	October 11, 1991
Cuba	March 2, 1905
	June 18, 1926
Cyprus	September 14, 1999
Czech Republic	March 29, 1926
	August 28, 1935
Denmark	July 31, 1974
Dominica	May 25, 2000
Dominican Republic	August 2, 1910
Ecuador	November 12, 1873
	May 29, 1941
Egypt	April 22, 1875
El Salvador	July 10, 1911
Estonia	November 15, 1924
	May 7, 1935
Fiji	June 24, 1935
	August 17, 1973
Finland	May 11, 1980
France	February 1, 2002
Gambia	June 24, 1935
Germany	August 29, 1980
	March 11, 1993

Country	Entered Into Force
Ghana	June 24, 1935
Greece	November 1, 1932 September 2, 1937
Grenada	September 14, 1999
Guatemala	August 15, 1903 March 13, 1941
Guyana	June 24, 1935
Haiti	June 28, 1905
Honduras	July 10, 1912 June 5, 1928
Hong Kong	January 21, 1998
Hungary	March 18, 1997
Iceland	January 6, 1902 February 19, 1906
India	July 21, 1999
Iraq	April 23, 1936
Ireland	December 15, 1984
Israel	December 5, 1963
Italy	September 24, 1984
Jamaica	July 7, 1991
Japan	March 26, 1980
Jordan	July 29, 1995
Kenya	June 24, 1935 August 19, 1965
Kiribati	January 21, 1977
Korea	December 20, 1999
Latvia	March 1, 1924 March 29, 1935
Lesotho	June 24, 1935
Liberia	November 21, 1939
Liechtenstein	June 28, 1937
Lithuania	March 31, 2003
Luxembourg	February 1, 2002
Malawi	June 24, 1935 April 4, 1967
Malaysia	June 2, 1997
Malta	June 24, 1935
Marchall Islands	May 1, 2004
Mauritius	June 24, 1935
Mexico	January 25, 1980 May 21, 2001
Micronesia	June 25, 2004
Monaco	March 28, 1940
Nauru	August 30, 1935
Netherlands	September 15, 1983
New Zealand	December 8, 1970
Nicaragua	July 14, 1907
Nigeria	June 24, 1935
Norway	March 7, 1980
Pakistan	March 9, 1942
Panama	May 8, 1905
Papua New Guinea	August 30, 1935
Paraguay	March 9, 2001
Peru	August 25, 2003
Philippines	November 22, 1996
Poland	September 17, 1999 June 5, 1936

Country	Entered Into Force
Portugal	November 14, 1908
Romania	April 7, 1925
	July 27, 1937
Saint Christopher and Nevis	February 23, 2000
Saint Lucia	February 2, 2000
Saint Vincent and the Grenadines	September 8, 1999
San Marino	July 8, 1908
	June 28, 1935
Seychelles	June 24, 1935
Sierra Leone	June 24, 1935
Singapore	June 24, 1935
	June 10, 1969
Slovac Republic	March 29, 1926
	August 28, 1935
Solomon Islands	January 21, 1977
South Africa	June 25, 2001
Spain	June 16, 1971
	June 2, 1978
	July 2, 1993
	July 25, 1999
Sri Lanka	January 12, 2001
Suriname	July 11, 1889
	August 28, 1904
Swaziland	June 24, 1935
	July 28, 1970
Sweden	December 3, 1963
	September 24, 1984
Switzerland	September 10, 1997
Tanzania	June 24, 1935
	December 6, 1965
Thailand	March 24, 1924
Tonga	August 1, 1966
	April 13, 1977
Trinidad and Tobago	November 29, 1999
Turkey	January 1, 1981
Tuvalu	January 21, 1977
	April 25, 1980
United Kingdom	January 21, 1977
	December 23, 1986
Uruguay	April 11, 1984
Venezuela	April 14, 1923
Yugoslavia	June 12, 1902
Zambia	June 24, 1935
Zimbabwe	April 26, 2000

b. Extradition Treaty Between the United States and Saint Kitts and Nevis [1]

Signed at Basseterre, September 18, 1996; Ratification advised by the Senate, October 21, 1998; Ratified by the President, January 20, 1999; Ratified by Saint Kitts and Nevis, January 19, 2000; Entered into force, February 23, 2000

EXTRADITION TREATY BETWEEN THE GOVERNMENT OF THE UNITED STATES OF AMERICA AND THE GOVERNMENT OF SAINT KITTS AND NEVIS

The Government of the United States of America and the Government of Saint Kitts and Nevis,

RECALLING the Extradition Treaty between the Government of the United States of America and the Government of the United Kingdom of Great Britain and Northern Ireland, signed at London June 8, 1972,

NOTING that both the Government of the United States of America and the Government of Saint Kitts and Nevis currently apply the terms of that Treaty, and

DESIRING to provide for more effective cooperation between the two States in the suppression of crime, and, for that purpose, to conclude a new treaty for the extradition of accused or convicted offenders,

HAVE AGREED AS FOLLOWS:

ARTICLE 1

OBLIGATION TO EXTRADITE

The Contracting States agree to extradite to each other, pursuant to the provisions of this Treaty, persons sought for prosecution or persons who have been convicted of an extraditable offense by the authorities in the Requesting State.

ARTICLE 2

EXTRADITABLE OFFENSES

1. An offense shall be an extraditable offense if it is punishable under the laws in both Contracting States by deprivation of liberty for a period of more than one year or by a more severe penalty.

2. An offense shall also be an extraditable offense if it consists of an attempt or a conspiracy to commit, aiding or abetting, counselling or procuring the commission of, or being an accessory before or after the fact to, any offense described in paragraph 1.

[1] TIAS 12805. The full text of the Extradition Treaty between the United States of America and Saint Kitts and Nevis is set out in this volume as a model of the other 111 extradition treaties that were in force for the United States as of December 31, 2005.

3. For the purposes of this Article, an offense shall be an extraditable offense:

(a) whether or not the laws in the Contracting States place the offense within the same category of offenses or describe the offense by the same terminology; or

(b) whether or not the offense is one for which United States federal law requires the showing of such matters as interstate transportation, or use of the mails or of other facilities affecting interstate or foreign commerce, such matters being merely for the purpose of establishing jurisdiction in a United States federal court.

4. Where the offense was committed outside of the territory of the Requesting State, if the laws in the Requested State:

(a) provide for punishment of an offense committed outside of its territory in similar circumstances, extradition shall be granted in accordance with this treaty; or

(b) do not provide for punishment of an offense committed outside of its territory in similar circumstances, extradition may nonetheless be granted in the discretion of the executive authority of the Requested State, provided that all other requirements of this Treaty are met.

5. If extradition has been granted for an extraditable offense, it may also be granted for any other offense specified in the request even if the latter offense is punishable by less than one year's deprivation of liberty, provided that all other requirements for extradition are met.

Article 3

Nationality

If all conditions in this Treaty relating to extradition are met, extradition shall not be refused based on the nationality of the person sought.

Article 4

Political and Military Offenses

1. Extradition shall not be granted if the offense for which extradition is requested is a political offense.

2. For the purposes of this Treaty, the following offenses shall not be considered to be political offenses:

(a) a murder or other violent crime against the person of a Head of State of one of the Contracting States, or of a member of the Head of State's family;

(b) an offense for which both Contracting States have the obligation pursuant to a multilateral international agreement to extradite the person sought or to submit the case to their competent authorities for decision as to prosecution; and

(c) a conspiracy or attempt to commit any of the foregoing offenses, or aiding or abetting a person who commits or attempts to commit such offenses.

3. Notwithstanding the terms of paragraph 2 of this Article, extradition shall not be granted if the executive authority of the Requested State determines that the request was politically motivated.

4. The executive authority of the Requested State may refuse extradition for offenses under military law which are not offenses under ordinary criminal law.

Article 5

Prior Prosecution

1. Extradition shall not be granted when the person sought has been convicted or acquitted in the Requested State for the offense for which extradition is requested.

2. Extradition shall not be precluded by the fact that the authorities in the Requested State have decided not to prosecute the person sought for the acts for which extradition is requested, or to discontinue any criminal proceedings which have been instituted against the person sought for those acts.

Article 6

Extradition Procedures and Required Documents

1. All requests for extradition shall be submitted through the diplomatic channel.

2. All requests shall be supported by:

(a) documents, statements, or other types of information which describe the identity, and probable location of the person sought;

(b) information describing the facts of the offense and the procedural history of the case;

(c) information as to:

(i) the provisions of the laws describing the essential elements of the offense for which extradition is requested;

(ii) the provisions of the law describing the punishment for the offense; and

(iii) the provisions of law describing any time limit on the prosecution; and

(d) the documents, statements, or other types of information specified in paragraph 3 or paragraph 4 of this Article, as applicable.

3. A request for extradition of a person who is sought for prosecution shall also be supported by:

(a) a copy of the warrant or order of arrest, if any, issued by a judge or other competent authority of the Requesting State;

(b) a document setting forth the charges; and

(c) such information as would provide a reasonable basis to believe that the person sought committed the offense for which extradition is requested.

4. A request for extradition relating to a person who has been convicted of the offense for which extradition is sought shall also be supported by:

(a) a copy of the judgment of conviction or, if such copy is not available, a statement by a judicial authority that the person has been convicted;

(b) information establishing that the person sought is the person to whom the conviction refers;

(c) a copy of the sentence imposed, if the person sought has been sentenced, and a statement establishing to what extent the sentence has been carried out; and

(d) in the case of a person who has been convicted in absentia, the documents required by paragraph 3.

Article 7

Admissibility of Documents

The documents which accompany an extradition request shall be received and admitted as evidence in extradition proceedings if:

(a) in the case of a request from the United States, they are authenticated by an officer of the United States Department of State and are certified by the principal diplomatic or consular officer of Saint Kitts and Nevis resident in the United States;

(b) in the case of a request from Saint Kitts and Nevis, they are certified by the principal diplomatic or consular officer of the United States resident in Saint Kitts and Nevis, as provided by the extradition laws of the United States; or

(c) they are certified or authenticated in any other manner accepted by the law of the Requested State.

Article 8

Lapse of Time

Extradition shall not be denied because of the prescriptive laws of either the Requesting State or the Requested State.

Article 9

Provisional Arrest

1. In case of urgency, a Contracting State may initiate the process of extradition by requesting the provisional arrest of the person sought. A request for provisional arrest may be transmitted through the diplomatic channel or directly between the United States Department of Justice and the Attorney General in Saint Kitts and Nevis. Such a request may also be transmitted through the facilities of the International Criminal Police Organization (INTERPOL), or through such other means as may be settled by arrangement between the Contracting States.

2. The application for provisional arrest shall contain:

(a) a description of the person sought;

(b) the location of the person sought, if known;

(c) a brief statement of the facts of the case, including, if possible, the time and location of the offense;

(d) a description of the laws violated;

(e) a statement of the existence of a warrant of arrest or a finding of guilt or judgment of conviction against the person sought; and

(f) a statement that a request for extradition for the person sought will follow.

3. The Requesting State shall be notified without delay of the disposition of its application and the reasons for any denial.

4. Provisional arrest shall be terminated if, within a period of 45 days after the apprehension of the person sought, the Requested State has not received the request for extradition and the documents mentioned in Article 6. This period may be extended, upon the Requesting State's application, for up to an additional 15 days after the apprehension of the person sought.

5. The fact that the person sought has been discharged from custody pursuant to paragraph 4 of this Article shall not prejudice the subsequent rearrest and extradition of that person if the extradition request and supporting documents are delivered at a later date.

Article 10

Decision and Surrender

1. The Requested State shall promptly notify the Requesting State through the diplomatic channel of its decision on the request for extradition.

2. If the request is denied in whole or in part, the Requested State shall provide an explanation of the reasons for the denial. The Requested State shall provide copies of pertinent judicial decisions upon request.

3. If the request for extradition is granted, the authorities of the Contracting States shall agree on the time and place for the surrender of the person sought.

4. If the person sought is not removed from the territory of the Requested State within the time prescribed by the law of that State, that person may be discharged from custody, and the Requested State may subsequently refuse extradition for the same offense.

Article 11

Temporary and Deferred Surrender

1. If the extradition request is granted in the case of a person who is being proceeded against or is serving a sentence in the Requested State, the Requested State may temporarily surrender the person sought to the Requesting State for the purpose of prosecution. The person so surrendered shall be kept in custody in the Requesting State and shall be returned to the Requested State after the conclusion of the proceedings against that person, in accordance with conditions to be determined by mutual agreement of the Contracting States.

2. The Requested State may postpone the extradition proceedings against a person who is being prosecuted or who is serving a sentence in that State. The postponement may continue until the prosecution of the person sought has been concluded or until such person has served any sentence imposed.

ARTICLE 12

REQUESTS FOR EXTRADITION MADE BY SEVERAL STATES

If the Requested State receives requests from the other Contracting State and from any other State or States for the extradition of the same person, either for the same offense or for different offenses, the executive authority of the Requested State shall determine to which State it will surrender the person. In making its decision, the Requested State shall consider all relevant factors, including but not limited to:

(a) whether the requests were made pursuant to treaty;
(b) the place where each offense was committed;
(c) the respective interests of the Requesting States;
(d) the gravity of the offenses;
(e) the nationality of the victim;
(f) the possibility of further extradition between the Requesting States; and
(g) the chronological order in which the requests were received from the Requesting States.

ARTICLE 13

SEIZURE AND SURRENDER OF PROPERTY

1. To the extent permitted under its law, the Requested State may seize and surrender to the Requesting State all articles, documents, and evidence connected with the offense in respect of which extradition is granted. The items mentioned in this Article may be surrendered even when the extradition cannot be effected due to the death, disappearance, or escape of the person sought.

2. The Requested State may condition the surrender of the property upon satisfactory assurances from the Requesting State that the property will be returned to the Requested State as soon as practicable. The Requested State may also defer the surrender of such property if it is needed as evidence in the Requested State.

3. The rights of third parties in such property shall be duly respected.

ARTICLE 14

RULE OF SPECIALITY

1. A person extradited under this Treaty may not be detained, tried, or punished in the Requesting State except for:

(a) the offense for which extradition has been granted or a differently denominated offense based on the same facts on which extradition was granted, provided such offense is extraditable, or is a lesser included offense;

(b) an offense committed after the extradition of the person; or

(c) an offense for which the executive authority of the Requested State consents to the person's detention, trial, or punishment. For the purpose of this subparagraph:

(i) the Requested State may require the submission of the documents called for in Article 6; and

(ii) the person extradited may be detained by the Requesting State for 90 days while the request is being processed. This time period may be extended by the Requested State upon request of the Requesting State.

2. A person extradited under this Treaty may not be extradited to a third State for an offense committed prior to his surrender unless the surrendering State consents.

3. Paragraphs 1 and 2 of this Article shall not prevent the detention, trial, or punishment of an extradited person, or the extradition of that person to a third State, if:

(a) that person leaves the territory of the Requesting State after extradition and voluntarily returns to it; or

(b) that person does not leave the territory of the Requesting State within 10 days of the day on which that person is free to leave.

Article 15

Waiver of Extradition

If the person sought consents to surrender to the Requesting State, the Requested State may surrender the person as expeditiously as possible without further proceedings.

Article 16

Transit

1. Either Contracting State may authorize transportation through its territory of a person surrendered to the other State by a third State. A request for transit shall be transmitted through the diplomatic channel or directly between the Department of Justice in the United States and the Attorney General in Saint Kitts and Nevis. Such a request may also be transmitted through the facilities of the International Criminal Police Organization (INTERPOL), or through such other means as may be settled by arrangement between the Contracting States. It shall contain a description of the person being transported and a brief statement of the facts of the case. A person in transit may be detained in custody during the period of transit.

2. No authorization is required where air transportation is used and no landing is scheduled on the territory of the Contracting State. If an unscheduled landing occurs on the territory of the other Contracting State, the other Contracting State may require the request for transit as provided in paragraph 1. That Contracting State may detain the person to be transported until the request for transit is received and the transit is effected, so long as the request is received within 96 hours of the unscheduled landing.

Article 17

Representation and Expenses

1. The Requested State shall advise, assist, appear in court on behalf of the Requesting State, and represent the interests of the Requesting State, in any proceedings arising out of a request for extradition.

2. The Requesting State shall bear the expenses related to the translation of documents and the transportation of the person surrendered. The Requested State shall pay all other expenses incurred in that State by reason of the extradition proceedings.

3. Neither State shall make any pecuniary claim against the other State arising out of the arrest, detention, examination, or surrender of persons sought under this Treaty.

Article 18

Consultation

The Department of Justice of the United States and the Attorney General of Saint Kitts and Nevis may consult with each other directly in connection with the processing of individual cases and in furtherance of maintaining and improving procedures for the implementation of this Treaty. Issues considered in such consultations shall include training and technical assistance.

Article 19

Application

Subject to Article 20(3), this Treaty shall apply to offenses committed before as well as after the date it enters into force.

Article 20

Ratification and Entry into Force

1. This Treaty shall be subject to ratification; the instruments of ratification shall be exchanged at Washington as soon as possible.

2. This Treaty shall enter into force upon the exchange of the instruments of ratification.

3. Upon the entry into force of this Treaty, the Treaty on Extradition signed at London June 8, 1972 shall cease to have any effect between the United States and Saint Kitts and Nevis. Nevertheless, the prior Treaty shall apply to any extradition proceedings in which the extradition documents have already been submitted to the courts of the Requested State at the time this Treaty enters into force, except that Article 15 of this Treaty shall be applicable to such proceedings. Article 14 of this Treaty shall apply to persons found extraditable under the prior Treaty.

ARTICLE 21

TERMINATION

Either Contracting State may terminate this Treaty at any time by giving written notice to the other Contracting State, and the termination shall be effective six months after the date of receipt of such notice.

IN WITNESS WHEREOF, the undersigned, being duly authorized by their respective Governments have signed this Treaty.

DONE at Basseterre, St. Kitts, in duplicate, this 18th day of September, 1996.

11. Return of Stolen Vehicles Treaties

a. Countries With Which the United States Has a Treaty for the Return of Stolen Vehicles

Country	Entered Into Force
Belize	August 16, 2002
Dominican Republic	August 3, 2001
Mexico	June 28, 1983
Panama	September 13, 2001

b. Treaty for the Return of Stolen Vehicles Between the United States and Belize [1]

Signed at Belmopan, October 3, 1996; Ratification advised by the Senate, October 18, 2000; Entered into force, August 16, 2002

TREATY BETWEEN THE GOVERNMENT OF BELIZE AND THE GOVERNMENT OF THE UNITED STATES OF AMERICA FOR THE RETURN OF STOLEN VEHICLES

The Government of the United States of America and the Government of Saint Kitts and Nevis,

RECALLING the Extradition Treaty between the Government of the United States of America and the Government of the United Kingdom of Great Britain and Northern Ireland, signed at London June 8, 1972,

The Government of Belize and the Government of the United States of America (hereinafter, "the Parties");

RECOGNIZING the growing problem of transnational theft of vehicles;

CONSIDERING the difficulties faced by innocent owners in securing the return of vehicles stolen in the territory of one Party that are recovered in the territory of the other Party; and

DESIRING to eliminate such difficulties and to regularize procedures for the expeditious return of such vehicles;

HAVE AGREED AS FOLLOWS:

ARTICLE 1

For purposes of this Treaty:

(1) A "vehicle" means any automobile, truck, bus, motorcycle, motorhome, or trailer.

(2) A vehicle shall be considered "stolen" when possession thereof has been obtained without the consent of the owner or other person legally authorized to use such vehicle. A vehicle shall also be considered "stolen" when:

(a) it is unlawfully appropriated by the person who had rented it from an enterprise legally authorized for that purpose and in the normal course of business, or

(b) it is unlawfully appropriated by a person with whom it has been deposited by official or judicial action.

(3) A vehicle shall not be presumed to have been stolen when it is exported in accordance with the Protocol to this Treaty.

(4) All references to "days" shall mean calendar days.

[1] The full text of the Treaty between Belize and the United States of America for the Return of Stolen Vehicles is set out in this volume as a model of the other three stolen vehicles return treaties that were in force for the United States as of December 31, 2005.

ARTICLE 2

Each Party agrees to return, in accordance with the terms of this Treaty, vehicles that are:

(1) registered, titled, or otherwise documented in the territory of the other Party;

(2) stolen in the territory of the other Party or from one of its nationals; and

(3) found in the territory of the first Party.

ARTICLE 3

1. Whenever police, customs, or other authorities of a Party impound or seize a vehicle and they have reason to believe that such vehicle is registered, titled, or otherwise documented in the territory of the other Party, the first Party shall, within 30 days of such impoundment or seizure, notify, in writing, the Embassy of the other Party that its authorities have custody of the vehicle.

2. Such notification shall include all available identifying information about the vehicle listed in Annex 1.

ARTICLE 4

Authorities of a Party who have impounded or seized a vehicle that may be subject to return in accordance with this Treaty shall take reasonable steps regarding the safekeeping of the vehicle, including preventing the obliteration or modification of identifying information such as vehicle identification numbers. The said authorities shall not thereafter operate, auction, dismantle, or otherwise alter or dispose of the vehicle. However, this Treaty shall not preclude the said authorities from operating, auctioning, dismantling, or otherwise altering or disposing of the vehicle if—

(1) No request for the return of the vehicle is received within 60 days of receipt of a notification made pursuant to Article 3;

(2) A determination is made in accordance with Article 7(1) that a request for the return of the vehicle does not meet the requirements of this Treaty, and notification of such determination has been made in accordance with Article 7(3);

(3) The vehicle has not been retrieved, within the time period stated in Article 7 (2), by the person identified in the request for return as the owner or the owner's authorized representative after the vehicle has been made available as provided in Article 7 (2); or

(4) There is no obligation under this Treaty, pursuant to Article 8 (2) or Article 8 (3), to return the vehicle.

ARTICLE 5

1. After a Party receives a notification made pursuant to Article 3, that Party may submit a request for the return of the vehicle.

2. The request for return shall be transmitted under seal of a consular officer of the Requesting Party and shall follow the form appended in Annex 2. The request shall be transmitted under cover of a note to the foreign ministry of the Requested Party. A request shall be made only after receipt by the consular officer of certified copies of the following documents:

(a) The title of ownership to the vehicle, if the vehicle is subject to titling, but, if the title is not available, a certified statement from the titling authority that the vehicle is titled and specifying the person or entity to whom it is titled;

(b) The certificate of registration of the vehicle, if the vehicle is subject to registration, but, if the registration document is not available, a certified statement from the registering authority that the vehicle is registered and specifying the person or entity to whom it is registered;

(c) The bill of sale or other documentation that establishes ownership of the vehicle, in the event the vehicle is not titled or registered;

(d) Documentation that establishes the transfer of ownership of the vehicle, if subsequent to the theft of the vehicle the owner at the time of the theft has transferred ownership to a third party;

(e) The report of the theft issued by a competent authority of the Requesting Party. In the event that the theft is reported by the victim to the competent authority after the vehicle is seized or otherwise comes into possession of the Requested Party, the person seeking its return shall furnish a document justifying the reasons for the delay in reporting the theft and may provide any supporting documentation therefor; and

(f) In cases in which the person requesting the return of a vehicle is not the owner, a power of attorney granted in the presence of a notary public by the owner or his legal representative, authorizing that person to recover the vehicle.

3. No further legalization or authentication of documents shall be required by the Requested Party.

Article 6

If a Party learns, through means other than a notification made pursuant to Article 3, that the authorities of the other Party may have impounded, seized, or otherwise taken possession of a vehicle that may be registered, titled, or otherwise documented in the territory of the first Party, that Party:

(1) may, through a note to the foreign ministry of the other Party, seek official confirmation of this and may request the other Party to provide the notification described in Article 3, in which case the other Party shall either provide the notification or explain, in writing, why notification is not required; and

(2) may also, in appropriate cases, submit a request for the return of the vehicle as described in Article 5.

Article 7

1. Except as provided in Article 8, the Requested Party shall, within 30 days of receiving a request for the return of a stolen vehicle, determine whether the request for return meets the requirements of this Treaty for the return of the vehicle and shall notify the Embassy of the Requesting Party of its determination.

2. If the Requested Party determines that the request for the return of a stolen vehicle meets the requirements of this Treaty, the Requested Party shall, within 15 days of such determination, make

the vehicle available to the person identified in the request for return as the owner or the owner's authorized representative. The vehicle shall remain available for the person identified in the request for return as the owner or the owner's authorized representative to take delivery for at least 90 days. The Requested Party shall take necessary measures to permit the owner or the owner's authorized representative to take delivery of the vehicle and return with it to the territory of the Requesting Party.

3. If the Requested Party determines that the request for return does not meet the requirements of this Treaty, it shall provide written notification to the Embassy of the Requesting Party, including grounds for its decision.

Article 8

1. If a vehicle whose return is requested is being held in connection with a criminal investigation or prosecution, its return pursuant to this Treaty shall be effected when its presence is no longer required for purposes of that investigation or prosecution. The Requested Party shall, however, take all practicable measures to assure that substitute pictorial or other evidence is used wherever possible in such investigation or prosecution so that the vehicle may be returned as soon as possible.

2. If the ownership or custody of a vehicle whose return is requested is the subject of a pending judicial action in the territory of the Requested Party, its return pursuant to this Treaty shall be effected at the conclusion of that judicial action. However, a Party shall have no obligation under this Treaty to return the vehicle if such judicial action results in a final decision that awards the vehicle to a person other than the person identified in the request for return as the owner of the vehicle or the owner's authorized representative. Such judicial action may include adjudication by an administrative panel specifically designated by the Requested Party to review the question of ownership or custody of vehicles, so long as:

(1) the Requested Party gives the Requesting Party at least 60 days written notice of such administrative proceeding; and

(2) the decision of such administrative panel may be appealed, by any person claiming ownership or custody of a vehicle, to a court of law.

3. A Party shall have no obligation under this Treaty to return a vehicle whose return is requested if the vehicle is subject to forfeiture under its laws because it was used in its territory for the commission of a crime with the consent or complicity of the owner, or represents the proceeds of such a crime. The Requested Party shall not forfeit the vehicle without giving the owner or the owner's authorized representative reasonable notice and an opportunity to contest such forfeiture in accordance with its laws.

4. A Party shall have no obligation under this Treaty to return a stolen vehicle if no request for return is received within 60 days of receipt of a notification made pursuant to Article 3.

5. If the return of a stolen vehicle whose return is requested is postponed pursuant to this Article, the Requested Party shall so

notify the Embassy of the Requesting Party in writing within 30 days of receiving a request for the return of the vehicle.

ARTICLE 9

1. The Requested Party shall not impose any import or export duties, taxes, fines, or other monetary penalties or charges on vehicles returned in accordance with this Treaty, or on their owners or authorized representatives as a condition for the return of such vehicles.

2. Reasonable expenses incurred in the return of the vehicle in accordance with this Treaty, including towing costs, storage costs, maintenance costs, transportation costs, and costs of translation of documents required under this Treaty, shall be borne by the person seeking its return and shall be paid prior to the return of the vehicle.

3. In particular cases, the expenses of return may include the costs of any repairs or reconditioning of a vehicle that were necessary to permit the vehicle to be moved to a storage area or to maintain it in the condition in which it was found. The person seeking the return of a vehicle shall not be responsible for the costs of any other work performed on the vehicle while it was in the custody of the authorities of the Requested Party.

4. Provided that the Requested Party complies with the provisions of this Treaty with respect to recovery, storage, safekeeping, and, where appropriate, return of a vehicle, no person shall be entitled to compensation from the Requested Party for any damage caused to or sustained by the vehicle while it is in the custody of the Requested Party.

ARTICLE 10

The mechanisms for the recovery and return of stolen vehicles under this Treaty shall be in addition to those available under the laws of the Requested Party. Nothing in this Treaty shall impair any rights for the recovery of stolen vehicles under applicable law.

ARTICLE 11

1. Any differences regarding the interpretation or application of this Treaty shall be resolved through consultations between the Parties.

2. This Treaty shall be subject to ratification. It shall enter into force on the date of exchange of instruments of ratification.

3. The annexes and protocol attached hereto shall be considered an integral part of the Treaty.

4. This Treaty may be terminated by either Party upon a minimum of 90 days written notification.

DONE at Belmopan, this third day of October 1996, in duplicate, both texts being equally authentic.

Annex 1

Identifying Information to be Provided in a Notification Made Pursuant to Article 3

1. Vehicle Identification Number (VIN);
2. Name of manufacturer of vehicle;
3. Vehicle model and year of manufacture, if known;
4. Color of vehicle;
5. Licence plate number (LPN) of vehicle and jurisdiction of issuance (if available);
6. City/other jurisdiction tag or sticker number and name of city/other jurisdiction (if available);
7. A description of the condition of the vehicle, including its operability, if known, and repairs that appear necessary;
8. The current location of the vehicle;
9. The identity of the authority with physical custody of the vehicle and a contact point, including name, address, and telephone number of the official with recovery information;
10. Any information that indicates whether the vehicle was being used in connection with the commission of a crime;
11. Whether it appears that the vehicle may be subject to forfeiture under the laws of the notifying Party.

Annex 2

Request for the Return of a Stolen Vehicle

The Embassy of [country name] respectfully requests that (the appropriate authority of [country name]) return the vehicle described below to (its owner/its owner's authorized representative) in accordance with the Treaty Between the Government of the United States of America and the Government of Belize for the Return of Stolen Vehicles:

Make:
Model (Year):
Type:
Vehicle Identification Number:
Licence Plates:
Registered Owner:

The Embassy of [country name] certifies that it has examined the following documents which have been presented by (identity of person submitting documents) as evidence of (his or her ownership of the vehicle/ownership of the vehicle by the person for whom he or she is acting as authorized representative) and found them to be properly certified under the laws of (appropriate jurisdiction).

a. (document description)
b. (document description)
c. (document description)
d. (document description)

Complimentary closing
Place and date
Attachments

Protocol

In considering the provisions of the Treaty between the Government of Belize and the Government of the United States of America for the Return of Stolen Vehicles, the two Governments developed certain common understandings, which will provide guidance to authorities of the two Governments concerning the Treaty's implementation.

The Government of the United States of America has informed the Government of Belize that the laws and regulations of the United States require that, in order for a vehicle to be exported legally from the United States, documentation concerning the vehicle must be presented to the appropriate U.S. Customs Office and the Customs Office will issue a validation stamp when the title of the vehicle is authenticated.

Accordingly, in implementing its obligations under the Treaty, the Government of Belize shall not presume that a vehicle has been stolen from the United States if it has been exported from the United States in accordance with U.S. legal requirements and the person claiming the vehicle in Belize presents documentation from U.S. Customs.

J. HUMAN RIGHTS

CONTENTS

1. Universal Declaration of Human Rights [1]

Adopted and proclaimed by General Assembly resolution 217 A (III) of 10 December 1948

PREAMBLE

WHEREAS recognition of the inherent dignity and of the equal and inalienable rights of all members of the human family is the foundation of freedom, justice and peace in the world,

WHEREAS disregard and contempt for human rights have resulted in barbarous acts which have outraged the conscience of mankind, and the advent of a world in which human beings shall enjoy freedom of speech and belief and freedom from fear and want has been proclaimed as the highest aspiration of the common people,

WHEREAS it is essential, if man is not to be compelled to have recourse, as a last resort, to rebellion against tyranny and oppression, that human rights should be protected by the rule of law,

WHEREAS it is essential to promote the development of friendly relations between nations,

WHEREAS the people of the United Nations have in the Charter reaffirmed their faith in fundamental human rights, in the dignity and worth of the human person and in the equal rights of men and women and have determined to promote social progress and better standards of life in larger freedom,

WHEREAS Member States have pledged themselves to achieve, in co-operation with the United Nations, the promotion of universal respect for and observance of human rights and fundamental freedoms,

WHEREAS a common understanding of these rights and freedoms is of the greatest importance for the full realization of this pledge,

NOW, THEREFORE,

THE GENERAL ASSEMBLY

PROCLAIMS this Universal Declaration of Human Rights as a common standard of achievement for all peoples and all nations, to the end that every individual and every organ of society, keeping this Declaration constantly in mind, shall strive by teaching and education to promote respect for these rights and freedoms and by progressive measures, national and international to secure their universal and effective recognition and observance, both among the peoples of Member States themselves and among the peoples of territories under their jurisdiction.

[1] The Universal Declaration of Human Rights is a resolution adopted by the U.N. General Assembly and is not a treaty.

Article 1

All human beings are born free and equal in dignity and rights. They are endowed with reason and conscience and should act towards one another in a spirit of brotherhood.

Article 2

Everyone is entitled to all the rights and freedoms set forth in this Declaration, without distinction of any kind, such as race, colour, sex, language, religion, political or other opinion, national or social origin, property, birth or other status.

Furthermore, no distinction shall be made on the basis of the political, jurisdictional or international status of the country or territory to which a person belongs, whether it be independent, trust, non-selfgoverning or under any other limitation of sovereignty.

Article 3

Everyone has the right to life, liberty and the security of person.

Article 4

No one shall be held in slavery or servitude; slavery and the slave trade shall be prohibited in all their forms.

Article 5

No one shall be subjected to torture or to cruel, inhuman or degrading treatment or punishment.

Article 6

Everyone has the right to recognition everywhere as a person before the law.

Article 7

All are equal before the law and are entitled without any discrimination to equal protection of the law. All are entitled to equal protection against any discrimination in violation of this Declaration and against any incitement to such discrimination.

Article 8

Everyone has the right to an effective remedy by the competent national tribunals for acts violating the fundamental rights granted him by the Constitution or by law.

Article 9

No one shall be subjected to arbitrary arrest, detention or exile.

Article 10

Everyone is entitled in full equality to a fair and public hearing by an independent and impartial tribunal, in the determination of his rights and obligations and of any criminal charge against him.

ARTICLE 11

1. Everyone charged with a penal offence has the right to be presumed innocent until proved guilty according to law in a public trial at which he has had all the guarantees necessary for his defence.

2. No one shall be held guilty of any penal offence on account of any act or omission which did not constitute a penal offence, under national or international law, at the time when it was committed. Nor shall a heavier penalty be imposed than the one that was applicable at the time the penal offence was committed.

ARTICLE 12

No one shall be subjected to arbitrary interference with his privacy, family, home or correspondence, nor to attacks upon his honour and reputation. Everyone has the right to the protection of the law against such interference or attacks.

ARTICLE 13

1. Everyone has the right to freedom of movement and residence within the borders of each State.

2. Everyone has the right to leave any country including his own, and to return to his country.

ARTICLE 14

1. Everyone has the right to seek and to enjoy in other countries asylum from persecution.

2. This right may not be invoked in the case of prosecutions genuinely arising from non-political crimes or from acts contrary to the purposes and principles of the United Nations.

ARTICLE 15

1. Everyone has the right to a nationality.

2. No one shall be arbitrarily deprived of his nationality nor denied the right to change his nationality.

ARTICLE 16

1. Men and women of full age, without any limitation due to race, nationality or religion, have the right to marry and to found a family. They are entitled to equal rights as to marriage, during marriage and at its dissolution.

2. Marriage shall be entered into only with the free and full consent of the intending spouses.

3. The family is the natural and fundamental group unit of society and is entitled to protection by society and the State.

ARTICLE 17

1. Everyone has the right to own property alone as well as in association with others.

2. No one shall be arbitrarily deprived of his property.

Article 18

Everyone has the right to freedom of thought, conscience and religion; this right includes freedom to change his religion or belief, and freedom, either alone or in community with others and in public or private, to manifest his religion or belief in teaching, practice, worship and observance.

Article 19

Everyone has the right to freedom of opinion and expression; this right includes freedom to hold opinions without interference and to seek, receive and impart information and ideas through any media and regardless of frontiers.

Article 20

1. Everyone has the right to freedom of peaceful assembly and association.
2. No one may be compelled to belong to an association.

Article 21

1. Everyone has the right to take part in the government of his country, directly or through freely chosen representatives.
2. Everyone has the right of equal access to public service in his country.
3. The will of the people shall be the basis of the authority of government; this will shall be expressed in periodic and genuine elections which shall be by universal and equal suffrage and shall be held by secret vote or by equivalent free voting procedures.

Article 22

Everyone, as a member of society, has the right to social security and is entitled to realization, through national effort and international co-operation and in accordance with the organization and resources of each State, of the economic, social and cultural rights indispensable for his dignity and the free development of his personality.

Article 23

1. Everyone has the right to work, to free choice of employment, to just and favourable conditions of work and to protection against unemployment.
2. Everyone, without any discrimination, has the right to equal pay for equal work.
3. Everyone who works has the right to just and favourable remuneration ensuring for himself and his family an existence worthy of human dignity, and supplemented, if necessary, by other means of social protection.
4. Everyone has the right to form and to join trade unions for the protection of his interests.

Article 24

Everyone has the right to rest and leisure, including reasonable limitation of working hours and periodic holidays with pay.

Article 25

1. Everyone has the right to a standard of living adequate for the health and well-being of himself and of his family, including food, clothing, housing and medical care and necessary social services, and the right to security in the event of unemployment, sickness disability, widowhood, old age or other lack of livelihood in circumstances beyond his control.

2. Motherhood and childhood are entitled to special care and assistance. All children, whether born in or out of wedlock, shall enjoy the same social protection.

Article 26

1. Everyone has the right to education. Education shall be free, at least in the elementary and fundamental stages. Elementary education shall be compulsory. Technical and professional education shall be made generally available and higher education shall be equally accessible to all on the basis of merit.

2. Education shall be directed to the full development of the human personality and to the strengthening of respect for human rights and fundamental freedoms. It shall promote understanding, tolerance and friendship among all nations, racial or religious groups, and shall further the activities of the United Nations for the maintenance of peace.

3. Parents have a prior right to choose the kind of education that shall be given to their children.

Article 27

1. Everyone has the right freely to participate in the cultural life of the community, to enjoy the arts and to share in scientific advancement and its benefits.

2. Everyone has the right to the protection of the moral and material interests resulting from any scientific, literary or artistic production of which he is the author.

Article 28

Everyone is entitled to a social and international order in which the rights and freedoms set forth in this Declaration can be fully realized.

Article 29

1. Everyone has duties to the community in which alone the free and full development of his personality is possible.

2. In the exercise of his rights and freedoms, everyone shall be subject only to such limitations as are determined by law solely for the purpose of securing due recognition and respect for the rights and freedoms of others and of meeting the just requirements of morality, public order and the general welfare in a democratic society.

3. These rights and freedoms may in no case be exercised contrary to the purposes and principles of the United Nations.

Article 30

Nothing in this Declaration may be interpreted as implying for any State, group or person any right to engage in any activity or to perform any act aimed at the destruction of any of the rights and freedoms set forth herein.

2. United Nations Convention on the Prevention and Punishment of the Crime of Genocide

Adopted by the United Nations General Assembly in General Assemly resolution 260 A(III) at Paris, December 9, 1948; Signed by the United States, December 11, 1948; Open for negotiation until December 31, 1949; Entered into force for participating countries, January 12, 1951; Senate gave advice and consent to ratification with reservations, declaration and understandings, February 19, 1986; Entered into force with respect to the United States, February 23, 1989[1]

The Contracting Parties,

HAVING CONSIDERED the declaration made by the General Assembly of the United Nations in its resolution 96 (I) dated 11 December 1946 that genocide is a crime under international law, contrary to the spirit and aims of the United Nations and condemned by the civilized world.

RECOGNIZING that at all periods of history genocide has inflicted great losses on humanity, and

BEING CONVINCED that, in order to liberate mankind from such an odious scourge, international co-operation is required,

HEREBY AGREE AS HEREINAFTER PROVIDE:

ARTICLE I

The Contracting Parties confirm that genocide, whether committed in time of peace or time of war, is a crime under international law which they undertake to prevent and to punish.

ARTICLE II

In the present Convention, genocide[2] means any of the following acts committed with intent to destroy, in whole or in part, a national, ethnical, racial or religious group, as such:

(a) Killing members of the group;

(b) Causing serious bodily or mental harm to members of the group;

(c) Deliberately inflicting on the group conditions of life calculated to bring about its physical destruction in whole or in part;

(d) Imposing measures intended to prevent births within the group;

(e) Forcibly transferring children of the group to another group.

---

[1] Article III of the Senate's Resolution of Ratification of this Convention provided that the President would not deposit the instrument of ratification until implementing legislation had been enacted. Such legislation, the Genocide Convention Implementation Act of 1987 (Public Law 100–606; 102 Stat. 3045), was enacted into law on November 5, 1988.

[2] See also: S.Res. 347, adopted February 19, 1986, expressing the sense of the Senate of "the desire of the United States to amend the Convention to include acts constituting political genocide within the definition of the term 'genocide'".

Article III

The following acts shall be punishable:

(a) Genocide;
(b) Conspiracy to commit genocide;
(c) Direct and public incitement to commit genocide;
(d) Attempt to commit genocide;
(e) Complicity in genocide.

Article IV

Persons committing genocide or any of the other acts enumerated in article III shall be punished, whether they are constitutionally responsible rulers, public officials or private individuals.

Article V

The Contracting Parties undertake to enact, in accordance with their respective Constitutions, the necessary legislation to give effect to the provisions of the present Convention and, in particular, to provide effective penalties for persons guilty of genocide or any of the other acts enumerated in article III.

Article VI

Persons charged with genocide or any of the other acts enumerated in article III shall be tried by a competent tribunal of the State in the territory of which the act was committed, or by such international penal tribunal as may have jurisdiction with respect to these Contracting Parties which shall have accepted its jurisdiction.

Article VII

Genocide and the other acts enumerated in article III shall not be considered as political crimes for the purpose of extradition.

The Contracting Parties pledge themselves in such cases to grant extradition in accordance with their laws and treaties in force.

Article VIII

Any Contracting Party may call upon the competent organs of the United Nations to take such action under the Charter of the United Nations as they consider appropriate for the prevention and suppression of acts of genocide or any of the other acts enumerated in article III.

Article IX

Disputes between the Contracting Parties relating to the interpretation, application or fulfillment of the present Convention, including those relating to the responsibility of a State for genocide or for any of the other acts enumerated in article III, shall be submitted to the International Court of Justice at the request of any of the parties to the dispute.

Article X

The present Convention, of which the Chinese, English, French, Russian and Spanish texts are equally authentic, shall bear the date of 9 December 1948.

Article XI

The present Convention shall be open until 31 December 1949 for signature on behalf of any Member of the United Nations and of any non-member State to which an invitation to sign has been addressed by the General Assembly.

The present Convention shall be ratified, and the instruments of ratification shall be deposited with the Secretary-General of the United Nations.

After 1 January 1950, the present Convention may be acceded to on behalf of any Member of the United Nations and of any non-member State which has received an invitation as aforesaid.

Instruments of accession shall be deposited with the Secretary-General of the United Nations.

Article XII

Any Contracting Party may at any time, by notification addressed to the Secretary-General of the United Nations, extend the application of the present Convention to all or any of the territories for the conduct of whose foreign relations that Contracting Party is responsible.

Article XIII

On the day when the first twenty instruments of ratification or accession have been deposited, the Secretary-General shall draw up a *procès-verbal* and to each of the non-member States contemplated in article XI.

The present Convention shall come into force on the ninetieth day following the date of deposit of the twentieth instrument of ratification or accession.

Any ratification or accession effected subsequent to the latter date shall become effective on the ninetieth day following the deposit of the instrument of ratification or accession.

Article XIV

The present Convention shall remain in effect for a period of ten years as from the date of its coming into force.

It shall thereafter remain in force for successive periods of five years for such Contracting Parties as have not denounced it at least six months before the expiration of the current period.

Denunciation shall be effected by a written notification addressed to the Secretary-General of the United Nations.

ARTICLE XV

If, as a result of denunciations, the number of Parties to the present Convention should become less than sixteen, the Convention shall cease to be in force as from the date on which the last of these denunciations shall become effective.

ARTICLE XVI

A request for the revision of the present Convention may be made at any time by any Contracting Party by means of a notification in writing addressed to the Secretary-General.

The General Assembly shall decide upon the steps, if any, to be taken in respect of such request.

ARTICLE XVII

The Secretary-General of the United Nations shall notify all Members of the United Nations and the non-member States contemplated in article XI of the following:

(a) Signatures, ratifications and accessions received in accordance with article XI;

(b) Notifications received in accordance with article XII;

(c) The date upon which the present Convention comes into force in accordance with article XIII;

(d) Denunciations received in accordance with article XIV;

(e) The abrogation of the Convention in accordance with article XV;

(f) Notifications received in accordance with article XVI.

ARTICLE XVIII

The original of the present Convention shall be deposited in the archives of the United Nations.

A certified copy of the Convention shall be transmitted to each Member of the United Nations and to each of the non-member States contemplated in article XI.

ARTICLE XIX

The present Convention shall be registered by the Secretary-General of the United Nations on the date of its coming into force.

3. Senate Resolution of Ratification of Genocide Convention Including Reservations, Understandings and Declaration

S. Res. 347, agreed to by the Senate on February 19, 1986

Resolved, (two-thirds of the Senators present concurring therein), That the Senate advise and consent to the ratification of the International Convention on the Prevention and Punishment of the Crime of Genocide, adopted unanimously by the General Assembly of the United Nations in Paris on December 9, 1948 (Executive O, Eighty-first Congress, first session), *Provided that:*

I. The Senate's advice and consent is subject to the following reservations:

(1) That with reference to Article IX of the Convention, before any dispute to which the United States is a party may be submitted to the jurisdiction of the International Court of Justice under this article, the specific consent of the United States is required in each case.

(2) That nothing in the Convention requires or authorizes legislation or other action by the United States of America prohibited by the Constitution of the United States as interpreted by the United States.

II. The Senate's advice and consent is subject to the following understandings, which shall apply to the obligations of the United States under the Convention:

(1) That the term "intent to destroy, in whole or in part, a national, ethnical, racial, or religious group as such" appearing in Article II means the specific intent to destroy, in whole or in substantial part, a national, ethnical, racial, or religious group as such by the acts specified in Article II.

(2) That the term "mental harm" in Article II(b) means permanent impairment of mental faculties through drugs, torture or similar techniques.

(3) That the pledge to grant extradition in accordance with a state's laws and treaties in force found in Article VII extends only to acts which are criminal under the laws of both the requesting and the requested state and nothing in Article VI affects the right of any state to bring to trial before its own tribunals any of its nationals for acts committed outside a state.

(4) That acts in the course of armed conflicts committed without the specific intent required by Article II are not sufficient to constitute genocide as defined by this Convention.

(5) That with regard to the reference to an international penal tribunal in Article VI of the Convention, the United States declares that it reserves the right to effect its participation in any such tribunal only by a treaty entered into specifically for that purpose with the advice and consent of the Senate.

III. The Senate's advice and consent is subject to the following declaration:

That the President will not deposit the instrument of ratification until after the implementing legislation referred to in Article V has been enacted.[1]

[1] The Genocide Convention Implementation Act of 1987 (Public Law 100–606; 102 Stat. 3045) was signed into law November 5, 1988. See *Legislation on Foreign Relations Through 2005*, vol. II–A, sec. H.

4. International Covenant on Civil and Political Rights [1]

Adopted at New York, December 16, 1966; Entered into force generally, March 23, 1976; Ratification advised by the Senate, April 2, 1992; Entered into force for the United States, September 8, 1992

The States Parties to the Present Covenant,

CONSIDERING that, in accordance with the principles proclaimed in the Charter of the United Nations, recognition of the inherent dignity and of the equal and inalienable rights of all members of the human family is the foundation of freedom, justice and peace in the world,

RECOGNIZING that these rights derive from the inherent dignity of the human person,

RECOGNIZING that, in accordance with the Universal Declaration of Human Rights, the ideal of free human beings enjoying civil and political freedom and freedom from fear and want can only be achieved if conditions are created whereby everyone may enjoy his civil and political rights, as well as his economic, social and cultural rights,

CONSIDERING the obligation of States under the Charter of the United Nations to promote universal respect for, and observance of, human rights and freedoms,

REALIZING that the individual, having duties to other individuals and to the community to which he belongs, is under a responsibility to strive for the promotion and observance of the rights recognized in the present Covenant,

AGREE UPON THE FOLLOWING ARTICLES:

PART I

ARTICLE 1

1. All peoples have the right of self-determination. By virtue of that right they freely determine their political status and freely pursue their economic, social and cultural development.

2. All peoples may, for their own ends, freely dispose of their natural wealth and resources without prejudice to any obligations arising out of international economic co-operation, based upon the principle of mutual benefit, and international law. In no case may a people be deprived of its own means of subsistence.

3. The States Parties to the present Covenant, including those having responsibility for the administration of Non-Self-Governing and Trust Territories, shall promote the realization of the right of self-determination, and shall respect that right, in conformity with the provisions of the Charter of the United Nations.

[1] For a list of states that are parties, see Department of State publication, *Treaties in Force.*

PART II

ARTICLE 2

1. Each State Party to the present Covenant undertakes to respect and to ensure to all individuals within its territory and subject to its jurisdiction the rights recognized in the present Covenant, without distinction of any kind, such as race, colour, sex, language, religion, political or other opinion, national or social origin, property, birth or other status.

2. Where not already provided for by existing legislative or other measures, each State Party to the present Covenant undertakes to take the necessary steps, in accordance with its constitutional processes and with the provisions of the present Covenant, to adopt such legislative or other measures as may be necessary to give effect to the rights recognized in the present Covenant.

3. Each State Party to the present Covenant undertakes:

(a) To ensure that any person whose rights or freedoms as herein recognized are violated shall have an effective remedy, notwithstanding that the violation has been committed by persons acting in an official capacity;

(b) To ensure that any person claiming such a remedy shall have his right thereto determined by competent judicial, administrative or legislative authorities, or by any other competent authority provided for by the legal system of the State, and to develop the possibilities of judicial remedy;

(c) To ensure that the competent authorities shall enforce such remedies when granted.

ARTICLE 3

The States Parties to the present Covenant undertake to ensure the equal right of men and women to the enjoyment of all civil and political rights set forth in the present Covenant.

ARTICLE 4

1. In time of public emergency which threatens the life of the nation and the existence of which is officially proclaimed, the States Parties to the present Covenant may take measures derogating from their obligations under the present Covenant to the extent strictly required by the exigencies of the situation, provided that such measures are not inconsistent with their other obligations under international law and do not involve discrimination solely on the ground of race, colour, sex, language, religion or social origin.

2. No derogation from articles 6, 7, 8 (paragraphs 1 and 2), 11, 15, 16 and 18 may be made under this provision.

3. Any State Party to the present Covenant availing itself of the right of derogation shall immediately inform the other States Parties to the present Covenant, through the intermediary of the Secretary-General of the United Nations, of the provisions from which it has derogated and of the reasons by which it was actuated. A further communication shall be made, through the same intermediary, on the date on which it terminates such derogation.

ARTICLE 5

1. Nothing in the present Covenant may be interpreted as implying for any State, group or person any right to engage in any activity or perform any act aimed at the destruction of any of the rights and freedoms recognized herein or at their limitation to a greater extent than is provided for in the present Covenant.

2. There shall be no restriction upon or derogation from any of the fundamental human rights recognized or existing in any State Party to the present Covenant pursuant to law, conventions, regulations or custom on the pretext that the present Covenant does not recognize such rights or that it recognizes them to a lesser extent.

Part III

ARTICLE 6

1. Every human being has the inherent right to life. This right shall be protected by law. No one shall be arbitrarily deprived of his life.

2. In countries which have not abolished the death penalty, sentence of death may be imposed only for the most serious crimes in accordance with the law in force at the time of the commission of the crime and not contrary to the provisions of the present Covenant and to the Convention on the Prevention and Punishment of the Crime of Genocide. This penalty can only be carried out pursuant to a final judgement rendered by a competent court.

3. When deprivation of life constitutes the crime of genocide, it is understood that nothing in this article shall authorize any State Party to the present Covenant to derogate in any way from any obligation assumed under the provisions of the Convention on the Prevention and Punishment of the Crime of Genocide.

4. Anyone sentenced to death shall have the right to seek pardon or commutation of the sentence. Amnesty, pardon or commutation of the sentence of death may be granted in all cases.

5. Sentence of death shall not be imposed for crimes committed by persons below eighteen years of age and shall not be carried out on pregnant women.

6. Nothing in this article shall be invoked to delay or to prevent the abolition of capital punishment by any State Party to the present Covenant.

ARTICLE 7

No one shall be subjected to torture or to cruel, inhuman or degrading treatment or punishment. In particular, no one shall be subjected without his free consent to medical or scientific experimentation.

ARTICLE 8

1. No one shall be held in slavery; slavery and the slave-trade in all their forms shall be prohibited.

2. No one shall be held in servitude.

3. (a) No one shall be required to perform forced or compulsory labour;

(b) Paragraph 3(a) shall not be held to preclude, in countries where imprisonment with hard labour may be imposed as a punishment for a crime, the performance of hard labour in pursuance of a sentence to such punishment by a competent court;

(c) For the purpose of this paragraph the term "forced or compulsory labour" shall not include:

(i) Any work or service, not referred to in sub-paragraph (b), normally required of a person who is under detention in consequence of a lawful order of a court, or of a person during conditional release from such detention;

(ii) Any service of a military character and, in countries where conscientious objection is recognized, any national service required by law of conscientious objectors;

(iii) Any service exacted in cases of emergency or calamity threatening the life or well-being of the community;

(iv) Any work or service which forms part of normal civil obligations.

ARTICLE 9

1. Everyone has the right to liberty and security of person. No one shall be subjected to arbitrary arrest or detention. No one shall be deprived of his liberty except on such grounds and in accordance with such procedure as are established by law.

2. Anyone who is arrested shall be informed, at the time of arrest, of the reasons for his arrest and shall be promptly informed of any charges against him.

3. Anyone arrested or detained on a criminal charge shall be brought promptly before a judge or other officer authorized by law to exercise judicial power and shall be entitled to trial within a reasonable time or to release. It shall not be the general rule that persons awaiting trial shall be detained in custody, but release may be subject to guarantees to appear for trial, at any other stage of the judicial proceedings, and, should occasion arise, for execution of the judgement.

4. Anyone who is deprived of his liberty by arrest or detention shall be entitled to take proceedings before a court, in order that that court may decide without delay on the lawfulness of his detention and order his release if the detention is not lawful.

5. Anyone who has been the victim of unlawful arrest or detention shall have an enforceable right to compensation.

ARTICLE 10

1. All persons deprived of their liberty shall be treated with humanity and with respect for the inherent dignity of the human person.

2. (a) Accused persons shall, save in exceptional circumstances, be segregated from convicted persons and shall be subject to separate treatment appropriate to their status as unconvicted persons;

(b) Accused juvenile persons shall be separated from adults and brought as speedily as possible for adjudication.

3. The penitentiary system shall comprise treatment of prisoners the essential aim of which shall be their reformation and social rehabilitation. Juvenile offenders shall be segregated from adults and be accorded treatment appropriate to their age and legal status.

ARTICLE 11

No one shall be imprisoned merely on the ground of inability to fulfill a contractual obligation.

ARTICLE 12

1. Everyone lawfully within the territory of a State shall, within that territory, have the right to liberty of movement and freedom to choose his residence.

2. Everyone shall be free to leave any country, including his own.

3. The above-mentioned rights shall not be subject to any restrictions except those which are provided by law, are necessary to protect national security, public order (ordre public), public health or morals or the rights and freedoms of others, and are consistent with the other rights recognized in the present Covenant.

4. No one shall be arbitrarily deprived of the right to enter his own country.

ARTICLE 13

An alien lawfully in the territory of a State Party to the present Covenant may be expelled therefrom only in pursuance of a decision reached in accordance with law and shall, except where compelling reasons of national security otherwise require, be allowed to submit the reasons against his expulsion and to have his case reviewed by, and be represented for the purpose before, the competent authority or a person or persons especially designated by the competent authority.

ARTICLE 14

1. All persons shall be equal before the courts and tribunals. In the determination of any criminal charge against him, or of his rights and obligations in a suit at law, everyone shall be entitled to a fair and public hearing by a competent, independent and impartial tribunal established by law. The Press and the public may be excluded from all or part of a trial for reasons of morals, public order (ordre public) or national security in a democratic society, or when the interest of the private lives of the parties so requires, or to the extent strictly necessary in the opinion of the court in special circumstances where publicity would prejudice the interests of justice; but any judgement rendered in a criminal case or in a suit at law shall be made public except where the interest of juvenile persons otherwise requires or the proceedings concern matrimonial disputes or the guardianship of children.

2. Everyone charged with a criminal offence shall have the right to be presumed innocent until proved guilty according to law.

3. In the determination of any criminal charge against him, everyone shall be entitled to the following minimum guarantees, in full equality:

(a) To be informed promptly and in detail in a language which he understands of the nature and cause of the charge against him;

(b) To have adequate time and facilities for the preparation of his defence and to communicate with counsel of his own choosing;

(c) To be tried without undue delay;

(d) To be tried in his presence, and to defend himself in person or through legal assistance of his own choosing; to be informed, if he does not have legal assistance, of this right; and to have legal assistance assigned to him, in any case where the interests of justice so require, and without payment by him in any such case if he does not have sufficient means to pay for it;

(e) To examine, or have examined, the witnesses against him and to obtain the attendance and examination of witnesses on his behalf under the same conditions as witnesses against him;

(f) To have the free assistance of an interpreter if he cannot understand or speak the language used in court;

(g) Not to be compelled to testify against himself or to confess guilt.

4. In the case of juvenile persons, the procedure shall be such as will take account of their age and the desirability of promoting their rehabilitation.

5. Everyone convicted of a crime shall have the right to his conviction and sentence being reviewed by a higher tribunal according to law.

6. When a person has by a final decision been convicted of a criminal offence and when subsequently his conviction has been reversed or he has been pardoned on the ground that a new or newly discovered fact shows conclusively that there has been a miscarriage of justice, the person who has suffered punishment as a result of such conviction shall be compensated according to law, unless it is proved that the non-disclosure of the unknown fact in time is wholly or partly attributable to him.

7. No one shall be liable to be tried or punished again for an offence for which he has already been finally convicted or acquitted in accordance with the law and penal procedure of each country.

ARTICLE 15

1. No one shall be held guilty of any criminal offence on account of any act or omission which did not constitute a criminal offence, under national or international law, at the time when it was committed. Nor shall a heavier penalty be imposed than the one that was applicable at the time when the criminal offence was committed. If, subsequent to the commission of the offence, provision is made by law for the imposition of a lighter penalty, the offender shall benefit thereby.

2. Nothing in this article shall prejudice the trial and punishment of any person for any act or omission which, at the time when it was committed, was criminal according to the general principles of law recognized by the community of nations.

ARTICLE 16

Everyone shall have the right to recognition everywhere as a person before the law.

ARTICLE 17

1. No one shall be subjected to arbitrary or unlawful interference with his privacy, family, home or correspondence, nor to unlawful attacks on his honour and reputation.

2. Everyone has the right to the protection of the law against such interference or attacks.

ARTICLE 18

1. Everyone shall have the right to freedom of thought, conscience and religion. This right shall include freedom to have or to adopt a religion or belief of his choice, and freedom, either individually or in community with others and in public or private to manifest his religion or belief in worship, observance, practice and teaching.

2. No one shall be subject to coercion which would impair his freedom to have or to adopt a religion or belief of his choice.

3. Freedom to manifest one's religion or beliefs may be subject only to such limitations as are prescribed by law and are necessary to protect public safety, order, health, or morals or the fundamental rights and freedoms of others.

4. The States Parties to the present Covenant undertake to have respect for the liberty of parents and, when applicable, legal guardians to ensure the religious and moral education of their children in conformity with their own convictions.

ARTICLE 19

1. Everyone shall have the right to hold opinions without interference.

2. Everyone shall have the right to freedom of expression; this right shall include freedom to seek, receive and impart information and ideas of all kinds, regardless of frontiers, either orally, in writing or in print, in the form of art, or through any other media of his choice.

3. The exercise of the rights provided for in paragraph 2 of this article carries with it special duties and responsibilities. It may therefore be subject to certain restrictions, but these shall only be such as are provided by law and are necessary:

(a) For respect of the rights or reputations of others;

(b) For the protection of national security or of public order (ordre public), or of public health or morals.

ARTICLE 20

1. Any propaganda for war shall be prohibited by law.

2. Any advocacy of national, racial or religious hatred that constitutes incitement to discrimination, hostility or violence shall be prohibited by law.

ARTICLE 21

The right of peaceful assembly shall be recognized. No restrictions may be placed on the exercise of this right other than those imposed in conformity with the law and which are necessary in a democratic society in the interests of national security or public safety, public order (ordre public), the protection of public health or morals or the protection of the rights and freedoms of others.

ARTICLE 22

1. Everyone shall have the right to freedom of association with others, including the right to form and join trade unions for the protection of his interests.

2. No restrictions may be placed on the exercise of this right other than those which are prescribed by law and which are necessary in a democratic society in the interests of national security or public safety, public order (ordre public), the protection of public health or morals or the protection of the rights and freedoms of others. This Article shall not prevent the imposition of lawful restrictions on members of the armed forces and of the police in their exercise of this right.

3. Nothing in this article shall authorize States Parties to the International Labour Organisation Convention of 1948 concerning Freedom of Association and Protection of the Right to Organize to take legislative measures which would prejudice, or to apply the law in such a manner as to prejudice, the guarantees provided for in that Convention.

ARTICLE 23

1. The family is the natural and fundamental group unit of society and is entitled to protection by society and the State.

2. The right of men and women of marriageable age to marry and to found a family shall be recognized.

3. No marriage shall be entered into without the free and full consent of the intending spouses.

4. States Parties to the present Covenant shall take appropriate steps to ensure equality of rights and responsibilities of spouses as to marriage, during marriage and at its dissolution. In the case of dissolution, provision shall be made for the necessary protection of any children.

ARTICLE 24

1. Every child shall have, without any discrimination as to race, colour, sex, language, religion, national or social origin, property or birth, the right to such measures of protection as are required by his status as a minor, on the part of his family, society and the State.

2. Every child shall be registered immediately after birth and shall have a name.

3. Every child has the right to acquire a nationality.

ARTICLE 25

Every citizen shall have the right and the opportunity, without any of the distinctions mentioned in article 2 and without unreasonable restrictions:

(a) To take part in the conduct of public affairs, directly or through freely chosen representatives;

(b) To vote and to be elected at genuine periodic elections which shall be by universal and equal suffrage and shall be held by secret ballot, guaranteeing the free expression of the will of the electors;

(c) To have access, on general terms of equality, to public service in his country.

ARTICLE 26

All persons are equal before the law and are entitled without any discrimination to the equal protection of the law. In this respect, the law shall prohibit any discrimination and guarantee to all persons equal and effective protection against discrimination on any ground such as race, colour, sex, language, religion, political or other opinion, national or social origin, property, birth or other status.

ARTICLE 27

In those States in which ethnic, religious or linguistic minorities exist, persons belonging to such minorities shall not be denied the right, in community with the other members of their group, to enjoy their own culture, to profess and practice their own religion, or to use their own language.

PART IV

ARTICLE 28

1. There shall be established a Human Rights Committee (hereafter referred to in the present Covenant as the Committee). It shall consist of eighteen members and shall carry out the functions hereinafter provided.
2. The Committee shall be composed of nationals of the States Parties to the present Covenant who shall be persons of high moral character and recognized competence in the field of human rights, consideration being given to the usefulness of the participation of some persons having legal experience.
3. The members of the Committee shall be elected and shall serve in their personal capacity.

ARTICLE 29

1. The members of the Committee shall be elected by secret ballot from a list of persons possessing the qualifications prescribed in article 28 and nominated for the purpose by the States Parties to the present Covenant.
2. Each State Party to the present Covenant may nominate not more than two persons. These persons shall be nationals of the nominating State.
3. A person shall be eligible for renomination.

ARTICLE 30

1. The initial election shall be held no later than six months after the date of the entry into force of the presented Covenant.

2. At least four months before the date of each election to the Committee, other than an election to fill a vacancy declared in accordance with article 34, the Secretary-General of the United Nations shall address a written invitation to the States Parties to the present Covenant to submit their nominations for membership of the Committee within three months.

3. The Secretary-General of the United Nations shall prepare a list in alphabetical order of all the persons thus nominated, with an indication of the States Parties which have nominated them, and shall submit it to the States Parties to the present Covenant no later than one month before the date of each election.

4. Elections of the members of the Committee shall be held at a meeting of the States Parties to the present Covenant convened by the Secretary-General of the United Nations at the Headquarters of the United Nations. At that meeting, for which two thirds of the States Parties to the present Covenant shall constitute a quorum, the persons elected to the Committee shall be those nominees who obtain the largest number of votes and an absolute majority of the votes of the representatives of States Parties present and voting.

ARTICLE 31

1. The Committee may not include more than one national of the same State.

2. In the election of the Committee, consideration shall be given to equitable geographical distribution of membership and to the representation of the different forms of civilization and of the principal legal systems.

ARTICLE 32

1. The members of the Committee shall be elected for a term of four years. They shall be eligible for re-election if renominated. However, the terms of nine of the members elected at the first election shall expire at the end of two years; immediately after the first election, the names of these nine members shall be chosen by lot by the Chairman of the meeting referred to in article 30, paragraph 4.

2. Elections at the expiry of office shall be held in accordance with the preceding articles of this part of the present Covenant.

ARTICLE 33

1. If, in the unanimous opinion of the other members, a member of the Committee has ceased to carry out his functions for any cause other than absence of a temporary character, the Chairman of the Committee shall notify the Secretary-General of the United Nations, who shall then declare the seat of that member to be vacant.

2. In the event of the death or the resignation of a member of the Committee, the Chairman shall immediately notify the Secretary-General of the United Nations, who shall declare the seat

vacant from the date of death or the date on which the resignation takes effect.

ARTICLE 34

1. When a vacancy is declared in accordance with article 33 and if the term of office of the member to be replaced does not expire within six months of the declaration of the vacancy, the Secretary-General of the United Nations shall notify each of the States Parties to the present Covenant, which may within two months submit nominations in accordance with article 29 for the purpose of filling the vacancy.

2. The Secretary-General of the United Nations shall prepare a list in alphabetical order of the persons thus nominated and shall submit it to the States Parties to the present Covenant. The election to fill the vacancy shall then take place in accordance with the relevant provisions of this part of the present Covenant.

3. A member of the Committee elected to fill a vacancy declared in accordance with article 33 shall hold office for the remainder of the term of the member who vacated the seat on the Committee under the provisions of that article.

ARTICLE 35

The members of the Committee shall, with the approval of the General Assembly of the United Nations, receive emoluments from United Nations resources on such terms and conditions as the General Assembly may decide, having regard to the importance of the Committee's responsibilities.

ARTICLE 36

The Secretary-General of the United Nations shall provide the necessary staff and facilities for the effective performance of the functions of the Committee under the present Covenant.

ARTICLE 37

1. The Secretary-General of the United Nations shall convene the initial meeting of the Committee at the Headquarters of the United Nations.

2. After its initial meeting, the Committee shall meet at such times as shall be provided in its rules of procedure.

3. The Committee shall normally meet at the Headquarters of the United Nations or at the United Nations Office at Geneva.

ARTICLE 38

Every member of the Committee shall, before taking up his duties, make a solemn declaration in open committee that he will perform his functions impartially and conscientiously.

ARTICLE 39

1. The Committee shall elect its officers for a term of two years. They may be re-elected.

2. The Committee shall establish its own rules of procedure, but these rules shall provide, inter alia, that:

(a) Twelve members shall constitute a quorum;

(b) Decisions of the Committee shall be made by a majority vote of the members present.

ARTICLE 40

1. The States Parties to the present Covenant undertake to submit reports on the measures they have adopted which give effect to the rights recognized herein and on the progress made in the enjoyment of those rights:

(a) Within one year of the entry into force of the present Covenant for the States Parties concerned;

(b) Thereafter whenever the Committee so requests.

2. All reports shall be submitted to the Secretary-General of the United Nations, who shall transmit them to the Committee for consideration. Reports shall indicate the factors and difficulties, if any, affecting the implementation of the present Covenant.

3. The Secretary-General of the United Nations may, after consultation with the Committee, transmit to the specialized agencies concerned copies of such parts of the reports as may fall within their field of competence.

4. The Committee shall study the reports submitted by the States Parties to the present Covenant. It shall transmit its reports, and such general comments as it may consider appropriate, to the States Parties. The Committee may also transmit to the Economic and Social Council these comments along with the copies of the reports it has received from States Parties to the present Covenant.

5. The States Parties to the present Covenant may submit to the Committee observations on any comments that may be made in accordance with paragraph 4 of this article.

ARTICLE 41

1. A State Party to the present Covenant may at any time declare under this article that it recognizes the competence of the Committee to receive and consider communications to the effect that a State Party claims that another State Party is not fulfilling its obligations under the present Covenant. Communications under this article may be received and considered only if submitted by a State Party which has made a declaration recognizing in regard to itself the competence of the Committee. No communication shall be received by the Committee if it concerns a State Party which has not made such a declaration. Communications received under this article shall be dealt with in accordance with the following procedure:

(a) If a State Party to the present Covenant considers that another State Party is not giving effect to the provisions of the present Covenant, it may, by written communication, bring the matter to the attention of that State Party. Within three months after the receipt of the communication, the receiving State shall afford the State which sent the communication an explanation or any other statement in writing clarifying the matter, which should include, to the extent possible and pertinent, reference to domestic procedures and remedies taken, pending, or available in the matter.

(b) If the matter is not adjusted to the satisfaction of both States Parties concerned within six months after the receipt by the receiving State of the initial communication, either State shall have the right to refer the matter to the Committee, by notice given to the Committee and to the other State.

(c) The Committee shall deal with a matter referred to it only after it has ascertained that all available domestic remedies have been invoked and exhausted in the matter, in conformity with the generally recognized principles of international law. This shall not be the rule where the application of the remedies is unreasonably prolonged.

(d) The Committee shall hold closed meetings when examining communications under this article.

(e) Subject to the provisions of sub-paragraph (c), the Committee shall make available its good offices to the States Parties concerned with a view to a friendly solution of the matter on the basis of respect for human rights and fundamental freedoms as recognized in the present Covenant.

(f) In any matter referred to it, the Committee may call upon the States Parties concerned, referred to in sub-paragraph (b), to supply any relevant information.

(g) The States Parties concerned, referred to in sub-paragraph (b), shall have the right to be represented when the matter is being considered in the Committee and to make submissions orally and/or in writing.

(h) The Committee shall, within twelve months after the date of receipt of notice under sub-paragraph (b), submit a report:

(i) If a solution within the terms of sub-paragraph (e) is reached, the Committee shall confine its report to a brief statement of the facts and of the solution reached;

(ii) If a solution within the terms of sub-paragraph (e) is not reached, the Committee shall confine its report to a brief statement of the facts; the written submissions and record of the oral submissions made by the States Parties concerned shall be attached to the report.

In every matter, the report shall be communicated to the States Parties concerned.

2. The provisions of this article shall come into force when ten States Parties to the present Covenant have made declarations under paragraph 1 of this article. Such declarations shall be deposited by the States Parties with the Secretary-General of the United Nations, who shall transmit copies thereof to the other States Parties. A declaration may be withdrawn at any time by notification to the Secretary-General. Such a withdrawal shall not prejudice the consideration of any matter which is the subject of a communication already transmitted under this article; no further communication by any State Party shall be received after the notification of withdrawal of the declaration has been received by the Secretary-General, unless the State Party concerned has made a new declaration.

ARTICLE 42

1. (a) If a matter referred to the Committee in accordance with article 41 is not resolved to the satisfaction of the States Parties concerned, the Committee may, with the prior consent of the States Parties concerned, appoint an ad hoc Conciliation Commission (hereinafter referred to as the Commission). The good offices of the Commission shall be made available to the States Parties concerned with a view to an amicable solution of the matter on the basis of respect for the present Covenant;

(b) The Commission shall consist of five persons acceptable to the States Parties concerned. If the States Parties concerned fail to reach agreement within three months on all or part of the composition of the Commission the members of the Commission concerning whom no agreement has been reached shall be elected by secret ballot by a two-thirds majority vote of the Committee from among its members.

2. The members of the Commission shall serve in their personal capacity. They shall not be nationals of the States Parties concerned, or of a State not party to the present Covenant, or of a State Party which has not made a declaration under article 41.

3. The Commission shall elect its own Chairman and adopt its own rules of procedure.

4. The meetings of the Commission shall normally be held at the Headquarters of the United Nations or at the United Nations Office at Geneva. However, they may be held at such other convenient places as the Commission may determine in consultation with the Secretary-General of the United Nations and the States Parties concerned.

5. The secretariat provided in accordance with article 36 shall also service the commissions appointed under this article.

6. The information received and collated by the Committee shall be made available to the Commission and the Commission may call upon the States Parties concerned to supply any other relevant information.

7. When the Commission has fully considered the matter, but in any event not later than twelve months after having been seized of the matter, it shall submit to the Chairman of the Committee a report for communication to the States Parties concerned.

(a) If the Commission is unable to complete its consideration of the matter within twelve months, it shall confine its report to a brief statement of the status of its consideration of the matter;

(b) If an amicable solution to the matter on the basis of respect for human rights as recognized in the present Covenant is reached, the Commission shall confine its report to a brief statement of the facts and of the solution reached.

(c) If a solution within the terms of sub-paragraph (b) is not reached, the Commission's report shall embody its findings on all questions of fact relevant to the issues between the States Parties concerned, and its views on the possibilities of an amicable solution of the matter. This report shall also contain the written submissions and a record of the oral submissions made by the States Parties concerned.

(d) If the Commission's report is submitted under sub-paragraph (c), the States Parties concerned shall, within three months of the receipt of the report, notify the Chairman of the Committee whether or not they accept the contents of the report of the Commission.

8. The provisions of this article are without prejudice to the responsibilities of the Committee under article 41.

9. The States Parties concerned shall share equally all the expenses of the members of the Commission in accordance with estimates to be provided by the Secretary-General of the United Nations.

10. The Secretary-General of the United Nations shall be empowered to pay the expenses of the members of the Commission, if necessary, before reimbursement by the States Parties concerned, in accordance with paragraph 9 of this article.

ARTICLE 43

The members of the Committee, and of the ad hoc conciliation commissions which may be appointed under article 42, shall be entitled to the facilities, privileges and immunities of experts on mission for the United Nations as laid down in the relevant sections of the Convention on the Privileges and Immunities of the United Nations.

ARTICLE 44

The provisions for the implementation of the present Covenant shall apply without prejudice to the procedures prescribed in the field of human rights by or under the constituent instruments and the conventions of the United Nations and of the specialized agencies and shall not prevent the States Parties to the present Covenant from having recourse to other procedures for settling a dispute in accordance with general or special international agreements in force between them.

ARTICLE 45

The Committee shall submit to the General Assembly of the United Nations through the Economic and Social Council, an annual report on its activities.

PART V

ARTICLE 46

Nothing in the present Covenant shall be interpreted as impairing the provisions of the Charter of the United Nations and of the constitutions of the specialized agencies which define the respective responsibilities of the various organs of the United Nations and of the specialized agencies in regard to the matters dealt with in the present Covenant.

ARTICLE 47

Nothing in the present Covenant shall be interpreted as impairing the inherent right of all peoples to enjoy and utilize fully and freely their natural wealth and resources.

PART VI

ARTICLE 48

1. The present Covenant is open for signature by any State Member of the United Nations or member of any of its specialized agencies, by any State Party to the Statute of the International Court of Justice, and by any other State which has been invited by the General Assembly of the United Nations to become a party to the present Covenant.

2. The present Covenant is subject to ratification. Instruments of ratification shall be deposited with the Secretary-General of the United Nations.

3. The present Covenant shall be open to accession by any State referred to in paragraph 1 of this article.

4. Accession shall be effected by the deposit of an instrument of accession with the Secretary-General of the United Nations.

5. The Secretary-General of the United Nations shall inform all States which have signed this Covenant or acceded to it of the deposit of each instrument of ratification or accession.

ARTICLE 49

1. The present Covenant shall enter into force three months after the date of the deposit with the Secretary-General of the United Nations of the thirty-fifth instrument of ratification or instrument of accession.

2. For each State ratifying the present Covenant or acceding to it after the deposit of the thirty-fifth instrument of ratification or instrument of accession, the present Covenant shall enter into force three months after the date of the deposit of its own instrument of ratification or instrument of accession.

ARTICLE 50

The provisions of the present Covenant shall extend to all parts of federal States without any limitations or exceptions.

ARTICLE 51

1. Any State Party to the present Covenant may propose an amendment and file it with the Secretary-General of the United Nations. The Secretary-General of the United Nations shall thereupon communicate any proposed amendments to the States Parties to the present Covenant with a request that they notify him whether they favour a conference of States Parties for the purpose of considering and voting upon the proposals. In the event that at least one third of the States Parties favours such a conference, the Secretary-General shall convene the conference under the auspices of the United Nations. Any amendment adopted by a majority of the States Parties present and voting at the conference shall be submitted to the General Assembly of the United Nations for approval.

2. Amendments shall come into force when they have been approved by the General Assembly of the United Nations and accepted by a two-thirds majority of the States Parties to the present Covenant in accordance with their respective constitutional processes.

3. When amendments come into force, they shall be binding on those States Parties which have accepted them, other States Parties still being bound by the provisions of the present Covenant and any earlier amendment which they have accepted.

ARTICLE 52

Irrespective of the notifications made under article 48, paragraph 5, the Secretary-General of the United Nations shall inform all States referred to in paragraph 1 of the same article of the following particulars:

(a) Signatures, ratifications and accessions under article 48;

(b) The date of the entry into force of the present Covenant under article 49 and the date of the entry into force of any amendments under article 51.

ARTICLE 53

1. The present Covenant, of which the Chinese, English, French, Russian and Spanish texts are equally authentic, shall be deposited in the archives of the United Nations.

2. The Secretary-General of the United Nations shall transmit certified copies of the present Covenant to all States referred to in article 48.

IN FAITH WHEREOF the undersigned, being duly authorized thereto by their respective Governments, have signed the present Covenant, opened for signature at New York, on the nineteenth day of December, one thousand nine hundred and sixty-six.

5. ILO Convention No. 105 Concerning the Abolition of Forced Labor [1]

Adopted at the 40th session of the General Conference of the International Labor Organization, Geneva, June 25, 1957; Entered into force generally, January 17, 1959; Ratification advised by the Senate, May 14, 1991; Entered into force for the United States, September 25, 1992

The General Conference of the International Labour Organisation,

Having been convened at Geneva by the Governing Body of the International Labour Office, and having met in its fortieth session on 5 June 1957, and

Having considered the question of forced labour, which is the fourth item on the agenda of the session, and

Having noted the provisions of the Forced Labour Convention, 1930, and

Having noted that the Slavery Convention, 1926, provides that all necessary measures shall be taken to prevent compulsory or forced labour from developing into conditions analogous to slavery and that the Supplementary Convention on the Abolition of Slavery, the Slave Trade, and Institutions and Practices Similar to Slavery, 1956, provides for the complete abolition of debt bondage and serfdom, and

Having noted that the Protection of Wages Convention, 1949, provides that wages shall be paid regularly and prohibits methods of payment which deprive the worker of a genuine possibility of terminating his employment, and

Having decided upon the adoption of further proposals with regard to the abolition of certain forms of forced or compulsory labour constituting a violation of the rights of man referred to in the Charter of the United Nations and enunciated by the Universal Declaration of Human Rights, and

Having determined that these proposals shall take the form of an international Convention,

Adopts this twenty-fifth day of June of the year one thousand nine hundred and fifty-seven the following Convention, which may be cited as the Abolition of Forced Labour Convention, 1957:

Article 1

Each Member of the International Labour Organisation which ratifies this Convention undertakes to suppress and not to make use of any form of forced or compulsory labour:

[1] 320 UNTS 291. For a list of states that are parties, see Department of State publication, *Treaties in Force*.

(a) As a means of political coercion or education or as a punishment for holding or expressing political views or views ideologically opposed to the established political, social or economic system;

(b) As a method of mobilising and using labour for purposes of economic development;

(c) As a means of labour discipline;

(d) As a punishment for having participated in strikes;

(e) As a means of racial, social, national or religious discrimination.

ARTICLE 2

Each Member of the International Labour Organisation which ratifies this Convention undertakes to take effective measures to secure the immediate and complete abolition of forced or compulsory labour as specified in article 1 of this Convention.

ARTICLE 3

The formal ratifications of this Convention shall be communicated to the Director-General of the International Labour Office for registration.

ARTICLE 4

1. This Convention shall be binding only upon those Members of the International Labour Organisation whose ratifications have been registered with the Director-General.

2. It shall come into force twelve months after the date on which the ratifications of two Members have been registered with the Director-General.

3. Thereafter, this Convention shall come into force for any Member twelve months after the date on which its ratification has been registered.

ARTICLE 5

1. A Member which has ratified this Convention may denounce it after the expiration of ten years from the date on which the Convention first comes into force, by an act communicated to the Director-General of the International Labour Office for registration. Such denunciation shall not take effect until one year after the date on which it is registered.

2. Each Member which has ratified this Convention and which does not, within the year following the expiration of the period of ten years mentioned in the preceding paragraph, exercise the right of denunciation provided for in this article, will be bound for another period of five years and, thereafter, may denounce this Convention at the expiration of each period of five years under the terms provided for in this article.

ARTICLE 6

1. The Director-General of the International Labour Office shall notify all Members of the International Labour Organisation of the

registration of all ratifications and denunciations communicated to him by the Members of the Organisation.

2. When notifying the Members of the Organisation of the registration of the second ratification communicated to him the Director-General shall draw the attention of the Members of the Organisation to the date upon which the Convention will come into force.

ARTICLE 7

The Director-General of the International Labour Office shall communicate to the Secretary-General of the United Nations for registration in accordance with Article 102 of the Charter of the United Nations full particulars of all ratifications and acts of denunciation registered by him in accordance with the provisions of the preceding articles.

ARTICLE 8

At such times as it may consider necessary the Governing Body of the International Labour Office shall present to the General Conference a report on the working of the Convention and shall examine the desirability of placing on the agenda of the Conference the question of its revision in whole or in part.

1. Should the Conference adopt a new Convention revising this Convention in whole or in part, then, unless the new Convention otherwise provides:

(a) The ratification by a Member of the new revising Convention shall ipso jure involve the immediate denunciation of this Convention, notwithstanding the provisions of article 5 above, if and when the new revising Convention shall have come into force;

(b) As from the date when the new revising Convention comes into force this Convention shall cease to be open to ratification by the Members.

2. This Convention shall in any case remain in force in its actual form and content for those Members which have ratified it but have not ratified the revising Convention.

ARTICLE 10[2]

The English and French versions of the text of this Convention are equally authoritative.

The foregoing is the authentic text of the Convention duly adopted by the General Conference of the International Labour Organisation during its fortieth session which was held at Geneva and declared closed the twenty-seventh day of June 1957.

IN FAITH WHEREOF we have appended our signatures this fourth day of July 1957.

[2] The Convention did not include an Article 9.

6. ILO Convention No. 144 Concerning Tripartite Consultations to Promote the Implementation of International Labor Standards [1]

Adopted at the 61st session of the General Conference of the International Labor Organization, Geneva, June 21, 1976; Entered into force generally, May 16, 1978; Ratification advised by the Senate, February 1, 1988; Entered into force for the United States, June 15, 1989

The General Conference of the International Labour Organisation,

Having been convened at Geneva by the Governing Body of the International Labour Office, and having met in its Sixty-first Session on 2 June 1976, and

Recalling the terms of existing international labour Conventions and Recommendations—in particular the Freedom of Association and Protection of the Right to Organise Convention, 1948, the Right to Organise and Collective Bargaining Convention, 1949, and the Consultation (Industrial and National Levels) Recommendation, 1960—which affirm the right of employers and workers to establish free and independent Organisations and call for measures to promote effective consultation at the national level between public authorities and employers' and workers' Organisations, as well as the provisions of numerous international labour Conventions and Recommendations which provide for the consultation of employers' and workers' Organisations on measures to give effect thereto, and

Having considered the fourth item on the agenda of the session which is entitled "Establishment of tripartite machinery to promote the implementation of international labour standards", and having decided upon the adoption of certain proposals concerning tripartite consultation to promote the implementation of international labour standards, and

Having determined that these proposals shall take the form of an international Convention,

adopts this twenty-first day of June of the year one thousand nine hundred and seventy-six the following Convention, which may be cited as the Tripartite Consultation (International Labour Standards) Convention, 1976:

ARTICLE 1

In this Convention the term representative Organisations means the most representative Organisations of employers and workers enjoying the right of freedom of association.

---

[1] For a list of states that are parties, see Department of State publication, *Treaties in Force.*

ARTICLE 2

1. Each Member of the International Labour Organisation which ratifies this Convention undertakes to operate procedures which ensure effective consultations, with respect to the matters concerning the activities of the International Labour Organisation set out in Article 5, paragraph 1, below, between representatives of the government, of employers and of workers.

2. The nature and form of the procedures provided for in paragraph 1 of this Article shall be determined in each country in accordance with national practice, after consultation with the representative Organisations, where such Organisations exist and such procedures have not yet been established.

ARTICLE 3

1. The representatives of employers and workers for the purposes of the procedures provided for in this Convention shall be freely chosen by their representative Organisations, where such Organisations exist.

2. Employers and workers shall be represented on an equal footing on any bodies through which consultations are undertaken.

ARTICLE 4

1. The competent authority shall assume responsibility for the administrative support of the procedures provided for in this Convention.

2. Appropriate arrangements shall be made between the competent authority and the representative Organisations, where such Organisations exist, for the financing of any necessary training of participants in these procedures.

ARTICLE 5

1. The purpose of the procedures provided for in this Convention shall be consultations on—

(a) government replies to questionnaires concerning items on the agenda of the International Labour Conference and government comments on proposed texts to be discussed by the Conference;

(b) the proposals to be made to the competent authority or authorities in connection with the submission of Conventions and Recommendations pursuant to article 19 of the Constitution of the International Labour Organisation;

(c) the re-examination at appropriate intervals of unratified Conventions and of Recommendations to which effect has not yet been given, to consider what measures might be taken to promote their implementation and ratification as appropriate;

(d) questions arising out of reports to be made to the International Labour Office under Article 22 of the Constitution of the International Labour Organisation;

(e) proposals for the denunciation of ratified Conventions.

2. In order to ensure adequate consideration of the matters referred to in paragraph 1 of this Article, consultation shall be undertaken at appropriate intervals fixed by agreement, but at least once a year.

Article 6

When this is considered appropriate after consultation with the representative Organisations, where such Organisations exist, the competent authority shall issue an annual report on the working of the procedures provided for in this Convention.

Article 7

The formal ratifications of this Convention shall be communicated to the Director-General of the International Labour Office for registration.

Article 8

1. This Convention shall be binding only upon those Members of the International Labour Organisation whose ratifications have been registered with the Director-General.
2. It shall come into force twelve months after the date on which the ratifications of two Members have been registered with the Director-General.
3. Thereafter, this Convention shall come into force for any Member twelve months after the date on which its ratification has been registered.

Article 9

1. A Member which has ratified this Convention may denounce it after the expiration of ten years from the date on which the Convention first comes into force, by an act communicated to the Director-General of the International Labour Office for registration. Such denunciation shall not take effect until one year after the date on which it is registered.
2. Each Member which has ratified this Convention and which does not, within the year following the expiration of the period of ten years mentioned in the preceding paragraph, exercise the right of denunciation provided for in this Article, will be bound for another period of ten years and, thereafter, may denounce this Convention at the expiration of each period of ten years under the terms provided for in this Article.

Article 10

1. The Director-General of the International Labour Office shall notify all Members of the International Labour Organisation of the registration of all ratifications and denunciations communicated to him by the Members of the Organisation.
2. When notifying the Members of the Organisation of the registration of the second ratification communicated to him, the Director-General shall draw the attention of the Members of the Organisation to the date upon which the Convention will come into force.

ARTICLE 11

The Director-General of the International Labour Office shall communicate to the Secretary-General of the United Nations for registration in accordance with Article 102 of the Charter of the United Nations full particulars of all ratifications and acts of denunciation registered by him in accordance with the provisions of the preceding Articles.

ARTICLE 12

At such times as it may consider necessary the Governing Body of the International Labour Office shall present to the General Conference a report on the working of this Convention and shall examine the desirability of placing on the agenda of the Conference the question of its revision in whole or in part.

ARTICLE 13

1. Should the Conference adopt a new Convention revising this Convention in whole or in part, then, unless the new Convention otherwise provides:

(a) the ratification by a Member of the new revising Convention shall ipso jure involve the immediate denunciation of this Convention, notwithstanding the provisions of Article 9 above, if and when the new revising Convention shall have come into force;

(b) as from the date when the new revising Convention comes into force this Convention shall cease to be open to ratification by the Members.

2. This Convention shall in any case remain in force in its actual form and content for those Members which have ratified it but have not ratified the revising Convention.

ARTICLE 14

The English and French versions of the text of this Convention are equally authoritative.

7. ILO Convention Concerning the Prohibition and Immediate Action for the Elimination of the Worst Forms of Child Labour [1]

Adopted at the 87th session of the General Conference of the International Labor Organization, Geneva, June 17, 1999; Ratification advised by the Senate, November 5, 1999; Entered into force generally, November 19, 2000; Entered into force for the United States, December 2, 2000

The General Conference of the International Labour Organization,

Having been convened at Geneva by the Governing Body of the International Labour Office, and having met in its 87th Session on 1 June 1999, and

Considering the need to adopt new instruments for the prohibition and elimination of the worst forms of child labour, as the main priority for national and international action, including international cooperation and assistance, to complement the Convention and the Recommendation concerning Minimum Age for Admission to Employment, 1973, which remain fundamental instruments on child labour, and

Considering that the effective elimination of the worst forms of child labour requires immediate and comprehensive action, taking into account the importance of free basic education and the need to remove the children concerned from all such work and to provide for their rehabilitation and social integration while addressing the needs of their families, and

Recalling the resolution concerning the elimination of child labour adopted by the International Labour Conference at its 83rd Session in 1996, and

Recognizing that child labour is to a great extent caused by poverty and that the long-term solution lies in sustained economic growth leading to social progress, in particular poverty alleviation and universal education, and

Recalling the Convention on the Rights of the Child adopted by the United Nations General Assembly on 20 November 1989, and

Recalling the ILO Declaration on Fundamental Principles and Rights at Work and its Follow-up, adopted by the International Labour Conference at its 86th Session in 1998, and

Recalling that some of the worst forms of child labour are covered by other international instruments, in particular the Forced Labour Convention, 1930, and the United Nations Supplementary Convention on the Abolition of Slavery, the Slave Trade, and Institutions and Practices Similar to Slavery, 1956, and

Having decided upon the adoption of certain proposals with regard to child labour, which is the fourth item on the agenda of the session, and

[1] For a list of states that are parties, see Department of State publication, *Treaties in Force.*

Having determined that these proposals shall take the form of an international Convention;

adopts this seventeenth day of June of the year one thousand nine hundred and ninety-nine the following Convention, which may be cited as the Worst Forms of Child Labour Convention, 1999.

Article 1

Each Member which ratifies this Convention shall take immediate and effective measures to secure the prohibition and elimination of the worst forms of child labour as a matter of urgency.

Article 2

For the purposes of this Convention, the term child shall apply to all persons under the age of 18.

Article 3

For the purposes of this Convention, the term the worst forms of child labour comprises:

(a) all forms of slavery or practices similar to slavery, such as the sale and trafficking of children, debt bondage and serfdom and forced or compulsory labour, including forced or compulsory recruitment of children for use in armed conflict;

(b) the use, procuring or offering of a child for prostitution, for the production of pornography or for pornographic performances;

(c) the use, procuring or offering of a child for illicit activities, in particular for the production and trafficking of drugs as defined in the relevant international treaties;

(d) work which, by its nature or the circumstances in which it is carried out, is likely to harm the health, safety or morals of children.

Article 4

1. The types of work referred to under Article 3(d) shall be determined by national laws or regulations or by the competent authority, after consultation with the organizations of employers and workers concerned, taking into consideration relevant international standards, in particular Paragraphs 3 and 4 of the Worst Forms of Child Labour Recommendation, 1999.

2. The competent authority, after consultation with the organizations of employers and workers concerned, shall identify where the types of work so determined exist.

3. The list of the types of work determined under paragraph 1 of this Article shall be periodically examined and revised as necessary, in consultation with the organizations of employers and workers concerned.

Article 5

Each Member shall, after consultation with employers' and workers' organizations, establish or designate appropriate mechanisms to monitor the implementation of the provisions giving effect to this Convention.

Article 6

1. Each Member shall design and implement programmes of action to eliminate as a priority the worst forms of child labour.

2. Such programmes of action shall be designed and implemented in consultation with relevant government institutions and employers' and workers' organizations, taking into consideration the views of other concerned groups as appropriate.

Article 7

1. Each Member shall take all necessary measures to ensure the effective implementation and enforcement of the provisions giving effect to this Convention including the provision and application of penal sanctions or, as appropriate, other sanctions.

2. Each Member shall, taking into account the importance of education in eliminating child labour, take effective and time-bound measures to:

(a) prevent the engagement of children in the worst forms of child labour;

(b) provide the necessary and appropriate direct assistance for the removal of children from the worst forms of child labour and for their rehabilitation and social integration;

(c) ensure access to free basic education, and, wherever possible and appropriate, vocational training, for all children removed from the worst forms of child labour;

(d) identify and reach out to children at special risk; and

(e) take account of the special situation of girls.

3. Each Member shall designate the competent authority responsible for the implementation of the provisions giving effect to this Convention.

Article 8

Members shall take appropriate steps to assist one another in giving effect to the provisions of this Convention through enhanced international cooperation and/or assistance including support for social and economic development, poverty eradication programmes and universal education.

Article 9

The formal ratifications of this Convention shall be communicated to the Director-General of the International Labour Office for registration.

Article 10

1. This Convention shall be binding only upon those Members of the International Labour Organization whose ratifications have been registered with the Director-General of the International Labour Office.

2. It shall come into force 12 months after the date on which the ratifications of two Members have been registered with the Director-General.

3. Thereafter, this Convention shall come into force for any Member 12 months after the date on which its ratification has been registered.

ARTICLE 11

1. A Member which has ratified this Convention may denounce it after the expiration of ten years from the date on which the Convention first comes into force, by an act communicated to the Director-General of the International Labour Office for registration. Such denunciation shall not take effect until one year after the date on which it is registered.

2. Each Member which has ratified this Convention and which does not, within the year following the expiration of the period of ten years mentioned in the preceding paragraph, exercise the right of denunciation provided for in this Article, will be bound for another period of ten years and, thereafter, may denounce this Convention at the expiration of each period of ten years under the terms provided for in this Article.

ARTICLE 12

1. The Director-General of the International Labour Office shall notify all Members of the International Labour Organization of the registration of all ratifications and acts of denunciation communicated by the Members of the Organization.

2. When notifying the Members of the Organization of the registration of the second ratification, the Director-General shall draw the attention of the Members of the Organization to the date upon which the Convention shall come into force.

ARTICLE 13

The Director-General of the International Labour Office shall communicate to the Secretary-General of the United Nations, for registration in accordance with article 102 of the Charter of the United Nations, full particulars of all ratifications and acts of denunciation registered by the Director-General in accordance with the provisions of the preceding Articles.

ARTICLE 14

At such times as it may consider necessary, the Governing Body of the International Labour Office shall present to the General Conference a report on the working of this Convention and shall examine the desirability of placing on the agenda of the Conference the question of its revision in whole or in part.

ARTICLE 15

1. Should the Conference adopt a new Convention revising this Convention in whole or in part, then, unless the new Convention otherwise provides—

(a) the ratification by a Member of the new revising Convention shall ipso jure involve the immediate denunciation of this Convention, notwithstanding the provisions of Article 11 above, if and when the new revising Convention shall have come into force;

(b) as from the date when the new revising Convention comes into force, this Convention shall cease to be open to ratification by the Members.

2. This Convention shall in any case remain in force in its actual form and content for those Members which have ratified it but have not ratified the revising Convention.

ARTICLE 16

The English and French versions of the text of this Convention are equally authoritative.

8. ILO Convention Concerning Safety and Health in Mines[1]

Adopted at the 82nd session of the General Conference of the International Labor Organization, Geneva, June 22, 1995; Entered into force generally, June 5, 1998; Ratification advised by the Senate, September 20, 2000; Entered into force for the United States, February 9, 2002

The General Conference of the International Labour Organization,

Having been convened at Geneva by the Governing Body of the International Labour Office, and having met in its Eighty-Second Session on 6 June 1995, and

Noting the relevant International Labour Conventions and Recommendations and, in particular, the Abolition of Forced Labour Convention, 1957; the Radiation Protection Convention and Recommendation, 1960; the Guarding of Machinery Convention and Recommendation, 1963; the Employment Injury Benefits Convention and Recommendation, 1964; the Minimum Age (Underground Work) Convention and Recommendation, 1965; the Medical Examination of Young Persons (Underground Work) Convention, 1965; the Working Environment (Air Pollution, Noise and Vibration) Convention and Recommendation, 1977; the Occupational Safety and Health Convention and Recommendation, 1981; the Occupational Health Services Convention and Recommendation, 1985; the Asbestos Convention and Recommendation, 1986; the Safety and Health in Construction Convention and Recommendation, 1988; the Chemicals Convention and Recommendation, 1990; and the Prevention of Major Industrial Accidents Convention and Recommendation, 1993, and

Considering that workers have a need for, and a right to, information, training and genuine consultation on and participation in the preparation and implementation of safety and health measures concerning the hazards and risks they face in the mining industry, and

Recognizing that it is desirable to prevent any fatalities, injuries or ill health affecting workers or members of the public, or damage to the environment arising from mining operations, and

Having regard to the need for cooperation between the International Labour Organization, the World Health Organization, the International Atomic Energy Agency and other relevant institutions and noting the relevant instruments, codes of practice, codes and guidelines issued by these organizations, and

Having decided upon the adoption of certain proposals with regard to safety and health in mines, which is the fourth item on the agenda of the session, and

Having determined that these proposals shall take the form of an international Convention;

---

[1] For a list of states that are parties, see Department of State publication, *Treaties in Force.*

adopts this twenty-second day of June of the year one thousand nine hundred and ninety-five the following Convention, which may be cited as the Safety and Health in Mines Convention, 1995:

Part I. Definitions

ARTICLE 1

1. For the purpose of this Convention, the term mine covers—

(a) surface or underground sites where the following activities, in particular, take place:

(i) exploration for minerals, excluding oil and gas, that involves the mechanical disturbance of the ground;

(ii) extraction of minerals, excluding oil and gas;

(iii) preparation, including crushing, grinding, concentration or washing of the extracted material; and

(b) all machinery, equipment, appliances, plant, buildings and civil engineering structures used in conjunction with the activities referred to in (a) above.

2. For the purpose of this Convention, the term employer means any physical or legal person who employs one or more workers in a mine and, as the context requires, the operator, the principal contractor, contractor or subcontractor.

Part II. Scope and Means of Application

ARTICLE 2

1. This Convention applies to all mines.

2. After consultations with the most representative organizations of employers and workers concerned, the competent authority of a Member which ratifies the Convention:

(a) may exclude certain categories of mines from the application of the Convention, or certain provisions thereof, if the overall protection afforded at these mines under national law and practice is not inferior to that which would result from the full application of the provisions of the Convention;

(b) shall, in the case of exclusion of certain categories of mines pursuant to clause (a) above, make plans for progressively covering all mines.

3. A Member which ratifies the Convention and avails itself of the possibility afforded in paragraph 2(a) above shall indicate, in its reports on the application of the Convention submitted under article 22 of the Constitution of the International Labour Organization, any particular category of mines thus excluded and the reasons for the exclusion.

ARTICLE 3

In the light of national conditions and practice and after consultations with the most representative organizations of employers and workers concerned, the Member shall formulate, carry out and periodically review a coherent policy on safety and health in mines, particularly with regard to the measures to give effect to the provisions of the Convention.

ARTICLE 4

1. The measures for ensuring application of the Convention shall be prescribed by national laws and regulations.

2. Where appropriate, these national laws and regulations shall be supplemented by:

(a) technical standards, guidelines or codes of practice; or

(b) other means of application consistent with national practice, as identified by the competent authority.

ARTICLE 5

1. National laws and regulations pursuant to Article 4, paragraph 1, shall designate the competent authority that is to monitor and regulate the various aspects of safety and health in mines.

2. Such national laws and regulations shall provide for:

(a) the supervision of safety and health in mines;

(b) the inspection of mines by inspectors designated for the purpose by the competent authority;

(c) the procedures for reporting and investigating fatal and serious accidents, dangerous occurrences and mine disasters, each as defined by national laws or regulations;

(d) the compilation and publication of statistics on accidents, occupational diseases and dangerous occurrences, each as defined by national laws or regulations;

(e) the power of the competent authority to suspend or restrict mining activities on safety and health grounds, until the condition giving rise to the suspension or restriction has been corrected; and

(f) the establishment of effective procedures to ensure the implementation of the rights of workers and their representatives to be consulted on matters and to participate in measures relating to safety and health at the workplace.

3. Such national laws and regulations shall provide that the manufacture, storage, transport and use of explosives and initiating devices at the mine shall be carried out by or under the direct supervision of competent and authorized persons.

4. Such national laws and regulations shall specify:

(a) requirements relating to mine rescue, first aid and appropriate medical facilities;

(b) an obligation to provide and maintain adequate self-rescue respiratory devices for workers in underground coal mines and, where necessary, in other underground mines;

(c) protective measures to secure abandoned mine workings so as to eliminate or minimize risks to safety and health;

(d) requirements for the safe storage, transportation and disposal of hazardous substances used in the mining process and waste produced at the mine; and

(e) where appropriate, an obligation to supply sufficient sanitary conveniences and facilities to wash, change and eat, and to maintain them in hygienic condition.

5. Such national laws and regulations shall provide that the employer in charge of the mine shall ensure that appropriate plans of workings are prepared before the start of operation and, in the

event of any significant modification, that such plans are brought up to date periodically and kept available at the mine site.

Part III. Preventive and Protective Measures at the Mine

A. RESPONSIBILITIES OF EMPLOYERS

ARTICLE 6

In taking preventive and protective measures under this Part of the Convention the employer shall assess the risk and deal with it in the following order of priority:

(a) eliminate the risk;

(b) control the risk at source;

(c) minimize the risk by means that include the design of safe work systems; and

(d) in so far as the risk remains, provide for the use of personal protective equipment, having regard to what is reasonable, practicable and feasible, and to good practice and the exercise of due diligence.

ARTICLE 7

Employers shall take all necessary measures to eliminate or minimize the risks to safety and health in mines under their control, and in particular:

(a) ensure that the mine is designed, constructed and provided with electrical, mechanical and other equipment, including a communication system, to provide conditions for safe operation and a healthy working environment;

(b) ensure that the mine is commissioned, operated, maintained and decommissioned in such a way that workers can perform the work assigned to them without endangering their safety and health or that of other persons;

(c) take steps to maintain the stability of the ground in areas to which persons have access in the context of their work;

(d) whenever practicable, provide, from every underground workplace, two exits, each of which is connected to separate means of egress to the surface;

(e) ensure the monitoring, assessment and regular inspection of the working environment to identify the various hazards to which the workers may be exposed and to assess their level of exposure;

(f) ensure adequate ventilation for all underground workings to which access is permitted;

(g) in respect of zones susceptible to particular hazards, draw up and implement an operating plan and procedures to ensure a safe system of work and the protection of workers;

(h) take measures and precautions appropriate to the nature of a mine operation to prevent, detect and combat the start and spread of fires and explosions; and

(i) ensure that when there is serious danger to the safety and health of workers, operations are stopped and workers are evacuated to a safe location.

ARTICLE 8

The employer shall prepare an emergency response plan, specific to each mine, for reasonably foreseeable industrial and natural disasters.

ARTICLE 9

Where workers are exposed to physical, chemical or biological hazards the employer shall:

(a) inform the workers, in a comprehensible manner, of the hazards associated with their work, the health risks involved and relevant preventive and protective measures;

(b) take appropriate measures to eliminate or minimize the risks resulting from exposure to those hazards;

(c) where adequate protection against risk of accident or injury to health including exposure to adverse conditions cannot be ensured by other means, provide and maintain at no cost to the worker suitable protective equipment, clothing as necessary and other facilities defined by national laws or regulations; and

(d) provide workers who have suffered from an injury or illness at the workplace with first aid, appropriate transportation from the workplace and access to appropriate medical facilities.

ARTICLE 10

The employer shall ensure that:

(a) adequate training and retraining programmes and comprehensible instructions are provided for workers, at no cost to them, on safety and health matters as well as on the work assigned;

(b) in accordance with national laws and regulations, adequate supervision and control are provided on each shift to secure the safe operation of the mine;

(c) a system is established so that the names of all persons who are underground can be accurately known at any time, as well as their probable location;

(d) all accidents and dangerous occurrences, as defined by national laws or regulations, are investigated and appropriate remedial action is taken; and

(e) a report, as specified by national laws and regulations, is made to the competent authority on accidents and dangerous occurrences.

ARTICLE 11

On the basis of general principles of occupational health and in accordance with national laws and regulations, the employer shall ensure the provision of regular health surveillance of workers exposed to occupational health hazards specific to mining.

ARTICLE 12

Whenever two or more employers undertake activities at the same mine, the employer in charge of the mine shall coordinate the implementation of all measures concerning the safety and health of workers and shall be held primarily responsible for the safety of the operations. This shall not relieve individual employers from responsibility for the implementation of all measures concerning the safety and health of their workers.

B. RIGHTS AND DUTIES OF WORKERS AND THEIR REPRESENTATIVES

ARTICLE 13

1. Under the national laws and regulations referred to in Article 4, workers shall have the following rights:

(a) to report accidents, dangerous occurrences and hazards to the employer and to the competent authority;

(b) to request and obtain, where there is cause for concern on safety and health grounds, inspections and investigations to be conducted by the employer and the competent authority;

(c) to know and be informed of workplace hazards that may affect their safety or health;

(d) to obtain information relevant to their safety or health, held by the employer or the competent authority;

(e) to remove themselves from any location at the mine when circumstances arise which appear, with reasonable justification, to pose a serious danger to their safety or health; and

(f) to collectively select safety and health representatives.

2. The safety and health representatives referred to in paragraph 1(f) above shall, in accordance with national laws and regulations, have the following rights:

(a) to represent workers on all aspects of workplace safety and health, including where applicable, the exercise of the rights provided in paragraph 1 above;

(b) to:

(i) participate in inspections and investigations conducted by the employer and by the competent authority at the workplace; and

(ii) monitor and investigate safety and health matters;

(c) to have recourse to advisers and independent experts;

(d) to consult with the employer in a timely fashion on safety and health matters, including policies and procedures;

(e) to consult with the competent authority; and

(f) to receive, relevant to the area for which they have been selected, notice of accidents and dangerous occurrences.

3. Procedures for the exercise of the rights referred to in paragraphs 1 and 2 above shall be specified:

(a) by national laws and regulations; and

(b) through consultations between employers and workers and their representatives.

4. National laws and regulations shall ensure that the rights referred to in paragraphs 1 and 2 above can be exercised without discrimination or retaliation.

ARTICLE 14

Under national laws and regulations, workers shall have the duty, in accordance with their training:

(a) to comply with prescribed safety and health measures;

(b) to take reasonable care for their own safety and health and that of other persons who may be affected by their acts or omissions at work, including the proper care and use of protective clothing, facilities and equipment placed at their disposal for this purpose;

(c) to report forthwith to their immediate supervisor any situation which they believe could present a risk to their safety or health or that of other persons, and which they cannot properly deal with themselves; and

(d) to cooperate with the employer to permit compliance with the duties and responsibilities placed on the employer pursuant to the Convention.

C. COOPERATION

ARTICLE 15

Measures shall be taken, in accordance with national laws and regulations, to encourage cooperation between employers and workers and their representatives to promote safety and health in mines.

PART IV. IMPLEMENTATION

ARTICLE 16

The Member shall:

(a) take all necessary measures, including the provision of appropriate penalties and corrective measures, to ensure the effective enforcement of the provisions of the Convention; and

(b) provide appropriate inspection services to supervise the application of the measures to be taken in pursuance of the Convention and provide these services with the resources necessary for the accomplishment of their tasks.

PART V. FINAL PROVISIONS

ARTICLE 17

The formal ratifications of this Convention shall be communicated to the Director-General of the International Labour Office for registration.

ARTICLE 18

1. This Convention shall be binding only upon those Members of the International Labour Organization whose ratifications have been registered with the Director-General of the International Labour Office.

2. It shall come into force 12 months after the date on which the ratifications of two Members have been registered with the Director-General.

3. Thereafter, this Convention shall come into force for any Member 12 months after the date on which its ratification has been registered.

ARTICLE 19

1. A Member which has ratified this Convention may denounce it after the expiration of ten years from the date on which the Convention first comes into force, by an act communicated to the Director-General of the International Labour Office for registration. Such denunciation shall not take effect until one year after the date on which it is registered.

2. Each Member which has ratified this Convention and which does not, within the year following the expiration of the period of ten years mentioned in the preceding paragraph, exercise the right of denunciation provided for in this Article, will be bound for another period of ten years and, thereafter, may denounce this Convention at the expiration of each period of ten years under the terms provided for in this Article.

ARTICLE 20

1. The Director-General of the International Labour Office shall notify all Members of the International Labour Organization of the registration of all ratifications and denunciations communicated by the Members of the Organization.

2. When notifying the Members of the Organization of the registration of the second ratification, the Director-General shall draw the attention of the Members of the Organization to the date upon which the Convention shall come into force.

ARTICLE 21

The Director-General of the International Labour Office shall communicate to the Secretary-General of the United Nations, for registration in accordance with article 102 of the Charter of the United Nations, full particulars of all ratifications and acts of denunciation registered by the Director-General in accordance with the provisions of the preceding Articles.

ARTICLE 22

At such times as it may consider necessary, the Governing Body of the International Labour Office shall present to the General Conference a report on the working of this Convention and shall examine the desirability of placing on the agenda of the Conference the question of its revision in whole or in part.

ARTICLE 23

1. Should the Conference adopt a new Convention revising this Convention in whole or in part, then, unless the new Convention otherwise provides—

(a) the ratification by a Member of the new revising Convention shall ipso jure involve the immediate denunciation of this Convention, notwithstanding the provisions of Article 19 above, if and when the new revising Convention shall have come into force;

(b) as from the date when the new revising Convention comes into force, this Convention shall cease to be open to ratification by the Members.

2. This Convention shall in any case remain in force in its actual form and content for those Members which have ratified it but have not ratified the revising Convention.

ARTICLE 24

The English and French versions of the text of this Convention are equally authoritative.

9. Optional Protocols to the Convention on the Rights of the Child

a. Optional Protocol to the Convention on the Rights of the Child on the Involvement of Children in Armed Conflict[1]

Adopted at New York, May 25, 2000; Entered into force generally, February 12, 2002; Ratification advised by the Senate, June 18, 2002; Entered into force for the United States, January 23, 2003

The States Parties to the present Protocol,

ENCOURAGED by the overwhelming support for the Convention on the Rights of the Child, demonstrating the widespread commitment that exists to strive for the promotion and protection of the rights of the child,

REAFFIRMING that the rights of children require special protection, and calling for continuous improvement of the situation of children without distinction, as well as for their development and education in conditions of peace and security,

DISTURBED by the harmful and widespread impact of armed conflict on children and the long-term consequences it has for durable peace, security and development,

CONDEMNING the targeting of children in situations of armed conflict and direct attacks on objects protected under international law, including places that generally have a significant presence of children, such as schools and hospitals,

NOTING the adoption of the Rome Statute of the International Criminal Court, in particular, the inclusion therein as a war crime, of conscripting or enlisting children under the age of 15 years or using them to participate actively in hostilities in both international and non-international armed conflicts,

CONSIDERING therefore that to strengthen further the implementation of rights recognized in the Convention on the Rights of the Child there is a need to increase the protection of children from involvement in armed conflict,

NOTING that article 1 of the Convention on the Rights of the Child specifies that, for the purposes of that Convention, a child means every human being below the age of 18 years unless, under the law applicable to the child, majority is attained earlier,

CONVINCED that an optional protocol to the Convention that raises the age of possible recruitment of persons into armed forces and their participation in hostilities will contribute effectively to the implementation of the principle that the best interests of the child are to be a primary consideration in all actions concerning children,

[1] For a list of states that are parties, see Department of State publication, *Treaties in Force.*

NOTING that the twenty-sixth International Conference of the Red Cross and Red Crescent in December 1995 recommended, inter alia, that parties to conflict take every feasible step to ensure that children below the age of 18 years do not take part in hostilities,

WELCOMING the unanimous adoption, in June 1999, of International Labour Organization Convention No. 182 on the Prohibition and Immediate Action for the Elimination of the Worst Forms of Child Labour, which prohibits, inter alia, forced or compulsory recruitment of children for use in armed conflict,

CONDEMNING with the gravest concern the recruitment, training and use within and across national borders of children in hostilities by armed groups distinct from the armed forces of a State, and recognizing the responsibility of those who recruit, train and use children in this regard,

RECALLING the obligation of each party to an armed conflict to abide by the provisions of international humanitarian law,

STRESSING that the present Protocol is without prejudice to the purposes and principles contained in the Charter of the United Nations, including Article 51, and relevant norms of humanitarian law,

BEARING IN MIND that conditions of peace and security based on full respect of the purposes and principles contained in the Charter and observance of applicable human rights instruments are indispensable for the full protection of children, in particular during armed conflicts and foreign occupation,

RECOGNIZING the special needs of those children who are particularly vulnerable to recruitment or use in hostilities contrary to the present Protocol owing to their economic or social status or gender,

MINDFUL of the necessity of taking into consideration the economic, social and political root causes of the involvement of children in armed conflicts,

CONVINCED of the need to strengthen international cooperation in the implementation of the present Protocol, as well as the physical and psychosocial rehabilitation and social reintegration of children who are victims of armed conflict,

ENCOURAGING the participation of the community and, in particular, children and child victims in the dissemination of informational and educational programmes concerning the implementation of the Protocol,

HAVE AGREED AS FOLLOWS:

ARTICLE 1

States Parties shall take all feasible measures to ensure that members of their armed forces who have not attained the age of 18 years do not take a direct part in hostilities.

ARTICLE 2

States Parties shall ensure that persons who have not attained the age of 18 years are not compulsorily recruited into their armed forces.

ARTICLE 3

1. States Parties shall raise in years the minimum age for the voluntary recruitment of persons into their national armed forces from that set out in article 38, paragraph 3, of the Convention on the Rights of the Child, taking account of the principles contained in that article and recognizing that under the Convention persons under the age of 18 years are entitled to special protection.

2. Each State Party shall deposit a binding declaration upon ratification of or accession to the present Protocol that sets forth the minimum age at which it will permit voluntary recruitment into its national armed forces and a description of the safeguards it has adopted to ensure that such recruitment is not forced or coerced.

3. States Parties that permit voluntary recruitment into their national armed forces under the age of 18 years shall maintain safeguards to ensure, as a minimum, that:

(a) Such recruitment is genuinely voluntary;

(b) Such recruitment is carried out with the informed consent of the person's parents or legal guardians;

(c) Such persons are fully informed of the duties involved in such military service;

(d) Such persons provide reliable proof of age prior to acceptance into national military service.

4. Each State Party may strengthen its declaration at any time by notification to that effect addressed to the Secretary-General of the United Nations, who shall inform all States Parties. Such notification shall take effect on the date on which it is received by the Secretary-General.

5. The requirement to raise the age in paragraph 1 of the present article does not apply to schools operated by or under the control of the armed forces of the States Parties, in keeping with articles 28 and 29 of the Convention on the Rights of the Child.

ARTICLE 4

1. Armed groups that are distinct from the armed forces of a State should not, under any circumstances, recruit or use in hostilities persons under the age of 18 years.

2. States Parties shall take all feasible measures to prevent such recruitment and use, including the adoption of legal measures necessary to prohibit and criminalize such practices.

3. The application of the present article shall not affect the legal status of any party to an armed conflict.

ARTICLE 5

Nothing in the present Protocol shall be construed as precluding provisions in the law of a State Party or in international instruments and international humanitarian law that are more conducive to the realization of the rights of the child.

ARTICLE 6

1. Each State Party shall take all necessary legal, administrative and other measures to ensure the effective implementation and enforcement of the provisions of the present Protocol within its jurisdiction.

2. States Parties undertake to make the principles and provisions of the present Protocol widely known and promoted by appropriate means, to adults and children alike.

3. States Parties shall take all feasible measures to ensure that persons within their jurisdiction recruited or used in hostilities contrary to the present Protocol are demobilized or otherwise released from service. States Parties shall, when necessary, accord to such persons all appropriate assistance for their physical and psychological recovery and their social reintegration.

ARTICLE 7

1. States Parties shall cooperate in the implementation of the present Protocol, including in the prevention of any activity contrary thereto and in the rehabilitation and social reintegration of persons who are victims of acts contrary thereto, including through technical cooperation and financial assistance. Such assistance and cooperation will be undertaken in consultation with the States Parties concerned and the relevant international organizations.

2. States Parties in a position to do so shall provide such assistance through existing multilateral, bilateral or other programmes or, inter alia, through a voluntary fund established in accordance with the rules of the General Assembly.

ARTICLE 8

1. Each State Party shall, within two years following the entry into force of the present Protocol for that State Party, submit a report to the Committee on the Rights of the Child providing comprehensive information on the measures it has taken to implement the provisions of the Protocol, including the measures taken to implement the provisions on participation and recruitment.

2. Following the submission of the comprehensive report, each State Party shall include in the reports it submits to the Committee on the Rights of the Child, in accordance with article 44 of the Convention, any further information with respect to the implementation of the Protocol. Other States Parties to the Protocol shall submit a report every five years.

3. The Committee on the Rights of the Child may request from States Parties further information relevant to the implementation of the present Protocol.

ARTICLE 9

1. The present Protocol is open for signature by any State that is a party to the Convention or has signed it.

2. The present Protocol is subject to ratification and is open to accession by any State. Instruments of ratification or accession shall be deposited with the Secretary-General of the United Nations.

3. The Secretary-General, in his capacity as depositary of the Convention and the Protocol, shall inform all States Parties to the Convention and all States that have signed the Convention of each instrument of declaration pursuant to article 3.

Article 10

1. The present Protocol shall enter into force three months after the deposit of the tenth instrument of ratification or accession.

2. For each State ratifying the present Protocol or acceding to it after its entry into force, the Protocol shall enter into force one month after the date of the deposit of its own instrument of ratification or accession.

Article 11

1. Any State Party may denounce the present Protocol at any time by written notification to the Secretary-General of the United Nations, who shall thereafter inform the other States Parties to the Convention and all States that have signed the Convention. The denunciation shall take effect one year after the date of receipt of the notification by the Secretary-General. If, however, on the expiry of that year the denouncing State Party is engaged in armed conflict, the denunciation shall not take effect before the end of the armed conflict.

2. Such a denunciation shall not have the effect of releasing the State Party from its obligations under the present Protocol in regard to any act that occurs prior to the date on which the denunciation becomes effective. Nor shall such a denunciation prejudice in any way the continued consideration of any matter that is already under consideration by the Committee on the Rights of the Child prior to the date on which the denunciation becomes effective.

Article 12

1. Any State Party may propose an amendment and file it with the Secretary-General of the United Nations. The Secretary-General shall thereupon communicate the proposed amendment to States Parties with a request that they indicate whether they favour a conference of States Parties for the purpose of considering and voting upon the proposals. In the event that, within four months from the date of such communication, at least one third of the States Parties favour such a conference, the Secretary-General shall convene the conference under the auspices of the United Nations. Any amendment adopted by a majority of States Parties present and voting at the conference shall be submitted to the General Assembly of the United Nations for approval.

2. An amendment adopted in accordance with paragraph 1 of the present article shall enter into force when it has been approved by the General Assembly and accepted by a two-thirds majority of States Parties.

3. When an amendment enters into force, it shall be binding on those States Parties that have accepted it, other States Parties still being bound by the provisions of the present Protocol and any earlier amendments they have accepted.

Article 13

1. The present Protocol, of which the Arabic, Chinese, English, French, Russian and Spanish texts are equally authentic, shall be deposited in the archives of the United Nations.

2. The Secretary-General of the United Nations shall transmit certified copies of the present Protocol to all States Parties to the Convention and all States that have signed the Convention.

b. Optional Protocol to the Convention on the Rights of the Child on the Sale of Children, Child Prostitution, and Child Pornography [1]

Adopted at New York, May 25, 2000; Entered into force generally, January 18, 2002; Ratification advised by the Senate, June 18, 2002; Entered into force for the United States, January 23, 2003

The States Parties to the present Protocol,

CONSIDERING that, in order further to achieve the purposes of the Convention on the Rights of the Child and the implementation of its provisions, especially articles 1, 11, 21, 32, 33, 34, 35 and 36, it would be appropriate to extend the measures that States Parties should undertake in order to guarantee the protection of the child from the sale of children, child prostitution and child pornography,

CONSIDERING also that the Convention on the Rights of the Child recognizes the right of the child to be protected from economic exploitation and from performing any work that is likely to be hazardous or to interfere with the child's education, or to be harmful to the child's health or physical, mental, spiritual, moral or social development,

GRAVELY CONCERNED at the significant and increasing international traffic in children for the purpose of the sale of children, child prostitution and child pornography,

DEEPLY CONCERNED at the widespread and continuing practice of sex tourism, to which children are especially vulnerable, as it directly promotes the sale of children, child prostitution and child pornography,

RECOGNIZING that a number of particularly vulnerable groups, including girl children, are at greater risk of sexual exploitation and that girl children are disproportionately represented among the sexually exploited,

CONCERNED about the growing availability of child pornography on the Internet and other evolving technologies, and recalling the International Conference on Combating Child Pornography on the Internet, held in Vienna in 1999, in particular its conclusion calling for the worldwide criminalization of the production, distribution, exportation, transmission, importation, intentional possession and advertising of child pornography, and stressing the importance of closer cooperation and partnership between Governments and the Internet industry,

BELIEVING that the elimination of the sale of children, child prostitution and child pornography will be facilitated by adopting a holistic approach, addressing the contributing factors, including underdevelopment, poverty, economic disparities, inequitable socio-economic structure, dysfunctioning families, lack of education,

---

[1] For a list of states that are parties, see Department of State publication, *Treaties in Force.*

urban-rural migration, gender discrimination, irresponsible adult sexual behaviour, harmful traditional practices, armed conflicts and trafficking in children,

BELIEVING also that efforts to raise public awareness are needed to reduce consumer demand for the sale of children, child prostitution and child pornography, and believing further in the importance of strengthening global partnership among all actors and of improving law enforcement at the national level,

NOTING the provisions of international legal instruments relevant to the protection of children, including the Hague Convention on Protection of Children and Cooperation in Respect of Intercountry Adoption, the Hague Convention on the Civil Aspects of International Child Abduction, the Hague Convention on Jurisdiction, Applicable Law, Recognition, Enforcement and Cooperation in Respect of Parental Responsibility and Measures for the Protection of Children, and International Labour Organization Convention No. 182 on the Prohibition and Immediate Action for the Elimination of the Worst Forms of Child Labour,

ENCOURAGED by the overwhelming support for the Convention on the Rights of the Child, demonstrating the widespread commitment that exists for the promotion and protection of the rights of the child,

RECOGNIZING the importance of the implementation of the provisions of the Programme of Action for the Prevention of the Sale of Children, Child Prostitution and Child Pornography and the Declaration and Agenda for Action adopted at the World Congress against Commercial Sexual Exploitation of Children, held in Stockholm from 27 to 31 August 1996, and the other relevant decisions and recommendations of pertinent international bodies,

TAKING due account of the importance of the traditions and cultural values of each people for the protection and harmonious development of the child,

HAVE AGREED AS FOLLOWS:

ARTICLE 1

States Parties shall prohibit the sale of children, child prostitution and child pornography as provided for by the present Protocol.

ARTICLE 2

For the purposes of the present Protocol:

(a) Sale of children means any act or transaction whereby a child is transferred by any person or group of persons to another for remuneration or any other consideration;

(b) Child prostitution means the use of a child in sexual activities for remuneration or any other form of consideration;

(c) Child pornography means any representation, by whatever means, of a child engaged in real or simulated explicit sexual activities or any representation of the sexual parts of a child for primarily sexual purposes.

ARTICLE 3

1. Each State Party shall ensure that, as a minimum, the following acts and activities are fully covered under its criminal or penal law, whether such offences are committed domestically or transnationally or on an individual or organized basis:

(a) In the context of sale of children as defined in article 2:

(i) Offering, delivering or accepting, by whatever means, a child for the purpose of:

a. Sexual exploitation of the child;

b. Transfer of organs of the child for profit;

c. Engagement of the child in forced labour;

(ii) Improperly inducing consent, as an intermediary, for the adoption of a child in violation of applicable international legal instruments on adoption;

(b) Offering, obtaining, procuring or providing a child for child prostitution, as defined in article 2;

(c) Producing, distributing, disseminating, importing, exporting, offering, selling or possessing for the above purposes child pornography as defined in article 2.

2. Subject to the provisions of the national law of a State Party, the same shall apply to an attempt to commit any of the said acts and to complicity or participation in any of the said acts.

3. Each State Party shall make such offences punishable by appropriate penalties that take into account their grave nature.

4. Subject to the provisions of its national law, each State Party shall take measures, where appropriate, to establish the liability of legal persons for offences established in paragraph 1 of the present article. Subject to the legal principles of the State Party, such liability of legal persons may be criminal, civil or administrative.

5. States Parties shall take all appropriate legal and administrative measures to ensure that all persons involved in the adoption of a child act in conformity with applicable international legal instruments.

ARTICLE 4

1. Each State Party shall take such measures as may be necessary to establish its jurisdiction over the offences referred to in article 3, paragraph 1, when the offences are commited in its territory or on board a ship or aircraft registered in that State.

2. Each State Party may take such measures as may be necessary to establish its jurisdiction over the offences referred to in article 3, paragraph 1, in the following cases:

(a) When the alleged offender is a national of that State or a person who has his habitual residence in its territory;

(b) When the victim is a national of that State.

3. Each State Party shall also take such measures as may be necessary to establish its jurisdiction over the aforementioned offences when the alleged offender is present in its territory and it does not extradite him or her to another State Party on the ground that the offence has been committed by one of its nationals.

4. The present Protocol does not exclude any criminal jurisdiction exercised in accordance with internal law.

ARTICLE 5

1. The offences referred to in article 3, paragraph 1, shall be deemed to be included as extraditable offences in any extradition treaty existing between States Parties and shall be included as extraditable offences in every extradition treaty subsequently concluded between them, in accordance with the conditions set forth in such treaties.

2. If a State Party that makes extradition conditional on the existence of a treaty receives a request for extradition from another State Party with which it has no extradition treaty, it may consider the present Protocol to be a legal basis for extradition in respect of such offences. Extradition shall be subject to the conditions provided by the law of the requested State.

3. States Parties that do not make extradition conditional on the existence of a treaty shall recognize such offences as extraditable offences between themselves subject to the conditions provided by the law of the requested State.

4. Such offences shall be treated, for the purpose of extradition between States Parties, as if they had been committed not only in the place in which they occurred but also in the territories of the States required to establish their jurisdiction in accordance with article 4.

5. If an extradition request is made with respect to an offence described in article 3, paragraph 1, and the requested State Party does not or will not extradite on the basis of the nationality of the offender, that State shall take suitable measures to submit the case to its competent authorities for the purpose of prosecution.

ARTICLE 6

1. States Parties shall afford one another the greatest measure of assistance in connection with investigations or criminal or extradition proceedings brought in respect of the offences set forth in article 3, paragraph 1, including assistance in obtaining evidence at their disposal necessary for the proceedings.

2. States Parties shall carry out their obligations under paragraph 1 of the present article in conformity with any treaties or other arrangements on mutual legal assistance that may exist between them. In the absence of such treaties or arrangements, States Parties shall afford one another assistance in accordance with their domestic law.

ARTICLE 7

States Parties shall, subject to the provisions of their national law:

(a) Take measures to provide for the seizure and confiscation, as appropriate, of:

(i) Goods, such as materials, assets and other instrumentalities used to commit or facilitate offences under the present protocol;

(ii) Proceeds derived from such offences;

(b) Execute requests from another State Party for seizure or confiscation of goods or proceeds referred to in subparagraph (a);

(c) Take measures aimed at closing, on a temporary or definitive basis, premises used to commit such offences.

ARTICLE 8

1. States Parties shall adopt appropriate measures to protect the rights and interests of child victims of the practices prohibited under the present Protocol at all stages of the criminal justice process, in particular by:

(a) Recognizing the vulnerability of child victims and adapting procedures to recognize their special needs, including their special needs as witnesses;

(b) Informing child victims of their rights, their role and the scope, timing and progress of the proceedings and of the disposition of their cases;

(c) Allowing the views, needs and concerns of child victims to be presented and considered in proceedings where their personal interests are affected, in a manner consistent with the procedural rules of national law;

(d) Providing appropriate support services to child victims throughout the legal process;

(e) Protecting, as appropriate, the privacy and identity of child victims and taking measures in accordance with national law to avoid the inappropriate dissemination of information that could lead to the identification of child victims;

(f) Providing, in appropriate cases, for the safety of child victims, as well as that of their families and witnesses on their behalf, from intimidation and retaliation;

(g) Avoiding unnecessary delay in the disposition of cases and the execution of orders or decrees granting compensation to child victims.

2. States Parties shall ensure that uncertainty as to the actual age of the victim shall not prevent the initiation of criminal investigations, including investigations aimed at establishing the age of the victim.

3. States Parties shall ensure that, in the treatment by the criminal justice system of children who are victims of the offences described in the present Protocol, the best interest of the child shall be a primary consideration.

4. States Parties shall take measures to ensure appropriate training, in particular legal and psychological training, for the persons who work with victims of the offences prohibited under the present Protocol.

5. States Parties shall, in appropriate cases, adopt measures in order to protect the safety and integrity of those persons and/or organizations involved in the prevention and/or protection and rehabilitation of victims of such offences.

6. Nothing in the present article shall be construed to be prejudicial to or inconsistent with the rights of the accused to a fair and impartial trial.

ARTICLE 9

1. States Parties shall adopt or strengthen, implement and disseminate laws, administrative measures, social policies and programmes to prevent the offences referred to in the present Protocol. Particular attention shall be given to protect children who are especially vulnerable to such practices.

2. States Parties shall promote awareness in the public at large, including children, through information by all appropriate means, education and training, about the preventive measures and harmful effects of the offences referred to in the present Protocol. In fulfilling their obligations under this article, States Parties shall encourage the participation of the community and, in particular, children and child victims, in such information and education and training programmes, including at the international level.

3. States Parties shall take all feasible measures with the aim of ensuring all appropriate assistance to victims of such offences, including their full social reintegration and their full physical and psychological recovery.

4. States Parties shall ensure that all child victims of the offences described in the present Protocol have access to adequate procedures to seek, without discrimination, compensation for damages from those legally responsible.

5. States Parties shall take appropriate measures aimed at effectively prohibiting the production and dissemination of material advertising the offences described in the present Protocol.

ARTICLE 10

1. States Parties shall take all necessary steps to strengthen international cooperation by multilateral, regional and bilateral arrangements for the prevention, detection, investigation, prosecution and punishment of those responsible for acts involving the sale of children, child prostitution, child pornography and child sex tourism. States Parties shall also promote international cooperation and coordination between their authorities, national and international non-governmental organizations and international organizations.

2. States Parties shall promote international cooperation to assist child victims in their physical and psychological recovery, social reintegration and repatriation.

3. States Parties shall promote the strengthening of international cooperation in order to address the root causes, such as poverty and underdevelopment, contributing to the vulnerability of children to the sale of children, child prostitution, child pornography and child sex tourism.

4. States Parties in a position to do so shall provide financial, technical or other assistance through existing multilateral, regional, bilateral or other programmes.

ARTICLE 11

Nothing in the present Protocol shall affect any provisions that are more conducive to the realization of the rights of the child and that may be contained in:

(a) The law of a State Party;

(b) International law in force for that State.

Article 12

1. Each State Party shall, within two years following the entry into force of the present Protocol for that State Party, submit a report to the Committee on the Rights of the Child providing comprehensive information on the measures it has taken to implement the provisions of the Protocol.

2. Following the submission of the comprehensive report, each State Party shall include in the reports they submit to the Committee on the Rights of the Child, in accordance with article 44 of the Convention, any further information with respect to the implementation of the present Protocol. Other States Parties to the Protocol shall submit a report every five years.

3. The Committee on the Rights of the Child may request from States Parties further information relevant to the implementation of the present Protocol.

Article 13

1. The present Protocol is open for signature by any State that is a party to the Convention or has signed it.

2. The present Protocol is subject to ratification and is open to accession by any State that is a party to the Convention or has signed it. Instruments of ratification or accession shall be deposited with the Secretary-General of the United Nations.

Article 14

1. The present Protocol shall enter into force three months after the deposit of the tenth instrument of ratification or accession.

2. For each State ratifying the present Protocol or acceding to it after its entry into force, the Protocol shall enter into force one month after the date of the deposit of its own instrument of ratification or accession.

Article 15

1. Any State Party may denounce the present Protocol at any time by written notification to the Secretary-General of the United Nations, who shall thereafter inform the other States Parties to the Convention and all States that have signed the Convention. The denunciation shall take effect one year after the date of receipt of the notification by the Secretary-General.

2. Such a denunciation shall not have the effect of releasing the State Party from its obligations under the present Protocol in regard to any offence that occurs prior to the date on which the denunciation becomes effective. Nor shall such a denunciation prejudice in any way the continued consideration of any matter that is already under consideration by the Committee on the Rights of the Child prior to the date on which the denunciation becomes effective.

ARTICLE 16

1. Any State Party may propose an amendment and file it with the Secretary-General of the United Nations. The Secretary-General shall thereupon communicate the proposed amendment to States Parties with a request that they indicate whether they favour a conference of States Parties for the purpose of considering and voting upon the proposals. In the event that, within four months from the date of such communication, at least one third of the States Parties favour such a conference, the Secretary-General shall convene the conference under the auspices of the United Nations. Any amendment adopted by a majority of States Parties present and voting at the conference shall be submitted to the General Assembly of the United Nations for approval.

2. An amendment adopted in accordance with paragraph 1 of the present article shall enter into force when it has been approved by the General Assembly and accepted by a two-thirds majority of States Parties.

3. When an amendment enters into force, it shall be binding on those States Parties that have accepted it, other States Parties still being bound by the provisions of the present Protocol and any earlier amendments they have accepted.

ARTICLE 17

1. The present Protocol, of which the Arabic, Chinese, English, French, Russian and Spanish texts are equally authentic, shall be deposited in the archives of the United Nations.

2. The Secretary-General of the United Nations shall transmit certified copies of the present Protocol to all States Parties to the Convention and all States that have signed the Convention.

K. FINANCIAL INSTITUTIONS

CONTENTS

1. International Monetary Fund

a. Articles of Agreement (amended)

CONTENTS

SCHEDULES

1. International Monetary Fund

a. Articles of Agreement [1] (amended)

Articles of agreement between the United States and other powers respecting the International Monetary Fund

Formulated at the United Nations Monetary and Financial Conference, Bretton Woods, New Hampshire, July 1 to July 22, 1944; Signed at Washington, December 27, 1945; Instrument of acceptance by the United States deposited, December 20, 1945, Effective December 27, 1945; Amended May 31, 1968,[2] April 30, 1976,[3] and June 28, 1990 [4]

The Governments on whose behalf the present Agreement is signed agree as follows:

INTRODUCTORY ARTICLE

(i) The International Monetary Fund is established and shall operate in accordance with the provisions of this Agreement as originally adopted and subsequently amended.

(ii) To enable the Fund to conduct its operations and transactions, the Fund shall maintain a General Department and a Special Drawing Rights Department. Membership in the Fund shall give the right to participation in the Special Drawing Rights Department.

(iii) Operations and transactions authorized by this Agreement shall be conducted through the General Department, consisting in accordance with the provisions of this Agreement of the General Resources Account, the Special Disbursement Account, and the Investment Account; except that operations and transactions involving special drawing rights shall be conducted through the Special Drawing Rights Department.

ARTICLE I—PURPOSES

The purposes of the International Monetary Fund are:

(i) To promote international monetary cooperation through a permanent institution which provides the machinery for consultation and collaboration on international monetary problems.

(ii) To facilitate the expansion and balanced growth of international trade, and to contribute thereby to the promotion and maintenance of high levels of employment and real income and to the development of the productive resources of all members as primary objectives of economic policy.

---

[1] 60 Stat. 1401; TIAS 1501; 3 Bevans 1351; 2 UNTS 39. For a list of states that are parties to the Fund, see Department of State publication, *Treaties in Force*.

[2] Entered into force July 28, 1969. 20 UST 2775; TIAS 6748.

[3] Entered into force April 1, 1978. 29 UST 2203; TIAS 8937.

[4] Entered into force November 11, 1992. TIAS 11898.

(iii) To promote exchange stability, to maintain orderly exchange arrangements among members, and to avoid competitive exchange depreciation.

(iv) To assist in the establishment of a multilateral system of payments in respect of current transactions between members and in the elimination of foreign exchange restrictions which hamper the growth of world trade.

(v) To give confidence to members by making the general resources of the Fund temporarily available to them under adequate safeguards, thus providing them with opportunity to correct maladjustments in their balance of payments without resorting to measures destructive of national or international prosperity.

(vi) In accordance with the above, to shorten the duration and lessen the degree of disequilibrium in the international balances of payments of members.

The Fund shall be guided in all its policies and decisions by the purposes set forth in this Article.

ARTICLE II—MEMBERSHIP

SECTION 1. ORIGINAL MEMBERS

The original members of the Fund shall be those of the countries represented at the United Nations Monetary and Financial Conference whose governments accept membership before December 31, 1945.

SECTION 2. OTHER MEMBERS

Membership shall be open to other countries at such times and in accordance with such terms as may be prescribed by the Board of Governors. These terms, including the terms for subscriptions, shall be based on principles consistent with those applied to other countries that are already members.

ARTICLE III—QUOTAS AND SUBSCRIPTIONS

SECTION 1. QUOTAS AND PAYMENT OF SUBSCRIPTIONS

Each member shall be assigned a quota expressed in special drawing rights. The quotas of the members represented at the United Nations Monetary and Financial Conference which accept membership before December 31, 1945 shall be those set forth in Schedule A. The quotas of other members shall be determined by the Board of Governors. The subscription of each member shall be equal to its quota and shall be paid in full to the Fund at the appropriate depository.

SECTION 2. ADJUSTMENT OF QUOTAS

(a) The Board of Governors shall at intervals of not more than five years conduct a general review, and if it deems it appropriate propose an adjustment, of the quotas of the members. It may also, if it thinks fit, consider at any other time the adjustment of any particular quota at the request of the member concerned.

(b) The Fund may at any time propose an increase in the quotas of those members of the Fund that were members on August 31, 1975 in proportion to their quotas on that date in a cumulative amount not in excess of amounts transferred under Article V, Section 12(f)(i) and (j) from the Special Disbursement Account to the General Resources Account.

(c) An eighty-five percent majority of the total voting power shall be required for any change in quotas.

(d) The quota of a member shall not be changed until the member has consented and until payment has been made unless payment is deemed to have been made in accordance with Section 3(b) of this Article.

SECTION 3. PAYMENTS WHEN QUOTAS ARE CHANGED

(a) Each member which consents to an increase in its quota under Section 2(a) of this Article shall, within a period determined by the Fund, pay to the Fund twenty-five percent of the increase in special drawing rights, but the Board of Governors may prescribe that this payment may be made, on the same basis for all members, in whole or in part in the currencies of other members specified, with their concurrence, by the Fund, or in the member's own currency. A non-participant shall pay in the currencies of other members specified by the Fund, with their concurrence, a proportion of the increase corresponding to the proportion to be paid in special drawing rights by participants. The balance of the increase shall be paid by the member in its own currency. The Fund's holdings of a member's currency shall not be increased above the level at which they would be subject to charges under Article V, Section 8(b)(ii), as a result of payments by other members under this provision.

(b) Each member which consents to an increase in its quota under Section 2(b) of this Article shall be deemed to have paid to the Fund an amount of subscription equal to such increase.

(c) If a member consents to a reduction in its quota, the Fund shall, within sixty days, pay to the member an amount equal to the reduction. The payment shall be made in the member's currency and in such amount of special drawing rights or the currencies of other members specified, with their concurrence, by the Fund as is necessary to prevent the reduction of the Fund's holdings of the currency below the new quota, provided that in exceptional circumstances the Fund may reduce its holdings of the currency below the new quota by payment to the member in its own currency.

(d) A seventy percent majority of the total voting power shall be required for any decision under (a) above, except for the determination of a period and the specification of currencies under that provision.

SECTION 4. SUBSTITUTION OF SECURITIES FOR CURRENCY

The Fund shall accept from any member, in place of any part of the member's currency in the General Resources Account which in the judgment of the Fund is not needed for its operations and transactions, notes or similar obligations issued by the member or the depository designated by the member under Article XIII, Section 2, which shall be non-negotiable, non-interest bearing and payable at their face value on demand by crediting the account of the Fund in the designated depository. This Section shall apply not only to currency subscribed by members but also to any currency otherwise due to, or acquired by, the Fund and to be placed in the General Resources Account.

ARTICLE IV—OBLIGATIONS REGARDING EXCHANGE ARRANGEMENTS

SECTION 1. GENERAL OBLIGATIONS OF MEMBERS

Recognizing that the essential purpose of the international monetary system is to provide a framework that facilitates the exchange of goods, services, and capital among countries, and that sustains sound economic growth, and that a principal objective is the continuing development of the orderly underlying conditions that are necessary for financial and economic stability, each member undertakes to collaborate with the Fund and other members to assure orderly exchange arrangements and to promote a stable system of exchange rates. In particular, each member shall:

(i) endeavor to direct its economic and financial policies toward the objective of fostering orderly economic growth with reasonable price stability, with due regard to its circumstances;

(ii) seek to promote stability by fostering orderly underlying economic and financial conditions and a monetary system that does not tend to produce erratic disruptions;

(iii) avoid manipulating exchange rates or the international monetary system in order to prevent effective balance of payments adjustment or to gain an unfair competitive advantage over other members; and

(iv) follow exchange policies compatible with the undertakings under this Section.

SECTION 2. GENERAL EXCHANGE ARRANGEMENTS

(a) Each member shall notify the Fund, within thirty days after the date of the second amendment of this Agreement, of the exchange arrangements it intends to apply in fulfillment of its obligations under Section 1 of this Article, and shall notify the Fund promptly of any changes in its exchange arrangements.

(b) Under an international monetary system of the kind prevailing on January 1, 1976, exchange arrangements may include (i) the maintenance by a member of a value for its currency in terms of the special drawing right or another denominator, other than gold, selected by the member, or (ii) cooperative arrangements by which members maintain the value of their currencies in relation to the value of the currency or currencies of other members, or (iii) other exchange arrangements of a member's choice.

(c) To accord with the development of the international monetary system, the Fund, by an eighty-five percent majority of the total voting power, may make provision for general exchange arrangements without limiting the right of members to have exchange arrangements of their choice consistent with the purposes of the Fund and the obligations under Section 1 of this Article.

SECTION 3. SURVEILLANCE OVER EXCHANGE ARRANGEMENTS

(a) The Fund shall oversee the international monetary system in order to ensure its effective operation, and shall oversee the compliance of each member with its obligations under Section 1 of this Article.

(b) In order to fulfill its functions under (a) above, the Fund shall exercise firm surveillance over the exchange rate policies of members, and shall adopt specific principles for the guidance of all members with respect to those policies. Each member shall provide the Fund with the information necessary for such surveillance, and, when requested by the Fund, shall consult with it on the member's exchange rate policies. The principles adopted by the Fund shall be consistent with cooperative arrangements by which members maintain the value of their currencies in relation to the value of the currency or currencies of other members, as well as with other exchange arrangements of a member's choice consistent with the purposes of the Fund and Section 1 of this Article. These principles shall respect the domestic social and political policies of members, and in applying these principles the Fund shall pay due regard to the circumstances of members.

SECTION 4. PAR VALUES

The Fund may determine, by an eighty-five percent majority of the total voting power, that international economic conditions permit the introduction of a widespread system of exchange arrangements based on stable but adjustable par values. The Fund shall make the determination on the basis of the underlying stability of the world economy, and for this purpose shall take into account price movements and rates of expansion in the economies of members. The determination shall be made in light of the evolution of the international monetary system, with particular reference to sources of liquidity, and, in order to ensure the effective operation of a system of par values, to arrangements under which both members in surplus and members in deficit in their balances of payments take prompt, effective, and symmetrical action to achieve adjustment, as well as to arrangements for intervention and the treatment of imbalances. Upon making such determination, the Fund shall notify members that the provisions of Schedule C apply.

SECTION 5. SEPARATE CURRENCIES WITHIN A MEMBER'S TERRITORIES

(a) Action by a member with respect to its currency under this Article shall be deemed to apply to the separate currencies of all territories in respect of which the member has accepted this Agreement under Article XXXI, Section 2(g) unless the member declares that its action relates either to the metropolitan currency alone, or only to one or more specified separate currencies, or to the metropolitan currency and one or more specified separate currencies.

(b) Action by the Fund under this Article shall be deemed to relate to all currencies of a member referred to in (a) above unless the Fund declares otherwise.

Article V—Operations and Transactions of the Fund

SECTION 1. AGENCIES DEALING WITH THE FUND

Each member shall deal with the Fund only through its Treasury, central bank, stabilization fund, or other similar fiscal agency, and the Fund shall deal only with or through the same agencies.

SECTION 2. LIMITATION ON THE FUND'S OPERATIONS AND TRANSACTIONS

(a) Except as otherwise provided in this Agreement, transactions on the account of the Fund shall be limited to transactions for the purpose of supplying a member, on the initiative of such member, with special drawing rights or the currencies of other members from the general resources of the Fund, which shall be held in the General Resources Account, in exchange for the currency of the member desiring to make the purchase.

(b) If requested, the Fund may decide to perform financial and technical services, including the administration of resources contributed by members, that are consistent with the purposes of the Fund. Operations involved in the performance of such financial services shall not be on the account of the Fund. Services under this subsection shall not impose any obligation on a member without its consent.

SECTION 3. CONDITIONS GOVERNING USE OF THE FUND'S GENERAL RESOURCES

(a) The Fund shall adopt policies on the use of its general resources, including policies on stand-by or similar arrangements, and may adopt special policies for special balance of payments problems, that will assist members to solve their balance of payments problems in a manner consistent with the provisions of this Agreement and that will establish adequate safeguards for the temporary use of the general resources of the Fund.

(b) A member shall be entitled to purchase the currencies of other members from the Fund in exchange for an equivalent amount of its own currency subject to the following conditions:

(i) the member's use of the general resources of the Fund would be in accordance with the provisions of this Agreement and the policies adopted under them;

(ii) the member represents that it has a need to make the purchase because of its balance of payments or its reserve position or developments in its reserves;

(iii) the proposed purchase would be a reserve tranche purchase, or would not cause the Fund's holdings of the purchasing member's currency to exceed two hundred percent of its quota;

(iv) the Fund has not previously declared under Section 5 of this Article, Article VI, Section 1, or Article XXVI, Section 2(a) that the member desiring to purchase is ineligible to use the general resources of the Fund.

(c) The Fund shall examine a request for a purchase to determine whether the proposed purchase would be consistent with the provisions of this Agreement and the policies adopted under them, provided that requests for reserve tranche purchases shall not be subject to challenge.

(d) The Fund shall adopt policies and procedures on the selection of currencies to be sold that take into account, in consultation with members, the balance of payments and reserve position of members and developments in the exchange markets, as well as the desirability of promoting over time balanced positions in the Fund, provided that if a member represents that it is proposing to purchase the currency of another member because the purchasing member wishes to obtain an equivalent amount of its own currency offered by the other member, it shall be entitled to purchase the currency of the other member unless the Fund has given notice under Article VII, Section 3 that its holdings of the currency have become scarce.

(e)(i) Each member shall ensure that balances of its currency purchased from the Fund are balances of a freely usable currency or can be exchanged at the time of purchase for a freely usable currency of its choice at an exchange rate between the two currencies equivalent to the exchange rate between them on the basis of Article XIX, Section 7(a).

(ii) Each member whose currency is purchased from the Fund or is obtained in exchange for currency purchased from the Fund shall collaborate with the Fund and other members to enable such balances of its currency to be exchanged, at the time of purchase, for the freely usable currencies of other members.

(iii) An exchange under (i) above of a currency that is not freely usable shall be made by the member whose currency is purchased unless that member and the purchasing member agree on another procedure.

(iv) A member purchasing from the Fund the freely usable currency of another member and wishing to exchange it at the time of purchase for another freely usable currency shall make the exchange with the other member if requested by that member. The exchange shall be made for a freely usable currency selected by the other member at the rate of exchange referred to in (i) above.

(f) Under policies and procedures which it shall adopt, the Fund may agree to provide a participant making a purchase in accordance with this Section with special drawing rights instead of the currencies of other members.

SECTION 4. WAIVER OF CONDITIONS

The Fund may in its discretion, and on terms which safeguard its interests, waive any of the conditions prescribed in Section 3(b)(iii) and (iv) of this Article, especially in the case of members with a record of avoiding large or continuous use of the Fund's general resources. In making a waiver it shall take into consideration periodic or exceptional requirements of the member requesting the waiver. The Fund shall also take into consideration a member's willingness to pledge as collateral security acceptable assets having a value sufficient in the opinion of the Fund to protect its interests and may require as a condition of waiver the pledge of such collateral security.

SECTION 5. INELIGIBILITY TO USE THE FUND'S GENERAL RESOURCES

Whenever the Fund is of the opinion that any member is using the general resources of the Fund in a manner contrary to the purposes of the Fund, it shall present to the member a report setting forth the views of the Fund and prescribing a suitable time for reply. After presenting such a report to a member, the Fund may limit the use of its general resources by the member. If no reply to the report is received from the member within the prescribed time, or if the reply received is unsatisfactory, the Fund may continue to limit the member's use of the general resources of the Fund or may, after giving reasonable notice to the member, declare it ineligible to use the general resources of the Fund.

SECTION 6. OTHER PURCHASES AND SALES OF SPECIAL DRAWING RIGHTS BY THE FUND

(a) The Fund may accept special drawing rights offered by a participant in exchange for an equivalent amount of the currencies of other members.

(b) The Fund may provide a participant, at its request, with special drawing rights for an equivalent amount of the currencies of other members. The Fund's holdings of a member's currency shall not be increased as a result of these transactions above the level at which the holdings would be subject to charges under Section 8(b)(ii) of this Article.

(c) The currencies provided or accepted by the Fund under this Section shall be selected in accordance with policies that take into account the principles of Section 3(d) or 7(i) of this Article. The Fund may enter into transactions under this Section only if a member whose currency is provided or accepted by the Fund concurs in that use of its currency.

SECTION 7. REPURCHASE BY A MEMBER OF ITS CURRENCY HELD BY THE FUND

(a) A member shall be entitled to repurchase at any time the Fund's holdings of its currency that are subject to charges under Section 8(b) of this Article.

(b) A member that has made a purchase under Section 3 of this Article will be expected normally, as its balance of payments and reserve position improves, to repurchase the Fund's holdings of its currency that result from the purchase and are subject to charges under Section 8(b) of this Article. A member shall repurchase these holdings if, in accordance with policies on repurchase that the Fund shall adopt and after consultation with the member, the Fund represents to the member that it should repurchase because of an improvement in its balance of payments and reserve position.

(c) A member that has made a purchase under Section 3 of this Article shall repurchase the Fund's holdings of its currency that result from the purchase and are subject to charges under Section 8(b) of this Article not later than five years after the date on which the purchase was made. The Fund may prescribe that repurchase shall be made by a member in installments during the period beginning three years and ending five years after the date of a purchase. The Fund, by an eighty-five percent majority of the total voting power, may change the periods for repurchase under this subsection, and any period so adopted shall apply to all members.

(d) The Fund, by an eighty-five percent majority of the total voting power, may adopt periods other than those that apply in accordance with (c) above, which shall be the same for all members, for the repurchase of holdings of currency acquired by the Fund pursuant to a special policy on the use of its general resources.

(e) A member shall repurchase, in accordance with policies that the Fund shall adopt by a seventy percent majority of the total voting power, the Fund's holdings of its currency that are not acquired as a result of purchases and are subject to charges under Section 8(b)(ii) of this Article.

(f) A decision prescribing that under a policy on the use of the general resources of the Fund the period for repurchase under (c) or (d) above shall be shorter than the one in effect under the policy shall apply only to holdings acquired by the Fund subsequent to the effective date of the decision.

(g) The Fund, on the request of a member, may postpone the date of discharge of a repurchase obligation, but not beyond the maximum period under (c) or (d) above or under policies adopted by the Fund under (e) above, unless the Fund determines, by a seventy percent majority of the total voting power, that a longer period for repurchase which is consistent with the temporary use of the general resources of the Fund is justified because discharge on the due date would result in exceptional hardship for the member.

(h) The Fund's policies under Section 3(d) of this Article may be supplemented by policies under which the Fund may decide after consultation with a member to sell under Section 3(b) of this Article its holdings of the member's currency that have not been repurchased in accordance with this Section 7, without prejudice to any action that the Fund may be authorized to take under any other provision of this Agreement.

(i) All repurchases under this Section shall be made with special drawing rights or with the currencies of other members specified by the Fund. The Fund shall adopt policies and procedures with regard to the currencies to be used by members in making repurchases that take into account the principles in Section 3(d) of this Article. The Fund's holdings of a member's currency that is used in repurchase shall not be increased by the repurchase above the level at which they would be subject to charges under Section 8(b)(ii) of this Article.

(j)(i) If a member's currency specified by the Fund under (i) above is not a freely usable currency, the member shall ensure that the repurchasing member can obtain it at the time of the repurchase in exchange for a freely usable currency selected by the member whose currency has been specified. An exchange of currency under this provision shall take place at an exchange rate between the two currencies equivalent to the exchange rate between them on the basis of Article XIX, Section 7(a).

(ii) Each member whose currency is specified by the Fund for repurchase shall collaborate with the Fund and other members to enable repurchasing members, at the time of the repurchase, to obtain the specified currency in exchange for the freely usable currencies of other members.

(iii) An exchange under (j)(i) above shall be made with the member whose currency is specified unless that member and the repurchasing member agree on another procedure.

(iv) If a repurchasing member wishes to obtain, at the time of the repurchase, the freely usable currency of another member specified by the Fund under (i) above, it shall, if requested by the other member, obtain the currency from the other member in exchange for a freely usable currency at the rate of exchange referred to in (j)(i) above. The Fund may adopt regulations on the freely usable currency to be provided in an exchange.

SECTION 8. CHARGES

(a)(i) The Fund shall levy a service charge on the purchase by a member of special drawing rights or the currency of another member held in the General Resources Account in exchange for its own currency, provided that the Fund may levy a lower service charge on reserve tranche purchases than on other purchases. The service charge on reserve tranche purchases shall not exceed one-half of one percent.

(ii) The Fund may levy a charge for stand-by or similar arrangements. The Fund may decide that the charge for an arrangement shall be offset against the service charge levied under (i) above on purchases under the arrangement.

(b) The Fund shall levy charges on its average daily balances of a member's currency held in the General Resources Account to the extent that they

(i) have been acquired under a policy that has been the subject of an exclusion under Article XXX(c), or

(ii) exceed the amount of the member's quota after excluding any balances referred to in (i) above.

The rates of charge normally shall rise at intervals during the period in which the balances are held.

(c) If a member fails to make a repurchase required under Section 7 of this Article, the Fund, after consultation with the member on the reduction of the Fund's holdings of its currency, may impose such charges as the Fund deems appropriate on its holdings of the member's currency that should have been repurchased.

(d) A seventy percent majority of the total voting power shall be required for the determination of the rates of charge under (a) and (b) above, which shall be uniform for all members, and under (c) above.

(e) A member shall pay all charges in special drawing rights, provided that in exceptional circumstances the Fund may permit a member to pay charges in the currencies of other members specified by the Fund, after consultation with them, or in its own currency. The Fund's holdings of a member's currency shall not be increased as a result of payments by other members under this provision above the level at which they would be subject to charges under (b)(ii) above.

SECTION 9. REMUNERATION

(a) The Fund shall pay remuneration on the amount by which the percentage of quota prescribed under (b) or (c) below exceeds the Fund's average daily balances of a member's currency held in the General Resources Account other than balances acquired under a policy that has been the subject of an exclusion under Article XXX(c). The rate of remuneration, which shall be determined by the Fund by a seventy percent majority of the total voting power, shall be the same for all members and shall be not more than, nor less than four-fifths of, the rate of interest under Article XX, Section 3. In establishing the rate of remuneration, the Fund shall take into account the rates of charge under Article V, Section 8(b).

(b) The percentage of quota applying for the purposes of (a) above shall be:

(i) for each member that became a member before the second amendment of this Agreement, a percentage of quota corresponding to seventy-five percent of its quota on the date of the second amendment of this Agreement, and for each member that became a member after the date of the second amendment of this Agreement, a percentage of quota calculated by dividing the total of the amounts corresponding to the percentages of quota that apply to the other members on the date on which the member became a member by the total of the quotas of the other members on the same date; plus

(ii) the amounts it has paid to the Fund in currency or special drawing rights under Article III, Section 3(a) since the date applicable under (b)(i) above; and minus

(iii) the amounts it has received from the Fund in currency or special drawing rights under Article III, Section 3(c) since the date applicable under (b)(i) above.

(c) The Fund, by a seventy percent majority of the total voting power, may raise the latest percentage of quota applying for the purposes of (a) above to each member to:

(i) a percentage, not in excess of one hundred percent, that shall be determined for each member on the basis of the same criteria for all members, or

(ii) one hundred percent for all members.

(d) Remuneration shall be paid in special drawing rights, provided that either the Fund or the member may decide that the payment to the member shall be made in its own currency.

SECTION 10. COMPUTATIONS

(a) The value of the Fund's assets held in the accounts of the General Department shall be expressed in terms of the special drawing right.

(b) All computations relating to currencies of members for the purpose of applying the provisions of this Agreement, except Article IV and Schedule C, shall be at the rates at which the Fund accounts for these currencies in accordance with Section 11 of this Article.

(c) Computations for the determination of amounts of currency in relation to quota for the purpose of applying the provisions of this

Agreement shall not include currency held in the Special Disbursement Account or in the Investment Account.

SECTION 11. MAINTENANCE OF VALUE

(a) The value of the currencies of members held in the General Resources Account shall be maintained in terms of the special drawing right in accordance with exchange rates under Article XIX, Section 7(a).

(b) An adjustment in the Fund's holdings of a member's currency pursuant to this Section shall be made on the occasion of the use of that currency in an operation or transaction between the Fund and another member and at such other times as the Fund may decide or the member may request. Payments to or by the Fund in respect of an adjustment shall be made within a reasonable time, as determined by the Fund, after the date of adjustment, and at any other time requested by the member.

SECTION 12. OTHER OPERATIONS AND TRANSACTIONS

(a) The Fund shall be guided in all its policies and decisions under this Section by the objectives set forth in Article VIII, Section 7 and by the objective of avoiding the management of the price, or the establishment of a fixed price, in the gold market.

(b) Decisions of the Fund to engage in operations or transactions under (c), (d), and (e) below shall be made by an eighty-five percent majority of the total voting power.

(c) The Fund may sell gold for the currency of any member after consulting the member for whose currency the gold is sold, provided that the Fund's holdings of a member's currency held in the General Resources Account shall not be increased by the sale above the level at which they would be subject to charges under Section 8(b)(ii) of this Article without the concurrence of the member, and provided that, at the request of the member, the Fund at the time of sale shall exchange for the currency of another member such part of the currency received as would prevent such an increase. The exchange of a currency for the currency of another member shall be made after consultation with that member, and shall not increase the Fund's holdings of that member's currency above the level at which they would be subject to charges under Section 8(b)(ii) of this Article. The Fund shall adopt policies and procedures with regard to exchanges that take into account the principles applied under Section 7(i) of this Article. Sales under this provision to a member shall be at a price agreed for each transaction on the basis of prices in the market.

(d) The Fund may accept payments from a member in gold instead of special drawing rights or currency in any operations or transactions under this Agreement. Payments to the Fund under this provision shall be at a price agreed for each operation or transaction on the basis of prices in the market.

(e) The Fund may sell gold held by it on the date of the second amendment of this Agreement to those members that were members on August 31, 1975 and that agree to buy it, in proportion to their quotas on that date. If the Fund intends to sell gold under

(c) above for the purpose of (f)(ii) below, it may sell to each developing member that agrees to buy it that portion of the gold which, if sold under (c) above, would have produced the excess that could have been distributed to it under (f)(iii) below. The gold that would be sold under this provision to a member that has been declared ineligible to use the general resources of the Fund under Section 5 of this Article shall be sold to it when the ineligibility ceases, unless the Fund decides to make the sale sooner. The sale of gold to a member under this subsection (e) shall be made in exchange for its currency and at a price equivalent at the time of sale to one special drawing right per 0.888 671 gram of fine gold.

(f) Whenever under (c) above the Fund sells gold held by it on the date of the second amendment of this Agreement, an amount of the proceeds equivalent at the time of sale to one special drawing right per 0.888 671 gram of fine gold shall be placed in the General Resources Account and, except as the Fund may decide otherwise under (g) below, any excess shall be held in the Special Disbursement Account. The assets held in the Special Disbursement Account shall be held separately from the other accounts of the General Department, and may be used at any time:

(i) to make transfers to the General Resources Account for immediate use in operations and transactions authorized by provisions of this Agreement other than this Section;

(ii) for operations and transactions that are not authorized by other provisions of this Agreement but are consistent with the purposes of the Fund. Under this subsection (f)(ii) balance of payments assistance may be made available on special terms to developing members in difficult circumstances, and for this purpose the Fund shall take into account the level of per capita income;

(iii) for distribution to those developing members that were members on August 31, 1975, in proportion to their quotas on that date, of such part of the assets that the Fund decides to use for the purposes of (ii) above as corresponds to the proportion of the quotas of these members on the date of distribution to the total of the quotas of all members on the same date, provided that the distribution under this provision to a member that has been declared ineligible to use the general resources of the Fund under Section 5 of this Article shall be made when the ineligibility ceases, unless the Fund decides to make the distribution sooner.

Decisions to use assets pursuant to (i) above shall be taken by a seventy percent majority of the total voting power, and decisions pursuant to (ii) and (iii) above shall be taken by an eighty-five percent majority of the total voting power.

(g) The Fund may decide, by an eighty-five percent majority of the total voting power, to transfer a part of the excess referred to in (f) above to the Investment Account for use pursuant to the provisions of Article XII, Section 6(f).

(h) Pending uses specified under (f) above, the Fund may invest a member's currency held in the Special Disbursement Account in marketable obligations of that member or in marketable obligations of international financial organizations. The income of investment and interest received under (f)(ii) above shall be placed in the Special Disbursement Account. No investment shall be made without the concurrence of the member whose currency is used to make the investment. The Fund shall invest only in obligations denominated in special drawing rights or in the currency used for investment.

(i) The General Resources Account shall be reimbursed from time to time in respect of the expenses of administration of the Special Disbursement Account paid from the General Resources Account by transfers from the Special Disbursement Account on the basis of a reasonable estimate of such expenses.

(j) The Special Disbursement Account shall be terminated in the event of the liquidation of the Fund and may be terminated prior to liquidation of the Fund by a seventy percent majority of the total voting power. Upon termination of the account because of the liquidation of the Fund, any assets in this account shall be distributed in accordance with the provisions of Schedule K. Upon termination prior to liquidation of the Fund, any assets in this account shall be transferred to the General Resources Account for immediate use in operations and transactions. The Fund, by a seventy percent majority of the total voting power, shall adopt rules and regulations for the administration of the Special Disbursement Account.

ARTICLE VI—CAPITAL TRANSFERS

SECTION 1. USE OF THE FUND'S GENERAL RESOURCES FOR CAPITAL TRANSFERS

(a) A member may not use the Fund's general resources to meet a large or sustained outflow of capital except as provided in Section 2 of this Article, and the Fund may request a member to exercise controls to prevent such use of the general resources of the Fund. If, after receiving such a request, a member fails to exercise appropriate controls, the Fund may declare the member ineligible to use the general resources of the Fund.

(b) Nothing in this Section shall be deemed:

(i) to prevent the use of the general resources of the Fund for capital transactions of reasonable amount required for the expansion of exports or in the ordinary course of trade, banking, or other business; or

(ii) to affect capital movements which are met out of a member's own resources, but members undertake that such capital movements will be in accordance with the purposes of the Fund.

SECTION 2. SPECIAL PROVISIONS FOR CAPITAL TRANSFERS

A member shall be entitled to make reserve tranche purchases to meet capital transfers.

SECTION 3. CONTROLS OF CAPITAL TRANSFERS

Members may exercise such controls as are necessary to regulate international capital movements, but no member may exercise these controls in a manner which will restrict payments for current transactions or which will unduly delay transfers of funds in settlement of commitments, except as provided in Article VII, Section 3(b) and in Article XIV, Section 2.

Article VII—Replenishment and Scarce Currencies

Section 1. Measures to replenish the Fund's holdings of scarce currencies

The Fund may, if it deems such action appropriate to replenish its holdings of any member's currency in the General Resources Account needed in connection with its transactions, take either or both of the following steps:

(i) propose to the member that, on terms and conditions agreed between the Fund and the member, the latter lend its currency to the Fund or that, with the concurrence of the member, the Fund borrow such currency from some other source either within or outside the territories of the member, but no member shall be under any obligation to make such loans to the Fund or to concur in the borrowing of its currency by the Fund from any other source;

(ii) require the member, if it is a participant, to sell its currency to the Fund for special drawing rights held in the General Resources Account, subject to Article XIX, Section 4. In replenishing with special drawing rights, the Fund shall pay due regard to the principles of designation under Article XIX, Section 5.

Section 2. General scarcity of currency

If the Fund finds that a general scarcity of a particular currency is developing, the Fund may so inform members and may issue a report setting forth the causes of the scarcity and containing recommendations designed to bring it to an end. A representative of the member whose currency is involved shall participate in the preparation of the report.

Section 3. Scarcity of the Fund's holdings

(a) If it becomes evident to the Fund that the demand for a member's currency seriously threatens the Fund's ability to supply that currency, the Fund, whether or not it has issued a report under Section 2 of this Article, shall formally declare such currency scarce and shall thenceforth apportion its existing and accruing supply of the scarce currency with due regard to the relative needs of members, the general international economic situation, and any other pertinent considerations. The Fund shall also issue a report concerning its action.

(b) A formal declaration under (a) above shall operate as an authorization to any member, after consultation with the Fund, temporarily to impose limitations on the freedom of exchange operations in the scarce currency. Subject to the provisions of Article IV and Schedule C, the member shall have complete jurisdiction in determining the nature of such limitations, but they shall be no more restrictive than is necessary to limit the demand for the scarce currency to the supply held by, or accruing to, the member in question, and they shall be relaxed and removed as rapidly as conditions permit.

(c) The authorization under (b) above shall expire whenever the Fund formally declares the currency in question to be no longer scarce.

SECTION 4. ADMINISTRATION OF RESTRICTIONS

Any member imposing restrictions in respect of the currency of any other member pursuant to the provisions of Section 3(b) of this Article shall give sympathetic consideration to any representations by the other member regarding the administration of such restrictions.

SECTION 5. EFFECT OF OTHER INTERNATIONAL AGREEMENTS ON RESTRICTIONS

Members agree not to invoke the obligations of any engagements entered into with other members prior to this Agreement in such manner as will prevent the operation of the provisions of this Article.

ARTICLE VIII—GENERAL OBLIGATIONS OF MEMBERS

SECTION 1. INTRODUCTION

In addition to the obligations assumed under other articles of this Agreement, each member undertakes the obligations set out in this Article.

SECTION 2. AVOIDANCE OF RESTRICTIONS ON CURRENT PAYMENTS

(a) Subject to the provisions of Article VII, Section 3(b) and Article XIV, Section 2, no member shall, without the approval of the Fund, impose restrictions on the making of payments and transfers for current international transactions.

(b) Exchange contracts which involve the currency of any member and which are contrary to the exchange control regulations of that member maintained or imposed consistently with this Agreement shall be unenforceable in the territories of any member. In addition, members may, by mutual accord, cooperate in measures for the purpose of making the exchange control regulations of either member more effective, provided that such measures and regulations are consistent with this Agreement.

SECTION 3. AVOIDANCE OF DISCRIMINATORY CURRENCY PRACTICES

No member shall engage in, or permit any of its fiscal agencies referred to in Article V, Section 1 to engage in, any discriminatory currency arrangements or multiple currency practices, whether within or outside margins under Article IV or prescribed by or under Schedule C, except as authorized under this Agreement or approved by the Fund. If such arrangements and practices are engaged in at the date when this Agreement enters into force, the member concerned shall consult with the Fund as to their progressive removal unless they are maintained or imposed under Article XIV, Section 2, in which case the provisions of Section 3 of that Article shall apply.

SECTION 4. CONVERTIBILITY OF FOREIGN-HELD BALANCES

(a) Each member shall buy balances of its currency held by another member if the latter, in requesting the purchase, represents:

(i) that the balances to be bought have been recently acquired as a result of current transactions; or

(ii) that their conversion is needed for making payments for current transactions.

The buying member shall have the option to pay either in special drawing rights, subject to Article XIX, Section 4, or in the currency of the member making the request.

(b) The obligation in (a) above shall not apply when:

(i) the convertibility of the balances has been restricted consistently with Section 2 of this Article or Article VI, Section 3;

(ii) the balances have accumulated as a result of transactions effected before the removal by a member of restrictions maintained or imposed under Article XIV, Section 2;

(iii) the balances have been acquired contrary to the exchange regulations of the member which is asked to buy them;

(iv) the currency of the member requesting the purchase has been declared scarce under Article VII, Section 3(a); or

(v) the member requested to make the purchase is for any reason not entitled to buy currencies of other members from the Fund for its own currency.

SECTION 5. FURNISHING OF INFORMATION

(a) The Fund may require members to furnish it with such information as it deems necessary for its activities, including, as the minimum necessary for the effective discharge of the Fund's duties, national data on the following matters:

(i) official holdings at home and abroad of (1) gold, (2) foreign exchange;

(ii) holdings at home and abroad by banking and financial agencies, other than official agencies, of (1) gold, (2) foreign exchange;

(iii) production of gold;

(iv) gold exports and imports according to countries of destination and origin;

(v) total exports and imports of merchandise, in terms of local currency values, according to countries of destination and origin;

(vi) international balance of payments, including (1) trade in goods and services, (2) gold transactions, (3) known capital transactions, and (4) other items;

(vii) international investment position, i.e., investments within the territories of the member owned abroad and investments abroad owned by persons in its territories so far as it is possible to furnish this information;

(viii) national income;

(ix) price indices, i.e., indices of commodity prices in wholesale and retail markets and of export and import prices;

(x) buying and selling rates for foreign currencies;

(xi) exchange controls, i.e., a comprehensive statement of exchange controls in effect at the time of assuming membership in the Fund and details of subsequent changes as they occur; and

(xii) where official clearing arrangements exist, details of amounts awaiting clearance in respect of commercial and financial transactions, and of the length of time during which such arrears have been outstanding.

(b) In requesting information the Fund shall take into consideration the varying ability of members to furnish the data requested. Members shall be under no obligation to furnish information in such detail that the affairs of individuals or corporations are disclosed. Members undertake, however, to furnish the desired information in as detailed and accurate a manner as is practicable and, so far as possible, to avoid mere estimates.

(c) The Fund may arrange to obtain further information by agreement with members. It shall act as a centre for the collection and exchange of information on monetary and financial problems, thus facilitating the preparation of studies designed to assist members in developing policies which further the purposes of the Fund.

SECTION 6. CONSULTATION BETWEEN MEMBERS REGARDING EXISTING INTERNATIONAL AGREEMENTS

Where under this Agreement a member is authorized in the special or temporary circumstances specified in the Agreement to maintain or establish restrictions on exchange transactions, and there are other engagements between members entered into prior to this Agreement which conflict with the application of such restrictions, the parties to such engagements shall consult with one another with a view to making such mutually acceptable adjustments as may be necessary. The provisions of this Article shall be without prejudice to the operation of Article VII, Section 5.

SECTION 7. OBLIGATION TO COLLABORATE REGARDING POLICIES ON RESERVE ASSETS

Each member undertakes to collaborate with the Fund and with other members in order to ensure that the policies of the member with respect to reserve assets shall be consistent with the objectives of promoting better international surveillance of international liquidity and making the special drawing right the principal reserve asset in the international monetary system.

ARTICLE IX—STATUS, IMMUNITIES AND PRIVILEGES

SECTION 1. PURPOSES OF ARTICLE

To enable the Fund to fulfill the functions with which it is entrusted, the status, immunities, and privileges set forth in this Article shall be accorded to the Fund in the territories of each member.

SECTION 2. STATUS OF THE FUND

The Fund shall possess full juridical personality, and in particular, the capacity:

(i) to contract;

(ii) to acquire and dispose of immovable and movable property; and

(iii) to institute legal proceedings.

SECTION 3. IMMUNITY FROM JUDICIAL PROCESS

The Fund, its property and its assets, wherever located and by whomsoever held, shall enjoy immunity from every form of judicial process except to the extent that it expressly waives its immunity for the purpose of any proceedings or by the terms of any contract.

SECTION 4. IMMUNITY FROM OTHER ACTION

Property and assets of the Fund, wherever located and by whomsoever held, shall be immune from search, requisition, confiscation, expropriation, or any other form of seizure by executive or legislative action.

SECTION 5. IMMUNITY OF ARCHIVES

The archives of the Fund shall be inviolable.

SECTION 6. FREEDOM OF ASSETS FROM RESTRICTIONS

To the extent necessary to carry out the activities provided for in this Agreement, all property and assets of the Fund shall be free from restrictions, regulations, controls, and moratoria of any nature.

SECTION 7. PRIVILEGE FOR COMMUNICATIONS

The official communications of the Fund shall be accorded by members the same treatment as the official communications of other members.

SECTION 8. IMMUNITIES AND PRIVILEGES OF OFFICERS AND EMPLOYEES

All Governors, Executive Directors, Alternates, members of committees, representatives appointed under Article XII, Section 3(j), advisors of any of the foregoing persons, officers, and employees of the Fund:

(i) shall be immune from legal process with respect to acts performed by them in their official capacity except when the Fund waives this immunity;

(ii) not being local nationals, shall be granted the same immunities from immigration restrictions, alien registration requirements, and national service obligations and the same facilities as regards exchange restrictions as are accorded by members to the representatives, officials, and employees of comparable rank of other members; and

(iii) shall be granted the same treatment in respect of traveling facilities as is accorded by members to representatives, officials, and employees of comparable rank of other members.

SECTION 9. IMMUNITIES FROM TAXATION

(a) The Fund, its assets, property, income, and its operations and transactions authorized by this Agreement shall be immune from all taxation and from all customs duties. The Fund shall also be immune from liability for the collection or payment of any tax or duty.

(b) No tax shall be levied on or in respect of salaries and emoluments paid by the Fund to Executive Directors, Alternates, officers, or employees of the Fund who are not local citizens, local subjects, or other local nationals.

(c) No taxation of any kind shall be levied on any obligation or security issued by the Fund, including any dividend or interest thereon, by whomsoever held:

(i) which discriminates against such obligation or security solely because of its origin; or

(ii) if the sole jurisdictional basis for such taxation is the place or currency in which it is issued, made payable or paid, or the location of any office or place of business maintained by the Fund.

SECTION 10. APPLICATION OF ARTICLE

Each member shall take such action as is necessary in its own territories for the purpose of making effective in terms of its own law the principles set forth in this Article and shall inform the Fund of the detailed action which it has taken.

ARTICLE X—RELATIONS WITH OTHER INTERNATIONAL ORGANIZATIONS

The Fund shall cooperate within the terms of this Agreement with any general international organization and with public international organizations having specialized responsibilities in related fields. Any arrangements for such cooperation which would involve a modification of any provision of this Agreement may be effected only after amendment to this Agreement under Article XXVIII.

ARTICLE XI—RELATIONS WITH NON-MEMBER COUNTRIES

SECTION 1. UNDERTAKINGS REGARDING RELATIONS WITH NON-MEMBER COUNTRIES

Each member undertakes:

(i) not to engage in, nor to permit any of its fiscal agencies referred to in Article V, Section 1 to engage in, any transactions with a non-member or with persons in a non-member's territories which would be contrary to the provisions of this Agreement or the purposes of the Fund;

(ii) not to cooperate with a non-member or with persons in a non-member's territories in practices which would be contrary to the provisions of this Agreement or the purposes of the Fund; and

(iii) to cooperate with the Fund with a view to the application in its territories of appropriate measures to prevent transactions with non-members or with persons in their territories which would be contrary to the provisions of this Agreement or the purposes of the Fund.

SECTION 2. RESTRICTIONS ON TRANSACTIONS WITH NON-MEMBER COUNTRIES

Nothing in this Agreement shall affect the right of any member to impose restrictions on exchange transactions with non-members or with persons in their territories unless the Fund finds that such restrictions prejudice the interests of members and are contrary to the purposes of the Fund.

ARTICLE XII—ORGANIZATION AND MANAGEMENT

SECTION 1. STRUCTURE OF THE FUND

The Fund shall have a Board of Governors, an Executive Board, a Managing Director, and a staff, and a Council if the Board of Governors decides, by an eighty-five percent majority of the total voting power, that the provisions of Schedule D shall be applied.

SECTION 2. BOARD OF GOVERNORS

(a) All powers under this Agreement not conferred directly on the Board of Governors, the Executive Board, or the Managing Director shall be vested in the Board of Governors. The Board of Governors shall consist of one Governor and one Alternate appointed by each member in such manner as it may determine. Each Governor and each Alternate shall serve until a new appointment is made. No Alternate may vote except in the absence of his principal. The Board of Governors shall select one of the Governors as Chairman.

(b) The Board of Governors may delegate to the Executive Board authority to exercise any powers of the Board of Governors, except the powers conferred directly by this Agreement on the Board of Governors.

(c) The Board of Governors shall hold such meetings as may be provided for by the Board of Governors or called by the Executive Board. Meetings of the Board of Governors shall be called whenever requested by fifteen members or by members having one-quarter of the total voting power.

(d) A quorum for any meeting of the Board of Governors shall be a majority of the Governors having not less than two-thirds of the total voting power.

(e) Each Governor shall be entitled to cast the number of votes allotted under Section 5 of this Article to the member appointing him.

(f) The Board of Governors may by regulation establish a procedure whereby the Executive Board, when it deems such action to be in the best interests of the Fund, may obtain a vote of the Governors on a specific question without calling a meeting of the Board of Governors.

(g) The Board of Governors, and the Executive Board to the extent authorized, may adopt such rules and regulations as may be necessary or appropriate to conduct the business of the Fund.

(h) Governors and Alternates shall serve as such without compensation from the Fund, but the Fund may pay them reasonable expenses incurred in attending meetings.

(i) The Board of Governors shall determine the remuneration to be paid to the Executive Directors and their Alternates and the salary and terms of the contract of service of the Managing Director.

(j) The Board of Governors and the Executive Board may appoint such committees as they deem advisable. Membership of committees need not be limited to Governors or Executive Directors or their Alternates.

SECTION 3. EXECUTIVE BOARD

(a) The Executive Board shall be responsible for conducting the business of the Fund, and for this purpose shall exercise all the powers delegated to it by the Board of Governors.

(b) The Executive Board shall consist of Executive Directors with the Managing Director as chairman. Of the Executive Directors:

(i) five shall be appointed by the five members having the largest quotas; and

(ii) fifteen shall be elected by the other members.

For the purpose of each regular election of Executive Directors, the Board of Governors, by an eighty-five percent majority of the total voting power, may increase or decrease the number of Executive Directors in (ii) above. The number of Executive Directors in (ii) above shall be reduced by one or two, as the case may be, if Executive Directors are appointed under (c) below, unless the Board of Governors decides, by an eighty-five percent majority of the total voting power, that this reduction would hinder the effective discharge of the functions of the Executive Board or of Executive Directors or would threaten to upset a desirable balance in the Executive Board.

(c) If, at the second regular election of Executive Directors and thereafter, the members entitled to appoint Executive Directors under (b)(i) above do not include the two members, the holdings of whose currencies by the Fund in the General Resources Account have been, on the average over the preceding two years, reduced below their quotas by the largest absolute amounts in terms of the special drawing right, either one or both of such members, as the case may be, may appoint an Executive Director.

(d) Elections of elective Executive Directors shall be conducted at intervals of two years in accordance with the provisions of Schedule E, supplemented by such regulations as the Fund deems appropriate. For each regular election of Executive Directors, the Board of Governors may issue regulations making changes in the proportion of votes required to elect Executive Directors under the provisions of Schedule E.

(e) Each Executive Director shall appoint an Alternate with full power to act for him when he is not present. When the Executive Directors appointing them are present, Alternates may participate in meetings but may not vote.

(f) Executive Directors shall continue in office until their successors are appointed or elected. If the office of an elected Executive Director becomes vacant more than ninety days before the end of his term, another Executive Director shall be elected for the remainder of the term by the members that elected the former Executive Director. A majority of the votes cast shall be required for election. While the office remains vacant, the Alternate of the former Executive Director shall exercise his powers, except that of appointing an Alternate.

(g) The Executive Board shall function in continuous session at the principal office of the Fund and shall meet as often as the business of the Fund may require.

(h) A quorum for any meeting of the Executive Board shall be a majority of the Executive Directors having not less than one-half of the total voting power.

(i)(i) Each appointed Executive Director shall be entitled to cast the number of votes allotted under Section 5 of this Article to the member appointing him.

(ii) If the votes allotted to a member that appoints an Executive Director under (c) above were cast by an Executive Director together with the votes allotted to other members as a result of the last regular election of Executive Directors, the member may agree with each of the other members that the number of votes allotted to it shall be cast by the appointed Executive Director. A member making such an agreement shall not participate in the election of Executive Directors.

(iii) Each elected Executive Director shall be entitled to cast the number of votes which counted towards his election.

(iv) When the provisions of Section 5(b) of this Article are applicable, the votes which an Executive Director would otherwise be entitled to cast shall be increased or decreased correspondingly. All the votes which an Executive Director is entitled to cast shall be cast as a unit.

(v) When the suspension of the voting rights of a member is terminated under Article XXVI, Section 2(b), and the member is not entitled to appoint an Executive Director, the member may agree with all the members that have elected an Executive Director that the number of votes allotted to that member shall be cast by such Executive Director, provided that, if no regular election of Executive Directors has been conducted during the period of the suspension, the Executive Director in whose election the member had participated prior to the suspension, or his successor elected in accordance with paragraph 3(c) (i) of Schedule L or with (f) above, shall be entitled to cast the number of votes allotted to the member. The member shall be deemed to have participated in the election of the Executive Director entitled to cast the number of votes allotted to the member.

(j) The Board of Governors shall adopt regulations under which a member not entitled to appoint an Executive Director under (b) above may send a representative to attend any meeting of the Executive Board when a request made by, or a matter particularly affecting, that member is under consideration.

SECTION 4. MANAGING DIRECTOR AND STAFF

(a) The Executive Board shall select a Managing Director who shall not be a Governor or an Executive Director. The Managing Director shall be chairman of the Executive Board, but shall have no vote except a deciding vote in case of an equal division. He may participate in meetings of the Board of Governors, but shall not vote at such meetings. The Managing Director shall cease to hold office when the Executive Board so decides.

(b) The Managing Director shall be chief of the operating staff of the Fund and shall conduct, under the direction of the Executive Board, the ordinary business of the Fund. Subject to the general control of the Executive Board, he shall be responsible for the organization, appointment, and dismissal of the staff of the Fund.

(c) The Managing Director and the staff of the Fund, in the discharge of their functions, shall owe their duty entirely to the Fund and to no other authority. Each member of the Fund shall respect the international character of this duty and shall refrain from all attempts to influence any of the staff in the discharge of these functions.

(d) In appointing the staff the Managing Director shall, subject to the paramount importance of securing the highest standards of efficiency and of technical competence, pay due regard to the importance of recruiting personnel on as wide a geographical basis as possible.

SECTION 5. VOTING

(a) Each member shall have two hundred fifty votes plus one additional vote for each part of its quota equivalent to one hundred thousand special drawing rights.

(b) Whenever voting is required under Article V, Section 4 or 5, each member shall have the number of votes to which it is entitled under (a) above adjusted

(i) by the addition of one vote for the equivalent of each four hundred thousand special drawing rights of net sales of its currency from the general resources of the Fund up to the date when the vote is taken, or

(ii) by the subtraction of one vote for the equivalent of each four hundred thousand special drawing rights of its net purchases under Article V, Section 3(b) and (f) up to the date when the vote is taken,

provided that neither net purchases nor net sales shall be deemed at any time to exceed an amount equal to the quota of the member involved.

(c) Except as otherwise specifically provided, all decisions of the Fund shall be made by a majority of the votes cast.

SECTION 6. RESERVES, DISTRIBUTION OF NET INCOME, AND INVESTMENT

(a) The Fund shall determine annually what part of its net income shall be placed to general reserve or special reserve, and what part, if any, shall be distributed.

(b) The Fund may use the special reserve for any purpose for which it may use the general reserve, except distribution.

(c) If any distribution is made of the net income of any year, it shall be made to all members in proportion to their quotas.

(d) The Fund, by a seventy percent majority of the total voting power, may decide at any time to distribute any part of the general reserve. Any such distribution shall be made to all members in proportion to their quotas.

(e) Payments under (c) and (d) above shall be made in special drawing rights, provided that either the Fund or the member may decide that the payment to the member shall be made in its own currency.

(f)(i) The Fund may establish an Investment Account for the purposes of this subsection (f). The assets of the Investment Account shall be held separately from the other accounts of the General Department.

(ii) The Fund may decide to transfer to the Investment Account a part of the proceeds of the sale of gold in accordance with Article V, Section 12(g) and, by a seventy percent majority of the total voting power, may decide to transfer to the Investment Account, for immediate investment, currencies held in the General Resources Account. The amount of these transfers shall not exceed the total amount of the general reserve and the special reserve at the time of the decision.

(iii) The Fund may invest a member's currency held in the Investment Account in marketable obligations of that member or in marketable obligations of international financial organizations. No investment shall be made without the concurrence of the member whose currency is used to make the investment. The Fund shall invest only in obligations denominated in special drawing rights or in the currency used for investment.

(iv) The income of investment may be invested in accordance with the provisions of this subsection (f). Income not invested shall be held in the Investment Account or may be used for meeting the expenses of conducting the business of the Fund.

(v) The Fund may use a member's currency held in the Investment Account to obtain the currencies needed to meet the expenses of conducting the business of the Fund.

(vi) The Investment Account shall be terminated in the event of liquidation of the Fund and may be terminated, or the amount of the investment may be reduced, prior to liquidation of the Fund by a seventy percent majority of the total voting power. The Fund, by a seventy percent majority of the total voting power, shall adopt rules and regulations regarding administration of the Investment Account, which shall be consistent with (vii), (viii), and (ix) below.

(vii) Upon termination of the Investment Account because of liquidation of the Fund, any assets in this account shall be distributed in accordance with the provisions of Schedule K, provided that a portion of these assets corresponding to the proportion of the assets transferred to this account under Article V, Section 12(g) to the total of the assets transferred to this account shall be deemed to be assets held in the Special Disbursement Account and shall be distributed in accordance with Schedule K, paragraph 2(a)(ii).

(viii) Upon termination of the Investment Account prior to liquidation of the Fund, a portion of the assets held in this account corresponding to the proportion of the assets transferred to this account under Article V, Section 12(g) to the total of the assets transferred to the account shall be transferred to the Special Disbursement Account if it has not been terminated, and the balance of the assets held in the Investment Account shall be transferred to the General Resources Account for immediate use in operations and transactions.

(ix) On a reduction of the amount of the investment by the Fund, a portion of the reduction corresponding to the proportion of the assets transferred to the Investment Account under Article V, Section 12(g) to the total of the assets transferred to this account shall be transferred to the Special Disbursement Account if it has not been terminated, and the balance of the reduction shall be transferred to the General Resources Account for immediate use in operations and transactions.

SECTION 7. PUBLICATION OF REPORTS

(a) The Fund shall publish an annual report containing an audited statement of its accounts, and shall issue, at intervals of three months or less, a summary statement of its operations and transactions and its holdings of special drawing rights, gold, and currencies of members.

(b) The Fund may publish such other reports as it deems desirable for carrying out its purposes.

SECTION 8. COMMUNICATION OF VIEWS TO MEMBERS

The Fund shall at all times have the right to communicate its views informally to any member on any matter arising under this Agreement. The Fund may, by a seventy percent majority of the total voting power, decide to publish a report made to a member regarding its monetary or economic conditions and developments which directly tend to produce a serious disequilibrium in the international balance of payments of members. If the member is not entitled to appoint an Executive Director, it shall be entitled to representation in accordance with Section 3(j) of this Article. The Fund shall not publish a report involving changes in the fundamental structure of the economic organization of members.

ARTICLE XIII—OFFICES AND DEPOSITORIES

SECTION 1. LOCATION OF OFFICES

The principal office of the Fund shall be located in the territory of the member having the largest quota, and agencies or branch offices may be established in the territories of other members.

SECTION 2. DEPOSITORIES

(a) Each member shall designate its central bank as a depository for all the Fund's holdings of its currency, or if it has no central bank it shall designate such other institution as may be acceptable to the Fund.

(b) The Fund may hold other assets, including gold, in the depositories designated by the five members having the largest quotas and in such other designated depositories as the Fund may select. Initially, at least one-half of the holdings of the Fund shall be held in the depository designated by the member in whose territories the Fund has its principal office and at least forty percent shall be held in the depositories designated by the remaining four members referred to above. However, all transfers of gold by the Fund shall be made with due regard to the costs of transport and anticipated requirements of the Fund. In an emergency the Executive Board may transfer all or any part of the Fund's gold holdings to any place where they can be adequately protected.

SECTION 3. GUARANTEE OF THE FUND'S ASSETS

Each member guarantees all assets of the Fund against loss resulting from failure or default on the part of the depository designated by it.

ARTICLE XIV—TRANSITIONAL ARRANGEMENTS

SECTION 1. NOTIFICATION TO THE FUND

Each member shall notify the Fund whether it intends to avail itself of the transitional arrangements in Section 2 of this Article, or whether it is prepared to accept the obligations of Article VIII, Sections 2, 3, and 4. A member availing itself of the transitional arrangements shall notify the Fund as soon thereafter as it is prepared to accept these obligations.

SECTION 2. EXCHANGE RESTRICTIONS

A member that has notified the Fund that it intends to avail itself of transitional arrangements under this provision may, notwithstanding the provisions of any other articles of this Agreement, maintain and adapt to changing circumstances the restrictions on payments and transfers for current international transactions that were in effect on the date on which it became a member. Members shall, however, have continuous regard in their foreign exchange policies to the purposes of the Fund, and, as soon as conditions permit, they shall take all possible measures to develop such commercial and financial arrangements with other members as will facilitate international payments and the promotion of a stable system of exchange rates. In particular, members shall withdraw restrictions maintained under this Section as soon as they are satisfied that they will be able, in the absence of such restrictions, to settle their balance of payments in a manner which will not unduly encumber their access to the general resources of the Fund.

SECTION 3. ACTION OF THE FUND RELATING TO RESTRICTIONS

The Fund shall make annual reports on the restrictions in force under Section 2 of this Article. Any member retaining any restrictions inconsistent with Article VIII, Sections 2, 3, or 4 shall consult the Fund annually as to their further retention. The Fund may, if it deems such action necessary in exceptional circumstances, make representations to any member that conditions are favorable for the withdrawal of any particular restriction, or for the general abandonment of restrictions, inconsistent with the provisions of any other articles of this Agreement. The member shall be given a suitable time to reply to such representations. If the Fund finds that the member persists in maintaining restrictions which are inconsistent with the purposes of the Fund, the member shall be subject to Article XXVI, Section 2(a).

ARTICLE XV—SPECIAL DRAWING RIGHTS

SECTION 1. AUTHORITY TO ALLOCATE SPECIAL DRAWING RIGHTS

To meet the need, as and when it arises, for a supplement to existing reserve assets, the Fund is authorized to allocate special drawing rights to members that are participants in the Special Drawing Rights Department.

SECTION 2. VALUATION OF THE SPECIAL DRAWING RIGHT

The method of valuation of the special drawing right shall be determined by the Fund by a seventy percent majority of the total voting power, provided, however, that an eighty-five percent majority of the total voting power shall be required for a change in the principle of valuation or a fundamental change in the application of the principle in effect.

ARTICLE XVI—GENERAL DEPARTMENT AND SPECIAL DRAWING RIGHTS DEPARTMENT

SECTION 1. SEPARATION OF OPERATIONS AND TRANSACTIONS

All operations and transactions involving special drawing rights shall be conducted through the Special Drawing Rights Department. All other operations and transactions on the account of the Fund authorized by or under this Agreement shall be conducted through the General Department. Operations and transactions pursuant to Article XVII, Section 2 shall be conducted through the General Department as well as the Special Drawing Rights Department.

SECTION 2. SEPARATION OF ASSETS AND PROPERTY

All assets and property of the Fund, except resources administered under Article V, Section 2(b), shall be held in the General Department, provided that assets and property acquired under Article XX, Section 2 and Articles XXIV and XXV and Schedules H and I shall be held in the Special Drawing Rights Department. Any assets or property held in one Department shall not be available to discharge or meet the liabilities, obligations, or losses of the Fund incurred in the conduct of the operations and transactions of the other Department, except that the expenses of conducting the business of the Special Drawing Rights Department shall be paid by the Fund from the General Department which shall be reimbursed in special drawing rights from time to time by assessments under Article XX, Section 4 made on the basis of a reasonable estimate of such expenses.

SECTION 3. RECORDING AND INFORMATION

All changes in holdings of special drawing rights shall take effect only when recorded by the Fund in the Special Drawing Rights Department. Participants shall notify the Fund of the provisions of this Agreement under which special drawing rights are used. The Fund may require participants to furnish it with such other information as it deems necessary for its functions.

Article XVII—Participants and Other Holders of Special Drawing Rights

SECTION 1. PARTICIPANTS

Each member of the Fund that deposits with the Fund an instrument setting forth that it undertakes all the obligations of a participant in the Special Drawing Rights Department in accordance with its law and that it has taken all steps necessary to enable it to carry out all of these obligations shall become a participant in the Special Drawing Rights Department as of the date the instrument is deposited, except that no member shall become a participant before the provisions of this Agreement pertaining exclusively to the Special Drawing Rights Department have entered into force and instruments have been deposited under this Section by members that have at least seventy-five percent of the total of quotas.

SECTION 2. FUND AS A HOLDER

The Fund may hold special drawing rights in the General Resources Account and may accept and use them in operations and transactions conducted through the General Resources Account with participants in accordance with the provisions of this Agreement or with prescribed holders in accordance with the terms and conditions prescribed under Section 3 of this Article.

SECTION 3. OTHER HOLDERS

The Fund may prescribe:

(i) as holders, non-members, members that are non-participants, institutions that perform functions of a central bank for more than one member, and other official entities;

(ii) the terms and conditions on which prescribed holders may be permitted to hold special drawing rights and may accept and use them in operations and transactions with participants and other prescribed holders; and

(iii) the terms and conditions on which participants and the Fund through the General Resources Account may enter into operations and transactions in special drawing rights with prescribed holders.

An eighty-five percent majority of the total voting power shall be required for prescriptions under (i) above. The terms and conditions prescribed by the Fund shall be consistent with the provisions of this Agreement and the effective functioning of the Special Drawing Rights Department.

Article XVIII—Allocation and Cancellation of Special Drawing Rights

SECTION 1. PRINCIPLES AND CONSIDERATIONS GOVERNING ALLOCATION AND CANCELLATION

(a) In all its decisions with respect to the allocation and cancellation of special drawing rights the Fund shall seek to meet the long-term global need, as and when it arises, to supplement existing reserve assets in such manner as will promote the attainment of its purposes and will avoid economic stagnation and deflation as well as excess demand and inflation in the world.

(b) The first decision to allocate special drawing rights shall take into account, as special considerations, a collective judgment that there is a global need to supplement reserves, and the attainment of a better balance of payments equilibrium, as well as the likelihood of a better working of the adjustment process in the future.

SECTION 2. ALLOCATION AND CANCELLATION

(a) Decisions of the Fund to allocate or cancel special drawing rights shall be made for basic periods which shall run consecutively and shall be five years in duration. The first basic period shall begin on the date of the first decision to allocate special drawing rights or such later date as may be specified in that decision. Any allocations or cancellations shall take place at yearly intervals.

(b) The rates at which allocations are to be made shall be expressed as percentages of quotas on the date of each decision to allocate. The rates at which special drawing rights are to be cancelled shall be expressed as percentages of net cumulative allocations of special drawing rights on the date of each decision to cancel. The percentages shall be the same for all participants.

(c) In its decision for any basic period the Fund may provide, notwithstanding (a) and (b) above, that:

(i) the duration of the basic period shall be other than five years; or

(ii) the allocations or cancellations shall take place at other than yearly intervals; or

(iii) the basis for allocations or cancellations shall be the quotas or net cumulative allocations on dates other than the dates of decisions to allocate or cancel.

(d) A member that becomes a participant after a basic period starts shall receive allocations beginning with the next basic period in which allocations are made after it becomes a participant unless the Fund decides that the new participant shall start to receive allocations beginning with the next allocation after it becomes a participant. If the Fund decides that a member that becomes a participant during a basic period shall receive allocations during the remainder of that basic period and the participant was not a member on the dates established under (b) or (c) above, the Fund shall determine the basis on which these allocations to the participant shall be made.

(e) A participant shall receive allocations of special drawing rights made pursuant to any decision to allocate unless:

(i) the Governor for the participant did not vote in favor of the decision; and

(ii) the participant has notified the Fund in writing prior to the first allocation of special drawing rights under that decision that it does not wish special drawing rights to be allocated to it under the decision. On the request of a participant, the Fund may decide to terminate the effect of the notice with respect to allocations of special drawing rights subsequent to the termination.

(f) If on the effective date of any cancellation the amount of special drawing rights held by a participant is less than its share of the special drawing rights that are to be cancelled, the participant shall eliminate its negative balance as promptly as its gross reserve position permits and shall remain in consultation with the Fund for this purpose. Special drawing rights acquired by the participant after the effective date of the cancellation shall be applied against its negative balance and cancelled.

SECTION 3. UNEXPECTED MAJOR DEVELOPMENTS

The Fund may change the rates or intervals of allocation or cancellation during the rest of a basic period or change the length of a basic period or start a new basic period, if at any time the Fund finds it desirable to do so because of unexpected major developments.

SECTION 4. DECISIONS ON ALLOCATIONS AND CANCELLATIONS

(a) Decisions under Section 2(a), (b), and (c) or Section 3 of this Article shall be made by the Board of Governors on the basis of proposals of the Managing Director concurred in by the Executive Board.

(b) Before making any proposal, the Managing Director, after having satisfied himself that it will be consistent with the provisions of Section 1(a) of this Article, shall conduct such consultations as will enable him to ascertain that there is broad support among participants for the proposal. In addition, before making a proposal for the first allocation, the Managing Director shall satisfy himself that the provisions of Section 1(b) of this Article have been met and that there is broad support among participants to begin allocations; he shall make a proposal for the first allocation as soon after the establishment of the Special Drawing Rights Department as he is so satisfied.

(c) The Managing Director shall make proposals:

(i) not later than six months before the end of each basic period;

(ii) if no decision has been taken with respect to allocation or cancellation for a basic period, whenever he is satisfied that the provisions of (b) above have been met;

(iii) when, in accordance with Section 3 of this Article, he considers that it would be desirable to change the rate or intervals of allocation or cancellation or change the length of a basic period or start a new basic period; or

(iv) within six months of a request by the Board of Governors or the Executive Board;

provided that, if under (i), (iii), or (iv) above the Managing Director ascertains that there is no proposal which he considers to be consistent with the provisions of Section 1 of this Article that has broad support among participants in accordance with (b) above, he shall report to the Board of Governors and to the Executive Board.

(d) An eighty-five percent majority of the total voting power shall be required for decisions under Section 2(a), (b), and (c) or Section 3 of this Article except for decisions under Section 3 with respect to a decrease in the rates of allocation.

ARTICLE XIX—OPERATIONS AND TRANSACTIONS IN SPECIAL DRAWING RIGHTS

SECTION 1. USE OF SPECIAL DRAWING RIGHTS

Special drawing rights may be used in the operations and transactions authorized by or under this Agreement.

SECTION 2. OPERATIONS AND TRANSACTIONS BETWEEN PARTICIPANTS

(a) A participant shall be entitled to use its special drawing rights to obtain an equivalent amount of currency from a participant designated under Section 5 of this Article.

(b) A participant, in agreement with another participant, may use its special drawing rights to obtain an equivalent amount of currency from the other participant.

(c) The Fund, by a seventy percent majority of the total voting power, may prescribe operations in which a participant is authorized to engage in agreement with another participant on such terms and conditions as the Fund deems appropriate. The terms and conditions shall be consistent with the effective functioning of the Special Drawing Rights Department and the proper use of special drawing rights in accordance with this Agreement.

(d) The Fund may make representations to a participant that enters into any operation or transaction under (b) or (c) above that in the judgment of the Fund may be prejudicial to the process of designation according to the principles of Section 5 of this Article or is otherwise inconsistent with Article XXII. A participant that persists in entering into such operations or transactions shall be subject to Article XXIII, Section 2(b).

SECTION 3. REQUIREMENT OF NEED

(a) In transactions under Section 2(a) of this Article, except as otherwise provided in (c) below, a participant will be expected to use its special drawing rights only if it has a need because of its balance of payments or its reserve position or developments in its reserves, and not for the sole purpose of changing the composition of its reserves.

(b) The use of special drawing rights shall not be subject to challenge on the basis of the expectation in (a) above, but the Fund may make representations to a participant that fails to fulfill this expectation. A participant that persists in failing to fulfill this expectation shall be subject to Article XXIII, Section 2(b).

(c) The Fund may waive the expectation in (a) above in any transactions in which a participant uses special drawing rights to obtain an equivalent amount of currency from a participant designated under Section 5 of this Article that would promote reconstitution by the other participant under Section 6(a) of this Article; prevent or reduce a negative balance of the other participant; or offset the effect of a failure by the other participant to fulfill the expectation in (a) above.

SECTION 4. OBLIGATION TO PROVIDE CURRENCY

(a) A participant designated by the Fund under Section 5 of this Article shall provide on demand a freely usable currency to a participant using special drawing rights under Section 2(a) of this Article. A participant's obligation to provide currency shall not extend beyond the point at which its holdings of special drawing rights in excess of its net cumulative allocation are equal to twice its net cumulative allocation or such higher limit as may be agreed between a participant and the Fund.

(b) A participant may provide currency in excess of the obligatory limit or any agreed higher limit.

SECTION 5. DESIGNATION OF PARTICIPANTS TO PROVIDE CURRENCY

(a) The Fund shall ensure that a participant will be able to use its special drawing rights by designating participants to provide currency for specified amounts of special drawing rights for the purposes of Sections 2(a) and 4 of this Article. Designations shall be made in accordance with the following general principles supplemented by such other principles as the Fund may adopt from time to time:

(i) A participant shall be subject to designation if its balance of payments and gross reserve position is sufficiently strong, but this will not preclude the possibility that a participant with a strong reserve position will be designated even though it has a moderate balance of payments deficit. Participants shall be designated in such manner as will promote over time a balanced distribution of holdings of special drawing rights among them.

(ii) Participants shall be subject to designation in order to promote reconstitution under Section 6(a) of this Article, to reduce negative balances in holdings of special drawing rights, or to offset the effect of failures to fulfill the expectation in Section 3(a) of this Article.

(iii) In designating participants, the Fund normally shall give priority to those that need to acquire special drawing rights to meet the objectives of designation under (ii) above.

(b) In order to promote over time a balanced distribution of holdings of special drawing rights under (a)(i) above, the Fund shall apply the rules for designation in Schedule F or such rules as may be adopted under (c) below.

(c) The rules for designation may be reviewed at any time and new rules shall be adopted if necessary. Unless new rules are adopted, the rules in force at the time of the review shall continue to apply.

SECTION 6. RECONSTITUTION

(a) Participants that use their special drawing rights shall reconstitute their holdings of them in accordance with the rules for reconstitution in Schedule G or such rules as may be adopted under (b) below.

(b) The rules for reconstitution may be reviewed at any time and new rules shall be adopted if necessary. Unless new rules are adopted or a decision is made to abrogate rules for reconstitution, the rules in force at the time of review shall continue to apply. A seventy percent majority of the total voting power shall be required for decisions to adopt, modify, or abrogate the rules for reconstitution.

SECTION 7. EXCHANGE RATES

(a) Except as otherwise provided in (b) below, the exchange rates for transactions between participants under Section 2(a) and (b) of this Article shall be such that participants using special drawing rights shall receive the same value whatever currencies might be provided and whichever participants provide those currencies, and the Fund shall adopt regulations to give effect to this principle.

(b) The Fund, by an eighty-five percent majority of the total voting power, may adopt policies under which in exceptional circumstances the Fund, by a seventy percent majority of the total voting power, may authorize participants entering into transactions under Section 2(b) of this Article to agree on exchange rates other than those applicable under (a) above.

(c) The Fund shall consult a participant on the procedure for determining rates of exchange for its currency.

(d) For the purpose of this provision the term participant includes a terminating participant.

ARTICLE XX—SPECIAL DRAWING RIGHTS DEPARTMENT INTEREST AND CHARGES

SECTION 1. INTEREST

Interest at the same rate for all holders shall be paid by the Fund to each holder on the amount of its holdings of special drawing rights. The Fund shall pay the amount due to each holder whether or not sufficient charges are received to meet the payment of interest.

SECTION 2. CHARGES

Charges at the same rate for all participants shall be paid to the Fund by each participant on the amount of its net cumulative allocation of special drawing rights plus any negative balance of the participant or unpaid charges.

SECTION 3. RATE OF INTEREST AND CHARGES

The Fund shall determine the rate of interest by a seventy percent majority of the total voting power. The rate of charges shall be equal to the rate of interest.

SECTION 4. ASSESSMENTS

When it is decided under Article XVI, Section 2 that reimbursement shall be made, the Fund shall levy assessments for this purpose at the same rate for all participants on their net cumulative allocations.

SECTION 5. PAYMENT OF INTEREST, CHARGES, AND ASSESSMENTS

Interest, charges, and assessments shall be paid in special drawing rights. A participant that needs special drawing rights to pay any charge or assessment shall be obligated and entitled to obtain them, for currency acceptable to the Fund, in a transaction with the Fund conducted through the General Resources Account. If sufficient special drawing rights cannot be obtained in this way, the participant shall be obligated and entitled to obtain them with a freely usable currency from a participant which the Fund shall specify. Special drawing rights acquired by a participant after the date for payment shall be applied against its unpaid charges and cancelled.

Article XXI—Administration of the General Department and the Special Drawing Rights Department

(a) The General Department and the Special Drawing Rights Department shall be administered in accordance with the provisions of Article XII, subject to the following provisions:

(i) For meetings of or decisions by the Board of Governors on matters pertaining exclusively to the Special Drawing Rights Department only requests by, or the presence and the votes of, Governors appointed by members that are participants shall be counted for the purpose of calling meetings and determining whether a quorum exists or whether a decision is made by the required majority.

(ii) For decisions by the Executive Board on matters pertaining exclusively to the Special Drawing Rights Department only Executive Directors appointed or elected by at least one member that is a participant shall be entitled to vote. Each of these Executive Directors shall be entitled to cast the number of votes allotted to the member which is a participant that appointed him or to the members that are participants whose votes counted towards his election. Only the presence of Executive Directors appointed or elected by members that are participants and the votes allotted to members that are participants shall be counted for the purpose of determining whether a quorum exists or whether a decision is made by the required majority. For the purposes of this provision, an agreement under Article XII, Section 3(i)(ii) by a member that is a participant shall entitle an appointed Executive Director to vote and cast the number of votes allotted to the member.

(iii) Questions of the general administration of the Fund, including reimbursement under Article XVI, Section 2, and any question whether a matter pertains to both Departments or exclusively to the Special Drawing Rights Department shall be decided as if they pertained exclusively to the General Department. Decisions with respect to the method of valuation of the special drawing right, the acceptance and holding of special drawing rights in the General Resources Account of the General Department and the use of them, and other decisions affecting the operations and transactions conducted through both the General Resources Account of the General Department and the Special Drawing Rights Department shall be made by the majorities required for decisions on matters pertaining exclusively to each Department. A decision on a matter pertaining to the Special Drawing Rights Department shall so indicate.

(b) In addition to the privileges and immunities that are accorded under Article IX of this Agreement, no tax of any kind shall be levied on special drawing rights or on operations or transactions in special drawing rights.

(c) A question of interpretation of the provisions of this Agreement on matters pertaining exclusively to the Special Drawing Rights Department shall be submitted to the Executive Board pursuant to Article XXIX(a) only on the request of a participant. In any case where the Executive Board has given a decision on a question of interpretation pertaining exclusively to the Special Drawing Rights Department only a participant may require that the question be referred to the Board of Governors under Article XXIX(b). The Board of Governors shall decide whether a Governor appointed by a member that is not a participant shall be entitled to vote in the Committee on Interpretation on questions pertaining exclusively to the Special Drawing Rights Department.

(d) Whenever a disagreement arises between the Fund and a participant that has terminated its participation in the Special Drawing Rights Department or between the Fund and any participant during the liquidation of the Special Drawing Rights Department with respect to any matter arising exclusively from participation in the Special Drawing Rights Department, the disagreement shall be submitted to arbitration in accordance with the procedures in Article XXIX(c).

Article XXII—General Obligations of Participants

In addition to the obligations assumed with respect to special drawing rights under other articles of this Agreement, each participant undertakes to collaborate with the Fund and with other participants in order to facilitate the effective functioning of the Special Drawing Rights Department and the proper use of special drawing rights in accordance with this Agreement and with the objective of making the special drawing right the principal reserve asset in the international monetary system.

Article XXIII—Suspension of Operations and Transactions in Special Drawing Rights

Section 1. Emergency provisions

In the event of an emergency or the development of unforeseen circumstances threatening the activities of the Fund with respect to the Special Drawing Rights Department, the Executive Board, by an eighty-five percent majority of the total voting power, may suspend for a period of not more than one year the operation of any of the provisions relating to operations and transactions in special drawing rights, and the provisions of Article XXVII, Section 1(b), (c), and (d) shall then apply.

Section 2. Failure to fulfill obligations

(a) If the Fund finds that a participant has failed to fulfill its obligations under Article XIX, Section 4, the right of the participant to use its special drawing rights shall be suspended unless the Fund otherwise decides.

(b) If the Fund finds that a participant has failed to fulfill any other obligation with respect to special drawing rights, the Fund may suspend the right of the participant to use special drawing rights it acquires after the suspension.

(c) Regulations shall be adopted to ensure that before action is taken against any participant under (a) or (b) above, the participant shall be informed immediately of the complaint against it and given an adequate opportunity for stating its case, both orally and in writing. Whenever the participant is thus informed of a complaint relating to (a) above, it shall not use special drawing rights pending the disposition of the complaint.

(d) Suspension under (a) or (b) above or limitation under (c) above shall not affect a participant's obligation to provide currency in accordance with Article XIX, Section 4.

(e) The Fund may at any time terminate a suspension under (a) or (b) above, provided that a suspension imposed on a participant under (b) above for failure to fulfill the obligations under Article XIX, Section 6(a) shall not be terminated until one hundred eighty days after the end of the first calendar quarter during which the participant complies with the rules for reconstitution.

(f) The right of a participant to use its special drawing rights shall not be suspended because it has become ineligible to use the Fund's general resources under Article V, Section 5, Article VI, Section 1, or Article XXVI, Section 2(a). Article XXVI, Section 2 shall not apply because a participant has failed to fulfill any obligations with respect to special drawing rights.

Article XXIV—Termination of Participation

SECTION 1. RIGHT TO TERMINATE PARTICIPATION

(a) Any participant may terminate its participation in the Special Drawing Rights Department at any time by transmitting a notice in writing to the Fund at its principal office. Termination shall become effective on the date the notice is received.

(b) A participant that withdraws from membership in the Fund shall be deemed to have simultaneously terminated its participation in the Special Drawing Rights Department.

SECTION 2. SETTLEMENT ON TERMINATION

(a) When a participant terminates its participation in the Special Drawing Rights Department, all operations and transactions by the terminating participant in special drawing rights shall cease except as otherwise permitted under an agreement made pursuant to (c) below in order to facilitate a settlement or as provided in Sections 3, 5, and 6 of this Article or in Schedule H. Interest and charges that accrued to the date of termination and assessments levied before that date but not paid shall be paid in special drawing rights.

(b) The Fund shall be obligated to redeem all special drawing rights held by the terminating participant, and the terminating participant shall be obligated to pay to the Fund an amount equal to its net cumulative allocation and any other amounts that may be due and payable because of its participation in the Special Drawing Rights Department. These obligations shall be set off against each other and the amount of special drawing rights held by the terminating participant that is used in the setoff to extinguish its obligation to the fund shall be cancelled.

(c) A settlement shall be made with reasonable despatch by agreement between the terminating participant and the Fund with respect to any obligation of the terminating participant or the Fund after the setoff in (b) above. If agreement on a settlement is not reached promptly the provisions of Schedule H shall apply.

SECTION 3. INTEREST AND CHARGES

After the date of termination the Fund shall pay interest on any outstanding balance of special drawing rights held by a terminating participant, and the terminating participant shall pay charges on any outstanding obligation owed to the Fund at the times and rates prescribed under Article XX. Payment shall be made in special drawing rights. A terminating participant shall be entitled to obtain special drawing rights with a freely usable currency to pay charges or assessments in a transaction with a participant specified by the Fund or by agreement from any other holder, or to dispose of special drawing rights received as interest in a transaction with any participant designated under Article XIX, Section 5 or by agreement with any other holder.

SECTION 4. SETTLEMENT OF OBLIGATION TO THE FUND

Currency received by the Fund from a terminating participant shall be used by the Fund to redeem special drawing rights held by participants in proportion to the amount by which each participant's holdings of special drawing rights exceed its net cumulative allocation at the time the currency is received by the Fund. Special drawing rights so redeemed and special drawing rights obtained by a terminating participant under the provisions of this Agreement to meet any installment due under an agreement on settlement or under Schedule H and set off against that installment shall be cancelled.

SECTION 5. SETTLEMENT OF OBLIGATION TO A TERMINATING PARTICIPANT

Whenever the Fund is required to redeem special drawing rights held by a terminating participant, redemption shall be made with currency provided by participants specified by the Fund. These participants shall be specified in accordance with the principles in Article XIX, Section 5. Each specified participant shall provide at its option the currency of the terminating participant or a freely usable currency to the Fund and shall receive an equivalent amount of special drawing rights. However, a terminating participant may use its special drawing rights to obtain its own currency, a freely usable currency, or any other asset from any holder, if the Fund so permits.

SECTION 6. GENERAL RESOURCES ACCOUNT TRANSACTIONS

In order to facilitate settlement with a terminating participant, the Fund may decide that a terminating participant shall:

(i) use any special drawing rights held by it after the setoff in Section 2(b) of this Article, when they are to be redeemed, in a transaction with the Fund conducted through the General Resources Account to obtain its own currency or a freely usable currency at the option of the Fund; or

(ii) obtain special drawing rights in a transaction with the Fund conducted through the General Resources Account for a currency acceptable to the Fund to meet any charges or installment due under an agreement or the provisions of Schedule H.

Article XXV—Liquidation of the Special Drawing Rights Department

(a) The Special Drawing Rights Department may not be liquidated except by decision of the Board of Governors. In an emergency, if the Executive Board decides that liquidation of the Special Drawing Rights Department may be necessary, it may temporarily suspend allocations or cancellations and all operations and transactions in special drawing rights pending decision by the Board of Governors. A decision by the Board of Governors to liquidate the Fund shall be a decision to liquidate both the General Department and the Special Drawing Rights Department.

(b) If the Board of Governors decides to liquidate the Special Drawing Rights Department, all allocations or cancellations and all operations and transactions in special drawing rights and the activities of the Fund with respect to the Special Drawing Rights Department shall cease except those incidental to the orderly discharge of the obligations of participants and of the Fund with respect to special drawing rights, and all obligations of the Fund and of participants under this Agreement with respect to special drawing rights shall cease except those set out in this Article, Article XX, Article XXI(d), Article XXIV, Article XXIX(c), and Schedule H, or any agreement reached under Article XXIV subject to paragraph 4 of Schedule H, and Schedule I.

(c) Upon liquidation of the Special Drawing Rights Department, interest and charges that accrued to the date of liquidation and assessments levied before that date but not paid shall be paid in special drawing rights. The Fund shall be obligated to redeem all special drawing rights held by holders, and each participant shall be obligated to pay the Fund an amount equal to its net cumulative allocation of special drawing rights and such other amounts as may be due and payable because of its participation in the Special Drawing Rights Department.

(d) Liquidation of the Special Drawing Rights Department shall be administered in accordance with the provisions of Schedule I.

Article XXVI—Withdrawal from Membership

Section 1. Right of members to withdraw

Any member may withdraw from the Fund at any time by transmitting a notice in writing to the Fund at its principal office. Withdrawal shall become effective on the date such notice is received.

Section 2. Compulsory withdrawal

(a) If a member fails to fulfill any of its obligations under this Agreement, the Fund may declare the member ineligible to use the general resources of the Fund. Nothing in this Section shall be deemed to limit the provisions of Article V, Section 5 or Article VI, Section 1.

(b) If, after the expiration of a reasonable period following a declaration of ineligibility under (a) above, the member persists in its failure to fulfill any of its obligations under this Agreement, the Fund may, by a seventy percent majority of the total voting power, suspend the voting rights of the member. During the period of the suspension, the provisions of Schedule L shall apply. The Fund may, by a seventy percent majority of the total voting power, terminate the suspension at any time.

(c) If, after the expiration of a reasonable period following a decision of suspension under (b) above, the member persists in its failure to fulfill any of its obligations under this Agreement, that member may be required to withdraw from membership in the Fund by a decision of the Board of Governors carried by a majority of the Governors having eighty-five percent of the total voting power.

(d) Regulations shall be adopted to ensure that before action is taken against any member under (a), (b), or (c) above, the member shall be informed in reasonable time of the complaint against it and given an adequate opportunity for stating its case, both orally and in writing.

SECTION 3. SETTLEMENT OF ACCOUNTS WITH MEMBERS WITHDRAWING

When a member withdraws from the Fund, normal operations and transactions of the Fund in its currency shall cease and settlement of all accounts between it and the Fund shall be made with reasonable despatch by agreement between it and the Fund. If agreement is not reached promptly, the provisions of Schedule J shall apply to the settlement of accounts.

Article XXVII—Emergency Provisions

SECTION 1. TEMPORARY SUSPENSION

(a) In the event of an emergency or the development of unforeseen circumstances threatening the activities of the Fund, the Executive Board, by an eighty-five percent majority of the total voting power, may suspend for a period of not more than one year the operation of any of the following provisions:

(i) Article V, Sections 2, 3, 7, 8(a)(i) and (e);
(ii) Article VI, Section 2;
(iii) Article XI, Section 1;
(iv) Schedule C, paragraph 5.

(b) A suspension of the operation of a provision under (a) above may not be extended beyond one year except by the Board of Governors which, by an eighty-five percent majority of the total voting power, may extend a suspension for an additional period of not more than two years if it finds that the emergency or unforeseen circumstances referred to in (a) above continue to exist.

(c) The Executive Board may, by a majority of the total voting power, terminate such suspension at any time.

(d) The Fund may adopt rules with respect to the subject matter of a provision during the period in which its operation is suspended.

SECTION 2. LIQUIDATION OF THE FUND

(a) The Fund may not be liquidated except by decision of the Board of Governors. In an emergency, if the Executive Board decides that liquidation of the Fund may be necessary, it may temporarily suspend all operations and transactions, pending decision by the Board of Governors.

(b) If the Board of Governors decides to liquidate the Fund, the Fund shall forthwith cease to engage in any activities except those incidental to the orderly collection and liquidation of its assets and the settlement of its liabilities, and all obligations of members under this Agreement shall cease except those set out in this Article, in Article XXIX(c), in Schedule J, paragraph 7, and in Schedule K.

(c) Liquidation shall be administered in accordance with the provisions of Schedule K.

ARTICLE XXVIII—AMENDMENTS

(a) Any proposal to introduce modifications in this Agreement, whether emanating from a member, a Governor, or the Executive Board, shall be communicated to the chairman of the Board of Governors who shall bring the proposal before the Board of Governors. If the proposed amendment is approved by the Board of Governors, the Fund shall, by circular letter or telegram, ask all members whether they accept the proposed amendment. When three-fifths of the members, having eighty-five percent of the total voting power, have accepted the proposed amendment, the Fund shall certify the fact by a formal communication addressed to all members.

(b) Notwithstanding (a) above, acceptance by all members is required in the case of any amendment modifying:

(i) the right to withdraw from the Fund (Article XXVI, Section 1);

(ii) the provision that no change in a member's quota shall be made without its consent (Article III, Section 2(d)); and

(iii) the provision that no change may be made in the par value of a member's currency except on the proposal of that member (Schedule C, paragraph 6).

(c) Amendments shall enter into force for all members three months after the date of the formal communication unless a shorter period is specified in the circular letter or telegram.

ARTICLE XXIX—INTERPRETATION

(a) Any question of interpretation of the provisions of this Agreement arising between any member and the Fund or between any members of the Fund shall be submitted to the Executive Board for its decision. If the question particularly affects any member not entitled to appoint an Executive Director, it shall be entitled to representation in accordance with Article XII, Section 3(j).

(b) In any case where the Executive Board has given a decision under (a) above, any member may require, within three months from the date of the decision, that the question be referred to the Board of Governors, whose decision shall be final. Any question referred to the Board of Governors shall be considered by a Committee on Interpretation of the Board of Governors. Each Committee member shall have one vote. The Board of Governors shall establish the membership, procedures, and voting majorities of the Committee. A decision of the Committee shall be the decision of the Board of Governors unless the Board of Governors, by an eighty-five percent majority of the total voting power, decides otherwise. Pending the result of the reference to the Board of Governors the Fund may, so far as it deems necessary, act on the basis of the decision of the Executive Board.

(c) Whenever a disagreement arises between the Fund and a member which has withdrawn, or between the Fund and any member during liquidation of the Fund, such disagreement shall be submitted to arbitration by a tribunal of three arbitrators, one appointed by the Fund, another by the member or withdrawing member, and an umpire who, unless the parties otherwise agree, shall be appointed by the President of the International Court of Justice or such other authority as may have been prescribed by regulation adopted by the Fund. The umpire shall have full power to settle all questions of procedure in any case where the parties are in disagreement with respect thereto.

ARTICLE XXX—EXPLANATION OF TERMS

In interpreting the provisions of this Agreement the Fund and its members shall be guided by the following provisions:

(a) The Fund's holdings of a member's currency in the General Resources Account shall include any securities accepted by the Fund under Article III, Section 4.

(b) Stand-by arrangement means a decision of the Fund by which a member is assured that it will be able to make purchases from the General Resources Account in accordance with the terms of the decision during a specified period and up to a specified amount.

(c) Reserve tranche purchase means a purchase by a member of special drawing rights or the currency of another member in exchange for its own currency which does not cause the Fund's holdings of the member's currency in the General Resources Account to exceed its quota, provided that for the purposes of this definition the Fund may exclude purchases and holdings under:

(i) policies on the use of its general resources for compensatory financing of export fluctuations;

(ii) policies on the use of its general resources in connection with the financing of contributions to international buffer stocks of primary products; and

(iii) other policies on the use of its general resources in respect of which the Fund decides, by an eighty-five percent majority of the total voting power, that an exclusion shall be made.

(d) Payments for current transactions means payments which are not for the purpose of transferring capital, and includes, without limitation:

(1) all payments due in connection with foreign trade, other current business, including services, and normal short-term banking and credit facilities;

(2) payments due as interest on loans and as net income from other investments;

(3) payments of moderate amount for amortization of loans or for depreciation of direct investments; and

(4) moderate remittances for family living expenses.

The Fund may, after consultation with the members concerned, determine whether certain specific transactions are to be considered current transactions or capital transactions.

(e) Net cumulative allocation of special drawing rights means the total amount of special drawing rights allocated to a participant less its share of special drawing rights that have been cancelled under Article XVIII, Section 2(a).

(f) A freely usable currency means a member's currency that the Fund determines (i) is, in fact, widely used to make payments for international transactions, and (ii) is widely traded in the principal exchange markets.

(g) Members that were members on August 31, 1975 shall be deemed to include a member that accepted membership after that date pursuant to a resolution of the Board of Governors adopted before that date.

(h) Transactions of the Fund means exchanges of monetary assets by the Fund for other monetary assets. Operations of the Fund means other uses or receipts of monetary assets by the Fund.

(i) Transactions in special drawing rights means exchanges of special drawing rights for other monetary assets. Operations in special drawing rights means other uses of special drawing rights.

Article XXXI—Final Provisions

Section 1. Entry into Force

This Agreement shall enter into force when it has been signed on behalf of governments having sixty-five percent of the total of the quotas set forth in Schedule A and when the instruments referred to in Section 2(a) of this Article have been deposited on their behalf, but in no event shall this Agreement enter into force before May 1, 1945.

Section 2. Signature

(a) Each government on whose behalf this Agreement is signed shall deposit with the Government of the United States of America an instrument setting forth that it has accepted this Agreement in accordance with its law and has taken all steps necessary to enable it to carry out all of its obligations under this Agreement.

(b) Each country shall become a member of the Fund as from the date of the deposit on its behalf of the instrument referred to in (a) above, except that no country shall become a member before this Agreement enters into force under Section 1 of this Article.

(c) The Government of the United States of America shall inform the governments of all countries whose names are set forth in

Schedule A, and the governments of all countries whose membership is approved in accordance with Article II, Section 2, of all signatures of this Agreement and of the deposit of all instruments referred to in (a) above.

(d) At the time this Agreement is signed on its behalf, each government shall transmit to the Government of the United States of America one one-hundredth of one percent of its total subscription in gold or United States dollars for the purpose of meeting administrative expenses of the Fund. The Government of the United States of America shall hold such funds in a special deposit account and shall transmit them to the Board of Governors of the Fund when the initial meeting has been called. If this Agreement has not come into force by December 31, 1945, the Government of the United States of America shall return such funds to the governments that transmitted them.

(e) This Agreement shall remain open for signature at Washington on behalf of the governments of the countries whose names are set forth in Schedule A until December 31, 1945.

(f) After December 31, 1945, this Agreement shall be open for signature on behalf of the government of any country whose membership has been approved in accordance with Article II, Section 2.

(g) By their signature of this Agreement, all governments accept it both on their own behalf and in respect of all their colonies, overseas territories, all territories under their protection, suzerainty, or authority, and all territories in respect of which they exercise a mandate.

(h) Subsection (d) above shall come into force with regard to each signatory government as from the date of its signature.

[The signature and depositary clause reproduced below followed the text of Article XX in the original Articles of Agreement]

DONE at Washington, in a single copy which shall remain deposited in the archives of the Government of the United States of America, which shall transmit certified copies to all governments whose names are set forth in Schedule A and to all governments whose membership is approved in accordance with Article II, Section 2.

Schedule A—Quotas[5]

[In millions of U.S. dollars]

Country	Quota	Country	Quota
Australia	200	India	400
Belgium	225	Iran	25
Bolivia	10	Iraq	8
Brazil	150	Liberia	.5
Canada	300	Luxembourg	10
Chile	50	Mexico	90
China	550	Netherlands	275
Colombia	50	New Zealand	50
Costa Rica	5	Nicaragua	2
Cuba	50	Norway	50
Czechoslovakia	125	Panama	.5

[5] Subsequent changes in membership and quotas are not reflected in Schedule A.

Schedule A—Quotas[5]

[In millions of U.S. dollars]

Denmark	(*)	Paraguay	2
Dominican Republic	5	Peru	25
Ecuador	5	Philippine Commonwealth.	15
Egypt	45	Poland	125
El Salvador	2.5	Union of South Africa	100
Ethiopia	6	Union of Soviet Socialist Republics	1,200
France	450	United Kingdom	1,300
Greece	40	United States	2,750
Guatemala	5	Uruguay	15
Haiti	5	Venezuela	15
Hondouras	2.5	Yugoslavia	60
Iceland	1		

*The quota of Denmark shall be determined by the Fund after the Danish Government has declared its readiness to sign this Agreement but before signature takes place.

SCHEDULE B—TRANSITIONAL PROVISIONS WITH RESPECT TO REPURCHASE, PAYMENT OF ADDITIONAL SUBSCRIPTIONS, GOLD, AND CERTAIN OPERATIONAL MATTERS

1. Repurchase obligations that have accrued pursuant to Article V, Section 7(b) before the date of the second amendment of this Agreement and that remain undischarged at that date shall be discharged not later than the date or dates at which the obligations had to be discharged in accordance with the provisions of this Agreement before the second amendment.

2. A member shall discharge with special drawing rights any obligation to pay gold to the Fund in repurchase or as a subscription that is outstanding at the date of the second amendment of this Agreement, but the Fund may prescribe that these payments may be made in whole or in part in the currencies of other members specified by the Fund. A non-participant shall discharge an obligation that must be paid in special drawing rights pursuant to this provision with the currencies of other members specified by the Fund.

3. For the purposes of 2 above 0.888 671 gram of fine gold shall be equivalent to one special drawing right, and the amount of currency payable under 2 above shall be determined on that basis and on the basis of the value of the currency in terms of the special drawing right at the date of discharge.

4. A member's currency held by the Fund in excess of seventy-five percent of the member's quota at the date of the second amendment of this Agreement and not subject to repurchase under 1 above shall be repurchased in accordance with the following rules:

(i) Holdings that resulted from a purchase shall be repurchased in accordance with the policy on the use of the Fund's general resources under which the purchase was made.

(ii) Other holdings shall be repurchased not later than four years after the date of the second amendment of this Agreement.

5. Repurchases under 1 above that are not subject to 2 above, repurchases under 4 above, and any specification of currencies under 2 above shall be in accordance with Article V, Section 7(i).

6. All rules and regulations, rates, procedures, and decisions in effect at the date of the second amendment of this Agreement shall remain in effect until they are changed in accordance with the provisions of this Agreement.

7. To the extent that arrangements equivalent in effect to (a) and (b) below have not been completed before the date of the second amendment of this Agreement, the Fund shall

(a) sell up to 25 million ounces of fine gold held by it on August 31, 1975 to those members that were members on that date and that agree to buy it, in proportion to their quotas on that date. The sale to a member under this sub-paragraph (a) shall be made in exchange for its currency and at a price equivalent at the time of sale to one special drawing right per 0.888 671 gram of fine gold, and

(b) sell up to 25 million ounces of fine gold held by it on August 31, 1975 for the benefit of developing members that were members on that date, provided, however, that the part of any profits or surplus value of the gold that corresponds to the proportion of such a member's quota on August 31, 1975 to the total of the quotas of all members on that date shall be transferred directly to each such member. The requirements under Article V, Section 12(c) that the Fund consult a member, obtain a member's concurrence, or exchange a member's currency for the currencies of other members in certain circumstances shall apply with respect to currency received by the Fund as a result of sales of gold under this provision, other than sales to a member in return for its own currency, and placed in the General Resources Account.

Upon the sale of gold under this paragraph 7, an amount of the proceeds in the currencies received equivalent at the time of sale to one special drawing right per 0.888 671 gram of fine gold shall be placed in the General Resources Account and other assets held by the Fund under arrangements pursuant to (b) above shall be held separately from the general resources of the Fund. Assets that remain subject to disposition by the Fund upon termination of arrangements pursuant to (b) above shall be transferred to the Special Disbursement Account.

Schedule C—Par Values

1. The Fund shall notify members that par values may be established for the purposes of this Agreement, in accordance with Article IV, Sections 1, 3, 4, and 5 and this Schedule, in terms of the special drawing right, or in terms of such other common denominator as is prescribed by the Fund. The common denominator shall not be gold or a currency.

2. A member that intends to establish a par value for its currency shall propose a par value to the Fund within a reasonable time after notice is given under 1 above.

3. Any member that does not intend to establish a par value for its currency under 1 above shall consult with the Fund and ensure that its exchange arrangements are consistent with the purposes of the Fund and are adequate to fulfill its obligations under Article IV, Section 1.

4. The Fund shall concur in or object to a proposed par value within a reasonable period after receipt of the proposal. A proposed par value shall not take effect for the purposes of this Agreement if the Fund objects to it, and the member shall be subject to 3 above. The Fund shall not object because of the domestic social or political policies of the member proposing the par value.

5. Each member that has a par value for its currency undertakes to apply appropriate measures consistent with this Agreement in order to ensure that the maximum and the minimum rates for spot exchange transactions taking place within its territories between its currency and the currencies of other members maintaining par values shall not differ from parity by more than four and one-half percent or by such other margin or margins as the Fund may adopt by an eighty-five percent majority of the total voting power.

6. A member shall not propose a change in the par value of its currency except to correct, or prevent the emergence of, a fundamental disequilibrium. A change may be made only on the proposal of the member and only after consultation with the Fund.

7. When a change is proposed, the Fund shall concur in or object to the proposed par value within a reasonable period after receipt of the proposal. The Fund shall concur if it is satisfied that the change is necessary to correct, or prevent the emergence of, a fundamental disequilibrium. The Fund shall not object because of the domestic social or political policies of the member proposing the change. A proposed change in par value shall not take effect for the purposes of this Agreement if the Fund objects to it. If a member changes the par value of its currency despite the objection of the Fund, the member shall be subject to Article XXVI, Section 2. Maintenance of an unrealistic par value by a member shall be discouraged by the Fund.

8. The par value of a member's currency established under this Agreement shall cease to exist for the purposes of this Agreement if the member informs the Fund that it intends to terminate the par value. The Fund may object to the termination of a par value by a decision taken by an eighty-five percent majority of the total voting power. If a member terminates a par value for its currency despite the objection of the Fund, the member shall be subject to Article XXVI, Section 2. A par value established under this Agreement shall cease to exist for the purposes of this Agreement if the member terminates the par value despite the objection of the Fund, or if the Fund finds that the member does not maintain rates for a substantial volume of exchange transactions in accordance with 5 above, provided that the Fund may not make such finding unless it has consulted the member and given it sixty days notice of the Fund's intention to consider whether to make a finding.

9. If the par value of the currency of a member has ceased to exist under 8 above, the member shall consult with the Fund and ensure that its exchange arrangements are consistent with the purposes of the Fund and are adequate to fulfill its obligations under Article IV, Section 1.

10. A member for whose currency the par value has ceased to exist under 8 above may, at any time, propose a new par value for its currency.

11. Notwithstanding 6 above, the Fund, by a seventy percent majority of the total voting power, may make uniform proportionate changes in all par values if the special drawing right is the common denominator and the changes will not affect the value of the special drawing right. The par value of a member's currency shall, however, not be changed under this provision if, within seven days after the Fund's action, the member informs the Fund that it does not wish the par value of its currency to be changed by such action.

SCHEDULE D—COUNCIL

1. (a) Each member that appoints an Executive Director and each group of members that has the number of votes allotted to them cast by an elected Executive Director shall appoint to the Council one Councillor, who shall be a Governor, Minister in the government of a member, or person of comparable rank, and may appoint not more than seven Associates. The Board of Governors may change, by an eighty-five percent majority of the total voting power, the number of Associates who may be appointed. A Councillor or Associate shall serve until a new appointment is made or until the next regular election of Executive Directors, whichever shall occur sooner.

(b) Executive Directors, or in their absence their Alternates, and Associates shall be entitled to attend meetings of the Council, unless the Council decides to hold a restricted session. Each member and each group of members that appoints a Councillor shall appoint an Alternate who shall be entitled to attend a meeting of the Council when the Councillor is not present, and shall have full power to act for the Councillor.

2. (a) The Council shall supervise the management and adaptation of the international monetary system, including the continuing operation of the adjustment process and developments in global liquidity, and in this connection shall review developments in the transfer of real resources to developing countries.

(b) The Council shall consider proposals pursuant to Article XXVIII(a) to amend the Articles of Agreement.

3. (a) The Board of Governors may delegate to the Council authority to exercise any powers of the Board of Governors except the powers conferred directly by this Agreement on the Board of Governors.

(b) Each Councillor shall be entitled to cast the number of votes allotted under Article XII, Section 5 to the member or group of members appointing him. A Councillor appointed by a group of members may cast separately the votes allotted to each member in the group. If the number of votes allotted to a member cannot be cast by an Executive Director, the member may make arrangements with a Councillor for casting the number of votes allotted to the member.

(c) The Council shall not take any action pursuant to powers delegated by the Board of Governors that is inconsistent with any action taken by the Board of Governors and the Executive Board shall not take any action pursuant to powers delegated by the Board of Governors that is inconsistent with any action taken by either the Board of Governors or the Council.

4. The Council shall select a Councillor as chairman, shall adopt regulations as may be necessary or appropriate to perform its functions, and shall determine any aspect of its procedure. The Council shall hold such meetings as may be provided for by the Council or called by the Executive Board.

5. (a) The Council shall have powers corresponding to those of the Executive Board under the following provisions: Article XII, Section 2(c), (f), (g), and (j); Article XVIII, Section 4(a) and Section 4(c)(iv); Article XXIII, Section 1; and Article XXVII, Section l(a).

(b) For decisions by the Council on matters pertaining exclusively to the Special Drawing Rights Department, only Councillors appointed by a member that is a participant or a group of members at least one member of which is a participant shall be entitled to vote. Each of these Councillors shall be entitled to cast the number of votes allotted to the member which is a participant that appointed him or to the members that are participants in the group of members that appointed him, and may cast the votes allotted to a participant with which arrangements have been made pursuant to the last sentence of 3(b) above.

(c) The Council may by regulation establish a procedure whereby the Executive Board may obtain a vote of the Councillors on a specific question without a meeting of the Council when in the judgment of the Executive Board an action must be taken by the Council which should not be postponed until the next meeting of the Council and which does not warrant the calling of a special meeting.

(d) Article IX, Section 8 shall apply to Councillors, their Alternates, and Associates, and to any other person entitled to attend a meeting of the Council.

(e) For the purposes of (b) and 3(b) above, an agreement under Article XII, Section 3(i)(ii) by a member, or by a member that is a participant, shall entitle a Councillor to vote and cast the number of votes allotted to the member.

(f) When an Executive Director is entitled to cast the number of votes allotted to a member pursuant to Article XII, Section 3(i)(v), the Councillor appointed by the group whose members elected such Executive Director shall be entitled to vote and cast the number of votes allotted to such member. The member shall be deemed to have participated in the appointment of the Councillor entitled to vote and cast the number of votes allotted to the member.

6. The first sentence of Article XII, Section 2(a) shall be deemed to include a reference to the Council.

SCHEDULE E—ELECTION OF EXECUTIVE DIRECTORS

1. The election of the elective Executive Directors shall be by ballot of the Governors eligible to vote.

2. In balloting for the Executive Directors to be elected, each of the Governors eligible to vote shall cast for one person all of the votes to which he is entitled under Article XII, Section 5(a). The fifteen persons receiving the greatest number of votes shall be Executive Directors, provided that no person who received less than four percent of the total number of votes that can be cast (eligible votes) shall be considered elected.

3. When fifteen persons are not elected in the first ballot, a second ballot shall be held in which there shall vote only (a) those Governors who voted in the first ballot for a person not elected, and (b) those Governors whose votes for a person elected are deemed under 4 below to have raised the votes cast for that person above nine percent of the eligible votes. If in the second ballot there are more candidates than the number of Executive Directors to be elected, the person who received the lowest number of votes in the first ballot shall be ineligible for election.

4. In determining whether the votes cast by a Governor are to be deemed to have raised the total of any person above nine percent of the eligible votes, the nine percent shall be deemed to include, first, the votes of the Governor casting the largest number of votes for such person, then the votes of the Governor casting the next largest number, and so on until nine percent is reached.

5. Any Governor, part of whose votes must be counted in order to raise the total of any person above four percent, shall be considered as casting all of his votes for such person even if the total votes for such person thereby exceed nine percent.

6. If, after the second ballot, fifteen persons have not been elected, further ballots shall be held on the same principles until fifteen persons have been elected, provided that after fourteen persons are elected, the fifteenth may be elected by a simple majority of the remaining votes and shall be deemed to have been elected by all such votes.

SCHEDULE F—DESIGNATION

During the first basic period the rules for designation shall be as follows:

(a) Participants subject to designation under Article XIX, Section 5(a)(i) shall be designated for such amounts as will promote over time equality in the ratios of the participants' holdings of special drawing rights in excess of their net cumulative allocations to their official holdings of gold and foreign exchange.

(b) The formula to give effect to (a) above shall be such that participants subject to designation shall be designated:

(i) in proportion to their official holdings of gold and foreign exchange when the ratios described in (a) above are equal; and

(ii) in such manner as gradually to reduce the difference between the ratios described in (a) above that are low and the ratios that are high.

Schedule G—Reconstitution

1. During the first basic period the rules for reconstitution shall be as follows:

(a)(i) A participant shall so use and reconstitute its holdings of special drawing rights that, five years after the first allocation and at the end of each calendar quarter thereafter, the average of its total daily holdings of special drawing rights over the most recent five-year period will be not less than thirty percent of the average of its daily net cumulative allocation of special drawing rights over the same period.

(ii) Two years after the first allocation and at the end of each calendar month thereafter the Fund shall make calculations for each participant so as to ascertain whether and to what extent the participant would need to acquire special drawing rights between the date of the calculation and the end of any five-year period in order to comply with the requirement in (a)(i) above. The Fund shall adopt regulations with respect to the bases on which these calculations shall be made and with respect to the timing of the designation of participants under Article XIX, Section 5(a)(ii), in order to assist them to comply with the requirement in (a)(i) above.

(iii) The Fund shall give special notice to a participant when the calculations under (a)(ii) above indicate that it is unlikely that the participant will be able to comply with the requirement in (a)(i) above unless it ceases to use special drawing rights for the rest of the period for which the calculation was made under (a)(ii) above.

(iv) A participant that needs to acquire special drawing rights to fulfill this obligation shall be obligated and entitled to obtain them, for currency acceptable to the Fund, in a transaction with the Fund conducted through the General Resources Account. If sufficient special drawing rights to fulfill this obligation cannot be obtained in this way, the participant shall be obligated and entitled to obtain them with a freely usable currency from a participant which the Fund shall specify.

(b) Participants shall also pay due regard to the desirability of pursuing over time a balanced relationship between their holdings of special drawing rights and their other reserves.

2. If a participant fails to comply with the rules for reconstitution, the Fund shall determine whether or not the circumstances justify suspension under Article XXIII, Section 2(b).

Schedule H—Termination of Participation

1. If the obligation remaining after the setoff under Article XXIV, Section 2(b) is to the terminating participant and agreement on settlement between the Fund and the terminating participant is not reached within six months of the date of termination, the Fund shall redeem this balance of special drawing rights in equal half-yearly installments within a maximum of five years of the date of termination. The Fund shall redeem this balance as it may determine, either (a) by the payment to the terminating participant of the amounts provided by the remaining participants to the Fund in accordance with Article XXIV, Section 5, or (b) by permitting the

terminating participant to use its special drawing rights to obtain its own currency or a freely usable currency from a participant specified by the Fund, the General Resources Account, or any other holder.

2. If the obligation remaining after the setoff under Article XXIV, Section 2(b) is to the Fund and agreement on settlement is not reached within six months of the date of termination, the terminating participant shall discharge this obligation in equal half-yearly installments within three years of the date of termination or within such longer period as may be fixed by the Fund. The terminating participant shall discharge this obligation, as the Fund may determine, either (a) by the payment to the Fund of a freely usable currency, or (b) by obtaining special drawing rights, in accordance with Article XXIV, Section 6, from the General Resources Account or in agreement with a participant specified by the Fund or from any other holder, and the setoff of these special drawing rights against the installment due.

3. Installments under either 1 or 2 above shall fall due six months after the date of termination and at intervals of six months thereafter.

4. In the event of the Special Drawing Rights Department going into liquidation under Article XXV within six months of the date a participant terminates its participation, the settlement between the Fund and that government shall be made in accordance with Article XXV and Schedule I.

SCHEDULE I—ADMINISTRATION OF LIQUIDATION OF THE SPECIAL DRAWING RIGHTS DEPARTMENT

1. In the event of liquidation of the Special Drawing Rights Department, participants shall discharge their obligations to the Fund in ten half-yearly installments, or in such longer period as the Fund may decide is needed, in a freely usable currency and the currencies of participants holding special drawing rights to be redeemed in any installment to the extent of such redemption, as determined by the Fund. The first half-yearly payment shall be made six months after the decision to liquidate the Special Drawing Rights Department.

2. If it is decided to liquidate the Fund within six months of the date of the decision to liquidate the Special Drawing Rights Department, the liquidation of the Special Drawing Rights Department shall not proceed until special drawing rights held in the General Resources Account have been distributed in accordance with the following rule:

> After the distributions made under 2(a) and (b) of Schedule K, the Fund shall apportion its special drawing rights held in the General Resources Account among all members that are participants in proportion to the amounts due to each participant after the distribution under 2(b). To determine the amount due to each member for the purpose of apportioning the remainder of its holdings of each currency under 2(d) of Schedule K, the Fund shall deduct the distribution of special drawing rights made under this rule.

3. With the amounts received under 1 above, the Fund shall redeem special drawing rights held by holders in the following manner and order:

(a) Special drawing rights held by governments that have terminated their participation more than six months before the date the Board of Governors decides to liquidate the Special Drawing Rights Department shall be redeemed in accordance with the terms of any agreement under Article XXIV or Schedule H.

(b) Special drawing rights held by holders that are not participants shall be redeemed before those held by participants, and shall be redeemed in proportion to the amount held by each holder.

(c) The Fund shall determine the proportion of special drawing rights held by each participant in relation to its net cumulative allocation. The Fund shall first redeem special drawing rights from the participants with the highest proportion until this proportion is reduced to that of the second highest proportion; the Fund shall then redeem the special drawing rights held by these participants in accordance with their net cumulative allocations until the proportions are reduced to that of the third highest proportion; and this process shall be continued until the amount available for redemption is exhausted.

4. Any amount that a participant will be entitled to receive in redemption under 3 above shall be set off against any amount to be paid under 1 above.

5. During liquidation the Fund shall pay interest on the amount of special drawing rights held by holders, and each participant shall pay charges on the net cumulative allocation of special drawing rights to it less the amount of any payments made in accordance with 1 above. The rates of interest and charges and the time of payment shall be determined by the Fund. Payments of interest and charges shall be made in special drawing rights to the extent possible. A participant that does not hold sufficient special drawing rights to meet any charges shall make the payment with a currency specified by the Fund. Special drawing rights received as charges in amounts needed for administrative expenses shall not be used for the payment of interest, but shall be transferred to the Fund and shall be redeemed first and with the currencies used by the Fund to meet its expenses.

6. While a participant is in default with respect to any payment required by 1 or 5 above, no amounts shall be paid to it in accordance with 3 or 5 above.

7. If after the final payments have been made to participants each participant not in default does not hold special drawing rights in the same proportion to its net cumulative allocation, those participants holding a lower proportion shall purchase from those holding a higher proportion such amounts in accordance with arrangements made by the Fund as will make the proportion of their holdings of special drawing rights the same. Each participant in default shall pay to the Fund its own currency in an amount equal to its default. The Fund shall apportion this currency and residual claims among participants in proportion to the amount of special drawing rights held by each and these special drawing rights shall

be cancelled. The Fund shall then close the books of the Special Drawing Rights Department and all of the Fund's liabilities arising from the allocations of special drawing rights and the administration of the Special Drawing Rights Department shall cease.

8. Each participant whose currency is distributed to other participants under this Schedule guarantees the unrestricted use of such currency at all times for the purchase of goods or for payments of sums due to it or to persons in its territories. Each participant so obligated agrees to compensate other participants for any loss resulting from the difference between the value at which the Fund distributed its currency under this Schedule and the value realized by such participants on disposal of its currency.

SCHEDULE J—SETTLEMENT OF ACCOUNTS WITH MEMBERS WITHDRAWING

1. The settlement of accounts with respect to the General Resources Account shall be made according to 1 to 6 of this Schedule. The Fund shall be obligated to pay to a member withdrawing an amount equal to its quota, plus any other amounts due to it from the Fund, less any amounts due to the Fund, including charges accruing after the date of its withdrawal; but no payment shall be made until six months after the date of withdrawal. Payments shall be made in the currency of the withdrawing member, and for this purpose the Fund may transfer to the General Resources Account holdings of the member's currency in the Special Disbursement Account or in the Investment Account in exchange for an equivalent amount of the currencies of other members in the General Resources Account selected by the Fund with their concurrence.

2. If the Fund's holdings of the currency of the withdrawing member are not sufficient to pay the net amount due from the Fund, the balance shall be paid in a freely usable currency, or in such other manner as may be agreed. If the Fund and the withdrawing member do not reach agreement within six months of the date of withdrawal, the currency in question held by the Fund shall be paid forthwith to the withdrawing member. Any balance due shall be paid in ten half-yearly installments during the ensuing five years. Each such installment shall be paid, at the option of the Fund, either in the currency of the withdrawing member acquired after its withdrawal or in a freely usable currency.

3. If the Fund fails to meet any installment which is due in accordance with the preceding paragraphs, the withdrawing member shall be entitled to require the Fund to pay the installment in any currency held by the Fund with the exception of any currency which has been declared scarce under Article VII, Section 3.

4. If the Fund's holdings of the currency of a withdrawing member exceed the amount due to it, and if agreement on the method of settling accounts is not reached within six months of the date of withdrawal, the former member shall be obligated to redeem such excess currency in a freely usable currency. Redemption shall be made at the rates at which the Fund would sell such currencies

at the time of withdrawal from the Fund. The withdrawing member shall complete redemption within five years of the date of withdrawal, or within such longer period as may be fixed by the Fund, but shall not be required to redeem in any half-yearly period more than one-tenth of the Fund's excess holdings of its currency at the date of withdrawal plus further acquisitions of the currency during such half-yearly period. If the withdrawing member does not fulfill this obligation, the Fund may in an orderly manner liquidate in any market the amount of currency which should have been redeemed.

5. Any member desiring to obtain the currency of a member which has withdrawn shall acquire it by purchase from the Fund, to the extent that such member has access to the general resources of the Fund and that such currency is available under 4 above.

6. The withdrawing member guarantees the unrestricted use at all times of the currency disposed of under 4 and 5 above for the purchase of goods or for payment of sums due to it or to persons within its territories. It shall compensate the Fund for any loss resulting from the difference between the value of its currency in terms of the special drawing right on the date of withdrawal and the value realized in terms of the special drawing right by the Fund on disposal under 4 and 5 above.

7. If the withdrawing member is indebted to the Fund as the result of transactions conducted through the Special Disbursement Account under Article V, Section 12(f)(ii), the indebtedness shall be discharged in accordance with the terms of the indebtedness.

8. If the Fund holds the withdrawing member's currency in the Special Disbursement Account or in the Investment Account, the Fund may in an orderly manner exchange in any market for the currencies of members the amount of the currency of the withdrawing member remaining in each account after use under 1 above, and the proceeds of the exchange of the amount in each account shall be kept in that account. Paragraph 5 above and the first sentence of 6 above shall apply to the withdrawing member's currency.

9. If the Fund holds obligations of the withdrawing member in the Special Disbursement Account pursuant to Article V, Section 12(h), or in the Investment Account, the Fund may hold them until the date of maturity or dispose of them sooner. Paragraph 8 above shall apply to the proceeds of such disinvestment.

10. In the event of the Fund going into liquidation under Article XXVII, Section 2 within six months of the date on which the member withdraws, the accounts between the Fund and that government shall be settled in accordance with Article XXVII, Section 2 and Schedule K.

Schedule K—Administration of Liquidation

1. In the event of liquidation the liabilities of the Fund other than the repayment of subscriptions shall have priority in the distribution of the assets of the Fund. In meeting each such liability the Fund shall use its assets in the following order:

(a) the currency in which the liability is payable;

(b) gold;

(c) all other currencies in proportion, so far as may be practicable, to the quotas of the members.

2. After the discharge of the Fund's liabilities in accordance with 1 above, the balance of the Fund's assets shall be distributed and apportioned as follows:

(a)(i) The Fund shall calculate the value of gold held on August 31, 1975 that it continues to hold on the date of the decision to liquidate. The calculation shall be made in accordance with 9 below and also on the basis of one special drawing right per 0.888 671 gram of fine gold on the date of liquidation. Gold equivalent to the excess of the former value over the latter shall be distributed to those members that were members on August 31, 1975 in proportion to their quotas on that date.

(ii) The Fund shall distribute any assets held in the Special Disbursement Account on the date of the decision to liquidate to those members that were members on August 31, 1975 in proportion to their quotas on that date. Each type of asset shall be distributed proportionately to members.

(b) The Fund shall distribute its remaining holdings of gold among the members whose currencies are held by the Fund in amounts less than their quotas in the proportions, but not in excess of, the amounts by which their quotas exceed the Fund's holdings of their currencies.

(c) The Fund shall distribute to each member one-half the Fund's holdings of its currency but such distribution shall not exceed fifty percent of its quota.

(d) The Fund shall apportion the remainder of its holdings of gold and each currency

(i) among all members in proportion to, but not in excess of, the amounts due to each member after the distributions under (b) and (c) above, provided that distribution under 2(a) above shall not be taken into account for determining the amounts due, and

(ii) any excess holdings of gold and currency among all the members in proportion to their quotas.

3. Each member shall redeem the holdings of its currency apportioned to other members under 2(d) above, and shall agree with the Fund within three months after a decision to liquidate upon an orderly procedure for such redemption.

4. If a member has not reached agreement with the Fund within the three-month period referred to in 3 above, the Fund shall use the currencies of other members apportioned to that member under 2(d) above to redeem the currency of that member apportioned to other members. Each currency apportioned to a member which has not reached agreement shall be used, so far as possible, to redeem its currency apportioned to the members which have made agreements with the Fund under 3 above.

5. If a member has reached agreement with the Fund in accordance with 3 above, the Fund shall use the currencies of other members apportioned to that member under 2(d) above to redeem the currency of that member apportioned to other members which have made agreements with the Fund under 3 above. Each amount so redeemed shall be redeemed in the currency of the member to which it was apportioned.

6. After carrying out the steps in the preceding paragraphs, the Fund shall pay to each member the remaining currencies held for its account.

7. Each member whose currency has been distributed to other members under 6 above shall redeem such currency in the currency of the member requesting redemption, or in such other manner as may be agreed between them. If the members involved do not otherwise agree, the member obligated to redeem shall complete redemption within five years of the date of distribution, but shall not be required to redeem in any half-yearly period more than one-tenth of the amount distributed to each other member. If the member does not fulfill this obligation, the amount of currency which should have been redeemed may be liquidated in an orderly manner in any market.

8. Each member whose currency has been distributed to other members under 6 above guarantees the unrestricted use of such currency at all times for the purchase of goods or for payment of sums due to it or to persons in its territories. Each member so obligated agrees to compensate other members for any loss resulting from the difference between the value of its currency in terms of the special drawing right on the date of the decision to liquidate the Fund and the value in terms of the special drawing right realized by such members on disposal of its currency.

9. The Fund shall determine the value of gold under this Schedule on the basis of prices in the market.

10. For the purposes of this Schedule, quotas shall be deemed to have been increased to the full extent to which they could have been increased in accordance with Article III, Section 2(b) of this Agreement.

Schedule L—Suspension of Voting Rights

In the case of a suspension of voting rights of a member under Article XXVI, Section 2(b), the following provisions shall apply:

1. The member shall not:

(a) participate in the adoption of a proposed amendment of this Agreement, or be counted in the total number of members for that purpose, except in the case of an amendment requiring acceptance by all members under Article XXVIII(b) or pertaining exclusively to the Special Drawing Rights Department;

(b) appoint a Governor or Alternate Governor, appoint or participate in the appointment of a Councillor or Alternate Councillor, or appoint, elect, or participate in the election of an Executive Director.

2. The number of votes allotted to the member shall not be cast in any organ of the Fund. They shall not be included in the calculation of the total voting power, except for purposes of the acceptance of a proposed amendment pertaining exclusively to the Special Drawing Rights Department.

3. (a) The Governor and Alternate Governor appointed by the member shall cease to hold office.

(b) The Councillor and Alternate Councillor appointed by the member, or in whose appointment the member has participated, shall cease to hold office, provided that, if such Councillor was entitled to cast the number of votes allotted to other members whose voting rights have not been suspended, another Councillor and Alternate Councillor shall be appointed by such other members under Schedule D, and, pending such appointment, the Councillor and Alternate Councillor shall continue to hold office, but for a maximum of thirty days from the date of suspension.

(c) The Executive Director appointed or elected by the member, or in whose election the member has participated, shall cease to hold office, unless such Executive Director was entitled to cast the number of votes allotted to other members whose voting rights have not been suspended. In the latter case:

(i) if more than ninety days remain before the next regular election of Executive Directors, another Executive Director shall be elected for the remainder of the term by such other members by a majority of the votes cast; pending such election, the Executive Director shall continue to hold office, but for a maximum of thirty days from the date of suspension;

(ii) if not more than ninety days remain before the next regular election of Executive Directors, the Executive Director shall continue to hold office for the remainder of the term.

4. The member shall be entitled to send a representative to attend any meeting of the Board of Governors, the Council, or the Executive Board, but not any meeting of their committees, when a request made by, or a matter particularly affecting, the member is under consideration.

b. General Arrangements to Borrow

(1) Original Decision of the Executive Directors of the International Monetary Fund

Partial text of Decision No. 1289–(62/1), January 5, 1962

> NOTE.—On February 24, 1983, in Decision No. 7337–(83/37), the Executive Board of the International Monetary Fund approved provisions for enlarging and revising this Decision on the General Arrangements to Borrow (GAB), and for increasing the amounts of the participant's credit arrangements. This Decision became effective on December 26, 1983. The complete text of the revised Decision to the GAB with the Annex containing the increases in the participant's credit arrangements follows at item (3).
>
> The retained provisions of this decision, as reproduced below, reflect the wording of the text prior to its being amended. The text which reads the same in both versions of the Decision has been omitted from this Decision but has been printed in the revision.
>
> See also Decision No. 11428—(97/6) creating the New Arrangements to Borrow (NAB), item c. (1). The NAB doubles the amount of resources available to the IMF under the GAB. Although the NAB do not replace the existing GAB, the NAB would typically be the first and principal recourse in the event of a need to provide supplementary resources to the IMF.

Preamble

In order to enable the International Monetary Fund to fulfill more effectively its role in the international monetary system in the new conditions of widespread convertibility, including greater freedom for short-term capital movements, the main industrial countries have agreed that they will, in a spirit of broad and willing cooperation, strengthen the Fund by general arrangements under which they will stand ready to lend their currencies to the Fund up to specified amounts under Article VII, Section 2 of the Articles of Agreement when supplementary resources are needed to forestall or cope with an impairment of the international monetary system in the aforesaid conditions. In order to give effect to these intentions, the following terms and conditions are adopted under Article VII, Section 2 of the Articles of Agreement.

Paragraph 1. *Definitions*

* * * * * * *

(vi) "amount of a credit arrangement" means the maximum amount expressed in units of its currency that a participant undertakes to lend to the Fund under a credit arrangement;

* * * * * * *

(ix) "drawer" means a member that purchases borrowed currency from the Fund in an exchange transaction or in an exchange transaction under a standby arrangement;

Paragraph 2. *Credit Arrangements*

A member or institution that adheres to this Decision undertakes to lend its currency to the Fund on the terms and conditions of this Decision up to the amount in units of its currency set forth in the Annex to this Decision or established in accordance with Paragraph 3(b).

Paragraph 3. *Adherence*

(a) * * *

(b) Any member or institution not specified in the Annex that wishes to become a participant may at any time, after consultation with the Fund, give notice of its willingness to adhere to this Decision, and, if the Fund shall so agree and no participant object, the member or institution may adhere in accordance with Paragraph 3(c). When giving notice of its willingness to adhere under this Paragraph 3(b) a member or institution shall specify the amount, expressed in terms of its currency, of the credit arrangement which it is willing to enter into, provided that the amount shall not be less than the equivalent at the date of adherence of one hundred million United States dollars of the weight and fineness in effect on July 1, 1944.

* * * * * * *

Paragraph 6. *Initial Procedure*

When a participating member or a member whose institution is a participant approaches the Fund on an exchange transaction or stand-by arrangement and the Managing Director, after consultation, considers that the exchange transaction or stand-by arrangement is necessary in order to forestall or cope with an impairment of the international monetary system, and that the Fund's resources need to be supplemented for this purpose, he shall initiate the procedure for making calls under Paragraph 7.

Paragraph 7. *Calls*

(a) The Managing Director shall make a proposal for calls for an exchange transaction or for future calls for exchange transactions under a stand-by arrangement only after consultation with Executive Directors and participants. A proposal shall become effective only if it is accepted by participants and the proposal is then approved by the Executive Directors. Each participant shall notify the

Fund of the acceptance of a proposal involving a call under its credit arrangement.

* * * * * * *

(d) If a participant on which calls may be made pursuant to Paragraph 7(a) for a drawer's purchases under a stand-by arrangement gives notice to the Fund that in the participant's opinion, based on the present and prospective balance of payments and reserve position, calls should no longer be made on the participant or that calls should be for a smaller amount, the Managing Director may propose to other participants that substitute amounts be made available under their credit arrangements, and this proposal shall be subject to the procedure of Paragraph 7(a). The proposal as originally approved under Paragraph 7(a) shall remain effective unless and until a proposal for substitute amounts is approved in accordance with Paragraph 7(a).

* * * * * * *

Paragraph 9. *Interest and Charges*

(a) The Fund shall pay a charge of one-half of one percent on transfers made in accordance with Paragraph 7(e).

(b) The Fund shall pay interest on its indebtedness at the rate of one and one-half percent per annum. In the event that this becomes different from a basic rate determined as follows:

> the charge levied by the Fund pursuant to Article V, Section 8(a) plus the charge levied by the Fund pursuant to Article V, Section 8(c)(i), as changed from time to time under Article V, Section 8(e), during the first year after a purchase or exchange from the Fund, minus one-half of one percent.

The interest payable by the Fund shall be changed by the same amount as from the date when the difference in the basic rate takes effect. Interest shall be paid as soon as possible after July 31, October 31, January 31, and April 30.

(c) Interest and charges shall be paid in gold to the extent that this can be effected in bars. Any balance not so paid shall be paid in United States dollars.

(d) Gold payable to a participant in accordance with Paragraph 9(b) or Paragraph 11 shall be delivered at any gold depository of the Fund chosen by the participant at which the Fund has sufficient gold for making the payment. Such delivery shall be free of any charges or costs for the participant.

Paragraph 10. *Use of Borrowed Currency*

The Fund's policies and practices on the use of its resources and stand-by arrangements, including those relating to the period of use, shall apply to purchases of currency borrowed by the Fund.

Paragraph 11. *Repayment by the Fund*

(a) Subject to the other provisions of this Paragraph 11, the Fund, five years after a transfer by a participant, shall repay the participant an amount equivalent to the transfer calculated in accordance with Paragraph 12. If the drawer for whose purchase participants make transfers is committed to repurchase at a fixed date earlier than five years after its purchase, the Fund shall repay the participants at that date. Repayment under this Paragraph 11(a) or under Paragraph 11(c) shall be, as determined by the Fund, in the participant's currency whenever feasible, or in gold, or, after consultation with the participant, in other currencies that are convertible in fact. Repayments to a participant under the subsequent provisions of this Paragraph 11 shall be credited against transfers by the participant for a drawer's purchases in the order in which repayment must be made under this Paragraph 11(a).

(b)[1] Before the date prescribed in Paragraph 11(a), the Fund, after consultation with a participant, may make repayment to the participant, in part or in full. The Fund shall have the option to make repayment under this Paragraph 11(b) in the participant's currency, or in special drawing rights in an amount that does not increase the participant's holding of special drawing rights above the limit under Article XIX, Section 4, of the Articles of Agreement unless the participant agrees to accept special drawing rights above that limit in such repayment, or with the agreement of the participant, in other currencies that are actually convertible.

(c) Whenever a drawer repurchases, the Fund shall promptly repay an equivalent amount, except in any of the following cases:

(i) The repurchase is under Article V, Section 7(b) and can be identified as being in respect of a purchase of currency other than borrowed currency.

(ii) The repurchase is in discharge of a commitment entered into on a purchase of currency other than borrowed currency.

(iii) The repurchase entitles the drawer to augmented rights under a stand-by arrangement pursuant to Section II of Decision No. 876–(59/15) of the Executive Directors, provided that, to the extent that the drawer does not exercise such augmented rights, the Fund shall promptly repay an equivalent amount on the expiration of the stand-by arrangement.

(d) Whenever the Fund decides in agreement with a drawer that the problem for which the drawer made its purchases has been overcome, the drawer shall complete repurchase, and the Fund shall complete repayment and be entitled to use its holdings of the drawer's currency below 75 percent of the drawer's quota in order to complete such repayment.

(e) Repayments under Paragraph 11 (c) and (d) shall be made in the order established under Paragraph 11(a) and in proportion to the Fund's indebtedness to the participants that made transfers in respect of which repayment is being made.

(f) Before the date prescribed in Paragraph 11(a) a participant may give notice representing that there is a balance of payments need for repayment of part or all of the Fund's indebtedness and requesting such repayment. The Fund shall give the overwhelming benefit of any doubt to the participant's representation. Repayment shall be made after consultation with the participant in the currencies of other members that are convertible in fact, or made in

[1] Executive Board Decision No. 6241–(79/156), August 24, 1979, amended subpara. (b). Previously, subpara. (b) read as follows:

"(b) Before the date prescribed in Paragraph 11(a), the Fund, after consultation with a participant, may make repayment to the participant, in part or in full, with any increases in the Fund's holdings of the participant's currency that exceed the Fund's working requirements, and participants shall accept such repayment.".

gold, as determined by the Fund. If the Fund's holdings of currencies in which repayment should be made are not wholly adequate, individual participants shall be requested, and will be expected to provide the necessary balance under their credit arrangements. If, not withstanding the expectation that the participants will provide the necessary balance, they fail to do so, repayment shall be made to the extent necessary in the currency of the drawer for whose purchases the participant requesting repayment made transfers. For all of the purposes of this Paragraph 11, transfers under this Paragraph 11(f) shall be deemed to have been made at the same time and for the same purchases as the transfers by the participant obtaining repayment under this Paragraph 11(f).

(g) * * *[2]

(h) * * *[2]

(i) When any repayment is made to a participant, the amount that can be called for under its credit arrangement in accordance with this Decision shall be restored *pro tanto* but not beyond the amount of the credit arrangement.

Paragraph 12. *Rates of Exchange*

(a) The value of any transfer shall be calculated as of the date of the transfer in terms of a stated number of fine ounces of gold or of the United States dollar of the weight and fineness in effect on July 1, 1944, and the Fund shall be obliged to repay an equivalent value.

(b) For all of the purposes of this Decision, the equivalent in currency of any number of fine ounces of gold or of the United States dollar of the weight and fineness in effect on July 1, 1944, or *vice versa,* shall be calculated at the rate of exchange at which the Fund holds such currency at the date as of which the calculation is made; provided however that the provisions of Decision No. 321–(54/32) of the Executive Directors on Transactions and Computations Involving Fluctuating Currencies, as amended by Decision No. 1245–(61/45) and Decision No. 1283–(61/56), shall determine the rate of exchange for any currency to which that decision, as amended, has been applied.

* * * * * * *

Paragraph 14. *Notices*

Notice to or by a participating member under this Decision shall be in writing or by cable and shall be given to or by the fiscal agency of the participating member designated in accordance with Article V, Section 1 of the Articles and Rule G1 of the Rules and Regulations of the Fund. Notice to or by a participating institution shall be in writing or by cable and shall be given to or by the participating institution.

* * * * * * *

Paragraph 17. *Withdrawal from Membership*

If a participating member or a member whose institution is a participant withdraws from membership in the Fund, the partici-

[2] Paras. (g) and (h) became paras. (f) and (g) in the revised Decision.

pant's credit arrangement shall cease at the same time as the withdrawal takes effect. The Fund's indebtedness under the credit arrangement shall be treated as an amount due from the Fund for the purpose of Article XV, Section 3, and Schedule D of the Articles.

Paragraph 18. *Suspension of Exchange Transactions and Liquidation*

(a) The right of the Fund to make calls under Paragraph 7 and the obligation to make repayments under Paragraph 11 shall be suspended during any suspension of exchange transactions under Article XVI of the Articles.

(b) * * *

Paragraph 19. *Period and Renewal*

(a)[3] This Decision shall continue in existence for four years from its effective date.

* * * * * * *

Paragraph 20. *Interpretation*

Any question of interpretation raised in connection with this Decision which does not fall within the purview of Article XVIII of the Articles shall be settled to the mutual satisfaction of the Fund, the participant raising the question, and all other participants. For the purpose of this Paragraph 20 participants shall be deemed to include those former participants to which Paragraphs 8 through 14, 17 and 18(b) continue to apply pursuant to Paragraph 19(c) to the extent that any such former participant is affected by a question of interpretation that is raised.

Annex

Participants and Amounts of Credit Arrangements

	Units of Participant's Currency
1. United States of America (US$)	2,000,000,000
2. Deutsche Bundesbank (DM)	4,000,000
3. United Kingdom (£)	357,142,857
4. France (NF)	2,715,381,428
5. Italy (Lit)	343,750,000,000
6. Japan (Yen)	90,000,000,000
7. Canada (Can$)	216,216,000
8. Netherlands (f.)	724,000,000
9. Belgium (BF)	7,500,000,000
10. Sveriges Riksbank (Sweden) (SKr)	517,320,000

[3] This Decision has been renewed by the Executive Directors nine times, the most recent of which was November 12, 2002, for five years dating from December 2003.

The foregoing is the text of a decision of the Executive Board taken at Meeting 62/1, January 5, 1962.

ROMAN L. HORNE, *Secretary*.

(2) Letter from M. Wilfrid Baumgartner, Minister of Finance, France, to Douglas Dillon, Secretary of the Treasury, United States

MINISTÈRE DES FINANCES
Le Ministre, le 15 Décembre 1961.

The Honorable DOUGLAS DILLON,
Secretary of the Treasury.

DEAR MR. SECRETARY:

The purpose of this letter is to set forth the understandings reached during the recent discussions in Paris with respect to the procedure to be followed by the Participating Countries and Institutions (hereinafter referred to as "the participants") in connection with borrowings by the International Monetary Fund of Supplementary Resources under credit arrangements which we expect will be established pursuant to a decision of the Executive Directors of the Fund.

This procedure, which would apply after the entry into force of that decision with respect to the participants which adhere to it in accordance with their laws, and which would remain in effect during the period of the decision, is as follows:

A. A participating country which has need to draw currencies from the International Monetary Fund or to seek a stand-by agreement with the Fund in circumstances indicating that the Supplementary Resources might be used, shall consult with the Managing Director of the Fund first and then with the other participants.

B. If the Managing Director makes a proposal for Supplementary Resources to be lent to the Fund, the participants shall consult on this proposal and inform the Managing Director of the amounts of their currencies which they consider appropriate to lend to the Fund, taking into account the recommendations of the Managing Director and their present and prospective balance of payments and reserve positions. The participants shall aim at reaching unanimous agreement.

C. If it is not possible to reach unanimous agreement, the question whether the participants are prepared to facilitate, by lending their currencies, an exchange transaction or stand-by arrangement of the kind covered by the special borrowing arrangements and requiring the Fund's resources to be supplemented in the general order of magnitude proposed by the Managing Director, will be decided by a poll of the participants.

The prospective drawer will not be entitled to vote. A favorable decision shall require the following majorities of the participants which take part in the vote, it being understood that abstentions may be justified only for balance of payments reasons as stated in paragraph D:

(1) a two-thirds majority of the number of participants voting; and

(2) a three-fifth majority of the weighted votes of the participants voting, weighted on the basis of the commitments to the Supplementary Resources.

D. If the decision in paragraph C is favorable, there shall be further consultations among the participants, and with the Managing Director, concerning the amounts of the currencies of the respective participants which will be loaned to the Fund in order to attain a total in the general order of magnitude agreed under paragraph C. If during the consultations a participant gives notice that in its opinion, based on its present and prospective balance of payments and reserve position, calls should not be made on it, or that calls should be for a smaller amount than that proposed, the participants shall consult among themselves and with the Managing Director as to the additional amounts of their currencies which they could provide so as to reach the general order of magnitude agreed under paragraph C.

E. When agreement is reached under paragraph D, each participant shall inform the Managing Director of the calls which it is prepared to meet under its credit arrangement with the Fund.

F. If a participant which has loaned its currency to the Fund under its credit arrangement with the Fund subsequently requests a reversal of its loan which leads to further loans to the Fund by other participants, the participant seeking such reversal shall consult with the Managing Director and with the other participants.

For the purpose of the consultative procedures described above, participants will designate representatives who shall be empowered to act with respect to proposals for use of the Supplementary Resources.

It is understood that in the event of any proposals for calls under the credit arrangements or if other matters should arise under the Fund decision requiring consultations among the participants, a consultative meeting will be held among all the participants. The representative of France shall be responsible for calling the first meeting, and at that time the participants will determine who shall be the Chairman. The Managing Director of the Fund or his representative shall be invited to participate in these consultative meetings.

It is understood that in order to further the consultations envisaged, participants should, to the fullest extent practicable, use the facilities of the international organizations to which they belong in keeping each other informed of developments in their balances of payments that could give rise to the use of the Supplementary Resources.

These consultative arrangements, undertaken in a spirit of international cooperation, are designed to insure the stability of the international payments system.

I shall appreciate a reply confirming that the foregoing represents the understandings which have been reached with respect to the procedure to be followed in connection with borrowings by the International Monetary Fund under the credit arrangements to which I have referred.

I am sending identical letters to the other participants—that is, Belgium, Canada, Germany, Italy, Japan, The Netherlands, Sweden, the United Kingdom. Attached is a verbatim text of this letter in English. The French and English texts and the replies of the participants in both languages, shall be equally authentic. I shall notify all of the participants of the confirmations [1] received in response to this letter.

W. BAUMGARTNER.

[1] Acceptance by the United States, Belgium, Canada, Germany, Italy, Japan, the Netherlands, Sweden, the United Kingdom, and France.

(3) General Arrangements to Borrow: Revision

Decision No. 7337–(83/37) of the Executive Directors of the International Monetary Fund, February 24, 1983, as amended[1]

GENERAL ARRANGEMENTS TO BORROW: REVISED TEXT

Preamble

In order to enable the International Monetary Fund to fulfill more effectively its role in the international monetary system, the main industrial countries have agreed that they will, in a spirit of broad and willing cooperation, strengthen the Fund by general arrangements under which they will stand ready to make loans to the Fund up to specified amounts under Article VII, Section 1 of the Articles of Agreement when supplementary resources are needed to forestall or cope with an impairment of the international monetary system. In order to give effect to these intentions, the following terms and conditions are adopted under Article VII, Section 1 of the Articles of Agreement.

Paragraph 1. *Definitions*

As used in this Decision the term:

(i) "Articles" means the Articles of Agreement of the International Monetary Fund;

(ii) "credit arrangement" means an undertaking to lend to the Fund on the terms and conditions of this Decision;

(iii) "participant" means a participating member of a participating institution;

(iv) "participating institution" means an official institution of a member that has entered into a credit arrangement with the Fund with the consent of the member;

(v) "participating member" means a member of the Fund that has entered into a credit arrangement with the Fund;

(vi) "amount of a credit arrangement" means the maximum amount expressed in special drawing rights that a participant undertakes to lend to the Fund under a credit arrangement;

(vii) "call" means a notice by the Fund to a participant to make a transfer under its credit arrangement to the Fund's account;

(viii) "borrowed currency" means currency transferred to the Fund's account under a credit arrangement;

(ix) "drawer" means a member that purchases borrowed currency from the Fund in an exchange transaction or in an exchange transaction under a standby or extended arrangement;

[1] Decision No. 7337–(83/37) became effective December 26, 1983. Decision No. 10175–(92/129) of October 28, 1992, amended this Decision, effective December 22, 1992. Decision No. 7337–(83/37) has been renewed for periods of five years from December 26, 1988 (Decision No. 8733–(87/159); December 26, 1993 (Decision No. 10176–(92/129); December 26, 1998 (Decision No. 11609–(97/112); and December 26, 2003 (Decision No. 12879–(02/113).

(x) "indebtedness" of the Fund means the amount it is committed to repay under a credit arrangement.

Paragraph 2. *Credit Arrangements*

A member or institution that adheres to this Decision undertakes to lend its currency to the Fund on the terms and conditions of this Decision up to the amount in special drawing rights set forth in the Annex to this Decision or established in accordance with Paragraph 3(b).

Paragraph 3. *Adherence*

(a) Any member or institution specified in the Annex may adhere to this Decision in accordance with Paragraph 3(c).

(b) Any member or institution not specified in the Annex that wishes to become a participant may at any time, after consultation with the Fund, give notice of its willingness to adhere to this Decision, and, if the Fund shall so agree and no participant object, the member or institution may adhere in accordance with Paragraph 3(c). When giving notice of its willingness to adhere under this Paragraph 3(b) a member or institution shall specify the amount, expressed in terms of the special drawing right, of the credit arrangement which it is willing to enter into, provided that the amount shall not be less than the amount of the credit arrangement of the participant with the smallest credit arrangement.

(c) A member or institution shall adhere to this Decision by depositing with the Fund an instrument setting forth that it has adhered in accordance with its law and has taken all steps necessary to enable it to carry out the terms and conditions of this Decision. On the deposit of the instrument the member or institution shall be a participant as of the date of the deposit or of the effective date of this Decision, whichever shall be later.

Paragraph 4. *Entry into Force*

This Decision shall become effective when it has been adhered to by at least seven of the members or institutions included in the Annex with credit arrangements amounting in all to not less than the equivalent of five and one-half billion United States dollars of the weight and fineness in effect on July 1, 1944.

Paragraph 5. *Changes in Amounts of Credit Arrangements*

The amounts of participants' credit arrangements may be reviewed from time to time in the light of developing circumstances and changed with the agreement of the Fund and all participants.

Paragraph 6. *Initial Procedure*

When a participating member or a member whose institution is a participant approaches the Fund on an exchange transaction or stand-by arrangement and the Managing Director, after consultation, considers that the exchange transaction or stand-by or extended arrangement is necessary in order to forestall or cope with an impairment of the international monetary system, and that the Fund's resources need to be supplemented for this purpose, he shall initiate the procedure for making calls under Paragraph 7.

Paragraph 7. *Calls*

(a) The Managing Director shall make a proposal for calls for an exchange transaction or for future calls for exchange transactions under a stand-by or extended arrangement only after consultation with Executive Directors and participants. A proposal shall become effective only if it is accepted by participants and the proposal is then approved by the Executive Board. Each participant shall notify the Fund of the acceptance of a proposal involving a call under its credit arrangement.

(b) The currencies and amounts to be called under one or more of the credit arrangements shall be based on the present and prospective balance of payments and reserve positions of participating members or members whose institutions are participants and on the Fund's holdings of currencies.

(c) Unless otherwise provided in a proposal for future calls approved under Paragraph 7(a), purchases of borrowed currency under a stand-by arrangement shall be made in the currencies of participants in proportion to the amounts in the proposal.

(d) If a participant on which calls may be made pursuant to Paragraph 7(a) for a drawer's purchases under a stand-by or extended arrangement gives notice to the Fund that in the participant's opinion, based on the present and prospective balance of payments and reserve position, calls should no longer be made on the participant or that calls should be for a smaller amount, the Managing Director may propose to other participants that substitute amounts be made available under their credit arrangements, and this proposal shall be subject to the procedure of Paragraph 7(a). The proposal as originally approved under Paragraph 7(a) shall remain effective unless and until a proposal for substitute amounts is approved in accordance with Paragraph 7(a).

(e) When the Fund makes a call pursuant to this Paragraph 7, the participant shall promptly make the transfer in accordance with the call.

Paragraph 8. *Evidence of Indebtedness*

(a) The Fund shall issue to a participant, on its request, nonnegotiable instruments evidencing the Fund's indebtedness to the participant. The form of the instruments shall be agreed between the Fund and the participant.

(b) Upon repayment of the amount of any instrument issued under Paragraph 8(a) and all accrued interest, the instrument shall be returned to the Fund for cancellation. If less than the amount of any such instrument is repaid, the instrument shall be returned to the Fund and a new instrument for the remainder of the amount shall be substituted with the same maturity date as in the old instrument.

Paragraph 9. *Interest*

(a) The Fund shall pay interest on its indebtedness at a rate equal to the combined market interest rate computed by the Fund from time to time for the purpose of determining the rate at which it pays interest on holdings of special drawing rights. A change in the method of calculating the combined market interest rate shall apply only if the Fund and at least two thirds of the participants having three fifths of the total amount of the credit arrangements so agree; provided that it a participant so requests at the time this agreement is reached, the change shall not apply to the Funds's indebtedness to that participant outstanding at the date the change becomes effective.

(b) Interest shall accrue daily and shall be paid as soon as possible after each July 31, October 31, January 31, and April 30.

(c) Interest due to a participant shall be paid, as determined by the Fund, in special drawing rights, or in the participant's currency, or in other currencies that are actually convertible.

Paragraph 10. *Use of Borrowed Currency*

The Fund's policies and practices under Article V, Sections 3 and 7 on the use of its general resources and stand-by and extended arrangements, including those relating to the period of use, shall apply to purchases of currency borrowed by the Fund. Nothing in this Decision shall affect the authority of the Fund with respect to requests for the use if its resources by individual members, and access to these resources by members shall be determined by the Fund's policies and practices, and shall not depend on whether the Fund can borrow under this Decision.

Paragraph 11. *Repayment by the Fund*

(a) Subject to the other provisions of this Paragraph 11, the Fund, five years after a transfer by a participant, shall repay the participant an amount equivalent to the transfer calculated in accordance with Paragraph 12. If the drawer for whose purchase participants make transfers is committed to repurchase at a fixed date earlier than five years after its purchase, the Fund shall repay the participants at that date. Repayment under this Paragraph 11(a) or under Paragraph 11(c) shall be, as determined by the Fund, in the participant's currency whenever feasible, or in special drawing rights, or, after consultation with the participant, in other currencies that are convertible. Repayments to a participant under Paragraph 11(b) and (e) shall be credited against transfers by the participant for a drawer's purchases in the order in which repayment must be made under this Paragraph 11(a). in gold

(b) Before the date prescribed in Paragraph 11(a), the Fund, after consultation with a participant, may make repayment to the participant in part or in full. The Fund shall have the option to make repayment under this Paragraph 11(b) in the participant's currency, or in special drawing rights in an amount that does not increase the participant's holding of special drawing rights above the limit under Article XIX, Section 4, of the Articles of Agreement unless the participant agrees to accept special drawing rights above that limit in such repayment, or, with the agreement of the participant, in other currencies that are actually convertible.

(c) Whenever a reduction in the Fund's holdings of a drawer's currency is attributed to a purchase of borrowed currency, the Fund shall promptly repay an equivalent amount. If the Fund is indebted to a participant as a result of transfers to finance a reserve tranche purchase by a drawer and the Fund's holding of the drawer's currency that are not subject to repurchase are reduced as a result of net sales of that currency during a quarterly period covered by an operational budget, the Fund shall repay at the beginning of the next quarterly period an amount equivalent to that reduction, up to the amount of the indebtedness to the participant.

(d) Repayments under Paragraph 11(c) shall be made in proportion to the Fund's indebtedness to the participants that made transfers in respect of which repayment is being made.

(e) Before the date prescribed in Paragraph 11(a) a participant may give notice representing that there is a balance of payments need for repayment of part or all of the Fund's indebtedness and requesting such repayment. The Fund shall give the overwhelming benefit of any doubt to the participant's representation. Repayment shall be made after consultation with the participant in the currencies in which repayment should be made are not wholly adequate, individual participants shall be requested, and will be expected, to provide the necessary balance under their credit arrangements. If, notwithstanding the expectation that the participants will provide the necessary balance, they fail to do so, repayment shall be made to the extent necessary in the currency of the drawer for whose purchases the participant requesting repayment made transfers. For all of the purposes of this Paragraph 11 transfers under this Paragraph 11(e) shall be deemed to have been made at the same time and for the same purchases as the transfers by the participant obtaining repayment under this Paragraph 11(e).

(f) All repayments to a participant in a currency other than its own shall be guided, to the maximum extent practicable, by the present and prospective balance of payments and reserve position of the members whose currencies are to be used in repayment.

(g) The Fund shall at no time reduce its holdings of a drawer's currency below an amount equal to the Fund's indebtedness to the participants resulting from transfers for the drawer's purchases.

(h) When any repayment is made to a participant, the amount that can be called for under its credit arrangement in accordance with this Decision shall be restored pro tanto.

(i) The Fund shall be deemed to have discharged its obligations to a participating institution to make repayment in accordance with the provisions of this Paragraph or to pay interest in accordance with the provisions of Paragraph 9 if the Fund transfers an equivalent amount in special drawing rights to the member in which the institution is established.

Paragraph 12. *Rates of Exchange*

(a) The value of any transfer shall be calculated as of the date of the dispatch of the instruction for the transfer. The calculation shall be made in terms of the special drawing right in accordance with Article XIX, Section 7(a) of the Articles, and the Fund shall be obliged to repay an equivalent value.

(b) For all of the purposes of this Decision, the value of a currency in terms of the special drawing right shall be calculated by the Fund in accordance with Rule O-2 of the Fund's Rules and Regulations.

Paragraph 13. *Transferability*

A participant may not transfer all or part of its claim to repayment under a credit arrangement except with the prior consent of the Fund and on such terms and conditions as the Fund may approve.

Paragraph 14. *Notices*

Notice to or by a participating member under this Decision shall be in writing or by rapid means of communication and shall be given to or by the fiscal agency of the participating member designated in accordance with Article V, Section 1 of the Articles and Rule G–1 of the Rules and Regulations of the Fund. Notice to or by a participating institution shall be in writing or by rapid means of communication and shall be given to or by the participating institution.

Paragraph 15. *Amendment*

This Decision may be amended during the period prescribed in Paragraph 19(a) only by a decision of the Fund and with the concurrence of all participants. Such concurrence shall not be necessary for the modification of the Decision on its renewal pursuant to Paragraph 19(b).

Paragraph 16. *Withdrawal of Adherence*

A participant may withdraw its adherence to this Decision in accordance with Paragraph 19(b) but may not withdraw within the period described in Paragraph 19(a) except with the agreement of the Fund and all participants.

Paragraph 17. *Withdrawal from Membership*

If a participating member or a member whose institution is a participant withdraws from membership in the Fund, the participant's credit arrangement shall cease at the same time as the withdrawal takes effect. The Fund's indebtedness under the credit arrangement shall be treated as an amount due from the Fund for the purpose of Article XXVI, Section 3, and Schedule J of the Articles.

Paragraph 18. *Suspension of Exchange Transactions and Liquidation*

(a) The right of the Fund to make calls under Paragraph 7 and the obligation to make repayments under Paragraph 11 shall be suspended during any suspension of exchange transactions under Article XXVII of the Articles.

(b) In the event of liquidation of the Fund, credit arrangements shall cease and the Fund's indebtedness shall constitute liabilities under Schedule K of the Articles. For the purpose of Paragraph 1(a) of Schedule K, the currency in which the liability of the Fund shall be payable shall be first the participant's currency and then the currency of the drawer for whose purchases transfers were made by the participant.

Paragraph 19. *Period and Renewal*

(a)[2] This Decision shall continue in existence for four years from its effective date. A new period of five years shall begin on the effective date of Decision No. 7337–(83/37), adopted February 24, 1983. References in Paragraph 19(b) to the period prescribed in Paragraph 19(a) shall refer to this new period and to any subsequent renewal periods that may be decided pursuant to Paragraph 19(b). When considering a renewal of this Decision for the period following the five-year period refereed to in Paragraph 19(a), the Fund and the participants shall review the functioning of this Decision, including the provisions of Paragraph 21.

(b) This Decision may be renewed for such periods and with such modifications, subject to Paragraph 5, as the Fund may decide. The Fund shall adopt a decision on renewal and modification, if any, not later than twelve months before the end of the period prescribed in Paragraph 19(a). Any participant may advise the Fund not less than six months before the end of the period prescribed in Paragraph 19(a) that it will withdraw its adherence to the Decision as renewed. In the absence of such notice, a participant shall be deemed to continue to adhere to the Decision as renewed. Withdrawal of adherence in accordance with this Paragraph 19(b) by a participant, whether or not included in the Annex, shall not preclude its subsequent adherence in accordance with Paragraph 3(b).

(c) If this Decision is terminated or not renewed, Paragraphs 8 through 14, 17 and 18(b) shall nevertheless continue to apply in connection with any indebtedness of the Fund under credit arrangements in existence at the date of the termination or expiration of the Decision until repayment is completed. If a participant withdraws its adherence to this Decision in accordance with Paragraph 16 or Paragraph 19(b), it shall cease to be a participant under the Decision, but Paragraphs 8 through 14, 17 and 18(b) of the Decision as of the date of the withdrawal shall nevertheless continue to apply to any indebtedness of the Fund under the former credit arrangement until repayment has been completed.

Paragraph 20. *Interpretation*

Any question of interpretation raised in connection with this Decision which does not fall within the purview of Article XXIX of the Articles shall be settled to the mutual satisfaction of the Fund, the participant raising the question, and all other participants. For the purpose of this Paragraph 20 participants shall be deemed to include those former participants to which Paragraphs 8 through 14, 17 and 18(b) continue to apply pursuant to Paragraph 19(c) to the extent that any such former participant is affected by a question of interpretation that is raised.

Paragraph 21. *Use of Credit Arrangements for Nonparticipants*

(a) The Fund may make calls in accordance with Paragraphs 6 and 7 for exchange transactions requested by members that are not participants if the exchange transactions are (i) transactions in the

[2]This Decision has been renewed by the Executive Directors nine times, the most recent of which was November 12, 2002, for five years dating from December 2003.

upper credit tranches, (ii) transactions under stand-by arrangements, (iii) transactions under extended arrangements, or (iv) transactions in the first credit trance in conjunction with a stand-by or an extended arrangement. All the provisions of this Decision relating to calls shall apply, except as otherwise provided in Paragraph 21(b).

(b) The Managing Director may initiate the procedure for making calls under Paragraph 7 in connection with requests referred to in Paragraph 21(a) if, after consultation, he considers that the Fund faces an inadequacy of resources to meet actual and expected requests for financing that reflect the existence of an exceptional situation associated with balance of payments problems of members of a character or aggregate size that could threaten the stability of the international monetary system. In making proposals for calls pursuant to Paragraph 21(a) and (b), the Managing Director shall pay due regard to potential calls pursuant to other provisions of this Decision.

Paragraph 22. *Participation of the Swiss National Bank* [Abrogated—1992] [3]

Paragraph 23. *Associated Borrowing Arrangements*

(a) A borrowing arrangement between the Fund and a member that is not a participant, or an official institution of such a member, under which the member or the official institution undertakes to make loans to the Fund for the same purposes as, and on terms comparable to, those made by participants under this Decision, may, with the concurrence of all participants, authorize the Fund to make calls on participants in accordance with Paragraphs 6 and 7 for exchange transactions with that member, or to make requests under Paragraph 11(e) in connection with an early repayment of a claim under the borrowing arrangement, or both. For the purposes of this Decision such calls or requests shall be treated as if they were calls or requests in respect of a participant.

---

[3] Decision No. 10175–(92/129) of October 28, 1992, abrogated para. 22. Para. 22 formerly read as follows:

"(a) Notwithstanding any other provision of this Decision, the Swiss National Bank (hereinafter called the Bank) may become a participant by adhering to this Decision in accordance with Paragraph 3(c) and accepting, by its adherence, a credit arrangement in an amount equivalent to one thousand and twenty million special drawing rights. Upon adherence, the Bank shall be deemed to be a participating institution, and all the provisions of this Decision relating to participating institutions shall apply in respect of the Bank, subject to, and as supplemented by, Paragraph 22(b),(c),(d),(e), and (f).

"(b) Under its credit arrangement, the Bank undertakes to lend any currency, specified by the Managing Director after consultation with the Bank at the time of a call, that the Fund has determined to be a freely usable currency pursuant to Article XXX(f) of the Articles.

"(c) In relation to the Bank, the references to the balance of payments and reserve position in Paragraph 7(b) and (d), and Paragraph 11(e), shall be understood to refer to the position of the Swiss Confederation.

"(d) In relation to the Bank, the references to a participant's currency in Paragraph 9(c), Paragraph 11(a) and (b), and Paragraph 18(b) shall be understood to refer to any currency, specified by the Managing Director after consultation with the Bank at the time of payment by the Fund, that the Fund has determined to be a freely usable currency pursuant to Article XXX(f) of the Articles.

"(e) Payment of special drawing rights to the Bank pursuant to Paragraph 9(c) and Paragraph 11 shall be made only while the Bank is a prescribed holder pursuant to Article XVII of the Articles.

"(f) The Bank shall accept as binding a decision of the Fund on any question of interpretation raised in connection with this Decision which falls within the purview of Article XXIX of the Articles, to the same extent as that decision is binding on other participants.".

(b) Nothing in this Decision shall preclude the Fund from entering into any other types of borrowing arrangements, including an arrangement between the Fund and a lender, involving an association with participants, that does not contain the authorizations referred to in Paragraph 23(a).

ANNEX

Participants and Amounts of Credit Arrangements

	Amount in Units of Participant's Currency
I. Prior to the Effective Date of Decision No. 7337–(83/37)	
1. United States of America (US$)	2,000,000,000
2. Deutsche Bundesbank (DM)	4,000,000,000
3. United Kingdom (£)	357,142,857
4. France (F)	2,715,381,428
5. Italy (Lit)	343,750,000,000
6. Japan (Yen)	340,000,000,000
7. Canada (Can$)	216,216,000
8. Netherlands (f.)	724,000,000
9. Belgium (BF)	7,500,000,000
10. Sveriges Riksbank (SKr)	517,320,000

	Amount in Special Drawing Rights
II. From the Effective Date of Decision No. 7337–(83/37)	
1. United States of America	4,250,000,000
2. Deutsche Bundesbank	2,380,000,000
3. Japan	2,125,000,000
4. France	1,700,000,000
5. United Kingdom	1,700,000,000
6. Italy	1,105,000,000
7. Canada	892,500,000
8. Netherlands	850,000,000
9. Belgium	595,000,000
10. Sveriges Riksbank	382,500,000
11. Swiss National Bank*	1,020,000,0
	17,000,000,000

*With effect from the date on which the Swiss National Bank adheres to this Decision in accordance with Paragraph 22.

(4) Borrowing Arrangement with Saudi Arabia in Association with the General Arrangements to Borrow

Pursuant to Article VII, Section 1 of the Articles of Agreement, the Managing Director is authorized to send to the Minister of Finance of Saudi Arabia a letter proposing a borrowing agreement with Saudi Arabia, as set forth in the attachment. When a reply is received from the Minister accepting the proposal, the Managing Director's letter and the reply shall constitute an agreement between Saudi Arabia and the Fund, which shall enter into force on the date on which the revised and enlarged General Arrangements to Borrow authorized by Decision No. 7337–(83/37) become effective.

Decision No. 7403–(83/73)
May 20, 1983

ATTACHMENT

YOUR EXCELLENCY: I refer to Decision No. 7337–(83/87) of the Executive Board of the International Monetary Fund (the Fund), providing for a revision and enlargement of the General Arrangements to Borrow (the GAB), and to the desire of Saudi Arabia to strength the Fund by providing supplementary resources, in association with and for the same purposes as the GAB. Accordingly, pursuant to Article VII of the Articles of Agreement of the Fund (the Articles) and Executive Board Decision No. 7403–(83/73), adopted May 20, 1983, I have been authorized to propose on behalf of the Fund that Saudi Arabia enter into an Agreement with the Fund as set forth below:

Paragraph 1. *The Credit Arrangement*

During the period specified in Paragraph 2 and any renewal thereof, Saudi Arabia will stand ready to lend Saudi riyals to the Fund up to a maximum amount equivalent to one thousand five hundred million SDRs (SDR 1,500,000,000), on the terms and conditions set forth in this Agreement, to assist the Fund in the financing of purchases by members for the same purposes and in the same circumstances as are prescribed in the GAB. This amount may be changed by agreement between Saudi Arabia and the Fund.

Paragraph 2. *Period of Credit Arrangement and Renewal*

(a) Amounts of resources may be called by the Fund hereunder during a period of five years from the date this Agreement enters into force, unless the Fund's right to make calls is terminated earlier in accordance with this Agreement.

(b) When a renewal of the GAB Decision is under consideration, the Fund and Saudi Arabia shall consult regarding the renewal of the credit arrangement under this Agreement or the conclusion of such other credit arrangement as may be found appropriate at that time.

(c) Notwithstanding the termination of the credit arrangement under this Agreement, the provisions of Paragraphs 4 through 13 shall continue to apply until all the obligations of the Fund under this Agreement have been discharged.

Paragraph 3. *Calls*

(a) Calls may be made only pursuant to a proposal of the Managing Director that has become effective in accordance with (d) below.

(b) The Managing Director may make a proposal for calls for purchases, including future calls for purchases under stand-by or extended arrangements, (i) if he considers that a proposal for calls or future calls for the same purchases could be made under the GAB and (ii) after consultation with Saudi Arabia at the same time and in the same manner as he consults GAB participants.

(c) In deciding whether to make a proposal and the amount to be called thereunder, the Managing Director shall take into account the present and prospective balance of payments and reserve position of Saudi Arabia and the Fund's holdings of Saudi riyals.

(d) A proposal for calls shall become effective only when Saudi Arabia has notified the Fund that it accepts the proposal and the proposal has been approved by the Executive Board of the Fund. Calls shall be made as and when amounts of Saudi riyals are needed by the Fund to finance purchases covered by the proposal.

(e) When the Fund makes a call, Saudi Arabia shall transfer to the account of the Fund, free of any charge or commission, an amount of Saudi Riyals equivalent to the amount of the call. The transfer shall be made on the date specified in the call. Saudi Arabia shall exchange the riyals for a freely usable currency of its choice in accordance with Article V, Section 3 of the Articles.

(f) If Saudi Arabia represents to the Fund that, in view of the present and prospective balance of payments and reserve position of Saudi Arabia, future calls under a proposal that has become effective as provided in (d) above should no longer be made or be made for a smaller amount and the Fund, after giving the overwhelming benefit of any doubt to the representation, determines that it is justified, the Fund shall comply with Saudi Arabia's representation.

Paragraph 4. *Evidence of Indebtedness*

The Fund shall issue to Saudi Arabia, at its request, a nonnegotiable instrument or instruments in a form to be agreed with Saudi Arabia, evidencing the Fund's outstanding indebtedness to Saudi Arabia under this agreement. Upon repayment of an amount of indebtedness evidenced by an instrument and all accrued interest thereon, the instrument shall be returned to the Fund for cancellation, and if any balance of the indebtedness remains outstanding, the Fund shall issue a new instrument for the remainder of the amount, with the same maturity date.

Paragraph 5. *Interest*

(a) The Fund shall pay interest on its outstanding indebtedness at a rate equal to the combined market interest rate computed by the Fund from time to time under its Rules and Regulations for the purpose of determining the rate at which it pays interest on holdings of SDRs. If the Fund changes the method of computing the combined market interest rate, the new method will apply to amounts borrowed hereunder only if it is applied to borrowing by the Fund under the GAB, and Saudi Arabia agrees.

(b) Interest shall accrue daily and shall be paid as soon as possible after each July 31, October 31, January 31, and April 30.

Paragraph 6. *Repayment by the Fund*

(a) Subject to the other provisions of this Agreement, the Fund shall repay an amount equal to each amount transferred by Saudi Arabia hereunder five years after the date the transfer was made. To the extent the member whose purchase the amount was used to finance is committed to repurchase by installments on fixed dates falling earlier than five years after that date, the Fund shall repay the amount in corresponding installments on those fixed dates.

(b) Whenever a reduction in the Fund's holdings of currency of a purchasing member is attributed to a purchase financed with an amount transferred by Saudi Arabia hereunder, the Fund shall promptly make a corresponding repayment to Saudi Arabia. If the amount was used to finance a reserve tranche purchase, and the Fund's holdings of the purchasing member's currency not subject to repurchase are reduced as a result of net sales of the currency during a quarterly period covered by an operational budget, the Fund shall make a corresponding repayment to Saudi Arabia at the beginning of the next quarterly period. The amount repaid under this subparagraph (b) shall bear the same proportion to the amount of the reduction as the amount transferred under this Agreement bears to the amount of the purchase.

(c) Before the date repayment is due under (a) or (b) above, the Fund, after consultation with Saudi Arabia, may repay all or part of its outstanding indebtedness hereunder.

(d) If Saudi Arabia represents to the Fund that it has a balance of payments need for repayment before the due date of all or part of such outstanding indebtedness and requests such repayment, and the Fund after giving Saudi Arabia's representation the overwhelming benefit of any doubt determines that there is such a need, the Fund shall make early repayment as requested by Saudi Arabia's representation the overwhelming benefit of any doubt determines that there is such a need, the Fund shall make early repayment as requested by Saudi Arabia.

(e) Amounts repaid under (c) and (d) shall be credited against outstanding indebtedness in the order in which such indebtedness would fall due under (a) above.

(f) The Fund shall at no time reduce its holdings of the currency of a member whose purchases were financed by borrowing hereunder below an amount equal to the outstanding amount of such borrowing plus any outstanding amount borrowed under the GAB to finance purchases by the same member.

(g) When any repayment is made to Saudi Arabia, the amount that the Fund may call for under the credit arrangement shall be restored pro tanto.

Paragraph 7. *Media of Payment*

(a) Payments of interest and repayments of principal shall be made, as determined by the Fund after consultation with Saudi Arabia, in Saudi riyals, in SDRs, or in currencies that are actually convertible; provided that (i) unless Saudi Arabia agrees, SDRs shall not be used in early repayment under Paragraph 6(c) if the effect would be to increase Saudi Arabia's holdings of SDRs above the limit specified in Article XIX, Section 4 of the Articles, and (ii) Saudi riyals shall not be used in early repayment on balance of payments grounds under Paragraph 6(d).

(b) Currencies other than Saudi riyals to be used in payment of interest and repayment of principal shall be selected by the Fund from those that can be used in net sales under the operational budget of the Fund in effect at the time the payment is made.

Paragraph 8. *Rates of Exchange*

All amounts under this Agreement shall be denominated in SDRs, as valued by the Fund from time to time. The value in terms of SDRs of Saudi riyals to be transferred by Saudi Arabia to the Fund and of payments to be made by the Fund to Saudi Arabia in currencies shall be determined in accordance with Rule O–2 of the Rules and Regulations of the Fund.

Paragraph 9. *Transferability*

Saudi Arabia may transfer all or part of its claims under this Agreement only with the prior consent of the Fund and on such terms and conditions as the Fund may approve.

Paragraph 10. *Withdrawal from Membership*

If Saudi Arabia withdraws from membership in the Fund, no further calls shall be made hereunder. The Fund's outstanding indebtedness hereunder shall be treated as an amount due from the Fund for the purpose of Article XXVI, Section 3, and Schedule J of the Articles.

Paragraph 11. *Suspension of Exchange Transactions and Liquidation*

(a) The right of the Fund to make calls and its obligation to make repayment hereunder shall be suspended during any suspension of exchange transactions under Article XXVII of the Articles.

(b) In the event of liquidation of the Fund, no further calls shall be made by the Fund hereunder. The Fund's outstanding indebtedness shall constitute a liability under Schedule K of the Articles. For the purpose of Paragraph 1(a) of Schedule K, the currency in which each amount of the Fund's indebtedness is payable shall be first Saudi riyals and then any currency that is actually convertible.

Paragraph 12. *Amendments*

(a) This Agreement may be amended at any time, by agreement between Saudi Arabia and the Fund.

(b) If the revised and enlarged GAB is modified while this Agreement is in effect, Saudi Arabia and the Fund will consult with each other with a view to determining whether consequential modifications should be made in the provisions of this Agreement.

(c) If, after consultation with the Fund and the GAB participants, Saudi Arabia proposes that the credit arrangement under this Agreement be converted into or replaced by an arrangement of the type referred to in Paragraph 23(a) or Paragraph 3(b) of the revised GAB Decision, as the case may be, the Fund will consider the steps to be taken, subject to the concurrence of the GAB participants as necessary, to effect such conversion or replacement.

Paragraph 13. *Interpretation; Settlement of Disputes*

Any question of interpretation arising in connection with this Agreement that does not fall within the purview of Article XXIX of the Articles, and any dispute arising hereunder, shall be settled to the mutual satisfaction of Saudi Arabia and the Fund.

If the foregoing proposal is acceptable to Saudi Arabia, this communication and your reply indicating Saudi Arabia's acceptance shall constitute an Agreement between Saudi Arabia and the Fund, which shall enter into force on the date on which the revised and enlarged GAB authorized by Decision No. 7337–(83/37) of the Executive Board of the Fund becomes effective.

Very truly yours,

J. DE LAROSIÈRE

c. New Arrangements to Borrow

(1) Decision of the Executive Directors of the International Monetary Fund

Decision No. 11428–(97/6), January 27, 1997; amended by Executive Board Decision No. 12880–(02/113); and by Executive Board Decision No. 12881–(02/113), November 12, 2002

Preamble

In order to enable the International Monetary Fund to fulfill more effectively its role in the international monetary system, a number of countries with the financial capacity to support the international monetary system have agreed to make available to the Fund resources in the form of loans up to specified amounts when supplementary resources are needed to forestall or cope with an impairment of the international monetary system or to deal with an exceptional situation that poses a threat to the stability of that system. In order to give effect to these intentions, the following terms and conditions are adopted under Article VII, Section 1 of the Articles of Agreement.

Paragraph 1. *Definitions*

(a) As used in this decision the term:

(i) "amount of a credit arrangement" means the maximum amount expressed in special drawing rights that a participant undertakes to lend to the Fund under a credit arrangement;

(ii) "Articles" means the Articles of Agreement of the International Monetary Fund;

(iii) "available commitment" means a participant's credit arrangement less any committed or drawn balances;

(iv) "borrowed currency" or "currency borrowed" means currency transferred to the Fund's account under a credit arrangement;

(v) "call" means a notice by the Fund to a participant to make a transfer under its credit arrangement to the Fund's account;

(vi) "credit arrangement" means an undertaking to lend to the Fund on the terms and conditions of this decision;

(vii) "currency actually convertible" means currency included in the Fund's quarterly operational budget for transfers;

(viii) "drawer" means a member that purchases borrowed currency from the Fund in an exchange transaction, including an exchange transaction under a stand-by or extended arrangement;

(ix) "indebtedness" of the Fund means the amount it is committed to repay under a credit arrangement;

(x) "member" means a member of the Fund;

(xi) "participant" means a participating member or a participating institution;

(xii) "participating institution" means an official institution of a member that has entered into a credit arrangement with the Fund with the consent of the member, or an official institution of a nonmember that has entered into a credit arrangement with the Fund;

(xiii) "participating member" means a member that has entered into a credit arrangement with the Fund.

(b) For the purposes of this decision, the Hong Kong Monetary Authority (HKMA) shall be regarded as an official institution of the member whose territories include Hong Kong, provided that:

(i) loans by the HKMA and payments by the Fund to the HKMA under this decision shall be made in principle in the currency of the United States of America, unless the currency of another member is agreed between the Fund and the HKMA;

(ii) the participation of the HKMA shall not give rise to the application of paragraph 6 A to the member whose territories include Hong Kong; and

(iii) the references to the balance of payments and reserve position in paragraphs 7 A(c), 7 B(b) and 11(e) shall be understood to refer to the balance of payments and reserve position of Hong Kong.

Paragraph 2. *Credit Arrangements*

(a) A member or institution that adheres to this decision undertakes to make loans to the Fund on the terms and conditions of this decision up to the amount in special drawing rights set forth in the Annex to this decision or established in accordance with paragraph 3(b).

(b) Unless otherwise agreed with the Fund, loans under this decision shall be made in the currency of the participant. If the participant is an institution of a nonmember, the Fund and the participant shall agree on which member's currency or members' currencies shall be used for the loans. Agreements under this paragraph shall be subject to the concurrence of any member whose currency shall be used in the loans.

Paragraph 3. *Adherence*

(a) Any member or institution specified in the Annex may adhere to this decision in accordance with paragraph 3(c).

(b) Any member or institution not specified in the Annex, including an institution of a nonmember, may apply to become a participant at the time of renewal of this decision in accordance with paragraph 19. Any such member or institution that wishes to become a participant shall, after consultation with the Fund, give notice of its willingness to adhere to this decision, and, if the Fund and participants representing 80 percent of total credit arrangements under the renewed decision shall so agree, the member or institution may adhere in accordance with paragraph 3(c). When giving notice of its willingness to adhere under this paragraph 3(b), a member or institution shall specify the amount, expressed in special drawing rights, of the credit arrangement which it is willing to enter into, provided that the amount shall not be less than the credit arrangement of the participant with the smallest credit arrangement. The admission of a new participant shall lead to a proportional reduction in the credit arrangements of all existing participants whose credit arrangements are above that of the participant with the smallest credit arrangement: such proportional reduction in the credit arrangements of participants shall be in an aggregate amount equal to the amount of the new participant's credit arrangement less any increase in total credit arrangements decided in accordance with paragraph 5(a), provided that no participant's credit arrangement shall be reduced below the minimum amount set out in the Annex.

(c) A member or institution shall adhere to this decision by depositing with the Fund an instrument setting forth that it has adhered in accordance with its law and has taken all steps necessary to enable it to carry out the terms and conditions of this decision. On the deposit of the instrument the member or institution shall be a participant as of the date of the deposit or of the effective date of this decision, whichever is later.

Paragraph 4. *Entry into Force*

This decision shall become effective when it has been adhered to by members or institutions included in the Annex with credit arrangements amounting to not less than SDR 28.9 billion, including the five members or institutions with the largest credit arrangements specified in the Annex.

Paragraph 5. *Changes in Amounts of Credit Arrangements*

(a) When a member or institution is authorized under paragraph 3(b) to adhere to this decision, the total amount of credit arrangements may be increased by the Fund with the agreement of participants representing 85 percent of total credit arrangements; the increase shall not exceed the amount of the new participant's credit arrangement.

(b) The amounts of participants' individual credit arrangements may be reviewed from time to time in the light of developing circumstances and changed with the agreement of the Fund and of participants representing 85 percent of total credit arrangements, including each participant whose credit arrangement is changed. This provision may be amended only with the consent of all participants.

Paragraph 6. *Initiation of Procedure*

A. Participants

When a participating member or a member whose institution is a participant approaches the Fund on an exchange transaction or a stand-by or extended arrangement and the Managing Director, after consultation, considers that the exchange transaction or stand-by or extended arrangement is necessary in order to forestall or cope with an impairment of the international monetary system, and that the Fund's resources need to be supplemented for this purpose, the Managing Director may initiate the procedure set out in paragraph 7A.

B. Nonparticipants

The Managing Director may initiate the procedure set out in paragraph 7A for exchange transactions requested by members that are not participants if (a), the exchange transactions are (i) transactions in the upper credit tranches, (ii) transactions under stand-by arrangements extending beyond the first credit tranche, (iii) transactions under extended arrangements, or (iv) transactions in the first credit tranche in conjunction with a stand-by arrangement or an extended arrangement, and (b), after consultation, the Managing Director considers that the Fund's resources need to be supplemented to meet actual and expected requests for financing that reflect the existence of an exceptional situation associated with balance of payments problems of members of a character or aggregate size that could threaten the stability of the international monetary system. In making proposals for calls pursuant to paragraph 6B, the Managing Director shall pay due regard to potential calls pursuant to paragraph 6A.

Paragraph 7. *Proposals and Calls*

A. Proposals

(a) The Managing Director shall make a proposal for calls under this decision only after consultation with Executive Directors and participants.

(b) In making a proposal for resources to be lent to the Fund, the Managing Director shall identify the prospective drawer, the amount, and the period during which the resources requested in the proposal may be called.

(c) If a participant determines that it will not be able to meet calls under a proposal because of its present and prospective balance of payments and reserve position, which would normally be reflected in the member's exclusion from the list of countries that are included in the Fund's quarterly operational budget for transfers of their currencies, it shall so notify the Fund and the other participants. If the participant is an institution of a nonmember, the participant shall consult with the Fund on that nonmember's balance of payments and reserve position before making a determination under this provision. A participant shall exercise restraint and shall take into account the views of the Fund and other participants in making such a determination.

(d) Unless otherwise specified under paragraph 7A(e), a proposal shall be for calls proportional to the amount of each participant's credit arrangement.

(e) The Managing Director may make a proposal for calls that are not proportional to the amount of each participant's credit arrangement under the following circumstances:

(i) If proportional calls sufficient to provide the total amount sought from participants to finance the proposed exchange transactions cannot be made because at least one participant's available commitment is insufficient to meet such a proportional call, the Managing Director may ask every participant whose available commitment would have been sufficient to meet fully such a proportional call to provide the amount under such a proportional call; provided that, if the Managing

Director asks every such participant to provide such amount, the Managing Director shall also ask every participant whose available commitment would have been insufficient to meet such a proportional call to provide an amount to the extent of its available commitment. If necessary, the Managing Director may also ask for an amount in addition to that provided under the prior sentence from a participant whose available commitment exceeds the amount it would provide under such a proportional call.

(ii) If proportional calls sufficient to provide the total amount sought from participants to finance the proposed exchange transactions cannot be made because at least one participant lacks sufficient amounts of the type of currency or currencies needed for the proposed exchange transactions, the Managing Director may ask every participant that is in a position to provide the currency or currencies needed to provide the amount under such a proportional call, up to the amount of its available commitment or the amount that it is in a position to provide, whichever is less. If necessary, the Managing Director may also ask a participant whose available commitment exceeds the resources it would provide under such a proportional call and that remains in a position to provide the type of currency or currencies needed to provide an amount of the currency or currencies needed in addition to that provided under the prior sentence.

(f) The concurrence of every participant that would undertake to provide proportionately more resources than at least one other participant shall be required before the proposal can be accepted under Paragraph 7A(g).

(g) If there is not unanimity among the participants, the question whether the participants are prepared to facilitate, by making loans to the Fund, the exchange transactions or stand-by or extended arrangement specified in the proposal will be decided by a poll of the participants. A favorable decision shall require an 80 percent majority of total credit arrangements of participants eligible to vote. The decision shall be notified to the Fund.

(h) Neither the prospective drawer nor its participating institution nor participants that have notified that they will not meet calls under a proposal shall be eligible to vote on the proposal.

(i) A proposal shall become effective only if it is accepted by participants pursuant to paragraph 7A(g) and is then approved by the Executive Board.

(j) After a proposal has been accepted, commitments and drawings shall not be affected by a subsequent change in the amounts of the credit arrangements.

B. Calls

(a) Unless otherwise provided in a proposal for future calls approved under paragraph 7A, each call shall be made in proportion to the amounts in the proposal.

(b) Except with the participant's consent, calls may not be made on a participant, on which calls could otherwise be made pursuant to this paragraph, when, based on its present and prospective balance of payments and reserve position, the member is not included and is not being proposed by the Managing Director to be included in the list of countries in the quarterly operational budget for transfers of its currency. If the participant is an institution of a nonmember, its ability to meet calls under this decision shall be determined by the Fund, after consultation with the participant, on the basis of that nonmember's present and prospective balance of payments and reserve position. In the event that a call is not made on a participant, the Managing Director may propose to the other participants that substitute amounts be made available under their credit arrangements, and this proposal shall be subject to the procedure of paragraph 7A.

(c) When the Fund makes a call pursuant to this paragraph, the participant shall promptly make the transfer in accordance with the call.

Paragraph 8. *Evidence of Indebtedness*

(a) The Fund shall issue to a participant, on its request, nonnegotiable instruments evidencing the Fund's indebtedness to the participant. The form of the instruments shall be agreed between the Fund and the participant.

(b) Upon repayment of the amount of any instrument issued under paragraph 8(a) and all accrued interest, the instrument shall be returned to the Fund for cancellation. If less than the amount of any such instrument is repaid, the instrument shall be returned to the Fund and a new instrument for the remainder of the amount shall be substituted with the same maturity date as in the old instrument.

Paragraph 9. *Interest*

(a) The Fund shall pay interest on its indebtedness under this decision at a rate equal to the combined market interest rate computed by the Fund from time to time for the purpose of determining the rate at which it pays interest on holdings of special drawing rights or any such higher rate as may be agreed between the Fund and participants representing 80 percent of the total credit arrangements.

(b) A change in the method of calculating the combined market interest rate shall apply to the Fund's indebtedness under this decision only if the Fund and participants representing 80 percent of the total credit arrangements so agree; provided that, if a participant so requests at the time this agreement is reached, the change shall not apply to the Fund's indebtedness to that participant outstanding at the date the change becomes effective.

(c) Interest shall accrue daily and shall be paid as soon as possible after each July 31, October 31, January 31, and April 30.

(d) Interest due to a participant shall be paid, as determined by the Fund in consultation with the participant, in special drawing rights, in the participant's currency, in the currency borrowed, or in other currencies that are actually convertible.

Paragraph 10. *Use of Borrowed Currency*

The Fund's policies and practices under Article V, Sections 3 and 7 on the use of its general resources and stand-by arrangements and extended arrangements, including those relating to the period of use, shall apply to purchases of currency borrowed by the Fund. Nothing in this decision shall affect the authority of the Fund with respect to requests for the use of its resources by individual members, and access to these resources by members shall be determined by the Fund's policies and practices, and shall not depend on whether the Fund can borrow under this decision.

Paragraph 11. *Repayment by the Fund*

(a) Subject to the other provisions of this paragraph 11, the Fund, five years after a transfer by a participant, shall repay the participant an amount equivalent to the transfer calculated in accordance with paragraph 12. If the drawer for whose purchase participants make transfers is committed to repurchase at a fixed date earlier than five years after its purchase, the Fund shall repay the participants at that date. Repayment under this paragraph 11(a) or under paragraph 11(c) shall be, as determined by the Fund, in the currency borrowed whenever feasible, in the currency of the participant, in special drawing rights in an amount that does not increase the participant's holdings of special drawing rights above the limit under Article XIX, Section 4, of the Articles of Agreement unless the participant agrees to accept special drawing rights above that limit in such repayment, or, after consultation with the participant, in other currencies that are actually convertible. Repayments to a participant under paragraph 11(b) and 11(e) shall be credited against transfers by the participant for a drawer's purchases in the order in which repayment must be made under this paragraph 11(a).

(b) Before the date prescribed in paragraph 11(a), the Fund, after consultation with the participants, may make repayment in part or in full to one or several participants. The Fund shall have the option to make repayment under this paragraph 11(b) in the participant's currency, in the currency borrowed, in special drawing rights in an amount that does not increase the participant's holdings of special drawing rights above the limit under Article XIX, Section 4, of the Articles of Agreement unless the participant agrees to accept special drawing rights above that limit in such repayment, or, with the agreement of the participant, in other currencies that are actually convertible.

(c) Whenever a reduction in the Fund's holdings of a drawer's currency is attributed to a purchase of currency borrowed under this decision, the Fund shall promptly repay an equivalent amount. If the Fund is indebted to a participant as a result of transfers to finance a reserve tranche purchase by a drawer and the Fund's holdings of the drawer's currency that are not subject to repurchase are reduced as a result of net sales of that currency during a quarterly period covered by an operational budget, the Fund shall repay at the beginning of the next quarterly period an amount equivalent to that reduction, up to the amount of the indebtedness to the participant.

(d) Repayment under paragraph 11(c) shall be made in proportion to the Fund's indebtedness to the participants that made transfers in respect of which repayment is being made.

(e) Before the date prescribed in paragraph 11(a), a participant may give notice representing that there is a balance of payments need for repayment of part or all of the Fund's indebtedness and requesting such repayment. If a reversal of its loan may lead to further loans to the Fund by other participants, the participant seeking such reversal shall consult with the Managing Director and with the other participants before giving notice. The Fund shall give the overwhelming benefit of any doubt to the participant's representation. Repayment shall be made after consultation with the participant in the currencies of other members that are actually convertible, or in special drawing rights, as determined by the Fund. If the Fund's holdings of currencies in which repayment should be made are not wholly adequate, individual participants may be requested to provide the necessary balance under their credit arrangements subject to the limit of their available commitments. For all of the purposes of this paragraph 11, transfers under this paragraph 11(e) shall be deemed to have been made at the same time and for the same purchases as the transfers by the participant obtaining repayment under this paragraph 11(e).

(f) When a repayment is made to a participant, the amount that can be called for under its credit arrangement in accordance with this decision shall be restored pro tanto.

(g) The Fund shall be deemed to have discharged its obligations to a participating institution to make repayment in accordance with the provisions of this paragraph or to pay interest in accordance with the provisions of paragraph 9 if the Fund transfers an equivalent amount in special drawing rights to the member in which the institution is established.

Paragraph 12. *Rates of Exchange*

(a) The value of any transfer shall be calculated as of the date of the dispatch of the instructions for the transfer. The calculation shall be made in terms of the special drawing right in accordance with Article XIX, Section 7(a) of the Articles, and the Fund shall be obliged to repay an equivalent value.

(b) For all of the purposes of this decision, the value of a currency in terms of the special drawing right shall be calculated by the Fund in accordance with Rule O–2 of the Fund's Rules and Regulations.

Paragraph 13. *Transferability*

A participant may not transfer all or part of its claim to repayment under a credit arrangement except with the prior consent of the Fund and on such terms and conditions as the Fund may approve.

Paragraph 14. *Notices*

Notice to or by a participating member under this decision shall be in writing or by rapid means of communication and shall be given to or by the fiscal agency of the participating member designated in accordance with Article V, Section 1 of the Articles and Rule G–1 of the Rules and Regulations of the Fund. Notice to or by a participating institution shall be in writing or by rapid means of communication and shall be given to or by the participating institution.

Paragraph 15. *Amendment*

(a) Except as provided in paragraphs 5(b), 15(b) and 16, this decision may be amended during the period prescribed in paragraph 19(a) and any subsequent renewal periods that may be decided pursuant to paragraph 19(b) only by a decision of the Fund and with the concurrence of participants representing 85 percent of total credit arrangements. Such concurrence shall not be necessary for the modification of the decision on its renewal pursuant to paragraph 19(b).

(b) If in its view an amendment materially affects the interest of a participant that voted against the amendment, the participant shall have the right to withdraw its adherence to this decision by giving notice to the Fund and the other participants within 90 days from the date the amendment was adopted. This provision may be amended only with the consent of all participants.

Paragraph 16. *Withdrawal of Adherence*

Without prejudice to paragraph 15(b), a participant may withdraw its adherence to this decision in accordance with paragraph 19(b) but may not withdraw within the period prescribed in paragraph 19(a) except with the agreement of the Fund and all participants. This provision may be amended only with the consent of all participants.

Paragraph 17. *Withdrawal from Membership*

If a participating member or a member whose institution is a participant withdraws from membership in the Fund, the participant's credit arrangement shall cease at the same time as the withdrawal takes effect. The Fund's indebtedness under the credit arrangement shall be treated as an amount due from the Fund for the purpose of Article XXVI, Section 3, and Schedule J of the Articles.

Paragraph 18. *Suspension of Exchange Transactions and Liquidation*

(a) The right of the Fund to make calls under paragraph 7 and the obligation to make repayments under paragraph 11 shall be suspended during any suspension of exchange transactions under Article XXVII of the Articles.

(b) In the event of liquidation of the Fund, credit arrangements shall cease and the Fund's indebtedness shall constitute liabilities under Schedule K of the Articles. For the purpose of paragraph 1(a) of Schedule K, the currency in which the liability of the Fund shall be payable shall be first the currency borrowed, then the participant's currency and finally the currency of the drawer for whose purchases transfers were made by the participants.

Paragraph 19. *Period and Renewal*

(a) This decision shall continue in existence for five years from its effective date. When considering a renewal of this decision for the period following the five-year period referred to in this paragraph 19(a), the Fund and the participants shall review the functioning of this decision and shall consult on any possible modifications.

(b) This decision may be renewed for such period or periods and with such modifications, subject to paragraphs 5(b), 15(b) and 16, as the Fund may decide. The Fund shall adopt a decision on renewal and modification, if any, not later than twelve months before the end of the period prescribed in paragraph 19(a). Any participant may advise the Fund not less than six months before the end of the period prescribed in paragraph 19(a) that it will withdraw its adherence to the decision as renewed. In the absence of such notice, a participant shall be deemed to continue to adhere to the decision as renewed. Withdrawal of adherence in accordance with this paragraph 19(b) by a participant, whether or not included in the Annex, shall not preclude its subsequent adherence in accordance with paragraph 3(b).

(c) If this decision is terminated or not renewed, paragraphs 8 through 14, 17 and 18(b) shall nevertheless continue to apply in connection with any indebtedness of the Fund under credit arrangements in existence at the date of the termination or expiration of the decision until repayment is completed. If a participant withdraws its adherence to this decision in accordance with paragraph 15(b), paragraph 16, or paragraph 19(b), it shall cease to be a participant under the decision, but paragraphs 8 through 14, 17 and 18(b) of the decision as of the date of the withdrawal shall nevertheless continue to apply to any indebtedness of the Fund under the former credit arrangement until repayment has been completed.

Paragraph 20. *Interpretation*

Any question of interpretation raised in connection with this decision which does not fall within the purview of Article XXIX of the Articles shall be settled to the mutual satisfaction of the Fund, the participant raising the question, and all other participants. For the purpose of this paragraph 20 participants shall be deemed to include those former participants to which paragraphs 8 through 14, 17 and 18(b) continue to apply pursuant to paragraph 19(c) to the extent that any such former participant is affected by a question of interpretation that is raised.

Paragraph 21. *Relationship with the General Arrangements to Borrow and Associated Borrowing Arrangements*

(a) When considering whether to activate the New Arrangements to Borrow or the General Arrangements to Borrow, the Fund shall be guided by the following principles: the New Arrangements to Borrow shall be the facility of first and principal recourse except that:

(i) in the event of a request for a drawing on the Fund by a participating member, or a member whose institution is a participant, in both the General Arrangements to Borrow and the New Arrangements to Borrow, a proposal for calls may be made under either of the arrangements; and

(ii) in the event that a proposal for calls under the New Arrangements to Borrow is not accepted under paragraph 7A, a proposal for calls may be made under the General Arrangements to Borrow.

(b) Outstanding drawings and commitments under the New Arrangements to Borrow and the General Arrangements to Borrow shall not exceed SDR 34 billion, or such other amount of total credit arrangements as may be in effect in accordance with this decision. The available commitment of a participant under the New Arrangements to Borrow shall be reduced pro tanto by any outstanding drawings on, and commitments of, the participant under the General Arrangements to Borrow. The available commitment of a participant under the General Arrangements to Borrow shall be reduced pro tanto by the extent to which its credit arrangement under the General Arrangements to Borrow exceeds its available commitment under the New Arrangements to Borrow.

(c) References to drawings and commitments under the General Arrangements to Borrow shall include drawings and commitments under the Associated Borrowing Arrangements referred to in paragraph 23 of the General Arrangements to Borrow.

Paragraph 22. *Other Borrowing Arrangements*

Nothing in this decision shall preclude the Fund from entering into any other types of borrowing arrangements.

Annex

Participants and Amount of Credit Arrangements

The size of each participant's credit arrangement listed below has initially been based in principle on its relative economic strength as reflected in its quota in the Fund. Credit arrangements are subject to a minimum of SDR 340 million. Amounts have been adjusted between some participants subject to the condition that the total for the participants involved in an adjustment does not change and the minimum is observed. The amounts, in terms of SDRs of the individual credit arrangements and their total will remain in effect unless and until changed in accordance with this decision.

The size of the Hong Kong Monetary Authority's (HKMA) credit arrangement has not been calculated on the basis of the quota of the member whose territories include Hong Kong. The same principle explains the special provision on activation of the New Arrangements to Borrow to meet requests from such member.

	Amounts in Millions of Special Drawing Rights
Australia	810
Austria	412
Belgium	967

	Amounts in Millions of Special Drawing Rights
Canada	1396
Chile *	340
Denmark	371
Deutsche Bundesbank	3557
Finland	340
France	2577
Hong Kong Monetary Authority	340
Italy	1772
Japan	3557
Korea	340
Kuwait	345
Luxembourg	340
Malaysia	340
Netherlands	1316
Norway	383
Saudi Arabia	1780
Singapore	340
Spain	672
Sveriges Riksbank	859
Swiss National Bank	1557
Thailand	340
United Kingdom of Great Britain and Northern Ireland	2577
United States of America	6712

* The Fund agreed to Chile's request to adhere to the NAB decision. Adherence will become effective when participants representing 80 percent of total credit arrangements under the NAB decision so agree (Decision No. 12881-(02/113), November 12, 2002).

ATTACHMENT TO SM/96/307

NAB Meetings

In the course of establishing the new arrangements to borrow (NAB), understandings were reached on procedures and administrative arrangements for meetings of participants. These understandings are intended to complement, but do not supersede or modify, the provisions related to the activation of the new arrangements to borrow, as specified in the Fund decision.

Frequency, timing, subject matter, and level of representation

Participants agreed that, in addition to any meetings needed for activation, renewal, or amendment of the NAB, it would be appropriate for participants to meet once a year at the time of the annual Fund/Bank meetings to discuss matters pertaining to the NAB. The objective of these meetings would be to review and discuss macroeconomic and financial markets developments, especially those that could have an impact on the stability of the financial system and lead to a possible need for the Fund to seek supplementary resources for the purposes set out in the preamble of the NAB. Participants would be represented by a minister or central bank governor or both. The principal representative could appoint deputies to meet in their stead. The level of the meeting (Ministerial or Deputy) would be determined each year in light of the issues at hand.

Chairmanship

The Chairmanship of the NAB grouping would rotate annually in the English alphabetical order of the participants, as listed in the Annex to the decision, beginning with the first name on that list.[2] The Chair would, in consultation with participants, be responsible for determining the agenda of the meeting, which will be devoted to the matters set out above. These consultations would also serve to determine the level of representation (Ministerial or Deputy) that would be most appropriate for the meeting in question.

Support

IMF headquarters staff would, under the direction of the Chair, provide secretariat support for the group. This would entail providing logistic support and maintaining an archive of documents concerning the deliberations and decisions taken under the new arrangements to borrow.

[2] In the event that the Chair was unable to perform its functions, a substitute would be provided by the participant immediately above the Chair on the list of participants in the Annex, or, if that substitute were not available, by the participant immediately below the Chair in that list.

(2) Transferability of Claims

Decision No. 11428–(97/6) of the Executive Directors of the International Monetary Fund, January 27, 1997

Pursuant to paragraph 13 of the New Arrangements to Borrow (NAB), the Fund consents in advance to the transfer of outstanding claims to repayments under the NAB on the terms and conditions set out below:

1. All or part of any claim under the NAB may be transferred at any time to a participant in the NAB.

2. As from the value date of the transfer, the transferred claim shall be held by the transferee on the same terms and conditions as claims originating under its credit arrangement, except that the transferee shall acquire the right to request early repayment of the transferred claim on balance of payments grounds pursuant to paragraph 11(e) of the NAB only if, at the time of the transfer, (i) the transferee is a member, or the institution of a member, whose balance of payment and reserve position is considered sufficiently strong for its currency to be usable in net transfers in the Fund's operational budget; or (ii) the transferee is the institution of a nonmember, and the balance of payments and reserve position of the nonmember is, in the opinion of the Fund, sufficiently strong to justify such acquisition.

3. The price for the claim transferred shall be as agreed between the transferee and the transferor.

4. The transferor of a claim shall inform the Fund promptly of the claim that is being transferred, the name of the transferee, the amount of the claim that is being transferred, the agreed price for transfer of the claim, and the value date of the transfer.

5. The transfer shall be registered by the Fund if it is in accordance with the terms and conditions of this decision. The transfer shall be effective as of the value date agreed between the transferee and the transferor.

6. If all or part of a claim is transferred during a quarterly period as described in paragraph 9(c) of the NAB, the Fund shall pay interest to the transferee on the amount of the claim transferred for the whole of that period.

7. If requested, the Fund shall assist in seeking to arrange transfers.

8. This decision shall become effective on the date of effectiveness of the NAB.

2. Articles of Agreement Establishing the International Bank for Reconstruction and Development (Amended)

CONTENTS

2. Articles of Agreement Establishing the International Bank for Reconstruction and Development

Articles of agreement between the United States and others respecting the International Bank for Reconstruction and Development, formulated at the United Nations Monetary and Financial Conference, Bretton Woods, New Hampshire, July 1 to July 22, 1944; Signed at Washington, December 27, 1945; Instrument of acceptance by the United States deposited, December 20, 1945; Entered into force, December 27, 1945;[1] Article III amended December 16, 1965[2]

The governments on whose behalf the present Agreement is signed agree as follows:

INTRODUCTORY ARTICLE

The International Bank for Reconstruction and Development is established and shall operate in accordance with the following provisions:

ARTICLE I—PURPOSES

The purposes of the Bank are:

(i) To assist in the reconstruction and development of territories of members by facilitating the investment of capital for productive purposes, including the restoration of economies destroyed or disrupted by war, the reconversion of productive facilities to peacetime needs and the encouragement of the development of productive facilities and resources in less developed countries.

(ii) To promote private foreign investment by means of guarantees or participations in loans and other investments made by private investors; and when private capital is not available on reasonable terms, to supplement private investment by providing, on suitable conditions, finance for productive purposes out of its own capital, funds raised by it and its other resources.

(iii) To promote the long-range balanced growth of international trade and the maintenance of equilibrium in balances of payments by encouraging international investment for the development of the productive resources of members, thereby assisting in raising productivity, the standard of living and conditions of labor in their territories.

(iv) To arrange the loans made or guaranteed by it in relation to international loans through other channels so that the more useful and urgent projects, large and small alike, will be dealt with first.

[1] 60 Stat. 1440; TIAS 1503; 3 Bevans 1390; 2 UNTS 134. For a list of states that are parties to this Agreement, see Department of State publication, *Treaties in Force*.

[2] 16 UST 1942; TIAS 5929. Done at Washington, December 16, 1965; Entered into force, December 17, 1965.

(v) To conduct its operations with due regard to the effect of international investment on business conditions in the territories of members and, in the immediate postwar years, to assist in bringing about a smooth transition from a wartime to a peacetime economy.

The Bank shall be guided in all its decisions by the purposes set forth above.

ARTICLE II—MEMBERSHIP IN AND CAPITAL OF THE BANK

SECTION 1. MEMBERSHIP

(a) The original members of the Bank shall be those members of the International Monetary Fund which accept membership in the Bank before the date specified in Article XI, Section 2(e).

(b) Membership shall be open to other members of the Fund, at such times and in accordance with such terms as may be prescribed by the Bank.

SECTION 2. AUTHORIZED CAPITAL [3]

(a) The authorized capital stock of the Bank shall be $10,000,000,000, in terms of United States dollars of the weight and fineness in effect on July 1, 1944. The capital stock shall be divided into 100,000 shares having a par value of $100,000 each, which shall be available for subscription only by members.

(b) The capital stock may be increased when the Bank deems it advisable by a three-fourths majority of the total voting power.

SECTION 3. SUBSCRIPTION OF SHARES

(a) Each member shall subscribe shares of the capital stock of the Bank. The minimum number of shares to be subscribed by the original members shall be those set forth in Schedule A. The minimum number of shares to be subscribed by other members shall be determined by the Bank, which shall reserve a sufficient proportion of its capital stock for subscription by such members.

(b) The Bank shall prescribe rules laying down the conditions under which members may subscribe shares of the authorized capital stock of the Bank in addition to their minimum subscriptions.

(c) If the authorized capital stock of the Bank is increased, each member shall have a reasonable opportunity to subscribe, under such conditions as the Bank shall decide, a portion of the increase of stock equivalent to the proportion which its stock theretofore subscribed bears to the total capital stock of the Bank, but no member shall be obligated to subscribe any part of the increased capital.

---

[3] There have been three General Capital Increases to the authorized capital of the Bank. In 1959, a general increase of $10 billion was authorized, doubling to $20 billion, the authorized capital stock of the Bank. A second increase in the amount of $40 billion was approved in 1980. In 1988, a Third General Capital Increase of $74.8 billion was approved by the Board of Governors, raising the total authorized capital to $171.4 billion.

In addition to the General Capital Increases, there have been Selective Capital Increases for the years and in the amounts as follows: 1959—$1 billion; 1963—$1 billion; 1965—$2 billion; 1970—$3 billion; 1977—$8.4 billion; 1980—$4 billion; and 1984—$8.4 billion.

SECTION 4. ISSUE PRICE OF SHARES

Shares included in the minimum subscriptions of original members shall be issued at par. Others shares shall be issued at par unless the Bank by a majority of the total voting power decides in special circumstances to issue them on other terms.

SECTION 5. DIVISION AND CALLS OF SUBSCRIBED CAPITAL

The subscription of each member shall be divided into two parts as follows:

(i) twenty percent shall be paid or subject to call under Section 7(i) of this Article as needed by the bank for its operations;

(ii) the remaining eighty percent shall be subject to call by the Bank only when required to meet obligations of the Bank created under Article IV, Sections 1(a), (ii) and (iii).

Calls on unpaid subscriptions shall be uniform on all shares.

SECTION 6. LIMITATION ON LIABILITY

Liability on shares shall be limited to the unpaid portion of the issue price of the shares.

SECTION 7. METHOD OF PAYMENT OF SUBSCRIPTIONS FOR SHARES

Payment of subscriptions for shares shall be made in gold or United States dollars and in the currencies of the members as follows:

(i) under Section 5(i) of this Article, two percent of the price of each share shall be payable in gold or United States dollars, and, when calls are made, the remaining eighteen percent shall be paid in the currency of the member;

(ii) when a call is made under Section 5(iii) of this Article, payment may be made at the option of the member either in gold, in United States dollars or in the currency required to discharge the obligations of the Bank for the purpose for which the call is made;

(iii) when a member makes payments in any currency under (i) and (ii) above, such payments shall be made in amounts equal in value to the member's liability under the call. This liability shall be a proportionate part of the subscribed capital stock of the Bank as authorized and defined in Section 2 of this Article.

SECTION 8. TIME OF PAYMENT OF SUBSCRIPTIONS

(a) The two percent payable on each share in gold or United States dollars under Section 7(i) of this Article, shall be paid within sixty days of the date on which the Bank begins operations, provided that—

(i) any original member of the Bank whose metropolitan territory has suffered from enemy occupation or hostilities during the present war shall be granted the right to postpone payment of one-half percent until five years after that date;

(ii) an original member who cannot make such a payment because it has not recovered possession of its gold reserves which are still seized or immobilized as a result of the war may postpone all payment until such date as the Bank shall decide.

(b) The remainder of the price of each share payable under Section 7(i) of this Article shall be paid as and when called by the Bank, provided that—

(i) the Bank shall, within one year of its beginning operations, call not less than eight percent of the price of the share in addition to the payment of two percent referred to in (a) above;

(ii) not more than five percent of the price of the share shall be called in any period of three months.

SECTION 9. MAINTENANCE OF VALUE OF CERTAIN CURRENCY HOLDINGS OF THE BANK

(a) Whenever (i) the par value of a member's currency is reduced, or (ii) the foreign exchange value of a member's currency has, in the opinion of the Bank, depreciated to a significant extent within that member's territories, the member shall pay to the Bank within a reasonable time an additional amount of its own currency sufficient to maintain the value, as of the time of initial subscription, of the amount of the currency of such member which is held by the Bank and derived from currency originally paid in the Bank by the member under Article II, Section 7(i), from currency referred to in Article IV, Section 2(b), or from any additional currency furnished under the provisions of the present paragraph, and which has not been repurchased by the member for gold or for the currency of any member which is acceptable to the Bank.

(b) Whenever the par value of a member's currency is increased, the Bank shall return to such member within a reasonable time an amount of that member's currency equal to the increase in the value of the amount of such currency described in (a) above.

(c) The provisions of the preceding paragraphs may be waived by the Bank when a uniform proportionate change in the par values of the currencies of all its members is made by the International Monetary Fund.

SECTION 10. RESTRICTION ON DISPOSAL OF SHARES

Shares shall not be pledged or encumbered in any manner whatever and they shall be transferable only to the Bank.

ARTICLE III—GENERAL PROVISIONS RELATING TO LOANS AND GUARANTEES

SECTION. 1. USE OF RESOURCES

(a) The resources and the facilities of the Bank shall be used exclusively for the benefit of members with equitable consideration to projects for development and projects for reconstruction alike.

(b) for the purpose of facilitating the restoration and reconstruction of the economy of members whose metropolitan territories have suffered great devastation from enemy occupation or hostilities, the Bank, in determining the conditions and terms of loans made to such members, shall pay special regard to lightening the financial burden and expediting the completion of such restoration and reconstruction.

SECTION 2. DEALINGS BETWEEN MEMBERS AND THE BANK

Each member shall deal with the Bank only through its treasury, central bank, stabilization fund or other similar fiscal agency, and the Bank shall deal with members only by or through the same agencies.

SECTION 3. LIMITATIONS ON GUARANTEES AND BORROWINGS OF THE BANK

The total amount outstanding of guarantees, participations in loans and direct loans made by the Bank shall not be increased at any time, if by such increase the total would exceed one hundred percent of the unimpaired subscribed capital, reserves and surplus of the Bank.

SECTION 4. CONDITIONS ON WHICH THE BANK MAY GUARANTEE OR MAKE LOANS

The Bank may guarantee, participate in, or make loans to any member or any political subdivision thereof and any business, industrial, and agricultural enterprise in the territories of a member, subject to the following conditions:

(i) When the member in whose territories the project is located is not itself the borrower, the member or the central bank or some comparable agency of the member which is acceptable to the Bank, fully guarantees the repayment of the principal and the payment of interest and other charges on the loan.

(ii) The Bank is satisfied that in the prevailing market conditions the borrower would be unable otherwise to obtain the loan under conditions which in the opinion of the Bank are reasonable for the borrower.

(iii) A competent committee, as provided for in Article V, Section 7, has submitted a written report recommending the project after a careful study of the merits of the proposal.

(iv) In the opinion of the Bank the rate of interest and other charges are reasonable and such rate, charges and the schedule for repayment of principal are appropriate to the project.

(v) In making or guaranteeing a loan, the Bank shall pay due regard to the prospects that the borrower, and, if the borrower is not a member, that the guarantor, will be in position to meet its obligations under the loan; and the Bank shall act prudently in the interests both of the particular member in whose territories the project is located and of the members as a whole.

(vi) In guaranteeing a loan made by other investors, the Bank receives suitable compensation for its risk.

(vii) Loans made or guaranteed by the Bank shall, except in special circumstances, be for the purpose of specific projects of reconstruction or development.

SECTION 5. USE OF LOANS GUARANTEED, PARTICIPATED IN OR MADE BY THE BANK

(a) The Bank shall impose no conditions that the proceeds of a loan shall be spent in the territories of any particular member or members.

(b) The Bank shall make arrangements to ensure that the proceeds of any loan are used only for the purposes for which the loan was granted, with due attention to considerations of economy and efficiency and without regard to political or other non-economic influences or considerations.

(c) In the case of loans made by the Bank, it shall open an account in the name of the borrower and the amount of the loan shall be credited to this account in the currency or currencies in which the loan is made. The borrower shall be permitted by the Bank to draw on this account only to meet expenses in connection with the project as they are actually incurred.

SECTION 6. LOANS TO THE INTERNATIONAL FINANCE CORPORATION [4]

(a) The Bank may make, participate in, or guarantee loans to the International Finance Corporation, an affiliate of the Bank, for use in its lending operations. The total amount outstanding of such loans, participations and guarantees shall not be increased if, at the time or as a result thereof, the aggregate amount of debt (including the guarantee of any debt) incurred by the said Corporation from any source and then outstanding shall exceed an amount equal to four times its unimpaired subscribed capital and surplus.

(b) The provisions of Article III, Sections 4 and 5(c) and of Article IV, Section 3 shall not apply to loans, participations and guarantees authorized by this Section.

ARTICLE IV—OPERATIONS

SECTION 1. METHODS OF MAKING OR FACILITATING LOANS

(a) The Bank may make or facilitate loans which satisfy the general conditions of Article III in any of the following ways:

(i) By making or participating in direct loans out of its own funds corresponding to its unimpaired paid-up capital and surplus and, subject to Section 6 of this Article, to its reserves.

(ii) By making or participating in direct loans out of funds raised in the market of a member, or otherwise borrowed by the Bank.

(iii) By guaranteeing in whole or in part loans made by private investors through the usual investment channels.

(b) The Bank may borrow funds under (a)(ii) above or guarantee loans under (a)(iii) above only with the approval of the member in whose markets the funds are raised and the member in whose currency the loan is denominated, and only if those members agree that the proceeds may be exchanged for the currency of any other member without restriction.

---

[4] Sec. 6 was added by amendment, effective December 17, 1965 (16 UST 1942; TIAS 5929).

SECTION 2. AVAILABILITY AND TRANSFERABILITY OF CURRENCIES

(a) Currencies paid into the Bank under Article II, Section 7(i), shall be loaned only with the approval in each case of the member whose currency is involved; provided, however, that if necessary, after the Bank's subscribed capital has been entirely called, such currencies shall, without restriction by the members whose currencies are offered, be used or exchanged for the currencies required to meet contractual payments of interest, other charges or amortization on the Bank's own borrowings, or to meet the Bank's liabilities with respect to such contractual payments on loans guaranteed by the Bank.

(b) Currencies received by the Bank from borrowers and guarantors in payment on account of principal of direct loans made with currencies referred to in (a) above shall be exchanged for the currencies of other members or reloaned only with the approval for the currencies of other members or reloaned only with the approval in each case of the members whose currencies are involved; provided, however, that if necessary, after the Bank's subscribed capital has been entirely called, such currencies shall, without restriction by the members whose currencies are offered, be used or exchanged for the currencies required to meet contractual payments of interest, other charges or amortization on the Bank's own borrowings, or to meet the Bank's liabilities with respect to such contractual payments on loans guaranteed by the Bank.

(c) Currencies received by the Bank from borrowers or guarantors in payment on account of principal of direct loans made by the Bank under Section 1(a)(ii) of this Article, shall be held and used, without restriction by the members, to make amortization payments, or to anticipate payment of or repurchase part or all of the Bank's own obligations.

(d) All other currencies available to the Bank, including those raised in the market or otherwise borrowed under Section 1(a)(ii) of this Article, those obtained by the sale of gold, those received as payments of interest and other charges for direct loans made under Sections 1(a) (i) and (ii), and those received as payments of commissions and other charges under Section 1(a)(iii), shall be used or exchanged for other currencies or gold required in the operations of the Bank without restriction by the members whose currencies are offered.

(e) Currencies raised in the markets of members by borrowers on loans guaranteed by the Bank under Section 1(a)(iii) of this Article, shall also be used or exchanged for other currencies without restriction by such members.

SECTION 3. PROVISION OF CURRENCIES FOR DIRECT LOANS

The following provisions shall apply to direct loans under Sections 1(a) (i) and (ii) of this Article:

(a) The Bank shall furnish the borrower with such currencies of members, other than the member in whose territories the project is located, as are needed by the borrower for expenditures to be made in the territories of such other members to carry out the purposes of the loan.

(b) The Bank may, in exceptional circumstances when local currency required for the purposes of the loan cannot be raised by the borrower on reasonable terms, provide the borrower as part of the loan with an appropriate amount of that currency.

(c) The Bank, if the project gives rise indirectly to an increased need for foreign exchange by the member in whose territories the project is located, may in exceptional circumstances provide the borrower as part of the loan with an appropriate amount of gold or foreign exchange not in excess of the borrower's local expenditure in connection with the purposes of the loan.

(d) The Bank may, in exceptional circumstances, at the request of a member in whose territories a portion of the loan is spent, repurchase with gold or foreign exchange a part of that member's currency thus spent but in no case shall the part so repurchased exceed the amount by which the expenditure of the loan in those territories gives rise to an increased need for foreign exchange.

SECTION 4. PAYMENT PROVISIONS FOR DIRECT LOANS

Loan contracts under Section 1(a) (i) or (ii) of this Article shall be made in accordance with the following payment provisions:

(a) The terms and conditions of interest and amortization payments, maturity and dates of payment of each loan shall be determined by the Bank. The Bank shall also determine the rate and any other terms and conditions of commission to be charged in connection with such loan.

In the case of loans made under Section 1(a)(ii) of this Article during the first ten years of the Bank's operations, this rate of commission shall be not less than one percent per annum and not greater than one and one-half percent per annum, and shall be charged on the outstanding portion of any such loan. At the end of this period of ten years, the rate of commission may be reduced by the Bank with respect both to the outstanding portions of loans already made and to future loans, if the reserves accumulated by the Bank under Section 6 of the Article and out of other earnings are considered by it sufficient to justify a reduction. In the case of future loans the Bank shall also have discretion to increase the rate of commission beyond the above limit, if experience indicates that an increase is advisable.

(b) All loan contracts shall stipulate the currency or currencies in which payments under the contract shall be made to the Bank. At the option of the borrower, however, such payments may be made in gold, or subject to the agreement of the Bank, in the currency of a member other than that prescribed in the contract.

(i) In the case of loans made under Section 1(a)(i) of this Article, the loan contracts shall provide that payments to the Bank of interest, other charges and amortization shall be made in the currency loaned, unless the member whose currency is loaned agrees that such payments shall be made in some other specified currency or currencies. These payments, subject to the provisions of Article II, Section 9(c), shall be equivalent to the value of such contractual payments at the time the loans were made, in terms of a currency specified for the purpose by the Bank by a three-fourths majority of the total voting power.

(ii) In the case of loans made under Section 1(a)(ii) of this Article, the total amount outstanding and payable to the bank in any one currency shall at no time exceed the total amount of the outstanding borrowings made by the Bank under Section 1 (a)(ii) and payable in the same currency.

(c) If a member suffers from an acute exchange stringency, so that the service of any loan contracted by that member or guaranteed by it or by one of its agencies cannot be provided in the stipulated manner, the member concerned may apply to the Bank for a relaxation of the conditions of payment. If the Bank is satisfied that some relaxation is in the interests of the particular member and of the operations of the Bank and of its members as a whole, it may take action under either, or both, of the following paragraphs with respect to the whole, or part, of the annual service:

(i) The Bank may, in its discretion, make arrangements with the member concerned to accept service payments on the loan in the member's currency for periods not to exceed three years upon appropriate terms regarding the use of such currency and the maintenance of its foreign exchange value; and for the repurchase of such currency on appropriate terms.

(ii) The Bank may modify the terms of amortization or extend the life of the loan, or both.

SECTION 5. GUARANTEES

(a) In guaranteeing a loan placed through the usual investment channels, the Bank shall charge a guarantee commission payable periodically on the amount of the loan outstanding at a rate determined by the Bank. During the first ten years of the Bank's operations, this rate shall be not less than one percent per annum and not greater than one and one-half percent per annum. At the end of this period of ten years, the rate of commission may be reduced by the Bank with respect both to the outstanding portions of loans already guaranteed and to future loans if the reserves accumulated by the Bank under Section 6 of this Article and out of other earnings are considered by it sufficient to justify a reduction. In the case of future loans the Bank shall also have discretion to increase the rate of commission beyond the above limit, if experience indicates that an increase is advisable.

(b) Guarantee commissions shall be paid directly to the Bank by the borrower.

(c) Guarantees by the Bank shall provide that the Bank may terminate its liability with respect to interest if, upon default by the borrower and by the guarantor, if any, the Bank offers to purchase, at par and interest accrued to a date designated in the offer, the bonds or other obligations guaranteed.

(d) The Bank shall have power to determine any other terms and conditions of the guarantee.

SECTION 6. SPECIAL RESERVE

The amount of commissions received by the Bank under Sections 4 and 5 of this Article shall be set aside as a special reserve, which shall be kept available for meeting liabilities of the Bank in accordance with Section 7 of this Article. The special reserve shall be held in such liquid form, permitted under this Agreement, as the Executive Directors may decide.

SECTION 7. METHODS OF MEETING LIABILITIES OF THE BANK IN CASE OF DEFAULTS

In case of default on loans made, participated in, or guaranteed by the Bank:

(a) The Bank shall make such arrangements as may be feasible to adjust the obligations under the loans, including arrangements under or analogous to those provided in Section 4(c) of this Article.

(b) The payments in discharge of the Bank's liabilities on borrowings or guarantees under Section 1(a) (ii) and (iii) of this Article shall be charged—

(i) first, against the special reserve provided in Section 6 of this Article;

(ii) then, to the extent necessary and at the discretion of the Bank, against the other reserves, surplus and capital available to the Bank.

(c) Whenever necessary to meet contractual payments of interest, other charges or amortization on the Bank's own borrowings, or to meet the Bank's liabilities with respect to similar payments on loans guaranteed by it, the Bank may call an appropriate amount of the unpaid subscriptions of members in accordance with Article II, Sections 5 and 7. Moreover, if it believes that a default may be of long duration, the Bank may call an additional amount of such unpaid subscriptions not to exceed in any one year one percent of the total subscriptions of the members of the following purposes:

(i) To redeem prior to maturity, or otherwise discharge its liability on, all or part of the outstanding principal of any loan guaranteed by it in respect of which the debtor is in default.

(ii) To repurchase, or otherwise discharge its liability on, all or part of its own outstanding borrowings.

SECTION 8. MISCELLANEOUS OPERATIONS

In addition to the operations specified elsewhere in this Agreement, the Bank shall have the power:

(i) To buy and sell securities it has issued and to buy and sell securities which it has guaranteed or in which it has invested, provided that the Bank shall obtain the approval of the member in whose territories the securities are to be bought or sold.

(ii) To guarantee securities in which it has invested for the purpose of facilitating their sale.

(iii) To borrow the currency of any member with the approval of that member.

(iv) To buy and sell such other securities as the directors by a three-fourths majority of the total voting power may deem proper for the investment of all or part of the special reserve under section 6 of this Article.

In exercising the powers conferred by this section, the Bank may deal with any person, partnership, association, corporation or other legal entity in the territories of any member.

SECTION 9. WARNING TO BE PLACED ON SECURITIES

Every security guaranteed or issued by the Bank shall bear on its face a conspicuous statement to the effect that it is not an obligation of any government unless expressly stated on the security.

SECTION 10. POLITICAL ACTIVITY PROHIBITED

The Bank and its officers shall not interfere in the political affairs of any member; nor shall they be influenced in their decisions by the political character of the member or members concerned. Only economic considerations shall be relevant to their decisions, and these considerations shall be weighed impartially in order to achieve the purposes stated in Article I.

ARTICLE V—ORGANIZATION AND MANAGEMENT

SECTION 1. STRUCTURE OF THE BANK

The Bank shall have a Board of Governors, Executive Directors, a President and such other officers and staff to perform such duties as the Bank may determine.

SECTION 2. BOARD OF GOVERNORS

(a) All the powers of the Bank shall be vested in the Board of Governors consisting of one governor and one alternate appointed by each member in such manner as it may determine. Each governor and each alternate shall serve for five years, subject to the pleasure of the member appointing him, and may be reappointed. No alternate may vote except in the absence of his principal. The Board shall select one of the governors as Chairman.

(b) The Board of Governors may delegate to the Executive Directors authority to exercise any powers of the Board, except the power to:

(i) Admit new members and determine the conditions of their admission;

(ii) Increase or decrease the capital stock;

(iii) Suspend a member;

(iv) Decide appeals from interpretations of this Agreement given by the Executive Directors;

(v) Make arrangements to cooperate with other international organizations (other than informal arrangements of a temporary and administrative character);

(vi) Decide to suspend permanently the operations of the Bank and to distribute its assets;

(vii) Determine the distribution of the net income of the Bank.

(c) The Board of Governors shall hold an annual meeting and such other meetings as may be provided for by the Board or called by the Executive Directors. Meetings of the Board shall be called by the directors whenever requested by five members or by members having one-quarter of the total voting power.

(d) A quorum for any meeting of the Board of Governors shall be a majority of the governors, exercising not less than two-thirds of the total voting power.

(e) The Board of Governors may by regulation establish a procedure whereby the Executive Directors, when they deem such action to be in the best interests of the Bank, may obtain a vote of the Governors on a specific question without calling a meeting of the Board.

(f) The Board of Governors, and the Executive Directors to the extent authorized, may adopt such rules and regulations as may be necessary or appropriate to conduct the business of the Bank.

(g) Governors and alternates shall serve as such without compensation from the Bank, but the Bank shall pay them reasonable expenses incurred in attending meetings.

(h) The Board of Governors shall determine the remuneration to be paid to the Executive Directors and the salary and terms of the contract of service of the President.

SECTION 3. VOTING

(a) Each member shall have two hundred and fifty votes plus one additional vote for each share of stock held.

(b) Except as otherwise specifically provided, all matters before the Bank shall be decided by a majority of the votes cast.

SECTION 4. EXECUTIVE DIRECTORS

(a) The Executive Directors shall be responsible for the conduct of the general operations of the Bank, and for this purpose, shall exercise all the powers delegated to them by the Board of Governors.

(b) There shall be twelve Executive Directors, who need not be governors, and of whom—

(i) five shall be appointed, one by each of the five members having the largest number of shares;

(ii) seven shall be elected according to Schedule B by all the governors other than those appointed by the five members referred to in (i) above.

For the purpose of this paragraph "members" means governments of countries whose names are set forth in Schedule A, whether they are original members or become members in accordance with Article II, Section 1(b). When governments of other countries become members, the Board of Governors may, by a four-fifths majority of the total voting power, increase the total number of directors by increasing the number of directors to be elected.

Executive Directors shall be appointed or elected every two years.

(c) Each Executive Director shall appoint an alternate with full power to act for him when he is not present. When the Executive Directors appointing them are present, alternates may participate in meetings but shall not vote.

(d) Directors shall continue in office until their successors are appointed or elected. If the office of an elected director becomes vacant more than ninety days before the end of his term, another director shall be elected for the remainder of the term by the governors who elected the former director. A majority of the votes cast shall be required for election. While the office remains vacant, the alternate of the former director shall exercise his powers, except that of appointing an alternate.

(e) The Executive Directors shall function in continuous session at the principal office of the Bank and shall meet as often as the business of the Bank may require.

(f) A quorum for any meeting of the Executive Directors shall be a majority of the directors, exercising not less than one half of the total voting power.

(g) Each appointed director shall be entitled to cast the number of votes allotted under Section 3 of this Article to the member appointing him. Each elected director shall be entitled to cast the number of votes which counted toward his election. All the votes which a director is entitled to cast shall be cast as a unit.

(h) The Board of Governors shall adopt regulations under which a member not entitled to appoint a director under (b) above may send a representative to attend any meeting of the Executive Directors when a request made by, or a matter particularly affecting, that member is under consideration.

(i) The Executive Directors may appoint such committees as they deem advisable. Membership of such committees need not be limited to governors or directors or their alternates.

SECTION 5. PRESIDENT AND STAFF

(a) The Executive Directors shall select a President who shall not be a governor or an Executive Director or an alternate for either. The President shall be Chairman of the Executive Directors, but shall have no vote except a deciding vote in case of an equal division. He may participate in meetings of the Board of Governors, but shall not vote at such meetings. The President shall cease to hold office when the Executive Directors so decide.

(b) The President shall be chief of the operating staff of the Bank and shall conduct, under the direction of the Executive Directors, the ordinary business of the Bank. Subject to the general control of the Executive Directors, he shall be responsible for the organization, appointment and dismissal of the officers and staff.

(c) The President, officers and staff of the Bank, in the discharge of their offices, owe their duty entirely to the Bank and to no other authority. Each member of the Bank shall respect the international character of this duty and shall refrain from all attempts to influence any of them in the discharge of their duties.

(d) In appointing the officers and staff the President shall, subject to the paramount importance of securing the highest standards of efficiency and of technical competence, pay due regard to the importance of recruiting personnel on as wide a geographical basis as possible.

SECTION 6. ADVISORY COUNCIL

(a) There shall be an Advisory Council of not less than seven persons selected by the Board of Governors including representatives of banking, commercial, industrial, labor, and agricultural interests, and with as wide a national representation as possible. In those fields where specialized international organizations exist, the members of the Council representative of those fields shall be elected in agreement with such organizations. The Council shall advise the Bank on matters of general policy. The Council shall meet annually and on such other occasions as the Bank may request.

(b) Councilors shall serve for two years and may be reappointed. They shall be paid their reasonable expenses incurred on behalf of the Bank.

SECTION 7. LOAN COMMITTEES

The committees required to report on loans under Article III, Section 4, shall be appointed by the Bank. Each such committee shall include an expert selected by the governor representing the member in whose territories the project is located and one or more members of the technical staff of the Bank.

SECTION 8. RELATIONSHIP TO OTHER INTERNATIONAL ORGANIZATIONS

(a) The bank, within the terms of this Agreement, shall cooperate with any general international organization, and with public international organizations having specialized responsibilities in related fields. Any arrangements for such cooperation which would involve a modification of any provision of this Agreement may be affected only after amendment to this Agreement under Article VIII.

(b) In making decisions on applications for loans or guarantees relating to matters directly within the competence of any international organization of the types specified in the preceding paragraph and participated in primarily by members of the Bank, the Bank shall give consideration to the views and recommendations of such organization.

SECTION 9. LOCATION OF OFFICES

(a) The principal office of the Banks shall be located in the territory of the member holding the greatest number of shares.

(b) The Bank may establish agencies or branch offices in the territories of any member of the Bank.

SECTION 10. REGIONAL OFFICES AND COUNCILS

(a) The Bank may establish regional offices and determine the location of, and the areas to be covered by, each regional office.

(b) Each regional office shall be advised by a regional council representative of the entire area and selected in such manner as the Bank may decide.

SECTION 11. DEPOSITORIES

(a) Each member shall designate its central bank as a depository for all the Bank's holdings of its currency or, if it has no central bank, it shall designate such other institution as may be acceptable to the Bank.

(b) The Bank may hold other assets, including gold, in depositories designated by the five members having the largest number of shares and in such other designated depositories as the Bank may select. Initially, at least one-half of the gold holdings of the Bank shall be held in the depository designated by the member in whose territory the Bank has its principal office, and at least forty percent shall be held in the depositories designated by the remaining four members referred to above, each of such depositors to hold, initially, not less than the amount of gold paid on the shares of the member designating it. However, all transfers of gold by the Bank shall be made with due regard to the costs of transport and anticipated requirements of the Bank. In an emergency the Executive Directors may transfer all or any part of the Bank's gold holdings to any place where they can be adequately protected.

SECTION 12. FORM OF HOLDINGS OF CURRENCY

The Bank shall accept from any member, in place of any part of the member's currency, paid in to the Bank under Article II, Section 7(i), or to meet amortization payments on loans made with such currency, and not needed by the Bank in its operations, notes or similar obligations issued by the government of the member or the depository designated by such member, which shall be non-negotiable, non-interest-bearing and payable at their par value on demand by credit to the account of the Bank in the designated depository.

SECTION 13. PUBLICATION OF REPORTS AND PROVISION OF INFORMATION

(a) The Bank shall publish an annual report containing an audited statement of its accounts and shall circulate to members at intervals of three months or less a summary statement of its financial position and a profit and loss statement showing the results of its operations.

(b) The Bank may publish such other reports as it deems desirable to carry out its purposes.

(c) Copies of all reports, statements and publications made under this section shall be distributed to members.

SECTION 14. ALLOCATION OF NET INCOME

(a) The Board of Governors shall determine annually what part of the Bank's net income, after making provision for reserves, shall be allocated to surplus and what part, if any, shall be distributed.

(b) If any part is distributed, up to two percent non-cumulative shall be paid, as a first charge against the distribution for any year, to each member on the basis of the average amount of the loans outstanding during the year made under Article IV, Section 1(a)(i), out of currency corresponding to its subscription. If two percent is paid as a first charge, any balance remaining to be distributed shall be paid to all members in proportion to their shares. Payments to each member shall be made in its own currency, or if that currency is not available, in other currency acceptable to the member. If such payments are made in currencies other than the member's own currency, the transfer of the currency and its use by the receiving member after payment shall be without restriction by the members.

ARTICLE VI—WITHDRAWAL AND SUSPENSION OF MEMBERSHIP: SUSPENSION OF OPERATION

SECTION 1. RIGHT OF MEMBERS TO WITHDRAW

Any member may withdraw from the Bank at any time by transmitting a notice in writing to the Bank at its principal office. Withdrawal shall become effective on the date such notice is received.

SECTION 2. SUSPENSION OF MEMBERSHIP

If a member fails to fulfill any of its obligations to the Bank, the Bank may suspend its membership by decision of a majority of the governors, exercising a majority of the total voting power. The member so suspended shall automatically cease to be a member one year from the date of its suspension unless a decision is taken by the same majority to restore the member to good standing.

While under suspension, a member shall not be entitled to exercise any rights under this Agreement, except the right to withdrawal, but shall remain subject to all obligations.

SECTION 3. CESSATION OF MEMBERSHIP IN INTERNATIONAL MONETARY FUND

Any member which ceases to be a member of the International Monetary Fund shall automatically cease after three months to be a member of the Bank unless the Bank by three-fourths of the total voting power has agreed to allow it to remain a member.

SECTION 4. SETTLEMENT OF ACCOUNTS WITH GOVERNMENTS CEASING TO BE MEMBERS

(a) When a government ceases to be a member, it shall remain liable for its direct obligations to the Bank and for its contingent liabilities to the Bank so long as any part of the loans or guarantees contracted before it ceased to be a member are outstanding; but it shall cease to incur liabilities with respect to loans and guarantees entered into thereafter by the Bank and to share either in the income or the expenses of the Bank.

(b) At the time a government ceases to be a member, the Bank shall arrange for the purchase of its share as a part of the settlement of accounts with such government in accordance with the provisions of (c) and (d) below. For this purpose the repurchase price of the shares shall be the value shown by the books of the Bank on the day the government ceases to be a member.

(c) The payment for shares repurchased by the Bank under this section shall be governed by the following conditions:

(i) Any amount due to the government for its shares shall be withheld so long as the government, its central bank or any of its agencies remains liable, as borrower or guarantor, to the Bank and such amount may, at the option of the Bank, be applied on any such liability as it matures. No amount shall be withheld on account of the liability of the government resulting from its subscription for shares under Article II, Section 5(ii). In any event, no amount due to a member for its shares shall be paid until six months after the date upon which the government ceases to be a member.

(ii) Payments for shares may be made from time to time, upon their surrender by the government, to the extent by which the amount due as the repurchase price in (b) above exceeds the aggregate of liabilities on loans and guarantees in (c)(i) above until the former member has received the full repurchase price.

(iii) Payments shall be made in the currency of the country receiving payment or at the option of the Bank in gold.

(iv) If losses are sustained by the Bank on any guarantees, participation in loans, or loans which were outstanding on the date when the government ceased to be a member, and the amount of such losses exceeds the amount of the reserve provided against losses on the date when the government ceased to be a member, such government shall be obligated to repay upon demand the amount by which the repurchase price of its shares would have been reduced, if the losses had been taken into account when the repurchase price was determined. In addition, the former member government shall remain liable on any call for unpaid subscriptions under Article II, Section 5(ii), to the extent that it would have been required to respond if the impairment of capital had occurred and the call had been made at the time the repurchase price of its shares was determined.

(d) If the Bank suspends permanently its operations under Section 5(b) of this Article, within six months of the date upon which any government ceases to be a member, all rights of such government shall be determined by the provisions of Section 5 of this Article.

SECTION 5. SUSPENSION OF OPERATIONS AND SETTLEMENT OF OBLIGATIONS

(a) In an emergency the Executive Directors may suspend temporarily operations in respect to new loans and guarantees pending an opportunity for further consideration and action by the Board of Governors.

(b) The Bank may suspend permanently its operations in respect of new loans and guarantees by vote of a majority of the Governors, exercising a majority of the total voting power. After such suspension of operations the Bank shall forthwith cease all activities, except those incident to the orderly realization, conservation, and preservation of its assets and settlement of its obligations.

(c) The liability of all members for uncalled subscriptions to the capital stock of the Bank and in respect of the depreciation of their own currencies shall continue until all claims of creditors, including all contingent claims shall have been discharged.

(d) All creditors holding direct claims shall be paid out of the assets of the Bank, and then out of payments to the Bank on calls on unpaid subscriptions. Before making any payments to creditors holding direct claims the Executive Directors shall make such arrangements as are necessary, in their judgment, to insure a distribution to holders of contingent claims ratably with creditors holding direct claims.

(e) No distribution shall be made to members on account of their subscriptions to the capital stock of the Bank until—

(i) all liabilities to creditors have been discharged or provided for, and

(ii) a majority of the governors, exercising a majority of the total voting power, have decided to make a distribution.

(f) After a decision to make a distribution has been taken under (e) above, the Executive Directors, may by a two-thirds majority vote, make successive distributions of the assets of the Bank to members until all of the assets have been distributed. This distribution shall be subject to the prior settlement of all outstanding claims of the Bank against each member.

(g) Before any distribution of assets is made, the Executive Directors shall fix the proportionate share of each member according to the ratio of its shareholding to the total outstanding shares of the Bank.

(h) The Executive Directors shall value the assets to be distributed as at the date of distribution and then proceed to distribute in the following manner:

(i) There shall be paid to each member in its own obligations or those of its official agencies or legal entities within its territories, insofar as they are available for distribution, an amount equivalent in value to its proportionate share of the total amount to be distributed.

(ii) Any balance due to a member after payment has been made under (i) above shall be paid, in its own currency, insofar as it is held by the Bank, up to an amount equivalent in value to such balance.

(iii) Any balance due to a member after payment has been made under (i) and (ii) above shall be paid in gold or currency acceptable to the member, insofar as they are held by the Bank, up to an amount equivalent in value to such balance.

(iv) Any remaining assets held by the Bank after payments have been made to members under (i), (ii), and (iii) above shall be distributed *pro rata* among the members.

(i) Any member receiving assets distributed by the Bank in accordance with (h) above, shall enjoy the same rights with respect to such assets as the Bank enjoyed prior to their distribution.

ARTICLE VII—STATUS, IMMUNITIES AND PRIVILEGES

SECTION 1. PURPOSES OF ARTICLE

To enable the Bank to fulfill the functions with which it is entrusted, the status, immunities and privileges set forth in this Article shall be accorded to the Bank in the territories of each member.

SECTION 2. STATUS OF THE BANK

The Bank shall possess full juridical personality, and, in particular the capacity—

(i) to contract;

(ii) to acquire and dispose of immovable and movable property;

(iii) to institute legal proceedings.

SECTION 3. POSITION OF THE BANK WITH REGARD TO JUDICIAL PROCESS

Actions may be brought against the Bank only in a court of competent jurisdiction in the territories of a member in which the Bank has an office, has appointed an agent for the purpose of accepting service or notice of process, or has issued or guaranteed securities. No actions shall, however, be brought by members or persons acting for or deriving claims from members. The property and assets of the Bank shall, wheresoever located and by whomsoever held, be immune from all forms of seizure, attachment or execution before the delivery of final judgment against the Bank.

SECTION 4. IMMUNITY OF ASSETS FROM SEIZURE

Property and assets of the Bank, wherever located and by whomsoever held, shall be immune from search, requisition, confiscation, expropriation or any other form of seizure by executive or legislative action.

SECTION 5. IMMUNITY OF ARCHIVES

The archives of the Bank shall be inviolable.

SECTION 6. FREEDOM OF ASSETS FROM RESTRICTIONS

To the extent necessary to carry out the operations provided for in this Agreement and subject to the provisions of this Agreement, all property and assets of the Bank shall be free from restrictions, regulations, controls, and moratoria of any nature.

SECTION 7. PRIVILEGE FOR COMMUNICATIONS

The official communications of the Bank shall be accorded by each member the same treatment that it accords to the official communications of other members.

SECTION 8. IMMUNITIES AND PRIVILEGES OF OFFICERS AND EMPLOYEES

All governors, executive directors, alternates, officers and employees of the Bank—

(i) shall be immune from legal process with respect to acts performed by them in their official capacity except when the Bank waives this immunity;

(ii) not being local nationals, shall be accorded the same immunities from immigration restrictions, alien registration requirements and national service obligations and the same facilities as regards exchange restrictions as are accorded by members to the representatives, officials, and employees of comparable rank of other members;

(iii) shall be granted the same treatment in respect of travelling facilities as is accorded by members to representatives, officials and employees of comparable rank of other members.

SECTION 9. IMMUNITIES FROM TAXATION

(a) The Bank, its assets, property, income and its operations and transactions authorized by this Agreement, shall be immune from all taxation and from all customs duties. The Bank shall also be immune from liability for the collection or payment of any tax or duty.

(b) No tax shall be levied on or in respect of salaries and emoluments paid by the Bank to executive directors, alternates, officials or employees of the Bank who are not local citizens, local subjects, or other local nationals.

(c) No taxation of any kind shall be levied on any obligation or security issued by the Bank (including any dividend or interest thereon) by whomsoever held—

(i) Which discriminates against such obligation or security solely because it is issued by the Bank; or

(ii) if the sole jurisdictional basis for such taxation is the place or currency in which it is issued, made payable or paid, or the location of any office or place of business maintained by the Bank.

(d) No taxation of any kind shall be levied on any obligation or security guaranteed by the bank (including any dividend or interest thereon) by whomsoever held—

(i) which discriminates against such obligation or security solely because it is guaranteed by the Bank; or

(ii) if the sole jurisdictional basis for such taxation is the location of any office or place of business maintained by the Bank.

SECTION 10. APPLICATION OF ARTICLE

Each member shall take such action as is necessary in its own territories for the purpose of making effective in terms of its own law the principles set forth in this Article and shall inform the Bank of the detailed action which it has taken.

ARTICLE VIII—AMENDMENTS

(a) Any proposal to introduce modifications in this Agreement, whether emanating from a member, a governor or the Executive Directors, shall be communicated to the Chairman of the Board of Governors who shall bring the proposal before the Board. If the proposed amendment is approved by the Board the Bank shall, by circular letter or telegram, ask all members whether they accept the proposed amendment. When three-fifths of the members having four-fifths of the total voting power, have accepted the proposed amendments, the Bank shall certify the fact by formal communication address to all members.

(b) Notwithstanding (a) above, acceptance by all members is required in the case of any amendment modifying—

(i) the right to withdraw from the Bank provided in Article VI, Section 1;

(ii) the right secured by Article II, Section 3(c);

(iii) the limitation on liability provided in Article II, Section 6.

(c) Amendments shall enter into force for all members three months after the date of the formal communication unless a shorter period is specified in the circular letter or telegram.

ARTICLE IX—INTERPRETATION

(a) Any question of interpretation of the provisions of this Agreement arising between any member and the Bank or between any members of the Bank shall be submitted to the Executive Directors for their decision. If the question particularly affects any member not entitled to appoint an executive director, it shall be entitled to representation in accordance with Article V, Section 4(h).

(b) In any case where the Executive Directors have given a decision under (a) above, any member may require that the question be referred to the Board of Governors, whose decision shall be final. Pending the result of the reference to the Board, the Bank may, so far as it deems necessary, act on the basis of the decision of the Executive Directors.

(c) Whenever a disagreement arises between the Bank and a country which has ceased to be a member, or between the Bank and any member during the permanent suspension of the Bank, such disagreement shall be submitted to arbitration by a tribunal of three arbitrators, one appointed by the Bank, another by the country involved and an umpire who, unless the parties otherwise agree, shall be appointed by the President of the Permanent Court of International Justice or such other authority as may have been prescribed by regulation adopted by the Bank. The umpire shall have full power to settle all questions of procedure in any case where the parties are in disagreement with respect thereto.

ARTICLE X—APPROVAL DEEMED GIVEN

Whenever the approval of any member is required before any act may be done by the Bank, except in Article VIII, approval shall be deemed to have been given unless the member presents an objection within such reasonable period as the Bank may fix in notifying the member of the proposed act.

ARTICLE XI—FINAL PROVISIONS

SECTION 1. ENTRY INTO FORCE

This Agreement shall enter into force when it has been signed on behalf of governments whose minimum subscriptions comprise not less than sixty-five percent of the total subscriptions set forth in Schedule A and when the instruments referred to in Section 2(a) of this Article have been deposited on their behalf, but in no event shall this Agreement enter into force before May 1, 1945.

SECTION 2. SIGNATURE

(a) Each government on whose behalf this Agreement is signed shall deposit with the Government of the United States of America an instrument setting forth that it has accepted this Agreement in accordance with its law and has taken all steps necessary to enable it to carry out all of its obligations under this Agreement.

(b) Each government shall become a member of the Bank as from the date of the deposit on its behalf of the instrument referred to in (a) above, except that no government shall become a member before this Agreement enters into force under Section 1 of this Article.

(c) The Government of the United States of America shall inform the governments of all countries whose names are set forth in Schedule A, and all governments whose membership is approved in accordance with Article II, Section 1(b), of all signatures of this Agreement and of the deposit of all instruments referred to in (a) above.

(d) At the time this Agreement is signed on its behalf, each government shall transmit to the Government of the United States of America one one-hundredth of one percent of the price of each share in gold or United States dollars for the purpose of meeting administrative expenses of the Bank. This payment shall be credited on account of the payment to be made in accordance with Article II, Section 8(a). The Government of the United States of America shall hold such funds in a special deposit account and shall transmit them to the Board of Governors of the Bank when the initial meeting has been called under Section 3 of this Article. If this Agreement has not come into force by December 31, 1945, the Government of the United States of America shall return such funds to the governments that transmitted them.

(e) This Agreement shall remain open for signature at Washington on behalf of the governments of the countries whose names are set forth in Schedule A until December 31, 1945.

(f) After December 31, 1945, this Agreement shall be open for signature on behalf of the government of any country whose membership has been approved in accordance with Article II, Section 1(b).

(g) By their signature of this Agreement, all governments accept it both on their own behalf and in respect of all their colonies, overseas territories, all territories under their protection, suzerainty, or authority and all territories in respect of which they exercise a mandate.

(h) In the case of governments whose metropolitan territories have been under enemy occupation, the deposit of the instrument referred to in (a) above may be delayed until one hundred and eighty days after the date on which these territories have been liberated. If, however, it is not deposited by any such government before the expiration of this period, the signature affixed on behalf of that government shall become void and the portion of its subscription paid under (d) above shall be returned to it.

(i) Paragraphs (d) and (h) shall come into force with regard to each signatory government as from the date of its signature.

SECTION 3. INAUGURATION OF THE BANK

(a) As soon as this Agreement enters into force under Section 1 of this Article, each member shall appoint a governor and the member to whom the largest number of shares is allocated in Schedule A shall call the first meeting of the Board of Governors.

(b) At the first meeting of the Board of Governors, arrangements shall be made for the selection of provisional executive directors. The governments of the five countries, to which the largest number of shares are allocated in Schedule A, shall appoint provisional executive directors. If one or more of such governments have not become members, the executive directorships which they would be entitled to fill shall remain vacant until they become members, or until January 1, 1946, whichever is the earlier. Seven provisional executive directors shall be elected in accordance with the provisions of Schedule B and shall remain in office until the date of the first regular election of executive directors which shall be held as soon as practicable after January 1, 1946.

(c) The Board of Governors may delegate to the provisional executive directors any powers except those which may not be delegated to the Executive Directors.

(d) The Bank shall notify members when it is ready to commence operations.

DONE at Washington, in a single copy which shall remain deposited in the Archives of the Government of the United States of America, which shall transmit certified copies to all governments whose names are set forth in Schedule A and to all governments whose Membership is approved in accordance with Article II, Section 1(b).

* * * * * * *

Schedule A—Subscriptions [1]

[millions of dollars]

Australia	200	India	400
Belgium	225	Iran	24
Bolivia	7	Iraq	6
Brazil	105	Liberia	.5
Canada	325	Luxembourg	10
Chile	35	Mexico	65
China	600	Netherlands	275
Colombia	35	New Zealand	50
Costa Rica	2	Nicaragua	.8
Cuba	35	Norway	50
Czechoslovakia	125	Panama	.2
Denmark	(2)	Paraguay	.8
Dominican Republic	2	Peru	17.5
Ecuador	3.2	Philippine Commonwealth	15
Egypt	40	Poland	125
El Salvador	1	Union of South Africa	100
Ethiopia	3	Union of Soviet Socialist Republics	1,200
France	450	United Kingdom	1,300
Greece	25	United States	3,175
Guatemala	2	Uruguay	10.5
Haiti	2	Venezuela	10.5
Honduras	1	Yugoslavia	40
Iceland	1		
		Total	9,100

[1] Subsequent changes in membership and quotas are not reflected in Schedule A.

[2] The quota of Denmark shall be determined by the Bank after Denmark accepts membership in accordance with these Articles of Agreement.

SCHEDULE B—ELECTION OF EXECUTIVE DIRECTORS

1. The election of the elective executive directors shall be by ballot of the governors eligible to vote under Article V, Section 4(b).

2. In balloting for the elective executive directors, each governor eligible to vote shall cast for one person all of the votes to which the member appointing him is entitled under Section 3 of Article V. The seven persons receiving the greatest number of votes shall be executive directors, except that no person who receives less than fourteen percent of the total of the votes which can be cast (eligible votes) shall be considered elected.

3. When seven persons are not elected on the first ballot, a second ballot shall be held in which the person who received the lowest number of votes shall be ineligible for election and in which there shall vote only (a) those governors who voted in the first ballot for a person not elected and (b) those governors whose votes for a person elected are deemed under 4 below to have raised the votes cast for that person above fifteen percent of the eligible votes.

4. In determining whether the votes cast by a governor are to be deemed to have raised the total of any person above fifteen percent of the eligible votes, the fifteen percent shall be deemed to include, first, the votes of the governor casting the largest number of votes for such person, then the votes of the governor casting the next largest number, and so on until fifteen percent is reached.

5. Any governor, part of whose votes must be counted in order to raise the total of any person above fourteen percent, shall be considered as casting all of his votes for such person even if the total votes for such person thereby exceed fifteen percent.

6. If, after the second ballot, seven persons have not been elected, further ballots shall be held on the same principles until seven persons have been elected, provided that after six persons are elected, the seventh may be elected by a simple majority of the remaining votes and shall be deemed to have been elected by all such votes.

3. Articles of Agreement Establishing the International Development Association

CONTENTS

3. Articles of Agreement Establishing the International Development Association

Articles of agreement approved at Washington by the Executive Directors of the International Bank for Reconstruction and Development, January 26, 1960; Signed for the United States, August 9, 1960; Instrument of acceptance by the United States deposited, August 9, 1960; Entered into force September 24, 1960[1]

The Governments on whose behalf this Agreement is signed,

CONSIDERING:

That mutual cooperation for constructive economic purposes, healthy development of the world economy and balanced growth of international trade foster international relationships conducive to the maintenance of peace and world prosperity;

That an acceleration of economic development which will promote higher standards of living and economic and social progress in the less-developed countries is desirable not only in the interests of those countries but also in the interests of the international community as a whole;

That achievement of these objectives would be facilitated by an increase in the international flow of capital, public and private, to assist in the development of the resources of the less-developed countries,

do hereby agree as follows:

INTRODUCTORY ARTICLE

The INTERNATIONAL DEVELOPMENT ASSOCIATION (hereinafter called "the Association") is established and shall operate in accordance with the following provisions:

ARTICLE I—PURPOSES

The purposes of the Association are to promote economic development, increase productivity and thus raise standards of living in the less-developed areas of the world included within the Association's membership, in particular by providing finance to meet their important developmental requirements on terms which are more flexible and bear less heavily on the balance of payments than those of conventional loans, thereby furthering the developmental objectives of the International Bank for Reconstruction and Development (hereinafter called "the Bank") and supplementing its activities.

The Association shall be guided in all its decisions by the provisions of this Article.

[1] 11 UST 2284; TIAS 4607; 439 UNTS 249. For a list of states that are parties to this Agreement, see Department of State publication, *Treaties in Force*.

ARTICLE II—MEMBERSHIP; INITIAL SUBSCRIPTIONS

SECTION 1. MEMBERSHIP

(a) The original members of the Association shall be those members of the Bank listed in Schedule A hereto which, on or before the date specified in Article XI, Section 2(c), accept membership in the Association.

(b) Membership shall be open to other members of the Bank at such times and in accordance with such terms as the Association may determine.

SECTION 2. INITIAL SUBSCRIPTIONS

(a) Upon accepting membership, each member shall subscribe funds in the amount assigned to it. Such subscriptions are herein referred to as initial subscriptions.

(b) The initial subscription assigned to each original member shall be in the amount set forth opposite its name in Schedule A, expressed in terms of United States dollars of the weight and fineness in effect on January 1, 1960.

(c) Ten percent of the initial subscription of each original member shall be payable in gold or freely convertible currency as follows: fifty percent within thirty days after the date on which the Association shall begin operations pursuant to Article XI, Section 4, or on the date on which the original member becomes a member, whichever shall be later; twelve and one-half percent one year after the beginning of operations of the Association; and twelve and one-half percent each year thereafter at annual intervals until the ten percent portion of the initial subscription shall have been paid in full.

(d) The remaining ninety percent of the initial subscription of each original member shall be payable in gold or freely convertible currency in the case of members listed in Part I of Schedule A, and in the currency of the subscribing member in the case of members listed in Part II of Schedule A. This ninety percent portion of initial subscriptions of original members shall be payable in five equal annual installments as follows: the first such installment within thirty days after the date on which the Association shall begin operations pursuant to Article XI, Section 4, or on the date on which the original member becomes a member, whichever shall be later; the second installment one year after the beginning of operations of the Association, and succeeding installments each year thereafter at annual intervals until the ninety percent portion of the initial subscription shall have been paid in full.

(e) The Association shall accept from any member, in place of any part of the member's currency paid in or payable by the member under the preceding subsection (d) or under Section 2 of Article IV and not needed by the Association in its operations, notes or similar obligations issued by the government of the member or the depository designated by such member, which shall be non-negotiable, non-interest-bearing and payable at their par value on demand to the account of the Association in the designated depository.

(f) For the purposes of this Agreement the Association shall regard as "freely convertible currency":

(i) currency of a member which the Association determines, after consultation with the International Monetary Fund, is adequately convertible into the currencies of other members for the purposes of the Association's operations; or

(ii) currency of a member which such member agrees, on terms satisfactory to the Association, to exchange for the currencies of other members for the purposes of the Association's operations.

(g) Except as the Association may otherwise agree, each member listed in Part I of Schedule A shall maintain, in respect of its currency paid in by it as freely convertible currency pursuant to subsection (d) of this Section, the same convertibility as existed at the time of payment.

(h) The conditions on which the initial subscriptions of members other than original members may be made, and the amounts and the terms of payment thereof, shall be determined by the Association pursuant to Section 1(b) of this Article.

SECTION 3. LIMITATION ON LIABILITY

No member shall be liable, by reason of its membership, for obligations of the Association.

ARTICLE III—ADDITIONS TO RESOURCES

SECTION 1. ADDITIONAL SUBSCRIPTIONS

(a) The Association shall at such time as it deems appropriate in the light of the schedule for completion of payments on initial subscriptions of original members, and at intervals of approximately five years thereafter, review the adequacy of its resources and, if it deems desirable, shall authorize a general increase in subscriptions.[2] Notwithstanding the foregoing, general or individual increases in subscriptions may be authorized at any time, provided that an individual increase shall be considered only at the request of the member involved. Subscriptions pursuant to this Section are herein referred to as additional subscriptions.

(b) Subject to the provisions of paragraph (c) below, when additional subscriptions are authorized, the amounts authorized for subscription and the terms and conditions relating thereto shall be as determined by the Association.

(c) When any additional subscription is authorized, each member shall be given an opportunity to subscribe, under such conditions as shall be reasonably determined by the Association, an amount which will enable it to maintain its relative voting power, but no member shall be obligated to subscribe.

(d) All decisions under this Section shall be made by a two-thirds majority of the total voting power.

[2] The resources of the Association have been replenished fourteen times. The fourteenth replenishment (IDA XIV) negotiations, totaling $18 billion, on February 22, 2005. The U.S. share of IDA XIV is 13 percent.

SECTION 2. SUPPLEMENTARY RESOURCES PROVIDED BY A MEMBER IN THE CURRENCY OF ANOTHER MEMBER

(a) The Association may enter into arrangements, on such terms and conditions consistent with the provisions of this Agreement as may be agreed upon, to receive from any member, in addition to the amounts payable by such member on account of its initial or any additional subscription, supplementary resources in the currency of another member, provided that the Association shall not enter into any such arrangement unless the Association is satisfied that the member whose currency is involved agrees to the use of such currency as supplementary resources and to the terms and conditions governing such use. The arrangements under which any such resources are received may include provisions regarding the disposition of earnings on the resources and regarding the disposition of the resources in the event that the member providing them ceases to be a member or the Association permanently suspends its operations.

(b) The Association shall deliver to the contributing member a Special Development Certificate setting forth the amount and currency of the resources so contributed and the terms and conditions of the arrangement relating to such resources. A Special Development Certificate shall not carry any voting rights and shall be transferable only to the Association.

(c) Nothing in this Section shall preclude the Association from accepting resources from a member in its own currency on such terms as may be agreed upon.

ARTICLE IV—CURRENCIES

SECTION 1. USE OF CURRENCIES

(a) Currency of any member listed in Part II of Schedule A, whether or not freely convertible, received by the Association pursuant to Article II, Section 2(d), in payment of the ninety percent portion payable thereunder in the currency of such member, and currency of such member derived therefrom as principal, interest or other charges, may be used by the Association for administrative expenses incurred by the Association in the territories of such member and, insofar as consistent with sound monetary policies in payment for goods and services produced in the territories of such member and required for projects financed by the Association and located in such territories; and in addition when and to the extent justified by the economic and financial situation of the member concerned as determined by agreement between the member and the Association, such currency shall be freely convertible or otherwise usable for projects financed by the Association and located outside the territories of the member.

(b) The usability of currencies received by the Association in payment of subscriptions other than initial subscriptions of original members, and currencies derived therefrom as principal, interest or other charges, shall be governed by the terms and conditions on which such subscriptions are authorized.

(c) The usability of currencies received by the Association as supplementary resources other than subscriptions, and currencies derived therefrom, as principal, interest or other charges, shall be governed by the terms of the arrangements pursuant to which such currencies are received.

(d) All other currencies received by the Association may be freely used and exchanged by the Association and shall not be subject to any restriction by the member whose currency is used or exchanged; provided that the foregoing shall not preclude the Association from entering into any arrangements with the member in whose territories any project financed by the Association is located restricting the use by the Association of such member's currency received as principal, interest or other charges in connection with such financing.

(e) The Association shall take appropriate steps to ensure that, over reasonable intervals of time, the portions of the subscriptions paid under Article II, Section 2(d) by members listed in Part I of Schedule A shall be used by the Association on an approximately *pro rata* basis, provided, however, that such portions of such subscriptions as are paid in gold or in a currency other than that of the subscribing member may be used more rapidly.

SECTION 2. MAINTENANCE OF VALUE OF CURRENCY HOLDINGS

(a) Whenever the par value of a member's currency is reduced or the foreign exchange value of a member's currency has, in the opinion of the Association, depreciated to a significant extent within that member's territories, the member shall pay to the Association within a reasonable time an additional amount of its own currency sufficient to maintain the value, as of the time of subscription, of the amount of the currency of such member paid in to the Association by the member under Article II, Section 2(d), and currency furnished under the provisions of the present paragraph, whether or not such currency is held in the form of notes accepted pursuant to Article II, Section 2(e), provided, however, that the foregoing shall apply only so long as and to the extent that such currency shall not have been initially disbursed or exchanged for the currency of another member.

(b) Whenever the par value of a member's currency is increased, or the foreign exchange value of a member's currency has, in the opinion of the Association, appreciated to a significant extent within that member's territories, the Association shall return to such member within a reasonable time an amount of that member's currency equal to the increase in the value of the amount of such currency to which the provisions of paragraph (a) of this Section are applicable.

(c) The provisions of the preceding paragraph may be waived by the Association when a uniform proportionate change in the par value of the currencies of all its members is made by the International Monetary Fund.

(d) Amounts furnished under the provisions of paragraph (a) of this Section to maintain the value of any currency shall be convertible and usable to the same extent as such currency.

Article V—Operations

SECTION 1. USE OF RESOURCES AND CONDITIONS OF FINANCING

(a) The Association shall provide financing to further development in the less-developed areas of the world included within the Association's membership.

(b) Financing provided by the Association shall be for purposes which in the opinion of the Association are of high developmental priority in the light of the needs of the area or area concerned and, except in special circumstances, shall be for specific projects.

(c) The Association shall not provide financing if in its opinion such financing is available from private sources on terms which are reasonable for the recipient or could be provided by a loan of the type made by the Bank.

(d) The Association shall not provide financing except upon the recommendation of a competent committee, made after a careful study of the merits of the proposal. Each such committee shall be appointed by the Association and shall include a nominee of the Governor or Governors representing the member or members in whose territories the project under consideration is located and one or more members of the technical staff of the Association. The requirement that the committee include the nominee of a Governor or Governors shall not apply in the case of financing provided to a public international or regional organization.

(e) The Association shall not provide financing for any project if the member in whose territories the project is located objects to such financing, except that it shall not be necessary for the Association to assure itself that individual members do not object in the case of financing provided to a public international or regional organization.

(f) The Association shall impose no conditions that the proceeds of its financing shall be spent in the territories of any particular member or members. The foregoing shall not preclude the Association from complying with any restrictions on the use of funds imposed in accordance with the provisions of these Articles, including restrictions attached to supplementary resources pursuant to agreement between the Association and the contributor.

(g) The Association shall make arrangements to ensure that the proceeds of any financing are used only for the purposes for which the financing was provided, with due attention to considerations of economy, efficiency and competitive international trade and without regard to political or other noneconomic influences or considerations.

(h) Funds to be provided under any financing operation shall be made available to the recipient only to meet expenses in connection with the project as they are actually incurred.

SECTION 2. FORM AND TERMS OF FINANCING

(a) Financing by the Association shall take the form of loans. The Association may, however, provide other financing, either

(i) out of funds subscribed pursuant to Article III, Section 1, and funds derived therefrom as principal, interest or other charges, if the authorization for such subscriptions expressly provides for such financing;

or

(ii) in special circumstances, out of supplementary resources furnished to the Association, and funds derived therefrom as principal, interest or other charges, if the arrangements under which such resources are furnished expressly authorize such financing.

(b) Subject to the foregoing paragraph, the Association may provide financing in such forms and on such terms as it may deem appropriate, having regard to the economic position and prospects of the area or areas concerned and to the nature and requirements of the project.

(c) The Association may provide financing to a member, the government of a territory included within the Association's membership, a political subdivision of any of the foregoing, a public or private entity in the territories of a member or members, or to a public international or regional organization.

(d) In the case of a loan to an entity other than a member, the Association may, in its discretion, require a suitable governmental or other guarantee or guarantees.

(e) The Association, in special cases, may make foreign exchange available for local expenditures.

SECTION 3. MODIFICATIONS OF TERMS OF FINANCING

The Association may, when and to the extent it deems appropriate in the light of all relevant circumstances, including the financial and economic situation and prospects of the member concerned, and on such conditions as it may determine, agree to a relaxation or other modification of the terms on which any of its financing shall have been provided.

SECTION 4. COOPERATION WITH OTHER INTERNATIONAL ORGANIZATIONS AND MEMBERS PROVIDING DEVELOPMENT ASSISTANCE

The Association shall cooperate with those public international organizations and members which provide financial and technical assistance to the less-developed areas of the world.

SECTION 5. MISCELLANEOUS OPERATIONS

In addition to the operations specified elsewhere in this Agreement, the Association may:

(i) borrow funds with the approval of the member in whose currency the loan is denominated;

(ii) guarantee securities in which it has invested in order to facilitate their sale;

(iii) buy and sell securities it has issued or guaranteed or in which it has invested;

(iv) in special cases, guarantee loans from other sources for purposes not inconsistent with the provisions of these Articles;

(v) provide technical assistance and advisory services at the request of a member; and

(vi) exercise such other powers incidental to its operations as shall be necessary or desirable in furtherance of its purposes.

SECTION 6. POLITICAL ACTIVITY PROHIBITED

The Association and its officers shall not interfere in the political affairs of any member; nor shall they be influenced in their decisions by the political character of the member or members concerned. Only economic considerations shall be relevant to their decisions, and these considerations shall be weighed impartially in order to achieve the purposes stated in this Agreement.

ARTICLE VI—ORGANIZATION AND MANAGEMENT

SECTION 1. STRUCTURE OF THE ASSOCIATION

The Association shall have a Board of Governors, Executive Directors, a President and such other officers and staff to perform such duties as the Association may determine.

SECTION 2. BOARD OF GOVERNORS

(a) All the powers of the Association shall be vested in the Board of Governors.

(b) Each Governor and Alternate Governor of the Bank appointed by a member of the Bank which is also a member of the Association shall *ex officio* be a Governor and Alternate Governor, respectively, of the Association. No Alternate Governor may vote except in the absence of his principal. The Chairman of the Board of Governors of the Bank shall *ex officio* be Chairman of the Board of Governors of the Association except that if the Chairman of the Board of Governors of the Bank shall represent a state which is not a member of the Association, then the Board of Governors shall select one of the Governors as Chairman of the Board of Governors. Any Governor or Alternate Governor shall cease to hold office if the member by which he was appointed shall cease to be a member of the Association.

(c) The Board of Governors may delegate to the Executive Directors authority to exercise any of its powers, except the power to:

(i) admit new members and determine the conditions of their admission;

(ii) authorize additional subscriptions and determine the terms and conditions relating thereto;

(iii) suspend a member;

(iv) decide appeals from interpretations of this Agreement given by the Executive Directors;

(v) make arrangements pursuant to Section 7 of this Article to cooperate with other international organizations (other than informal arrangements of a temporary and administrative character);

(vi) decide to suspend permanently the operations of the Association and to distribute its assets;

(vii) determine the distribution of the Association's net income pursuant to Section 12 of this Article; and

(viii) approve proposed amendments to this Agreement.

(d) The Board of Governors shall hold an annual meeting and such other meetings as may be provided for by the Board of Governors or called by the Executive Directors.

(e) The annual meeting of the Board of Governors shall be held in conjunction with the annual meeting of the Board of Governors of the Bank.

(f) A quorum for any meeting of the Board of Governors shall be a majority of the Governors, exercising not less than two-thirds of the total voting power.

(g) The Association may by regulation establish a procedure whereby the Executive Directors may obtain a vote of the Governors on a specific question without calling a meeting of the Board of Governors.

(h) The Board of Governors, and the Executive Directors to the extent authorized, may adopt such rules and regulations as may be necessary or appropriate to conduct the business of the Association.

(i) Governors and Alternate Governors shall serve as such without compensation from the Association.

SECTION 3. VOTING

(a) Each original member shall, in respect of its initial subscription, have 500 votes plus one additional vote for each $5,000 of its initial subscription. Subscriptions other than initial subscriptions of original members shall carry such voting rights as the Board of Governors shall determine pursuant to the provisions of Article II, Section 1(b) or Article III, Section 1 (b) and (c), as the case may be. Additions to resources other than subscriptions under Article II, Section 1(b) and additional subscriptions under Article III, Section 1, shall not carry voting rights.

(b) Except as otherwise specifically provided, all matters before the Association shall be decided by a majority of the votes cast.

SECTION 4. EXECUTIVE DIRECTORS

(a) The Executive Directors shall be responsible for the conduct of the general operations of the Association, and for this purpose shall exercise all the powers given to them by this Agreement or delegated to them by the Board of Governors.

(b) The Executive Directors of the Association shall be composed *ex officio* of each Executive Director of the Bank who shall have been (i) appointed by a member of the Bank which is also a member of the Association, or (ii) elected in an election in which the votes of at least one member of the Bank which is also a member of the Association shall have counted toward his election. The Alternate to each such Executive Director of the Bank shall *ex officio* be an Alternate Director of the Association. Any Director shall cease to hold office if the member by which he was appointed, or if all the members whose votes counted toward his election, shall cease to be members of the Association.

(c) Each Director who is an appointed Executive Director of the Bank shall be entitled to cast the number of votes which the member by which he was appointed is entitled to cast in the Association. Each Director who is an elected Executive Director of the Bank shall be entitled to cast the number of votes which the member or members of the Association whose votes counted toward his election in the Bank are entitled to cast in the Association. All the votes which a Director is entitled to cast shall be cast as a unit.

(d) An Alternate Director shall have full power to act in the absence of the Director who shall have appointed him. When a Director is present, his Alternate may participate in meetings but shall not vote.

(e) A quorum for any meeting of the Executive Directors shall be a majority of the Directors exercising not less than one-half of the total voting power.

(f) The Executive Directors shall meet as often as the business of the Association may require.

(g) The Board of Governors shall adopt regulations under which a member of the Association not entitled to appoint an Executive Director of the Bank may send a representative to attend any meeting of the Executive Directors of the Association when a request made by, or a matter particularly affecting, that member is under consideration.

SECTION 5. PRESIDENT AND STAFF

(a) The President of the Bank shall be *ex officio* President of the Association. The President shall be Chairman of the Executive Directors of the Association but shall have no vote except a deciding vote in case of an equal division. He may participate in meetings of the Board of Governors but shall not vote at such meetings.

(b) The President shall be chief of the operating staff of the Association. Under the direction of the Executive Directors he shall conduct the ordinary business of the Association and under their general control shall be responsible for the organization, appointment and dismissal of the officers and staff. To the extent practicable, officers and staff of the Bank shall be appointed to serve concurrently as officers and staff of the Association.

(c) The President, officers and staff of the Association, in the discharge of their offices, owe their duty entirely to the Association and to no other authority. Each member of the Association shall respect the international character of this duty and shall refrain from all attempts to influence any of them in the discharge of their duties.

(d) In appointing officers and staff the President shall, subject to the paramount importance of securing the highest standards of efficiency and of technical competence, pay due regard to the importance of recruiting personnel on as wide a geographical basis as possible.

SECTION 6. RELATIONSHIP TO THE BANK

(a) The Association shall be an entity separate and distinct from the Bank and the funds of the Association shall be kept separate and apart from those of the Bank. The Association shall not borrow from or lend to the Bank, except that this shall not preclude the Association from investing funds not needed in its financing operations in obligations of the Bank.

(b) The Association may make arrangements with the Bank regarding facilities, personnel, and services and arrangements for reimbursement of administrative expenses paid in the first instance by either organization on behalf of the other.

(c) Nothing in this Agreement shall make the Association liable for the acts or obligations of the Bank, or the Bank liable for the acts or obligations of the Association.

SECTION 7. RELATIONS WITH OTHER INTERNATIONAL ORGANIZATIONS

The Association shall enter into formal arrangements with the United Nations and may enter into such arrangements with other public international organizations having specialized responsibilities in related fields.

SECTION 8. LOCATION OF OFFICES

The principal office of the Association shall be the principal office of the Bank. The Association may establish other offices in the territories of any member.

SECTION 9. DEPOSITORIES

Each member shall designate its central bank as a depository in which the Association may keep holdings of such member's currency or other assets of the Association, or, if it has no central bank, it shall designate for such purpose such other institution as may be acceptable to the Association. In the absence of any different designation, the depository designated for the Bank shall be the depository for the Association.

SECTION 10. CHANNEL OF COMMUNICATION

Each member shall designate an appropriate authority with which the Association may communicate in connection with any matter arising under this Agreement. In the absence of any different designation, the channel of communication designated for the Bank shall be the channel for the Association.

SECTION 11. PUBLICATION OF REPORTS AND PROVISION OF INFORMATION

(a) The Association shall publish an annual report containing an audited statement of its accounts and shall circulate to members at appropriate intervals a summary statement of its financial position and of the results of its operation.

(b) The Association may publish such other reports as it deems desirable to carry out its purposes.

(c) Copies of all reports, statements, and publications made under this Section shall be distributed to members.

SECTION 12. DISPOSITION OF NET INCOME

The Board of Governors shall determine from time to time the disposition of the Association's net income, having due regard to provisions for reserves and contingencies.

ARTICLE VII—WITHDRAWAL; SUSPENSION OF MEMBERSHIP; SUSPENSION OF OPERATIONS

SECTION 1. WITHDRAWAL BY MEMBERS

Any member may withdraw from membership in the Association at any time by transmitting a notice in writing to the Association at its principal office. Withdrawal shall become effective upon the date such notice is received.

SECTION 2. SUSPENSION OF MEMBERSHIP

(a) If a member fails to fulfill any of its obligations to the Association, the Association may suspend its membership by decision of a majority of the Governors, exercising a majority of the total voting power. The member so suspended shall automatically cease to be a member one year from the date of its suspension unless a decision is taken by the same majority to restore the member to good standing.

(b) While under suspension, a member shall not be entitled to exercise any rights under this Agreement except the right of withdrawal, but shall remain subject to all obligations.

SECTION 3. SUSPENSION OR CESSATION OF MEMBERSHIP IN THE BANK

Any member which is suspended from membership in, or ceases to be a member of, the Bank shall automatically be suspended from membership in, or cease to be a member of, the Association, as the case may be.

SECTION 4. RIGHTS AND DUTIES OF GOVERNMENTS CEASING TO BE MEMBERS

(a) When a government ceases to be a member, it shall have no rights under this Agreement except as provided in this Section and in Article X(c), but it shall, except as in this Section otherwise provided, remain liable for all financial obligations undertaken by it to the Association, whether as a member, borrower, guarantor or otherwise.

(b) When a government ceases to be a member, the Association and the government shall proceed to a settlement of accounts. As part of such settlement of accounts, the Association and the government may agree on the amounts to be paid to the government on account of its subscription and on the time and currencies of payment. The term "subscription" when used in relation to any member government shall for the purposes of this Article be deemed to include both the initial subscription and any additional subscription of such member government.

(c) If no such agreement is reached within six months from the date when the government ceased to be a member, or such other time as may be agreed upon by the Association and the government, the following provision shall apply:

(i) The government shall be relieved of any further liability to the Association on account of its subscription, except that the government shall pay to the Association forthwith amounts due and unpaid on the date when the government ceased to be a member and which in the opinion of the Association are needed by it to meet its commitments as of that date under its financing operations.

(ii) The Association shall return to the government funds paid in by the government on account of its subscription or derived therefrom as principal repayments and held by the Association on the date when the government ceased to be a member, except to the extent that in the opinion of the Association such funds will be needed by it to meet its commitments as of that date under its financing operations.

(iii) The Association shall pay over to the government a *pro rata* share of all principal repayments received by the Association after the date on which the government ceases to be a member on loans contracted prior thereto, except those made out of supplementary resources provided to the Association under arrangements specifying special liquidation rights. Such share shall be such proportion of the total principal amount of such loans as the total amount paid by the government on account of its subscription and not returned to it pursuant to clause (ii) above shall bear to the total amount paid by all members on account of their subscriptions which shall have been used or in the opinion of the Association will be needed by it to meet its commitments under its financing operations as of the date on which the government ceases to be a member. Such payments by the Association shall be made in installments when and as such principal repayments are received by the Association, but not more frequently than annually. Such installments shall be paid in the currencies received by the Association except that the Association may in its discretion make payment in the currency of the government concerned.

(iv) Any amount due to the government on account of its subscription may be withheld so long as that government, or the government of any territory included within its membership, or any political subdivision or any agency of any of the foregoing remains liable, as borrower or guarantor, to the Association, and such amount may, at the option of the Association, be applied against any such liability as it matures.

(v) In no event shall the government receive under this paragraph (c) an amount exceeding, in the aggregate, the lesser of the two following: (a) the amount paid by the government on account of its subscription, or (b) such proportion of the net assets of the Association, as shown on the books of the Association as of the date on which the government ceased to be a member, as the amount of its subscription shall bear to the aggregate amount of the subscriptions of all members.

(vi) All calculations required hereunder shall be made on such basis as shall be reasonably determined by the Association.

(d) In no event shall any amount due to a government under this Section be paid until six months after the date upon which the government ceases to be a member. If within six months of the date upon which any government ceases to be a member the Association suspends operations under Section 5 of this Article, all rights of such government shall be determined by the provisions of such Section 5 and such government shall be considered a member of the Association for purposes of such Section 5, except that it shall have no voting rights.

SECTION 5. SUSPENSION OF OPERATIONS AND SETTLEMENT OF OBLIGATIONS

(a) The Association may permanently suspend its operations by vote of a majority of the Governors exercising a majority of the total voting power. After such suspension of operations the Association shall forthwith cease all activities, except those incident to the orderly realization, conservation and preservation of its assets and settlement of it obligations. Until final settlement of such obligations and distribution of such assets, the Association shall remain in existence and all mutual rights and obligations of the Association and its members under this Agreement shall continue unimpaired, except that no member shall be suspended or shall withdraw and that no distribution shall be made to members except as in this Section provide.

(b) No distribution shall be made to members on account of their subscriptions until all liabilities to creditors shall have been discharged or provided for and until the Board Governors, by a vote of a majority of the Governors exercising a majority of the total voting power, shall have decided to make such distribution.

(c) Subject to the foregoing, and to any special arrangements for the disposition of supplementary resources agreed upon in connection with the provision of such resources to the Association, the Association shall distribute its assets to members *pro rata* in proportion to amounts paid in by them on account of their subscriptions. Any distribution pursuant to the foregoing provision of this paragraph (c) shall be subject, in the case of any members, to prior settlement of all outstanding claims by the Association against such member. Such distribution shall be made at such times, in such currencies, and in cash or other assets as the Association shall deem fair and equitable. Distribution to the several members need not be uniform in respect of the type of assets distributed or of the currencies in which they are expressed.

(d) Any member receiving assets distributed by the Association pursuant to this Section or Section 4 shall enjoy the same rights with respect to such assets as the Association enjoyed prior to their distribution.

ARTICLE VIII—STATUS, IMMUNITIES AND PRIVILEGES

SECTION 1. PURPOSES OF ARTICLE

To enable the Association to fulfill the functions with which it is entrusted, the status, immunities and privileges provided in this Article shall be accorded to the Association in the territories of each member.

SECTION 2. STATUS OF THE ASSOCIATION

The Association shall possess full juridical personality and, in particular, the capacity:

(i) to contract;

(ii) to acquire and dispose of immovable and movable property;

(iii) to institute legal proceedings.

SECTION 3. POSITION OF THE ASSOCIATION WITH REGARD TO JUDICIAL PROCESS

Actions may be brought against the Association only in a court of competent jurisdiction in the territories of a member in which the Association has an office, has appointed an agent for the purpose of accepting service or notice of process, or has issued or guaranteed securities. No actions shall, however, be brought by members or persons acting for or deriving claims from members. The property and assets of the Association shall, wheresoever located and by whomsoever held, be immune from all forms of seizure, attachment or execution before the delivery of final judgment against the Association.

SECTION 4. IMMUNITY OF ASSETS FROM SEIZURE

Property and assets of the Association, wherever located and by whomsoever held, shall be immune from search, requisition, confiscation, expropriation or any other form of seizure by executive or legislative action.

SECTION 5. IMMUNITY OF ARCHIVES

The archives of the Association shall be inviolable.

SECTION 6. FREEDOM OF ASSETS FROM RESTRICTIONS

To the extent necessary to carry out the operations provided for in this Agreement and subject to the provisions of this Agreement, all property and assets of the Association shall be free from restrictions, regulations, controls and moratoria of any nature.

SECTION 7. PRIVILEGE FOR COMMUNICATIONS

The official communications of the Association shall be accorded by each member the same treatment that it accords to the official communications of other members.

SECTION 8. IMMUNITIES AND PRIVILEGES OF OFFICERS AND EMPLOYEES

All Governors, Executive Directors, Alternates, officers and employees of the Association—

(i) shall be immune from legal process with respect to acts performed by them in their official capacity except when the Association waives this immunity;

(ii) not being local nationals, shall be accorded the same immunities from immigration restrictions, alien registration requirements and national service obligations and the same facilities as regards exchange restrictions as are accorded by members to the representatives, officials, and employees of comparable rank of other members;

(iii) shall be granted the same treatment in respect of traveling facilities as is accorded by members to representatives, officials and employees of comparable rank of other members.

SECTION 9. IMMUNITIES FROM TAXATION

(a) The Association, its assets, property, income and its operations and transactions authorized by this Agreement, shall be immune from all taxation and from all customs duties. The Association shall also be immune from liability for the collection or payment of any tax or duty.

(b) No tax shall be levied on or in respect of salaries and emoluments paid by the Association to Executive Directors, Alternates, officials or employees of the Association who are not local citizens, local subjects, or other local nationals.

(c) No taxation of any kind shall be levied on any obligation or security issued by the Association (including any dividend or interest thereon) by whomsoever held

(i) which discriminates against such obligation or security solely because it is issued by the Association; or

(ii) if the sole jurisdictional basis for such taxation is the place or currency in which it is issued, made payable or paid, or the location of any office or place of business maintained by the Association.

(d) No taxation of any kind shall be levied on any obligation or security guaranteed by the Association (including any dividend or interest thereon) by whomsoever held

(i) which discriminates against such obligation or security solely because it is guaranteed by the Association; or

(ii) if the sole jurisdictional basis for such taxation is the location of any office or place of business maintained by the Association.

SECTION 10. APPLICATION OF ARTICLE

Each member shall take such action as is necessary in its own territories for the purpose of making effective in terms of its own law the principles set forth in this Article and shall inform the Association of the detailed action which it has taken.

ARTICLE IX—AMENDMENTS

(a) Any proposal to introduce modifications in this Agreement, whether emanating from a member, a Governor or the Executive Directors, shall be communicated to the Chairman of the Board of Governors who shall bring the proposal before the Board. If the proposed amendment is approved by the Board, the Association shall, by circular letter or telegram, ask all members whether they accept the proposed amendment. When three-fifths of the members, having four-fifths of the total voting power, have accepted the proposed amendments, the Association shall certify the fact by formal communication addressed to all members.

(b) Notwithstanding (a) above, acceptance by all members is required in the case of any amendment modifying

(i) the right to withdraw from the Association provided in Article VII, Section I;

(ii) the right secured by Article III, Section 1(c);

(iii) the limitation on liability provided in Article II, Section 3.

(c) Amendments shall enter into force for all members three months after the date of the formal communication unless a shorter period is specified in the circular letter or telegram.

Article X—Interpretation and Arbitration

(a) Any question of interpretation of the provisions of this Agreement arising between any member and the Association or between any members of the Association shall be submitted to the Executive Directors for their decision. If the question particularly affects any member of the Association not entitled to appoint an Executive Director of the Bank, it shall be entitled to representation in accordance with Article VI, Section 4(g).

(b) In any case where the Executive Directors have given a decision under (a) above, any member may require that the question be referred to the Board of Governors, whose decision shall be final. Pending the result of the reference to the Board of Governors, the Association may, so far as it deems necessary, act on the basis of the decision of the Executive Directors.

(c) Whenever a disagreement arises between the Association and a country which has ceased to be a member, or between the Association and any member during the permanent suspension of the Association, such disagreement shall be submitted to arbitration by a tribunal of three arbitrators, one appointed by the Association, another by the country involved and an umpire who, unless the parties otherwise agree, shall be appointed by the President of the International Court of Justice or such other authority as may have been prescribed by regulation adopted by the Association. The umpire shall have full power to settle all questions of procedure in any case where the parties are in disagreement with respect thereto.

Article XI—Final Provision

SECTION 1. ENTRY INTO FORCE

This Agreement shall enter into force when it has been signed on behalf of governments whose subscriptions comprise not less than sixty-five percent of the total subscriptions set forth in Schedule A and when the instruments referred to in Section 2(a) of this Article have been deposited on their behalf, but in no event shall this Agreement enter into force before September 15, 1960.

SECTION 2. SIGNATURE

(a) Each government on whose behalf this Agreement is signed shall deposit with the Bank an instrument setting forth that it has accepted this Agreement in accordance with its law and has taken all steps necessary to enable it to carry out all of its obligations under this Agreement.

(b) Each government shall become a member of the Association as from the date of the deposit on its behalf of the instrument referred to in paragraph (a) above except that no government shall become a member before this Agreement enters into force under Section 1 of this Article.

(c) This Agreement shall remain open for signature until the close of business on December 31, 1960, at the principal office of the Bank, on behalf of the governments of the states whose names are set forth in Schedule A, provided that, if this Agreement shall not have entered into force by that date, the Executive Directors of the Bank may extend the period during which this Agreement shall remain open for signature by not more than six months.

(d) After this Agreement shall have entered into force, it shall be open for signature on behalf of the government of any state whose membership shall have been approved pursuant to Article II, Section 1(b).

SECTION 3. TERRITORIAL APPLICATION

By its signature of this Agreement, each government accepts it both on its own behalf and in respect of all territories for whose international relations such government is responsible except those which are excluded by such government by written notice to the Association.

SECTION 4. INAUGURATION OF THE ASSOCIATION

(a) As soon as this Agreement enters into force under Section 1 of this Article the President shall call a meeting of the Executive Directors.

(b) The Association shall begin operations on the date when such meeting is held.

(c) Pending the first meeting of the Board of Governors, the Executive Directors may exercise all the powers of the Board of Governors except those reserved to the Board of Governors under this Agreement.

SECTION 5. REGISTRATION

The Bank is authorized to register this Agreement with the Secretariat of the United Nations in accordance with Article 102 of the Charter of the United Nations and the Regulations thereunder adopted by the General Assembly.

DONE at Washington, in a single copy which shall remain deposited in the archives of the International Bank for Reconstruction and Development, which has indicated by its signature below its agreement to the act as depository of this Agreement, to register this Agreement with the Secretariat of the United Nations and to notify all governments whose names are set forth in Schedule A of the date when this Agreement shall have entered into force under Article XI, Section 1 hereof.

Schedule A—Initial Subscriptions

[US $ Millions]*

Part I

Country	Amount	Country	Amount
Australia	20.18	Japan	33.59
Austria	5.04	Luxembourg	1.01
Belgium	22.70	Netherlands	22.74
Canada	37.83	Norway	6.72
Denmark	8.74	Sweden	10.99
Finland	3.83	Union of South Africa	10.99
France	52.96	United Kingdom	131.14
Germany	52.96	United States	320.29
Italy	18.16		
		Subtotal	763.07

Part II

Country	Amount	Country	Amount
Afghanistan	1.01	Israel	1.68
Argentina	18.33	Jordan	0.30
Bolivia	1.06	Korea	1.26
Brazil	18.83	Lebanon	0.45
Burma	2.02	Libya	1.01
Ceylon	3.03	Malaya	2.52
Chile	3.53	Mexico	8.74
China	30.26	Morocco	3.53
Colombia	3.53	Nicaragua	0.30
Costa Rica	0.20	Pakistan	10.09
Cuba	4.71	Panama	0.02
Dominican Republic	0.40	Paraguay	0.30
Ecuador	0.65	Peru	1.77
El Salvador	0.30	Philippines	5.04
Ethiopia	0.50	Saudi Arabia	3.70
Ghana	2.36	Spain	10.09
Greece	2.52	Sudan	1.01
Guatemala	0.40	Thailand	3.03
Haiti	0.76	Tunisia	1.51
Honduras	0.30	Turkey	5.80
Iceland	0.10	United Arab Republic	6.03
India	40.35	Uruguay	1.06
Indonesia	11.10	Venezuela	7.06
Iran	4.54	Viet-Nam	1.51
Iraq	0.76	Yugoslavia	4.04
Ireland	3.03		
		Subtotal	236.93
		Total	1,000.00

*In terms of United States dollars of the weight and fineness in effect on January 1, 1960.

4. Articles of Agreement Establishing the International Finance Corporation (Amended)

CONTENTS

4. Articles of Agreement Establishing the International Finance Corporation (Amended)

Open for signature at the International Bank for Reconstruction and Development, Washington; Signed on behalf of the United States, December 5, 1955; Acceptance of the United States deposited, December 5, 1955; Entered into force, July 20, 1956;[1] Amended, September 1, 1961[2] and August 25, 1965[2]

The governments on whose behalf this Agreement is signed agree as follows:

INTRODUCTORY ARTICLE

The INTERNATIONAL FINANCE CORPORATION (hereinafter called the Corporation) is established and shall operate in accordance with the following provisions:

ARTICLE I—PURPOSE

The purpose of the Corporation is to further economic development by encouraging the growth of productive private enterprise in member countries, particularly in the less developed areas, thus supplementing the activities of the International Bank for Reconstruction and Development (hereinafter called the Bank). In carrying out this purpose, the Corporation shall—

(i) in association with private investors, assist in financing the establishment, improvement and expansion of productive private enterprises which would contribute to the development of its member countries by making investments, without guarantee of repayment by the member government concerned, in cases where sufficient private capital is not available on reasonable terms;

(ii) seek to bring together investment opportunities, domestic and foreign private capital, and experienced management; and

(iii) seek to stimulate, and to help create conditions conducive to, the flow of private capital, domestic and foreign, into productive investment member countries.

The Corporation shall be guided in all its decisions by the provisions of this Article.

[1] 7 UST 2197; TIAS 3620; 264 UNTS 117. For a list of states that are parties to the Corporation, see Department of State publication, *Treaties in Force*.

[2] Amendments:
September 1, 1961 (12 UST 2945: TIAS 4894; 439 UNTS 318).
September 1, 1965 (24 UST 1760; TIAS 7683).

Article II—Membership and Capital

SECTION 1. MEMBERSHIP

(a) The original members of the Corporation shall be those members of the Bank listed in Schedule A hereto which shall, on or before the date specified in Article IX, Section 2(c), accept membership in the Corporation.

(b) Membership shall be open to other members of the Bank at such times and in accordance with such terms as may be prescribed by the Corporation.

SECTION 2. CAPITAL STOCK

(a) The authorized capital stock of the Corporation shall be $100,000,000, in terms of United States dollars.[3]

(b) The authorized capital stock shall be divided into 100,000 shares having a par value of one thousand United States dollars each. Any such shares not initially subscribed by original members shall be available for subsequent subscription in accordance with Section 3(d) of this Article.

(c) The amount of capital stock at any time authorized may be increased by the Board of Governors as follows:

(i) by a majority of the votes cast, in case such increase is necessary for the purpose of issuing shares of capital stock on initial subscription by members other than original members, provided that the aggregate of any increases authorized pursuant to this subparagraph shall not exceed 10,000 shares;

(ii) in any other case, by a three-fourths majority of the total voting power.

(d) In case of an increase authorized pursuant to paragraph (c)(ii) above, each member shall have a reasonable opportunity to subscribe, under such conditions as the Corporation shall decide, to a proportion of the increase of stock equivalent to the proportion which its stock theretofore subscribed bears to the total capital stock of the Corporation, but no member shall be obligated to subscribe to any part of the increased capital.

(e) Issuance of shares of stock, other than those subscribed either on initial subscription or pursuant to paragraph (d) above, shall require a three-fourths majority of the total voting power.

(f) Shares of stock of the Corporation shall be available for subscription only by, and shall be issued only to, members.

SECTION 3. SUBSCRIPTIONS

(a) Each original member shall subscribe to the number of shares of stock set forth opposite its name in Schedule A. The number of shares of stock to be subscribed by other members shall be determined by the Corporation.

---

[3] On September 3, 1963, the Board increased the authorized capital stock of the IFC to $110 million, divided into 110,000 shares of $1,000 each. In 1977 the Board increased the authorized capital of the IFC by $540 million bringing the total to $650 million, divided into 650,000 shares of $1,000 each. In 1985, the Board increased the authorized capital stock of the IFC by an additional $650 million (thereby doubling IFC capital stock). On May 4, 1992, the Board increased the authorized capital stock of the IFC by an additional $1 billion bringing the total to $2.3 billion.

(b) Shares of stock initially subscribed by original members shall be issued at par.

(c) The initial subscription of each original member shall be payable in full within 30 days after either the date on which the Corporation shall begin operations pursuant to Article IX, Section 3(b), or the date on which such original member becomes a member, whichever shall be later, or at such date thereafter as the Corporation shall determine. Payment shall be made in gold or United States dollars in response to a call by the Corporation which shall specify the place or places of payment.

(d) The price and other terms of subscription of shares of stock to be subscribed, otherwise than on initial subscription by original members, shall be determined by the Corporation.

SECTION 4. LIMITATION ON LIABILITY

No member shall be liable, by reason of its membership, for obligations of the Corporation.

SECTION 5. RESTRICTION ON TRANSFERS AND PLEDGES OF SHARES

Shares of stock shall not be pledged or encumbered in any manner whatever, and shall be transferable only to the Corporation.

ARTICLE III—OPERATIONS

SECTION 1. FINANCING OPERATIONS

The Corporation may make investments of its funds in productive private enterprises in the territories of its members. The existence of a government or other public interest in such an enterprise shall not necessarily preclude the Corporation from making an investment therein.

SECTION 2.[4] FORMS OF FINANCING

The Corporation may make investments of its funds in such form or forms as it may deem appropriate in the circumstances.[2]

SECTION 3. OPERATIONAL PRINCIPLES

The operations of the Corporation shall be conducted in accordance with the following principles:

---

[4] Amended language. The purpose of the amended language is to authorize the Corporation to make investments of its funds in capital stock and to limit the exercise of voting rights by the Corporation unless exercise of such rights is deemed necessary by the Corporation to protect its interests. See sec. 5 of the International Finance Corporation Act (Public Law 84–350), in *Legislation on Foreign Relations*, vol. III, sec. I.

The resolution to amend the Articles was adopted on September 1, 1961, and on September 21, 1961, the Governors resolved that the amendment should be effective forthwith.

Sec. 2 formerly read as follows:

"(a) The Corporation's financing shall not take the form of investments in capital stock. Subject to the foregoing, the Corporation may make investments of its funds in such form or forms as it may deem appropriate in the circumstances, including (but without limitation) investments according to the holder thereof the right to participate in earnings, and the right to subscribe to, or to convert the investment into, capital stock.

"(b) The Corporation shall not itself exercise any right to subscribe to, or convert any investment into, capital stock.".

Sec. 3(iv) formerly read: "the Corporation shall not assume responsibility for managing any enterprise in which it has invested.".

(i) the Corporation shall not undertake any financing for which in its opinion sufficient private capital could be obtained on reasonable terms;

(ii) the Corporation shall not finance an enterprise in the territories of any member if the member objects to such financing;

(iii) the Corporation shall impose no conditions that the proceeds of any financing by it shall be spent in the territories of any particular country;

(iv)[4] the Corporation shall not assume responsibility for managing any enterprise in which it has invested and shall not exercise voting rights for such purpose or for any other purpose which, in its opinion, properly is within the scope of managerial control;

(v) the Corporation shall undertake its financing on terms and conditions which it considers appropriate, taking into account the requirements of the enterprise, the risks being undertaken by the Corporation and the terms and conditions normally obtained by private investors for similar financing;

(vi) the Corporation shall seek to resolve its funds by selling its investments to private investors whenever it can appropriately do so on satisfactory terms;

(vii) the Corporation shall seek to maintain a reasonable diversification in its investments.

SECTION 4. PROTECTION OF INTERESTS

Nothing in this Agreement shall prevent the Corporation, in the event of actual or threatened default on any of its investments, actual or threatened insolvency of the enterprise in which such investment shall have been made, or other situations which, in the opinion of the Corporation, threaten to jeopardize such investment, from taking such action and exercising such rights as it may deem necessary for the protection of its interests.

SECTION 5. APPLICABILITY OF CERTAIN FOREIGN EXCHANGE RESTRICTIONS

Funds received by or payable to the Corporation in respect of an investment of the Corporation made in any member's territories pursuant to Section 1 of this Article shall not be free, solely by reason of any provision of this Agreement, from general applicable foreign exchange restrictions, regulations and controls in force in the territories of that member.

SECTION 6. MISCELLANEOUS OPERATIONS

In addition to the operations specified elsewhere in this Agreement, the Corporation shall have the power to—

(i)[5] borrow funds, and in that connection to furnish such collateral or other security therefor as it shall determine; provided, however, that before making a public sale of its obligations in the markets of a member, the Corporation shall have obtained the approval of that member and of the member in whose currency the obligations are to be denominated; if and

[5] An amendment adopted August 25, 1965 added clause (i).

so long as the Corporation shall be indebted on loans from or guaranteed by the Bank, the total amount outstanding of borrowings incurred or guarantees given by the Corporation shall not be increased if, at the time or as a result thereof, the aggregate amount of debt (including the guarantee of any debt) incurred by the Corporation from any source and then outstanding shall exceed an amount equal to four times its unimpaired subscribed capital and surplus;

(ii) invest funds not needed in its financing operations in such obligations as it may determine and invest funds held by it for pension or similar purposes in any marketable securities, all without being subject to the restrictions imposed by other sections of this Article;

(iii) guarantee securities in which it has invested in order to facilitate their sale;

(iv) buy and sell securities it has issued or guaranteed or in which it has invested;

(v) exercise such other powers incidental to its business as shall be necessary or desirable in furtherance of its purposes.

SECTION 7. VALUATION OF CURRENCIES

Whenever it shall become necessary under this Agreement to value any currency in terms of the value of another currency, such valuation shall be as reasonably determined by the Corporation after consultation with the International Monetary Fund.

SECTION 8. WARNING TO BE PLACED ON SECURITIES

Every security issued or guaranteed by the Corporation shall bear on its face a conspicuous statement to the effect that it is not an obligation of the Bank or, unless expressly stated on the security, of any government.

SECTION 9. POLITICAL ACTIVITY PROHIBITED

The Corporation and its officers shall not interfere in the political affairs of any member; nor shall they be influenced in their decisions by the political character of the member or members concerned. Only economic considerations shall be relevant to their decisions, and these considerations shall be weighed impartially in order to achieve the purposes stated in this Agreement.

ARTICLE IV—ORGANIZATION AND MANAGEMENT

SECTION 1. STRUCTURE OF THE CORPORATION

The Corporation shall have a Board of Governors, a Board of Directors, a Chairman of the Board of Directors, a President and such other officers and staff to perform such duties as the Corporation may determine.

SECTION 2. BOARD OF GOVERNORS

(a) All the powers of the Corporation shall be vested in the Board of Governors.

(b) Each governor and alternate governor of the Bank appointed by a member of the Bank which is also a member of the Corporation shall *ex officio* be a Governor or Alternate Governor, respectively, of the Corporation. No Alternate Governor may vote except in the absence of his principal. The Board of Governors shall select one of the Governors as Chairman of the Board of Governors. Any Governor or Alternate Governor shall cease to hold office if the member by which he was appointed shall cease to be a member of the Corporation.

(c) The Board of Governors may delegate to the Board of Directors authority to exercise any of its powers, except the power to—

(i) admit new members and determine the conditions of their admission;

(ii) increase or decrease the capital stock;

(iii) suspend a member;

(iv) decide appeals from interpretation of this Agreement given by the Board of Directors;

(v) make arrangements to cooperate with other international organizations (other than informal arrangements of a temporary and administrative character);

(vi) decide to suspend permanently the operations of the Corporation and to distribute its assets;

(vii) declare dividends;

(viii) amend this Agreement.

(d) The Board of Governors shall hold an annual meeting and such other meetings as may be provided for by the Board of Governors or called by the Board of Directors.

(e) The annual meeting of the Board of Governors shall be held in conjunction with the annual meeting of the Board of Governors of the Bank.

(f) A quorum for any meeting of the Board of Governors shall be a majority of the governors, exercising not less than two-thirds of the total voting power.

(g) The Corporation may by regulation establish a procedure whereby the Board of Directors may obtain a vote of the governors on a specific question without calling a meeting of the Board of Governors.

(h) The Board of Governors, and the Board of Directors to the extent authorized, may adopt such rules and regulations as may be necessary or appropriate to conduct the business of the Corporation.

(i) Governors and Alternate Governors shall serve as such without compensation from the Corporation.

SECTION 3. VOTING

(a) Each member shall have two hundred and fifty votes plus one additional vote for each share of stock held.

(b) Except as otherwise expressly provided, all matters before the Corporation shall be decided by a majority of the votes cast.

SECTION 4. BOARD OF DIRECTORS

(a) The Board of Directors shall be responsible for the conduct of the general operations of the Corporation, and for this purpose shall exercise all the powers given to it by this Agreement or delegated to it by the Board of Governors.

(b) The Board of Directors of the Corporation shall be composed *ex officio* of each Executive Director of the Bank who shall have been either (i) appointed by a member of the Bank which is also a member of the Corporation, or (ii) elected in an election in which the votes of at least one member of the Bank which is also a member of the Corporation shall have counted toward his election. The Alternate to each such Executive Director of the Bank shall *ex officio* be an Alternate Director of the Corporation. Any Director shall cease to hold office if the member by which he was appointed, or if all the members whose votes counted toward his election, shall cease to be members of the Corporation.

(c) Each Director who is an appointed Executive Director of the Bank shall be entitled to cast the number of votes which the member by which he was so appointed is entitled to cast in the Corporation. Each Director who is an elected Executive Director of the Bank shall be entitled to cast the number of votes which the member or members of the Corporation whose votes counted toward his election in the Bank are entitled to cast in the Corporation. All the votes which a director is entitled to cast shall be cast as a unit.

(d) An Alternate Director shall have full power to act in the absence of the Director who shall have appointed him. When a Director is present his Alternate may participate in meetings but shall not vote.

(e) A quorum for any meeting of the Board of Directors shall be a majority of the Directors exercising not less than one-half of the total voting power.

(f) The Board of Directors shall meet as often as the business of the Corporation may require.

(g) The Board of Governors shall adopt regulations under which a member of the Corporation not entitled to appoint an Executive Director of the Bank may send a representative to attend any meeting of the Board of Directors of the Corporation when a request made by, or a matter particularly affecting, that member is under consideration.

SECTION 5. CHAIRMAN, PRESIDENT AND STAFF

(a) The President of the Bank shall be *ex officio* Chairman of the Board of Directors of the Corporation, but shall have no vote except a deciding vote in case of an equal division. He may participate in meetings of the Board of Governors but shall not vote at such meetings.

(b) The President of the Corporation shall be appointed by the Board of Directors on the recommendation of the Chairman. The President shall be chief of the operating staff of the Corporation. Under the direction of the Board of Directors and the general supervision of the Chairman, he shall conduct the ordinary business of the Corporation and under their general control shall be responsible for the organization, appointment and dismissal of the officers and staff. The President may participate in meetings of the Board of Directors but shall not vote at such meetings. The President shall cease to hold office by decision of the Board of Directors in which the Chairman concurs.

(c) The President, officers and staff of the Corporation, in the discharge of their offices, owe their duty entirely to the Corporation and to no other authority. Each member of the Corporation shall respect the international character of this duty and shall refrain from all attempts to influence any of them in the discharge of their duties.

(d) Subject to the paramount importance of securing the highest standards of efficiency and of technical competence, due regard shall be paid, in appointing the officers and staff of the Corporation, to the importance of recruiting personnel on as wide a geographical basis as possible.

SECTION 6. RELATIONSHIP TO THE BANK

(a) The Corporation shall be an entity separate and distinct from the Bank and the funds of the Corporation shall be kept separate and apart from those of the Bank.[6] The provisions of this section shall not prevent the Corporation from making arrangements with the Bank regarding facilities, personnel and services and arrangements for reimbursement of administrative expenses paid in the first instance by either organization on behalf of the other.

(b) Nothing in this Agreement shall make the Corporation liable for the acts or obligations of the Bank, or the Bank liable for the acts or obligations of the Corporation.

SECTION 7. RELATIONS WITH OTHER INTERNATIONAL ORGANIZATIONS

The Corporation, acting through the Bank, shall enter into formal arrangements with the United Nations, and may enter into such arrangements with other public international organizations having specialized responsibilities in related fields.

SECTION 8. LOCATION OF OFFICES

The principal office of the Corporation shall be in the same locality as the principal office of the Bank. The Corporation may establish other offices in the territories of any member.

SECTION 9. DEPOSITORIES

Each member shall designate its central bank as a depository in which the Corporation may keep holdings of such member's currency or other assets of the Corporation or, if it has no central bank, it shall designate for such purpose such other institution as may be acceptable to the Corporation.

SECTION 10. CHANNEL OF COMMUNICATION

Each member shall designate an appropriate authority with which the Corporation may communicate in connection with any matter arising under this Agreement.

[6] Original text included the following: "The Corporation shall not lend to or borrow from the Bank.". Amendment adopted August 25, 1965, deleted this sentence.

SECTION 11. PUBLICATION OF REPORTS AND PROVISION OF INFORMATION

(a) The Corporation shall publish an annual report containing an audited statement of its accounts and shall circulate to members at appropriate intervals a summary statement of its financial position and a profit and loss statement showing the results of its operations.

(b) The Corporation may publish such other reports as it deems desirable to carry out its purposes.

(c) Copies of all reports, statements and publications made under this section shall be distributed to members.

SECTION 12. DIVIDENDS

(a) The Board of Governors may determine from time to time what part of the Corporation's net income and surplus, after making appropriate provision for reserves, shall be distributed as dividends.

(b) Dividends shall be distributed *pro rata* in proportion to capital stock held by members.

(c) Dividends shall be paid in such manner and in such currency or currencies as the Corporation shall determine.

ARTICLE V—WITHDRAWAL; SUSPENSION OF MEMBERSHIP; SUSPENSION OF OPERATIONS

SECTION 1. WITHDRAWAL BY MEMBERS

Any member may withdraw from membership in the Corporation at any time by transmitting a notice in writing to the Corporation at its principal office. Withdrawal shall become effective upon the date such notice is received.

SECTION 2. SUSPENSION OF MEMBERSHIP

(a) If a member fails to fulfill any of its obligations to the Corporation, the Corporation may suspend its membership by decision of a majority of the governors, exercising a majority of the total voting power. The member so suspended shall automatically cease to be a member one year from the date of its suspension unless a decision is taken by the same majority to restore the member to good standing.

(b) While under suspension, a member shall not be entitled to exercise any rights under this Agreement except the right of withdrawal, but shall remain subject to all obligations.

SECTION 3. SUSPENSION OR CESSATION OF MEMBERSHIP IN THE BANK

Any member which is suspended from membership in, or ceases to be a member of, the Bank shall automatically be suspended from membership in, or cease to be a member of, the Corporation, as the case may be.

SECTION 4. RIGHTS AND DUTIES OF GOVERNMENTS CEASING TO BE MEMBERS

(a) When a government ceases to be a member it shall remain liable for all amounts due from it to the Corporation. The Corporation shall arrange for the repurchase of such government's capital stock as a part of the settlement of accounts with it in accordance with the provisions of this section, but the government shall have no other rights under this Agreement except as provided in this section and in Article VIII(c).

(b) The Corporation and the government may agree on the repurchase of the capital stock of the government on such terms as may be appropriate under the circumstances, without regard to the provisions of paragraph (c) below. Such agreement may provide, among other things, for a final settlement of all obligations of the government to the Corporation.

(c) If such agreement shall not have been made within six months after the government ceases to be a member or such other time as the Corporation and such government may agree, the repurchase price of the government's capital stock shall be the value thereof shown by the books of the Corporation on the day when the government ceases to be a member. The repurchase of the capital stock shall be subject to the following conditions:

(i) payments for shares of stock may be made from time to time, upon their surrender by the government, in such installments, at such times and in such available currency or currencies as the Corporation reasonably determines, taking into account the financial position of the Corporation;

(ii) any amount due to the government for its capital stock shall be withheld so long as the government or any of its agencies remains liable to the Corporation for payment of any amount and such amount may, at the option of the Corporation, be set off, as it becomes payable, against the amount due from the Corporation;

(iii) if the Corporation sustains a net loss on the investments made pursuant to Article III, Section 1, and held by it on the date when the government ceases to be a member, and the amount of such loss exceeds the amount of the reserves provided therefor on such date, such government shall repay on demand the amount by which the repurchase price of its shares of stock would have been reduced if such loss had been taken into account when the repurchase price was determined.

(d) In no event shall any amount due to a government for its capital stock under this section be paid until six months after the date upon which the government ceases to be a member. If within six months of the date upon which any government ceases to be a member the Corporation suspends operations under Section 5 of this Article, all rights of such government shall be determined by the provisions of such Section 5 and such government shall be considered still a member of the Corporation for purposes of such Section 5, except that it shall have no voting rights.

SECTION 5. SUSPENSION OF OPERATIONS AND SETTLEMENT OF OBLIGATIONS

(a) The Corporation may permanently suspend its operations by vote of a majority of the Governors exercising a majority of the total voting power. After such suspension of operations the Corporation shall forthwith cease all activities, except those incident to the orderly realization, conservation and preservation of its assets and settlement of its obligations. Until final settlement of such obligations and distribution of such assets, the Corporation shall remain in existence and all mutual rights and obligations of the Corporation and its members under this Agreement shall continue unimpaired, except that no member shall be suspended or withdraw and that no distribution shall be made to members except as in this section provided.

(b) No distribution shall be made to members on account of their subscriptions to the capital stock of the Corporation until all liabilities to creditors shall have been discharged or provided for and until the Board of Governors, by vote of a majority of the Governors exercising a majority of the total voting power, shall have decided to make such distribution.

(c) Subject to the foregoing, the Corporation shall distribute the assets of the Corporation to members *pro rata* in proportion to capital stock held by them, subject, in the case of any member, to prior settlement of all outstanding claims by the Corporation against such member. Such distribution shall be made at such times, in such currencies, and in cash or other assets as the Corporation shall deem fair and equitable. The shares distributed to the several members need not necessarily be uniform in respect of the type of assets distributed or of the currencies in which they are expressed.

(d) Any member receiving assets distributed by the Corporation pursuant to this section shall enjoy the same rights with respect to such assets as the Corporation enjoyed prior to their distribution.

ARTICLE VI—STATUS, IMMUNITIES AND PRIVILEGES

SECTION 1. PURPOSES OF ARTICLE

To enable the Corporation to fulfill the functions with which it is entrusted, the status, immunities and privileges set forth in this Article shall be accorded to the Corporation in the territories of each member.

SECTION 2. STATUS OF THE CORPORATION

The Corporation shall possess full juridical personality and, in particular, the capacity—

(i) to contract;

(ii) to acquire and dispose of immovable and movable property;

(iii) to institute legal proceedings.

SECTION 3. POSITION OF THE CORPORATION WITH REGARD TO JUDICIAL PROCESS

Actions may be brought against the Corporation only in a court of competent jurisdiction in the territories of a member in which the Corporation has an office, has appointed an agent for the purpose of accepting service or notice of process, or has issued or guaranteed securities. No actions shall, however, be brought by members or persons acting for or deriving claims from members. The property and assets of the Corporation shall, wheresoever located and by whomsoever held, be immune from all forms of seizure, attachment or execution before the delivery of final judgment against the Corporation.

SECTION 4. IMMUNITY OF ASSETS FROM SEIZURE

Property and assets of the Corporation, wherever located and by whomsoever held, shall be immune from search, requisition, confiscation, expropriation or any other form of seizure by executive or legislative action.

SECTION 5. IMMUNITY OF ARCHIVES

The archives of the Corporation shall be inviolable.

SECTION 6. FREEDOM OF ASSETS FROM RESTRICTIONS

To the extent necessary to carry out the operations provided for in this Agreement and subject to the provisions of Article III, Section 5, and other provisions of this Agreement, all property and assets of the Corporation shall be free from restrictions, regulations, controls and moratoria of any nature.

SECTION 7. PRIVILEGE FOR COMMUNICATIONS

The official communications of the Corporation shall be accorded by each member the same treatment that it accords to the official communications of other members.

SECTION 8. IMMUNITIES AND PRIVILEGES OF OFFICERS AND EMPLOYEES

All governors, directors, alternates, officers and employees of the Corporation—

(i) shall be immune from legal process with respect to acts performed by them in their official capacity;

(ii) not being local nationals, shall be accorded the same immunities from immigration restrictions, alien registration requirements and national service obligations and the same facilities as regards exchange restrictions as are accorded by members to the representatives, officials, and employees of comparable rank of other members;

(iii) shall be granted the same treatment in respect of traveling facilities as is accorded by members to representatives, officials and employees of comparable rank of other members.

SECTION 9. IMMUNITIES FROM TAXATION

(a) The Corporation, its assets, property, income and its operations and transactions authorized by this Agreement, shall be immune from all taxation and from all customs duties. The Corporation shall also be immune from liability for the collection or payment of any tax or duty.

(b) No tax shall be levied on or in respect of salaries and emoluments paid by the Corporation to Directors, Alternates, officials or employees of the Corporation who are not local citizens, local subjects, or other local nationals.

(c) No taxation of any kind shall be levied on any obligation or security issued by the Corporation (including any dividend or interest thereon) by whomsoever held—

(i) which discriminates against such obligation or security solely because it is issued by the Corporation; or

(ii) if the sole jurisdictional basis for such taxation is the place or currency in which it is issued, made payable or paid, or the location of any office or place of business maintained by the Corporation.

(d) No taxation of any kind shall be levied on any obligation or security guaranteed by the Corporation (including any dividend or interest thereon) by whomsoever held—

(i) which discriminates against such obligation or security solely because it is guaranteed by the Corporation; or

(ii) if the sole jurisdictional basis for such taxation is the location of any office or place of business maintained by the Corporation.

SECTION 10. APPLICATION OF ARTICLE

Each member shall take such action as is necessary in its own territories for the purpose of making effective in terms of its own law the principles set forth in this Article and shall inform the Corporation of the detailed action which it has taken.

SECTION 11. WAIVER

The Corporation in its discretion may waive any of the privileges and immunities conferred under this Article to such extent and upon such conditions as it may determine.

ARTICLE VII—AMENDMENTS

(a) This Agreement may be amended by vote of three-fifths of the Governors exercising four-fifths of the total voting power.

(b) Notwithstanding paragraph (a) above, the affirmative vote of all Governors is required in the case of any amendment modifying—

(i) the right to withdraw from the Corporation provided in Article V, Section 1;

(ii) the preemptive right secured by Article II, Section 2(d);

(iii) the limitation on liability provided in Article II, Section 4.

(c) Any proposal to amend this Agreement, whether emanating from a member, a Governor or the Board of Directors, shall be communicated to the Chairman of the Board of Governors who shall bring the proposal before the Board of Governors. When an amendment has been duly adopted, the Corporation shall so certify by formal communication addressed to all members. Amendments shall enter into force for all members three months after the date of the formal communication unless the Board of Governors shall specify a shorter period.

Article VIII—Interpretation and Arbitration

(a) Any question of interpretation of the provisions of this Agreement arising between any member and the Corporation or between any members of the Corporation shall be submitted to the Board of Directors for its decision. If the question particularly affects any member of the Corporation not entitled to appoint an Executive Director of the Bank, it shall be entitled to representation in accordance with Article IV, Section 4(g).

(b) In any case where the Board of Directors has given a decision under (a) above, any member may require that the question be referred to the Board of Governors, whose decision be final. Pending the result of the reference to the Board of Governors, the Corporation may, so far as it deems necessary, act on the basis of the decision of the Board of Directors.

(c) Whenever a disagreement arises between the Corporation and a country which has ceased to be a member, or between the Corporation and any member during the permanent suspension of the Corporation, such disagreement shall be submitted to arbitration by a tribunal of three arbitrators, one appointed by the Corporation, another by the country involved and an umpire who, unless the parties otherwise agree, shall be appointed by the President of the International Court of Justice or such other authority as may have been prescribed by regulation adopted by the Corporation. The umpire shall have full power to settle all questions of procedure in any case where the parties are in disagreement with respect thereto.

Article IX—Final Provisions

SECTION 1. ENTRY INTO FORCE

This Agreement shall enter into force when it has been signed on behalf of not less than 30 governments whose subscriptions comprise not less than 75 percent of the total subscriptions set forth in Schedule A and when the instruments referred to in Section 2(a) of this Article have been deposited on their behalf, but in no event shall this Agreement enter into force before October 1, 1955.

SECTION 2. SIGNATURE

(a) Each government on whose behalf this Agreement is signed shall deposit with the Bank an instrument setting forth that it has accepted this Agreement without reservation in accordance with its law and has taken all steps necessary to enable it to carry out all of its obligations under this Agreement.

(b) Each government shall become a member of the Corporation as from the date of the deposit on its behalf of the instrument referred to in paragraph (a) above except that no government shall become a member before this Agreement enters into force under Section 1 of this Article.

(c) This Agreement shall remain open for signature until the close of business on December 31, 1956, at the principal office of the Bank on behalf of the governments of the countries whose names are set forth in Schedule A.

(d) After this Agreement shall have entered into force, it shall be open for signature on behalf of the government of any country whose membership has been approved pursuant to Article II, Section 1(b).

SECTION 3. INAUGURATION OF THE CORPORATION

(a) As soon as this Agreement enters into force under Section 1 of this Article the Chairman of the Board of Directors shall call a meeting of the Board of Directors.

(b) The Corporation shall begin operations on the date when such meeting is held.

(c) Pending the first meeting of the Board of Governors, the Board of Directors may exercise all the powers of the Board of Governors except those reserved to the Board of Governors under this Agreement.

DONE at Washington, in a single copy which shall remain deposited in the archives of the International Bank for Reconstruction and Development, which has indicated by its signature below its agreement to act as depository of this Agreement and to notify all governments whose names are set forth in Schedule A of the date when this Agreement shall enter into force under Article IX, Section 1 hereof.

* * * * * * *

5. Convention Establishing the Multilateral Investment Guarantee Agency

CONTENTS

5. Convention Establishing the Multilateral Investment Guarantee Agency[1]

Done at Seoul; Opened for signature at the International Bank for Reconstruction and Development, October 1985; Ratified by, and entered into force for, the United States, April 12, 1988

CONVENTION ESTABLISHING THE MULTILATERAL INVESTMENT GUARANTEE AGENCY

PREAMBLE

The Contracting States

CONSIDERING the need to strengthen international cooperation for economic development and to foster the contribution to such development of foreign investment in general and private foreign investment in particular;

RECOGNIZING that the flow of foreign investment to developing countries would be facilitated and further encouraged by alleviating concerns to non-commercial risks;

DESIRING to enhance the flow to developing countries of capital and technology for productive purposes under conditions consistent with their development needs, policies and objectives, on the basis of fair and stable standards for the treatment of foreign investment;

CONVINCED that the Multilateral Investment Guarantee Agency can play an important role in the encouragement of foreign investment complementing national and regional investment guarantee programs and private insurers of non-commercial risk; and

REALIZING that such Agency should, to the extent possible, meet its obligations without resort to its callable capital and that such an objective would be served by continued improvement in investment conditions,

HAVE AGREED AS FOLLOWS:

CHAPTER I—ESTABLISHMENT, STATUS, PURPOSES AND DEFINITIONS

ARTICLE 1. ESTABLISHMENT AND STATUS OF THE AGENCY

(a) There is hereby established the Multilateral Investment Agency (hereinafter called the Agency).

(b) The Agency shall possess full juridical personality and, in particular, the capacity to:

(i) contract;

(ii) acquire and dispose of movable and immovable property; and

(iii) institute legal proceedings.

[1] TIAS 12089. For states that are parties to this Convention, see Department of State publication, *Treaties in Force*.

ARTICLE 2. OBJECTIVE AND PURPOSES

The objective of the Agency shall be to encourage the flow of investments for productive purposes among member countries, and in particular to developing member countries, thus supplementing the activities of the INTERNATIONAL BANK FOR RECONSTRUCTION AND DEVELOPMENT (hereinafter referred to as the Bank), the International Finance Corporation and other international development finance institutions.

To serve its objective, the Agency shall:

(a) issue guarantees, including coinsurance and reinsurance, against non-commercial risks in respect of investments in a member country which flow from other member countries;

(b) carry out appropriate complementary activities to promote the flow of investments to and among developing member countries; and

(c) exercise such other incidental powers as shall be necessary or desirable in the furtherance of its objective.

The Agency shall be guided in all its decisions by the provisions of this Article.

ARTICLE 3. DEFINITIONS

For the purposes of this Convention:

(a) "Member" means a State with respect to which this Convention has entered into force in accordance with Article 61.

(b) "Host country" or "host government" means a member, its government, or any public authority of a member in whose territories, as defined in Article 66, an investment which has been guaranteed or reinsured, or is considered for guarantee or reinsurance, by the Agency is to be located.

(c) A "developing member country" means a member which is listed as such in Schedule A hereto as this Schedule may be amended from time to time by the Council of Governors referred to in Article 30 (hereinafter called the Council).

(d) A "special majority" means an affirmative vote of not less than two-thirds of the total voting power representing not less than fifty-five percent of the subscribed shares of the capital stock of the Agency.

(e) A "freely usable currency" means (i) any currency designated as such by the International Monetary Fund from time to time and (ii) any other freely available and effectively usable currency which the Board of Directors referred to in Article 30 (hereinafter called the Board) may designate for the purposes of this Convention after consultation with the International Monetary Fund and with the approval of the country of such currency.

CHAPTER II—MEMBERSHIP AND CAPITAL

ARTICLE 4. MEMBERSHIP [2]

(a) Membership in the Agency shall be open to all members of the Bank and to Switzerland.

[2] Title IV of H.R. 3570 (Multilateral Investment Guarantee Agency Act) as introduced in the House of Representatives on December 11, 1987, and as enacted into law by sec. 101(e) of the

Continued

(b) Original members shall be the States which are listed in Schedule A hereto and become parties to this Convention on or before October 30, 1987.

ARTICLE 5. CAPITAL

(a) The authorized capital stock of the Agency shall be one billion Special Drawing Rights (SDR 1,000,000,000). The capital stock shall be divided into 100,000 shares having an par value of SDR 10,000 each, which shall be available for subscription by members. All payment obligations of members with respect to capital stock shall be settled on the basis of the average value of the SDR in terms of United States dollars for the period January 1, 1981 to June 30, 1985, such value being 1.082 United States dollars per SDR.

(b) The capital stock shall increase on the admission of a new member to the extent that the then authorized shares are insufficient to provide the shares to be subscribed by such member pursuant to Article 6.

(c) The Council, by special majority, may at any time increase the capital stock of the Agency.

ARTICLE 6. SUBSCRIPTION OF SHARES

Each original member of the Agency shall subscribe at par to the number of shares of capital stock set forth opposite its name in Schedule A hereto. Each other member shall subscribe to such number of shares of capital stock on such terms and conditions as may be determined by the Council, but in no event at an issue price of less than par. No member shall subscribe to less than fifty shares. The Council may prescribe rules by which members may subscribe to additional shares of the authorized capital stock.

ARTICLE 7. DIVISION AND CALLS OF SUBSCRIBED CAPITAL

The initial subscription of each member shall be paid as follows:

(i) Within ninety days from the date on which this Convention enters into force with respect to such member, ten percent of the price of each share shall be paid in cash as stipulated in Section (a) of Article 8 and an additional ten percent in the form of non-negotiable, non-interest-bearing promissory notes or similar obligations to be encashed pursuant to a decision of the Board in order to meet the Agency's obligations.

(ii) The remainder shall be subject to call by the Agency when required to meet its obligations.

ARTICLE 8. PAYMENT OF SUBSCRIPTION OF SHARES

(a) Payments of subscriptions shall be made in freely usable currencies except that payments by developing member countries may be made in their own currencies up to twenty-five percent of the paid-in cash portion of their subscriptions payable under Article 7 (i).

Continuing Appropriations, 1988 (Public Law 100–202; 101 Stat. 1329–134), authorized U.S. membership in the Multilateral Investment Guarantee Agency. For text, see *Legislation on Foreign Relations Through 2005*, vol. III, sec. I.

(b) Calls on any portion of unpaid subscriptions shall be uniform on all shares.

(c) If the amount received by the Agency on a call shall be insufficient to meet the obligations which have necessitated the call, the Agency may make further successive calls on unpaid subscriptions until the aggregate amount received by it shall be sufficient to meet such obligations.

(d) Liability on shares shall be limited to the unpaid portion of the issue price.

ARTICLE 9. VALUATION OF CURRENCIES

Whenever it shall be necessary for the purposes of this Convention to determine the value of one currency in terms of another, such value shall be as reasonably determined by the Agency, after consultation with the International Monetary Fund.

ARTICLE 10. REFUNDS

(a) The Agency shall, as soon as practicable, return to members amounts paid on calls on subscribed capital if and to the extent that:

(i) the call shall have been made to pay a claim resulting from a guarantee or reinsurance contract and thereafter the Agency shall have recovered its payment, in whole or in part, in a freely usable currency; or

(ii) the call shall have been made because of a default in payment by a member and thereafter such member shall have made good such default in whole or in part; or

(iii) the Council, by special majority, determines that the financial position of the Agency permits all or part of such amounts to be returned out of the Agency's revenues.

(b) Any refund effected under this Article to a member shall be made in freely usable currency in the proportion of the payments made by that member to the total amount paid pursuant to calls made prior to such refund.

(c) The equivalent of amounts refunded under this Article to a member shall become part of the callable capital obligations of the member under Article 7 (ii).

CHAPTER III—OPERATIONS

ARTICLE 11. COVERED RISKS

(a) Subject to the provisions of Sections (b) and (c) below, the Agency may guarantee eligible investments against a loss resulting from one or more of the following types of risk:

(i) CURRENCY TRANSFER

any introduction attributable to the host government of restrictions on the transfer outside the host country of its currency into a freely usable currency or another currency acceptable to the holder of the guarantee, including a failure of the host government to act within a reasonable period of time on an application by such holder for such transfer;

(ii) EXPROPRIATION AND SIMILAR MEASURES

any legislative action or administrative action or omission attributable to the host government which has the effect of depriving the holder of a guarantee of his ownership or control of, or a substantial benefit from, his investment, with the exception of non-discriminatory measures of general application which governments normally take for the purpose of regulating economic activity in their territories;

(iii) BREACH OF CONTRACT

any repudiation or breach by the host government of a contract with the holder of a guarantee, when (a) the holder of a guarantee does not have recourse to a judicial or arbitral forum to determine the claim of repudiation or breach, or (b) a decision by such forum is not rendered within such reasonable period of time as shall be prescribed in the contracts of guarantee pursuant to the Agency's regulations, or (c) such a decision cannot be enforced; and

(iv) WAR AND CIVIL DISTURBANCE

any military action or civil disturbance in any territory of the host country to which this Convention shall be applicable as provided in Article 66.

(b) Upon the joint application of the investor and the host country, the Board, by special majority, may approve the extension of coverage under this Article to specific non-commercial risks other than those referred to in Section (a) above, but in no case to the risk of devaluation or depreciation of currency.

(c) Losses resulting from the following shall not be covered:

(i) any host government action or omission to which the holder of the guarantee has agreed or for which he has been responsible; and

(ii) any host government action or omission or any other event occurring before the conclusion of the contract of guarantee.

ARTICLE 12. ELIGIBLE INVESTMENTS

(a) Eligible investment shall include equity interests, including medium- or long-term loans made or guaranteed by holders of equity in the enterprise concerned, and such forms of direct investment as may be determined by the Board.

(b) The Board, by special majority, may extend eligibility to any other medium- or long-term form of investment, except that loans other than those mentioned in Section (a) above may be eligible only if they are related to a specific investment covered or to be covered by the Agency.

(c) Guarantees shall be restricted to investments the implementation of which begins subsequent to the registration of the application for the guarantee by the Agency. Such investments may include:

(i) any transfer of foreign exchange made to modernize, expand, or develop an existing investment; and

(ii) the use of earnings from existing investments which could otherwise be transferred outside the host country.

(d) In guaranteeing an investment, the Agency shall satisfy itself as to:

(i) the economic soundness of the investment and its contribution to the development of the host country;

(ii) compliance of the investment with the host country's laws and regulations;

(iii) consistency of the investment with the declared development objectives and priorities of the host country; and

(iv) the investment conditions in the host country, including the availability of fair and equitable treatment and legal protection for the investment.

ARTICLE 13. ELIGIBLE INVESTORS

(a) Any natural person and any juridical person may be eligible to receive the Agency's guarantee provided that:

(i) such natural person is a national of a member other than the host country;

(ii) such juridical person is incorporated and has its principal place of business in a member or the majority of its capital is owned by a member or members or nationals thereof, provided that such member is not the host country in any of the above cases; and

(iii) such juridical person, whether or not it is privately owned, operates on a commercial basis.

(b) In case the investor has more than one nationality, for the purposes of Section (a) above the nationality of a member shall prevail over the nationality of a non-member, and the nationality of the host country shall prevail over the nationality of any other member.

(c) Upon the joint application of the investor and the host country, the Board, by special majority, may extend eligibility to a natural person who is a national of the host country or a juridical person which is incorporated in the host country or the majority of whose capital is owned by its nationals, provided that the assets invested are transferred from outside the host country.

ARTICLE 14. ELIGIBLE HOST COUNTRIES

Investments shall be guaranteed under this Chapter only if they are to be made in the territory of a developing member country.

ARTICLE 15. HOST COUNTRY APPROVAL

The Agency shall not conclude any contract of guarantee before the host government has approved the issuance of the guarantee by the Agency against the risks designated for cover.

ARTICLE 16. TERMS AND CONDITIONS

The terms and conditions of each contract of guarantee shall be determined by the Agency subject to such rules and regulations as the Board shall issue, provided that the Agency shall not cover the total loss of the guaranteed investment. Contracts of guarantee shall be approved by the President under the direction of the Board.

ARTICLE 17. PAYMENT OF CLAIMS

The President under the direction of the Board shall decide on the payment of claims to a holder of guarantee in accordance with the contract of guarantee and such policies as the Board may adopt. Contracts of guarantee shall require holders of guarantees to seek, before a payment is made by the Agency, such administrative remedies as may be appropriate under the circumstances, provided that they are readily available to them under the laws of the host country. Such contracts may require the lapse of certain reasonable periods between the occurrence of events giving rise to claims and payments of claims.

ARTICLE 18. SUBROGATION

(a) Upon paying or agreeing to pay compensation to a holder of a guarantee, the Agency shall be subrogated to such rights or claims related to the guaranteed investment as the holder of a guarantee may have had against the host country and other obligors. The contract of guarantee shall provide the terms and conditions of such subrogation.

(b) The rights of the Agency pursuant to Section (a) above shall be recognized by all members.

(c) Amounts in the currency of the host country acquired by the Agency as subrogee pursuant to Section (a) above shall be accorded, with respect to use and conversion, treatment by the host country as favorable as the treatment to which such funds would be entitled in the hands of the holder of the guarantee. In any case, such amounts may be used by the Agency for the payment of its administrative expenditures and other costs. The Agency shall also seek to enter into arrangements with host countries on other uses of such currencies to the extent that they are not freely usable.

ARTICLE 19. RELATIONSHIP TO NATIONAL AND REGIONAL ENTITIES

The Agency shall cooperate with, and seek to complement the operations of, national entities of members and regional entities the majority of whose capital is owned by members, which carry out activities similar to those of the Agency, with a view to maximizing both the efficiency of their respective services and their contribution to increased flows of foreign investment. To this end, the Agency may enter into arrangements with such entities on the details of such cooperation, including in particular the modalities of reinsurance and coinsurance.

ARTICLE 20. REINSURANCE OF NATIONAL AND REGIONAL ENTITIES

(a) The Agency may issue reinsurance in respect of a specific investment against a loss resulting from one or more of the non-commercial risks underwritten by a member or agency thereof or by a regional investment guarantee agency the majority of whose capital is owned by members. The Board, by special majority, shall from time to time prescribe maximum amounts of contingent liability which may be assumed by the Agency with respect to reinsurance contracts. In respect of specific investment which have been completed more than twelve months prior to receipt of the application for reinsurance by the Agency, the maximum amount shall initially be set at ten percent of the aggregate contingent liability of the Agency under this Chapter. The conditions of eligibility specified in Articles 11 to 14 shall apply to reinsurance operations, except that the reinsured investments need not be implemented subsequent to the application for reinsurance.

(b) The mutual rights and obligations of the Agency and a reinsured member or agency shall be stated in contracts of reinsurance subject to such rules and regulations as the Board shall issue. The Board shall approve each contract for reinsurance covering an investment which has been made prior to receipt of the application for reinsurance by the Agency, with a view to minimizing risks, assuring that the Agency receives premiums commensurate with its risk, and assuring that the reinsured entity is appropriately committed toward promoting new investment in developing member countries.

(c) The Agency shall, to the extent possible, assure that it or the reinsured entity shall have the rights of subrogation and arbitration equivalent to those the Agency would have if it were the primary guarantor. The terms and conditions of reinsurance shall require that administrative remedies are sought in accordance with Article 17 before a payment is made by the Agency. Subrogation shall be effective with respect to the host country concerned only after its approval of the reinsurance by the Agency. The Agency shall include in the contracts of reinsurance provisions requiring the reinsured to pursue with due diligence the rights or claims related to the reinsured investment.

ARTICLE 21. COOPERATION WITH PRIVATE INSURERS AND WITH REINSURERS

(a) The Agency may enter into arrangements with private insurers in member countries to enhance its own operations and encourage such insurers to provide coverage of non-commercial risks in developing member countries on conditions similar to those applied by the Agency. Such arrangements may include the provision of reinsurance by the Agency under the conditions and procedures specified in Article 20.

(b) The Agency may reinsure with any appropriate reinsurance entity, in whole or in part, any guarantee or guarantees issued by it.

(c) The Agency will in particular seek to guarantee investments for which comparable coverage on reasonable terms is not available from private insurers and reinsurers.

ARTICLE 22. LIMITS OF GUARANTEE

(a) Unless determined otherwise by the Council by special majority, the aggregate amount of contingent liabilities which may be assumed by the Agency under this Chapter shall not exceed one hundred and fifty percent of the amount of the Agency's unimpaired subscribed capital and its reserves plus such portion of its reinsurance cover as the Board may determine. The Board shall from time to time review the risk profile of the Agency's portfolio in the light of its experience with claims, degree of risk diversification, reinsurance cover and other relevant factors with a view to ascertaining whether changes in the maximum aggregate amount of contingent liabilities should be recommended to the Council. The maximum amount determined by the Council shall not under any circumstance exceed five times the amount of the Agency's unimpaired subscribed capital, its reserves and such portion of its reinsurance cover as may be deemed appropriate.

(b) Without prejudice to the general limit of guarantee referred to in Section (a) above, the Board may prescribe:

(i) maximum aggregate amounts of contingent liability which may be assumed by the Agency under this Chapter for all guarantees issued to investors of each individual member. In determining such maximum amounts, the Board shall give due consideration to the share of the respective member in the capital of the Agency and the need to apply more liberal limitations in respect of investments originating in developing member countries; and

(ii) maximum aggregate amounts of contingent liability which may be assumed by the Agency with respect to such risk diversification factors as individual projects, individual host countries and types of investment or risk.

ARTICLE 23. INVESTMENT PROMOTION

(a) The Agency shall carry out research, undertake activities to promote investment flows and disseminate information on investment opportunities in developing member countries, with a view to improving the environment for foreign investment flows to such countries. The Agency may, upon the request of a member, provide technical advice and assistance to improve the investment conditions in the territories of that member. In performing these activities, the Agency shall:

(i) be guided by relevant investment agreements among member countries;

(ii) seek to remove impediments, in both developed and developing member countries; and

(iii) coordinate with other agencies concerned with the promotion of foreign investment, and in particular the International Finance Corporation.

(b) The Agency also shall:

(i) encourage the amicable settlement of disputes between investors and host countries;

(ii) endeavor to conclude agreements with developing member countries, and in particular with prospective host countries, which will assure that the Agency, with respect to investment guaranteed by it, has treatment at least as favorable as that agreed by the member concerned for the most favored investment guarantee agency or State in an agreement relating to investment, such agreements to be approved by special majority of the Board; and

(iii) promote and facilitate the conclusion of agreements, among its members, on the promotion and protection of investments.

(c) The Agency shall give particular attention in its promotional efforts to the importance of increasing the flow of investments among developing member countries.

ARTICLE 24. GUARANTEES OF SPONSORED INVESTMENTS

In addition to the guarantee operations undertaken by the Agency under this Chapter, the Agency may guarantee investments under the sponsorship arrangements provided for in Annex I to this Convention.

CHAPTER IV—FINANCIAL PROVISIONS

ARTICLE 25. FINANCIAL MANAGEMENT

The Agency shall carry out its activities in accordance with sound business and prudent financial management practices with a view to maintaining under all circumstances its ability to meet its financial obligations.

ARTICLE 26. PREMIUMS AND FEES

The Agency shall establish and periodically review the rates of premiums, fees and other charges, if any, applicable to each type of risk.

ARTICLE 27. ALLOCATION OF NET INCOME

(a) Without prejudice to the provisions of Section (a) (iii) of Article 10, the Agency shall allocate net income to reserves until such reserves reach five times the subscribed capital of the Agency.

(b) After the reserves of the Agency have reached the level prescribed in Section (a) above, the Council shall decide whether, and to what extent, the Agency's net income shall be allocated to reserves, be distributed to the Agency's members or be used otherwise. Any distribution of net income to the Agency's members shall be made in proportion to the share of each member in the capital of the Agency in accordance with a decision of the Council acting by special majority.

ARTICLE 28. BUDGET

The President shall prepare an annual budget of revenues and expenditures of the Agency for approval by the Board.

ARTICLE 29. ACCOUNTS

The Agency shall publish an Annual Report which shall include statements of its accounts and of the accounts of the Sponsorship Trust Fund referred to in Annex I to this Convention, as audited by independent auditors. The Agency shall circulate to members at appropriate intervals a summary statement of its financial position and a profit and loss statement showing the results of its operations.

CHAPTER V—ORGANIZATION AND MANAGEMENT

ARTICLE 30. STRUCTURE OF THE AGENCY

The Agency shall have a Council of Governors, a Board of Directors, a President and staff to perform such duties as the Agency may determine.

ARTICLE 31. THE COUNCIL

(a) All the powers of the Agency shall be vested in the Council, except such powers as are, by the terms of this Convention, specifically conferred upon another organ of the Agency. The Council may delegate to the Board the exercise of any of its powers, except the power to:

(i) admit new members and determine the conditions of their admission;

(ii) suspend a member;

(iii) decide on any increase or decrease in the capital;

(iv) increase the limit of the aggregate amount of contingent liabilities pursuant to Section (a) of Article 22;

(v) designate a member as a developing member country pursuant to Section (c) of Article 3;

(vi) classify a new member as belonging to Category One or Category Two for voting purposes pursuant to Section (a) of Article 39 or reclassify an existing member for the same purposes;

(vii) determine the compensation of Directors and their Alternates;

(viii) cease operations and liquidate the Agency;

(ix) distribute assets to members upon liquidation; and

(x) amend this Convention, its Annexes and Schedules.

(b) The Council shall be composed of one Governor and one Alternate appointed by each member in such manner as it may determine. No Alternate may vote except in the absence of his principal. The Council shall select one of the Governors as Chairman.

(c) The Council shall hold an annual meeting and such other meetings as may be determined by the Council or called by the Board. The Board shall call a meeting of the Council whenever requested by five members or by members having twenty-five percent of the total voting power.

ARTICLE 32. THE BOARD

(a) The Board shall be responsible for the general operations of the Agency and shall take, in the fulfillment of this responsibility, any action required or permitted under this Convention.

(b) The Board shall consist of not less than twelve Directors. The number of Directors may be adjusted by the Council to take into account charges in membership. Each Director may appoint an Alternate with full power to act for him in case of the Director's absence or inability to act. The President of the Bank shall be *ex officio* Chairman of the Board, but shall have not vote except a deciding vote in case of an equal division.

(c) The Council shall determine the term of office of the Directors. The first Board shall be constituted by the Council at its inaugural meeting.

(d) The Board shall meet at the call of its Chairman acting on his own initiative or upon request of three Directors.

(e) Until such time as the Council may decide that the Agency shall have a resident Board which functions in continuous session, the Directors and Alternates shall receive compensation only for the cost of attendance at the meetings of the Board and the discharge of other official functions on behalf of the Agency. Upon the establishment of a Board in continuous session, the Directors and Alternates shall receive such remuneration as may be determined by the Council.

ARTICLE 33. PRESIDENT AND STAFF

(a) The President shall, under the general control of the Board, conduct the ordinary business of the Agency. He shall be responsible for the organization, appointment and dismissal of the staff.

(b) The President shall be appointed by the Board on the nomination of its Chairman. The Council shall determine the salary and terms of the contract of service of the President.

(c) In the discharge of their offices, the President and the staff owe their duty entirely to the Agency and to no other authority. Each member of the Agency shall respect the international character of this duty and shall refrain from all attempts to influence the President or the staff in the discharge of their duties.

(d) In appointing the staff, the President shall, subject to the paramount importance of securing the highest standards of efficiency and of technical competence, pay due regard to the importance of recruiting personnel on as wide a geographical basis as possible.

(e) The President and staff shall maintain at all times the confidentiality of information obtained in carrying out the Agency's operations.

ARTICLE 34. POLITICAL ACTIVITY PROHIBITED

The Agency, its President and staff shall not interfere in the political affairs of any member. Without prejudice to the right of the Agency to take into account all the circumstances surrounding an investment, they shall not be influenced in their decisions by the political character of the member or members concerned. Considerations relevant to their decisions shall be weighed impartially in order to achieve the purposes stated in Article 2.

ARTICLE 35. RELATIONS WITH INTERNATIONAL ORGANIZATIONS

The Agency shall, within the terms of this Convention, cooperate with the United Nations and with other inter-governmental organizations having specialized responsibilities in related fields, including in particular the Bank and the International Finance Corporation.

ARTICLE 36. LOCATION OF PRINCIPAL OFFICE

(a) The principal office of the Agency shall be located in Washington, D.C., unless the Council, by special majority, decides to establish it in another location.

(b) The Agency may establish other offices as may be necessary for its work.

ARTICLE 37. DEPOSITORIES FOR ASSETS

Each member shall designate its central bank as a depository in which the Agency may keep holdings of such member's currency or other assets of the Agency or, if it has no central bank, it shall designate for such purpose such other institution as may be acceptable to the Agency.

ARTICLE 38. CHANNEL OF COMMUNICATION

(a) Each member shall designate an appropriate authority with which the Agency may communicate in connection with any matter arising under this Convention. The Agency may rely on statements of such authority as being statements of the member. The Agency, upon the request of a member, shall consult with that member with respect to matters dealt with in Articles 19 to 21 and related to entities or insurers of that member.

(b) Whenever the approval of any member is required before any act may be done by the Agency, approval shall be deemed to have been given unless the member presents an objection within such reasonable period as the Agency may fix in notifying the member of the proposed act.

CHAPTER VI—VOTING, ADJUSTMENTS OF SUBSCRIPTIONS AND REPRESENTATION

ARTICLE 39. VOTING AND ADJUSTMENTS OF SUBSCRIPTIONS

(a) In order to provide for voting arrangements that reflect the equal interest in the Agency of the two Categories of States listed in Schedule A of this Convention, as well as the importance of each member's financial participation, each member shall have 177 membership votes plus one subscription vote for each share of stock held by that member.

(b) If at any time within three years after the entry into force of this Convention the aggregate sum of membership and subscription votes of members which belong to either of the two Categories of States listed in Schedule A of this Convention is less than forty percent of the total voting power, members from such a Category shall have such number of supplementary votes as shall be necessary for the aggregate voting power of the Category to equal such a percentage of the total voting power. Such supplementary votes shall be distributed among the members of such Category in the proportion that the subscription votes of each bears to the aggregate of subscription votes for the Category. Such supplementary votes shall be subject to automatic adjustment to ensure that such percentage is maintained and shall be canceled at the end of the above-mentioned three-year period.

(c) During the third year following the entry into force of this Convention, the Council shall review the allocation of shares and shall be guided in its decision by the following principles:

(i) the votes of members shall reflect actual subscriptions to the Agency's capital and the membership votes as set out in Section (a) of this Article;

(ii) shares allocated to countries which shall not have signed the Convention shall be made available for reallocation to such members and in such manner as to make possible voting parity between the above-mentioned Categories; and

(iii) the Council will take measures that will facilitate members' ability to subscribe to shares allocated to them.

(d) Within the three-year period provided for in Section (b) of this Article, all decisions of the Council and Board shall be taken by special majority, except that decisions requiring a higher majority under this Convention shall be taken by such higher majority.

(e) In case the capital stock of the Agency is increased pursuant to Section (c) of Article 5, each member which so requests shall be authorized to subscribe a proportion of the increase equivalent to the proportion which its stock theretofore subscribed bears to the total capital stock of the Agency, but no member shall be obligated to subscribe any part of the increased capital.

(f) The Council shall issue regulations regarding the making of additional subscriptions under Section (e) of this Article. Such regulations shall prescribe reasonable time limits for the submission by members of requests to make such subscriptions.

ARTICLE 40. VOTING IN THE COUNCIL

(a) Each Governor shall be entitled to cast the votes of the member he represents. Except as otherwise specified in this Convention, decisions of the Council shall be taken by a majority of the votes cast.

(b) A quorum for any meeting of the Council shall be constituted by a majority of the Governors exercising not less than two-thirds of the total voting power.

(c) The Council may by regulation establish a procedure whereby the Board, when its deems such action to be in the best interests of the Agency, may request a decision of the Council on a specific questions without calling a meeting of the Council.

ARTICLE 41. ELECTION OF DIRECTORS

(a) Directors shall be elected in accordance with Schedule B.

(b) Directors shall continue in office until their successors are elected. If the office of a Director becomes vacant more than ninety days before the end of his term, another Director shall be elected for the remainder of the term by the Governors who elected the former Director. A majority of the votes cast shall be required for election. While the office remains vacant, the Alternate of the former Director shall exercise his powers, except that of appointing an Alternate.

ARTICLE 42. VOTING IN THE BOARD

(a) Each Director shall be entitled to cast the number of votes of the members whose votes counted towards his election. All the votes which a Director is entitled to cast shall be cast as a unit. Except as otherwise specified in this Convention, decisions of the Board shall be taken by a majority of the votes cast.

(b) A quorum for a meeting of the Board shall be constituted by a majority of the Directors exercising not less than one-half of the total voting power.

(c) The Board may by regulation establish a procedure whereby its Chairman, when he deems such action to be in the best interests of the Agency, may request a decision of the Board on a specific question without calling a meeting of the Board.

Chapter VII—Privileges and Immunities

ARTICLE 43. PURPOSES OF CHAPTER

To enable the Agency to fulfill its functions, the immunities and privileges set forth in this Chapter shall be accorded to the Agency in the territories of each member.

ARTICLE 44. LEGAL PROCESS

Actions other than those within the scope of Articles 57 and 58 may be brought against the Agency only in a court of competent jurisdiction in the territories of a member in which the Agency has an office or has appointed an agent for the purpose of accepting service or notice of process. No such action against the Agency shall be brought (i) by members of persons acting for or deriving claims from members or (ii) in respect of personnel matters. The property and assets of the Agency shall, wherever located and by whomsoever held, be immune from all forms of seizure, attachment or execution before the delivery of the final judgment or award against the Agency.

ARTICLE 45. ASSETS

(a) The property and assets of the Agency, wherever located and by whomsoever held, shall be immune from search, requisition, confiscation, expropriation or any other form of seizure by executive or legislative action.

(b) To the extent necessary to carry out its operations under this Convention, all property and assets of the Agency shall be free from restrictions, regulations, controls and moratoria of any nature; provided that property and assets acquired by the Agency as successor to or subrogee of a holder of a guarantee, a reinsured entity or an investor insured by a reinsured entity shall be free from applicable foreign exchange restrictions, regulations and controls in force in the territories of the member concerned to the extent that the holder, entity or investor to whom the Agency was subrogated was entitled to such treatment.

(c) For purposes of this Chapter, the term "assets" shall include the assets of the Sponsorship Trust Fund referred to in Annex I to this Convention and other assets administered by the Agency in furtherance of its objective.

ARTICLE 46. ARCHIVES AND COMMUNICATIONS

(a) The archives of the Agency shall be inviolable, wherever they may be.

(b) The official communications of the Agency shall be accorded by each member the same treatment that is accorded to the official communications of the Bank.

ARTICLE 47. TAXES

(a) The Agency, its assets, property and income, and its operations and transactions authorized by this Convention, shall be immune from all taxes and customs duties. The Agency shall also be immune from liability for the collection or payment of any tax or duty.

(b) Except in the case of local nationals, no tax shall be levied on or in respect of expense allowances paid by the Agency to Governors and their Alternates or on or in respect of their salaries, expense allowances or other emoluments paid by the Agency to the Chairman of the Board, Directors, their Alternates, the President or staff of the Agency.

(c) No taxation of any kind shall be levied on any investment guaranteed or reinsured by the Agency (including any earnings therefrom) or any insurance policies reinsured by the Agency (including any premiums and other revenues therefrom) by whomsoever held: (i) which discriminates against such investment or insurance policy solely because it is guaranteed or reinsured by the Agency; or (ii) if the sole jurisdictional basis for such taxation is the location of any office or place of business maintained by the Agency.

ARTICLE 48. OFFICIALS OF THE AGENCY

All Governors, Directors, Alternates, the President and staff of the Agency:

(i) shall be immune from legal process with respect to acts performed by them in their official capacity;

(ii) not being local nationals, shall be accorded the same immunities from immigration restrictions, alien registration requirements and national service obligations, and the same facilities as regards exchange restrictions as are accorded by the members concerned to the representatives, officials and employees of comparable rank of other members; and

(iii) shall be granted the same treatment in respect of travelling facilities as is accorded by the members concerned to representatives, officials and employees of comparable rank of other members.

ARTICLE 49. APPLICATION OF THIS CHAPTER

Each member shall take such action as is necessary in its own territories for the purpose of making effective in terms of its own law the principles set forth in this Chapter and shall inform the Agency of the detailed action which it has taken.

ARTICLE 50. WAIVER

The immunities, exemptions and privileges provided in this Chapter are granted in the interests of the Agency and may be waived, to such extent and upon such conditions as the Agency may determine, in cases where such a waiver would not prejudice its interests. The Agency shall waive the immunity of any of its staff in cases where, in its opinion, the immunity would impede the course of justice and can be waived without prejudice to the interests of the Agency.

Chapter VIII—Withdrawal, Suspension of Membership and Cessation of Operations

ARTICLE 51. WITHDRAWAL

Any member may, after the expiration of three years following the date upon which this Convention has entered into force with respect to such member, withdraw from the Agency at any time by giving notice in writing to the Agency at its principal office. The Agency shall notify the Bank, as depository of this Convention, of the receipt of such notice. Any withdrawal shall become effective ninety days following the date of the receipt of such notice by the Agency. A member may revoke such notice as long as it has not become effective.

ARTICLE 52. SUSPENSION OF MEMBERSHIP

(a) If a member fails to fulfill any of its obligations under this Convention, the Council may, by a majority of its members exercising a majority of the total voting power, suspend its membership.

(b) While under suspension a member shall have no rights under this Convention, except for the right of withdrawal and other rights provided in this Chapter and Chapter IX, but shall remain subject to all its obligations.

(c) For purposes of determining eligibility for a guarantee or reinsurance to be issued under Chapter III or Annex I to this Convention, a suspended member shall not be treated as a member of the Agency.

(d) The suspended member shall automatically cease to be a member one year from the date of its suspension unless the Council decides to extend the period of suspension or to restore the member to good standing.

ARTICLE 53. RIGHTS AND DUTIES OF STATES CEASING TO BE MEMBERS

(a) When a State ceases to be a member, it shall remain liable for all its obligations, including its contingent obligations, under this Convention which shall have been in effect before the cessation of its membership.

(b) Without prejudice to Section (a) above, the Agency shall enter into an arrangement with such State for the settlement of their respective claims and obligations. Any such arrangement shall be approved by the Board.

ARTICLE 54. SUSPENSION OF OPERATIONS

(a) The Board may, whenever it deems it justified, suspend the issuance of new guarantees for a specified period.

(b) In an emergency, the Board may suspend all activities of the Agency for a period not exceeding the duration of such emergency, provided that necessary arrangements shall be made for the protection of the interests of the Agency and of third parties.

(c) The decision to suspend operations shall have no effect on the obligations of the members under this Convention or on the obligations of the Agency towards holders of a guarantee or reinsurance policy or towards third parties.

ARTICLE 55. LIQUIDATION

(a) The Council, by special majority, may decide to cease operations and to liquidate the Agency. Thereupon the Agency shall forthwith cease all activities, except those incident to the orderly realization, conservation and preservation of assets and settlement of obligations. Until final settlement and distribution of assets, the Agency shall remain in existence and all rights and obligations of members under this Convention shall continue unimpaired.

(b) No distribution of assets shall be made to members until all liabilities to holders of guarantees and other creditors shall have been discharged or provided for and until the Council shall have decided to make such distribution.

(c) Subject to the foregoing, the Agency shall distribute its remaining assets to members in proportion to each member's share in the subscribed capital. The Agency shall also distribute any remaining assets of the Sponsorship Trust Fund referred to in Annex I to this Convention to sponsoring members in the proportion which the investments sponsored by each bears to the total of sponsored investments. No member shall be entitled to its share in the assets of the Agency or the Sponsorship Trust Fund unless that member has settled all outstanding claims by the Agency against it. Every distribution of assets shall be made at such times as the Council shall determine and in such manner as it shall deem fair and equitable.

CHAPTER IX—SETTLEMENT OF DISPUTES

ARTICLE 56. INTERPRETATION AND APPLICATION OF THE CONVENTION

(a) Any question of interpretation or application of the provisions of this Convention arising between any member of the Agency and the Agency or among members of the Agency shall be submitted to the Board for its decision. Any member which is particularly affected by the question and which is not otherwise represented by a national in the Board may send a representative to attend any meeting of the Board at which such question is considered.

(b) In any case where the Board has given a decision under Section (a) above, any member may require that the question be referred to the Council, whose decision shall be final. Pending the result of the referral to the Council, the Agency may, so far as it deems necessary, act on the basis of the decision of the Board.

ARTICLE 57. DISPUTES BETWEEN THE AGENCY AND MEMBERS

(a) Without prejudice to the provisions of Article 56 and of Section (b) of this Article, any dispute between the Agency and a member or an agency thereof and any dispute between the Agency and a country (or agency thereof) which has ceased to be a member, shall be settled in accordance with the procedure set out in Annex II to this Convention.

(b) Disputes concerning claims of the Agency acting as subrogee of an investor shall be settled in accordance with either (i) the procedure set out in Annex II to this Convention, or (ii) an agreement to be entered into between the Agency and the member concerned on an alternative method or methods for the settlement of such disputes. In the latter case, Annex II to this Convention shall serve as a basis for such an agreement which shall, in each case, be approved by the Board by special majority prior to the undertaking by the Agency of operations in the territories of the member concerned.

ARTICLE 58. DISPUTES INVOLVING HOLDERS OF A GUARANTEE OR REINSURANCE

Any dispute arising under a contract of guarantee or reinsurance between the parties thereto shall be submitted to arbitration for final determination in accordance with such rules as shall be provided for or referred to in the contract of guarantee or reinsurance.

CHAPTER X—AMENDMENTS

ARTICLE 59. AMENDMENT BY COUNCIL

(a) This Convention and its Annexes may be amended by vote of three-fifths of the Governors exercising four-fifths of the total voting power, provided that:

(i) any amendment modifying the right to withdraw from the Agency provided in Article 51 or the limitation on liability provided in Section (d) of Article 8 shall require the affirmative vote of all Governors; and

(ii) any amendment modifying the loss-sharing arrangement provided in Articles 1 and 3 of Annex I to this Convention which will result in an increase in any member's liability thereunder shall require the affirmative vote of the Governor of each such member.

(b) Schedules A and B to this Convention may be amended by the Council by special majority.

(c) If an amendment affects any provision of Annex I to this Convention, total votes shall include the additional votes allotted under Article 7 of such Annex to sponsoring members and countries hosting sponsored investments.

ARTICLE 60. PROCEDURE

Any proposal to amend this Convention, whether emanating from a member or a Governor or a Director, shall be communicated to the Chairman of the Board who shall bring the proposal before the Board. If the proposed amendment is recommended by the Board, it shall be submitted to the Council for approval in accordance with Article 59. When an amendment has been duly approved by the Council, the Agency shall so certify by formal communication addressed to all members. Amendments shall enter into force for all members ninety days after the date of the formal communication unless the Council shall specify a different date.

Chapter XI—Final Provisions

ARTICLE 61. ENTRY INTO FORCE

(a) This Convention shall be open for signature on behalf of all members of the Bank and Switzerland and shall be subject to ratification, acceptance or approval by the signatory States in accordance with their constitutional procedures.

(b) This Convention shall enter into force on the day when not less than five instruments of ratification, acceptance or approval shall have been deposited on behalf of signatory States in Category One, and not less than fifteen such instruments shall have been deposited on behalf of signatory States in Category Two; provided that total subscriptions of these States amount to not less than one-third of the authorized capital of the Agency as prescribed in Article 5.

(c) For each State which deposits its instrument of ratification, acceptance or approval after this Convention shall have entered into force, this Convention shall enter into force on the date of such deposit.

(d) If this Convention shall not have entered into force within two years after its opening for signature, the President of the Bank shall convene a conference of interested countries to determine the future course of action.

ARTICLE 62. INAUGURAL MEETING

Upon entry into force of this Convention, the President of the Bank shall call the inaugural meeting of the Council. This meeting shall be held at the principal office of the Agency within sixty days from the date on which this Convention has entered into force or as soon as practicable thereafter.

ARTICLE 63. DEPOSITORY

Instruments of ratification, acceptance or approval of this Convention and amendments thereto shall be deposited with the Bank which shall act as the depository of this Convention. The depository shall transmit certified copies of this Convention to States members of the Bank and to Switzerland.

ARTICLE 64. REGISTRATION

The depository shall register this Convention with the Secretariat of the United Nations in accordance with Article 102 of the Charter of the United Nations and the Regulations thereunder adopted by the General Assembly.

ARTICLE 65. NOTIFICATION

The depository shall notify all signatory States and, upon the entry into force of this Convention, the Agency of the following:

(a) signatures of this Convention;

(b) deposits of instruments of ratification, acceptance and approval in accordance with Article 63;

(c) the date on which this Convention enters into force in accordance with Article 61;

(d) exclusions from territorial application pursuant to Article 66; and

(e) withdrawal of a member from the Agency pursuant to Article 51.

ARTICLE 66. TERRITORIAL APPLICATION

This Convention shall apply to all territories under the jurisdiction of a member including the territories for whose international relations a member is responsible, except those which are excluded by such member by written notice to the depository of this Convention either at the time of ratification, acceptance or approval or subsequently.

ARTICLE 67. PERIODIC REVIEWS

(a) The Council shall periodically undertake comprehensive reviews of the activities of the Agency as well as the results achieved with a view to introducing any changes required to enhance the Agency's ability to serve its objectives.

(b) The first such review shall take place five years after the entry into force of this Convention. The dates of subsequent reviews shall be determined by the Council.

DONE at Seoul, in a single copy which shall remain deposited in the archives of the International Bank for Reconstruction and Development, which has indicated by its signature below its agreement to fulfill the functions with which it is charged under this Convention.

ANNEX I—GUARANTEES OF SPONSORED INVESTMENTS UNDER ARTICLE 24

ARTICLE 1. SPONSORSHIP

(a) Any member may sponsor for guarantee an investment to be made by an investor of any nationality or by investors of any or several nationalities.

(b) Subject to the provisions of Section (b) and (c) of Article 3 of this Annex, each sponsoring member shall share with the other sponsoring members in losses under guarantees of sponsored investments, when and to the extent that such losses cannot be covered out of the Sponsorship Trust Fund referred to in Article 2 of this Annex, in the proportion which the amount of maximum contingent liability under the guarantees of investments sponsored by it bears to the total amount of maximum contingent liability under the guarantees of investments sponsored by all members.

(c) In its decisions on the issuance of guarantees under this Annex, the Agency shall pay due regard to the prospects that the sponsoring member will be in a position to meet its obligations under this Annex and shall give priority to investments which are co-sponsored by the host countries concerned.

(d) The Agency shall periodically consult with sponsoring members with respect to its operations under this Annex.

ARTICLE 2. SPONSORSHIP TRUST FUND

(a) Premiums and other revenues attributable to guarantees of sponsored investments, including returns on the investment of such premiums and revenues, shall be held in a separate account which shall be called the Sponsorship Trust Fund.

(b) All administrative expenses and payments on claims attributable to guarantees issued under this Annex shall be paid out of the Sponsorship Trust Fund.

(c) The assets of the Sponsorship Trust Fund shall be held and administered for the joint account of sponsoring members and shall be kept separate and apart from the assets of the Agency.

ARTICLE 3. CALLS ON SPONSORING MEMBERS

(a) To the extent that any amount is payable by the Agency on account of a loss under a sponsored guarantee and such amount cannot be paid out of assets of the Sponsorship Trust Fund, the Agency shall call on each sponsoring member to pay into such Fund its share of such amount as shall be determined in accordance with Section (b) of Article 1 of this Annex.

(b) No member shall be liable to pay any amount on a call pursuant to the provisions of this Article if as a result total payments made by that member will exceed the total amount of guarantees covering investments sponsored by it.

(c) Upon the expiry of any guarantee covering an investment sponsored by a member, the liability of that member shall be decreased by an amount equivalent to the amount of such guarantee; such liability shall also be decreased on a pro rata basis upon payment by the Agency of any claim related to a sponsored investment and shall otherwise continue in effect until the expiry of all guarantees of sponsored investments outstanding at the time of such payment.

(d) If any sponsoring member shall not be liable for an amount of a call pursuant to the provisions of this Article because of the limitation contained in Sections (b) and (c) above, or if any sponsoring member shall default in payment of an amount due in response to any such call, the liability for payment of such amount shall be shared pro rata by the other sponsoring members. Liability of members pursuant to this Section shall be subject to the limitation set forth in Sections (b) and (c) above.

(e) Any payment by a sponsoring member pursuant to a call in accordance with this Article shall be made promptly and in freely usable currency.

ARTICLE 4. VALUATION OF CURRENCIES AND REFUNDS

The provisions on valuation of currencies and refunds contained in this Convention with respect to capital subscriptions shall be applied *mutatis mutandis* to funds paid by members on account of sponsored investments.

ARTICLE 5. REINSURANCE

(a) The Agency may, under the conditions set forth in Article 1 of this Annex, provide reinsurance to a member, an agency thereof, a regional agency as defined in Section (a) of Article 20 of this Convention or a private insurer in a member country. The provisions of this Annex concerning guarantees and of Articles 20 and 21 of this Convention shall be applied *mutatis mutandis* to reinsurance provided under this Section.

(b) The Agency may obtain reinsurance for investments guaranteed by it under this Annex and shall meet the cost of such reinsurance out of the Sponsorship Trust Fund. The Board may decide whether and to what extent the loss-sharing obligation of sponsoring members referred to in Section (b) of Article 1 of this Annex may be reduced on account of the reinsurance cover obtained.

ARTICLE 6. OPERATIONAL PRINCIPLES

Without prejudice to the provisions of this Annex, the provisions with respect to guarantee operations under Chapter III of this Convention and to financial management under Chapter IV of this Convention shall applied *mutatis mutandis* to guarantees of sponsored investments except that (i) such investments shall qualify for sponsorship if made in the territories of any member, and in particular of any developing member, by an investor or investors eligible under Section (a) of Article 1 of this Annex, and (ii) the Agency shall not be liable with respect to its own assets for any guarantee or reinsurance issued under this Annex and each contract of guarantee or reinsurance concluded pursuant to this Annex shall expressly so provide.

ARTICLE 7. VOTING

For decisions relating to sponsored investments, each sponsoring member shall have one additional vote for each 10,000 Special Drawing Rights equivalent of the amount guaranteed or reinsured on the basis of its sponsorship, and each member hosting a sponsored investment shall have one additional vote for each 10,000 Special Drawing Rights equivalent of the amount guaranteed or reinsured with respect to any sponsored investment hosted by it. Such additional votes shall be cast only for decisions related to sponsored investments and shall otherwise be disregarded in determining the voting power of members.

ANNEX II—SETTLEMENT OF DISPUTES BETWEEN A MEMBER AND THE AGENCY UNDER ARTICLE 57

ARTICLE 1. APPLICATION OF THE ANNEX

All disputes within the scope of Article 57 of this Convention shall be settled in accordance with the procedure set out in this Annex, except in the cases where the Agency has entered into an agreement with a member pursuant to Section (b) (ii) of Article 57.

ARTICLE 2. NEGOTIATION

The parties to a dispute within the scope of this Annex shall attempt to settle such dispute by negotiation before seeking conciliation or arbitration. Negotiation shall be deemed to have been exhausted if the parties fail to reach a settlement within a period of one hundred and twenty days from the date of the request to enter into negotiation.

ARTICLE 3. CONCILIATION

(a) If the dispute is not resolved through negotiation, either party may submit the dispute to arbitration in accordance with the provisions of Article 4 of this Annex, unless the parties, by mutual consent, have decided to resort first to the conciliation procedure provided for in this Article.

(b) The agreement for recourse to conciliation shall specify the matter in dispute, the claims of the parties in respect thereof and, if available, the name of the conciliator agreed upon by the parties. In the absence of agreement on the conciliator, the parties may jointly request either the Secretary-General of the International Centre for Settlement of Investment Disputes (hereinafter called ICSID) or the President of the International Court of Justice to appoint a conciliator. The conciliation procedure shall terminate if the conciliator has not been appointed within ninety days after the agreement for recourse to conciliation.

(c) Unless otherwise provided in this Annex or agreed upon by the parties, the conciliator shall determine the rules governing the conciliation procedure and shall be guided in this regard by the conciliation rules adopted pursuant to the Convention on the Settlement of Investment Disputes between States and Nationals of Other States.

(d) The parties shall cooperate in good faith with the conciliator and shall, in particular, provide him with all information and documentation which would assist him in the discharge of his functions; they shall give their most serious consideration to his recommendations.

(e) Unless otherwise agreed upon by the parties, the conciliator shall, within a period not exceeding one hundred and eighty days from the date of his appointment, submit to the parties a report recording the results of his efforts and setting out the issues controversial between the parties and his proposals for their settlement.

(f) Each party shall, within sixty days from the date of the receipt of the report, express in writing its views on the report to the other party.

(g) Neither party to a conciliation proceeding shall be entitled to have recourse to arbitration unless:

(i) the conciliator shall have failed to submit his report within the period established in Section (e) above; or

(ii) the parties shall have failed to accept all of the proposals contained in the report within sixty days after its receipt; or

(iii) the parties, after an exchange of views on the report, shall have failed to agree on a settlement of all controversial issues within sixty days after receipt of the conciliator's report; or

(iv) a party shall have failed to express its views on the report as prescribed in Section (f) above.

(h) Unless the parties agree otherwise, the fees of the conciliator shall be determined on the basis of the rates applicable to ICSID conciliation. These fees and the other costs of the conciliation proceedings shall be borne equally by the parties. Each party shall defray its own expenses.

ARTICLE 4. ARBITRATION

(a) Arbitration proceedings shall be instituted by means of a notice by the party seeking arbitration (the claimant) addressed to the other party or parties to the dispute (the respondent). The notice shall specify the nature of the dispute, the relief sought and the name of the arbitrator appointed by the claimant. The respondent shall, within thirty days after the date of receipt of the notice, notify the claimant of the name of the arbitrator appointed by it. The two parties shall, within a period of thirty days from the date of appointment of the second arbitrator, select a third arbitrator, who shall act as President of the Arbitral Tribunal (the Tribunal).

(b) If the Tribunal shall not have been constituted within sixty days form the date of the notice, the arbitrator not yet appointed or the President not yet selected shall be appointed, at the joint request of the parties, by the Secretary-General of ICSID. If there is no such joint request, or if the Secretary-General shall fail to make the appointment within thirty days of the request, either party may request the President of the International Court of Justice to make the appointment.

(c) No party shall have the right change the arbitrator appointed by it once the hearing of the dispute has commenced. In case any arbitrator (including the President of the Tribunal) shall resign, die, or become incapacitated, a successor shall be appointed in the manner followed in the appointment of his predecessor and such successor shall have the same powers and duties of the arbitrator he succeeds.

(d) The Tribunal shall convene first at such time and place as shall be determined by the President. Thereafter, the Tribunal shall determine the place and dates of its meetings.

(e) Unless otherwise provided in this Annex or agreed upon by the parties, the Tribunal shall determine its procedure and shall be guided in this regard by the arbitration rules adopted pursuant to the Convention on the Settlement of Investment Disputes between States and Nationals of Other States.

(f) The Tribunal shall be the judge of its own competence except that, if an objection is raised before the Tribunal to the effect that the dispute falls within the jurisdiction of the Board or the Council under Article 56 or within the jurisdiction of a judicial or arbitral body designated in an agreement under Article 1 of this Annex and the Tribunal is satisfied that the objection is genuine, the objection shall be referred by the Tribunal to the Board or the Council or the designated body, as the case may be, and arbitration proceedings shall be stayed until a decision has been reached on the matter, which shall be binding upon the Tribunal.

(g) The Tribunal shall, in any dispute within the scope of this Annex, apply the provisions of this Convention, any relevant agreement between the parties to the dispute, the Agency's by-laws and regulations, the applicable rules of international law, the domestic law of the member concerned as well as the applicable provisions of the investment contract, if any. Without prejudice to the provisions of this Convention, the Tribunal may decide a dispute *ex aequo et bono* if the Agency and the member concerned so agree. The Tribunal may not bring a finding of *non liquet* on the ground of silence or obscurity of the law.

(h) The Tribunal shall afford a fair hearing to all the parties. All decisions of the Tribunal shall be taken by a majority vote and shall state the reasons on which they are based. The award of the Tribunal shall be in writing, and shall be signed by at least two arbitrators and a copy thereof shall be transmitted to each party. The award shall be final and binding upon the parties and shall not be subject to appeal, annulment or revision.

(i) If any dispute shall arise between the parties as to the meaning or scope of any award, either party may, within sixty days after the award was rendered, request interpretation of the award by an application in writing to the President of the Tribunal which rendered the award. The President shall, if possible, submit the request to the Tribunal which rendered the award and shall convene such Tribunal within sixty days after receipt of the application. If this shall not be possible, a new Tribunal shall be constituted in accordance with the provisions of Sections (a) to (d) above. The Tribunal may stay enforcement of the award pending its decision on the requested interpretation.

(j) Each member shall recognize an award rendered pursuant to this Article as binding and enforceable within its territories as if it were a final judgment of a court in that member. Execution of the award shall be governed by the laws concerning the execution of judgments in force in the State in whose territories such execution is sought and shall not derogate from the law in force relating to immunity from execution.

(k) Unless the parties shall agree otherwise, the fees and remuneration payable to arbitrators shall be determined on the basis of the rates applicable to ICSID arbitration. Each party shall defray its own costs associated with the arbitration proceedings. The costs of the Tribunal shall be borne by the parties in equal proportion unless the Tribunal decides otherwise. Any question concerning the division of the costs of the Tribunal or the procedure for payment of such costs shall be decided by the Tribunal.

ARTICLE 5. SERVICE OF PROCESS

Service of any notice or process in connection with any proceeding under this Annex shall be made in writing. It shall be made by the Agency upon the authority designated by the member concerned pursuant to Article 38 of this Convention and by that member at the principal office of the Agency.

SCHEDULE A—MEMBERSHIP AND SUBSCRIPTIONS

Country	Number of Shares	Subscription (millions of SDR)
CATEGORY ONE		
Australia	1,713	17.13
Austria	775	7.75
Belgium	2,030	20.30
Canada	2,965	29.65
Denmark	718	7.18
Finland	600	6.00
France	4,860	48.60
Germany, Federal Republic of	5,071	50.71
Iceland	90	0.90
Ireland	369	3.69
Italy	2,820	28.20
Japan	5,095	50.95
Luxembourg	116	1.16
Netherlands	2,169	21.69
New Zealand	513	5.13
Norway	699	6.99
South Africa	943	9.43
Sweden	1,049	10.49
Switzerland	1,500	15.00
United Kingdom	4,860	48.60
United States	20,519	205.19
Subtotal	59,473	594.73
CATEGORY TWO *		
Afghanistan	118	1.18
Algeria	649	6.49
Antigua and Barbuda	50	0.50
Argentina	1,254	12.54
Bahamas	100	1.00
Bahrian	77	0.77
Bangladesh	340	3.40
Barbados	68	0.68
Belize	50	0.50
Benin	61	0.61
Bhutan	50	0.50
Bolivia	125	1.25
Botswana	50	0.50
Brazil	1,479	14.79
Burkina Faso	61	0.61
Burma	178	1.78
Burundi	74	0.74
Cameroon	107	1.07
Cape Verde	50	0.50
Central African Republic	60	0.60
Chad	60	0.60
Chile	485	4.85
China	3,138	31.38

Country	Number of Shares	Subscription (millions of SDR)
Colombia	437	4.37
Comoros	50	0.50
Congo, People's Republic of the	65	0.65
Costa Rica	117	1.17
Cyprus	104	1.04
Djibouti	50	0.50
Dominica	50	0.50
Dominican Republic	147	1.47
Ecuador	182	1.82
Egypt, Arab Republic of	459	4.59
El Salvador	122	1.22
Equatorial Guinea	50	0.50
Ethiopia	70	0.70
Fiji	71	0.71
Gabon	96	0.96
Gambia, The	50	0.50
Ghana	245	2.45
Greece	280	2.80
Grenada	50	0.50
Guatemala	140	1.40
Guinea	91	0.91
Guinea-Bissau	50	0.50
Guyana	84	0.84
Haiti	75	0.75
Honduras	101	1.01
Hungary	564	5.64
India	3,048	30.48
Indonesia	1,049	10.49
Iran, Islamic Republic of	1,659	16.59
Iraq	350	3.50
Israel	474	4.74
Ivory Coast	176	1.76
Jamaica	181	1.81
Jordan	97	0.97
Kampuchea, Democratic	93	0.93
Kenya	172	1.72
Korea, Republic of	449	4.49
Kuwait	930	9.30
Lao People's Democratic Republic	60	0.60
Lebanon	142	1.42
Lesotho	50	0.50
Liberia	84	0.84
Libyan Arab Jamahiriya	549	5.49
Madagascar	100	1.00
Malawi	77	0.77
Malaysia	579	5.79
Maldives	50	0.50
Mali	81	0.81
Malta	75	0.75
Mauritania	63	0.63
Mauritius	87	0.87
Mexico	1,192	11.92
Morocco	348	3.48

Country	Number of Shares	Subscription (millions of SDR)
Mozambique	97	0.97
Nepal	69	0.69
Nicaragua	102	1.02
Niger	62	0.62
Nigeria	844	8.44
Oman	94	0.94
Pakistan	660	6.60
Panama	131	1.31
Papua New Guinea	96	0.96
Paraguay	80	0.80
Peru	373	3.73
Philippines	484	4.84
Portugual	382	3.82
Qatar	137	1.37
Romania	555	5.55
Rwanda	75	0.75
Saint Christopher and Nevis	50	0.50
Saint Lucia	50	0.50
Saint Vincent	50	0.50
Sao Tome and Principe	50	0.50
Saudi Arabia	3,137	31.37
Senegal	145	1.45
Seychelles	50	0.50
Sierra Leone	75	0.75
Singapore	154	1.54
Solomon Islands	50	0.50
Somalia	78	0.78
Spain	1,285	12.85
Sri Lanka	271	2.71
Sudan	206	2.06
Suriname	82	0.82
Syrian Arab Republic	168	1.68
Swaziland	58	0.58
Tanzania	141	1.41
Thailand	421	4.21
Togo	77	0.77
Trinidad and Tobago	203	2.03
Tunisia	156	1.56
Turkey	462	4.62
United Arab Emirates	372	3.72
Uganda	132	1.32
Uruguay	202	2.02
Vanuatu	50	0.50
Venezuela	1,427	14.27
Viet Nam	220	2.20
Western Samoa	50	0.50
Yemen Arab Republic	67	0.67
Yemen, People's Democratic Republic of	115	1.15
Yugoslavia	635	6.35
Zaire	338	3.38
Zambia	318	3.18
Zimbabwe	236	2.36

Country	Number of Shares	Subscription (millions of SDR)
Subtotal	40,527	405.27
Total	100,000	1,000.00

*Countries listed under Category Two are developing member countries for the purposes of this Convention.

SCHEDULE B—ELECTION OF DIRECTORS

1. Candidates for the office of Director shall be nominated by the Governors, provided that a Governor may nominate only one person.

2. The election of Directors shall be by ballot of the Governors.

3. In balloting for the Directors, every Governor shall cast for one candidate all the votes which the member represented by him is entitled to cast under Section (a) of Article 40.

4. One-fourth of the number of Directors shall be elected separately, one by each of the Governors of members having the largest number of shares. If the total number of Directors is not divisible by four, the number of Directors so elected shall be one-fourth of the next lower number that is divisible by four.

5. The remaining Directors shall be elected by the other Governors in accordance with the provision of paragraphs 6 to 11 of this Schedule.

6. If the number of candidates nominated equals the number of such remaining Directors to be elected, all the candidates shall be elected in the first ballot; except that a candidate or candidates having received less than the minimum percentage of total votes determined by the Council for such election shall not be elected if any candidate shall have received more than the maximum percentage of total votes determined by the Council.

7. If the number of candidates nominated exceeds the number of such remaining Directors to be elected, the candidates receiving the largest number of votes shall be elected with the exception of any candidate who has received less than the minimum percentage of the total votes determined by the Council.

8. If all of such remaining Directors are not elected in the first ballot, a second ballot shall be held. The candidate or candidates not elected in the first ballot shall again be eligible for election.

9. In the second ballot, voting shall be limited to (i) those Governors having voted in the first ballot for a candidate not elected and (ii) those Governors having voted in the first ballot for an elected candidate who had already received the maximum percentage of total votes determined by the Council before taking their votes into account.

10. In determining when an elected candidate has received more than the maximum percentage of the votes, the votes of the Governor casting the largest number of votes for such candidate shall

be counted first, then the votes of the Governor casting the next largest number, and so on until such percentage is reached.

11. If not all the remaining Directors have been elected after the second ballot, further ballots shall be held on the same principles until all the remaining Directors are elected, provided that when only one Director remains to be elected, this Director may be elected by a simple majority of the remaining votes and shall be deemed to have been elected by all such votes.

6. Instrument for the Establishment of the Restructured Global Environment Facility (Amended)

CONTENTS

6. Instrument for the Establishment of the Restructured Global Environment Facility

Done at Geneva, with the acceptance by representatives of 73 States, March 1994; Formally adopted by the three Implementing Agencies of the Global Environment Facility: the United Nations Development Programme, the United Nations Environment Programme, and the World Bank; Entered into force, July 7, 1994; Amended at the Second GEF Assembly in Beijing, October 2002; Entered into effect on adoption by the United Nations Development Programme, the United Nations Environment Programme, and the World Bank, June 19, 2003

PREAMBLE

Whereas:

(a) The Global Environment Facility (GEF or the Facility) was established in the International Bank for Reconstruction and Development (IBRD or World Bank) as a pilot program in order to assist in the protection of the global environment and promote thereby environmentally sound and sustainable economic development, by resolution of the Executive Directors of the World Bank and related interagency arrangements between the United Nations Development Programme (UNDP), the United Nations Environment Programme (UNEP), and the World Bank;

(b) In April 1992, Participants in the GEF agreed that its structure and modalities should be modified. Agenda 21 (the action plan of the 1992 United Nations Conference on Environment and Development), the United Nations Framework Convention on Climate Change and the Convention on Biological Diversity subsequently called for the restructuring of the Facility;

(c) Representatives of the States participating at present in the Facility and of other States wishing to participate in it have requested that the Facility be restructured in order to take account of these developments, to establish the GEF as one of the principal mechanisms for global environment funding, to ensure a governance that is transparent and democratic in nature, to promote universality in its participation and to provide for full cooperation in its implementation among UNDP, UNEP and the World Bank (together referred to hereinafter as the Implementing Agencies), and to benefit from the evaluation of experience with the operation of the Facility since its establishment;

(d) It is necessary to replenish the resources for these purposes under a restructured Facility which includes a new GEF Trust Fund on the basis of this Instrument;

(e) It is desirable to terminate the existing Global Environment Trust Fund (GET) and to transfer any funds, receipts, assets and liabilities held in it upon termination to the new GEF Trust Fund;

(f) The Implementing Agencies have reached a common understanding of principles for cooperation as set forth in the present Instrument, subject to approval of their participation by their respective governing bodies;

It is resolved as follows:

I. Basic Provisions

Restructuring and Purpose of GEF

1. The restructured GEF shall be established in accordance with the present Instrument. This Instrument, having been accepted by representatives of the States participating in the GEF at their meeting in Geneva, Switzerland, from March 14 to 16, 1994, shall be adopted by the Implementing Agencies in accordance with their respective rules and procedural requirements.

2. The GEF shall operate, on the basis of collaboration and partnership among the Implementing Agencies, as a mechanism for international cooperation for the purpose of providing new and additional grant and concessional funding to meet the agreed incremental costs of measures to achieve agreed global environmental benefits in the following focal areas:

(a) biological diversity;

(b) climate change;

(c) international waters;

(d) land degradation, primarily desertification and deforestation;

(e) ozone layer depletion; and

(f) persistent organic pollutants.

3. The agreed incremental costs of activities to achieve global environmental benefits concerning chemicals management as they relate to the above focal areas shall be eligible for funding. The agreed incremental costs of other relevant activities under Agenda 21 that may be agreed by the Council shall also be eligible for funding insofar as they achieve global environmental benefits by protecting the global environment in the focal areas.

4. The GEF shall ensure the cost-effectiveness of its activities in addressing the targeted global environmental issues, shall fund programs and projects which are country-driven and based on national priorities designed to support sustainable development and shall maintain sufficient flexibility to respond to changing circumstances in order to achieve its purposes.

5. The GEF operational policies shall be determined by the Council in accordance with paragraph 20(f) and with respect to GEF-financed projects shall provide for full disclosure of all non-confidential information, and consultation with, and participation as appropriate of, major groups and local communities throughout the project cycle.

6. In partial fulfillment of its purposes, the GEF shall, on an interim basis, operate the financial mechanism for the implementation of the United Nations Framework Convention on Climate Change and shall be, on an interim basis, the institutional structure which carries out the operation of the financial mechanism for the implementation of the Convention on Biological Diversity, in accordance with such cooperative arrangements or agreements as

may be made pursuant to paragraphs 27 and 31. The GEF shall be available to continue to serve for the purposes of the financial mechanisms for the implementation of those conventions if it is requested to do so by their Conferences of the Parties. The GEF shall also be available to serve as an entity entrusted with the operation of the financial mechanism of the Stockholm Convention on Persistent Organic Pollutants. In such respects, the GEF shall function under the guidance of, and be accountable to, the Conferences of the Parties which shall decide on policies, program priorities and eligibility criteria for the purposes of the conventions. The GEF shall also be available to meet the agreed full costs of activities under Article 12, paragraph 1, of the United Nations Framework Convention on Climate Change.

PARTICIPATION

7. Any State member of the United Nations or of any of its specialized agencies may become a Participant in the GEF by depositing with the Secretariat an instrument of participation substantially in the form set out in Annex A. In the case of a State contributing to the GEF Trust Fund, an instrument of commitment shall be deemed to serve as an instrument of participation. Any Participant may withdraw from the GEF by depositing with the Secretariat an instrument of termination of participation substantially in the form set out in Annex A.

ESTABLISHMENT OF GEF TRUST FUND

8. The new GEF Trust Fund shall be established, and the World Bank shall be invited to serve as the Trustee of the Fund. The GEF Trust Fund shall consist of the contributions received in accordance with the present Instrument, the balance of funds transferred from the GET pursuant to paragraph 32, and any other assets and receipts of the Fund. In serving as the Trustee of the Fund, the World Bank shall serve in a fiduciary and administrative capacity, and shall be bound by its Articles of Agreement, by-laws, rules and decisions, as specified in Annex B.

ELIGIBILITY

9. GEF funding shall be made available for activities within the focal areas defined in paragraphs 2 and 3 of this Instrument in accordance with the following eligibility criteria:

(a) GEF grants that are made available within the framework of the financial mechanisms of the conventions referred to in paragraph 6 shall be in conformity with the eligibility criteria decided by the Conference of the Parties of each convention, as provided under the arrangements or agreements referred to in paragraph 27.

(b) All other GEF grants shall be made available to eligible recipient countries and, where appropriate, for other activities promoting the purposes of the Facility in accordance with this paragraph and any additional eligibility criteria determined by the Council. A country shall be an eligible recipient of GEF grants if it is eligible to borrow from the World Bank (IBRD and/or IDA) or if it is an eligible recipient of UNDP technical assistance through its country Indicative Planning Figure (IPF). GEF grants for activities within a focal area addressed by a convention referred to in paragraph 6 but outside the framework of the financial mechanism of the convention, shall only be made available to eligible recipient countries that are party to the convention concerned.

(c) GEF concessional financing in a form other than grants that is made available within the framework of the financial mechanism of the conventions referred to in paragraph 6 shall be in conformity with eligibility criteria decided by the Conference of the Parties of each convention, as provided under the arrangements or agreements referred to in paragraph 27. GEF concessional financing in a form other than grants may also be made available outside those frameworks on terms to be determined by the Council.

II. Contributions and Other Financial Provisions for Replenishment

10. Contributions to the GEF Trust Fund for the first replenishment period shall be made to the Trustee by Contributing Participants in accordance with the financial provisions for replenishment as specified in Annex C. The Trustee's responsibility for mobilization of resources pursuant to paragraph 20(e) of this Instrument and paragraph 4(a) of Annex B shall be initiated for subsequent replenishments at the request of the Council.

III. Governance and Structure

11. The GEF shall have an Assembly, a Council and a Secretariat. In accordance with paragraph 24, a Scientific and Technical Advisory Panel (STAP) shall provide appropriate advice.

12. The Implementing Agencies shall establish a process for their collaboration in accordance with an interagency agreement to be concluded on the basis of the principles set forth in Annex D.

Assembly

13. The Assembly shall consist of Representatives of all Participants. The Assembly shall meet once every three years. Each Participant may appoint one Representative and one Alternate to the Assembly in such manner as it may determine. Each Representative and each Alternate shall serve until replaced. The Assembly shall elect its Chairperson from among the Representatives.

14. The Assembly shall:

(a) review the general policies of the Facility;

(b) review and evaluate the operation of the Facility on the basis of reports submitted by the Council;

(c) keep under review the membership of the Facility; and

(d) consider, for approval by consensus, amendments to the present Instrument on the basis of recommendations by the Council.

COUNCIL

15. The Council shall be responsible for developing, adopting and evaluating the operational policies and programs for GEF-financed activities, in conformity with the present Instrument and fully taking into account reviews carried out by the Assembly. Where the GEF serves for the purposes of the financial mechanisms of the conventions referred to in paragraph 6, the Council shall act in conformity with the policies, program priorities and eligibility criteria decided by the Conference of the Parties for the purposes of the convention concerned.

16. The Council shall consist of 32 Members, representing constituency groupings formulated and distributed taking into account the need for balanced and equitable representation of all Participants and giving due weight to the funding efforts of all donors. There shall be 16 Members from developing countries, 14 Members from developed countries and 2 Members from the countries of central and eastern Europe and the former Soviet Union, in accordance with Annex E. There shall be an equal number of Alternate Members. The Member and Alternate representing a constituency shall be appointed by the Participants in each constituency. Unless the constituency decides otherwise, each Member of the Council and each Alternate shall serve for three years or until a new Member is appointed by the constituency, whichever comes first. A Member or Alternate may be reappointed by the constituency. Members and Alternates shall serve without compensation. The Alternate Member shall have full power to act for the absent Member.

17. The Council shall meet semi-annually or as frequently as necessary at the seat of the Secretariat to enable it to discharge its responsibilities. Two-thirds of the Members of the Council shall constitute a quorum.

18. At each meeting, the Council shall elect a Chairperson from among its Members for the duration of that meeting. The elected Chairperson shall conduct deliberations of the Council at that meeting on issues related to Council responsibilities listed in paragraphs 20(b), (g), (i), (j) and (k). The position of elected Chairperson shall alternate from one meeting to another between recipient and non-recipient Council Members. The Chief Executive Officer of the Facility (CEO) shall conduct deliberations of the Council on issues related to Council responsibilities listed in paragraphs 20(c), (e), (f) and (h). The elected Chairperson and the CEO shall jointly conduct deliberations of the Council on issues related to paragraph 20(a).

19. Costs of Council meetings, including travel and subsistence of Council Members from developing countries, in particular the Least Developed Countries, shall be disbursed from the administrative budget of the Secretariat as necessary.

20. The Council shall:

(a) keep under review the operation of the Facility with respect to its purposes, scope and objectives;

(b) ensure that GEF policies, programs, operational strategies and projects are monitored and evaluated on a regular basis;

(c) review and approve the work program referred to in paragraph 29, monitor and evaluate progress in the implementation of the work program and provide related guidance to the Secretariat, the Implementing Agencies and the other bodies referred to in paragraph 28, recognizing that the Implementing Agencies will retain responsibility for the further preparation of individual projects approved in the work program;

(d) arrange for Council Members to receive final project documents and within four weeks transmit to the CEO any concerns they may have prior to the CEO endorsing a project document for final approval by the Implementing Agency;

(e) direct the utilization of GEF funds, review the availability of resources from the GEF Trust Fund and cooperate with the Trustee to mobilize financial resources;

(f) approve and periodically review operational modalities for the Facility, including operational strategies and directives for project selection, means to facilitate arrangements for project preparation and execution by organizations and entities referred to in paragraph 28, additional eligibility and other financing criteria in accordance with paragraphs 9(b) and 9(c) respectively, procedural steps to be included in the project cycle, and the mandate, composition and role of STAP;

(g) act as the focal point for the purpose of relations with the Conferences of the Parties to the conventions referred to in paragraph 6, including consideration, approval and review of the arrangements or agreements with such Conferences, receipt of guidance and recommendations from them and compliance with requirements under these arrangements or agreements for reporting to them;

(h) in accordance with paragraphs 26 and 27, ensure that GEF-financed activities relating to the conventions referred to in paragraph 6 conform with the policies, program priorities and eligibility criteria decided by the Conference of the Parties for the purposes of the convention concerned;

(i) appoint the CEO in accordance with paragraph 21, oversee the work of the Secretariat, and assign specific tasks and responsibilities to the Secretariat;

(j) review and approve the administrative budget of the GEF and arrange for periodic financial and performance audits of the Secretariat and the Implementing Agencies with regard to activities undertaken for the Facility;

(k) in accordance with paragraph 31, approve an annual report and keep the UN Commission on Sustainable Development apprised of its activities; and

(l) exercise such other operational functions as may be appropriate to fulfill the purposes of the Facility.

Secretariat

21. The GEF Secretariat shall service and report to the Assembly and the Council. The Secretariat, which shall be headed by the CEO/Chairperson of the Facility, shall be supported administratively by the World Bank and shall operate in a functionally independent and effective manner. The CEO shall be appointed to serve

for three years on a full time basis by the Council on the joint recommendation of the Implementing Agencies. Such recommendation shall be made after consultation with the Council. The CEO may be reappointed by the Council. The CEO may be removed by the Council only for cause. The staff of the Secretariat shall include staff members seconded from the Implementing Agencies as well as individuals hired competitively on an as needed basis by one of the Implementing Instrument for the Establishment of the Restructured Global Environment Facility Agencies. The CEO shall be responsible for the organization, appointment and dismissal of Secretariat staff. The CEO shall be accountable for the performance of the Secretariat functions to the Council. The Secretariat shall, on behalf of the Council, exercise the following functions:

(a) implement effectively the decisions of the Assembly and the Council;

(b) coordinate the formulation and oversee the implementation of program activities pursuant to the joint work program, ensuring liaison with other bodies as required, particularly in the context of the cooperative arrangements or agreements referred to in paragraph 27;

(c) in consultation with the Implementing Agencies, ensure the implementation of the operational policies adopted by the Council through the preparation of common guidelines on the project cycle. Such guidelines shall address project identification and development, including the proper and adequate review of project and work program proposals, consultation with and participation of local communities and other interested parties, monitoring of project implementation and evaluation of project results;

(d) review and report to the Council on the adequacy of arrangements made by the Implementing Agencies in accordance with the guidelines referred to in paragraph (c) above, and if warranted, recommend to the Council and the Implementing Agencies additional arrangements for project preparation and execution under paragraphs 20(f) and 28;

(e) chair interagency group meetings to ensure the effective execution of the Council's decisions and to facilitate coordination and collaboration among the Implementing Agencies;

(f) coordinate with the Secretariats of other relevant international bodies, in particular the Secretariats of the conventions referred to in paragraph 6, the Secretariats of the Montreal Protocol on Substances that Deplete the Ozone Layer and its Multilateral Fund and the United Nations Convention to Combat Desertification in Countries Experiencing Serious Drought and/or Desertification, Particularly in Africa;

(g) report to the Assembly, the Council and other institutions as directed by the Council;

(h) provide the Trustee with all relevant information to enable it to carry out its responsibilities; and

(i) perform any other functions assigned to the Secretariat by the Council.

Implementing Agencies

22. The Implementing Agencies of the GEF shall be UNDP, UNEP, and the World Bank. The Implementing Agencies shall be accountable to the Council for their GEF-financed activities, including the preparation and cost-effectiveness of GEF projects, and for the implementation of the operational policies, strategies and decisions of the Council within their respective areas of competence and in accordance with an interagency agreement to be concluded on the basis of the principles of cooperation set forth in Annex D to the present Instrument. The Implementing Agencies shall cooperate with the Participants, the Secretariat, parties receiving assistance under the GEF, and other interested parties, including local communities and non-governmental organizations, to promote the purposes of the Facility.

23. The CEO shall periodically convene meetings with the heads of the Implementing Agencies to promote interagency collaboration and communication, and to review operational policy issues regarding the implementation of GEF-financed activities. The CEO shall transmit their conclusions and recommendations to the Council for its consideration.

Scientific and Technical Advisory Panel (STAP)

24. UNEP shall establish, in consultation with UNDP and the World Bank and on the basis of guidelines and criteria established by the Council, the Scientific and Technical Advisory Panel (STAP) as an advisory body to the Facility. UNEP shall provide the STAP's Secretariat and shall operate as the liaison between the Facility and the STAP.

IV. Principles of Decision-Making

25. (a) Procedure

The Assembly and the Council shall each adopt by consensus regulations as may be necessary or appropriate to perform their respective functions transparently; in particular, they shall determine any aspect of their respective procedures, including the admission of observers and, in the case of the Council, provision for executive sessions.

(b) Consensus

Decisions of the Assembly and the Council shall be taken by consensus. In the case of the Council if, in the consideration of any matter of substance, all practicable efforts by the Council and its Chairperson have been made and no consensus appears attainable, any Member of the Council may require a formal vote.

(c) Formal Vote

(i) Unless otherwise provided in this Instrument, decisions requiring a formal vote by the Council shall be taken by a double weighted majority; that is, an affirmative vote representing both a 60 percent majority of the total number of Participants and a 60 percent majority of the total contributions.

(ii) Each Member of the Council shall cast the votes of the Participant or Participants he/she represents. A Member of the

Council appointed by a group of Participants may cast separately the votes of each Participant in the constituency he/she represents.

(iii) For the purpose of voting power, total contributions shall consist of the actual cumulative contributions made to the GEF Trust Fund as specified in Annex C (Attachment 1) and in subsequent replenishments of the GEF Trust Fund, contributions made to the GET, and the grant equivalent of co-financing and parallel financing made under the GEF pilot program, or agreed with the Trustee, until the effective date of the GEF Trust Fund. Until the effective date of the GEF Trust Fund, advance contributions made under paragraph 7(c) of Annex C shall be deemed to be contributions to the GET.

V. Relationship and Cooperation With Conventions

26. The Council shall ensure the effective operation of the GEF as a source of funding activities under the conventions referred to in paragraph 6. The use of the GEF resources for purposes of such conventions shall be in conformity with the policies, program priorities and eligibility criteria decided by the Conference of the Parties of each of those conventions.

27. The Council shall consider and approve cooperative arrangements or agreements with the Conferences of the Parties to the conventions referred to in paragraph 6, including reciprocal arrangements for representation in meetings. Such arrangements or agreements shall be in conformity with the relevant provisions of the convention concerned regarding its financial mechanism and shall include procedures for determining jointly the aggregate GEF funding requirements for the purpose of the convention. With regard to each convention referred to in paragraph 6, until the first meeting of its Conference of the Parties, the Council shall consult the convention's interim body.

VI. Cooperation With Other Bodies

28. The Secretariat and the Implementing Agencies under the guidance of the Council shall cooperate with other international organizations to promote achievement of the purposes of the GEF. The Implementing Agencies may make arrangements for GEF project preparation and execution by multilateral development banks, specialized agencies and programs of the United Nations, other international organizations, bilateral development agencies, national institutions, non-governmental organizations, private sector entities and academic institutions, taking into account their comparative advantages in efficient and cost-effective project execution. Such arrangements shall be made in accordance with national priorities. Pursuant to paragraph 20(f), the Council may request the Secretariat to make similar arrangements in accordance with national priorities. In the event of disagreements among the Implementing Agencies or between an Implementing Agency and any entity concerning project preparation or execution, an Implementing Agency or any entity referred to in this paragraph may request the Secretariat to seek to resolve such disagreements.

VII. Operational Modalities

29. The Secretariat shall coordinate the preparation of and determine the content of a joint work program for the GEF among the Implementing Agencies, including an indication of the financial resources required for the program, for approval by the Council. The work program shall be prepared in accordance with paragraph 4 and in cooperation with eligible recipients and any executing agency referred to in paragraph 28.

30. GEF projects shall be subject to endorsement by the CEO before final project approval. If at least four Council Members request that a project be reviewed at a Council meeting because in their view the project is not consistent with the Instrument or GEF policies and procedures, the CEO shall submit the project document to the next Council meeting, and shall only endorse the project for final approval by the Implementing Agency if the Council finds that the project is consistent with the Instrument and GEF policies and procedures.

VIII. Reporting

31. The Council shall approve an annual report on the activities of the GEF. The report shall be prepared by the Secretariat and circulated to all Participants. It shall contain information on the activities carried out under the GEF, including a list of project ideas submitted for consideration and a review of the project activities funded by the Facility and their outcomes. The report shall contain all the information necessary to meet the principles of accountability and transparency that shall characterize the Facility as well as the requirements arising from the reporting arrangements agreed with each Conference of the Parties to the conventions referred to in paragraph 6. The report shall be conveyed to each of these Conferences of the Parties, the United Nations Commission on Sustainable Development and any other international organization deemed appropriate by the Council.

IX. Transitional and Final Provisions

Termination of the GET

32. The World Bank shall be invited to terminate the existing Global Environment Trust Fund (GET) on the effective date of the establishment of the new GEF Trust Fund, and any funds, receipts, assets and liabilities held in the GET upon termination, including the administration of any cofinancing by the Trustee in accordance with the provisions of Resolution No. 91-5 of the Executive Directors of the World Bank, shall be transferred to the new GEF Trust Fund. Pending the termination of the GET under this provision, projects financed from the GET resources shall continue to be processed and approved subject to the rules and procedures applicable to the GET.

INTERIM PERIOD

33. The Council may, pursuant to the provisions of this Instrument, be convened during the period from the adoption of this Instrument and its annexes by the Implementing Agencies until the effective date of the establishment of the new GEF Trust Fund: (a) to appoint, by consensus, the CEO in order to enable him/her to assume the work of the Secretariat; and (b) to prepare the Council's rules of procedure and the operational modalities for the Facility. The first meeting of the Council shall be organized by the secretariat of the GEF pilot program. Administrative expenses during this interim period shall be covered by the existing GET.

AMENDMENT AND TERMINATION

34. Amendment or termination of the present Instrument may be approved by consensus by the Assembly upon the recommendation of the Council, after taking into account the views of the Implementing Agencies and the Trustee, and shall become effective after adoption by the Implementing Agencies and the Trustee in accordance with their respective rules and procedural requirements. This paragraph shall apply to the amendment of any annex to this Instrument unless the annex concerned provides otherwise.

35. The Trustee may at any time terminate its role as trustee in accordance with paragraph 14 of Annex B, and an Implementing Agency may at any time terminate its role as implementing agency, after consultation with the other Implementing Agencies and after giving the Council six months' notice in writing.

ANNEX A

Notification of Participation/Termination of Participation [1]

The Government of ____________________ hereby notifies the Chief Executive Officer of the Global Environment Facility ("the Facility") that it will participate [terminate its participation] in the Facility.

____________ ____________________________________

(Date) (Name and Office)

ANNEX B

Role and Fiduciary Responsibilities of the Trustee of the GEF Trust Fund

1. The World Bank shall be the Trustee of the GEF Trust Fund (the Fund) referred to in paragraph 8 of the Instrument and in this capacity shall, as legal owner, hold in trust the funds, assets and receipts which constitute the Fund, and manage and use them only for the purpose of, and in accordance with, the provisions of the Instrument keeping them separate and apart from all other accounts and assets of, or administered by, the Trustee.

[1] The notification is to be signed on behalf of the Government by a duly authorized representative thereof. Participation, and termination of participation, will take effect upon deposit of the notification with the CEO. In the case of a State contributing to the GEF Trust Fund, an instrument of commitment (Attachment 2 of Annex C) shall be deemed to serve as a notification of participation.

2. The Trustee shall be accountable to the Council for the performance of its fiduciary responsibilities as set forth in this Annex.

3. The Trustee shall administer the Fund in accordance with the applicable provisions of the Instrument and such decisions as the Council may take under the Instrument and shall be bound in the performance of its duties by the applicable provisions of the Trustee's Articles of Agreement, by-laws, rules and decisions (hereinafter referred to as "the rules of the Trustee").

4. The responsibilities of the Trustee shall include in particular:

(a) the mobilization of resources for the Fund and the preparation of such studies and arrangements as may be required for this purpose;

(b) the financial management of the Fund, including the investment of its liquid assets, the disbursement of funds to the implementing and other executing agencies as well as the preparation of the financial reports regarding the investment and use of the Fund's resources;

(c) the maintenance of appropriate records and accounts of the Fund, and providing for their audit, in accordance with the rules of the Trustee; and

(d) the monitoring of the application of budgetary and project funds in accordance with paragraph 21(h) of the Instrument and paragraph 11 of this Annex so as to ensure that the resources of the Fund are being used in accordance with the Instrument and the decisions taken by the Council, including the regular reporting to the Council on the status of the Fund's resources.

5. The Trustee shall exercise the same care in the discharge of its functions under this Annex as it exercises with respect to its own affairs and shall have no further liability in respect thereof. To this end, the Trustee shall apply such considerations of economy and efficiency as may be required for the investment and disbursement of funds from the Fund, consistent with the rules of the Trustee and the decisions of the Council.

6. All amounts in respect of which the Trustee is authorized to make commitments or disbursements under the Instrument shall be used by the Trustee on the basis of the work program approved by the Council for the activities of the Facility, including the reasonable expenses incurred by the Implementing Agencies and any executing agency in the performance of their responsibilities, in accordance with the Instrument and the decisions taken by the Council. All amounts in respect of which the Trustee is authorized to make transfers to the Implementing Agencies and any executing agency shall be transferred as agreed between the Trustee and the transferee.

7. The Trustee may enter into arrangements and agreements with any national or international entity as may be needed in order to administer and manage financing for the purpose of, and on terms consistent with, the Instrument. Upon the request of the Council, the Trustee will, for the purposes of paragraph 27 of the Instrument, formalize the arrangements or agreements that have been considered and approved by the Council with the Conferences of the Parties of the conventions referred to in paragraph 6 of the Instrument.

8. Pending transfers to the Implementing Agencies or an executing agency, the Trustee may invest the funds held in the Fund in such form as it may decide, including pooled investments (in which separate accounts shall be held for the funds of the Fund) with other funds owned, or administered, by it. The income of such investments shall be credited to the Fund, and the Trustee shall be reimbursed annually from the resources of the Fund for the reasonable expenses incurred by it for the administration of the Fund and for expenses incurred in administratively supporting the Secretariat. The reimbursement shall be made on the basis of estimated cost, subject to end of year adjustment.

9. The Trustee shall make all necessary arrangements to avoid commitments on behalf of the Fund in excess of the resources available to such Fund.

10. In order to enable the Trustee to carry out its functions enumerated in this Annex, the Chief Executive Officer of the Facility (CEO) shall cooperate fully with the Trustee and shall observe the rules of the Trustee specified in paragraph 3 above, in the activities of the Secretariat relating to the administration of the Fund under the provisions of the Instrument and its Annexes.

11. To ensure that the resources of the Fund are being used in accordance with the Instrument and the decisions taken by the Council, the Trustee shall work with the Implementing Agencies and the CEO to address and resolve any concerns it may have about inconsistencies between the uses of Fund resources and such Instrument and decisions. The CEO shall inform the Council of any concerns that the Trustee or an Implementing Agency may have which are not satisfactorily resolved.

12. Should it appear to the Council or the Trustee that there is an inconsistency between the decisions of the Council and the rules of the Trustee, the Council and the Trustee shall consult each other with a view to avoiding the inconsistency.

13. The privileges and immunities accorded to the Trustee under its Articles of Agreement shall apply to the property, assets, archives, income, operations and transactions of the Fund.

14. The provisions of this Annex may be amended by the Executive Directors of the Trustee only with the agreement of the Council and the other Implementing Agencies. The provisions of this Annex may be terminated when the Executive Directors of the Trustee so decide after consultation with the Council and the other Implementing Agencies and after giving the Council six months' notice in writing. In case of termination, the Trustee shall take all necessary action for winding up its activities in an expeditious manner, in accordance with such decision. The decision shall also provide for meeting the commitments of the Facility already made for grants and transfers, and for the disposition of any remaining funds, receipts, assets or liabilities of the Fund upon termination.

Annex C

GEF Trust Fund: Financial Provisions for Replenishment

Contributions

1. The Bank, acting as Trustee for the GEF Trust Fund, is authorized to accept contributions to the Fund for the period from July 1, 1994 to June 30, 1997:

(a) by way of grant from each Participant in the amount specified for each participant in Attachment 1; and

(b) other contributions on terms consistent with the present Annex.

Instruments of Commitment

2. (a) Participants contributing to the GEF Trust Fund (Contributing Participants) shall be expected to deposit with the Trustee an instrument of commitment substantially in the form set out in Attachment 2 (Instrument of Commitment).

(b) When a Contributing Participant agrees to pay a part of its contribution without qualification and the remainder is subject to enactment by its legislature of the necessary appropriation legislation, it shall deposit a qualified instrument of commitment in a form acceptable to the Trustee (Qualified Instrument of Commitment); such Participant undertakes to exercise its best efforts to obtain legislative approval for the full amount of its contribution by the payment dates set out in paragraph 3.

3. (a) Contributions to the GEF Trust Fund under paragraph 1 (a) shall be paid, at the option of each Contributing Participant, in cash by November 30, 1994 or in installments.

(b) Payment in cash under paragraph (a) above shall be made on terms agreed between the Contributing Participant and the Trustee that shall be no less favorable to the GEF Trust Fund than payment in installment.

(c) Payment in installments that a Contributing Participant agrees to make without qualification shall be paid to the Trustee in four equal installments by November 30, 1994, November 30, 1995, November 30, 1996 and November 30, 1997, provided that:

(i) the Trustee and each Contributing Participant may agree to earlier payment;

(ii) if the GEF Trust Fund shall not have become effective by October 31, 1994, payment of the first such installment may be postponed by the Contributing Participant for not more than 30 days after the date on which this Annex becomes effective;

(iii) the Trustee may agree to postpone the payment of any installment, or part thereof, if the amount paid, together with any unused balance of previous payments by the Contributing Participant, shall be at least equal to the amount estimated by the Trustee to be required from the Contributing Participant, up to the date of the next installment, for meeting commitments under the GEF Trust Fund; and

(iv) if any Contributing Participant shall deposit an Instrument of Commitment with the Trustee after the date on which the first installment of the contributions is due, payment of any installment, or part thereof, shall be made to the Trustee within 30 days after the date of such deposit.

(d) If a Contributing Participant has deposited a Qualified Instrument of Commitment and thereafter notifies the Trustee that an installment, or part thereof, is unqualified after the date when it was due, then payment of such installment, or part thereof, shall be made within 30 days of such notification.

Mode of Payment in Installments

4. (a) Payments shall be made, at the option of each Contributing Participant, in cash on terms agreed between the Contributing Participant and the Trustee that shall be no less favorable to the GEF Trust Fund than payment in installments or by the deposit of notes or similar obligations issued by the government of the Contributing Participant or the depository designated by the Contributing Participant, which shall be nonnegotiable, non-interest bearing and payable at their par value on demand to the account of the Trustee.

(b) The Trustee shall encash the notes or similar obligations quarterly in equal proportions in terms of their unit of denomination, as needed for disbursement and transfers referred to in paragraph 8 and the operational and administrative requirements for liquidity of the Trustee and the Implementing Agencies, as determined by the Trustee. At the request of a Contributing Participant that is also an eligible recipient under the GEF Trust Fund, the Trustee may permit postponement of encashment for up to two years in light of exceptionally difficult budgetary circumstances of the Contributing Participant.

(c) In respect of each contribution under paragraph 1 (b), payment shall be made in accordance with the terms on which such contributions are accepted by the Trustee.

Currency of Denomination and Payment

5. (a) Contributing Participants shall denominate their contributions in Special Drawing Rights (SDRs) or a currency that is freely convertible as determined by the Trustee, except that if a Contributing Participant's economy experienced a rate of inflation in excess of fifteen percent per annum on average in the period 1990 to 1992 as determined by the Trustee as of the date of adoption of this Annex, its contribution shall be denominated in SDRs.

(b) Contributing Participants shall make payments in SDRs, a currency used for the valuation of the SDR, or with the agreement of the Trustee in another freely convertible currency, and the Trustee may exchange the amounts received for such currencies as it may decide.

(c) Each Contributing Participant shall maintain, in respect of its currency paid to the Trustee and the currency of such Contributing Participant derived therefrom, the same convertibility as existed on the date of adoption of this Annex.

Effective Date

6. (a) The GEF Trust Fund shall become effective and the resources to be contributed pursuant to this Annex shall become payable to the Trustee on the date when Contributing Participants

whose contributions aggregate not less than SDR 980.53 million shall have deposited with the Trustee Instruments of Commitment or Qualified Instruments of Commitment (the effective date), provided that this date shall not be later than October 31, 1994, or such later date as the Trustee may determine.

(b) If the Trustee determines that the effective date is likely to be unduly delayed, it shall convene promptly a meeting of the Contributing Participants to review the situation and to consider the steps to be taken to prevent an interruption of GEF financing.

ADVANCE CONTRIBUTION

7. (a) In order to avoid an interruption in the GEF's ability to make financing commitments pending the effectiveness of the GEF Trust Fund, and if the Trustee will have received Instruments of Commitment from Contributing Participants whose contributions aggregate not less than SDR 280.15 million, the Trustee may deem, prior to the effective date, one-quarter of the total amount of each contribution for which an Instrument of Commitment has been deposited with the Trustee as an advance contribution, unless the Contributing Participant specifies otherwise in its Instrument of Commitment. Advance contributions shall be paid to the GEF under Resolution 91–5 adopted by the Executive Directors of the World Bank and shall be governed by the provisions of that Resolution until the effective date.

(b) The Trustee shall specify when advance contributions pursuant to paragraph (a) above are to be paid to the Trustee.

(c) The terms and conditions applicable to contributions under this Annex shall apply also to advance contributions until the effective date, when such contributions shall be deemed to constitute payment towards the amount due from each Contributing Participant for its contribution.

COMMITMENT OR TRANSFER AUTHORITY

8. (a) Contributions shall become available for commitment by the Trustee, for disbursement or transfer as needed pursuant to the work program approved by the Council under paragraph 20(c) of the Instrument, upon receipt of payment by the Trustee, except as provided in subparagraph (c) below.

(b) The Trustee shall promptly inform Contributing Participants if a Participant that has deposited a Qualified Instrument of Commitment and whose contribution represents more than 20 percent of the total amount of the resources to be contributed pursuant to this Annex has not unqualified at least 50 percent of the total amount of its contribution by November 30, 1995, or 30 days after the effective date, whichever is later, and at least 75 percent of the total amount of its contribution by November 30, 1996, or 30 days after the effective date, whichever is later, and the total amount thereof by November 30, 1997, or 30 days after the effective date, whichever is later.

(c) Within 30 days of the dispatch of notice by the Trustee under paragraph (b) above, each other Contributing Participant may notify the Trustee in writing that the commitment by the Trustee of the second, third or fourth tranche, whichever is applicable, of such

Participant's contribution shall be deferred while, and to the extent that, any part of the contribution referred to in subparagraph (b) remains qualified; during such period, the Trustee shall make no commitments in respect of the resources to which the notice pertains unless the right of the Contributing Participant is waived pursuant to paragraph (d) below.

(d) The right of a Contributing Participant under paragraph (c) above may be waived in writing, and it shall be deemed waived if the Trustee receives no written notice pursuant to such subparagraph within the period specified therein.

(e) The Trustee shall consult with the Contributing Participants where, in its judgment:

(i) there is a substantial likelihood that the total amount of the contribution referred to in paragraph (b) above could not be committed to the Trustee without qualification by June 30, 1998, or

(ii) as a result of Contributing Participants exercising their rights under paragraph (b), the Trustee is or may shortly be precluded from entering into new commitments for disbursement or transfer.

(f) Commitment and transfer authority shall be increased by:

(i) the income of investment of resources held in the GEF Trust Fund pending disbursement or transfer by the Trustee;

(ii) uncommitted resources transferred to the Trustee upon termination of the GET;

(iii) the amount of undisbursed commitments that have been cancelled; and

(iv) payments received by the Trustee as repayment, interest or charges on loans made by the GEF Trust Fund.

(g) Commitment and transfer authority shall be reduced for the reimbursement of administrative costs charged against the resources of the GEF Trust Fund, as determined by the Trustee on the basis of the work program and budget approved by the Council.

(h) The Trustee may enter into agreements to provide financing from the GEF Trust Fund, conditional on such financing becoming effective and binding on the GEF Trust Fund when resources become available for commitment by the Trustee.

Annex C—Attachment 1

Global Environment Facility Trust Fund

Contributions (in millions)

Contributing Participants	SDR Amounts	National Currency Amounts [a]
Group I [b, c]		
Australia	20.84	42.76
Austria	14.28	231.51
Canada	61.78	111.11
Denmark	25.08	§
Finland	15.45	124.00
France	102.26	806.71
Germany	171.30	394.76

Global Environment Facility Trust Fund—Continued

Contributions (in millions)

Contributing Participants	SDR Amounts	National Currency Amounts [a]
Italy	81.86	159,803.25
Japan	295.95	45,698.09
Netherlands	50.97	§
New Zealand	4.00	10.35
Norway	21.93	216.42
Portugal	4.00	§
Spain	12.36	2,180.10
Sweden	41.60	450.04
Group II [b]		
Brazil	4.00	§
China	4.00	§
Côte d'Ivoire	4.00	§
Egypt	4.00	§
India	6.00	
Mexico	4.00	§
Pakistan	4.00	
Turkey	4.00	§
Group III [b]		
Ireland	1.71	1.64
Other*	6.48	
Unallocated**	42.83	

[a] Calculated by converting the SDR amount to the national currency using an average of daily exchange rates over the period February 1, 1993, to October 31, 1993.

[b] Group I consists of non-recipient donors that participated in the replenishment meetings. Group II consists of recipient donors that participated in the replenishment meetings. Group III consists of other donors.

[c] The following table shows background information and explanations regarding the breakdown of Group I contributions according to contributions based on IDA10 basic shares, Supplementary Contributions towards meeting adjusted IDA10 shares, and additional Supplementary Contributions.

*Includes the enhanced value of contributions through accelerated encashments, not included in the figures above and new and additional contributions made to the GET and expected to be available for the GEF I.

**It is expected that other donors will make contributions amounting to US$60 million (SDR 42.83 million), which represents 3% of the original replenishment target of US$2,000 million.

§ These countries are denominating their contributions in SDRs.

‡ Calculated by converting the SDR amount into US$, using an average of daily exchange rates over the period February 1, 1993, to October 31, 1993.[2]

Explanatory Note: Donors agreed that a core replenishment of US$2 billion (SDR 1427.52 million) should be built on IDA10 shares. Since IDA10 basic shares of non-recipient donors participating in the replenishment meetings add up to 87.81% in order to avoid a funding gap, IDA10 basic shares were adjusted on a prorata basis to increase the shares of non-recipient donors participating in the replenishment meetings to 95% with the remaining

[2] No such corresponding symbol appears in Annex C, Attachment 1 chart.

5% set aside for nonrecipient donors not participating in the replenishment discussions, as well as for recipient donors. Donors agreed to aim to make basic contributions to the GEF Trust Fund in accordance with these adjusted shares. The first column shows contributions based on IDA10 basic shares. Column 3 shows additional contributions towards reaching the adjusted IDA10 shares.

Contributions to the Global Environment Facility Trust Fund

Background Information

Contributing Participants	Contributions based on IDA 10 Basic Shares		Supplementary Contributions towards meeting adj. IDA 10 shares SDR m	Additional Supplementary Contributions SDR m	Total Contributions	
	SDR m	% [a]			SDR millions	National Currency millions [b]
Australia	20.84	1.46	....	....	20.84	42.76
Austria	12.85	0.90	1.05	0.37	14.28	231.51
Canada	57.10	4.00	4.68	....	61.78	111.11
Denmark	18.56	1.30	1.52	5.00	25.08	§
Finland	14.28	1.00	1.17	....	15.45	124.00
France*	100.21	7.02	2.05	....	102.26	806.71
Germany	157.03	11.00	12.86	1.41	171.30	394.76
Italy	75.66	5.30	6.20	....	81.86‡	159,803.25
Japan	266.95	18.70	21.86	7.14	295.95	45,698.09
Netherlands	47.11	3.30	3.86	....	50.97	§
New Zealand	1.71	0.12	0.14	2.15	4.00	10.35
Norway	20.27	1.42	1.66	....	21.93	216.42
Portugal	1.71	0.12	0.14	2.15	4.00	§
Spain	11.42	0.80	0.94	....	12.36	2,180.10
Sweden	37.40	2.62	3.06	1.14	41.60	450.04
Switzerland	24.84	1.74	2.03	5.10	31.97	§
United Kingdom	87.79	6.15	7.19	1.06	96.04	89.55
United States	297.78	20.86	9.14	....	306.92	430.00

[a] IDA10 basic shares as agreed by IDA deputies in December 1992.

[b] Calculated by converting the SDR amount of the total contribution to the national currency, using an average of daily exchange rates over the period February 1, 1993, to October 31, 1993.

‡ This SDR amount includes the effect of early encashment.

§ These countries are denominating their contributions in SDRs.

*At the 12-month exchange rate, from November 1, 1992–October 31, 1993, the total contribution of French francs (FF) 806.71 million to the GEF Trust Fund is equivalent to SDR 103.58 million. The IDA10 basic share is SDR 100.50 million; hence the supplementary contribution is SDR 3.08 million.

Memorandum Item: In addition to the above contributions, the following countries have indicated their intention to provide cofinancing or parallel financing on grant or concessional terms in support of the GEF: Austria (SDR 6 million); Denmark; France (FF 440 million); and Norway.

ANNEX C—ATTACHMENT 2

Global Environment Facility Trust Fund

Instrument of Commitment

Reference is made to Resolution No. 94–2 of the Executive Directors of the International Bank for Reconstruction and Development entitled "Global Environment Facility Trust Fund: Restructuring and First Replenishment of the Global Environment Facility," which was adopted on May 24, 1994 ("the Resolution").

The Government of ____________________ hereby notifies the Bank as Trustee of the Global Environment Facility Trust Fund that it will participate in the Global Environment Facility Trust Fund and pursuant to paragraph 2(a) of Annex C of the Instrument referred to in paragraph 1 of the Resolution it will make the contribution authorized for it in accordance with the terms of the Resolution in the amount of ____________________.

____________ ________________________________

(Date) (Name and Office)

ANNEX D

Principles of Cooperation Among the Implementing Agencies

I. GENERAL PRINCIPLES

1. At the United Nations Conference on Environment and Development, Governments recognized that new forms of cooperation are required to achieve better integration among national and local government, industry, science, environmental groups and the public in developing and implementing effective approaches to integrating environment and development. The responsibility for bringing about changes lies primarily with Governments in consultation with national major groups and local communities, and in collaboration with national, regional and international organizations, including in particular UNDP, UNEP and the World Bank.

2. In this context, the GEF has a special role to play in providing new and additional grant and concessional funding to meet the agreed incremental costs of measures to achieve agreed global environmental benefits in accordance with paragraphs 2 and 3 of the Instrument.

3. By designating UNDP, UNEP and the World Bank as the Implementing Agencies of the GEF, the Participants have recognized that the three agencies have key roles to play in the implementation of GEF-financed activities within their respective spheres of competence, and in facilitating cooperation in GEF-financed activities by multilateral development banks, United Nations agencies and programs, other international institutions, national institutions and bilateral development agencies, local communities, nongovernmental organizations, the private sector and the academic community in accordance with paragraph 28 of the Instrument.

4. For their part, the three agencies recognize the need for institutional arrangements in conformity with, and providing input to

the fulfillment of, GEF objectives, based on a results oriented approach and in a spirit of partnership, and consistent with the principles of universality, democracy, transparency, cost-effectiveness and accountability.

5. The Implementing Agencies will put these principles into practice by ensuring the development and implementation of programs and projects which are country-driven and based on national priorities designed to support sustainable development. Actions needed to attain global environmental benefits are strongly influenced by existing national policies and sub regional and regional cooperative mechanisms. GEF financing will need to be coordinated with appropriate national policies and strategies as well as with development financing. To the extent that the GEF operates a funding mechanism for global environmental conventions, the Implementing Agencies will focus on joint programming and implementation with eligible countries, either directly or, where appropriate, at a sub regional or regional level, of the program priorities and criteria adopted by the Conference of the Parties to each Convention.

6. In developing joint work programs and in project preparation, the Implementing Agencies will, through country-driven initiatives, collaborate with eligible countries in the identification of projects for GEF funding through a jointly operated Project Preparation Assistance Program. Priority will be given to integrating global environmental concerns with national ones in the framework of national sustainable development strategies.

7. The Implementing Agencies will ensure the cost-effectiveness and sustainability of their activities in addressing the targeted global environmental issues. In this context, one important feature of adhering to these principles is that the least-cost sustainable means of meeting many global environmental objectives lie in a combination of investment, technical assistance, and policy actions at the national and regional level. The experience and mandate of each Implementing Agency will contribute to bringing to light, when assessing specific project interventions, the range of possible policy, technical assistance and investment options. In addition, each Implementing Agency will strive to promote measures to achieve global environmental benefits within the context of its regular work programs.

8. The Implementing Agencies are committed to facilitating continued effective participation, as appropriate, of major groups and local communities and to promoting opportunities for mobilizing outside resources in support of GEF activities.

9. Collaboration among the Implementing Agencies will be sufficiently flexible to promote introduction of modifications as the need arises. Within an overall cooperative framework, the Implementing Agencies will strive for innovative approaches to strengthening their collaboration and effectiveness, in particular at the country level, and an efficient division of labor that maximizes the synergy among them and recognizes their terms of reference and comparative advantages.

II. Emphasis of Each Implementing Agency

10. The Implementing Agencies recognize that in carrying out their responsibilities there will be areas of shared interest and work effort focusing primarily on the integration of GEF objectives and activities with national sustainable development strategies. In addition to collaboration in promoting an efficient and effective response to issues of shared interest, the agencies' partnership will recognize distinctive areas of emphasis.

11. Areas of particular emphasis for each of the Implementing Agencies will be as follows:

(a) UNDP will play the primary role in ensuring the development and management of capacity building programs and technical assistance projects. Through its global network of field offices, UNDP will draw upon its experience in human resources development, institutional strengthening, and non-governmental and community participation to assist countries in promoting, designing and implementing activities consistent with the purpose of the GEF and national sustainable development strategies. Also drawing on its intercountry programming experience, UNDP will contribute to the development of regional and global projects within the GEF work program in cooperation with the other Implementing Agencies.

(b) UNEP will play the primary role in catalyzing the development of scientific and technical analysis and in advancing environmental management in GEF-financed activities. UNEP will provide guidance on relating the GEF-financed activities to global, regional and national environmental assessments, policy frameworks and plans, and to international environmental agreements. UNEP will also be responsible for establishing and supporting the Scientific and Technical Advisory Panel (STAP) as an advisory body to the GEF.

(c) The World Bank will play the primary role in ensuring the development and management of investment projects. The World Bank will draw upon its investment experience in eligible countries to promote investment opportunities and to mobilize private sector resources that are consistent with GEF objectives and national sustainable development strategies.

III. Process of Collaboration

12. The Implementing Agencies will be accountable to the Council for their GEF-financed activities in accordance with paragraph 22 of the Instrument.

13. Responsibility for facilitating and coordinating GEF-financed activities will be vested in the Secretariat in accordance with paragraph 21 of the Instrument. The Secretariat, in addition to servicing the Assembly and the Council, will provide a focal point for coordinating the GEF-financed activities of the Implementing Agencies, including interaction of the Implementing Agencies with the Council, coordination of the preparation of the GEF joint work program, oversight of the implementation of program activities pursuant to the joint work program, preparation and monitoring of budgets, and ensuring liaison with other bodies as appropriate.

14. In order to facilitate the collaboration between the agencies and ensure the effective development and execution of the GEF joint work program, an ongoing interagency process is essential. Such a process will be embodied in an interagency committee, which will function on two distinct levels:

(a) As an institutionalized high-level forum focusing on strategic operational issues, common direction and broad guidance of the interagency collaborative process. This forum will consist of the heads of agency or their representatives and will be convened by the Chief Executive Officer of the Facility (CEO). It will meet regularly as needed, and no less than once a year.

(b) As a staff level interagency group which will collaborate with the Secretariat in the preparation of a joint work program, focus on all pertinent issues concerning the operations of the Facility, its projects, communication and outreach, and other initiatives. This interagency group will be chaired by the Secretariat in accordance with paragraph 21(e) of the Instrument. Other ad hoc interagency groups may be established as deemed necessary.

ANNEX E

Constituencies of the GEF Council

1. GEF Participants shall be grouped in 32 constituencies, with 18 constituencies composed of recipient countries (referred to as "recipient constituencies"), and 14 constituencies composed principally of non-recipient countries (referred to as "non-recipient constituencies").

2. The 18 recipient constituencies shall be distributed among the following geographic regions, bearing in mind the possibility of mixed constituencies:

Africa 6
Asia and Pacific 6
Latin America and Caribbean 4
Central, Eastern Europe and Former Soviet Union 2

3. For each geographic region referred to in paragraph 2, recipient constituencies shall be formed through a process of consultation among the GEF recipient country Participants in the region in accordance with their own criteria. It is expected that in this consultation process a number of criteria will be taken into account, including:

(a) Equitable and balanced representation from within the geographic region;

(b) Commonality of global, regional and sub regional environmental concerns;

(c) Policies and efforts towards sustainable development;

(d) Natural resource endowment and environmental vulnerability;

(e) Contributions to the GEF as defined in paragraph 25(c) (iii) of the Instrument; and

(f) All other relevant and environment-related factors.

4. The non-recipient constituencies shall be formed through a process of consultation among interested Participants. It is expected that grouping of non-recipient countries will be primarily

guided by total contributions as defined in paragraph 25(c) (iii) of the Instrument.

5. Consultations to form the constituencies shall take place following the acceptance of the Instrument by representatives of the States participating in the GEF. The GEF Secretariat will provide assistance to facilitate these consultations at the regional level. The Secretariat shall be informed of the initial composition of each constituency no later than May 15, 1994.

6. The grouping of constituencies as communicated to the Secretariat, including any adjustments pursuant to paragraph 8 of this Annex, shall be subject to confirmation by the Council after the effective date of the establishment of the GEF Trust Fund, taking into account the instruments deposited in accordance with Annex A to the Instrument.

7. The Participant or Participants in each constituency shall appoint a Member and an Alternate to represent the constituency in the Council. The names and addresses of the Members and Alternates for each constituency shall be communicated to the Secretariat no later than two weeks prior to the first meeting of the Council pursuant to paragraph 33 of the Instrument, and shall be subject to confirmation by the Participant or Participants in each constituency upon the confirmation of the constituencies by the Council under paragraph 6 above.

8. Any State that becomes a Participant in accordance with paragraph 7 of the Instrument after the formation of constituencies pursuant to paragraphs 3 to 6 above shall, after consultation with the Participants in the constituency concerned, notify the Secretariat as regards the constituency in which it wishes to be grouped and shall be grouped in that constituency subject to agreement by the Participants in that constituency and subsequent confirmation by the Council at its next meeting.

9. Each Council Member or Alternate shall represent the Participant or Participants in the constituency by which that Member or Alternate was appointed, subject to any adjustments pursuant to paragraph 8 above, and any termination of participation in accordance with paragraph 7 of the Instrument.

10. If the office of a Council Member or Alternate becomes vacant before the expiration of the term of office of the Member or Alternate, the Participant or Participants in the constituency concerned shall appoint a new Member or Alternate, whose name and address shall be communicated to the Secretariat no later than two weeks prior to the next meeting of the Council.

11. In accordance with paragraph 25(a) of the Instrument, the Council may adopt procedures to give effect to the provisions of this Annex.

7. Articles of Agreement Establishing the Inter-American Development Bank (Amended)

CONTENTS

7. Articles of Agreement Establishing the Inter-American Development Bank (Amended)[1]

Done at Washington, April 8, 1959; Instrument of acceptance by the United States deposited with the General Secretariat of the Organization of American States, October 14, 1959; Entered into force, December 30, 1959; Amended[2] January 28, 1964, March 31, 1968, March 23, 1972, June 1, 1976, and January 27, 1977

The countries on whose behalf this Agreement is signed agree to create the Inter-American Development Bank, which shall operate in accordance with the following provisions:

ARTICLE I. PURPOSE AND FUNCTIONS

SECTION 1. PURPOSE

The purpose of the Bank shall be to contribute to the acceleration of the process of economic and social[3] development of the regional developing[3] member countries, individually and collectively.

SECTION 2. FUNCTIONS

(a) To implement its purpose, the Bank shall have the following functions:

(i) to promote the investment of public and private capital for development purposes;

(ii) to utilize its own capital, funds raised by it in financial markets, and other available resources, for financing the development of the member countries, giving priority to those loans and guarantees that will contribute most effectively to their economic growth;

(iii) to encourage private investment in projects, enterprises, and activities contributing to economic development and to supplement private investment when private capital is not available on reasonable terms and conditions;

(iv) to cooperate with the member countries to orient their development policies toward a better utilization of their resources, in a manner consistent with the objectives of making their economies more complementary and of fostering the orderly growth of their foreign trade; and

---

[1] 10 UST 3029; TIAS 4387; 389 UNTS 69. For a list of states that are parties to this Agreement, see Department of State publication, *Treaties in Force.*

[2] Amendments:

January 28, 1964 (21 UST 1570; TIAS 6920); Entered into force April 28, 1964.
March 31, 1968 (19 UST 7381; TIAS 6591); Entered into force June 30, 1968.
March 23, 1972 (23 UST 2455; TIAS 7437; 851 UNTS 283); Entered into force March 27, 1972.
June 1, 1976 (27 UST 3547; TIAS 8383); Entered into force June 1, 1976.
January 27, 1977 (TIAS).

[3] Action of the Board of Governors on June 1, 1976 (TIAS 8383) amended sec. 1 by adding the words "and social" and "regional developing".

(v) to provide technical assistance for the preparation, financing, and implementation of development plans and projects, including the study of priorities and the formulation of specific project proposals.

(b) In carrying out its functions, the Bank shall cooperate as far as possible with national and international institutions and the private sources supplying investment capital.

ARTICLE II. MEMBERSHIP IN AND CAPITAL OF THE BANK

SECTION 1. MEMBERSHIP

(a) The original members of the Bank shall be those members of the Organization of American States which, by the date specified in Article XV, Section 1(a), shall accept membership in the Bank.

(b)[4] Membership shall be open to other members of the Organization of American States and to Canada, Bahamas and Guyana, at such times and in accordance with such terms as the Bank may determine.

Nonregional countries which are members of the International Monetary Fund, and Switzerland, may also be admitted to the Bank, at such times, and under such general rules as the Board of Governors shall have established. Such general rules may be amended only by decision of the Board of Governors by a two-thirds majority of the total number of governors, including two-thirds of the governors of nonregional members, representing not less than three-fourths of the total voting power of the member countries.

SECTION 1A.[5] CATEGORIES OF RESOURCES

The resources of the Bank shall consist of the ordinary capital resources, provided for in this article, and the inter-regional capital resources, provided for in Article IIA, and the resources of the Fund for Special Operations established by Article IV (hereinafter called the Fund).

SECTION 2.[6] AUTHORIZED ORDINARY CAPITAL

(a) The authorized ordinary capital stock of the Bank initially shall be in the amount of eight hundred fifty million dollars ($850,000,000)[7] in terms of United States dollars of the weight and fineness in effect on January 1, 1959 and shall be divided into 85,000 shares having a par value of $10,000 each, which shall be

---

[4] Action of the Board of Governors on March 23, 1972 (TIAS 7437) amended subsec. (b); further amended and restated on June 1, 1976 (TIAS 8383).

[5] Action of the Board of Governors on June 1, 1976 (TIAS 8383) added sec. 1A.

[6] Action of the Board of Governors on June 1, 1976 (TIAS 8383) amended sec. 2.

[7] On January 28, 1964, the Board of Governors increased the authorized capital stock of the Bank to two billion one hundred and fifty million dollars ($2,150,000,000); on June 20, 1968, to three billion one hundred and fifty million dollars ($3,150,000,000); and on December 30, 1971, to five billion one hundred and fifty million dollars ($5,150,000,000). Due to the devaluation of the U.S. dollar and other member currency, a special adjustment process occurred during 1972 and 1973 which increased the resources available for ordinary capital lending to $6.2 billion (as of December 31, 1974, in terms of current U.S. dollars). In 1976, the authorized ordinary capital of the Bank was again increased by $2.9 billion bringing the total to $9.1 billion. In 1979, the ordinary capital of the Bank was increased by $8 billion. In 1983, the authorized capital stock (ordinary and inter-regional capital resources) was increased by an additional $15 billion with the approval of the Sixth General Increase of Resources for the period 1983 through 1986. In April 1989, as part of the seventh replenishment, the ordinary capital stock was increased by $26.5 billion. In April 1995, as part of the eighth replenishment, the ordinary capital stock was increased by $40 billion, bringing the total to $101 billion.

available for subscription by members in accordance with Section 3 of this article.

(b) The authorized ordinary capital stock shall be divided into paid-in shares and callable shares. The equivalent of four hundred million dollars ($400,000,000) shall be paid in, and four hundred fifty million dollars ($450,000,000) shall be callable for the purposes specified in Section 4(a)(ii) of this article.

(c) The ordinary capital stock indicated in (a) of this section shall be increased by five hundred million dollars ($500,000,000) in terms of United States dollars of the weight and fineness existing on January 1, 1959, provided that:

(i) the date for payment of all subscriptions established in accordance with Section 4 of this article shall have passed; and

(ii) a regular or special meeting of the Board of Governors, held as soon as possible after the date referred to in subparagraph (i) of this paragraph, shall have approved the above-mentioned increase of five hundred million dollars ($500,000,000) by a three-fourths majority of the total voting power of the member countries.

(d) The increase of capital stock provided for in the preceding paragraph shall be in the form of callable capital.

(e) Notwithstanding the provisions of paragraphs (c) and (d) of this section and subject to the provisions of Article VIII, Section 4(b), the authorized ordinary capital stock may be increased when the Board of Governors deems it advisable and in a manner agreed upon by a three-fourths majority of the total voting power of the member countries, including a two-thirds majority of the governors of regional members.

(f) Whenever the authorized inter-regional capital stock is increased pursuant to Article IIA, Section 1(c), and a member exercises the option provided for in Article II, Section 3(f), ordinary capital stock shall be increased in the amount required to allow such member to exercise that option and the inter-regional capital stock available for subscription by that member shall be reduced in an equivalent amount and be appropriately canceled.

SECTION 3.[8] SUBSCRIPTION OF SHARES

(a) Each regional member shall subscribe to shares of the ordinary capital stock of the Bank, and nonregional members may subscribe thereto in accordance with the terms of paragraph (b) of this section and in accordance with such terms as the Board of Governors shall establish. The number of shares to be subscribed by the original members shall be those set forth in Annex A of this Agreement, which specifies the obligations of each member as to both paid-in and callable capital. The number of shares to be subscribed by other members shall be determined by the Bank.

(b) In case of an increase in ordinary capital pursuant to Section 2, paragraph (c) or (e) of this article, or an increase in inter-regional capital pursuant to Article IIA, Section 1(c), or an increase in both ordinary and inter-regional capital, each member shall have a right to subscribe, under such conditions as the Bank shall

[8] Action of the Board of Governors on June 1, 1976 (TIAS 8383) amended and restated sec. 3.

decide, to a proportion of the increase of stock equivalent to the proportion which its stock theretofore subscribed bears to the total capital stock of the Bank. No member, however, shall be obligated to subscribe to any part of such increased capital.

(c) Shares of ordinary capital stock initially subscribed by original members shall be issued at par. Other shares shall be issued at par unless the Bank decides in special circumstances to issue them on other terms.

(d) The liability of the member countries on ordinary capital shares shall be limited to the unpaid portion of their issue price.

(e) Shares of ordinary capital stock shall not be pledged or encumbered in any manner, and they shall be transferable only to the Bank.

(f) Any member having the right to subscribe to the interregional capital stock of the Bank under paragraph (b) of this section, shall have the option of waiving that right and subscribing in lieu thereof to an equivalent amount of ordinary capital stock.

SECTION 4. PAYMENT OF SUBSCRIPTIONS

(a) Payment of the subscriptions to the ordinary[9] capital stock of the Bank as set forth in Annex A shall be made as follows:

(i) Payment of the amount subscribed by each country to the paid-in capital stock of the Bank shall be made in three installments, the first of which shall be 20 percent, and the second and third each 40 percent, of such amount. The first installment shall be paid by each country at any time on or after the date on which this Agreement is signed, and the instrument of acceptance or ratification deposited, on its behalf in accordance with Article XV, Section 1, but not later than September 30, 1960. The remaining two installments shall be paid on such dates as are determined by the Bank, but not sooner than September 30, 1961, and September 30, 1962, respectively.

Of each installment, 50 percent shall be paid in gold and/or dollars and 50 percent in the currency of the member.

(ii) The callable portion of the subscription for ordinary[9] capital shares in the Bank shall be subject to call only when required to meet the obligations of the Bank created under Article III, Section 4(ii) and (v)[9] on borrowing of funds for inclusion in the Bank's ordinary capital resources or guarantees chargeable to such resources. In the event of such a call, payment may be made at the option of the member either in gold, in United States dollars, or in the currency required to discharge the obligations of the Bank for the purpose for which the call is made.

Calls on unpaid subscriptions shall be uniform in percentage on all shares.

(b) Each payment of a member in its own currency under paragraph (a)(i) of this section shall be in such amount as, in the opinion of the Bank, is equivalent to the full value of terms of United States dollars of the weight and fineness in effect on January 1,

---

[9] Action of the Board of Governors on June 1, 1976 (TIAS 8383) inserted "ordinary" in two places in subsec. (a) and struck out "(iii)" and inserted in lieu thereof "(v)".

1959, of the portion of the subscription being paid. The initial payment shall be in such amount as the member considers appropriate hereunder but shall be subject to such adjustment, to be effected within 60 days of the date on which the payment was due, as the Bank shall determine to be necessary to constitute the full dollar value equivalent as provided in this paragraph.

(c) Unless otherwise determined by the Board of Governors by a three-fourths majority of the total voting power of the member countries, the liability of members of payment of the second and third installments of the paid-in portion of their subscriptions to the capital stock shall be conditional upon payment of not less than 90 percent of the total obligations of the members due for—

(i) the first and second installments, respectively, of the paid-in portion of the subscriptions; and

(ii) the initial payment and all prior calls on the subscription quotas to the Fund.

SECTION 5. ORDINARY CAPITAL RESOURCES

As used in this Agreement, the term "ordinary capital resources" of the Bank shall be deemed to include the following:

(i) authorized ordinary [10] capital, including both paid-in and callable shares, subscribed pursuant to Sections 2 and 3 of this article;

(ii) all funds raised by borrowings under the authority of Article VII, Section 1(i) to which the commitment set forth in Section 4(a)(ii) of this article is applicable;

(iii) all funds received in repayment of loans made with the resources indicated in (i) and (ii) of this section;

(iv) all income derived from loans made from the aforementioned funds or from guarantees to which the commitment set forth in Section 4(a)(ii) of this article is applicable; and

(v) [11] all other income derived from any of the resources mentioned above.

ARTICLE IIA. INTER-REGIONAL CAPITAL OF THE BANK [12]

SECTION 1. AUTHORIZED INTER-REGIONAL CAPITAL

(a) The initial authorized inter-regional capital stock of the Bank shall be four hundred twenty million dollars ($420,000,000) [13] in terms of United States dollars of the weight and fineness in effect on January 1, 1959 and shall be divided into 42,000 shares having a par value of $10,000 each, which shall be available for subscription by members in accordance with Section 2 of this article.

(b) The authorized inter-regional capital stock shall be divided into paid-in shares and callable shares. Of the initial authorized inter-regional capital stock, the equivalent of seventy million dollars ($70,000,000) shall be paid-in, and three hundred fifty million dollars ($350,000,000) shall be callable for the purposes specified in Section 3(c) of this article.

---

[10] Action of the Board of Governors on June 1, 1976 (TIAS 8383) inserted "ordinary".

[11] Action of the Board of Governors on June 1, 1976 (TIAS 8383) added subpara. (v).

[12] Action of the Board of Governors on June 1, 1976 (TIAS 8383) added Article IIA.

[13] In 1976, 1980, and 1983, the Board of Governors increased the inter-regional capital stock of the Bank.

(c) Subject to the provisions of Article VIII, Section 4(b), the authorized inter-regional capital stock may be increased when the Board of Governors deems it advisable and in a manner agreed upon by a two-thirds majority of the total number of governors, including two-thirds of the governors of regional members, representing not less than three-fourths of the total voting power of the member countries.

(d) Whenever the authorized ordinary capital stock is increased pursuant to Article II, Section 2(e), and a member exercises the option provided for in Article IIA, Section 2(g), inter-regional capital stock shall be increased in the amount required to allow such member to exercise that option and the ordinary capital stock available for subscription by that member shall be reduced in an equivalent amount and be appropriately canceled.

SECTION 2. SUBSCRIPTION OF SHARES OF INTER-REGIONAL CAPITAL

(a) Each nonregional member shall subscribe to shares of the inter-regional capital stock, and regional members may subscribe thereto in accordance with the terms of Article II, Section 3(b), and in accordance with such terms as the Board of Governors shall establish, subject to the provisions of this section.

(b) The subscription of each original nonregional member shall be such number of shares of paid-in and callable inter-regional capital stock as may be determined by the Bank. The subscription, including the manner of its payment, of any new nonregional member shall be determined by the Bank with due regard to the conditions of the existing subscriptions.

(c) Regional members may subscribe to the inter-regional capital stock on such terms as the Bank may determine, giving due regard to the conditions established for subscriptions by nonregional members.

(d) Shares of the initial authorized inter-regional capital stock shall be issued at par. Other shares will be issued at par unless the Bank decides in special circumstances to issue them on other terms.

(e) The liability of the member countries on inter-regional capital shares shall be limited to the unpaid portion of their issue price.

(f) Shares of inter-regional capital stock shall not be pledged or encumbered in any manner, and they shall be transferable only to the Bank.

(g) Any member having the right to subscribe to the ordinary capital stock of the Bank under Article II, Section 3(b), shall have the option of waiving that right and subscribing in lieu thereof to an equivalent amount of inter-regional capital stock.

SECTION 3. PAYMENT OF SUBSCRIPTIONS TO INTER-REGIONAL CAPITAL

(a) Payment of the amount subscribed by each country to the paid-in inter-regional capital stock shall be made entirely in the currency of the respective member, which shall make arrangements satisfactory to the Bank to assure that, subject to the provisions of Article V, Section 1(c), its currency shall be freely convertible into the currencies of other countries for the purposes of the Bank's operations.

(b) Each payment of a member under paragraph (a) of this section shall be in such amount as, in the opinion of the Bank, is equivalent to the full value in terms of United States dollars of the weight and fineness in effect on January 1, 1959, of the portion of the subscription being paid. The initial payment shall be in such amount as the member considers appropriate hereunder but shall be subject to such adjustment, to be effected within 60 days of the date on which the payment was due, as the Bank shall determine to be necessary to constitute the full dollar value equivalent as provided in this paragraph.

(c) The callable portion of the subscription for inter-regional capital shares of the Bank shall be subject to call only when required to meet the obligations of the Bank created under Article III, Section 4 (iv) and (v), on borrowings of funds for inclusion in the Bank's inter-regional capital resources or guarantees chargeable to such resources. In the event of such a call, payment may be made at the option of the member either in fully convertible currency of a member country or in the currency required to discharge the obligations of the Bank for the purpose for which the call is made.

Calls on unpaid subscriptions of inter-regional callable capital shall be uniform in percentage on all such shares.

SECTION 4. INTER-REGIONAL CAPITAL RESOURCES

As used in this Agreement, the term "inter-regional capital resources" of the Bank shall be deemed to include the following:

(i) Authorized inter-regional capital, including both paid-in and callable shares, subscribed pursuant to Section 2 of this article;

(ii) all funds raised by borrowings under the authority of Article VII, Section 1(i) to which the commitment set forth in Section 3(c) of this article is applicable;

(iii) all funds received in repayment of loans made with the resources indicated in (i) and (ii) of this section;

(iv) all income derived from loans made from the aforementioned funds or from guarantees to which the commitment set forth in Section 3(c) of this article is applicable; and

(v) all other income derived from any of the resources mentioned above.

ARTICLE III. OPERATIONS

SECTION 1. USE OF RESOURCES

The resources and facilities of the Bank shall be used exclusively to implement the purpose and functions enumerated in Article I of this Agreement.

SECTION 2.[14] CATEGORIES OF OPERATIONS

(a) The operations of the Bank shall be divided into ordinary operations, inter-regional resources operations, and special operations.

[14] Action of the Board of Governors on June 1, 1976 (TIAS 8383) amended and restated sec. 2.

(b) The ordinary operations shall be those financed from the Bank's ordinary capital resources, as defined in Article II, Section 5. The inter-regional resources operations shall be those financed from the Bank's inter-regional capital resources, as defined in Article IIA, Section 4. Both types of operations shall relate exclusively to loans made, participated in, or guaranteed by the Bank which are repayable only in the respective currency or currencies in which the loans were made. Such operations shall be subject to the terms and conditions that the Bank deems advisable, consistent with the provisions of this agreement.

(c) The special operations shall be those financed from the resources of the Fund in accordance with the provisions of Article IV.

SECTION 3.[15] BASIC PRINCIPLE OF SEPARATION

(a) Subject to the amending provisions of Article XII(a)(ii), the ordinary capital resources, as defined in Article II, Section 5, the inter-regional capital resources, as defined in Article IIA, Section 4, and the resources of the Fund, as defined in Article IV, Section 3(h), shall at all times and in all respects be held, used, obligated, invested, or otherwise disposed of entirely separate from each other.

(b) The ordinary capital resources and the inter-regional capital resources shall under no circumstances be charged with, or used to discharge, obligations, liabilities or losses arising out of operations for which the resources of the Fund were originally used or committed.

(c) The ordinary capital resources shall under no circumstances be charged with, or used to discharge, obligations, liabilities or losses chargeable to the inter-regional capital resources, and, except as provided in Article VII, Section 3(d), the inter-regional capital resources shall under no circumstances be charged with, or used to discharge, obligations, liabilities or losses chargeable to the ordinary capital resources.

(d) The financial statements of the Bank shall show separately the ordinary operations, the inter-regional resources operations, and the special operations, and the Bank shall establish such other administrative rules as may be necessary to ensure the effective separation of the three types of operations.

(e) Expenses pertaining directly to ordinary operations shall be charged to the ordinary capital resources. Expenses pertaining directly to inter-regional resources operations shall be charged to the inter-regional capital resources. Expenses pertaining directly to special operations shall be charged to the resources of the Fund. Other expenses shall be charged as the Bank determines.

SECTION 4. METHODS OF MAKING OR GUARANTEEING LOANS

Subject to the conditions stipulated in this article, the Bank may make or guarantee loans to any member, or any agency or political subdivision thereof, and to any enterprise in the territory of a member in any of the following ways:

[15] Action of the Board of Governors on June 1, 1976 (TIAS 8383) amended and restated sec. 3.

(i) by making or participating in direct loans with funds corresponding to the unimpaired paid-in ordinary[16] capital and, except as provided in Section 13 of this article, to its reserves and undistributed surplus; or with the unimpaired resources of the Fund;

(ii) By making or participating in direct loans with funds raised by the Bank in capital markets, or borrowed or acquired in any other manner for inclusion in the ordinary capital resources of the Bank or the resources of the Fund;

(iii)[16] by making or participating in direct loans with funds corresponding to the unimpaired paid-in inter-regional capital, including any reserves or undistributed surplus pertaining to such resources;

(iv)[16] by making or participating in direct loans with funds raised by the Bank in capital markets, or borrowed or acquired in any other manner, for inclusion in the inter-regional capital resources of the Bank; and

(v)[16] by guaranteeing, with the ordinary capital resources, the inter-regional capital resources, or the resources of the Fund, in whole or in part loans made, except in special cases, by private investors.

SECTION 5.[17] LIMITATIONS ON OPERATIONS

(a) The total amount outstanding of loans and guarantees made by the Bank in its ordinary operations shall not at any time exceed the total amount of the unimpaired subscribed ordinary capital of the Bank, plus the unimpaired reserves and surplus included in the ordinary capital resources of the Bank, as defined in Article II, Section 5, exclusive of income assigned to the special reserve established pursuant to Section 13 of this article and other income of the ordinary capital resources assigned by decision of the Board of Governors to reserves not available for loans or guarantees.

(b) The total amount outstanding of loans and guarantees made by the Bank in its inter-regional resources operations shall not at any time exceed the total amount of the unimpaired subscribed inter-regional capital of the Bank, plus the unimpaired reserves and surplus included in the inter-regional capital resources of the Bank, as defined in Article IIA, Section 4, exclusive of income of the inter-regional capital resources assigned by decision of the Board of Governors to reserves not available for loans or guarantees.

(c) In the case of loans made out of funds borrowed by the Bank to which the obligations provided for in Article II, Section 4(a)(ii), are applicable, the total amount of principal outstanding and payable to the Bank in a specific currency shall at no time exceed the total amount of principal of the outstanding borrowings by the Bank for inclusion in its ordinary capital resources that are payable in the same currency.

(d) In the case of loans made out of funds borrowed by the Bank to which the obligations provided for in Article IIA, Section 3(c),

---

[16] Action by the Board of Governors on June 1, 1976 (TIAS 8383) inserted "ordinary" in para. (i), redesignated para. (iii) as para. (v), and added paras. (iii) and (iv).

[17] Action by the Board of Governors on June 1, 1976 (TIAS 8383) amended and restated sec. 5.

are applicable, the total amount of principal outstanding and payable to the Bank in a specific currency shall at no time exceed the total amount of principal of the outstanding borrowings by the Bank for inclusion in its inter-regional capital resources that are payable in the same currency.

SECTION 6. DIRECT LOAN FINANCING

In making direct loans or participating in them, the Bank may provide financing in any of the following ways:

(a) By furnishing the borrower currencies of members, other than the currency of the member in whose territory the project is to be carried out, that are necessary to meet the foreign exchange costs of the project.

(b) By providing financing to meet expenses related to the purposes of the loan in the territories of the member in which the project is to be carried out. Only in special cases, particularly when the project indirectly gives rise to an increase in the demand for foreign exchange in that country, shall the financing granted by the Bank to meet local expenses be provided in gold or in currencies other than that of such member; in such cases, the amount of the financing granted by the Bank for this purpose shall not exceed a reasonable portion of the local expenses incurred by the borrower.

SECTION 7. RULES AND CONDITIONS FOR MAKING OR GUARANTEEING LOANS

(a) The Bank may make or guarantee loans subject to the following rules and conditions:

(i) the applicant for the loan shall have submitted a detailed proposal and the staff of the Bank shall have presented a written report recommending the proposal after a study of its merits. In special circumstances, the Board of Executive Directors, by a majority of the total voting power of the member countries, may require that a proposal be submitted to the Board for decision in the absence of such a report;

(ii) in considering a request for a loan or guarantee, the Bank shall take into account the ability of the borrower to obtain the loan from private sources of financing on terms which, in the opinion of the Bank, are reasonable for the borrower, taking into account all pertinent factors;

(iii) in making or guaranteeing a loan, the Bank shall pay due regard to the prospects that the borrower and its guarantor, if any, will be in a position to meet their obligations under the loan contract;

(iv) in the opinion of the Bank, the rate of interest, other charges and the schedule for repayment of principal are appropriate for the project in question;

(v) in guaranteeing a loan made by other investors, the Bank shall receive suitable compensation for its risk; and

(vi) loans made or guaranteed by the Bank shall be principally for financing specific projects, including those forming part of a national or regional development program. However, the Bank may make or guarantee overall loans to development institutions or similar agencies of the members in order that the latter may facilitate the financing of specific development projects whose individual financing requirements are not, in the opinion of the Bank, large enough to warrant the direct supervision of the Bank.

(b) The Bank shall not finance any undertaking in the territory of a member if that member objects to such financing.

SECTION 8. OPTIONAL CONDITIONS FOR MAKING OR GUARANTEEING LOANS

(a) In the case of loans or guarantees of loans to nongovernmental entities, the Bank may, when it deems it advisable, require that the member in whose territory the project is to be carried out, or a public institution or a similar agency of the member acceptable to the Bank, guarantee the repayment of the principal and the payment of interest and other charges on the loan.

(b) The Bank may attach such other conditions to the making of loans or guarantees as it deems appropriate, taking into account both the interest of the members directly involved in the particular loan or guarantee proposal and the interests of the members as a whole.

SECTION 9. USE OF LOANS MADE OR GUARANTEED BY THE BANK

(a) Except as provided in Article V, Section 1, the Bank shall impose no condition that the proceeds of a loan shall be spent in the territory of any particular country nor that such proceeds shall not be spent in the territories of any particular member or members; provided, however, that with respect to any increase of the resources of the Bank the question of restriction of procurement by the Bank or any member with regard to those members which do not participate in an increase under the terms and conditions specified by the Board of Governors may be determined by the Board of Governors.[18]

(b) The Bank shall take the necessary measures to insure that the proceeds of any loan made, guaranteed, or participated in by the Bank are used only for the purposes for which the loan was granted, with due attention to considerations of economy and efficiency.

SECTION 10. PAYMENT PROVISIONS FOR DIRECT LOANS

Direct loan contracts made by the Bank in conformity with Section 4[19] of this article shall establish:

(a) All the terms and conditions of each loan, including among others, provision for payment of principal, interest and other charges, maturities, and dates of payment; and

(b) The currency or currencies in which payments shall be made to the Bank.

---

[18] Action by the Board of Governors on June 1, 1976 (TIAS 8383) added the words to this point beginning with "provided, however,".

[19] Action by the Board of Governors on June 1, 1976 (TIAS 8383) struck out "(i) or (ii)" which formerly appeared at this point.

SECTION 11. GUARANTEES

(a) In guaranteeing a loan the Bank shall charge a guarantee fee, at a rate determined by the Bank, payable periodically on the amount of the loan outstanding.

(b) Guarantee contracts concluded by the Bank shall provide that the Bank may terminate its liability with respect to interest if, upon default by the borrower and by the guarantor, if any, the Bank offers to purchase, at par and interest accrued to a date designated in the offer, the bonds or other obligations guaranteed.

(c) In issuing guarantees, the Bank shall have power to determine any other terms and conditions.

SECTION 12. SPECIAL COMMISSION

On all loans, participations, or guarantees made out of or by commitment of the ordinary capital resources of the Bank, the latter shall charge a special commission. The special commission, payable periodically, shall be computed on the amount outstanding on each loan, participation, or guarantee and shall be at the rate of one percent per annum, unless the Bank, by a two-thirds majority of the total voting power of the member countries, decides to reduce the rate of commission.

SECTION 13. SPECIAL RESERVE

The amount of commissions received by the Bank under Section 12 of this article shall be set aside as a special reserve, which shall be kept for meeting liabilities of the Bank in accordance with Article VII, Section 3(b)(i). The special reserves shall be held in such liquid form, permitted under this Agreement, as the Board of Executive Directors may decide.

Article IV. Fund for Special Operations

SECTION 1. ESTABLISHMENT, PURPOSE, AND FUNCTIONS

A Fund for Special Operations is established for the making of loans on terms and conditions appropriate for dealing with special circumstances arising in specific countries or with respect to specific projects.

The Fund, whose administration shall be entrusted to the Bank, shall have the purpose and functions set forth in Article I of this Agreement.

SECTION 2. APPLICABLE PROVISIONS

The Fund shall be governed by the provisions of the present article and all other provisions of this Agreement, excepting those inconsistent with the provisions of the present article and those expressly applying only to other[20] operations of the Bank.

[20] Action by the Board of Governors on June 1, 1976 (TIAS 8383) struck out "the ordinary", inserted in lieu thereof "other" in sec. 2, and inserted "Bahamas and Guyana," in sec. 3(b).

SECTION 3. RESOURCES

(a) The original members of the Bank shall contribute to the resources of the Fund in accordance with the provisions of this section.

(b) Members of the Organization of American States that join the Bank after the date specified in Article XV, Section 1(a), Canada, Bahamas and Guyana,[20] and countries that are admitted in accordance with Article II, Section 1(b), shall contribute to the Fund with such quotas, and under terms, as may be determined by the Bank.[21]

(c) The Fund shall be established with initial resources in the amount of one hundred and fifty million dollars ($150,000,000)[22] in terms of United States dollars of the weight and fineness in effect on January 1, 1959, which shall be contributed by the original members of the Bank in accordance with the quotas specified in Annex B.

(d) Payment of the quotas shall be made as follows:

(i) Fifty percent of its quota shall be paid by each member at any time on or after the date on which this Agreement is signed, and the instrument of acceptance or ratification deposited, on its behalf in accordance with Article XV, Section 1, but not later than September 30, 1960.

(ii) The remaining 50 percent shall be paid at any time subsequent to one year after the Bank has begun operations, in such amounts and at such times as are determined by the Bank; provided, however, that the total amount of all quotas shall be made due and payable not later than the date fixed for payment of the third installment of the subscriptions to the paid-in capital stock of the Bank.

(iii) The payments required under this section shall be distributed among the members in proportion to their quotas and shall be made one-half in gold and/or United States dollars, and one-half in the currency of the contributing member.

(e) Each payment of a member in its own currency under the preceding paragraph shall be in such amount as, in the opinion of the Bank, is equivalent to the full value, in terms of United States dollars of the weight and fineness in effect on January 1, 1959, of the portion of the quota being paid. The initial payment shall be in such amount as the member considers appropriate hereunder but shall be subject to such adjustment, to be effected within 60 days of the date on which payment was due, as the Bank shall determine to be necessary to constitute the full dollar value equivalent as provided in this paragraph.

[21] Action by the Board of Governors on March 23, 1972 (TIAS 7437) amended and restated subsec. (b).

[22] The Board of Governors increased the authorized resources of the Fund for Special Operations (FSO) on January 28, 1964, to $223.158 million; on March 31, 1965, to $1.123 billion; on December 29, 1967, to $2.323 billion; on October 16, 1969, to $2.328 billion; and on May 3, 1972 to $2.388 billion. In addition, on December 31, 1970, the Board of Governors approved a resolution providing for a further increase of $1.5 billion, an amount that increased the authorized resources of the FSO to $3.888 billion. Effective in 1976, the authorized resources of the Fund were again increased to $5.4 billion. In 1980 the authorized resources of the Fund were increased by $1.75 billion, raising the total resources to $7.655 billion. The Board of Governors approved a further increase of $703 million in 1983, followed by another increase of $200 million in April 1989. In April 1994, the Board of Governors approved an additional increase of $1 billion, bringing total FSO resources to over $10 billion.

(f) Unless otherwise determined by the Board of Governors by a three-fourths majority of the total voting power of the member countries, the liability of members for payment of any call on the unpaid portion of their subscription quotas to the Fund shall be conditional upon payment of not less than 90 percent of the total obligations of the members for—

(i) the initial payment and all prior calls on such quota subscriptions to the Fund; and

(ii) any installments due on the paid-in portion of the subscriptions to the capital stock of the Bank.

(g) The resources of the Fund shall be increased through additional contributions by the members when the Board of Governors considers it advisable by a three-fourths majority of the total voting power of the member countries. The provisions of Article II, Section 3(b), shall apply to such increases, in terms of the proportion between the quota in effect for each member and the total amount of the resources of the Fund contributed by members. No member, however, shall be obligated to contribute any part of such increase.[23]

(h) As used in this Agreement, the term "resources of the Fund" shall be deemed to include the following:

(i) contributions by members pursuant to paragraphs (c) and (g) of this section;

(ii) all funds raised by borrowing to which the commitment stipulated in Article II, Section 4(a)(ii), and Article IIA, Section 3(c), are[24] not applicable, i.e., those that are specifically chargeable to the resources of the Fund;

(iii) all funds received in repayment of loans made from the resources mentioned above;

(iv) all income derived from operations using or committing any of the resources mentioned above; and

(v) any other resources at the disposal of the Fund.

SECTION 4. OPERATIONS

(a) The operations of the Fund shall be those financed from its own resources, as defined in Section 3(h) of the present article.

(b) Loans made with resources of the Fund may be partially or wholly repayable in the currency of the member in whose territory the project being financed will be carried out. The part of the loan not repayable in the currency of the member shall be paid in the currency or currencies in which the loan was made.

SECTION 5. LIMITATION ON LIABILITY

In the operations of the Fund, the financial liability of the Bank shall be limited to the resources and reserves of the Fund, and the liability of members shall be limited to the unpaid portion of their respective quotas that has become due and payable.

---

[23] Action by the Board of Governors on June 1, 1976 (TIAS 8383) added this sentence.

[24] Action by the Board of Governors on June 1, 1976 (TIAS 8383) inserted ", and Article IIA, Section 3(c), are".

SECTION 6. LIMITATION ON DISPOSITION OF QUOTAS

The rights of members of the Bank resulting from their contributions to the Fund may not be transferred or encumbered, and members shall have no right of reimbursement of such contributions except in cases of loss of the status of membership or of termination of the operations of the Fund.

SECTION 7. DISCHARGE OF FUND LIABILITIES ON BORROWINGS

Payments in satisfaction of any liability on borrowing of funds for inclusion in the resources of the Fund shall be charged—

(i) first, against any reserve established for this purpose; and

(ii) then, against any other funds available in the resources of the Fund.

SECTION 8. ADMINISTRATION

(a) Subject to the provisions of this Agreement, the authorities of the Bank shall have full powers to administer the Fund.

(b) There shall be a Vice President of the Bank in charge of the Fund. The Vice President shall participate in the meetings of the Board of Executive Directors of the Bank, without vote, whenever matters relating to the Fund are discussed.

(c) In the operations of the Fund the Bank shall utilize to the fullest extent possible the same personnel, experts, installations, offices, equipment, and services as it uses for its other[25] operations.

(d) The Bank shall publish a separate annual report showing the results of the Fund's financial operations, including profits or losses. At the annual meeting of the Board of Governors there shall be at least one session devoted to consideration of this report. In addition, the Bank shall transmit to the members a quarterly summary of the Fund's operations.

SECTION 9. VOTING

(a) In making decisions concerning operations of the Fund, each member country of the Bank shall have the voting power in the Board of Governors accorded to it pursuant to Article VIII, Section 4 (a) and (c),[26] and each Director shall have the voting power in the Board of Executive Directors accorded to him pursuant to Article VIII, Section 4 (a) and (d).[26]

(b) All decisions of the Bank concerning the operations of the Fund shall be adopted by a two-thirds majority of the total voting power of the member countries, unless otherwise provided in this article.

SECTION 10. DISTRIBUTION OF NET PROFITS

The Board of Governors of the Bank shall determine what portion of the net profits of the Fund shall be distributed among the

[25] Action by the Board of Governors on June 1, 1976 (TIAS 8383) struck out "ordinary" and inserted in lieu thereof "other".

[26] Action taken by the Board of Directors on June 1, 1976, struck out "(b)" and "(c)" and inserted in lieu thereof "(c)" and "(d)", respectively.

members after making provision for reserves. Such net profits shall be shared in proportion to the quotas of the members.

SECTION 11. WITHDRAWAL OF CONTRIBUTIONS

(a) No country may withdraw its contribution and terminate its relations with the Fund while it is still a member of the Bank.

(b) The provisions of Article IX, Section 3, with respect to the settlement of accounts with countries that terminate their membership in the Bank also shall apply to the Fund.

SECTION 12. SUSPENSION AND TERMINATION

The provisions of Article X also shall apply to the Fund with substitution of terms relating to the Fund and its resources and respective creditors for those relating to the Bank and its capital resources and respective creditors.

ARTICLE V. CURRENCIES

SECTION 1.[27] USE OF CURRENCIES

(a) The currency of any member held by the Bank in its ordinary capital resources, in its inter-regional capital resources, or in the resources of the Fund, however acquired, may be used by the Bank and by any recipient from the Bank, without restriction by the member, to make payments for goods and services produced in the territory of such member.

(b) Members may not maintain or impose restrictions of any kind upon the use by the Bank or by any recipient from the Bank, or payments in any country, of the following:

(i) gold and dollars received by the Bank in payment of the 50 percent portion of each member's subscription to shares of the Bank's ordinary capital and of the 50 percent portion of each member's quota for contribution to the Fund, pursuant to the provisions of Article II and Article IV, respectively, and currency received by the Bank in payment of the equivalent portion of each member's subscription to shares of the inter-regional capital pursuant to the provisions of Article IIA;

(ii) currencies of members purchased with the resources referred to in (i) of this paragraph;

(iii) currencies obtained by borrowings, pursuant to the provisions of Article VII, Section 1(i), for inclusion in the capital resources of the Bank;

(iv) gold and dollars received by the Bank in payment on account of principal, interest, and other charges, of loans made from the gold and dollar funds referred to in (i) of this paragraph; currencies received by the Bank in payment on account of principal, interest, and other charges, of loans made from the portion of the inter-regional capital referred to in (i) of this paragraph; currencies received in payment of principal, interest, and other charges, of loans made from currencies referred to in (ii) and (iii) of this paragraph; and currencies received in

[27] Action by the Board of Governors on June 1, 1976 (TIAS 8383) amended and restated sec. 1.

payment of commissions and fees on all guarantees made by the Bank; and

(v) currencies, other than the member's own currency, received from the Bank pursuant to Article VII, Section 4(d), and Article IV, Section 10, in distribution of net profits.

(c) A member's currency held by the Bank, whether in its ordinary capital resources, in its inter-regional capital resources, or in the resources of the Fund, not covered by paragraph (b) of this section, also may be used by the Bank or any recipient from the Bank for payments in any country without restriction of any kind, unless the member notifies the Bank of its desire that such currency or a portion thereof be restricted to the uses specified in paragraph (a) of this section.

(d) Members may not place any restrictions on the holding and use by the Bank, for making amortization payments or anticipating payment of, or repurchasing part or all of, the Bank's own obligations, of currencies received by the Bank in repayment of direct loans made from borrowed funds included in the ordinary or inter-regional capital resources of the Bank.

(e) Gold or currency held by the Bank in its ordinary capital resources, in its inter-regional capital resources, or in the resources of the Fund shall not be used by the Bank to purchase other currencies unless authorized by a two-thirds majority of the total voting power of the member countries. Any currencies purchased pursuant to the provisions of this paragraph shall not be subject to maintenance of value under Section 3 of this article.

SECTION 2. VALUATION OF CURRENCIES

Whenever it shall become necessary under this Agreement to value any currency in terms of another currency, or in terms of gold, such valuation shall be determined by the Bank after consultation with the International Monetary Fund.

SECTION 3. MAINTENANCE OF VALUE OF THE CURRENCY HOLDINGS OF THE BANK

(a) Whenever the par value in the International Monetary Fund of a member's currency is reduced or the foreign exchange value of a member's currency has, in the opinion of the Bank, depreciated to a significant extent, the member shall pay to the Bank within a reasonable time an additional amount of its own currency sufficient to maintain the value of all the currency of the member held by the Bank in its ordinary capital resources, in its inter-regional capital resources,[28] or in the resources of the Fund, excepting currency derived from borrowings by the Bank. The standard of value for this purpose shall be the United States dollar of the weight and fineness in effect on January 1, 1959.

(b) Whenever the par value in the International Monetary Fund of a member's currency is increased or the foreign exchange value of such member's currency has, in the opinion of the Bank, appreciated to a significant extent, the Bank shall return to such member within a reasonable time an amount of that member's currency

[28] Action by the Board of Governors on June 1, 1976 (TIAS 8383) inserted "in its inter-regional capital resources," in subsecs. (a) and (b), and added subsec. (d).

equal to the increase in the value of the amount of such currency which is held by the Bank in its ordinary capital resources, in its inter-regional capital resources,[28] or in the resources of the Fund, excepting currency derived from borrowings by the Bank. The standard of value for this purpose shall be the same as that established in the preceding paragraph.

(c) The provisions of this section may be waived by the Bank when a uniform proportionate change in the par value of the currencies of all the Bank's members is made by the International Monetary Fund.

(d)[28] Notwithstanding any other provisions of this section, the terms and conditions of any increase in the resources of the Fund pursuant to Article IV, Section 3(g), may include maintenance of value provisions other than those provided for in this section which would apply to the resources of the Fund contributed by such increase.

SECTION 4. METHODS OF CONSERVING CURRENCIES

The Bank shall accept from any member promissory notes or similar securities issued by the government of the member, or by the depository designated by such member, in lieu of any part of the currency of the member representing the 50 percent portion of its subscription to the Bank's authorized ordinary[29] capital and the 50 percent portion of its subscription to the resources of the Fund, which, pursuant to the provisions of Article II and Article IV, respectively, are payable by each member in its national currency, provided such currency is not required by the Bank for the conduct of its operations. Such[29] notes or securities shall be non-negotiable, non-interest-bearing, and payable to the Bank at their par value on demand. On the same conditions, the Bank shall also accept such notes or securities in lieu of any part of the subscription of a member to the inter-regional capital with respect to which part the terms of the subscription do not require payment in cash.[29]

ARTICLE VI. TECHNICAL ASSISTANCE

SECTION 1. PROVISION OF TECHNICAL ADVICE AND ASSISTANCE

The Bank may, at the request of any member or members, or of private firms that may obtain loans from it, provide technical advice and assistance in its field of activity, particularly on—

(i) the preparation, financing, and execution of development plans and projects, including the consideration of priorities, and the formulation of loan proposals on specific national or regional development projects; and

(ii) the development and advanced training, through seminars and other forms of instruction, of personnel specializing in the formulation and implementation of development plans and projects.

---

[29] Action by the Board of Governors on June 1, 1976 (TIAS 8383) inserted "ordinary", struck out "promissory" which previously appeared after "Such", and added the final sentence in sec. 4.

SECTION 2. COOPERATIVE AGREEMENTS ON TECHNICAL ASSISTANCE

In order to accomplish the purposes of this article, the Bank may enter into agreements on technical assistance with other national or international institutions, either public or private.

SECTION 3. EXPENSES

(a) The Bank may arrange with member countries or firms receiving technical assistance, for reimbursement of the expenses of furnishing such assistance on terms which the Bank deems appropriate.

(b) The expenses of providing technical assistance not paid by the recipients shall be met from the net income of the ordinary capital resources, of the inter-regional capital resources,[30] or of the Fund. However, during the first three years of the Bank's operations, up to three percent, in total, of the initial resources of the Fund may be used to meet such expenses.

ARTICLE VII. MISCELLANEOUS POWERS AND DISTRIBUTION OF PROFITS

SECTION 1. MISCELLANEOUS POWERS OF THE BANK

In addition to the powers specified elsewhere in this Agreement, the Bank shall have the power to—

(i) borrow funds and in that connection to furnish such collateral or other security therefore as the Bank shall determine, provided that, before making a sale of its obligations in the markets of a country, the Bank shall have obtained the approval of that country and of the member in whose currency the obligations are denominated. In addition, in the case of borrowings of funds to be included in the Bank's ordinary capital resources or inter-regional capital resources,[31] the Bank shall obtain agreement of such countries that the proceeds may be exchanged for the currency of any other country without restriction;

(ii) buy and sell securities it has issued or guaranteed or in which it has invested, provided that the Bank shall obtain the approval of the country in whose territories the securities are to be bought or sold;

(iii) with the approval of a two-thirds majority of the total voting power of the member countries, invest funds not needed in its operations in such obligations as it may determine;

(iv) guarantee securities in its portfolio for the purpose of facilitating their sale; and

(v) exercise such other powers as shall be necessary or desirable in furtherance of its purpose and functions, consistent with the provisions of this Agreement.

---

[30] Action of the Board of Governors on June 1, 1976 (TIAS 8383) struck out "Bank" and inserted in lieu thereof "ordinary capital resources, of the inter-regional capital resources,".

[31] Action by the Board of Governors on June 1, 1976 (TIAS 8383) inserted "or inter-regional capital resources,".

SECTION 2. WARNING TO BE PLACED ON SECURITIES

Every security issued or guaranteed by the Bank shall bear on its face a conspicuous statement to the effect that it is not an obligation of any government, unless it is in fact the obligation of a particular government, in which case it shall so state.

SECTION 3.[32] METHODS OF MEETING LIABILITIES OF THE BANK IN CASE OF DEFAULTS

(a) The Bank, in the event of actual or threatened default on loans made or guaranteed by the Bank using its ordinary capital resources or its inter-regional capital resources, shall take such action as it deems appropriate with respect to modifying the terms of the loan, other than the currency of repayment.

(b) The payments in discharge of the Bank's liabilities on borrowings or guarantees under Article III, Section 4 (ii) and (v) chargeable against the ordinary capital resources of the Bank shall be charged:

(i) first, against the special reserve provided for in Article III, Section 13; and

(ii) then, to the extent necessary and at the discretion of the Bank, against the other reserves, surplus, and funds corresponding to the capital paid in for ordinary capital shares.

(c) Whenever necessary to meet contractual payments of interest, other charges, or amortization on the Bank's borrowings payable out of its ordinary capital resources, or to meet the Bank's liabilities with respect to similar payments on loans guaranteed by it chargeable to its ordinary capital resources, the Bank may call upon the members to pay an appropriate amount of their callable ordinary capital subscriptions, in accordance with Article II, Section 4(a)(ii). Moreover, if the Bank believes that a default may be of long duration, it may call an additional part of such subscriptions not to exceed in any one year one percent of the total subscriptions of the members of the ordinary capital resources, for the following purposes:

(i) to redeem prior to maturity, or otherwise discharge its liability on, all or part of the outstanding principal of any loan guaranteed by it chargeable to its ordinary capital resources in respect of which the debtor is in default; and

(ii) to repurchase, or otherwise discharge its liability on, all or part of its own outstanding obligations payable out of its ordinary capital resources.

(d)[33] The Bank's liabilities on all borrowings of funds for inclusion in its ordinary capital resources which were outstanding at December 31, 1974 shall be payable out of both the ordinary capital resources and the inter-regional capital resources, including, notwithstanding the provisions of Article IIA, Section 3(c), the callable inter-regional capital subscriptions, provided, however, that the Bank shall use its best efforts to discharge its liabilities on such

[32] Action by the Board of Governors on June 1, 1976 (TIAS 8383) amended and restated sec. 3.

[33] Action by the Board of Governors on June 1, 1976 (TIAS 8383) added subsecs. (d), (e), and (f).

outstanding borrowings out of its ordinary capital resources pursuant to paragraphs (b) and (c) of this section before discharging such liabilities out of its inter-regional capital resources pursuant to paragraphs (e) and (f) of this section, for which purpose appropriate substitution shall be made in such paragraphs of the term ordinary capital for inter-regional capital.

(e)[33] The payments in discharge of the Bank's liabilities on borrowings or guarantees under Article III, Section 4 (iv) and (v) chargeable against the inter-regional capital resources of the Bank shall be charged:

(i) first, against any reserve established for this purpose; and

(ii) then, to the extent necessary and at the discretion of the Bank, against the other reserves, surplus, and funds corresponding to the capital paid in for inter-regional capital shares.

(f)[33] Whenever necessary to meet contractual payments of interest, other charges, or amortization on the Bank's borrowings payable out of its inter-regional capital resources, or to meet the Bank's liabilities with respect to similar payments on loans guaranteed by it chargeable to its inter-regional capital resources, the Bank may call upon the members to pay an appropriate amount of their callable inter-regional capital subscriptions, in accordance with Article IIA, Section 3(c). Moreover, if the Bank believes that a default may be of long duration, it may call an additional part of such subscriptions not to exceed in any one year one percent of the total subscriptions of the members to the inter-regional capital resources, for the following purposes:

(i) to redeem prior to maturity, or otherwise discharge its liability on, all or part of the outstanding principal of any loan guaranteed by it chargeable to its inter-regional capital resources in respect of which the debtor is in default; and

(ii) to repurchase, or otherwise discharge its liability on, all or part of its own outstanding obligations payable out of its inter-regional capital resources.

SECTION 4.[34] DISTRIBUTION OF NET PROFITS AND SURPLUS

(a) The Board of Governors may determine periodically what part of the net profits and of the surplus of the ordinary capital resources and of the inter-regional capital resources shall be distributed. Such distributions may be made only when the reserves have reached a level which the Board of Governors considers adequate.

(b) When approving the statements of profit and loss, pursuant to Article VIII, Section 2(b)(viii), the Board of Governors may by decision of a two-thirds majority of the total number of governors representing not less than three-fourths of the total voting power of the member countries transfer part of the net profits for the respective fiscal year of the ordinary capital resources or of the inter-regional capital resources to the Fund.

Before the Board of Governors determines to make a transfer to the Fund, it shall have received a report from the Board of Executive Directors on the desirability of such a transfer, which shall

[34] Action by the Board of Governors on June 1, 1976 (TIAS 8383) amended and restated sec. 4.

take into consideration, *inter alia,* (1) whether the reserves have reached a level that is adequate; (2) whether the transferred funds are needed for the operation of the Fund; and (3) the impact, if any, on the Bank's ability to borrow.

(c) The distributions referred to in paragraph (a) of this section shall be made from the ordinary capital resources in proportion to the number of ordinary capital shares held by each member and from the inter-regional capital resources in proportion to the number of inter-regional capital shares held by each member and likewise the net profits transferred to the Fund pursuant to paragraph (b) of this section shall be credited to the total contribution quotas of each member in the Fund in the foregoing proportions.

(d) Payments pursuant to paragraph (a) of this section shall be made in such manner and in such currency or currencies as the Board of Governors shall determine. If such payments are made to a member in currencies other than its own, the transfer of such currencies and their use by the receiving country shall be without restriction by any member.

ARTICLE VIII. ORGANIZATION AND MANAGEMENT

SECTION 1. STRUCTURE OF THE BANK

The Bank shall have a Board of Governors, a Board of Executive Directors, a President, an Executive Vice President, a Vice President in charge of the Fund, and such other officers and staff as may be considered necessary.

SECTION 2. BOARD OF GOVERNORS

(a) All the powers of the Bank shall be vested in the Board of Governors. Each member shall appoint one governor and one alternate, who shall serve for five years, subject to termination of appointment at any time, or to reappointment, at the pleasure of the appointing member. No alternate may vote except in the absence of his principal. The Board shall select one of the governors as Chairman, who shall hold office until the next regular meeting of the Board.

(b) The Board of Governors may delegate to the Board of Executive Directors all its powers except power to—

(i) admit new members and determine the conditions of their admission;

(ii) increase or decrease the authorized ordinary capital stock and inter-regional[35] capital stock of the Bank and the contributions to the Fund;

(iii) elect the President of the Bank and determine his remuneration;

(iv) suspend a member, pursuant to Article IX, Section 2;

(v) determine the remuneration of the executive directors and their alternates;

(vi) hear and decide any appeals from interpretations of this Agreement given by the Board of Executive Directors;

[35] Action by the Board of Governors on June 1, 1976 (TIAS 8383) inserted "ordinary capital stock and inter-regional" in para. (ii), and struck out "Bank" and inserted in lieu thereof "ordinary capital resources and of the inter-regional capital resources" in para. (ix).

(vii) authorize the conclusion of general agreements for cooperation with other international organizations;

(viii) approve, after reviewing the auditor's reports, the general balance sheets and the statements of profit and loss of the institution;

(ix) determine the reserves and the distribution of the net profits of the ordinary capital resources and of the inter-regional capital resources[35] and of the Fund;

(x) select outside auditors to certify to the general balance sheets and the statements of profit and loss of the institution;

(xi) amend this Agreement; and

(xii) decide to terminate the operations of the Bank and to distribute its assets.

(c) The Board of Governors shall retain full power to exercise authority over any matter delegated to the Board of Executive Directors under paragraph (b) above.

(d) The Board of Governors shall, as a general rule, hold a meeting annually. Other meetings may be held when the Board of Governors so provides or when called by the Board of Executive Directors. Meetings of the Board of Governors also shall be called by the Board of Executive Directors whenever requested by five members of the Bank or by members having one-fourth of the total voting power of the member countries.

(e) A quorum for any meeting of the Board of Governors shall be an absolute majority of the total number of governors including an absolute majority of the governors of regional members,[36] representing not less than two-thirds of the total voting power of the member countries.

(f) The Board of Governors may establish a procedure whereby the Board of Executive Directors, when it deems such action appropriate, may submit a specific question to a vote of the governors without calling a meeting of the Board of Governors.

(g) The Board of Governors, and the Board of Executive Directors to the extent authorized, may adopt such rules and regulations as may be necessary or appropriate to conduct the business of the Bank.

(h) Governors and alternates shall serve as such without compensation from the Bank, but the Bank may pay them reasonable expenses incurred in attending meetings of the Board of Governors.

SECTION 3. BOARD OF EXECUTIVE DIRECTORS[37]

(a) The Board of Executive Directors shall be responsible for the conduct of the operations of the Bank, and for this purpose may exercise all the powers delegated to it by the Board of Governors.

---

[36] Action by the Board of Governors on June 1, 1976 (TIAS 8383) inserted "including an absolute majority of the governors of regional members,".

[37] Action by the Board of Governors on June 1, 1976 (TIAS 8383) amended and restated sec. 3. Action by the Board of Governors on April 28, 1964 (21 UST 157; TIAS 6920) added subsec. (j). Subsequently, action by the Board of Governors on March 23, 1972 (TIAS 7437) repealed subsec. (j). It formerly read as follows:

"(j) Upon the admission to the Bank of new members, having votes totalling not less than 22,000, the Board of Governors may, by a two-thirds majority of the total number of governors representing not less than three-fourths of the total voting power of the member countries, increase by one the number of Executive Directors to be elected.".

(b) (i) Executive directors shall be persons of recognized competence and wide experience in economic and financial matters but who shall not be governors.

(ii)[38] One executive director shall be appointed by the member country having the largest number of shares in the Bank, two executive directors shall be elected by the governors of the nonregional member countries, and not less than eight others shall be elected by the governors of the remaining member countries. The number of executive directors to be elected in the last category, and the procedure for the election of all the elective directors shall be determined by regulations adopted by the Board of Governors by a three-fourths majority of the total voting power of the member countries, including, with respect to provisions relating exclusively to the election of directors by nonregional member countries, a two-thirds majority of the governors of the nonregional members, and, with respect to provisions relating exclusively to the number and election of directors by the remaining member countries, by a two-thirds majority of the governors of regional members. Any change in the aforementioned regulations shall require the same majority of votes for its approval.

(iii) Executive directors shall be appointed or elected for terms of three years and may be reappointed or reelected for successive terms.

(c) Each executive director shall appoint an alternate who shall have full power to act for him when he is not present. Directors and alternates shall be citizens of the member countries. None of the elected directors and their alternates may be of the same citizenship, except in the case of countries that are not borrowers. Alternates may participate in meetings but may vote only when they are acting in place of their principals.

(d) Directors shall continue in office until their successors are appointed or elected. If the office of an elected director becomes vacant more than 180 days before the end of his term, a successor shall be elected for the remainder of the term by the governors who elected the former director. An absolute majority of the votes cast shall be required for election. While the office remains vacant, the alternate shall have all the powers of the former director except the power to appoint an alternate.

(e) The Board of Executive Directors shall function in continuous session at the principal office of the Bank and shall meet as often as the business of the Bank may require.

(f) A quorum for any meeting of the Board of Executive Directors shall be an absolute majority of the total number of directors, including an absolute majority of regional members,[39] representing not less than two-thirds of the total voting power of the member countries.

(g) A member of the Bank may send a representative to attend any meeting of the Board of Executive Directors when a matter especially affecting that member is under consideration. Such right of representation shall be regulated by the Board of Governors.

---

[38] Action by the Board of Governors on June 1, 1976 (TIAS 8383) amended and restated para. (ii).

[39] Action by the Board of Governors on June 1, 1976 (TIAS 8383) inserted ", including an absolute majority of regional members,".

(h) The Board of Executive Directors may appoint such committees as it deems advisable. Membership of such committees need not be limited to governors, directors, or alternates.

(i) The Board of Executive Directors shall determine the basic organization of the Bank, including the number and general responsibilities of the chief administrative and professional positions of the staff, and shall approve the budget of the Bank.

SECTION 4.[40] VOTING

(a) Each member country shall have 135 votes plus one vote for each share of ordinary capital stock and for each share of inter-regional capital stock of the Bank held by that country, provided, however, that, in connection with any increase in the authorized ordinary or inter-regional capital stock, the Board of Governors may determine that the capital stock authorized by such increase shall not have voting rights and that such increase of stock shall not be subject to the preemptive rights established in Article II, Section 3(b).

(b) No increase in the subscription of any member to either the ordinary capital stock or the inter-regional capital stock shall become effective, and any right to subscribe thereto is hereby waived, which would have the effect of reducing the voting power (i) of the regional developing members below 53.5 percent of the total voting power of the member countries; (ii) of the member having the largest number of shares below 34.5 percent of such total voting power; or (iii) of Canada below 4 percent of such total voting power.

(c) In voting in the Board of Governors, each governor shall be entitled to cast the votes of the member country which he represents. Except as otherwise specifically provided in this Agreement, all matters before the Board of Governors shall be decided by a majority of the total voting power of the member countries.

(d) In voting in the Board of Executive Directors:

(i) the appointed director shall be entitled to cast the number of votes of the member country which appointed him;

(ii) each elected director shall be entitled to cast the number of votes that counted toward his election, which votes shall be cast as a unit; and

(iii) except as otherwise specifically provided in this Agreement, all matters before the Board of Executive Directors shall be decided by a majority of the total voting power of the member countries.

SECTION 5. PRESIDENT, EXECUTIVE VICE PRESIDENT, AND STAFF

(a)[41] The Board of Governors, by a majority of the total voting power of the member countries, including an absolute majority of the governors of regional members, shall elect a President of the Bank who, while holding office, shall not be a governor or an executive director or alternate for either.

---

[40] Action by the Board of Governors on June 1, 1976 (TIAS 8383) amended and restated sec. 4.

[41] Action by the Board of Governors on June 1, 1976 (TIAS 8383) amended and restated subsec. (a).

Under the direction of the Board of Executive Directors, the President of the Bank shall conduct the ordinary business of the Bank and shall be chief of its staff. He also shall be the presiding officer at meetings of the Board of Executive Directors, but shall have no vote, except that it shall be his duty to cast a deciding vote when necessary to break a tie.

The President of the Bank shall be the legal representative of the Bank. The term of office of the President of the Bank shall be five years, and he may be reelected to successive terms. He shall cease to hold office when the Board of Governors so decides by a majority of the total voting power of the member countries, including a majority of the total voting power of the regional member countries.

(b) The Executive Vice President shall be appointed by the Board of Executive Directors on the recommendation of the President of the Bank. Under the direction of the Board of Executive Directors and the President of the Bank, the Executive Vice President shall exercise such authority and perform such functions in the administration of the Bank as may be determined by the Board of the Executive Directors. In the absence or incapacity of the President of the Bank, the Executive Vice President shall exercise the authority and perform the functions of the President.

The Executive Vice President shall participate in meetings of the Board of Executive Directors but shall have no vote at such meetings, except that he shall cast the deciding vote, as provided in paragraph (a) of this section, when he is acting in place of the President of the Bank.

(c) In addition to the Vice President referred to in Article IV, Section 8(b), the Board of Executive Directors may, on recommendation of the President of the Bank, appoint other vice presidents who shall exercise such authority and perform such functions as the Board of Executive Directors may determine.

(d) The President, officers, and staff of the Bank, in the discharge of their offices, owe their duty entirely to the Bank and shall recognize no other authority. Each member of the Bank shall respect the international character of this duty.

(e) The paramount consideration in the employment of the staff and in the determination of the conditions of service shall be the necessity of securing the highest standards of efficiency, competence, and integrity. Due regard shall also be paid to the importance of recruiting the staff on as wide a geographical basis as possible, taking into account the regional character of the institution.[42]

(f) The Bank, its officers and employees, shall not interfere in the political affairs of any member, nor shall they be influenced in their decisions by the political character of the member or members concerned. Only economic considerations shall be relevant to their decisions, and these considerations shall be weighted impartially in order to achieve the purpose and functions stated in Article I.

[42] Action by the Board of Governors on June 1, 1976 (TIAS 8383) inserted "taking into account the regional character of the institution".

SECTION 6. PUBLICATION OF REPORTS AND PROVISION OF INFORMATION

(a)[43] The Bank shall publish an annual report containing separate audited statements of the accounts of the ordinary capital resources and of the inter-regional capital resources. It shall also transmit quarterly to the members summary statements of the financial position and profit-and-loss statements showing separately the results of its ordinary operations and its inter-regional resources operations.

(b) The Bank may also publish such other reports as it deems desirable to carry out its purpose and functions.

ARTICLE IX. WITHDRAWAL AND SUSPENSION OF MEMBERS

SECTION 1. RIGHT TO WITHDRAW

Any member may withdraw from the Bank by delivering to the Bank at its principal office written notice of its intention to do so. Such withdrawal shall become finally effective on the date specified in the notice but in no event less than six months after the notice is delivered to the Bank. However, at any time before the withdrawal becomes finally effective, the member may notify the Bank in writing of the cancellation of its notice of intention to withdraw.

After withdrawing, a member shall remain liable for all direct and contingent obligations to the Bank to which it was subject at the date of delivery of the withdrawal notice, including those specified in Section 3 of this article. However, if the withdrawal becomes finally effective, the member shall not incur any liability for obligations resulting from operations of the Bank effected after the date on which the withdrawal notice was received by the Bank.

SECTION 2. SUSPENSION OF MEMBERSHIP

If a member fails to fulfill any of its obligations to the Bank, the Bank may suspend its membership by decision of the Board of Governors by a three-fourths majority of the total voting power of the member countries, including a two-thirds majority of the total number of governors, which, in the case of suspension of a regional member country, shall include a two-thirds majority of the governors of regional members and, in the case of suspension of a non-regional member country, a two-thirds majority of the governors of non-regional members.[44]

The member so suspended shall automatically cease to be a member of the Bank one year from the date of its suspension unless the Board of Governors decides by the same majority to terminate the suspension.

While under suspension, a member shall not be entitled to exercise any rights under this Agreement, except the right of withdrawal, but shall remain subject to all its obligations.

[43] Action by the Board of Governors on June 1, 1976 (TIAS 8383) amended and restated subsec. (a).

[44] Action by the Board of Governors on June 1, 1976 (TIAS 8383) amended and restated this paragraph.

SECTION 3. SETTLEMENT OF ACCOUNTS

(a) After a country ceases to be a member, it no longer shall share in the profits or losses of the Bank, nor shall it incur any liability with respect to loans and guarantees entered into by the Bank thereafter. However, it shall remain liable for all amounts it owes the Bank and for its contingent liabilities to the Bank so long as any part of the loans or guarantees contracted by the Bank before the date on which the country ceased to be a member remains outstanding.

(b) When a country ceases to be a member, the Bank shall arrange for the repurchase of such country's capital stock as a part of the settlement of accounts pursuant to the provisions of this section; but the country shall have no other rights under this Agreement except as provided in this section and in Article XIII, Section 2.

(c) The Bank and the country ceasing to be a member may agree on the repurchase of the capital stock on such terms as are deemed appropriate in the circumstances, without regard to the provisions of the following paragraph. Such agreement may provide, among other things, for a final settlement of all obligations of the country to the Bank.

(d) If the agreement referred to in the preceding paragraph has not been consummated within six months after the country ceases to be a member or such other time as the Bank and such country may agree upon, the repurchase price of such country's capital stock shall be its book value, according to the books of the Bank, on the date when the country ceased to be a member. Such repurchase shall be subject to the following conditions:

(i) As a prerequisite for payment, the country ceasing to be a member shall surrender its stock certificates, and such payment may be made in such installments, at such times and in such available currencies as the Bank determines, taking into account the financial position of the Bank.

(ii) Any amount which the Bank owes the country for the repurchase of its capital stock shall be withheld to the extent that the country or any of its subdivisions or agencies remains liable to the Bank as a result of loan or guarantee operations. The amount withheld may, at the option of the Bank, be applied on any such liability as it matures. However, no amount shall be withheld on account of the country's contingent liability for future calls on its subscription pursuant to Article II, Section 4(a)(ii), or Article IIA, Section 3(c).[45]

(iii) If the Bank sustains net losses on any loans or participations, or as a result of any guarantees, outstanding on the date the country ceased to be a member, and the amount of such losses exceeds the amount of the reserves provided therefor on such date, such country shall repay on demand the amount by which the repurchase price of its shares would have been reduced, if the losses had been taken into account when the book value of the shares, according to the books of the Bank, was

[45] Action by the Board of Governors on June 1, 1976 (TIAS 8383) inserted "or Article IIA, Section 3(c)".

determined. In addition, the former member shall remain liable on any call pursuant to Article II, Section 4(a)(ii), or Article IIA, Section 3(c),[45] to the extent that it would have been required to respond if the impairment of capital had occurred and the call had been made at the time the repurchase price of its share had been determined.

(e) In no event shall any amount due to a country for its shares under this section be paid until six months after the date upon which the country ceases to be a member. If within that period the Bank terminates operations, all rights of such country shall be determined by the provisions of Article X, and such country shall be considered still a member of the Bank for the purposes of such article except that it shall have no voting rights.

ARTICLE X. SUSPENSION AND TERMINATION OF OPERATIONS

SECTION 1. SUSPENSION OF OPERATIONS

In an emergency the Board of Executive Directors may suspend operations in respect of new loans and guarantees until such time as the Board of Governors may have an opportunity to consider the situation and take pertinent measures.

SECTION 2.[46] TERMINATION OF OPERATIONS

The Bank may terminate its operations by a decision of the Board of Governors by a three-fourths majority of the total voting power of the member countries, including a two-thirds majority of the governors of regional members. After such termination of operations the Bank shall forthwith cease all activities, except those incident to the conservation, preservation, and realization of its assets and settlement of its obligations.

SECTION 3. LIABILITY OF MEMBERS AND PAYMENT OF CLAIMS

(a) The liability of all members arising from the subscriptions to the capital stock of the Bank and in respect to the depreciation of their currencies shall continue until all direct and contingent obligations shall have been discharged.

(b) All creditors holding direct claims shall be paid out of the assets of the Bank to which such claims are chargeable[47] and then out of payments to the Bank on unpaid or callable subscriptions to which such claims are chargeable.[47] Before making any payments to creditors holding direct claims, the Board of Executive Directors shall make such arrangements as are necessary, in its judgment, to ensure a pro rata distribution among holders of direct and contingent claims.

SECTION 4. DISTRIBUTION OF ASSETS

(a)[48] No distribution of assets shall be made to members on account of their subscriptions to the capital stock of the Bank until

[46] Action by the Board of Governors on June 1, 1976 (TIAS 8383) amended and restated sec. 2.

[47] Action by the Board of Governors on June 1, 1976 (TIAS 8383) inserted "to which such claims are chargeable".

[48] Action by the Board of Governors on June 1, 1976 (TIAS 8383) amended and restated subsec. (a).

all liabilities to creditors chargeable to such capital stock shall have been discharged or provided for. Moreover, such distribution must be approved by a decision of the Board of Governors by a three-fourths majority of the total voting power of the member countries, including a two-thirds majority of the governors of regional members.

(b) Any distribution of the assets of the Bank to the members shall be in proportion to capital stock held by each member and shall be effected at such times and under such conditions as the Bank shall deem fair and equitable. The shares of assets distributed need not be uniform as to type of assets. No member shall be entitled to receive its share in such a distribution of assets until it has settled all of its obligations to the Bank.

(c) Any member receiving assets distributed pursuant to this article shall enjoy the same rights with respect to such assets as the Bank enjoyed prior to their distribution.

ARTICLE XI. IMMUNITIES AND PRIVILEGES

SECTION 1. SCOPE OF ARTICLE

To enable the Bank to fulfill its purpose and the functions with which it is entrusted, the status, immunities, and privileges set forth in this article shall be accorded to the Bank in the territories of each member.

SECTION 2. LEGAL STATUS

The Bank shall possess juridical personality and, in particular, full capacity—

(a) to contract;

(b) to acquire and dispose of immovable and movable property; and

(c) to institute legal proceedings.

SECTION 3. JUDICIAL PROCEEDINGS

Actions may be brought against the Bank only in a court of competent jurisdiction in the territories of a member in which the Bank has an office, has appointed an agent for the purpose of accepting service or notice of processes, or has issued or guaranteed securities.

No action shall be brought against the Bank by members or persons acting for or deriving claims from members. However, member countries shall have recourse to such special procedures to settle controversies between the Bank and its members as may be prescribed in this Agreement, in the bylaws and regulations of the Bank or in contracts entered into with the Bank.

Property and assets of the Banks shall, wheresoever located and by whomsoever held, be immune from all forms of seizure, attachment or execution before the delivery of final judgment against the Bank.

SECTION 4. IMMUNITY OF ASSETS

Property and assets of the Bank, wheresoever located and by whomsoever held, shall be considered public international property and shall be immune from search, requisition, confiscation, expropriation or any other form of taking or foreclosure by executive or legislative action.

SECTION 5. INVIOLABILITY OF ARCHIVES

The archives of the Bank shall be inviolable.

SECTION 6. FREEDOM OF ASSETS FROM RESTRICTIONS

To the extent necessary to carry out the purpose and functions of the Bank and to conduct operations in accordance with this Agreement, all property and other assets of the Bank shall be free from restrictions, regulations, controls and moratoria of any nature, except as may otherwise be provided in this Agreement.

SECTION 7. PRIVILEGE FOR COMMUNICATIONS

The official communications of the Bank shall be accorded by each member the same treatment that it accords to the official communications of other members.

SECTION 8. PERSONAL IMMUNITIES AND PRIVILEGES

All governors, executive directors, alternates, officers and employees of the Bank shall have the following privileges and immunities:

(a) Immunity from legal process with respect to acts performed by them in their official capacity, except when the Bank waives this immunity.

(b) When not local nationals, the same immunities from immigration restrictions, alien registration requirements and national service obligations and the same facilities as regards exchange provisions as are accorded by members to the representatives, officials, and employees of comparable rank of other members.

(c) The same privileges in respect of traveling facilities as are accorded by members to representatives, officials, and employees of comparable rank of other members.

SECTION 9. IMMUNITIES FROM TAXATION

(a) The Bank, its property, other assets, income, and the operations and transactions it carries out pursuant to this Agreement, shall be immune from all taxation and from all customs duties. The Bank shall also be immune from any obligation relating to the payment, withholding or collection of any tax, or duty.

(b) No tax shall be levied on or in respect of salaries and emoluments paid by the Bank to executive directors, alternates, officials or employees of the Bank who are not local citizens or other local nationals.

(c) No tax of any kind shall be levied on any obligation or security issued by the Bank, including any dividend or interest thereon, by whomsoever held—

(i) which discriminates against such obligation or security solely because it is issued by the Bank; or

(ii) if the sole jurisdictional basis for such taxation is the place or currency in which it is issued, made payable or paid, or the location of any office or place of business maintained by the Bank.

(d) No tax of any kind shall be levied on any obligation or security guaranteed by the Bank, including any dividend or interest thereon, by whomsoever held—

(i) which discriminates against such obligation or security solely because it is guaranteed by the Bank; or

(ii) if the sole jurisdictional basis for such taxation is the location of any office or place of business maintained by the Bank.

SECTION 10. IMPLEMENTATION

Each member, in accordance with its juridical system, shall take such action as is necessary to make effective in its own territories the principles set forth in this article, and shall inform the Bank of the action which it has taken on the matter.

ARTICLE XII. AMENDMENTS

(a)[49] (i) This agreement may be amended only by decision of the Board of Governors by a majority of the total number of governors, including two-thirds of the governors of regional members, representing not less than three-fourths of the total voting power of the member countries, provided, however, that the voting majorities provided in Article II, Section 1(b), may be amended only by the voting majorities stated therein.

(ii) The relevant articles of the Agreement may be amended as provided in paragraph (a)(i) above to provide for the merger of the inter-regional capital stock and the ordinary capital stock at such time as the Bank shall have discharged its liabilities on all its ordinary capital borrowing which were outstanding at December 31, 1974.

(b)[49] Notwithstanding the provisions of (a) above, the unanimous agreement of the Board of Governors shall be required for the approval of any amendment modifying:

(i) the right to withdraw from the Bank as provided in Article IX, Section 1;

(ii) the right to purchase capital stock of the Bank and to contribute to the Fund as provided in Article II, Section 3(b) and in Article IV, Section 3(g), respectively; and

(iii) the limitation on liability as provided in Article II, Section 3(d), Article IIA, Section 2(e), and Article IV, Section 5.

(c) Any proposal to amend this Agreement, whether emanating from a member or the Board of Executive Directors, shall be communicated to the Chairman of the Board of Governors, who shall bring the proposal before the Board of Governors. When an amendment has been adopted, the Bank shall so certify in an official communication addressed to all members. Amendments shall enter into force for all members three months after the date of the official communication unless the Board of Governors shall specify a different period.

[49] Action by the Board of Governors on June 1, 1976 (TIAS 8383) amended and restated subsecs. (a) and (b).

Article XIII. Interpretation and Arbitration

SECTION 1. INTERPRETATION

(a) Any question of interpretation of the provisions of this Agreement arising between any member and the Bank or between any members of the Bank shall be submitted to the Board of Executive Directors for decision.

Members especially affected by the question under consideration shall be entitled to direct representation before the Board of Executive Directors as provided in Article VIII, Section 3(g).

(b) In any case where the Board of Executive Directors has given a decision under (a) above, any member may require that the question be submitted to the Board of Governors, whose decision shall be final. Pending the decision of the Board of Governors, the Bank may, so far as it deems it necessary, act on the basis of the decision of the Board of Executive Directors.

SECTION 2. ARBITRATION

If a disagreement should arise between the Bank and a country which has ceased to be a member, or between the Bank and any member after adoption of a decision to terminate the operation of the Bank such disagreement shall be submitted to arbitration by a tribunal of three arbitrators. One of the arbitrators shall be appointed by the Bank, another by the country concerned, and the third, unless the parties otherwise agree, by the Secretary General of the Organization of American States. If all efforts to reach an unanimous agreement fail, decisions shall be made by a majority vote of the three arbitrators.

The third arbitrator shall be empowered to settle all questions of procedure in any case where the parties are in disagreement with respect thereto.

Article XIV. General Provisions

SECTION 1. PRINCIPAL OFFICE

The principal office of the Bank shall be located in Washington, District of Columbia, United States of America.

SECTION 2. RELATIONS WITH OTHER ORGANIZATIONS

The Bank may enter into arrangements with other organizations with respect to the exchange of information or for other purposes consistent with this Agreement.

SECTION 3. CHANNEL OF COMMUNICATION

Each member shall designate an official entity for purposes of communication with the Bank on matters connected with this Agreement.

SECTION 4. DEPOSITORIES

Each member shall designate its central bank as a depository in which the Bank may keep its holdings of such member's currency and other assets of the Bank. If a member has no central bank, it shall, in agreement with the Bank, designate another institution for such purpose.

ARTICLE XV. FINAL PROVISIONS

SECTION 1. SIGNATURE AND ACCEPTANCE

(a) This Agreement shall be deposited with the General Secretariat of the Organization of American States, where it shall remain open until December 31, 1959, for signature by the representatives of the countries listed in Annex A. Each signatory country shall deposit with the General Secretariat of the Organization of American States an instrument setting forth that it has accepted or ratified this Agreement in accordance with its own laws and has taken the steps necessary to enable it to fulfill all of its obligations under this Agreement.

(b) The General Secretariat of the Organization of American States shall send certified copies of this Agreement to the members of the Organization and duly notify them of each signature and deposit of the instrument of acceptance or ratification made pursuant to the foregoing paragraph, as well as the date thereof.

(c) At the time the instrument of acceptance or ratification is deposited on its behalf, each country shall deliver to the General Secretariat of the Organization of American States, for the purpose of meeting administrative expenses of the Bank, gold or United States dollars equivalent to one-tenth of one percent of the purchase price of the shares of the Bank subscribed by it and of its quota in the Fund. This payment shall be credited to the member on account of its subscription and quota prescribed pursuant to Articles II, Section 4(a)(i), and IV, Section 3(d)(i). At any time on or after the date on which its instrument of acceptance or ratification is deposited, any member may make additional payments to be credited to the member on account of its subscription and quota prescribed pursuant to Articles II and IV. The General Secretariat of the Organization of American States shall hold all funds paid under this paragraph in a special deposit account or accounts and shall make such funds available to the Bank not later than the time of the first meeting of the Board of Governors held pursuant to Section 3 of this article. If this Agreement has not come into force by December 31, 1959, the General Secretariat of the Organization of American States shall return such funds to the countries that delivered them.

(d) On or after the date on which the Bank commences operations, the General Secretariat of the Organization of American States may receive the signature and the instrument of acceptance or ratification of this Agreement from any country whose membership has been approved in accordance with Article II, Section 1(b).

SECTION 2. ENTRY INTO FORCE

(a) This Agreement shall enter into force when it has been signed and instruments of acceptance or ratification have been deposited, in accordance with Section 1(a) of this article, by representatives of countries whose subscriptions comprise not less than 85 percent of the total subscriptions set forth in Annex A.

(b) Countries whose instruments of acceptance or ratification were deposited prior to the date on which the agreement entered into force shall become members on that date. Other countries shall become members on the dates on which their instruments of acceptance or ratification are deposited.

SECTION 3. COMMENCEMENT OF OPERATIONS

(a) The Secretary General of the Organization of American States shall call the first meeting of the Board of Governors as soon as this Agreement enters into force under Section 2 of this article.

(b) At the first meeting of the Board of Governors arrangements shall be made for the selection of the executive directors and their alternates in accordance with the provisions of Article VIII, Section 3, and for the determination of the date on which the Bank shall commence operations. Notwithstanding the provisions of Article VII, Section 3, the governors, if they deem it desirable, may provide that the first term to be served by such directors may be less than three years.

DONE at the city of Washington, District of Columbia, United States of America, in a single original, dated April 8, 1959, whose English, French, Portuguese, and Spanish texts are equally authentic.

ANNEX A—SUBSCRIPTIONS TO AUTHORIZED CAPITAL STOCK OF THE BANK[50]

[In shares of US $10,000 of the weight and fineness in effect on Jan. 1, 1959]

Country	Paid-in capital shares	Call-able shares	Total sub-scrip-tion
Argentina	5,157	5,157	10,314
Bolivia	414	414	828
Brazil	5,157	5,157	10,314
Chile	1,416	1,416	2,832
Colombia	1,415	1,415	2,830
Costa Rica	207	207	414
Cuba[51]	1,842	1,842	3,684
Dominican Republic	276	276	552
Ecuador	276	276	552
El Salvador	207	207	414
Guatemala	276	276	552
Haiti	207	207	414
Honduras	207	207	414
Mexico	3,315	3,315	6,630
Nicaragua	207	207	414
Panama	207	207	414
Paraguay	207	207	414
Peru	691	691	1,382
United States of America	15,000	20,000	35,000
Uruguay	553	553	1,106
Venezuela	2,763	2,763	5,526
Total	40,000	45,000	85,000

[50] Subsequent changes in membership subscriptions are not reflected in Annex A.

[51] Cuba's shares are carried as "unassigned" as it never became a member of the Inter-American Development Bank.

Annex B—Contribution Quotas for the Fund for Special Operations[52]

[In thousands of U.S. dollars of the weight and fineness in effect on Jan. 1, 1959]

Country:	Quota
Argentina	10,314
Bolivia	828
Brazil	10,314
Chile	2,832
Colombia	2,830
Costa Rica	414
Cuba[53]	3,684
Dominican Republic	552
Ecuador	552
El Salvador	414
Guatemala	552
Haiti	414
Honduras	414
Mexico	6,630
Nicaragua	414
Panama	414
Paraguay	414
Peru	1,382
United States of America	100,000
Uruguay	1,106
Venezuela	5,526
Total	150,000

[52] Subsequent changes in membership quotas are not reflected in Annex B.

[53] Cuba's shares are carried as "unassigned" as it never became a member of the Inter-American Development Bank.

8. Inter-American Investment Corporation

Done at Washington, November 19, 1984; Entered into force, March 23, 1986

ARTICLES OF AGREEMENT OF THE INTER-AMERICAN INVESTMENT CORPORATION, AS AMENDED [1]

The countries on behalf of which this Agreement is signed agree to create the Inter-American Investment Corporation, which shall be governed by the following provisions:

ARTICLE I—PURPOSE AND FUNCTIONS

SECTION 1. PURPOSE

The purpose of the Corporation shall be to promote the economic development of its regional developing member countries by encouraging the establishment, expansion, and modernization of private enterprises, preferably those that are small and medium-scale, in such a way as to supplement the activities of the Inter-American Development Bank (hereinafter referred to as "the Bank").

Enterprises with partial share participation by government or other public entities, whose activities strengthen the private sector of the economy, are eligible for financing by the Corporation.

SECTION 2. FUNCTIONS

In order to accomplish its purpose, the Corporation shall undertake the following functions in support of the enterprises referred to in Section 1:

(a) Assist, alone or in association with other lenders or investors, in the financing of the establishment, expansion and modernization of enterprises, utilizing such instruments and/or mechanisms as the Corporation deems appropriate in each instance;

(b) Facilitate their access to private and public capital, domestic and foreign, and to technical and managerial know-how;

(c) Stimulate the development of investment opportunities conducive to the flow of private and public capital, domestic and foreign, into investments in the member countries;

(d) Take in each case the proper and necessary measures for their financing, bearing in mind their needs and principles based on prudent administration of the resources of the Corporation; and

(e) Provide technical cooperation for the preparation, financing and execution of projects, including the transfer of appropriate technology.

[1] TIAS 12087. Amendments made by resolutions effective October 3, 1995, July 4, 2001 and June 12, 2002. For states that are parties to this Agreement, see Department of State publication, *Treaties in Force.*

SECTION 3. POLICIES

The activities of the Corporation shall be conducted in accordance with the operating, financial and investment policies set forth in detail in Regulations approved by the Board of Executive Directors of the Corporation, which Regulations may be amended by said Board.

ARTICLE II—MEMBERS AND CAPITAL

SECTION 1. MEMBERS [2]

(a) The founding members of the Corporation shall be those member countries of the Bank that have signed this Agreement by the date specified in Article XI, Section 1(a) and made the initial payment required in Section 3(b) of this Article;

(b) The other member countries of the Bank and non-member countries of the Bank may accede to this Agreement on such date and in accordance with such conditions as the Board of Governors of the Corporation may determine by a majority representing at least two-thirds of the votes of the members, which shall include two-thirds of the Governors.

(c) The word "members" as used in this Agreement shall refer to member countries of the Bank and non-member countries of the Bank which are members of the Corporation.

SECTION 2. RESOURCES

(a) The initial authorized capital stock of the Corporation shall be two hundred million dollars of the United States of America (US$200,000,000).

(b) The authorized capital stock shall be divided into twenty thousand (20,000) shares having a par value of ten thousand dollars of the United States of America (US$10,000) each. Any shares not initially subscribed by the founding members in accordance with Section 3(a) of this Article shall be available for subsequent subscription in accordance with Section 3(d) hereof.

(c) The Board of Governors may increase the authorized capital stock by a majority representing at least three-fourths of the votes of the members, which shall include two-thirds of the Governors.

(d) In addition to the authorized capital referred to above, the Board of Governors may, after the date in which the initial authorized capital has been fully paid in, authorize the issue of callable capital and establish the terms and conditions for the subscription thereof, as follows:

(i) such decision shall be approved by a majority representing at least three-fourths of the votes of the members which shall include two-thirds of the Governors; and

(ii) the callable capital shall be divided into shares with a par value of ten thousand dollars of the United States of America (US$10,000) each.

---

[2] Title II of S. 2416 as introduced in the Senate on March 13, 1984, and enacted into law by reference in Public Law 98–473 (98 Stat. 1885), authorized U.S. membership in the Inter-American Investment Corporation. For text of the IIC Act, see *Legislation on Foreign Relations Through 2005*, vol. III, sec. I.

(e) The callable capital shares shall be subject to call only when required to meet the obligations of the Corporation created under Article III, Section 7(a). In the event of such a call, payment may be made at the option of the member in United States dollars, or in the currency required to discharge the obligations of the Corporation for the purpose for which the call is made. Calls on the shares shall be uniform and proportionate for all shares. Obligations of the members to make payments on any such calls are independent of each other and failure of one or more members to make payments on any such calls shall not excuse any other member from its obligation to make payment. Successive calls may be made if necessary to meet the obligations of the Corporation.

(f) The other resources of the Corporation shall consist of:

(i) amounts accruing by way of dividends, commissions, interest, and other funds derived from the investments of the Corporation;

(ii) amounts received upon the sale of investments or the repayment of loans;

(iii) amounts raised by the Corporation by means of borrowings; and

(iv) other contributions and funds entrusted to its administration.

SECTION 3. SUBSCRIPTIONS

(a) Each founding member shall subscribe the number of shares specified in Annex A.[3]

(b) The payment for capital stock, set forth in Annex A, by each founding member shall be made in four annual, equal and consecutive installments each of twenty-five percent of such amount. The first installment shall be paid by each member in full within three months after the date on which the Corporation begins operation pursuant to Article XI, Section 3 below, or the date on which such founding member accedes to this Agreement, or by such date or dates thereafter as the Board of Executive Directors of the Corporation specifies. The remaining three installments shall be paid on such dates as are determined by the Board of Executive Directors of the Corporation but not earlier than December 31, 1985, December 31, 1986, and December 31, 1987, respectively. The payment of each of the last three installments of capital subscribed by each of the member countries shall be subject to fulfillment of such legal requirements as may be appropriate in the respective countries. Payment shall be made in United States dollars. The Corporation shall specify the place or places of payment.

(c) Shares initially subscribed by the founding members shall be issued at par.

(d) The conditions governing the subscription of shares to be issued after the initial share subscription by the founding members which shall not have been subscribed under Article II, Section 2(b), as well as the dates of payment thereof, shall be determined by the Board of Executive Directors of the Corporation.

---

[3] Public Law 98–473 (98 Stat. 1885) authorized the initial U.S. subscription of $51 million (5,100 shares).

SECTION 4. RESTRICTION ON TRANSFERS AND PLEDGE OF SHARES

Shares of the Corporation may not be pledged, encumbered or transferred in any manner whatever except to the Corporation, unless the Board of Governors of the Corporation approves a transfer between members by a majority of the Governors representing four-fifths of the votes of the members.

SECTION 5. PREFERENTIAL SUBSCRIPTION RIGHT

In case of an increase in capital, in accordance with Section 2(c) and (d) of this Article, each member shall be entitled, subject to such terms as may be established by the Corporation, to a percentage of the increased shares equivalent to the proportion which its shares heretofore subscribed bears to the total capital of the Corporation. However, no member shall be obligated to subscribe to any part of the increased capital.

SECTION 6. LIMITATION ON LIABILITY

The liability of members on the shares subscribed by them shall be limited to the unpaid portion of their price at issuance. No member shall be liable, by reason of its membership, for obligations of the Corporation.

ARTICLE III—OPERATIONS

SECTION 1. OPERATING PROCEDURES.

In order to accomplish its purposes, the Corporation is authorized to:

(a) Identify and promote projects which meet criteria of economic feasibility and efficiency, with preference given to projects that have one or more of the following characteristics:

(i) they promote the development and use of material and human resources in the developing countries which are members of the Corporation;

(ii) they provide incentives for the creation of jobs;

(iii) they encourage savings and the use of capital in productive investments;

(iv) they contribute to the generation and/or savings of foreign exchange;

(v) they foster management capability and technology transfer; and

(vi) they promote broader public ownership of enterprises through the participation of as many investors as possible in the capital stock of such enterprises.

(b) Make direct investments, through the granting of loans, and preferably through the subscription and purchase of shares or convertible debt instruments, in enterprises located in regional developing member countries, and make indirect investments in such enterprises through other financial institutions, both of which investments require the significant generation of local added value.

(c) Promote the participation of other sources of financing and/or expertise through appropriate means, including the organization of loan syndicates, the underwriting of securities and participations, joint ventures, and other forms of association such as licensing arrangements, marketing or management contracts;

(d) Conduct cofinancing operations and assist domestic financial institutions, international institutions and bilateral investment institutions;

(e) Provide technical cooperation, financial and general management assistance, and act as financial agent of enterprises;

(f) Help to establish, expand, improve and finance development finance companies in the private sector and other institutions to assist in the development of said sector;

(g) Promote the underwriting of shares and securities issues, and extend such underwriting provided the appropriate conditions are met, either individually or jointly with other financial entities;

(h) Administer funds of other private, public or semi-public institutions; for this purpose, the Corporation may sign management and trustee contracts;

(i) Conduct currency transactions essential to the activities of the Corporation; and

(j) Issue bonds, certificates of indebtedness and participation certificates, and enter into credit agreements.

SECTION 2. OTHER FORMS OF INVESTMENTS

The Corporation may make investments of its funds in such form or forms as it may deem appropriate in the circumstances, in accordance with Section 7(b) below.

SECTION 3. OPERATING PRINCIPLES

The operations of the Corporation shall be governed by the following principles:

(a) It shall not establish as a condition that the proceeds of its financing be used to procure goods and services originating in a predetermined country;

(b) It shall not assume responsibility for managing any enterprise in which it has invested and shall not exercise its voting rights for such purpose or for any other purpose which, in its opinion, is properly within the scope of managerial control;

(c) It shall provide financing on terms and conditions which it considers appropriate taking into account the requirements of the enterprises, the risks assumed by the Corporation and the terms and conditions normally obtained by private investors for similar financings;

(d) It shall seek to revolve its funds by selling its investments, provided such sale can be made in an appropriate form and under satisfactory conditions to the extent possible in accordance with Section 1(a)(vi) above;

(e) It shall seek to maintain a reasonable diversification in its investments;

(f) It shall apply financial, technical, economic, legal and institutional feasibility criteria to justify investments and the adequacy of the guarantees offered; and

(g) It shall not undertake any financing for which, in its opinion, sufficient capital could be obtained on adequate terms.

SECTION 4. LIMITATIONS

(a) With the exception of the investment of liquid assets of the Corporation referred to in Section 7(b) of this Article, investments of the Corporation shall be made only in enterprises located in developing regional member countries; such investments shall be made following sound rules of financial management.

(b) The Corporation shall not provide financing or undertake other investments in an enterprise in the territory of a member country if its government objects to such financing or investment.

SECTION 5. PROTECTION OF INTERESTS

Nothing in this Agreement shall prevent the Corporation from taking such action and exercising such rights as it may deem necessary for the protection of its interests in the event of default on any of its investments, actual or threatened insolvency of enterprises in which such investments have been made, or other situations which, in the opinion of the Corporation, threaten to jeopardize such investments.

SECTION 6. APPLICABILITY OF CERTAIN FOREIGN EXCHANGE RESTRICTIONS

Funds received by or payable to the Corporation in respect of an investment of the Corporation made in any member's territories shall not be free, solely by reason of any provision of this Agreement from generally applicable foreign exchange restrictions, regulations and controls in force in the territories of that member.

SECTION 7. OTHER POWERS

The Corporation shall also have the power to:

(a) Borrow funds and for that purpose furnish such collateral or other security as the Corporation shall determine, provided that the total amount outstanding on borrowing incurred or guarantees given by the Corporation, regardless of source, shall not exceed an amount equal to three times the sum of its subscribed capital, earned surplus and reserves;

(b) Invest funds not immediately needed in its financial operations, as well as funds held by it for other purposes, in such marketable obligations and securities as the Corporation may determine;

(c) Guarantee securities in which it has invested in order to facilitate their sale;

(d) Buy and/or sell securities it has issued or guaranteed or in which it has invested.

(e) Handle, on such terms as the Corporation may determine, any specific matters incidental to its business as may be entrusted to the Corporation by its shareholders or third parties, and discharge the duties of trustee in respect of trusts; and

(f) Exercise all other powers inherent and which may be necessary or useful for the accomplishment of its purposes, including the signing of contracts and conducting of necessary legal actions.

SECTION 8. POLITICAL ACTIVITY PROHIBITED

The Corporation and its officers shall not interfere in the political affairs of any member; nor shall they be influenced in their decisions by the political character of the member or members concerned. Only economic considerations shall be relevant to decisions of the Corporation, and these considerations shall be weighed impartially in order to achieve the purposes stated in this Agreement.

ARTICLE IV—ORGANIZATION AND MANAGEMENT

SECTION 1. STRUCTURE OF THE CORPORATION

The Corporation shall have a Board of Governors, a Board of Executive Directors, a Chairman of the Board of Executive Directors, a General Manager and such other officers and staff as may be determined by the Board of Executive Directors of the Corporation.

SECTION 2. BOARD OF GOVERNORS

(a) All the powers of the Corporation shall be vested in the Board of Governors.

(b) Each Governor and Alternate Governor of the Inter-American Development Bank appointed by a member country of the Bank which is also a member of the Corporation shall unless the respective country indicates to the contrary, be a Governor or Alternate Governor ex-officio, respectively, of the Corporation. No Alternate Governor may vote except in the absence of his principal. The Board of Governors shall select one of the Governors as Chairman of the Board of Governors. A Governor and Alternate Governor shall cease to hold office if the member by which they were appointed ceases to be a member of the Corporation.

(c) The Board of Governors may delegate all its powers to the Board of Executive Directors, except the power to:

(i) admit new members and determine the conditions of their admission;

(ii) increase or decrease the capital stock;

(iii) suspend a member;

(iv) consider and decide appeals on interpretations of this Agreement made by the Board of Executive Directors;

(v) approve, after receipt of the auditors report, the general balance sheets and the statements of profit and loss of the institution;

(vi) rule on reserves and the distribution of net income, and declare dividends;

(vii) engage the services of external auditors to examine the general balance sheets and the statements of profit and loss of the institution;

(viii) amend this Agreement; and

(ix) decide to suspend permanently the operations of the Corporation and to distribute its assets.

(d) The Board of Governors shall hold an annual meeting, which shall be held in conjunction with the annual meeting of the Board of Governors of the Inter-American Development Bank. It may meet on other occasions by call of the Board of Executive Directors.

(e) A quorum for any meeting of the Board of Governors shall be a majority of the Governors representing at least two-thirds of the votes of the members. The Board of Governors may establish a procedure whereby the Board of Executive Directors, if it deems appropriate, may submit a specific question to a vote of the Government without calling a meeting of the Board of Governors.

(f) The Board of Governors and the Board of Executive Directors, to the extent the latter is authorized, may issue such rules and regulations as may be necessary or appropriate to conduct the business of the Corporation.

(g) Governors and Alternate Governors shall serve as such without compensation from the Corporation.

SECTION 3. VOTING

(a) Each member shall have one vote for each fully paid share held by it and for each callable share subscribed.

(b) Except as otherwise provided, all matters before the Board of Governors or the Board of Executive Directors shall be decided by a majority of the votes of the members.

SECTION 4. BOARD OF EXECUTIVE DIRECTORS

(a) The Board of Executive Directors shall be responsible for the conduct of the operations of the Corporation and for this purpose shall exercise all the powers given it by this Agreement or delegated to it by the Board of Governors.

(b) The Executive Directors and Alternates shall be elected or appointed among the Executive Directors and Alternates of the Bank except when:

(i) a member country or a group of member countries of the Corporation is represented in the Board of Executive Directors of the Bank by an Executive Director and an Alternate which are citizens of countries which are not members of the Corporation; and

(ii) given the different structure of participation and composition, the member countries referred to in (c)(iii) below, as per the rotation arrangement agreed upon among said member countries, designate their own representatives for the positions corresponding to them in the Board of Executive Directors of the Corporation, whenever they could not be adequately represented by Directors or Alternates of the Bank.

(c) The Board of Executive Directors of the Corporation shall be composed as follows:

(i) one Executive Director shall be appointed by the member country having the largest number of shares in the Corporation;

(ii) nine Executive Directors shall be elected by the Governors for the regional developing member countries;

(iii) two Executive Directors shall be elected by the Governors for the remaining member countries.

The procedure for the election of Executive Directors shall be set forth in the Regulations to be adopted by the Board of Governors by a majority of at least two-thirds of the votes of the members.

One additional Executive Director may be elected by the Governors for the member countries mentioned in (iii) above under such conditions and within the term to be established under said Regulations and, in the event that such conditions were not met, by the Governors for the regional developing member countries, in conformity with the provisions of said Regulations.

Each Executive Director may designate an Alternate Director who shall have full power to act for him when he is not present.

(d) No Executive Director may simultaneously serve as a Governor of the Corporation.

(e) Elected Executive Directors shall be elected for terms of three years and may be reelected for successive terms.

(f) Each Director shall be entitled to cast the number of votes which the member or members of the Corporation whose votes counted towards his nomination or election are entitled to cast.

(g) All the votes which a Director is entitled to cast shall be cast as a unit.

(h) In the event of the temporary absence of an Executive Director and his Alternate, the Executive Director or, in his absence the Alternate Director may appoint a person to represent him.

(i) A Director shall cease to hold office if all the members whose votes counted toward his nomination or election cease to be members of the Corporation.

(j) The Board of Executive Directors shall operate at the headquarters of the Corporation, or exceptionally at such other location as shall be designated by said Board, and shall meet as frequently as the business of the institution requires.

(k) A quorum for any meeting of the Board of Executive Directors shall be a majority of the Directors representing not less than two-thirds of the votes of the members.

(l) Every member of the Corporation may send a representative to attend every meeting of the Board of Executive Directors, when a matter especially affecting that member is under consideration. Such right of representation shall be regulated by the Board of Governors.

SECTION 5. BASIC ORGANIZATION

The Board of Executive Director shall determine the basic organization of the Corporation, including the number and general responsibilities of the principal administrative and professional positions, and shall adopt the budget of the institution.

SECTION 6. EXECUTIVE COMMITTEE OF THE BOARD OF EXECUTIVE DIRECTORS

(a) The Executive Committee of the Board of Executive Directors shall be composed as follows:

(i) one person who is the Director or Alternate appointed by the member country having the largest number of shares in the Corporation;

(ii) two persons from among the Directors representing the regional developing member countries of the Corporation; and

(iii) one person from the Directors representing the other member countries.

The election of members of the Executive Committee and their Alternates in categories (ii) and (iii) above shall be made by the members of each respective group pursuant to procedures to be worked out within each group;

(b) The Chairman of the Board of Executive Directors shall preside over meetings of said Committee. In his absence, a member of the Committee chosen by a process of rotation shall preside over meetings.

(c) The Committee shall consider all loans and investments by the Corporation in enterprises in the member countries.

(d) All loans and investments shall require the vote of a majority of the Committee for approval. A quorum for any meeting of the Committee shall be three. An absence or abstention shall be considered a negative vote.

(e) A report with respect to each operation approved by the Committee shall be submitted to the Board of Executive Directors. At the request of any Director, such operation shall be presented to the Board for a vote. In the absence of such request within the period established by the Board, an operation shall be deemed approved by the Board.

(f) In the event that there is a tie vote regarding a proposed operation, such proposal shall be returned to Management for further review and analysis; if upon reconsideration in the Committee, a tie vote shall again occur, the Chairman of the Board of Executive Directors shall have the right to cast the deciding vote in the Committee.

(g) In the event that the Committee shall reject an operation, the Board of Executive Directors, upon the request of any Director, may require that Management's report on such operation, together with a summary of the Committee's review, be submitted to the Board for discussion and possible recommendation with regard to the technical and policy issues related to the operation and to comparable operations in the future.

SECTION 7. CHAIRMAN, GENERAL MANAGER AND OFFICERS

(a) The President of the Bank shall be ex-officio Chairman of the Board of Executive Directors of the Corporation. He shall preside over meetings of the Board of Executive Directors but without the right to vote except in the event of a tie. He may participate in meetings of the Board of Governors, but shall not vote at such meetings.

(b) The General Manager of the Corporation shall be appointed by the Board of Executive Directors, by a four-fifths majority of the total voting power, on the recommendation of the Chairman of the Board of Executive Directors, for such term as he shall indicate. The General Manager shall be chief of the officers and staff of the Corporation. Under the direction of the Board of Executive Directors and the general supervision of the Chairman of the Board of Executive Directors, he will conduct the ordinary business of the

Corporation and in consultation with the Board of Executive Directors and the Chairman of the Board of Executive Directors, shall be responsible for the organization, appointment and dismissal of the officers and staff. The General Manager may participate in meetings of the Board of Executive Directors but shall not vote at such meetings. The General Manager shall cease to hold office by resignation or by decision of the Board of Executive Directors, by a three-fifths majority of the total voting power, in which the Chairman of the Board of Executive Directors concurs.

(c) Whenever activities must be carried out that require specialized knowledge or cannot be handled by the regular staff of the Corporation, the Corporation shall obtain technical assistance from the staff of the Bank, or if it is unavailable, the services of experts and consultants may be engaged on a temporary basis.

(d) The officers and staff of the Corporation owe their duty entirely to the Corporation in the discharge of their office and shall recognize no other authority. Each member country shall respect the international character of such obligation.

(e) The Corporation shall have due regard for the need to assure the highest standards of efficiency, competence and integrity as the paramount consideration in appointing the staff of the Corporation and in establishing their conditions of service. Due regard shall also be paid to the importance of recruiting the staff on as wide a geographic basis as possible, taking into account the regional character of the institution.

SECTION 8. RELATIONS WITH THE BANK

(a) The Corporation shall be an entity separate and distinct from the Bank. The funds of the Corporation shall be kept separate and apart from those of the Bank. The provisions of this Section shall not prevent the Corporation from making arrangements with the Bank regarding facilities, personnel, services and others concerning reimbursement of administrative expenses paid by either organization on behalf of the other.

(b) The Corporation shall seek insofar as possible to utilize the facilities, installations and personnel of the Bank.

(c) Nothing in this Agreement shall make the Corporation liable for the acts or obligations of the Bank, or the Bank liable for the acts or obligations of the Corporation.

SECTION 9. PUBLICATION OF ANNUAL REPORTS AND CIRCULATION OF REPORTS

(a) The Corporation shall publish an annual report containing an audited statement of its accounts. It shall also send the members a quarterly summary of its financial position and a profit and loss statement indicating the results of its operations.

(b) The Corporation may also publish any such other reports as it deems appropriate in order to carry out its purpose and functions.

SECTION 10. DIVIDENDS

(a) The Board of Governors may determine what part of the Corporation's net income and surplus, after making provision for reserves, shall be distributed as dividends.

(b) Dividends shall be distributed pro rata in proportion to paid-in capital stock held by each member.

(c) Dividends shall be paid in such manner and in such currency or currencies as the Corporation may determine.

ARTICLE V—WITHDRAWAL AND SUSPENSION OF MEMBERS

SECTION 1. RIGHT OF WITHDRAWAL

(a) Any member may withdraw from the Corporation by notifying the Corporation's principal office in writing of its intention to do so. Such withdrawal shall become effective on the date specified in the notice but in no event prior to six months from the date on which such notice was delivered to the Corporation. At any time before the withdrawal becomes effective, the member may, upon written notice to the Corporation, renounce its intention to withdraw.

(b) Even after withdrawing, a member shall remain liable for all obligations to the Corporation to which it was subject at the date of delivery of the withdrawal notice, including those specified in Section 3 of this Article. However, if the withdrawal becomes effective, a member shall not incur any liability for obligations resulting from operations of the Corporation effected after the date on which the withdrawal notice was received by the latter.

SECTION 2. SUSPENSION OF MEMBERSHIP

(a) A member that fails to fulfill any of its obligations to the Corporation under this Agreement may be suspended by decision of the Board of Governors by a majority representing at least three-fourths of the votes of the members, which shall include two-thirds of the Governors.

(b) A member so suspended shall automatically cease to be a member of the Corporation within one year from the date of suspension unless the Board of Governors decides, by the same majority specified in paragraph (a) preceding, to lift the suspension.

(c) While under suspension, a member may exercise none of the rights conferred upon it by this Agreement, except the right of withdrawal, but it shall remain subject to fulfillment of all its obligations.

SECTION 3. TERMS OF WITHDRAWAL FROM MEMBERSHIP

(a) From the time its membership ceases, a member shall no longer share in the profits or losses of the institution and shall incur no liability with respect to loans and guarantees entered into by the Corporation thereafter. The Corporation shall arrange for the repurchase of such member's capital stock as part of the settlement of accounts with it in accordance with the provisions of this Section.

(b) The Corporation and a member may agree on the withdrawal from membership and the repurchase of shares of said member on terms appropriate under the circumstances. If such agreement is not reached within three months after the date on which such member expresses its desire to withdraw from membership, or within a term agreed upon between both parties, the repurchase price of the member's shares shall be equal to the book value thereof on the date when the member ceases to belong to the institution, such book value to be determined by the Corporation's audited financial statements.

(c) Payment for shares shall be made, upon surrender of the corresponding share certificates, in such installments and at such times and in such available currencies as the Corporation shall determine, taking into account its financial position.

(d) No amount due to a former member for its shares under this Section may be paid until one month after the date upon which such member ceases to belong to the institution. If, within that period the Corporation suspends operations, the rights of such member shall be determined by the provisions of Article VI and the member shall be considered still a member of the Corporation for purposes of said Article, except that it shall have no voting rights.

ARTICLE VI—SUSPENSION AND TERMINATION OF OPERATIONS

SECTION 1. SUSPENSION OF OPERATIONS

In an emergency the Board of Executive Directors may suspend operations in respect of new investments, loans and guarantees until such time as the Board of Governors has the opportunity to consider the situation and take pertinent measures.

SECTION 2. TERMINATION OF OPERATIONS

(a) The Corporation may terminate its operations by decision of the Board of Governors by a majority representing at least three-fourths of the votes of the members, which shall include two-thirds of the Governors. Upon termination of operations, the Corporation shall forthwith cease all activities except those incident to the conservation, preservation and realization of its assets and settlement of its obligations.

(b) Until final settlement of such obligations and distribution of such assets, the Corporation shall remain in existence and all mutual rights and obligations of the Corporation and its members under this Agreement shall continue unimpaired, except that no member shall be suspended or withdraw and that no distribution shall be made to members except as provided in this Article.

SECTION 3. LIABILITY OF MEMBERS AND PAYMENT OF DEBTS

(a) The liability of members arising from capital subscriptions shall remain in force until the Corporation's obligations, including contingent obligations, are settled.

(b) All creditors holding direct claims shall be paid out of the assets of the Corporation to which such obligations are chargeable and then out of payments to the Corporation on unpaid capital subscriptions to which such claims are chargeable. Before making any payments to creditors holding direct claims, the Board of Executive Directors shall make such arrangements as are necessary in its judgment to ensure a pro rata distribution among holders of direct and contingent claims.

SECTION 4. DISTRIBUTION OF ASSETS

(a) No distribution of assets shall be made to members on account of the shares held by them in the Corporation until all liabilities to creditors chargeable to such shares have been discharged or provided for. Moreover, such distribution must be approved by a decision of the Board of Governors by a majority representing at least three-fourths of the votes of the members, which shall include two-thirds of the Governors.

(b) Any distribution of assets to the members shall be in proportion to the number of shares held and shall be effected at such times and under such conditions as the Corporation deems fair and equitable. The proportions of assets distributed need not be uniform as to type of assets. No member shall be entitled to receive its proportion in such distribution of assets until it has settled all its obligations to the Corporation.

(c) Any member receiving assets distributed pursuant to this Article shall enjoy the same rights with respect to such assets as the Corporation enjoyed prior to their distribution.

ARTICLE VII—JURIDICAL PERSONALITY, IMMUNITIES, EXEMPTIONS AND PRIVILEGES

SECTION 1. SCOPE

To enable the Corporation to fulfill its purpose and the functions with which it is entrusted, the status, immunities, exemptions and privileges set forth in this Article shall be accorded to the Corporation in the territories of each member country.

SECTION 2. JURIDICAL PERSONALITY

The Corporation shall possess juridical personality and, in particular, full capacity:

(a) to contract;

(b) to acquire and dispose of immovable and movable property; and

(c) to institute legal and administrative proceedings.

SECTION 3. JUDICIAL PROCEEDINGS

(a) Actions may be brought against the Corporation only in a court of competent jurisdiction in the territories of a member country in which the Corporation has an office, has appointed an agent for the purpose of accepting service or notice of process, or has issued or guaranteed securities. No action shall be brought against the Corporation by member or persons acting for or deriving claims from member countries. However, such countries or persons shall have recourse to such special procedures to settle controversies between the Corporation and its member countries as may be prescribed in this Agreement, in the by-laws and regulations of the Corporation or in contracts entered into with the Corporation.

(b) Property and assets of the Corporation shall, wheresoever located and by whomsoever held, be immune from all forms of seizure, attachment or execution before the delivery of final judgment against the Corporation.

SECTION 4. IMMUNITY OF ASSETS

Property and assets of the Corporation, wheresoever located and by whomsoever held, shall be immune from search, requisition, confiscation, expropriation or any other form of taking or foreclosure by executive or legislative action.

SECTION 5. INVIOLABILITY OF ARCHIVES

The archives of the Corporation shall be inviolable.

SECTION 6. FREEDOM OF ASSETS FROM RESTRICTIONS

To the extent necessary to enable the Corporation to carry out its purpose and functions and to conduct its operations in accordance with this Agreement, all property and other assets of the Corporation shall be free from restrictions, regulations, controls and moratoria of any nature, except as may otherwise be provided in this Agreement.

SECTION 7. PRIVILEGE FOR COMMUNICATIONS

The official communications of the Corporation shall be accorded by each member country the same treatment that it accords to the official communications of other members.

SECTION 8. PERSONAL IMMUNITIES AND PRIVILEGES

All Governors, Executive Directors, Alternates, officers, and employees of the Corporation shall have the following privileges and immunities:

(a) Immunity from legal process with respect to acts performed by them in their official capacity, except when the Corporation waives this immunity;

(b) When not local nationals, the same immunities from immigration restrictions, alien registration requirements and military service obligations and the same facilities as regards exchange provisions as are accorded by a member country to the representatives, officials, and employees of comparable rank of other member countries; and

(c) The same privileges in respect of traveling facilities as are accorded by member countries to representatives, officials, and employees of comparable rank of other member countries.

SECTION 9. IMMUNITIES FROM TAXATION

(a) The Corporation, its property, other assets, income, and the operations and transactions it carries out pursuant to this Agreement, shall be immune from all taxation and from all customs duties. The Corporation shall also be immune from any obligation relating to the payment, withholding or collection of any tax or duty.

(b) No tax shall be levied on or in respect of salaries and emoluments paid by the Corporation to officials or employees of the Corporation who are not local citizens or other local nationals.

(c) No tax of any kind shall be levied on any obligation or security issued by the Corporation, including any dividend or interest thereon, by whomsoever held:

(i) which discriminates against such obligation or security solely because it is issued by the Corporation; or

(ii) if the sole jurisdictional basis for such taxation is the place or currency in which it is issued, made payable or paid, or the location of any office or place of business maintained by the Corporation.

(d) No tax of any kind shall be levied on any obligation or security guaranteed by the Corporation including any dividend or interest thereon, by whomsoever held:

(i) which discriminates against such obligation or security solely because it is guaranteed by the Corporation; or

(ii) if the sole jurisdictional basis for such taxation is the location of any office or place of business maintained by the Corporation.

SECTION 10. IMPLEMENTATION

Each member country, in accordance with its juridical system, shall take such action as is necessary to make effective in its own territories the principles set forth in this Article, and shall inform the Corporation of the action which it has taken on the matter.

SECTION 11. WAIVER

The Corporation in its discretion may waive any of the privileges or immunities conferred under this Article to such extent and upon such conditions as it may determine.

ARTICLE VIII—AMENDMENTS

SECTION 1. AMENDMENTS

(a) This Agreement may be amended only by decision of the Board of Governors by a majority representing at least four-fifths of the votes of the members, which shall include two-thirds of the Governors.

(b) Notwithstanding the provisions of (a) above, the unanimous agreement of the Board of Governors shall be required for the approval of any amendment modifying:

(i) the right to withdraw from the Corporation as provided in Article V, Section 1;

(ii) the right to purchase shares of the Corporation as provided in Article II, Section 5; and

(iii) the limitation on liability as provided in Article II, Section 6.

(c) Any proposal to amend this Agreement, whether emanating from a member country or the Board of Executive Directors, shall be communicated to the Chairman of the Board of Governors, who shall bring the proposal before the Board of Governors. When an amendment has been adopted, the Corporation shall so certify in an official communication addressed to all members. Amendments shall enter into force for all members three months after the date of the official communication unless the Board of Governors shall specify a different period.

Article IX—Interpretation and Arbitration

SECTION 1. INTERPRETATION

(a) Any question of interpretation of the provisions of this Agreement arising between any member and the Corporation or between members shall be submitted to the Board of Executive Director for decision. Members especially affected by the question under consideration shall be entitled to direct representation before the Board of Executive Directors as provided in Article IV, Section 4, paragraph (l).

(b) In any case where the Board of Executive Directors has given a decision under the above paragraph, any member may require that the question be submitted to the Board of Governors, whose decision shall be final. Pending the decision of the Board of Governors, the Corporation may, insofar as it deems it necessary, act on the basis of the decision of the Board of Executive Directors.

SECTION 2. ARBITRATION

If a disagreement should arise between the Corporation and a member which has ceased to be such, or between the Corporation and any member after adoption of a decision to terminate the operations of the institution, such disagreement shall be submitted to arbitration by a tribunal of three arbitrators. One of the arbitrators shall be appointed by the Corporation, another by the member concerned, and the third, unless the parties otherwise agree, by the President of the International Court of Justice. If all efforts to reach a unanimous agreement fail, decisions shall be reached by a majority vote of the three arbitrators. The third arbitrator shall be empowered to settle all questions of procedure in any case where the parties are in disagreement with respect thereto.

Article X—General Provisions

SECTION 1. HEADQUARTERS OF THE CORPORATION

The headquarters of the Corporation shall be located in the same locality as the headquarters of the Bank. The Board of Executive Directors of the Corporation may establish other offices in the territories of any of its member countries by a majority representing at least two-thirds of the votes of the members.

SECTION 2. RELATIONS WITH OTHER ORGANIZATIONS

The Corporation may enter into agreements with other organizations for purposes consistent with this Agreement.

SECTION 3. CHANNELS OF COMMUNICATION

Each member shall designate an official entity for purposes of communication with the Corporation on matters connected with this Agreement.

ARTICLE XI—FINAL PROVISIONS

SECTION 1. SIGNATURE AND ACCEPTANCE

(a) This Agreement shall be deposited with the Bank, where it shall remain open for signature by the representatives of the countries listed in Annex A until December 31, 1985 or such later date as shall be established by the Board of Executive Directors of the Corporation. In case this Agreement shall not have entered into force, a later date may be determined by the representatives of the signatory countries of the Final Act of the Negotiations on the Creation of the Inter-American Investment Corporation. Each signatory of this Agreement shall deposit with the Bank an instrument setting forth that it has accepted or ratified this Agreement in accordance with its own laws and has taken the steps necessary to enable it to fulfill all of its obligations under this Agreement.

(b) The Bank shall send certified copies of this Agreement to its members and duly notify them of each signature and deposit of the instrument of acceptance or ratification made pursuant to the foregoing paragraph, as well as the date thereof.

(c) On or after the date on which the Corporation commences operations, the Bank may receive the signature and the instrument of acceptance or ratification of this Agreement from any country, whose membership has been approved in accordance with Article II, Section 1(b).

SECTION 2. ENTRY INTO FORCE

(a) This Agreement shall enter into force when it has been signed and instruments of acceptance or ratification have been deposited, in accordance with Section 1 of this Article, by representatives of countries whose subscriptions comprise not less than two-thirds of the total subscriptions set forth in Annex A, which shall include:

(i) the subscription of the member country with the largest number of shares; and

(ii) subscriptions of regional developing member countries with a total of shares greater than all other subscriptions.

(b) Countries whose instruments of acceptance or ratification were deposited prior to the date on which the agreement entered into force, shall become members on that date. Other countries shall become members on the dates on which their instruments of acceptance or ratification are deposited.

SECTION 3. COMMENCEMENT OF OPERATIONS

As soon as this Agreement enters into force under Section 2 of this Article, the President of the Bank shall call a meeting of the Board of Governors. The Corporation shall begin operations on the date when such meeting is held.

DONE at the city of Washington, District of Columbia, United States of America, in a single original, dated November 19, 1984, whose English, French, Portuguese, and Spanish texts are equally authentic and which shall remain deposited in the archives of the Inter-American Development Bank, which has indicated by its signature below its agreement to act as depository of this Agreement and to notify all those governments of the countries whose names are set forth in Annex A of the date when this Agreement shall enter into force, in accordance with Section 2 of Article XI.

* * * * * * *

9. Articles of Agreement Establishing the Asian Development Bank

CONTENTS

9. Articles of Agreement Establishing the Asian Development Bank

Done at Manila, December 4, 1965; Open for signature at the United Nations Economic Commission for Asia and the Far East, at Bangkok, until January 31, 1966; Acceptance by the United States, with a declaration; Deposited with the Secretary-General of the United Nations, August 16, 1966; Entered into force, August 22, 1966[1]

The Contracting Parties

CONSIDERING the importance of closer economic co-operation as a means for achieving the most efficient utilization of resources and for accelerating the economic development of Asia and the Far East;

REALIZING the significance of making additional development financing available for the region by mobilizing such funds and other resources both from within and outside the region, and by seeking to create and foster conditions conducive to increased domestic savings and greater flow of development funds into the region;

RECOGNIZING the desirability of promoting the harmonious growth of the economics of the region and the expansion of external trade of member countries;

CONVINCED that the establishment of a financial institution that is Asian in its basic character would serve these ends;

HAVE AGREED to establish hereby the Asian Development Bank (hereinafter called the "Bank") which shall operate in accordance with the following:

ARTICLES OF AGREEMENT

CHAPTER I—PURPOSE, FUNCTIONS, AND MEMBERSHIP

ARTICLE 1. PURPOSE

The purpose of the Bank shall be to foster economic growth and co-operation in the region of Asia and the Far East (hereinafter referred to as the "region") and to contribute to the acceleration of the process of economic development of the developing member countries in the region, collectively and individually. Wherever used in this Agreement, the terms "region of Asia and the Far East" and "region" shall comprise the territories of Asia and the Far East included in the Terms of References of the United Nations Economic Commission for Asia and the Far East.

[1] 17 UST 1418; TIAS 6103; 571 UNTS 123. For a list of states that are parties to this Agreement, see Department of State publication, *Treaties in Force*.

Procès Verbal of rectification to the English text of this Agreement signed at New York November 2, 1967 (18 UST 2935; TIAS 6387; 608 UNTS 380).

ARTICLE 2. FUNCTIONS

To fulfill its purpose, the Bank shall have the following functions:

(i) to promote investment in the region of public and private capital for development purposes;

(ii) to utilize the resources at its disposal for financing development of the developing member countries in the region, giving priority to those regional, sub-regional as well as national projects and programmes which will contribute most effectively to the harmonious economic growth of the region as a whole, and having special regard to the needs of the smaller or less-developed member countries in the region;

(iii) to meet requests from members in the region to assist them in the coordination of their development policies and plans with a view to achieving better utilization of their resources, making their economies more complementary, and promoting the orderly expansion of their foreign trade, in particular, intra-regional trade;

(iv) to provide technical assistance for the preparation, financing and execution of development projects and programmes, including the formulation of specific project proposals;

(v) to co-operate, in such manner as the Bank may deem appropriate, within the terms of this Agreement, with the United Nations, its organs and subsidiary bodies including, in particular, the Economic Commission for Asia and the Far East, and with public international organizations and other international institutions, as well as national entities whether public or private, which are concerned with the investment of development funds in the region, and to interest such institutions and entities in new opportunities for investment and assistance; and

(vi) to undertake such other activities and provide such other services as may advance its purpose.

ARTICLE 3. MEMBERSHIP

1. Membership in the Bank shall be open to: (i) members and associate members of the United Nations Economic Commission for Asia and the Far East; and (ii) other regional countries and non-regional developed countries which are members of the United Nations or of any of its specialized agencies.

2. Countries eligible for membership under paragraph 1 of this Article which do not become members in accordance with Article 64 of this Agreement may be admitted, under such terms and conditions as the Bank may determine, to membership in the Bank upon the affirmative vote of two-thirds of the total number of Governors, representing not less than three-fourths of the total voting power of the members.

3. In the case of associate members of the United Nations Economic Commission for Asia and the Far East which are not responsible for the conduct of their international relations, application for membership in the Bank shall be presented by the member of the bank responsible for the international relations of the applicant

and accompanied by an undertaking by such member that, until the applicant itself assumes such responsibility, the member shall be responsible for all obligations that may be incurred by the applicant by reason of admission to membership in the Bank and enjoyment of the benefits of such membership. "Country" as used in this Agreement shall include a territory which is an associate member of the United Nations Economic Commission for Asia and the Far East.

CHAPTER II—CAPITAL

ARTICLE 4. AUTHORIZED CAPITAL

1. The authorized capital stock of the Bank shall be one billion dollars ($1,000,000,000)[2] in terms of United States dollars of the weight and fineness in effect on 31 January 1966. The dollar wherever referred to in this Agreement shall be understood as being a United States dollar of the above value. The authorized capital stock shall be divided into one hundred thousand (100,000) shares having a par value of ten thousand dollars ($10,000) each, which shall be available for subscription only by members in accordance with the provisions of Article 5 of this Agreement.

2. The original authorized capital stock shall be divided into paid-in shares and callable shares. Shares having an aggregate par value of five hundred million dollars ($500,000,000) shall be paid-in shares, and shares having an aggregate par value of five hundred million dollars ($500,000,000) shall be callable shares.

3. The authorized capital stock of the Bank may be increased by the Board of Governors, at such time and under such terms and conditions as it may deem advisable, by a vote of two-thirds of the total number of Governors, representing not less than three-fourths of the total voting power of the members.

ARTICLE 5. SUBSCRIPTION OF SHARES

1. Each member shall subscribe to shares of the capital stock of the Bank. Each subscription to the original authorized capital stock shall be for paid-in shares and callable shares in equal parts. The initial number of shares to be subscribed by countries which become members in accordance with Article 64 of this Agreement shall be that set forth in Annex A hereof. The initial number of shares to be subscribed by countries which are admitted to membership in accordance with paragraph 2 of Article 3 of this Agreement shall be determined by the Board of Governors; provided, however, that no such subscription shall be authorized which

---

[2] On November 25, 1966, the Board of Governors increased the authorized capital stock of the Bank by $100 million, divided into 10,000 shares having a par value of $10,000 each of which 5,000 were paid-in shares and 5,000 callable shares.

On November 30, 1971, the Board of Governors approved an increase in the authorized capital stock of the Bank by $1,650 million divided into 165,000 shares having a par value of $10,000 each. Of the newly authorized shares, 20 percent would be paid-in and 80 percent callable.

On October 29, 1976, the Board of Governors approved an increase in the authorized capital stock of the Bank by $5 billion. Of the newly authorized shares, 90 percent would be callable and 10 percent paid-in. Effective September 30, 1977, the total authorized capital of the Bank was $8.7 billion.

In 1984, the Board of Governors increased ADB authorized capital stock by an additional $8.1 billion to $14.473 billion.

On May 26, 1994, the Board of Governors increased ADB authorized capital stock by an additional $25.8 billion to $48 billion.

would have the effect of reducing the percentage of capital stock held by regional members below sixty (60) percent of the total subscribed capital stock.

2. The Board of Governors shall at intervals of not less than five (5) years review the capital stock of the Bank. In case of an increase in the authorized capital stock, each member shall have a reasonable opportunity to subscribe, under such terms and conditions as the Board of Governors shall determine, to a proportion of the increase of stock equivalent to the proportion which its stock theretofore subscribed bears to the total subscribed capital stock immediately prior to such increase; provided, however, that the foregoing provision shall not apply in respect of any increase or portion of an increase in the authorized capital stock intended solely to give effect to determinations of the Board of Governors under paragraphs 1 and 3 of this Article. No member shall be obligated to subscribe to any part of an increase of capital stock.

3. The Board of Governors may, at the request of a member, increase the subscription of such member on such terms and conditions as the Board may determine; provided, however, that no such increase in the subscription of any member shall be authorized which would have the effect of reducing the percentage of capital stock held by regional members below sixty (60) percent of the total subscribed capital stock. The Board of Governors shall pay special regard to the request of any regional member having less than six (6) percent of the subscribed capital stock to increase its proportionate share thereof.

4. Shares of stock initially subscribed by members shall be issued at par. Other shares shall be issued at par unless the Board of Governors by a vote of a majority of the total number of Governors, representing a majority of the total voting power of the members, decides in special circumstances to issue them on other terms.

5. Shares of stock shall not be pledged or encumbered in any manner whatsoever, and they shall not be transferable except to the Bank in accordance with Chapter VII of this Agreement.

6. The liability of the members on shares shall be limited to the unpaid portion of their issue price.

7. No member shall be liable, by reason of its membership, for obligations of the Bank.

ARTICLE 6. PAYMENT OF SUBSCRIPTIONS

1. Payment of the amount initially subscribed by each Signatory to this Agreement which becomes a member in accordance with Article 64 to the paid-in capital stock of the Bank shall be made in five (5) installments of twenty (20) percent each of such amount. The first installment shall be paid by each member within thirty (30) days after entry into force of this Agreement, or on or before the date of deposit on its behalf of its instrument of ratification or acceptance in accordance with paragraph 1 of Article 64, whichever is later. The second installment shall become due one (1) year from the entry into force of this Agreement. The remaining three (3) installments shall each become due successively one (1) year from the date on which the preceding installment becomes due.

2. Of each installment for the payment of initial subscriptions to the original paid-in capital stock:

(a) fifty (50) percent shall be paid in gold or convertible currency; and

(b) fifty (50) percent in the currency of the number.

3. The Bank shall accept from any member promissory notes or other obligations issued by the Government of the member, or by the depository designated by such member, in lieu of the amount to be paid in the currency of the member pursuant to paragraph 2(b) of this Article, provided such currency is not required by the Bank for the conduct of its operations. Such notes or obligations shall be non-negotiable, non-interest-bearing, and payable to the Bank at par value upon demand. Subject to the provisions of paragraph (2)(ii) of Article 24, demands upon such notes or obligations payable in convertible currencies shall, over reasonable periods of time, be uniform in percentage on all such notes or obligations.

4. Each payment of a member in its own currency under paragraph 2(b) of this Article shall be in such amount as the Bank, after such consultation with the International Monetary Fund as the Bank may consider necessary and utilizing the par value established with the International Monetary Fund, if any, determines to be equivalent to the full value in terms of dollars of the portion of the subscription being paid. The initial payment shall be in such amount as the member considers appropriate hereunder but shall be subject to such adjustment, to be effected within ninety (90) days of the date on which such payment was due, as the Bank shall determine to be necessary to constitute the full dollar equivalent of such payment.

5. Payment of the amount subscribed to the callable capital stock of the Bank shall be subject to call only as when required by the Bank to meet its obligations incurred under sub-paragraphs (ii) and (iv) of Article 11 on borrowings of funds for inclusion in its ordinary capital resources or on guarantees chargeable to such resources.

6. In the event of the call referred to in paragraph 5 of this Article, payment may be made at the option of the member in gold, convertible currency or in the currency required to discharge the obligations of the Bank for the purposes of which the call is made. Calls on unpaid subscriptions shall be uniform in percentage on all callable shares.

7. The Bank shall determine the place for any payment under this Article, provided that, until the inaugural meeting of its Board of Governors, the payment of the first installment referred to in paragraph 1 of this Article shall be made to the Secretary-General of the United Nations, as Trustee for the Bank.

ARTICLE 7. ORDINARY CAPITAL RESOURCES

As used in this Agreement, the term "ordinary capital resources" of the Bank shall include the following:

(i) authorized capital stock of the Bank, including both paid-in and callable shares, subscribed pursuant to Article 5 of this Agreement, except such part thereof as may be set aside into one or more Special Funds in accordance with paragraph 1(i) of Article 19 of this Agreement;

(ii) funds raised by borrowings of the Bank by virtue of powers conferred by sub-paragraph (i) of Article 21 of this Agreement, to which the commitment to calls provided for in paragraph 5 of Article 6 of this Agreement is applicable;

(iii) funds received in repayment of loans or guarantees made with the resources indicated in (i) and (ii) of this Article;

(iv) income derived from loans made from the aforementioned funds or from guarantees to which the commitment to calls set forth in paragraph 5 of Article 6 of this Agreement is applicable; and

(v) any other funds or income received by the Bank which do not form part of its Special Funds resources referred to in Article 20 of this Agreement.

CHAPTER III—OPERATIONS

ARTICLE 8. USE OF RESOURCES

The resources and facilities of the Bank will be used exclusively to implement the purpose and functions set forth respectively in Articles 1 and 2 of this Agreement.

ARTICLE 9. ORDINARY AND SPECIAL OPERATIONS

1. The operations of the Bank shall consist of ordinary operations and special operations.
2. Ordinary operations shall be those financed from the ordinary capital resources of the Bank.
3. Special operations shall be those financed from the Special Funds resources referred to in Article 20 of this Agreement.

ARTICLE 10. SEPARATION OF OPERATIONS

1. To ordinary capital resources and the Special Funds resources of the Bank shall at all times and in all respects be held, used, committed, invested or otherwise disposed of entirely separate from each other. The financial statements of the Bank shall show the ordinary operations and special operations separately.
2. The ordinary capital resources of the Bank shall under no circumstances be charged with, or used to discharge, losses or liabilities arising out of special operations or other activities for which Special Funds resources were originally used or committed.
3. Expenses appertaining directly to ordinary operations shall be charged to the ordinary capital resources of the Bank. Expenses appertaining directly to the special operations shall be charged to the Special Funds resources. Any other expenses shall be charged as the Bank shall determine.

ARTICLE 11. RECIPIENTS AND METHODS OF OPERATION

Subject to the conditions stipulated in this Agreement, the Bank may provide or facilitate financing to any member, or any agency, instrumentality or political subdivision thereof, or any entity or enterprise operating in the territory of a member, as well as to international or regional agencies or entities concerned with economic development of the region. The Bank may carry out its operations in any of the following ways:

(i) by making or participating in direct loans with its unimpaired paid-in capital and, except as provided in Article 17 of this Agreement, with its reserves and undistributed surplus; or with the unimpaired Special Funds resources;

(ii) by making or participating in direct loans with funds raised by the Bank in capital markets or borrowed or otherwise acquired by the Bank for inclusion in its ordinary capital resources;

(iii) by investment of funds referred to in (i) and (ii) of this Article in the equity capital of an institution or enterprise, provided no such investment shall be made until after the Board of Governors, by a vote of a majority of a total number of Governors, representing a majority of the total voting power of the members, shall have determined that the Bank is in a position to commence such type of operations; or

(iv) by guaranteeing, whether as primary or secondary obligor, in whole or in part, loans for economic development participated in by the Bank.

ARTICLE 12. LIMITATIONS ON ORDINARY OPERATIONS

1. The total amount outstanding of loans, equity investments and guarantees made by the Bank in its ordinary operations shall not at any time exceed the total amount of its unimpaired subscribed capital, reserves and surplus included in its ordinary capital resources, exclusive of the special reserve provided for by Article 17 of this Agreement and other reserves not available for ordinary operations.

2. In the case of loans made with funds borrowed by the Bank to which the commitment to calls provided for by paragraph 5 of Article 6 of this Agreement is applicable, the total amount of principal outstanding and payable to the Bank in a specific currency shall not at any time exceed the total amount of the principal of outstanding borrowings by the Bank that are payable in the same currency.

3. In the case of funds invested in equity capital out of the ordinary capital resources of the Bank, the total amount invested shall not exceed ten (10) percent of the aggregate amount of the unimpaired paid-in capital stock of the Bank actually paid up at any given time together with the reserves the surplus included in its ordinary capital resources, exclusive of the special reserve provided in Article 17 of this Agreement.

4. The amount of any equity investment shall not exceed such percentage of the equity capital of the entity or enterprise concerned as the Board of Directors shall in each specific case determine to be appropriate. The Bank shall not seek to obtain by such an investment a controlling interest in the entity or enterprise concerned, except where necessary to safeguard the investment of the Bank.

ARTICLE 13. PROVISION OF CURRENCIES FOR DIRECT LOANS

In making direct loans or participating in them, the Bank may provide financing in any of the following ways:

(i) by furnishing the borrower with currencies other than the currency of the member in whose territory the project concerned is to be carried out (the latter currency hereinafter to be called "local currency"), which are necessary to meet the foreign exchange costs of such project; or

(ii) by providing financing to meet local expenditures on the project concerned, where it can do so by supplying local currency without selling any of its holdings in gold or convertible currencies. In special cases when, in the opinion of the Bank, the project causes or is likely to cause undue loss or strain on the balance of payments of the member in whose territory the project is to be carried out, the financing granted by the Bank to meet local expenditures may be provided in currencies other than that of such member; in such cases, the amount of the financing granted by the Bank for this purpose shall not exceed a reasonable portion of the total local expenditure incurred by the borrower.

ARTICLE 14. OPERATING PRINCIPLES

The operations of the Bank shall be conducted in accordance with the following principles:

(i) The operations of the Bank shall provide principally for the financing of specific projects, including those forming part of a national sub-regional or regional development programme. They may, however, include loans to, or guarantees of loans made to, national development banks or other suitable entities, in order that the latter may finance specific development projects whose individual financing requirements are not, in the opinion of the Bank, large enough to warrant the direct supervision of the Bank;

(ii) In selecting suitable projects, the Bank shall always be guided by the provisions of sub-paragraph (ii) of Article 2 of this Agreement;

(iii) The Bank shall not finance any undertaking in the territory of a member if that member objects to such financing;

(iv) Before a loan is granted, the applicant shall have submitted an adequate loan proposal and the President of the Bank shall have presented to the Board of Directors a written report regarding the proposal, together with his recommendations, on the basis of a staff study;

(v) In considering an application for a loan or guarantee, the Bank shall pay due regard to the ability of the borrower to obtain financing or facilities elsewhere on terms and conditions that the Bank considers reasonable for the recipient, taking into account all pertinent factors;

(vi) In making or guaranteeing a loan, the Bank shall pay due regard to the prospects that the borrower and its guarantor, if any, will be in a position to meet their obligations under the loan contract;

(vii) In making or guaranteeing a loan, the rate of interest, other charges and the schedule for repayment of principal shall be such as are, in the opinion of the Bank, appropriate for the loan concerned;

(viii) In guaranteeing a loan made by other investors, or in underwriting the sale of securities, the Bank shall receive suitable compensation for its risk;

(ix) The proceeds of any loan, investment or other financing undertaken in the ordinary operations of the Bank or with Special Funds established by the Bank pursuant to paragraph 1(i) of Article 19, shall be used only for procurement in member countries of goods and services produced in member countries, except in any case in which the Board of Directors, by a vote of the Directors representing not less than two-thirds of the total voting power of the members, determines to permit procurement in a non-member country or of goods and services produced in a non-member country in special circumstances making such procurement appropriate, as in the case of a non-member country in which a significant amount of financing has been provided to the Bank;

(x) In the case of a direct loan made by the Bank, the borrower shall be permitted by the Bank to draw its funds only to meet expenditures in connexion with the project as they are actually incurred;

(xi) The Bank shall take the necessary measures to ensure that the proceeds of any loan made, guaranteed or participated in by the Bank are used only for the purposes for which the loan was granted and with due attention to considerations of economy and efficiency;

(xii) The Bank shall pay due regard to the desirability of avoiding a disproportionate amount of its resources being used for the benefit of any member;

(xiii) The Bank shall seek to maintain reasonable diversification in its investments in equity capital; it shall not assume responsibility for managing any entity or enterprise in which it has an investment, except where necessary to safeguard its investments; and

(xiv) The Bank shall be guided by sound banking principles in its operations.

ARTICLE 15. TERMS AND CONDITIONS FOR DIRECT LOANS AND GUARANTEES

1. In the case of direct loans made or participated in or loans guaranteed by the Bank, the contract shall establish, in conformity with the operating principles set forth in Article 14 of this Agreement and subject to the other provisions of this Agreement, the terms and conditions for the loan or the guarantee concerned, including those relating to payment of principal, interest and other charges, maturities, and dates of payment in respect to the loan, or the fees and other charges in respect of the guarantee, respectively. In particular, the contract shall provide that, subject to paragraph 3 of this Article, all payments to the Bank under the contract shall be made in the currency loaned, unless, in the case of a direct loan made or a loan guaranteed as part of special operations with funds provided under paragraph 1(ii) of Article 19, the rules and regulations of the Bank provide otherwise. Guarantees by the Bank shall also provide that the Bank may terminate its liability with respect to interest if, upon default by the borrower and

the guarantor, if any, the Bank offers to purchase at par and interest accrued to a date designated in the offer, the bonds or other obligations guaranteed.

2. Where the recipient of loans or guarantees of loans is not itself a member, the Bank may, when it deems it advisable, require that the member in whose territory the project concerned is to be carried out, or a public agency or any instrumentality of that member acceptable to the Bank, guarantee the repayment of the principal and the payment of interest and other charges on the loan in accordance with the terms thereof.

3. The loan or guarantee contract shall expressly state the currency in which all payments to the Bank thereunder shall be made. At the option of the borrower, however, such payments may always be made in gold or convertible currency.

ARTICLE 16. COMMISSION AND FEES

1. The Bank shall charge, in addition to interest, a commission on direct loans made or participated in as part of its ordinary operations. This commission, payable periodically, shall be computed on the amount outstanding on each loan or participation and shall be at the rate of not less than one (1) percent per annum, unless the Bank, after the first five (5) years of its operations, decides to reduce this minimum rate by a two-thirds majority of its members, representing not less than three-fourths of the total voting power of the members.

2. In guaranteeing a loan as part of its ordinary operations, the Bank shall charge a guarantee fee, at a rate determined by the Board of Directors, payable periodically on the amount of the loan outstanding.

3. Other charges of the Bank in its ordinary operations and any commission, fees or other charges in its special operations shall be determined by the Board of Directors.

ARTICLE 17. SPECIAL RESERVE

The amount of commissions and guarantee fees received by the Bank pursuant to Article 16 of this Agreement shall be set aside as a special reserve which shall be kept for meeting liabilities of the Bank in accordance with Article 18 of this Agreement. The special reserve shall be held in such liquid form as the Board of Directors may decide.

ARTICLE 18. METHODS OF MEETING LIABILITIES OF THE BANK

1. In cases of default on loans made, participated in or guaranteed by the Bank in its ordinary operations, the Bank shall take such action as it deems appropriate with respect to modifying the terms of the loan, other than the currency of repayment.

2. The payments in discharge of the Bank's liabilities on borrowings or guarantees under sub-paragraphs (ii) and (iv) or Article 11 chargeable to the ordinary capital resources shall be charged:

(i) First, against the special reserve provided for in Article 17;

(ii) Then, to the extent necessary and at the discretion of the Bank, against the other reserves, surplus and capital available to the Bank.

3. Whenever necessary to meet contractual payments of interest, other charges or amortization on borrowings of the Bank in its ordinary operations, or to meet its liabilities with respect to similar payments in respect of loans guaranteed by it, chargeable to its ordinary capital resources, the Bank may call an appropriate amount of the uncalled subscribed callable capital in accordance with paragraphs 6 and 7 of Article 6 of this Agreement.

4. In cases of default in respect of a loan made from borrowed funds or guaranteed by the Bank as part of its ordinary operations, the Bank may, if it believes that the default may be of long duration, call an additional amount of such callable capital not to exceed in any one (1) year one (1) percent of the total subscriptions of the members to such capital, for the following purposes:

(i) To redeem before maturity, or otherwise discharge, the Bank's liability on all or part of the outstanding principal of any loan guaranteed by it in respect of which the debtor is in default; and

(ii) To repurchase, or otherwise discharge, the Bank's liability on all or part of its own outstanding borrowing.

5. If the Bank's subscribed callable capital stock shall be entirely called pursuant to paragraphs 3 and 4 of this Article, the Bank may, if necessary for the purposes specified in paragraph 3 of this Article, use or exchange the currency of any member without restriction, including any restriction imposed pursuant to paragraphs 2 (i) and (ii) of Article 24.

ARTICLE 19. SPECIAL FUNDS

1. The Bank may:

(i) set aside, by a vote of two-thirds of the total number of Governors, representing at least three-fourths of the total voting power of the members, not more than ten (10) percent each of the portion of the unimpaired paid-in capital of the Bank paid by members pursuant to paragraph 2(a) of Article 6 and of the portion thereof paid pursuant to paragraph 2(b) of Article 6, and establish therewith one or more Special Funds; and

(ii) accept the administration of Special Funds which are designed to serve the purpose and come within the functions of the Bank.

2. Special Funds established by the Bank pursuant to paragraph 1(i) of this Article may be used to guarantee or make loans of high developmental priority, with longer maturities, longer deferred commencement of repayment and lower interest rates than those established by the Bank for its ordinary operations. Such Funds may also be used on such other terms and conditions, not inconsistent with the applicable provisions of this Agreement nor with the character of such Funds as revolving funds, as the Bank in establishing such Funds may direct.

3. Special Funds accepted by the Bank under paragraph 1(ii) of this Article may be used in any manner and on any terms and conditions not inconsistent with the purpose of the Bank and with the agreement relating to such Funds.

4. The Bank shall adopt such special rules and regulations as may be required for the establishment, administration, and use of each Special Fund. Such rules and regulations shall be consistent with the provisions of this Agreement, excepting those provisions expressly applicable only to ordinary operations of the Bank.

ARTICLE 20. SPECIAL FUNDS RESOURCES

As used in this Agreement, the term "Special Funds resources" shall refer to the resources of any Special Fund and shall include:

(a) resources set aside from the paid-in capital to a Special Fund or otherwise initially contributed to any Special Fund;

(b) funds accepted by the Bank for inclusion in any Special Fund;

(c) funds repaid in respect of loans or guarantees financed from the resources of any Special Fund which, under the rules and regulations of the Bank governing that Special Fund, are received by such Special Fund;

(d) income derived from operations of the Bank in which any of the aforementioned resources or funds are used or committed if, under the rules and regulations of the Bank governing the Special Fund concerned, that income accrues to such Special Fund; and

(e) any other resources placed at the disposal of any Special Fund.

CHAPTER IV—BORROWING AND OTHER MISCELLANEOUS POWERS

ARTICLE 21. GENERAL POWERS

In addition to the powers specified elsewhere in this Agreement, the Bank shall have the power to:

(i) borrow funds in member countries or elsewhere, and in this connexion to furnish such collateral or other security therefor as the Bank shall determine, provided always that:

(a) before making a sale of its obligations in the territory of a country, the Bank shall have obtained its approval;

(b) where the obligations of the Bank are to be denominated in the currency of a member, the Bank shall have obtained its approval;

(c) the Bank shall obtain the approval of the countries referred to in sub-paragraphs (a) and (b) of this paragraph that the proceeds may be exchanged for the currency of any member without restriction; and

(d) before determining to sell its obligations in a particular country, the Bank shall consider the amount of previous borrowing, if any, in that country, the amount of previous borrowing in other countries, and the possible availability of funds in such other countries; and shall give due regard to the general principle that its borrowings should to the greatest extent possible be diversified as to country of borrowing;

(ii) buy and sell securities the Bank has issued or guaranteed or in which it has invested, provided always that it shall have obtained the approval of any country in whose territory the securities are to be bought or sold;

(iii) guarantee securities in which it has invested in order to facilitate their sale;

(iv) underwrite, or participate in the underwriting of, securities issued by any entity or enterprise for purposes consistent with the purpose of the Bank;

(v) invest funds, not needed in its operations, in the territories of members in such obligations of members or nationals thereof as it may determine, and invest funds held by the Bank for pensions or similar purposes in the territories of members in marketable securities issued by members or nationals thereof;

(vi) provide technical advice and assistance which serve its purpose and come within its functions, and where expenditures incurred in furnishing such services are not reimbursable, charge the net income of the Bank therewith; in the first five (5) years of its operations, the Bank may use up to two (2) per cent of its paid-in capital for furnishing such services on a non-reimbursable basis; and

(vii) exercise such other powers and establish such rules and regulations as may be necessary or appropriate in furtherance of its purpose and functions, consistent with the provisions of this Agreement.

ARTICLE 22. NOTICE TO BE PLACED ON SECURITIES

Every security issued or guaranteed by the Bank shall bear on its face a conspicuous statement to the effect that it is not an obligation of any Government, unless it is in fact the obligation of a particular Government, in which case it shall so state.

CHAPTER V—CURRENCIES

ARTICLE 23. DETERMINATION OF CONVERTIBILITY

Whenever it shall become necessary under this Agreement to determine whether any currency is convertible, such determination shall be made by the Bank after consultation with the International Monetary Fund.

ARTICLE 24. USE OF CURRENCIES

1. Members may not maintain or impose any restrictions on the holding or use by the Bank or by any recipient from the Bank, for payments in any country, of the following:

(i) gold or convertible currencies received by the Bank in payment of subscriptions to its capital stock, other than that paid to the Bank by members pursuant to paragraph 2(b) of Article 6 and restricted pursuant to paragraph 2 (i) and (ii) of this Article;

(ii) currencies of members purchased with the gold or convertible currencies referred to in the preceding sub-paragraph;

(iii) currencies obtained by the Bank by borrowing, pursuant to sub-paragraph (i) of Article 21 of this Agreement, for inclusion in its ordinary capital resources;

(iv) gold or currencies received by the Bank in payment on account of principal, interest, dividends or other changes in respect of loans or investments made out of any of the funds referred to in sub-paragraphs (i) to (iii) of this paragraph or in payment of fees in respect of guarantees made by the Bank; and

(v) currencies, other than the member's own currency, received by the member from the Bank in distribution of the net income of the Bank in accordance with Article 40 of this Agreement.

2. Members may not maintain or impose any restriction on the holding or use by the Bank or by any recipient from the Bank, for payments in any country, of currency of a member received by the Bank which does not come within the provisions of the preceding paragraph unless:

(i) a developing member country, after consultation with and subject to periodic review by the Bank, restricts in whole or in part the use of such currency to payments for goods or services produced and intended for use in its territory; or

(ii) any other member whose subscription has been determined in Part A of Annex A hereof and whose exports of industrial products do not represent a substantial proportion of its total exports, deposits with its instrument of ratification or acceptance a declaration that it desires the use of the portion of its subscription paid pursuant to paragraph 2(b) of Article 6 to be restricted, in whole or in part, to payments for goods or services produced in its territory; provided that such restrictions be subject to periodic review by and consultation with the Bank and that any purchases of goods or services in the territory of that member, subject to the usual consideration of competitive tendering, shall be first charged against the portion of its subscription paid pursuant to paragraph 2(b) of Article 6; or

(iii) such currency forms part of the Special Funds resources of the Bank available under paragraph 1(ii) of Article 19 and its use is subject to special rules and regulations.

3. Members may not maintain or impose any restrictions on the holding or use by the Bank, for making amortization payments or anticipatory payments or for repurchasing in whole or in part the Bank's own obligations, of currencies received by the Bank in repayment of direct loans made out of its ordinary capital resources, provided, however, that until the Bank's subscribed callable capital stock has been entirely called, such holding or use shall be subject to any limitations imposed pursuant to paragraph 2(i) of this Article except in respect of obligations payable in the currency of the member concerned.

4. Gold or currencies held by the Bank shall not be used by the Bank to purchase other currencies of members or non-members except:

(i) in order to meet its obligation in the ordinary course of its business; or

(ii) pursuant to a decision of the Board of Directors adopted by a vote of the Directors representing not less than two-thirds of the total voting powers of the members.

5. Nothing herein contained shall prevent the Bank from using the currency of any member for administrative expenses by the Bank in the territory of such member.

ARTICLE 25. MAINTENANCE OF VALUE OF THE CURRENCY HOLDINGS OF THE BANK

1. Whenever (a) the par value in the International Monetary Fund of the currency of a member is reduced in terms of the dollar defined in Article 4 of this Agreement, or (b) in the opinion of the Bank, after consultation with the International Monetary Fund, the foreign exchange value of a member's currency has depreciated to a significant extent, that member shall pay to the Bank within a reasonable time an additional amount of its currency required to maintain the value of all such currency held by the Bank, excepting (a) currency derived by the Bank from its borrowings, and (b) unless otherwise provided in the agreement establishing such Funds, Special Funds resources accepted by the Bank under paragraph 1(ii) of Article 19.

2. Whenever (a) the par value in the International Monetary Fund of the currency of a member is increased in terms of the said dollar, or (b) in the opinion of the Bank, after consultation with the International Monetary Fund, the foreign exchange value of a member's currency has appreciated to a significant extent, the Bank shall pay to that member within a reasonable time an amount of that currency required to adjust the value of all such currency held by the Bank excepting (a) currency derived by the Bank from its borrowings, and (b) unless otherwise provided in the agreement establishing such Funds, Special Funds resources accepted by the Bank under paragraph 1(ii) of Article 19.

3. The Bank may waive the provisions of this Article when a uniform proportionate change in the par value of the currencies of all its members takes place.

CHAPTER VI—ORGANIZATION AND MANAGEMENT

ARTICLE 26. STRUCTURE

The Bank shall have a Board of Governors, a Board of Directors, a President, one or more Vice-Presidents and such other officers and staff as may be considered necessary.

ARTICLE 27. BOARD OF GOVERNORS: COMPOSITION

1. Each member shall be represented on the Board of Governors and shall appoint one Governor and one alternate. Each Governor and alternate shall serve at the pleasure of the appointing member. No alternate may vote except in the absence of his principal. At its annual meeting, the Board shall designate one of the Governors as Chairman who shall hold office until the election of the next Chairman and the next annual meeting of the Board.

2. Governors and alternates shall serve as such without remuneration from the Bank, but the Bank may pay them reasonable expenses incurred in attending meetings.

ARTICLE 28. BOARD OF GOVERNORS: POWERS

1. All the powers of the Bank shall be vested in the Board of Governors.

2. The Board of Governors may delegate to the Board of Directors any or all its powers, except the power to:

(i) admit new members and determine the conditions of their admission;

(ii) increase or decrease the authorized capital stock of the Bank;

(iii) suspend a member;

(iv) decide appeals from interpretations or applications of this Agreement given by the Board of Directors;

(v) authorize the conclusion of general agreements for co-operation with other international organizations;

(vi) elect the Directors and the President of the Bank;

(vii) determine the remuneration of the Directors and their alternates and the salary and other terms of the contract of service of the President;

(viii) approve, after reviewing the auditors' report, the general balance sheet and the statement of profit and loss of the Bank;

(ix) determine the reserves and the distribution of the net profits of the Bank;

(x) amend this Agreement;

(xi) decide to terminate the operations of the Bank and to distribute its assets; and

(xii) exercise such other powers as are expressly assigned to the Board of Governors in this Agreement.

3. The Board of Governors shall retain full power to exercise authority over any matter delegated to the Board of Directors under paragraph 2 of this Article.

4. For the purposes of this Agreement, the Board of Governors may, by a vote of two-thirds of the total number of Governors, representing not less than three-fourths of the total voting power of the members, from time to time determine which countries or members of the Bank are to be regarded as developing countries or members, taking into account appropriate economic considerations.

ARTICLE 29. BOARD OF GOVERNORS: PROCEDURE

1. The Board of Governors shall hold an annual meeting and such other meetings as may be provided for by the Board or called by the Board of Directors. Meetings of the Board of Governors shall be called, by the Board of Directors, whenever requested by five (5) members of the Bank.

2. A majority of the Governors shall constitute a quorum for any meeting of the Board of Governors, provided such majority represents not less than two-thirds of the total voting power of the members.

3. The Board of Governors may by regulation establish a procedure whereby the Board of Directors may, when the latter deems such action advisable, obtain a vote of the Governors on a specific question without calling a meeting of the Board of Governors.

4. The Board of Governors, and the Board of Directors to the extent authorized, may establish such subsidy bodies as may be necessary or appropriate to conduct the business of the Bank.

ARTICLE 30. BOARD OF DIRECTORS: COMPOSITION

1. (i) The Board of Directors shall be composed of ten (10) members who shall not be members of the Board of Governors, and of whom:

(a) seven (7) shall be elected by the Governors representing regional members; and

(b) three (3) by the Governors representing non-regional members.

Directors shall be persons of high competence in economic and financial matters and shall be elected in accordance with Annex B hereof.

(ii) At the Second Annual Meeting of the Board of Governors after its inaugural meeting, the Board of Governors shall review the size and composition of the Board of Directors, and shall increase the number of Directors as appropriate, paying special regard to the desirability, in the circumstances at that time, of increasing representation in the Board of Directors of smaller less developed member countries. Decisions under this paragraph should be made by a vote of a majority of the total number of Governors, representing not less than two-thirds of the total voting power of the members.

2. Each Director shall appoint an alternate with full power to act for him when he is not present. Directors and alternates shall be nationals of member countries. No two or more Directors may be of the same nationality nor may any two or more alternates be of the same nationality. An alternate may participate in meetings of the Board but may vote only when he is acting in place of his principal.

3. Directors shall hold office for a term of two (2) years and may be re-elected. They shall continue in office until their successors shall have been chosen and qualified. If the office of a Director becomes vacant more than one hundred and eighty (180) days before the end of his term, a successor shall be chosen in accordance with Annex B hereof, for the remainder of the term, by the Governors who elected the former Director. A majority of the votes cast by such Governors shall be required for such election. If the office of a Director becomes vacant one hundred and eighty (180) days or less before the end of his term, a successor may similarly be chosen for the remainder of the term, by the Governors who elected the former Director, in which election a majority of the votes cast by such Governors shall be required. While the office remains vacant, the alternate of the former Director shall exercise the powers of the latter, except that of appointing an alternate.

ARTICLE 31. BOARD OF DIRECTORS: POWERS

The Board of Directors shall be responsible for the direction of the general operations of the Bank and, for this purpose, shall, in addition to the powers assigned to it expressly by this Agreement, exercise all the powers delegated to it by the Board of Governors, and in particular:

(i) prepare the work of the Board of Governors;

(ii) in conformity with the general directions of the Board of Governors, take decisions concerning loans, guarantees, investments in equity capital, borrowing by the Bank, furnishing of technical assistance and other operations of the Bank;

(iii) submit the accounts for each financial year for approval of the Board of Governors at each annual meeting; and

(iv) approve the budget of the Bank.

ARTICLE 32. BOARD OF DIRECTORS: PROCEDURE

1. The Board of Directors shall normally function at the principal office of the Bank and shall meet as often as the business of the Bank may require.

2. A majority of the Directors shall constitute a quorum for any meeting of the Board of Directors, provided such majority represents not less than two-thirds of the total voting power of the members.

3. The Board of Governors shall adopt regulations under which, if there is no Director of its nationality, a member may send a representative to attend, without right to vote, any meeting of the Board of Directors when a matter particularly affecting that member is under consideration.

ARTICLE 33. VOTING

1. The total voting power of each member shall consist of the sum of its basic votes and proportional votes.

(i) The basic votes of each member shall consist of such number of votes as results from the equal distribution among all the members of twenty (20) percent of the aggregate sum of the basic votes and proportional votes of all the members.

(ii) The number of the proportional votes of each member shall be equal to the number of shares of the capital stock of the Bank held by that member.

2. In voting in the Board of Governors, each Governor shall be entitled to cast the votes of the member he represents. Except as otherwise expressly provided in this Agreement, all matters before the Board of Governors shall be decided by a majority of the voting power represented at the meeting.

3. In voting in the Board of Directors, each Director shall be entitled to cast the number of votes that counted towards his election which votes need not be cast as a unit. Except as otherwise expressly provided in this Agreement, all matters before the Board of Directors shall be decided by a majority of the voting power represented at the meeting.

ARTICLE 34. THE PRESIDENT

1. The Board of Governors, by a vote of a majority of the total number of Governors, representing not less than a majority of the total voting power of the members, shall elect a President of the Bank. He shall be a national of a regional member country. The

President, while holding office, shall not be a Governor or a Director or an alternate for either.

2. The term of office of the President shall be five (5) years. He may be re-elected. He shall, however, cease to hold office when the Board of Governors so decides by a vote of two-thirds of the total number of Governors, representing not less than two-thirds of the total voting power of the members. If the office of the President for any reason becomes vacant more than one hundred and eighty (180) days before the end of his term, a successor shall be elected for the unexpired portion of such term by the Board of Governors in accordance with the provisions of paragraph 1 of this Article. If such office for any reason becomes vacant one hundred and eighty (180) days or less before the end of the term, a successor may similarly be elected for the unexpired portion of such term by the Board of Governors.

3. The President shall be Chairman of the Board of Directors but shall have no vote, except a deciding vote in case of an equal division. He may participate in meetings of the Board of Governors but shall not vote.

4. The President shall be the legal representative of the Bank.

5. The President shall be chief of the staff of the Bank and shall conduct, under the direction of the Board of Directors, the current business of the Bank. He shall be responsible for the organization, appointment and dismissal of the officers and staff in accordance with regulations adopted by the Board of Directors.

6. In appointing the officers and staff, the President shall, subject to the paramount importance of securing the highest standards of efficiency and technical competence, pay due regard to the recruitment of personnel on as wide a regional geographical basis as possible.

ARTICLE 35. VICE-PRESIDENT(S)

1. One or more Vice-Presidents shall be appointed by the Board of Directors on the recommendation of the President. Vice-President(s) shall hold office for such term, exercise such authority and perform such functions in the administration of the Bank, as may be determined by the Board of Directors. In the absence of incapacity of the President, the Vice-President or, if there be more than one, the ranking Vice-President, shall exercise the authority and perform the functions of the President.

2. Vice-President(s) may participate in meetings of the Board of Directors but shall have no vote at such meetings, except that the Vice-President or ranking Vice-President, as the case may be, shall cast the deciding vote when acting in place of the President.

ARTICLE 36. PROHIBITION OF POLITICAL ACTIVITY: THE INTERNATIONAL CHARACTER OF THE BANK

1. The Bank shall not accept loans or assistance that may in any way prejudice, limit, deflect or otherwise alter its purpose or functions.

2. The Bank, its President, Vice-President(s), officers and staff shall not interfere in the political affairs of any member, nor shall they be influenced in their decisions by the political character of

the member concerned. Only economic considerations shall be relevant to their decisions. Such considerations shall be weighed impartially in order to achieve and carry out the purpose and functions of the Bank.

3. The President, Vice-President(s), officers and staff of the Bank, in the discharge of their offices, owe their duty entirely to the Bank and to no other authority. Each member of the Bank shall respect the international character of this duty and shall refrain from all attempts to influence any of them in the discharge of their duties.

ARTICLE 37. OFFICE OF THE BANK

1. The principal office of the Bank shall be located in Manila, Philippines.

2. The Bank may establish agencies or branch offices elsewhere.

ARTICLE 38. CHANNEL OF COMMUNICATIONS, DEPOSITORIES

1. Each member shall designate an appropriate official entity with which the Bank may communicate in connexion with any matter arising under this Agreement.

2. Each member shall designate its central bank, or such other agency as may be agreed upon with the Bank, as a depository with which the Bank may keep its holdings of currency of that member as well as other assets of the Bank.

ARTICLE 39. WORKING LANGUAGE, REPORTS

1. The working language of the Bank shall be English.

2. The Bank shall transmit to its members an Annual Report containing an audited statement of its accounts and shall publish such Report. It shall also transmit quarterly to its members a summary statement of its financial position and a profit and loss statement showing the results of its operations.

3. The Bank may also publish such other reports as it deems desirable in the carrying out of its purpose and functions. Such reports shall be transmitted to the members of the Bank.

ARTICLE 40. ALLOCATION OF NET INCOME

1. The Board of Governors shall determine annually what part of the net income of the Bank, including the net income accruing to Special Funds, shall be allocated, after making provision for reserves, to surplus and what part, if any, shall be distributed to the members.

2. The distribution referred to in the preceding paragraph shall be made in proportion to the number of shares held by each member.

3. Payments shall be made in such manner and in such currency as the Board of Governors shall determine.

CHAPTER VII—WITHDRAWAL AND SUSPENSION OF MEMBERS, TEMPORARY SUSPENSION AND TERMINATION OF OPERATIONS OF THE BANK

ARTICLE 41. WITHDRAWAL

1. Any member may withdraw from the Bank at any time by delivering a notice in writing to the Bank at its principal office.

2. Withdrawal by a member shall become effective, and its membership shall cease, on the date specified in its notice but in no event less than six (6) months after the date that notice has been received by the Bank. However, at any time before the withdrawal becomes finally effective, the member may notify the Bank in writing of the cancellation of its notice of intention to withdraw.

3. A withdrawing member shall remain liable for all direct and contingent obligations to the Bank to which it was subject at the date of delivery of the withdrawal notice. If the withdrawal becomes finally effective, the member shall not incur any liability for obligations resulting from operations of the Bank effected after the date on which the withdrawal notice was received by the Bank.

ARTICLE 42. SUSPENSION OF MEMBERSHIP

1. If a member fails to fulfill any of its obligations to the Bank, the Board of Governors may suspend such member by a vote of two-thirds of the total number of Governors, representing not less than three-fourths of the total voting power of the members.

2. The member so suspended shall cease to be a member of the Bank one (1) year from the date of its suspension unless the Board of Governors, during that one-year period, decides by the same majority necessary for suspension to restore the member to good standing.

3. While under suspension, a member shall not be entitled to exercise any rights under this Agreement, except the right of withdrawal, but shall remain subject to all its obligations.

ARTICLE 43. SETTLEMENT OF ACCOUNTS

1. After the date on which a country ceases to be a member, it shall remain liable for its direct obligations to the Bank and for its contingent liabilities to the Bank so long as any part of the loans or guarantees contracted before it ceased to be a member is outstanding; but it shall not incur liabilities with respect to loans and guarantees entered into thereafter by the Bank nor share either in the income or the expenses of the Bank.

2. At the time a country ceases to be a member, the Bank shall arrange for the repurchase of such country's shares by the Bank as a part of the settlement of accounts with such country in accordance with the provisions of paragraphs 3 and 4 of this Article. For this purpose, the repurchase price of the shares shall be the value shown by the books of the Bank on the date the country ceases to be a member.

3. The payment for shares repurchased by the Bank under this Article shall be governed by the following conditions:

(i) Any amount due to the country concerned for its shares shall be withheld so long as that country, its central bank or any of its agencies, instrumentalities or political subdivisions remains liable, as borrower or guarantor, to the Bank and such amount may, at the option of the Bank, be applied on any such liability as it matures. No amount shall be withheld on account of the contingent liability of the country for future calls on its subscription for shares in accordance with paragraph 5 of Article 6 of this Agreement. In any event, no amount due to a member for its shares shall be paid until six (6) months after the date on which the country ceases to be a member.

(ii) Payments for shares may be made from time to time, upon surrender of the corresponding stock certificates by the country concerned, to the extent by which the amount due as the repurchase price in accordance with paragraph 2 of this Article exceeds the aggregate amount of liabilities on loans and guarantees referred to in subparagraph (i) of this paragraph, until the former member has received the full repurchase price.

(iii) Payments shall be made in such available currency as the Bank determines, taking into account its financial position.

(iv) If losses are sustained by the Bank on any guarantees or loans which were outstanding on the date when a country ceased to be a member and the amount of such losses exceeds the amount of the reserve provided against losses on that date, the country concerned shall repay, upon demand, the amount by which the repurchase price of its shares would have been reduced if the losses had been taken into account when the repurchase price was determined. In addition, the former member shall remain liable on any call for unpaid subscriptions in accordance with paragraph 5 of Article 6 of this Agreement, to the same extent that it would have been required to respond if the impairment of capital had occurred and the call had been made at the time the repurchase price of its shares was determined.

4. If the Bank terminates its operations pursuant to Article 45 of this Agreement within six (6) months of the date upon which any country ceases to be a member, all rights of the country concerned shall be determined in accordance with the provisions of Articles 45 to 47 of this Agreement. Such country shall be considered as still a member for purposes of such Articles but shall have no voting rights.

ARTICLE 44. TEMPORARY SUSPENSION OF OPERATIONS

In an emergency, the Board of Directors may temporarily suspend operations in respect of new loans and guarantees, pending an opportunity for further consideration and action by the Board of Governors.

ARTICLE 45. TERMINATION OF OPERATIONS

1. The Bank may terminate its operations by a resolution of the Board of Governors approved by a vote of two-thirds of the total number of Governors, representing not less than three-fourths of the total voting power of the members.

2. After such termination, the Bank shall forthwith cease all activities except those incident to the orderly realization, conservation and preservation of its assets and settlement of its obligations.

ARTICLE 46. LIABILITY OF MEMBERS AND PAYMENT OF CLAIMS

1. In the event of termination of operations of the Bank, the liability of all members for uncalled subscriptions to the capital stock of the Bank and in respect of the depreciation of their currencies shall continue until all claims of creditors, including all contingent claims, shall have been discharged.

2. All creditors holding direct claims shall first be paid out of the assets of the Bank and then out of payments to the Bank on unpaid or callable subscriptions. Before making any payments to creditors holding direct claims, the Board of Directors shall make such arrangements as are necessary, in its judgment, to insure a pro rata distribution among holders of direct and contingent claims.

ARTICLE 47. DISTRIBUTION OF ASSETS

1. No distribution of assets shall be made to members on account of their subscriptions to the capital stock of the Bank until all liabilities to creditors shall have been discharged or provided for. Moreover, such distribution must be approved by the Board of Governors by a vote of two-thirds of the total number of Governors, representing not less than three-fourths of the total voting power of the members.

2. Any distribution of the assets of the Bank to the members shall be in proportion to the capital stock held by each member and shall be effected at such times and under such conditions as the Bank shall deem fair and equitable. The shares of assets distributed need not be uniform as to type of asset. No member shall be entitled to receive his share in such a distribution of assets until it has settled all of its obligations to the Bank.

3. Any member receiving assets distributed pursuant to this article shall enjoy the same rights with respect to such assets as the Bank enjoyed prior to their distribution.

CHAPTER VIII—STATUS, IMMUNITIES, EXEMPTIONS, AND PRIVILEGES

ARTICLE 48. PURPOSE OF CHAPTER

To enable the Bank effectively to fulfill its purpose and carry out the functions entrusted to it, the status, immunities, exemptions and privileges set forth in this Chapter shall be accorded to the Bank in the territory of each member.

ARTICLE 49. LEGAL STATUS

The Bank shall possess full juridical personality and, in particular, full capacity:

(i) to contract;

(ii) to acquire, and dispose of, immovable and movable property; and

(iii) to institute legal proceedings.

ARTICLE 50. IMMUNITY FROM JUDICIAL PROCEEDINGS

1. The Bank shall enjoy immunity from every form of legal process, except in cases arising out of or in connexion with the exercise of its powers to borrow money, to guarantee obligations, or to buy and sell or underwrite the sale of securities, in which cases actions may be brought against the Bank in a court of competent jurisdiction in the territory of a country in which the Bank has its principal or a branch office, or has appointed an agent for the purpose of accepting service or notice of process, or has issued or guaranteed securities.

2. Notwithstanding the provisions of paragraph 1 of this article, no action shall be brought against the Bank by any member, or by any agency or instrumentality of a member, or by any entity or person directly or indirectly acting for or deriving claims from a member or from any agency or instrumentality of a member. Members shall have recourse to such special procedures for the settlement of controversies between the Bank and its members as may be prescribed in this Agreement, in the bylaws and regulations of the Bank, or in contracts entered into with the Bank.

3. Property and assets of the Bank shall, wheresoever located and by whomsoever held, be immune from all forms of seizure, attachment or execution before the delivery of final judgment against the Bank.

ARTICLE 51. IMMUNITY OF ASSETS

Property and assets of the Bank, wheresoever located and by whomsoever held, shall be immune from search, requisition, confiscation, expropriation or any other form of taking or foreclosure by executive or legislative action.

ARTICLE 52. IMMUNITY OF ARCHIVES

The archives of the Bank and, in general, all documents belonging to it, or held by it, shall be inviolable, wherever located.

ARTICLE 53. FREEDOM OF ASSETS FROM RESTRICTIONS

To the extent necessary to carry out the purpose and functions of the Bank effectively, and subject to the provisions of this Agreement, all property and assets of the Bank shall be free from restrictions, regulations, controls, and moratoria of any nature.

ARTICLE 54. PRIVILEGE FOR COMMUNICATIONS

Official communications of the Bank shall be accorded by each member treatment not less favorable than that it accords to the official communications of any other member.

ARTICLE 55. IMMUNITIES AND PRIVILEGES OF BANK PERSONNEL

All Governors, Directors, alternates, officers and employees of the Bank, including experts performing missions for the Bank:

(i) shall be immune from legal process with respect to acts performed by them in their official capacity, except when the Bank waives the immunity;

(ii) where they are not local citizens or nationals, shall be accorded the same immunities from immigration restrictions, alien registration requirements and national service obligations, and the same facilities as regards exchange regulations, as are accorded by members to the representatives, officials and employees of comparable rank of other members; and

(iii) shall be granted the same treatment in respect of traveling facilities as is accorded by members to representatives, officials and employees of comparable rank of other members.

ARTICLE 56. EXEMPTION FROM TAXATION

1. The Bank, its assets, property, income and its operations and transactions, shall be exempt from all taxation and from all customs duties. The Bank shall also be exempt from any obligation for the payment, withholding or collection of any tax or duty.

2. No tax shall be levied on or in respect of salaries and emoluments paid by the Bank to Directors, alternates, officers or employees of the Bank, including experts performing missions for the Bank, except where a member deposits with its instrument of ratification or acceptance a declaration[3] that such member retains for itself and its political subdivisions the right to tax salaries and emoluments paid by the Bank to citizens or nationals of such member.

3. No tax of any kind shall be levied on any obligation or security issued by the Bank, including any dividend or interest thereon, by whomsoever held:

(i) which discriminates against such obligation or security solely because it is issued by the Bank; or

(ii) if the sole jurisdictional basis for such taxation is the place or currency in which it is issued, made payable or paid, or the location of any office or place of business maintained by the Bank.

4. No tax of any kind shall be levied on any obligation or security guaranteed by the Bank, including any dividend or interest thereon, by whomsoever held:

(i) which discriminates against such obligation or security solely because it is guaranteed by the Bank; or

(ii) if the sole jurisdictional basis for such taxation is the location of any office or place of business maintained by the Bank.

ARTICLE 57. IMPLEMENTATION

Each member, in accordance with its juridical system, shall promptly take such action as is necessary to make effective in its own territory the provisions set forth in this Chapter and shall inform the Bank of the action which it has taken on the matter.

---

[3] Acceptance deposited, August 16, 1966, with a declaration that "the United States of America retains for itself and for all political subdivisions of the United States of America the right to tax salaries and emoluments paid by the Asian Development Bank to any citizen or national of the United States of America," in accordance with article 56(2) of the agreement.

ARTICLE 58. WAIVER OF IMMUNITIES, EXEMPTIONS, AND PRIVILEGES

The Bank at its discretion may waive any of the privileges, immunities and exemptions conferred under this Chapter in any case or instance, in such manner and upon such conditions as it may determine to be appropriate in the best interests of the Bank.

CHAPTER IX—AMENDMENTS, INTERPRETATIONS, ARBITRATION

ARTICLE 59. AMENDMENTS

1. This Agreement may be amended only by a resolution of the Board of Governors approved by a vote of two-thirds of the total number of Governors, representing not less than three-fourths of the total voting power of the members.

2. Notwithstanding the provisions of paragraph 1 of this Article, the unanimous agreement of the Board of Governors shall be required for the approval of any amendment modifying:

(i) the right to withdraw from the Bank;

(ii) the limitations on liability provided in paragraphs 6 and 7 of Article 5; and

(iii) the rights pertaining to purchase of capital stock provided in paragraph 2 of Article 5.

3. Any proposal to amend this Agreement, whether emanating from a member of the Board of Directors shall be communicated to the Chairman of the Board of Governors, who shall bring the proposal before the Board of Governors. When an amendment has been adopted, the Bank shall so certify in an official communication addressed to all members. Amendments shall enter into force for all members three (3) months after the date of the official communication unless the Board of Governors specifies therein a different period.

ARTICLE 60. INTERPRETATION OR APPLICATION

1. Any question of interpretation or application of the provisions of this Agreement arising between any member and the Bank, or between two or more members of the Bank, shall be submitted to the Board of Directors for decision. If there is no Director of its nationality on that Board, a member particularly affected by the question under consideration shall be entitled to direct representation in the Board of Directors during such consideration; the representative of such member shall, however, have no vote. Such right of representation shall be regulated by the Board of Governors.

2. In any case where the Board of Directors has given a decision under paragraph 1 of this Article, any member may require that the question be referred to the Board of Governors, whose decision shall be final. Pending the decision of the Board of Governors, the Bank may, so far as it deems it necessary, act on the basis of the decision of the Board of Directors.

ARTICLE 61. ARBITRATION

If a disagreement should arise between the Bank and a country which has ceased to be a member, or between the Bank and any member, after adoption of a resolution to terminate the operations of the Bank, such disagreement shall be submitted to arbitration by a tribunal of three arbitrators. One of the arbitrators shall be appointed by the Bank, another by the country concerned, and the third, unless the parties otherwise agree, by the President of the International Court of Justice or such other authority as may have been prescribed by regulations adopted by the Board of Governors. A majority vote of the arbitrators shall be sufficient to reach a decision which shall be final and binding upon the parties. The third arbitrator shall be empowered to settle all questions of procedure in any case where the parties are in disagreement with respect thereto.

ARTICLE 62. APPROVAL DEEMED GIVEN

Whenever the approval of any member is required before any act may be done by the Bank, approval shall be deemed to have been given unless the member presents an objection within such reasonable period as the Bank may fix in notifying the members of the proposed act.

CHAPTER X—FINAL PROVISIONS

ARTICLE 63. SIGNATURE AND DEPOSIT

1. The original of this Agreement in a single copy in the English language shall remain open for signature at the United Nations Economic Commission for Asia and the Far East, in Bangkok, until 31 January 1966 by Governments of countries listed in Annex A to this Agreement. This document shall thereafter be deposited with the Secretary-General of the United Nations (hereinafter called the "Depository").

2. The Depository shall send certified copies of this Agreement to all the Signatories and other countries which become members of the Bank.

ARTICLE 64. RATIFICATION OR ACCEPTANCE

1. This Agreement shall be subject to ratification or acceptance by the Signatories. Instruments of ratification or acceptance shall be deposited with the Depository not later than 30 September 1966. The Depository shall duly notify the other Signatories of each deposit and the date thereof.

2. A Signatory whose instrument of ratification or acceptance is deposited before the date on which this Agreement enters into force, shall become a member of the Bank on that date. Any other Signatory which complies with the provisions of the preceding paragraph, shall become a member of the Bank on the date on which its instrument of ratification or acceptance is deposited.

ARTICLE 65. ENTRY INTO FORCE

This Agreement shall enter into force when instruments of ratification or acceptance have been deposited by at least fifteen (15) Signatories (including not less than ten [10] regional countries) whose initial subscriptions, as set forth in Annex A to this Agreement, in the aggregate comprise not less than sixty-five (65) percent of the authorized capital stock of the Bank.

ARTICLE 66. COMMENCEMENT OF OPERATIONS

1. As soon as this Agreement enters into force, each member shall appoint a Governor, and the Executive Secretary of the United Nations Economic Commission for Asia and the Far East shall call the inaugural meeting of the Board of Governors.

2. At its inaugural meeting, the Board of Governors:

(i) shall make arrangements for the election of Directors of the Bank in accordance with paragraph 1 of Article 30 of this Agreement; and

(ii) shall make arrangements for the determination of the date on which the Bank shall commence its operations.

3. The Bank shall notify its members of the date of the commencement of its operations.

DONE at the City of Manila, Philippines, on 4 December 1965, in a single copy in the English language which shall be brought to the United Nations Economic Commission for Asia and the Far East, in Bangkok, and thereafter deposited with the Secretary-General of the United Nations, New York, in accordance with Article 63 of this Agreement.

ANNEX A—INITIAL SUBSCRIPTIONS TO THE AUTHORIZED CAPITAL STOCK FOR COUNTRIES WHICH MAY BECOME MEMBERS IN ACCORDANCE WITH ARTICLE 64

Part A. Regional Countries

I

Country	Amount of subscription (millions U.S. dollars)
1. Afghanistan	3.36
2. Australia	85.00
3. Cambodia	3.00
4. Ceylon	8.52
5. China, Republic of	16.00
6. India	93.00
7. Iran	60.00
8. Japan	200.00
9. Korea, Republic of	30.00
10. Laos	.42
11. Malaysia	20.00
12. Nepal	2.16
13. New Zealand	22.56
14. Pakistan	32.00
15. Philippines	35.00
16. Republic of Viet-Nam	7.00
17. Singapore	4.00
18. Thailand	20.00
19. Western Samoa	.06
Total	642.08

II

The following regional countries may become Signatories of this Agreement in accordance with Article 63, provided that at the time of signing, they shall respectively subscribe to the capital stock of the Bank in the following amounts:

Country	Amount of subscription (millions U.S. dollars)
1. Burma	7.74
2. Mongolia	.18
Total	7.92

Part B. Non-Regional Countries

I

Country	Amount of subscription (millions U.S. dollars)
1. Belgium	5.00
2. Canada	25.00
3. Denmark	5.00
4. Germany, Federal Republic of	30.00
5. Italy	10.00
6. Netherlands	11.00
7. United Kingdom	10.00
8. United States	200.00
Total	296.00

II

The following non-regional countries which participated in the meeting of the Preparatory Committee on the Asian Development Bank in Bangkok from 21 October to 1 November 1965 and which there indicated interest in membership in the Bank, may become Signatories of this Agreement in accordance with Article 63, provided that at the time of signing, each such country shall subscribe to the capital stock of the Bank in an amount which shall not be less than five million dollars ($5,000,000):

1. Austria
2. Finland
3. Norway
4. Sweden

III

On or before 31 January 1966, any of the non-regional countries listed in Part B(I) of this Annex may increase the amount of its subscription by so informing the Executive Secretary of the United Nations Economic Commission for Asia and the Far East in Bangkok, provided, however, that the total amount of the initial subscriptions of the non-regional countries listed in Part (B) (I) and (II) of this Annex shall not exceed the amount of three hundred and fifty million dollars ($350,000,000).

ANNEX B—ELECTION OF DIRECTORS

SECTION A. ELECTION OF DIRECTORS BY GOVERNORS REPRESENTING REGIONAL MEMBERS [4]

(1) Each Governor representing a regional member shall cast all votes of the member he represents for a single person.

(2) The seven (7) persons receiving the highest number of votes shall be Directors, except that no person who receives less than ten (10) percent of the total voting power of regional members shall be considered as elected.

(3) If seven (7) persons are not elected at the first ballot, a second ballot shall be held in which the person who received the lowest number of votes in the preceding ballot shall be ineligible and in which votes shall be cast only by:

(a) Governors who voted in the preceding ballot for a person who is not elected; and

(b) Governors whose votes for a person who is elected are deemed, in accordance with paragraph (4) of this Section, to have raised the votes cast for that person above eleven (11) percent of the total voting power of regional members.

(4)(a) In determining whether the votes cast by a Governor shall be deemed to have raised the total number of votes for any person above eleven (11) percent, the said eleven (11) percent shall be deemed to include, first, the votes of the Governor casting the highest number of votes for that person, and then, in diminishing order, the votes of each Governor casting the next highest number until eleven (11) percent is attained.

(b) Any Governor, part of whose votes must be counted in order to raise the votes cast for any person above (10) percent, shall be considered as casting all his votes for that person even if the total number of votes cast for that person thereby exceeds eleven (11) percent.

(5) If, after the second ballot, seven (7) persons are not elected, further ballots shall be held in conformity with the principles and procedures laid down in this Section, except that after six (6) persons are elected, the seventh may be elected—notwithstanding the provisions of paragraph (2) of this Section—by a simple majority of the remaining votes of regional members. All such remaining votes shall be deemed to have counted toward the election of the seventh Director.

(6) In case of an increase in the number of Directors to be elected by Governors representing regional members, the minimum and maximum percentages specified in paragraphs (2), (3), and (4) of

[4] On April 10, 1969, the Board of Governors changed the minimum and maximum percentages specified in subsecs. (2), (3) and (4) of sec. A to 8 percent and 10 percent.

Section A of this Annex shall be correspondingly adjusted by the Board of Governors.

SECTION B. ELECTION OF DIRECTORS BY GOVERNORS REPRESENTING NON-REGIONAL MEMBERS [5]

(1) Each Governor representing a non-regional member shall cast all votes of the member he represents for a single person.

(2) The three (3) persons receiving the highest number of votes shall be Directors, except that no person who receives less than twenty-five (25) percent of the total voting power of non-regional members shall be considered as elected.

(3) If three (3) persons are not elected at the first ballot, a second ballot shall be held in which the person who received the lowest number of votes in the preceding ballot shall be ineligible and in which votes shall be cast only by:

(a) Governors who voted in the preceding ballot for a person who is not elected; and

(b) Governors whose votes for a person who is elected are deemed, in accordance with paragraph (4) of this Section, to have raised the votes cast for that person above twenty-six (26) percent of the total voting power of non-regional members.

(4)(a) In determining whether the votes cast by a Governor shall be deemed to have raised the total number of votes for any person above twenty-six (26) percent, the said twenty-six (26) percent shall be deemed to include, first, the votes of the Governor casting the highest number of votes for that person, and then in diminishing order, the votes of each Governor casting the next highest number until twenty-six (26) percent is attained.

(b) Any Governor, part of whose votes must be counted in order to raise the votes cast for any person above twenty-five (25) percent, shall be considered as casting all his votes for that person even if the total number of votes cast for that person thereby exceeds twenty-six (26) percent.

(5) If, after the second ballot, three (3) persons are not elected, further ballots shall be held in conformity with the principles and procedures laid down in this Section, except that after two (2) persons are elected, a third may be elected—provided that subscriptions from non-regional members shall have reached a minimum total of three hundred forty-five million dollars ($345,000,000) , and notwithstanding the provisions of paragraph (2) of this Section—by a simple majority of the remaining votes. All such remaining votes shall be deemed to have counted toward the election of the third Director.

(6) In case of an increase in the number of Directors to be elected by Governors representing non-regional members, the minimum and maximum percentages specified in paragraphs (2), (3) and (4) of Section B of this Annex shall be correspondingly adjusted by the Board of Governors.

---

[5] On April 10, 1969, the Board of Governors changed the minimum and maximum percentages specified in subsecs. (2), (3) and (4) of sec. B to 16 percent and 19 percent. On February 19, 1971, the Board of Governors changed the minimum percentage from 16 percent to 17 percent.

10. Articles of Agreement Establishing the African Development Fund

CONTENTS

10. Articles of Agreement Establishing the African Development Fund

Articles of agreement done at Abidjan, November 29, 1972; Signed for the United States, November 18, 1976; Instrument of acceptance by the United States deposited with the African Development Bank, November 18, 1976; Entered into force for the United States, November 18, 1976; Amended, July 4, 2003[1]

The States parties to this Agreement and the African Development Bank have agreed to establish hereby the African Development Fund which shall be governed by the following provisions:

CHAPTER I—DEFINITIONS

ARTICLE 1

(1) The following terms wherever used in this Agreement shall have the following meanings, unless the context shall otherwise specify or require:

"Fund" shall mean the African Development Fund established by this Agreement.

"Bank" shall mean the African Development Bank.

"member" shall mean a member of the Bank.

"participant" shall mean the Bank and any State which shall become a party to this Agreement.

"State participant" shall mean a participant other than the Bank.

"original participant" shall mean the Bank and each State participant which becomes a participant pursuant to Article 57(1).

"subscription" shall mean amounts subscribed by participants pursuant to Articles 5, 6 or 7.

"unit of account" shall mean a unit of account having a value of 0.81851265 gramme of fine gold.

"freely convertible currency" shall mean currency of a participant which the Fund determines, after consultation with the International Monetary Fund, is adequately convertible into other currencies for the purpose of the Fund's operations.

"President", "Board of Governors" and "Board of Directors" shall mean respectively the President, Board of Governors and Board of Directors of the Fund and in the case of the governors and directors shall include alternate governors and alternate directors when acting as governors and directors respectively.

"regional" shall mean located in the continent of Africa or the African islands.

(2) Reference to Chapters, Articles, paragraphs and Schedules shall mean the Chapters, Articles and paragraphs of, or Schedules to this Agreement.

[1] 28 UST 4547; TIAS 8605.

(3) The headings of the Chapters and Articles are inserted for convenience of reference only and are not part of this Agreement.

CHAPTER II—PURPOSE AND PARTICIPATION

ARTICLE 2. PURPOSE

The purpose of the Fund shall be to assist the Bank in making an increasingly effective contribution to the economic and social development of the Bank's members and to the promotion of co-operation (including regional and sub-regional co-operation) and increased international trade, particularly among such members. It shall provide finance on concessional terms for purposes which are of primary importance for and serve such development.

ARTICLE 3. PARTICIPATION

(1) The participants in the Fund shall be the Bank and those States which shall have become parties to this Agreement in accordance with its terms.

(2) The original State participants shall be those States listed in Schedule A which shall have become parties to this Agreement pursuant to Article 57(1).

(3) A State which is not an original participant may become a participant and a party to this Agreement upon such terms, not inconsistent with this Agreement, as the Board of Governors shall determine by a unanimous resolution adopted by the affirmative vote of the total voting power of the participants. Such participation shall be open only to those States which are members of the United Nations or any of its specialized agencies or are parties to the Statute of the International Court of Justice.

(4) A State may authorize an entity or agency acting on its behalf to sign this Agreement and to represent it in all matters relating to this Agreement with the exception of the matters referred to in Article 55.

CHAPTER III—RESOURCES

ARTICLE 4. RESOURCES[2]

The resources of the Fund shall consist of:

(i) subscriptions by the Bank;

---

[2] The initial authorized capital resources of the Fund were $89 million. Following a special general increase of $36.9 million and initial subscriptions by two additional countries, the total resources by the end of 1975 amounted to $150.7 million. The First Replenishment of the Fund's resources, effective July 15, 1976, equaling $269.9 million, plus the accession of three additional countries, brought the total resources to $453.3 million. A Second Replenishment in 1979, and the addition of four new members, contributed $758 million to the resources of the Fund. In 1983, the Third Replenishment plus two new members provided $1,154 million authorized capital. The Fourth Replenishment (AFDF IV) in 1986, targeted $1.5 billion (U.S. contribution—$225 million) to finance the 1985–1987 lending program. A Fifth Replenishment in 1987, adopted a $2.7 billion target level of funding (U.S. contribution—$315 million) to administer the Funds 1988–1990 programs. A Sixth Replenishment in 1991, adopted a $3.42 billion target level of funding (U.S. contribution—$405 million) to administer the Funds, 1991–1993. A Seventh Replenishment in 1996, adopted a $3.2 billion target level of funding (U.S. contribution—$200 million) to administer the Funds, 1996–1998. An Eighth Replenishment in 1999, adopted a $3.38 billion target level of funding (U.S. contribution—$300 million) to administer the Funds, 1999–2001. A Ninth Replenishment in 2002, adopted a $3.5 billion target level of funding (U.S. contribution—$280 million) to administer the Funds, 2002–2004. A Tenth Replenishment in 2004, adopted a $5.4 billion target level of funding (U.S. contribution—$406 million) to administer the Funds, 2005–2007.

(ii) subscriptions by State participants;
(iii) other resources received by the Fund; and
(iv) funds derived from operations or otherwise accruing to the Fund.

ARTICLE 5. SUBSCRIPTIONS BY THE BANK

The Bank shall pay to the Fund as its initial subscription the amount, expressed in units of account, set forth opposite its name in Schedule A, utilizing for that purpose the funds standing to the credit of the "African Development Fund" of the Bank. Payment shall be made on the same terms and conditions as are specified in Article 6(2) for the payment of the initial subscription of State participants. The Bank will thereafter subscribe such other amounts as the Board of Governors of the Bank may determine, on such terms and conditions as shall be agreed with the Fund.

ARTICLE 6. INITIAL SUBSCRIPTIONS OF STATE PARTICIPANTS

(1) Upon becoming a participant each State participant shall subscribe funds in the amount assigned to it. Such subscriptions are hereinafter referred to as initial subscriptions.

(2) The initial subscription assigned to each original State participant shall be in the amount set forth opposite its name in Schedule A, and shall be expressed in units of account and payable in freely convertible currency. Payment shall be made in three equal annual instalments as follows: the first such instalment shall be paid within thirty days after the Fund shall begin operations pursuant to Article 60 or on date on which the original State participant becomes a party to this Agreement, whichever is later; the second instalment within one year thereafter and the third instalment within one year after the payment or the due date of the second instalment, whichever is earlier. The Fund may request earlier payment or either or both of the second and third instalments if the operations of the Fund shall require it, but such earlier payment shall be entirely voluntary on the part of each participant.

(3) The initial subscriptions of State participants other than original participants shall also be expressed in units of account and payable in freely convertible currency. The amount and terms of payment of such subscription shall be determined by the Fund pursuant to Article 3(3).

(4) Except as the Fund may otherwise agree, each State participant shall maintain the free convertibility of its currency paid in by it pursuant to this Article.

(5) Notwithstanding the foregoing provisions of this Article, a State participant may defer for a period of not more than three months the making of any payment required by this Article when budgetary or other circumstances necessitate such delay.

ARTICLE 7. ADDITIONAL SUBSCRIPTIONS BY STATE PARTICIPANTS

(1) The Fund shall at such time as it deems appropriate in the light of the schedule of payments of the initial subscriptions of original participants and of its own operations, and at appropriate intervals thereafter, review the adequacy of its resources and, if it

deems it desirable, may authorize a general increase in the subscriptions of State participants on such terms and conditions as the Fund shall determine. Notwithstanding the foregoing, the Fund may authorize general or individual increases in such subscriptions at any time, provided that an individual increase shall be considered only at the request of the State participant involved.

(2) When any additional individual subscription is authorized pursuant to paragraph (1), each State participant shall be given an opportunity to subscribe, under no less favourable conditions, reasonably determined by the Fund, than those prescribed under paragraph (1), an amount which will enable it to maintain its relative voting power as among State participants.

(3) No State participant shall be obliged to subscribe additional amounts in the case of general or individual increases in subscriptions.

(4) All authorizations for, and determinations in respect of, general increases under paragraph (1) shall be by an eighty-five percent majority of the total voting power of the participants.

ARTICLE 8. OTHER RESOURCES

(1) Subject to the following provisions of this Article, the Fund may enter into arrangements to receive other resources, including grants and loans, from members, participants, States which are not participants and from any public or private entity or entities.

(2) Such arrangements shall be on terms and conditions which are consistent with the Fund's purposes, operations and policies and which will not impose an undue administrative or financial burden on the Fund or the Bank.

(3) Such arrangements, other than those for grants for technical assistance, shall be on terms which will permit the Fund to comply with the requirements of Article 15 (4) and (5).

(4) Such arrangements shall be approved by the Board of Directors, in the case of arrangements with a State which is not a member or a participant or with an agency of such State, by an eighty-five percent majority of the total voting power of the participants.

(5) The Fund shall not accept any loan (except temporary accommodations required for its operations) which is not on concessional terms and shall not borrow in any market or, as a borrower, guarantor, or otherwise, participate in the issue of securities in any market and shall not issue negotiable or transferable obligations evidencing indebtedness for loans received pursuant to paragraph (1).

ARTICLE 9. PAYMENT OF SUBSCRIPTIONS

The Fund shall accept any part of a participant's subscription payable by the participant under Article 5, 6 or 7 or under Article 13 and not needed by the Fund in its operations, in the form of notes, letters of credit or similar obligations issued by the participant or the depository, if any, designated by the participant pursuant to Article 33. Such notes or other obligations shall be non-negotiable, non-interest-bearing and payable at their par value on demand to the account of the Fund in the designated depository, or if there is none, as the Fund shall direct. Notwithstanding the issuance or acceptance of any such note, letter of credit or other obligation, the obligation of the participant under Articles 5, 6 and 7 and Article 13 shall continue to subsist. Amounts held by the Fund in respect of subscriptions of participants which do not avail themselves of the provisions of this Article may be deposited or invested by the Fund to produce income to help defray its administrative and other expenses. The Fund shall draw down all subscriptions on a *pro rata* basis, as far as practicable over reasonable periods of time, to finance expenditures regardless of the form in which such subscriptions are made.

ARTICLE 10. LIMITATION OF LIABILITY

No participant shall be liable, by reason of its participation, for acts or obligations of the Fund.

CHAPTER IV—CURRENCIES

ARTICLE 11. USE OF CURRENCIES

(1) Currencies received in payment of, or under Article 13 in respect of, subscriptions made pursuant to Article 5 and Article 6(2) may be used and exchanged by the Fund for any of its operations and, subject to the approval of the Board of Directors, for the temporary investment of funds not needed in its operations.

(2) The use of currencies received in payment of, or under Article 13 in respect of, subscriptions under Article 6(3) and Article 7 (1) and (2) or as other resources under Article 8 shall be governed by the terms and conditions pursuant to which such currencies are received or, in the case of currencies received under Article 13, the use shall be governed by the terms and conditions on which the currencies whose value is so maintained were received.

(3) All other currencies received by the Fund may be freely used and exchanged by the Fund for any of its operations and, subject to the approval of the Board of Directors, for the temporary investment of funds not needed in its operations.

(4) No restriction shall be imposed which is contrary to the provisions of this Article.

ARTICLE 12. VALUATION OF CURRENCIES

(1) Whenever it shall be necessary under this Agreement to determine the value of any currency in terms of another currency or currencies or of the unit of account, such valuation shall be reasonably made by the Fund after consultation with the International Monetary Fund.

(2) In the case of a currency which does not have a par value established with the International Monetary Fund, the value of such currency in terms of the unit of account shall be determined from time to time by the Fund pursuant to paragraph (1) of this Article and the value so determined shall be treated as if it were the par value of such currency for the purpose of this Agreement, including, without limitation, Article 13 (1) and (2).

ARTICLE 13. MAINTENANCE OF VALUE OF CURRENCY HOLDINGS

(1) Whenever the par value in the International Monetary Fund of the currency of a State participant is reduced in terms of the unit of account, or its foreign exchange value has, in the opinion of the Fund, depreciated to a significant extent within that participant's territory, that participant shall pay to the Fund within a reasonable time an amount of its currency required to maintain the value, as of the time of subscription, of the amount of such currency paid in to the Fund by that participant pursuant to Article 6 and pursuant to the provisions of the present paragraph, whether or not such currency is held in the form of notes, letters of credit or other obligations accepted pursuant to Article 9, provided that the foregoing shall apply only so long as and to the extent that such currency shall not have been initially disbursed or exchanged for another currency.

(2) Whenever the par value of the currency of a State participant is increased in terms of the unit of account or its foreign exchange value has, in the opinion of the Fund, appreciated to a significant extent within that participant's territory, the Fund shall return to that participant within a reasonable time an amount of such currency equal to the increase in the value of the amount of such currency to which the provisions of paragraph (1) are applicable.

(3) The Fund may waive or declare inoperative the provisions of this Article when a uniform change in the par value of the currencies of all State participants is made by the International Monetary Fund.

CHAPTER V—OPERATIONS

ARTICLE 14. USE OF RESOURCES

(1) The Fund shall provide financing for projects and programmes to further economic and social development in the territory of members. The Fund shall provide such financing for the benefit of those members whose economic situation and prospects require such financing to be on concessional terms.

(2) Financing provided by the Fund shall be for purposes which in the opinion of the Fund are of high developmental priority in the light of the needs of the area or areas concerned and shall, except in special circumstances, be for specific projects or groups of projects, particularly those forming part of a national or regional or sub-regional programme, including provisions of financing for national development banks or other suitable institutions for relending for specific projects approved by the Fund.

ARTICLE 15. CONDITIONS OF FINANCING

(1) The Fund shall not provide financing for any project in the territory of a member if that member objects thereto, except that it shall not be necessary for the Fund to assure itself that individual members do not object in the case of financing provided to a public international, regional or sub-regional organization.

(2) (a) The Fund shall not provide financing if, in its opinion, such financing is available from other sources on terms that the Fund considers as reasonable for the recipient.

(b) In making financing available for entities other than members, the Fund shall take all necessary steps to ensure that the concessional benefits of its financing accrue only to members or other entities which should, taking into account all the relevant circumstances, receive some or all of those benefits.

(3) Before financing is provided, the applicant shall have presented an adequate proposal through the President of the Bank and the President shall have presented to the Board of Directors of the Fund a written report recommending such financing, on the basis of a staff study of its merits.

(4) (a) The Fund shall impose no conditions that the proceeds of its financing shall be spent in the territories of any particular State participant or member, but such proceeds shall be used only for procurement in the territories of State participants or members, of goods produced in and services supplied from the territories of State participants or members, provided that, in the case of funds received pursuant to Article 8 from a State which is not a participant or member, the territories of that State shall also be eligible sources of procurement from such funds, and may be eligible sources of procurement from such other funds received under that Article as the Board of Directors shall determine.

(b) Procurement shall be on the basis of international competition among eligible suppliers except in cases where the Board of Directors determines that such international competition would not be justified.

(5) The Fund shall make arrangements to ensure that the proceeds of any financing are used only for the purposes for which the financing was provided, with due attention to considerations of economy, efficiency and competitive international trade and without regard to political or other non-economic influences or considerations.

(6) Funds to be provided under any financing operations shall be made available to the recipient only to meet expenses in connection with the project as they are actually incurred.

(7) The Fund shall be guided by sound development banking principles in its operations.

(8) The Fund shall not engage in refinancing operations.

(9) In making a loan, the Fund shall pay due regard to the prospects that the borrower and the guarantor, if any, will be able to meet their obligations.

(10) In considering an application for financing, the Fund shall pay due regard to the relevant self-help measures being taken by the recipient and, where the recipient is not a member, by both the recipient and the member or members whose territories the project or programme is intended to serve.

(11) The Fund shall adopt such measures as shall be required to ensure the effective application of this Article.

ARTICLE 16. FORM AND TERMS OF FINANCING

(1) Financing by the Fund from resources provided under Articles 5, 6 and 7, and from repayments of, and income arising from, such financing, shall take the form of loans. The Fund may provide

other financing, including grants, out of resources received pursuant to arrangements under Article 8 expressly authorizing such financing.

(2) (a) Subject to the provisions of the foregoing paragraph, financing by the Fund shall be on such concessional terms as may be appropriate.

(b) Where the borrower is a member, or an inter-governmental body to which one or more members belong, the Fund shall, in establishing the terms of financing, take account primarily of the economic circumstances and prospects of the member or members for whose benefit the financing is being provided and, in addition, of the nature and requirements of the project or programme concerned.

(3) The Fund may provide financing for: (a) any member or any geographical or administrative subdivision or agency thereof: (b) any institution or undertaking in the territory of any member; and (c) any regional or sub-regional agency or institution concerned with development in the territories of members. All such financing shall, in the opinion of the Fund, be for the furtherance of the purposes of this Agreement. Where the borrower is not itself a member, the Fund shall require a suitable governmental or other guarantee or guarantees.

(4) The Fund may make foreign exchange available to meet local expenditure on a project when and to the extent which, in the opinion of the Fund, this is necessary or appropriate for the purposes of the loan, having regard to the economic position and prospects of the member or members for whose benefit the financing is being provided, and to the nature and requirements of the project.

(5) Loans shall be repayable in the currency or currencies loaned, or in such other freely convertible currency or currencies as the Fund shall determine.

(6) Before any financing is made available to or for the benefit of a member or for a project in the territory of a member, the Fund shall be satisfied that such member has taken all such administrative and legislative measures in respect of its territory as are necessary to give effect to the provisions of Article 11(4) and Chapter VIII as if the member were a State participant, and it shall be a term of such financing that such administrative and legislative measures shall be maintained, and that in the event of any dispute between the Fund and a member, and in the absence of any other provision therefor, the provisions of Article 53 shall have effect, as if the member were a State participant in the circumstances to which that Article applies.

ARTICLE 17. REVIEW AND EVALUATION

A comprehensive and continuing review of completed projects, programmes and activities financed by the Fund shall be carried out to aid the Board of Directors and the President in determining the effectiveness of the Fund in accomplishing its purposes. The President, with the agreement of the Board of Directors, shall make arrangements for carrying out this review and its results shall be reported through the President to the Board of Directors.

ARTICLE 18. CO-OPERATION WITH OTHER INTERNATIONAL ORGANIZATIONS, OTHER INSTITUTIONS AND STATES

In furtherance of its purposes, the Fund shall seek to co-operate, and may enter into arrangements for co-operation, with other international organizations, regional and sub-regional organizations, other institutions and States, provided that no such arrangement shall be made with a State which is not a member or a participant or with an agency of such State unless it shall have been approved by an eighty-five percent majority of the total voting power of the participants.

ARTICLE 19. TECHNICAL ASSISTANCE

In furtherance of its purposes, the Fund may provide technical assistance, but such assistance will normally be on a reimbursable basis if it is not provided from special technical assistance grants or other means made available to the Fund for the purpose.

ARTICLE 20. MISCELLANEOUS OPERATIONS

In addition to the powers provided for elsewhere in this Agreement, the Fund may undertake such other activities incidental to its operations as shall be necessary or desirable in furtherance of its purposes and consistent with the provisions of this Agreement.

ARTICLE 21. POLITICAL ACTIVITY PROHIBITED

Neither the Fund, nor any officials or other persons acting on its behalf, shall interfere in the political affairs of any member; nor shall they be influenced in their decisions by the political character of the member or members concerned. Only considerations relevant to the economic and social development of members shall be relevant to such decisions, and these considerations shall be weighed impartially to achieve the purposes stated in this Agreement.

CHAPTER VI—ORGANIZATION AND MANAGEMENT

ARTICLE 22. ORGANIZATION OF THE FUND

The Fund shall have a Board of Governors, a Board of Directors and a President. The Fund will utilise the officers, staff, organization, services and facilities of the Bank to carry out its functions and, if the Board of Directors recognizes that there is need for additional personnel, will have such personnel who shall be engaged by the President pursuant to Article 30(4)(v).

ARTICLE 23. BOARD OF GOVERNORS: POWERS

(1) All the powers of the Fund shall be vested in the Board of Governors.

(2) The Board of Governors may delegate to the Board of Directors all its powers, except the power to:

(i) admit new participants and determine the terms of their admission;

(ii) authorize increases in subscription under Article 7 and determine the terms and conditions relating thereto;

(iii) suspend a participant;

(iv) decide appeals from decisions made by the Board of Directors concerning the interpretation or application of this Agreement;

(v) authorize the conclusion of general arrangements for cooperation with other international organizations, other than arrangements of a temporary or administrative character;

(vi) select external auditors to audit the accounts of the Fund and certify the balance sheet and statement of the income and expenditures of the Fund;

(vii) approve, after reviewing the report of the auditors; the balance sheet and the statement of the income and expenditures of the Fund;

(viii) amend this Agreement;

(ix) decide to terminate the operations of the Fund and distribute its assets; and

(x) exercise such other powers as are expressly assigned to the Board of Governors in this Agreement.

(3) The Board of Governors may at any time revoke the delegation of any matter to the Board of Directors.

ARTICLE 24. BOARD OF GOVERNORS: COMPOSITION

(1) The governors and alternate governors of the Bank shall be *ex officio* governors and alternate governors respectively of the Fund. The President of the Bank shall notify to the Fund as necessary the names of such governors and alternates.

(2) Each State participant which is not a member shall appoint one governor and one alternate governor who shall serve at the pleasure of the appointing participant.

(3) No alternate may vote except in the absence of his principal.

(4) Subject to the provisions of Article 60(4), governors and alternates shall serve as such without payment of remuneration or expenses by the Fund.

ARTICLE 25. BOARD OF GOVERNORS: PROCEDURE

(1) The Board of Governors shall hold an annual meeting and such other meetings as may be provided for by the Board or called by the Board of Directors. The Chairman of the Board of Governors of the Bank shall be *ex officio* Chairman of the Board of Governors of the Fund.

(2) The annual meeting of the Board of Governors shall be held in conjunction with the annual meeting of the Board of Governors of the Bank.

(3) A quorum for any meeting of the Board of Governors shall be a majority of the total number of governors, representing not less than three-fourths of the total voting power of the participants.

(4) The Board of Governors may by regulation establish a procedure whereby the Board of Directors may, when it deems such action advisable, obtain a vote of the governors on a specific question without calling a meeting of the Board of Governors.

(5) The Board of Governors, and the Board of Directors to the extent authorized by the Board of Governors, may establish such subsidiary committees as may be necessary or appropriate to conduct the business of the Fund.

(6) The Board of Governors, and the Board of Directors to the extent authorized by the Board of Governors or by this Agreement, may adopt such regulations, not inconsistent with this Agreement, as shall be necessary or appropriate for the conduct of the business of the Fund.

ARTICLE 26. BOARD OF DIRECTORS: FUNCTIONS

Without prejudice to the powers of the Board of Governors provided for in Article 23, the Board of Directors shall be responsible for the direction of the general operations of the Fund and for this purpose shall exercise any functions expressly given to it in this Agreement or delegated to it by the Board of Governors and, in particular, shall:

(i) prepare the work of the Board of Governors;

(ii) in conformity with the general directives of the Board of Governors, take decisions regarding individual loans and other forms of financing to be provided by the fund under this Agreement;

(iii) adopt such rules, regulations or other measures as may be required to ensure that proper and adequate audited accounts and records are kept in relation to the operations of the Fund;

(iv) ensure that the Fund is served in the most efficient and economical manner;

(v) submit to the Board of Governors, for approval at each annual meeting, the accounts for each financial year in a form which distinguishes, to the extent necessary, between the accounts of the general operations of the Fund and of such operations as are financed from contributions made available to the Fund under Article 8;

(vi) submit to the Board of Governors for approval at each annual meeting an annual report; and

(vii) approve the budget and general lending programme and policies of the Fund, in accordance with the resources respectively available for these purposes.

ARTICLE 27. BOARD OF DIRECTORS: COMPOSITION

(1) There shall be a Board of Directors composed of twelve directors.

(2) The State participants shall, pursuant to Schedule B, select six directors and six alternate directors.

(3) The Bank shall, pursuant to Schedule B, designate six directors and their alternates from the Board of Directors of the Bank.

(4) An alternate director of the Fund may attend all meetings of the Board of Directors but shall neither participate nor vote except in the absence of his principal.

(5) The Board of Directors shall invite the other directors of the Bank and their alternates to attend meetings of the Board of Directors as observers and any such Bank director or, in his absence, his alternate may participate in the discussion of any proposed project designed to benefit the country which he represents in the Board of Directors of the Bank.

(6) (a) A director designated by the Bank shall hold office until his successor shall have been designated pursuant to Schedule B and shall have assumed office. If a director designated by the Bank shall cease to be a director of the Bank he shall cease to be a director of the Fund.

(b) The term of office of directors selected by State participants shall be three years, but shall terminate whenever a general increase in subscriptions pursuant to Article 7(1) becomes effective. Such directors shall be eligible for a further term or terms of office. They shall continue in office until their successors have been selected and have assumed office. If the office of such a director shall become vacant before the expiration of his term of office, the vacancy shall be filled by a new director selected by the State participant or participants whose votes his predecessor was entitled to cast. Such successor director shall hold office for the remainder of the term of office of his predecessor.

(c) While the office of a director remains vacant the alternate of the former director shall exercise the powers of the latter except that of appointing an alternate, other than a temporary alternate to represent him at meetings when he cannot be present.

(7) If a State shall become a State participant pursuant to Article 3(3), or a State participant shall increase its subscription, or if for any other reason the voting rights of individual State participants should change between the times provided for the selection of directors representing State participants:

(i) There shall be no change in directors as a result thereof, provided that if a director shall cease to have any voting rights, his term of office and that of his alternate shall terminate forthwith;

(ii) Voting rights of State participants and of the directors selected by them shall be adjusted as of the effective date of the increase in subscription or the new subscription or other change in voting rights, as the case may be; and

(iii) If such a new State participant shall have voting rights, it may designate a director then representing one or more State participants to represent it and cast its votes until the next general selection of State participant directors.

(8) Directors and alternates shall serve as such without payment of remuneration or expenses by the Fund.

ARTICLE 28. BOARD OF DIRECTORS: PROCEDURE

(1) The Board of Directors shall meet as often as the business of the Fund may require. The Chairman shall call a meeting of the Board of Directors whenever requested to do so by four directors.

(2) A quorum for any meeting of the Board of Directors shall be a majority of the total number of directors having not less than three-fourths of the total voting power of the participants.

ARTICLE 29. VOTING

(1) The Bank, and the State participants as a group, shall each have 1,000 votes.

(2) Each governor of the Fund who is a governor of the Bank shall have, and shall be entitled to cast, such proportionate share

of the Bank's votes as shall have been notified to the Fund by the President of the Bank.

(3) Each State participant shall have a proportionate share of the aggregate votes of the State participants based on the subscriptions of such participant made pursuant to Article 6 and, to the extent agreed by the State participants in connection with additional subscriptions authorized under Article 7 (1) and (2), on such additional subscriptions. However, the total votes to be allocated to regional members that are State participants shall not exceed one per cent of the total votes of State participants. In voting in the Board of Governors, each governor representing a State participant shall be entitled to cast the votes of the participant he represents.

(4) In voting in the Board of Directors, directors designated by the Bank shall together have 1,000 votes and directors selected by the State participants shall together have 1,000 votes. Each director designated by the Bank shall have the number of votes allocated to him by the Bank as set forth in the notification of his designation, given pursuant to Part I of Schedule B. Each director selected by one or more State participants shall have the number of votes held by the participant or participants which selected him.

(5) Each Bank director shall cast his votes as a unit. A director representing more than one State participant may cast separately the votes of the States he represents.

(6) Notwithstanding any of the other provisions of this Agreement, if a State shall be or become both a State participant and a member it shall, but solely for the purposes of this Agreement, be treated in all respects as if it were not a member.

(7) Except as otherwise provided in this Agreement, all matters before the Board of Governors or the Board of Directors shall be decided by a three-fourths majority of the total voting power of the participants.

ARTICLE 30. THE PRESIDENT

(1) The President of the Bank shall be *ex officio* President of the Fund. He shall be Chairman of the Board of Directors but shall have no vote. He may participate in meetings of the Board of Governors but shall not vote.

(2) The President shall be the legal representative of the Fund.

(3) In the event that the President of the Bank is absent or his office should become vacant, the person for the time being designated to perform the duties of President of the Bank shall act as President of the Fund.

(4) Subject to Article 26, the President shall conduct the ordinary business of the Fund and, in particular shall:

(i) propose the operating and administrative budgets;

(ii) propose the overall financing programme;

(iii) arrange for the study and appraisal of projects and programmes for financing by the Fund in accordance with Article 15(3);

(iv) draw, as needed, on the officers, staff, organization, services and facilities of the Bank to carry out the business of the Fund and shall be responsible to the Board of Directors for ensuring and controlling the proper organization, staffing and services provided under Article 22; and

(v) engage the services of such personnel, including consultants and experts, as may be needed by the Fund, and may terminate such services.

ARTICLE 31. RELATIONSHIP TO THE BANK

(1) The Fund shall reimburse the Bank for the fair value of its use of the officers, staff, organization, services and facilities of the Bank, in accordance with arrangements made between the Fund and the Bank.

(2) The Fund shall be an entity juridically separate and distinct from the Bank and assets of the Fund shall be kept separate and apart from those of the Bank.

(3) Nothing in this Agreement shall make the Fund liable for the acts or obligations of the Bank, or the Bank liable for the acts or obligations of the Fund.

ARTICLE 32. OFFICE OF THE FUND

The office of the Fund shall be the principal office of the Bank.

ARTICLE 33. DEPOSITORIES

Each State participant shall designate its central bank or such other institution as may be acceptable to the Fund as a depository in which the Fund may keep holdings of such participant's currency or other assets of the Fund. In the absence of any different designation, the depository for each member shall be the depository designated by it for the purposes of the Agreement establishing the Bank.

ARTICLE 34. CHANNEL OF COMMUNICATION

Each State participant shall designate an appropriate authority with which the Fund may communicate in connection with any matter arising under this Agreement. In the absence of any different designation, the channel of communication designated by a member for the Bank shall be its channel for the Fund.

ARTICLE 35. PUBLICATION OF REPORTS AND PROVISION OF INFORMATION

(1) The Fund shall publish an annual report containing an audited statement of its accounts and shall circulate to participants and members at appropriate intervals a summary statement of its financial position and an income and expenditures statement showing the results of its operations.

(2) The Fund may publish such other reports as it deems desirable to carry out its purposes.

(3) Copies of all reports, statements and publications made under this Article shall be distributed to participants and members.

ARTICLE 36. ALLOCATION OF NET INCOME

The Board of Governors shall determine from time to time the disposition of the Fund's net income, having due regard to provision for reserves and contingencies.

CHAPTER VII—WITHDRAWAL; SUSPENSION OF PARTICIPATION; TERMINATION OF OPERATIONS

ARTICLE 37. WITHDRAWAL BY PARTICIPANTS

Any participant may withdraw from participation in the Fund at any time by transmitting a notice in writing to the Fund at its principal office. Withdrawal shall become effective upon the date such notice is received or upon such date, not more than six months thereafter, as may be specified in such notice.

ARTICLE 38. SUSPENSION OF PARTICIPANT

(1) If a participant fails to fulfill any of its obligations to the Fund, the Fund may suspend its participation by decision of the Board of Governors.

The participant so suspended shall automatically cease to be a participant one year from the date of its suspension unless a decision is taken by the Board of Governors to restore the participant to good standing.

(2) While under suspension, a participant shall not be entitled to exercise any rights under this Agreement except the right of withdrawal, but shall remain subject to all obligations.

ARTICLE 39. RIGHTS AND DUTIES OF STATES CEASING TO BE PARTICIPANTS

(1) When a State ceases to be a participant, it shall have no rights under this Agreement except as provided in this Article and in Article 53 but it shall, except as in this Article otherwise provided, remain liable for all financial obligations undertaken by it to the Fund, whether as a participant, borrower, guarantor or otherwise.

(2) When a State ceases to be a participant, the Fund and the State shall proceed to a settlement of accounts. As part of such settlement of accounts, the Fund and the State may agree on the amounts to be paid to the State on account of its subscription and on the time and currencies of payment. The term "subscription" when used in relation to any participant shall for the purposes of this Article and Article 40 be deemed to include both the initial subscription and any addition subscription of such participant.

(3) Pending such agreement, and in any event if no such agreement is reached within six months from the date when the State ceased to be a participant or such other time as may be agreed upon by the Fund and the State, the following provisions shall apply:

(i) The State shall be relieved of any further liability to the Fund on account of its subscription, except that the State shall pay to the Fund on their due dates amounts of its subscription unpaid on the date when the State ceased to be a participant and which in the opinion of the Fund are needed by it to meet its commitments as of that date under its financing operations.

(ii) The Fund shall return to the State funds paid in by the State on account of its subscription or derived therefrom as principal repayments and held by the Fund on the date when the State ceased to be a participant, except to the extent that in the opinion of the Fund such funds will be needed by it to meet its commitments as of that date under its financing operations.

(iii) The Fund shall pay to the State a *pro rata* share of all principal repayments received by the Fund after the date on which the State ceases to be a participant on loans contracted prior thereto, except those made out of resources provided to the Fund under arrangements specifying special liquidation rights. Such share shall be such proportion of the total principal amount of such loans as the total amount paid by the State on account of its subscription and not returned to it pursuant to sub-paragraph (ii) above shall bear to the total amount paid by all participants on account of their subscriptions which shall have been used or in the opinion of the Fund will be needed by it to meet its commitments under its financing operations as of the date on which the State ceases to be a participant. Such payment by the Fund shall be made in installments when and as such principal repayments are received by the Fund, but not more frequently than annually. Such installments shall be paid in the currencies received by the Fund except that the Fund may in its discretion make payment in the currency of the State concerned.

(iv) Any amount due to the State on account of its subscription may be withheld so long as that State, or any sub-division or any agency of any of the foregoing remains liable, as borrower or guarantor, to the Fund, and such amount may at the option of the Fund, be applied against any such liability as it matures.

(v) In no event shall the State receive under this paragraph an amount exceeding, in the aggregate, the lesser of the two following:

(1) the amount paid by the State on account of its subscription, or

(2) such proportion of the net assets of the Fund, as shown on the books of the Fund as of the date on which the State ceased to be a participant, as the amount of its subscription shall bear to the aggregate amount of the subscriptions of all participants.

(vi) All calculations required hereunder shall be made on such basis as shall be reasonably determined by the Fund.

(4) In no event shall any amount due to a State under this Article be paid until six months after the date upon which the State ceases to be a participant. If within six months of the date upon which any State ceases to be a participant the Fund terminates its operations under Article 40, all rights of such State shall be determined by the provisions of such Article 40, and such State shall be considered a participant in the Fund for purposes of such Article 40, except that it shall have no voting rights.

ARTICLE 40. TERMINATION OF OPERATIONS AND SETTLEMENT OF OBLIGATIONS

(1) The Fund may terminate its operations by vote of the Board of Governors. Withdrawal by the Bank or all the State participants pursuant to Article 37 shall constitute a termination of operations

by the Fund. After such termination of operations the Fund shall forthwith cease all activities, except those incidental to the orderly realization, conservation and preservation of its assets and settlement of its obligations. Until final settlement of such obligations and distribution of such assets, the Fund shall remain in existence and all mutual rights and obligations of the Fund and the participants under this Agreement shall continue unimpaired, except that no participant shall be suspended or shall withdraw and that no distribution shall be made to participants except as in this Article provided.

(2) No distribution shall be made to participants on account of their subscriptions until all liabilities to creditors shall have been discharged or provided for and until the Board of Governors shall have decided to make such distribution.

(3) Subject to the foregoing and to any special arrangements for the disposition of resources agreed upon in connection with the provision of such resources to the Fund, the Fund shall distribute its assets to participants *pro rata* in proportion to amounts paid in by them on account of their subscriptions. Any distribution pursuant to the foregoing provision of this paragraph shall be subject, in the case of any participant, to prior settlement of all outstanding claims by the Fund against such participant. Such distribution shall be made at such times, in such currencies, and in cash or other assets as the Fund shall deem fair and equitable. Distribution to the several participants need not be uniform in respect of the type of assets distributed or of the currencies in which they are expressed.

(4) Any participant receiving assets distributed by the Fund pursuant to this Article or Article 39 shall enjoy the same rights with respect to such assets as the Fund enjoyed prior to their distribution.

CHAPTER VIII—STATUS; IMMUNITIES; EXEMPTIONS AND PRIVILEGES

ARTICLE 41. PURPOSE OF CHAPTER

To enable the Fund effectively to fulfill its purpose and carry out the functions entrusted to it, the status, immunities, exemptions and privileges set forth in this Chapter shall be accorded to the Fund in the territory of each State participant, and each State participant shall inform the Fund of the specific action which it has taken for such purpose.

ARTICLE 42. STATUS

The Fund shall possess full juridical personality and, in particular, full capacity:

(i) to contract;

(ii) to acquire, and dispose of, immovable and movable property; and

(iii) to institute legal proceedings.

ARTICLE 43. LEGAL PROCESS

(1) The Fund shall enjoy immunity from every form of legal process, except in cases arising out of or in connection with the exercise

of its powers to receive loans in accordance with Article 8, in which case actions may be brought against the Fund in a court of competent jurisdiction in the territory of a country in which the Fund has its office, or has appointed an agent for the purpose of accepting service or notice of process, or has otherwise agreed to be sued.

(2) Notwithstanding the provisions of paragraph (1), no action shall be brought against the Fund by any participant, or by any agency or instrumentality of a participant, or by any entity or person directly or indirectly acting for or deriving claims from a participant or from any agency or instrumentality of a participant. Participants shall have recourse to such special procedures for the settlement of disputes between the Fund and its participants as may be prescribed in this Agreement, in the by-laws and regulations of the Fund, or in contracts entered into with the Fund.

(3) The Fund shall also make provisions for appropriate modes of settlement of disputes in cases which do not come within the provisions of paragraph (2) and of Articles 52 and 53 and which are subject to the immunity of the Fund by virtue of paragraph (1) of this Article.

(4) Where by virtue of any of the provisions of this Agreement the Fund does not enjoy immunity from legal process, the Fund, and its property and assets wherever located and by whomsoever held, shall nevertheless be immune from all forms of seizure, attachment or execution before the delivery of final judgment against the Fund.

ARTICLE 44. IMMUNITY OF ASSETS

Property and assets of the Fund, wherever located and by whomsoever held, shall be immune from search, requisition, confiscation, expropriation or any other form of taking or foreclosure by executive or legislative action.

ARTICLE 45. IMMUNITY OF ARCHIVES

The archives of the Fund, and, in general, all documents belonging to it, or held by it, shall be inviolable, wherever located.

ARTICLE 46. FREEDOM OF ASSETS FROM RESTRICTION

To the extent necessary to carry out the purpose and functions of the Fund, and subject to the provisions of this Agreement, all property and other assets of the Fund shall be free from restriction by financial controls, regulations, or moratoria of any kind.

ARTICLE 47. PRIVILEGE FOR COMMUNICATIONS

Official communications of the Fund shall be accorded by each State participant the same treatment as it accords to the official communications of other international financial institutions of which it is a member.

ARTICLE 48. IMMUNITIES AND PRIVILEGES OF OFFICIALS AND PERSONNEL

All governors and directors, and their alternates, the President and personnel, including experts performing missions for the Fund:

(i) Shall be immune from legal process with respect to acts performed by them in their official capacity;

(ii) When they are not local nationals, shall be accorded no less favourable immunities from immigration restrictions, alien registration requirements and national service obligations, and no less favourable facilities as regards exchange regulations than are accorded by the State participant concerned to the representatives, officials and employees of comparable rank of any other international financial institution of which it is a member; and

(iii) Shall be granted no less favourable treatment in respect of traveling facilities than is accorded by the State participant concerned to representatives, officials and employees of comparable rank of any other international financial institution of which it is a member.

ARTICLE 49. EXEMPTION FROM TAXATION

(1) The Fund, its assets, property, income, operation and transactions shall be exempt from all direct taxation, and from all customs duties, or taxes having equivalent effect, on goods imported or exported for its official use. The Fund shall also be exempt from any obligation for the payment, withholding or collection of any tax or duty.

(2) Notwithstanding the provisions of paragraph (1), the Fund shall not claim exemption from taxes which are no more than charges for services rendered.

(3) Articles imported under an exemption provided for by paragraph (1) shall not be sold in the territory of the State participant which granted the exemption except under conditions agreed with that participant.

(4) No tax shall be levied on or in respect of salaries and emoluments paid by the Fund to the President and personnel including experts performing missions for it.

ARTICLE 50. WAIVER BY THE FUND

(1) The immunities, exemptions and privileges provided in this Chapter are granted in the interests of the Fund. The Board of Directors may waive, to such extent and upon such conditions, as it may determine, the immunities, exemptions and privileges provided in this Chapter in cases where its action would in its opinion further the interests of the Fund.

(2) Regardless of the provisions of paragraph 1, the President shall have the right and the duty to waive the immunity of any of the personnel, including experts performing missions for the fund, in cases where, in his opinion, the immunity would impede the course of justice and can be waived without prejudice to the interests of the Fund.

CHAPTER IX—AMENDMENTS

ARTICLE 51

(1) Any proposal to introduce modifications to this Agreement, whether emanating from a participant, a governor or the Board of

Directors, shall be communicated to the Chairman of the Board of Governors, who shall bring the proposal before that Board. If the proposed amendment is approved by the Board, the Fund shall, by circular letter or telegram, ask the participants whether they accept the proposed amendment. When three-fourths of the participants having eighty-five percent of the voting power have accepted the proposed amendment, the Fund shall certify the fact by formal communication addressed to the participants. Amendments shall enter into force for all participants three months after the date of the formal communication provided for in this paragraph unless the Board of Governors specifies a different period or date.

(2) Notwithstanding the provisions of paragraph (1), the unanimous approval of the Board of Governors shall be required for the approval of any amendment modifying:

(i) the limitation on liability provided for in Article 10;

(ii) the provisions of Article 7 (2) and (3) relating to the subscription of additional funds;

(iii) the right to withdraw from the Fund; and

(iv) the voting majority requirements contained in the Agreement.

Chapter X—Interpretation and Arbitration

ARTICLE 52. INTERPRETATION

(1) Any question of interpretation or application of the provisions of this Agreement arising between any participant and the Fund or between any participants shall be submitted to the Board of Directors for decision. If there is no director of its nationality on that Board, a State participant particularly affected by the question under consideration shall be entitled to direct representation in such cases. Such right of representation shall be regulated by the Board of Governors.

(2) In any case where the Board of Directors has given a decision under paragraph (1), any participant may require that the question be referred to the Board of Governors, whose decision shall be final. Pending the decision of the Board of Governors, the Fund may, so far as it deems necessary, act on the basis on the decision of the Board of Directors.

ARTICLE 53. ARBITRATION

In the case of a dispute between the Fund and a State which has ceased to be a participant, or between the Fund and any participant upon the termination of the operations of the Fund, such dispute shall be submitted to arbitration by a tribunal of three arbitrators. One of the arbitrators shall be appointed by the Fund, another by the participant or former participant concerned, and the two parties shall appoint the third arbitrator, who shall be the Chairman. If within forty-five days of receipt of the request for arbitration either party has not appointed an arbitrator or if within thirty days of the appointment of two arbitrators the third arbitrator has not been appointed, either party may request the President of the International Court of Justice, or such other authority as may have been prescribed by regulations adopted by the Board of Governors, to appoint an arbitrator. The procedure of the arbitration shall be fixed by the arbitrators, but the third arbitrator shall have full power to settle all questions of procedure in any case of disagreement with respect thereto. A majority vote of the arbitrators shall be sufficient to reach a decision, which shall be final and binding upon the parties.

CHAPTER XI—FINAL PROVISIONS

ARTICLE 54. SIGNATURE

The original of this Agreement shall remain open until 31 March 1973 for signature by the Bank and by the States whose names are set forth in Schedule A.

ARTICLE 55. RATIFICATION, ACCEPTANCE OR APPROVAL

(1) This Agreement shall be subject to ratification, acceptance or approval by the signatories.

(2) Instruments of ratification, acceptance or approval shall be deposited with the Bank at its principal office by each signatory before 31 December 1973, provided that, if this Agreement shall not have entered into force by that date in accordance with Article 56, the Board of Directors of the Bank may extend the period for deposit of instruments of ratification, acceptance or approval by not more than six months.

ARTICLE 56. ENTRY INTO FORCE

This Agreement shall enter into force on the date on which the Bank and eight signatory States whose initial subscriptions, as set forth in Schedule A to this Agreement, comprise in aggregate not less than 55 million units of account, have deposited their instruments of ratification, acceptance or approval.

ARTICLE 57. PARTICIPATION

(1) A signatory whose instrument of ratification, acceptance or approval is deposited on or before the date on which this Agreement enters into force shall become a participant on that date. A signatory whose instrument of ratification, acceptance or approval is deposited thereafter and before the date prescribed in or pursuant to Article 55(2) shall become a participant on the date of such deposit.

(2) A State which is not an original participant may become a participant pursuant to Article 3(3), and, notwithstanding the provisions of Articles 54 and 55, such participation shall be effected by signing this Agreement and by depositing with the Bank an instrument of ratification, acceptance or approval, which shall take effect on the date of such deposit.

ARTICLE 58. RESERVATIONS

A State may, when depositing its instrument of ratification, acceptance or approval, declare:

(i) that in its territory the immunity conferred by Article 43(1) and by Article 48(i) shall not apply in relation to a civil action arising out of an accident caused by a motor vehicle belonging to the Fund or operated on its behalf, or to a traffic offense committed by the driver of such a vehicle;

(ii) that it retains for itself and its political sub-divisions the right to tax salaries and emoluments paid by the Fund to that State's citizens, nationals or residents;

(iii) that it understands that the Fund will not normally claim exemption from excise duties levied by that State on goods originating in its territory, and from taxes on the sale of movable and immovable property, which form part of the price to be paid, but that where the Fund is making important purchases for official use of property on which such duties and taxes have been charged or are chargeable, whenever possible, appropriate administrative arrangements will be made by that State for the remission or return of the amount of duty or tax; and

(iv) that the provisions of Article 49(3) shall apply to articles in respect of which a remission or return of duty or tax has been made by that State pursuant to the arrangements referred to in subparagraph (iii).

ARTICLE 59. NOTIFICATION

The Bank shall notify all signatories of:

(a) any signature;

(b) any deposit of an instrument of ratification, acceptance or approval;

(c) the date of entry into force of this Agreement; and

(d) any declarations or reservations made at the time of deposit of an instrument of ratification, acceptance or approval.

ARTICLE 60. INAUGURAL MEETING

(1) As soon as this Agreement enters into force, each State participant shall appoint a governor, and the Chairman of the Board of Governors shall call the inaugural meeting of the Board of Governors.

(2) At the inaugural meeting:

(i) twelve directors of the Fund shall be designated and selected pursuant to Article 27 (2) and (3); and

(ii) arrangements shall be made for determining the date on which the Fund shall commence operations.

(3) The Fund shall notify all participants of the date of commencement of its operations.

(4) Reasonable and necessary expenses incurred by the Bank in establishing the Fund, including subsistence expenses of governors and their alternates in attending the Inaugural Meeting, shall be reimbursed by the Fund.

IN WITNESS WHEREOF the undersigned, being thereunto duly authorized, have signed this Agreement.

DONE at Abidjan, this twenty-ninth day of November, one thousand nine hundred and seventy-two, in the English and French languages, both being equally authentic, in a single copy, which shall remain deposited with the Bank.

The Bank shall transmit certified copies of this Agreement to each signatory.

SCHEDULE A

1. ORIGINAL PARTICIPANTS

The following States shall be eligible to become original participants: Belgium, Brazil, Canada, Denmark, Finland, Federal Republic of Germany, Italy, Japan, The Netherlands, Norway, Spain, Sweden, Switzerland, The United Kingdom, The United States of America and Yugoslavia.

Any of the aforementioned States which, after 31 December 1973, makes a subscription of at least 15 million United States dollars shall, nevertheless, be deemed an original participant provided it signs and ratifies this Agreement on or before 31 December 1974.

2. INITIAL SUBSCRIPTIONS

The Bank and the following States which have signed this Agreement have subscribed the following amounts:

	Subscriptions in Units of Account
African Development Bank	5,000,000
Belgium	3,000,000
Brazil	2,000,000
Canada	15,000,000
Denmark	5,000,000
Federal Republic of Germany	7,447,630
Finland	2,000,000
Italy	10,000,000
Japan	15,000,000
Netherlands	4,000,000
Norway	5,000,000
Spain	2,000,000
Sweden	5,000,000
Swiss Confederation	3,000,000
United Kingdom	5,211,420
Yugoslavia	2,000,000
Total	90,659,050

SCHEDULE B—DESIGNATION AND SELECTION OF DIRECTORS

PART I—DESIGNATION OF DIRECTORS BY THE BANK

(1) The President of the Bank shall give to the Fund, on the occasion of each designation by the Bank of directors of the Fund, a notification setting forth:

(i) the names of the directors so designated; and

(ii) the number of votes which each such director shall be entitled to cast.

(2) When there shall be a vacancy in the office of a director designated by the Bank, the President shall notify to the Fund the name of the person designated by the Bank as his successor.

PART II—SELECTION OF DIRECTORS BY GOVERNORS REPRESENTING STATE PARTICIPANTS

(1) In balloting for the selection of directors, each governor representing a State participant shall cast for one person all of the votes to which the State appointing him is entitled. The six persons receiving the greatest number of votes shall be directors, except that no person who receives less than 12 percent of the total of the votes of such governors shall be considered elected.

(2) When six persons are not elected on the first ballot, a second ballot shall be held in which the person who received the lowest number of votes shall be ineligible for election and in which there shall vote only (a) those governors who voted in the first ballot for a person not elected and (b) those governors whose votes for a person elected are deemed under (3) below to have raised the votes cast for that person above fifteen percent of the eligible votes.

(3) In determining whether the votes cast by a governor are to be deemed to have raised the total of any person above fifteen percent of the eligible votes, the fifteen percent shall be deemed to include, first, the votes of the governor casting the largest number of votes for such person, then the votes of the governor casting the next largest number, and so on until 15 percent is reached.

(4) Any governor, part of whose votes must be counted in order to raise the total of any person above 12 percent, shall be considered as casting all of his votes for such person even if the total votes for such person thereby exceeded fifteen percent.

(5) If, after the second ballot, six persons have not been elected, further ballots shall be held on the same principles until six persons have been elected, provided that after five persons are elected, the sixth may be elected by a simple majority of the remaining votes and shall be deemed to have been elected by all such votes.

(6) The Governors representing State participants may change the foregoing rules by a 75 percent majority of the total voting power of such governors.

(7) There shall be a new selection of directors representing State participants at each of the first three annual meetings of the Board of Governors.

(8) Each director shall appoint an alternate who shall have full power to act for him when he is not present. Directors and their alternates shall be nationals of State participants.

11. Convention on the Settlement of Investment Disputes Between States and Nationals of Other States [1]

Convention approved by the Executive Directors of the International Bank for Reconstruction and Development for submission to member governments, at Washington, March 18, 1965; [2] Open for signature at IBRD, and signed on behalf of the United States, August 27, 1965; Ratification advised by the Senate, May 16, 1966; Ratified by the President, June 1, 1966; Instrument of ratification of the United States deposited with IBRD, June 10, 1966; Proclaimed by the President, September 30, 1966; Entered into force, October 14, 1966

PREAMBLE

The Contracting States

CONSIDERING, The need for international cooperation for economic development, and the role of private international investment therein;

BEARING IN MIND, The possibility that from time to time disputes may arise in connection with such investment between Contracting States and nationals of other Contracting States;

RECOGNIZING, That while such disputes would usually be subjected to national legal processes, international methods of settlement may be appropriate in certain cases;

ATTACHING PARTICULAR IMPORTANCE, To the availability of facilities for international conciliation or arbitration to which Contracting States and nationals of other Contracting States may submit such disputes if they so desire;

DESIRING, To establish such facilities under the auspices of the International Bank for Reconstruction and Development;

RECOGNIZING, That mutual consent by the parties to submit such disputes to conciliation or to arbitration through such facilities constitutes a binding agreement which requires in particular that due consideration be given to any recommendation or conciliators, and that any arbitral award be complied with; and

---

[1] 17 UST 1270; TIAS 6090; 575 UNTS 159. For a list of states which are parties to this convention, see Department of State publication, *Treaties in Force*.

[2] Partial text of Resolution 65–14, approving the submission of the Convention, reads as follows:

"Now, therefore, the Executive Directors hereby resolve as follows:

"(1) The text of the Convention on the Settlement of Investment Disputes Between States and Nationals of Other States formulated by the Executive Directors in the form presented to this meeting and the report of the Executive Directors thereon are hereby approved for submission to member governments of the Bank;

"(2) The President of the Bank shall transmit said report and the text of the said convention to all member governments of the Bank;

"(3) The President and the General Counsel of the Bank shall sign a copy of said convention on behalf of the Bank to indicate the Bank's agreement to fulfill the functions with which it is charged under the convention;

"(4) The copy of the Convention so signed on behalf of the Bank shall remain deposited in the archives of the Bank and shall be open for signature on behalf of governments in accordance with its terms.".

DECLARING, That no Contracting State shall by the mere fact of its ratification, acceptance or approval of this Convention and without its consent be deemed to be under any obligation to submit any particular dispute to conciliation or arbitration,

HAVE AGREED AS FOLLOWS:

CHAPTER I—INTERNATIONAL CENTRE FOR SETTLEMENT OF INVESTMENT DISPUTES

SECTION 1—ESTABLISHMENT AND ORGANIZATION

ARTICLE 1

(1) There is hereby established the International Centre for Settlement of Investment Disputes (hereinafter called the Centre).

(2) The purpose of the Centre shall be to provide facilities for conciliation and arbitration of investment disputes between Contracting States and nationals of other Contracting States in accordance with the provisions of this Convention.

ARTICLE 2

The seat of the Centre shall be at the principal office of the International Bank for Reconstruction and Development (hereinafter called the Bank). The seat may be moved to another place by decision of the Administrative Council adopted by a majority of two-thirds of its members.

ARTICLE 3

The Centre shall have an Administrative Council and a Secretariat and shall maintain a Panel of Conciliators and a Panel of Arbitrators.

SECTION 2—THE ADMINISTRATIVE COUNCIL

ARTICLE 4

(1) The Administrative Council shall be composed of one representative of each Contracting State. An alternate may act as representative in case of his principal's absence from a meeting or inability to act.

(2) In the absence of a contrary designation, each governor and alternate governor of the Bank appointed by a Contracting State shall be *ex officio* its representative and its alternate respectively.

ARTICLE 5

The president of the Bank shall be *ex officio* Chairman of the Administrative Council (hereinafter called the Chairman) but shall have no vote. During his absence or inability to act and during any vacancy in the office of President of the Bank, the person for the time being acting as President shall act as Chairman of the Administrative Council.

ARTICLE 6

(1) Without prejudice to the powers and functions vested in it by other provisions of this Convention, the Administrative Council shall:

(a) adopt the administrative and financial regulations of the Centre;

(b) adopt the rules of procedure for the institution of conciliation and arbitration proceedings;

(c) adopt the rules of procedure for conciliation and arbitration proceedings (hereinafter called the Conciliation Rules and the Arbitration Rules);

(d) approve arrangements with the Bank for the use of the Bank's administrative facilities and services;

(e) determine the conditions of service of the Secretary-General and of any Deputy Secretary-General;

(f) adopt the annual budget of revenues and expenditures of the Centre;

(g) approve the annual report on the operation of the Centre.

The decisions referred to in sub-paragraphs (a), (b), (c) and (f) above shall be adopted by a majority of two-thirds of the members of the Administrative Council.

(2) The Administrative Council may appoint such committees as it considers necessary.

(3) The Administrative Council shall also exercise such other powers and perform such other functions as it shall determine to be necessary for the implementation of the provisions of this Convention.

ARTICLE 7

(1) The Administrative Council shall hold an annual meeting and such other meetings as may be determined by the Council, or convened by the Chairman, or convened by the Secretary-General at the request of not less than five members of the Council.

(2) Each member of the Administrative Council shall have one vote and, except as otherwise herein provided, all matters before the Council shall be decided by a majority of the votes cast.

(3) A quorum for any meeting of the Administrative Council shall be a majority of its members.

(4) The Administrative Council may establish, by a majority of two-thirds of its members, a procedure whereby the Chairman may seek a vote of the Council without convening a meeting of the Council. The vote shall be considered valid only if the majority of the members of the Council cast their votes within the time limit fixed by the said procedure.

ARTICLE 8

Members of the Administrative Council and the Chairman shall serve without remuneration from the Centre.

SECTION 3—THE SECRETARIAT

ARTICLE 9

The Secretariat shall consist of a Secretary-General, one or more Deputy Secretaries-General and staff.

ARTICLE 10

(1) The Secretary-General and any Deputy Secretary-General shall be elected by the Administrative Council by a majority of two-thirds of its members upon the nomination of the Chairman for a term of service not exceeding six years and shall be eligible for re-election. After consulting the members of the Administration Council, the Chairman shall propose one or more candidates for each such office.

(2) The offices of Secretary-General and Deputy Secretary-General shall be incompatible with the exercise of any political function. Neither the Secretary-General nor any Deputy Secretary-General may hold any other employment or engage in any other occupation except with the approval of the Administrative Council.

(3) During the Secretary-General's absence or inability to act, and during any vacancy of the office of Secretary-General, the Deputy Secretary-General shall act as Secretary-General. If there shall be more than one Deputy Secretary-General, the Administrative Council shall determine in advance the order in which they shall act as Secretary-General.

ARTICLE 11

The Secretary-General shall be the legal representative and the principal officer of the Centre and shall be responsible for its administration, including the appointment of staff, in accordance with the provisions of this Convention and the rules adopted by the Administrative Council. He shall perform the function of registrar and shall have the power to authenticate arbitral awards rendered pursuant to this Convention, and to certify copies thereof.

SECTION 4—THE PANELS

ARTICLE 12

The Panel of Conciliators and the Panel of Arbitrators shall each consist of qualified persons, designated as hereinafter provided, who are willing to serve thereon.

ARTICLE 13

(1) Each Contracting State may designate to each Panel four persons who may but need not be its nationals.

(2) The Chairman may designate ten persons to each Panel. The persons so designated to a Panel shall each have a different nationality.

ARTICLE 14

(1) Persons designated to serve on the Panels shall be persons of high moral character and recognized competence in the fields of

law, commerce, industry or finance, who may be relied upon to exercise independent judgment. Competence in the field of law shall be of particular importance in the case of persons on the Panel of Arbitrators.

(2) The Chairman, in designating persons to serve on the Panels, shall in addition pay due regard to the importance of assuring representation on the Panels of the principal legal systems of the world and of the main forms of economic activity.

ARTICLE 15

(1) Panel members shall serve for renewable periods of six years.

(2) In case of death or resignation of a member of a Panel, the authority which designated the member shall have the right to designate another person to serve for the remainder of that member's term.

(3) Panel members shall continue in office until their successors have been designated.

ARTICLE 16

(1) A person may serve on both Panels.

(2) If a person shall have been designated to serve on the same Panel by more than one Contracting State, or by one or more Contracting States and the Chairman, he shall be deemed to have been designated by the authority which first designated him or, if one such authority is the State of which he is a national, by that State.

(3) All designations shall be notified to the Secretary-General and shall take effect from the date on which the notification is received.

SECTION 5—FINANCING THE CENTRE

ARTICLE 17

If the expenditure of the Centre cannot be met out of charges for the use of its facilities, or out of other receipts, the excess shall be borne by Contracting States which are members of the Bank in proportion to their respective subscriptions to the capital stock of the Bank, and by Contracting States which are not members of the Bank in accordance with rules adopted by the Administrative Council.

SECTION 6—STATUS, IMMUNITIES, AND PRIVILEGES

ARTICLE 18

The Centre shall have full international legal personality. The legal capacity of the Centre shall include the capacity:

(a) to contract;

(b) to acquire and dispose of movable and immovable property;

(c) to institute legal proceedings.

ARTICLE 19

To enable the Centre to fulfill its functions, it shall enjoy in the territories of each Contracting State the immunities and privileges set forth in this Section.

ARTICLE 20

The Centre, its property and assets shall enjoy immunity from all legal process, except when the Centre waives this immunity.

ARTICLE 21

The Chairman, the members of the Administrative Council, persons acting as conciliators or arbitrators or members of a Committee appointed pursuant to paragraph (3) of Article 52, and the officers and employees of the Secretariat,

(a) shall enjoy immunity from legal process with respect to acts performed by them in the exercise of their functions, except when the Centre waives this immunity;

(b) not being local nationals, shall enjoy the same immunities from immigration restrictions, alien registration requirements and national service obligations, the same facilities as regards exchange restrictions and the same treatment in respect of traveling facilities as are accorded by Contracting States to the representatives, officials and employees of comparable rank of other Contracting States.

ARTICLE 22

The provisions of Article 21 shall apply to persons appearing in proceedings under this Convention as parties, agents, counsel, advocates, witnesses or experts; provided, however, that sub-paragraph (b) thereof shall apply only in connection with their travel to and from, and their stay at, the place where the proceedings are held.

ARTICLE 23

(1) The archives of the Centre shall be inviolable, wherever they may be.

(2) With regard to its official communications, the Centre shall be accorded by each Contracting State treatment not less favourable than that accorded to other international organizations.

ARTICLE 24

(1) The Centre, its assets, property and income, and its operations and transactions authorized by this Convention shall be exempt from all taxation and customs duties. The Centre shall also be exempt from liability for the collection of payment of any taxes or customs duties.

(2) Except in the case of local nationals, no tax shall be levied on or in respect of expenses allowances paid by the Centre to the Chairman or members of the Administrative Council, or on or in respect of salaries, expense allowances or other emoluments paid by the Centre to officials or employees of the Secretariat.

(3) No tax shall be levied on or in respect of fees or expense allowances received by persons acting as conciliators, or arbitrators, or members of a Committee appointed pursuant to paragraph (3) of Article 52, in proceedings under this Convention, if the sole jurisdictional basis for such tax is the location of the Centre or the place where such proceedings are conducted or the place where such fees or allowances are paid.

CHAPTER II—JURISDICTION OF THE CENTRE

ARTICLE 25

(1) The jurisdiction of the Centre shall extend to any legal dispute arising directly out of an investment, between a Contracting State (or any constituent subdivision or agency of a Contracting State designated to the Centre by that State) and a national of another Contracting State, which the parties to the dispute consent in writing to submit to the Centre. When the parties have given their consent, no party may withdraw its consent unilaterally.

(2) "National of another Contracting State" means:

(a) any natural person who had the nationality of a Contracting State other than the State party to the dispute on the date on which the parties consented to submit such dispute to conciliation or arbitration as well as on the date on which the request was registered pursuant to paragraph (3) of Article 28 or paragraph (3) of Article 36, but does not include any person who on either date also had the nationality of the Contracting State party to the dispute; and

(b) any juridical person which had the nationality of a Contracting State other than the State party to the dispute on the date on which the parties consented to submit such dispute to conciliation or arbitration and any juridical person which had the nationality of the Contracting State party to the dispute on that date and which, because of foreign control, the parties have agreed should be treated as a national of another Contracting State for the purposes of this Convention.

(3) Consent by a constituent subdivision or agency of a Contracting State shall require the approval of that State unless that State notifies the Centre that no such approval is required.

(4) Any contracting State may, at the time of ratification, acceptance or approval of this Convention or at any time thereafter, notify the Centre of the class or classes of disputes which it would or would not consider submitting to the jurisdiction of the Centre. The Secretary-General shall forthwith transmit such notification to all Contracting States. Such notification shall not constitute the consent required by paragraph (1).

ARTICLE 26

Consent of the parties to arbitration under this Convention shall, unless otherwise stated, be deemed consent to such arbitration to the exclusion of any other remedy. A Contracting State may require the exhaustion of local administrative or judicial remedies as a condition of its consent to arbitration under this Convention.

ARTICLE 27

(1) No Contracting State shall give diplomatic protection, or bring an international claim, in respect of a dispute which one of its nationals and another Contracting State shall have consented to submit or shall have submitted to arbitration under this Convention, unless such other Contracting State shall have failed to abide by and comply with the award rendered in such dispute.

(2) Diplomatic protection, for the purposes of paragraph (1), shall not include informal diplomatic exchanges for the sole purpose of facilitating a settlement of the dispute.

CHAPTER III—CONCILIATION

SECTION 1—REQUEST FOR CONCILIATION

ARTICLE 28

(1) Any Contracting State or any national of a Contracting State wishing to institute conciliation proceedings shall address a request to that effect in writing to the Secretary-General who shall send a copy of the request to the other party.

(2) The request shall contain information concerning the issues in dispute, the identity of the parties and their consent to conciliation in accordance with the rules of procedure for the institution of conciliation and arbitration proceedings.

(3) The Secretary-General shall register the request unless he finds, on the basis of the information contained in the request, that the dispute is manifestly outside the jurisdiction of the Centre. He shall forthwith notify the parties of registration or refusal to register.

SECTION 2—CONSTITUTION OF THE CONCILIATION COMMISSION

ARTICLE 29

(1) The Conciliation Commission (hereinafter called the Commission) shall be constituted as soon as possible after registration of a request pursuant to Article 28.

(2) (a) The Commission shall consist of a sole conciliator or any uneven number of conciliators appointed as the parties shall agree.

(b) Where the parties do not agree upon the number of conciliators and the method of their appointment, the Commission shall consist of three conciliators, one conciliator appointed by each party and the third, who shall be the president of the Commission, appointed by agreement of the parties.

ARTICLE 30

If the Commission shall not have been constituted within 90 days after notice of registration of the request has been dispatched by the Secretary-General in accordance with paragraph (3) of Article 28, or such other period as the parties may agree, the Chairman shall, at the request of either party and after consulting both parties as far as possible, appoint the conciliator or conciliators not yet appointed.

ARTICLE 31

(1) Conciliators may be appointed from outside the Panel of Conciliators, except in the case of appointments by the Chairman pursuant to Article 30.

(2) Conciliators appointed from outside the Panel of Conciliators shall possess the qualities stated in paragraph (1) of Article 14.

SECTION 3—CONCILIATION PROCEEDINGS

ARTICLE 32

(1) The Commission shall be the judge of its own competence.

(2) Any objection by a party to the dispute that that dispute is not within the jurisdiction of the Centre, or for other reasons is not within the competence of the Commission, shall be considered by the Commission which shall determine whether to deal with it as a preliminary question or to join the merits of the dispute.

ARTICLE 33

Any conciliation proceeding shall be conducted in accordance with the provisions of this Section and, except as the parties otherwise agree, in accordance with the Conciliation Rules in effect on the date on which the parties consented to conciliation. If any question of procedure arises which is not covered by this Section or the Conciliation Rules or any rules agreed by the parties, the Commission shall decide the question.

ARTICLE 34

(1) It shall be the duty of the Commission to clarify the issues in dispute between the parties and to endeavour to bring about agreement between them upon mutually acceptable terms. To that end, the Commission may at any stage of the proceedings and from time to time recommend terms of settlement to the parties. The parties shall cooperate in good faith with the Commission in order to enable the Commission to carry out its functions, and shall give their most serious consideration to its recommendations.

(2) If the parties reach agreement, the Commission shall draw up a report noting the issues in dispute and recording that the parties have reached agreement. If, at any stage of the proceedings, it appears to the Commission that there is no likelihood of agreement between the parties, it shall close the proceedings and shall draw up a report noting the submission of the dispute and recording the failure of the parties to reach agreement. If one party fails to appear or participate in the proceedings, the Commission shall close the proceedings and shall draw up a report noting that party's failure to appear or participate.

ARTICLE 35

Except as the parties to the dispute shall otherwise agree, neither party to a conciliation proceeding shall be entitled in any other proceeding, whether before arbitrators or in a court of law or otherwise, to invoke or rely on any views expressed or statements or admissions or offers of settlement made by the other party in the conciliation proceedings, or the report or any recommendations made by the Commission.

CHAPTER IV—ARBITRATION

SECTION 1—REQUEST FOR ARBITRATION

ARTICLE 36

(1) Any Contracting State or any national of a Contracting State wishing to institute arbitration proceedings shall address a request to that effect in writing to the Secretary-General who shall send a copy of the request to the other party.

(2) The request shall contain information concerning the issues in dispute, the identity of the parties and their consent to arbitration in accordance with the rules of procedure for the institution of conciliation and arbitration proceedings.

(3) The Secretary-General shall register the request unless he finds, on the basis of the information contained in the request, that the dispute is manifestly outside the jurisdiction of the Centre. He shall forthwith notify the parties of registration or refusal to register.

SECTION 2—CONSTITUTION OF THE TRIBUNAL

ARTICLE 37

(1) The Arbitral Tribunal (hereinafter called the Tribunal) shall be constituted as soon as possible after registration of a request pursuant to Article 36.

(2) (a) The Tribunal shall consist of a sole arbitrator or any uneven number of arbitrators appointed as the parties shall agree.

(b) Where the parties do not agree upon the number of arbitrators and the method of their appointment, the Tribunal shall consist of three arbitrators, one arbitrator appointed by each party and the third, who shall be the president of the Tribunal, appointed by agreement of the parties.

ARTICLE 38

If the Tribunal shall not have been constituted within 90 days after notice of registration of the request has been dispatched by the Secretary-General in accordance with paragraph (3) of Article 36, or such other period as the parties may agree, the Chairman shall, at the request of either party and after consulting both parties as far as possible, appoint the arbitrator or arbitrators not yet appointed. Arbitrators appointed by the Chairman pursuant to this Article shall not be nationals of the Contracting State party to the dispute or of the Contracting State whose national is a party to the dispute.

ARTICLE 39

The majority of the arbitrators shall be nationals of States other than the Contracting State party to the dispute and the Contracting State whose national is a party to the dispute; provided, however, that the foregoing provisions of this Article shall not apply if the sole arbitrator or each individual member of the Tribunal has been appointed by agreement of the parties.

ARTICLE 40

(1) Arbitrators may be appointed from outside the Panel of Arbitrators, except in the case of appointments by the Chairman pursuant to Article 38.

(2) Arbitrators appointed from outside the Panel of Arbitrators shall possess the qualities stated in paragraph (1) of Article 14.

SECTION 3—POWERS AND FUNCTIONS OF THE TRIBUNAL

ARTICLE 41

(1) The Tribunal shall be the judge of its own competence.

(2) Any objection by a party to the dispute that that dispute is not within the jurisdiction of the Centre, or for other reasons is not within the competence of the Tribunal, shall be considered by the Tribunal which shall determine whether to deal with it as a preliminary question or to join it to the merits of the dispute.

ARTICLE 42

(1) The Tribunal shall decide a dispute in accordance with such rules of law as may be agreed by the parties. In the absence of such agreement, the Tribunal shall apply the law of the Contracting State party to the dispute (including its rules on the conflict of laws) and such rules of international law as may be applicable.

(2) The Tribunal may not bring in a finding of *non liquet* on the ground of silence or obscurity of the law.

(3) The provisions of paragraphs (1) and (2) shall not prejudice the power of the Tribunal to decide a dispute *ex aequo et bono* if the parties so agree.

ARTICLE 43

Except as the parties otherwise agree, the Tribunal may, if it deems it necessary at any stage of the proceedings,

(a) call upon the parties to produce documents or other evidence, and

(b) visit the scene connected with the dispute, and conduct such inquires there as it may deem appropriate.

ARTICLE 44

Any arbitration proceeding shall be conducted in accordance with the provisions of this section and, except as the parties otherwise agree, in accordance with the Arbitration Rules in effect on the date on which the parties consented to arbitration. If any question of procedure arises which is not covered by this Section or the Arbitration Rules or any rules agreed by the parties, the Tribunal shall decide the question.

ARTICLE 45

(1) Failure of a party to appear or to present his case shall not be deemed an admission of the other party's assertions.

(2) If a party fails to appear or to present his case at any stage of the proceedings the other party may request the Tribunal to deal with the questions submitted to it and to render an award. Before rendering an award, the Tribunal shall notify, and grant a period of grace to, the party failing to appear or to present its case, unless it is satisfied that that party does not intend to do so.

ARTICLE 46

Except as the parties otherwise agree, the Tribunal shall, if requested by a party, determine any incidental or additional claims or counter-claims arising directly out of the subject-matter of the dispute provided that they are within the scope of the consent of the parties and are otherwise within the jurisdiction of the Centre.

ARTICLE 47

Except as the parties otherwise agree, the Tribunal may, if it considers that the circumstances so require, recommend any provisional measures which should be taken to preserve the respective rights of either party.

SECTION 4—THE AWARD

ARTICLE 48

(1) The Tribunal shall decide questions by a majority of the votes of all its members.

(2) The award of the Tribunal shall be in writing and shall be signed by the members of the Tribunal who voted for it.

(3) The award shall deal with every question submitted to the Tribunal, and shall state the reasons upon which it is based.

(4) Any member of the Tribunal may attach his individual opinion to the award, whether he dissents from the majority or not, or a statement of his dissent.

(5) The Centre shall not publish the award without the consent of the parties.

ARTICLE 49

(1) The Secretary-General shall promptly dispatch certified copies of the award to the parties. The award shall be deemed to have been rendered on the date on which the certified copies were dispatched.

(2) The Tribunal upon the request of a party made within 45 days after the date on which the award was rendered may after notice to the other party decide any question which it had omitted to decide in the award, and shall rectify any clerical, arithmetical or similar error in the award. Its decision shall become part of the award and shall be notified to the parties in the same manner as the award. The periods of time provided for under paragraph (2) of Article 51 and paragraph (2) of Article 52 shall run from the date on which the decision was rendered.

SECTION 5—INTERPRETATION, REVISION AND ANNULMENT OF THE AWARD

ARTICLE 50

(1) If any dispute shall arise between the parties as to the meaning or scope of an award, either party may request interpretation of the award by an application in writing addressed to the Secretary-General.

(2) The request shall, if possible, be submitted to the Tribunal which rendered the award. If this shall not be possible, a new Tribunal shall be constituted in accordance with Section 2 of this Chapter. The Tribunal may, if it considers that the circumstances so require, stay enforcement of the award pending its decision.

ARTICLE 51

(1) Either party may request revision of the award by an application in writing addressed to the Secretary-General on the ground of discovery of some fact of such a nature as decisively to affect the award, provided that when the award was rendered that fact was unknown to the Tribunal and to the applicant and that the applicant's ignorance of that fact was not due to negligence.

(2) The application shall be made within 90 days after the discovery of such fact and in any event within three years after the date on which the award was rendered.

(3) The request shall, if possible, be submitted to the Tribunal which rendered the award. If this shall not be possible, a new Tribunal shall be constituted in accordance with Section 2 of this Chapter.

(4) The Tribunal may, if it considers that the circumstances so require, stay enforcement of the award pending its decision. If the applicant requests a stay of enforcement of the award in his application, enforcement shall be stayed provisionally until the Tribunal rules on such request.

ARTICLE 52

(1) Either party may request annulment of the award by an application in writing addressed to the Secretary-General on one or more of the following grounds:

(a) that the Tribunal was not properly constituted;

(b) that the Tribunal has manifestly exceeded its powers;

(c) that there was corruption on the part of a member of the Tribunal;

(d) that there has been a serious departure from a fundamental rule of procedure; or

(e) that the award has failed to state the reasons on which it is based.

(2) The application shall be made within 120 days after the date on which the award was rendered except that when annulment is requested on the ground of corruption such application shall be made within 120 days after discovery of the corruption and in any event within three years after the date on which the award was rendered.

(3) On receipt of the request the Chairman shall forthwith appoint from the Panel of Arbitrators an *ad hoc* Committee of three persons. None of the members of the Committee shall have been a member of the Tribunal which rendered the award, shall be of the same nationality as any such member, shall be a national of the State party to the dispute or of the State whose national is a party to the dispute, shall have been designated to the Panel of Arbitrators by either of those States, or shall have acted as a conciliator in the same dispute. The Committee shall have the authority to annul the award or any part thereof on any of the grounds set forth in paragraph (1).

(4) The provisions of Articles 41–45, 48, 49, 53 and 54, and of Chapters VI and VII shall apply *mutatis mutandis* to proceedings before the Committee.

(5) The Committee may, if it considers that the circumstances so require, stay enforcement of the award pending its decision. If the applicant requests a stay of enforcement of the award in this application, enforcement shall be stayed provisionally until the Committee rules on such request.

(6) If the award is annulled the dispute shall, at the request of either party, be submitted to a new Tribunal constituted in accordance with Section 2 of this Chapter.

SECTION 6—RECOGNITION AND ENFORCEMENT OF THE AWARD

ARTICLE 53

(1) The award shall be binding on the parties and shall not be subject to any appeal or to any other remedy except those provided for in this Convention. Each party shall abide by and comply with the terms of the award except to the extent that enforcement shall have been stayed pursuant to the relevant provisions of this Convention.

(2) For the purposes of this Section, "award" shall include any decision interpreting, revising or annulling such award pursuant to Articles 50, 51 or 52.

ARTICLE 54

(1) Each Contracting State shall recognize an award rendered pursuant to this Convention as binding and enforce the pecuniary obligations imposed by that award within its territories as if it were a final judgment of a court in that State. A Contracting State with a federal constitution may enforce such an award in or through its federal courts and may provide that such courts shall treat the award as if it were a final judgment of the courts of a constituent state.

(2) A party seeking recognition or enforcement in the territories of a Contracting State shall furnish to a competent court or other authority which such State shall have designated for this purpose a copy of the award certified by the Secretary-General. Each Contracting State shall notify the Secretary-General of the designation of the competent court or other authority for this purpose and of any subsequent change in such designation.

(3) Execution of the award shall be governed by the laws concerning the execution of judgments in force in the State in whose territories such execution is sought.

ARTICLE 55

Nothing in Article 54 shall be construed as derogating from the law in force in any Contracting State relating to immunity of that State or of any foreign State from execution.

CHAPTER V—REPLACEMENT AND DISQUALIFICATION OF CONCILIATORS AND ARBITRATORS

ARTICLE 56

(1) After a Commission or a Tribunal has been constituted and proceedings have begun, its composition shall remain unchanged; provided, however, that if a conciliator or an arbitrator should die, become incapacitated, or resign, the resulting vacancy shall be filled in accordance with the provisions of Section 2 of Chapter III or Section 2 of Chapter IV.

(2) A member of a Commission or Tribunal shall continue to serve in that capacity not withstanding that he shall have ceased to be a member of the panel.

(3) If a conciliator or arbitrator appointed by a party shall have resigned without the consent of the Commission or Tribunal of which he was a member, the Chairman shall appoint a person from the appropriate Panel to fill the resulting vacancy.

ARTICLE 57

A party may propose to a Commission or Tribunal the disqualification of any of its members on account of any fact indicating a manifest lack of the qualities required by paragraph (1) of Article 14. A party to arbitration proceedings may, in addition, propose the disqualification of an arbitrator on the ground that he was ineligible for appointment to the Tribunal under Section 2 of Chapter IV.

ARTICLE 58

The decision on any proposal to disqualify a conciliator or arbitrator shall be taken by the other members of the Commission or Tribunal as the case may be, provided that where those members are equally divided, or in the case of a proposal to disqualify a sole conciliator or arbitrator, or a majority of the conciliators or arbitrators, the Chairman shall take that decision. If it is decided that the proposal is well-founded the conciliator or arbitrator to whom the decision relates shall be replaced in accordance with the provisions of Section 2 of Chapter III or Section 2 of Chapter IV.

CHAPTER VI—COST OF PROCEEDINGS

ARTICLE 59

The charges payable by the parties for the use of the facilities of the Centre shall be determined by the Secretary-General in accordance with the regulations adopted by the Administrative Council.

ARTICLE 60

(1) Each Commission and each Tribunal shall determine the fees and expenses of its members within limits established from time to time by the Administrative Council and after consultation with the Secretary-General.

(2) Nothing in paragraph (1) of this Article shall preclude the parties from agreeing in advance with the Commission or Tribunal concerned upon the fees and expenses of its members.

ARTICLE 61

(1) In the case of conciliation proceeding the fees and expenses of members of the Commission as well as the charges for the use of the facilities of the Centre, shall be borne equally by the parties. Each party shall bear any other expenses it incurs in connection with the proceedings.

(2) In the case of arbitration proceedings the Tribunal shall, except as the parties otherwise agree, assess the expenses incurred by the parties in connection with the proceedings, and shall decide how and by whom those expenses, the fees and expenses of the members of the Tribunal and the charges for the use of the facilities of the Centre shall be paid. Such decision shall form part of the award.

CHAPTER VII—PLACE OF PROCEEDINGS

ARTICLE 62

Counciliation and arbitration proceedings shall be held at the seat of the Centre except as hereinafter provided.

ARTICLE 63

Conciliation and arbitration proceedings may be held, if the parties so agree,

(a) at the seat of the Permanent Court of Arbitration or of any other appropriate institution, whether private or public, with which the Centre may make arrangements for that purpose; or

(b) at any other place approved by the Commission or Tribunal after consultation with the Secretary-General.

CHAPTER VIII—DISPUTES BETWEEN CONTRACTING STATES

ARTICLE 64

Any dispute arising between Contracting States concerning the interpretation or application of this Convention which is not settled by negotiation shall be referred to the International Court of Justice by the application of any party to such dispute, unless the States concerned agree to another method of settlement.

CHAPTER IX—AMENDMENT

ARTICLE 65

Any Contracting State may propose amendment of this Convention. The text of a proposed amendment shall be communicated to the Secretary-General not less than 90 days prior to the meeting of the Administrative Council at which such amendment is to be considered and shall forthwith be transmitted by him to all the members of the Administrative Council.

ARTICLE 66

(1) If the Administrative Council shall so decide by a majority of two-thirds of its members, the proposed amendment shall be circulated to all Contracting States for ratification, acceptance or approval. Each amendment shall enter into force 30 days after dispatch by the depositary of this Convention of a notification to Contracting States that all Contracting States have ratified, accepted or approved the amendment.

(2) No amendment shall affect the rights and obligations under this Convention of any Contracting State or of any of its constituent subdivisions or agencies, or of any national of such State arising out of consent to the jurisdiction of the Centre given before the date of entry into force of the amendment.

CHAPTER X—FINAL PROVISIONS

ARTICLE 67

This Convention shall be open for signature on behalf of States members of the Bank. It shall also be open for signature on behalf of any other State which is a party to the Statute of the International Court of Justice and which the Administrative Council, by a vote of two-thirds of its members, shall have invited to sign the Convention.

ARTICLE 68

(1) This Convention shall be subject to ratification, acceptance or approval by the signatory States in accordance with their respective constitutional procedures.

(2) This Convention shall enter into force 30 days after the date of deposit of the twentieth instrument of ratification, acceptance or approval. It shall enter into force for each State which subsequently deposits its instrument of ratification, acceptance or approval 30 days after the date of such deposit.

ARTICLE 69

Each Contracting State shall take such legislative or other measures as may be necessary for making the provisions of this Convention effective in its territories.

ARTICLE 70

This Convention shall apply to all territories for whose international relations a Contracting State is responsible, except those which are excluded by such State by written notice to the depositary of this Convention either at the time of ratification, acceptance or approval or subsequently.

ARTICLE 71

Any Contracting State may denounce this Convention by written notice to the depositary of this Convention. The denunciation shall take effect six months after receipt of such notice.

ARTICLE 72

Notice by a Contracting State pursuant to Articles 70 or 71 shall not affect the rights or obligations under this Convention of that State or of any of its constituent subdivisions or agencies or of any national of that State arising out of consent to the jurisdiction of the Centre given by one of them before such notice was received by the depositary.

ARTICLE 73

Instruments of ratification, acceptance or approval of this Convention and of amendments thereto shall be deposited with the Bank which shall act as the depositary of this Convention. The depositary shall transmit certified copies of this Convention to States members of the Bank and to any other State invited to sign the Convention.

ARTICLE 74

The depositary shall register this Convention with the Secretariat of the United Nations in accordance with Article 102 of the Charter of the United Nations and the Regulations thereunder adopted by the General Assembly.

ARTICLE 75

The depositary shall notify all signatory States of the following:

(a) signatures in accordance with Article 67;

(b) deposits of instruments of ratification, acceptance and approval in accordance with Article 73;

(c) the date on which this Convention enters into force in accordance with Article 68;

(d) exclusions from territorial application pursuant to Article 70;

(e) the date on which any amendment of this Convention enters into force in accordance with Article 66; and

(f) denunciations in accordance with Article 71.

DONE at Washington in the English, French and Spanish languages, all three texts being equally authentic, in a single copy which shall remain deposited in the archives of the International Bank for Reconstruction and Development, which has indicated by its signature below its agreement to fulfill the functions with which it is charged under this Convention.

12. Agreement Establishing the European Bank for Reconstruction and Development (Amended) [1]

Agreement signed at Paris, May 29, 1990; Entered into force, March 18, 1991

The contracting parties,

COMMITTED to the fundamental principles of multiparty democracy, the rule of law, respect for human rights and market economics;

RECALLING the Final Act of the Helsinki Conference on Security and Cooperation in Europe, and in particular its Declaration on Principles;

WELCOMING the intent of Central and Eastern European countries to further the practical implementation of multiparty democracy, strengthening democratic institutions, the rule of law and respect for human rights and their willingness to implement reforms in order to evolve towards market-oriented economies;

CONSIDERING the importance of close and coordinated cooperation in order to promote the economic progress of Central and Eastern European countries to help their economies become more internationally competitive and assist them in their reconstruction and development and thus to reduce, where appropriate, any risks related to the financing of their economies;

CONVINCED that the establishment of a multilateral financial institution which is European in its basic character and broadly international in its membership would help serve these ends and would constitute a new and unique structure of cooperation in Europe;

HAVE AGREED to establish hereby the European Bank for Reconstruction and Development (hereinafter called "the Bank") which shall operate in accordance with the following:

CHAPTER I

PURPOSE, FUNCTIONS AND MEMBERSHIP

ARTICLE 1

PURPOSE

In contributing to economic progress and reconstruction, the purpose of the Bank shall be to foster the transition towards open market-oriented economies and to promote private and entrepreneurial initiative in the Central and Eastern European countries committed to and applying the principles of multiparty democracy,

[1] A Resolution of the Board of Governors adopted on January 31, 2004, amended sec. 1 of the Agreement, effective October 15, 2006. For a list of states that are parties to this convention, see Department of State publication, *Treaties in Force*.

pluralism and market economics. The purpose of the Bank may also be carried out in Mongolia subject to the same conditions. Accordingly, any reference in this Agreement and its annexes to "Central and Eastern European countries", "countries from Central and Eastern Europe", "recipient country (or countries)" or "recipient member country (or countries)" shall refer to Mongolia as well.

ARTICLE 2

FUNCTIONS

1. To fulfill on a long-term basis its purpose of fostering the transition of Central and Eastern European countries towards open market-oriented economies and the promotion of private and entrepreneurial initiative, the Bank shall assist the recipient member countries to implement structural and sectoral economic reforms, including demonopolization, decentralization and privatization, to help their economies become fully integrated into the international economy by measures;

(i) to promote, through private and other interested investors, the establishment, improvement and expansion of productive, competitive and private sector activity, in particular small and medium sized enterprises;

(ii) to mobilize domestic and foreign capital and experienced management to the end described in (i);

(iii) to foster productive investment, including in the service and financial sectors, and in related infrastructure where that is necessary to support private and entrepreneurial initiative, thereby assisting in making a competitive environment and raising productivity, the standard of living and conditions of labour;

(iv) to provide technical assistance for the preparation, financing and implementation of relevant projects, whether individual or in the context of specific investment programmes;

(v) to stimulate and encourage the development of capital markets;

(vi) to give support to sound and economically viable projects involving more than one recipient member country;

(vii) to promote in the full range of its activities environmentally sound and sustainable development; and

(viii) to undertake such other activities and provide such other services as may further these functions.

2. In carrying out the functions referred to in paragraph 1 of this Article, the Bank shall work in close cooperation with all its members and, in such manner as it may deem appropriate within the terms of this Agreement, with the International Monetary Fund, the International Bank for Reconstruction and Development, the International Finance Corporation, the Multilateral Investment Guarantee Agency, and the Organisation for Economic Cooperation and Development, and shall cooperate with the United Nations and its Specialised Agencies and other related bodies, and any entity, whether public or private, concerned with the economic development of, and investment in, Central and Eastern European countries.

ARTICLE 3

MEMBERSHIP

1. Membership in the Bank shall be open:

(i) to (1) European countries and (2) non-European countries which are members of the International Monetary Fund; and

(ii) to the European Economic Community and the European Investment Bank.

2. Countries eligible for membership under paragraph 1 of this Article, which do not become members in accordance with Article 61 of this Agreement, may be admitted, under such terms and conditions as the Bank may determine, to membership in the Bank upon the affirmative vote of not less than two-thirds of the Governors, representing not less than three-fourths of the total voting power of the members.

CHAPTER II

CAPITAL

ARTICLE 4

AUTHORIZED CAPITAL STOCK

1. The original authorized capital stock shall be ten thousand million (10,000,000,000) ECU. It shall be divided into one million (1,000,000) shares, having a par value of ten thousand (10,000) ECU each, which shall be available for subscription only by members in accordance with the provisions of Article 5 of this Agreement.

2. The original capital stock shall be divided into paid-in shares and callable shares. The initial total aggregate par value of paid-in shares shall be three thousand million (3,000,000,000) ECU.

3. The authorized capital stock may be increased at such time and under such terms as may seem advisable, by a vote of not less than two-thirds of the Governors, representing not less than three-fourths of the total voting power of the members.

ARTICLE 5

SUBSCRIPTION OF SHARES

1. Each member shall subscribe to shares of the capital stock of the Bank, subject to fulfillment of the member's legal requirements. Each subscription to the original authorized capital stock shall be for paid-in shares and callable shares in the proportion of three (3) to seven (7). The initial number of shares available to be subscribed to by Signatories to this Agreement which become members in accordance with Article 61 of this Agreement shall be that set forth in Annex A. No member shall have an initial subscription of less than one hundred (100) shares.

2. The initial number of shares to be subscribed to by countries which are admitted to membership in accordance with paragraph 2 of Article 3 of this Agreement shall be determined by the Board of Governors; provided, however, that no such subscription shall be

authorized which would have the effect of reducing the percentage of capital stock held by countries which are members of the European Economic Community, together with the European Economic Community and the European Investment Bank, below the majority of the total subscribed capital stock.

3. The Board of Governors shall at intervals of not more than five (5) years review the capital stock of the Bank. In case of an increase in the authorized capital stock, each member shall have a reasonable opportunity to subscribe, under such uniform terms and conditions as the Board of Governors shall determine, to a proportion of the increase in stock equivalent to the proportion which its stock subscribed bears to the total subscribed capital stock immediately prior to such increase. No member shall be obliged to subscribe to any part of an increase of capital stock.

4. Subject to the provisions of paragraph 3 of this Article, the Board of Governors may, at the request of a member, increase the subscription of that member, or allocate shares to that member within the authorized capital stock which are not taken up by other members; provided, however, that such increase shall not have the effect of reducing the percentage of capital stock held by countries which are members of the European Economic Community, together with the European Economic Community and the European Investment Bank, below the majority of the total subscribed capital stock.

5. Shares of stock initially subscribed to by members shall be issued at par. Other shares shall be issued at par unless the Board of Governors, by a vote of not less than two-thirds of the Governors, representing not less than two-thirds of the total voting power of the members, decides to issue them in special circumstances on other terms.

6. Shares of stock shall not be pledged or encumbered in any manner whatsoever, and they shall not be transferable except to the Bank in accordance with Chapter VII of this Agreement.

7. The liability of the members on shares shall be limited to the unpaid portion of their issue price. No member shall be liable, by reason of its membership, for obligations of the Bank.

Article 6

PAYMENT OF SUBSCRIPTIONS

1. Payment of the paid-in shares of the amount initially subscribed to by each Signatory to this Agreement, which becomes a member in accordance with Article 61 of this Agreement, shall be made in five (5) instalments of twenty (20) per cent each of such amount. The first instalment shall be paid by each member within sixty (60) days after the date of the entry into force of this Agreement, or after the date of deposit of its instrument of ratification, acceptance or approval in accordance with Article 61, if this latter is later than the date of the entry into force. The remaining four (4) instalments shall each become due successively one year from the date on which the preceding instalment became due and shall each, subject to the legislative requirements of each member, be paid.

2. Fifty (50) per cent of payment of each instalment pursuant to paragraph 1 of this Article, or by a member admitted in accordance with paragraph 2 of Article 3 of this Agreement, may be made in promissory notes or other obligations issued by such member and denominated in ECU, in United States dollars or in Japanese yen, to be drawn down as the Bank needs funds for disbursement as a result of its operations. Such notes or obligations shall be non-negotiable, non-interest-bearing and payable to the Bank at par value upon demand. Demands upon such notes or obligations shall, over reasonable periods of time, be made so that the value of such demands in ECU at the time of demand from each member is proportional to the number of paid-in shares subscribed to any held by each such member depositing such notes or obligations.

3. All payment obligations of a member in respect of subscription to shares in the initial capital stock shall be settled either in ECU, in United States dollars or in Japanese yen on the basis of the average exchange rate of the relevant currency in terms of the ECU for the period from 30 September 1989 to 31 March 1990 inclusive.

4. Payment of the amount subscribed to the callable capital stock of the Bank shall be subject to call, taking account of Article 17 and 42 of this Agreement, only as and when required by the Bank to meet its liabilities.

5. In the event of a call referred to in paragraph 4 of this Article, payments shall be made by the member in ECU, in United States dollars or in Japanese yen. Such calls shall be uniform in ECU value upon each callable share calculated at the time of the call.

6. The Bank shall determine the place for any payment under this Article not later than one month after the inaugural meeting of its Board of Governors, provided that, before such determination, the payment of the first instalment referred to in paragraph 1 of this Article shall be made to the European Investment Bank, as trustees for the Bank.

7. For subscriptions other than those described in paragraphs 1, 2 and 3 of this Article, payments by a member in respect of subscription to paid-in shares in the authorized capital stock shall be made in ECU, in United States dollars or in Japanese yen whether in cash or in promissory notes or in other obligations.

8. For the purposes of this Article, payment or denomination in ECU shall include payment or denomination in any fully convertible currency which is equivalent on the date of payment or encashment of the value of the relevant obligation in ECU.

Article 7

ORDINARY CAPITAL RESOURCES

As used in this Agreement, the term “ordinary capital resources” of the Bank shall include the following:

(i) authorized capital stock of the Bank, including both paid-in and callable shares, subscribed to pursuant to Article 5 of this Agreement;

(ii) funds raised by borrowings of the Bank by virtue of powers conferred by subparagraph (i) of Article 20 of this Agreement, to which the commitment to calls provided for in paragraph 4 of Article 6 of this Agreement is applicable;

(iii) funds received in repayment of loans or guarantees and proceeds from the disposal of equity investment made with the resources indicated in sub-paragraphs (i) and (ii) of this Article;

(iv) income derived from loans and equity investment, made from the resources indicated in sub-paragraphs (i) and (ii) of this Article, and income derived from guarantees and underwriting not forming part of the special operations of the Bank; and

(v) any other funds or income received by the Bank which do not form part of its Special Funds resources referred to in Article 19 of this Agreement.

CHAPTER III

OPERATIONS

ARTICLE 8

RECIPIENT COUNTRIES AND USE OF RESOURCES

1. The resources and facilities of the Bank shall be used exclusively to implement the purpose and carry out the functions set forth, respectively, in Articles 1 and 2 of this Agreement.

2. The Bank may conduct its operations in countries from Central and Eastern Europe which are proceeding steadily in the transition towards market oriented economies and the promotion of private and entrepreneurial initiative, and which apply, by concrete steps and otherwise, to principles as set forth in Article 1 of this Agreement.

3. In cases where a member might be implementing policies which are inconsistent with Article 1 of this Agreement, or in exceptional circumstances, the Board of Directors shall consider whether access by a member to Bank resources should be suspended or otherwise modified and may make recommendations accordingly to the Board of Governors. Any decision on these matters shall be taken by the Board of Governors by a majority of not less than two-thirds of the Governors, representing not less than three-fourths of the total voting power of the members.

4. (i) Any potential recipient country may request that the Bank provide access to its resources for limited purposes over a period of three (3) years beginning after the entry into force of this Agreement. Any such request shall be attached as an integral part of this Agreement as soon as it is made.

(ii) During such a period:

(a) the Bank shall provide to such a country, and to enterprises in its territory, upon their request, technical assistance and other types of assistance directed to finance its private sector, to facilitate the transition of state-owned enterprises to private ownership and control, and to help enterprises operating competitively and moving to participation in the market oriented economy, subject to the proportion set forth in paragraph 3 of Article 11 of this Agreement;

(b) the total amount of any assistance thus provided shall not exceed the total amount of cash disbursed and promissory notes issued by that country for its shares.

(iii) At the end of this period, the decision to allow such a country access beyond the limits specified in subparagraphs (a) and (b) shall be taken by the Board of Governors by a majority of not less than three-fourths of the Governors representing not less than eighty-five (85) per cent of the total voting power of the members.

Article 9

ORDINARY AND SPECIAL OPERATIONS

The operations of the Bank shall consist of ordinary operations financed from the ordinary capital resources of the Bank referred to in Article 7 of this Agreement and special operations financed from the Special Funds resources referred to in Article 19 of this Agreement. The two types of operations may be combined.

Article 10

SEPARATION OF OPERATIONS

1. The ordinary capital resources and the Special Funds resources of the Bank shall at all times and in all respects be held, used, committed, invested or otherwise disposed of entirely separately from each other. The financial statements of the Bank shall show the reserves of the Bank, together with its ordinary operations, and, separately, its special operations.
2. The ordinary capital resources of the Bank shall under no circumstances be charged with, or used to discharge, losses or liabilities arising out of special operations or other activities for which Special Funds resources were originally used or committed.
3. Expenses appertaining directly to ordinary operations shall be charged to the ordinary capital resources of the Bank. Expenses appertaining directly to special operations shall be charged to Special Funds resources. Any other expenses shall, subject to paragraph 1 of Article 18 of this Agreement, be charged as the Bank shall determine.

Article 11

METHODS OF OPERATION

1. The Bank shall carry out its operations in furtherance of its purpose and functions as set out in Articles 1 and 2 of this Agreement in any or all of the following ways:

(i) by making, or cofinancing together with multilateral institutions, commercial banks or other interested sources, or participating in, loans to private sector enterprises, loans to any state-owned enterprise operating competitively and moving to participation in the market oriented economy, and loans to any state-owned enterprise to facilitate its transition to private ownership and control; in particular to facilitate or enhance the participation of private and/or foreign capital in such enterprises;

(ii)(a) by investment in the equity capital of private sector enterprises;

(b) by investment in the equity capital of any state-owned enterprise operating competitively and moving to participation in the market oriented economy, and investment in the equity capital of any state-owned enterprise to facilitate its transition to private ownership and control; in particular to facilitate or enhance the participation of private and/or foreign capital in such enterprises; and

(c) by underwriting, where other means of financing are not appropriate, the equity issue of securities by both private sector enterprises and such state-owned enterprise referred to in (b) above for the ends mentioned in that subparagraph;

(iii) by facilitating access to domestic and international capital markets by private sector enterprises or by other enterprises referred to in subparagraph (i) of this paragraph for the ends mentioned in that subparagraph, through the provision of guarantees, where other means of financing are not appropriate, and through financial advice and other forms of assistance;

(iv) by deploying Special Funds resources in accordance with the agreements determining their use; and

(v) by making or participating in loans and providing technical assistance for the reconstruction or development of infrastructure, including environmental programmes, necessary for private sector development and the transition to a market-oriented economy.

For the purposes of this paragraph, a state-owned enterprise shall not be regarded as operating competitively unless it operates autonomously in a competitive market environment and unless it is subject to bankruptcy laws.

2. (i) The Board of Directors shall review at least annually the Bank's operations and lending strategy in each recipient country to ensure that the purpose and functions of the Bank, as set out in Articles 1 and 2 of this Agreement, are fully served. Any decision pursuant to such a review shall be taken by a majority of not less than two-thirds of the Directors, representing not less than three-fourths of the total voting power of the members.

(ii) The said review shall involve the consideration of, *inter alia*, each recipient country's progress made on decentralization, demonopolization and privatization and the relative shares of the Bank's lending to private enterprises, to state-owned enterprises in the process of transition to participation in the market-oriented economy or privatization, for infrastructure, for technical assistance, and for other purposes.

3. (i) Not more than forty (40) per cent of the amount of the Bank's total committed loans, guarantees and equity investments, without prejudice to its other operations referred to in this Article, shall be provided to the state sector. Such percentage limit shall apply initially over a two (2) year period, from the date of commencement of the Bank's operations, taking one year with another, and thereafter in respect of each subsequent financial year.

(ii) For any country, not more than forty (40) per cent of the amount of the Bank's total committed loans, guarantees and equity investments over a period of five (5) years, taking one year with another, and without prejudice to the Bank's other operations referred to in this Article, shall be provided to the state sector.

(iii) For the purposes of this paragraph,

(a) the state sector includes national and local governments, their agencies, and enterprises owned or controlled by any of them;

(b) a loan or guarantee to, or equity investment in, a state-owned enterprise which is implementing a programme to achieve private ownership and control shall not be considered as made to the state sector;

(c) loans to a financial intermediary for onlending to the private sector shall not be considered as made the state sector.

ARTICLE 12

LIMITATIONS ON ORDINARY OPERATIONS

1. The total amount of outstanding loans, equity investments and guarantees made by the Bank in its ordinary operations shall not be increased at any time, if by such increase the total amount of its unimpaired subscribed capital, reserves and surpluses included in its ordinary capital resources would be exceeded.

2. The amount of any equity investment shall not normally exceed such percentage of the equity capital of the enterprise concerned as shall be determined, by a general rule, to be appropriate by the Board of Directors. The Bank shall not seek to obtain by such an investment a controlling interest in the enterprise concerned and shall not exercise such control or assume direct responsibility for managing any enterprise in which it has an investment, except in the event of actual or threatened default on any of its investments, actual or threatened insolvency of the enterprise in which such investment shall have been made, or other situations which, in the opinion of the Bank, threaten to jeopardize such investment, in which case the Bank may take such action and exercise such rights as it may deem necessary for the protection of its interests.

3. The amount of the Bank's disbursed equity investments shall not at any time exceed an amount corresponding to its total unimpaired paid-in subscribed capital, surpluses and general reserve.

4. The Bank shall not issue guarantees for export credits nor undertake insurance activities.

ARTICLE 13

OPERATING PRINCIPLES

The Bank shall operate in accordance with the following principles:

(i) the Bank shall apply sound banking principles to all its operations;

(ii) the operations of the Bank shall provide for the financing of specific projects, whether individual or in the context of specific investment programmes, and for technical assistance, designed to fulfill its purpose and functions as set out in Articles 1 and 2 of this Agreement;

(iii) the Bank shall not finance any undertaking in the territory of a member if that member objects to such financing;

(iv) the Bank shall not allow a disproportionate amount of its resources to be used for the benefit of any member;

(v) the Bank shall seek to maintain reasonable diversification in all its investments;

(vi) before a loan, guarantee or equity investment is granted, the application shall have submitted an adequate proposal and the President of the Bank shall have presented to the Board of Directors a written report regarding the proposal, together with recommendations, on the basis of a staff study;

(vii) the Bank shall not undertake any financing, or provide any facilities, when the applicant is able to obtain sufficient financing or facilities elsewhere on terms and conditions that the Bank considers reasonable;

(viii) in providing or guaranteeing financing, the Bank shall pay due regard to the prospect that the borrower and its guarantor, if any, will be in a position to meet their obligations under the financing contract;

(ix) in case of a direct loan made by the Bank, the borrower shall be permitted by the Bank to draw its funds only to meet expenditure as it is actually incurred;

(x) the Bank shall seek to revolve its funds by selling its investments to private investors whenever it can appropriately do so on satisfactory terms;

(xi) in its investments in individual enterprises, the Bank shall undertake its financing on terms and conditions which it considers appropriate, taking into account the requirements of the enterprise, the risks being undertaken by the Bank, and the terms and conditions normally obtained by private investors for similar financing;

(xii) the Bank shall place no restriction upon the procurement of goods and services from any country from the proceeds of any loan, investment or other financing undertaken in the ordinary or special operations of the Bank, and shall, in all appropriate cases, make its loans and other operations conditional on international invitations to tender being arranged; and

(xiii) the Bank shall take the necessary measures to ensure that the proceeds of any loan made, guaranteed or participated in by the Bank, or any equity investment, are used only for the purposes for which the loan or the equity investment was granted and with due attention to considerations of economy and efficiency.

Article 14

TERMS AND CONDITIONS FOR LOANS AND GUARANTEES

1. In the case of loans made, participated in, or guaranteed by the Bank, the contract shall establish the terms and conditions for the loan or the guarantee concerned, including those relating to payment of principal, interest and other fees, charges, maturities and date of payment in respect of the loan or the guarantee, respectively. In setting such terms and conditions ,the Bank shall take fully into account the need to safeguard its income.

2. Where the recipient of loans or guarantees of loans is not itself a member, but is a state-owned enterprise, the Bank may, when it appears desirable, bearing in mind the different approaches appropriate to public and state-owned enterprise in transition to private ownership and control, require the member or members in whose territory the project concerned is to be carried out, or a public agency or any instrumentality of such member or members acceptable to the Bank, to guarantee the repayment of the principal and the payment of interest and other fees and charges of the loan in accordance with the terms thereof. The Board of Directors shall review annually the Bank's practice in this matter, paying due attention to the Bank's creditworthiness.

3. The loan or guarantee contract shall expressly state the currency or currencies, or ECU, in which all payments to the Bank thereunder shall be made.

Article 15

COMMISSION AND FEES

1. The Bank shall charge, in addition to interest, a commission on loans made or participated in as part of its ordinary operations. The terms and conditions of this commission shall be determined by the Board of Directors.

2. In guaranteeing a loan as part of its ordinary operations, or in underwriting the sale of securities, the Bank shall charge fees, payable at rates and times determined by the Board of Directors, to provide suitable compensation for its risks.

3. The Board of Directors may determine any other charges of the Bank in its ordinary operations and any commission, fees or other charges in its special operations.

Article 16

SPECIAL RESERVE

1. The amount of commissions and fees received by the Bank pursuant to Article 15 of this Agreement shall be set aside as a special reserve which shall be kept for meeting the losses of the Bank in accordance with Article 17 of this Agreement. The special reserve shall be held in such liquid form as the Bank may decide.

2. If the Board of Directors determines that the size of the special reserve is adequate, it may decide that all or part of the said commission or fees shall henceforth form part of the income of the Bank.

ARTICLE 17

METHODS OF MEETING THE LOSSES OF THE BANK

1. In the Bank's ordinary operations, in cases of arrears or default on loans made, participated in, or guaranteed by the Bank, and in cases of losses on underwriting and in equity investment, the Bank shall take such action as its deems appropriate. The Bank shall maintain appropriate provisions against possible losses.

2. Losses arising in the Bank's ordinary operations shall be charged:

(i) first, to the provisions referred to in paragraph 1 of this Article;

(ii) second, to net income;

(iii) third, against the special reserve provided for in Article 16 of this Agreement;

(iv) fourth, against its general reserve and surpluses;

(v) fifth, against the unimpaired paid-in capital; and

(vi) last, against an appropriate amount of the uncalled subscribed callable capital which shall be called in accordance with the provisions of paragraphs 4 and 5 of Article 6 of this Agreement.

ARTICLE 18

SPECIAL FUNDS

1. The Bank may accept the administration of Special Funds which are designed to serve the purpose and come within the functions of the Bank. The full cost of administering any such Special Fund shall be charged to that Special Fund.

2. Special Funds accepted by the Bank may be used in any manner and on any terms and conditions consistent with the purpose and the functions of the Bank, with the other applicable provisions of this Agreement, and with the agreement or agreements relating to such Funds.

3. The Bank shall adopt such rules and regulations as may be required for the establishment, administration and use of each Special Fund. Such rules and regulations shall be consistent with the provisions of this Agreement, except for those provisions expressly applicable only to ordinary operations of the Bank.

ARTICLE 19

SPECIAL FUNDS RESOURCES

The term "special Funds resources" shall refer to the resources of any Special Fund and shall include:

(i) funds accepted by the Bank for inclusion in any Special Fund;

(ii) funds repaid in respect of loans or guarantees, and the proceeds of equity investments, financed from the resources of any Special Fund which, under the rules and regulations governing that Special Fund, are received by such Special Fund; and

(iii) income derived from investment of Special Fund resources.

CHAPTER IV

BORROWING AND OTHER MISCELLANEOUS POWERS

ARTICLE 20

GENERAL POWERS

1. The Bank shall have, in addition to the powers specified elsewhere in this agreement, the power to:

(i) borrow funds in member countries or elsewhere, provided always that:

(a) before making a sale of its obligations in the territory of a country, the Bank shall have obtained its approval; and

(b) where the obligations of the Bank are to be denominated in the currency of a member, the Bank shall have obtained its approval;

(ii) invest or deposit funds not needed in its operations;

(iii) buy and sell securities, in the secondary market, which the Bank has issued or guaranteed or in which it has invested;

(iv) guarantee securities in which it has invested in order to facilitate their sale;

(v) underwrite, or participate in the underwriting of, securities issued by any enterprise for purposes consistent with the purpose and functions of the Bank;

(vi) provide technical advice and assistance which service its purpose and come within its function;

(vii) exercise such other powers and adopt such rules and regulations as may be necessary or appropriate in furtherance of its purpose and functions, consistent with the provisions of this Agreement; and

(viii) conclude agreements of cooperation with any public or private entity or entities.

2. Every security issued or guaranteed by the Bank shall bear on its face a conspicuous statement to the effect that it is not an obligation of any Government or member, unless it is in fact the obligation of a particular Government or member, in which case it shall so state.

CHAPTER V

CURRENCIES

ARTICLE 21

DETERMINATION AND USE OF CURRENCIES

1. Whenever it shall become necessary under this Agreement to determine whether any currency is fully convertible for the purposes of this Agreement, such determination shall be made by the Bank, taking into account the paramount need to preserve its own

financial interests, after consultation, if necessary, with the International Monetary Fund.

2. Members shall not impose any restrictions on the receipt, holding, use or transfer by the Bank of the following:

(i) currencies or ECU received by the Bank in payment of subscriptions to its capital stock, in accordance with Article 6 of this Agreement;

(ii) currencies obtained by the Bank by borrowing;

(iii) currencies and other resources administered by the Bank as contributions to Special Funds; and

(iv) currencies received by the Bank in payment on account of principal, interest, dividends or other charges in respect of loans or investments, or the proceeds of disposal of such investments made out of any of the funds referred to in subparagraphs (i) to (iii) of this paragraph, or in payment of commission, fees or other charges.

CHAPTER VI

ORGANIZATION AND MANAGEMENT

Article 22

STRUCTURE

The Bank shall have a Board of Governors, a Board of Directors, a President, one or more Vice-Presidents and such other officers and staff as may be considered necessary.

Article 23

BOARD OF GOVERNORS: COMPOSITION

1. Each member shall be represented on the Board of Governors and shall appoint one Governor and one Alternate. Each Governor and Alternate shall serve at the pleasure of the appointing member. No Alternate may vote except in the absence of his or her principal. At each of its annual meetings, the Board shall elect on of the Governors as Chairman who shall hold office until the election of the next Chairman.

2. Governors and Alternates shall serve as such without remuneration from the Bank.

Article 24

BOARD OF GOVERNORS: POWERS

1. All the powers of the Bank shall be vested in the Board of Governors.

2. The Board of Governors may delegate to the Board of Directors any or all of its powers, except the power to:

(i) admit new members and determine the conditions of their admission;

(ii) increase or decrease the authorized capital stock of the Bank;

(iii) suspend a member;

(iv) decide appeals from interpretations or applications of this Agreement given by the Board of Directors;

(v) authorize the conclusion of general agreements for co-operation with other international organizations;

(vi) elect the Directors and the President of the Bank;

(vii) determine the remuneration of the Directors and Alternate Directors and the Salary and other terms of the contract of service of the President;

(viii) approve, after reviewing the auditors' report, the general balance sheet and the statement of profit and loss of the Bank;

(ix) determine the reserves and the allocation and distribution of the net profits of the Bank;

(x) amend this Agreement;

(xi) decide to terminate the operations of the Bank and to distribute its assets; and

(xii) exercise such other powers as are expressly assigned to the Board of Governors in this Agreement.

3. The Board of Governors shall retain full power to exercise authority over any matter delegated or assigned to the Board of Directors under paragraph 2 of this Article, or elsewhere in this Agreement.

ARTICLE 25

BOARD OF GOVERNORS: PROCEDURE

1. The Board of Governors shall hold an annual meeting and such other meetings as may be provided for by the Board or called by the Board of Directors. Meetings of the Board of Governors shall be called, by the Board of Directors, whenever requested by not less than five (5) members of the Bank or members holding not less than one quarter of the total voting power of the members.

2. Two-thirds of the Governors shall constitute a quorum for any meeting of the Board of Governors, provided such majority represents not less than two-thirds of the total voting power of the members.

3. The Board of Governors may by regulations establish a procedure whereby the Board of Directors may, when the latter deems such action advisable, obtain a vote of the Governors on a specific questions without calling a meeting of the Board of Governors.

4. The Board of Governors, and the Board of Directors to the extent authorized, may adopt such rules and regulations and establish such subsidiary bodies as may be necessary or appropriate to conduct the business of the Bank.

ARTICLE 26

BOARD OF DIRECTORS: COMPOSITION

1. The Board of Directors shall be composed of twenty-three (23) members who shall not be members of the Board of Governors, and of whom:

(i) Eleven (11) shall be elected by the Governors representing Belgium, Denmark, France, the Federal Republic of Germany,

Greece, Ireland, Italy, Luxembourg, the Netherlands, Portugal, Spain, the United Kingdom, the European Economic Community and the European Investment Bank; and

(ii) Twelve (12) shall be elected by the Governors representing other members, of whom:

(a) four (4), by the Governors representing those countries listed in Annex A as Central and Eastern European countries eligible for assistance from the Bank;

(b) four (4), by the Governors representing those countries listed in Annex A as other European countries;

(c) four (4), by the Governors representing those countries listed in Annex A as non-European countries.

Directors, as well as representing members whose Governors have elected them, may also represent members who assign their votes to them.

2. Directors shall be persons of high competence in economic and financial matters and shall be elected in accordance with Annex B.

3. The Board of Governors may increase or decrease the size, or revise the composition, of the Board of Directors, in order to take into account changes in the number of members of the Bank, by an affirmative vote of not less than two-thirds of the Governors, representing not less than three-fourths of the total voting powers for subsequent elections, the number and composition of the second Board of Directors shall be as set out in paragraph 1 of this Article.

4. Each Director shall appoint an Alternate with full power to act for him or her when he or she is not present. Directors and Alternates shall be nationals of member countries. No member shall be represented by more than one Director. An Alternate may participate in meetings of the Board but may vote only when he or she is acting in place of his or her principal.

5. Directors shall hold office for a term of three (3) years and may be reelected; provided that the first Board of Directors shall be elected by the Board of Governors at its inaugural meeting, and shall hold office until the next immediately following annual meeting of the Board of Governors or, if that Board shall so decide at that annual meeting, until its next subsequent annual meeting. They shall continue in office until their successors shall have been chosen and assumed office. If the office of a Director becomes vacant more than one hundred and eighty (180) days before the end of his or her term, a successor shall be chosen in accordance with Annex B, for the remainder of the term, by the Governors who elected the former Director. A majority of the votes cast by such Governors shall be required for such election. If the office of a Director becomes vacant one hundred and eighty (180) days or less before the end of his or her term, a successor may similarly be chosen for the remainder of the term, by the votes cast by such Governors who elected the former Director, in which election a majority of the votes cast by such Governors shall be required. While the office remains vacant, the Alternate of the former Director shall exercise the powers of the latter, except that of appointing an Alternate.

Article 27

BOARD OF DIRECTORS: POWERS

Without prejudice to the powers of the Board of Governors as provided in Article 24 of this Agreement, the Board of Directors shall be responsible for the direction of the general operations of the Bank and, for this purpose, shall, in addition to the powers assigned to it expressly by this Agreement, exercise all the powers delegated to it by the Board of Governors, and in particular:

(i) prepare the work of the Board of Governors;

(ii) in conformity with the general directions of the Board of Governors, establish policies and take decisions concerning loans, guarantees, investments in equity capital, borrowing by the Bank, the furnishing of technical assistance, and other operations of the Bank;

(iii) submit the audited accounts for each financial year for approval of the Board of Governors at each annual meeting; and

(iv) approve the budget of the Bank.

Article 28

BOARD OF DIRECTORS: PROCEDURE

1. The Board of Directors shall normally function at the principal office of the Bank and shall meet as often as the business of the Bank may require.

2. A majority of the Directors shall constitute a quorum for any meeting of the Board of Directors, provided such majority represents not less than two-thirds of the total voting power of the members.

3. The Board of Governors shall adopt regulations under which, if there is no Director of its nationality, a member may send a representative to attend, without right to vote, any meeting of the Board of Directors when a matter particularly affecting that member is under consideration.

Article 29

VOTING

1. The voting power of each member shall be equal to the number of its subscribed shares in the capital stock of the Bank. In the event of any member failing to pay any part of the amount due in respect of its obligations in relation to paid-in shares under Article 6 of this Agreement, such member shall be unable for so long as such failure continues to exercise that percentage of its voting power which corresponds to the percentage which the amount due but unpaid bears to the total amount of paid-in shares subscribed to by that member in the capital stock of the Bank.

2. In voting in the Board of Governors, each Governor shall be entitled to cast the votes of the member he or she represents. Except as otherwise expressly provided in this Agreement, all matters before the Board of Governors shall be decided by a majority of the voting power of the members voting.

3. In voting in the Board of Directors each Director shall be entitled to cast the number of votes to which the Governors who have elected him or her are entitled and those to which any Governors who have assigned their votes to him or her, pursuant to Section D of Annex B, are entitled. A Director representing more than one member may cast separately the votes of the members he or she represents. Except as otherwise expressly provided in this Agreement, and except for general policy decisions in which cases such policy decisions shall be taken by a majority of not less than two-thirds of the total voting power of the members voting, all matters before the Board of Directors shall be decided by a majority of the voting power of the members voting.

ARTICLE 30

THE PRESIDENT

1. The Board of Governors, by a vote of a majority of the total number of Governors, representing not less than a majority of the total voting power of the members, shall elect a President of the Bank. The President, while holding office, shall not be a Governor or a Director or an Alternate for either.

2. The term of office of the President shall be four (4) years. He or she may be re-elected. He or she shall, however, cease to hold office when the Board of Governors so decides by an affirmative vote of not less than two-thirds of the Governors, representing not less than two-thirds of the total voting power of the members. If the office of the President for any reason becomes vacant, the Board of Governors, in accordance with the provisions of paragraph 1 of this Article, shall elect a successor for up to four (4) years.

3. The President shall not vote, except that he or she may cast a deciding vote in case of any equal division. He or she may participate in meetings of the Board of Governors and shall chair the meetings of the Board of Directors.

4. The President shall be the legal representative of the Bank.

5. The President shall be chief of the staff of the Bank. He or she shall be responsible for the organization, appointment and dismissal of the officers and staff in accordance with regulations to be adopted by the Board of Directors. In appointing officers and staff, he or she shall, subject to the paramount importance of efficiency and technical competence, pay due regard to recruitment on a wide geographical basis among members of the Bank.

6. The President shall conduct, under the direction of the Board of Directors, the current business of the Bank.

ARTICLE 31

VICE-PRESIDENT(S)

1. One or more Vice-Presidents shall be appointed by the Board of Directors on the recommendation of the President. A Vice-President shall hold office for such term, exercise such authority and perform such functions in the administration of the Bank, as may

be determined by the Board of Directors. In the absence or incapacity of the President, a Vice-President shall exercise the authority and perform the functions of the President.

2. A Vice-President may participate in meetings of the Board of Directors but shall have not vote at such meetings, except that he or she may cast the deciding vote when acting in place of the President.

ARTICLE 32

INTERNATIONAL CHARACTER OF THE BANK

1. The Bank shall not accept Special Funds or other loans or assistance that may in any way prejudice, deflect or otherwise alter its purpose or functions.

2. The Bank, its President, Vice-President(s), officers and staff shall in their decisions take into account only considerations relevant to the Bank's purpose, functions and operations, as set out in this Agreement. Such considerations shall be weighed impartially in order to achieve and carry out the purpose and functions of the Bank.

3. The President, Vice-President(s), officers and staff of the Bank, in the discharge of their offices, shall owe their duty entirely to the Bank and to no other authority. Each member of the Bank shall respect the international character of this duty and shall refrain from all attempts to influence any of them in the discharge of their duties.

ARTICLE 33

LOCATION OF OFFICES

1. The principal office of the Bank shall be located in London.

2. The Bank may establish agencies or branch offices in the territory of any member of the Bank.

ARTICLE 34

DEPOSITORIES AND CHANNELS OF COMMUNICATION

1. Each member shall designate its central bank, or such other institution as may be agreed upon with the Bank, as a depository for all the Bank's holdings of its currency as well as other assets of the Bank.

2. Each member shall designate an appropriate official entity with which the Bank may communicate in connection with any matter arising under this Agreement.

ARTICLE 35

PUBLICATION OF REPORTS AND PROVISION OF INFORMATION

1. The Bank shall public an annual report containing an audited statement of its accounts and shall circulate to members at intervals of three (3) months or less a summary statement of its financial position and a profit and loss statement showing the results of its operations. The financial accounts shall be kept in ECU.

2. The Bank shall report annually on the environmental impact of its activities and may publish such other reports as it deems desirable to advance its purpose.

3. Copies of all reports, statements and publications made under this Article shall be distributed to members.

Article 36

ALLOCATION AND DISTRIBUTION OF NET INCOME

1. The Board of Governors shall determine at least annually what part of the Bank's net income, after making provisions for reserves and, if necessary, against possible losses under paragraph 1 of Article 17 of this Agreement, shall be allocated to surplus or other purposes and what part, if any, shall be distributed. Any such decision on the allocation of the Bank's net income to other purposes shall be taken by a majority of not less than two-thirds of the Governors, representing not less than two-thirds of the total voting power of the members. No such allocation, and no distribution, shall be made until the general reserve amounts to at least ten (10) per cent of the authorized capital stock.

2. Any distribution referred to in the preceding paragraph shall be made in proportion to the number of paid-in shares held by each member; provided that in calculating such number account shall be taken only of payments received in cash and promissory notes encashed in respect of such shares on or before the end of the relevant financial year.

3. Payments to each member shall be made in such manner as the Board of Governors shall determine. Such payments and their use by the receiving country shall be without restriction by any member.

CHAPTER VII

WITHDRAWAL AND SUSPENSION OF MEMBERSHIP: TEMPORARY SUSPENSION AND TERMINATION OF OPERATIONS

Article 37

RIGHT OF MEMBERS TO WITHDRAW

1. Any member may withdraw from the Bank at any time by transmitting a notice in writing to the Bank at its principal office.

2. Withdrawal by a member shall become effective, and its membership shall cease, on the date specified in its notice but in no event less than six (6) months after such notice is received by the Bank. However, at any time before the withdrawal becomes finally effective, the member may notify the Bank in writing of the cancellation of its notice of intention to withdraw.

Article 38

SUSPENSION OF MEMBERSHIP

1. If a member fails to fulfill any of its obligations to the Bank, the Bank may suspend its membership by decision of a majority of

not less than two-thirds of the Governors, representing not less than two-thirds of the total voting power of the members. The member so suspended shall automatically cease to be a member one year from the date of its suspension unless a decision is taken by not less than the same majority to restore the member to good standing.

2. While under suspension, a member shall not be entitled to exercise any rights under this Agreement, except the right of withdrawal, but shall remain subject to all its obligations.

ARTICLE 39

SETTLEMENT OF ACCOUNTS WITH FORMER MEMBERS

1. After the date on which a member ceases to be a member, such former member shall remain liable for its direct obligations to the Bank and for its contingent liabilities to the Bank so long as any part of the loans, equity investments or guarantees contracted before it ceased to be a member are outstanding; but it shall cease to incur such liabilities with respect to loans, equity investments and guarantees entered into thereafter by the Bank and to share either in the income or the expenses of the Bank.

2. At the time a member ceases to be a member, the Bank shall arrange for the repurchase of such former member's shares as a part of the settlement of accounts with such former member in accordance with the provisions of this Article. For this purpose, the repurchase price of the shares shall be the value shown by the books of the Bank on the date of cessation of membership, with the original purchase price of each share being its maximum value.

3. The payment for shares repurchased by the Bank under this Article shall be governed by the following conditions:

(i) any amount due to the former member for its shares shall be withheld so long as the former member, its central bank or any of its agencies or instrumentalities remains liable, as borrower or guarantor, to the Bank and such amount may, at the option of the Bank, be applied on any such liability as it matures. No amount shall be withheld on account of the liability of the former member resulting from its subscription for shares in accordance with paragraphs 4, 5 and 7 of Article 6 of this Agreement. In any event, no amount due to a member for its shares shall be paid until six (6) months after the date upon which the member ceases to be a member;

(ii) payments for shares may be made from time to time, upon their surrender by the former member, to the extent by which the amount due as the repurchase price in accordance with paragraph 2 of this Article exceeds the aggregate amount of liabilities on loans, equity investments and guarantees in subparagraph (i) of this paragraph until the former member has received the full repurchase price;

(iii) payments shall be made on such conditions and in such fully convertible currencies, or ECU, and on such dates, as the Bank determines; and

(iv) if losses are sustained by the Bank on any guarantees, participations in loans, or loans which were outstanding on the date when the member ceased to be a member, or if a net loss is sustained by the Bank on equity investment held by it on such date, and the amount of such losses on the date when the member ceased to be a member, such former member shall repay, upon demand, the amount by which the repurchase price of its shares would have been reduced if the losses had been taken into account when the repurchase price was determined. In addition, the former member shall remain liable on any call for unpaid subscriptions under paragraph 4 of Article 6 of this Agreement, to the extent that it would have been required to respond if the impairment of capital had occurred and the call had been made at the time the repurchase price of its shares was determined.

4. If the Bank terminates its operations pursuant to Article 41 of this Agreement within six (6) months of the date upon which any member ceases to be a member, all rights of such former members shall be determined in accordance with the provisions of Articles 41 to 43 of this Agreement.

ARTICLE 40

TEMPORARY SUSPENSION OF OPERATIONS

In an emergency, the Board of Directors may suspend temporarily operations in respect of new loans, guarantees, underwriting, technical assistance and equity investments pending an opportunity for further consideration and action by the Board of Governors.

ARTICLE 41

TERMINATION OF OPERATIONS

The Bank may terminate its operations by the affirmative vote of not less than two-thirds of the Governors, representing not less than three-fourths of the total voting power of the members. Upon such termination of operations the Bank shall forthwith cease all activities, except those incident to the orderly realization, conservation and preservation of its assets and settlement of its obligations.

ARTICLE 42

LIABILITY OF MEMBERS AND PAYMENT OF CLAIMS

1. In the event of termination of the operations of the Bank, the liability of all members for uncalled subscriptions to the capital stock of the Bank shall continue until all claims of creditors, including all contingent claims, shall have been discharged.

2. Creditors on ordinary operations holding direct claims shall be paid first out of the assets of the Bank, secondly out of the payments to be made to the Bank in respect of unpaid paid-in shares, and then out of payments to be made to the Bank in respect of callable capital stock. Before making any payments to creditors holding direct claims, the Board of Directors shall make such arrangements as are necessary, in its judgment, to ensure a *pro rata* distribution among holders of direct and holders of contingent claims.

ARTICLE 43

DISTRIBUTION OF ASSETS

1. No distribution under this Chapter shall be made to members on account of their subscriptions to the capital stock of the Bank until:

(i) all liabilities to creditors have been discharged or provided for; and

(ii) the Board of Governors has decided by a vote of not less than two-thirds of the Governors, representing not less than three-fourths of the total voting power of the members, to make a distribution.

2. Any distribution of the assets of the Bank to the members shall be in proportion to the capital stock held by each member and shall be effected at such times and under such conditions as the Bank shall deem fair and equitable. The shares of assets distributed need not be uniform as to type of assets. No member shall be entitled to receive its share in such a distribution of assets until it has settled all of its obligations to the Bank.

3. Any member receiving assets distributed pursuant to this Article shall enjoy the same rights with respect to such assets as the Bank enjoyed prior to their distribution.

CHAPTER VIII

STATUS, IMMUNITIES, PRIVILEGES AND EXEMPTIONS

ARTICLE 44

PURPOSES OF CHAPTER

To enable the Bank to fulfill its purpose and the functions with which it is entrusted, the status, immunities, privileges and exemptions set forth in this Chapter shall be accorded to the Bank in the territory of each member country.

ARTICLE 45

STATUS OF THE BANK

The Bank shall possess full legal personality and, in particular, the full legal capacity:

(i) to contract;

(ii) to acquire, and dispose of, immovable and movable property; and

(iii) to institute legal proceedings.

ARTICLE 46

POSITION OF THE BANK WITH REGARD TO JUDICIAL PROCESS

Actions may be brought against the Bank only in a court of competent jurisdiction in the territory of a country in which the Bank has an office, has appointed an agent for the purpose of accepting service or notice of process, or has issued or guaranteed securities.

No actions shall, however, be brought by members or persons acting for or deriving claims from members. The property and assets of the Bank shall, wheresoever located and by whomsoever held, be immune from all forms of seizure, attachment or execution before the delivery of final judgment against the Bank.

ARTICLE 47

IMMUNITY OF ASSETS FROM SEIZURE

Property and assets of the Bank, wheresoever located and by whomsoever held, shall be immune from search, requisition, confiscation, expropriation or any other form of taking or foreclosure by executive or legislative action.

ARTICLE 48

IMMUNITY OF ARCHIVES

The archives of the Bank, and in general all documents belonging to it or held by it, shall be inviolable.

ARTICLE 49

FREEDOM OF ASSETS FROM RESTRICTIONS

To the extent necessary to carry out the purpose and functions of the Bank and subject to the provisions of this Agreement, all property and assets of the Bank shall be free from restrictions, regulations, controls and moratoria of any nature.

ARTICLE 50

PRIVILEGE FOR COMMUNICATIONS

The official communications of the Bank shall be accorded by each member the same treatment that it accords to the official communications of any other member.

ARTICLE 51

IMMUNITIES OF OFFICERS AND EMPLOYEES

All Governors, Directors, Alternates, officers and employees of the Bank and experts performing missions for the Bank shall be immune from legal process with respect to acts performed by them in their official capacity, except when the Bank waives this immunity, and shall enjoy inviolability of all their official papers and documents. This immunity shall not apply, however, to civil liability in the case of damage arising from a road traffic accident caused by any such Governor, Director, Alternate, officer, employee or expert.

Article 52

PRIVILEGES OF OFFICERS AND EMPLOYEES

1. All Governors, Directors, Alternates, officers and employees of the Bank and experts of the Bank performing missions for the Bank:

(i) not being local nationals, shall be accorded the same immunities from immigration restrictions, alien registration requirements and national service obligations, and the same facilities as regards exchange regulations, as are accorded by members to the representatives, officials, and employees of comparable rank of other members; and

(ii) shall be granted the same treatment in respect of travelling facilities as is accorded by members to representatives, officials and employees of comparable rank of other members.

2. The spouses and immediate dependents of those Directors, Alternate Directors, officers, employees and experts of the Bank who are resident in the country in which the principal office of the Bank is located shall be accorded opportunity to take employment in that country. The spouses and immediate dependents of those Directors, Alternate Directors, officers, employees and experts of the Bank who are resident in a country in which any agency or branch office of the Bank is located should, wherever possible, in accordance with the national law of that country, be accorded similar opportunity in that country. The Bank shall negotiate specific agreements implementing the provisions of this paragraph with the country in which the principal office of the Bank is located and, as appropriate, with the other countries concerned.

Article 53

EXEMPTION FROM TAXATION

1. Within the scope of its official activities the Bank, its assets, property, and income shall be exempt from all direct taxes.

2. When purchases or services of substantial value and necessary for the exercise of the official activities of the Bank are made or used by the Bank and when the price of such purchases or services includes taxes or duties, the member that has levied the taxes or duties shall, if they are identifiable, take appropriate measures to grant exemption from such taxes or duties or to provide for their reimbursement.

3. Goods imported by the Bank and necessary for the exercise of its official activities shall be exempt from all import duties and taxes, and from all import prohibitions and restrictions. Similarly goods exported by the Bank and necessary for the exercise of its official activities shall be exempt from all export duties and taxes, and from all export prohibitions and restrictions.

4. Goods acquired or imported and exempted under this Article shall not be sold, hired out, lent or given away against payment or free of charge, except in accordance with conditions laid down by the members which have granted exemptions or reimbursements.

5. The provisions of this Article shall not apply to taxes or duties which are no more than charges for public utility services.

6. Directors, Alternate Directors, officers and employees of the Bank shall be subject to an internal effective tax for the benefit of the Bank on salaries and emoluments paid by the Bank, subject to conditions to be laid down and rules to be adopted by the Board of Governors within a period of one year from the date of entry into force of this Agreement. From the date on which this tax is applied, such salaries and emoluments shall be exempt from national income tax. The members may, however, take into account the salaries and emoluments thus exempt when assessing the amount of tax to be applied to income from other sources.

7. Notwithstanding the provisions of paragraph 6 of this Article, a member may deposit, with its instrument of ratification, acceptance or approval, a declaration that such member retains for itself, its political subdivisions or its local authorities the right to tax salaries and emoluments paid by the Bank to citizens or nationals of such member. The Bank shall be exempt from any obligation for the payment, withholding or collection of such taxes. The Bank shall not make any reimbursement for such taxes.

8. Paragraph 6 of this Article shall not apply to pensions and annuities paid by the Bank.

9. No tax of any kind shall be levied on any obligation or security issued by the Bank, including any dividend or interest thereon, by whomsoever held:

(i) which discriminates against such obligation or security solely because it is issued by the Bank, or

(ii) if the sole jurisdictional basis for such taxation is the place or currency in which it is issued, made payable or paid, or the location of any office or place of business maintained by the Bank.

10. No tax of any kind shall be levied on any obligation or security guaranteed by the Bank, including any dividend or interest thereon, by whomsoever held:

(i) which discriminates against such obligation or security solely because it is guaranteed by the Bank, or

(ii) if the sole jurisdictional basis for such taxation is the location any office or place of business maintained by the Bank.

Article 54

IMPLEMENTATION OF CHAPTER

Each member shall promptly take such action as is necessary for the purpose of implementing the provisions of this Chapter and shall inform the Bank of the detailed action which it has taken.

Article 55

WAIVER OF IMMUNITIES, PRIVILEGES AND EXEMPTIONS

The immunities, privileges and exemptions conferred under this Chapter are granted in the interest of the Bank. The Board of Directors may waive to such extend and upon such conditions as it may determine any of the immunities, privileges and exemptions conferred under this Chapter in cases where such action would, in its opinion, be appropriate in the best interests of the Bank. The

President shall have the right and the duty to waive any immunity, privilege or exemption in respect of any officer, employee or expert of the Bank, other than the President or a Vice-President, where, in his or her opinion, the immunity, privilege or exemption would impede the course of justice and can be waived without prejudice to the interests of the Bank. In similar circumstances and under the same conditions, the Board of Directors shall have the right and the duty to waive any immunity, privilege or exemption in respect of the President and each Vice-President.

CHAPTER IX

AMENDMENTS, INTERPRETATION, ARBITRATION

ARTICLE 56

AMENDMENTS

1. any proposal to amend this Agreement, whether emanating from a member, a Governor or the Board of Directors, shall be communicated to the Chairman of the Board of Governors who shall bring the proposal before that Board. If the proposed amendment is approved by the Board the Bank shall, by any rapid means of communication, ask all members whether they accept the proposed amendment. When not less than three-fourths of the members (including at least two countries from central and Eastern Europe listed in Annex A), having not less than four-fifths of the total voting power of the members, have accepted the proposed amendment, the Bank shall certify that fact by formal communication addressed to all members.

2. Notwithstanding paragraph 1 of this Article:

(i) acceptance by all members shall be required in the case of any amendment modifying:

(a) the right to withdraw from the Bank;

(b) the rights pertaining to purchase of capital stock provided for in paragraph 3 of Article 5 of this Agreement;

(c) the limitations on liability provided for in paragraph 7 of Article 5 of this Agreement; and

(d) the purpose and functions of the Bank defined by Articles 1 and 2 of this Agreement;

(ii) acceptance by not less than three-fourths of the members having not less than eighty-five (85) per cent of the total voting power of the members shall be required in the case of any amendment modifying paragraph 4 of Article 8 of this Agreement.

When the requirements for accepting any such proposed amendments have been met, the Bank shall certify that fact by formal communication addressed to all members.

3. Amendments shall enter into force for all members three (3) months after the date of the formal communication provided for in paragraphs 1 and 2 of this Article unless the Board of Governors specifies a different period.

ARTICLE 57

INTERPRETATION AND APPLICATION

1. Any question of interpretation or application of the provisions of this Agreement arising between any member and the Bank, or between any members of the Bank, shall be submitted to the Board of Directors for its decision. If there is no Director of its nationality in that Board, a member particularly affected by the question under consideration shall be entitled to direct representation in the meeting of the Board of Directors during such consideration. The representative of such member shall, however, have no vote. Such right of representation shall be regulated by the Board of Governors.

2. In any case where the Board of Directors has given a decision under paragraph 1 of this Article, any member may require that the question be referred to the Board of Governors, whose decision shall be final. Pending the decision of the Board of Governors, the Bank may, so far as it deems it necessary, act on the basis of the decision of the Board of Directors.

ARTICLE 58

ARBITRATION

If a disagreement should arise between the Bank and a member which has ceased to be a member, or between the Bank and any member after adoption of a decision to terminate the operations of the Bank, such disagreement shall be submitted to arbitration by a tribunal of three (3) arbitrators, one appointed by the Bank, another by the member or former member concerned, and the third, unless the parties otherwise agree, by the President of the International Court of Justice or such other authority as may have been prescribed by regulations adopted by the Board of Governors. A majority vote of the arbitrators shall be sufficient to reach a decision which shall be final and binding upon the parties. The third arbitrator shall have full power to settle all questions of procedure in any case where the parties are in disagreement with respect thereto.

ARTICLE 59

APPROVAL DEEMED GIVEN

Whenever the approval or the acceptance of any member is required before any act may be done by the Bank, except under Article 56 of this Agreement, approval or acceptance shall be deemed to have been given unless the member presents an objection within such reasonable period as the Bank may fix in notifying the member of the proposed act.

CHAPTER X

FINAL PROVISIONS

ARTICLE 60

SIGNATURE AND DEPOSIT

1. This Agreement, deposited with the Government of the French Republic (hereinafter called "the Depository"), shall remain open until 31 December 1990 for signature by the prospective members whose names are set forth in Annex A to this Agreement.

2. The Depository shall communicate certified copies of this agreement to all the Signatories.

ARTICLE 61

RATIFICATION, ACCEPTANCE OR APPROVAL

1. The Agreement shall be subject to ratification, acceptance or approval by the Signatories. Instruments of ratification, acceptance or approval shall, subject to paragraph 2 of this Article, be deposited with the Depository not later than 31 March 1991. The Depository shall duly notify the other Signatories of each deposit and the date thereof.

2. Any Signatory may become a party to this Agreement by depositing an instrument of ratification, acceptance or approval until one year after the date of its entry into force or, if necessary, until such later date as may be decided by a majority of Governors, representing a majority of the total voting power of the members.

3. A Signatory whose instrument referred to in paragraph 1 of this Article is deposited before the date on which this Agreement enters into force shall become a member of the Bank on that date. Any other Signatory which complies with the provisions of the preceding paragraph shall become a member of the Bank on the date on which its instrument of ratification, acceptance or approval is deposited.

ARTICLE 62

ENTRY INTO FORCE

1. This Agreement shall enter into force when instruments of ratification, acceptance or approval have been deposited by Signatories whose initial subscriptions represent not less than two thirds of the total subscriptions set forth in Annex A, including at least two countries from Central and Eastern Europe listed in Annex A.

2. If this Agreement has not entered into force by 31 March 1991, the Depository may convene a conference of interested prospective members to determine the future course of action and decide a new date by which instruments of ratification, acceptance or approval shall be deposited.

ARTICLE 63

INAUGURAL MEETING AND COMMENCEMENT OF OPERATIONS

1. As soon as this Agreement enters into force under Article 62 of this Agreement, each member shall appoint a Governor. The Depository shall call the first meeting of the Board of Governors within sixty (60) days of entry into force of this Agreement under Article 62 or as soon as possible thereafter.

2. At its first meeting, the Board of Governors:

(i) shall elect the President;

(ii) shall elect the Directors of the Bank in accordance with Article 26 of this Agreement;

(iii) shall make arrangements for determining the date of the commencement of the Bank's operations; and

(iv) shall make such other arrangements as appear to it necessary to prepare for the commencement of the Bank's operations.

3. The Bank shall notify its members of the date of commencement of its operations.

DONE at Paris on 29 May 1990 in a single original, whose English, French, German and Russian texts are equally authentic, which shall be deposited in the archives of the Depository which shall transmit a duly certified copy to each of the other prospective members whose names are set forth in Annex A.

ANNEX A

INITIAL SUBSCRIPTIONS TO THE AUTHORIZED CAPITAL STOCK FOR PROSPECTIVE MEMBERS WHICH MAY BECOME MEMBERS IN ACCORDANCE WITH ARTICLE 61

	Number of shares	Capital subscription (in million ECUs)
A—European Communities		
a)		
Belgium	22,800	228.00
Denmark	12,000	120.00
France	85,175	851.75
Germany, Federal Republic of	85,175	851.75
Greece	6,500	65.00
Ireland	3,000	30.00
Italy	85,175	851.75
Luxembourg	2,000	22.00
Netherlands	24,800	248.00
Portugal	4,200	42.00
Spain	34,000	340.00
United Kingdom	85,175	851.75
b)		
European Economic Community	30,000	300.00
European Investment Bank	30,000	300.00

	Number of shares	Capital subscription (in million ECUs)
B—Other European Countries		
Austria	22,800	228.00
Cyprus	1,000	10.00
Finland	12,500	125.00
Iceland	1,000	10.00
Israel	6,500	65.00
Liechtenstein	200	2.00
Malta	100	1.00
Norway	12,500	125.00
Sweden	22,800	228.00
Switzerland	22,800	228.00
Turkey	11,500	115.00
C—Recipient countries		
Bulgaria	7,900	79.00
Czechoslovakia	12,800	128.00
German Democratic Republic	15,500	155.00
Hungary	7,900	79.00
Poland	12,800	128.00
Romania	4,800	48.00
Union of Soviet Socialist Republics	60,000	600.00
Yugoslavia	12,800	128.00
D—Non-European Countries		
Australia	10,000	100.00
Canada	34,000	340.00
Egypt	1,000	10.00
Japan	85,175	851.75
Korea, Republic of	6,500	65.00
Mexico	3,000	30.00
Morocco	1,000	10.00
New Zealand	1,000	10.00
United States of America	100,000	1,000.00
E—Non-allocated shares	125	1.25
TOTAL	1,000,000	10,000.00

(*) Prospective members are listed under the above categories only for the purpose of this Agreement. Recipient countries are referred to elsewhere in this Agreement as Central and Eastern European countries.

ANNEX B

Section A—Election of Directors by Governors Representing Belgium, Denmark, France, the Federal Republic of Germany, Greece, Ireland, Italy, Luxembourg, the Netherlands, Portugal, Spain, the United Kingdom, the European Economic Community and the European Investment Bank (hereinafter referred to as Section A Governors).

1. The provisions set out below in this Section shall apply exclusively to this Section.

2. Candidates for the office of Director shall be nominated by Section A Governors, provided that a Governor may nominate only one person. The election of Directors shall be by ballot of Section A Governors.

3. Each Governor eligible to vote shall cast for one person all of the votes to which the member appointing him or her is entitled under paragraphs 1 and 2 of Article 29 of this Agreement.

4. Subject to paragraph 10 of this Section the 11 persons receiving the highest number of votes shall be Directors, except that no person who receives less than 4.5 per cent of the total of the votes which can be cast (eligible votes) in Section A shall be considered elected.

5. Subject to paragraph 10 of this Section, if 11 persons are not elected on the first ballot, a second ballot shall be held in which, unless there were no more than 11 candidates, the person who received the lowest number of votes in the first ballot shall be ineligible for election and in which there shall note only:

(a) those Governors who voted in the first ballot for a person not elected and

(b) those Governors whose votes for a person elected are deemed under paragraphs 6 and 7 below of this Section to have raised the votes cast for that person above 5.5 per cent of the eligible votes.

6. In determining whether the votes cast by a Governor are deemed to have raised the total votes cast for any person above 5.5 per cent of the eligible votes, the 5.5 per cent shall be deemed to include, first, the votes of the Governor casting the largest number of votes for such person, then the votes of the Governor casting the next largest number and so on, until 5.5 per cent is reached.

7. Any Governor, part of whose votes must be counted in order to raise the total of votes cast for any person above 4.5 per cent shall be considered as casting all of his or her votes for such person, even if the total votes for such person thereby exceed 5.5 per cent and shall not be eligible to vote in a further ballot.

8. Subject to paragraph 10 of this Section, if, after the second ballot, 11 persons have not been elected, further ballots shall be held in conformity with the principles and procedures laid down in this Section, until 11 persons have been elected, provided that, if at any stage 10 persons are elected, notwithstanding the provisions of paragraph 4 of this Section, the 11th may be elected by a simple majority of the remaining votes cast.

9. In the case of an increase or decrease in the number of Directors to be elected by Section A Governors, the minimum and maximum percentages specified in paragraphs 4, 5, 6 and 7 of this Section shall be appropriately adjusted by the Board of Governors.

10. So long as any Signatory, or group of Signatories, whose share of the total amount of capital subscriptions provided in Annex A is more than 2.4 per cent, has not deposited its instrument or their instruments of ratification, approval or acceptance, there shall be no election for one Director in respect of each such

Signatory or group of Signatories. The Governor or Governors representing such a Signatory or group of Signatories shall elect a Director in respect of each Signatory or group of Signatories, immediately after the Signatory becomes a member or the group of Signatories become members. Such Director shall be deemed to have been elected by the Board of Governors at its inaugural meeting, in accordance with paragraph 3 of Article 26 of this Agreement, if he or she is elected during the period in which the first Board of Directors shall hold office.

SECTION B—ELECTION OF DIRECTORS BY GOVERNORS REPRESENTING OTHER COUNTRIES.

SECTION B (i)—ELECTION OF DIRECTORS BY GOVERNORS REPRESENTING THOSE COUNTRIES LISTED IN ANNEX A AS CENTRAL AND EASTERN EUROPEAN COUNTRIES (RECIPIENT COUNTRIES) (HEREINAFTER REFERRED TO AS SECTION B (i) GOVERNORS).

1. The provisions set out below in this Section shall apply exclusively to this Section.

2. Candidates for the office of Director shall be nominated by Section B (i) Governors, provided that a Governor may nominate only person. The election of Directors shall be by ballot of Section B (i) Governors.

3. Each Governor eligible to vote shall cast for one person all of the votes to which the member appointing him or her is entitled under paragraphs 1 and 2 of Article 29 of this Agreement.

4. Subject to paragraph 10 of this Section, the 4 persons receiving the highest number of votes shall be Directors, except that no person who receives less than 12 per cent of the total of the votes which can be cast (eligible votes) in Section B (i) shall be considered elected.

5. Subject to paragraph 10 of this Section, if 4 persons are not elected on the first ballot, a second ballot shall be held in which, unless there were no more than 4 candidates, the person who received the lowest number of votes in the first ballot shall be ineligible for election and in which there shall vote only:

(a) those Governors who voted in the first ballot for a person not elected and

(b) those Governors whose votes for a person elected are deemed under paragraphs 6 and 7 below of this Section to have raised the votes cast for that person above 13 per cent of the eligible votes.

6. In determining whether the vote cast by a Governor are deemed to have raised the total votes cast for any person above 13 per cent of the eligible votes, the 13 per cent shall be deemed to include, first, the votes of the Governor casting the largest number of votes for such person, then the votes of the Governor casting the next largest number and so on, until 13 per cent is reached.

7. Any Governor, part of whose votes must be counted in order to raise the total of votes cast for any person above 12 per cent shall be considered as casting all of his or her votes for such person, even if the total votes for such person thereby exceed 13 per cent and shall not be eligible to vote in a further ballot.

8. Subject to paragraph 10 of this Section, if, after the second ballot, 4 persons have not been elected, further ballots shall be held in conformity with the principles and procedures laid down in this Section, until 4 persons have been elected, provided that, if at any stage 3 persons are elected, notwithstanding the provisions of paragraph 4 of this Section, the 4th may be elected by a simple majority of the remaining votes cast.

9. In the case of an increase or decrease in the number of Directors to be elected by Section B (i) Governors, the minimum and maximum percentages specified in paragraphs 4, 5, 6 and 7 of this Section shall be appropriately adjusted by the Board of Governors.

10. So long as any Signatory, or group of Signatories, whose share of the total amount of capital subscriptions provided in Annex A is more than 2.8 per cent, has not deposited its instrument or their instruments of ratification, approval or acceptance, there shall be no election for one Director in respect of each such Signatory or group of Signatories. The Governor or Governors representing such a Signatory group or Signatories shall elect a Director in respect of each Signatory or group of Signatories, immediately after the Signatory becomes a member or the group of Signatories become members. Such Director shall be deemed to have been elected by the Board of Governors at its inaugural meeting, in accordance with paragraph 3 of Article 26 of this Agreement, if he or she is elected during the period in which the first Board of Directors shall hold office.

SECTION B (ii)—ELECTION OF DIRECTORS BY GOVERNORS REPRESENTING THOSE COUNTRIES LISTED IN ANNEX A AS OTHER EUROPEAN COUNTRIES (HEREINAFTER REFERRED TO AS SECTION B (ii) GOVERNORS).

1. The provisions set out below in this Section shall apply exclusively to this Section.

2. Candidates for the office of Director shall be nominated by Section A Governors, provided that a Governor may nominate only one person. The election of Directors shall be by ballot of Section A Governors.

3. Each Governor eligible to vote shall cast for one person all of the votes to which the member appointing him or her is entitled under paragraphs 1 and 2 of Article 29 of this Agreement.

4. Subject to paragraph 10 of this Section the 11 persons receiving the highest number of votes shall be Directors, except that no person who receives less than 4.5 per cent of the total of the votes which can be cast (eligible votes) in Section A shall be considered elected.

5. Subject to paragraph 10 of this Section, if 11 persons are not elected on the first ballot, a second ballot shall be held in which, unless there were no more than 11 candidates, the person who received the lowest number of votes in the first ballot shall be ineligible for election and in which there shall note only:

(a) those Governors who voted in the first ballot for a person not elected and

(b) those Governors whose votes for a person elected are deemed under paragraphs 6 and 7 below of this Section to have raised the votes cast for that person above 5.5 per cent of the eligible votes.

6. In determining whether the votes cast by a Governor are deemed to have raised the total votes cast for any person above 5.5 per cent of the eligible votes, the 5.5 per cent shall be deemed to include, first, the votes of the Governor casting the largest number of votes for such person, then the votes of the Governor casting the next largest number and so on, until 5.5 per cent is reached.

7. Any Governor, part of whose votes must be counted in order to raise the total of votes cast for any person above 4.5 per cent shall be considered as casting all of his or her votes for such person, even if the total votes for such person thereby exceed 5.5 per cent and shall not be eligible to vote in a further ballot.

8. Subject to paragraph 10 of this Section, if, after the second ballot, 11 persons have not been elected, further ballots shall be held in conformity with the principles and procedures laid down in this Section, until 11 persons have been elected, provided that, if at any stage 10 persons are elected, notwithstanding the provisions of paragraph 4 of this Section, the 11th may be elected by a simple majority of the remaining votes cast.

9. In the case of an increase or decrease in the number of Directors to be elected by Section A Governors, the minimum and maximum percentages specified in paragraphs 4, 5, 6 and 7 of this Section shall be appropriately adjusted by the Board of Governors.

10. So long as any Signatory, or group of Signatories, whose share of the total amount of capital subscriptions provided in Annex A is more than 2.4 per cent, has not deposited its instrument or their instruments of ratification, approval or acceptance, there shall be no election for one Director in respect of each such Signatory or group of Signatories. The Governor or Governors representing such a Signatory or group of Signatories shall elect a Director in respect of each Signatory or group of Signatories, immediately after the Signatory becomes a member or the group of Signatories become members. Such Director shall be deemed to have been elected by the Board of Governors at its inaugural meeting, in accordance with paragraph 3 of Article 26 of this Agreement, if he or she is elected during the period in which the first Board of Directors shall hold office.

SECTION B (iii)—ELECTION OF DIRECTORS BY GOVERNORS REPRESENTING THOSE COUNTRIES LISTED IN ANNEX A AS NON-EUROPEAN COUNTRIES (HEREINAFTER REFERRED TO AS SECTION B (iii) GOVERNORS).

1. The provisions set out below in this Section shall apply exclusively to this Section.

2. Candidates for the office of Director shall be nominated by Section B (iii) Governors, provided that a Governor may nominate only person. The election of Directors shall be by ballot of Section B (iii) Governors.

3. Each Governor eligible to vote shall cast for one person all of the votes to which the member appointing him or her is entitled under paragraphs 1 and 2 of Article 29 of this Agreement.

4. Subject to paragraph 10 of this Section, the 4 persons receiving the highest number of votes shall be Directors, except that no person who receives less than 8 per cent of the votes which can be cast (eligible votes) in Section B (iii) shall be considered elected.

5. Subject to paragraph 10 of this Section, if 4 persons are not elected on the first ballot, a second ballot shall be held in which, unless there were no more than 4 candidates, the person who received the lowest number of votes in the first ballot shall be ineligible for election and in which there shall vote only:

(a) those Governors who voted in the first ballot for a person not elected and

(b) those Governors whose votes for a person elected are deemed under paragraphs 6 and 7 below of this Section to have raised the votes cast for that person above 9 per cent of the eligible votes.

6. In determining whether the vote cast by a Governor are deemed to have raised the total votes cast for any person above 9 per cent of the eligible votes, the 9 per cent shall be deemed to include, first, the votes of the Governor casting the largest number of votes for such person, then the votes of the Governor casting the next largest number and so on, until 9 per cent is reached.

7. Any Governor, part of whose votes must be counted in order to raise the total of votes cast for any person above 8 per cent shall be considered as casting all of his or her votes for such person, even if the total votes for such person thereby exceed 9 per cent and shall not be eligible to vote in a further ballot.

8. Subject to paragraph 10 of this Section, if, after the second ballot, 4 persons have not been elected, further ballots shall be held in conformity with the principles and procedures laid down in this Section, until 4 persons have been elected, provided that, if at any stage 3 persons are elected, notwithstanding the provisions of paragraph 4 of this Section, the 4th may be elected by a simple majority of the remaining votes cast.

9. In the case of an increase or decrease in the number of Directors to be elected by Section B (iii) Governors, the minimum and maximum percentages specified in paragraphs 4, 5, 6 and 7 of this Section shall be appropriately adjusted by the Board of Governors.

10. So long as any Signatory, or group of Signatories, whose share of the total amount of capital subscriptions provided in Annex A is more than 5 per cent, has not deposited its instrument or their instruments of ratification, approval or acceptance, there shall be no election for one Director in respect of each such Signatory or group of Signatories. The Governor or Governors representing such a Signatory group or Signatories shall elect a Director in respect of each Signatory or group of Signatories, immediately after the Signatory becomes a member or the group of Signatories become members. Such Director shall be deemed to have been elected by the Board of Governors at its inaugural meeting, in accordance with paragraph 3 of Article 26 of this Agreement, if he or she is elected during the period in which the first Board of Directors shall hold office.

SECTION C—ARRANGEMENTS FOR THE ELECTION OF DIRECTORS REPRESENTING COUNTRIES NOT LISTED IN ANNEX A.

If the Board of Governors decides, in accordance with paragraph 3 of Article 26 of this Agreement, to increase or decrease the size, or revise the composition, of the Board of Directors, in order to take into account changes in the number of members of the Bank, the Board of Governors shall first consider whether any amendments are required to this Annex, and may make any such amendments as its deems necessary as part of such decision.

SECTION D—ASSIGNMENT OF VOTES.

Any Governors who does not participate in voting for the election or whose vote does not contribute to the election of a Director under Section A or Section B (i) or Section B (ii) or Section B (iii) of this Annex may assign the votes to which he or she is entitled to an elected Director, provided that such Governor shall first have obtained the agreement of all those Governors who have elected that Director to such assignment.

A decision by any Governor not to participate in voting for the election of a Director shall not affect the calculation of the eligible votes to be made under Section A, Section B (i), Section B (ii) or Section B (iii) of this Annex.

LETTER FROM THE HEAD OF THE SOVIET DELEGATION

To the Chairman of the Conference on the Establishment of the European Bank for Reconstruction and Development

MR. CHAIRMAN,

As you know, the initiative of the President of France M. F. Mitterand to establish the European Bank for Reconstruction and Development for the purpose of facilitating the transition of Central and Eastern European countries towards market-oriented economies has found understanding and support on behalf of the Soviet authorities. The Soviet delegation participated in the sessions of talks on drafting the constituent documents of the Bank. As a result the constituent countries have reached considerable progress in drawing up the Agreement establishing the European Bank for Reconstruction and Development.

At the same time, certain difficulties largely stem from fears of a number of countries that due to the size of its economy the Soviet Union may become the principal recipient of credits of the Bank and therefore will narrow its capacity to extend aid to other Central and Eastern European Countries.

In this connexion I would like to assure you, dear Mr. Chairman, that the intentions of the Soviet Union to become an equal member of the Bank account primarily for its will to establish a new institution of multilateral co-operation so as to foster historical reforms on the European continent.

I would like to inform you that my government is prepared to limit its access to the Bank's resources, pursuant to paragraph 4 of Article 8 of the Articles of Agreement of the Bank, for a period of three years starting from the entry into force of the Articles of Agreement of the Bank.

During that period, the Soviet Union wishes that the Bank will provide technical assistance and other types of assistance directed to finance its private sector, to facilitate the transition of state owned enterprises to private sector ownership and control and to help enterprises operating competitively and moving to participation in the market-oriented economy, subject to the proportion set forth in paragraph 3 of Article 11 of this Agreement. The total amount of any assistance thus provided by the Bank would not exceed the total amount of the cash disbursed and the promissory notes issued by the Soviet Union for its shares.

I am confident, that continuing economic reforms in the Soviet Union will inevitably promote the expansion of the Bank's activities into the territory of the Soviet Union. However, the USSR, being interested in securing the multilateral character of the Bank, will not choose that at any time in future the Soviet borrowings will exceed an amount consistent with maintaining the necessary diversity in the bank's operations and prudent limits on its exposure.

Please accept, Mr. Chairman, the assurances of my highest consideration.

HEAD OF SOVIET DELEGATION
CHAIRMAN OF THE BOARD OF THE STATE BANK OF THE USSR
Victor V. GERASHCHENKO

13. Agreement Between the United States and the United Mexican States Concerning the Establishment of a Border Environment Cooperation Commission and a North American Development Bank (Amended) [1]

Agreement signed at Washington, November 16 and 18, 1993; Entered into force, January 1, 1994

The Government of the United States of America and the Government of the United Mexican States ("the Parties"):

CONVINCED of the importance of the conservation, protection and enhancement of their environments and the essential role of cooperation in these areas in achieving sustainable development for the well-being of present and future generations;

RECOGNIZING the bilateral nature of many transboundary environmental issues, and that such issues can be most effectively addressed jointly;

ACKNOWLEDGING that the border region of the United States and Mexico is experiencing environmental problems that must be addressed in order to promote sustainable development;

RECOGNIZING the need for environmental infrastructure in the border region, especially in the areas of water pollution, wastewater treatment, municipal solid waste, and related matters;

AFFIRMING that, to the extent practicable, environmental infrastructure projects should be financed by the private sector, but that the urgency of the environmental problems in the border region requires that the Parties be prepared to assist in supporting these projects;

AFFIRMING that, to the extent practicable, environmental infrastructure projects in the border region should be operated and maintained through user fees paid by polluters and those who benefit from the projects, and should be subject to local or private control;

NOTING that the International Boundary and Water Commission, established pursuant to the Treaty between the United States and Mexico Relating to Utilization of Waters of the Colorado and Tijuana Rivers and of the Rio Grande, signed at Washington February 3, 1944, plays an important role in efforts to preserve the health and vitality of the river waters of the border region;

RECOGNIZING that there is a need to establish a new organization to strengthen cooperation among interested parties and to facilitate the financing, construction, operation and maintenance of environmental infrastructure projects in the border region;

[1] TIAS 12516. The Agreement, also known as the "Charter", was amended on August 6, 2004. For a list of states that are parties to this convention, see Department of State publication, *Treaties in Force*.

AFFIRMING the desirability of encouraging increased investment in the environmental infrastructure in the border region, whether or not such investment is made under the auspices of this Agreement;

CONVINCED of the need to collaborate with states and localities, nongovernmental organizations, and other members of the public in the effort to address environmental problems in the border region;

SEEKING to assist community adjustment and investment in the United States and Mexico;

REAFFIRMING the importance of the environmental goals and objectives embodied in the Agreement on Cooperation for the Protection and Improvement of the Environment in the Border Area, signed at La Paz, Baja California Sur, August 14, 1983; and

WISHING to follow upon the goals and objectives of the North American Free Trade Agreement, signed at Washington, Ottawa, and Mexico December 8, 11, 14, and 17, 1992, and the North American Agreement on Environmental Cooperation, signed at Mexico, Washington, and Ottawa September 8, 9, 12, and 14, 1993;

HAVE AGREED AS FOLLOWS:

CHAPTER I—INTERNATIONAL CENTRE FOR SETTLEMENT OF INVESTMENT DISPUTES

SECTION 1—ESTABLISHMENT AND ORGANIZATION

ARTICLE 1

INTRODUCTORY ARTICLE

The Parties agree to establish the Border Environment Cooperation Commission and the North American Development Bank, which shall operate in accordance with the following provisions:

CHAPTER I—BORDER ENVIRONMENT COOPERATION COMMISSION

ARTICLE I—PURPOSE AND FUNCTIONS

SECTION 1. PURPOSE

(a) The purpose of the Commission shall be to help preserve, protect and enhance the environment of the border region in order to advance the well-being of the people of the United States and Mexico.

(b) In carrying out this purpose, the Commission shall cooperate as appropriate with the North American Development Bank and other national and international institutions, and with private sources supplying investment capital for environmental infrastructure projects in the border region.

SECTION 2. FUNCTIONS

(a) In carrying out this purpose, the Commission may do any or all of the following:

(1) with their concurrence, assist states and localities and other public entities and private investors in:

(A) coordinating environmental infrastructure projects in the border region;

(B) preparing, developing, implementing, and overseeing environmental infrastructure projects in the border region, including the design, siting and other technical aspects of such projects;

(C) analyzing the financial feasibility or the environmental aspects, or both, of environmental infrastructure projects in the border region;

(D) evaluating social and economic benefits of environmental infrastructure projects in the border region; and

(E) organizing, developing and arranging public and private financing for environmental infrastructure projects in the border region;

(2) certify, by a decision of the Board of Directors in accordance with Article II, Section 3 of this Chapter, environmental infrastructure projects in the border region to be submitted for financing to the North American Development Bank, or to other sources of financing that request such certification.

(b) The Commission may carry out the functions in this section with respect to an environmental infrastructure project outside the border region upon a decision by the Board of Directors that the project would remedy a transboundary environmental or health problem.

Article II—Operations

Section 1. Use of Resources

The resources and facilities of the Commission shall be used exclusively to implement the purpose and functions enumerated in Article I of this Chapter.

Section 2. Requests for Assistance

(a) The Commission may seek and accept requests from states and localities, other public entities and private investors for assistance in carrying out the activities enumerated in Article I of this Chapter.

(b) Upon receipt of a request for assistance pursuant to paragraph (a) of this Section, the Commission may provide any and all such assistance as it deems appropriate. In providing such assistance, the Commission shall give preference to environmental infrastructure projects relating to water pollution, wastewater treatment, water conservation, municipal solid waste, and related matters.

(c) In providing such assistance, the Commission shall consult, as appropriate, with the North American Development Bank.

Section 3. Applications for Certification

(a) The Commission may accept applications from states and localities, other public entities and private investors for certification of environmental infrastructure projects in the border region with respect to which an applicant will be seeking financial assistance from the North American Development Bank or other sources of financing requesting such certification.

(b) The Board of Directors may certify for such financing any project that meets or agrees to meet the technical, environmental, financial or other criteria applied, either generally or specifically, by the Commission to that project. To be eligible for certification, a project shall observe or be capable of observing the environmental and other laws of the place where it is to be located or executed.

(c) For each project located in the border region and having significant environmental effects,

(1) an environmental assessment shall be presented as part of the application process, and the Board of Directors shall examine potential environmental benefits, environmental risks, and costs, as well as available alternatives and the environmental standards and objectives of the affected area; and

(2) the Board of Directors, in consultation with affected states and localities, shall determine that the project meets the necessary conditions to achieve a high level of environmental protection for the affected area.

(d) In making certifications pursuant to this Section, the Board of Directors shall give preference to environmental infrastructure projects relating to water pollution, wastewater treatment, water conservation, municipal solid waste, and related matters.

SECTION 4. RELATIONSHIP WITH THE PUBLIC

The Commission shall establish procedures in English and Spanish:

(a) ensuring, to the extent possible, public availability of documentary information on all projects for which a request for assistance or an application for certification is made;

(b) for giving written notice of and providing members of the public reasonable opportunity to comment on any general guidelines which may be established by the Commission for environmental infrastructure projects for which it provides assistance, and on all applications for certification received by the Commission; and

(c) whereby the Board of Directors could receive complaints from groups affected by projects that the Commission has assisted or certified and could obtain independent assessments as to whether the terms of this Chapter or the procedures established by the Board of Directors pursuant to this Chapter have been observed.

SECTION 5. REIMBURSEMENT, FEES AND CHARGES

(a) The Commission may arrange for reimbursement of the costs of furnishing assistance on terms which the Commission deems appropriate.

(b) The Commission may establish reasonable fees or other charges for its assistance, including the processing of applications for certification.

Article III—Organization and Management

Section 1. Location of Offices

The Commission shall have its offices in the border region.

Section 2. Structure of the Commission

The Commission shall have a Board of Directors as specified in Chapter III, a General Manager, a Deputy General Manager, and such other officers and staff to perform such duties as the Commission may determine.

Section 3. General Manager

(a) The Board of Directors shall appoint a General Manager and a Deputy General Manager. The General Manager, under the direction of the Board of Directors, shall conduct the business of the Commission and shall be chief of its staff. The General Manager or his or her designee shall be the legal representative of the Commission. The General Manager and the Deputy General Manager each ordinarily shall serve a nonrenewable term of five years. The Board of Directors may remove the General Manager or the Deputy General Manager at any time. The offices of General Manager and Deputy General Manager shall alternate between nationals of the Parties. The General Manager and the Deputy General Manager shall be nationals of different Parties at all times.

(b) The General Manager shall exercise all the powers delegated to him or her by the Board of Directors. The General Manager may participate in meetings of the Board of Directors, but shall not vote at such meetings. Subject to the general control of the Board of Directors, the General Manager shall be responsible for the organization, appointment and dismissal of the officers and staff of the Commission.

(c) The General Manager, officers and staff of the Commission, in the discharge of their offices, shall owe their duty entirely to the Commission and to no other authority. The Parties shall respect the international character of this duty and shall refrain from all attempts to influence any of them in the discharge of their duties.

(d) In appointing the officers and staff, the General Manager shall, subject to the paramount importance of securing the highest standards of efficiency and technical competence, seek to achieve at each level a balanced proportion of nationals of each Party.

(e) The General Manager shall submit to the Board of Directors for its approval an annual program and budget for the Commission.

Section 4. Relationship to the International Boundary and Water Commission

(a) The Commission may enter into arrangements with the International Boundary and Water Commission ("IBWC") regarding facilities, personnel and services and arrangements for reimbursement of administrative and other expenses paid by one organization on behalf of the other.

(b) Nothing in this Chapter shall make the Commission liable for the acts or obligations of the IBWC, or the IBWC liable for the acts or obligations of the Commission.

(c) The Parties shall call upon the Commission and the IBWC to cooperate, as appropriate, with each other in planning, developing and carrying out border sanitation and other environmental activities.

SECTION 5. FUNDING

Each Party shall contribute an equal share of the budget of the Commission, subject to the availability of appropriated funds and in accordance with its domestic legal requirements. The Commission shall establish an account or accounts to receive such contributions from the Parties.

SECTION 6. CHANNEL OF COMMUNICATION

Each Party shall designate an appropriate authority with which the Commission may communicate in connection with any matter arising under this Chapter.

SECTION 7. ANNUAL REPORTS

(a) The Commission shall submit to the Parties an annual report in English and Spanish on its operations. The report shall be prepared by the General Manager and shall be approved by the Board of Directors. The annual report shall include an audited statement of the Commission's accounts.

(b) Copies of the annual report prepared under this section shall be made available to the public.

SECTION 8. LIMITATIONS ON DISCLOSURE

(a) Notwithstanding any other provision of this Chapter, the Commission, including its officers and staff, shall not make public information with respect to which a Party has notified the Commission that public disclosure would impede its law enforcement.

(b) The Commission shall establish regulations to protect from disclosure business or proprietary information and information the disclosure of which would violate personal privacy or the confidentiality of government decision-making.

(c) A party that requests assistance or submits an application to the Commission may request that information contained therein be designated confidential by the Commission, and may request an advance determination from the Commission as to whether such information is entitled to confidentiality pursuant to subsection (b) above. If the Commission determines that such information is not entitled to confidentiality pursuant to subsection (b) above, the party may withdraw its request or application prior to further action by the Commission. Upon such withdrawal, the Commission shall not keep any copy of the information and shall not make public that it received such a request or application.

Article IV—Status, Immunities and Privileges

Section 1. Scope of Article

To enable the Commission to fulfill its purpose and the functions with which it is entrusted, the status, immunities and privileges set forth in this Article shall be accorded to the Commission in the territories of each Party.

Section 2. Legal Status

(a) The Commission shall possess juridical personality and, in particular, full capacity:

(i) to contract;

(ii) to acquire and dispose of immovable and movable property; and

(iii) to institute legal proceedings.

(b) The Commission may exercise such other powers as shall be necessary in furtherance of its purpose and functions, consistent with the provisions of this Chapter.

Section 3. Judicial Proceedings

The Commission, its property and its assets, wherever located, and by whomsoever held, shall enjoy the same immunity from suit and every form of judicial process as is enjoyed by foreign governments, except to the extent that the Commission may expressly waive its immunity for the purposes of any proceedings or by the terms of any contract.

Section 4. Immunity of Assets

Property and assets of the Commission, wheresoever located and by whomsoever held, shall be considered public international property and shall be immune from search, requisition, confiscation, expropriation or any other form of taking or foreclosure by executive or legislative action.

Section 5. Inviolability of Archives

The archives of the Commission shall be inviolable.

Section 6. Freedom of Assets from Restrictions

To the extent necessary to carry out the purpose and functions of the Commission and to conduct its operations in accordance with this Chapter, all property and other assets of the Commission shall be free from restrictions, regulations, controls and moratoria of any nature, except as may otherwise be provided in this Chapter.

Section 7. Privilege for Communications

The official communications of the Commission shall be accorded by each Party the same treatment that it accords to the official communications of the other Party.

SECTION 8. PERSONAL IMMUNITIES AND PRIVILEGES

The directors, General Manager, Deputy General Manager, officers and staff of the Commission shall have the following privileges and immunities:

(a) immunity from legal process with respect to acts performed by them in their official capacity except when the Commission expressly waives this immunity;

(b) when not local nationals, the same immunities from immigration restrictions, alien registration requirements and national service obligations and the same facilities as regards exchange provisions as are accorded by each Party to the representatives, officials, and employees of comparable rank of the other Party; and

(c) the same privileges in respect of traveling facilities as are accorded by each Party to representatives, officials, and employees of comparable rank of the other Party.

SECTION 9. IMMUNITIES FROM TAXATION

(a) The Commission, its property, other assets, income, and the operations it carries out pursuant to this Chapter shall be immune from all taxation and from all customs duties. The Commission shall also be immune from any obligation relating to the payment, withholding or collection of any tax or customs duty.

(b) No tax shall be levied on or in respect of salaries and emoluments paid by the Commission to officers or staff of the Commission who are not local nationals of the country where the Commission has its principal office.

SECTION 10. IMPLEMENTATION

Each Party, in accordance with its juridical system, shall take such action as is necessary to make effective in its own territories the principles set forth in this Article, and shall inform the Commission of the action which it has taken on the matter.

ARTICLE V—TERMINATION OF OPERATIONS

(a) The Parties, by mutual agreement, may terminate the operations of the Commission. A Party may withdraw from the Commission by delivering to the Commission at its principal office a written notice of its intention to do so. Such withdrawal shall become finally effective on the date specified in the notice but in no event less than six months after the notice is delivered to the Commission. However, at any time before the withdrawal becomes finally effective, the Party may notify the Commission in writing of the cancellation of its notice of intention to withdraw. The Commission shall terminate its operations on the effective date of any notice of withdrawal from the Commission.

(b) After such termination of operations the Commission shall forthwith cease all activities, except those incident to the conservation, preservation, and realization of its assets and settlement of its obligations.

CHAPTER II—NORTH AMERICAN DEVELOPMENT BANK

ARTICLE I—PURPOSES AND FUNCTIONS

SECTION 1. PURPOSES

The purposes of the North American Development Bank shall be:

(a) to provide financing for projects certified by the Board of Directors in accordance with Articles I and II of Chapter I, and, as the Board of Directors deems appropriate, to otherwise assist the Commission in fulfilling its purposes and functions;

(b) to provide financing endorsed by the United States, as appropriate, for community adjustment and investment in support of the purposes of the North American Free Trade Agreement; and

(c) to provide financing endorsed by Mexico, as appropriate, for community adjustment and investment in support of the purpose of the North American Free Trade Agreement.

SECTION 2. FUNCTIONS

To implement its purposes, the Bank shall utilize its own capital resources, funds raised by it in financial markets, and other available resources and shall fulfill the following functions:

(a) to promote the investment of public and private capital contributing to its purposes;

(b) to encourage private investment in projects, enterprises, and activities contributing to its purposes, and to supplement private investment when private capital is not available on reasonable terms and conditions; and

(c) to provide, under the direction of the Board of Directors, technical and other assistance for the financing and the implementation of the plans and projects.

In carrying out its functions, the Bank shall cooperate as appropriate with national and international institutions and with private sources supplying investment capital.

ARTICLE II—CAPITAL OF THE BANK

SECTION 1. AUTHORIZED CAPITAL

(a) The authorized capital stock of the Bank initially shall be in the amount of $3,000,000,000 in United States dollars and shall be divided into 300,000 shares having a par value of $10,000 each, which shall be available for subscription by the Parties in accordance with Section 2 of this Article.

(b) The authorized capital stock shall be divided into paid-in shares and callable shares. $450,000,000 shall be paid-in shares, and $2,550,000,000 shall be callable for the purposes specified in Section 3 (d) of this Article.

(c) The authorized capital stock may be increased when the directors from the federal governments of the Parties on the Board of Directors by a unanimous vote deem it advisable, subject to the domestic legal requirements of the Parties.

SECTION 2. SUBSCRIPTION OF SHARES

(a) Each Party shall subscribe to shares of the capital stock of the Bank. The number of shares to be subscribed by the Parties shall be those set forth in Annex A of this Agreement, which specifies the obligation of each Party as to both paid-in and callable capital.

(b) Shares of capital stock subscribed by the Parties shall be issued at par, unless the Board of Directors decides in special circumstances to issue them on other terms.

(c) The liability of the Parties on capital shares shall be limited to the unpaid portion of their issue price.

(d) Shares of capital stock shall not be pledged or encumbered in any manner, and they shall be transferable only to the Bank.

SECTION 3. PAYMENT OF SUBSCRIPTIONS

Payment of the subscriptions to the capital stock of the Bank as set forth in Annex A shall be made as follows:

(a) As soon as possible after this Agreement enters into force pursuant to Article I of Chapter IV, but no later than thirty days thereafter, each Party shall deposit with the Bank an Instrument of Subscription in which it agrees to pay in either Party's currency to the Bank the amount of paid-in capital set forth for it in Annex A, and to accept the obligations of callable shares ("Unqualified Subscription"). Payment of the paid-in capital shall be due according to a schedule to be established by the Board of Directors after entry into force of this Agreement.

(b) Notwithstanding the provisions of paragraph (a) of this Section regarding Unqualified Subscriptions, as an exceptional case, a Party may deposit an Instrument of Subscription in which it agrees that payment of all installments of paid-in capital, and its obligations with respect to all callable shares, are subject to subsequent budgetary legislation ("Qualified Subscription"). In such an instrument, the Party shall undertake to seek to obtain the necessary legislation to pay the full amount of paid-in capital and to accept the full amount of corresponding obligations for callable shares, by the payment dates determined in accordance with paragraph (a) of this Section. Payment of an installment due after any such date shall be made within sixty days after the requisite legislation has been obtained.

(c) If any Party which has made a Qualified Subscription has not obtained the legislation to make payment in full of any installment (or to accept obligations in respect of callable shares) by the dates determined in accordance with paragraph (a) of this Section, then a Party which has paid the corresponding installment on time and in full, may, after consultation with the Board of Directors, direct the Bank in writing to restrict commitments against that installment. That restriction shall not exceed the percentage which the unpaid portion of the installment, due from the Party that has made the Qualified Subscription, bears to the entire amount of the installment to be paid by the Party, and shall be in effect only for the time that unpaid portion remains unpaid.

(d) The callable portion of the subscription for capital shares of the Bank shall be subject to call only when required to meet the obligations of the Bank created under Article III, Section 2 (b) and (c) of this Chapter on borrowings of funds for inclusion in the Bank's capital resources or guarantees chargeable to such resources. In the event of such a call, payment shall be made in either Party's currency. Calls on unpaid subscriptions shall be uniform in percentage on all shares.

SECTION 4. CAPITAL RESOURCES

As used in this Chapter, the term "capital resources" of the Bank shall be deemed to include the following:

(a) authorized capital, including both paid-in and callable shares, subscribed pursuant to Section 2 and 3 of this Article;

(b) all funds raised by borrowings under the authority of Article V, Section 1 (a) of this Chapter to which the commitment set forth in Section 3 (d) of this Article is applicable;

(c) all funds received in repayment of loans made with the resources indicated in paragraphs (a) and (b) of this section;

(d) all income derived from loans made from the aforementioned funds or from guarantees to which the commitment set forth in Section 3(d) of this Article is applicable; and

(e) all other income derived from any of the resources mentioned above.

ARTICLE III—GENERAL OPERATIONS

SECTION 1. USE OF RESOURCES

The resources and facilities of the Bank shall be used exclusively to implement the purposes and functions enumerated in Article I of this Chapter.

SECTION 2. METHODS OF MAKING OR GUARANTEEING LOANS

Subject to the conditions stipulated in this Article, the Bank may make or guarantee loans to either Party, or any agency or political subdivision thereof, and to any entity in the territory of a Party, in any of the following ways:

(a) by making or participating in direct loans with funds corresponding to the unimpaired paid-in capital and to its reserves and undistributed surplus;

(b) by making or participating in direct loans with funds raised by the Bank in capital markets, or borrowed or acquired in any other manner, for inclusion in the capital resources of the Bank; and

(c) by guaranteeing in whole or in part loans made to, or securities issued in connection with, projects.

SECTION 3. GRANTS

Subject to the conditions stipulated in this Article, the Bank shall make grants with funds corresponding to the Bank's unimpaired paid-in capital, reserves and undistributed surplus to either Party, or any agency or political subdivision thereof, and to any entity in the territory of a Party for purposes specified in Article I, Section 1(a) of this Chapter.

SECTION 4. LIMITATIONS ON OPERATIONS

The total amount outstanding of loans and guarantees made by the Bank in its operations shall not at any time exceed the total amount of the unimpaired subscribed capital of the Bank, plus the unimpaired reserves and undistributed surplus included in the capital resources of the Bank, as defined in Article II, Section 4 of this Chapter, exclusive of income on the capital resources that is assigned by decision of the Board of Directors to reserves not available for loans or guarantees.

SECTION 5. DIRECT LOAN AND GRANT FINANCING

In making grants or in making direct loans or participating in them, the Bank may provide financing in the currencies of the Parties to meet the costs and expenses related to the purposes of the grant or loan.

SECTION 6. RULES AND CONDITIONS FOR MAKING OR GUARANTEEING LOANS

(a) The Bank may make or guarantee loans, subject to the following rules and conditions:

(1) in considering a request for a loan or a guarantee, the Bank shall take into account the ability of the borrower to obtain the loan from private sources of financing on terms which, in the opinion of the Bank, are reasonable for the borrower, taking into account all pertinent factors;

(2) in making or guaranteeing a loan, the Bank shall pay due regard to prospects that the borrower and its guarantor, if any, will be in a position to meet their obligations under the loan contract;

(3) in the opinion of the Bank, the rate of interest, other charges and the schedule for repayment of principal are appropriate for the purposes or project in question; and

(4) in guaranteeing a loan made by other investors, the Bank shall receive suitable compensation for its risk.

(b) In addition to the rules and conditions set forth in paragraph (a) of this Section, the following rules and conditions shall apply to loans or guarantees made pursuant to a certification from the Board of Directors in accordance with Articles I and II of Chapter I:

(1) the Bank management shall have submitted a detailed financial proposal to the Board of Directors, and the Board of Directors shall have certified the project relating to such proposal;

(2) in approving a loan or guarantee for a project, the Board of Directors shall find that the project is economically/financially sound, and pay due regard to the prospects that the

project will generate sufficient revenues, by user fees or otherwise, to be self-sustaining or that funds will be available from other sources to meet debt servicing obligations; and

(3) loans made or guaranteed by the Bank shall be for financing specific projects.

SECTION 7. OPTIONAL CONDITIONS FOR MAKING OR GUARANTEEING LOANS

(a) In the case of loans or guarantees of loans to nongovernmental entities, the Bank may, when it deems it advisable, require that the Party in whose territory the project is to be carried out, or a public institution or a similar agency of the Party acceptable to the Bank, guarantee the repayment of the principal and the payment of interest and other charges on the loan.

(b) The Bank may attach such other conditions to the making of loans or guarantees as it deems appropriate.

SECTION 8. USE OF PROCEEDS

(a) The Bank shall impose no condition that the proceeds of a loan guaranteed or made, or a grant made, for the purposes specified in Article 1, Section 1(a) of this Chapter shall be spent in the territory of either Party.

(b) The Bank shall take the necessary measures to ensure that the proceeds of any loan made, guaranteed, or participated in, or any grant made, by the Bank are used only for the purposes for which the loan was granted, or the grant was made, with due attention to considerations of economy and efficiency.

SECTION 9. TERMS FOR DIRECT LOANS

Direct loan contracts made by the Bank in conformity with Section 5 and 6 of this Article shall establish:

(a) All the terms and conditions of each loan, including among others, provision for payment of principal, interest and other charges, maturities, and dates of payment; and

(b) The currency or currencies in which payment shall be made to the Bank.

SECTION 10. TERMS FOR GUARANTEES

(a) In making any guarantee pursuant to Section 2(c) of this Article, the Bank shall charge a guarantee fee, at a rate determined by the Bank, payable periodically on the amount of the loan outstanding.

(b) Guarantee contracts concluded by the Bank shall provide that the Bank may terminate its liability with respect to interest if, upon default by the borrower and by the guarantor, if any, the Bank offers to purchase, at par and interest accrued to a date designated in the offer, the bonds or other obligations guaranteed.

(c) In issuing guarantees, the Bank shall have power to determine any other terms and conditions.

SECTION 11. RULES AND CONDITIONS FOR MAKING GRANTS

(a) Before the Board of Directors may approve a grant (excluding technical assistance expenditures) for an environmental project in accordance with the purposes specified in Article 1, Section 1(a) of this Chapter, (i) the Bank management shall have submitted a detailed financial proposal to the Board of Directors, and (ii) the Board of Directors shall have certified the project relating to such proposal in accordance with Articles I and II of Chapter I.

(b) The Bank may attach such other conditions to the making of grants for the purposes specified in Article 1, Section 1(a) of this Chapter as it deems appropriate.

SECTION 12. RELATIONSHIP WITH OTHER ENTITIES

(a) The Bank may make arrangements or agreements with other entities, including multilateral development banks, regarding facilities, personnel and services and arrangements for reimbursement of administrative expenses paid by either entity on behalf of the other.

(b) Nothing in this Agreement shall make the Bank liable for the acts or obligations of an entity referred to in paragraph (a) of this Section, or any such entity liable for the acts or obligations of the Bank.

ARTICLE IV—COMMUNITY ADJUSTMENT AND INVESTMENT OPERATIONS

SECTION 1. COMMUNITY ADJUSTMENT AND INVESTMENT GRANTS

(a) Subject to the conditions stipulated in this Article and Article III of this Chapter, the Bank shall make grants to the United States or any agency or political subdivision thereof, and to any entity in the territory of the United States for purposes of community adjustment and investment specified in Article I, Section 1(b) of this Chapter.

(b) Subject to the conditions stipulated in this Article and Article III of this Chapter, the Bank shall make grants to Mexico or any agency or political subdivision thereof, and to any entity in the territory of Mexico for purposes of community adjustment and investment specified in Article I, Section 1(c) of this Chapter.

SECTION 2. RULES AND CONDITIONS FOR MAKING COMMUNITY ADJUSTMENT AND INVESTMENT GRANTS

(a) Notwithstanding Article VI of Chapter III, and subject to the limitations specified in Sections 5(a) and 5(b) of this Article, the Bank shall make grants for the purposes of community adjustment and investment specified in Article I, Section 1(b) of this Chapter pursuant to an endorsement by the United States. (b) Notwithstanding Article VI of Chapter III, and subject to the limitations specified in Sections 5(c) and 5(d) of this Article, the Bank shall make grants for the purposes of community adjustment and investment specified in Article I Section 1(c) of this Chapter pursuant to an endorsement by Mexico.

SECTION 3. METHODS OF MAKING COMMUNITY ADJUSTMENT AND INVESTMENT LOANS

Section 2 of Article III of this Chapter shall apply to any loans made or guaranteed by the Bank for the purposes specified in Article 1, Sections 1(b) or 1(c) of this Chapter.

SECTION 4. RULES AND CONDITIONS FOR MAKING OR GUARANTEEING COMMUNITY ADJUSTMENT AND INVESTMENT LOANS

In addition to the rules and conditions set forth in Section 6(a) of Article III of this Chapter and the optional rules and conditions set forth in Section 7 of Article III of this Chapter:

(a) loans and guarantees made for the purposes of community adjustment and investment specified in Article I, Section 1(b) of this Chapter shall require an endorsement from the United States; and

(b) loans and guarantees made for the purposes of community adjustment and investment specified in Article 1, Section 1(c) of this Chapter shall require an endorsement from Mexico.

SECTION 5. LIMITATIONS ON COMMUNITY ADJUSTMENT AND INVESTMENT OPERATIONS

In addition to the limitations on operations set forth in Section 4 of Article III of this Chapter:

(a) The total amount of loans, guarantees and grants provided for the purposes of community adjustment and investment specified in Article I, Section 1(b) of this Chapter, shall not exceed 10 percent of the sum of the paid-in capital actually paid to the Bank by the United States, and the amount of callable shares for which the United States has an unqualified subscription.

(b) The total amount of grants made pursuant to Section 1(a) of this Article, plus 15 percent of the total amount of loans and guarantees made for the purposes of community adjustment and investment specified in Article 1 Section 1(b) of this Chapter, shall not exceed 10 percent of the paid-in capital actually paid to the Bank by the United States.

(c) The total amount of loans, guarantees and grants provided for the purposes of community adjustment and investment specified in Article I, Section 1(c) of this Chapter, shall not exceed 10 percent of the sum of the paid-in capital actually paid to the Bank by Mexico, and the amount of callable shares for which Mexico has an unqualified subscription.

(d) The total amount of grants made pursuant to Section 1(b) of this Article, plus 15 percent of the total amount of loans and guarantees made for the purposes of community adjustment and investment specified in Article 1, Section 1(c) of this Chapter, shall not exceed 10 percent of the paid-in capital actually paid to the Bank by Mexico.

SECTION 6. APPLICABILITY OF ARTICLE III TO COMMUNITY ADJUSTMENT AND INVESTMENT OPERATIONS

Sections 1, 2, 4, 5, 6(a), 7, 8(b), 9 and 10 of Article III of this Chapter shall apply to Bank operations for the purposes specified in Article I, Sections 1(b) and 1(c) of this Chapter.

ARTICLE V—CURRENCIES

SECTION 1. USE OF CURRENCIES

(a) The Parties may not maintain or impose restrictions of any kind upon the use by the Bank or by any recipient from the Bank, for payment in any country, of the following:

(1) currencies received by the Bank in payment of each Party's subscription to shares of the Bank's capital;

(2) currencies of the Parties purchased with the resources referred to in (1) of this paragraph;

(3) currencies obtained by borrowings, pursuant to the provisions of Article V, Section 1(a) of this Chapter, for inclusion in the capital resources of the Bank;

(4) currencies received by the Bank in payment on account of principal, interest, or other charges in respect of loans made from the funds referred to in (1), (2) or (3) of this paragraph; and currencies received in payment of commissions and fees on all guarantees made by the Bank; and

(5) currencies received from the Bank pursuant to Article V Section 4(c) of this Chapter, in distribution of net profits.

(b) A Party's currency held by the Bank in its capital resources, which is not covered by paragraph (a) of this section, also may be used by the Bank or any recipient from the Bank for payments in any country without restriction of any kind.

(c) The Parties may not place any restrictions on the holding and use by the Bank, for making amortization payments or anticipating payment of, or repurchasing part or all of the Bank's own obligations, of currencies received by the Bank in repayment of direct loans made from borrowed funds included in the capital resources of the Bank.

SECTION 2. VALUATION OF CURRENCIES

(a) The amount of a currency other than the U.S. dollar paid for purposes of Section 3(a), (b) or (d) of Article II of this Chapter or Section 3 of this Article to discharge a U.S. dollar-denominated obligation shall be that amount which will yield to the Bank the U.S. dollar amount of such obligation.

(b) Whenever it shall become necessary under this Chapter to value any currency in terms of another currency, such valuation shall be determined by the Bank after consultation, if necessary, with the International Monetary Fund.

SECTION 3. METHODS OF CONSERVING CURRENCIES

The Bank shall accept from either Party promissory notes or similar securities issued by the government of the Party, or by the depository designated by such Party, in lieu of any part of the currency of the Party representing the paid-in portion of its subscription to the Bank's authorized capital, provided such currency is not required by the Bank for the conduct of its operations. Such notes or securities shall be non-negotiable, non-interest BECC-bearing, and payable to the Bank at their par value on demand. On the same conditions, the Bank shall also accept such notes or securities in lieu of any part of the subscription of a Party with respect to which part the terms of the subscription do not require payment in cash.

ARTICLE VI—MISCELLANEOUS POWERS AND DISTRIBUTION OF PROFITS

SECTION 1. MISCELLANEOUS POWERS OF THE BANK

In addition to the powers specified elsewhere in this Chapter, the Bank shall have the power to:

(a) borrow funds and in that connection to furnish such collateral or other security therefor as the Bank shall determine, provided that, before making a sale of its obligations in the markets of a Party, the Bank shall have obtained the approval of that country and of the Party in whose currency the obligations are denominated;

(b) invest funds not needed in its operations in such obligations as it may determine;

(c) guarantee securities in its portfolio for the purpose of facilitating their sale; and

(d) exercise such other powers as shall be necessary or desirable in furtherance of its purposes and functions, consistent with the provisions of this Chapter.

SECTION 2. WARNING TO BE PLACED ON SECURITIES

Every security issued or guaranteed by the Bank shall bear on its face a conspicuous statement to the effect that it is not an obligation of any government, unless it is in fact the obligation of a particular government, in which case it shall so state.

SECTION 3. METHODS OF MEETING THE LOSSES OF THE BANK

(a) In case of arrears or default on loans made, participated in, or guaranteed by the Bank, the Bank shall take such action as it deems appropriate. The Bank shall maintain appropriate provisions against possible losses.

(b) Losses arising in the Bank's operations shall be charged first, to the provisions referred to in paragraph (a); second, to net income; third, against its general reserve and surpluses; and fourth, against the unimpaired paid-in capital.

(c) Whenever necessary to meet contractual payments of interest, other charges, or amortization on the Bank's borrowings payable out of its capital resources, or to meet the Bank's liabilities with respect to similar payments on loans guaranteed by it chargeable to its capital resources, the Bank may call upon both Parties to pay an appropriate amount of their callable capital subscriptions, in accordance with Article II, Section 3 of this Chapter. Moreover, if the

Bank believes that a default may be of long duration, it may call an additional part of such subscriptions not to exceed in any one year one percent of the total subscriptions of the Parties to the capital resources, for the following purposes:

(1) to redeem prior to maturity, or otherwise discharge its liability on, all or part of the outstanding principal of any loan guaranteed by it chargeable to its capital resources in respect of which the debtor is in default; and

(2) to repurchase, or otherwise discharge its liability on, all or part of its own outstanding obligations payable out of its capital resources.

SECTION 4. DISTRIBUTION OR TRANSFER OF NET PROFITS AND SURPLUS

(a) The Board of Directors may determine periodically what part of the net profits and of the surplus of the capital resources shall be distributed. Such distributions may be made only when the reserves have reached a level which the Board of Directors considers adequate.

(b) The distributions referred to in paragraph (a) of this section shall be made from the capital resources in proportion to the payments on capital stock made by each Party.

(c) Payments pursuant to paragraph (a) of this section shall be made in such manner and in such currency or currencies as the Board of Directors shall determine. If such payments are made to a Party in currencies other than its own, the transfer of such currencies and their use by the receiving country shall be without restriction by either Party.

ARTICLE VII—ORGANIZATION AND MANAGEMENT

SECTION 1. STRUCTURE OF THE BANK

The Bank shall have a Board of Directors as specified in Chapter III, a Managing Director, a Deputy Managing Director, and such other officers and staff as may be considered necessary.

SECTION 2. DECISION-MAKING

All decisions of the Board of Directors shall be made as provided in Article VI of Chapter III.

SECTION 3. MANAGING DIRECTOR AND STAFF

(a) The Board of Directors shall appoint a Managing Director and a Deputy Managing Director of the Bank. The Managing Director, under the direction of the Board of Directors, shall conduct the business of the Bank and shall be chief of its staff. The Managing Director or his or her designee shall be the legal representative of the Bank. The Managing Director and Deputy Managing Director each ordinarily shall serve a nonrenewable term of five years. The Board of Directors may remove the Managing Director or the Deputy Managing Director at any time. The offices of the Managing Director and the Deputy Managing Director shall alternate between the nationals of the Parties. The Managing Director and the Deputy Managing Director shall be nationals of different Parties at all times.

(b) The Managing Director, officers and staff of the Bank, in the discharge of their offices, shall owe their duty entirely to the Bank and to no other authority. The Parties shall respect the international character of this duty and shall refrain from all attempts to influence any of them in the discharge of their duties.

(c) In appointing the officers and staff, the Managing Director shall, subject to the paramount importance of securing the highest standards of efficiency and technical competence, seek to achieve, at each level, a balance in the number of nationals from each Party.

(d) The Bank, its officers and staff shall not interfere in the political affairs of either Party, nor shall they be influenced in their decisions by the political character of the Party or Parties concerned. Only economic/financial considerations shall be relevant to their decisions, and these considerations shall be weighed impartially in order to achieve the purposes and functions stated in Article I of this Chapter.

Section 4. Publication of Reports and Provision of Information

(a) The Bank shall publish an annual report containing an audited statement of its accounts. It shall also transmit quarterly to the Parties a summary statement of its financial position and profit-and-loss statement showing the results of its operations.

(b) The Bank may also publish such other reports as it deems desirable to inform the public of its activities and to carry out its purposes and functions.

Article VIII—Suspension and Termination of Operations

Section 1. Suspension of Operations

In an emergency the Board of Directors may suspend operations in respect of loans, guarantees and grants until such time as the Board of Directors may have an opportunity to consider the situation and take pertinent measures.

Section 2. Termination of Operations

(a) The Parties, by mutual agreement, may terminate the operations of the Bank. A Party may withdraw from the Bank by delivering to the Bank at its principal office a written notice of its intention to do so. Such withdrawal shall become finally effective on the date specified in the notice but in no event less than six months after the notice is delivered to the Bank. However, at any time before the withdrawal becomes finally effective, the Party may notify the Bank in writing of the cancellation of its notice of intention to withdraw. The Bank shall terminate its operations on the effective date of any notice of withdrawal from the Bank.

(b) After such termination of operations the Bank shall forthwith cease all activities, except those incident to the conservation, preservation, and realization of its assets and settlement of its obligations.

SECTION 3. LIABILITY OF THE PARTIES AND PAYMENT OF CLAIMS

(a) The liability of the Parties arising from their subscriptions to the capital stock of the Bank shall continue until all direct and contingent obligations shall have been discharged.

(b) All creditors holding direct claims shall be paid out of the assets of the Bank and then out of payments to the Bank on unpaid or callable subscriptions. Before making any payments to creditors holding direct claims, the Board of Directors shall make such arrangements as are necessary, in its judgment, to ensure a pro rata distribution among holders of direct and contingent claims.

SECTION 4. DISTRIBUTION OF ASSETS

(a) No distribution of assets shall be made to either Party on account of their subscription to the capital stock of the Bank until all liabilities to creditors chargeable to such capital stock shall have been discharged or provided for. Moreover, such distribution must be approved by a decision of the Board of Directors.

(b) Any distribution of the assets of the Bank to the Parties shall be in proportion to payments on capital stock made by each Party and shall be effected at such times and under such conditions as the Bank shall deem fair and equitable. The shares of assets distributed need not be uniform as to type of assets. No Party shall be entitled to receive its shares in such a distribution of assets until it has settled all of its obligations to the Bank.

(c) A Party receiving assets distributed pursuant to this Article shall enjoy the same rights with respect to such assets as the Bank enjoyed prior to their distribution.

ARTICLE IX—STATUS, IMMUNITIES AND PRIVILEGES

SECTION 1. SCOPE OF ARTICLE

To enable the Bank to fulfill its purposes and the functions with which it is entrusted, the status, immunities, and privileges set forth in this Article shall be accorded to the Bank in the territories of each Party.

SECTION 2. LEGAL STATUS

The Bank shall possess juridical personality and, in particular, full capacity:

(a) to contract;

(b) to acquire and dispose of immovable and movable property; and

(c) to institute legal proceedings.

SECTION 3. JUDICIAL PROCEEDINGS

Actions may be brought against the Bank only in a court of competent jurisdiction in the territories of a Party in which the Bank has an office, has appointed an agent for the purpose of accepting service or notice of process, or has issued or guaranteed securities.

No action shall be brought against the Bank by the Parties or persons acting for or deriving claims from the Parties. However, the Parties shall have recourse to such special procedures to settle controversies between the Bank and its Parties as may be prescribed in this Chapter, in the by-laws and regulations of the Bank or in contracts or other agreements entered into with the Bank.

Property and assets of the Bank shall, wheresoever located and by whomsoever held, be immune from all forms of seizure, attachment or execution before the delivery of final judgment against the Bank.

SECTION 4. IMMUNITY OF ASSETS

Property and assets of the Bank, wheversoever located and by whomsoever held, shall be considered public international property and shall be immune from search, requisition, confiscation, expropriation or any other form of taking or foreclosure by executive or legislative action.

SECTION 5. INVIOLABILITY OF ARCHIVES

The archives of the Bank shall be inviolable.

SECTION 6. FREEDOM OF ASSETS FROM RESTRICTIONS

To the extent necessary to carry out the purposes and functions of the Bank and to conduct its operations in accordance with this Chapter, all property and other assets of the Bank shall be free from restrictions, regulations, controls and moratoria of any nature, except as may otherwise be provided in this Chapter.

SECTION 7. PRIVILEGE FOR COMMUNICATIONS

The official communications of the Bank shall be accorded by each Party the same treatment that it accords to the official communications of the other Party.

SECTION 8. PERSONAL IMMUNITIES AND PRIVILEGES

The directors, Managing Director, Deputy Managing Director, officers, and staff of the Bank shall have the following privileges and immunities:

(a) immunity from legal process with respect to acts performed by them in their official capacity, except when the Bank expressly waives this immunity;

(b) when not local nationals, the same immunities from immigration restrictions, alien registration requirements and national service obligations and the same facilities as regards exchange provisions as are accorded by the Parties to the representatives, officials, and employees of comparable rank of the other Party; and

(c) the same privileges in respect of traveling facilities as are accorded by the Parties to representatives, officials, and employees of comparable rank of members of the other Party.

Section 9. Immunities from Taxation

(a) The Bank, its property, other assets, income, and the operations it carries out pursuant to this Chapter shall be immune from all taxation and from all customs duties. The Bank shall also be immune from any obligation relating to the payment, withholding or collection of any tax or customs duty.

(b) No tax shall be levied on or in respect of any salaries or emoluments paid by the Bank to directors, officers or staff of the Bank who are not local nationals of the country where the Bank has its principal office.

(c) No tax of any kind shall be levied on any obligation or security issued by the Bank, including any dividend or interest thereon, by whomsoever held:

(1) which discriminates against such obligation or security solely because it is issued by the Bank; or

(2) if the sole jurisdictional basis for such taxation is the place or currency in which it is issued, made payable or paid, or the location of any office or place of business maintained by the Bank.

(d) No tax of any kind shall be levied on any obligation or security guaranteed by the Bank, including any dividend or interest thereon, by whomsoever held:

(1) which discriminates against such obligation or security solely because it is guaranteed by the Bank; or

(2) if the sole jurisdictional basis for such taxation is the location of any office or place of business maintained by the Bank.

Section 10. Implementation

Each Party, in accordance with its juridical system, shall take such action as is necessary to make effective in its own territories the principles set forth in this Article, and shall inform the Bank of the action that it has taken on the matter.

Article X—General Provisions

Section 1. Principal Office

The principal office of the Bank shall be located in a place to be mutually agreed by the Parties so as to facilitate the operations of the Bank.

Section 2. Relations with Other Organizations

The Bank may enter into arrangements or agreements with other organizations with respect to the exchange of information or for other purposes consistent with this Chapter.

Section 3. Channel of Communication

Each Party shall designate an official entity for purposes of communication with the Bank on matters connected with this Chapter.

Section 4. Depositories

Each Party shall designate its central bank to serve as a depository in which the Bank may keep its holdings of such Party's currency and other assets of the Bank. However, with the agreement of the Bank, a Party may designate another institution for such purpose.

Section 5. Commencement of Operations

The Parties shall call the first meeting of the Board of Directors as soon as this Agreement enters into force under Article I of Chapter V of this Agreement.

CHAPTER III—BECC–NADB BOARD OF DIRECTORS

Article I—Board of Directors

All the powers of the Commission and the Bank shall be vested in the Board of Directors of the Border Environment Cooperation Commission and the North American Development Bank.

Article II—Board Members

The Board of Directors shall have the following ten, appointed directors:

(1) the Secretary of the United States Department of the Treasury, or his/her delegate, who shall serve ex officio;

(2) the Secretary of Finance and Public Credit of Mexico, or his/her delegate, who shall serve ex officio;

(3) the Administrator of the Environmental Protection Agency of the United States, or his/her delegate, who shall serve ex officio;

(4) the Secretary of the Environment and Natural Resources of Mexico, or his/her delegate, who shall serve ex officio;

(5) the Secretary of the United States Department of State, or his/her delegate, who shall serve ex officio;

(6) the Secretary of the Ministry of External Affairs of Mexico, or his/her delegate, who shall serve ex officio;

(7) a representative of one of the U.S. border states, appointed by the United States in such manner as it may determine;

(8) a representative of one of the Mexican border states, appointed by Mexico in such manner as it may determine;

(9) a member of the United States public who is a resident of the border region, appointed by the United States in such manner as it may determine; and

(10) a member of the Mexican public who is a resident of the border region, appointed by Mexico in such manner as it may determine.

Article III—Chairperson

Each of the Parties, on an alternating basis, shall select one of the directors as Chairperson of the Board of Directors for a one-year term.

Article IV—Powers Reserved to the Board

The Board of Directors may delegate to the General Manager of the Commission or the Managing Director of the Bank the authority to exercise any powers of the Board of Directors, except the power to:

(a) certify environmental infrastructure projects in accordance with Article II, Section 3 of Chapter I;

(b) approve financing by the Bank for purposes specified in Article 1 Section 1(a) of Chapter II;

(c) approve the annual program, budget and report of the Commission and the Bank; and

(d) determine the salary and terms of contract of service for the General Manager and Deputy General Manager of the Commission, and the Managing Director and Deputy Managing Director of the Bank.

Article V—Board Meetings

The Board of Directors shall meet publicly at least twice each calendar year. The Board of Directors shall determine the location of its meetings. One public meeting each year shall be designated the Annual Meeting of the Board of Directors. A quorum for any meeting of the Board of Directors shall be a majority of the directors appointed by each of the Parties.

Article VI—Voting

Subject to Section 1(c) of Article II in Chapter II, all decisions of the Board of Directors shall require the approval of a majority of the directors appointed by each Party; provided that, in the case of any decision relating to or affecting project certification or financing, such majority shall include the directors representing the U.S. Department of the Treasury, Secretaría de Hacienda y Crédito Público, the Environmental Protection Agency of the United States, and SEMARNAT in order to ensure appropriate consideration of financial, technical and environmental matters. A written record of such decisions shall be made public in English and Spanish.

Article VII—General

Section 1. Rules and Regulations

The Board of Directors may adopt such rules and regulations as may be necessary or appropriate to conduct the business of the Commission and the Bank.

Section 2. Compensation

Directors shall serve as such without compensation for their services from the Commission or the Bank.

Section 3. Committees

The Board of Directors may establish such committees for the Commission or the Bank as it deems advisable.

CHAPTER IV—ENTRY INTO FORCE, AMENDMENT AND INTERPRETATION

Article I—Entry into Force

This Agreement shall enter into force on January 1, 1994, immediately after entry into force of the North American Free Trade Agreement, on an exchange of written notifications certifying the completion of necessary legal procedures.

Article II—Amendment

The Parties may agree on any modification of or addition to this Agreement. When so agreed, and approved in accordance with the applicable legal procedures of each Party, a modification or addition shall constitute an integral part of this Agreement.

Article III—Interpretation and Consultation

Section 1. Interpretation

The Parties shall at all times endeavor to agree on the interpretation and application of this Agreement, and shall make every effort to resolve any matter that might affect the implementation of this Agreement.

Section 2. Consultation

Upon the written request of either Party or the Board of Directors in English and Spanish, the Parties shall consult regarding the interpretation or application of this Agreement. These consultations shall take place within 30 days after a written request for consultation.

CHAPTER V—DEFINITIONS AND OTHER ARRANGEMENTS

Article I—Relations to Other Agreements or Arrangements

(a) Nothing in this Agreement shall prejudice other agreements or arrangements between the Parties, including those relating to conservation or the environment.

(b) Nothing in this Agreement shall be construed to limit the right of any public entity or private person of a Party to seek investment capital or other sources of finance, or to propose, construct or operate an environmental infrastructure project in the border region without the assistance or certification of the Board of Directors.

Article II—Definitions

For purposes of this Agreement, it shall be understood that:

Bank means the North American Development Bank established pursuant to Chapter II of this Agreement;

Board of Directors means the Board of Directors of the Border Environment Cooperation Commission and the North American Development Bank established pursuant to Chapter III of this Agreement;

Border region means the area in the United States that is within 100 kilometers of the international border between the United States and Mexico, and the area in Mexico that is within 300 kilometers of the international border between the United States and Mexico;

Commission means the Border Environment Cooperation Commission established pursuant to Chapter I of this Agreement;

Environmental infrastructure project means a project that will prevent, control or reduce environmental pollutants or contaminants, improve the drinking water supply, or protect flora and fauna so as to improve human health, promote sustainable development, or contribute to a higher quality of life;

Mexico means the United Mexican States;

Mexican border states means Baja California, Chihuahua, Coahuila, Nuevo Leon, Sonora and Tamaulipas;

National means a natural person who is citizen or permanent resident of a Party, including:

1) with respect to Mexico, a national or a citizen according to Articles 30 and 34, respectively of the Mexican Constitution; and

2) with respect to the United States, "national of the United States" as defined in the existing provisions of the Immigration and Nationality Act.

Nongovernmental organization means any scientific, professional, business, non-profit or public interest organization or association which is neither affiliated with, nor under the direction of, a government;

North American Development Bank means the bank established by the Parties pursuant to Chapter II of this Agreement;

United States means the United States of America; and

U.S. border states means Arizona, California, New Mexico and Texas.

The English and Spanish versions of this Agreement are equally authentic.

ANNEX A

INITIAL SUBSCRIPTIONS TO THE AUTHORIZED CAPITAL STOCK OF THE BANK

(in shares of US$10,000 each)

	Paid-in Capital Shares	Callable Shares	Total Subscription
United States	22,500	127,500	150,000
Mexico	22,500	127,500	150,000
TOTAL	45,000	255,000	300,000

L. FOREIGN ECONOMIC POLICY: TARIFF AND TRADE LAWS

CONTENTS

1. International Trade Functions

a. Agreement on Trade Relations Between the United States of America and the Hungarian People's Republic

Treaty done at Budapest, March 17, 1978; Presidential Proclamation 4560, April 7, 1978, 43 F.R. 15125; Entered into force, July 7, 1978

BY THE PRESIDENT OF THE UNITED STATES OF AMERICA

A PROCLAMATION

As President of the United States of America, acting through my representatives, I entered into the negotiation of an agreement on trade relations between the United States of America and the Hungarian People's Republic with representatives of the Hungarian People's Republic;

The negotiations were conducted in accordance with the requirements of the Trade Act of 1974 (P.L. 93–618, January 3, 1975; 88 Stat. 1978) ("the Act");

An "Agreement on Trade Relations Between the United States of America and the Hungarian People's Republic," in English and Hungarian, was signed on March 17, 1978, by representatives of the two Governments, and is annexed to this Proclamation;

The Agreement conforms to the requirements relating to bilateral commercial agreements specified in Section 405(b) of the Act;

Article XI of the Agreement provides that it shall enter into force on the date of exchange of written notices of acceptance by the Governments of the United States of America and the Hungarian People's Republic; and

Section 405(c) of the Act provides that a bilateral commercial agreement and a proclamation implementing such agreement shall take effect only if approved by the Congress;

NOW, THEREFORE, I, JIMMY CARTER, President of the United States of America, proclaim as follows:

(1) This Proclamation shall become effective, said Agreement shall enter into force according to its terms, and nondiscriminatory treatment shall be extended to the products of the Hungarian People's Republic in accordance with the terms of the said Agreement, on the date of exchange of written notices of acceptance in accordance with Article XI of the said Agreement; and

(2) General Headnote 3(e) of the Tariff Schedules of the United States is amended by deleting therefrom "Hungary" as of the effective date of this proclamation and a notice thereof shall be published in the FEDERAL REGISTER promptly thereafter.

IN WITNESS WHEREOF, I have signed this Proclamation this seventh day of April, in the year of our Lord one thousand nine hundred seventy-eight, and of the Independence of the United States of America the two hundred second.

JIMMY CARTER.

AGREEMENT ON TRADE RELATIONS BETWEEN THE UNITED STATES OF AMERICA AND THE HUNGARIAN PEOPLE'S REPUBLIC [1]

The Government of the United States of America and the Government of the Hungarian People's Republic;

DESIRING to develop further the friendship between the American and Hungarian peoples;

NOTING the steady improvement in relations between the two countries;

RECOGNIZING that the development of economic and commercial relations can contribute to a general strengthening of their relations;

ACKNOWLEDGING that favorable conditions for the further long-term expansion of trade and economic cooperation exist between the two countries and can be further expanded to the benefit of both countries;

DESIRING to develop long-term trade and economic cooperation based upon the principles of sovereign equality and mutual benefit;

REAFFIRMING the importance of the principles of the General Agreement on Tariffs and Trade for the trade policies of the two countries;

DETERMINED to give full effect to the Final Act of the Conference on Security and Cooperation in Europe signed on August 1, 1975;

HAVE AGREED as follows:

ARTICLE I—MOST FAVORED NATION TREATMENT

NONDISCRIMINATORY TRADE

1. The Parties shall apply between themselves the provisions of the General Agreement on Tariffs and Trade and the Protocol for the Accession of Hungary of August 8, 1973, as those provisions apply to each Party, provided that to the extent that any provision of the General Agreement or its Protocols is inconsistent with any provision of the Agreement, the latter shall apply.

2. The Parties agree to maintain a satisfactory balance of concession in trade and services during the period of this Agreement, and in particular to reciprocate satisfactorily reductions by the other Party in tariffs and non-tariff barriers to trade that result from multilateral negotiations.

ARTICLE II—EXPANSION OF TRADE

1. The Parties shall take appropriate measures to encourage and facilitate the exchange of goods and services on the basis of mutual

[1] 29 UST 2711; TIAS 8967.

advantage, and to secure favorable conditions for the continuous, long-term development of trade relations, between firms, enterprises and companies of the two countries.

2. The Parties recognize the significant role which economic, industrial and technical cooperation may play in the further development of their economic and trade relations. They confirm their readiness to encourage, promote and facilitate these forms of cooperation between interested firms, enterprises and companies of their respective countries in the fields of industry, agriculture trade and technology.

3. Commercial transactions will be effected on the basis of contracts to be concluded between firms, enterprises and companies of the two countries in accordance with applicable laws and regulations. Such contracts, including contracts for services, especially those for commercial, technical, financial, transportation and insurance services, will generally be concluded on the basis of commercial considerations on terms customary in international commercial practice.

Article III—Business Facilitation

1. Each party acknowledges that favorable conditions exist for the facilitation of business and the exchange of economic and commercial information in both countries. The Parties, through their laws and regulations, will continue to provide further business facilities, especially those indicated in this Article, to support the development of their mutual trade.

2. Firms, enterprises and companies of each Party shall be afforded access to all courts and, when applicable, to administrative bodies of the other Party as plaintiff or defendants, or otherwise, in accordance with the laws in force in the territory of such other Party, on the basis of most-favored-nation treatment.

3. Each Party shall permit firms, enterprises and companies of the other Party to advertise and promote its products and services and provide technical services, in compliance with the respective laws and regulations of each Party.

4. Each Party reaffirms its commitments made in the International Convention to Facilitate the Importation of Commercial Samples and Advertising Material, done at Geneva on November 7, 1952.

5. Firms, enterprises and companies of each Party may initiate and maintain contact with present and potential buyers, users and suppliers for authorized purposes, including the exchange of technical and economic information and for the purposes specified in contracts between firms, enterprises and companies of each Party, in accordance with laws and regulations in force.

6. Each Party shall permit and facilitate the entry, exit and safety within its territory of foreign employees and foreign representatives of the other Party's firms, enterprises and companies, subject to applicable laws and regulations.

7. Each Party will continue to publish and to make available economic and commercial information to promote trade and to help firms, enterprises and companies engaged in commercial activities.

8. Each Party will encourage the participation of its firms, enterprises and companies in trade promotional events such as fairs, exhibitions, missions and seminars in the other country. Similarly, each Party will encourage firms, enterprises and companies of the other Party to participate in trade promotional events in its territory. Subject to the laws in force within their territories, the Parties agree to allow the import and re-export on a duty free basis of all articles for use in promotional events, provided that such articles are not sold or other wise transferred.

9. Each Party agrees to provide its good offices to assist in the solution of business facilitation problems. For this purpose, each Party will designate appropriate organizations within its government to which firms, enterprises and companies of the other Party will have ready access in order to present business facilitation problems in cases where all normal channels have been exhausted.

10. Neither Party shall take measures which would unreasonably impair the contractual rights or other interests acquired within its territory by firms, enterprises and companies of the other Party.

11. Representation of the firms, enterprises and companies of one Party in the territory of the other shall be facilitated in accordance with the following provisions.

A. Each Party recognizes the value of representation in its territory of firms, enterprises and companies of the other Party, either by local firms, enterprises and companies on the basis of agency contracts, or by commercial representations, as defined in Article X paragraph 2, subject to laws and regulations of each Party.

B. They agree to facilitate the establishment and operation of such agency or commercial representations. Applications for any authorizations required for the establishment and operation of commercial representations shall be acted upon without delay.

C. Firms, enterprises and companies of each Party that have or desire to open commercial representations in the territory of the other Party shall be accorded treatment no less favorable than that accorded to firms, enterprises and companies of any third country.

D. Firms, enterprises and companies operating commercial representations may hire, directly compensate at lawful rates, and terminate the employment of nationals of the host country or of third countries, in accordance with laws and regulations in force in the host country. Persons other than local nationals may be employed in accordance with laws applicable to the entry and sojourn of aliens.

E. Commercial representations shall be permitted to import office equipment and automobiles for their operation, subject to applicable customs regulations. In the event of termination of the operation of a commercial representation, it shall be permitted to export equipment properly imported under this Article.

F. Each Party shall permit foreign employees of commercial representations of the other Party to reside in its territory along with their families, subject to its laws and regulations applicable to the entry and sojourn of aliens. Foreign employees of commercial representations shall be permitted to secure housing and office facilities.

G. Each Party shall normally issue multiple entry and exit visas to foreign employees of commercial representations and their families who are assigned in that capacity in its territory; such persons shall be permitted to import personal effects for personal use and not for any other person nor for sale duty free in accordance with applicable customs procedures. They shall be permitted to export their imported personal effects duty free.

H. The Parties recognize the value of facilitating the work of other persons who may be assigned in their territory in connection with activities related to this Agreement. To this end, the two preceding subparagraphs of this Article shall apply with respect to:

i. Foreign employees of joint ventures involving firms, enterprises and companies of both Parties who are assigned in the territory of the other Party for purposes of the joint venture; and

ii. Employees or other representatives of firms, enterprises or companies of either Party who are assigned in the territory of the other Party pursuant to sales or other contracts between firms, enterprises and companies of the Parties.

Article IV—Financial Provisions Relating to Trade

1. Firms, enterprises and companies of either Party will conduct their financial transactions with the firms, enterprises and companies of the other Party, including those specified in paragraphs 2 through 5, in accordance with applicable laws and regulations of each Party.

2. Financial transactions between firms, enterprises and companies of the two countries shall be carried out in United States dollars or any other freely convertible currency unless the parties to the transaction agree otherwise.

3. Each Party shall grant any authorizations which may be necessary to the firms, enterprises and companies of the other Party on the basis of most-favored-nation treatment with respect to:

A. Transactions involving payments, remittances and transfers of convertible currencies or financial instruments representative thereof between the territories of the two Parties, as well as between the territory of that Party and that of any third country;

B. Rates of exchange and matters relating thereto;

C. Opening and maintaining accounts in local and any convertible currency in financial institutions and with respect to use of such currencies.

4. Expenditures in the territory of a Party by firms, enterprises and companies of the other Party may be made in local currency received in an authorized manner.

5. Except in time of declared national emergency, neither Party shall place restrictions upon the export from its territory of freely

convertible currencies or deposits, or instruments representative thereof, by the firms, enterprises and companies or Government of the other Party, provided such currencies, deposits, or instruments were received in an authorized manner.

ARTICLE V—INDUSTRIAL PROPERTY, COPYRIGHTS AND INDUSTRIAL RIGHTS AND PROCESSES

1. Each Party reaffirms the commitments made with respect to industrial property in the Paris Convention for the Protection of Industrial Property as revised at Stockholm on July 14, 1967.

2. Each Party reaffirms the commitments made in the Universal Copyright Convention of September 6, 1952, as revised at Paris on July 24, 1971.

3. Each Party shall provide to the firms, enterprises and companies of the other Party national treatment of most-favored-nation treatment, whichever is more favorable, with respect to legal protection of other industrial rights and processes.

ARTICLE VI—GOVERNMENT COMMERCIAL OFFICES

1. In order to promote the expansion of trade and economic cooperation between the Parties, each Party will permit and facilitate the establishment and operation of a government commercial office of the other Party as an integral part of its Embassy. This office may be located in premises separate from those occupied by the Embassy. The opening of branches of such government commercial offices shall be the subject of separate arrangements between the Parties. Representatives of firms, companies and enterprises of either Party shall have for commercial purposes full access to these offices.

2. Government commercial offices, and their respective officers and staff members, to the extent that they enjoy diplomatic immunity, shall not function as agents or principals in commercial transactions, or enter into contractual agreements on behalf of commercial organizations, or engage in other commercial activities inconsistent with their diplomatic status. They may, however, engage in general trade promotion activity.

ARTICLE VII—MARKET DISRUPTION SAFEGUARDS

1. The Parties agree to consult promptly at the request of either Party whenever either actual or prospective imports of products originating in the territory of the other Party cause or threaten to cause or significantly contribute to market disruption. Market disruption exists within a domestic industry whenever imports of an article, like or directly competitive with an article produced by such domestic industry, are increasing rapidly, either absolutely or relatively, so as to be a significant cause of material injury, or threat thereof, to such domestic industry.

2. Either Party may impose restrictions, limitations or price measures on imports originating in the territory of the other Party to prevent or remedy actual or threatened market disruption.

3. The procedures for application of this Article are set forth in the Annex.

Article VIII—Settlement of Commercial Disputes

1. The Parties encourage the prompt and equitable settlement of commercial disputes between their firms, enterprises and companies.

2. Both Parties endorse the adoption of arbitration for the settlement of such disputes not otherwise amicably resolved. The Parties encourage their respective firms, enterprises and companies to provide in their contracts for arbitration under internationally recognized place of arbitration rules. Such agreements may specify a place of arbitration in a country other than the Hungarian People's Republic or the United States of America that is a Party to the 1958 Convention for the Recognition and Enforcement of Foreign Arbitral Awards. Parties to the contract may provide for any other place or rules of arbitration.

Article IX—National Security

The provisions of this Agreement shall not limit the right of either Party to take any action for the protection of its security interests.

Article X—Definitions

1. As used in this Agreement, the term "firms, enterprises and companies" of the United States means nationals, firms and companies of the United States, engaged in commercial activities. "Firms, enterprises and companies" of the Hungarian People's Republic means firms, enterprises, companies and other legal persons authorized under the laws and regulations of the Hungarian People's Republic to carry on foreign trade or other activities mentioned in the respective paragraphs.

2. As used in this Agreement, the term "commercial representations" shall mean, in the case of representations established in the United States, any form of lawful business or commercial representation, other than representation by a U.S. firm, enterprise or company pursuant to an agency contract.

In the case of commercial representations established in the Hungarian People's Republic, the term shall mean direct commercial representations as provided for in Decree 8 of 1974 of the Minister of Foreign Trade, section 1, paragraph 3.

Article XI—Entry into Force, Duration and Review

1. This Agreement, including its Annex and the three attached letters, which are integral parts of the Agreement, shall enter into force on the date of exchange of written notices of acceptance by the two Governments,[2] and shall remain in force as provided in paragraph 2 of this Article.

2. A. The initial term of this Agreement shall be three years, subject to subparagraph B. of this paragraph.

---

[2] July 7, 1978.

B. If either Party encounters or foresees a problem concerning its domestic legal authority to carry out any of its obligations under this Agreement, such Party shall request immediate consultations with the other Party. Once consultations have been requested, the other Party shall enter into such consultations as soon as possible concerning the circumstances that have arisen with a view to finding a solution to avoid action under subparagraph C.

C. If either Party does not have domestic legal authority to carry out its obligations under this Agreement, either Party may suspend the application of this Agreement or, with the agreement of the other Party, any part of this Agreement. In that event, the Parties will, to the fullest extent practicable and consistent with domestic law, seek to minimize disruption to existing trade relations between the two countries.

D. This Agreement shall be extended for successive periods of three years each unless either Party has given written notice to the other Party of the termination of this Agreement at least 30 days prior to its expiration.

3. The Parties agree to consult at the request of either Party to review the operation of this Agreement and other relevant aspects of the relations between the Parties.

IN WITNESS WHEREOF, the authorized representatives of the Parties have signed this Agreement.

DONE at Budapest on this seventeenth day of March, 1978, in two original copies, in the English and Hungarian languages, both texts being equally authentic.

ANNEX

1. A. In the consultations provided for under Article VII the Parties shall present and examine the factors relating to those imports that may be causing or threatening to cause, or significantly contributing to market disruption, as described in paragraph 1 of the Article VII, and seek means of preventing or remedying such market disruption. They shall take due account of any contracts between firms, enterprises and companies of the two countries concluded prior to the request for consultations and shall seek not to impair unreasonably rights of importers and exporters under such contracts. Such consultations shall provide for a review of the production, market, and trade situation of the product involved and may include such factors as trends in domestic production, profits of firms within the industry, the employment situation, sales, inventories, rates of increase of imports, market share, level and prices of imports, sources of supply, the situation of the exporter and any other aspect which may contribute to the examination of the situation. In the consultation the partners shall take due account whether newly marketed or well established products are involved; the mere appearance of a new product or products on the market may not necessarily be interpreted as a significant cause of material injury or as significantly contributing to market disruption. Such consultations shall be initiated promptly and concluded within ninety days of the request, unless otherwise agreed.

B. Unless a different solution is agreed upon, restrictions or limitations determined by the importing Party to be necessary to prevent or remedy the market disruption in question shall be implemented. The other Party shall then be free to deviate from its obligations to the first Party in respect of substantially equivalent trade as provided in the General Agreement on Tariffs and Trade.

C. In critical circumstances, where delay would cause damage difficult to repair, such preventive or remedial action may be taken provisionally without prior consultation on the condition that consultation shall be effected immediately after taking such action.

2. A. In accordance with applicable laws and regulations, each Party shall take appropriate measures to ensure that export from its country of the products concerned do not exceed the quantities or vary from the restrictions established for imports of such products into the other country pursuant to paragraph 1 of this Annex.

B. Each Party may take appropriate measures with respect to imports into its country to ensure that imports of products originating in the other country comply with such quantitative limitations or other restrictions.

b. Agreement on Trade Relations Between the United States of America and the People's Republic of China

Done at Beijing, July 7, 1979; Presidential Proclamation 4697, October 23, 1979, 44 F.R. 61161; Entered into force, February 1, 1980

BY THE PRESIDENT OF THE UNITED STATES OF AMERICA

A PROCLAMATION

As President of the United States of America, acting through my representatives, I entered into the negotiation of an agreement on trade relations between the United States of America and the People's Republic of China with representatives of the People's Republic of China;

The negotiations were conducted in accordance with the requirements of the Trade Act of 1974 (P.L. 93–618, January 3, 1975; 88 Stat. 1978) ("the Act");

An "Agreement on Trade Relations between the United States of America and the People's Republic of China", in English and Chinese, was signed on July 7, 1979, by representatives of the two Governments, and is annexed to this Proclamation;

The Agreement conforms to the requirements relating to bilateral commercial agreements specified in section 405(b) of the Act;

Article X of the Agreement provides that it shall come into force on the date on which the Contracting Parties have exchanged notifications that each has completed the legal procedures necessary for this purpose; and

Section 405(c) of the Act provides that a bilateral commercial agreement and a proclamation implementing such agreement shall take effect only if approved by the Congress;

NOW, THEREFORE, I, JIMMY CARTER, President of the United States of America, proclaim as follows:

(1) This Proclamation shall become effective, said Agreement shall enter into force according to its terms, and nondiscriminatory treatment shall be extended to the products of the People's Republic of China in accordance with the terms of the said Agreement, on the date on which the Contracting Parties have exchanged notifications that each has completed the legal procedures necessary for this purpose in accordance with Article X of the said Agreement

(2) General Headnote 3(e) of the Tariff Schedules of the United States is amended by deleting therefrom "China (any part of which may be under Communist domination or control)" and "Tibet" as of the effective date of this proclamation and a notice thereof shall be published in the FEDERAL REGISTER promptly thereafter.

IN WITNESS WHEREOF, I have hereunto set my hand this twenty-third day of October, in the year of our Lord nineteen hundred and seventy-nine, and of the Independence of the United States of America the two hundred and fourth.

JIMMY CARTER.

AGREEMENT ON TRADE RELATIONS BETWEEN THE UNITED STATES OF AMERICA AND THE PEOPLE'S REPUBLIC OF CHINA [1]

The Government of the United States of America and the Government of the People's Republic of China;

ACTING in the spirit of the Joint Communique on the Establishment of Diplomatic Relations between the United States of America and the People's Republic of China;

DESIRING to enhance friendship between both peoples;

WISHING to develop further economic and trade relations between both countries on the basis of the principles of equality and mutual benefit as well as nondiscriminatory treatment;

HAVE AGREED AS FOLLOWS:

ARTICLE I

1. The Contracting Parties undertake to adopt all appropriate measures to create the most favorable conditions for strengthening, in all aspects, economic and trade relations between the two countries so as to promote the continuous, long-term development of trade between the two countries.

2. In order to strive for a balance in their economic interests, the Contracting Parties shall make every effort to foster the mutual expansion of their reciprocal trade and to contribute, each by its own means, to attaining the harmonious development of such trade.

3. Commercial transactions will be effected on the basis of contracts between firms, companies and corporations, and trading organizations of the two countries. They will be concluded on the basis of customary international trade practice and commercial considerations such as price, quality, delivery and terms of payment.

ARTICLE II

1. With a view to establishing their trade relations on a nondiscriminatory basis, the Contracting Parties shall accord each other most-favored-nation treatment with respect to products originating in or destined for the other Contracting Party, i.e., any advantage, favor, privilege, or immunity they grant to like products originating in or destined for any other country or region, in all matters regarding:

(A) Customs duties and charges of all kinds applied to the import, export, re-export or transit of products, including the rules, formalities and procedures for collection of such duties and charges;

[1] 31 UST 4651; TIAS 9630.

(B) Rules, formalities and procedures concerning customs clearance, transit, warehousing and transshipment of imported and exported products;

(C) Taxes and other internal charges levied directly or indirectly on imported or exported products or services;

(D) All laws, regulations and requirements affecting all aspects of internal sale, purchase, transportation, distribution or use of imported products; and

(E) Administrative formalities for the issuance of import and export licenses.

2. In the event either Contracting Party applies quantitative restrictions to certain products originating in or exported to any third country or region, it shall afford to all like products originating in or exported to the other country treatment which is equitable to that afforded to such third country or region.

3. The Contracting Parties note, and shall take into consideration in the handling of their bilateral trade relations, that, at its current state of economic development, China is a developing country.

4. The principles of Paragraph 1 of this Article will be applied by the Contracting Parties in the same way as they are applied under similar circumstances under any multilateral trade agreement to which either Contracting Party is a party on the date of entry into force of this Agreement.

5. The Contracting Parties agree to reciprocate satisfactorily concessions with regard to trade and services, particularly tariff and non-tariff barriers to trade, during the term of this Agreement.

Article III

For the purpose of promoting economic and trade relations between their two countries, the Contracting Parties agree to:

A. Accord firms, companies and corporations, and trading organizations of the other Party treatment no less favorable than is afforded to any third country or region;

B. Promote visits by personnel, groups and delegations from economic, trade and industrial circles; encourage commercial exchanges and contacts; and support the holding of fairs, exhibitions and technical seminars in each other's country;

C. Permit and facilitate, subject to their respective laws and regulations and in accordance with physical possibilities, the stationing of representatives, or the establishment of business offices, by firms, companies and corporations, and trading organizations of the other Party in its own territory; and

D. Subject to their respective laws and regulations and physical possibilities, further support trade promotions and improve all conveniences, facilities and related services for the favorable conduct of business activities by firms, companies and corporations, and trading organizations of the two countries, including various facilities in respect of office space and residential housing, telecommunications, visa issuance, internal business travel, customs formalities for entry and re-export of personal effects, office articles and commercial samples, and observance of contracts.

Article IV

The Contracting Parties affirm that government trade offices contribute importantly to the development of their trade and economic relations. They agree to encourage and support the trade promotion activities of these offices. Each Party undertakes to provide facilities as favorable as possible for the operation of these offices in accordance with their respective physical possibilities.

Article V

1. Payments for transactions between the United States of America and the People's Republic of China shall either be effected in freely convertible currencies mutually accepted by firms, companies and corporations, and trading organizations of the two countries, or made otherwise in accordance with agreements signed by and between the two parties to the transaction. Neither Contracting Party may impose restrictions on such payments except in time of declared national emergency.

2. The Contracting Parties agree, in accordance with their respective laws, regulations and procedures, to facilitate the availability of official export credits on the most favorable terms appropriate under the circumstances for transactions in support of economic and technological projects and products between firms, companies and corporations, and trading organizations of the two countries. Such credits will be the subject of separate arrangements by the concerned authorities of the two Contracting Parties.

3. Each Contracting Party shall provide, on the basis of most-favored-nation treatment, and subject to its respective laws and regulations, all necessary facilities for financial, currency and banking transactions by nationals, firms, companies and corporations, and trading organizations of the other Contracting Party on terms as favorable as possible. Such facilities shall include all required authorizations for international payments, remittances and transfers, and uniform application of rates of exchange.

4. Each Contracting Party will look with favor towards participation by financial institutions of the other country in appropriate aspects of banking services related to international trade and financial relations. Each Contracting Party will permit those financial institutions of the other country established in its territory to provide such services on a basis no less favorable than that accorded to financial institutions of other countries.

Article VI

1. Both Contracting Parties in their trade relations recognize the importance of effective protection of patents, trademarks and copyrights.

2. Both Contracting Parties agree that on the basis of reciprocity legal or natural persons of either Party may apply for registration of trademarks and acquire exclusive rights thereto in the territory of the other Party in accordance with its laws and regulations.

3. Both Contracting Parties agree that each Party shall seek, under its laws and with due regard to international practice, to ensure to legal or natural persons of the other Party protection of patents and trademarks equivalent to the patent and trademark protection correspondingly accorded by the other Party.

4. Both Contacting Parties shall permit and facilitate enforcement of provisions concerning protection of industrial property in contracts between firms, companies and corporations, and trading organizations of their respective countries, and shall provide means, in accordance with their respective laws, to restrict unfair competition involving unauthorized use of such rights.

5. Both Contracting Parties agree that each Party shall take appropriate measures, under its laws and regulations and with due regard to international practice, to ensure to legal or natural persons of the other Party protection of copyrights equivalent to the copyright protection correspondingly accorded by the other Party.

Article VII

1. The Contracting Parties shall exchange information on any problems that may arise from their bilateral trade, and shall promptly hold friendly consultations to seek mutually satisfactory solutions to such problems. No action shall be taken by either Contracting Party before such consultations are held.

2. However, if consultations do not result in a mutually satisfactory solution within a reasonable period of time, either Contracting Party may take such measures as it deems appropriate. In an exceptional case where a situation does not admit any delay, either Contracting Party may take preventive or remedial action provisionally, on the condition that consultation shall be effected immediately after taking such action.

3. When either Contracting Party takes measures under this Article, it shall ensure that the general objectives of this Agreement are not prejudiced.

Article VIII

1. The Contracting Parties encourage the prompt and equitable settlement of any disputes arising from or in relation to contracts between their respective firms, companies and corporations, and trading organizations, through friendly consultations, conciliation or other mutually acceptable means.

2. If such disputes cannot be settled promptly by any one of the above-mentioned means, the parties to the dispute may have recourse to arbitration for settlement in accordance with provisions specified in their contracts or other agreements to submit to arbitration. Such arbitration may be conducted by an arbitration institution in the People's Republic of China, the United States of America, or a third country. The arbitration rules of procedure of the relevant arbitration institution are applicable, and the arbitration rules of the United Nations Commission on International Trade Law recommended by the United Nations, or other international arbitration rules, may also be used where acceptable to the parties to the dispute and to the arbitration institution.

3. Each Contracting Party shall seek to ensure that arbitration awards are recognized and enforced by their competent authorities where enforcement is sought, in accordance with applicable laws and regulations.

ARTICLE IX

The provisions of this Agreement shall not limit the right of either Contracting Party to take any action for the protection of its security interests.

ARTICLE X

1. This Agreement shall come into force on the date on which the Contracting Parties have exchanged notifications that each has completed the legal procedures necessary for this purpose, and shall remain in force for three years.
2. This Agreement shall be extended for successive terms of three years if neither Contracting Party notifies the other of its intent to terminate this Agreement at least 30 days before the end of a term.
3. If either Contracting Party does not have domestic legal authority to carry out its obligations under this Agreement, either Contracting Party may suspend application of this Agreement, or, with the agreement of the other Contracting Party, any part of this Agreement. In that event, the Parties will seek, to the fullest extent practicable in accordance with domestic law, to minimize unfavorable effects on existing trade relations between the two countries.
4. The Contracting Parties agree to consult at the request of either Contracting Party to review the operation of this Agreement and other relevant aspects of the relations between the two Parties.

IN WITNESS WHEREOF; the authorized representatives of the Contracting Parties have signed this Agreement.

DONE at Beijing in two original copies this seventh day of July, 1979, in English and Chinese, both texts being equally authentic.

2. Hostage Return and Economic Relations with Iran

a. Declaration of the Government of the Democratic and Popular Republic of Algeria

The Government of the Democratic and Popular Republic of Algeria, having been requested by the Governments of the Islamic Republic of Iran and the United States of America to serve as an intermediary in seeking a mutually acceptable resolution of the crisis in their relations arising out of the detention of the 52 United States nationals in Iran, has consulted extensively with the two governments as to the commitments which each is willing to make in order to resolve the crisis within the framework of the four points stated in the resolution of November 2, 1980, of the Islamic Consultative Assembly of Iran. On the basis of formal adherences received from Iran and the United States, the Government of Algeria now declares that the following interdependent commitments have been made by the two governments:

GENERAL PRINCIPLES

The undertakings reflected in this Declaration are based on the following general principles:

A. Within the framework of and pursuant to the provisions of the two Declarations of the Government of the Democratic and Popular Republic of Algeria, the United States will restore the financial position of Iran, in so far as possible, to that which existed prior to November 14, 1979. In this context, the United States commits itself to ensure the mobility and free transfer of all Iranian assets within its jurisdiction, as set forth in Paragraphs 49.

B. It is the purpose of both parties, within the framework of and pursuant to the provisions of the two Declarations of the Government of the Democratic and Popular Republic of Algeria, to terminate all litigation as between the Government of each party and the nationals of the other, and to bring about the settlement and termination of all such claims through binding arbitration. Through the procedures provided in the Declaration, relating to the Claims Settlement Agreement, the United States agrees to terminate all legal proceedings in the United States courts involving claims of United States persons and institutions against Iran and its state enterprises, to nullify all attachments and judgments obtained therein, to prohibit all further litigation based on such claims, and to bring about the termination of such claims through binding arbitration.

Point I. Non-Intervention in Iranian Affairs

1. The United States pledges that it is and from now on will be the policy of the United States not to intervene, directly or indirectly, politically or militarily, in Iran's internal affairs.

Points II and III. Return of Iranian Assets and Settlement of U.S. Claims

2. Iran and the United States (hereinafter "the parties") will immediately select a mutually agreeable central bank (hereinafter "the Central Bank") to act, under the instructions of the Government of Algeria and the Central Bank of Algeria (hereinafter "The Algerian Central Bank") as depositary of the escrow and security funds hereinafter prescribed and will promptly enter into depositary arrangements with the Central Bank in accordance with the terms of this declaration. All funds places in escrow with the Central Bank pursuant to this declaration shall be held in an account in the name of the Algerian Central Bank. Certain procedures for implementing the obligations set forth in this Declaration and in the Declaration of the Democratic and Popular Republic of Algeria concerning the settlement of claims by the Government of the United States and the Government of the Islamic Republic of Iran (hereinafter "the Claims Settlement Agreement") are separately set forth in certain Undertakings of the Government of the United States of America and the Government of the Islamic Republic of Iran with respect to the Declaration of the Democratic and Popular Republic of Algeria.

3. The depositary arrangement shall provide that, in the event that the Government of Algeria certifies to the Algerian Central Bank that the 52 U.S. nationals have safely departed from Iran, the Algerian Central Bank will thereupon instruct the Central Bank to transfer immediately all monies or other assets in escrow with the Central Bank pursuant to this declaration, provided that at any time prior to the making of such certification by the Government of Algeria, each of the two parties, Iran and the United States, shall have the right on seventy-two hours notice to terminate its commitments under this declaration.

If such notice is given by the United States and the foregoing certification is made by the Government of Algeria within the seventy-two hour period of notice, the Algerian Central Bank will thereupon instruct the Central Bank to transfer such monies and assets. If the seventy-two hour period of notice by the United States expires without such a certification having been made, or if the notice of termination is delivered by Iran, the Algerian Central Bank will thereupon instruct the Central Bank to return all such monies and assets to the United States, and thereafter the commitments reflected in this declaration shall be of no further force and effect.

ASSETS IN THE FEDERAL RESERVE BANK

4. Commencing upon completion of the requisite escrow arrangements with the Central Bank, the United States will bring about the transfer to the Central Bank of all gold bullion which is owned by Iran and which is in the custody of the Federal Reserve Bank of New York, together with all other Iranian assets (or the cash equivalent thereof) in the custody of the Federal Reserve Bank of New York, to be held by the Central Bank in escrow until such time as their transfer or return is required by Paragraph 3 above.

ASSETS IN FOREIGN BRANCHES OF U.S. BANKS

5. Commencing upon the completion of the requisite escrow arrangements with the Central Bank, the United States will bring about the transfer to the Central Bank, to the account of the Algerian Central Bank, of all Iranian deposits and securities which on or after November 14, 1979, stood upon the books of overseas banking offices of U.S. banks, together with interest thereon through December 31, 1980, to be held by the Central Bank, to the account of the Algerian Central Bank, in escrow until such time as their transfer or return is required in accordance with Paragraph 3 of this Declaration.

ASSETS IN U.S. BRANCHES OF U.S. BANKS

6. Commencing with the adherence by Iran and the United States to this declaration and the claims settlement agreement attached hereto, and following the conclusion of arrangements with the Central Bank for the establishment of the interest-bearing security account specified in that agreement and Paragraph 7 below, which arrangements will be concluded within 30 days from the date of this Declaration, the United States will act to bring about the transfer to the Central Bank, within six months from such date, of all Iranian deposits and securities in U.S. banking institutions in the United States, together with interest thereon, to be held by the Central Bank in escrow until such time as their transfer or return is required by Paragraph 3.

7. As funds are received by the Central Bank pursuant to Paragraph 6 above, the Algerian Central Bank shall direct the Central Bank to (1) transfer one-half of each such receipt to Iran and (2) place the other half in a special interest-bearing security account in the Central Bank, until the balance in the security account has reached the level of $1 billion. After the $1 billion balance has been achieved, the Algerian Central Bank shall direct all funds received pursuant to Paragraph 6 to be transferred to Iran. All funds in the security account are to be used for the sole purpose of securing the payment of, and paying, claims against Iran in accordance with the claims settlement agreement. Whenever the Central Bank shall thereafter notify Iran that the balance in the security account has fallen below $500 million, Iran shall promptly make new deposits sufficient to maintain a minimum balance of $500 million in the account. The account shall be so maintained until the President of the Arbitral Tribunal established pursuant to the claims settlement agreement has certified to the Central Bank of Algeria that all arbitral awards against Iran have been satisfied in accordance with the claims settlement agreement, at which point any amount remaining in the security account shall be transferred to Iran.

OTHER ASSETS IN THE U.S. AND ABROAD

8. Commencing with the adherence of Iran and the United States to this declaration and the attached claims settlement agreement and the conclusion of arrangements for the establishment of the security account, which arrangements will be concluded within 30 days from the date of this Declaration, the United States will act

to bring about the transfer to the Central Bank of all Iranian financial assets (meaning funds or securities) which are located in the United States and abroad, apart from those assets referred to in Paragraphs 5 and 6 above, to be held by the Central Bank in escrow until their transfer or return is required by Paragraph 3 above.

9. Commencing with the adherence by Iran and the United States to this declaration and the attached claims settlement agreement and the making by the Government of Algeria of the certification described in Paragraph 3 above, the United States will arrange, subject to the provisions of U.S. law applicable prior to November 14, 1979, for the transfer to Iran of all Iranian properties which are located in the United States and abroad and which are not within the scope of the preceding paragraphs.

NULLIFICATION OF SANCTIONS AND CLAIMS

10. Upon the making by the Government of Algeria of the certification described in Paragraph 3 above, the United States will revoke all trade sanctions which were directed against Iran in the period November 4, 1979, to date.

11. Upon the making by the Government of Algeria of the certification described in Paragraph 3 above, the United States will promptly withdraw all claims now pending against Iran before the International Court of Justice and will thereafter bar and preclude the prosecution against Iran of any pending or future claims of the United States or a United States national arising out of events occurring before the date of this declaration related to (A) the seizure of the 52 United States nationals on November 4, 1979, (B) their subsequent detention, (C) injury to United States property or property of the United States nationals within the United States Embassy compound in Tehran after November 3, 1979, and (D) injury to the United States nationals or their property as a result of popular movements in the course of the Islamic Revolution in Iran which were not an act of the Government of Iran. The United States will also bar and preclude the prosecution against Iran in the courts of the United States of any pending or future claim asserted by persons other than the United States nationals arising out of the events specified in the preceding sentence.

Point IV. Return of the Assets of the Family of the Former Shah

12. Upon the making by the Government of Algeria of the certification described in Paragraph 3 above, the United States will freeze, and prohibit any transfer of, property and assets in the United States within the control of the estate of the former Shah or of any close relative of the former Shah served as a defendant in U.S. litigation brought by Iran to recover such property and assets as belonging to Iran. As to any such defendant, including the estate of the former Shah, the freeze order will remain in effect until such litigation is finally terminated. Violation of the freeze order shall be subject to the civil and criminal penalties prescribed by U.S. law.

13. Upon the making by the Government of Algeria of the certification described in Paragraph 3 above, the United States will order all persons within U.S. jurisdiction to report to the U.S. Treasury

within 30 days, for transmission to Iran, all information known to them, as of November 3, 1979, and as of the date of the order, with respect to the property and assets referred to in Paragraph 12. Violation of the requirement will be subject to the civil and criminal penalties prescribed by U.S. law.

14. Upon the making by the Government of Algeria of the certification described in Paragraph 3 above, the United States will make known, to all appropriate U.S. courts, that in any litigation of the kind described in Paragraph 12 above the claims of Iran should not be considered legally barred either by sovereign immunity principles or by the act of state doctrine and that Iranian decrees and judgments relating to such assets should be enforced by such courts in accordance with United States law.

15. As to any judgment of a U.S. court which calls for the transfer of any property or assets to Iran, the United States hereby guarantees the enforcement of the final judgment to the extent that the property or assets exist within the United States.

16. If any dispute arises between the parties as to whether the United States has fulfilled any obligation imposed upon it by Paragraphs 1215, inclusive, Iran may submit the dispute to binding arbitration by the tribunal established by, and in accordance with the provisions of, the claims settlement agreement. If the tribunal determines that Iran has suffered a loss as a result of a failure by the United States to fulfill such obligation, it shall make an appropriate award in favor of Iran which may be enforced by Iran in the courts of any nation in accordance with its laws.

SETTLEMENT OF DISPUTES

17. If any other dispute arises between the parties as to the interpretation or performance of any provision of this declaration, either party may submit the dispute to binding arbitration by the tribunal established by, and by accordance with the provisions of, the claims settlement agreement. Any decision of the tribunal with respect to such dispute, including any award of damages to compensate for a loss resulting from a breach of this declaration or the claims settlement agreement, may be enforced by the prevailing party in the courts of any nation in accordance with its laws.

Initialed on January 19, 1981.

By WARREN M. CHRISTOPHER,
Deputy Secretary of State
of the Government of the United States.

By virtue of the powers vested in him by his Government as deposited with the Government of Algeria.

b. Declaration of the Government of the Democratic and Popular Republic of Algeria Concerning the Settlement of Claims by the Government of the United States of America and the Government of the Islamic Republic of Iran

The Government of the Democratic and Popular Republic of Algeria, on the basis of formal notice of adherence received from the Government of the Islamic Republic of Iran and the Government of the United States of America, now declares that Iran and the United States have agreed as follows:

ARTICLE I

Iran and the United States will promote the settlement of the claims described in Article II by the parties directly concerned. Any such claims not settled within six months from the date of entry into force of this agreement shall be submitted to binding third-party arbitration in accordance with the terms of this agreement. The aforementioned six months' period may be extended once by three months at the request of either party.

ARTICLE II

1. An International Arbitral Tribunal (the Iran-United States Claims Tribunal) is hereby established for the purpose of deciding claims of nationals of the United States against Iran and claims of nationals of Iran against the United States, and any counterclaim which arises out of the same contract, transaction or occurrence that constitutes the subject matter of that national's claim, if such claims and counterclaims are outstanding on the date of this agreement, whether or not filed with any court, and arise out of debts, contracts (including transactions which are the subject of letters of credit or bank guarantees), expropriations or other measures affecting property rights, excluding claims described in Paragraph 11 of the Declaration of the Government of Algeria of January 19, 1981, and claims arising out of the actions of the United States in response to the conduct described in such paragraph, and excluding claims arising under a binding contract between the parties specifically providing that any disputes thereunder shall be within the sole jurisdiction of the competent Iranian courts in response to the Majlis position.

2. The Tribunal shall also have jurisdiction over official claims of the United States and Iran against each other arising out of contractual arrangements between them for the purchase and sale of goods and services.

3. The Tribunal shall have jurisdiction, as specified in Paragraphs 16–17 of the Declaration of the Government of Algeria of January 19, 1981, over any dispute as to the interpretation of performance of any provision of that declaration.

ARTICLE III

1. The Tribunal shall consist of nine members or such larger multiple of three as Iran and the United States may agree are necessary to conduct its business expeditiously. Within ninety days after the entry into force of this agreement, each government shall appoint one-third of the members. Within thirty days after their appointment, the members so appointed shall by mutual agreement select the remaining third of the members and appoint one of the remaining third President of the Tribunal. Claims may be decided by the full Tribunal or by a panel of three members of the Tribunal as the President shall determine. Each such panel shall be composed by the President and shall consist of one member appointed by each of the three methods set forth above.

2. Members of the Tribunal shall be appointed and the Tribunal shall conduct its business in accordance with the arbitration rules of the United Nations Commission on International Trade Law (UNCITRAL) except to the extent modified by the parties or by the Tribunal to ensure that this agreement can be carried out. The UNCITRAL rules for appointing members of three-member Tribunals shall apply *mutatis mutandis* to the appointment of the Tribunal.

3. Claims of nationals of the United States and Iran that are within the scope of this agreement shall be presented to the Tribunal either by claimants themselves, or, in the case of claims of less than $250,000, by the Government of such national.

4. No claim may be filed with the Tribunal more than one year after the entry into force of this agreement or six months after the date the President is appointed, whichever is later. These deadlines do not apply to the procedures contemplated by Paragraphs 16 and 17 of the Declaration of the Government of Algeria of January 19, 1981.

ARTICLE IV

1. All decisions and awards of the Tribunal shall be final and binding.

2. The President of the Tribunal shall certify, as prescribed in Paragraph 7 of the Declaration of the Government of Algeria of January 19, 1981, when all arbitral awards under this agreement have been satisfied.

3. Any award which the Tribunal may render against either government shall be enforceable against such government in the courts of any nation in accordance with its laws.

ARTICLE V

The Tribunal shall decide all cases on the basis of respect for law, applying such choice of law rules and principles of commercial and international law as the Tribunal determines to be applicable, taking into account relevant usages of the trade, contract provisions and changed circumstances.

ARTICLE VI

1. The seat of the Tribunal shall be The Hague, The Netherlands, or any other place agreed by Iran and the United States.

2. Each government shall designate an agent at the seat of the Tribunal to represent it to the Tribunal and to receive notices or other communications directed to it or to its nationals, agencies, instrumentalities, or entities in connection with proceedings before the Tribunal.

3. The expenses of the Tribunal shall be borne equally by the two governments.

4. Any question concerning the interpretation or application of this agreement shall be decided by the Tribunal upon the request of either Iran or the United States.

ARTICLE VII

For the purposes of this agreement:

1. A "national" of Iran or of the United States, as the case may be, means (a) a natural person who is a citizen of Iran or the United States; and (b) a corporation or other legal entity which is organized under the laws of Iran or the United States or any of its states or territories, the District of Columbia or the Commonwealth of Puerto Rico, if, collectively, natural persons who are citizens of such country hold, directly, or indirectly, an interest in such corporation or entity equivalent to fifty percent or more of its capital stock.

2. "Claims of nationals" of Iran or the United States, as the case may be, means claims owned continuously, from the date on which the claim arose to the date on which this agreement enters into force, by nationals of that state, including claims that are owned indirectly by such nationals through ownership of capital stock or other proprietary interests in juridical persons, provided that the ownership interests of such nationals, collectively, were sufficient at the time the claim arose to control the corporation or other entity, and provided, further, that the corporation or other entity is not itself entitled to bring a claim under the terms of this agreement. Claims referred to the Arbitral Tribunal shall, as of the date of filings of such claims with the Tribunal, be considered excluded from the jurisdiction of the courts of Iran, or of the United States, or of any other court.

3. "Iran" means the Government of Iran, any political subdivision of Iran, and any agency, instrumentality, or entity controlled by the Government of Iran or any political subdivision thereof.

4. The "United States" means the Government of the United States, any political subdivision of the United States, any agency, instrumentality or entity controlled by the Government of the United States or any political subdivision thereof.

ARTICLE VIII

This agreement shall enter into force when the Government of Algeria has received from both Iran and the United States a notification of adherence to the agreement.

Initialed on January 19, 1981.

By WARREN M. CHRISTOPHER,
Deputy Secretary of State
of the Government of the United States.

By virtue of the powers vested in him by his Government as deposited with the Government of Algeria.

3. World Trade Organization and the General Agreement on Tariffs and Trade

a. The General Agreement on Tariffs and Trade, 1947, as amended

CONTENTS

a. The General Agreement on Tariffs and Trade, 1947,[1] as amended[2]

Final act signed at Geneva at the conclusion of the second session of the Preparatory Committee of the United Nations Conference on Trade and Employment, October 30, 1947; Opened for signature at Geneva, October 30, 1947; Entered into force for the United States January 1, 1948

GENERAL AGREEMENT ON TARIFFS AND TRADE

The Governments of the Commonwealth of Australia, the Kingdom of Belgium, the United States of Brazil, Burma, Canada, Ceylon, the Republic of Chile, the Republic of China, the Republic of Cuba, the Czechoslovak Republic, the French Republic, India, Lebanon, the Grand-Duchy of Luxemburg, the Kingdom of the Netherlands, New Zealand, the Kingdom of Norway, Pakistan, Southern Rhodesia, Syria, the Union of South Africa, the United Kingdom of Great Britain and Northern Ireland, and the United States of America:

RECOGNIZING that their relations in the field of trade and economic endeavour should be conducted with a view to raising standards of living, ensuring full employment and a large and steadily growing volume of real income and effective demand, developing

[1] 61 Stat. parts (5) and (6); TIAS 1700; 4 Bevans 639; 5561 UNTS. The abbreviation "GATT" is used in the footnotes in referring to the General Agreement on Tariffs and Trade. The General Agreement is reproduced here as amended by various protocols, including those parts of the Protocol Amending the Preamble and Parts II and III and the Procès-Verbal of Rectification concerning that Protocol which became effective for two-thirds of the contracting parties, including the United States, on October 7, 1957, and February 15, 1961 (Article XIV).

[2] The Protocols and Procès-Verbal of Rectification modifying the GATT are as follows:

(a) Protocol modifying certain provisions of the General Agreement. Signed at Havana March 24, 1948; entered into force for the United States April 15, 1948. 62 Stat. 1992; TIAS 1763; 4 Bevans 708; 62 UNTS 30.

(b) Special Protocol modifying Article XIV of the General Agreement. Signed at Havana March 24, 1948; entered into force for the United States April 19, 1948. 62 Stat. 2000; TIAS 1764; 4 Bevans 712; 62 UNTS 40.

(c) Special Protocol relating to Article XXIV of the General Agreement. Signed at Havana March 24, 1948; entered into force for the United States June 7, 1948. 62 Stat. 2013; TIAS 1765; 4 Bevans 719; 62 UNTS 56.

(d) Protocol modifying Part II and Article XXVI of the General Agreement. Signed at Geneva September 14, 1948; entered into force for the United States December 14, 1948, 62 Stat. 3679; TIAS 1890; 4 Bevans 769; 62 UNTS 80.

(e) Protocol modifying Article XXVI of the General Agreement. Dated at Annecy August 13, 1949; entered into force for the United States March 28, 1950. 2 UST 1583; TIAS 2300; 62 UNTS 113.

(f) Protocol modifying Part I and Article XXIX of the General Agreement. Signed at Geneva September 14, 1948; entered into force for the United States September 24, 1952. 3 UST 5355; TIAS 2744; 138 UNTS 334.

(g) Protocol amending the Preamble and Parts II and III of the General Agreement. Done at Geneva March 10, 1955; entered into force for the United States October 7, 1957. 8 UST 1767; TIAS 3930; 278 UNTS 168.

(h) Fourth Protocol of rectifications and modifications to the Annexes and to the text of the Schedules to the GATT. Done at Geneva March 7, 1955. 10 UST 217; TIAS 4186; 324 UNTS 300.

(i) Amendment: December 3, 1955. 19 UST 4638; TIAS 6452; 278 UNTS 246.

(j) Protocol to introduce Part IV. Done at Geneva February 8, 1965; signed by the United States February 8, 1965; entered into force June 27, 1966. 17 UST 1977; TIAS 6139; 572 UNTS 320.

the full use of the resources of the world and expanding the production and exchange of goods.

BEING DESIROUS of contributing to these objectives by entering into reciprocal and mutually advantageous arrangements directed to the substantial reduction of tariffs and other barriers to trade and to the elimination of discriminatory treatment in international commerce,

HAVE THROUGH THEIR REPRESENTATIVES AGREED AS FOLLOWS:

PART I

ARTICLE I—GENERAL MOST-FAVOURED-NATION TREATMENT

1. With respect to customs duties and charges of any kind imposed on or in connection with importation or exportation or imposed on the international transfer of payments for imports or exports, and with respect to the method of levying such duties and charges, and with respect to all rules and formalities in connection with importation and exportation, and with respect to all matters referred to in paragraphs 2 and 4 of Article III, any advantage, favour, privilege or immunity granted by any contracting party to any product originating in or destined for any other country shall be accorded immediately and unconditionally to the like product originating in or destined for the territories of all other contracting parties.

2. The provisions of paragraph 1 of this Article shall not require the elimination of any preferences in respect of import duties or charges which do not exceed the levels provided for in paragraph 4 of this Article and which fall within the following descriptions:

(a) preferences in force exclusively between two or more of the territories listed in Annex A, subject to the conditions set forth therein;

(b) preferences in force exclusively between two or more territories which on July 1, 1939, were connected by common sovereignty or relations of protection or suzerainty and which are listed in Annexes B, C and D, subject to the conditions set forth therein;

(c) preferences in force exclusively between the United States of America and the Republic of Cuba;

(d) preferences in force exclusively between neighbouring countries listed in Annexes E and F.

3.[3] The provisions of paragraph 1 shall not apply to preferences between the countries formerly a part of the Ottoman Empire and detached from it on July 24, 1923, provided such preferences are approved under subparagraph 5 (a)[4] of Article XXV, which shall be applied in this respect in the light of paragraph 1 of Article XXIX.

4. The margin of preference on any product in respect of which a preference is permitted under paragraph 2 of this Article but is not specifically set forth as a maximum margin of preference in the appropriate Schedule annexed to this Agreement shall not exceed:

[3] Part A of Protocol Modifying Part I and Article XXIX of the GATT (3 UST 5356) added para. 3 and renumbered para. 3 as para. 4.

[4] As signed; should probably read "paragraph 5".

(a) in respect of duties or charges on any product described in such Schedule, the difference between the most-favored-nation and preferential rates provided for therein; if no preferential rate is provided for, the preferential rate shall for the purposes of this paragraph be taken to be that in force on April 10, 1947, and, if no most-favoured-nation rate is provided for, the margin shall not exceed the difference between the most-favoured-nation and preferential rates existing on April 10, 1947;

(b) in respect of duties or charges on any product not described in the appropriate Schedule, the difference between the most-favoured-nation and preferential rates existing on April 10, 1947.

In the case of the contracting parties named in Annex G, the date of April 10, 1947, referred to in sub-paragraphs (a) and (b) of this paragraph shall be replaced by the respective dates set forth in that Annex.

ARTICLE II—SCHEDULES OF CONCESSIONS

1. (a) Each contracting party shall accord to the commerce of the other contracting parties treatment no less favourable than that provided for in the appropriate Part of the appropriate Schedule annexed to this Agreement.

(b) The products described in Part I of the Schedule relating to any contracting party, which are the products of territories of other contracting parties, shall, on their importation into the territory to which the Schedule relates, and subject to the terms, conditions or qualifications set forth in that Schedule, be exempt from ordinary customs duties in excess of those set forth and provided for therein. Such products shall also be exempt from all other duties or charges of any kind imposed on or in connection with importation in excess of those imposed on the date of this Agreement or those directly and mandatorily required to be imposed thereafter by legislation in force in the importing territory on that date.

(c) The products described in Part II of the Schedule relating to any contracting party which are the products of territories entitled under Article I to receive preferential treatment upon importation into the territory to which the Schedule relates shall, on their importation into such territory, and subject to the terms, conditions or qualifications set forth in that Schedule, be exempt from ordinary customs duties in excess of those set forth and provided for in Part II of that Schedule. Such products shall also be exempt from all other duties or charges of any kind imposed on or in connection with importation in excess of those imposed on the date of this Agreement or those directly and mandatorily required to be imposed thereafter by legislation in force in the importing territory on that date. Nothing in this Article shall prevent any contracting party from maintaining its requirements existing on the date of this Agreement as to the eligibility of goods for entry at preferential rates of duty.

2. Nothing in this Article shall prevent any contracting party from imposing at any time on the importation of any product:

(a) a charge equivalent to an internal tax imposed consistently with the provisions of paragraph 2 of Article III in respect of the like domestic product or in respect of an article from which the imported product has been manufactured or produced in whole or in part;

(b) any anti-dumping or countervailing duty applied consistently with the provisions of Article VI;

(c) fees or other charges commensurate with the cost of services rendered.

3. No contracting party shall alter its method of determining dutiable value or of converting currencies so as to impair the value of any of the concessions provided for in the appropriate Schedule annexed to this Agreement.

4. If any contracting party establishes, maintains or authorizes, formally or in effect, a monopoly of the importation of any product described in the appropriate Schedule annexed to this Agreement, such monopoly shall not, except as provided for in that Schedule or as otherwise agreed between the parties which initially negotiated the concession, operate so as to afford protection on the average in excess of the amount of protection provided for in that Schedule. The provisions of this paragraph shall not limit the use by contracting parties of any form of assistance to domestic producers permitted by other provisions of this Agreement.

5. If any contracting party considers that a product is not receiving from another contracting party the treatment which the first contracting party believes to have been contemplated by a concession provided for in the appropriate Schedule annexed to this Agreement, it shall bring the matter directly to the attention of the other contracting party. If the latter agrees that the treatment contemplated was that claimed by the first contracting party, but declares that such treatment cannot be accorded because a court or other proper authority has ruled to the effect that the product involved cannot be classified under the tariff laws of such contracting party so as to permit the treatment contemplated in this Agreement, the two contracting parties, together with any other contracting parties substantially interested, shall enter promptly into further negotiations with a view to a compensatory adjustment of the matter.

6. (a) The specific duties and charges included in the Schedules relating to contracting parties members of the International Monetary Fund, and margins of preference in specific duties and charges maintained by such contracting parties, are expressed in the appropriate currency at the par value accepted or provisionally recognized by the Fund at the date of this Agreement. Accordingly, in case this par value is reduced consistently with the Articles of Agreement of the International Monetary Fund by more than twenty per centum, such specific duties and charges and margins of preference may be adjusted to take account of such reduction; *Provided,* That the CONTRACTING PARTIES (i.e., the contracting parties acting jointly as provided for in Article XXV) concur that such adjustments will not impair the value of the concessions provided for in the appropriate Schedule or elsewhere in this Agreement, due account being taken of all factors which may influence the need for, or urgency of, such adjustments.

(b) Similar provisions shall apply to any contracting party not a member of the Fund, as from the date on which such contracting party becomes a member of the Fund or enters into a special exchange agreement in pursuance of Article XV.

7. The Schedules annexed to this Agreement are hereby made an integral part of Part I of this Agreement.

PART II

ARTICLE III—NATIONAL TREATMENT ON INTERNAL TAXATION AND REGULATION[5]

1. The contracting parties recognize that internal taxes and other internal charges, and laws, regulations and requirements affecting the internal sale, offering for sale, purchase, transportation, distribution or use of products, and internal quantitative regulations requiring the mixture, processing or use of products in specified amounts or proportions, should not be applied to imported or domestic products so as to afford protection to domestic production.

2. The products of the territory of any contracting party imported into the territory of any other contracting party shall not be subject, directly or indirectly to internal taxes or other internal charges of any kind in excess of those applied, directly or indirectly, to like domestic products. Moreover, no contracting party shall otherwise apply internal taxes or other internal charges to imported or domestic products in a manner contrary to the principles set forth in paragraph 1.

3. With respect to any existing tax which is inconsistent with the provisions of paragraph 2, but which is specifically authorized under a trade agreement, in force on April 10, 1947, in which the import duty on the taxed product is bound against increase, the contracting party imposing the tax shall be free to postpone the application of the provisions of paragraph 2 to such tax until such time as it can obtain release from the obligations of such trade agreement in order to permit the increase of such duty to the extent necessary to compensate for the elimination of the protective element of the tax.

4. The products of the territory of any contracting party imported into the territory of any other contracting party shall be accorded treatment no less favorable than that accorded to like products of national origin in respect of all laws, regulations and requirements affecting their internal sale, offering for sale, purchase, transportation, distribution or use. The provisions of this paragraph shall not prevent the application of differential internal transportation charges which are based exclusively on the economic operation of the means of transport and not on the nationality of the product.

5. No contracting party shall establish or maintain any internal quantitative regulation relating to the mixture, processing or use of products in specified amounts or proportions which requires, directly or indirectly, that any specified amount or proportion of any product which is the subject of the regulation must be supplied

[5] The Protocol Modifying Part II and Article XXVI of the GATT (62 Stat. 3679) amended Article III.

from domestic sources. Moreover, no contracting party shall otherwise apply internal quantitative regulations in a manner contrary to the principles set forth in paragraph 1.

6. The provisions of paragraph 5 shall not apply to any internal quantitative regulation in force in the territory of any contracting party on July 1, 1939, April 10, 1947, or March 24, 1948, at the option of that contracting party; *Provided,* That any such regulation which is contrary to the provisions of paragraph 5 shall not be modified to the detriment of imports and shall be treated as a customs duty for the purpose of negotiation.

7. No internal quantitative regulation relating to the mixture, processing or use of products in specified amounts or proportions shall be applied in such a manner as to allocate any such amount or proportion among external sources of supply.

8. (a) The provisions of this Article shall not apply to laws, regulations or requirements governing the procurement by governmental agencies of products purchased for governmental purposes and not with a view to commercial resale or with a view to use in the production of goods for commercial sale.

(b) The provisions of this Article shall not prevent the payment of subsidies exclusively to domestic producers, including payments to domestic producers derived from the proceeds of internal taxes or charges applied consistently with the provisions of this Article and subsidies effected through governmental purchases of domestic products.

9. The contracting parties recognize that internal maximum price control measures, even though conforming to the other provisions of this Article, can have effects prejudicial to the interests of contracting parties supplying imported products. Accordingly, contracting parties applying such measures shall take account of the interests of exporting contracting parties with a view to avoiding to the fullest practicable extent such prejudicial effects.

10. The provisions of this Article shall not prevent any contracting party from establishing or maintaining internal quantitative regulations relating to exposed cinematograph films and meeting the requirements of Article IV.

ARTICLE IV—SPECIAL PROVISIONS RELATING TO CINEMATOGRAPH FILMS

If any contracting party establishes or maintains internal quantitative regulations relating to exposed cinematograph films, such regulations shall take the form of screen quotas which shall conform to the following requirements:

(a) Screen quotas may require the exhibition of cinematograph films of national origin during a specified minimum proportion of the total screen time actually utilized, over a specified period of not less than one year, in the commercial exhibition of all films of whatever origin, and shall be computed on the basis of screen time per theatre per year or the equivalent thereof;

(b) With the exception of screen time reserved for films of national origin under a screen quota, screen time including that released by administrative action from screen time reserved for films of national origin, shall not be allocated formally or in effect among sources of supply;

(c) Notwithstanding the provisions of sub-paragraph (b) of this Article, any contracting party may maintain screen quotas conforming to the requirements of sub-paragraph (a) of this Article which reserve a minimum proportion of screen time for films of a specified origin other than that of the contracting party imposing such screen quotas; *Provided,* That no such minimum proportion of screen time shall be increased above the level in effect on April 10, 1947;

(d) Screen quotas shall be subject to negotiation for their limitation, liberalization or elimination.

ARTICLE V—FREEDOM OF TRANSIT

1. Goods (including baggage), and also vessels and other means of transport, shall be deemed to be in transit across the territory of a contracting party when the passage across such territory, with or without trans-shipment, warehousing, breaking bulk, or change in the mode of transport, is only a portion of a complete journey beginning and terminating beyond the frontier of the contracting party across whose territory the traffic passes. Traffic of this nature is termed in this Article "traffic in transit".

2. There shall be freedom of transit through the territory of each contracting party, via the routes most convenient for international transit, for traffic in transit to or from the territory of other contracting parties. No distinction shall be made which is based on the flag of vessels, the place of origin, departure, entry, exit or destination, or on any circumstances relating to the ownership of goods, of vessels or of other means of transport.

3. Any contracting party may require that traffic in transit through its territory be entered at the proper custom house, but, except in cases of failure to comply with applicable customs laws and regulations, such traffic coming from or going to the territory of other contracting parties shall not be subject to any unnecessary delays or restrictions and shall be exempt from customs duties and from all transit duties or other charges imposed in respect of transit, except charges for transportation of those commensurate with administrative expenses entailed by transit or with the cost of services rendered.

4. All charges and regulations imposed by contracting parties on traffic in transit to or from the territories of other contracting parties shall be reasonable, having regard to the conditions of the traffic.

5. With respect to all charges, regulations and formalities in connection with transit, each contracting party shall accord to traffic in transit to or from the territory of any other contracting party treatment no less favourable than the treatment accorded to traffic in transit to or from any third country.

6. Each contracting party shall accord to products which have been in transit through the territory of any other contracting party treatment no less favourable than that which would have been accorded to such products had they been transported from their place of origin to their destination without going through the territory of

such other contracting party. Any contracting party shall, however, be free to maintain its requirements of direct consignment existing on the date of this Agreement, in respect of any goods in regard to which such direct consignment is a requisite condition of eligibility for entry of the goods at preferential rates of duty or has relation to the contracting party's prescribed method of valuation for duty purposes.

7. The provisions of this Article shall not apply to the operation of aircraft in transit, but shall apply to air transit of goods (including baggage).

ARTICLE VI—ANTIDUMPING AND COUNTERVAILING DUTIES [6]

1. The contracting parties recognize that dumping, by which products of one country are introduced into the commerce of another country at less than the normal value of the products, is to be condemned if it causes or threatens material injury to an established industry in the territory of a contracting party or materially retards the establishment of a domestic industry. For the purposes of this Article, a product is to be considered as being introduced into the commerce of an importing country at less than its normal value, if the price of the product exported from one country to another

(a) is less than the comparable price, in the ordinary course of trade, for the like product when destined for consumption in the exporting country, or,

(b) in the absence of such domestic price, is less than either

(i) the highest comparable price for the like product for export to any third country in the ordinary course of trade, or

(ii) the cost of production of the product in the country of origin plus a reasonable addition for selling cost and profit.

Due allowance shall be made in each case for differences in conditions and terms of sale, for differences in taxation, and for other differences affecting price comparability.

2. In order to offset or prevent dumping, a contracting party may levy on any dumped product an anti-dumping duty not greater in amount than the margin of dumping in respect of such product. For the purposes of this Article, the margin of dumping is the price difference determined in accordance with the provisions of paragraph 1.

3. No countervailing duty shall be levied on any product of the territory of any contracting party imported into the territory of another contracting party in excess of an amount equal to the estimated bounty or subsidy determined to have been granted, directly or indirectly, on the manufacture, production or export of such product in the country of origin or exportation, including any special subsidy to the transportation of a particular product. The term "countervailing duty" shall be understood to mean a special duty levied for the purpose of offsetting any bounty or subsidy bestowed,

[6] The Protocol Modifying Part II and Article XXVI of the GATT (62 Stat. 3679) amended Article VI.

directly or indirectly, upon the manufacture, production or export of any merchandise.

4. No product of the territory or any contracting party imported into the territory of any other contracting party shall be subject to anti-dumping or countervailing duty by reason of the exemption of such product from duties or taxes borne by the like product when destined for consumption in the country of origin or exportation, or by reason of the refund of such duties or taxes.

5. No product of the territory of any contracting party imported into the territory of any other contracting party shall be subject to both anti-dumping and countervailing duties to compensate for the same situation of dumping or export subsidization.

6.[7] (a) No contracting party shall levy any anti-dumping or countervailing duty on the importation of any product of the territory of another contracting party unless it determines that the effect of the dumping or subsidization, as the case may be, is such as to cause or threaten material injury to an established domestic industry, or is such as to retard materially the establishment of a domestic industry.

(b) The CONTRACTING PARTIES may waive the requirement of subparagraph (a) of this paragraph so as to permit a contracting party to levy an anti-dumping or countervailing duty on the importation of any product for the purpose of offsetting dumping or subsidization which causes or threatens material injury to an industry in the territory of another contracting party exporting the product concerned to the territory of the importing contracting party. The CONTRACTING PARTIES shall waive the requirements of sub-paragraph (a) of this paragraph, so as to permit the levying of a countervailing duty, in cases in which they find that a subsidy is causing or threatening material injury to an industry in the territory of another contracting party exporting the product concerned to the territory of the importing contracting party.

(c) In exceptional circumstances, however, where delay might cause damage which would be difficult to repair, a contracting party may levy a countervailing duty for the purpose referred to in subparagraph (b) of this paragraph without the prior approval of the CONTRACTING PARTIES; *Provided,* That such action shall be reported immediately to the CONTRACTING PARTIES and that the countervailing duty shall be withdrawn promptly if the CONTRACTING PARTIES disapprove.

7. A system for the stabilization of the domestic price or of the return to domestic producers of a primary commodity, independently of the movements of export prices, which results at times in the sale of the commodity for export at a price lower than the comparable price charged for the like commodity to buyers in the domestic market, shall be presumed not to result in material injury within the meaning of paragraph 6 if it is determined by consultation among the contracting parties substantially interested in the commodity concerned that:

---

[7] Sec. D of the Protocol Amending the Preamble and Parts II and III of the GATT (8 UST 1769) amended subsec. (a).

(a) the system has also resulted in the sale of the commodity for export at a price higher than the comparable price charged for the like commodity to buyers in the domestic market, and

(b) the system is so operated, either because of the effective regulation of production, or otherwise, as not to stimulate exports unduly or otherwise seriously prejudice the interests of other contracting parties.

ARTICLE VII—VALUATION FOR CUSTOMS PURPOSES [8]

1.[8] The contracting parties recognize the validity of the general principles of valuation set forth in the following paragraphs of this Article, and they undertake to give effect to such principles, in respect of all products subject to duties or other charges or restrictions on importation and exportation based upon or regulated in any manner by value. Moreover, they shall, upon a request by another contracting party review the operation of any of their laws or regulations relating to value for customs purposes in the light of these principles. The CONTRACTING PARTIES may request from contracting parties reports on steps taken by them in pursuance of the provisions of this Article.

2.[8] (a) The value for customs purposes of imported merchandise should be based on the actual value of the imported merchandise on which duty is assessed, or of like merchandise, and should not be based on the value of merchandise of national origin or on arbitrary or fictitious values.

(b) "Actual value" should be the price at which, at a time and place determined by the legislation of the country of importation, such or like merchandise is sold or offered for sale in the ordinary course of trade under fully competitive conditions. To the extent to which the price of such or like merchandise is governed by the quantity in a particular transaction, the price to be considered should uniformly be related to either (i) comparable quantities, or (ii) quantities not less favourable to importers than those in which the greater volume of the merchandise is sold in the trade between the countries of exportation and importation.

(c) When the actual value is not ascertainable in accordance with sub-paragraph (b) of this paragraph, the value for customs purposes should be based on the nearest ascertainable equivalent of such value.

3. The value for customs purposes of any imported product should not include the amount of any internal tax, applicable within the country of origin or export, from which the imported product has been exempted or has been or will be relieved by means of refund.

4. (a) Except as otherwise provided for in this paragraph, where it is necessary for the purposes of paragraph 2 of this Article for a contracting party to convert into its own currency a price expressed in the currency of another country, the conversion rate of exchange to be used shall be based, for each currency involved, on the par value as established pursuant to the Articles of Agreement

---

[8] Sec. E of the Protocol Amending the Preamble and Parts I and II of the GATT (8 UST 1770) amended paras. 1 and 2.

of the International Monetary Fund or on the rate of exchange recognized by the Fund, or on the par value established in accordance with a special exchange agreement entered into pursuant to Article XV of this Agreement.

(b) Where no such established par value and no such recognized rate of exchange exist, the conversion rate shall reflect effectively the current value of such currency in commercial transactions.

(c) The CONTRACTING PARTIES, in agreement with the International Monetary Fund, shall formulate rules governing the conversion by contracting parties of any foreign currency in respect of which multiple rates of exchange are maintained consistently with the Articles of Agreement of the International Monetary Fund. Any contracting party may apply such rules in respect of such foreign currencies for the purposes of paragraph 2 of this Article as an alternative to the use of par values. Until such rules are adopted by the CONTRACTING PARTIES, any contracting party may employ, in respect of any such foreign currency, rules of conversion for the purposes of paragraph 2 of this Article which are designed to reflect effectively the value of such foreign currency in commercial transactions.

(d) Nothing in this paragraph shall be construed to require any contracting party to alter the method of converting currencies for customs purposes which is applicable in its territory on the date of this Agreement, if such alteration would have the effect of increasing generally the amounts of duty payable.

5. The bases and methods for determining the value of products subject to duties or other charges or restrictions based upon or regulated in any manner by value should be stable and should be given sufficient publicity to enable traders to estimate, with a reasonable degree of certainty, the value for customs purposes.

ARTICLE VIII—FEES AND FORMALITIES CONNECTED WITH IMPORTATION AND EXPORTATION

1.[9] (a) All fees and charges of whatever character (other than import and export duties and other than taxes within the purview of Article III) imposed by contracting parties on or in connection with importation or exportation shall be limited in amount to the approximate cost of services rendered and shall not represent an indirect protection to domestic products or a taxation of imports or exports for fiscal purposes.

(b) The contracting parties recognize the need for reducing the number and diversity of fees and charges referred to in sub-paragraph (a).

(c) The contracting parties also recognize the need for minimizing the incidence and complexity of import and export formalities and for decreasing and simplifying import and export documentation requirements.

2.[9] A contracting party shall, upon request by another contracting party or by the CONTRACTING PARTIES, review the operation of its laws and regulations in the light of the provisions of this Article.

[9] Sec. F of the Protocol Amending the Preamble and Parts II and III of the GATT (8 UST 1770) amended paras. 1 and 2.

3. No contracting party shall impose substantial penalties for minor breaches of customs regulations or procedural requirements. In particular, no penalty in respect of any omission or mistake in customs documentation which is easily rectifiable and obviously made without fraudulent intent or gross negligence shall be greater than necessary to serve merely as a warning.

4. The provisions of this Article shall extend to fees, charges, formalities and requirements imposed by governmental authorities in connection with importation and exportation, including those relating to:

(a) consular transactions, such as consular invoices and certificates;
(b) quantitative restrictions;
(c) licensing;
(d) exchange control;
(e) statistical services;
(f) documents, documentation and certification;
(g) analysis and inspection; and
(h) quarantine, sanitation and fumigation.

Article IX—Marks of Origin

1. Each contracting party shall accord to the products of the territories of other contracting parties treatment with regard to marking requirements no less favourable than the treatment accorded to like products of any third country.

2.[10] The contracting parties recognize that, in adopting and enforcing laws and regulations relating to marks of origin, the difficulties and inconveniences which such measures may cause to the commerce and industry of exporting countries should be reduced to a minimum, due regard being had to the necessity of protecting consumers against fraudulent or misleading indications.

3. Whenever it is administratively practicable to do so, contracting parties should permit required marks of origin to be affixed at the time of importation.

4. The laws and regulations of contracting parties relating to the marking of imported products shall be such as to permit compliance without seriously damaging the products, or materially reducing their value, or unreasonably increasing their cost.

5. As a general rule, no special duty or penalty should be imposed by any contracting party for failure to comply with marking requirements prior to importation unless corrective marking is unreasonably delayed or deceptive marks have been affixed or the required marking has been intentionally omitted.

6. The contracting parties shall co-operate with each other with a view to preventing the use of trade names in such manner as to misrepresent the true origin of a product, to the detriment of such distinctive regional or geographical names of products of the territory of a contracting party as are protected by its legislation. Each contracting party shall accord full and sympathetic consideration to such requests or representations as may be made by any other contracting party regarding the application of the undertaking set

[10] Sec. G of the Protocol Amending the Preamble and Parts II and III of the GATT (8 UST 1771) added para. 2 and renumbered paras. 2 through 5 as paras. 3 through 6.

forth in the preceding sentence to names of products which have been communicated to it by the other contracting party.

ARTICLE X—PUBLICATION AND ADMINISTRATION OF TRADE REGULATIONS

1. Laws, regulations, judicial decisions and administrative rulings of general application, made effective by any contracting party, pertaining to the classification or the valuation of products for customs purposes, or to rates of duty, taxes or other charges, or to requirements, restrictions or prohibitions on imports or exports or on the transfer of payments therefor, or affecting their sale, distribution, transportation, insurance, warehousing, inspection, exhibition processing, mixing or other use, shall be published promptly in such a manner as to enable governments and traders to become acquainted with them. Agreements affecting international trade policy which are in force between the government or a governmental agency of any contracting party and the government or governmental agency of any other contracting party shall also be published. The provisions of this paragraph shall not require any contracting party to disclose confidential information which would impede law enforcement or otherwise be contrary to the public interest or would prejudice the legitimate commercial interests of particular enterprises, public or private.

2. No measure of general application taken by any contracting party effecting an advance in a rate of duty or other charge on imports under an established and uniform practice, or imposing a new or more burdensome requirement, restriction or prohibition on imports, or on the transfer of payments therefor, shall be enforced before such measure has been officially published.

3. (a) Each contracting party shall administer in a uniform, impartial and reasonable manner all its laws, regulations, decisions and rulings of the kind described in paragraph 1 of this Article.

(b) Each contracting party shall maintain, or institute as soon as practicable, judicial, arbitral or administrative tribunals or procedures for the purpose, *inter alia,* of the prompt review and correction of administrative action relating to customs matters. Such tribunals or procedures shall be independent of the agencies entrusted with administrative enforcement and their decisions shall be implemented by, and shall govern the practice of, such agencies unless an appeal is lodged with a court or tribunal of superior jurisdiction within the time prescribed for appeals to be lodged by importers; *Provided,* That the central administration of such agency may take steps to obtain a review of the matter in another proceeding if there is good cause to believe that the decision is inconsistent with established principles of law or the actual facts.

(c) The provisions of sub-paragraph (b) of this paragraph, shall not require the elimination or substitution of procedures in force in the territory of a contracting party on the date of this Agreement which in fact provide for an objective and impartial review of administrative action even though such procedures are not fully or formally independent of the agencies entrusted with administrative enforcement. Any contracting party employing such procedures shall, upon request, furnish the contracting parties with full information thereon in order that they may determine whether such procedures conform to the requirements of this sub-paragraph.

ARTICLE XI—GENERAL ELIMINATION OF QUANTITATIVE RESTRICTIONS

1. No prohibitions or restrictions other than duties, taxes or other charges, whether made effective through quotas, import or export licenses or other measures, shall be instituted or maintained by any contracting party on the importation of any product of the territory of any other contracting party or on the exportation or sale for export of any product destined for the territory of any other contracting party.

2. The provisions of paragraph 1 of this Article shall not extend to the following:

(a) Export prohibitions or restrictions temporarily applied to prevent or relieve critical shortages of foodstuffs or other products essential to the exporting contracting party;

(b) Import and export prohibitions or restrictions necessary to the application of standards or regulations for the classification, grading or marketing of commodities in international trade;

(c) Import restrictions on any agricultural or fisheries product, imported in any form, necessary to the enforcement of governmental measures which operate:

(i) to restrict the quantities of the like domestic product permitted to be marketed or produced, or, if there is no substantial domestic production of the like product, of a domestic product for which the imported product can be directly substituted; or

(ii) to remove a temporary surplus of the like domestic product, or, if there is no substantial domestic production of the like product, of a domestic product for which the imported product can be directly substituted, by making the surplus available to certain groups of domestic consumers free of charge or at prices below the current market level; or

(iii) to restrict the quantities permitted to be produced of any animal product the production of which is directly dependent, wholly or mainly, on the imported commodity, if the domestic production of that commodity is relatively negligible.

Any contracting party applying restrictions on the importation of any product pursuant to sub-paragraph (c) of this paragraph shall give public notice of the total quantity or value of the product permitted to be imported during a specified future period and of any change in such quantity or value. Moreover, any restrictions applied under (i) above shall not be such as will reduce the total of imports relative to the total of domestic production, as compared with the proportion which might reasonably be expected to rule between the two in the absence of restriction. In determining this proportion, the contracting party shall pay due regard to the proportion prevailing during a previous representative period and to any special factors which may have affected or may be affecting the trade in the product concerned.

ARTICLE XII—RESTRICTIONS TO SAFEGUARD THE BALANCE OF PAYMENTS [11]

1. Notwithstanding the provisions of paragraph 1 of Article XI, any contracting party, in order to safeguard for the external financial position and its balance of payments, may restrict the quantity or value of merchandise permitted to be imported, subject to the provisions of the following paragraphs of this Article.

2. (a) Import restrictions instituted, maintained or intensified by a contracting party under this article shall not exceed those necessary:

(i) to forestall the imminent threat of, or to stop, a serious decline in its monetary reserves, or

(ii) in the case of a contracting party with very low monetary reserves, to achieve a reasonable rate of increase in its reserves.

Due regard shall be paid in either case to any special factors which may be affecting the reserves of such contracting party or its need for reserves, including, where special external credits or other resources are available to it, the need to provide for the appropriate use of such credits or resources.

(b) Contracting parties applying restrictions under sub-paragraph (a) of this paragraph shall progressively relax them as such conditions improve, maintaining them only to the extent that the conditions specified in that sub-paragraph still justify their application. They shall eliminate the restrictions when conditions would no longer justify their institution or maintenance under that sub-paragraph.

3. (a) Contracting parties undertake, in carrying out their domestic policies, to pay due regard to the need for maintaining or restoring equilibrium in their balance of payments on a sound and lasting basis and to the desirability of avoiding an uneconomic employment of productive resources. They recognize that in order to achieve these ends, it is desirable so far as possible to adopt measures which expand rather than contract international trade.

(b) Contracting parties applying restrictions under this Article may determine the incidence of the restrictions on imports of different products or classes of products in such a way as to give priority to the importance of those products which are more essential.

(c) Contracting parties applying restrictions under this Article undertake:

(i) to avoid unnecessary damage to the commercial or economic interests of any other contracting party;

(ii) not to apply restrictions so as to prevent unreasonably the importation of any description of goods in minimum commercial quantities the exclusion of which would impair regular channels of trade; and

[11] Sec. I of the Protocol Amending the Preamble and Parts II and III of the GATT (8 UST 1771) amended Article XII.

(iii) not to apply restrictions which would prevent the importation of commercial samples or prevent compliance with patent, trade mark, copyright, or similar procedures.

(d) The contracting parties recognize that, as a result of domestic policies directed towards the achievement and maintenance of full and productive employment or towards the development of economic resources, a contracting party may experience a high level of demand for imports involving a threat to its monetary reserves of the sort referred to in paragraph 2(a) of this Article. Accordingly, a contracting party otherwise complying with the provisions of this Article shall not be required to withdraw or modify restrictions on the ground that a change in those policies would render unnecessary restrictions which it is applying under this Article.

4. (a) Any contracting party applying new restrictions or raising the general level of its existing restrictions by a substantial intensification of the measures applied under this Article shall immediately after instituting or intensifying such restrictions (or, in circumstances in which prior consultation is practicable, before doing so) consult with the CONTRACTING PARTIES as to the nature of its balance of payments difficulties, alternative corrective measures which may be available, and the possible effect of the restrictions on the economies of other contracting parties.

(b) On a date to be determined by them, the CONTRACTING PARTIES shall review all restriction still applied under this Article on that date. Beginning one year after that date, contracting parties applying import restrictions under this Article shall enter into consultations of the type provided for in sub-paragraph (a) of this paragraph with the CONTRACTING PARTIES annually.

(c)(i) If, in the course of consultations with a contracting party under sub-paragraph (a) or (b) above, the CONTRACTING PARTIES find that the restrictions are not consistent with the provisions of this Article or with those of Article XIII (subject to the provisions of Article XIV), they shall indicate the nature of the inconsistency and may advise that the restrictions be suitably modified.

(ii) If, however, as a result of the consultations, the CONTRACTING PARTIES determine that the restrictions are being applied in a manner involving an inconsistency of a serious nature with the provisions of this Article or with those of Article XIII (subject to the provisions of Article XIV) and that damage to the trade of any contracting party is caused or threatened thereby, they shall so inform the contracting party applying the restrictions and shall make appropriate recommendations for securing conformity with such provisions within a specified period of time. If such contracting party does not comply with these recommendations within the specified period, the CONTRACTING PARTIES may release any contracting party the trade of which is adversely affected by the restrictions from such obligations under this Agreement towards the contracting party applying the restrictions as they determine to be appropriate in the circumstances.

(d) The CONTRACTING PARTIES shall invite any contracting party which is applying restrictions under this Article to enter into consultations with them at the request of any contracting party which can establish a *prima facie* case that the restrictions are inconsistent with the provisions of this Article or with those of Article

XIII (subject to the provisions of Article XIV) and that its trade is adversely affected thereby. However, no such invitation shall be issued unless the CONTRACTING PARTIES have ascertained that direct discussions between the contracting parties concerned have not been successful. If, as a result of the consultations with the CONTRACTING PARTIES, no agreement is reached and they determine that the restrictions are being applied inconsistently with such provisions, and that damage to the trade of the contracting party initiating the procedure is caused or threatened thereby, they shall recommend the withdrawal or modification of the restrictions. If the restrictions are not withdrawn or modified within such time as the CONTRACTING PARTIES may prescribe, they may release the contracting party initiating the procedure from such obligation under this Agreement towards the contracting party applying the restrictions as they determine to be appropriate in the circumstances.

(e) In proceeding under this paragraph, the CONTRACTING PARTIES shall have due regard to any special external factors adversely affecting the export trade of the contracting party applying restrictions.

(f) Determinations under this paragraph shall be rendered expeditiously and, if possible, within sixty days of the initiation of the consultations.

5. If there is a persistent and widespread application of import restrictions under this Article, indicating the existence of a general disequilibrium which is restricting international trade, the CONTRACTING PARTIES shall initiate discussions to consider whether other measures might be taken, either by those contracting parties the balances of payments of which are under pressure or by those the balances of payments of which are tending to be exceptionally favourable, or by any appropriate intergovernmental organization, to remove the underlying causes of the disequilibrium. On the invitation of the CONTRACTING PARTIES, contracting parties shall participate in such discussions.

ARTICLE XIII—NON-DISCRIMINATORY ADMINISTRATION OF QUANTITATIVE RESTRICTIONS

1. No prohibition or restriction shall be applied by any contracting party on the importation of any product of the territory of any other contracting party or on the exportation of any product destined for the territory of any other contracting party, unless the importation of the like product of all third countries or the exportation of the like product to all third countries is similarly prohibited or restricted.

2. In applying import restrictions to any product, contracting parties shall aim at a distribution of trade in such product approaching as closely as possible the shares which the various contracting parties might be expected to obtain in the absence of such restrictions, and to this end shall observe the following provisions:

(a) Wherever practicable, quotas representing the total amount of permitted imports (whether allocated among supplying countries or not) shall be fixed, and notice given of their amount in accordance with paragraph 3(b) of this Article;

(b) In cases in which quotas are not practicable, the restrictions may be applied by means of import licenses or permits without a quota;

(c) Contracting parties shall not, except for purposes of operating quotas allocated in accordance with subparagraph (d) of this paragraph, require that import licenses or permits be utilized for the importation of the product concerned from a particular country or source;

(d) In cases in which a quota is allocated among supplying countries, the contracting party applying the restrictions may seek agreement with respect to the allocation of shares in the quota with all other contracting parties having a substantial interest in supplying the product concerned. In cases in which this method is not reasonably practicable, the contracting party concerned shall allot to contracting parties having a substantial interest in supplying the product shares based upon the proportions, supplied by such contracting parties during a previous representative period, of the total quantity or value of imports of the product, due account being taken of any special factors which may have affected or may be affecting the trade in the product. No conditions or formalities shall be imposed which would prevent any contracting party from utilizing fully the share of any such total quantity or value which has been allotted to it, subject to importation being made within any prescribed period to which the quota may relate.

3. (a) In cases in which import licenses are issued in connection with import restrictions, the contracting party applying the restrictions shall provide, upon the request of any contracting party having an interest in the trade in the product concerned, all relevant information concerning the administration of the restrictions, the import licenses granted over a recent period and the distribution of such licenses among supplying countries; *Provided,* That there shall be no obligation to supply information as to the names of importing or supplying enterprises.

(b) In the case of import restrictions involving the fixing of quotas, the contracting party applying the restrictions shall give public notice of the total quantity or value of the product or products which will be permitted to be imported during a specified future period and of any change in such quantity or value. Any supplies of the product in question which were *en route* at the time at which public notice was given shall not be excluded from entry; *Provided,* That they may be counted so far as practicable, against the quantity permitted to be imported in the period in question, and also, where necessary, against the quantities permitted to be imported in the next following period or periods; and *Provided further,* That if any contracting party customarily exempts from such restrictions products entered for consumption or withdrawn from warehouse for consumption during a period of thirty days after the day of such public notice, such practice shall be considered full compliance with this sub-paragraph.

(c) In the case of quotas allocated among supplying countries, the contracting party applying the restrictions shall promptly inform all other contracting parties having an interest in supplying the product concerned of the shares in the quota currently allocated, by quantity or value, to the various supplying countries and shall give public notice thereof.

4. With regard to restrictions applied in accordance with paragraph 2(d) of this Article or under paragraph 2(c) of Article XI, the selection of a representative period for any product and the appraisal of any special factors affecting the trade in the product shall be made initially by the contracting party applying the restriction; *Provided,* That such contracting party shall, upon the request of any other contracting party having a substantial interest in supplying that product or upon the request of the CONTRACTING PARTIES, consult promptly with the other contracting party or the CONTRACTING PARTIES regarding the need for an adjustment of the proportion determined or of the base period selected, or for the reappraisal of the special factors involved, or for the elimination of conditions, formalities or any other provisions established unilaterally relating to the allocation of an adequate quota or its unrestricted utilization.

5. The provisions of this Article shall apply to any tariff quota instituted or maintained by any contracting party, and, in so far as applicable, the principles of this Article shall also extend to export restrictions.

ARTICLE XIV—EXCEPTIONS TO THE RULE OF NON-DISCRIMINATION [12]

1. A contracting party which applies restrictions under Article XII or under Section B of Article XVIII may, in the application of such restrictions, deviate from the provisions of Article XIII in a manner having equivalent effect to restrictions on payments and transfers for current international transactions that contracting party may at that time apply under Article VIII or XIV of the Articles of Agreement of the International Monetary Fund, or under analogous provisions of a special exchange agreement entered into pursuant to paragraph 6 of Article XV.

2. A contracting party which is applying import restrictions under Article XII or under Section B of Article XVIII may, with the consent of the CONTRACTING PARTIES temporarily deviate from the provisions of Article XIII in respect of a small part of its external trade where the benefits to the contracting party or contracting parties concerned substantially outweigh any injury which may result to the trade of other contracting parties.

3. The provisions of Article XIII shall not preclude a group of territories having a common quota in the International Monetary Fund from applying against imports from other countries, but not among themselves, restrictions in accordance with the provisions of Article XII or of Section B of Article XVIII on condition that such restrictions are in all other respects consistent with the provisions of Article XIII.

4. A contracting party applying import restrictions under Article XII or under Section B of Article XVIII shall not be precluded by Articles XI to XV or Section B of Article XVIII of this Agreement

[12] Text as amended February 15, 1961, on which date Annex J was deleted. Originally amended and restated by special Protocol Modifying Article XIV of the GATT (62 Stat. 2006). Further amended and restated by Section J of the Protocol Amending the Preamble and Parts II and III of the GATT (8 UST 1775).

from applying measures to direct its exports in such a manner as to increase its earnings of currencies which it can use without deviation from the provisions of Article XIII.

5. A contracting party shall not be precluded by Articles XI to XV, inclusive, or by Section B of Article XVIII, of this Agreement from applying quantitative restrictions:

(a) having equivalent effect to exchange restrictions authorized under Section 3(b) of Article VII of the Articles of Agreement of the International Monetary Fund, or

(b) under the preferential arrangements provided for in Annex A of this Agreement, pending the outcome of the negotiations referred to therein.

ARTICLE XV—EXCHANGE ARRANGEMENTS

1. The CONTRACTING PARTIES shall seek co-operation with the International Monetary Fund to the end that the CONTRACTING PARTIES and the Fund may pursue a coordinated policy with regard to exchange questions within the jurisdiction of the fund and questions of quantitative restrictions and other trade measures within the jurisdiction of the CONTRACTING PARTIES.

2. In all cases in which the CONTRACTING PARTIES are called upon to consider or deal with problems concerning monetary reserves, balances of payments or foreign exchange arrangements, they shall consult fully with the International Monetary Fund. In such consultations, the CONTRACTING PARTIES shall accept all findings of statistical and other facts presented by the fund relating to foreign exchange, monetary reserves and balances of payments, and shall accept the determination of the Fund as to whether action by a contracting party in exchange matters is in accordance with the Articles of Agreement of the International Monetary Fund, or with the terms of a special exchange agreement between that contracting party and the CONTRACTING PARTIES. The CONTRACTING PARTIES, in reaching their final decision in cases involving the criteria set forth in paragraph 2(a) of Article XII or in paragraph 9 [13] of Article XVIII, shall accept the determination of the Fund as to what constitutes a serious decline in the contracting party's monetary reserves, a very low level of its monetary reserves or a reasonable rate of increase in its monetary reserves, and as to the financial aspects of other matters covered in consultation in such cases.

3. The CONTRACTING PARTIES shall seek agreement with the Fund regarding procedures for consultation under paragraph 2 of this Article.

4. Contracting parties shall not, by exchange action, frustrate the intent of the provisions of this Agreement, nor, by trade action, the intent of the provisions of the Articles of Agreement of the International Monetary Fund.

5. If the CONTRACTING PARTIES consider, at any time, that exchange restrictions on payments and transfers in connection with imports are being applied by a contracting party in a manner inconsistent with the exceptions provided for in this Agreement for quantitative restrictions, they shall report thereon to the Fund.

---

[13] Sec. K of the Protocol Amending the Preamble and Parts II and III of the GATT (8 UST 1776) added the reference to para. 9.

6. Any contracting party which is not a member of the fund shall, within a time to be determined by the CONTRACTING PARTIES after consultation with the Fund, become a member of the Fund, or, failing that, enter into a special exchange agreement with the CONTRACTING PARTIES. A contracting party which ceases to be a member of the fund shall forthwith enter into a special exchange agreement with the CONTRACTING PARTIES. Any special exchange agreement entered into by a contracting party under this paragraph shall thereupon become part of its obligations under this Agreement.

7. (a) A special exchange agreement between a contracting party and the CONTRACTING PARTIES under paragraph 6 of this Article shall provide to the satisfaction of the CONTRACTING PARTIES that the objectives of this Agreement will not be frustrated as a result of action in exchange matters by the contracting party in question.

(b) The terms of any such agreement shall not impose obligations on the contracting party in exchange matters generally more restrictive than those imposed by the Articles of Agreement of the International Monetary Fund on members of the Fund.

8. A contracting party which is not a member of the Fund shall furnish such information within the general scope of section 5 of Article VIII of the Articles of Agreement of the International Monetary Fund as the CONTRACTING PARTIES may require in order to carry out their functions under this Agreement.

9. Nothing in this Agreement shall preclude: [14]

(a) the use by a contracting party of exchange controls or exchange restrictions in accordance with the Articles of Agreement of the International Monetary Fund or with that contracting party's special exchange agreement with the CONTRACTING PARTIES, or

(b) the use by a contracting party of restrictions or controls on imports or exports, the sole effect of which, additional to the effects permitted under Articles XI, XII, XIII and XIV, is to make effective such exchange controls or exchange restrictions.

ARTICLE XVI—SUBSIDIES

SECTION A—SUBSIDIES IN GENERAL

1. If any contracting party grants or maintains any subsidy, including any form of income or price support, which operates directly or indirectly to increase exports of any product from, or to reduce imports of any product into, its territory, it shall notify the contracting parties in writing of the extent and nature of the subsidization, of the estimated effect of the subsidization on the quantity of the affected product or products imported into or exported from its territory and of the circumstances making the subsidization necessary. In any case in which it is determined that serious prejudice to the interests of any other contracting party is caused or threatened by any such subsidization, the contracting party granting the subsidy shall, upon request, discuss with the other

[14] Part D of the Protocol Modifying Part II and Article XXVI of the GATT (62 Stat. 3683) amended this paragraph.

contracting party or parties concerned, or with the CONTRACTING PARTIES, the possibility of limiting the subsidization.

SECTION B—ADDITIONAL PROVISIONS ON EXPORT SUBSIDIES [15]

2. The contracting parties recognize that the granting by a contracting party of a subsidy on the export of any product may have harmful effects for other CONTRACTING PARTIES, both importing and exporting, may cause undue disturbance to their normal commercial interests, and may hinder the achievement of the objectives of this Agreement.

3. Accordingly, contracting parties should seek to avoid the use of subsidies on the export of primary products. If, however, a contracting party grants directly or indirectly any form of subsidy which operates to increase the export of any primary product from its territory, such subsidy shall not be applied in a manner which results in that contracting party having more than an equitable share of world export trade in that product, account being taken of the shares of the contracting parties in such trade in the product during a previous representative period, and any special factors which may have affected or may be affecting such trade in the product.

4. Further, as from 1 January 1958 or the earliest practicable date thereafter, contracting parties shall cease to grant either directly or indirectly any form of subsidy on the export of any product other than a primary product which subsidy results in the sale of such product for export at a price lower than the comparable price charged for the like product to buyers in the domestic market. Until 31 December 1957 no contracting party shall extend the scope of any such subsidization beyond that existing on 1 January 1955 by the introduction of new, or the extension of existing, subsidies.

5. The CONTRACTING PARTIES shall review the operation of the provisions of this Article from time to time with a view to examining its effectiveness, in the light of actual experience, in promoting the objectives of this Agreement and avoiding subsidization seriously prejudicial to the trade or interests of contracting parties.

ARTICLE XVII—STATE TRADING ENTERPRISES [16]

1. (a) Each contracting party undertakes that if it establishes or maintains a State enterprise, wherever located, or grants to any enterprise, formally or in effect, exclusive or special privileges, such enterprise shall, in its purchases or sales involving either imports or exports, act in a manner consistent with the general principles of nondiscriminatory treatment prescribed in this Agreement for governmental measures affecting imports or exports by private traders.

---

[15] Sec. L of the Protocol Amending the Preamble and Parts II and III of the GATT (8 UST 1776) added sec. B.

[16] Sec. M of the Protocol Amending the Preamble and Parts II and III of the GATT (8 UST 1777) added paras. 3 and 4 and the title to Article XVII.

(b) The provision of sub-paragraph (a) of this paragraph shall be understood to require that such enterprises shall, having due regard to the other provisions of this Agreement, make any such purchases or sales solely in accordance with commercial considerations, including price, quality, availability, marketability, transportation and other conditions of purchase or sale, and shall afford the enterprises of the other contracting parties adequate opportunity, in accordance with customary business practice, to compete for participation in such purchases or sales.

(c) No contracting party shall prevent any enterprise (whether or not an enterprise described in sub-paragraph (a) of this paragraph) under its jurisdiction from acting in accordance with the principles of sub-paragraphs (a) and (b) of this paragraph.

2. The provisions of paragraph 1 of this article shall not apply to imports of products for immediate or ultimate consumption in governmental use and not otherwise for resale or use in the production of goods for sale. With respect to such imports, each contracting party shall accord to the trade of the other contracting parties fair and equitable treatment.

3.[16] The contracting parties recognize that enterprises of the kind described in paragraph 1(a) of this Article might be operated so as to create serious obstacles to trade; thus negotiations on a reciprocal and mutually advantageous basis designed to limit or reduce such obstacles are of importance to the expansion of international trade.

4.[16] (a) Contracting parties shall notify the CONTRACTING PARTIES of the products which are imported into or exported from their territories by enterprises of the kind described in paragraph 1(a) of this Article.

(b) A contracting party establishing, maintaining or authorizing an import monopoly of a product, which is not the subject of a concession under Article II, shall, on the request of another contracting party having a substantial trade in the product concerned, inform the CONTRACTING PARTIES of the import markup on the product during a recent representative period, or, when it is not possible to do so, of the price charged on the resale of the product.

(c) The CONTRACTING PARTIES may, at the request of a contracting party which has reason to believe that its interests under this Agreement are being adversely affected by the operations of an enterprise of the kind described in paragraph 1(a), request the contracting party establishing, maintaining or authorizing such enterprise to supply information about its operations related to the carrying out of the provisions of this Agreement.

(d) The provisions of this paragraph shall not require any contracting party to disclose confidential information which would impede law enforcement or otherwise be contrary to the public interest or would prejudice the legitimate commercial interests of particular enterprises.

ARTICLE XVIII—GOVERNMENTAL ASSISTANCE TO ECONOMIC DEVELOPMENT [17]

1. The contracting parties recognize that the attainment of the objectives of this Agreement will be facilitated by the progressive development of their economies, particularly of those contracting parties the economies of which can only support low standards of living and are in the early stages of development.

2. The contracting parties recognize further that it may be necessary for those contracting parties, in order to implement programmes and policies of economic development designed to raise the general standard of living of their people, to take protective or other measures affecting imports, and that such measures are justified in so far as they facilitate the attainment of the objectives of this Agreement. They agree, therefore, that those contracting parties should enjoy additional facilities to enable them (a) to maintain sufficient flexibility in their tariff structure to be able to grant the tariff protection required for the establishment of a particular industry and (b) to apply quantitative restrictions for balance of payments purposes in a manner which takes full account of the continued high level of demand for imports likely to be generated by their programmes of economic development.

3. The contracting parties recognize finally that with those additional facilities which are provided for in Sections A and B of this Article, the provisions of this Agreement would normally be sufficient to enable contracting parties to meet the requirements of their economic development. They agree, however, that there may be circumstances where no measure consistent with those provisions is practicable to permit a contracting party in the process of economic development to grant the governmental assistance required to promote the establishment of particular industries with a view to raising the general standard of living of its people. Special procedures are laid down in Sections C and D of this Article to deal with those cases.

4. (a) Consequently, a contracting party the economy of which can only support low standards of living and is in the early stages of development shall be free to deviate temporarily from the provisions of the other Articles of this Agreement, as provided in Sections A, B and C of this Article.

(b) A contracting party the economy of which is in the process of development but which does not come within the scope of sub-paragraph (a) above, may submit applications to the CONTRACTING PARTIES under Section D of this Article.

5. The contracting parties recognize that the export earnings of contracting parties the economies of which are of the type described in paragraph 4 (a) and (b) above, and which depend on exports of a small number of primary commodities may be seriously reduced by a decline in the sale of such commodities. Accordingly, when the exports of primary commodities by such a contracting party are seriously affected by measures taken by another contracting party, it

---

[17] Sec. N of the Protocol Amending the Preamble and Parts II and III of the GATT (8 UST 1778) amended Article XVIII. Previously amended by sec. E of the Protocol Modifying Part II and Article XXVI of the GATT (62 Stat. 3684).

may have resort to the consultation provisions of Article XXII of this Agreement.

6. The CONTRACTING PARTIES shall review annually all measures applied pursuant to the provisions of Sections C and D of this Article.

SECTION A

7. (a) If a contracting party coming within the scope of paragraph 4(a) of this Article considers it desirable, in order to promote the establishment of a particular industry with a view to raising the general standard of living of its people, to modify or withdraw a concession included in the appropriate Schedule annexed to this Agreement, it shall notify the CONTRACTING PARTIES to this effect and enter into negotiations with any contracting party with which such concession was initially negotiated, and with any other contracting party determined by the CONTRACTING PARTIES to have a substantial interest therein. If agreement is reached between such contracting parties concerned, they shall be free to modify or withdraw concessions under the appropriate Schedules to this Agreement in order to give effect to such agreement, including any compensatory adjustments involved.

(b) If agreement is not reached within sixty days after the notification provided for in sub-paragraph (a) above, the contracting party which proposes to modify or withdraw the concession may refer the matter to the CONTRACTING PARTIES, which shall promptly examine it. If they find that the contracting party which proposes to modify or withdraw the concession has made every effort to reach an agreement and that the compensatory adjustment offered by it is adequate, that contracting party shall be free to modify or withdraw the concession if at the same time, it gives effect to the compensatory adjustment. If the CONTRACTING PARTIES do not find that the compensation offered by a contracting party proposing to modify or withdraw the concession is adequate, but find that it has made every reasonable effort to offer adequate compensation, that contracting party shall be free to proceed with such modification or withdrawal. If such action is taken, any other contracting party referred to in sub-paragraph (a) above shall be free to modify or withdraw substantially equivalent concessions initially negotiated with the contracting party which has taken the action.

SECTION B

8. The contracting parties recognize that contracting parties coming within the scope of paragraph 4(a) of this Article tend, when they are in rapid process of development, to experience balance of payments difficulties arising mainly from efforts to expand their internal markets as well as from the instability in their terms of trade.

9. In order to safeguard its external financial position and to ensure a level of reserves adequate for the implementation of its programme of economic development, a contracting party coming within the scope of paragraph 4(a) of this Article may, subject to the provisions of paragraphs 10 to 12, control the general level of its

imports by restricting the quantity or value of merchandise permitted to be imported; *Provided* that the import restrictions instituted, maintained or intensified shall not exceed those necessary.

(a) to forestall the threat of, or to stop, a serious decline in its monetary reserves, or

(b) in the case of a contracting party with inadequate monetary reserves, to achieve a reasonable rate of increase in its reserves.

Due regard shall be paid in either case to any special factors which may be affecting the reserves of the contracting party or its need for reserves, including, where special external credits or other resources are available to it, the need to provide for the appropriate use of such credits or resources.

10. In applying these restrictions, the contracting party may determine their incidence on imports of different products or classes of products in such a way as to give priority to the importation of those products which are more essential in the light of its policy of economic development; *Provided* that the restrictions are so applied as to avoid unnecessary damage to the commercial or economic interests of any other contracting party and not to prevent unreasonably the importation of any description of goods in minimum commercial quantities the exclusion of which would impair regular channels of trade; and *Provided further* that the restrictions are not so applied as to prevent the importation of commercial samples or to prevent compliance with patent, trademark, copyright or similar procedures.

11. In carrying out its domestic policies, the contracting party concerned shall pay due regard to the need for restoring equilibrium in its balance of payments on a sound and lasting basis and to the desirability of assuring an economic employment of productive resources. It shall progressively relax any restrictions applied under this Section as conditions improve, maintaining them only to the extent necessary under the terms of paragraph 9 of this Article and shall eliminate them when conditions no longer justify such maintenance; *Provided* that no contracting party shall be required to withdraw or modify restrictions on the ground that a change in its development policy would render unnecessary the restrictions which it is applying under this Section.

12. (a) Any contracting party applying new restrictions or raising the general level of its existing restrictions by a substantial intensification of the measures applied under this Section, shall immediately after instituting or intensifying such restrictions (or, in circumstances in which prior consultation is practicable, before doing so) consult with the CONTRACTING PARTIES as to the nature of its balance of payments difficulties, alternative corrective measures which may be available, and the possible effect of the restrictions on the economies of other contracting parties.

(b) On a date to be determined by them, the CONTRACTING PARTIES shall review all restrictions still applied under this Section on that date. Beginning two years after that date, contracting parties applying restrictions under this Section shall enter into consultations of the type provided for in sub-paragraph (a) above with the CONTRACTING PARTIES at intervals of approximately, but not less than, two years according to a programme to be drawn up each year by the CONTRACTING PARTIES; *Provided* that no consultation under this sub-paragraph shall take place within two years after the conclusion of a consultation of a general nature under any other provision of this paragraph.

(c)(i) If, in the course of consultations with a contracting party under sub-paragraph (a) or (b) of this paragraph, the CONTRACTING PARTIES find that the restrictions are not consistent with the provisions of this Section or with those of Article XIII (subject to the provisions of Article XIV), they shall indicate the nature of the inconsistency and may advise that the restrictions be suitably modified.

(ii) If, however, as a result of the consultations, the CONTRACTING PARTIES determine that the restrictions are being applied in a manner involving an inconsistency of a serious nature with the provisions of this Section or with those of Article XIII (subject to the provisions of Article XIV) and that damage to the trade of any contracting party is caused or threatened thereby, they shall so inform the contracting party applying the restrictions and shall make appropriate recommendations for securing conformity with such provisions within a specified period. If such contracting party does not comply with these recommendations within the specified period, the CONTRACTING PARTIES may release any contracting party the trade of which is adversely affected by the restrictions from such obligations under this Agreement towards the contracting party applying the restrictions as they determine to be appropriate in the circumstances.

(d) The CONTRACTING PARTIES shall invite any contracting party which is applying restrictions under this Section to enter into consultations with them at the request of any contracting party which can establish a *prima facie* case that the restrictions are inconsistent with the provisions of this Section or with those of Article XIII (subject to the provisions of Article XIV) and that its trade is adversely affected thereby. However, no such invitation shall be issued unless the CONTRACTING PARTIES have ascertained that direct discussions between the contracting parties concerned have not been successful. If, as a result of the consultations with the CONTRACTING PARTIES no agreement is reached and they determine that the restrictions are being applied inconsistently with such provisions, and that damage to the trade of the contracting party initiating the procedure is caused or threatened thereby, they shall recommend the withdrawal or modification of the restrictions. If the restrictions are not withdrawn or modified within such time as the CONTRACTING PARTIES may prescribe, they may release the contracting party initiating the procedure from such obligations under this Agreement towards the contracting party applying the restrictions as they determine to be appropriate in the circumstances.

(e) If a contracting party against which action has been taken in accordance with the last sentence of sub-paragraph (c)(ii) or (d) of this paragraph, finds that the release of obligations authorized by the CONTRACTING PARTIES adversely affects the operation of its programme and policy of economic development, it shall be free, not later than sixty days after such action is taken to give written notice to the Executive Secretary to the CONTRACTING PARTIES of its intention to withdraw from this Agreement and such withdrawal shall take effect on the sixtieth day following the day on which the notice is received by him.

(f) In proceeding under this paragraph, the CONTRACTING PARTIES shall have due regard to the factors referred to in paragraph 2 of this Article. Determinations under this paragraph shall be rendered expeditiously and, if possible, within sixty days of the initiation of the consultations.

SECTION C

13. If a contracting party coming within the scope of paragraph 4(a) of this Article finds that governmental assistance is required to promote the establishment of a particular industry with a view to raising the general standard of living of its people, but that no measure consistent with the other provisions of this Agreement is practicable to achieve that objective, it may have recourse to the provisions and procedures set out in this Section.

14. The contracting party concerned shall notify the CONTRACTING PARTIES of the special difficulties which it meets in the achievement of the objective outlined in paragraph 13 of this Article and shall indicate the specific measure affecting imports which it proposes to introduce in order to remedy these difficulties. It shall not introduce that measure before the expiration of the time-limit laid down in paragraph 15 or 17, as the case may be, or if the measure affects imports of a product which is the subject of a concession included in the appropriate Schedule annexed to this Agreement, unless it has secured the concurrence of the CONTRACTING PARTIES in accordance with the provisions of paragraph 18; *Provided* that, if the industry receiving assistance has already started production, the contracting party may, after informing the CONTRACTING PARTIES, take such measures as may be necessary to prevent, during that period, imports of the product or products concerned from increasing substantially above a normal level.

15. If, within thirty days of the notification of the measure, the CONTRACTING PARTIES do not request the contracting party concerned to consult with them, that contracting party shall be free to deviate from the relevant provisions of the other Articles of this Agreement to the extent necessary to apply the proposed measure.

16. If it is requested by the CONTRACTING PARTIES to do so, the contracting party concerned shall consult with them as to the purpose of the proposed measure, as to alternative measures which may be available under this Agreement, and as to the possible effect of the measure proposed on the commercial and economic interests of other contracting parties. If, as a result of such consultation, the CONTRACTING PARTIES agree that there is no measure consistent with the other provisions of this Agreement which is practicable in order to achieve the objective outlined in paragraph 13 of this Article, and concur in the proposed measure, the contracting party concerned shall be released from its obligations under the relevant provisions of the other Articles of this Agreement to the extent necessary to apply that measure.

17. If, within ninety days after the date of the notification of the proposed measure under paragraph 14 of this Article, the CONTRACTING PARTIES have not concurred in such measure, the contracting party concerned may introduce the measure proposed after informing the CONTRACTING PARTIES.

18. If the proposed measure affects a product which is the subject of a concession included in the appropriate Schedule annexed to this Agreement, the contracting party concerned shall enter into consultations with any other contracting party with which the concession was initially negotiated, and with any other contracting party determined by the CONTRACTING PARTIES to have a substantial interest therein. The CONTRACTING PARTIES shall concur in the measure if they agree that there is no measure consistent with the other provisions of this Agreement which is practicable in order to achieve the objective set forth in paragraph 13 of this Article, and if they are satisfied:

(a) that agreement has been reached with such other contracting parties as a result of the consultations referred to above, or

(b) if no such agreement has been reached within sixty days after the notification provided for in paragraph 14 has been received by the CONTRACTING PARTIES, that the contracting party having recourse to this Section has made all reasonable efforts to reach an agreement and that the interests of other contracting parties are adequately safeguarded.

The contracting party having recourse to this Section shall thereupon be released from its obligations under the relevant provisions of the other Articles of this Agreement to the extent necessary to permit it to apply the measure.

19. If a proposed measure of the type described in paragraph 13 of this Article concerns an industry the establishment of which has in the initial period been facilitated by incidental protection afforded by restrictions imposed by the contracting party concerned for balance of payments purposes under the relevant provisions of this Agreement, that contracting party may resort to the provisions and procedures of this Section, *Provided* that it shall not apply the proposed measure without the concurrence of the CONTRACTING PARTIES.

20. Nothing in the preceding paragraphs of this Section shall authorize any deviation from the provisions of Articles I, II and XIII of this Agreement. The provisos to paragraph 10 of this Article shall also be applicable to any restriction under this Section.

21. At any time while a measure is being applied under paragraph 17 of this Article any contracting party substantially affected by it may suspend the application to the trade of the contracting party having recourse to this Section of such substantially equivalent concessions or other obligations under this Agreement the suspension of which the CONTRACTING PARTIES do not disapprove; *Provided* that sixty days' notice of such suspension is given to the CONTRACTING PARTIES not later than six months after the measure has been introduced or changed substantially to the detriment of the contracting party affected. Any such contracting party shall afford adequate opportunity for consultation in accordance with the provisions of Article XXII of this Agreement.

SECTION D

22. A contracting party coming within the scope of subparagraph 4(b) of this Article desiring, in the interest of the development of its economy, to introduce a measure of the type described in paragraph 13 of this Article in respect of the establishment of a particular industry may apply to the CONTRACTING PARTIES for approval of such measure. The CONTRACTING PARTIES shall promptly consult with such contracting party and shall, in making their decision be guided by the considerations set out in paragraph 16. If the CONTRACTING PARTIES concur in the proposed measure the contracting party concerned shall be released from its obligations under the relevant provisions of the other Articles of this agreement to the extent necessary to permit it to apply the measure. If the proposed measure affects a product which is the subject of a concession included in the appropriate Schedule annexed to this Agreement, the provisions of paragraph 18 shall apply.

23. Any measure applied under this Section shall comply with the provisions of paragraph 20 of this Article.

ARTICLE XIX—EMERGENCY ACTION ON IMPORTS OF PARTICULAR PRODUCTS

1. (a) If, as a result of unforeseen developments and of the effect of the obligations incurred by a contracting party under this Agreement, including tariff concessions, any product is being imported into the territory of that contracting party in such increased quantities and under such conditions as to cause or threaten serious injury to domestic producers in that territory of like or directly competitive products, the contracting party shall be free, in respect of such product, and to the extent and for such time as may be necessary to prevent or remedy such injury, to suspend the obligation in whole or in part or to withdraw or modify the concession.

(b) If any product, which is the subject of a concession with respect to a preference, is being imported into the territory of a contracting party in the circumstances set forth in sub-paragraph (a) of this paragraph, so as to cause or threaten serious injury to domestic producers of like or directly competitive products in the territory of a contracting party which receives or received such preference, the importing contracting party shall be free, if that other contracting party so requests, to suspend the relevant obligation in whole or in part or to withdraw or modify the concession in respect of the product, to the extent and for such time as may be necessary to prevent or remedy such injury.

2. Before any contracting party shall take action pursuant to the provisions of paragraph 1 of this Article, it shall give notice in writing to the CONTRACTING PARTIES as far in advance as may be practicable and shall afford the CONTRACTING PARTIES and those contracting parties having a substantial interest as exporters of the product concerned an opportunity to consult with it in respect of the proposed action. When such notice is given in relation to a concession with respect to a preference, the notice shall name the contracting party which has requested the action. In critical circumstances, where delay would cause damage which it would be difficult to repair, action under paragraph 1 of this Article may be

taken provisionally without prior consultation, on the condition that consultation shall be effected immediately after taking such action.

3. (a) If agreement among the interested contracting parties with respect to the action is not reached, the contracting party which proposes to take or continue the action shall, nevertheless, be free to do so, and if such action is taken or continued, the affected contracting parties shall then be free, not later than ninety days after such action is taken, to suspend, upon the expiration of thirty days from the day on which written notice of such suspension is received by the CONTRACTING PARTIES, the application to the trade of the contracting party taking such action, or in the case envisaged in paragraph 1(b) of this Article, to the trade of the contracting party requesting such action, of such substantially equivalent concessions or other obligations[18] under this Agreement the suspension of which the CONTRACTING PARTIES do not disapprove.

(b) Notwithstanding the provisions of sub-paragraph (a) of this paragraph, where action is taken under paragraph 2 of this Article without prior consultation and causes or threatens serious injury in the territory of a contracting party to the domestic producers of products affected by the action, that contracting party shall, where delay would cause damage difficult to repair, be free to suspend, upon the taking of the action and throughout the period of consultation, such concessions or other obligations as may be necessary to prevent or remedy the injury.

ARTICLE XX—GENERAL EXCEPTIONS

Subject to the requirement that such measures are not applied in a manner which would constitute a means of arbitrary or unjustifiable discrimination between countries where the same conditions prevail, or a disguised restriction on international trade, nothing in this Agreement shall be construed to prevent the adoption or enforcement by any contracting party of measures:

(a) necessary to protect public morals;

(b) necessary to protect human, animal or plant life or health;

(c) relating to the importation or exportation of gold or silver;

(d) necessary to secure compliance with laws or regulations which are not inconsistent with the provisions of this Agreement, including those relating to customs enforcement, the enforcement of monopolies operated under paragraph 4 of Article II and Article XVII, the protection of patents, trademarks and copyrights, and the prevention of deceptive practices;

(e) relating to the products of prison labour;

(f) imposed for the protection of national treasures of artistic, historic or archaeological value;

(g) relating to the conservation of exhaustible natural resources if such measures are made effective in conjunction with restrictions on domestic production or consumption;

---

[18] Sec. O of the Protocol Amending the Preamble and Parts II and III of the GATT (8 UST 1786) struck out "obligations or concessions" and inserted in lieu thereof "concessions or other obligations".

(h)[19] undertaken in pursuance of obligations under any intergovernmental commodity agreement which conforms to criteria submitted to the CONTRACTING PARTIES and not disapproved by them or which is itself so submitted and not so disapproved;

(i) involving restrictions on exports of domestic materials necessary to assure essential quantities of such materials to a domestic processing industry during periods when the domestic price of such materials is held below the world price as part of a governmental stabilization plan; *Provided* that such restrictions shall not operate to increase the exports of or the protection afforded to such domestic industry, and shall not depart from the provisions of this Agreement relating to non-discrimination;

(j)[19] essential to the acquisition or distribution of products in general or local short supply; *Provided* that any such measures shall be consistent with the principle that all contracting parties are entitled to an equitable share of the international supply of such products, and that any such measures, which are inconsistent with the other provisions of this Agreement shall be discontinued as soon as the conditions giving rise to them have ceased to exist. The CONTRACTING PARTIES shall review the need for this sub-paragraph not later than 30 June 1960.

ARTICLE XXI—SECURITY EXCEPTIONS

Nothing in this Agreement shall be construed

(a) to require any contracting party to furnish any information the disclosure of which it considers contrary to its essential security interests; or

(b) to prevent any contracting party from taking any action which it considers necessary for the protection of its essential security interests

(i) relating to fissionable materials or the materials from which they are derived;

(ii) relating to the traffic in arms, ammunition and implements of war and to such traffic in other goods and materials as is carried on directly or indirectly for the purpose of supplying a military establishment;

(iii) taken in time of war or other emergency in international relations; or

(c) to prevent any contracting party from taking any action in pursuance of its obligations under the United Nations Charter for the maintenance of international peace and security.

ARTICLE XXII—CONSULTATION[20]

1. Each contracting party shall accord sympathetic consideration to, and shall afford adequate opportunity for consultation regarding, such representations as may be made by another contracting

[19] Sec. P of the Protocol Amending the Preamble and Parts II and III of the GATT (8 UST 1786) amended para. (h) and added para. (j).

[20] Sec. Q of the Protocol Amending the Preamble and Parts II and III of the GATT (8 UST 1787) amended Article XXII.

party with respect to any matter affecting the operation of this Agreement.

2. The CONTRACTING PARTIES may, at the request of a contracting party, consult with any contracting party or parties in respect of any matter for which it has not been possible to find a satisfactory solution through consultation under paragraph 1.

ARTICLE XXIII—NULLIFICATION OR IMPAIRMENT

1. If any contracting party should consider that any benefit accruing to it directly or indirectly under this Agreement is being nullified or impaired or that the attainment of any objective of the Agreement is being impeded as the result of (a) the failure of another contracting party to carry out its obligations under this Agreement, or (b) the application by another contracting party of any measure, whether or not it conflicts with the provisions of this Agreement, or (c) the existence of any other situation, the contracting party may, with a view to the satisfactory adjustment of the matter, make written representations or proposals to the other contracting party or parties which it considers to be concerned. Any contracting party thus approached shall give sympathetic consideration to the representations or proposals made to it.

2. If no satisfactory adjustment is effected between the contracting parties concerned within a reasonable time, or if the difficulty is of the type described in paragraph 1(c) of this Article, the matter may be referred to the CONTRACTING PARTIES. The CONTRACTING PARTIES shall promptly investigate any matter so referred to them and shall make appropriate recommendations to the contracting parties which they consider to be concerned, or give a ruling on the matter, as appropriate. The CONTRACTING PARTIES may consult with contracting parties, with the Economic and Social Council of the United Nations and with any appropriate inter-governmental organization in cases where they consider such consultation necessary. If the CONTRACTING PARTIES consider that the circumstances are serious enough to justify such action, they may authorize a contracting party or parties to suspend the application to any other contracting party or parties of such concessions or other obligations under this Agreement as they determine to be appropriate in the circumstances.[21] If the application to any contracting party of any concession or other obligation is in fact suspended, that contracting party shall then be free, not later than sixty days after such action is taken to give written notice to the Executive Secretary to the CONTRACTING PARTIES of its intention to withdraw from this Agreement and such withdrawal shall take effect upon the sixtieth day following the day on which such notice is received by him.[21]

---

[21] Sec. R of the Protocol Amending the Preamble and Parts II and III of the GATT (8 UST 1787) added these sentences.

PART III

ARTICLE XXIV—TERRITORIAL APPLICATION—FRONTIER TRAFFIC—CUSTOMS UNIONS AND FREE-TRADE AREAS[22]

1. The provisions of this Agreement shall apply to the metropolitan customs territories of the contracting parties and to any other customs territories in respect of which this Agreement has been accepted under Article XXVI or is being applied under Article XXXIII or pursuant to the Protocol of Provisional Application. Each such customs territory shall, exclusively for the purposes of the territorial application of this Agreement, be treated as though it were a contracting party; *Provided* that the provisions of this paragraph shall not be construed to create any rights or obligations as between two or more customs territories in respect of which this Agreement has been accepted under Article XXVI or is being applied under Article XXXIII or pursuant to the Protocol of Provisional Application by a single contracting party.

2. For purposes of this Agreement customs territory shall be understood to mean any territory with respect to which separate tariffs or other regulations of commerce are maintained for a substantial part of the trade of such territory with other territories.

3. The provisions of this Agreement shall not be construed to prevent:

(a) advantages accorded by any contracting party to adjacent countries in order to facilitate frontier traffic;

(b) advantages accorded to the trade with the Free Territory of Trieste by countries contiguous to that territory, provided that such advantages are not in conflict with the Treaties of Peace arising out of the Second World War.

4.[23] The contracting parties recognize the desirability of increasing freedom of trade by the development, through voluntary agreements, of closer integration between the economies of the countries parties to such agreements. They also recognize that the purpose of a customs union or of a free-trade area should be to facilitate trade between the constituent territories and not to raise barriers to the trade of other contracting parties with such territories.

5. Accordingly, the provisions of this Agreement shall not prevent, as between the territories of contracting parties, the formation of a customs union or of a free-trade area or the adoption of an interim agreement necessary for the formation of a customs union or of a free-trade area; *Provided* that:

(a) with respect to a customs union, or an interim agreement leading to the formation of a customs union, the duties and other regulations of commerce imposed at the institution of any such union or interim agreement in respect of trade with contracting parties not parties to such union or agreement shall not on the whole be higher or more restrictive than the general incidence of the duties and regulations of commerce applicable in the constituent territories prior to the formation of such

---

[22] The Special Protocol Relating to Article XXIV of the GATT (62 Stat. 2013) amended Article XXIV.

[23] Sec. S of the Protocol Amending the Preamble and Parts II and III of the GATT (8 UST 1788) amended para. 4.

union or the adoption of such interim agreement, as the case may be;

(b) with respect to a free-trade area, or an interim agreement leading to the formation of a free-trade area, the duties and other regulations of commerce maintained in each of the constituent territories and applicable at the formation of such free-trade area or the adoption of such interim agreement to the trade of contracting parties not included in such area or not parties to such agreement shall not be higher or more restrictive than the corresponding duties and other regulations of commerce existing in the same constituent territories prior to the formation of the free-trade area, or interim agreement, as the case may be; and

(c) any interim agreement referred to in sub-paragraphs (a) and (b) shall include a plan and schedule for the formation of such a customs union or of such a free-trade area within a reasonable length of time.

6. If, in fulfilling the requirements of sub-paragraphs 5(a), a contracting party proposes to increase any rate of duty inconsistently with the provisions of Article II, the procedure set forth in Article XXVIII shall apply. In providing for compensatory adjustment, due account shall be taken of the compensation already afforded by the reductions brought about in the corresponding duty of the other constituents of the union.

7. (a) Any contracting party deciding to enter into a customs union or free-trade area, or an interim agreement leading to the formation of such a union or area, shall promptly notify the CONTRACTING PARTIES and shall make available to them such information regarding the proposed union or area as will enable them to make such reports and recommendations to contracting parties as they may deem appropriate.

(b) If, after having studied the plan and schedule included in an interim agreement referred to in paragraph 5 in consultation with the parties to that agreement and taking due account of the information made available in accordance with the provisions of sub-paragraph (a), the CONTRACTING PARTIES find that such agreement is not likely to result in the formation of a customs union or of a free-trade area within the period contemplated by the parties to the agreement or that such period is not a reasonable one, the CONTRACTING PARTIES shall make recommendations to the parties to the agreement. The parties shall not maintain or put into force, as the case may be, such agreement if they are not prepared to modify it in accordance with these recommendations.

(c) Any substantial change in the plan or schedule referred to in paragraph 5(c) shall be communicated to the CONTRACTING PARTIES, which may request the contracting parties concerned to consult with them if the change seems likely to jeopardize or delay unduly the formation of the customs union or of the free-trade area.

8. For the purposes of this Agreement:

(a) A customs union shall be understood to mean the substitution of a single customs territory for two or more customs territories, so that

(i) duties and other restrictive regulations of commerce (except, where necessary, those permitted under Article XI,

XII, XIII, XIV, XV and XX) are eliminated with respect to substantially all the trade between the constituent territories of the union or at least with respect to substantially all the trade in products originating in such territories, and,

(ii) subject to the provisions of paragraph 9, substantially the same duties and other regulations of commerce are applied by each of the members of the union to the trade of territories not included in the union;

(b) A free-trade area shall be understood to mean a group of two or more customs territories in which the duties and other restrictive regulations of commerce (except, where necessary, those permitted under Articles XI, XII, XIII, XIV, XV, and XX) are eliminated on substantially all the trade between the constituent territories in products originating in such territories.

9. The preferences referred to in paragraph 2 of Article I shall not be affected by the formation of a customs union or of a free-trade area but may be eliminated or adjusted by means of negotiations with contracting parties affected. This procedure of negotiations with affected contracting parties shall, in particular, apply to the elimination of preferences required to conform with the provisions of paragraph 8(a)(i) and paragraph 8(b).

10. The CONTRACTING PARTIES may by a two-thirds majority approve proposals which do not full comply with the requirements of paragraphs 5 to 9 inclusive, provided that such proposals lead to the formation of a customs union or a free-trade area in the sense of this Article.

11. Taking into account the exceptional circumstances arising out of the establishment of India and Pakistan as independent States and recognizing the fact that they have long constituted an economic unit, the contracting parties agree that the provisions of this Agreement shall not prevent the two countries from entering into special arrangements with respect to the trade between them, pending the establishment of their mutual trade relations on a definitive basis.

12. Each contracting party shall take such reasonable measures as may be available to it to ensure observance of the provisions of this Agreement by the regional and local governments and authorities within its territory.

ARTICLE XXV—JOINT ACTION BY THE CONTRACTING PARTIES

1. Representatives of the contracting parties shall meet from time to time for the purpose of giving effect to those provisions of this Agreement which involve joint action and, generally, with a view to facilitating the operation and furthering the objectives of this Agreement. Wherever reference is made in this Agreement to the contracting parties acting jointly they are designated as the CONTRACTING PARTIES.

2. The Secretary-General of the United Nations is requested to convene the first meeting of the CONTRACTING PARTIES, which shall take place not later than March 1, 1948.

3. Each contracting party shall be entitled to have one vote at all meetings of the CONTRACTING PARTIES.

4. Except as otherwise provided for in this Agreement, decisions of the CONTRACTING PARTIES shall be taken by a majority of the votes cast.

5.[24] In exceptional circumstances not elsewhere provided for in this Agreement, the CONTRACTING PARTIES may waive an obligation imposed upon a contracting party by this Agreement; *Provided* that any such decision shall be approved by a two-thirds majority of the votes cast and that such majority shall comprise more than half of the contracting parties. The CONTRACTING PARTIES may also by such a vote

(i) define certain categories of exceptional circumstances to which other voting requirements shall apply for the waiver of obligations, and

(ii) prescribe such criteria as may be necessary for the application of this sub-paragraph.[25]

ARTICLE XXVI—ACCEPTANCE, ENTRY INTO FORCE AND REGISTRATION[26]

1. The date of this Agreement shall be 30 October 1947.

2. This Agreement shall be open for acceptance by any contracting party which, on 1 March 1955, was a contracting party or was negotiating with a view to accession to this Agreement.

3. This Agreement, done in a single English original and in a single French original, both texts authentic, shall be deposited with the Secretary-General of the United Nations, who shall furnish certified copies thereof to all interested governments.

4. Each government accepting this Agreement shall deposit an instrument of acceptance with the Executive Secretary of the CONTRACTING PARTIES who will inform all interested governments of the date of deposit of each instrument of acceptance and of the day on which this Agreement enters into force under paragraph 6 of this Article.

5. (a) Each government accepting this Agreement does so in respect of its metropolitan territory and of the other territories for which it has international responsibility, except such separate customs territories as it shall notify to the Executive Secretary to the CONTRACTING PARTIES at the time of its own acceptance.

(b) Any government, which has so notified the Executive Secretary under the exceptions in sub-paragraph (a) of this paragraph, may at any time give notice to the Executive Secretary that its acceptance shall be effective in respect of any separate customs territory or territories so excepted and such notice shall take effect on the thirtieth day following the day on which it is received by the Executive Secretary.

(c) If any of the customs territories, in respect of which a contracting party has accepted this Agreement, possesses or acquires full autonomy in the conduct of its external commercial relations

---

[24] The Protocol Modifying Certain Provisions of the GATT (62 Stat. 1992) amended para. 5. The Protocol Amending the Preamble and Parts II and III of the GATT (8 UST 1788) deleted subparas. (b), (c) and (d).

[25] As signed; should probably read "paragraph".

[26] Sec. U of the Protocol Amending the Preamble and Parts II and III of the GATT (8 UST 1788) amended Article XXVI.

and of the other matters provided for in this Agreement, such territory shall, upon sponsorship through a declaration by the responsible contracting party establishing the above-mentioned fact, be deemed to be a contracting party.

6. This Agreement shall enter into force, as among the governments which have accepted it, on the thirtieth day following the day on which instruments of acceptance have been deposited with the Executive Secretary to the CONTRACTING PARTIES on behalf of governments named in Annex H, the territories of which account for 85 per centum of the total external trade of the territories of such governments, computed in accordance with the applicable column of percentages set forth therein. The instrument of acceptance of each other government shall take effect on the thirtieth day following the day on which such instrument has been deposited.

7. The United Nations is authorized to effect registration of this Agreement as soon as it enters into force.

ARTICLE XXVII—WITHHOLDING OR WITHDRAWAL OF CONCESSIONS

Any contracting party shall at any time be free to withhold or to withdraw in whole or in part any concession, provided for in the appropriate Schedule annexed to this Agreement, in respect of which such contracting party determines that it was initially negotiated with a government which has not become, or has ceased to be, a contracting party. A contracting party taking such action shall notify the CONTRACTING PARTIES and, upon request, consult with contracting parties which have a substantial interest in the product concerned.[27]

ARTICLE XXVIII—MODIFICATION OF SCHEDULES[28]

1. On the first day of each three-year period, the first period beginning on 1 January 1958 (or on the first day of any other period that may be specified by the CONTRACTING PARTIES by two-thirds of the votes cast) a contracting party (hereafter in this Article referred to as the "applicant contracting party") may, by negotiation and agreement with any contracting party with which such concession was initially negotiated and with any other contracting party determined by the CONTRACTING PARTIES to have a principal supplying interest (which two preceding categories of contracting parties, together with the applicant contracting party, are in this Article hereinafter referred to as the "contracting parties primarily concerned"), and subject to consultation with any other contracting party determined by the CONTRACTING PARTIES to have a substantial interest in such concession, modify or withdraw a concession included in the appropriate Schedule annexed to this Agreement.

2. In such negotiations and agreement, which may include provision for compensatory adjustment with respect to other products, the contracting parties concerned shall endeavour to maintain a general level of reciprocal and mutually advantageous concessions

---

[27] Sec. V of the Protocol Amending the Preamble and Parts II and III of the GATT (8 UST 1789) amended this sentence. Further amended by the Protocol Modifying Article XXVI of the Agreement of October 30, 1947 (2 UST 1583).

[28] Sec. W of the Protocol Amending the Preamble and Parts II and III of the GATT (18 UST 1790) amended Article XXVIII.

not less favourable to trade than that provided for in this Agreement prior to such negotiations.

3. (a) If agreement between the contracting parties primarily concerned cannot be reached before 1 January 1958 or before the expiration of a period envisaged in paragraph 1 of this Article, the contracting party which propose to modify or withdraw the concession shall, nevertheless, be free to do so and if such action is taken any contracting party with which such concession was initially negotiated, any contracting party determined under paragraph 1 to have a principal supplying interest and any contracting party determined under paragraph 1 to have a substantial interest shall then be free not later than six months after such action is taken, to withdraw, upon the expiration of thirty days from the day on which written notice of such withdrawal is received by the CONTRACTING PARTIES, substantially equivalent concessions initially negotiated with the applicant contracting party.

(b) If agreement between the contracting parties primarily concerned is reached but any other contracting party determined under paragraph 1 of this Article to have a substantial interest is not satisfied, such other contracting party shall be free, not later than six months after action under such agreement is taken, to withdraw, upon the expiration of thirty days from the day on which written notice of such withdrawal is received by the CONTRACTING PARTIES, substantially equivalent concessions initially negotiated with the applicant contracting party.

4. The CONTRACTING PARTIES may, at any time, in special circumstances, authorize a contracting party to enter into negotiations for modification or withdrawal of a concession included in the appropriate Schedule annexed to this Agreement subject to the following procedures and conditions:

(a) Such negotiations and any related consultations shall be conducted in accordance with the provisions of paragraphs 1 and 2 of this Article.

(b) If agreement between the contracting parties primarily concerned is reached in the negotiations, the provisions of paragraph 3(b) of this Article shall apply.

(c) If agreement between the contracting parties primarily concerned is not reached within a period of sixty days after negotiations have been authorized, or within such longer period as the CONTRACTING PARTIES may have prescribed the applicant contracting party may refer the matter to the CONTRACTING PARTIES.

(d) Upon such reference, the CONTRACTING PARTIES shall promptly examine the matter and submit their views to the contracting parties primarily concerned with the aim of achieving a settlement. If a settlement is reached, the provisions of paragraph 3(b) shall apply as if agreement between the contracting parties primarily concerned had been reached. If no settlement is reached between the contracting parties primarily concerned, the applicant contracting party shall be free to modify or withdraw the concession, unless the CONTRACTING PARTIES determine that the applicant contracting party has unreasonably failed to offer adequate compensation. If such action is taken, any contracting party with which the concession was initially negotiated, any contracting party determined under paragraph 4(a) to have a principal supplying interest and any contracting party determined under paragraph 4(a) to have a substantial interest, shall be free, not later than six months after such action is taken, to modify or withdraw, upon the expiration of thirty days from the day on which written notice of such withdrawal is received by the CONTRACTING PARTIES, substantially equivalent concessions initially negotiated with the applicant contracting party.

5. Before 1 January 1958 and before the end of any period envisaged in paragraph 1 a contracting party may elect by notifying the CONTRACTING PARTIES to reserve the right, for the duration of the next period, to modify the appropriate Schedule in accordance with the procedures of paragraphs 1 to 3. If a contracting party so elects, other contracting parties shall have the right, during the same period, to modify or withdraw, in accordance with the same procedures, concessions initially negotiated with that contracting party.

ARTICLE XXVIII bis—TARIFF NEGOTIATIONS[29]

1. The contracting parties recognize that customs duties often constitute serious obstacles to trade; thus negotiations on a reciprocal and mutually advantageous basis, directed to the substantial reduction of the general level of tariffs and other charges on imports and exports and in particular to the reduction of such high tariffs as discourage the importation even of minimum quantities, and conducted with due regard to the objectives of this Agreement and the varying needs of individual contracting parties, are of great importance to the expansion of international trade. The CONTRACTING PARTIES may therefore sponsor such negotiations from time to time.

2. (a) Negotiations under this Article may be carried out on a selective product-by-product basis or by the application of such multilateral procedures as may be accepted by the contracting parties concerned. Such negotiations may be directed towards the reduction of duties, the binding of duties at then existing levels or undertakings that individual duties or the average duties on specified categories of products shall not exceed specified levels. The binding against increase of low duties or of duty-free treatment shall, in principle, be recognized as a concession equivalent in value to the reduction of high duties.

(b) The contracting parties recognize that in general the success of multilateral negotiations would depend on the participation of all contracting parties which conduct a substantial proportion of their external trade with one another.

3. Negotiations shall be conducted on a basis which affords adequate opportunity to take into account:

(a) the needs of individual contracting parties and individual industries;

(b) the needs of less-developed countries for a more flexible use of tariff protection to assist their economic development and the special needs of these countries to maintain tariffs for revenue purposes; and

[29] The Protocol Amending the Preamble and Parts II and III of the GATT (8 UST 1792) added Article XXVIII.

(c) all other relevant circumstances, including the fiscal, developmental, strategic and other needs of the contracting parties concerned.

ARTICLE XXIX—THE RELATION OF THIS AGREEMENT TO THE HAVANA CHARTER[30]

1. The contracting parties undertake to observe to the fullest extent of their executive authority the general principles of Chapters I to VI inclusive and of Chapter IX of the Havana Charter pending their acceptance of it in accordance with their constitutional procedures.

2. Part II of this Agreement shall be suspended on the day on which the Havana Charter enters into force.

3. If by September 30, 1949, the Havana Charter has not entered into force, the contracting parties shall meet before December 31, 1949, to agree whether this Agreement shall be amended, supplemented or maintained.

4. If at any time the Havana Charter should cease to be in force, the CONTRACTING PARTIES shall meet as soon as practicable thereafter to agree whether this Agreement shall be supplemented, amended or maintained. Pending such agreement, Part II of this Agreement shall again enter into force; *Provided* that the provisions of Part II other than Article XXIII shall be replaced, *mutatis mutandis,* in the form in which they then appeared in the Havana Charter; and *Provided further* that no contracting party shall be bound by any provisions which did not bind it at the time when the Havana Charter ceased to be in force.

5. If any contracting party has not accepted the Havana Charter by the date upon which it enters into force, the CONTRACTING PARTIES shall confer to agree whether, and if so in what way, this Agreement in so far as it affects relations between such contracting party and other contracting parties, shall be supplemented or amended. Pending such agreement the provisions of Part II of this Agreement shall, notwithstanding the provisions of paragraph 2 of this Article, continue to apply as between such contracting party and other contracting parties.

6. Contracting parties which are Members of the International Trade Organization shall not invoke the provisions of this Agreement so as to prevent the operation of any provision of the Havana Charter. The application of the principle underlying this paragraph to any contracting party which is not a Member of the International Trade Organization shall be the subject of an agreement pursuant to paragraph 5 of this Article.

ARTICLE XXX—AMENDMENTS

1. Except where provision for modification is made elsewhere in this Agreement, amendments to the provisions of Part I of this Agreement or to the provisions of Article XXIX or of this Article

[30] Part C of the Protocol Modifying Part I and Article XXIX of the GATT (3 UST 5357) amended Article XXIX.

shall become effective upon acceptance by all the contracting parties, and other amendments to this Agreement shall become effective, in respect of those contracting parties which accept them, upon acceptance by two thirds of the contracting parties and thereafter for each other contracting party upon acceptance by it.

2. Any contracting party accepting an amendment to this Agreement shall deposit an instrument of acceptance with the Secretary-General of the United Nations within such period as the CONTRACTING PARTIES may specify. The CONTRACTING PARTIES may decide that any amendment made effective under this Article is of such a nature that any contracting party which has not accepted it within a period specified by the CONTRACTING PARTIES shall be free to withdraw from this Agreement, or to remain a contracting party with the consent of the CONTRACTING PARTIES.

ARTICLE XXXI—WITHDRAWAL [31]

Without prejudice to the provisions of paragraph 12 of Article XVIII or of Article XXIII or of paragraph 2 of Article XXX, any contracting party may withdraw from this Agreement, or may separately withdraw on behalf of any of the separate customs territories for which it has international responsibility and which at the time possesses full autonomy in the conduct of its external commercial relations and of the other matters provided for in this Agreement. The withdrawal shall take effect upon the expiration of six months from the day on which written notice of withdrawal is received by the Secretary-General of the United Nations.

ARTICLE XXXII—CONTRACTING PARTIES [32]

1. The contracting parties to this Agreement shall be understood to mean those governments which are applying the provisions of this Agreement under Articles XXVI or XXXIII or pursuant to the Protocol of Provisional Application.

2. At any time after the entry into force of this Agreement pursuant to paragraph 6 of Article XXVI, those contracting parties which have accepted this Agreement pursuant to paragraph 4 of Article XXVI may decide that any contracting party which has not so accepted it shall cease to be a contracting party.

ARTICLE XXXIII—ACCESSION [33]

A government not party to this Agreement, or a government acting on behalf of a separate customs territory possessing full autonomy in the conduct of its external commercial relations and of the other matters provided for in this Agreement, may accede to this Agreement, on its own behalf or on behalf of that territory, on terms to be agreed between such government and the CONTRACTING PARTIES. Decisions of the CONTRACTING PARTIES under this paragraph shall be taken by a two-thirds majority.

---

[31] Sec. Y of the Protocol Amending the Preamble and Parts II and III of the GATT (8 UST 1793) amended Article XXXI.

[32] The Protocol Modifying Certain Provisions of the GATT (62 Stat. 1992) amended Article XXXII.

[33] The Protocol Modifying Certain Provisions of the GATT (62 Stat. 1992) amended Article XXXIII.

ARTICLE XXXIV—ANNEXES

The annexes to this Agreement are hereby made an integral part of this Agreement.

ARTICLE XXXV—NON-APPLICATION OF THE AGREEMENT BETWEEN PARTICULAR CONTRACTING PARTIES[34]

1. This Agreement, or alternatively Article II of this Agreement shall not apply as between any contracting party and any other contracting party if:

(a) the two contracting parties have not entered into tariff negotiations with each other, and

(b) either of the contracting parties, at the time either becomes a contracting party, does not consent to such application.

2. The CONTRACTING PARTIES may review the operation of this Article in particular cases at the request of any contracting party and make appropriate recommendations.

PART IV—TRADE AND DEVELOPMENT[35]

ARTICLE XXXVI—PRINCIPLES AND OBJECTIVES

1. The contracting parties,

(a) recalling that the basic objectives of this Agreement include the raising of standards of living and the progressive development of the economies of all contracting parties, and considering that the attainment of these objectives is particularly urgent for less-developed contracting parties;

(b) considering that export earnings of the less-developed contracting parties can play a vital part in their economic development and that the extent of this contribution depends on the prices paid by the less-developed contracting parties for essential imports, the volume of their exports, and the prices received for these exports;

(c) noting, that there is a wide gap between standards of living in less-developed countries and in other countries;

(d) recognizing that individual and joint action is essential to further the development of the economies of less-developed contracting parties and to bring about a rapid advance in the standards of living in these countries;

(e) recognizing that international trade as a means of achieving economic and social advancement should be governed by such rules and procedures—and measures in conformity with such rules and procedures—as are consistent with the objectives set forth in this Article;

(f) noting that the CONTRACTING PARTIES may enable less-developed contracting parties to use special measures to promote their trade and development;

agree as follows:

---

[34] Protocol Modifying Certain Provisions of the GATT (62 Stat. 1992) added Article XXXV. Further amended by sec. Z of the Protocol Amending the Preamble and Parts II and III of the GATT (8 UST 1793).

[35] Sec. 1A of the Protocol to Introduce Part IV (17 UST 1977) added Part IV.

2. There is need for a rapid and sustained expansion of the export earnings of the less-developed contracting parties.

3. There is need for positive efforts designed to ensure that less-developed contracting parties secure a share in the growth in international trade commensurate with the needs of their economic development.

4. Given the continued dependence of many less-developed contracting parties on the exportation of a limited range of primary products, there is need to provide in the largest possible measure more favourable and acceptable conditions of access to world markets for these products, and whenever appropriate to devise measures designed to stabilize and improve conditions of world markets in these products, including in particular measures designed to attain stable, equitable and remunerative prices, thus permitting an expansion of world trade and demand and a dynamic and steady growth of the real export earnings of these countries so as to provide them with expanding resources for their economic development.

5. The rapid expansion of the economies of the less-developed contracting parties will be facilitated by a diversification of the structure of their economies and the avoidance of an excess dependence on the export of primary products. There is, therefore, need for increased access in the largest possible measure to markets under favourable conditions for processed and manufactured products currently or potentially of particular export interest to less developed contracting parties.

6. Because of the chronic deficiency in the export proceeds and other foreign exchange earnings of less-developed contracting parties, there are important inter-relationships between trade and financial assistance to development. There is, therefore, need for close and continuing collaboration between the CONTRACTING PARTIES and the international lending agencies so that they can contribute most effectively to alleviating the burdens these less-developed contracting parties assume in the interest of their economic development.

7. There is need for appropriate collaboration between the CONTRACTING PARTIES, other intergovernmental bodies and the organs and agencies of the United Nations system, whose activities relate to the trade and economic development of less-developed countries.

8. The developed contracting parties do not expect reciprocity for commitments made by them in trade negotiations to reduce or remove tariffs and other barriers to the trade of less-developed contracting parties.

9. The adoption of measures to give effect to these principles and objectives shall be a matter of conscious and purposeful effort on the part of the contracting parties both individually and jointly.

ARTICLE XXXVII—COMMITMENTS

1. The developed contracting parties shall to the fullest extent possible—that is, except when compelling reasons, which may include legal reasons, make it impossible—give effect to the following provisions:

(a) accord high priority to the reduction and elimination of barriers to products currently or potentially of particular export interest to less-developed contracting parties including customs duties and other restrictions which differentiate unreasonably between such products in their primary and in their processed forms:

(b) refrain from introducing, or increasing the incidence of, customs duties or non-tariff import barriers on products currently or potentially of particular export interest to less-developed contracting parties; and

(c)(i) refrain from imposing new fiscal measures, and

(ii) in any adjustments of fiscal policy accord high priority to the reduction and elimination of fiscal measures,

which would hamper, or which hamper, significantly the growth of consumption of primary products, in raw or processed form, wholly or mainly produced in the territories of less-developed contracting parties, and which are applied specifically to those products.

2. (a) Whenever it is considered that effect is not being given to any of the provisions of sub-paragraph (a), (b), or (c) of paragraph 1, the matter shall be reported to the CONTRACTING PARTIES either by the contracting party not so giving effect to the relevant provisions or by any other interested contracting party.

(b)(i) The CONTRACTING PARTIES shall, if requested so to do by any interested contracting party, and without prejudice to any bilateral consultations that may be undertaken, consult with the contracting party concerned and all interested contracting parties with respect to the matter with a view to reaching solutions satisfactory to all contracting parties concerned in order to further the objectives set forth in Article XXXVI. In the course of these consultations, the reasons given in cases where effect was not being given to the provisions of sub-paragraph (a), (b), or (c) of paragraph 1 shall be examined.

(ii) As the implementation of the provisions of sub-paragraph (a), (b), or (c) of paragraph 1 by individual contracting parties may in some cases be more readily achieved where action is taken jointly with other developed contracting parties, such consultation might, where appropriate, be directed towards this end.

(iii) the consultations by the CONTRACTING PARTIES might also, in appropriate cases, be directed towards agreement on joint action designed to further the objectives of this Agreement as envisaged in paragraph 1 of Article XXV.

3. The developed contracting parties shall:

(a) make every effort, in cases where a government directly or indirectly determines the resale price of products wholly or mainly produced in the territories of less-developed contracting parties, to maintain trade margins at equitable levels;

(b) give active consideration to the adoption of other measures designed to provide greater scope for the development of imports from less-developed contracting parties and collaborate in appropriate international action to this end;

(c) have special regard to the trade interests of less-developed contracting parties when considering the application of other measures permitted under this Agreement to meet particular problems and explore all possibilities of constructive remedies before applying such measures where they would affect essential interests of those contracting parties.

4. Less-developed contracting parties agree to take appropriate action in implementation of the provisions of Part IV for the benefit of the trade of other less-developed contracting parties, insofar as such action is consistent with their individual present and future development, financial and trade needs taking into account past trade developments as well as the trade interests of less-developed contracting parties as a whole.

5. In the implementation of the commitments set forth in paragraphs 1 to 4 each contracting party shall afford to any other interested contracting party or contracting parties full and prompt opportunity for consultations under the normal procedures of this agreement with respect to any matter or difficulty which may arise.

ARTICLE XXXVIII—JOINT ACTION

1. The contracting parties shall collaborate jointly, within the framework of this Agreement and elsewhere, as appropriate, to further the objectives set forth in Article XXXVI.

2. In particular, the CONTRACTING PARTIES shall:

(a) where appropriate, take action, including action through international arrangements, to provide improved and acceptable conditions of access to world markets for primary products of particular interest to less-developed contracting parties and to devise measures designed to stabilize and improve conditions of world markets in these products including measures designed to attain stable, equitable and remunerative prices for exports of such products;

(b) seek appropriate collaboration in matters of trade and development policy with the United Nations and its organs and agencies, including any institutions that may be created on the basis of recommendations by the United Nations Conference on Trade and Development;

(c) collaborate in analyzing the development plans and policies of individual less-developed contracting parties and in examining trade and aid relationships with a view to devising concrete measures to promote the development of export potential and to facilitate access to export markets for the products of the industries thus developed and, in this connexion seek appropriate collaboration with governments and international organizations, and in particular with organizations having competence in relation to financial assistance for economic development, in systematic studies of trade and aid relationships in individual less-developed contracting parties aimed at obtaining a clear analysis of export potential, market prospects and any further action that may be required;

(d) keep under continuous review the development of world trade with special reference to the rate of growth of the trade of less-developed contracting parties and make such recommendations to contracting parties as may, in the circumstances, be deemed appropriate;

(e) collaborate in seeking feasible methods to expand trade for the purpose of economic development, through international harmonization and adjustment of national policies and regulations, through technical and commercial standards affecting production, transportation and marketing, and through export promotion by the establishment of facilities for the increased flow of trade information and the development of market research; and

(f) establish such institutional arrangements as may be necessary to further the objectives set forth in Article XXXVI and to give effect to the provisions of this Part.

ANNEX A—LIST OF TERRITORIES REFERRED TO IN PARAGRAPH 2(a) OF ARTICLE I

United Kingdom of Great Britain and Northern Ireland.
Dependent territories of the United Kingdom of Great Britain and Northern Ireland.
Canada.
Commonwealth of Australia.
Dependent territories of the Commonwealth of Australia.
New Zealand.
Dependent territories of New Zealand.
Union of South Africa including South West Africa.
Ireland.
India (as on April 10, 1947).
Newfoundland.
Southern Rhodesia.
Burma.
Ceylon.

Certain of the territories listed above have two or more preferential rates in force for certain products. Any such territory may, by agreement with the other contracting parties which are principal suppliers of such products at the most-favoured-nation rate, substitute for such preferential rates a single preferential rate which shall not on the whole be less favourable to suppliers at the most-favoured-nation rate than the preferences in force prior to such substitution.

The imposition of an equivalent margin of tariff preference to replace a margin of preference in an internal tax existing on April 10, 1947, exclusively between two or more of the territories listed in this Annex or to replace the preferential quantitative arrangements described in the following paragraph, shall not be deemed to constitute an increase in a margin of tariff preference.

The preferential arrangements referred to in paragraph 5(b) of Article XIV are those existing in the United Kingdom on April 10, 1947, under contractual agreements with the Governments of Canada, Australia and New Zealand, in respect to chilled and frozen beef and veal, frozen mutton and lamb, chilled and frozen pork, and bacon. It is the intention, without prejudice to any action taken under part I(h) of Article XX, that these arrangements shall be eliminated or replaced by tariff preferences, and that negotiations to this end shall take place as soon as practicable among the countries substantially concerned or involved.

The film hire tax in force in New Zealand on April 10, 1947, shall, for the purposes of this Agreement, be treated as a customs duty under Article I. The renters' film quota in force in New Zealand on April 10, 1947, shall, for the purposes of this Agreement, be treated as a screen quota under Article IV.

The Dominions of India and Pakistan have not been mentioned separately in the above list since they had not come into existence as such on the base date of April 10, 1947.

ANNEX B—LIST OF TERRITORIES OF THE FRENCH UNION REFERRED TO IN PARAGRAPH 2(b) OF ARTICLE I [36]

France.
French Equatorial Africa (Treaty Basin of the Congo [37] and other territories).
French West Africa.
Cameroons under French Trusteeship.[37]
French Somali Coast and Dependencies.
French Establishments in Oceania.
French Establishments in the Condominium of the New Hebrides.[37]
Indo-China.
Madagascar and Dependencies.
Morocco (French zone).[37]
New Caledonia and Dependencies.
Saint-Pierre and Miquelon.
Togo under French Trusteeship.[37]
Tunisia.

ANNEX C—LIST OF TERRITORIES OF THE CUSTOMS UNION OF BELGIUM, LUXEMBURG AND THE NETHERLANDS REFERRED TO IN PARAGRAPH 2(b) OF ARTICLE I

The Economic Union of Belgium and Luxemburg.
Belgian Congo.
Ruanda Urundi.
Netherlands.
New Guinea.
Surinam.
Netherlands Antilles.
Republic of Indonesia.

For imports into the metropolitan territories constituting the Customs Union.

ANNEX D—LIST OF TERRITORIES REFERRED TO IN PARAGRAPH 2(b) OF ARTICLE I AS RESPECTS THE UNITED STATES OF AMERICA

United States of America (customs territory).
Dependent territories of the United States of America.
Republic of the Philippines.

The imposition of an equivalent margin of tariff preference to replace a margin of preference in an internal tax existing on April 10, 1947, exclusively between two or more of the territories listed

---

[36] The Fourth Protocol of Rectifications and modifications to the annexes and to the text of the schedules to the GATT (10 UST 217) amended Annex B.

[37] For imports into Metropolitan France and Territories of the French Union.

in this Annex shall not be deemed to constitute an increase in a margin of tariff presence.

ANNEX E—LIST OF TERRITORIES COVERED BY PREFERENTIAL ARRANGEMENTS BETWEEN CHILE AND NEIGHBOURING COUNTRIES REFERRED TO IN PARAGRAPH 2(d) OF ARTICLE I

Preferences in force exclusively between Chile on the one hand, and

1. Argentina.
2. Bolivia.
3. Peru.

on the other hand.

ANNEX F—LIST OF TERRITORIES COVERED BY PREFERENTIAL ARRANGEMENTS BETWEEN LEBANON AND SYRIA AND NEIGHBORING COUNTRIES REFERRED TO IN PARAGRAPH 2(d) OF ARTICLE I

Preferences in force exclusively between the Lebano-Syrian Customs Union, on the one hand, and

1. Palestine.
2. Transjordan.

on the other hand.

ANNEX G—DATES ESTABLISHING MAXIMUM MARGINS OF PREFERENCE REFERRED TO IN PARAGRAPH 4 OF ARTICLE I [38]

Australia	October 15, 1946.
Canada	July 1, 1939.
France	January 1, 1939.
Lebano-Syrian Customs Union	November 30, 1938.
Union of South Africa	July 1, 1938.
Southern Rhodesia	May 1, 1941.

ANNEX H—PERCENTAGE SHARES OF TOTAL EXTERNAL TRADE TO BE USED FOR THE PURPOSE OF MAKING THE DETERMINATION REFERRED TO IN ARTICLE XXVI [39]

(Based on the average of 1949–1953)

If, prior to the accession of the Government to Japan to the General Agreement, the present Agreement has been accepted by contracting parties the external trade of which under column I accounts for the percentage of such trade specified in paragraph 6 of Article XXVI, column I shall be applicable for the purposes of that paragraph. If the present Agreement has not been so accepted prior to the accession of the Government of Japan, column II shall be applicable for the purposes of that paragraph.

---

[38] The authentic text erroneously reads "Paragraph 3". The reference to Article I was intended to be a reference to the last paragraph of Article I, which originally consisted of only three numbered paragraphs.

[39] Sec. AA of the Protocol Amending the Preamble and Parts II and III of the GATT (8 UST 1794) amended Annex H.

	Contracting parties on—			Contracting parties on—	
	Mar. 1, 1955 (Column I)	Mar. 1, 1955 and Japan (Column II)		Mar. 1, 1955 (Column I)	Mar. 1, 1955 and Japan (Column II)
Australia	3.1	3.0	Indonesia	1.3	1.3
Austria	.9	.8	Italy	2.9	2.8
Belgium-Luxemburg	4.3	4.2	Netherlands, Kingdom of the.	4.7	4.6
Brazil	2.5	2.4	New Zealand	1.0	1.0
Burma	.3	.3	Nicaragua	.1	.1
Canada	6.7	6.5	Norway	1.1	1.1
Ceylon	.5	.5	Pakistan	.9	.8
Chile	.6	.6	Peru	.4	.4
Cuba	1.1	1.1	Rhodesia and Nyasaland	.6	.6
Czechoslovakia	1.4	1.4	Sweden	2.5	2.4
Denmark	1.4	1.4	Turkey	.6	.6
Dominican Republic	.1	.1	Union of South Africa	1.8	1.8
Finland	1.0	1.0	United Kingdom	20.3	19.8
France	8.7	8.5	United States of America	20.6	20.1
Germany, Federal Republic of.	5.3	5.2	Uruguay	.4	.4
Greece	.4	.4	Japan	....	2.3
Haiti	.1	.1			
India	2.4	2.4	Total	100.0	100.0

Note: These percentages have been computed taking into account the trade of all territories in respect of which the General Agreement on Tariffs and Trade is applied.

ANNEX I—NOTES AND SUPPLEMENTARY PROVISIONS[40]

AD ARTICLE I

Paragraph 1

The obligations incorporated in paragraph 1 of Article I by reference to paragraphs 2 and 4 of Article III and those incorporated in paragraph 2(b) of Article II by reference to Article VI shall be considered as falling within Part II for the purposes of the Protocol of Provisional Application.

The cross-references, in the paragraph immediately above and in paragraph 1 of Article I, to paragraphs 2 and 4 of Article III shall only apply after Article III has been modified by the entry into force of the amendment provided for in the Protocol Modifying Part II and Article XXVI of the General Agreement on Tariffs and Trade, dated September 14, 1948.

Paragraph 4

The term "margin of preference" means the absolute difference between the most-favoured-nation rate of duty and the preferential

[40] The Protocol Amending the Preamble and Parts II and III of the GATT (8 UST 1795–1809) amended Annex I.

rate of duty for the like product, and not the proportionate relation between those rates. As examples:

(1) If the most-favoured-nation rate were 36 per cent *ad valorem* and the preferential rate were 24 per cent *ad valorem*, and not one-third of the most-favoured-nation rate;

(2) If the most-favoured-nation rate were 36 per cent *ad valorem* and the preferential rate were expressed as two-thirds of the most-favoured-nation rate, the margin of preference would be 12 per cent *ad valorem;*

(3) If the most-favoured-nation rate were 2 francs per kilogramme and the preferential rate were 1.50 francs per kilogramme, the margin of preference would be 0.50 francs per kilogramme.

The following kinds of customs action, taken in accordance with established uniform procedures, would not be contrary to a general binding of margins of preference:

(i) The re-application to an imported product of a tariff classification or rate of duty, properly applicable to such product, in cases in which the application of such classification or rate to such product was temporarily suspended or inoperative on April 10, 1947; and

(ii) The classification of a particular product under a tariff item other than that under which importations of that product were classified on April 10, 1947, in cases in which the tariff law clearly contemplates that such product may be classified under more than one tariff item.

AD ARTICLE II

Paragraph 2(a)

The cross-reference, in paragraph 2(a) of Article II, to paragraph 2 of Article III shall only apply after Article III has been modified by the entry into force of the amendment provided for in the Protocol Modifying Part II and Article XXVI of the General Agreement on Tariffs and Trade, dated September 14, 1948.

Paragraph 2(b)

See the note relating to paragraph 1 of Article I.

Paragraph 4

Except where otherwise specifically agreed between the contracting parties which initially negotiated the concession, the provisions of this paragraph will be applied in the light of the provisions of Article 31 of the Havana Charter.

AD ARTICLE III

Any internal tax or other internal charge, or any law, regulation or requirement of the kind referred to in paragraph 1 which applies to any imported product and to the like domestic product and is collected or enforced in the case of the imported product at the time or point of importation, is nevertheless to be regarded as an internal tax or other internal charge, or a law, regulation or requirement of the kind referred to in paragraph 1, and is accordingly subject to the provisions of Article III.

Paragraph 1

The application of paragraph 1 to internal taxes imposed by local governments and authorities within the territory of a contracting party is subject to the provisions of the final paragraph of article XXIV. The term "reasonable measures" in the last-mentioned paragraph would not require, for example, the repeal of existing national legislation authorizing local governments to impose internal taxes which, although technically inconsistent with the letter of Article III, are not in fact inconsistent with its spirit, if such repeal would result in a serious financial hardship for the local governments or authorities concerned. With regard to taxation by local governments or authorities which is inconsistent with both the letter and spirit of Article III, the term "reasonable measures" would permit a contracting party to eliminate the inconsistent taxation gradually over a transition period, if abrupt action would create serious administrative and financial difficulties.

Paragraph 2

A tax conforming to the requirements of the first sentence of paragraph 2 would be considered to be inconsistent with the provisions of the second sentence only in cases where competition was involved between, on the one hand, the taxed product and, on the other hand, a directly competitive or substitutable product which was not similarly taxed.

Paragraph 5

Regulations consistent with the provisions of the first sentence of paragraph 5 shall not be considered to be contrary to the provisions of the second sentence in any case in which all of the products subject to the regulations are produced domestically in substantial quantities. A regulation cannot be justified as being consistent with the provisions of the second sentence on the ground that the proportion or amount allocated to each of the products which are the subject of the regulation constitutes an equitable relationship between imported and domestic products.

AD ARTICLE V

Paragraph 5

With regard to transportation charges, the principle laid down in paragraph 5 refers to like products being transported on the same route under like conditions.

AD ARTICLE VI

Paragraph 1

1. Hidden dumping by associated houses (that is, the sale by an importer at a price below that corresponding to the price invoiced by an exporter with whom the importer is associated, and also below the price in the exporting country) constitutes a form of price dumping with respect to which the margin of dumping may be calculated on the basis of the price at which the goods are resold by the importer.

2. It is recognized that, in the case of imports from a country which has a complete or substantially complete monopoly of its trade and where all domestic prices are fixed by the State, special difficulties may exist in determining price comparability for the purposes of paragraph 1, and in such cases importing contracting parties may find it necessary to take into account the possibility that a strict comparison with domestic prices in such a country may not always be appropriate.

Paragraphs 2 and 3

Note 1.—As in many other cases in customs administration, a contracting party may require reasonable security (bond or cash deposit) for the payment of anti-dumping or countervailing duty pending final determination of the facts in any case of suspected dumping or subsidization.

Note 2.—Multiple currency practices can in certain circumstances constitute a subsidy to exports which may be met by countervailing duties under paragraph 3 or can constitute a form of dumping by means of a partial depreciation of a country's currency which may be met by action under paragraph 2. By "multiple currency practices" is meant practices by governments or sanctioned by governments.

Paragraph 6(b)

Waivers under the provisions of this sub-paragraph shall be granted only on application by the contracting party proposing to levy an anti-dumping or countervailing duty, as the case may be.

AD ARTICLE VII

Paragraph 1

The expression "or other charges" is not to be regarded as including internal taxes or equivalent charges imposed on or in connexion with imported products.

Paragraph 2

1. It would be in conformity with Article VII to presume that "actual value" may be represented by the invoice price, plus any non-included charges for legitimate costs which are proper elements of "actual value" and plus any abnormal discount or other reduction from the ordinary competitive price.

2. It would be in conformity with Article VII, paragraph 2(b), for a contracting party to construe the phrase "in the ordinary course of trade . . . under fully competitive conditions", as excluding any transaction wherein the buyer and seller are not independent of each other and price is not the sole consideration.

3. The standard of "fully competitive conditions" permits a contracting party to exclude from consideration prices involving special discounts limited to exclusive agents.

4. The wording of sub-paragraphs (a) and (b) permits a contracting party to determine the value for customs purposes, uniformly either (1) on the basis of a particular exporter's prices of the imported merchandise, or (2) on the basis of the general price level of like merchandise.

AD ARTICLE VIII

1. While Article VIII does not cover the use of multiple rates of exchange as such, paragraphs 1 and 4 condemn the use of exchange taxes or fees as a device for implementing multiple currency practices; if, however, a contracting party is using multiple currency exchange fees for balance of payments reasons with the approval of the International Monetary Fund, the provisions of paragraph 9(a) of Article XV fully safeguard its position.

2. It would be consistent with paragraph 1 if on the importation of products from the territory of a contracting party into the territory of another contracting party, the production of certificates of origin should only be required to the extent that is strictly indispensable.

AD ARTICLES XI, XII, XIII, XIV AND XVIII

Throughout Articles XI, XII, XIII, XIV and XVIII the terms "import restrictions" or "export restrictions" include restrictions made effective through state-trading operations.

AD ARTICLE XI

Paragraph 2(c)

The term "in any form" in this paragraph covers the same products when in early stage of processing and still perishable, which compete directly with the fresh product and if freely imported would tend to make the restriction on the fresh product ineffective.

Paragraph 2, last sub-paragraph

The term "special factors" includes changes in relative productive efficiency as between domestic and foreign producers, or as between different foreign producers, but not changes artificially brought about by means not permitted under the Agreement.

AD ARTICLE XII

The CONTRACTING PARTIES shall make provision for the utmost secrecy in the conduct of any consultation under the provisions of this Article.

Paragraph 3(c)(i)

Contracting parties applying restrictions shall endeavour to avoid causing serious prejudice to exports of a commodity on which the economy of a contracting party is largely dependent.

Paragraph 4(b)

It is agreed that the date shall be within ninety days after the entry into force of the amendments of this Article effected by the Protocol Amending the Preamble and Parts II and III of this Agreement. However, should the CONTRACTING PARTIES find that conditions were not suitable for the application of the provisions of this sub-paragraph at the time envisaged, they may determine a later date; *Provided* that such date is not more than thirty days after such time as the obligations of Article VIII, Sections 2, 3, and 4 of the Articles of Agreement of the International Monetary Fund become applicable to contracting parties, members of the Fund, the combined foreign trade of which constitutes at least fifty per centum of the aggregate foreign trade of all contracting parties.

Paragraph 4(e)

It is agreed that paragraph 4(e) does not add any new criteria for the imposition or maintenance of quantitative restrictions for balance of payments reasons. It is solely intended to ensure that all external factors such as changes in the terms of trade, quantitative restrictions, excessive tariffs and subsidies, which may be contributing to the balance of payments difficulties of the contracting party applying restrictions will be fully taken into account.

AD ARTICLE XIII

Paragraph 2(d)

No mention was made of "commercial considerations" as a rule for the allocation of quotas because it was considered that its application by governmental authorities might not always be practicable. Moreover, in cases where it is practicable, a contracting party could apply these considerations in the process of seeking agreement, consistently with the general rule laid down in the opening sentence of paragraph 2.

Paragraph 4

See note relating to "special factors" in connection with the last subparagraph of paragraph 2 of Article XI.

AD ARTICLE XIV

Paragraph 1

The provisions of this paragraph shall not be so construed as to preclude full consideration by the CONTRACTING PARTIES, in the consultations provided for in paragraph 4 of Article XII and in paragraph 12 of Article XVIII, of the nature, effects and reasons for discrimination in the field of import restrictions.[40]

Paragraph 2

One of the situations contemplated in paragraph 2 is that of a contracting party holding balances acquired as a result of current transactions which it finds itself unable to use without a measure of discrimination.

AD ARTICLE XV

Paragraph 4

The word "frustrate" is intended to indicate, for example, that infringements of the letter of any Article of this Agreement by exchange action shall not be regarded as a violation of that Article if, in practice, there is no appreciable departure from the intent of the Article. Thus, a contracting party which, as part of its exchange

[40] Text as amended February 15, 1961.

control operated in accordance with the Articles of Agreement of the International Monetary Fund, requires payment to be received for its exports in its own currency or in the currency of one or more members of the International Monetary Fund will not thereby be deemed to contravene Article XI or Article XIII. Another example would be that of a contracting party which specifies on an import license the country from which the goods may be imported, for the purpose not of introducing any additional element of discrimination in its import licensing system but of enforcing permissible exchange controls.

AD ARTICLE XVI

The exemption of an exported product from duties or taxes borne by the like product when destined for domestic consumption, or the remission of such duties or taxes in amounts not in excess of those which have accrued, shall not be deemed to be a subsidy.

Section B

1. Nothing in Section B shall preclude the use by a contracting party of multiple rates of exchange in accordance with the Articles of Agreement of the International Monetary Fund.

2. For the purposes of Section B, a "primary product" is understood to be any product of farm, forest or fishery, or any mineral, in its natural form or which has undergone such processing as is customarily required to prepare it for marketing in substantial volume in international trade.

Paragraph 3

1. The fact that a contracting party has not exported the product in question during the previous representative period would not in itself preclude that contracting party from establishing its right to obtain a share of the trade in the product concerned.

2. A system for the stabilization of the domestic price or of the return to domestic producers of a primary product independently of the movements of export prices, which results at times in the sale of the product for export at a price lower than the comparable price charged for the like product to buyers in the domestic market, shall be considered not to involve a subsidy on exports within the meaning of paragraph 3 if the CONTRACTING PARTIES determine that:

(a) the system has also resulted, or is so designed as to result, in the sale of the product for export at a price higher than the comparable price charged for the like product to buyers in the domestic market; and

(b) the system is so operated, or is designed so to operate, either because of the effective regulation of production or otherwise, as not to stimulate exports unduly or otherwise seriously to prejudice the interests of other contracting parties.

Notwithstanding such determination by the CONTRACTING PARTIES, operations under such a system shall be subject to the provisions of paragraph 3 where they are wholly or partly financed out of government funds in addition to the funds collected from producers in respect of the product concerned.

Paragraph 4

The intention of paragraph 4 is that the contracting parties should seek before the end of 1957 to reach agreement to abolish all remaining subsidies as from 1 January 1958; or, failing this, to reach agreement to extend the application of the standstill until the earliest date thereafter by which they can expect to reach such agreement.

AD ARTICLE XVII

Paragraph 1

The operations of Marketing Boards, which are established by contracting parties and are engaged in purchasing or selling, are subject to the provisions of sub-paragraphs (a) and (b).

The activities of Marketing Boards which are established by contracting parties and which do not purchase or sell but lay down regulations covering private trade are governed by the relevant Articles of this Agreement.

The charging by a state enterprise of different prices for its sales of a product in different markets is not precluded by the provisions of this Article, provided that such different prices are charged for commercial reasons, to meet conditions of supply and demand in export markets.

Paragraph 1(a)

Governmental measures imposed to ensure standards of quality and efficiency in the operation of external trade, or privileges granted for the exploitation of national natural resources but which do not empower the government to exercise control over the trading activities of the enterprise in question, do not constitute "exclusive or special privileges".

Paragraph 1(b)

A country receiving a "tied loan" is free to take this loan into account as a "commercial consideration" when purchasing requirements abroad.

Paragraph 2

The term "goods" is limited to products as understood in commercial practice, and is not intended to include the purchase or sale of services.

Paragraph 3

Negotiations which contracting parties agree to conduct under this paragraph may be directed towards the reduction of duties and other charges on imports and exports or towards the conclusion of any other mutually satisfactory arrangement consistent with the provisions of this Agreement. (See paragraph 4 of Article II and the note to that paragraph.)

Paragraph 4(b)

The term "import mark-up" in this paragraph shall represent the margin by which the price charged by the import monopoly for the imported product (exclusive of internal taxes within the purview of

Article III, transportation, distribution, and other expenses incident to the purchase, sale or further processing, and a reasonable margin of profit) exceeds the landed cost.

AD ARTICLE XVIII

The CONTRACTING PARTIES and the contracting parties concerned shall preserve the utmost secrecy in respect of matters arising under this Article.

Paragraphs 1 and 4

1. When they consider whether the economy of a contracting party "can only support low standards of living", the CONTRACTING PARTIES shall take into consideration the normal position of that economy and shall not base their determination on exceptional circumstances such as those which may result from the temporary existence of exceptionally favourable conditions for the staple export product or products of such contracting party.

2. The phrase "in the early stages of development" is not meant to apply only to contracting parties which have just started their economic development, but also to contracting parties the economies of which are undergoing a process of industrialization to correct an excessive dependence on primary production.

Paragraphs 2, 3, 7, 13 and 22

The reference to the establishment of particular industries shall apply not only to the establishment of a new industry, but also to the establishment of a new branch of production in an existing industry and to the substantial transformation of an existing industry, and to the substantial expansion of an existing industry supplying a relatively small proportion of the domestic demand. It shall also cover the reconstruction of an industry destroyed or substantially damaged as a result of hostilities or natural disasters.

Paragraph 7(b)

A modification or withdrawal, pursuant to paragraph 7(b), by a contracting party, other than the applicant contracting party, referred to in paragraph 7(a), shall be made within six months of the day in which the action is taken by the applicant contracting party, and shall become effective on the thirtieth day following the day on which such modification or withdrawal has been notified to the CONTRACTING PARTIES.

Paragraph 11

The second sentence in paragraph 11 shall not be interpreted to mean that a contracting party is required to relax or remove restrictions if such relaxation or removal would thereupon produce conditions, justifying the intensification or institution, respectively, of restrictions under paragraph 9 of Article XVIII.

Paragraph 12(b)

The date referred to in paragraph 12(b) shall be the date determined by the CONTRACTING PARTIES in accordance with the provisions of paragraph 4(b) of Article XII of this Agreement.

Paragraphs 13 and 14

It is recognized that, before deciding on the introduction of a measure and notifying the contracting parties in accordance with paragraph 14, a contracting party may need a reasonable period of time to assess the competitive position of the industry concerned.

Paragraphs 15 and 16

It is understood that the CONTRACTING PARTIES shall invite a contracting party proposing to apply a measure under Section C to consult with them pursuant to paragraph 16 if they are requested to do so by a contracting party the trade of which would be appreciably affected by the measure in question.

Paragraphs 16, 18, 19 and 22

1. It is understood that the CONTRACTING PARTIES may concur in a proposed measure subject to specific conditions or limitations. If the measure as applied does not conform to the terms of the concurrence it will to that extent be deemed a measure in which the CONTRACTING PARTIES have not concurred. In cases in which the CONTRACTING PARTIES have concurred in a measure for a specified period, the contracting party concerned, if it finds that the maintenance of the measure for a further period of time is required to achieve the objective for which the measure was originally taken, may apply to the CONTRACTING PARTIES for an extension of that period in accordance with the provisions and procedures of Section C or D, as the case may be.

2. It is expected that the CONTRACTING PARTIES will, as a rule, refrain from concurring in a measure which is likely to cause serious prejudice to exports of a commodity on which the economy of a contracting party is largely dependent.

Paragraphs 18 and 22

The phrase "that the interests of other contracting parties are adequately safeguarded" is meant to provide latitude sufficient to permit consideration in each case of the most appropriate method of safeguarding those interests. The appropriate method may, for instance, take the form of an additional concession to be applied by the contracting party having recourse to Section C or D during such time as the deviation from the other Articles of the Agreement would remain in force or of the temporary suspension by any other contracting party referred to in paragraph 18 of a concession substantially equivalent to the impairment due to the introduction of the measure in question. Such contracting party would have the right to safeguard its interests through such a temporary suspension of a concession; *Provided* that this right will not be exercised when, in the case of a measure imposed by a contracting party coming within the scope of paragraph 4(a), the CONTRACTING PARTIES have determined that the extent of the compensatory concession proposed was adequate.

Paragraph 19

The provisions of paragraph 19 are intended to cover the cases where an industry has been in existence beyond the "reasonable period of time" referred to in the note to paragraphs 13 and 14, and should not be so construed as to deprive a contracting party coming within the scope of paragraph 4(a) of Article XVIII, of its right to resort to the other provisions of Section C, including paragraph 17, with regard to a newly established industry even though it has benefited from incidental protection afforded by balance of payments import restrictions.

Paragraph 21

Any measure taken pursuant to the provisions of paragraph 21 shall be withdrawn forthwith if the action taken in accordance with paragraph 17 is withdrawn or if the CONTRACTING PARTIES concur in the measure proposed after the expiration of the ninety-day time limit specified in paragraph 17.

AD ARTICLE XX

Sub-paragraph (h)

The exception provided for in this sub-paragraph extends to any commodity agreement which conforms to the principles approved by the Economic and Social Council in its Resolution 30 (IV) of 28 March 1947.

AD ARTICLE XXIV

Paragraph 9

It is understood that the provisions of Article I would require that, when a product which has been imported into the territory of a member of a customs union or free-trade area at a preferential rate of duty is re-exported to the territory of another member of such union or area, the latter member should collect a duty equal to the difference between the duty already paid and any higher duty that would be payable if the product were being imported directly into its territory.

Paragraph 11

Measures adopted by India and Pakistan in order to carry out definitive trade arrangements between them, once they have been agreed upon, might depart from particular provisions of this Agreement, but these measures would in general be consistent with the objectives of the Agreement.

AD ARTICLE XXVIII

The CONTRACTING PARTIES and each contracting party concerned should arrange to conduct the negotiations and consultations with the greatest possible secrecy in order to avoid premature disclosure of details of prospective tariff changes. The CONTRACTING PARTIES shall be informed immediately of all changes in national tariffs resulting from recourse to this Article.

Paragraph 1

1. If the CONTRACTING PARTIES specify a period other than a three-year period, a contracting party may act pursuant to paragraph 1 or paragraph 3 of Article XXVIII on the first day following

the expiration of such other period and, unless the CONTRACTING PARTIES have again specified another period, subsequent periods will be three-year periods following the expiration of such specified period.

2. The provision that on 1 January 1958, and on other days determined pursuant to paragraph 1, a contracting party "may . . . modify, or withdraw a concession" means that on such day, and on the first day after the end of each period, the legal obligation of such contracting party under Article II is altered; it does not mean that the changes in its customs tariff should necessarily be made effective on that day. If a tariff change resulting from negotiations undertaken pursuant to this Article is delayed, the entry into force of any compensatory concessions may be similarly delayed.

3. Not earlier than six months, nor later than three months, prior to 1 January 1958, or to the termination date of any subsequent period, a contracting party wishing to modify or withdraw any concession embodied in the appropriate Schedule, should notify the CONTRACTING PARTIES to this effect. The CONTRACTING PARTIES shall then determine the contracting party or contracting parties with which the negotiations or consultations referred to in paragraph 1 shall take place. Any contracting party so determined shall participate in such negotiations or consultations with the applicant contracting party with the aim of reaching agreement before the end of the period. Any extension of the assured life of the Schedules shall relate to the Schedules as modified after such negotiations, in accordance with paragraphs 1, 2, and 3 of Article XXVIII. If the CONTRACTING PARTIES are arranging for multilateral tariff negotiations to take place within the period of six months before 1 January 1958, or before any other day determined pursuant to paragraph 1, they shall include in the arrangements for such negotiations suitable procedures for carrying out the negotiations referred to in this paragraph.

4. The object of providing for the participation in the negotiations of any contracting party with a principal supplying interest, in addition to any contracting party with which the concession was initially negotiated, is to ensure that a contracting party with a larger share in trade affected by the concession than a contracting party with which the concession was initially negotiated shall have an effective opportunity to protect the contractual right which it enjoys under this Agreement. On the other hand, it is not intended that the scope of the negotiations should be such as to make negotiations and agreement under Article XXVIII unduly difficult nor to create complications in the application of this Article in the future to concessions which result from negotiations thereunder. Accordingly, the CONTRACTING PARTIES should only determine that a contracting party has a principal supplying interest if that contracting party has had, over a reasonable period of time prior to the negotiations, a larger share in the market of the applicant contracting party than a contracting party with which the concession was initially negotiated or would, in the judgment of the CONTRACTING PARTIES, have had such a share in the absence of discriminatory quantitative restrictions maintained by the applicant contracting party. It would therefore not be appropriate for the CONTRACTING PARTIES to determine that more than one contracting party, or in

those exceptional cases where there is near equality more than two contracting parties, had a principal supplying interest.

5. Notwithstanding the definition of a principal supplying interest in note 4 of paragraph 1, the CONTRACTING PARTIES may exceptionally determine that a contracting party has a principal supplying interest if the concession in question affects trade which constitutes a major part of the total exports of such contracting party.

6. It is not intended that provision for participation in the negotiations of any contracting party with a principal supplying interest, and for consultation with any contracting party having a substantial interest in the concession which the applicant contracting party is seeking to modify or withdraw, should have the effect that it should have to pay compensation or suffer retaliation greater than the withdrawal or modification sought, judged in the light of the conditions of trade at the time of the proposed withdrawal or modification, making allowance for any discriminatory quantitative restrictions maintained by the applicant contracting party.

7. The expression "substantial interest" is not capable of a precise definition and accordingly may present difficulties for the CONTRACTING PARTIES. It is, however, intended to be construed to cover only those contracting parties which have, or in the absence of discriminatory quantitative restrictions affecting their exports could reasonably be expected to have, a significant share in the market of the contracting party seeking to modify or withdraw the concession.

Paragraph 4

1. Any request for authorization to enter into negotiations shall be accompanied by all relevant statistical and other data. A decision on such request shall be made within thirty days of its submission.

2. It is recognized that to permit certain contracting parties, depending in large measure on a relatively small number of primary commodities and relying on the tariff as an important aid for furthering diversification of their economies or as an important source of revenue, normally to negotiate for the modification or withdrawal of concessions only under paragraph 1 of Article XXVIII, might cause them at such a time to make modifications or withdrawals which in the long run would prove unnecessary. To avoid such a situation the CONTRACTING PARTIES shall authorize any such contracting party, under paragraph 4, to enter into negotiations unless they consider this would result in, or contribute substantially toward, such an increase in tariff levels as to threaten the stability of the Schedules to this Agreement or lead to undue disturbance of international trade.

3. It is expected that negotiations authorized under paragraph 4 for modification or withdrawal of a single item, or a very small group of items, could normally be brought to a conclusion in sixty days. It is recognized, however, that such a period will be inadequate for cases involving negotiations for the modification or withdrawal of a larger number of items and in such cases, therefore, it would be appropriate for the CONTRACTING PARTIES to prescribe a longer period.

4. The determination referred to in paragraph 4(d) shall be made by the CONTRACTING PARTIES within thirty days of the submission of the matter to them, unless the applicant contracting party agrees to a longer period.

5. In determining under paragraph 4(d) whether an applicant contracting party has unreasonably failed to offer adequate compensation, it is understood that the CONTRACTING PARTIES will take due account of the special position of a contracting party which has bound a high proportion of its tariffs at very low rates of duty and to this extent has less scope than other contracting parties to make compensatory adjustment.

AD ARTICLE XXVIII bis

Paragraph 3

It is understood that the reference to fiscal needs would include the revenue aspect of duties and particularly duties imposed primarily for revenue purposes or duties imposed on products which can be substituted for products subject to revenue duties to prevent the avoidance of such duties.

AD ARTICLE XXIX

Paragraph 1

Chapters VII and VIII of the Havana Charter have been excluded from paragraph 1 because they generally deal with the organization, functions and procedures of the International Trade Organization.

AD PART IV

The words "developed contracting parties" and the words "less-developed contracting parties" as used in Part IV are to be understood to refer to developed and less-developed countries which are parties to the General Agreement on Tariffs and Trade.

AD ARTICLE XXXVI

Paragraph 1

This Article is based upon the objectives set forth in Article I as it will be amended by Section A of paragraph 1 of the Protocol Amending Part I and Articles XXIX and XXX when that Protocol enters into force.

Paragraph 4

The term "primary products" includes agricultural products, *vide* paragraph 2 of the note Ad Article XVI, Section B.

Paragraph 5

A diversification programme would generally include the intensification of activities for the processing of primary products and the development of manufacturing industries, taking into account the situation of the particular contracting party and the world outlook for production and consumption of different commodities.

Paragraph 8

It is understood that the phrase "do not expect reciprocity" means, in accordance with the objectives set forth in this Article, that the less-developed contracting parties should not be expected, in the course of trade negotiations, to make contributions which are inconsistent with their individual development, financial and trade needs, taking into consideration past trade developments.

This paragraph would apply in the event of action under Section A of Article XVIII, Article XXVIII, Article XXVIII bis (Article XXIX after the amendment set forth in Section A of paragraph 1 of the Protocol Amending Part I and Articles XXIX and XXX shall have become effective), Article XXXIII, or any other procedure under this Agreement.

AD ARTICLE XXXVII

Paragraph 1(a)

This paragraph would apply in the event of negotiations for reduction or elimination of tariffs or other restrictive regulations of commerce under Articles XXVIII, XXVIII bis (XXIX after the amendment set forth in Section A of paragraph 1 of the Protocol Amending Part I and Articles XXIX and XXX shall have become effective), and Article XXXIII, as well as in connexion with other action to effect such reduction or elimination which contracting parties may be able to undertake.

Paragraph 3(b)

The other measures referred to in this paragraph might include steps to promote domestic structural changes, to encourage the consumption of particular products, or to introduce measures of trade promotion.

PROTOCOL OF PROVISIONAL APPLICATION OF THE GENERAL AGREEMENT OF TARIFFS AND TRADE [41]

1. The Governments of the COMMONWEALTH OF AUSTRALIA, the KINGDOM OF BELGIUM (in respect of its metropolitan territory), CANADA, the FRENCH REPUBLIC (in respect of its metropolitan territory), the GRAND-DUCHY OF LUXEMBURG, the KINGDOM OF THE NETHERLANDS (in respect of its metropolitan territory), the UNITED KINGDOM OF GREAT BRITAIN AND NORTHERN IRELAND (in respect of its metropolitan territory), and the UNITED STATES OF AMERICA, undertake, provided that this Protocol shall have been signed on behalf of all the foregoing Governments not later than November 15, 1947, to apply provisionally on and after January 1, 1948:

(a) Parts I and III of the General Agreement on Tariffs and Trade, and

(b) Part II of that Agreement to the fullest extent not inconsistent with existing legislation.

2. The foregoing Governments shall make effective such provisional application of the General Agreement, in respect of any of their territories other than their metropolitan territories, on or

---

[41] 61 Stat., part (61), page A2051.

after January 1, 1948, upon the expiration of thirty days from the day on which notice of such application is received by the Secretary-General of the United Nations.

3. Any other Government signatory to this Protocol shall make effective such provisional application of the General Agreement, on or after January 1, 1948, upon the expiration of thirty days from the day of signature of this Protocol on behalf of such Government.

4. This Protocol shall remain open for signature at the Headquarters of the United Nations, (a) until November 15, 1947, on behalf of any Government named in paragraph 1 of this Protocol which has not signed it on this day, and (b) until June 30, 1948, on behalf of any other Government signatory to the Final Act adopted at the conclusion of the Second Session of the Preparatory Committee of the United Nations Conference on Trade and Employment which has not signed it on this day.

5. Any Government applying this Protocol shall be free to withdraw such application, and such withdrawal shall take effect upon the expiration of sixty days from the day on which written notice of such withdrawal is received by the Secretary-General of the United Nations.

6. The original of this Protocol shall be deposited with the Secretary-General of the United Nations, who will furnish certified copies thereof to all interested Governments.

IN WITNESS WHEREOF the respective Representatives, after having communicated their full powers, found to be in good and due form, have signed this Protocol.

DONE at Geneva, in a single copy, in the English and French languages, both texts authentic, this thirtieth day of October, one thousand nine hundred and forty-seven.

b. The General Agreement on Tariffs and Trade, 1994 [1]

Signed at Marrakesh April 15, 1994

GENERAL AGREEMENT ON TARIFFS AND TRADE 1994

1. The General Agreement on Tariffs and Trade 1994 ("GATT 1994") shall consist of:

(a) the provisions in the General Agreement on Tariffs and Trade, dated 30 October 1947, annexed to the Final Act Adopted at the Conclusion of the Second Session of the Preparatory Committee of the United Nations Conference on Trade and Employment (excluding the Protocol of Provisional Application), as rectified, amended or modified by the terms of legal instruments which have entered into force before the date of entry into force of the WTO Agreement;

(b) the provisions of the legal instruments set forth below that have entered into force under the GATT 1947 before the date of entry into force of the WTO Agreement:

(i) protocols and certifications relating to tariff concessions;

(ii) protocols of accession (excluding the provisions (a) concerning provisional application and withdrawal of provisional application and (b) providing that Part II of GATT 1947 shall be applied provisionally to the fullest extent not inconsistent with legislation existing on the date of the Protocol);

(iii) decisions on waivers granted under Article XXV of GATT 1947 and still in force on the date of entry into force of the WTO Agreement;

(iv) other decisions of the CONTRACTING PARTIES to GATT 1947;

(c) the Understandings set forth below:

(i) Understanding on the Interpretation of Article II:1(b) of the General Agreement on Tariffs and Trade 1994;

(ii) Understanding on the Interpretation of Article XVII of the General Agreement on Tariffs and Trade 1994;

(iii) Understanding on Balance-of-Payments Provisions of the General Agreement on Tariffs and Trade 1994;

(iv) Understanding on the Interpretation of Article XXIV of the General Agreement on Tariffs and Trade 1994;

(v) Understanding in Respect of Waivers of Obligations under the General Agreement on Tariffs and Trade 1994;

(vi) Understanding on the Interpretation of Article XXVIII of the General Agreement on Tariffs and Trade 1994; and

(d) the Marrakesh Protocol to GATT 1994.

[1] 1867 UNTS 187.

2. *Explanatory Notes*

(a) The references to "contracting party" in the provisions of GATT 1994 shall be deemed to read "Member". The references to "less-developed contracting party" and "developed contracting party" shall be deemed to read "developing country Member" and "developed country Member". The references to "Executive Secretary" shall be deemed to read "Director-General of the WTO".

(b) The references to the CONTRACTING PARTIES acting jointly in Articles XV:1, XV:2, XV:8, XXXVIII and the Notes Ad Article XII and XVIII; and in the provisions on special exchange agreements in Articles XV:2, XV:3, XV:6, XV:7 and XV:9 of GATT 1994 shall be deemed to be references to the WTO. The other functions that the provisions of GATT 1994 assign to the CONTRACTING PARTIES acting jointly shall be allocated by the Ministerial Conference.

(c)(i) The text of GATT 1994 shall be authentic in English, French and Spanish.

(ii) The text of GATT 1994 in the French language shall be subject to the rectifications of terms indicated in Annex A to document MTN.TNC/41.

(iii) The authentic text of GATT 1994 in the Spanish language shall be the text in Volume IV of the Basic Instruments and Selected Documents series, subject to the rectifications of terms indicated in Annex B to document MTN.TNC/41.

3.(a) The provisions of Part II of GATT 1994 shall not apply to measures taken by a Member under specific mandatory legislation, enacted by that Member before it became a contracting party to GATT 1947, that prohibits the use, sale or lease of foreign-built or foreign-reconstructed vessels in commercial applications between points in national waters or the waters of an exclusive economic zone. This exemption applies to: (a) the continuation or prompt renewal of a non-conforming provision of such legislation; and (b) the amendment to a non-conforming provision of such legislation to the extent that the amendment does not decrease the conformity of the provision with Part II of GATT 1947. This exemption is limited to measures taken under legislation described above that is notified and specified prior to the date of entry into force of the WTO Agreement. If such legislation is subsequently modified to decrease its conformity with Part II of GATT 1994, it will no longer qualify for coverage under this paragraph.

(b) The Ministerial Conference shall review this exemption not later than five years after the date of entry into force of the WTO Agreement and thereafter every two years for as long as the exemption is in force for the purpose of examining whether the conditions which created the need for the exemption still prevail.

(c) A Member whose measures are covered by this exemption shall annually submit a detailed statistical notification consisting of a five-year moving average of actual and expected deliveries of relevant vessels as well as additional information on the use, sale, lease or repair of relevant vessels covered by this exemption.

(d) A Member that considers that this exemption operates in such a manner as to justify a reciprocal and proportionate limitation on the use, sale, lease or repair of vessels constructed in the territory of the Member invoking the exemption shall be free to introduce such a limitation subject to prior notification to the Ministerial Conference.

(e) This exemption is without prejudice to solutions concerning specific aspects of the legislation covered by this exemption negotiated in sectoral agreements or in other fora.

c. Agreement on Implementation of Article VI of the General Agreement on Tariffs and Trade 1994

Signed at Marrakesh, April 15, 1994; Entered into force, January 1, 1995

AGREEMENT ON IMPLEMENTATION OF ARTICLE VI OF THE GENERAL AGREEMENT ON TARIFFS AND TRADE 1994

Members hereby *agree as follows:*

PART I

ARTICLE 1—PRINCIPLES

An anti dumping measure shall be applied only under the circumstances provided for in Article VI of GATT 1994 and pursuant to investigations initiated and conducted in accordance with the provisions of this Agreement. The following provisions govern the application of Article VI of GATT 1994 in so far as action is taken under anti dumping legislation or regulations.

ARTICLE 2—DETERMINATION OF DUMPING

2.1 For the purpose of this Agreement, a product is to be considered as being dumped, i.e. introduced into the commerce of another country at less than its normal value, if the export price of the product exported from one country to another is less than the comparable price, in the ordinary course of trade, for the like product when destined for consumption in the exporting country.

2.2 When there are no sales of the like product in the ordinary course of trade in the domestic market of the exporting country or when, because of the particular market situation or the low volume of the sales in the domestic market of the exporting country , such sales do not permit a proper comparison, the margin of dumping shall be determined by comparison with a comparable price of the like product when exported to an appropriate third country, provided that this price is representative, or with the cost of production in the country of origin plus a reasonable amount for administrative, selling and general costs and for profits.

2.2.1 Sales of the like product in the domestic market of the exporting country or sales to a third country at prices below per unit (fixed and variable) costs of production plus administrative, selling and general costs may be treated as not being in the ordinary course of trade by reason of price and may be disregarded in determining normal value only if the authorities determine that such sales are made within an extended period of time in substantial quantities and are at prices which do not provide for the recovery of all costs within a reasonable period of time. If prices which are below per unit costs at the time of sale are above weighted average per unit costs for the period of investigation, such prices shall be considered to provide for recovery of costs within a reasonable period of time.

2.2.1.1 For the purpose of paragraph 2, costs shall normally be calculated on the basis of records kept by the exporter or producer under investigation, provided that such records are in accordance with the generally accepted accounting principles of the exporting country and reasonably reflect the costs associated with the production and sale of the product under consideration. Authorities shall consider all available evidence on the proper allocation of costs, including that which is made available by the exporter or producer in the course of the investigation provided that such allocations have been historically utilized by the exporter or producer, in particular in relation to establishing appropriate amortization and depreciation periods and allowances for capital expenditures and other development costs. Unless already reflected in the cost allocations under this sub paragraph, costs shall be adjusted appropriately for those non recurring items of cost which benefit future and/or current production, or for circumstances in which costs during the period of investigation are affected by start up operations.

2.2.2 For the purpose of paragraph 2, the amounts for administrative, selling and general costs and for profits shall be based on actual data pertaining to production and sales in the ordinary course of trade of the like product by the exporter or producer under investigation. When such amounts cannot be determined on this basis, the amounts may be determined on the basis of:

(i) the actual amounts incurred and realized by the exporter or producer in question in respect of production and sales in the domestic market of the country of origin of the same general category of products;

(ii) the weighted average of the actual amounts incurred and realized by other exporters or producers subject to investigation in respect of production and sales of the like product in the domestic market of the country of origin;

(iii) any other reasonable method, provided that the amount for profit so established shall not exceed the profit normally realized by other exporters or producers on sales of products of the same general category in the domestic market of the country of origin.

2.3 In cases where there is no export price or where it appears to the authorities concerned that the export price is unreliable because of association or a compensatory arrangement between the exporter and the importer or a third party, the export price may be constructed on the basis of the price at which the imported products are first resold to an independent buyer, or if the products are not resold to an independent buyer, or not resold in the condition as imported, on such reasonable basis as the authorities may determine.

2.4 A fair comparison shall be made between the export price and the normal value. This comparison shall be made at the same level of trade, normally at the ex factory level, and in respect of sales made at as nearly as possible the same time. Due allowance shall be made in each case, on its merits, for differences which affect price comparability, including differences in conditions and terms of sale, taxation, levels of trade, quantities, physical characteristics, and any other differences which are also demonstrated to affect price comparability. In the cases referred to in paragraph 3, allowances for costs, including duties and taxes, incurred between importation and resale, and for profits accruing, should also be made. If in these cases price comparability has been affected, the authorities shall establish the normal value at a level of trade equivalent to the level of trade of the constructed export price, or shall make due allowance as warranted under this paragraph. The authorities shall indicate to the parties in question what information is necessary to ensure a fair comparison and shall not impose an unreasonable burden of proof on those parties.

2.4.1 When the comparison under paragraph 4 requires a conversion of currencies, such conversion should be made using the rate of exchange on the date of sale , provided that when a sale of foreign currency on forward markets is directly linked to the export sale involved, the rate of exchange in the forward sale shall be used. Fluctuations in exchange rates shall be ignored and in an investigation the authorities shall allow exporters at least 60 days to have adjusted their export prices to reflect sustained movements in exchange rates during the period of investigation.

2.4.2 Subject to the provisions governing fair comparison in paragraph 4, the existence of margins of dumping during the investigation phase shall normally be established on the basis of a comparison of a weighted average normal value with a weighted average of prices of all comparable export transactions or by a comparison of normal value and export prices on a transaction to transaction basis. A normal value established on a weighted average basis may be compared to prices of individual export transactions if the authorities find a pattern of export prices which differ significantly among different purchasers, regions or time periods, and if an explanation is provided as to why such differences cannot be taken into account appropriately by the use of a weighted average to weighted average or transaction to transaction comparison.

2.5 In the case where products are not imported directly from the country of origin but are exported to the importing Member from an intermediate country, the price at which the products are sold from the country of export to the importing Member shall normally be compared with the comparable price in the country of export. However, comparison may be made with the price in the country of origin, if, for example, the products are merely transshipped through the country of export, or such products are not produced in the country of export, or there is no comparable price for them in the country of export.

2.6 Throughout this Agreement the term "like product" ("produit similaire") shall be interpreted to mean a product which is identical, i.e. alike in all respects to the product under consideration, or in the absence of such a product, another product which, although not alike in all respects, has characteristics closely resembling those of the product under consideration.

2.7 This Article is without prejudice to the second Supplementary Provision to paragraph 1 of Article VI in Annex I to GATT 1994.

ARTICLE 3—DETERMINATION OF INJURY

3.1 A determination of injury for purposes of Article VI of GATT 1994 shall be based on positive evidence and involve an objective examination of both (a) the volume of the dumped imports and the effect of the dumped imports on prices in the domestic market for like products, and (b) the consequent impact of these imports on domestic producers of such products.

3.2 With regard to the volume of the dumped imports, the investigating authorities shall consider whether there has been a significant increase in dumped imports, either in absolute terms or relative to production or consumption in the importing Member. With regard to the effect of the dumped imports on prices, the investigating authorities shall consider whether there has been a significant price undercutting by the dumped imports as compared with the price of a like product of the importing Member, or whether the effect of such imports is otherwise to depress prices to a significant degree or prevent price increases, which otherwise would have occurred, to a significant degree. No one or several of these factors can necessarily give decisive guidance.

3.3 Where imports of a product from more than one country are simultaneously subject to anti dumping investigations, the investigating authorities may cumulatively assess the effects of such imports only if they determine that (a) the margin of dumping established in relation to the imports from each country is more than de minimis as defined in paragraph 8 of Article 5 and the volume of imports from each country is not negligible and (b) a cumulative assessment of the effects of the imports is appropriate in light of the conditions of competition between the imported products and the conditions of competition between the imported products and the like domestic product.

3.4 The examination of the impact of the dumped imports on the domestic industry concerned shall include an evaluation of all relevant economic factors and indices having a bearing on the state of the industry, including actual and potential decline in sales, profits, output, market share, productivity, return on investments, or utilization of capacity; factors affecting domestic prices; the magnitude of the margin of dumping; actual and potential negative effects on cash flow, inventories, employment, wages, growth, ability to raise capital or investments. This list is not exhaustive, nor can one or several of these factors necessarily give decisive guidance.

3.5 It must be demonstrated that the dumped imports are, through the effects of dumping, as set forth in paragraphs 2 and 4, causing injury within the meaning of this Agreement. The demonstration of a causal relationship between the dumped imports and the injury to the domestic industry shall be based on an examination of all relevant evidence before the authorities. The authorities shall also examine any known factors other than the dumped imports which at the same time are injuring the domestic industry, and the injuries caused by these other factors must not be attributed to the dumped imports. Factors which may be relevant in this respect include, inter alia, the volume and prices of imports not sold at dumping prices, contraction in demand or changes in the patterns of consumption, trade restrictive practices of and competition between the foreign and domestic producers, developments in technology and the export performance and productivity of the domestic industry.

3.6 The effect of the dumped imports shall be assessed in relation to the domestic production of the like product when available data permit the separate identification of that production on the basis of such criteria as the production process, producers' sales and profits. If such separate identification of that production is not possible, the effects of the dumped imports shall be assessed by the examination of the production of the narrowest group or range of products, which includes the like product, for which the necessary information can be provided.

3.7 A determination of a threat of material injury shall be based on facts and not merely on allegation, conjecture or remote possibility. The change in circumstances which would create a situation in which the dumping would cause injury must be clearly foreseen and imminent. In making a determination regarding the existence of a threat of material injury, the authorities should consider, inter alia, such factors as:

(i) a significant rate of increase of dumped imports into the domestic market indicating the likelihood of substantially increased importation;

(ii) sufficient freely disposable, or an imminent, substantial increase in, capacity of the exporter indicating the likelihood of substantially increased dumped exports to the importing Member's market, taking into account the availability of other export markets to absorb any additional exports;

(iii) whether imports are entering at prices that will have a significant depressing or suppressing effect on domestic prices, and would likely increase demand for further imports; and

(iv) inventories of the product being investigated.

No one of these factors by itself can necessarily give decisive guidance but the totality of the factors considered must lead to the conclusion that further dumped exports are imminent and that, unless protective action is taken, material injury would occur.

3.8 With respect to cases where injury is threatened by dumped imports, the application of anti dumping measures shall be considered and decided with special care.

ARTICLE 4—DEFINITION OF DOMESTIC INDUSTRY

4.1 For the purposes of this Agreement, the term "domestic industry" shall be interpreted as referring to the domestic producers as a whole of the like products or to those of them whose collective output of the products constitutes a major proportion of the total domestic production of those products, except that:

(i) when producers are related to the exporters or importers or are themselves importers of the allegedly dumped product, the term "domestic industry" may be interpreted as referring to the rest of the producers;

(ii) in exceptional circumstances the territory of a Member may, for the production in question, be divided into two or more competitive markets and the producers within each market may be regarded as a separate industry if (a) the producers within such market sell all or almost all of their production of the product in question in that market, and (b) the demand in that market is not to any substantial degree supplied by producers of the product in question located elsewhere in the territory. In such circumstances, injury may be found to exist even where a major portion of the total domestic industry is not injured, provided there is a concentration of dumped imports into such an isolated market and provided further that the dumped imports are causing injury to the producers of all or almost all of the production within such market.

4.2 When the domestic industry has been interpreted as referring to the producers in a certain area, i.e. a market as defined in paragraph 1(ii), anti dumping duties shall be levied only on the products in question consigned for final consumption to that area. When the constitutional law of the importing Member does not permit the levying of anti dumping duties on such a basis, the importing Member may levy the anti dumping duties without limitation only if (a) the exporters shall have been given an opportunity to cease exporting at dumped prices to the area concerned or otherwise give assurances pursuant to Article 8 and adequate assurances in this regard have not been promptly given, and (b) such duties cannot be levied only on products of specific producers which supply the area in question.

4.3 Where two or more countries have reached under the provisions of paragraph 8(a) of Article XXIV of GATT 1994 such a level of integration that they have the characteristics of a single, unified market, the industry in the entire area of integration shall be taken to be the domestic industry referred to in paragraph 1.

4.4 The provisions of paragraph 6 of Article 3 shall be applicable to this Article.

ARTICLE 5—INITIATION AND SUBSEQUENT INVESTIGATION

5.1 Except as provided for in paragraph 6, an investigation to determine the existence, degree and effect of any alleged dumping shall be initiated upon a written application by or on behalf of the domestic industry.

5.2 An application under paragraph 1 shall include evidence of (a) dumping, (b) injury within the meaning of Article VI of GATT 1994 as interpreted by this Agreement and (c) a causal link between the dumped imports and the alleged injury. Simple assertion, unsubstantiated by relevant evidence, cannot be considered sufficient to meet the requirements of this paragraph. The application shall contain such information as is reasonably available to the applicant on the following:

(i) the identity of the applicant and a description of the volume and value of the domestic production of the like product by the applicant. Where a written application is made on behalf of the domestic industry, the application shall identify the industry on behalf of which the application is made by a list of all known domestic producers of the like product (or associations of domestic producers of the like product) and, to the extent possible, a description of the volume and value of domestic production of the like product accounted for by such producers;

(ii) a complete description of the allegedly dumped product, the names of the country or countries of origin or export in question, the identity of each known exporter or foreign producer and a list of known persons importing the product in question;

(iii) information on prices at which the product in question is sold when destined for consumption in the domestic markets of the country or countries of origin or export (or, where appropriate, information on the prices at which the product is sold from the country or countries of origin or export to a third country or countries, or on the constructed value of the product) and information on export prices or, where appropriate, on the prices at which the product is first resold to an independent buyer in the territory of the importing Member;

(iv) information on the evolution of the volume of the allegedly dumped imports, the effect of these imports on prices of the like product in the domestic market and the consequent impact of the imports on the domestic industry, as demonstrated by relevant factors and indices having a bearing on the state of the domestic industry, such as those listed in paragraphs 2 and 4 of Article 3.

5.3 The authorities shall examine the accuracy and adequacy of the evidence provided in the application to determine whether there is sufficient evidence to justify the initiation of an investigation.

5.4 An investigation shall not be initiated pursuant to paragraph 1 unless the authorities have determined, on the basis of an examination of the degree of support for, or opposition to, the application expressed by domestic producers of the like product, that the application has been made by or on behalf of the domestic industry. The application shall be considered to have been made "by or on behalf of the domestic industry" if it is supported by those domestic producers whose collective output constitutes more than 50 per cent of the total production of the like product produced by that portion of the domestic industry expressing either support for or opposition to the application. However, no investigation shall be initiated when domestic producers expressly supporting the application account for less than 25 per cent of total production of the like product produced by the domestic industry.

5.5 The authorities shall avoid, unless a decision has been made to initiate an investigation, any publicizing of the application for the initiation of an investigation. However, after receipt of a properly documented application and before proceeding to initiate an investigation, the authorities shall notify the government of the exporting Member concerned.

5.6 If, in special circumstances, the authorities concerned decide to initiate an investigation without having received a written application by or on behalf of a domestic industry for the initiation of such investigation, they shall proceed only if they have sufficient evidence of dumping, injury and a causal link, as described in paragraph 2, to justify the initiation of an investigation.

5.7 The evidence of both dumping and injury shall be considered simultaneously (a) in the decision whether or not to initiate an investigation, and (b) thereafter, during the course of the investigation, starting on a date not later than the earliest date on which in accordance with the provisions of this Agreement provisional measures may be applied.

5.8 An application under paragraph 1 shall be rejected and an investigation shall be terminated promptly as soon as the authorities concerned are satisfied that there is not sufficient evidence of either dumping or of injury to justify proceeding with the case. There shall be immediate termination in cases where the authorities determine that the margin of dumping is de minimis, or that the volume of dumped imports, actual or potential, or the injury, is negligible. The margin of dumping shall be considered to be de minimis if this margin is less than 2 per cent, expressed as a percentage of the export price. The volume of dumped imports shall normally be regarded as negligible if the volume of dumped imports from a particular country is found to account for less than 3 per cent of imports of the like product in the importing Member, unless countries which individually account for less than 3 per cent of the imports of the like product in the importing Member collectively account for more than 7 per cent of imports of the like product in the importing Member.

5.9 An anti dumping proceeding shall not hinder the procedures of customs clearance.

5.10 Investigations shall, except in special circumstances, be concluded within one year, and in no case more than 18 months, after their initiation.

Article 6—Evidence

6.1 All interested parties in an anti dumping investigation shall be given notice of the information which the authorities require and ample opportunity to present in writing all evidence which they consider relevant in respect of the investigation in question.

6.1.1 Exporters or foreign producers receiving questionnaires used in an anti dumping investigation shall be given at least 30 days for reply. Due consideration should be given to any request for an extension of the 30 day period and, upon cause shown, such an extension should be granted whenever practicable.

6.1.2 Subject to the requirement to protect confidential information, evidence presented in writing by one interested party shall be made available promptly to other interested parties participating in the investigation.

6.1.3 As soon as an investigation has been initiated, the authorities shall provide the full text of the written application received under paragraph 1 of Article 5 to the known exporters and to the authorities of the exporting Member and shall make it available, upon request, to other interested parties involved. Due regard shall be paid to the requirement for the protection of confidential information, as provided for in paragraph 5.

6.2 Throughout the anti dumping investigation all interested parties shall have a full opportunity for the defence of their interests. To this end, the authorities shall, on request, provide opportunities for all interested parties to meet those parties with adverse interests, so that opposing views may be presented and rebuttal arguments offered. Provision of such opportunities must take account of the need to preserve confidentiality and of the convenience to the parties. There shall be no obligation on any party to attend a meeting, and failure to do so shall not be prejudicial to that party's case. Interested parties shall also have the right, on justification, to present other information orally.

6.3 Oral information provided under paragraph 2 shall be taken into account by the authorities only in so far as it is subsequently reproduced in writing and made available to other interested parties, as provided for in subparagraph 1.2.

6.4 The authorities shall whenever practicable provide timely opportunities for all interested parties to see all information that is relevant to the presentation of their cases, that is not confidential as defined in paragraph 5, and that is used by the authorities in an anti dumping investigation, and to prepare presentations on the basis of this information.

6.5 Any information which is by nature confidential (for example, because its disclosure would be of significant competitive advantage to a competitor or because its disclosure would have a significantly adverse effect upon a person supplying the information or upon a person from whom that person acquired the information), or which is provided on a confidential basis by parties to an investigation shall, upon good cause shown, be treated as such by the authorities. Such information shall not be disclosed without specific permission of the party submitting it.

6.5.1 The authorities shall require interested parties providing confidential information to furnish non confidential summaries thereof. These summaries shall be in sufficient detail to permit a reasonable understanding of the substance of the information submitted in confidence. In exceptional circumstances, such parties may indicate that such information is not susceptible of summary. In such exceptional circumstances, a statement of the reasons why summarization is not possible must be provided.

6.5.2 If the authorities find that a request for confidentiality is not warranted and if the supplier of the information is either unwilling to make the information public or to authorize its disclosure in generalized or summary form, the authorities may disregard such information unless it can be demonstrated to their satisfaction from appropriate sources that the information is correct.

6.6 Except in circumstances provided for in paragraph 8, the authorities shall during the course of an investigation satisfy themselves as to the accuracy of the information supplied by interested parties upon which their findings are based.

6.7 In order to verify information provided or to obtain further details, the authorities may carry out investigations in the territory of other Members as required, provided they obtain the agreement of the firms concerned and notify the representatives of the government of the Member in question, and unless that Member objects to the investigation. The procedures described in Annex I shall apply to investigations carried out in the territory of other Members. Subject to the requirement to protect confidential information, the authorities shall make the results of any such investigations available, or shall provide disclosure thereof pursuant to paragraph 9, to the firms to which they pertain and may make such results available to the applicants.

6.8 In cases in which any interested party refuses access to, or otherwise does not provide, necessary information within a reasonable period or significantly impedes the investigation, preliminary and final determinations, affirmative or negative, may be made on the basis of the facts available. The provisions of Annex II shall be observed in the application of this paragraph.

6.9 The authorities shall, before a final determination is made, inform all interested parties of the essential facts under consideration which form the basis for the decision whether to apply definitive measures. Such disclosure should take place in sufficient time for the parties to defend their interests.

6.10 The authorities shall, as a rule, determine an individual margin of dumping for each known exporter or producer concerned of the product under investigation. In cases where the number of exporters, producers, importers or types of products involved is so large as to make such a determination impracticable, the authorities may limit their examination either to a reasonable number of interested parties or products by using samples which are statistically valid on the basis of information available to the authorities at the time of the selection, or to the largest percentage of the volume of the exports from the country in question which can reasonably be investigated.

6.10.1 Any selection of exporters, producers, importers or types of products made under this paragraph shall preferably be chosen in consultation with and with the consent of the exporters, producers or importers concerned.

6.10.2 In cases where the authorities have limited their examination, as provided for in this paragraph, they shall nevertheless determine an individual margin of dumping for any exporter or producer not initially selected who submits the necessary information in time for that information to be considered during the course of the investigation, except where the number of exporters or producers is so large that individual examinations would be unduly burdensome to the authorities and prevent the timely completion of the investigation. Voluntary responses shall not be discouraged.

6.11 For the purposes of this Agreement, "interested parties" shall include:

(i) an exporter or foreign producer or the importer of a product subject to investigation, or a trade or business association a majority of the members of which are producers, exporters or importers of such product;

(ii) the government of the exporting Member; and

(iii) a producer of the like product in the importing Member or a trade and business association a majority of the members of which produce the like product in the territory of the importing Member.

This list shall not preclude Members from allowing domestic or foreign parties other than those mentioned above to be included as interested parties.

6.12 The authorities shall provide opportunities for industrial users of the product under investigation, and for representative consumer organizations in cases where the product is commonly sold at the retail level, to provide information which is relevant to the investigation regarding dumping, injury and causality.

6.13 The authorities shall take due account of any difficulties experienced by interested parties, in particular small companies, in supplying information requested, and shall provide any assistance practicable.

6.14 The procedures set out above are not intended to prevent the authorities of a Member from proceeding expeditiously with regard to initiating an investigation, reaching preliminary or final determinations, whether affirmative or negative, or from applying provisional or final measures, in accordance with relevant provisions of this Agreement.

ARTICLE 7—PROVISIONAL MEASURES

7.1 Provisional measures may be applied only if:

(i) an investigation has been initiated in accordance with the provisions of Article 5, a public notice has been given to that effect and interested parties have been given adequate opportunities to submit information and make comments;

(ii) a preliminary affirmative determination has been made of dumping and consequent injury to a domestic industry; and

(iii) the authorities concerned judge such measures necessary to prevent injury being caused during the investigation.

7.2 Provisional measures may take the form of a provisional duty or, preferably, a security by cash deposit or bond equal to the amount of the anti dumping duty provisionally estimated, being not greater than the provisionally estimated margin of dumping. Withholding of appraisement is an appropriate provisional measure, provided that the normal duty and the estimated amount of the anti dumping duty be indicated and as long as the withholding of appraisement is subject to the same conditions as other provisional measures.

7.3 Provisional measures shall not be applied sooner than 60 days from the date of initiation of the investigation.

7.4 The application of provisional measures shall be limited to as short a period as possible, not exceeding four months or, on decision of the authorities concerned, upon request by exporters representing a significant percentage of the trade involved, to a period not exceeding six months. When authorities, in the course of an investigation, examine whether a duty lower than the margin of dumping would be sufficient to remove injury, these periods may be six and nine months, respectively.

7.5 The relevant provisions of Article 9 shall be followed in the application of provisional measures.

ARTICLE 8—PRICE UNDERTAKINGS

8.1 Proceedings may be suspended or terminated without the imposition of provisional measures or anti dumping duties upon receipt of satisfactory voluntary undertakings from any exporter to revise its prices or to cease exports to the area in question at dumped prices so that the authorities are satisfied that the injurious effect of the dumping is eliminated. Price increases under such undertakings shall not be higher than necessary to eliminate the margin of dumping. It is desirable that the price increases be less than the margin of dumping if such increases would be adequate to remove the injury to the domestic industry.

8.2 Price undertakings shall not be sought or accepted from exporters unless the authorities of the importing Member have made a preliminary affirmative determination of dumping and injury caused by such dumping.

8.3 Undertakings offered need not be accepted if the authorities consider their acceptance impractical, for example, if the number of actual or potential exporters is too great, or for other reasons, including reasons of general policy. Should the case arise and where practicable, the authorities shall provide to the exporter the reasons which have led them to consider acceptance of an undertaking as inappropriate, and shall, to the extent possible, give the exporter an opportunity to make comments thereon.

8.4 If an undertaking is accepted, the investigation of dumping and injury shall nevertheless be completed if the exporter so desires or the authorities so decide. In such a case, if a negative determination of dumping or injury is made, the undertaking shall automatically lapse, except in cases where such a determination is due in large part to the existence of a price undertaking. In such cases, the authorities may require that an undertaking be maintained for a reasonable period consistent with the provisions of this Agreement. In the event that an affirmative determination of dumping and injury is made, the undertaking shall continue consistent with its terms and the provisions of this Agreement.

8.5 Price undertakings may be suggested by the authorities of the importing Member, but no exporter shall be forced to enter into such undertakings. The fact that exporters do not offer such undertakings, or do not accept an invitation to do so, shall in no way prejudice the consideration of the case. However, the authorities are free to determine that a threat of injury is more likely to be realized if the dumped imports continue.

8.6 Authorities of an importing Member may require any exporter from whom an undertaking has been accepted to provide periodically information relevant to the fulfilment of such an undertaking and to permit verification of pertinent data. In case of violation of an undertaking, the authorities of the importing Member may take, under this Agreement in conformity with its provisions, expeditious actions which may constitute immediate application of provisional measures using the best information available. In such cases, definitive duties may be levied in accordance with this

Agreement on products entered for consumption not more than 90 days before the application of such provisional measures, except that any such retroactive assessment shall not apply to imports entered before the violation of the undertaking.

ARTICLE 9—IMPOSITION AND COLLECTION OF ANTI DUMPING DUTIES

9.1 The decision whether or not to impose an anti dumping duty in cases where all requirements for the imposition have been fulfilled, and the decision whether the amount of the anti dumping duty to be imposed shall be the full margin of dumping or less, are decisions to be made by the authorities of the importing Member. It is desirable that the imposition be permissive in the territory of all Members, and that the duty be less than the margin if such lesser duty would be adequate to remove the injury to the domestic industry.

9.2 When an anti dumping duty is imposed in respect of any product, such anti dumping duty shall be collected in the appropriate amounts in each case, on a non discriminatory basis on imports of such product from all sources found to be dumped and causing injury, except as to imports from those sources from which price undertakings under the terms of this Agreement have been accepted. The authorities shall name the supplier or suppliers of the product concerned. If, however, several suppliers from the same country are involved, and it is impracticable to name all these suppliers, the authorities may name the supplying country concerned. If several suppliers from more than one country are involved, the authorities may name either all the suppliers involved, or, if this is impracticable, all the supplying countries involved.

9.3 The amount of the anti dumping duty shall not exceed the margin of dumping as established under Article 2.

9.3.1 When the amount of the anti dumping duty is assessed on a retrospective basis, the determination of the final liability for payment of anti dumping duties shall take place as soon as possible, normally within 12 months, and in no case more than 18 months, after the date on which a request for a final assessment of the amount of the anti dumping duty has been made. Any refund shall be made promptly and normally in not more than 90 days following the determination of final liability made pursuant to this sub paragraph. In any case, where a refund is not made within 90 days, the authorities shall provide an explanation if so requested.

9.3.2 When the amount of the anti dumping duty is assessed on a prospective basis, provision shall be made for a prompt refund, upon request, of any duty paid in excess of the margin of dumping. A refund of any such duty paid in excess of the actual margin of dumping shall normally take place within 12 months, and in no case more than 18 months, after the date on which a request for a refund, duly supported by evidence, has been made by an importer of the product subject to the anti dumping duty. The refund authorized should normally be made within 90 days of the above noted decision.

9.3.3 In determining whether and to what extent a reimbursement should be made when the export price is constructed in accordance with paragraph 3 of Article 2, authorities should take account of any change in normal value, any change in costs incurred between importation and resale, and any movement in the resale price which is duly reflected in subsequent selling prices, and should calculate the export price with no deduction for the amount of anti dumping duties paid when conclusive evidence of the above is provided.

9.4 When the authorities have limited their examination in accordance with the second sentence of paragraph 10 of Article 6, any anti dumping duty applied to imports from exporters or producers not included in the examination shall not exceed:

(i) the weighted average margin of dumping established with respect to the selected exporters or producers or,

(ii) where the liability for payment of anti dumping duties is calculated on the basis of a prospective normal value, the difference between the weighted average normal value of the selected exporters or producers and the export prices of exporters or producers not individually examined,

provided that the authorities shall disregard for the purpose of this paragraph any zero and de minimis margins and margins established under the circumstances referred to in paragraph 8 of Article 6. The authorities shall apply individual duties or normal values to imports from any exporter or producer not included in the examination who has provided the necessary information during the course of the investigation, as provided for in subparagraph 10.2 of Article 6.

9.5 If a product is subject to anti dumping duties in an importing Member, the authorities shall promptly carry out a review for the purpose of determining individual margins of dumping for any exporters or producers in the exporting country in question who have not exported the product to the importing Member during the period of investigation, provided that these exporters or producers can show that they are not related to any of the exporters or producers in the exporting country who are subject to the anti dumping duties on the product. Such a review shall be initiated and carried out on an accelerated basis, compared to normal duty assessment and review proceedings in the importing Member. No anti dumping duties shall be levied on imports from such exporters or producers while the review is being carried out. The authorities may, however, withhold appraisement and/or request guarantees to ensure that, should such a review result in a determination of dumping in respect of such producers or exporters, anti dumping duties can be levied retroactively to the date of the initiation of the review.

Article 10—Retroactivity

10.1 Provisional measures and anti dumping duties shall only be applied to products which enter for consumption after the time when the decision taken under paragraph 1 of Article 7 and paragraph 1 of Article 9, respectively, enters into force, subject to the exceptions set out in this Article.

10.2 Where a final determination of injury (but not of a threat thereof or of a material retardation of the establishment of an industry) is made or, in the case of a final determination of a threat of injury, where the effect of the dumped imports would, in the absence of the provisional measures, have led to a determination of injury, anti dumping duties may be levied retroactively for the period for which provisional measures, if any, have been applied.

10.3 If the definitive anti dumping duty is higher than the provisional duty paid or payable, or the amount estimated for the purpose of the security, the difference shall not be collected. If the definitive duty is lower than the provisional duty paid or payable, or the amount estimated for the purpose of the security, the difference shall be reimbursed or the duty recalculated, as the case may be.

10.4 Except as provided in paragraph 2, where a determination of threat of injury or material retardation is made (but no injury has yet occurred) a definitive anti dumping duty may be imposed only from the date of the determination of threat of injury or material retardation, and any cash deposit made during the period of the application of provisional measures shall be refunded and any bonds released in an expeditious manner.

10.5 Where a final determination is negative, any cash deposit made during the period of the application of provisional measures shall be refunded and any bonds released in an expeditious manner.

10.6 A definitive anti dumping duty may be levied on products which were entered for consumption not more than 90 days prior to the date of application of provisional measures, when the authorities determine for the dumped product in question that:

(i) there is a history of dumping which caused injury or that the importer was, or should have been, aware that the exporter practises dumping and that such dumping would cause injury, and

(ii) the injury is caused by massive dumped imports of a product in a relatively short time which in light of the timing and the volume of the dumped imports and other circumstances (such as a rapid build up of inventories of the imported product) is likely to seriously undermine the remedial effect of the definitive anti dumping duty to be applied, provided that the importers concerned have been given an opportunity to comment.

10.7 The authorities may, after initiating an investigation, take such measures as the withholding of appraisement or assessment as may be necessary to collect anti dumping duties retroactively, as provided for in paragraph 6, once they have sufficient evidence that the conditions set forth in that paragraph are satisfied.

10.8 No duties shall be levied retroactively pursuant to paragraph 6 on products entered for consumption prior to the date of initiation of the investigation.

Article 11—Duration and Review of Anti Dumping Duties and Price Undertakings

11.1 An anti dumping duty shall remain in force only as long as and to the extent necessary to counteract dumping which is causing injury.

11.2 The authorities shall review the need for the continued imposition of the duty, where warranted, on their own initiative or, provided that a reasonable period of time has elapsed since the imposition of the definitive anti dumping duty, upon request by any interested party which submits positive information substantiating the need for a review. Interested parties shall have the right to request the authorities to examine whether the continued imposition of the duty is necessary to offset dumping, whether the injury would be likely to continue or recur if the duty were removed or varied, or both. If, as a result of the review under this paragraph, the authorities determine that the anti dumping duty is no longer warranted, it shall be terminated immediately.

11.3 Notwithstanding the provisions of paragraphs 1 and 2, any definitive anti dumping duty shall be terminated on a date not later than five years from its imposition (or from the date of the most recent review under paragraph 2 if that review has covered both dumping and injury, or under this paragraph), unless the authorities determine, in a review initiated before that date on their own initiative or upon a duly substantiated request made by or on behalf of the domestic industry within a reasonable period of time prior to that date, that the expiry of the duty would be likely to lead to continuation or recurrence of dumping and injury. The duty may remain in force pending the outcome of such a review.

11.4 The provisions of Article 6 regarding evidence and procedure shall apply to any review carried out under this Article. Any such review shall be carried out expeditiously and shall normally be concluded within 12 months of the date of initiation of the review.

11.5 The provisions of this Article shall apply mutatis mutandis to price undertakings accepted under Article 8.

Article 12—Public Notice and Explanation of Determinations

12.1 When the authorities are satisfied that there is sufficient evidence to justify the initiation of an anti dumping investigation pursuant to Article 5, the Member or Members the products of which are subject to such investigation and other interested parties known to the investigating authorities to have an interest therein shall be notified and a public notice shall be given.

12.1.1 A public notice of the initiation of an investigation shall contain, or otherwise make available through a separate report , adequate information on the following:

(i) the name of the exporting country or countries and the product involved;

(ii) the date of initiation of the investigation;

(iii) the basis on which dumping is alleged in the application;

(iv) a summary of the factors on which the allegation of injury is based;

(v) the address to which representations by interested parties should be directed;

(vi) the time limits allowed to interested parties for making their views known.

12.2 Public notice shall be given of any preliminary or final determination, whether affirmative or negative, of any decision to accept an undertaking pursuant to Article 8, of the termination of such an undertaking, and of the termination of a definitive anti dumping duty. Each such notice shall set forth, or otherwise make available through a separate report, in sufficient detail the findings and conclusions reached on all issues of fact and law considered material by the investigating authorities. All such notices and reports shall be forwarded to the Member or Members the products of which are subject to such determination or undertaking and to other interested parties known to have an interest therein.

12.2.1 A public notice of the imposition of provisional measures shall set forth, or otherwise make available through a separate report, sufficiently detailed explanations for the preliminary determinations on dumping and injury and shall refer to the matters of fact and law which have led to arguments being accepted or rejected. Such a notice or report shall, due regard being paid to the requirement for the protection of confidential information, contain in particular:

(i) the names of the suppliers, or when this is impracticable, the supplying countries involved;

(ii) a description of the product which is sufficient for customs purposes;

(iii) the margins of dumping established and a full explanation of the reasons for the methodology used in the establishment and comparison of the export price and the normal value under Article 2;

(iv) considerations relevant to the injury determination as set out in Article 3;

(v) the main reasons leading to the determination.

12.2.2 A public notice of conclusion or suspension of an investigation in the case of an affirmative determination providing for the imposition of a definitive duty or the acceptance of a price undertaking shall contain, or otherwise make available through a separate report, all relevant information on the matters of fact and law and reasons which have led to the imposition of final measures or the acceptance of a price undertaking, due regard being paid to the requirement for the protection of confidential information. In particular, the notice or report shall contain the information described in subparagraph 2.1, as well as the reasons for the acceptance or rejection of relevant arguments or claims made by the exporters and importers, and the basis for any decision made under subparagraph 10.2 of Article 6.

12.2.3 A public notice of the termination or suspension of an investigation following the acceptance of an undertaking pursuant to Article 8 shall include, or otherwise make available through a separate report, the non confidential part of this undertaking.

12.3 The provisions of this Article shall apply mutatis mutandis to the initiation and completion of reviews pursuant to Article 11 and to decisions under Article 10 to apply duties retroactively.

Article 13—Judicial Review

Each Member whose national legislation contains provisions on anti dumping measures shall maintain judicial, arbitral or administrative tribunals or procedures for the purpose, inter alia, of the prompt review of administrative actions relating to final determinations and reviews of determinations within the meaning of Article 11. Such tribunals or procedures shall be independent of the authorities responsible for the determination or review in question.

Article 14—Anti Dumping Action on Behalf of a Third Country

14.1 An application for anti dumping action on behalf of a third country shall be made by the authorities of the third country requesting action.

14.2 Such an application shall be supported by price information to show that the imports are being dumped and by detailed information to show that the alleged dumping is causing injury to the domestic industry concerned in the third country. The government of the third country shall afford all assistance to the authorities of the importing country to obtain any further information which the latter may require.

14.3 In considering such an application, the authorities of the importing country shall consider the effects of the alleged dumping on the industry concerned as a whole in the third country; that is to say, the injury shall not be assessed in relation only to the effect of the alleged dumping on the industry's exports to the importing country or even on the industry's total exports.

14.4 The decision whether or not to proceed with a case shall rest with the importing country. If the importing country decides that it is prepared to take action, the initiation of the approach to the Council for Trade in Goods seeking its approval for such action shall rest with the importing country.

Article 15—Developing Country Members

It is recognized that special regard must be given by developed country Members to the special situation of developing country Members when considering the application of anti dumping measures under this Agreement. Possibilities of constructive remedies provided for by this Agreement shall be explored before applying anti dumping duties where they would affect the essential interests of developing country Members.

PART II

Article 16—Committee on Anti Dumping Practices

16.1 There is hereby established a Committee on Anti Dumping Practices (referred to in this Agreement as the "Committee") composed of representatives from each of the Members. The Committee shall elect its own Chairman and shall meet not less than twice a year and otherwise as envisaged by relevant provisions of this Agreement at the request of any Member. The Committee shall carry out responsibilities as assigned to it under this Agreement or by the Members and it shall afford Members the opportunity of consulting on any matters relating to the operation of the Agreement or the furtherance of its objectives. The WTO Secretariat shall act as the secretariat to the Committee.

16.2 The Committee may set up subsidiary bodies as appropriate.

16.3 In carrying out their functions, the Committee and any subsidiary bodies may consult with and seek information from any source they deem appropriate. However, before the Committee or a subsidiary body seeks such information from a source within the jurisdiction of a Member, it shall inform the Member involved. It shall obtain the consent of the Member and any firm to be consulted.

16.4 Members shall report without delay to the Committee all preliminary or final anti dumping actions taken. Such reports shall be available in the Secretariat for inspection by other Members. Members shall also submit, on a semi annual basis, reports of any anti dumping actions taken within the preceding six months. The semi-annual reports shall be submitted on an agreed standard form.

16.5 Each Member shall notify the Committee (a) which of its authorities are competent to initiate and conduct investigations referred to in Article 5 and (b) its domestic procedures governing the initiation and conduct of such investigations.

Article 17—Consultation and Dispute Settlement

17.1 Except as otherwise provided herein, the Dispute Settlement Understanding is applicable to consultations and the settlement of disputes under this Agreement.

17.2 Each Member shall afford sympathetic consideration to, and shall afford adequate opportunity for consultation regarding, representations made by another Member with respect to any matter affecting the operation of this Agreement.

17.3 If any Member considers that any benefit accruing to it, directly or indirectly, under this Agreement is being nullified or impaired, or that the achievement of any objective is being impeded, by another Member or Members, it may, with a view to reaching a mutually satisfactory resolution of the matter, request in writing consultations with the Member or Members in question. Each Member shall afford sympathetic consideration to any request from another Member for consultation.

17.4 If the Member that requested consultations considers that the consultations pursuant to paragraph 3 have failed to achieve a mutually agreed solution, and if final action has been taken by the administering authorities of the importing Member to levy definitive anti dumping duties or to accept price undertakings, it may refer the matter to the Dispute Settlement Body ("DSB"). When a provisional measure has a significant impact and the Member that requested consultations considers that the measure was taken contrary to the provisions of paragraph 1 of Article 7, that Member may also refer such matter to the DSB.

17.5 The DSB shall, at the request of the complaining party, establish a panel to examine the matter based upon:

(i) a written statement of the Member making the request indicating how a benefit accruing to it, directly or indirectly, under this Agreement has been nullified or impaired, or that the achieving of the objectives of the Agreement is being impeded, and

(ii) the facts made available in conformity with appropriate domestic procedures to the authorities of the importing Member.

17.6 In examining the matter referred to in paragraph 5:

(i) in its assessment of the facts of the matter, the panel shall determine whether the authorities' establishment of the facts was proper and whether their evaluation of those facts was unbiased and objective. If the establishment of the facts was proper and the evaluation was unbiased and objective, even though the panel might have reached a different conclusion, the evaluation shall not be overturned;

(ii) the panel shall interpret the relevant provisions of the Agreement in accordance with customary rules of interpretation of public international law. Where the panel finds that a relevant provision of the Agreement admits of more than one permissible interpretation, the panel shall find the authorities' measure to be in conformity with the Agreement if it rests upon one of those permissible interpretations.

17.7 Confidential information provided to the panel shall not be disclosed without formal authorization from the person, body or authority providing such information. Where such information is requested from the panel but release of such information by the panel is not authorized, a non confidential summary of the information, authorized by the person, body or authority providing the information, shall be provided.

PART III

ARTICLE 18—FINAL PROVISIONS

18.1 No specific action against dumping of exports from another Member can be taken except in accordance with the provisions of GATT 1994, as interpreted by this Agreement.

18.2 Reservations may not be entered in respect of any of the provisions of this Agreement without the consent of the other Members.

18.3 Subject to subparagraphs 3.1 and 3.2, the provisions of this Agreement shall apply to investigations, and reviews of existing measures, initiated pursuant to applications which have been made on or after the date of entry into force for a Member of the WTO Agreement.

18.3.1 With respect to the calculation of margins of dumping in refund procedures under paragraph 3 of Article 9, the rules used in the most recent determination or review of dumping shall apply.

18.3.2 For the purposes of paragraph 3 of Article 11, existing anti dumping measures shall be deemed to be imposed on a date not later than the date of entry into force for a Member of the WTO Agreement, except in cases in which the domestic legislation of a Member in force on that date already included a clause of the type provided for in that paragraph.

18.4 Each Member shall take all necessary steps, of a general or particular character, to ensure, not later than the date of entry into force of the WTO Agreement for it, the conformity of its laws, regulations and administrative procedures with the provisions of this Agreement as they may apply for the Member in question.

18.5 Each Member shall inform the Committee of any changes in its laws and regulations relevant to this Agreement and in the administration of such laws and regulations.

18.6 The Committee shall review annually the implementation and operation of this Agreement taking into account the objectives thereof. The Committee shall inform annually the Council for Trade in Goods of developments during the period covered by such reviews.

18.7 The Annexes to this Agreement constitute an integral part thereof.

ANNEX I

PROCEDURES FOR ON THE SPOT INVESTIGATIONS PURSUANT TO PARAGRAPH 7 OF ARTICLE 6

1. Upon initiation of an investigation, the authorities of the exporting Member and the firms known to be concerned should be informed of the intention to carry out on the spot investigations.
2. If in exceptional circumstances it is intended to include non governmental experts in the investigating team, the firms and the authorities of the exporting Member should be so informed. Such non governmental experts should be subject to effective sanctions for breach of confidentiality requirements.
3. It should be standard practice to obtain explicit agreement of the firms concerned in the exporting Member before the visit is finally scheduled.
4. As soon as the agreement of the firms concerned has been obtained, the investigating authorities should notify the authorities of the exporting Member of the names and addresses of the firms to be visited and the dates agreed.
5. Sufficient advance notice should be given to the firms in question before the visit is made.
6. Visits to explain the questionnaire should only be made at the request of an exporting firm. Such a visit may only be made if (a) the authorities of the importing Member notify the representatives of the Member in question and (b) the latter do not object to the visit.
7. As the main purpose of the on the spot investigation is to verify information provided or to obtain further details, it should be carried out after the response to the questionnaire has been received unless the firm agrees to the contrary and the government of the exporting Member is informed by the investigating authorities of the anticipated visit and does not object to it; further, it

should be standard practice prior to the visit to advise the firms concerned of the general nature of the information to be verified and of any further information which needs to be provided, though this should not preclude requests to be made on the spot for further details to be provided in the light of information obtained.

8. Enquiries or questions put by the authorities or firms of the exporting Members and essential to a successful on the spot investigation should, whenever possible, be answered before the visit is made.

ANNEX II

BEST INFORMATION AVAILABLE IN TERMS OF PARAGRAPH 8 OF ARTICLE 6

1. As soon as possible after the initiation of the investigation, the investigating authorities should specify in detail the information required from any interested party, and the manner in which that information should be structured by the interested party in its response. The authorities should also ensure that the party is aware that if information is not supplied within a reasonable time, the authorities will be free to make determinations on the basis of the facts available, including those contained in the application for the initiation of the investigation by the domestic industry.

2. The authorities may also request that an interested party provide its response in a particular medium (e.g. computer tape) or computer language. Where such a request is made, the authorities should consider the reasonable ability of the interested party to respond in the preferred medium or computer language, and should not request the party to use for its response a computer system other than that used by the party. The authority should not maintain a request for a computerized response if the interested party does not maintain computerized accounts and if presenting the response as requested would result in an unreasonable extra burden on the interested party, e.g. it would entail unreasonable additional cost and trouble. The authorities should not maintain a request for a response in a particular medium or computer language if the interested party does not maintain its computerized accounts in such medium or computer language and if presenting the response as requested would result in an unreasonable extra burden on the interested party, e.g. it would entail unreasonable additional cost and trouble.

3. All information which is verifiable, which is appropriately submitted so that it can be used in the investigation without undue difficulties, which is supplied in a timely fashion, and, where applicable, which is supplied in a medium or computer language requested by the authorities, should be taken into account when determinations are made. If a party does not respond in the preferred medium or computer language but the authorities find that the circumstances set out in paragraph 2 have been satisfied, the failure to respond in the preferred medium or computer language should not be considered to significantly impede the investigation.

4. Where the authorities do not have the ability to process information if provided in a particular medium (e.g. computer tape), the

information should be supplied in the form of written material or any other form acceptable to the authorities.

5. Even though the information provided may not be ideal in all respects, this should not justify the authorities from disregarding it, provided the interested party has acted to the best of its ability.

6. If evidence or information is not accepted, the supplying party should be informed forthwith of the reasons therefor, and should have an opportunity to provide further explanations within a reasonable period, due account being taken of the time limits of the investigation. If the explanations are considered by the authorities as not being satisfactory, the reasons for the rejection of such evidence or information should be given in any published determinations.

7. If the authorities have to base their findings, including those with respect to normal value, on information from a secondary source, including the information supplied in the application for the initiation of the investigation, they should do so with special circumspection. In such cases, the authorities should, where practicable, check the information from other independent sources at their disposal, such as published price lists, official import statistics and customs returns, and from the information obtained from other interested parties during the investigation. It is clear, however, that if an interested party does not cooperate and thus relevant information is being withheld from the authorities, this situation could lead to a result which is less favourable to the party than if the party did cooperate.

d. Final Act Embodying the Results of the Uruguay Round of Multilateral Trade Negotiations

Signed at Marrakesh, April 15, 1994; Entered into force, January 1, 1995

FINAL ACT EMBODYING THE RESULTS OF THE URUGUAY ROUND OF MULTILATERAL TRADE NEGOTIATIONS

1. Having met in order to conclude the Uruguay Round of Multilateral Trade Negotiations, representatives of the governments and of the European Communities, members of the Trade Negotiations Committee, *agree* that the Agreement Establishing the World Trade Organization (referred to in this Final Act as the "WTO Agreement"), the Ministerial Declarations and Decisions, and the Understanding on Commitments in Financial Services, as annexed hereto, embody the results of their negotiations and form an integral part of this Final Act.

2. By signing the present Final Act, the representatives *agree*

(a) to submit, as appropriate, the WTO Agreement for the consideration of their respective competent authorities with a view to seeking approval of the Agreement in accordance with their procedures; and

(b) to adopt the Ministerial Declarations and Decisions.

3. The representatives *agree* on the desirability of acceptance of the WTO Agreement by all participants in the Uruguay Round of Multilateral Trade Negotiations (hereinafter referred to as "participants") with a view to its entry into force by 1 January 1995, or as early as possible thereafter. Not later than late 1994, Ministers will meet, in accordance with the final paragraph of the Punta del Este Ministerial Declaration, to decide on the international implementation of the results, including the timing of their entry into force.

4. The representatives *agree* that the WTO Agreement shall be open for acceptance as a whole, by signature or otherwise, by all participants pursuant to Article XIV thereof. The acceptance and entry into force of a Plurilateral Trade Agreement included in Annex 4 of the WTO Agreement shall be governed by the provisions of that Plurilateral Trade Agreement.

5. Before accepting the WTO Agreement, participants which are not contracting parties to the General Agreement on Tariffs and Trade must first have concluded negotiations for their accession to the General Agreement and become contracting parties thereto. For participants which are not contracting parties to the General Agreement as of the date of the Final Act, the Schedules are not definitive and shall be subsequently completed for the purpose of their accession to the General Agreement and acceptance of the WTO Agreement.

6. This Final Act and the texts annexed hereto shall be deposited with the Director-General to the CONTRACTING PARTIES to the General Agreement on Tariffs and Trade who shall promptly furnish to each participant a certified copy thereof.

e. Agreement Establishing the World Trade Organization

Signed at Marrakesh, April 15, 1994; Entered into force, January 1, 1995

AGREEMENT ESTABLISHING THE WORLD TRADE ORGANIZATION

The Parties to this Agreement,

RECOGNIZING that their relations in the field of trade and economic endeavour should be conducted with a view to raising standards of living, ensuring full employment and a large and steadily growing volume of real income and effective demand, and expanding the production of and trade in goods and services, while allowing for the optimal use of the world's resources in accordance with the objective of sustainable development, seeking both to protect and preserve the environment and to enhance the means for doing so in a manner consistent with their respective needs and concerns at different levels of economic development,

RECOGNIZING further that there is need for positive efforts designed to ensure that developing countries, and especially the least developed among them, secure a share in the growth in international trade commensurate with the needs of their economic development,

BEING DESIROUS of contributing to these objectives by entering into reciprocal and mutually advantageous arrangements directed to the substantial reduction of tariffs and other barriers to trade and to the elimination of discriminatory treatment in international trade relations,

RESOLVED, therefore, to develop an integrated, more viable and durable multilateral trading system encompassing the General Agreement on Tariffs and Trade, the results of past trade liberalization efforts, and all of the results of the Uruguay Round of Multilateral Trade Negotiations,

DETERMINED to preserve the basic principles and to further the objectives underlying this multilateral trading system,

AGREE AS FOLLOWS:

ARTICLE I—ESTABLISHMENT OF THE ORGANIZATION

The World Trade Organization (hereinafter referred to as "the WTO") is hereby established.

ARTICLE II—SCOPE OF THE WTO

1. The WTO shall provide the common institutional framework for the conduct of trade relations among its Members in matters related to the agreements and associated legal instruments included in the Annexes to this Agreement.

2. The agreements and associated legal instruments included in Annexes 1, 2 and 3 (hereinafter referred to as "Multilateral Trade Agreements") are integral parts of this Agreement, binding on all Members.

3. The agreements and associated legal instruments included in Annex 4 (hereinafter referred to as "Plurilateral Trade Agreements") are also part of this Agreement for those Members that have accepted them, and are binding on those Members. The Plurilateral Trade Agreements do not create either obligations or rights for Members that have not accepted them.

4. The General Agreement on Tariffs and Trade 1994 as specified in Annex 1A (hereinafter referred to as "GATT 1994") is legally distinct from the General Agreement on Tariffs and Trade, dated 30 October 1947, annexed to the Final Act Adopted at the Conclusion of the Second Session of the Preparatory Committee of the United Nations Conference on Trade and Employment, as subsequently rectified, amended or modified (hereinafter referred to as "GATT 1947").

Article III—Functions of the WTO

1. The WTO shall facilitate the implementation, administration and operation, and further the objectives, of this Agreement and of the Multilateral Trade Agreements, and shall also provide the framework for the implementation, administration and operation of the Plurilateral Trade Agreements.

2. The WTO shall provide the forum for negotiations among its Members concerning their multilateral trade relations in matters dealt with under the agreements in the Annexes to this Agreement. The WTO may also provide a forum for further negotiations among its Members concerning their multilateral trade relations, and a framework for the implementation of the results of such negotiations, as may be decided by the Ministerial Conference.

3. The WTO shall administer the Understanding on Rules and Procedures Governing the Settlement of Disputes (hereinafter referred to as the "Dispute Settlement Understanding" or "DSU") in Annex 2 to this Agreement.

4. The WTO shall administer the Trade Policy Review Mechanism (hereinafter referred to as the "TPRM") provided for in Annex 3 to this Agreement.

5. With a view to achieving greater coherence in global economic policy-making, the WTO shall cooperate, as appropriate, with the International Monetary Fund and with the International Bank for Reconstruction and Development and its affiliated agencies.

Article IV—Structure of the WTO

1. There shall be a Ministerial Conference composed of representatives of all the Members, which shall meet at least once every two years. The Ministerial Conference shall carry out the functions of the WTO and take actions necessary to this effect. The Ministerial Conference shall have the authority to take decisions on all matters under any of the Multilateral Trade Agreements, if so requested by a Member, in accordance with the specific requirements

for decision-making in this Agreement and in the relevant Multilateral Trade Agreement.

2. There shall be a General Council composed of representatives of all the Members, which shall meet as appropriate. In the intervals between meetings of the Ministerial Conference, its functions shall be conducted by the General Council. The General Council shall also carry out the functions assigned to it by this Agreement. The General Council shall establish its rules of procedure and approve the rules of procedure for the Committees provided for in paragraph 7.

3. The General Council shall convene as appropriate to discharge the responsibilities of the Dispute Settlement Body provided for in the Dispute Settlement Understanding. The Dispute Settlement Body may have its own chairman and shall establish such rules of procedure as it deems necessary for the fulfilment of those responsibilities.

4. The General Council shall convene as appropriate to discharge the responsibilities of the Trade Policy Review Body provided for in the TPRM. The Trade Policy Review Body may have its own chairman and shall establish such rules of procedure as it deems necessary for the fulfilment of those responsibilities.

5. There shall be a Council for Trade in Goods, a Council for Trade in Services and a Council for Trade-Related Aspects of Intellectual Property Rights (hereinafter referred to as the "Council for TRIPS"), which shall operate under the general guidance of the General Council. The Council for Trade in Goods shall oversee the functioning of the Multilateral Trade Agreements in Annex 1A. The Council for Trade in Services shall oversee the functioning of the General Agreement on Trade in Services (hereinafter referred to as "GATS"). The Council for TRIPS shall oversee the functioning of the Agreement on Trade-Related Aspects of Intellectual Property Rights (hereinafter referred to as the "Agreement on TRIPS"). These Councils shall carry out the functions assigned to them by their respective agreements and by the General Council. They shall establish their respective rules of procedure subject to the approval of the General Council. Membership in these Councils shall be open to representatives of all Members. These Councils shall meet as necessary to carry out their functions.

6. The Council for Trade in Goods, the Council for Trade in Services and the Council for TRIPS shall establish subsidiary bodies as required. These subsidiary bodies shall establish their respective rules of procedure subject to the approval of their respective Councils.

7. The Ministerial Conference shall establish a Committee on Trade and Development, a Committee on Balance-of-Payments Restrictions and a Committee on Budget, Finance and Administration, which shall carry out the functions assigned to them by this Agreement and by the Multilateral Trade Agreements, and any additional functions assigned to them by the General Council, and may establish such additional Committees with such functions as it may deem appropriate. As part of its functions, the Committee on Trade and Development shall periodically review the special provisions in the Multilateral Trade Agreements in favour of the

least-developed country Members and report to the General Council for appropriate action. Membership in these Committees shall be open to representatives of all Members.

8. The bodies provided for under the Plurilateral Trade Agreements shall carry out the functions assigned to them under those Agreements and shall operate within the institutional framework of the WTO. These bodies shall keep the General Council informed of their activities on a regular basis.

ARTICLE V—RELATIONS WITH OTHER ORGANIZATIONS

1. The General Council shall make appropriate arrangements for effective cooperation with other intergovernmental organizations that have responsibilities related to those of the WTO.

2. The General Council may make appropriate arrangements for consultation and cooperation with non-governmental organizations concerned with matters related to those of the WTO.

ARTICLE VI—THE SECRETARIAT

1. There shall be a Secretariat of the WTO (hereinafter referred to as "the Secretariat") headed by a Director-General.

2. The Ministerial Conference shall appoint the Director-General and adopt regulations setting out the powers, duties, conditions of service and term of office of the Director-General.

3. The Director-General shall appoint the members of the staff of the Secretariat and determine their duties and conditions of service in accordance with regulations adopted by the Ministerial Conference.

4. The responsibilities of the Director-General and of the staff of the Secretariat shall be exclusively international in character. In the discharge of their duties, the Director-General and the staff of the Secretariat shall not seek or accept instructions from any government or any other authority external to the WTO. They shall refrain from any action which might adversely reflect on their position as international officials. The Members of the WTO shall respect the international character of the responsibilities of the Director-General and of the staff of the Secretariat and shall not seek to influence them in the discharge of their duties.

ARTICLE VII—BUDGET AND CONTRIBUTIONS

1. The Director-General shall present to the Committee on Budget, Finance and Administration the annual budget estimate and financial statement of the WTO. The Committee on Budget, Finance and Administration shall review the annual budget estimate and the financial statement presented by the Director-General and make recommendations thereon to the General Council. The annual budget estimate shall be subject to approval by the General Council.

2. The Committee on Budget, Finance and Administration shall propose to the General Council financial regulations which shall include provisions setting out:

(a) the scale of contributions apportioning the expenses of the WTO among its Members; and

(b) the measures to be taken in respect of Members in arrears.

The financial regulations shall be based, as far as practicable, on the regulations and practices of GATT 1947.

3. The General Council shall adopt the financial regulations and the annual budget estimate by a two-thirds majority comprising more than half of the Members of the WTO.

4. Each Member shall promptly contribute to the WTO its share in the expenses of the WTO in accordance with the financial regulations adopted by the General Council.

ARTICLE VIII—STATUS OF THE WTO

1. The WTO shall have legal personality, and shall be accorded by each of its Members such legal capacity as may be necessary for the exercise of its functions.

2. The WTO shall be accorded by each of its Members such privileges and immunities as are necessary for the exercise of its functions.

3. The officials of the WTO and the representatives of the Members shall similarly be accorded by each of its Members such privileges and immunities as are necessary for the independent exercise of their functions in connection with the WTO.

4. The privileges and immunities to be accorded by a Member to the WTO, its officials, and the representatives of its Members shall be similar to the privileges and immunities stipulated in the Convention on the Privileges and Immunities of the Specialized Agencies, approved by the General Assembly of the United Nations on 21 November 1947.

5. The WTO may conclude a headquarters agreement.

ARTICLE IX—DECISION-MAKING

1. The WTO shall continue the practice of decision-making by consensus followed under GATT 1947. Except as otherwise provided, where a decision cannot be arrived at by consensus, the matter at issue shall be decided by voting. At meetings of the Ministerial Conference and the General Council, each Member of the WTO shall have one vote. Where the European Communities exercise their right to vote, they shall have a number of votes equal to the number of their member States which are Members of the WTO. Decisions of the Ministerial Conference and the General Council shall be taken by a majority of the votes cast, unless otherwise provided in this Agreement or in the relevant Multilateral Trade Agreement.

2. The Ministerial Conference and the General Council shall have the exclusive authority to adopt interpretations of this Agreement and of the Multilateral Trade Agreements. In the case of an interpretation of a Multilateral Trade Agreement in Annex 1, they shall exercise their authority on the basis of a recommendation by the Council overseeing the functioning of that Agreement. The decision to adopt an interpretation shall be taken by a three-fourths majority of the Members. This paragraph shall not be used in a manner that would undermine the amendment provisions in Article X.

3. In exceptional circumstances, the Ministerial Conference may decide to waive an obligation imposed on a Member by this Agreement or any of the Multilateral Trade Agreements, provided that any such decision shall be taken by three fourths of the Members unless otherwise provided for in this paragraph.

(a) A request for a waiver concerning this Agreement shall be submitted to the Ministerial Conference for consideration pursuant to the practice of decision-making by consensus. The Ministerial Conference shall establish a time-period, which shall not exceed 90 days, to consider the request. If consensus is not reached during the time-period, any decision to grant a waiver shall be taken by three fourths of the Members.

(b) A request for a waiver concerning the Multilateral Trade Agreements in Annexes 1A or 1B or 1C and their annexes shall be submitted initially to the Council for Trade in Goods, the Council for Trade in Services or the Council for TRIPS, respectively, for consideration during a time-period which shall not exceed 90 days. At the end of the time-period, the relevant Council shall submit a report to the Ministerial Conference.

4. A decision by the Ministerial Conference granting a waiver shall state the exceptional circumstances justifying the decision, the terms and conditions governing the application of the waiver, and the date on which the waiver shall terminate. Any waiver granted for a period of more than one year shall be reviewed by the Ministerial Conference not later than one year after it is granted, and thereafter annually until the waiver terminates. In each review, the Ministerial Conference shall examine whether the exceptional circumstances justifying the waiver still exist and whether the terms and conditions attached to the waiver have been met. The Ministerial Conference, on the basis of the annual review, may extend, modify or terminate the waiver.

5. Decisions under a Plurilateral Trade Agreement, including any decisions on interpretations and waivers, shall be governed by the provisions of that Agreement.

Article X—Amendments

1. Any Member of the WTO may initiate a proposal to amend the provisions of this Agreement or the Multilateral Trade Agreements in Annex 1 by submitting such proposal to the Ministerial Conference. The Councils listed in paragraph 5 of Article IV may also submit to the Ministerial Conference proposals to amend the provisions of the corresponding Multilateral Trade Agreements in Annex 1 the functioning of which they oversee. Unless the Ministerial Conference decides on a longer period, for a period of 90 days after the proposal has been tabled formally at the Ministerial Conference any decision by the Ministerial Conference to submit the proposed amendment to the Members for acceptance shall be taken by consensus. Unless the provisions of paragraphs 2, 5 or 6 apply, that decision shall specify whether the provisions of paragraphs 3 or 4 shall apply. If consensus is reached, the Ministerial Conference shall forthwith submit the proposed amendment to the Members for acceptance. If consensus is not reached at a meeting of the Ministerial Conference within the established period, the Ministerial

Conference shall decide by a two-thirds majority of the Members whether to submit the proposed amendment to the Members for acceptance. Except as provided in paragraphs 2, 5 and 6, the provisions of paragraph 3 shall apply to the proposed amendment, unless the Ministerial Conference decides by a three-fourths majority of the Members that the provisions of paragraph 4 shall apply.

2. Amendments to the provisions of this Article and to the provisions of the following Articles shall take effect only upon acceptance by all Members:

Article IX of this Agreement;
Articles I and II of GATT 1994;
Article II:1 of GATS;
Article 4 of the Agreement on TRIPS.

3. Amendments to provisions of this Agreement, or of the Multilateral Trade Agreements in Annexes 1A and 1C, other than those listed in paragraphs 2 and 6, of a nature that would alter the rights and obligations of the Members, shall take effect for the Members that have accepted them upon acceptance by two thirds of the Members and thereafter for each other Member upon acceptance by it. The Ministerial Conference may decide by a three-fourths majority of the Members that any amendment made effective under this paragraph is of such a nature that any Member which has not accepted it within a period specified by the Ministerial Conference in each case shall be free to withdraw from the WTO or to remain a Member with the consent of the Ministerial Conference.

4. Amendments to provisions of this Agreement or of the Multilateral Trade Agreements in Annexes 1A and 1C, other than those listed in paragraphs 2 and 6, of a nature that would not alter the rights and obligations of the Members, shall take effect for all Members upon acceptance by two thirds of the Members.

5. Except as provided in paragraph 2 above, amendments to Parts I, II and III of GATS and the respective annexes shall take effect for the Members that have accepted them upon acceptance by two thirds of the Members and thereafter for each Member upon acceptance by it. The Ministerial Conference may decide by a three-fourths majority of the Members that any amendment made effective under the preceding provision is of such a nature that any Member which has not accepted it within a period specified by the Ministerial Conference in each case shall be free to withdraw from the WTO or to remain a Member with the consent of the Ministerial Conference. Amendments to Parts IV, V and VI of GATS and the respective annexes shall take effect for all Members upon acceptance by two thirds of the Members.

6. Notwithstanding the other provisions of this Article, amendments to the Agreement on TRIPS meeting the requirements of paragraph 2 of Article 71 thereof may be adopted by the Ministerial Conference without further formal acceptance process.

7. Any Member accepting an amendment to this Agreement or to a Multilateral Trade Agreement in Annex 1 shall deposit an instrument of acceptance with the Director-General of the WTO within the period of acceptance specified by the Ministerial Conference.

8. Any Member of the WTO may initiate a proposal to amend the provisions of the Multilateral Trade Agreements in Annexes 2 and

3 by submitting such proposal to the Ministerial Conference. The decision to approve amendments to the Multilateral Trade Agreement in Annex 2 shall be made by consensus and these amendments shall take effect for all Members upon approval by the Ministerial Conference. Decisions to approve amendments to the Multilateral Trade Agreement in Annex 3 shall take effect for all Members upon approval by the Ministerial Conference.

9. The Ministerial Conference, upon the request of the Members parties to a trade agreement, may decide exclusively by consensus to add that agreement to Annex 4. The Ministerial Conference, upon the request of the Members parties to a Plurilateral Trade Agreement, may decide to delete that Agreement from Annex 4.

10. Amendments to a Plurilateral Trade Agreement shall be governed by the provisions of that Agreement.

Article XI—Original Membership

1. The contracting parties to GATT 1947 as of the date of entry into force of this Agreement, and the European Communities, which accept this Agreement and the Multilateral Trade Agreements and for which Schedules of Concessions and Commitments are annexed to GATT 1994 and for which Schedules of Specific Commitments are annexed to GATS shall become original Members of the WTO.

2. The least-developed countries recognized as such by the United Nations will only be required to undertake commitments and concessions to the extent consistent with their individual development, financial and trade needs or their administrative and institutional capabilities.

Article XII—Accession

1. Any State or separate customs territory possessing full autonomy in the conduct of its external commercial relations and of the other matters provided for in this Agreement and the Multilateral Trade Agreements may accede to this Agreement, on terms to be agreed between it and the WTO. Such accession shall apply to this Agreement and the Multilateral Trade Agreements annexed thereto.

2. Decisions on accession shall be taken by the Ministerial Conference. The Ministerial Conference shall approve the agreement on the terms of accession by a two-thirds majority of the Members of the WTO.

3. Accession to a Plurilateral Trade Agreement shall be governed by the provisions of that Agreement.

Article XIII—Non-Application of Multilateral Trade Agreements between Particular Members

1. This Agreement and the Multilateral Trade Agreements in Annexes 1 and 2 shall not apply as between any Member and any other Member if either of the Members, at the time either becomes a Member, does not consent to such application.

2. Paragraph 1 may be invoked between original Members of the WTO which were contracting parties to GATT 1947 only where Article XXXV of that Agreement had been invoked earlier and was effective as between those contracting parties at the time of entry into force for them of this Agreement.

3. Paragraph 1 shall apply between a Member and another Member which has acceded under Article XII only if the Member not consenting to the application has so notified the Ministerial Conference before the approval of the agreement on the terms of accession by the Ministerial Conference.

4. The Ministerial Conference may review the operation of this Article in particular cases at the request of any Member and make appropriate recommendations.

5. Non-application of a Plurilateral Trade Agreement between parties to that Agreement shall be governed by the provisions of that Agreement.

Article XIV—Acceptance, Entry into Force and Deposit

1. This Agreement shall be open for acceptance, by signature or otherwise, by contracting parties to GATT 1947, and the European Communities, which are eligible to become original Members of the WTO in accordance with Article XI of this Agreement. Such acceptance shall apply to this Agreement and the Multilateral Trade Agreements annexed hereto. This Agreement and the Multilateral Trade Agreements annexed hereto shall enter into force on the date determined by Ministers in accordance with paragraph 3 of the Final Act Embodying the Results of the Uruguay Round of Multilateral Trade Negotiations and shall remain open for acceptance for a period of two years following that date unless the Ministers decide otherwise. An acceptance following the entry into force of this Agreement shall enter into force on the 30th day following the date of such acceptance.

2. A Member which accepts this Agreement after its entry into force shall implement those concessions and obligations in the Multilateral Trade Agreements that are to be implemented over a period of time starting with the entry into force of this Agreement as if it had accepted this Agreement on the date of its entry into force.

3. Until the entry into force of this Agreement, the text of this Agreement and the Multilateral Trade Agreements shall be deposited with the Director-General to the CONTRACTING PARTIES to GATT 1947. The Director-General shall promptly furnish a certified true copy of this Agreement and the Multilateral Trade Agreements, and a notification of each acceptance thereof, to each government and the European Communities having accepted this Agreement. This Agreement and the Multilateral Trade Agreements, and any amendments thereto, shall, upon the entry into force of this Agreement, be deposited with the Director-General of the WTO.

4. The acceptance and entry into force of a Plurilateral Trade Agreement shall be governed by the provisions of that Agreement. Such Agreements shall be deposited with the Director-General to the CONTRACTING PARTIES to GATT 1947. Upon the entry into

force of this Agreement, such Agreements shall be deposited with the Director-General of the WTO.

ARTICLE XV—WITHDRAWAL

1. Any Member may withdraw from this Agreement. Such withdrawal shall apply both to this Agreement and the Multilateral Trade Agreements and shall take effect upon the expiration of six months from the date on which written notice of withdrawal is received by the Director-General of the WTO.

2. Withdrawal from a Plurilateral Trade Agreement shall be governed by the provisions of that Agreement.

ARTICLE XVI—MISCELLANEOUS PROVISIONS

1. Except as otherwise provided under this Agreement or the Multilateral Trade Agreements, the WTO shall be guided by the decisions, procedures and customary practices followed by the CONTRACTING PARTIES to GATT 1947 and the bodies established in the framework of GATT 1947.

2. To the extent practicable, the Secretariat of GATT 1947 shall become the Secretariat of the WTO, and the Director-General to the CONTRACTING PARTIES to GATT 1947, until such time as the Ministerial Conference has appointed a Director-General in accordance with paragraph 2 of Article VI of this Agreement, shall serve as Director-General of the WTO.

3. In the event of a conflict between a provision of this Agreement and a provision of any of the Multilateral Trade Agreements, the provision of this Agreement shall prevail to the extent of the conflict.

4. Each Member shall ensure the conformity of its laws, regulations and administrative procedures with its obligations as provided in the annexed Agreements.

5. No reservations may be made in respect of any provision of this Agreement. Reservations in respect of any of the provisions of the Multilateral Trade Agreements may only be made to the extent provided for in those Agreements. Reservations in respect of a provision of a Plurilateral Trade Agreement shall be governed by the provisions of that Agreement.

6. This Agreement shall be registered in accordance with the provisions of Article 102 of the Charter of the United Nations.

DONE at Marrakesh this fifteenth day of April one thousand nine hundred and ninety-four, in a single copy, in the English, French and Spanish languages, each text being authentic.

Explanatory Notes:

The terms “country” or “countries” as used in this Agreement and the Multilateral Trade Agreements are to be understood to include any separate customs territory Member of the WTO.

In the case of a separate customs territory Member of the WTO, where an expression in this Agreement and the Multilateral Trade Agreements is qualified by the term “national”, such expression shall be read as pertaining to that customs territory, unless otherwise specified.

LIST OF ANNEXES

ANNEX 1

ANNEX 1A: Multilateral Agreements on Trade in Goods
General Agreement on Tariffs and Trade 1994
Agreement on Agriculture
Agreement on the Application of Sanitary and Phytosanitary Measures
Agreement on Textiles and Clothing
Agreement on Technical Barriers to Trade
Agreement on Trade-Related Investment Measures
Agreement on Implementation of Article VI of the General Agreement on Tariffs and Trade 1994
Agreement on Implementation of Article VII of the General Agreement on Tariffs and Trade 1994
Agreement on Preshipment Inspection
Agreement on Rules of Origin
Agreement on Import Licensing Procedures
Agreement on Subsidies and Countervailing Measures
Agreement on Safeguards
ANNEX 1B: General Agreement on Trade in Services and Annexes
ANNEX 1C: Agreement on Trade-Related Aspects of Intellectual Property Rights

ANNEX 2

Understanding on Rules and Procedures Governing the Settlement of Disputes

ANNEX 3

Trade Policy Review Mechanism

ANNEX 4—PLURILATERAL TRADE AGREEMENTS

Agreement on Trade in Civil Aircraft
Agreement on Government Procurement
International Dairy Agreement
International Bovine Meat Agreement

4. International Telecommunication Union

a. Constitution of the International Telecommunication Union, as amended [1]

Done at Geneva, December 22, 1992; Entered into force generally, July 1, 1994; Advise and consent of the Senate, October 23, 1997; Entered into force for the United States, October 26, 1997

CONSTITUTION OF THE INTERNATIONAL TELECOMMUNICATION UNION

PREAMBLE

1. While fully recognizing the sovereign right of each State to regulate its telecommunication and having regard to the growing importance of telecommunication for the preservation of peace and the economic and social development of all States, the States Parties to this Constitution, as the basic instrument of the International Telecommunication Union, and to the Convention of the International Telecommunication Union (hereinafter referred to as "the Convention") which complements it, with the object of facilitating peaceful relations, international cooperation among peoples and economic and social development by means of efficient telecommunication services, have agreed as follows:

CHAPTER I—BASIC PROVISIONS

ARTICLE 1—PURPOSES OF THE UNION

1. The purposes of the Union are:

(a) to maintain and extend international cooperation among all its Member States for the improvement and rational use of telecommunications of all kinds;

(abis) to promote and enhance participation of entities and organizations in the activities of the Union and foster fruitful cooperation and partnership between them and Member States for the fulfillment of the overall objectives as embodied in the purposes of the Union;

(b) to promote and to offer technical assistance to developing countries in the field of telecommunications, and also to promote the mobilization of the material, human and financial resources needed for its implementation, as well as access to information;

[1] For states that are parties to the Constitution, see Department of State publication, *Treaties in Force*. The Constitution was amended at Kyoto, October 14, 1994; at Minneapolis, 1998, and at Marrakesh, 2002.

(c) to promote the development of technical facilities and their most efficient operation with a view to improving the efficiency of telecommunication services, increasing their usefulness and making them, so far as possible, generally available to the public;

(d) to promote the extension of the benefits of the new telecommunication technologies to all the world's inhabitants;

(e) to promote the use of telecommunication services with the objective of facilitating peaceful relations;

(f) to harmonize the actions of Member States and promote fruitful and constructive cooperation and partnership between Member States and Sector Members in the attainment of those ends;

(g) to promote, at the international level, the adoption of a broader approach to the issues of telecommunications in the global information economy and society, by cooperating with other world and regional intergovernmental organizations and those non-governmental organizations concerned with telecommunications.

2. To this end, the Union shall in particular:

(a) effect allocation of bands of the radio-frequency spectrum, the allotment of radio frequencies and the registration of radio-frequency assignments and, for space services, of any associated orbital position in the geostationary-satellite orbit or of any associated characteristics of satellites in other orbits, in order to avoid harmful interference between radio stations of different countries;

(b) coordinate efforts to eliminate harmful interference between radio stations of different countries and to improve the use made of the radio-frequency spectrum for radiocommunication services and of the geostationary-satellite and other satellite orbits;

(c) facilitate the worldwide standardization of telecommunications, with a satisfactory quality of service;

(d) foster international cooperation and solidarity in the delivery of technical assistance to the developing countries and the creation, development and improvement of telecommunication equipment and networks in developing countries by every means at its disposal, including through its participation in the relevant programmes of the United Nations and the use of its own resources, as appropriate;

(e) coordinate efforts to harmonize the development of telecommunication facilities, notably those using space techniques, with a view to full advantage being taken of their possibilities;

(f) foster collaboration among Member States and Sector Members with a view to the establishment of rates at levels as low as possible consistent with an efficient service and taking into account the necessity for maintaining independent financial administration of telecommunications on a sound basis;

(g) promote the adoption of measures for ensuring the safety of life through the cooperation of telecommunication services;

(h) undertake studies, make regulations, adopt resolutions, formulate recommendations and opinions, and collect and publish information concerning telecommunication matters;

(i) promote, with international financial and development organizations, the establishment of preferential and favourable lines of credit to be used for the development of social projects aimed, inter alia, at extending telecommunication services to the most isolated areas in countries.

(j) promote participation of concerned entities in the activities of the Union and cooperation with regional and other organizations for the fulfillment of the purposes of the Union.

ARTICLE 2—COMPOSITION OF THE UNION

The International Telecommunication Union is an intergovernmental organization in which Member States and Sector Members, having well-defined rights and obligations, cooperate for the fulfillment of the purposes of the Union. It shall, having regard to the principle of universality and the desirability of universal participation in the Union, be composed of:

(a) any State which is a Member State of the International Telecommunication Union as a Party to any International Telecommunication Convention prior to the entry into force of this Constitution and the Convention;

(b) any other State, a Member of the United Nations, which accedes to this Constitution and the Convention in accordance with Article 53 of this Constitution;

(c) any other State, not a Member of the United Nations, which applies for membership of the Union and which, after having secured approval of such application by two-thirds of the Member States of the Union, accedes to this Constitution and the Convention in accordance with Article 53 of this Constitution. If such application for membership is made during the interval between two plenipotentiary conferences, the Secretary-General shall consult the Member States of the Union; a Member State shall be deemed to have abstained if it has not replied within four months after its opinion has been requested.

ARTICLE 3—RIGHTS AND OBLIGATIONS OF MEMBER STATES AND SECTOR MEMBERS

1. Member States and Sector Members shall have the rights and shall be subject to the obligations provided for in this Constitution and the Convention.

2. Rights of Member States in respect of their participation in the conferences, meetings and consultations of the Union are:

(a) all Member States shall be entitled to participate in conferences, shall be eligible for election to the Council and shall have the right to nominate candidates for election as officials of the Union or as members of the Radio Regulations Board;

(b) subject to the provisions of Nos. 169 and 210 of this Constitution, each Member State shall have one vote at all plenipotentiary conferences, all world conferences and all Sector assemblies and study group meetings and, if it is a Member State of the Council, all sessions of that Council. At regional conferences, only the Member States of the region concerned shall have the right to vote;

(c) subject to the provisions of Nos. 169 and 210 of this Constitution, each Member State shall also have one vote in all consultations carried out by correspondence. In the case of consultations regarding regional conferences, only the Member States of the region concerned shall have the right to vote.

3. In respect of their participation in activities of the Union, Sector Members shall be entitled to participate fully in the activities of the Sector of which they are members, subject to relevant provisions of this Constitution and the Convention:

(a) they may provide chairmen and vice-chairmen of Sector assemblies and meetings and world telecommunication development conferences;

(b) they shall be entitled, subject to the relevant provisions of the Convention and relevant decisions adopted in this regard by the Plenipotentiary Conference, to take part in the adoption of Questions and Recommendations and in decisions relating to the working methods and procedures of the Sector concerned.

ARTICLE 4—INSTRUMENTS OF THE UNION

1. The instruments of the Union are:

—this Constitution of the International Telecommunication Union,

—the Convention of the International Telecommunication Union, and

—the Administrative Regulations.

2. This Constitution, the provisions of which are complemented by those of the Convention, is the basic instrument of the Union.

3. The provisions of both this Constitution and the Convention are further complemented by those of the Administrative Regulations, enumerated below, which regulate the use of telecommunications and shall be binding on all Member States:

—International Telecommunication Regulations,

—Radio Regulations.

4. In the case of inconsistency between a provision of this Constitution and a provision of the Convention or of the Administrative Regulations, the Constitution shall prevail. In the case of inconsistency between a provision of the Convention and a provision of the Administrative Regulations, the Convention shall prevail.

ARTICLE 5—DEFINITIONS

Unless the context otherwise requires:

(a) the terms used in this Constitution and defined in its Annex, which forms an integral part of this Constitution, shall have the meanings assigned to them in that Annex;

(b) the terms—other than those defined in the Annex to this Constitution—used in the Convention and defined in the Annex thereto, which forms an integral part of the Convention, shall have the meanings assigned to them in that Annex;

(c) other terms defined in the Administrative Regulations shall have the meanings therein assigned to them.

ARTICLE 6—EXECUTION OF THE INSTRUMENTS OF THE UNION

1. The Member States are bound to abide by the provisions of this Constitution, the Convention and the Administrative Regulations in all telecommunication offices and stations established or operated by them which engage in international services or which are capable of causing harmful interference to radio services of other countries, except in regard to services exempted from these obligations in accordance with the provisions of Article 48 of this Constitution.

2. The Member States are also bound to take the necessary steps to impose the observance of the provisions of this Constitution, the Convention and the Administrative Regulations upon operating agencies authorized by them to establish and operate telecommunications and which engage in international services or which operate stations capable of causing harmful interference to the radio services of other countries.

ARTICLE 7—STRUCTURE OF THE UNION

The Union shall comprise:

(a) the Plenipotentiary Conference, which is the supreme organ of the Union;

(b) the Council, which acts on behalf of the Plenipotentiary Conference;

(c) world conferences on international telecommunications;

(d) the Radiocommunication Sector, including world and regional radiocommunication conferences, radiocommunication assemblies and the Radio Regulations Board;

(e) the Telecommunication Standardization Sector, including world telecommunication standardization assemblies;

(f) the Telecommunication Development Sector, including world and regional telecommunication development conferences;

(g) the General Secretariat.

ARTICLE 8—PLENIPOTENTIARY CONFERENCE

1. The Plenipotentiary Conference shall be composed of delegations representing Member States. It shall be convened every four years.

2. On the basis of proposals by Member States and taking account of reports by the Council, the Plenipotentiary Conference shall:

(a) determine the general policies for fulfilling the purposes of the Union prescribed in Article 1 of this Constitution;

(b) consider the reports by the Council on the activities of the Union since the previous plenipotentiary conference and on the policy and strategic planning of the Union;

(c) in the light of its decisions taken on the reports referred to in No. 50 above, establish the strategic plan for the Union and the basis for the budget of the Union, and determine related financial limits, until the next plenipotentiary conference, after considering all relevant aspects of the work of the Union in that period;

(cbis) establish, using the procedures described in Nos. 161D to 161G of this Constitution, the total number of contributory units for the period up to the next plenipotentiary conference on the basis of the classes of contribution announced by Member States;

(d) provide any general directives dealing with the staffing of the Union and, if necessary, fix the basic salaries, the salary scales and the system of allowances and pensions for all the officials of the Union;

(e) examine the accounts of the Union and finally approve them, if appropriate;

(f) elect the Member States which are to serve on the Council;

(g) elect the Secretary-General, the Deputy Secretary-General and the Directors of the Bureau of the Sectors as elected officials of the Union;

(h) elect the members of the Radio Regulations Board;

(i) consider and adopt, if appropriate, proposals for amendments to this Constitution and the Convention, put forward by Member States, in accordance with the provisions of Article 55 of this Constitution and the relevant provisions of the Convention, respectively;

(j) conclude or revise, if necessary, agreements between the Union and other international organizations, examine any provisional agreements with such organizations concluded by the Council on behalf of the Union, and take such measures in connection therewith as it deems appropriate;

(jbis) adopt and amend the General Rules of conferences, assemblies and meetings of the Union;

(k) deal with such other telecommunication questions as may be necessary.

3. Exceptionally, in the interval between two ordinary Plenipotentiary Conferences, it shall be possible to convene an extraordinary Plenipotentiary Conference with a restricted agenda to deal with specific matters:

(a) by a decision of the preceding ordinary Plenipotentiary Conference;

(b) should two-thirds of the Member States individually so request the Secretary-General;

(c) at the proposal of the Council with the approval of at least two-thirds of the Member States.

Article 9—Principles Concerning Elections and Related Matters

1. The Plenipotentiary Conference, at any elections referred to in Nos. 54 to 56 of this Constitution, shall ensure that:

(a) the Member States of the Council are elected with due regard to the need for equitable distribution of the seats on the Council among all regions of the world;

(b) the Secretary-General, the Deputy Secretary-General and the Directors of the Bureau shall be elected among the candidates proposed by Member States as their nationals and shall all be nationals of different Member States, and at their election due consideration should be given to equitable geographical distribution amongst the regions of the world; due consideration should also be given to the principles embodied in No. 154 of this Constitution;

(c) the members of the Radio Regulations Board shall be elected in their individual capacity from among the candidates proposed by Member States as their nationals. Each Member State may propose only one candidate. The members of the Radio Regulations Board shall not be nationals of the same Member State as the Director of the Radiocommunication Bureau; at their election, due consideration should be given to equitable geographical distribution amongst the regions of the world and to the principles embodied in No. 93 of this Constitution.

2. Provisions relating to taking up duties, vacancy and re-eligibility are contained in the Convention.

Article 10—The Council

1. The Council shall be composed of Member States elected by the Plenipotentiary Conference in accordance with the provisions of No. 61 of this Constitution.

2. Each Member State of the Council shall appoint a person to serve on the Council who may be assisted by one or more advisers.

3. In the interval between Plenipotentiary Conferences, the Council shall act, as governing body of the Union, on behalf of the Plenipotentiary Conference within the limits of the powers delegated to it by the latter.

4.(1) The Council shall take all steps to facilitate the implementation by the Member States of the provisions of this Constitution, of the Convention, of the Administrative Regulations, of the decisions of the Plenipotentiary Conference, and, where appropriate, of the decisions of other conferences and meetings of the Union, and perform any duties assigned to it by the Plenipotentiary Conference.

(2) The Council shall consider broad telecommunication policy issues in accordance with the guidelines given by the Plenipotentiary Conference to ensure that the Union's policies and strategy fully respond to changes in the telecommunication environment.

(2bis) The Council shall prepare a report on the policy and strategic planning recommended for the Union, together with their financial implications, using the specific data prepared by the Secretary-General under No. 74A below.

(3) It shall ensure the efficient coordination of the work of the Union and exercise effective financial control over the General Secretariat and the three Sectors.

(4) It shall contribute, in accordance with the purposes of the Union, to the development of telecommunications in the developing countries by every means at its disposal, including through the participation of the Union in the appropriate programmes of the United Nations.

Article 11—General Secretariat

1.(1) The General Secretariat shall be directed by a Secretary-General, assisted by one Deputy Secretary-General.

(2) The functions of the Secretary-General are specified in the Convention. In addition, the Secretary-General shall:

(a) coordinate the Union's activities, with the assistance of the Coordination Committee;

(b) prepare, with the assistance of the Coordination Committee, and provide to the Member States and Sector Members, such specific information as may be required for the preparation of a report on the policies and strategic plan for the Union, and coordinate the implementation of the plan; this report shall be communicated to the Member States and Sector Members for review during the last two regularly scheduled sessions of the Council before a plenipotentiary conference;

(c) take all the actions required to ensure economic use of the Union's resources and be responsible to the Council for all the administrative and financial aspects of the Union's activities;

(d) act as the legal representative of the Union.

(3) The Secretary-General may act as depositary of special arrangements established in conformity with Article 42 of this Constitution.

2. The Deputy Secretary-General shall be responsible to the Secretary-General; he shall assist the Secretary-General in the performance of his duties and undertake such specific tasks as may be entrusted to him by the Secretary-General. He shall perform the duties of the Secretary-General in the absence of the latter.

CHAPTER II—RADIOCOMMUNICATION SECTOR

Article 12—Functions and Structure

1.(1) The functions of the Radiocommunication Sector shall be, bearing in mind the particular concerns of developing countries, to fulfill the purposes of the Union, as stated in Article 1 of this Constitution, relating to radiocommunication:

—by ensuring the rational, equitable, efficient and economical use of the radio-frequency spectrum by all radiocommunication services, including those using the geostationary-satellite or other satellite orbits, subject to the provisions of Article 44 of this Constitution, and

—by carrying out studies without limit of frequency range and adopting recommendations on radiocommunication matters.

(2) The precise responsibilities of the Radiocommunication Sector and the Telecommunication Standardization Sector shall be subject to continuing review, in close cooperation, with regard to matters of common interest to both Sectors, in accordance with the relevant provisions of the Convention. Close coordination shall be carried out between the Radiocommunication, Telecommunication Standardization and Telecommunication Development Sectors.

2. The Radiocommunication Sector shall work through:

(a) world and regional radiocommunication conferences;

(b) the Radio Regulations Board;

(c) radiocommunication assemblies;

(d) radiocommunication study groups;

(dbis) the radiocommunication advisory group;

(e) the Radiocommunication Bureau, headed by the elected Director.

3. The Radiocommunication Sector shall have as members:

(a) of right, the administrations of all Member States;

(b) any entity or organization which becomes a Sector Member in accordance with the relevant provisions of the Convention.

ARTICLE 13—RADIOCOMMUNICATION CONFERENCES AND RADIOCOMMUNICATION ASSEMBLIES

1. A world radiocommunication conference may partially or, in exceptional cases, completely, revise the Radio Regulations and may deal with any question of a worldwide character within its competence and related to its agenda; its other duties are specified in the Convention.

2. World radiocommunication conferences shall normally be convened every two to three years; however, following the application of the relevant provisions of the Convention, such a conference need not be convened or an additional one may be convened.

3. Radiocommunication assemblies shall also normally be convened every two to three years, and may be associated in place and time with world radiocommunication conferences so as to improve the efficiency and effectiveness of the Radiocommunication Sector. Radiocommunication assemblies shall provide the necessary technical bases for the work of the world radiocommunication conferences and respond to all requests from world radiocommunication conferences. The duties of the radiocommunication assemblies are specified in the Convention.

4. The decisions of a world radiocommunication conference, of a radiocommunication assembly and of a regional radiocommunication conference shall in all circumstances be in conformity with this Constitution and the Convention. The decisions of a radiocommunication assembly or of a regional radiocommunication conference shall also in all circumstances be in conformity with the Radio Regulations. When adopting resolutions and decisions, the conferences shall take into account the foreseeable financial implications and should avoid adopting resolutions and decisions which might give rise to expenditure in excess of the financial limits laid down by the Plenipotentiary Conference.

ARTICLE 14—RADIO REGULATIONS BOARD

1. The Radio Regulations Board shall consist of elected members thoroughly qualified in the field of radiocommunications and possessing practical experience in the assignment and utilization of frequencies. Each member shall be familiar with the geographic, economic and demographic conditions within a particular area of the world. They shall perform their duties for the Union independently and on a part-time basis.

1bis. The Radio Regulations Board is composed of not more than either 12 members, or of a number corresponding to 6% of the total number of Member States, whichever is the greater.

2. The duties of the Radio Regulations Board shall consist of:

(a) the approval of Rules of Procedure, which include technical criteria, in accordance with the Radio Regulations and with any decision which may be taken by competent radiocommunication conferences. These Rules of Procedure shall be used by the Director and the Bureau in the application of the Radio Regulations to register frequency assignments made by Member States. These Rules shall be developed in a transparent manner and shall be open to comment by administrations and, in case of continuing disagreement, the matter shall be submitted to the next world radiocommunication conference;

(b) the consideration of any other matter that cannot be resolved through the application of the above Rules of Procedure;

(c) the performance of any additional duties, concerned with the assignment and utilization of frequencies, as indicated in No. 78 of this Constitution, in accordance with the procedures provided for in the Radio Regulations, and as prescribed by a competent conference or by the Council with the consent of a majority of the Member States, in preparation for, or in pursuance of the decisions of, such a conference.

3. (1) In the exercise of their Board duties, the members of the Radio Regulations Board shall serve, not as representing their respective Member States nor a region, but as custodians of an international public trust. In particular, each member of the Board shall refrain from intervening in decisions directly concerning the member's own administration.

(2) No member of the Board shall request or receive instructions relating to the exercise of his duties for the Union from any government or a member thereof, or from any public or private organization or person. Members of the Board shall refrain from taking any action or from participating in any decision which may be incompatible with their status defined in No. 98 above.

(3) Member States and Sector Members shall respect the exclusively international character of the duties of the members of the Board and refrain from attempting to influence them in the performance of their Board duties.

4. The working methods of the Radio Regulations Board are defined in the Convention.

Article 15—PP–98 Radiocommunication Study Groups and Advisory Group

The respective duties of the radiocommunication study groups and advisory group are specified in the Convention.

Article 16—Radiocommunication Bureau

The functions of the Director of the Radiocommunication Bureau are specified in the Convention.

CHAPTER III—TELECOMMUNICATION STANDARDIZATION SECTOR

ARTICLE 17—FUNCTIONS AND STRUCTURE

1. (1) The functions of the Telecommunication Standardization Sector shall be, bearing in mind the particular concerns of the developing countries, to fulfill the purposes of the Union relating to telecommunication standardization, as stated in Article 1 of this Constitution, by studying technical, operating and tariff questions and adopting recommendations on them with a view to standardizing telecommunications on a worldwide basis.

(2) The precise responsibilities of the Telecommunication Standardization and Radiocommunication Sectors shall be subject to continuing review, in close cooperation, with regard to matters of common interest to both Sectors, in accordance with the relevant provisions of the Convention. Close coordination shall be carried out between the Radiocommunication, Telecommunication Standardization and Telecommunication Development Sectors.

2. The Telecommunication Standardization Sector shall work through:

(a) world telecommunication standardization assemblies;

(b) telecommunication standardization study groups;

(bbis) the telecommunication standardization advisory group;

(c) the Telecommunication Standardization Bureau headed by the elected Director.

3. The Telecommunication Standardization Sector shall have as members:

(a) of right, the administrations of all Member States;

(b) any entity or organization which becomes a Sector Member in accordance with the relevant provisions of the Convention.

ARTICLE 18—PP–98 WORLD TELECOMMUNICATION STANDARDIZATION ASSEMBLIES

1. The duties of world telecommunication standardization assemblies are specified in the Convention.

2. World telecommunication standardization assemblies shall be convened every four years; however, an additional assembly may be held in accordance with the relevant provisions of the Convention.

3. Decisions of world telecommunication standardization assemblies must in all circumstances be in conformity with this Constitution, the Convention and the Administrative Regulations. When adopting resolutions and decisions, the assemblies shall take into account the foreseeable financial implications and should avoid adopting resolutions and decisions which might give rise to expenditure in excess of the financial limits laid down by the Plenipotentiary Conference.

ARTICLE 19—PP–98 TELECOMMUNICATION STANDARDIZATION STUDY GROUPS AND ADVISORY GROUP

The respective duties of the telecommunication standardization study groups and advisory group are specified in the Convention.

Article 20—Telecommunication Standardization Bureau

The functions of the Director of the Telecommunication Standardization Bureau are specified in the Convention.

CHAPTER IV—Telecommunication Development Sector

Article 21—Functions and Structure

1. (1) The functions of the Telecommunication Development Sector shall be to fulfill the purposes of the Union as stated in Article 1 of this Constitution and to discharge, within its specific sphere of competence, the Union's dual responsibility as a United Nations specialized agency and executing agency for implementing projects under the United Nations development system or other funding arrangements so as to facilitate and enhance telecommunications development by offering, organizing and coordinating technical cooperation and assistance activities.

(2) The activities of the Radiocommunication, Telecommunication Standardization and Telecommunication Development Sectors shall be the subject of close cooperation with regard to matters relating to development, in accordance with the relevant provisions of this Constitution.

2. Within the foregoing framework, the specific functions of the Telecommunication Development Sector shall be to:

(a) raise the level of awareness of decision-makers concerning the important role of telecommunications in the national economic and social development programme, and provide information and advice on possible policy and structural options;

(b) promote, especially by means of partnership, the development, expansion and operation of telecommunication networks and services, particularly in developing countries, taking into account the activities of other relevant bodies, by reinforcing capabilities for human resources development, planning, management, resource mobilization, and research and development;

(c) enhance the growth of telecommunications through cooperation with regional telecommunications organizations and with global and regional development financing institutions, monitoring the status of projects included in its development programme to ensure that they are properly executed;

(d) activate the mobilization of resources to provide assistance in the field of telecommunications to developing countries by promoting the establishment of preferential and favourable lines of credit, and cooperating with international and regional financial and development institutions;

(e) promote and coordinate programmes to accelerate the transfer of appropriate technologies to the developing countries in the light of changes and developments in the networks of the developed countries;

(f) encourage participation by industry in telecommunication development in developing countries, and offer advice on the choice and transfer of appropriate technology;

(g) offer advice, carry out or sponsor studies, as necessary, on technical, economic, financial, managerial, regulatory and policy issues, including studies of specific projects in the field of telecommunications;

(h) collaborate with the other Sectors, the General Secretariat and other concerned bodies in developing a general plan for international and regional telecommunication networks so as to facilitate the coordination of their development with a view to the provision of telecommunication services;

(i) in carrying out the above functions, give special attention to the requirements of the least developed countries.

3. The Telecommunication Development Sector shall work through:

(a) world and regional telecommunication development conferences;

(b) telecommunication development study groups;

(bbis) the telecommunication development advisory group;

(c) the Telecommunication Development Bureau headed by the elected Director.

4. The Telecommunication Development Sector shall have as members:

(a) of right, the administrations of all Member States;

(b) any entity or organization which becomes a Sector Member in accordance with the relevant provisions of the Convention.

ARTICLE 22—TELECOMMUNICATION DEVELOPMENT CONFERENCES

1. Telecommunication development conferences shall be a forum for the discussion and consideration of topics, projects and programmes relevant to telecommunication development and for the provision of direction and guidance to the Telecommunication Development Bureau.

2. Telecommunication development conferences shall comprise:

(a) world telecommunication development conferences;

(b) regional telecommunication development conferences.

3. There shall be, between two Plenipotentiary Conferences, one world telecommunication development conference and, subject to resources and priorities, regional telecommunication development conferences.

4. Telecommunication development conferences shall not produce Final Acts. Their conclusions shall take the form of resolutions, decisions, recommendations or reports. These conclusions must in all circumstances be in conformity with this Constitution, the Convention and the Administrative Regulations. When adopting resolutions and decisions, the conferences shall take into account the foreseeable financial implications and should avoid adopting resolutions and decisions which might give rise to expenditure in excess of the financial limits laid down by the Plenipotentiary Conference.

5. The duties of telecommunication development conferences are specified in the Convention.

Article 23—PP–98 Telecommunication Development Study Groups and Advisory Group

The respective duties of telecommunication development study groups and advisory group are specified in the Convention.

Article 24—Telecommunication Development Bureau

The functions of the Director of the Telecommunication Development Bureau are specified in the Convention.

CHAPTER V—Other Provisions Concerning the Functioning of the Union

Article 25—World Conferences on International Telecommunications

1. A world conference on international telecommunications may partially, or in exceptional cases, completely revise the International Telecommunication Regulations and may deal with any question of a worldwide character within its competence and related to its agenda.

2. Decisions of world conferences on international telecommunications shall in all circumstances be in conformity with this Constitution and the Convention. When adopting resolutions and decisions, the conferences shall take into account the foreseeable financial implications and should avoid adopting resolutions and decisions which might give rise to expenditure in excess of the financial limits laid down by the Plenipotentiary Conference.

Article 26—Coordination Committee

1. The Coordination Committee shall consist of the Secretary-General, the Deputy Secretary-General and the Directors of the three Bureau. It shall be presided over by the Secretary-General, and in his absence by the Deputy Secretary-General.

2. The Coordination Committee shall act as an internal management team which advises and gives the Secretary-General practical assistance on all administrative, financial, information system and technical cooperation matters which do not fall under the exclusive competence of a particular Sector or of the General Secretariat and on external relations and public information. In its considerations, the Committee shall keep fully in view the provisions of this Constitution, the Convention, the decisions of the Council and the interests of the Union as a whole.

Article 27—Elected Officials and Staff of the Union

1. (1) In the performance of their duties, neither the elected officials nor the staff of the Union shall seek or accept instructions from any government or from any other authority outside the Union. They shall refrain from acting in any way which is incompatible with their status as international officials.

(2) Member States and Sector Members shall respect the exclusively international character of the duties of these elected officials and of the staff of the Union, and refrain from trying to influence them in the performance of their work.

(3) No elected official or any member of the staff of the Union shall participate in any manner or have any financial interest whatsoever in any enterprise concerned with telecommunications, except as part of their duties. However, the term "financial interest" is not to be construed as applying to the continuation of retirement benefits accruing in respect of previous employment or service.

(4) In order to ensure the efficient operation of the Union, any Member State a national of which has been elected Secretary-General, Deputy Secretary-General or Director of a Bureau shall refrain, as far as possible, from recalling that national between two plenipotentiary conferences.

2. The paramount consideration in the recruitment of staff and in the determination of the conditions of service shall be the necessity of securing for the Union the highest standards of efficiency, competence and integrity. Due regard shall be paid to the importance of recruiting the staff on as wide a geographical basis as possible.

ARTICLE 28—FINANCES OF THE UNION

1. The expenses of the Union shall comprise the costs of:

(a) the Council;

(b) the General Secretariat and the Sectors of the Union;

(c) Plenipotentiary Conferences and world conferences on international telecommunications.

2. The expenses of the Union shall be met from:

(a) the contributions of its Member States and Sector Members;

(b) other revenues as identified in the Convention or in the Financial Regulations.

2bis. Each Member State and Sector Member shall pay a sum equivalent to the number of units in the class of contribution it has chosen in accordance with Nos. 160 to 161I below.

2ter. Expenses incurred by the regional conferences referred to in No. 43 of this Constitution shall be borne:

(a) by all the Member States of the region concerned, in accordance with their class of contribution;

(b) by any Member States of other regions which have participated in such conferences, in accordance with their class of contribution;

(c) by authorized Sector Members and other authorized organizations which have participated in such conferences, in accordance with the provisions of the Convention.

3. (1) Member States and Sector Members shall be free to choose their class of contribution for defraying Union expenses.

(2) The choice by Member States shall be made at a plenipotentiary conference in accordance with the scale of classes of contribution and conditions contained in the Convention and with the procedures described below.

(3) The choice by Sector Members shall be made in accordance with the scale of classes of contribution and conditions contained in the Convention and with the procedures described below.

3bis. (1) At its session preceding the plenipotentiary conference, the Council shall fix the provisional amount of the contributory unit, on the basis of the draft financial plan for the corresponding period and total number of contributory units.

(2) The Secretary-General shall inform the Member States and Sector Members of the provisional amount of the contributory unit as determined under No. 161B above and invite the Member States to notify, no later than one week prior to the date set for the opening of the plenipotentiary conference, the class of contribution they have provisionally chosen.

(3) The plenipotentiary conference shall, during its first week, determine the provisional upper limit of the amount of the contributory unit resulting from the steps taken by the Secretary-General in pursuance of Nos. 161B and 161C above, and taking account of any changes in class of contribution notified by Member States to the Secretary-General as well as classes of contribution remaining unchanged.

(4) Bearing in mind the draft financial plan as revised, the plenipotentiary conference shall, as soon as possible, determine the definitive upper limit of the amount of the contributory unit and set the date, which shall be a date within the penultimate week of the plenipotentiary conference, by which Member States, upon invitation by the Secretary-General, shall announce their definitive choice of class of contribution.

(5) Member States which have failed to notify the Secretary-General of their decision by the date set by the plenipotentiary conference shall retain the class of contribution previously chosen.

(6) The plenipotentiary conference shall then approve the definitive financial plan on the basis of the total number of contributory units corresponding to the definitive classes of contribution chosen by the Member States and classes of contribution of the Sector Members at the date on which the financial plan is approved.

3ter. (1) The Secretary-General shall inform the Sector Members of the definitive upper limit of the amount of the contributory unit and invite them to notify, within three months from the closing date of the plenipotentiary conference, the class of contribution they have chosen.

(2) Sector Members which have failed to notify the Secretary-General of their decision within this three-month period shall retain the class of contribution previously chosen.

(3) Amendments to the scale of classes of contribution adopted by a plenipotentiary conference shall apply for the selection of the class of contribution during the following plenipotentiary conference.

(4) The class of contribution chosen by a Member State or a Sector Member is applicable as of the first biennial budget after a plenipotentiary conference.

(SUP)

5. When choosing its class of contribution, a Member State shall not reduce it by more than two classes of contribution and the Council shall indicate to it the manner in which the reduction shall be gradually implemented over the period between plenipotentiary conferences. However, under exceptional circumstances such as natural disasters necessitating international aid programmes, the

Plenipotentiary Conference may authorize a greater reduction in the number of contributory units when so requested by a Member State which has established that it can no longer maintain its contribution at the class originally chosen.

5bis. Under exceptional circumstances such as natural disasters necessitating international aid programmes, the Council may authorize a reduction in the number of contributory units when so requested by a Member State which has established that it can no longer maintain its contribution at the class originally chosen.

5ter. Member States and Sector Members may at any time choose a class of contribution higher than the one already adopted by them.

(SUP)

8. Member States and Sector Members shall pay in advance their annual contributory shares, calculated on the basis of the biennial budget approved by the Council as well as of any adjustment adopted by the Council.

9. A Member State which is in arrears in its payments to the Union shall lose its right to vote as defined in Nos. 27 and 28 of this Constitution for so long as the amount of its arrears equals or exceeds the amount of the contribution due for the two preceding years.

10. Specific provisions governing the financial contributions by Sector Members and by other international organizations are contained in the Convention.

ARTICLE 29—LANGUAGES

1. (1) The official and working languages of the Union shall be Arabic, Chinese, English, French, Russian and Spanish.

(2) In accordance with the relevant decisions of the Plenipotentiary Conference, these languages shall be used for drawing up and publishing documents and texts of the Union, in versions equivalent in form and content, as well as for reciprocal interpretation during conferences and meetings of the Union.

(3) In case of discrepancy or dispute, the French text shall prevail.

2. When all participants in a conference or in a meeting so agree, discussions may be conducted in fewer languages than those mentioned above.

ARTICLE 30—SEAT OF THE UNION

The seat of the Union shall be at Geneva.

ARTICLE 31—LEGAL CAPACITY OF THE UNION

The Union shall enjoy in the territory of each of its Member States such legal capacity as may be necessary for the exercise of its functions and the fulfillment of its purposes.

ARTICLE 32—GENERAL RULES OF CONFERENCES, ASSEMBLIES AND MEETINGS OF THE UNION

1. The General Rules of conferences, assemblies and meetings of the Union adopted by the Plenipotentiary Conference shall apply to

the preparation of conferences and assemblies and to the organization of the work and conduct of the discussions of conferences, assemblies and meetings of the Union, as well as to the election of Member States of the Council, of the Secretary-General, of the Deputy Secretary-General, of the Directors of the Bureau of the Sectors and of the members of the Radio Regulations Board.

2. Conferences, assemblies and the Council may adopt such rules as they consider to be essential in addition to those in Chapter II of the General Rules of conferences, assemblies and meetings of the Union. Such additional rules must, however, be compatible with this Constitution, the Convention and the aforesaid Chapter II; those adopted by conferences or assemblies shall be published as documents of the conference or assembly concerned.

CHAPTER VI—GENERAL PROVISIONS RELATING TO TELECOMMUNICATIONS

ARTICLE 33—THE RIGHT OF THE PUBLIC TO USE THE INTERNATIONAL TELECOMMUNICATION SERVICE

Member States recognize the right of the public to correspond by means of the international service of public correspondence. The services, the charges and the safeguards shall be the same for all users in each category of correspondence without any priority or preference.

ARTICLE 34—STOPPAGE OF TELECOMMUNICATIONS

1. Member States reserve the right to stop, in accordance with their national law, the transmission of any private telegram which may appear dangerous to the security of the State or contrary to its laws, to public order or to decency, provided that they immediately notify the office of origin of the stoppage of any such telegram or any part thereof, except when such notification may appear dangerous to the security of the State.

2. Member States also reserve the right to cut off, in accordance with their national law, any other private telecommunications which may appear dangerous to the security of the State or contrary to its laws, to public order or to decency.

ARTICLE 35—SUSPENSION OF SERVICES

Each Member State reserves the right to suspend the international telecommunication service, either generally or only for certain relations and/or for certain kinds of correspondence, outgoing, incoming or in transit, provided that it immediately notifies such action to each of the other Member States through the Secretary-General.

ARTICLE 36—RESPONSIBILITY

Member States accept no responsibility towards users of the international telecommunication services, particularly as regards claims for damages.

Article 37—Secrecy of Telecommunications

1. Member States agree to take all possible measures, compatible with the system of telecommunication used, with a view to ensuring the secrecy of international correspondence.

2. Nevertheless, they reserve the right to communicate such correspondence to the competent authorities in order to ensure the application of their national laws or the execution of international conventions to which they are parties.

Article 38—Establishment, Operation and Protection of Telecommunication Channels and Installations

1. Member States shall take such steps as may be necessary to ensure the establishment, under the best technical conditions, of the channels and installations necessary to carry on the rapid and uninterrupted exchange of international telecommunications.

2. So far as possible, these channels and installations must be operated by the methods and procedures which practical operating experience has shown to be the best. They must be maintained in proper operating condition and kept abreast of scientific and technical progress.

3. Member States shall safeguard these channels and installations within their jurisdiction.

4. Unless other conditions are laid down by special arrangements, each Member State shall take such steps as may be necessary to ensure maintenance of those sections of international telecommunication circuits within its control.

5. Member States recognize the necessity of taking practical measures to prevent the operation of electrical apparatus and installations of all kinds from disrupting the operation of telecommunication installations within the jurisdiction of other Member States.

Article 39—Notification of Infringements

In order to facilitate the application of the provisions of Article 6 of this Constitution, Member States undertake to inform and, as appropriate, assist one another with regard to infringements of the provisions of this Constitution, of the Convention and of the Administrative Regulations.

Article 40—Priority of Telecommunications Concerning Safety of Life

International telecommunication services must give absolute priority to all telecommunications concerning safety of life at sea, on land, in the air or in outer space, as well as to epidemiological telecommunications of exceptional urgency of the World Health Organization.

Article 41—Priority of Government Telecommunications

Subject to the provisions of Articles 40 and 46 of this Constitution, government telecommunications (see Annex to this Constitution, No. 1014) shall enjoy priority over other telecommunications to the extent practicable upon specific request by the originator.

Article 42—Stoppage of Telecommunications

Member States reserve for themselves, for the operating agencies recognized by them and for other agencies duly authorized to do so, the right to make special arrangements on telecommunication matters which do not concern Member States in general. Such arrangements, however, shall not be in conflict with the terms of this Constitution, of the Convention or of the Administrative Regulations, so far as concerns the harmful interference which their operation might cause to the radio services of other Member States, and in general so far as concerns the technical harm which their operation might cause to the operation of other telecommunication services of other Member States.

Article 43—Regional Conferences, Arrangements and Organizations

Member States reserve the right to convene regional conferences, to make regional arrangements and to form regional organizations, for the purpose of settling telecommunication questions which are susceptible of being treated on a regional basis. Such arrangements shall not be in conflict with either this Constitution or the Convention.

CHAPTER VII—Special Provisions for Radio

Article 44—Use of the Radio-Frequency Spectrum and of the Geostationary-Satellite and Other Satellite Orbits

1. Member States shall endeavour to limit the number of frequencies and the spectrum used to the minimum essential to provide in a satisfactory manner the necessary services. To that end, they shall endeavour to apply the latest technical advances as soon as possible.

2. In using frequency bands for radio services, Member States shall bear in mind that radio frequencies and any associated orbits, including the geostationary-satellite orbit, are limited natural resources and that they must be used rationally, efficiently and economically, in conformity with the provisions of the Radio Regulations, so that countries or groups of countries may have equitable access to those orbits and frequencies, taking into account the special needs of the developing countries and the geographical situation of particular countries.

Article 45—Harmful Interference

1. All stations, whatever their purpose, must be established and operated in such a manner as not to cause harmful interference to the radio services or communications of other Member States or of recognized operating agencies, or of other duly authorized operating agencies which carry on a radio service, and which operate in accordance with the provisions of the Radio Regulations.

2. Each Member State undertakes to require the operating agencies which it recognizes and the other operating agencies duly authorized for this purpose to observe the provisions of No. 197 above.

3. Further, the Member States recognize the necessity of taking all practicable steps to prevent the operation of electrical apparatus and installations of all kinds from causing harmful interference to the radio services or communications mentioned in No. 197 above.

Article 46—Distress Calls and Messages

Radio stations shall be obliged to accept, with absolute priority, distress calls and messages regardless of their origin, to reply in the same manner to such messages, and immediately to take such action in regard thereto as may be required.

Article 47—False or Deceptive Distress, Urgency, Safety or Identification Signals

Member States agree to take the steps required to prevent the transmission or circulation of false or deceptive distress, urgency, safety or identification signals, and to collaborate in locating and identifying stations under their jurisdiction transmitting such signals.

Article 48—Installations for National Defence Services

1. Member States retain their entire freedom with regard to military radio installations.

2. Nevertheless, these installations must, so far as possible, observe statutory provisions relative to giving assistance in case of distress and to the measures to be taken to prevent harmful interference, and the provisions of the Administrative Regulations concerning the types of emission and the frequencies to be used, according to the nature of the service performed by such installations.

3. Moreover, when these installations take part in the service of public correspondence or other services governed by the Administrative Regulations, they must, in general, comply with the regulatory provisions for the conduct of such services.

CHAPTER VIII—Relations With the United Nations, Other International Organizations and Non-Member States

Article 49—Relations With the United Nations

The relationship between the United Nations and the International Telecommunication Union is defined in the Agreement concluded between these two organizations.

Article 50—Relations With Other International Organizations

In furtherance of complete international coordination on matters affecting telecommunication, the Union should cooperate with international organizations having related interests and activities.

Article 51—Relations With Non-Member States

Each Member State reserves for itself and for the recognized operating agencies the right to fix the conditions on which it admits telecommunications exchanged with a State which is not a Member

State of the Union. If a telecommunication originating in the territory of such a State is accepted by a Member State, it must be transmitted and, in so far as it follows the telecommunication channels of a Member State, the obligatory provisions of this Constitution, of the Convention and of the Administrative Regulations and the usual charges shall apply to it.

CHAPTER IX—FINAL PROVISIONS

ARTICLE 52—RATIFICATION, ACCEPTANCE OR APPROVAL

1. This Constitution and the Convention shall be simultaneously ratified, accepted or approved by any signatory Member State, in accordance with its constitutional rules, in one single instrument. This instrument shall be deposited, in as short a time as possible, with the Secretary-General. The Secretary-General shall notify the Member States of each deposit of any such instrument.

2. (1) During a period of two years from the date of entry into force of this Constitution and the Convention, a signatory Member State, even though it may not have deposited an instrument of ratification, acceptance or approval, in accordance with No. 208 above, shall enjoy the rights conferred on Member States in Nos. 25 to 28 of this Constitution.

(2) From the end of a period of two years from the date of entry into force of this Constitution and the Convention, a signatory Member State which has not deposited an instrument of ratification, acceptance or approval, in accordance with No. 208 above, shall no longer be entitled to vote at any conference of the Union, at any session of the Council, at any meeting of any of the Sectors of the Union, or during any consultation by correspondence conducted in accordance with the provisions of this Constitution and of the Convention until it has so deposited such an instrument. Its rights, other than voting rights, shall not be affected.

3. After the entry into force of this Constitution and the Convention in accordance with Article 58 of this Constitution, an instrument of ratification, acceptance or approval, shall become effective on the date of its deposit with the Secretary-General.

ARTICLE 53—ACCESSION

1. A Member State which is not a signatory to this Constitution and the Convention, or, subject to the provisions of Article 2 of this Constitution, any other State referred to in that Article, may accede to this Constitution and the Convention at any time. Such accession shall be made simultaneously in the form of one single instrument covering both this Constitution and the Convention.

2. The instrument of accession shall be deposited with the Secretary-General, who shall notify the Member States of each deposit of any such instrument when it is received and shall forward to each of them a certified copy thereof.

3. After the entry into force of this Constitution and the Convention in accordance with Article 58 of this Constitution, an instrument of accession shall become effective on the date of its deposit with the Secretary-General, unless otherwise specified therein.

Article 54—Administrative Regulations

1. The Administrative Regulations, as specified in Article 4 of this Constitution, are binding international instruments and shall be subject to the provisions of this Constitution and the Convention.

2. Ratification, acceptance or approval of this Constitution and the Convention, or accession to these instruments, in accordance with Articles 52 and 53 of this Constitution, shall also constitute consent to be bound by the Administrative Regulations adopted by competent world conferences prior to the date of signature of this Constitution and the Convention. Such consent is subject to any reservation made at the time of signature of the Administrative Regulations or revisions thereof to the extent that the reservation is maintained at the time of deposit of the instrument of ratification, acceptance, approval or accession.

2bis. The Administrative Regulations referred to in No. 216 above shall remain in force, subject to such revisions as may be adopted in application of Nos. 89 and 146 of this Constitution and brought into force. Any revision of the Administrative Regulations, either partial or complete, shall enter into force on the date or dates specified therein only for the Member States which, prior to such date or dates, have notified the Secretary-General of their consent to be bound by that revision.

(SUP)

3bis. A Member State shall notify its consent to be bound by a partial or complete revision of the Administrative Regulations by depositing with the Secretary-General an instrument of ratification, acceptance or approval of that revision or of accession thereto or by notifying the Secretary-General of its consent to be bound by that revision.

3ter. Any Member State may also notify the Secretary-General that its ratification, acceptance or approval of, or accession to, amendments to this Constitution or the Convention in accordance with Article 55 of the Constitution or Article 42 of the Convention shall constitute consent to be bound by any revision of the Administrative Regulations, either partial or complete, adopted by a competent conference prior to the signature of the said amendments to this Constitution or to the Convention.

3quater. The notification referred to in No. 217B above shall be given at the time of the deposit by the Member State of its instrument of ratification, acceptance or approval of, or accession to, the amendments to this Constitution or to the Convention.

3penter. Any revision of the Administrative Regulations shall apply provisionally, as from the date of entry into force of the revision, in respect of any Member State that has signed the revision and has not notified the Secretary-General of its consent to be bound in accordance with Nos. 217A and 217B above. Such provisional application only takes effect if the Member State in question did not oppose it at the time of signature of the revision.

4. Such provisional application shall continue for a Member State until it notifies the Secretary-General of its decision concerning its consent to be bound by any such revision.

(SUP)

5bis. If a Member State fails to notify the Secretary-General of its decision concerning its consent to be bound under No. 218 above within thirty-six months following the date or dates of entry into force of the revision, that Member State shall be deemed to have consented to be bound by that revision.

5ter. Any provisional application within the meaning of No. 217D or any consent to be bound within the meaning of No. 221A shall be subject to any reservation as may have been made by the Member State concerned at the time of signature of the revision. Any consent to be bound within the meaning of Nos. 216A, 217A, 217B and 218 above shall be subject to any reservation as may have been made by the Member State concerned at the time of signature of the Administrative Regulations or revision thereto, provided that it maintains the reservation when notifying the Secretary-General of its consent to be bound.

(SUP)

7. The Secretary-General shall inform Member States promptly of any notification received pursuant to this Article.

Article 55—Provisions for Amending this Constitution

1. Any Member State may propose any amendment to this Constitution. Any such proposal shall, in order to ensure its timely transmission to, and consideration by, all the Member States, reach the Secretary General not later than eight months prior to the opening date fixed for the plenipotentiary conference. The Secretary General shall, as soon as possible, but not later than six months prior to the latter date, publish any such proposal for the information of all the Member States.

2. Any proposed modification to any amendment submitted in accordance with No. 224 above may, however, be submitted at any time by a Member State or by its delegation at the plenipotentiary conference.

3. The quorum required at any Plenary Meeting of the Plenipotentiary Conference for consideration of any proposal for amending this Constitution or modification thereto shall consist of more than one half of the delegations accredited to the Plenipotentiary Conference.

4. To be adopted, any proposed modification to a proposed amendment as well as the proposal as a whole, whether or not modified, shall be approved, at a Plenary Meeting, by at least two-thirds of the delegations accredited to the Plenipotentiary Conference which have the right to vote.

5. Unless specified otherwise in the preceding paragraphs of this Article, which shall prevail, the General Rules of conferences, assemblies and meetings of the Union shall apply.

6. Any amendments to this Constitution adopted by a plenipotentiary conference shall, as a whole and in the form of one single amending instrument, enter into force at a date fixed by the conference between Member States having deposited before that date their instrument of ratification, acceptance or approval of, or accession to, both this Constitution and the amending instrument. Ratification, acceptance or approval of, or accession to, only a part of such an amending instrument shall be excluded.

7. The Secretary-General shall notify all Member States of the deposit of each instrument of ratification, acceptance, approval or accession.

8. After entry into force of any such amending instrument, ratification, acceptance, approval or accession in accordance with Articles 52 and 53 of this Constitution shall apply to the Constitution as amended.

9. After entry into force of any such amending instrument, the Secretary-General shall register it with the Secretariat of the United Nations, in accordance with the provisions of Article 102 of the Charter of the United Nations. No. 241 of this Constitution shall also apply to any such amending instrument.

ARTICLE 56—SETTLEMENT OF DISPUTES

1. Member States may settle their disputes on questions relating to the interpretation or application of this Constitution, of the Convention or of the Administrative Regulations by negotiation, through diplomatic channels, or according to procedures established by bilateral or multilateral treaties concluded between them for the settlement of international disputes, or by any other method mutually agreed upon.

2. If none of these methods of settlement is adopted, any Member State party to a dispute may have recourse to arbitration in accordance with the procedure defined in the Convention.

3. The Optional Protocol on the Compulsory Settlement of Disputes Relating to this Constitution, to the Convention, and to the Administrative Regulations shall be applicable as between Member States parties to that Protocol.

ARTICLE 57—DENUNCIATION OF THIS CONSTITUTION AND THE CONVENTION

1. Each Member State which has ratified, accepted, approved or acceded to this Constitution and the Convention shall have the right to denounce them. In such a case, this Constitution and the Convention shall be denounced simultaneously in one single instrument, by a notification addressed to the Secretary-General. Upon receipt of such notification, the Secretary-General shall advise the other Member States thereof.

2. Such denunciation shall take effect at the expiration of a period of one year from the date of receipt of its notification by the Secretary-General.

ARTICLE 58—ENTRY INTO FORCE AND RELATED MATTERS

1. This Constitution and the Convention, adopted by the Additional Plenipotentiary Conference (Geneva, 1992), shall enter into force on 1 July 1994 between Member States having deposited before that date their instrument of ratification, acceptance, approval or accession.

2. Upon the date of entry into force specified in No. 238 above, this Constitution and the Convention shall, as between Parties thereto, abrogate and replace the International Telecommunication Convention (Nairobi, 1982).

3. In accordance with the provisions of Article 102 of the Charter of the United Nations, the Secretary-General of the Union shall register this Constitution and the Convention with the Secretariat of the United Nations.

4. The original of this Constitution and the Convention drawn up in the Arabic, Chinese, English, French, Russian and Spanish languages shall remain deposited in the archives of the Union. The Secretary-General shall forward, in the languages requested, a certified true copy to each of the signatory Member States.

5. In the event of any discrepancy among the various language versions of this Constitution and the Convention, the French text shall prevail.

ANNEX—DEFINITION OF CERTAIN TERMS USED IN THIS CONSTITUTION, THE CONVENTION AND THE ADMINISTRATIVE REGULATIONS OF THE INTERNATIONAL TELECOMMUNICATION UNION

For the purpose of the above instruments of the Union, the following terms shall have the meanings defined below:

Member State: A State which is considered to be a Member of the International Telecommunication Union in application of Article 2 of this Constitution.

Sector Member: An entity or organization authorized in accordance with Article 19 of the Convention to participate in the activities of a Sector.

Administration: Any governmental department or service responsible for discharging the obligations undertaken in the Constitution of the International Telecommunication Union, in the Convention of the International Telecommunication Union and in the Administrative Regulations.

Harmful Interference: Interference which endangers the functioning of a radionavigation service or of other safety services or seriously degrades, obstructs or repeatedly interrupts a radiocommunication service operating in accordance with the Radio Regulations.

Public Correspondence: Any telecommunication which the offices and stations must, by reason of their being at the disposal of the public, accept for transmission.

Delegation: The totality of the delegates and, should the case arise, any representatives, advisers, attachés, or interpreters sent by the same Member State.

Each Member State shall be free to make up its delegation as it wishes. In particular, it may include in its delegation, inter alia, in the capacity of delegates, advisers or attachés, persons belonging to any entity or organization authorized in accordance with the relevant provisions of the Convention.

Delegate: A person sent by the government of a Member State to a plenipotentiary conference, or a person representing a government or an administration of a Member State at another conference or at a meeting of the Union.

Operating Agency: Any individual, company, corporation or governmental agency which operates a telecommunication installation intended for an international telecommunication service or capable of causing harmful interference with such a service.

Recognized Operating Agency: Any operating agency, as defined above, which operates a public correspondence or broadcasting service and upon which the obligations provided for in Article 6 of this Constitution are imposed by the Member State in whose territory the head office of the agency is situated, or by the Member State which has authorized this operating agency to establish and operate a telecommunication service on its territory.

Radiocommunication: Telecommunication by means of radio waves.

Broadcasting Service: A radiocommunication service in which the transmissions are intended for direct reception by the general public. This service may include sound transmissions, television transmissions or other types of transmission.

International Telecommunication Service: The offering of a telecommunication capability between telecommunication offices or stations of any nature that are in or belong to different countries.

Telecommunication: Any transmission, emission or reception of signs, signals, writing, images and sounds or intelligence of any nature by wire, radio, optical or other electromagnetic systems.

Telegram: Written matter intended to be transmitted by telegraphy for delivery to the addressee. This term also includes radiotelegrams unless otherwise specified.

Government Telecommunications: Telecommunications originating with any:

—Head of State;

—Head of government or members of a government;

—Commanders-in-Chief of military forces, land, sea or air;

—diplomatic or consular agents;

—the Secretary-General of the United Nations; Heads of the principal organs of the United Nations;

—the International Court of Justice,

or replies to government telecommunications mentioned above.

Private Telegrams: Telegrams other than government or service telegrams.

Telegraphy: A form of telecommunication in which the transmitted information is intended to be recorded on arrival as a graphic document; the transmitted information may sometimes be presented in an alternative form or may be stored for subsequent use.

Note: A graphic document records information in a permanent form and is capable of being filed and consulted; it may take the form of written or printed matter or of a fixed image.

Telephony: A form of telecommunication primarily intended for the exchange of information in the form of speech.

b. Convention of the International Telecommunication Union, as amended [1]

Done at Geneva December, 22, 1992; Entered into force generally, July 1, 1994; Advise and consent of the Senate, October 23, 1997; Entered into force for the United States, October 26, 1997

CONVENTION OF THE INTERNATIONAL TELECOMMUNICATION UNION

CHAPTER I—FUNCTIONING OF THE UNION

SECTION 1

ARTICLE 1—PLENIPOTENTIARY CONFERENCE

1. (1) The Plenipotentiary Conference shall be convened in accordance with the relevant provisions of Article 8 of the Constitution of the International Telecommunication Union (hereinafter referred to as "the Constitution").

(2) If practicable, the precise place and the exact dates of a plenipotentiary conference shall be set by the preceding plenipotentiary conference; failing this, they shall be fixed by the Council with the concurrence of the majority of the Member States.

2. (1) The precise place and the exact dates of the next Plenipotentiary Conference, or either one of these, may be changed:

(a) when at least one-quarter of the Member States have individually proposed a change to the Secretary-General; or

(b) on a proposal of the Council.

(2) Any such change shall require the concurrence of a majority of the Member States.

ARTICLE 2—ELECTIONS AND RELATED MATTERS

THE COUNCIL

1. Except in the case of vacancies arising in the circumstances described in Nos. 10 to 12 below, the Member States elected to the Council shall hold office until the date on which a new Council is elected. They shall be eligible for reelection.

2. (1) If, between two plenipotentiary conferences, a seat becomes vacant on the Council, it shall pass by right to the Member State from the same region as the Member State whose seat is vacated which had obtained at the previous election the largest number of votes among those not elected.

(2) When for any reason a vacant seat cannot be filled according to the procedure of No. 8 above, the Chairman of the Council shall invite the other Member States of the region to seek election within

[1] For states that are parties to the Convention, see Department of State publication, *Treaties in Force*. The Convention was amended at Kyoto, October 14, 1994; at Minneapolis, 1998, and at Marrakesh, 2002.

one month of such an invitation being issued. At the end of this period, the Chairman of the Council shall invite Member States to elect a new Member State of the Council. The election shall be carried out by secret ballot by correspondence. The same majority as indicated above will be required. The new Member State of the Council shall hold office until the election of the new Council by the next competent plenipotentiary conference.

3. A seat on the Council shall be considered vacant:

(a) when a Member State of the Council does not have a representative in attendance at two consecutive ordinary sessions of the Council;

(b) when a Member State resigns its membership of the Council.

ELECTED OFFICIALS

1. The Secretary-General, the Deputy Secretary-General and the Directors of the Bureau shall take up their duties on the dates determined by the Plenipotentiary Conference at the time of their election. They shall normally remain in office until dates determined by the following Plenipotentiary Conference, and they shall be eligible for re-election once only.

2. If the post of Secretary-General falls vacant, the Deputy Secretary-General shall succeed to it and shall remain in office until a date determined by the following Plenipotentiary Conference. When under these conditions the Deputy Secretary-General succeeds to the office of the Secretary-General, the post of Deputy Secretary-General shall be considered to fall vacant on that same date and the provisions of No. 15 below shall be applied.

3. If the post of Deputy Secretary-General falls vacant more than 180 days prior to the date set for the convening of the next Plenipotentiary Conference, the Council shall appoint a successor for the balance of the term.

4. If the posts of the Secretary-General and the Deputy Secretary-General fall vacant simultaneously, the Director who has been longest in office shall discharge the duties of Secretary-General for a period not exceeding 90 days. The Council shall appoint a Secretary-General and, if the vacancies occur more than 180 days prior to the date set for the convening of the next Plenipotentiary Conference, a Deputy Secretary-General. An official thus appointed by the Council shall serve for the balance of the term for which his predecessor was elected.

5. If the post of a Director becomes unexpectedly vacant, the Secretary-General shall take the necessary steps to ensure that the duties of that Director are carried out until the Council shall appoint a new Director at its next ordinary session following the occurrence of such a vacancy. A Director so appointed shall serve until the date fixed by the next Plenipotentiary Conference.

6. Subject to the relevant provisions of Article 27 of the Constitution, the Council shall provide for the filling of any vacancy in the post of Secretary-General or Deputy Secretary-General in the situation described in the relevant provisions of the present Article at an ordinary session, if held within 90 days after a vacancy occurs,

or at a session convened by the Chairman within the periods specified in those provisions.

7. Any period of service in the post of an elected official pursuant to an appointment under Nos. 14 to 18 above shall not affect eligibility for election or re-election to such a post.

MEMBERS OF THE RADIO REGULATIONS BOARD

1. The members of the Radio Regulations Board shall take up their duties on the dates determined by the Plenipotentiary Conference at the time of their election. They shall remain in office until dates determined by the following Plenipotentiary Conference, and shall be eligible for re-election once only.

2. If, in the interval between two plenipotentiary conferences, a member of the Board resigns or is no longer in a position to perform his duties, the Secretary-General, in consultation with the Director of the Radiocommunication Bureau, shall invite the Member States of the region concerned to propose candidates for the election of a replacement at the next session of the Council. However, if the vacancy occurs more than 90 days before a session of the Council or after the session of the Council preceding the next plenipotentiary conference, the Member State concerned shall designate, as soon as possible and within 90 days, another national as a replacement who will remain in office until the new member elected by the Council takes office or until the new members of the Board elected by the next plenipotentiary conference take office, as appropriate. The replacement shall be eligible for election by the Council or by the Plenipotentiary Conference, as appropriate.

3. A member of the Radio Regulations Board is considered no longer in a position to perform his duties after three consecutive absences from the Board meetings. The Secretary-General shall, after consultation with the Board's Chairman as well as the member of the Board and the Member State concerned, declare existence of a vacancy in the Board and shall proceed as stipulated in No. 21 above.

ARTICLE 3—PP–98 OTHER CONFERENCES AND ASSEMBLIES

1. In conformity with the relevant provisions of the Constitution, the following world conferences and assemblies of the Union shall normally be convened within the period between two plenipotentiary conferences:

(a) one or two world radiocommunication conferences;
(b) one world telecommunication standardization assembly;
(c) one world telecommunication development conference;
(d) one or two radiocommunication assemblies.

2. Exceptionally, within the period between Plenipotentiary Conferences:

(SUP)

—an additional world telecommunication standardization assembly may be convened.

3. These actions shall be taken:

(a) by a decision of a Plenipotentiary Conference;

(b) on the recommendation of the previous world conference or assembly of the Sector concerned, if approved by the Council; in the case of a radiocommunication assembly, the recommendation of the assembly shall be transmitted to the following world radiocommunication conference for comments for the attention of the Council;

(c) at the request of at least one-quarter of the Member States, which shall individually address their requests to the Secretary-General; or

(d) on a proposal of the Council.

4. A regional radiocommunication conference shall be convened:

(a) by a decision of a Plenipotentiary Conference;

(b) on the recommendation of a previous world or regional radiocommunication conference if approved by the Council;

(c) at the request of at least one-quarter of the Member States belonging to the region concerned, which shall individually address their requests to the Secretary-General; or

(d) on a proposal of the Council.

5. (1) The precise place and the exact dates of a world or regional conference or an assembly of a Sector may be fixed by a plenipotentiary conference.

(2) In the absence of such a decision, the Council shall determine the precise place and the exact dates of a world conference or an assembly of a Sector with the concurrence of a majority of the Member States, and of a regional conference with the concurrence of a majority of the Member States belonging to the region concerned; in both cases the provisions of No. 47 below shall apply.

6. (1) The precise place and the exact dates of a conference or assembly may be changed:

(a) at the request of at least one-quarter of the Member States in the case of a world conference or an assembly of a Sector, or of at least one-quarter of the Member States belonging to the region concerned in the case of a regional conference. Their requests shall be addressed individually to the Secretary-General, who shall transmit them to the Council for approval; or

(b) on a proposal of the Council.

(2) In the cases specified in Nos. 44 and 45 above, the changes proposed shall not be finally adopted until accepted by a majority of the Member States, in the case of a world conference or an assembly of a Sector, or by a majority of the Member States belonging to the region concerned, in the case of a regional conference, subject to the provisions of No. 47 below.

7. In the consultations referred to in Nos. 42, 46, 118, 123 and 138 of this Convention and in Nos. 26, 28, 29, 31 and 36 of the General Rules of conferences, assemblies and meetings of the Union, Member States which have not replied within the time-limits specified by the Council shall be regarded as not participating in the consultations, and in consequence shall not be taken into account in computing the majority. If the number of replies does not exceed one-half of the Member States consulted, a further consultation shall take place, the results of which shall be decisive regardless of the number of votes cast.

8. (1) World conferences on international telecommunications shall be held upon decision by the Plenipotentiary Conference.

(2) The provisions for the convening of, the adoption of the agenda of, and the participation in a world radiocommunication conference shall, as appropriate, equally apply to world conferences on international telecommunications.

SECTION 2

ARTICLE 4—THE COUNCIL

1. (1) The number of Member States of the Council shall be determined by the Plenipotentiary Conference which is held every four years.

(2) This number shall not exceed 25% of the total number of Member States.

2. (1) The Council shall hold an ordinary session annually at the seat of the Union.

(2) During this session it may decide to hold, exceptionally, an additional session.

(3) Between ordinary sessions, it may be convened, as a general rule at the seat of the Union, by the Chairman at the request of a majority of its Member States, or on the initiative of the Chairman under the conditions provided for in No. 18 of this Convention.

3. The Council shall take decisions only in session. Exceptionally, the Council in session may agree that any specific issue shall be decided by correspondence.

4. At the beginning of each ordinary session, the Council shall elect its own Chairman and Vice-Chairman from among the representatives of its Member States, taking into account the principle of rotation between the regions. They shall serve until the opening of the next ordinary session and shall not be eligible for re-election. The Vice-Chairman shall serve as Chairman in the absence of the latter.

5. The person appointed to serve on the Council by a Member State of the Council shall, so far as possible, be an official serving in, or directly responsible to, or for, their telecommunication administration and qualified in the field of telecommunication services.

6. Only the travelling, subsistence and insurance expenses incurred by the representative of each Member State of the Council, belonging to the category of developing countries, the list of which is established by the United Nations Development Programme, in that capacity at Council sessions, shall be borne by the Union.

7. The representative of each Member State of the Council shall have the right to attend, as an observer, all meetings of the Sectors of the Union.

8. The Secretary-General shall act as Secretary of the Council.

9. The Secretary-General, the Deputy Secretary-General and the Directors of the Bureau may participate as of right in the deliberations of the Council, but without taking part in the voting. Nevertheless, the Council may hold meetings confined to the representatives of its Member States.

9bis. A Member State which is not a Member State of the Council may, with prior notice to the Secretary General, send one observer at its own expense to meetings of the Council, its committees and its working groups. An observer shall not have the right to vote.

9ter. Sector Members may be represented as observers at meetings of the Council, its committees and its working groups, subject to the conditions established by the Council, including conditions relating to the number of such observers and the procedures for appointing them.

10. The Council shall consider each year the report prepared by the Secretary-General on implementation of the strategic plan adopted by the Plenipotentiary Conference and shall take appropriate action.

10bis. While at all times respecting the financial limits as adopted by the Plenipotentiary Conference, the Council may, as necessary, review and update the strategic plan which forms the basis of the corresponding operational plans and inform the Member States and Sector Members accordingly.

10ter. The Council shall adopt its own Rules of Procedure.

11. The Council shall, in the interval between two Plenipotentiary Conferences, supervise the overall management and administration of the Union; it shall in particular:

(1) receive and review the specific data for strategic planning that is provided by the Secretary-General as noted in No. 74A of the Constitution and, in the last but one ordinary session of the Council before the next plenipotentiary conference, initiate the preparation of a draft new strategic plan for the Union, drawing upon input from Member States, Sector Members and the Sector advisory groups, and produce a coordinated draft new strategic plan at least four months before that plenipotentiary conference;

(1bis) establish a calendar for the development of strategic and financial plans for the Union, and of operational plans for each Sector and for the General Secretariat, so as to allow for the development of appropriate linkage among the plans;

(1ter) approve and revise the Staff Regulations and the Financial Regulations of the Union and any other regulations as it may consider necessary, taking account of current practice of the United Nations and of the specialized agencies applying the common system of pay, allowances and pensions;

(2) adjust as necessary:

(a) the basic salary scales for staff in the professional and higher categories, excluding the salaries for posts filled by election, to accord with any changes in the basic salary scales adopted by the United Nations for the corresponding common system categories;

(b) the basic salary scales for staff in the general services categories to accord with changes in the rates applied by the United Nations and the specialized agencies at the seat of the Union;

(c) the post adjustment for professional and higher categories, including posts filled by election, in accordance with decisions of the United Nations for application at the seat of the Union;

(d) the allowances for all staff of the Union, in accordance with any changes adopted in the United Nations common system;

(3) take decisions to ensure equitable geographical distribution and representation of women in the Professional and higher categories in the staff of the Union and monitor the implementation of such decisions;

(4) decide on proposals for major organizational changes within the General Secretariat and the Bureau of the Sectors of the Union consistent with the Constitution and this Convention, submitted to it by the Secretary-General following their consideration by the Coordination Committee;

(5) examine and decide on plans concerning Union posts and staff and human resources development programmes covering several years, and give guidelines for the staffing of the Union, including on staffing levels and structures, taking into account the guidelines given by the Plenipotentiary Conference and the relevant provisions of Article 27 of the Constitution;

(6) adjust, as necessary, the contributions payable by the Union and its staff to the United Nations Joint Staff Pension Fund, in accordance with the Fund's rules and regulations, as well as the cost of living allowances to be granted to beneficiaries of the Union Staff Superannuation and Benevolent Funds on the basis of the practice followed by the Fund;

(7) review and approve the biennial budget of the Union, and consider the budget forecast (included in the financial operating report prepared by the Secretary-General under No. 101 of this Convention) for the two-year period following a given budget period, taking account of the decisions of the Plenipotentiary Conference in relation to No. 50 of the Constitution and of the financial limits set by the Plenipotentiary Conference in accordance with No. 51 of the Constitution; it shall ensure the strictest possible economy but be mindful of the obligation upon the Union to achieve satisfactory results as expeditiously as possible. In so doing, the Council shall take into account the priorities established by the Plenipotentiary Conference as expressed in the strategic plan for the Union, the views of the Coordination Committee as contained in the report by the Secretary General mentioned in No. 86 of this Convention and the financial operating report mentioned in No. 101 of this Convention;

(8) arrange for the annual audit of the accounts of the Union prepared by the Secretary-General and approve them, if appropriate, for submission to the next Plenipotentiary Conference;

(9) arrange for the convening of the conferences and assemblies of the Union and provide, with the consent of a majority of the Member States in the case of a world conference or assembly, or of a majority of the Member States belonging to the region concerned in the case of a regional conference, appropriate directives to the General Secretariat and the Sectors of the Union with regard to their technical and other assistance

in the preparation for and organization of conferences and assemblies;

(10) take decisions in relation to No. 28 of this Convention;

(11) decide upon the implementation of any decisions which have been taken by conferences and which have financial implications;

(12) to the extent permitted by the Constitution, this Convention and the Administrative Regulations, take any other action deemed necessary for the proper functioning of the Union;

(13) take any necessary steps, with the agreement of a majority of the Member States, provisionally to resolve questions not covered by the Constitution, this Convention and the Administrative Regulations and which cannot await the next competent conference for settlement;

(14) be responsible for effecting the coordination with all international organizations referred to in Articles 49 and 50 of the Constitution and to this end, conclude, on behalf of the Union, provisional agreements with the international organizations referred to in Article 50 of the Constitution and in Nos. 260 and 261 of the Convention, and with the United Nations in application of the Agreement between the United Nations and the International Telecommunication Union; these provisional agreements shall be submitted to the Plenipotentiary Conference in accordance with the relevant provision of Article 8 of the Constitution;

(15) send to Member States, within 30 days after each of its sessions, summary records on the activities of the Council and other documents deemed useful;

(16) submit to the Plenipotentiary Conference a report on the activities of the Union since the previous Plenipotentiary Conference and any appropriate recommendations.

SECTION 3

ARTICLE 5—GENERAL SECRETARIAT

1. The Secretary-General shall:

(a) be responsible for the overall management of the Union's resources; he may delegate the management of part of these resources to the Deputy Secretary-General and the Directors of the Bureau, in consultation as necessary with the Coordination Committee;

(b) coordinate the activities of the General Secretariat and the Sectors of the Union, taking into account the views of the Coordination Committee, with a view to assuring the most effective and economical use of the resources of the Union;

(c) prepare, with the assistance of the Coordination Committee, and submit to the Council a report indicating changes in the telecommunication environment since the last plenipotentiary conference and containing recommended action relating to the Union's future policies and strategy, together with their financial implications;

(cbis) coordinate implementation of the strategic plan adopted by the Plenipotentiary Conference and prepare an annual report on this implementation for review by the Council;

(d) organize the work of the General Secretariat and appoint the staff of that Secretariat in accordance with the directives of the Plenipotentiary Conference and the rules established by the Council;

(dbis) prepare annually a four-year rolling operational plan of activities to be undertaken by the staff of the General Secretariat consistent with the strategic plan, covering the subsequent year and the following three-year period, including financial implications, taking due account of the financial plan as approved by the plenipotentiary conference; this four-year operational plan shall be reviewed by the advisory groups of all three Sectors, and shall be reviewed and approved annually by the Council;

(e) undertake administrative arrangements for the Bureau of the Sectors of the Union and appoint their staff on the basis of the choice and proposals of the Director of the Bureau concerned, although the final decision for appointment or dismissal shall rest with the Secretary-General;

(f) report to the Council any decisions taken by the United Nations and the specialized agencies which affect common system conditions of service, allowances and pensions;

(g) ensure the application of any regulations adopted by the Council;

(h) provide legal advice to the Union;

(i) supervise, for administrative management purposes, the staff of the Union with a view to assuring the most effective use of personnel and the application of the common system conditions of employment for the staff of the Union. The staff appointed to assist directly the Directors of the Bureau shall be under the administrative control of the Secretary-General and shall work under the direct orders of the Directors concerned but in accordance with administrative guidelines given by the Council;

(j) in the interest of the Union as a whole and in consultation with the Directors of the Bureau concerned, temporarily reassign staff members from their appointed position as necessary to meet fluctuating work requirements at headquarters;

(k) make, in agreement with the Director of the Bureau concerned, the necessary administrative and financial arrangements for the conferences and meetings of each Sector;

(l) taking into account the responsibilities of the Sectors, undertake appropriate secretariat work preparatory to and following conferences of the Union;

(m) prepare recommendations for the first meeting of the Heads of delegations referred to in No. 342 of this Convention), taking into account the results of any regional consultation;

(n) provide, where appropriate in cooperation with the inviting government, the secretariat of conferences of the Union, and provide the facilities and services for meetings of the Union, in collaboration, as appropriate, with the Director concerned, drawing from the Union's staff as he deems necessary in accordance with No. 93 above. The Secretary-General may also, when so requested, provide the secretariat of other telecommunication meetings on a contractual basis;

(o) take necessary action for the timely publication and distribution of service documents, information bulletins, and other documents and records prepared by the General Secretariat and the Sectors, communicated to the Union or whose publication is requested by conferences or the Council; the list of documents to be published shall be maintained by the Council, following consultation with the conference concerned, with respect to service documents and other documents whose publication is requested by conferences;

(p) publish periodically, with the help of information put at his disposal or which he may collect, including that which he may obtain from other international organizations, a journal of general information and documentation concerning telecommunication;

(q) after consultation with the Coordination Committee and making all possible economies, prepare and submit to the Council a biennial draft budget covering the expenditures of the Union, taking account of the financial limits laid down by the Plenipotentiary Conference. This draft shall consist of a consolidated budget, including cost-based budgets for the three Sectors, prepared in accordance with the budget guidelines issued by the Secretary-General, and comprising two versions. One version shall be for zero growth of the contributory unit, the other for a growth less than or equal to any limit fixed by the Plenipotentiary Conference, after any drawing on the Reserve Account. The budget resolution, after approval by the Council, shall be sent for information to all Member States;

(r) with the assistance of the Coordination Committee, prepare an annual financial operating report in accordance with the Financial Regulations and submit it to the Council. A recapitulative financial operating report and accounts shall be prepared and submitted to the next Plenipotentiary Conference for examination and final approval;

(s) with the assistance of the Coordination Committee, prepare an annual report on the activities of the Union which, after approval by the Council, shall be sent to all Member States;

(sbis) manage the special arrangements referred to in No. 76A of the Constitution, the cost of this management being borne by the signatories of the arrangement in a manner agreed between them and the Secretary-General.

(t) perform all other secretarial functions of the Union;

(u) perform any other functions entrusted to him by the Council.

2. The Secretary-General or the Deputy Secretary-General may participate, in a consultative capacity, in conferences of the Union; the Secretary-General or his representative may participate in a consultative capacity in all other meetings of the Union.

Section 4

Article 6—Coordination Committee

1. (1) The Coordination Committee shall assist and advise the Secretary-General on all matters mentioned under the relevant

provisions of Article 26 of the Constitution and the relevant Articles of this Convention.

(2) The Committee shall be responsible for ensuring coordination with all the international organizations mentioned in Articles 49 and 50 of the Constitution as regards representation of the Union at conferences of such organizations.

(3) The Committee shall examine the progress of the work of the Union and assist the Secretary-General in the preparation of the report referred to in No. 86 of this Convention for submission to the Council.

2. The Committee shall endeavour to reach conclusions unanimously. In the absence of the support of the majority in the Committee, its Chairman may in exceptional circumstances take decisions, on the Chairman's own responsibility, when judging that the decision of the matters in question is urgent and cannot await the next session of the Council. In such circumstances the Chairman shall report promptly in writing on such matters to the Member States of the Council, setting forth the reasons for such action together with any other written views submitted by other members of the Committee. If in such circumstances the matters are not urgent, but nevertheless important, they shall be submitted for consideration by the next session of the Council.

3. The Chairman shall convene the Committee at least once a month; the Committee may also be convened when necessary at the request of two of its members.

4. A report shall be made of the proceedings of the Coordination Committee and will be made available on request to Member States of the Council.

SECTION 5

ARTICLE 7—WORLD RADIOCOMMUNICATION CONFERENCE

1. In accordance with No. 90 of the Constitution, a world radiocommunication conference shall be convened to consider specific radiocommunication matters. A world radiocommunication conference shall deal with those items which are included in its agenda adopted in accordance with the relevant provisions of this Article.

2. (1) The agenda of a world radiocommunication conference may include:

(a) the partial or, exceptionally, complete revision of the Radio Regulations referred to in Article 4 of the Constitution;

(b) any other question of a worldwide character within the competence of the conference;

(c) an item concerning instructions to the Radio Regulations Board and the Radiocommunication Bureau regarding their activities, and a review of those activities;

(d) the identification of topics to be studied by the radiocommunication assembly and the radiocommunication study groups, as well as matters that the assembly shall consider in relation to future radiocommunication conferences.

(2) The general scope of this agenda should be established four to six years in advance, and the final agenda shall be established by the Council preferably two years before the conference, with the

concurrence of a majority of the Member States, subject to the provisions of No. 47 of this Convention. These two versions of the agenda shall be established on the basis of the recommendations of the world radiocommunication conference, in accordance with No. 126 of this Convention.

(3) This agenda shall include any question which a Plenipotentiary Conference has directed to be placed on the agenda.

3. (1) This agenda may be changed:

(a) at the request of at least one-quarter of the Member States. Such requests shall be addressed individually to the Secretary-General, who shall transmit them to the Council for approval; or

(b) on a proposal of the Council.

(2) The proposed changes to the agenda of a world radiocommunication conference shall not be finally adopted until accepted by a majority of the Member States, subject to the provisions of No. 47 of this Convention.

4. The conference shall also:

(1) consider and approve the report of the Director of the Bureau on the activities of the Sector since the last conference;

(2) recommend to the Council items for inclusion in the agenda of a future conference and give its views on such agendas for at least a four-year cycle of radiocommunication conferences, together with an estimate of the financial implications;

(3) include, in its decisions, instructions or requests, as appropriate, to the Secretary-General and the Sectors of the Union.

5. The Chairman and Vice-Chairmen of the radiocommunication assembly, or of relevant study groups, may participate in the associated world radiocommunication conference.

ARTICLE 8—RADIOCOMMUNICATION ASSEMBLY

1. A radiocommunication assembly shall deal with and issue, as appropriate, recommendations on questions adopted pursuant to its own procedures or referred to it by the Plenipotentiary Conference, any other conference, the Council or the Radio Regulations Board.

1bis. The radiocommunication assembly is authorized to adopt the working methods and procedures for the management of the Sector's activities in accordance with No. 145A of the Constitution.

2. With regard to No. 129 above, the radiocommunication assembly shall:

(1) consider the reports of study groups prepared in accordance with No. 157 of this Convention and approve, modify or reject the draft recommendations contained in those reports, and consider the reports of the radiocommunication advisory group prepared in accordance with No. 160H of this Convention;

(2) bearing in mind the need to keep the demands on the resources of the Union to a minimum, approve the programme of work arising from the review of existing questions and new

questions and determine the priority, urgency, estimated financial implications and time-scale for the completion of their study;

(3) decide, in the light of the approved programme of work derived from No. 132 above, on the need to maintain, terminate or establish study groups, and allocate to each of them the questions to be studied;

(4) group questions of interest to the developing countries as far as possible, in order to facilitate their participation in the study of those questions;

(5) give advice on matters within its competence in response to requests from a world radiocommunication conference;

(6) report to the following world radiocommunication conference on the progress in matters that may be included in the agenda of future radiocommunication conferences.

(7) decide on the need to maintain, terminate or establish other groups and appoint their chairmen and vice-chairmen;

(8) establish the terms of reference for the groups referred to in No. 136A above; such groups shall not adopt questions or recommendations.

3. A radiocommunication assembly shall be presided over by a person designated by the government of the country in which the meeting is held or, in the case of a meeting held at the seat of the Union, by a person elected by the assembly itself. The Chairman shall be assisted by Vice-Chairmen elected by the assembly.

4. A radiocommunication assembly may assign specific matters within its competence, except those relating to the procedures contained in the Radio Regulations, to the radiocommunication advisory group indicating the action required on those matters.

ARTICLE 9—REGIONAL RADIOCOMMUNICATION CONFERENCES

The agenda of a regional radiocommunication conference may provide only for specific radiocommunication questions of a regional nature, including instructions to the Radio Regulations Board and the Radiocommunication Bureau regarding their activities in respect of the region concerned, provided such instructions do not conflict with the interests of other regions. Only items included in its agenda may be discussed by such a conference. The provisions contained in Nos. 118 to 123 of this Convention shall apply to a regional radiocommunication conference, but only with regard to the Member States of the region concerned.

ARTICLE 10—RADIO REGULATIONS BOARD

(SUP)

2. In addition to the duties specified in Article 14 of the Constitution, the Board shall:

(1) consider reports from the Director of the Radiocommunication Bureau on investigations of harmful interference carried out at the request of one or more of the interested administrations, and formulate recommendations with respect thereto;

(2) also, independently of the Radiocommunication Bureau, at the request of one or more of the interested administrations,

consider appeals against decisions made by the Radiocommunication Bureau regarding frequency assignments.

3. The members of the Board shall participate, in an advisory capacity, in radiocommunication conferences. In this case, they shall not participate in these conferences as members of their national delegations.

3bis. Two members of the Board, designated by the Board, shall participate, in an advisory capacity, in plenipotentiary conferences and radiocommunication assemblies. In these cases, the two members designated by the Board shall not participate in these conferences or assemblies as members of their national delegations.

4. Only the travelling, subsistence and insurance expenses incurred by the members of the Board in the exercise of their duties for the Union shall be borne by the Union.

4bis. The members of the Board shall, while in the exercise of their duties for the Union, as specified in the Constitution and Convention, or while on mission for the Union, enjoy functional privileges and immunities equivalent to those granted to the elected officials of the Union by each Member State, subject to the relevant provisions of the national legislation or other applicable legislation in each Member State. Such functional privileges and immunities are granted to members of the Board for the purposes of the Union and not for their personal advantage. The Union may and shall withdraw the immunity granted to a member of the Board whenever it considers that such immunity is contrary to the orderly administration of justice and its withdrawal is not prejudicial to the interests of the Union.

5. The working methods of the Board shall be as follows:

(1) The members of the Board shall elect from their own members a Chairman and a Vice-Chairman for a period of one year. Thereafter the Vice-Chairman shall succeed the Chairman each year and a new Vice-Chairman shall be elected. In the absence of the Chairman and Vice-Chairman, the Board shall elect a temporary Chairman for the occasion from among its members.

(2) The Board shall normally hold up to four meetings a year, of up to five days' duration, generally at the seat of the Union, at which at least two-thirds of its members shall be present, and may carry out its duties using modern means of communication. However, if the Board deems necessary, depending upon the matters to be considered, it may increase the number of its meetings. Exceptionally, the meetings may be of up to two weeks' duration.

(3) The Board shall endeavour to reach its decisions unanimously. If it fails in that endeavour, a decision shall be valid only if at least two-thirds of the members of the Board vote in favour thereof. Each member of the Board shall have one vote; voting by proxy is not allowed.

(4) The Board may make such internal arrangements as it considers necessary in conformity with the provisions of the Constitution, this Convention and the Radio Regulations. Such arrangements shall be published as part of the Board's Rules of Procedure.

ARTICLE 11—RADIOCOMMUNICATION STUDY GROUPS

1. Radiocommunication study groups are set up by a radiocommunication assembly.

2. (1) The radiocommunication study groups shall study questions adopted in accordance with a procedure established by the radiocommunication assembly and prepare draft recommendations to be adopted in accordance with the procedure set forth in Nos. 246A to 247 of this Convention.

(1bis) The radiocommunication study groups shall also study topics identified in resolutions and recommendations of world radiocommunication conferences. The results of such studies shall be included in recommendations or in the reports prepared in accordance with No. 156 below.

(2) The study of the above questions and topics shall, subject to No. 158 below, focus on the following:

(a) use of the radio-frequency spectrum in terrestrial and space radiocommunication and of the geostationary-satellite and other satellite orbits;

(b) characteristics and performance of radio systems;

(c) operation of radio stations;

(d) radiocommunication aspects of distress and safety matters.

(3) These studies shall not generally address economic questions, but when they involve comparing technical or operational alternatives, economic factors may be taken into consideration.

3. The radiocommunication study groups shall also carry out preparatory studies of the technical, operational and procedural matters to be considered by world and regional radiocommunication conferences and elaborate reports thereon in accordance with a programme of work adopted in this respect by a radiocommunication assembly or following instructions by the Council.

4. Each study group shall prepare for the radiocommunication assembly a report indicating the progress of work, the recommendations adopted in accordance with the consultation procedure contained in No. 149 above and any draft new or revised recommendations for consideration by the assembly.

5. Taking into account No. 79 of the Constitution, the tasks enumerated in Nos. 151 to 154 above and in No. 193 of this Convention in relation to the Telecommunication Standardization Sector shall be kept under continuing review by the Radiocommunication Sector and the Telecommunication Standardization Sector with a view to reaching common agreement on changes in the distribution of matters under study. The two Sectors shall cooperate closely and adopt procedures to conduct such a review and reach agreements in a timely and effective manner. If agreement is not reached, the matter may be submitted through the Council to the Plenipotentiary Conference for decision.

6. In the performance of their studies, the radiocommunication study groups shall pay due attention to the study of questions and to the formulation of recommendations directly connected with the

establishment, development and improvement of telecommunications in developing countries at both the regional and international levels. They shall conduct their work giving due consideration to the work of national, regional and other international organizations concerned with radiocommunication and cooperate with them, keeping in mind the need for the Union to maintain its preeminent position in the field of telecommunications.

7. For the purpose of facilitating the review of activities in the Radiocommunication Sector, measures should be taken to foster cooperation and coordination with other organizations concerned with radiocommunication and with the Telecommunication Standardization Sector and the Telecommunication Development Sector. A radiocommunication assembly shall determine the specific duties, conditions of participation and rules of procedure for these measures.

ARTICLE 11A—RADIOCOMMUNICATION ADVISORY GROUP PURPOSES OF THE UNION

1. The radiocommunication advisory group shall be open to representatives of administrations of Member States and representatives of Sector Members and to chairmen of the study groups and other groups, and will act through the Director.

2. The radiocommunication advisory group shall:

(1) review priorities, programmes, operations, financial matters and strategies related to radiocommunication assemblies, study groups and other groups and the preparation of radiocommunication conferences, and any specific matters as directed by a conference of the Union, a radiocommunication assembly or the Council;

(1bis) review the implementation of the operational plan of the preceding period in order to identify areas in which the Bureau has not achieved or was not able to achieve the objectives laid down in that plan, and advise the Director on the necessary corrective measures;

(2) review progress in the implementation of the programme of work established under No. 132 of this Convention;

(3) provide guidelines for the work of study groups;

(4) recommend measures, inter alia, to foster cooperation and coordination with other standards bodies, with the Telecommunication Standardization Sector, the Telecommunication Development Sector and the General Secretariat;

(5) adopt its own working procedures compatible with those adopted by the radiocommunication assembly;

(6) prepare a report for the Director of the Radiocommunication Bureau indicating action in respect of the above items;

(7) prepare a report for the Radiocommunication Assembly on the matters assigned to it in accordance with No. 137A of this Convention and transmit it to the Director for submission to the assembly.

ARTICLE 12—RADIOCOMMUNICATION BUREAU

1. The Director of the Radiocommunication Bureau shall organize and coordinate the work of the Radiocommunication Sector. The

duties of the Bureau are supplemented by those specified in provisions of the Radio Regulations.

2. The Director shall, in particular,

(1) in relation to radiocommunication conferences:

(a) coordinate the preparatory work of the study groups and other groups and the Bureau, communicate to the Member States and Sector Members the results of this preparatory work, collect their comments and submit a consolidated report to the conference which may include proposals of a regulatory nature;

(b) participate as of right, but in an advisory capacity, in the deliberations of radiocommunication conferences, of the radiocommunication assembly and of the radiocommunication study groups and other groups. The Director shall make all necessary preparations for radiocommunication conferences and meetings of the Radiocommunication Sector in consultation with the General Secretariat in accordance with No. 94 of this Convention and, as appropriate, with the other Sectors of the Union, and with due regard for the directives of the Council in carrying out these preparations;

(c) provide assistance to the developing countries in their preparations for radiocommunication conferences.

(2) in relation to the Radio Regulations Board:

(a) prepare and submit draft Rules of Procedure for approval by the Radio Regulations Board; they shall include, inter alia, calculation methods and data required for the application of the provisions of the Radio Regulations;

(b) distribute to all Member States the Rules of Procedure of the Board, collect comments thereon received from administrations and submit them to the Board;

(c) process information received from administrations in application of the relevant provisions of the Radio Regulations and regional agreements and their associated Rules of Procedure and prepare it, as appropriate, in a form suitable for publication;

(d) apply the Rules of Procedure approved by the Board, prepare and publish findings based on those Rules, and submit to the Board any review of a finding which is requested by an administration and which cannot be resolved by the use of those Rules of Procedure;

(e) in accordance with the relevant provisions of the Radio Regulations, effect an orderly recording and registration of frequency assignments and, where appropriate, the associated orbital characteristics, and keep up to date the Master International Frequency Register; review entries in that Register with a view to amending or eliminating, as appropriate, those which do not reflect actual frequency usage, in agreement with the administration concerned;

(f) assist in the resolution of cases of harmful interference, at the request of one or more of the interested administrations, and where necessary, make investigations and prepare, for consideration by the Board, a report including draft recommendations to the administrations concerned;

(g) act as executive secretary to the Board;

(3) coordinate the work of the radiocommunication study groups and other groups and be responsible for the organization of that work;

(3bis) provide the necessary support for the radiocommunication advisory group, and report each year to Member States and Sector Members and to the Council on the results of the work of the advisory group.

(3ter) take practical measures to facilitate the participation of developing countries in the radiocommunication study groups and other groups.

(4) also undertake the following:

(a) carry out studies to furnish advice with a view to the operation of the maximum practicable number of radio channels in those portions of the spectrum where harmful interference may occur, and with a view to the equitable, effective and economical use of the geostationary-satellite and other satellite orbits, taking into account the needs of Member States requiring assistance, the specific needs of developing countries, as well as the special geographical situation of particular countries;

(b) exchange with Member States and Sector Members data in machine-readable and other forms, prepare and keep up to date any documents and databases of the Radiocommunication Sector, and arrange, with the Secretary-General, as appropriate, for their publication in the working languages of the Union in accordance with No. 172 of the Constitution;

(c) maintain such essential records as may be required;

(d) submit to the world radiocommunication conference a report on the activities of the Radiocommunication Sector since the last conference; if a world radiocommunication conference is not planned, a report on the activities of the Sector covering the period since the last conference shall be submitted to the Council and, for information, to Member States and Sector Members;

(e) prepare a cost-based budget estimate for the requirements of the Radiocommunication Sector and transmit it to the Secretary-General for consideration by the Coordination Committee and inclusion in the Union's budget.

(f) prepare annually a rolling four-year operational plan that covers the subsequent year and the following three-year period, including financial implications of activities to be undertaken by the Bureau in support of the Sector as a whole; this four-year operational plan shall be reviewed by the radiocommunication advisory group in accordance with Article 11A of this Convention, and shall be reviewed and approved annually by the Council;

3. The Director shall choose the technical and administrative personnel of the Bureau within the framework of the budget as approved by the Council. The appointment of the technical and administrative personnel is made by the Secretary-General in agreement with the Director. The final decision for appointment or dismissal rests with the Secretary-General.

4. The Director shall provide technical support, as necessary, to the Telecommunication Development Sector within the framework of the Constitution and this Convention.

SECTION 6: TELECOMMUNICATION STANDARDIZATION SECTOR

ARTICLE 13—PP–98—WORLD TELECOMMUNICATION STANDARDIZATION ASSEMBLY

1. In accordance with No. 104 of the Constitution, a world telecommunication standardization assembly shall be convened to consider specific matters related to telecommunication standardization.

1bis. The world telecommunication standardization assembly is authorized to adopt the working methods and procedures for the management of the Sector's activities in accordance with No. 145A of the Constitution.

2. The questions to be studied by a world telecommunication standardization assembly, on which recommendations shall be issued, shall be those adopted pursuant to its own procedures or referred to it by the Plenipotentiary Conference, any other conference, or the Council.

3. In accordance with No. 104 of the Constitution, the assembly shall:

(a) consider the reports of study groups prepared in accordance with No. 194 of this Convention and approve, modify or reject draft recommendations contained in those reports, and consider the reports of the telecommunication standardization advisory group in accordance with Nos. 197H and 197I of this Convention;

(b) bearing in mind the need to keep the demands on the resources of the Union to a minimum, approve the programme of work arising from the review of existing questions and new questions and determine the priority, urgency, estimated financial implications and time-scale for the completion of their study;

(c) decide, in the light of the approved programme of work derived from No. 188 above, on the need to maintain, terminate or establish study groups and allocate to each of them the questions to be studied;

(d) group, as far as practicable, questions of interest to the developing countries to facilitate their participation in these studies;

(e) consider and approve the report of the Director on the activities of the Sector since the last conference.

(f) decide on the need to maintain, terminate or establish other groups and appoint their chairmen and vice-chairmen;

(g) establish the terms of reference for the groups referred to in No. 191 bis above; such groups shall not adopt questions or recommendations.

4. A world telecommunication standardization assembly may assign specific matters within its competence to the telecommunication standardization advisory group indicating the action required on those matters.

5. A world telecommunication standardization assembly shall be presided over by a chairman designated by the government of the country in which the meeting is held or, in the case of a meeting held at the seat of the Union, by a chairman elected by the assembly itself. The chairman shall be assisted by vice-chairmen elected by the assembly.

Article 14—Telecommunication Standardization Study Groups

1. (1) Telecommunication standardization study groups shall study questions adopted in accordance with a procedure established by the world telecommunication standardization assembly and prepare draft recommendations to be adopted in accordance with the procedure set forth in Nos. 246A to 247 of this Convention.

(2) The study groups shall, subject to No. 195 below, study technical, operating and tariff questions and prepare recommendations on them with a view to standardizing telecommunications on a worldwide basis, including recommendations on interconnection of radio systems in public telecommunication networks and on the performance required for these interconnections. Technical or operating questions specifically related to radiocommunication as enumerated in Nos. 151 to 154 of this Convention shall be within the purview of the Radiocommunication Sector.

(3) Each study group shall prepare for the world telecommunication standardization assembly a report indicating the progress of work, the recommendations adopted in accordance with the consultation procedure contained in No. 192 above, and any draft new or revised recommendations for consideration by the assembly.

2. Taking into account No. 105 of the Constitution, the tasks enumerated in No. 193 above and those enumerated in Nos. 151 to 154 of this Convention in relation to the Radiocommunication Sector shall be kept under continuing review by the Telecommunication Standardization Sector and the Radiocommunication Sector with a view to reaching common agreement on changes in the distribution of matters under study. The two Sectors shall cooperate closely and adopt procedures to conduct such a review and reach agreements in a timely and effective manner. If agreement is not reached, the matter may be submitted through the Council to the Plenipotentiary Conference for decision.

3. In the performance of their studies, the telecommunication standardization study groups shall pay due attention to the study of questions and to the formulation of recommendations directly connected with the establishment, development and improvement of telecommunications in developing countries at both the regional and international levels. They shall conduct their work giving due

consideration to the work of national, regional and other international standardization organizations, and cooperate with them, keeping in mind the need for the Union to maintain its pre-eminent position in the field of worldwide standardization for telecommunications.

4. For the purpose of facilitating the review of activities in the Telecommunication Standardization Sector, measures should be taken to foster cooperation and coordination with other organizations concerned with telecommunication standardization and with the Radiocommunication Sector and the Telecommunication Development Sector. A world telecommunication standardization assembly shall determine the specific duties, conditions of participation and rules of procedure for these measures.

Article 14A—Telecommunication Standardization Advisory Group

1. The telecommunication standardization advisory group shall be open to representatives of administrations of Member States and representatives of Sector Members and to chairmen of the study groups and other groups.

2. The telecommunication standardization advisory group shall:

(1) review priorities, programmes, operations, financial matters and strategies for activities in the Telecommunication Standardization Sector;

(1bis) review the implementation of the operational plan of the preceding period in order to identify areas in which the Bureau has not achieved or was not able to achieve the objectives laid down in that plan, and advise the Director on the necessary corrective measures;

(2) review progress in the implementation of the programme of work established under No. 188 of this Convention;

(3) provide guidelines for the work of study groups;

(4) recommend measures, inter alia, to foster cooperation and coordination with other relevant bodies, with the Radiocommunication Sector, the Telecommunication Development Sector and the General Secretariat;

(5) adopt its own working procedures compatible with those adopted by the world telecommunication standardization assembly;

(6) prepare a report for the Director of the Telecommunication Standardization Bureau indicating action in respect of the above items.

(7) prepare a report for the world telecommunication standardization assembly on the matters assigned to it in accordance with No. 191A and transmit it to the Director for submission to the assembly.

Article 15—Telecommunication Standardization Bureau

1. The Director of the Telecommunication Standardization Bureau shall organize and coordinate the work of the Telecommunication Standardization Sector.

2. The Director shall, in particular:

(a) update annually the work programme approved by the world telecommunication standardization assembly, in consultation with the chairmen of the telecommunication standardization study groups and other groups;

(b) participate, as of right, but in an advisory capacity, in the deliberations of world telecommunication standardization assemblies and of the telecommunication standardization study groups and other groups. The Director shall make all necessary preparations for assemblies and meetings of the Telecommunication Standardization Sector in consultation with the General Secretariat in accordance with No. 94 of this Convention and, as appropriate, with the other Sectors of the Union, and with due regard for the directives of the Council concerning these preparations;

(c) process information received from administrations in application of the relevant provisions of the International Telecommunication Regulations or decisions of the world telecommunication standardization assembly and prepare it, where appropriate, in a suitable form for publication;

(d) exchange with Member States and Sector Members data in machine-readable and other forms, prepare and, as necessary, keep up to date any documents and databases of the Telecommunication Standardization Sector, and arrange with the Secretary-General, where appropriate, for their publication in the working languages of the Union in accordance with No. 172 of the Constitution;

(e) submit to the world telecommunication standardization assembly a report on the activities of the Sector since the last assembly; the Director shall also submit to the Council and to the Member States and Sector Members such a report covering the two-year period since the last assembly, unless a second assembly is convened;

(f) prepare a cost-based budget estimate for the requirements of the Telecommunication Standardization Sector and transmit it to the Secretary-General for consideration by the Coordination Committee and inclusion in the Union's budget.

(g) prepare annually a rolling four-year operational plan that covers the subsequent year and the following three-year period, including financial implications of activities to be undertaken by the Bureau in support of the Sector as a whole; this four-year operational plan shall be reviewed by the telecommunication standardization advisory group in accordance with Article 14A of this Convention, and shall be reviewed and approved annually by the Council;

(h) provide the necessary support for the telecommunication standardization advisory group, and report each year to Member States and Sector Members and to the Council on the results of its work;

(i) provide assistance to developing countries in the preparatory work for world standardization assemblies, particularly with regard to matters of a priority nature for those countries.

3. The Director shall choose the technical and administrative personnel of the Telecommunication Standardization Bureau within

the framework of the budget as approved by the Council. The appointment of the technical and administrative personnel is made by the Secretary-General in agreement with the Director. The final decision on appointment or dismissal rests with the Secretary-General.

4. The Director shall provide technical support, as necessary, to the Telecommunication Development Sector within the framework of the Constitution and this Convention.

SECTION 7: TELECOMMUNICATION DEVELOPMENT SECTOR

ARTICLE 16—TELECOMMUNICATION DEVELOPMENT CONFERENCES

1. The world telecommunication development conference is authorized to adopt the working methods and procedures for the management of the Sector's activities in accordance with No. 145A of the Constitution.

1bis. In accordance with No. 118 of the Constitution, the duties of the telecommunication development conferences shall be as follows:

(a) world telecommunication development conferences shall establish work programmes and guidelines for defining telecommunication development questions and priorities and shall provide direction and guidance for the work programme of the Telecommunication Development Sector. They may set up study groups, as necessary;

(abis) decide on the need to maintain, terminate or establish other groups and appoint their chairmen and vice-chairmen;

(ater) establish the terms of reference for the groups referred to in No. 209A above; such groups shall not adopt questions or recommendations.

(b) regional telecommunication development conferences shall consider questions and priorities relating to telecommunication development, taking into account the needs and characteristics of the region concerned, and may also submit recommendations to world telecommunication development conferences;

(c) the telecommunication development conferences should fix the objectives and strategies for the balanced worldwide and regional development of telecommunications, giving particular consideration to the expansion and modernization of the networks and services of the developing countries as well as the mobilization of the resources required for this purpose. They shall serve as a forum for the study of policy, organizational, operational, regulatory, technical and financial questions and related aspects, including the identification and implementation of new sources of funding;

(d) world and regional telecommunication development conferences, within their respective sphere of competence, shall consider reports submitted to them and evaluate the activities of the Sector; they may also consider telecommunication development aspects related to the activities of the other Sectors of the Union.

2. The draft agenda of telecommunication development conferences shall be prepared by the Director of the Telecommunication Development Bureau and be submitted by the Secretary-General to the Council for approval with the concurrence of a majority of the Member States in the case of a world conference, or of a majority of the Member States belonging to the region concerned in the case of a regional conference, subject to the provisions of No. 47 of this Convention.

3. A telecommunication development conference may assign specific matters within its competence to the telecommunication development advisory group, indicating the recommended action on those matters.

ARTICLE 17—TELECOMMUNICATION DEVELOPMENT STUDY GROUPS

1. Telecommunication development study groups shall deal with specific telecommunication questions of general interest to developing countries, including the matters enumerated in No. 211 above. Such study groups shall be limited in number and created for a limited period of time, subject to the availability of resources, shall have specific terms of reference on questions and matters of priority to developing countries and shall be task-oriented.

2. Taking into account No. 119 of the Constitution, the Radiocommunication, Telecommunication Standardization and Telecommunication Development Sectors shall keep the matters under study under continuing review with a view to reaching agreement on the distribution of work, avoiding duplication of effort and improving coordination. The Sectors shall adopt procedures to conduct such reviews and reach such agreement in a timely and effective manner.

3. Each telecommunication development study group shall prepare for the world telecommunication development conference a report indicating the progress of work and any draft new or revised recommendations for consideration by the conference.

4. Telecommunication development study groups shall study questions and prepare draft recommendations to be adopted in accordance with the procedures set out in Nos. 246A to 247 of this Convention.

ARTICLE 17A—TELECOMMUNICATION DEVELOPMENT ADVISORY GROUP

1. The telecommunication development advisory group shall be open to representatives of administrations of Member States and representatives of Sector Members and to chairmen and vice-chairmen of study groups and other groups.

2. The telecommunication development advisory group shall:

(1) review priorities, programmes, operations, financial matters and strategies for activities in the Telecommunication Development Sector;

(1bis) review the implementation of the operational plan of the preceding period in order to identify areas in which the Bureau has not achieved or was not able to achieve the objectives laid down in that plan, and advise the Director on the necessary corrective measures.

(2) review progress in the implementation of the programme of work established under No. 209 of this Convention;

(3) provide guidelines for the work of study groups;

(4) recommend measures, inter alia, to foster cooperation and coordination with the Radiocommunication Sector, the Telecommunication Standardization Sector and the General Secretariat, as well as with other relevant development and financial institutions.

(5) adopt its own working procedures compatible with those adopted by the world telecommunication development conference.

(6) prepare a report for the Director of the Telecommunication Development Bureau indicating action in respect of the above items.

(6bis) prepare a report for the world telecommunication development conference on the matters assigned to it in accordance with No. 213A of this Convention and transmit it to the Director for submission to the conference.

3. Representatives of bilateral cooperation and development aid agencies and multilateral development institutions may be invited by the Director to participate in the meetings of the advisory group.

Article 18—Telecommunication Development Bureau

1. The Director of the Telecommunication Development Bureau shall organize and coordinate the work of the Telecommunication Development Sector.

2. The Director shall, in particular:

(a) participate as of right, but in an advisory capacity, in the deliberations of the telecommunication development conferences and of the telecommunication development study groups and other groups. The Director shall make all necessary preparations for conferences and meetings of the Telecommunication Development Sector in consultation with the General Secretariat in accordance with No. 94 of this Convention and, as appropriate, with the other Sectors of the Union, and with due regard for the directives of the Council in carrying out these preparations;

(b) process information received from administrations in application of the relevant resolutions and decisions of the Plenipotentiary Conference and telecommunication development conferences and prepare it, where appropriate, in a suitable form for publication;

(c) exchange with members data in machine-readable and other forms, prepare and, as necessary, keep up to date any documents and databases of the Telecommunication Development Sector, and arrange with the Secretary-General, as appropriate, for their publication in the working languages of the Union in accordance with No. 172 of the Constitution;

(d) assemble and prepare for publication, in cooperation with the General Secretariat and the other Sectors of the Union, both technical and administrative information that might be especially useful to developing countries in order to help them to improve their telecommunication networks. Their attention shall also be drawn to the possibilities offered by the international programmes under the auspices of the United Nations;

(e) submit to the world telecommunication development conference a report on the activities of the Sector since the last conference; the Director shall also submit to the Council and to the Member States and Sector Members such a report covering the two-year period since the last conference;

(f) prepare a cost-based budget estimate for the requirements of the Telecommunication Development Sector and transmit it to the Secretary-General for consideration by the Coordination Committee and inclusion in the Union's budget;

(g) prepare annually a rolling four-year operational plan that covers the subsequent year and the following three-year period, including financial implications of activities to be undertaken by the Bureau in support of the Sector as a whole; this four-year operational plan shall be reviewed by the telecommunication development advisory group in accordance with Article 17A of this Convention, and shall be reviewed and approved annually by the Council;

(h) provide the necessary support for the telecommunication development advisory group, and report each year to the Member States and Sector Members and to the Council on the results of its work.

3. The Director shall work collegially with the other elected officials in order to ensure that the Union's catalytic role in stimulating telecommunication development is strengthened and shall make the necessary arrangements with the Director of the Bureau concerned for initiating suitable action, including the convening of information meetings on the activities of the Sector concerned.

4. At the request of the Member States concerned, the Director, with the assistance of the Directors of the other Bureau and, where appropriate, the Secretary-General, shall study and offer advice concerning their national telecommunication problems; where a comparison of technical alternatives is involved, economic factors may be taken into consideration.

5. The Director shall choose the technical and administrative personnel of the Telecommunication Development Bureau within the framework of the budget as approved by the Council. The appointment of the personnel is made by the Secretary-General in agreement with the Director. The final decision for appointment or dismissal rests with the Secretary-General.

(SUP)

SECTION 8

ARTICLE 19—PARTICIPATION OF ENTITIES AND ORGANIZATIONS OTHER THAN ADMINISTRATIONS IN THE UNION'S ACTIVITIES

1. The Secretary-General and the Directors of the Bureau shall encourage the enhanced participation in the activities of the Union of the following entities and organizations:

(a) recognized operating agencies, scientific or industrial organizations and financial or development institutions which are approved by the Member State concerned;

(b) other entities dealing with telecommunication matters which are approved by the Member State concerned;

(c) regional and other international telecommunication, standardization, financial or development organizations.

2. The Directors of the Bureau shall maintain close working relations with those entities and organizations which are authorized to participate in the activities of one or more of the Sectors of the Union.

3. Any request from an entity listed in No. 229 above to participate in the work of a Sector, in accordance with the relevant provisions of the Constitution and this Convention, approved by the Member State concerned shall be forwarded by the latter to the Secretary-General.

4. Any request from an entity referred to in No. 230 above submitted by the Member State concerned shall be handled in conformity with a procedure established by the Council. Such a request shall be reviewed by the Council with respect to its conformity with the above procedure.

4bis. Alternatively, a request from an entity listed in No. 229 or 230 above to become a Sector Member may be sent direct to the Secretary-General. Those Member States authorizing such entities to send a request directly to the Secretary-General shall inform the latter accordingly. Entities whose Member State has not provided such notice to the Secretary-General shall not have the option of direct application. The Secretary-General shall regularly update and publish a list of those Member States that have authorized entities under their jurisdiction or sovereignty to apply directly.

4ter. Upon receipt, directly from an entity, of a request under No. 234A above, the Secretary-General shall, on the basis of criteria defined by the Council, ensure that the function and purposes of the candidate are in conformity with the purposes of the Union. The Secretary-General shall then, without delay, inform the applicant's Member State inviting approval of the application. If the Secretary-General receives no objection from the Member State within four months, a reminder telegram shall be sent. If the Secretary-General receives no objection within four months after the date of dispatch of the reminder telegram, the application shall be regarded as approved. If an objection is received from the Member State by the Secretary-General, the applicant shall be invited by the Secretary-General to contact the Member State concerned.

quater. When authorizing direct application, a Member State may notify the Secretary-General that it assigns authority to the Secretary-General to approve any application by an entity under its jurisdiction or sovereignty.

5. Any request from any entity or organization listed in No. 231 above (other than those referred to in Nos. 260 and 261 of this Convention) to participate in the work of a Sector shall be sent to the Secretary-General and acted upon in accordance with procedures established by the Council.

6. Any request from an organization referred to in Nos. 260 to 262 of this Convention to participate in the work of a Sector shall

be sent to the Secretary-General, and the organization concerned shall be included in the lists referred to in No. 237 below.

7. The Secretary-General shall compile and maintain lists of all entities and organizations referred to in Nos. 229 to 231 and Nos. 260 to 262 of this Convention that are authorized to participate in the work of each Sector and shall, at appropriate intervals, publish and distribute these lists to all Member States and Sector Members concerned and to the Director of the Bureau concerned. That Director shall advise such entities and organizations of the action taken on their requests, and shall inform the relevant Member States.

8. The conditions of participation in the Sectors by entities and organizations contained in the lists referred to in No. 237 above are specified in this Article, in Article 33 and in other relevant provisions of this Convention. The provisions of Nos. 25 to 28 of the Constitution do not apply to them.

9. A Sector Member may act on behalf of the Member State which has approved it, provided that the Member State informs the Director of the Bureau concerned that it is authorized to do so.

10. Any Sector Member has the right to denounce such participation by notifying the Secretary-General. Such participation may also be denounced, where appropriate, by the Member State concerned or, in case of the Sector Member approved pursuant to No. 234C above, in accordance with criteria and procedures determined by the Council. Such denunciation shall take effect at the end of one year from the date when notification is received by the Secretary-General.

11. The Secretary-General shall delete from the list of entities and organizations any entity or organization that is no longer authorized to participate in the work of a Sector, in accordance with criteria and procedures determined by the Council.

12. The assembly or conference of a Sector may decide to admit entities or organizations to participate as Associates in the work of a given study group or subgroups thereof following the principles set out below:

(1) An entity or organization referred to in Nos. 229 to 231 above may apply to participate in the work of a given study group as an Associate.

(2) In cases where a Sector has decided to admit Associates, the Secretary-General shall apply to the applicants the relevant provisions of this Article, taking account of the size of the entity or organization and any other relevant criteria.

(3) Associates admitted to participate in a given study group are not entered in the list referred to in No. 237 above.

(4) The conditions governing participation in the work of a study group are specified in Nos. 248B and 483A of this Convention.

ARTICLE 20—CONDUCT OF BUSINESS OF STUDY GROUPS

1. The radiocommunication assembly, the world telecommunication standardization assembly and the world telecommunication development conference shall appoint the chairman and one vice-chairman or more for each study group. In appointing chairmen and vice-chairmen, particular consideration shall be given to the

requirements of competence and equitable geographical distribution, and to the need to promote more efficient participation by the developing countries.

2. If the workload of any study group requires, the assembly or conference shall appoint such additional vice-chairmen as it deems necessary.

3. If, in the interval between two assemblies or conferences of the Sector concerned, a study group Chairman is unable to carry out his duties and only one Vice-Chairman has been appointed, then that Vice-Chairman shall take the Chairman's place. In the case of a study group for which more than one Vice-Chairman has been appointed, the study group at its next meeting shall elect a new Chairman from among those Vice-Chairmen and, if necessary, a new Vice-Chairman from among the members of the study group. It shall likewise elect a new Vice-Chairman if one of the Vice-Chairmen is unable to carry out his duties during that period.

4. Study groups shall conduct their work as far as possible by correspondence, using modern means of communication.

5. The Director of the Bureau of each Sector, on the basis of the decisions of the competent conference or assembly, after consultation with the Secretary-General and coordination as required by the Constitution and Convention, shall draw up the general plan of study group meetings.

5bis. (1) Member States and Sector Members shall adopt questions to be studied in accordance with procedures established by the relevant conference or assembly, as appropriate, including the indication whether or not a resulting recommendation shall be the subject of a formal consultation of Member States.

(2) Recommendations resulting from the study of the above questions are adopted by a study group in accordance with procedures established by the relevant conference or assembly, as appropriate. Those recommendations which do not require formal consultation of Member States for their approval shall be considered as approved.

(3) A recommendation requiring formal consultation of Member States shall be either treated in accordance with No. 247 below or transmitted to the relevant conference or assembly, as appropriate.

(4) Nos. 246A and 246B above shall not be used for questions and recommendations having policy or regulatory implications such as:

(a) questions and recommendations approved by the Radiocommunication Sector relevant to the work of radiocommunication conferences, and other categories of questions and recommendations that may be decided by the radiocommunication assembly;

(b) questions and recommendations approved by the Telecommunication Standardization Sector which relate to tariff and accounting issues, and relevant numbering and addressing plans;

(c) questions and recommendations approved by the Telecommunication Development Sector which relate to regulatory, policy and financial issues;

(d) questions and recommendations where there is any doubt about their scope.

6. Study groups may initiate action for obtaining approval from Member States for recommendations completed between two assemblies or conferences. The procedures to be applied for obtaining such approval shall be those approved by the competent assembly or conference, as appropriate.

6bis. Recommendations approved in application of Nos. 246B or 247 above shall have the same status as ones approved by the conference or assembly itself.

7. Where necessary, joint working parties may be established for the study of questions requiring the participation of experts from several study groups.

7bis. Following a procedure developed by the Sector concerned, the Director of a Bureau may, in consultation with the chairman of the study group concerned, invite an organization which does not participate in the Sector to send representatives to take part in the study of a specific matter in the study group concerned or its subordinate groups.

7ter. An Associate, as referred to in No. 241A of this Convention, will be permitted to participate in the work of the selected study group without taking part in any decision-making or liaison activity of that study group.

8. The Director of the relevant Bureau shall send the final reports of the study groups to the administrations, organizations and entities participating in the Sector. Such reports shall include a list of the recommendations approved in conformity with No. 247 above. These reports shall be sent as soon as possible and, in any event, in time for them to be received at least one month before the date of the next session of the conference concerned.

ARTICLE 21—RECOMMENDATIONS FROM ONE CONFERENCE TO ANOTHER

1. Any conference may submit to another conference of the Union recommendations within its field of competence.

2. Such recommendations shall be sent to the Secretary-General in good time for assembly, coordination and communication, as laid down in No. 320 of this Convention.

ARTICLE 22—RELATIONS BETWEEN SECTORS AND WITH INTERNATIONAL ORGANIZATIONS

1. The Directors of the Bureau may agree, after appropriate consultation and coordination as required by the Constitution, the Convention and the decisions of the competent conferences or assemblies, to organize joint meetings of study groups of two or three Sectors, in order to study and prepare draft recommendations on questions of common interest. Such draft recommendations shall be submitted to the competent conferences or assemblies of the Sectors concerned.

2. Conferences or meetings of a Sector may be attended in an advisory capacity by the Secretary-General, the Deputy Secretary-General, the Directors of the Bureau of the other Sectors, or their representatives, and members of the Radio Regulations Board. If necessary, they may invite, in an advisory capacity, representatives

of the General Secretariat or of any other Sector which has not considered it necessary to be represented.

3. When a Sector is invited to participate in a meeting of an international organization, its Director is authorized to make arrangements for its representation in an advisory capacity, taking into account the provisions of No. 107 of this Convention.

CHAPTER II—Specific Provisions Regarding Conferences and Assemblies

Article 23—Invitation and Admission to Plenipotentiary Conferences when There is an Inviting Government

1. The following shall be admitted to plenipotentiary conferences:

(a) delegations;

(b) the elected officials, in an advisory capacity;

(c) the Radio Regulations Board, in accordance with No. 141A of this Convention, in an advisory capacity;

(d) observers of the following organizations, agencies and entities:

(i) the United Nations;

(ii) regional telecommunication organizations mentioned in Article 43 of the Constitution;

(iii) intergovernmental organizations operating satellite systems;

(iv) the specialized agencies of the United Nations and the International Atomic Energy Agency;

(e) observers from the Sector Members referred to in Nos. 229 and 231 of this Convention.

(2) The General Secretariat and the three Bureau of the Union shall be represented at the conference in an advisory capacity.

Article 24—Invitation and Admission to Radiocommunication Conferences when There is an Inviting Government

1. The following shall be admitted to radiocommunication conferences:

(a) delegations;

(b) observers of organizations and agencies referred to in Nos. 269A to 269D of this Convention;

(c) observers of other international organizations invited by the government and admitted by the conference in accordance with the relevant provisions of Chapter I of the General Rules of conferences, assemblies and meetings of the Union;

(d) observers representing Sector Members of the Radiocommunication Sector duly authorized by the Member State concerned;

(e) observers of Member States participating in a non-voting capacity in a regional radiocommunication conference of a region other than that to which the said Member States belong;

(f) in an advisory capacity, the elected officials, when the conference is discussing matters coming within their competence, and the members of the Radio Regulations Board.

ARTICLE 25—INVITATION AND ADMISSION TO RADIOCOMMUNICATION ASSEMBLIES, WORLD TELECOMMUNICATION STANDARDIZATION ASSEMBLIES AND TELECOMMUNICATION DEVELOPMENT CONFERENCES WHEN THERE IS AN INVITING GOVERNMENT

1. The following shall be admitted to the assembly or conference:

(a) delegations;

(b) observers of the following organizations and agencies:

(i) regional telecommunication organizations mentioned in Article 43 of the Constitution;

(ii) intergovernmental organizations operating satellite systems;

(iii) any other regional organization or other international organization dealing with matters of interest to the assembly or conference;

(iv) the United Nations;

(v) the specialized agencies of the United Nations and the International Atomic Energy Agency;

(c) representatives of Sector Members concerned.

2. The elected officials, the General Secretariat and the Bureau of the Union, as appropriate, shall be represented at the assembly or conference in an advisory capacity. Two members of the Radio Regulations Board, designated by the Board, shall participate in radiocommunication assemblies in an advisory capacity.

SUP

ARTICLE 31—CREDENTIALS FOR CONFERENCES

1. The delegation sent by a Member State to a plenipotentiary conference, a radiocommunication conference or a world conference on international telecommunications shall be duly accredited in accordance with Nos. 325 to 331 below.

2. (1) Accreditation of delegations to Plenipotentiary Conferences shall be by means of instruments signed by the Head of State, by the Head of Government or by the Minister for Foreign Affairs.

(2) Accreditation of delegations to the other conferences referred to in No. 324 above shall be by means of instruments signed by the Head of State, by the Head of Government, by the Minister for Foreign Affairs or by the Minister responsible for questions dealt with during the conference.

(3) Subject to confirmation prior to the signature of the Final Acts, by one of the authorities mentioned in Nos. 325 or 326 above, a delegation may be provisionally accredited by the head of the diplomatic mission of the Member State concerned to the host government. In the case of a conference held in the Swiss Confederation, a delegation may also be provisionally accredited by the head of the permanent delegation of the Member State concerned to the United Nations Office at Geneva.

3. Credentials shall be accepted if they are signed by one of the competent authorities mentioned in Nos. 325 to 327 above, and fulfill one of the following criteria:

—they confer full powers on the delegation;

—they authorize the delegation to represent its government, without restrictions;

—they give the delegation, or certain members thereof, the right to sign the Final Acts.

4. (1) A delegation whose credentials are found to be in order by the Plenary Meeting shall be entitled to exercise the right to vote of the Member State concerned, subject to the provisions of Nos. 169 and 210 of the Constitution, and to sign the final acts.

(2) A delegation whose credentials are found not to be in order by the Plenary Meeting shall not be entitled to exercise the right to vote or to sign the Final Acts until the situation has been rectified.

5. Credentials shall be deposited with the secretariat of the conference as early as possible; to that end, Member States should send their credentials, prior to the opening date of the conference, to the Secretary-General who shall transmit them to the secretariat of the conference as soon as the latter has been established. The committee referred to in No. 68 of the General Rules of conferences, assemblies and meetings of the Union shall be entrusted with the verification thereof and shall report on its conclusions to the Plenary Meeting within the time specified by the latter. Pending the decision of the Plenary Meeting thereon, any delegation shall be entitled to participate in the conference and to exercise the right to vote of the Member State concerned.

6. As a general rule, Member States should endeavour to send their own delegations to conferences of the Union. However, if a Member State is unable, for exceptional reasons, to send its own delegation, it may give the delegation of another Member State powers to vote and sign on its behalf. Such powers must be conveyed by means of an instrument signed by one of the authorities mentioned in Nos. 325 or 326 above.

7. A delegation with the right to vote may give to another delegation with the right to vote a mandate to exercise its vote at one or more meetings at which it is unable to be present. In such a case it shall, in good time, notify the Chairman of the conference in writing.

8. A delegation may not exercise more than one proxy vote.

9. Credentials and transfers of powers sent by telegram shall not be accepted. Nevertheless, replies sent by telegram to requests by the Chairman or the secretariat of the conference for clarification of credentials shall be accepted.

10. A Member State or an authorized entity or organization intending to send a delegation or representatives to a telecommunication standardization assembly, a telecommunication development conference or a radiocommunication assembly shall so inform the Director of the Bureau of the Sector concerned, indicating the names and functions of the members of the delegation or of the representatives.

Article 32—Rules of Procedure of Conferences and Other Meetings

1. The General Rules of conferences, assemblies and meetings of the Union are adopted by the Plenipotentiary Conference. The provisions governing the procedure for amending those Rules and the

entry into force of amendments are contained in the Rules themselves.

2. The General Rules of conferences, assemblies and meetings of the Union shall apply without prejudice to the amendment provisions contained in Article 55 of the Constitution and in Article 42 of this Convention.

ARTICLE 32A—RIGHT TO VOTE

1. At all meetings of a conference, assembly or other meeting, the delegation of a Member State duly accredited by that Member State to take part in the work of the conference, assembly or other meeting shall be entitled to one vote in accordance with Article 3 of the Constitution.

2. The delegation of a Member State shall exercise the right to vote under the conditions described in Article 31 of this Convention.

3. When a Member State is not represented by an administration at a radiocommunication assembly, a world telecommunication standardization assembly or a telecommunication development conference, the representatives of the recognized operating agencies of the Member State concerned shall, as a whole, and regardless of their number, be entitled to a single vote, subject to the provisions of No. 239 of this Convention. The provisions of Nos. 335 to 338 of this Convention concerning the transfer of powers shall apply to the above conferences and assemblies.

ARTICLE 32B—RESERVATIONS

1. As a general rule, any delegation whose views are not shared by the remaining delegations shall endeavour, as far as possible, to conform to the opinion of the majority.

2. Any Member State that, during a plenipotentiary conference, reserves its right to make reservations as specified in its declaration when signing the final acts, may make reservations regarding an amendment to the Constitution or to this Convention until such time as its instrument of ratification, acceptance or approval of or accession to the amendment has been deposited with the Secretary-General.

3. If any decision appears to a delegation to be such as to prevent its government from consenting to be bound by the revision of the Administrative Regulations, this delegation may make reservations, final or provisional, regarding that decision, at the end of the conference adopting that revision; any such reservations may be made by a delegation on behalf of a Member State which is not participating in the competent conference and which has given that delegation proxy powers to sign the final acts in accordance with the provisions of Article 31 of this Convention.

4. A reservation made following a conference shall only be valid if the Member State which made it formally confirms it when notifying its consent to be bound by the amended or revised instrument adopted by the conference at the close of which it made the reservation in question.

(SUP)

CHAPTER III—DELETED

CHAPTER IV—OTHER PROVISIONS

ARTICLE 33—FINANCES

1. (1) The scale from which each Member State, subject to the provisions of No. 468A below, and Sector Member, subject to the provisions of No. 468B below, shall choose its class of contribution, in conformity with the relevant provisions of Article 28 of the Constitution, shall be as follows:

40 unit class 8 unit class
35 unit class 5 unit class
30 unit class 4 unit class
28 unit class 3 unit class
25 unit class 2 unit class
23 unit class 1 1/2 unit class
20 unit class 1 unit class
18 unit class 1/2 unit class
15 unit class 1/4 unit class
13 unit class 1/8 unit class
10 unit class 1/16 unit class

(1bis) Only Member States listed by the United Nations as least developed countries and those determined by the Council may select the 1/8 and 1/16 unit classes of contribution.

(1ter) Sector Members may not select a class of contribution lower than 1/2 unit, with the exception of Sector Members of the Telecommunication Development Sector, which may select the 1/4, 1/8 and 1/16 unit classes. However, the 1/16 unit class is reserved for Sector Members of developing countries as determined by the list established by the United Nations Development Programme (UNDP) to be reviewed by the ITU Council.

(2) In addition to the classes of contribution listed in No. 468 above, any Member State or Sector Member may choose a number of contributory units over 40.

(3) The Secretary-General shall communicate promptly to each Member State not represented at the Plenipotentiary Conference the decision of each Member State as to the class of contribution to be paid by it.

(SUP)

2. (1) Every new Member State and Sector Member shall, in respect of the year of its accession or admission, pay a contribution calculated as from the first day of the month of accession or admission, as the case may be.

(2) Should a Member State denounce the Constitution and this Convention or a Sector Member denounce its participation in a Sector, its contribution shall be paid up to the last day of the month in which such denunciation takes effect in accordance with No. 237 of the Constitution or No. 240 of this Convention, respectively.

3. The amounts due shall bear interest from the beginning of the fourth month of each financial year of the Union at 3% (three per cent) per annum during the following three months, and at 6% (six per cent) per annum from the beginning of the seventh month.

(SUP)

4. (1) The organizations referred to in Nos. 269A to 269E of this Convention and other organizations of an international character (unless they have been exempted by the Council, subject to reciprocity) and Sector Members which participate, in accordance with the provisions of this Convention, in a plenipotentiary conference, in a conference, assembly or meeting of a Sector of the Union, or in a world conference on international telecommunications, shall share in defraying the expenses of the conferences, assemblies and meetings in which they participate on the basis of the cost of these conferences and meetings and in accordance with the Financial Regulations. Nevertheless, Sector Members will not be charged separately for their attendance at a conference, assembly or meeting of their respective Sectors, except in the case of regional radiocommunication conferences.

(2) Any Sector Member appearing in the lists mentioned in No. 237 of this Convention shall share in defraying the expenses of the Sector in accordance with Nos. 480 and 480A below.

(SUP)

(5) The amount of the contribution per unit payable towards the expenses of each Sector concerned shall be set at 1/5 of the contributory unit of the Member States. These contributions shall be considered as Union income. They shall bear interest in accordance with the provisions of No. 474 above.

(5bis) When a Sector Member contributes to defraying the expenses of the Union under No. 159 of the Constitution, the Sector for which the contribution is made should be identified.

4bis. Associates as described in No. 241A of this Convention shall share in defraying the expenses of the Sector and the study group and subordinate groups in which they participate, as determined by the Council.

5. The Council shall determine criteria for the application of cost recovery for some products and services of the Union.

6. The Union shall maintain a reserve account in order to provide working capital to meet essential expenditures and to maintain sufficient cash reserves to avoid resorting to loans as far as possible. The amount of the reserve account shall be fixed annually by the Council on the basis of expected requirements. At the end of each biennial budgetary period all budget credits which have not been expended or encumbered will be placed in the reserve account. Other details of this account are described in the Financial Regulations.

7. (1) The Secretary-General may, in agreement with the Coordination Committee, accept voluntary contributions in cash or kind, provided that the conditions attached to such voluntary contributions are consistent, as appropriate, with the purposes and programmes of the Union and with the programmes adopted by a conference and in conformity with the Financial Regulations, which shall contain special provisions for the acceptance and use of such voluntary contributions.

(2) Such voluntary contributions shall be reported by the Secretary-General to the Council in the financial operating report as well as in a summary indicating for each case the origin, proposed use and action taken with respect to each voluntary contribution.

ARTICLE 34—FINANCIAL RESPONSIBILITIES OF CONFERENCES

1. Before adopting proposals or taking decisions with financial implications, the conferences of the Union shall take account of all the Union's budgetary provisions with a view to ensuring that they will not result in expenses beyond the credits which the Council is empowered to authorize.

2. No decision of a conference shall be put into effect if it will result in a direct or indirect increase in expenses beyond the credits that the Council is empowered to authorize.

ARTICLE 35—LANGUAGES

1. (1) Languages other than those mentioned in the relevant provisions of Article 29 of the Constitution may be used:

(a) if an application is made to the Secretary-General to provide for the use of an additional language or languages, oral or written, on a permanent or an ad hoc basis, provided that the additional cost so incurred shall be borne by those Member States which have made or supported the application;

(b) if, at conferences and meetings of the Union, after informing the Secretary-General or the Director of the Bureau concerned, any delegation itself makes arrangements at its own expense for oral translation from its own language into any one of the languages referred to in the relevant provision of Article 29 of the Constitution.

(2) In the case provided for in No. 491 above, the Secretary-General shall comply to the extent practicable with the application, having first obtained from the Member States concerned an undertaking that the cost incurred will be duly repaid by them to the Union.

(3) In the case provided for in No. 492 above, the delegation concerned may, furthermore, if it wishes, arrange at its own expense for oral translation into its own language from one of the languages referred to in the relevant provision of Article 29 of the Constitution.

2. Any of the documents referred to in the relevant provisions of Article 29 of the Constitution may be published in languages other than those specified therein, provided that the Member States requesting such publication undertake to defray the whole of the cost of translation and publication involved.

CHAPTER V—VARIOUS PROVISIONS RELATED TO THE OPERATION OF TELECOMMUNICATION SERVICES

ARTICLE 36—CHARGES AND FREE SERVICES

The provisions regarding charges for telecommunications and the various cases in which free services are accorded are set forth in the Administrative Regulations.

ARTICLE 37—RENDERING AND SETTLEMENT OF ACCOUNTS

1. The settlement of international accounts shall be regarded as current transactions and shall be effected in accordance with the current international obligations of the Member States and Sector

Members concerned in those cases where their governments have concluded arrangements on this subject. Where no such arrangements have been concluded, and in the absence of special agreements made under Article 42 of the Constitution, these settlements shall be effected in accordance with the Administrative Regulations.

2. Administrations of Member States and Sector Members which operate international telecommunication services shall come to an agreement with regard to the amount of their debits and credits.

3. The statement of accounts with respect to debits and credits referred to in No. 498 above shall be drawn up in accordance with the provisions of the Administrative Regulations, unless special arrangements have been concluded between the parties concerned.

Article 38—Monetary Unit

In the absence of special arrangements concluded between Member States, the monetary unit to be used in the composition of accounting rates for international telecommunication services and in the establishment of international accounts shall be:

—either the monetary unit of the International Monetary Fund
—or the gold franc,

both as defined in the Administrative Regulations. The provisions for application are contained in Appendix 1 to the International Telecommunication Regulations.

Article 39—Intercommunication

1. Stations performing radiocommunication in the mobile service shall be bound, within the limits of their normal employment, to exchange radiocommunications reciprocally without distinction as to the radio system adopted by them.

2. Nevertheless, in order not to impede scientific progress, the provisions of No. 501 above shall not prevent the use of a radio system incapable of communicating with other systems, provided that such incapacity is due to the specific nature of such system and is not the result of devices adopted solely with the object of preventing intercommunication.

3. Notwithstanding the provisions of No. 501 above, a station may be assigned to a restricted international service of telecommunication, determined by the purpose of such service, or by other circumstances independent of the system used.

Article 40—Secret Language

1. Government telegrams and service telegrams may be expressed in secret language in all relations.

2. Private telegrams in secret language may be admitted between all Member States with the exception of those which have previously notified, through the Secretary-General, that they do not admit this language for that category of correspondence.

3. Member States which do not admit private telegrams in secret language originating in or destined for their own territory must let them pass in transit, except in the case of suspension of service provided for in Article 35 of the Constitution.

CHAPTER VI—ARBITRATION AND AMENDMENT

ARTICLE 41—ARBITRATION: PROCEDURE (SEE ARTICLE 56 OF THE CONSTITUTION)

1. The party which appeals to arbitration shall initiate the arbitration procedure by transmitting to the other party to the dispute a notice of the submission of the dispute to arbitration.

2. The parties shall decide by agreement whether the arbitration is to be entrusted to individuals, administrations or governments. If within one month after notice of submission of the dispute to arbitration, the parties have been unable to agree upon this point, the arbitration shall be entrusted to governments.

3. If arbitration is to be entrusted to individuals, the arbitrators must neither be nationals of a State party to the dispute, nor have their domicile in the States parties to the dispute, nor be employed in their service.

4. If arbitration is to be entrusted to governments, or to administrations thereof, these must be chosen from among the Member States which are not involved in the dispute, but which are parties to the agreement, the application of which caused the dispute.

5. Within three months from the date of receipt of the notification of the submission of the dispute to arbitration, each of the two parties to the dispute shall appoint an arbitrator.

6. If more than two parties are involved in the dispute, an arbitrator shall be appointed in accordance with the procedure set forth in Nos. 510 and 511 above, by each of the two groups of parties having a common position in the dispute.

7. The two arbitrators thus appointed shall choose a third arbitrator who, if the first two arbitrators are individuals and not governments or administrations, must fulfill the conditions indicated in No. 509 above, and in addition must not be of the same nationality as either of the other two arbitrators. Failing an agreement between the two arbitrators as to the choice of a third arbitrator, each of these two arbitrators shall nominate a third arbitrator who is in no way concerned in the dispute. The Secretary-General shall then draw lots in order to select the third arbitrator.

8. The parties to the dispute may agree to have their dispute settled by a single arbitrator appointed by agreement; or alternatively, each party may nominate an arbitrator, and request the Secretary-General to draw lots to decide which of the persons so nominated is to act as the single arbitrator.

9. The arbitrator or arbitrators shall be free to decide upon the venue and the rules of procedure to be applied to the arbitration.

10. The decision of the single arbitrator shall be final and binding upon the parties to the dispute. If the arbitration is entrusted to more than one arbitrator, the decision made by the majority vote of the arbitrators shall be final and binding upon the parties.

11. Each party shall bear the expense it has incurred in the investigation and presentation of the arbitration. The costs of arbitration other than those incurred by the parties themselves shall be divided equally between the parties to the dispute.

12. The Union shall furnish all information relating to the dispute which the arbitrator or arbitrators may need. If the parties to

the dispute so agree, the decision of the arbitrator or arbitrators shall be communicated to the Secretary-General for future reference purposes.

ARTICLE 42—PROVISIONS FOR AMENDING THIS CONVENTION

1. Any Member State may propose any amendment to this Convention. Any such proposal shall, in order to ensure its timely transmission to, and consideration by, all the Member States, reach the Secretary-General not later than eight months prior to the opening date fixed for the Plenipotentiary Conference. The Secretary-General shall, as soon as possible, but not later than six months prior to the latter date, forward any such proposal to all the Member States.

2. Any proposed modification to any amendment submitted in accordance with No. 519 above may, however, be submitted at any time by a Member State or by its delegation at the Plenipotentiary Conference.

3. The quorum required at any Plenary Meeting of the Plenipotentiary Conference for consideration of any proposal for amending this Convention or modification thereto shall consist of more than one half of the delegations accredited to the Plenipotentiary Conference.

4. To be adopted, any proposed modification to a proposed amendment as well as the proposal as a whole, whether or not modified, shall be approved, at a Plenary Meeting, by more than half of the delegations accredited to the Plenipotentiary Conference which have the right to vote.

5. Unless specified otherwise in the preceding paragraphs of this Article, which shall prevail, the General Rules of conferences, assemblies and meetings of the Union shall apply.

6. Any amendments to this Convention adopted by a plenipotentiary conference shall, as a whole and in the form of one single amending instrument, enter into force at a date fixed by the conference between Member States having deposited before that date their instrument of ratification, acceptance or approval of, or accession to, both this Convention and the amending instrument. Ratification, acceptance or approval of, or accession to, only a part of such an amending instrument shall be excluded.

7. Notwithstanding No. 524 above, the Plenipotentiary Conference may decide that an amendment to this Convention is necessary for the proper implementation of an amendment to the Constitution. In that case, the amendment to this Convention shall not enter into force prior to the entry into force of the amendment to the Constitution.

8. The Secretary-General shall notify all Member States of the deposit of each instrument of ratification, acceptance, approval or accession.

9. After entry into force of any such amending instrument, ratification, acceptance, approval or accession in accordance with Articles 52 and 53 of the Constitution shall apply to this Convention as amended.

10. After the entry into force of any such amending instrument, the Secretary-General shall register it with the Secretariat of the

United Nations, in accordance with the provisions of Article 102 of the Charter of the United Nations. No. 241 of the Constitution shall also apply to any such amending instrument.

ANNEX—DEFINITION OF CERTAIN TERMS USED IN THIS CONVENTION AND THE ADMINISTRATIVE REGULATIONS OF THE INTERNATIONAL TELECOMMUNICATION UNION

For the purpose of the above instruments of the Union, the following terms shall have the meanings defined below:

Expert: A person sent by either:

(a) the Government or the administration of his country, or

(b) an entity or an organization authorized in accordance with Article 19 of this Convention, or

(c) an international organization

to participate in tasks of the Union relevant to his area of professional competence.

Observer: A person sent by:

—the United Nations, a specialized agency of the United Nations, the International Atomic Energy Agency, a regional telecommunication organization, or an intergovernmental organization operating satellite systems, to participate, in an advisory capacity, in a plenipotentiary conference, a conference or a meeting of a Sector,

—an international organization to participate, in an advisory capacity, in a conference or a meeting of a Sector,

—the government of a Member State to participate, in a non-voting capacity, in a regional conference, or

—a Sector Member referred to in Nos. 229 or 231 of the Convention or an organization of an international character representing such Sector Members,

in accordance with the relevant provisions of this Convention.

Mobile Service: A radiocommunication service between mobile and land stations, or between mobile stations.

Scientific or Industrial Organization: Any organization, other than a governmental establishment or agency, which is engaged in the study of telecommunication problems or in the design or manufacture of equipment intended for telecommunication services.

Radiocommunication: Telecommunication by means of radio waves.

Note 1: Radio waves are electromagnetic waves of frequencies arbitrarily lower than 3 000 GHz, propagated in space without artificial guide.

Note 2: For the requirements of Nos. 149 to 154 of this Convention, the term "radiocommunication" also includes telecommunications using electromagnetic waves of frequencies above 3 000 GHz, propagated in space without artificial guide.

Service Telecommunication: A telecommunication that relates to public international telecommunications and that is exchanged among the following:

—administrations,

—recognized operating agencies, and

—the Chairman of the Council, the Secretary-General, the Deputy Secretary-General, the Directors of the Bureau, the members of the Radio Regulations Board, and other representatives or authorized officials of the Union, including those working on official matters outside the seat of the Union.

5. World Intellectual Property Organization Copyright Treaty[1]

Done at Geneva, December 20, 1996; Advise and consent of the Senate provided, October 21, 1998; Entered into force, March 6, 2002

PREAMBLE

The Contracting Parties,

DESIRING to develop and maintain the protection of the rights of authors in their literary and artistic works in a manner as effective and uniform as possible,

RECOGNIZING the need to introduce new international rules and clarify the interpretation of certain existing rules in order to provide adequate solutions to the questions raised by new economic, social, cultural and technological developments,

RECOGNIZING the profound impact of the development and convergence of information and communication technologies on the creation and use of literary and artistic works,

EMPHASIZING the outstanding significance of copyright protection as an incentive for literary and artistic creation,

RECOGNIZING the need to maintain a balance between the rights of authors and the larger public interest, particularly education, research and access to information, as reflected in the Berne Convention,

HAVE AGREED AS FOLLOWS:

ARTICLE 1—RELATION TO THE BERNE CONVENTION

(1) This Treaty is a special agreement within the meaning of Article 20 of the Berne Convention for the Protection of Literary and Artistic Works, as regards Contracting Parties that are countries of the Union established by that Convention. This Treaty shall not have any connection with treaties other than the Berne Convention, nor shall it prejudice any rights and obligations under any other treaties.

(2) Nothing in this Treaty shall derogate from existing obligations that Contracting Parties have to each other under the Berne Convention for the Protection of Literary and Artistic Works.

(3) Hereinafter, "Berne Convention" shall refer to the Paris Act of July 24, 1971 of the Berne Convention for the Protection of Literary and Artistic Works.

[1] For states that are parties to the Treaty, see Department of State publication, *Treaties in Force.*

(4)[2] Contracting Parties shall comply with Articles 1 to 21 and the Appendix of the Berne Convention.

Article 2—Scope of Copyright Protection

Copyright protection extends to expressions and not to ideas, procedures, methods of operation or mathematical concepts as such.

Article 3—Application of Articles 2 to 6 of the Berne Convention[3]

Contracting Parties shall apply mutatis mutandis the provisions of Articles 2 to 6 of the Berne Convention in respect of the protection provided for in this Treaty.

Article 4—Computer Programs[4]

Computer programs are protected as literary works within the meaning of Article 2 of the Berne Convention. Such protection applies to computer programs, whatever may be the mode or form of their expression.

Article 5—Compilations of Data (Databases)[5]

Compilations of data or other material, in any form, which by reason of the selection or arrangement of their contents constitute intellectual creations, are protected as such. This protection does not extend to the data or the material itself and is without prejudice to any copyright subsisting in the data or material contained in the compilation.

Article 6—Right of Distribution[6]

(1) Authors of literary and artistic works shall enjoy the exclusive right of authorizing the making available to the public of the

[2] Agreed statements concerning Article 1(4): The reproduction right, as set out in Article 9 of the Berne Convention, and the exceptions permitted thereunder, fully apply in the digital environment, in particular to the use of works in digital form. It is understood that the storage of a protected work in digital form in an electronic medium constitutes a reproduction within the meaning of Article 9 of the Berne Convention.

[3] Agreed statements concerning Article 3: It is understood that in applying Article 3 of this Treaty, the expression "country of the Union" in Articles 2 to 6 of the Berne Convention will be read as if it were a reference to a Contracting Party to this Treaty, in the application of those Berne Articles in respect of protection provided for in this Treaty. It is also understood that the expression "country outside the Union" in those Articles in the Berne Convention will, in the same circumstances, be read as if it were a reference to a country that is not a Contracting Party to this Treaty, and that "this Convention" in Articles 2(8), 2bis(2), 3, 4 and 5 of the Berne Convention will be read as if it were a reference to the Berne Convention and this Treaty. Finally, it is understood that a reference in Articles 3 to 6 of the Berne Convention to a "national of one of the countries of the Union" will, when these Articles are applied to this Treaty, mean, in regard to an intergovernmental organization that is a Contracting Party to this Treaty, a national of one of the countries that is member of that organization.

[4] Agreed statements concerning Article 4: The scope of protection for computer programs under Article 4 of this Treaty, read with Article 2, is consistent with Article 2 of the Berne Convention and on a par with the relevant provisions of the TRIPS Agreement.

[5] Agreed statements concerning Article 5: The scope of protection for compilations of data (databases) under Article 5 of this Treaty, read with Article 2, is consistent with Article 2 of the Berne Convention and on a par with the relevant provisions of the TRIPS Agreement.

[6] Agreed statements concerning Articles 6 and 7: As used in these Articles, the expressions "copies" and "original and copies," being subject to the right of distribution and the right of rental under the said Articles, refer exclusively to fixed copies that can be put into circulation as tangible objects.

Continued

original and copies of their works through sale or other transfer of ownership.

(2) Nothing in this Treaty shall affect the freedom of Contracting Parties to determine the conditions, if any, under which the exhaustion of the right in paragraph (1) applies after the first sale or other transfer of ownership of the original or a copy of the work with the authorization of the author.

ARTICLE 7—RIGHT OF RENTAL[6]

(1) Authors of

(i) computer programs;

(ii) cinematographic works; and

(iii) works embodied in phonograms, as determined in the national law of Contracting Parties,

shall enjoy the exclusive right of authorizing commercial rental to the public of the originals or copies of their works.

(2) Paragraph (1) shall not apply

(i) in the case of computer programs, where the program itself is not the essential object of the rental; and

(ii) in the case of cinematographic works, unless such commercial rental has led to widespread copying of such works materially impairing the exclusive right of reproduction.

(3) Notwithstanding the provisions of paragraph (1), a Contracting Party that, on April 15, 1994, had and continues to have in force a system of equitable remuneration of authors for the rental of copies of their works embodied in phonograms may maintain that system provided that the commercial rental of works embodied in phonograms is not giving rise to the material impairment of the exclusive right of reproduction of authors.

ARTICLE 8—RIGHT OF COMMUNICATION TO THE PUBLIC[7]

Without prejudice to the provisions of Articles 11(1)(ii), 11bis(1)(i) and (ii), 11ter(1)(ii), 14(1)(ii) and 14bis(1) of the Berne Convention, authors of literary and artistic works shall enjoy the exclusive right of authorizing any communication to the public of their works, by wire or wireless means, including the making available to the public of their works in such a way that members of the public may access these works from a place and at a time individually chosen by them.

ARTICLE 9—DURATION OF THE PROTECTION OF PHOTOGRAPHIC WORKS

In respect of photographic works, the Contracting Parties shall not apply the provisions of Article 7(4) of the Berne Convention.

As used in these Articles, the expressions "copies" and "original and copies," being subject to the right of distribution and the right of rental under the said Articles, refer exclusively to fixed copies that can be put into circulation as tangible objects.

It is understood that the obligation under Article 7(1) does not require a Contracting Party to provide an exclusive right of commercial rental to authors who, under that Contracting Party's law, are not granted rights in respect of phonograms. It is understood that this obligation is consistent with Article 14(4) of the TRIPS Agreement.

[7] Agreed statements concerning Article 8: It is understood that the mere provision of physical facilities for enabling or making a communication does not in itself amount to communication within the meaning of this Treaty or the Berne Convention. It is further understood that nothing in Article 8 precludes a Contracting Party from applying Article 11bis(2).

ARTICLE 10—LIMITATIONS AND EXCEPTIONS[8]

(1) Contracting Parties may, in their national legislation, provide for limitations of or exceptions to the rights granted to authors of literary and artistic works under this Treaty in certain special cases that do not conflict with a normal exploitation of the work and do not unreasonably prejudice the legitimate interests of the author.

(2) Contracting Parties shall, when applying the Berne Convention, confine any limitations of or exceptions to rights provided for therein to certain special cases that do not conflict with a normal exploitation of the work and do not unreasonably prejudice the legitimate interests of the author.

ARTICLE 11—OBLIGATIONS CONCERNING TECHNOLOGICAL MEASURES

Contracting Parties shall provide adequate legal protection and effective legal remedies against the circumvention of effective technological measures that are used by authors in connection with the exercise of their rights under this Treaty or the Berne Convention and that restrict acts, in respect of their works, which are not authorized by the authors concerned or permitted by law.

ARTICLE 12—OBLIGATIONS CONCERNING RIGHTS MANAGEMENT INFORMATION[9]

(1) Contracting Parties shall provide adequate and effective legal remedies against any person knowingly performing any of the following acts knowing, or with respect to civil remedies having reasonable grounds to know, that it will induce, enable, facilitate or conceal an infringement of any right covered by this Treaty or the Berne Convention:

(i) to remove or alter any electronic rights management information without authority;

(ii) to distribute, import for distribution, broadcast or communicate to the public, without authority, works or copies of works knowing that electronic rights management information has been removed or altered without authority.

(2) As used in this Article, "rights management information" means information which identifies the work, the author of the work, the owner of any right in the work, or information about the terms and conditions of use of the work, and any numbers or codes

[8] Agreed statements concerning Article 10: It is understood that the provisions of Article 10 permit Contracting Parties to carry forward and appropriately extend into the digital environment limitations and exceptions in their national laws which have been considered acceptable under the Berne Convention. Similarly, these provisions should be understood to permit Contracting Parties to devise new exceptions and limitations that are appropriate in the digital network environment.

It is also understood that Article 10(2) neither reduces nor extends the scope of applicability of the limitations and exceptions permitted by the Berne Convention.

[9] Agreed statements concerning Article 12: It is understood that the reference to "infringement of any right covered by this Treaty or the Berne Convention" includes both exclusive rights and rights of remuneration.

It is further understood that Contracting Parties will not rely on this Article to devise or implement rights management systems that would have the effect of imposing formalities which are not permitted under the Berne Convention or this Treaty, prohibiting the free movement of goods or impeding the enjoyment of rights under this Treaty.

that represent such information, when any of these items of information is attached to a copy of a work or appears in connection with the communication of a work to the public.

ARTICLE 13—APPLICATION IN TIME

Contracting Parties shall apply the provisions of Article 18 of the Berne Convention to all protection provided for in this Treaty.

ARTICLE 14—PROVISIONS ON ENFORCEMENT OF RIGHTS

(1) Contracting Parties undertake to adopt, in accordance with their legal systems, the measures necessary to ensure the application of this Treaty.

(2) Contracting Parties shall ensure that enforcement procedures are available under their law so as to permit effective action against any act of infringement of rights covered by this Treaty, including expeditious remedies to prevent infringements and remedies which constitute a deterrent to further infringements.

ARTICLE 15—ASSEMBLY

(1)(a) The Contracting Parties shall have an Assembly.

(b) Each Contracting Party shall be represented by one delegate who may be assisted by alternate delegates, advisors and experts.

(c) The expenses of each delegation shall be borne by the Contracting Party that has appointed the delegation. The Assembly may ask the World Intellectual Property Organization (hereinafter referred to as "WIPO") to grant financial assistance to facilitate the participation of delegations of Contracting Parties that are regarded as developing countries in conformity with the established practice of the General Assembly of the United Nations or that are countries in transition to a market economy.

(2)(a) The Assembly shall deal with matters concerning the maintenance and development of this Treaty and the application and operation of this Treaty.

(b) The Assembly shall perform the function allocated to it under Article 17(2) in respect of the admission of certain intergovernmental organizations to become party to this Treaty.

(c) The Assembly shall decide the convocation of any diplomatic conference for the revision of this Treaty and give the necessary instructions to the Director General of WIPO for the preparation of such diplomatic conference.

(3)(a) Each Contracting Party that is a State shall have one vote and shall vote only in its own name.

(b) Any Contracting Party that is an intergovernmental organization may participate in the vote, in place of its Member States, with a number of votes equal to the number of its Member States which are party to this Treaty. No such intergovernmental organization shall participate in the vote if any one of its Member States exercises its right to vote and vice versa.

(4) The Assembly shall meet in ordinary session once every two years upon convocation by the Director General of WIPO.

(5) The Assembly shall establish its own rules of procedure, including the convocation of extraordinary sessions, the requirements

of a quorum and, subject to the provisions of this Treaty, the required majority for various kinds of decisions.

Article 16—International Bureau

The International Bureau of WIPO shall perform the administrative tasks concerning the Treaty.

Article 17—Eligibility for Becoming Party to the Treaty

(1) Any Member State of WIPO may become party to this Treaty.

(2) The Assembly may decide to admit any intergovernmental organization to become party to this Treaty which declares that it is competent in respect of, and has its own legislation binding on all its Member States on, matters covered by this Treaty and that it has been duly authorized, in accordance with its internal procedures, to become party to this Treaty.

(3) The European Community, having made the declaration referred to in the preceding paragraph in the Diplomatic Conference that has adopted this Treaty, may become party to this Treaty.

Article 18—Rights and Obligations under the Treaty

Subject to any specific provisions to the contrary in this Treaty, each Contracting Party shall enjoy all of the rights and assume all of the obligations under this Treaty.

Article 19—Signature of the Treaty

This Treaty shall be open for signature until December 31, 1997, by any Member State of WIPO and by the European Community.

Article 20—Entry into Force of the Treaty

This Treaty shall enter into force three months after 30 instruments of ratification or accession by States have been deposited with the Director General of WIPO.

Article 21—Effective Date of Becoming Party to the Treaty

This Treaty shall bind:

(i) the 30 States referred to in Article 20, from the date on which this Treaty has entered into force;

(ii) each other State from the expiration of three months from the date on which the State has deposited its instrument with the Director General of WIPO;

(iii) the European Community, from the expiration of three months after the deposit of its instrument of ratification or accession if such instrument has been deposited after the entry into force of this Treaty according to Article 20, or, three months after the entry into force of this Treaty if such instrument has been deposited before the entry into force of this Treaty;

(iv) any other intergovernmental organization that is admitted to become party to this Treaty, from the expiration of three months after the deposit of its instrument of accession.

Article 22—No Reservations to the Treaty

No reservation to this Treaty shall be admitted.

Article 23—Denunciation of the Treaty

This Treaty may be denounced by any Contracting Party by notification addressed to the Director General of WIPO. Any denunciation shall take effect one year from the date on which the Director General of WIPO received the notification.

Article 24—Languages of the Treaty

(1) This Treaty is signed in a single original in English, Arabic, Chinese, French, Russian and Spanish languages, the versions in all these languages being equally authentic.

(2) An official text in any language other than those referred to in paragraph (1) shall be established by the Director General of WIPO on the request of an interested party, after consultation with all the interested parties. For the purposes of this paragraph, "interested party" means any Member State of WIPO whose official language, or one of whose official languages, is involved and the European Community, and any other intergovernmental organization that may become party to this Treaty, if one of its official languages is involved.

Article 25—Depositary

The Director General of WIPO is the depositary of this Treaty.

6. Trademark Law Treaty [1]

Done at Geneva, October 27, 1994; Entered into force, August 1, 1996; Ratification advised by the Senate, June 26, 1998; Entered into force for the United States, August 12, 2000

ARTICLE 1—ABBREVIATED EXPRESSIONS

For the purposes of this Treaty, unless expressly stated otherwise:

(i) "Office" means the agency entrusted by a Contracting Party with the registration of marks;

(ii) "registration" means the registration of a mark by an Office;

(iii) "application" means an application for registration;

(iv) references to a "person" shall be construed as references to both a natural person and a legal entity;

(v) "holder" means the person whom the register of marks shows as the holder of the registration;

(vi) "register of marks" means the collection of data maintained by an Office, which includes the contents of all registrations and all data recorded in respect of all registrations, irrespective of the medium in which such data are stored;

(vii) "Paris Convention" means the Paris Convention for the Protection of Industrial Property, signed at Paris on March 20, 1883, as revised and amended;

(viii) "Nice Classification" means the classification established by the Nice Agreement Concerning the International Classification of Goods and Services for the Purposes of the Registration of Marks, signed at Nice on June 15, 1957, as revised and amended;

(ix) "Contracting Party" means any State or intergovernmental organization party to this Treaty;

(x) references to an "instrument of ratification" shall be construed as including references to instruments of acceptance and approval;

(xi) "Organization" means the World Intellectual Property Organization;

(xii) "Director General" means the Director General of the Organization;

(xiii) "Regulations" means the Regulations under this Treaty that are referred to in Article 17.

ARTICLE 2—MARKS TO WHICH THE TREATY APPLIES

(1) *Nature of Marks*

[1] 2037 UNTS 35. For states that are parties to the Treaty, see Department of State publication, *Treaties in Force*.

(a) This Treaty shall apply to marks consisting of visible signs, provided that only those Contracting Parties which accept for registration three-dimensional marks shall be obliged to apply this Treaty to such marks.

(b) This Treaty shall not apply to hologram marks and to marks not consisting of visible signs, in particular, sound marks and olfactory marks.

(2) *Kinds of Marks*

(a) This Treaty shall apply to marks relating to goods (trademarks) or services (service marks) or both goods and services.

(b) This Treaty shall not apply to collective marks, certification marks and guarantee marks.

Article 3—Application

(1) *Indications or Elements Contained in or Accompanying an Application; Fee*

(a) Any Contracting Party may require that an application contain some or all of the following indications or elements:

(i) a request for registration;

(ii) the name and address of the applicant;

(iii) the name of a State of which the applicant is a national if he is the national of any State, the name of a State in which the applicant has his domicile, if any, and the name of a State in which the applicant has a real and effective industrial or commercial establishment, if any;

(iv) where the applicant is a legal entity, the legal nature of that legal entity and the State, and, where applicable, the territorial unit within that State, under the law of which the said legal entity has been organized;

(v) where the applicant has a representative, the name and address of that representative;

(vi) where an address for service is required under Article 4(2)(b), such address;

(vii) where the applicant wishes to take advantage of the priority of an earlier application, a declaration claiming the priority of that earlier application, together with indications and evidence in support of the declaration of priority that may be required pursuant to Article 4 of the Paris Convention;

(viii) where the applicant wishes to take advantage of any protection resulting from the display of goods and/or services in an exhibition, a declaration to that effect, together with indications in support of that declaration, as required by the law of the Contracting Party;

(ix) where the Office of the Contracting Party uses characters (letters and numbers) that it considers as being standard and where the applicant wishes that the mark be registered and published in standard characters, a statement to that effect;

(x) where the applicant wishes to claim color as a distinctive feature of the mark, a statement to that effect as well as the name or names of the color or colors claimed and an indication, in respect of each color, of the principal parts of the mark which are in that color;

(xi) where the mark is a three-dimensional mark, a statement to that effect;

(xii) one or more reproductions of the mark;

(xiii) a transliteration of the mark or of certain parts of the mark;

(xiv) a translation of the mark or of certain parts of the mark;

(xv) the names of the goods and/or services for which the registration is sought, grouped according to the classes of the Nice Classification, each group preceded by the number of the class of that Classification to which that group of goods or services belongs and presented in the order of the classes of the said Classification;

(xvi) a signature by the person specified in paragraph (4);

(xvii) a declaration of intention to use the mark, as required by the law of the Contracting Party.

(b) The applicant may file, instead of or in addition to the declaration of intention to use the mark referred to in subparagraph (a)(xvii), a declaration of actual use of the mark and evidence to that effect, as required by the law of the Contracting Party.

(c) Any Contracting Party may require that, in respect of the application, fees be paid to the Office.

(2) *Presentation.* As regards the requirements concerning the presentation of the application, no Contracting Party shall refuse the application,

(i) where the application is presented in writing on paper, if it is presented, subject to paragraph (3), on a form corresponding to the application Form provided for in the Regulations,

(ii) where the Contracting Party allows the transmittal of communications to the Office by telefacsimile and the application is so transmitted, if the paper copy resulting from such transmittal corresponds, subject to paragraph (3), to the application Form referred to in item (i).

(3) *Language.* Any Contracting Party may require that the application be in the language, or in one of the languages, admitted by the Office. Where the Office admits more than one language, the applicant may be required to comply with any other language requirement applicable with respect to the Office, provided that the application may not be required to be in more than one language.

(4) *Signature*

(a) The signature referred to in paragraph (1)(a)(xvi) may be the signature of the applicant or the signature of his representative.

(b) Notwithstanding subparagraph (a), any Contracting Party may require that the declarations referred to in paragraph (1)(a)(xvii) and (b) be signed by the applicant himself even if he has a representative.

(5) *Single Application for Goods and/or Services in Several Classes.* One and the same application may relate to several goods

and/or services, irrespective of whether they belong to one class or to several classes of the Nice Classification.

(6) *Actual Use.* Any Contracting Party may require that, where a declaration of intention to use has been filed under paragraph (1)(a)(xvii), the applicant furnish to the Office within a time limit fixed in its law, subject to the minimum time limit prescribed in the Regulations, evidence of the actual use of the mark, as required by the said law.

(7) *Prohibition of Other Requirements.* No Contracting Party may demand that requirements other than those referred to in paragraphs (1) to (4) and (6) be complied with in respect of the application. In particular, the following may not be required in respect of the application throughout its pendency:

(i) the furnishing of any certificate of, or extract from, a register of commerce;

(ii) an indication of the applicant's carrying on of an industrial or commercial activity, as well as the furnishing of evidence to that effect;

(iii) an indication of the applicant's carrying on of an activity corresponding to the goods and/or services listed in the application, as well as the furnishing of evidence to that effect;

(iv) the furnishing of evidence to the effect that the mark has been registered in the register of marks of another Contracting Party or of a State party to the Paris Convention which is not a Contracting Party, except where the applicant claims the application of Article 6quinquies of the Paris Convention.

(8) *Evidence.* Any Contracting Party may require that evidence be furnished to the Office in the course of the examination of the application where the Office may reasonably doubt the veracity of any indication or element contained in the application.

Article 4—Representation; Address for Service

(1) *Representatives Admitted to Practice.* Any Contracting Party may require that any person appointed as representative for the purposes of any procedure before the Office be a representative admitted to practice before the Office.

(2) *Mandatory Representation; Address for Service*

(a) Any Contracting Party may require that, for the purposes of any procedure before the Office, any person who has neither a domicile nor a real and effective industrial or commercial establishment on its territory be represented by a representative.

(b) Any Contracting Party may, to the extent that it does not require representation in accordance with subparagraph (a), require that, for the purposes of any procedure before the Office, any person who has neither a domicile nor a real and effective industrial or commercial establishment on its territory have an address for service on that territory.

(3) *Power of Attorney*

(a) Whenever a Contracting Party allows or requires an applicant, a holder or any other interested person to be represented by a representative before the Office, it may require that the representative be appointed in a separate communication (hereinafter referred to as "power of attorney") indicating the name of, and signed by, the applicant, the holder or the other person, as the case may be.

(b) The power of attorney may relate to one or more applications and/or registrations identified in the power of attorney or, subject to any exception indicated by the appointing person, to all existing and future applications and/or registrations of that person.

(c) The power of attorney may limit the powers of the representative to certain acts. Any Contracting Party may require that any power of attorney under which the representative has the right to withdraw an application or to surrender a registration contain an express indication to that effect.

(d) Where a communication is submitted to the Office by a person who refers to himself in the communication as a representative but where the Office is, at the time of the receipt of the communication, not in possession of the required power of attorney, the Contracting Party may require that the power of attorney be submitted to the Office within the time limit fixed by the Contracting Party, subject to the minimum time limit prescribed in the Regulations. Any Contracting Party may provide that, where the power of attorney has not been submitted to the Office within the time limit fixed by the Contracting Party, the communication by the said person shall have no effect.

(e) As regards the requirements concerning the presentation and contents of the power of attorney, no Contracting Party shall refuse the effects of the power of attorney,

(i) where the power of attorney is presented in writing on paper, if it is presented, subject to paragraph (4), on a form corresponding to the power of attorney Form provided for in the Regulations,

(ii) where the Contracting Party allows the transmittal of communications to the Office by telefacsimile and the power of attorney is so transmitted, if the paper copy resulting from such transmittal corresponds, subject to paragraph (4), to the power of attorney Form referred to in item (i).

(4) *Language.* Any Contracting Party may require that the power of attorney be in the language, or in one of the languages, admitted by the Office.

(5) *Reference to Power of Attorney.* Any Contracting Party may require that any communication made to the Office by a representative for the purposes of a procedure before the Office contain a reference to the power of attorney on the basis of which the representative acts.

(6) *Prohibition of Other Requirements.* No Contracting Party may demand that requirements other than those referred to in paragraphs (3) to (5) be complied with in respect of the matters dealt with in those paragraphs.

(7) *Evidence.* Any Contracting Party may require that evidence be furnished to the Office where the Office may reasonably doubt the veracity of any indication contained in any communication referred to in paragraphs (2) to (5).

Article 5—Filing Date

(1) *Permitted Requirements*

(a) Subject to subparagraph (b) and paragraph (2), a Contracting Party shall accord as the filing date of an application the date on which the Office received the following indications and elements in the language required under Article 3(3):

(i) an express or implicit indication that the registration of a mark is sought;

(ii) indications allowing the identity of the applicant to be established;

(iii) indications sufficient to contact the applicant or his representative, if any, by mail;

(iv) a sufficiently clear reproduction of the mark whose registration is sought;

(v) the list of the goods and/or services for which the registration is sought;

(vi) where Article 3(1)(a)(xvii) or (b) applies, the declaration referred to in Article 3(1)(a)(xvii) or the declaration and evidence referred to in Article 3(1)(b), respectively, as required by the law of the Contracting Party, those declarations being, if so required by the said law, signed by the applicant himself even if he has a representative.

(b) Any Contracting Party may accord as the filing date of the application the date on which the Office received only some, rather than all, of the indications and elements referred to in subparagraph (a) or received them in a language other than the language required under Article 3(3).

(2) *Permitted Additional Requirement*

(a) A Contracting Party may provide that no filing date shall be accorded until the required fees are paid.

(b) A Contracting Party may apply the requirement referred to in subparagraph (a) only if it applied such requirement at the time of becoming party to this Treaty.

(3) *Corrections and Time Limits.* The modalities of, and time limits for, corrections under paragraphs (1) and (2) shall be fixed in the Regulations.

(4) *Prohibition of Other Requirements.* No Contracting Party may demand that requirements other than those referred to in paragraphs (1) and (2) be complied with in respect of the filing date.

Article 6—Single Registration for Goods and/or Services in Several Classes

Where goods and/or services belonging to several classes of the Nice Classification have been included in one and the same application, such an application shall result in one and the same registration.

Article 7—Division of Application and Registration

(1) *Division of Application*

(a) Any application listing several goods and/or services (hereinafter referred to as "initial application") may,

(i) at least until the decision by the Office on the registration of the mark,

(ii) during any opposition proceedings against the decision of the Office to register the mark,

(iii) during any appeal proceedings against the decision on the registration of the mark, be divided by the applicant or at his request into two or more applications (hereinafter referred to as "divisional applications") by distributing among the latter the goods and/or services listed in the initial application. The divisional applications shall preserve the filing date of the initial application and the benefit of the right of priority, if any.

(b) Any Contracting Party shall, subject to subparagraph (a), be free to establish requirements for the division of an application, including the payment of fees.

(2) *Division of Registration.* Paragraph (1) shall apply, mutatis mutandis, with respect to a division of a registration. Such a division shall be permitted

(i) during any proceedings in which the validity of the registration is challenged before the Office by a third party,

(ii) during any appeal proceedings against a decision taken by the Office during the former proceedings, provided that a Contracting Party may exclude the possibility of the division of registrations if its law allows third parties to oppose the registration of a mark before the mark is registered.

ARTICLE 8—SIGNATURE

(1) *Communication on Paper.* Where a communication to the Office of a Contracting Party is on paper and a signature is required, that Contracting Party

(i) shall, subject to item (iii), accept a handwritten signature,

(ii) shall be free to allow, instead of a handwritten signature, the use of other forms of signature, such as a printed or stamped signature, or the use of a seal,

(iii) may, where the natural person who signs the communication is its national and such person's address is in its territory, require that a seal be used instead of a handwritten signature,

(iv) may, where a seal is used, require that the seal be accompanied by an indication in letters of the name of the natural person whose seal is used.

(2) *Communication by Telefacsimile*

(a) Where a Contracting Party allows the transmittal of communications to the Office by telefacsimile, it shall consider the communication signed if, on the printout produced by the telefacsimile, the reproduction of the signature, or the reproduction of the seal together with, where required under paragraph (1)(iv), the indication in letters of the name of the natural person whose seal is used, appears.

(b) The Contracting Party referred to in subparagraph (a) may require that the paper whose reproduction was transmitted by telefacsimile be filed with the Office within a certain period, subject to the minimum period prescribed in the Regulations.

(3) *Communication by Electronic Means.* Where a Contracting Party allows the transmittal of communications to the Office by electronic means, it shall consider the communication signed if the latter identifies the sender of the communication by electronic means as prescribed by the Contracting Party.

(4) *Prohibition of Requirement of Certification.* No Contracting Party may require the attestation, notarization, authentication, legalization or other certification of any signature or other means of self-identification referred to in the preceding paragraphs, except, if the law of the Contracting Party so provides, where the signature concerns the surrender of a registration.

ARTICLE 9—CLASSIFICATION OF GOODS AND/OR SERVICES

(1) *Indications of Goods and/or Services.* Each registration and any publication effected by an Office which concerns an application or registration and which indicates goods and/or services shall indicate the goods and/or services by their names, grouped according to the classes of the Nice Classification, and each group shall be preceded by the number of the class of that Classification to which that group of goods or services belongs and shall be presented in the order of the classes of the said Classification.

(2) *Goods or Services in the Same Class or in Different Classes*

(a) Goods or services may not be considered as being similar to each other on the ground that, in any registration or publication by the Office, they appear in the same class of the Nice Classification.

(b) Goods or services may not be considered as being dissimilar from each other on the ground that, in any registration or publication by the Office, they appear in different classes of the Nice Classification.

ARTICLE 10—CHANGES IN NAMES OR ADDRESSES

(1) *Changes in the Name or Address of the Holder*

(a) Where there is no change in the person of the holder but there is a change in his name and/or address, each Contracting Party shall accept that a request for the recordal of the change by the Office in its register of marks be made in a communication signed by the holder or his representative and indicating the registration number of the registration concerned and the change to be recorded. As regards the requirements concerning the presentation of the request, no Contracting Party shall refuse the request,

(i) where the request is presented in writing on paper, if it is presented, subject to subparagraph (c), on a form corresponding to the request Form provided for in the Regulations,

(ii) where the Contracting Party allows the transmittal of communications to the Office by telefacsimile and the request is so transmitted, if the paper copy resulting from such transmittal corresponds, subject to subparagraph (c), to the request Form referred to in item (i).

(b) Any Contracting Party may require that the request indicate

(i) the name and address of the holder;

(ii) where the holder has a representative, the name and address of that representative;

(iii) where the holder has an address for service, such address.

(c) Any Contracting Party may require that the request be in the language, or in one of the languages, admitted by the Office.

(d) Any Contracting Party may require that, in respect of the request, a fee be paid to the Office.

(e) A single request shall be sufficient even where the change relates to more than one registration, provided that the registration numbers of all registrations concerned are indicated in the request.

(2) *Change in the Name or Address of the Applicant.* Paragraph (1) shall apply, mutatis mutandis, where the change concerns an application or applications, or both an application or applications and a registration or registrations, provided that, where the application number of any application concerned has not yet been issued or is not known to the applicant or his representative, the request otherwise identifies that application as prescribed in the Regulations.

(3) *Change in the Name or Address of the Representative or in the Address for Service.* Paragraph (1) shall apply, mutatis mutandis, to any change in the name or address of the representative, if any, and to any change relating to the address for service, if any.

(4) *Prohibition of Other Requirements.* No Contracting Party may demand that requirements other than those referred to in paragraphs (1) to (3) be complied with in respect of the request referred to in this Article. In particular, the furnishing of any certificate concerning the change may not be required.

(5) *Evidence.* Any Contracting Party may require that evidence be furnished to the Office where the Office may reasonably doubt the veracity of any indication contained in the request.

Article 11—Change in Ownership

(1) *Change in the Ownership of a Registration*

(a) Where there is a change in the person of the holder, each Contracting Party shall accept that a request for the recordal of the change by the Office in its register of marks be made in a communication signed by the holder or his representative, or by the person who acquired the ownership (hereinafter referred to as "new owner") or his representative, and indicating the registration number of the registration concerned and the change to be recorded. As regards the requirements concerning the presentation of the request, no Contracting Party shall refuse the request,

(i) where the request is presented in writing on paper, if it is presented, subject to paragraph (2)(a), on a form corresponding to the request Form provided for in the Regulations,

(ii) where the Contracting Party allows the transmittal of communications to the Office by telefacsimile and the request is so transmitted, if the paper copy resulting from such transmittal corresponds, subject to paragraph (2)(a), to the request Form referred to in item (i).

(b) Where the change in ownership results from a contract, any Contracting Party may require that the request indicate that fact and be accompanied, at the option of the requesting party, by one of the following:

(i) a copy of the contract, which copy may be required to be certified, by a notary public or any other competent public authority, as being in conformity with the original contract;

(ii) an extract of the contract showing the change in ownership, which extract may be required to be certified, by a notary public or any other competent public authority, as being a true extract of the contract;

(iii) an uncertified certificate of transfer drawn up in the form and with the content as prescribed in the Regulations and signed by both the holder and the new owner;

(iv) an uncertified transfer document drawn up in the form and with the content as prescribed in the Regulations and signed by both the holder and the new owner.

(c) Where the change in ownership results from a merger, any Contracting Party may require that the request indicate that fact and be accompanied by a copy of a document, which document originates from the competent authority and evidences the merger, such as a copy of an extract from a register of commerce, and that that copy be certified by the authority which issued the document or by a notary public or any other competent public authority, as being in conformity with the original document.

(d) Where there is a change in the person of one or more but not all of several co-holders and such change in ownership results from a contract or a merger, any Contracting Party may require that any co-holder in respect of which there is no change in ownership give his express consent to the change in ownership in a document signed by him.

(e) Where the change in ownership does not result from a contract or a merger but from another ground, for example, from operation of law or a court decision, any Contracting Party may require that the request indicate that fact and be accompanied by a copy of a document evidencing the change and that that copy be certified as being in conformity with the original document by the authority which issued the document or by a notary public or any other competent public authority.

(f) Any Contracting Party may require that the request indicate

(i) the name and address of the holder;

(ii) the name and address of the new owner;

(iii) the name of a State of which the new owner is a national if he is the national of any State, the name of a State in which the new owner has his domicile, if any, and the name of a State in which the new owner has a real and effective industrial or commercial establishment, if any;

(iv) where the new owner is a legal entity, the legal nature of that legal entity and the State, and, where applicable, the territorial unit within that State, under the law of which the said legal entity has been organized;

(v) where the holder has a representative, the name and address of that representative;

(vi) where the holder has an address for service, such address;

(vii) where the new owner has a representative, the name and address of that representative;

(viii) where the new owner is required to have an address for service under Article 4(2)(b), such address.

(g) Any Contracting Party may require that, in respect of the request, a fee be paid to the Office.

(h) A single request shall be sufficient even where the change relates to more than one registration, provided that the holder and the new owner are the same for each registration and that the registration numbers of all registrations concerned are indicated in the request.

(i) Where the change of ownership does not affect all the goods and/or services listed in the holder's registration, and the applicable law allows the recording of such change, the Office shall create a separate registration referring to the goods and/or services in respect of which the ownership has changed.

(2) *Language; Translation*

(a) Any Contracting Party may require that the request, the certificate of transfer or the transfer document referred to in paragraph (1) be in the language, or in one of the languages, admitted by the Office.

(b) Any Contracting Party may require that, if the documents referred to in paragraph (1)(b)(i) and (ii), (c) and (e) are not in the language, or in one of the languages, admitted by the Office, the request be accompanied by a translation or a certified translation of the required document in the language, or in one of the languages, admitted by the Office.

(3) *Change in the Ownership of an Application.* Paragraphs (1) and (2) shall apply, mutatis mutandis, where the change in ownership concerns an application or applications, or both an application or applications and a registration or registrations, provided that, where the application number of any application concerned has not yet been issued or is not known to the applicant or his representative, the request otherwise identifies that application as prescribed in the Regulations.

(4) *Prohibition of Other Requirements.* No Contracting Party may demand that requirements other than those referred to in paragraphs (1) to (3) be complied with in respect of the request referred to in this Article. In particular, the following may not be required:

(i) subject to paragraph (1)(c), the furnishing of any certificate of, or extract from, a register of commerce;

(ii) an indication of the new owner's carrying on of an industrial or commercial activity, as well as the furnishing of evidence to that effect;

(iii) an indication of the new owner's carrying on of an activity corresponding to the goods and/or services affected by the change in ownership, as well as the furnishing of evidence to either effect;

(iv) an indication that the holder transferred, entirely or in part, his business or the relevant goodwill to the new owner, as well as the furnishing of evidence to either effect.

(5) *Evidence.* Any Contracting Party may require that evidence, or further evidence where paragraph (1)(c) or (e) applies, be furnished to the Office where that Office may reasonably doubt the veracity of any indication contained in the request or in any document referred to in the present Article.

ARTICLE 12—CORRECTION OF A MISTAKE

(1) *Correction of a Mistake in Respect of a Registration*

(a) Each Contracting Party shall accept that the request for the correction of a mistake which was made in the application or other request communicated to the Office and which mistake is reflected in its register of marks and/or any publication by the Office be made in a communication signed by the holder or his representative and indicating the registration number of the registration concerned, the mistake to be corrected and the correction to be entered. As regards the requirements concerning the presentation of the request, no Contracting Party shall refuse the request,

(i) where the request is presented in writing on paper, if it is presented, subject to subparagraph (c), on a form corresponding to the request Form provided for in the Regulations,

(ii) where the Contracting Party allows the transmittal of communications to the Office by telefacsimile and the request is so transmitted, if the paper copy resulting from such transmittal corresponds, subject to subparagraph (c), to the request Form referred to in item (i).

(b) Any Contracting Party may require that the request indicate

(i) the name and address of the holder;

(ii) where the holder has a representative, the name and address of that representative;

(iii) where the holder has an address for service, such address.

(c) Any Contracting Party may require that the request be in the language, or in one of the languages, admitted by the Office.

(d) Any Contracting Party may require that, in respect of the request, a fee be paid to the Office.

(e) A single request shall be sufficient even where the correction relates to more than one registration of the same person, provided that the mistake and the requested correction are the same for each registration and that the registration numbers of all registrations concerned are indicated in the request.

(2) *Correction of a Mistake in Respect of an Application.* Paragraph (1) shall apply, mutatis mutandis, where the mistake concerns an application or applications, or both an application or applications and a registration or registrations, provided that, where the application number of any application concerned has not yet been issued or is not known to the applicant or his representative, the request otherwise identifies that application as prescribed in the Regulations.

(3) *Prohibition of Other Requirements.* No Contracting Party may demand that requirements other than those referred to in paragraphs (1) and (2) be complied with in respect of the request referred to in this Article.

(4) *Evidence.* Any Contracting Party may require that evidence be furnished to the Office where the Office may reasonably doubt that the alleged mistake is in fact a mistake.

(5) *Mistakes Made by the Office.* The Office of a Contracting Party shall correct its own mistakes, ex officio or upon request, for no fee.

(6) *Uncorrectable Mistakes.* No Contracting Party shall be obliged to apply paragraphs (1), (2) and (5) to any mistake which cannot be corrected under its law.

ARTICLE 13—DURATION AND RENEWAL OF REGISTRATION

(1) *Indications or Elements Contained in or Accompanying a Request for Renewal; Fee*

(a) Any Contracting Party may require that the renewal of a registration be subject to the filing of a request and that such request contain some or all of the following indications:

(i) an indication that renewal is sought;

(ii) the name and address of the holder;

(iii) the registration number of the registration concerned;

(iv) at the option of the Contracting Party, the filing date of the application which resulted in the registration concerned or the registration date of the registration concerned;

(v) where the holder has a representative, the name and address of that representative;

(vi) where the holder has an address for service, such address;

(vii) where the Contracting Party allows the renewal of a registration to be made for some only of the goods and/or services which are recorded in the register of marks and such a renewal is requested, the names of the recorded goods and/or services for which the renewal is requested or the names of the recorded goods and/or services for which the renewal is not requested, grouped according to the classes of the Nice Classification, each group preceded by the number of the class of that Classification to which that group of goods or services belongs and presented in the order of the classes of the said Classification;

(viii) where a Contracting Party allows a request for renewal to be filed by a person other than the holder or his representative and the request is filed by such a person, the name and address of that person;

(ix) a signature by the holder or his representative or, where item (viii) applies, a signature by the person referred to in that item.

(b) Any Contracting Party may require that, in respect of the request for renewal, a fee be paid to the Office. Once the fee has been paid in respect of the initial period of the registration or of any renewal period, no further payment may be required for the maintenance of the registration in respect of that period. Fees associated with the furnishing of a declaration and/or evidence of use shall not be regarded, for the purposes of this subparagraph, as payments required for the maintenance of the registration and shall not be affected by this subparagraph.

(c) Any Contracting Party may require that the request for renewal be presented, and the corresponding fee referred to in subparagraph (b) be paid, to the Office within the period fixed by the law of the Contracting Party, subject to the minimum periods prescribed in the Regulations.

(2) *Presentation.* As regards the requirements concerning the presentation of the request for renewal, no Contracting Party shall refuse the request,

(i) where the request is presented in writing on paper, if it is presented, subject to paragraph (3), on a form corresponding to the request Form provided for in the Regulations,

(ii) where the Contracting Party allows the transmittal of communications to the Office by telefacsimile and the request is so transmitted, if the paper copy resulting from such transmittal corresponds, subject to paragraph (3), to the request Form referred to in item (i).

(3) *Language.* Any Contracting Party may require that the request for renewal be in the language, or in one of the languages, admitted by the Office.

(4) *Prohibition of Other Requirements.* No Contracting Party may demand that requirements other than those referred to in paragraphs (1) to (3) be complied with in respect of the request for renewal. In particular, the following may not be required:

(i) any reproduction or other identification of the mark;

(ii) the furnishing of evidence to the effect that the mark has been registered, or that its registration has been renewed, in the register of marks of any other Contracting Party;

(iii) the furnishing of a declaration and/or evidence concerning use of the mark.

(5) *Evidence.* Any Contracting Party may require that evidence be furnished to the Office in the course of the examination of the request for renewal where the Office may reasonably doubt the veracity of any indication or element contained in the request for renewal.

(6) *Prohibition of Substantive Examination.* No Office of a Contracting Party may, for the purposes of effecting the renewal, examine the registration as to substance.

(7) *Duration.* The duration of the initial period of the registration, and the duration of each renewal period, shall be 10 years.

Article 14—Observations in Case of Intended Refusal

An application or a request under Articles 10 to 13 may not be refused totally or in part by an Office without giving the applicant or the requesting party, as the case may be, an opportunity to make observations on the intended refusal within a reasonable time limit.

Article 15—Obligation to Comply with the Paris Convention

Any Contracting Party shall comply with the provisions of the Paris Convention which concern marks.

Article 16—Service Marks

Any Contracting Party shall register service marks and apply to such marks the provisions of the Paris Convention which concern trademarks.

Article 17—Regulations

(1) *Content*

(a) The Regulations annexed to this Treaty provide rules concerning

(i) matters which this Treaty expressly provides to be "prescribed in the Regulations";

(ii) any details useful in the implementation of the provisions of this Treaty;

(iii) any administrative requirements, matters or procedures.

(b) The Regulations also contain Model International Forms.

(2) *Conflict Between the Treaty and the Regulations.* In the case of conflict between the provisions of this Treaty and those of the Regulations, the former shall prevail.

Article 18—Revision; Protocols

(1) *Revision.* This Treaty may be revised by a diplomatic conference.

(2) *Protocols.* For the purposes of further developing the harmonization of laws on marks, protocols may be adopted by a diplomatic conference insofar as those protocols do not contravene the provisions of this Treaty.

Article 19—Becoming Party to the Treaty

(1) *Eligibility.* The following entities may sign and, subject to paragraphs (2) and (3) and Article 20(1) and (3), become party to this Treaty:

(i) any State member of the Organization in respect of which marks may be registered with its own Office;

(ii) any intergovernmental organization which maintains an Office in which marks may be registered with effect in the territory in which the constituting treaty of the intergovernmental organization applies, in all its member States or in those of its member States which are designated for such purpose in the relevant application, provided that all the member

States of the intergovernmental organization are members of the Organization;

(iii) any State member of the Organization in respect of which marks may be registered only through the Office of another specified State that is a member of the Organization;

(iv) any State member of the Organization in respect of which marks may be registered only through the Office maintained by an intergovernmental organization of which that State is a member;

(v) any State member of the Organization in respect of which marks may be registered only through an Office common to a group of States members of the Organization.

(2) *Ratification or Accession.* Any entity referred to in paragraph (1) may deposit

(i) an instrument of ratification, if it has signed this Treaty,

(ii) an instrument of accession, if it has not signed this Treaty.

(3) *Effective Date of Deposit*

(a) Subject to subparagraph (b), the effective date of the deposit of an instrument of ratification or accession shall be,

(i) in the case of a State referred to in paragraph (1)(i), the date on which the instrument of that State is deposited;

(ii) in the case of an intergovernmental organization, the date on which the instrument of that intergovernmental organization is deposited;

(iii) in the case of a State referred to in paragraph (1)(iii), the date on which the following condition is fulfilled: the instrument of that State has been deposited and the instrument of the other, specified State has been deposited;

(iv) in the case of a State referred to in paragraph (1)(iv), the date applicable under (ii), above;

(v) in the case of a State member of a group of States referred to in paragraph (1)(v), the date on which the instruments of all the States members of the group have been deposited.

(b) Any instrument of ratification or accession (referred to in this subparagraph as "instrument") of a State may be accompanied by a declaration making it a condition to its being considered as deposited that the instrument of one other State or one intergovernmental organization, or the instruments of two other States, or the instruments of one other State and one intergovernmental organization, specified by name and eligible to become party to this Treaty, is or are also deposited. The instrument containing such a declaration shall be considered to have been deposited on the day on which the condition indicated in the declaration is fulfilled. However, when the deposit of any instrument specified in the declaration is, itself, accompanied by a declaration of the said kind, that instrument shall be considered as deposited on the day on which the condition specified in the latter declaration is fulfilled.

(c) Any declaration made under paragraph (b) may be withdrawn, in its entirety or in part, at any time. Any such withdrawal shall become effective on the date on which the notification of withdrawal is received by the Director General.

Article 20—Effective Date of Ratifications and Accessions

(1) *Instruments to Be Taken Into Consideration.* For the purposes of this Article, only instruments of ratification or accession that are deposited by entities referred to in Article 19(1) and that have an effective date according to Article 19(3) shall be taken into consideration.

(2) *Entry Into Force of the Treaty.* This Treaty shall enter into force three months after five States have deposited their instruments of ratification or accession.

(3) *Entry Into Force of Ratifications and Accessions Subsequent to the Entry Into Force of the Treaty.* Any entity not covered by paragraph (2) shall become bound by this Treaty three months after the date on which it has deposited its instrument of ratification or accession.

Article 21—Reservations

(1) *Special Kinds of Marks.* Any State or intergovernmental organization may declare through a reservation that, notwithstanding Article 2(1)(a) and (2)(a), any of the provisions of Articles 3(1) and (2), 5, 7, 11 and 13 shall not apply to associated marks, defensive marks or derivative marks. Such reservation shall specify those of the aforementioned provisions to which the reservation relates.

(2) *Modalities.* Any reservation under paragraph (1) shall be made in a declaration accompanying the instrument of ratification of, or accession to, this Treaty of the State or intergovernmental organization making the reservation.

(3) *Withdrawal.* Any reservation under paragraph (1) may be withdrawn at any time.

(4) *Prohibition of Other Reservations.* No reservation to this Treaty other than the reservation allowed under paragraph (1) shall be permitted.

Article 22—Transitional Provisions

(1) *Single Application for Goods and Services in Several Classes; Division of Application*

(a) Any State or intergovernmental organization may declare that, notwithstanding Article 3(5), an application may be filed with the Office only in respect of goods or services which belong to one class of the Nice Classification.

(b) Any State or intergovernmental organization may declare that, notwithstanding Article 6, where goods and/or services belonging to several classes of the Nice Classification have been included in one and the same application, such application shall result in two or more registrations in the register of marks, provided that each and every such registration shall bear a reference to all other such registrations resulting from the said application.

(c) Any State or intergovernmental organization that has made a declaration under subparagraph (a) may declare that, notwithstanding Article 7(1), no application may be divided.

(2) *Single Power of Attorney for More Than One Application and/or Registration.* Any State or intergovernmental organization may declare that, notwithstanding Article 4(3)(b), a power of attorney may only relate to one application or one registration.

(3) *Prohibition of Requirement of Certification of Signature of Power of Attorney and of Signature of Application.* Any State or intergovernmental organization may declare that, notwithstanding Article 8(4), the signature of a power of attorney or the signature by the applicant of an application may be required to be the subject of an attestation, notarization, authentication, legalization or other certification.

(4) *Single Request for More Than One Application and/or Registration in Respect of a Change in Name and/or Address, a Change in Ownership or a Correction of a Mistake.* Any State or intergovernmental organization may declare that, notwithstanding Article 10(1)(e), (2) and (3), Article 11(1)(h) and (3) and Article 12(1)(e) and (2), a request for the recordal of a change in name and/or address, a request for the recordal of a change in ownership and a request for the correction of a mistake may only relate to one application or one registration.

(5) *Furnishing, on the Occasion of Renewal, of Declaration and/or Evidence Concerning Use.* Any State or intergovernmental organization may declare that, notwithstanding Article 13(4)(iii), it will require, on the occasion of renewal, the furnishing of a declaration and/or of evidence concerning use of the mark.

(6) *Substantive Examination on the Occasion of Renewal.* Any State or intergovernmental organization may declare that, notwithstanding Article 13(6), the Office may, on the occasion of the first renewal of a registration covering services, examine such registration as to substance, provided that such examination shall be limited to the elimination of multiple registrations based on applications filed during a period of six months following the entry into force of the law of such State or organization that introduced, before the entry into force of this Treaty, the possibility of registering service marks.

(7) *Common Provisions*

(a) A State or an intergovernmental organization may make a declaration under paragraphs (1) to (6) only if, at the time of depositing its instrument of ratification of, or accession to, this Treaty, the continued application of its law would, without such a declaration, be contrary to the relevant provisions of this Treaty.

(b) Any declaration under paragraphs (1) to (6) shall accompany the instrument of ratification of, or accession to, this Treaty of the State or intergovernmental organization making the declaration.

(c) Any declaration made under paragraphs (1) to (6) may be withdrawn at any time.

(8) *Loss of Effect of Declaration*

(a) Subject to subparagraph (c), any declaration made under paragraphs (1) to (5) by a State regarded as a developing country in conformity with the established practice of the General Assembly of the United Nations, or by an intergovernmental organization each member of which is such a State, shall lose its effect at the end of a period of eight years from the date of entry into force of this Treaty.

(b) Subject to subparagraph (c), any declaration made under paragraphs (1) to (5) by a State other than a State referred to in subparagraph (a), or by an intergovernmental organization other than an intergovernmental organization referred to in subparagraph (a), shall lose its effect at the end of a period of six years from the date of entry into force of this Treaty.

(c) Where a declaration made under paragraphs (1) to (5) has not been withdrawn under paragraph (7)(c), or has not lost its effect under subparagraph (a) or (b), before October 28, 2004, it shall lose its effect on October 28, 2004.

(9) *Becoming Party to the Treaty.* Until December 31, 1999, any State which, on the date of the adoption of this Treaty, is a member of the International (Paris) Union for the Protection of Industrial Property without being a member of the Organization may, notwithstanding Article 19(1)(i), become a party to this Treaty if marks may be registered with its own Office.

Article 23—Denunciation of the Treaty

(1) *Notification.* Any Contracting Party may denounce this Treaty by notification addressed to the Director General.

(2) *Effective Date.* Denunciation shall take effect one year from the date on which the Director General has received the notification. It shall not affect the application of this Treaty to any application pending or any mark registered in respect of the denouncing Contracting Party at the time of the expiration of the said one-year period, provided that the denouncing Contracting Party may, after the expiration of the said one-year period, discontinue applying this Treaty to any registration as from the date on which that registration is due for renewal.

Article 24—Languages of the Treaty; Signature

(1) *Original Texts; Official Texts*

(a) This Treaty shall be signed in a single original in the English, Arabic, Chinese, French, Russian and Spanish languages, all texts being equally authentic.

(b) At the request of a Contracting Party, an official text in a language not referred to in subparagraph (a) that is an official language of that Contracting Party shall be established by the Director General after consultation with the said Contracting Party and any other interested Contracting Party.

(2) *Time Limit for Signature.* This Treaty shall remain open for signature at the headquarters of the Organization for one year after its adoption.

Article 25—Depositary

The Director General shall be the depositary of this Treaty.

7. Bilateral Investment Treaties

a. Countries With Which the United States Has a Bilateral Investment Treaty

Country	Entered Into Force
Albania	January 4, 1998
Argentina	October 12, 1994
Armenia	March 29, 1996
Azerbaijan	August 2, 2001
Bahrain	May 30, 2001
Bangladesh	July 25, 1989
Bolivia	June 6, 2001
Bulgaria	June 2, 1994
Cameroon	April 6, 1989
Congo, Democratic of	July 28, 1989
Congo, Republic of	August 13, 1994
Croatia	June 20, 2001
Czech Republic	December 19, 1992
Ecuador	May 11, 1997
Egypt	June 27, 1992
Estonia	February 16, 1997
Georgia	August 17, 1997
Grenada	March 3, 1989
Honduras	July 11, 2001
Jamaica	March 7, 1997
Jordan	June 12, 2003
Kazakhstan	January 12, 1994
Kyrgyzstan	January 12, 1994
Latvia	December 26, 1996
Lithuania	November 22, 2001
Moldova	November 25, 1994
Mongolia	January 1, 1997
Morocco	May 29, 1991
Mozambique	March 3, 2005
Panama	May 30, 1991, as amended May 14, 2001
Poland	August 6, 1994
Romania	January 15, 1994
Senegal	October 25, 1990
Slovakia	December 19, 1992
Sri Lanka	May 1, 1993
Trinidad and Tobago	December 26, 1996
Tunisia	February 7, 1993
Turkey	May 18, 1990
Ukraine	November 16, 1996

b. Treaty Between the United States and Jordan Concerning the Encouragement and Reciprocal Protection of Investment[1]

Signed at Amman, July 1, 1997; Ratification advised by the Senate, October 18, 2000; Entered into force, June 12, 2003

The Government of the United States of America and the Government of the Hashemite Kingdom of Jordan (hereinafter the Contracting "Parties");

DESIRING to establish more effective cooperation in the area of mutual legal assistance in criminal matters;

DESIRING to promote greater economic cooperation between them, with respect to investment nationals and companies of one Contracting Party in the territory of the other Contracting Party;

RECOGNIZING that agreement upon the treatment to be accorded such investment will stimulate the flow of private capital and the economic development of the Contracting Parties;

AGREEING that a stable framework for investment will maximize effective utilization of economic resources and improve living standards;

RECOGNIZING that the development of economic and business ties can promote respect for internationally recognized worker rights;

AGREEING that these objectives can be achieved without relaxing health, safety and environmental measures of general application; and

HAVING resolved to conclude a Treaty concerning the encouragement and reciprocal protection of investment;

HAVE AGREED as follows:

ARTICLE I

DEFINITIONS

For the purpose of this Treaty,

(a) "company" means any entity constituted or organized under applicable law, whether or not for profit, and whether privately or governmentally owned or controlled, and includes a corporation, trust, partnership, sole proprietorship, branch, joint venture, association, or other organization;

(b) "company of a Contracting Party" means that a company constituted or organized under the laws of that Contracting Party;

[1] The full text of the Treaty Concerning the Encouragement and Reciprocal Protection of Investment Between Jordan and the United States of America is set out in this volume as a model of the other 38 Bilateral Investment Treaties (BIT) that were in force for the United States as of December 31, 2005.

(c) "national" of a Contracting Party means a natural person who is a national of that Contracting Party under its applicable law;

(d) "investment" of a national or company means every kind of investment owned or controlled directly or indirectly by that national or company, and includes investment consisting or taking the form of:

(i) a company;

(ii) shares, stock, and other forms of equity participation and bonds, debentures, and other forms of debt interests, in a company;

(iii) contractual rights, such as under turnkey, construction or management contracts, production or revenue-sharing contracts, concessions, or other similar contracts;

(iv) tangible property, including real property; and intangible property, including rights, such as leases, mortgages, liens and pledges;

(v) intellectual property, including;

copyrights and related rights,
industrial property rights,
patents,
rights in plant varieties,
utility models,
industrial designs or models,
rights in semiconductor layout design,
indications of origin,
trade secrets, including know-how,
confidential business information,
trade and service marks, and
trade names; and

(vi) rights conferred pursuant to law, such as licenses and permits;

any change in the form of an investment does not affect its character as an investment;

(e) "covered investment" means an investment of a national or company of a Contracting Party in the territory of the other Contracting Party;

(f) "state enterprise" means an investment of a national or company of a Contracting Party in the territory of the other Contracting Party;

(g) "investment authorization" means an authorization granted by the foreign investment authority of a Contracting Party to a covered investment or a national or company of the other Contracting Party;

(h) "investment agreement" means a written agreement between the national authorities of a Contracting Party and a covered investment or a national or company of the other Contracting Party that (i) grants rights with respect to natural resources or other assets controlled by the national authorities and (ii) the investment, national or company relies upon in establishing or acquiring a covered investment;

(i) "ICSID Convention" means the convention on the Settlement of Investment Disputes between States and Nationals of Other States, done at Washington, March 18, 1965;

(j) "Centre" means the International Centre for Settlement of Investment Disputes Established by the ICSID Convention; and

(k) "UNCITRAL Arbitration Rules" means the arbitration rules of the United Nations Commission on International Trade Law.

ARTICLE II

TREATMENT AND PROTECTION OF INVESTMENT

1. With respect to the establishment, acquisition, expansion, management, conduct, operation and sale or other disposition of covered investments, each Contracting Party shall accord treatment no less favorable than that it accords, in like situations, to investments in its territory of its own nationals or companies (hereinafter "national treatment") or to investments in its territory of nationals or companies of a third country (hereinafter "most favored nation treatment"), whichever is most favorable (hereinafter "national and most favored nation treatment"). Each Contracting Party shall ensure that its state enterprises, in the provision of their goods or services, accord national and most favored nation treatment to covered investments.

2. (a) A Contracting Party may adopt or maintain exceptions to the obligations of paragraph 1 in the sectors or with respect to the matters specified in the Annex to this Treaty. In adopting such an exception, a Contracting Party may not require the divestment, in whole or in part, of covered investments existing at the time the exception becomes effective.

(b) The obligations of paragraph 1 do not apply to procedures provided in multilateral agreements concluded under the auspices of the World Intellectual Property Organization relating to the acquisition or maintenance of intellectual property rights.

3. (a) Each Contracting Party shall at all times accord to covered investments fair and equitable treatment and full protection and security, and shall in no case accord treatment less favorable than that required by international law.

(b) Neither Contracting Party shall in any way impair by unreasonable and discriminatory measures the management, conduct, operation, and sale or other disposition of covered investments.

4. Each Contracting Party shall provide effective means of asserting claims and enforcing rights with respect to covered investments.

5. Each Contracting Party shall ensure that its laws, regulations, administrative practices and procedures of general application, and adjudicatory decisions, that pertain to or affect covered investments are promptly published or otherwise made publicly available.

ARTICLE III

EXPROPRIATION AND COMPENSATION THEREFORE

1. Neither Contracting Party shall expropriate or nationalize a covered investment either directly or indirectly through measures

tantamount to expropriation or nationalization ("expropriation") except for a public purpose; in a non-discriminatory manner; upon payment of prompt, adequate and effective compensation; and in accordance with due process of law and the general principles of treatment provided for in Article II (3).

2. Compensation shall be paid without delay; be equivalent to the fair market value of the expropriated investment immediately before the expropriatory action was taken ("the date of expropriation"); and fully realizable and freely transferable. The fair market value shall not reflect any change in value occurring because the expropriatory action had become known before the date of expropriation.

3. If the fair market value is denominated in a freely usable currency, the compensation paid shall be no less than the fair market value on the date of expropriation, plus interest at a commercially reasonable rate for that currency, accrued from the date of expropriation until the date of payment.

4. If the fair market value is denominated in a currency that is not freely usable, the compensation paid—converted into the currency of payment at the market rate of exchange prevailing on the date of payment—shall be no less than:

(a) the fair market value on the date of expropriation, converted into a freely usable currency at the market rate of exchange prevailing on that date, plus

(b) interest, at a commercially reasonable rate for that freely usable currency, accrued from the date of expropriation until the date of payment.

Article IV

Compensation for Damages Due to War and Similar Events

1. Each Contracting Party shall accord national and most favored nation treatment to covered investments as regards any measure relating to losses that investments suffer in its territory owing to war or other armed conflict, revolution, state of national emergency, insurrection, civil disturbance, or similar events.

2. Each Contracting Party shall accord restitution, or pay compensation in accordance with paragraphs 2 through 4 of Article III, in the event that covered investments suffer losses in its territory, owing to war or other armed conflict, revolution, state of national emergency, insurrection, civil disturbance, or similar events, that result from:

(a) requisitioning of all or part of such investments by the Contracting Party's forces or authorities, or

(b) destruction of all or part of such investments by the Contracting Party's forces or authorities that was not required by the necessity of the situation.

Article V

Transfers

1. Each Contracting Party shall permit all transfers relating to a covered investment to be made freely and without delay into and out of its territory. Such transfers include:

(a) contributions to capital;

(b) profits, dividends, capital gains, and proceeds from the sale of all or any part of the investment or from the partial or complete liquidation of the investment;

(c) interest, royalty payments, management fees, and technical assistance and other fees;

(d) payments made under a contract, including a loan agreement;

(e) compensation pursuant to Articles III and IV, and payments arising out of an investment dispute;

(f) earnings of a national of one Contracting Party earned in the territory of the other Contracting Party in earned in the territory of the other Contracting Party in connection with a covered investment of that national; and

(g) other forms of income.

2. Each Contracting Party shall permit returns in kind to be made as authorized or specified in an investment authorization, investment agreement, or other written agreement between the Contracting Party and a covered investment or a national or company of the other Contracting Party.

3. Each Contracting Party shall permit returns in kind to be made as authorized or specified in an investment authorization, investment agreement, or other written agreement between the Contracting Party and a covered investment or a national or company of the other Contracting Party.

4. Notwithstanding paragraphs 1 through 3, a Contracting Party may prevent a transfer through the equitable, non-discriminatory and good faith application of its laws relating to:

(a) bankruptcy, insolvency or the protection of the rights of creditors;

(b) issuing, trading or dealing in securities;

(c) criminal or penal offenses; or

(d) ensuring compliance with orders or judgments in adjudicatory proceedings.

Article VI

Performance Requirements

Neither Contracting Party shall mandate or enforce, as a condition for the establishment, acquisition, expansion, management, conduct or operation of a covered investment, any requirement (including any commitment or undertaking in connection with the receipt of a governmental permission or authorization):

(a) to achieve a particular level or percentage of local content, or to purchase, use or otherwise give a preference to products or services of domestic origin or from any domestic source;

(b) to limit imports by the investment of products or services in relation to a particular volume or value of production, exports or foreign exchange earnings;

(c) to export a particular type, level or percentage of products or services, either generally or to a specific market region;

(d) to limit sales by the investment of products or services in the Contracting Party's territory in relation to a particular value or value of production, exports or foreign exchange earnings;

(e) to transfer technology, a production process or other proprietary knowledge to a national or company in the Contracting Party's territory, except pursuant to an order, commitment or undertaking that is enforced by a court, administrative tribunal or competition authority to remedy an alleged or adjudicated violation of competition laws; or

(f) to carry out a particular type, level or percentage of research and development in the Contracting Party's territory.

Such requirements do not include conditions for the receipt or continued receipt of an advantage.

Article VII

Entry, Sojourn and Employment of Aliens

1. (a) Subject to its laws relating to the entry, sojourn and employment of aliens, each Contracting Party shall permit to enter and to remain in its territory nationals of the other Contracting Party for the purpose of establishing, developing, administering or advising on the operation of an investment to which they, or a company of the other Contracting Party that employs them, have committed or are in the process of committing a substantial amount of capital or other resources.

(b) Neither Contracting Party shall, in granting entry under paragraph 1(a), require a labor certification test or other procedures of similar effect, or apply any numerical restriction.

2. Each Contracting Party shall permit covered investments to engage top managerial personnel of their choice regardless of nationality.

Article VIII

Consultations

The Contracting Parties agree to consult promptly, on the request of either, to resolve any disputes in connection with the Treaty, or to discuss any matter relating to the interpretation or application of the Treaty or to the realization of the objectives of the Treaty.

Article IX

Settlement of Disputes Between One Contracting Party and a National or Company of the Other Contracting Party

1. For purposes of this Treaty, an investment dispute is a dispute between a Contracting Party and a national or company of the

other Contracting Party arising out of or relating to an investment authorization, an investment agreement or an alleged breach of any right conferred, created or recognized by this Treaty with respect to a covered investment. In the event of an investment dispute, the parties to the dispute should initially seek a resolution through consultation and negotiation.

2. A national or company that is a party to an investment dispute may submit the dispute of resolution under one of the following alternatives:

(a) to the courts or administrative tribunals of the Party that is a party to the dispute; or

(b) in accordance with any applicable, previously agreed dispute-settlement procedures; or

(c) in accordance with the terms of paragraph 3.

3. (a) Provided that the national or company concerned has not submitted the dispute for resolution under paragraph 2 (a) or (b), and that three months have elapsed from the date on which the dispute arouse, the national or company concerned may submit the dispute for settlement by binding arbitration:

(i) to the Centre, if the Centre is available; or

(ii) to the Additional Facility of the Centre, if the Centre is not available; or

(iii) in accordance with the UNCITRAL Arbitration Rules; or

(iv) if agreed by both parties to the dispute, to any other arbitration institution or in accordance with any other arbitration rules.

(b) a national or company, notwithstanding that it may have submitted a dispute to binding arbitration under paragraph 3 (a), may seek interim injunctive relief, not involving the payment of damages, before the judicial or administrative tribunals of the Contracting Party that is a party to the dispute, prior to the institution of the arbitral proceeding or during the proceeding, for the preservation of its rights and interests.

4. Each Contracting Party hereby consents to the submission of any investment dispute for settlement by binding arbitration in accordance with the choice of the national or company under paragraph 3 (a) (i), (ii), and (iii) or the mutual agreement of both parties to the dispute under paragraph 3 (a) (iv). This consent and the submission of the dispute by a national or company under paragraph 3 (a) shall satisfy the requirements of:

(a) Chapter II of the ICSID Convention (Jurisdiction of the Centre) and the Additional Facility Rules for written consent of the parties to the dispute; and

(b) Article II of the United Nations Convention on the Recognition and Enforcement of Foreign Arbitral Awards, done at New York, June 10, 1958, for an "agreement in writing."

5. Any arbitration under paragraph 3 (a) (ii), (iii) or (iv) shall be held in a state that is a party to the United Nations Convention on the Recognition and Enforcement of Foreign Arbitral Awards, done at New York, June 10, 1958.

6. Any arbitral award rendered pursuant to this Article shall be final and binding on the parties to the dispute. Each Contracting Party shall carry out without delay the provisions of any such

award and provide in its territory for the enforcement of such award.

7. In any proceeding involving an investment dispute, a Contracting Party shall not assert, as a defense, counterclaim, right of set-off or for any other reason, that indemnification or other compensation for all or part of the alleged damages has been received or will be received pursuant to an insurance or guarantee contract.

8. For purposes of Article 2(2) (b) of the ICSID Convention and this Article, a company of a Contracting Party that, immediately before the occurrence of the event or events giving rise to an investment dispute, was a covered investment, shall be treated as a company of the other Contracting Party.

Article X

Settlement of Disputes Between the Contracting Parties

1. Any dispute between the Contracting Parties concerning the interpretation or application of the Treaty, that is not resolved through consultations or other diplomatic channels, shall be submitted upon the request of either Contracting Party to an arbitral tribunal for binding decision in accordance with the applicable rules of international law. In the absence of an agreement by the Contracting Parties to the contrary, the UNCITRAL Arbitration Rules shall govern, except to the extent these rules are (a) modified by the Contracting Parties or (b) modified by the arbitrators unless either Contracting Party objects to the proposed modification.

2. Within two months of receipt of a request, each Contracting Party shall appoint an arbitrator. The two arbitrators shall select a third arbitrator as chairman, who shall be a national of a third state. The UNCITRAL Arbitration Rules applicable to appointing members of three-member panels shall apply mutatis mutandis to the appointment of the arbitral panel except that the appointing authority referenced in those rules shall be the Secretary General of the Centre.

3. Unless otherwise agreed, all submissions shall be made and all hearings shall be completed within six months of the date of selection of the third arbitrator, and the arbitral panel shall render its decisions within two months of the date of the final submissions or the date of the closing of the hearings, whichever is later.

4. Expenses incurred by the Chairman and other arbitrators, and other costs of the proceedings, shall be paid for equally by the Contracting Parties. However, the arbitral panel may, at its discretion, direct that a higher proportion of the costs be paid by one of the Contracting Parties.

Article XI

Preservation of Legal Rights

This Treaty shall not derogate from any of the following that entitle covered investments to treatment more favorable than that accorded by this Treaty:

(a) laws and regulations, administrative practices or procedures, or administrative or adjudicatory decisions of a Contracting Parties;

(b) international legal obligations or

(c) obligations assumed by a Contracting Party, including those contained in an investment authorization or an investment agreement.

Article XII

Denial of Benefits

Each Contracting Party reserves the right to deny to a company of the other Contracting Party the benefits of this Treaty if nationals of a third country own or control the company and:

(a) the denying Contracting Party does not maintain normal economic relations with the third country; or

(b) the company has no substantial business activities in the territory of the Contracting Party under whose laws it is constituted or organized.

Article XIII

Taxation

1. No provision of this Treaty shall impose obligations with respect to tax matters, except that:

(a) Articles III, IX and X will apply with respect to expropriation; and

(b) Article IX will apply with respect to an investment agreement or an investment authorization.

2. A national or company, that asserts in an investment dispute that a tax matter involves an expropriation, may submit that dispute to arbitration pursuant to Article IX(3) only if:

(a) the national or company concerned has first referred to the competent tax authorities of both Contracting Parties the issue of whether the tax matter involves an expropriation; and

(b) the competent tax authorities have not both determined within nine months from the time the national or company referred the issue, that the matter does not involve an expropriation.

Article XIV

Measures Not Precluded by This Treaty

1. This Treaty shall not preclude a Contracting Party from applying measures necessary for the fulfillment of its obligations with respect to the maintenance or restoration of international peace or security, or the protection of its own essential security interests.

2. This Treaty shall not preclude a Contracting Party from prescribing special formalities in connection with covered investments, such as a requirement that such investments be legally constituted

under the laws and regulations of that Contracting Party, or a requirement that transfers of currency or other monetary instruments be reported, proved that such formalities shall not impair the substance of any of the rights set forth in this Treaty.

ARTICLE XV

APPLICATION OF THIS TREATY TO POLITICAL SUBDIVISIONS AND STATE ENTERPRISES OF THE CONTRACTING PARTIES

1. (a) The obligations of this Treaty shall apply to the political subdivisions of the Contracting Parties.

(b) With respect to the treatment accorded by a State, Territory or possession of the United States of America, national treatment means treatment no less favorable than the treatment accorded thereby, in like situations, to investments of nationals of the United States of America resident in, and companies legally constituted under the laws and regulations of, other States, Territories or possessions of the United States of America.

2. A Contracting Party's obligations under this Treaty shall apply to a stat enterprise in the exercise of any regulatory, administrative or other governmental authority delegated to it by that Contracting Party.

ARTICLE XVI

ENTRY INTO FORCE, DURATION AND TERMINATION

1. This Treaty shall enter into forces thirty days after the date of exchange of instruments of ratification. It shall remain in force for a period of then years and shall continue in force unless terminated in accordance with paragraph 2. It shall apply to covered investments existing at the time of entry into force as well as to those established or acquired thereafter.

2. A Contracting Party may terminate this Treaty at the end of the initial ten year period or at any time thereafter by giving one year's written notice to the other Contracting Party.

3. For ten years from the date of termination, all other Articles shall continue to apply to covered investments established or acquired prior to the date of termination, except insofar as those Articles extend to the establishment or acquisition of covered investments.

4. The Annex and Protocol shall form an integral part of the Treaty.

IN WITNESS WHEREOF, the respective plenipotentiaries have signed this Treaty.

DONE in duplicate at ______________ this ________, 1997, in the English and Arabic languages, each text being equally authentic.

For the Government of the United States of America:

WESLEY W. EGAN, JR.
[SIGNATURE]

For the Government of the Hashemite Kingdom of Jordan:

HANI AL-MULKI
[SIGNATURE]

ANNEX

1. The Government of the United States of America may adopt or maintain exceptions to the obligation to accord national treatment to covered investment in the sectors or with respect to the matters specified below:

atomic energy; customhouse brokers; licenses for broadcast, common carrier, or aeronautical radio stations; COMSAT; subsidies or grants, including governments-supported loans, guarantees and insurance; state and local measures exempt from Article 1102 of the North American Free Trade Agreement pursuant to Article 1108 thereof; and landing of submarine cables.

Most favored nation treatment shall be accorded in the sectors and matters indicated above.

2. The Government of the United States of America may adopt or maintain exceptions to the obligations to accord national treatment to covered investments in the sectors or with respect to the matters specified below:

fisheries; air and maritime transport, and related activities; banking, insurance, securities, and other financial services; and minerals leases on government land.

3. The Government of the Hashemite Kingdom of Jordan may adopt or maintain exception to the obligations to accord national treatment to covered investments in the sectors and with respect to the matters specified below:

air transport; ownership of bus transport companies; ownership of construction contracting companies, but not including cross-border provision of construction services; small scale commerce with total invested capital of no more than US$50,000 (or its equivalent in national currency), as adjusted annually for the first five years that the treaty is in force by the annual percentage change in the GDP deflator of the United States of America; ownership of banks and insurance companies; ownership of companies engaged in telecommunications systems operations, but not including activities such as maintenance, equipment production, equipment and spare parts sales, or other telecommunications related services; extraction concessions for minerals, including oil, natural gas and oil shale; farming (not including animal husbandry) on large tracts of land (greater than 500 acres or its equivalent in dunums); ownership of agricultural land; ownership of land in the Jordan valley and ownership of land for non-business related purposes.

Most favored nation treatment shall be accorded in the sectors and matters indicated above.

4. Notwithstanding paragraphs 1 and 3, each Party agrees to accord national treatment to covered investment in the following sectors:

leasing of pipeline rights-of-way on government land.

PROTOCOL

1. With respect to Article I (d), the Contracting Parties confirm with their mutual understanding that either Contracting Party may require approvals or impose format requirements in connection with a change in the form of an investment, provided that such approvals or formal requirements are otherwise consistent with this Treaty.

2. With regard to Article III (2), the term "without delay" does not necessarily mean instantaneous. The intent is that the Contracting Party diligently and expeditiously carry out necessary formalities.

8. Conventions for the Avoidance of Double Taxation and the Prevention of Fiscal Evasion with Respect to Taxes on Income

a. Countries With Which the United States has a Convention for the Avoidance of Double Taxation and the Prevention of Fiscal Evasion With Respect to Taxes on Income

Country	Entered Into Force
Australia	October 31, 1983
Austria	July 1, 1983
Barbados	November 3, 1984, as amended December 29, 1993 and December 20, 2004
Belguim	July 9, 1970, as modified August 3, 1989
Canada	August 16, 1984, as amended August 16, 1984 and August 16, 1984
China	April 30, 1984, as amended November 21, 1986
Cyprus	December 31, 1985
Czech Republic	December 23, 1993
Denmark	March 31, 2000
Egypt	December 31, 1981
Estonia	December 30, 1999
Finland	December 30, 1990
France	December 30, 1995
Germany	August 21, 1991
Greece	December 30, 1953
Hungary	September 18, 1979
Iceland	December 26, 1975
India	December 18, 1990
Indonesia	December 30, 1990, as amended December 23, 1996
Ireland	December 17, 1997, as amended September 24, 1999
Israel	December 30, 1994, as amended May 30, 1980 and January 26, 1993
Italy	December 30, 1985
Jamaica	December 29, 1981, as amended December 29, 1981
Japan	July 9, 1972
Kazakhstan	December 30, 1996
Korea, Republic of	October 20, 1979
Latvia	December 30, 1999
Lithuania	December 30, 1999

Country	Entered Into Force
Luxembourg	December 20, 2000
Mexico	December 28, 1993, as modified October 26, 1995 and July 3, 2003
Morocco	December 30, 1981
Netherlands	December 31, 1993, as amended December 30, 1993 and December 28, 2004
New Zealand	November 2, 1983
Norway	November 29, 1972, as amended December 15, 1981
Pakistan	May 21, 1959
Philippines	October 16, 1982
Poland	July 22, 1976
Portugal	December 18, 1995
Romania	January 1, 1974
Russia	December 16, 1993
Saudi Arabia	January 31, 2000
Slovak Republic	December 30, 1993
Slovenia	June 22, 2001
South Africa	December 28, 1997
Spain	November 21, 1990
Sweden	October 26, 1995
Switzerland	December 19, 1997
Thailand	December 15, 1997
Trinidad and Tobago	December 30, 1970
Tunisia	December 26, 1990
Turkey	December 19, 1997
Ukraine	June 5, 2000
United Kingdom	March 31, 2003
Venezuela	December 30, 1999

b. Convention Between the United States and Denmark for the Avoidance of Double Taxation and the Prevention of Fiscal Evasion With Respect to Taxes on Income [1]

Signed at Washington, August 19, 1999; Ratification advised by the Senate, November 5, 1999; Entered into force, March 31, 2000

The Government of the United States of America and the Government of the Kingdom of Denmark, desiring to conclude a Convention for the avoidance of double taxation and the prevention of fiscal evasion with respect to taxes on income, have agreed as follows:

ARTICLE 1

GENERAL SCOPE

1. Except as otherwise provided in this Convention, this Convention shall apply to persons who are residents of one or both of the Contracting States.

2. This Convention shall not restrict in any manner any benefit now or hereafter accorded:

a) by the laws of either Contracting State; or

b) by any other agreement between the Contracting States.

3. Notwithstanding the provisions of subparagraph 2b):

a) the provisions of Article 25 (Mutual Agreement Procedure) of this Convention exclusively shall apply to any dispute concerning whether a measure is within the scope of this Convention, and the procedures under this Convention exclusively shall apply to that dispute; and

b) unless the competent authorities determine that a taxation measure is not within the scope of this Convention, the non-discrimination obligations of this Convention exclusively shall apply with respect to that measure, except for such national treatment or most-favored-nation obligations as may apply to trade in goods under the General Agreement on Tariffs and Trade. No national treatment or most-favored-nation obligation under any other agreement shall apply with respect to that measure.

c) For the purpose of this paragraph, a "measure" is a law, regulation, rule, procedure, decision, administrative action, or any similar provision or action.

4. Notwithstanding any provision of the Convention except paragraph 5 of this Article, a Contracting State may tax its residents

[1] The full text of the Convention Between the Government of the United States of America and the Government of the Kingdom of Denmark for the Avoidance of Double Taxation and the Prevention of Fiscal Evasion with Respect to Taxes on Income is set out in this volume as a model of the other 53 Tax Conventions that were in force for the United States as of December 31, 2005.

(as determined under Article 4 (Residence)), and by reason of citizenship may tax its citizens, as if the Convention had not come into effect. For this purpose, the term "citizen" shall include a former citizen or long-term resident whose loss of such status had as one of its principal purposes the avoidance of tax (as defined under the laws of the Contracting State of which the person was a citizen or long-term resident), but only for a period of 10 years following such loss.

5. The provisions of paragraph 4 shall not affect:

a) the benefits conferred by a Contracting State under paragraph 2 of Article 9 (Associated Enterprises), paragraphs 7 and 8 of Article 13 (Capital Gains), paragraphs 1 (c), 2 and 5 of Article 18 (Pensions, Social Security, Annuities, Alimony and Child Support Payments), and Articles 23 (Relief from Double Taxation), 24 (Non-Discrimination), and 25 (Mutual Agreement Procedure); and

b) the benefits conferred by a Contracting State under Articles 19 (Government Service), 20 (Students and Trainees) and 28 (Diplomatic Agents and Consular Officers), upon individuals who are neither citizens of, nor have been admitted for permanent residence in, that State.

Article 2

Taxes Covered

1. The existing taxes to which this Convention applies are:

a) in the United States:

(i) the Federal income taxes imposed by the Internal Revenue Code (but excluding social security taxes); and

(ii) the Federal excise taxes imposed with respect to private foundations;

b) in Denmark:

(i) the income tax to the State (indkomstskatten til staten);

(ii) the municipal income tax (den kommunale indkomstskat);

(iii) the income tax to the county municipalities (den amtskommunale indkomstskat); and

(iv) taxes imposed under the Hydrocarbon Tax Act (skatter i henhold til kulbrinteskatteloven).

2. The Convention shall apply also to any identical or substantially similar taxes which are imposed after the date of signature of the Convention in addition to, or in place of, the existing taxes. The competent authorities of the Contracting States shall notify each other of any significant changes that have been made in their respective taxation laws or other laws affecting their obligations under the Convention, and of any official published material concerning the application of this Convention, including explanations, regulations, rulings, or judicial decisions.

Article 3

General Definitions

1. For the purposes of this Convention, unless the context otherwise requires:

a) the term "person" includes an individual, an estate, a trust, a partnership, a company and any other body of persons;

b) the term "company" means any body corporate or any entity which is treated as a body corporate for tax purposes according to the laws of the state in which it is organized;

c) the terms "enterprise of a Contracting State" and "enterprise of the other Contracting State" mean respectively an enterprise carried on by a resident of a Contracting State, and an enterprise carried on by a resident of the other Contracting State; the terms also include an enterprise carried on by a resident of a Contracting State through an entity that is treated as fiscally transparent in that Contracting State;

d) the term "international traffic" means any transport by a ship or aircraft, except when such transport is solely between places in a Contracting State;

e) the term "competent authority" means:

(i) in the United States: the Secretary of the Treasury or his delegate; and

(ii) in Denmark: the Minister for Taxation or his authorized representative;

f) the term "United States" means the United States of America, and includes the states thereof and the District of Columbia; such term also includes the territorial sea thereof and the seabed and subsoil of the submarine areas adjacent to that territorial sea, over which the United States exercises sovereign rights in accordance with international law; the term, however, does not include Puerto Rico, the Virgin Islands, Guam or any other United States possession or territory.

g) the term "Denmark" means the Kingdom of Denmark, including any area outside the territorial sea of Denmark which in accordance with international law has been or may hereafter be designated under Danish laws as an area within which Denmark may exercise sovereign rights with respect to the exploration and exploitation of the natural resources of the seabed or its subsoil and the superjacent waters and with respect to other activities for the exploration and economic exploitation of the area; the term "Denmark" does not comprise the Faroe Islands or Greenland;

h) the term "national of a Contracting State," means:

(i) any individual possessing the nationality or citizenship of that State; and

(ii) any legal person, partnership or association deriving its status as such from the laws in force in that State;

i) the term "qualified governmental entity" means:

(i) any person or body of persons that constitutes a governing body of a Contracting State, or of a political subdivision or local authority of a Contracting State;

(ii) a person that is wholly owned, directly or indirectly, by a Contracting State or political subdivision or local authority of a Contracting State, provided it is organized under the laws of the Contracting State, its earnings are credited to its own account with no portion of its income inuring to the benefit of any private person, and its assets vest in the Contracting State, political subdivision or local authority upon dissolution; and

(iii) a pension trust or fund of a person described in clause (i) or (ii) that is constituted and operated exclusively to administer or provide pension benefits described in Article 19 (Government Service); provided that an entity described in clause (ii) or (iii) does not carry on commercial activities.

2. As regards the application of the Convention at any time by a Contracting State any term not defined therein shall, unless the context otherwise requires, or the competent authorities agree to a common meaning pursuant to the provisions of Article 25 (Mutual Agreement Procedure), have the meaning which it has at that time under the law of that State for the purposes of the taxes to which the Convention applies, any meaning under the applicable tax laws of that State prevailing over a meaning given to the term under other laws of that State.

Article 4

Residence

1. Except as provided in this paragraph, for the purposes of this Convention, the term "resident of a Contracting State" means any person who, under the laws of that State, is liable to tax therein by reason of his domicile, residence, citizenship, place of management, place of incorporation, or any other criterion of a similar nature.

a) The term "resident of a Contracting State" does not include any person who is liable to tax in that State in respect only of income from sources in that State or of profits attributable to a permanent establishment in that State.

b) A legal person organized under the laws of a Contracting State and that is generally exempt from tax in that State and is established and maintained in that State either:

(i) exclusively for a religious, charitable, educational, scientific, or other similar purpose; or

(ii) to provide pensions or other similar benefits to employees, including self-employed individuals, pursuant to a plan is to be treated for purposes of this paragraph as a resident of that Contracting State.

c) A qualified governmental entity is to be treated as a resident of the Contracting State where it is established.

d) An item of income, profit or gain derived through an entity that is fiscally transparent under the laws of either Contracting State shall be considered to be derived by a resident of a State to the extent that the item is treated for purposes of the taxation law of such Contracting State as the income, profit or gain of a resident.

2. Where by reason of the provisions of paragraph 1 an individual is a resident of both Contracting States, then his status shall be determined as follows:

a) the individual shall be deemed to be a resident of the State in which he has a permanent home available to him; if such individual has a permanent home available to him in both States, he shall be deemed to be a resident of the State with which his personal and economic relations are closer (center of vital interests);

b) if the State in which the individual has his center of vital interests cannot be determined, or if he has no permanent home available to him in either State, he shall be deemed to be a resident of the State in which he has an habitual abode;

c) if the individual has an habitual abode in both States or in neither of them, he shall be deemed to be a resident of the State of which he is a national;

d) if he is a national of both States or of neither of them, the competent authorities of the Contracting States shall endeavor to settle the question by mutual agreement.

3. Where by reason of the provisions of paragraph 1 a person other than an individual is a resident of both Contracting States, the competent authorities of the Contracting States shall by mutual agreement endeavor to settle the question and to determine the mode of application of the Convention to such person.

4. A United States citizen or an alien lawfully admitted for permanent residence in the United States is a resident of the United States, but only if such person has a substantial presence, permanent home or habitual abode in the United States.

Article 5

Permanent Establishment

1. For the purposes of this Convention, the term "permanent establishment" means a fixed place of business through which the business of an enterprise is wholly or partly carried on.

2. The term "permanent establishment" includes especially:

a) a place of management;

b) a branch;

c) an office;

d) a factory;

e) a workshop; and

f) a mine, an oil or gas well, a quarry, or any other place of extraction of natural resources.

3. A building site or construction or installation project, or an installation or drilling rig or ship used for the exploration of natural resources, constitutes a permanent establishment only if it lasts, or the activity continues for, more than 12 months. For the purpose of this paragraph, activities carried on by an enterprise related to another enterprise, within the meaning of Article 9 (Associated Enterprises), shall be regarded as carried on by the enterprise to which it is related if the activities in question:

a) are substantially the same as those carried on by the last-mentioned enterprise; and

b) are concerned with the same project or operation; except to the extent that those activities are carried on at the same time.

4. Notwithstanding the preceding provisions of this Article, the term "permanent establishment" shall be deemed not to include:

a) the use of facilities solely for the purpose of storage, display, or delivery of goods or merchandise belonging to the enterprise;

b) the maintenance of a stock of goods or merchandise belonging to the enterprise solely for the purpose of storage, display, or delivery;

c) the maintenance of a stock of goods or merchandise belonging to the enterprise solely for the purpose of processing by another enterprise;

d) the maintenance of a fixed place of business solely for the purpose of purchasing goods or merchandise, or of collecting information, for the enterprise;

e) the maintenance of a fixed place of business solely for the purpose of carrying on, for the enterprise, any other activity of a preparatory or auxiliary character;

f) the maintenance of a fixed place of business solely for any combination of the activities mentioned in subparagraphs a) to e) of this paragraph, provided that the overall activity of the fixed place of business resulting from the combination is of a preparatory or auxiliary character.

5. Notwithstanding the provisions of paragraphs 1 and 2, where a person—other than an agent of an independent status to whom paragraph 6 applies—is acting on behalf of an enterprise and has and habitually exercises in a Contracting State an authority to conclude contracts in the name of the enterprise, that enterprise shall be deemed to have a permanent establishment in that State in respect of any activities which that person undertakes for the enterprise, unless the activities of such person are limited to those mentioned in paragraph 4 which, if exercised through a fixed place of business, would not make this fixed place of business a permanent establishment under the provisions of that paragraph.

6. An enterprise shall not be deemed to have a permanent establishment in a Contracting State merely because it carries on business in that State through a broker, general commission agent, or any other agent of an independent status, provided that such persons are acting in the ordinary course of their business as independent agents.

7. The fact that a company that is a resident of a Contracting State controls or is controlled by a company that is a resident of the other Contracting State, or which carries on business in that other State (whether through a permanent establishment or otherwise), shall not constitute either company a permanent establishment of the other.

ARTICLE 6

INCOME FROM REAL PROPERTY

1. Income derived by a resident of a Contracting State from real property (including income from agriculture or forestry) situated in the other Contracting State may be taxed in that other State.

2. The term "real property" shall have the meaning which it has under the law of the Contracting State in which the property in question is situated. The term shall in any case include property accessory to real property, livestock and equipment used in agriculture and forestry, rights to which the provisions of general law respecting landed property apply, usufruct of real property, and rights to variable or fixed payments as consideration for the working of, or the right to work, mineral deposits, sources and other natural resources; ships, boats and aircraft shall not be regarded as real property.

3. The provisions of paragraph 1 shall apply to income derived from the direct use, letting, or use in any other form of real property.

4. The provisions of paragraphs 1 and 3 shall also apply to the income from real property of an enterprise and to income from real property used for the performance of independent personal services.

5. A resident of a Contracting State who is liable to tax in the other Contracting State on income from real property situated in the other Contracting State may elect for any taxable year to compute the tax on such income on a net basis as if such income were business profits attributable to a permanent establishment in such other State. Any such election shall be binding for the taxable year of the election and all subsequent taxable years unless the competent authority of the Contracting State in which the property is situated agrees to terminate the election.

ARTICLE 7

BUSINESS PROFITS

1. The business profits of an enterprise of a Contracting State shall be taxable only in that State unless the enterprise carries on business in the other Contracting State through a permanent establishment situated therein. If the enterprise carries on business as aforesaid, the business profits of the enterprise may be taxed in the other State but only so much of them as is attributable to that permanent establishment.

2. Subject to the provisions of paragraph 3, where an enterprise of a Contracting State carries on business in the other Contracting State through a permanent establishment situated therein, there shall in each Contracting State be attributed to that permanent establishment the business profits which it might be expected to make if it were a distinct and independent enterprise engaged in the same or similar activities under the same or similar conditions. For this purpose, the business profits to be attributed to the permanent establishment shall include only the profits derived from the assets or activities of the permanent establishment.

3. In determining the business profits of a permanent establishment, there shall be allowed as deductions expenses which are incurred for the purposes of the permanent establishment, including a reasonable allocation of executive and general administrative expenses, research and development expenses, interest, and other expenses incurred for the purposes of the enterprise as a whole (or the part thereof which includes the permanent establishment), whether incurred in the State in which the permanent establishment is situated or elsewhere.

4. No business profits shall be attributed to a permanent establishment by reason of the mere purchase by that permanent establishment of goods or merchandise for the enterprise.

5. For the purposes of the preceding paragraphs, the profits to be attributed to the permanent establishment shall be determined by the same method year by year unless there is good and sufficient reason to the contrary.

6. Where business profits include items of income which are dealt with separately in other Articles of this Convention, then the provisions of those Articles shall not be affected by the provisions of this Article.

7. For the purposes of this Convention, the term "business profits" means income from any trade or business, including income derived by an enterprise from the performance of personal services, and from the rental of tangible personal property.

8. In applying paragraphs 1 and 2 of Article 7 (Business Profits), paragraph 6 of Article 10 (Dividends), paragraph 3 of Article 11 (Interest), paragraph 3 of Article 12 (Royalties), paragraph 3 of Article 13 (Capital Gains), Article 14 (Independent Personal Services), and paragraph 2 of Article 21 (Other Income), any income or gain attributable to a permanent establishment or fixed base during its existence is taxable in the Contracting State where such permanent establishment or fixed base is situated even if the payments are deferred until such permanent establishment or fixed base has ceased to exist.

Article 8

Shipping and Air Transport

1. Profits of an enterprise of a Contracting State from the operation in international traffic of ships or aircraft shall be taxable only in that State.

2. For the purposes of this Article, profits from the operation of ships or aircraft include profits derived from the rental of ships or aircraft on a full (time or voyage) basis. They also include profits from the rental of ships or aircraft on a bareboat basis if such ships or aircraft are operated in international traffic by the lessee, or if the rental income is incidental to profits from the operation of ships or aircraft in international traffic. Profits derived by an enterprise from the inland transport of property or passengers within either Contracting State, shall be treated as profits from the operation of ships or aircraft in international traffic if such transport is undertaken as part of international traffic.

3. Profits of an enterprise of a Contracting State from the use, maintenance or rental of containers (including trailers, barges, and

related equipment for the transport of containers) used in international traffic shall be taxable only in that State.

4. The provisions of paragraphs 1 and 3 shall also apply to profits from the participation in a consortium, a pool, a joint business, or an international operating agency.

5. Notwithstanding the provisions of subparagraph 2f) and paragraph 3 of Article 5 (Permanent Establishment), the profits of an enterprise of a Contracting State from the transport by ships or aircraft of supplies or personnel to a location where offshore activities in connection with the exploration or exploitation of natural resources are being carried on in the other Contracting State, or from the operation of tugboats and similar vessels in connection with such activities, shall be taxable only in the first-mentioned State.

Article 9

Associated Enterprises

1. Where

a) an enterprise of a Contracting State participates, directly or indirectly, in the management, control, or capital of an enterprise of the other Contracting State, or

b) the same persons participate directly or indirectly in the management, control, or capital of an enterprise of a Contracting State and an enterprise of the other Contracting State, and in either case conditions are made or imposed between the two enterprises in their commercial or financial relations which differ from those which would be made between independent enterprises, then any profits which, but for those conditions, would have accrued to one of the enterprises, but by reason of those conditions, have not so accrued, may be included in the profits of that enterprise and taxed accordingly.

2. Where a Contracting State includes in the profits of an enterprise of that State, and taxes accordingly, profits on which an enterprise of the other Contracting State has been charged to tax in that other State, and the other Contracting State agrees that the profits so included are profits that would have accrued to the enterprise of the first-mentioned State if the conditions made between the two enterprises had been those which would have been made between independent enterprises, then that other State shall make an appropriate adjustment to the amount of the tax charged therein on those profits. In determining such adjustment, due regard shall be had to the other provisions of this Convention and the competent authorities of the Contracting States shall if necessary consult each other.

Article 10

Dividends

1. Dividends paid by a resident of a Contracting State to a resident of the other Contracting State may be taxed in that other State.

2. However, such dividends may also be taxed in the Contracting State of which the company paying the dividends is a resident and

according to the laws of that State, but if the beneficial owner of the dividends is a resident of the other Contracting State the tax so charged shall not exceed:

a) 5 percent of the gross amount of the dividends if the beneficial owner is a company which holds directly at least 10 percent of the share capital of the company paying the dividends;

b) 15 percent of the gross amount of the dividends in all other cases. This paragraph shall not affect the taxation of the company in respect of the profits out of which the dividends are paid.

3. Subparagraph a) of paragraph 2 shall not apply in the case of dividends paid by a United States Regulated Investment Company (RIC) or United States Real Estate Investment Trust (REIT). In the case of dividends from a RIC, subparagraph b) of paragraph 2 shall apply. In the case of dividends paid by a REIT, subparagraph b) of paragraph 2 shall apply only if:

a) the beneficial owner of the dividends is an individual holding an interest of not more than 10 percent in the REIT;

b) the dividends are paid with respect to a class of stock that is publicly traded and the beneficial owner of the dividends is a person holding an interest of not more than 5 percent of any class of the REIT's stock; or

c) the beneficial owner of the dividends is a person holding an interest of not more than 10 percent in the REIT and the REIT is diversified.

4. Notwithstanding paragraph 2, dividends may not be taxed in the Contracting State of which the payor is a resident if the beneficial owner of the dividends is a resident of the other Contracting State that is a qualified governmental entity that does not control the payor of the dividend.

5. The term "dividends" as used in this Article means income from shares or other rights, not being debt-claims, participating in profits, as well as income that is subject to the same taxation treatment as income from shares by the laws of the State of which the payor is a resident.

6. The provisions of paragraphs 1 and 2 shall not apply if the beneficial owner of the dividends, being a resident of a Contracting State, carries on business in the other Contracting State of which the payor is a resident, through a permanent establishment situated therein, or performs in that other State independent personal services from a fixed base situated therein, and the dividends are attributable to such permanent establishment or fixed base. In such case, the provisions of Article 7 (Business Profits) or Article 14 (Independent Personal Services), as the case may be, shall apply.

7. A Contracting State may not impose any tax on dividends paid by a resident of the other State, except insofar as the dividends are paid to a resident of the first-mentioned State or the dividends are attributable to a permanent establishment or a fixed base situated in that State, nor may it impose tax on a corporation's undistributed profits, except as provided in paragraph 8, even if the dividends paid or the undistributed profits consist wholly or partly of profits or income arising in that State.

8. A corporation that is a resident of one of the States and that has a permanent establishment in the other State or that is subject to tax in the other State on a net basis on its income that may be taxed in the other State under Article 6 (Income from Real Property) or under paragraph 1 of Article 13 (Capital Gains) may be subject in that other State to a tax in addition to the tax allowable under the other provisions of this Convention. Such tax, however, may be imposed on only the portion of the business profits of the corporation attributable to the permanent establishment and the portion of the income referred to in the preceding sentence that is subject to tax under Article 6 (Income from Real Property) or under paragraph 1 of Article 13 (Capital Gains) that, in the case of the United States, represents the dividend equivalent amount of such profits or income and, in the case of Denmark, is an amount that is analogous to the dividend equivalent amount.

9. The tax referred to in paragraph 8 may not be imposed at a rate in excess of the rate specified in subparagraph a) of paragraph 2.

Article 11

Interest

1. Interest arising in a Contracting State and beneficially owned by a resident of the other Contracting State shall be taxable only in that other State.

2. The term "interest" as used in this Article means income from debt-claims of every kind, whether or not secured by mortgage, and whether or not carrying a right to participate in the debtor's profits, and in particular, income from government securities and income from bonds or debentures, including premiums or prizes attaching to such securities, bonds, or debentures, and all other income that is subjected to the same taxation treatment as income from money lent by the taxation law of the Contracting State in which the income arises. Income dealt with in Article 10 (Dividends) and penalty charges for late payment shall not be regarded as interest for the purposes of this Article.

3. The provisions of paragraph 1 shall not apply if the beneficial owner of the interest, being a resident of a Contracting State, carries on business in the other Contracting State in which the interest arises, through a permanent establishment situated therein, or performs in that other State independent personal services from a fixed base situated therein, and the interest is attributable to such permanent establishment or fixed base. In such case the provisions of Article 7 (Business Profits) or Article 14 (Independent Personal Services), as the case may be, shall apply.

4. Where, by reason of a special relationship between the payor and the beneficial owner or between both of them and some other person, the amount of the interest, having regard to the debt-claim for which it is paid, exceeds the amount which would have been agreed upon by the payor and the beneficial owner in the absence of such relationship, the provisions of this Article shall apply only to the last-mentioned amount. In such case, the excess part of the payments shall remain taxable according to the laws of each State, due regard being had to the other provisions of this Convention.

5. Notwithstanding the provisions of paragraph 1:

a) interest paid by a resident of a Contracting State and that is determined with reference to receipts, sales, income, profits or other cash flow of the debtor or a related person, to any change in the value of any property of the debtor or a related person or to any dividend, partnership distribution or similar payment made by the debtor to a related person, and paid to a resident of the other State also may be taxed in the Contracting State in which it arises, and according to the laws of that State, but if the beneficial owner is a resident of the other Contracting State, the gross amount of the interest may be taxed at a rate not exceeding the rate prescribed in subparagraph b) of paragraph 2 of Article 10 (Dividends); and

b) interest that is an excess inclusion with respect to a residual interest in a real estate mortgage investment conduit may be taxed by each State in accordance with its domestic law.

Article 12

Royalties

1. Royalties arising in a Contracting State and beneficially owned by a resident of the other Contracting State shall be taxable only in that other State.

2. The term "royalties" as used in this Article means:

a) any consideration for the use of, or the right to use, any copyright of literary, artistic, scientific or other work (including computer software, cinematographic films, audio or video tapes or disks, and other means of image or sound reproduction), any patent, trademark, design or model, plan, secret formula or process, or other like right or property, or for information concerning industrial, commercial or scientific experience; and

b) gain derived from the alienation of any property described in subparagraph a), provided that such gain is contingent on the productivity, use or disposition of the property.

3. The provisions of paragraph 1 shall not apply if the beneficial owner of the royalties, being a resident of a Contracting State, carries on business in the other Contracting State in which the royalties arise, through a permanent establishment situated therein, or performs in that other State independent personal services from a fixed base situated therein, and the royalties are attributable to such permanent establishment or fixed base. In such case the provisions of Article 7 (Business Profits) or Article 14 (Independent Personal Services), as the case may be, shall apply.

4. Where, by reason of a special relationship between the payor and the beneficial owner or between both of them and some other person, the amount of the royalties, having regard to the use, right, or information for which they are paid, exceeds the amount which would have been agreed upon by the payor and the beneficial owner in the absence of such relationship, the provisions of this Article shall apply only to the last-mentioned amount. In such case, the excess part of the payments shall remain taxable according to the laws of each Contracting State, due regard being had to the other provisions of this Convention.

Article 13

Capital Gains

1. Gains derived by a resident of a Contracting State that are attributable to the alienation of real property situated in the other Contracting State may be taxed in that other State.

2. For the purposes of this Article, the term "real property situated in the other Contracting State" shall include:

a) real property referred to in Article 6 (Income from Real Property);

b) a United States real property interest; and

c) an equivalent interest in real property situated in Denmark.

3. Gains from the alienation of personal property that are attributable to a permanent establishment that an enterprise of a Contracting State has in the other Contracting State or that are attributable to a fixed base that is available to a resident of a Contracting State in the other Contracting State for the purpose of performing independent personal services, and gains from the alienation of such a permanent establishment (alone or with the whole enterprise) or of such a fixed base, may be taxed in that other State.

4. Notwithstanding the provisions of paragraph 3, gains derived by an enterprise of a Contracting State from the alienation of ships, boats, aircraft, or containers operated or used in international traffic or personal property pertaining to the operation or use of such ships, boats, aircraft, or containers shall be taxable only in that State.

5. Gains derived by an enterprise of a Contracting State from the deemed alienation of an installation, drilling rig, or ship used in the other Contracting State for the exploration for or exploitation of oil and gas resources may be taxed in that other State in accordance with its law, but only to the extent of any depreciation taken in that other State.

6. Gains from the alienation of any property, other than that referred to in paragraphs 1 through 5, shall be taxable only in the Contracting State of which the alienator is a resident.

7. If a resident of a Contracting State is subject to income taxation in both Contracting States on a disposition of property and is treated as having alienated property with respect to which a gain is recognized under the income tax laws of the other Contracting State, then the resident not otherwise required to do so may elect in his annual return of income for the year of the alienation to be liable to tax in the residence State in that year as if he had, immediately before that time, sold and repurchased such property for an amount equal to its fair market value at that time. Such an election shall apply to all property described in this paragraph that is alienated by the resident in the taxable year for which the election is made or at any time thereafter.

8. Where a resident of a Contracting State alienates property in the course of a corporate or other organization, reorganization, amalgamation, division or similar transaction and profit, gain or income with respect to such alienation is not recognized for the

purpose of taxation in that State, the competent authority of the other Contracting State may agree, if requested to do so by the person who acquires the property, in order to avoid double taxation and subject to terms and conditions satisfactory to such competent authority, to defer the recognition of the profit, gain or income with respect to such property for the purpose of taxation in that other State until such time and in such manner as may be stipulated in the agreement.

Article 14

Independent Personal Services

1. Income derived by an individual who is a resident of a Contracting State in respect of the performance of personal services of an independent character shall be taxable only in that State, unless the individual has a fixed base regularly available to him in the other Contracting State for the purpose of performing his activities. If he has such a fixed base, the income attributable to the fixed base that is derived in respect of services performed in that other State also may be taxed by that other State.

2. For purposes of paragraph 1, the income that is taxable in the other Contracting State shall be determined under the principles of paragraph 3 of Article 7 (Business Profits).

Article 15

Dependent Personal Services

1. Subject to the provisions of Articles 16 (Directors' Fees), 18 (Pensions, Social Security, Annuities, Alimony and Child Support Payments), and 19 (Government Service), salaries, wages and other remuneration derived by a resident of a Contracting State in respect of an employment shall be taxable only in that State unless the employment is exercised in the other Contracting State. If the employment is so exercised, such remuneration as is derived therefrom may be taxed in that other State.

2. Notwithstanding the provisions of paragraph 1, remuneration derived by a resident of a Contracting State in respect of an employment exercised in the other Contracting State shall be taxable only in the first-mentioned State if:

a) the recipient is present in the other State for a period or periods not exceeding in the aggregate 183 days in any twelve month period commencing or ending in the taxable year concerned; and

b) the remuneration is paid by, or on behalf of, an employer who is not a resident of the other State; and

c) the remuneration is not borne by a permanent establishment or a fixed base which the employer has in the other State.

3. Notwithstanding the preceding provisions of this Article, remuneration described in paragraph 1 that is derived by a resident of a Contracting State in respect of an employment as a member of the regular complement of a ship or aircraft operated in international traffic shall be taxable only in that State.

Article 16

Directors' Fees

Directors' fees and other similar payments derived by a resident of a Contracting State in his capacity as a member of the board of directors of a company which is a resident of the other Contracting State may be taxed in that other State.

Article 17

Artistes and Sportsmen

1. Income derived by a resident of a Contracting State as an entertainer, such as a theater, motion picture, radio, or television artiste, or a musician, or as a sportsman, from his personal activities as such exercised in the other Contracting State, which income would be exempt from tax in that other Contracting State under the provisions of Articles 14 (Independent Personal Services) and 15 (Dependent Personal Services), may be taxed in that other State, except where the amount of the gross receipts derived by such entertainer or sportsman, including expenses reimbursed to him, or borne on his behalf, from such activities does not exceed twenty thousand United States dollars ($20,000) or its equivalent in Danish kroner for the taxable year concerned.

2. Where income in respect of activities exercised by an entertainer or a sportsman in his capacity as such accrues not to the entertainer or sportsman himself but to another person, that income may, notwithstanding the provisions of Articles 7 (Business Profits) and 14 (Independent Personal Services), be taxed in the Contracting State in which the activities of the entertainer or sportsman are exercised, unless the entertainer or sportsman establishes that neither the entertainer or sportsman nor persons related thereto participate directly or indirectly in the profits of that other person in any manner, including the receipt of deferred remuneration, bonuses, fees, dividends, partnership distributions, or other distributions.

Article 18

Pensions, Social Security, Annuities, Alimony and Child Support Payments

1. Subject to the provisions of paragraph 2 of Article 19 (Government Service),

a) Except as provided in subparagraph b), pension distributions arising in a Contracting State and beneficially owned by a resident of the other Contracting State shall be taxable only in the State in which they arise;

b) If, prior to the time of entry into force of this Convention, a person was a resident of a Contracting State and was receiving pension distributions arising in the other Contracting State, that person shall be taxable on pension distributions referred to in subparagraph a) only in the first-mentioned Contracting State;

c) Pension distributions shall be deemed to arise in a Contracting State only if paid by a pension scheme established in that State.

d) For purposes of this paragraph, pension distributions means pension distributions and other similar remuneration, whether paid periodically or as a single sum.

2. Notwithstanding the provisions of paragraph 1, payments made by a Contracting State under provisions of the social security or similar legislation of that Contracting State to a resident of the other Contracting State or to a citizen of the United States shall be taxable only in the first mentioned State.

3. Annuities derived and beneficially owned by an individual resident of a Contracting State shall be taxable only in that State. The term "annuities" as used in this paragraph means a stated sum paid periodically at stated times during a specified number of years or for life under an obligation to make the payments in return for adequate and full consideration (other than services rendered).

4. Alimony paid by a resident of a Contracting State, and deductible therein, to a resident of the other Contracting State shall be taxable only in that other Contracting State. The term "alimony" as used in this paragraph means periodic payments made pursuant to a written separation agreement or a decree of divorce, separate maintenance, or compulsory support, which payments are taxable to the recipient under the laws of the State of which he is a resident.

5. Periodic payments, not dealt with in paragraph 4, for the support of a child made pursuant to a written separation agreement or a decree of divorce, separate maintenance, or compulsory support, paid by a resident of a Contracting State to a resident of the other Contracting State, shall be taxable only in the first-mentioned Contracting State.

Article 19

Government Service

1. Notwithstanding the provisions of Articles 14 (Independent Personal Services), 15 (Dependent Personal Services), 16 (Directors' Fees) and 17 (Artistes and Sportsmen):

a) Salaries, wages and other remuneration, other than a pension, paid from the public funds of a Contracting State or a political subdivision or a local authority thereof to an individual in respect of services rendered to that State or subdivision or authority in the discharge of functions of a governmental nature shall, subject to the provisions of subparagraph b), be taxable only in that State;

b) such remuneration, however, shall be taxable only in the other Contracting State if the services are rendered in that State and the individual is a resident of that State who:

(i) is a national of that State; or

(ii) did not become a resident of that State solely for the purpose of rendering the services.

2. a) Any pension paid from the public funds of a Contracting State or a political subdivision or a local authority thereof to an individual in respect of services rendered to that State or subdivision or authority in the discharge of functions of a governmental nature (other than a payment described in paragraph 2 of Article 18 (Pensions, Social Security, Annuities, Alimony and Child Support Payments)) shall, subject to the provisions of subparagraph b), be taxable only in that State;

b) such pension, however, shall be taxable only in the other Contracting State if the individual is a resident or a national of that State.

3. The provisions of Articles 15 (Dependent Personal Services), 16 (Directors' Fees), 17 (Artistes and Sportsmen) and 18 (Pensions, Social Security, Annuities, Alimony and Child Support Payments) shall apply to remuneration and pensions in respect of services rendered in connection with a business carried on by a Contracting State or a political subdivision or a local authority thereof.

ARTICLE 20

STUDENTS AND TRAINEES

Payments received by a student, apprentice, or business trainee who is, or was immediately before visiting a Contracting State, a resident of the other Contracting State, and who is present in the first-mentioned State for the purpose of his full-time education at an accredited educational institution, or for his full-time training, shall not be taxed in that State, provided that such payments arise outside that State, and are for the purpose of his maintenance, education or training. The exemption from tax provided by this Article shall apply to an apprentice or business trainee only for a period of time not exceeding three years from the date he first arrives in the first-mentioned Contracting State for the purpose of his training. The provisions of this paragraph shall not apply to income from research if such research is undertaken not in the public interest but primarily for the private benefit of a specific person or persons.

ARTICLE 21

OTHER INCOME

1. Items of income beneficially owned by a resident of a Contracting State, wherever arising, not dealt with in the foregoing Articles of this Convention shall be taxable only in that State.

2. The provisions of paragraph 1 shall not apply to income, other than income from real property as defined in paragraph 2 of Article 6 (Income from Real Property), if the beneficial owner of such income, being a resident of a Contracting State, carries on business in the other Contracting State through a permanent establishment situated therein, or performs in the other State independent personal services from a fixed base situated therein, and the income is attributable to such permanent establishment or fixed base. In such case the provisions of Article 7 (Business Profits) or Article 14 (Independent Personal Services), as the case may be, shall apply.

Article 22

Limitation of Benefits

1. A resident of a Contracting State shall be entitled to the benefits of this Convention only to the extent provided in this Article.

2. A resident of a Contracting State shall be entitled to all the benefits of this Convention only if such resident is:

a) an individual;

b) a Contracting State, a political subdivision, or local authority thereof, or an agency or instrumentality of that State, subdivision, or authority;

c) a company if:

(i) all the shares in the class or classes of shares representing more than 50 percent of the vote and value are listed on a recognized stock exchange and are substantially and regularly traded on one or more recognized stock exchanges;

(ii) one or more taxable nonstock corporations entitled to benefits under paragraph g) own shares representing more than 50 percent of the voting power of the company and all other shares are listed on a recognized stock exchange and are substantially and regularly traded on one or more recognized stock exchanges; or

(iii) at least 50 percent of each class of shares in the company is owned, directly or indirectly, by five or fewer companies entitled to benefits under clause (i) or (ii), or any combination thereof, provided that in the case of indirect ownership, each intermediate owner is a person entitled to benefits of the Convention under this paragraph;

d) a charitable organization or other legal person described in subparagraph b)(i) of paragraph 1 of Article 4 (Residence);

e) a legal person, whether or not exempt from tax, organized under the laws of a Contracting State to provide a pension or other similar benefits to employees, including self-employed individuals, pursuant to a plan, provided that more than 50 percent of the person's beneficiaries, members or participants are individuals resident in either Contracting State; or

f) a person, other than an individual, if

(i) on at least half the days of the taxable year, persons described in subparagraphs a), b), c), d), or e) own, directly or indirectly (through a chain of ownership in which each person is entitled to the benefits of the Convention under this paragraph), at least 50 percent of the beneficial interest in such person (or, in the case of a company, at least 50 percent of the vote and value of the company's shares); and

(ii) less than 50 percent of the person's gross income for the taxable year is paid or accrued, in the form of deductible payments, directly or indirectly, to persons who are not residents of either Contracting State (unless the payment is attributable to a permanent establishment situated in either State);

g) in the case of Denmark, a taxable nonstock corporation if

(i) the amount paid or accrued in the form of deductible payments in the taxable year and in each of the preceding three taxable years, directly or indirectly, to persons who are not entitled to benefits under subparagraphs a), b), c)(i), c)(iii) by virtue of c)(i), d) or e), does not exceed 50% of the amount of its gross income (excluding its tax-exempt income); and

(ii) the amount paid or accrued, in the form of both deductible payments and non-deductible distributions, in the taxable year and in each of the preceding three taxable years, directly or indirectly, to persons who are not entitled to benefits under subparagraphs a), b), c)(i), c(iii) by virtue of c(i), d), or e), does not exceed 50% of the amount of its total income (including its tax-exempt income).

3. a) A resident of a Contracting State not otherwise entitled to benefits shall be entitled to the benefits of this Convention with respect to an item of income derived from the other Contracting State if:

(i) the resident is engaged in the active conduct of a trade or business in the first-mentioned Contracting State;

(ii) the income is connected with or incidental to the trade or business in the first-mentioned Contracting State; and

(iii) the trade or business is substantial in relation to the activity in the other State generating the income.

b) For purposes of this paragraph, the business of making or managing investments will not be considered an active trade or business, unless the activity is banking, insurance or securities activities carried on by a bank, insurance company, or registered securities dealer.

c) Whether a trade or business is substantial for purposes of this paragraph will be determined based on all the facts and circumstances. In any case, however, a trade or business will be deemed substantial if, for the preceding taxable year, or for the average of the three preceding taxable years, the asset value, the gross income, and the payroll expense that are related to the trade or business in the first-mentioned State equal at least 7.5 percent of the resident's (and any related parties') proportionate share of the asset value, gross income and payroll expense, respectively, that are related to the activity that generated the income in the other State, and the average of the three ratios exceeds 10 percent. In determining the above ratios, assets, income, and payroll expense shall be taken into account only to the extent of the resident's direct or indirect ownership interest in the activity in the other State. If neither the resident nor any of its associated enterprises has an ownership interest in the activity in the other State, the resident's trade or business in the first-mentioned State shall be considered substantial in relation to such activity.

d) Income is derived in connection with a trade or business if the activity in the other State generating the income is a line of business that forms part of or is complementary to the trade or business. Income is incidental to a trade or business if it facilitates the conduct of the trade or business in the other State.

4. a) A company that is a resident of a Contracting State shall also be entitled to all of the benefits of the Convention if:

(i) at least 95 percent of the aggregate vote and value of all its shares is owned, directly or indirectly, by seven or fewer persons that are residents of Member States of the European Union, or of the European Economic Area, or of parties to the North American Free Trade Agreement (NAFTA) that, in any case, meet the requirements of subparagraph c), or any combination thereof; and

(ii) less than 50 percent of the company's gross income for the taxable year is paid or accrued, in the form of deductible payments, directly or indirectly, to persons who are not residents of Member States of the European Union, or of the European Economic Area, or of parties to the North American Free Trade Agreement that, in any case, meet the requirements of subparagraph c), or any combination thereof.

b) However, a company otherwise entitled to benefits under subparagraph a) will not be entitled to the benefits of this Convention if that company, or a company that controls such company, has outstanding a class of shares:

(i) the terms of which, or which is subject to other arrangements that, entitle its holders to a portion of the income of the company derived from the other Contracting State that is larger than the portion such holders would receive absent such terms or arrangements; and

(ii) 50 percent or more of the vote or value of which is owned by persons who are not residents of a Member State of the European Union or the European Economic Area or a party to the North American Free Trade Agreement that, in any case, meet the requirements of subparagraph c), or any combination thereof.

c) For purposes of subparagraphs a) and b), a person will be treated as a resident of a Member State of the European Union or of the European Economic Area or of a party to the North American Free Trade Agreement only if such person:

(i) would be entitled to the benefits of a comprehensive income tax convention in force between any Member State of the European Union or of the European Economic Area or a party to the North American Free Trade Agreement and the Contracting State from which the benefits of this Convention are claimed, provided that if such other convention does not contain a comprehensive limitation on benefits article (including provisions similar to those of subparagraphs c) and f) of paragraph 2 and paragraph 3 of this Article), the person would be entitled to the benefits of this Convention under the principles of paragraph 2 if such person were a resident of one of the Contracting States under Article 4 (Residence) of this Convention; and

(ii) with respect to income referred to in Articles 10 (Dividends), 11 (Interest) or 12 (Royalties), would be entitled under such other convention to a rate of tax with respect to the particular class of income for which benefits are being claimed under this Convention that is at least as low as the rate applicable under this Convention.

5. A resident of one of the Contracting States that derives from the other Contracting State income mentioned in Article 8 (Shipping and Air Transport) and that is not entitled to the benefits of this Convention because of the foregoing paragraphs, shall nevertheless be entitled to the benefits of this Convention with respect to such income if at least 50% of the beneficial interest in such person (or in the case of a company, at least 50% of the aggregate vote and value of the stock of such company) is owned directly or indirectly:

a) by persons described in subparagraphs a), b), c), d), or e) of paragraph 2, or citizens of the United States, or individuals who are residents of a third state; or

b) by a company or combination of companies the stock of which is primarily and regularly traded on an established securities market in a third state, provided that such third state grants an exemption under similar terms for profits as mentioned in Article 8 (Shipping and Air Transport) of this Convention to citizens and corporations of the other Contracting State either under its national law or in common agreement with that other Contracting State or under a convention between that third state and the other Contracting State.

6. The following rules and definitions shall apply for purposes of this Article:

a) in measuring "gross income", as used in subparagraph f) of paragraph 2, the term means gross income for the first taxable period preceding the current taxable period, provided that the amount of gross income for the first taxable period preceding the current taxable period shall be deemed to be no less than the average of the annual amounts of gross income for the four taxable periods preceding the current taxable period;

b) the term "deductible payments"

(i) as used in subparagraphs f) and g) of paragraph 2 and subparagraph a) of paragraph 4 includes payments for interest or royalties, but does not include payments at arm's length for the purchase or use of or the right to use tangible property in the ordinary course of business or remuneration at arm's length for services performed in the Contracting State in which the person making such payments is a resident; and

(ii) as used in subparagraph g) of paragraph 2 also includes deductible distributions made by a taxable nonstock corporation. Types of payments may be added to, or eliminated from, the exceptions mentioned in the preceding definition of "deductible payments" by mutual agreement of the competent authorities;

c) For the purposes of this Article, the term "recognized stock exchange" means:

(i) the NASDAQ System owned by the National Association of Securities Dealers, Inc. and any stock exchange registered with the U.S. Securities and Exchange Commission as a national securities exchange for purposes of the U.S. Securities Exchange Act of 1934;

(ii) the Copenhagen Stock Exchange and the stock exchanges of Amsterdam, Brussels, Frankfurt, Hamburg, London, Paris, Stockholm, Sydney, Tokyo and Toronto;

(iii) any other stock exchanges agreed upon by the competent authorities of both Contracting States;

d) the term "engaged in the active conduct of a trade or business" in a Contracting State as used in paragraph 3, applies to a person that is directly so engaged, or is a partner in a partnership that is so engaged, or is so engaged through one or more associated enterprises (wherever resident);

e) the term "taxable nonstock corporation" as used in paragraph 2 means a foundation that is taxable in accordance with paragraph 1 of Article 1 of the Danish Act on Taxable Nonstock Corporations (fonde der beskattes efter fondsbeskatningsloven).

f) (i) For the purposes of paragraph 2, the shares in a class of shares are considered to be substantially and regularly traded on one or more recognized stock exchanges in a taxable year if:

(1) trades in such class are effected on one or more of such stock exchanges other than in de minimis quantities during every quarter; and

(2) the aggregate number of shares or units of that class traded on such stock exchange or exchanges during the previous taxable year is at least 6 percent of the average number of shares or units outstanding in that class (including shares held by taxable nonstock corporations) during that taxable year.

(ii) For purposes of determining whether a company satisfies the requirements of clause (c)(ii) of paragraph 2, clause (i) of this subparagraph shall be applied as if all the shares issued by the company were one class of shares, and shares held by taxable nonstock corporations will be considered outstanding for purposes of determining whether 6 percent of the outstanding shares have been traded during a taxable year.

7. A resident of a Contracting State that is not entitled to the benefits of the Convention under the provisions of the preceding paragraphs of this Article shall, nevertheless, be granted the benefits of the Convention if the competent authority of the other Contracting State so determines.

Article 23

Relief from Double Taxation

1. In accordance with the provisions and subject to the limitations of the law of the United States (as it may be amended from time to time without changing the general principle hereof), the United States shall allow to a resident or citizen of the United States as a credit against the United States tax on income:

a) the income tax paid or accrued to Denmark by or on behalf of such resident or citizen; and

b) in the case of a United States company owning at least 10 percent of the voting stock of a company that is a resident of Denmark and from which the United States company receives dividends, the income tax paid or accrued to Denmark by or on behalf of the payor with respect to the profits out of which the dividends are paid.

c) (i) Subject to the provisions of clause (ii), in the case of a resident or national of the United States subject to the taxes imposed by the Hydrocarbon Tax Act that are referred to in subparagraph b)(iv) of paragraph 1 of Article 2 (Taxes Covered), the United States shall allow as a credit against the United States tax on income, the appropriate amount of tax paid or accrued to Denmark by or on behalf of such resident or national pursuant to the Hydrocarbon Tax Act on oil and gas extraction income from oil or gas wells in Denmark. However, the appropriate amount allowed as a credit shall not exceed the product of the maximum statutory United States tax rate applicable to such resident or national for such taxable year, and the amount of income separately assessed under the Hydrocarbon Tax Act.

(ii) The appropriate amount is also subject to any other limitations imposed by the law of the United States, as it may be amended from time to time, that apply to creditable taxes under section 901 or 903 of the Internal Revenue Code for persons claiming benefits under this Convention. Any taxes paid on income assessed separately under the Hydrocarbon Tax Act in excess of the appropriate amount may be used only as a credit in another taxable year, and only against United States tax on income assessed separately under the Hydrocarbon Tax Act.

(iii) The provisions of clauses (i) and (ii) shall apply separately, in the same way, to the amount of tax paid or accrued to Denmark pursuant to the Hydrocarbon Tax Act on (1) Danish source oil related income not described in clause (i); and (2) other Danish source income.

For the purposes of this Article, the Danish taxes referred to in paragraphs 1(b) and 2 of Article 2 (Taxes Covered) shall be considered income taxes and shall be allowed as a credit against the United States tax on income, subject to all the provisions and limitations of this paragraph.

2. Where a United States citizen is a resident of Denmark:

a) with respect to items of income that under the provisions of this Convention are exempt from United States tax or that are subject to a reduced rate of United States tax when derived by a resident of Denmark who is not a United States citizen, Denmark shall allow as a credit against Danish tax only the tax paid, if any, that the United States may impose under the provisions of this Convention, other than taxes that may be imposed solely by reason of citizenship under the saving clause of paragraph 4 of Article 1 (General Scope);

b) for purposes of computing United States tax on those items of income referred to in subparagraph a), the United States shall allow as a credit against United States tax the income tax paid to Denmark after the credit referred to in subparagraph a); the credit so allowed shall not reduce the portion of the United States tax that is creditable against the Danish tax in accordance with subparagraph a); and

c) for the exclusive purpose of relieving double taxation in the United States under subparagraph b), items of income referred to in subparagraph a) shall be deemed to arise in Denmark to the extent necessary to avoid double taxation of such income under subparagraph b).

3. In the case of Denmark, double taxation shall be avoided as follows:

a) When a resident of Denmark derives income which, in accordance with the provisions of this Convention, may be taxed in the United States, Denmark shall allow as a deduction from the tax on the income of that resident an amount equal to the income tax paid in the United States;

b) Such deduction shall not, however, exceed that part of the income tax, as computed before the deduction is given, which is attributable to the income that may be taxed in the United States.

c) When a resident of Denmark derives income which, in accordance with the provisions of this Convention, shall be taxable only in the United States, Denmark may include this income in the tax base but shall allow as a deduction from income tax that part of the income tax which is attributable to the income derived from the United States.

For the purposes of this paragraph, the United States taxes referred to in paragraphs 1(a) and 2 of Article 2 (Taxes Covered) shall be considered income taxes, and shall be allowed as a credit against the Danish tax on income.

Article 24

Non-Discrimination

1. Nationals of a Contracting State shall not be subjected in the other Contracting State to any taxation or any requirement connected therewith that is more burdensome than the taxation and connected requirements to which citizens of that other State in the same circumstances, particularly with respect to taxation of worldwide income, are or may be subjected. This provision shall also apply to persons who are not residents of one or both of the Contracting States.

2. The taxation on a permanent establishment or fixed base that a resident or enterprise of a Contracting State has in the other Contracting State shall not be less favorably levied in that other State than the taxation levied on enterprises or residents of that other State carrying on the same activities. The provisions of this paragraph shall not be construed as obliging a Contracting State to grant to residents of the other Contracting State any personal allowances, reliefs, and reductions for taxation purposes on account of civil status or family responsibilities which it grants to its own residents.

3. Except where the provisions of paragraph 1 of Article 9 (Associated Enterprises), paragraph 4 of Article 11 (Interest), or paragraph 4 of Article 12 (Royalties) apply, interest, royalties and other disbursements paid by an enterprise of a Contracting State to a

resident of the other Contracting State shall, for the purpose of determining the taxable profits of such enterprise, be deductible under the same conditions as if they had been paid to a resident of the first-mentioned State. Similarly, any debts of an enterprise of a Contracting State to a resident of the other Contracting State shall, for the purpose of determining the taxable capital of the first mentioned resident, be deductible under the same conditions as if they had been contracted to a resident of the first-mentioned State.

4. Enterprises of a Contracting State, the capital of which is wholly or partly owned or controlled, directly or indirectly, by one or more residents of the other Contracting State, shall not be subjected in the first-mentioned State to any taxation or any requirement connected therewith that is more burdensome than the taxation and connected requirements to which other similar enterprises of the first-mentioned State are or may be subjected.

5. Nothing in this Article shall be construed as preventing either Contracting State from imposing a tax as described in paragraph 8 of Article 10 (Dividends).

6. The provisions of this Article shall, notwithstanding the provisions of Article 2 (Taxes Covered), apply to taxes of every kind and description imposed by a Contracting State or a political subdivision or local authority thereof.

Article 25

Mutual Agreement Procedure

1. Where a person considers that the actions of one or both of the Contracting States result or will result for him in taxation not in accordance with the provisions of this Convention, he may, irrespective of the remedies provided by the domestic law of those States and the time limits prescribed in such laws for presentation of claims for refund, present his case to the competent authority of the Contracting State of which he is a resident or national.

2. The competent authority shall endeavour, if the objection appears to it to be justified and if it is not itself able to arrive at a satisfactory solution, to resolve the case by mutual agreement with the competent authority of the other Contracting State, with a view to the avoidance of taxation which is not in accordance with the Convention. Any agreement reached shall be implemented notwithstanding any time limits in the domestic law of the Contracting States. Assessment and collection procedures shall be suspended during the pendency of any mutual agreement proceeding.

3. The competent authorities of the Contracting States shall endeavour to resolve by mutual agreement any difficulties or doubts arising as to the interpretation or application of the Convention. In particular the competent authorities of the Contracting States may agree:

a) to the same attribution of income, deductions, credits, or allowances of an enterprise of a Contracting State to its permanent establishment situated in the other Contracting State;

b) to the same allocation of income, deductions, credits, or allowances between persons;

c) to the same characterization of particular items of income, including the same characterization of income that is assimilated to income from shares by the taxation law of one of the Contracting States and that is treated as a different class of income in the other State;

d) to the same characterization of persons;

e) to the same application of source rules with respect to particular items of income;

f) to a common meaning of a term;

g) to advance pricing arrangements; and

h) to the application of the provisions of domestic law regarding penalties, fines, and interest in a manner consistent with the purposes of the Convention.

They may also consult together for the elimination of double taxation in cases not provided for in the Convention.

4. The competent authorities also may agree to increases in any specific dollar amounts referred to in the Convention to reflect economic or monetary developments.

5. The competent authorities of the Contracting States may communicate with each other directly for the purpose of reaching an agreement in the sense of the preceding paragraphs.

Article 26

Exchange of Information

1. The competent authorities of the Contracting States shall exchange such information as is relevant for carrying out the provisions of this Convention or of the domestic laws of the Contracting States concerning taxes covered by the Convention insofar as the taxation thereunder is not contrary to the Convention, including information relating to the assessment or collection of, the enforcement or prosecution in respect of, or the determination of appeals in relation to, the taxes covered by the Convention. The exchange of information is not restricted by Article 1 (General Scope). Any information received by a Contracting State shall be treated as secret in the same manner as information obtained under the domestic laws of that State and shall be disclosed only to persons or authorities (including courts and administrative bodies) involved in the assessment, collection, or administration of, the enforcement or prosecution in respect of, or the determination of appeals in relation to, the taxes covered by the Convention or the oversight of the above. Such persons or authorities shall use the information only for such purposes. They may disclose the information in public court proceedings or in judicial decisions.

2. In no case shall the provisions of paragraph 1 be construed so as to impose on a Contracting State the obligation:

a) to carry out administrative measures at variance with the laws and administrative practice of that or of the other Contracting State;

b) to supply information which is not obtainable under the laws or in the normal course of the administration of that or of the other Contracting State; or

c) to supply information which would disclose any trade, business, industrial, commercial, or professional secret or trade process, or information the disclosure of which would be contrary to public policy (ordre public).

3. Notwithstanding paragraph 2, the competent authority of the requested State shall have the authority to obtain and provide information held by financial institutions, nominees or persons acting in an agency or fiduciary capacity, or respecting interests in a person. If information is requested by a Contracting State in accordance with this Article, the other Contracting State shall obtain that information in the same manner and to the same extent as if the tax of the first mentioned State were the tax of that other State and were being imposed by that other State, notwithstanding that the other State may not, at that time, need such information for purposes of its own tax. If specifically requested by the competent authority of a Contracting State, the competent authority of the other Contracting State shall provide information under this Article in the form of depositions of witnesses and authenticated copies of unedited original documents (including books, papers, statements, records, accounts, and writings), to the same extent such depositions and documents can be obtained under the laws and administrative practices of that other State with respect to its own taxes.

4. For purposes of this Article, the Convention shall apply, notwithstanding the provisions of Article 2 (Taxes Covered), to taxes of every kind imposed by a Contracting State.

Article 27

Administrative Assistance

1. The Contracting States undertake to lend assistance to each other in the collection of taxes referred to in Article 2 (Taxes Covered), together with interest, costs, additions to such taxes, and civil penalties, referred to in this Article as a "revenue claim."

2. An application for assistance in the collection of a revenue claim shall include a certification by the competent authority of the applicant State that, under the laws of that State, the revenue claim has been finally determined. For the purposes of this Article, a revenue claim is finally determined when the applicant State has the right under its internal law to collect the revenue claim and all administrative and judicial rights of the taxpayer to restrain collection in the applicant State have lapsed or been exhausted.

3. A revenue claim of the applicant State that has been finally determined may be accepted for collection by the competent authority of the requested State and, subject to the provisions of paragraph 7, if accepted shall be collected by the requested State as though such revenue claim were the requested State's own revenue claim finally determined in accordance with the laws applicable to the collection of the requested State's own taxes.

4. Where an application for collection of a revenue claim in respect of a taxpayer is accepted

a) by the United States, the revenue claim shall be treated by the United States as an assessment under United States laws against the taxpayer as of the time the application is received; and

b) by Denmark, the revenue claim shall be treated by Denmark as an assessment under Danish laws against the taxpayer as of the time the application is received.

5. Nothing in this Article shall be construed as creating or providing any rights of administrative or judicial review of the applicant State's finally determined revenue claim by the requested State, based on any such rights that may be available under the laws of either Contracting State. If, at any time pending execution of a request for assistance under this Article, the applicant State loses the right under its internal law to collect the revenue claim, the competent authority of the applicant State shall promptly withdraw the request for assistance in collection.

6. Subject to this paragraph, amounts collected by the requested State pursuant to this Article shall be forwarded to the competent authority of the applicant State. Unless the competent authorities of the Contracting States otherwise agree, the ordinary costs incurred in providing collection assistance shall be borne by the requested State and any extraordinary costs so incurred shall be borne by the applicant State.

7. A revenue claim of an applicant State accepted for collection shall not have in the requested State any priority accorded to the revenue claims of the requested State.

8. No assistance shall be provided under this Article for a revenue claim in respect of a taxpayer to the extent that the taxpayer can demonstrate that

a) where the taxpayer is an individual, the revenue claim relates to a taxable period in which the taxpayer was a citizen of the requested State, and

b) where the taxpayer is an entity that is a company, estate or trust, the revenue claim relates to a taxable period in which the taxpayer derived its status as such an entity from the laws in force in the requested State.

9. Each of the Contracting States shall endeavor to collect on behalf of the other Contracting State such amounts as may be necessary to ensure that relief granted by the Convention from taxation imposed by that other State does not inure to the benefit of persons not entitled thereto.

10. Nothing in this Article shall be construed as imposing on either Contracting State the obligation to carry out administrative measures of a different nature from those used in the collection of its own taxes or that would be contrary to its public policy (ordre public).

11. The competent authorities of the Contracting States shall agree upon the mode of application of this Article, including agreement to ensure comparable levels of assistance to each of the Contracting States.

12. The requested State shall not be obliged to accede to the request of the applicant State:

a) if the applicant State has not pursued all appropriate collection action in its own jurisdiction; or

b) in those cases where the administrative burden for the requested State is disproportionate to the benefit to be derived by the applicant State.

ARTICLE 28

DIPLOMATIC AGENTS AND CONSULAR OFFICERS

Nothing in this Convention shall affect the fiscal privileges of diplomatic agents or consular officers under the general rules of international law or under the provisions of special agreements.

ARTICLE 29

ENTRY INTO FORCE

1. The Contracting States shall notify each other when the requirements for the entry into force of this Convention have been complied with.

2. The Convention shall enter into force on the date of the receipt of the later of such notifications, and its provisions shall have effect:

a) in respect of taxes withheld at source, for amounts paid or credited on or after the first day of the second month next following the date on which the Convention enters into force;

b) in respect of other taxes, for taxable periods beginning on or after the first day of January next following the date on which the Convention enters into force.

3. Subject to paragraph 4, the Convention between Denmark and the United States for the Avoidance of Double Taxation and the Prevention of Fiscal Evasion with Respect to Taxes on Income signed at Washington, D.C., on May 6, 1948 (hereinafter referred to as "the 1948 Convention") shall cease to have effect when the provisions of this Convention take effect in accordance with paragraph 2 or 4.

4. Where the 1948 Convention would have afforded any person any greater relief from tax than this Convention, the 1948 Convention shall, at the election of any person that was entitled to benefits under the prior Convention, continue to have effect in its entirety for one year after the date on which the provisions of this Convention would otherwise first have effect pursuant to paragraph 2.

5. The 1948 Convention shall terminate on the last date on which it has effect in accordance with the foregoing provisions of this Article.

ARTICLE 30

TERMINATION

This Convention shall remain in force until terminated by a Contracting State. Either Contracting State may terminate the Convention by giving notice of termination through diplomatic channels. In such event, the Convention shall cease to have effect:

a) in respect of taxes withheld at source, for amounts paid or credited after the expiration of the 6-month period beginning on the date on which notice of termination was given; and

b) in respect of other taxes, for taxable periods beginning on or after the expiration of the 6-month period beginning on the date on which notice of termination was given.

IN WITNESS WHEREOF, the respective plenipotentiaries have signed this Treaty.

DONE in duplicate at ________________ this ________, 1997, in the English and Arabic languages, each text being equally authentic.

For the Government of the United States of America:

WESLEY W. EGAN, JR.
[SIGNATURE]

For the Government of the Hashemite Kingdom of Jordan:

HANI AL-MULKI
[SIGNATURE]

IN WITNESS WHEREOF, the undersigned, being duly authorized by their respective Governments, have signed this Convention.

DONE at Washington in the English language, this 19th day of August, 1999.

For the Government of the United States of America:

(S) DONALD C. LUBICK

For the Government of the Kingdom of Denmark

(S) LARS MOELLER

PROTOCOL

At the signing today of the Convention between the Government of the United States of America and the Government of the Kingdom of Denmark for the Avoidance of Double Taxation and the Prevention of Fiscal Evasion with Respect to Taxes on Income ("the Convention"), the undersigned have agreed on the following provisions, which shall form an integral part of the Convention.

1. Scandinavian Airlines System (SAS) is a consortium within the meaning of Article 8 (Shipping and Air Transport), its participating members being SAS Danmark A/S, SAS Norge ASA and SAS Sverige AB. In order to avoid the problems inherent in operating in the United States through a consortium, the members of the consortium in 1946 established a New York corporation, Scandinavian Airlines System, Inc. (SAS, Inc.) to act on their behalf in the United States pursuant to an agency agreement dated September 18, 1946. A similar agreement was entered into by SAS directly and SAS, Inc., on March 14, 1951. Pursuant to the agency agreement, SAS, Inc., is authorized to perform only such functions as SAS assigns to it, all in connection with international air traffic. Under that agreement, all revenues collected by SAS, Inc., are automatically credited to SAS. Operation expenses incurred by SAS, Inc., are debited to SAS in accordance with the terms of the agency agreement. SAS is obligated under the terms of the agency agreement to reimburse SAS, Inc. for all of its expenses irrespective of the revenues of SAS, Inc. SAS, Inc., does not perform any functions except those connected with or incidental to the business of SAS as an operator of aircraft in international traffic.

In view of the special nature of the SAS consortium and in view of the agency agreement as described above, the United States for purposes of Article 8 (Shipping and Air Transport) of the Convention shall treat all of the income earned by SAS, Inc., that is derived from the operation in international traffic of aircraft as the income of the SAS consortium.

2. This Convention may be extended either in its entirety or with any necessary modifications to any part of Denmark to which the Convention does not apply and which imposes taxes substantially similar in character to those to which the Convention applies. Such extension shall take effect from such date, shall be subject to such modification and conditions as may be specified in a supplementary Convention agreed between the Contracting States, and shall enter into force in accordance with their constitutional procedures.

3. Articles 7 (Business Profits) and 24 (Non-Discrimination) shall not prevent Denmark from continuing to tax permanent establishments of United States insurance companies in accordance with section 12, paragraph 3, of the Danish Company Tax law nor shall it prevent the United States from continuing to tax permanent establishments of Danish insurance companies in accordance with section 842(b) of the Internal Revenue Code.

4. a) A payment shall be treated as a pension distribution under paragraph 1 of Article 18 (Pensions, Social Security, Annuities, Alimony and Child Support Payments) if it is a payment under a pension scheme recognized for tax purposes in the Contracting State where the pension scheme is established.

b) For this purpose, pension schemes recognized for tax purposes shall include the following and any identical or substantially similar schemes which are imposed after the date of signature of the Convention:

(i) Under United States law, qualified plans under section 401(a) of the Internal Revenue Code, individual retirement plans (including individual retirement plans that are part of a simplified employee pension plan that satisfies section 408(k), individual retirement accounts, individual retirement annuities, section 408(p) accounts, and Roth IRAs under section 408A), section 403(a) qualified annuity plans, and section 403(b) plans.

(ii) Under the law of Denmark, pension schemes under Section I of the Act on Taxation of Pension Schemes (pensionsbeskatningslovens afsnit I).

IN WITNESS WHEREOF, the undersigned, being duly authorized by their respective Governments, have signed this Protocol.

DONE at Washington in the English language, this 19th day of August, 1999.

For the Government of the United States of America:

(S) DONALD C. LUBICK

For the Government of the Kingdom of Denmark

(S) LARS MOELLER

9. Friendship Treaties [1]

a. Countries with which the United States has a Friendship Treaty

Country	Entered Into Force
Afghanistan	March 26, 1936
Argentina	December 20, 1854
Austria	May 27, 1931
Belguim	October 3, 1963
Bolivia	November 9, 1862
Brazil	March 18, 1829
Brunei	July 11, 1853
China (Taiwan)	November 30, 1948
Cook Islands	September 8, 1953
Costa Rica	May 26, 1852
Denmark	August 10, 1826
Ecuador	April 9, 1842
Estonia	May 22, 1926
Finland	August 10, 1934
Germany	July 14, 1956
Greece	October 10, 13, 1954
Honduras	July 19, 1928
Ireland	September 14, 1950
Israel	April 3, 1954
Italy	July 26, 1949
Japan	October 30, 1953
Kiribati	September 23, 1983
Korea, Republic of	November 7, 1957
Latvia	July 25, 1928
Liberia	November 21, 1939
Luxembourg	March 28, 1963
Mexico	May 30, 1848
Nepal	April 25, 1947
Netherlands	November 21, 1946
Norway	September 13, 1932
Pakistan	February 12, 1961
Paraguay	March 7, 1860
Spain	April 14, 1903
Suriname	February 10, 1963
Sweden	November 8, 1855
Tuvalu	September 23, 1983
Venezuela	May 31, 1836
Yemen	May 4, 1946

[1] Friendship treaties generally encompass additional matters in the relationship between the United States and the other party, including such items as commerce, navigation, and consular rights.

b. Treaty of Friendship, Commerce and Navigation Between the United States and the Netherlands, With Protocol[1]

Signed at the Hague, March 27, 1956; Entered into force, December 5, 1957

WHEREAS a treaty of friendship, commerce and navigation between the United States of America and the Kingdom of the Netherlands, together with a protocol and an exchange of notes relating thereto, was signed at The Hague on March 27, 1956;

WHEREAS the originals of the said treaty and protocol in the English and Netherlands languages and the text of the exchange of notes signed in the English language are word for word as follows:

The United States of America and the Kingdom of the Netherlands,

desirous of strengthening the bonds of peace and friendship traditionally existing between them and of encouraging closer economic and cultural relations between their peoples, and being cognizant of the contributions which may be made toward these ends by arrangements promoting mutually advantageous commercial intercourse, encouraging mutually beneficial investments, and establishing mutual rights and privileges,

have resolved to conclude a Treaty of Friendship, Commerce and Navigation, based in general upon the principles of national and unconditional most-favored-nation treatment reciprocally accorded,

and for that purpose have appointed as their Plenipotentiaries:

the President of the United States of America:

H.E. Mr. H. Freeman Matthews, Ambassador extraordinary and plenipotentiary of the United States of America at The Hague,

and Her Majesty the Queen of the Netherlands:

H.E. Dr. J.W. Beyen, Minister of Foreign Affairs, and

H.E. Dr. J. M. A. H. Luns, Minister without Portfolio, who, having communicated to each other their full powers found to be in due form, have agreed as follows:

ARTICLE I

1. Each Party shall at all times accord fair and equitable treatment to the nationals and companies of the other Party, and to their property, enterprises and other interests.

2. Between the territories of the two Parties there shall be, in accordance with the provisions of the present Treaty, freedom of commerce and navigation.

---

[1] TIAS 3942. The full text of the Treaty of Friendship, Commerce and Navigation Between the Government of the United States of America and the Government of the Netherlands, with Protocol, is set out in this volume as a model of the other 37 Friendship Treaties that were in force for the United States as of December 31, 2005.

ARTICLE II

1. Nationals of either Party shall be permitted to enter the territories of the other Party and to remain therein:

(a) for the purpose of carrying on trade between the territories of the two Parties and engaging in related commercial activities;

(b) for the purpose of developing and directing the operations of an enterprise in which they have invested, or in which they are actively in the process of investing, a substantial amount of capital; and

(c) for other purposes subject to the laws relating to the entry and sojourn of aliens.

2. Each Party undertakes to make available the best facilities practicable for travel by tourists and other visitors with respect to their entry, sojourn and departure, and for the distribution of information for tourists.

3. Nationals of either Party, within the territories of the other Party, shall be permitted:

(a) to travel therein freely, and to reside at places of their choice;

(b) to enjoy liberty of conscience;

(c) to hold both private and public religious services;

(d) to gather and to transmit material for dissemination to the public abroad; and

(e) to communicate with other persons inside and outside such territories by mail, telegraph and other means open to general public use.

4. The provisions of the present Article shall be subject to the right of either Party to apply measures that are necessary to maintain public order and protect the public health, morals and safety.

ARTICLE III

1. Nationals of either Party within the territories of the other Party shall be free from molestations of every kind, and shall receive the most constant protection and security. They shall be accorded in like circumstances treatment no less favorable than that accorded nationals of such other Party for the protection and security of their persons and their rights. The treatment accorded in this respect shall in no case be less favorable than that accorded nationals of any third country or that required by international law.

2. If, within the territories of either Party, a national of the other Party is taken into custody, the nearest consular representative of his country shall on the demand of such national be immediately notified and shall have the right to visit and communicate with such national. Such national shall:

(a) receive reasonable and humane treatment;

(b) be promptly informed of the accusations against him;

(c) be brought to trial as promptly as is consistent with proper preparation of his defense; and

(d) enjoy all means reasonably necessary to his defense, including the services of competent counsel of his choice.

ARTICLE IV

1. Nationals of either Party shall be accorded national treatment in the application of laws and regulations within the territories of the other Party that establish a pecuniary compensation or other benefit or service, on account of disease, injury or death arising out of and in the course of employment or due to the nature of employment.

2. In addition to the rights and privileges provided in paragraph 1 of the present Article, nationals of either Party shall, within the territories of the other Party, be accorded national treatment in the application of laws and regulations establishing compulsory systems of social security, under which benefits are paid without an individual test of financial need in the following cases:

(a) sickness, including temporary disability for work, and maternity;

(b) invalidity, or occupational disability;

(c) death of father, spouse, or any other person liable for maintenance;

(d) unemployment.

ARTICLE V

1. Nationals and companies of either Party shall be accorded national treatment with respect to access to the courts of justice and to administrative tribunals and agencies within the territories of the other Party, in all degrees of jurisdiction, both in pursuit and in defense of their rights. It is understood that companies of either Party not engaged in activities within the territories of the other Party shall enjoy such access therein without any requirement of registration or domestication.

2. (a) Contracts entered into between nationals or companies of either Party and nationals or companies of the other Party, that provide for the settlement by arbitration of controversies, shall not be deemed unenforceable within the territories of such other Party merely on the grounds that the place designated for the arbitration proceedings is outside such territories or that the nationality of one or more of the arbitrators is not that of such other Party.

(b) In conformity with subparagraphs (1) and (2) hereof, awards duly rendered pursuant to any such contracts, which are final and enforceable under the laws of the place where rendered, shall be deemed conclusive in enforcement proceedings brought before the courts of competent jurisdiction of either Party.

(1) As regards recognition and enforcement in the United States of America, such awards shall be entitled in any court in any State thereof only to the same measure of recognition and enforcement as awards rendered in other States thereof.

(2) As regards enforcement in the Kingdom of the Netherlands, such awards shall be dealt with in the same way as awards as referred to in the Convention on the execution of foreign arbitral awards concluded at Geneva on September 26, 1927.

Article VI

1. Property of nationals and companies of either Party shall receive the most constant protection and security within the territories of the other Party.

2. The dwellings, offices, warehouses, factories and other premises of nationals and companies of either Party located within the territories of the other Party shall not be subject to molestation or to entry without just cause. Official searches and examinations of such premises and their contents, when necessary, shall be made only according to law and with careful regard for the convenience of the occupants and the conduct of business.

3. Neither Party shall take unreasonable or discriminatory measures that would impair the rights or interests within its territories of nationals and companies of the other Party, whether in their capital, or in their enterprises and the property thereof, or in the skills, arts or technology which they have supplied.

4. Property of nationals and companies of either Party shall not be taken within the territories of the other Party except for a public interest, nor shall it be taken without the prompt payment of just compensation. Such compensation shall be in an effectively realizable form and shall represent the equivalent of the property taken; and adequate provision shall have been made at or prior to the time of taking for the determination and payment thereof.

5. Nationals and companies of either Party shall in no case be accorded, within the territories of the other Party, less than national treatment and most-favored-nation treatment with respect to the matters set forth in paragraphs 2 and 4 of the present Article. Moreover, enterprises in which nationals and companies of either Party have a substantial interest shall be accorded, within the territories of the other Party, not less than national treatment and most-favored-nation treatment in all matters relating to the taking of privately owned enterprises into public ownership and to the placing of such enterprises under public control or administration.

Article VII

1. Nationals and companies of either Party shall be accorded national treatment with respect to engaging in all types of commercial, industrial, financial and other activity for gain (business activities) within the territories of the other Party, whether directly or by agent or through the medium of any form of lawful juridical entity. Accordingly, such nationals and companies shall be permitted within such territories:

(a) to establish and maintain branches, agencies, offices, factories and other establishments appropriate to the conduct of their business;

(b) either directly or indirectly through one or more intermediaries, to organize companies under the general company laws of such other Party and to acquire the controlling interest in companies of such other Party;

(c) to control and manage enterprises which they have established or acquired. Moreover, enterprises which they control, whether in the form of individual proprietorships, companies or otherwise, shall in all that relates to the conduct of the activities thereof, be accorded treatment no less favorable than that accorded like enterprises controlled by nationals and companies of such other Party.

2. Each Party reserves the right to limit the extent to which aliens may within its territories establish, acquire interests in, or carry on enterprises engaged in communications, air or water transport, banking involving depository or fiduciary functions, or the exploitation of land or other natural resources. However, new limitations imposed by either Party upon the extent to which aliens are accorded national treatment, with respect to carrying on such activities within its territories, shall not be applied as against enterprises which are engaged in such activities therein at the time such new limitations are adopted and which are owned or controlled by nationals and companies of the other Party. Moreover, neither Party shall deny to transportation, communications and banking companies of the other Party the right to maintain branches and agencies, in conformity with the applicable laws and regulations, to perform functions necessary for essentially international operations in which they engage.

3. The provisions of paragraph 1 of the present Article shall not prevent either Party from prescribing special formalities in connection with the establishment of alien-controlled enterprises within its territories; but such formalities may not impair the substance of the rights set forth in said paragraph.

4. Nationals and companies of either Party, as well as enterprises controlled by such nationals and companies, shall in any event be accorded most-favored-nation treatment with reference to the matters treated in the present Article.

Article VIII

1. Nationals and companies of either Party shall be permitted to engage, within the territories of the other Party, accountants and other technical experts, executive personnel, attorneys, agents and other specialists of their choice. Moreover, such nationals and companies shall be permitted to engage accountants and other technical experts regardless of the extent to which they may have qualified for the practice of a profession within the territories of such other Party, for the particular purpose of making examinations, audits and technical investigations for, and rendering reports to, such nationals and companies in connection with the planning and operation of their enterprises, and enterprises in which they have a financial interest, within such territories.

2. Nationals and companies of either Party shall be accorded national treatment and most favored-nation treatment with respect to engaging in scientific, educational, religious and philanthropic activities within the territories of the other Party, and shall be accorded the right to form associations for that purpose under the laws of such other Party.

ARTICLE IX

1. Nationals and companies of the Kingdom of the Netherlands shall be accorded, within the territories of the United States of America:

(a) national treatment with respect to leasing land, buildings and other real property appropriate to the conduct of activities in which they are permitted to engage pursuant to Articles VII and VIII and for residential purposes and with respect to occupying and using such property; and

(b) other rights in real property permitted by the applicable laws of the States, Territories and possessions of the United States of America.

2. Nationals and companies of the United States of America shall be accorded, within the territories of the Kingdom of the Netherlands, national treatment with respect to acquiring by purchase, lease, or otherwise, and with respect to owning, occupying and using land, buildings and other real property. However, in the case of any such national domiciled in, or any such company constituted under the laws of, any State, Territory or possession of the United States of America that accords less than national treatment to nationals and companies of the Kingdom of the Netherlands in this respect, the Kingdom of the Netherlands shall not be obligated to accord to such national or company treatment more favorable in this respect than such State, Territory or possession accords to nationals and companies of the Kingdom of the Netherlands.

3. Nationals and companies of either Party shall be accorded within the territories of the other Party national treatment and most-favored-nation treatment with respect to acquiring, by purchase, lease, or otherwise, and with respect to owning and possessing, personal property of all kinds, both tangible and intangible. However, either Party may impose restrictions on alien ownership of materials dangerous from the standpoint of public safety and alien ownership of interests in enterprises carrying on particular types of activity, but only to the extent that this can be done without impairing the rights and privileges secured by Article VII or by other provisions of the present Treaty.

4. Nationals and companies of either Party shall be accorded national treatment within the territories of the other Party with respect to acquiring property of all kinds by testate or intestate succession or through judicial process. Should they because of their alienage be ineligible to continue to own any such property, they shall be allowed a reasonable period in which to dispose of it, in a normal manner at its market value.

5. Nationals and companies of either Party shall be accorded within the territories of the other Party national treatment and most-favored-nation treatment with respect to disposing of property of all kinds. Furthermore, with respect to the acquisition, ownership, use and disposition of property of all kinds within the territories of either Party, companies constituted under the laws of that Party, which are controlled by nationals and companies of the other Party, shall be accorded treatment no less favorable than that accorded within such territories to companies of such other Party or

to companies similarly constituted which are controlled by nationals and companies of any third country.

ARTICLE X

1. Nationals and companies of either Party shall be accorded, within the territories of the other Party, national treatment with respect to obtaining and maintaining patents of invention, and with respect to rights in trade marks, trade names, trade labels and industrial property of every kind.

2. The Parties agree as to the desirability of furthering, through cooperative or other appropriate means, the interchange and use of scientific and technical knowledge, particularly in the interest of increasing productivity and improving standards of living within their respective territories.

ARTICLE XI

1. Nationals of either Party residing within the territories of the other Party, and nationals and companies of either Party engaged in trade or other gainful pursuit or in scientific, educational, religious or philanthropic activities within the territories of the other Party, shall not be subject to the payment of taxes, fees or charges imposed upon or applied to income, capital, transactions, activities or any other object, or to requirements with respect to the levy and collection thereof, within the territories of such other Party, more burdensome than those borne by nationals and companies of such other Party.

2. With respect to nationals of either Party who are neither resident nor engaged in trade or other gainful pursuit within the territories of the other Party, and with respect to companies of either Party which are not engaged in trade or other gainful pursuit within the territories of the other Party, it shall be the aim of such other Party to apply in general the principle set forth in paragraph 1 of the present Article.

3. Nationals and companies of either Party shall in no case be subject, within the territories of the other Party, to the payment of taxes, fees or charges imposed upon or applied to income, capital, transactions, activities or any other object, or to requirements with respect to the levy and collection thereof, more burdensome than those borne by nationals, residents and companies of any third country.

4. In the case of companies and of non-resident nationals of either Party engaged in trade or other gainful pursuit within the territories of the other Party, such other Party shall not impose or apply any tax, fee or charge upon any income, capital or other basis in excess of that reasonably allocable or apportionable to its territories, nor grant deductions and exemptions less than those reasonably allocable or apportionable to its territories. A comparable rule shall apply also in the case of companies organized and operated exclusively for scientific, educational, religious or philanthropic purposes.

5. Each Party reserves the right to:

(a) extend specific tax advantages on the basis of reciprocity;

(b) accord special tax advantages by virtue of agreements for the avoidance of double taxation or the mutual protection of revenue; and

(c) accord to its own nationals and to residents of contiguous countries more favorable exemptions of a personal nature with respect to income and inheritance taxes than are accorded to other non-resident persons.

Article XII

1. Nationals and companies of either Party shall be accorded by the other Party national treatment and most-favored-nation treatment with respect to payments, remittances and transfers of funds or financial instruments between the territories of the two Parties as well as between the territories of such other Party and of any third country.

2. Neither Party shall impose exchange restrictions as defined in paragraph 5 of the present Article except to the extent necessary to maintain or restore adequacy in its monetary reserves, particularly in relation to its external commercial and financial requirements. It is understood that the provisions of the present Article do not alter the obligations either Party may have to the International Monetary Fund or preclude imposition of particular restrictions whenever the Fund specifically authorizes or requests a Party to impose such particular restrictions.

3. If either Party imposes exchange restrictions in accordance with paragraph 2 of the present Article, it shall, after making whatever provision may be necessary to assure the availability of foreign exchange for goods and services essential to the health and welfare of its people, make reasonable provision for the withdrawal, in foreign exchange in the currency of the other Party, of:

(a) the compensation referred to in Article VI, paragraph 4,

(b) earnings, whether in the form of salaries, interest, dividends, commissions, royalties, payments for technical services, or otherwise, and

(c) amounts for amortization of loans, depreciation of direct investments, and capital transfers to the extent feasible, giving consideration to special needs for other transactions. If more than one rate of exchange is in force, the rate applicable to such withdrawals shall be a rate which is specifically approved by the International Monetary Fund for such transactions or, in the absence of a rate so approved, an effective rate which, inclusive of any taxes or surcharges on exchange transfers, is just and reasonable.

4. Exchange restrictions shall not be imposed by either Party in a manner unnecessarily detrimental or arbitrarily discriminatory to the claims, investments, transport, trade, and other interests of nationals and companies of the other Party, nor to the competitive position thereof. Each Party shall afford the other Party adequate opportunity for consultation at any time regarding application of the present Article.

5. The term "exchange restrictions" as used in the present Article includes all restrictions, regulations, charges, taxes, or other requirements imposed by either Party which burden or interfere with

payments, remittances, or transfers of funds or of financial instruments between the territories of the two Parties.

6. Questions arising under the present Treaty concerning exchange control are governed by the provisions of the present Article.

ARTICLE XIII

Commercial travelers representing nationals and companies of either Party engaged in business within the territories thereof shall, upon their entry into and departure from the territories of the other Party and during their sojourn therein, be accorded most-favored-nation treatment in respect of the customs and other matters, including, subject to the exceptions in paragraph 5 of Article XI, taxes and charges applicable to them, their samples and the taking of orders, and regulations governing the exercise of their functions.

ARTICLE XIV

1. Each Party shall accord most-favored-nation treatment to products of the other Party, from whatever place and by whatever type of carrier arriving, and to products destined for exportation to the territories of such other Party, by whatever route and by whatever type of carrier, with respect to customs duties and charges of any kind imposed on or in connection with importation or exportation or imposed on the international transfer of payments for imports or exports, and with respect to the method of levying such duties and charges, and with respect to all rules and formalities in connection with importation and exportation.

2. Neither Party shall impose restrictions or prohibitions on the importation of any product of the other Party, or on the exportation of any product to the territories of the other Party, unless the importation of the like product of, or the exportation of the like product to, all third countries is similarly restricted or prohibited.

3. If either Party imposes quantitative restrictions on the importation or exportation of any product in which the other Party has an important interest:

(a) it shall as a general rule give prior public notice of the total amount of the product, by quantity or value, that may be imported or exported during a specified period, and of any change in such amount or period; and

(b) if it makes allotments to any third country, it shall afford such other Party a share proportionate to the amount of the product, by quantity or value, supplied by or to it during a previous representative period, due consideration being given to any special factors affecting the trade in such product.

4. Either Party may impose prohibitions or restrictions on sanitary or other customary grounds of a non-commercial nature, or in the interest of preventing deceptive or unfair practices, provided such prohibitions or restrictions do not arbitrarily discriminate against the commerce of the other Party.

5. Nationals and companies of either Party shall be accorded national treatment and most-favored-nation treatment by the other

Party with respect to all matters relating to importation and exportation.

6. Notwithstanding the provisions of paragraphs 2 and 3 (b) of the present Article, a Party may apply restrictions or controls on importation and exportation of goods that have effect equivalent to, or which are necessary to make effective, exchange restrictions applied pursuant to Article XII. However, such restrictions or controls shall depart no more than necessary from the aforesaid paragraphs and shall be conformable with a policy designed to promote the maximum development of nondiscriminatory foreign trade and to expedite the attainment both of a balance-of-payments position and of monetary reserves which will obviate the necessity of such restrictions.

ARTICLE XV

1. Each Party shall promptly publish laws, regulations and administrative rulings of general application pertaining to rates of duty, taxes or other charges, to the classification of articles for customs purposes, and to requirements or restrictions on imports and exports or the transfer of payments therefore, or affecting their sale, distribution or use; and shall administer such laws, regulations and rulings in a uniform, impartial and reasonable manner. As a general practice, new administrative requirements or restrictions affecting imports, with the exception of those imposed on sanitary grounds or for reasons of public safety, shall not go into effect before the expiration of a reasonable time, in the light of circumstances.

2. Each Party shall provide an appeals procedure under which nationals and companies of the other Party, and importers of products of such other Party, shall be able to obtain prompt and impartial review, and correction when warranted, of administrative action relating to customs matters, including the imposition of fines and penalties, confiscations, and rulings on questions of customs classification and valuation by the administrative authorities.

3. Penalties imposed by either Party for infractions of the customs and shipping laws and regulations concerning documentation shall be no greater than necessary to serve merely as a warning in the case of clerical errors and of errors made without fraudulent intent or gross negligence.

4. With reference to marking requirements applicable to imported products, each Party shall as a general practice:

(a) allow required marks of origin to be affixed after importation;

(b) not permit markings that result in misrepresenting the true origin of the products; and

(c) not apply requirements that entail an expense which is economically prohibitive or that result in seriously damaging the product.

5. Neither Party shall impose any measure of a discriminatory nature that hinders or prevents the importer or exporter of products of either country from obtaining marine insurance on such products in companies of either Party.

Article XVI

1. Products of either Party shall be accorded, within the territories of the other Party, national treatment and most-favored-nation treatment in all matters affecting internal taxation, sale, distribution, storage and use.

2. Articles produced by nationals and companies of either Party within the territories of the other Party, or by companies of the latter Party controlled by such nationals and companies, shall be accorded therein treatment no less favorable than that accorded to like articles of national origin by whatever person or company produced, in all matters affecting exportation, taxation, sale, distribution, storage and use.

Article XVII

1. Each Party undertakes:

(a) that enterprises owned or controlled by its Government, and that monopolies or agencies granted exclusive or special privileges within its territories, shall make their purchases and sales involving either imports or exports affecting the commerce of the other Party solely in accordance with commercial considerations, including price, quality, availability marketability, transportation and other conditions of purchase or sale; and

(b) that the nationals, companies and commerce of such other Party shall be afforded adequate opportunity, in accordance with customary business practice, to compete for participation in such purchases and sales.

2. Each Party shall accord to the nationals, companies and commerce of the other Party fair and equitable treatment, as compared with that accorded to the nationals, companies and commerce of any third country, with respect to:

(a) the governmental purchase of supplies;

(b) the awarding of concessions and other government contracts; and

(c) the sale of any service sold by the Government or by any monopoly or agency granted exclusive or special privileges.

Article XVIII

1. The Parties recognize that conditions of competitive equality should be maintained in situations in which publicly owned or controlled trading or manufacturing enterprises of either Party engage in competition, within the territories thereof, with privately owned and controlled enterprises of nationals and companies of the other Party. Accordingly, such state-owned enterprises should not be given special economic privileges in order to injure the competitive position of such private enterprises. However, this principle shall not be construed to prevent either Party from making such special concessions in aid of state-owned enterprises as it deems necessary during periods of economic crisis, especially to relieve unemployment. This principle, moreover, is without prejudice to special advantages given in connection with:

(a) manufacturing goods for government use, or supplying goods and services to the Government for government use; or

(b) supplying, at prices substantially below competitive prices, the needs of particular population groups for essential goods and services not otherwise practically obtainable by such groups.

2. No enterprise of either Party, including corporations, associations, and government agencies and instrumentalities, which is publicly owned or controlled shall, to the extent that it engages in commercial, industrial, shipping or other business activities within the territories of the other Party, claim or enjoy, either for itself or for its property, immunity therein from taxation, suit, execution of judgment or other liability to which privately owned and controlled enterprises are subject therein.

ARTICLE XIX

1. Vessels under the flag of either Party, and carrying the papers required by its laws in proof of nationality, shall be deemed to be vessels of that Party both on the high seas and within the ports, places and waters of the other Party.

2. Vessels of either Party shall have liberty, on equal terms with vessels of the other Party and on equal terms with vessels of any third country, to come with their cargoes to all ports, places and waters of such other Party open to foreign commerce and navigation. Such vessels and cargoes shall in all respects be accorded national treatment and most-favored-nation treatment within the ports, places and waters of such other Party; but each Party may reserve exclusive rights and privileges to its own vessels with respect to the coasting trade and inland navigation.

3. Vessels of either Party shall be accorded national treatment and most-favored-nation treatment with respect to the right to carry all cargo that may be carried by vessel to or from the territories of the other Party.

4. Goods carried by vessels under the flag of either Party to or from the territories of the other Party shall enjoy the same favors as when transported in vessels sailing under the flag of such other Party. This applies especially with regard to customs duties and all other fees and charges, to bounties, drawbacks and other privileges of this nature, as well as to the administration of the customs and to transport to and from port by rail and other means of transportation.

5. If a vessel of either Party runs aground or is wrecked on the coasts of the other Party, or if it is in distress and must put into a port of the other Party, the latter Party shall extend to the vessel as well as to the crew, the passengers, the personal property of crew and passengers, and to the cargo of the vessel, the same protection and assistance as would have been extended to a vessel under its own flag in like circumstances; and shall permit the vessel after repairs to proceed with its voyage upon conformity with the laws applicable alike to vessels under its own flag. Articles salvaged from the vessel shall be exempt from all customs duties unless they pass into internal consumption; but articles not entered

for consumption may be subject to measures for the protection of the revenue pending their exit from the country.

6. The term "vessels", as used herein, means all types of vessels, whether privately owned or operated, or publicly owned or operated, except vessels of war. This term does not, except with reference to paragraphs 1 and 5 of the present Article and Article XX, include fishing vessels.

Article XX

1. In all ports of either Party the masters of all vessels under the flag of the other Party, whose crews have ceased to be fully constituted on account of illness or for any other cause, shall be permitted to engage such seamen as may be necessary for the continuation of the voyage.

2. Nationals of either Party who are seamen may be sent to ports of the other Party to join national vessels, in care of consular officers, either individually or in groups on the basis of seamen's papers issued in lieu of passports. Likewise, nationals of either Party shall be permitted to travel through the territory of the other Party on their way to join vessels or to be repatriated on the basis of seamen's papers used in lieu of passports.

Article XXI

There shall be freedom of transit through the territories of each Party by the routes most convenient for international transit:

(a) for nationals of the other Party, together with their baggage;

(b) for other persons, together with their baggage, en route to or from the territories of such other Party; and

(c) for products of any origin en route to or from the territories of such other Party. Such persons and things in transit shall be exempt from customs duties, from duties imposed by reason of transit, and from unreasonable charges and requirements; and shall be free from unnecessary delays and restrictions. They shall, however, be subject to measures referred to in paragraph 4 of Article II, and to nondiscriminatory regulations necessary to prevent abuse of the transit privilege.

Article XXII

1. The present Treaty shall not preclude the application of measures by either Party:

(a) regulating the importation or exportation of gold or silver;

(b) relating to fissionable materials, to radioactive by-products of the utilization or processing thereof, or to materials that are the source of fissionable materials;

(c) regulating the production of or traffic in arms, ammunition and implements of war, or traffic in other materials carried on directly or indirectly for the purpose of supplying a military establishment;

(d) necessary to fulfil its obligations for the maintenance or restoration of international peace and security, or necessary to protect its essential security interests;

(e) denying to any company in which nationals of any third country or countries enjoy directly or indirectly the controlling interest, the advantages of the present Treaty, except with respect to recognition of juridical status and with respect to access to courts; and

(f) regarding its national fisheries and the landing of the products thereof.

2. The most-favored-nation provisions of the present Treaty shall not apply to advantages accorded by:

(a) the United States of America or its Territories and possessions to one another, to the Republic of Cuba, to the Republic of the Philippines, to the Trust Territory of the Pacific Islands or to the Panama Canal Zone; or

(b) by the Parts of the Kingdom of the Netherlands to one another, by the Netherlands to its Benelux-partners (Belgium, including its Overseas and Trust Territories, and Luxembourg), or by the Kingdom of the Netherlands to the Republic of Indonesia.

3. The most-favored-nation treatment provisions of the present Treaty shall not apply to advantages accorded by either Party to adjacent countries in order to facilitate frontier traffic, or by virtue of a customs union or free trade area of which either Party may become a member, after having informed the other Party of its plans and having afforded it opportunity to express its views thereon.

4. The provisions of the present Treaty relating to the treatment of goods shall not preclude action by either Party which is required or specifically permitted under the General Agreement on Tariffs and Trade during such time as such Party is a contracting party to the General Agreement. Similarly, the most-favored-nation provisions of the present Treaty shall not apply to special advantages accorded by virtue of the aforesaid Agreement.

5. Nationals of either Party admitted into the territories of the other Party for limited purposes shall not enjoy rights to engage in gainful occupations in contravention of limitations expressly imposed, according to law, as a condition of their admittance.

6. Nothing in the present Treaty shall be deemed to grant or imply any right to engage in political activities.

Article XXIII

1. The term "national treatment" means treatment accorded within the territories of a Party upon terms no less favorable than the treatment accorded therein, in like situations, to nationals, companies, products, vessels or other objects, as the case may be, of such Party.

2. The term "most-favored-nation treatment" means treatment accorded within the territories of a Party upon terms no less favorable than the treatment accorded therein, in like situations, to nationals, companies, products, vessels or other objects, as the case may be, of any third country.

3. As used in the present Treaty, the term "companies" means corporations, partnerships, companies, foundations, associations, and other legal entities or juridical person, whether or not with

limited liability and whether or not for pecuniary profit. Companies constituted under the applicable laws and regulations within the territories of either Party shall be deemed companies thereof and shall have their juridical status recognized within the territories of the other Party.

4. National treatment accorded under the provisions of the present Treaty to companies shall:

(a) as regards companies of the Kingdom of the Netherlands, in any State, Territory or possession of the United States of America, be the treatment accorded therein to companies created or organized in other States, Territories and possessions of the United States of America; and

(b) as regards companies of the United States of America, in any Part of the Kingdom of the Netherlands, be the treatment accorded therein to companies created or organized in any other Part of the Kingdom. Furthermore, in any Part of the Kingdom of the Netherlands outside Europe, national treatment accorded to nationals of the United States of America shall be the treatment accorded in such Part to Netherlands nationals not born in that Part.

Article XXIV

The territories to which the present Treaty extends shall comprise all areas of land and water under the jurisdiction of each Party, as well as any territory for which it has international responsibility, other than the Panama Canal Zone and the Trust Territory of the Pacific Islands, provided that it shall not apply with respect to Surinam or the Netherlands Antilles, respectively, until one month after the receipt by the Government of the United States of America of notifications of such application by the Kingdom of the Netherlands.

Article XXV

1. Each Party shall accord sympathetic consideration to, and shall afford adequate opportunity for consultation regarding, such representations as the other Party may make with respect to any matter affecting the operation of the present Treaty.

2. Any dispute between the Parties as to the interpretation or application of the present Treaty, not satisfactorily adjusted by diplomacy, shall be submitted to the International Court of Justice, unless the Parties agree to settlement by some other pacific means.

Article XXVI

The present Treaty shall replace the convention of commerce and navigation signed at Washington August 26, 1852, and the agreement in regard to trade marks effected by exchange of notes signed at Washington February 10 and 16, 1883.

Article XXVII

1. The present Treaty shall be ratified, and the ratifications thereof shall be exchanged at Washington as soon as possible.

2. The present Treaty shall enter into force one month after the day of exchange of ratifications. It shall remain in force for ten years and shall continue in force thereafter until terminated as provided herein.

3. Either Party may, by giving one year's written notice to the other Party, terminate the present Treaty at the end of the initial ten-year period or at any time thereafter with respect to all the territories to which it applies or with respect to Surinam or the Netherlands Antilles.

In witness whereof the respective Plenipotentiaries have signed the present Treaty and have affixed hereunto their seals.

Done in duplicate, in the English and Netherlands languages, both texts being equally authentic, at The Hague, this 27th day of March, one thousand nine hundred fifty-six.

For the United States of America:

H. Freeman Matthews

For the Kingdom of the Netherlands:

J W Beyen, J M A H Luns

Protocol

At the time of signing the Treaty of Friendship, Commerce and Navigation between the United States of America and the Kingdom of the Netherlands, the undersigned Plenipotentiaries, duly authorized by their respective Governments, have further agreed on the following provisions, which shall be considered integral parts of the aforesaid Treaty:

1. The spouse and unmarried minor children of a person permitted entry under the provisions of Article II, paragraph 1(a) and (b), shall also be permitted entry if accompanying him or following to join him.

2. The provisions of Article II, paragraph 1 (b), shall be construed to extend to persons who represent nationals and companies of the same nationality which have invested or are actively in the process of investing a substantial amount of capital in an enterprise in the territories of the other Party, and who are employed by such nationals and companies in a responsible capacity.

3. With respect to Article II, paragraph 1, and the first sentence of Article VIII, paragraph 1, nationals of the United States of America shall be accorded in any Part of the Kingdom of the Netherlands outside Europe the treatment accorded therein to Netherlands nationals not born in that Part.

4. The provisions of Article IV, paragraph 2, refer only to laws or regulations which either are national laws or regulations or are based in whole or in part on requirements of national laws or regulations. Moreover, that paragraph shall not be construed to prevent a Party from relieving aliens temporarily resident within its territories from coverage under its contributory social security system.

5. The term "access" as used in Article V, paragraph 1, comprehends, among other things, legal aid, cost-free access to the courts and exemption from security for costs.

6. The provisions of Article VI, paragraph 4, providing for the payment of compensation shall extend to interests held directly or indirectly by nationals and companies of either Party in property which is taken within the territories of the other Party.

7. The provisions of Article VII do not obligate either Party to permit nationals and companies of the other Party to carry on businesses in its territories without fulfilling the requirements which are generally applicable by law.

8. The activities referred to in Article VII, paragraph 1, do not include the practice of professions.

9. With reference to Article VII, paragraph 1, it is understood that either Party may, consistently with the terms and intent of the Treaty, apply special requirements to alien insurance companies with a view to assuring that such companies maintain standards of accountability and solvency comparable with those required of like domestic companies, so long as such requirements do not have the effect of discrimination in substance against such alien companies.

10. It is agreed that, on a reciprocity basis, the first sentence of Article VII, paragraph 2, shall not apply to the establishment of, or the acquisition of interests in, or the control, operation and management of, companies of either Party for engaging in the exploration for and exploitation of petroleum and other mineral resources within the territories of that Party, by nationals or companies of the other Party.

11. The provisions of the first sentence of Article VIII, paragraph 1, shall not be construed to affect the right of the Netherlands to require that aliens may not be employed in the Netherlands unless the appropriate permits have been granted. However, in keeping with the terms of that paragraph, the regulations governing employment shall be applied in a liberal fashion.

12. Nothing in the present Treaty shall be construed to supersede any provision of the Convention between the Kingdom of the Netherlands and the United States of America with respect to taxes on income and certain other taxes, signed at Washington April 29, 1948.

13. The treatment provided in Article XII, paragraph 1, as clarified by reference to Article XXIII, paragraphs 1 and 2, is designed only to preclude discrimination on the ground of nationality and does not, for instance, preclude different treatment of different currencies or the application of residence requirements.

14. Either Party may impose restrictions on the introduction of foreign capital as may be necessary to protect its monetary reserves as provided in Article XII, paragraph 2, or to prevent serious monetary disturbances arising from speculative financial operations.

15. It is understood that for the purposes of Article XVII, paragraph 1, availability of means of payment is considered to be a commercial consideration.

16. The provisions of Article XVII, paragraph 2 (b) and (c), and of Article XIX, paragraph 3, shall not apply to postal services.

17. It is understood that the word "cargoes" as used in paragraph 2 and the word "cargo" as used in paragraph 3, of Article XIX, shall be deemed to comprehend passengers as well as goods.

18. With reference to Article XXII, paragraph 1 (d), it is understood that it is not the purpose of the security reservation to create a basis for unduly prolonged departures from any provision of the Treaty. On the other hand, each Party determines, according to its own best judgment, the measures deemed necessary to protect its essential security interests.

19. The provisions of Article XXII, paragraph 2, shall apply in the case of Puerto Rico regardless of any change that may take place in its political status.

20. Article XXIV does not apply to territories under the authority of either Party solely as a military base or by reason of temporary military occupation.

IN WITNESS WHEREOF the respective Plenipotentiaries have signed the present Protocol and have affixed hereunto their seals.

DONE in duplicate, in the English and Netherlands languages, both texts being equally authentic, at The Hague, this 27th day of March, one thousand nine hundred fifty-six.

For the United States of America:

H. FREEMAN MATTHEWS

For the Kingdom of the Netherlands:

J W BEYEN, J M A H LUNS

10. Bilateral Free Trade Agreements

a. Countries With Which the United States Has a Bilateral Free Trade Agreement

Country	Entered Into Force
Australia	January 1, 2005
Chile	January 1, 2004
Israel	August 19, 1985
Jordan	December 17, 2001
Canada, Mexico (NAFTA)	January 1, 1994
Singapore	January 1, 2004

b. United States-Chile Free Trade Agreement[1]

Signed at Miami, June 6, 2003; Entered into force January 1, 2004

The Government of the United States of America and the Government of the Republic of Chile, resolved to:

STRENGTHEN the special bonds of friendship and cooperation between their nations;

CONTRIBUTE to the harmonious development and expansion of world trade and provide a catalyst to broader international cooperation;

CREATE an expanded and secure market for the goods and services produced in their territories;

AVOID distortions in their reciprocal trade;

ESTABLISH clear and mutually advantageous rules governing their trade;

ENSURE a predictable commercial framework for business planning and investment;

BUILD on their respective rights and obligations under the Marrakesh Agreement establishing the World Trade Organization and other multilateral and bilateral instruments of cooperation;

ENHANCE the competitiveness of their firms in global markets;

FOSTER creativity and innovation, and promote trade in goods and services that are the subject of intellectual property rights;

CREATE new employment opportunities and improve working conditions and living standards in their respective territories;

BUILD on their respective international commitments and strengthen their cooperation on labor matters;

PROTECT, enhance, and enforce basic workers' rights;

IMPLEMENT this Agreement in a manner consistent with environmental protection and conservation;

PROMOTE sustainable development;

CONSERVE, protect, and improve the environment, including through managing natural resources in their respective territories and through multilateral environmental agreements to which they are both parties;

PRESERVE their flexibility to safeguard the public welfare; and

CONTRIBUTE to hemispheric integration and the fulfillment of the objectives of the Free Trade Area of the Americas;

HAVE AGREED AS FOLLOWS:

---

[1] The full text of the United States-Chile Free Trade Agreement, with annexes, is set out in this volume as a model of the other six Free Trade Agreements that were in force for the United States as of December 31, 2005.

Chapter One

Initial Provisions

ARTICLE 1.1: ESTABLISHMENT OF A FREE TRADE AREA

The Parties to this Agreement, consistent with Article XXIV of the General Agreement on Tariffs and Trade 1994 and Article V of the General Agreement on Trade in Services, hereby establish a free trade area.

ARTICLE 1.2: OBJECTIVES

1. The objectives of this Agreement, as elaborated more specifically through its principles and rules, including national treatment, most-favored-nation treatment, and transparency, are to:

(a) encourage expansion and diversification of trade between the Parties;

(b) eliminate barriers to trade in, and facilitate the cross-border movement of, goods and services between the Parties;

(c) promote conditions of fair competition in the free trade area;

(d) substantially increase investment opportunities in the territories of the Parties;

(e) provide adequate and effective protection and enforcement of intellectual property rights in each Party's territory;

(f) create effective procedures for the implementation and application of this Agreement, for its joint administration, and for the resolution of disputes; and

(g) establish a framework for further bilateral, regional, and multilateral cooperation to expand and enhance the benefits of this Agreement.

2. The Parties shall interpret and apply the provisions of this Agreement in the light of its objectives set out in paragraph 1 and in accordance with applicable rules of international law.

ARTICLE 1.3: RELATION TO OTHER AGREEMENTS

The Parties affirm their existing rights and obligations with respect to each other under the WTO Agreement and other agreements to which both Parties are party.

ARTICLE 1.4: EXTENT OF OBLIGATIONS

The Parties shall ensure that all necessary measures are taken in order to give effect to the provisions of this Agreement, including their observance, except as otherwise provided in this Agreement, by state governments.

Chapter Two

General Definitions

ARTICLE 2.1: DEFINITIONS OF GENERAL APPLICATION

For purposes of this Agreement, unless otherwise specified:

central level of government means:

(a) for the United States, the federal level of government; and

(b) for Chile, the national level of government;

Commission means the Free Trade Commission established under Article 21.1 (The Free Trade Commission);

covered investment means, with respect to a Party, an investment in its territory of an investor of the other Party in existence as of the date of entry into force of this Agreement or established, acquired, or expanded thereafter;

customs authority means the competent authority that is responsible under the law of a Party for the administration of customs laws and regulations;

customs duty includes any customs or import duty and a charge of any kind imposed in connection with the importation of a good, including any form of surtax or surcharge in connection with such importation, but does not include any:

(a) charge equivalent to an internal tax imposed consistently with Article III:2 of the GATT 1994; in respect of like, directly competitive, or substitutable goods of the Party, or in respect of goods from which the imported good has been manufactured or produced in whole or in part;

(b) antidumping or countervailing duty; and

(c) fee or other charge in connection with importation commensurate with the cost of services rendered;

Customs Valuation Agreement means the Agreement on Implementation of Article VII of the General Agreement on Tariffs and Trade 1994, which is part of the WTO Agreement;

days means calendar days;

enterprise means any entity constituted or organized under applicable law, whether or not for profit, and whether privately-owned or governmentally-owned, including any corporation, trust, partnership, sole proprietorship, joint venture, or other association;

enterprise of a Party means an enterprise constituted or organized under the law of a Party;

existing means in effect on the date of entry into force of this Agreement;

GATS means the General Agreement on Trade in Services, which is part of the WTO Agreement;

GATT 1994 means the General Agreement on Tariffs and Trade 1994, which is part of the WTO Agreement;

goods of a Party means domestic products as these are understood in the GATT 1994 or such goods as the Parties may agree, and includes originating goods of that Party. A good of a Party may include materials of other countries;

Harmonized System (HS) means the Harmonized Commodity Description and Coding System, including its General Rules of Interpretation, Section Notes, and Chapter Notes, as adopted and implemented by the Parties in their respective tariff laws;

heading means the first four digits in the tariff classification number under the Harmonized System;

measure includes any law, regulation, procedure, requirement, or practice;

national means a natural person who has the nationality of a Party according to Annex 2.1 or a permanent resident of a Party;

originating means qualifying under the rules of origin set out in Chapter Four (Rules of Origin and Origin Procedures);

person means a natural person or an enterprise;

person of a Party means a national or an enterprise of a Party;

preferential tariff treatment means the duty rate applicable under this Agreement to an originating good;

procurement means the process by which a government obtains the use of or acquires goods or services, or any combination thereof, for governmental purposes and not with a view to commercial sale or resale, or use in the production or supply of goods or services for commercial sale or resale;

regional level of government means, for the United States, a state of the United States, the District of Columbia, or Puerto Rico. For Chile, as a unitary state, "regional level of government" is not applicable;

Safeguards Agreement means the Agreement on Safeguards, which is part of the WTO Agreement;

SPS Agreement means the Agreement on the Application of Sanitary and Phytosanitary Measures, which is part of the WTO Agreement;

state enterprise means an enterprise that is owned, or controlled through ownership interests, by a Party;

subheading means the first six digits in the tariff classification number under the Harmonized System;

TBT Agreement means the Agreement on Technical Barriers to Trade, which is part of the WTO Agreement;

territory means for a Party the territory of that Party as set out in Annex 2.1;

TRIPS Agreement means the Agreement on Trade-Related Aspects of Intellectual Property Rights, which is part of the WTO Agreement; and

WTO Agreement means the Marrakesh Agreement Establishing the World Trade Organization, done on April 15, 1994.

Chapter Three

National Treatment and Market Access for Goods

ARTICLE 3.1: SCOPE AND COVERAGE

Except as otherwise provided, this Chapter applies to trade in goods of a Party.

Section A—National Treatment

ARTICLE 3.2: NATIONAL TREATMENT

1. Each Party shall accord national treatment to the goods of the other Party in accordance with Article III of GATT 1994, including

its interpretative notes, and to this end Article III of GATT 1994, and its interpretative notes, are incorporated into and made part of this Agreement, *mutatis mutandis*.

2. The provisions of paragraph 1 regarding national treatment shall mean, with respect to a regional level of government, treatment no less favorable than the most favorable treatment that regional level of government accords to any like, directly competitive, or substitutable goods, as the case may be, of the Party of which it forms a part.[2]

3. Paragraphs 1 and 2 shall not apply to the measures set out in Annex 3.2.

Section B—Tariff Elimination

Article 3.3: Tariff Elimination

1. Except as otherwise provided in this Agreement, neither Party may increase any existing customs duty, or adopt any customs duty, on an originating good.

2. Except as otherwise provided in this Agreement, each Party shall progressively eliminate its customs duties on originating goods in accordance with Annex 3.3.

3. The United States shall eliminate customs duties on any non-agricultural originating goods that, after the date of entry into force of this Agreement, are designated as articles eligible for duty-free treatment under the U.S. *Generalized System of Preferences,* effective from the date of such designation.

4. On the request of either Party, the Parties shall consult to consider accelerating the elimination of customs duties set out in their Schedules to Annex 3.3. An agreement between the Parties to accelerate the elimination of a customs duty on a good shall supercede any duty rate or staging category determined pursuant to their Schedules to Annex 3.3 for such good when approved by each Party in accordance with Article 21.1(3)(b) (The Free Trade Commission) and its applicable legal procedures.

5. For greater certainty, a Party may:

(a) raise a customs duty back to the level established in its Schedule to Annex 3.3 following a unilateral reduction; or

(b) maintain or increase a customs duty as authorized by the Dispute Settlement Body of the WTO.

Article 3.4: Used Goods

On entry into force of this Agreement, Chile shall cease applying the 50 percent surcharge established in the *Regla General Complementaria N° 3* of *Arancel Aduanero* with respect to originating goods of the other Party that benefit from preferential tariff treatment.

[2] For greater certainty, "goods of the Party" includes goods produced in a state or region of that Party.

ARTICLE 3.5: CUSTOMS VALUATION OF CARRIER MEDIA

1. For purposes of determining the customs value of carrier media bearing content, each Party shall base its determination on the cost or value of the carrier media alone.

2. For purposes of the effective imposition of any internal taxes, direct or indirect, each Party shall determine the tax basis according to its domestic law.

Section C—Special Regimes

ARTICLE 3.6: WAIVER OF CUSTOMS DUTIES

1. Neither Party may adopt any new waiver of customs duties, or expand with respect to existing recipients or extend to any new recipient the application of an existing waiver of customs duties, where the waiver is conditioned, explicitly or implicitly, on the fulfillment of a performance requirement.

2. Neither Party may, explicitly or implicitly, condition on the fulfillment of a performance requirement the continuation of any existing waiver of customs duties.

3. This Article shall not apply to measures subject to Article 3.8.

ARTICLE 3.7: TEMPORARY ADMISSION OF GOODS

1. Each Party shall grant duty-free temporary admission for:

(a) professional equipment, including equipment for the press or television, software and broadcasting and cinematographic equipment, necessary for carrying out the business activity, trade or profession of a business person who qualifies for temporary entry pursuant to the laws of the importing Party;

(b) goods intended for display or demonstration;

(c) commercial samples and advertising films and recordings; and

(d) goods admitted for sports purposes,

regardless of their origin.

2. Each Party shall, at the request of the person concerned and for reasons deemed valid by its customs authority, extend the time limit for temporary admission beyond the period initially fixed.

3. Neither Party may condition the duty-free temporary admission of goods referred to in paragraph 1, other than to require that such goods:

(a) be used solely by or under the personal supervision of a national or resident of the other Party in the exercise of the business activity, trade, profession, or sport of that person;

(b) not be sold or leased while in its territory;

(c) be accompanied by a security in an amount no greater than the charges that would otherwise be owed on entry or final importation, releasable on exportation of the good;

(d) be capable of identification when exported;

(e) be exported on the departure of the person referenced in subparagraph (a), or within such other period, related to the purpose of the temporary admission, as the Party may establish, or within one year, unless extended;

(f) be admitted in no greater quantity than is reasonable for their intended use; and

(g) be otherwise admissible into the Party's territory under its laws.

4. If any condition that a Party imposes under paragraph 3 has not been fulfilled, the Party may apply the customs duty and any other charge that would normally be owed on the good plus any other charges or penalities provided for under its domestic law.

5. Each Party, through its customs authority, shall adopt procedures providing for the expeditious release of goods admitted under this Article. To the extent possible, such procedures shall provide that when such a good accompanies a national or resident of the other Party who is seeking temporary entry, the good shall be released simultaneously with the entry of that national or resident.

6. Each Party shall permit a good temporarily admitted under this Article to be exported through a customs port other than that through which it was admitted.

7. Each Party, through its customs authority, consistent with domestic law, shall relieve the importer or other person responsible for a good admitted under this Article from any liability for failure to export the good on presentation of satisfactory proof to customs authorities that the good has been destroyed within the original period fixed for temporary admission or any lawful extension.

8. Subject to Chapters Ten (Investment) and Eleven (Cross-Border Trade in Services):

(a) each Party shall allow a vehicle or container used in international traffic that enters its territory from the territory of the other Party to exit its territory on any route that is reasonably related to the economic and prompt departure of such vehicle or container;

(b) neither Party may require any bond or impose any penalty or charge solely by reason of any difference between the port of entry and the port of departure of a vehicle or container;

(c) neither Party may condition the release of any obligation, including any bond, that it imposes in respect of the entry of a vehicle or container into its territory on its exit through any particular port of departure; and

(d) neither Party may require that the vehicle or carrier bringing a container from the territory of the other Party into its territory be the same vehicle or carrier that takes such container to the territory of the other Party.

9. For purposes of paragraph 8, **vehicle** means a truck, a truck tractor, tractor, trailer unit or trailer, a locomotive, or a railway car or other railroad equipment.

ARTICLE 3.8: DRAWBACK AND DUTY DEFERRAL PROGRAMS

1. Except as otherwise provided in this Article, neither Party may refund the amount of customs duties paid, or waive or reduce the amount of customs duties owed, on a good imported into its territory, on condition that the good is:

(a) subsequently exported to the territory of the other Party;

(b) used as a material in the production of another good that is subsequently exported to the territory of the other Party; or

(c) substituted by an identical or similar good used as a material in the production of another good that is subsequently exported to the territory of the other Party.

2. Neither Party may, on condition of export, refund, waive, or reduce:

(a) an antidumping or countervailing duty;

(b) a premium offered or collected on an imported good arising out of any tendering system in respect of the administration of quantitative import restrictions, tariff rate quotas, or tariff preference levels; or

(c) customs duties paid or owed on a good imported into its territory and substituted by an identical or similar good that is subsequently exported to the territory of the other Party.

3. Where a good is imported into the territory of a Party pursuant to a duty deferral program and is subsequently exported to the territory of the other Party, or is used as a material in the production of another good that is subsequently exported to the territory of the other Party, or is substituted by an identical or similar good used as a material in the production of another good that is subsequently exported to the territory of the other Party, the Party from whose territory the good is exported shall assess the customs duties as if the exported good had been withdrawn for domestic consumption.

4. This Article does not apply to:

(a) a good entered under bond for transportation and exportation to the territory of the other Party;

(b) a good exported to the territory of the other Party in the same condition as when imported into the territory of the Party from which the good was exported (testing, cleaning, repacking, inspecting, sorting, marking, or preserving a good shall not be considered to change the good's condition). Where such a good has been commingled with fungible goods and exported in the same condition, its origin for purposes of this subparagraph may be determined on the basis of such inventory management methods as first-in, first-out or last-in, first-out. Nothing in this subparagraph shall be construed to permit a Party to waive, refund, or reduce a customs duty contrary to paragraph 2(c);

(c) a good imported into the territory of a Party that is deemed to be exported from its territory, or used as a material in the production of another good that is deemed to be exported to the territory of the other Party, or is substituted by an identical or similar good used as a material in the production of another good that is deemed to be exported to the territory of the other Party, by reason of

(i) delivery to a duty-free shop,

(ii) delivery for ship's stores or supplies for ships or aircraft, or

(iii) delivery for use in joint undertakings of the Parties and that will subsequently become the property of the Party into whose territory the good was deemed to be exported;

(d) a refund of customs duties by a Party on a particular good imported into its territory and subsequently exported to the territory of the other Party, where that refund is granted by reason of the failure of such good to conform to sample or specification, or by reason of the shipment of such good without the consent of the consignee; or

(e) an originating good that is imported into the territory of a Party and is subsequently exported to the territory of the other Party, or used as a material in the production of another good that is subsequently exported to the territory of the other Party, or is substituted by an identical or similar good used as a material in the production of another good that is subsequently exported to the territory of the other Party.

5. This Article shall take effect beginning eight years after the date of entry into force of this Agreement, and thereafter a Party may refund, waive, or reduce duties paid or owed under the Party's duty drawback or deferral programs according to the following schedule:

(a) no more than 75 percent in year nine;

(b) no more than 50 percent in year 10;

(c) no more than 25 percent in year 11; and

(d) zero in year 12 and thereafter.

6. For purposes of this Article:

good means "good" as defined in Article 4.18 (Definitions);

identical or similar goods means "identical goods" and "similar goods", respectively, as defined in the Customs Valuation Agreement;

material means "material" as defined in Article 4.18 (Definitions); and

used means used or consumed in the production of goods.

ARTICLE 3.9: GOODS RE-ENTERED AFTER REPAIR OR ALTERATION

1. Neither Party may apply a customs duty to a good, regardless of its origin, that reenters its territory after that good has been temporarily exported from its territory to the territory of the other Party for repair or alteration, regardless of whether such repair or alteration could be performed in its territory.

2. Neither Party may apply a customs duty to a good, regardless of its origin, admitted temporarily from the territory of the other Party for repair or alteration.

3. For purposes of this Article, **repair or alteration** does not include an operation or process that:

(a) destroys a good's essential characteristics or creates a new or commercially different good; or

(b) transforms an unfinished good into a finished good.

ARTICLE 3.10: DUTY-FREE ENTRY OF COMMERCIAL SAMPLES OF NEGLIGIBLE VALUE AND PRINTED ADVERTISING MATERIALS

Each Party shall grant duty-free entry to commercial samples of negligible value, and to printed advertising materials, imported from the territory of the other Party, regardless of their origin, but may require that:

(a) such samples be imported solely for the solicitation of orders for goods, or services provided from the territory, of the other Party or a non-Party; or

(b) such advertising materials be imported in packets that each contain no more than one copy of each such material and that neither such materials nor packets form part of a larger consignment.

Section D—Non-Tariff Measures

Article 3.11: Import and Export Restrictions

1. Except as otherwise provided in this Agreement, neither Party may adopt or maintain any prohibition or restriction on the importation of any good of the other Party or on the exportation or sale for export of any good destined for the territory of the other Party, except in accordance with Article XI of GATT 1994 and its interpretative notes and to this end Article XI of GATT 1994 and its interpretative notes are incorporated into and made a part of this Agreement, *mutatis mutandis.*

2. The Parties understand that the GATT rights and obligations incorporated by paragraph 1 prohibit, in any circumstances in which any other form of restriction is prohibited, a Party from adopting or maintaining:

(a) export and import price requirements, except as permitted in enforcement of countervailing and antidumping orders and undertakings;

(b) import licensing conditioned on the fulfilment of a performance requirement; or

(c) voluntary export restraints not consistent with Article VI of GATT 1994, as implemented under Article 18 of the SCM Agreement and Article 8.1 of the AD Agreement.

3. In the event that a Party adopts or maintains a prohibition or restriction on the importation from or exportation to a non-Party of a good, nothing in this Agreement shall be construed to prevent the Party from:

(a) limiting or prohibiting the importation from the territory of the other Party of such good of that non-Party; or

(b) requiring as a condition of export of such good of the Party to the territory of the other Party, that the good not be re-exported to the non-Party, directly or indirectly, without being consumed in the territory of the other Party.

4. In the event that a Party adopts or maintains a prohibition or restriction on the importation of a good from a non-Party, the Parties, on the request of either Party, shall consult with a view to avoiding undue interference with or distortion of pricing, marketing, and distribution arrangements in the other Party.

5. Paragraphs 1 through 4 shall not apply to the measures set out in Annex 3.2.

Article 3.12: Administrative Fees and Formalities

1. Each Party shall ensure, in accordance with Article VIII:1 of GATT 1994 and its interpretive notes, that all fees and charges of whatever character (other than customs duties, charges equivalent

to an internal tax or other internal charge applied consistently with Article III:2 of GATT 1994, and antidumping and countervailing duties) imposed on or in connection with importation or exportation are limited in amount to the approximate cost of services rendered and do not represent an indirect protection to domestic goods or a taxation of imports or exports for fiscal purposes.

2. Neither Party may require consular transactions, including related fees and charges, in connection with the importation of any good of the other Party.

3. Each Party shall make available through the Internet or a comparable computerbased telecommunications network a current list of the fees and charges it imposes in connection with importation or exportation.

4. The United States shall eliminate its merchandise processing fee on originating goods of Chile.

ARTICLE 3.13: EXPORT TAXES

Neither Party may adopt or maintain any duty, tax, or other charge on the export of any good to the territory of the other Party, unless such duty, tax, or charge is adopted or maintained on any such good when destined for domestic consumption.

ARTICLE 3.14: LUXURY TAX

Chile shall eliminate the Luxury Tax established in Article 46 of Decreto Ley 825 of 1974, according to the schedule set out in Annex 3.14.

Section E—Other Measures

ARTICLE 3.15: DISTINCTIVE PRODUCTS

1. Chile shall recognize Bourbon Whiskey and Tennessee Whiskey, which is a straight Bourbon Whisky authorized to be produced only in the State of Tennessee, as distinctive products of the United States. Accordingly, Chile shall not permit the sale of any product as Bourbon Whiskey or Tennessee Whiskey, unless it has been manufactured in the United States in accordance with the laws and regulations of the United States governing the manufacture of Bourbon Whiskey and Tennessee Whiskey.

2. The United States shall recognize *Pisco Chileno* (Chilean Pisco), *Pajarete,* and *Vino Asoleado,* which is authorized in Chile to be produced only in Chile, as distinctive products of Chile. Accordingly, the United States shall not permit the sale of any product as *Pisco Chileno* (Chilean Pisco), *Pajarete,* or *Vino Asoleado,* unless it has been manufactured in Chile in accordance with the laws and regulations of Chile governing the manufacture of *Pisco, Pajarete,* and *Vino Asoleado.*

Section F—Agriculture

ARTICLE 3.16: AGRICULTURAL EXPORT SUBSIDIES

1. The Parties share the objective of the multilateral elimination of export subsidies for agricultural goods and shall work together

toward an agreement in the World Trade Organization to eliminate those subsidies and prevent their reintroduction in any form.

2. Except as provided in paragraph 3, neither Party shall introduce or maintain any export subsidy on any agricultural good destined for the territory of the other Party.

3. Where an exporting Party considers that a non-Party is exporting an agricultural good to the territory of the other Party with the benefit of export subsidies, the importing Party shall, on written request of the exporting Party, consult with the exporting Party with a view to agreeing on specific measures that the importing Party may adopt to counter the effect of such subsidized imports. If the importing Party adopts the agreed-upon measures, the exporting Party shall refrain from applying any export subsidy to exports of such good to the territory of the importing Party.

Article 3.17: Agricultural Marketing and Grading Standards

1. Where a Party adopts or maintains a measure respecting the classification, grading, or marketing of a domestic agricultural good, or a measure to expand, maintain, or develop its domestic market for an agricultural good, it shall accord treatment to a like good of the other Party that is no less favorable than it accords under the measure to the domestic agricultural good, regardless of whether the good is intended for direct consumption or for processing.

2. Paragraph 1 shall be without prejudice to the rights of either Party under the WTO Agreement or under this Agreement regarding measures respecting the classification, grading, or marketing of an agricultural good.

3. The Parties hereby establish a Working Group on Agricultural Trade, comprising representatives of the Parties, which shall meet annually or as otherwise agreed. The Working Group shall review, in coordination with the Committee on Technical Barriers to Trade established in Article 7.8 (Committee on Technical Barriers to Trade), the operation of agricultural grade and quality standards and programs of expansion and development that affect trade between the Parties, and shall resolve any issues that may arise regarding the operation of those standards and programs. The Group shall report to the Committee on Trade in Goods established in Article 3.23.

4. Each Party shall recognize the other Party's grading programs for beef, as set out in Annex 3.17.

Article 3.18: Agricultural Safeguard Measures

1. Notwithstanding Article 3.3(2), each Party may impose a safeguard measure in the form of additional import duties, consistent with paragraphs 2 through 7, on an originating agricultural good listed in its section of Annex 3.18. The sum of any such additional duty and any import duties or other charges applied pursuant to Article 3.3(2) shall not exceed the lesser of:

(a) the prevailing most-favored-nation (MFN) applied rate; or

(b) the MFN applied rate of duty in effect on the day immediately preceding the date of entry into force of this Agreement.

2. A Party may impose a safeguard measure only if the unit import price of the good enters the Party's customs territory at a level below a trigger price for that good as set out in that Party's section of Annex 3.18.

(a) The unit import price shall be determined on the basis of the C.I.F. import price of the good in U.S. dollars for goods entering Chile, and on the basis of the F.O.B. import price of the good in U.S. dollars for goods entering the United States.

(b) The trigger prices for the goods eligible for a safeguard measure, which reflect historic unit import values for the products concerned, are listed in Annex 3.18. The Parties may mutually agree to periodically evaluate and update the trigger prices.

3. The additional duties under paragraph 2 shall be set in accordance with the following schedule:

(a) if the difference between the unit import price of the item expressed in terms of domestic currency (the "import price") and the trigger price as defined under paragraph 2(b) is less than or equal to 10 percent of the trigger price, no additional duty shall be imposed;

(b) if the difference between the import price and the trigger price is greater than 10 percent but less than or equal to 40 percent of the trigger price, the additional duty shall equal 30 percent of the difference between the MFN rate applicable under paragraph 1 and the preferential tariff rate;

(c) if the difference between the import price and the trigger price is greater than 40 percent but less than or equal to 60 percent of the trigger price, the additional duty shall equal 50 percent of the difference between the MFN rate applicable under paragraph 1 and the preferential tariff rate;

(d) if the difference between the import price and the trigger price is greater than 60 percent but less than or equal to 75 percent, the additional duty shall equal 70 percent of the difference between the MFN rate applicable under paragraph 1 and the preferential tariff rate; and

(e) if the difference between the import price and the trigger price is greater than 75 percent of the trigger price, the additional duty shall equal 100 percent of the difference between the MFN rate applicable under paragraph 1 and the preferential tariff rate.

4. Neither Party may, with respect to the same good, at the same time:

(a) impose a safeguard measure under this Article; and

(b) take a safeguard action under Section A of Chapter Eight (Trade Remedies).

5. Neither Party may impose a safeguard measure on a good that is subject to a measure that the Party has imposed pursuant to Article XIX of GATT 1994 and the Safeguards Agreement, and neither Party may continue maintaining a safeguard measure on a good that becomes subject to a measure that the Party imposes pursuant to Article XIX of GATT 1994 and the Safeguards Agreement.

6. A Party may impose a safeguard measure only during the 12-year period beginning on the date of entry into force of this Agreement. Neither Party may impose a safeguard measure on a good once the good achieves duty-free status under this Agreement. Neither Party may impose a safeguard measure that increases a zero in-quota duty on a good subject to a tariff-rate quota.

7. Each Party shall implement any safeguard measure in a transparent manner. Within 60 days after imposing a measure, a Party shall notify the other Party, in writing, and shall provide it relevant data concerning the measure. On request, the Party imposing the measure shall consult with the other Party with respect to the conditions of application of the measure.

8. The general operation of the agricultural safeguard provisions and the trigger prices for their implementation may be the subject of discussion and review in the Committee on Trade in Goods.

9. For purposes of this Article, **safeguard measure** means an agricultural safeguard measure described in paragraph 1.

Section G—Textiles and Apparel

Article 3.19: Bilateral Emergency Actions

1. If, as a result of the elimination of a duty provided for in this Agreement, a textile or apparel good benefiting from preferential tariff treatment under this Agreement is being imported into the territory of a Party in such increased quantities, in absolute terms or relative to the domestic market for that good, and under such conditions as to cause serious damage, or actual threat thereof, to a domestic industry producing a like or directly competitive good, the importing Party may, to the extent and for such time as may be necessary to prevent or remedy such damage and to facilitate adjustment, take emergency action, consisting of an increase in the rate of duty on the good to a level not to exceed the lesser of:

(a) the most-favored-nation (MFN) applied rate of duty in effect at the time the action is taken; and

(b) the MFN applied rate of duty in effect on the date of entry into force of this Agreement.

2. In determining serious damage, or actual threat thereof, the importing Party:

(a) shall examine the effect of increased imports from the other Party on the particular industry, as reflected in changes in such relevant economic variables as output, productivity, utilization of capacity, inventories, market share, exports, wages, employment, domestic prices, profits and investment, none of which is necessarily decisive; and

(b) shall not consider changes in technology or consumer preference as factors supporting a determination of serious damage or actual threat thereof.

3. The importing Party may take an emergency action under this Article only following an investigation by its competent authorities.

4. The importing Party shall deliver to the other Party, without delay, written notice of its intent to take emergency action, and, on request of the other Party, shall enter into consultations with that Party.

5. The following conditions and limitations shall apply to any emergency action taken under this Article:

(a) no emergency action may be maintained for a period exceeding three years;

(b) no emergency action may be taken or maintained beyond the period ending eight years after duties on a good have been eliminated pursuant to this Agreement;

(c) no emergency action may be taken by an importing Party against any particular good of the other Party more than once; and

(d) on termination of the action, the good will return to duty-free status.

6. The Party taking an emergency action under this Article shall provide to the Party against whose good the action is taken mutually agreed trade liberalizing compensation in the form of concessions having substantially equivalent trade effects or equivalent to the value of the additional duties expected to result from the emergency action. Such concessions shall be limited to textile and apparel goods, unless the Parties otherwise agree. If the Parties are unable to agree on compensation, the Party against whose good the emergency action is taken may take tariff action having trade effects substantially equivalent to the trade effects of the emergency action taken under this Article. Such tariff action may be taken against any goods of the Party taking the emergency action. The Party taking the tariff action shall apply such action only for the minimum period necessary to achieve the substantially equivalent trade effects. The importing Party's obligation to provide trade compensation and the exporting Party's right to take tariff action shall terminate when the emergency action terminates.

7. Nothing in this Agreement shall be construed to limit a Party's right to restrain imports of textile and apparel goods in a manner consistent with the Agreement on Textiles and Clothing or the Safeguards Agreement. However, a Party may not take or maintain an emergency action under this Article against a textile or apparel good that is subject, or becomes subject, to a safeguard measure that a Party takes pursuant to either such WTO agreement.

ARTICLE 3.20: RULES OF ORIGIN AND RELATED MATTERS

Application of Chapter Four

1. Except as provided in this Section, Chapter Four (Rules of Origin and Origin Procedures) applies to textile and apparel goods.

2. The rules of origin set forth in this Agreement shall not apply in determining the country of origin of a textile or apparel good for non-preferential purposes.

Consultations

3. On the request of either Party, the Parties shall consult to consider whether the rules of origin applicable to particular textile and apparel goods should be revised to address issues of availability of supply of fibers, yarns or fabrics in the territories of the Parties.

4. In the consultations referred to in paragraph 3, each Party shall consider all data presented by the other Party showing substantial production in its territory of the particular good. The Parties shall consider that substantial production has been shown if a Party demonstrates that its domestic producers are capable of supplying commercial quantities of the good in a timely manner.

5. The Parties shall endeavor to conclude consultations within 60 days of a request. An agreement between the Parties resulting from the consultations shall supersede any prior rule of origin for such good when approved by the Parties in accordance with Article 24.2 (Amendments).

De Minimis

6. A textile or apparel good provided for in Chapters 50 through 63 of the Harmonized System that is not an originating good, because certain fibers or yarns used in the production of the component of the good that determines the tariff classification of the good do not undergo an applicable change in tariff classification set out in Annex 4.1 (Specific Rules of Origin), shall nonetheless be considered to be an originating good if the total weight of all such fibers or yarns in that component is not more than seven percent of the total weight of that component. Notwithstanding the preceding sentence, a good containing elastomeric yarns in the component of the good that determines the tariff classification of the good shall be considered to be an originating good only if such yarns are wholly formed in the territory of a Party.

Treatment of Sets

7. Notwithstanding the good specific rules in Annex 4.1 (Specific Rules of Origin), textile and apparel goods classifiable as goods put up in sets for retail sale as provided for in General Rule of Interpretation 3 of the Harmonized System shall not be regarded as originating goods unless each of the goods in the set is an originating good or the total value of the non-originating goods in the set does not exceed 10 percent of the customs value of the set.

Preferential Tariff Treatment for Non-Originating Cotton and Man-made Fiber Fabric Goods (Tariff Preference Levels)

8. Subject to paragraph 9, the following goods, if they meet the applicable conditions for preferential tariff treatment under this Agreement other than the condition that they be originating goods, shall be accorded preferential tariff treatment as if they were originating goods:

(a) cotton or man-made fiber fabric goods provided for in Chapters 52, 54, 55, 58, and 60 of the Harmonized System that are wholly formed in the territory of a Party from yarn produced or obtained outside the territory of a Party; and

(b) cotton or man-made fiber fabric goods provided for in Annex 4.1 (Specific Rules of Origin) that are wholly formed in the territory of a Party from yarn spun in the territory of a Party from fiber produced or obtained outside the territory of a Party.

9. The treatment described in paragraph 8 shall be limited to goods imported into the territory of a Party up to an annual total quantity of 1,000,000 SME.

Preferential Tariff Treatment for Non-Originating Cotton and Man-made Fiber Apparel Goods (Tariff Preference Levels)

10. Subject to paragraph 11, cotton or man-made fiber apparel goods provided for in Chapters 61 and 62 of the Harmonized System that are both cut (or knit to shape) and sewn or otherwise assembled in the territory of a Party from fabric or yarn produced or obtained outside the territory of a Party, and that meet the applicable conditions for preferential tariff treatment under this Agreement other than the condition that they be originating goods, shall be accorded preferential tariff treatment as if they were originating goods.

11. The treatment described in paragraph 10 shall be limited as follows:

(a) in each of the first 10 years after the date of entry into force of this Agreement, the treatment shall apply to goods described in that paragraph imported into the territory of a Party up to a quantity of 2,000,000 SME; and

(b) in the eleventh year, and for each year thereafter, the treatment shall apply to goods described in that paragraph imported into the territory of a Party up to a quantity of 1,000,000 SME.

Certification for Tariff Preference Level

12. A Party, through its competent authorities, may require that an importer claiming preferential tariff treatment for a textile or apparel good under paragraph 8 or 10 present to such competent authorities at the time of importation a certification of eligibility for preferential tariff treatment under such paragraph. A certification of eligibility shall be prepared by the importer and shall consist of information demonstrating that the good satisfies the requirements for preferential tariff treatment under paragraph 8 or 10.

ARTICLE 3.21: CUSTOMS COOPERATION

1. The Parties shall cooperate for purposes of:

(a) enforcing or assisting in the enforcement of their laws, regulations, and procedures implementing this Agreement affecting trade in textile and apparel goods;

(b) ensuring the accuracy of claims of origin; and

(c) preventing circumvention of laws, regulations, and procedures of either Party or international agreements affecting trade in textile and apparel goods.

2. On the request of the importing Party, the exporting Party shall conduct a verification for purposes of enabling the importing Party to determine that a claim of origin for a textile or apparel good is accurate. The exporting Party shall conduct such a verification, regardless of whether an importer claims preferential tariff treatment for the good. The exporting Party also may conduct such a verification on its own initiative.

3. Where the importing Party has a reasonable suspicion that an exporter or producer of the exporting Party is engaging in unlawful activity relating to trade in textile and apparel goods, the importing Party may request the exporting Party to conduct a verification for purposes of enabling the importing Party to determine that the exporter or producer is complying with applicable customs laws, regulations, and procedures regarding trade in textile and apparel goods, including laws, regulations, and procedures that the exporting Party adopts and maintains pursuant to this Agreement and laws, regulations, and procedures of either Party implementing other international agreements regarding trade in textile and apparel goods, and to determine that claims of origin regarding textile or apparel goods exported or produced by that person are accurate. For purposes of this paragraph, a reasonable suspicion of unlawful activity shall be based on factors including relevant factual information of the type set forth in Article 5.5 (Cooperation) or that, with respect to a particular shipment, indicates circumvention by the exporter or producer of applicable customs laws, regulations, or procedures regarding trade in textile and apparel goods, including laws, regulations, or procedures adopted to implement this Agreement, or international agreements affecting trade in textile and apparel goods.

4. The importing Party, through its competent authorities, may undertake or assist in a verification conducted pursuant to paragraph 2 or 3, including by conducting, along with the competent authorities of the exporting Party, visits in the territory of the exporting Party to the premises of an exporter, producer, or any other enterprise involved in the movement of textile or apparel goods from the territory of the exporting Party to the territory of the importing Party.

5. Each Party shall provide to the other Party, consistent with its laws, regulations, and procedures, production, trade, and transit documents and other information necessary to conduct verifications under paragraphs 2 and 3. Any documents or information exchanged between the Parties in the course of such a verification shall be considered confidential, as provided for in Article 5.6 (Confidentiality).

6. While a verification is being conducted, the importing Party may take appropriate action, which may include suspending the application of preferential tariff treatment to:

(a) the textile or apparel good for which a claim of origin has been made, in the case of a verification under paragraph 2; or

(b) the textile and apparel goods exported or produced by the person subject to a verification under paragraph 3, where the reasonable suspicion of unlawful activity relates to those goods.

7. The Party conducting a verification under paragraph 2 or 3 shall provide the other Party with a written report on the results of the verification, which shall include all documents and facts supporting any conclusion that the Party reaches.

8. (a) If the importing Party is unable to make the determination described in paragraph 2 within 12 months after its request for a verification, it may take action as permitted under its law with respect to the textile and apparel good subject to the verification, and

with respect to similar goods exported or produced by the person that exported or produced the good.

(b) If the importing Party is unable to make the determinations described in paragraph 3 within 12 months after its request for a verification, it may take action as permitted under its law with respect to any textile or apparel goods exported or produced by the person subject to the verification.

9. Prior to commencing appropriate action under paragraph 8, the importing Party shall notify the other Party. The importing Party may continue to take appropriate action under paragraph 8 until it receives information sufficient to enable it to make the determination described in paragraph 2 or 3, as the case may be.

10. Chile shall implement its obligations under paragraphs 2, 3, 6, 7, 8, and 9 no later than two years after the date of entry into force of this Agreement. Before Chile fully implements those provisions, if the importing Party requests a verification, the verification shall be conducted principally by that Party, including through means described in paragraph 4. Nothing in this paragraph shall be construed to waive or limit the importing Party's rights under paragraphs 6 and 8.

11. On the request of either Party, the Parties shall enter into consultations to resolve any technical or interpretive difficulties that may arise under this Article or to discuss ways to improve the effectiveness of their cooperative efforts. In addition, either Party may request technical or other assistance from the other Party in implementing this Article. The Party receiving such a request shall make every effort to respond favorably and promptly to it.

ARTICLE 3.22: DEFINITIONS

For purposes of this Section:

claim of origin means a claim that a textile or apparel good is an originating good or a good of a Party;

exporting Party means the Party from whose territory a textile or apparel good is exported;

importing Party means the Party into whose territory a textile or apparel good is imported;

SME means square meter equivalents, as calculated in accordance with the conversion factors set out in the *Correlation: Textile and Apparel Categories with the Harmonized Tariff Schedule of the United States, 2002* (or successor publication), published by the United States Department of Commerce, International Trade Administration, Office of Textiles and Apparel, Trade and Data Division, Washington, D.C.; and

textile or apparel good means a good listed in the Annex to the Agreement on Textiles and Clothing.

Section H—Institutional Provisions

ARTICLE 3.23: COMMITTEE ON TRADE IN GOODS

1. The Parties hereby establish a Committee on Trade in Goods, comprising representatives of each Party.

2. The Committee shall meet on the request of either Party or the Commission to consider any matter arising under this Chapter, Chapter Four (Rules of Origin and Origin Procedures), or Chapter Five (Customs Administration).

3. The Committee's functions shall include:

(a) promoting trade in goods between the Parties, including through consultations on accelerating tariff elimination under this Agreement and other issues as appropriate; and

(b) addressing barriers to trade in goods between the Parties, especially those related to the application of non-tariff measures, and, if appropriate, referring such matters to the Commission for its consideration.

Section I—Definitions

ARTICLE 3.24: DEFINITIONS

For purposes of this Chapter:

AD Agreement means the *Agreement on Implementation of Article VI of the General Agreement on Tariffs and Trade 1994,* which is part of the WTO Agreement;

advertising films and recordings means recorded visual media or audio materials, consisting essentially of images and/or sound, showing the nature or operation of goods or services offered for sale or lease by a person established or resident in the territory of a Party, provided that such materials are of a kind suitable for exhibition to prospective customers but not for broadcast to the general public, and provided that they are imported in packets that each contain no more than one copy of each film or recording and that do not form part of a larger consignment;

Agreement on Textiles and Clothing means the Agreement on Textiles and Clothing, which is part of the WTO Agreement;

agricultural goods means those goods referred to in Article 2 of the Agreement on Agriculture, which is part of the WTO Agreement;

articles eligible for duty-free treatment under the U.S. Generalized System of Preferences does not include articles eligible only when imported from least-developed beneficiary developing countries or from beneficiary sub-Saharan African countries under the African Growth and Opportunity Act;

carrier media means any good of heading 8523 or 8524;

commercial samples of negligible value means commercial samples having a value, individually or in the aggregate as shipped, of not more than one U.S. dollar, or the equivalent amount in Chilean currency, or so marked, torn, perforated, or otherwise treated that they are unsuitable for sale or for use except as commercial samples;

consular transactions means requirements that goods of a Party intended for export to the territory of the other Party must first be submitted to the supervision of the consul of the importing Party in the territory of the exporting Party for the purpose of obtaining consular invoices or consular visas for commercial invoices, certificates of origin, manifests, shippers' export declarations, or any other customs documentation required on or in connection with importation;

consumed means:

(a) actually consumed; or

(b) further processed or manufactured so as to result in a substantial change in value, form, or use of the good or in the production of another good;

duty-free means free of customs duty;

duty deferral program includes measures such as those governing foreign-trade zones, regímenes de zonas francas y regímenes aduaneros especiales, temporary importations under bond, bonded warehouses, and inward processing programs;

export subsidies shall have the meaning assigned to that term in Article 1(e) of the WTO Agreement on Agriculture, including any amendment of that article;

goods intended for display or demonstration includes their component parts, ancillary apparatus, and accessories;

goods temporarily admitted for sports purposes means sports requisites for use in sports contests, demonstrations, or training in the territory of the Party into whose territory such goods are admitted;

import licensing means an administrative procedure requiring the submission of an application or other documentation (other than that generally required for customs clearance purposes) to the relevant administrative body as a prior condition for importation into the territory of the importing Party;

performance requirement means a requirement that:

(a) a given level or percentage of goods or services be exported;

(b) domestic goods or services of the Party granting a waiver of customs duties or an import license be substituted for imported goods or services;

(c) a person benefitting from a waiver of customs duties or an import license purchase other goods or services in the territory of the Party granting the waiver of customs duties or the import license, or accord a preference to domestically produced goods or services;

(d) a person benefitting from a waiver of customs duties or an import license produce goods or supply services, in the territory of the Party granting the waiver of customs duties or the import license, with a given level or percentage of domestic content; or

(e) relates in any way the volume or value of imports to the volume or value of exports or to the amount of foreign exchange inflows.

printed advertising materials means those goods classified in Chapter 49 of the Harmonized System, including brochures, pamphlets, leaflets, trade catalogues, yearbooks published by trade associations, tourist promotional materials, and posters, that are used to promote, publicize, or advertise a good or service, are essentially intended to advertise a good or service, and are supplied free of charge; and

SCM Agreement means the Agreement on Subsidies and Countervailing Measures, which is part of the WTO Agreement.

Chapter Four

Rules of Origin and Origin Procedures

Section A—Rules of Origin

ARTICLE 4.1: ORIGINATING GOODS

1. Except as otherwise provided in this Chapter, a good is originating where:

(a) the good is wholly obtained or produced entirely in the territory of one or both of the Parties;

(b) the good is produced entirely in the territory of one or both of the Parties and

(i) each of the non-originating materials used in the production of the good undergoes an applicable change in tariff classification specified in Annex 4.1, or

(ii) the good otherwise satisfies any applicable regional value content or other requirements specified in Annex 4.1, and the good satisfies all other applicable requirements of this Chapter; or

(c) the good is produced entirely in the territory of one or both of the Parties exclusively from originating materials.

2. A good shall not be considered to be an originating good and a material shall not be considered to be an originating material by virtue of having undergone:

(a) simple combining or packaging operations; or

(b) mere dilution with water or with another substance that does not materially alter the characteristics of the good or material.

ARTICLE 4.2: REGIONAL VALUE CONTENT

1. Where Annex 4.1 specifies a regional value content test to determine whether a good is originating, each Party shall provide that the person claiming preferential tariff treatment for the good may calculate regional value content on the basis of one or the other of the following methods:

(a) Builddown method $RVC = (AV - VNM)/AV \times 100$

(b) Buildup method $RVC = VOM/AV \times 100$

where RVC is the regional value content, expressed as a percentage;

AV is the adjusted value;

VNM is the value of non-originating materials used by the producer in the production of the good; and

VOM is the value of originating materials used by the producer in the production of the good.

ARTICLE 4.3: VALUE OF MATERIALS

1. Each Party shall provide that for purposes of calculating the regional value content of a good, and for purposes of applying the de minimis rule, the value of a material:

(a) for a material that is imported by the producer of the good, is the adjusted value of the material with respect to that importation;

(b) for a material acquired in the territory where the good is produced, is the producer's price actually paid or payable for the material, except for materials within the meaning of subparagraph (c);

(c) for a material provided to the producer without charge, or at a price reflecting a discount or similar reduction, is determined by computing the sum of:

(i) all expenses incurred in the growth, production, or manufacture of the material, including general expenses; and

(ii) an amount for profit; and

(d) for a material that is self-produced, is determined by computing the sum of:

(i) all expenses incurred in the production of the material, including general expenses; and

(ii) an amount for profit.

2. Each Party shall provide that the person claiming preferential tariff treatment for a good may adjust the value of materials as follows:

(a) for originating materials, the following expenses may be added to the value of the material where not included under paragraph 1:

(i) the costs of freight, insurance, packing, and all other costs incurred in transporting the material to the location of the producer;

(ii) duties, taxes, and customs brokerage fees on the material paid in the territory of one or both of the Parties, other than duties and taxes that are waived, refunded, refundable, or otherwise recoverable, including credit against duty or tax paid or payable; and

(iii) the cost of waste and spoilage resulting from the use of the material in the production of the good, less the value of renewable scrap or byproduct.

(b) for non-originating materials, the following expenses may be deducted from the value of the material where included under paragraph 1:

(i) the costs of freight, insurance, packing, and all other costs incurred in transporting the material to the location of the producer;

(ii) duties, taxes, and customs brokerage fees on the material paid in the territory of one or both of the Parties, other than duties and taxes that are waived, refunded, refundable, or otherwise recoverable, including credit against duty or tax paid or payable;

(iii) the cost of waste and spoilage resulting from the use of the material in the production of the good, less the value of renewable scrap or byproducts; and

(iv) the cost of originating materials used in the production of the nonoriginating material in the territory of a Party.

ARTICLE 4.4: ACCESSORIES, SPARE PARTS, AND TOOLS

Each Party shall provide that accessories, spare parts, or tools delivered with a good that form part of the good's standard accessories, spare parts, or tools, shall be regarded as a material used in the production of the good, provided that:

(a) the accessories, spare parts, or tools are classified with and not invoiced separately from the good; and

(b) the quantities and value of the accessories, spare parts, or tools are customary for the good.

ARTICLE 4.5: FUNGIBLE GOODS AND MATERIALS

1. Each Party shall provide that the person claiming preferential tariff treatment for a good may claim that a fungible good or material is originating based on either the physical segregation of each fungible good or material, or through the use of any inventory management method, such as averaging, last-in, first-out, or first-in, first-out, recognized in the Generally Accepted Accounting Principles of the Party in which the production is performed or otherwise accepted by the Party in which the production is performed.

2. Each Party shall provide that the inventory management method selected under paragraph 1 for particular fungible goods or materials shall continue to be used for those goods or materials throughout the fiscal year of the person that selected the inventory management method.

ARTICLE 4.6: ACCUMULATION

1. Each Party shall provide that originating goods or materials of a Party, incorporated into a good in the territory of the other Party, shall be considered to originate in the territory of the other Party.

2. Each Party shall provide that a good is originating where the good is produced in the territory of one or both Parties by one or more producers, provided that the good satisfies the requirements in Article 4.1 and all other applicable requirements in this Chapter.

ARTICLE 4.7: DE MINIMIS RULE

1. Each Party shall provide that a good that does not undergo a change in tariff classification pursuant to Annex 4.1 is nonetheless originating if the value of all nonoriginating materials that are used in the production of the good and that do not undergo the applicable change in tariff classification does not exceed 10 percent of the adjusted value of the good, provided that the value of such nonoriginating materials shall be included in the value of non-originating materials for any applicable regional value content requirement and that the good meets all other applicable requirements in this Chapter.

2. Paragraph 1 does not apply to:

(a) a non-originating material provided for in Chapter 4 of the Harmonized System, or a non-originating dairy preparation containing over 10 percent by weight of milk solids provided for in subheadings 1901.90 or 2106.90 of the Harmonized System, that is used in the production of a good provided for in Chapter 4 of the Harmonized System;

(b) a non-originating material provided for in Chapter 4 of the Harmonized System, or non-originating dairy preparations containing over 10 percent by weight of milk solids provided for in subheading 1901.90 of the Harmonized System, that are used in the production of the following goods: infant preparations containing over 10 percent in weight of milk solids provided for in subheading 1901.10 of the Harmonized System; mixes and doughs, containing over 25 percent by weight of butterfat, not put up for retail sale, provided for in subheading 1901.20 of the Harmonized System; dairy preparations containing over 10 percent by weight of milk solids provided for in subheadings 1901.90 or 2106.90 of the Harmonized System; goods provided for in heading 2105 of the Harmonized System; beverages containing milk provided for in subheading 2202.90 of the Harmonized System; or animal feeds containing over 10 percent by weight of milk solids provided for in subheading 2309.90 of the Harmonized System;

(c) a non-originating material provided for in heading 0805 of the Harmonized System or subheadings 2009.11 through 2009.30 of the Harmonized System that is used in the production of a good provided for in subheadings 2009.11 through 2009.30 of the Harmonized System, or in fruit or vegetable juice of any single fruit or vegetable, fortified with minerals or vitamins, concentrated or unconcentrated, provided for in subheadings 2106.90 or 2202.90 of the Harmonized System;

(d) a non-originating material provided for in Chapter 15 of the Harmonized System that is used in the production of a good provided for in headings 1501 through 1508, 1512, 1514, or 1515 of the Harmonized System;

(e) a non-originating material provided for in heading 1701 of the Harmonized System that is used in the production of a good provided for in headings 1701 through 1703 of the Harmonized System;

(f) a non-originating material provided for in Chapter 17 or in heading 1805 of the Harmonized System that is used in the production of a good provided for in subheading 1806.10 of the Harmonized System;

(g) a non-originating material provided for in headings 2203 through 2208 of the Harmonized System that is used in the production of a good provided for in heading 2207 or 2208 of the Harmonized System; and

(h) a non-originating material used in the production of a good provided for in Chapters 1 through 21 of the Harmonized System unless the non-originating material is provided for in a different subheading than the good for which origin is being determined under this Article.

3. With respect to a textile and apparel good provided for in Chapters 50 through 63 of the Harmonized System, Article 3.20(6) (Rules of Origin and Related Matters) applies in place of paragraph 1.

ARTICLE 4.8: INDIRECT MATERIALS USED IN PRODUCTION

Each Party shall provide that an indirect material shall be considered to be an originating material without regard to where it is produced.

ARTICLE 4.9: PACKAGING MATERIALS AND CONTAINERS FOR RETAIL SALE

Each Party shall provide that packaging materials and containers in which a good is packaged for retail sale, if classified with the good, shall be disregarded in determining whether all non-originating materials used in the production of the good undergo the applicable change in tariff classification set out in Annex 4.1, and, if the good is subject to a regional value content requirement, the value of such packaging materials and containers shall be taken into account as originating or non-originating materials, as the case may be, in calculating the regional value content of the good.

ARTICLE 4.10: PACKING MATERIALS AND CONTAINERS FOR SHIPMENT

Each Party shall provide that packing materials and containers for shipment shall be disregarded in determining whether:

(a) the non-originating materials used in the production of the good undergo an applicable change in tariff classification set out in Annex 4.1; and

(b) the good satisfies a regional value content requirement.

ARTICLE 4.11: TRANSIT AND TRANSSHIPMENT

1. Each Party shall provide that a good shall not be considered an originating good if the good undergoes subsequent production or any other operation outside the territories of the Parties, other than unloading, reloading, or any other process necessary to preserve the good in good condition or to transport the good to the territory of a Party.

2. The importing Party may require that a person claiming that a good is originating demonstrate, to the satisfaction of the Party's customs authority, that any subsequent operations on the good performed outside the territories of the Parties comply with the requirements in paragraph 1.

Section B—Origin Procedures

ARTICLE 4.12: CLAIMS OF ORIGIN

1. Each Party shall require that an importer claiming preferential tariff treatment for a good:

(a) make a written declaration in the importation document that the good qualifies as originating;

(b) be prepared to submit, on the request of the importing Party's customs authority, a certificate of origin or information demonstrating that the good qualifies as originating;

(c) promptly make a corrected declaration and pay any duties owing where the importer has reason to believe that the certificate or other information on which the declaration was based is incorrect.

2. Each Party, where appropriate, may request that an importer claiming preferential tariff treatment for a good demonstrate to the Party's customs authority that the good qualifies as originating under Section A, including that the good satisfies the requirements in Article 4.11.

3. Each Party shall provide that, where an originating good was imported into the territory of that Party but no claim for preferential tariff treatment was made at the time of importation, the importer of the good may, no later than one year after the date on which the good was imported, apply for a refund of any excess duties paid as the result of the good not having been accorded preferential tariff treatment, on presentation of:

(a) a written declaration that the good qualified as originating at the time of importation;

(b) a copy of a certificate of origin or other information demonstrating that the good qualifies as originating; and

(c) such other documentation relating to the importation of the good as the importing Party may require.

Article 4.13: Certificates of Origin

1. Each Party shall provide that an importer may satisfy a request under Article 4.12(1)(b) by providing a certificate of origin that sets forth a valid basis for a claim that a good is originating. Each Party shall provide that the certificate of origin need not be in a prescribed format, and that the certificate may be submitted electronically.

2. Each Party shall provide that a certificate of origin may be issued by the importer, exporter, or producer of the good. Where an exporter or importer is not the producer of the good, each Party shall provide that the exporter or importer may issue a certificate of origin based on:

(a) a certificate of origin issued by the producer; or

(b) knowledge of the exporter or importer that the good qualifies as an originating good.

3. Each Party shall provide that a certificate of origin may cover the importation of one or more goods or several importations of identical goods within a period specified in the certificate.

4. Each Party shall provide that a certificate of origin is valid for four years from the date on which the certificate was issued.

5. A Party may require that a certificate of origin for a good imported into its territory be completed in either Spanish or English.

6. For an originating good that is imported into the territory of a Party on or after the date of entry into force of this Agreement, each Party shall accept a certificate of origin issued by the importer, exporter, or producer of the good prior to that date, unless the Party possesses information indicating that the certificate is invalid.

7. Neither Party may require a certificate of origin or information demonstrating that the good qualifies as originating for:

(a) the importation of goods with a customs value not exceeding US $2,500, or the equivalent amount in Chilean currency, or such higher amount as may be established by the importing Party; or

(b) the importation of other goods as may be identified in the importing Party's laws governing claims of origin under this Agreement, unless the importation can be considered to have been carried out or planned for the purpose of evading compliance with the Party's laws governing claims of origin under this Agreement.

ARTICLE 4.14: OBLIGATIONS RELATING TO IMPORTATIONS

1. Each Party shall provide that the importer is responsible for submitting a certificate of origin or other information demonstrating that the good qualifies as originating, for the truthfulness of the information and data contained therein, for submitting any supporting documents requested by the Party's customs authority, and for the truthfulness of the information contained in those documents.

2. Each Party shall provide that the fact that the importer has issued a certificate of origin based on information provided by the exporter or the producer shall not relieve the importer of the responsibility referred to in paragraph 1.

3. Each Party shall provide that an importer claiming preferential tariff treatment for a good imported into the Party's territory shall maintain, for a period of five years after the date of importation of the good, a certificate of origin or other information demonstrating that the good qualifies as originating, and all other documents that the Party may require relating to the importation of the good, including records associated with:

(a) the purchase, cost, value of, and payment for, the good;

(b) where appropriate, the purchase, cost, value of, and payment for, all materials, including recovered goods and indirect materials, used in the production of the good; and

(c) where appropriate, the production of the good in its exported form.

ARTICLE 4.15: OBLIGATIONS RELATING TO EXPORTATIONS

1. For purposes of cooperation under Article 5.5 (Cooperation), each Party shall provide that an exporter or producer that issues a certificate of origin for a good exported from the Party's territory shall provide a copy of the certificate to the Party's customs authority upon its request.

2. Each Party shall provide that an exporter or producer that has issued a certificate of origin for a good exported from the Party's territory shall maintain, for a period of at least five years after the date the certificate was issued, all records and supporting documents related to the origin of the good, including:

(a) purchase, cost, value of, and payment for, the good;

(b) where appropriate, the purchase, cost, value of, and payment for, all materials, including recovered goods, used in the production of the good; and

(c) where appropriate, the production of the good in the form in which it was exported.

3. Each Party shall provide that where an exporter or producer has issued a certificate of origin, and has reason to believe that the

certificate contains or is based on incorrect information, the exporter or producer shall immediately notify, in writing, every person to whom the exporter or producer issued the certificate of any change that could affect the accuracy or validity of the certificate. Neither Party may impose penalties on an exporter or producer in its territory for issuing an incorrect certificate if it voluntarily provides written notification in conformity with this paragraph.

ARTICLE 4.16: PROCEDURES FOR VERIFICATION OF ORIGIN

1. Each Party shall grant any claim for preferential tariff treatment made in accordance with this Section, unless the Party possesses information indicating that the importer's claim fails to comply with any requirement under Section A or Article 3.20 (Rules of Origin and Related Matters), except as otherwise provided in Article 3.21 (Customs Cooperation).

2. To determine whether a good imported into its territory qualifies as originating, the importing Party may, through its customs authority, verify the origin in accordance with its customs laws and regulations.

3. Where a Party denies a claim for preferential tariff treatment, it shall issue a written determination containing findings of fact and the legal basis for its determination. The Party shall issue the determination within a period established under its law.

4. A Party shall not subject an importer to penalties where the importer that made an incorrect declaration voluntarily makes a corrected declaration.

5. Where a Party determines through verification that an importer has certified more than once, falsely or without substantiation, that a good qualifies as originating, the Party may suspend preferential tariff treatment to identical goods imported by that person until the importer proves that it has complied with the Party's laws and regulations governing claims of origin under this Agreement.

6. Each Party that carries out a verification of origin in which Generally Accepted Accounting Principles are pertinent shall apply those principles in the manner that they are applied in the territory of the Party from which the good was exported.

ARTICLE 4.17: COMMON GUIDELINES

By the date of entry into force of this Agreement, the Parties shall agree on and publish common guidelines for the interpretation, application, and administration of this Chapter and the relevant provisions of Chapter Three (National Treatment and Market Access for Goods). As appropriate, the Parties may subsequently agree to modify the common guidelines.

Section C—Definitions

ARTICLE 4.18: DEFINITIONS

For purposes of this Chapter:

adjusted value means the value determined in accordance with Articles 1 through 8, Article 15, and the corresponding interpretative notes of the Customs Valuation Agreement, adjusted, if necessary, to exclude any costs, charges, or expenses incurred for transportation, insurance, and related services incident to the international shipment of the merchandise from the country of exportation to the place of importation;

exporter means a person who exports goods from the territory of a Party;

fungible goods or materials means goods or materials that are interchangeable for commercial purposes and whose properties are essentially identical;

Generally Accepted Accounting Principles means the principles, rules, and procedures, including both broad and specific guidelines, that define the accounting practices accepted in the territory of a Party;

good means any merchandise, product, article, or material;

goods wholly obtained or produced entirely in the territory of one or both of the Parties means:

(a) mineral goods extracted in the territory of one or both of the Parties;

(b) vegetable goods, as such goods are defined in the Harmonized System, harvested in the territory of one or both of the Parties;

(c) live animals born and raised in the territory of one or both of the Parties;

(d) goods obtained from hunting, trapping, or fishing in the territory of one or both of the Parties;

(e) goods (fish, shellfish, and other marine life) taken from the sea by vessels registered or recorded with a Party and flying its flag;

(f) goods produced on board factory ships from the goods referred to in subparagraph (e) provided such factory ships are registered or recorded with that Party and fly its flag;

(g) goods taken by a Party or a person of a Party from the seabed or beneath the seabed outside territorial waters, provided that a Party has rights to exploit such seabed;

(h) goods taken from outer space, provided they are obtained by a Party or a person of a Party and not processed in the territory of a non-Party;

(i) waste and scrap derived from

(i) production in the territory of one or both of the Parties, or

(ii) used goods collected in the territory of one or both of the Parties, provided such goods are fit only for the recovery of raw materials;

(j) recovered goods derived in the territory a Party from used goods, and utilized in the Party's territory in the production of remanufactured goods; and

(k) goods produced in the territory of one or both of the Parties exclusively from goods referred to in subparagraphs (a) through (i), or from their derivatives, at any stage of production;

importer means a person who imports goods into the territory of a Party;

indirect material means a good used in the production, testing, or inspection of a good but not physically incorporated into the good, or a good used in the maintenance of buildings or the operation of equipment associated with the production of a good, including:

(a) fuel and energy;

(b) tools, dies, and molds;

(c) spare parts and materials used in the maintenance of equipment and buildings;

(d) lubricants, greases, compounding materials, and other materials used in production or used to operate equipment and buildings;

(e) gloves, glasses, footwear, clothing, safety equipment, and supplies;

(f) equipment, devices, and supplies used for testing or inspecting the goods;

(g) catalysts and solvents; and

(h) any other goods that are not incorporated into the good but whose use in the production of the good can reasonably be demonstrated to be a part of that production;

issued means prepared by and, where required under a Party's domestic law or regulation, signed by the importer, exporter, or producer of the good;

location of the producer means site of production of a good;

material means a good that is used in the production of another good, including a part, ingredient, or indirect material;

non-originating good or non-originating material means a good or material that does not qualify as originating under this Chapter;

packing materials and containers for shipment means the goods used to protect a good during its transportation, and does not include the packaging materials and containers in which a good is packaged for retail sale;

producer means a person who engages in the production of a good in the territory of a Party;

production means growing, mining, harvesting, fishing, raising, trapping, hunting, manufacturing, processing, assembling, or disassembling a good;

recovered goods means materials in the form of individual parts that are the result of: (1) the complete disassembly of used goods into individual parts; and (2) the cleaning, inspecting, testing, or other processing of those parts as necessary for improvement to sound working condition one or more of the following processes: welding, flame spraying, surface machining, knurling, plating, sleeving, and rewinding in order for such parts to be assembled with other parts, including other recovered parts in the production of a remanufactured good of Annex 4.18;

remanufactured goods means industrial goods assembled in the territory of a Party, listed in Annex 4.18, that: (1) are entirely or partially comprised of recovered goods; and (2) have the same life expectancy and meet the same performance standards as new goods; and (3) enjoy the same factory warranty as such new goods;

self-produced material means an originating material that is produced by a producer of a good and used in the production of that good; and

value means the value of a good or material for purposes of calculating customs duties or for purposes of applying this Chapter.

Chapter Five

Customs Administration

Article 5.1: Publication

1. Each Party shall publish its customs laws, regulations, and administrative procedures on the Internet or a comparable computer-based telecommunications network.

2. Each Party shall designate one or more inquiry points to address inquiries from interested persons concerning customs matters, and shall make available on the Internet information concerning procedures for making such inquiries.

3. To the extent possible, each Party shall publish in advance any regulations of general application governing customs matters that it proposes to adopt and provide interested persons the opportunity to comment on such proposed regulations prior to their adoption.

Article 5.2: Release of Goods

Each Party shall:

(a) adopt or maintain procedures providing for the release of goods within a period of time no greater than that required to ensure compliance with its customs laws and, to the extent possible, within 48 hours of arrival;

(b) adopt or maintain procedures allowing, to the extent possible, goods to be released at the point of arrival, without temporary transfer to warehouses or other locations;

(c) adopt or maintain procedures allowing the release of goods prior to, and without prejudice to, the final determination by its customs authority of the applicable customs duties, taxes and fees;[3] and

(d) otherwise endeavor to adopt or maintain simplified procedures for the release of goods.

Article 5.3: Automation

Each Party's customs authority shall:

(a) endeavor to use information technology that expedites procedures; and

(b) in deciding on the information technology to be used for this purpose, take into account international standards.

---

[3] A Party may require an importer to provide sufficient guarantee in the form of a surety, a deposit, or some other appropriate instrument, covering the ultimate payment of the customs duties for which the goods may be liable.

Article 5.4: Risk Assessment

Each Party shall endeavor to adopt or maintain risk management systems that enable its customs authority to concentrate inspection activities on high risk goods and that simplify the clearance and movement of low risk goods.

Article 5.5: Cooperation

1. Each Party shall endeavor to provide the other Party with advance notice of any significant modification of administrative policy regarding the implementation of its customs laws that is likely to substantially affect the operation of this Agreement.

2. The Parties shall cooperate in achieving compliance with their laws and regulations pertaining to:

(a) the implementation and operation of the provisions of this Agreement relating to the importation of goods, including Chapter Three (National Treatment and Market Access for Goods), Chapter Four (Rules of Origin and Origin Procedures), and this Chapter;

(b) the implementation and operation of the Customs Valuation Agreement;

(c) restrictions or prohibitions on imports or exports; or

(d) such other customs matters as the Parties may agree.

3. Where a Party has a reasonable suspicion of unlawful activity related to its laws or regulations governing importations, the Party may request that the other Party provide specific confidential information normally collected by the other Party in association with the importation of goods pertaining to trade transactions relevant to that activity. The Party shall make its request in writing, shall identify the requested information with sufficient specificity for the other Party to locate it, and shall specify the purposes for which the information is sought.

4. The other Party shall respond by providing any information that it has collected that is material to the request.

5. For purposes of paragraph 3, a reasonable suspicion of unlawful activity means a suspicion based on relevant factual information obtained from public or private sources, including:

(a) historical evidence that a specific importer, exporter, producer, or other enterprise involved in the movement of goods from the territory of one Party to the territory of the other Party has not complied with a Party's laws or regulations governing importations;

(b) historical evidence that some or all of the enterprises involved in the movement from the territory of one Party to the territory of the other Party of goods within a specific product sector have not complied with a Party's laws or regulations governing importations; or

(c) other information that the Parties agree is sufficient in the context of a particular request.

6. Each Party shall endeavor to provide the other Party with any other information that would assist in determining whether imports from or exports to the other Party are in compliance with the other Party's laws or regulations governing importations, in particular those related to the prevention of unlawful activities.

7. Each Party shall endeavor to provide the other with technical advice and assistance for the purpose of improving risk assessment techniques, simplifying and expediting customs procedures, advancing technical skills, and enhancing the use of technologies that can lead to improved compliance with laws and regulations governing importations.

8. Building on the procedures established in this Article, the Parties shall use best efforts to explore additional avenues of cooperation to enhance each Party's ability to enforce its laws and regulations governing importations, including by:

(a) concluding a mutual assistance agreement between their respective customs authorities within six months after the date of entry into force of this Agreement; and

(b) considering whether to establish additional channels of communication to facilitate the secure and rapid exchange of information and to improve coordination on customs issues.

Article 5.6: Confidentiality

1. Where a Party providing information to the other Party in accordance with this Chapter designates the information as confidential, the other Party shall maintain the confidentiality of the information. The Party providing the information may, in accordance with its domestic law, require written assurances from the other Party that the information will be held in confidence, will be used only for the purposes specified in the other Party's request for information, and will not be disclosed without the Party's specific permission.

2. A Party may decline to provide information requested by the other Party where the other Party has failed to act in conformity with assurances provided under paragraph 1.

3. Each Party shall adopt or maintain procedures in which confidential information, including information the disclosure of which could prejudice the competitive position of the person providing the information, submitted in connection with the Party's administration of its customs laws shall be protected from unauthorized disclosure.

Article 5.7: Express Shipments

Each Party shall adopt or maintain separate, expedited customs procedures for express shipments, while maintaining appropriate customs control and selection, including procedures:

(a) in which the information necessary for the release of an express shipment may be submitted, and processed by the Party's customs authority, prior to the arrival of the shipment;

(b) allowing a shipper to submit a single manifest covering all goods contained in a shipment transported by the express shipment service, through, if possible, electronic means;

(c) that, to the extent possible, minimize the documentation required for the release of express shipments; and

(d) that, under normal circumstances, allow for an express shipment that has arrived at a point of entry to be released no later than six hours after the submission of the information necessary for release.

ARTICLE 5.8: REVIEW AND APPEAL

Each Party shall ensure that with respect to its determinations on customs matters, importers in its territory have access to:

(a) administrative review independent of the official or office that issued the determination; and

(b) judicial review of the determination or decision taken at the final level of administrative review.

ARTICLE 5.9: PENALTIES

Each Party shall adopt or maintain measures that provide for the imposition of civil, administrative, and, where appropriate, criminal sanctions for violations of its customs laws and regulations, including those governing tariff classification, customs valuation, rules of origin, and the entitlement to preferential tariff treatment under this Agreement.

ARTICLE 5.10: ADVANCE RULINGS

1. Each Party, through its customs authority, shall issue written advance rulings prior to the importation of a good into its territory at the written request of an importer in its territory, or an exporter or producer in the territory of the other Party, on the basis of the facts and circumstances provided by the requester, concerning:

(a) tariff classification;

(b) the application of customs valuation criteria for a particular case, in accordance with the application of the provisions set forth in the Customs Valuation Agreement;

(c) duty drawback;

(d) whether a good qualifies as an originating good under Chapter Four (Rules of Origin and Origin Procedures); and

(e) whether a good qualifies for duty-free treatment in accordance with Article 3.9 (Goods Re-entered after Repair or Alteration).

2. Each Party shall provide that its customs authority shall issue advance rulings within 150 days of a request, provided that the requester has submitted all necessary information.

3. Each Party shall provide that advance rulings shall be in force from their date of issuance, or such other date specified by the ruling, for at least three years, provided that the facts or circumstances on which the ruling is based remain unchanged.

4. The issuing Party may modify or revoke an advance ruling where facts or circumstances warrant, such as where the information on which the ruling is based is false or inaccurate.

5. Where an importer claims that the treatment accorded to an imported good should be governed by an advance ruling, the customs authority may evaluate whether the facts and circumstances of the importation are consistent with the facts and circumstances upon which the advance ruling was based.

6. Each Party shall make its advance rulings publicly available, subject to confidentiality requirements in its domestic law, for purposes of promoting the consistent application of advance rulings to other goods.

7. If a requester provides false information or omits relevant circumstances or facts in its request for an advance ruling, or does not act in accordance with the ruling's terms and conditions, the importing Party may apply appropriate measures, including civil, criminal, and administrative actions, penalties, or other sanctions.

ARTICLE 5.11: IMPLEMENTATION

1. With respect to the obligations of Chile, Articles 5.1(1) and (2), 5.7(b), and 5.10(1)(b) shall enter into force three years after the date of entry into force of this Agreement.

2. Within 120 days after the date of entry into force of this Agreement, the Parties shall consult on the procedures that Chile needs to adopt to implement Article 5.10(1)(b) and on related technical assistance to be provided by the United States, and shall establish a work program outlining the steps needed for Chile to implement Article 5.10(1)(b).

3. Not later than 18 months after the date of entry into force of this Agreement, the Parties shall consult to discuss the progress made by Chile in implementing Article 5.10(1)(b) and to consider whether to engage in further cooperative efforts.

Chapter Six

Sanitary and Phytosanitary Measures

Objectives

The objectives of this Chapter are to protect human, animal, and plant health conditions in the Parties' territories, enhance the Parties' implementation of the SPS Agreement, provide a forum for addressing bilateral sanitary and phytosanitary matters, resolve trade issues, and thereby expand trade opportunities.

ARTICLE 6.1: SCOPE AND COVERAGE

This Chapter applies to all sanitary and phytosanitary measures of a Party that may, directly or indirectly, affect trade between the Parties.

ARTICLE 6.2: GENERAL PROVISIONS

1. Further to Article 1.3 (Relation to Other Agreements), the Parties affirm their existing rights and obligations with respect to each other under the SPS Agreement.

2. Neither Party may have recourse to dispute settlement under this Agreement for any matter arising under this Chapter.

ARTICLE 6.3: COMMITTEE ON SANITARY AND PHYTOSANITARY MATTERS

1. The Parties hereby agree to establish a Committee on Sanitary and Phytosanitary Matters comprising representatives of each Party who have responsibility for sanitary and phytosanitary matters.

2. The Parties shall establish the Committee not later than 30 days after the date of entry into force of this Agreement through an exchange of letters identifying the primary representative of

each Party to the Committee and establishing the Committee's terms of reference.

3. The objectives of the Committee shall be to enhance the implementation by each Party of the SPS Agreement, protect human, animal, and plant life and health, enhance consultation and cooperation on sanitary and phytosanitary matters, and facilitate trade between the Parties.

4. The Committee shall seek to enhance any present or future relationships between the Parties' agencies with responsibility for sanitary and phytosanitary matters.

5. The Committee shall provide a forum for:

(a) enhancing mutual understanding of each Party's sanitary and phytosanitary measures and the regulatory processes that relate to those measures;

(b) consulting on matters related to the development or application of sanitary and phytosanitary measures that affect, or may affect, trade between the Parties;

(c) consulting on issues, positions, and agendas for meetings of the WTO SPS Committee, the various *Codex* committees (including the *Codex Alimentarius Commission*), the *International Plant Protection Convention,* the *International Office of Epizootics,* and other international and regional fora on food safety and human, animal, and plant health;

(d) coordinating technical cooperation programs on sanitary and phytosanitary matters;

(e) improving bilateral understanding related to specific implementation issues concerning the SPS Agreement; and

(f) reviewing progress on addressing sanitary and phytosanitary matters that may arise between the Parties' agencies with responsibility for such matters.

6. The Committee shall meet at least once a year unless the Parties otherwise agree.

7. The Committee shall perform its work in accordance with the terms of reference referenced in paragraph 2. The Committee may revise the terms of reference and may develop procedures to guide its operation.

8. Each Party shall ensure that appropriate representatives with responsibility for the development, implementation, and enforcement of sanitary and phytosanitary measures from its relevant trade and regulatory agencies or ministries participate in meetings of the Committee. The official agencies and ministries of each Party responsible for such measures shall be set out in the Committee's terms of reference.

9. The Committee may agree to establish ad hoc working groups in accordance with the Committee's terms of reference.

Article 6.4: Definitions

For purposes of this Chapter, **sanitary or phytosanitary measure** means any measure referred to in Annex A, paragraph 1, of the SPS Agreement.

Chapter Seven

Technical Barriers to Trade

Objectives

The objectives of this Chapter are to increase and facilitate trade through the improvement of the implementation of the TBT Agreement, the elimination of unnecessary technical barriers to trade, and the enhancement of bilateral cooperation.

Article 7.1: Scope and Coverage

1. Except as provided in paragraphs 2 and 3 of this Article, this Chapter applies to all standards, technical regulations, and conformity assessment procedures that may, directly or indirectly, affect trade in goods between the Parties. Notwithstanding Article 1.4 (Extent of Obligations), this Chapter applies only to central government bodies.

2. Technical specifications prepared by governmental bodies for production or consumption requirements of such bodies are not subject to the provisions of this Chapter, but are addressed in Chapter Nine (Government Procurement), according to its coverage.

3. This Chapter does not apply to sanitary and phytosanitary measures as defined in Annex A of the SPS Agreement.

Article 7.2: Affirmation of Agreement on Technical Barriers to Trade

Further to Article 1.3 (Relation to Other Agreements), the Parties affirm their existing rights and obligations with respect to each other under the TBT Agreement.

Article 7.3: International Standards

In determining whether an international standard, guide, or recommendation within the meaning of Articles 2, 5, and Annex 3 of the TBT Agreement exists, each Party shall apply the principles set out in Decisions and Recommendations adopted by the Committee since 1 January 1995, G/TBT/1/Rev.7, 28 November 2000, Section IX (Decision of the Committee on Principles for the Development of International Standards, Guides and Recommendations with relation to Articles 2, 5 and Annex 3 of the Agreement), issued by the WTO Committee on Technical Barriers to Trade.

Article 7.4: Trade Facilitation

The Parties shall intensify their joint work in the field of standards, technical regulations, and conformity assessment procedures with a view to facilitating access to each other's markets. In particular, the Parties shall seek to identify bilateral initiatives that are appropriate for particular issues or sectors. Such initiatives may include cooperation on regulatory issues, such as convergence or equivalence of technical regulations and standards, alignment with international standards, reliance on a supplier's declaration of conformity, and use of accreditation to qualify conformity assessment bodies, as well as cooperation through mutual recognition.

Article 7.5: Technical Regulations

1. Where a Party provides for the acceptance of a foreign technical regulation as equivalent to a particular technical regulation of its own, and the Party does not accept a technical regulation of the other Party as equivalent to that technical regulation, it shall, at the request of the other Party, explain the reasons for not accepting the technical regulation of the other Party as equivalent.

2. Where a Party does not provide for the acceptance of foreign technical regulations as equivalent to its own, that Party may, at the request of the other Party, explain the reasons for not accepting the other Party's technical regulations as equivalent.

Article 7.6: Conformity Assessment

1. The Parties recognize that a broad range of mechanisms exists to facilitate the acceptance of conformity assessment results, including:

(a) the importing Party's reliance on a supplier's declaration of conformity;

(b) voluntary arrangements between conformity assessment bodies from each Party's territory;

(c) agreements on mutual acceptance of the results of conformity assessment procedures with respect to specified regulations conducted by bodies located in the territory of the other Party;

(d) accreditation procedures for qualifying conformity assessment bodies;

(e) government designation of conformity assessment bodies; and

(f) recognition by one Party of the results of conformity assessments performed in the other Party's territory.

The Parties shall intensify their exchange of information on the range of mechanisms to facilitate the acceptance of conformity assessment results.

2. Where a Party does not accept the results of a conformity assessment procedure performed in the territory of the other Party, it shall, on request of the other Party, explain its reasons.

3. Each Party shall accredit, approve, license, or otherwise recognize conformity assessment bodies in the territory of the other Party on terms no less favorable than those it accords to conformity assessment bodies in its territory. If a Party accredits, approves, licenses, or otherwise recognizes a body assessing conformity with a particular technical regulation or standard in its territory and it refuses to accredit, approve, license, or otherwise recognize a body assessing conformity with that technical regulation or standard in the territory of the other Party, it shall, on request, explain the reasons for its refusal.

4. Where a Party declines a request from the other Party to engage in or conclude negotiations to reach agreement on facilitating recognition in its territory of the results of conformity assessment

procedures conducted by bodies in the territory of the other Party, it shall, on request, explain its reasons.

ARTICLE 7.7: TRANSPARENCY

1. Further to Article 20.2 (Publication), each Party shall allow persons of the other Party to participate in the development of standards, technical regulations, and conformity assessment procedures. Each Party shall permit persons of the other Party to participate in the development of such measures on terms no less favorable than those accorded to its own persons.

2. Each Party shall recommend that non-governmental standardizing bodies in its territory observe paragraph 1.

3. In order to enhance the opportunity for persons to provide meaningful comments, a Party publishing a notice under Article 2.9 or 5.6 of the TBT Agreement shall:

(a) include in the notice a statement describing the objective of the proposal and the rationale for the approach the Party is proposing; and

(b) transmit the proposal electronically to the other Party through the inquiry point established under Article 10 of the TBT Agreement at the same time as it notifies WTO Members of the proposal pursuant to the TBT Agreement.

Each Party should allow at least 60 days from the transmission under subparagraph (b) for persons and the other Party to make comments in writing on the proposal.

4. Where a Party makes a notification under Article 2.10 or 5.7 of the TBT Agreement, it shall at the same time transmit the notification to the other Party, electronically, through the inquiry point referenced in paragraph 3(b).

5. Each Party shall publish, in print or electronically, or otherwise make available to the public, its responses to significant comments at the same time as the publication of the final technical regulation or conformity assessment procedure.

6. Each Party shall, on request of the other Party, provide information regarding the objective of, and rationale for, a standard, technical regulation, or conformity assessment procedure that the Party has adopted or is proposing to adopt.

7. Each Party shall implement this Article as soon as is practicable and in no event later than five years from the date of entry into force of this Agreement.

ARTICLE 7.8: COMMITTEE ON TECHNICAL BARRIERS TO TRADE

1. The Parties hereby establish the Committee on Technical Barriers to Trade, comprising representatives of each Party, pursuant to Annex 7.8.

2. The Committee's functions shall include:

(a) monitoring the implementation and administration of this Chapter;

(b) promptly addressing any issue that a Party raises related to the development, adoption, application, or enforcement of standards, technical regulations, or conformity assessment procedures;

(c) enhancing cooperation in the development and improvement of standards, technical regulations, and conformity assessment procedures;

(d) where appropriate, facilitating sectoral cooperation among governmental and non-governmental conformity assessment bodies in the Parties' territories;

(e) exchanging information on developments in non-governmental, regional, and multilateral fora engaged in activities related to standardization, technical regulations, and conformity assessment procedures;

(f) taking any other steps the Parties consider will assist them in implementing the TBT Agreement and in facilitating trade in goods between them;

(g) at a Party's request, consulting on any matter arising under this Chapter;

(h) reviewing this Chapter in light of any developments under the TBT Agreement, and developing recommendations for amendments to this Chapter in light of those developments; and

(i) as it considers appropriate, reporting to the Commission on the implementation of this Chapter.

3. Where the Parties have had recourse to consultations under paragraph 2(g) such consultations shall, on the agreement of the Parties, constitute consultations under Article 22.4 (Consultations).

4. A Party shall, on request, give favorable consideration to any sector-specific proposal the other Party makes for further cooperation under this Chapter.

5. The Committee shall meet at least once a year unless the Parties otherwise agree.

ARTICLE 7.9: INFORMATION EXCHANGE

Any information or explanation that is provided on request of a Party pursuant to the provisions of this Chapter shall be provided in print or electronically within a reasonable period of time.

ARTICLE 7.10: DEFINITIONS

For purposes of this Chapter, **technical regulation, standard, conformity assessment procedures**, and **central government body** shall have the meanings assigned to those terms in Annex 1 of the TBT Agreement.

Chapter Eight

Trade Remedies

Section A—Safeguards

ARTICLE 8.1: IMPOSITION OF A SAFEGUARD MEASURE

1. A Party may impose a safeguard measure described in paragraph 2, during the transition period only, if as a result of the reduction or elimination of a duty pursuant to this Agreement,[4] a

[4] The Parties note that many of Chile's products received duty-free treatment under the U.S. Generalized System of Preferences prior to the entry into force of this Agreement.

good originating in the territory of the other Party is being imported into the Party's territory in such increased quantities, in absolute terms or relative to domestic production, and under such conditions as to constitute a substantial cause of serious injury, or threat thereof, to a domestic industry producing a like or directly competitive good.

2. If the conditions in paragraph 1 are met, a Party may to the extent as may be necessary to prevent or remedy serious injury, or threat thereof, and facilitate adjustment:

(a) suspend the further reduction of any rate of duty provided for under this Agreement on the good; or

(b) increase the rate of duty on the good to a level not to exceed the lesser of

(i) the most-favored-nation (MFN) applied rate of duty in effect at the time the action is taken, or

(ii) the MFN applied rate of duty in effect on the day immediately preceding the date of entry into force of this Agreement.[5]

ARTICLE 8.2: STANDARDS FOR A SAFEGUARD MEASURE

1. A Party may apply a safeguard measure, including any extension thereof, for no longer than three years. Regardless of its duration, such measure shall terminate at the end of the transition period.

2. In order to facilitate adjustment in a situation where the expected duration of a safeguard measure is over one year, the Party applying the measure shall progressively liberalize it at regular intervals during the period of application.

3. Neither Party may impose a safeguard measure more than once on the same good.

4. Neither Party may impose a safeguard measure on a good that is subject to a measure that the Party has imposed pursuant to Article XIX of GATT 1994 and the Safeguards Agreement, and neither Party may continue maintaining a safeguard measure on a good that becomes subject to a measure that the Party imposes pursuant to Article XIX of GATT 1994 and the Safeguards Agreement.

5. On the termination of a safeguard measure, the rate of duty shall be no higher than the rate that, according to the Party's Schedule to Annex 3.3 (Tariff Elimination), would have been in effect one year after the imposition of the measure. Beginning on January 1 of the year following the termination of the action, the Party that has applied the measure shall:

(a) apply the rate of duty set out in the Party's Schedule to Annex 3.3 (Tariff Elimination) as if the safeguard measure had never been applied; or

(b) eliminate the tariff in equal annual stages ending on the date set out in the Party's Schedule to Annex 3.3 (Tariff Elimination) for the elimination of the tariff.

---

[5] The Parties understand that neither tariff rate quotas nor quantitative restrictions would be a permissible form of safeguard measure.

Article 8.3: Investigation Procedures and Transparency Requirements

1. A Party shall impose a safeguard measure only following an investigation by the Party's competent authorities in accordance with Articles 3 and 4.2(c) of the Safeguards Agreement; and to this end, Articles 3 and 4.2(c) of the Safeguards Agreement are incorporated into and made a part of this Agreement, *mutatis mutandis.*

2. In the investigation described in paragraph 1, a Party shall comply with the requirements of Article 4.2(a) of the Safeguards Agreement; and to this end, Article 4.2(a) of the Safeguards Agreement is incorporated into and made a part of this Agreement, *mutatis mutandis.*

Article 8.4: Notification

1. A Party shall promptly notify the other Party, in writing, on:

(a) initiating an investigation under Article 8.3;

(b) making a finding of serious injury or threat thereof caused by increased imports under Article 8.1;

(c) taking a decision to impose or extend a safeguard measure; and

(d) taking a decision to modify a safeguard measure previously undertaken.

2. A Party shall provide to the other Party a copy of the public version of the report of its competent authorities required under Article 8.3(1).

Article 8.5: Compensation

1. The Party taking a safeguard measure shall, in consultation with the other Party, provide to the other Party mutually agreed trade liberalizing compensation in the form of concessions having substantially equivalent trade effects or equivalent to the value of the additional duties expected to result from the measure. Such consultations shall begin within 30 days of the imposition of the measure.

2. If the Parties are unable to reach agreement on compensation within 30 days after the consultations commence, the exporting Party shall be free to suspend the application of substantially equivalent concessions to the trade of the Party applying the safeguard measure.

3. A Party shall notify the other Party in writing at least 30 days before suspending concessions under paragraph 2.

4. The obligation to provide compensation under paragraph 1 and the right to suspend substantially equivalent concessions under paragraph 2 shall terminate on the later of: (a) the termination of the safeguard measure; or (b) the date on which the rate of duty returns to the rate of duty set out in the Party's Schedule to Annex 3.3 (Tariff Elimination).

Article 8.6: Global Actions

1. Each Party retains its rights and obligations under Article XIX of GATT 1994 and the Safeguards Agreement.

2. This Agreement does not confer any additional rights or obligations on the Parties with regard to actions taken pursuant to Article XIX of GATT 1994 and the Safeguards Agreement.

ARTICLE 8.7: DEFINITIONS

For purposes of this Section:

domestic industry means, with respect to an imported good, the producers as a whole of the like or directly competitive good or those producers whose collective production of the like or directly competitive good constitutes a major proportion of the total domestic production of such good;

safeguard measure means a safeguard measure described in Article 8.1(2);

serious injury means a significant overall impairment in the position of a domestic industry;

substantial cause means a cause which is important and not less than any other cause;

threat of serious injury means serious injury that, on the basis of facts and not merely on allegation, conjecture, or remote possibility, is clearly imminent; and

transition period means the 10-year period beginning on the date of entry into force of this Agreement, except that **transition period** shall mean the 12-year period beginning on the date of entry into force of this Agreement in any case in which a safeguard measure is applied against an agricultural good and the Schedule to Annex 3.3 (Tariff Elimination) of the Party applying the measure provides for the Party to eliminate its tariffs on the good over 12 years.

Section B—Antidumping and Countervailing Duties

ARTICLE 8.8: ANTIDUMPING AND COUNTERVAILING DUTIES

1. Each Party retains its rights and obligations under the WTO Agreement with regard to the application of antidumping and countervailing duties.

2. No provisions of this Agreement, including the provisions of Chapter Twenty-Two (Dispute Settlement), shall be construed as imposing any rights or obligations on the Parties with respect to antidumping or countervailing duty measures.

Chapter Nine

Government Procurement

Objectives

The objectives of this Chapter are to recognize the importance of conducting government procurement in accordance with the fundamental principles of openness, transparency, and due process; and to strive to provide comprehensive coverage of procurement markets by eliminating market access barriers to the supply of goods and services, including construction services.

Article 9.1: Scope and Coverage

1. This Chapter applies to any measure adopted or maintained by a Party relating to procurement by an entity listed in Annex 9.1:

(a) by any contractual means, including purchase and rental or lease, with or without an option to buy, build-operate-transfer contracts, and public works concession contracts; and

(b) subject to the conditions specified in Annex 9.1.

2. This Chapter does not apply to:

(a) non-contractual agreements or any form of assistance provided by a Party or a state enterprise, including grants, loans, equity infusions, fiscal incentives, subsidies, guarantees, cooperative agreements, government provision of goods and services to persons or to a regional or local level of government, and purchases for the direct purpose of providing foreign assistance;

(b) purchases funded by international grants, loans, or other assistance, where the provision of such assistance is subject to conditions inconsistent with the provisions of this Chapter;

(c) hiring of government employees and related employment measures; and

(d) acquisition of fiscal agency or depository services, liquidation and management services for regulated financial institutions, and sale and distribution services for government debt.

3. Each Party shall ensure that its procuring entities listed in Annex 9.1 comply with this Chapter in conducting procurement covered by this Chapter.

4. Where an entity awards a contract that is not covered by this Chapter, nothing in this Chapter shall be construed to cover any good or service component of that contract.

5. No entity may prepare, design, or otherwise structure or divide, in any stage of the procurement, any procurement in order to avoid the obligations of this Chapter.

6. Nothing in this Chapter shall prevent either Party from developing new procurement policies, procedures, or contractual means, provided they are not inconsistent with this Chapter.

Article 9.2: General Principles

National Treatment and Non-Discrimination

1. With respect to any measure governing procurement covered by this Chapter, each Party shall accord to the goods and services of the other Party, and to the suppliers of the other Party of such goods and services, treatment no less favorable than the most favorable treatment the Party accords to its own goods, services, and suppliers.

2. With respect to any measure governing procurement covered by this Chapter, neither Party may:

(a) treat a locally established supplier less favorably than another locally established supplier on the basis of degree of foreign affiliation or ownership; or

(b) discriminate against a locally established supplier on the basis that the goods or services offered by that supplier for a particular procurement are goods or services of the other Party.

Determination of Origin

3. For purposes of paragraphs 1 and 2, determination of the origin of goods shall be made on a non-preferential basis.

Offsets

4. An entity shall not consider, seek, or impose offsets at any stage of a procurement.

Measures Not Specific to Procurement

5. Paragraphs 1 and 2 do not apply to measures respecting customs duties or other charges of any kind imposed on or in connection with importation, the method of levying such duties and charges or other import regulations, including restrictions and formalities, or measures affecting trade in services other than measures specifically governing procurement covered by this Chapter.

ARTICLE 9.3: PUBLICATION OF PROCUREMENT MEASURES

Each Party shall promptly publish:

(a) its measures of general application specifically governing procurement covered by this Chapter; and

(b) any changes in such measures in the same manner as the original publication.

ARTICLE 9.4: PUBLICATION OF NOTICE OF INTENDED PROCUREMENT

1. For each procurement covered by this Chapter, an entity shall publish in advance a notice inviting interested suppliers to submit tenders for that procurement ("notice of intended procurement"), except as provided in Article 9.9(2). Each such notice shall be accessible during the entire period established for tendering for the relevant procurement.

2. Each notice of intended procurement shall include a description of the intended procurement, any conditions that suppliers must fulfill to participate in the procurement, the name of the entity issuing the notice, the address where suppliers may obtain all documents relating to the procurement, the time limits for submission of tenders, and the dates for delivery of the goods or services to be procured.

ARTICLE 9.5: TIME LIMITS FOR THE TENDERING PROCESS

1. An entity shall prescribe time limits for the tendering process that allow sufficient time for suppliers to prepare and submit responsive tenders, taking into account the nature and complexity of the procurement. An entity shall provide no less than 30 days between the date on which it publishes the notice of intended procurement and the deadline for submitting tenders.

2. Notwithstanding paragraph 1, where there are no qualification requirements for suppliers, entities may establish a time limit of less than 30 days, but in no case less than 10 days, in the following circumstances:

(a) where the entity has published a notice containing the information specified in Article 9.4(2) at least 30 days and not more than 12 months in advance;

(b) in the case of the second or subsequent publications of notices for procurement of a recurring nature;

(c) where an entity procures commercial goods or services that are sold or offered for sale to, and customarily purchased and used by, non-governmental buyers for non-governmental purposes; or

(d) where an unforeseen state of urgency duly substantiated by the entity renders impracticable the time limits specified in paragraph 1.

Article 9.6: Information on Intended Procurements

1. An entity shall provide interested suppliers tender documentation that includes all the information necessary to permit suppliers to prepare and submit responsive tenders. The documentation shall include all criteria that the entity will consider in awarding the contract, including all cost factors, and the weights or, where appropriate, the relative values, that the entity will assign to these criteria in evaluating tenders.

2. Where an entity does not publish all the tender documentation by electronic means, the entity shall, on request of any supplier, promptly make the documentation available in written form to the supplier.

3. Where an entity, during the course of a procurement, modifies the criteria referred to in paragraph 1, it shall transmit all such modifications in writing:

(a) to all suppliers that are participating in the procurement at the time the criteria are modified, if the identities of such suppliers are known, and in all other cases, in the same manner as the original information was transmitted; and

(b) in adequate time to allow such suppliers to modify and re-submit their tenders, as appropriate.

Article 9.7: Technical Specifications

1. An entity shall not prepare, adopt, or apply any technical specification with the purpose or the effect of creating unnecessary obstacles to trade between the Parties.

2. Any technical specification prescribed by an entity shall be, where appropriate:

(a) specified in terms of performance requirements rather than design or descriptive characteristics; and

(b) based on international standards, where applicable, otherwise on national technical regulations, recognized national standards, or building codes.

3. An entity shall not prescribe technical specifications that require or refer to a particular trademark or trade name, patent, design or type, specific origin or producer or supplier unless there is no sufficiently precise or intelligible way of otherwise describing the procurement requirements and provided that, in such cases, words such as "or equivalent" are included in the tender documentation.

4. An entity shall not seek or accept, in a manner that would have the effect of precluding competition, advice that may be used in the preparation or adoption of any technical specification for a specific procurement from a person that may have a commercial interest in that procurement.

5. For greater certainty, this Article is not intended to preclude a Party from preparing, adopting, or applying technical specifications to promote the conservation of natural resources.

Article 9.8: Conditions for Participation

1. Where an entity requires suppliers to satisfy registration, qualification, or any other requirements or conditions for participation ("conditions for participation") in order to participate in a procurement, the entity shall publish a notice inviting suppliers to apply for participation. The entity shall publish the notice sufficiently in advance to provide interested suppliers sufficient time to prepare and submit applications and for the entity to evaluate and make its determinations based on such applications.

2. Each entity shall:

(a) limit any conditions for participation in a procurement to those that are essential to ensure that the potential supplier has the legal, technical, and financial capacity to fulfill the requirements and technical specifications of the procurement;

(b) base qualification decisions solely on the conditions for participation that it has specified in advance in notices or tender documentation; and

(c) recognize as qualified all suppliers of the other Party that meet the requisite conditions for participation in a procurement covered by this Chapter.

3. Entities may establish publicly available lists of suppliers qualified to participate in procurements. Where an entity requires suppliers to qualify for such a list in order to participate in a procurement, and a supplier that has not yet qualified applies to be included on the list, the entity shall promptly start the qualification procedures for the supplier and shall allow the supplier to participate in the procurement, provided there is sufficient time to complete the procedures within the time period established for tendering.

4. No entity may impose the condition that, in order for a supplier to participate in a procurement, the supplier has previously been awarded one or more contracts by an entity of that Party or that the supplier has prior work experience in the territory of that Party. An entity shall judge a supplier's financial and technical capacities on the basis of its global business activities including both its activity in the territory of the Party of the supplier, and its activity, if any, in the territory of the Party of the entity.

5. An entity shall promptly communicate to any supplier that has applied for qualification its decision on whether that supplier is qualified. Where an entity rejects an application for qualification or ceases to recognize a supplier as qualified, that entity shall, on request of the supplier, promptly provide it a written explanation of the reasons for its decision.

6. Nothing in this Article shall preclude an entity from excluding a supplier from a procurement on grounds such as bankruptcy or false declarations.

ARTICLE 9.9: TENDERING PROCEDURES

1. Entities shall award contracts by means of open tendering procedures, in the course of which any interested supplier may submit a tender.

2. Provided that the tendering procedure is not used to avoid competition or to protect domestic suppliers, entities may award contracts by means other than open tendering procedures in the following circumstances, where applicable:

(a) in the absence of tenders that conform to the essential requirements in the tender documentation provided in a prior invitation to tender, including any conditions for participation, on condition that the requirements of the initial procurement are not substantially modified in the contract as awarded;

(b) where, for works of art, or for reasons connected with the protection of exclusive rights, such as patents or copyrights, or proprietary information, or where there is an absence of competition for technical reasons, the goods or services can be supplied only by a particular supplier and no reasonable alternative or substitute exists;

(c) for additional deliveries by the original supplier that are intended either as replacement parts, extensions, or continuing services for existing equipment, software, services or installations, where a change of supplier would compel the entity to procure goods or services not meeting requirements of interchangeability with existing equipment, software, services, or installations;

(d) for goods purchased on a commodity market;

(e) where an entity procures a prototype or a first good or service that is developed at its request in the course of, and for, a particular contract for research, experiment, study, or original development. When such contracts have been fulfilled, subsequent procurements of such goods or services shall be subject to Articles 9.2 through 9.8 and Article 9.17;

(f) where additional construction services that were not included in the initial contract but that were within the objectives of the original tender documentation have, due to unforeseeable circumstances, become necessary to complete the construction services described therein. However, the total value of contracts awarded for additional construction services may not exceed 50 percent of the amount of the initial contract; or

(g) in so far as is strictly necessary where, for reasons of extreme urgency brought about by events unforeseeable by the entity, the goods or services could not be obtained in time by means of an open tendering procedure and the use of an open tendering procedure would result in serious injury to the entity, or the entity's program responsibilities, or the Party. For purposes of this subparagraph, lack of advance planning by an entity or its concerns relating to the amount of funds available to it within a particular period do not constitute unforeseeable events.

3. An entity shall maintain a record or prepare a written report providing specific justification for any contract awarded by means other than open tendering procedures, as provided in paragraph 2.

Article 9.10: Awarding of Contracts

1. An entity shall require that in order to be considered for award, a tender must be submitted in writing and must, at the time it is submitted:

(a) conform to the essential requirements of the tender documentation; and

(b) be submitted by a supplier that has satisfied the conditions for participation that the entity has provided to all participating suppliers.

2. Unless an entity determines that it is not in the public interest to award a contract, it shall award the contract to the supplier that the entity has determined to be fully capable of undertaking the contract and whose tender is determined to be the most advantageous in terms of the requirements and evaluation criteria set out in the tender documentation.

3. No entity may cancel a procurement, or terminate or modify awarded contracts, in order to avoid the obligations of this Chapter.

Article 9.11: Information on Awards

Information Provided to Suppliers

1. Subject to Article 9.15, an entity shall promptly inform suppliers participating in a tendering procedure of its contract award decision. On request, an entity shall provide a supplier whose tender was not selected for award the reasons for not selecting its tender and the relative advantages of the tender the entity selected.

Publication of Award Information

2. After awarding a contract covered by this Chapter, an entity shall promptly publish a notice that includes at least the following information about the award:

(a) the name of the entity;

(b) a description of the goods or services procured;

(c) the name of the winning supplier;

(d) the value of the contract award; and

(e) where the entity has not used open tendering procedures, an indication of the circumstances justifying the procedures used.

Maintenance of Records

3. An entity shall maintain records and reports relating to tendering procedures and contract awards covered by this Chapter, including the records and reports provided for in Article 9.9(3), for a period of at least three years.

ARTICLE 9.12: ENSURING INTEGRITY IN PROCUREMENT PRACTICES

Each Party shall adopt the necessary legislative or other measures to establish that it is a criminal offense under its law for:

(a) a procurement official of that Party to solicit or accept, directly or indirectly, any article of monetary value or other benefit, for that procurement official or for another person, in exchange for any act or omission in the performance of that procurement official's procurement functions;

(b) any person to offer or grant, directly or indirectly, to a procurement official of that Party, any article of monetary value or other benefit, for that procurement official or for another person, in exchange for any act or omission in the performance of that procurement official's procurement functions; and

(c) any person intentionally to offer, promise or give any undue pecuniary or other advantage, whether directly or through intermediaries, to a foreign procurement official, for that foreign procurement official or for a third party, in order that the foreign procurement official act or refrain from acting in relation to the performance of procurement duties, in order to obtain or retain business or other improper advantage.

ARTICLE 9.13: DOMESTIC REVIEW OF SUPPLIER CHALLENGES

Independent Review Authorities

1. Each Party shall establish or designate at least one impartial administrative or judicial authority that is independent from its entities to receive and review challenges that suppliers submit relating to the Party's measures implementing this Chapter in connection with a procurement covered by this Chapter and make appropriate findings and recommendations. Where a challenge by a supplier is initially reviewed by a body other than such an impartial authority, the Party shall ensure that the supplier may appeal the initial decision to an impartial administrative or judicial authority that is independent of the entity that is the subject of the challenge.

2. Each Party shall provide that an authority it establishes or designates under paragraph 1 has authority to take prompt interim measures pending the resolution of a challenge to preserve the supplier's opportunity to participate in the procurement and to ensure that the Party complies with its measures implementing this Chapter, including by suspending the contract award or the performance of a contract that has already been awarded.

3. Each Party shall ensure that its review procedures are published and are timely, transparent, effective, and consistent with due process principles.

4. Each Party shall ensure that all documents related to a challenge to a procurement covered by this Chapter are made available to any authority it establishes or designates under paragraph 1.

5. Notwithstanding other review procedures provided for or developed by each of the Parties, each Party shall ensure that any authority it establishes or designates under paragraph 1 provides at least the following:

(a) an opportunity for the supplier to review relevant documents and to be heard by the authority in a timely manner;

(b) sufficient time for the supplier to prepare and submit written challenges, which in no case shall be less than 10 days from the time when the basis of the complaint became known or reasonably should have become known to the supplier;

(c) a requirement that the entity respond in writing to the supplier's challenge;

(d) an opportunity for the supplier to reply to the entity's response to the challenge; and

(e) prompt delivery in writing of the decisions relating to the challenge, with an explanation of the grounds for each decision.

6. Each Party shall ensure that a supplier's submission of a challenge will not prejudice the supplier's participation in ongoing or future procurements.

ARTICLE 9.14: MODIFICATIONS AND RECTIFICATIONS

1. Either Party may modify its coverage under this Chapter provided that it:

(a) notifies the other Party in writing and the other Party does not object in writing within 30 days of the notification; and

(b) offers within 30 days acceptable compensatory adjustments to the other Party to maintain a level of coverage comparable to that existing prior to the modification, except as provided in paragraphs 2 and 3.

2. Either Party may make rectifications of a purely formal nature to its coverage under this Chapter, or minor amendments to its Schedules to Annex 9.1, Sections (A) through (C), provided that it notifies the other Party in writing and the other Party does not object in writing within 30 days of the notification. A Party that makes such a rectification or minor amendment shall not be required to provide compensatory adjustments.

3. A Party need not provide compensatory adjustments in those circumstances where the Parties agree that the proposed modification covers an entity over which a Party has effectively eliminated its control or influence. Where the Parties do not agree that such government control or influence has been effectively eliminated, the objecting Party may request further information or consultations with a view to clarifying the nature of any government control or influence and reaching agreement on the entity's continued coverage under this Chapter.

4. Where the Parties are in agreement on the proposed modification, rectification, or minor amendment, including where a Party has not objected within 30 days under paragraph 1 or 2, the Commission shall give effect to the agreement by modifying forthwith the relevant Section of Annex 9.1.

ARTICLE 9.15: NON-DISCLOSURE OF INFORMATION

1. The Parties, their entities, and their review authorities shall not disclose confidential information the disclosure of which would prejudice legitimate commercial interests of a particular person or

might prejudice fair competition between suppliers, without the formal authorization of the person that provided the information to the Party.

2. Nothing in this Chapter shall be construed as requiring a Party or its entities to disclose confidential information the disclosure of which would impede law enforcement or otherwise be contrary to the public interest.

Article 9.16: Exceptions

Provided that such measures are not applied in a manner that would constitute a means of arbitrary or unjustifiable discrimination between Parties where the same conditions prevail or a disguised restriction on trade between the Parties, nothing in this Chapter shall be construed to prevent a Party from adopting or maintaining measures:

(a) necessary to protect public morals, order, or safety;

(b) necessary to protect human, animal, or plant life or health;

(c) necessary to protect intellectual property; or

(d) relating to goods or services of handicapped persons, of philanthropic institutions, or of prison labor.

The Parties understand that subparagraph (b) includes environmental measures necessary to protect human, animal, or plant life or health.

Article 9.17: Public Information

1. In order to facilitate access to information on commercial opportunities under this Chapter, each Party shall ensure that electronic databases that provide current information on all procurements covered by this Chapter that are conducted by entities listed in Annex 9.1(A), including information that can be disaggregated by detailed categories of goods and services, are made available to interested suppliers of the other Party, through the Internet or a comparable computer-based telecommunications network. Each Party shall, on request of the other Party, provide information on:

(a) the classification system used to disaggregate information on procurement of different goods and services in such databases; and

(b) the procedures for obtaining access to such databases.

2. Entities listed in Annex 9.1(A) shall publish notices of intended procurement in a government-wide, single point of entry electronic publication that is accessible through the Internet or a comparable computer-based telecommunications network. For entities listed in Annex 9.1(B), each Party shall facilitate a reasonable means for suppliers of the other Party to easily identify procurement opportunities, which should include a single point of entry.

3. Each Party shall encourage its entities to publish, as early as possible in the fiscal year, information regarding the entity's procurement plans.

Article 9.18: Committee on Procurement

The Parties hereby establish a Committee on Procurement comprising representatives of each Party. On request, the Committee shall meet to address matters related to the implementation of this Chapter, such as:

(a) bilateral cooperation relating to the development and use of electronic communications in government procurement systems, including developments that may lead to reducing the time limits for tendering set out in Article 9.5;

(b) exchange of statistics and other information to assist the Parties in monitoring the implementation and operation of this Chapter;

(c) consideration of further negotiations aimed at broadening the coverage of this Chapter, including with respect to sub-federal or sub-central entities and state-owned enterprises; and

(d) efforts to increase understanding of their respective government procurement systems, with a view to maximizing access to government procurement opportunities for small business suppliers. To that end, either Party may request the other to provide trade-related technical assistance, including training of government personnel or interested suppliers on specific elements of each Party's government procurement system.

Article 9.19: Further Negotiations

On request of either Party, the Parties shall enter into negotiations with a view to extending coverage under this Chapter on a reciprocal basis, if a Party provides, through an international agreement entered into after entry into force of this Agreement, access to its procurement market for suppliers of a non-Party beyond what it provides under this Agreement to suppliers of the other Party.

Article 9.20: Definitions

For purposes of this Chapter:

build-operate-transfer contract and public works concession contract mean any contractual arrangement, the primary purpose of which is to provide for the construction or rehabilitation of physical infrastructure, plant, buildings, facilities, or other government-owned works and under which, as consideration for a supplier's execution of a contractual arrangement, the entity grants to the supplier, for a specified period of time, temporary ownership or a right to control and operate, and demand payment for the use of, such works for the duration of the contract;

entity means an entity listed in Annex 9.1;

in writing or written means any expression of information in words, numbers, or other symbols, including electronic expressions, that can be read, reproduced, and stored;

international standard means a standard that has been developed in conformity with the document referenced in Article 7.3 (International Standards);

offsets means conditions imposed or considered by an entity prior to, or in the course of, its procurement process that encourage local development or improve a Party's balance of payments accounts by means of requirements of local content, licensing of technology, investment, counter-trade, or similar requirements;

procurement official means a person who performs procurement functions;

publish means to disseminate information in an electronic or paper medium that is distributed widely and is readily accessible to the general public;

supplier means a person that provides or could provide goods or services to an entity; and

technical specification means a specification that lays down the characteristics of goods to be procured or their related processes and production methods, or the characteristics of services to be procured or their related operating methods, including the applicable administrative provisions, and a requirement relating to conformity assessment procedures that an entity prescribes. A technical specification may also include or deal exclusively with terminology, symbols, packaging, marking or labeling requirements, as they apply to a good, process, service or production or operating method.

Chapter Ten

Investment

Section A—Investment

Article 10.1: Scope and Coverage [6]

1. This Chapter applies to measures adopted or maintained by a Party relating to:

(a) investors of the other Party;

(b) covered investments; and

(c) with respect to Articles 10.5 and 10.12, all investments in the territory of the Party.

2. In the event of any inconsistency between this Chapter and another Chapter, the other Chapter shall prevail to the extent of the inconsistency.

3. A requirement by a Party that a service provider of the other Party post a bond or other form of financial security as a condition of providing a service into its territory does not of itself make this Chapter applicable to the provision of that cross-border service. This Chapter applies to that Party's treatment of the posted bond or financial security.

4. This Chapter does not apply to measures adopted or maintained by a Party to the extent that they are covered by Chapter Twelve (Financial Services).

Article 10.2: National Treatment

1. Each Party shall accord to investors of the other Party treatment no less favorable than that it accords, in like circumstances, to its own investors with respect to the establishment, acquisition, expansion, management, conduct, operation, and sale or other disposition of investments in its territory.

[6] For greater certainty, the provisions of this chapter do not bind either Party in relation to any act or fact that took place or any situation that ceased to exist before the date of entry into force of this Agreement. Also, for greater certainty, this chapter is subject to and shall be interpreted in accordance with Annexes 10–A through 10–H.

2. Each Party shall accord to covered investments treatment no less favorable than that it accords, in like circumstances, to investments in its territory of its own investors with respect to the establishment, acquisition, expansion, management, conduct, operation, and sale or other disposition of investments.

3. The treatment to be accorded by a Party under paragraphs 1 and 2 means, with respect to a regional level of government, treatment no less favorable than the most favorable treatment accorded, in like circumstances, by that regional level of government to investors, and to investments of investors, of the Party of which it forms a part.

ARTICLE 10.3: MOST-FAVORED-NATION TREATMENT

1. Each Party shall accord to investors of the other Party treatment no less favorable than that it accords, in like circumstances, to investors of any non-Party with respect to the establishment, acquisition, expansion, management, conduct, operation, and sale or other disposition of investments in its territory.

2. Each Party shall accord to covered investments treatment no less favorable than that it accords, in like circumstances, to investments in its territory of investors of any non-Party with respect to the establishment, acquisition, expansion, management, conduct, operation, and sale or other disposition of investments.

ARTICLE 10.4: MINIMUM STANDARD OF TREATMENT [7]

1. Each Party shall accord to covered investments treatment in accordance with customary international law, including fair and equitable treatment and full protection and security.

2. For greater certainty, paragraph 1 prescribes the customary international law minimum standard of treatment of aliens as the minimum standard of treatment to be afforded to covered investments. The concepts of "fair and equitable treatment" and "full protection and security" do not require treatment in addition to or beyond that which is required by that standard, and do not create additional substantive rights. The obligation in paragraph 1 to provide:

(a) "fair and equitable treatment" includes the obligation not to deny justice in criminal, civil, or administrative adjudicatory proceedings in accordance with the principle of due process embodied in the principal legal systems of the world; and

(b) "full protection and security" requires each Party to provide the level of police protection required under customary international law.

3. A determination that there has been a breach of another provision of this Agreement, or of a separate international agreement, does not establish that there has been a breach of this Article.

4. Notwithstanding Article 10.7(5)(b), each Party shall accord to investors of the other Party, and to covered investments, non-discriminatory treatment with respect to measures it adopts or maintains relating to losses suffered by investments in its territory owing to armed conflict or civil strife.

[7] For greater certainty, Article 10.4 shall be interpreted in accordance with Annex 10–A.

5. Notwithstanding paragraph 4, if an investor of a Party, in the situations referred to in that paragraph, suffers a loss in the territory of the other Party resulting from:

(a) requisitioning of its covered investment or part thereof by the latter's forces or authorities; or

(b) destruction of its covered investment or part thereof by the latter's forces or authorities, which was not required by the necessity of the situation,

the latter Party shall provide the investor restitution or compensation, which in either case shall be prompt, adequate, and effective, and, with respect to compensation, shall be in accordance with Article 10.9(2) through (4).

6. Paragraph 4 does not apply to existing measures relating to subsidies or grants that would be inconsistent with Article 10.2 but for Article 10.7(5)(b).

ARTICLE 10.5: PERFORMANCE REQUIREMENTS

Mandatory Performance Requirements

1. Neither Party may impose or enforce any of the following requirements, or enforce any commitment or undertaking, in connection with the establishment, acquisition, expansion, management, conduct, operation, or sale or other disposition of an investment of an investor of a Party or of a non-Party in its territory:

(a) to export a given level or percentage of goods or services;

(b) to achieve a given level or percentage of domestic content;

(c) to purchase, use, or accord a preference to goods produced in its territory, or to purchase goods from persons in its territory;

(d) to relate in any way the volume or value of imports to the volume or value of exports or to the amount of foreign exchange inflows associated with such investment;

(e) to restrict sales of goods or services in its territory that such investment produces or supplies by relating such sales in any way to the volume or value of its exports or foreign exchange earnings;

(f) to transfer a particular technology, a production process, or other proprietary knowledge to a person in its territory; or

(g) to supply exclusively from the territory of the Party the goods that it produces or the services that it supplies to a specific regional market or to the world market.

Advantages Subject to Performance Requirements

2. Neither Party may condition the receipt or continued receipt of an advantage, in connection with the establishment, acquisition, expansion, management, conduct, operation, or sale or other disposition of an investment in its territory of an investor of a Party or of a non-Party, on compliance with any of the following requirements:

(a) to achieve a given level or percentage of domestic content;

(b) to purchase, use, or accord a preference to goods produced in its territory, or to purchase goods from persons in its territory;

(c) to relate in any way the volume or value of imports to the volume or value of exports or to the amount of foreign exchange inflows associated with such investment; or

(d) to restrict sales of goods or services in its territory that such investment produces or supplies by relating such sales in any way to the volume or value of its exports or foreign exchange earnings.

Exceptions and Exclusions

3. (a) Nothing in paragraph 2 shall be construed to prevent a Party from conditioning the receipt or continued receipt of an advantage, in connection with an investment in its territory of an investor of a Party or of a non-Party, on compliance with a requirement to locate production, supply a service, train or employ workers, construct or expand particular facilities, or carry out research and development, in its territory.

(b) Paragraph 1(f) does not apply:

(i) when a Party authorizes use of an intellectual property right in accordance with Article 31[8] of the TRIPS Agreement, or to measures requiring the disclosure of proprietary information that fall within the scope of, and are consistent with, Article 39 of the TRIPS Agreement; or

(ii) when the requirement is imposed or the commitment or undertaking is enforced by a court, administrative tribunal, or competition authority to remedy a practice determined after judicial or administrative process to be anticompetitive under the Party's competition laws.[9]

(c) Provided that such measures are not applied in an arbitrary or unjustifiable manner, or do not constitute a disguised restriction on international trade or investment, paragraphs 1(b), (c), and (f), and 2(a) and (b), shall not be construed to prevent a Party from adopting or maintaining measures, including environmental measures:

(i) necessary to secure compliance with laws and regulations that are not inconsistent with this Agreement;

(ii) necessary to protect human, animal, or plant life or health; or

(iii) related to the conservation of living or non-living exhaustible natural resources.

(d) Paragraphs 1(a), (b), and (c), and 2(a) and (b), do not apply to qualification requirements for goods or services with respect to export promotion and foreign aid programs.

(e) Paragraphs 1(b), (c), (f), and (g), and 2(a) and (b), do not apply to procurement.

(f) Paragraphs 2(a) and (b) do not apply to requirements imposed by an importing Party relating to the content of goods necessary to qualify for preferential tariffs or preferential quotas.

4. For greater certainty, paragraphs 1 and 2 do not apply to any requirement other than the requirements set out in those paragraphs.

---

[8] The reference to "Article 31" includes footnote 7 to Article 31.

[9] The Parties recognize that a patent does not necessarily confer market power.

5. This Article does not preclude enforcement of any commitment, undertaking, or requirement between private parties, where a Party did not impose or require the commitment, undertaking, or requirement.

ARTICLE 10.6: SENIOR MANAGEMENT AND BOARDS OF DIRECTORS

1. Neither Party may require that an enterprise of that Party that is a covered investment appoint to senior management positions individuals of any particular nationality.

2. A Party may require that a majority of the board of directors, or any committee thereof, of an enterprise of that Party that is a covered investment, be of a particular nationality, or resident in the territory of the Party, provided that the requirement does not materially impair the ability of the investor to exercise control over its investment.

ARTICLE 10.7: NON-CONFORMING MEASURES [10]

1. Articles 10.2, 10.3, 10.5, and 10.6 do not apply to:

(a) any existing non-conforming measure that is maintained by a Party at:

(i) the central level of government, as set out by that Party in its Schedule to Annex I,

(ii) a regional level of government, as set out by that Party in its Schedule to Annex I, or

(iii) a local level of government;

(b) the continuation or prompt renewal of any non-conforming measure referred to in subparagraph (a); or

(c) an amendment to any non-conforming measure referred to in subparagraph (a) to the extent that the amendment does not decrease the conformity of the measure, as it existed immediately before the amendment, with Articles 10.2, 10.3, 10.5, and 10.6.

2. Articles 10.2, 10.3, 10.5, and 10.6 do not apply to any measure that a Party adopts or maintains with respect to sectors, subsectors, or activities, as set out in its Schedule to Annex II.

3. Neither Party may, under any measure adopted after the date of entry into force of this Agreement and covered by its Schedule to Annex II, require an investor of the other Party, by reason of its nationality, to sell or otherwise dispose of an investment existing at the time the measure becomes effective.

4. Articles 10.2 and 10.3 do not apply to any measure that is an exception to, or derogation from, the obligations under Article 17.1(6) (General Provisions) as specifically provided for in that Article.

5. Articles 10.2, 10.3, and 10.6 do not apply to:

(a) procurement; or

(b) subsidies or grants provided by a Party, including government-supported loans, guarantees, and insurance.

[10] For greater certainty, Article 10.7 is subject to Annex 10–B.

ARTICLE 10.8: TRANSFERS[11]

1. Each Party shall permit all transfers relating to a covered investment to be made freely and without delay into and out of its territory. Such transfers include:

(a) contributions to capital;

(b) profits, dividends, interest, capital gains, royalty payments, management fees, and technical assistance and other fees;

(c) proceeds from the sale of all or any part of the covered investment or from the partial or complete liquidation of the covered investment;

(d) payments made under a contract entered into by the investor, or the covered investment, including payments made pursuant to a loan agreement;

(e) payments made pursuant to Article 10.4(4) and (5) and Article 10.9; and

(f) payments arising under Section B.

2. Each Party shall permit returns in kind relating to a covered investment to be made as authorized or specified in an investment authorization or other written agreement[12] between the Party and a covered investment or an investor of the other Party.

3. Each Party shall permit transfers relating to a covered investment to be made in a freely usable currency at the market rate of exchange prevailing on the date of transfer.

4. Neither Party may require its investors to transfer, or penalize its investors that fail to transfer, the income, earnings, profits, or other amounts derived from, or attributable to, investments in the territory of the other Party.

5. Notwithstanding paragraphs 1 through 3, a Party may prevent a transfer through the equitable, nondiscriminatory, and good faith application of its laws relating to:

(a) bankruptcy, insolvency, or the protection of the rights of creditors;

(b) issuing, trading, or dealing in securities, futures, or derivatives;

(c) criminal or penal offenses;

(d) financial reporting or record keeping of transfers when necessary to assist law enforcement or financial regulatory authorities; or

(e) ensuring compliance with orders or judgments in judicial or administrative proceedings.

6. Notwithstanding paragraph 2, a Party may restrict transfers of returns in kind in circumstances where it could otherwise restrict such transfers under this Agreement, including as set out in paragraph 5.

[11] For greater certainty, Article 10.8 is subject to Annex 10–C.

[12] Notwithstanding any other provision of this chapter, this paragraph takes effect on the date of entry into force of this Agreement.

Article 10.9: Expropriation and Compensation[13]

1. Neither Party may expropriate or nationalize a covered investment either directly or indirectly through measures equivalent to expropriation or nationalization ("expropriation"), except:

(a) for a public purpose;

(b) in a non-discriminatory manner;

(c) on payment of prompt, adequate, and effective compensation in accordance with paragraphs 2 through 4; and

(d) in accordance with due process of law and Article 10.4(1) through (3).

2. Compensation shall:

(a) be paid without delay;

(b) be equivalent to the fair market value of the expropriated investment immediately before the expropriation took place ("the date of expropriation");

(c) not reflect any change in value occurring because the intended expropriation had become known earlier; and

(d) be fully realizable and freely transferable.

3. If the fair market value is denominated in a freely usable currency, the compensation paid shall be no less than the fair market value on the date of expropriation, plus interest at a commercially reasonable rate for that currency, accrued from the date of expropriation until the date of payment.

4. If the fair market value is denominated in a currency that is not freely usable, the compensation paid—converted into the currency of payment at the market rate of exchange prevailing on the date of payment—shall be no less than:

(a) the fair market value on the date of expropriation, converted into a freely usable currency at the market rate of exchange prevailing on that date, plus

(b) interest, at a commercially reasonable rate for that freely usable currency, accrued from the date of expropriation until the date of payment.

5. This Article does not apply to the issuance of compulsory licenses granted in relation to intellectual property rights in accordance with the TRIPS Agreement, or to the revocation, limitation, or creation of intellectual property rights, to the extent that such revocation, limitation, or creation is consistent with Chapter Seventeen (Intellectual Property Rights).

Article 10.10: Special Formalities and Information Requirements

1. Nothing in Article 10.2 shall be construed to prevent a Party from adopting or maintaining a measure that prescribes special formalities in connection with covered investments, such as a requirement that investors be residents of the Party or that covered investments be legally constituted under the laws or regulations of the Party, provided that such formalities do not materially impair the protections afforded by a Party to investors of the other Party and covered investments pursuant to this Chapter.

[13] For greater certainty, Article 10.9 shall be interpreted in accordance with Annex 10–A and Annex 10–D.

2. Notwithstanding Articles 10.2 and 10.3, a Party may require an investor of the other Party, or a covered investment, to provide information concerning that investment solely for informational or statistical purposes. The Party shall protect such information that is confidential from any disclosure that would prejudice the competitive position of the investor or the covered investment. Nothing in this paragraph shall be construed to prevent a Party from otherwise obtaining or disclosing information in connection with the equitable and good faith application of its domestic law.

Article 10.11: Denial of Benefits

1. A Party may deny the benefits of this Chapter to an investor of the other Party that is an enterprise of such other Party and to investments of that investor if an investor of a non-Party owns or controls the enterprise and the denying Party:

(a) does not maintain diplomatic relations with the non-Party; or

(b) adopts or maintains measures with respect to the non-Party or an investor of the non-Party that prohibit transactions with the enterprise or that would be violated or circumvented if the benefits of this Chapter were accorded to the enterprise or to its investments.

2. Subject to Article 22.4 (Consultations), a Party may deny the benefits of this Chapter to:

(a) an investor of the other Party that is an enterprise of such other Party and to investments of that investor if an investor of a non-Party owns or controls the enterprise and the enterprise has no substantial business activities in the territory of the other Party; or

(b) an investor of the other Party that is an enterprise of such other Party and to investments of that investor if an investor of the denying Party owns or controls the enterprise and the enterprise has no substantial business activities in the territory of the other Party.

Article 10.12: Investment and Environment

Nothing in this Chapter shall be construed to prevent a Party from adopting, maintaining, or enforcing any measure otherwise consistent with this Chapter that it considers appropriate to ensure that investment activity in its territory is undertaken in a manner sensitive to environmental concerns.

Article 10.13: Implementation

The Parties shall consult annually, or as otherwise agreed, to review the implementation of this Chapter and consider any investment matter of mutual interest, including consideration of the development of procedures that could contribute to greater transparency of measures described in Article 10.7(1)(c).

Section B—Investor-State Dispute Settlement

ARTICLE 10.14: CONSULTATION AND NEGOTIATION

In the event of an investment dispute, the claimant and the respondent should initially seek to resolve the dispute through consultation and negotiation, which may include the use of non-binding, third-party procedures.

ARTICLE 10.15: SUBMISSION OF A CLAIM TO ARBITRATION [14]

1. In the event that a disputing party considers that an investment dispute cannot be settled by consultation and negotiation:

(a) the claimant, on its own behalf, may submit to arbitration under this Section a claim

(i) that the respondent has breached

(A) an obligation under Section A or Annex 10–F,

(B) an investment authorization, or

(C) an investment agreement; and

(ii) that the claimant has incurred loss or damage by reason of, or arising out of, that breach; and

(b) the claimant, on behalf of an enterprise of the respondent that is a juridical person that the claimant owns or controls directly or indirectly, may submit to arbitration under this Section a claim

(i) that the respondent has breached

(A) an obligation under Section A or Annex 10–F,

(B) an investment authorization, or

(C) an investment agreement; and

(ii) that the enterprise has incurred loss or damage by reason of, or arising out of, that breach.

2. For greater certainty, a claimant may submit to arbitration under this Section a claim that the respondent has breached an obligation under Section A or Annex 10–F through the actions of a designated monopoly or a state enterprise exercising delegated government authority as described in Article 16.3(3)(a) (Designated Monopolies) and Article 16.4(2) (State Enterprises), respectively.

3. Without prejudice to Article 12.1(2) (Scope and Coverage), no claim may be submitted under this Section that alleges a violation of any provision of this Agreement other than an obligation under Section A or Annex 10–F.

4. At least 90 days before submitting any claim to arbitration under this Section, a claimant shall deliver to the respondent a written notice of its intention to submit the claim to arbitration ("notice of intent"). The notice shall specify:

(a) the name and address of the claimant and, where a claim is submitted on behalf of an enterprise, the name, address, and place of incorporation of the enterprise;

(b) for each claim, the provision of this Agreement, investment authorization, or investment agreement alleged to have been breached and any other relevant provisions;

(c) the legal and factual basis for each claim; and

[14] For greater certainty, Article 10.15 is subject to Annex 10–E.

(d) the relief sought and the approximate amount of damages claimed.

5. Provided that six months have elapsed since the events giving rise to the claim, a claimant may submit a claim referred to in paragraph 1:

(a) under the ICSID Convention, provided that both the non-disputing Party and the respondent are parties to the ICSID Convention;

(b) under the ICSID Additional Facility Rules, provided that either the nondisputing Party or the respondent, but not both, is a party to the ICSID Convention;

(c) under the UNCITRAL Arbitration Rules; or

(d) if the disputing parties agree, to any other arbitration institution or under any other arbitration rules.

6. A claim shall be deemed submitted to arbitration under this Section when the claimant's notice of or request for arbitration ("notice of arbitration"):

(a) referred to in paragraph 1 of Article 36 of the ICSID Convention is received by the Secretary-General;

(b) referred to in Article 2 of Schedule C of the ICSID Additional Facility Rules is received by the Secretary-General;

(c) referred to in Article 3 of the UNCITRAL Arbitration Rules, together with the statement of claim referred to in Article 18 of the UNCITRAL Arbitration Rules, are received by the respondent; or

(d) referred to under any other arbitral institution or arbitral rules selected under paragraph 5(d) is received by the respondent.

7. The arbitration rules applicable under paragraph 5, and in effect on the date the claim or claims were submitted to arbitration under this Section, shall govern the arbitration except to the extent modified by this Agreement.

8. The claimant shall provide with the notice of arbitration referred to in paragraph 6:

(a) the name of the arbitrator that the claimant appoints; or

(b) the claimant's written consent for the Secretary-General to appoint the claimant's arbitrator.

Article 10.16: Consent of Each Party to Arbitration

1. Each Party consents to the submission of a claim to arbitration under this Section in accordance with this Agreement.

2. The consent under paragraph 1 and the submission of a claim to arbitration under this Section shall satisfy the requirements of:

(a) Chapter II of the ICSID Convention (Jurisdiction of the Centre) and the ICSID Additional Facility Rules for written consent of the parties to the dispute;

(b) Article II of the New York Convention for an "agreement in writing;" and

(c) Article I of the Inter-American Convention for an "agreement."

Article 10.17: Conditions and Limitations on Consent of Each Party

1. No claim may be submitted to arbitration under this Section if more than three years have elapsed from the date on which the claimant first acquired, or should have first acquired, knowledge of the breach alleged under Article 10.15(1) and knowledge that the claimant (for claims brought under Article 10.15(1)(a)) or the enterprise (for claims brought under Article 10.15(1)(b)) has incurred loss or damage.

2. No claim may be submitted to arbitration under this Section unless:

(a) the claimant consents in writing to arbitration in accordance with the procedures set out in this Agreement; and

(b) the notice of arbitration referred to in Article 10.15(6) is accompanied,

(i) for claims submitted to arbitration under Article 10.15(1)(a), by the claimant's written waiver, and

(ii) for claims submitted to arbitration under Article 10.15(1)(b), by the claimant's and the enterprise's written waivers of any right to initiate or continue before any administrative tribunal or court under the law of either Party, or other dispute settlement procedures, any proceeding with respect to the events alleged to give rise to the claimed breach.

3. Notwithstanding paragraph 2(b), the claimant (for claims brought under Article 10.15(1)(a)) and the claimant or the enterprise (for claims brought under Article 10.15(1)(b)) may initiate or continue an action that seeks interim injunctive relief and does not involve the payment of monetary damages before a judicial or administrative tribunal of the respondent, provided that the action is brought for the sole purpose of preserving the claimant's or the enterprise's rights and interests during the pendency of the arbitration.

Article 10.18: Selection of Arbitrators

1. Unless the disputing parties otherwise agree, the tribunal shall comprise three arbitrators, one arbitrator appointed by each of the disputing parties and the third, who shall be the presiding arbitrator, appointed by agreement of the disputing parties.

2. The Secretary-General shall serve as appointing authority for an arbitration under this Section.

3. If a tribunal has not been constituted within 75 days from the date that a claim is submitted to arbitration under this Section, the Secretary-General, on the request of a disputing party, shall appoint, in his or her discretion, the arbitrator or arbitrators not yet appointed.

4. For purposes of Article 39 of the ICSID Convention and Article 7 of Schedule C to the ICSID Additional Facility Rules, and without prejudice to an objection to an arbitrator on a ground other than nationality:

(a) the respondent agrees to the appointment of each individual member of a tribunal established under the ICSID Convention or the ICSID Additional Facility Rules;

(b) a claimant referred to in Article 10.15(1)(a) may submit a claim to arbitration under this Section, or continue a claim, under the ICSID Convention or the ICSID Additional Facility Rules, only on condition that the claimant agrees in writing to the appointment of each individual member of the tribunal; and

(c) a claimant referred to in Article 10.15(1)(b) may submit a claim to arbitration under this Section, or continue a claim, under the ICSID Convention or the ICSID Additional Facility Rules, only on condition that the claimant and the enterprise agree in writing to the appointment of each individual member of the tribunal.

ARTICLE 10.19: CONDUCT OF THE ARBITRATION

1. The disputing parties may agree on the legal place of any arbitration under the arbitral rules applicable under Article 10.15(5)(b), (c), or (d). If the disputing parties fail to reach agreement, the tribunal shall determine the place in accordance with the applicable arbitral rules, provided that the place shall be in the territory of a State that is a party to the New York Convention.

2. The non-disputing Party may make oral and written submissions to the tribunal regarding the interpretation of this Agreement.

3. The tribunal shall have the authority to accept and consider amicus curiae submissions from a person or entity that is not a disputing party (the "submitter"). The submissions shall be provided in both Spanish and English, and shall identify the submitter and any Party, other government, person, or organization, other than the submitter, that has provided, or will provide, any financial or other assistance in preparing the submission.

4. Without prejudice to a tribunal's authority to address other objections as a preliminary question, such as an objection that a dispute is not within a tribunal's competence, a tribunal shall address and decide as a preliminary question any objection by the respondent that, as a matter of law, a claim submitted is not a claim for which an award in favor of the claimant may be made under Article 10.25.

(a) Such objection shall be submitted to the tribunal as soon as possible after the tribunal is constituted, and in no event later than the date the tribunal fixes for the respondent to submit its counter-memorial (or, in the case of an amendment to the notice of arbitration referred to in Article 10.15(6), the date the tribunal fixes for the respondent to submit its response to the amendment).

(b) On receipt of an objection under this paragraph, the tribunal shall suspend any proceedings on the merits, establish a schedule for considering the objection consistent with any schedule it has established for considering any other preliminary question, and issue a decision or award on the objection, stating the grounds therefor.

(c) In deciding an objection under this paragraph, the tribunal shall assume to be true claimant's factual allegations in support of any claim in the notice of arbitration (or any amendment thereof) and, in disputes brought under the UNCITRAL Arbitration Rules, the statement of claim referred to in Article 18 of the UNCITRAL Arbitration Rules. The tribunal may also consider any relevant facts not in dispute.

(d) The respondent does not waive any objection as to competence or any argument on the merits merely because the respondent did or did not raise an objection under this paragraph or make use of the expedited procedure set out in the following paragraph.

5. In the event that the respondent so requests within 45 days after the tribunal is constituted, the tribunal shall decide on an expedited basis an objection under paragraph 4 or any objection that the dispute is not within the tribunal's competence. The tribunal shall suspend any proceedings on the merits and issue a decision or award on the objection(s), stating the grounds therefor, no later than 150 days after the date of the request. However, if a disputing party requests a hearing, the tribunal may take an additional 30 days to issue the decision or award. Regardless of whether a hearing is requested, a tribunal may, on a showing of extraordinary cause, delay issuing its decision or award by an additional brief period of time, which may not exceed 30 days.

6. When it decides a respondent's objection under paragraph 4 or 5, the tribunal may, if warranted, award to the prevailing disputing party reasonable costs and attorneys' fees incurred in submitting or opposing the objection. In determining whether such an award is warranted, the tribunal shall consider whether either the claimant's claim or the respondent's objection was frivolous, and shall provide the disputing parties a reasonable opportunity to comment.

7. A respondent may not assert as a defense, counterclaim, right of set-off, or for any other reason that the claimant has received or will receive indemnification or other compensation for all or part of the alleged damages pursuant to an insurance or guarantee contract.

8. A tribunal may order an interim measure of protection to preserve the rights of a disputing party, or to ensure that the tribunal's jurisdiction is made fully effective, including an order to preserve evidence in the possession or control of a disputing party or to protect the tribunal's jurisdiction. A tribunal may not order attachment or enjoin the application of a measure alleged to constitute a breach referred to in Article 10.15. For purposes of this paragraph, an order includes a recommendation.

9. (a) At the request of a disputing party, a tribunal shall, before issuing an award on liability, transmit its proposed award to the disputing parties and to the non-disputing Party. Within 60 days after the tribunal transmits its proposed award, only the disputing parties may submit written comments to the tribunal concerning any aspect of its proposed award. The tribunal shall consider any such comments and issue its award not later than 45 days after the expiration of the 60-day comment period.

(b) Subparagraph (a) shall not apply in any arbitration for which an appeal has been made available pursuant to paragraph 10.

10. If a separate multilateral agreement enters into force as between the Parties that establishes an appellate body for purposes of reviewing awards rendered by tribunals constituted pursuant to international trade or investment agreements to hear investment disputes, the Parties shall strive to reach an agreement that would have such appellate body review awards rendered under Article 10.25 in arbitrations commenced after the appellate body's establishment.

ARTICLE 10.20: TRANSPARENCY OF ARBITRAL PROCEEDINGS

1. Subject to paragraphs 2 and 4, the respondent shall, after receiving the following documents, promptly transmit them to the non-disputing Party and make them available to the public:

(a) the notice of intent referred to in Article 10.15(4);

(b) the notice of arbitration referred to in Article 10.15(6);

(c) pleadings, memorials, and briefs submitted to the tribunal by a disputing party and any written submissions submitted pursuant to Article 10.19(2) and (3) and Article 10.24;

(d) minutes or transcripts of hearings of the tribunal, where available; and

(e) orders, awards, and decisions of the tribunal.

2. The tribunal shall conduct hearings open to the public and shall determine, in consultation with the disputing parties, the appropriate logistical arrangements. However, any disputing party that intends to use information designated as confidential business information or information that is privileged or otherwise protected from disclosure under a Party's law in a hearing shall so advise the tribunal. The tribunal shall make appropriate arrangements to protect the information from disclosure.

3. Nothing in this Section requires a respondent to disclose confidential business information or information that is privileged or otherwise protected from disclosure under a Party's law or to furnish or allow access to information that it may withhold in accordance with Article 23.2 (Essential Security) or Article 23.5 (Disclosure of Information).

4. Confidential business information or information that is privileged or otherwise protected from disclosure under a Party's law shall, if such information is submitted to the tribunal, be protected from disclosure in accordance with the following procedures:

(a) Subject to subparagraph (d), neither the disputing parties nor the tribunal shall disclose to the non-disputing Party or to the public any confidential business information or information that is privileged or otherwise protected from disclosure under a Party's law where the disputing party that provided the information clearly designates it in accordance with subparagraph (b);

(b) Any disputing party claiming that certain information constitutes confidential business information or information that is privileged or otherwise protected from disclosure under a Party's law shall clearly designate the information at the time it is submitted to the tribunal;

(c) A disputing party shall, at the same time that it submits a document containing information claimed to be confidential business information or information that is privileged or otherwise protected from disclosure under a Party's law, submit a redacted version of the document that does not contain the information. Only the redacted version shall be provided to the nondisputing Party and made public in accordance with paragraph 1; and

(d) The tribunal shall decide any objection regarding the designation of information claimed to be confidential business information or information that is privileged or otherwise protected from disclosure under a Party's law. If the tribunal determines that such information was not properly designated, the disputing party that submitted the information may:

(i) withdraw all or part of its submission containing such information; or

(ii) agree to resubmit complete and redacted documents with corrected designations in accordance with the tribunal's determination and subparagraph (c).

In either case, the other disputing party shall, whenever necessary, resubmit complete and redacted documents which either remove the information withdrawn under subparagraph (d)(i) by the disputing party that first submitted the information or redesignate the information consistent with the designation under subparagraph (d)(ii) of the disputing party that first submitted the information.

5. Nothing in this Section authorizes a respondent to withhold from the public information required to be disclosed by its laws.

Article 10.21: Governing Law

1. Subject to paragraph 3, when a claim is submitted under Article 10.15(1)(a)(i)(A) or Article 10.15(1)(b)(i)(A), the tribunal shall decide the issues in dispute in accordance with this Agreement and applicable rules of international law.

2. Subject to paragraph 3, when a claim is submitted under Article 10.15(1)(a)(i)(B) or (C), or Article 10.15(1)(b)(i)(B) or (C), the tribunal shall decide the issues in dispute in accordance with the rules of law specified in the pertinent investment agreement or investment authorization, or as the disputing parties may otherwise agree. If the rules of law have not been specified or otherwise agreed, the tribunal shall apply the law of the respondent (including its rules on the conflict of laws), the terms of the investment agreement or investment authorization, such rules of international law as may be applicable, and this Agreement.

3. A decision of the Commission declaring its interpretation of a provision of this Agreement under Article 21.1 (Free Trade Commission) shall be binding on a tribunal established under this Section, and any award must be consistent with that decision.

Article 10.22: Interpretation of Annexes

1. Where a respondent asserts as a defense that the measure alleged to be a breach is within the scope of a non-conforming measure set out in Annex I or Annex II, the tribunal shall, on request of the respondent, request the interpretation of the Commission on

the issue. The Commission shall submit in writing any decision declaring its interpretation under Article 21.1 (Free Trade Commission) to the tribunal within 60 days of delivery of the request.

2. A decision issued by the Commission under paragraph 1 shall be binding on the tribunal, and any award must be consistent with that decision. If the Commission fails to issue such a decision within 60 days, the tribunal shall decide the issue.

Article 10.23: Expert Reports

Without prejudice to the appointment of other kinds of experts where authorized by the applicable arbitration rules, a tribunal, at the request of a disputing party or, unless the disputing parties disapprove, on its own initiative, may appoint one or more experts to report to it in writing on any factual issue concerning environmental, health, safety, or other scientific matters raised by a disputing party in a proceeding, subject to such terms and conditions as the disputing parties may agree.

Article 10.24: Consolidation

1. Where two or more claims have been submitted separately to arbitration under Article 10.15(1) and the claims have a question of law or fact in common and arise out of the same events or circumstances, any disputing party may seek a consolidation order in accordance with the agreement of all the disputing parties sought to be covered by the order or the terms of paragraphs 2 through 10.

2. A disputing party that seeks a consolidation order under this Article shall deliver, in writing, a request to the Secretary-General and to all the disputing parties sought to be covered by the order and shall specify in the request:

(a) the names and addresses of all the disputing parties sought to be covered by the order;

(b) the nature of the order sought; and

(c) the grounds on which the order is sought.

3. Unless the Secretary-General finds within 30 days after receiving a request under paragraph 2 that the request is manifestly unfounded, a tribunal shall be established under this Article.

4. Unless all the disputing parties sought to be covered by the order otherwise agree, a tribunal established under this Article shall comprise three arbitrators:

(a) one arbitrator appointed by agreement of the claimants;

(b) one arbitrator appointed by the respondent; and

(c) the presiding arbitrator appointed by the Secretary-General, provided, however, that the presiding arbitrator shall not be a national of either Party.

5. If, within 60 days after the Secretary-General receives a request made under paragraph 2, the respondent fails or the claimants fail to appoint an arbitrator in accordance with paragraph 4, the Secretary-General, on the request of any disputing party sought to be covered by the order, shall appoint the arbitrator or arbitrators not yet appointed. If the respondent fails to appoint an arbitrator, the Secretary-General shall appoint a national of the respondent, and if the claimants fail to appoint an arbitrator, the

Secretary-General shall appoint a national of the non-disputing Party.

6. Where a tribunal established under this Article is satisfied that two or more claims that have been submitted to arbitration under Article 10.15(1) have a question of law or fact in common, and arise out of the same events or circumstances, the tribunal may, in the interest of fair and efficient resolution of the claims, and after hearing the disputing parties, by order:

(a) assume jurisdiction over, and hear and determine together, all or part of the claims;

(b) assume jurisdiction over, and hear and determine one or more of the claims, the determination of which it believes would assist in the resolution of the others; or

(c) instruct a tribunal previously established under Article 10.18 to assume jurisdiction over, and hear and determine together, all or part of the claims, provided that

(i) that tribunal, at the request of any claimant not previously a disputing party before that tribunal, shall be reconstituted with its original members, except that the arbitrator for the claimants shall be appointed pursuant to paragraphs 4(a) and 5; and

(ii) that tribunal shall decide whether any prior hearing shall be repeated.

7. Where a tribunal has been established under this Article, a claimant that has submitted a claim to arbitration under Article 10.15(1) and that has not been named in a request made under paragraph 2 may make a written request to the tribunal that it be included in any order made under paragraph 6, and shall specify in the request:

(a) the name and address of the claimant;

(b) the nature of the order sought; and

(c) the grounds on which the order is sought.

The claimant shall deliver a copy of its request to the Secretary-General.

8. A tribunal established under this Article shall conduct its proceedings in accordance with the UNCITRAL Arbitration Rules, except as modified by this Section.

9. A tribunal established under Article 10.18 shall not have jurisdiction to decide a claim, or a part of a claim, over which a tribunal established or instructed under this Article has assumed jurisdiction.

10. On application of a disputing party, a tribunal established under this Article, pending its decision under paragraph 6, may order that the proceedings of a tribunal established under Article 10.18 be stayed, unless the latter tribunal has already adjourned its proceedings.

ARTICLE 10.25: AWARDS

1. Where a tribunal makes a final award against a respondent, the tribunal may award, separately or in combination, only:

(a) monetary damages and any applicable interest;

(b) restitution of property, in which case the award shall provide that the respondent may pay monetary damages and any applicable interest in lieu of restitution.

A tribunal may also award costs and attorneys' fees in accordance with this Section and the applicable arbitration rules.

2. Subject to paragraph 1, where a claim is submitted to arbitration under Article 10.15(1)(b):

(a) an award of restitution of property shall provide that restitution be made to the enterprise;

(b) an award of monetary damages and any applicable interest shall provide that the sum be paid to the enterprise; and

(c) the award shall provide that it is made without prejudice to any right that any person may have in the relief under applicable domestic law.

3. A tribunal may not award punitive damages.

4. An award made by a tribunal shall have no binding force except between the disputing parties and in respect of the particular case.

5. Subject to paragraph 6 and the applicable review procedure for an interim award, a disputing party shall abide by and comply with an award without delay.

6. A disputing party may not seek enforcement of a final award until:

(a) in the case of a final award made under the ICSID Convention

(i) 120 days have elapsed from the date the award was rendered and no disputing party has requested revision or annulment of the award; or

(ii) revision or annulment proceedings have been completed; and

(b) in the case of a final award under the ICSID Additional Facility Rules, the UNCITRAL Arbitration Rules, or the rules selected pursuant to Article 10.15(5)(d)

(i) 90 days have elapsed from the date the award was rendered and no disputing party has commenced a proceeding to revise, set aside, or annul the award, or

(ii) a court has dismissed or allowed an application to revise, set aside, or annul the award and there is no further appeal.

7. Each Party shall provide for the enforcement of an award in its territory.

8. If the respondent fails to abide by or comply with a final award, on delivery of a request by the non-disputing Party, a panel shall be established under Article 22.6 (Request for an Arbitral Panel). The requesting Party may seek in such proceedings:

(a) a determination that the failure to abide by or comply with the final award is inconsistent with the obligations of this Agreement; and

(b) if the Parties agree, a recommendation that the respondent abide by or comply with the final award.

9. A disputing party may seek enforcement of an arbitration award under the ICSID Convention, the New York Convention, or the Inter-American Convention regardless of whether proceedings have been taken under paragraph 8.

10. A claim that is submitted to arbitration under this Section shall be considered to arise out of a commercial relationship or transaction for purposes of Article I of the New York Convention and Article I of the Inter-American Convention.

ARTICLE 10.26: SERVICE OF DOCUMENTS

Delivery of notice and other documents on a Party shall be made to the place named for that Party in Annex 10–G.

Section C—Definitions

ARTICLE 10.27: DEFINITIONS

For purposes of this Chapter:

Centre means the International Centre for Settlement of Investment Disputes (ICSID) established by the ICSID Convention;

claimant means an investor of a Party that is a party to an investment dispute with the other Party;

disputing parties means the claimant and the respondent;

disputing party means either the claimant or the respondent;

enterprise means an "enterprise" as defined in Article 2.1 (Definitions of General Application), and a branch of an enterprise;

enterprise of a Party means an enterprise constituted or organized under the law of a Party, and a branch located in the territory of a Party and carrying out business activities there;

freely usable currency means "freely usable currency" as determined by the International Monetary Fund under its Articles of Agreement;

ICSID Additional Facility Rules means the Rules Governing the Additional Facility for the Administration of Proceedings by the Secretariat of the International Centre for Settlement of Investment Disputes;

ICSID Convention means the Convention on the Settlement of Investment Disputes between States and Nationals of other States, done at Washington, March 18, 1965;

Inter-American Convention means the Inter-American Convention on International Commercial Arbitration, done at Panama, January 30, 1975;

investment means every asset that an investor owns or controls, directly or indirectly, that has the characteristics of an investment, including such characteristics as the commitment of capital or other resources, the expectation of gain or profit, or the assumption of risk. Forms that an investment may take include:

(a) an enterprise;

(b) shares, stock, and other forms of equity participation in an enterprise;

(c) bonds, debentures, loans, and other debt instruments;[15]

(d) futures, options, and other derivatives;

[15] Some forms of debt, such as bonds, debentures, and long-term notes, are more likely to have the characteristics of an investment, while other forms of debt, such as claims to payments that are immediately due and result from the sale of goods or services, are less likely to have such characteristics.

(e) rights under contract, including turnkey, construction, management, production, concession, or revenue-sharing contracts;

(f) intellectual property rights;

(g) rights conferred pursuant to domestic law, such as concessions, licenses, authorizations, and permits;[16] and

(h) other tangible or intangible, movable or immovable property, and related property rights, such as leases, mortgages, liens, and pledges;

but investment does not mean an order or judgment entered in a judicial or administrative action;

investment agreement means a written agreement[17] that takes effect at least two years after the date of entry into force of this Agreement between a national authority[18] of a Party and a covered investment or an investor of the other Party:

(a) that grants rights with respect to natural resources or other assets that a national authority controls; and

(b) that the covered investment or the investor relies on in establishing or acquiring a covered investment;

investment authorization means an authorization that the foreign investment authority of a Party grants to a covered investment or an investor of the other Party;[19]

investor of a non-Party means, with respect to a Party, an investor that attempts to make, is making, or has made an investment in the territory of that Party, that is not an investor of either Party;

investor of a Party means a Party or state enterprise thereof, or a national or an enterprise of a Party, that attempts to make, is making, or has made an investment in the territory of the other Party; provided, however, that a natural person who is a dual national shall be deemed to be exclusively a national of the State of his/her dominant and effective nationality;

monopoly means "monopoly" as defined in Article 16.9 (Definitions);

New York Convention means the United Nations Convention on the Recognition and Enforcement of Foreign Arbitral Awards, done at New York, June 10, 1958;

non-disputing Party means the Party that is not a party to an investment dispute;

---

[16] Whether a particular right conferred pursuant to domestic law, as referred to in para. (g), has the characteristics of an investment depends on such factors as the nature and extent of the rights that the holder has under the domestic law of the Party. Among such rights that do not have the characteristics of an investment are those that do not create any rights protected under domestic law. For greater certainty, the foregoing is without prejudice to whether any asset associated with such right has the characteristics of an investment.

[17] For purposes of this definition, "written agreement" means an agreement in writing, executed and entered into by both parties or their representatives, which sets forth an exchange of rights and obligations, for value. Neither a unilateral act of an administrative or judicial authority, such as a decree, order, or judgment, nor a consent decree, shall be considered a written agreement.

[18] For purposes of this definition, "national authority" means (a) for the United States, an authority at the central level of government; and (b) for Chile, an authority at the ministerial level of government. "National authority" does not include state enterprises.

[19] The Parties recognize that neither Party has a foreign investment authority, as of the date this Agreement enters into force.

respondent means the Party that is a party to an investment dispute;

Secretary-General means the Secretary-General of ICSID;

tribunal means an arbitration tribunal established under Article 10.18 or 10.24; and

UNCITRAL Arbitration Rules means the arbitration rules of the United Nations Commission on International Trade Law.

Chapter Eleven

Cross-Border Trade in Services

Article 11.1: Scope and Coverage

1. This Chapter applies to measures adopted or maintained by a Party affecting cross-border trade in services by service suppliers of the other Party. Such measures include measures affecting:

(a) the production, distribution, marketing, sale, and delivery of a service;

(b) the purchase or use of, or payment for, a service;

(c) the access to and use of distribution, transport, or telecommunications networks and services in connection with the supply of a service;

(d) the presence in its territory of a service supplier of the other Party; and

(e) the provision of a bond or other form of financial security as a condition for the supply of a service.

2. For purposes of this Chapter, "measures adopted or maintained by a Party" means measures adopted or maintained by:

(a) central, regional, or local governments and authorities; and

(b) non-governmental bodies in the exercise of powers delegated by central, regional, or local governments or authorities.

3. Articles 11.4, 11.7, and 11.8 also apply to measures by a Party affecting the supply of a service in its territory by an investor of the other Party as defined in Article 10.27 (Definitions) or a covered investment.[20]

4. This Chapter does not apply to:

(a) financial services, as defined in Article 12.19 (Definitions), except as provided in paragraph 3;

(b) air services, including domestic and international air transportation services, whether scheduled or non-scheduled, and related services in support of air services, other than:

(i) aircraft repair and maintenance services during which an aircraft is withdrawn from service, and

(ii) specialty air services;

(c) procurement; or

(d) subsidies or grants provided by a Party or a state enterprise, including government-supported loans, guarantees, and insurance.

[20] The Parties understand that nothing in this chapter, including this paragraph, is subject to investor-state dispute settlement pursuant to sec. B of Chapter Ten (Investment).

5. This Chapter does not impose any obligation on a Party with respect to a national of the other Party seeking access to its employment market, or employed on a permanent basis in its territory, and does not confer any right on that national with respect to that access or employment.

6. This Chapter does not apply to services supplied in the exercise of governmental authority. A "service supplied in the exercise of governmental authority" means any service which is supplied neither on a commercial basis, nor in competition with one or more service suppliers.

ARTICLE 11.2: NATIONAL TREATMENT

1. Each Party shall accord to service suppliers[21] of the other Party treatment no less favorable than that it accords, in like circumstances, to its own service suppliers.

2. The treatment to be accorded by a Party under paragraph 1 means, with respect to a regional level of government, treatment no less favorable than the most favorable treatment accorded, in like circumstances, by that regional level of government to service suppliers of the Party of which it forms a part.

ARTICLE 11.3: MOST-FAVORED-NATION TREATMENT

Each Party shall accord to service suppliers[22] of the other Party treatment no less favorable than that it accords, in like circumstances, to service suppliers of a non-Party.

ARTICLE 11.4: MARKET ACCESS

Neither Party may, either on the basis of a regional subdivision or on the basis of its entire territory, adopt or maintain measures that:

(a) impose limitations on:

(i) the number of service suppliers,[23] whether in the form of numerical quotas, monopolies, exclusive service suppliers, or the requirement of an economic needs test,

(ii) the total value of service transactions or assets in the form of numerical quotas or the requirement of an economic needs test,

(iii) the total number of service operations or on the total quantity of services output expressed in terms of designated numerical units in the form of quotas or the requirement of an economic needs test,[24] or

(iv) the total number of natural persons that may be employed in a particular service sector or that a service supplier may employ and who are necessary for, and directly related to, the supply of a specific service in the form of a numerical quotas or the requirement of an economic needs test; or

---

21 The Parties understand that "service suppliers" has the same meaning as "services and service suppliers" in Article XVII:1 of GATS.

22 The Parties understand that "service suppliers" has the same meaning as "services and service suppliers" in Article II:1 of GATS.

23 The Parties understand that "service suppliers" has the same meaning as "service and service suppliers" in Article XVI of GATS.

24 This clause does not cover measures of a Party which limit inputs for the supply of services.

(b) restrict or require specific types of legal entity or joint venture through which a service supplier may supply a service.

Article 11.5: Local Presence

Neither Party may require a service supplier of the other Party to establish or maintain a representative office or any form of enterprise, or to be resident, in its territory as a condition for the cross-border supply of a service.

Article 11.6: Non-conforming Measures

1. Articles 11.2, 11.3, 11.4, and 11.5 do not apply to:

(a) any existing non-conforming measure that is maintained by a Party at:

(i) the central level of government, as set out by that Party in its Schedule to Annex I,

(ii) a regional level of government, as set out by that Party in its Schedule to Annex I, or

(iii) a local level of government;

(b) the continuation or prompt renewal of any non-conforming measure referred to in subparagraph (a); or

(c) an amendment to any non-conforming measure referred to in subparagraph (a) to the extent that the amendment does not decrease the conformity of the measure, as it existed immediately before the amendment, with Articles 11.2, 11.3 , 11.4, or 11.5.

2. Articles 11.2, 11.3, 11.4, and 11.5 do not apply to any measure that a Party adopts or maintains with respect to sectors, sub-sectors, or activities, as set out in its Schedule to Annex II.

3. Annex 11.6 sets out specific commitments by the Parties.

Article 11.7: Transparency in Development and Application of Regulations[25]

Further to Chapter Twenty (Transparency):

(a) each Party shall maintain or establish appropriate mechanisms for responding to inquiries from interested persons regarding their regulations relating to the subject matter of this Chapter;[26]

(b) at the time it adopts final regulations relating to the subject matter of this Chapter, each Party shall, to the extent possible, including upon request, address in writing substantive comments received from interested persons with respect to the proposed regulations; and

(c) to the extent possible, each Party shall allow a reasonable period of time between publication of final regulations and their effective date.

---

[25] For greater certainty, "regulations" includes regulations establishing or applying to licensing authorization or criteria.

[26] Chile's implementation of its obligation to establish appropriate mechanisms for small administrative agencies may need to take into account resource and budget constraints.

ARTICLE 11.8: DOMESTIC REGULATION

1. Where a Party requires authorization for the supply of a service, the competent authorities of that Party shall, within a reasonable period of time after the submission of an application considered complete under domestic laws and regulations, inform the applicant of the decision concerning the application. At the request of the applicant, the competent authorities of the Party shall provide, without undue delay, information concerning the status of the application. This obligation shall not apply to authorization requirements that are within the scope of Article 11.6(2).

2. With a view to ensuring that measures relating to qualification requirements and procedures, technical standards, and licensing requirements do not constitute unnecessary barriers to trade in services, each Party shall endeavor to ensure, as appropriate for individual sectors, that any such measures that it adopts or maintains are:

(a) based on objective and transparent criteria, such as competence and the ability to supply the service;

(b) not more burdensome than necessary to ensure the quality of the service; and

(c) in the case of licensing procedures, not in themselves a restriction on the supply of the service.

3. If the results of the negotiations related to Article VI:4 of GATS (or the results of any similar negotiations undertaken in other multilateral fora in which both Parties participate) enter into effect, this Article shall be amended, as appropriate, after consultations between the Parties, to bring those results into effect under this Agreement. The Parties agree to coordinate on such negotiations as appropriate.

ARTICLE 11.9: MUTUAL RECOGNITION

1. For the purposes of the fulfillment, in whole or in part, of its standards or criteria for the authorization, licensing, or certification of services suppliers, and subject to the requirements of paragraph 4, a Party may recognize the education or experience obtained, requirements met, or licenses or certifications granted in a particular country. Such recognition, which may be achieved through harmonization or otherwise, may be based upon an agreement or arrangement with the country concerned or may be accorded autonomously.

2. Where a Party recognizes, autonomously or by agreement or arrangement, the education or experience obtained, requirements met, or licenses or certifications granted in the territory of a non-Party, nothing in Article 11.3 shall be construed to require the Party to accord such recognition to the education or experience obtained, requirements met, or licenses or certifications granted in the territory of the other Party.

3. A Party that is a party to an agreement or arrangement of the type referred to in paragraph 1, whether existing or future, shall afford adequate opportunity for the other Party, if the other Party is interested, to negotiate its accession to such an agreement or arrangement or to negotiate comparable ones with it. Where a Party

accords recognition autonomously, it shall afford adequate opportunity for the other Party to demonstrate that education, experience, licenses, or certifications obtained or requirements met in that other Party's territory should be recognized.

4. A Party shall not accord recognition in a manner which would constitute a means of discrimination between countries in the application of its standards or criteria for the authorization, licensing, or certification of services suppliers, or a disguised restriction on trade in services.

5. Annex 11.9 applies to measures adopted or maintained by a Party relating to the licensing or certification of professional service suppliers as set out in the provisions of that Annex.

Article 11.10: Implementation

The Parties shall consult annually, or as otherwise agreed, to review the implementation of this Chapter and consider other trade in services issues of mutual interest. Among other issues, the Parties will consult with a view to determining the feasibility of removing any remaining citizenship or permanent residency requirement for the licensing or certification of each other's services suppliers. Such consultations will also include consideration of the development of procedures that could contribute to greater transparency of measures described in Article 11.6(1)(c).

Article 11.11: Denial of Benefits

1. A Party may deny the benefits of this Chapter to a service supplier of the other Party if the service is being supplied by an enterprise owned or controlled by nationals of a non-Party, and the denying Party:

(a) does not maintain diplomatic relations with the non-Party; or

(b) adopts or maintains measures with respect to the non-Party that prohibit transactions with the enterprise or that would be violated or circumvented if the benefits of this Chapter were accorded to the enterprise.

2. Subject to Article 22.4 (Consultations), a Party may deny the benefits of this Chapter to:

(a) service suppliers of the other Party where the service is being supplied by an enterprise that is owned or controlled by persons of a non-Party and the enterprise has no substantial business activities in the territory of the other Party, or

(b) service suppliers of the other Party where the service is being supplied by an enterprise that is owned or controlled by persons of the denying Party and the enterprise has no substantial business activities in the territory of the other Party.

Article 11.12: Definitions

For purposes of this Chapter:

cross-border trade in services or **cross-border supply of services** means the supply of a service:

(a) from the territory of one Party into the territory of the other Party;

(b) in the territory of one Party by a person of that Party to a person of the other Party; or

(c) by a national of a Party in the territory of the other Party,

but does not include the supply of a service in the territory of a Party by an investor of the other Party as defined in Article 10.27 (Investment-Definitions) or a covered investment;

enterprise means an "enterprise" as defined in Article 2.1 (Definitions of General Application), and a branch of an enterprise;

enterprise of a Party means an enterprise constituted or organized under the law of a Party, and a branch located in the territory of a Party and carrying out business activities there;

professional services means services, the provision of which requires specialized post-secondary education, or equivalent training or experience, and for which the right to practice is granted or restricted by a Party, but does not include services provided by trades-persons or vessel and aircraft crew members;

service supplier of a Party means a person of a Party that seeks to supply or supplies a service; and

specialty air services means any non-transportation air services, such as aerial fire-fighting, sightseeing, spraying, surveying, mapping, photography, parachute jumping, glider towing, and helicopter-lift for logging and construction, and other airborne agricultural, industrial, and inspection services.

Chapter Twelve

Financial Services

Article 12.1: Scope and Coverage

1. This Chapter applies to measures adopted or maintained by a Party relating to:

(a) financial institutions of the other Party;

(b) investors of the other Party, and investments of such investors, in financial institutions in the Party's territory; and

(c) cross-border trade in financial services.

2. Articles 10.8 through 10.12 and 11.11 are hereby incorporated into and made a part of this Chapter. Section B of Chapter Ten (Investment) is hereby incorporated into and made a part of this Chapter solely for breaches by a Party of Articles 10.8 through 10.11, as incorporated into this Chapter.[27] No other provision of Chapter Ten (Investment) or Chapter Eleven (Cross Border Trade in Services) shall apply to a measure described in paragraph 1.

3. This Chapter does not apply to measures adopted or maintained by a Party relating to:

(a) activities or services forming part of a public retirement plan or statutory system of social security; or

(b) activities or services conducted for the account or with the guarantee or using the financial resources of the Party, including its public entities,

[27] For greater certainty, the provisions of chapter Ten (Investment) hereby incorporated include, are subject to, and shall be interpreted in conformity with, Annexes 10–A through 10–H of that chapter, as applicable.

except that this Chapter shall apply if a Party allows any of the activities or services referred to in subparagraphs (a) or (b) to be conducted by its financial institutions in competition with a public entity or a financial institution.

ARTICLE 12.2: NATIONAL TREATMENT

1. Each Party shall accord to investors of the other Party treatment no less favorable than that it accords to its own investors, in like circumstances, with respect to the establishment, acquisition, expansion, management, conduct, operation, and sale or other disposition of financial institutions and investments in financial institutions in its territory.

2. Each Party shall accord to financial institutions of the other Party and to investments of investors of the other Party in financial institutions treatment no less favorable than that it accords to its own financial institutions, and to investments of its own investors in financial institutions, in like circumstances, with respect to the establishment, acquisition, expansion, management, conduct, operation, and sale or other disposition of financial institutions and investments.

3. For purposes of the national treatment obligations in Article 12.5(1), a Party shall accord to cross-border financial service suppliers of the other Party treatment no less favorable than that it accords to its own financial service suppliers, in like circumstances, with respect to the supply of the relevant service.

ARTICLE 12.3: MOST-FAVORED-NATION TREATMENT

1. Each Party shall accord to investors of the other Party, financial institutions of the other Party, investments of investors in financial institutions, and cross-border financial service suppliers of the other Party treatment no less favorable than that it accords to the investors, financial institutions, investments of investors in financial institutions and crossborder financial service suppliers of a non-Party, in like circumstances.

2. A Party may recognize prudential measures of a non-Party in the application of measures covered by this Chapter. Such recognition may be:

(a) accorded unilaterally;

(b) achieved through harmonization or other means; or

(c) based upon an agreement or arrangement with the non-Party.

3. A Party according recognition of prudential measures under paragraph 2 shall provide adequate opportunity to the other Party to demonstrate that circumstances exist in which there are or will be equivalent regulation, oversight, implementation of regulation, and, if appropriate, procedures concerning the sharing of information between the Parties.

4. Where a Party accords recognition of prudential measures under paragraph 2(c) and the circumstances set out in paragraph 3 exist, the Party shall provide adequate opportunity to the other Party to negotiate accession to the agreement or arrangement, or to negotiate a comparable agreement or arrangement.

ARTICLE 12.4: MARKET ACCESS FOR FINANCIAL INSTITUTIONS

Neither Party may, with respect to investors of the other Party, either on the basis of a regional subdivision or on the basis of its entire territory adopt or maintain measures that:

(a) impose limitations on:

(i) the number of financial institutions whether in the form of numerical quotas, monopolies, exclusive financial service suppliers, or the requirements of an economic needs test,

(ii) the total value of financial service transactions or assets in the form of numerical quotas or the requirement of an economic needs test,

(iii) the total number of financial service operations or on the total quantity of financial services output expressed in terms of designated numerical units in the form of quotas or the requirement of an economic needs test, or

(iv) the total number of natural persons that may be employed in a particular financial service sector or that a financial institution may employ and who are necessary for, and directly related to, the supply of a specific financial service in the form of a numerical quota or the requirement of an economic needs test; or

(b) restrict or require specific types of legal entity or joint venture through which a financial institution may supply a service.

ARTICLE 12.5: CROSS-BORDER TRADE

1. Each Party shall permit, under terms and conditions that accord national treatment, cross-border financial service suppliers of the other Party to supply the financial services specified in Annex 12.5.

2. Each Party shall permit persons located in its territory, and its nationals wherever located, to purchase financial services from cross-border financial service suppliers of the other Party located in the territory of the other Party. This obligation does not require a Party to permit such suppliers to do business or solicit in its territory. Each Party may define "doing business" and "solicitation" for purposes of this Article as long as such definitions are not inconsistent with the obligations of paragraph 1.

3. Without prejudice to other means of prudential regulation of cross-border trade in financial services, a Party may require the registration of cross-border financial service suppliers of the other Party and of financial instruments.

ARTICLE 12.6: NEW FINANCIAL SERVICES [28]

1. Each Party shall permit a financial institution of the other Party, on request or notification to the relevant regulator, where

[28] The Parties understand that nothing in Article 12.6 prevents a financial institution of a Party from applying to the other Party to consider authorizing the supply of a financial service that is supplied within neither Party's territory. Such application shall be subject to the domestic law of the Party to which the application is made and, for greater certainty, shall not be subject to the obligations of Article 12.6.

required, to supply any new financial service that the first Party would permit its own financial institutions, in like circumstances, to supply under its domestic law, provided that the introduction of the financial service does not require the Party to adopt a new law or modify an existing law.

2. A Party may determine the institutional and juridical form through which the new financial service may be supplied and may require authorization for the supply of the service. Where a Party would permit the new financial service and authorization is required, the decision shall be made within a reasonable time and authorization may only be refused for prudential reasons.

Article 12.7: Treatment of Certain Information

Nothing in this Chapter requires a Party to furnish or allow access to:

(a) information related to the financial affairs and accounts of individual customers of financial institutions or cross-border financial service suppliers; or

(b) any confidential information, the disclosure of which would impede law enforcement or otherwise be contrary to the public interest or prejudice legitimate commercial interests of particular enterprises.

Article 12.8: Senior Management and Boards of Directors

1. Neither Party may require financial institutions of the other Party to engage individuals of any particular nationality as senior managerial or other essential personnel.

2. Neither Party may require that more than a minority of the board of directors of a financial institution of the other Party be composed of nationals of the Party, persons residing in the territory of the Party, or a combination thereof.

Article 12.9: Non-Conforming Measures

1. Articles 12.2 through 12.5 and 12.8 and Section A of Annex 12.9 do not apply to:

(a) any existing non-conforming measure that is maintained by a Party at:

(i) the central level of government, as set out by that Party in its Schedule to Annex III,

(ii) a regional level of government, as set out by that Party in its Schedule to Annex III, or

(iii) a local level of government;

(b) the continuation or prompt renewal of any non-conforming measure referred to in subparagraph (a); or

(c) an amendment to any non-conforming measure referred to in subparagraph (a) to the extent that the amendment does not decrease the conformity of the measure, as it existed immediately before the amendment, with Articles 12.2, 12.3, 12.4, and 12.8 and Section A of Annex 12.9.

2. Articles 12.2 through 12.5 and 12.8 and Section A of Annex 12.9 do not apply to any measure that a Party adopts or maintains with respect to sectors, subsectors, or activities, as set out in its Schedule to Annex III.

3. Annex 12.9 sets out certain specific commitments by each Party.

4. Where a Party has set out in its Schedule to Annexes I and II a measure that does not conform to Articles 10.2, 10.3, 11.2, 11.3, or 11.4 pursuant to paragraphs 1 and 2 of Articles 10.7 and 11.6, that measure shall be deemed to constitute a non-conforming measure, pursuant to paragraphs 1 and 2 of this Article, with respect to Article 12.2, Article 12.3, or Article 12.4, or Section A of Annex 12.9, as the case may be, to the extent that the measure, sector, sub-sector, or activity set out in the Schedule of non-conforming measures is covered by this Chapter.

ARTICLE 12.10: EXCEPTIONS

1. Notwithstanding any other provision of this Chapter or of Chapters Ten (Investment), Eleven (Cross-Border Trade in Services), Thirteen (Telecommunications), Fifteen (Electronic Commerce), and Sixteen (Competition Policy, Designated Monopolies, and State Enterprises), including specifically Article 13.16 (Telecommunications—Relationship to Other Chapters), a Party shall not be prevented from adopting or maintaining measures for prudential reasons,[29] including for the protection of investors, depositors, policy holders, or persons to whom a fiduciary duty is owed by a financial institution or crossborder financial service supplier, or to ensure the integrity and stability of the financial system. Where such measures do not conform with the provisions of this Agreement referred to in this paragraph, they shall not be used as a means of avoiding the Party's commitments or obligations under such provisions.[30]

2. Nothing in this Chapter or Chapters Ten (Investment), Eleven (Cross-Border Trade in Services), Thirteen (Telecommunications), Fifteen (Electronic Commerce), and Sixteen (Competition Policy, Designated Monopolies, and State Enterprises), including specifically Article 13.16 (Telecommunications—Relationship to Other Chapters), applies to nondiscriminatory measures of general application taken by any public entity in pursuit of monetary and related credit policies or exchange rate policies. This paragraph shall not affect a Party's obligations under Article 10.5 (Performance Requirements) with respect to measures covered by Chapter Ten (Investment) or Article 10.8 (Transfers).

3. Notwithstanding Article 10.8 (Transfers), as incorporated into this Chapter, a Party may prevent or limit transfers by a financial institution or cross-border financial service supplier to, or for the benefit of, an affiliate of or person related to such institution or supplier, through the equitable, non-discriminatory and good faith application of measures relating to maintenance of the safety, soundness, integrity, or financial responsibility of financial institutions or cross-border financial service suppliers. This paragraph

[29] It is understood that the term "prudential reasons" includes the maintenance of the safety, soundness, integrity, or financial responsibility of individual financial institutions or cross-border financial service suppliers.

[30] The Parties understand that a Party may take measures for prudential reasons through regulatory or administrative authorities, in addition to those who have regulatory responsibilities with respect to financial institutions, such as ministries or departments of labor.

does not prejudice any other provision of this Agreement that permits a Party to restrict transfers.

4. For greater certainty, nothing in this Chapter shall be construed to prevent the adoption or enforcement by a Party of measures necessary to secure compliance with laws or regulations that are not inconsistent with this Chapter, including those relating to the prevention of deceptive and fraudulent practices or to deal with the effects of a default on financial services contracts, subject to the requirement that such measures are not applied in a manner which would constitute a means of arbitrary or unjustifiable discrimination between countries where like conditions prevail, or a disguised restriction on investment in financial institutions or cross-border trade in financial services as covered by this Chapter.

ARTICLE 12.11: TRANSPARENCY

1. The Parties recognize that transparent regulations and policies and reasonable, objective, and impartial administration governing the activities of financial institutions and financial service suppliers are important in facilitating both access of financial institutions and financial service suppliers to, and their operations in, each other's markets.

2. In lieu of Article 20.2 (Publication), each Party shall, to the extent practicable:

(a) publish in advance any regulations of general application relating to the subject matter of this Chapter that it proposes to adopt; and

(b) provide interested persons and the other Party a reasonable opportunity to comment on such proposed regulations.

3. Each Party's regulatory authorities shall make available to interested persons their requirements, including any documentation required, for completing applications relating to the supply of financial services.

4. On the request of an applicant, the regulatory authority shall inform the applicant of the status of its application. If such authority requires additional information from the applicant, it shall notify the applicant without undue delay.

5. A regulatory authority shall make an administrative decision on a completed application of an investor in a financial institution, a financial institution, or a cross-border financial service supplier of the other Party relating to the supply of a financial service within 120 days, and shall promptly notify the applicant of the decision. An application shall not be considered complete until all relevant hearings are held and all necessary information is received. Where it is not practicable for a decision to be made within 120 days, the regulatory authority shall notify the applicant without undue delay and shall endeavor to make the decision within a reasonable time thereafter.

6. Each Party shall maintain or establish appropriate mechanisms that will respond to inquiries from interested persons regarding measures of general application covered by this Chapter.

7. Each Party shall ensure that the rules of general application adopted or maintained by self-regulatory organizations of the Party

are promptly published or otherwise made available in such a manner as to enable interested persons to become acquainted with them.

8. To the extent practicable, each Party should allow reasonable time between publication of final regulations and their effective date.

9. At the time it adopts final regulations, a Party should, to the extent practicable, address in writing substantive comments received from interested persons with respect to the proposed regulations.

Article 12.12: Self-Regulatory Organizations

Where a Party requires a financial institution or a cross-border financial service supplier of the other Party to be a member of, participate in, or have access to, a self-regulatory organization to provide a financial service in or into the territory of that Party, the Party shall ensure observance of the obligations of Articles 12.2 and 12.3 by such self-regulatory organization.

Article 12.13: Payment and Clearing Systems

Under terms and conditions that accord national treatment, each Party shall grant to financial institutions of the other Party established in its territory access to payment and clearing systems operated by public entities, and to official funding and refinancing facilities available in the normal course of ordinary business. This paragraph is not intended to confer access to the Party's lender of last resort facilities.

Article 12.14: Expedited Availability of Insurance Services

The Parties recognize the importance of maintaining and developing regulatory procedures to expedite the offering of insurance services by licensed suppliers.

Article 12.15: Financial Services Committee

1. The Parties hereby establish the Financial Services Committee. The principal representative of each Party shall be an official of the Party's authority responsible for financial services set out in Annex 12.15.

2. In accordance with Article 21.1(2)(d) (The Free Trade Commission), the Committee shall:

(a) supervise the implementation of this Chapter and its further elaboration;

(b) consider issues regarding financial services that are referred to it by a Party; and

(c) participate in the dispute settlement procedures in accordance with Articles 12.17 and 12.18.

3. The Committee shall meet annually, or as otherwise agreed, to assess the functioning of this Agreement as it applies to financial services. The Committee shall inform the Commission of the results of each meeting.

Article 12.16: Consultations

1. A Party may request in writing consultations with the other Party regarding any matter arising under this Agreement that affects financial services. The other Party shall give sympathetic consideration to the request. The Parties shall report the results of their consultations to the Committee.

2. Officials from the authorities specified in Annex 12.15 shall participate in the consultations under this Article.

3. Nothing in this Article shall be construed to require regulatory authorities participating in consultations under paragraph 1 to disclose information or take any action that would interfere with specific regulatory, supervisory, administrative, or enforcement matters.

4. Nothing in this Article shall be construed to require a Party to derogate from its relevant law regarding sharing of information among financial regulators or the requirements of an agreement or arrangement between financial authorities of the Parties.

Article 12.17: Dispute Settlement

1. Chapter Twenty-Two (Dispute Settlement) applies as modified by this Article to the settlement of disputes arising under this Chapter.

2. For purposes of Article 22.4 (Consultations), consultations held under Article 12.16 with respect to a measure or matter shall be deemed to constitute consultations under Article 22.4(1), unless the Parties otherwise agree. Upon initiation of consultations, the Parties shall provide information and give confidential treatment under Article 22.4(4)(b) to the information exchanged. If the matter has not been resolved within 45 days after commencing consultations under Article 12.16 or 90 days after the delivery of the request for consultations under Article 12.16, whichever is earlier, the complaining Party may request in writing the establishment of an arbitral panel. The Parties shall report the results of their consultations to the Commission.

3. The Parties shall establish by January 1, 2005, and maintain a roster of up to 10 individuals who are willing and able to serve as financial services panelists, up to four of whom shall be non-Party nationals. The roster members shall be appointed by mutual agreement of the Parties, and may be reappointed. Once established, a roster shall remain in effect for a minimum of three years, and shall remain in effect thereafter until the Parties constitute a new roster.

4. Financial services roster members shall:

(a) have expertise or experience in financial services law or practice, which may include the regulation of financial institutions;

(b) be chosen strictly on the basis of objectivity, reliability, and sound judgment;

(c) be independent of, and not affiliated with or take instructions from, either Party; and

(d) comply with a code of conduct to be established by the Commission.

5. Where a Party claims that a dispute arises under this Chapter, Article 22.9 (Panel Selection) shall apply, except that, unless the Parties otherwise agree, the panel shall be composed entirely of panelists meeting the qualifications in paragraph 4.

6. In any dispute where a panel finds a measure to be inconsistent with the obligations of this Agreement and the measure affects:

(a) only the financial services sector, the complaining Party may suspend benefits only in the financial services sector;

(b) the financial services sector and any other sector, the complaining Party may suspend benefits in the financial services sector that have an effect equivalent to the effect of the measure in the Party's financial services sector; or

(c) only a sector other than the financial services sector, the complaining Party may not suspend benefits in the financial services sector.

Article 12.18: Investment Disputes in Financial Services

1. Where an investor of one Party submits a claim under Article 10.15 (Submission of a Claim to Arbitration) to arbitration under Section B of Chapter Ten (Investment) against the other Party and the respondent invokes Article 12.10, on request of the respondent, the tribunal shall refer the matter in writing to the Committee for a decision. The tribunal may not proceed pending receipt of a decision or report under this Article.

2. In a referral pursuant to paragraph 1, the Committee shall decide the issue of whether and to what extent Article 12.10 is a valid defense to the claim of the investor. The Committee shall transmit a copy of its decision to the tribunal and to the Commission. The decision shall be binding on the tribunal.

3. Where the Committee has not decided the issue within 60 days of the receipt of the referral under paragraph 1, the respondent or the Party of the claimant may request the establishment of an arbitral panel under Article 22.6 (Request for an Arbitral Panel). The panel shall be constituted in accordance with Article 12.17. Further to Article 22.13 (Final Report), the panel shall transmit its final report to the Committee and to the tribunal. The report shall be binding on the tribunal.

4. Where no request for the establishment of a panel pursuant to paragraph 3 has been made within 10 days of the expiration of the 60-day period referred to in paragraph 3, the tribunal may proceed to decide the matter.

Article 12.19: Definitions

For purposes of this Chapter:

cross-border financial service supplier of a Party means a person of a Party that is engaged in the business of supplying a financial service within the territory of the Party and that seeks to supply or supplies a financial service through the cross-border supply of such services;

cross-border trade in financial services or **cross-border supply of financial services** means the supply of a financial service:

(a) from the territory of one Party into the territory of the other Party,

(b) in the territory of a Party by a person of that Party to a person of the other Party, or

(c) by a national of a Party in the territory of the other Party,

but does not include the supply of a service in the territory of a Party by an investment in that territory;

financial institution means any financial intermediary or other enterprise that is authorized to do business and regulated or supervised as a financial institution under the law of the Party in whose territory it is located;

financial institution of the other Party means a financial institution, including a branch, located in the territory of a Party that is controlled by persons of the other Party;

financial service means any service of a financial nature. Financial services include all insurance and insurance-related services, and all banking and other financial services (excluding insurance), as well as services incidental or auxiliary to a service of a financial nature. Financial services include the following activities:

Insurance and insurance-related services

(a) Direct insurance (including co-insurance):

(i) life

(ii) non-life

(b) Reinsurance and retrocession;

(c) Insurance intermediation, such as brokerage and agency;

(d) Service auxiliary to insurance, such as consultancy, actuarial, risk assessment, and claim settlement services.

Banking and other financial services (excluding insurance)

(e) Acceptance of deposits and other repayable funds from the public;

(f) Lending of all types, including consumer credit, mortgage credit, factoring and financing of commercial transactions;

(g) Financial leasing;

(h) All payment and money transmission services, including credit, charge and debit cards, travelers checks, and bankers drafts;

(i) Guarantees and commitments;

(j) Trading for own account or for account of customers, whether on an exchange, in an over-the-counter market, or otherwise, the following:

(i) money market instruments (including checks, bills, certificates of deposits);

(ii) foreign exchange;

(iii) derivative products including, futures and options;

(iv) exchange rate and interest rate instruments, including products such as swaps, forward rate agreements;

(v) transferable securities;

(vi) other negotiable instruments and financial assets, including bullion;

(k) Participation in issues of all kinds of securities, including underwriting and placement as agent (whether publicly or privately) and provision of services related to such issues;

(l) Money broking;

(m) Asset management, such as cash or portfolio management, all forms of collective investment management, pension fund management, custodial, depository, and trust services;

(n) Settlement and clearing services for financial assets, including securities, derivative products, and other negotiable instruments;

(o) Provision and transfer of financial information, and financial data processing and related software by suppliers of other financial services;

(p) Advisory, intermediation, and other auxiliary financial services on all the activities listed in subparagraphs (e) through (o), including credit reference and analysis, investment and portfolio research and advice, advice on acquisitions and on corporate restructuring and strategy;

financial service supplier of a Party means a person of a Party that is engaged in the business of supplying a financial service within the territory of that Party;

investment means "investment" as defined in Article 10.27 (Definitions), except that, with respect to "loans" and "debt instruments" referred to in that Article:

(a) a loan to or debt instrument issued by a financial institution is an investment only where it is treated as regulatory capital by the Party in whose territory the financial institution is located; and

(b) a loan granted by or debt instrument owned by a financial institution, other than a loan to or debt instrument of a financial institution referred to in subparagraph (a), is not an investment;

for greater certainty, a loan granted by or debt instrument owned by a cross-border financial service supplier, other than a loan to or debt instrument issued by a financial institution, is an investment if such loan or debt instrument meets the criteria for investments set out in Article 10.27 (Definitions);

investor of a Party means a Party or state enterprise thereof, or a person of a Party, that attempts to make, is making, or has made an investment in the territory of the other Party; provided, however, that a natural person who is a dual national shall be deemed to be exclusively a national of the State of his/her dominant and effective nationality;

new financial service means a financial service not supplied in the Party's territory that is supplied within the territory of the other Party, and includes any new form of delivery of a financial service or the sale of a financial product that is not sold in the Party's territory;

person of a Party means "person of a Party" as defined in Article 2.1 (General Definitions) and, for greater certainty, does not include a branch of an enterprise of a non-Party;

public entity means a central bank or monetary authority of a Party, or any financial institution owned or controlled by a Party;

self-regulatory organization means any non-governmental body, including any securities or futures exchange or market, clearing agency, other organization or association, that exercises its own or delegated regulatory or supervisory authority over financial service suppliers or financial institutions; and

tribunal means an arbitration tribunal established under Article 10.18 (Selection of Arbitrators).

Chapter Thirteen

Telecommunications

Article 13.1: Scope and Coverage

1. This Chapter applies to:

(a) measures adopted or maintained by a Party relating to access to and use of the public telecommunications network and services;

(b) measures adopted or maintained by a Party relating to obligations of major suppliers of public telecommunications services;

(c) measures adopted or maintained by a Party relating to the provision of information services; and

(d) other measures relating to public telecommunication networks or services.

2. Except to ensure that enterprises operating broadcast stations and cable systems have continued access to and use of public telecommunications networks and services, this Chapter does not apply to any measure adopted or maintained by a Party relating to cable or broadcast distribution of radio or television programming.

3. Nothing in this Chapter shall be construed to:

(a) require a Party or require a Party to compel any enterprise to establish, construct, acquire, lease, operate, or provide telecommunications networks or telecommunications services, where such networks or services are not offered to the public generally;

(b) require a Party to compel any enterprise exclusively engaged in the cable or broadcast distribution of radio or television programming to make available its cable or broadcast facilities as a public telecommunications network; or

(c) prevent a Party from prohibiting persons operating private networks from using their networks to provide public telecommunications networks or services to third persons.

ARTICLE 13.2: ACCESS TO AND USE OF PUBLIC TELECOMMUNICATIONS NETWORKS AND SERVICES[31]

1. Each Party shall ensure that enterprises of the other Party have access to and use of any public telecommunications service, including leased circuits, offered in its territory or across its borders, on reasonable and non-discriminatory terms and conditions, including as set out in paragraphs 2 through 6.

2. Each Party shall ensure that such enterprises are permitted to:

(a) purchase or lease, and attach terminal or other equipment that interfaces with the public telecommunications network;

(b) provide services to individual or multiple end-users over any leased or owned circuit(s);

(c) connect owned or leased circuits with public telecommunications networks and services in the territory, or across the borders, of that Party or with circuits leased or owned by another person;

(d) perform switching, signaling, processing, and conversion functions; and

(e) use operating protocols of their choice.

3. Each Party shall ensure that enterprises of the other Party may use public telecommunications services for the movement of information in its territory or across its borders and for access to information contained in databases or otherwise stored in machine-readable form in the territory of either Party.

4. Further to Article 23.1 (General Exceptions) and notwithstanding paragraph 3, a Party may take such measures as are necessary to:

(a) ensure the security and confidentiality of messages; or

(b) protect the privacy of non-public personal data of subscribers to public telecommunications services,

subject to the requirement that such measures are not applied in a manner that would constitute a means of arbitrary or unjustifiable discrimination or disguised restriction on trade in services.

5. Each Party shall ensure that no condition is imposed on access to and use of public telecommunications networks or services, other than that necessary to:

(a) safeguard the public service responsibilities of providers of public telecommunications networks or services, in particular their ability to make their networks or services available to the public generally; or

(b) protect the technical integrity of public telecommunications networks or services.

6. Provided that conditions for access to and use of public telecommunications networks or services satisfy the criteria set out in paragraph 5, such conditions may include:

(a) a requirement to use specified technical interfaces, including interface protocols, for interconnection with such networks or services; and

[31] For greater certainty, access to unbundled network elements, including access to leased circuits as an unbundled network element, is addressed in Article 13.4(3).

(b) a licensing, permit, registration, or notification procedure which, if adopted or maintained, is transparent and applications filed thereunder are processed expeditiously.

ARTICLE 13.3: OBLIGATIONS RELATING TO INTERCONNECTION WITH SUPPLIERS OF PUBLIC TELECOMMUNICATIONS SERVICES

1. Each Party shall ensure that suppliers of public telecommunications services in its territory provide, directly or indirectly, interconnection with the suppliers of public telecommunications services of the other Party.

2. In carrying out paragraph 1, each Party shall ensure, in accordance with its domestic law and regulations, that suppliers of public telecommunications services in its territory take reasonable steps to protect the confidentiality of commercially sensitive information of, or relating to, suppliers and end-users of public telecommunications services and only use such information for the purpose of providing those services.

ARTICLE 13.4: ADDITIONAL OBLIGATIONS RELATING TO CONDUCT OF MAJOR SUPPLIERS OF PUBLIC TELECOMMUNICATIONS SERVICES[32]

Treatment by Major Suppliers

1. Subject to Annex 13.4(1), each Party shall ensure that major suppliers in its territory accord suppliers of public telecommunications services of the other Party non-discriminatory treatment regarding:

(a) the availability, provisioning, rates, or quality of like public telecommunications services; and

(b) the availability of technical interfaces necessary for interconnection.

Competitive Safeguards

2. (a) Each Party shall maintain appropriate measures for the purpose of preventing suppliers who, alone or together, are a major supplier in its territory from engaging in or continuing anti-competitive practices.

(b) For purposes of subparagraph (a), examples of anti-competitive practices include:

(i) engaging in anti-competitive cross-subsidization;

(ii) using information obtained from competitors with anti-competitive results; and

(iii) not making available, on a timely basis, to suppliers of public telecommunications services, technical information about essential facilities and commercially relevant information which are necessary for them to provide public telecommunications services.

Unbundling of Network Elements

3. (a) Each Party shall provide its competent body the authority to require that major suppliers in its territory provide suppliers of

[32] For purposes of this Agreement, this Article does not apply to suppliers of commercial mobile services. Nothing in this Agreement shall be construed to preclude an authority from imposing measures set forth in this Article upon suppliers of commercial mobile services.

public telecommunications services of the other Party access to network elements on an unbundled basis for the supply of those services on terms and conditions and at cost-oriented rates that are reasonable and non-discriminatory.

(b) Which network elements will be required to be made available in its territory, and which suppliers may obtain such elements, will be determined in accordance with national law and regulation(s).

(c) In determining the network elements to be made available, each Party's competent body shall consider, at a minimum, in accordance with national law and regulation:

(i) whether access to such network elements as are proprietary in nature is necessary, and whether the failure to provide access to such network elements would impair the ability of suppliers of public telecommunications services of the other Party to provide the services they seek to offer; or

(ii) other factors as established in national law or regulation,

as that body construes these factors.

Co-Location

4. (a) Each Party shall ensure that major suppliers in its territory provide to suppliers of public telecommunications services of the other Party physical co-location of equipment necessary for interconnection or access to unbundled network elements on terms, conditions, and at cost-oriented rates that are reasonable and non-discriminatory.

(b) Where physical co-location is not practical for technical reasons or because of space limitations, each Party shall ensure that major suppliers in its territory provide:

(i) alternative solutions; or

(ii) facilitate virtual co-location,

on terms, conditions, and at cost-oriented rates that are reasonable and non-discriminatory.

(c) Each Party may determine which premises shall be subject to subparagraphs (a) and (b).

Resale

5. Each Party shall ensure that major suppliers in its territory:

(a) offer for resale, at reasonable rates,[33] to suppliers of public telecommunications services of the other Party, public telecommunications services that such major supplier provides at retail to end users that are not suppliers of public telecommunications services; and

(b) subject to Annex 13.4(5)(b), do not impose unreasonable or discriminatory conditions or limitations on the resale of such services.

Number Portability

6. Each Party shall ensure that major suppliers in its territory provide number portability to the extent technically feasible, on a timely basis, and on reasonable terms and conditions.

[33] The standard of reasonableness in this paragraph is satisfied, among others, by wholesale rates or cost-oriented rates set pursuant to domestic law and regulations.

Dialing Parity

7. Each Party shall ensure that major suppliers in its territory provide dialing parity to suppliers of public telecommunications services of the other Party and afford suppliers of public telecommunications services of the other Party non-discriminatory access to telephone numbers and related services with no unreasonable dialing delays.

Interconnection

8. (a) General Terms and Conditions

Each Party shall ensure that major suppliers in its territory provide interconnection for the facilities and equipment of suppliers of public telecommunications services of the other Party:

(i) at any technically feasible point in the major supplier's network;

(ii) under non-discriminatory terms, conditions (including technical standards and specifications), and rates;

(iii) of a quality no less favorable than that provided by such major supplier for its own like services, or for like services of non-affiliated service suppliers or for like services of its subsidiaries or other affiliates;

(iv) in a timely fashion, on terms, conditions (including technical standards and specifications), and cost-oriented rates that are transparent, reasonable, having regard to economic feasibility, and sufficiently unbundled so that the supplier need not pay for network components or facilities that it does not require for the service to be provided; and

(v) on request, at points in addition to the network termination points offered to the majority of users, subject to charges that reflect the cost of construction of necessary additional facilities.

(b) Options for Interconnecting with Major Suppliers

Each Party shall ensure that suppliers of public telecommunications services of the other Party may interconnect their facilities and equipment with those of major suppliers in its territory pursuant to at least one of the following options:

(i) a reference interconnection offer or other standard interconnection offer containing the rates, terms, and conditions that the major supplier offers generally to suppliers of public telecommunications services; or

(ii) the terms and conditions of an existing interconnection agreement or through negotiation of a new interconnection agreement.

(c) Public Availability of Interconnection Offers

Each Party shall require each major supplier in its territory to make publicly available a reference interconnection offer or other standard interconnection offer containing the rates, terms, and conditions that the major supplier offers generally to suppliers of public telecommunications services.

(d) Public Availability of the Procedures for Interconnection

Each Party shall make publicly available the applicable procedures for interconnection negotiations with major suppliers in its territory.

(e) Public Availability of Interconnection Agreements with Major Suppliers

Each Party shall:

(i) require major suppliers in its territory to file all interconnection agreements to which they are party with its telecommunications regulatory body, and

(ii) make publicly available interconnection agreements in force between major suppliers in its territory and other suppliers of public telecommunications services in such territory.

Leased Circuits Services[34]

9. (a) Each Party shall ensure that major suppliers in its territory provide enterprises of the other Party leased circuits services that are public telecommunications services, on terms, conditions, and at rates that are reasonable and non-discriminatory.

(b) In carrying out subparagraph (a), each Party shall provide its telecommunications regulatory body the authority to require major suppliers in its territory to offer leased circuits that are part of the public telecommunications services to enterprises of the other Party at flat-rate prices that are cost-oriented.

Article 13.5: Submarine Cable Systems

1. Each Party shall ensure that enterprises in its territory that operate submarine cable systems accord non-discriminatory treatment for access to submarine cable systems.

2. Whether to apply paragraph 1 may be based on classification by a Party of such submarine cable system within its territory as a public telecommunications service supplier.

Article 13.6: Conditions for Supplying Information Services

1. Neither Party may require an enterprise in its territory that it classifies as a supplier of information services (which supplies such services over facilities that it does not own) to:

(a) supply those services to the public generally;

(b) cost-justify its rates for such services;

(c) file a tariff for such services;

(d) interconnect its networks with any particular customer for the supply of such services; or

(e) conform with any particular standard or technical regulation for interconnection for the supply of such services other than for interconnection to a public telecommunications network.

2. Notwithstanding paragraph 1, a Party may take appropriate action, including any of the actions described in paragraph 1, to remedy a practice of an information services supplier that the Party has found in a particular case to be anti-competitive under its law or regulation(s), or to otherwise promote competition or safeguard the interests of consumers.

[34] For greater certainty, access to unbundled network elements, including access to leased circuits as an unbundled network element, is addressed in Article 13.4(3).

Article 13.7: Independent Telecommunications Regulatory Bodies

1. Each Party shall ensure that its telecommunications regulatory body is separate from, and not accountable to, any supplier of public telecommunications services. To this end, each Party shall ensure that its telecommunications regulatory body does not hold a financial interest or maintain an operating role in any such supplier.

2. Each Party shall ensure that the decisions and procedures of its telecommunications regulatory body are impartial with respect to all interested persons. To this end, each Party shall ensure that any financial interest that it holds in a supplier of public telecommunications services does not influence the decisions and procedures of its telecommunications regulatory body.

Article 13.8: Universal Service

Each Party shall administer any universal service obligation that it maintains or adopts in a transparent, non-discriminatory, and competitively neutral manner and shall ensure that its universal service obligation is not more burdensome than necessary for the kind of universal service that it has defined.

Article 13.9: Licensing Procedures

1. When a Party requires a supplier of public telecommunications services to have a license, the Party shall make publicly available:

(a) the licensing criteria and procedures it applies, and the time it normally requires to act on an application, for issuing a license; and

(b) the terms and conditions of all licenses it has issued.

2. Each Party shall ensure that, upon request, an applicant receives the reasons for the denial of a license.

Article 13.10: Allocation and Use of Scarce Resources

1. Each Party shall administer its procedures for allocating and using scarce telecommunications resources, including frequencies, numbers, and rights of way, in an objective, timely, transparent, and non-discriminatory manner.

2. Each Party shall make publicly available the current state of allocated frequency bands but shall not be required to provide detailed identification of frequencies allocated for specific uses.

3. Decisions on allocating and assigning spectrum and frequency management are not measures that are inconsistent with Article 11.4 (Market Access), which is applied to Chapter Ten (Investment) through Article 11.1(3) (Scope and Coverage). Accordingly, each Party retains the right to exercise its spectrum and frequency management policies, which may affect the number of suppliers of public telecommunications services, provided that this is done in a manner that is consistent with the provisions of this Agreement. The Parties also retain the right to allocate frequency bands taking into account existing and future needs.

ARTICLE 13.11: ENFORCEMENT

Each Party shall ensure that its competent authority is authorized to enforce domestic measures relating to the obligations set out in Articles 13.2 through 13.5. Such authority shall include the ability to impose effective sanctions, which may include financial penalties, injunctive relief (on an interim or final basis), or the modification, suspension, and revocation of licenses.

ARTICLE 13.12: PROCEDURES FOR RESOLVING DOMESTIC TELECOMMUNICATIONS DISPUTES

Further to Articles 20.4 (Administrative Proceedings) and 20.5 (Review and Appeal), each Party shall ensure the following:

Recourse to Telecommunications Regulatory Bodies

(a) (i) Each Party shall ensure that enterprises of the other Party may have recourse to a national telecommunications regulatory body or other relevant body to resolve disputes arising under domestic measures addressing a matter set out in Articles 13.2 through 13.5.

(ii) Each Party shall ensure that suppliers of public telecommunications services of the other Party that have requested interconnection with a major supplier in its territory may have recourse, within a reasonable and publicly available period of time after the supplier requests interconnection, to a national telecommunications regulatory body or other relevant body to resolve disputes regarding the terms, conditions, and rates for interconnection with such major supplier.

Reconsideration

(b) Each Party shall ensure that an enterprise that is aggrieved or whose interests are adversely affected by a determination or decision of a national telecommunications regulatory body or other relevant body may petition the body to reconsider its determination or decision. Neither Party may permit such a petition to constitute grounds for non-compliance with such determination or decision of the telecommunications regulatory body or other relevant body unless an appropriate authority stays such determination or decision.

Judicial Review

(c) Each Party shall ensure that any enterprise aggrieved by a determination or decision of the national telecommunications regulatory body or other relevant body may obtain judicial review of such determination or decision by an impartial and independent judicial authority.

ARTICLE 13.13: TRANSPARENCY

Further to Article 20.2 (Publication), each Party shall make publicly available its measures relating to access to and use of public telecommunications services including its measures relating to:

(a) tariffs and other terms and conditions of service;

(b) specifications for technical interfaces;

(c) bodies responsible for preparing, amending, and adopting standards-related measures affecting access and use;

(d) conditions for attaching terminal or other equipment to the public telecommunications network; and

(e) notification, permit, registration, or licensing requirements, if any.

ARTICLE 13.14: FLEXIBILITY IN THE CHOICE OF TECHNOLOGIES

Each Party shall endeavor to not prevent suppliers of public telecommunications services from having the flexibility to choose the technologies that they use to supply their services, including commercial mobile wireless services.

ARTICLE 13.15: FORBEARANCE

The Parties recognize the importance of relying on market forces to achieve wide choices in the supply of telecommunications services. To this end, where provided for under domestic law, each Party may forbear from applying regulation to a telecommunication service that the Party classifies as a public telecommunications service if its telecommunications regulatory body determines that:

(a) enforcement of such regulation is not necessary to prevent unreasonable or discriminatory practices;

(b) enforcement of such regulation is not necessary for the protection of consumers; and

(c) forbearance is consistent with the public interest, including promoting and enhancing competition among suppliers of public telecommunications services.

ARTICLE 13.16: RELATIONSHIP TO OTHER CHAPTERS

In the event of any inconsistency between this Chapter and another Chapter, this Chapter shall prevail to the extent of the inconsistency.

ARTICLE 13.17: DEFINITIONS

For purposes of this Chapter:

commercial mobile services means public telecommunications services supplied through mobile wireless means;

cost-oriented means based on cost, and may include a reasonable profit, and may involve different cost methodologies for different facilities or services;

dialing parity means the ability of a subscriber to use of an equal number of digits to access a public telecommunications service, regardless of the public telecommunications services supplier chosen by such end-user;

enterprise means an "enterprise" as defined in Article 2.1 (Definitions of General Application) and includes a branch of an enterprise;

end-user means a final consumer of or subscriber to a public telecommunications service, including any service supplier other than a supplier of public telecommunications services;

essential facilities means facilities of a public telecommunications network or service that:

(a) are exclusively or predominantly provided by a single or limited number of suppliers, and

(b) cannot feasibly be economically or technically substituted in order to provide a service;

information service means the offering of a capability for generating, acquiring, storing, transforming, processing, retrieving, utilizing, or making available information via telecommunications, and includes electronic publishing, but does not include any use of any such capability for the management, control, or operation of a telecommunications system or the management of a telecommunications service;

interconnection means linking with suppliers providing public telecommunications services in order to allow the users of one supplier to communicate with users of another supplier and to access services provided by another supplier;

leased circuit means telecommunications facilities between two or more designated points that are made available solely to, or dedicated exclusively for use by, a particular customer or other users of the customer's choosing;

major supplier means a supplier of public telecommunications services that has the ability to materially affect the terms of participation (having regard to price and supply) in the relevant market for public telecommunications services as a result of:

(a) control over essential facilities; or

(b) use of its position in the market;

network element means a facility or equipment used in supplying a public telecommunications service, including features, functions, and capabilities provided by means of such facility or equipment;

non-discriminatory means treatment no less favorable than that accorded to any other user of like public telecommunications services in like circumstances;

number portability means the ability of end-users of public telecommunications services to retain, at the same location, existing telephone numbers without impairment of quality, reliability, or convenience when switching like suppliers of public telecommunications services;

physical co-location means physical access to and control over space in order to install, maintain, or repair equipment, at premises owned or controlled and used by a major supplier to provide public telecommunications services;

private network means a telecommunications network that is used exclusively for intraenterprise communications;

public telecommunications network means telecommunications infrastructure which a Party requires to provide public telecommunications services between defined network termination points;

public telecommunications service means any telecommunications service which a Party requires, explicitly or in effect, to be offered to the public generally. Such services may include, inter alia, telephone and data transmission typically involving customer-supplied information between two or more points without any end-to-end change in the form or content of the customer's information, but does not include the offering of information services;

reference interconnection offer means an interconnection offer that a major supplier extends and that is filed with or approved by a telecommunications regulatory body and that is sufficiently detailed to enable a supplier of public telecommunications services that is willing to accept its rates, terms, and conditions to obtain interconnection without having to engage in negotiations with the major supplier concerned;

telecommunications means the transmission and reception of signals by any electromagnetic means, including by photonic means;

telecommunications regulatory body means a body responsible for the regulation of telecommunications; and

user means an end-user or a supplier of public telecommunications services.

Chapter Fourteen

Temporary Entry for Business Persons

Article 14.1: General Principles

1. Further to Article 1.2 (Objectives), this Chapter reflects the preferential trading relationship between the Parties, the mutual desire of the Parties to facilitate temporary entry of business persons under the provisions of Annex 14.3 on a reciprocal basis and of establishing transparent criteria and procedures for temporary entry, and the need to ensure border security and to protect the domestic labor force and permanent employment in their respective territories.

2. This Chapter does not apply to measures regarding citizenship, nationality, permanent residence, or employment on a permanent basis.

Article 14.2: General Obligations

1. Each Party shall apply its measures relating to the provisions of this Chapter in accordance with Article 14.1(1) and, in particular, shall apply expeditiously those measures so as to avoid unduly impairing or delaying trade in goods or services or conduct of investment activities under this Agreement.

2. For greater certainty, nothing in this Chapter shall be construed to prevent a Party from applying measures to regulate the entry of natural persons into, or their temporary stay in, its territory, including those measures necessary to protect the integrity of, and to ensure the orderly movement of natural persons across, its borders, provided that such measures are not applied in such a manner as to unduly impair or delay trade in goods or services or conduct of investment activities under this Agreement. The sole fact of requiring a visa for natural persons shall not be regarded as unduly impairing or delaying trade in goods or services or conduct of investment activities under this Agreement.

Article 14.3: Grant of Temporary Entry

1. Each Party shall grant temporary entry to business persons who are otherwise qualified for entry under applicable measures relating to public health and safety and national security, in accordance with this Chapter, including the provisions of Annex 14.3.

2. A Party may refuse to issue an immigration document authorizing employment to a business person where the temporary entry of that person might affect adversely:

(a) the settlement of any labor dispute that is in progress at the place or intended place of employment; or

(b) the employment of any person who is involved in such dispute.

3. When a Party refuses pursuant to paragraph 2 to issue an immigration document authorizing employment, it shall:

(a) inform in writing the business person of the reasons for the refusal; and

(b) promptly notify the other Party in writing of the reasons for the refusal.

4. Each Party shall limit any fees for processing applications for temporary entry of business persons in a manner consistent with Article 14.2(1).

Article 14.4: Provision of Information

1. Further to Article 20.2 (Publication), each Party shall:

(a) provide to the other Party such materials as will enable it to become acquainted with its measures relating to this Chapter; and

(b) no later than six months after the date of entry into force of this Agreement, prepare, publish, and make available in its own territory, and in the territory of the other Party, explanatory material, including references to applicable laws and regulations, in a consolidated document regarding the requirements for temporary entry under this Chapter in such a manner as will enable business persons of the other Party to become acquainted with them.

2. Each Party shall collect and maintain, and make available upon request to the other Party in accordance with its domestic law, data respecting the granting of temporary entry under this Chapter to business persons of the other Party who have been issued immigration documentation, with a view towards including data specific to each occupation, profession, or activity.

Article 14.5: Committee on Temporary Entry

1. The Parties hereby establish a Committee on Temporary Entry, comprising representatives of each Party, including immigration officials.

2. The Committee shall:

(a) establish a schedule for its meetings;

(b) establish procedures to exchange information on measures that affect the temporary entry of business persons under this Chapter;

(c) consider the development of measures to further facilitate temporary entry of business persons on a reciprocal basis under the provisions of Annex 14.3;

(d) consider the implementation and administration of this Chapter; and

(e) consider the development of common criteria and interpretations for the implementation of this Chapter.

ARTICLE 14.6: DISPUTE SETTLEMENT

1. A Party may not initiate proceedings under Article 22.5 (Commission—Good Offices, Conciliation, and Mediation) regarding a refusal to grant temporary entry under this Chapter or a particular case arising under Article 14.2 unless:

(a) the matter involves a pattern of practice; and

(b) the business person has exhausted the available administrative remedies regarding the particular matter.

2. The remedies referred to in paragraph (1)(b) shall be deemed to be exhausted if a final determination in the matter has not been issued by the competent authority within one year of the institution of an administrative proceeding, and the failure to issue a determination is not attributable to delay caused by the business person.

ARTICLE 14.7: RELATION TO OTHER CHAPTERS

1. Except for this Chapter, Chapters One (Initial Provisions), Two (General Definitions), Twenty-One (Administration of the Agreement), Twenty-Two (Dispute Settlement), and Twenty-Four (Final Provisions), and Articles 20.1 (Contact Points), 20.2 (Publication), 20.3 (Notification and Provision of Information), and 20.4 (Administrative Proceedings), no provision of this Agreement shall impose any obligation on a Party regarding its immigration measures.

2. Nothing in this Chapter shall be construed to impose obligations or commitments with respect to other Chapters of this Agreement.

ARTICLE 14.8: TRANSPARENCY IN DEVELOPMENT AND APPLICATION OF REGULATIONS[35]

1. Further to Chapter Twenty (Transparency), each Party shall establish or maintain appropriate mechanisms to respond to inquiries from interested persons regarding regulations relating to the temporary entry of business persons.

2. Further to Article 20.2 (Publication), to the extent possible, each Party shall, on request, provide to interested persons a concise statement addressing comments received on proposed regulations relating to the temporary entry of business persons at the time that it adopts the final regulations.

3. Further to Article 20.2 (Publication), to the extent possible, each Party shall allow a reasonable period of time between the date

[35] For greater certainty, "regulations" includes regulations establishing or applying to licensing authorization or criteria.

it publishes final regulations governing entry of business persons and the date they take effect.

4. Each Party shall, within a reasonable period after an application requesting temporary entry is considered complete under its domestic laws and regulations, inform the applicant of the decision concerning the application. At the request of the applicant, the Party shall provide, without undue delay, information concerning the status of the application.

ARTICLE 14.9: DEFINITIONS

For purposes of this Chapter:

business person means a national of a Party who is engaged in trade in goods, the supply of services, or the conduct of investment activities;

immigration measure means any law, regulation, or procedure affecting the entry and sojourn of aliens;

national has the same meaning as the term "natural person who has the nationality of a Party" as defined in Annex 2.1 (Country-Specific Definitions);

professional means a national of a Party who is engaged in a specialty occupation requiring:

(a) theoretical and practical application of a body of specialized knowledge, and

(b) attainment of a post-secondary degree in the specialty requiring four or more years of study[36] (or the equivalent of such a degree) as a minimum for entry into the occupation; and

temporary entry means entry into the territory of a Party by a business person of the other Party without the intent to establish permanent residence.

Chapter Fifteen

Electronic Commerce

ARTICLE 15.1: GENERAL PROVISIONS

1. The Parties recognize the economic growth and opportunity provided by electronic commerce and the importance of avoiding unnecessary barriers to its use and development.

2. Nothing in this Chapter shall be construed to prevent a Party from imposing internal taxes, directly or indirectly, on digital products, provided they are imposed in a manner consistent with this Agreement.

3. This Chapter is subject to any other relevant provisions, exceptions, or nonconforming measures set forth in other Chapters or Annexes of this Agreement.

[36] Chile recognizes the Baccalaureate Degree, Master's Degree, and the Doctoral Degree conferred by institutions in the United States as such degrees. The United States recognizes the licenciatura degree and titulo professional and higher degrees conferred by institutions in Chile as such degrees.

ARTICLE 15.2: ELECTRONIC SUPPLY OF SERVICES

The Parties recognize that the supply of a service using electronic means falls within the scope of the obligations contained in the relevant provisions of Chapter Eleven (Cross-Border Trade in Services) and Chapter Twelve (Financial Services), subject to any nonconforming measures or exceptions applicable to such obligations.[37]

ARTICLE 15.3: CUSTOMS DUTIES ON DIGITAL PRODUCTS

Neither Party may apply customs duties on digital products of the other Party.

ARTICLE 15.4: NON-DISCRIMINATION FOR DIGITAL PRODUCTS

1. A Party shall not accord less favorable treatment to a digital product than it accords to other like digital products, on the basis that:

(a) the digital product receiving less favorable treatment is created, produced, published, stored, transmitted, contracted for, commissioned, or first made available on commercial terms in the territory of the other Party; or

(b) the author, performer, producer, developer, or distributor of such digital products is a person of the other Party.[38]

2. (a) A Party shall not accord less favorable treatment to a digital product created, produced, published, stored, transmitted, contracted for, commissioned, or first made available on commercial terms in the territory of the other Party than it accords to a like digital product created, produced, published, stored, transmitted, contracted for, commissioned, or first made available on commercial terms in the territory of a non-Party.

(b) A Party shall not accord less favorable treatment to digital products whose author, performer, producer, developer, or distributor is a person of the other Party than it accords to like digital products whose author, performer, producer, developer, or distributor is a person of a non-Party.

3. A Party may maintain an existing measure that does not conform with paragraph 1 or 2 for one year after the date of entry into force of this Agreement. A Party may maintain the measure thereafter, if the treatment the Party accords under the measure is no less favorable than the treatment the Party accorded under the measure on the date of entry into force of this Agreement, and the Party has set out the measure in its Schedule to Annex 15.4. A Party may amend such a measure only to the extent that the amendment does not decrease the conformity of the measure, as it existed immediately before the amendment, with paragraphs 1 and 2.

---

[37] For greater certainty, nothing in this chapter imposes obligations to allow the electronic supply of a service nor the electronic transmission of content associated with those services except in accordance with the provisions of Chapter Eleven (Cross-Border Trade in Services) or Chapter Twelve (Financial Services), including their Annexes (Non-Conforming Measures).

[38] For greater certainty, if one or more of the criteria of para. 1(a) or (b) is satisfied, the obligation to accord no less favorable treatment to that digital product applies even if one or more of the activities listed in para. 1(a) occurs outside of the territory of the other Party, or one or more persons listed in para. 1(b) are persons of the other Party or a non-Party.

ARTICLE 15.5: COOPERATION

Having in mind the global nature of electronic commerce, the Parties recognize the importance of:

(a) working together to overcome obstacles encountered by small and medium enterprises in the use of electronic commerce;

(b) sharing information and experiences on regulations, laws, and programs in the sphere of electronic commerce, including those related to data privacy, consumer confidence, cyber-security, electronic signatures, intellectual property rights, and electronic government;

(c) working to maintain cross-border flows of information as an essential element for a vibrant electronic commerce environment;

(d) encouraging the development by the private sector of methods of selfregulation, including codes of conduct, model contracts, guidelines, and enforcement mechanisms that foster electronic commerce; and

(e) actively participating in international fora, at both a hemispheric and multilateral level, with the purpose of promoting the development of electronic commerce.

ARTICLE 15.6: DEFINITIONS

For purposes of this Chapter:

digital products means computer programs, text, video, images, sound recordings, and other products that are digitally encoded and transmitted electronically, regardless of whether a Party treats such products as a good or a service under its domestic law;[39]

electronic means means employing computer processing; and

electronic transmission or **transmitted electronically** means the transfer of digital products using any electromagnetic or photonic means.

Chapter Sixteen

Competition Policy, Designated Monopolies, and State Enterprises

ARTICLE 16.1: ANTICOMPETITIVE BUSINESS CONDUCT

1. Each Party shall adopt or maintain competition laws that proscribe anticompetitive business conduct, with the objective of promoting economic efficiency and consumer welfare, and shall take appropriate action with respect to such conduct.

2. Each Party shall maintain an authority responsible for the enforcement of its national competition laws. The enforcement policy of each Party's national competition authorities is not to discriminate on the basis of the nationality of the subjects of their proceedings. Each Party shall ensure that:

[39] For greater certainty, digital products do not include digitized representations of financial instruments, including money. The definition of digital products is without prejudice to the ongoing WTO discussions on whether trade in digital products transmitted electronically is a good or a service.

(a) before it imposes a sanction or remedy against any person for violating its competition law, it affords the person the right to be heard and to present evidence, except that it may provide for the person to be heard and present evidence within a reasonable time after it imposes an interim sanction or remedy; and

(b) an independent court or tribunal imposes or, at the person's request, reviews any such sanction or remedy.

3. Nothing in this Chapter shall be construed to infringe each Party's autonomy in developing its competition policies or in deciding how to enforce its competition laws.

ARTICLE 16.2: COOPERATION

The Parties agree to cooperate in the area of competition policy. The Parties recognize the importance of cooperation and coordination between their respective authorities to further effective competition law enforcement in the free trade area. Accordingly, the Parties shall cooperate on issues of competition law enforcement, including notification, consultation, and exchange of information relating to the enforcement of the Parties' competition laws and policies.

ARTICLE 16.3: DESIGNATED MONOPOLIES

1. Nothing in this Chapter shall be construed to prevent a Party from designating a monopoly.

2. Where a Party designates a monopoly and the designation may affect the interests of persons of the other Party, the Party shall:

(a) at the time of the designation endeavor to introduce such conditions on the operation of the monopoly as will minimize or eliminate any nullification or impairment of benefits in the sense of Annex 22.2 (Nullification or Impairment); and

(b) provide written notification, in advance wherever possible, to the other Party of the designation and any such conditions.

3. Each Party shall ensure that any privately-owned monopoly that it designates after the date of entry into force of this Agreement and any government monopoly that it designates or has designated:

(a) acts in a manner that is not inconsistent with the Party's obligations under this Agreement wherever such a monopoly exercises any regulatory, administrative, or other governmental authority that the Party has delegated to it in connection with the monopoly good or service, such as the power to grant import or export licenses, approve commercial transactions, or impose quotas, fees, or other charges;

(b) acts solely in accordance with commercial considerations in its purchase or sale of the monopoly good or service in the relevant market, including with regard to price, quality, availability, marketability, transportation, and other terms and conditions of purchase or sale, except to comply with any terms of its designation that are not inconsistent with subparagraph (c) or (d);

(c) provides non-discriminatory treatment to covered investments, to goods of the other Party, and to service suppliers of the other Party in its purchase or sale of the monopoly good or service in the relevant market; and

(d) does not use its monopoly position to engage, either directly or indirectly, including through its dealings with its parent, subsidiaries, or other enterprises with common ownership, in anticompetitive practices in a nonmonopolized market in its territory that adversely affect covered investments.

4. This Article does not apply to procurement.

Article 16.4: State Enterprises

1. Nothing in this Agreement shall be construed to prevent a Party from establishing or maintaining a state enterprise.

2. Each Party shall ensure that any state enterprise that it establishes or maintains acts in a manner that is not inconsistent with the Party's obligations under this Agreement wherever such enterprise exercises any regulatory, administrative, or other governmental authority that the Party has delegated to it, such as the power to expropriate, grant licenses, approve commercial transactions, or impose quotas, fees, or other charges.

3. Each Party shall ensure that any state enterprise that it establishes or maintains accords non-discriminatory treatment in the sale of its goods or services to covered investments.

Article 16.5: Differences in Pricing

The charging of different prices in different markets, or within the same market, where such differences are based on normal commercial considerations, such as taking account of supply and demand conditions, is not in itself inconsistent with Articles 16.3 and 16.4.

Article 16.6: Transparency and Information Requests

1. The Parties recognize the value of transparency of government competition policies.

2. On request, each Party shall make available to the other Party public information concerning its:

(a) competition law enforcement activities; and

(b) state enterprises and designated monopolies, public or private, at any level of government.

Requests under subparagraph (b) shall indicate the entities or localities involved, specify the particular products and markets concerned, and include indicia of practices that may restrict trade or investment between the Parties.

3. On request, each Party shall make available to the other Party public information concerning exemptions provided under its competition laws. Requests shall specify the particular goods and markets of interest and include indicia that the exemption may restrict trade or investment between the Parties.

ARTICLE 16.7: CONSULTATIONS

To foster understanding between the Parties, or to address specific matters that arise under this Chapter, each Party shall, on request of the other Party, enter into consultations regarding representations made by the other Party. In its request, the Party shall indicate, if relevant, how the matter affects trade or investment between the Parties. The Party addressed shall accord full and sympathetic consideration to the concerns of the other Party.

ARTICLE 16.8: DISPUTES

Neither Party may have recourse to dispute settlement under this Agreement for any matter arising under Article 16.1, 16.2, or 16.7.

ARTICLE 16.9: DEFINITIONS

For purposes of this Chapter:

a **delegation** includes a legislative grant, and a government order, directive, or other act, transferring to the monopoly or state enterprise, or authorizing the exercise by the monopoly or state enterprise of, governmental authority;

designate means to establish, designate, or authorize, formally or in effect, a monopoly or to expand the scope of a monopoly to cover an additional good or service;

government monopoly means a monopoly that is owned, or controlled through ownership interests, by the national government of a Party or by another such monopoly;

in accordance with commercial considerations means consistent with normal business practices of privately-held enterprises in the relevant business or industry;

market means the geographic and commercial market for a good or service;

monopoly means an entity, including a consortium or government agency, that in any relevant market in the territory of a Party is designated as the sole provider or purchaser of a good or service, but does not include an entity that has been granted an exclusive intellectual property right solely by reason of such grant; and

non-discriminatory treatment means the better of national treatment and most-favored-nation treatment, as set out in the relevant provisions of this Agreement.

Chapter Seventeen

Intellectual Property Rights

The Parties,

DESIRING to reduce distortions and impediments to trade between the Parties;

DESIRING to enhance the intellectual property systems of the two Parties to account for the latest technological developments and to ensure that measures and procedures to enforce intellectual property rights do not themselves become barriers to legitimate trade;

DESIRING to promote greater efficiency and transparency in the administration of intellectual property systems of the Parties;

DESIRING to build on the foundations established in existing international agreements in the field of intellectual property, including the World Trade Organization (WTO) Agreement on Trade-Related Aspects of Intellectual Property Rights (TRIPS Agreement) and affirming the rights and obligations set forth in the TRIPS Agreement;

RECOGNIZING the principles set out in the Declaration on the TRIPS Agreement on Public Health, adopted on November 14, 2001, by the WTO at the Fourth WTO Ministerial Conference, held in Doha, Qatar;

EMPHASIZING that the protection and enforcement of intellectual property rights is a fundamental principle of this Chapter that helps promote technological innovation as well as the transfer and dissemination of technology to the mutual advantage of technology producers and users, and that encourages the development of social and economic well-being;

CONVINCED of the importance of efforts to encourage private and public investment for research, development, and innovation;

RECOGNIZING that the business community of each Party should be encouraged to participate in programs and initiatives for research, development, innovation, and the transfer of technology implemented by the other Party;

RECOGNIZING the need to achieve a balance between the rights of right holders and the legitimate interests of users and the community with regard to protected works;

AGREE AS FOLLOWS:

ARTICLE 17.1: GENERAL PROVISIONS

1. Each Party shall give effect to the provisions of this Chapter and may, but shall not be obliged to, implement in its domestic law more extensive protection than is required by this Chapter, provided that such protection does not contravene the provisions of this Chapter.

2. Before January 1, 2007, each Party shall ratify or accede to the *Patent Cooperation Treaty* (1984).

3. Before January 1, 2009, each Party shall ratify or accede to:

(a) the *International Convention for the Protection of New Varieties of Plants* (1991);

(b) the *Trademark Law Treaty* (1994); and

(c) the *Convention Relating to the Distribution of Programme-Carrying Signals Transmitted by Satellite* (1974).

4. Each Party shall undertake reasonable efforts to ratify or accede to the following agreements in a manner consistent with its domestic law:

(a) the *Patent Law Treaty* (2000);

(b) the *Hague Agreement Concerning the International Registration of Industrial Designs* (1999); and

(c) the *Protocol Relating to the Madrid Agreement Concerning the International Registration of Marks* (1989).

5. Nothing in this Chapter concerning intellectual property rights shall derogate from the obligations and rights of one Party with respect to the other by virtue of the TRIPS Agreement or multilateral intellectual property agreements concluded or administered under the auspices of the World Intellectual Property Organization (WIPO).

6. In respect of all categories of intellectual property covered in this Chapter, each Party shall accord to persons of the other Party treatment no less favorable than it accords to its own persons with regard to the protection[40] and enjoyment of such intellectual property rights and any benefits derived from such rights. With respect to secondary uses of phonograms by means of analog communications and free over-the-air radio broadcasting, however, a Party may limit the rights of the performers and producers of the other Party to the rights its persons are accorded within the jurisdiction of the other Party.

7. Each Party may derogate from paragraph 6 in relation to its judicial and administrative procedures, including the designation of an address for service or the appointment of an agent within the jurisdiction of that Party, only where such derogations are necessary to secure compliance with laws and regulations that are not inconsistent with the provisions of this Chapter and where such practices are not applied in a manner that would constitute a disguised restriction on trade.

8. Paragraphs 6 and 7 do not apply to procedures provided in multilateral agreements concluded under the auspices of WIPO relating to the acquisition or maintenance of intellectual property rights.

9. This Chapter does not give rise to obligations in respect of acts that occurred before the date of entry into force of this Agreement.

10. Except as otherwise provided for in this Chapter, this Chapter gives rise to obligations in respect of all subject matter existing at the date of entry into force of this Agreement, and which is protected by a Party on that date, or which meets or comes subsequently to meet the criteria for protection under the terms of this Chapter. In respect of paragraphs 10 and 11, copyright and related rights obligations with respect to existing works and phonograms shall be determined solely under Article 17.7(7).

11. Neither Party shall be obligated to restore protection to subject matter which on the date of entry into force of this Chapter has fallen into the public domain in that Party.

12. Each Party shall ensure that all laws, regulations, and procedures concerning the protection or enforcement of intellectual property rights, and all final judicial decisions and administrative rulings of general applicability pertaining to the enforcement of such rights, shall be in writing and shall be published,[41] or where such

[40] For purposes of paras. 6 and 7, "protection" shall include matters affecting the availability, acquisition, scope, maintenance, and enforcement of intellectual property rights as well as matters affecting the use of intellectual property rights specifically covered by this chapter. For purposes of paras. 6 and 7, "protection" shall also include the prohibition on circumvention of effective technological measures pursuant to Article 17.7(5) and the provisions concerning rights management information pursuant to Article 17.7(6).

[41] The requirement for publication is satisfied by making the written document available to the public via the Internet.

publication is not practicable, made publicly available, in a national language in such a manner as to enable the other Party and right holders to become acquainted with them, with the object of making the protection and enforcement of intellectual property rights transparent. Nothing in this paragraph shall require a Party to disclose confidential information the disclosure of which would impede law enforcement or otherwise be contrary to the public interest or would prejudice the legitimate commercial interests of particular enterprises, public or private.

13. Nothing in this Chapter prevents a Party from adopting measures necessary to prevent anticompetitive practices that may result from the abuse of the intellectual property rights set forth in this Chapter.

14. For the purposes of strengthening the development and protection of intellectual property, and implementing the obligations of this Chapter, the Parties will cooperate, on mutually agreed terms and subject to the availability of appropriated funds, by means of:

(a) educational and dissemination projects on the use of intellectual property as a research and innovation tool, as well as on the enforcement of intellectual property;

(b) appropriate coordination, training, specialization courses, and exchange of information between the intellectual property offices and other institutions of the Parties; and

(c) enhancing the knowledge, development, and implementation of the electronic systems used for the management of intellectual property.

ARTICLE 17.2: TRADEMARKS

1. Each Party shall provide that trademarks shall include collective, certification, and sound marks, and may include geographical indications[42] and scent marks. Neither Party is obligated to treat certification marks as a separate category in its domestic law, provided that the signs as such are protected.

2. Each Party shall afford an opportunity for interested parties to oppose the application for a trademark.

3. Pursuant to Article 20 of the TRIPS Agreement, each Party shall ensure that any measures mandating the use of the term customary in common language as the common name for a good ("common name") including, *inter alia*, requirements concerning the relative size, placement, or style of use of the trademark in relation to the common name, do not impair the use or effectiveness of trademarks used in relation to such good.

4. Each Party shall provide that the owner of a registered trademark shall have the exclusive right to prevent third parties not

[42] A geographical indication is capable of constituting a trademark to the extent that the geographical indication consists of any sign, or any combination of signs, capable of identifying a good or service as originating in the territory of a Party, or a region or locality in that territory, where a given quality, reputation, or other characteristic of the good or service is essentially attributable to its geographical origin.

having the owner's consent from using in the course of trade identical or similar signs, including subsequent geographical indications, for goods or services that are related to those goods or services in respect of which the trademark is registered, where such use would result in a likelihood of confusion.[43]

5. Each Party may provide limited exceptions to the rights conferred by a trademark, such as fair use of descriptive terms, provided that such exceptions take account of the legitimate interests of the owner of the trademark and of third parties.

6. Article *6bis of the Paris Convention for the Protection of Industrial Property* (1967) (Paris Convention) shall apply, *mutatis mutandis*, to goods or services which are not similar to those identified by a well-known trademark, whether registered or not, provided that use of that trademark in relation to those goods or services would indicate a connection between those goods or services and the owner of the trademark and provided that the interests of the owner of the trademark are likely to be damaged by such use.

7. Each Party shall, according to its domestic law, provide for appropriate measures to prohibit or cancel the registration of a trademark identical or similar to a well-known trademark, if the use of that trademark by the registration applicant is likely to cause confusion, or to cause mistake, or to deceive or risk associating the trademark with the owner of the well-known trademark, or constitutes unfair exploitation of the reputation of the trademark. Such measures to prohibit or cancel registration shall not apply when the registration applicant is the owner of the well-known trademark.

8. In determining whether a trademark is well-known, a Party shall not require that the reputation of the trademark extend beyond the sector of the public that normally deals with the relevant goods or services.

9. Each Party recognizes the importance of the *Joint Recommendation Concerning Provisions on the Protection of Well-Known Marks* (1999), adopted by the Assembly of the Paris Union for the Protection of Industrial Property and the General Assembly of WIPO and shall be guided by the principles contained in this Recommendation.

10. Each Party shall provide a system for the registration of trademarks, which shall include:

(a) providing to the applicant a communication in writing, which may be electronic, of the reasons for any refusal to register a trademark;

(b) providing to the applicant an opportunity to respond to communications from the trademark authorities, contest an initial refusal, and appeal judicially any final refusal to register; and

(c) a requirement that decisions in opposition or cancellation proceedings be reasoned and in writing.

11. Each Party shall work to provide, to the maximum degree practical, a system for the electronic application, processing, registration, and maintenance of trademarks.

---

[43] It is understood that likelihood of confusion is to be determined under the domestic trademark law of each Party.

12. In relation to trademarks, Parties are encouraged to classify goods and services according to the classification of the *Nice Agreement Concerning the International Classification of Goods and Services for the Purposes of the Registration of Marks* (1979). In addition, each Party shall provide that:

(a) each registration or publication which concerns a trademark application or registration and which indicates the relevant goods or services shall indicate the goods or services by their names; and

(b) goods or services may not be considered as being similar to each other simply on the ground that, in any registration or publication, they appear in the same class of any classification system, including the Nice Classification. Conversely, goods or services may not be considered as being dissimilar from each other simply on the ground that, in any registration or publication, they appear in different classes of any classification system, including the Nice Classification.

Article 17.3: Domain Names on the Internet

1. Each Party shall require that the management of its country-code top level domain (ccTLD) provide an appropriate procedure for the settlement of disputes, based on the principles established in the *Uniform Domain-Name Dispute-Resolution Policy* (UDRP), in order to address the problem of trademark cyber-piracy.

2. Each Party shall, in addition, require that the management of its respective ccTLD provide online public access to a reliable and accurate database of contact information for domain-name registrants, in accordance with each Party's law regarding protection of personal data.

Article 17.4: Geographical Indications [44]

1. Geographical indications, for the purposes of this Article, are indications which identify a good as originating in the territory of a Party, or a region or locality in that territory, where a given quality, reputation, or other characteristic of the good is essentially attributable to its geographical origin. Any sign or combination of signs (such as words, including geographical and personal names, letters, numerals, figurative elements, and colors), in any form whatsoever, shall be eligible for protection or recognition as a geographical indication.

2. Chile shall:

(a) provide the legal means to identify and protect geographical indications of United States persons that meet the criteria in paragraph 1; and

(b) provide to United States geographical indications of wines and spirits the same recognition as Chile accords to wines and spirits under the Chilean geographical indications registration system.

3. The United States shall:

[44] For the purposes of this Article, persons of a Party shall also mean government agencies.

(a) provide the legal means to identify and protect the geographical indications of Chile that meet the criteria in paragraph 1; and

(b) provide to Chilean geographical indications of wines and spirits the same recognition as the United States accords to wines and spirits under the Certificate of Label Approval (COLA) system as administered by the Alcohol and Tobacco Tax and Trade Bureau, Department of Treasury (TTB), or any successor agencies. Names that Chile desires to be included in the regulation set forth in 27 CFR Part 12 (Foreign Non-generic), or any successor to that regulation, will be governed by paragraph 4 of this Article.

4. Each Party shall provide the means for persons of the other Party to apply for protection or petition for recognition of geographical indications. Each Party shall accept applications or petitions, as the case may be, without the requirement for intercession by a Party on behalf of its persons.

5. Each Party shall process applications or petitions, as the case may be, for geographical indications with a minimum of formalities.

6. Each Party shall make the regulations governing filing of such applications or petitions, as the case may be, available to the public in both printed and electronic form.

7. Each Party shall ensure that applications or petitions, as the case may be, for geographical indications are published for opposition, and shall provide procedures to effect opposition of geographical indications that are the subject of applications or petitions. Each Party shall also provide procedures to cancel any registration resulting from an application or a petition.

8. Each Party shall ensure that measures governing the filing of applications or petitions, as the case may be, for geographical indications set out clearly the procedures for these actions. Such procedures shall include contact information sufficient for applicants or petitioners to obtain specific procedural guidance regarding the processing of applications or petitions.

9. The Parties acknowledge the principle of exclusivity incorporated in the Paris Convention and TRIPS Agreement, with respect to rights in trademarks.

10. After the date of entry into force of this Agreement, each Party shall ensure that grounds for refusing protection or registration of a geographical indication include the following:

(a) the geographical indication is confusingly similar to a pre-existing pending good faith application for a trademark or a pre-existing trademark registered in that Party; or

(b) the geographical indication is confusingly similar to a pre-existing trademark, the rights to which have been acquired through use in good faith in that Party.

11. Within six months of the entry into force of this Agreement, each Party shall communicate to the public the means by which it intends to implement paragraphs 2 through 10.

ARTICLE 17.5: COPYRIGHT[45]

1. Each Party shall provide that authors[46] of literary and artistic works have the right[47] to authorize or prohibit all reproductions of their works, in any manner or form, permanent or temporary (including temporary storage in electronic form).

2. Without prejudice to the provisions of Articles 11(1)(ii), 11*bis*(1)(i) and (ii), 11*ter*(1)(ii), 14(1)(ii), and 14*bis*(1) of the *Berne Convention for the Protection of Literary and Artistic Works* (1971) (Berne Convention), each Party shall provide to authors of literary and artistic works the right to authorize or prohibit the communication to the public of their works, by wire or wireless means, including the making available to the public of their works in such a way that members of the public may access these works from a place and at a time individually chosen by them.[48]

3. Each Party shall provide to authors of literary and artistic works the right to authorize the making available to the public of the original and copies[49] of their works through sale or other transfer of ownership.

4. Each Party shall provide that where the term of protection of a work (including a photographic work) is calculated:

(a) on the basis of the life of a natural person, the term shall be not less than the life of the author and 70 years after the author's death; and

(b) on a basis other than the life of a natural person, the term shall be

(i) not less than 70 years from the end of the calendar year of the first authorized publication of the work, or

(ii) failing such authorized publication within 50 years from the creation of the work, not less than 70 years from the end of the calendar year of the creation of the work.

ARTICLE 17.6: RELATED RIGHTS[50]

1. Each Party shall provide that performers and producers of phonograms[51] have the right to authorize or prohibit all reproductions of their performances or phonograms, in any manner or form, permanent or temporary (including temporary storage in electronic form).

---

[45] Except as provided in Article 17.12(2), each Party shall give effect to this Article upon the date of entry into force of this Agreement.

[46] References to "authors" in this chapter refer also to any successors in interest.

[47] With respect to copyrights and related rights in this chapter, a right to authorize or prohibit or a right to authorize shall mean an exclusive right.

[48] It is understood that the mere provision of physical facilities for enabling or making a communication does not in itself amount to communication within the meaning of this chapter or the Berne Convention. It is further understood that nothing in this Article precludes a Party from applying Article 11*bis*(2) of the Berne Convention.

[49] The expressions "copies" and "original and copies", being subject to the right of distribution under this paragraph, refer exclusively to fixed copies that can be put into circulation as tangible objects, i.e., for this purpose, "copies" means physical copies.

[50] Except as provided in Article 17.12(2), each Party shall give effect to this Article upon the date of entry into force of this Agreement.

[51] References to "performers and producers of phonograms" in this chapter refer also to any successors in interest.

2. Each Party shall provide to performers and producers of phonograms the right to authorize the making available to the public of the original and copies[52] of their performances or phonograms through sale or other transfer of ownership.

3. Each Party shall accord the rights provided under this Chapter to the performers and producers of phonograms who are persons of the other Party and to performances or phonograms first published or first fixed in a Party. A performance or phonogram shall be considered first published in any Party in which it is published within 30 days of its original publication.[53]

4. Each Party shall provide to performers the right to authorize or prohibit:

(a) the broadcasting and communication to the public of their unfixed performances except where the performance is already a broadcast performance, and

(b) the fixation of their unfixed performances.

5. (a) Each Party shall provide to performers and producers of phonograms the right to authorize or prohibit the broadcasting or any communication to the public of their fixed performances or phonograms, by wire or wireless means, including the making available to the public of those performances and phonograms in such a way that members of the public may access them from a place and at a time individually chosen by them.

(b) Notwithstanding paragraph 5(a) and Article 17.7(3), the right to authorize or prohibit the broadcasting or communication to the public of performances or phonograms through analog communication and free over-the-air broadcasting, and the exceptions or limitations to this right for such activities, shall be a matter of domestic law. Each Party may adopt exceptions and limitations, including compulsory licenses, to the right to authorize or prohibit the broadcasting or communication to the public of performances or phonograms in respect of other noninteractive transmissions in accordance with Article 17.7(3). Such compulsory licenses shall not prejudice the right of the performer or producer of a phonogram to obtain equitable remuneration.

6. Neither Party shall subject the enjoyment and exercise of the rights of performers and producers of phonograms provided for in this Chapter to any formality.

7. Each Party shall provide that where the term of protection of a performance or phonogram is to be calculated on a basis other than the life of a natural person, the term shall be:

(a) not less than 70 years from the end of the calendar year of the first authorized publication of the performance or phonogram, or

(b) failing such authorized publication within 50 years from the fixation of the performance or phonogram, not less than 70 years from the end of the calendar year of the fixation of the performance or phonogram.

---

[52] The expressions "copies" and "original and copies", being subject to the right of distribution under this paragraph, refer exclusively to fixed copies that can be put into circulation as tangible objects, i.e., for this purpose, "copies" means physical copies.

[53] For the application of Article 17.6(3), fixation means the finalization of the master tape or its equivalent.

8. For the purposes of Articles 17.6 and 17.7, the following definitions apply with respect to performers and producers of phonograms:

(a) **performers** means actors, singers, musicians, dancers, and other persons who act, sing, deliver, declaim, play in, interpret, or otherwise perform literary or artistic works or expressions of folklore;

(b) **phonogram** means the fixation of the sounds of a performance or of other sounds, or of a representation of sounds, other than in the form of a fixation incorporated in a cinematographic or other audiovisual work;[54]

(c) **fixation** means the embodiment of sounds, or of the representations thereof, from which they can be perceived, reproduced, or communicated through a device;

(d) **producer of a phonogram** means the person, or the legal entity, who or which takes the initiative and has the responsibility for the first fixation of the sounds of a performance or other sounds, or the representations of sounds;

(e) **publication of a fixed performance or a phonogram** means the offering of copies of the fixed performance or the phonogram to the public, with the consent of the right holder, and provided that copies are offered to the public in reasonable quantity;

(f) **broadcasting** means the transmission by wireless means for public reception of sounds or of images and sounds or of the representations thereof; such transmission by satellite is also broadcasting; transmission of encrypted signals is broadcasting where the means for decrypting are provided to the public by the broadcasting organization or with its consent; and

(g) **communication to the public of a performance or a phonogram** means the transmission to the public by any medium, otherwise than by broadcasting, of sounds of a performance or the sounds or the representations of sounds fixed in a phonogram. For the purposes of Article 17.6(5) "communication to the public" includes making the sounds or representations of sounds fixed in a phonogram audible to the public.

ARTICLE 17.7: OBLIGATIONS COMMON TO COPYRIGHT AND RELATED RIGHTS[55]

1. Each Party shall establish that in cases where authorization is needed from both the author of a work embodied in a phonogram and a performer or producer owning rights in the phonogram, the need for the authorization of the author does not cease to exist because the authorization of the performer and producer is also required. Likewise, each Party shall establish that in cases where authorization is needed from both the author of a work embodied in a phonogram and a performer or producer owning rights in the

[54] It is understood that the definition of phonogram provided in this chapter does not suggest that rights in the phonogram are in any way affected through their incorporation into a cinematographic or other audiovisual work.

[55] Except as provided in Article 17.12(2), each Party shall give effect to this Article upon the date of entry into force of this Agreement.

phonogram, the need for the authorization of the performer or producer does not cease to exist because the authorization of the author is also required.

2. (a) Each Party shall provide that for copyright and related rights:

(i) any person owning any economic right, i.e., not a moral right, may freely and separately transfer such right by contract; and

(ii) any person who has acquired or owns any such economic right by virtue of a contract, including contracts of employment underlying the creation of works and phonograms, shall be permitted to exercise that right in its own name and enjoy fully the benefits derived from that right.

(b) Each Party may establish:

(i) which contracts of employment underlying the creation of works or phonograms shall, in the absence of a written agreement, result in a transfer of economic rights by operation of law; and

(ii) reasonable limits to the provisions in paragraph 2(a) to protect the interests of the original right holders, taking into account the legitimate interests of the transferees.

3. Each Party shall confine limitations or exceptions to rights to certain special cases which do not conflict with a normal exploitation of the work, performance, or phonogram, and do not unreasonably prejudice the legitimate interests of the right holder.[56]

4. In order to confirm that all federal or central government agencies use computer software only as authorized, each Party shall issue appropriate laws, orders, regulations, or administrative or executive decrees to actively regulate the acquisition and management of software for such government use. Such measures may take the form of procedures such as preparing and maintaining inventories of software present on agencies' computers and inventories of software licenses.

5. In order to provide adequate legal protection and effective legal remedies against the circumvention of effective technological measures that are used by authors, performers, and producers of phonograms in connection with the exercise of their rights and that restrict unauthorized acts in respect of their works, performances, and phonograms, protected by copyright and related rights:

(a) each Party shall provide that any person who knowingly[57] circumvents without authorization of the right holder

---

[56] Article 17.7(3) permits a Party to carry forward and appropriately extend into the digital environment limitations and exceptions in its domestic laws which have been considered acceptable under the Berne Convention. Similarly, these provisions permit a Party to devise new exceptions and limitations that are appropriate in the digital network environment. For works, other than computer software, and other subject-matter, such exceptions and limitations may include temporary acts of reproduction which are transient or incidental and an integral and essential part of a technological process and whose sole purpose is to enable (a) a lawful transmission in a network between third parties by an intermediary; or (b) a lawful use of a work or other subject-matter to be made; and which have no independent economic significance.

Article 17.7(3) neither reduces nor extends the scope of applicability of the limitations and exceptions permitted by the Berne Convention, the *WIPO Copyright Treaty* (1996), and the *WIPO Performances and Phonograms Treaty* (1996).

[57] For purposes of para. 5, knowledge may be demonstrated through reasonable evidence taking into account the facts and circumstances surrounding the alleged illegal act.

or law consistent with this Agreement any effective technological measure that controls access to a protected work, performance, or phonogram shall be civilly liable and, in appropriate circumstances, shall be criminally liable, or said conduct shall be considered an aggravating circumstance of another offense.[58] No Party is required to impose civil or criminal liability for a person who circumvents any effective technological measure that protects any of the exclusive rights of copyright or related rights in a protected work, but does not control access to such work.

(b) each Party shall also provide administrative or civil measures, and, where the conduct is willful and for prohibited commercial purposes, criminal measures with regard to the manufacture, import, distribution, sale, or rental of devices, products, or components or the provision of services which:

(i) are promoted, advertised, or marketed for the purpose of circumvention of any effective technological measure, or

(ii) do not have a commercially significant purpose or use other than to circumvent any effective technological measure, or

(iii) are primarily designed, produced, adapted, or performed for the purpose of enabling or facilitating the circumvention of any effective technological measures.

Each Party shall ensure that due account is given, inter alia, to the scientific or educational purpose of the conduct of the defendant in applying criminal measures under any provisions implementing this subparagraph. A Party may exempt from criminal liability, and if carried out in good faith without knowledge that the conduct is prohibited, from civil liability, acts prohibited under this subparagraph that are carried out in connection with a nonprofit library, archive or educational institution.

(c) Each Party shall ensure that nothing in subparagraphs (a) and (b) affects rights, remedies, limitations, or defenses with respect to copyright or related rights infringement.

(d) Each Party shall confine limitations and exceptions to measures implementing subparagraphs (a) and (b) to certain special cases that do not impair the adequacy of legal protection or the effectiveness of legal remedies against the circumvention of effective technological measures. In particular, each Party may establish exemptions and limitations to address the following situations and activities in accordance with subparagraph (e):

(i) when an actual or likely adverse effect on noninfringing uses with respect to a particular class of works or exceptions or limitation to copyright or related rights with respect to a class of users is demonstrated or recognized through a legislative or administrative proceeding established by law, provided that any limitation or exception adopted in reliance upon this subparagraph (d)(i) shall

[58] Para. 5 does not obligate a Party to require that the design of, or the design and selection of parts and components for, a consumer electronics, telecommunications, or computing product provide for a response to any particular technological measure, so long as such product does not otherwise violate any measure implementing para. 5(b).

have effect for a period of not more than three years from the date of conclusion of such proceeding;

(ii) noninfringing reverse engineering activities with regard to a lawfully obtained copy of a computer program, carried out in good faith with respect to particular elements of that computer program that have not been readily available to that person,[59] for the sole purpose of achieving interoperability of an independently created computer program with other programs;[60]

(iii) noninfringing good faith activities, carried out by a researcher who has lawfully obtained a copy, performance, or display of a work, and who has made a reasonable attempt to obtain authorization for such activities, to the extent necessary for the sole purpose of identifying and analyzing flaws and vulnerabilities of encryption technologies;[61]

(iv) the inclusion of a component or part for the sole purpose of preventing the access of minors to inappropriate online content in a technology, product, service, or device that does not itself violate any measures implementing subparagraphs (a) and (b);

(v) noninfringing good faith activities that are authorized by the owner of a computer, computer system, or computer network for the sole purpose of testing, investigating, or correcting the security of that computer, computer system, or computer network;

(vi) noninfringing activities for the sole purpose of identifying and disabling a capability to carry out undisclosed collection or dissemination of personally identifying information reflecting the online activities of a natural person in a way that has no other effect on the ability of any person to gain access to any work;

(vii) lawfully authorized activities carried out by government employees, agents, or contractors for the purpose of law enforcement, intelligence, or similar government activities; and

(viii) access by a nonprofit library, archive, or educational institution to a work not otherwise available to it, for the sole purpose of making acquisition decisions.

(e) Each Party may apply the exceptions and limitations for the situations and activities set forth in subparagraph (d) as follows:

(i) any measure implementing subparagraph (a) may be subject to the exceptions and limitations with respect to each situation and activity set forth in subparagraph (d).

---

[59] For greater certainty, elements of a computer program are not readily available to a person seeking to engage in noninfringing reverse engineering when they cannot be obtained from the literature on the subject, from the copyright holder, or from sources in the public domain.

[60] Such activity occurring in the course of research and development is not excluded from this exception.

[61] Such activity occurring in the course of research and development is not excluded from this exception.

(ii) any measure implementing subparagraph (b), as it applies to effective technological measures that control access to a work, may be subject to exceptions and limitations with respect to the activities set forth in subparagraphs (d)(ii), (iii), (iv), (v), and (vii).

(iii) any measure implementing subparagraph (b), as it applies to effective technological measures that protect any copyright or any rights related to copyright, may be subject to exceptions and limitations with respect to the activities set forth in subparagraph (d)(ii) and (vii).

(f) **Effective technological measure** means any technology, device, or component that, in the normal course of its operation, controls access to a work, performance, phonogram, or any other protected material, or that protects any copyright or any rights related to copyright, and cannot, in the usual case, be circumvented accidentally.

6. In order to provide adequate and effective legal remedies to protect rights management information:

(a) each Party shall provide that any person who without authority, and knowing, or, with respect to civil remedies, having reasonable grounds to know, that it will induce, enable, facilitate, or conceal an infringement of any copyright or related right,

(i) knowingly removes or alters any rights management information;

(ii) distributes or imports for distribution rights management information knowing that the rights management information has been altered without authority; or

(iii) distributes, imports for distribution, broadcasts, communicates, or makes available to the public copies of works or phonograms, knowing that rights management information has been removed or altered without authority,

shall be liable, upon the suit of any injured person, and subject to the remedies in Article 17.11(5). Each Party shall provide for application of criminal procedures and remedies at least in cases where acts prohibited in the subparagraph are done willfully and for purposes of commercial advantage. A Party may exempt from criminal liability prohibited acts done in connection with a nonprofit library, archive, educational institution, or broadcasting entity established without a profit-making purpose.

(b) **Rights management information** means:

(i) information which identifies a work, performance, or phonogram; the author of the work, the performer of the performance, or the producer of the phonogram; or the owner of any right in the work, performance, or phonogram;

(ii) information about the terms and conditions of the use of the work, performance, or phonogram; and

(iii) any numbers or codes that represent such information,

when any of these items is attached to a copy of the work, performance, or phonogram or appears in conjunction with the communication or making available of a work, performance, or phonogram to the public. Nothing in paragraph 6(a) requires the owner of any right in the work, performance, or phonogram to attach rights management information to copies of the owner's work, performance, or phonogram or to cause rights management information to appear in connection with a communication of the work, performance, or phonogram to the public.

7. Each Party shall apply Article 18 of the Berne Convention, *mutatis mutandis*, to all the protections of copyright and related rights and effective technological measures and rights management information in Articles 17.5, 17.6, and 17.7.

ARTICLE 17.8: PROTECTION OF ENCRYPTED PROGRAM-CARRYING SATELLITE SIGNALS

1. Each Party shall make it:

(a) a civil or criminal offense to manufacture, assemble, modify, import, export, sell, lease, or otherwise distribute a tangible or intangible device or system, knowing[62] that the device or system's principal function is solely to assist in decoding an encrypted program-carrying satellite signal without the authorization of the lawful distributor of such signal; and

(b) a civil or criminal offense willfully to receive or further distribute an encrypted program-carrying satellite signal knowing that it has been decoded without the authorization of the lawful distributor of the signal.

2. Each Party shall provide that any person injured by any activity described in subparagraphs 1(a) or 1(b), including any person that holds an interest in the encrypted programming signal or the content of that signal, shall be permitted to initiate a civil action under any measure implementing such subparagraphs.

ARTICLE 17.9: PATENTS

1. Each Party shall make patents available for any invention, whether a product or a process, in all fields of technology, provided that the invention is new, involves an inventive step, and is capable of industrial application. For purposes of this Article, a Party may treat the terms "inventive step" and "capable of industrial application" as being synonymous with the terms "non-obvious" and "useful" respectively.

2. Each Party will undertake reasonable efforts, through a transparent and participatory process, to develop and propose legislation within 4 years from the entry into force of this Agreement that makes available patent protection for plants that are new, involve an inventive step, and are capable of industrial application.

3. Each Party may provide limited exceptions to the exclusive rights conferred by a patent, provided that such exceptions do not unreasonably conflict with a normal exploitation of the patent and do not unreasonably prejudice the legitimate interests of the patent owner, taking account of the legitimate interests of third parties.

---

[62] For purposes of para. 1, knowledge may be demonstrated through reasonable evidence, taking into account the facts and circumstances surrounding the alleged illegal act.

4. If a Party permits the use by a third party of the subject matter of a subsisting patent to support an application for marketing approval or sanitary permit of a pharmaceutical product, the Party shall provide that any product produced under such authority shall not be made, used, or sold in the territory of the Party other than for purposes related to meeting requirements for marketing approval or the sanitary permit, and if export is permitted, the product shall only be exported outside the territory of the Party for purposes of meeting requirements for issuing marketing approval or sanitary permits in the exporting Party.

5. A Party may revoke or cancel a patent only when grounds exist that would have justified a refusal to grant the patent.[63]

6. Each Party shall provide for the adjustment of the term of a patent, at the request of the patent owner, to compensate for unreasonable delays that occur in granting the patent. For the purposes of this paragraph, an unreasonable delay shall be understood to include a delay in the issuance of the patent of more than five years from the date of filing of the application in the Party, or three years after a request for examination of the application has been made, whichever is later, provided that periods of time attributable to actions of the patent applicant need not be included in the determination of such delays.

7. Neither Party shall use a public disclosure to bar patentability based upon a lack of novelty or inventive step if the public disclosure (a) was made or authorized by, or derived from, the patent applicant and (b) occurs within 12 months prior to the date of filing of the application in the Party.

Article 17.10: Measures Related to Certain Regulated Products

1. If a Party requires the submission of undisclosed information concerning the safety and efficacy of a pharmaceutical or agricultural chemical product which utilizes a new chemical entity, which product has not been previously approved, to grant a marketing approval or sanitary permit for such product, the Party shall not permit third parties not having the consent of the person providing the information to market a product based on this new chemical entity, on the basis of the approval granted to the party submitting such information. A Party shall maintain this prohibition for a period of at least five years from the date of approval for a pharmaceutical product and ten years from the date of approval for an agricultural chemical product.[64] Each Party shall protect such information against disclosure except where necessary to protect the public.

2. With respect to pharmaceutical products that are subject to a patent, each Party shall:

[63] Fraud in obtaining a patent may constitute grounds for revocation or cancellation.

[64] Where a Party, on the date of its implementation of the TRIPS Agreement, had in place a system for protecting pharmaceutical or agricultural chemical products not involving new chemical entities from unfair commercial use which conferred a period of protection shorter than that specified in para. 1, that Party may retain such system notwithstanding the obligations of para. 1.

(a) make available an extension of the patent term to compensate the patent owner for unreasonable curtailment of the patent term as a result of the marketing approval process;

(b) make available to the patent owner the identity of any third party requesting marketing approval effective during the term of the patent; and

(c) not grant marketing approval to any third party prior to the expiration of the patent term, unless by consent or acquiescence of the patent owner.

ARTICLE 17.11: ENFORCEMENT OF INTELLECTUAL PROPERTY RIGHTS

General Obligations

1. Each Party shall ensure that procedures and remedies set forth in this Article for enforcement of intellectual property rights are established in accordance with its domestic law.[65] Such administrative and judicial procedures and remedies, both civil and criminal, shall be made available to the holders of such rights in accordance with the principles of due process that each Party recognizes as well as with the foundations of its own legal system.

2. This Article does not create any obligation:

(a) to put in place a judicial system for the enforcement of intellectual property rights distinct from that already existing for the enforcement of law in general, or

(b) with respect to the distribution of resources for the enforcement of intellectual property rights and the enforcement of law in general. The distribution of resources for the enforcement of intellectual property rights shall not excuse a Party from compliance with the provisions of this Article.

3. Final decisions on the merits of a case of general application shall be in writing and shall state the reasons or the legal basis upon which decisions are based.

4. Each Party shall publicize or make available to the public information that each Party might collect regarding its efforts to provide effective enforcement of intellectual property rights, including statistical information.

5. Each Party shall make available the civil remedies set forth in this Article for the acts described in the Articles 17.7(5) and 17.7(6).

6. In civil, administrative, and criminal proceedings involving copyright or related rights, each Party shall provide that:

(a) the natural person or legal entity whose name is indicated as the author, producer, performer, or publisher of the work, performance, or phonogram in the usual manner,[66] shall, in the absence of proof to the contrary, be presumed to be the designated right holder in such work, performance, or phonogram.

[65] Nothing in this chapter prevents a Party from establishing or maintaining appropriate judicial or administrative procedural formalities for this purpose that do not impair each Party's rights and obligations under this Agreement.

[66] Each Party may establish the means by which it shall determine what constitutes the "usual manner" for a particular physical support.

(b) it shall be presumed, in the absence of proof to the contrary, that the copyright or related right subsists in such subject matter. A Party may require, as a condition for according such presumption of subsistence, that the work appear on its face to be original and that it bear a publication date not more than 70 years prior to the date of the alleged infringement.

Civil and Administrative Procedures[67] *and Remedies*

7. Each Party shall make available to right holders[68] civil judicial procedures concerning the enforcement of any intellectual property right.

8. Each Party shall provide that:

(a) In civil judicial proceedings, the judicial authorities shall have the authority to order the infringer to pay the right holder:

(i) damages adequate to compensate for the injury the right holder has suffered because of an infringement of that person's intellectual property right by an infringer engaged in infringing activity, and

(ii) at least in the case of infringements of trademark, copyright, or related rights, the profits of the infringer that are attributable to the infringement and are not already taken into account in determining injury.

(b) In determining injury to the right holder, the judicial authorities shall, *inter alia*, consider the legitimate retail value of the infringed goods.

9. In civil judicial proceedings, each Party shall, at least with respect to works protected by copyright or related rights and trademark counterfeiting, establish pre-established damages, prescribed by each Party's domestic law, that the judicial authorities deem reasonable in light of the goals of the intellectual property system and the objectives set forth in this Chapter.

10. Each Party shall provide that, except in exceptional circumstances, its judicial authorities have the authority to order, at the conclusion of civil judicial proceedings concerning infringement of copyright or related rights and trademark counterfeiting, that the prevailing right holder shall be paid the court costs or fees and reasonable attorney's fees by the infringing party.

11. In civil judicial proceedings concerning copyright and related rights infringement and trademark counterfeiting, each Party shall provide that its judicial authorities shall have the authority to order the seizure of suspected infringing goods, and of material and implements by means of which such goods are produced where necessary to prevent further infringement.

12. In civil judicial proceedings, each Party shall provide that:

(a) its judicial authorities shall have the authority to order, at their discretion, the destruction, except in exceptional cases, of the goods determined to be infringing goods;

---

[67] For the purposes of this Article, civil judicial procedures mean those procedures as applied to the protection and enforcement of intellectual property rights.

[68] For the purposes of this Article, the term "right holder" shall include duly authorized licensees as well as federations and associations having legal standing and authorization to assert such rights.

(b) the charitable donation of goods that infringe copyright and related rights shall not be ordered by the judicial authorities without the authorization of the right holder other than in special cases that do not conflict with the normal exploitation of the work, performance, or phonogram, and do not unreasonably prejudice the legitimate interests of the right holder;

(c) the judicial authorities shall have the authority to order, at their discretion, that material and implements actually used in the manufacture of the infringing goods be destroyed. In considering such requests, the judicial authorities shall take into account, *inter alia*, the need for proportionality between the gravity of the infringement and remedies ordered, as well as the interests of third parties holding an ownership, possessory, contractual, or secured interest; and

(d) in regard to counterfeited trademarked goods, the simple removal of the trademark unlawfully affixed shall not permit release of the goods into the channels of commerce. However, such goods may be donated to charity when the removal of the trademark eliminates the infringing characteristic of the good and the good is no longer identifiable with the removed trademark.

13. In civil judicial proceedings, each Party shall provide that the judicial authorities shall have the authority to order the infringer to provide any information the infringer may have regarding persons involved in the infringement, and regarding the distribution channels of infringing goods. Judicial authorities shall also have the authority to impose fines or imprisonment on infringers who do not comply with such orders, in accordance with each Party's domestic law.

14. To the extent that any civil remedy can be ordered as a result of administrative procedures on the merits of a case, such procedures shall conform to principles equivalent in substance to those set forth in paragraphs 1 through 13.

Provisional Measures

15. Each Party shall provide that requests for relief *inaudita altera parte* shall be acted upon expeditiously in accordance with the judicial procedural rules of that Party.

16. Each Party shall provide that:

(a) its judicial authorities have the authority to require the applicant for any provisional measure to provide any reasonably available evidence in order to satisfy themselves to a sufficient degree of certainty that the applicant is the holder of the right in question[69] and that infringement of such right is imminent, and to order the applicant to provide a reasonable security or equivalent assurance in an amount that is sufficient to protect the defendant and prevent abuse, set at a level so as not to unreasonably deter recourse to such procedures.

(b) in the event that judicial or other authorities appoint experts, technical or otherwise, that must be paid by the parties, such costs shall be set at a reasonable level taking into account the work performed, or if applicable, based on standardized

[69] In accordance with the provisions in para. 6(a).

fees, and shall not unreasonably deter recourse to provisional relief.

Special Requirements Related to Border Measures

17. Each Party shall provide that any right holder initiating procedures for suspension by the customs authorities of the release of suspected counterfeit trademark or pirated copyright goods[70] into free circulation is required to provide adequate evidence to satisfy the competent authorities that, under the laws of the Party of importation, there is *prima facie* an infringement of the right holder's intellectual property right and to supply sufficient information to make the suspected goods reasonably recognizable to the customs authorities. The sufficient information required shall not unreasonably deter recourse to these procedures.

18. Each Party shall provide the competent authorities with the authority to require an applicant to provide a reasonable security or equivalent assurance sufficient to protect the defendant and the competent authorities and to prevent abuse. Such security or equivalent assurance shall not unreasonably deter recourse to these procedures.

19. Where the competent authorities have made a determination that goods are counterfeit or pirated, a Party shall grant the competent authorities the authority to inform the right holder, at the right holder's request, of the names and addresses of the consignor, the importer, and the consignee, and of the quantity of the goods in question.

20. Each Party shall provide that the competent authorities are permitted to initiate border measures *ex officio*, without the need for a formal complaint from a person or right holder. Such measures shall be used when there is reason to believe or suspect that goods being imported, destined for export, or moving in transit are counterfeit or pirated. In case of goods in transit, each Party, in conformity with other international agreements subscribed to by it, may provide that *ex officio* authority shall be exercised prior to sealing the container, or other means of conveyance, with the customs seal, as applicable.[71]

21. Each Party shall provide that:

(a) goods that have been found to be pirated or counterfeit by the competent authorities shall be destroyed, except in exceptional cases.

---

[70] For the purposes of paras. 17 through 19:

(a) **counterfeit trademark goods** means any goods, including packaging, bearing without authorization a trademark which is identical to the trademark validly registered in respect of such goods, or which cannot be distinguished in its essential aspects from such a trademark, and which thereby infringes the rights of the owner of the trademark in question under the law of the country of importation;

(b) **pirated copyright goods** means any goods which are copies made without the consent of the right holder or person duly authorized by the right holder in the country of production and which are made directly or indirectly from an article where the making of that copy would have constituted an infringement of a copyright or a related right under the law of the country of importation.

[71] The Parties recognize their obligations with respect to technological cooperation and other matters set forth in chapter five (Customs Administration), concerning, inter alia, improved customs enforcement, including with respect to intellectual property rights.

(b) in regard to counterfeit trademark goods, the simple removal of the trademark unlawfully affixed shall not be sufficient to permit the release of goods into the channels of commerce.

(c) in no event shall the competent authorities engage in, or permit, the re-exportation of counterfeit or pirated goods, nor shall they permit such goods to be subject to other customs procedures.

Criminal Procedures and Remedies

22. Each Party shall provide for application of criminal procedures and penalties at least in cases of willful trademark counterfeiting or piracy, on a commercial scale, of works, performances, or phonograms protected by copyright or related rights. Specifically, each Party shall ensure that:

(a) (i) willfull infringement[72] of copyright and related rights for a commercial advantage or financial gain, is subject to criminal procedures and penalties;[73]

(ii) copyright or related rights piracy on a commercial scale includes the willful infringing reproduction or distribution, including by electronic means, of copies with a significant aggregate monetary value, calculated based on the legitimate retail value of the infringed goods;

(b) available remedies include sentences of imprisonment and/or monetary fines that are sufficient to provide a deterrent to future infringements and present a level of punishment consistent with the gravity of the offense, which shall be applied by the judicial authorities in light of, *inter alia*, these criteria;

(c) judicial authorities have the authority to order the seizure of suspected counterfeit or pirated goods, assets legally traceable to the infringing activity, documents and related materials, and implements that constitute evidence of the offense. Each Party shall further provide that its judicial authorities have the authority to seize items in accordance with its domestic law. Items that are subject to seizure pursuant to a search order need not be individually identified so long as they fall within general categories specified in the order;

(d) judicial authorities have the authority to order, among other measures, the forfeiture of any assets legally traceable to the infringing activity, and the forfeiture and destruction of all counterfeit and pirated goods and, at least with respect to copyright and related rights piracy, any related materials and implements actually used in the manufacture of the pirated goods. Parties shall not make compensation available to the infringer for any such forfeiture or destruction; and

(e) Appropriate authorities, as determined by each Party, have the authority, in cases of copyright and related rights piracy and trademark counterfeiting, to exercise legal action *ex*

---

[72] For purposes of para. 22, evidence of reproduction or distribution of a copyrighted work, by itself, shall not be sufficient to establish willful infringement.

[73] For purposes of para. 22, commercial advantage or financial gain shall be understood to exclude *de minimis* infringements. Nothing in this Agreement prevents prosecutors from exercising any discretion that they may have to decline to pursue cases.

officio without the need for a formal complaint by a person or right holder.

Limitations on Liability for Internet Service Providers

23. (a) For the purpose of providing enforcement procedures that permit effective action against any act of infringement of copyright[74] covered under this Chapter, including expeditious remedies to prevent infringements and criminal and civil remedies, each Party shall provide, consistent with the framework set forth in this Article:

(i) legal incentives for service providers to cooperate with copyright owners in deterring the unauthorized storage and transmission of copyrighted materials; and

(ii) limitations in its law regarding the scope of remedies available against service providers for copyright infringements that they do not control, initiate, or direct, and that take place through systems or networks controlled or operated by them or on their behalf, as set forth below.

(b) These limitations shall preclude monetary relief and provide reasonable limitations on court-ordered relief to compel or restrain certain actions for the following functions and shall be confined to those functions:

(i) transmitting, routing, or providing connections for material without modification of its content;[75]

(ii) caching carried out through an automatic process;

(iii) storage at the direction of a user of material residing on a system or network controlled or operated by or for the provider, including e-mails and its attachments stored in the provider's server, and web pages residing on the provider's server; and

(iv) referring or linking users to an online location by using information location tools, including hyperlinks and directories. These limitations shall apply only where the provider does not initiate the transmission, or select the material or its recipients (except to the extent that a function described in subparagraph (iv) in itself entails some form of selection). This paragraph does not preclude the availability of other defenses to copyright infringement that are of general applicability, and qualification for the limitations as to each function shall be considered separately from qualification for the limitations as to other functions.

(c) With respect to function (b)(ii), the limitations shall be conditioned on the service provider:

(i) complying with conditions on user access and rules regarding the updating of the cached material imposed by the supplier of the material;

(ii) not interfering with technology consistent with widely accepted industry standards lawfully used at the originating site to obtain information about the use of the material, and not modifying its content in transmission to subsequent users; and

[74] For purposes of para. 23, "copyright" shall also include related rights.

[75] Modification of the content of material shall not include technological manipulation of material for the purpose of facilitating network transmission, such as division into packets.

(iii) expeditiously removing or disabling access, upon receipt of an effective notification of claimed infringement in accordance with subparagraph (f), to cached material that has been removed or access to which has been disabled at the originating site.

With respect to functions (b)(iii) and (iv), the limitations shall be conditioned on the service provider:

(i) not receiving a financial benefit directly attributable to the infringing activity, in circumstances where it has the right and ability to control such activity;

(ii) expeditiously removing or disabling access to the material residing on its system or network upon obtaining actual knowledge of the infringement or becoming aware of facts or circumstances from which the infringement was apparent, including through effective notifications of claimed infringement in accordance with subparagraph (f); and

(iii) publicly designating a representative to receive such notifications.

(d) Eligibility for application of the limitations in this paragraph shall be conditioned on the service provider:

(i) adopting and reasonably implementing[76] a policy that provides for termination in appropriate circumstances of the accounts of repeat infringers; and

(ii) accommodating and not interfering with standard technical measures that lawfully protect and identify copyrighted material, that are developed through an open, voluntary process by a broad consensus of interested parties, approved by relevant authorities, as applicable, that are available on reasonable and nondiscriminatory terms, and that do not impose substantial costs on service providers or substantial burdens on their systems or networks.

Eligibility for application of the limitations in this paragraph may not be conditioned on the service provider monitoring its service, or affirmatively seeking facts indicating infringing activity, except to the extent consistent with such technical measures.

(e) If the service provider qualifies for the limitation with respect to function (b)(i), court-ordered relief to compel or restrain certain actions shall be limited to measures to terminate specified accounts, or to take reasonable steps to block access to a specific, non-domestic online location. If the service provider qualifies for the limitations with respect to any other function in subparagraph (b), court-ordered relief to compel or restrain certain actions shall be limited to removing or disabling access to the infringing material, terminating specified accounts, and other remedies that a court may find necessary provided that such other remedies are the least burdensome to the service provider and users or subscribers among comparably effective forms of relief. Any such relief shall be issued with due regard for the relative burden to the service provider, to users or subscribers and harm to the copyright owner, the technical feasibility and effectiveness of the remedy and whether less burdensome, comparably effective enforcement methods are

[76] A Party may determine in its domestic law that "reasonably implementing" entails, inter alia, making such policy continuously available to its users of its system or network.

available. Except for orders ensuring the preservation of evidence, or other orders having no material adverse effect on the operation of the service provider's communications network, such relief shall be available only where the service provider has received notice and an opportunity to appear before the judicial authority.

(f) For purposes of the notice and take down process for functions (b)(ii), (iii), and (iv), each Party shall establish appropriate procedures through an open and transparent process which is set forth in domestic law, for effective notifications of claimed infringement, and effective counter-notifications by those whose material is removed or disabled through mistake or misidentification. At a minimum, each Party shall require that an effective notification of claimed infringement be a written communication, physically or electronically[77] signed by a person who represents, under penalty of perjury or other criminal penalty, that he is an authorized representative of a right holder in the material that is claimed to have been infringed, and containing information that is reasonably sufficient to enable the service provider to identify and locate material that the complaining party claims in good faith to be infringing and to contact that complaining party. At a minimum, each Party shall require that an effective counter-notification contain the same information, *mutatis mutandis*, as a notification of claimed infringement, and in addition, contain a statement that the subscriber making the counter-notification consents to the jurisdiction of the courts of the Party. Each Party shall also provide for monetary remedies against any person who makes a knowing material misrepresentation in a notification or counter-notification which causes injury to any interested party as a result of a service provider relying on the misrepresentation.

(g) If the service provider removes or disables access to material in good faith based on claimed or apparent infringement, it shall be exempted from liability for any resulting claims, provided that, in the case of material residing on its system or network, it takes reasonable steps promptly to notify the supplier of the material that it has done so and, if the supplier makes an effective counter-notification and is subject to jurisdiction in an infringement suit, to restore the material online unless the original notifying party seeks judicial relief within a reasonable time.

(h) Each Party shall establish an administrative or judicial procedure enabling copyright owners who have given effective notification of claimed infringement to obtain expeditiously from a service provider information in its possession identifying the alleged infringer.

(i) **Service provider** means, for purposes of function (b)(i), a provider of transmission, routing, or connections for digital online communications without modification of their content between or among points specified by the user of material of the user's choosing, or for purposes of functions (b)(ii) through (iv) a provider or operator of facilities for online services (including in cases where network access is provided by another provider) or network access.

---

[77] In accordance with domestic law.

Article 17.12: Final Provisions

1. Except as otherwise provided in this Chapter, each Party shall give effect to the provisions of this Chapter upon the date of entry into force of this Agreement.

2. In those cases in which the full implementation of the obligations contained in this Chapter requires a Party to amend its domestic legislation or additional financial resources, those amendments and financial resources shall be in force or available as soon as practicable, and in no event later than:

(a) two years from the date of entry into force of this Agreement, with respect to the obligations in Article 17.2 on trademarks, Article 17.4(1) through17.4(9) on geographical indications, Article 17.9(1), 17.9(3) through 17.9(7) on patents, and Articles 17.5(1) and 17.6(1) on temporary copies;

(b) four years from the date of entry into force of this Agreement, with respect to the obligations in Article 17.11 on enforcement (including border measures), and Article 17.6(5) with respect to the right of communication to the public, and non-interactive digital transmissions, for performers and producers of phonograms; and

(c) five years from the date of entry into force of this Agreement, with respect to the obligations in Article 17.7(5) on effective technological measures.

Chapter Eighteen

Labor

Article 18.1: Statement of Shared Commitment

1. The Parties reaffirm their obligations as members of the International Labor Organization (ILO) and their commitments under the ILO Declaration on Fundamental Principles and Rights at Work and its Follow-up (1998). Each Party shall strive to ensure that such labor principles and the internationally recognized labor rights set forth in Article 18.8 are recognized and protected by its domestic law.

2. Recognizing the right of each Party to establish its own domestic labor standards, and to adopt or modify accordingly its labor laws, each Party shall strive to ensure that its laws provide for labor standards consistent with the internationally recognized labor rights set forth in Article 18.8 and shall strive to improve those standards in that light.

Article 18.2: Enforcement of Labor Laws

1. (a) A Party shall not fail to effectively enforce its labor laws, through a sustained or recurring course of action or inaction, in a manner affecting trade between the Parties, after the date of entry into force of this Agreement.

(b) The Parties recognize that each Party retains the right to exercise discretion with respect to investigatory, prosecutorial, regulatory, and compliance matters and to make decisions regarding the allocation of resources to enforcement with respect to other labor matters determined to have higher priorities. Accordingly, the Parties understand that a Party is in compliance with subparagraph (a) where a course of action or inaction reflects a reasonable exercise of such discretion, or results from a bona fide decision regarding the allocation of resources.

2. The Parties recognize that it is inappropriate to encourage trade or investment by weakening or reducing the protections afforded in domestic labor laws. Accordingly, each Party shall strive to ensure that it does not waive or otherwise derogate from, or offer to waive or otherwise derogate from, such laws in a manner that weakens or reduces adherence to the internationally recognized labor rights referred to in Article 18.8 as an encouragement for trade with the other Party, or as an encouragement for the establishment, acquisition, expansion, or retention of an investment in its territory.

3. Nothing in this Chapter shall be construed to empower a Party's authorities to undertake labor law enforcement activities in the territory of the other Party.

Article 18.3: Procedural Guarantees and Public Awareness

1. Each Party shall ensure that persons with a legally recognized interest under its law in a particular matter have appropriate access to judicial tribunals of general, labor or other specific jurisdiction, quasi-judicial tribunals, or administrative tribunals, as appropriate, for the enforcement of the Party's labor laws.

2. Each Party shall ensure that its proceedings for the enforcement of its labor laws are fair, equitable, and transparent.

3. Each Party shall provide that the parties to such proceedings may seek remedies to ensure the enforcement of their rights under domestic labor laws.

4. For greater certainty, decisions by each Party's judicial tribunals of general, labor, or other specific jurisdiction, quasi-judicial tribunals, or administrative tribunals, as appropriate, or pending decisions, as well as related proceedings, shall not be subject to revision or reopened under the provisions of this Chapter.

5. Each Party shall promote public awareness of its labor laws.

Article 18.4: Labor Affairs Council

1. The Parties hereby establish a Labor Affairs Council, comprising cabinet-level or equivalent representatives of the Parties, or their designees.

2. The Council shall meet within the first year after the date of entry into force of this Agreement and thereafter as often as it considers necessary to oversee the implementation of and review progress under this Chapter, including the activities of the Labor Cooperation Mechanism established under Article 18.5, and to pursue the labor objectives of this Agreement. Each meeting of the Council shall include a public session, unless the Parties otherwise agree.

3. Each Party shall designate an office within its labor ministry that shall serve as a point of contact with the other Party, and with the public, for purposes of carrying out the work of the Council.

4. The Council shall establish its work program and procedures and may, in carrying out its work, establish governmental working or expert groups and consult with or seek advice of non-governmental organizations or persons, including independent experts.

5. All decisions of the Council shall be taken by mutual agreement of the Parties and shall be made public, unless the Council decides otherwise.

6. Each Party may convene a national consultative or advisory committee, as appropriate, comprising members of its public, including representatives of its labor and business organizations and other persons to provide views regarding the implementation of this Chapter.

7. Each Party's point of contact shall provide for the submission, receipt, and consideration of public communications on matters related to this Chapter, and shall make such communications available to the other Party and the public. Each Party shall review such communications, as appropriate, in accordance with its domestic procedures.

Article 18.5: Labor Cooperation Mechanism

Recognizing that cooperation provides enhanced opportunities for the Parties to promote respect for the principles embodied in the *ILO Declaration on Fundamental Principles and Rights at Work and its Follow-up (1998)*, compliance with *ILO Convention 182 Concerning the Prohibition and Immediate Action for the Elimination of the Worst Forms of Child Labor (1999)*, and to advance other common commitments, the Parties hereby establish a Labor Cooperation Mechanism, as set out in Annex 18.5.

Article 18.6: Cooperative Consultations

1. A Party may request consultations with the other Party regarding any matter arising under this Chapter by delivering a written request to the point of contact that the other Party has designated under Article 18.4(3).

2. The Parties shall consult promptly after delivery of the request. The requesting Party shall provide specific and sufficient information in the request for the other Party to respond.

3. The Parties shall make every attempt to arrive at a mutually satisfactory resolution of the matter and may seek advice or assistance from any person or body they deem appropriate in order to fully examine the matter at issue.

4. If the Parties fail to resolve a matter through consultations, either Party may request that the Council be convened to consider the matter by delivering a written request to the other Party's point of contact.

5. The Council shall promptly convene and shall endeavor to resolve the matter, including, where appropriate, by consulting outside experts and having recourse to such procedures as good offices, conciliation, or mediation.

6. If the matter concerns whether a Party is conforming to its obligations under Article 18.2(1)(a), and the Parties have failed to resolve the matter within 60 days of a request under paragraph 1, the complaining Party may request consultations under Article

22.4 (Consultations) or a meeting of the Commission under Article 22.5 (Commission—Good Offices, Conciliation, and Mediation) and, as provided in Chapter Twenty-Two (Dispute Settlement), thereafter have recourse to the other provisions of that Chapter.

7. Neither Party may have recourse to dispute settlement under this Agreement for any matter arising under any provision of this Chapter other than Article 18.2(1)(a).

8. Neither Party may have recourse to dispute settlement under this Agreement for a matter arising under Article 18.2(1)(a) without first pursuing resolution of the matter in accordance with this Article.

ARTICLE 18.7: LABOR ROSTER

1. The Parties shall establish within six months after the date of entry into force of this Agreement and maintain a roster of up to 12 individuals who are willing and able to serve as panelists in disputes arising under Article 18.2(1)(a). Unless the Parties otherwise agree, four members of the roster shall be selected from among individuals who are non-Party nationals. Labor roster members shall be appointed by mutual agreement of the Parties and may be reappointed. Once established, a roster shall remain in effect for a minimum of three years, and shall remain in effect thereafter until the Parties constitute a new roster.

2. Labor roster members shall:

(a) have expertise or experience in labor law or its enforcement, or in the resolution of disputes arising under international agreements;

(b) be chosen strictly on the basis of objectivity, reliability, and sound judgment;

(c) be independent of, and not affiliated with or take instructions from, either Party; and

(d) comply with a code of conduct to be established by the Commission.

3. Where a Party claims that a dispute arises under Article 18.2(1)(a), Article 22.9 (Panel Selection) shall apply, except that the panel shall be composed entirely of panelists meeting the qualifications in paragraph 2.

ARTICLE 18.8: DEFINITIONS

For purposes of this Chapter:

labor laws means a Party's statutes or regulations, or provisions thereof, that are directly related to the following internationally recognized labor rights:

(a) the right of association;

(b) the right to organize and bargain collectively;

(c) a prohibition on the use of any form of forced or compulsory labor;

(d) a minimum age for the employment of children and the prohibition and elimination of the worst forms of child labor; and

(e) acceptable conditions of work with respect to minimum wages, hours of work, and occupational safety and health.

For greater certainty, the setting of standards and levels in respect of minimum wages by each Party shall not be subject to obligations under this Chapter. Each Party's obligations under this Chapter pertain to enforcing the level of the general minimum wage established by that Party.

statutes or regulations means:

(a) for the United States, acts of the Congress or regulations promulgated pursuant to acts of the Congress that are enforceable by action of the federal government; and

(b) for Chile, acts or regulations promulgated pursuant to acts that are enforceable by the agency charged with enforcing Chile's labor laws.

Chapter Nineteen

Environment

Objectives

The objectives of this Chapter are to contribute to the Parties' efforts to ensure that trade and environmental policies are mutually supportive and to collaboratively promote the optimal use of resources in accordance with the objective of sustainable development; and to strive to strengthen the links between the Parties' trade and environment policies and practices to further the trade expanding goals of this Agreement, including through promoting non-discriminatory measures, avoiding disguised barriers to trade, and eliminating trade distortions where the result can directly benefit both trade and the environment.

Article 19.1: Levels of Protection

Recognizing the right of each Party to establish its own levels of domestic environmental protection and environmental development policies and priorities, and to adopt or modify accordingly its environmental laws, each Party shall ensure that its laws provide for high levels of environmental protection and shall strive to continue to improve those laws.

Article 19.2: Enforcement of Environmental Laws

1. (a) A Party shall not fail to effectively enforce its environmental laws, through a sustained or recurring course of action or inaction, in a manner affecting trade between the Parties, after the date of entry into force of this Agreement.

(b) The Parties recognize that each Party retains the right to exercise discretion with respect to investigatory, prosecutorial, regulatory, and compliance matters and to make decisions regarding the allocation of resources to enforcement with respect to other environmental matters determined to have higher priorities. Accordingly, the Parties understand that a Party is in compliance with subparagraph (a) where a course of action or inaction reflects a reasonable exercise of such discretion, or results from a bona fide decision regarding the allocation of resources.

2. The Parties recognize that it is inappropriate to encourage trade or investment by weakening or reducing the protections afforded in domestic environmental laws. Accordingly, each Party shall strive to ensure that it does not waive or otherwise derogate from, or offer to waive or otherwise derogate from, such laws in a manner that weakens or reduces the protections afforded in those laws as an encouragement for trade with the other Party, or as an encouragement for the establishment, acquisition, expansion, or retention of an investment in its territory.

3. Nothing in this Chapter shall be construed to empower a Party's authorities to undertake environmental law enforcement activities in the territory of the other Party.

Article 19.3: Environment Affairs Council

1. The Parties hereby establish an Environment Affairs Council comprising cabinet level or equivalent representatives of the Parties, or their designees. The Council shall meet once a year, or more often if the Parties agree, to discuss the implementation of, and progress under, this Chapter. Meetings of the Council shall include a public session, unless the Parties otherwise agree.

2. In order to share innovative approaches for addressing environmental issues of interest to the public, the Council shall ensure a process for promoting public participation in its work, including by seeking advice from the public in developing agendas for Council meetings and by engaging in a dialogue with the public on those issues.

3. The Council shall seek appropriate opportunities for the public to participate in the development and implementation of cooperative environmental activities, including through the United States-Chile Environmental Cooperation Agreement, as set out in Annex 19.3.

4. All decisions of the Council shall be taken by mutual agreement and shall be made public, unless the Council decides otherwise, or as otherwise provided in this Agreement.

Article 19.4: Opportunities for Public Participation

1. Each Party shall provide for the receipt and consideration of public communications on matters related to this Chapter. Each Party shall promptly make available to the other Party and to its public all communications it receives and shall review and respond to them in accordance with its domestic procedures.

2. Each Party shall make best efforts to respond favorably to requests for consultations by persons or organizations in its territory regarding the Party's implementation of this Chapter.

3. Each Party may convene, or consult an existing, national consultative or advisory committee, comprising members of its public, including representatives of business and environmental organizations, and other persons, to advise it on the implementation of this Chapter.

Article 19.5: Environmental Cooperation

1. The Parties recognize the importance of strengthening capacity to protect the environment and promote sustainable development in concert with strengthening trade and investment relations between them. The Parties agree to undertake cooperative environmental activities, in particular through:

(a) pursuing, through their relevant ministries or agencies, the specific cooperative projects that the Parties have identified and set out in Annex 19.3; and

(b) promptly negotiating a United States-Chile Environmental Cooperation Agreement to establish priorities for further cooperative environmental activities, as elaborated in Annex 19.3,

while recognizing the ongoing importance of environmental cooperation undertaken outside this Agreement.

2. Each Party shall take into account public comments and recommendations it receives regarding cooperative environmental activities the Parties undertake pursuant to this Chapter.

3. The Parties shall, as they deem appropriate, share information on their experiences in assessing and taking into account positive or negative environmental effects of trade agreements and policies.

Article 19.6: Environmental Consultations

1. A Party may request consultations with the other Party regarding any matter arising under this Chapter by delivering a written request to the other Party.

2. The Parties shall consult promptly after delivery of the request. The requesting Party shall provide specific and sufficient information in the request for the other Party to respond.

3. The Parties shall make every attempt to arrive at a mutually satisfactory resolution of the matter and may seek advice or assistance from any person or body they deem appropriate in order to fully examine the matter at issue.

4. If the Parties fail to resolve the matter through consultations, either Party may request that the Council be convened to consider the matter by delivering a written request to the other Party.

5. The Council shall promptly convene and shall endeavor to resolve the matter, including, where appropriate, by consulting governmental or outside experts and having recourse to such procedures as good offices, conciliation, or mediation.

6. If the matter concerns whether a Party is conforming to its obligations under Article 19.2(1)(a), and the Parties have failed to resolve the matter within 60 days of a request for consultations under paragraph 1, the complaining Party may request consultations under Article 22.4 (Consultations) or a meeting of the Commission under Article 22.5 (Commission—Good Offices, Conciliation, and Mediation) and, as provided in Chapter Twenty-Two (Dispute Settlement), thereafter have recourse to the other provisions of that Chapter.

7. The Council may, where appropriate, provide information to the Commission regarding any consultations held on the matter.

8. Neither Party may have recourse to dispute settlement under this Agreement for any matter arising under any provision of this Chapter other than Article 19.2(1)(a).

9. Neither Party may have recourse to dispute settlement under this Agreement for a matter arising under Article 19.2(1)(a) without first pursuing resolution of the matter in accordance with this Article.

10. In cases where the Parties agree that a matter arising under this Chapter is more properly covered by another agreement to which the Parties are party, they shall refer the matter for appropriate action in accordance with that agreement.

Article 19.7: Environment Roster

1. The Parties shall establish within six months after the date of entry into force of this Agreement and maintain a roster of at least 12 individuals who are willing and able to serve as panelists in disputes arising under Article 19.2(1)(a). Unless the Parties otherwise agree, four members of the roster shall be selected from among individuals who are non-Party nationals. Environment roster members shall be appointed by mutual agreement of the Parties, and may be reappointed. Once established, a roster shall remain in effect for a minimum of three years, and shall remain in effect thereafter until the Parties constitute a new roster.

2. Environment roster members shall:

(a) have expertise or experience in environmental law or its enforcement, international trade, or the resolution of disputes arising under international trade agreements;

(b) be chosen strictly on the basis of objectivity, reliability, and sound judgment;

(c) be independent of, and not affiliated with or take instructions from, either Party; and

(d) comply with a code of conduct to be established by the Commission.

3. Where a Party claims that a dispute arises under Article 19.2(1)(a), Article 22.9 (Panel Selection) shall apply, except that:

(a) where the Parties so agree, the panel shall be composed entirely of panelists meeting the qualifications in paragraph 2; and

(b) if the Parties cannot so agree, each Party may select panelists meeting the qualifications set out in paragraph 2 or in Article 22.8 (Qualifications of Panelists).

Article 19.8: Procedural Matters

1. Each Party shall ensure that judicial, quasi-judicial, or administrative proceedings are available under its law to sanction or remedy violations of its environmental laws.

(a) Such proceedings shall be fair, open, and equitable, and to this end shall comply with due process of law, and be open to the public (except where the administration of justice otherwise requires).

(b) Each Party shall provide appropriate and effective remedies or sanctions for a violation of its environmental laws that:

(i) take into consideration the nature and gravity of the violation, any economic benefit the violator has derived from the violation, the economic condition of the violator, and other relevant factors; and

(ii) may include compliance agreements, penalties, fines, imprisonment, injunctions, the closure of facilities, and the cost of containing or cleaning up pollution.

2. Each Party shall ensure that interested persons may request the Party's competent authorities to investigate alleged violations of its environmental laws and that the competent authorities give such requests due consideration in accordance with its law.

3. Each Party shall ensure that persons with a legally recognized interest under its law in a particular matter have appropriate access to judicial, quasi-judicial, or administrative proceedings for the enforcement of the Party's environmental laws.

4. Each Party shall provide persons appropriate and effective rights of access to remedies in accordance with its laws, which may include the right:

(a) to sue another person under that Party's jurisdiction for damages under that Party's environmental laws;

(b) to seek sanctions or remedies such as monetary penalties, emergency closures, or orders to mitigate the consequences of violations of its environmental laws;

(c) to request the competent authorities to take appropriate action to enforce the Party's environmental laws in order to protect the environment or to avoid environmental harm; or

(d) to seek injunctions where a person suffers, or may suffer, loss, damage, or injury as a result of conduct by another person under that Party's jurisdiction contrary to that Party's environmental laws or from tortious conduct that harms human health or the environment.

ARTICLE 19.9: RELATIONSHIP TO ENVIRONMENTAL AGREEMENTS

The Parties recognize the importance of multilateral environmental agreements, including the appropriate use of trade measures in such agreements to achieve specific environmental goals. Recognizing that in paragraph 31(i) of the *Ministerial Declaration adopted on November 14, 2001 in Doha*, WTO members have agreed to negotiations on the relationship between existing WTO rules and specific trade obligations set out in multilateral environmental agreements, the Parties shall consult on the extent to which the outcome of the negotiations applies to this Agreement.

ARTICLE 19.10: PRINCIPLES OF CORPORATE STEWARDSHIP

Recognizing the substantial benefits brought by international trade and investment as well as the opportunity for enterprises to implement policies for sustainable development that seek to ensure coherence between social, economic and environmental objectives, each Party should encourage enterprises operating within its territory or jurisdiction to voluntarily incorporate sound principles of corporate stewardship in their internal policies, such as those principles or agreements that have been endorsed by both Parties.

ARTICLE 19.11: DEFINITIONS

For purposes of this Chapter:

environmental law means any statute or regulation of a Party, or provision thereof, the primary purpose of which is the protection of the environment, or the prevention of a danger to human life or health, through:

(a) the prevention, abatement, or control of the release, discharge, or emission of pollutants or environmental contaminants;

(b) the control of environmentally hazardous or toxic chemicals, substances, materials, and wastes, and the dissemination of information related thereto; or

(c) the protection or conservation of wild flora and fauna, including endangered species, their habitat, and specially protected natural areas,

in the Party's territory, but does not include any statute or regulation, or provision thereof, directly related to worker safety or health.

For greater certainty, **environmental law** does not include any statute or regulation, or provision thereof, the primary purpose of which is managing the commercial harvest or exploitation, or subsistence or aboriginal harvesting, of natural resources.

For purposes of the definition of "environmental law," the primary purpose of a particular statutory or regulatory provision shall be determined by reference to its primary purpose, rather than to the primary purpose of the statute or regulation of which it is part.

For the United States, **statute or regulation** means an act of Congress or regulation promulgated pursuant to an act of Congress that is enforceable by action of the federal government.

For the United States, **territory** means its territory as set out in Annex 2.1 as well as other areas with respect to which it exercises sovereignty, sovereign rights, or jurisdiction.

Chapter Twenty

Transparency

ARTICLE 20.1: CONTACT POINTS

1. Each Party shall designate a contact point to facilitate communications between the Parties on any matter covered by this Agreement.

2. On the request of the other Party, the contact point shall identify the office or official responsible for the matter and assist, as necessary, in facilitating communication with the requesting Party.

ARTICLE 20.2: PUBLICATION

1. Each Party shall ensure that its laws, regulations, procedures, and administrative rulings of general application respecting any matter covered by this Agreement are promptly published or otherwise made available in such a manner as to enable interested persons and the other Party to become acquainted with them.

2. To the extent possible, each Party shall:

(a) publish in advance any such measure that it proposes to adopt; and

(b) provide interested persons and the other Party a reasonable opportunity to comment on such proposed measures.

ARTICLE 20.3: NOTIFICATION AND PROVISION OF INFORMATION

1. To the maximum extent possible, each Party shall notify the other Party of any proposed or actual measure that the Party considers might materially affect the operation of this Agreement or otherwise substantially affect the other Party's interests under this Agreement.

2. On request of the other Party, a Party shall promptly provide information and respond to questions pertaining to any actual or proposed measure, whether or not the other Party has been previously notified of that measure.

3. Any notification or information provided under this Article shall be without prejudice as to whether the measure is consistent with this Agreement.

ARTICLE 20.4: ADMINISTRATIVE PROCEEDINGS

With a view to administering in a consistent, impartial, and reasonable manner all measures of general application affecting matters covered by this Agreement, each Party shall ensure that in its administrative proceedings applying measures referred to in Article 20.2 to particular persons, goods, or services of the other Party in specific cases that:

(a) wherever possible, persons of the other Party that are directly affected by a proceeding are provided reasonable notice, in accordance with domestic procedures, when a proceeding is initiated, including a description of the nature of the proceeding, a statement of the legal authority under which the proceeding is initiated, and a general description of any issues in controversy;

(b) such persons are afforded a reasonable opportunity to present facts and arguments in support of their positions prior to any final administrative action, when time, the nature of the proceeding, and the public interest permit; and

(c) its procedures are in accordance with domestic law.

ARTICLE 20.5: REVIEW AND APPEAL

1. Each Party shall establish or maintain judicial, quasi-judicial, or administrative tribunals or procedures for the purpose of the prompt review and, where warranted, correction of final administrative actions regarding matters covered by this Agreement. Such tribunals shall be impartial and independent of the office or authority entrusted with administrative enforcement and shall not have any substantial interest in the outcome of the matter.

2. Each Party shall ensure that, in any such tribunals or procedures, the parties to the proceeding are provided with the right to:

(a) a reasonable opportunity to support or defend their respective positions; and

(b) a decision based on the evidence and submissions of record or, where required by domestic law, the record compiled by the administrative authority.

3. Each Party shall ensure, subject to appeal or further review as provided in its domestic law, that such decisions shall be implemented by, and shall govern the practice of, the office or authority with respect to the administrative action that is the subject of the decision.

ARTICLE 20.6: DEFINITIONS

For purposes of this Chapter:

administrative ruling of general application means an administrative ruling or interpretation that applies to all persons and fact situations that fall generally within its ambit and that establishes a norm of conduct but does not include:

(a) a determination or ruling made in an administrative or quasi-judicial proceeding that applies to a particular person, good, or service of the other Party in a specific case; or

(b) a ruling that adjudicates with respect to a particular act or practice.

Chapter Twenty-One

Administration of the Agreement

ARTICLE 21.1: THE FREE TRADE COMMISSION

1. The Parties hereby establish the Free Trade Commission, comprising cabinet-level representatives of the Parties or their designees.

2. The Commission shall:

(a) supervise the implementation of this Agreement;

(b) oversee the further elaboration of this Agreement;

(c) seek to resolve disputes that may arise regarding the interpretation or application of this Agreement;

(d) supervise the work of all committees and working groups established under this Agreement;

(e) establish the amounts of remuneration and expenses that will be paid to panelists; and

(f) consider any other matter that may affect the operation of this Agreement.

3. The Commission may:

(a) establish and delegate responsibilities to committees and working groups;

(b) in accordance with Annex 21.1, further the implementation of the Agreement's objectives by approving any modifications of:

(i) the Schedules attached to Annex 3.3 (Tariff Elimination), by accelerating tariff elimination,

(ii) the rules of origin established in Annex 4.1 (Specific Rules of Origin),

(iii) the Common Guidelines referenced in Article 4.17 (Common Guidelines), and

(iv) the Sections of Annex 9.1 (Government Procurement);

(c) seek the advice of non-governmental persons or groups; and

(d) take such other action in the exercise of its functions as the Parties may agree.

4. The Commission shall establish its rules and procedures. All decisions of the Commission shall be taken by mutual agreement.

5. The Commission shall convene at least once a year in regular session. Regular sessions of the Commission shall be chaired successively by each Party.

Article 21.2: Administration of Dispute Settlement Proceedings

1. Each Party shall designate an office that shall provide administrative assistance to panels established under Chapter Twenty-Two (Dispute Settlement) and perform such other functions as the Commission may direct.

2. Each Party shall be responsible for the operation and costs of its designated office, and shall notify the Commission of the location of its office.

Chapter Twenty-Two

Dispute Settlement

Article 22.1: Cooperation

The Parties shall at all times endeavor to agree on the interpretation and application of this Agreement, and shall make every attempt through cooperation and consultations to arrive at a mutually satisfactory resolution of any matter that might affect its operation.

Article 22.2: Scope of Application

Except as otherwise provided in this Agreement, the dispute settlement provisions of this Chapter shall apply:

(a) with respect to the avoidance or settlement of all disputes between the Parties regarding the interpretation or application of this Agreement;

(b) wherever a Party considers that a measure of the other Party is inconsistent with the obligations of this Agreement or that the other Party has otherwise failed to carry out its obligations under this Agreement; and

(c) wherever a Party considers that a measure of the other Party causes nullification or impairment in the sense of Annex 22.2.

Article 22.3: Choice of Forum

1. Where a dispute regarding any matter arises under this Agreement and under another free trade agreement to which both Parties are party or the WTO Agreement, the complaining Party may select the forum in which to settle the dispute.

2. Once the complaining Party has requested a panel under an agreement referred to in paragraph 1, the forum selected shall be used to the exclusion of the others.

ARTICLE 22.4: CONSULTATIONS

1. Either Party may request in writing consultations with the other Party with respect to any actual or proposed measure or any other matter that it considers might affect the operation of this Agreement.

2. The requesting Party shall set out the reasons for the request, including identification of the measure or other matter at issue and an indication of the legal basis for the complaint, and shall deliver the request to the other Party.

3. Consultations on matters regarding perishable goods shall commence within 15 days of the date of delivery of the request.

4. The Parties shall make every attempt to arrive at a mutually satisfactory resolution of any matter through consultations under this Article or other consultative provisions of this Agreement. To this end, the Parties shall:

(a) provide sufficient information to enable a full examination of how the actual or proposed measure or other matter might affect the operation and application of this Agreement; and

(b) treat any confidential information exchanged in the course of consultations on the same basis as the Party providing the information.

5. In consultations under this Article, a Party may request the other Party to make available personnel of its government agencies or other regulatory bodies who have expertise in the matter subject to consultations.

ARTICLE 22.5: COMMISSION—GOOD OFFICES, CONCILIATION, AND MEDIATION

1. A Party may request in writing a meeting of the Commission if the Parties fail to resolve a matter pursuant to Article 22.4 within:

(a) 60 days of delivery of a request for consultations;

(b) 15 days of delivery of a request for consultations in matters regarding perishable goods; or

(c) such other period as they may agree.

2. A Party may also request in writing a meeting of the Commission where consultations have been held pursuant to Article 18.6 (Cooperative Consultations), Article 19.6 (Environmental Consultations) or Article 7.8 (Committee on Technical Barriers to Trade).

3. The requesting Party shall state in the request the measure or other matter complained of and deliver the request to the other Party.

4. Unless it decides otherwise, the Commission shall convene within 10 days of delivery of the request and shall endeavor to resolve the dispute promptly. The Commission may:

(a) call on such technical advisers or create such working groups or expert groups as it deems necessary;

(b) have recourse to good offices, conciliation, mediation, or such other dispute resolution procedures; or

(c) make recommendations,

as may assist the Parties to reach a mutually satisfactory resolution of the dispute.

Article 22.6: Request for an Arbitral Panel

1. If the Parties fail to resolve a matter within:

(a) 30 days of the Commission convening pursuant to Article 22.5;

(b) 75 days after a Party has delivered a request for consultations under Article 22.4, if the Commission has not convened pursuant to Article 22.5(4);

(c) 30 days after a Party has delivered a request for consultations under Article 22.4 in a matter regarding perishable goods, if the Commission has not convened pursuant to Article 22.5(4); or

(d) such other period as the Parties agree, either Party may request in writing the establishment of an arbitral panel to consider the matter. The requesting Party shall state in the request the measure or other matter complained of and indicate the provisions of this Agreement that it considers relevant, and shall deliver the request to the other Party. An arbitral panel shall be established upon delivery of a request.

2. Unless the Parties otherwise agree, the panel shall be established and perform its functions in a manner consistent with the provisions of this Chapter.

3. Notwithstanding paragraphs 1 and 2, an arbitral panel may not be established to review a proposed measure.

Article 22.7: Roster

1. The Parties shall establish within six months of the entry into force of this Agreement and maintain a roster of at least 20 individuals who are willing and able to serve as panelists. Unless the Parties otherwise agree, six roster members shall be selected from among individuals who are non-Party nationals. The roster members shall be appointed by mutual agreement of the Parties, and may be reappointed. Once established, a roster shall remain in effect for a minimum of three years, and shall remain in effect thereafter until the Parties constitute a new roster.

2. Roster members shall:

(a) have expertise or experience in law, international trade, other matters covered by this Agreement, or the resolution of disputes arising under international trade agreements;

(b) be chosen strictly on the basis of objectivity, reliability, and sound judgment;

(c) be independent of, and not be affiliated with or take instructions from, any Party; and

(d) comply with a code of conduct to be established by the Commission.

ARTICLE 22.8: QUALIFICATIONS OF PANELISTS

All panelists shall meet the qualifications set out in Article 22.7(2). Individuals may not serve as panelists for a dispute in which they have participated pursuant to Article 22.5(4)(a).

ARTICLE 22.9: PANEL SELECTION

1. The Parties shall apply the following procedures in selecting a panel:

(a) the panel shall comprise three members;

(b) the Parties shall endeavor to agree on the chair of the panel within 15 days of the delivery of the request for the establishment of the panel. If the Parties are unable to agree on the chair within this period, the chair shall be selected by lot within three days from among the roster members who are non-Party nationals;

(c) within 15 days of selection of the chair, each Party shall select one panelist;

(d) if a Party fails to select its panelist within such period, the panelist shall be selected by lot within three days from among the roster members who are nationals of the Party; and

(e) each Party shall endeavor to select panelists who have expertise or experience relevant to the subject matter of the dispute.

2. Panelists shall normally be selected from the roster. A Party may exercise a peremptory challenge against any individual not on the roster who is proposed as a panelist by the other Party within 15 days after the individual has been proposed.

3. If a Party believes that a panelist is in violation of the code of conduct, the Parties shall consult and if they agree, the panelist shall be removed and a new panelist shall be selected in accordance with this Article.

ARTICLE 22.10: RULES OF PROCEDURE

1. The Commission shall establish, by the date of entry into force of this Agreement, Rules of Procedure, which shall ensure:

(a) a right to at least one hearing before the panel, which, subject to subparagraph (e), shall be open to the public;

(b) an opportunity for each Party to provide initial and rebuttal submissions;

(c) that each Party's written submissions, written versions of its oral statement, and written responses to a request or questions from the panel will be made public within 10 days after they are submitted, subject to subparagraph (e);

(d) that the panel will consider requests from non-governmental entities located in the Parties' territories to provide written views regarding the dispute that may assist the panel in evaluating the submissions and arguments of the Parties; and

(e) the protection of confidential information.

2. Unless the Parties otherwise agree, the panel shall conduct its proceedings in accordance with the Rules of Procedure and may,

after consulting with the Parties, adopt additional procedural rules not inconsistent with the Rules of Procedure.

3. The Commission may modify the Rules of Procedure.

4. Unless the Parties otherwise agree within 20 days from the date of the delivery of the request for the establishment of the panel, the terms of reference shall be:

> "To examine, in the light of the relevant provisions of this Agreement, the matter referenced in the panel request and to make findings, determinations and recommendations as provided in Article 22.12(3) and to deliver the written reports referred to in Articles 22.12 and 22.13."

5. If the complaining Party wishes to argue that a matter has nullified or impaired benefits, the terms of reference shall so indicate.

6. If a Party wishes the panel to make findings as to the degree of adverse trade effects on a Party of any measure or other matter found not to conform with the obligations of this Agreement or to have caused nullification or impairment in the sense of Annex 22.2, the terms of reference shall so indicate.

Article 22.11: Experts and Technical Advice

1. On request of a Party, or, unless the Parties disapprove, on its own initiative, the panel may seek information and technical advice, including information and technical advice concerning environmental, labor, health, safety, or other technical matters raised by a Party in a proceeding, from any person or body that it deems appropriate.

2. Before a panel seeks information or technical advice, it shall establish appropriate procedures in consultation with the Parties. The panel shall provide the Parties:

(a) advance notice of, and an opportunity to provide comments to the panel on, proposed requests for information and technical advice pursuant to paragraph 1; and

(b) a copy of any information or technical advice submitted in response to a request pursuant to paragraph 1 and an opportunity to provide comments.

3. Where the panel takes the information or technical advice into account in the preparation of its report, it shall also take into account any comments by the Parties on the information or technical advice.

Article 22.12: Initial Report

1. Unless the Parties otherwise agree, the panel shall base its report on the relevant provisions of this Agreement and the submissions and arguments of the Parties.

2. If the Parties agree, the panel may make recommendations for resolution of the dispute.

3. Unless the Parties otherwise agree, the panel shall, within 120 days after the last panelist is selected, present to the Parties an initial report containing:

(a) findings of fact, including any findings pursuant to a request under Article 22.10(6);

(b) its determination as to whether a Party has not conformed with its obligations under this Agreement or that a Party's measure is causing nullification or impairment in the sense of Annex 22.2, or any other determination requested in the terms of reference; and

(c) its recommendations, if the Parties have requested them, for resolution of the dispute.

4. Panelists may furnish separate opinions on matters not unanimously agreed.

5. A Party may submit written comments to the panel on its initial report within 14 days of presentation of the report or within such other period as the Parties may agree.

6. After considering any written comments on the initial report, the panel may reconsider its report and make any further examination it considers appropriate.

Article 22.13: Final Report

1. The panel shall present a final report to the Parties, including any separate opinions on matters not unanimously agreed, within 30 days of presentation of the initial report, unless the Parties otherwise agree. The Parties shall release the final report to the public within 15 days thereafter, subject to the protection of confidential information.

2. No panel may, either in its initial report or its final report, disclose which panelists are associated with majority or minority opinions.

Article 22.14: Implementation of Final Report

1. On receipt of the final report of a panel, the Parties shall agree on the resolution of the dispute, which normally shall conform with the determinations and recommendations, if any, of the panel.

2. If, in its final report, the panel determines that a Party has not conformed with its obligations under this Agreement or that a Party's measure is causing nullification or impairment in the sense of Annex 22.2, the resolution, whenever possible, shall be to eliminate the non-conformity or the nullification or impairment.[78]

3. Where appropriate, the Parties may agree on a mutually satisfactory action plan to resolve the dispute, which normally shall conform with the determinations and recommendations, if any, of the panel. If the Parties agree on such an action plan, the complaining Party may have recourse to Article 22.15(2) or Article 22.16(1), as the case may be, only if it considers that the Party complained against has failed to carry out the action plan.

Article 22.15: Non-Implementation—Suspension of Benefits

1. If a panel has made a determination of the type described in Article 22.14(2) and the Parties are unable to reach agreement on a resolution pursuant to Article 22.14 within 45 days of receiving

[78] Compensation, the payment of monetary assessments, and the suspension of benefits are intended as temporary measures pending the elimination of any non-conformity or nullification or impairment that the panel has found.

the final report, or such other period as the Parties agree, the Party complained against shall enter into negotiations with the other Party with a view to developing mutually acceptable compensation.

2. If the Parties:

(a) are unable to agree on compensation within 30 days after the period for developing such compensation has begun; or

(b) have agreed on compensation or on a resolution pursuant to Article 22.14 and the complaining Party considers that the other Party has failed to observe the terms of the agreement,

the complaining Party may at any time thereafter provide written notice to the other Party that it intends to suspend the application to the other Party of benefits of equivalent effect. The notice shall specify the level of benefits that the Party proposes to suspend. Subject to paragraph 5, the complaining Party may begin suspending benefits 30 days after the later of the date on which it provides notice under this paragraph or the panel issues its determination under paragraph 3, as the case may be.

3. If the Party complained against considers that:

(a) the level of benefits proposed to be suspended is manifestly excessive; or

(b) it has eliminated the non-conformity or the nullification or impairment that the panel has found,

it may, within 30 days after the complaining Party provides notice under paragraph 2, request that the panel be reconvened to consider the matter. The Party complained against shall deliver its request in writing to the other Party. The panel shall reconvene as soon as possible after delivery of the request and shall present its determination to the Parties within 90 days after it reconvenes to review a request under subparagraph (a) or (b), or within 120 days for a request under subparagraphs (a) and (b). If the panel determines that the level of benefits proposed to be suspended is manifestly excessive, it shall determine the level of benefits it considers to be of equivalent effect.

4. The complaining Party may suspend benefits up to the level the panel has determined under paragraph 3 or, if the panel has not determined the level, the level the Party has proposed to suspend under paragraph 2, unless the panel has determined that the Party complained against has eliminated the non-conformity or the nullification or impairment.

5. The complaining Party may not suspend benefits if, within 30 days after it provides written notice of intent to suspend benefits or, if the panel is reconvened under paragraph 3, within 20 days after the panel provides its determination, the Party complained against provides written notice to the other Party that it will pay an annual monetary assessment. The Parties shall consult, beginning no later than 10 days after the Party complained against provides notice, with a view to reaching agreement on the amount of the assessment. If the Parties are unable to reach an agreement within 30 days after consultations begin, the amount of the assessment shall be set at a level, in U.S. dollars, equal to 50 percent of the level of the benefits the panel has determined under paragraph 3 to be of equivalent effect or, if the panel has not determined the

level, 50 percent of the level that the complaining Party has proposed to suspend under paragraph 2.

6. Unless the Commission otherwise decides, a monetary assessment shall be paid to the complaining Party in U.S. currency, or in an equivalent amount of Chilean currency, in equal, quarterly installments beginning 60 days after the Party complained against gives notice that it intends to pay an assessment. Where the circumstances warrant, the Commission may decide that an assessment shall be paid into a fund established by the Commission and expended at the direction of the Commission for appropriate initiatives to facilitate trade between the Parties, including by further reducing unreasonable trade barriers or by assisting a Party in carrying out its obligations under the Agreement.

7. If the Party complained against fails to pay a monetary assessment, the complaining Party may suspend the application to the Party complained against of benefits in accordance with paragraph 4.

8. This Article shall not apply with respect to a matter described in Article 22.16(1).

ARTICLE 22.16: NON-IMPLEMENTATION IN CERTAIN DISPUTES

1. If, in its final report, a panel determines that a Party has not conformed with its obligations under Article 18.2(1)(a) (Enforcement of Labor Laws) or Article 19.2(1)(a) (Enforcement of Environmental Laws), and the Parties:

(a) are unable to reach agreement on a resolution pursuant to Article 22.14 within 45 days of receiving the final report; or

(b) have agreed on a resolution pursuant to Article 22.14 and the complaining Party considers that the other Party has failed to observe the terms of the agreement,

the complaining Party may at any time thereafter request that the panel be reconvened to impose an annual monetary assessment on the other Party. The complaining Party shall deliver its request in writing to the other Party. The panel shall reconvene as soon as possible after delivery of the request.

2. The panel shall determine the amount of the monetary assessment in U.S. dollars within 90 days after it reconvenes under paragraph 1. In determining the amount of the assessment, the panel shall take into account:

(a) the bilateral trade effects of the Party's failure to effectively enforce the relevant law;

(b) the pervasiveness and duration of the Party's failure to effectively enforce the relevant law;

(c) the reasons for the Party's failure to effectively enforce the relevant law;

(d) the level of enforcement that could reasonably be expected of the Party given its resource constraints;

(e) the efforts made by the Party to begin remedying the non-enforcement after the final report of the panel, including through the implementation of any mutually agreed action plan; and

(f) any other relevant factors.

The amount of the assessment shall not exceed 15 million dollars annually, adjusted for inflation as specified in Annex 22.16.

3. On the date on which the panel determines the amount of the monetary assessment under paragraph 2, or at any time thereafter, the complaining Party may provide notice in writing to the other Party demanding payment of the monetary assessment. The monetary assessment shall be payable in U.S. currency, or in an equivalent amount of Chilean currency, in equal, quarterly, installments beginning 60 days after the complaining Party provides such notice.

4. Assessments shall be paid into a fund established by the Commission and shall be expended at the direction of the Commission for appropriate labor or environmental initiatives, including efforts to improve or enhance labor or environmental law enforcement, as the case may be, in the territory of the Party complained against, consistent with its law. In deciding how to expend monies paid into the fund, the Commission shall consider the views of interested persons in the Parties' territories.

5. If the Party complained against fails to pay a monetary assessment, the complaining Party may take other appropriate steps to collect the assessment or otherwise secure compliance. These steps may include suspending tariff benefits under the Agreement as necessary to collect the assessment, while bearing in mind the Agreement's objective of eliminating barriers to bilateral trade and while seeking to avoid unduly affecting parties or interests not party to the dispute.

Article 22.17: Compliance Review

1. Without prejudice to the procedures set out in Article 22.15(3), if the Party complained against considers that it has eliminated the non-conformity or the nullification or impairment that the panel has found, it may refer the matter to the panel by providing written notice to the other Party. The panel shall issue its report on the matter within 90 days after the Party complained against provides notice.

2. If the panel decides that the Party complained against has eliminated the nonconformity or the nullification or impairment, the complaining Party shall promptly reinstate any benefits it has suspended under Article 22.15 or 22.16 and the Party complained against shall no longer be required to pay any monetary assessment it has agreed to pay under Article 22.15(5) or that has been imposed on it under Article 22.16(1).

Article 22.18: Five-Year Review

The Commission shall review the operation and effectiveness of Articles 22.15 and 22.16 not later than five years after the Agreement enters into force, or within six months after benefits have been suspended or monetary assessments have been imposed in five proceedings initiated under this Chapter, whichever occurs first.

Article 22.19: Referral of Matters from Judicial or Administrative Proceedings

1. If an issue of interpretation or application of this Agreement arises in any domestic judicial or administrative proceeding of a Party that any Party considers would merit its intervention, or if a court or administrative body solicits the views of a Party, that Party shall notify the other Party. The Commission shall endeavor to agree on an appropriate response as expeditiously as possible.

2. The Party in whose territory the court or administrative body is located shall submit any agreed interpretation of the Commission to the court or administrative body in accordance with the rules of that forum.

3. If the Commission is unable to agree, either Party may submit its own views to the court or administrative body in accordance with the rules of that forum.

Article 22.20: Private Rights

Neither Party may provide for a right of action under its domestic law against the other Party on the ground that a measure of the other Party is inconsistent with this Agreement.

Article 22.21: Alternative Dispute Resolution

1. Each Party shall, to the maximum extent possible, encourage and facilitate the use of arbitration and other means of alternative dispute resolution for the settlement of international commercial disputes between private parties in the free trade area.

2. To this end, each Party shall provide appropriate procedures to ensure observance of agreements to arbitrate and for the recognition and enforcement of arbitral awards in such disputes.

3. A Party shall be deemed to be in compliance with paragraph 2 if it is a party to and is in compliance with the 1958 *United Nations Convention on the Recognition and Enforcement of Foreign Arbitral Awards or the 1975 Inter-American Convention on International Commercial Arbitration.*

Chapter Twenty-Three

Exceptions

Article 23.1: General Exceptions

1. For purposes of Chapters Three through Seven (National Treatment and Market Access for Goods, Rules of Origin and Origin Procedures, Customs Administration, Sanitary and Phytosanitary Measures, and Technical Barriers to Trade), Article XX of GATT 1994 and its interpretive notes are incorporated into and made part of this Agreement, *mutatis mutandis.* The Parties understand that the measures referred to in Article XX(b) of GATT 1994 include environmental measures necessary to protect human, animal, or plant life or health, and that Article XX(g) of GATT 1994 applies to measures relating to the conservation of living and non-living exhaustible natural resources.

2. For purposes of Chapters Eleven, Thirteen, and Fifteen[79] (Cross-Border Trade in Services, Telecommunications, and Electronic Commerce), Article XIV of GATS (including its footnotes) is incorporated into and made part of this Agreement.[80] The Parties understand that the measures referred to in Article XIV(b) of GATS include environmental measures necessary to protect human, animal, or plant life or health.

ARTICLE 23.2: ESSENTIAL SECURITY

Nothing in this Agreement shall be construed:

(a) to require a Party to furnish or allow access to any information the disclosure of which it determines to be contrary to its essential security interests; or

(b) to preclude a Party from applying measures that it considers necessary for the fulfillment of its obligations under the United Nations Charter with respect to the maintenance or restoration of international peace or security, or the protection of its own essential security interests.

ARTICLE 23.3: TAXATION

1. Except as set out in this Article, nothing in this Agreement shall apply to taxation measures.

2. Nothing in this Agreement shall affect the rights and obligations of either Party under any tax convention. In the event of any inconsistency between this Agreement and any such convention, that convention shall prevail to the extent of the inconsistency. In the case of a tax convention between the Parties, the competent authorities under that convention shall have sole responsibility for determining whether any inconsistency exists between this Agreement and that convention.

3. Notwithstanding paragraph 2:

(a) Article 3.2 (Market Access—National Treatment) and such other provisions of this Agreement as are necessary to give effect to that Article shall apply to taxation measures to the same extent as does Article III of the GATT 1994; and

(b) Articles 3.13 (Market Access—Export Taxes) and 3.14 (Market Access—Luxury Tax) shall apply to taxation measures.

4. Subject to paragraph 2:

(a) Article 11.2 (Cross-Border Trade in Services—National Treatment) and Article 12.2 (Financial Services—National Treatment) shall apply to taxation measures on income, capital gains, or on the taxable capital of corporations that relate to the purchase or consumption of particular services, except that nothing in this subparagraph shall prevent a Party from conditioning the receipt or continued receipt of an advantage relating to the purchase or consumption of particular services on requirements to provide the service in its territory; and

[79] This Article is without prejudice to whether digital products should be classified as goods or services.

[80] If Article XIV of GATS is amended, this Article shall be amended, as appropriate, after consultations between the Parties.

(b) Articles 10.2 (Investment—National Treatment) and 10.3 (Investment—Most-Favored-Nation Treatment), Articles 11.2 (Cross-Border Trade in Services—National Treatment) and 11.3 (Cross-Border Trade in Services—Most-Favored Nation Treatment), and Articles 12.2 (Financial Services—National Treatment) and 12.3 (Financial Services—Most-Favored-Nation Treatment) shall apply to all taxation measures, other than those on income, capital gains, or on the taxable capital of corporations, taxes on estates, inheritances, gifts, and generation-skipping transfers, except that nothing in those Articles shall apply:

(c) any most-favored-nation obligation with respect to an advantage accorded by a Party pursuant to a tax convention;

(d) to a non-conforming provision of any existing taxation measure;

(e) to the continuation or prompt renewal of a non-conforming provision of any existing taxation measure;

(f) to an amendment to a non-conforming provision of any existing taxation measure to the extent that the amendment does not decrease its conformity, at the time of the amendment, with any of those Articles;

(g) to the adoption or enforcement of any taxation measure aimed at ensuring the equitable or effective imposition or collection of taxes (as permitted by Article XIV(d) of GATS);

(h) to a provision that conditions the receipt, or continued receipt, of an advantage relating to the contributions to, or income of, pension trusts or pension plans on a requirement that the Party maintain continuous jurisdiction over the pension trust or pension plan; or

(i) to any excise tax on insurance premiums adopted by Chile to the extent that such tax would, if levied by the United States, be covered by subparagraphs (d), (e), or (f).

5. Subject to paragraph 2 and without prejudice to the rights and obligations of the Parties under paragraph 3, Article 10.5(2), (3), and (4) (Investment—Performance Requirements) shall apply to taxation measures.

6. Article 10.9 (Expropriation and Compensation) and Article 10.15 (Submission of a Claim to Arbitration) shall apply to a taxation measure alleged to be an expropriation or a breach of an investment agreement or investment authorization. However, no investor may invoke Article 10.9 as the basis of a claim where it has been determined pursuant to this paragraph that the measure is not an expropriation. An investor that seeks to invoke Article 10.9 with respect to a taxation measure must first refer to the competent authorities set out in Annex 23.3 at the time that it gives its notice of intent under Article 10.15(4) the issue of whether that taxation measure involves an expropriation. If the competent authorities do not agree to consider the issue or, having agreed to consider it, fail to agree that the measure is not an expropriation within a period of six months of such referral, the investor may submit its claim to arbitration under Article 10.15.

Article 23.4: Balance of Payments Measures on Trade in Goods

Should a Party decide to impose measures for balance of payments purposes, it shall do so only in accordance with that Party's rights and obligations under GATT 1994, including the *Declaration on Trade Measures Taken for Balance of Payments Purposes* (1979 Declaration) and the *Understanding on the Balance of Payments Provisions of the GATT 1994* (BOP Understanding). In adopting such measures, the Party shall immediately consult with the other Party and shall not impair the relative benefits accorded to the other Party under this Agreement.[81]

Article 23.5: Disclosure of Information

Nothing in this Agreement shall be construed to require a Party to furnish or allow access to information the disclosure of which would impede law enforcement or would be contrary to the Party's law protecting personal privacy or the financial affairs and accounts of individual customers of financial institutions.

Article 23.6: Definitions

For purposes of this Chapter:

tax convention means a convention for the avoidance of double taxation or other international taxation agreement or arrangement; and

taxes and taxation measures do not include:

(a) a customs duty; or

(b) the measures listed in exceptions (b) and (c) of the definition of customs duty.

Chapter Twenty-Four

Final Provisions

Article 24.1: Annexes, Appendices, and Footnotes

The Annexes, Appendices, and footnotes to this Agreement constitute an integral part of this Agreement.

Article 24.2: Amendments

1. The Parties may agree on any modification of or addition to this Agreement.

2. When so agreed, and approved in accordance with the applicable legal procedures of each Party, a modification or addition shall constitute an integral part of this Agreement.

Article 24.3: Amendment of the WTO Agreement

If any provision of the WTO Agreement that the Parties have incorporated into this Agreement is amended, the Parties shall consult on whether to amend this Agreement.

---

[81] For greater certainty, this Article applies to balance of payments measures imposed on trade in goods.

ARTICLE 24.4: ENTRY INTO FORCE AND TERMINATION

1. The entry into force of this Agreement is subject to the completion of necessary domestic legal procedures by each Party.

2. This Agreement shall enter into force 60 days after the date on which the Parties exchange written notification that such procedures have been completed, or after such other period as the Parties may agree.

3. Either Party may terminate this Agreement by written notification to the other Party. This Agreement shall expire 180 days after the date of such notification.

ARTICLE 24.5: AUTHENTIC TEXTS

The English and Spanish texts of this Agreement are equally authentic.

IN WITNESS WHEREOF, the undersigned, being duly authorized by their respective Governments, have signed this Agreement.

DONE at Miami, in duplicate, this sixth day of June, 2003.

M. LAW OF THE SEAS AND SELECTED MARITIME LEGISLATION

CONTENTS

NOTE.—Conventions and agreements referred to by Acts in this section may be researched according to the conventional citations to such materials or by consulting the compilation *Treaties and Other International Agreements on Fisheries, Oceanographic Resources, and Wildlife Involving the United States.* U.S. Congress. Senate. Committee on Commerce, Science, and Transportation. Prepared by the Congressional Research Service, Library of Congress. Washington, U.S. Govt. Printing Off., 1977 (95th Congress, 1st Session. Committee Print, October 1977).

See also the *Marine Mammal Commission Compendium of Selected Treaties, International Agreements, and Other Relevant Documents on Marine Resources, Wildlife, and the Environment.*

1. Law of the Seas

a. Convention on the Territorial Sea and the Contiguous Zone

Done at Geneva, April 29, 1958; Ratification advised by the Senate, May 26, 1960; Ratified by the President, March 24, 1961; Ratification of the United States deposited with the Secretary-General of the United Nations, April 12, 1961; Proclaimed by the President, September 8, 1964; Entered into force, September 10, 1964

ANNEX I [1]

CONVENTION ON THE TERRITORIAL SEA AND THE CONTIGUOUS ZONE [2]

The States Parties to this Convention have agreed as follows:

PART I—TERRITORIAL SEA

SECTION I. GENERAL

Article 1

1. The sovereignty of a State extends, beyond its land territory and its internal waters, to a belt of sea adjacent to its coast, described as the territorial sea.
2. This sovereignty is exercised subject to the provisions of these articles and to other rules of international law.

Article 2

The sovereignty of a coastal State extends to the air space over the territorial sea as well as to its bed and subsoil.

SECTION II. LIMITS OF THE TERRITORIAL SEA

Article 3

Except where otherwise provided in these articles, the normal baseline for measuring the breadth of the territorial sea is the low-water line along the coast as marked on large-scale charts officially recognized by the coastal State.

[1] The text of the Convention printed herein constituted Annex I to the Final Act of the United Nations Conference on the Law of the Sea, which was certified by the Legal Counsel, for the Secretary-General of the United Nations. For a list of states which are parties to the Convention, see Department of State publication, *Treaties in Force.*
[2] 15 UST 1606; TIAS 5639; 516 UNTS 205.

Article 4

1. In localities where the coast line is deeply indented and cut into, or if there is a fringe of islands along the coast in its immediate vicinity, the method of straight baselines joining appropriate points may be employed in drawing the baseline from which the breadth of the territorial sea is measured.

2. The drawing of such baselines must not depart to any appreciable extent from the general direction of the coast, and the sea areas lying within the lines must be sufficiently closely linked to the land domain to be subject to the regime of internal waters.

3. Baselines shall not be drawn to and from low-tide elevations, unless lighthouses or similar installations which are permanently above sea level have been built on them.

4. Where the method of straight baselines is applicable under the provisions of paragraph 1, account may be taken, in determining particular baselines, of economic interests peculiar to the region concerned, the reality and the importance of which are clearly evidenced by a long usage.

5. The system of straight baselines may not be applied by a State in such a manner as to cut off the high seas the territorial sea of another State.

6. The coastal State must clearly indicate straight baselines on charts, to which due publicity must be given.

Article 5

1. Waters on the landward side of the baseline of the territorial sea form part of the internal waters of the State.

2. Where the establishment of a straight baseline in accordance with article 4 has the effect of enclosing as internal waters areas which previously had been considered as part of the territorial sea or of the high seas, a right of innocent passage, as provided in articles 14 to 23, shall exist in those waters.

Article 6

The outer limit of the territorial sea is the line every point of which is at a distance from the nearest point of the baseline equal to the breadth of the territorial sea.

Article 7

1. This article relates only to bays the coasts of which belong to a single State.

2. For the purposes of these articles, a bay is a well-marked indentation whose penetration is in such proportion to the width of its mouth as to contain landlocked waters and constitute more than a mere curvature of the coast. An indentation shall not, however, be regarded as a bay unless its area is as large as, or larger than, that of the semi-circle whose diameter is a line drawn across the mouth of that indentation.

3. For the purpose of measurement, the area of an indentation is that lying between the low-water mark around the shore of the indentation and a line joining the low-water marks of its natural

entrance points. Where, because of the presence of islands, an indentation has more than one mouth, the semi-circle shall be drawn on a line as long as the sum total of the lengths of the lines across the different mouths. Islands within an indentation shall be included as if they were part of the water areas of the indentation.

4. If the distance between the low-water marks of the natural entrance points of a bay does not exceed twenty-four miles, a closing line may be drawn between these two low-water marks, and the waters enclosed thereby shall be considered as internal waters.

5. Where the distance between the low-water marks of the natural entrance points of a bay exceeds twenty-four miles, a straight baseline of twenty-four miles shall be drawn within the bay in such a manner as to enclose the maximum area of water that is possible with a line of that length.

6. The foregoing provisions shall not apply to so-called "historic" bays, or in any case where the straight baseline system provided for in article 4 is applied.

Article 8

For the purpose of delimiting the territorial sea, the outermost permanent harbour works which form an integral part of the harbour system shall be regarded as forming part of the coast.

Article 9

Roadsteads which are normally used for the loading, unloading and anchoring of ships, and which would otherwise be situated wholly or partly outside the outer limit of the territorial sea, are included in the territorial sea. The coastal State must clearly demarcate such roadsteads and indicate then on charts together with their boundaries, to which due publicity must be given.

Article 10

1. An island is a naturally-formed area of land, surrounded by water, which is above water at high-tide.

2. The territorial sea of an island is measured in accordance with the provisions of these articles.

Article 11

1. A low-tide elevation is a naturally-formed area of land which is surrounded by and above water at low-tide but submerged at high-tide. Where a low-tide elevation is situated wholly or partly at a distance not exceeding the breadth of the territorial sea from the mainland or an island, the low-water line on that elevation may be used as the baseline for measuring the breadth of the territorial sea.

2. Where a low-tide elevation is wholly situated at a distance exceeding the breadth of the territorial sea from the mainland or an island, it has no territorial sea of its own.

Article 12

1. Where the coasts of two States are opposite or adjacent to each other, neither of the two States is entitled, failing agreement between them to the contrary, to extend its territorial sea beyond the median line every point of which is equidistant from the nearest points on the baselines from which the breadth of the territorial seas of each of the two States is measured. The provisions of this paragraph shall not apply, however, where it is necessary by reason of historic title or other special circumstances to delimit the territorial seas of the two States in a way which is at variance with this provision.

2. The line of delimitation between the territorial seas of two States lying opposite to each other or adjacent to each other shall be marked on large-scale charts officially recognized by the coastal States.

Article 13

If a river flows directly into the sea, the baseline shall be a straight line across the mouth of the river between points on the low-tide line of its banks.

SECTION III. RIGHT OF INNOCENT PASSAGE

Sub-section A. Rules Applicable to All Ships

Article 14

1. Subject to the provisions of these articles, ships of all States, whether coastal or not, shall enjoy the right of innocent passage through the territorial sea.

2. Passage means navigation through the territorial sea for the purpose either of traversing that sea without entering internal waters, or of proceeding to internal waters, or of making for the high seas from internal waters.

3. Passage includes stopping and anchoring, but only insofar as the same are incidental to ordinary navigation or are rendered necessary by *force majeure* or by distress.

4. Passage is innocent so long as it is not prejudicial to the peace, good order or security of the coastal State. Such passage shall take place in conformity with these articles and with other rules of international law.

5. Passage of foreign fishing vessels shall not be considered innocent if they do not observe such laws and regulations as the coastal State may make and publish in order to prevent these vessels from fishing in the territorial sea.

6. Submarines are required to navigate on the surface and to show their flag.

Article 15

1. The coastal State must not hamper innocent passage through the territorial sea.

2. The coastal State is required to give appropriate publicity to any dangers to navigation, of which it has knowledge, within its territorial sea.

Article 16

1. The coastal State may take the necessary steps in its territorial sea to prevent passage which is not innocent.

2. In the case of ships proceeding to internal waters, the coastal State shall also have the right to take the necessary steps to prevent any breach of the conditions to which admission of those ships to those waters in subject.

3. Subject to the provisions of paragraph 4, the coastal State may, without discrimination amongst foreign ships, suspend temporarily in specified areas of its territorial sea the innocent passage of foreign ships if such suspension is essential for the protection of its security. Such suspension shall take effect only after having been duly published.

4. There shall be no suspension of the innocent passage of foreign ships through straits which are used for international navigation between one part of the high seas and another part of the high seas or the territorial sea of a foreign State.

Article 17

Foreign ships exercising the right of innocent passage shall comply with the laws and regulations enacted by the coastal State in conformity with these articles and other rules of international law and, in particular, with such laws and regulations relating to transport and navigation.

Sub-section B. Rules Applicable to Merchant Ships

Article 18

1. No charge may be levied upon foreign ships by reason only of their passage through the territorial sea.

2. Charges may be levied upon a foreign ship passing through the territorial sea as payment only for specific services rendered to the ship. These charges shall be levied without discrimination.

Article 19

1. The criminal jurisdiction of the coastal State should not be exercised on board a foreign ship passing through the territorial sea to arrest any person or to conduct any investigation in connexion with any crime committed on board the ship during its passage, save only in the following cases:

(a) If the consequences of the crime extend to the coastal State; or

(b) If the crime is of a kind to disturb the peace of the country or the good order of the territorial sea; or

(c) If the assistance of the local authorities has been requested by the captain of the ship or by the consul of the country whose flag the ship flies; or

(d) If it is necessary for the suppression of illicit traffic in narcotic drugs.

2. The above provisions do not affect the right of the coastal State, to take any steps authorized by its laws for the purpose of

an arrest or investigation on board a foreign ship passing through the territorial sea after leaving internal waters.

3. In the cases provided for in paragraphs 1 and 2 of this article, the coastal State shall, if the captain so requests, advise the consular authority of the flag State before taking any steps, and shall facilitate contact between such authority and the ship's crew. In cases of emergency this notification may be communicated while the measures are being taken.

4. In considering whether or how an arrest should be made, the local authorities shall pay due regard to the interest of navigation.

5. The coastal State may not take any steps on board a foreign ship passing through the territorial sea to arrest any person or to conduct any investigation in connexion with any crime committed before the ship entered the territorial sea, if the ship, proceeding from a foreign port, is only passing through the territorial sea without entering internal waters.

Article 20

1. The coastal State should not stop or divert a foreign ship passing through the territorial sea for the purpose of exercising civil jurisdiction in relation to a person on board the ship.

2. The coastal State may not levy execution against or arrest the ship for the purpose of any civil proceedings, save only in respect of obligations or liabilities assumed or incurred by the ship itself in the course or for the purpose of its voyage through the waters of the coastal State.

3. The provisions of the previous paragraph are without prejudice to the right of the coastal State, in accordance with its laws, to levy execution against or to arrest, for the purpose of any civil proceedings, a foreign ship lying in the territorial sea, or passing through the territorial sea after leaving internal waters.

Sub-section C. Rules Applicable to Government Ships Other Than Warships

Article 21

The rules contained in sub-sections A and B shall also apply to government ships operated for commercial purposes.

Article 22

1. The rule contained in sub-section A and in article 18 shall apply to government ships operated for non-commercial purposes.

2. With such exceptions as are contained in the provisions referred to in the preceding paragraph, nothing in these articles affects the immunities which such ships enjoy under these articles or other rules of international law.

Sub-section D. Rule Applicable to Warships

Article 23

If any warship does not comply with the regulations of the coastal State concerning passage through the territorial sea and disregards any request for compliance which is made to it, the coastal State may require the warship to leave the territorial sea.

PART II—CONTIGUOUS ZONE

Article 24

1. In a zone of the high sea contiguous to its territorial sea, the coastal State may exercise the control necessary to:

(a) Prevent infringement of its customs, fiscal, immigration or sanitary regulations within its territory or territorial sea;

(b) Punish infringement of the above regulations committed within its territory or territorial sea.

2. The contiguous zone may not extend beyond twelve miles from the baseline from which the breadth of the territorial sea is measured.

3. Where the coasts of two States are opposite or adjacent to each other, neither of the two States is entitled, failing agreement between them to the contrary, to extend its contiguous zone beyond the median line every point of which is equidistant from the nearest points on the baselines from which the breadth of the territorial seas of the two States is measured.

PART III—FINAL ARTICLES

Article 25

The provisions of this Convention shall not affect conventions or other international agreements already in force, as between States Parties to them.

Article 26

This convention shall, until 31 October 1958, be open for signature by all States Members of the United Nations or of any of the specialized agencies, and by any other State invited by the General Assembly of the United Nations to become a Party to the Convention.

Article 27

This Convention is subject to ratification. The instruments of ratification shall be deposited with the Secretary-General of the United Nations.

Article 28

This Convention shall be open for accession by any States belonging to any of the categories mentioned in article 26. The instruments of accession shall be deposited with the Secretary-General of the United Nations.

Article 29

1. This Convention shall come into force on the thirtieth day following the date of deposit of the twenty-second instrument of ratification or accession with the Secretary-General of the United Nations.

2. For each State ratifying or acceding to the Convention after the deposit of the twenty-second instrument of ratification or accession, the Convention shall enter into force on the thirtieth day after deposit by such State of its instrument of ratification or accession.

Article 30

1. After the expiration of a period of five years from the date on which this Convention shall enter into force, a request for the revision of this Convention may be made at any time by any Contracting Party by means of a notification in writing addressed to the Secretary-General of the United Nations.

2. The General Assembly of the United Nations shall decide upon the steps, if any, to be taken in respect of such request.

Article 31

The Secretary-General of the United Nations shall inform all States Members of the United Nations and the other States referred to in article 26:

(a) Of signatures to this Convention and of the deposit of instruments of ratification or accession, in accordance with articles 26, 27 and 28;

(b) Of the date on which this Convention will come into force, in accordance with article 29;

(c) Of requests for revision in accordance with article 30.

Article 32

The original of this Convention, of which the Chinese, English, French, Russian and Spanish texts are equally authentic, shall be deposited with the Secretary-General of the United Nations, who shall send certified copies thereof to all States referred to in article 26.

IN WITNESS WHEREOF the undersigned Plenipotentiaries, being duly authorized thereto by their respective Governments, have signed this Convention.

DONE at Geneva, this twenty-ninth day of April one thousand nine hundred and fifty-eight.

b. Convention on the High Seas

Done at Geneva, April 29, 1958; Ratification advised by the Senate, May 26, 1960; Ratified by the President, March 24, 1961; Ratification of the United States deposited with the Secretary-General of the United Nations, April 12, 1961; Proclaimed by the President, November 9, 1962; Entered into force, September 30, 1962

ANNEX II [1]

CONVENTION ON THE HIGH SEAS [2]

The States Parties to this Convention,

DESIRING to codify the rules of international law relating to the high seas,

RECOGNIZING that the United Nations Conference on the Law of the Sea, held at Geneva from 24 February to 27 April 1958, adopted the following provisions as generally declaratory of established principles of international law,

HAVE AGREED AS FOLLOWS:

ARTICLE 1

The term "high seas" means all parts of the sea that are not included in the territorial sea or in the internal waters of a State.

ARTICLE 2

The High seas being open to all nations, no State may validly purport to subject any part of them to its sovereignty. Freedom of the high seas is exercised under the conditions laid down by these articles and by the other rules of international law. It comprises, *inter alia,* both for coastal and non-coastal States:

(1) Freedom of navigation;
(2) Freedom of fishing;
(3) Freedom to lay submarine cables and pipelines;
(4) Freedom to fly over the high seas.

These freedoms, and others which are recognized by the general principles of international law shall be exercised by all States with reasonable regard to the interests of other States in their exercise of the freedom of the high seas.

ARTICLE 3

1. In order to enjoy the freedom of the seas on equal terms with coastal States, States having no sea-coast should have free access

---

[1] The text of the Convention printed herein constituted Annex II to the Final Act of the United Nations Conference on the Law of the Sea, which was certified by the Legal Counsel, for the Secretary-General of the United Nations. For a list of states which are parties to the Convention, see Department of State publication, *Treaties in Force.*

[2] 13 UST 2312; TIAS 5200; 450 UNTS 82.

to the sea. To this end States situated between the sea and a State having no sea-coast shall by common agreement with the latter and in the conformity with existing international convention accord:

(a) To the State having no sea-coast, on a basis of reciprocity, free transit through their territory; and

(b) To ships flying the flag of that State treatment equal to that accorded to their own ships, or to the ships of any other States, as regards access to seaports and the use of such ports.

2. States situated between the sea and a State having no sea-coast shall settle, by mutual agreement with the latter, and taking into account the rights of the coastal State or State of transit and the special conditions of the State having no sea-coast, all matters relating to freedom of transit and equal treatment in ports, in case such States are not already parties to existing international conventions.

Article 4

Every State, whether coastal or not, has the right to sail ships under its flag on the high seas.

Article 5

1. Each State shall fix the conditions for the grant of its nationality to ships, for the registration of ships in its territory, and for the right to fly its flag. Ships have the nationality of the State whose flag they are entitled to fly. There must exist a genuine link between the State and the ship; in particular, the State must effectively exercise its jurisdiction and control in administrative, technical and social matters over ships flying its flag.

2. Each State shall issue to ships to which it has granted the right to fly its flag documents to that effect.

Article 6

1. Ships shall sail under the flag of one State only and, save in exceptional cases expressly provided for in international treaties or in these articles, shall be subject to its exclusive jurisdiction on the high seas. A ship may not change its flag during a voyage or while in a port of call, save in the case of a real transfer of ownership or change of registry.

2. A ship which sails under the flags of two or more States, using them according to convenience, may not claim any of the nationalities in question with respect to any other State, and may be assimilated to a ship without nationality.

Article 7

The provision of the preceding articles do not prejudice the question of ships employed on the official service of an inter-governmental organization flying the flag of the organization.

Article 8

1. Warships on the high seas have complete immunity from the jurisdiction of any State other than the flag State.

2. For the purposes of these articles, the term "warship" means a ship belonging to the naval forces of a State and bearing the external marks distinguishing warships of its nationality, under the command of an officer duly commissioned by the government and whose name appears in the Navy List, and manned by a crew who are under regular naval discipline.

Article 9

Ships owned or operated by a State and used only on government non-commercial service shall, on the high seas, have complete immunity from the jurisdiction of any State other than the flag State.

Article 10

1. Every State shall take such measures for ships under its flag as are necessary to ensure safety at sea with regard *inter alia* to:

(a) The use of signals, the maintenance of communications and the prevention of collisions;

(b) The manning of ships and labour conditions for crews taking into account the applicable international labour instruments;

(c) The construction, equipment and seaworthiness of ships.

2. In taking such measures each State is required to conform to generally accepted international standards and to take any steps which may be necessary to ensure their observance.

Article 11

1. In the event of a collision or of any other incident of navigation concerning a ship on the high seas, involving the penal or disciplinary responsibility of the master or of any other person in the service of the ship, no penal or disciplinary proceedings may be instituted against such persons except before the judicial or administrative authorities either of the flag State or of the State of which such person is a national.

2. In disciplinary matters, the State which has issued a master's certificate or a certificate of competence or license shall alone be competent, after due legal process, to pronounce the withdrawal of such certificates, even if the holder is not a national of the State which issued them.

3. No arrest or detention of the ship, even as a measure of investigation, shall be ordered by any authorities other than those of the flag State.

Article 12

1. Every State shall require the master of a ship sailing under its flag, in so far as he can do so without serious danger to the ship, the crew, or the passengers,

(a) To render assistance to any person found at sea in danger of being lost;

(b) To proceed with all possible speed to the rescue of persons in distress if informed of their need of assistance, in so far as such action may reasonably be expected of him;

(c) After a collision, to render assistance to the other ship, her crew and her passengers and, where possible to inform the other ship of the name of his own ship, her port of registry and the nearest port at which she will call.

2. Every coastal State promote the establishment and maintenance of an adequate and effective search and rescue service regarding safety on and over the sea and—where circumstances so require—by way of mutual regional arrangements co-operate with neighbouring States for this purpose.

Article 13

Every State shall adopt effective measures to prevent and punish the transport of slaves in ships authorized to fly its flag, and to prevent the unlawful use of its flag for that purpose. Any slave taking refuge on board any ship, whatever its flag, shall *ipso facto* be free.

Article 14

All States shall co-operate to the fullest possible extent in the repression of piracy on the high seas or in any other place outside the jurisdiction of any State.

Article 15

Piracy consists of any of the following acts:

(1) Any illegal acts of violence, detention or any act depredation, committed for private ends by the crew or the passengers of a private ship or a private aircraft, and directed:

(a) On the high seas, against another ship or aircraft, or against persons or property on board such ship or aircraft;

(b) Against a ship, aircraft, persons or property in a place outside the jurisdiction of any State;

(2) Any act of voluntary participation in the operation of a ship or of an aircraft with knowledge of facts making it a pirate ship or aircraft;

(3) Any act of inciting or of intentionally facilitating an act described in sub-paragraph 1 or sub-paragraph 2 of this article.

Article 16

The acts of piracy, as defined in article 15, committed by a warship, government ship or government aircraft whose crew has mutinied and taken control of the ship or aircraft are assimilated to acts committed by a private ship.

Article 17

A ship or aircraft is considered a pirate ship or aircraft if it is intended by the persons in dominant control to be used for the purpose of committing one of the acts referred to in article 15. The same applies if the ship or aircraft has been used to commit any such act, so long as it remains under the control of the persons guilty of that act.

ARTICLE 18

A ship or aircraft may retain its nationality although it has become a pirate ship or aircraft. The retention or loss of nationality is determined by the law of the State from which such nationality was derived.

ARTICLE 19

On the high seas, or in any other place outside the jurisdiction of any State, every State may seize a pirate ship or aircraft, or a ship taken by piracy and under the control of pirates, and arrest the persons and seize the property on board. The courts of the State which carried out the seizure may decide upon the penalties to be imposed, and may also determine the action to be taken with regard to the ships, aircraft or property, subject to the rights of third parties acting in good faith.

ARTICLE 20

Where the seizure of a ship or aircraft on suspicion of piracy has been effected without adequate grounds, the State making the seizure shall be liable to the State the nationality of which is possessed by the ship or aircraft, for any loss or damage caused by the seizure.

ARTICLE 21

A seizure on account of piracy may only be carried out by warships or military aircraft, or other ships or aircraft on government service authorized to that effect.

ARTICLE 22

1. Except where acts of interference derive from powers conferred by treaty, a warship which encounters a foreign merchant ship on the high seas is not justified in boarding her unless there is reasonable ground for suspecting:

(a) That the ship is engaged in piracy; or

(b) That the ship is engaged in the slave trade; or

(c) That, though flying a foreign flag or refusing to show its flag, the ship is, in reality, of the same nationality as the warship.

2. In the cases provided for in sub-paragraphs (a), (b) and (c) above, the warship may proceed to verify the ship's right to fly its flag. To this end, it may send a boat under the command of an officer to the suspected ship. If suspicion remains after the documents have been checked, it may proceed to a further examination on board the ship, which must be carried out with all possible consideration.

3. If the suspicions prove to be unfounded, and provided that the ship boarded has not committed any act justifying them, it shall be compensated for any loss or damage that may have been sustained.

ARTICLE 23

1. The hot pursuit of a foreign ship may be undertaken when the competent authorities of the coastal State have good reason to believe that the ship has violated the laws and regulations of that State. Such pursuit must be commenced when the foreign ship or one of its boats is within the internal waters or the territorial sea or the contiguous zone of the pursuing State, and may only be continued outside the territorial sea or the contiguous zone if the pursuit has not been interrupted. It is not necessary that, at the time when the foreign ship within the territorial sea or the contiguous zone receives that order to stop, the ship given the order should likewise be within the territorial sea or the contiguous zone. If the foreign ship is within a contiguous zone, as defined in article 24 of the Convention on the Territorial Sea and the Contiguous Zone, the pursuit may only be undertaken if there has been a violation of the rights for the protection of which the zone was established.

2. The right of hot pursuit ceases as soon as the ship pursued enters the territorial sea of its own country or of a third State.

3. Hot pursuit is not deemed to have begun unless the pursuing ship has satisfied itself by such practicable means as may be available that the ship pursued or one of its boats or other craft working as a team and using the ship pursued as a mother ship are within the limits of the territorial sea, or as the case may be within the contiguous zone. The pursuit may only be commenced after a visual or auditory signal to stop has been given at a distance which enables it to be seen or heard by the foreign ship.

4. The right of hot pursuit may be exercised only by warships or military aircraft, or other ships or aircraft on government service specially authorized to that effect.

5. Where hot pursuit is effected by an aircraft:

(a) The provisions of paragraph 1 to 3 of this article shall apply *mutatis mutandis;*

(b) The aircraft giving the order to stop must itself actively pursue the ship until a ship or aircraft of the coastal State, summoned by the aircraft, arrives to take over the pursuit, unless the aircraft is itself able to arrest the ship. It does not suffice to justify an arrest on the high seas that the ship was merely sighted by the aircraft as an offender or suspected offender, if it was not both ordered to stop and pursued by the aircraft itself or other aircraft or ships which continue the pursuit without interruption.

6. The release of a ship arrested within the jurisdiction of a State and escorted to a port of that State for the purposes of an enquiry before the competent authorities may not be claimed solely on the ground that the ship, in the course of its voyage, was escorted across a portion of the high seas, if the circumstances rendered this necessary.

7. Where a ship has been stopped or arrested on the high seas in circumstances which do not justify the exercise of the right of hot pursuit, it shall be compensated for any loss or damage that may have been thereby sustained.

ARTICLE 24

Every State shall draw up regulations to prevent pollution of the seas by the discharge of oil from ships or pipelines or resulting from the exploitation and exploration of the seabed and its subsoil, taking account of existing treaty provisions on the subject.

ARTICLE 25

1. Every State shall take measures to prevent pollution of the seas from the dumping of radioactive waste, taking into account any standards and regulations which may be formulated by the competent international organizations.

2. All States shall co-operate with the competent international organizations in taking measures for the prevention of pollution of the seas or air space above, resulting from any activities with radio-active materials or other harmful agents.

ARTICLE 26

1. All States shall be entitled to lay submarine cables and pipelines on the bed of the high seas.

2. Subject to its right to take reasonable measures for the exploration of the continental shelf and the exploitation of its natural resources, the coastal State may not impede the laying or maintenance of such cables or pipelines.

3. When laying such cables or pipelines the State in question shall pay due regard to cables or pipelines already in position on the seabed. In particular, possibilities of repairing existing cables or pipelines shall not be prejudiced.

ARTICLE 27

Every State shall take the necessary legislative measures to provide that the breaking or injury by a ship flying its flag or by a person subject to its jurisdiction of a submarine cable beneath the high seas done willfully or through culpable negligence, in such a manner as to be liable to interrupt or obstruct telegraphic or telephonic communications, and similarly the breaking or injury of a submarine, pipeline or high-voltage power cable shall be a punishable offense. This provision shall not apply to any break or injury caused by persons who acted merely with the legitimate object of saving their lives or their ships, after having taken all necessary precautions to avoid such break or injury.

ARTICLE 28

Every State shall take the necessary legislative measures to provide that, if persons subject to its jurisdiction who are the owners of a cable or pipeline beneath the high seas, in laying or repairing that cable or pipeline, cause a break in or injury to another cable or pipeline, they shall bear the cost of the repairs.

ARTICLE 29

Every State shall take the necessary legislative measures to ensure that the owners of ships who can prove that they have sacrificed an anchor, a net or any other fishing gear, in order to avoid injuring a submarine cable or pipeline, shall be indemnified by the owner of the cable or pipeline, provided that the owner of the ship has taken all reasonable precautionary measures beforehand.

ARTICLE 30

The provisions of this Convention shall not affect conventions or other international agreements already in force, as between States parties to them.

ARTICLE 31

This Convention shall, until October 1958, be open for signature by all States Members of the United Nations or of any of the specialized agencies, and by any other State invited by the General Assembly of the United Nations to become a Party to the Convention.

ARTICLE 32

This Convention is subject to ratification. The instruments of ratification shall be deposited with the Secretary-General of the United Nations.

ARTICLE 33

This Convention shall be open for accession by any States belonging to any of the categories mentioned in article 31. The instruments of accession shall be deposited with the Secretary-General of the United Nations.

ARTICLE 34

1. This Convention shall come into force on the thirtieth day following the date of deposit of the twenty-second instrument of ratification or accession with the Secretary-General of the United Nations.

2. For each State ratifying or acceding to the Convention after the deposit of the twenty-second instrument of ratification or accession, the Convention shall enter into force on the thirtieth day after deposit by such State of its instrument of ratification or accession.

ARTICLE 35

1. After the expiration of a period of five years from the date on which this Convention shall enter into force, a request for the revision of this Convention may be made at any time by any Contracting Party by means of a notification in writing addressed to the Secretary-General of the United Nations.

2. The General Assembly of the United Nations shall decide upon the steps, if any, to be taken in respect of such request.

Article 36

The Secretary-General of the United Nations shall inform all States Members of the United Nations and the other States referred to in article 31:

(a) Of signatures to this Convention and of the deposit of instruments of ratification or accession, in accordance with articles 31, 32 and 33;

(b) Of the date on which this Convention will come into force, in accordance with article 34;

(c) Of requests for revision in accordance with article 35.

Article 37

The original of this Convention, of which the Chinese, English, French, Russian and Spanish texts are equally authentic, shall be deposited with the Secretary-General of the United Nations, who shall send certified copies thereof to all States referred to in article 31.

In witness whereof the undersigned Plenipotentiaries being duly authorized thereto by their respective Governments, have signed this Convention.

Done at Geneva, this twenty-ninth day of April one thousand nine hundred and fifty-eight.

c. Convention on Fishing and Conservation of the Living Resources of the High Seas

Done at Geneva, April 29, 1958; Ratification, subject to an understanding, advised by the Senate, May 26, 1960; Ratified, subject to the said understanding, by the President, March 24, 1961; Ratification of the United States, with the said understanding, deposited with the Secretary-General of the United Nations, April 12, 1961; Proclaimed by the President, March 31, 1966; Entered into force, March 20, 1966

ANNEX III[1]

CONVENTION ON FISHING AND CONSERVATION OF THE LIVING RESOURCES OF THE HIGH SEAS[2]

The States Parties to this Convention,

CONSIDERING that the development of modern techniques for the exploitation of the living resources of the sea, increasing man's ability to meet the need of the world's expanding population for food, has exposed some of these resources to the danger of being over-exploited.

CONSIDERING ALSO that the nature of the problems involved in the conservation of the living resources of the high seas is such that there is a clear necessity that they be solved, whenever possible on the basis of international co-operation through the concerted action of all the States concerned.

HAVE AGREED AS FOLLOWS:

ARTICLE 1

1. All States have the right for their nationals to engage in fishing on the high seas, subject (a) to their treaty obligation, (b) to the interests and the rights of coastal States as provided for in this Convention, and (c) to the provisions contained in the following articles concerning conservation of the living resources of the high seas.

2. All States have the duty to adopt, or to co-operate with other States in adopting, such measures for their respective nationals as may be necessary for the conservation of the living resources of the high seas.

ARTICLE 2

As employed in this Convention, the expression "conservation of the living resources of the high seas" means the aggregate of the measures rendering possible the optimum sustainable yield from

[1] The text of the Convention printed herein constituted Annex III of the Final Act of the United Nations Conference of the Law of the Sea which was certified by the Legal Counsel, for the Secretary-General of the United Nations.

[2] 17 UST 138; TIAS 5969; 559 UNTS 285.

those resources so as to secure a maximum supply of food and other marine products. Conservation programmes should be formulated with a view to securing the first place a supply of food for human consumption.

ARTICLE 3

A State whose nationals are engaged in fishing any stock or stocks of fish or other living marine resources in any area of the high seas where the nationals of other States are not thus engaged shall adopt, for its own nationals, measures in that area when necessary for the purpose of the conservation of the living resources affected.

ARTICLE 4

1. If the nationals of two or more States are engaged in fishing the same stock or stocks of fish or other living marine resources in any area or areas of the high seas, these States shall, at the request of any of them, enter into negotiations with a view to prescribing by agreement for their nationals the necessary measures for the conservation of the living resources affected.

2. If the States concerned do not reach agreement within twelve months, any of the parties may initiate the procedure contemplated by article 9.

ARTICLE 5

1. If, subsequent to the adoption of the measures referred to in articles 3 and 4, nationals of other States engage in fishing the same stock or stocks of fish or other living marine resources in any area or areas of the high seas, the other States shall apply the measures, which shall not be discriminatory in form or in fact, to their own nationals not later than seven months after the date on which the measures shall have been notified to the Director-General of the Food and Agriculture Organization of the United Nations. The Director-General shall notify such measures to any State which so requests and, in any case, to any State specified by the State initiating the measure.

2. If these other States do not accept the measures so adopted and if no agreement can be reached within twelve months, any of the interested parties may initiate the procedure contemplated by article 9. Subject to paragraph 2 of article 10, the measures adopted shall remain obligatory pending the decision of the special commission.

ARTICLE 6

1. A coastal State has a special interest in the maintenance of the productivity of the living resources in any area of the high seas adjacent to its territorial sea.

2. A coastal State is entitled to take part on an equal footing in any system of research and regulation for purposes of conservation of the living resources of the high seas in that area, even though its nationals do not carry on fishing there.

3. A State whose nationals are engaged in fishing in any area of the high seas adjacent to the territorial sea of a coastal State shall, at the request of that coastal State, enter in negotiations with a view to prescribing by agreement the measures necessary for the conservation of the living resources of the high seas in that area.

4. A State whose nationals are engaged in fishing in any area of the high seas adjacent to the territorial sea of a coastal State shall not enforce conservation measures in that area which are opposed to those which have been adopted by the coastal State, but may enter into negotiations with the coastal State with a view to prescribing by agreement the measures necessary for the conservation of the living resources of the high seas in that area.

5. If the States concerned do not reach agreement with respect to conservation measures within twelve months, any of the parties may initiate the procedure contemplated by article 9.

ARTICLE 7

1. Having regard to the provisions of paragraph 1 of article 6, any coastal State may, with a view to the maintenance of the productivity of the living resources of the sea, adopt unilateral measures of conservation appropriate to any stock of fish or other marine resources in any area of the high seas adjacent to its territorial sea, provided that negotiations to that effect with the other States concerned have not led to an agreement within six months.

2. The measures which the coastal State adopts under the previous paragraph shall be valid as to other States only if the following requirements are fulfilled:

(a) That there is a need for urgent application of conservation measures in the light of the existing knowledge of the fishery;

(b) That the measures adopted are based on appropriate scientific findings; and

(c) That such measures do not discriminate in form or in fact against foreign fishermen.

3. These measures shall remain in force pending the settlement, in accordance with the relevant provisions of this Convention, of any disagreement as to their validity.

4. If the measures are not accepted by the other States concerned, any of the parties may initiate the procedure contemplated by article 9. Subject to paragraph 2 of article 10, the measures adopted shall remain obligatory pending the decision of the special commission.

5. The principles of geographical demarcation as defined in article 12 of the Convention on the Territorial Sea and the Contiguous Zone shall be adopted when coasts of different States are involved.

ARTICLE 8

1. Any State which, even if its nationals are not engaged in fishing in an area of the high seas not adjacent to its coast, has a special interest in the conservation of the living resources of the high seas in that area, may request the State or States whose nationals are engaged in fishing there to take the necessary measures of conservation under articles 3 and 4 respectively, at the same time

mentioning the scientific reasons which in its opinion make such measures necessary, and indicating its special interest.

2. If no agreement is reached within twelve months, such State may initiate the procedure contemplated by article 9.

ARTICLE 9

1. Any dispute which may arise between States under articles 4, 5, 6, 7, and 8 shall, at the request of any of the parties, be submitted for settlement to a special commission of five members, unless the parties agree to seek a solution by another method of peaceful settlements, as provided for in Article 33 of the Charter of the United Nations.

2. The members of the commission, one of whom shall be designated as chairman, shall be named by agreement between the States in dispute within three months of the request for settlement in accordance with the provisions of this article. Failing agreement they shall, upon the request of any State party, be named by the Secretary-General of the United Nations, within a further three-month period, in consultation with the States in dispute and with the President of the International Court of Justice and the Director-General of the Food and Agriculture Organization of the United Nations, from amongst well-qualified persons being nationals of the States not involved in the dispute and specializing in legal, administrative or scientific questions relating to fisheries, depending upon the nature of the dispute to be settled. Any vacancy arising after the original appointment shall be filled in the same manner as provided for the initial selection.

3. Any State party to proceedings under these articles shall have the right to name one of its nationals to the special commission, with the right to participate fully in the proceedings on the same footing as a member of the commission but without the right to vote or to take part in the writing of the commission's decision.

4. The commission shall determine its own procedure, assuring each party to the proceedings a full opportunity to be heard and to present its case. It shall also determine how the costs and expenses shall be divided between the parties to the dispute, failing agreement by the parties on this matter.

5. The special commission shall render its decision within a period of five months from the time it is appointed unless it decides, in case of necessity, to extend the time limit for a period not exceeding three months.

6. The special commission shall, in reaching its decisions, adhere to these articles and to any special agreements between the disputing parties regarding settlement of the dispute.

7. Decisions of the commission shall be by majority vote.

ARTICLE 10

1. The special commission shall, in disputes arising under article 7, apply the criteria listed in paragraph 2 of that article. In disputes under articles 4, 5, 6 and 8 the commission shall apply the following criteria, according to the issues involved in the dispute:

(a) Common to the determination of disputes arising under articles 4, 5 and 6 are the requirements:

(i) That scientific findings demonstrate the necessity of conservation measures;

(ii) That the specific measures are based on scientific findings and are practicable; and

(iii) That the measures do not discriminate, in form or in fact, against fishermen of other States.

(b) Applicable to the determination of disputes arising under article 8 is the requirement that scientific findings demonstrate the necessity for conservation measures, or that the conservation program is adequate, as the case may be.

2. The special commission may decide that pending its award the measures in dispute shall not be applied, provided that, in the case of disputes under article 7, the measures shall only be suspended when it is apparent to the commission on the basis of *prima facie* evidence that the need for the urgent application of such measures does not exist.

ARTICLE 11

The decisions of the special commission shall be binding on the States concerned and the provisions of paragraph 2 of Article 94 of the Charter of the United Nations shall be applicable to those decisions. If the decisions are accompanied by any recommendations, they shall receive the greatest possible consideration.

ARTICLE 12

1. If the factual basis of the award of the special commission is altered by substantial changes in the conditions of the stock or stocks of fish or other living marine resources or in methods of fishing, any of the States concerned may request the other States to enter into negotiations with a view to prescribing by agreement the necessary modifications in the measures of conservation.

2. If no agreement is reached within a reasonable period of time, any of the States concerned may again resort to the procedure contemplated by article 9 provided that at least two years have elapsed from the original award.

ARTICLE 13

1. The regulation of fisheries conducted by means of equipment embedded in the floor of the sea in areas of the high seas adjacent to the territorial sea of a State may be undertaken by that State where such fisheries have long been maintained and conducted by its nationals, provided that non-nationals are permitted to participate in such activities on an equal footing with nationals except in areas where such fisheries have by long usage been exclusively enjoyed by such nationals. Such regulations will not, however, affect the general status of the areas as high seas.

2. In this article, the expression “fisheries conducted by means of equipment embedded in the floor of the sea” means those fisheries using gear with supporting members embedded in the sea floor, constructed on a site and left there to operate permanently or, if removed, restored each season on the same site.

ARTICLE 14

In articles 1, 3, 4, 5, 6 and 8, the term "nationals" means fishing boats or craft of any size having the nationality of the State concerned, according to the law of that State, irrespective of the nationality of the members of their crews.

ARTICLE 15

The Convention shall, until 31 October 1958, be open for signature by all States Members of the United Nations or any of the specialized agencies, and by any other State invited by the General Assembly of the United Nations to become a Party to the Convention.

ARTICLE 16

This Convention is subject to ratification. The instruments of ratification shall be deposited with the Secretary-General of the United Nations.

ARTICLE 17

This Convention shall be open for accession by any States belonging to any of the categories mentioned in article 15. The instruments of accession shall be deposited with the Secretary-General of the United Nations.

ARTICLE 18

1. This Convention shall come into force on the thirtieth day following the date of deposit of the twenty-second instrument of ratification or accession with the Secretary-General of the United Nations.

2. For each State ratifying or acceding to the Convention after the deposit of the twenty-second instrument of ratification or accession, the Convention shall enter into force on the thirtieth day after deposit by such State of its instrument of ratification or accession.

ARTICLE 19

1. At the time of signature, ratification or accession, any State may make reservations to articles of the Convention other than to articles 6, 7, 9, 10, 11 and 12.

2. Any Contracting State making a reservation in accordance with the preceding paragraph may at any time withdraw the reservation by a communication to that effect addressed to the Secretary-General of the United Nations.

ARTICLE 20

1. After the expiration of a period of five years from the date on which this Convention shall enter into force, a request for the revision of this Convention may be made at any time by any Contracting Party by means of a notification in writing addressed to the Secretary-General of the United Nations.

2. The General Assembly of the United Nations shall decide upon the steps, if any, to be taken in respect of such request.

ARTICLE 21

The Secretary-General of the United Nations shall inform all States Members of the United Nations and the other States referred to in article 15:

(a) Of signatures to this Convention and of the deposit of instruments of ratification or accession, in accordance with articles 15, 16 and 17;

(b) Of the date on which this Convention will come into force, in accordance with article 18;

(c) Of requests for revision in accordance with article 20;

(d) Of reservations to this Convention, in accordance with article 19.

ARTICLE 22

The original of this Convention, of which the Chinese, English, French, Russian and Spanish texts are equally authentic, shall be deposited with the Secretary-General of the United Nations, who shall send certified copies thereof to all States referred to in article 15.

IN WITNESS WHEREOF the undersigned Plenipotentiaries, being duly authorized thereto by their respective Governments, have signed this Convention.

DONE at Geneva, this twenty-ninth day of April one thousand nine hundred and fifty-eight.

RESERVATION AS STATED IN THE PROCLAMATION

Whereas the Senate of the United States of America by their resolution of May 26, 1960, two-thirds of the Senators present concurring therein, did advise and consent to the ratification of the said Convention subject to the understanding "that such ratification shall not be construed to impair the applicability of the principle of 'absentention', as defined in paragraph A.1 of the documents of record in the proceedings of the Conference above referred to, identified as A/CONF.13/C.3/L69, 8 April 1958";

Whereas paragraph A.1 of document A/CONF.13/C.3/L69, 8 April 1958, of the United Nations Conferences on the Law of the Sea reads as follows:

"Where the nationals of a coastal State, alone or with the nationals of one or more other States, are (a) fishing a stock of fish in an area of the high seas adjacent to the territorial sea of the coastal State with such intensity that an increase in fishing effort will not result in a substantial increase in the yield which can be maintained year after year, and (b) where the maintenance of the current yield, or when possible, the further development of it is dependent upon a conservation programme carried out by those States, involving research and limitations upon the size or quantity of the fish which may be caught, then (c) States whose nationals are not fishing the stock regularly or which have not theretofore done so within a reasonable period of time, shall abstain from fishing such stock, provided, however, that this shall not apply to any coastal State with respect to fishing any stock in waters adjacent to its territorial sea."

d. Convention on the Continental Shelf

Done at Geneva, April 29, 1958; Ratification advised by the Senate, May 26, 1960; Ratified by the President, March 24, 1961; Ratification of the United States deposited with the Secretary-General of the United Nations, April 12, 1961; Proclaimed by the President, May 25, 1964; Entered into force, June 10, 1964

ANNEX IV[1]

CONVENTION ON THE CONTINENTAL SHELF[2]

The States Parties to this Convention,

HAVE AGREED AS FOLLOWS:

ARTICLE 1

For the purpose of these articles, the term "continental shelf" is used as referring (a) to the seabed and subsoil of the submarine areas adjacent to the coast but outside the area of the territorial sea, to a depth of 200 metres or, beyond that limit, to where the depth of the superjacent waters admits of the exploitation of the natural resources of the said areas; (b) to the seabed and subsoil of similar submarine areas adjacent to the coasts of islands.

ARTICLE 2

1. The coastal State exercises over the continental shelf sovereign rights for the purpose of exploring it and exploiting its natural resources.
2. The rights referred to in paragraph 1 of this article are exclusive in the sense that if the coastal State does not explore the continental shelf or exploit its natural resources, no one may undertake these activities, or make a claim to the continental shelf, without the express consent of the coastal State.
3. The rights of the coastal State over the continental shelf do not depend on occupation, effective or notional, or on any express proclamation.
4. The natural resources referred to in these articles consist of the mineral and other non-living resources of the seabed and subsoil together with living organisms belonging to sedentary species, that is to say, organisms which, at the harvestable stage, either are immobile on or under the seabed or are unable to move except in constant physical contact with the seabed or the subsoil.

---

[1] The text of the convention printed herein constituted Annex IV to the Final Act of the United Nations Conference on the Law of the Sea, which was certified by the Legal Counsel, for the Secretary-General of the United Nations.

[2] 15 UST 471; TIAS 5578; 499 UNTS 311.

ARTICLE 3

The rights of the coastal State over the continental shelf do not affect the legal status of the superjacent waters as high seas, or that of the airspace above those waters.

ARTICLE 4

Subject to its right to take reasonable measures for the exploration of the continental shelf and the exploitation of its natural resources, the coastal State may not impede the laying or maintenance of submarine cables or pipe lines on the continental shelf.

ARTICLE 5

1. The exploration of the continental shelf and the exploitation of its natural resources must not result in any unjustifiable interference with navigation, fishing or the conservation of the living resources of the sea, nor result in any interference with fundamental oceanographic or other scientific research carried out with the intention of open publication.

2. Subject to the provisions of paragraphs 1 and 6 of this article, the coastal State is entitled to construct and maintain or operate on the continental shelf installations and other devices necessary for its exploration and the exploitation of its natural resources, and to establish safety zones around such installations and devices and to take in those zones measures necessary for their protection.

3. The safety zones referred to in paragraph 2 of this article may extend to a distance of 500 metres around the installations and other devices which have been erected, measured from each point of their outer edge. Ships of all nationalities must respect these safety zones.

4. Such installations and devices, though under the jurisdiction of the coastal State, do not possess the status of islands. They have no territorial sea of their own, and their presence does not affect the delimitation of the territorial sea of the coastal State.

5. Due notice must be given of the construction of any such installation, and permanent means for giving warning of their presence must be maintained. Any installations which are abandoned or disused must be entirely removed.

6. Neither the installations or devices, nor the safety zones around them, may be established where interference may be caused to the use of recognized sea lanes essential to international navigation.

7. The coastal State is obliged to undertake, in the safety zones, all appropriate measures for the protection of the living resources of the sea from harmful agents.

8. The consent of the coastal State shall be obtained in respect of any research concerning the continental shelf and undertaken there. Nevertheless the coastal State shall not normally withhold its consent if the request is submitted by a qualified institution with a view to purely scientific research into the physical or biological characteristics of the continental shelf, subject to the proviso

that the coastal State shall have the right, if it so desires, to participate or to be represented in the research, and that in any event the results shall be published.

Article 6

1. Where the same continental shelf is adjacent to the territories of two or more States whose coasts are opposite each other, the boundary of the continental shelf appertaining to such States shall be determined by agreement between them. In the absence of agreement, and unless another boundary line is justified by special circumstances, the boundary is the median line, every point of which is equidistant from the nearest points of the baselines from which the breadth of the territorial sea of each State is measured.

2. Where the same continental shelf is adjacent to the territories of two adjacent States, the boundary of the continental shelf shall be determined by agreement between them. In the absence of agreement, and unless another boundary line is justified by special circumstances, the boundary shall be determined by application of the principle of equidistance from the nearest points of the baselines from which the breadth of the territorial sea of each State is measured.

3. In delimiting the boundaries of the continental shelf, any lines which are drawn in accordance with the principles set out in paragraphs 1 and 2 of this article should be defined with reference to charts and geographical features as they exist at a particular date, and reference should be made to fixed permanent identifiable points on the land.

Article 7

The provisions of these articles shall not prejudice the right of the coastal State to exploit the subsoil by means of tunnelling irrespective of the depth of water above the topsoil.

Article 8

The Convention shall until 31 October 1958, be open for signature by all States Members of the United Nations or of any of the specialized agencies, and by any other State invited by the General Assembly of the United Nations to become a Party to the Convention.

Article 9

This Convention is subject to ratification. The instruments of ratification shall be deposited with the Secretary-General of the United Nations.

Article 10

This Convention shall be open for accession by any States belonging to any of the categories mentioned in article 8. The instruments of accession shall be deposited with the Secretary-General of the United Nations.

Article 11

1. This Convention shall come into force on the thirtieth day following the date of deposit of the twenty-second instrument of ratification or accession with the Secretary-General of the United Nations.

2. For each State ratifying or acceding to the Convention after the deposit of the twenty-second instrument of ratification or accession, the Convention shall enter into force on the thirtieth day after deposit by such State of its instrument of ratification or accession.

Article 12

1. At the time of signature, ratification or accession, any State may make reservations to articles of the Convention other than to articles 1 to 3 inclusive.

2. Any Contracting State making a reservation in accordance with the preceding paragraph may at any time withdraw the reservation by a communication to that effect addressed to the Secretary-General of the United Nations.

Article 13

1. After the expiration of a period of five years from the date on which this Convention shall enter into force, a request for the revision of this Convention may be made at any time by any Contracting Party by means of a notification in writing addressed to the Secretary-General of the United Nations.

2. The General Assembly of the United Nations shall decide upon the steps, if any, to be taken in respect of such request.

Article 14

The Secretary-General of the United Nations shall inform all States Members of the United Nations and the other States referred to in article 8:

(a) Of signatures to this Convention and of the deposit of instruments of ratification or accession with articles 8, 9 and 10;

(b) Of the date on which this Convention will come into force, in accordance with article 11;

(c) Of requests for revision in accordance with article 13; and

(d) Of reservations to this Convention, in accordance with article 12.

Article 15

The original of this Convention of which the Chinese, English, French, Russian and Spanish texts are equally authentic, shall be deposited with the Secretary-General of the United Nations, who shall send certified copies thereof to all States referred to in article 8.

In witness whereof the undersigned Plenipotentiaries, being duly authorized thereto by their respective Governments, have signed this Convention.

Done at Geneva, this twenty-ninth day of April one thousand nine hundred and fifty-eight.

2. Convention for the Prohibition of Fishing with Long Driftnets in the South Pacific

Done at Wellington, November 24, 1989; Entered into force, May 17, 1991; Entered into force for the United States, February 28, 1992

CONVENTION FOR THE PROHIBITION OF FISHING WITH LONG DRIFTNETS IN THE SOUTH PACIFIC [1]

The Parties to this Convention,

RECOGNISING the importance of marine living resources to the people of the South Pacific region;

PROFOUNDLY CONCERNED at the damage now being done by pelagic driftnet fishing to the albacore tuna resource and to the environment and economy of the South Pacific region;

CONCERNED ALSO for the navigational threat posed by driftnet fishing;

NOTING that the increasing fishing capacity induced by large scale driftnet fishing threatens the fish stocks in the South Pacific;

MINDFUL OF the relevant rules of international law, including the provisions of the United Nations Convention on the Law of the Sea done at Montego Bay on 10 December 1982, in particular Parts V, VII and XVI;

RECALLING the Declaration of the South Pacific Forum at Tarawa, 11 July 1989 that a Convention should be adopted to ban the use of driftnets in the South Pacific region;

RECALLING ALSO the Resolution of the 29th South Pacific Conference at Guam, which called for an immediate ban on the practice of driftnet fishing in the South Pacific Commission region;

HAVE AGREED AS FOLLOWS:

ARTICLE 1

DEFINITIONS

For the purposes of this Convention and its Protocols:

(a) the "Convention Area",

(i) subject to sub-paragraph (ii) of this paragraph, shall be the area lying within 10 degrees North latitude and 50 degrees South latitude and 130 degrees East longitude and 120 degrees West longitude, and shall also include all waters under the fisheries jurisdiction of any Party to this Convention.

[1] 1899 UNTS 3. For a list of parties to the Convention, see Department of State publication *Treaties in Force.*

(ii) In the case of a State or Territory which is Party to the Convention by virtue of paragraph 1(b) or 1(c) of Article 10, it shall include only waters under the fisheries jurisdiction of that Party, adjacent to the Territory referred to in paragraph 1(b) or 1(c) of Article 10;

(b) "driftnet" means a gillnet or other net or a combination of nets which is more than 2.5 kilometres in length the purpose of which is to enmesh, entrap or entangle fish by drifting on the surface of or in the water;

(c) "driftnet fishing activities" means:

(i) catching, taking or harvesting fish with the use of a driftnet;

(ii) attempting to catch, take or harvest fish with the use of a driftnet;

(iii) engaging in any other activity which can reasonably be expected to result in the catching, taking or harvesting of fish with the use of a driftnet, including searching for and locating fish to be taken by that method;

(iv) any operations at sea in support of, or in preparation for any activity described in this paragraph, including operations of placing, searching for or recovering fish aggregation devices or associated electronic equipment such as radio beacons;

(v) aircraft use, relating to the activities described in this paragraph, except for flights in emergencies involving the health or safety of crew members or the safety of a vessel; or

(vi) transporting, transhipping and processing any driftnet catch, and cooperation in the provision of food, fuel and other supplies for vessels equipped for or engaged in driftnet fishing;

(d) the "FFA" means the South Pacific Forum Fisheries Agency; and

(e) "fishing vessel" means any vessel or boat equipped for or engaged in searching for, catching, processing or transporting fish or other marine organisms.

Article 2

MEASURES REGARDING NATIONALS AND VESSELS

Each Party undertakes to prohibit its nationals and vessels documented under its laws from engaging in driftnet fishing activities within the Convention Area.

Article 3

MEASURES AGAINST DRIFTNET FISHING ACTIVITIES

(1) Each Party undertakes:

(a) not to assist or encourage the use of driftnets within the Convention Area; and

(b) to take measures consistent with international law to restrict driftnet fishing activities within the Convention Area, including but not limited to:

(i) prohibiting the use of driftnets within areas under its fisheries jurisdiction; and

(ii) prohibiting the transhipment of driftnet catches within areas under its jurisdiction.

(2) Each Party may also take measures consistent with international law to:

(a) prohibit the landing of driftnet catches within its territory;

(b) prohibit the processing of driftnet catches in facilities under its jurisdiction;

(c) prohibit the importation of any fish or fish product, whether processed or not, which was caught using a driftnet;

(d) restrict port access and port servicing facilities for driftnet fishing vessels; and

(e) prohibit the possession of driftnets on board any fishing vessel within areas under its fisheries jurisdiction.

(3) Nothing in this Convention shall prevent a Party from taking measures against driftnet fishing activities which are stricter than those required by the Convention.

ARTICLE 4

ENFORCEMENT

(1) Each Party shall take appropriate measures to ensure the application of the provisions of this Convention.

(2) The Parties undertake to collaborate to facilitate surveillance and enforcement of measures taken by Parties pursuant to this Convention.

(3) The Parties undertake to take measures leading to the withdrawal of good standing on the Regional Register of Foreign Fishing Vessels maintained by the FFA against any vessel engaging in driftnet fishing activities.

ARTICLE 5

CONSULTATION WITH NON-PARTIES

(1) The Parties shall seek to consult with any State which is eligible to become a Party to this Convention on any matter relating to driftnet fishing activities which appear to affect adversely the conservation of marine living resources within the Convention Area or the implementation of the Convention or its Protocols.

(2) The Parties shall seek to reach agreement with any State referred to in paragraph 1 of this Article, concerning the prohibitions established pursuant to Articles 2 and 3.

ARTICLE 6

INSTITUTIONAL ARRANGEMENTS

(1) The FFA shall be responsible for carrying out the following functions:

(a) the collection, preparation and dissemination of information on driftnet fishing activities within the Convention Area;

(b) the facilitation of scientific analyses on the effects of driftnet fishing activities within the Convention Area, including consultations with appropriate regional and international organisations; and

(c) The preparation and transmission to the Parties of an annual report on any driftnet fishing activities within the Convention Area and the measures taken to implement this Convention or its Protocols.

(2) Each Party shall expeditiously convey to the FFA:

(a) information on the measures adopted by it pursuant to the implementation of the Convention; and

(b) information on, and scientific analyses on the effects of, driftnet fishing activities relevant to the Convention Area.

(3) All Parties, including States or Territories not members of the FFA and the FFA shall cooperate to promote the effective implementation of this Article.

Article 7

REVIEW AND CONSULTATION AMONG PARTIES

(1) Without prejudice to the conduct of consultations among Parties by other means, the FFA, at the request of three Parties, shall convene meetings of the Parties to review the implementation of this Convention and its Protocols.

(2) Parties to the Protocols shall be invited to any such meeting and to participate in a manner to be determined by the Parties to the Convention.

Article 8

CONSERVATION AND MANAGEMENT MEASURES

Parties to this Convention shall cooperate with each other and with appropriate distant water fishing nations and other entities or organisations in the development of conservation and management measures for South Pacific albacore tuna within the Convention Area.

Article 9

PROTOCOLS

This Convention may be supplemented by Protocols or associated instruments to further its objectives.

Article 10

SIGNATURE, RATIFICATION AND ACCESSION

(1) This Convention shall be open for signature by:

(a) any member of the FFA; and

(b) any State in respect of any Territory situated within the Convention Area for which it is internationally responsible; or

(c) any Territory situated within the Convention Area which has been authorised to sign the Convention and to assume rights and obligations under it by the Government of the State which is internationally responsible for it.

(2) This Convention is subject to ratification by members of the FFA and the other States and Territories referred to in paragraph 1 of this Article. The instruments of ratification shall be deposited with the Government of New Zealand which shall be the Depositary.

(3) This Convention shall remain open for accession by the members of the FFA and the other States and Territories referred to in paragraph 1 of this Article. The instruments of accession shall be deposited with the Depositary.

ARTICLE 11

RESERVATIONS

This Convention shall not be subject to reservations.

ARTICLE 12

AMENDMENTS

(1) Any Party may propose amendments to this Convention.

(2) Amendments shall be adopted by consensus among the Parties.

(3) Any amendments adopted shall be submitted by the Depositary to all Parties for ratification, approval or acceptance.

(4) An amendment shall enter into force thirty days after receipt by the Depositary of instruments of ratification, approval or acceptance from all Parties.

ARTICLE 13

ENTRY INTO FORCE

(1) This Convention shall enter into force on the date of deposit of the fourth instrument of ratification or accession.

(2) For any member of the FFA or a State or Territory which ratifies or accedes to this Convention after the date of deposit of the fourth instrument of ratification or accession, the Convention shall enter into force on the date of deposit of its instrument of ratification or accession.

ARTICLE 14

CERTIFICATION AND REGISTRATION

(1) The original of this Convention and its Protocols shall be deposited with the Depositary, which shall transmit certified copies to all States and Territories eligible to become Party to the Convention and to all States eligible to become Party to a Protocol to the Convention.

(2) The Depositary shall register this Convention and its Protocols in accordance with Article 102 of the Charter of the United Nations.

DONE at Wellington this twenty-fourth day of November 1989 in the English and French languages, each text being equally authentic.

IN WITNESS WHEREOF the undersigned, being duly authorised by their Governments, have signed this Convention.

PROTOCOL I

The Parties to this Protocol,

NOTING the provisions of the Convention for the Prohibition of Fishing with Long driftnets in the South Pacific ("the Convention")

HAVE AGREED AS FOLLOWS:

ARTICLE 1

APPLICATION OF THE CONVENTION

Nothing in this Protocol shall affect or prejudice the views or positions of any Party with respect to the law of the sea.

ARTICLE 2

MEASURES REGARDING NATIONALS AND VESSELS

Each Party undertakes to prohibit its nationals and fishing vessels documented under its laws from using driftnets within the Convention Area.

ARTICLE 3

TRANSMISSION OF INFORMATION

Each Party shall expeditiously convey to the FFA:

(a) information on the measures adopted by it pursuant to the implementation of this Protocol; and

(b) information on, and scientific analyses on the effects of, driftnet fishing activities relevant to the Convention Area.

ARTICLE 4

CONSERVATION AND MANAGEMENT MEASURES

Parties to this Protocol shall cooperate with Parties to the Convention in the development of conservation and management measures for South Pacific albacore tuna within the Convention Area.

ARTICLE 5

ENFORCEMENT

Each Party shall take appropriate measures to ensure the application of the provisions of this Protocol.

ARTICLE 6

WITHDRAWAL

At any time after three years from the date on which this Protocol has entered into force for a Party, that Party may withdraw from the Protocol by giving written notice to the Depositary. The Depositary shall immediately inform all Parties to the Convention or its Protocols of receipt of a withdrawal notice. Withdrawal shall take effect one year after receipt of such notice by the Depositary.

ARTICLE 7

FINAL CLAUSES

(1) This Protocol shall be open for signature by any State whose nationals or fishing vessels documented under its laws fish within the Convention Area or by any other State invited to sign by the Parties to the Convention.

(2) This Protocol shall be subject to ratification. Instruments of ratification shall be deposited with the Government of New Zealand, which shall be the Depositary.

(3) This Protocol shall enter into force for each State on the date of deposit of its instrument of ratification with the Depositary.

(4) This Protocol shall not be subject to reservations.

DONE at Noumea this twentieth day of October 1990.

IN WITNESS WHEREOF the undersigned, being duly authorised by their Governments, have signed this Protocol.

PROTOCOL II

The Parties to this Protocol,

NOTING the provisions of the Convention for the Prohibition of Fishing with Long driftnets in the South Pacific ("the Convention")

HAVE AGREED AS FOLLOWS:

ARTICLE 1

APPLICATION OF THE CONVENTION

Noting in this Protocol shall affect or prejudice the views or positions of any Party with respect to the law of the sea.

ARTICLE 2

MEASURES REGARDING NATIONALS AND VESSELS

Each Party undertakes to prohibit its nationals and fishing vessels documented under its laws from using driftnets within the Convention Area.

ARTICLE 3

MEASURES AGAINST DRIFTNET FISHING ACTIVITIES

(1) Each Party undertakes:

(a) not to assist or encourage the use of driftnets within the Convention Area; and

(b) to take measures consistent with international law to restrict driftnet fishing activities, including but not limited to:

(i) prohibiting the use of driftnets within areas under its fisheries jurisdiction; and

(ii) prohibiting the transhipment of driftnet catches within areas under its jurisdiction.

(2) Each Party may also take measures consistent with international law to:

(a) prohibit the landing of driftnet catches within its territory;

(b) prohibit the processing of driftnet catches in facilities under its jurisdiction;

(c) prohibit the importation of any fish or fish product, whether processed or not, which was caught using a driftnet;

(d) restrict port access and port servicing facilities for driftnet fishing vessels; and

(e) prohibit the possession of driftnets on board any fishing vessel within areas under its fisheries jurisdiction.

(3) Nothing in this Protocol shall prevent a Party from taking measures consistent with international law against driftnet fishing activities which are stricter than those required by the Protocol.

Article 4

TRANSMISSION OF INFORMATION

Each Party shall expeditiously convey to the FFA:

(a) information on the measures adopted by it pursuant to the implementation of this Protocol; and

(b) information on, and scientific analyses on the effects of, driftnet fishing activities relevant to the Convention Area.

Article 5

ENFORCEMENT

Each Party shall take appropriate measures to ensure the application of the provisions of this Protocol.

Article 6

WITHDRAWAL

At any time after three years from the date on which this Protocol has entered into force for a Party, that Party may withdraw from the Protocol by giving written notice to the Depositary. The Depositary shall immediately inform all Parties to the Convention or its Protocols of receipt of a withdrawal notice. Withdrawal shall take effect one year after receipt of such notice by the Depositary.

Article 7

FINAL CLAUSES

(1) This Protocol shall be open for signature by any State the waters under the jurisdiction of which are contiguous with or adjacent to the Convention Area or by any other State invited to sign by the Parties to the Convention.

(2) This Protocol shall be subject to ratification. Instruments of ratification shall be deposited with the Government of New Zealand, which shall be the Depositary.

(3) This Protocol shall enter into force for each State on the date of deposit of its instruments of ratification with the Depositary.

(4) This Protocol shall not be subject to reservations.

DONE at Noumea this twentieth day of October 1990.

IN WITNESS WHEREOF the undersigned, being duly authorised by their Governments, have signed this Protocol.

3. Inter-American Convention for the Protection of Sea Turtles

Done at Caracas, Venezuela, December 1, 1996; Signed by the United States of America, subject to ratification, December 13, 1996; Ratification advised by the Senate, September 20, 2000; Entered into force, May 2, 2001

INTER-AMERICAN CONVENTION FOR THE PROTECTION AND CONSERVATION OF SEA TURTLES

PREAMBLE

The Parties to this Convention:

RECOGNIZING the rights and duties of States established in international law, as reflected in the United Nations Convention on the Law of the Sea of 10 December 1982, relating to the conservation and management of living marine resources;

INSPIRED by the principles contained in the 1992 Rio Declaration on Environment and Development;

CONSIDERING the principles and recommendations set forth in the Code of Conduct for Responsible Fishing adopted by the Conference of the Food and Agriculture Organization (FAO) of the United Nations in its 28th Session (1995);

RECALLING that Agenda 21, adopted in 1992 by the United Nations Conference on Environment and Development, recognizes the need to protect and restore endangered marine species and to conserve their habitats;

UNDERSTANDING that, in accordance with the best available scientific evidence, species of sea turtles in the Americas are threatened or endangered, and that some of these species may face an imminent risk of extinction;

ACKNOWLEDGING the importance of having the States in the Americas adopt an agreement to address this situation through an instrument that also facilitates the participation of States from other regions interested in the worldwide protection and conservation of sea turtles, taking into account the widely migratory nature of these species;

RECOGNIZING that sea turtles are subject to capture, injury or mortality as a direct or indirect result of human-related activities;

CONSIDERING that coastal zone management measures are indispensable for protecting populations of sea turtles and their habitats;

RECOGNIZING the individual environmental, socio-economic and cultural conditions in the States in the Americas;

RECOGNIZING that sea turtles migrate widely throughout marine areas and that their protection and conservation require cooperation and coordination among States within the range of such species;

RECOGNIZING also the programs and activities that certain States are currently carrying out for the protection and conservation of sea turtles and their habitats;

DESIRING to establish, through this Convention, appropriate measures for the protection and conservation of sea turtles throughout their range in the Americas, as well as their habitats;

HAVE AGREED AS FOLLOWS:

ARTICLE I

DEFINITIONS

For the purposes of this Convention:

1. "Sea turtle" means any of the species listed in Annex I.
2. "Sea turtle habitats" means all those aquatic and terrestrial environments which sea turtles use at any stage of their life cycles.
3. "Parties" means States which have consented to be bound by this Convention and for which this Convention is in force.
4. "States in the Americas" means the States of North, Central and South America and the Caribbean Sea, as well as other States that have continental or insular territories in this region.

ARTICLE II

OBJECTIVE

The objective of this Convention is to promote the protection, conservation and recovery of sea turtle populations and of the habitats on which they depend, based on the best available scientific evidence, taking into account the environmental, socioeconomic and cultural characteristics of the Parties.

ARTICLE III

AREA OF APPLICATION OF THE CONVENTION

The area of application of this Convention (the Convention Area) comprises the land territory in the Americas of each of the Parties, as well as the maritime areas of the Atlantic Ocean, the Caribbean Sea and the Pacific Ocean, with respect to which each of the Parties exercises sovereignty, sovereign rights or jurisdiction over living marine resources in accordance with international law, as reflected in the United Nations Convention on the Law of the Sea.

ARTICLE IV

MEASURES

1. Each Party shall take appropriate and necessary measures, in accordance with international law and on the basis of the best

available scientific evidence, for the protection, conservation and recovery of sea turtle populations and their habitats:

a. In its land territory and in maritime areas with respect to which it exercises sovereignty, sovereign rights or jurisdiction included within the Convention Area; and

b. Notwithstanding Article III, with respect to vessels on the high seas that are authorized to fly its flag.

2. Such measures shall include:

a. The prohibition of the intentional capture, retention or killing of, and domestic trade in, sea turtles, their eggs, parts or products;

b. Compliance with the obligations established under the Convention on International Trade in Endangered Species of Wild Fauna and Flora relating to sea turtles, their eggs, parts or products;

c. To the extent practicable, the restriction of human activities that could seriously affect sea turtles, especially during the periods of reproduction, nesting and migration;

d. The protection, conservation and, if necessary, the restoration of sea turtle habitats and nesting areas, as well as the establishment of necessary restrictions on the use of such zones, including the designation of protected areas, as provided in Annex II;

e. The promotion of scientific research relating to sea turtles and their habitats, as well as to other relevant matters that will provide reliable information useful for the adoption of the measures referred to in this Article;

f. The promotion of efforts to enhance sea turtle populations, including research into the experimental reproduction, raising and reintroduction of sea turtles into their habitats in order to determine the feasibility of these practices to increase populations, without putting sea turtles at risk;

g. The promotion of environmental education and dissemination of information in an effort to encourage the participation of government institutions, nongovernmental organizations and the general public of each State, especially those communities that are involved in the protection, conservation and recovery of sea turtle populations and their habitats;

h. The reduction, to the greatest extent practicable, of the incidental capture, retention, harm or mortality of sea turtles in the course of fishing activities, through the appropriate regulation of such activities, as well as the development, improvement and use of appropriate gear, devices or techniques, including the use of turtle excluder devices (TEDs) pursuant to the provisions of Annex III, and the corresponding training, in keeping with the principle of the sustainable use of fisheries resources; and

i. Any other measure, in accordance with international law, which the Parties deem appropriate to achieve the objective of this Convention.

3. With respect to such measures:

a. Each Party may allow exceptions to Paragraph 2(a) to satisfy economic subsistence needs of traditional communities, taking into account the recommendations of the Consultative

Committee established pursuant to Article VII, provided that such exceptions do not undermine efforts to achieve the objective of this Convention. In making its recommendations, the Consultative Committee shall consider, inter alia, the status of the sea turtle populations in question, the views of any Party regarding such populations, impacts on such populations on a regional level, and methods used to take the eggs or turtles to cover such needs;

b. A Party allowing such an exception shall:

(i) establish a management program that includes limits on levels of intentional taking;

(ii) include in its Annual Report, referred to in Article XI, information concerning its management program;

c. Parties may establish, by mutual agreement, bilateral, subregional or regional management plans.

d. The Parties may, by consensus, approve exceptions to the measures set forth in paragraph 2(c)–(i) to account of circumstances warranting special consideration, provided that such exceptions do not undermine the objective of this Convention.

4. When an emergency situation is identified that undermines efforts to achieve the objective of this Convention and that requires collective action, the Parties shall consider the adoption of appropriate and adequate measures to address the situation. These measures shall be of a temporary nature and shall be based on the best available scientific evidence.

Article V

Meetings of the Parties

1. For the first three years following the entry into force of this Convention, the Parties shall hold an ordinary meeting at least once per year to consider matters pertaining to the implementation of the provisions of this Convention. Following that, the Parties shall hold ordinary meetings at least once every two years.

2. The Parties may also hold extraordinary meetings when deemed necessary. These meetings shall be convened at the request of any Party, provided that such request is supported by a majority of the Parties.

3. At such meetings, the Parties shall, among other things:

a. Evaluate compliance with the provisions of this Convention;

b. Examine the reports and consider the recommendations of the Consultative Committee and the Scientific Committee, established pursuant to Articles VII and VIII, regarding the implementation of this Convention;

c. Adopt such additional conservation and management measures as deemed appropriate to achieve the objective of this Convention. If the Parties consider it necessary, such measures may be included in an Annex to this Convention;

d. Consider, and as necessary adopt, amendments to this Convention, in accordance with Article XXIV.

e. Review reports of the Secretariat, if established, relating to its budget and activities.

4. At their first meeting, the Parties shall adopt rules of procedure for meetings of the Parties as well as for meetings of the Consultative Committee and the Scientific Committee, and shall consider other matters relating to those committees.

5. Decisions reached at meetings of the Parties shall be adopted by consensus.

6. The Parties may invite other interested States, relevant international organizations, as well as the private sector, scientific institutions and nongovernmental organizations with recognized expertise in matters pertaining to this Convention to attend their meetings as observers and to participate in activities under this Convention.

ARTICLE VI

SECRETARIAT

1. At their first meeting, the Parties shall consider the establishment of a Secretariat with the following functions:

a. Providing assistance in convening and organizing the meetings specified in Article V;

b. Receiving from the Parties the annual reports referred to in Article XI and placing them at the disposal of the other Parties and of the Consultative Committee and the Scientific Committee;

c. Publishing and disseminating the recommendations and decisions adopted at the meetings of the Parties in accordance with rules of procedures adopted by the Parties;

d. Disseminating and promoting the exchange of information and educational materials regarding efforts undertaken by the Parties to increase public awareness of the need to protect and conserve sea turtles and their habitats, while maintaining the economic profitability of diverse artisanal, commercial, and subsistence fishing operations, as well as the sustainable use of fisheries resources. This information shall concern, inter alia:

(i) environmental education and local community involvement;

(ii) the results of research related to the protection and conservation of sea turtles and their habitats and the socioeconomic and environmental effects of the measures adopted pursuant to this Convention;

e. Seeking economic and technical resources to carry out research and to implement the measures adopted within the framework of this Convention;

f. Performing such other functions as the Parties may assign.

2. When deciding in this regard, the Parties shall consider the possibility of appointing the Secretariat from among competent international organizations that are willing and able to perform the functions provided for in this Article. The Parties shall determine the means of financing necessary to carry out the functions of the Secretariat.

Article VII

Consultative Committee

1. At their first meeting, the Parties shall establish a Consultative Committee of Experts, hereinafter referred to as "the Consultative Committee", which shall be constituted as follows:

a. Each Party may appoint one representative to the Consultative Committee, who may be accompanied at each meeting by advisors;

b. The Parties shall also appoint, by consensus, three representatives with recognized expertise in matters pertaining to this Convention, from each of the following groups:

(i) the scientific community;

(ii) the private sector; and

(iii) nongovernmental organizations.

2. The functions of the Consultative Committee shall be to:

a. Review and analyze the reports referred to in Article XI, and any other information relating to the protection and conservation of populations of sea turtles and their habitats;

b. Solicit from any Party additional relevant information relating to the implementation of the measures set forth in this Convention or adopted pursuant thereto;

c. Examine reports concerning the environmental, socio-economic and cultural impact on affected communities resulting from the measures set forth in this Convention or adopted pursuant thereto;

d. Evaluate the efficiency of the different measures proposed to reduce the capture and incidental mortality of sea turtles, as well as the efficiency of different kinds of TEDs;

e. Present a report to the Parties on its work, including, as appropriate, recommendations on the adoption of additional conservation and management measures to promote the objective of this Convention;

f. Consider reports of the Scientific Committee;

g. Perform such other functions as the Parties may assign.

3. The Consultative Committee shall meet at least once a year for the first three years after the entry into force of the Convention, and after that in accordance with decisions made by the Parties.

4. The Parties may establish expert groups to advise the Consultative Committee.

Article VIII

Scientific Committee

1. At their first meeting, the Parties shall establish a Scientific Committee which shall be comprised of representatives designated by the Parties and which shall meet, preferably, prior to the meetings of the Consultative Committee.

2. The functions of the Scientific Committee shall be to:

a. Examine and, as appropriate, conduct research on sea turtles covered by this Convention, including research on their biology and population dynamics;

b. Evaluate the environmental impact on sea turtles and their habitats of activities such as fishing operations and the exploitation of marine resources, coastal development, dredging, pollution, clogging of estuaries and reef deterioration, among other things, as well as the potential impact of activities undertaken as a result of exceptions to the measures allowed in accordance with this Convention;

c. Analyze relevant research conducted by the Parties;

d. Formulate recommendations for the protection and conservation of sea turtles and their habitats;

e. Make recommendations on scientific and technical matters at the request of any Party regarding specific matters related to this Convention;

f. Perform such other scientific functions as the Parties may assign.

Article IX

Monitoring Programs

1. During the year following the entry into force of this Convention, each Party shall establish, within its territory and in maritime areas with respect to which it exercises sovereignty, sovereign rights or jurisdiction, a program to ensure monitoring of the application of the measures to protect and conserve sea turtles and their habitats set forth in this Convention or adopted pursuant thereto.

2. The program referred to in the preceding paragraph shall include, where appropriate, mechanisms and arrangements for the participation by observers designated by each Party or by agreement among them in monitoring activities.

3. In implementing the program, each Party may act with the support or cooperation of other interested States and relevant international organizations, as well as non-governmental organizations.

Article X

Compliance

Each Party shall ensure, within its territory and in maritime areas with respect to which it exercises sovereignty, sovereign rights or jurisdiction, effective compliance with measures to protect and conserve sea turtles and their habitats set forth in this Convention or adopted pursuant thereto.

Article XI

Annual Reports

1. Each Party shall prepare an annual report, in accordance with Annex IV, on the programs it has adopted to protect and conserve sea turtles and their habitats, as well as any program it may have adopted relating to the utilization of these species in accordance with Article IV(3).

2. Each Party shall provide, either directly or through the Secretariat, if established, its annual report to the other Parties and to

the Consultative and Scientific Committees at least 30 days prior to the next ordinary meeting of the Parties and shall also make such annual reports available to other States or interested entities that so request.

Article XII

International Cooperation

1. The Parties shall promote bilateral and multilateral cooperative activities to further the objective of this Convention and, when they deem it appropriate, shall seek the support of relevant international organizations.

2. Such activities may include the training of advisors and educators; the exchange and training of technicians, sea turtle managers and researchers; the exchange of scientific information and educational materials; the development of joint research programs, studies, seminars and workshops; and other activities on which the Parties may agree.

3. The Parties shall cooperate to develop and to facilitate access to information and training regarding the use and transfer of environmentally sustainable technologies, consistent with the objective of this Convention. They shall also develop endogenous scientific and technological capabilities.

4. The Parties shall promote international cooperation in the development and improvement of fishing gear and techniques, taking into account the specific conditions of each region, in order to maintain the productivity of commercial fisheries and to ensure the protection, conservation and recovery of sea turtle populations.

5. The cooperative activities shall include rendering assistance, including technical assistance, to Parties that are developing States, in order to assist them in complying with their obligations under this Convention.

Article XIII

Financial Resources

1. At their first meeting, the Parties shall assess the need for and possibilities of obtaining financial resources, including the establishment of a special fund for purposes such as the following:

a. Meeting the expenses that could be required for the potential establishment of the Secretariat, pursuant to Article VI;

b. Assisting the Parties that are developing States in fulfilling their obligations under this Convention, including providing access to the technology deemed most appropriate.

Article XIV

Coordination

The Parties shall seek to coordinate their activities under this Convention with relevant international organizations, whether global, regional or subregional.

Article XV

Trade Measures

1. In implementing this Convention, the Parties shall act in accordance with the provisions of the Agreement establishing the World Trade Organization (WTO), as adopted at Marrakesh in 1994, including its annexes.

2. In particular, and with respect to the subject matter of this Convention, the Parties shall act in accordance with the provisions of the Agreement on Technical Barriers to Trade contained in Annex 1 of the WTO Agreement, as well as Article XI of the General Agreement on Tariffs and Trade of 1994.

3. The Parties shall endeavor to facilitate trade in fish and fishery products associated with this Convention, in accordance with their international obligations.

Article XVI

Settlement of Disputes

1. Any Party may consult with one or more other Parties about any dispute related to the interpretation or application of the provisions of this Convention to reach a solution satisfactory to all parties to the dispute as quickly as possible.

2. If a dispute is not settled through such consultation within a reasonable period, the Parties in question shall consult among themselves as soon as possible in order to settle the dispute through any peaceful means they may decide upon in accordance with international law, including, where appropriate, those provided for in the United Nations Convention on the Law of the Sea.

Article XVII

Rights of the Parties

1. No provision of this Convention may be interpreted in such a way as to prejudice or undermine the sovereignty, sovereign rights or jurisdiction exercised by any Party in accordance with international law.

2. No provision of this Convention, nor measures or activities performed in its implementation, may be interpreted in such a way as to allow a Party to make a claim, or to exercise sovereignty, sovereign rights or jurisdiction in contravention of international law.

Article XVIII

Implementation at the National Level

Each Party shall adopt measures in its respective national laws for implementation of the provisions of this Convention and to ensure effective compliance by means of policies, plans and programs for the protection and conservation of sea turtles and their habitats.

Article XIX

Non-Parties

1. The Parties shall encourage:

a. any eligible State to become party to this Convention;

b. any other State to become party to a complementary protocol as envisioned in Article XX.

2. The Parties shall also encourage all States not Party to this Convention to adopt laws and regulations consistent with the provisions of this Convention.

Article XX

Complementary Protocols

In order to promote the protection and conservation of sea turtles outside the Convention Area where these species also exist, the Parties should negotiate with States that are not eligible to become party to this Convention a complementary protocol or protocols, consistent with the objective of this Convention, to which all interested States may become party.

Article XXI

Signature and Ratification

1. This Convention shall be open for signature at Caracas, Venezuela, by States in the Americas from December 1, 1996, until December 31, 1998.

2. This Convention is subject to ratification by the Signatories in accordance with their domestic laws and procedures. Instruments of ratification shall be deposited with the Government of Venezuela, which shall be the Depositary.

Article XXII

Entry into Force and Accession

1. This Convention shall enter into force ninety days after the date of deposit of the eighth instrument of ratification.

2. After the Convention has entered into force, it shall be open for accession by States in the Americas. This Convention shall enter into force for any such State on the date of its deposit of an instrument of accession with the Depositary.

Article XXIII

Reservations

Signature and ratification of, or accession to, this Convention may not be made subject to any reservation.

ARTICLE XXIV

AMENDMENTS

1. Any Party may propose an amendment to this Convention by providing the Depositary the text of a proposed amendment at least 60 days in advance of the next meeting of the Parties. The Depositary shall promptly circulate any amendment proposed to all the Parties.

2. Amendments to this Convention, adopted in accordance with the provisions of Article V(5), shall enter into force when the Depositary has received instruments of ratification from all Parties.

ARTICLE XXV

WITHDRAWAL

Any Party may withdraw from this Convention at any time after 12 months from the date on which this Convention entered into force with respect to that Party by giving written notice of withdrawal to the Depositary. The Depositary shall inform the other Parties of the withdrawal within 30 days of receipt of such notice. The withdrawal shall become effective six months after receipt of such notice.

ARTICLE XXVI

STATUS OF ANNEXES

1. The Annexes to this Convention are an integral part hereof. All references to this Convention shall be understood as including its Annexes.

2. Unless the Parties decide otherwise, the Annexes to this Convention may be amended, by consensus, at any meeting of the Parties. Unless otherwise agreed, amendments to an Annex shall enter into force for all Parties one year after adoption.

ARTICLE XXVII

AUTHENTIC TEXTS AND CERTIFIED COPIES

1. The English, French, Portuguese, and Spanish texts of this Convention are equally authentic.

2. The original texts of this Convention shall be deposited with the Government of Venezuela, which shall send certified copies thereof to the Signatory States and to the Parties hereto, and to the Secretary General of the United Nations for registration and publication, pursuant to Article 102 of the Charter of the United Nations.

IN WITNESS WHEREOF, the undersigned, having been duly authorized by their respective governments, have signed this Convention.

DONE at Caracas on this first day of December, 1996.

ANNEX I

SEA TURTLES [1]

1. Caretta caretta (Linnaeus, 1758)
    Tortuga caguama, cabezuda, cahuama
    Loggerhead turtle
    Tortue caouanne
    Cabeçuda, mestiça

2. Chelonia mydas (Linnaeus, 1758), including populations of this species in the Eastern or American Pacific alternatively classified by specialists as Chelonia mydas agassizii (Carr, 1952), or as Chelonia agassizii (Bocourt, 1868).
    Tortuga blanca, aruana, verde
    Green sea turtle
    Tortue verte
    Tartaruga verde
    Soepschildpad, krapé

   Common alternate names in the Eastern Pacific:
    Tortuga prieta
    East Pacific green turtle, black turtle
    Tortue verte du Pacifique est

3. Dermochelys coriacea (Vandelli, 1761)
    Tortuga laod, gigante, de cuero
    Leatherback turtle
    Tortue luth
    Tartaruga gigante, de couro
    Lederschildpad, aitkanti

4. Eretmochelys imbricata (Linnaeus, 1766)
    Tortuga de carey
    Hawksbill sea turtle
    Tortue caret
    Tartaruga de pente
    Karét.

5. Lepidochelys kempii (Garman, 1880)
    Tortuga lora
    Kemp's ridley turtle
    Tortue de Kemp

6. Lepidochelys olivacea (Eschscholtz, 1829)
    Tortuga golfina
    Olive ridley turtle
    Tortue olivâtre
    Tartaruga oliva
    Warana

ANNEX II

PROTECTION AND CONSERVATION OF SEA TURTLE HABITATS

Each Party shall consider and may adopt, as necessary and in accordance with its laws, regulations, policies, plans and programs,

[1] Due to the wide variety of common names, even within the same State, this list should not be considered exhaustive.

measures to protect and conserve sea turtle habitats within its territory and in maritime areas with respect to which it exercises sovereignty, sovereign rights or jurisdiction, such as:

1. Requiring assessments of the environmental impact of marine and coastal development activities that may affect sea turtle habitats, including: dredging of canals and estuaries; construction of sea walls, piers and marinas; extraction of raw materials; operation of aquaculture facilities; siting of industrial facilities; use of reefs; deposit of dredged materials and trash; and other related activities;

2. Managing and, when necessary, regulating the use of beaches and coastal dunes with respect to the location and design of buildings, the use of artificial lighting and the transit of vehicles in nesting areas;

3. Establishing protected areas and taking other measures to regulate the use of areas where sea turtles nest or regularly occur, including permanent or temporary closures, modification of fishing gear, and, to the greatest extent practicable, restrictions on vessel traffic.

Annex III

Use of Turtle Excluder Devices

1. "Shrimp trawl vessel" means any vessel used to catch shrimp species with trawl nets.

2. "Turtle Excluder Device" or "TED" means a device designed to increase the selectivity of shrimp trawl nets in order to reduce the incidental capture of sea turtles in shrimp fishing operations.

3. Each Party shall require shrimp trawl vessels subject to its jurisdiction that operate within the Convention Area to use recommended TEDs that are properly installed and functional.

4. Each Party, in accordance with the best available scientific evidence, may allow exceptions to use of TEDs as required in Paragraph 3 only in the following circumstances:

a. For shrimp trawl vessels whose nets are retrieved exclusively by manual rather than mechanical means, and shrimp vessels with trawl nets for which no TEDs have been developed. A Party allowing such exception shall adopt other measures to reduce the incidental mortality of sea turtles that are equally effective and that do not undermine efforts to achieve the objective of this Convention, such as limits on tow times, closed seasons and closed fishing areas where sea turtles occur.

b. For shrimp trawl vessels:

(i) exclusively using other trawl gear that has been demonstrated not to pose a risk of incidental mortality of sea turtles; or

(ii) operating under conditions where there is no likelihood of interaction with sea turtles;

provided that the Party allowing such exception provides to the other Parties, either directly or through the Secretariat, if established, documented scientific evidence demonstrating the lack of such risk or likelihood;

c. For shrimp trawl vessels conducting scientific research under a program approved by the Party;

d. Where the presence of algae, seaweed, debris, or other special conditions, temporary or permanent, make the use of TEDs impracticable in a specific area, provided that:

(i) a Party allowing this exception shall adopt other measures to protect sea turtles in the area in question, such as limits on tow times;

(ii) only in extraordinary emergency situations of a temporary nature may a Party allow this exception to apply to more than a small number of the vessels subject to its jurisdiction that would otherwise be required to use TEDs pursuant to this Annex;

(iii) a Party allowing this exception shall provide to the other Parties, either directly or through the Secretariat, if established, information concerning the special conditions and the number of shrimp trawl vessels operating in the area in question.

5. Any Party may comment upon information provided by any other Party pursuant to Paragraph 4. Where appropriate, the Parties shall seek guidance from the Consultative Committee and the Scientific Committee to resolve differences of view. If the Consultative Committee so recommends, and the Parties agree, a Party that has allowed an exception pursuant to Paragraph 4 shall reconsider the allowance or extent of such an exception.

6. The Parties may, by consensus, approve other exceptions to the use of TEDs as required in Paragraph 3, in accordance with the best available scientific evidence and based on recommendations of the Consultative Committee and the Scientific Committee, to account for circumstances warranting special consideration, provided that such exceptions do not undermine efforts to achieve the objective of this Convention.

7. For the purposes of this Convention:

a. Recommended TEDs shall be those TEDs determined by the Parties, with advice from the Consultative Committee, to reduce the incidental capture of sea turtles in shrimp trawl fishing operations to the greatest extent practicable;

b. At their first meeting, the Parties shall develop an initial list of recommended TEDs, which they may modify at subsequent meetings;

c. Until the first meeting of the Parties, each Party shall determine, in accordance with its laws and regulations, which TEDs to require for use by shrimp trawl vessels subject to its jurisdiction in order to reduce the incidental capture of sea turtles in shrimp trawl fishing operations to the greatest extent practicable, based on consultations with other Parties.

8. At the request of any other Party or of the Consultative Committee or the Scientific Committee, each Party shall provide, either directly or through the Secretariat, if established, scientific information relevant to the achievement of the objective of this Convention.

Annex IV

Annual Reports

The annual reports referred to in Article XI(1) shall include the following:

a. A general description of the program to protect and conserve sea turtles and their habitats, including any laws or regulations adopted to achieve the objective of this Convention;

b. Any pertinent new laws or regulations adopted during the preceding year;

c. A summary of actions taken, and the results thereof, to implement measures for the protection and conservation of sea turtles and their habitats, such as: operation of turtle camps; improvement and development of new fishing gear to reduce incidental sea turtle capture and mortality; scientific research, including marking, migration, and repopulation studies; environmental education; programs to establish and manage protected areas; cooperative activities with other Parties; and any other activities designed to achieve the objective of this Convention;

d. A summary of the actions taken to enforce its laws and regulations, including penalties imposed for violations;

e. A detailed description of any exceptions allowed, in accordance with this Convention, during the preceding year, including monitoring and mitigation measures related to these exceptions, and, in particular, any relevant information on the number of turtles, nests, and eggs, as well as sea turtle habitats, affected by the allowance of these exceptions;

f. Any other information the Party may deem relevant.

N. ENERGY AND NATURAL RESOURCES

CONTENTS

1. Nuclear Energy

a. Treaty Establishing the International Atomic Energy Agency

Done at New York, October 26, 1956; Entered into force, July 29, 1957

STATUTE OF THE INTERNATIONAL ATOMIC ENERGY AGENCY[1]

ARTICLE I: ESTABLISHMENT OF THE AGENCY

The Parties hereto establish an International Atomic Energy Agency (hereinafter referred to as "the Agency") upon the terms and conditions hereinafter set forth.

ARTICLE II: OBJECTIVES

The Agency shall seek to accelerate and enlarge the contribution of atomic energy to peace, health and prosperity throughout the world. It shall ensure, so far as it is able, that assistance provided by it or at its request or under its supervision or control is not used in such a way as to further any military purpose.

ARTICLE III: FUNCTIONS

A. The Agency is authorized:

1. To encourage and assist research on, and development and practical application of, atomic energy for peaceful uses throughout the world; and, if requested to do so, to act as an intermediary for the purposes of securing the performance of services or the supplying of materials, equipment, or facilities by one member of the Agency for another; and to perform any operation or service useful in research on, or development or practical application of, atomic energy for peaceful purposes;
2. To make provision, in accordance with this Statute, for materials, services, equipment, and facilities to meet the needs of research on, and development and practical application of, atomic energy for peaceful purposes, including the production of electric power, with due consideration for the needs of the under-developed areas of the world;
3. To foster the exchange of scientific and technical information on peaceful uses of atomic energy;
4. To encourage the exchange of training of scientists and experts in the field of peaceful uses of atomic energy;
5. To establish and administer safeguards designed to ensure that special fissionable and other materials, services, equipment, facilities, and information made available by the Agency

[1] TIAS 3873. As amended, October 4, 1961, September 28, 1970, and September 27, 1984. For a list of states that are parties to the Agreement, see Department of State publication, *Treaties in Force*.

or at its request or under its supervision or control are not used in such a way as to further any military purpose; and to apply safeguards, at the request of the parties, to any bilateral or multilateral arrangement, or at the request of a State, to any of that State's activities in the field of atomic energy;

6. To establish or adopt, in consultation and, where appropriate, in collaboration with the competent organs of the United Nations and with the specialized agencies concerned, standards of safety for protection of health and minimization of danger to life and property (including such standards for labour conditions), and to provide for the application of these standards to its own operation as well as to the operations making use of materials, services, equipment, facilities, and information made available by the Agency or at its request or under its control or supervision; and to provide for the application of these standards, at the request of the parties, to operations under any bilateral or multilateral arrangements, or, at the request of a State, to any of that State's activities in the field of atomic energy;

7. To acquire or establish any facilities, plant and equipment useful in carrying out its authorized functions, whenever the facilities, plant, and equipment otherwise available to it in the area concerned are inadequate or available only on terms it deems unsatisfactory.

B. In carrying out its functions, the Agency shall:

1. Conduct its activities in accordance with the purposes and principles of the United Nations to promote peace and international co-operation, and in conformity with policies of the United Nations furthering the establishment of safeguarded worldwide disarmament and in conformity with any international agreements entered into pursuant to such policies;

2. Establish control over the use of special fissionable materials received by the Agency, in order to ensure that these materials are used only for peaceful purposes;

3. Allocate its resources in such a manner as to secure efficient utilization and the greatest possible general benefit in all areas of the world, bearing in mind the special needs of the under-developed areas of the world;

4. Submit reports on its activities annually to the General Assembly of the United Nations and, when appropriate, to the Security Council: if in connection with the activities of the Agency there should arise questions that are within the competence of the Security Council, the Agency shall notify the Security Council, as the organ bearing the main responsibility for the maintenance of international peace and security, and may also take the measures open to it under this Statute, including those provided in paragraph C of Article XII;

5. Submit reports to the Economic and Social Council and other organs of the United Nations on matters within the competence of these organs.

C. In carrying out its functions, the Agency shall not make assistance to members subject to any political, economic, military, or other conditions incompatible with the provisions of this Statute.

D. Subject to the provisions of this Statute and to the terms of agreements concluded between a State or a group of States and the Agency which shall be in accordance with the provisions of the Statute, the activities of the Agency shall be carried out with due observance of the sovereign rights of States.

ARTICLE IV: MEMBERSHIP

A. The initial members of the Agency shall be those States Members of the United Nations or of any of the specialized agencies which shall have signed this Statute within ninety days after it is opened for signature and shall have deposited an instrument of ratification.

B. Other members of the Agency shall be those States, whether or not Members of the United Nations or of any of the specialized agencies, which deposit an instrument of acceptance of this Statute after their membership has been approved by the General Conference upon the recommendation of the Board of Governors. In recommending and approving a State for membership, the Board of Governors and the General Conference shall determine that the State is able and willing to carry out the obligations of membership in the Agency, giving due consideration to its ability and willingness to act in accordance with the purposes and principles of the Charter of the United Nations.

C. The Agency is based on the principle of the sovereign equality of all its members, and all members, in order to ensure to all of them the rights and benefits resulting from membership, shall fulfill in good faith the obligation assumed by them in accordance with this Statute.

ARTICLE V: GENERAL CONFERENCE

A. A General Conference consisting of representatives of all members shall meet in regular annual session and in such special sessions as shall be convened by the Director General at the request of the Board of Governors or of a majority of members. The sessions shall take place at the headquarters of the Agency unless otherwise determined by the General Conference.

B. At such sessions, each member shall be represented by one delegate who may be accompanied by alternates and by advisers. The cost of attendance of any delegation shall be borne by the member concerned.

C. The General Conference shall elect a President and such other officers as may be required at the beginning of each session. They shall hold office for the duration of the session. The General Conference, subject to the provisions of this Statute, shall adopt its own rules of procedure. Each member shall have one vote. Decisions pursuant to paragraph H of article XIV, paragraph C of article XVIII and paragraph B of article XIX shall be made by a two-thirds majority of the members present and voting. Decisions on other questions, including the determination of additional questions or categories of questions to be decided by a two-thirds majority, shall be made by a majority of the members present and voting. A majority of members shall constitute a quorum.

D. The General Conference may discuss any questions or any matters within the scope of this Statute or relating to the powers and functions of any organs provided for in this Statute, and may make recommendations to the membership of the Agency or to the Board of Governors or to both on any such questions or matters.

E. The General Conference shall:

1. Elect members of the Board of Governors in accordance with article VI;

2. Approve States for membership in accordance with article IV;

3. Suspend a member from the privileges and rights of membership in accordance with article XIX;

4. Consider the annual report of the Board;

5. In accordance with article XIV, approve the budget of the Agency recommended by the Board or return it with recommendations as to its entirety or parts to the Board. for resubmission to the General Conference;

6. Approve reports to be submitted to the United Nations as required by the relationship agreement between the Agency and the United Nations, except reports referred to in paragraph C of article XII, or return them to the Board with its recommendations;

7. Approve any agreement or agreements between the Agency and the United Nations and other organizations as provided in article XVI or return such agreements with its recommendations to the Board, for resubmission to the General Conference;

8. Approve rules and limitations regarding the exercise of borrowing powers by the Board, in accordance with paragraph G of article XIV; approve rules regarding the acceptance of voluntary contributions to the Agency; and approve, in accordance with paragraph F of article XIV, the manner in which the general fund referred to in that paragraph may be used;

9. Approve amendments to this Statute in accordance with paragraph C of article XVIII;

10. Approve the appointment of the Director General in accordance with paragraph A of article VII.

F. The General Conference shall have the authority:

1. To take decisions on any matter specifically referred to the General Conference for this purpose by the Board;

2. To propose matters for consideration by the Board and request from the Board reports on any matter relating to the functions of the Agency.

ARTICLE VI: BOARD OF GOVERNORS

A. The Board of Governors shall be composed as follows:

1. The outgoing Board of Governors shall designate for membership on the Board the ten members most advanced in the technology of atomic energy including the production of source materials, and the member most advanced in the technology of atomic energy including the production of source materials in each of the following areas in which none of the aforesaid ten is located:

1. North America

2. Latin America
3. Western Europe
4. Eastern Europe
5. Africa
6. Middle East and South Asia
7. South East Asia and the Pacific
8. Far East.

2. The General Conference shall elect to membership of the Board of Governors:

(a) Twenty members, with due regard to equitable representation on the Board as a whole of the members in the areas listed in sub-paragraph A.1 of this article, so that the Board shall at all times include in this category five representatives of the area of Latin America, four representatives of the area of Western Europe, three representatives of the area of Eastern Europe, four representatives of the area of Africa, two representatives of the area of the Middle East and South Asia, one representative of the area of South East Asia and the Pacific, and one representative of the area of the Far East. No member in this category in any one term of office will be eligible for reelection in the same category for the following term of office; and

(b) One further member from among the members in the following areas: Middle East and South Asia, South East Asia and the Pacific, Far East;

(c) One further member from among the members in the following areas: Africa, Middle East and South Asia, South East Asia and the Pacific.

B. The designations provided for in sub-paragraph A–l of this article shall take place not less than sixty days before each regular annual session of the General Conference. The elections provided for in sub-paragraph A–2 of this article shall take place at regular annual sessions of the General Conference.

C. Members represented on the Board of Governors in accordance with sub-paragraph A–l of this article shall hold office from the end of the next regular annual session of the General Conference after their designation until the end of the following regular annual session of the General Conference.

D. Members represented on the Board of Governors in accordance with sub-paragraph A–2 of this article shall hold office from the end of the regular annual session of the General Conference at which they are elected until the end of the second regular annual session of the General Conference thereafter.

E. Each member of the Board of Governors shall have one vote. Decisions on the amount of the Agency's budget shall be made by a two-thirds majority of those present and voting, as provided in paragraph H of article XIV. Decisions on other questions, including the determination of additional questions or categories of questions to be decided by a two thirds majority, shall be made by a majority of those present and voting. Two-thirds of all members of the Board shall constitute a quorum.

F. The Board of Governors shall have authority to carry out the functions of the Agency in accordance with this Statute, subject to its responsibilities to the General Conference as provided in this Statute.

G. The Board of Governors shall meet at such times as it may determine. The meetings shall take place at the headquarters of the Agency unless otherwise determined by the Board.

H. The Board of Governors shall elect a Chairman and other officers from among its members and, subject to the provisions of this Statute, shall adopt its own rules of procedure.

I. The Board of Governors may establish such committees as it deems advisable. The Board may appoint persons to represent it in its relations with other organizations.

J. The Board of Governors shall prepare an annual report to the General Conference concerning the affairs of the Agency and any projects approved by the Agency. The Board shall also prepare for submission to the General Conference such reports as the Agency is or may be required to make to the United Nations or to any other organization the work of which is related to that of the Agency. These reports, along with the annual reports, shall be submitted to members of the Agency at least one month before the regular annual session of the General Conference.

Article VII: Staff

A. The staff of the Agency shall be headed by a Director General. The Director General shall be appointed by the Board of Governors with the approval of the General Conference for a term of four years. He shall be the chief administrative officer of the Agency.

B. The Director General shall be responsible for the appointment, organization, and functioning of the staff and shall be under the authority of and subject to the control of the Board of Governors. He shall perform his duties in accordance with regulations adopted by the Board.

C. The staff shall include such qualified scientific and technical and other personnel as may be required to fulfill the objectives and functions of the Agency. The Agency shall be guided by the principle that its permanent staff shall be kept to a minimum.

D. The paramount consideration in the recruitment and employment of the staff and in the determination of the conditions of service shall be to secure employees of the highest standards of efficiency, technical competence, and integrity. Subject to this consideration, due regard shall be paid to the contributions of members to the Agency and to the importance of recruiting the staff on as wide a geographical basis as possible.

E. The terms and conditions on which the staff shall be appointed, remunerated, and dismissed shall be in accordance with regulations made by the Board of Governors, subject to the provisions of this Statute and to general rules approved by the General Conference on the recommendation of the Board.

F. In the performance of their duties, the Director General and the staff shall not seek or receive instructions from any source external to the Agency. They shall refrain from any action which might reflect on their position as officials of the Agency; subject to their responsibilities to the Agency, they shall not disclose any industrial secret or other confidential information coming to their knowledge by reason of their official duties for the Agency. Each member undertakes to respect the international character of the responsibilities of the Director General and the staff and shall not seek to influence them in the discharge of their duties.

G. In this article the term "staff" includes guards.

Article VIII: Exchange of Information

A. Each member should make available such information as would, in the judgement of the member, be helpful to the Agency.

B. Each member shall make available to the Agency all scientific information developed as a result of assistance extended by the Agency pursuant to article XI.

C. The Agency shall assemble and make available in an accessible form the information made available to it under paragraphs A and B of this article. It shall take positive steps to encourage the exchange among its members of information relating to the nature and peaceful uses of atomic energy and shall serve as an intermediary among its members for this purpose.

Article IX: Supplying of Materials

A. Members may make available to the Agency such quantities of special fissionable materials as they deem advisable and on such terms as shall be agreed with the Agency. The materials made available to the Agency may, at the discretion of the member making them available, be stored either by the member concerned or, with the agreement of the Agency, in the Agency's depots.

B. Members may also make available to the Agency source materials as defined in article XX and other materials. The Board of Governors shall determine the quantities of such materials which the Agency will accept under agreements provided for in article XIII.

C. Each member shall notify the Agency of the quantities, form, and composition of special fissionable materials, source materials, and other materials which that member is prepared, in conformity with its laws, to make available immediately or during a period specified by the Board of Governors.

D. On request of the Agency a member shall, from the materials which it has made available, without delay deliver to another member or group of members such quantities of such materials as the Agency may specify, and shall without delay deliver to the Agency itself such quantities of such materials as are really necessary for operations and scientific research in the facilities of the Agency.

E. The quantities, form and composition of materials made available by any member may be changed at any time by the member with the approval of the Board of Governors.

F. An initial notification in accordance with paragraph C of this article shall be made within three months of the entry into force of this Statute with respect to the member concerned. In the absence of a contrary decision of the Board of Governors, the materials initially made available shall be for the period of the calendar year succeeding the year when this Statute takes effect with respect to the member concerned. Subsequent notifications shall likewise, in the absence of a contrary action by the Board, relate to the period of the calendar year following the notification and shall be made no later than the first day of November of each year.

G. The Agency shall specify the place and method of delivery and, where appropriate, the form and composition, of materials which it has requested a member to deliver from the amounts which that member has notified the Agency it is prepared to make available. The Agency shall also verify the quantities of materials delivered and shall report those quantities periodically to the members.

H. The Agency shall be responsible for storing and protecting materials in its possession. The Agency shall ensure that these materials shall be safeguarded against

1. hazards of the weather,
2. unauthorized removal or diversion,
3. damage or destruction, including sabotage, and
4. forcible seizure. In storing special fissionable materials in its possession, the Agency shall ensure the geographical distribution of these materials in such a way as not to allow concentration of large amounts of such materials in any one country or region of the world.

I. The Agency shall as soon as practicable establish or acquire such of the following as may be necessary:

1. Plant, equipment, and facilities for the receipt, storage, and issue of materials;
2. Physical safeguards;
3. Adequate health and safety measures;
4. Control laboratories for the analysis and verification of materials received;
5. Housing and administrative facilities for any staff required for the foregoing.

J. The materials made available pursuant to this article shall be used as determined by the Board of Governors in accordance with the provisions of this Statute. No member shall have the right to require that the materials it makes available to the Agency be kept separately by the Agency or to designate the specific project in which they must be used.

Article X: Services, Equipment, and Facilities

Members may make available to the Agency services, equipment, and facilities which may be of assistance in fulfilling the Agency's objectives and functions.

Article XI: Agency Projects

A. Any member or group of members of the Agency desiring to set up any project for research on, or development or practical application of, atomic energy for peaceful purposes may request the assistance of the Agency in securing special fissionable and other materials, services, equipment, and facilities necessary for this purpose. Any such request shall be accompanied by an explanation of the purpose and extent of the project and shall be considered by the Board of Governors.

B. Upon request, the Agency may also assist any member or group of members to make arrangements to secure necessary financing from outside sources to carry out such projects. In extending this assistance, the Agency will not be required to provide any guarantees or to assume any financial responsibility for the project.

C. The Agency may arrange for the supplying of any materials, services, equipment, and facilities necessary for the project by one or more members or may itself undertake to provide any or all of these directly, taking into consideration the wishes of the member or members making the request.

D. For the purpose of considering the request, the Agency may send into the territory of the member or group of members making the request a person or persons qualified to examine the project. For this purpose the Agency may, with the approval of the member or group of members making the request, use members of its own staff or employ suitably qualified nationals of any member.

E. Before approving a project under this article, the Board of Governors shall give due consideration to:

1. The usefulness of the project, including its scientific and technical feasibility;
2. The adequacy of plans, funds, and technical personnel to assure the effective execution of the project;
3. The adequacy of proposed health and safety standards for handling and storing materials and for operating facilities;
4. The inability of the member or group of members making the request to secure the necessary finances, materials, facilities, equipment, and services;
5. The equitable distribution of materials and other resources available to the Agency;
6. The special needs of the under-developed areas of the world; and
7. Such other matters as may be relevant.

F. Upon approving a project, the Agency shall enter into an agreement with the member or group of members submitting the project, which agreement shall:

1. Provide for allocation to the project of any required special fissionable or other materials;
2. Provide for transfer of special fissionable materials from their then place of custody, whether the materials be in the custody of the Agency or of the member making them available for use in Agency projects, to the member or group of members submitting the project, under conditions which ensure the safety of any shipment required and meet applicable health and safety standards;
3. Set forth the terms and conditions, including charges, on which any materials, services, equipment, and facilities are to be provided by the Agency itself, and, if any such materials, services, equipment, and facilities are to be provided by a member, the terms and conditions as arranged for by the member or group of members submitting the project and the supplying member;
4. Include undertakings by the member or group of members submitting the project: (a) that the assistance provided shall not be used in such a way as to further any military purpose;

and (b) that the project shall be subject to the safeguards provided for in article XII, the relevant safeguards being specified in the agreement;

5. Make appropriate provision regarding the rights and interests of the Agency and the member or members concerned in any inventions or discoveries, or any patents therein, arising from the project;

6. Make appropriate provision regarding settlement of disputes;

7. Include such other provisions as may be appropriate.

G. The provisions of this article shall also apply where appropriate to a request for materials, services, facilities, or equipment in connection with an existing project.

Article XII: Agency Safeguards

A. With respect to any Agency project, or other arrangement where the Agency is requested by the parties concerned to apply safeguards, the Agency shall have the following rights and responsibilities to the extent relevant to the project or arrangement:

1. To examine the design of specialized equipment and facilities, including nuclear reactors, and to approve it only from the view-point of assuring that it will not further any military purpose, that it complies with applicable health and safety standards, and that it will permit effective application of the safeguards provided for in this article;

2. To require the observance of any health and safety measures prescribed by the Agency;

3. To require the maintenance and production of operating records to assist in ensuring accountability for source and special fissionable materials used or produced in the project or arrangement;

4. To call for and receive progress reports;

5. To approve the means to be used for the chemical processing of irradiated materials solely to ensure that this chemical processing will not lend itself to diversion of materials for military purposes and will comply with applicable health and safety standards; to require that special fissionable materials recovered or produced as a by-product be used for peaceful purposes under continuing Agency safeguards for research or in reactors, existing or under construction, specified by the member or members concerned; and to require deposit with the Agency of any excess of any special fissionable materials recovered or produced as a by-product over what is needed for the above-stated uses in order to prevent stockpiling of these materials, provided that thereafter at the request of the member or members concerned special fissionable materials so deposited with the Agency shall be returned promptly to the member or members concerned for use under the same provisions as stated above.

6. To send into the territory of the recipient State or States inspectors, designated by the Agency after consultation with the State or States concerned, who shall have access at all times to all places and data and to any person who by reason

of his occupation deals with materials, equipment, or facilities which are required by this Statute to be safeguarded, as necessary to account for source and special fissionable materials supplied and fissionable products and to determine whether there is compliance with the undertaking against use in furtherance of any military purpose referred to in sub-paragraph F–4 of article Xl, with the health and safety measures referred to in sub-paragraph A–2 of this article, and with any other conditions prescribed in the agreement between the Agency and the State or States concerned. Inspectors designated by the Agency shall be accompanied by representatives of the authorities of the State concerned, if that State so requests, provided that the inspectors shall not thereby be delayed or otherwise impeded in the exercise of their functions;

7. In the event of non-compliance and failure by the recipient State or States to take requested corrective steps within a reasonable time, to suspend or terminate assistance and withdraw any materials and equipment made available by the Agency or a member in furtherance of the project.

B. The Agency shall, as necessary, establish a staff of inspectors. The Staff of inspectors shall have the responsibility of examining all operations conducted by the Agency itself to determine whether the Agency is complying with the health and safety measures prescribed by it for application to projects subject to its approval, supervision or control, and whether the Agency is taking adequate measures to prevent the source and special fissionable materials in its custody or used or produced in its own operations from being used in furtherance of any military purpose. The Agency shall take remedial action forthwith to correct any non-compliance or failure to take adequate measures.

C. The staff of inspectors shall also have the responsibility of obtaining and verifying the accounting referred to in sub-paragraph A–6 of this article and of determining whether there is compliance with the undertaking referred to in sub-paragraph F–4 of article XI, with the measures referred to in sub-paragraph A–2 of this article, and with all other conditions of the project prescribed in the agreement between the Agency and the State or States concerned. The inspectors shall report any non-compliance to the Director General who shall thereupon transmit the report to the Board of Governors. The Board shall call upon the recipient State or States to remedy forthwith any non-compliance which it finds to have occurred. The Board shall report the non-compliance to all members and to the Security Council and General Assembly of the United Nations. In the event of failure of the recipient State or States to take fully corrective action within a reasonable time, the Board may take one or both of the following measures: direct curtailment or suspension of assistance being provided by the Agency or by a member, and call for the return of materials and equipment made available to the recipient member or group of members. The Agency may also, in accordance with article XIX, suspend any non-complying member from the exercise of the privileges and rights of membership.

ARTICLE XIII: REIMBURSEMENT OF MEMBERS

Unless otherwise agreed upon between the Board of Governors and the member furnishing to the Agency materials, services, equipment, or facilities, the Board shall enter into an agreement with such member providing for reimbursement for the items furnished.

ARTICLE XIV: FINANCE

A. The Board of Governors shall submit to the General Conference the annual budget estimates for the expenses of the Agency. To facilitate the work of the Board in this regard, the Director General shall initially prepare the budget estimates. If the General Conference does not approve the estimates, it shall return them together with its recommendations to the Board. The Board shall then submit further estimates to the General Conference for its approval.

B. Expenditures of the Agency shall be classified under the following categories:

1. Administrative expenses: these shall include:

(a) Costs of the staff of the Agency other than the staff employed in connection with materials, services, equipment, and facilities referred to in sub-paragraph B–2 below; costs of meetings; and expenditures required for the preparation of Agency projects and for the distribution of information;

(b) Costs of implementing the safeguards referred to in article XII in relation to Agency projects or, under sub-paragraph A–5 of article III, in relation to any bilateral or multilateral arrangement, together with the costs of handling and storage of special fissionable material by the Agency other than the storage and handling charges referred to in paragraph E below;

2. Expenses, other than those included in sub-paragraph 1 of this paragraph, in connection with any materials, facilities, plant, and equipment acquired or established by the Agency in carrying out its authorized functions, and the costs of materials, services, equipment, and facilities provided by it under agreements with one or more members.

C. In fixing the expenditures under sub-paragraph B–l (b) above, the Board of Governors shall deduct such amounts as are recoverable under agreements regarding the application of safeguards between the Agency and parties to bilateral or multilateral arrangements.

D. The Board of Governors shall apportion the expenses referred to in sub-paragraph B–1 above, among members in accordance with a scale to be fixed by the General Conference. In fixing the scale the General Conference shall be guided by the principles adopted by the United Nations in assessing contributions of Member States to the regular budget of the United Nations.

E. The Board of Governors shall establish periodically a scale of charges, including reasonable uniform storage and handling charges, for materials, services, equipment, and facilities furnished to members by the Agency. The scale shall be designed to produce revenues for the Agency adequate to meet the expenses and costs referred to in sub-paragraph B–2 above, less any voluntary contributions which the Board of Governors may, in accordance with paragraph F, apply for this purpose. The proceeds of such charges shall be placed in a separate fund which shall be used to pay members for any materials, services, equipment, or facilities furnished by them and to meet other expenses referred to in sub-paragraph B–2 above which may be incurred by the Agency itself

F. Any excess of revenues referred to in paragraph E over the expenses and costs there referred to, and any voluntary contributions to the Agency, shall be placed in a general fund which may be used as the Board of Governors, with the approval of the General Conference, may determine.

G. Subject to rules and limitations approved by the General Conference, the Board of Governors shall have the authority to exercise borrowing powers on behalf of the Agency without, however, imposing on members of the Agency any liability in respect of loans entered into pursuant to this authority, and to accept voluntary contributions made to the Agency.

H. Decisions of the General Conference on financial questions and of the Board of Governors on the amount of the Agency's budget shall require a two-thirds majority of those present and voting.

Article XV: Privileges and Immunities

A. The Agency shall enjoy in the territory of each member such legal capacity and such privileges and immunities as are necessary for the exercise of its functions.

B. Delegates of members together with their alternates and advisers, Governors appointed to the Board together with their alternates and advisers, and the Director General and the staff of the Agency, shall enjoy such privileges and immunities as are necessary in the independent exercise of their functions in connection with the Agency.

C. The legal capacity, privileges, and immunities referred to in this article shall be defined in a separate agreement or agreements between the Agency, represented for this purpose by the Director General acting under instructions of the Board of Governors. and the members.

Article XVI: Relationship with Other Organizations

A. The Board of Governors, with the approval of the General Conference, is authorized to enter into an agreement or agreements establishing an appropriate relationship between the Agency and the United Nations and any other organizations the work of which is related to that of the Agency.

B. The agreement or agreements establishing the relationship of the Agency and the United Nations shall provide for:

1. Submission by the Agency of reports as provided for in sub-paragraphs B–4 and B–5 of article III;
2. Consideration by the Agency of resolutions relating to it adopted by the General Assembly or any of the Councils of the United Nations and the submission of reports, when requested, to the appropriate organ of the United Nations on the action

taken by the Agency or by its members in accordance with this Statute as a result of such consideration.

ARTICLE XVII: SETTLEMENT OF DISPUTES

A. Any question or dispute concerning the interpretation or application of this Statute which is not settled by negotiation shall be referred to the International Court of Justice in conformity with the Statute of the Court, unless the parties concerned agree on another mode of settlement.

B. The General Conference and the Board of Governors are separately empowered, subject to authorization from the General Assembly of the United Nations, to request the International Court of Justice to give an advisory opinion on any legal question arising within the scope of the Agency's activities.

ARTICLE XVIII: AMENDMENTS AND WITHDRAWALS

A. Amendments to this Statute may be proposed by any member. Certified copies of the text of any amendment proposed shall be prepared by the Director General and communicated by him to all members at least ninety days in advance of its consideration by the General Conference.

B. At the fifth annual session of the General Conference following the coming into force of this Statute, the question of a general review of the provisions of this Statute shall be placed on the agenda of that session. On approval by a majority of the members present and voting, the review will take place at the following General Conference. Thereafter, proposals on the question of a general review of this Statute may be submitted for decision by the General Conference under the same procedure.

C. Amendments shall come into force for all members when:

(i) Approved by the General Conference by a two-thirds majority of those present and voting after consideration of observations submitted by the Board of Governors on each proposed amendment, and

(ii) Accepted by two-thirds of all the members in accordance with their respective constitutional processes. Acceptance by a member shall be effected by the deposit of an instrument of acceptance with the depositary Government referred to in paragraph C of article XXI.

D. At any time after five years from the date when this Statute shall take effect in accordance with paragraph E of article XXI or whenever a member is unwilling to accept an amendment to this Statute, it may withdraw from the Agency by notice in writing to that effect given to the depositary Government referred to in paragraph C of article XXI, which shall promptly inform the Board of Governors and all members.

E. Withdrawal by a member from the Agency shall not affect its contractual obligations entered into pursuant to article XI or its budgetary obligations for the year in which it withdraws.

ARTICLE XIX: SUSPENSION OF PRIVILEGES

A. A member of the Agency which is in arrears in the payment of its financial contributions to the Agency shall have no vote in the Agency if the amount of its arrears equals or exceeds the amount of the contributions due from it for the preceding two years. The General Conference may, nevertheless, permit such a member to vote if it is satisfied that the failure to pay is due to conditions beyond the control of the member.

B. A member which has persistently violated the provisions of this Statute or of any agreement entered into by it pursuant to this Statute may be suspended from the exercise of the privileges and rights of membership by the General Conference acting by a two-thirds majority of the members present and voting upon recommendation by the Board of Governors.

ARTICLE XX: DEFINITIONS

As used in this Statute:

1. The term "special fissionable material" means plutonium-239; uranium-233; uranium enriched in the isotopes 235 or 233; any material containing one or more of the foregoing; and such other fissionable material as the Board of Governors shall from time to time deter mine; but the term "special fissionable material" does not include source material.
2. The term "uranium enriched in the isotopes 235 or 233" means uranium containing the isotopes 235 or 233 or both in an amount such that the abundance ratio of the sum of these isotopes to the isotope 238 is greater than the ratio of the isotope 235 to the isotope 238 occurring in nature.
3. The term "source material" means uranium containing the mixture of isotopes occurring in nature; uranium depleted in the isotope 235; thorium; any of the foregoing in the form of metal, alloy, chemical compound, or concentrate; any other material containing one or more of the foregoing in such concentration as the Board of Governors shall from time to time determine; and such other material as the Board of Governors shall from time to time determine.

ARTICLE XXI: SIGNATURE, ACCEPTANCE, AND ENTRY INTO FORCE

A. This Statute shall be open for signature on 26 October 1956 by all States Members of the United Nations or of any of the specialized agencies and shall remain open for signature by those States for a period of ninety days.

B. The signatory States shall become parties to this Statute by deposit of an instrument of ratification.

C. Instruments of ratification by signatory States and instruments of acceptance by States whose membership has been approved under paragraph B of article IV of this Statute shall be deposited with the Government of the United States of America, hereby designated as depositary Government.

D. Ratification or acceptance of this Statute shall be effected by States in accordance with their respective constitutional processes.

E. This Statute, apart from the Annex, shall come into force when eighteen States have deposited instruments of ratification in accordance with paragraph B of this article, provided that such eighteen States shall include at least three of the following States: Canada, France, the Union of Soviet Socialist Republics, the United

Kingdom of Great Britain and Northern Ireland, and the United States of America. Instruments of ratification and instruments of acceptance deposited thereafter shall take effect on the date of their receipt.

F. The depositary Government shall promptly inform all States signatory to this Statute of the date of each deposit of ratification and the date of entry into force of the Statute. The depositary Government shall promptly inform all signatories and members of the dates on which States subsequently become parties thereto.

G. The Annex to this Statute shall come into force on the first day this Statute is open for signature.

Article XXII: Registration with the United Nations

A. This Statute shall be registered by the depositary Government pursuant to Article 102 of the Charter of the United Nations.

B. Agreements between the Agency and any member or members, agreements between the Agency and any other organization or organizations, and agreements between members subject to approval of the Agency, shall be registered with the Agency. Such agreements shall be registered by the Agency with the United Nations if registration is required under Article 102 of the Charter of the United Nations.

Article XXIII: Authentic Texts and Certified Copies

This Statute, done in the Chinese, English, French, Russian and Spanish languages, each being equally authentic, shall be deposited in the archives of the depositary Government. Duly certified copies of this Statute shall be transmitted by the depositary Government to the Governments of the other signatory States and to the Governments of States admitted to membership under paragraph B of article IV.

In witness whereof the undersigned, duly authorized, have signed this Statute.

Done at the Headquarters of the United Nations, this twenty-sixth day of October, one thousand nine hundred and fifty-six.

Annex: Preparatory Commission

A. A Preparatory Commission shall come into existence on the first day this Statute is open for signature. It shall be composed of one representative each of Australia, Belgium, Brazil, Canada, Czechoslovakia, France, India, Portugal, Union of South Africa, Union of Soviet Socialist Republics, United Kingdom of Great Britain and Northern Ireland, and United States of America, and one representative each of six other States to be chosen by the International Conference on the Statute of the International Atomic Energy Agency. The Preparatory Commission shall remain in existence until this Statute comes into force and thereafter until the General Conference has convened and a Board of Governors has been selected in accordance with article VI.

B. The expenses of the Preparatory Commission may be met by a loan provided by the United Nations and for this purpose the Preparatory Commission shall make the necessary arrangements with the appropriate authorities of the United Nations, including arrangements for repayment of the loan by the Agency. Should these funds be insufficient, the Preparatory Commission may accept advances from Governments. Such advances may be set off against the contributions of the Governments concerned to the Agency.

C. The Preparatory Commission shall:

1. Elect its own officers, adopt its own rules of procedure, meet as often as necessary, determine its own place of meeting and establish such committees as it deems necessary;

2. Appoint an executive secretary and staff as shall be necessary, who shall exercise such powers and perform such duties as the Commission may determine;

3. Make arrangements for the first session of the General Conference, including the preparation of a provisional agenda and draft rules of procedure, such session to be held as soon as possible after the entry into force of this Statute;

4. Make designations for membership on the first Board of Governors in accordance with sub-paragraphs A–1 and A–2 and paragraph B of article VI;

5. Make studies, reports, and recommendations for the first session of the General Conference and for the first meeting of the Board of Governors on subjects of concern to the Agency requiring immediate attention, including (a) the financing of the Agency; (b) the programmes and budget for the first year of the Agency; (c) technical problems relevant to advance planning of Agency operations; (d) the establishment of a permanent Agency staff; and (e) the location of the permanent headquarters of the Agency;

6. Make recommendations for the first meeting of the Board of Governors concerning the provisions of a headquarters agreement defining the status of the Agency and the rights and obligations which will exist in the relationship between the Agency and the host Government;

7. (a) Enter into negotiations with the United Nations with a view to the preparation of a draft agreement in accordance with article XVI of this Statute, such draft agreement to be submitted to the first session of the General Conference and to the first meeting of the Board of Governors; and

(b) make recommendations to the first session of the Conference and to the first meeting of the Board of Governors concerning the relationship of the Agency to other international organizations as contemplated in article XVI of this Statute.

b. Export and Import of Nuclear Equipment and Material Regulations

Regulations of the Nuclear Regulatory Commission, 10 CFR Part 110, May 19, 1978, 43 F.R. 21641; as amended at 45 F.R. 18906, March 24, 1980; 45 F.R. 51184, August 1, 1980; 49 F.R. 47197–47203, December 3, 1984; 49 F.R. 49841, December 24, 1984; 50 F.R. 20743, May 20, 1985; 51 F.R. 12600, April 14, 1986; 51 F.R. 27826, August 4, 1986; 51 F.R. 47208, December 31, 1986; 52 F.R. 9655, March 26, 1987; 52 F.R. 49374, December 31, 1987; 53 F.R. 4112, February 12, 1988; 53 F.R. 17916, May 19, 1988; 53 F.R. 19263, May 27, 1988; 53 F.R. 43422, October 27, 1988; 55 F.R. 30450, July 26, 1990; 55 F.R. 34519, August 23, 1990; 56 F.R. 24684, May 31, 1991; 56 F.R. 38336, August 13, 1991; 56 F.R. 40692, August 15, 1991; 57 F.R. 18393, April 30, 1992; 57 F.R. 55080, November 24, 1992; 57 F.R. 62605, December 31, 1992; 58 F.R. 13001, March 9, 1993; 58 F.R. 57963, October 28, 1993; 59 F.R. 48997, September 26, 1994; 59 F.R. 50689, October 5, 1994; 60 F.R. 37562, July 21, 1995; 60 F.R. 55183, October 30, 1995; 61 F.R. 35602, July 8, 1996; 62 F.R. 27495, May 20, 1997; 62 F.R. 52190, October 6, 1997; 62 F.R. 59277, November 3, 1997; 63 F.R. 1900, January 13, 1998; 63 F.R. 15744, April 1, 1998; 64 F.R. 48955, September 9, 1999; 65 F.R. 70289, November 22, 2000; 67 F.R. 67101, November 4, 2002; 67 F.R. 70835, November 27, 2002; 68 F.R. 31589, May 28, 2003; 68 F.R. 58824, October 10, 2003; 69 F.R. 2281, January 14, 2004; 69 F.R. 18803, April 9, 2004; 70 F.R. 29936, May 25, 2005; 70 F.R. 37991, July 1, 2005; 70 F.R. 37991, July 1, 2005; 70 F.R. 41939, July 21, 2005; 70 F.R. 46066, August 9, 2005

SUBPART A—GENERAL PROVISIONS

§ 110.1 Purpose and scope.

(a) The regulations in this part prescribe licensing, enforcement, and rulemaking procedures and criteria, under the Atomic Energy Act, for the export of nuclear equipment and material, as set out in Sec. 110.8 and 110.9, and the import of nuclear equipment and material, as set out in Sec. 110.9a. This part also gives notice to all persons who knowingly provide to any licensee, applicant, contractor, or subcontractor, components, equipment, materials, or other goods or services, that relate to a licensee's or applicant's activities subject to this part, that they may be individually subject to NRC enforcement action for violation of Sec. 110.7b.

(b) The regulations in this part apply to all persons in the United States except:

(1) The Departments of Defense and Energy for activities authorized by sections 54, 64, 82, and 91 of the Atomic Energy Act, except when the Department of Energy seeks an export license under section 111 of the Atomic Energy Act;

(2) Persons who export or import U.S. Munitions List nuclear items, such as uranium depleted in the isotope-235 and incorporated in defense articles. These persons are subject to the controls of the Department of State pursuant to 22 CFR 120–130 "International Traffic in Arms Regulations" (ITAR), under the Arms Export Control Act, as authorized by section 110 of

the International Security and Development Cooperation Act of 1980;[1]

(3) Persons who export uranium depleted in the isotope-235 and incorporated in commodities solely to take advantage of high density or pyrophoric characteristics. These persons are subject to the controls of the Department of Commerce under the Export Administration Act, as authorized by section 110 of the International Security and Development Cooperation Act of 1980;

(4) Persons who export nuclear referral list commodities. These persons are subject to the licensing authority of the Department of Commerce pursuant to 15 CFR part 799, such as bulk zirconium, rotor and bellows equipment, maraging steel, nuclear reactor related equipment, including process control systems and simulators; and

(5) Persons who import deuterium, nuclear grade graphite, or nuclear equipment other than production or utilization facilities. A uranium enrichment facility is not a production facility.

(6) Shipments which are only passing through the U.S. (in bond shipments) do not require an NRC import or export license; however, they must comply with the Department of Transportation/IAEA packaging, and state transportation requirements.

§ 110.2 Definitions.

As used in this part,

"Agreement for cooperation" means any agreement with another nation or group of nations concluded under section 123 of the Atomic Energy Act, as amended.

"Atomic Energy Act" means the Atomic Energy Act of 1954, as amended (42 U.S.C. 2011).

"Byproduct material" means

(1) Any radioactive material (except special nuclear material) yielded in, or made radioactive by, exposure to the radiation incident to the process of producing or using special nuclear material (as in a reactor); and

(2) The tailings or wastes produced by the extraction or concentration or uranium or thorium from ore (see 10 CFR 20.1003).

"Classified information means National Security Information classified under Executive Order 12356.

"Commission" means the United States Nuclear Regulatory Commission or its duly authorized representatives.

"Common defense and security" means the common defense and security of the United States.

"Conversion facility" means any facility for the transformation from one uranium chemical species to another, including: conversion of uranium ore concentrates to UO3, conversion of UO3 to UO2, conversion of uranium oxides to UF4 or UF6, conversion of

[1] These exports are subject to the controls of the State Department and the Commerce Department under the general authority of the Arms Export Control Act and the Export Administration Act. The Commerce Department also has export licensing authority over additional nuclear-related commodities, such as advanced computers, bulk zirconium and beryllium.

UF4 to UF6, conversion of UF6 to UF4, conversion of UF4 to uranium metal, and conversion of uranium fluorides to UO2.

"Depleted uranium" means uranium having a percentage of uranium-235 less than the naturally occurring distribution of U–235 found in natural uranium (less than 0.711 weight percent U–235). It is obtained from spent (used) fuel elements or as byproduct tails or residues from uranium isotope separation.

"Deuterium" means deuterium and any deuterium compound, including heavy water, in which the ratio of deuterium atoms to hydrogen atoms exceeds 1:5000.

"Disposal" means permanent isolation of radioactive material from the surrounding environment.

"Dual-use" means equipment and materials that may be used in nuclear or non-nuclear applications.

"Effective kilograms of special nuclear material" means:

(1) For plutonium and uranium-233, their weight in kilograms;

(2) For uranium enriched 1 percent or greater in the isotope U–235, its element weight in kilograms multiplied by the square of its enrichment expressed as a decimal weight fraction; and

(3) For uranium enriched below 1 percent in the isotope U–235, its element weight in kilograms multiplied by 0.0001.

"Embargoed" means that no nuclear material or equipment can be exported to certain countries under an NRC general license because there is a U.S. trade embargo in effect.

"Exceptional circumstances" means, with respect to exports from the United States of radioactive material listed in Table 1 of Appendix P of this part:

(1) Cases of considerable health or medical need as acknowledged by the U.S. Government and the government of the importing country;

(2) Cases where there is an imminent radiological hazard or security threat presented by one or more radioactive sources; and

(3) Cases in which the exporting facility or U.S. Government maintains control of the radioactive material throughout the period the material is outside of the U.S. and removes the material at the conclusion of this period.

"Executive Branch" means the Departments of State, Energy, Defense and Commerce and the Arms Control and Disarmament Agency.

"Export" means to physically transfer nuclear equipment or material to a person or an international organization in a foreign country, except DOE distributions as authorized in Section 111 of the Atomic Energy Act or Section 110 of the International Security and Development Cooperation Act of 1980.

"General license" means an export or import license effective without the filing of a specific application with the Commission or the issuance of licensing documents to a particular person.

"Heels" means small quantities of natural, depleted or low-enriched uranium (to a maximum of 20 percent), in the form of UF6 left in emptied transport cylinders being returned to suppliers after delivery of the product.

"High-enriched uranium" means uranium enriched to 20 percent or greater in the isotope uranium-235.

"IAEA" means the International Atomic Energy Agency.

"Import" means import into the United States.

"Incidental radioactive material" means any radioactive material not otherwise subject to specific licensing under this part that is contained in or a contaminant of any non-radioactive material that:

(1) For purposes unrelated to the regulations in this part, is exported or imported for recycling or resource recovery of the non-radioactive component; and

(2) Will not be processed for separation of the radioactive component before the recycling or resource recovery occurs or as part of the resource recovery process.

The term does not include material that contains or is contaminated with "hazardous waste" as defined in section 1004(5) of the Solid Waste Disposal Act, 42 U.S.C. 6903(5).

"Individual shipment" means a shipment consisting of one lot of freight tendered to a carrier by one consignor at one place at one time for delivery to one consignee on one bill of lading. This lot may consist of:

(1) Only one item or

(2) A number of containers all listed on the same set of shipping documents. This one lot of freight or "distinct" shipment can be transported on the same carrier with other distinct shipments containing the same items as long as each shipment is covered by separate sets of shipping documents.

The phrase "introduced into a hearing" means the introduction or incorporation of testimony or documentary matter into the record of a hearing.

"License" means a general or specific export or import license issued pursuant to this part.

"Licensee" means a person authorized by a specific or a general license to export or import nuclear equipment or material pursuant to this part.

"Low-enriched uranium" means uranium enriched below 20 percent in the isotope uranium-235.

"Management" means storage, packaging, or treatment of radioactive waste.

"Natural uranium" means uranium as found in nature, containing about 0.711 percent of Uranium 235, 99.283 percent of uranium-238, and a trace (0.006 percent) of uranium-234.

"NPT" means the Treaty on the Non-Proliferation of Nuclear Weapons (TIAS 6839).

"Non-nuclear weapon State" means any State not a nuclear weapon State as defined in the Treaty on the Non-Proliferation of Nuclear Weapons.

"Nuclear weapon State" means any State which has manufactured and exploded a nuclear weapon or other nuclear explosive device prior to January 1, 1967.

"Non-Proliferation Act" means the Nuclear Non-Proliferation Act of 1978 (Pub. L. 95–242).

"NRC Public Document Room" means the facility at One White Flint North, 11555 Rockville Pike (first floor), Rockville, Maryland, where certain public records of the NRC that were made available for public inspection in paper or microfiche prior to the implementation of the NRC Agencywide Documents Access and Management System, commonly referred to as ADAMS, will remain available for public inspection. It is also the place where NRC makes computer terminals available to access the Publicly Available Records System (PARS) component of ADAMS on the NRC Web site, http://www.nrc.gov, and where copies can be viewed or ordered for a fee as set forth in Sec. 9.35 of this chapter. The facility is staffed with reference librarians to assist the public in identifying and locating documents and in using the NRC Web site and ADAMS. The NRC Public Document Room is open from 7:45 am to 4:15 pm, Monday through Friday, except on Federal holidays. Reference service and access to documents may also be requested by telephone (301–415–4737 or 800–397–4209) between 8:30 am and 4:15 pm, or by e-mail (PDR@nrc.gov), facsimile (301–415–3548), or letter (NRC Public Document Room, One White Flint North, 11555 Rockville Pike (first floor), Rockville, Maryland 20852-2738).

"NRC records" means any documentary material made by, in the possession of, or under the control of the Commission under Federal law or in connection with the transaction of public business as evidence of any of the Commission's activities.

NRC Web site, http://www.nrc.gov, is the Internet uniform resource locator name for the Internet address of the Web site where NRC will ordinarily make available its public records for inspection.

"Nuclear grade graphite for nuclear end use" means graphite having a purity level better than (i.e., less than) 5 parts per million boron equivalent, as measured according to ASTM standard C1233-98 and intended for use in a nuclear reactor. (Nuclear grade graphite for non-nuclear end use is regulated by the Department of Commerce.)

"Nuclear reactor" means an apparatus, other than an atomic weapon or nuclear explosive device, designed or used to sustain nuclear fission in a self-supporting chain reaction.

"Nuclear reactor internals" means the major structures within a reactor vessel that have one or more functions such as supporting the core, maintaining fuel alignment, directing primary coolant flow, providing radiation shields for the reactor vessel, and guiding in-core instrumentation.

"Nuclear Referral List (NRL)" means the nuclear-related, dual-use commodities on the Commerce Control List that are subject to the nuclear non-proliferation export licensing controls of the Department of Commerce. They are contained in 15 CFR part 774 of the Department of Commerce's Export Administration Regulations and are designated by the symbol (NP) as the reason for control.

"Obligations" means the commitments entered into by the U.S. Government under Atomic Energy Act (AEA) section 123 agreements for cooperation in the peaceful uses of atomic energy. Imports and exports of material or equipment pursuant to such agreements are subject to these commitments, which in some cases involve an exchange of information on imports, exports, retransfers with foreign governments, peaceful end-use assurances, and other conditions placed on the transfer of the material or equipment. The U.S. Government informs the licensee of obligations attached to material or equipment being imported into the U.S. and approves changes to those obligations.

"Packaging" means one or more receptacles and wrappers and their contents, excluding any special nuclear material, source material or byproduct material, but including absorbent material, spacing structures, thermal insulation, radiation shielding, devices for cooling and for absorbing mechanical shock, external fittings, neutron moderators, nonfissile neutron absorbers and other supplementary equipment.

"Participant" means a person, identified in a hearing notice or other Commission order, who takes part in a hearing conducted by the Commission under this part, including any person to whom the Commission grants a hearing or leave to intervene in an export or import licensing hearing, either as a matter of right or as a matter of discretion.

"Person" means any individual, corporation, partnership, firm, association, trust, estate, institution, group, Government agency other than the Commission or, with respect to imports, the Department of Energy; any State or political entity within a State; any foreign government or political entity of such government; and any authorized representative of the foregoing.

"Physical security" means measures to reasonably ensure that source or special nuclear material will only be used for authorized purposes and to prevent theft or sabotage.

"Production facility" means any nuclear reactor or plant specially designed or used to produce special nuclear material through the irradiation of source material or special nuclear material, the chemical reprocessing of irradiated source or special nuclear material, or the separation of isotopes, other than a uranium enrichment facility.

"Public health and safety" means the public health and safety of the United States.

"Radioactive material" means source, byproduct, or special nuclear material.

"Radioactive waste" means any waste that contains or is contaminated with source, byproduct, or special nuclear material, including any such waste that contains or is contaminated with "hazardous waste" as defined in section 1004(5) of the Solid Waste Disposal Act, 42 U.S.C. 6903(5), but such term does not include radioactive material that is—

(1) Contained in a sealed source, or device containing a sealed source, that is being returned to any manufacturer qualified to receive and possess the sealed source or the device containing a sealed source;

(2) A contaminant on service equipment (including service tools) used in nuclear facilities, if the service equipment is being shipped for use in another nuclear facility and not for waste management purposes or disposal; or

(3) Generated or used in a United States Government waste research and development testing program under international arrangements.

"Restricted destinations" means countries that are not parties to the NPT or are listed for reasons recommended by the executive branch.

"Retransfer" means the transport from one foreign country to another of nuclear equipment or nuclear material previously exported from the United States, or of special nuclear material produced through the use of source material or special nuclear material previously exported from the United States.

"Sealed source" means any special nuclear material or byproduct material encased in a capsule designed to prevent leakage or escape of that nuclear material.

"Secretary" means the Secretary of the Commission.

"Source material" means:

(1) Natural or depleted uranium, or thorium, other than special nuclear material; or

(2) Ores that contain by weight 0.05 percent or more of uranium, thorium or depleted uranium.

"Special nuclear material" means plutonium, uranium-233 or uranium enriched above 0.711 percent by weight in the isotope uranium-235.

"Specific activity" means the radioactivity of a radionuclide per unit mass of that nuclide, expressed in the SI unit of Terabequerels per gram (TBq/g). Values of specific activity are found in Appendix A to part 71 of this chapter.

"Specific license" means an export or import license issued to a named person upon an application filed pursuant to this part.

"Storage" means the temporary holding of radioactive material.

"Target" means material subjected to irradiation in an accelerator or nuclear reactor to induce a reaction or produce nuclear material.

"Transfer" means the transfer of possession from one person to another person.

"Transport" means the physical movement of material from one location to another.

"Treatment means any method, technique, or process, including storage for radioactive decay, designed to change the physical, chemical or biological characteristics or composition of any radioactive material.

"Tritium" means not only tritium but also includes compounds and mixtures containing tritium in which the ratio of tritium to hydrogen by atoms exceeds one part in 1,000.

United States, when used in a geographical sense, includes Puerto Rico and all territories and possessions of the United States.

"Uranium enrichment facility" means:

(1) Any facility used for separating the isotopes of uranium or enriching uranium in the isotope 235, except laboratory scale facilities designed or used for experimental or analytical purposes only; or

(2) Any equipment or device, or important component part especially designed for such equipment or device, capable of separating the isotopes of uranium or enriching uranium in the isotope 235.

"Utilization facility" means:

(1) Any nuclear reactor, other than one that is a production facility and

(2) Any of the following major components of a nuclear reactor:

(i) Reactor pressure vessel (designed to contain the core of a nuclear reactor);

(ii) Reactor primary coolant pump;

(iii) "On-line" reactor fuel charging and discharging machine; and

(iv) Complete reactor control rod system.

(3) A utilization facility does not include the steam turbine generator portion of a nuclear power plant.

§ 110.3 Interpretations.

Except as authorized by the Commission in writing, no interpretation of the meaning of the regulations in this part other than a written interpretation by the Commission's General Counsel is binding upon the Commission.

§ 110.4 Inquiries.

Except where otherwise specified in this part, all communications and reports concerning the regulations in this part should be addressed to the Deputy Director of the NRC's Office of International Programs, either by telephone to (301) 415–2344; by mail to the U.S. Nuclear Regulatory Commission, Washington, DC 20555–0001; by hand delivery to the NRC's offices at 11555 Rockville Pike, Rockville, Maryland; or, where practicable, by electronic submission, for example, via Electronic Information Exchange, or CD–ROM. Electronic submissions must be made in a manner that enables the NRC to receive, read, authenticate, distribute, and archive the submission, and process and retrieve it a single page at a time. Detailed guidance on making electronic submissions can be obtained by visiting the NRC's Web site at http://www.nrc.gov/site-help/eie.html, by calling (301) 415–6030, by e-mail to EIE@nrc.gov, or by writing the Office of Information Services, U.S. Nuclear Regulatory Commission, Washington, DC 20555–0001. The guidance discusses, among other topics, the formats the NRC can accept, the use of electronic signatures, and the treatment of nonpublic information.

§ 110.5 License requirements.

Except as provided under subpart B of this part, no person may export any nuclear equipment or material listed in Sec. 110.8 and Sec. 110.9, or import any nuclear equipment or material listed in Sec. 110.9a, unless authorized by a general or specific license issued under this part.

§ 110.6 Retransfers.

(a) Retransfer of any nuclear equipment or material listed in Sec. 110.8 and 110.9, including special nuclear material produced through the use of U.S.-origin source material or special nuclear material, requires authorization by the Department of Energy, unless, the export to the new destination is authorized under a special or general license or an exemption from licensing requirements. Under certain agreements for cooperation, Department of Energy authorization also is required for the retransfer of special nuclear material produced through the use of non-U.S.-supplied nuclear material in U.S.-supplied utilization facilities. Department of

Energy authorization is also required for the retransfer of obligated nuclear equipment and material (see definition of "obligated" in Sec. 110.2).

(b) Requests for authority to retransfer are processed by the Department of Energy, Office of Arms Control and Nonproliferation Technology Support, Washington, DC 20585.

§ 110.7 Information collection requirement: OMB approval.

(a) The Nuclear Regulatory Commission has submitted the information collection requirements contained in this part to the Office of Management and Budget (OMB) for approval as required by the Paperwork Reduction Act (44 U.S.C. 3501 et seq.). The NRC may not conduct or sponsor, and a person is not required to respond to, a collection of information unless it displays a currently valid OMB control number. OMB has approved the information collection requirements contained in this part under control numbers 3150–0036.

(b) The approved information collection requirements contained in this part appear in Sec. 110.7a, 110.23, 110.26, 110.27, 110.31, 110.32, 110.50, 110.51, 110.52, and 110.53

(c) This part contains information collection requirements in addition to those approved under the control number specified in paragraph (a) of this section. These information collection requirements and the control numbers under which they are approved are as follows:

(1) In Sec. 110.19, 110.20, 110.21, 110.22, 110.23, 110.31, and 110.32, NRC Form 7 is approved under control number 3150–0027.

(2) [Reserved]

§ 110.7a Completeness and accuracy of information.

(a) Information provided to the Commission by an applicant for a license or by a licensee or information required by statute or by the Commission's regulations, orders, or license conditions to be maintained by the applicant or the licensee shall be complete and accurate in all material respects.

(b) Each applicant or licensee shall notify the Commission of information identified by the applicant or licensee as having for the regulated activity a significant implication for public health and safety or common defense and security. An applicant or licensee violates this paragraph only if the applicant or licensee fails to notify the Commission of information that applicant or licensee has identified as having a significant implication for public health and safety or common defense and security. Notification shall be provided to the Administrator of the appropriate Regional Office within two working days of identifying the information. This requirement is not applicable to information which is already required to be provided to the Commission by other reporting or updating requirements.

§ 110.8 List of nuclear equipment and material under NRC export licensing authority.

(a) Nuclear reactors and especially designed or prepared equipment and components for nuclear reactors. (See Appendix A to this part.)

(b) Plants for the separation of isotopes of uranium (source material or special nuclear material) including gas centrifuge plants, gaseous diffusion plants, aerodynamic enrichment plants, chemical exchange or ion exchange enrichment plants, laser based enrichment plants, plasma separation enrichment plants, electromagnetic enrichment plants, and especially designed or prepared equipment, other than analytical instruments, for the separation of isotopes of uranium. (See appendices to this part for lists of: gas centrifuge equipment—Appendix B; gaseous diffusion equipment—Appendix C; aerodynamic enrichment equipment—Appendix D; chemical exchange or ion exchange enrichment equipment—Appendix E; laser based enrichment equipment—Appendix F; plasma separation enrichment equipment—Appendix G; and electromagnetic enrichment equipment—Appendix H.)

(c) Plants for the separation of the isotopes of lithium and especially designed or prepared assemblies and components for these plants. (See Appendix N to this part.)

(d) Plants for the reprocessing of irradiated nuclear reactor fuel elements and especially designed or prepared assemblies and components for these plants. (See Appendix I to this part.)

(e) Plants for the fabrication of nuclear reactor fuel elements and especially designed or prepared assemblies and components for these plants. (See Appendix O to this part.)

(f) Plants for the conversion of uranium and plutonium and especially designed or prepared assemblies and components for these plants. (See Appendix J to this part.)

(g) Plants for the production, separation, or purification of heavy water, deuterium, and deuterium compounds and especially designed or prepared assemblies and components for these plants. (See Appendix K to this part.)

(h) Plants for the production of special nuclear material using accelerator-driven subcritical assembly systems capable of continuous operation above 5 MWe thermal.

(i) Other nuclear-related commodities are under the export licensing authority of the Department of Commerce.

§ 110.9 List of nuclear material under NRC export licensing authority.

(a) Special Nuclear Material.
(b) Source Material.
(c) Byproduct Material.
(d) Deuterium.
(e) Nuclear grade graphite for nuclear end use.

§ 110.9a List of nuclear equipment and material under NRC import licensing authority.

(a) Production and utilization facilities.
(b) Special nuclear material.

(c) Source material.
(d) Byproduct material.

SUBPART B—EXEMPTIONS

§ 110.10 General.

(a) In response to a request or on its own initiative, the Commission may grant an exemption from the regulations in this part, if it determines that the exemption:

(1) Is authorized by law;

(2) Is not inimical to the common defense and security; and

(3) Does not constitute an unreasonable risk to the public health and safety.

(b) An exemption from statutory licensing requirements, as authorized by sections 57d, 62, and 81 of the Atomic Energy Act, will be granted only after coordination with the Executive Branch.

(c) The granting of an exemption does not relieve any person from complying with the regulations of other Government agencies applicable to exports or imports under their authority.

§ 110.11 Export of IAEA safeguards samples.

A person is exempt from the requirements for a license to export special nuclear material set forth in sections 53 and 54d. of the Atomic Energy Act and from the regulations in this part to the extent that the person exports special nuclear material in IAEA safeguards samples, if the samples are exported in accordance with § 75.42(e)(1) of this chapter, or a comparable Department of Energy order, and are in quantities not exceeding a combined total of 100 grams of contained plutonium, U–233 and U–235 per facility per year. This exemption does not relieve any person from complying with Parts 71 or 73 of this chapter or any Commission order pursuant to section 201(a) of the Energy Reorganization Act of 1974 (42 U.S.C. 5841(a)).

SUBPART C—LICENSES

SOURCE: 49 FR 47198, December. 3, 1984, unless otherwise noted.

§ 110.19 Types of licenses.

(a) Licenses for the export and import of nuclear equipment and material in this part consist of two types: General licenses and Specific licenses. Except as provided in paragraph (b) of this section, a general license is effective without the filing of an application with the Commission or the issuance of licensing documents to a particular person. A specific license is issued to a named person and is effective upon approval by the Commission of an application filed pursuant to the regulations in this part and issuance of licensing documents to the applicant. Issuance of a specific or general license under this part does not relieve a person from complying with applicable regulations of the Environmental Protection Agency for any export or import that contains or is contaminated with hazardous waste.

(b) A person using a general license under this part as authority to export incidental radioactive material that is contained in or a contaminant of a shipment that exceeds 100 kilograms in total weight shall file a completed NRC Form 7 before the export takes place.

§ 110.20 General license information.

(a) A person may use an NRC general license as authority to export or import nuclear equipment or material (including incidental radioactive material), if the nuclear equipment or material to be exported or imported is covered by the NRC general licenses described in Sec. 110.21 through 110.30.

(1) A person using a general license under this part as authority to export incidental radioactive material that is contained in or a contaminant of a shipment that exceeds 100 kilograms in total weight shall file a completed NRC Form 7 before the export takes place.

(2) If an export or import is not covered by the NRC general licenses described in Sec. 110.21 through 110.30, a person must file an application with the Commission for a specific license in accordance with Sec. 110.31 through 110.32.

(b) In response to a petition or on its own initiative, the Commission may issue a general license for export or import if it determines that any exports or imports made under the general license will not be inimical to the common defense and security or constitute an unreasonable risk to the public health and safety and otherwise meet applicable statutory requirements. A general license is issued as a regulation after a rulemaking proceeding under subpart K of this part. Issuance of a general license is coordinated with the Executive Branch.

(c) A general license does not relieve a person from complying with the regulations of other Government agencies applicable to exports or imports under their authority.

(d) A general license for export may not be used if the exporter knows, or has reason to believe, that the material will be used in any activity related to isotope separation, chemical reprocessing, heavy water production or the fabrication of nuclear fuel containing plutonium, unless these activities are generically authorized under an appropriate agreement for cooperation.

(e) A person who uses an NRC general license as the authority to export or import may cite on the shipping documents the section of this part which authorizes the described export or import under general license, as a means of expediting U.S. Customs Service's processing of the shipment.

(f) As specified in Sec. 110.21 through 110.26, 110.28, 110.29, and 110.30 only certain countries are eligible recipients of equipment or material under NRC general licenses to export. The Commission will closely monitor these countries and may at any time remove a country from a general license in response to significant adverse developments in the country involved. A key factor in this regard is the nonproliferation credentials of the importing country.

§ 110.21 General license for the export of special nuclear material.

(a) Except as provided in paragraph (d) of this section, a general license is issued to any person to export the following to any country not listed in Sec. 110.28:

(1) Low-enriched uranium as residual contamination (17.5 parts per million or less) in any item or substance.

(2) Plutonium containing 80 percent or more by weight of plutonium-238 in cardiac pacemakers.

(3) Special nuclear material, other than Pu-236 and Pu-238, in sensing components in instruments, if no more than 3 grams of enriched uranium or 0.1 gram of Pu or U–233 are contained in each sensing component.

(4) Pu-236 and Pu-238 when contained in a device, or a source for use in a device, in quantities of less than 3.7 × 10-3 TBq (100 millicuries) of alpha activity (189 micrograms Pu-236, 5.88 milligrams Pu-238) per device or source.

(b) Except as provided in paragraph (d) of this section, a general license is issued to any person to export the following to any country not listed in Sec. 110.28 or Sec. 110.29:

(1) Special nuclear material, other than Pu-236 and Pu-238, in individual shipments of 0.001 effective kilogram or less (e.g., 1.0 gram of plutonium, U–233 or U–235, or 10 kilograms of 1 percent enriched uranium), not to exceed 0.1 effective kilogram per year to any one country.

(2) Special nuclear material in fuel elements as replacements for damaged or defective unirradiated fuel elements previously exported under a specific license, subject to the same terms as the original export license and the condition that the replaced fuel elements must be returned to the United States within a reasonable time period.

(3) Uranium, enriched to less than 20 percent in U–235, in the form of UF6 heels in cylinders being returned to suppliers in EURATOM.

(c) Except as provided in paragraph (d) of this section, a general license is issued to any person to export Pu-236 or Pu-238 to any country listed in Sec. 110.30 in individual shipments of 1 gram or less, not to exceed 100 grams per year to any one country.

(d) The general licenses in paragraphs (a), (b), and (c) of this section do not authorize the export of special nuclear material in radioactive waste.

(e) Persons using the general licenses in paragraphs (a), (b), and (c) of this section as authority to export special nuclear material as incidental radioactive material shall file a completed NRC Form 7 before the export takes place if the total weight of the shipment exceeds 100 kilograms.

§ 110.22 General license for the export of source material.

(a) Except as provided in paragraph (e) of this section, a general license is issued to any person to export the following to any country not listed in Sec. 110.28:

(1) Uranium or thorium, other than U–230, U–232, Th-227, and Th-228, in any substance in concentrations of less than 0.05 percent by weight.

(2) Thorium, other than Th-227 and Th-228, in incandescent gas mantles or in alloys in concentrations of 5 percent or less.

(3) Th-227, Th-228, U–230, and U–232 when contained in a device, or a source for use in a device, in quantities of less than 3.7 × 10-3 TBq (100 millicuries) of alpha activity (3.12

micrograms Th-227, 122 micrograms Th-228, 3.7 micrograms U–230, 4.7 milligrams U–232) per device or source.

(b) Except as provided in paragraph (e) of this section, a general license is issued to any person to export uranium or thorium, other than U–230, U–232, Th-227, or Th-228, in individual shipments of 10 kilograms or less to any country not listed in Sec. 110.28 or Sec. 110.29, not to exceed 1,000 kilograms per year to any one country or 500 kilograms per year to any one country when the uranium or thorium is of Canadian origin.

(c) A general license is issued to any person to export uranium, enriched to less than 20 percent in U–235, in the form of UF6 heels in cylinders being returned to suppliers in EURATOM.

(d) Except as provided in paragraph (e) of this section, a general license is issued to any person to export uranium or thorium, other than U–230, U–232, Th-227, or Th-228, in individual shipments of 1 kilogram or less to any country listed in Sec. 110.29, not to exceed 100 kilograms per year to any one country.

(e) Except as provided in paragraph (e) of this section, a general license is issued to any person to export U–230, U–232, Th-227, or Th-228 in individual shipments of 10 kilograms or less to any country listed in Sec. 110.30, not to exceed 1,000 kilograms per year to any one country or 500 kilograms per year to any one country when the uranium or thorium is of Canadian origin.

(f) Paragraphs (a), (b), (c), and (d) of this section do not authorize the export under general license of source material in radioactive waste.

(g) Persons using the general licenses in paragraphs (a), (b), (c), and (d) of this section as authority to export source material as incidental radioactive material shall file a completed NRC Form 7 before the export takes place if the total weight of the shipment exceeds 100 kilograms.

§ 110.23 General license for the export of byproduct material.

(a) A general license is issued to any person to export byproduct material (see appendix L to this part) except that:

(1) This section does not authorize the export of byproduct material to any embargoed country listed in Sec. 110.28, or byproduct material in radioactive waste, or tritium for recovery or recycle purposes.

(2) Actinium-225 and -227, americium-241 and -242m, californium-248, -249, -250, -251, -252, -253, and -254, curium-240, -241, -242, -243, -244, -245, -246 and -247, einsteinium-252, -253, -254 and -255, fermium-257, gadolinium-148, mendelevium-258, neptunium-235 and -237, polonium-210, and radium-223 must be contained in a device, or a source for use in a device, in quantities of less than 3.7 × 10-3 TBq (100 millicuries) of alpha activity per device or source, unless the export is to a country listed in Sec. 110.30. Individual shipments must be less than the TBq values specified in Category 2 of Table 1 of Appendix P to this Part. Exports of americium and neptunium are subject to the reporting requirements listed in paragraph (b) of this section.

(3) For americium-241, exports must not exceed 0.6 TBq (16 curies) per device or 60 TBq (1,600 curies) to any one country listed in Sec. 110.29, and must be contained in industrial process control equipment or petroleum exploration equipment in quantities of less than 0.6 TBq (16 curies) per device and per shipment, not to exceed 60 TBq (1,600 curies) per year to any one country. Individual shipments to all countries other than those listed in Sec. 110.28 and 110.29 must be less than 0.6 TBq (16 curies) per shipment, consistent with Appendix P to this part.

(4) For neptunium-235 and -237, exports must not exceed individual shipments of one gram, not to exceed 10 grams per year to any one country.

(5) For polonium-210, the material must be contained in static eliminators and may not exceed 3.7 TBq (100 curies) per individual shipment.

(6) For tritium in any dispersed form, except for recovery or recycle purposes (e.g., luminescent light sources and paint, accelerator targets, calibration standards, labeled compounds), exports must not exceed the quantity of 0.37 TBq (10 curies (1.03 milligrams)) or less per item, not to exceed 37 TBq (1,000 curies (103 milligrams)) per shipment or 370 TBq (10,000 curies (1.03 grams)) per year to any one country. Exports of tritium to the countries listed in Sec. 110.30 must not exceed the quantity of 1.48 TBq (40 curies (4.12 milligrams)) or less per item, not to exceed 37 TBq (1,000 curies (103 milligrams)) per shipment or 370 TBq (10,000 curies (1.03 grams)) per year to any, one country, and exports of tritium in luminescent safety devices installed in aircraft must not exceed a quantity of 1.48 TBq (40 curies (4.12 milligrams)) or less per light source.

(b) Persons making exports under the general license established by paragraph (a) of this section shall submit by February 1 of each year one copy of a report of all americium and neptunium shipments during the previous calendar year. The report must include:

(1) A description of the material, including quantity;

(2) Approximate shipment dates; and

(3) A list of recipient countries, end users, and intended use keyed to the items shipped.

(c) Persons using a general license issued under paragraph (a) of this section as authority to export byproduct material as incidental radioactive material shall file a completed NRC Form 7 before the export takes place if the total weight of the shipment exceeds 100 kilograms.

§ 110.24 General license for the export of deuterium.

(a) A general license is issued to any person to export deuterium in individual shipments of 10 kilograms or less (50 kilograms of heavy water) to any country not listed in Sec. 110.28 or Sec. 110.29. No person may export more than 200 kilograms (1000 kilograms of heavy water) per year to any one country.

(b) A general license is issued to any person to export deuterium in individual shipments of 1 kilogram or less (5 kilograms of heavy water) to any country listed in Sec. 110.29. No person may export more than 5 kilograms (25 kilograms of heavy water) per year to any one country.

§ 110.26 General license for the export of nuclear reactor components.

(a) A general license is issued to any person to export to the following countries any nuclear reactor component described in paragraphs (5) through (9) of appendix A to this part if—

(1) The component is of U.S. origin,

(2) The component will be used in a light or heavy water-moderated power or research reactor in those countries, or

(3) The component is in semifabricated form and will be undergoing final fabrication or repair in those countries for subsequent return to the United States for use in a nuclear power or research reactor in the United States:

Austria
Belgium
Bulgaria
Canada
Czech Republic
Denmark
Finland
France
German
Indonesia
Ireland
Italy
Japan
Latvia
Lithuania
Luxembourg
Netherlands
New Zealand
Philippines
Portugal
Republic of Korea
Romania
Spain
Sweden
Switzerland
Taiwan
United Kingdom

(b) This general license does not authorize the export of components, in final or semi-fabricated form, for research reactors capable of continuous operation above 5 MWe thermal.

(c) This general license does not authorize the export of essentially complete reactors through piecemeal exports of facility components. When individual exports of components would amount in the aggregate to export of an essentially complete nuclear reactor, a facility export license is required.

(d) Persons making exports under the general license established by paragraph (a) of this section shall submit by February 1 of each year one copy of a report of all components shipped during the previous calendar year. This report must include:

(1) A description of the components keyed to the categories listed in appendix A to this part.

(2) Approximate shipment dates.

(3) A list of recipient countries and endusers keyed to the items shipped.

§ 110.27 General license for imports.

(a) Except as provided in paragraphs (b), (c), and (f) of this section, a general license is issued to any person to import byproduct, source, or special nuclear material if the consignee is authorized to receive and possess the material under:

(1) A contract with the Department of Energy;

(2) An exemption from licensing requirements issued by the Commission; or

(3) A general or specific NRC or Agreement State license issued by the Commission or a State with which the Commission has entered into an agreement under Section 274b. of the Atomic Energy Act.

(b) The general license in paragraph (a) of this section does not authorize the import of source or special nuclear material in the form of irradiated fuel that exceeds 100 kilograms per shipment.

(c) Paragraph (a) of this section does not authorize the import under general license of radioactive waste, other than radioactive waste that is being returned to a United States Government or military facility in the United States which is authorized to possess the material.

(d) A person importing formula quantities of strategic special nuclear material (as defined in Sec. 73.2 of this chapter) under this general license shall provide the notifications required by Sec. 73.27 and Sec. 73.72 of this chapter.

(e) A general license is issued to any person to import the major components of a utilization facility as defined in Sec. 110.2 for end-use at a utilization facility licensed by the Commission.

(f) Individual import shipments of radioactive material listed in Appendix P must be less than the amounts specified in Category 2 in Table 1 of Appendix P to this part.

§ 110.28 Embargoed destinations.

Cuba
Iran
Iraq
Libya
North Korea
Syria
Sudan

§ 110.29 Restricted destinations.

Afghanistan
Andorra
Angola
Burma (Myanmar)
Djibouti
India
Israel
Oman
Pakistan

§ 110.30 Members of the Nuclear Suppliers Group.

Argentina
Australia
Austria
Belarus
Belgium
Brazil
Bulgaria
Canada
Cyprus
Czech Republic
Denmark
Finland
France
Germany
Greece
Hungary
Ireland
Italy
Japan
Latvia
Luxembourg
Netherlands
New Zealand
Norway
Poland
Portugal
Republic of Korea
Romania
Russia
Slovak Republic
Slovenia
South Africa
Spain
Sweden
Switzerland
Turkey
Ukraine
United Kingdom

§ 110.30 Application for a specific license.

(a) A person shall file an application for a specific license to export or import with the Deputy Director of the NRC's Office of International Programs, using an appropriate method listed in Sec. 110.4.

(b) An application for a specific license to export or import must be accompanied by the appropriate fee in accordance with the fee schedule in Sec. 170.21 and Sec. 170.31 of this chapter. A license application will not be processed unless the specified fee is received.

(c) A license application should be filed on NRC Form 7, except that an import license application and a production or utilization facility export license application should be filed by letter.

(d) Each person shall provide in the license application, as appropriate, the information specified in Sec. 110.32. The Commission also may require the submission of additional information if necessary to complete its review.

(e) An application may cover multiple shipments and destinations.

(f) The applicant shall withdraw an application when it is no longer needed. The Commission's official files retain all documents related to a withdrawn application.

§ 110.32 Information required in an application for a specific license/NRC Form 7.

(a) Name and address of applicant.

(b) Name and address of supplier of equipment or material.

(c) Country of origin of equipment or material, and any other countries that have processed the material prior to its import into the U.S.[1]

(d) Names and addresses of all intermediate and ultimate consignees, other than intermediate consignees performing shipping services only.

(e) Dates of proposed first and last shipments.

(f) Description of the equipment or material including, as appropriate, the following:

(1) Maximum quantity of material in grams or kilograms (terabequerels or TBq for byproduct material) and its chemical and physical form.

(2) For enriched uranium, the maximum weight percentage of enrichment and maximum weight of contained U–235.

(3) For nuclear equipment, total dollar value.

(4) For nuclear reactors, the name of the facility and its design power level.

(5) For proposed exports or imports of radioactive waste, and for proposed exports of incidental radioactive material—the volume, classification (as defined in Sec. 61.55 of this chapter), physical and chemical characteristics, route of transit of shipment, and ultimate disposition (including forms of management) of the waste.

---

[1] Note: This is meant to include all obligations attached to the material, according to the definition of obligations in Sec. 110.2. Licensees must keep records of obligations attached to material which they own or is in their possession.

(6) For proposed imports of radioactive waste—the industrial or other process responsible for generation of the waste, and the status of the arrangements for disposition, e.g., any agreement by a low-level waste compact or State to accept the material for management purposes or disposal.

(7) Description of end use by all consignees in sufficient detail to permit accurate evaluation of the justification for the proposed export or import, including the need for shipment by the dates specified.

(g) For proposed imports of material listed in Table 1 of Appendix P to this part, a copy of the applicant's authorization to receive and possess the radioactive material to be imported for each recipient.

(h) For proposed exports of material listed in Table 1 of Appendix P to this part, pertinent documentation that the recipient of the material has the necessary authorization under the laws and regulations of the importing country to receive and possess the material. Pertinent documentation shall consist of a copy of the recipient's authorization to receive and possess the material to be exported or a confirmation from the government of the importing country that the recipient is so authorized. The recipient authorization shall include the following information:

(1) Name of the recipient

(2) Recipient location and legal address or principal place of business

(3) Relevant radionuclides and radioactivity being imported or that the recipient is authorized to receive and possess

(4) Uses, if appropriate

(5) The expiration date of the recipient's authorization (if any)

Subpart D—Review of License Applications

§ 110.40 Commission review.[2]

(a) Immediately after receipt of a license application for an export or import requiring a specific license under this part, the Commission will initiate its licensing review and, to the maximum extent feasible, will expeditiously process the application concurrently with any applicable review by the Executive Branch.

(b) The Commissioners shall review a license application for export of the following:

(1) A production or utilization facility.

(2) More than one effective kilogram of high-enriched uranium, plutonium or U–233.

(3) Nuclear grade graphite for nuclear end use.

(4) 1,000 kilograms or more of deuterium oxide (heavy water), other than exports of heavy water to Canada.

---

[2] Editorial Note: Sec. 110.40 was amended at 70 FR 37992, July 1, 2005. The amendment, however, could not be incorporated due to inaccurate amendatory instruction. At 70 FR 46066, August 9, 2005, the July 1, 2005 amendment was corrected. The correction, however, could not be incorporated due to inaccurate amendatory instruction.

(5) An export involving assistance to end uses related to isotope separation, chemical reprocessing, heavy water production, advanced reactors, or the fabrication of nuclear fuel containing plutonium, except for exports of source material or low-enriched uranium to EURATOM or Japan for enrichment up to 5 percent in the isotope uranium-235, and those categories of exports which the Commission has approved in advance as constituting permitted incidental assistance.

(6) The initial export to a country since March 10, 1978 of source or special nuclear material for nuclear end use.

(7) An export involving over:

(i) 10 grams of plutonium, U–233 or high-enriched uranium;

(ii) 1 effective kilogram of low-enriched uranium;

(iii) Nuclear grade graphite for nuclear end use;

(iv) 250 kilograms of source material or heavy water; or

(v) 1,000 curies of tritium, to any country listed in Sec. 110.28 or Sec. 110.29.

(8) Any export subject to special limitations as determined by the staff or a majority of the Commissioners.

(c) If the Commission has not completed action on a license application within 60 days after receipt of the Executive Branch judgment, as provided for in Sec. 110.41, or the license application when an Executive Branch judgment is not required, it will inform the applicant in writing of the reason for delay and, as appropriate, provide followup reports.

§ 110.41 Executive Branch review.

(a) An application for a license to export the following will be promptly forwarded to the Executive Branch for review:

(1) A production or utilization facility.

(2) More than one effective kilogram of high-enriched uranium or 10 grams of plutonium or U–233.

(3) Nuclear grade graphite for nuclear end use.

(4) More than 3.7 TBq (100 curies) of tritium, and deuterium oxide (heavy water), other than exports of heavy water to Canada.

(5) One kilogram or more of source or special nuclear material to be exported under the US–IAEA Agreement for Cooperation.

(6) An export involving assistance to end uses related to isotope separation, chemical reprocessing, heavy water production, advanced reactors, or the fabrication of nuclear fuel containing plutonium, except for exports of source material or low-enriched uranium to EURATOM and Japan for enrichment up to 5 percent in the isotope uranium-235, and those categories of exports approved in advance by the Executive Branch as constituting permitted incidental assistance.

(7) The initial export of nuclear material or equipment to a foreign reactor.

(8) An export involving radioactive waste.

(9) An export to any country listed in Sec. 110.28 or Sec. 110.29.

(10) An export subject to special limitations as determined by the Commission or the Executive Branch.

(b) The Executive Branch will be requested to:

(1) Provide its judgment as to whether the proposed export would be inimical to the common defense and security, along with supporting rationale and information.

(2) Where applicable, confirm that the proposed export would be under the terms of an agreement for cooperation; and

(3) Address the extent to which the export criteria in Sec. 110.42 are met, if applicable, and the extent to which the recipient country or group of countries has adhered to the provisions of any applicable agreement for cooperation.

(c) The Commission may request the Executive Branch to address specific concerns and provide additional data and recommendations as necessary.

§ 110.42 Export licensing criteria.

(a) The review of license applications for export for peaceful nuclear uses of production or utilization facilities[3] or for export for peaceful nuclear uses of special nuclear or source material requiring a specific license under this part is governed by the following criteria:

(1) IAEA safeguards as required by Article III (2) of the NPT will be applied with respect to any such facilities or material proposed to be exported, to any such material or facilities previously exported and subject to the applicable agreement for cooperation, and to any special nuclear material used in or produced through the use thereof.

(2) No such material or facilities proposed to be exported or previously exported and subject to the applicable agreement for cooperation, and no special nuclear material produced through the use of such material or facilities, will be used for any nuclear explosive device or for research on or development of any nuclear explosive device.

(3) Adequate physical security measures will be maintained with respect to such material or facilities proposed to be exported and to any special nuclear material used in or produced through the use thereof. Physical security measures will be deemed adequate if such measures provide a level of protection equivalent to that set forth in Sec. 110.44.

(4) No such material or facilities proposed to be exported, and no special nuclear material produced through the use of such material, will be retransferred to the jurisdiction of any other country or group of countries unless the prior approval of the United States is obtained for such retransfer.

(5) No such material proposed to be exported and no special nuclear material produced through the use of such material will be reprocessed, and no irradiated fuel elements containing

[3] Exports of nuclear reactors, reactor pressure vessels, reactor primary coolant pumps, "on-line" reactor fuel charging and discharging machines, and complete reactor control rod systems, as specified in paras. (1) through (4) of appendix A to this part, are subject to the export licensing criteria in Sec. 110.42(a). Exports of nuclear reactor components, as specified in paras. (5) through (9) of appendix A to this part, when exported separately from the items described in paras. (1) through (4) of appendix A of this part, are subject to the export licensing criteria in Sec. 110.42(b).

such material removed from a reactor will be altered in form or content, unless the prior approval of the United States is obtained for such reprocessing or alteration.

(6) With respect to exports of such material or facilities to nonnuclear weapon states, IAEA safeguards will be maintained with respect to all peaceful activities in, under the jurisdiction of, or carried out under the control of such state at the time of export. This criterion will not be applied if the Commission has been notified by the President in writing that failure to approve an export because this criterion has not been met would be seriously prejudicial to the achievement of United States nonproliferation objectives or otherwise jeopardize the common defense and security, in which case the provisions of section 128 of the Atomic Energy Act regarding Congressional review will apply.

(7) The proposed export of a facility or of more than 0.003 effective kilograms of special nuclear material, other than plutonium containing 80 percent or more by weight of plutonium-238, would be under the terms of an agreement for cooperation.

(8) The proposed export is not inimical to the common defense and security and, in the case of facility exports, does not constitute an unreasonable risk to the public health and safety in the United States.

(9)(i) With respect to exports of high-enriched uranium to be used as a fuel or target in a nuclear research or test reactor, the Commission determines that:

(A) There is no alternative nuclear reactor fuel or target enriched to less than 20 percent in the isotope U–235 that can be used in that reactor;

(B) The proposed recipient of the uranium has provided assurances that, whenever an alternative nuclear reactor fuel or target can be used in that reactor, it will use that alternative fuel or target in lieu of highly-enriched uranium; and

(C) The United States Government is actively developing an alternative nuclear reactor fuel or target that can be used in that reactor.

(ii) A fuel or target "can be used" in a nuclear research or test reactor if—

(A) The fuel or target has been qualified by the Reduced Enrichment Research and Test Reactor Program of the Department of Energy; and

(B) Use of the fuel or target will permit the large majority of ongoing and planned experiments and isotope production to be conducted in the reactor without a large percentage increase in the total cost of operating the reactor.

(b) The review of license applications for the export of nuclear equipment, other than a production or utilization facility, and for deuterium and nuclear grade graphite for nuclear end use, is governed by the following criteria:

(1) IAEA safeguards as required by Article III (2) of the NPT will be applied with respect to such equipment or material.

(2) No such equipment or material will be used for any nuclear explosive device or for research on or development of any nuclear explosive device.

(3) No such equipment or material will be retransferred to the jurisdiction of any other country or group of countries without the prior consent of the United States.

(4) The proposed export is not inimical to the common defense and security.

(c) Except where paragraph (d) is applicable, the review of license applications for export of byproduct material or for export of source material for non-nuclear end uses requiring a specific license under this part is governed by the criterion that the proposed export is not inimical to the common defense and security.

(d) The review of license applications for the export of radioactive waste requiring a specific license under this part is governed by the following criteria:

(1) The proposed export is not inimical to the common defense and security.

(2) The receiving country, after being advised of the information required by Sec. 110.32(f)(5), finds that it has the administrative and technical capacity and regulatory structure to manage and dispose of the waste and consents to the receipt of the radioactive waste.

In the case of radioactive waste containing a nuclear material to which paragraph (a) or (b) of this section is applicable, the criteria in this paragraph (d) shall be in addition to the criteria provided in paragraph (a) or (b) of this section.

(e) In making its findings under paragraphs (a)(8) and (c) of this section for proposed exports of radioactive material listed in Appendix P to this part, the NRC shall consider:

(1) Whether the foreign recipient is authorized based on the authorization or confirmation required by Sec. 110.32(h) to receive and possess the material under the laws and regulations of the importing country;

(2) Whether the importing country has the appropriate technical and administrative capability, resources and regulatory structure to manage the material in a safe and secure manner;

(3) For proposed exports of Category 1 amounts of radioactive material listed in Table 1 of Appendix P to this part, whether the government of the importing country provides consent to the United States Government for the import of the material;

(4) In cases where the importing country does not have the technical and administrative capability described in paragraph (e)(2) of this section, and in cases where there is insufficient evidence of the recipient's authorization to receive and possess the material to be exported, described in paragraph (e)(1) of this section, whether exceptional circumstances exist, and if so, whether the export should be licensed in light of those exceptional circumstances and the risks, if any, to the common defense and security of the proposed export;

(5) For proposed exports under exceptional circumstances of Category 1 or Category 2 amounts of radioactive material listed in Table 1 of Appendix P to this part, whether the government of the importing country provides consent to the United States Government for the import of the material;

(6) For proposed exports of radioactive material listed in Table 1 of Appendix P to this part under the exceptional circumstance in which there is a considerable health or medical need as acknowledged by the U.S. Government and the importing country, whether the United States and the importing country have, to the extent practicable, made arrangements for the safe and secure management of the radioactive sources during and at the end of their useful life;

(7) Based upon the available information, whether the foreign recipient has engaged in clandestine or illegal procurement of radioactive material listed in Table 1 of Appendix P to the part;

(8) Based upon available information, whether an import or export authorization for radioactive material listed in Table 1 of Appendix P to this part has been denied to the recipient or importing country, or whether the recipient or importing country has diverted any import or export of radioactive material previously authorized; and

(9) Based upon available information, whether there is a risk of diversion or malicious acts involving radioactive material in Table 1 of Appendix P to this part.

§ 110.43 Import licensing criteria.

The review of license applications for imports requiring a specific license under this part is governed by the following criteria:

(a) The proposed import is not inimical to the common defense and security.

(b) The proposed import does not constitute an unreasonable risk to the public health and safety.

(c) Any applicable requirements of subpart A of part 51 of this chapter are satisfied.

(d) With respect to the import of radioactive waste, an appropriate facility has agreed to accept the waste for management or disposal.

(e) With respect to proposed imports of radioactive material listed in Appendix P to this part, the NRC shall consider whether the U.S. recipient is authorized to possess the material under a contract with the Department of Energy or a license issued by the Commission or a State with which the Commission has entered into an agreement under Section 274b of the AEA.

(f) In making its findings under paragraphs (a) and (b) of this section for proposed imports of radioactive material listed in Appendix P to this part, the NRC shall consider:

(1) Based upon available information, whether the applicant has been engaged in clandestine or illegal procurement of radioactive material listed in Table 1 of Appendix P to this part;

(2) Based upon available information, whether an import or export authorization for radioactive material has been denied to the applicant or whether the applicant has diverted any import or export of radioactive material previously authorized; and

(3) Based upon available information, whether a risk of diversion or malicious acts involving the radioactive material listed in Table 1 of Appendix P to this part.

§ 110.44 Physical security standards.

(a) Physical security measures in recipient countries must provide protection at least comparable to the recommendations in the current version of IAEA publication INFCIRC/225/Rev. 4 (corrected), June 1999, "The Physical Protection of Nuclear Material and Nuclear Facilities," and is incorporated by reference in this part. This incorporation by reference was approved by the Director of the Federal Register in accordance with 5 U.S.C. 552(a) and 1 CFR part 51. Notice of any changes made to the material incorporated by reference will be published in the Federal Register. Copies of INFCIRC/225/Rev. 4 may be obtained from the Deputy Director, Office of International Programs, U.S. Nuclear Regulatory Commission, Washington, DC 20555–0001, and are available for inspection at the NRC library, 11545 Rockville Pike, Rockville, Maryland 20852–2738. A copy is available for inspection at the library of the Office of the Federal Register, 800 N. Capitol Street, NW, Suite 700, Washington DC.

(b) Commission determinations on the adequacy of physical security measures are based on—

(1) Receipt of written assurances from recipient countries that physical security measures providing protection at least comparable to the recommendations set forth in INFCIRC/225/Rev. 4 (corrected).

(2) Information obtained through country visits, information exchanges, or other sources. Determinations are made on a country-wide basis and are subject to continuing review. Appendix M to this part describes the different categories of nuclear material to which physical security measures are applied.

§ 110.45 Issuance or denial of licenses.

(a) The Commission will issue an export license if it has been notified by the State Department that it is the judgment of the Executive Branch that the proposed export will not be inimical to the common defense and security; and:

(1) Finds, based upon a reasonable judgment of the assurances provided and other information available to the Federal government, that the applicable criteria in Sec. 110.42, or their equivalent, are met. (If an Executive Order provides an exemption pursuant to section 126a of the Atomic Energy Act, proposed exports to EURATOM countries are not required to meet the criteria in Sec. 110.42(a) (4) and (5)); or

(2) Finds that there are no material changed circumstances associated with an export license application (except for byproduct material applications) from those existing at the time of issuance of a prior license to export to the same country, if

the prior license was issued under the provisions of paragraph (a)(1) of this section.

(b) The Commission will issue an import license if it finds that:

(1) The proposed import will not be inimical to the common defense and security;

(2) The proposed import will not constitute an unreasonable risk to the public health and safety;

(3) The requirements of subpart A of part 51 of this chapter (to the extent applicable to the proposed import) have been satisfied; and

(4) With respect to a proposed import of radioactive waste, an appropriate facility has agreed to accept the waste for management or disposal.

(5) With respect to a proposed import of radioactive material listed in Table 1 of Appendix P to this part, the U.S. recipient is authorized to receive and possess the material under a contract with the Department of Energy or a license issued by the Commission or a State with which the Commission has entered into an agreement under Section 274b. of the Atomic Energy Act.

(c) With respect to a proposed import of radioactive material listed in Table 1 of Appendix P to this part:

(1) If the Commission authorizes a proposed import of Category 1 or Category 2 amounts of radioactive material, it will take appropriate steps to ensure that a copy of the recipient authorization, or confirmation by the U.S. Government that the recipient is authorized to receive and possess the source or sources to be exported, is provided to the Government of the exporting country or to the exporting facility.

(2) If the Commission authorizes a proposed import of Category 1 amounts of radioactive material, it will take appropriate steps to ensure that a copy of the consent of the United States Government to the import is provided to the government of the exporting country in cases where it is requested by such government.

(d) If, after receiving the Executive Branch judgement that the issuance of a proposed export license will not be inimical to the common defense and security, the Commission does not issue the proposed license on a timely basis because it is unable to make the statutory determinations required under the Atomic Energy Act, the Commission will publicly issue a decision to that effect and will submit the license application to the President. The Commission's decision will include an explanation of the basis for the decision and any dissenting or separate views. The provisions in this paragraph do not apply to Commission decisions regarding license applications for the export of byproduct material or radioactive waste requiring a specific license.

(e) The Commission will deny: (1) Any export license application for which the Executive Branch judgment does not recommend approval; (2) any byproduct material export license application for which the Commission is unable to make the finding in paragraph (a)(1) of this section; or (3) any import license application for which the Commission is unable to make the finding in paragraph (b) of this section. The applicant will be notified in writing of the reason for denial.

§ 110.46 Conduct resulting in termination of nuclear exports.

(a) Except as provided in paragraph (c) of this section, no license will be issued to export nuclear equipment or material, other than byproduct material, to any non-nuclear weapon state that is found by the President to have, after March 10, 1978:

(1) Detonated a nuclear explosive device;

(2) Terminated or abrogated IAEA safeguards;

(3) Materially violated an IAEA safeguards agreement; or

(4) Engaged in activities involving source or special nuclear material and having direct significance for the manufacture or acquisition of nuclear explosive devices, and failed to take steps which represent sufficient progress toward terminating such activities.

(b) Except as provided in paragraph (c) of this section, no license will be issued to export nuclear equipment or material, other than byproduct material, to any country or group of countries that is found by the President to have, after March 10, 1978:

(1) Materially violated an agreement for cooperation with the United States or the terms of any other agreement under which nuclear equipment or material has been exported;

(2) Assisted, encouraged or induced any non-nuclear weapon state to engage in activities involving source or special nuclear material and having direct significance for the manufacture or acquisition of nuclear explosive devices, and failed to take steps which represent sufficient progress toward terminating such assistance, encouragement or inducement; or

(3) Entered into an agreement for the transfer of reprocessing equipment, materials or technology to the sovereign control of a non-nuclear weapon state, except in connection with an international fuel cycle evaluation in which the United States is a participant or pursuant to an international agreement or understanding to which the United States subscribes.

(c) Under section 129 of the Atomic Energy Act, the President may waive the requirement for the termination of exports to a country described in paragraph (a) or (b) of this section after determining in writing that the cessation of exports would seriously prejudice the achievement of United States nonproliferation objectives or otherwise jeopardize the common defense and security. If the President makes this determination, the Commission will issue licenses to export to that country, if other applicable statutory provisions are met.

Subpart E—License Terms and Related Provisions

§ 110.50 Terms.

(a) General and specific licenses. (1) Each license is subject to all applicable provisions of the Atomic Energy Act and to all applicable rules, regulations, decisions and orders of the Commission.

(2) Each license is subject to amendment, suspension, revocation or incorporation of separate conditions when required by amendments of the Atomic Energy Act or other applicable law, or by other rules, regulations, decisions or orders issued in accordance with the terms of the Atomic Energy Act or other applicable law.

(3) Each license authorizes export or import only and does not authorize any person to receive title to, acquire, receive, possess, deliver, use, transport or transfer nuclear equipment or material.

(4) Each nuclear material license authorizes the export or import of only the nuclear material and accompanying packaging and fuel element hardware.

(5) No nuclear equipment license confers authority to export or import nuclear material.

(6) Each nuclear equipment export license authorizes the export of only those items required for use in the foreign nuclear installation for which the items are intended.

(7) A licensee shall not proceed to export or import and shall notify the Commission promptly if he knows or has reason to believe that the packaging requirements of part 71 of this chapter have not been met.

(b) Specific licenses. (1) Each specific license will have an expiration date.

(2) A licensee may export or import only for the purpose stated in the license application.

(3) Unless a license specifically authorizes the export of foreign-origin nuclear material or equipment, a licensee may not ship such material or equipment until;

(i) The licensee has given at least 40 days advance notice of the intended shipment in writing to the Deputy Director, Office of International Programs (OIP), and

(ii) The Deputy Director, OIP, has

(A) Obtained confirmation, through either the Department of Energy or State, that the foreign government in question has given its consent to the intended shipment pursuant to its agreement for cooperation with the United States, and

(B) Communicated this in writing to the licensee.

(4) A licensee authorized to export or import the radioactive material listed in Appendix P to this part is responsible for notifying NRC and, in cases of exports, the government of the importing country in advance of each shipment. A list of points of contact in importing countries is available at NRC's Office of International Programs website, accessible on the NRC Public Web Site by the following links to What We Do—International Programs. The NRC's office responsible for receiving advance notifications for all export and import shipments is the NRC Operations Center. Specific details on where to send the information will be listed in each specific export and import license. Notifications must be received by the NRC at least 7 days in advance of each shipment, to the extent practical, but in no case less than 24 hours in advance of each shipment. Notifications may be electronic or in writing on business stationary, and must contain or be accompanied by the information which follows.

(i) For export notifications:

(A) Part 110 export license number and expiration date;

(B) Name of the individual and licensee making the notification, address, and telephone number;

(C) Foreign recipient name, address, and end use location(s) (if different than recipient's address);

(D) Radionuclides and activity level in TBq, both for single and aggregate shipments;

(E) Make, model and serial number, for any Category 1 and 2 sealed sources, if available;

(F) End use in the importing country, if known;

(G) Shipment date;

(H) A copy of the foreign recipient's authorization or confirmation of that authorization from the government of the importing country as required by Sec. 110.32(h).

(ii) For import notifications:

(A) Part 110 import license number and expiration date;

(B) Name of individual and licensee making the notification, address, and telephone number;

(C) Recipient name, location, and address (if different than above);

(D) Radionuclides and activity level in TBq, both for single and aggregate shipments;

(E) Make, model and serial number, radionuclide, and activity level for any Category 1 and 2 sealed sources, if available;

(F) End use in the U.S.;

(G) Shipment date from exporting facility and estimated arrival date at the end use location;

(H) NRC or Agreement State license number to possess the import in the U.S. and expiration date.

(5) A licensee authorized to export or import nuclear material is responsible for compliance with applicable requirements of parts 40, 70, 71, and 73 of this chapter, unless a domestic licensee of the Commission has assumed that responsibility and the Commission has been so notified.

(6) A license may be transferred, disposed of or assigned to another person only with the approval of the Commission by license amendment.

(7) Advance notifications containing the above information must be controlled, handled, and transmitted in accordance with Sec. 2.390 of this chapter and other applicable NRC requirements governing protection of sensitive information.

§ 110.51 Amendment and renewal of licenses.

(a) A licensee may submit a request to renew a license or to amend a license.

(b) If an application to renew a license is submitted 30 days or more before the license expires, the license remains valid until the Commission acts on the renewal application. An expired license is not renewable.

(c) An amendment is not required for:

(1) Changes in value (but not amount or quantity);

(2) Changes in the mailing addresses within the same countries of intermediate or ultimate consignees; or

(3) The addition of intermediate consignees in any of the importing countries specified in the license (for a nuclear equipment license only).

(d) In acting upon license renewal and amendment applications, the Commission will use, as appropriate, the same procedures and criteria it uses for original license applications.

§ 110.52 Revocation, suspension, and modification.

(a) A license may be revoked, suspended, or modified for a condition which would warrant denial of the original license application.

(b) The Commission may require further information from a licensee to determine whether a license should be revoked, suspended, or modified.

(c) Except when the common defense and security or public health and safety requires otherwise, no license will be revoked, suspended, or modified before the licensee is informed in writing of the grounds for such action and afforded the opportunity to reply and be heard under procedures patterned on those in subpart I.

§ 110.53 United States address, records, and inspections.

(a) Each licensee shall have an office in the United States where papers may be served and where records required by the Commission will be maintained.

(b)(1) Each licensee shall maintain records concerning his exports or imports. The licensee shall retain these records for five years after each export or import, except that byproduct material records must be retained for three years after each export or import.

(2) Records which must be maintained pursuant to this part may be the original or a reproduced copy of microform if such reproduced copy or microform is duly authenticated by authorized personnel and the microform is capable of producing a clear and legible copy after storage for the period specified by Commission regulations. The record may also be stored in electronic media with the capability for producing legible, accurate, and complete records during the required retention period. Records such as letters, drawings, specifications, must include all pertinent information such as stamps, initials, and signatures. The licensee shall maintain adequate safeguards against tampering with and loss of records.

(c) Each licensee shall permit the Commission to inspect his records, premises, and activities pertaining to his exports and imports when necessary to fulfill the requirements of the Atomic Energy Act.

Subpart F—Violations and Enforcement

§ 110.60 Violations.

(a) The Commission may obtain an injunction or other court order to prevent a violation of the provisions of—

(1) The Atomic Energy Act of 1954, as amended;

(2) Title II of the Energy Reorganization Act of 1974, as amended; or

(3) A regulation or order issued pursuant to those Acts.

(b) The Commission may obtain a court order for the payment of a civil penalty imposed under section 234 of the Atomic Energy Act:

(1) For violations of—

(i) Sections 53, 57, 62, 63, 81, 82, 101, 103, 104, 107, or 109 of the Atomic Energy Act of 1954, as amended;

(ii) Section 206 of the Energy Reorganization Act;

(iii) Any rule, regulation, or order issued pursuant to the sections specified in paragraph (b)(1)(i) of this section;

(iv) Any term, condition, or limitation of any license issued under the sections specified in paragraph (b)(1)(i) of this section.

(2) For any violation for which a license may be revoked under section 186 of the Atomic Energy Act of 1954, as amended.

§ 110.62 Order to show cause.

(a) In response to an alleged violation, described in § 110.60, the Commission may institute a proceeding to revoke, suspend, or modify a license by issuing an order to show cause:

(1) Stating the alleged violation and proposed enforcement action; and

(2) Informing the licensee of his right, within 20 days or other specified time, to file a written answer and demand a hearing.

(b) An answer consenting to the proposed enforcement action shall constitute a waiver by the licensee of a hearing and of all rights to seek further Commission or judicial review.

(c) The order to show cause may be omitted and an order issued to revoke, suspend, or modify the license in cases where the Commission determines that the violation is willful or that the public health, safety, or interest so requires.

§ 110.63 Order for revocation, suspension, or modification.

(a) In response to an alleged violation described in § 110.60, the Commission may revoke, suspend, or modify a license by issuing an order:

(1) Stating the violation and the effective date of the proposed enforcement action; and

(2) Informing the licensee of his right, within 20 days or other specified time, to file a written answer and demand a hearing.

(b) If an answer is not filed within the time specified, the enforcement action will become effective and permanent as proposed.

(c) If a timely answer is filed, the Commission, after considering the answer, will issue an order dismissing the proceeding, staying the effectiveness of the order or taking other appropriate action.

(d) The order may be made effective immediately, with reasons stated, pending further hearing and order, when the Commission determines that the violation is willful or that the public health, safety, or interest so requires.

§ 110.64 Civil penalty.

(a) In response to a violation, the Commission may institute a proceeding to impose a civil penalty under section 234 of the Atomic Energy Act by issuing a notice to the licensee:

(1) Stating the alleged violation and the amount of the proposed penalty;

(2) Informing the licensee of his right, within 20 days or other specified time, to file a written answer; and

(3) Advising that a delinquent payment for a subsequently imposed penalty may be referred to the Attorney General for collection pursuant to section 234c. of the Atomic Energy Act.

(b) If an answer is not filed within the time specified, the Commission will issue an order imposing the proposed penalty.

(c) If a timely answer is filed, the Commission, after considering the answer, will issue an order dismissing the proceeding or imposing a penalty subject to any required hearing.

(d) If an order imposing a civil penalty is issued, the licensee may request a hearing within 20 days or other specified time.

(e) Except when the matter has been referred to the Attorney General for collection, payment of penalties shall be made by check, draft, or money order payable to the Treasurer of the United States, and mailed to the Secretary, U.S. Nuclear Regulatory Commission, Washington, DC 20555–0001.

(f) An enforcement action to impose a civil penalty will not itself revoke, modify, or suspend any license under this part.

§ 110.65 Settlement and compromise.

At any time after issuance of an order for any enforcement action under this subpart, an agreement may be entered into for settlement of the proceeding or compromise of a penalty. Upon approval by the Commission, or presiding officer if a hearing has been requested, the terms of the settlement or compromise will be embodied in the order disposing of the enforcement action.

§ 110.66 Enforcement hearing.

(a) If the licensee demands a hearing, the Commission will issue an order specifying the time and place.

(b) A hearing pursuant to this subpart will be conducted under the procedures in Subpart G of Part 2.

§ Sec. 110.67 Criminal penalties.

(a) Section 223 of the Atomic Energy Act of 1954, as amended, provides for criminal sanctions for willful violation of, attempted violation of, or conspiracy to violate, any regulation issued under sections 161b, 161i, or 161o of the Act. For purposes of section 223, all the regulations in part 110 are issued under one or more of sections 161b, 161i, or 161o, except for the sections listed in paragraph (b) of this section.

(b) The regulations in part 110 that are not issued under sections 161b, 161i, or 161o for the purposes of section 223 are as follows:

Sec. 110.1, 110.2, 110.3, 110.4, 110.7, 110.10, 110.11, 110.30, 110.31, 110.32, 110.40, 110.41, 110.42, 110.43, 110.44, 110.45, 110.46, 110.51, 110.52, 110.60, 110.61, 110.62, 110.63, 110.64,

110.65, 110.66, 110.67, 110.70, 110.71, 110.72, 110.73, 110.80, 110.81, 110.82, 110.83, 110.84, 110.85, 110.86, 110.87, 110.88, 110.89, 110.90, 110.91, 110.100, 110.101, 110.102, 110.103, 110.104, 110.105, 110.106, 110.107, 110.108, 110.109, 110.110, 110.111, 110.112, 110.113, 110.120, 110.122, 110.124, 110.130, 110.131, 110.132, 110.133, 110.134, and 110.135.

Subpart G—Public Notification and Availability of Documents and Records

§ 110.70 Public notice of receipt of an application.

(a) The Commission will notice the receipt of each license application for an export or import for which a specific license is required by making a copy available at the NRC Web site, http://www.nrc.gov.

(b) The Commission will also publish in the Federal Register a notice of receipt of an application for a license to export the following:

(1) A production or utilization facility.

(2) Five effective kilograms or more of plutonium, high-enriched uranium or uranium-233.

(3) 10,000 kilograms or more of heavy water.

(4) Nuclear grade graphite for nuclear end use.

(5) Radioactive waste.

(Note: Does not apply to exports of heavy water to Canada.)

(c) The Commission will also publish in the Federal Register a notice of receipt of a license application for an import of radioactive waste for which a specific license is required.

§ 110.71 Notice of withdrawal of an application.

The Commission will notice the withdrawal of an application by making a copy available at the NRC Web site, http://www.nrc.gov.

§ 110.72 Public availability of documents.

Unless exempt from disclosure under part 9 of this chapter, the following documents pertaining to each license and license application for an import or export requiring a specific license under this part will be made available at the NRC Web site, http://www.nrc.gov, and/or at the NRC Public Document Room:

(a) The license application and any requests for amendments;

(b) Commission correspondence with the applicant or licensee;

(c) Federal Register notices;

(d) The Commission letter requesting Executive Branch views;

(e) Correspondence from the State Department with Executive Branch views;

(f) Correspondence from foreign governments and international organizations;

(g) Filings pursuant to subpart I and Commission and Executive Branch responses, if any;

(h) If a hearing is held, the hearing record and decision;

(i) A statement of staff conclusions; and

(j) The license, requests for license amendments and amendments.

§ 110.73 Availability of NRC records.

(a) Commission records under this part will be made available to the public only in accordance with part 9 of this chapter.

(b) Proprietary information provided under this part may be protected under Part 9 and Sec. 2.390(b), (c), and (d) of this chapter.

SUBPART H—PUBLIC PARTICIPATION PROCEDURES CONCERNING LICENSE APPLICATION

§ 110.80 Basis for hearings.

The procedures in this part will constitute the exclusive basis for hearings on export license applications.

§ 110.81 Written comments.

(a) The Commission encourages written comments from the public regarding export and import license applications. The Commission will consider and, if appropriate, respond to these comments.

(b) If possible, these comments should be submitted within 30 days after public notice of receipt of the application and addressed to the Secretary, U.S. Nuclear Regulatory Commission, Washington, DC 20555–0001, Attention: Rulemakings and Adjudications Staff.

(c) The Commission will provide the applicant with a copy of the comments and, if appropriate, a reasonable opportunity for response.

§ 110.82 Hearing request or intervention petition.

(a) A person may request a hearing or petition for leave to intervene on a license application for an import or export requiring a specific license.

(b) Hearing requests and intervention petitions must:

(1) State the name, address and telephone number of the requestor or petitioner;

(2) Set forth the issues sought to be raised;

(3) Explain why a hearing or an intervention would be in the public interest and how a hearing or intervention would assist the Commission in making the determinations required by Sec. 110.45.

(4) Specify, when a person asserts that his interest may be affected, both the facts pertaining to his interest and how it may be affected, with particular reference to the factors in Sec. 110.84.

(c) Hearing requests and intervention petitions will be considered timely only if filed not later than:

(1) 30 days after notice of receipt in the Federal Register, for those applications published in the Federal Register;

(2) 30 days after notice of receipt in the Public Document Room, for all other applications; or

(3) Such other time as may be provided by the Commission.

§ 110.83 Answers and replies.

(a) Unless otherwise specified by the Commission, an answer to a hearing request or intervention petition may be filed within 30 days after the request or petition has been served.

(b) Unless otherwise specified by the Commission, a reply to an answer may be filed within 10 days after all timely answers have been filed.

(c) Answers and replies should address the factors in § 110.84.

§ 110.84 Commission action on a hearing request or intervention petition.

(a) In an export licensing proceeding, or in an import licensing proceeding in which a hearing request or intervention petition does not assert or establish an interest which may be affected, the Commission will consider:

(1) Whether a hearing would be in the public interest; and

(2) Whether a hearing would assist the Commission in making the statutory determinations required by the Atomic Energy Act.

(b) If a hearing request or intervention petition asserts an interest which may be affected, the Commission will consider:

(1) The nature of the alleged interest;

(2) How that interest relates to issuance or denial; and

(3) The possible effect of any order on that interest, including whether the relief requested is within the Commission's authority, and, if so, whether granting relief would redress the alleged injury.

(c) Untimely hearing requests or intervention petitions may be denied unless good cause for failure to file on time is established. In reviewing untimely requests or petitions, the Commission will also consider:

(1) The availability of other means by which the requestor's or petitioner's interest, if any, will be protected or represented by other participants in a hearing; and

(2) The extent to which the issues will be broadened or action on the application delayed.

(d) Before granting or denying a hearing request or intervention petition, the Commission will review the Executive Branch's views on the license application and may request further information from the petitioner, requester, the Commission staff, the Executive Branch or others.

(e) The Commission will deny a request or petition that pertains solely to matters outside its jurisdiction.

(f) If an issue has been adequately explored in a previous licensing hearing conducted pursuant to this part, a request for a new hearing in connection with that issue will be denied unless:

(1) A hearing request or intervention petition establishes that an interest may be affected; or

(2) The Commission determines that changed circumstances or new information warrant a new hearing.

(g) After consideration of the factors covered by paragraphs (a) through (f), the Commission will issue a notice or order granting or denying a hearing request or intervention petition. Upon the affirmative vote of two Commissioners a hearing will be ordered. A notice granting a hearing will be published in the FEDERAL REGISTER and will specify whether the hearing will be oral or consist of written comments. A denial notice will set forth the reasons for denial.

§ 110.85 Notice of hearing consisting of written comments.

(a) A notice of hearing consisting of written comments will:

(1) State the issues to be considered;

(2) Provide the names and addresses of participants;

(3) Specify the time limits for participants and others to submit written views and respond to any written comments; and

(4) State any other instructions the Commission deems appropriate.

(b) The Secretary will give notice of any hearing under this section and § 110.86 to any person who so requests.

§ 110.86 Notice of oral hearing.

(a) A notice of oral hearing will:

(1) State the time, place and issues to be considered;

(2) Provide names and addresses of participants;

(3) Designate the presiding officer;

(4) Specify the time limit for participants and others to indicate whether they wish to present views; and

(5) State any other instructions the Commission deems appropriate.

(b) If the Commission is not the presiding officer, the notice of oral hearing will also state:

(1) When the jurisdiction of the presiding officer commences and terminates;

(2) The powers of the presiding officer; and

(3) Instructions to the presiding officer to certify promptly the completed hearing record to the Commission without preliminary decision or findings, unless the Commission directs otherwise.

§ 110.87 Conditions in a notice or order.

(a) A notice or order granting a hearing or permitting intervention may restrict irrelevant or duplicative testimony, or require common interests to be represented by a single spokesman.

(b) If a participant's interests do not extend to all the issues in the hearing, the notice or order may limit his participation accordingly.

(c) Unless authorized by the Commission, the granting of participation will not broaden the hearing issues.

§ 110.88 Authority of the Secretary.

The Secretary is authorized to prescribe time schedules and other procedural arrangements, when not covered by this part, and rule on related procedural requests.

§ 110.89 Filing and service.

(a) Hearing requests, intervention petitions, answers, replies and accompanying documents must be filed with the Commission by delivery or by mail or telegram to the Secretary, U.S. Nuclear Regulatory Commission, Washington, DC 20555–0001, Attention: Rulemakings and Adjudications Staff. Filing by mail or telegram is complete upon deposit in the mail or with a telegraph company.

(b) All filing and Commission notices and orders must be served upon the applicant; the General Counsel, U.S. Nuclear Regulatory Commission, Washington, DC 20555; the Executive Secretary, Department of State, Washington, DC 20520; and participants if any. Hearing requests, intervention petitions, and answers and replies must be served by the person filing those pleadings.

(c) Service is completed by:

(1) Delivering the paper to the person; or leaving it in his office with someone in charge; or, if there is no one in charge, leaving it in a conspicuous place in the office; or, if he has no office or it is closed, leaving it at his usual place of residence with some occupant of suitable age and discretion;

(2) Depositing it with a telegraph company, properly addressed and with charges prepaid;

(3) Depositing it in the United States mail, properly stamped and addressed; or

(4) Any other manner authorized by law, when service cannot be made as provided in paragraphs (c)(1) through (3) of this section.

(d) Proof of service, stating the name and address of the person served and the manner and date of service, shall be shown, and may be made by:

(1) Written acknowledgment of the person served or an authorized representative; or

(2) The certificate or affidavit of the person making the service.

(e) The Commission may make special provisions for service when circumstances warrant.

§ 110.90 Computation of time.

(a) In computing time, the first day of a designated time period is not included and the last day is included. If the last day is a Saturday, Sunday or legal holiday at the place where the required action is to be accomplished, the time period will end on the next day which is not a Saturday, Sunday or legal holiday.

(b) In time periods of 7 days or less, Saturdays, Sundays and holidays are not counted.

(c) Whenever an action is required within a prescribed period by a paper served pursuant to § 110.89, 3 days shall be added to the prescribed period if service is by mail.

(d) An interpretation of this section is contained in § 8.3 of this chapter.

§ 110.91 Commission consultations.

The Commission may consult at any time on a license application with the staff, Executive Branch or other persons.

SUBPART I—HEARINGS

§ 110.100 Public hearings.

Hearings under this part will be public unless the Commission directs otherwise.

§ 110.101 Filing and service.

Filing and service of hearing documents shall be pursuant to § 110.89.

§ 110.102 Hearing docket.

For each hearing, the Secretary will maintain a docket which will include the hearing transcript, exhibits and all papers filed or issued pursuant to the hearing.

§ 110.103 Acceptance of hearing documents.

(a) Each document filed or issued must be clearly legible and bear the docket number, license application number and hearing title.

(b) Each document shall be filed in one original and signed by the participant or his authorized representative, with his address and date of signature indicated. The signature is a representation that the document is submitted with full authority, the signator knows its contents and that, to the best of his knowledge, the statements made in it are true.

(c) A document not meeting the requirements of this section may be returned with an explanation for nonacceptance and, if so, will not be docketed.

§ 110.104 Presiding officer.

(a) The full Commission will ordinarily be the presiding officer at a hearing under this part. However, the Commission may provide in a hearing notice that one or more Commissioners, or any other person as provided by law, will preside.

(b) A participant may submit a written motion for the disqualification of any person presiding. The motion shall be supported by affidavit setting forth the alleged grounds for disqualification. If the presiding officer does not grant the motion or the person does not disqualify himself, the Commission will decide the matter.

(c) If any presiding officer designated by the Commission deems himself disqualified, he shall withdraw by notice on the record after notifying the Commission.

(d) If a presiding officer becomes unavailable, the Commission will designate a replacement.

(e) Any motion concerning the designation of a replacement presiding officer shall be made within 5 days after the designation.

(f) Unless otherwise ordered by the Commission, the jurisdiction of a presiding officer other than the Commission commences as designated in the hearing notice and terminates upon certification of the hearing record to the Commission, or when the presiding officer is disqualified.

§ 110.105 Responsibility and power of the presiding officer in an oral hearing.

(a) The presiding officer in any oral hearing shall conduct a fair hearing, develop a record that will contribute to informed decision-making, and within the framework of the Commission's orders, have the power necessary to achieve these ends, including the power to:

(1) Take action to avoid unnecessary delay and maintain order;

(2) Dispose of procedural requests;

(3) Question participants and witnesses, and entertain suggestions as to questions which may be asked of participants and witnesses;

(4) Order consolidation of participants;

(5) Establish the order of presentation;

(6) Hold conferences before or during the hearing;

(7) Establish reasonable time limits;

(8) Limit the number of witnesses; and

(9) Strike or reject duplicative or irrelevant presentations.

(b) Where the Commission itself does not preside:

(1) The presiding officer may certify questions or refer rulings to the Commission for decision;

(2) Any hearing order may be modified by the Commission; and

(3) The presiding officer will certify the completed hearing record to the Commission, which may then issue its opinion on the hearing or provide that additional testimony be presented.

§ 110.106 Participation in a hearing.

(a) Unless otherwise limited by this part or by the Commission, participants in a hearing may submit:

(1) Initial and concluding written statements of position on the issues;

(2) Written questions to the presiding officer; and

(3) Written response and rebuttal testimony to the statements of other participants.

(b) Participants in an oral hearing may also submit oral statements, questions, responses and rebuttal testimony.

(c) A participant in an import licensing hearing establishing that his interest may be affected, may be accorded additional procedural rights under Subpart G of Part 2 with respect to resolution of domestic factual issues regarding the public health, safety and environment of the United States, and the protection of the United States public against domestic theft, diversion or sabotage, to the extent that such issues are separable from the nondomestic issues associated with the license application.

§ 110.107 Presentation of testimony in an oral hearing.

(a) All direct testimony in an oral hearing shall be filed no later than 7 days before the hearing or as otherwise ordered or allowed.

(b) Written testimony will be received into evidence in exhibit form.

(c) Unless proscribed under § 110.87, members of groups which are designated as participants may testify in their individual capacities.

(d) Participants may present their own witnesses.

(e) Testimony by the Commission and the Executive Branch will be presented only by persons officially designated for that purpose.

(f) Participants and witnesses will be questioned orally or in writing and only by the presiding officer. Questions may be addressed to individuals or to panels or to participants or witnesses.

(g) The presiding officer may accept written testimony from a person unable to appear at the hearing, and may request him to respond to questions.

(h) No subpoenas will be granted at the request of participants for attendance and testimony of participants or witnesses or the production of evidence.

§ 110.108 Appearance in an oral hearing.

(a) A participant may appear in a hearing on his own behalf or be represented by an authorized representative.

(b) A person appearing shall file a written notice stating his name, address and telephone number, and if an authorized representative, the basis of his eligibility and the name and address of the participant on whose behalf he appears.

(c) A person may be excluded from a hearing for disorderly, dilatory or contemptuous conduct, provided he is informed of the grounds and given an opportunity to respond.

§ 110.109 Motions and requests.

(a) Motions and requests shall be addressed to the presiding officer and, if written, also filed with the Secretary and served on other participants.

(b) Other participants may respond to the motion or request. Responses to written motions or requests shall be filed within 5 days after service.

(c) When the Commission does not preside, in response to a motion or request, the presiding officer may refer a ruling or certify a question to the Commission for decision and notify the participants.

(d) Unless otherwise ordered by the Commission, a motion or request, or the certification of a question or referral of a ruling, shall not stay or extend any aspect of the hearing.

§ 110.110 Default.

When a participant fails to act within a specified time, the presiding officer may consider him in default, issue an appropriate ruling and proceed without further notice to the defaulting participant.

§ 110.111 Waiver of a rule or regulation.

(a) A participant may petition that a Commission rule or regulation be waived with respect to the license application under consideration.

(b) The sole ground for a waiver shall be that, because of special circumstances concerning the subject of the hearing, application of a rule or regulation would not serve the purposes for which it was adopted.

(c) Waiver petition shall specify why application of the rule or regulation would not serve the purposes for which it was adopted.

(d) Other participants may, within 10 days, file a response to a waiver petition.

(e) When the Commission does not preside, the presiding officer will certify the waiver petition to the Commission, which, in response, will grant or deny the waiver or direct any further proceedings.

(f) Regardless of whether a waiver is granted or denied, a separate petition for rulemaking may be filed pursuant to subpart K of this part.

§ 110.112 Reporter and transcript for an oral hearing.

(a) A reporter designated by the Commission will record an oral hearing and prepare the official hearing transcript.

(b) Except for any classified portions, transcripts will be made available at the NRC Web site, http://www.nrc.gov, and/or at the NRC Public Document Room.

(c) Corrections of the official transcript may be made only as specified by the Secretary.

§ 110.113 Commission action.

(a) Upon completion of a hearing, the Commission will issue a written opinion including its decision on the license application, the reasons for the decision and any dissenting views.

(b) While the Commission will consider fully the hearing record, the licensing decision will be based on all relevant information, including information which might go beyond that in the hearing record.

(c) If the Commission considers information not in the hearing record in reaching its licensing decision, the hearing participants will be informed and, if not classified or otherwise privileged, the information will be made available at the NRC Web site, http://www.nrc.gov, and furnished to the participants.

(d) The Commission may issue a license before completion of a hearing if it finds that:

(1) Prompt issuance is required in the public interest, particularly the common defense and security; and

(2) A participant establishing that his interest may be affected has been provided a fair opportunity to present his views.

(e) The Commission may:

(1) Defer any hearing;

(2) Consolidate applications for hearing;

(3) Narrow or broaden the hearing issues; and

(4) Take other action, as appropriate.

SUBPART J—SPECIAL PROCEDURES FOR CLASSIFIED INFORMATION IN HEARINGS

§ 110.120 Purpose and scope.

(a) This subpart contains special procedures concerning access to, and introduction of, classified information into hearings under this part.

(b) These procedures do not in any way apply to classified information exchanged between the Executive Branch and the Commission not introduced into a hearing. Such information will be declassified to the maximum extent feasible. The public statements of the Commission staff and Executive Branch will, to the extent consistent with classification requirements, reflect consideration of any such classified information.

§ 110.121 Security clearances and access to classified information.

(a) No person without a security clearance will have access to classified information.

(b) Only the Commission will act upon an application for access to classified information.

(c) To the extent practicable, applications for access to classified information shall describe the information to which access is desired and its level of classification (confidential, secret or other); the reasons for requesting access; the names of individuals for whom access is requested; and the reasons why access is requested for those individuals.

(d) The Commission will consider requests for appropriate security clearances in reasonable numbers; conduct its review and grant or deny these in accordance with Part 10 of this chapter; and make a reasonable charge to cover costs.

(e) The Commission will not grant security clearances for access to classified information, unless it determines that the available unclassified information is inadequate on the subject matter involved.

(f) When an applicant demonstrates that access to classified information not introduced into a hearing may be needed to prepare a participant's position on the hearing issues, the Commission may issue an order granting access to this information to the participant, his authorized representative or other persons. Access will be subject to the conditions in paragraphs (e) and (j) and will not be granted unless required security clearances have been obtained.

(g) Once classified information has been introduced into a hearing, the Commission will grant access to a participant, his authorized representative or such other persons as the Commission determines may be needed by the participant to prepare his position on the hearing issues. Access will be subject to the conditions in paragraph (e) and (j) and will not be granted unless required security clearances have been obtained.

(h) For good cause, the Commission may postpone action upon an application for access to classified information.

(i) The Commission will grant access to classified information only up to the level for which the persons described in paragraph (f) and (g) of this section are cleared and only upon an adequate commitment by them not to disclose such information subject to penalties as provided by law.

(j) The Commission will not in any circumstances grant access to classified information:

(1) Unless it determines that the grant is not inimical to the common defense and security; and

(2) Which it has received from another Government agency, without the prior consent of the originating agency.

(k) Upon completion of a hearing, the Commission will terminate all security clearances granted pursuant to the hearing and may require the disposal of classified information to which access has been granted or the observance of other procedures to safeguard this information.

§ 110.122 Classification assistance.

On the request of any hearing participant or the presiding officer (if other than the Commission), the Commission will designate a representative to advise and assist the presiding officer or the participants with respect to security classification of information and the protective requirements to be observed.

§ 110.123 Notice of intent to introduce classified information.

(a) A participant shall seek the required security clearances, where necessary, and file with the Secretary a notice of intent to introduce classified information into a hearing at the earliest possible time after the notice of hearing.

(b) If a participant has not filed a notice of intent in accordance with this section, he may introduce classified information only if he gives to the other participants and the Commission prompt written notice of intent and only as permitted by the Commission when it determines that the public interest will not be prejudiced.

(c) The notice of intent shall be unclassified and, to the extent consistent with classification requirements, state:

(1) The subject matter of the classified information, which it is anticipated will be involved;

(2) The highest level of classification of the information (confidential, secret or other);

(3) When it is anticipated that the information would be introduced; and

(4) The relevance and materiality of the information to the hearing issues.

§ 110.124 Rearrangement or suspension of a hearing.

When a participant gives notice of intent to introduce classified information and other participants do not have the required security clearances, subject to § 110.121, the Commission may:

(a) Suspend or rearrange the normal order of the hearing to give other participants an opportunity to obtain the required security clearances with minimum delay in the conduct of the hearing; or

(b) Take such other action as it determines to be in the public interest.

§ 110.125 Unclassified statements required.

(a) It is the obligation of hearing participants to introduce information in unclassified form wherever possible, and to declassify, to the maximum extent feasible, any classified information introduced into the hearing. This obligation rests on each participant whether or not any other participant has the required security clearances.

(b) When classified information is offered for introduction into a hearing.

(1) The participant offering it shall, to the extent consistent with classification requirements, submit to the presiding officer and other participants an unclassified statement describing the substance of the classified information as accurately and completely as possible;

(2) In accordance with procedures agreed upon by the participants or prescribed by the presiding officer, and after notice to all participants and opportunity to be heard on the notice, the presiding officer will determine whether an unclassified statement may be substituted for the classified information in the hearing record without prejudice to the interest of any participant or the public;

(3) If the Commission determines that the unclassified statement (together with such unclassified modifications as it finds are necessary or appropriate to protect the interest of other participants and the public) adequately sets forth information in the classified matter which is relevant and material to the issues in the hearing, it will direct that the classified matter be excluded from the record of the hearing; and

(4) The Commission may postpone any of the procedures in this section until all other evidence has been received. However, a participant shall not postpone service of any unclassified statement required in this section.

§ 110.126 Protection of classified information.

Nothing in this subpart shall relieve any person from safeguarding classified information as required by law and rules, regulations or orders of any Government agency.

Subpart K—Rulemaking

§ 110.130 Initiation of rulemaking.

The Commission may initiate action to amend the regulations in this part on its own initiative or in response to a petition.

§ 110.131 Petition for rulemaking.

(a) A petition for rulemaking should be addressed to the Secretary of the Commission, for the attention of the Secretary's Rulemakings and Adjudications Staff. The petition should be sent using an appropriate method listed in Sec. 110.4.

(b) The petition shall state the basis for the requested amendment.

(c) The petition may request the Commission to suspend all or part of any licensing proceeding under this part pending disposition of the petition.

(d) The Secretary will assign a docket number to the petition, place a copy in the Public Document Room and notice its receipt in the Federal Register.

(e) Publication may be limited by order of the Commission to the extent required by section 181 of the Atomic Energy Act.

§ 110.132 Commission action on a petition.

(a) The Commission may grant or deny the petition in whole or in part.

(b) If the petition is granted, a notice of proposed rulemaking or a notice of rulemaking will be published in the FEDERAL REGISTER.

(c) If the petition is denied, the petitioner will be informed of the grounds.

(d) Commission action on a petition will normally follow, when ever appropriate, receipt and evaluation of Executive Branch views.

(e) The Commission, in exercising the discretion authorized by section 4(a)(1) of the Administrative Procedure Act (5 U.S.C. 553(a)(1)), will decide what, if any, public rulemaking procedures will be followed.

§ 110.133 Notice of proposed rulemaking.

(a) When the Commission proposes to amend the regulations in this part, it will normally publish a notice of proposed rulemaking in the FEDERAL REGISTER.

(b) A notice of proposed rulemaking will include:

(1) The authority for the proposed rule;

(2) The substance and purpose of the proposed rule;

(3) Directions for public participation;

(4) The time and place of any public hearing; and

(5) If a hearing is to be held by other than the Commission, designated of a presiding officer and instructions for the conduct of the hearing.

(c) A notice of proposed rulemaking will be published not less than 15 days before any hearing, unless the Commission for good cause provides otherwise in the notice.

§ 110.134 Public participation.

(a) The Commission may hold an oral hearing on a proposed rule or permit any person to participate in a rulemaking proceeding through the submission of written comments.

(b) When it is in the public interest and is authorized by law, public rulemaking procedures may be omitted and a notice of rulemaking published pursuant to § 110.135.

§ 110.135 Notice of rulemaking.

(a) Upon approval of an amendment, the Commission will publish in the FEDERAL REGISTER a notice of rulemaking which includes a statement of its basis and purpose, effective date and, where appropriate, any significant variations from the amendment as proposed in any notice of proposed rulemaking.

(b) The effective date of an amendment will normally be no earlier than 30 days after publication of the notice of rulemaking, unless the Commission for good cause provides otherwise in the notice.

APPENDIX A TO PART 110—ILLUSTRATIVE LIST OF NUCLEAR REACTOR EQUIPMENT UNDER NRC EXPORT LICENSING AUTHORITY[5]

* * * * * * *

APPENDIX B TO PART 110—ILLUSTRATIVE LIST OF GAS CENTRIFUGE ENRICHMENT PLANT COMPONENTS UNDER NRC'S EXPORT LICENSING AUTHORITY[5]

* * * * * * *

APPENDIX C TO PART 110—ILLUSTRATIVE LIST OF GASEOUS DIFFUSION ENRICHMENT PLANT ASSEMBLIES AND COMPONENTS UNDER NRC EXPORT LICENSING AUTHORITY[5]

* * * * * * *

APPENDIX D TO PART 110—ILLUSTRATIVE LIST OF AERODYNAMIC ENRICHMENT PLANT EQUIPMENT AND COMPONENTS UNDER NRC EXPORT LICENSING AUTHORITY[5]

* * * * * * *

APPENDIX E TO PART 110—ILLUSTRATIVE LIST OF CHEMICAL EXCHANGE OR ION EXCHANGE ENRICHMENT PLANT EQUIPMENT AND COMPONENTS UNDER NRC EXPORT LICENSING AUTHORITY[5]

* * * * * * *

APPENDIX F TO PART 110—ILLUSTRATIVE LIST OF LASER-BASED ENRICHMENT PLANT EQUIPMENT AND COMPONENTS UNDER NRC EXPORT LICENSING AUTHORITY[5]

* * * * * * *

APPENDIX G TO PART 110—ILLUSTRATIVE LIST OF PLASMA SEPARATION ENRICHMENT PLANT EQUIPMENT AND COMPONENTS UNDER NRC EXPORT LICENSING AUTHORITY[5]

* * * * * * *

APPENDIX H TO PART 110—ILLUSTRATIVE LIST OF ELECTROMAGNETIC ENRICHMENT PLANT EQUIPMENT AND COMPONENTS UNDER NRC EXPORT LICENSING AUTHORITY[5]

* * * * * * *

APPENDIX I TO PART 110—ILLUSTRATIVE LIST OF REPROCESSING PLANT COMPONENTS UNDER NRC EXPORT LICENSING AUTHORITY[5]

* * * * * * *

APPENDIX J TO PART 110—ILLUSTRATIVE LIST OF URANIUM CONVERSION PLANT EQUIPMENT AND PLUTONIUM CONVERSION PLANT EQUIPMENT UNDER NRC EXPORT LICENSING AUTHORITY[5]

* * * * * * *

[5] Appendixes A through P can be found at 10 CFR 110, Appendix.

Appendix K to Part 110—Illustrative List of Equipment and Components Under NRC Export Licensing Authority for Use in a Plant for the Production of Heavy Water, Deuterium and Deuterium Compounds [5]

* * * * * * *

Appendix L to Part 110—Illustrative List of Byproduct Materials Under NRC Export/Import Licensing Authority [5]

* * * * * * *

Appendix M—Categorization of Nuclear Material [5]

* * * * * * *

Appendix N to Part 110—Illustrative List of Lithium Isotope Separation Facilities, Plants and Equipment Under NRC's Export Licensing Authority [5]

* * * * * * *

Appendix O to Part 110—Illustrative List of Fuel Element Fabrication Plant Equipment and Components Under NRC's Export Licensing Authority [5]

* * * * * * *

Appendix P to Part 110—Category 1 and 2 Radioactive Material [5]

* * * * * * *

c. Amendment to Procedures Established Pursuant to the Nuclear Non-Proliferation Act of 1978

Procedures established by the Department of State, the Department of Energy, and the Department of Commerce dated May 1, 1984, 49 F.R. 20780

> NOTE.—On June 7, 1978, procedures were established pursuant to the Nuclear Non-Proliferation Act of 1978 (Public Law 95–242) at 43 FR 25326. This amendment to those procedures adds a new part, entitled "Approvals Under Section 109b(3) of the Atomic Energy Act," establishing component retransfer approval procedures, eliminates the requirement for a Department of Energy retransfer approval under section 131 of the Atomic Energy Act in most cases where a Nuclear Regulatory Commission export license has already authorized the retransfer, eliminates possible duplicative reviews of the same export transaction by generally authorizing certain transactions if the same transaction is authorized by a different export procedure involving the same agencies; and makes minor modifications to the procedures under section 309(c) of the Nuclear Non-Proliferation Act, required by enactment of the Export Administration Act of 1979. For simplicity and ease of use, the entire text of the procedures as amended is set forth below.

Part A. General Provisions

Section 1. Authority and Scope

a. The procedures herein are established by:

(i) The Department of Energy pursuant to section 102 and 402(a) of the Nuclear Non-Proliferation Act of 1978 (the "NNPA") and section 54, 57b(2), 64, 82, 109b, 111b(1), and 131 of the Atomic Energy Act of 1954, as amended (the "AEA");

(ii) The Department of State pursuant to section 102 of the NNPA and sections 109b and 126a(1) of the AEA;

(iii) The Department of Commerce pursuant to section 309(c) of the NNPA, and the general policies and procedures set forth in the Export Administration Act of 1979, as amended.

b. These procedures apply to agency activities with respect to the matters dealt with by sections 54, 57b(2), 64, 82, 109, 111b(1), 126a and 131 of the AEA and sections 309(c) and 402(a) of the NNPA, and the Export Administration Act of 1979, as amended.

c. These procedures have been agreed to by the Secretaries of State, Energy, Defense, and Commerce, the Director of the Arms Control and Disarmament Agency, and the Nuclear Regulatory Commission, or by the authorized designee acting on behalf of any of the foregoing.

Section 2. Responsible Officials

a. Department of State, Washington, D.C. 20520—The Deputy Assistant Secretary for Nuclear Energy and Energy Technology Affairs in the Bureau of Oceans and International Environmental and Scientific Affairs.

b. Department of Energy, Washington, D.C. 20545—For sections 57b and 126a of the AEA and section 309(c) of the NNPA, the Assistant Secretary for Defense Programs. For sections 54, 64, 109b, 111b and 131 of the AEA and section 402 of the NNPA, the Deputy Assistant Secretary for International Affairs.

c. Department of Defense, Washington, D.C. 20301—The Assistant Secretary for International Security Policy.

d. Department of Commerce, Washington, D.C. 20230—The Deputy Assistant Secretary for Export Administration.

e. Arms Control and Disarmament Agency, Washington, D.C. 20451—The Assistant Director for Nuclear and Weapons Control.

f. The Nuclear Regulatory Commission, Washington, D.C. 20555—The Director, Office of International Programs.

Section 3. Offices for Coordination

a. Department of State—The Office of Export and Import Control in the Nuclear Energy and Energy Technology Division of the Bureau of Oceans and International Environmental and Scientific Affairs.

b. Department of Energy—For Parts B, D, and F of these procedures, the Office of International Security Affairs in Defense Programs. For Parts C and E of these procedures, the Office of Nuclear Non-Proliferation Policy, in the Office of International Affairs.

c. Department of Defense—The Office of the Assistant Secretary for International Security Policy.

d. Department of Commerce—The Office of Export Administration.

e. Arms Control and Disarmament Agency—The International Nuclear Affairs Division of the Bureau of Nuclear and Weapons Control.

f. Nuclear Regulatory Commission—The Office of International Programs, Assistant Director for Export/Import and International Safeguards.

Section 4. Coordination and Monitoring

The Interagency Subgroup on Nuclear Export Coordination (SNEC) shall, without prejudice to its authority to carry out other functions, monitor and facilitate the interagency processing of the activities referred to in section 1(b), and serve as a forum for exchanging and coordinating views. This Subgroup shall meet as frequently as necessary, normally every three weeks. This Subgroup shall establish such procedures as are necessary for its effective functioning.

Section 5. Resolution of Interagency Disagreements

a. If, after appropriate consultation, any agency listed in section 2 does not agree with a proposed Executive branch action covered by these procedures, the steps set forth below may be followed, normally in the order indicated, to facilitate resolution of the disagreement:

(i) Consideration in the SNEC;

(ii) Consideration in the Interagency Group on Non-Proliferation and Peaceful Nuclear Cooperation;

(iii) Any procedures of the National Security Council that are appropriate;

(iv) Referral to the President.

b. Recourse to the steps in this section shall be taken expeditiously. An agency wishing to have recourse to any of the steps above shall so indicate immediately to the offices specified in section 3. The agency concerned shall normally give five days notice before initiating action under steps (ii), (iii), or (iv).

c. Nothing in this section shall derogate from the statutory authority of any agency. If any agency considers that all statutory requirements have been met and wishes to proceed with an action within its jurisdiction covered by these procedures notwithstanding the existence of an interagency disagreement, it shall normally provide all other concerned agencies with five working days notice.

Section 6. Content of Judgments, Findings and Considerations Under These Procedures

Judgments, findings and determinations under these procedures shall address the matters required by the applicable section of the law.

Section 7. Technical Provisions

a. Except as otherwise provided, these procedures take effect on May 1, 1984.

b. The processing of any action subject to these procedures shall not be delayed because of the entry into effect of these procedures. Clearances obtained or matters resolved under procedures previously in effect need not be reconsidered for the sole purpose of complying with new procedural requirements.

c. Nothing in these procedures shall affect the ability of any agency to protect classified or proprietary information pursuant to applicable law.

d. These procedures may be amended at any time subject to agreement among the agencies specified in section 1(c).

Part B. Executive Branch Judgments Under Section 128a(1) of the Atomic Energy Act

Section 8. Procedures

a. The Nuclear Regulatory Commission shall promptly transmit any properly completed export license application to the offices listed in paragraphs a through e of section 3.

b. As promptly as possible, but in no event later than 15 days after the receipt of each license application the offices listed in paragraphs b through e of section 3 shall review the submission and shall advise the Office of Export and Import Control:

(i) Whether that agency believes that any additional information is required in connection with preparation of the Executive branch judgment. In the event that such information is required, the Office of Export and Import Control shall seek to obtain and provide the information as promptly as possible. If additional information required is essential to further Executive branch processing, the Office of Export and Import Control may return the application to the Nuclear Regulatory Commission, in which event the schedule of actions and deadlines set out herein shall recommence upon receipt by the Office of a substantively complete application;

(ii) Whether that agency believes a license application appears to raise issues which will require more extensive consideration than is normally necessary in Executive branch processing of similar license applications. If such issues appear to be present, the Office of Export and Import Control will normally schedule consideration of these issues at the earliest possible meeting of the SNEC and shall as promptly as possible initiate appropriate steps, including those required to obtain any necessary policy decisions and to initiate any necessary diplomatic consultations;

(iii) Of their preliminary views on the license application, if so requested by the Office of Export and Import Control.

If the Department of Energy is the license applicant it shall not be subject to the requirements of this paragraph.

c. No later than five working days after receipt of its copy of a license application from the Nuclear Regulatory Commission, the Department of Energy (Office of International Security Affairs) shall, as appropriate, if the proposed export appears to be consistent with the applicable agreement for cooperation, request confirmation in writing from the nation or group of nations under the agreement for cooperation of which the export is to take place, that among other things:

(i) The export will be subject to the terms and conditions of the agreement for cooperation;

(ii) The ultimate consignee and any intermediate consignee is authorized to receive the export; and

(iii) Physical security measures will be maintained with respect to the export that as a minimum provide protection comparable to that set forth in document INFCIRC 225/Rev. 1 of the International Atomic Energy Agency, entitled, "The Physical Protection of Nuclear Material."[1]

If any such confirmation is not received within fifty-five days after receipt of the license application by the Office of Export and Import Control in the Department of State, the Office may return the application to the Nuclear Regulatory Commission, in which event the schedule of actions and deadlines set out herein shall recommence after receipt of the confirmation and return to the Office by the Nuclear Regulatory Commission of the application.

[1] Many recipients have provided a generic confirmation concerning physical security measures.

d. If the proposed export involves material that has been identified as material with respect to which the United States has agreed to consult with or obtain the approval of any other nation or group of nations prior to its export, the Department of State shall take appropriate action in this regard.

e. If the license application is for an export of high enriched uranium, plutonium or uranium-233, equal to or exceeding formula quantities (as defined in 10 CFR 73.30) the Department of Energy shall prepare an analysis of the technical and economic justification for the use of such material, including whether the quantities requested are necessary for the efficient and continuous operation of the facility involved. This analysis shall be provided to the Office of Export and Import Control of the Department of State within 30 days after receipt by the Department of Energy of its copy of the export license application or as soon thereafter as possible. This analysis shall be provided to concerned agencies and shall be taken into consideration in preparing the Executive branch judgment.

f. As promptly as possible following receipt of the information in paragraph b, and no later than 30 days after its receipt of the license application, proposed general license or proposed exemption, the Office of Export and Import Control shall prepare and transmit to the offices listed in paragraphs b through e of section 3, a proposed Executive branch judgment on the application.

g. No later than ten days after the date of receipt of a proposed Executive branch judgment, the designees of the Secretaries of Energy, Defense, and Commerce, and the Director of the Arms Control and Disarmament Agency, shall each provide the Office of Export and Import Control their written views on the proposed Executive branch judgment transmitted pursuant to paragraph f. When providing its views, the Department of Energy shall transmit a copy of any confirmation obtained pursuant to paragraph c. If a required confirmation or approval is not available at that time, the Department of Energy shall so advise the Office of Export and Import Control. Upon receipt of the required confirmation, the Department of Energy shall forward it as expeditiously as possible to the Office of Export and Import Control and shall simultaneously advise the Nuclear Regulatory Commission. In the event of any disagreement which cannot be resolved between agencies, the provisions in section 5 shall be followed.

h. An Executive branch judgment shall normally address the matters required by section 126a(1) of the AEA with respect to both any intermediate destinations and the final destination of the export that are identified in the license application. Notice of any transfer of the export between intermediate destinations and the final destination shall be received by the Department of Energy. No further action shall be required under Part E for approval of transfers between intermediate and final destinations specified in an application for an export license and for which the license is granted except in the instances set forth in section 16. In such instances, an appropriate request for approval of the transfer shall be submitted to the Department of Energy for action pursuant to the procedures in Part E.

i. A single Executive branch judgment may address more than a single application.

j. An Executive branch judgment may address the matters required by section 126a(1) of the AEA by expressing the view that there is no material changed circumstance associated with a new license application from those existing at the time of issuance of a previous license for an export to the same country, where the previous license was subject to full analysis by the Executive branch.

k. An Executive branch judgment may address any or all of the matters required by section 126a(1) of the AEA by reference to an analysis previously submitted to the Nuclear Regulatory Commission if the offices in paragraphs a through e of section 3 agree that there is no material changed circumstance with respect of such matter or matters.

l. No later than 60 days after receipt of a license application by the Department of State, the Department shall transmit to the Nuclear Regulatory Commission the Executive branch judgment on the license application.

m. Any time period in this section may be extended by the Deputy Assistant Secretary of State for Nuclear Energy and Energy Technology: *Provided,* That the time period in paragraph 1 may be extended only if in the view of the Secretary of State or his designee it is in the national interest to allow additional time, in which case he shall notify the Committee on Foreign Relations of the Senate, the Committee on Foreign Affairs of the House of Representatives, and the offices listed in paragraphs b through f of section 3 of such extension.

n. The Office of Export and Import Control shall maintain for at least five years records of steps set forth above and the dates on which they were taken.

o. This section shall also apply, to the extent relevant, to proposed general licenses and proposed exemptions from licensing requirements.

Section 9. Exports for Which Executive Branch Review Is Not Required

a. Pursuant to the authority in section 126a(1) of the AEA to determine that any export in a category would not be inimical to the common defense and security because it lacks significance for nuclear explosive purposes, the following categories of exports defined in subsection 110.41(d) of tile 10 of the Code of Federal Regulations shall not normally require case-by-case Executive branch review under these procedures.

b. Pursuant to the authority in section 126a(2) of the AEA to deem that the relevant export license requirements are met if there are no material changed circumstances from those existing at the time of the last application for an export to the same country, the following exports to France, Spain and countries that are parties to the Treaty on the Non-Proliferation of Nuclear Weapons (the "NPT") or for which the Treaty for Prohibition of Nuclear Weapons in Latin America is in force, and for which the requirements of section 126 were previously found to be met, shall not require Executive branch review under these procedures, unless the Executive branch informs the Nuclear Regulatory Commission to the contrary:

(1) Low-enriched uranium: a low-enriched uranium reload for a reactor in a country that has in force either a bilateral agreement for cooperation with the United States or an applicable supply agreement pursuant to the Agreement for Cooperation between the United States and the International Atomic Energy Agency;

(2) Equipment: all exports for use in reactors in countries that have provided the assurances required under section 109b of the AEA on a generic basis.

c. This section shall not apply to exports with end uses related to isotope separation, chemical reprocessing, heavy water production, plutonium handling, such types of advanced technology reactors as may be agreed by the agencies listed in section 1(c), and initial exports of nuclear material or equipment to foreign nuclear reactors, and is subject to other limitations which the Executive branch or the Nuclear Regulatory Commission, may, from time to time, deem necessary.

Part C. Foreign Distributions Under Sections 54, 64, and 82 of the Atomic Energy Act

Section 10. Procedures

a. The Office of Non-Proliferation Policy of the Department of Energy shall transmit requests for distributions of nuclear material to the offices listed in paragraphs a, c, e, and f of section 3. If appropriate or if requested by another agency, an analysis shall be prepared setting forth a statement of the purpose of the distribution, reference to the applicable agreements for cooperation, other pertinent information and a recommended course of action. When the proposed distribution appears to raise issues which will require more extensive consideration than is normally necessary for Executive branch processing of similar requests, as analysis addressing these issues will be prepared, and the Office of Non-Proliferation Policy will initiate as promptly as possible appropriate steps, including those required in order to obtain any necessary policy decisions and to initiate any necessary diplomatic consultations.

b. No later than 30 days following receipt of the request or of any analysis that may be prepared, the designees of the Secretaries of State and Defense, the Director of the Arms Control and Disarmament Agency and the Nuclear Regulatory Commission shall provide the Office of Non-Proliferation Policy with their concurrence or such other views, comments or proposed courses of action which they consider appropriate. In the event of any disagreement which cannot be resolved between agencies, the provisions in section 5 shall be followed.

c. No later than 30 days following the expiration of the time limit set forth in paragraph b, the Office of Non-Proliferation Policy shall determine whether to authorize the proposed distribution: *Provided,* That if recourse is made to the procedures in section 5, this period shall be 60 days.

d. Any time period in this section may be extended by the Deputy Assistant Secretary for International Energy Cooperation and Nuclear Non-Proliferation Policy or his designee.

Section 11. Exports for Which Further Executive Branch Review is Not Required

The Department of Energy, without further interagency concurrence or consultation may, to the extent authorized in sections 54, 64 and 82 of the AEA, distribute material referred to in paragraph a of section 9, subject to the qualifications and conditions contained in paragraph c of that section.

Part D. Direct or Indirect Production of Special Nuclear Material Abroad Pursuant to Section 57b of the Atomic Energy Act

Section 12. Procedures

a. Following receipt by the Department of Energy of any application for specific authorization under Part 810 of title 10 of the Code of Federal Regulations, the Office of International Security Affairs of the Department of Energy shall conduct a preliminary review to determine whether the application involves is properly submitted under and subject to the provisions of that Part and to determine whether the application involves sensitive nuclear technology. When this review is completed, the Office of International Security Affairs shall transmit any application which is properly submitted and subject to Part 810 to the offices listed in paragraphs a and c through f of section 3, along with any conclusion that sensitive nuclear technology is involved.

b. The Office of International Security Affairs shall prepare an analysis and preliminary staff recommendation concerning each application transmitted pursuant to paragraph a, which shall also be transmitted to the offices indicated in that paragraph. The analysis shall specify whether the application appears to raise issues which will require more extensive considerations than is normally necessary for Executive branch processing of similar applications, and the Assistant Secretary for Defense Programs or his designee shall as promptly as possible initiate appropriate steps, including those required in order to obtain any necessary policy decisions and to initiate any necessary diplomatic consultations.

c. No later than 30 days after receipt of the analysis, the designees of the Secretary of State, Defense, Commerce, the Director of the Arms Control and Disarmament Agency, and the Nuclear Regulatory Commission shall provide the Office of International Security Affairs of the Department of Energy with written concurrence in the preliminary staff recommendation of such other views, comments or proposed courses of action which they consider appropriate, including such analysis as may be needed to support their position. In the event of any disagreement which cannot be resolved among the agencies, the provisions in section 5 shall be followed.

d. No later than 30 days following receipt of the concurrence or views as provided in paragraph c, the Assistant Secretary for Defense Programs shall provide the Secretary of Energy with a recommendation, including the views of the agencies listed in paragraph c, concerning his action on the application: *Provided*, That if recourse is made to the procedures in section 5, this period shall be 60 days.

e. Any time period in this section may be extended by the Assistant Secretary for Defense Programs or his designees.

Section 13. Continued Effect of Part 810 Procedures

a. The regulations set forth in Part 810 of title 10 of the Code of Federal Regulations, "Unclassified Activities in Foreign Atomic Energy Programs," continue in effect.

b. Any amendment of Part 810 shall be made in accordance with these procedures.

Section 14. Coordination of Reviews

Where an activity involving technology controlled pursuant to section 57(b)(2) of the AEA and requiring specific authorization pursuant to 10 CFR Part 810 is part of an export or activity licensed by another agency of the United States Government, the Department of Energy shall make every effort to coordinate its review with that of the other agency with a view toward expediting the reviewing process and fostering consistent government decision-making.

Part E. Subsequent Arrangements Under Section 131 of the Atomic Energy Act; Approvals Under Section 109b(3) of the Atomic Energy Act

Section 15. Procedures for Review of Subsequent Arrangement and Procedures and Criteria for Review of Component Retransfers

a. Any request from a nation or group of nations for a subsequent arrangement as defined in section 131a(2) of the AEA; or (2) approval of a retransfer of a component; or (3) for an enrichment authorization under section 402(a) of the NNPA shall, if it appears consistent with applicable law and agreements and if submitted in appropriate form, be transmitted promptly by the Office of Non-Proliferation Policy of the Department of Energy to the offices listed in paragraphs a, and c through f of section 3, together with any supporting documents. All references to the term "subsequent arrangement" shall, for purposes of this Part, be deemed to include an enrichment authorization. All references to the term "component" shall, for the purposes of this Part, mean any component, item or substance listed in Appendix A to Part 110 of title 10 of the Code of Federal Regulations other than a production or utilization facility or source, special nuclear or by-product material as defined in section 110.2 of that Part.

b. As promptly as possible, but no later than 15 days after receipt of each request for a subsequent arrangement or a component retransfer approval, the offices listed in paragraphs a, and c through f of section 3 shall review the request and shall advise the Office of Non-Proliferation Policy:

(i) Whether that agency believes that any additional information is required. In the event that such information is required, the Office of Non-Proliferation Policy shall seek to obtain and provide the information as promptly as possible;

(ii) Whether that agency believes the request appears to raise issues which will require more extensive consideration than is normally necessary in Executive branch processing of similar requests. If such issues appear to be present, the Office of Non-Proliferation Policy will normally schedule consideration of these issues at the earliest possible meeting of the Subgroup on Nuclear Export Coordination and shall as promptly as possible initiate appropriate steps, including those required to obtain any necessary policy decisions and to begin any necessary diplomatic consultations; and

(iii) Of their preliminary view, if so requested by the Office of Non-Proliferation Policy.

c. The Office of Non-Proliferation Policy shall (if a request for a subsequent arrangement is involved, no later than 15 days after the expiration of the time limit set forth in paragraph b)[2] prepare and transmit to the offices listed in paragraphs a, and c through f of section 3, a proposed subsequent arrangement, proposed denial of a subsequent arrangement, other proposed course of action with respect to the subsequent arrangement, or a proposed approval or denial of a component retransfer request. Where appropriate, a single transmittal may be used to fulfill the requirements of the foregoing sentence and of paragraph a. In the transmittal of a proposed subsequent arrangement pursuant to this paragraph, the Office of Non-Proliferation shall advise the Office of Export and Import Control of the Department of State if, in the view of the Department of Energy, a proposed subsequent arrangement is likely to involve negotiations of a policy nature pertaining to arrangements for the storage or disposition of irradiated fuel elements or approvals for the transfer, for which prior approval is required under an agreement for cooperation, by a recipient of source or special nuclear material, production or utilization facilities, or nuclear technology. This transmittal shall also specify any steps deemed appropriate to expedite a proposed subsequent arrangement in the instances specified in section 131a(3) of the AEA. The transmittal of a proposed subsequent arrangement or component retransfer approval may include analysis where necessary in the judgment of the Office of Non-Proliferation Policy to facilitate review. Upon the request of any recipient office within 10 days after receipt of a proposed subsequent arrangement or proposed component retransfer approval, the Office of Non-Proliferation Policy shall prepare and transmit an analysis.

d. No later than 20 days after receipt of the proposed subsequent arrangement or component retransfer approval pursuant to paragraph c, the designees of the Secretary of State, the Secretary of Defense, the Secretary of Commerce, the Director of the Arms Control and Disarmament Agency, and the Nuclear Regulatory Commission shall, as appropriate, provide the Office of Non-Proliferation Policy with their concurrences or such other views, comments, or proposed courses. With respect to subsequent arrangement, the response of the designee of the Director of the Arms Control and Disarmament Agency shall also include a declaration of any intention of the Director to prepare a Nuclear Proliferation Assessment Statement pursuant to section 131a of the AEA. Any such statement shall be prepared within 60 days of the receipt by the Direc-

[2] A subsequent arrangement may be initiated in certain circumstances by the Department of Energy, in which case paras. a and b are not applicable.

tor or his designee of a copy of the proposed subsequent arrangement. In the event of any disagreement concerning a proposed subsequent arrangement or component retransfer approval which cannot be resolved between agencies, the provisions of section 5 shall be followed.

e. In the case of a proposed subsequent arrangement, no later than 20 days after the expiration of the time limit set forth in paragraph d, but, if the Director of the Arms Control and Disarmament Agency has declared his intention to prepare a Nuclear Proliferation Assessment Statement, only after receipt of the Statement or the expiration of the time authorized in section 131c of the AEA for the preparation of the Statement, whichever occurs first, the Secretary of Energy, or his designee, after making the determination required by section 131a(1) of the AEA and pursuant to any required judgment, under section 131b(2) of the AEA, shall decide whether to enter into the proposed subsequent arrangement: *Provided,* That if recourse is made to the provisions in section 5, this period shall be 60 days.

f. In the case of a proposed component retransfer approval request, the Deputy Assistant Secretary for International Affairs shall approve the retransfer if, with the concurrence of the Deputy Assistant Secretary of State for Nuclear Energy and Technology. he finds, based on a reasonable judgment of the assurances provided and other information available to the Federal Government, that the following criteria or their equivalent are met:

(1) IAEA safeguards as required by article III(2) of the NPT will be applied with respect to such component;

(2) The component will not be used for any nuclear explosive device or for research on or development of any nuclear explosive device;

(3) The component will be further retransferred only to nations or groups of nations for which consent has been given pursuant to section 19 or upon prior consent of the United States; and

(4) The retransfer will not be inimical to the common defense and security of the United States

Action pursuant to paragraph f shall be taken no later than 20 days after the expiration of the time period in paragraph d: *Provided* that if recourse is made to the provisions in section 5, this period shall be 45 days.

g. After discharging the Department of Energy's responsibilities under paragraph e of these procedures, the Secretary of Energy or his designee shall cause to be published in the FEDERAL REGISTER notice of any proposed subsequent arrangement together with his written determination that the arrangement will not be inimical to the common defense and security. He shall also report to Congress with respect to any proposed subsequent arrangement of the types specified in section 131b(1) of the AEA. No subsequent arrangement shall take effect until the applicable time period or periods in section 131 of the AEA have elapsed.

h. Except for the time limits for the preparation of a Nuclear Proliferation Assessment Statement, any time period in this section may be extended by the Deputy Assistant Secretary for International Energy Cooperation and Nuclear Non-Proliferation Policy or his designee.

Section 16. Retransfers Within the Scope of an Export License and Other Subsequent Arrangements and Component Retransfers for Which Further Executive Branch Review is Not Required

a. The Secretary of Energy, with the concurrence of the Secretary of State, and having consulted the Director of the Arms Control and Disarmament Agency, and the Nuclear Regulatory Commission and the Secretary of Defense, hereby determines that a subsequent arrangement or component retransfer which is limited to a retransfer where an applicable export license has authorized transfer of the material involved for the same purpose and to the same destination for which the retransfer is to be made will not be inimical to the common defense and security and is hereby approved without any further requirement for a request for approval, unless the retransfer does not occur in the same general time period as contemplated by the export license. The foregoing approval does not apply to any such subsequent arrangement subject to section 131b of the AEA. The foregoing subsequent arrangement shall take effect on May 31, 1984 and may be withdrawn in whole or in part, or with respect to any specific destination if the Departments of Energy and State, after consultation with the Departments of Defense and Commerce, the Arms Control and Disarmament Agency and the Nuclear Regulatory Commission, determine that a material change in circumstances so warrants.

b. The Secretary of Energy, with the concurrence of the Secretary of State, and having consulted the Director of the Arms Control and Disarmament Agency, and the Nuclear Regulatory Commission and the Secretary of Defense, may enter into a proposed subsequent arrangement or approve a component retransfer which is limited to items specified in paragraph a or b of section 9, subject to the qualifications and conditions contained in those paragraphs and paragraph c of that section.

Section 17. Elimination of Duplicative Reviews

a. Where a subsequent arrangement (other than a subsequent arrangement subject to subsection b or f of section 131) is part of an export licensed by an agency of the United States Government, the Secretary of Energy, with the concurrence of the Secretary of State and having consulted the Director of the Arms Control and Disarmament Agency, and the Nuclear Regulatory Commission and the Secretary of Defense, hereby determines that the subsequent arrangement will not be inimical to the common defense and security and is hereby approved, provided that the Executive branch has concurred in such license.

b. Where a proposed export requires approval for enrichment pursuant to section 402(a) of the NNPA and the proposed export for enrichment is licensed by the Nuclear Regulatory Commission, the Secretary of Energy, with the concurrence of the Secretary of State and having consulted the Director of the Arms Control and Disarmament Agency, and the Nuclear Regulatory Commission and the Secretary of Defense, hereby approves such enrichment.

c. This section shall take effect on May 31, 1984 and the approval contained herein may be withdrawn in whole or in part, or with respect to any specific destination if the Departments of Energy and State after consultation with the Department of Defense and Commerce, the Arms Control and Disarmament Agency and the Nuclear Regulatory Commission, determine that a material change in circumstances so warrants.

Section 18. Generally Approved Retransfers

a. Where the prior consent of the United States for the retransfer of a component is an export license criterion under section 109(3) of the AEA, it is hereby determined that such retransfer will not be arrangement will not be inimical to the common defense and security and United States consent is hereby granted, without any further requirement for a request for approval, for the retransfer of the component from the nation or group of nations to which export was licensed to the jurisdiction of another nation or group of nations.

(1) If the component will be used in a facility the export of which was licensed pursuant to section 126 of the AEA; or

(2) If the Nuclear Regulatory Commission has in effect a general license for the export from the United States of all components to the retransferee nation or group of nations; or

(3) If the Nuclear Regulatory Commission has in effect a general license for the export from the United States of components for use in the facility in which the components will be used; or

(4) If the Nuclear Regulatory Commission has in effect a general license authorizing the export from the United States of an equal or larger quantity of the same component to the same nation or group of nations as the retransferee.

b. The Secretary of Energy, with the concurrence of the Secretary of State, and having consulted the Director of the Arms Control and Disarmament Agency, and the Nuclear Regulatory Commission and the Secretary of Defense, hereby determines that a subsequent arrangement, which is limited to a retransfer to a destination to which a Nuclear Regulatory Commission general export license that is in effect authorizes export from the United States of the same material, will not be inimical to the common defense and security and is hereby authorized without any further requirement for a request for approval. The foregoing subsequent arrangement. The foregoing subsequent arrangement shall take effect on May 31, 1984.

c. The approvals in paragraphs a and b shall not apply if the retransfer is for any of the purposes set forth in paragraph c of section 9 and may be withdrawn in whole or in part, or with respect to any specific destination, if the Departments of Energy and State, after consultation with the Departments of Defense and Commerce, the Arms Control and Disarmament Agency and the Nuclear Regulatory Commission, determine that a material change in circumstances so warrants.

Section 19. Reports on Retransfers

a. Any consent to retransfer source or special nuclear material granted in a subsequent arrangement entered into pursuant to these procedures is granted on the express condition that the retransfer nation or group of nations, or its agent, normally within 30 days of the time the retransfer occurs, submit a properly completed Department of Energy Form S–10 to the Director of the Office of Non-Proliferation Policy, Office of International Affairs, Department of Energy, Washington, D.C. 20545.

b. Any consent to retransfer any component pursuant to these procedures is granted on the express condition that the retransferor nation or group of nations, or its agent, normally within 30 days after a generally approved retransfer occurs or at the time a request for specific retransfer approval is made submit to the Director of the Office of Non-Proliferation Policy, Office of International Affairs, Department of Energy, Washington, D.C. 20545, a report containing: (1) The name, address and citizenship of the person submitting the report; (2) a description of the component involved in the retransfer; (3) the name of the retransferor nation or group of nations and the entity under its jurisdiction having possession of the component; (4) the name of the retransferee nation or group of nations and the entity under its jurisdiction having possession of the component; (5) the actual or proposed time when the retransfer is to occur; and (6) the end use of the component.

Part F. Export Items Under Section 309c of the Nuclear Non-Proliferation Act

Section 20. Procedures

a. A list of commodities licensed by the Department of Commerce which, if used for purposes other than those for which the export is intended, could be of significance for nuclear explosive purposes, is published in the Department of Commerce's Export Administration Regulations and shall be revised as appropriate by the Departments of Commerce and Energy in consultation with the Departments of State and Defense, the Arms Control and Disarmament Agency, and the Nuclear Regulatory Commission.

b. Export license applications for commodities on the list referred to in paragraph 1, as well as any other applications which may involve possible nuclear uses, shall be reviewed by the Department of Commerce in consultation with the Department of Energy. When either the Department of Commerce or the Department of Energy believes that—because of the proposed destination of the export, its timing, or other relevant considerations—a particular application should be reviewed by other agencies, or denied, such application shall be referred to the SNEC. The SNEC shall promptly consider any such application and provide its advice and recommendations to the Department of Commerce. Disagreements shall be handled in accordance with the provisions of section 5.

c. Reviewing agencies shall promptly, but not later than 30 days after receipt from the Department of Commerce of an application, provide their views thereon to the Department of Commerce. If, however, it is not possible to provide views within this time or if, at any point during review, it appears that final action on an application will not be completed within 60 days of receipt by the Department of Commerce, any agency which requires additional time shall inform the Department of Commerce at the earliest possible time of the issues involved and provide an estimate of the time needed to complete its review. In accordance with section 17(d)(2) of the Export Administration Act of 1979, if action is not completed within 180 days of receipt of the application by the Department of Commerce, the applicant shall have the rights of appeal and court action provided in section 10(j) of such Act.

d. If the SNEC recommends denial of an application, the reasons therefor shall be articulated for the record. If the Department of Commerce agrees with the recommendation, that Department, in accordance with section 10(f)(2) of the Export Administration Act of 1979, shall, to the maximum extent consistent with the national security and foreign policy of the United States, inform the applicant in writing of the negative considerations raised with respect to such license application. Before final action is taken on the application, the applicant shall be afforded the opportunity to respond within 15 days to such negative considerations. If appropriate, the applicant's response will be made available to the SNEC for further review and advice. In the event of any disagreement which cannot be resolved between agencies, the provisions in section 5 shall be followed.

d. Convention on the Physical Protection of Nuclear Material

Done at Vienna, October 26, 1979; Ratification advised by the Senate, July 30, 1981; Entered into force, February 8, 1987

CONVENTION ON THE PHYSICAL PROTECTION OF NUCLEAR MATERIAL [1]

The States Parties to this Convention,

RECOGNIZING the right of all States to develop and apply nuclear energy for peaceful purposes and their legitimate interests in the potential benefits to be derived from the peaceful application of nuclear energy,

CONVINCED of the need for facilitating international co-operation in the peaceful application of nuclear energy,

DESIRING to avert the potential dangers posed by the unlawful taking and use of nuclear material,

CONVINCED that offences relating to nuclear material are a matter of grave concern and that there is an urgent need to adopt appropriate and effective measures to ensure the prevention, detection and punishment of such offences,

AWARE OF THE NEED FOR international co-operation to establish, in conformity with the national law of each State Party and with this Convention, effective measures for the physical protection of nuclear material,

CONVINCED that this Convention should facilitate the safe transfer of nuclear material,

STRESSING also the importance of the physical protection of nuclear material in domestic use, storage and transport,

RECOGNIZING the importance of effective physical protection of nuclear material used for military purposes, and understanding that such material is and will continue to be accorded stringent physical protection,

HAVE AGREED AS FOLLOWS:

ARTICLE 1

For the purposes of this Convention:

1. "nuclear material" means plutonium except that with isotopic concentration exceeding 80% in plutonium-238; uranium-233; uranium enriched in the isotope 235 or 233; uranium containing the mixture of isotopes as occurring in nature other than in the form of ore or ore-residue; any material containing one or more of the foregoing;

[1] TIAS 11080. For a list of states that are parties to the Agreement, see Department of State publication, *Treaties in Force.*

2. "uranium enriched in the isotope 235 or 233" means uranium containing the isotope 235 or 233 or both in an amount such that the abundance ratio of the sum of these isotopes to the isotope 238 is greater than the ratio of the isotope 235 to the isotope 238 occurring in nature;

3. "international nuclear transport" means the carriage of a consignment of nuclear material by any means of transportation intended to go beyond the territory of the State where the shipment originates beginning with the departure from a facility of the shipper in that State and ending with the arrival at a facility of the receiver within the State of ultimate destination.

ARTICLE 2

1. This Convention shall apply to nuclear material used for peaceful purposes while in international nuclear transport.

2. With the exception of articles 3 and 4 and paragraph 3 of article 5, this Convention shall also apply to nuclear material used for peaceful purposes while in domestic use, storage and transport.

3. Apart from the commitments expressly undertaken by States Parties in the articles covered by paragraph 2 with respect to nuclear material used for peaceful purposes while in domestic use, storage and transport, nothing in this Convention shall be interpreted as affecting the sovereign rights of a State regarding the domestic use, storage and transport of such nuclear material.

ARTICLE 3

Each State Party shall take appropriate steps within the framework of its national law and consistent with international law to ensure as far as practicable that, during international nuclear transport, nuclear material within its territory, or on board a ship or aircraft under its jurisdiction insofar as such ship or aircraft is engaged in the transport to or from that State, is protected at the levels described in Annex I.

ARTICLE 4

1. Each State Party shall not export or authorize the export of nuclear material unless the State Party has received assurances that such material will be protected during the international nuclear transport at the levels described in Annex I.

2. Each State Party shall not import or authorize the import of nuclear material from a State not party to this Convention unless the State Party has received assurances that such material will during the international nuclear transport be protected at the levels described in Annex I.

3. A State Party shall not allow the transit of its territory by land or internal waterways or through its airports or seaports of nuclear material between States that are not parties to this Convention unless the State Party has received assurances as far as practicable that this nuclear material will be protected during international nuclear transport at the levels described in Annex I.

4. Each State Party shall apply within the framework of its national law the levels of physical protection described in Annex I to

nuclear material being transported from a part of that State to another part of the same State through international waters or airspace.

5. The State Party responsible for receiving assurances that the nuclear material will be protected at the levels described in Annex I according to paragraphs 1 to 3 shall identify and inform in advance States which the nuclear material is expected to transit by land or internal waterways, or whose airports or seaports it is expected to enter.

6. The responsibility for obtaining assurances referred to in paragraph 1 may be transferred, by mutual agreement, to the State Party involved in the transport as the importing State.

7. Nothing in this article shall be interpreted as in any way affecting the territorial sovereignty and jurisdiction of a State, including that over its airspace and territorial sea.

ARTICLE 5

1. States Parties shall identify and make known to each other directly or through the International Atomic Energy Agency their central authority and point of contact having responsibility for physical protection of nuclear material and for co-ordinating recovery and response operations in the event of any unauthorized removal, use or alteration of nuclear material or in the event of credible threat thereof.

2. In the case of theft, robbery or any other unlawful taking of nuclear material or of credible threat thereof, States Parties shall, in accordance with their national law, provide co-operation and assistance to the maximum feasible extent in the recovery and protection of such material to any State that so requests. In particular:

   1. a State Party shall take appropriate steps to inform as soon as possible other States, which appear to it to be concerned, of any theft, robbery or other unlawful taking of nuclear material or credible threat thereof and to inform, where appropriate, international organizations;
   2. as appropriate, the States Parties concerned shall exchange information with each other or international organizations with a view to protecting threatened nuclear material, verifying the integrity of the shipping container, or recovering unlawfully taken nuclear material and shall:
      1. co-ordinate their efforts through diplomatic and other agreed channels;
      2. render assistance; if requested;
      3. ensure the return of nuclear material stolen or missing as a consequence of the above-mentioned events.

The means of implementation of this co-operation shall be determined by the States Parties concerned.

3. States Parties shall co-operate and consult as appropriate, with each other directly or through international organizations, with a view to obtaining guidance on the design, maintenance and improvement of systems of physical protection of nuclear material in international transport.

ARTICLE 6

1. States Parties shall take appropriate measures consistent with their national law to protect the confidentiality of any information which they receive in confidence by virtue of the provisions of this Convention form another State Party or through participation in an activity carried out for the implementation of this Convention. If States Parties provide information to international organizations in confidence, steps shall be taken to ensure that the confidentiality of such information is protected.

2. States Parties shall not be required by this Convention to provide any information which they are not permitted to communicate pursuant to national law or which would jeopardize the security of the State concerned or the physical protection of nuclear material.

ARTICLE 7

1. The intentional commission of:

1. an act without lawful authority which constitutes the receipt, possession, use, transfer, alteration, disposal or dispersal of nuclear material and which causes or is likely to cause death or serious injury to any person or substantial damage to property;

2. a theft or robbery of nuclear material;

3. an embezzlement or fraudulent obtaining of nuclear material;

4. an act constituting a demand for nuclear material by threat or use of force or by any other form of intimidation;

5. a threat:

1. to use nuclear material to cause death or serious injury to any person or substantial property damage, or

2. to commit an offence described in sub-paragraph (b) in order to compel a natural or legal person, international organization or State to do or to refrain from doing any act;

6. an attempt to commit any offence described in paragraphs (a), (b) or (c); and

7. an act which constitutes participation in any offence described in paragraphs (a) to (f) shall be made a punishable offence by each State Party under its national law.

2. Each State Party shall make the offences described in this article punishable by appropriate penalties which take into account their grave nature.

ARTICLE 8

1. Each State Party shall take such measures as may be necessary to establish its jurisdiction over the offences set forth in article 7 in the following cases;

1. when the offence is committed in the territory of that State or on board a ship or aircraft registered in that State;

2. when the alleged offender is a national of that State.

2. Each State Party shall likewise take such measures as may be necessary to establish its jurisdiction over these offences in cases where the alleged offender is presented in its territory and it does

not extradite him pursuant to article 11 to any of the States mentioned in paragraph 1.

3. This Convention does not exclude any criminal jurisdiction exercised in accordance with national law.

4. In addition to the States Parties mentioned in paragraphs 1 and 2, each State Party may, consistent with international law, establish its jurisdiction over the offences set forth in article 7 when it is involved in international nuclear transport as the exporting or importing State.

Article 9

Upon being satisfied that the circumstances so warrant, the State Party in whose territory the alleged offender is present shall take appropriate measures, including detention, under its national law to ensure his presence for the purpose of prosecution or extradition. Measures taken according to this article shall be notified without delay to the States required to establish jurisdiction pursuant to article 8 and, where appropriate, all other States concerned.

Article 10

The State Party in whose territory the alleged offender is present shall, if it does not extradite him, submit, without exception whatsoever and without undue delay, the case to its competent authorities for the purpose of prosecution, through proceedings in accordance with the laws of that State.

Article 11

1. The offences in article 7 shall be deemed to be included as extraditable offences in any extradition treaty existing between States Parties. States Parties undertake to include those offences as extraditable offences in every future extradition treaty to be concluded between them.

2. If a State Party which makes extradition conditional on the existence of a treaty receives a request for extradition from another State Party with which it has no extradition treaty, it may at its option consider this Convention as the legal basis for extradition in respect of those offences. Extradition shall be subject to the other conditions provided by the law of the requested State.

3. States Parties which do not make extradition conditional on the existence of a treaty shall recognize those offences as extraditable offences between themselves subject to the conditions provided by the law of the requested State.

4. Each of the offences shall be treated, for the purpose of extradition between States Parties, as if it had been committed not only in the place in which it occurred but also in the territories of the States Parties required to establish their jurisdiction in accordance with paragraph 1 of article 8.

Article 12

Any person regarding whom proceedings are being carried out in connection with any of the offences set forth in article 7 shall be guaranteed fair treatment at all stages of the proceedings.

ARTICLE 13

1. States Parties shall afford one another the greatest measure of assistance in connection with criminal proceedings brought in respect of the offences set forth in article 7, including the supply of evidence at their disposal necessary for the proceedings. The law of the State requested shall apply in all cases.

2. The provisions of paragraph 1 shall not affect obligations under any other treaty, bilateral or multilateral, which governs or will govern, in whole or in part, mutual assistance in criminal matters.

ARTICLE 14

1. Each State Party shall inform the depositary of its laws and regulations which give effect to this Convention. The depositary shall communicate such information periodically to all States Parties.

2. The State Party where an alleged offender is prosecuted shall, wherever practicable, first communicate the final outcome of the proceedings to the States directly concerned. The State Party shall also communicate the final outcome to the depositary who shall inform all States.

3. Where an offence involves nuclear material used for peaceful purposes in domestic use, storage or transport, and both the alleged offender and the nuclear material remain in the territory of the State Party in which the offence was committed, nothing in this Convention shall be interpreted as requiring that State Party to provide information concerning criminal proceedings arising out of such an offence.

ARTICLE 15

The Annexes constitute an integral part of this Convention.

ARTICLE 16

1. A conference of States Parties shall be convened by the depositary of five years after the entry into force of this Convention to review the implementation of the Convention and its adequacy as concerns the preamble, the whole of the operative part and the annexes in the light of the then prevailing situation.

2. At intervals of not less than five years thereafter, the majority of States Parties may obtain, by submitting a proposal to this effect to the depositary, the convening of further conferences with the same objective.

ARTICLE 17

1. In the event of a dispute between two or more States Parties concerning the interpretation or application of this Convention, such States Parties shall consult with a view to the settlement of the dispute by negotiation, or by any other peaceful means of settling disputes acceptable to all parties to the dispute.

2. Any dispute of this character which cannot be settled in the manner prescribed in paragraph 1 shall, at the request of any party to such dispute, be submitted to arbitration or referred to the

International Court of Justice for decision. Where a dispute is submitted to arbitration, if, within six months from the date of the request, the parties to the dispute are unable to agree on the organization of the arbitration, a party may request the President of the International Court of Justice or the Secretary-General of the United Nations to appoint one or more arbitrators. In case of conflicting requests by the parties to the dispute, the request to the Secretary-General of the United Nations shall have priority.

3. Each State Party may at the time of signature, ratification, acceptance or approval of this Convention or accession thereto declare that it does not consider itself bound by either or both of the dispute settlement procedures provided for in paragraph 2. The other States Parties shall not be bound by a dispute settlement procedure provided for in paragraph 2, with respect to a State Party which has made a reservation to that procedure.

4. Any State Party which has made a reservation in accordance with paragraph 3 may at any time withdraw that reservation by notification to the depositary.

Article 18

1. This Convention shall be open for signature by all States at the Headquarters of the International Atomic Energy Agency in Vienna and at the Headquarters of the United Nations in New York from 3 March 1980 until its entry into force.

2. This Convention is subject to ratification, acceptance or approval by the signatory States.

3. After its entry into force, this Convention will be open for accession by all States.

4. 1. This Convention shall be open for signature or accession by international organizations and regional organizations of an integration or other nature, provided that any such organization is constituted by sovereign States and has competence in respect of the negotiation, conclusion and application of international agreements in matters covered by this Convention.

2. In matters within their competence, such organizations shall, on their own behalf, exercise the rights and fulfill the responsibilities which this Convention attributes to States Parties.

3. When becoming party to this Convention such an organization shall communicate to the depository a declaration indicating which States are members thereof and which articles of this Convention do not apply to it.

4. Such an organization shall not hold any vote additional to those of its Member States.

5. Instruments of ratification, acceptance, approval or accession shall be deposited with depositary.

Article 19

1. This Convention shall enter into force on the thirtieth day following the date of deposit of the twenty-first instrument of ratification, acceptance or approval with the depositary.

2. For each State ratifying, accepting, approving or acceding to the Convention after the date of deposit of the twenty-first instrument of ratification, acceptance or approval, the Convention shall

enter into force on the thirtieth day after the deposit by such State of its instrument of ratification, acceptance, approval or accession.

ARTICLE 20

1. Without prejudice to article 16 a State Party may propose amendments to this Convention. The proposed amendment shall be submitted to the depositary who shall circulate it immediately to all States Parties. If a majority of States Parties request the depositary to convene a conference to consider the proposed amendments, the depositary shall invite all States Parties to attend such a conference to being not sooner than thirty days after the invitations are issued. Any amendment adopted at the conference by a two-thirds majority of all States Parties shall be promptly circulated by the depositary to all States Parties.

2. The amendment shall enter into force for each State Party that deposits its instrument of ratification, acceptance or approval of the amendment on the thirtieth day after the date on which two thirds of the States Parties have deposited their instruments of ratification, acceptance or approval with the depositary. Thereafter, the amendment shall enter into force for any other State Party on the day on which that State Party deposits its instrument of ratification, acceptance or approval of the amendment.

ARTICLE 21

1. Any State Party any denounce this Convention by written notification to the depositary.

2. Denunciation shall take effect one hundred and eighty days following the date on which notification is received by the depositary.

ARTICLE 22

The depositary shall promptly notify all States of:

1. each signature of this Convention;
2. each deposit of an instrument of ratification, acceptance, approval or accession;
3. any reservation or withdrawal in accordance with article 17;
4. any communication made by an organization in accordance with paragraph 4(c) of article 18;
5. the entry into force of this Convention;
6. the entry into force of any amendment to this Convention; and
7. any denunciation made under article 21.

ARTICLE 23

The original of this Convention, of which the Arabic, Chinese, English, French, Russian and Spanish texts are equally authentic, shall be deposited with the Director General of the International Atomic Energy Agency who shall send certified copies thereof to all States.

IN WITNESS WHEREOF, the undersigned, being duly authorized, have signed this Convention, opened for signature at Vienna and at New York on 3 March 1980.

ANNEX I

Levels of Physical Protection to be Applied in International Transport of Nuclear Materials as Categorized in Annex II

1. Levels of physical protection for nuclear material during storage incidental to international nuclear transport include:

   1. For Category III materials, storage within an area to which access is controlled;

   2. For Category II materials, storage within an area under constant surveillance by guards or electronic devices, surrounded by a physical barrier with a limited number of points of entry under appropriate control or any area with an equivalent level of physical protection;

   3. For Category I material, storage within a protected area as defined for Category II above, to which, in addition, access is restricted to persons whose trustworthiness has been determined, and which is under surveillance by guards who are in close communication with appropriate response forces. Specific measures taken in this context should have as their object the detection and prevention of any assault, unauthorized access or unauthorized removal of material.

2. Levels of physical protection for nuclear material during international transport include:

   1. For Category II and III materials, transportation shall take place under special precautions including prior arrangements among sender, receiver, and carrier, and prior agreement between natural or legal persons subject to the jurisdiction and regulation of exporting and importing States, specifying time, place and procedures for transferring transport responsibility;

   2. For Category I materials, transportation shall take place under special precautions identified above for transportation of Category II and III materials, and in addition, under constant surveillance by escorts and under conditions which assure close communication with appropriate response forces;

   3. For natural uranium other than in the form of ore or ore-residue; transportation protection for quantities exceeding 500 kilograms uranium shall include advance notification of shipment specifying mode of transport, expected time of arrival and confirmation of receipt of shipment.

ANNEX II

Table: Categorization of Nuclear Material

Material	Form	Category I	Category II	Category III[c]
1. Plutonium[a]	Unirradiated[b]	2 kg or more.	Less than 2 kg but more than 500 g.	500 g or less but more than 15 g
2. Uranium-235	Unirradiated[b] .... uranium enriched to 20% ^{235}U or more. uranium enriched to 10% ^{235}U but less than 20%. uranium enriched above natural, but less than 10% ^{235}U.	5 kg or more. Less than 5 kg but more than 1 kg.	10 kg or more. 1 kg or less but more than 15 g.	Less than 10 kg but more than 1 kg 10 kg or more
3. Uranium-233	Unirradiatedb[b] ..	2 kg or more.	Less than 2 kg but more than 500 g.	500 g or less but more than 15 g
4. Irradiated fuel	Depleted or natural uranium, thorium or low-enriched fuel (less than 10% fossile content)[d, e].			

[a] All plutonium except that with isotopic concentration exceeding 80% in plutonium-238.

[b] Material not irradiated in a reactor or material irradiated in a reactor but with a radiation level equal to or less than 100 rads/hour at one metre unshielded.

[c] Quantities not falling in Category III and natural uranium should be protected in accordance with prudent management practice.

[d] Although this level of protection is recommended, it would be open to States, upon evaluation of the specific circumstances, to assign a different category of physical protection.

[e] Other fuel which by virtue of its original fissile material content is classified as Category I and II before irradiation may be reduced one category level while the radiation level from the fuel exceeds 100 rads/hour at one metre unshielded.

FINAL ACT

Meeting of Governmental Representatives to Consider the Drafting of a Convention on the Physical Protection of Nuclear Material

1. The Meeting of Governmental Representatives to Consider the Drafting of a Convention on the Physical Protection of Nuclear Material met in Vienna at the Headquarters of the International Atomic Energy Agency from 31 October to 10 November 1977, from 10 to 20 April 1978, from 5 to 16 February and from 15 to 26 October 1979. Informal consultations between Governmental Representatives took place from 4 to 7 September 1978 and from 24 to 25 September 1979.

2. Representatives of 58 States and one organization participated, namely, representatives of:

Algeria	Cuba	Guatemala
Korea, Republic of	Philippines	Union of Soviet Socialist Republics
Argentina	Czechoslovakia	Holy See
Libyan Arab Jamahiriya	Poland	United Arab Emirates
Australia	Denmark	Hungary
Luxembourg	Qatar	United Kingdom of Great Britain and Northern Ireland
Austria	Ecuador	India
Mexico	Romania	United States of America
Belgium	Egypt	Indonesia
Netherlands	South Africa	Venezuela
Brazil	Finland	Ireland
Niger	Spain	Yugoslavia
Bulgaria	France	Israel
Norway	Sweden	Zaire
Canada	German Democratic Republic	Italy
Pakistan	Switzerland	European Atomic Energy Community
Chile	Germany, Federal Republic of	Japan
Panama	Tunisia	
Colombia	Greece	
Paraguay	Turkey	
Costa Rica		
Peru		

3. The following States and international organizations participated as observers:

Iran
Lebanon
Malaysia
Thailand
Nuclear Energy Agency of the Organisation for Economic Co-operation and Development

4. The Meeting elected Ambassador D.L. Siazon Jr. (Philippines) as Chairman. For the meetings in April 1978 and February 1979 Mr. R.A. Estrada-Oyuela (Argentina) was elected Chairman.

5. The Meetings elected as Vice-Chairmen:

Mr. K. Willuhn of the German Democratic Republic, who at the meeting in February 1979 was succeeded by Mr. H. Rabold of the German Democratic Republic;

Mr. R.J.S. Harry, Netherlands, who at the meeting of October 1979 was succeeded by Mr. G. Dahlhoff of the Federal Republic of Germany;

Mr. R.A. Estrada-Oyuela, Argentina, who at the meeting of October 1979 was succeeded by Mr. L.A. Olivieri of Argentina.

Mr. L.W. Herron (Australia) was elected Rapporteur. For the meeting in October 1979 Mr. N.R. Smith (Australia) was elected Rapporteur.

6. Secretariat services were provided by the International Atomic Energy Agency. The Director General of the Agency was represented by the Director of the Legal Division of the Agency, Mr. D.M. Edwards and, in succession to him, Mr. L.W. Herron.

7. The Meeting set up the following groups:

1. Working Group on Technical Issues
   Chairman: Mr. R.J.S. Harry, Netherlands
2. Working Group on Legal Issues
   Chairman: Mr. R.A. Estrada-Oyuela, Argentina
3. Working Group on Scope of Convention
   Chairman: Mr. K. Willuhn, German Democratic Republic
4. Drafting Committee
   Chairman: Mr. De Castro Neves, Brazil
   Members: Representatives of Australia, Brazil, Canada, Chile, Czechoslovakia, Egypt, France, Federal Republic of Germany, Italy, Japan, Mexico, Qatar, Tunisia, Union of Soviet Socialist Republics, United States of America.

8. The Meeting had before it the following documents:

1. Draft Convention on the Physical Protection of Nuclear Materials, Facilities and Transports, as contained in document CPNM/1;
2. IAEA document INFCIRC/225/Rev.1: The Physical Protection of Nuclear Material;
3. IAEA document INFCIRC/254: Communications Received from Certain Member States regarding Guidelines for the Export of Nuclear Material, Equipment or Technology.

9. The Meeting completed consideration of a Convention, the text of which is attached as Annex I[*]. Certain delegations expressed reservations with regard to particular provisions in the text. These are recorded in the documents and in the Daily Reports of the Meeting. It was agreed that the text will be referred by delegations to their authorities for consideration.

10. The Meeting recommended that the text of the Convention be transmitted for information to the twenty-third General Conference of the International Atomic Energy Agency.

11. The Convention will, in accordance with its terms, be opened for signature from 3 March 1980 at the Headquarters of the International Atomic Energy Agency in Vienna and at the Headquarters of the United Nations in New York.

Vienna, 26 October 1979

(signed)
D.L. SIAZON JR.

[1] The text of the Convention was transmitted to the twenty-third (1979) regular session of the General Conference of the International Atomic Energy Agency, pursuant to paragraph 11 of the Final Act, as document INFCIRC/274.

[*] Since the Convention has been opened for signature it is not attached here as Annex I; it is reproduced as the first part of this document.

e. Convention on Nuclear Safety

Done at Vienna, September 20, 1994; Entered into force generally, October 24, 1996; Ratification advised by the Senate, March 25, 1999; Entered into force for the United States, July 10, 1999

CONVENTION ON NUCLEAR SAFETY [1]

Preamble

The Contracting Parties

1. AWARE of the importance to the international community of ensuring that the use of nuclear energy is safe, well regulated and environmentally sound;

2. REAFFIRMING the necessity of continuing to promote a high level of nuclear safety worldwide;

3. REAFFIRMING that responsibility for nuclear safety rests with the State having jurisdiction over a nuclear installation;

4. DESIRING to promote an effective nuclear safety culture;

5. AWARE that accidents at nuclear installations have the potential for transboundary impacts;

6. KEEPING in mind the Convention on the Physical Protection of Nuclear Material (1979), the Convention on Early Notification of a Nuclear Accident (1986), and the Convention on Assistance in the Case of a Nuclear Accident or Radiological Emergency (1986);

7. AFFIRMING the importance of international co-operation for the enhancement of nuclear safety through existing bilateral and multilateral mechanisms and the establishment of this incentive Convention;

8. RECOGNIZING that this Convention entails a commitment to the application of fundamental safety principles for nuclear installations rather than of detailed safety standards and that there are internationally formulated safety guidelines which are updated from time to time and so can provide guidance on contemporary means of achieving a high level of safety;

9. AFFIRMING the need to begin promptly the development of an international convention on the safety of radioactive waste management as soon as the ongoing process to develop waste management safety fundamentals has resulted in broad international agreement;

10. RECOGNIZING the usefulness of further technical work in connection with the safety of other parts of the nuclear fuel cycle, and that this work may, in time, facilitate the development of current or future international instruments;

HAVE AGREED AS FOLLOWS:

[1] For a list of states that are parties to the Agreement, see Department of State publication, *Treaties in Force.*

CHAPTER 1. OBJECTIVES, DEFINITIONS AND SCOPE OF APPLICATION

ARTICLE 1. OBJECTIVES

The objectives of this Convention are:

1. to achieve and maintain a high level of nuclear safety worldwide through the enhancement of national measures and international co-operation including, where appropriate, safety-related technical co-operation;
2. to establish and maintain effective defences in nuclear installations against potential radiological hazards in order to protect individuals, society and the environment from harmful effects of ionizing radiation from such installations;
3. to prevent accidents with radiological consequences and to mitigate such consequences should they occur.

ARTICLE 2. DEFINITIONS

For the purpose of this Convention:

1. "nuclear installation" means for each Contracting Party any land-based civil nuclear power plant under its jurisdiction including such storage, handling and treatment facilities for radioactive materials as are on the same site and are directly related to the operation of the nuclear power plant. Such a plant ceases to be a nuclear installation when all nuclear fuel elements have been removed permanently from the reactor core and have been stored safely in accordance with approved procedures, and a decommissioning programme has been agreed to by the regulatory body.
2. "regulatory body" means for each Contracting Party any body or bodies given the legal authority by that Contracting Party to grant licences and to regulate the siting, design, construction, commissioning, operation or decommissioning of nuclear installations.
3. "licence" means any authorization granted by the regulatory body to the applicant to have the responsibility for the siting, design, construction, commissioning, operation or decommissioning of a nuclear installation.

ARTICLE 3. SCOPE OF APPLICATION

This Convention shall apply to the safety of nuclear installations.

CHAPTER 2. OBLIGATIONS

1. General Provisions

ARTICLE 4. IMPLEMENTING MEASURES

Each Contracting Party shall take, within the framework of its national law, the legislative, regulatory and administrative measures and other steps necessary for implementing its obligations under this Convention.

ARTICLE 5. REPORTING

Each Contracting Party shall submit for review, prior to each meeting referred to in Article 20, a report on the measures it has taken to implement each of the obligations of this Convention

ARTICLE 6. EXISTING NUCLEAR INSTALLATIONS

Each Contracting Party shall take the appropriate steps to ensure that the safety of nuclear installations existing at the time the Convention enters into force for that Contracting Party is reviewed as soon as possible. When necessary in the context of this Convention, the Contracting Party shall ensure that all reasonably practicable improvements are made as a matter of urgency to upgrade the safety of the nuclear installation. If such upgrading cannot be achieved, plans should be implemented to shut down the nuclear installation as soon as practically possible. The timing of the shutdown may take into account the whole energy context and possible alternatives as well as the social, environmental and economic impact.

2. Legislation and Regulation

ARTICLE 7. LEGISLATIVE AND REGULATORY FRAMEWORK

1. Each Contracting Party shall establish and maintain a legislative and regulatory framework to govern the safety of nuclear installations.

2. The legislative and regulatory framework shall provide for:

1. the establishment of applicable national safety requirements and regulations;

2. a system of licensing with regard to nuclear installations and the prohibition of the operation of a nuclear installation without a licence:

3. a system of regulatory inspection and assessment of nuclear installations to ascertain compliance with applicable regulations and the terms of licences;

4. the enforcement of applicable regulations and of the terms of licences, including suspension, modification or revocation.

ARTICLE 8. REGULATORY BODY

1. Each Contracting Party shall establish or designate a regulatory body entrusted with the implementation of the legislative and regulatory framework referred to in Article 7, and provided with adequate authority, competence and financial and human resources to fulfill its assigned responsibilities.

2. Each Contracting Party shall take the appropriate steps to ensure an effective separation between the functions of the regulatory body and those of any other body or organization concerned with the promotion or utilization of nuclear energy.

ARTICLE 9. RESPONSIBILITY OF THE LICENCE HOLDER

Each Contracting Party shall ensure that prime responsibility for the safety of a nuclear installation rests with the holder of the relevant licence and shall take the appropriate steps to ensure that each such licence holder meets its responsibility.

3. General Safety Considerations

ARTICLE 10. PRIORITY TO SAFETY

Each Contracting Party shall take the appropriate steps to ensure that all organizations engaged in activities directly related to nuclear installations shall establish policies that give due priority to nuclear safety.

ARTICLE 11. FINANCIAL AND HUMAN RESOURCES

1. Each Contracting Party shall take the appropriate steps to ensure that adequate financial resources are available to support the safety of each nuclear installation throughout its life.
2. Each Contracting Party shall take the appropriate steps to ensure that sufficient numbers of qualified staff with appropriate education, training and retraining are available for all safety-related activities in or for each nuclear installation, throughout its life.

ARTICLE 12. HUMAN FACTORS

Each Contracting Party shall take the appropriate steps to ensure that the capabilities and limitations of human performance are taken into account throughout the life of a nuclear installation.

ARTICLE 13. QUALITY ASSURANCE

Each Contracting Party shall take the appropriate steps to ensure that quality assurance programmes are established and implemented with a view to providing confidence that specified requirements for all activities important to nuclear safety are satisfied throughout the life of a nuclear installation.

ARTICLE 14. ASSESSMENT AND VERIFICATION OF SAFETY

Each Contracting Party shall take the appropriate steps to ensure that:

1. comprehensive and systematic safety assessments are carried out before the construction and commissioning of a nuclear installation and throughout its life. Such assessments shall be well documented, subsequently updated in the light of operating experience and significant new safety information, and reviewed under the authority of the regulatory body;
2. verification by analysis, surveillance, testing and inspection is carried out to ensure that the physical state and the operation of a nuclear installation continue to be in accordance with its design, applicable national safety requirements, and operational limits and conditions.

ARTICLE 15. RADIATION PROTECTION

Each Contracting Party shall take the appropriate steps to ensure that in all operational states the radiation exposure to the workers and the public caused by a nuclear installation shall be kept as low as reasonably achievable and that no individual shall be exposed to radiation doses which exceed prescribed national dose limits.

ARTICLE 16. EMERGENCY PREPAREDNESS

1. Each Contracting Party shall take the appropriate steps to ensure that there are on-site and off-site emergency plans that are routinely tested for nuclear installations and cover the activities to be carried out in the event of an emergency.

For any new nuclear installation, such plans shall be prepared and tested before it commences operation above a low power level agreed by the regulatory body.

2. Each Contracting Party shall take the appropriate steps to ensure that, insofar as they are likely to be affected by a radiological emergency, its own population and the competent authorities of the States in the vicinity of the nuclear installation are provided with appropriate information for emergency planning and response.

3. Contracting Parties which do not have a nuclear installation on their territory, insofar as they are likely to be affected in the event of a radiological emergency at a nuclear installation in the vicinity, shall take the appropriate steps for the preparation and testing of emergency plans for their territory that cover the activities to be carried out in the event of such an emergency.

4. Safety of Installations

ARTICLE 17. SITING

Each Contracting Party shall take the appropriate steps to ensure that appropriate procedures are established and implemented:

1. for evaluating all relevant site-related factors likely to affect the safety of a nuclear installation for its projected lifetime;
2. for evaluating the likely safety impact of a proposed nuclear installation on individuals, society and the environment;
3. for re-evaluating as necessary all relevant factors referred to in sub-paragraphs (i) and (ii) so as to ensure the continued safety acceptability of the nuclear installation;
4. for consulting Contracting Parties in the vicinity of a proposed nuclear installation, insofar as they are likely to be affected by that installation and, upon request providing the necessary information to such Contracting Parties, in order to enable them to evaluate and make their own assessment of the likely safety impact on their own territory of the nuclear installation.

ARTICLE 18. DESIGN AND CONSTRUCTION

Each Contracting Party shall take the appropriate steps to ensure that:

1. the design and construction of a nuclear installation provides for several reliable levels and methods of protection (defense in depth) against the release of radioactive materials, with a view to preventing the occurrence of accidents and to mitigating their radiological consequences should they occur;
2. the technologies incorporated in the design and construction of a nuclear installation are proven by experience or qualified by testing or analysis;

3. the design of a nuclear installation allows for reliable, stable and easily manageable operation, with specific consideration of human factors and the man-machine interface.

ARTICLE 19. OPERATION

Each Contracting Party shall take the appropriate steps to ensure that:

1. the initial authorization to operate a nuclear installation is based upon an appropriate safety analysis and a commissioning programme demonstrating that the installation, as constructed, is consistent with design and safety requirements;
2. operational limits and conditions derived from the safety analysis, tests and operational experience are defined and revised as necessary for identifying safe boundaries for operation;
3. operation, maintenance, inspection and testing of a nuclear installation are conducted in accordance with approved procedures;
4. procedures are established for responding to anticipated operational occurrences and to accidents;
5. necessary engineering and technical support in all safety-related fields is available throughout the lifetime of a nuclear installation;
6. incidents significant to safety are reported in a timely manner by the holder of the relevant licence to the regulatory body;
7. programmes to collect and analyse operating experience are established, the results obtained and the conclusions drawn are acted upon and that existing mechanisms are used to share important experience with international bodies and with other operating organizations and regulatory bodies;
8. the generation of radioactive waste resulting from the operation of a nuclear installation is kept to the minimum practicable for the process concerned, both in activity and in volume, and any necessary treatment and storage of spent fuel and waste directly related to the operation and on the same site as that of the nuclear installation take into consideration conditioning and disposal.

CHAPTER 3. MEETINGS OF THE CONTRACTING PARTIES

ARTICLE 20. REVIEW MEETINGS

1. The Contracting Parties shall hold meetings (hereinafter referred to as "review meetings") for the purpose of reviewing the reports submitted pursuant to Article 5 in accordance with the procedures adopted under Article 22.

2. Subject to the provisions of Article 24 sub-groups comprised of representatives of Contracting Parties may be established and may function during the review meetings as deemed necessary for the purpose of reviewing specific subjects contained in the reports.

3. Each Contracting Party shall have a reasonable opportunity to discuss the reports submitted by other Contracting Parties and to seek clarification of such reports.

ARTICLE 21. TIMETABLE

1. A preparatory meeting of the Contracting Parties shall be held not later than six months after the date of entry into force of this Convention.

2. At this preparatory meeting, the Contracting Parties shall determine the date for the first review meeting. This review meeting shall be held as soon as possible, but not later than thirty months after the date of entry into force of this Convention.

3. At each review meeting, the Contracting Parties shall determine the date for the next such meeting. The interval between review meetings shall not exceed three years.

ARTICLE 22. PROCEDURAL ARRANGEMENTS

1. At the preparatory meeting held pursuant to Article 21 the Contracting Parties shall prepare and adopt by consensus Rules of Procedure and Financial Rules. The Contracting Parties shall establish in particular and in accordance with the Rules of Procedure:

1. guidelines regarding the form and structure of the reports to be submitted pursuant to Article 5;
2. a date for the submission of such reports;
3. the process for reviewing such reports.

2. At review meetings the Contracting Parties may, if necessary, review the arrangements established pursuant to sub-paragraphs (i)–(iii) above, and adopt revisions by consensus unless otherwise provided for in the Rules of Procedure. They may also amend the Rules of Procedure and the Financial Rules, by consensus.

ARTICLE 23. EXTRAORDINARY MEETINGS

An extraordinary meeting of the Contracting Parties shall be held:

1. if so agreed by a majority of the Contracting Parties present and voting at a meeting, abstentions being considered as voting; or
2. at the written request of a Contracting Party, within six months of this request having been communicated to the Contracting Parties and notification having been received by the secretariat referred to in Article 28, that the request has been supported by a majority of the Contracting Parties.

ARTICLE 24. ATTENDANCE

1. Each Contracting Party shall attend meetings of the Contracting Parties and be represented at such meetings by one delegate, and by such alternates, experts and advisers as it deems necessary.

2. The Contracting Parties may invite, by consensus, any intergovernmental organization which is competent in respect of matters governed by this Convention to attend, as an observer, any meeting, or specific sessions thereof. Observers shall be required to accept in writing, and in advance, the provisions of Article 27.

ARTICLE 25. SUMMARY REPORTS

The Contracting Parties shall adopt, by consensus, and make available to the public a document addressing issues discussed and conclusions reached during a meeting.

ARTICLE 26. LANGUAGES

1. The languages of meetings of the Contracting Parties shall be Arabic, Chinese, English, French, Russian and Spanish unless otherwise provided in the Rules of Procedure.

2. Reports submitted pursuant to Article 5 shall be prepared in the national language of the submitting Contracting Party or in a single designated language to be agreed in the Rules of Procedure. Should the report be submitted in a national language other than the designated language, a translation of the report into the designated language shall be provided by the Contracting Party.

3. Notwithstanding the provisions of paragraph 2, if compensated, the secretariat will assume the translation into the designated language of reports submitted in any other language of the meeting.

ARTICLE 27. CONFIDENTIALITY

1. The provisions of this Convention shall not affect the rights and obligations of the Contracting Parties under their law to protect information from disclosure. For the purposes of this Article, "information" includes, inter alia, (i) personal data; (ii) information protected by intellectual property rights or by industrial or commercial confidentiality; and (iii) information relating to national security or to the physical protection of nuclear materials or nuclear installations.

2. When, in the context of this Convention, a Contracting Party provides information identified by it as protected as described in paragraph 1, such information shall be used only for the purposes for which it has been provided and its confidentiality shall be respected.

3. The content of the debates during the reviewing of the reports by the Contracting Parties at each meeting shall be confidential.

ARTICLE 28. SECRETARIAT

1. The International Atomic Energy Agency, (hereinafter referred to as the "Agency") shall provide the secretariat for the meetings of the Contracting Parties.

2. The secretariat shall:

1. convene, prepare and service the meetings of the Contracting Parties;

2. transmit to the Contracting Parties information received or prepared in accordance with the provisions of this Convention.

The costs incurred by the Agency in carrying out the functions referred to in sub-paragraphs (i) and (ii) above shall be borne by the Agency as part of its regular budget.

3. The Contracting Parties may, by consensus, request the Agency to provide other services in support of meetings of the Contracting Parties. The Agency may provide such services if they can

be undertaken within its programme and regular budget. Should this not be possible, the Agency may provide such services if voluntary funding is provided from another source.

CHAPTER 4. FINAL CLAUSES AND OTHER PROVISIONS

ARTICLE 29. RESOLUTION OF DISAGREEMENTS

In the event of a disagreement between two or more Contracting Parties concerning the interpretation or application of this Convention, the Contracting Parties shall consult within the framework of a meeting of the Contracting Parties with a view to resolving the disagreement.

ARTICLE 30. SIGNATURE, RATIFICATION, ACCEPTANCE, APPROVAL, ACCESSION

1. This Convention shall be open for signature by all States at the Headquarters of the Agency in Vienna from 20 September 1994 until its entry into force.
2. This Convention is subject to ratification, acceptance or approval by the signatory States.
3. After its entry into force, this Convention shall be open for accession by all States.
4.
    i. This Convention shall be open for signature or accession by regional organizations of an integration or other nature, provided that any such organization is constituted by sovereign States and has competence in respect of the negotiation, conclusion and application of international agreements in matters covered by this Convention.
    ii. In matters within their competence, such organizations shall, on their own behalf, exercise the rights and fulfill the responsibilities which this Convention attributes to States Parties
    iii. When becoming party to this Convention, such an organization shall communicate to the Depositary referred to in Article 34, a declaration indicating which States are members thereof, which articles of this Convention apply to it, and the extent of its competence in the field covered by those articles.
    iv. Such an organization shall not hold any vote additional to those of its Member States.
5. Instruments of ratification, acceptance, approval or accession shall be deposited with the Depositary.

ARTICLE 31. ENTRY INTO FORCE

1. This Convention shall enter into force on the ninetieth day after the date of deposit with the Depositary of the twenty-second instrument of ratification, acceptance or approval, including the instruments of seventeen States, each having at least one nuclear installation which has achieved criticality in a reactor core.
2. For each State or regional organization of an integration of other nature which ratifies, accepts, approves or accedes to this Convention after the date of deposit of the last instrument required to satisfy the conditions set forth in paragraph 1, this Convention

shall enter into force on the ninetieth day after the date of deposit with the Depositary of the appropriate instrument by such a State or organization.

ARTICLE 32. AMENDMENTS TO THE CONVENTION

1. Any Contracting party may propose an amendment to this Convention. Proposed amendments shall be considered at a review meeting or an extraordinary meeting.

2. The text of any proposed amendment and the reasons for it shall be provided to the Depositary who shall communicate the proposal to the Contracting Parties promptly and at least ninety days before the meeting for which it is submitted for consideration. Any comments received on such a proposal shall be circulated by the Depositary to the Contracting Parties.

3. The Contracting Parties shall decide after consideration of the proposed amendment whether to adopt it by consensus, or, in the absence of consensus, to submit it to a Diplomatic Conference. A decision to submit a proposed amendment to a Diplomatic Conference shall require a two-thirds majority vote of the Contracting parties present and voting at the meeting, provided that at least one half of the Contracting Parties are present at the time of voting. Abstentions shall be considered as voting.

4. The Diplomatic Conference to consider and adopt amendments to this Convention shall be convened by the Depositary and held no later than one year after the appropriate decision taken in accordance with paragraph 3 of this Article. The Diplomatic Conference shall make every effort to ensure amendments are adopted by consensus. Should this not be possible, amendments shall be adopted with a two-thirds majority of all Contracting Parties.

5. Amendments to this Convention adopted pursuant to paragraphs 3 and 4 above shall be subject to ratification, acceptance, approval, or confirmation by the Contracting Parties and shall enter into force for those Contracting Parties which have ratified, accepted, approved or confirmed them on the ninetieth day after the receipt by the Depositary of the relevant instruments by at least three fourths of the Contracting Parties. For a Contracting Party which subsequently ratifies, accepts, approves or confirms the said amendments, the amendments will enter into force on the ninetieth day after that Contracting Party has deposited its relevant instrument.

ARTICLE 33. DENUNCIATION

1. Any Contracting Party may denounce this Convention by written notification to the Depositary.

2. Denunciation shall take effect one year following the date of the receipt of the notification by the Depositary, or on such later date as may be specified in the notification.

ARTICLE 34. DEPOSITORY

1. The Director General of the Agency shall be the Depositary of this Convention.

2. The Depositary shall inform the Contracting Parties of:

1. the signature of this Convention and of the deposit of instruments of ratification, acceptance, approval or accession, in accordance with Article 30;

2. the date on which the Convention enters into force, in accordance with Article 31;

3. the notifications of denunciation of the Convention and the date thereof, made in accordance with Article 33;

4. the proposed amendments to this Convention submitted by Contracting Parties, the amendments adopted by the relevant Diplomatic Conference or by the meeting of the Contracting Parties, and the date of entry into force of the said amendments, in accordance with Article 32.

ARTICLE 35. AUTHENTIC TEXTS

The original of this Convention of which the Arabic, Chinese, English, French, Russian and Spanish texts are equally authentic, shall be deposited with the Depositary, who shall send certified copies thereof to the Contracting Parties.

2. Agreement on an International Energy Program

Done at Paris, November 18, 1974; Entered into force provisionally, November 18, 1974; Amendment approved by the Governing Board of the International Emergency Agency at Paris, February 5, 1975; Entered into force for the United States, March 21, 1975; Entered into force definitively, January 19, 1976

AGREEMENT ON AN INTERNATIONAL ENERGY PROGRAM [1]

The Governments of the Republic of Austria, the Kingdom of Belgium, Canada, the Kingdom of Denmark, the Federal Republic of Germany, Ireland, the Italian Republic, Japan, the Grand Duchy of Luxembourg, the Kingdom of the Netherlands, Spain, the Kingdom of Sweden, the Swiss Confederation, the Republic of Turkey, the United Kingdom of Great Britain and Northern Ireland, and the United States of America,

DESIRING to promote secure oil supplies on reasonable and equitable terms,

DETERMINED to take common effective measures to meet oil supply emergencies by developing an emergency self-sufficiency in oil supplies, restraining demand and allocating available oil among their countries on an equitable basis,

DESIRING to promote cooperative relations with oil producing countries and with other oil consuming countries, including those of the developing world, through a purposeful dialogue, as well as through other forms of cooperation, to further the opportunities for a better understanding between consumer and producer countries.

MINDFUL of the interests of other oil consuming countries including those of the developing world,

DESIRING to play a more active role in relation to the oil industry by establishing a comprehensive international information system and a permanent framework for consultation with oil companies,

DETERMINED to reduce their dependence on imported oil by undertaking long term cooperative efforts on conservation of energy, on accelerated development of alternative sources of energy, on research and development in the energy field and on uranium enrichment,

CONVINCED that those objectives can only be reached through continued cooperative efforts within effective organs,

EXPRESSING the intention that such organs be created within the framework of the Organization for Economic Co-operation and Development,

---

[1] 27 UST 1685; TIAS 8278. Entered into force for the United States January 19, 1976. For a list of states that are parties to the Agreement, see Department of State publication, *Treaties in Force*.

RECOGNIZING that other member countries of the Organization for Economic Co-operation and Development may desire to join in their efforts,

CONSIDERING the special responsibility of governments for energy supply,

CONCLUDE that it is necessary to establish an International Energy Program to be implemented through an International Energy Agency, and to that end,

HAVE AGREED AS FOLLOWS:

ARTICLE 1

1. The Participating Countries shall implement the International Energy Program as provided for in this Agreement through the International Energy Agency, described in Chapter IX, hereinafter referred to as the "Agency."

2. The term "Participating Countries" means States to which this Agreement applies provisionally and States for which the Agreement has entered into and remains in force.

3. The term "group" means the Participating Countries as a group:

CHAPTER I—EMERGENCY SELF-SUFFICIENCY

ARTICLE 2

1. The Participating Countries shall establish a common emergency self-sufficiency in oil supplies. To this end, each Participating Country shall maintain emergency reserves sufficient to sustain consumption for at least 60 days with no net oil imports. Both consumption and net oil imports shall be reckoned at the average daily level of the previous calendar year.

2. The Governing Board shall, acting by special majority not later than July 1st, 1975, decide the date from which the emergency reserve commitment of each Participating Country shall, for the purpose of calculating its supply right referred to in Article 7, be deemed to be raised to a level of 90 days. Each Participating Country shall increase its actual level or emergency reserves to 90 days and shall endeavour to do so by the date so decided.

3. The term "emergency reserve commitment" means the emergency reserves equivalent to 60 days of net oil imports as set out in paragraph 1 and, from the date to be decided according to paragraph 2, to 90 days of net oil imports as set out in paragraph 2.

ARTICLE 3

1. The emergency reserve commitment set out in Article 2 may be satisfied by

Oil stocks.

Fuel switching capacity.

Stand-by oil production.

In accordance with the provisions of the Annex which forms an integral part of this Agreement.

2. The Governing Board shall, acting by majority, not later than July 1st, 1975, decide the extent to which the emergency reserve

commitment may be satisfied by the elements mentioned in paragraph 1.

ARTICLE 4

1. The Standing Group on Emergency Questions shall, on a continuing basis, review the effectiveness of the measures taken by each Participating Country to meet its emergency reserve commitment.

2. The Standing Group on Emergency Questions shall report to the Management Committee, which shall make proposals, as appropriate, to the Governing Board. The Governing Board may, acting by majority, adopt recommendations to Participating Countries.

CHAPTER II—DEMAND RESTRAINT

ARTICLE 5

1. Each Participating Country shall at all times have ready a program of contingent oil demand restraint measures enabling it to reduce its rate of final consumption in accordance with Chapter IV.

2. The Standing Group on Emergency Questions shall, on a continuing basis, review and assess:

Each Participating Country's program of demand restraint measures.

The effectiveness of measures actually taken by each Participating Country.

3. The Standing Group on Emergency Questions shall report to the Management Committee, which shall make proposals, as appropriate, to the Governing Board. The Governing Board may, acting by majority, adopt recommendations to Participating Countries.

CHAPTER III—ALLOCATION

ARTICLE 6

1. Each Participating Country shall take the necessary measures in order that allocation of oil will be carried out pursuant to this Chapter and Chapter IV.

2. The Standing Group on Emergency Questions shall, on a continuing basis, review and assess:

Each Participating Country's measures in order that allocation of oil will be carried out pursuant to this chapter and Chapter IV.

The effectiveness of measures actually taken by each Participating Country.

3. The Standing Group on Emergency Questions shall report to the Management Committee, which shall make proposals, as appropriate, to the Governing Board. The Governing Board may, acting by majority, adopt recommendations to Participating Countries.

4. The Governing Board shall, acting by majority, decide promptly on the practical procedures for the allocation of oil and on the procedures and modalities for the participation of oil companies therein within the framework of this Agreement.

ARTICLE 7

1. When allocation of oil is carried out pursuant to Article 13, 14, or 15, each Participating Country shall have a supply right equal to its permissible consumption less its emergency reserve drawdown obligation.

2. A Participating Country whose supply right exceeds the sum of its normal domestic production and actual net imports available during an emergency shall have an allocation right which entitles it to additional net imports equal to that excess.

3. A Participating Country in which the sum of normal domestic production and actual net imports available during an emergency exceeds its supply right shall have an allocation obligation which requires it to supply, directly or indirectly, the quantity of oil equal to that excess to other Participating Countries. This would not preclude any Participating Country from maintaining exports of oil to non-participating countries.

4. The term "permissible consumption" means the average daily rate of final consumption allowed when emergency demand restraint at the applicable level has been activated; possible further voluntary demand restraint by any Participating Country shall not affect its allocation right or obligation.

5. The term "emergency reserve drawdown obligation" means the emergency reserve commitment of any Participating Country divided by the total emergency reserve commitment of the group and multiplied by the group supply shortfall.

6. The term "group supply shortfall" means the shortfall for the group as measured by the aggregate permissible consumption for the group minus the daily rate of oil supplies available to the group during an emergency.

7. The term "oil supplies available to the group" means:

All crude oil available to the group.

All petroleum products imported from outside the group, and all finished products and refinery feedstocks which are produced in association with natural gas and oil and are available to the group.

8. The term "final consumption" means total domestic consumption of all finished petroleum products.

ARTICLE 8

1. When allocation of oil to a Participating Country is carried out pursuant to Article 17, that Participating Country shall:

Sustain from its final consumption the reduction in its oil supplies up to a level equal to 7 per cent of its final consumption during the base period.

Have an allocation right equal to the reduction in its oil supplies which results in a reduction of its final consumption over and above that level.

2. The obligation to allocate this amount of oil is shared among the other Participating Countries on the basis of their final consumption during the base period.

3. The Participating Countries may meet their allocation obligations by any measures of their own choosing, including demand restraint measures or use of emergency reserves.

ARTICLE 9

1. For purposes of satisfying allocation rights and allocation obligations, the following elements will be included:

All crude oil,

All petroleum products,

All refinery feedstocks, and

All finished products produced in association with natural gas and crude oil.

2. To calculate a Participating Country's allocation right, petroleum products normally imported by that Participating Country, whether from other Participating Countries or from non-participating countries, shall be expressed in crude oil equivalent and treated as though they were imports of crude oil to that Participating Country.

3. Insofar as possible, normal channels of supply will be maintained as well as the normal supply proportions between crude oil and products and among different categories of crude oil and products.

4. When allocation takes place, an objective of the Program shall be that available crude oil and products shall, insofar as possible, be shared within the refining and distributing industries as well as between refining and distributing companies in accordance with historical supply patterns.

ARTICLE 10

1. The objectives of the Program shall include ensuring fair treatment for all Participating Countries and basing the price for allocated oil on the price conditions prevailing for comparable commercial transactions.

2. Questions relating to the price of oil allocated during an emergency shall be examined by the Standing Group on Emergency Questions

ARTICLE 11

1. It is not an objective of the Program to seek to increase, in an emergency, the share of world oil supply that the group had under normal market conditions. Historical oil trade patterns should be preserved as far as is reasonable, and due account should be taken of the position of individual non-participating countries.

2. In order to maintain the principles set out in paragraph 1, the Management Committee shall make proposals, as appropriate, to the Governing Board, which, acting by majority, shall decide on such proposals.

CHAPTER IV—ACTIVATION

Activation

ARTICLE 12

Whenever the group as a whole or any Participating Country sustains or can reasonably be expected to sustain a reduction in its oil supplies, the emergency measures, which are the mandatory demand restraint referred to in Chapter II and the allocation of available oil referred to in Chapter III, shall be activated in accordance with this Chapter.

ARTICLE 13

Whenever the group sustains or can reasonably be expected to sustain a reduction in the daily rate of its oil supplies at least equal to 7 per cent of the average daily rate of its final consumption during the base period, each Participating Country shall implement demand restraint measures sufficient to reduce its final consumption by an amount equal to 7 percent of its final consumption during the base period, and allocation of available oil among the Participating Countries shall take place in accordance with Articles 7, 9, 10 and 11.

ARTICLE 14

Whenever the group sustains or can reasonably be expected to sustain a reduction in the daily rate of its oil supplies at least equal to 12 per cent of the average daily rate of its final consumption during the base period, each Participating Country shall implement demand restraint measures sufficient to reduce its final consumption by an amount equal to 10 per cent of its final consumption during the base period, and allocation of available oil among the Participating Countries shall take place in accordance with Articles 7, 9, 10 and 11.

ARTICLE 15

When cumulative daily emergency reserve drawdown obligations as defined in Article 7 have reached 50 per cent of emergency reserve commitments and a decision has been taken in accordance with Article 20, each Participating Country shall take the measures so decided, and allocation of available oil among the Participating Countries shall take place in accordance with Articles 7, 9, 10 and 11.

ARTICLE 16

When demand restraint is activated in accordance with this Chapter, a Participating Country may substitute for demand restraint measures use of emergency reserves held in excess of its emergency reserve commitment as provided in the Program.

ARTICLE 17

1. Whenever any Participating Country sustains or can reasonably be expected to sustain a reduction in the daily rate of its oil supplies which results in a reduction of the daily rate of its final consumption by an amount exceeding 7 per cent of the average daily rate of its final consumption during the base period, allocation of available oil to that Participating Country shall take place in accordance with Articles 8 to 11.

2. Allocation of available oil shall also take place when the conditions in paragraph 1 are fulfilled in a major region of a Participating Country whose oil market is incompletely integrated. In this

case, the allocation obligation of other Participating Countries shall be reduced by the theoretical allocation obligation of any other major region or regions of the Participating Country concerned.

ARTICLE 18

1. The term "base period" means the most recent four quarters with a delay of one quarter necessary to collect information. While emergency measures are applied with regard to the group or to a Participating Country, the base period shall remain fixed.

2. The Standing Group on Emergency Questions shall examine the base period set out in paragraph 1, taking into account in particular such factors as growth, seasonal variations in consumption and cyclical changes and shall, not later than April 1st, 1975, report to the Management Committee. The Management Committee shall make proposals, as appropriate, to the Governing Board, which, acting by majority, shall decide on these proposals not later than January 1, 1975.

ARTICLE 19

1. The Secretariat shall make a finding when a reduction of oil supplies as mentioned in Article 13, 14 or 17 has occurred or can reasonably be expected to occur, and shall establish the amount of the reduction or expected reduction for each Participating Country and for the group. The Secretariat shall keep the Management Committee informed of its deliberations, and shall immediately report its finding to the members of the Committee and inform the Participating Countries thereof. The report shall include information on the nature of the reduction.

2. Within 48 hours of the Secretariat's reporting a finding, the Committee shall meet to review the accuracy of the data compiled and the information provided. The Committee shall report to the Governing Board within a further 48 hours. The report shall set out the views expressed by the members of the Committee, including any views regarding the handling of the emergency.

3. Within 48 hours of receiving the Management Committee's report, the Governing Board shall meet to review the finding of the Secretariat in the light of that report. The activation of emergency measures shall be considered confirmed and Participating Countries shall implement such measures within 15 days of such confirmation unless the Governing Board, acting by special majority, decides within a further 48 hours to activate the emergency measures, to activate them only in part or to fix another time limit for their implementation.

4. If, according to the finding of the Secretariat, the conditions of more than one of the Articles 14, 13 and 17 are fulfilled, any decision not to activate emergency measures shall be taken separately for each Article and in the above order. If the conditions in Article 17 are fulfilled with regard to more than one Participating Country any decision not to activate allocation shall be taken separately with respect to each Country.

5. Decisions pursuant to paragraphs 3 and 4 may at any time be reversed by the Governing Board, acting by majority.

6. In making its finding under this Article, the Secretariat shall consult with oil companies to obtain their views regarding the situation and the appropriateness of the measures to be taken.

7. An international advisory board from the oil industry shall be convened, not later than the activation of emergency measures, to assist the Agency in ensuring the effective operation of such measures.

ARTICLE 20

1. The Secretariat shall make a finding when cumulative daily emergency reserve drawdown obligations have reached or can reasonably be expected to reach 50 percent of emergency reserve commitments. The Secretariat shall immediately report its finding to the members of the Management Committee and inform the Participating Countries thereof. The report shall include information on the oil situation.

2. Within 72 hours of the Secretariat's reporting such a finding, the Management Committee shall meet to review the data compiled and the information provided. On the basis of available information the Committee shall report to the Governing Board within a further 48 hours proposing measures required for meeting the necessities of the situation, including the increase in the level of mandatory demand restraint that may be necessary. The report shall set out the views expressed by the members of the Committee.

3. The Governing Board shall meet within 48 hours of receiving the Committee's report and proposal. The Governing Board shall review the finding of the Secretariat and the report of the Management Committee and shall within a further 48 hours, acting by special majority, decide on the measures required for meeting the necessities of the situation, including the increase in the level of mandatory demand restraint that may be necessary.

ARTICLE 21

1. Any Participating Country may request the Secretariat to make a finding under Article 19 or 20.

2. If, within 72 hours of such request, the Secretariat does not make such a finding, the Participating Country may request the Management Committee to meet and consider the situation in accordance with the provisions of this Agreement.

3. The Management Committee shall meet within 48 hours of such request in order to consider the situation. It shall, at the request of any Participating Country, report to the Governing Board within a further 48 hours. The report shall set out the views expressed by the members of the Committee and by the Secretariat, including any views regarding the handling of the situation.

4. The Governing Board shall meet within 48 hours of receiving the Management Committee's report. If it finds, acting by majority, that the conditions set out in Article 13, 14, 15 or 17 are fulfilled, emergency measures shall be activated accordingly.

ARTICLE 22

The Governing Board may at any time decide by unanimity to activate any appropriate emergency measures not provided for in this Agreement, if the situation so requires.

Deactivation

ARTICLE 23

1. The Secretariat shall make a finding when a reduction of supplies as mentioned in Article 13, 14 or 17 has decreased or can reasonably be expected to decrease below the level referred to in the relevant Article. The Secretariat shall keep the Management Committee informed of its deliberations and shall immediately report its finding to the members of the Committee and inform the Participating Countries thereof.

2. Within 72 hours of the Secretariat's reporting a finding, the Management Committee shall meet to review the data compiled and the information provided. It shall report to the Governing Board within a further 48 hours. The report shall set out the views expressed by the members of the Committee, including any views regarding the handling of the emergency.

3. Within 48 hours of receiving the Committee's report, the Governing Board shall meet to review the finding of the Secretariat in the light of the report from the Management Committee. The deactivation of emergency measures or the applicable reduction of the demand restraint level shall be considered confirmed unless the Governing Board, acting by special majority, decides within a further 48 hours to maintain the emergency measures or to deactivate them only in part.

4. In making its findings under this Article, the Secretariat shall consult with the international advisory board, mentioned in Article 19, paragraph 7, to obtain its views regarding the situation and the appropriateness of the measures to be taken.

5. Any Participating Country may request the Secretariat to make a finding under this Article.

ARTICLE 24

When emergency measures are in force, and the Secretariat has not made a finding under Article 23, the Governing Board, acting by special majority, may at any time decide to deactivate the measures either wholly or in part.

CHAPTER V—INFORMATION SYSTEM ON THE INTERNATIONAL OIL MARKET

ARTICLE 25

1. The Participating Countries shall establish an Information System consisting of two sections:

—a General Section on the situation in the international oil market and activities of oil companies,

—a Special Section designed to ensure the efficient operation of the measures described in Chapters I to IV.

2. The System shall be operated on a permanent basis, both under normal conditions and during emergencies, and in a manner which ensures the confidentiality of the information made available.

3. The Secretariat shall be responsible for the operation of the Information System and shall make the information compiled available to the Participating Countries.

ARTICLE 26

The term "oil companies" means international companies, national companies, non-integrated companies and other entities which play a significant role in the international oil industry.

General Section

ARTICLE 27

1. Under the General Section of the Information System, the Participating Countries shall, on a regular basis, make available to the Secretariat information on the precise data identified in accordance with Article 29 on the following subjects relating to oil companies operating within their respective jurisdictions:

(a) Corporate structure;

(b) Financial structure, including balance sheets, profit and loss accounts, and taxes paid;

(c) Capital investments realized;

(d) Terms of arrangements for access to major sources of crude oil;

(e) Current rates of production and anticipated changes therein;

(f) Allocations of available crude supplies to affiliates and other customers (criteria and realizations);

(g) Stocks;

(h) Cost of crude oil and oil products;

(i) Prices, including transfer prices to affiliates;

(j) Other subjects, as decided by the Governing Board, acting by unanimity.

2. Each Participating Country shall take appropriate measures to ensure that all oil companies operating within its jurisdiction make such information available to it as is necessary to fulfill its obligations under paragraph 1, taking into account such relevant information as is already available to the public or to Governments.

3. Each Participating Country shall provide information on a nonproprietary basis and on a company and/or country basis as appropriate, and in such manner and degree as will not prejudice competition or conflict with the legal requirements of any Participating Country relating to competition.

4. No Participating Country shall be entitled to obtain, through the General Section, any information on the activities of a company operating within its jurisdiction which could not be obtained by it from that company by application of its laws or through its institutions and customs if that company were operating solely within its jurisdiction.

ARTICLE 28

Information provided on a "non-proprietary basis" means information which does not constitute or relate to patents, trademarks, scientific or manufacturing processes or developments, individual sales, tax returns, customer lists or geological and geophysical information, including maps.

ARTICLE 29

1. Within 60 days of the first day of the provisional application of this Agreement, and as appropriate thereafter, the Standing Group on the Oil Market shall submit a report to the Management Committee identifying the precise data within the list of subjects in Article 27, paragraph 1, which are required for the efficient operation of the General Section, and specifying the procedures for obtaining such data on a regular basis.

2. The Management Committee shall review the report and make proposals to the Governing Board which, within 30 days of the submission of the report to the Management Committee, and acting by majority, shall take the decisions necessary for the establishment and efficient operation of the General Section.

ARTICLE 30

In preparing its reports under Article 29, the Standing Group on the Oil Market shall

Consult with oil companies to ensure that the System is compatible with industry operations;

Identify specific problems and issues which are of concern to Participating Countries;

Identify specific data which are useful and necessary to resolve such problems and issues;

Work out precise standards for the harmonization of the required information in order to ensure comparability of the data;

Work out procedures to ensure the confidentiality of the information.

ARTICLE 31

1. The Standing Group on the Oil Market shall on a continuing basis review the operation of the General Section.

2. In the event of changes in the conditions of the international oil market, the Standing Group on the Oil Market shall report to the Management Committee. The Committee shall make proposals on appropriate changes to the Governing Board which, acting by majority, shall decide on such proposals.

Special Section

ARTICLE 32

1. Under the Special Section of the Information System, the Participating Countries shall make available to the Secretariat all information which is necessary to ensure the efficient operation of emergency measures.

2. Each Participating Country shall take appropriate measures to ensure that all oil companies operating within its jurisdiction make such information available to it as is necessary to enable it to fulfill its obligations under paragraph 1 and under Article 33.

3. The Secretariat shall, on the basis of this information and other information available, continuously survey the supply of oil to and the consumption of oil within the group and each Participating Country.

ARTICLE 33

Under the Special Section, the Participating Countries shall, on a regular basis, make available to the Secretariat information on the precise data identified in accordance with Article 34 on the following subjects.

(a) Oil consumption and supply;

(b) Demand restraint measures;

(c) Levels of emergency Reserves;

(d) Availability and utilization of transportation facilities;

(e) Current and projected levels of international supply and demand;

(f) Other subjects, as decided by the Governing Board, acting by unanimity.

ARTICLE 34

1. Within 30 days of the first day of the provisional application of this Agreement, the Standing Group on Emergency Questions shall submit a report to the Management Committee identifying the precise data within the list of subjects in Article 33 which are required under the Special Section to ensure the efficient operation of emergency measures and specifying the procedures for obtaining such data on a regular basis, including accelerated procedures in times of emergency.

2. The Management Committee shall review the report and make proposals to the Governing Board which, within 30 days of the submission of the report to the Management Committee, and acting by majority, shall take the decisions necessary for the establishment and efficient operation of the Special Section.

ARTICLE 35

In preparing its report under Article 34, the Standing Group on Emergency Questions shall

Consult with oil companies to ensure that the System is compatible with industry operations;

Work out precise standards for the harmonization of the required information in order to ensure comparability of the data;

Work out procedures to ensure the confidentiality of the information.

ARTICLE 36

The Standing Group on Emergency Questions shall on a continuing basis review the operation of the Special Section and shall, as appropriate, report to the Management Committee. The Committee shall make proposals on appropriate changes to the Governing Board, which, acting by majority, shall decide on such proposals.

CHAPTER VI—FRAMEWORK FOR CONSULTATION WITH OIL COMPANIES

ARTICLE 37

1. The Participating Countries shall establish within the Agency a permanent framework for consultation within which one or more Participating Countries may, in an appropriate manner, consult with and request information from individual oil companies on all important aspects of the oil industry, and within which the Participating Countries may share among themselves on a cooperative basis the results of such consultations.

2. The framework for consultation shall be established under the auspices of the Standing Group on the Oil Market.

3. Within 60 days of the first day of the provisional application of this Agreement, and as appropriate thereafter, the Standing Group on the Oil Market, after consultation with oil companies, shall submit a report to the Management Committee on the procedures for such consultations. The Management Committee shall review the report and make proposals to the Governing Board, which, within 30 days of the submission of the report to the Management Committee, and acting by majority, shall decide on such procedures.

ARTICLE 38

1. The Standing Group on the Oil Market shall present a report to the Management Committee on consultations held with any oil company within 30 days thereof.

2. The Management Committee shall consider the report and may make proposals on appropriate cooperative action to the Governing Board, which shall decide on such proposals.

ARTICLE 39

1. The Standing Group on the Oil Market shall, on a continuing basis, evaluate the results of the consultations with and the information collected from oil companies.

2. On the basis of these evaluations, the Standing Group may examine and assess the international oil situation and the position of the oil industry and shall report to the Management Committee.

3. The Management Committee shall review such reports and make proposals on appropriate cooperative action to the Governing Board, which shall decide on such proposals.

ARTICLE 40

The Standing Group on the Oil Market shall submit annually a general report to the Management Committee on the functioning of the framework for consultation with oil companies.

Chapter VII—Long Term Cooperation on Energy

ARTICLE 41

1. The Participating Countries are determined to reduce over the longer term their dependence on imported oil for meeting their total energy requirements.

2. To this end, the Participating Countries will undertake national programs and promote the adoption of cooperative programs, including, as appropriate, the sharing of means and efforts, while concerting national policies, in the areas set out in Article 42.

ARTICLE 42

1. The Standing Group on Long Term Cooperation shall examine and report to the Management Committee on cooperative action. The following areas shall in particular be considered:

(a) Conservation of energy, including cooperative programs on

Exchange of national experiences and information on energy conservation;

Ways and means for reducing the growth of energy consumption through conservation.

(b) Development of alternative sources of energy such as domestic oil, coal, natural gas, nuclear energy and hydroelectric power, including cooperative programs on

Exchange of information on such matters as resources, supply and demand, price and taxation;

Ways and means for reducing the growth of consumption of imported oil through the development of alternative sources of energy;

Concrete projects, including jointly financed projects;

Criteria, quality objectives and standards for environmental protection.

(c) Energy research and development, including as a matter of priority cooperative programs on

Coal technology;

Solar energy;

Radioactive waste management;

Controlled thermonuclear fusion;

Production of hydrogen from water;

Nuclear safety;

Waste heat utilization;

Conservation of energy;

Municipal and industrial waste utilization for energy conservation;

Overall energy system analysis and general studies.

(d) "Uranium enrichment, including cooperative programs"

To monitor developments of natural and enriched uranium supply;

To facilitate development of natural uranium resources and enrichment services;

To encourage such consultations as may be required to deal with international issues that may arise in relation to the expansion of enriched uranium supply;

To arrange for the requisite collection, analysis and dissemination data related to the planning of enrichment services.

2. In examining the areas of cooperative action, the Standing Group shall take due account of ongoing activities elsewhere.

3. Program developed under paragraph 1 may be jointly financed. Such joint financing may take place in accordance with Article 64, paragraph 2.

ARTICLE 43

1. The Management Committee shall review the reports of the Standing Group and make appropriate proposals to the Governing Board, which shall decide on these proposals not later than July 1st, 1975.

2. The Governing Board shall take into account possibilities for cooperation within a broader framework.

CHAPTER VIII—RELATIONS WITH PRODUCER COUNTRIES AND WITH OTHER CONSUMER COUNTRIES

ARTICLE 44

The Participating Countries will endeavour to promote cooperative relations with oil producing countries and with other oil consuming countries, including developing countries. They will keep under review developments in the energy field with a view to identifying opportunities for, and promoting a purposeful dialogue, as well as other forms of cooperation, with producer countries and with other consumer countries.

ARTICLE 45

To achieve the objectives set out in Article 44, the Participating Countries will give full consideration to the needs and interests of other oil consuming countries, particularly those of the developing countries.

ARTICLE 46

The Participating Countries will, in the context of the Program, exchange views on their relations with oil producing countries. To this end, the Participating Countries should inform each other of cooperative action on their part with producer countries which is relevant to the objectives of the Program.

ARTICLE 47

The Participating Countries will, in the context of the Program

Seek, in the light of their continuous review of developments in the international energy situation and its effect on the world economy, opportunities and means of encouraging stable international trade in oil and of promoting secure oil supplies on reasonable and equitable terms for each Participating Country;

Consider, in the light of work going on in other international organisations, other possible fields of cooperation including the prospects for cooperation in accelerated industrialisation and socio-economic development in the principal producing areas and the implications of this for international trade and investment;

Keep under review the prospects for cooperation with oil producing countries on energy questions of mutual interest, such as conservation of energy, the development of alternative sources, and research and development.

ARTICLE 48

1. The Standing Group on Relations with Producer and other Consumer Countries will examine and report to the Management Committee on the matters described in this Chapter.

2. The Management Committee may make proposals on appropriate cooperative action regarding these matters to the Governing Board, which shall decide on such proposals.

CHAPTER IX—INSTITUTIONAL AND GENERAL PROVISIONS

ARTICLE 49

1. The Agency shall have the following organs:

A Governing Board;
A Management Committee;
Standing Groups on
Emergency Questions
The Oil Market
Long Term Cooperation
Relations with Producer and Other Consumer Countries

2. The Governing Board or the Management Committee may, acting by majority, establish any other organ necessary for the implementation of the Program.

3. The Agency shall have a Secretariat to assist the organs mentioned in paragraphs 1 and 2.

Governing Board

ARTICLE 50

1. The Governing Board shall be composed of one or more ministers or their delegates from each Participating Country.

2. The Governing Board, acting by majority, shall adopt its own rules of procedure. Unless otherwise decided in the rules procedure, these rules shall also apply to the Management Committee and the Standing Groups.

3. The Governing Board, acting by majority, shall elect its Chairman and Vice Chairmen.

ARTICLE 51

1. The Governing Board shall adopt decisions and make recommendations which are necessary for the proper functioning of the Program.

2. The Governing Board shall review periodically and take appropriate action concerning developments in the international energy situation, including problems relating to the oil supplies of any Participating Country or Countries, and the economic and monetary implications of these developments. In its activities concerning

the economic and monetary implications of developments in the international energy situation, the Governing Board shall take into account the competence and activities of international institutions responsible for overall economic and monetary questions.

3. The Governing Board, acting by majority, may delegate any of its functions to any other organ of the Agency.

ARTICLE 52

1. Subject to Article 61, paragraph 2, and Article 65, decisions adopted pursuant to this Agreement by the Governing Board or by any other organ by delegation from the Board shall be binding on the Participating Countries.

2. Recommendations shall not be binding.

Management Committee

ARTICLE 53

1. The Management Committee shall be composed of one or more senior representatives of the Government of each Participating Country.

2. The Management Committee shall carry out the functions assigned to it in this Agreement and any other function delegated to it by the Governing Board.

3. The Management Committee may examine and make proposals to the Governing Board, as appropriate, on any matter within the scope of this Agreement.

4. The Management Committee shall be convened upon the request of any Participating Country.

5. The Management Committee, acting by majority, shall elect its Chairman and Vice-Chairmen.

Standing Groups

ARTICLE 54

1. Each Standing Group shall be composed of one or more representatives of the Government of each Participating Country.

2. The Management Committee, acting by majority, shall elect the Chairmen and Vice-Chairmen of the Standing Groups.

ARTICLE 55

1. The Standing Group on Emergency Questions shall carry out the functions assigned to it in Chapters I to V and the Annex and any other function delegated to it by the Governing Board.

2. The Standing Group may review and report to the Management Committee on any matter within the scope of Chapters I to V and the Annex.

3. The Standing Group may consult with oil companies on any matter within its competence.

ARTICLE 56

1. The Standing Group on the Oil Market shall carry out the functions assigned to it in Chapters V and VI and any other function delegated to it by the Governing Board.

2. The Standing Group may review and report to the Management Committee on any matter within the scope of Chapters V and VI.

3. The Standing Group may consult with oil companies on any matter within its competence.

ARTICLE 57

1. The Standing Group on Long Term Cooperation shall carry out the functions assigned to it in Chapter VII and any other function delegated to it by the Governing Board.

2. The Standing Group may review and report to the Management Committee on any matter within the scope of Chapter VII.

ARTICLE 58

1. The Standing Group on Relations with Producer and other Consumer Countries shall carry out the functions assigned to it in Chapter VIII and any other function delegated to it by the Governing Board.

2. The Standing Group may review and report to the Management Committee on any matter within the scope of Chapter VIII.

3. The Standing Group may consult with oil companies on any matter within its competence.

Secretariat

ARTICLE 59

1. The Secretariat shall be composed of an Executive Director and such staff as is necessary.

2. The Executive Director shall be appointed by the Governing Board.

3. In the performance of their duties under this Agreement the Executive Director and the staff shall be responsible to and report to the organs of the Agency.

4. The Governing Board, acting by majority, shall make all decisions necessary for the establishment and the functioning of the Secretariat.

ARTICLE 60

The Secretariat shall carry out the functions assigned to it in this Agreement and any other function assigned to it by the Governing Board.

Voting

ARTICLE 61

1. The Governing Board shall adopt decisions and recommendations for which no express voting provision is made in this Agreement, as follows:

(a) by majority:

Decisions on the management of the Program, including decisions applying provisions of this Agreement which already impose specific obligations on Participating Countries

Decisions on procedural questions
Recommendations

(b) by unanimity:

All other decisions, including in particular decisions which impose on Participating Countries new obligations not already specified in this Agreement.

2. Decisions mentioned in paragraph 1(b) may provide:

(a) that they shall not be binding on one or more Participating Countries;

(b) that they shall be binding only under certain conditions.

ARTICLE 62

1. Unanimity shall require all of the votes of the Participating Countries present and voting. Countries abstaining shall be considered as not voting.

2. When majority or special majority is required, the Participating Countries shall have the following voting weights:[2]

	General voting weights	Oil consumption voting weights	Combined voting weights
Austria	3	1	1
Belgium	3	2	4
Canada	3	5	5
Denmark	3	1	8
Germany	3	8	14
Ireland	3	0	3
Italy	3	6	9
Japan	3	15	18
Luxembourg	3	0	3
The Netherlands	3	2	5
New Zealand	3	0	3
Spain	3	2	5
Sweden	3	2	5
Switzerland	3	1	4
Turkey	3	1	4
United Kingdom	3	6	9
United States	3	48	51
Total	51	100	151

3. Majority shall require 60 per cent of the total combined voting weights and 50 per cent of the general voting weights cast.

4. Special majority shall require:

(a) 60 per cent of the total combined voting weights and 39 general voting weights for:[2]

The decision under Article 2, paragraph 2, relating to the increase in the emergency reserve commitment;

Decisions under Article 19, paragraph 3, not to activate the emergency measures referred to in Articles 13 and 14;

Decisions under Article 20, paragraph 3, on the measures referred for meeting the necessities of the situation;

[2] As amended on February 5, 1975 by decision of the Governing Board with the accession of New Zealand to the Agreement (27 UST 1817).

Decisions under Article 23, paragraph 3, to maintain the emergency measures referred to in Articles 13 and 14;

Decisions under Article 24 to deactivate the emergency measures referred to in Articles 13 and 14.

(b) 45 general voting weights for:[2]

Decisions under Article 19, paragraph 3, not to activate the emergency measures referred to in Article 17;

Decisions under Article 23, paragraph 3, to maintain the emergency measures referred to in Article 17;

Decisions under Article 24 to deactivate the emergency measures referred to in Article 17.

5. The Governing Board, acting by unanimity, shall decide on the necessary increase, decrease, and redistribution of the voting weights referred to in paragraph 2, as well as on amendment of the voting requirements set out in paragraphs 3 and 4 in the event that

A Country accedes to this Agreement in accordance with Article 71, or

A Country withdraws from this Agreement in accordance with Article 68, paragraph 2, or Article 69, paragraph 2.

6. The Governing Board shall review annually the number and distribution of voting weights specified in paragraph 2, and, on the basis of such review, acting by unanimity, shall decide whether such voting weights should be increased or decreased, or redistributed, or both, because a change in any Participating Country's share in total oil consumption has occurred or for any other reason.

7. Any change in paragraph 2, 3 or 4 shall be based on the concepts underlying those paragraphs and paragraph 6.

Relations with other entities

ARTICLE 63

In order to achieve the objectives of the Program, the Agency may establish appropriate relations with non-participating countries, international organizations, whether governmental or non-governmental, other entities and individuals.

Financial arrangements

ARTICLE 64

1. The expenses of the Secretariat and all other common expenses shall be shared among all Participating Countries according to a scale of contributions elaborated according to the principles and rules set out in the Annex to the "OECD Resolution of the Council on Determination of the Scale of Contributions by Member Countries to the Budget of the Organization of December 10th, 1963. After the first year of application of this Agreement, the Governing Board shall review this scale of contributions and, acting by unanimity", shall decide upon any appropriate changes in accordance with Article 73.

2. Special expenses incurred in connection with special activities carried out pursuant to Article 65 shall be shared by the Participating Countries taking part in such special activities in such proportions as shall be determined by unanimous agreement between them.

3. The Executive Director shall, in accordance with the financial regulations adopted by the Governing Board and not later than October 1st of each year, submit to the Governing Board a draft budget including personnel requirements. The Governing Board, acting by majority, shall adopt the budget.

4. The Governing Board, acting by majority, shall take all other necessary decisions regarding the financial administration of the Agency.

5. The financial year shall begin on January 1st and end on December 31st of each year. At the end of each financial year, revenues and expenditures shall be submitted to audit.

Special activities

ARTICLE 65

1. Any two or more Participating Countries may decide to carry out within the scope of this Agreement special activities, other than activities which are required to be carried out by all Participating Countries under Chapter I to V. Participating Countries which do not wish to take part in such special activities shall abstain from taking part in such decisions and shall not be bound by them. Participating Countries carrying out such activities shall keep the Governing Board informed thereof.

2. For the implementation of such special activities, the Participating Countries concerned may agree upon voting procedures other than those provided for in Articles 61 and 62.

Implementation of the Agreement

ARTICLE 66

Each Participating Country shall take the necessary measures, including any necessary legislative measures, to implement this Agreement and decisions taken by the Governing Board.

CHAPTER X—FINAL PROVISIONS

ARTICLE 67

1. Each Signatory State shall, not later than May 1st, 1975, notify the Government of Belgium that, having complied with its constitutional procedures, it consents to be bound by this Agreement.

2. On the tenth day following the day on which at least six States holding at least 60 per cent of the combined voting weights mentioned in Article 62 have deposited a notification of consent to be bound or an instrument of accession, this Agreement shall enter into force for such States.

3. For each Signatory State which deposits its notification thereafter, this Agreement shall enter into force on the tenth day following the day of deposit.

4. The Governing Board, acting by majority, may upon request from any Signatory State decide to extend, with respect to that State, the time limit for notification beyond May 1st, 1975.

ARTICLE 68

1. Notwithstanding the provisions of Article 67, this Agreement shall be applied provisionally by all Signatory States, to the extent possible not inconsistent with their legislation, as from November 18, 1974 following the first meeting of the Governing Board.

2. Provisional application of the Agreement shall continue until:

The Agreement enters into force for the State concerned in accordance with Article 67, or

60 days after the Government of Belgium receives notification that the State concerned will not consent to be bound by the Agreement, or

The time limit for notification of consent by the State concerned referred to in Article 67 expires.

ARTICLE 69

1. This Agreement shall remain in force for a period of ten years from the date of its entry into force and shall continue in force thereafter unless and until the Governing Board, acting by majority, decides on its termination.

2. Any Participating Country may terminate the application of this Agreement for its part upon twelve months' written notice to the Government of Belgium to that effect, given not less than three years after the first day of the provisional application of this Agreement.

ARTICLE 70

1. Any State may, at the time of signature, notification of consent to be bound in accordance with Article 67, accession or at any later date, declare by notification addressed to the Government of Belgium that this Agreement shall apply to all or any of the territories for whose international relations it is responsible, or to any territories within its frontiers for whose oil supplies it is legally responsible.

2. Any declaration made pursuant to paragraph 1 may, in respect of any territory mentioned in such declaration, be withdrawn in accordance with the provisions of Article 69, paragraph 2.

ARTICLE 71

1. This Agreement shall be open for accession by any Member of the Organisation for Economic Co-operation and Development which is able and willing to meet the requirements of the Program. The Governing Board, acting by majority, shall decide on any request for accession.

2. This Agreement shall enter into force for any State whose request for accession has been granted on the tenth day following the deposit of its instrument of accession with the Government of Belgium, or on the date of entry into force of the Agreement pursuant to Article 67, paragraph 2, whichever is the later.

3. Until May 1st, 1975, accession may take place on a provisional basis under the conditions set out in Article 68.

ARTICLE 72

1. This Agreement shall be open for accession by the European Communities.

2. This Agreement shall not in any way impede the further implementation of the treaties establishing the European Communities.

ARTICLE 73

This Agreement may at any time be amended by the Governing Board, acting by unanimity. Such amendment shall come into force in a manner determined by the Governing Board, acting by unanimity and making provision for Participating Countries to comply with their respective constitutional procedures.

ARTICLE 74

This Agreement shall be subject to a general review after May 1st, 1980.

ARTICLE 75

The Government of Belgium shall notify all Participating Countries of the deposit of each notification of consent to be bound in accordance with Article 67, and of each instrument of accession, of the entry into force of this Agreement or any amendment thereto, of any denunciation thereof, and of any other declaration or notification received.

ARTICLE 76

The original of this Agreement, of which the English, French and German texts are equally authentic, shall be deposited with the Government of Belgium, and a certified copy thereof shall be furnished to each other Participating Country by the Government of Belgium.

ANNEX—EMERGENCY RESERVES

ARTICLE 1

1. Total oil stocks are measured according to the OECD and EEC definitions, revised as follows:

A. Stocks included:

Crude oil, major products and unfinished oils held
In refinery tanks.
In bulk terminals.
In pipeline tankage.
In barges.
In intercoastal tankers.
In oil tankers in port.
In inland ship bunkers.
In storage tank bottoms.
In working stocks.

By large consumers as required by law or otherwise controlled by Governments.

B. Stocks excluded:

(a) Crude oil not yet produced.

(b) Crude oil, major products and unfinished oils held

In pipelines.
In rail tank cars.
In truck tank cars.
In seagoing ships' bunkers.
In service stations and retail stores.
By other consumers.
In tankers at sea.
As military stocks.

2. That portion of oil stocks which can be credited toward each participating Country's emergency reserve commitment is its total oil stocks under the above definition minus those stocks which can be technically determined as being absolutely unavailable in even the most severe emergency. The Standing Group on Emergency Questions shall examine this concept and report on criteria for the measurement of absolutely unavailable stocks.

3. Until a decision has been taken on this matter, each Participating Country shall subtract 10 per cent from its total stocks in measuring its emergency reserves.

The Standing Group on Emergency Questions shall examine and report to the Management Committee on:

(a) the modalities of including naphtha for uses other than motor and aviation gasoline in the consumption against which stocks are measured,

(b) the possibility of creating common rules for the treatment of marine bunkers in an emergency, and of including marine bunkers in the consumption against which stocks are measured,

(c) the possibility of creating common rules concerning demand restraint for aviation bunkers,

(d) the possibility of crediting towards emergency reserve commitments some portion of oil at sea at the time of activation of emergency measures,

(e) the possibility of increasing supplies available in an emergency through savings in the distribution system.

ARTICLE 2

1. Fuel switching capacity is defined as normal oil consumption that may be replaced by other fuels in an emergency, provided that this capacity is subject to government control in an emergency, can be brought into operation within one month, and that secure supplies of the alternative fuel are available for use.

2. The supply of alternative fuel shall be expressed in terms of oil equivalent.

3. Stocks of an alternative fuel reserved for fuel switching purposes may be credited towards emergency reserve commitments insofar as they can be used during the period of self-sufficiency.

4. Stand-by production of an alternative fuel reserved for fuel switching purposes will be credited toward emergency reserve commitments on the same basis as stand-by oil production, subject to the provisions of Article 4 of this Annex.

5. The Standing Group on Emergency Questions shall examine and report to the Management Committee on

(a) the appropriateness of the time limit of one month mentioned in paragraph 1,

(b) the basis of accounting for the fuel switching capacity based on stocks of an alternative fuel, subject to the provisions of paragraph 3.

ARTICLE 3

A Participating Country may credit towards its emergency reserve commitment oil stocks in another country provided that the Government of that other country has an agreement with the Government of the Participating Country that it shall impose no impediment to the transfer of those stocks in an emergency to the Participating Country.

ARTICLE 4

1. Stand-by oil production is defined as a Participating Country's potential oil production in excess of normal oil production within its jurisdiction—

Which is subject to government control, and

Which can be brought into use during an emergency within the period of self-sufficiency.

2. The Standing Group on Emergency Questions shall examine and report to the Management Committee on

(a) the concept of and methods of measurement of stand-by oil production as referred to in paragraph 1,

(b) the appropriateness of "the period of self-sufficiency" as a time limit,

(c) the question of whether a given quantity of standby oil production is of greater value for purposes of emergency self-sufficiency than the same quantity of oil stocks, the amount of a possible credit for standby production, and the method of its calculation.

ARTICLE 5

Stand-by oil production available to a Participating Country within the jurisdiction of another country may be credited towards its emergency reserve commitment on the same basis as stand-by oil production within its own jurisdiction, subject to the provisions of Article 4 of this Annex provided that the Government of that other country has an agreement with the Government of the Participating Country that it shall impose no impediment to the supply of oil from that stand-by capacity to the Participating Country in an emergency.

ARTICLE 6

The Standing Group on Emergency Questions shall examine and report to the Management Committee on the possibility of crediting towards a Participating Country's emergency reserve commitment mentioned in Article 2, paragraph 2, of the Agreement, long term investments which have the effect of reducing the Participating Countries dependence on imported oil.

ARTICLE 7

1. The Standing Group on Emergency Questions shall examine and report to the Management Committee regarding the reference period set out in Article 2, paragraph 1, of the Agreement, in particular taking into account such factors as growth, seasonal variations in consumption and cyclical changes.

2. A decision by the Governing Board to change the definition of the reference period mentioned in paragraph 1 shall be taken by unanimity.

ARTICLE 8

The Standing Group on Emergency Questions shall examine and report to the Management Committee on all elements of Chapters I to IV of the Agreement to eliminate possible mathematical and statistical anomalies.

ARTICLE 9

The reports from the Standing Group on Emergency Questions on the matters mentioned in this Annex shall be submitted to the Management Committee by April 1st, 1975. The Management Committee shall make proposals, as appropriate, to the Governing Board, which acting by majority not later than July 1st, 1975, shall decide on these proposals, except as provided for in Article 7, paragraph 2 of this Annex.

3. Convention on Early Notification of a Nuclear Accident

Done at Vienna, September 26, 1986; Entered into force generally, October 27, 1986; Entered into force for the United States, October 20, 1988

CONVENTION ON EARLY NOTIFICATION OF A NUCLEAR ACCIDENT [1]

The States Parties to this Convention

AWARE that nuclear activities are being carried out in a number of States,

NOTING that comprehensive measures have been and are being take to ensure a high level of safety in nuclear activities, aimed at preventing nuclear accidents and minimizing the consequences of any such accident, should it occur,

DESIRING to strengthen further international co-operation in the safe development and use of nuclear energy,

CONVINCED of the need for States to provide relevant information about nuclear accidents as early as possible in order that transboundary radiological consequences can be minimized,

NOTING the usefulness of bilateral and multilateral arrangements on information exchange in this area,

HAVE AGREED AS FOLLOWS:

ARTICLE 1

SCOPE OF APPLICATION

1. This Convention shall apply in the event of any accident involving facilities or activities of a State Party or of persons or legal entities under its jurisdiction or control, referred to in paragraph 2 below, from which a release of radioactive material occurs or is likely to occur and which has resulted or may result in an international transboundary release that could be of radiological safety significance for another State.

2. The facilities and activities referred to in paragraph 1 are the following:

a. any nuclear reactor wherever located;

b. any nuclear fuel cycle facility;

c. any radioactive waste management facility;

d. the transport and storage of nuclear fuels or radioactive wastes;

e. the manufacture, use, storage, disposal and transport of radioisotopes for agricultural, industrial, medical and related scientific and research purposes; and

f. the use of radioisotopes for power generation in space objects.

---

[1] 1439 UNTS 175. For a list of states that are parties to the Convention, see Department of State publication, *Treaties in Force*.

ARTICLE 2

NOTIFICATION AND INFORMATION

In the event of an accident specified in article 1 (hereinafter referred to as a "nuclear accident"), the State Party referred to in that article shall:

a. forthwith notify, directly or though the International Atomic Energy Agency (hereinafter referred to as the "Agency"), those States which are or may be physically affected as specified in article 1 and the Agency of the nuclear accident, its nature, the time of its occurrence and its exact location where appropriate; and

b. promptly provide the States referred to in sub-paragraph (a), directly or through the Agency, and the Agency with such available information relevant to minimizing the radiological consequences in those States, as specified in article 5.

ARTICLE 3

OTHER NUCLEAR ACCIDENTS

With a view to minimizing the radiological consequences, States Parties may notify in the event of nuclear accidents other than those specified in article 1.

ARTICLE 4

FUNCTIONS OF THE AGENCY

The Agency shall:

a. forthwith inform States Parties, Member States, other States which are or may be physically affected as specified in article 1 and relevant international intergovernmental organizations (hereinafter referred to as "international organizations") of a notification received pursuant to sub-paragraph (a) of article 2; and

b. promptly provide any State Party, Member State or relevant international organization, upon request, with the information received pursuant to sub-paragraph (b) of article 2.

ARTICLE 5

INFORMATION TO BE PROVIDED

1. The information to be provided pursuant to sub-paragraph (b) of article 2 shall comprise the following data as then available to the notifying State Party:

a. the time, exact location where appropriate, and the nature of the nuclear accident;

b. the facility or activity involved;

c. the assumed or established cause and the foreseeable development of the nuclear accident relevant to the transboundary release of the radioactive materials;

d. the general characteristics of the radioactive release, including, as far as is practicable and appropriate, the nature, probable physical and chemical form and the quantity, composition and effective height of the radioactive release;

e. information on current and forecast meteorological and hydrological conditions, necessary for forecasting the transboundary release of the radioactive materials;

f. the results of environmental monitoring relevant to the transboundary release of the radioactive materials;

g. the off-site protective measures taken or planned;

h. the predicted behaviour over time of the radioactive release.

2. Such information shall be supplemented at appropriate intervals by further relevant information on the development of the emergency situation, including its foreseeable or actual termination.

3. Information received pursuant to subparagraph (b) of article 2 may used without restriction, except when such information is provided in confidence by the notifying State Party.

Article 6

Consultations

A State Party providing information pursuant to sub-paragraph (b) of article 2 shall, as far as is reasonably practicable, respond promptly to a request for further information or consultations sought by an affected State Party with a view to minimizing the radiological consequences in that State.

Article 7

Competent authorities and points of contact

1. Each State Party shall make known to the Agency and to other States Parties, directly or through the Agency, its competent authorities and point of contact responsible for issuing and receiving the notification and information referred to in article 2. Such points of contact and a focal point within the Agency shall be available continuously.

2. Each State Party shall promptly inform the Agency of any changes that may occur in the information referred to in paragraph 1.

3. The Agency shall maintain an up-to-date list of such national authorities and points of contact as well as points of contact of relevant international organizations and shall provide it to States Parties and Member States and to relevant international organizations.

Article 8

Assistance to States Parties

The Agency shall, in accordance with its Statute and upon a request of a State Party which does not have nuclear activities itself and borders on a State having an active nuclear programme but not Party, conduct investigations into the feasibility and establishment of an appropriate radiation monitoring system in order to facilitate the achievement of the objectives of this Convention.

ARTICLE 9

BILATERAL AND MULTILATERAL ARRANGEMENTS

In furtherance of their mutual interests, States Parties may consider, where deemed appropriate, the conclusion of bilateral or multilateral arrangements relating to the subject matter of this Convention.

ARTICLE 10

RELATIONSHIP TO OTHER INTERNATIONAL AGREEMENTS

This Convention shall not affect the reciprocal rights and obligations of State Parties under existing international agreements which relate to the matters covered by this Convention, or under future international agreements concluded in accordance with the object and purpose of this Convention.

ARTICLE 11

SETTLEMENT OF DISPUTES

1. In the event of a dispute between States Parties, or between a State Party and the Agency, concerning the interpretation or application of this Convention, the parties to the dispute shall consult with a view to the settlement of the dispute by negotiation or by any other peaceful means of settling disputes acceptable to them.

2. If a dispute of this character between States Parties cannot be settled within one year from the request for consultation pursuant to paragraph 1, it shall, at the request of any party to such a dispute, be submitted to arbitration or referred to the International Court of Justice for decision. Where a dispute is submitted to arbitration, if, within six months from the date of the request, the parties to the dispute are unable to agree on the organization of the arbitration, a party may request the President of the International Court of Justice or the Secretary- General of the United Nations to appoint one or more arbitrators. In cases of conflicting requests by the parties to the dispute, the request to the Secretary-General of the United Nations shall have priority.

3. When signing, ratifying, accepting, approving or acceding to this Convention, a State may declare that it does not consider itself bound by either or both of the dispute settlement procedures provided for in paragraph 2. The other States Parties shall not be bound by a dispute settlement procedure provided for in paragraph 2 with respect to a State Party for which such a declaration is in force.

4. A State Party which has made a declaration in accordance with paragraph 3 may at any time withdraw it by notification to the depositary.

Article 12

Entry into force

1. This Convention shall be open for signature by all States and Namibia, represented by the United Nations Council for Namibia, at the Headquarters of the International Atomic Energy Agency in Vienna and at the Headquarters of the United Nations in New York, from 26 September 1986 and 6 October 1986 respectively, until its entry into force or for twelve months, whichever period is longer.

2. A State and Namibia, represented by the United Nations Council for Namibia, may express its consent to be bound by this Convention either by signature, or be deposit of an instrument of ratification, acceptance or approval following signature made subject to ratification, acceptance or approval, or by deposit of an instrument of accession. The instruments of ratification, acceptance, approval or accession shall be deposited with the depositary.

3. This Convention shall enter into force thirty days after consent to be bound has been expressed by three States.

4. For each State expressing consent to be bound by this Convention after its entry into force, this Convention shall enter into force for that State thirty days after the date of expression of consent.

5.

a. This Convention shall be open for accession, as provided for in this article, by international organizations and regional integration organizations constituted by sovereign States, which have competence in respect of the negotiation, conclusion and application of international agreements in matters covered by this Convention.

b. In matters within their competence such organizations shall, on their own behalf, exercise the rights and fulfil the obligations which this Convention attributes to States Parties.

c. When depositing its instrument of accession, such an organization shall communicate to the depositary a declaration indicating the extent of its competence in respect of matters covered by this Convention.

d. Such an organization shall not hold any vote additional to those of its Member States.

Article 13

Provisional application

A State may, upon signature or at any later date before this Convention enters into force for it, declare that it will apply this Convention provisionally.

Article 14

Amendments

1. A State Party may propose amendments to this Convention. The proposed amendment shall be submitted to the depositary who shall circulate it immediately to all other States Parties.

2. If a majority of the States Parties request the depositary to convene a conference to consider the proposed amendments, the depositary shall invite all States Parties to attend such a conference to begin not sooner than thirty days after the invitations are issued. Any amendment adopted at the conference by a two-thirds majority of all States Parties shall be laid down in a protocol which is open to signature in Vienna and New York by all States Parties.

3. The protocol shall enter into force thirty days after consent to be bound has been expressed by three States. For each State expressing consent to be bound by the protocol after its entry into force, the protocol shall enter into force for the State thirty days after the date of expression of consent.

ARTICLE 15

DENUNCIATION

1. A State Party may denounce this Convention by written notification to the depositary.

2. Denunciation shall take effect on year following the date on which the notification is received by the depositary.

ARTICLE 16

DEPOSITARY

1. The Director General of the Agency shall be the depositary of this Convention.

2. The Director General of the Agency shall promptly notify States Parties and all other States of:

a. each signature of this Convention or any protocol of amendment;

b. each deposit of an instrument of ratification, acceptance, approval or accession concerning this Convention of any protocol of amendment;

c. any declaration or withdrawal thereof in accordance with article 11;

d. any declaration of provisional application of this Convention in accordance with article 13;

e. the entry into force of this Convention and of any amendment thereto; and

f. any denunciation made under article 15.

ARTICLE 17

AUTHENTIC TEXTS AND CERTIFIED COPIES

The original of this Convention, of which the Arabic, Chinese, English, French, Russian and Spanish texts are equally authentic, shall be deposited with the Director General of the International Atomic Energy Agency who shall send certified copies to States Parties and all other States.

IN WITNESS WHEREOF the undersigned, being duly authorized, have signed this Convention, open for signature as provided for in paragraph 1 of article 12.

ADOPTED by the General Conference of the International Atomic Energy Agency meeting in special session at Vienna on the twenty-sixth day of September one thousand nine hundred and eighty-six.

4. Convention on Assistance in the Case of a Nuclear Accident or Radiological Emergency

Done at Vienna, September 26, 1986; Entered into force generally, February 26, 1987; Entered into force for the United States, October 20, 1988

CONVENTION ON ASSISTANCE IN THE CASE OF A NUCLEAR ACCIDENT OR RADIOLOGICAL EMERGENCY [1]

The States Parties to this Convention

AWARE that nuclear activities are being carried out in a number of States,

NOTING that comprehensive measures have been and are being taken to ensure a high level of safety in nuclear activities, aimed at preventing nuclear accidents and minimizing the consequences of any such accident, should it occur,

DESIRING to strengthen further international co-operation in the safe development and use of nuclear energy,

CONVINCED of the need for an international framework which will facilitate the prompt provision of assistance in the event of a nuclear accident or radiological emergency to mitigate its consequences,

NOTING the usefulness of bilateral and multilateral arrangements on mutual assistance in this area,

NOTING the activities of the International Atomic Energy Agency in developing guidelines for mutual emergency assistance arrangements in connection with a nuclear accident or radiological emergency,

HAVE AGREED AS FOLLOWS:

ARTICLE 1

GENERAL PROVISIONS

1. The States Parties shall cooperate between themselves and with the International Atomic Energy Agency (hereinafter referred to as the "Agency") in accordance with the provisions of this Convention to facilitate prompt assistance in the event of a nuclear accident or radiological emergency to minimize its consequences and to protect life, property and the environment from the effects of radioactive releases.

2. To facilitate such cooperation States Parties may agree on bilateral or multilateral arrangements or, where appropriate, a combination of these, for preventing or minimizing injury and damage which may result in the event of a nuclear accident or radiological emergency.

[1] 1457 UNTS 133. For a list of states that are parties to the Convention, see Department of State publication, *Treaties in Force.*

3. The States Parties request the Agency, acting within the framework of its Statute, to use its best endeavours in accordance with the provisions of this Convention to promote, facilitate and support the cooperation between States Parties provided for in this Convention.

Article 2

Provision of assistance

1. If a State Party needs assistance in the event of a nuclear accident or radiological emergency, whether or not such accident or emergency originates within its territory, jurisdiction or control, it may call for such assistance from any other State Party, directly or through the Agency, and from the Agency, or, where appropriate, from other international intergovernmental organizations (hereinafter referred to as "international organizations").

2. A State Party requesting assistance shall specify the scope and type of assistance required and, where practicable, provide the assisting party with such information as may be necessary for that party to determine the extent to which it is able to meet the request. In the event that it is not practicable for the requesting State Party to specify the scope and type of assistance required, the requesting State Party and the assisting party shall, in consultation, decide upon the scope and type of assistance required.

3. Each State Party to which a request for such assistance is directed shall promptly decide and notify the requesting Slate Party, directly or through the Agency, whether it is in a position to render the assistance requested, and the scope and terms of the assistance that might be rendered.

4. States Parties shall, within the limits of their capabilities, identify and notify the Agency of experts, equipment and materials which could be made available for the provision of assistance to other States Parties in the event of a nuclear accident or radiological emergency as well as the terms, especially financial, under which such assistance could be provided.

5. Any State Party may request assistance relating to medical treatment or temporary relocation into the territory of another State Party of people involved in a nuclear accident or radiological emergency.

6. The Agency shall respond, in accordance with its Statute and as provided for in this Convention, to a requesting State Party's or a Member State's request for assistance in the event of a nuclear accident or radiological emergency by:

   1. making available appropriate resources allocated for this purpose;
   2. transmitting promptly the request to other States and international organizations which, according to the Agency's information, may possess the necessary resources; and
   3. if so requested by the requesting State, co-ordinating the assistance at the international level which may thus become available.

Article 3

Direction and control of assistance

Unless otherwise agreed:

1. the overall direction, control, co-ordination and supervision of the assistance shall be the responsibility within its territory of the requesting State. The assisting party should, where the assistance involves personnel, designate in consultation with the requesting State, the person who should be in charge of and retain immediate operational supervision over the personnel and the equipment provided by it. The designated person should exercise such supervision in cooperation with the appropriate authorities of the requesting State;
2. the requesting State shall provide, to the extent of its capabilities, local facilities and services for the proper and effective administration of the assistance. It shall also ensure the protection of personnel, equipment and materials brought into its territory by or on behalf of the assisting party for such purpose;
3. ownership of equipment and materials provided by either party during the periods of assistance shall be unaffected, and their return shall be ensured;
4. a State Party providing assistance in response to a request under paragraph 5 of article 2 shall co-ordinate that assistance within its territory.

Article 4

Competent authorities and points of contact

1. Each State Party shall make known to the Agency and to other States Parties, directly or through the Agency, its competent authorities and point of contact authorized to make and receive requests for and to accept offers of assistance. Such points of contact and a focal point within the Agency shall be available continuously.

2. Each State Party shall promptly inform the Agency of any changes that may occur in the information referred to in paragraph 1.

3. The Agency shall regularly and expeditiously provide to States Parties, Member States and relevant international organizations the information referred to in paragraphs 1 and 2.

Article 5

Functions of the Agency

The States Parties request the Agency, in accordance with paragraph 3 of article 1 and without prejudice to other provisions of this Convention, to:

1. collect and disseminate to States Parties and Member States information concerning:
    1. experts, equipment and materials which could be made available in the event of nuclear accidents or radiological emergencies;

2. methodologies, techniques and available results of research relating to response to nuclear accidents or radiological emergencies;

2. assist a State Party or a Member State when requested in any of the following or other appropriate matters:

1. preparing both emergency plans in the case of nuclear accidents and radiological emergencies and the appropriate legislation;

2. developing appropriate training programmes for personnel to deal with nuclear accidents and radiological emergencies;

3. transmitting requests for assistance and relevant information in the event of a nuclear accident or radiological emergency;

4. developing appropriate radiation monitoring programmes, procedures and standards;

5. conducting investigations into the feasibility of establishing appropriate radiation monitoring systems;

3. make available to a State Party or a Member State requesting assistance in the event of a nuclear accident or radiological emergency appropriate resources allocated for the purpose of conducting an initial assessment of the accident or emergency;

4. offer its good offices to the States Parties and Member States in the event of a nuclear accident or radiological emergency;

5. establish and maintain liaison with relevant international organizations for the purposes of obtaining and exchanging relevant information and data, and make a list of such organizations available to States Parties, Member States and the aforementioned organizations.

Article 6

Confidentiality and public statements

1. The requesting State and the assisting party shall protect the confidentiality of any confidential information that becomes available to either of them in connection with the assistance in the event of a nuclear accident or radiological emergency. Such information shall be used exclusively for the purpose of the assistance agreed upon.

2. The assisting party shall make every effort to coordinate with the requesting State before releasing information to the public on the assistance provided in connection with a nuclear accident or radiological emergency.

Article 7

Reimbursement of costs

1. An assisting party may offer assistance without costs to the requesting Slate. When considering whether to offer assistance on such a basis, the assisting party shall take into account:

1. the nature of the nuclear accident or radiological emergency;

2. the place of origin of the nuclear accident or radiological emergency;

3. the needs of developing countries;

4. the particular needs of countries without nuclear facilities; and

5. any other relevant factors.

2. When assistance is provided wholly or partly on a reimbursement basis, the requesting State shall reimburse the assisting party for the costs incurred for the services rendered by persons or organizations acting on its behalf, and for all expenses in connection with the assistance to the extent that such expenses are not directly defrayed by the requesting State. Unless otherwise agreed, reimbursement shall be provided promptly after the assisting party has presented its request for reimbursement to the requesting State, and in respect of costs other than local costs, shall be freely transferrable.

3. Notwithstanding paragraph 2, the assisting party may at any time waive, or agree to the postponement of, the reimbursement in whole or in part. In considering such waiver or postponement, assisting parties shall give due consideration to the needs of developing countries.

Article 8

Privileges, immunities and facilities

1. The requesting State shall afford to personnel of the assisting party and personnel acting on its behalf the necessary privileges, immunities and facilities for the performance of their assistance functions.

2. The requesting State shall afford the following privileges and immunities to personnel of the assisting party or personnel acting on its behalf who have been duly notified to and accepted by the requesting State:

1. immunity from arrest, detention and legal process, including criminal, civil and administrative jurisdiction, of the requesting State, in respect of acts or omissions in the performance of their duties; and

2. exemption from taxation, duties or other charges, except those which are normally incorporated in the price of goods or paid for services rendered, in respect of the performance of their assistance functions.

3. The requesting State shall:

1. afford the assisting party exemption from taxation, duties or other charges on the equipment and property brought into the territory of the requesting State by the assisting party for the purpose of the assistance; and

2. provide immunity from seizure, attachment or requisition of such equipment and property.

4. The requesting State shall ensure the return of such equipment and property. If requested by the assisting party, the requesting State shall arrange, to the extent it is able to

do so, for the necessary decontamination of recoverable equipment involved in the assistance before its return.

5. The requesting State shall facilitate the entry into, stay in and departure from its national territory of personnel notified pursuant to paragraph 2 and of equipment and property involved in the assistance.

6. Nothing in this article shall require the requesting State to provide its nationals or permanent residents with the privileges and immunities provided for in the foregoing paragraphs.

7. Without prejudice to the privileges and immunities, all beneficiaries enjoying such privileges and immunities under this article have a duty to respect the laws and regulations of the requesting State. They shall also have the duty not to interfere in the domestic affairs of the requesting State.

8. Nothing in this article shall prejudice rights and obligations with respect to privileges and immunities afforded pursuant to other international agreements or the rules of customary international law.

9. When signing, ratifying, accepting, approving or acceding to this Convention, a State may declare that it does not consider itself bound in whole or in part by paragraphs 2 and 3.

10. A State Party which has made a declaration in accordance with paragraph 9 may at any time withdraw it by notification to the depositary.

Article 9

Transit of personnel, equipment and property

Each State Party shall, at the request of the requesting State or the assisting party, seek to facilitate the transit through its territory of duly notified personnel, equipment and property involved in the assistance to and from the requesting State.

Article 10

Claims and compensation

1. The States Parties shall closely cooperate in order to facilitate the settlement of legal proceedings and claims under this article.

2. Unless otherwise agreed, a requesting State shall in respect of death or of injury to persons, damage to or loss of property, or damage to the environment caused within its territory or other area under its jurisdiction or control in the course of providing the assistance requested:

1. not bring any legal proceedings against the assisting party or persons or other legal entities acting on its behalf;

2. assume responsibility for dealing with legal proceedings and claims brought by third parties against the assisting party or against persons or other legal entities acting on its behalf;

3. hold the assisting party or persons or other legal entities acting on its behalf harmless in respect of legal proceedings and claims referred to in sub-paragraph (b); and

4. compensate the assisting party or persons or other legal entities acting on its behalf for:

1. death of or injury to personnel of the assisting party or persons acting on its behalf;

2. loss of or damage to non-consumable equipment or materials related to the assistance;

except in cases of wilful misconduct by the individuals who caused the death, injury, loss or damage.

3. This article shall not prevent compensation or indemnity available under any applicable international agreement or national law of any State.

4. Nothing in this article shall require the requesting State to apply paragraph 2 in whole or in part to its nationals or permanent residents.

5. When signing, ratifying, accepting, approving or acceding to this Convention, a State may declare:

1. that it does not consider itself bound in whole or in part by paragraph 2;

2. that it will not apply paragraph 2 in whole or in part in cases of gross negligence by the individuals who caused the death, injury, loss or damage.

6. A State Party which has made a declaration in accordance with paragraph 5 may at any time withdraw it by notification to the depositary.

Article 11

Termination of assistance

The requesting State or the assisting party may at any time, after appropriate consultations and by notification in writing, request the termination of assistance received or provided under this Convention. Once such a request has been made, the parties involved shall consult with each other to make arrangements for the proper conclusion of the assistance.

Article 12

Relationship to other international agreements

This Convention shall not affect the reciprocal rights and obligations of States Parties under existing international agreements which relate to the matters covered by this Convention, or under future international agreements concluded in accordance with the object and purpose of this Convention.

Article 13

Settlement of disputes

1. In the event of a dispute between States Parties, or between a State Party and the Agency, concerning the interpretation or application of this Convention, the parties to the dispute shall consult with a view to the settlement of the dispute by negotiation or by any other peaceful means of settling disputes acceptable to them.

2. If a dispute of this character between States Parties cannot be settled within one year from the request for consultation pursuant to paragraph 1, it shall, at the request of any party to such dispute,

be submitted to arbitration or referred to the International Court of Justice for decision. Where a dispute is submitted to arbitration, if, within six months from the date of the request, the parties to the dispute are unable to agree on the organization of the arbitration, a party may request the President of The International Court of Justice or the Secretary-General of the United Nations to appoint one or more arbitrators. In cases of conflicting requests by the parties to the dispute, the request to the Secretary-General of the United Nations shall have priority.

3. When signing, ratifying, accepting, approving or acceding to this Convention, a State may declare that it does not consider itself bound by either or both of the dispute settlement procedures provided for in paragraph 2. The other States Parties shall not be bound by a dispute settlement procedure provided for in paragraph 2 with respect to a State Party for which such a declaration is in force.

4. A State Party which has made a declaration in accordance with paragraph 3 may at any time withdraw it by notification to the depositary.

Article 14

Entry into force

1. This Convention shall be open for signature by all States and Namibia, represented by the United Nations Council for Namibia, at the Headquarters of the International Atomic Energy Agency in Vienna and at the Headquarters of the United Nations in New York, from 26 September 1986 and 6 October 1986 respectively, until its entry into force or for twelve months, whichever period is longer.

2. A State and Namibia, represented by the United Nations Council for Namibia, may express its consent to be bound by this Convention either by signature, or by deposit of an instrument of ratification, acceptance or approval following signature made subject to ratification, acceptance or approval, or by deposit of an instrument of accession. The instruments of ratification, acceptance, approval or accession shall be deposited with the depositary.

3. This Convention shall enter into force thirty days after consent to be bound has been expressed by three States.

4. For each State expressing consent to be bound by this Convention after its entry into force, this Convention shall enter into force for that State thirty days after the date of expression of consent.

5.

> 1. This Convention shall be open for accession, as provided for in this article, by international organizations and regional integration organizations constituted by sovereign States, which have competence in respect of the negotiation, conclusion and application of international agreements in matters covered by this Convention.
>
> 2. In matters within their competence such organizations shall, on their own behalf, exercise the rights and fulfil the obligations which this Convention attributes to States Parties.

3. When depositing its instrument of accession, such an organization shall communicate to the depositary a declaration indicating the extent of its competence in respect of matters covered by this Convention.

4. Such an organization shall not hold any vote additional to those of its Member States.

ARTICLE 15

PROVISIONAL APPLICATION

A State may, upon signature or at any later date before this Convention enters into force for it, declare that it will apply this Convention provisionally.

ARTICLE 16

AMENDMENTS

1. A State Party may propose amendments to this Convention. The proposed amendment shall be submitted to the depositary who shall circulate it immediately to all other States Parties.

2. If a majority of the States Parties request the depositary to convene a conference to consider the proposed amendments, the depositary shall invite all States Parties to attend such a conference to begin not sooner than thirty days after the invitations are issued. Any amendment adopted at the conference by a two-thirds majority of all States Parties shall be laid down in a protocol which is open to signature in Vienna and New York by all States Parties.

3. The protocol shall enter into force thirty days after consent to be bound has been expressed by three States. For each State expressing consent to be bound by the protocol after its entry into force, the protocol shall enter into force for that State thirty days after the date of expression of consent.

ARTICLE 17

DENUNCIATION

1. A State Party may denounce this Convention by written notification to the depositary.

2. Denunciation shall take effect one year following the date on which the notification is received by the depositary.

ARTICLE 18

DEPOSITARY

1. The Director General of the Agency shall be the depositary of this Convention.

2. The Director General of the Agency shall promptly notify States Parties and all other States of:

1. each signature of this Convention or any protocol of amendment;

2. each deposit of an instrument of ratification, acceptance, approval or accession concerning this Convention or any protocol of amendment;

3. any declaration or withdrawal thereof in accordance with articles 8, 10 and 13;

4. any declaration of provisional application of this Convention in accordance with article 15;

5. the entry into force of this Convention and of any amendment thereto; and

6. any denunciation made under article 17.

ARTICLE 19

AUTHENTIC TEXTS AND CERTIFIED COPIES

The original of this Convention, of which the Arabic, Chinese, English, French, Russian and Spanish texts are equally authentic, shall be deposited with the Director General of the International Atomic Energy Agency who shall send certified copies to States Parties and all other States.

IN WITNESS WHEREOF the undersigned, being duly authorized, have signed this Convention, open for signature as provided for in paragraph 1 of article 14.

ADOPTED by the General Conference of the International Atomic Energy Agency meeting in special session at Vienna on the twenty-sixth day of September one thousand nine hundred and eighty-six.

5. Joint Convention on the Safety of Spent Fuel Management and on the Safety of Radioactive Waste Management

Done at Vienna, September 5, 1997; Entered into force generally, June 18, 2001; Ratification advised by the Senate, April 2, 2003; Entered into force for the United States, July 14, 2003

JOINT CONVENTION ON THE SAFETY OF SPENT FUEL MANAGEMENT AND ON THE SAFETY OF RADIOACTIVE WASTE MANAGEMENT [1]

PREAMBLE

The Contracting Parties

(i) RECOGNIZING that the operation of nuclear reactors generates spent fuel and radioactive waste and that other applications of nuclear technologies also generate radioactive waste;

(ii) RECOGNIZING that the same safety objectives apply both to spent fuel and radioactive waste management;

(iii) REAFFIRMING the importance to the international community of ensuring that sound practices are planned and implemented for the safety of spent fuel and radioactive waste management;

(iv) RECOGNIZING the importance of informing the public on issues regarding the safety of spent fuel and radioactive waste management;

(v) DESIRING to promote an effective nuclear safety culture worldwide;

(vi) REAFFIRMING that the ultimate responsibility for ensuring the safety of spent fuel and radioactive waste management rests with the State;

(vii) RECOGNIZING that the definition of a fuel cycle policy rests with the State, some States considering spent fuel as a valuable resource that may be reprocessed, others electing to dispose of it;

(viii) RECOGNIZING that spent fuel and radioactive waste excluded from the present Convention because they are within military or defence programmes should be managed in accordance with the objectives stated in this Convention;

(ix) AFFIRMING the importance of international co-operation in enhancing the safety of spent fuel and radioactive waste management through bilateral and multilateral mechanisms, and through this incentive Convention;

(x) MINDFUL of the needs of developing countries, and in particular the least developed countries, and of States with economies in transition and of the need to facilitate existing mechanisms to assist in the fulfillment of their rights and obligations set out in this incentive Convention;

---

[1] For a list of states that are parties to the Convention, see Department of State publication, *Treaties in Force*.

(xi) CONVINCED that radioactive waste should, as far as is compatible with the safety of the management of such material, be disposed of in the State in which it was generated, whilst recognizing that, in certain circumstances, safe and efficient management of spent fuel and radioactive waste might be fostered through agreements among Contracting parties to use facilities in one of them for the benefit of the other Parties, particularly where waste originates from joint projects;

(xii) RECOGNIZING that any State has the right to ban import into its territory of foreign spent fuel and radioactive waste;

(xiii) KEEPING in mind the Convention on Nuclear Safety (1994), the Convention on Early Notification of a Nuclear Accident (1986), the Convention on Assistance in the Case of a Nuclear Accident or Radiological Emergency (1986), the Convention on the Physical Protection of Nuclear Material (1980), the Convention on the Prevention of Marine Pollution by Dumping of Wastes and Other Matter as amended (1994) and other relevant international instruments;

(xiv) KEEPING in mind the principles contained in the interagency "International Basic Safety Standards for Protection against Ionizing Radiation and for the Safety of Radiation Sources" (1996), in the IAEA Safety Fundamentals entitled "The Principles of Radioactive Waste Management" (1995), and in the existing international standards relating to the safety of the transport of radioactive materials;

(xv) RECALLING Chapter 22 of Agenda 21 by the United Nations Conference on Environment and Development in Rio de Janeiro adopted in 1992, which reaffirms the paramount importance of the safe and environmentally sound management of radioactive waste;

(xvi) RECOGNIZING the desirability of strengthening the international control system applying specifically to radioactive materials as referred to in Article 1(3) of the Basel Convention on the Control of Transboundary Movements of Hazardous Wastes and Their Disposal (1989);

HAVE AGREED AS FOLLOWS:

CHAPTER 1. OBJECTIVES, DEFINITIONS AND SCOPE OF APPLICATION

ARTICLE 1. OBJECTIVES

The objectives of this Convention are:

(i) to achieve and maintain a high level of safety worldwide in spent fuel and radioactive waste management, through the enhancement of national measures and international co-operation, including where appropriate, safety-related technical co-operation;

(ii) to ensure that during all stages of spent fuel and radioactive waste management there are effective defenses against potential hazards so that individuals, society and the environment are protected from harmful effects of ionizing radiation, now and in the future, in such a way that the needs and aspirations of the present generation are met without compromising the ability of future generations to meet their needs and aspirations;

(iii) to prevent accidents with radiological consequences and to mitigate their consequences should they occur during any stage of spent fuel or radioactive waste management.

Article 2. Definitions

For the purposes of this Convention:

(a) "closure" means the completion of all operations at some time after the emplacement of spent fuel or radioactive waste in a disposal facility. This includes the final engineering or other work required to bring the facility to a condition that will be safe in the long term;

(b) "decommissioning" means all steps leading to the release of a nuclear facility, other than a disposal facility, from regulatory control. These steps include the processes of decontamination and dismantling;

(c) "discharges" means planned and controlled releases into the environment, as a legitimate practice, within limits authorized by the regulatory body, of liquid or gaseous radioactive materials that originate from regulated nuclear facilities during normal operation;

(d) "disposal" means the emplacement of spent fuel or radioactive waste in an appropriate facility without the intention of retrieval;

(e) "licence" means any authorization, permission or certification granted by a regulatory body to carry out any activity related to management of spent fuel or of radioactive waste;

(f) "nuclear facility" means a civilian facility and its associated land, buildings and equipment in which radioactive materials are produced, processed, used, handled, stored or disposed of on such a scale that consideration of safety is required;

(g) "operating lifetime" means the period during which a spent fuel or a radioactive waste management facility is used for its intended purpose. In the case of a disposal facility, the period begins when spent fuel or radioactive waste is first emplaced in the facility and ends upon closure of the facility;

(h) "radioactive waste" means radioactive material in gaseous, liquid or solid form for which no further use is foreseen by the Contracting Party or by a natural or legal person whose decision is accepted by the Contracting Party, and which is controlled as radioactive waste by a regulatory body under the legislative and regulatory framework of the Contracting Party;

(i) "radioactive waste management" means all activities, including decommissioning activities, that relate to the handling, pretreatment, treatment, conditioning, storage, or disposal of radioactive waste, excluding off-site transportation. It may also involve discharges;

(j) "radioactive waste management facility" means any facility or installation the primary purpose of which is radioactive waste management, including a nuclear facility in the process of being decommissioned only if it is designated by the Contracting Party as a radioactive waste management facility;

(k) "regulatory body" means any body or bodies given the legal authority by the Contracting Party to regulate any aspect of the safety of spent fuel or radioactive waste management including the granting of licences;

(l) "reprocessing" means a process or operation, the purpose of which is to extract radioactive isotopes from spent fuel for further use;

(m) "sealed source" means radioactive material that is permanently sealed in a capsule or closely bonded and in a solid form, excluding reactor fuel elements;

(n) "spent fuel" means nuclear fuel that has been irradiated in and permanently removed from a reactor core;

(o) "spent fuel management" means all activities that relate to the handling or storage of spent fuel, excluding off-site transportation. It may also involve discharges;

(p) "spent fuel management facility" means any facility or installation the primary purpose of which is spent fuel management;

(q) "State of destination" means a State to which a transboundary movement is planned or takes place;

(r) "State of origin" means a State from which a transboundary movement is planned to be initiated or is initiated;

(s) "State of transit" means any State, other than a State of origin or a State of destination, through whose territory a transboundary movement is planned or takes place;

(t) "storage" means the holding of spent fuel or of radioactive waste in a facility that provides for its containment, with the intention of retrieval;

(u) "transboundary movement" means any shipment of spent fuel or of radioactive waste from a State of origin to a State of destination.

Article 3. Scope of Application

1. This Convention shall apply to the safety of spent fuel management when the spent fuel results from the operation of civilian nuclear reactors. Spent fuel held at reprocessing facilities as part of a reprocessing activity is not covered in the scope of this Convention unless the Contracting Party declares reprocessing to be part of spent fuel management.

2. This Convention shall also apply to the safety of radioactive waste management when the radioactive waste results from civilian applications. However, this Convention shall not apply to waste that contains only naturally occurring radioactive materials and that does not originate from the nuclear fuel cycle, unless it constitutes a disused sealed source or it is declared as radioactive waste for the purposes of this Convention by the Contracting Party.

3. This Convention shall not apply to the safety of management of spent fuel or radioactive waste within military or defence programmes, unless declared as spent fuel or radioactive waste for the purposes of this Convention by the Contracting Party. However, this Convention shall apply to the safety of management of spent

fuel and radioactive waste from military or defence programmes if and when such materials are transferred permanently to and managed within exclusively civilian programmes.

4. This Convention shall also apply to discharges as provided for in Articles 4, 7, 11, 14, 24 and 26.

Chapter 2. Safety of Spent Fuel Management

Article 4. General Safety Requirements

Each Contracting Party shall take the appropriate steps to ensure that at all stages of spent fuel management, individuals, society and the environment are adequately protected against radiological hazards. In so doing, each Contracting Party shall take the appropriate steps to:

(i) ensure that criticality and removal of residual heat generated during spent fuel management are adequately addressed;

(ii) ensure that the generation of radioactive waste associated with spent fuel management is kept to the minimum practicable, consistent with the type of fuel cycle policy adopted;

(iii) take into account interdependencies among the different steps in spent fuel management;

(iv) provide for effective protection of individuals, society and the environment, by applying at the national level suitable protective methods as approved by the regulatory body, in the framework of its national legislation which has due regard to internationally endorsed criteria and standards;

(v) take into account the biological, chemical and other hazards that may be associated with spent fuel management;

(vi) strive to avoid actions that impose reasonably predictable impacts on future generations greater than those permitted for the current generation;

(vii) aim to avoid imposing undue burdens on future generations.

Article 5. Existing Facilities

Each Contracting Party shall take the appropriate steps to review the safety of any spent fuel management facility existing at the time the Convention enters into force for that Contracting Party and to ensure that, if necessary, all reasonably practicable improvements are made to upgrade the safety of such a facility.

Article 6. Siting of Proposed Facilities

1. Each Contracting Party shall take the appropriate steps to ensure that procedures are established and implemented for a proposed spent fuel management facility:

(i) to evaluate all relevant site-related factors likely to affect the safety of such a facility during its operating lifetime;

(ii) to evaluate the likely safety impact of such a facility on individuals, society and the environment;

(iii) to make information on the safety of such a facility available to members of the public;

(iv) to consult Contracting Parties in the vicinity of such a facility, insofar as they are likely to be affected by that facility, and provide them, upon their request, with general data relating to the facility to enable them to evaluate the likely safety impact of the facility upon their territory.

2. In so doing, each Contracting Party shall take the appropriate steps to ensure that such facilities shall not have unacceptable effects on other Contracting Parties by being sited in accordance with the general safety requirements of Article 4.

ARTICLE 7. DESIGN AND CONSTRUCTION OF FACILITIES

Each Contracting Party shall take the appropriate steps to ensure that:

(i) the design and construction of a spent fuel management facility provide for suitable measures to limit possible radiological impacts on individuals, society and the environment, including those from discharges or uncontrolled releases;

(ii) at the design stage, conceptual plans and, as necessary, technical provisions for the decommissioning of a spent fuel management facility are taken into account;

(iii) the technologies incorporated in the design and construction of a spent fuel management facility are supported by experience, testing or analysis.

ARTICLE 8. ASSESSMENT OF SAFETY OF FACILITIES

Each Contracting Party shall take the appropriate steps to ensure that:

(i) before construction of a spent fuel management facility, a systematic safety assessment and an environmental assessment appropriate to the hazard presented by the facility and covering its operating lifetime shall be carried out;

(ii) before the operation of a spent fuel management facility, updated and detailed versions of the safety assessment and of the environmental assessment shall be prepared when deemed necessary to complement the assessments referred to in paragraph (i).

ARTICLE 9. OPERATION OF FACILITIES

Each Contracting Party shall take the appropriate steps to ensure that:

(i) the licence to operate a spent fuel management facility is based upon appropriate assessments as specified in Article 8 and is conditional on the completion of a commissioning programme demonstrating that the facility, as constructed, is consistent with design and safety requirements;

(ii) operational limits and conditions derived from tests, operational experience and the assessments, as specified in Article 8, are defined and revised as necessary;

(iii) operation, maintenance, monitoring, inspection and testing of a spent fuel management facility are conducted in accordance with established procedures;

(iv) engineering and technical support in all safety-related fields are available throughout the operating lifetime of a spent fuel management facility;

(v) incidents significant to safety are reported in a timely manner by the holder of the licence to the regulatory body;

(vi) programmes to collect and analyse relevant operating experience are established and that the results are acted upon, where appropriate;

(vii) decommissioning plans for a spent fuel management facility are prepared and updated, as necessary, using information obtained during the operating lifetime of that facility, and are reviewed by the regulatory body.

ARTICLE 10. DISPOSAL OF SPENT FUEL

If, pursuant to its own legislative and regulatory framework, a Contracting Party has designated spent fuel for disposal, the disposal of such spent fuel shall be in accordance with the obligations of Chapter 3 relating to the disposal of radioactive waste.

CHAPTER 3. SAFETY OF RADIOACTIVE WASTE MANAGEMENT

ARTICLE 11. GENERAL SAFETY REQUIREMENTS

Each Contracting Party shall take the appropriate steps to ensure that at all stages of radioactive waste management individuals, society and the environment are adequately protected against radiological and other hazards.

In so doing, each Contracting Party shall take the appropriate steps to:

(i) ensure that criticality and removal of residual heat generated during radioactive waste management are adequately addressed;

(ii) ensure that the generation of radioactive waste is kept to the minimum practicable;

(iii) take into account interdependencies among the different steps in radioactive waste management;

(iv) provide for effective protection of individuals, society and the environment, by applying at the national level suitable protective methods as approved by the regulatory body, in the framework of its national legislation which has due regard to internationally endorsed criteria and standards;

(v) take into account the biological, chemical and other hazards that may be associated with radioactive waste management;

(vi) strive to avoid actions that impose reasonably predictable impacts on future generations greater than those permitted for the current generation;

(vii) aim to avoid imposing undue burdens on future generations.

ARTICLE 12. EXISTING FACILITIES AND PAST PRACTICES

Each Contracting Party shall in due course take the appropriate steps to review:

(i) the safety of any radioactive waste management facility existing at the time the Convention enters into force for that Contracting Party and to ensure that, if necessary, all reasonably practicable improvements are made to upgrade the safety of such a facility;

(ii) the results of past practices in order to determine whether any intervention is needed for reasons of radiation protection bearing in mind that the reduction in detriment resulting from the reduction in dose should be sufficient to justify the harm and the costs, including the social costs, of the intervention.

ARTICLE 13. SITING OF PROPOSED FACILITIES

1. Each Contracting Party shall take the appropriate steps to ensure that procedures are established and implemented for a proposed radioactive waste management facility:

(i) to evaluate all relevant site-related factors likely to affect the safety of such a facility during its operating lifetime as well as that of a disposal facility after closure;

(ii) to evaluate the likely safety impact of such a facility on individuals, society and the environment, taking into account possible evolution of the site conditions of disposal facilities after closure;

(iii) to make information on the safety of such a facility available to members of the public;

(iv) to consult Contracting Parties in the vicinity of such a facility, insofar as they are likely to be affected by that facility, and provide them, upon their request, with general data relating to the facility to enable them to evaluate the likely safety impact of the facility upon their territory.

2. In so doing, each Contracting Party shall take the appropriate steps to ensure that such facilities shall not have unacceptable effects on other Contracting Parties by being sited in accordance with the general safety requirements of Article 11.

ARTICLE 14. DESIGN AND CONSTRUCTION OF FACILITIES

Each Contracting Party shall take the appropriate steps to ensure that:

(i) the design and construction of a radioactive waste management facility provide for suitable measures to limit possible radiological impacts on individuals, society and the environment, including those from discharges or uncontrolled releases;

(ii) at the design stage, conceptual plans and, as necessary, technical provisions for the decommissioning of a radioactive waste management facility other than a disposal facility are taken into account;

(iii) at the design stage, technical provisions for the closure of a disposal facility are prepared;

(iv) the technologies incorporated in the design and construction of a radioactive waste management facility are supported by experience, testing or analysis.

ARTICLE 15. ASSESSMENT OF SAFETY OF FACILITIES

Each Contracting Party shall take the appropriate steps to ensure that:

(i) before construction of a radioactive waste management facility, a systematic safety assessment and an environmental assessment appropriate to the hazard presented by the facility and covering its operating lifetime shall be carried out;

(ii) in addition, before construction of a disposal facility, a systematic safety assessment and an environmental assessment for the period following closure shall be carried out and the results evaluated against the criteria established by the regulatory body;

(iii) before the operation of a radioactive waste management facility, updated and detailed versions of the safety assessment and of the environmental assessment shall be prepared when deemed necessary to complement the assessments referred to in paragraph (i).

ARTICLE 16. OPERATION OF FACILITIES

Each Contracting Party shall take the appropriate steps to ensure that:

(i) the licence to operate a radioactive waste management facility is based upon appropriate assessments as specified in Article 15 and is conditional on the completion of a commissioning programme demonstrating that the facility, as constructed, is consistent with design and safety requirements;

(ii) operational limits and conditions, derived from tests, operational experience and the assessments as specified in Article 15 are defined and revised as necessary;

(iii) operation, maintenance, monitoring, inspection and testing of a radioactive waste management facility are conducted in accordance with established procedures. For a disposal facility the results thus obtained shall be used to verify and to review the validity of assumptions made and to update the assessments as specified in Article 15 for the period after closure;

(iv) engineering and technical support in all safety-related fields are available throughout the operating lifetime of a radioactive waste management facility;

(v) procedures for characterization and segregation of radioactive waste are applied;

(vi) incidents significant to safety are reported in a timely manner by the holder of the licence to the regulatory body;

(vii) programmes to collect and analyse relevant operating experience are established and that the results are acted upon, where appropriate;

(viii) decommissioning plans for a radioactive waste management facility other than a disposal facility are prepared and updated, as necessary, using information obtained during the operating lifetime of that facility, and are reviewed by the regulatory body;

(ix) plans for the closure of a disposal facility are prepared and updated, as necessary, using information obtained during the operating lifetime of that facility and are reviewed by the regulatory body.

Article 17. Institutional Measures after Closure

Each Contracting Party shall take the appropriate steps to ensure that after closure of a disposal facility:

(i) records of the location, design and inventory of that facility required by the regulatory body are preserved;

(ii) active or passive institutional controls such as monitoring or access restrictions are carried out, if required; and

(iii) if, during any period of active institutional control, an unplanned release of radioactive materials into the environment is detected, intervention measures are implemented, if necessary.

Chapter 4. General Safety Provisions

Article 18. Implementing Measures

Each Contracting Party shall take, within the framework of its national law, the legislative, regulatory and administrative measures and other steps necessary for implementing its obligations under this Convention.

Article 19. Legislative and Regulatory Framework

1. Each Contracting Party shall establish and maintain a legislative and regulatory framework to govern the safety of spent fuel and radioactive waste management.

2. This legislative and regulatory framework shall provide for:

(i) the establishment of applicable national safety requirements and regulations for radiation safety;

(ii) a system of licensing of spent fuel and radioactive waste management activities;

(iii) a system of prohibition of the operation of a spent fuel or radioactive waste management facility without a licence;

(iv) a system of appropriate institutional control, regulatory inspection and documentation and reporting;

(v) the enforcement of applicable regulations and of the terms of the licences;

(vi) a clear allocation of responsibilities of the bodies involved in the different steps of spent fuel and of radioactive waste management.

3. When considering whether to regulate radioactive materials as radioactive waste, Contracting Parties shall take due account of the objectives of this Convention.

Article 20. Regulatory Body

1. Each Contracting Party shall establish or designate a regulatory body entrusted with the implementation of the legislative and regulatory framework referred to in Article 19, and provided with adequate authority, competence and financial and human resources to fulfill its assigned responsibilities.

2. Each Contracting Party, in accordance with its legislative and regulatory framework, shall take the appropriate steps to ensure the effective independence of the regulatory functions from other functions where organizations are involved in both spent fuel or radioactive waste management and in their regulation.

Article 21. Responsibility of the Licence Holder

1. Each Contracting Party shall ensure that prime responsibility for the safety of spent fuel or radioactive waste management rests with the holder of the relevant licence and shall take the appropriate steps to ensure that each such licence holder meets its responsibility.

2. If there is no such licence holder or other responsible party, the responsibility rests with the Contracting Party which has jurisdiction over the spent fuel or over the radioactive waste.

Article 22. Human and Financial Resources

Each Contracting Party shall take the appropriate steps to ensure that:

(i) qualified staff are available as needed for safety-related activities during the operating lifetime of a spent fuel and a radioactive waste management facility;

(ii) adequate financial resources are available to support the safety of facilities for spent fuel and radioactive waste management during their operating lifetime and for decommissioning;

(iii) financial provision is made which will enable the appropriate institutional controls and monitoring arrangements to be continued for the period deemed necessary following the closure of a disposal facility.

Article 23. Quality Assurance

Each Contracting Party shall take the necessary steps to ensure that appropriate quality assurance programmes concerning the safety of spent fuel and radioactive waste management are established and implemented.

Article 24. Operational Radiation Protection

1. Each Contracting Party shall take the appropriate steps to ensure that during the operating lifetime of a spent fuel or radioactive waste management facility:

(i) the radiation exposure of the workers and the public caused by the facility shall be kept as low as reasonably achievable, economic and social factors being taken into account;

(ii) no individual shall be exposed, in normal situations, to radiation doses which exceed national prescriptions for dose limitation which have due regard to internationally endorsed standards on radiation protection; and

(iii) measures are taken to prevent unplanned and uncontrolled releases of radioactive materials into the environment.

2. Each Contracting Party shall take appropriate steps to ensure that discharges shall be limited:

(i) to keep exposure to radiation as low as reasonably achievable, economic and social factors being taken into account; and

(ii) so that no individual shall be exposed, in normal situations, to radiation doses which exceed national prescriptions for dose limitation which have due regard to internationally endorsed standards on radiation protection.

3. Each Contracting Party shall take appropriate steps to ensure that during the operating lifetime of a regulated nuclear facility, in the event that an unplanned or uncontrolled release of radioactive materials into the environment occurs, appropriate corrective measures are implemented to control the release and mitigate its effects.

ARTICLE 25. EMERGENCY PREPAREDNESS

1. Each Contracting Party shall ensure that before and during operation of a spent fuel or radioactive waste management facility there are appropriate on-site and, if necessary, off-site emergency plans. Such emergency plans should be tested at an appropriate frequency.

2. Each Contracting Party shall take the appropriate steps for the preparation and testing of emergency plans for its territory insofar as it is likely to be affected in the event of a radiological emergency at a spent fuel or radioactive waste management facility in the vicinity of its territory.

ARTICLE 26. DECOMMISSIONING

Each Contracting Party shall take the appropriate steps to ensure the safety of decommissioning of a nuclear facility. Such steps shall ensure that:

(i) qualified staff and adequate financial resources are available;

(ii) the provisions of Article 24 with respect to operational radiation protection, discharges and unplanned and uncontrolled releases are applied;

(iii) the provisions of Article 25 with respect to emergency preparedness are applied; and

(iv) records of information important to decommissioning are kept.

CHAPTER 5. MISCELLANEOUS PROVISIONS

ARTICLE 27. TRANSBOUNDARY MOVEMENT

1. Each Contracting Party involved in transboundary movement shall take the appropriate steps to ensure that such movement is undertaken in a manner consistent with the provisions of this Convention and relevant binding international instruments.

In so doing:

(i) a Contracting Party which is a State of origin shall take the appropriate steps to ensure that transboundary movement is authorized and takes place only with the prior notification and consent of the State of destination;

(ii) transboundary movement through States of transit shall be subject to those international obligations which are relevant to the particular modes of transport utilized;

(iii) a Contracting Party which is a State of destination shall consent to a transboundary movement only if it has the administrative and technical capacity, as well as the regulatory structure, needed to manage the spent fuel or the radioactive waste in a manner consistent with this Convention;

(iv) a Contracting Party which is a State of origin shall authorize a transboundary movement only if it can satisfy itself in accordance with the consent of the State of destination that the requirements of subparagraph (iii) are met prior to transboundary movement;

(v) a Contracting Party which is a State of origin shall take the appropriate steps to permit re-entry into its territory, if a transboundary movement is not or cannot be completed in conformity with this Article, unless an alternative safe arrangement can be made.

2. A Contracting Party shall not licence the shipment of its spent fuel or radioactive waste to a destination south of latitude 60 degrees South for storage or disposal.

3. Nothing in this Convention prejudices or affects:

(i) the exercise, by ships and aircraft of all States, of maritime, river and air navigation rights and freedoms, as provided for in international law;

(ii) rights of a Contracting Party to which radioactive waste is exported for processing to return, or provide for the return of, the radioactive waste and other products after treatment to the State of origin;

(iii) the right of a Contracting Party to export its spent fuel for reprocessing;

(iv) rights of a Contracting Party to which spent fuel is exported for reprocessing to return, or provide for the return of, radioactive waste and other products resulting from reprocessing operations to the State of origin.

Article 28. Disused Sealed Sources

1. Each Contracting Party shall, in the framework of its national law, take the appropriate steps to ensure that the possession, remanufacturing or disposal of disused sealed sources takes place in a safe manner.

2. A Contracting Party shall allow for reentry into its territory of disused sealed sources if, in the framework of its national law, it has accepted that they be returned to a manufacturer qualified to receive and possess the disused sealed sources.

Chapter 6. Meetings of the Contracting Parties

Article 29. Preparatory Meeting

1. A preparatory meeting of the Contracting Parties shall be held not later than six months after the date of entry into force of this Convention.

2. At this meeting, the Contracting Parties shall:

(i) determine the date for the first review meeting as referred to in Article 30. This review meeting shall be held as soon as possible, but not later than thirty months after the date of entry into force of this Convention;

(ii) prepare and adopt by consensus Rules of Procedure and Financial Rules;

(iii) establish in particular and in accordance with the Rules of Procedure:

(a) guidelines regarding the form and structure of the national reports to be submitted pursuant to Article 32;

(b) a date for the submission of such reports;

(c) the process for reviewing such reports.

3. Any State or regional organization of an integration or other nature which ratifies, accepts, approves, accedes to or confirms this Convention and for which the Convention is not yet in force, may attend the preparatory meeting as if it were a Party to this Convention.

Article 30. Review Meetings

1. The Contracting Parties shall hold meetings for the purpose of reviewing the reports submitted pursuant to Article 32.

2. At each review meeting the Contracting Parties:

(i) shall determine the date for the next such meeting, the interval between review meetings not exceeding three years;

(ii) may review the arrangements established pursuant to paragraph 2 of Article 29, and adopt revisions by consensus unless otherwise provided for in the Rules of Procedure. They may also amend the Rules of Procedure and Financial Rules by consensus.

3. At each review meeting each Contracting Party shall have a reasonable opportunity to discuss the reports submitted by other Contracting Parties and to seek clarification of such reports.

Article 31. Extraordinary Meetings

An extraordinary meeting of the Contracting Parties shall be held:

(i) if so agreed by a majority of the Contracting Parties present and voting at a meeting; or

(ii) at the written request of a Contracting Party, within six months of this request having been communicated to the Contracting Parties and notification having been received by the secretariat referred to in Article 37 that the request has been supported by a majority of the Contracting Parties.

Article 32. Reporting

1. In accordance with the provisions of Article 30, each Contracting Party shall submit a national report to each review meeting of Contracting Parties. This report shall address the measures taken to implement each of the obligations of the Convention. For each Contracting Party the report shall also address its:

(i) spent fuel management policy;

(ii) spent fuel management practices;

(iii) radioactive waste management policy;

(iv) radioactive waste management practices;

(v) criteria used to define and categorize radioactive waste.

2. This report shall also include:

(i) a list of the spent fuel management facilities subject to this Convention, their location, main purpose and essential features;

(ii) an inventory of spent fuel that is subject to this Convention and that is being held in storage and of that which has been disposed of. This inventory shall contain a description of the material and, if available, give information on its mass and its total activity;

(iii) a list of the radioactive waste management facilities subject to this Convention, their location, main purpose and essential features;

(iv) an inventory of radioactive waste that is subject to this Convention that:

(a) is being held in storage at radioactive waste management and nuclear fuel cycle facilities;

(b) has been disposed of; or

(c) has resulted from past practices. This inventory shall contain a description of the material and other appropriate information available, such as volume or mass, activity and specific radionuclides;

(v) a list of nuclear facilities in the process of being decommissioned and the status of decommissioning activities at those facilities.

Article 33. Attendance

1. Each Contracting Party shall attend meetings of the Contracting Parties and be represented at such meetings by one delegate, and by such alternates, experts and advisers as it deems necessary.

2. The Contracting Parties may invite, by consensus, any intergovernmental organization which is competent in respect of matters governed by this Convention to attend, as an observer, any meeting, or specific sessions thereof. Observers shall be required to accept in writing, and in advance, the provisions of Article 36.

Article 34. Summary Reports

The Contracting Parties shall adopt, by consensus, and make available to the public a document addressing issues discussed and conclusions reached during meetings of the Contracting Parties.

Article 35. Languages

1. The languages of meetings of the Contracting Parties shall be Arabic, Chinese, English, French, Russian and Spanish unless otherwise provided in the Rules of Procedure.

2. Reports submitted pursuant to Article 32 shall be prepared in the national language of the submitting Contracting Party or in a single designated language to be agreed in the Rules of Procedure. Should the report be submitted in a national language other than the designated language, a translation of the report into the designated language shall be provided by the Contracting Party.

3. Notwithstanding the provisions of paragraph 2, the secretariat, if compensated, will assume the translation of reports submitted in any other language of the meeting into the designated language.

Article 36. Confidentiality

1. The provisions of this Convention shall not affect the rights and obligations of the Contracting Parties under their laws to protect information from disclosure. For the purposes of this article, "information" includes, inter alia, information relating to national security or to the physical protection of nuclear materials, information protected by intellectual property rights or by industrial or commercial confidentiality, and personal data.

2. When, in the context of this Convention, a Contracting Party provides information identified by it as protected as described in paragraph 1, such information shall be used only for the purposes for which it has been provided and its confidentiality shall be respected.

3. With respect to information relating to spent fuel or radioactive waste falling within the scope of this Convention by virtue of paragraph 3 of Article 3, the provisions of this Convention shall not affect the exclusive discretion of the Contracting Party concerned to decide:

(i) whether such information is classified or otherwise controlled to preclude release;

(ii) whether to provide information referred to in sub-paragraph (i) above in the context of the Convention; and

(iii) what conditions of confidentiality are attached to such information if it is provided in the context of this Convention.

4. The content of the debates during the reviewing of the national reports at each review meeting held pursuant to Article 30 shall be confidential.

Article 37. Secretariat

1. The International Atomic Energy Agency (hereinafter referred to as "the Agency") shall provide the secretariat for the meetings of the Contracting Parties.

2. The secretariat shall:

(i) convene, prepare and service the meetings of the Contracting Parties referred to in Articles 29, 30 and 31;

(ii) transmit to the Contracting Parties information received or prepared in accordance with the provisions of this Convention.

The costs incurred by the Agency in carrying out the functions referred to in sub-paragraphs (i) and (ii) above shall be borne by the Agency as part of its regular budget.

3. The Contracting Parties may, by consensus, request the Agency to provide other services in support of meetings of the Contracting Parties. The Agency may provide such services if they can be undertaken within its programme and regular budget. Should this not be possible, the Agency may provide such services if voluntary funding is provided from another source.

CHAPTER 7. FINAL CLAUSES AND OTHER PROVISIONS

ARTICLE 38. RESOLUTION OF DISAGREEMENTS

In the event of a disagreement between two or more Contracting Parties concerning the interpretation or application of this Convention, the Contracting Parties shall consult within the framework of a meeting of the Contracting Parties with a view to resolving the disagreement. In the event that the consultations prove unproductive, recourse can be made to the mediation, conciliation and arbitration mechanisms provided for in international law, including the rules and practices prevailing within the IAEA.

ARTICLE 39. SIGNATURE, RATIFICATION, ACCEPTANCE, APPROVAL, ACCESSION

1. This Convention shall be open for signature by all States at the Headquarters of the Agency in Vienna from 29 September 1997 until its entry into force.
2. This Convention is subject to ratification, acceptance or approval by the signatory States.
3. After its entry into force, this Convention shall be open for accession by all States.
4. (i) This Convention shall be open for signature subject to confirmation, or accession by regional organizations of an integration or other nature, provided that any such organization is constituted by sovereign States and has competence in respect of the negotiation, conclusion and application of international agreements in matters covered by this Convention.

(ii) In matters within their competence, such organizations shall, on their own behalf, exercise the rights and fulfil the responsibilities which this Convention attributes to States Parties.

(iii) When becoming party to this Convention, such an organization shall communicate to the Depositary referred to in Article 43, a declaration indicating which States are members thereof, which Articles of this Convention apply to it, and the extent of its competence in the field covered by those articles.

(iv) Such an organization shall not hold any vote additional to those of its Member States.

5. Instruments of ratification, acceptance, approval, accession or confirmation shall be deposited with the Depositary.

ARTICLE 40. ENTRY INTO FORCE

1. This Convention shall enter into force on the ninetieth day after the date of deposit with the Depositary of the twenty-fifth instrument of ratification, acceptance or approval, including the instruments of fifteen States each having an operational nuclear power plant.
2. For each State or regional organization of an integration or other nature which ratifies, accepts, approves, accedes to or confirms this Convention after the date of deposit of the last instrument required to satisfy the conditions set forth in paragraph 1, this Convention shall enter into force on the ninetieth day after the date of deposit with the Depositary of the appropriate instrument by such a State or organization.

Article 41. Amendments to the Convention

1. Any Contracting Party may propose an amendment to this Convention. Proposed amendments shall be considered at a review meeting or at an extraordinary meeting.

2. The text of any proposed amendment and the reasons for it shall be provided to the Depositary who shall communicate the proposal to the Contracting Parties at least ninety days before the meeting for which it is submitted for consideration. Any comments received on such a proposal shall be circulated by the Depositary to the Contracting Parties.

3. The Contracting Parties shall decide after consideration of the proposed amendment whether to adopt it by consensus, or, in the absence of consensus, to submit it to a Diplomatic Conference. A decision to submit a proposed amendment to a Diplomatic Conference shall require a two-thirds majority vote of the Contracting Parties present and voting at the meeting, provided that at least one half of the Contracting Parties are present at the time of voting.

4. The Diplomatic Conference to consider and adopt amendments to this Convention shall be convened by the Depositary and held no later than one year after the appropriate decision taken in accordance with paragraph 3 of this article. The Diplomatic Conference shall make every effort to ensure amendments are adopted by consensus. Should this not be possible, amendments shall be adopted with a two-thirds majority of all Contracting Parties.

5. Amendments to this Convention adopted pursuant to paragraphs 3 and 4 above shall be subject to ratification, acceptance, approval, or confirmation by the Contracting Parties and shall enter into force for those Contracting Parties which have ratified, accepted, approved or confirmed them on the ninetieth day after the receipt by the Depositary of the relevant instruments of at least two thirds of the Contracting Parties. For a Contracting Party which subsequently ratifies, accepts, approves or confirms the said amendments, the amendments will enter into force on the ninetieth day after that Contracting Party has deposited its relevant instrument.

Article 42. Denunciation

1. Any Contracting Party may denounce this Convention by written notification to the Depositary.

2. Denunciation shall take effect one year following the date of the receipt of the notification by the Depositary, or on such later date as may be specified in the notification.

Article 43. Depositary

1. The Director General of the Agency shall be the Depositary of this Convention.

2. The Depositary shall inform the Contracting Parties of:

(i) the signature of this Convention and of the deposit of instruments of ratification, acceptance, approval, accession or confirmation in accordance with Article 39;

(ii) the date on which the Convention enters into force, in accordance with Article 40;

(iii) the notifications of denunciation of the Convention and the date thereof, made in accordance with Article 42;

(iv) the proposed amendments to this Convention submitted by Contracting Parties, the amendments adopted by the relevant Diplomatic Conference or by the meeting of the Contracting Parties, and the date of entry into force of the said amendments, in accordance with Article 41.

ARTICLE 44. AUTHENTIC TEXTS

The original of this Convention of which the Arabic, Chinese, English, French, Russian and Spanish texts are equally authentic, shall be deposited with the Depositary, who shall send certified copies thereof to the Contracting Parties.

IN WITNESS WHEREOF the undersigned, being duly authorized to that effect, have signed this Convention.

DONE at Vienna on the fifth day of September, one thousand nine hundred and ninety-seven.

6. Montreal Protocol on Substances that Deplete the Ozone Layer, with annexes, as amended and adjusted

Done at Montreal, September 16, 1987; Entered into force, January 1, 1989; Amended and adjusted, June 29, 1990, June 19–21, 1991, November 23–25, 1992, December 7, 1995, September 15–17, 1997, and December 3, 1999

MONTREAL PROTOCOL ON SUBSTANCES THAT DEPLETE THE OZONE LAYER [1]

PREAMBLE

The Parties to this Protocol

BEING Parties to the Vienna Convention for the Protection of the Ozone Layer,

MINDFUL of their obligation under that Convention to take appropriate measures to protect human health and the environment against adverse effects resulting or likely to result from human activities which modify or are likely to modify the ozone layer,

RECOGNIZING that world-wide emissions of certain substances can significantly deplete and otherwise modify the ozone layer in a manner that is likely to result in adverse effects on human health and the environment,

CONSCIOUS of the potential climatic effects of emissions of these substances,

AWARE that measures taken to protect the ozone layer from depletion should be based on relevant scientific knowledge, taking into account technical and economic considerations,

DETERMINED to protect the ozone layer by taking precautionary measures to control equitably total global emissions of substances that deplete it, with the ultimate objective of their elimination on the basis of developments in scientific knowledge, taking into account technical and economic considerations and bearing in mind the developmental needs of developing countries,

ACKNOWLEDGING that special provision is required to meet the needs of developing countries, including the provision of additional financial resources and access to relevant technologies, bearing in mind that the magnitude of funds necessary is predictable, and the funds can be expected to make a substantial difference in the world's ability to address the scientifically established problem of ozone depletion and its harmful effects,

NOTING the precautionary measures for controlling emissions of certain chlorofluorocarbons that have already been taken at national and regional levels,

---

[1] For a list of states that are parties to the Convention, see Department of State publication, *Treaties in Force*.

CONSIDERING the importance of promoting international co-operation in the research, development and transfer of alternative technologies relating to the control and reduction of emissions of substances that deplete the ozone layer, bearing in mind in particular the needs of developing countries,

HAVE AGREED AS FOLLOWS:

ARTICLE 1: DEFINITIONS

For the purposes of this Protocol:

1. "Convention" means the Vienna Convention for the Protection of the Ozone Layer, adopted on 22 March 1985.
2. "Parties" means, unless the text otherwise indicates, Parties to this Protocol.
3. "Secretariat" means the Secretariat of the Convention.
4. "Controlled substance" means a substance in Annex A, Annex B, Annex C or Annex E to this Protocol, whether existing alone or in a mixture. It includes the isomers of any such substance, except as specified in the relevant Annex, but excludes any controlled substance or mixture which is in a manufactured product other than a container used for the transportation or storage of that substance.
5. "Production" means the amount of controlled substances produced, minus the amount destroyed by technologies to be approved by the Parties and minus the amount entirely used as feedstock in the manufacture of other chemicals. The amount recycled and reused is not to be considered as "production".
6. "Consumption" means production plus imports minus exports of controlled substances.
7. "Calculated levels" of production, imports, exports and consumption means levels determined in accordance with Article 3.
8. "Industrial rationalization" means the transfer of all or a portion of the calculated level of production of one Party to another, for the purpose of achieving economic efficiencies or responding to anticipated shortfalls in supply as a result of plant closures.

ARTICLE 2: CONTROL MEASURES

1. Incorporated in Article 2A.
2. Replaced by Article 2B.
3. Replaced by Article 2A.
4. Replaced by Article 2A.
5. Any Party may, for one or more control periods, transfer to another Party any portion of its calculated level of production set out in Articles 2A to 2F, and Article 2H, provided that the total combined calculated levels of production of the Parties concerned for any group of controlled substances do not exceed the production limits set out in those Articles for that group. Such transfer of production shall be notified to the Secretariat by each of the Parties concerned, stating the terms of such transfer and the period for which it is to apply.

5 *bis*. Any Party not operating under paragraph 1 of Article 5 may, for one or more control periods, transfer to another such Party any portion of its calculated level of consumption set out in Article 2F, provided that the calculated level of consumption of controlled substances in Group I of Annex A of the Party transferring the portion of its calculated level of consumption did not exceed 0.25 kilograms per capita in 1989 and that the total combined calculated levels of consumption of the Parties concerned do not exceed the consumption limits set out in Article 2F. Such transfer of consumption shall be notified to the Secretariat by each of the Parties concerned, stating the terms of such transfer and the period for which it is to apply.

6. Any Party not operating under Article 5, that has facilities for the production of Annex A or Annex B controlled substances under construction, or contracted for, prior to 16 September 1987, and provided for in national legislation prior to 1 January 1987, may add the production from such facilities to its 1986 production of such substances for the purposes of determining its calculated level of production for 1986, provided that such facilities are completed by 31 December 1990 and that such production does not raise that Party's annual calculated level of consumption of the controlled substances above 0.5 kilograms per capita.

7. Any transfer of production pursuant to paragraph 5 or any addition of production pursuant to paragraph 6 shall be notified to the Secretariat, no later than the time of the transfer or addition.

8. (a) Any Parties which are Member States of a regional economic integration organization as defined in Article 1 (6) of the Convention may agree that they shall jointly fulfil their obligations respecting consumption under this Article and Articles 2A to 2I provided that their total combined calculated level of consumption does not exceed the levels required by this Article and Articles 2A to 2I.

(b) The Parties to any such agreement shall inform the Secretariat of the terms of the agreement before the date of the reduction in consumption with which the agreement is concerned.

(c) Such agreement will become operative only if all Member States of the regional economic integration organization and the organization concerned are Parties to the Protocol and have notified the Secretariat of their manner of implementation.

9. (a) Based on the assessments made pursuant to Article 6, the Parties may decide whether:

(i) Adjustments to the ozone depleting potentials specified in Annex A, Annex B, Annex C and/or Annex E should be made and, if so, what the adjustments should be; and

(ii) Further adjustments and reductions of production or consumption of the controlled substances should be undertaken and, if so, what the scope, amount and timing of any such adjustments and reductions should be;

(b) Proposals for such adjustments shall be communicated to the Parties by the Secretariat at least six months before the meeting of the Parties at which they are proposed for adoption;

(c) In taking such decisions, the Parties shall make every effort to reach agreement by consensus. If all efforts at consensus have been exhausted, and no agreement reached, such decisions shall, as a last resort, be adopted by a two-thirds majority vote of the Parties present and voting representing a majority of the Parties operating under Paragraph 1 of Article 5 present and voting and a majority of the Parties not so operating present and voting;

(d) The decisions, which shall be binding on all Parties, shall forthwith be communicated to the Parties by the Depositary. Unless otherwise provided in the decisions, they shall enter into force on the expiry of six months from the date of the circulation of the communication by the Depositary.

10. Based on the assessments made pursuant to Article 6 of this Protocol and in accordance with the procedure set out in Article 9 of the Convention, the Parties may decide:

(a) whether any substances, and if so which, should be added to or removed from any annex to this Protocol, and

(b) the mechanism, scope and timing of the control measures that should apply to those substances;

11. Notwithstanding the provisions contained in this Article and Articles 2A to 2I Parties may take more stringent measures than those required by this Article and Articles 2A to 2I.

Article 2A: CFCs

1. Each Party shall ensure that for the twelve-month period commencing on the first day of the seventh month following the date of entry into force of this Protocol, and in each twelve-month period thereafter, its calculated level of consumption of the controlled substances in Group I of Annex A does not exceed its calculated level of consumption in 1986. By the end of the same period, each Party producing one or more of these substances shall ensure that its calculated level of production of the substances does not exceed its calculated level of production in 1986, except that such level may have increased by no more than ten per cent based on the 1986 level. Such increase shall be permitted only so as to satisfy the basic domestic needs of the Parties operating under Article 5 and for the purposes of industrial rationalization between Parties.

2. Each Party shall ensure that for the period from 1 July 1991 to 31 December 1992 its calculated levels of consumption and production of the controlled substances in Group I of Annex A do not exceed 150 per cent of its calculated levels of production and consumption of those substances in 1986; with effect from 1 January 1993, the twelve-month control period for these controlled substances shall run from 1 January to 31 December each year.

3. Each Party shall ensure that for the twelve-month period commencing on 1 January 1994, and in each twelve-month period thereafter, its calculated level of consumption of the controlled substances in Group I of Annex A does not exceed, annually, twenty-five per cent of its calculated level of consumption in 1986. Each Party producing one or more of these substances shall, for the same periods, ensure that its calculated level of production of the substances does not exceed, annually, twenty-five per cent of its calculated level of production in 1986. However, in order to satisfy the basic domestic needs of the Parties operating under paragraph 1 of Article 5, its calculated level of production may exceed that limit by up to ten per cent of its calculated level of production in 1986.

4. Each Party shall ensure that for the twelve-month period commencing on 1 January 1996, and in each twelve-month period thereafter, its calculated level of consumption of the controlled substances in Group I of Annex A does not exceed zero. Each Party producing one or more of these substances shall, for the same periods, ensure that its calculated level of production of the substances does not exceed zero. However, in order to satisfy the basic domestic needs of the Parties operating under paragraph 1 of Article 5, its calculated level of production may exceed that limit by a quantity equal to the annual average of its production of the controlled substances in Group I of Annex A for basic domestic needs for the period 1995 to 1997 inclusive. This paragraph will apply save to the extent that the Parties decide to permit the level of production or consumption that is necessary to satisfy uses agreed by them to be essential.

5. Each Party shall ensure that for the twelve-month period commencing on 1 January 2003 and in each twelve-month period thereafter, its calculated level of production of the controlled substances in Group I of Annex A for the basic domestic needs of the Parties operating under paragraph 1 of Article 5 does not exceed eighty per cent of the annual average of its production of those substances for basic domestic needs for the period 1995 to 1997 inclusive.

6. Each Party shall ensure that for the twelve-month period commencing on 1 January 2005 and in each twelve-month period thereafter, its calculated level of production of the controlled substances in Group I of Annex A for the basic domestic needs of the Parties operating under paragraph 1 of Article 5 does not exceed fifty per cent of the annual average of its production of those substances for basic domestic needs for the period 1995 to 1997 inclusive.

7. Each Party shall ensure that for the twelve-month period commencing on 1 January 2007 and in each twelve-month period thereafter, its calculated level of production of the controlled substances in Group I of Annex A for the basic domestic needs of the Parties operating under paragraph 1 of Article 5 does not exceed fifteen per cent of the annual average of its production of those substances for basic domestic needs for the period 1995 to 1997 inclusive.

8. Each Party shall ensure that for the twelve-month period commencing on 1 January 2010 and in each twelve-month period thereafter, its calculated level of production of the controlled substances in Group I of Annex A for the basic domestic needs of the Parties operating under paragraph 1 of Article 5 does not exceed zero.

9. For the purposes of calculating basic domestic needs under paragraphs 4 to 8 of this Article, the calculation of the annual average of production by a Party includes any production entitlements that it has transferred in accordance with paragraph 5 of Article 2, and excludes any production entitlements that it has acquired in accordance with paragraph 5 of Article 2.

ARTICLE 2B: HALONS

1. Each Party shall ensure that for the twelve-month period commencing on 1 January 1992, and in each twelve-month period

thereafter, its calculated level of consumption of the controlled substances in Group II of Annex A does not exceed, annually, its calculated level of consumption in 1986. Each Party producing one or more of these substances shall, for the same periods, ensure that its calculated level of production of the substances does not exceed, annually, its calculated level of production in 1986. However, in order to satisfy the basic domestic needs of the Parties operating under paragraph 1 of Article 5, its calculated level of production may exceed that limit by up to ten per cent of its calculated level of production in 1986.

2. Each Party shall ensure that for the twelve-month period commencing on 1 January 1994, and in each twelve-month period thereafter, its calculated level of consumption of the controlled substances in Group II of Annex A does not exceed zero. Each Party producing one or more of these substances shall, for the same periods, ensure that its calculated level of production of the substances does not exceed zero. However, in order to satisfy the basic domestic needs of the Parties operating under paragraph 1 of Article 5, its calculated level of production may, until 1 January 2002 exceed that limit by up to fifteen per cent of its calculated level of production in 1986; thereafter, it may exceed that limit by a quantity equal to the annual average of its production of the controlled substances in Group II of Annex A for basic domestic needs for the period 1995 to 1997 inclusive. This paragraph will apply save to the extent that the Parties decide to permit the level of production or consumption that is necessary to satisfy uses agreed by them to be essential.

3. Each Party shall ensure that for the twelve-month period commencing on 1 January 2005 and in each twelve-month period thereafter, its calculated level of production of the controlled substances in Group II of Annex A for the basic domestic needs of the Parties operating under paragraph 1 of Article 5 does not exceed fifty per cent of the annual average of its production of those substances for basic domestic needs for the period 1995 to 1997 inclusive.

4. Each Party shall ensure that for the twelve-month period commencing on 1 January 2010 and in each twelve-month period thereafter, its calculated level of production of the controlled substances in Group II of Annex A for the basic domestic needs of the Parties operating under paragraph 1 of Article 5 does not exceed zero.

ARTICLE 2C: OTHER FULLY HALOGENATED CFCS

1. Each Party shall ensure that for the twelve-month period commencing on 1 January 1993, its calculated level of consumption of the controlled substances in Group I of Annex B does not exceed, annually, eighty per cent of its calculated level of consumption in 1989. Each Party producing one or more of these substances shall, for the same period, ensure that its calculated level of production of the substances does not exceed, annually, eighty per cent of its calculated level of production in 1989. However, in order to satisfy the basic domestic needs of the Parties operating under paragraph 1 of Article 5, its calculated level of production may exceed that limit by up to ten per cent of its calculated level of production in 1989.

2. Each Party shall ensure that for the twelve-month period commencing on 1 January 1994, and in each twelve-month period thereafter, its calculated level of consumption of the controlled substances in Group I of Annex B does not exceed, annually, twenty-five per cent of its calculated level of consumption in 1989. Each Party producing one or more of these substances shall, for the same periods, ensure that its calculated level of production of the substances does not exceed, annually, twenty-five per cent of its calculated level of production in 1989. However, in order to satisfy the basic domestic needs of the Parties operating under paragraph 1 of Article 5, its calculated level of production may exceed that limit by up to ten per cent of its calculated level of production in 1989.

3. Each Party shall ensure that for the twelve-month period commencing on 1 January 1996, and in each twelve-month period thereafter, its calculated level of consumption of the controlled substances in Group I of Annex B does not exceed zero. Each Party producing one or more of these substances shall, for the same periods, ensure that its calculated level of production of the substances does not exceed zero. However, in order to satisfy the basic domestic needs of the Parties operating under paragraph 1 of Article 5, its calculated level of production may, until 1 January 2003 exceed that limit by up to fifteen per cent of its calculated level of production in 1989; thereafter, it may exceed that limit by a quantity equal to eighty per cent of the annual average of its production of the controlled substances in Group I of Annex B for basic domestic needs for the period 1998 to 2000 inclusive. This paragraph will apply save to the extent that the Parties decide to permit the level of production or consumption that is necessary to satisfy uses agreed by them to be essential.

4. Each Party shall ensure that for the twelve-month period commencing on 1 January 2007 and in each twelve-month period thereafter, its calculated level of production of the controlled substances in Group I of Annex B for the basic domestic needs of the Parties operating under paragraph 1 of Article 5 does not exceed fifteen per cent of the annual average of its production of those substances for basic domestic needs for the period 1998 to 2000 inclusive.

5. Each Party shall ensure that for the twelve-month period commencing on 1 January 2010 and in each twelve-month period thereafter, its calculated level of production of the controlled substances in Group I of Annex B for the basic domestic needs of the Parties operating under paragraph 1 of Article 5 does not exceed zero.

ARTICLE 2D: CARBON TETRACHLORIDE

1. Each Party shall ensure that for the twelve-month period commencing on 1 January 1995, its calculated level of consumption of the controlled substance in Group II of Annex B does not exceed, annually, fifteen per cent of its calculated level of consumption in 1989. Each Party producing the substance shall, for the same period, ensure that its calculated level of production of the substance does not exceed, annually, fifteen per cent of its calculated level of production in 1989. However, in order to satisfy the basic domestic needs of the Parties operating under paragraph 1 of Article 5, its

calculated level of production may exceed that limit by up to ten per cent of its calculated level of production in 1989.

2. Each Party shall ensure that for the twelve-month period commencing on 1 January 1996, and in each twelve-month period thereafter, its calculated level of consumption of the controlled substance in Group II of Annex B does not exceed zero. Each Party producing the substance shall, for the same periods, ensure that its calculated level of production of the substance does not exceed zero. However, in order to satisfy the basic domestic needs of the Parties operating under paragraph 1 of Article 5, its calculated level of production may exceed that limit by up to fifteen per cent of its calculated level of production in 1989. This paragraph will apply save to the extent that the Parties decide to permit the level of production or consumption that is necessary to satisfy uses agreed by them to be essential.

ARTICLE 2E: 1,1,1-TRICHLOROETHANE (METHYL CHLOROFORM)

1. Each Party shall ensure that for the twelve-month period commencing on 1 January 1993, its calculated level of consumption of the controlled substance in Group III of Annex B does not exceed, annually, its calculated level of consumption in 1989. Each Party producing the substance shall, for the same period, ensure that its calculated level of production of the substance does not exceed, annually, its calculated level of production in 1989. However, in order to satisfy the basic domestic needs of the Parties operating under paragraph 1 of Article 5, its calculated level of production may exceed that limit by up to ten per cent of its calculated level of production in 1989.

2. Each Party shall ensure that for the twelve-month period commencing on 1 January 1994, and in each twelve-month period thereafter, its calculated level of consumption of the controlled substance in Group III of Annex B does not exceed, annually, fifty per cent of its calculated level of consumption in 1989. Each Party producing the substance shall, for the same periods, ensure that its calculated level of production of the substance does not exceed, annually, fifty per cent of its calculated level of production in 1989. However, in order to satisfy the basic domestic needs of the Parties operating under paragraph 1 of Article 5, its calculated level of production may exceed that limit by up to ten per cent of its calculated level of production in 1989.

3. Each Party shall ensure that for the twelve-month period commencing on 1 January 1996, and in each twelve-month period thereafter, its calculated level of consumption of the controlled substance in Group III of Annex B does not exceed zero. Each Party producing the substance shall, for the same periods, ensure that its calculated level of production of the substance does not exceed zero. However, in order to satisfy the basic domestic needs of the Parties operating under paragraph 1 of Article 5, its calculated level of production may exceed that limit by up to fifteen per cent of its calculated level of production for 1989. This paragraph will apply save to the extent that the Parties decide to permit the level of production or consumption that is necessary to satisfy uses agreed by them to be essential.

ARTICLE 2F: HYDROCHLOROFLUOROCARBONS

1. Each Party shall ensure that for the twelve-month period commencing on 1 January 1996, and in each twelve-month period thereafter, its calculated level of consumption of the controlled substances in Group I of Annex C does not exceed, annually, the sum of:

(a) Two point eight per cent of its calculated level of consumption in 1989 of the controlled substances in Group I of Annex A; and

(b) Its calculated level of consumption in 1989 of the controlled substances in Group I of Annex C.

2. Each Party shall ensure that for the twelve month period commencing on 1 January 2004, and in each twelve-month period thereafter, its calculated level of consumption of the controlled substances in Group I of Annex C does not exceed, annually, sixty-five per cent of the sum referred to in paragraph 1 of this Article.

3. Each Party shall ensure that for the twelve-month period commencing on 1 January 2010, and in each twelve-month period thereafter, its calculated level of consumption of the controlled substances in Group I of Annex C does not exceed, annually, thirty-five per cent of the sum referred to in paragraph 1 of this Article.

4. Each Party shall ensure that for the twelve-month period commencing on 1 January 2015, and in each twelve-month period thereafter, its calculated level of consumption of the controlled substances in Group I of Annex C does not exceed, annually, ten per cent of the sum referred to in paragraph 1 of this Article.

5. Each Party shall ensure that for the twelve-month period commencing on 1 January 2020, and in each twelve-month period thereafter, its calculated level of consumption of the controlled substances in Group I of Annex C does not exceed, annually, zero point five per cent of the sum referred to in paragraph 1 of this Article. Such consumption shall, however, be restricted to the servicing of refrigeration and air conditioning equipment existing at that date.

6. Each Party shall ensure that for the twelve-month period commencing on 1 January 2030, and in each twelve-month period thereafter, its calculated level of consumption of the controlled substances in Group I of Annex C does not exceed zero.

7. As of 1 January 1996, each Party shall endeavour to ensure that:

(a) The use of controlled substances in Group I of Annex C is limited to those applications where other more environmentally suitable alternative substances or technologies are not available;

(b) The use of controlled substances in Group I of Annex C is not outside the areas of application currently met by controlled substances in Annexes A, B and C, except in rare cases for the protection of human life or human health; and

(c) Controlled substances in Group I of Annex C are selected for use in a manner that minimizes ozone depletion, in addition to meeting other environmental, safety and economic considerations.

8. Each Party producing one or more of these substances shall ensure that for the twelve-month period commencing on 1 January

2004, and in each twelve-month period thereafter, its calculated level of production of the controlled substances in Group I of Annex C does not exceed, annually, the average of:

(a) The sum of its calculated level of consumption in 1989 of the controlled substances in Group I of Annex C and two point eight per cent of its calculated level of consumption in 1989 of the controlled substances in Group I of Annex A; and

(b) The sum of its calculated level of production in 1989 of the controlled substances in Group I of Annex C and two point eight per cent of its calculated level of production in 1989 of the controlled substances in Group I of Annex A. However, in order to satisfy the basic domestic needs of the Parties operating under paragraph 1 of Article 5, its calculated level of production may exceed that limit by up to fifteen per cent of its calculated level of production of the controlled substances in Group I of Annex C as defined above.

Article 2G: Hydrobromofluorocarbons

Each Party shall ensure that for the twelve-month period commencing on 1 January 1996, and in each twelve-month period thereafter, its calculated level of consumption of the controlled substances in Group II of Annex C does not exceed zero. Each Party producing the substances shall, for the same periods, ensure that its calculated level of production of the substances does not exceed zero. This paragraph will apply save to the extent that the Parties decide to permit the level of production or consumption that is necessary to satisfy uses agreed by them to be essential.

Article 2H: Methyl bromide

1. Each Party shall ensure that for the twelve-month period commencing on 1 January 1995, and in each twelve-month period thereafter, its calculated level of consumption of the controlled substance in Annex E does not exceed, annually, its calculated level of consumption in 1991. Each Party producing the substance shall, for the same period, ensure that its calculated level of production of the substance does not exceed, annually, its calculated level of production in 1991. However, in order to satisfy the basic domestic needs of the Parties operating under paragraph 1 of Article 5, its calculated level of production may exceed that limit by up to ten per cent of its calculated level of production in 1991.

2. Each Party shall ensure that for the twelve-month period commencing on 1 January 1999, and in the twelve-month period thereafter, its calculated level of consumption of the controlled substance in Annex E does not exceed, annually, seventy-five per cent of its calculated level of consumption in 1991. Each Party producing the substance shall, for the same periods, ensure that its calculated level of production of the substance does not exceed, annually, seventy-five per cent of its calculated level of production in 1991. However, in order to satisfy the basic domestic needs of the Parties operating under paragraph 1 of Article 5, its calculated level of production may exceed that limit by up to ten per cent of its calculated level of production in 1991.

3. Each Party shall ensure that for the twelve-month period commencing on 1 January 2001, and in the twelve-month period thereafter, its calculated level of consumption of the controlled substance in Annex E does not exceed, annually, fifty per cent of its calculated level of consumption in 1991. Each Party producing the substance shall, for the same periods, ensure that its calculated level of production of the substance does not exceed, annually, fifty per cent of its calculated level of production in 1991. However, in order to satisfy the basic domestic needs of the Parties operating under paragraph 1 of Article 5, its calculated level of production may exceed that limit by up to ten per cent of its calculated level of production in 1991.

4. Each Party shall ensure that for the twelve-month period commencing on 1 January 2003, and in the twelve-month period thereafter, its calculated level of consumption of the controlled substance in Annex E does not exceed, annually, thirty per cent of its calculated level of consumption in 1991. Each Party producing the substance shall, for the same periods, ensure that its calculated level of production of the substance does not exceed, annually, thirty per cent of its calculated level of production in 1991. However, in order to satisfy the basic domestic needs of the Parties operating under paragraph 1 of Article 5, its calculated level of production may exceed that limit by up to ten per cent of its calculated level of production in 1991.

5. Each Party shall ensure that for the twelve-month period commencing on 1 January 2005, and in each twelve-month period thereafter, its calculated level of consumption of the controlled substance in Annex E does not exceed zero. Each Party producing the substance shall, for the same periods, ensure that its calculated level of production of the substance does not exceed zero. However, in order to satisfy the basic domestic needs of the Parties operating under paragraph 1 of Article 5, its calculated level of production may, until 1 January 2002 exceed that limit by up to fifteen per cent of its calculated level of production in 1991; thereafter, it may exceed that limit by a quantity equal to the annual average of its production of the controlled substance in Annex E for basic domestic needs for the period 1995 to 1998 inclusive. This paragraph will apply save to the extent that the Parties decide to permit the level of production or consumption that is necessary to satisfy uses agreed by them to be critical uses.

5 *bis*. Each Party shall ensure that for the twelve-month period commencing on 1 January 2005 and in each twelve-month period thereafter, its calculated level of production of the controlled substance in Annex E for the basic domestic needs of the Parties operating under paragraph 1 of Article 5 does not exceed eighty per cent of the annual average of its production of the substance for basic domestic needs for the period 1995 to 1998 inclusive.

5 *ter*. Each Party shall ensure that for the twelve-month period commencing on 1 January 2015 and in each twelve-month period thereafter, its calculated level of production of the controlled substance in Annex E for the basic domestic needs of the Parties operating under paragraph 1 of Article 5 does not exceed zero.

6. The calculated levels of consumption and production under this Article shall not include the amounts used by the Party for quarantine and pre-shipment applications.

ARTICLE 2I: BROMOCHLOROMETHANE

Each Party shall ensure that for the twelve-month period commencing on 1 January 2002, and in each twelve-month period thereafter, its calculated level of consumption and production of the controlled substance in Group III of Annex C does not exceed zero. This paragraph will apply save to the extent that the Parties decide to permit the level of production or consumption that is necessary to satisfy uses agreed by them to be essential.

ARTICLE 3: CALCULATION OF CONTROL LEVELS

For the purposes of Articles 2, 2A to 2I and 5, each Party shall, for each group of substances in Annex A, Annex B, Annex C or Annex E determine its calculated levels of:

(a) Production by:

(i) multiplying its annual production of each controlled substance by the ozone depleting potential specified in respect of it in Annex A, Annex B, Annex C or Annex E;

(ii) adding together, for each such Group, the resulting figures;

(b) Imports and exports, respectively, by following, mutatis mutandis, the procedure set out in subparagraph (a); and

(c) Consumption by adding together its calculated levels of production and imports and subtracting its calculated level of exports as determined in accordance with subparagraphs (a) and (b). However, beginning on 1 January 1993, any export of controlled substances to non-Parties shall not be subtracted in calculating the consumption level of the exporting Party.

ARTICLE 4: CONTROL OF TRADE WITH NON-PARTIES

1. As of 1 January 1990, each party shall ban the import of the controlled substances in Annex A from any State not party to this Protocol.

1 *bis*. Within one year of the date of the entry into force of this paragraph, each Party shall ban the import of the controlled substances in Annex B from any State not party to this Protocol.

1 *ter*. Within one year of the date of entry into force of this paragraph, each Party shall ban the import of any controlled substances in Group II of Annex C from any State not party to this Protocol.

1 *qua*. Within one year of the date of entry into force of this paragraph, each Party shall ban the import of the controlled substance in Annex E from any State not party to this Protocol.

1 *quin*. As of 1 January 2004, each Party shall ban the import of the controlled substances in Group I of Annex C from any State not party to this Protocol.

1 *sex*. Within one year of the date of entry into force of this paragraph, each Party shall ban the import of the controlled substance in Group III of Annex C from any State not party to this Protocol.

2. As of 1 January 1993, each Party shall ban the export of any controlled substances in Annex A to any State not party to this Protocol.

2 *bis*. Commencing one year after the date of entry into force of this paragraph, each Party shall ban the export of any controlled substances in Annex B to any State not party to this Protocol.

2 *ter*. Commencing one year after the date of entry into force of this paragraph, each Party shall ban the export of any controlled substances in Group II of Annex C to any State not party to this Protocol.

2 *qua*. Commencing one year of the date of entry into force of this paragraph, each Party shall ban the export of the controlled substance in Annex E to any State not party to this Protocol.

2 *quin*. As of 1 January 2004, each Party shall ban the export of the controlled substances in Group I of Annex C to any State not party to this Protocol.

2 *sex*. Within one year of the date of entry into force of this paragraph, each Party shall ban the export of the controlled substance in Group III of Annex C to any State not party to this Protocol.

3. By 1 January 1992, the Parties shall, following the procedures in Article 10 of the Convention, elaborate in an annex a list of products containing controlled substances in Annex A. Parties that have not objected to the annex in accordance with those procedures shall ban, within one year of the annex having become effective, the import of those products from any State not party to this Protocol.

3 *bis*. Within three years of the date of the entry into force of this paragraph, the Parties shall, following the procedures in Article 10 of the Convention, elaborate in an annex a list of products containing controlled substances in Annex B. Parties that have not objected to the annex in accordance with those procedures shall ban, within one year of the annex having become effective, the import of those products from any State not party to this Protocol.

3 *ter*. Within three years of the date of entry into force of this paragraph, the Parties shall, following the procedures in Article 10 of the Convention, elaborate in an annex a list of products containing controlled substances in Group II of Annex C. Parties that have not objected to the annex in accordance with those procedures shall ban, within one year of the annex having become effective, the import of those products from any State not party to this Protocol.

4. By 1 January 1994, the Parties shall determine the feasibility of banning or restricting, from States not party to this Protocol, the import of products produced with, but not containing, controlled substances in Annex A. If determined feasible, the Parties shall, following the procedures in Article 10 of the Convention, elaborate in an annex a list of such products. Parties that have not objected to the annex in accordance with those procedures shall ban, within one year of the annex having become effective, the import of those products from any State not party to this Protocol.

4 *bis*. Within five years of the date of the entry into force of this paragraph, the Parties shall determine the feasibility of banning or restricting, from States not party to this Protocol, the import of products produced with, but not containing, controlled substances

in Annex B. If determined feasible, the Parties shall, following the procedures in Article 10 of the Convention, elaborate in an annex a list of such products. Parties that have not objected to the annex in accordance with those procedures shall ban or restrict, within one year of the annex having become effective, the import of those products from any State not party to this Protocol.

4 *ter*. Within five years of the date of entry into force of this paragraph, the Parties shall determine the feasibility of banning or restricting, from States not party to this Protocol, the import of products produced with, but not containing, controlled substances in Group II of Annex C. If determined feasible, the Parties shall, following the procedures in Article 10 of the Convention, elaborate in an annex a list of such products. Parties that have not objected to the annex in accordance with those procedures shall ban or restrict, within one year of the annex having become effective, the import of those products from any State not party to this Protocol.

5. Each Party undertakes to the fullest practicable extent to discourage the export to any State not party to this Protocol of technology for producing and for utilizing controlled substances in Annexes A, B, C and E.

6. Each Party shall refrain from providing new subsidies, aid, credits, guarantees or insurance programmes for the export to States not party to this Protocol of products, equipment, plants or technology that would facilitate the production of controlled substances in Annexes A, B, C and E.

7. Paragraphs 5 and 6 shall not apply to products, equipment, plants or technology that improve the containment, recovery, recycling or destruction of controlled substances, promote the development of alternative substances, or otherwise contribute to the reduction of emissions of controlled substances in Annexes A, B, C and E.

8. Notwithstanding the provisions of this Article, imports and exports referred to in paragraphs 1 to 4 ter of this Article may be permitted from, or to, any State not party to this Protocol, if that State is determined, by a meeting of the Parties, to be in full compliance with Article 2, Articles 2A to 2I and this Article, and have submitted data to that effect as specified in Article 7.

9. For the purposes of this Article, the term "State not party to this Protocol" shall include, with respect to a particular controlled substance, a State or regional economic integration organization that has not agreed to be bound by the control measures in effect for that substance.

10. By 1 January 1996, the Parties shall consider whether to amend this Protocol in order to extend the measures in this Article to trade in controlled substances in Group I of Annex C and in Annex E with States not party to the Protocol.

Article 4A: Control of trade with Parties

1. Where, after the phase-out date applicable to it for a controlled substance, a Party is unable, despite having taken all practicable steps to comply with its obligation under the Protocol, to cease production of that substance for domestic consumption, other than for uses agreed by the Parties to be essential, it shall ban the export

of used, recycled and reclaimed quantities of that substance, other than for the purpose of destruction.

2. Paragraph 1 of this Article shall apply without prejudice to the operation of Article 11 of the Convention and the noncompliance procedure developed under Article 8 of the Protocol.

Article 4B: Licensing

1. Each Party shall, by 1 January 2000 or within three months of the date of entry into force of this Article for it, whichever is the later, establish and implement a system for licensing the import and export of new, used, recycled and reclaimed controlled substances in Annexes A, B, C and E.

2. Notwithstanding paragraph 1 of this Article, any Party operating under paragraph 1 of Article 5 which decides it is not in a position to establish and implement a system for licensing the import and export of controlled substances in Annexes C and E, may delay taking those actions until 1 January 2005 and 1 January 2002, respectively.

3. Each Party shall, within three months of the date of introducing its licensing system, report to the Secretariat on the establishment and operation of that system.

4. The Secretariat shall periodically prepare and circulate to all Parties a list of the Parties that have reported to it on their licensing systems and shall forward this information to the Implementation Committee for consideration and appropriate recommendations to the Parties.

Article 5: Special situation of developing countries

1. Any Party that is a developing country and whose annual calculated level of consumption of the controlled substances in Annex A is less than 0.3 kilograms per capita on the date of the entry into force of the Protocol for it, or any time thereafter until 1 January 1999, shall, in order to meet its basic domestic needs, be entitled to delay for ten years its compliance with the control measures set out in Articles 2A to 2E, provided that any further amendments to the adjustments or Amendment adopted at the Second Meeting of the Parties in London, 29 June 1990, shall apply to the Parties operating under this paragraph after the review provided for in paragraph 8 of this Article has taken place and shall be based on the conclusions of that review.

1 *bis*. The Parties shall, taking into account the review referred to in paragraph 8 of this Article, the assessments made pursuant to Article 6 and any other relevant information, decide by 1 January 1996, through the procedure set forth in paragraph 9 of Article 2:

(a) With respect to paragraphs 1 to 6 of Article 2F, what base year, initial levels, control schedules and phase-out date for consumption of the controlled substances in Group I of Annex C will apply to Parties operating under paragraph 1 of this Article;

(b) With respect to Article 2G, what phase-out date for production and consumption of the controlled substances in Group

II of Annex C will apply to Parties operating under paragraph 1 of this Article; and

(c) With respect to Article 2H, what base year, initial levels and control schedules for consumption and production of the controlled substance in Annex E will apply to Parties operating under paragraph 1 of this Article.

2. However, any Party operating under paragraph 1 of this Article shall exceed neither an annual calculated level of consumption of the controlled substances in Annex A of 0.3 kilograms per capita nor an annual calculated level of consumption of controlled substances of Annex B of 0.2 kilograms per capita.

3. When implementing the control measures set out in Articles 2A to 2E, any Party operating under paragraph 1 of this Article shall be entitled to use:

(a) For controlled substances under Annex A, either the average of its annual calculated level of consumption for the period 1995 to 1997 inclusive or a calculated level of consumption of 0.3 kilograms per capita, whichever is the lower, as the basis for determining its compliance with the control measures relating to consumption.

(b) For controlled substances under Annex B, the average of its annual calculated level of consumption for the period 1998 to 2000 inclusive or a calculated level of consumption of 0.2 kilograms per capita, whichever is the lower, as the basis for determining its compliance with the control measures relating to consumption.

(c) For controlled substances under Annex A, either the average of its annual calculated level of production for the period 1995 to 1997 inclusive or a calculated level of production of 0.3 kilograms per capita, whichever is the lower, as the basis for determining its compliance with the control measures relating to production.

(d) For controlled substances under Annex B, either the average of its annual calculated level of production for the period 1998 to 2000 inclusive or a calculated level of production of 0.2 kilograms per capita, whichever is the lower, as the basis for determining its compliance with the control measures relating to production.

4. If a Party operating under paragraph 1 of this Article, at any time before the control measures obligations in Articles 2A to 2I become applicable to it, finds itself unable to obtain an adequate supply of controlled substances, it may notify this to the Secretariat. The Secretariat shall forthwith transmit a copy of such notification to the Parties, which shall consider the matter at their next Meeting, and decide upon appropriate action to be taken.

5. Developing the capacity to fulfil the obligations of the Parties operating under paragraph 1 of this Article to comply with the control measures set out in Articles 2A to 2E and Article 2I, and any control measures in Articles 2F to 2H that are decided pursuant to paragraph 1 bis of this Article, and their implementation by those same Parties will depend upon the effective implementation of the financial co-operation as provided by Article 10 and the transfer of technology as provided by Article 10A.

6. Any Party operating under paragraph 1 of this Article may, at any time, notify the Secretariat in writing that, having taken all practicable steps it is unable to implement any or all of the obligations laid down in Articles 2A to 2E and Article 2I, or any or all obligations in Articles 2F to 2H that are decided pursuant to paragraph 1 bis of this Article, due to the inadequate implementation of Articles 10 and 10A. The Secretariat shall forthwith transmit a copy of the notification to the Parties, which shall consider the matter at their next Meeting, giving due recognition to paragraph 5 of this Article and shall decide upon appropriate action to be taken.

7. During the period between notification and the Meeting of the Parties at which the appropriate action referred to in paragraph 6 above is to be decided, or for a further period if the Meeting of the Parties so decides, the non-compliance procedures referred to in Article 8 shall not be invoked against the notifying Party.

8. A Meeting of the Parties shall review, not later than 1995, the situation of the Parties operating under paragraph 1 of this Article, including the effective implementation of financial co-operation and transfer of technology to them, and adopt such revisions that may be deemed necessary regarding the schedule of control measures applicable to those Parties.

8 *bis*. Based on the conclusions of the review referred to in paragraph 8 above:

(a) With respect to the controlled substances in Annex A, a Party operating under paragraph 1 of this Article shall, in order to meet its basic domestic needs, be entitled to delay for ten years its compliance with the control measures adopted by the Second Meeting of the Parties in London, 29 June 1990, and reference by the Protocol to Articles 2A and 2B shall be read accordingly;

(b) With respect to the controlled substances in Annex B, a Party operating under paragraph 1 of this Article shall, in order to meet its basic domestic needs, be entitled to delay for ten years its compliance with the control measures adopted by the Second Meeting of the Parties in London, 29 June 1990, and reference by the Protocol to Articles 2C to 2E shall be read accordingly.

8 *ter*. Pursuant to paragraph 1 bis above:

(a) Each Party operating under paragraph 1 of this Article shall ensure that for the twelve-month period commencing on 1 January 2016, and in each twelve-month period thereafter, its calculated level of consumption of the controlled substances in Group I of Annex C does not exceed, annually, its calculated level of consumption in 2015. As of 1 January 2016 each Party operating under paragraph 1 of this Article shall comply with the control measures set out in paragraph 8 of Article 2F and, as the basis for its compliance with these control measures, it shall use the average of its calculated levels of production and consumption in 2015;

(b) Each Party operating under paragraph 1 of this Article shall ensure that for the twelve-month period commencing on 1 January 2040, and in each twelve-month period thereafter, its calculated level of consumption of the controlled substances in Group I of Annex C does not exceed zero;

(c) Each Party operating under paragraph 1 of this Article shall comply with Article 2G;

(d) With regard to the controlled substance contained in Annex E:

(i) As of 1 January 2002 each Party operating under paragraph 1 of this Article shall comply with the control measures set out in paragraph 1 of Article 2H and, as the basis for its compliance with these control measures, it shall use the average of its annual calculated level of consumption and production, respectively, for the period of 1995 to 1998 inclusive;

(ii) Each Party operating under paragraph 1 of this Article shall ensure that for the twelve-month period commencing on 1 January 2005, and in each twelve-month period thereafter, its calculated levels of consumption and production of the controlled substance in Annex E do not exceed, annually, eighty per cent of the average of its annual calculated levels of consumption and production, respectively, for the period of 1995 to 1998 inclusive;

(iii) Each Party operating under paragraph 1 of this Article shall ensure that for the twelve-month period commencing on 1 January 2015 and in each twelve-month period thereafter, its calculated levels of consumption and production of the controlled substance in Annex E do not exceed zero. This paragraph will apply save to the extent that the Parties decide to permit the level of production or consumption that is necessary to satisfy uses agreed by them to be critical uses;

(iv) The calculated levels of consumption and production under this subparagraph shall not include the amounts used by the Party for quarantine and pre-shipment applications.

9. Decisions of the Parties referred to in paragraph 4, 6 and 7 of this Article shall be taken according to the same procedure applied to decision-making under Article 10.

Article 6: Assessment and review of control measures

Beginning in 1990, and at least every four years thereafter, the Parties shall assess the control measures provided for in Article 2 and Articles 2A to 2I on the basis of available scientific, environmental, technical and economic information. At least one year before each assessment, the Parties shall convene appropriate panels of experts qualified in the fields mentioned and determine the composition and terms of reference of any such panels. Within one year of being convened, the panels will report their conclusions, through the Secretariat, to the Parties.

Article 7: Reporting of data

1. Each Party shall provide to the Secretariat, within three months of becoming a Party, statistical data on its production, imports and exports of each of the controlled substances in Annex A

for the year 1986, or the best possible estimates of such data where actual data are not available.

2. Each Party shall provide to the Secretariat statistical data on its production, imports and exports of each of the controlled substances

—in Annex B and Annexes I and II of Group C for the year 1989;

—in Annex E, for the year 1991,

or the best possible estimates of such data where actual data are not available, not later than three months after the date when the provisions set out in the Protocol with regard to the substances in Annexes B, C and E respectively enter into force for that Party.

3. Each Party shall provide to the Secretariat statistical data on its annual production (as defined in paragraph 5 of Article 1) of each of the controlled substances listed in Annexes A, B, C and E and, separately, for each substance,

—Amounts used for feedstocks,

—Amounts destroyed by technologies approved by the Parties, and

—Imports from and exports to Parties and non-Parties respectively,

for the year during which provisions concerning the substances in Annexes A, B, C and E respectively entered into force for that Party and for each year thereafter. Each Party shall provide to the Secretariat statistical data on the annual amount of the controlled substance listed in Annex E used for quarantine and pre-shipment applications. Data shall be forwarded not later than nine months after the end of the year to which the data relate.

3 *bis*. Each Party shall provide to the Secretariat separate statistical data of its annual imports and exports of each of the controlled substances listed in Group II of Annex A and Group I of Annex C that have been recycled.

4. For Parties operating under the provisions of paragraph 8 (a) of Article 2, the requirements in paragraphs 1, 2, 3 and 3 bis of this Article in respect of statistical data on imports and exports shall be satisfied if the regional economic integration organization concerned provides data on imports and exports between the organization and States that are not members of that organization.

Article 8: Non-compliance

The Parties, at their first meeting, shall consider and approve procedures and institutional mechanisms for determining non-compliance with the provisions of this Protocol and for treatment of Parties found to be in non-compliance.

Article 9: Research, development, public awareness and exchange of information

1. The Parties shall co-operate, consistent with their national laws, regulations and practices and taking into account in particular the needs of developing countries, in promoting, directly or

through competent international bodies, research, development and exchange of information on:

(a) best technologies for improving the containment, recovery, recycling, or destruction of controlled substances or otherwise reducing their emissions;

(b) possible alternatives to controlled substances, to products containing such substances, and to products manufactured with them; and

(c) costs and benefits of relevant control strategies.

2. The Parties, individually, jointly or through competent international bodies, shall co-operate in promoting public awareness of the environmental effects of the emissions of controlled substances and other substances that deplete the ozone layer.

3. Within two years of the entry into force of this Protocol and every two years thereafter, each Party shall submit to the Secretariat a summary of the activities it has conducted pursuant to this Article.

ARTICLE 10: FINANCIAL MECHANISM

1. The Parties shall establish a mechanism for the purposes of providing financial and technical co-operation, including the transfer of technologies, to Parties operating under paragraph 1 of Article 5 of this Protocol to enable their compliance with the control measures set out in Articles 2A to 2E and Article 2I, and any control measures in Articles 2F to 2H that are decided pursuant to paragraph 1 bis of Article 5 of the Protocol. The mechanism, contributions to which shall be additional to other financial transfers to Parties operating under that paragraph, shall meet all agreed incremental costs of such Parties in order to enable their compliance with the control measures of the Protocol. An indicative list of the categories of incremental costs shall be decided by the meeting of the Parties.

2. The mechanism established under paragraph 1 shall include a Multilateral Fund. It may also include other means of multilateral, regional and bilateral co-operation.

3. The Multilateral Fund shall:

(a) Meet, on a grant or concessional basis as appropriate, and according to criteria to be decided upon by the Parties, the agreed incremental costs;

(b) Finance clearing-house functions to:

(i) Assist Parties operating under paragraph 1 of Article 5, through country specific studies and other technical co-operation, to identify their needs for co-operation;

(ii) Facilitate technical co-operation to meet these identified needs;

(iii) Distribute, as provided for in Article 9, information and relevant materials, and hold workshops, training sessions, and other related activities, for the benefit of Parties that are developing countries; and

(iv) Facilitate and monitor other multilateral, regional and bilateral co-operation available to Parties that are developing countries;

(c) Finance the secretarial services of the Multilateral Fund and related support costs.

4. The Multilateral Fund shall operate under the authority of the Parties who shall decide on its overall policies.

5. The Parties shall establish an Executive Committee to develop and monitor the implementation of specific operational policies, guidelines and administrative arrangements, including the disbursement of resources, for the purpose of achieving the objectives of the Multilateral Fund. The Executive Committee shall discharge its tasks and responsibilities, specified in its terms of reference as agreed by the Parties, with the co-operation and assistance of the International Bank for Reconstruction and Development (World Bank), the United Nations Environment Programme, the United Nations Development Programme or other appropriate agencies depending on their respective areas of expertise. The members of the Executive Committee, which shall be selected on the basis of a balanced representation of the Parties operating under paragraph 1 of Article 5 and of the Parties not so operating, shall be endorsed by the Parties.

6. The Multilateral Fund shall be financed by contributions from Parties not operating under paragraph 1 of Article 5 in convertible currency or, in certain circumstances, in kind and/or in national currency, on the basis of the United Nations scale of assessments. Contributions by other Parties shall be encouraged. Bilateral and, in particular cases agreed by a decision of the Parties, regional co-operation may, up to a percentage and consistent with any criteria to be specified by decision of the Parties, be considered as a contribution to the Multilateral Fund, provided that such co-operation, as a minimum:

(a) Strictly relates to compliance with the provisions of this Protocol;

(b) Provides additional resources; and

(c) Meets agreed incremental costs.

7. The Parties shall decide upon the programme budget of the Multilateral Fund for each fiscal period and upon the percentage of contributions of the individual Parties thereto.

8. Resources under the Multilateral Fund shall be disbursed with the concurrence of the beneficiary Party.

9. Decisions by the Parties under this Article shall be taken by consensus whenever possible. If all efforts at consensus have been exhausted and no agreement reached, decisions shall be adopted by a two-thirds majority vote of the Parties present and voting, representing a majority of the Parties operating under paragraph 1 of Article 5 present and voting and a majority of the Parties not so operating present and voting.

10. The financial mechanism set out in this Article is without prejudice to any future arrangements that may be developed with respect to other environmental issues.

ARTICLE 10A: TRANSFER OF TECHNOLOGY

Each Party shall take every practicable step, consistent with the programmes supported by the financial mechanism, to ensure:

(a) that the best available, environmentally safe substitutes and related technologies are expeditiously transferred to Parties operating under paragraph 1 of Article 5; and

(b) that the transfers referred to in subparagraph (a) occur under fair and most favourable conditions.

ARTICLE 11: MEETINGS OF THE PARTIES

1. The Parties shall hold meetings at regular intervals. The Secretariat shall convene the first meeting of the Parties not later than one year after the date of the entry into force of this Protocol and in conjunction with a meeting of the Conference of the Parties to the Convention, if a meeting of the latter is scheduled within that period.

2. Subsequent ordinary meetings of the parties shall be held, unless the Parties otherwise decide, in conjunction with meetings of the Conference of the Parties to the Convention. Extraordinary meetings of the Parties shall be held at such other times as may be deemed necessary by a meeting of the Parties, or at the written request of any Party, provided that within six months of such a request being communicated to them by the Secretariat, it is supported by at least one third of the Parties.

3. The Parties, at their first meeting, shall:

(a) adopt by consensus rules of procedure for their meetings;

(b) adopt by consensus the financial rules referred to in paragraph 2 of Article 13;

(c) establish the panels and determine the terms of reference referred to in Article 6;

(d) consider and approve the procedures and institutional mechanisms specified in Article 8; and

(e) begin preparation of workplans pursuant to paragraph 3 of Article 10.

4. The functions of the meetings of the Parties shall be to:

(a) review the implementation of this Protocol;

(b) decide on any adjustments or reductions referred to in paragraph 9 of Article 2;

(c) decide on any addition to, insertion in or removal from any annex of substances and on related control measures in accordance with paragraph 10 of Article 2;

(d) establish, where necessary, guidelines or procedures for reporting of information as provided for in Article 7 and paragraph 3 of Article 9;

(e) review requests for technical assistance submitted pursuant to paragraph 2 of Article 10;

(f) review reports prepared by the secretariat pursuant to subparagraph (c) of Article 12;

(g) assess, in accordance with Article 6, the control measures;

(h) consider and adopt, as required, proposals for amendment of this Protocol or any annex and for any new annex;

(i) consider and adopt the budget for implementing this Protocol; and

(j) consider and undertake any additional action that may be required for the achievement of the purposes of this Protocol.

5. The United Nations, its specialized agencies and the International Atomic Energy Agency, as well as any State not party to this Protocol, may be represented at meetings of the Parties as observers. Any body or agency, whether national or international, governmental or non-governmental, qualified in fields relating to the protection of the ozone layer which has informed the secretariat of its wish to be represented at a meeting of the Parties as an observer may be admitted unless at least one third of the Parties present object. The admission and participation of observers shall be subject to the rules of procedure adopted by the Parties.

Article 12: Secretariat

For the purposes of this Protocol, the Secretariat shall:

(a) arrange for and service meetings of the Parties as provided for in Article 11;

(b) receive and make available, upon request by a Party, data provided pursuant to Article 7;

(c) prepare and distribute regularly to the Parties reports based on information received pursuant to Articles 7 and 9;

(d) notify the Parties of any request for technical assistance received pursuant to Article 10 so as to facilitate the provision of such assistance;

(e) encourage non-Parties to attend the meetings of the Parties as observers and to act in accordance with the provisions of this Protocol;

(f) provide, as appropriate, the information and requests referred to in subparagraphs (c) and (d) to such non-party observers; and

(g) perform such other functions for the achievement of the purposes of this Protocol as may be assigned to it by the Parties.

Article 13: Financial provisions

1. The funds required for the operation of this Protocol, including those for the functioning of the Secretariat related to this Protocol, shall be charged exclusively against contributions from the Parties.

2. The Parties, at their first meeting, shall adopt by consensus financial rules for the operation of this Protocol.

Article 14: Relationship of this protocol to the convention

Except as otherwise provided in this Protocol, the provisions of the Convention relating to its protocols shall apply to this Protocol.

Article 15: Signature

This Protocol shall be open for signature by States and by regional economic integration organizations in Montreal on 16 September 1987, in Ottawa from 17 September 1987 to 16 January 1988, and at United Nations Headquarters in New York from 17 January 1988 to 15 September 1988.

ARTICLE 16: ENTRY INTO FORCE

1. This Protocol shall enter into force on 1 January 1989, provided that at least eleven instruments of ratification, acceptance, approval of the Protocol or accession thereto have been deposited by States or regional economic integration organizations representing at least two-thirds of 1986 estimated global consumption of the controlled substances, and the provisions of paragraph 1 of Article 17 of the Convention have been fulfilled. In the event that these conditions have not been fulfilled by that date, the Protocol shall enter into force on the ninetieth day following the date on which the conditions have been fulfilled.

2. For the purposes of paragraph 1, any such instrument deposited by a regional economic integration organization shall not be counted as additional to those deposited by member States of such organization.

3. After the entry into force of this Protocol, any State or regional economic integration organization shall become a Party to it on the ninetieth day following the date of deposit of its instrument of ratification, acceptance, approval or accession.

ARTICLE 17: PARTIES JOINING AFTER ENTRY INTO FORCE

Subject to Article 5, any State or regional economic integration organization which becomes a Party to this Protocol after the date of its entry into force, shall fulfil forthwith the sum of the obligations under Article 2, as well as under Articles 2A to 2I and Article 4, that apply at that date to the States and regional economic integration organizations that became Parties on the date the Protocol entered into force.

ARTICLE 18: RESERVATIONS

No reservations may be made to this Protocol.

ARTICLE 19: WITHDRAWAL

Any Party may withdraw from this Protocol by giving written notification to the Depositary at any time after four years of assuming the obligations specified in paragraph 1 of Article 2A. Any such withdrawal shall take effect upon expiry of one year after the date of its receipt by the Depositary, or on such later date as may be specified in the notification of the withdrawal.

ARTICLE 20: AUTHENTIC TEXTS

The original of this Protocol, of which the Arabic, Chinese, English, French, Russian and Spanish texts are equally authentic, shall be deposited with the Secretary-General of the United Nations.

IN WITNESS WHEREOF the undersigned, being duly authorized to that effect, have signed this protocol.

DONE at Montreal this sixteenth day of September, one thousand nine hundred and eighty seven.

Annex A: Controlled substances

Group	Substance	Ozone-Depleting Potential*
Group I		
$CFCl_3$	(CFC–11)	1.0
CF_2Cl_2	(CFC–12)	1.0
$C_2F_3Cl_3$	(CFC–113)	0.8
$C_2F_4Cl_2$	(CFC–114)	1.0
C_2F_5Cl	(CFC–115)	0.6
Group II		
CF_2BrCl	(halon-1211)	3.0
CF_3Br	(halon-1301)	10.0
$C_2F_4Br_2$	(halon-2402)	6.0

*These ozone depleting potentials are estimates based on existing knowledge and will be reviewed and revised periodically.

Annex B: Controlled substances

Group	Substance	Ozone-Depleting Potential
Group I		
CF_3Cl	(CFC–13)	1.0
C_2FCl_5	(CFC–111)	1.0
$C_2F_2Cl_4$	(CFC–112)	1.0
C_3FCl_7	(CFC–211)	1.0
$C_3F_2Cl_6$	(CFC–212)	1.0
$C_3F_3Cl_5$	(CFC–213)	1.0
$C_3F_4Cl_4$	(CFC–214)	1.0
$C_3F_5Cl_3$	(CFC–215)	1.0
$C_3F_6Cl_2$	(CFC–216)	1.0
C3F7Cl	(CFC–217)	1.0
Group II		
CCl_4	carbon tetrachloride	1.1
Group III		
$C_2H_3Cl_3$*	1,1,1-trichloroethane* (methyl chloroform)	0.1

*This formula does not refer to 1,1,2-trichloroethane.

Annex C: Controlled substances

Group	Substance	Number of isomers	Ozone-Depleting Potential
Group I			
$CHFCl_2$	(HCFC–21)**	1	0.04
CHF_2Cl	(HCFC–22)**	1	0.055
CH_2FCl	(HCFC–31)	1	0.02

ANNEX C: CONTROLLED SUBSTANCES—CONTINUED

Group	Substance	Number of isomers	Ozone-Depleting Potential
C_2HFCl_4	(HCFC–121)	2	0.01–0.04
$C_2HF_2Cl_3$	(HCFC–122)	3	0.02–0.08
$C_2HF_3Cl_2$	(HCFC–123)	3	0.02–0.06
$CHCl_2CF_3$	(HCFC–123)**	—	0.02
C_2HF_4Cl	(HCFC–124)	2	0.02–0.04
$CHFClCF_3$	(HCFC–124)**	—	0.022
$C_2H_2FCl_3$	(HCFC–131)	3	0.007–0.05
$C_2H_2F_2Cl_2$	(HCFC–132)	4	0.008–0.05
$C_2H_2F_3Cl$	(HCFC–133)	3	0.02–0.06
$C_2H_3FCl_2$	(HCFC–141)	3	0.005–0.07
CH_3CFCl_2	(HCFC–141b)**	—	0.11
$C_2H_3F_2Cl$	(HCFC–142)	3	0.008–0.07
CH_3CF_2Cl	(HCFC–142b)**	—	0.065
C_2H_4FCl	(HCFC–151)	2	0.003–0.005
C_3HFCl_6	(HCFC–221)	5	0.015–0.07
$C_3HF_2Cl_5$	(HCFC–222)	9	0.01–0.09
$C_3HF_3Cl_4$	(HCFC–223)	12	0.01–0.08
$C_3HF_4Cl_3$	(HCFC–224)	12	0.01–0.09
$C_3HF_5Cl_2$	(HCFC–225)	9	0.02–0.07
$CF_3CF_2CHCl_2$	(HCFC–225ca)**	—	0.025
CF_2ClCF_2CHClF	(HCFC–225cb)**	—	0.033
C_3HF_6Cl	(HCFC–226)	5	0.02–0.10
$C_3H_2FCl_5$	(HCFC–231)	9	0.05–0.09
$C_3H_2F_2Cl_4$	(HCFC–232)	16	0.008–0.10
$C_3H_2F_3Cl_3$	(HCFC–233)	18	0.007–0.23
$C_3H_2F_4Cl_2$	(HCFC–234)	16	0.01–0.28
$C_3H_2F_5Cl$	(HCFC–235)	9	0.03–0.52
$C_3H_3FCl_4$	(HCFC–241)	12	0.004–0.09
$C_3H_3F_2Cl_3$	(HCFC–242)	18	0.005–0.13
$C_3H_3F_3Cl_2$	(HCFC–243)	18	0.007–0.12
$C_3H_3F_4Cl$	(HCFC–244)	12	0.009–0.14
$C_3H_4FCl_3$	(HCFC–251)	12	0.001–0.01
$C_3H_4F_2Cl_2$	(HCFC–252)	16	0.005–0.04
$C_3H_4F_3Cl$	(HCFC–253)	12	0.003–0.03
$C_3H_5FCl_2$	(HCFC–261)	9	0.002–0.02
$C_3H_5F_2Cl$	(HCFC–262)	9	0.002–0.02
C_3H_6FCl	(HCFC–271)	5	0.001–0.03
Group II			
$CHFBr_2$	1		1.00
CHF_2Br	(HBFC–22B1)	1	0.74
CH_2FBr	1		0.73
C_2HFBr_4		2	0.3–0.8
$C_2HF_2Br_3$		3	0.5–1.8
$C_2HF_3Br_2$		3	0.4–1.6
C_2HF_4Br		2	0.7–1.2
$C_2H_2FBr_3$		3	0.1–1.1
$C_2H_2F_2Br_2$		4	0.2–1.5
$C_2H_2F_3Br$		3	0.7–1.6
$C_2H_3FBr_2$		3	0.1–1.7
$C_2H_3F_2Br$		3	0.2–1.1
C_2H_4FBr		2	0.07–0.1
C_3HFBr6		5	0.3–1.5
$C_3HF_2Br_5$		9	0.2–1.9

ANNEX C: CONTROLLED SUBSTANCES—CONTINUED

Group	Substance	Number of isomers	Ozone-Depleting Potential
$C_3HF_3Br_4$		12	0.3–1.8
$C_3HF_4Br_3$		12	0.5–2.2
$C_3HF_5Br_2$		9	0.9–2.0
C_3HF_6Br		5	0.7–3.3
$C_3H_2FBr_5$		9	0.1–1.9
$C_3H_2F_2Br_4$		16	0.2–2.1
$C_3H_2F_3Br_3$		18	0.2–5.6
$C_3H_2F_4Br_2$		16	0.3–7.5
$C_3H_2F_5Br$		8	0.9–14.0
$C_3H_3FBr_4$		12	0.08–1.9
$C_3H_3F_2Br_3$		18	0.1–3.1
$C_3H_3F_3Br_2$		18	0.1–2.5
$C_3H_3F_4Br$		12	0.3–4.4
$C_3H_4FBr_3$		12	0.03–0.3
$C_3H_4F_2Br_2$		16	0.1–1.0
$C_3H_4F_3Br$		12	0.07–0.8
$C_3H_5FBr_2$		9	0.04–0.4
$C_3H_5F_2Br$		9	0.07–0.8
C_3H_6FBr		5	0.02–0.7
Group III			
CH_2BrCl	bromochloromethane	1	0.12

*Where a range of ODPs is indicated, the highest value in that range shall be used for the purposes of the Protocol. The ODPs listed as a single value have been determined from calculations based on laboratory measurements. Those listed as a range are based on estimates and are less certain. The range pertains to an isomeric group. The upper value is the estimate of the ODP of the isomer with the highest ODP, and the lower value is the estimate of the ODP of the isomer with the lowest ODP.

**Identifies the most commercially viable substances with ODP values listed against them to be used for the purposes of the Protocol.

ANNEX D:* A LIST OF PRODUCTS** CONTAINING CONTROLLED SUBSTANCES SPECIFIED IN ANNEX A

Products	Customs code number
1. Automobile and truck air conditioning units (whether incorporated in vehicles or not)	—
2. Domestic and commercial refrigeration and air conditioning/heat pump equipment***	—
e.g. Refrigerators	—
Freezers	—
Dehumidifiers	—
Water coolers	—
Ice machines	—
Air conditioning and heat pump units	—
3. Aerosol products, except medical aerosols	—
4. Portable fire extinguisher	—
5. Insulation boards, panels and pipe covers	—

Annex D:* A list of products** containing controlled substances specified in Annex A—Continued

Products	Customs code number
6. Pre-polymers	—

*This Annex was adopted by the Third Meeting of the Parties in Nairobi, 21 June 1991 as required by paragraph 3 of Article 4 of the Protocol.

**Though not when transported in consignments of personal or household effects or in similar non-commercial situations normally exempted from customs attention.

***When containing controlled substances in Annex A as a refrigerant and/or in insulating material of the product.

Annex E: Controlled substance

Group	Substance	Ozone-Depleting Potential
Group I		
CH_3Br	methyl bromide	0.6

7. U.N. Convention to Combat Desertification in those Countries Experiencing Serious Drought and/or Desertification, Particularly in Africa

Done at Paris, June 17, 1994; Entered into force generally, December 26, 1996; Ratification advised by the Senate, October 18, 2000; Entered into force for the United States, February 15, 2001

UNITED NATIONS CONVENTION TO COMBAT DESERTIFICATION IN THOSE COUNTRIES EXPERIENCING SERIOUS DROUGHT AND/OR DESERTIFICATION, PARTICULARLY IN AFRICA [1]

The Parties to this Convention,

AFFIRMING that human beings in affected or threatened areas are at the centre of concerns to combat desertification and mitigate the effects of drought,

REFLECTING the urgent concern of the international community, including States and international organizations, about the adverse impacts of desertification and drought,

AWARE that arid, semi-arid and dry sub-humid areas together account for a significant proportion of the Earth's land area and are the habitat and source of livelihood for a large segment of its population,

ACKNOWLEDGING that desertification and drought are problems of global dimension in that they affect all regions of the world and that joint action of the international community is needed to combat desertification and/or mitigate the effects of drought,

NOTING the high concentration of developing countries, notably the least developed countries, among those experiencing serious drought and/or desertification, and the particularly tragic consequences of these phenomena in Africa,

NOTING ALSO that desertification is caused by complex interactions among physical, biological, political, social, cultural and economic factors,

CONSIDERING the impact of trade and relevant aspects of international economic relations on the ability of affected countries to combat desertification adequately,

CONSCIOUS that sustainable economic growth, social development and poverty eradication are priorities of affected developing countries, particularly in Africa, and are essential to meeting sustainability objectives,

MINDFUL that desertification and drought affect sustainable development through their interrelationships with important social problems such as poverty, poor health and nutrition, lack of food

[1] For a list of states that are parties to the Convention, see Department of State publication, *Treaties in Force.*

security, and those arising from migration, displacement of persons and demographic dynamics,

APPRECIATING the significance of the past efforts and experience of States and international organizations in combating desertification and mitigating the effects of drought, particularly in implementing the Plan of Action to Combat Desertification which was adopted at the United Nations Conference on Desertification in 1977,

REALIZING that, despite efforts in the past, progress in combating desertification and mitigating the effects of drought has not met expectations and that a new and more effective approach is needed at all levels within the framework of sustainable development,

RECOGNIZING the validity and relevance of decisions adopted at the United Nations Conference on Environment and Development, particularly of Agenda 21 and its chapter 12, which provide a basis for combating desertification,

REAFFIRMING in this light the commitments of developed countries as contained in paragraph 13 of chapter 33 of Agenda 21,

RECALLING General Assembly resolution 47/188, particularly the priority in it prescribed for Africa, and all other relevant United Nations resolutions, decisions and programmes on desertification and drought, as well as relevant declarations by African countries and those from other regions,

REAFFIRMING the Rio Declaration on Environment and Development which states, in its Principle 2, that States have, in accordance with the Charter of the United Nations and the principles of international law, the sovereign right to exploit their own resources pursuant to their own environmental and developmental policies, and the responsibility to ensure that activities within their jurisdiction or control do not cause damage to the environment of other States or of areas beyond the limits of national jurisdiction,

RECOGNIZING that national Governments play a critical role in combating desertification and mitigating the effects of drought and that progress in that respect depends on local implementation of action programmes in affected areas,

RECOGNIZING also the importance and necessity of international cooperation and partnership in combating desertification and mitigating the effects of drought,

RECOGNIZING further the importance of the provision to affected developing countries, particularly in Africa, of effective means, inter alia substantial financial resources, including new and additional funding, and access to technology, without which it will be difficult for them to implement fully their commitments under this Convention,

EXPRESSING concern over the impact of desertification and drought on affected countries in Central Asia and the Transcaucasus,

STRESSING the important role played by women in regions affected by desertification and/or drought, particularly in rural areas of developing countries, and the importance of ensuring the full participation of both men and women at all levels in programmes to combat desertification and mitigate the effects of drought,

EMPHASIZING the special role of non-governmental organizations and other major groups in programmes to combat desertification and mitigate the effects of drought,

BEARING in mind the relationship between desertification and other environmental problems of global dimension facing the international and national communities,

BEARING also in mind the contribution that combating desertification can make to achieving the objectives of the United Nations Framework Convention on Climate Change, the Convention on Biological Diversity and other related environmental conventions,

BELIEVING that strategies to combat desertification and mitigate the effects of drought will be most effective if they are based on sound systematic observation and rigorous scientific knowledge and if they are continuously re-evaluated,

RECOGNIZING the urgent need to improve the effectiveness and coordination of international cooperation to facilitate the implementation of national plans and priorities,

DETERMINED to take appropriate action in combating desertification and mitigating the effects of drought for the benefit of present and future generations,

HAVE AGREED AS FOLLOWS:

PART I—INTRODUCTION

ARTICLE 1

Use of terms

For the purposes of this Convention:

(a) "desertification" means land degradation in arid, semi-arid and dry sub-humid areas resulting from various factors, including climatic variations and human activities;

(b) "combating desertification" includes activities which are part of the integrated development of land in arid, semi-arid and dry sub-humid areas for sustainable development which are aimed at:

(i) prevention and/or reduction of land degradation;

(ii) rehabilitation of partly degraded land; and

(iii) reclamation of desertified land;

(c) "drought" means the naturally occurring phenomenon that exists when precipitation has been significantly below normal recorded levels, causing serious hydrological imbalances that adversely affect land resource production systems;

(d) "mitigating the effects of drought" means activities related to the prediction of drought and intended to reduce the vulnerability of society and natural systems to drought as it relates to combating desertification;

(e) "land" means the terrestrial bio-productive system that comprises soil, vegetation, other biota, and the ecological and hydrological processes that operate within the system;

(f) "land degradation" means reduction or loss, in arid, semi-arid and dry sub-humid areas, of the biological or economic productivity and complexity of rainfed cropland, irrigated cropland, or range, pasture, forest and woodlands resulting from land uses or from a process or combination of processes, including processes arising from human activities and habitation patterns, such as:

(i) soil erosion caused by wind and/or water;

(ii) deterioration of the physical, chemical and biological or economic properties of soil; and

(iii) long-term loss of natural vegetation;

(g) "arid, semi-arid and dry sub-humid areas" means areas, other than polar and sub-polar regions, in which the ratio of annual precipitation to potential evapotranspiration falls within the range from 0.05 to 0.65;

(h) "affected areas" means arid, semi-arid and/or dry sub-humid areas affected or threatened by desertification;

(i) "affected countries" means countries whose lands include, in whole or in part, affected areas;

(j) "regional economic integration organization" means an organization constituted by sovereign States of a given region which has competence in respect of matters governed by this Convention and has been duly authorized, in accordance with its internal procedures, to sign, ratify, accept, approve or accede to this Convention;

(k) "developed country Parties" means developed country Parties and regional economic integration organizations constituted by developed countries.

Article 2

Objective

1. The objective of this Convention is to combat desertification and mitigate the effects of drought in countries experiencing serious drought and/or desertification, particularly in Africa, through effective action at all levels, supported by international cooperation and partnership arrangements, in the framework of an integrated approach which is consistent with Agenda 21, with a view to contributing to the achievement of sustainable development in affected areas.

2. Achieving this objective will involve long-term integrated strategies that focus simultaneously, in affected areas, on improved productivity of land, and the rehabilitation, conservation and sustainable management of land and water resources, leading to improved living conditions, in particular at the community level.

Article 3

Principles

In order to achieve the objective of this Convention and to implement its provisions, the Parties shall be guided, inter alia, by the following:

(a) the Parties should ensure that decisions on the design and implementation of programmes to combat desertification and/or mitigate the effects of drought are taken with the participation of populations and local communities and that an enabling environment is created at higher levels to facilitate action at national and local levels;

(b) the Parties should, in a spirit of international solidarity and partnership, improve cooperation and coordination at subregional, regional and international levels, and better focus financial, human, organizational and technical resources where they are needed;

(c) the Parties should develop, in a spirit of partnership, cooperation among all levels of government, communities, nongovernmental organizations and landholders to establish a better understanding of the nature and value of land and scarce water resources in affected areas and to work towards their sustainable use; and

(d) the Parties should take into full consideration the special needs and circumstances of affected developing country Parties, particularly the least developed among them.

Part II—General Provisions

Article 4

General obligations

1. The Parties shall implement their obligations under this Convention, individually or jointly, either through existing or prospective bilateral and multilateral arrangements or a combination thereof, as appropriate, emphasizing the need to coordinate efforts and develop a coherent long-term strategy at all levels.

2. In pursuing the objective of this Convention, the Parties shall:

(a) adopt an integrated approach addressing the physical, biological and socio-economic aspects of the processes of desertification and drought;

(b) give due attention, within the relevant international and regional bodies, to the situation of affected developing country Parties with regard to international trade, marketing arrangements and debt with a view to establishing an enabling international economic environment conducive to the promotion of sustainable development;

(c) integrate strategies for poverty eradication into efforts to combat desertification and mitigate the effects of drought;

(d) promote cooperation among affected country Parties in the fields of environmental protection and the conservation of land and water resources, as they relate to desertification and drought;

(e) strengthen subregional, regional and international cooperation;

(f) cooperate within relevant intergovernmental organizations;

(g) determine institutional mechanisms, if appropriate, keeping in mind the need to avoid duplication; and

(h) promote the use of existing bilateral and multilateral financial mechanisms and arrangements that mobilize and channel substantial financial resources to affected developing country Parties in combating desertification and mitigating the effects of drought.

3. Affected developing country Parties are eligible for assistance in the implementation of the Convention.

ARTICLE 5

Obligations of affected country Parties

In addition to their obligations pursuant to article 4, affected country Parties undertake to:

(a) give due priority to combating desertification and mitigating the effects of drought, and allocate adequate resources in accordance with their circumstances and capabilities;

(b) establish strategies and priorities, within the framework of sustainable development plans and/or policies, to combat desertification and mitigate the effects of drought;

(c) address the underlying causes of desertification and pay special attention to the socio-economic factors contributing to desertification processes;

(d) promote awareness and facilitate the participation of local populations, particularly women and youth, with the support of non-governmental organizations, in efforts to combat desertification and mitigate the effects of drought; and

(e) provide an enabling environment by strengthening, as appropriate, relevant existing legislation and, where they do not exist, enacting new laws and establishing long-term policies and action programmes.

ARTICLE 6

Obligations of developed country Parties

In addition to their general obligations pursuant to article 4, developed country Parties undertake to:

(a) actively support, as agreed, individually or jointly, the efforts of affected developing country Parties, particularly those in Africa, and the least developed countries, to combat desertification and mitigate the effects of drought;

(b) provide substantial financial resources and other forms of support to assist affected developing country Parties, particularly those in Africa, effectively to develop and implement their own long-term plans and strategies to combat desertification and mitigate the effects of drought;

(c) promote the mobilization of new and additional funding pursuant to article 20, paragraph 2 (b);

(d) encourage the mobilization of funding from the private sector and other non-governmental sources; and

(e) promote and facilitate access by affected country Parties, particularly affected developing country Parties, to appropriate technology, knowledge and know-how.

ARTICLE 7

Priority for Africa

In implementing this Convention, the Parties shall give priority to affected African country Parties, in the light of the particular situation prevailing in that region, while not neglecting affected developing country Parties in other regions.

ARTICLE 8

Relationship with other conventions

1. The Parties shall encourage the coordination of activities carried out under this Convention and, if they are Parties to them, under other relevant international agreements, particularly the United Nations Framework Convention on Climate Change and the Convention on Biological Diversity, in order to derive maximum benefit from activities under each agreement while avoiding duplication of effort. The Parties shall encourage the conduct of joint programmes, particularly in the fields of research, training, systematic observation and information collection and exchange, to the extent that such activities may contribute to achieving the objectives of the agreements concerned.

2. The provisions of this Convention shall not affect the rights and obligations of any Party deriving from a bilateral, regional or international agreement into which it has entered prior to the entry into force of this Convention for it.

PART III—ACTION PROGRAMMES, SCIENTIFIC AND TECHNICAL COOPERATION AND SUPPORTING MEASURES

SECTION 1: ACTION PROGRAMMES

ARTICLE 9

Basic approach

1. In carrying out their obligations pursuant to article 5, affected developing country Parties and any other affected country Party in the framework of its regional implementation annex or, otherwise, that has notified the Permanent Secretariat in writing of its intention to prepare a national action programme, shall, as appropriate, prepare, make public and implement national action programmes, utilizing and building, to the extent possible, on existing relevant successful plans and programmes, and subregional and regional action programmes, as the central element of the strategy to combat desertification and mitigate the effects of drought. Such programmes shall be updated through a continuing participatory process on the basis of lessons from field action, as well as the results of research. The preparation of national action programmes shall be closely interlinked with other efforts to formulate national policies for sustainable development.

2. In the provision by developed country Parties of different forms of assistance under the terms of article 6, priority shall be given to supporting, as agreed, national, subregional and regional

action programmes of affected developing country Parties, particularly those in Africa, either directly or through relevant multilateral organizations or both.

3. The Parties shall encourage organs, funds and programmes of the United Nations system and other relevant intergovernmental organizations, academic institutions, the scientific community and non-governmental organizations in a position to cooperate, in accordance with their mandates and capabilities, to support the elaboration, implementation and follow-up of action programmes.

Article 10

National action programmes

1. The purpose of national action programmes is to identify the factors contributing to desertification and practical measures necessary to combat desertification and mitigate the effects of drought.

2. National action programmes shall specify the respective roles of government, local communities and land users and the resources available and needed. They shall, inter alia:

(a) incorporate long-term strategies to combat desertification and mitigate the effects of drought, emphasize implementation and be integrated with national policies for sustainable development;

(b) allow for modifications to be made in response to changing circumstances and be sufficiently flexible at the local level to cope with different socio-economic, biological and geo-physical conditions;

(c) give particular attention to the implementation of preventive measures for lands that are not yet degraded or which are only slightly degraded;

(d) enhance national climatological, meteorological and hydrological capabilities and the means to provide for drought early warning;

(e) promote policies and strengthen institutional frameworks which develop cooperation and coordination, in a spirit of partnership, between the donor community, governments at all levels, local populations and community groups, and facilitate access by local populations to appropriate information and technology;

(f) provide for effective participation at the local, national and regional levels of non- governmental organizations and local populations, both women and men, particularly resource users, including farmers and pastoralists and their representative organizations, in policy planning, decision-making, and implementation and review of national action programmes; and

(g) require regular review of, and progress reports on, their implementation.

3. National action programmes may include, inter alia, some or all of the following measures to prepare for and mitigate the effects of drought:

(a) establishment and/or strengthening, as appropriate, of early warning systems, including local and national facilities and joint systems at the subregional and regional levels, and mechanisms for assisting environmentally displaced persons;

(b) strengthening of drought preparedness and management, including drought contingency plans at the local, national, subregional and regional levels, which take into consideration seasonal to interannual climate predictions;

(c) establishment and/or strengthening, as appropriate, of food security systems, including storage and marketing facilities, particularly in rural areas;

(d) establishment of alternative livelihood projects that could provide incomes in drought prone areas; and

(e) development of sustainable irrigation programmes for both crops and livestock.

4. Taking into account the circumstances and requirements specific to each affected country Party, national action programmes include, as appropriate, inter alia, measures in some or all of the following priority fields as they relate to combating desertification and mitigating the effects of drought in affected areas and to their populations: promotion of alternative livelihoods and improvement of national economic environments with a view to strengthening programmes aimed at the eradication of poverty and at ensuring food security; demographic dynamics; sustainable management of natural resources; sustainable agricultural practices; development and efficient use of various energy sources; institutional and legal frameworks; strengthening of capabilities for assessment and systematic observation, including hydrological and meteorological services, and capacity building, education and public awareness.

ARTICLE 11

Subregional and regional action programmes

Affected country Parties shall consult and cooperate to prepare, as appropriate, in accordance with relevant regional implementation annexes, subregional and/or regional action programmes to harmonize, complement and increase the efficiency of national programmes. The provisions of article 10 shall apply mutatis mutandis to subregional and regional programmes. Such cooperation may include agreed joint programmes for the sustainable management of transboundary natural resources, scientific and technical cooperation, and strengthening of relevant institutions.

ARTICLE 12

International cooperation

Affected country Parties, in collaboration with other Parties and the international community, should cooperate to ensure the promotion of an enabling international environment in the implementation of the Convention. Such cooperation should also cover fields of technology transfer as well as scientific research and development, information collection and dissemination and financial resources.

ARTICLE 13

Support for the elaboration and implementation of action programmes

1. Measures to support action programmes pursuant to article 9 include, inter alia:

(a) financial cooperation to provide predictability for action programmes, allowing for necessary long-term planning;

(b) elaboration and use of cooperation mechanisms which better enable support at the local level, including action through non-governmental organizations, in order to promote the replicability of successful pilot programme activities where relevant;

(c) increased flexibility in project design, funding and implementation in keeping with the experimental, iterative approach indicated for participatory action at the local community level; and

(d) as appropriate, administrative and budgetary procedures that increase the efficiency of cooperation and of support programmes.

2. In providing such support to affected developing country Parties, priority shall be given to African country Parties and to least developed country Parties.

ARTICLE 14

Coordination in the elaboration and implementation of action programmes

1. The Parties shall work closely together, directly and through relevant intergovernmental organizations, in the elaboration and implementation of action programmes.

2. The Parties shall develop operational mechanisms, particularly at the national and field levels, to ensure the fullest possible coordination among developed country Parties, developing country Parties and relevant intergovernmental and non-governmental organizations, in order to avoid duplication, harmonize interventions and approaches, and maximize the impact of assistance. In affected developing country Parties, priority will be given to coordinating activities related to international cooperation in order to maximize the efficient use of resources, to ensure responsive assistance, and to facilitate the implementation of national action programmes and priorities under this Convention.

ARTICLE 15

Regional implementation annexes

Elements for incorporation in action programmes shall be selected and adapted to the socio-economic, geographical and climatic factors applicable to affected country Parties or regions, as well as to their level of development. Guidelines for the preparation of action programmes and their exact focus and content for particular subregions and regions are set out in the regional implementation annexes.

SECTION 2: SCIENTIFIC AND TECHNICAL COOPERATION

ARTICLE 16

Information collection, analysis and exchange

The Parties agree, according to their respective capabilities, to integrate and coordinate the collection, analysis and exchange of relevant short term and long term data and information to ensure systematic observation of land degradation in affected areas and to understand better and assess the processes and effects of drought and desertification. This would help accomplish, inter alia, early warning and advance planning for periods of adverse climatic variation in a form suited for practical application by users at all levels, including especially local populations. To this end, they shall, as appropriate:

(a) facilitate and strengthen the functioning of the global network of institutions and facilities for the collection, analysis and exchange of information, as well as for systematic observation at all levels, which shall, inter alia:

(i) aim to use compatible standards and systems;

(ii) encompass relevant data and stations, including in remote areas;

(iii) use and disseminate modern technology for data collection, transmission and assessment on land degradation; and

(iv) link national, subregional and regional data and information centres more closely with global information sources;

(b) ensure that the collection, analysis and exchange of information address the needs of local communities and those of decision makers, with a view to resolving specific problems, and that local communities are involved in these activities;

(c) support and further develop bilateral and multilateral programmes and projects aimed at defining, conducting, assessing and financing the collection, analysis and exchange of data and information, including, inter alia, integrated sets of physical, biological, social and economic indicators;

(d) make full use of the expertise of competent intergovernmental and non-governmental organizations, particularly to disseminate relevant information and experiences among target groups in different regions;

(e) give full weight to the collection, analysis and exchange of socio-economic data, and their integration with physical and biological data;

(f) exchange and make fully, openly and promptly available information from all publicly available sources relevant to combating desertification and mitigating the effects of drought; and

(g) subject to their respective national legislation and/or policies, exchange information on local and traditional knowledge, ensuring adequate protection for it and providing appropriate return from the benefits derived from it, on an equitable basis and on mutually agreed terms, to the local populations concerned.

Article 17

Research and development

1. The Parties undertake, according to their respective capabilities, to promote technical and scientific cooperation in the fields of combating desertification and mitigating the effects of drought through appropriate national, subregional, regional and international institutions. To this end, they shall support research activities that:

(a) contribute to increased knowledge of the processes leading to desertification and drought and the impact of, and distinction between, causal factors, both natural and human, with a view to combating desertification and mitigating the effects of drought, and achieving improved productivity as well as sustainable use and management of resources;

(b) respond to well defined objectives, address the specific needs of local populations and lead to the identification and implementation of solutions that improve the living standards of people in affected areas;

(c) protect, integrate, enhance and validate traditional and local knowledge, know-how and practices, ensuring, subject to their respective national legislation and/or policies, that the owners of that knowledge will directly benefit on an equitable basis and on mutually agreed terms from any commercial utilization of it or from any technological development derived from that knowledge;

(d) develop and strengthen national, subregional and regional research capabilities in affected developing country Parties, particularly in Africa, including the development of local skills and the strengthening of appropriate capacities, especially in countries with a weak research base, giving particular attention to multidisciplinary and participative socio-economic research;

(e) take into account, where relevant, the relationship between poverty, migration caused by environmental factors, and desertification;

(f) promote the conduct of joint research programmes between national, subregional, regional and international research organizations, in both the public and private sectors, for the development of improved, affordable and accessible technologies for sustainable development through effective participation of local populations and communities; and

(g) enhance the availability of water resources in affected areas, by means of, inter alia, cloud-seeding.

2. Research priorities for particular regions and subregions, reflecting different local conditions, should be included in action programmes. The Conference of the Parties shall review research priorities periodically on the advice of the Committee on Science and Technology.

ARTICLE 18

Transfer, acquisition, adaptation and development of technology

1. The Parties undertake, as mutually agreed and in accordance with their respective national legislation and/or policies, to promote, finance and/or facilitate the financing of the transfer, acquisition, adaptation and development of environmentally sound, economically viable and socially acceptable technologies relevant to combating desertification and/or mitigating the effects of drought, with a view to contributing to the achievement of sustainable development in affected areas. Such cooperation shall be conducted bilaterally or multilaterally, as appropriate, making full use of the expertise of intergovernmental and non-governmental organizations. The Parties shall, in particular:

(a) fully utilize relevant existing national, subregional, regional and international information systems and clearing-houses for the dissemination of information on available technologies, their sources, their environmental risks and the broad terms under which they may be acquired;

(b) facilitate access, in particular by affected developing country Parties, on favourable terms, including on concessional and preferential terms, as mutually agreed, taking into account the need to protect intellectual property rights, to technologies most suitable to practical application for specific needs of local populations, paying special attention to the social, cultural, economic and environmental impact of such technology;

(c) facilitate technology cooperation among affected country Parties through financial assistance or other appropriate means;

(d) extend technology cooperation with affected developing country Parties, including, where relevant, joint ventures, especially to sectors which foster alternative livelihoods; and

(e) take appropriate measures to create domestic market conditions and incentives, fiscal or otherwise, conducive to the development, transfer, acquisition and adaptation of suitable technology, knowledge, know-how and practices, including measures to ensure adequate and effective protection of intellectual property rights.

2. The Parties shall, according to their respective capabilities, and subject to their respective national legislation and/or policies, protect, promote and use in particular relevant traditional and local technology, knowledge, know-how and practices and, to that end, they undertake to:

(a) make inventories of such technology, knowledge, know-how and practices and their potential uses with the participation of local populations, and disseminate such information, where appropriate, in cooperation with relevant intergovernmental and non-governmental organizations;

(b) ensure that such technology, knowledge, know-how and practices are adequately protected and that local populations benefit directly, on an equitable basis and as mutually agreed, from any commercial utilization of them or from any technological development derived therefrom;

(c) encourage and actively support the improvement and dissemination of such technology, knowledge, know-how and practices or of the development of new technology based on them; and

(d) facilitate, as appropriate, the adaptation of such technology, knowledge, know-how and practices to wide use and integrate them with modern technology, as appropriate.

SECTION 3: SUPPORTING MEASURES

ARTICLE 19

Capacity building, education and public awareness

1. The Parties recognize the significance of capacity building—that is to say, institution building, training and development of relevant local and national capacities—in efforts to combat desertification and mitigate the effects of drought. They shall promote, as appropriate, capacity-building:

(a) through the full participation at all levels of local people, particularly at the local level, especially women and youth, with the cooperation of non-governmental and local organizations;

(b) by strengthening training and research capacity at the national level in the field of desertification and drought;

(c) by establishing and/or strengthening support and extension services to disseminate relevant technology methods and techniques more effectively, and by training field agents and members of rural organizations in participatory approaches for the conservation and sustainable use of natural resources;

(d) by fostering the use and dissemination of the knowledge, know-how and practices of local people in technical cooperation programmes, wherever possible;

(e) by adapting, where necessary, relevant environmentally sound technology and traditional methods of agriculture and pastoralism to modern socio-economic conditions;

(f) by providing appropriate training and technology in the use of alternative energy sources, particularly renewable energy resources, aimed particularly at reducing dependence on wood for fuel;

(g) through cooperation, as mutually agreed, to strengthen the capacity of affected developing country Parties to develop and implement programmes in the field of collection, analysis and exchange of information pursuant to article 16;

(h) through innovative ways of promoting alternative livelihoods, including training in new skills;

(i) by training of decision makers, managers, and personnel who are responsible for the collection and analysis of data for the dissemination and use of early warning information on drought conditions and for food production;

(j) through more effective operation of existing national institutions and legal frameworks and, where necessary, creation of new ones, along with strengthening of strategic planning and management; and

(k) by means of exchange visitor programmes to enhance capacity building in affected country Parties through a long-term, interactive process of learning and study.

2. Affected developing country Parties shall conduct, in cooperation with other Parties and competent intergovernmental and non-governmental organizations, as appropriate, an interdisciplinary review of available capacity and facilities at the local and national levels, and the potential for strengthening them.

3. The Parties shall cooperate with each other and through competent intergovernmental organizations, as well as with non-governmental organizations, in undertaking and supporting public awareness and educational programmes in both affected and, where relevant, unaffected country Parties to promote understanding of the causes and effects of desertification and drought and of the importance of meeting the objective of this Convention. To that end, they shall:

(a) organize awareness campaigns for the general public;

(b) promote, on a permanent basis, access by the public to relevant information, and wide public participation in education and awareness activities;

(c) encourage the establishment of associations that contribute to public awareness;

(d) develop and exchange educational and public awareness material, where possible in local languages, exchange and second experts to train personnel of affected developing country Parties in carrying out relevant education and awareness programmes, and fully utilize relevant educational material available in competent international bodies;

(e) assess educational needs in affected areas, elaborate appropriate school curricula and expand, as needed, educational and adult literacy programmes and opportunities for all, in particular for girls and women, on the identification, conservation and sustainable use and management of the natural resources of affected areas; and

(f) develop interdisciplinary participatory programmes integrating desertification and drought awareness into educational systems and in non-formal, adult, distance and practical educational programmes.

4. The Conference of the Parties shall establish and/or strengthen networks of regional education and training centres to combat desertification and mitigate the effects of drought. These networks shall be coordinated by an institution created or designated for that purpose, in order to train scientific, technical and management personnel and to strengthen existing institutions responsible for education and training in affected country Parties, where appropriate, with a view to harmonizing programmes and to organizing exchanges of experience among them. These networks shall cooperate closely with relevant intergovernmental and non-governmental organizations to avoid duplication of effort.

Article 20

Financial resources

1. Given the central importance of financing to the achievement of the objective of the Convention, the Parties, taking into account their capabilities, shall make every effort to ensure that adequate financial resources are available for programmes to combat desertification and mitigate the effects of drought.

2. In this connection, developed country Parties, while giving priority to affected African country Parties without neglecting affected developing country Parties in other regions, in accordance with article 7, undertake to:

(a) mobilize substantial financial resources, including grants and concessional loans, in order to support the implementation of programmes to combat desertification and mitigate the effects of drought;

(b) promote the mobilization of adequate, timely and predictable financial resources, including new and additional funding from the Global Environment Facility of the agreed incremental costs of those activities concerning desertification that relate to its four focal areas, in conformity with the relevant provisions of the Instrument establishing the Global Environment Facility;

(c) facilitate through international cooperation the transfer of technology, knowledge and know-how; and

(d) explore, in cooperation with affected developing country Parties, innovative methods and incentives for mobilizing and channelling resources, including those of foundations, non- governmental organizations and other private sector entities, particularly debt swaps and other innovative means which increase financing by reducing the external debt burden of affected developing country Parties, particularly those in Africa.

3. Affected developing country Parties, taking into account their capabilities, undertake to mobilize adequate financial resources for the implementation of their national action programmes.

4. In mobilizing financial resources, the Parties shall seek full use and continued qualitative improvement of all national, bilateral and multilateral funding sources and mechanisms, using consortia, joint programmes and parallel financing, and shall seek to involve private sector funding sources and mechanisms, including those of non-governmental organizations. To this end, the Parties shall fully utilize the operational mechanisms developed pursuant to article 14.

5. In order to mobilize the financial resources necessary for affected developing country Parties to combat desertification and mitigate the effects of drought, the Parties shall:

(a) rationalize and strengthen the management of resources already allocated for combating desertification and mitigating the effects of drought by using them more effectively and efficiently, assessing their successes and shortcomings, removing hindrances to their effective use and, where necessary, reorienting programmes in light of the integrated long- term approach adopted pursuant to this Convention;

(b) give due priority and attention within the governing bodies of multilateral financial institutions, facilities and funds, including regional development banks and funds, to supporting affected developing country Parties, particularly those in Africa, in activities which advance implementation of the Convention, notably action programmes they undertake in the framework of regional implementation annexes; and

(c) examine ways in which regional and subregional cooperation can be strengthened to support efforts undertaken at the national level.

6. Other Parties are encouraged to provide, on a voluntary basis, knowledge, know-how and techniques related to desertification and/or financial resources to affected developing country Parties.

7. The full implementation by affected developing country Parties, particularly those in Africa, of their obligations under the Convention will be greatly assisted by the fulfilment by developed country Parties of their obligations under the Convention, including in particular those regarding financial resources and transfer of technology. In fulfilling their obligations, developed country Parties should take fully into account that economic and social development and poverty eradication are the first priorities of affected developing country Parties, particularly those in Africa.

ARTICLE 21

Financial mechanisms

1. The Conference of the Parties shall promote the availability of financial mechanisms and shall encourage such mechanisms to seek to maximize the availability of funding for affected developing country Parties, particularly those in Africa, to implement the Convention. To this end, the Conference of the Parties shall consider for adoption inter alia approaches and policies that:

(a) facilitate the provision of necessary funding at the national, subregional, regional and global levels for activities pursuant to relevant provisions of the Convention;

(b) promote multiple-source funding approaches, mechanisms and arrangements and their assessment, consistent with article 20;

(c) provide on a regular basis, to interested Parties and relevant intergovernmental and non- governmental organizations, information on available sources of funds and on funding patterns in order to facilitate coordination among them;

(d) facilitate the establishment, as appropriate, of mechanisms, such as national desertification funds, including those involving the participation of non-governmental organizations, to channel financial resources rapidly and efficiently to the local level in affected developing country Parties; and

(e) strengthen existing funds and financial mechanisms at the subregional and regional levels, particularly in Africa, to support more effectively the implementation of the Convention.

2. The Conference of the Parties shall also encourage the provision, through various mechanisms within the United Nations system and through multilateral financial institutions, of support at

the national, subregional and regional levels to activities that enable developing country Parties to meet their obligations under the Convention.

3. Affected developing country Parties shall utilize, and where necessary, establish and/or strengthen, national coordinating mechanisms, integrated in national development programmes, that would ensure the efficient use of all available financial resources. They shall also utilize participatory processes involving non-governmental organizations, local groups and the private sector, in raising funds, in elaborating as well as implementing programmes and in assuring access to funding by groups at the local level. These actions can be enhanced by improved coordination and flexible programming on the part of those providing assistance.

4. In order to increase the effectiveness and efficiency of existing financial mechanisms, a Global Mechanism to promote actions leading to the mobilization and channelling of substantial financial resources, including for the transfer of technology, on a grant basis, and/or on concessional or other terms, to affected developing country Parties, is hereby established. This Global Mechanism shall function under the authority and guidance of the Conference of the Parties and be accountable to it.

5. The Conference of the Parties shall identify, at its first ordinary session, an organization to house the Global Mechanism. The Conference of the Parties and the organization it has identified shall agree upon modalities for this Global Mechanism to ensure inter alia that such Mechanism:

(a) identifies and draws up an inventory of relevant bilateral and multilateral cooperation programmes that are available to implement the Convention;

(b) provides advice, on request, to Parties on innovative methods of financing and sources of financial assistance and on improving the coordination of cooperation activities at the national level;

(c) provides interested Parties and relevant intergovernmental and non-governmental organizations with information on available sources of funds and on funding patterns in order to facilitate coordination among them; and

(d) reports to the Conference of the Parties, beginning at its second ordinary session, on its activities.

6. The Conference of the Parties shall, at its first session, make appropriate arrangements with the organization it has identified to house the Global Mechanism for the administrative operations of such Mechanism, drawing to the extent possible on existing budgetary and human resources.

7. The Conference of the Parties shall, at its third ordinary session, review the policies, operational modalities and activities of the Global Mechanism accountable to it pursuant to paragraph 4, taking into account the provisions of article 7. On the basis of this review, it shall consider and take appropriate action.

PART IV—INSTITUTIONS

ARTICLE 22

Conference of the Parties

1. A Conference of the Parties is hereby established.

2. The Conference of the Parties is the supreme body of the Convention. It shall make, within its mandate, the decisions necessary to promote its effective implementation. In particular, it shall:

(a) regularly review the implementation of the Convention and the functioning of its institutional arrangements in the light of the experience gained at the national, subregional, regional and international levels and on the basis of the evolution of scientific and technological knowledge;

(b) promote and facilitate the exchange of information on measures adopted by the Parties, and determine the form and timetable for transmitting the information to be submitted pursuant to article 26, review the reports and make recommendations on them;

(c) establish such subsidiary bodies as are deemed necessary for the implementation of the Convention;

(d) review reports submitted by its subsidiary bodies and provide guidance to them;

(e) agree upon and adopt, by consensus, rules of procedure and financial rules for itself and any subsidiary bodies;

(f) adopt amendments to the Convention pursuant to articles 30 and 31;

(g) approve a programme and budget for its activities, including those of its subsidiary bodies, and undertake necessary arrangements for their financing;

(h) as appropriate, seek the cooperation of, and utilize the services of and information provided by, competent bodies or agencies, whether national or international, intergovernmental or non-governmental;

(i) promote and strengthen the relationship with other relevant conventions while avoiding duplication of effort; and

(j) exercise such other functions as may be necessary for the achievement of the objective of the Convention.

3. The Conference of the Parties shall, at its first session, adopt its own rules of procedure, by consensus, which shall include decision-making procedures for matters not already covered by decision-making procedures stipulated in the Convention. Such procedures may include specified majorities required for the adoption of particular decisions.

4. The first session of the Conference of the Parties shall be convened by the interim secretariat referred to in article 35 and shall take place not later than one year after the date of entry into force of the Convention. Unless otherwise decided by the Conference of the Parties, the second, third and fourth ordinary sessions shall be held yearly, and thereafter, ordinary sessions shall be held every two years.

5. Extraordinary sessions of the Conference of the Parties shall be held at such other times as may be decided either by the Conference of the Parties in ordinary session or at the written request

of any Party, provided that, within three months of the request being communicated to the Parties by the Permanent Secretariat, it is supported by at least one third of the Parties.

6. At each ordinary session, the Conference of the Parties shall elect a Bureau. The structure and functions of the Bureau shall be determined in the rules of procedure. In appointing the Bureau, due regard shall be paid to the need to ensure equitable geographical distribution and adequate representation of affected country Parties, particularly those in Africa.

7. The United Nations, its specialized agencies and any State member thereof or observers thereto not Party to the Convention, may be represented at sessions of the Conference of the Parties as observers. Any body or agency, whether national or international, governmental or non-governmental, which is qualified in matters covered by the Convention, and which has informed the Permanent Secretariat of its wish to be represented at a session of the Conference of the Parties as an observer, may be so admitted unless at least one third of the Parties present object. The admission and participation of observers shall be subject to the rules of procedure adopted by the Conference of the Parties.

8. The Conference of the Parties may request competent national and international organizations which have relevant expertise to provide it with information relevant to article 16, paragraph (g), article 17, paragraph 1 (c) and article 18, paragraph 2(b).

ARTICLE 23

Permanent Secretariat

1. A Permanent Secretariat is hereby established.

2. The functions of the Permanent Secretariat shall be:

(a) to make arrangements for sessions of the Conference of the Parties and its subsidiary bodies established under the Convention and to provide them with services as required;

(b) to compile and transmit reports submitted to it;

(c) to facilitate assistance to affected developing country Parties, on request, particularly those in Africa, in the compilation and communication of information required under the Convention;

(d) to coordinate its activities with the secretariats of other relevant international bodies and conventions;

(e) to enter, under the guidance of the Conference of the Parties, into such administrative and contractual arrangements as may be required for the effective discharge of its functions;

(f) to prepare reports on the execution of its functions under this Convention and present them to the Conference of the Parties; and

(g) to perform such other secretariat functions as may be determined by the Conference of the Parties.

3. The Conference of the Parties, at its first session, shall designate a Permanent Secretariat and make arrangements for its functioning.

ARTICLE 24

Committee on Science and Technology

1. A Committee on Science and Technology is hereby established as a subsidiary body of the Conference of the Parties to provide it with information and advice on scientific and technological matters relating to combating desertification and mitigating the effects of drought. The Committee shall meet in conjunction with the ordinary sessions of the Conference of the Parties and shall be multidisciplinary and open to the participation of all Parties. It shall be composed of government representatives competent in the relevant fields of expertise. The Conference of the Parties shall decide, at its first session, on the terms of reference of the Committee.

2. The Conference of the Parties shall establish and maintain a roster of independent experts with expertise and experience in the relevant fields. The roster shall be based on nominations received in writing from the Parties, taking into account the need for a multidisciplinary approach and broad geographical representation.

3. The Conference of the Parties may, as necessary, appoint ad hoc panels to provide it, through the Committee, with information and advice on specific issues regarding the state of the art in fields of science and technology relevant to combating desertification and mitigating the effects of drought. These panels shall be composed of experts whose names are taken from the roster, taking into account the need for a multidisciplinary approach and broad geographical representation. These experts shall have scientific backgrounds and field experience and shall be appointed by the Conference of the Parties on the recommendation of the Committee. The Conference of the Parties shall decide on the terms of reference and the modalities of work of these panels.

ARTICLE 25

Networking of institutions, agencies and bodies

1. The Committee on Science and Technology shall, under the supervision of the Conference of the Parties, make provision for the undertaking of a survey and evaluation of the relevant existing networks, institutions, agencies and bodies willing to become units of a network. Such a network shall support the implementation of the Convention.

2. On the basis of the results of the survey and evaluation referred to in paragraph 1, the Committee on Science and Technology shall make recommendations to the Conference of the Parties on ways and means to facilitate and strengthen networking of the units at the local, national and other levels, with a view to ensuring that the thematic needs set out in articles 16 to 19 are addressed.

3. Taking into account these recommendations, the Conference of the Parties shall:

(a) identify those national, subregional, regional and international units that are most appropriate for networking, and recommend operational procedures, and a time frame, for them; and

(b) identify the units best suited to facilitating and strengthening such networking at all levels.

Part V—Procedures

Article 26

Communication of information

1. Each Party shall communicate to the Conference of the Parties for consideration at its ordinary sessions, through the Permanent Secretariat, reports on the measures which it has taken for the implementation of the Convention. The Conference of the Parties shall determine the timetable for submission and the format of such reports.

2. Affected country Parties shall provide a description of the strategies established pursuant to article 5 and of any relevant information on their implementation.

3. Affected country Parties which implement action programmes pursuant to articles 9 to 15 shall provide a detailed description of the programmes and of their implementation.

4. Any group of affected country Parties may make a joint communication on measures taken at the subregional and/or regional levels in the framework of action programmes.

5. Developed country Parties shall report on measures taken to assist in the preparation and implementation of action programmes, including information on the financial resources they have provided, or are providing, under the Convention.

6. Information communicated pursuant to paragraphs 1 to 4 shall be transmitted by the Permanent Secretariat as soon as possible to the Conference of the Parties and to any relevant subsidiary body.

7. The Conference of the Parties shall facilitate the provision to affected developing countries, particularly those in Africa, on request, of technical and financial support in compiling and communicating information in accordance with this article, as well as identifying the technical and financial needs associated with action programmes.

Article 27

Measures to resolve questions on implementation

The Conference of the Parties shall consider and adopt procedures and institutional mechanisms for the resolution of questions that may arise with regard to the implementation of the Convention.

Article 28

Settlement of disputes

1. Parties shall settle any dispute between them concerning the interpretation or application of the Convention through negotiation or other peaceful means of their own choice.

2. When ratifying, accepting, approving, or acceding to the Convention, or at any time thereafter, a Party which is not a regional

economic integration organization may declare in a written instrument submitted to the Depositary that, in respect of any dispute concerning the interpretation or application of the Convention, it recognizes one or both of the following means of dispute settlement as compulsory in relation to any Party accepting the same obligation:

(a) arbitration in accordance with procedures adopted by the Conference of the Parties in an annex as soon as practicable;

(b) submission of the dispute to the International Court of Justice.

3. A Party which is a regional economic integration organization may make a declaration with like effect in relation to arbitration in accordance with the procedure referred to in paragraph 2 (a).

4. A declaration made pursuant to paragraph 2 shall remain in force until it expires in accordance with its terms or until three months after written notice of its revocation has been deposited with the Depositary.

5. The expiry of a declaration, a notice of revocation or a new declaration shall not in any way affect proceedings pending before an arbitral tribunal or the International Court of Justice unless the Parties to the dispute otherwise agree.

6. If the Parties to a dispute have not accepted the same or any procedure pursuant to paragraph 2 and if they have not been able to settle their dispute within twelve months following notification by one Party to another that a dispute exists between them, the dispute shall be submitted to conciliation at the request of any Party to the dispute, in accordance with procedures adopted by the Conference of the Parties in an annex as soon as practicable.

Article 29

Status of annexes

1. Annexes form an integral part of the Convention and, unless expressly provided otherwise, a reference to the Convention also constitutes a reference to its annexes.

2. The Parties shall interpret the provisions of the annexes in a manner that is in conformity with their rights and obligations under the articles of this Convention.

Article 30

Amendments to the Convention

1. Any Party may propose amendments to the Convention.

2. Amendments to the Convention shall be adopted at an ordinary session of the Conference of the Parties. The text of any proposed amendment shall be communicated to the Parties by the Permanent Secretariat at least six months before the meeting at which it is proposed for adoption. The Permanent Secretariat shall also communicate proposed amendments to the signatories to the Convention.

3. The Parties shall make every effort to reach agreement on any proposed amendment to the Convention by consensus. If all efforts at consensus have been exhausted and no agreement reached, the

amendment shall, as a last resort, be adopted by a two-thirds majority vote of the Parties present and voting at the meeting. The adopted amendment shall be communicated by the Permanent Secretariat to the Depositary, who shall circulate it to all Parties for their ratification, acceptance, approval or accession.

4. Instruments of ratification, acceptance, approval or accession in respect of an amendment shall be deposited with the Depositary. An amendment adopted pursuant to paragraph 3 shall enter into force for those Parties having accepted it on the ninetieth day after the date of receipt by the Depositary of an instrument of ratification, acceptance, approval or accession by at least two thirds of the Parties to the Convention which were Parties at the time of the adoption of the amendment.

5. The amendment shall enter into force for any other Party on the ninetieth day after the date on which that Party deposits with the Depositary its instrument of ratification, acceptance or approval of, or accession to the said amendment.

6. For the purposes of this article and article 31, "Parties present and voting" means Parties present and casting an affirmative or negative vote.

ARTICLE 31

Adoption and amendment of annexes

1. Any additional annex to the Convention and any amendment to an annex shall be proposed and adopted in accordance with the procedure for amendment of the Convention set forth in article 30, provided that, in adopting an additional regional implementation annex or amendment to any regional implementation annex, the majority provided for in that article shall include a two-thirds majority vote of the Parties of the region concerned present and voting. The adoption or amendment of an annex shall be communicated by the Depositary to all Parties.

2. An annex, other than an additional regional implementation annex, or an amendment to an annex, other than an amendment to any regional implementation annex, that has been adopted in accordance with paragraph 1, shall enter into force for all Parties to the Convention six months after the date of communication by the Depositary to such Parties of the adoption of such annex or amendment, except for those Parties that have notified the Depositary in writing within that period of their non- acceptance of such annex or amendment. Such annex or amendment shall enter into force for Parties which withdraw their notification of non-acceptance on the ninetieth day after the date on which withdrawal of such notification has been received by the Depositary.

3. An additional regional implementation annex or amendment to any regional implementation annex that has been adopted in accordance with paragraph 1, shall enter into force for all Parties to the Convention six months after the date of the communication by the Depositary to such Parties of the adoption of such annex or amendment, except with respect to:

(a) any Party that has notified the Depositary in writing, within such six month period, of its non-acceptance of that additional regional implementation annex or of the amendment to the regional implementation annex, in which case such annex or amendment shall enter into force for Parties which withdraw their notification of non-acceptance on the ninetieth day after the date on which withdrawal of such notification has been received by the Depositary; and

(b) any Party that has made a declaration with respect to additional regional implementation annexes or amendments to regional implementation annexes in accordance with article 34, paragraph 4, in which case any such annex or amendment shall enter into force for such a Party on the ninetieth day after the date of deposit with the Depositary of its instrument of ratification, acceptance, approval or accession with respect to such annex or amendment.

4. If the adoption of an annex or an amendment to an annex involves an amendment to the Convention, that annex or amendment to an annex shall not enter into force until such time as the amendment to the Convention enters into force.

Article 32

Right to vote

1. Except as provided for in paragraph 2, each Party to the Convention shall have one vote.

2. Regional economic integration organizations, in matters within their competence, shall exercise their right to vote with a number of votes equal to the number of their member States that are Parties to the Convention. Such an organization shall not exercise its right to vote if any of its member States exercises its right, and vice versa.

Part VI—Final Provisions

Article 33

Signature

This Convention shall be opened for signature at Paris, on 14-15 October 1994, by States Members of the United Nations or any of its specialized agencies or that are Parties to the Statute of the International Court of Justice and by regional economic integration organizations. It shall remain open for signature, thereafter, at the United Nations Headquarters in New York until 13 October 1995.

Article 34

Ratification, acceptance, approval and accession

1. The Convention shall be subject to ratification, acceptance, approval or accession by States and by regional economic integration organizations. It shall be open for accession from the day after the date on which the Convention is closed for signature. Instruments of ratification, acceptance, approval or accession shall be deposited with the Depositary.

2. Any regional economic integration organization which becomes a Party to the Convention without any of its member States being

a Party to the Convention shall be bound by all the obligations under the Convention. Where one or more member States of such an organization are also Party to the Convention, the organization and its member States shall decide on their respective responsibilities for the performance of their obligations under the Convention. In such cases, the organization and the member States shall not be entitled to exercise rights under the Convention concurrently.

3. In their instruments of ratification, acceptance, approval or accession, regional economic integration organizations shall declare the extent of their competence with respect to the matters governed by the Convention. They shall also promptly inform the Depositary, who shall in turn inform the Parties, of any substantial modification in the extent of their competence.

4. In its instrument of ratification, acceptance, approval or accession, any Party may declare that, with respect to it, any additional regional implementation annex or any amendment to any regional implementation annex shall enter into force only upon the deposit of its instrument of ratification, acceptance, approval or accession with respect thereto.

Article 35

Interim arrangements

The secretariat functions referred to in article 23 will be carried out on an interim basis by the secretariat established by the General Assembly of the United Nations in its resolution 47/188 of 22 December 1992, until the completion of the first session of the Conference of the Parties.

Article 36

Entry into force

1. The Convention shall enter into force on the ninetieth day after the date of deposit of the fiftieth instrument of ratification, acceptance, approval or accession.

2. For each State or regional economic integration organization ratifying, accepting, approving or acceding to the Convention after the deposit of the fiftieth instrument of ratification, acceptance, approval or accession, the Convention shall enter into force on the ninetieth day after the date of deposit by such State or regional economic integration organization of its instrument of ratification, acceptance, approval or accession.

3. For the purposes of paragraphs 1 and 2, any instrument deposited by a regional economic integration organization shall not be counted as additional to those deposited by States members of the organization.

Article 37

Reservations

No reservations may be made to this Convention.

ARTICLE 38

Withdrawal

1. At any time after three years from the date on which the Convention has entered into force for a Party, that Party may withdraw from the Convention by giving written notification to the Depositary.

2. Any such withdrawal shall take effect upon expiry of one year from the date of receipt by the Depositary of the notification of withdrawal, or on such later date as may be specified in the notification of withdrawal.

ARTICLE 39

Depositary

The Secretary-General of the United Nations shall be the Depositary of the Convention.

ARTICLE 40

Authentic texts

The original of the present Convention, of which the Arabic, Chinese, English, French, Russian and Spanish texts are equally authentic, shall be deposited with the Secretary-General of the United Nations.

IN WITNESS WHEREOF the undersigned, being duly authorized to that effect, have signed the present Convention.

DONE AT Paris, this 17th day of June one thousand nine hundred and ninety-four.

ANNEX I—REGIONAL IMPLEMENTATION ANNEX FOR AFRICA [2]

ANNEX II—REGIONAL IMPLEMENTATION ANNEX FOR ASIA [2]

ANNEX III—REGIONAL IMPLEMENTATION ANNEX FOR LATIN AMERICA AND THE CARIBBEAN [2]

ANNEX IV—REGIONAL IMPLEMENTATION ANNEX FOR THE NORTHERN MEDITERRANEAN [2]

ANNEX V—REGIONAL IMPLEMENTATION ANNEX FOR CENTRAL AND EASTERN EUROPE [2]

[2] For text of annexes regarding regional implementation, see: http://www.unccd.int/convention/text/convention.php

8. Revised Text of the International Plant Protection Convention

Done at Rome, November 17, 1997; Ratification advised by the Senate, October 18, 2000; Entered into force, October 2, 2005

REVISED TEXT OF THE INTERNATIONAL PLANT PROTECTION CONVENTION [1]

PREAMBLE

The contracting parties,

RECOGNIZING the necessity for international cooperation in controlling pests of plants and plant products and in preventing their international spread, and especially their introduction into endangered areas;

RECOGNIZING that phytosanitary measures should be technically justified, transparent and should not be applied in such a way as to constitute either a means of arbitrary or unjustified discrimination or a disguised restriction, particularly on international trade;

DESIRING to ensure close coordination of measures directed to these ends;

DESIRING to provide a framework for the development and application of harmonized phytosanitary measures and the elaboration of international standards to that effect;

TAKING into account internationally approved principles governing the protection of plant, human and animal health, and the environment; and

NOTING the agreements concluded as a result of the Uruguay Round of Multilateral Trade Negotiations, including the Agreement on the Application of Sanitary and Phytosanitary Measures;

HAVE AGREED AS FOLLOWS:

ARTICLE I

PURPOSE AND RESPONSIBILITY

1. With the purpose of securing common and effective action to prevent the spread and introduction of pests of plants and plant products, and to promote appropriate measures for their control, the contracting parties undertake to adopt the legislative, technical and administrative measures specified in this Convention and in supplementary agreements pursuant to Article XVI.

[1] For a list of states that are parties to the Convention, see Department of State publication, *Treaties in Force*.

2. Each contracting party shall assume responsibility, without prejudice to obligations assumed under other international agreements, for the fulfilment within its territories of all requirements under this Convention.

3. The division of responsibilities for the fulfilment of the requirements of this Convention between member organizations of FAO and their member states that are contracting parties shall be in accordance with their respective competencies.

4. Where appropriate, the provisions of this Convention may be deemed by contracting parties to extend, in addition to plants and plant products, to storage places, packaging, conveyances, containers, soil and any other organism, object or material capable of harbouring or spreading plant pests, particularly where international transportation is involved.

ARTICLE II

USE OF TERMS

1. For the purpose of this Convention, the following terms shall have the meanings hereunder assigned to them:

"Area of low pest prevalence"—an area, whether all of a country, part of a country, or all or parts of several countries, as identified by the competent authorities, in which a specific pest occurs at low levels and which is subject to effective surveillance, control or eradication measures;

"Commission"—the Commission on Phytosanitary Measures established under Article XI;

"Endangered area"—an area where ecological factors favour the establishment of a pest whose presence in the area will result in economically important loss;

"Establishment"—perpetuation, for the foreseeable future, of a pest within an area after entry;

"Harmonized phytosanitary measures"—phytosanitary measures established by contracting parties based on international standards;

"International standards"—international standards established in accordance with Article X, paragraphs 1 and 2;

"Introduction"—the entry of a pest resulting in its establishment;

"Pest"—any species, strain or biotype of plant, animal or pathogenic agent injurious to plants or plant products;

"Pest risk analysis"—the process of evaluating biological or other scientific and economic evidence to determine whether a pest should be regulated and the strength of any phytosanitary measures to be taken against it;

"Phytosanitary measure"—any legislation, regulation or official procedure having the purpose to prevent the introduction and/or spread of pests;

"Plant products"—unmanufactured material of plant origin (including grain) and those manufactured products that, by their nature or that of their processing, may create a risk for the introduction and spread of pests;

"Plants"—living plants and parts thereof, including seeds and germplasm;

"Quarantine pest"—a pest of potential economic importance to the area endangered thereby and not yet present there, or present but not widely distributed and being officially controlled;

"Regional standards"—standards established by a regional plant protection organization for the guidance of the members of that organization;

"Regulated article"—any plant, plant product, storage place, packaging, conveyance, container, soil and any other organism, object or material capable of harbouring or spreading pests, deemed to require phytosanitary measures, particularly where international transportation is involved;

"Regulated non-quarantine pest"—a non-quarantine pest whose presence in plants for planting affects the intended use of those plants with an economically unacceptable impact and which is therefore regulated within the territory of the importing contracting party;

"Regulated pest"—a quarantine pest or a regulated non-quarantine pest;

"Secretary"—Secretary of the Commission appointed pursuant to Article XII;

"Technically justified"—justified on the basis of conclusions reached by using an appropriate pest risk analysis or, where applicable, another comparable examination and evaluation of available scientific information.

2. The definitions set forth in this Article, being limited to the application of this Convention, shall not be deemed to affect definitions established under domestic laws or regulations of contracting parties.

Article III

Relationship with other international agreements

Nothing in this Convention shall affect the rights and obligations of the contracting parties under relevant international agreements.

Article IV

General provisions relating to the organizational arrangements for national plant protection

1. Each contracting party shall make provision, to the best of its ability, for an official national plant protection organization with the main responsibilities set out in this Article.

2. The responsibilities of an official national plant protection organization shall include the following:

a) the issuance of certificates relating to the phytosanitary regulations of the importing contracting party for consignments of plants, plant products and other regulated articles;

b) the surveillance of growing plants, including both areas under cultivation (inter alia fields, plantations, nurseries, gardens, greenhouses and laboratories) and wild flora, and of plants and plant products in storage or in transportation, particularly with the object of reporting the occurrence, outbreak and spread of pests, and of controlling those pests, including the reporting referred to under Article VIII paragraph 1(a);

c) the inspection of consignments of plants and plant products moving in international traffic and, where appropriate, the inspection of other regulated articles, particularly with the object of preventing the introduction and/or spread of pests;

d) the disinfestation or disinfection of consignments of plants, plant products and other regulated articles moving in international traffic, to meet phytosanitary requirements;

e) the protection of endangered areas and the designation, maintenance and surveillance of pest free areas and areas of low pest prevalence;

f) the conduct of pest risk analyses;

g) to ensure through appropriate procedures that the phytosanitary security of consignments after certification regarding composition, substitution and reinfestation is maintained prior to export; and

h) training and development of staff.

3. Each contracting party shall make provision, to the best of its ability, for the following:

a) the distribution of information within the territory of the contracting party regarding regulated pests and the means of their prevention and control;

b) research and investigation in the field of plant protection;

c) the issuance of phytosanitary regulations; and

d) the performance of such other functions as may be required for the implementation of this Convention.

4. Each contracting party shall submit a description of its official national plant protection organization and of changes in such organization to the Secretary. A contracting party shall provide a description of its organizational arrangements for plant protection to another contracting party, upon request.

Article V

Phytosanitary certification

1. Each contracting party shall make arrangements for phytosanitary certification, with the objective of ensuring that exported plants, plant products and other regulated articles and consignments thereof are in conformity with the certifying statement to be made pursuant to paragraph 2(b) of this Article.

2. Each contracting party shall make arrangements for the issuance of phytosanitary certificates in conformity with the following provisions:

a) Inspection and other related activities leading to issuance of phytosanitary certificates shall be carried out only by or under the authority of the official national plant protection organization. The issuance of phytosanitary certificates shall be carried out by public officers who are technically qualified and duly authorized by the official national plant protection organization to act on its behalf and under its control with such knowledge and information available to those officers that the authorities of importing contracting parties may accept the phytosanitary certificates with confidence as dependable documents.

b) Phytosanitary certificates, or their electronic equivalent where accepted by the importing contracting party concerned, shall be as worded in the models set out in the Annex to this Convention. These certificates should be completed and issued taking into account relevant international standards.

c) Uncertified alterations or erasures shall invalidate the certificates.

3. Each contracting party undertakes not to require consignments of plants or plant products or other regulated articles imported into its territories to be accompanied by phytosanitary certificates inconsistent with the models set out in the Annex to this Convention. Any requirements for additional declarations shall be limited to those technically justified.

ARTICLE VI

REGULATED PESTS

1. Contracting parties may require phytosanitary measures for quarantine pests and regulated non-quarantine pests, provided that such measures are:

a) no more stringent than measures applied to the same pests, if present within the territory of the importing contracting party; and

b) limited to what is necessary to protect plant health and/or safeguard the intended use and can be technically justified by the contracting party concerned.

2. Contracting parties shall not require phytosanitary measures for non-regulated pests.

ARTICLE VII

REQUIREMENTS IN RELATION TO IMPORTS

1. With the aim of preventing the introduction and/or spread of regulated pests into their territories, contracting parties shall have sovereign authority to regulate, in accordance with applicable international agreements, the entry of plants and plant products and other regulated articles and, to this end, may:

a) prescribe and adopt phytosanitary measures concerning the importation of plants, plant products and other regulated articles, including, for example, inspection, prohibition on importation, and treatment;

b) refuse entry or detain, or require treatment, destruction or removal from the territory of the contracting party, of plants, plant products and other regulated articles or consignments thereof that do not comply with the phytosanitary measures prescribed or adopted under subparagraph (a);

c) prohibit or restrict the movement of regulated pests into their territories;

d) prohibit or restrict the movement of biological control agents and other organisms of phytosanitary concern claimed to be beneficial into their territories.

2. In order to minimize interference with international trade, each contracting party, in exercising its authority under paragraph 1 of this Article, undertakes to act in conformity with the following:

a) Contracting parties shall not, under their phytosanitary legislation, take any of the measures specified in paragraph 1 of this Article unless such measures are made necessary by phytosanitary considerations and are technically justified.

b) Contracting parties shall, immediately upon their adoption, publish and transmit phytosanitary requirements, restrictions and prohibitions to any contracting party or parties that they believe may be directly affected by such measures.

c) Contracting parties shall, on request, make available to any contracting party the rationale for phytosanitary requirements, restrictions and prohibitions.

d) If a contracting party requires consignments of particular plants or plant products to be imported only through specified points of entry, such points shall be so selected as not to unnecessarily impede international trade. The contracting party shall publish a list of such points of entry and communicate it to the Secretary, any regional plant protection organization of which the contracting party is a member, all contracting parties which the contracting party believes to be directly affected, and other contracting parties upon request. Such restrictions on points of entry shall not be made unless the plants, plant products or other regulated articles concerned are required to be accompanied by phytosanitary certificates or to be submitted to inspection or treatment.

e) Any inspection or other phytosanitary procedure required by the plant protection organization of a contracting party for a consignment of plants, plant products or other regulated articles offered for importation, shall take place as promptly as possible with due regard to their perishability.

f) Importing contracting parties shall, as soon as possible, inform the exporting contracting party concerned or, where appropriate, the re-exporting contracting party concerned, of significant instances of non-compliance with phytosanitary certification. The exporting contracting party or, where appropriate, the reexporting contracting party concerned, should investigate and, on request, report the result of its investigation to the importing contracting party concerned.

g) Contracting parties shall institute only phytosanitary measures that are technically justified, consistent with the pest risk involved and represent the least restrictive measures available, and result in the minimum impediment to the international movement of people, commodities and conveyances.

h) Contracting parties shall, as conditions change, and as new facts become available, ensure that phytosanitary measures are promptly modified or removed if found to be unnecessary.

i) Contracting parties shall, to the best of their ability, establish and update lists of regulated pests, using scientific names, and make such lists available to the Secretary, to regional plant protection organizations of which they are members and, on request, to other contracting parties.

j) Contracting parties shall, to the best of their ability, conduct surveillance for pests and develop and maintain adequate information on pest status in order to support categorization of pests, and for the development of appropriate phytosanitary measures. This information shall be made available to contracting parties, on request.

3. A contracting party may apply measures specified in this Article to pests which may not be capable of establishment in its territories but, if they gained entry, cause economic damage. Measures taken against these pests must be technically justified.

4. Contracting parties may apply measures specified in this Article to consignments in transit through their territories only where such measures are technically justified and necessary to prevent the introduction and/or spread of pests.

5. Nothing in this Article shall prevent importing contracting parties from making special provision, subject to adequate safeguards, for the importation, for the purpose of scientific research, education, or other specific use, of plants and plant products and other regulated articles, and of plant pests.

6. Nothing in this Article shall prevent any contracting party from taking appropriate emergency action on the detection of a pest posing a potential threat to its territories or the report of such a detection. Any such action shall be evaluated as soon as possible to ensure that its continuance is justified. The action taken shall be immediately reported to contracting parties concerned, the Secretary, and any regional plant protection organization of which the contracting party is a member.

Article VIII

International cooperation

1. The contracting parties shall cooperate with one another to the fullest practicable extent in achieving the aims of this Convention, and shall in particular:

a) cooperate in the exchange of information on plant pests, particularly the reporting of the occurrence, outbreak or spread of pests that may be of immediate or potential danger, in accordance with such procedures as may be established by the Commission;

b) participate, in so far as is practicable, in any special campaigns for combatting pests that may seriously threaten crop production and need international action to meet the emergencies; and

c) cooperate, to the extent practicable, in providing technical and biological information necessary for pest risk analysis.

2. Each contracting party shall designate a contact point for the exchange of information connected with the implementation of this Convention.

Article IX

Regional plant protection organizations

1. The contracting parties undertake to cooperate with one another in establishing regional plant protection organizations in appropriate areas.

2. The regional plant protection organizations shall function as the coordinating bodies in the areas covered, shall participate in various activities to achieve the objectives of this Convention and, where appropriate, shall gather and disseminate information.

3. The regional plant protection organizations shall cooperate with the Secretary in achieving the objectives of the Convention and, where appropriate, cooperate with the Secretary and the Commission in developing international standards.

4. The Secretary will convene regular Technical Consultations of representatives of regional plant protection organizations to:

a) promote the development and use of relevant international standards for phytosanitary measures; and

b) encourage inter-regional cooperation in promoting harmonized phytosanitary measures for controlling pests and in preventing their spread and/or introduction.

Article X

Standards

1. The contracting parties agree to cooperate in the development of international standards in accordance with the procedures adopted by the Commission.

2. International standards shall be adopted by the Commission.

3. Regional standards should be consistent with the principles of this Convention; such standards may be deposited with the Commission for consideration as candidates for international standards for phytosanitary measures if more broadly applicable.

4. Contracting parties should take into account, as appropriate, international standards when undertaking activities related to this Convention.

Article XI

Commission on Phytosanitary Measures

1. Contracting parties agree to establish the Commission on Phytosanitary Measures within the framework of the Food and Agriculture Organization of the United Nations (FAO).

2. The functions of the Commission shall be to promote the full implementation of the objectives of the Convention and, in particular, to:

a) review the state of plant protection in the world and the need for action to control the international spread of pests and their introduction into endangered areas;

b) establish and keep under review the necessary institutional arrangements and procedures for the development and adoption of international standards, and to adopt international standards;

c) establish rules and procedures for the resolution of disputes in accordance with Article XIII;

d) establish such subsidiary bodies of the Commission as may be necessary for the proper implementation of its functions;

e) adopt guidelines regarding the recognition of regional plant protection organizations;

f) establish cooperation with other relevant international organizations on matters covered by this Convention;

g) adopt such recommendations for the implementation of the Convention as necessary; and

h) perform such other functions as may be necessary to the fulfilment of the objectives of this Convention.

3. Membership in the Commission shall be open to all contracting parties.

4. Each contracting party may be represented at sessions of the Commission by a single delegate who may be accompanied by an alternate, and by experts and advisers. Alternates, experts and advisers may take part in the proceedings of the Commission but may not vote, except in the case of an alternate who is duly authorized to substitute for the delegate.

5. The contracting parties shall make every effort to reach agreement on all matters by consensus. If all efforts to reach consensus have been exhausted and no agreement is reached, the decision shall, as a last resort, be taken by a two-thirds majority of the contracting parties present and voting.

6. A member organization of FAO that is a contracting party and the member states of that member organization that are contracting parties shall exercise their membership rights and fulfil their membership obligations in accordance, mutatis mutandis, with the Constitution and General Rules of FAO.

7. The Commission may adopt and amend, as required, its own Rules of Procedure, which shall not be inconsistent with this Convention or with the Constitution of FAO.

8. The Chairperson of the Commission shall convene an annual regular session of the Commission.

9. Special sessions of the Commission shall be convened by the Chairperson of the Commission at the request of at least one-third of its members.

10. The Commission shall elect its Chairperson and no more than two Vice-Chairpersons, each of whom shall serve for a term of two years.

Article XII

Secretariat

1. The Secretary of the Commission shall be appointed by the Director-General of FAO.

2. The Secretary shall be assisted by such secretariat staff as may be required.

3. The Secretary shall be responsible for implementing the policies and activities of the Commission and carrying out such other functions as may be assigned to the Secretary by this Convention and shall report thereon to the Commission.

4. The Secretary shall disseminate:

a) international standards to all contracting parties within sixty days of adoption;

b) to all contracting parties, lists of points of entry under Article VII paragraph 2(d) communicated by contracting parties;

c) lists of regulated pests whose entry is prohibited or referred to in Article VII paragraph 2(i) to all contracting parties and regional plant protection organizations;

d) information received from contracting parties on phytosanitary requirements, restrictions and prohibitions referred to in Article VII paragraph 2(b), and descriptions of official national plant protection organizations referred to in Article IV paragraph 4.

5. The Secretary shall provide translations in the official languages of FAO of documentation for meetings of the Commission and international standards.

6. The Secretary shall cooperate with regional plant protection organizations in achieving the aims of the Convention.

Article XIII

Settlement of disputes

1. If there is any dispute regarding the interpretation or application of this Convention, or if a contracting party considers that any action by another contracting party is in conflict with the obligations of the latter under Articles V and VII of this Convention, especially regarding the basis of prohibiting or restricting the imports of plants, plant products or other regulated articles coming from its territories, the contracting parties concerned shall consult among themselves as soon as possible with a view to resolving the dispute.

2. If the dispute cannot be resolved by the means referred to in paragraph 1, the contracting party or parties concerned may request the Director-General of FAO to appoint a committee of experts to consider the question in dispute, in accordance with rules and procedures that may be established by the Commission.

3. This Committee shall include representatives designated by each contracting party concerned. The Committee shall consider the question in dispute, taking into account all documents and other forms of evidence submitted by the contracting parties concerned. The Committee shall prepare a report on the technical aspects of the dispute for the purpose of seeking its resolution. The preparation of the report and its approval shall be according to rules and procedures established by the Commission, and it shall be transmitted by the Director-General to the contracting parties concerned. The report may also be submitted, upon its request, to the competent body of the international organization responsible for resolving trade disputes.

4. The contracting parties agree that the recommendations of such a committee, while not binding in character, will become the basis for renewed consideration by the contracting parties concerned of the matter out of which the disagreement arose.

5. The contracting parties concerned shall share the expenses of the experts.

6. The provisions of this Article shall be complementary to and not in derogation of the dispute settlement procedures provided for in other international agreements dealing with trade matters.

Article XIV

Substitution of Prior Agreements

This Convention shall terminate and replace, between contracting parties, the International Convention respecting measures to be taken against the Phylloxera vastatrix of 3 November 1881, the additional Convention signed at Berne on 15 April 1889 and the International Convention for the Protection of Plants signed at Rome on 16 April 1929.

Article XV

Territorial Application

1. Any contracting party may at the time of ratification or adherence or at any time thereafter communicate to the Director-General of FAO a declaration that this Convention shall extend to all or any of the territories for the international relations of which it is responsible, and this Convention shall be applicable to all territories specified in the declaration as from the thirtieth day after the receipt of the declaration by the Director-General.

2. Any contracting party which has communicated to the Director-General of FAO a declaration in accordance with paragraph 1 of this Article may at any time communicate a further declaration modifying the scope of any former declaration or terminating the application of the provisions of the present Convention in respect of any territory. Such modification or termination shall take effect as from the thirtieth day after the receipt of the declaration by the Director-General.

3. The Director-General of FAO shall inform all contracting parties of any declaration received under this Article.

Article XVI

Supplementary Agreements

1. The contracting parties may, for the purpose of meeting special problems of plant protection which need particular attention or action, enter into supplementary agreements. Such agreements may be applicable to specific regions, to specific pests, to specific plants and plant products, to specific methods of international transportation of plants and plant products, or otherwise supplement the provisions of this Convention.

2. Any such supplementary agreements shall come into force for each contracting party concerned after acceptance in accordance with the provisions of the supplementary agreements concerned.

3. Supplementary agreements shall promote the intent of this Convention and shall conform to the principles and provisions of this Convention, as well as to the principles of transparency, non-discrimination and the avoidance of disguised restrictions, particularly on international trade.

Article XVII

Ratification and adherence

1. This Convention shall be open for signature by all states until 1 May 1952 and shall be ratified at the earliest possible date. The instruments of ratification shall be deposited with the Director-General of FAO, who shall give notice of the date of deposit to each of the signatory states.

2. As soon as this Convention has come into force in accordance with Article XXII it shall be open for adherence by non-signatory states and member organizations of FAO. Adherence shall be effected by the deposit of an instrument of adherence with the Director-General of FAO, who shall notify all contracting parties.

3. When a member organization of FAO becomes a contracting party to this Convention, the member organization shall, in accordance with the provisions of Article II paragraph 7 of the FAO Constitution, as appropriate, notify at the time of its adherence such modifications or clarifications to its declaration of competence submitted under Article II paragraph 5 of the FAO Constitution as may be necessary in light of its acceptance of this Convention. Any contracting party to this Convention may, at any time, request a member organization of FAO that is a contracting party to this Convention to provide information as to which, as between the member organization and its member states, is responsible for the implementation of any particular matter covered by this Convention. The member organization shall provide this information within a reasonable time.

Article XVIII

Non-contracting parties

The contracting parties shall encourage any state or member organization of FAO, not a party to this Convention, to accept this Convention, and shall encourage any non-contracting party to apply phytosanitary measures consistent with the provisions of this Convention and any international standards adopted hereunder.

Article XIX

Languages

1. The authentic languages of this Convention shall be all official languages of FAO.

2. Nothing in this Convention shall be construed as requiring contracting parties to provide and to publish documents or to provide copies of them other than in the language(s) of the contracting party, except as stated in paragraph 3 below.

3. The following documents shall be in at least one of the official languages of FAO:

a) information provided according to Article IV paragraph 4;

b) cover notes giving bibliographical data on documents transmitted according to Article VII paragraph 2(b);

c) information provided according to Article VII paragraph 2(b), (d), (i) and (j);

d) notes giving bibliographical data and a short summary of relevant documents on information provided according to Article VIII paragraph 1(a);

e) requests for information from contact points as well as replies to such requests, but not including any attached documents;

f) any document made available by contracting parties for meetings of the Commission.

ARTICLE XX

TECHNICAL ASSISTANCE

The contracting parties agree to promote the provision of technical assistance to contracting parties, especially those that are developing contracting parties, either bilaterally or through the appropriate international organizations, with the objective of facilitating the implementation of this Convention.

ARTICLE XXI

AMENDMENT

1. Any proposal by a contracting party for the amendment of this Convention shall be communicated to the Director-General of FAO.

2. Any proposed amendment of this Convention received by the Director-General of FAO from a contracting party shall be presented to a regular or special session of the Commission for approval and, if the amendment involves important technical changes or imposes additional obligations on the contracting parties, it shall be considered by an advisory committee of specialists convened by FAO prior to the Commission.

3. Notice of any proposed amendment of this Convention, other than amendments to the Annex, shall be transmitted to the contracting parties by the Director-General of FAO not later than the time when the agenda of the session of the Commission at which the matter is to be considered is dispatched.

4. Any such proposed amendment of this Convention shall require the approval of the Commission and shall come into force as from the thirtieth day after acceptance by two-thirds of the contracting parties. For the purpose of this Article, an instrument deposited by a member organization of FAO shall not be counted as additional to those deposited by member states of such an organization.

5. Amendments involving new obligations for contracting parties, however, shall come into force in respect of each contracting party only on acceptance by it and as from the thirtieth day after such acceptance. The instruments of acceptance of amendments involving new obligations shall be deposited with the Director-General of FAO, who shall inform all contracting parties of the receipt of acceptance and the entry into force of amendments.

6. Proposals for amendments to the model phytosanitary certificates set out in the Annex to this Convention shall be sent to the Secretary and shall be considered for approval by the Commission. Approved amendments to the model phytosanitary certificates set

out in the Annex to this Convention shall become effective ninety days after their notification to the contracting parties by the Secretary.

7. For a period of not more than twelve months from an amendment to the model phytosanitary certificates set out in the Annex to this Convention becoming effective, the previous version of the phytosanitary certificates shall also be legally valid for the purpose of this Convention.

Article XXII

Entry into force

As soon as this Convention has been ratified by three signatory states it shall come into force among them. It shall come into force for each state or member organization of FAO ratifying or adhering thereafter from the date of deposit of its instrument of ratification or adherence.

Article XXIII

Denunciation

1. Any contracting party may at any time give notice of denunciation of this Convention by notification addressed to the Director-General of FAO. The Director-General shall at once inform all contracting parties.

2. Denunciation shall take effect one year from the date of receipt of the notification by the Director-General of FAO.

9. Agreement Establishing the South Pacific Regional Environment Programme

Done at Apia, Western Samoa, June 16, 1993; Entered into force generally, August 31, 1995; Ratification advised by the Senate, September 5, 2002; Entered into force for the United States, August 13, 2005

AGREEMENT ESTABLISHING THE SOUTH PACIFIC REGIONAL ENVIRONMENT PROGRAMME

The Parties,

RECOGNISING the importance of protecting the environment and conserving the natural resources of the South Pacific region;

CONSCIOUS of their responsibility to preserve their natural heritage for the benefit and enjoyment of present and future generations and their role as custodians of natural resources of global importance;

RECOGNISING the special hydrological, geological, atmospheric and ecological characteristics of the region which require special care and responsible management;

SEEKING TO ENSURE that resource development takes proper account of the need to protect and preserve the unique environmental values of the region and of the principles of sustainable development;

RECOGNISING the need for co-operation within the region and with competent international, regional and sub-regional organisations in order to ensure coordination and co-operation in efforts to protect the environment and use the natural resources of the region on a sustainable basis;

WISHING TO ESTABLISH a comprehensive Programme to assist the region in maintaining and improving its environment and to act as the central coordinating point for environmental protection measures within the region;

RECALLING the decision taken at the Conference on the Human Environment in the South Pacific, held at Rarotonga, Cook Islands, on 8–11 March 1982, to establish the South Pacific Regional Environment Programme as a separate entity within the South Pacific Commission;

RECALLING with appreciation the role of UNEP, ESCAP, the South Pacific Forum and the South Pacific Conference in supporting the establishment and encouraging the development of the South Pacific Regional Environment Programme as a regional programme and as part of the UNEP Regional Seas Programme;

NOTING with satisfaction that the Convention for the Protection of the Natural Resources and Environment of the South Pacific Region, done at Noumea on 24 November 1986, and its related Protocols, and the Convention on Conservation of Nature in the South Pacific, done at Apia on 12 June 1976, entered into force in 1990;

APPRECIATIVE of the valuable efforts that have been undertaken by the South Pacific Regional Environment Programme to promote environmental protection within the region and the support given to the Programme by the South Pacific Commission;

TAKING INTO ACCOUNT the decisions of the Third and Fourth Intergovernmental Meetings of the South Pacific Regional Environment Programme, held in Noumea in September 1990 and July 1991, and the endorsement of the Thirtieth South Pacific Conference, held in Noumea in October 1990; and

DESIRING TO ACCORD the South Pacific Regional Environment Programme the full and formal legal status necessary to operate as an autonomous body, to manage fully its own affairs and to provide the basis for the continued operation of SPREP in accordance with the traditions of cooperation in the region;

HAVE AGREED AS FOLLOWS:

ARTICLE 1

ESTABLISHMENT OF SPREP

1. The South Pacific Regional Environment Programme (hereinafter referred to as SPREP) is hereby established as an intergovernmental organisation.

2. The organs of SPREP are the SPREP Meeting and the Secretariat.

3. The Secretariat shall be located in Apia, Western Samoa, unless the SPREP Meeting decides otherwise.

ARTICLE 2

PURPOSES

1. The purposes of SPREP are to promote co-operation in the South Pacific region and to provide assistance in order to protect and improve its environment and to ensure sustainable development for present and future generations. SPREP shall achieve these purposes through the Action Plan adopted from time to time by the SPREP Meeting, setting the strategies and objectives of SPREP.

2. The Action Plan shall include:

(a) co-ordinating regional activities addressing the environment;

(b) monitoring and assessing the state of the environment in the region including the impacts of human activities on the ecosystems of the region and encouraging development undertaken to be directed towards maintaining or enhancing environmental qualities;

(c) promoting and developing programmes, including research programmes, to protect the atmosphere and terrestrial, freshwater, coastal and marine ecosystems and species, while ensuring ecologically sustainable utilisation of resources;

(d) reducing, through prevention and management, atmospheric, land based, freshwater and marine pollution;

(e) strengthening national and regional capabilities and institutional arrangements;

(f) increasing and improving training, educational and public awareness activities; and

(g) promoting integrated legal, planning and management mechanisms.

ARTICLE 3

SPREP MEETINGS

1. The SPREP Meeting shall be open to the Membership of the Parties to this Agreement and, with the appropriate authorisation of the Party having responsibility for its international affairs, of each of the following:

American Samoa
French Polynesia
Guam
New Caledonia
Northern Mariana Islands
Palau
Tokelau
Wallis and Futuna.

2. The SPREP Meeting shall be held at such times as the SPREP Meeting may determine. A special SPREP Meeting may be held at any time as provided in the Rules of Procedure.

3. The SPREP Meeting shall be the plenary body and its functions shall be:

(a) to provide a forum for Members to consult on matters of common concern with regard to the protection and improvement of the environment of the South Pacific region and, in particular, to further the purposes of SPREP;

(b) to approve and review the Action Plan for SPREP and to determine the general policies of SPREP;

(c) to adopt the report of the Director on the operation of SPREP;

(d) to adopt the work programmes of SPREP and review progress in their implementation;

(e) to adopt the Budget estimates of SPREP;

(f) to make recommendations to Members;

(g) to appoint the Director;

(h) to give directions to the Director concerning the implementation of the Work Programme;

(i) to approve rules and conditions for the appointment of the staff of the Secretariat; and

(j) to carry out such other functions as are specified in this Agreement or are necessary for the effective functioning of SPREP.

4. The SPREP Meeting may establish such committees and subcommittees and other subsidiary bodies as it considers necessary.

5. In addition to the functions referred to in paragraph (3) of this Article, the SPREP Meeting shall, through such mechanisms as it considers appropriate, consult and co-operate with the Meetings of Parties to:

(a) the Convention on Conservation of Nature in the South Pacific adopted at Apia on 12 June 1976;

(b) the Convention for the Protection of the Natural Resources and Environment of the South Pacific Region adopted at Noumea on 24 November 1986 and related Protocols; and

(c) any other international or regional Agreement that may be concluded for the protection of the environment of the South Pacific region,

with a view to ensuring the achievement of the purpose of SPREP and of this Agreement and facilitating the achievement of the purposes of those Conventions.

ARTICLE 4

MEETING PROCEDURE

1. The SPREP Meeting shall elect from among its Members a Chairperson and such other officers as it decides, who shall remain in office until the next SPREP Meeting. In principle, the role of the Chairperson shall rotate as decided by the SPREP Meeting.

2. The SPREP Meeting shall adopt its own Rules of Procedure.

3. (a) The Parties shall ensure the full involvement of all Members in the work of the SPREP Meeting. The work of the SPREP Meeting shall be conducted on the basis of consensus of all Members, taking into account the practices and procedures of the South Pacific region.

(b) In the event that a decision is required in the SPREP Meeting, that decision shall be taken by a consensus of the Parties. The consensus of the Parties shall ensure that the views of all Members of the SPREP Meeting have been properly considered and taken into account in reaching that consensus.

4. The attendance by observers in SPREP Meetings shall be provided for in the Rules of Procedure.

5. The SPREP Meeting shall be convened by the Director.

6. The working languages of SPREP shall include English and French.

ARTICLE 5

BUDGET

1. The Budget estimates for SPREP shall be prepared by the Director.

2. Adoption of the Budget of SPREP and determination of all other questions relating to the Budget shall be by consensus.

3. The SPREP Meeting shall adopt financial regulations for the administration of SPREP. Such regulations may authorise SPREP to accept contributions from private and public sources.

ARTICLE 6

DIRECTOR

1. The Director of SPREP shall be the head of the Secretariat.

2. The Director shall appoint staff to the Secretariat in accordance with such rules and conditions as the SPREP Meeting may determine.

3. The Director shall report annually to the South Pacific Conference and the South Pacific Forum on the activities of SPREP.

4. The Director shall be responsible to the SPREP Meeting for the administration and management of SPREP and such other functions as the SPREP Meeting may decide.

ARTICLE 7

FUNCTIONS OF THE SECRETARIAT

1. The functions of the Secretariat shall be to implement the activities of SPREP, which shall include:

(a) to promote, undertake and co-ordinate the implementation of the SPREP Action Plan through the annual Programmes of Work, and review and report regularly on progress thereon to Members;

(b) to carry out research and studies as required to implement the SPREP Action Plan through the annual Programmes of Work;

(c) to advise and assist Members on the implementation of activities carried out under the SPREP Action Plan or consistent with its purpose;

(d) to provide a means of regular consultation among Members on the implementation of activities under the SPREP Action Plan and on other relevant issues;

(e) to co-ordinate and establish working arrangements with relevant national, regional and international organisations;

(f) to gather and disseminate relevant information for Members and other interested Governments and organisations;

(g) to promote the development and training of personnel of Members and to promote public awareness and education, including the publication of materials;

(h) to assist Members in the acquisition, interpretation and evaluation of scientific and technical data and information;

(i) to undertake such other activities and follow such procedures as the SPREP Meeting may decide; and

(j) to seek financial and technical resources for SPREP.

2. In addition to the functions described in paragraph (1) of this Article, the Secretariat shall be responsible for the co-ordination and implementation of any functions that the SPREP Meeting may agree to undertake relating to:

(a) the Convention on Conservation of Nature in the South Pacific;

(b) the Convention for the Protection of the Natural Resources and Environment of the South Pacific Region, the Protocol for the Prevention of Pollution of the South Pacific Region by Dumping, and the Protocol concerning Co-operation in Combating Pollution Emergencies in the South Pacific Region; and

(c) any other international or regional Agreement that may be concluded for the protection of the environment of the South Pacific region.

ARTICLE 8

LEGAL STATUS, PRIVILEGES AND IMMUNITIES

1. SPREP shall have such legal personality as is necessary for it to carry out its functions and responsibilities and, in particular, shall have the capacity to contract, to acquire and dispose of moveable and immoveable property and to sue and be sued.

2. SPREP, its officers and employees, together with representatives to the SPREP Meeting, shall enjoy such privileges and immunities necessary for the fulfillment of their functions, as may be agreed between SPREP and the Party in whose territory the Secretariat is located, and as may be provided by other Parties.

ARTICLE 9

SOVEREIGN RIGHTS AND JURISDICTION OF STATES

Nothing in this Agreement shall be interpreted as prejudicing the sovereignty of the Parties over their territory, territorial sea, internal or archipelagic waters, or their sovereign rights:

(a) in their exclusive economic zones and fishing zones for the purpose of exploring or exploiting, conserving and managing the natural resources, whether living or non-living, of the waters superjacent to the sea-bed and of the sea-bed and its subsoil, and with regard to other activities for the economic exploitation and exploration of the zone; or

(b) over their continental shelves for the purpose of exploring them and exploiting the natural resources thereof.

ARTICLE 10

SIGNATURE, RATIFICATION, ACCEPTANCE, APPROVAL AND ACCESSION

1. This Agreement shall be open for signature from the sixteenth day of June 1993 until the sixteenth day of June 1994, and shall thereafter remain open for accession, by:

Australia Niue
Cook Islands Papua New Guinea
Federated States of Micronesia Solomon Islands
Republic of Fiji Kingdom of Tonga
Republic of France Tuvalu
Republic of Kiribati United Kingdom of Great Britain and Northern Ireland on behalf of Pitcairn Islands
Republic of the Marshall Islands United States of America
Republic of Nauru Republic of Vanuatu
New Zealand Western Samoa

2. This Agreement is subject to ratification, acceptance, or approval by the Signatories.

3. Reservations to this Agreement shall not be permitted.

4. This Agreement shall enter into force thirty days from the date of deposit of the tenth instrument of ratification, acceptance, approval, or accession with the Depositary, and thereafter for each State, thirty days after the date of deposit of its instrument of ratification, acceptance, approval, or accession with the Depositary.

5. Following the expiry of the period when this Agreement is open for signature, and provided that this Agreement has entered into force, this Agreement shall be open for accession by any State other than those referred to in this Article which, desiring to accede to this Agreement, may so notify the Depositary, which shall in turn notify the Parties. In the absence of a written objection by a Party within six months of receipt of such notification, a State may accede by deposit of an instrument of accession with the Depositary, and accession shall take effect thirty days after the date of deposit.

6. The Government of Western Samoa is hereby designated as the Depositary.

7. The Depositary shall transmit certified copies of this Agreement to all Members and shall register this Agreement in accordance with Article 102 of the Charter of the United Nations.

ARTICLE 11

AMENDMENT AND WITHDRAWAL

1. Any Party may propose amendments to this Agreement for consideration by the SPREP Meeting. The text of any amendment shall be circulated to Members no less than six months in advance of the Meeting at which it is to be considered.

2. An amendment shall be adopted at a SPREP Meeting by consensus of all Parties attending the SPREP Meeting and shall enter into force thirty days after the receipt by the Depositary of instruments of ratification, acceptance or approval of that amendment by all Parties.

3. Any Party to this Agreement may withdraw from this Agreement by giving written notice to the Depositary. Withdrawal shall take effect one year after receipt of such notice by the Depositary.

IN WITNESS WHEREOF the undersigned, being duly authorised by their respective Governments, have signed this Agreement.

DONE at Apia this sixteenth day of June 1993 in a single copy in the English and French languages, the two texts being equally authentic.

O. AVIATION, SPACE, AND INTERNATIONAL SCIENTIFIC COOPERATION

CONTENTS

1. Aviation

a. Convention on International Civil Aviation, with protocols and amendments

Done at Chicago, December 7, 1944; Entered into force, April 4, 1947

CONVENTION ON INTERNATIONAL CIVIL AVIATION [1]

PREAMBLE

WHEREAS the future development of international civil can greatly help to create and preserve friendship and

RECOGNIZING the right of all States to develop and apply nuclear energy for peaceful purposes and their understanding among the nations and peoples of the world, yet its abuse can become a threat to the general security;

WHEREAS it is desirable to avoid friction and to promote that cooperation between nations and peoples upon which the peace of the world depends;

THEREFORE, the undersigned governments having agreed on certain principles and arrangements in order that international civil aviation may be developed in a safe and orderly manner and that international air transport services may be established on the basis of equality of opportunity and operated soundly transport and economically;

HAVE ACCORDINGLY CONCLUDED THIS CONVENTION TO THAT END.

PART I—AIR NAVIGATION

CHAPTER I—GENERAL PRINCIPLES

ARTICLE 1—SOVEREIGNTY

The contracting States recognize that every State has complete and exclusive sovereignty over the airspace above its territory.

ARTICLE 2—TERRITORY

For the purposes of this Convention the territory of a State shall be deemed to be the land areas and territorial waters adjacent thereto under the sovereignty, suzerainty, protection or mandate of such State.

[1] TIAS 1591. For a list of states that are parties to the Agreement, see Department of State publication, *Treaties in Force.* See also Annex 17 to the Convention, adopted on March 22, 1974 and most recently amended July 1, 2002. This Annex sets out the basis for the ICAO civil aviation security program and seeks to safeguard civil aviation and its facilities against acts of unlawful interference.

ARTICLE 3—CIVIL AND STATE AIRCRAFT

a) This Convention shall be applicable only to civil aircraft, and shall not be applicable to state aircraft.

b) Aircraft used in military, customs and police services shall be deemed to be state aircraft.

c) No state aircraft of a contracting State shall fly over the territory of another State or land thereon without authorization by special agreement or otherwise, and in accordance with the terms thereof.

d) The contracting States undertake, when issuing regulations for their state aircraft, that they will have due regard for the safety of navigation of civil aircraft.

ARTICLE 3 BIS

a) The contracting States recognize that every State must refrain from resorting to the use of weapons against civil aircraft in flight and that, in case of interception, the lives of persons on board and the safety of aircraft must not be endangered. This provision shall not be interpreted as modifying in any way the rights and obligations of States set forth in the Charter of the United Nations.

b) The contracting States recognize that every State, in the exercise of its sovereignty, is entitled to require the landing at some designated airport of a civil aircraft flying above its territory without authority or if there are reasonable grounds to conclude that it is being used for any purpose inconsistent with the aims of this Convention; it may also give such aircraft any other instructions to put an end to such violations. For this purpose, the contracting States may resort to any appropriate means consistent with relevant rules of international law, including the relevant provisions of this Convention, specifically paragraph a) of this Article. Each contracting State agrees to publish its regulations in force regarding the interception of civil aircraft.

c) Every civil aircraft shall comply with an order given in conformity with paragraph b) of this Article. To this end each contracting State shall establish all necessary provisions in its national laws or regulations to make such compliance mandatory for any civil aircraft registered in that State or operated by an operator who has his principal place of business or permanent residence in that State. Each contracting State shall make any violation of such applicable laws or regulations punishable by severe penalties and shall submit the case to its competent authorities in accordance with its laws or regulations.

d) Each contracting State shall take appropriate measures to prohibit the deliberate use of any civil aircraft registered in that State or operated by an operator who has his principal place of business or permanent residence in that State for any purpose inconsistent with the aims of this Convention. This provision shall not affect paragraph a) or paragraphs b) and c) of this Article.

ARTICLE 4—MISUSE OF CIVIL AVIATION

Each contracting State agrees not to use civil aviation for any purpose inconsistent with the aims of this Convention.

CHAPTER II—FLIGHT OVER TERRITORY OF CONTRACTING STATES

ARTICLE 5—RIGHT OF NON-SCHEDULED FLIGHT

Each contracting State agrees that all aircraft of the other contracting States, being aircraft not engaged in scheduled international air services shall have the right, subject to the observance of the terms of this Convention, to make flights into or in transit non-stop across its territory and to make stops for non-traffic purposes without the necessity of obtaining prior permission, and subject to the right of the State flown over to require landing. Each contracting State nevertheless reserves the right, for reasons of safety of flight, to require aircraft desiring to proceed over regions which are inaccessible or without adequate air navigation facilities to follow prescribed routes, or to obtain special permission for such flights.

Such aircraft, if engaged in the carriage of passengers, cargo, or mail for remuneration or hire on other than scheduled international air services, shall also, subject to the provisions of Article 7, have the privilege of taking on or discharging passengers, cargo, or mail, subject to the right of any State where such embarkation or discharge takes place to impose such regulations, conditions or limitations as it may consider desirable.

ARTICLE 6—SCHEDULED AIR SERVICES

No scheduled international air service may be operated over or into the territory of a contracting State, except with the special permission or other authorization of that State, and in accordance with the terms of such permission or authorization.

ARTICLE 7—SABOTAGE

Each contracting State shall have the right to refuse permission to the aircraft of other contracting States to take on in its territory passengers, mail and cargo carried for remuneration or hire and destined for another point within its territory. Each contracting State undertakes not to enter into any arrangements which specifically grant any such privilege on an exclusive basis to any other State or an airline of any other State, and not to obtain any such exclusive privilege from any other State.

ARTICLE 8—PILOTLESS AIRCRAFT

No aircraft capable of being flown without a pilot shall be flown without a pilot over the territory of a contracting State without special authorization by that State and in accordance with the terms of such authorization. Each contracting State undertakes to insure that the flight of such aircraft without a pilot in regions open to civil aircraft shall be so controlled as to obviate danger to civil aircraft.

ARTICLE 9—PROHIBITED AREAS

a) Each contracting State may, for reasons of military necessity or public safety, restrict or prohibit uniformly the aircraft of other States from flying over certain areas of its territory, provided that no distinction in this respect is made between the aircraft of the

State whose territory is involved, engaged in international scheduled airline services, and the aircraft of the other contracting States likewise engaged. Such prohibited areas shall be of reasonable extent and location so as not to interfere unnecessarily with air navigation. Descriptions of such prohibited areas in the territory of a contracting State, as well as any subsequent alterations therein, shall be communicated as soon as possible to the other contracting modification States and to the International Civil Aviation Organization.

b) Each contracting State reserves also the right, in exceptional circumstances or during a period of emergency, or in the interest of public safety, and with immediate effect, to restrict or prohibit flying over the whole or any dire part of its territory, on condition that such restriction or prohibition shall be applicable without distinction of nationality to aircraft of all other States.

c) Each contracting State, under such regulations as it may prescribe, may require any aircraft entering the areas contemplated in subparagraphs a) or b) above to effect a landing as soon as practicable thereafter at some designated airport within its territory.

ARTICLE 10—LANDING AT CUSTOMS AIRPORT

Except in a case where, under the terms of this Convention or a special authorization, aircraft are permitted to cross the territory of a contracting State without landing, every aircraft which enters the territory of a contracting State shall, if the regulations of that State so require, land at an airport designated by that State for the purpose of customs and other examination. On departure from the territory of a contracting State, such aircraft shall depart from a similarly designated customs airport. Particulars of all designated customs airports shall be published by the State and transmitted to the International Civil Aviation Organization established under Part II of this Convention for communication to all other contracting States.

ARTICLE 11—APPLICABILITY OF AIR REGULATIONS

Subject to the provisions of this Convention, the laws and regulations of a contracting State relating to the admission to or departure from its territory of aircraft engaged in international air navigation, or to the operation and navigation of aircraft while within its territory, shall be applied to the aircraft of all contracting States without distinction as to nationality, and shall be complied with by such aircraft upon entering or departing from or while within the territory of that State.

ARTICLE 12—RULES OF THE AIR

Each contracting State undertakes to adopt measures to insure that every aircraft flying over or maneuvering within its territory and that every aircraft carrying its nationality mark, wherever such aircraft may be, shall comply with the rules and regulations relating to the flight and maneuver of aircraft there in force. Each contracting State undertakes to keep its own regulations in these respects uniform, to the greatest possible extent, with those established from time to time under this Convention. Over the high seas, the rules in force shall be those established under this Convention. Each contracting State undertakes to insure the prosecution of all persons violating the regulations applicable.

ARTICLE 13—ENTRY AND CLEARANCE REGULATIONS

The laws and regulations of a contracting State as to the admission to or departure from its territory of passengers, crew or cargo of aircraft, such as regulations relating to entry, clearance, immigration, passports, customs, and quarantine shall be complied with by or on behalf of such passengers, crew or cargo upon entrance into or departure from, or while within the territory of that State.

ARTICLE 14—PREVENTION OF SPREAD OF DISEASE

Each contracting State agrees to take effective measures to prevent the spread by means of air navigation of cholera, typhus (epidemic), smallpox, yellow fever, plague, and such other communicable diseases as the contracting States shall from time to time decide to designate, and to that end contracting States will keep in close consultation with the agencies concerned with international regulations relating to sanitary measures applicable to aircraft. Such consultation shall be without prejudice to the application of any existing international convention on this subject to which the contracting States may be parties.

ARTICLE 15—AIRPORT AND SIMILAR CHARGES

Every airport in a contracting State which is open to public use by its national aircraft shall likewise, subject to the provisions of Article 68, be open under uniform conditions to the aircraft of all the other contracting States. The like uniform conditions shall apply to the use, by aircraft of every contracting State, of all air navigation facilities, including radio and meteorological services, which may be provided for public use for the safety and expedition of air navigation.

Any charges that may be imposed or permitted to be imposed by a contracting State for the use of such airports and air navigation facilities by the aircraft of any other contracting State shall not be higher,

a) As to aircraft not engaged in scheduled international air services, than those that would be paid by national aircraft of the same class engaged in similar operations, and

b) As to aircraft engaged in scheduled international air services, than those that would be paid by its national aircraft engaged in similar international air services.

All such charges shall be published and communicated to the International Civil Aviation Organization, provided that, upon representation by an interested contracting State, the charges imposed for the use of airports and other facilities shall be subject to review by the Council, which shall report and make recommendations thereon for the consideration of the State or States concerned. No fees, dues or other charges shall be imposed by any contracting State in respect solely of the right of transit over or entry into or exit from its territory of any aircraft of a contracting State or persons or property thereon.

ARTICLE 16—SEARCH OF AIRCRAFT

The appropriate authorities of each of the contracting States shall have the right, without unreasonable delay, to search aircraft of the other contracting States on landing or departure, to inspect the certificates and other documents prescribed by this Convention.

CHAPTER III—NATONALITY OF AIRCRAFT

ARTICLE 17—NATIONALITY OF AIRCRAFT

Aircraft have the nationality of the State in which they are registered.

ARTICLE 18—DUAL REGISTRATION

An aircraft cannot be validly registered in more than one State, but its registration may be changed from one State to another.

ARTICLE 19—NATIONAL LAWS GOVERNING REGISTRATION

The registration or transfer of registration of aircraft in any State shall be made in accordance with its laws and regulations.

ARTICLE 20—DISPLAY OF MARKS

Every aircraft engaged in international air navigation shall bear its appropriate nationality and registration marks.

ARTICLE 21—REPORT OF REGISTRATIONS

Each contracting State undertakes to supply to any other contracting State or to the International Civil Aviation Organization, on demand, information concerning the registration and ownership of any particular aircraft registered in that State. In addition, each contracting State shall furnish reports to the International Civil Aviation Organization, under such regulations as the latter may prescribe, giving such pertinent data as can be made available concerning the ownership and control of aircraft registered in that State and habitually engaged in international air navigation. The data thus obtained by the International Civil Aviation Organization shall be made available by it on request to the other contracting States.

CHAPTER IV—MEASURES TO FACILITATE AIR NAVIGATION

ARTICLE 22—FACILITATION OF FORMALITIES

Each contracting State agrees to adopt all practicable measures, through the issuance of special regulations or otherwise, to facilitate and expedite navigation by aircraft between the territories of contracting States, and to prevent unnecessary delays to aircraft, crews, passengers and cargo, especially in the administration of the laws relating to immigration, quarantine, customs and clearance.

ARTICLE 23—CUSTOMS AND IMMIGRATION PROCEDURES

Each contracting State undertakes, so far as it may find practicable, to establish customs and immigration procedures affecting international air navigation in accordance with practices which may be established or recommended from time to time, pursuant to this Convention. Nothing in this Convention shall be construed as preventing the establishment of customs-free airports.

ARTICLE 24—CUSTOMS DUTY

a) Aircraft on a flight to, from, or across the territory of another contracting State shall be admitted temporarily free of duty, subject to the customs regulations of the State. Fuel, lubricating oils, spare parts, regular equipment and aircraft stores on board an aircraft of a contracting State, on arrival in the territory of another contracting State and retained on board on leaving the territory of that State shall be exempt from customs duty, inspection fees or similar national or local duties and charges. This exemption shall not apply to any quantities or articles unloaded, except in accordance with the customs regulations of the State, which may require that they shall be kept under customs supervision.

b) Spare parts and equipment imported into the territory of a contracting State for incorporation in or use on an aircraft of another contracting State engaged in international air navigation shall be admitted free of customs duty, subject to compliance with the regulations of the State concerned, which may provide that the articles shall be kept under customs supervision and control.

ARTICLE 25—AIRCRAFT IN DISTRESS

Each contracting State undertakes to provide such measures of assistance to aircraft in distress in its territory as it may find practicable, and to permit, subject to control by its own authorities, the owners of the aircraft or authorities of the State in which the aircraft is registered to provide such measures of assistance as may be necessitated by the circumstances. Each contracting State, when undertaking search for missing aircraft, will collaborate in coordinated measures which may be recommended from time to time pursuant to this Convention.

ARTICLE 26—INVESTIGATION OF ACCIDENTS

In the event of an accident to an aircraft of a contracting State occurring in the territory of another contracting State, and involving death or serious injury, or indicating serious technical defect in the aircraft or air navigation facilities, the State in which the accident occurs will institute an inquiry into the circumstances of the accident, in accordance, so far as its laws permit, with the procedure which may be recommended by the International Civil Aviation Organization. The State in which the aircraft is registered shall be given the opportunity to appoint observers to be present at the inquiry and the State holding the inquiry shall communicate the report and findings in the matter to that State.

ARTICLE 27—EXEMPTION FROM SEIZURE ON PATENT CLAIMS

a) While engaged in international air navigation, any authorized entry of aircraft of a contracting State into the territory of another contracting State or authorized transit across the territory of such State with or without landings shall not entail any seizure or detention of the aircraft or any claim against the owner or operator thereof or any other interference therewith by or on behalf of such State or any person therein, on the ground that the construction, mechanism, parts, accessories or operation of the aircraft is an infringement of any patent, design, or model duly granted or registered in the State whose territory is entered by the aircraft, it being agreed that no deposit of security in connection with the foregoing exemption from seizure or detention of the aircraft shall in any case be required in the State entered by such aircraft.

b) The provisions of paragraph a) of this Article shall also be applicable to the storage of spare parts and spare equipment for the aircraft and the right to use and install the same in the repair of an aircraft of a contracting State in the territory of any other contracting State, provided that any patented part or equipment so stored shall not be sold or distributed internally in or exported commercially from the contracting State entered by the aircraft.

c) The benefits of this Article shall apply only to such States, parties to this Convention, as either 1) are parties to the International Convention for the Protection of Industrial Property and to any amendments thereof; or 2) have enacted patent laws which recognize and give adequate protection to inventions made by the nationals of the other States parties to this Convention.

ARTICLE 28—AIR NAVIGATION FACILITIES AND STANDARD SYSTEMS

Each contracting State undertakes, so far as it may find practicable, to:

a) Provide, in its territory, airports, radio services, meteorological services and other air navigation facilities to facilitate international air navigation, in accordance with the standards and practices recommended or established from time to time, pursuant to this Convention;

b) Adopt and put into operation the appropriate standard systems of communications procedure, codes, markings, signals, lighting and other operational practices and rules which may be recommended or established from time to time, pursuant to this Convention;

c) Collaborate in international measures to secure the publication of aeronautical maps and charts in accordance with standards which may be recommended or established from time to time, pursuant to this Convention.

CHAPTER V—CONDITIONS TO BE FULFILLED WITH RESPECT TO AIRCRAFT

ARTICLE 29—DOCUMENTS CARRIED IN AIRCRAFT

Every aircraft of a contracting State, engaged in inter-navigation, shall carry the following documents in conformity with the conditions prescribed in this Convention:

a) Its certificate of registration;

b) Its certificate of airworthiness;

c) The appropriate licenses for each member of the crew;

d) Its journey log book;

e) If it is equipped with radio apparatus, the aircraft radio station license;

f) If it carries passengers, a list of their names and places of embarkation and destination;

g) If it carries cargo, a manifest and detailed of the cargo.

ARTICLE 30—AIRCRAFT RADIO EQUIPMENT

a) Aircraft of each contracting State may, in or over the territory of other contracting States, carry radio transmitting apparatus only if a license to install and operate such apparatus has been issued by the appropriate authorities of the State in which the aircraft is registered. The use of radio transmitting apparatus in the territory of the contracting State whose territory is flown over shall be in accordance with the regulations prescribed by that State.

b) Radio transmitting apparatus may be used only by members of the flight crew who are provided with a special license for the purpose, issued by the appropriate authorities of the State in which the aircraft is registered.

ARTICLE 31—CERTIFICATES OF AIRWORTHINESS

Every aircraft engaged in international navigation shall be provided with a certificate of airworthiness issued or rendered valid by the State in which it is registered.

ARTICLE 32—LICENSES OF PERSONNEL

a) The pilot of every aircraft and the other members of the operating crew of every aircraft engaged in international navigation shall be provided with certificates of competency and licenses issued or rendered valid by the State in which the aircraft is registered.

b) Each contracting State reserves the right to refuse to recognize, for the purpose of flight above its own territory, certificates of competency and licenses granted to any of its nationals by another contracting State.

ARTICLE 33—RECOGNITION OF CERTIFICATES AND LICENSES

Certificates of airworthiness and certificates of competency and licenses issued or rendered valid by the contracting State in which the aircraft is registered, shall be recognized as valid by the other contracting States, provided that the requirements under which such certificates or licences were issued or rendered valid are equal to or above the minimum standards which may be established from time to time pursuant to this Convention.

ARTICLE 34—JOURNEY LOG BOOKS

There shall be maintained in respect of every aircraft engaged in international navigation a journey log book in which shall be entered particulars of the aircraft, its crew and of each journey, in such form as may be prescribed from time to time pursuant to this Convention.

ARTICLE 35—CARGO RESTRICTIONS

a) No munitions of war or implements of war may be carried in or above the territory of a State in aircraft engaged in international navigation, except by permission of such State. Each State shall determine by regulations what constitutes munitions of war or implements of war for the purposes of this Article, giving due consideration, for the purposes of uniformity, to such recommendations as the International Civil Aviation Organization may from time to time make.

b) Each contracting State reserves the right, for reasons of public order and safety, to regulate or prohibit the carriage in or above its territory of articles other than those enumerated in paragraph a): provided that no distinction is made in this respect between its national aircraft engaged in international navigation and the aircraft of the other States so engaged; and provided further that no restriction shall be imposed which may interfere with the carriage and use on aircraft of apparatus necessary for the operation or navigation of the aircraft or the safety of the personnel or passengers.

ARTICLE 36—PHOTOGRAPHIC APPARATUS

Each contracting State may prohibit or regulate the use of photographic apparatus in aircraft over its territory.

CHAPTER VI—INTERNATIONAL STANDARDS AND RECOMMENDED PRACTICES

ARTICLE 37—ADOPTION OF INTERNATIONAL STANDARDS AND PROCEDURES

Each contracting State undertakes to collaborate in securing the highest practicable degree of uniformity in regulations, standards, procedures, and organization in relation to aircraft, personnel, airways and auxiliary services in all matters in which such uniformity will facilitate and improve air navigation.

To this end the International Civil Aviation Organization shall adopt and amend from time to time, as may be necessary, international standards and recommended practices and procedures dealing with:

a) Communications systems and air navigation aids, including ground marking;
b) including ground marking;
c) Rules of the air and air traffic control practices;
d) Licensing of operating and mechanical personnel;
e) Airworthiness of aircraft;
f) Registration and identification of aircraft;
g) Collection and exchange of meteorological information;
h) Log books;
i) Aeronautical maps and charts;
j) Customs and immigration procedures;
k) Aircraft in distress and investigation of accidents;

and such other matters concerned with the safety, regularity, and efficiency of air navigation as may from time to time appear appropriate.

ARTICLE 38—DEPARTURES FROM INTERNATIONAL STANDARDS AND PROCEDURES

Any State which finds it impracticable to comply in all respects with any such international standard or procedure, or to bring its own regulations or practices into full accord with any international standard or procedure after amendment of the latter, or which deems it necessary to adopt regulations or practices differing in any particular respect from those established by an international standard, shall give immediate notification to the International Civil Aviation Organization of the differences between its own practice and that established by the international standard. In the case of amendments to international standards, any State which does not make the appropriate amendments to its own regulations or practices shall give notice to the Council within sixty days of the adoption of the amendment to the international standard, or indicate the action which it proposes to take. In any such case, the Council shall make immediate notification to all other states of the difference which exists between one or more features of an international standard and the corresponding national practice of that State.

ARTICLE 39—ENDORSEMENT OF CERTIFICATES AND LICENSES

a) Any aircraft or part thereof with respect to which there exists an international standard of airworthiness or performance, and which failed in any respect to satisfy that standard at the time of its certification, shall have endorsed on or attached to its airworthiness certificate a complete enumeration of the details in respect of which it so failed.

b) Any person holding a license who does not satisfy in full the conditions laid down in the international standard relating to the class of license or certificate which he holds shall have endorsed on or attached to his license a complete enumeration of the particulars in which he does not satisfy such conditions.

ARTICLE 40—VALIDITY OF ENDORSED CERTIFICATES AND LICENSES

No aircraft or personnel having certificates or licenses so endorsed shall participate in international navigation, except with the permission of the State or States whose territory is entered. The registration or use of any such aircraft, or of any certificated aircraft part, in any State other than that in which it was originally certificated shall be at the discretion of the State into which the aircraft or part is imported.

ARTICLE 41—RECOGNITION OF EXISTING STANDARDS OF AIR WORTHINESS

The provisions of this Chapter shall not apply to aircraft and aircraft equipment of types of which the prototype is submitted to the appropriate national authorities for certification prior to a date three years after the date of adoption of an international standard of airworthiness for such equipment.

ARTICLE 42—RECOGNITION OF EXISTING STANDARDS OF COMPETENCY OF PERSONNEL

The provisions of this Chapter shall not apply to personnel whose licenses are originally issued prior to a date one year after initial adoption of an international standard of qualification for such personnel; but they shall in any case apply to all personnel whose licenses remain valid five years after the date of adoption of such standard.

PART II—THE INTERNATIONAL CIVIL AVIATION ORGANIZATION

CHAPTER I—THE ORGANIZATION

ARTICLE 43—NAME AND COMPOSITION

An organization to be named the International Civil Aviation Organization is formed by the Convention. It is made up of an Assembly, a Council, and such other bodies as may be necessary.

ARTICLE 44—OBJECTIVES

The aims and objectives of the Organization are to develop the principles and techniques of international air navigation principles to foster the planning and development of international air transport so as to:

a) Insure the safe and orderly growth of international civil aviation throughout the world;

b) Encourage the arts of aircraft design and operation for peaceful purposes;

c) Encourage the development of airways, airports, and air navigation facilities for international civil aviation;

d) Meet the needs of the peoples of the world for safe, regular, efficient and economical air transport;

e) Prevent economic waste caused by unreasonable competition;

f) Insure that the rights of contracting States are fully respected and that every contracting State has a fair opportunity to operate international airlines;

g) Avoid discrimination between contracting States;

h) Promote safety of flight in international air navigation;

i) Promote generally the development of all aspects of international civil aeronautics.

ARTICLE 45—PERMANENT SEAT

The permanent seat of the Organization shall be at such place as shall be determined at the final meeting of the Interim Assembly of the Provisional International Civil Aviation Organization set up by the Interim Agreement on International Civil Aviation signed at Chicago on December 7, 1944. The seat may be temporarily transferred elsewhere by decision of the Council, and otherwise than temporarily by decision of the Assembly, such decision to be taken by the number of votes specified by the Assembly. The number of votes so specified will not be less than three-fifths of the total number of contracting States.

ARTICLE 46—FIRST MEETING OF ASSEMBLY

The first meeting of the Assembly shall be summoned by the Interim Council of the above-mentioned Provisional Organization as soon as the Convention has come into force, to meet at a time and place to be decided by the Interim Council.

ARTICLE 47—LEGAL CAPACITY

The Organization shall enjoy in the territory of each contracting State such legal capacity as may be necessary for the performance of its functions. Full juridical personality shall be granted wherever compatible with the constitution and laws of the State concerned.

CHAPTER III—THE ASSEMBLY

ARTICLE 48—MEETINGS OF ASSEMBLY AND VOTING

a) The Assembly shall meet not less than once in three years and shall be convened by the Council at a suitable time and place. An extraordinary meeting of the Assembly may be held at any time upon the call of the Council or at the request of not less than one-fifth of the total number of contracting States addressed to the Secretary General.

b) All contracting States shall have an equal right to be represented at the meetings of the Assembly and each contracting State shall be entitled to one vote. Delegates representing contracting States may be assisted by technical advisers who may participate in the meetings but shall have no vote.

c) A majority of the contracting States is required to constitute a quorum for the meetings of the Assembly. Unless otherwise provided in this Convention, decisions of the Assembly shall be taken by a majority of the votes cast.

ARTICLE 49—POWERS AND DUTIES OF ASSEMBLY

The powers and duties of the Assembly shall be to:

a) Elect at each meeting its President and other officers;

b) Elect the contracting States to be represented on the Council, in accordance with the provisions of Chapter IX;

c) Examine and take appropriate action on the reports of the Council and decide on any matter referred to it by the Council;

d) Determine its own rules of procedure and establish such subsidiary commissions as it may consider to be necessary or desirable;

e) Vote annual budgets and determine the financial arrangements of the Organization, in accordance with the provisions of Chapter XII;

f) Review expenditures and approve the accounts of the Organization;

g) Refer, at its discretion, to the Council, to subsidiary commissions, or to any other body any matter within its sphere of action;

h) Delegate to the Council the powers and authority necessary or desirable for the discharge of the duties of the Organization and revoke or modify the delegations of authority at any time;

i) Carry out the appropriate provisions of Chapter XIII;

j) Consider proposals for the modification or amendment of the provisions of this Convention and, if it approves of the proposals, recommend them to the contracting States in accordance with the provisions of Chapter XXI;

k) Deal with any matter within the sphere of action of the Organization not specifically assigned to the Council.

CHAPTER IX—THE COUNCIL

ARTICLE 50—COMPOSITION AND ELECTION OF COUNCIL

a) The Council shall be a permanent body responsible to the Assembly. It shall be composed of thirty-six contracting States elected by the Assembly. An election shall be held at the first meeting of the Assembly and thereafter every three years, and the members of the Council so elected shall hold office until the next following election.

b) In electing the members of the Council, the Assembly shall give adequate representation to 1) the States of chief importance in air transport; 2) the States not otherwise included which make the largest contribution to the provision of facilities for civil air navigation; and 3) the States not otherwise included whose designation will insure that all the major geographic areas of the world are represented on the Council. Any vacancy on the Council shall be filled by the Assembly as soon as possible; any contracting State so elected to the Council shall hold office for the unexpired portion of its predecessor's term of office.

c) No representative of a contracting State on the Council shall be actively associated with the operation of an international air service or financially interested in such a service.

ARTICLE 51—PRESIDENT OF COUNCIL

The Council shall elect its President for a term of three years. He may be reelected. He shall have no vote. The Council shall elect from among its members one or more Vice Presidents who shall retain their right to vote when serving as acting President. The President need not be selected from among the representatives of the members of the Council but, if a representative is elected, his seat shall be deemed vacant and it shall be filled by the State which he represented. The duties of the President shall be to:

a) Convene meetings of the Council, the Air Transport Committee, and the Air Navigation Commission;

b) Serve as representative of the Council; and

c) Carry out on behalf of the Council the functions which the Council assigns to him.

ARTICLE 52—VOTING IN COUNCIL

Decisions by the Council shall require approval by a majority of its members. The Council may delegate authority with respect to any particular matter to a committee of its members. Decisions of any committee of the Council may be appealed to the Council by any interested contracting State.

ARTICLE 53—PARTICIPATION WITHOUT A VOTE

Any contracting State may participate, without a vote, in the consideration by the Council and by its committees and of any question which especially affects its interests. No member of the Council shall vote in the consideration by the Council of a dispute to which it is a party.

ARTICLE 54—MANDATORY FUNCTIONS OF COUNCIL

The Council shall:

a) Submit annual reports to the Assembly;

b) Carry out the directions of the Assembly and discharge the duties and obligations which are laid on it by this Convention;

c) Determine its organization and rules of procedure;

d) Appoint and define the duties of an Air Transport Committee, which shall be chosen from among the representatives of the members of the Council, and which shall be responsible to it;

e) Establish an Air Navigation Commission, in accordance with the provisions of Chapter X;

f) Administer the finances of the Organization in accordance with the provisions of Chapters XII and XV;

g) Determine the emoluments of the President of the Council;

h) Appoint a chief executive officer who shall be called the Secretary General, and make provision for the appointment of such other personnel as may be necessary, in accordance with the provisions of Chapter XI;

i) Request, collect, examine and publish information to the advancement of air navigation and the operation of international air services, including information about the costs of operation and particulars of subsidies paid to airlines from public funds;

j) Report to contracting States any infraction of this Convention, as well as any failure to carry out recommendations or determinations of the Council;

k) Report to the Assembly any infraction of this Convention where a contracting State has failed to take appropriate action within a reasonable time after notice of the infraction;

1) Adopt, in accordance with the provisions of Chapter VI of this Convention, international standards and recommended practices; for convenience, designate them as Annexes to this Convention; and notify all contracting States of the action taken;

m) Consider recommendations of the Air Navigation Commission for amendment of the Annexes and take action in accordance with the provisions of Chapter XX;

n) Consider any matter relating to the Convention which any contracting State refers to it.

ARTICLE 55—PERMISSIVE FUNCTIONS OF COUNCIL

The Council may:

a) Where appropriate and as experience may show to be desirable, create subordinate air transport commissions on a regional or other basis and define groups of states or airlines with or through which it may deal to facilitate the carrying out of the aims of this Convention;

b) Delegate to the Air Navigation Commission duties additional to those set forth in the Convention and revoke or modify such delegations of authority at any time;

c) Conduct research into all aspects of air transport and air navigation which are of international importance, communicate the results of its research to the contracting States, and facilitate the exchange of information between contracting States on air transport and air navigation matters;

d) Study any matters affecting the organization and operation of international air transport, including the international ownership and operation of international air services on trunk routes, and submit to the Assembly plans in relation thereto:

e) Investigate, at the request of any contracting State, any situation which may appear to present avoidable obstacles to the development of international air navigation; and, after such investigation, issue such reports as may appear to it desirable.

CHAPTER X—THE AIR NAVIGATION COMMISSION

ARTICLE 56—NOMINATION AND APPOINTMENT OF COMMISSION

The Air Navigation Commission shall be composed of nineteen members appointed by the Council from among persons nominated by contracting States. These persons shall have suitable qualifications and experience in the science and practice of aeronautics. The Council shall request all contracting States to submit nominations. The President of the Air Navigation Commission shall be appointed by the Council.

ARTICLE 57—DUTIES OF COMMISSION

The Air Navigation Commission shall:

a) Consider, and recommend to the Council for adoption, modifications of the Annexes to this Convention;

b) Establish technical subcommissions on which any contracting State may be represented, if it so desires;

c) Advise the Council concerning the collection and communication to the contracting States of all information which it considers necessary and useful for the advancement of air navigation.

ARTICLE 58—APPOINTMENT OF PERSONNEL

Subject to any rules laid down by the Assembly and to the provisions of this Convention, the Council shall determine the method of appointment and of termination of appointment, the training, and the salaries, allowances, and conditions of service of the Secretary General and other personnel of the Organization, and may employ or make use of the services of nationals of any contracting State.

ARTICLE 59—INTERNATIONAL CHARACTER OF PERSONNEL

The President of the Council, the Secretary General, and other personnel shall not seek or receive instructions in regard to the discharge of their responsibilities from any authority external to the Organization. Each contracting State undertakes fully to respect the international character of the responsibilities of the personnel and not to seek to influence any of its nationals in the discharge of their responsibilities.

ARTICLE 60—IMMUNITIES AND PRIVILEGES OF PERSONNEL

Each contracting State undertakes, so far as possible under its constitutional procedure, to accord to the President of the Council, the Secretary General, and the other personnel of the Organization, the immunities and privileges which are accorded to corresponding personnel of other public international organizations. If a general international agreement on the immunities and privileges of international civil servants is arrived at, the immunities and privileges accorded to the President, the Secretary General, and the other personnel of the Organization shall be the immunities and privileges accorded under that general international agreement.

ARTICLE 61—BUDGET AND APPORTIONMENT OF EXPENSES

The Council shall submit to the Assembly annual budgets, annual statements of accounts and estimates of all receipts and expenditures. The Assembly shall vote the budgets with whatever modification it sees fit to prescribe, and, with the exception of assessments under Chapter XV to States consenting thereto, shall apportion the expenses of the Organization among the contracting States on the basis which it shall from time to time determine.

ARTICLE 62—SUSPENSION OF VOTING POWER

The Assembly may suspend the voting power in the Assembly and in the Council of any contracting State that fails to discharge within a reasonable period its financial obligations to the Organization.

ARTICLE 63—EXPENSES OF DELEGATIONS AND OTHER REPRESENTATIVES

Each contracting State shall bear the expenses of its own delegation to the Assembly and the remuneration, travel, and expenses of any person whom it appoints to serve on the Council, and of its nominees or representatives on any subsidiary committees or commissions of the Organization.

CHAPTER XIII—OTHER INTERNATIONAL ARRANGEMENTS

ARTICLE 64—SECURITY ARRANGEMENTS

The Organization may, with respect to air matters within its competence directly affecting world security, by vote of the Assembly enter into appropriate arrangements with any general organization set up by the nations of the world to preserve peace.

ARTICLE 65—ARRANGEMENTS WITH OTHER INTERNATIONAL BODIES

The Council, on behalf of the Organization, may enter into agreements with other international bodies for the maintenance of common services and for common arrangements concerning personnel and, with the approval of the Assembly, may enter into such other arrangements as may facilitate the work of the Organization.

ARTICLE 66—FUNCTIONS RELATING TO OTHER AGREEMENTS

a) The Organization shall also carry out the functions placed upon it by the International Air Services Transit Agreement and by the International Air Transport Agreement drawn up at Chicago on December 7, 1944, in accordance with the terms and conditions therein set forth.

b) Members of the Assembly and the Council who have not accepted the International Air Services Transit Agreement of the International Air Transport Agreement drawn up at Chicago on December 7, 1944 shall not have the right to vote on any questions referred to the Assembly or Council under the provisions of the relevant Agreement.

PART III—INTERNATIONAL AIR TRANSPORT

CHAPTER XIV—INFORMATION AND REPORTS

ARTICLE 67—FILE REPORTS WITH COUNCIL

Each contracting State undertakes that its international airlines shall, in accordance with requirements laid down by the Council, file with the Council traffic reports, cost statistics and financial statements showing among other things all receipts and the sources thereof.

CHAPTER XV—AIRPORTS AND OTHER AIR NAVIGATION FACILITIES

ARTICLE 68—DESIGNATION OF ROUTES AND AIRPORTS

Each contracting State may, subject to the provisions of this Convention, designate the route to be followed within its territory by any international air service and the airports which any such service may use.

ARTICLE 69—IMPROVEMENT OF AIR NAVIGATION FACILITIES

If the Council is of the opinion that the airports or other air navigation facilities, including radio and meteorological services, of a contracting State are not reasonably adequate for the safe, regular, efficient, and economical operation of international air services, present or contemplated, the Council shall consult with the State directly concerned, and other States affected, with a view to finding means by which the situation may be remedied, and may make recommendations for that situation purpose. No contracting State shall be guilty of an infraction of this Convention if it fails to carry out these recommendations.

ARTICLE 70—FINANCING OF AIR NAVIGATION FACILITIES

A contracting State, in the circumstances arising under the provisions of Article 69, may conclude an arrangement with the Council for giving effect to such recommendations. The State may elect to bear all of the costs involved in any such arrangement. If the State does not so elect, the Council may agree, at the request of the State, to provide for all or a portion of the costs.

ARTICLE 71—PROVISION AND MAINTENANCE OF FACILITIES BY COUNCIL

If a contracting State so requests, the Council may agree to provide, man, maintain, and administer any or all of the airports and other air navigation facilities including radio and meteorological services, required in its territory for the safe, regular, efficient and economical operation of the international air services of the other contracting States, and may specify just and reasonable charges for the use of the facilities provided.

ARTICLE 72—ACQUISITION OR USE OF LAND

Where land is needed for facilities financed in whole or in part by the Council at the request of a contracting State, that State shall either provide the land itself, retaining title if it wishes, or facilitate the use of the land by the Council on just and reasonable terms and in accordance with the laws of the State concerned.

ARTICLE 73—EXPENDITURE AND ASSESSMENT OF FUNDS

Within the limit of the funds which may be made available to it by the Assembly under Chapter XII, the Council may make current expenditures for the purposes of this Chapter from the general funds of the Organization. The Council shall assess the capital funds required for the purposes of this Chapter in previously agreed proportions over a reasonable period of time to the contracting States consenting thereto whose airlines use the facilities. The Council may also assess to States that consent any working funds that are required.

ARTICLE 74—TECHNICAL ASSISTANCE AND UTILIZATION OF REVENUES

When the Council. at the request of a contracting State, advances funds or provides airports or other facilities in whole or in part. the arrangement may provide. with the consent of that State. for technical assistance in the supervision and operation of the airports and other facilities, and for the payment. from the revenues derived from the operation of the airports and other facilities, of the operating expenses of the airports and the other facilities, and of interest and amortization charges.

ARTICLE 75—TAKING OVER OF FACILITIES FROM COUNCIL

A contracting State may at any time discharge any obligation into which it has entered under Article 70, and take over airports and other facilities which the Council has provided in its territory pursuant to the provisions of Articles 71 and 72, by paying to the

Council an amount which in the opinion of the Council is reasonable in the circumstances. If the State considers that the amount fixed by the Council is unreasonable it may appeal to the Assembly against the decision of the Council and the Assembly may confirm or amend the decision of the Council.

ARTICLE 76—RETURN OF FUNDS

Funds obtained by the Council through reimbursement under Article 75 and from receipts of interest and amortization payments under Article 74 shall, in the case of advances originally financed by States under Article 73, be returned to the States which were originally assessed in the proportion of their assessments, as determined by the Council.

CHAPTER XVI—JOINT OPERATING ORGANIZATIONS AND POOLED SERVICES

ARTICLE 77—JOINT OPERATING ORGANIZATIONS PERMITTED

Nothing in this Convention shall prevent two or more contracting States from constituting joint air transport operating organizations or international operating agencies and from pooling their air services on any routes or in any regions, but such organizations or agencies and such pooled services shall be subject to all the provisions of this Convention, including those relating to the registration of agreements with the Council. The Council shall determine in what manner the provisions of this Convention relating to nationality of aircraft shall apply to aircraft operated by international operating agencies.

ARTICLE 78—FUNCTION OF COUNCIL

The Council may suggest to contracting States concerned that they form joint organizations to operate air services on any routes or in any regions.

ARTICLE 79—PARTICIPATION IN OPERATING ORGANIZATIONS

A State may participate in joint operating organizations or in pooling arrangements, either through its government or through an airline company or companies designated by its government. The companies may, at the sole discretion of the State concerned, be state-owned or partly state-owned or privately owned.

PART IV—FINAL PROVISIONS

CHAPTER XVII—OTHER AERONAUTICAL AGREEMENTS AND ARRANGEMENTS

ARTICLE 80—PARIS AND HABANA CONVENTIONS

Each contracting State undertakes, immediately upon the coming into force of this Convention, to give notice of denunciation of the Convention relating to the Regulation of Aerial Navigation signed at Paris on October 13, 1919 or the Convention on Commercial Aviation signed at Habana on February 20, 1928, if it is a party to either. As between contracting States, this Convention supersedes the Conventions of Paris and Habana previously referred to.

ARTICLE 81—REGISTRATION OF EXISTING AGREEMENTS

All aeronautical agreements which are in existence on the coming into force of this Convention, and which are between a contracting State and any other State or between an airline of a contracting State and any other State or the airline of any State, shall be forthwith registered with the Council.

ARTICLE 82—ABROGATION OF INCONSISTENT ARRANGEMENTS

The contracting States accept this Convention as abrogating all obligations and understandings between them which are inconsistent with its terms, and undertake not to enter into any such obligations and understandings. A contracting State which, before becoming a member of the Organization has undertaken any obligations toward a non-contracting State or a national of a contracting State or of a non-contracting State inconsistent with the terms of this Convention, shall take immediate steps to procure its release from the obligations. If an airline of any contracting State has entered into any such inconsistent obligations, the State of which it is a national shall use its best efforts to secure their termination forthwith and shall in any event cause them to be terminated as soon as such action can lawfully be taken after the coming into force of this Convention.

ARTICLE 83—REGISTRATION OF NEW ARRANGEMENTS

Subject to the provisions of the preceding Article, any contracting State may make arrangements not inconsistent with the provisions of this Convention. Any such arrangement shall be forthwith registered with the Council, which shall make it public as soon as possible.

ARTICLE 83 BIS—TRANSFER OF CERTAIN FUNCTIONS AND DUTIES

a) Notwithstanding the provisions of Articles 12, 30, 3 1 and 32 a), when an aircraft registered in a contracting State is operated pursuant to an agreement for the lease, charter or interchange of the aircraft or any similar arrangement by an operator who has his principal place of business or, if he has no such place of business, his permanent residence in another contracting State, the State of registry may, by agreement with such other State, transfer to it all or part of its functions and duties as State of registry in respect of that aircraft under Articles 12, 30, 31 and 32 a). The State of registry shall be relieved of responsibility in respect of the functions and duties transferred.

b) The transfer shall not have effect in respect of other contracting States before either the agreement between States in which it is embodied has been registered with the Council and made public pursuant to Article 83 or the existence and scope of the agreement have been directly communicated to the authorities of the other contracting State or States concerned by a State party to the agreement.

c) The provisions of paragraphs a) and b) above shall also be applicable to cases covered by Article 77.

CHAPTER XVIII—DISPUTES AND DEFAULT

ARTICLE 84—SETTLEMENT OF DISPUTES

If any disagreement between two or more contracting States relating to the interpretation or application of this Convention and its Annexes cannot be settled by negotiation, it shall, on the application of any State concerned in the disagreement, be decided by the Council. No member of the Council shall vote in the consideration by the Council of any dispute to which it is a party. Any contracting State may, subject to Article 85, appeal from the decision of the Council to an ad hoc arbitral tribunal agreed upon with the other parties to the dispute or to the Permanent Court of International Justice. Any such appeal shall be notified to the Council within sixty days of receipt of notification of the decision of the Council.

ARTICLE 85—ARBITRATION PROCEDURE

If any contracting State party to a dispute in which the decision of the Council is under appeal has not accepted the Statute of the Permanent Court of International Justice and the contracting States parties to the dispute cannot agree on the choice of the arbitral tribunal, each of the contracting States parties to the dispute shall name a single arbitrator who shall name an umpire. If either contracting State party to the dispute fails to name an arbitrator within a period of three months from the date of the appeal, an arbitrator shall be named on behalf of that State by the President of the Council from a list of qualified and available persons maintained by the Council. If, within thirty days, the arbitrators cannot agree on an umpire, the President of the Council shall designate an umpire from the list previously referred to. The arbitrators and the umpire shall then jointly constitute an arbitral tribunal. Any arbitral tribunal established under this or the preceding Article shall settle its own procedure and give its decisions by majority vote, provided that the Council may determine procedural questions in the event of any delay which in the opinion of the Council is excessive.

ARTICLE 86—APPEALS

Unless the Council decides otherwise any decision by the Council on whether an international airline is operating in conformity with the provisions of this Convention shall remain in effect unless reversed on appeal. On any other matter, decisions of the Council shall, if appealed from, be suspended until the appeal is decided. The decisions of the Permanent Court of International Justice and of an arbitral tribunal shall be final and binding.

ARTICLE 87—PENALTY FOR NON-CONFORMITY OF AIRLINE

Each contracting State undertakes not to allow the operation of an airline of a contracting State through the airspace above its territory if the Council has decided that the airline enterprise concerned is not conforming to a final decision rendered in accordance with the previous Article.

ARTICLE 88—PENALTY FOR NON-CONFORMITY

The Assembly shall suspend the voting power in the Assembly and in the Council of any contracting State that is found in default under the provisions of this Chapter.

CHAPTER XIX—WAR

ARTICLE 89—WAR AND EMERGENCY CONDITIONS

In case of war, the provisions of this Convention shall not affect the freedom of action of any of the contracting States affected, whether as belligerents or as neutrals. The same principle shall apply in the case of any contracting State which a state of national emergency and notifies the fact to the Council.

CHAPTER XX—ANNEXES

ARTICLE 90—ADOPTION AND AMENDMENT OF ANNEXES

a) The adoption by the Council of the Annexes described in Article 54, subparagraph 1), shall require the vote of two-thirds of the Council at a meeting called for that purpose and shall then be submitted by the Council to each contracting State. Any such Annex or any amendment of an Annex shall become effective within three months after its submission to the contracting States or at the end of such longer period of time as the Council may prescribe, unless in the meantime a majority of the contracting States register their disapproval with the Council.

b) The Council shall immediately notify all contracting States of the coming into force of any Annex or amendment thereto.

CHAPTER XXI—RATIFICATIONS, ADHERENCES, AMENDMENTS, AND DENUCIATIONS

ARTICLE 91—RATIFICATION OF CONVENTION

a) This Convention shall be subject to ratification by the signatory States. The instruments of ratification shall be deposited in the archives of the Government of the United States of America, which shall give notice of the date of the deposit to each of the signatory and adhering States.

b) As soon as this Convention has been ratified or adhered to by twenty-six States it shall come into force between them on the thirtieth day after deposit of the twenty-sixth instrument. It shall come into force for each State ratifying thereafter on the thirtieth day after the deposit of its instrument of ratification.

c) It shall be the duty of the Government of the United States of America to notify the government of each of the signatory and adhering States of the date on which this Convention comes into force.

ARTICLE 92—ADHERENCE TO CONVENTION

a) This Convention shall be open for adherence by members of the United Nations and States associated with them, and States which remained neutral during the present world conflict.

b) Adherence shall be effected by a notification addressed to the Government of the United States of America and shall take effect as from the thirtieth day from the receipt of the notification by the Government of the United States of America, which shall notify all the contracting States.

ARTICLE 93—ADMISSION OF OTHER STATES

States other than those provided for in Articles 91 and 92 a) may, subject to approval by any general international organization set up by the nations of the world to preserve peace, be admitted to participation in this Convention by means of a four-fifths vote of the Assembly and on such conditions as the Assembly may prescribe: provided that in each case the assent of any State invaded or attacked during the present war by the State seeking admission shall be necessary.

ARTICLE 93 BIS

a) Notwithstanding the provisions of Articles 91, 92 and 93 above:

1) A State whose government the General Assembly of the United Nations has recommended be debarred from membership in international agencies established by or brought into relationship with the United Nations shall automatically cease to be a member of the International Civil Aviation Organization;

2) A State which has been expelled from membership in the United Nations shall automatically cease to be a member of the International Civil Aviation Organization unless the General Assembly of the United Nations attaches to its act of expulsion a recommendation to the contrary.

b) A State which ceases to be a member of the International Civil Aviation Organization as a result of the provisions of paragraph a) above may, after approval by the General Assembly of the United Nations, be readmitted to the International Civil Aviation Organization upon application and upon approval by a majority of the Council.

c) Members of the Organization which are suspended from the exercise of the rights and privileges of membership in the United Nations shall, upon the request of the latter, be suspended from the rights and privileges of membership in this Organization.

ARTICLE 94—AMENDMENT OF CONVENTION

a) Any proposed amendment to this Convention must be approved by a two-thirds vote of the Assembly and shall then come into force in respect of States which have ratified such amendment when ratified by the number of contracting States specified by the

Assembly. The number so specified shall not be less than two-thirds of the total number of contracting States.

b) If in its opinion the amendment is of such a nature as to justify this course, the Assembly in its resolution recommending adoption may provide that any State which has not ratified within a specified period after the amendment has come into force shall thereupon cease to be a member of the Organization and a party to the Convention.

ARTICLE 95—DENUNCIATION OF CONVENTION

a) Any contracting State may give notice of denunciation of this Convention three years after its coming into effect by notification addressed to the Government of the United States of America, which shall at once inform each of the contracting States.

b) Denunciation shall take effect one year from the date of the receipt of the notification and shall operate only as regards the State effecting the denunciation.

CHAPTER XXII—DEFINITIONS

ARTICLE 96

For the purpose of this Convention the expression:

a) "Air service" means any scheduled air service performed by aircraft for the public transport of passengers, mail or cargo.

b) "International air service" means an air service which passes through the air space over the territory of more than one State.

c) "Airline" means any air transport enterprise offering or operating an international air service.

d) "Stop for non-traffic purposes" means a landing for any purpose other than taking on or discharging passengers, cargo or mail.

SIGNATURE OF CONVENTION

IN WITNESS WHEREOF, the undersigned plenipotentiaries, having been duly authorized, sign this Convention on behalf of their respective governments on the dates appearing opposite their signatures.

DONE at Chicago the seventh day of December 1944 in the English language. The texts of this Convention drawn up in the English, French, Russian and Spanish languages are of equal authenticity. These texts shall be deposited in the archives of the Government of the United States of America, and certified copies shall be transmitted by that Government to the Governments of all the States which may sign or adhere to this Convention. This Convention shall be open for signature at Washington, D.C.

PROTOCOL ON THE AUTHENTIC TRILINGUAL TEXT OF THE CONVENTION ON CIVIL AVIATION (CHICAGO)[2]

The undersigned governments

CONSIDERING that the last paragraph of the Convention on International Civil Aviation, hereinafter called "the Convention", provides that a text of the Convention, drawn up in the English, French and Spanish languages, each of which shall be of equal authenticity, shall be open for signature;

CONSIDERING that the Convention was opened for signature, at Chicago, on the seventh day of December, 1944, in a text in the English language;

CONSIDERING, accordingly, that it is appropriate to make the necessary provision for the text to exist in three languages as contemplated in the Convention;

CONSIDERING that in making such provision, it should be taken into account that there exist amendments to the Convention in the English, French and Spanish languages, and that the text of the Convention in the French and Spanish languages should not incorporate those amendments because, in accordance with Article 94 a) of the Convention, each such amendment can come into force only in respect of any State which has ratified it;

HAVE AGREED AS FOLLOWS:

ARTICLE I

The text of the Convention in the French and Spanish languages annexed to this Protocol, together with the text of the Convention in the English language, constitutes the text equally authentic in the three languages as specifically referred to in the last paragraph of the Convention.

ARTICLE II

If a State party to this Protocol has ratified or in the future ratifies any amendment made to the Convention in accordance with Article 94 a) thereof, then the text of such amendment in the English, French and Spanish languages shall be deemed to refer to the text, equally authentic in the three languages, which amendment results from this Protocol.

ARTICLE III

1) The States members of the International Civil Aviation Organization may become parties to this Protocol either by:

a) signature without reservation as to acceptance, or

b) signature with reservation as to acceptance followed by acceptance, or

c) acceptance.

2) This Protocol shall remain open for signature at Buenos Aires until the twenty-seventh day of September 1968 and thereafter at Washington, D.C.

---

[2] Signed at Buenos Aires on September 24, 1968.

3) Acceptance shall be effected by the deposit of an instrument of acceptance with the Government of the United States of America.

4) Adherence to or ratification or approval of this Protocol shall be deemed to be acceptance thereof.

ARTICLE IV

1) This Protocol shall come into force on the thirtieth day after twelve States shall, in accordance with the provisions of Article 111, have signed it without reservation as to acceptance or accepted it.

2) As regards any State which shall subsequently become a party to this Protocol, in accordance with Article 111, the Protocol shall come into force on the date of its signature without reservation as to acceptance or of its acceptance.

ARTICLE V

Any future adherence of a State to the Convention shall be deemed to be acceptance of this Protocol.

ARTICLE VI

As soon as this Protocol comes into force, it shall be registered with the United Nations and with the International Civil Aviation Organization by the Government of the United States of America.

ARTICLE VII

1) This Protocol shall remain in force so long as the Convention is in force.

2) This Protocol shall cease to be in force for a State only when that State ceases to be a party to the Convention.

ARTICLE VIII

The Government of the United States of America shall give notice to all States members of the International Civil Aviation Organization and to the Organization itself:

a) of any signature of this Protocol and the date thereof, with an indication whether the signature is with or without reservation as to acceptance;

b) of the deposit of any instrument of acceptance and the date thereof;

c) of the date on which this Protocol comes into force in accordance with the provisions of Article IV, paragraph 1).

ARTICLE IX

This Protocol, drawn up in the English, French and Spanish languages, each text being equally authentic, shall be deposited in the archives of the Government of the United States of America, which shall transmit duly certified copies thereof to the Government of the States members of the International Civil Aviation Organization.

IN WITNESS WHEREOF, the undersigned Plenipotentiaries, duly authorized, have signed this Protocol.

PROTOCOL ON THE AUTHENTIC QUADRILINGUAL TEXT OF THE CONVENTION ON INTERNATIONAL CIVIL AVIATION (CHICAGO, 1944)[3]

The undersigned governments

CONSIDERING that the 21st Session of the Assembly of the International Civil Aviation Organization requested the Council of this Organization "to undertake the necessary measures for the preparation of the authentic text of the Convention on International Civil Aviation in the Russian language, with the aim of having it approved not later than the year 1977";

CONSIDERING that the English text of the Convention on International Civil Aviation was opened for signature at Chicago on 7 December 1944;

CONSIDERING that, pursuant to the Protocol signed at Buenos Aires on 24 September 1968 on the authentic trilingual text of the Convention on International Civil Aviation done at Chicago, 7 December 1944, the text of the Convention on International Civil Aviation (hereinafter called the Convention) was adopted in the French and Spanish languages and, together with the text of the Convention in the English language, constitutes the text equally authentic in the three languages as provided for in the final clause of the Convention;

CONSIDERING, accordingly, that it is appropriate to make the necessary provision for the text of the Convention to exist in the Russian language;

CONSIDERING that in making such provision account must be taken of the existing amendments to the Convention in the English, French and Spanish languages, the texts of which are equally authentic and that, according to Article 94 a) of the Convention, any amendment can come into force only in respect of any State which has ratified it;

HAVE AGREED AS FOLLOWS:

ARTICLE I

The text of the Convention and of the amendments thereto in the Russian language annexed to this Protocol, together with the text of the Convention and of the amendments thereto in the English, French and Spanish languages, constitutes the text Convention equally authentic in the four languages.

ARTICLE II

If a State party to this Protocol has ratified or in the future ratifies any amendment made to the Convention in accordance with Article 94 a) thereof, then the text of such amendment in the Russian, English, French and Spanish languages shall be deemed to refer to the text equally authentic in the four amendment languages, which results from this Protocol.

ARTICLE III

1) The States members of the International Civil Aviation Organization may become parties to this Protocol either by:

[3] Signed at Montreal on September 30 1977.

a) signature without reservation as to acceptance, or

b) signature with reservation as to acceptance followed by acceptance,

c) acceptance.

2) This Protocol shall remain open for signature at Montreal until the 5th of October 1977 and thereafter at Washington, D.C.

3) Acceptance shall be effected by the deposit of an instrument of acceptance with the Government of the United States of America.

4) Adherence to or ratification or approval of this Protocol shall be deemed to be acceptance thereof.

ARTICLE IV

1) This Protocol shall come into force on the thirtieth day after twelve States shall, in accordance with the provisions of Article 111, have signed it without reservation as to acceptance or accepted it and after entry into force of the amendment to the final clause of the Convention, which provides that the text of the Convention in the Russian language is of equal authenticity.

2) As regards any State which shall subsequently become party to this Protocol in accordance with Article 111, the Protocol shall come into force on the date of its signature without reservation as to acceptance or of its acceptance.

ARTICLE V

Any adherence of a State to the Convention after this Protocol has entered into force shall be deemed to be acceptance of this Protocol.

ARTICLE VI

Acceptance by a State of this Protocol shall not be regarded as ratification by it of any amendment to the Convention.

ARTICLE VII

As soon as this Protocol comes into force, it shall be registered with the United Nations and with the International Civil Aviation Organization by the Government of the United States of America.

ARTICLE VIII

1) This Protocol shall remain in force so long as the Convention is in force.

2) This Protocol shall cease to be in force for a State only when that State ceases to be a party to the Convention.

ARTICLE IX

The Government of the United States of America shall give notice to all States members of the International Civil Aviation Organization and to the Organization itself:

a) of any signature of this Protocol and the date thereof, with an indication whether the signature is with or without reservation as to acceptance;

b) of the deposit of any instrument of acceptance and the date thereof;

c) of the date on which this Protocol comes into force in accordance with the provisions of Article IV, paragraph 1.

ARTICLE X

This Protocol, drawn up in the English, French, Russian and Spanish languages, each text being equally authentic, shall be deposited in the archives of the Government of the United States of America, which shall transmit duly certified copies thereof to the Governments of the States members of the International Civil Aviation Organization.

IN WITNESS WHEREOF, the undersigned Plenipotentiaries, duly authorized, have signed this Protocol.

DONE at Montreal this thirtieth day of September, one thousand nine hundred and seventy-seven.

b. Convention for the Suppression of Unlawful Seizure of Aircraft

Done at The Hague, December 16, 1970; Ratification advised by the Senate, September 8, 1971; Ratification by the President, September 14, 1971; Ratification of the United States, deposited at Washington, September 14, 1971; Proclaimed by the President, October 18, 1971; Entered into force, October 14, 1971[1]

CONVENTION FOR THE SUPPRESSION OF UNLAWFUL SEIZURE OF AIRCRAFT[1]

PREAMBLE

The States Parties to This Convention

CONSIDERING that unlawful acts of seizure or exercise of control of aircraft in flight jeopardize the safety of persons and property, seriously affect the operation of air services, and undermine the confidence of the peoples of the world in the safety of civil aviation;

CONSIDERING that the occurrence of such acts is a matter of grave concern;

CONSIDERING that, for the purpose of deterring such acts, there is an urgent need to provide appropriate measures for punishment of offenders;

HAVE AGREED AS FOLLOWS:

ARTICLE 1

Any person who on board an aircraft in flight:

(a) unlawfully, by force or threat thereof, or by any other form of intimidation, seizes, or exercises control of, that aircraft, or attempts to perform any such act, or

(b) is an accomplice of a person who performs or attempts to perform any such act

commits an offence (hereinafter referred to as "the offence").

ARTICLE 2

Each Contracting State undertakes to make the offence punishable by severe penalties.

ARTICLE 3

1. For the purposes of this Convention, an aircraft is considered to be in flight at any time from the moment when all its external doors are closed following embarkation until the moment when any such door is opened for disembarkation. In the case of a forced landing, the flight shall be deemed to continue until the competent

[1] 22 UST 1641; TIAS 7192. For a list of states that are parties to the Convention, see Department of State publication, *Treaties in Force*.

authorities take over the responsibility for the aircraft and for persons and property on board.

2. This Convention shall not apply to aircraft used in military, customs or police services.

3. This Convention shall apply only if the place of take-off or the place of actual landing of the aircraft on board which the offence is committed is situated outside the territory of the State of registration of that aircraft; it shall be immaterial whether the aircraft is engaged in an international or domestic flight.

4. In the cases mentioned in Article 5, this Convention shall not apply if the place of take-off and the place of actual landing of the aircraft on board which the offence is committed are situated within the territory of the same State where that State is one of those referred to in that Article.

5. Notwithstanding paragraphs 3 and 4 of this Article, Articles 6, 7, 8 and 10 shall apply whatever the place of take-off or the place of actual landing of the aircraft, if the offender or the alleged offender is found in the territory of a State other than the State of registration of that aircraft.

Article 4

1. Each Contracting State shall take such measures as may be necessary to establish its jurisdiction over the offence and any other act of violence against passengers or crew committed by the alleged offender in connection with the offence, in the following cases:

(a) when the offence is committed on board an aircraft registered in that State;

(b) when the aircraft on board which the offence is committed lands in its territory with the alleged offender still on board;

(c) when the offence is committed on board an aircraft leased without crew to a lessee who has his principal place of business or, if the lessee has no such place of business, his permanent residence, in that State.

2. Each Contracting State shall likewise take such measures as may be necessary to establish its jurisdiction over the offence in the case where the alleged offender is present in its territory and it does not extradite him pursuant to Article 8 to any of the States mentioned in paragraph 1 of this Article.

3. This Convention does not exclude any criminal jurisdiction exercised in accordance with national law.

Article 5

The Contracting States which establish joint air transport operating organizations or international operating agencies, which operate aircraft which are subject to joint or international registration shall, by appropriate means, designate for each aircraft the State among them which shall exercise the jurisdiction and have the attributes of the State of registration for the purpose of this Convention and shall give notice thereof to the International Civil Aviation Organization which shall communicate the notice to all States Parties to this Convention.

ARTICLE 6

1. Upon being satisfied that the circumstances so warrant, any Contracting State in the territory of which the offender or the alleged offender is present, shall take him into custody or take other measures to ensure his presence. The custody and other measures shall be as provided in the law of that State but may only be continued for such time as is necessary to enable any criminal or extradition proceedings to be instituted.

2. Such State shall immediately make a preliminary enquiry into the facts.

3. Any person in custody pursuant to paragraph 1 of this Article shall be assisted in communicating immediately with the nearest appropriate representative of the State of which he is a national.

4. When a State, pursuant to this Article, has taken a person into custody, it shall immediately notify the State of registration of the aircraft, the State mentioned in Article 4, paragraph 1(c), the State of nationality of the detained person and, if it considers it advisable, any other interested States of the fact that such person is in custody and of the circumstances which warrant his detention. The State which makes the preliminary enquiry contemplated in paragraph 2 of this Article shall promptly report its findings to the said States and shall indicate whether it intends to exercise jurisdiction.

ARTICLE 7

The Contracting State in the territory of which the alleged offender is found shall, if it does not extradite him, be obliged, without exception whatsoever and whether or not the offence was committed in its territory, to submit the case to its competent authorities for the purpose of prosecution. Those authorities shall take their decision in the same manner as in the case of any ordinary offence of a serious nature under the law of that State.

ARTICLE 8

1. The offence shall be deemed to be included as an extraditable offence in any extradition treaty existing between Contracting States. Contracting States undertake to include the offence as an extraditable offence in every extradition treaty to be concluded between them.

2. If a Contracting State which makes extradition conditional on the existence of a treaty receives a request for extradition from another Contracting State with which it has no extradition treaty, it may at its option consider this Convention as the legal basis for extradition in respect of the offence. Extradition shall be subject to the other conditions provided by the law of the requested State.

3. Contracting States which do not make extradition conditional on the existence of a treaty shall recognize the offence as an extraditable offence between themselves subject to the conditions provided by the law of the requested State.

4. The offence shall be treated, for the purpose of extradition between Contracting States, as if it had been committed not only in the place in which it occurred but also in the territories of the

States required to establish their jurisdiction in accordance with Article 4, paragraph 1.

ARTICLE 9

1. When any of the acts mentioned in Article 1(a) has occurred or is about to occur, Contracting States shall take appropriate measures to restore control of the aircraft to its lawful commander or to preserve his control of the aircraft.

2. In the cases contemplated by the preceding paragraph, any Contracting State in which the aircraft or its passengers or crew are present shall facilitate the continuation of the journey of the passengers and crew as soon as practicable, and shall without delay return the aircraft and its cargo to the persons lawfully entitled to possession.

ARTICLE 10

1. Contracting States shall afford one another the greatest measure of assistance in connection with criminal proceedings brought in respect of the offence and other acts mentioned in Article 4. The law of the State requested shall apply in all cases.

2. The provisions of paragraph 1 of this Article shall not affect obligations under any other treaty, bilateral or multilateral, which governs or will govern, in whole or in part, mutual assistance in criminal matters.

ARTICLE 11

Each Contracting State shall in accordance with its national law report to the Council of the International Civil Aviation Organization as promptly as possible any relevant information in its possession concerning:

(a) the circumstances of the offence;

(b) the action taken pursuant to Article 9;

(c) the measures taken in relation to the offender or the alleged offender, and, in particular, the results of any extradition proceedings or other legal proceedings.

ARTICLE 12

1. Any dispute between two or more Contracting States concerning the interpretation or application of this Convention which cannot be settled through negotiation shall, at the request of one of them, be submitted to arbitration. If within six months from the date of the request for arbitration the Parties are unable to agree on the organization of the arbitration, any one of those Parties may refer the dispute to the International Court of Justice by request in conformity with the Statute of the Court.

2. Each State may at the time of signature or ratification of this Convention or accession thereto, declare that it does not consider itself bound by the preceding paragraph. The other Contracting States shall not be bound by the preceding paragraph with respect to any Contracting State having made such a reservation.

3. Any Contracting State having made a reservation in accordance with the preceding paragraph may at any time withdraw this reservation by notification to the Depositary Governments.

ARTICLE 13

1. This Convention shall be open for signature at The Hague on 16 December 1970, by States participating in the International Conference on Air Law held at The Hague from 1 to 16 December 1970 (hereinafter referred to as The Hague Conference). After 31 December 1970, the Convention shall be open to all States for signature in Moscow, London and Washington. Any State which does not sign this Convention before its entry into force in accordance with paragraph 3 of this Article may accede to it at any time.

2. This Convention shall be subject to ratification by the signatory States. Instruments of ratification and instruments of accession shall be deposited with the Governments of the Union of Soviet Socialist Republics, the United Kingdom of Great Britain and Northern Ireland, and the United States of America, which are hereby designated the Depositary Governments.

3. This Convention shall enter into force thirty days following the date of the deposit of instruments of ratification by ten States signatory to this Convention which participated in The Hague Conference.

4. For other States, this Convention shall enter into force on the date of entry into force of this Convention in accordance with paragraph 3 of this Article, or thirty days following the date of deposit of their instruments of ratification or accession, whichever is later.

5. The Depositary Governments shall promptly inform all signatory and acceding States of the date of each signature, the date of deposit of each instrument of ratification or accession, the date of entry into force of this Convention, and other notices.

6. As soon as this Convention comes into force, it shall be registered by the Depositary Governments pursuant to Article 102 of the Charter of the United Nations [2] and pursuant to Article 83 of the Convention on International Civil Aviation (Chicago, 1944).[3]

ARTICLE 14

1. Any Contracting State may denounce this Convention by written notification to the Depositary Governments.

2. Denunciation shall take effect six months following the date on which notification is received by the Depositary Governments.

IN WITNESS WHEREOF the undersigned Plenipotentiaries, being duly authorised thereto by their Governments, have signed this Convention.

DONE at The Hague, this sixteenth day of December, one thousand nine hundred and seventy, in three originals, each being drawn up in four authentic texts in the English, French, Russian and Spanish languages.

[2] TS 993; 59 Stat. 1052.
[3] TIAS 1591; 61 Stat. 1203.

c. Convention for the Suppression of Unlawful Acts Against the Safety of Civil Aviation

Done at Montreal, September 23, 1971; Entered into force, January 26, 1973

CONVENTION FOR THE SUPPRESSION OF UNLAWFUL ACTS AGAINST THE SAFETY OF CIVIL AVIATION [1]

The States Parties to this Convention

CONSIDERING that unlawful acts against the safety of civil aviation jeopardize the safety of persons and property, seriously affect the operation of air services, and undermine the confidence of the peoples of the world in the safety of civil aviation;

CONSIDERING that the occurrence of such acts is a matter of grave concern;

CONSIDERING that, for the purpose of deterring such acts, there is an urgent need to provide appropriate measures for punishment of offenders;

HAVE AGREED AS FOLLOWS:

ARTICLE 1

1. Any person commits an offence if he unlawfully and intentionally:

(a) performs an act of violence against a person on board an aircraft in flight if that act is likely to endanger the safety of that aircraft; or

(b) destroys an aircraft in service or causes damage to such an aircraft which renders it incapable of flight or which is likely to endanger its safety in flight; or

(c) places or causes to be placed on an aircraft in service, by any means whatsoever, a device or substance which is likely to destroy that aircraft, or to cause damage to it which renders it incapable of flight, or to cause damage to it which is likely to endanger its safety in flight; or

(d) destroys or damages air navigation facilities or interferes with their operation, if any such act is likely to endanger the safety of aircraft in flight; or

(e) communicates information which he knows to be false, thereby endangering the safety of an aircraft in flight.

2. Any person also commits an offence if he:

(a) attempts to commit any of the offences mentioned in paragraph 1 of this Article; or

(b) is an accomplice of a person who commits or attempts to commit any such offence.

[1] 24 UST 564; TIAS 7570. For a list of states that are parties to the Treaty, see Department of State publication, *Treaties in Force.*

ARTICLE 2

For the purposes of this Convention:

(a) an aircraft is considered to be in flight at any time from the moment when all its external doors are closed following embarkation until the moment when any such door is opened for disembarkation; in the case of a forced landing, the flight shall be deemed to continue until the competent authorities take over the responsibility for the aircraft and for persons and property on board;

(b) an aircraft is considered to be in service from the beginning of the preflight preparation of the aircraft by ground personnel or by the crew for a specific flight until twenty-four hours after any landing; the period of service shall, in any event, extend for the entire period during which the aircraft is in flight as defined in paragraph (a) of this Article.

ARTICLE 3

Each Contracting State undertakes to make the offences mentioned in Article 1 punishable by severe penalties.

ARTICLE 4

1. This Convention shall not apply to aircraft used in military, customs or police services.

2. In the cases contemplated in subparagraphs (a), (b), (c) and (e) of paragraph 1 of Article 1, this Convention shall apply, irrespective of whether the aircraft is engaged in an international or domestic flight, only if:

(a) the place of take-off or landing, actual or intended, of the aircraft is situated outside the territory of the State of registration of that aircraft; or

(b) the offence is committed in the territory of a State other than the State of registration of the aircraft.

3. Notwithstanding paragraph 2 of this Article, in the cases contemplated in subparagraphs (a), (b), (c) and (e) of paragraph 1 of Article 1, this Convention shall also apply if the offender or the alleged offender is found in the territory of a State other than the State of registration of the aircraft.

4. With respect to the States mentioned in Article 9 and in the cases mentioned in subparagraphs (a), (b), (c) and (e) of paragraph 1 of Article 1, this Convention shall not apply if the places referred to in subparagraph (a) of paragraph 2 of this Article are situated within the territory of the same State where that State is one of those referred to in Article 9, unless the offence is committed or the offender or alleged offender is found in the territory of a State other than that State.

5. In the cases contemplated in subparagraph (d) of paragraph 1 of Article 1, this Convention shall apply only if the air navigation facilities are used in international air navigation.

6. The provisions of paragraphs 2, 3, 4 and 5 of this Article shall also apply in the cases contemplated in paragraph 2 of Article 1.

ARTICLE 5

1. Each Contracting State shall take such measures as may be necessary to establish its jurisdiction over the offences in the following cases:

(a) when the offence is committed in the territory of that State;

(b) when the offence is committed against or on board an aircraft registered in that State;

(c) when the aircraft on board which the offence is committed lands in its territory with the alleged offender still on board;

(d) when the offence is committed against or on board an aircraft leased without crew to a lessee who has his principal place of business or, if the lessee has no such place of business, his permanent residence, in that State.

2. Each Contracting State shall likewise take such measures as may be necessary to establish its jurisdiction over the offences mentioned in Article 1, paragraph 1(a), (b) and (c), and in Article 1, paragraph 2, in so far as that paragraph relates to those offences, in the case where the alleged offender is present in its territory and it does not extradite him pursuant to Article 8 to any of the States mentioned in paragraph 1 of this Article. 3. This Convention does not exclude any criminal jurisdiction exercised in accordance with national law.

ARTICLE 6

1. Upon being satisfied that the circumstances so warrant, any Contracting State in the territory of which the offender or the alleged offender is present, shall take him into custody or take other measures to ensure his presence. The custody and other measures shall be as provided in the law of that State but may only be continued for such time as is necessary to enable any criminal or extradition proceedings to be instituted.

2. Such State shall immediately make a preliminary enquiry into the facts.

3. Any person in custody pursuant to paragraph 1 of this Article shall be assisted in communicating immediately with the nearest appropriate representative of the State of which he is a national.

4. When a State, pursuant to this Article, has taken a person into custody, it shall immediately notify the States mentioned in Article 5, paragraph 1, the State of nationality of the detained person and, if it considers it advisable, any other interested States of the fact that such person is in custody and of the circumstances which warrant his detention. The State which makes the preliminary enquiry contemplated in paragraph 2 of this Article shall promptly report its findings to the said States and shall indicate whether it intends to exercise jurisdiction.

ARTICLE 7

The Contracting State in the territory of which the alleged offender is found shall, if it does not extradite him, be obliged, without exception whatsoever and whether or not the offence was committed in its territory, to submit the case to its competent authorities for the purpose of prosecution. Those authorities shall take their decision in the same manner as in the case of any ordinary offence of a serious nature under the law of that State.

ARTICLE 8

1. The offences shall be deemed to be included as extraditable offences in any extradition treaty existing between Contracting States. Contracting States undertake to include the offences as extraditable offences in every extradition treaty to be concluded between them.

2. If a Contracting State which makes extradition conditional on the existence of a treaty receives a request for extradition from another Contracting State with which it has no extradition treaty, it may at its option consider this Convention as the legal basis for extradition in respect of the offences. Extradition shall be subject to the other conditions provided by the law of the requested State.

3. Contracting States which do not make extradition conditional on the existence of a treaty shall recognize the offences as extraditable offences between themselves subject to the conditions provided by the law of the requested State.

4. Each of the offences shall be treated, for the purpose of extradition between Contracting States, as if it had been committed not only in the place in which it occurred but also in the territories of the States required to establish their jurisdiction in accordance with Article 5, paragraph 1(b), (c) and (d).

ARTICLE 9

The Contracting States which establish joint air transport operating organisations or international operating agencies, which operate aircraft which are subject to joint or international registration shall, by appropriate means, designate for each aircraft the State among them which shall exercise the jurisdiction and have the attributes of the State of registration for the purpose of this Convention and shall give notice thereof to the International Civil Aviation Organization which shall communicate the notice to all States Parties to this Convention.

ARTICLE 10

1. Contracting States shall, in accordance with international and national law, endeavour to take all practicable measures for the purpose of preventing the offences mentioned in Article 1.

2. When, due to the commission of one of the offences mentioned in Article 1, a flight has been delayed or interrupted, any Contracting State in whose territory the aircraft or passengers or crew are present shall facilitate the continuation of the journey of the passengers and crew as soon as practicable, and shall without

delay return the aircraft and its cargo to the persons lawfully entitled to possession.

ARTICLE 11

1. Contracting States shall afford one another the greatest measure of assistance in connection with criminal proceedings brought in respect of the offences. The law of the State requested shall apply in all cases.

2. The provisions of paragraph 1 of this Article shall not affect obligations under any other treaty, bilateral or multilateral, which governs or will govern, in whole or in part, mutual assistance in criminal matters.

ARTICLE 12

Any Contracting State having reason to believe that one of the offences mentioned in Article 1 will be committed shall, in accordance with its national law, furnish any relevant information in its possession to those States which it believes would be the States mentioned in Article 5, paragraph 1.

ARTICLE 13

Each Contracting State shall in accordance with its national law report to the Council of the International Civil Aviation Organization as promptly as possible any relevant information in its possession concerning:

(a) the circumstances of the offence;

(b) the action taken pursuant to Article 10, paragraph 2;

(c) the measures taken in relation to the offender or the alleged offender and, in particular, the results of any extradition proceedings or other legal proceedings.

ARTICLE 14

1. Any dispute between two or more Contracting States concerning the interpretation or application of this Convention which cannot be settled through negotiation, shall, at the request of one of them, be submitted to arbitration. If within six months from the date of the request for arbitration the Parties are unable to agree on the organization of the arbitration, any one of those Parties may refer the dispute to the International Court of Justice by request in conformity with the Statute of the Court.

2. Each State may at the time of signature or ratification of this Convention or accession thereto, declare that it does not consider itself bound by the preceding paragraph. The other Contracting States shall not be bound by the preceding paragraph with respect to any Contracting State having made such a reservation.

3. Any Contracting State having made a reservation in accordance with the preceding paragraph may at any time withdraw this reservation by notification to the Depositary Governments.

ARTICLE 15

1. This Convention shall be open for signature at Montreal on 23 September 1971, by States participating in the International Conference on Air Law held at Montreal from 8 to 23 September 1971 (hereinafter referred to as the Montreal Conference). After 10 October 1971, the Convention shall be open to all States for signature in Moscow, London and Washington. Any State which does not sign this Convention before its entry into force in accordance with paragraph 3 of this Article may accede to it at any time.

2. This Convention shall be subject to ratification by the signatory States. Instruments of ratification and instruments of accession shall be deposited with the Governments of the Union of Soviet Socialist Republics, the United Kingdom of Great Britain and Northern Ireland, and the United States of America, which are hereby designated the Depositary Governments.

3. This Convention shall enter into force thirty days following the date of the deposit of instruments of ratification by ten States signatory to this Convention which participated in the Montreal Conference.

4. For other States, this Convention shall enter into force on the date of entry into force of this Convention in accordance with paragraph 3 of this Article, or thirty days following the date of deposit of their instruments of ratification or accession, whichever is later.

5. The Depositary Governments shall promptly inform all signatory and acceding States of the date of each signature, the date of deposit of each instrument of ratification or accession, the date of entry into force of this Convention, and other notices.

6. As soon as this Convention comes into force, it shall be registered by the Depositary Governments pursuant to Article 102 of the Charter of the United Nations and pursuant to Article 83 of the Convention on International Civil Aviation (Chicago, 1944).

ARTICLE 16

1. Any Contracting State may denounce this Convention by written notification to the Depositary Governments.

2. Denunciation shall take effect six months following the date on which notification is received by the Depositary Governments.

IN WITNESS WHEREOF the undersigned Plenipotentiaries, being duly authorized thereto by their Governments, have signed this Convention.

DONE at Montreal, this twenty-third day of September, one thousand nine hundred and seventy-one, in three originals, each being drawn up in four authentic texts in the English, French, Russian and Spanish languages.

d. Convention for the Unification of Certain Rules for International Carriage by Air

Done at Montreal, May 28, 1999; Ratification advised by the Senate, July 31, 2003; Entered into force, November 4, 2003

CONVENTION FOR THE UNIFICATION OF CERTAIN RULES FOR INTERNATIONAL CARRIAGE BY AIR

The States Parties to This Convention

RECOGNIZING the significant contribution of the Convention for the Unification of Certain Rules relating to International Carriage by Air signed in Warsaw on 12 October 1929, hereinafter referred to as the "Warsaw Convention", and other related instruments to the harmonization of private international air law;

RECOGNIZING the need to modernize and consolidate the Warsaw Convention and related instruments;

RECOGNIZING the importance of ensuring protection of the interests of consumers in international carriage by air and the need for equitable compensation based on the principle of restitution;

REAFFIRMING the desirability of an orderly development of international air transport operations and the smooth flow of passengers, baggage and cargo in accordance with the principles and objectives of the Convention on International Civil Aviation, done at Chicago on 7 December 1944;

CONVINCED that collective State action for further harmonization and codification of certain rules governing international carriage by air through a new Convention is the most adequate means of achieving an equitable balance of interests;

HAVE AGREED AS FOLLOWS:

CHAPTER I—GENERAL PROVISIONS

ARTICLE 1—SCOPE OF APPLICATION

1. This Convention applies to all international carriage of persons, baggage or cargo performed by aircraft for reward. It applies equally to gratuitous carriage by aircraft performed by an air transport undertaking.

2. For the purposes of this Convention, the expression international carriage means any carriage in which, according to the agreement between the parties, the place of departure and the place of destination, whether or not there be a break in the carriage or a transhipment, are situated either within the territories of two States Parties, or within the territory of a single State Party if there is an agreed stopping place within the territory of another State, even if that State is not a State Party. Carriage between two points within the territory of a single State Party without an

agreed stopping place within the territory of another State is not international carriage for the purposes of this Convention.

3. Carriage to be performed by several successive carriers is deemed, for the purposes of this Convention, to be one undivided carriage if it has been regarded by the parties as a single operation, whether it had been agreed upon under the form of a single contract or of a series of contracts, and it does not lose its international character merely because one contract or a series of contracts is to be performed entirely within the territory of the same State.

4. This Convention applies also to carriage as set out in Chapter V, subject to the terms contained therein.

Article 2—Carriage Performed by State and Carriage of Postal Items

1. This Convention applies to carriage performed by the State or by legally constituted public bodies provided it falls within the conditions laid down in Article 1.

2. In the carriage of postal items, the carrier shall be liable only to the relevant postal administration in accordance with the rules applicable to the relationship between the carriers and the postal administrations.

3. Except as provided in paragraph 2 of this Article, the provisions of this Convention shall not apply to the carriage of postal items.

Chapter II—Documentation and Duties of the Parties Relating to the Carriage of Passengers, Baggage and Cargo

Article 3—Passengers and Baggage

1. In respect of carriage of passengers, an individual or collective document of carriage shall be delivered containing:

(a) an indication of the places of departure and destination;

(b) if the places of departure and destination are within the territory of a single State Party, one or more agreed stopping places being within the territory of another State, an indication of at least one such stopping place.

2. Any other means which preserves the information indicated in paragraph 1 may be substituted for the delivery of the document referred to in that paragraph. If any such other means is used, the carrier shall offer to deliver to the passenger a written statement of the information so preserved.

3. The carrier shall deliver to the passenger a baggage identification tag for each piece of checked baggage.

4. The passenger shall be given written notice to the effect that where this Convention is applicable it governs and may limit the liability of carriers in respect of death or injury and for destruction or loss of, or damage to, baggage, and for delay.

5. Non-compliance with the provisions of the foregoing paragraphs shall not affect the existence or the validity of the contract of carriage, which shall, nonetheless, be subject to the rules of this Convention including those relating to limitation of liability.

ARTICLE 4—CARGO

1. In respect of the carriage of cargo, an air waybill shall be delivered.

2. Any other means which preserves a record of the carriage to be performed may be substituted for the delivery of an air waybill. If such other means are used, the carrier shall, if so requested by the consignor, deliver to the consignor a cargo receipt permitting identification of the consignment and access to the information contained in the record preserved by such other means.

ARTICLE 5—CONTENTS OF AIR WAYBILL OR CARGO RECEIPT

The air waybill or the cargo receipt shall include:

(a) an indication of the places of departure and destination;

(b) if the places of departure and destination are within the territory of a single State Party, one or more agreed stopping places being within the territory of another State, an indication of at least one such stopping place; and

(c) an indication of the weight of the consignment.

ARTICLE 6—DOCUMENT RELATING TO THE NATURE OF THE CARGO

The consignor may be required, if necessary, to meet the formalities of customs, police and similar public authorities to deliver a document indicating the nature of the cargo. This provision creates for the carrier no duty, obligation or liability resulting therefrom.

ARTICLE 7—DESCRIPTION OF AIR WAYBILL

1. The air waybill shall be made out by the consignor in three original parts.

2. The first part shall be marked "for the carrier"; it shall be signed by the consignor. The second part shall be marked "for the consignee"; it shall be signed by the consignor and by the carrier. The third part shall be signed by the carrier who shall hand it to the consignor after the cargo has been accepted.

3. The signature of the carrier and that of the consignor may be printed or stamped.

4. If, at the request of the consignor, the carrier makes out the air waybill, the carrier shall be deemed, subject to proof to the contrary, to have done so on behalf of the consignor.

ARTICLE 8—DOCUMENTATION FOR MULTIPLE PACKAGES

When there is more than one package:

(a) the carrier of cargo has the right to require the consignor to make out separate air waybills;

(b) the consignor has the right to require the carrier to deliver separate cargo receipts when the other means referred to in paragraph 2 of Article 4 are used.

ARTICLE 9—NON-COMPLIANCE WITH DOCUMENTARY REQUIREMENTS

Non-compliance with the provisions of Articles 4 to 8 shall not affect the existence or the validity of the contract of carriage, which shall, nonetheless, be subject to the rules of this Convention including those relating to limitation of liability.

Article 10—Responsibility for Particulars of Documentation

1. The consignor is responsible for the correctness of the particulars and statements relating to the cargo inserted by it or on its behalf in the air waybill or furnished by it or on its behalf to the carrier for insertion in the cargo receipt or for insertion in the record preserved by the other means referred to in paragraph 2 of Article 4. The foregoing shall also apply where the person acting on behalf of the consignor is also the agent of the carrier.

2. The consignor shall indemnify the carrier against all damage suffered by it, or by any other person to whom the carrier is liable, by reason of the irregularity, incorrectness or incompleteness of the particulars and statements furnished by the consignor or on its behalf.

3. Subject to the provisions of paragraphs 1 and 2 of this Article, the carrier shall indemnify the consignor against all damage suffered by it, or by any other person to whom the consignor is liable, by reason of the irregularity, incorrectness or incompleteness of the particulars and statements inserted by the carrier or on its behalf in the cargo receipt or in the record preserved by the other means referred to in paragraph 2 of Article 4.

Article 11—Evidentiary Value of Documentation

1. The air waybill or the cargo receipt is prima facie evidence of the conclusion of the contract, of the acceptance of the cargo and of the conditions of carriage mentioned therein.

2. Any statements in the air waybill or the cargo receipt relating to the weight, dimensions and packing of the cargo, as well as those relating to the number of packages, are prima facie evidence of the facts stated; those relating to the quantity, volume and condition of the cargo do not constitute evidence against the carrier except so far as they both have been, and are stated in the air waybill or the cargo receipt to have been, checked by it in the presence of the consignor, or relate to the apparent condition of the cargo.

Article 12—Right of Disposition of Cargo

1. Subject to its liability to carry out all its obligations under the contract of carriage, the consignor has the right to dispose of the cargo by withdrawing it at the airport of departure or destination, or by stopping it in the course of the journey on any landing, or by calling for it to be delivered at the place of destination or in the course of the journey to a person other than the consignee originally designated, or by requiring it to be returned to the airport of departure. The consignor must not exercise this right of disposition in such a way as to prejudice the carrier or other consignors and must reimburse any expenses occasioned by the exercise of this right.

2. If it is impossible to carry out the instructions of the consignor, the carrier must so inform the consignor forthwith.

3. If the carrier carries out the instructions of the consignor for the disposition of the cargo without requiring the production of the

part of the air waybill or the cargo receipt delivered to the latter, the carrier will be liable, without prejudice to its right of recovery from the consignor, for any damage which may be caused thereby to any person who is lawfully in possession of that part of the air waybill or the cargo receipt.

4. The right conferred on the consignor ceases at the moment when that of the consignee begins in accordance with Article 13. Nevertheless, if the consignee declines to accept the cargo, or cannot be communicated with, the consignor resumes its right of disposition.

Article 13—Delivery of the Cargo

1. Except when the consignor has exercised its right under Article 12, the consignee is entitled, on arrival of the cargo at the place of destination, to require the carrier to deliver the cargo to it, on payment of the charges due and on complying with the conditions of carriage.

2. Unless it is otherwise agreed, it is the duty of the carrier to give notice to the consignee as soon as the cargo arrives.

3. If the carrier admits the loss of the cargo, or if the cargo has not arrived at the expiration of seven days after the date on which it ought to have arrived, the consignee is entitled to enforce against the carrier the rights which flow from the contract of carriage.

Article 14—Enforcement of the Rights of Consignor and Consignee

The consignor and the consignee can respectively enforce all the rights given to them by Articles 12 and 13, each in its own name, whether it is acting in its own interest or in the interest of another, provided that it carries out the obligations imposed by the contract of carriage.

Article 15—Relations of Consignor and Consignee or Mutual Relations of Third Parties

1. Articles 12, 13 and 14 do not affect either the relations of the consignor and the consignee with each other or the mutual relations of third parties whose rights are derived either from the consignor or from the consignee.

2. The provisions of Articles 12, 13 and 14 can only be varied by express provision in the air waybill or the cargo receipt.

Article 16—Formalities of Customs, Police or Other Public Authorities

1. The consignor must furnish such information and such documents as are necessary to meet the formalities of customs, police and any other public authorities before the cargo can be delivered to the consignee. The consignor is liable to the carrier for any damage occasioned by the absence, insufficiency or irregularity of any such information or documents, unless the damage is due to the fault of the carrier, its servants or agents.

2. The carrier is under no obligation to enquire into the correctness or sufficiency of such information or documents.

Chapter III—Liability of the Carrier and Extent of Compensation for Damage

Article 17—Death and Injury of Passengers—Damage to Baggage

1. The carrier is liable for damage sustained in case of death or bodily injury of a passenger upon condition only that the accident which caused the death or injury took place on board the aircraft or in the course of any of the operations of embarking or disembarking.

2. The carrier liable for damage sustained in case of destruction or loss of, or of damage to, checked baggage upon condition only that the event which caused the destruction, loss or damage took place on board the aircraft or during any period within which the checked baggage was in the charge of the carrier. However, the carrier is not liable if and to the extent that the damage resulted from the inherent defect, quality or vice of the baggage. In the case of unchecked baggage, including personal items, the carrier is liable if the damage resulted from its fault or that of its servants or agents.

3. If the carrier admits the loss of the checked baggage, or if the checked baggage has not arrived at the expiration of twenty-one days after the date on which it ought to have arrived, the passenger is entitled to enforce against the carrier the rights which flow from the contract of carriage.

4. Unless otherwise specified, in this Convention the term "baggage" means both checked baggage and unchecked baggage.

Article 18—Damage to Cargo

1. The carrier is liable for damage sustained in the event of the destruction or loss of or damage to, cargo upon condition only that the event which caused the damage so sustained took place during the carriage by air.

2. However, the carrier is not liable if and to the extent it proves that the destruction, or loss of, or damage to, the cargo resulted from one or more of the following:

(a) inherent defect, quality or vice of that cargo;

(b) defective packing of that cargo performed by a person other than the carrier or its servants or agents;

(c) an act of war or an armed conflict;

(d) an act of public authority carried out in connection with the entry, exit or transit of the cargo.

3. The carriage by air within the meaning of paragraph 1 of this Article comprises the period during which the cargo is in the charge of the carrier.

4. The period of the carriage by air does not extend to any carriage by land, by sea or by inland waterway performed outside an airport. If, however, such carriage takes place in the performance of a contract for carriage by air, for the purpose of loading, delivery or transhipment, any damage is presumed, subject to proof to the contrary, to have been the result of an event which took place during the carriage by air. If a carrier, without the consent of the consignor, substitutes carriage by another mode of transport for the

whole or part of a carriage intended by the agreement between the parties to be carriage by air, such carriage by another mode of transport is deemed to be within the period of carriage by air.

Article 19—Delay

The carrier is liable for damage occasioned by delay in the carriage by air of passengers, baggage or cargo. Nevertheless, the carrier shall not be liable for damage occasioned by delay if it proves that it and its servants and agents took all measures that could reasonably be required to avoid the damage or that it was impossible for it or them to take such measures.

Article 20—Exoneration

If the carrier proves that the damage was caused or contributed to by the negligence or other wrongful act or omission of the person claiming compensation, or the person from whom he or she derives his or her rights, the carrier shall be wholly or partly exonerated from its liability to the claimant to the extent that such negligence or wrongful act or omission caused or contributed to the damage. When by reason of death or injury of a passenger compensation is claimed by a person other than the passenger, the carrier shall likewise be wholly or partly exonerated from its liability to the extent that it proves that the damage was caused or contributed to by the negligence or other wrongful act or omission of that passenger. This Article applies to all the liability provisions in this Convention, including paragraph 1 of Article 21.

Article 21—Compensation in Case of Death or Injury of Passengers

1. For damages arising under paragraph 1 of Article 17 not exceeding 100,000 Special Drawing Rights for each passenger, the carrier shall not be able to exclude or limit its liability.
2. The carrier shall not be liable for damages arising under paragraph 1 of Article 17 to the extent that they exceed for each passenger 100,000 Special Drawing Rights if the carrier proves that:
   (a) such damage was not due to the negligence or other wrongful act or omission of the carrier or its servants or agents; or
   (b) such damage was solely due to the negligence or other wrongful act or omission of a third party.

Article 22—Limits of Liability in Relation to Delay, Baggage and Cargo

1. In the case of damage caused by delay as specified in Article 19 in the carriage of persons, the liability of the carrier for each passenger is limited to 4,150 Special Drawing Rights.
2. In the carriage of baggage, the liability of the carrier in the case of destruction, loss, damage or delay is limited to 1,000 Special Drawing Rights for each passenger unless the passenger has made, at the time when the checked baggage was handed over to the carrier, a special declaration of interest in delivery at destination and has paid a supplementary sum if the case so requires. In that case

the carrier will be liable to pay a sum not exceeding the declared sum, unless it proves that the sum is greater than the passenger's actual interest in delivery at destination.

3. In the carriage of cargo, the liability of the carrier in the case of destruction, loss, damage or delay is limited to a sum of 17 Special Drawing Rights per kilogram, unless the consignor has made, at the time when the package was handed over to the carrier, a special declaration of interest in delivery at destination and has paid a supplementary sum if the case so requires. In that case the carrier will be liable to pay a sum not exceeding the declared sum, unless it proves that the sum is greater than the consignor's actual interest in delivery at destination.

4. In the case of destruction, loss, damage or delay of part of the cargo, or of any object contained therein, the weight to be taken into consideration in determining the amount to which the carrier's liability is limited shall be only the total weight of the package or packages concerned. Nevertheless, when the destruction, loss, damage or delay of a part of the cargo, or of an object contained therein, affects the value of other packages covered by the same air waybill, or the same receipt or, if they were not issued, by the same record preserved by the other means referred to in paragraph 2 of Article 4, the total weight of such package or packages shall also be taken into consideration in determining the limit of liability.

5. The foregoing provisions of paragraphs 1 and 2 of this Article shall not apply if it is proved that the damage resulted from an act or omission of the carrier, its servants or agents, done with intent to cause damage or recklessly and with knowledge that damage would probably result; provided that, in the case of such act or omission of a servant or agent, it is also proved that such servant or agent was acting within the scope of its employment.

6. The limits prescribed in Article 21 and in this Article shall not prevent the court from awarding, in accordance with its own law, in addition, the whole or part of the court costs and of the other expenses of the litigation incurred by the plaintiff, including interest. The foregoing provision shall not apply if the amount of the damages awarded, excluding court costs and other expenses of the litigation, does not exceed the sum which the carrier has offered in writing to the plaintiff within a period of six months from the date of the occurrence causing the damage, or before the commencement of the action, if that is later.

Article 23—Conversion of Monetary Units

1. The sums mentioned in terms of Special Drawing Right in this Convention shall be deemed to refer to the Special Drawing Right as defined by the International Monetary Fund. Conversion of the sums into national currencies shall, in case of judicial proceedings, be made according to the value of such currencies in terms of the Special Drawing Right at the date of the judgement. The value of a national currency, in terms of the Special Drawing Right, of a State Party which is a Member of the International Monetary Fund, shall be calculated in accordance with the method of valuation applied by the International Monetary Fund, in effect at the date of the judgement, for its operations and transactions. The

value of a national currency, in terms of the Special Drawing Right, of a State Party which is not a Member of the International Monetary Fund, shall be calculated in a manner determined by that State.

2. Nevertheless, those States which are not Members of the International Monetary Fund and whose law does not permit the application of the provisions of paragraph 1 of this Article may, at the time of ratification or accession or at any time thereafter, declare that the limit of liability of the carrier prescribed in Article 21 is fixed at a sum of 1,500,000 monetary units per passenger in judicial proceedings in their territories; 62,500 monetary units per passenger with respect to paragraph 1 of Article 22; 15,000 monetary units per passenger with respect to paragraph 2 of Article 22; and 250 monetary units per kilogram with respect to paragraph 3 of Article 22. This monetary unit corresponds to sixty-five and a half milligrams of gold of millesimal fineness nine hundred. These sums may be converted into the national currency concerned in round figures. The conversion of these sums into national currency shall be made according to the law of the State concerned.

3. The calculation mentioned in the last sentence of paragraph I of this Article and the conversion method mentioned in paragraph 2 of this Article shall be made in such manner as to express in the national currency of the State Party as far as possible the same real value for the amounts in Articles 21 and 22 as would result from the application of the first three sentences of paragraph 1 of this Article. States Parties shall communicate to the depositary the manner of calculation pursuant to paragraph 1 of this Article, or the result of the conversion in paragraph 2 of this Article as the case may be, when depositing an instrument of ratification, acceptance, approval of or accession to this Convention and whenever there is a change in either.

Article 24—Review of Limits

1. Without prejudice to the provisions of Article 25 of this Convention and subject to paragraph 2 below, the limits of liability prescribed in Articles 21, 22 and 23 shall be reviewed by the Depositary at five-year intervals, the first such review to take place at the end of the fifth year following the date of entry into force of this Convention, or if the Convention does not enter into force within five years of the date it is first open for signature, within the first year of its entry into force, by reference to an inflation factor which corresponds to the accumulated rate of inflation since the previous revision or in the first instance since the date of entry into force of the Convention. The measure of the rate of inflation to be used in determining the inflation factor shall be the weighted average of the annual rates of increase or decrease in the Consumer Price Indices of the States whose currencies comprise the Special Drawing Right mentioned in paragraph 1 of Article 23.

2. If the review referred to in the preceding paragraph concludes that the inflation factor has exceeded 10 percent, the Depositary shall notify States Parties of a revision of the limits of liability.

Any such revision shall become effective six months after its notification to the States Parties. If within three months after its notification to the States Parties a majority of the States Parties register their disapproval, the revision shall not become effective and the Depositary shall refer the matter to a meeting of the States Parties. The Depositary shall immediately notify all States Parties of the coming into force of any revision.

3. Notwithstanding paragraph 1 of this Article, the procedure referred to in paragraph 2 of this Article shall be applied at any time provided that one-third of the States Parties express a desire to that effect and upon condition that the inflation factor referred to in paragraph 1 has exceeded 30 percent since the previous revision or since the date of entry into force of this Convention if there has been no previous revision. Subsequent reviews using the procedure described in paragraph 1 of this Article will take place at five-year intervals starting at the end of the fifth year following the date of the reviews under the present paragraph.

Article 25—Stipulation on Limits

A carrier may stipulate that the contract of carriage shall be subject to higher limits of liability than those provided for in this Convention or to no limits of liability whatsoever.

Article 26—Invalidity of Contractual Provisions

Any provision tending to relieve the carrier of liability or to fix a lower limit than that which is laid down in this Convention shall be null and void, but the nullity of any such provision does not involve the nullity of the whole contract, which shall remain subject to the provisions of this Convention.

Article 27—Freedom to Contract

Nothing contained in this Convention shall prevent the carrier from refusing to enter into any contract of carriage, from waiving any defences available under the Convention, or from laying down conditions which do not conflict with the provisions of this Convention.

Article 28—Advance Payments

In the case of aircraft accidents resulting in death or injury of passengers, the carrier shall, if required by its national law, make advance payments without delay to a natural person or persons who are entitled to claim compensation in order to meet the immediate economic needs of such persons. Such advance payments shall not constitute a recognition of liability and may be offset against any amounts subsequently paid as damages by the carrier.

Article 29—Basis of Claims

In the carriage of passengers, baggage and cargo, any action for damages, however founded, whether under this Convention or in contract or in tort or otherwise, can only be brought subject to the conditions and such limits of liability as are set out in this Convention without prejudice to the question as to who are the persons who have the right to bring suit and what are their respective rights. In any such action, punitive, exemplary or any other non-compensatory damages shall not be recoverable.

Article 30—Servants, Agents—Aggregation of Claims

1. If an action is brought against a servant or agent of the carrier arising out of damage to which the Convention relates, such servant or agent, if they prove that they acted within the scope of their employment, shall be entitled to avail themselves of the conditions and limits of liability which the carrier itself is entitled to invoke under this Convention.

2. The aggregate of the amounts recoverable from the carrier, its servants and agents, in that case, shall not exceed the said limits.

3. Save in respect of the carriage of cargo, the provisions of paragraphs 1 and 2 of this Article shall not apply if it is proved that the damage resulted from an act or omission of the servant or agent done with intent to cause damage or recklessly and with knowledge that damage would probably result.

Article 31—Timely Notice of Complaints

1. Receipt by the person entitled to delivery of checked baggage or cargo without complaint is prima facie evidence that the same has been delivered in good condition and in accordance with the document of carriage or with the record preserved by the other means referred to in paragraph 2 of Article 3 and paragraph 2 of Article 4.

2. In the case of damage, the person entitled to delivery must complain to the carrier forthwith after the discovery of the damage, and, at the latest, within seven days from the date of receipt in the case of checked baggage and fourteen days from the date of receipt in the case of cargo. In the case of delay, the complaint must be made at the latest within twenty-one days from the date on which the baggage or cargo have been placed at his or her disposal.

3. Every complaint must be made in writing and given or dispatched within the times aforesaid.

4. If no complaint is made within the times aforesaid, no action shall lie against the carrier, save in the case of fraud on its part.

Article 32—Death of Person Liable

In the case of the death of the person liable, an action for damages lies in accordance with the terms of this Convention against those legally representing his or her estate.

Article 33—Jurisdiction

1. An action for damages must be brought, at the option of the plaintiff, in the territory of one of the States Parties, either before the court of the domicile of the carrier or of its principal place of business, or where it has a place of business through which the contract has been made or before the court at the place of destination.

2. In respect of damage resulting from the death or injury of a passenger, an action may be brought before one of the courts mentioned in paragraph 1 of this Article, or in the territory of a State Party in which at the time of the accident the passenger has his or her principal and permanent residence and to or from which the carrier operates services for the carriage of passengers by air, either on its own aircraft or on another carrier's aircraft pursuant to a commercial agreement, and in which that carrier conducts its business of carriage of passengers by air from premises leased or owned by the carrier itself or by another carrier with which it has a commercial agreement.

3. For the purposes of paragraph 2,

(a) "commercial agreement" means an agreement, other than an agency agreement, made between carriers and relating to the provision of their joint services for carriage of passengers by air;

(b) "principal and permanent residence" means the one fixed and permanent abode of the passenger at the time of the accident. The nationality of the passenger shall not be the determining factor in this regard.

4. Questions of procedure shall be governed by the law of the court seized of the case.

Article 34—Arbitration

1. Subject to the provisions of this Article, the parties to the contract of carriage for cargo may stipulate that any dispute relating to the liability of the carrier under this Convention shall be settled by arbitration. Such agreement shall be in writing.

2. The arbitration proceedings shall, at the option of the claimant, take place within one of the jurisdictions referred to in Article 33.

3. The arbitrator or arbitration tribunal shall apply the provisions of this Convention.

4. The provisions of paragraphs 2 and 3 of this Article shall be deemed to be part of every arbitration clause or agreement, and any term of such clause or agreement which is inconsistent therewith shall be null and void.

Article 35—Limitation of Actions

1. The right to damages shall be extinguished if an action is not brought within a period of two years, reckoned from the date of arrival at the destination, or from the date on which the aircraft ought to have arrived, or from the date on which the carriage stopped.

2. The method of calculating that period shall be determined by the law of the court seized of the case.

Article 36—Successive Carriage

1. In the case of carriage to be performed by various successive carriers and falling within the definition set out in paragraph 3 of Article 1, each carrier which accepts passengers, baggage or cargo is subject to the rules set out in this Convention and is deemed to

be one of the parties to the contract of carriage in so far as the contract deals with that part of the carriage which is performed under its supervision.

2. In the case of carriage of this nature, the passenger or any person entitled to compensation in respect of him or her can take action only against the carrier which performed the carriage during which the accident or the delay occurred, save in the case where, by express agreement, the first carrier has assumed liability for the whole journey.

3. As regards baggage or cargo, the passenger or consignor will have a right of action against the first carrier, and the passenger or consignee who is entitled to delivery will have a right of action against the last carrier, and further, each may take action against the carrier which performed the carriage during which the destruction, loss, damage or delay took place. These carriers will be jointly and severally liable to the passenger or to the consignor or consignee.

Article 37—Right of Recourse Against Third Parties

Nothing in this Convention shall prejudice the question whether a person liable for damage in accordance with its provisions has a right of recourse against any other person.

Chapter IV—Combined Carriage

Article 38—A Combined Carriage

1. In the case of combined carriage performed partly by air and partly by any other mode of carriage, the provisions of this Convention shall, subject to paragraph 4 of Article 18, apply only to the carriage by air, provided that the carriage by air falls within the terms of Article 1.

2. Nothing in this Convention shall prevent the parties in the case of combined carriage from inserting in the document of air carriage conditions relating to other modes of carriage, provided that the provisions of this Convention are observed as regards the carriage by air.

Chapter V—Carriage by Air Performed by a Person Other than the Contracting Carrier

Article 39—Contracting Carrier—Actual Carrier

The provisions of this Chapter apply when a person (hereinafter referred to as "the contracting carrier") as a principal makes a contract of carriage governed by this Convention with a passenger or consignor or with a person acting on behalf of the passenger or consignor, and another person (hereinafter referred to as "the actual carrier") performs, by virtue of authority from the contracting carrier, the whole or part of the carriage, but is not with respect to such part a successive carrier within the meaning of this Convention. Such authority shall be presumed in the absence of proof to the contrary.

Article 40—Respective Liability of Contracting and Actual Carriers

If an actual carrier performs the whole or part of carriage which, according to the contract referred to in Article 39, is governed by this Convention, both the contracting carrier and the actual carrier shall, except as otherwise provided in this Chapter, be subject to the rules of this Convention, the former for the whole of the carriage contemplated in the contract, the latter solely for the carriage which it performs.

Article 41—Mutual Liability

1. The acts and omissions of the actual carrier and of its servants and agents acting within the scope of their employment shall, in relation to the carriage performed by the actual carrier, be deemed to be also those of the contracting carrier.

2. The acts and omissions of the contracting carrier and of its servants and agents acting within the scope of their employment shall, in relation to the carriage performed by the actual carrier, be deemed to be also those of the actual carrier. Nevertheless, no such act or omission shall subject the actual carrier to liability exceeding the amounts referred to in Articles 21, 22, 23 and 24. Any special agreement under which the contracting carrier assumes obligations not imposed by this Convention or any waiver of rights or defences conferred by this Convention or any special declaration of interest in delivery at destination contemplated in Article 22 shall not affect the actual carrier unless agreed to by it.

Article 42—Addressee of Complaints and Instructions

Any complaint to be made or instruction to be given under this Convention to the carrier shall have the same effect whether addressed to the contracting carrier or to the actual carrier. Nevertheless, instructions referred to in Article 12 shall only be effective if addressed to the contracting carrier.

Article 43—Servants and Agents

In relation to the carriage performed by the actual carrier, any servant or agent of that carrier or of the contracting carrier shall, if they prove that they acted within the scope of their employment, be entitled to avail themselves of the conditions and limits of liability which are applicable under this Convention to the carrier whose servant or agent they are, unless it is proved that they acted in a manner that prevents the limits of liability from being invoked in accordance with this Convention.

Article 44—Aggregation of Damages

In relation to the carriage performed by the actual carrier, the aggregate of the amounts recoverable from that carrier and the contracting carrier, and from their servants and agents acting within the scope of their employment, shall not exceed the highest amount which could be awarded against either the contracting carrier or the actual carrier under this Convention, but none of the persons mentioned shall be liable for a sum in excess of the limit applicable to that person.

Article 45—Addressee of Claims

In relation to the carriage performed by the actual carrier, an action for damages may be brought, at the option of the plaintiff, against that carrier or the contracting carrier, or against both together or separately. If the action is brought against only one of those carriers, that carrier shall have the right to require the other carrier to be joined in the proceedings, the procedure and effects being governed by the law of the court seized of the case.

Article 46—Additional Jurisdiction

Any action for damages contemplated in Article 45 must be brought, at the option of the plaintiff, in the territory of one of the States Parties, either before a court in which an action may be brought against the contracting carrier, as provided in Article 33, or before the court having jurisdiction at the place where the actual carrier has its domicile or its principal place of business.

Article 47—Invalidity of Contractual Provisions

Any contractual provision tending to relieve the contracting carrier or the actual carrier of liability under this Chapter or to fix a lower limit than that which is applicable according to this Chapter shall be null and void, but the nullity of any such provision does not involve the nullity of the whole contract, which shall remain subject to the provisions of this Chapter.

Article 48—Mutual Relations of Contracting and Actual Carriers

Except as provided in Article 45, nothing in this Chapter shall affect the rights and obligations of the carriers between themselves, including any right of recourse or indemnification.

Chapter VI—Other Provisions

Article 49—Mandatory Application

Any clause contained in the contract of carriage and all special agreements entered into before the damage occurred by which the parties purport to infringe the rules laid down by this Convention, whether by deciding the law to be applied, or by altering the rules as to jurisdiction, shall be null and void.

Article 50—Insurance

States Parties shall require their carriers to maintain adequate insurance covering their liability under this Convention. A carrier may be required by the State Party into which it operates to furnish evidence that it maintains adequate insurance covering its liability under this Convention.

Article 51—Carriage Performed in Extraordinary Circumstances

The provisions of Articles 3 to 5, 7 and 8 relating to the documentation of carriage shall not apply in the case of carriage performed in extraordinary circumstances outside the normal scope of a carrier's business.

Article 52—Definition of Days

The expression "days" when used in this Convention means calendar days, not working days.

Chapter VII—Final Clauses

Article 53—Signature, Ratification and Entry into Force

1. This Convention shall be open for signature in Montreal on 28 May 1999 by States participating in the International Conference on Air Law held at Montreal from 10 to 28 May 1999. After 28 May 1999, the Convention shall be open to all States for signature at the headquarters of the International Civil Aviation Organization in Montreal until it enters into force in accordance with paragraph 6 of this Article.

2. This Convention shall similarly be open for signature by Regional Economic Integration Organisations. For the purpose of this Convention, a "Regional Economic Integration Organisation" means any organisation which is constituted by sovereign States of a given region which has competence in respect of certain matters governed by this Convention and has been duly authorized to sign and to ratify, accept, approve or accede to this Convention. A reference to a "State Party" or "States Parties" in this Convention, otherwise than in paragraph 2 of Article 1, paragraph 1(b) of Article 3, paragraph (b) of Article 5, Articles 23, 33, 46 and paragraph (b) of Article 57, applies equally to a Regional Economic Integration Organisation. For the purpose of Article 24, the references to "a majority of the States Parties" and "one-third of the States Parties" shall not apply to a Regional Economic Integration Organisation.

3. This Convention shall be subject to ratification by States and by Regional Economic Integration Organisations which have signed it.

4. Any State or Regional Economic Integration Organisation which does not sign this Convention may accept, approve or accede to it at any time.

5. Instruments of ratification, acceptance, approval or accession shall be deposited with the International Civil Aviation Organization, which is hereby designated the Depositary.

6. This Convention shall enter into force on the sixtieth day following the date of deposit of the thirtieth instrument of ratification, acceptance, approval or accession with the Depositary between the States which have deposited such instrument. An instrument deposited by a Regional Economic Integration Organisation shall not be counted for the purpose of this paragraph.

7. For other States and for other Regional Economic Integration Organisations, this Convention shall take effect sixty days following the date of deposit of the instrument of ratification, acceptance, approval or accession.

8. The Depositary shall promptly notify all signatories and States Parties of:

(a) each signature of this Convention and date thereof;

(b) each deposit of an instrument of ratification, acceptance, approval or accession and date thereof;

(c) the date of entry into force of this Convention;

(d) the date of the coming into force of any revision of the limits of liability established under this Convention;

(e) any denunciation under Article 54.

Article 54—Denunciation

1. Any State Party may denounce this Convention by written notification to the Depositary.

2. Denunciation shall take effect one hundred and eighty days following the date on which notification is received by the Depositary.

Article 55—Relationship with other Warsaw Convention Instruments

This Convention shall prevail over any rules which apply to international carriage by air:

1. between States Parties to this Convention by virtue of those States commonly being Party to

(a) the Convention for the Unification of Certain Rules relating to International Carriage by Air signed at Warsaw on 12 October 1929 (hereinafter called the Warsaw Convention);

(b) the Protocol to amend the Convention for the Unification of Certain Rules relating to International Carriage by Air signed at Warsaw on 12 October 1929, done at The Hague on 28 September 1955 (hereinafter called The Hague Protocol);

(c) the Convention, Supplementary to the Warsaw Convention, for the Unification of Certain Rules relating to International Carriage by Air Performed by a Person other than the Contracting Carrier, signed at Guadalajara on 18 September 1961 (hereinafter called the Guadalajara Convention);

(d) the Protocol to amend the Convention for the Unification of Certain Rules relating to International Carriage by Air signed at Warsaw on 12 October 1929 as amended by the Protocol done at The Hague on 28 September 1955, signed at Guatemala City on 8 March 1971 (hereinafter called the Guatemala City Protocol);

(e) Additional Protocol Nos. 1 to 3 and Montreal Protocol No. 4 to amend the Warsaw Convention as amended by The Hague Protocol or the Warsaw Convention as amended by both The Hague Protocol and the Guatemala City

Protocol, signed at Montreal on 25 September 1975 (hereinafter called the Montreal Protocols); or

2. within the territory of any single State Party to this Convention by virtue of that State being Party to one or more of the instruments referred to in sub-paragraphs (a) to (e) above.

ARTICLE 56—STATES WITH MORE THAN ONE SYSTEM OF LAW

1. If a State has two or more territorial units in which different systems of law are applicable in relation to matters dealt with in this Convention, it may at the time of signature, ratification, acceptance, approval or accession declare that this Convention shall extend to all its territorial units or only to one or more of them and may modify this declaration by submitting another declaration at any time.

2. Any such declaration shall be notified to the Depositary and shall state expressly the territorial units to which the Convention applies.

3. In relation to a State Party which has made such a declaration:

(a) references in Article 23 to "national currency" shall be construed as referring to the currency of the relevant territorial unit of that State; and

(b) the reference in Article 28 to "national law" shall be construed as referring to the law of the relevant territorial unit of that State.

ARTICLE 57—RESERVATIONS

No reservation may be made to this Convention except that a State Party may at any time declare by a notification addressed to the Depositary that this Convention shall not apply to:

(a) international carriage by air performed and operated directly by that State Party for non-commercial purposes in respect to its functions and duties as a sovereign State; and/or

(b) the carriage of persons, cargo and baggage for its military authorities on aircraft registered in or leased by that State Party, the whole capacity of which has been reserved by or on behalf of such authorities.

IN WITNESS WHEREOF the undersigned Plenipotentiaries, having been duly authorized, have signed this Convention.

DONE at Montreal on the 28th day of May of the year one thousand nine hundred and ninety-nine in the English, Arabic, Chinese, French, Russian and Spanish languages, all texts being equally authentic. This Convention shall remain deposited in the archives of the International Civil Aviation Organization, and certified copies thereof shall be transmitted by the Depositary to all States Parties to this Convention, as well as to all States Parties to the Warsaw Convention, The Hague Protocol, the Guadalajara Convention, the Guatemala City Protocol and the Montreal Protocols.

2. Space and International Scientific Cooperation

a. Treaty on Outer Space [1]

Done at Washington, London and Moscow, January 27, 1967; Ratification advised by the Senate, April 25, 1967; Ratification by the President, May 24, 1967; Ratifications of the Governments of the United States, the United Kingdom and the Union of Soviet Socialist Republics deposited with the said Governments at Washington, London and Moscow, October 10, 1967; Proclaimed by the President, October 10, 1967; Entered into force, October 10, 1967

TREATY ON PRINCIPLES GOVERNING THE ACTIVITIES OF STATES IN THE EXPLORATION AND USE OF OUTER SPACE, INCLUDING THE MOON AND OTHER CELESTIAL BODIES

The States Parties to this Treaty,

INSPIRED by the great prospects opening up before mankind as a result of man's entry into outer space,

RECOGNIZING the common interest of all mankind in the progress of the exploration and use of outer space for peaceful purposes,

BELIEVING that the exploration and use of outer space should be carried on for the benefit of all peoples irrespective of the degree of their economic or scientific development,

DESIRING to contribute to broad international cooperation in the scientific as well as the legal aspects of the exploration and use of outer space for peaceful purposes,

BELIEVING that such cooperation will contribute to the development of mutual understanding and to the strengthening of friendly relations between States and peoples,

RECALLING resolution 1962 (XVIII), entitled "Declaration of Legal Principles Governing the Activities of States in the Exploration and Use of Outer Space", which was adopted unanimously by the United Nations General Assembly on 13 December 1963.

RECALLING resolution 1884 (XVIII), calling upon States to refrain from placing in orbit around the Earth any objects carrying nuclear weapons or any other kinds of weapons of mass destruction or from installing such weapons on celestial bodies, which was adopted unanimously by the United Nations General Assembly on 17 October 1963.

TAKING account of United Nations General Assembly resolution 110 (II) of 3 November 1947, which condemned propaganda designed or likely to provoke or encourage any threat to the peace breach of the peace or act of aggression, and considering that the aforementioned resolution is applicable to outer space.

---

[1] 18 UST 2410: TIAS 6347. For a list of states that are parties to the Treaty, see Department of State publication, *Treaties in Force*.

CONVINCED that a Treaty on Principles Governing the Activities of States in the Exploration and Use of Outer Space, including the Moon and Other Celestial Bodies, will further the Purposes and Principles of the Charter of the United Nations,

HAVE AGREED ON THE FOLLOWING:

ARTICLE I

The exploration and use of outer space, including the moon and other celestial bodies, shall be carried out for the benefit and in the interests of all counties, irrespective of their degree of economic or scientific development, and shall be the province of all mankind.

Outer space, including the moon and other celestial bodies, shall be free for exploration and use by all States without discrimination of any kind, on a basis of equality and in accordance with international law, and there shall be free access to all areas of celestial bodies.

There shall be freedom of scientific investigation in outer space, including the moon and other celestial bodies, and States shall facilitate and encourage international cooperation in such investigation.

ARTICLE II

Outer space, including the moon and other celestial bodies, is not subject to national appropriation by claim of sovereignty, by means of use or occupation, or by any other means.

ARTICLE III

States Parties to the Treaty shall carry on activities in the exploration and use of outer space, including the moon and other celestial bodies, in accordance with international law, including the Charter of the United Nations, in the interest of maintaining international peace and security and promoting international cooperation and understanding.

ARTICLE IV

States Parties to the Treaty undertake not to place in orbit around the Earth any objects carrying nuclear weapons or any other kinds of weapons of mass destruction, install such weapons on celestial bodies, or station such weapons in outer space in any other manner.

The moon and other celestial bodies shall be used by all States Parties to the Treaty exclusively for peaceful purposes. The establishment of military bases, installations and fortifications, the testing of any type of weapons and the conduct of military maneuvers on celestial bodies shall be forbidden. The use of military personnel for scientific research or for any other peaceful purposes shall not be prohibited. The use of any equipment or facility necessary for peaceful exploration of the moon and other celestial bodies shall also not be prohibited.

Article V

States Parties to the Treaty shall regard astronauts as envoys of mankind in outer space and shall render to them all possible assistance in the event of accident, distress, or emergency landing on the territory of another State Party or on the high seas. When astronauts make such a landing, they shall be safely and promptly returned to the State of registry of their space vehicle.

In carrying on activities in outer space and on celestial bodies, the astronauts of one State Party shall render all possible assistance to the astronauts of other States Parties.

States Parties to the Treaty shall immediately inform the other States Parties to the Treaty or the Secretary-General of the United Nations of any phenomena they discover in outer space, including the moon and other celestial bodies, which could constitute a danger to the life or health of astronauts.

Article VI

States Parties to the Treaty shall bear international responsibility for national activities in outer space, including the moon and other celestial bodies, whether such activities are carried on by governmental agencies or by non-governmental entities, and for assuring that national activities are carried out in conformity with the provisions set forth in the present Treaty. The activities of non-governmental entities in outer space, including the moon and other celestial bodies, shall require authorization and continuing supervision by the appropriate State Party to the Treaty. When activities are carried on in outer space, including the moon and other celestial bodies, by an international organization, responsibility for compliance with this Treaty shall be borne by the international organization and by the States Parties to the Treaty participating in such organization.

Article VII

Each State Party to the Treaty that launches or procures the launching of an object into outer space, including the moon and other celestial bodies, and each State Party from whose territory or facility an object is launched, is internationally liable for damage to another State Party to the Treaty or to its natural or juridical persons by such object or its component parts on the Earth, in air space or in outer space, including the moon and other celestial bodies.

Article VIII

A State Party to the Treaty on whose registry an object launched into outer space is carried shall retain jurisdiction and control over such object, and over any personnel thereof, while in outer space or on a celestial body. Ownership of objects launched into outer space, including objects landed or constructed on a celestial body, and of their component parts, is not affected by their presence in outer space or on a celestial body or by their return to the Earth. Such objects or component parts found beyond the limits of the State Party to the Treaty on whose registry they are carried shall be returned to that State Party, which shall, upon request, furnish identifying data prior to their return.

Article IX

In the exploration and use of outer space, including the moon and other celestial bodies, States Parties to the Treaty shall be guided by the principle of co-operation and mutual assistance and shall conduct all their activities in outer space, including the moon and other celestial bodies, with due regard to the corresponding interests of all other States Parties to the Treaty. States Parties to the Treaty shall pursue studies of outer space, including the moon and other celestial bodies, and conduct exploration of them so as to avoid their harmful contamination and also adverse changes in the environment of the Earth resulting from the introduction of extraterrestrial matter and, where necessary, shall adopt appropriate measures for this purpose. If a State Party to the Treaty has reason to believe that an activity or experiment planned by it or its nationals in outer space, including the moon and other celestial bodies, would cause potentially harmful interference with activities of other States Parties in the peaceful exploration and use of outer space, including the moon and other celestial bodies, is shall undertake appropriate international consultations before proceeding with any such activity or experiment. A State Party to the Treaty which has reason to believe that an activity or experiment planned by another State Party in outer space, including the moon and other celestial bodies, would cause potentially harmful interference with activities in the peaceful exploration and use of outer space, including the moon and other celestial bodies, may request consultation concerning the activity or experiment.

Article X

In order to promote international co-operation in the exploration and use of outer space, including the moon and other celestial bodies, in conformity with the purposes of this Treaty, the States Parties to the Treaty shall consider on a basis of the equality any requests by other States Parties to the Treaty to be afforded an opportunity to observe the flight of space objects launched by those States.

The nature of such an opportunity for observation and conditions under which it could be afforded shall be determined by agreement between the States concerned.

Article XI

In order to promote international co-operation in the peaceful exploration and use of outer space, States Parties to the Treaty conducting activities in outer space, including the moon and other celestial bodies, agree to inform the Secretary-General of the United Nations as well as the public and the international scientific community to the greatest extent feasible and practicable, of the nature, conduct, locations and results of such activities. On receiving the said information, the Secretary-General of the United Nations should be prepared to disseminate it immediately and effectively.

Article XII

All stations, installations, equipment and space vehicles on the moon and other celestial bodies shall be open to representatives of other States Parties to the Treaty on a basis of reciprocity. Such representatives shall give reasonable advance notice of a projected visit, in order that appropriate consultations may be held and that maximum precautions may be taken to assure safety and to avoid interference with normal operations in the facility to be visited.

Article XIII

The provisions of this Treaty shall apply to the activities of States Parties to the Treaty in the exploration and use of outer space, including the moon and other celestial bodies, whether such activities are carried on by a single State Party to the Treaty or jointly with other States, including cases where they are carried on within the framework of international inter-governmental organizations.

Any practical questions arising in connection with activities carried on by international inter-governmental organizations in the exploration and use of outer space, including the moon and other celestial bodies, shall be resolved by the States Parties to the Treaty either with the appropriate international organization or with one or more States members of that international organization, which are Parties to this Treaty.

Article XIV

1. This Treaty shall be open to all States for signature. Any State which does not sign this Treaty before its entry into force in accordance with paragraph 3 of this article may accede to it at any time.
2. This Treaty shall be subject to ratification by signatory States. Instruments of ratification and instruments of accession shall be deposited with the Governments of the United States of America, the United Kingdom of Great Britain and Northern Ireland, and the Union of Soviet Socialist Republics, which are hereby designated the Depositary Governments.
3. This Treaty shall enter into force upon the deposit of instruments of ratification by five Governments including the Governments designated as Depositary Governments under this Treaty.
4. For States whose instruments of ratification or accession are deposited subsequent to the entry into force of this Treaty, is shall enter into force on the date of the deposit of their instruments of ratification or accession.
5. The Depositary Governments shall promptly inform all signatory and acceding States of the date of each signature, the date of deposit of each instrument of ratification of and accession to this Treaty, the date of its entry into force and other notices.
6. This Treaty shall be registered by the Depositary Governments pursuant to Article 102 of the Charter of the United Nations.

ARTICLE XV

Any State Party to the Treaty may propose amendments to this Treaty. Amendments shall enter into force for each State party to the Treaty accepting the amendment upon their acceptance by a majority of the States Parties to the Treaty and thereafter for each remaining State Party to the Treaty on the date of acceptance by it.

ARTICLE XVI

Any State Party to the Treaty may give notice of its withdrawal from the Treaty one year after its entry into force by written notification to the Depositary Governments. Such withdrawal shall take effect one year from the date of receipt of this notification.

ARTICLE XVII

This Treaty, of which the English, Russian, French, Spanish and Chinese texts are equally authentic, shall be deposited in the archives of the Depositary Governments. Duly certified copies of this Treaty shall be transmitted by the Depositary Governments to the Governments of the signatory and acceding States.

IN WITNESS WHEREOF the undersigned, duly authorized, have signed this Treaty.

DONE in triplicate, at the cities of Washington, London and Moscow, this twenty-seventh day of January one thousand nine hundred sixty-seven.

b. Astronaut Assistance and Return Agreement [1]

Signed at Washington, London and Moscow, April 22, 1968; Ratification advised by the Senate, October 8, 1968; Ratification by the President, October 18, 1968; Ratifications of the Governments of the United States, the United Kingdom and the Union of Soviet Socialist Republics deposited with the said Governments at Washington, London, and Moscow, December 3, 1968; Proclaimed by the President, December 3, 1968; Entered into force, December 3, 1968

AGREEMENT ON THE RESCUE OF ASTRONAUTS, THE RETURN OF ASTRONAUTS AND THE RETURN OF OBJECTS LAUNCHED INTO OUTER SPACE

The Contracting Parties,

NOTING the great importance of the Treaty on Principles Governing the Activities of States in the Exploration and Use of Outer Space, Including the Moon and Other Celestial Bodies, which calls for the rendering of all possible assistance to astronauts in the event of accident, distress or emergency landing, the prompt and safe return of astronauts, and the return of objects launched into outer space,

DESIRING to develop and give further concrete expression to those duties,

WISHING to promote international co-operation in the peaceful exploration and use of outer space,

PROMPTED by sentiments of humanity,

HAVE AGREED ON THE FOLLOWING:

ARTICLE 1

Each Contracting Party which receives information or discovers that the personnel of a spacecraft have suffered accident or are experiencing conditions of distress or have made an emergency or unintended landing in territory under its jurisdiction or on the high seas or in any other place not under the jurisdiction of any State shall immediately:

(a) Notify the launching authority or, if it cannot identify and immediately communicate with the launching authority, immediately make a public announcement by all appropriate means of communication at its disposal;

(b) Notify the Secretary-General of the United Nations, who should disseminate the information without delay by all appropriate means of communication at his disposal.

[1] 19 UST 7570; TIAS 6599; 672 UNTS 119. For a list of states that are parties to the Agreement, see Department of State publication, *Treaties in Force*.

ARTICLE 2

If, owing to accident, distress, emergency or unintended landing, the personnel of a spacecraft land in territory under the jurisdiction of the Contracting Party, it shall immediately take all possible steps to rescue them and render them all necessary assistance. It shall inform the launching authority and also the Secretary-General of the United Nations of the steps it is taking and of their progress. If assistance by the launching authority would help to effect a prompt rescue or would contribute substantially to the effectiveness of search and rescue operations, the launching authority shall co-operate with the Contracting Party with a view to the effective conduct of search and rescue operations. Such operations shall be subject to the direction and control of the Contracting Party, which shall act in close and continuing consultation with the launching authority.

ARTICLE 3

If the information is received or it is discovered that the personnel of a spacecraft have alighted on the high seas on in any other place not under the jurisdiction of any State, those Contracting Parties which are in a position to do so shall, if necessary, extend assistance in search and rescue operations for such personnel to assure their speedy rescue. They shall inform the launching authority and the Secretary-General of the United Nations of the steps they are taking and of their progress.

ARTICLE 4

If, owing to accident, distress, emergency or unintended landing, the personnel of a spacecraft land in territory under the jurisdiction of a Contracting Party or have been found on the high seas or in any other place under the jurisdiction of any State, they shall be safely and promptly returned to representatives of the launching authority.

ARTICLE 5

1. Each Contracting Party which receives information or discovers that a space object or its component parts had returned to Earth in territory under its jurisdiction or on the high seas or in any other place not under the jurisdiction of any State, shall notify the launching authority and the Secretary-General of the United Nations.

2. Each Contracting Party having jurisdiction over the territory on which a space object or its component parts has been discovered shall, upon the request of the launching authority and with assistance from that authority if requested, take such steps as it finds practicable to recover the object or component parts.

3. Upon request of the launching authority, objects launched into outer space or their component parts found beyond the territorial limits of the launching authority shall be returned to or held at the disposal or representatives of the launching authority, which shall, upon request, furnish identifying data prior to their return.

4. Notwithstanding paragraphs 2 and 3 of this article, a Contracting Party which has reason to believe that a space object or its component parts discovered in territory under its jurisdictions, or recovered by it elsewhere, is of a hazardous or deleterious nature may so notify the launching authority, which shall immediately take effective steps, under the direction and control of the said Contracting Party, to eliminate possible danger of harm.

5. Expenses incurred in fulfilling obligations to recover and return a space object or its component parts under paragraphs 2 and 3 of this article shall be borne by the launching authority.

ARTICLE 6

For the purposes of this Agreement, the term "launching authority" shall refer to the State responsible for launching, or, where an international inter-governmental organization is responsible for launching, that organization, provided that that organization declares its acceptance of the rights and obligations provided for in this Agreement and a majority of the States members of that organization are Contracting Parties to this Agreement and to the Treaty on Principles Governing the Activities of States in the Exploration and Use of Outer Space, including the Moon and Other Celestial Bodies.

ARTICLE 7

1. This Agreement shall be open to all States for signature. Any State which does not sign this Agreement before its entry into force in accordance with paragraph 3 of this article may accede to it at any time.

2. This Agreement shall be subject to ratification by signatory States. Instruments of ratification and instruments of accession shall be deposited with the Governments of the United States of America, the United Kingdom of Great Britain and Northern Ireland and the Union of Soviet Socialist Republics, which are hereby designated the Depositary Governments.

3. This Agreement shall enter into force upon the deposit of instruments of ratification by five Governments including the Governments designated as Depositary Governments under this Agreement.

4. For States whose instruments of ratification or accession are deposited subsequent to the entry into force of this Agreement, it shall enter into force on the date of the deposit of their instruments of ratification or accession.

5. The Depositary Governments shall promptly inform all signatory and acceding States of the date of each signature, the date of deposit of each instrument of ratification of and accession to this Agreement, the date of its entry into force and other notices.

6. This Agreement shall be registered by the Depository Governments pursuant to Article 102 of the Charter of the United Nations.

ARTICLE 8

Any State Party to the Agreement may propose amendments to this Agreement. Amendments shall enter into force for each State

Party to the Agreement accepting the amendments upon their acceptance by a majority of the State Parties to the Agreement and thereafter for each remaining State Party to the Agreement on the date of acceptance by it.

ARTICLE 9

Any State Party to the Agreement may give notice of its withdrawal from the Agreement one year after its entry into force by written notification to the Depositary Governments. Such withdrawal shall take effect one year from the date of receipt of this notification.

ARTICLE 10

This Agreement, of which the English, Russian, French, Spanish and Chinese texts are equally authentic, shall be deposited in the archives of the Depositary Governments. Duly certified copies of this Agreement shall be transmitted by the Depository Government to the Governments of the signatory and acceding States.

IN WITNESS WHEREOF the undersigned, duly authorized, have signed this Treaty.

DONE in triplicate, at the cities of Washington, London and Moscow, this twenty-second day of April one thousand nine hundred sixty-eight.

c. Convention on International Liability for Damage Caused by Space Objects

Done at Washington, London, and Moscow, March 29, 1972; Ratification advised by the Senate, October 6, 1972; Ratification by the President, May 18, 1973; Ratifications of the Governments of the United States, the United Kingdom, and the Union of Soviet Socialist Republics deposited with the said Governments at Washington, London and Moscow, October 9, 1973; Entered into force, October 9, 1973; Proclaimed by the President, November 21, 1973 [1]

CONVENTION ON INTERNATIONAL LIABILITY FOR DAMAGE CAUSED BY SPACE OBJECTS

The States Parties to this Convention,

RECOGNIZING the common interest of all mankind in furthering the exploration and use of outer space for peaceful purposes,

RECALLING the Treaty on Principles Governing the Activities of States in the Exploration and Use of Outer Space, including the Moon and Other Celestial Bodies,

TAKING into consideration that, notwithstanding the precautionary measures to be taken by States and international intergovernmental organizations involved in the launching of space objects, damage may on occasion be caused by such objects,

RECOGNIZING the need to elaborate effective international rules and procedures concerning liability for damage caused by space objects and to ensure, in particular, the prompt payment under the terms of this Convention of a full and equitable measure of compensation to victims of such damage,

BELIEVING that the establishment of such rules and procedures will contribute to the strengthening of international cooperation in the field of the exploration and use of outer space for peaceful purposes,

HAVE AGREED ON THE FOLLOWING:

ARTICLE I

For the purposes of this Convention:

(a) The term "damage" means loss of life, personal injury or other impairment of health; or loss of or damage to property of States or of persons, natural or juridical, or property of international intergovernmental organizations;

(b) The term "launching" includes attempted launching;

(c) The term "launching State" means:

(i) A State which launches or procures the launching of a space object;

[1] 24 UST 2389, TIAS 7762. For a list of states that are parties to the Convention, see Department of State publication, *Treaties in Force*.

(ii) A State from whose territory or facility a space object is launched;

(d) The term "space object" includes component parts of a space object as well as its launch vehicle and parts thereof.

ARTICLE II

A launching State shall be absolutely liable to pay compensation for damage caused by its space object on the surface of the Earth or to aircraft in flight.

ARTICLE III

In the event of damage being caused elsewhere than on the surface of the Earth to a space object of one launching State or to persons or property on board such a space object by a space object of another launching State, the latter shall be liable only if the damage is due to its fault or the fault of persons for whom it is responsible.

ARTICLE IV

1. In the event of damage being caused elsewhere than on the surface of the Earth to a space object of one launching State or to persons or property on board such a space object by a space object of another launching State, and of damage thereby being caused to a third State or to its natural or juridical persons, the first two States shall be jointly and severally liable to the third State, to the extent indicated by the following:

(a) If the damage has been caused to the third State on the surface of the Earth or to aircraft in flight, their liability to the third State shall be absolute;

(b) If the damage has been caused to a space object of the third State or to persons or property on board that space object elsewhere than on the surface of the Earth, their liability to the third State shall be based on the fault of either of the first two States or on the fault of persons for whom either is responsible.

2. In all cases of joint and several liability referred to in paragraph 1 of this article, the burden of compensation for the damage shall be apportioned between the first two States in accordance with the extent to which they were at fault; if the extent of the fault of each of these States cannot be established, the burden of compensation shall be apportioned equally between them. Such apportionment shall be without prejudice to the right of the third State to seek the entire compensation due under this Convention from any or all of the launching States which are jointly and severally liable.

ARTICLE V

1. Whenever two or more States jointly launch a space object, they shall be jointly and severally liable for any damage caused.

2. A launching State which has paid compensation for damage shall have the right to present a claim for indemnification to other participants in the joint launching. The participants in a joint

launching may conclude agreements regarding the apportioning among themselves of the financial obligation in respect of which they are jointly and severally liable. Such agreements shall be without prejudice to the right of a State sustaining damage to seek the entire compensation due under this Convention from any or all of the launching States which are jointly and severally liable.

3. A State from whose territory or facility a space object is launched shall be regarded as a participant in a joint launching.

ARTICLE VI

1. Subject to the provisions of paragraph 2 of this article, exoneration from absolute liability shall be granted to the extent that a launching State establishes that the damage has resulted either wholly or partially from gross negligence or from an act or omission done with intent to cause damage on the part of a claimant State or of natural or juridical persons it represents.

2. No exoneration whatever shall be granted in cases where the damage has resulted from activities conducted by a launching State which are not in conformity with international law including, in particular, the Chapter of the United Nations and the Treaty on Principles Governing the Activities of States in the Exploration and Use of Outer Space, including the Moon and Other Celestial Bodies.

ARTICLE VII

The provisions of this Convention shall not apply to damage caused by a space object of a launching State to:

(a) Nationals of that launching State;

(b) Foreign nationals during such time as they are participating in the operation of that space object from the time of its launching or at any stage thereafter until its descent, or during such time as they are in the immediate vicinity of a planned launching or recovery area as the result of an invitation by that launching State.

ARTICLE VIII

1. A State which suffers damage, or whose natural or juridical persons suffer damage, may present to a launching State a claim for compensation for such damage.

2. If the State of nationality has not presented a claim, another State may, in respect of damage sustained in its territory by any natural or juridical person, present a claim to a launching State.

3. If neither the State of nationality nor the State in whose territory the damage was sustained has presented a claim or notified its intention of presenting a claim, another State may, in respect of damage sustained by its permanent residents, present a claim to a launching State.

ARTICLE IX

A claim for compensation for damages shall be presented to a launching State through diplomatic channels. If a State does not maintain diplomatic relations with the launching State concerned, it may request another State to present its claim to that launching State or otherwise represent its interests under this Convention. It may also present its claim through the Secretary-General of the United Nations, provided the claimant State and the launching State are both Members of the United Nations.

ARTICLE X

1. A claim for compensation for damage may be presented to a launching State not later than one year following the date of the occurrence of the damage or the identification of the launching State which is liable.

2. If, however, a State does not know of the occurrence of the damage or has not been able to identify the launching State which is liable, it may present a claim within one year following the date on which it learned of the aforementioned facts; however, this period shall in no event exceed one year following the date on which the State could reasonably be expected to have learned of the facts through exercise of due diligence.

3. The time-limits specified in paragraphs 1 and 2 of this article shall apply even if the full extent of the damage may not be known. In this event, however, the claimant State shall be entitled to revise the claim and submit additional documentation after the expiration of such time-limits until one year after the full extent of the damage is known.

ARTICLE XI

1. Presentation of a claim to a launching State for compensation for damage under this Convention shall not require the prior exhaustion of any local remedies which may be available to a claimant State or to natural or juridical persons it represents.

2. Nothing in this Convention shall prevent a State, or natural or juridical persons it might represent, from pursuing a claim in the courts or administrative tribunals or agencies of a launching State. A State shall not, however, be entitled to present a claim under this Convention in respect of the same damage for which a claim is being pursued in the courts or administrative tribunals or agencies of a launching State or under another international agreement which is binding on the States concerned.

ARTICLE XII

The compensation which the launching State shall be liable to pay for damage under this Convention shall be determined in accordance with international law and the principles of justice and equity, in order to provide such reparation in respect of the damage as will restore the person, natural or juridical, State or international organization on whose behalf the claim is presented to the condition which would have existed if the damage had not occurred.

ARTICLE XIII

Unless the claimant State and the State from which compensation is due under this Convention agree on another form of compensation, the compensation shall be paid in the currency of the claimant State or, if that State so requests, in the currency of the State from which compensation is due.

ARTICLE XIV

If no settlement of a claim is arrived at through diplomatic negotiations as provided for in article IX, within one year from the date on which the claimant State notifies the launching State that it has submitted the documentation of its claim, the parties concerned shall establish a Claims Commission at the request of either party.

ARTICLE XV

1. The Claims Commission shall be composed of three members: one appointed by the claimant State, one appointed by the launching State and the third member, the Chairman, to be chosen by both parties jointly. Each party shall make its appointment within two months of the request for the establishment of the Claims Commission.

2. If no agreement is reached on the choice of the Chairman within four months of the request for the establishment of the Commission, either party may request the Secretary-General of the United Nations to appoint the Chairman within a further period of two months.

ARTICLE XVI

1. If one of the parties does not make its appointment within the stipulated period, the Chairman shall, at the request of the other party, constitute a single-member Claims Commission.

2. Any vacancy which may arise in the Commission for whatever reason shall be filled by the same procedure adopted for the original appointment.

3. The Commission shall determine its own procedure.

4. The Commission shall determine the place or places where it shall sit and all other administrative matters.

5. Except in the case of decisions and awards by a single-member Commission, all decisions and awards of the Commission shall be by majority vote.

ARTICLE XVII

No increase in the membership of the Claims Commission shall take place by reason of two or more claimant States or launching States being joined in any one proceeding before the Commission. The claimant States so joined shall collectively appoint one member of the Commission in the same manner and subject to the same conditions as would be the case for a single claimant State. When two or more launching States are so joined, they shall collectively appoint one member of the Commission in the same way. If the claimant States or the launching States do not make the appointment within the stipulated period, the Chairman shall constitute a single-member Commission.

ARTICLE XVIII

The Claims Commission shall decide the merits of the claim for compensation and determine the amount of compensation payable, if any.

ARTICLE XIX

1. The Claims Commission shall act in accordance with the provisions of article XII.
2. The decision of the Commission shall be final and binding if the parties have so agreed; otherwise the Commission shall render a final and recommendatory award, which the parties shall consider in good faith. The Commission shall state the reasons for its decision or award.
3. The Commission shall give its decision or award as promptly as possible and no later than one year from the date of its establishment, unless an extension of this period is found necessary by the Commission.
4. The Commission shall make its decision or award public. It shall deliver a certified copy of its decision or award to each of the parties and to the Secretary-General of the United Nations.

ARTICLE XX

The expenses in regard to the Claims Commission shall be borne equally by the parties, unless otherwise decided by the Commission.

ARTICLE XXI

If the damage caused by a space object presents a large-scale danger to human life or seriously interferes with the living conditions of the population or the functioning of vital centers, the States Parties, and in particular the launching State, shall examine the possibility of rendering appropriate and rapid assistance to the State which has suffered the damage, when it so requests. However, nothing in this article shall affect the rights or obligations of the States Parties under this Convention.

ARTICLE XXII

1. In this Convention, with the exception of articles XXIV to XXVII, references to States shall be deemed to apply to any international intergovernmental organization which conducts space activities if the organization declares its acceptance of the rights and obligations provided for in this Convention and if a majority of the States members of the organization are States Parties to this Convention and to the Treaty on Principles Governing the Activities of States in the Exploration and Use of Outer Space, including the Moon and Other Celestial Bodies.

2. States members of any such organization which are States Parties to this Convention shall take all appropriate steps to ensure that the organization makes a declaration in accordance with the preceding paragraph.

3. If an international intergovernmental organization is liable for damage by virtue of the provisions of this Convention, that organization and those of its members which are States Parties to this Convention shall be jointly and severally liable; provided, however, that:

(a) Any claim for compensation in respect to such damage shall be first presented to the organization;

(b) Only where the organization has not paid, within a period of six months, any sum agreed or determined to be due as compensation for such damage, may the claimant State invoke the liability of the members which are States Parties to this Convention for the payment of that sum.

4. Any claim, pursuant to the provisions of this Convention, for compensation in respect of damage caused to an organization which has made a declaration in accordance with paragraph 1 of this article shall be presented by a State member of the organization which is a State Party to this Convention.

ARTICLE XXIII

1. The provisions of this Convention shall not affect other international agreements in force insofar as relations between the States Parties to such agreements are concerned.

2. No provision of this Convention shall prevent States from concluding international agreements reaffirming, supplementing or extending its provisions.

ARTICLE XXIV

1. This Convention shall be open to all States for signature. Any State which does not sign this Convention before its entry into force in accordance with paragraph 3 of this article may accede to it at any time.

2. This Convention shall be subject to ratification by signatory States. Instruments of ratification and instruments of accession shall be deposited with the Governments of the United States of America, the United Kingdom of Great Britain and Northern Ireland and the Union of Soviet Socialist Republics, which are hereby designated the Depositary Governments.

3. This Convention shall enter into force on the deposit of the fifth instrument of ratification.

4. For States whose instruments of ratification or accession are deposited subsequent to the entry into force of this Convention, it shall enter into force on the date of the deposit of their instruments of ratification or accession.

5. The Depositary Governments shall promptly inform all signatory and acceding States of the date of each signature, the date of deposit of each instrument of ratification of and accession to this Convention, the date of its entry into force and other notices.

6. This Convention shall be registered by the Depositary Governments pursuant to Article 102 of the Charter of the United Nations.

ARTICLE XXV

Any State Party to this Convention may propose amendments to this Convention. Amendments shall enter into force for each State Party to the Convention accepting the amendments upon their acceptance by a majority of the States Parties to the Convention and thereafter for each remaining State Party to the Convention on the date of acceptance by it.

ARTICLE XXVI

Ten years after the entry into force of this Convention, the question of the review of this Convention shall be included in the provisional agenda of the United Nations General Assembly in order to consider, in the light of past application of the Convention, whether it requires revision. However, at any time after the Convention has been in force for five years, and at the request of one third of the States Parties to the Convention, and with the concurrence of the majority of the States Parties, a conference of the States Parties shall be convened to review this Convention.

ARTICLE XXVII

Any State Party to this Convention may give notice of its withdrawal from the Convention one year after its entry into force by written notification to the Depositary Governments. Such withdrawal shall take effect one year from the date of receipt of this notification.

ARTICLE XXVIII

This Convention, of which the English, Russian, French, Spanish and Chinese texts are equally authentic, shall be deposited in the archives of the Depositary Governments. Duly certified copies of this Convention shall be transmitted by the Depositary Governments to the Governments of the signatory and acceding States.

IN WITNESS WHEREOF the undersigned, duly authorized, have signed this Convention.

DONE in triplicate, at the cities of Washington, London and Moscow, this twenty-ninth day of March, one thousand nine hundred and seventy-two.

d. Agreement Concerning Cooperation on the Civil International Space Station

Done at Washington, January 29, 1998; Entered into force, March 27, 2001 [1]

AGREEMENT AMONG THE GOVERNMENT OF CANADA, GOVERNMENTS OF THE MEMBER STATES OF THE EUROPEAN SPACE AGENCY, THE GOVERNMENT OF JAPAN, THE GOVERNMENT OF THE RUSSIAN FEDERATION, AND THE GOVERNMENT OF THE UNITED STATES OF AMERICA CONCERNING COOPERATION ON THE CIVIL INTERNATIONAL SPACE STATION

The Government of Canada (hereinafter also "Canada"),

The Governments of the Kingdom of Belgium, the Kingdom of Denmark, the French Republic, the Federal Republic of Germany, the Italian Republic, the Kingdom of the Netherlands, the Kingdom of Norway, the Kingdom of Spain, the Kingdom of Sweden, the Swiss Confederation, and the United Kingdom of Great Britain and Northern Ireland, being Governments of Member States of the European Space Agency (hereinafter collectively "the European Governments" or "the European Partner"),

The Government of Japan (hereinafter also "Japan"),

The Government of the Russian Federation (hereinafter also "Russia"), and

The Government of the United States of America (hereinafter "the Government of the United States" or "the United States"),

RECALLING that in January 1984 the President of the United States directed the National Aeronautics and Space Administration (NASA) to develop and place into orbit a permanently manned Space Station and invited friends and allies of the United States to participate in its development and use and to share in the benefits thereof,

RECALLING the acceptance of the aforementioned invitation by the Prime Minister of Canada at the March 1985 Quebec Summit meeting with the President of the United States and the mutual confirmation of interest on cooperation at the March 1986 Washington, D.C. Summit meeting,

RECALLING the terms of the relevant Resolutions adopted on 31 January 1985 and 20 October 1995 by the European Space Agency (ESA) Council meeting at the ministerial level, and that, within the framework of ESA, and in accordance with its purpose as defined in Article II of the Convention establishing it, the Columbus programme and the European participation in the international Space Station development programme have been undertaken to develop and will develop elements of the civil international Space Station,

---

[1] For a list of states that are parties to the Convention, see Department of State publication, *Treaties in Force.*

RECALLING Japan's interest in the Space Station program manifested during the NASA Administrator's visits to Japan in 1984 and 1985 and Japan's participation in the U.S. space program through the First Materials Processing Test,

RECALLING ESA's and Canada's participation in the U.S. Space Transportation System through the European development of the first manned space laboratory, Spacelab, and the Canadian development of the Remote Manipulator System,

RECALLING the partnership created by the Agreement Among the Government of the United States of America, Governments of Member States of the European Space Agency, the Government of Japan, and the Government of Canada on Cooperation in the Detailed Design, Development, Operation, and Utilization of the Permanently Manned Civil Space Station (hereinafter "the 1988 Agreement"), done at Washington on 29 September 1988 and related Memoranda of Understanding between NASA and the Ministry of State for Science and Technology (MOSST) of Canada, NASA and ESA, and NASA and the Government of Japan,

RECOGNIZING that the 1988 Agreement entered into force on 30 January 1992 between the United States and Japan,

RECALLING that NASA, ESA, the Government of Japan and MOSST have been implementing cooperative activities to realize the partnership in the Space Station program in accordance with the 1988 Agreement and the related Memoranda of Understanding, and recognizing that upon its establishment on 1 March 1989, the Canadian Space Agency (CSA) assumed responsibility for the execution of the Canadian Space Station Program from MOSST,

CONVINCED that, in view of the Russian Federation's unique experience and accomplishments in the area of human space flight and long-duration missions, including the successful long-term operation of the Russian Mir Space Station, its participation in the partnership will considerably enhance the capabilities of the Space Station to the benefit of all the Partners,

RECALLING the invitation extended on 6 December 1993 by the Government of Canada, the European Governments, the Government of Japan, and the Government of the United States to the Government of the Russian Federation to become a Partner in the detailed design, development, operation and utilization of the Space Station within the framework established by the Space Station Agreements, and the positive response of the Government of the Russian Federation on 17 December 1993 to that invitation,

RECALLING the arrangements between the Chairman of the Government of the Russian Federation and the Vice President of the United States to promote cooperation on important human spaceflight activities, including the Russian-U.S. Mir-Shuttle program, to prepare for building the International Space Station,

RECALLING the Treaty on Principles Governing the Activities of States in the Exploration and Use of Outer Space, including the Moon and Other Celestial Bodies (hereinafter "the Outer Space Treaty"), which entered into force on 10 October 1967,

RECALLING the Agreement on the Rescue of Astronauts, the Return of Astronauts, and the Return of Objects Launched into Outer

Space (hereinafter “the Rescue Agreement”), which entered into force on 3 December 1968,

RECALLING the Convention on International Liability for Damage Caused by Space Objects (hereinafter “the Liability Convention”), which entered into force on 1 September 1972,

RECALLING the Convention on Registration of Objects Launched into Outer Space (hereinafter “the Registration Convention”), which entered into force on 15 September 1976,

CONVINCED that working together on the civil international Space Station will further expand cooperation through the establishment of a long-term and mutually beneficial relationship, and will further promote cooperation in the exploration and peaceful use of outer space,

RECOGNIZING that NASA and CSA, NASA and ESA, NASA and the Government of Japan, and NASA and the Russian Space Agency (RSA) have prepared Memoranda of Understanding (hereinafter “the MOUs”) in conjunction with their Governments’ negotiation of this Agreement, and that the MOUs provide detailed provisions in implementation of this Agreement,

RECOGNIZING, in light of the foregoing, that it is desirable to establish among the Government of Canada, the European Governments, the Government of Japan, the Government of the Russian Federation, and the Government of the United States a framework for the design, development, operation, and utilization of the Space Station,

HAVE AGREED AS FOLLOWS:

ARTICLE 1

OBJECT AND SCOPE

1. The object of this Agreement is to establish a long-term international cooperative framework among the Partners, on the basis of genuine partnership, for the detailed design, development, operation, and utilization of a permanently inhabited civil international Space Station for peaceful purposes, in accordance with international law. This civil international Space Station will enhance the scientific, technological, and commercial use of outer space. This Agreement specifically defines the civil international Space Station program and the nature of this partnership, including the respective rights and obligations of the Partners in this cooperation. This Agreement further provides for mechanisms and arrangements designed to ensure that its object is fulfilled.

2. The Partners will join their efforts, under the lead role of the United States for overall management and coordination, to create an integrated international Space Station. The United States and Russia, drawing on their extensive experience in human space flight, will produce elements which serve as the foundation for the international Space Station. The European Partner and Japan will produce elements that will significantly enhance the Space Station’s capabilities. Canada’s contribution will be an essential part

of the Space Station. This Agreement lists in the Annex the elements to be provided by the Partners to form the international Space Station.

3. The permanently inhabited civil international Space Station (hereinafter "the Space Station") will be a multi-use facility in low-earth orbit, with flight elements and Space Station-unique ground elements provided by all the Partners. By providing Space Station flight elements, each Partner acquires certain rights to use the Space Station and participates in its management in accordance with this Agreement, the MOUs, and implementing arrangements.

4. The Space Station is conceived as having an evolutionary character. The Partner States' rights and obligations regarding evolution shall be subject to specific provisions in accordance with Article 14.

ARTICLE 2

INTERNATIONAL RIGHTS AND OBLIGATIONS

1. The Space Station shall be developed, operated, and utilized in accordance with international law, including the Outer Space Treaty, the Rescue Agreement, the Liability Convention, and the Registration Convention.

2. Nothing in this Agreement shall be interpreted as:

(a) modifying the rights and obligations of the Partner States found in the treaties listed in paragraph 1 above, either toward each other or toward other States, except as otherwise provided in Article 16;

(b) affecting the rights and obligations of the Partner States when exploring or using outer space, whether individually or in cooperation with other States, in activities unrelated to the Space Station; or

(c) constituting a basis for asserting a claim to national appropriation over outer space or over any portion of outer space.

ARTICLE 3

DEFINITIONS

For the purposes of this Agreement, the following definitions shall apply:

(a) "this Agreement": the present Agreement, including the Annex;

(b) "the Partners" (or, where appropriate, "each Partner"): the Government of Canada; the European Governments listed in the Preamble which become parties to this Agreement, as well as any other European Government that may accede to this Agreement in accordance with Article 25(3), acting collectively as one Partner; the Government of Japan; the Government of the Russian Federation; and the Government of the United States;

(c) "Partner State": each Contracting Party for which this Agreement has entered into force, in accordance with Article 25.

ARTICLE 4

COOPERATING AGENCIES

1. The Partners agree that the Canadian Space Agency (hereinafter "CSA") for the Government of Canada, the European Space Agency (hereinafter "ESA") for the European Governments, the Russian Space Agency (hereinafter "RSA") for Russia, and the National Aeronautics and Space Administration (hereinafter "NASA") for the United States shall be the Cooperating Agencies responsible for implementing Space Station cooperation. The Government of Japan's Cooperating Agency designation for implementing Space Station cooperation shall be made in the Memorandum of Understanding between NASA and the Government of Japan referred to in paragraph 2 below.

2. The Cooperating Agencies shall implement Space Station cooperation in accordance with the relevant provisions of this Agreement, the respective Memoranda of Understanding (MOUs) between NASA and CSA, NASA and ESA, NASA and the Government of Japan, and NASA and RSA concerning cooperation on the civil international Space Station, and arrangements between or among NASA and the other Cooperating Agencies implementing the MOUs (implementing arrangements). The MOUs shall be subject to this Agreement, and the implementing arrangements shall be consistent with and subject to the MOUs.

3. Where a provision of an MOU sets forth rights or obligations accepted by a Cooperating Agency (or, in the case of Japan, the Government of Japan) not a party to that MOU, such provision may not be amended without the written consent of that Cooperating Agency (or, in the case of Japan, the Government of Japan).

ARTICLE 5

REGISTRATION; JURISDICTION AND CONTROL

1. In accordance with Article II of the Registration Convention, each Partner shall register as space objects the flight elements listed in the Annex which it provides, the European Partner having delegated this responsibility to ESA, acting in its name and on its behalf.

2. Pursuant to Article VIII of the Outer Space Treaty and Article II of the Registration Convention, each Partner shall retain jurisdiction and control over the elements it registers in accordance with paragraph 1 above and over personnel in or on the Space Station who are its nationals. The exercise of such jurisdiction and control shall be subject to any relevant provisions of this Agreement, the MOUs, and implementing arrangements, including relevant procedural mechanisms established therein.

ARTICLE 6

OWNERSHIP OF ELEMENTS AND EQUIPMENT

1. Canada, the European Partner, Russia, and the United States, through their respective Cooperating Agencies, and an entity designated by Japan at the time of the deposit of its instrument under

Article 25(2), shall own the elements listed in the Annex that they respectively provide, except as otherwise provided for in this Agreement. The Partners, acting through their Cooperating Agencies, shall notify each other regarding the ownership of any equipment in or on the Space Station.

2. The European Partner shall entrust ESA, acting in its name and on its behalf, with ownership over the elements it provides, as well as over any other equipment developed and funded under an ESA programme as a contribution to the Space Station, its operation or utilization.

3. The transfer of ownership of the elements listed in the Annex or of equipment in or on the Space Station shall not affect the rights and obligations of the Partners under this Agreement, the MOUs, or implementing arrangements.

4. Equipment in or on the Space Station shall not be owned by, and ownership of elements listed in the Annex shall not be transferred to, any non-Partner or private entity under the jurisdiction of a non-Partner without the prior concurrence of the other Partners. Any transfer of ownership of any element listed in the Annex shall require prior notification of the other Partners.

5. The ownership of equipment or material provided by a user shall not be affected by the mere presence of such equipment or material in or on the Space Station.

6. The ownership or registration of elements or the ownership of equipment shall in no way be deemed to be an indication of ownership of material or data resulting from the conduct of activities in or on the Space Station.

7. The exercise of ownership of elements and equipment shall be subject to any relevant provisions of this Agreement, the MOUs, and implementing arrangements, including relevant procedural mechanisms established therein.

Article 7

Management

1. Management of the Space Station will be established on a multilateral basis and the Partners, acting through their Cooperating Agencies, will participate and discharge responsibilities in management bodies established in accordance with the MOUs and implementing arrangements as provided below. These management bodies shall plan and coordinate activities affecting the design and development of the Space Station and its safe, efficient, and effective operation and utilization, as provided in this Agreement and the MOUs. In these management bodies, decision-making by consensus shall be the goal. Mechanisms for decision-making within these management bodies where it is not possible for the Cooperating Agencies to reach consensus are specified in the MOUs. Decision-making responsibilities which the Partners and their Cooperating Agencies have with respect to the elements they provide are specified in this Agreement and the MOUs.

2. The United States, acting through NASA, and in accordance with the MOUs and implementing arrangements, shall be responsible for management of its own program, including its utilization

activities. The United States, acting through NASA, and in accordance with the MOUs and implementing arrangements, shall also be responsible for: overall program management and coordination of the Space Station, except as otherwise provided in this Article and in the MOUs; overall system engineering and integration; establishment of overall safety requirements and plans; and overall planning for and coordination of the execution of the overall integrated operation of the Space Station.

3. Canada, the European Partner, Japan and Russia, acting through their Cooperating Agencies, and in accordance with the MOUs and implementing arrangements, shall each be responsible for: management of their own programs, including their utilization activities; system engineering and integration of the elements they provide; development and implementation of detailed safety requirements and plans for the elements they provide; and, consistent with paragraph 2 above, supporting the United States in the performance of its overall responsibilities, including participating in planning for and coordination of the execution of the integrated operation of the Space Station.

4. To the extent that a design and development matter concerns only a Space Station element provided by Canada, the European Partner, Japan, or Russia and is not covered in the agreed program documentation provided for in the MOUs, that Partner, acting through its Cooperating Agency, may make decisions related to that element.

ARTICLE 8

DETAILED DESIGN AND DEVELOPMENT

In accordance with Article 7 and other relevant provisions of this Agreement, and in accordance with the MOUs and implementing arrangements, each Partner, acting through its Cooperating Agency, shall design and develop the elements which it provides, including Space Station-unique ground elements adequate to support the continuing operation and full international utilization of the flight elements, and shall interact with the other Partners, through their Cooperating Agencies, to reach solutions on design and development of their respective elements.

ARTICLE 9

UTILIZATION

1. Utilization rights are derived from Partner provision of user elements, infrastructure elements, or both. Any Partner that provides Space Station user elements shall retain use of those elements, except as otherwise provided in this paragraph. Partners which provide resources to operate and use the Space Station, which are derived from their Space Station infrastructure elements, shall receive in exchange a fixed share of the use of certain user elements. Partners' specific allocations of Space Station user elements and of resources derived from Space Station infrastructure are set forth in the MOUs and implementing arrangements.

2. The Partners shall have the right to barter or sell any portion of their respective allocations. The terms and conditions of any barter or sale shall be determined on a case-by-case basis by the parties to the transaction.

3. Each Partner may use and select users for its allocations for any purpose consistent with the object of this Agreement and provisions set forth in the MOUs and implementing arrangements, except that:

(a) any proposed use of a user element by a non-Partner or private entity under the jurisdiction of a non-Partner shall require the prior notification to and timely consensus among all Partners through their Cooperating Agencies; and

(b) the Partner providing an element shall determine whether a contemplated use of that element is for peaceful purposes, except that this subparagraph shall not be invoked to prevent any Partner from using resources derived from the Space Station infrastructure.

4. In its use of the Space Station, each Partner, through its Cooperating Agency, shall seek through the mechanisms established in the MOUs to avoid causing serious adverse effects on the use of the Space Station by the other Partners.

5. Each Partner shall assure access to and use of its Space Station elements to the other Partners in accordance with their respective allocations.

6. For purposes of this Article, an ESA Member State shall not be considered a "non-Partner".

Article 10

Operation

The Partners, acting through their Cooperating Agencies, shall have responsibilities in the operation of the elements they respectively provide, in accordance with Article 7 and other relevant provisions of this Agreement, and in accordance with the MOUs and implementing arrangements. The Partners, acting through their Cooperating Agencies, shall develop and implement procedures for operating the Space Station in a manner that is safe, efficient, and effective for Space Station users and operators, in accordance with the MOUs and implementing arrangements. Further, each Partner, acting through its Cooperating Agency, shall be responsible for sustaining the functional performance of the elements it provides.

Article 11

Crew

1. Each Partner has the right to provide qualified personnel to serve on an equitable basis as Space Station crew members. Selections and decisions regarding the flight assignments of a Partner's crew members shall be made in accordance with procedures provided in the MOUs and implementing arrangements.

2. The Code of Conduct for the Space Station crew will be developed and approved by all the Partners in accordance with the individual Partner's internal procedures, and in accordance with the

MOUs. A Partner must have approved the Code of Conduct before it provides Space Station crew. Each Partner, in exercising its right to provide crew, shall ensure that its crew members observe the Code of Conduct.

Article 12

Transportation

1. Each of the Partners shall have the right of access to the Space Station using its respective government and private sector space transportation systems, if they are compatible with the Space Station. The United States, Russia, the European Partner, and Japan, through their respective Cooperating Agencies, shall make available launch and return transportation services for the Space Station (using such space transportation systems as the U.S. Space Shuttle, the Russian Proton and Soyuz, the European Ariane-5, and the Japanese H–II). Initially, the U.S. and Russian space transportation systems will be used to provide launch and return transportation services for the Space Station and, in addition, the other space transportation systems will be used as those systems become available. Access and launch and return transportation services shall be in accordance with the provisions of the relevant MOUs and implementing arrangements.

2. Those Partners providing launch and return transportation services to other Partners and their respective users on a reimbursable or other basis shall provide such services consistent with conditions specified in the relevant MOUs and implementing arrangements. Those Partners providing launch and return transportation services on a reimbursable basis shall provide such services to another Partner or the users of that Partner, in comparable circumstances, on the same basis they provide such services to any other Partner or the users of such other Partner. Partners shall use their best efforts to accommodate proposed requirements and flight schedules of the other Partners.

3. The United States, through NASA, working with the other Partners' Cooperating Agencies in management bodies, shall plan and coordinate launch and return transportation services for the Space Station in accordance with the integrated traffic planning process, as provided in the MOUs and implementing arrangements.

4. Each Partner shall respect the proprietary rights in and the confidentiality of appropriately marked data and goods to be transported on its space transportation system.

Article 13

Communications

1. The United States and Russia, through their Cooperating Agencies, shall provide the two primary data relay satellite system space and ground communications networks for command, control, and operations of Space Station elements and payloads, and other Space Station communication purposes. Other Partners may provide data relay satellite system space and ground communication networks, if they are compatible with the Space Station and with

Space Station use of the two primary networks. The provision of Space Station communications shall be in accordance with provisions in the relevant MOUs and implementing arrangements.

2. On a reimbursable basis, the Cooperating Agencies shall use their best efforts to accommodate, with their respective communication systems, specific Space Station-related requirements of one another, consistent with conditions specified in the relevant MOUs and implementing arrangements.

3. The United States, through NASA, working with the other Partners' Cooperating Agencies in management bodies, shall plan and coordinate space and ground communications services for the Space Station in accordance with relevant program documentation, as provided in the MOUs and implementing arrangements.

4. Measures to ensure the confidentiality of utilization data passing through the Space Station Information System and other communication systems being used in connection with the Space Station may be implemented, as provided in the MOUs. Each Partner shall respect the proprietary rights in, and the confidentiality of, the utilization data passing through its communication systems, including its ground network and the communication systems of its contractors, when providing communication services to another Partner.

ARTICLE 14

EVOLUTION

1. The Partners intend that the Space Station shall evolve through the addition of capability and shall strive to maximize the likelihood that such evolution will be effected through contributions from all the Partners. To this end, it shall be the object of each Partner to provide, where appropriate, the opportunity to the other Partners to cooperate in its proposals for additions of evolutionary capability. The Space Station together with its additions of evolutionary capability shall remain a civil station, and its operation and utilization shall be for peaceful purposes, in accordance with international law.

2. This Agreement sets forth rights and obligations concerning only the elements listed in the Annex, except that this Article and Article 16 shall apply to any additions of evolutionary capability. This Agreement does not commit any Partner State to participate in, or otherwise grant any Partner rights in, the addition of evolutionary capability.

3. Procedures for the coordination of the Partners' respective evolution studies and for the review of specific proposals for the addition of evolutionary capability are provided in the MOUs.

4. Cooperation between or among Partners regarding the sharing of addition(s) of evolutionary capability shall require, following the coordination and review provided for in paragraph 3 above, either the amendment of this Agreement, or a separate agreement to which the United States, to ensure that any addition is consistent with the overall program, and any other Partner providing a Space Station element or space transportation system on which there is an operational or technical impact, shall be parties.

5. Following the coordination and review provided for in paragraph 3 above, the addition of evolutionary capability by one Partner shall require prior notification of the other Partners, and an agreement with the United States to ensure that any addition is consistent with the overall program, and with any other Partner providing a Space Station element or space transportation system on which there is an operational or technical impact.

6. A Partner which may be affected by the addition of evolutionary capability under paragraph 4 or 5 above may request consultations with the other Partners in accordance with Article 23.

7. The addition of evolutionary capability shall in no event modify the rights and obligations of any Partner State under this Agreement and the MOUs concerning the elements listed in the Annex, unless the affected Partner State otherwise agrees.

Article 15

Funding

1. Each Partner shall bear the costs of fulfilling its respective responsibilities under this Agreement, including sharing on an equitable basis the agreed common system operations costs or activities attributed to the operation of the Space Station as a whole, as provided in the MOUs and implementing arrangements.

2. Financial obligations of each Partner pursuant to this Agreement are subject to its funding procedures and the availability of appropriated funds. Recognizing the importance of Space Station cooperation, each Partner undertakes to make its best efforts to obtain approval for funds to meet those obligations, consistent with its respective funding procedures.

3. In the event that funding problems arise that may affect a Partner's ability to fulfill its responsibilities in Space Station cooperation, that Partner, acting through its Cooperating Agency, shall notify and consult with the other Cooperating Agencies. If necessary, the Partners may also consult.

4. The Partners shall seek to minimize operations costs for the Space Station. In particular, the Partners, through their Cooperating Agencies, in accordance with the provisions of the MOUs, shall develop procedures intended to contain the common system operations costs and activities within approved estimated levels.

5. The Partners shall also seek to minimize the exchange of funds in the implementation of Space Station cooperation, including through the performance of specific operations activities as provided in the MOUs and implementing arrangements or, if the concerned Partners agree, through the use of barter.

Article 16

Cross-Waiver of Liability

1. The objective of this Article is to establish a cross-waiver of liability by the Partner States and related entities in the interest of encouraging participation in the exploration, exploitation, and use of outer space through the Space Station. This cross-waiver of liability shall be broadly construed to achieve this objective.

2. For the purposes of this Article:

(a) A "Partner State" includes its Cooperating Agency. It also includes any entity specified in the MOU between NASA and the Government of Japan to assist the Government of Japan's Cooperating Agency in the implementation of that MOU.

(b) The term "related entity" means:

(1) a contractor or subcontractor of a Partner State at any tier;

(2) a user or customer of a Partner State at any tier; or

(3) a contractor or subcontractor of a user or customer of a Partner State at any tier.

This subparagraph may also apply to a State, or an agency or institution of a State, having the same relationship to a Partner State as described in subparagraphs 2(b)(1) through 2(b)(3) above or otherwise engaged in the implementation of Protected Space Operations as defined in subparagraph 2 (f) below. "Contractors" and "subcontractors" include suppliers of any kind.

(c) The term "damage" means:

(1) bodily injury to, or other impairment of health of, or death of, any person;

(2) damage to, loss of, or loss of use of any property;

(3) loss of revenue or profits; or

(4) other direct, indirect or consequential damage.

(d) The term "launch vehicle" means an object (or any part thereof) intended for launch, launched from Earth, or returning to Earth which carries payloads or persons, or both.

(e) The term "payload" means all property to be flown or used on or in a launch vehicle or the Space Station.

(f) The term "Protected Space Operations" means all launch vehicle activities, Space Station activities, and payload activities on Earth, in outer space, or in transit between Earth and outer space in implementation of this Agreement, the MOUs, and implementing arrangements. It includes, but is not limited to:

(1) research, design, development, test, manufacture, assembly, integration, operation, or use of launch or transfer vehicles, the Space Station, or a payload, as well as related support equipment and facilities and services; and

(2) all activities related to ground support, test, training, simulation, or guidance and control equipment and related facilities or services.

"Protected Space Operations" also includes all activities related to evolution of the Space Station, as provided for in Article 14. "Protected Space Operations" excludes activities on Earth which are conducted on return from the Space Station to develop further a payload's product or process for use other than for Space Station related activities in implementation of this Agreement.

3. (a) Each Partner State agrees to a cross-waiver of liability pursuant to which each Partner State waives all claims against any of the entities or persons listed in subparagraphs 3(a)(1) through 3(a)(3) below based on damage arising out of Protected Space Operations. This cross-waiver shall apply only if the person, entity, or

property causing the damage is involved in Protected Space Operations and the person, entity, or property damaged is damaged by virtue of its involvement in Protected Space Operations. The cross-waiver shall apply to any claims for damage, whatever the legal basis for such claims against:

(1) another Partner State;

(2) a related entity of another Partner State;

(3) the employees of any of the entities identified in subparagraphs 3(a)(1) and 3(a)(2) above.

(b) In addition, each Partner State shall, by contract or otherwise, extend the cross-waiver of liability as set forth in subparagraph 3(a) above to its related entities by requiring them to:

(1) waive all claims against the entities or persons identified in subparagraphs 3(a)(1) through 3(a)(3) above; and

(2) require that their related entities waive all claims against the entities or persons identified in subparagraphs 3(a)(1) through 3(a)(3) above.

(c) For avoidance of doubt, this cross-waiver of liability includes a cross-waiver of liability arising from the Liability Convention where the person, entity, or property causing the damage is involved in Protected Space Operations and the person, entity, or property damaged is damaged by virtue of its involvement in Protected Space Operations.

(d) Notwithstanding the other provisions of this Article, this cross-waiver of liability shall not be applicable to:

(1) claims between a Partner State and its related entity or between its own related entities;

(2) claims made by a natural person, his/her estate, survivors or subrogees (except when a subrogee is a Partner State) for bodily injury to, or other impairment of health of, or death of such natural person;

(3) claims for damage caused by willful misconduct;

(4) intellectual property claims;

(5) claims for damage resulting from a failure of a Partner State to extend the cross-waiver of liability to its related entities, pursuant to subparagraph 3(b) above.

(e) With respect to subparagraph 3(d)(2) above, in the event that a subrogated claim of the Government of Japan is not based upon government employee accident compensation law, the Government of Japan shall fulfill its obligation to waive such subrogated claim by ensuring that any assisting entity specified pursuant to subparagraph 2(a) above indemnifies, in a manner consistent with Article 15(2) and in accordance with applicable laws and regulations of Japan, any entity or person identified in subparagraphs 3(a)(1) through 3(a)(3) above against liability arising from such subrogated claim by the Government of Japan. Nothing in this Article shall preclude the Government of Japan from waiving the foregoing subrogated claims.

(f) Nothing in this Article shall be construed to create the basis for a claim or suit where none would otherwise exist.

Article 17

Liability Convention

1. Except as otherwise provided in Article 16, the Partner States, as well as ESA, shall remain liable in accordance with the Liability Convention.

2. In the event of a claim arising out of the Liability Convention, the Partners (and ESA, if appropriate) shall consult promptly on any potential liability, on any apportionment of such liability, and on the defense of such claim.

3. Regarding the provision of launch and return services provided for in Article 12(2), the Partners concerned (and ESA, if appropriate) may conclude separate agreements regarding the apportionment of any potential joint and several liability arising out of the Liability Convention.

Article 18

Customs and Immigration

1. Each Partner State shall facilitate the movement of persons and goods necessary to implement this Agreement into and out of its territory, subject to its laws and regulations.

2. Subject to its laws and regulations, each Partner State shall facilitate provision of the appropriate entry and residence documentation for nationals and families of nationals of another Partner State who enter or exit or reside within the territory of the first Partner State in order to carry out functions necessary for the implementation of this Agreement.

3. Each Partner State shall grant permission for duty-free importation and exportation to and from its territory of goods and software which are necessary for implementation of this Agreement and shall ensure their exemption from any other taxes and duties collected by the customs authorities. This paragraph shall be implemented without regard to the country of origin of such necessary goods and software.

Article 19

Exchange of Data and Goods

1. Except as otherwise provided in this paragraph, each Partner, acting through its Cooperating Agency shall transfer all technical data and goods considered to be necessary (by both parties to any transfer) to fulfill the responsibilities of that Partner's Cooperating Agency under the relevant MOUs and implementing arrangements. Each Partner undertakes to handle expeditiously any request for technical data or goods presented by the Cooperating Agency of another Partner for the purposes of Space Station cooperation. This Article shall not require a Partner State to transfer any technical data and goods in contravention of its national laws or regulations.

2. The Partners shall make their best efforts to handle expeditiously requests for authorization of transfers of technical data and goods by persons or entities other than the Partners or their Cooperating Agencies (for example, company-to-company exchanges

which are likely to develop), and they shall encourage and facilitate such transfers in connection with the Space Station cooperation under this Agreement. Otherwise, such transfers are not covered by the terms and conditions of this Article. National laws and regulations shall apply to such transfers.

3. The Partners agree that transfers of technical data and goods under this Agreement shall be subject to the restrictions set forth in this paragraph. The transfer of technical data for the purposes of discharging the Partners' responsibilities with regard to interface, integration and safety shall normally be made without the restrictions set forth in this paragraph. If detailed design, manufacturing, and processing data and associated software is necessary for interface, integration or safety purposes, the transfer shall be made in accordance with paragraph 1 above, but the data and associated software may be appropriately marked as set out below. Technical data and goods not covered by the restrictions set forth in this paragraph shall be transferred without restriction, except as otherwise restricted by national laws or regulations.

(a) The furnishing Cooperating Agency shall mark with a notice, or otherwise specifically identify, the technical data or goods that are to be protected for export control purposes. Such a notice or identification shall indicate any specific conditions regarding how such technical data or goods may be used by the receiving Cooperating Agency and its contractors and subcontractors, including (1) that such technical data or goods shall be used only for the purposes of fulfilling the receiving Cooperating Agency's responsibilities under this Agreement and the relevant MOUs, and (2) that such technical data or goods shall not be used by persons or entities other than the receiving Cooperating Agency, its contractors or subcontractors, or for any other purposes, without the prior written permission of the furnishing Partner State, acting through its Cooperating Agency.

(b) The furnishing Cooperating Agency shall mark with a notice the technical data that are to be protected for proprietary rights purposes. Such notice shall indicate any specific conditions regarding how such technical data may be used by the receiving Cooperating Agency and its contractors and subcontractors, including (1) that such technical data shall be used, duplicated, or disclosed only for the purposes of fulfilling the receiving Cooperating Agency's responsibilities under this Agreement and the relevant MOUs, and (2) that such technical data shall not be used by persons or entities other than the receiving Cooperating Agency, its contractors or subcontractors, or for any other purposes, without the prior written permission of the furnishing Partner State, acting through its Cooperating Agency.

(c) In the event that any technical data or goods transferred under this Agreement are classified, the furnishing Cooperating Agency shall mark with a notice, or otherwise specifically identify, such technical data or goods. The requested Partner State may require that any such transfer shall be pursuant to a security of information agreement or arrangement which sets forth the conditions for transferring and protecting such technical data or goods. A transfer need not be conducted if the receiving Partner State does not provide for the protection of the secrecy of patent applications containing information that is classified or otherwise held in secrecy for national security purposes.

No classified technical data or goods shall be transferred under this Agreement unless both parties agree to the transfer.

4. Each Partner State shall take all necessary steps to ensure that technical data or goods received by it under subparagraphs 3(a), 3(b), or 3(c) above shall be treated by the receiving Partner State, its Cooperating Agency, and other persons and entities (including contractors and subcontractors) to which the technical data or goods are subsequently transferred in accordance with the terms of the notice or identification. Each Partner State and Cooperating Agency shall take all reasonably necessary steps, including ensuring appropriate contractual conditions in their contracts and subcontracts, to prevent unauthorized use, disclosure, or retransfer of, or unauthorized access to, such technical data or goods. In the case of technical data or goods received under subparagraph 3(c) above, the receiving Partner State or Cooperating Agency shall accord such technical data or goods a level of protection at least equivalent to the level of protection accorded by the furnishing Partner State or Cooperating Agency.

5. It is not the intent of the Partners to grant, through this Agreement or the relevant MOUs, any rights to a recipient beyond the right to use, disclose, or retransfer received technical data or goods consistent with conditions imposed under this Article.

6. Withdrawal from this Agreement by a Partner State shall not affect rights or obligations regarding the protection of technical data and goods transferred under this Agreement prior to such withdrawal, unless otherwise agreed in a withdrawal agreement pursuant to Article 28.

7. For the purposes of this Article, any transfer of technical data and goods by a Cooperating Agency to ESA shall be deemed to be destined to ESA, to all of the European Partner States, and to ESA's designated Space Station contractors and subcontractors, unless otherwise specifically provided for at the time of transfer.

8. The Partners, through their Cooperating Agencies, will establish guidelines for security of information.

Article 20

Treatment of Data and Goods in Transit

Recognizing the importance of the continuing operation and full international utilization of the Space Station, each Partner State shall, to the extent its applicable laws and regulations permit, allow the expeditious transit of data and goods of the other Partners, their Cooperating Agencies, and their users. This Article shall only apply to data and goods transiting to and from the Space Station, including but not limited to transit between its national border and a launch or landing site within its territory, and between a launch or landing site and the Space Station.

ARTICLE 21

INTELLECTUAL PROPERTY

1. For the purposes of this Agreement, "intellectual property" is understood to have the meaning of Article 2 of the Convention Establishing the World Intellectual Property Organization, done at Stockholm on 14 July 1967.

2. Subject to the provisions of this Article, for purposes of intellectual property law, an activity occurring in or on a Space Station flight element shall be deemed to have occurred only in the territory of the Partner State of that element's registry, except that for ESA-registered elements any European Partner State may deem the activity to have occurred within its territory. For avoidance of doubt, participation by a Partner State, its Cooperating Agency, or its related entities in an activity occurring in or on any other Partner's Space Station flight element shall not in and of itself alter or affect the jurisdiction over such activity provided for in the previous sentence.

3. In respect of an invention made in or on any Space Station flight element by a person who is not its national or resident, a Partner State shall not apply its laws concerning secrecy of inventions so as to prevent the filing of a patent application (for example, by imposing a delay or requiring prior authorization) in any other Partner State that provides for the protection of the secrecy of patent applications containing information that is classified or otherwise protected for national security purposes. This provision does not prejudice (a) the right of any Partner State in which a patent application is first filed to control the secrecy of such patent application or restrict its further filing; or (b) the right of any other Partner State in which an application is subsequently filed to restrict, pursuant to any international obligation, the dissemination of an application.

4. Where a person or entity owns intellectual property which is protected in more than one European Partner State, that person or entity may not recover in more than one such State for the same act of infringement of the same rights in such intellectual property which occurs in or on an ESA-registered element. Where the same act of infringement in or on an ESA-registered element gives rise to actions by different intellectual property owners by virtue of more than one European Partner State's deeming the activity to have occurred in its territory, a court may grant a temporary stay of proceeding in a later-filed action pending the outcome of an earlier-filed action. Where more than one action is brought, satisfaction of a judgment rendered for damages in any of the actions shall bar further recovery of damages in any pending or future action for infringement based upon the same act of infringement.

5. With respect to an activity occurring in or on an ESA-registered element, no European Partner State shall refuse to recognize a license for the exercise of any intellectual property right if that license is enforceable under the laws of any European Partner State, and compliance with the provisions of such license shall also bar recovery for infringement in any European Partner State.

6. The temporary presence in the territory of a Partner State of any articles, including the components of a flight element, in transit between any place on Earth and any flight element of the Space Station registered by another Partner State or ESA shall not in itself form the basis for any proceedings in the first Partner State for patent infringement.

ARTICLE 22

CRIMINAL JURISDICTION

In view of the unique and unprecedented nature of this particular international cooperation in space:

1. Canada, the European Partner States, Japan, Russia, and the United States may exercise criminal jurisdiction over personnel in or on any flight element who are their respective nationals.

2. In a case involving misconduct on orbit that: (a) affects the life or safety of a national of another Partner State or (b) occurs in or on or causes damage to the flight element of another Partner State, the Partner State whose national is the alleged perpetrator shall, at the request of any affected Partner State, consult with such State concerning their respective prosecutorial interests. An affected Partner State may, following such consultation, exercise criminal jurisdiction over the alleged perpetrator provided that, within 90 days of the date of such consultation or within such other period as may be mutually agreed, the Partner State whose national is the alleged perpetrator either:

   (1) concurs in such exercise of criminal jurisdiction, or

   (2) fails to provide assurances that it will submit the case to its competent authorities for the purpose of prosecution.

3. If a Partner State which makes extradition conditional on the existence of a treaty receives a request for extradition from another Partner State with which it has no extradition treaty, it may at its option consider this Agreement as the legal basis for extradition in respect of the alleged misconduct on orbit. Extradition shall be subject to the procedural provisions and the other conditions of the law of the requested Partner State.

4. Each Partner State shall, subject to its national laws and regulations, afford the other Partners assistance in connection with alleged misconduct on orbit.

5. This Article is not intended to limit the authorities and procedures for the maintenance of order and the conduct of crew activities in or on the Space Station which shall be established in the Code of Conduct pursuant to Article 11, and the Code of Conduct is not intended to limit the application of this Article.

Article 23

Consultations

1. The Partners, acting through their Cooperating Agencies, may consult with each other on any matter arising out of Space Station cooperation. The Partners shall exert their best efforts to settle such matters through consultation between or among their Cooperating Agencies in accordance with procedures provided in the MOUs.

2. Any Partner may request that government-level consultations be held with another Partner on any matter arising out of Space Station cooperation. The requested Partner shall accede to such request promptly. If the requesting Partner notifies the United States that the subject of such consultations is appropriate for consideration by all the Partners, the United States shall convene multilateral consultations at the earliest practicable time, to which it shall invite all the Partners.

3. Any Partner which intends to proceed with significant flight element design changes which may have an impact on the other Partners shall notify the other Partners accordingly at the earliest opportunity. A Partner so notified may request that the matter be submitted to consultations in accordance with paragraphs 1 and 2 above.

4. If an issue not resolved through consultations still needs to be resolved, the concerned Partners may submit that issue to an agreed form of dispute resolution such as conciliation, mediation, or arbitration.

Article 24

Space Station Cooperation Review

In view of the long-term, complex, and evolving character of their cooperation under this Agreement, the Partners shall keep each other informed of developments which might affect this cooperation. Beginning in 1999, and every three years thereafter, the Partners shall meet to deal with matters involved in their cooperation and to review and promote Space Station cooperation.

Article 25

Entry into Force

1. This Agreement shall remain open for signature by the States listed in the Preamble of this Agreement.

2. This Agreement is subject to ratification, acceptance, approval, or accession. Ratification, acceptance, approval, or accession shall be effected by each State in accordance with its constitutional processes. Instruments of ratification, acceptance, approval, or accession shall be deposited with the Government of the United States, hereby designated as the Depositary.

3. (a) This Agreement shall enter into force on the date on which the last instrument of ratification, acceptance, or approval of

Japan, Russia and the United States has been deposited. The Depositary shall notify all signatory States of this Agreement's entry into force.

(b) This Agreement shall not enter into force for a European Partner State before it enters into force for the European Partner. It shall enter into force for the European Partner after the Depositary receives instruments of ratification, acceptance, approval, or accession from at least four European signatory or acceding States, and, in addition, a formal notification by the Chairman of the ESA Council.

(c) Following entry into force of this Agreement for the European Partner, it shall enter into force for any European State listed in the Preamble that has not deposited its instrument of ratification, acceptance or approval upon deposit of such instrument. Any ESA Member State not listed in the Preamble may accede to this Agreement by depositing its instrument of accession with the Depositary.

4. Upon entry into force of this Agreement, the 1988 Agreement shall cease to be in force.

5. If this Agreement has not entered into force for a Partner within a period of two years after its signature, the United States may convene a conference of the signatories to this Agreement to consider what steps, including any modifications to this Agreement, are necessary to take account of that circumstance.

Article 26

Operative Effect as Between Certain Parties

Notwithstanding Article 25 (3)(a) above, this Agreement shall become operative as between the United States and Russia on the date they have expressed their consent to be bound by depositing their instruments of ratification, acceptance or approval. The Depositary shall notify all signatory States if this Agreement becomes operative between the United States and Russia pursuant to this Article.

Article 27

Amendments

This Agreement, including its Annex, may be amended by written agreement of the Governments of the Partner States for which this Agreement has entered into force. Amendments to this Agreement, except for those made exclusively to the Annex, shall be subject to ratification, acceptance, approval, or accession by those States in accordance with their respective constitutional processes. Amendments made exclusively to the Annex shall require only a written agreement of the Governments of the Partner States for which this Agreement has entered into force.

Article 28

Withdrawal

1. Any Partner State may withdraw from this Agreement at any time by giving to the Depositary at least one year's prior written

notice. Withdrawal by a European Partner State shall not affect the rights and obligations of the European Partner under this Agreement.

2. If a Partner gives notice of withdrawal from this Agreement, with a view toward ensuring the continuation of the overall program, the Partners shall endeavor to reach agreement concerning the terms and conditions of that Partner's withdrawal before the effective date of withdrawal.

3. (a) Because Canada's contribution is an essential part of the Space Station, upon its withdrawal, Canada shall ensure the effective use and operation by the United States of the Canadian elements listed in the Annex. To this end, Canada shall expeditiously provide hardware, drawings, documentation, software, spares, tooling, special test equipment, and/or any other necessary items requested by the United States.

(b) Upon Canada's notice of withdrawal for any reason, the United States and Canada shall expeditiously negotiate a withdrawal agreement. Assuming that such agreement provides for the transfer to the United States of those elements required for the continuation of the overall program, it shall also provide for the United States to give Canada adequate compensation for such transfer.

4. If a Partner gives notice of withdrawal from this Agreement, its Cooperating Agency shall be deemed to have withdrawn from its corresponding MOU with NASA, effective from the same date as its withdrawal from this Agreement.

5. Withdrawal by any Partner State shall not affect that Partner State's continuing rights and obligations under Articles 16, 17, and 19, unless otherwise agreed in a withdrawal agreement pursuant to paragraph 2 or 3 above.

IN WITNESS WHEREOF the undersigned, being duly authorized thereto by their respective Governments, have signed this Agreement.

DONE at Washington, this 29th day of January, 1998. The texts of this Agreement in the English, French, German, Italian, Japanese, and Russian languages shall be equally authentic. A single original text in each language shall be deposited in the archives of the Government of the United States. The Depositary shall transmit certified copies to all signatory States. Upon entry into force of this Agreement, the Depositary shall register it pursuant to Article 102 of the Charter of the United Nations.

ANNEX

SPACE STATION ELEMENTS TO BE PROVIDED BY THE PARTNERS

The Space Station elements to be provided by the Partners are summarized below and are further elaborated in the MOUs:

1. The Government of Canada, through CSA, shall provide:
   —as a Space Station infrastructure element, the Mobile Servicing Center (MSC);
   —as an additional flight element, the Special Purpose Dexterous Manipulator; and

—in addition to the flight elements above, Space Station-unique ground elements.

2. The European Governments, through ESA, shall provide:

—as a user element, the European pressurized laboratory (including basic functional outfitting);

—other flight elements to supply and to reboost the Space Station; and

—in addition to the flight elements above, Space Station-unique ground elements.

3. The Government of Japan shall provide:

—as a user element, the Japanese Experiment Module (including basic functional outfitting, as well as the Exposed Facility and the Experiment Logistics Modules);

—other flight elements to supply the Space Station; and

—in addition to the flight elements above, Space Station-unique ground elements.

4. The Government of Russia, through RSA, shall provide:

—Space Station infrastructure elements, including service and other modules;

—as user elements, research modules (including basic functional outfitting) and attached payload accommodation equipment;

—other flight elements to supply and to reboost the Space Station; and

—in addition to the flight elements above, Space Station-unique ground elements.

5. The Government of the United States, through NASA, shall provide:

—Space Station infrastructure elements, including a habitation module;

—as user elements, laboratory modules (including basic functional outfitting), and attached payload accommodation equipment;

—other flight elements to supply the Space Station; and

—in addition to the flight elements above, Space Station-unique ground elements.

e. U.S.–U.S.S.R. Agreement Concerning Cooperation in the Exploration and Use of Outer Space for Peaceful Purposes

Done at Moscow June 17, 1992; Entered into force June 17, 1992[1]

AGREEMENT BETWEEN THE UNITED STATES OF AMERICA AND THE UNION OF SOVIET SOCIALIST REPUBLICS CONCERNING COOPERATION IN THE EXPLORATION AND USE OF OUTER SPACE FOR PEACEFUL PURPOSES

The United States of America and the Union of Soviet Socialist Republics;

CONSIDERING the role which the USA and the USSR play in the exploration and use of outer space for peaceful purposes;

STRIVING for a further expansion of cooperation between the USA and the USSR in the exploration and use of outer space for peaceful purposes;

NOTING the positive cooperation which the parties have already experienced in this area;

DESIRING to make the results of scientific research gained from the exploration and use of outer space for peaceful purposes available for the benefit of the peoples of the two countries and of all peoples of the world;

TAKING into consideration the provisions of the Treaty on principles governing the activities of States in the exploration and use of outer space, including the moon and other celestial bodies,2 as well as the Agreement on the rescue of astronauts, the return of astronauts, and the return of objects launched into outer space;

IN ACCORDANCE WITH the Agreement between the United States of America and the Union of Soviet Socialist Republics on exchanges and cooperation in scientific, technical, educational, cultural, and other fields, signed April 11, 1972, and in order to develop further the principles of mutually beneficial cooperation between the two countries;

HAVE AGREED AS FOLLOWS:

ARTICLE 1

The Parties will develop cooperation in the fields of space meteorology; study of the natural environment; exploration of near earth space, the moon and the planets; and space biology and medicine; and, in particular, will cooperate to take all appropriate measures to encourage and achieve the fulfilment of the Summary of

[1] TIAS 12457. The Agreement has been extended through amendment, the most recent of which was July 3 and August 9, 2002.

Results of Discussion on Space Cooperation Between the US National Aeronautics and Space Administration and the Academy of Sciences of the USSR dated January 21, 1971.

ARTICLE 2

The Parties will carry out such cooperation by means of mutual exchanges of scientific information and delegations, through meetings of scientists and specialists of both countries, and also in such other ways as may be mutually agreed. Joint working groups may be created for the development and implementation of appropriate programs of cooperation.

ARTICLE 3

The Parties have agreed to carry out projects for developing compatible rendezvous and docking systems of United States and Soviet manned spacecraft and stations in order to enhance the safety of manned flight in space and to provide the opportunity for conducting joint scientific experiments in the future. It is planned that the first experimental flight to test these systems be conducted during 1975, envisaging the docking of a United States Apollo-type spacecraft and a Soviet Soyuz-type spacecraft with visits of astronauts in each other's spacecraft. The implementation of these projects will be carried out on the basis of principles and procedures which will be developed in accordance with the summary of results of the meeting between representatives of the US National Aeronautics and Space Administration and the USSR Academy of Sciences on the question of developing compatible systems for rendezvous and docking of manned spacecraft and space stations of the USA and the USSR dated April 6, 1972.

ARTICLE 4

The Parties will encourage international efforts to resolve problems of international law in the exploration and use of outer space for peaceful purposes with the aim of strengthening the legal order in space and further developing international space law and will cooperate in this field.

ARTICLE 5

The Parties may by mutual agreement determine other areas of cooperation in the exploration and use of outer space for peaceful purposes.

ARTICLE 6

This Agreement shall enter into force upon signature and shall remain in force for five years. It may be modified or extended by mutual agreement of the Parties.[2]

DONE at Moscow this 24th day of May 1972 in duplicate, in the English and Russian languages, both equally authentic.

---

[2] The Agreement has been extended through amendment, the most recent of which was July 3 and August 9, 2002.

USE OF THE INDEX

The index is organized by subject matter only. Each subject entry also includes the legal citation indicating the document to which it refers. These legal citations were not chosen on the basis of standard legal citation form, but rather for the amount of information they provided and for convenience in producing a computer-printed index.

Page references, wherever possible, indicate the exact page on which mention of the entry is made. Entries of a more general nature that refer to a large section or to an entire document are listed with the page on which the reference begins.

INDEX

A

E

F

G

I

N

O

P

R

T

U

W

○